BOOKS FOR PROFESSIONAL MARINERS

Marine engineering • Cargo work & stability • Ship handling • Ship's business
Tugs & towing • Maritime safety & security • Navigation

BOOKS FOR LEISURE SAILORS

Seamanship • Cruising • Voyages • Racing • Knots • Coffee Table Books
Electrical • Boat construction • Great Lakes • History

MARINE CHARTS

Paper • Digital • Chartbooks • Charting Tools
Canadian Hydrographic • Imray • NOAA

nauticalmind.com

Marine Booksellers & Chart Agents

249 Queen's Quay West Toronto, Ontario 416-203-1163 | 800-463-9951
books@nauticalmind.com

═══ *Established 1985 on Toronto's waterfront* ═══

MW00803511

A2 ALTITUDE CORRECTION TABLES 10°–90°—SUN, STARS, PLANETS

OCT.—MAR. SUN APR.—SEPT.

App. Alt.	Lower Limb	Upper Limb	App. Alt.	Lower Limb	Upper Limb
° ′	′	′	° ′	′	′
9 33	+10·8	−21·5	9 39	+10·6	−21·2
9 45	+10·9	−21·4	9 50	+10·7	−21·1
9 56	+11·0	−21·3	10 02	+10·8	−21·0
10 08	+11·1	−21·2	10 14	+10·9	−20·9
10 20	+11·2	−21·1	10 27	+11·0	−20·8
10 33	+11·3	−21·0	10 40	+11·1	−20·7
10 46	+11·4	−20·9	10 53	+11·2	−20·6
11 00	+11·5	−20·8	11 07	+11·3	−20·5
11 15	+11·6	−20·7	11 22	+11·4	−20·4
11 30	+11·7	−20·6	11 37	+11·5	−20·3
11 45	+11·8	−20·5	11 53	+11·6	−20·2
12 01	+11·9	−20·4	12 10	+11·7	−20·1
12 18	+12·0	−20·3	12 27	+11·8	−20·0
12 36	+12·1	−20·2	12 45	+11·9	−19·9
12 54	+12·2	−20·1	13 04	+12·0	−19·8
13 14	+12·3	−20·0	13 24	+12·1	−19·7
13 34	+12·4	−19·9	13 44	+12·2	−19·6
13 55	+12·5	−19·8	14 06	+12·3	−19·5
14 17	+12·6	−19·7	14 29	+12·4	−19·4
14 41	+12·7	−19·6	14 53	+12·5	−19·3
15 05	+12·8	−19·5	15 18	+12·6	−19·2
15 31	+12·9	−19·4	15 45	+12·7	−19·1
15 59	+13·0	−19·3	16 13	+12·8	−19·0
16 27	+13·1	−19·2	16 43	+12·9	−18·9
16 58	+13·2	−19·1	17 14	+13·0	−18·8
17 30	+13·3	−19·0	17 47	+13·1	−18·7
18 05	+13·4	−18·9	18 23	+13·2	−18·6
18 41	+13·5	−18·8	19 00	+13·3	−18·5
19 20	+13·6	−18·7	19 41	+13·4	−18·4
20 02	+13·7	−18·6	20 24	+13·5	−18·3
20 46	+13·8	−18·5	21 10	+13·6	−18·2
21 34	+13·9	−18·4	21 59	+13·7	−18·1
22 25	+14·0	−18·3	22 52	+13·8	−18·0
23 20	+14·1	−18·2	23 49	+13·9	−17·9
24 20	+14·2	−18·1	24 51	+14·0	−17·8
25 24	+14·3	−18·0	25 58	+14·1	−17·7
26 34	+14·4	−17·9	27 11	+14·2	−17·6
27 50	+14·5	−17·8	28 31	+14·3	−17·5
29 13	+14·6	−17·7	29 58	+14·4	−17·4
30 44	+14·7	−17·6	31 33	+14·5	−17·3
32 24	+14·8	−17·5	33 18	+14·6	−17·2
34 15	+14·9	−17·4	35 15	+14·7	−17·1
36 17	+15·0	−17·3	37 24	+14·8	−17·0
38 34	+15·1	−17·2	39 48	+14·9	−16·9
41 06	+15·2	−17·1	42 28	+15·0	−16·8
43 56	+15·3	−17·0	45 29	+15·1	−16·7
47 07	+15·4	−16·9	48 52	+15·2	−16·6
50 43	+15·5	−16·8	52 41	+15·3	−16·5
54 46	+15·6	−16·7	56 59	+15·4	−16·4
59 21	+15·7	−16·6	61 50	+15·5	−16·3
64 28	+15·8	−16·5	67 15	+15·6	−16·2
70 10	+15·9	−16·4	73 14	+15·7	−16·1
76 24	+16·0	−16·3	79 42	+15·8	−16·0
83 05	+16·1	−16·2	86 31	+15·9	−15·9
90 00			90 00		

STARS AND PLANETS

App Alt.	Corrⁿ
° ′	′
9 55	−5·3
10 07	−5·2
10 20	−5·1
10 32	−5·0
10 46	−4·9
10 59	−4·8
11 14	−4·7
11 29	−4·6
11 44	−4·5
12 00	−4·4
12 17	−4·3
12 35	−4·2
12 53	−4·1
13 12	−4·0
13 32	−3·9
13 53	−3·8
14 16	−3·7
14 39	−3·6
15 03	−3·5
15 29	−3·4
15 56	−3·3
16 25	−3·2
16 55	−3·1
17 27	−3·0
18 01	−2·9
18 37	−2·8
19 16	−2·7
19 56	−2·6
20 40	−2·5
21 27	−2·4
22 17	−2·3
23 11	−2·2
24 09	−2·1
25 12	−2·0
26 20	−1·9
27 34	−1·8
28 54	−1·7
30 22	−1·6
31 58	−1·5
33 43	−1·4
35 38	−1·3
37 45	−1·2
40 06	−1·1
42 42	−1·0
45 34	−0·9
48 45	−0·8
52 16	−0·7
56 09	−0·6
60 26	−0·5
65 06	−0·4
70 09	−0·3
75 32	−0·2
81 12	−0·1
87 03	0·0
90 00	

App. Alt. — Additional Corrⁿ

2023

VENUS

Jan. 1–May 1
Dec. 2–Dec. 31

°	′
60	+0·1

May 2–June 19
Oct. 10–Dec. 1

°	′
41	+0·2
76	+0·1

June 20–July 12
Sept. 16–Oct. 9

°	′
34	+0·3
60	+0·2
80	+0·1

July 13–July 28
Aug. 31–Sept. 15

°	′
29	+0·4
51	+0·3
68	+0·2
83	+0·1

July 29–Aug. 30

°	′
26	+0·5
46	+0·4
60	+0·3
73	+0·2
84	+0·1

MARS

Jan. 1–Feb. 11

°	′
41	+0·2
76	+0·1

Feb. 12–Dec. 31

°	′
60	+0·1

DIP

Ht. of Eye	Corrⁿ	Ht. of Eye	Ht. of Eye	Corrⁿ
m	′	ft.	m	′
2·4	−2·8	8·0	1·0	−1·8
2·6	−2·9	8·6	1·5	−2·2
2·8	−3·0	9·2	2·0	−2·5
3·0	−3·1	9·8	2·5	−2·8
3·2	−3·2	10·5	3·0	−3·0
3·4	−3·3	11·2	See table ←	
3·6	−3·4	11·9	m	′
3·8	−3·5	12·6	20	−7·9
4·0	−3·6	13·3	22	−8·3
4·3	−3·7	14·1	24	−8·6
4·5	−3·8	14·9	26	−9·0
4·7	−3·9	15·7	28	−9·3
5·0	−4·0	16·5		
5·2	−4·1	17·4	30	−9·6
5·5	−4·2	18·3	32	−10·0
5·8	−4·3	19·1	34	−10·3
6·1	−4·4	20·1	36	−10·6
6·3	−4·5	21·0	38	−10·8
6·6	−4·6	22·0		
6·9	−4·7	22·9	40	−11·1
7·2	−4·8	23·9	42	−11·4
7·5	−4·9	24·9	44	−11·7
7·9	−5·0	26·0	46	−11·9
8·2	−5·1	27·1	48	−12·2
8·5	−5·2	28·1		
8·8	−5·3	29·2	ft.	′
9·2	−5·4	30·4	2	−1·4
9·5	−5·5	31·5	4	−1·9
9·9	−5·6	32·7	6	−2·4
10·3	−5·7	33·9	8	−2·7
10·6	−5·8	35·1	10	−3·1
11·0	−5·9	36·3	See table ←	
11·4	−6·0	37·6	ft.	′
11·8	−6·1	38·9	70	−8·1
12·2	−6·2	40·1	75	−8·4
12·6	−6·3	41·5	80	−8·7
13·0	−6·4	42·8	85	−8·9
13·4	−6·5	44·2	90	−9·2
13·8	−6·6	45·5	95	−9·5
14·2	−6·7	46·9		
14·7	−6·8	48·4	100	−9·7
15·1	−6·9	49·8	105	−9·9
15·5	−7·0	51·3	110	−10·2
16·0	−7·1	52·8	115	−10·4
16·5	−7·2	54·3	120	−10·6
16·9	−7·3	55·8	125	−10·8
17·4	−7·4	57·4		
17·9	−7·5	58·9	130	−11·1
18·4	−7·6	60·5	135	−11·3
18·8	−7·7	62·1	140	−11·5
19·3	−7·8	63·8	145	−11·7
19·8	−7·9	65·4	150	−11·9
20·4	−8·0	67·1	155	−12·1
20·9	−8·1	68·8		
21·4		70·5		

App. Alt. = Apparent altitude = Sextant altitude corrected for index error and dip.

ALTITUDE CORRECTION TABLES 0°–10°—SUN,STARS,PLANETS A3

App. Alt.	OCT.—MAR. SUN Lower Limb	Upper Limb	APR.—SEPT. Lower Limb	Upper Limb	STARS PLANETS
° ′	′	′	′	′	′
0 00	− 17·5	− 49·8	− 17·8	− 49·6	− 33·8
0 03	16·9	49·2	17·2	49·0	33·2
0 06	16·3	48·6	16·6	48·4	32·6
0 09	15·7	48·0	16·0	47·8	32·0
0 12	15·2	47·5	15·4	47·2	31·5
0 15	14·6	46·9	14·8	46·6	30·9
0 18	− 14·1	− 46·4	− 14·3	− 46·1	− 30·4
0 21	13·5	45·8	13·8	45·6	29·8
0 24	13·0	45·3	13·3	45·1	29·3
0 27	12·5	44·8	12·8	44·6	28·8
0 30	12·0	44·3	12·3	44·1	28·3
0 33	11·6	43·9	11·8	43·6	27·9
0 36	− 11·1	− 43·4	− 11·3	− 43·1	− 27·4
0 39	10·6	42·9	10·9	42·7	26·9
0 42	10·2	42·5	10·5	42·3	26·5
0 45	9·8	42·1	10·0	41·8	26·1
0 48	9·4	41·7	9·6	41·4	25·7
0 51	9·0	41·3	9·2	41·0	25·3
0 54	− 8·6	− 40·9	− 8·8	− 40·6	− 24·9
0 57	8·2	40·5	8·4	40·2	24·5
1 00	7·8	40·1	8·0	39·8	24·1
1 03	7·4	39·7	7·7	39·5	23·7
1 06	7·1	39·4	7·3	39·1	23·4
1 09	6·7	39·0	7·0	38·8	23·0
1 12	− 6·4	− 38·7	− 6·6	− 38·4	− 22·7
1 15	6·0	38·3	6·3	38·1	22·3
1 18	5·7	38·0	6·0	37·8	22·0
1 21	5·4	37·7	5·7	37·5	21·7
1 24	5·1	37·4	5·3	37·1	21·4
1 27	4·8	37·1	5·0	36·8	21·1
1 30	− 4·5	− 36·8	− 4·7	− 36·5	− 20·8
1 35	4·0	36·3	4·3	36·1	20·3
1 40	3·6	35·9	3·8	35·6	19·9
1 45	3·1	35·4	3·4	35·2	19·4
1 50	2·7	35·0	2·9	34·7	19·0
1 55	2·3	34·6	2·5	34·3	18·6
2 00	− 1·9	− 34·2	− 2·1	− 33·9	− 18·2
2 05	1·5	33·8	1·7	33·5	17·8
2 10	1·1	33·4	1·4	33·2	17·4
2 15	0·8	33·1	1·0	32·8	17·1
2 20	0·4	32·7	0·7	32·5	16·7
2 25	− 0·1	32·4	− 0·3	32·1	16·4
2 30	+ 0·2	− 32·1	0·0	− 31·8	− 16·1
2 35	0·5	31·8	+ 0·3	31·5	15·8
2 40	0·8	31·5	0·6	31·2	15·4
2 45	1·1	31·2	0·9	30·9	15·2
2 50	1·4	30·9	1·2	30·6	14·9
2 55	1·7	30·6	1·4	30·4	14·6
3 00	+ 2·0	− 30·3	+ 1·7	− 30·1	− 14·3
3 05	2·2	30·1	2·0	29·8	14·1
3 10	2·5	29·8	2·2	29·6	13·8
3 15	2·7	29·6	2·5	29·3	13·6
3 20	2·9	29·4	2·7	29·1	13·4
3 25	3·2	29·1	2·9	28·9	13·1
3 30	+ 3·4	− 28·9	+ 3·1	− 28·7	− 12·9
3 30	+ 3·4	− 28·9	+ 3·1	− 28·7	− 12·9
3 35	3·6	28·7	3·3	28·5	12·7
3 40	3·8	28·5	3·6	28·2	12·5
3 45	4·0	28·3	3·8	28·0	12·3
3 50	4·2	28·1	4·0	27·8	12·1
3 55	4·4	27·9	4·1	27·7	11·9
4 00	+ 4·6	− 27·7	+ 4·3	− 27·5	− 11·7
4 05	4·8	27·5	4·5	27·3	11·5
4 10	4·9	27·4	4·7	27·1	11·4
4 15	5·1	27·2	4·9	26·9	11·2
4 20	5·3	27·0	5·0	26·8	11·0
4 25	5·4	26·9	5·2	26·6	10·9
4 30	+ 5·6	− 26·7	+ 5·3	− 26·5	− 10·7
4 35	5·7	26·6	5·5	26·3	10·6
4 40	5·9	26·4	5·6	26·2	10·4
4 45	6·0	26·3	5·8	26·0	10·3
4 50	6·2	26·1	5·9	25·9	10·1
4 55	6·3	26·0	6·1	25·7	10·0
5 00	+ 6·4	− 25·9	+ 6·2	− 25·6	− 9·8
5 05	6·6	25·7	6·3	25·5	9·7
5 10	6·7	25·6	6·5	25·3	9·6
5 15	6·8	25·5	6·6	25·2	9·5
5 20	7·0	25·3	6·7	25·1	9·3
5 25	7·1	25·2	6·8	25·0	9·2
5 30	+ 7·2	− 25·1	+ 6·9	− 24·9	− 9·1
5 35	7·3	25·0	7·1	24·7	9·0
5 40	7·4	24·9	7·2	24·6	8·9
5 45	7·5	24·8	7·3	24·5	8·8
5 50	7·6	24·7	7·4	24·4	8·7
5 55	7·7	24·6	7·5	24·3	8·6
6 00	+ 7·8	− 24·5	+ 7·6	− 24·2	− 8·5
6 10	8·0	24·3	7·8	24·0	8·3
6 20	8·2	24·1	8·0	23·8	8·1
6 30	8·4	23·9	8·2	23·6	7·9
6 40	8·6	23·7	8·3	23·5	7·7
6 50	8·7	23·6	8·5	23·3	7·6
7 00	+ 8·9	− 23·4	+ 8·7	− 23·1	− 7·4
7 10	9·1	23·2	8·8	23·0	7·2
7 20	9·2	23·1	9·0	22·8	7·1
7 30	9·3	23·0	9·1	22·7	6·9
7 40	9·5	22·8	9·2	22·6	6·8
7 50	9·6	22·7	9·4	22·4	6·7
8 00	+ 9·7	− 22·6	+ 9·5	− 22·3	− 6·6
8 10	9·9	22·4	9·6	22·2	6·4
8 20	10·0	22·3	9·7	22·1	6·3
8 30	10·1	22·2	9·9	21·9	6·2
8 40	10·2	22·1	10·0	21·8	6·1
8 50	10·3	22·0	10·1	21·7	6·0
9 00	+ 10·4	− 21·9	+ 10·2	− 21·6	− 5·9
9 10	10·5	21·8	10·3	21·5	5·8
9 20	10·6	21·7	10·4	21·4	5·7
9 30	10·7	21·6	10·5	21·3	5·6
9 40	10·8	21·5	10·6	21·2	5·5
9 50	10·9	21·4	10·6	21·2	5·4
10 00	+ 11·0	− 21·3	+ 10·7	− 21·1	− 5·3

Additional corrections for temperature and pressure are given on the following page.

For bubble sextant observations ignore dip and use the star corrections for Sun, planets and stars.

© British Crown Copyright 2022. All rights reserved.

A4 ALTITUDE CORRECTION TABLES—ADDITIONAL CORRECTIONS
ADDITIONAL REFRACTION CORRECTIONS FOR NON-STANDARD CONDITIONS

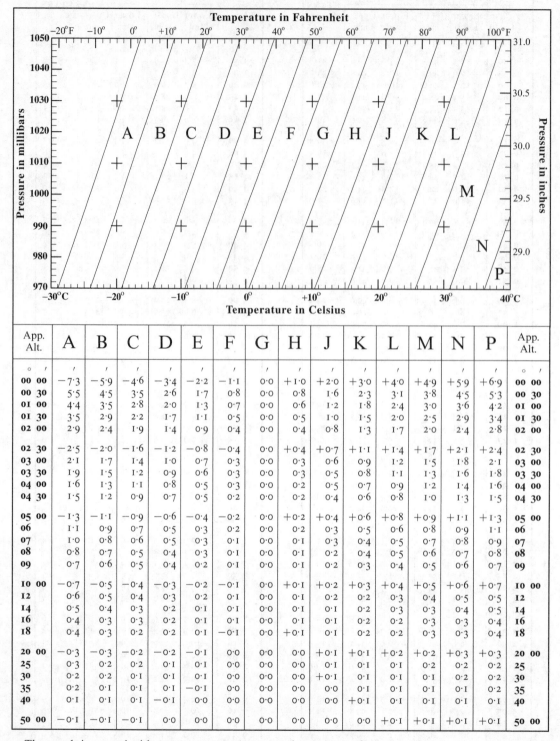

App. Alt.	A	B	C	D	E	F	G	H	J	K	L	M	N	P	App. Alt.
° ′	′	′	′	′	′	′	′	′	′	′	′	′	′	′	° ′
00 00	−7·3	−5·9	−4·6	−3·4	−2·2	−1·1	0·0	+1·0	+2·0	+3·0	+4·0	+4·9	+5·9	+6·9	00 00
00 30	5·5	4·5	3·5	2·6	1·7	0·8	0·0	0·8	1·6	2·3	3·1	3·8	4·5	5·3	00 30
01 00	4·4	3·5	2·8	2·0	1·3	0·7	0·0	0·6	1·2	1·8	2·4	3·0	3·6	4·2	01 00
01 30	3·5	2·9	2·2	1·7	1·1	0·5	0·0	0·5	1·0	1·5	2·0	2·5	2·9	3·4	01 30
02 00	2·9	2·4	1·9	1·4	0·9	0·4	0·0	0·4	0·8	1·3	1·7	2·0	2·4	2·8	02 00
02 30	−2·5	−2·0	−1·6	−1·2	−0·8	−0·4	0·0	+0·4	+0·7	+1·1	+1·4	+1·7	+2·1	+2·4	02 30
03 00	2·1	1·7	1·4	1·0	0·7	0·3	0·0	0·3	0·6	0·9	1·2	1·5	1·8	2·1	03 00
03 30	1·9	1·5	1·2	0·9	0·6	0·3	0·0	0·3	0·5	0·8	1·1	1·3	1·6	1·8	03 30
04 00	1·6	1·3	1·1	0·8	0·5	0·3	0·0	0·2	0·5	0·7	0·9	1·2	1·4	1·6	04 00
04 30	1·5	1·2	0·9	0·7	0·5	0·2	0·0	0·2	0·4	0·6	0·8	1·0	1·3	1·5	04 30
05 00	−1·3	−1·1	−0·9	−0·6	−0·4	−0·2	0·0	+0·2	+0·4	+0·6	+0·8	+0·9	+1·1	+1·3	05 00
06	1·1	0·9	0·7	0·5	0·3	0·2	0·0	0·2	0·3	0·5	0·6	0·8	0·9	1·1	06
07	1·0	0·8	0·6	0·5	0·3	0·1	0·0	0·1	0·3	0·4	0·5	0·7	0·8	0·9	07
08	0·8	0·7	0·5	0·4	0·3	0·1	0·0	0·1	0·2	0·4	0·5	0·6	0·7	0·8	08
09	0·7	0·6	0·5	0·4	0·2	0·1	0·0	0·1	0·2	0·3	0·4	0·5	0·6	0·7	09
10 00	−0·7	−0·5	−0·4	−0·3	−0·2	−0·1	0·0	+0·1	+0·2	+0·3	+0·4	+0·5	+0·6	+0·7	10 00
12	0·6	0·5	0·4	0·3	0·2	0·1	0·0	0·1	0·2	0·2	0·3	0·4	0·5	0·5	12
14	0·5	0·4	0·3	0·2	0·1	0·1	0·0	0·1	0·1	0·2	0·3	0·3	0·4	0·5	14
16	0·4	0·3	0·3	0·2	0·1	0·1	0·0	0·1	0·1	0·2	0·2	0·3	0·3	0·4	16
18	0·4	0·3	0·2	0·2	0·1	−0·1	0·0	+0·1	0·1	0·2	0·2	0·3	0·3	0·4	18
20 00	−0·3	−0·3	−0·2	−0·2	−0·1	0·0	0·0	0·0	+0·1	+0·1	+0·2	+0·2	+0·3	+0·3	20 00
25	0·3	0·2	0·2	0·1	0·1	0·0	0·0	0·0	0·1	0·1	0·1	0·2	0·2	0·2	25
30	0·2	0·2	0·1	0·1	0·1	0·0	0·0	0·0	+0·1	0·1	0·1	0·1	0·2	0·2	30
35	0·2	0·1	0·1	0·1	−0·1	0·0	0·0	0·0	0·0	0·1	0·1	0·1	0·1	0·2	35
40	0·1	0·1	0·1	−0·1	0·0	0·0	0·0	0·0	0·0	+0·1	0·1	0·1	0·1	0·1	40
50 00	−0·1	−0·1	−0·1	0·0	0·0	0·0	0·0	0·0	0·0	0·0	+0·1	+0·1	+0·1	+0·1	50 00

The graph is entered with arguments temperature and pressure to find a zone letter; using as arguments this zone letter and apparent altitude (sextant altitude corrected for index error and dip), a correction is taken from the table. This correction is to be applied to the sextant altitude in addition to the corrections for standard conditions (for the Sun, stars and planets from page A2-A3 and for the Moon from pages xxxiv and xxxv).

© British Crown Copyright 2022. All rights reserved.

2023
Nautical Almanac
COMMERCIAL EDITION

PUBLISHED BY:

Paradise Cay Publications, Inc.
PO Box 29
Arcata, CA 95518-0029
Tel: 1-707-822-9063
Fax: 1-707-822-9163
www.paracay.com

The name "Nautical Almanac Commercial Edition" is a trademark of Paradise Cay Publications, Inc.

© British Crown Copyright 2022. All rights reserved.

ISBN: 9781951116583

© British Crown Copyright 2022. All rights reserved.

Printed and distributed with permissions by Paradise Cay Publications

NOTE

Every care is taken to prevent errors in the production of this publication. As a final precaution it is recommended that the sequence of pages in this copy be examined on receipt. If faulty, it should be returned for replacement.

PREFACE

The first three sections of this book are a complete and accurate duplications from *The Nautical Almanac* produced jointly by Her Majesty's Nautical Almanac Office, United Kingdom Hydrographic Office, Admiralty Way, Taunton, Somerset, TA1 2DN, United Kingdom and the Nautical Almanac Office of the US Naval Observatory.

The material reproduced from the HM Nautical Almanac is protected by © British Crown Copyright. All rights reserved. No part of this publication may be reproduced, stored in a retrieval system or transmitted in any form by any means, electronic, mechanical, photocopying, recording or otherwise without prior permission of HM Nautical Almanac Office, United Kingdom Hydrographic Office, Admiralty Way, Taunton, Somerset, TA1 2DN, United Kingdom.

The following United States government work is excerpted from the above notice and no copyright is claimed for it in the United States: pages 6 and 7, and pages 286-317.

The UK Hydrographic Office makes the accompanying 2023 Nautical Almanac data available to Paradise Cay Publications Inc for use in accordance with Licence agreement GB CS-001-Paradise Cay Publications.

We gratefully acknowledge the United Kingdom Hydrographic Office and the United States Naval Observatory for permission to use the material contained in the almanac section of this publication.

CONDITIONS OF RELEASE

The supplied material is protected by Crown Copyright. No part of the supplied material may be reproduced, stored in a retrieval system or transmitted in any form or by any means, electronic, mechanical, photocopying, recording or otherwise except as required to fulfil the purpose above.

DISCLAIMER

Whilst the UK Hydrographic Office has endeavoured to ensure that the material supplied is suitable for the purpose, it accepts no liability (to the maximum extent permitted by law) for any damage or loss of any nature arising from its use. The material supplied is used entirely at the Recipient's own risk.

All material not originating from The Nautical Almanac is copyrighted © by Paradise Cay Publications, Inc. and may not be reproduced in any form or by any means without permission from Paradise Cay Publications, Inc. The front cover was designed by and is property of Paradise Cay Publications, Inc. All rights reserved. Copyright 2022 Paradise Cay Publications, Inc. The name "Nautical Almanac Commercial Edition" is a trademark of Paradise Cay Publications, Inc.

© British Crown Copyright 2022. All rights reserved.

THE NAUTICAL ALMANAC 2023

LIST OF CONTENTS

© British Crown Copyright 2022. All rights reserved.

CALENDAR, 2023

RELIGIOUS CALENDARS

Epiphany	Jan. 6	Low Sunday	Apr. 16
Septuagesima Sunday	Feb. 5	Rogation Sunday	May 14
Quinquagesima Sunday	Feb. 19	Ascension Day—Holy Thursday	May 18
Ash Wednesday	Feb. 22	Whit Sunday—Pentecost	May 28
Quadragesima Sunday	Feb. 26	Trinity Sunday	June 4
Palm Sunday	Apr. 2	Corpus Christi	June 8
Good Friday	Apr. 7	First Sunday in Advent	Dec. 3
Easter Day	Apr. 9	Christmas Day (Monday)	Dec. 25
First Day of Passover (Pesach)	Apr. 6	Day of Atonement (Yom Kippur)	Sept. 25
Feast of Weeks (Shavuot)	May 26	First day of Tabernacles (Succoth)	Sept. 30
Jewish New Year 5784 (Rosh Hashanah)	Sept. 16		
Ramadân, First day of (tabular)	Mar. 23	Islamic New Year (1445)	July 19

The Jewish and Islamic dates above are tabular dates, which begin at sunset on the previous evening and end at sunset on the date tabulated. In practice, the dates of Islamic fasts and festivals are determined by an actual sighting of the appropriate new moon.

CIVIL CALENDAR—UNITED KINGDOM

Accession of Queen Elizabeth II	Feb. 6	The Queen's Official Birthday†	June 10
St David (Wales)	Mar. 1	Birthday of Prince Philip, Duke of	
Commonwealth Day	Mar. 13	Edinburgh	June 10
St Patrick (Ireland)	Mar. 17	Remembrance Sunday	Nov. 12
Birthday of Queen Elizabeth II	Apr. 21	Birthday of the Prince of Wales	Nov. 14
St George (England)	Apr. 23	St Andrew (Scotland)	Nov. 30
Coronation Day	June 2		

PUBLIC HOLIDAYS

England and Wales—Jan. 2, Apr. 7, Apr. 10, May 1, May 29, Aug. 28, Dec. 25, Dec. 26
Northern Ireland—Jan. 2, Mar. 17, Apr. 7, Apr. 10, May 1, May 29, July 12, Aug. 28, Dec. 25, Dec. 26
Scotland—Jan. 2, Jan. 3, Apr. 7, May 1, May 29, Aug. 7, Dec. 25, Dec. 26

CIVIL CALENDAR—UNITED STATES OF AMERICA

New Year's Day	Jan. 1	Labor Day	Sept. 4
Martin Luther King's Birthday	Jan. 16	Columbus Day	Oct. 9
Washington's Birthday	Feb. 20	Election Day (in certain States)	Nov. 7
Memorial Day	May 29	Veterans Day	Nov. 11
Juneteenth National Independence Day	June 19	Thanksgiving Day	Nov. 23
Independence Day	July 4		

†Dates subject to confirmation

PHASES OF THE MOON

New Moon			First Quarter			Full Moon			Last Quarter		
d	h	m	d	h	m	d	h	m	d	h	m
						Jan. 6	23	08	Jan. 15	02	10
Jan. 21	20	53	Jan. 28	15	19	Feb. 5	18	29	Feb. 13	16	01
Feb. 20	07	06	Feb. 27	08	06	Mar. 7	12	40	Mar. 15	02	08
Mar. 21	17	23	Mar. 29	02	32	Apr. 6	04	35	Apr. 13	09	11
Apr. 20	04	13	Apr. 27	21	20	May 5	17	34	May 12	14	28
May 19	15	53	May 27	15	22	June 4	03	42	June 10	19	31
June 18	04	37	June 26	07	50	July 3	11	39	July 10	01	48
July 17	18	32	July 25	22	07	Aug. 1	18	32	Aug. 8	10	28
Aug. 16	09	38	Aug. 24	09	57	Aug. 31	01	36	Sept. 6	22	21
Sept. 15	01	40	Sept. 22	19	32	Sept. 29	09	58	Oct. 6	13	48
Oct. 14	17	55	Oct. 22	03	29	Oct. 28	20	24	Nov. 5	08	37
Nov. 13	09	27	Nov. 20	10	50	Nov. 27	09	16	Dec. 5	05	49
Dec. 12	23	32	Dec. 19	18	39	Dec. 27	00	33			

© British Crown Copyright 2022. All rights reserved.

DAYS OF THE WEEK AND DAYS OF THE YEAR

	JAN.		FEB.		MAR.		APR.		MAY		JUNE		JULY		AUG.		SEPT.		OCT.		NOV.		DEC.	
Day	Wk	Yr	Wk	Yr	Wk	Yr	Wk	Yr	Wk	Yr	Wk	Yr	Wk	Yr	Wk	Yr	Wk	Yr	Wk	Yr	Wk	Yr	Wk	Yr
1	Su.	1	W.	32	W.	60	Sa.	91	M.	121	Th.	152	Sa.	182	Tu.	213	F.	244	Su.	274	W.	305	F.	335
2	M.	2	Th.	33	Th.	61	Su.	92	Tu.	122	F.	153	Su.	183	W.	214	Sa.	245	M.	275	Th.	306	Sa.	336
3	Tu.	3	F.	34	F.	62	M.	93	W.	123	Sa.	154	M.	184	Th.	215	Su.	246	Tu.	276	F.	307	Su.	337
4	W.	4	Sa.	35	Sa.	63	Tu.	94	Th.	124	Su.	155	Tu.	185	F.	216	M.	247	W.	277	Sa.	308	M.	338
5	Th.	5	Su.	36	Su.	64	W.	95	F.	125	M.	156	W.	186	Sa.	217	Tu.	248	Th.	278	Su.	309	Tu.	339
6	F.	6	M.	37	M.	65	Th.	96	Sa.	126	Tu.	157	Th.	187	Su.	218	W.	249	F.	279	M.	310	W.	340
7	Sa.	7	Tu.	38	Tu.	66	F.	97	Su.	127	W.	158	F.	188	M.	219	Th.	250	Sa.	280	Tu.	311	Th.	341
8	Su.	8	W.	39	W.	67	Sa.	98	M.	128	Th.	159	Sa.	189	Tu.	220	F.	251	Su.	281	W.	312	F.	342
9	M.	9	Th.	40	Th.	68	Su.	99	Tu.	129	F.	160	Su.	190	W.	221	Sa.	252	M.	282	Th.	313	Sa.	343
10	Tu.	10	F.	41	F.	69	M.	100	W.	130	Sa.	161	M.	191	Th.	222	Su.	253	Tu.	283	F.	314	Su.	344
11	W.	11	Sa.	42	Sa.	70	Tu.	101	Th.	131	Su.	162	Tu.	192	F.	223	M.	254	W.	284	Sa.	315	M.	345
12	Th.	12	Su.	43	Su.	71	W.	102	F.	132	M.	163	W.	193	Sa.	224	Tu.	255	Th.	285	Su.	316	Tu.	346
13	F.	13	M.	44	M.	72	Th.	103	Sa.	133	Tu.	164	Th.	194	Su.	225	W.	256	F.	286	M.	317	W.	347
14	Sa.	14	Tu.	45	Tu.	73	F.	104	Su.	134	W.	165	F.	195	M.	226	Th.	257	Sa.	287	Tu.	318	Th.	348
15	Su.	15	W.	46	W.	74	Sa.	105	M.	135	Th.	166	Sa.	196	Tu.	227	F.	258	Su.	288	W.	319	F.	349
16	M.	16	Th.	47	Th.	75	Su.	106	Tu.	136	F.	167	Su.	197	W.	228	Sa.	259	M.	289	Th.	320	Sa.	350
17	Tu.	17	F.	48	F.	76	M.	107	W.	137	Sa.	168	M.	198	Th.	229	Su.	260	Tu.	290	F.	321	Su.	351
18	W.	18	Sa.	49	Sa.	77	Tu.	108	Th.	138	Su.	169	Tu.	199	F.	230	M.	261	W.	291	Sa.	322	M.	352
19	Th.	19	Su.	50	Su.	78	W.	109	F.	139	M.	170	W.	200	Sa.	231	Tu.	262	Th.	292	Su.	323	Tu.	353
20	F.	20	M.	51	M.	79	Th.	110	Sa.	140	Tu.	171	Th.	201	Su.	232	W.	263	F.	293	M.	324	W.	354
21	Sa.	21	Tu.	52	Tu.	80	F.	111	Su.	141	W.	172	F.	202	M.	233	Th.	264	Sa.	294	Tu.	325	Th.	355
22	Su.	22	W.	53	W.	81	Sa.	112	M.	142	Th.	173	Sa.	203	Tu.	234	F.	265	Su.	295	W.	326	F.	356
23	M.	23	Th.	54	Th.	82	Su.	113	Tu.	143	F.	174	Su.	204	W.	235	Sa.	266	M.	296	Th.	327	Sa.	357
24	Tu.	24	F.	55	F.	83	M.	114	W.	144	Sa.	175	M.	205	Th.	236	Su.	267	Tu.	297	F.	328	Su.	358
25	W.	25	Sa.	56	Sa.	84	Tu.	115	Th.	145	Su.	176	Tu.	206	F.	237	M.	268	W.	298	Sa.	329	M.	359
26	Th.	26	Su.	57	Su.	85	W.	116	F.	146	M.	177	W.	207	Sa.	238	Tu.	269	Th.	299	Su.	330	Tu.	360
27	F.	27	M.	58	M.	86	Th.	117	Sa.	147	Tu.	178	Th.	208	Su.	239	W.	270	F.	300	M.	331	W.	361
28	Sa.	28	Tu.	59	Tu.	87	F.	118	Su.	148	W.	179	F.	209	M.	240	Th.	271	Sa.	301	Tu.	332	Th.	362
29	Su.	29			W.	88	Sa.	119	M.	149	Th.	180	Sa.	210	Tu.	241	F.	272	Su.	302	W.	333	F.	363
30	M.	30			Th.	89	Su.	120	Tu.	150	F.	181	Su.	211	W.	242	Sa.	273	M.	303	Th.	334	Sa.	364
31	Tu.	31			F.	90			W.	151			M.	212	Th.	243			Tu.	304			Su.	365

ECLIPSES

There are two eclipses of the Sun.

1. *An annular-total eclipse of the Sun,* April 20. See map page 6. The eclipse begins at 01^h 34^m and ends at 06^h 59^m; the annular-total phase begins at 02^h 37^m and ends at 05^h 57^m. The maximum duration of totality is 1^m 21^s.

2. *An annular eclipse of the Sun,* October 14. See map on page 7. The eclipse begins at 15^h 04^m and ends at 20^h 55^m; the annular phase begins at 16^h 12^m and ends at 19^h 47^m. The maximum duration of annularity is 5^m 12^s.

3. *A partial eclipse of the Moon,* October 28. The eclipse begins at 19^h 34^m and ends at 20^h 54^m. The time of maximum eclipse is 20^h 14^m when 0·13 of the Moon's diameter is obscured. It is visible from most of Australia, Indonesia, Asia, East Antarctica, Africa, Europe, Iceland, Greenland, the easternmost part of South America and north-eastern Canada.

© British Crown Copyright 2022. All rights reserved.

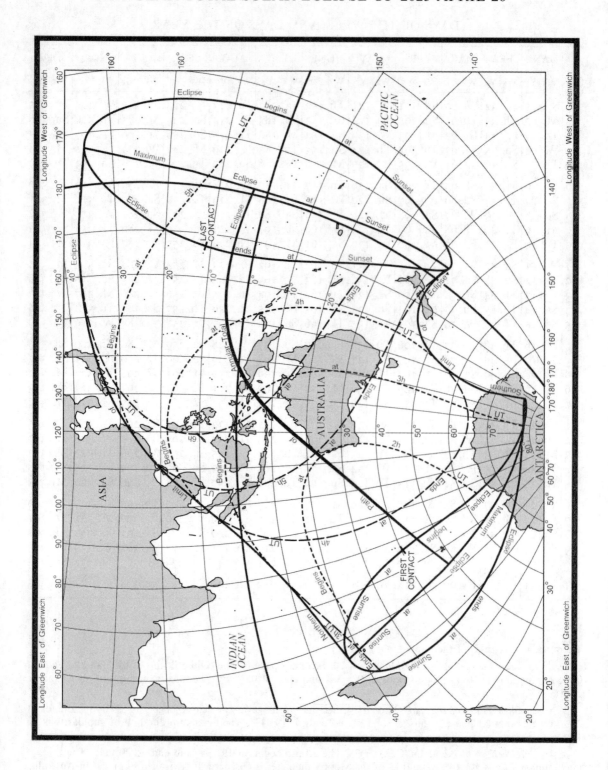

SOLAR ECLIPSE DIAGRAMS

The principal features shown on the above diagrams are: the paths of
total and annular eclipses; the northern and southern limits of partial
eclipse; the sunrise and sunset curves; dashed lines which show the
times of beginning and end of partial eclipse at hourly intervals.

© British Crown Copyright 2022. All rights reserved.

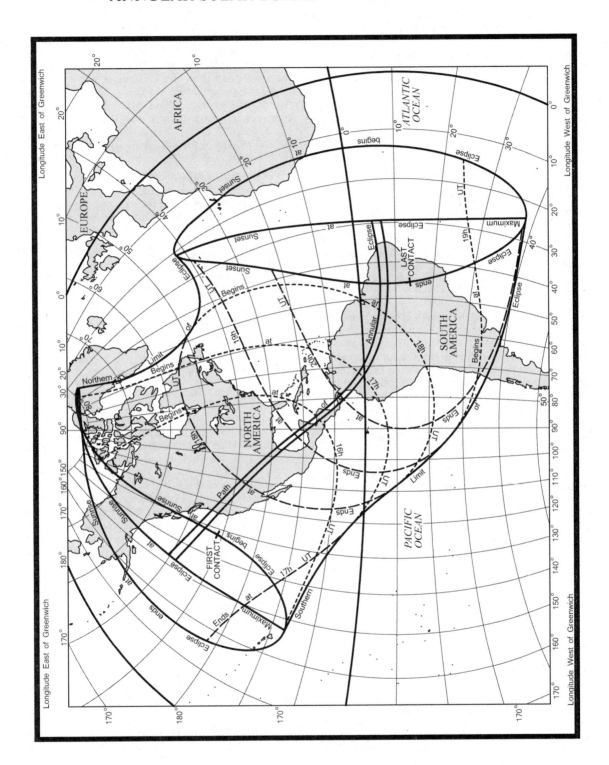

SOLAR ECLIPSE DIAGRAMS

Further details of the paths and times of central eclipse are given in
The Astronomical Almanac.

© British Crown Copyright 2022. All rights reserved.

VISIBILITY OF PLANETS

VENUS is a brilliant object in the evening sky from the beginning of the year until the beginning of the second week of August when it becomes too close to the Sun for observation. In the third week of August it reappears in the morning sky where it stays until the end of the year. Venus is in conjunction with Saturn on January 22, with Jupiter on March 2 and with Mercury on July 26.

MARS can be seen at the beginning of the year for more than half the night in Taurus (passing 8 deg. N of Aldebaran on February 5) and into Gemini in late March. Its eastward elongation gradually decreases until it can be seen in the evening sky, moving from Gemini (passing 5 deg. S of Pollux on May 10), through Cancer, Leo (passing 0.7 deg. N of Regulus on July 10) and into Virgo from mid August. From the beginning of October until the end of the year it is too close to the Sun for observation.

JUPITER can be seen at the beginning of the year in the evening sky in Pisces, moves into Cetus in early February and later in this month back into Pisces. From late March it becomes too close to the Sun for observation. It reappears in the morning sky in late April and moves into Aries in mid-May. Its westward elongation gradually increases until opposition on November 3. From early November its eastward elongation gradually decreases and it can be seen for more than half the night. Jupiter is in conjunction with Venus on March 2 and with Mercury on March 28.

SATURN can be seen in the evening sky from the beginning of the year in Capricornus. In late January it becomes too close to the Sun for observation until early March when it reappears in the morning sky in Aquarius. Its westward elongation gradually increases until August 27 when it is at opposition and is visible throughout the night. Its eastward elongation gradually decreases and by late November it can only be seen in the evening sky. Saturn is in conjunction with Venus on January 22.

MERCURY can only be seen low in the east before sunrise, or low in the west after sunset (about the time of beginning or end of civil twilight). It is visible in the mornings between the following approximate dates: January 13 (2.0) to March 7 (-0.9), May 11 (3.1) to June 24 (-1.5), September 14 (1.9) to October 8 (-1.2) and December 29 (1.5) to December 31 (0.8); the planet is brighter at the end of each period. It is visible in the evenings between the following approximate dates: January 1 (1.3) to January 2 (1.8), March 26 (-1.5) to April 23 (2.7), July 9 (-1.3) to August 30 (2.5) and November 5 (-0.6) to December 17 (1.6); the planet is brighter at the beginning of each period. The figures in parentheses are the magnitudes.

PLANET DIAGRAM

General Description. The diagram on the opposite page shows, in graphical form for any date during the year, the local mean time of meridian passage of the Sun, of the five planets Mercury, Venus, Mars, Jupiter, and Saturn, and of each 30° of SHA; intermediate lines corresponding to particular stars, may be drawn in by the user if desired. It is intended to provide a general picture of the availability of planets and stars for observation.

On each side of the line marking the time of meridian passage of the Sun a band, 45^m wide, is shaded to indicate that planets and most stars crossing the meridian within 45^m of the Sun are too close to the Sun for observation.

Method of use and interpretation. For any date, the diagram provides immediately the local mean times of meridian passage of the Sun, planets and stars, and thus the following information:

(a) whether a planet or star is too close to the Sun for observation;

(b) some indication of its position in the sky, especially during twilight;

(c) the proximity of other planets.

When the meridian passage of an outer planet occurs at midnight, the body is in opposition to the Sun and is visible all night; a planet may then be observable during both morning and evening twilights. As the time of meridian passage decreases, the body eventually ceases to be observable in the morning, but its altitude above the eastern horizon at sunset gradually increases; this continues until the body is on the meridian during evening twilight. From then onwards, the body is observable above the western horizon and its altitude at sunset gradually decreases; eventually the body becomes too close to the Sun for observation. When the body again becomes visible it is seen low in the east during morning twilight; its altitude at sunrise increases until meridian passage occurs during morning twilight. Then, as the time of meridian passage decreases to 0^h, the body is observable in the west during morning twilight with a gradually decreasing altitude, until it once again reaches opposition.

DO NOT CONFUSE

Mercury with Venus at the start of January when Venus is the brighter object and with Jupiter in late March when Jupiter is the brighter object.

Venus with Saturn in the second half of January, with Jupiter from late February until early March and with Mars from mid-June to mid-July; on all occasions Venus is the brighter object.

Mercury with Mars in mid-August where Mercury is the brighter object.

© British Crown Copyright 2022. All rights reserved.

LOCAL MEAN TIME OF MERIDIAN PASSAGE

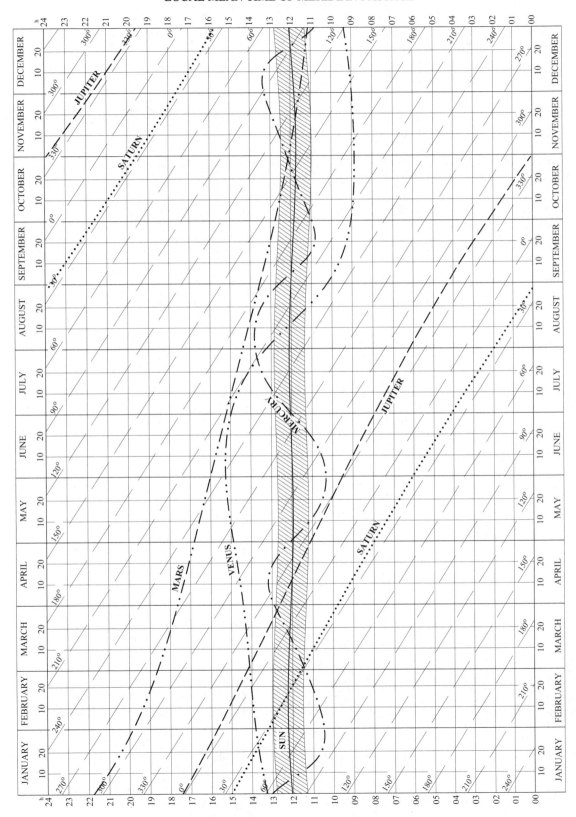

LOCAL MEAN TIME OF MERIDIAN PASSAGE

© British Crown Copyright 2022. All rights reserved.

UT	ARIES GHA	VENUS −3.9 GHA	Dec	MARS −1.2 GHA	Dec	JUPITER −2.3 GHA	Dec	SATURN +0.8 GHA	Dec
1 d h									
00	100 23.3	160 39.0	S22 02.2	33 29.7	N24 35.3	98 46.9	S 0 42.4	135 11.7	S15 12.9
01	115 25.8	175 38.2	01.6	48 32.6	35.3	113 49.1	42.2	150 13.9	12.8
02	130 28.2	190 37.3	01.1	63 35.5	35.2	128 51.3	42.1	165 16.2	12.7
03	145 30.7	205 36.5	22 00.5	78 38.4 ..	35.2	143 53.5 ..	42.0	180 18.4 ..	12.6
04	160 33.2	220 35.6	21 59.9	93 41.3	35.1	158 55.7	41.9	195 20.6	12.6
05	175 35.6	235 34.8	59.4	108 44.2	35.1	173 57.9	41.7	210 22.8	12.5
06	190 38.1	250 33.9	S21 58.8	123 47.1	N24 35.0	189 00.1	S 0 41.6	225 25.0	S15 12.4
07	205 40.6	265 33.0	58.2	138 50.0	35.0	204 02.3	41.5	240 27.3	12.3
08	220 43.0	280 32.2	57.6	153 52.9	34.9	219 04.5	41.3	255 29.5	12.2
09	235 45.5	295 31.3 ..	57.1	168 55.8 ..	34.9	234 06.7 ..	41.2	270 31.7 ..	12.1
10	250 48.0	310 30.5	56.5	183 58.7	34.9	249 08.8	41.1	285 33.9	12.1
11	265 50.4	325 29.6	55.9	199 01.6	34.8	264 11.0	40.9	300 36.1	12.0
12	280 52.9	340 28.8	S21 55.3	214 04.4	N24 34.8	279 13.2	S 0 40.8	315 38.3	S15 11.9
13	295 55.4	355 27.9	54.8	229 07.3	34.7	294 15.4	40.7	330 40.6	11.8
14	310 57.8	10 27.1	54.2	244 10.2	34.7	309 17.6	40.6	345 42.8	11.7
15	326 00.3	25 26.2 ..	53.6	259 13.1 ..	34.6	324 19.8 ..	40.4	0 45.0 ..	11.7
16	341 02.7	40 25.4	53.0	274 16.0	34.6	339 22.0	40.3	15 47.2	11.6
17	356 05.2	55 24.5	52.4	289 18.8	34.6	354 24.2	40.2	30 49.4	11.5
18	11 07.7	70 23.7	S21 51.8	304 21.7	N24 34.5	9 26.3	S 0 40.0	45 51.7	S15 11.4
19	26 10.1	85 22.8	51.3	319 24.6	34.5	24 28.5	39.9	60 53.9	11.3
20	41 12.6	100 22.0	50.7	334 27.4	34.4	39 30.7	39.8	75 56.1	11.2
21	56 15.1	115 21.1 ..	50.1	349 30.3 ..	34.4	54 32.9 ..	39.6	90 58.3 ..	11.2
22	71 17.5	130 20.3	49.5	4 33.2	34.3	69 35.1	39.5	106 00.5	11.1
23	86 20.0	145 19.4	48.9	19 36.0	34.3	84 37.3	39.4	121 02.8	11.0
2 00	101 22.5	160 18.6	S21 48.3	34 38.9	N24 34.3	99 39.5	S 0 39.2	136 05.0	S15 10.9
01	116 24.9	175 17.7	47.7	49 41.8	34.2	114 41.6	39.1	151 07.2	10.8
02	131 27.4	190 16.9	47.1	64 44.6	34.2	129 43.8	39.0	166 09.4	10.7
03	146 29.8	205 16.0 ..	46.5	79 47.5 ..	34.1	144 46.0 ..	38.8	181 11.6 ..	10.7
04	161 32.3	220 15.2	45.9	94 50.3	34.1	159 48.2	38.7	196 13.8	10.6
05	176 34.8	235 14.4	45.3	109 53.2	34.1	174 50.4	38.6	211 16.1	10.5
06	191 37.2	250 13.5	S21 44.7	124 56.1	N24 34.0	189 52.6	S 0 38.4	226 18.3	S15 10.4
07	206 39.7	265 12.7	44.1	139 58.9	34.0	204 54.8	38.3	241 20.5	10.3
08	221 42.2	280 11.8	43.5	155 01.8	33.9	219 56.9	38.2	256 22.7	10.2
09	236 44.6	295 11.0 ..	42.9	170 04.6 ..	33.9	234 59.1 ..	38.0	271 24.9 ..	10.2
10	251 47.1	310 10.1	42.3	185 07.5	33.8	250 01.3	37.9	286 27.1	10.1
11	266 49.6	325 09.3	41.7	200 10.3	33.8	265 03.5	37.8	301 29.4	10.0
12	281 52.0	340 08.4	S21 41.1	215 13.1	N24 33.8	280 05.7	S 0 37.7	316 31.6	S15 09.9
13	296 54.5	355 07.6	40.5	230 16.0	33.7	295 07.9	37.5	331 33.8	09.8
14	311 57.0	10 06.8	39.9	245 18.8	33.7	310 10.0	37.4	346 36.0	09.7
15	326 59.4	25 05.9 ..	39.3	260 21.7 ..	33.6	325 12.2 ..	37.3	1 38.2 ..	09.7
16	342 01.9	40 05.1	38.7	275 24.5	33.6	340 14.4	37.1	16 40.4	09.6
17	357 04.3	55 04.3	38.0	290 27.3	33.6	355 16.6	37.0	31 42.7	09.5
18	12 06.8	70 03.4	S21 37.4	305 30.2	N24 33.5	10 18.8	S 0 36.8	46 44.9	S15 09.4
19	27 09.3	85 02.6	36.8	320 33.0	33.5	25 20.9	36.7	61 47.1	09.3
20	42 11.7	100 01.8	36.2	335 35.8	33.4	40 23.1	36.6	76 49.3	09.2
21	57 14.2	115 00.9 ..	35.6	350 38.7 ..	33.4	55 25.3 ..	36.4	91 51.5 ..	09.2
22	72 16.7	130 00.1	35.0	5 41.5	33.4	70 27.5	36.3	106 53.7	09.1
23	87 19.1	144 59.2	34.4	20 44.3	33.3	85 29.7	36.2	121 56.0	09.0
3 00	102 21.6	159 58.4	S21 33.7	35 47.2	N24 33.3	100 31.8	S 0 36.0	136 58.2	S15 08.9
01	117 24.1	174 57.6	33.1	50 50.0	33.2	115 34.0	35.9	152 00.4	08.8
02	132 26.5	189 56.7	32.5	65 52.8	33.2	130 36.2	35.8	167 02.6	08.7
03	147 29.0	204 55.9 ..	31.9	80 55.6 ..	33.2	145 38.4 ..	35.6	182 04.8 ..	08.7
04	162 31.5	219 55.1	31.2	95 58.4	33.1	160 40.6	35.5	197 07.0	08.6
05	177 33.9	234 54.2	30.6	111 01.3	33.1	175 42.7	35.4	212 09.3	08.5
06	192 36.4	249 53.4	S21 30.0	126 04.1	N24 33.1	190 44.9	S 0 35.2	227 11.5	S15 08.4
07	207 38.8	264 52.6	29.4	141 06.9	33.0	205 47.1	35.1	242 13.7	08.3
08	222 41.3	279 51.8	28.7	156 09.7	33.0	220 49.3	35.0	257 15.9	08.2
09	237 43.8	294 50.9 ..	28.1	171 12.5 ..	32.9	235 51.4 ..	34.8	272 18.1 ..	08.2
10	252 46.2	309 50.1	27.5	186 15.3	32.9	250 53.6	34.7	287 20.3	08.1
11	267 48.7	324 49.3	26.8	201 18.1	32.9	265 55.8	34.6	302 22.5	08.0
12	282 51.2	339 48.4	S21 26.2	216 20.9	N24 32.8	280 58.0	S 0 34.4	317 24.8	S15 07.9
13	297 53.6	354 47.6	25.6	231 23.7	32.8	296 00.2	34.3	332 27.0	07.8
14	312 56.1	9 46.8	24.9	246 26.5	32.7	311 02.3	34.2	347 29.2	07.7
15	327 58.6	24 46.0 ..	24.3	261 29.3 ..	32.7	326 04.5 ..	34.0	2 31.4 ..	07.7
16	343 01.0	39 45.1	23.7	276 32.1	32.7	341 06.7	33.9	17 33.6	07.6
17	358 03.5	54 44.3	23.0	291 34.9	32.6	356 08.9	33.7	32 35.8	07.5
18	13 06.0	69 43.5	S21 22.4	306 37.7	N24 32.6	11 11.0	S 0 33.6	47 38.0	S15 07.4
19	28 08.4	84 42.7	21.7	321 40.5	32.6	26 13.2	33.5	62 40.3	07.3
20	43 10.9	99 41.8	21.1	336 43.3	32.5	41 15.4	33.3	77 42.5	07.2
21	58 13.3	114 41.0 ..	20.5	351 46.1 ..	32.5	56 17.6 ..	33.2	92 44.7 ..	07.1
22	73 15.8	129 40.2	19.8	6 48.9	32.5	71 19.7	33.1	107 46.9	07.1
23	88 18.3	144 39.4	19.2	21 51.7	32.4	86 21.9	32.9	122 49.1	07.0
Mer. Pass. 17 11.7		v −0.8 d 0.6		v 2.8 d 0.0		v 2.2 d 0.1		v 2.2 d 0.1	

Days: SUNDAY (1), MONDAY (2), TUESDAY (3)

STARS

Name	SHA	Dec
Acamar	315 12.8	S40 13.0
Achernar	335 21.3	S57 07.5
Acrux	173 05.9	S63 13.2
Adhara	255 06.8	S29 00.2
Aldebaran	290 41.2	N16 33.3
Alioth	166 14.5	N55 49.9
Alkaid	152 53.5	N49 11.7
Alnair	27 35.3	S46 51.2
Alnilam	275 39.1	S 1 11.3
Alphard	217 49.1	S 8 45.4
Alphecca	126 05.4	N26 38.1
Alpheratz	357 36.6	N29 13.1
Altair	62 01.9	N 8 55.7
Ankaa	353 08.8	S42 11.2
Antares	112 18.2	S26 28.9
Arcturus	145 49.6	N19 03.7
Atria	107 14.5	S69 03.9
Avior	234 14.8	S59 34.8
Bellatrix	278 24.3	N 6 22.2
Betelgeuse	270 53.6	N 7 24.7
Canopus	263 52.6	S52 42.5
Capella	280 23.9	N46 01.3
Deneb	49 27.4	N45 21.8
Denebola	182 26.6	N14 26.6
Diphda	348 49.0	S17 51.8
Dubhe	193 42.8	N61 37.4
Elnath	278 03.6	N28 37.6
Eltanin	90 43.5	N51 29.0
Enif	33 40.7	N 9 58.8
Fomalhaut	15 16.5	S29 30.3
Gacrux	171 53.5	S57 14.2
Gienah	175 45.3	S17 40.0
Hadar	148 38.6	S60 28.7
Hamal	327 52.9	N23 34.3
Kaus Aust.	83 35.1	S34 22.4
Kochab	137 20.4	N74 03.4
Markab	13 31.7	N15 19.7
Menkar	314 07.7	N 4 10.7
Menkent	147 59.7	S36 28.8
Miaplacidus	221 37.8	S69 48.4
Mirfak	308 30.3	N49 56.7
Nunki	75 50.2	S26 16.1
Peacock	53 08.9	S56 39.8
Pollux	243 19.0	N27 58.2
Procyon	244 52.3	N 5 09.9
Rasalhague	96 00.4	N12 32.5
Regulus	207 36.0	N11 51.3
Rigel	281 05.2	S 8 10.6
Rigil Kent.	139 42.9	S60 55.5
Sabik	102 05.0	S15 45.2
Schedar	349 32.9	N56 40.0
Shaula	96 13.1	S37 07.2
Sirius	258 27.4	S16 44.9
Spica	158 24.1	S11 16.8
Suhail	222 47.2	S43 31.3
Vega	80 34.8	N38 48.2
Zuben'ubi	136 58.1	S16 08.1

	SHA	Mer. Pass.
Venus	58 56.1	13 20
Mars	293 16.4	21 37
Jupiter	358 17.0	17 19
Saturn	34 42.5	14 53

© British Crown Copyright 2022. All rights reserved.

UT	SUN GHA	SUN Dec	MOON GHA	v	MOON Dec	d	HP
d h	° ′	° ′	° ′	′	° ′	′	′
1 00	179 12.0	S23 02.4	68 43.6	13.8	N12 03.2	13.4	56.3
01	194 11.7	02.2	83 16.4	13.8	12 16.6	13.3	56.3
02	209 11.4	02.0	97 49.2	13.8	12 29.9	13.3	56.2
03	224 11.1 ..	01.8	112 22.0	13.8	12 43.2	13.1	56.2
04	239 10.8	01.6	126 54.8	13.7	12 56.3	13.2	56.2
05	254 10.5	01.4	141 27.5	13.7	13 09.5	13.0	56.2
06	269 10.2	S23 01.2	156 00.2	13.7	N13 22.5	13.0	56.1
07	284 09.9	01.0	170 32.9	13.6	13 35.5	12.9	56.1
S 08	299 09.6	00.8	185 05.5	13.6	13 48.4	12.8	56.1
U 09	314 09.3 ..	00.6	199 38.1	13.6	14 01.2	12.8	56.0
N 10	329 09.0	00.4	214 10.7	13.6	14 14.0	12.7	56.0
D 11	344 08.7	00.2	228 43.3	13.5	14 26.7	12.6	56.0
A 12	359 08.4	S23 00.0	243 15.8	13.5	N14 39.3	12.5	56.0
Y 13	14 08.2	22 59.8	257 48.3	13.5	14 51.8	12.5	55.9
14	29 07.9	59.6	272 20.8	13.4	15 04.3	12.4	55.9
15	44 07.6 ..	59.3	286 53.2	13.4	15 16.7	12.3	55.9
16	59 07.3	59.1	301 25.6	13.4	15 29.0	12.2	55.9
17	74 07.0	58.9	315 58.0	13.3	15 41.2	12.1	55.8
18	89 06.7	S22 58.7	330 30.3	13.3	N15 53.3	12.1	55.8
19	104 06.4	58.5	345 02.6	13.2	16 05.4	12.0	55.8
20	119 06.1	58.3	359 34.8	13.2	16 17.4	11.9	55.8
21	134 05.8 ..	58.1	14 07.0	13.2	16 29.3	11.9	55.8
22	149 05.5	57.9	28 39.2	13.1	16 41.2	11.7	55.7
23	164 05.2	57.6	43 11.3	13.1	16 52.9	11.7	55.7
2 00	179 04.9	S22 57.4	57 43.4	13.1	N17 04.6	11.6	55.7
01	194 04.6	57.2	72 15.5	13.0	17 16.2	11.4	55.7
02	209 04.3	57.0	86 47.5	13.0	17 27.6	11.5	55.6
03	224 04.1 ..	56.8	101 19.5	12.9	17 39.1	11.3	55.6
04	239 03.8	56.6	115 51.4	12.9	17 50.4	11.2	55.6
05	254 03.5	56.3	130 23.3	12.8	18 01.6	11.2	55.6
06	269 03.2	S22 56.1	144 55.1	12.8	N18 12.8	11.0	55.5
07	284 02.9	55.9	159 26.9	12.8	18 23.8	11.0	55.5
08	299 02.6	55.7	173 58.7	12.7	18 34.8	10.9	55.5
M 09	314 02.3 ..	55.5	188 30.4	12.7	18 45.7	10.7	55.5
O 10	329 02.0	55.2	203 02.1	12.6	18 56.4	10.7	55.5
N 11	344 01.7	55.0	217 33.7	12.6	19 07.1	10.6	55.4
D 12	359 01.4	S22 54.8	232 05.3	12.5	N19 17.7	10.5	55.4
A 13	14 01.1	54.6	246 36.8	12.5	19 28.2	10.4	55.4
Y 14	29 00.8	54.3	261 08.3	12.4	19 38.6	10.4	55.4
15	44 00.6 ..	54.1	275 39.7	12.4	19 49.0	10.2	55.3
16	59 00.3	53.9	290 11.1	12.4	19 59.2	10.1	55.3
17	74 00.0	53.7	304 42.5	12.3	20 09.3	10.0	55.3
18	88 59.7	S22 53.4	319 13.8	12.2	N20 19.3	9.9	55.3
19	103 59.4	53.2	333 45.0	12.2	20 29.2	9.9	55.3
20	118 59.1	53.0	348 16.2	12.2	20 39.1	9.7	55.2
21	133 58.8 ..	52.7	2 47.4	12.1	20 48.8	9.6	55.2
22	148 58.5	52.5	17 18.5	12.0	20 58.4	9.5	55.2
23	163 58.2	52.3	31 49.5	12.1	21 07.9	9.4	55.2
3 00	178 58.0	S22 52.0	46 20.6	11.9	N21 17.3	9.4	55.2
01	193 57.7	51.8	60 51.5	12.0	21 26.7	9.2	55.2
02	208 57.4	51.6	75 22.5	11.8	21 35.9	9.1	55.1
03	223 57.1 ..	51.3	89 53.3	11.8	21 45.0	9.0	55.1
04	238 56.8	51.1	104 24.1	11.8	21 54.0	8.9	55.1
05	253 56.5	50.8	118 54.9	11.8	22 02.9	8.7	55.1
06	268 56.2	S22 50.6	133 25.7	11.6	N22 11.6	8.7	55.1
07	283 55.9	50.4	147 56.3	11.7	22 20.3	8.6	55.0
08	298 55.7	50.1	162 27.0	11.6	22 28.9	8.4	55.0
T 09	313 55.4 ..	49.9	176 57.6	11.5	22 37.3	8.4	55.0
U 10	328 55.1	49.6	191 28.1	11.5	22 45.7	8.2	55.0
E 11	343 54.8	49.4	205 58.6	11.4	22 53.9	8.2	55.0
S 12	358 54.5	S22 49.2	220 29.0	11.4	N23 02.1	8.0	55.0
D 13	13 54.2	48.9	234 59.4	11.4	23 10.1	7.9	54.9
A 14	28 53.9	48.7	249 29.8	11.3	23 18.0	7.8	54.9
Y 15	43 53.6 ..	48.4	264 00.1	11.2	23 25.8	7.6	54.9
16	58 53.4	48.2	278 30.3	11.2	23 33.4	7.6	54.9
17	73 53.1	47.9	293 00.5	11.2	23 41.0	7.4	54.9
18	88 52.8	S22 47.7	307 30.7	11.1	N23 48.4	7.4	54.9
19	103 52.5	47.4	322 00.8	11.1	23 55.8	7.2	54.8
20	118 52.2	47.2	336 30.9	11.0	24 03.0	7.1	54.8
21	133 51.9 ..	46.9	351 00.9	11.0	24 10.1	6.9	54.8
22	148 51.6	46.7	5 30.9	11.0	24 17.0	6.9	54.8
23	163 51.4	46.4	20 00.9	10.9	N24 23.9	6.7	54.8
	SD 16.3	d 0.2	SD 15.3		15.1		15.0

Lat.	Twilight Naut.	Twilight Civil	Sunrise	Moonrise 1	2	3	4
°	h m	h m	h m	h m	h m	h m	h m
N 72	08 23	10 40	■	10 20	□	□	□
N 70	08 04	09 48	■	10 47	09 50	□	□
68	07 49	09 16	10 26	11 08	10 36	□	□
66	07 37	08 52	10 26	11 25	11 07	10 34	□
64	07 26	08 34	09 49	11 39	11 30	11 18	10 52
62	07 17	08 18	09 22	11 50	11 48	11 47	11 49
60	07 09	08 05	09 02	12 00	12 03	12 10	12 22
N 58	07 02	07 54	08 45	12 09	12 16	12 28	12 47
56	06 55	07 44	08 31	12 17	12 28	12 43	13 07
54	06 50	07 35	08 19	12 24	12 38	12 57	13 23
52	06 44	07 27	08 08	12 30	12 47	13 08	13 37
50	06 39	07 20	07 58	12 35	12 55	13 19	13 50
45	06 28	07 05	07 38	12 48	13 12	13 40	14 15
N 40	06 18	06 52	07 22	12 58	13 26	13 58	14 36
35	06 09	06 40	07 08	13 07	13 38	14 13	14 53
30	06 00	06 30	06 56	13 14	13 48	14 26	15 08
20	05 44	06 11	06 35	13 28	14 06	14 48	15 33
N 10	05 28	05 54	06 17	13 40	14 22	15 07	15 55
0	05 12	05 38	06 00	13 51	14 37	15 25	16 15
S 10	04 53	05 20	05 43	14 02	14 52	15 43	16 36
20	04 31	05 00	05 24	14 14	15 08	16 03	16 58
30	04 02	04 36	05 03	14 28	15 27	16 26	17 24
35	03 44	04 21	04 50	14 36	15 38	16 39	17 39
40	03 22	04 03	04 35	14 45	15 51	16 55	17 56
45	02 52	03 41	04 18	14 56	16 05	17 13	18 18
S 50	02 08	03 12	03 56	15 10	16 24	17 37	18 45
52	01 42	02 57	03 45	15 16	16 33	17 48	18 58
54	01 03	02 40	03 34	15 23	16 42	18 00	19 13
56	////	02 19	03 20	15 31	16 54	18 15	19 31
58	////	01 51	03 04	15 39	17 06	18 33	19 53
S 60	////	01 08	02 44	15 49	17 22	18 54	20 21

Lat.	Sunset	Twilight Civil	Twilight Naut.	Moonset 1	2	3	4
°	h m	h m	h m	h m	h m	h m	h m
N 72	■	13 28	15 45	04 33	□	□	□
N 70	■	14 20	16 04	04 08	06 41	□	□
68	■	14 52	16 19	03 49	05 56	□	□
66	13 42	15 16	16 31	03 33	05 27	07 39	□
64	14 19	15 34	16 42	03 21	05 05	06 56	09 05
62	14 46	15 50	16 51	03 11	04 47	06 27	08 08
60	15 06	16 03	16 59	03 02	04 33	06 05	07 36
N 58	15 23	16 14	17 06	02 54	04 21	05 48	07 11
56	15 37	16 24	17 13	02 47	04 10	05 33	06 52
54	15 49	16 33	17 18	02 41	04 01	05 20	06 36
52	16 00	16 41	17 24	02 36	03 53	05 09	06 22
50	16 10	16 48	17 29	02 31	03 45	04 59	06 10
45	16 30	17 03	17 40	02 20	03 30	04 38	05 45
N 40	16 46	17 16	17 50	02 11	03 17	04 22	05 25
35	17 00	17 28	17 59	02 04	03 06	04 08	05 08
30	17 12	17 38	18 08	01 57	02 56	03 55	04 54
20	17 33	17 56	18 24	01 46	02 40	03 35	04 30
N 10	17 51	18 13	18 40	01 36	02 26	03 17	04 09
0	18 08	18 30	18 56	01 27	02 13	03 00	03 49
S 10	18 25	18 48	19 15	01 18	02 00	02 43	03 30
20	18 43	19 08	19 37	01 08	01 46	02 26	03 09
30	19 05	19 32	20 05	00 57	01 30	02 05	02 45
35	19 17	19 47	20 23	00 51	01 21	01 53	02 31
40	19 32	20 05	20 46	00 44	01 10	01 40	02 15
45	19 50	20 27	21 15	00 36	00 58	01 24	01 55
S 50	20 11	20 55	21 59	00 26	00 43	01 04	01 31
52	20 22	21 10	22 24	00 21	00 36	00 55	01 20
54	20 34	21 27	23 03	00 16	00 28	00 45	01 07
56	20 47	21 48	////	00 10	00 20	00 33	00 52
58	21 03	22 15	////	00 04	00 10	00 19	00 34
S 60	21 23	22 57	////	23 59	24 04	00 04	00 12

Day	SUN Eqn. of Time 00ʰ	SUN Eqn. of Time 12ʰ	SUN Mer. Pass.	MOON Mer. Pass. Upper	MOON Mer. Pass. Lower	Age	Phase
d	m s	m s	h m	h m	h m	d	%
1	03 11	03 26	12 03	20 02	07 39	09	74
2	03 40	03 54	12 04	20 48	08 25	10	83
3	04 08	04 21	12 04	21 37	09 13	11	89

© British Crown Copyright 2022. All rights reserved.

UT	ARIES GHA	VENUS −3.9 GHA	Dec	MARS −1.1 GHA	Dec	JUPITER −2.3 GHA	Dec	SATURN +0.8 GHA	Dec
4 00	103 20.7	159 38.5	S21 18.5	36 54.5	N24 32.4	101 24.1	S 0 32.8	137 51.3	S15 06.9
01	118 23.2	174 37.7	17.9	51 57.3	32.3	116 26.3	32.7	152 53.5	06.8
02	133 25.7	189 36.9	17.2	67 00.1	32.3	131 28.4	32.5	167 55.8	06.7
03	148 28.1	204 36.1	.. 16.6	82 02.9	.. 32.3	146 30.6	.. 32.4	182 58.0	.. 06.6
04	163 30.6	219 35.3	15.9	97 05.6	32.2	161 32.8	32.2	198 00.2	06.6
05	178 33.1	234 34.4	15.3	112 08.4	32.2	176 34.9	32.1	213 02.4	06.5
W 06	193 35.5	249 33.6	S21 14.6	127 11.2	N24 32.2	191 37.1	S 0 32.0	228 04.6	S15 06.4
E 07	208 38.0	264 32.8	14.0	142 14.0	32.1	206 39.3	31.8	243 06.8	06.3
D 08	223 40.5	279 32.0	13.3	157 16.7	32.1	221 41.5	31.7	258 09.0	06.2
N 09	238 42.9	294 31.2	.. 12.7	172 19.5	.. 32.1	236 43.6	.. 31.6	273 11.3	.. 06.1
E 10	253 45.4	309 30.3	12.0	187 22.3	32.0	251 45.8	31.4	288 13.5	06.0
S 11	268 47.8	324 29.5	11.3	202 25.1	32.0	266 48.0	31.3	303 15.7	06.0
D 12	283 50.3	339 28.7	S21 10.7	217 27.8	N24 32.0	281 50.1	S 0 31.1	318 17.9	S15 05.9
A 13	298 52.8	354 27.9	10.0	232 30.6	31.9	296 52.3	31.0	333 20.1	05.8
Y 14	313 55.2	9 27.1	09.4	247 33.4	31.9	311 54.5	30.9	348 22.3	05.7
15	328 57.7	24 26.3	.. 08.7	262 36.1	.. 31.8	326 56.7	.. 30.7	3 24.5	.. 05.6
16	344 00.2	39 25.4	08.0	277 38.9	31.8	341 58.8	30.6	18 26.7	05.5
17	359 02.6	54 24.6	07.4	292 41.7	31.8	357 01.0	30.4	33 29.0	05.5
18	14 05.1	69 23.8	S21 06.7	307 44.4	N24 31.7	12 03.2	S 0 30.3	48 31.2	S15 05.4
19	29 07.6	84 23.0	06.0	322 47.2	31.7	27 05.3	30.2	63 33.4	05.3
20	44 10.0	99 22.2	05.4	337 49.9	31.7	42 07.5	30.0	78 35.6	05.2
21	59 12.5	114 21.4	.. 04.7	352 52.7	.. 31.6	57 09.7	.. 29.9	93 37.8	.. 05.1
22	74 14.9	129 20.6	04.0	7 55.4	31.6	72 11.8	29.8	108 40.0	05.0
23	89 17.4	144 19.8	03.4	22 58.2	31.6	87 14.0	29.6	123 42.2	04.9
5 00	104 19.9	159 19.0	S21 02.7	38 00.9	N24 31.5	102 16.2	S 0 29.5	138 44.4	S15 04.9
01	119 22.3	174 18.1	02.0	53 03.7	31.5	117 18.3	29.3	153 46.7	04.8
02	134 24.8	189 17.3	01.3	68 06.4	31.5	132 20.5	29.2	168 48.9	04.7
03	149 27.3	204 16.5	.. 00.7	83 09.2	.. 31.4	147 22.7	.. 29.1	183 51.1	.. 04.6
04	164 29.7	219 15.7	21 00.0	98 11.9	31.4	162 24.8	28.9	198 53.3	04.5
05	179 32.2	234 14.9	20 59.3	113 14.7	31.4	177 27.0	28.8	213 55.5	04.4
T 06	194 34.7	249 14.1	S20 58.6	128 17.4	N24 31.3	192 29.2	S 0 28.6	228 57.7	S15 04.3
H 07	209 37.1	264 13.3	58.0	143 20.1	31.3	207 31.3	28.5	243 59.9	04.3
U 08	224 39.6	279 12.5	57.3	158 22.9	31.3	222 33.5	28.4	259 02.1	04.2
R 09	239 42.1	294 11.7	.. 56.6	173 25.6	.. 31.2	237 35.7	.. 28.2	274 04.3	.. 04.1
S 10	254 44.5	309 10.9	55.9	188 28.4	31.2	252 37.8	28.1	289 06.6	04.0
D 11	269 47.0	324 10.1	55.2	203 31.1	31.2	267 40.0	27.9	304 08.8	03.9
A 12	284 49.4	339 09.3	S20 54.5	218 33.8	N24 31.1	282 42.2	S 0 27.8	319 11.0	S15 03.8
Y 13	299 51.9	354 08.5	53.9	233 36.5	31.1	297 44.3	27.7	334 13.2	03.8
14	314 54.4	9 07.7	53.2	248 39.3	31.1	312 46.5	27.5	349 15.4	03.7
15	329 56.8	24 06.9	.. 52.5	263 42.0	.. 31.1	327 48.7	.. 27.4	4 17.6	.. 03.6
16	344 59.3	39 06.1	51.8	278 44.7	31.0	342 50.8	27.2	19 19.8	03.5
17	0 01.8	54 05.3	51.1	293 47.5	31.0	357 53.0	27.1	34 22.0	03.4
18	15 04.2	69 04.5	S20 50.4	308 50.2	N24 31.0	12 55.1	S 0 27.0	49 24.2	S15 03.3
19	30 06.7	84 03.7	49.7	323 52.9	30.9	27 57.3	26.8	64 26.5	03.2
20	45 09.2	99 02.9	49.0	338 55.6	30.9	42 59.5	26.7	79 28.7	03.2
21	60 11.6	114 02.1	.. 48.3	353 58.3	.. 30.9	58 01.6	.. 26.5	94 30.9	.. 03.1
22	75 14.1	129 01.3	47.6	9 01.0	30.8	73 03.8	26.4	109 33.1	03.0
23	90 16.6	144 00.5	46.9	24 03.8	30.8	88 06.0	26.2	124 35.3	02.9
6 00	105 19.0	158 59.7	S20 46.2	39 06.5	N24 30.8	103 08.1	S 0 26.1	139 37.5	S15 02.8
01	120 21.5	173 58.9	45.5	54 09.2	30.8	118 10.3	26.0	154 39.7	02.7
02	135 23.9	188 58.1	44.8	69 11.9	30.7	133 12.4	25.8	169 41.9	02.6
03	150 26.4	203 57.3	.. 44.1	84 14.6	.. 30.7	148 14.6	.. 25.7	184 44.1	.. 02.6
04	165 28.9	218 56.5	43.4	99 17.3	30.7	163 16.8	25.5	199 46.3	02.5
05	180 31.3	233 55.7	42.7	114 20.0	30.6	178 18.9	25.4	214 48.6	02.4
F 06	195 33.8	248 54.9	S20 42.0	129 22.7	N24 30.6	193 21.1	S 0 25.3	229 50.8	S15 02.3
R 07	210 36.3	263 54.1	41.3	144 25.4	30.6	208 23.3	25.1	244 53.0	02.2
I 08	225 38.7	278 53.3	40.6	159 28.1	30.5	223 25.4	25.0	259 55.2	02.1
D 09	240 41.2	293 52.5	.. 39.9	174 30.8	.. 30.5	238 27.6	.. 24.8	274 57.4	.. 02.0
A 10	255 43.7	308 51.7	39.2	189 33.5	30.5	253 29.7	24.7	289 59.6	02.0
Y 11	270 46.1	323 50.9	38.5	204 36.2	30.5	268 31.9	24.5	305 01.8	01.9
12	285 48.6	338 50.2	S20 37.8	219 38.9	N24 30.4	283 34.0	S 0 24.4	320 04.0	S15 01.8
13	300 51.1	353 49.4	37.1	234 41.6	30.4	298 36.2	24.3	335 06.2	01.7
14	315 53.5	8 48.6	36.4	249 44.3	30.4	313 38.4	24.1	350 08.4	01.6
15	330 56.0	23 47.8	.. 35.7	264 47.0	.. 30.3	328 40.5	.. 24.0	5 10.6	.. 01.5
16	345 58.4	38 47.0	34.9	279 49.7	30.3	343 42.7	23.8	20 12.9	01.4
17	1 00.9	53 46.2	34.2	294 52.4	30.3	358 44.8	23.7	35 15.1	01.3
18	16 03.4	68 45.4	S20 33.5	309 55.0	N24 30.3	13 47.0	S 0 23.5	50 17.3	S15 01.3
19	31 05.8	83 44.6	32.8	324 57.7	30.2	28 49.2	23.4	65 19.5	01.2
20	46 08.3	98 43.8	32.1	340 00.4	30.2	43 51.3	23.2	80 21.7	01.1
21	61 10.8	113 43.1	.. 31.4	355 03.1	.. 30.2	58 53.5	.. 23.1	95 23.9	.. 01.0
22	76 13.2	128 42.3	30.6	10 05.8	30.2	73 55.6	23.0	110 26.1	00.9
23	91 15.7	143 41.5	29.9	25 08.4	30.1	88 57.8	22.8	125 28.3	00.8
Mer. Pass. 16 59.9		*v* −0.8	*d* 0.7	*v* 2.7	*d* 0.0	*v* 2.2	*d* 0.1	*v* 2.2	*d* 0.1

STARS

Name	SHA	Dec
Acamar	315 12.8	S40 13.0
Achernar	335 21.3	S57 07.5
Acrux	173 01.8	S63 13.2
Adhara	255 06.8	S29 00.2
Aldebaran	290 41.2	N16 33.3
Alioth	166 14.4	N55 49.9
Alkaid	152 53.5	N49 11.7
Alnair	27 35.3	S46 51.2
Alnilam	275 39.1	S 1 11.3
Alphard	217 49.1	S 8 45.4
Alphecca	126 05.4	N26 38.1
Alpheratz	357 36.6	N29 13.1
Altair	62 01.9	N 8 55.7
Ankaa	353 08.9	S42 11.2
Antares	112 18.2	S26 28.9
Arcturus	145 49.6	N19 03.7
Atria	107 14.4	S69 03.9
Avior	234 14.8	S59 34.8
Bellatrix	278 24.3	N 6 22.2
Betelgeuse	270 53.6	N 7 24.7
Canopus	263 52.6	S52 42.5
Capella	280 23.9	N46 01.3
Deneb	49 27.4	N45 21.8
Denebola	182 26.6	N14 26.6
Diphda	348 49.0	S17 51.8
Dubhe	193 42.7	N61 37.4
Elnath	278 03.6	N28 37.6
Eltanin	90 43.5	N51 29.0
Enif	33 40.7	N 9 58.8
Fomalhaut	15 16.5	S29 30.3
Gacrux	171 53.4	S57 14.2
Gienah	175 45.2	S17 40.0
Hadar	148 38.6	S60 28.7
Hamal	327 53.0	N23 34.3
Kaus Aust.	83 35.1	S34 22.4
Kochab	137 20.4	N74 03.4
Markab	13 31.7	N15 19.7
Menkar	314 07.7	N 4 10.7
Menkent	147 59.7	S36 28.8
Miaplacidus	221 37.8	S69 48.4
Mirfak	308 30.3	N49 56.7
Nunki	75 50.2	S26 16.1
Peacock	53 08.9	S56 39.8
Pollux	243 19.0	N27 58.2
Procyon	244 52.2	N 5 09.9
Rasalhague	96 00.4	N12 32.5
Regulus	207 36.0	N11 51.3
Rigel	281 05.2	S 8 10.6
Rigil Kent.	139 42.9	S60 55.5
Sabik	102 05.0	S15 45.2
Schedar	349 33.0	N56 40.0
Shaula	96 13.0	S37 07.2
Sirius	258 27.3	S16 44.9
Spica	158 24.1	S11 16.8
Suhail	222 47.1	S43 31.4
Vega	80 34.8	N38 48.2
Zuben'ubi	136 58.0	S16 08.1

	SHA	Mer. Pass.
Venus	54 59.1	13 23
Mars	293 41.1	21 24
Jupiter	357 56.3	17 08
Saturn	34 24.6	14 43

© British Crown Copyright 2022. All rights reserved.

SUN and MOON

UT	SUN GHA	SUN Dec	MOON GHA	v	MOON Dec	d	HP
d h	° ′	° ′	° ′	′	° ′	′	′
4 00	178 51.1	S22 46.2	34 30.8	10.9	N24 30.6	6.6	54.8
01	193 50.8	45.9	49 00.7	10.8	24 37.2	6.5	54.7
02	208 50.5	45.7	63 30.5	10.8	24 43.7	6.4	54.7
03	223 50.2	45.4	78 00.3	10.7	24 50.1	6.3	54.7
04	238 49.9	45.1	92 30.0	10.7	24 56.4	6.1	54.7
05	253 49.7	44.9	106 59.7	10.6	25 02.5	6.0	54.7
06	268 49.4	S22 44.6	121 29.3	10.7	N25 08.5	5.9	54.7
W 07	283 49.1	44.4	135 59.0	10.6	25 14.4	5.7	54.7
E 08	298 48.8	44.1	150 28.6	10.5	25 20.1	5.7	54.6
D 09	313 48.5	43.9	164 58.1	10.5	25 25.8	5.5	54.6
N 10	328 48.2	43.6	179 27.6	10.5	25 31.3	5.4	54.6
E 11	343 48.0	43.3	193 57.1	10.4	25 36.7	5.2	54.6
S 12	358 47.7	S22 43.1	208 26.5	10.4	N25 41.9	5.2	54.6
D 13	13 47.4	42.8	222 55.9	10.4	25 47.1	5.0	54.6
A 14	28 47.1	42.5	237 25.3	10.3	25 52.1	4.8	54.6
Y 15	43 46.8	42.3	251 54.6	10.3	25 56.9	4.8	54.5
16	58 46.5	42.0	266 23.9	10.3	26 01.7	4.6	54.5
17	73 46.3	41.7	280 53.2	10.3	26 06.3	4.5	54.5
18	88 46.0	S22 41.5	295 22.5	10.2	N26 10.8	4.3	54.5
19	103 45.7	41.2	309 51.7	10.2	26 15.1	4.3	54.5
20	118 45.4	40.9	324 20.9	10.1	26 19.4	4.1	54.5
21	133 45.1	40.7	338 50.0	10.2	26 23.5	3.9	54.5
22	148 44.9	40.4	353 19.2	10.1	26 27.4	3.9	54.4
23	163 44.6	40.1	7 48.3	10.1	26 31.3	3.7	54.4
5 00	178 44.3	S22 39.9	22 17.4	10.0	N26 35.0	3.6	54.4
01	193 44.0	39.6	36 46.4	10.1	26 38.6	3.4	54.4
02	208 43.7	39.3	51 15.5	10.0	26 42.0	3.3	54.4
03	223 43.5	39.0	65 44.5	10.0	26 45.3	3.2	54.4
04	238 43.2	38.8	80 13.5	10.0	26 48.5	3.1	54.4
05	253 42.9	38.5	94 42.5	9.9	26 51.6	2.9	54.4
06	268 42.6	S22 38.2	109 11.4	10.0	N26 54.5	2.8	54.4
T 07	283 42.3	37.9	123 40.4	9.9	26 57.3	2.6	54.4
H 08	298 42.1	37.6	138 09.3	9.9	26 59.9	2.5	54.3
U 09	313 41.8	37.4	152 38.2	9.9	27 02.4	2.4	54.3
R 10	328 41.5	37.1	167 07.1	9.9	27 04.8	2.2	54.3
S 11	343 41.2	36.8	181 36.0	9.9	27 07.0	2.2	54.3
D 12	358 40.9	S22 36.5	196 04.9	9.9	N27 09.2	1.9	54.3
A 13	13 40.7	36.2	210 33.8	9.8	27 11.1	1.9	54.3
Y 14	28 40.4	36.0	225 02.6	9.9	27 13.0	1.7	54.3
15	43 40.1	35.7	239 31.5	9.8	27 14.7	1.6	54.3
16	58 39.8	35.4	254 00.3	9.9	27 16.3	1.4	54.3
17	73 39.6	35.1	268 29.2	9.8	27 17.7	1.3	54.3
18	88 39.3	S22 34.8	282 58.0	9.8	N27 19.0	1.2	54.2
19	103 39.0	34.5	297 26.8	9.9	27 20.2	1.0	54.2
20	118 38.7	34.2	311 55.7	9.8	27 21.2	0.9	54.2
21	133 38.4	34.0	326 24.5	9.8	27 22.1	0.8	54.2
22	148 38.2	33.7	340 53.3	9.9	27 22.9	0.6	54.2
23	163 37.9	33.4	355 22.2	9.8	27 23.5	0.5	54.2
6 00	178 37.6	S22 33.1	9 51.0	9.9	N27 24.0	0.4	54.2
01	193 37.3	32.8	24 19.9	9.8	27 24.4	0.2	54.2
02	208 37.1	32.5	38 48.7	9.9	27 24.6	0.1	54.2
03	223 36.8	32.2	53 17.6	9.8	27 24.7	0.1	54.2
04	238 36.5	31.9	67 46.5	9.8	27 24.6	0.2	54.2
05	253 36.2	31.6	82 15.3	9.9	27 24.4	0.3	54.2
06	268 36.0	S22 31.3	96 44.2	9.9	N27 24.1	0.4	54.1
07	283 35.7	31.0	111 13.1	10.0	27 23.7	0.6	54.1
08	298 35.4	30.7	125 42.1	9.9	27 23.1	0.7	54.1
F 09	313 35.1	30.4	140 11.0	9.9	27 22.4	0.9	54.1
R 10	328 34.9	30.1	154 39.9	10.0	27 21.5	0.9	54.1
I 11	343 34.6	29.8	169 08.9	10.0	27 20.6	1.2	54.1
D 12	358 34.3	S22 29.5	183 37.9	10.0	N27 19.4	1.2	54.1
A 13	13 34.1	29.2	198 06.9	10.0	27 18.2	1.4	54.1
Y 14	28 33.8	28.9	212 35.9	10.0	27 16.8	1.5	54.1
15	43 33.5	28.6	227 04.9	10.1	27 15.3	1.7	54.1
16	58 33.2	28.3	241 34.0	10.1	27 13.6	1.7	54.1
17	73 33.0	28.0	256 03.1	10.1	27 11.9	1.9	54.1
18	88 32.7	S22 27.7	270 32.2	10.2	N27 10.0	2.1	54.1
19	103 32.4	27.4	285 01.4	10.1	27 07.9	2.2	54.1
20	118 32.1	27.1	299 30.5	10.2	27 05.7	2.3	54.0
21	133 31.9	26.8	313 59.7	10.3	27 03.4	2.4	54.0
22	148 31.6	26.5	328 29.0	10.2	27 01.0	2.6	54.0
23	163 31.3	26.2	342 58.2	10.3	N26 58.4	2.7	54.0
SD	16.3	d 0.3	SD 14.9		14.8		14.7

Twilight, Sunrise and Moonrise

Lat.	Twilight Naut.	Civil	Sunrise	Moonrise 4	5	6	7
	h m	h m	h m	h m	h m	h m	h m
N 72	08 20	10 30	■	□	□	□	□
N 70	08 02	09 43	■	□	□	□	□
68	07 47	09 12	11 31	□	□	□	□
66	07 35	08 50	10 20	□	□	□	□
64	07 25	08 32	09 45	10 52	□	□	□
62	07 16	08 17	09 20	11 49	12 00	12 46	14 14
60	07 08	08 04	09 00	12 22	12 48	13 37	14 51
N 58	07 01	07 53	08 44	12 47	13 18	14 09	15 17
56	06 55	07 43	08 30	13 07	13 42	14 33	15 38
54	06 49	07 35	08 18	13 23	14 01	14 52	15 55
52	06 44	07 27	08 07	13 37	14 17	15 08	16 10
50	06 39	07 20	07 58	13 50	14 30	15 22	16 23
45	06 28	07 05	07 38	14 15	14 59	15 50	16 49
N 40	06 18	06 52	07 22	14 36	15 21	16 12	17 10
35	06 09	06 41	07 08	14 53	15 39	16 31	17 27
30	06 01	06 30	06 57	15 08	15 55	16 47	17 42
20	05 45	06 12	06 36	15 33	16 22	17 14	18 07
N 10	05 29	05 56	06 18	15 55	16 45	17 37	18 28
0	05 13	05 39	06 02	16 15	17 07	17 58	18 49
S 10	04 55	05 22	05 45	16 36	17 28	18 20	19 09
20	04 33	05 02	05 26	16 58	17 52	18 43	19 30
30	04 05	04 38	05 05	17 24	18 19	19 10	19 55
35	03 47	04 23	04 53	17 39	18 35	19 25	20 10
40	03 25	04 06	04 38	17 56	18 53	19 44	20 27
45	02 56	03 44	04 21	18 18	19 16	20 06	20 47
S 50	02 13	03 16	03 59	18 45	19 45	20 34	21 12
52	01 48	03 02	03 49	18 58	19 59	20 48	21 24
54	01 12	02 45	03 37	19 13	20 15	21 04	21 38
56	////	02 24	03 24	19 31	20 35	21 23	21 55
58	////	01 58	03 08	19 53	20 59	21 46	22 14
S 60	////	01 18	02 49	20 21	21 32	22 16	22 38

Sunset, Twilight and Moonset

Lat.	Sunset	Twilight Civil	Naut.	Moonset 4	5	6	7
	h m	h m	h m	h m	h m	h m	h m
N 72	■	13 41	15 51	□	□	□	□
N 70	■	14 28	16 09	□	□	□	□
68	12 40	14 59	16 24	□	□	□	□
66	13 51	15 21	16 36	□	□	□	□
64	14 26	15 39	16 46	09 05	□	□	□
62	14 51	15 54	16 58	08 08	09 44	10 46	11 04
60	15 11	16 07	17 03	07 36	08 56	09 54	10 26
N 58	15 27	16 18	17 10	07 11	08 26	09 22	09 59
56	15 41	16 27	17 16	06 52	08 03	08 59	09 38
54	15 53	16 36	17 22	06 36	07 44	08 39	09 21
52	16 03	16 44	17 27	06 22	07 28	08 23	09 06
50	16 13	16 51	17 32	06 10	07 14	08 09	08 53
45	16 33	17 07	17 43	05 45	06 46	07 41	08 26
N 40	16 49	17 19	17 53	05 25	06 24	07 18	08 05
35	17 02	17 30	18 02	05 08	06 06	07 00	07 47
30	17 14	17 40	18 10	04 54	05 51	06 44	07 32
20	17 34	17 58	18 26	04 30	05 24	06 17	07 06
N 10	17 52	18 15	18 41	04 09	05 01	05 53	06 44
0	18 09	18 31	18 57	03 49	04 40	05 32	06 23
S 10	18 26	18 49	19 16	03 30	04 19	05 10	06 02
20	18 44	19 08	19 37	03 09	03 56	04 47	05 39
30	19 05	19 32	20 05	02 45	03 30	04 19	05 13
35	19 18	19 47	20 23	02 31	03 14	04 03	04 57
40	19 32	20 04	20 45	02 15	02 56	03 45	04 39
45	19 49	20 26	21 14	01 55	02 35	03 22	04 17
S 50	20 11	20 54	21 56	01 31	02 07	02 53	03 50
52	20 21	21 08	22 21	01 20	01 54	02 39	03 36
54	20 33	21 25	22 56	01 07	01 38	02 22	03 20
56	20 46	21 45	////	00 52	01 20	02 03	03 02
58	21 01	22 11	////	00 34	00 58	01 38	02 39
S 60	21 20	22 50	////	00 12	00 29	01 05	02 08

SUN and MOON

Day	SUN Eqn. of Time 00h	12h	Mer. Pass.	MOON Mer. Pass. Upper	Lower	Age	Phase
d	m s	m s	h m	h m	h m	d	%
4	04 35	04 49	12 05	22 28	10 02	12	95
5	05 02	05 16	12 05	23 19	10 53	13	98
6	05 29	05 42	12 06	24 11	11 45	14	100

© British Crown Copyright 2022. All rights reserved.

UT (d h)	ARIES GHA	VENUS −3.9 GHA	Dec	MARS −1.0 GHA	Dec	JUPITER −2.3 GHA	Dec	SATURN +0.8 GHA	Dec	STARS Name	SHA	Dec
7 00	106 18.2	158 40.7	S20 29.2	40 11.1	N24 30.1	103 59.9	S 0 22.7	140 30.5	S15 00.7	Acamar	315 12.8	S40 13.0
01	121 20.6	173 39.9	28.5	55 13.8	30.1	119 02.1	22.5	155 32.7	00.7	Achernar	335 21.3	S57 07.5
02	136 23.1	188 39.1	27.7	70 16.5	30.0	134 04.3	22.4	170 34.9	00.6	Acrux	173 01.8	S63 13.3
03	151 25.6	203 38.4	.. 27.0	85 19.1	.. 30.0	149 06.4	.. 22.2	185 37.1	.. 00.5	Adhara	255 06.8	S29 00.2
04	166 28.0	218 37.6	26.3	100 21.8	30.0	164 08.6	22.1	200 39.4	00.4	Aldebaran	290 41.2	N16 33.3
05	181 30.5	233 36.8	25.6	115 24.5	30.0	179 10.7	22.0	215 41.6	00.3			
06	196 32.9	248 36.0	S20 24.8	130 27.1	N24 29.9	194 12.9	S 0 21.8	230 43.8	S15 00.2	Alioth	166 14.4	N55 49.8
S 07	211 35.4	263 35.2	24.1	145 29.8	29.9	209 15.0	21.7	245 46.0	00.1	Alkaid	152 53.4	N49 11.7
A 08	226 37.9	278 34.5	23.4	160 32.5	29.9	224 17.2	21.5	260 48.2	00.0	Alnair	27 35.3	S46 51.2
T 09	241 40.3	293 33.7	.. 22.6	175 35.1	.. 29.9	239 19.3	.. 21.4	275 50.4	15 00.0	Alnilam	275 39.1	S 1 11.3
U 10	256 42.8	308 32.9	21.9	190 37.8	29.8	254 21.5	21.2	290 52.6	14 59.9	Alphard	217 49.1	S 8 45.5
R 11	271 45.3	323 32.1	21.2	205 40.4	29.8	269 23.6	21.1	305 54.8	59.8			
D 12	286 47.7	338 31.3	S20 20.4	220 43.1	N24 29.8	284 25.8	S 0 20.9	320 57.0	S14 59.7	Alphecca	126 05.4	N26 38.1
A 13	301 50.2	353 30.6	19.7	235 45.8	29.8	299 27.9	20.8	335 59.2	59.6	Alpheratz	357 36.6	N29 13.1
Y 14	316 52.7	8 29.8	19.0	250 48.4	29.7	314 30.1	20.6	351 01.4	59.5	Altair	62 01.9	N 8 55.7
15	331 55.1	23 29.0	.. 18.2	265 51.1	.. 29.7	329 32.3	.. 20.5	6 03.6	.. 59.4	Ankaa	353 08.9	S42 11.2
16	346 57.6	38 28.2	17.5	280 53.7	29.7	344 34.4	20.4	21 05.8	59.4	Antares	112 18.2	S26 28.9
17	2 00.1	53 27.5	16.7	295 56.4	29.7	359 36.6	20.2	36 08.0	59.3			
18	17 02.5	68 26.7	S20 16.0	310 59.0	N24 29.6	14 38.7	S 0 20.1	51 10.3	S14 59.2	Arcturus	145 49.5	N19 03.7
19	32 05.0	83 25.9	15.3	326 01.7	29.6	29 40.9	19.9	66 12.5	59.1	Atria	107 14.4	S69 03.9
20	47 07.4	98 25.1	14.5	341 04.3	29.6	44 43.0	19.8	81 14.7	59.0	Avior	234 14.8	S59 34.8
21	62 09.9	113 24.4	.. 13.8	356 07.0	.. 29.6	59 45.2	.. 19.6	96 16.9	.. 58.9	Bellatrix	278 24.3	N 6 22.2
22	77 12.4	128 23.6	13.0	11 09.6	29.5	74 47.3	19.5	111 19.1	58.8	Betelgeuse	270 53.5	N 7 24.6
23	92 14.8	143 22.8	12.3	26 12.2	29.5	89 49.5	19.3	126 21.3	58.7			
8 00	107 17.3	158 22.1	S20 11.5	41 14.9	N24 29.5	104 51.6	S 0 19.2	141 23.5	S14 58.7	Canopus	263 52.6	S52 42.5
01	122 19.8	173 21.3	10.8	56 17.5	29.5	119 53.8	19.0	156 25.7	58.6	Capella	280 23.9	N46 01.3
02	137 22.2	188 20.5	10.0	71 20.1	29.4	134 55.9	18.9	171 27.9	58.5	Deneb	49 27.4	N45 21.8
03	152 24.7	203 19.7	.. 09.3	86 22.8	.. 29.4	149 58.1	.. 18.7	186 30.1	.. 58.4	Denebola	182 26.5	N14 26.5
04	167 27.2	218 19.0	08.5	101 25.4	29.4	165 00.2	18.6	201 32.3	58.3	Diphda	348 49.0	S17 51.8
05	182 29.6	233 18.2	07.8	116 28.0	29.4	180 02.4	18.5	216 34.5	58.2			
06	197 32.1	248 17.4	S20 07.0	131 30.7	N24 29.4	195 04.5	S 0 18.3	231 36.7	S14 58.1	Dubhe	193 42.7	N61 37.4
07	212 34.5	263 16.7	06.3	146 33.3	29.3	210 06.7	18.2	246 38.9	58.0	Elnath	278 03.6	N28 37.6
08	227 37.0	278 15.9	05.5	161 35.9	29.3	225 08.8	18.0	261 41.1	58.0	Eltanin	90 45.3	N51 29.0
S 09	242 39.5	293 15.1	.. 04.8	176 38.6	.. 29.3	240 11.0	.. 17.9	276 43.3	.. 57.9	Enif	33 40.7	N 9 58.8
U 10	257 41.9	308 14.4	04.0	191 41.2	29.3	255 13.1	17.7	291 45.6	57.8	Fomalhaut	15 16.5	S29 30.3
N 11	272 44.4	323 13.6	03.3	206 43.8	29.2	270 15.3	17.6	306 47.8	57.7			
D 12	287 46.9	338 12.8	S20 02.5	221 46.4	N24 29.2	285 17.4	S 0 17.4	321 50.0	S14 57.6	Gacrux	171 53.4	S57 14.2
A 13	302 49.3	353 12.1	01.7	236 49.0	29.2	300 19.6	17.3	336 52.2	57.5	Gienah	175 45.2	S17 40.1
Y 14	317 51.8	8 11.3	01.0	251 51.7	29.2	315 21.7	17.1	351 54.4	57.4	Hadar	148 38.5	S60 28.7
15	332 54.3	23 10.6	20 00.2	266 54.3	.. 29.2	330 23.8	.. 17.0	6 56.6	.. 57.3	Hamal	327 53.0	N23 34.3
16	347 56.7	38 09.8	19 59.4	281 56.9	29.1	345 26.0	16.8	21 58.8	57.3	Kaus Aust.	83 35.1	S34 22.4
17	2 59.2	53 09.0	58.7	296 59.5	29.1	0 28.1	16.7	37 01.0	57.2			
18	18 01.7	68 08.3	S19 57.9	312 02.1	N24 29.1	15 30.3	S 0 16.5	52 03.2	S14 57.1	Kochab	137 20.3	N74 03.3
19	33 04.1	83 07.5	57.2	327 04.7	29.1	30 32.4	16.4	67 05.4	57.0	Markab	13 31.7	N15 19.7
20	48 06.6	98 06.8	56.4	342 07.3	29.1	45 34.6	16.2	82 07.6	56.9	Menkar	314 07.7	N 4 10.7
21	63 09.0	113 06.0	.. 55.6	357 09.9	.. 29.0	60 36.7	.. 16.1	97 09.8	.. 56.8	Menkent	147 59.7	S36 28.8
22	78 11.5	128 05.2	54.8	12 12.5	29.0	75 38.9	15.9	112 12.0	56.7	Miaplacidus	221 37.8	S69 48.5
23	93 14.0	143 04.4	54.1	27 15.1	29.0	90 41.0	15.8	127 14.2	56.6			
9 00	108 16.4	158 03.7	S19 53.3	42 17.7	N24 29.0	105 43.2	S 0 15.6	142 16.4	S14 56.6	Mirfak	308 30.3	N49 56.7
01	123 18.9	173 03.0	52.5	57 20.3	29.0	120 45.3	15.5	157 18.6	56.5	Nunki	75 50.2	S26 16.1
02	138 21.4	188 02.2	51.8	72 22.9	28.9	135 47.5	15.3	172 20.8	56.4	Peacock	53 08.9	S56 39.8
03	153 23.8	203 01.4	.. 51.0	87 25.5	.. 28.9	150 49.6	.. 15.2	187 23.0	.. 56.3	Pollux	243 19.0	N27 58.2
04	168 26.3	218 00.7	50.2	102 28.1	28.9	165 51.7	15.0	202 25.2	56.2	Procyon	244 52.2	N 5 09.9
05	183 28.8	232 59.9	49.4	117 30.7	28.9	180 53.9	14.9	217 27.4	56.1			
06	198 31.2	247 59.2	S19 48.7	132 33.3	N24 28.9	195 56.0	S 0 14.8	232 29.6	S14 56.0	Rasalhague	96 00.4	N12 32.5
07	213 33.7	262 58.4	47.9	147 35.9	28.8	210 58.2	14.6	247 31.9	55.9	Regulus	207 36.0	N11 51.2
08	228 36.2	277 57.7	47.1	162 38.5	28.8	226 00.3	14.5	262 34.1	55.9	Rigel	281 05.1	S 8 10.6
M 09	243 38.6	292 56.9	.. 46.3	177 41.1	.. 28.8	241 02.5	.. 14.3	277 36.3	.. 55.8	Rigil Kent.	139 42.8	S60 55.5
O 10	258 41.1	307 56.2	45.5	192 43.7	28.8	256 04.6	14.2	292 38.5	55.7	Sabik	102 05.0	S15 45.2
N 11	273 43.5	322 55.4	44.8	207 46.3	28.8	271 06.7	14.0	307 40.7	55.6			
D 12	288 46.0	337 54.7	S19 44.0	222 48.9	N24 28.7	286 08.9	S 0 13.9	322 42.9	S14 55.5	Schedar	349 33.0	N56 40.0
A 13	303 48.5	352 53.9	43.2	237 51.4	28.7	301 11.0	13.7	337 45.1	55.4	Shaula	96 13.0	S37 07.2
Y 14	318 50.9	7 53.2	42.4	252 54.0	28.7	316 13.2	13.6	352 47.3	55.3	Sirius	258 27.3	S16 44.9
15	333 53.4	22 52.4	.. 41.6	267 56.6	.. 28.7	331 15.3	.. 13.4	7 49.5	.. 55.2	Spica	158 24.1	S11 16.8
16	348 55.9	37 51.7	40.8	282 59.2	28.7	346 17.5	13.3	22 51.7	55.1	Suhail	222 47.1	S43 31.4
17	3 58.3	52 50.9	40.0	298 01.8	28.7	1 19.6	13.1	37 53.9	55.0			
18	19 00.8	67 50.2	S19 39.3	313 04.3	N24 28.6	16 21.7	S 0 13.0	52 56.1	S14 55.0	Vega	80 34.8	N38 48.2
19	34 03.3	82 49.4	38.5	328 06.9	28.6	31 23.9	12.8	67 58.3	54.9	Zuben'ubi	136 58.0	S16 08.1
20	49 05.7	97 48.7	37.7	343 09.5	28.6	46 26.0	12.7	83 00.5	54.8			
21	64 08.2	112 47.9	.. 36.9	358 12.0	.. 28.6	61 28.2	.. 12.5	98 02.7	.. 54.7			
22	79 10.7	127 47.2	36.1	13 14.6	28.6	76 30.3	12.3	113 04.9	54.6			
23	94 13.1	142 46.4	35.3	28 17.2	28.6	91 32.4	12.2	128 07.1	54.5			
Mer.Pass.	16 48.1	v −0.8	d 0.8	v 2.6	d 0.0	v 2.1	d 0.1	v 2.2	d 0.1			

	SHA	Mer. Pass.
	° '	h m
Venus	51 04.8	13 27
Mars	293 57.6	21 11
Jupiter	357 34.3	16 58
Saturn	34 06.2	14 32

© British Crown Copyright 2022. All rights reserved.

UT	SUN GHA	SUN Dec	MOON GHA	v	Dec	d	HP
d h	° ′	° ′	° ′	′	° ′	′	′
7 00	178 31.1	S22 25.9	357 27.5	10.4	N26 55.7	2.8	54.0
01	193 30.8	25.6	11 56.9	10.3	26 52.9	2.9	54.0
02	208 30.5	25.3	26 26.2	10.4	26 50.0	3.1	54.0
03	223 30.3	. . 25.0	40 55.6	10.5	26 46.9	3.2	54.0
04	238 30.0	24.6	55 25.1	10.4	26 43.7	3.3	54.0
05	253 29.7	24.3	69 54.5	10.5	26 40.4	3.5	54.0
06	268 29.4	S22 24.0	84 24.0	10.6	N26 36.9	3.6	54.0
07	283 29.2	23.7	98 53.6	10.6	26 33.3	3.7	54.0
08	298 28.9	23.4	113 23.2	10.6	26 29.6	3.8	54.0
09	313 28.6	. . 23.1	127 52.8	10.7	26 25.8	4.0	54.0
10	328 28.4	22.8	142 22.5	10.7	26 21.8	4.1	54.0
11	343 28.1	22.4	156 52.2	10.8	26 17.7	4.2	54.0
12	358 27.8	S22 22.1	171 22.0	10.8	N26 13.5	4.3	54.0
13	13 27.6	21.8	185 51.8	10.8	26 09.2	4.5	54.0
14	28 27.3	21.5	200 21.6	10.9	26 04.7	4.6	54.0
15	43 27.0	. . 21.2	214 51.5	10.9	26 00.1	4.7	54.0
16	58 26.8	20.8	229 21.4	11.0	25 55.4	4.8	54.0
17	73 26.5	20.5	243 51.4	11.1	25 50.6	4.9	54.0
18	88 26.2	S22 20.2	258 21.5	11.1	N25 45.7	5.1	54.0
19	103 26.0	19.9	272 51.6	11.1	25 40.6	5.2	54.0
20	118 25.7	19.5	287 21.7	11.2	25 35.4	5.3	54.0
21	133 25.4	. . 19.2	301 51.9	11.2	25 30.1	5.4	54.0
22	148 25.2	18.9	316 22.1	11.3	25 24.7	5.5	54.0
23	163 24.9	18.6	330 52.4	11.4	25 19.2	5.6	54.0
8 00	178 24.6	S22 18.2	345 22.8	11.4	N25 13.6	5.8	54.0
01	193 24.4	17.9	359 53.2	11.4	25 07.8	5.9	54.0
02	208 24.1	17.6	14 23.6	11.5	25 01.9	6.0	54.0
03	223 23.8	. . 17.3	28 54.1	11.6	24 55.9	6.1	54.0
04	238 23.6	16.9	43 24.7	11.6	24 49.8	6.2	53.9
05	253 23.3	16.6	57 55.3	11.7	24 43.6	6.3	53.9
06	268 23.0	S22 16.3	72 26.0	11.7	N24 37.3	6.5	53.9
07	283 22.8	15.9	86 56.7	11.8	24 30.8	6.5	53.9
08	298 22.5	15.6	101 27.5	11.8	24 24.3	6.7	53.9
09	313 22.2	. . 15.3	115 58.3	11.9	24 17.6	6.7	53.9
10	328 22.0	14.9	130 29.2	12.0	24 10.9	6.9	53.9
11	343 21.7	14.6	145 00.2	12.0	24 04.0	7.0	53.9
12	358 21.4	S22 14.3	159 31.2	12.1	N23 57.0	7.1	53.9
13	13 21.2	13.9	174 02.3	12.1	23 49.9	7.2	53.9
14	28 20.9	13.6	188 33.4	12.2	23 42.7	7.3	53.9
15	43 20.7	. . 13.2	203 04.6	12.2	23 35.4	7.4	53.9
16	58 20.4	12.9	217 35.8	12.3	23 28.0	7.5	54.0
17	73 20.1	12.6	232 07.1	12.4	23 20.5	7.6	54.0
18	88 19.9	S22 12.2	246 38.5	12.4	N23 12.9	7.7	54.0
19	103 19.6	11.9	261 09.9	12.5	23 05.2	7.8	54.0
20	118 19.3	11.5	275 41.4	12.6	22 57.4	7.9	54.0
21	133 19.1	. . 11.2	290 13.0	12.6	22 49.5	8.1	54.0
22	148 18.8	10.8	304 44.6	12.6	22 41.4	8.1	54.0
23	163 18.6	10.5	319 16.2	12.8	22 33.3	8.2	54.0
9 00	178 18.3	S22 10.2	333 48.0	12.8	N22 25.1	8.3	54.0
01	193 18.0	09.8	348 19.8	12.8	22 16.8	8.4	54.0
02	208 17.8	09.5	2 51.6	12.9	22 08.4	8.5	54.0
03	223 17.5	. . 09.1	17 23.5	13.0	21 59.9	8.6	54.0
04	238 17.3	08.8	31 55.5	13.0	21 51.3	8.7	54.0
05	253 17.0	08.4	46 27.5	13.1	21 42.6	8.8	54.0
06	268 16.7	S22 08.1	60 59.6	13.2	N21 33.8	8.9	54.0
07	283 16.5	07.7	75 31.8	13.2	21 24.9	8.9	54.0
08	298 16.2	07.4	90 04.0	13.2	21 16.0	9.1	54.0
09	313 16.0	. . 07.0	104 36.2	13.4	21 06.9	9.1	54.0
10	328 15.7	06.7	119 08.6	13.4	20 57.8	9.3	54.0
11	343 15.5	06.3	133 41.0	13.4	20 48.5	9.3	54.0
12	358 15.2	S22 06.0	148 13.4	13.5	N20 39.2	9.4	54.0
13	13 14.9	05.6	162 45.9	13.6	20 29.8	9.5	54.0
14	28 14.7	05.2	177 18.5	13.6	20 20.3	9.6	54.0
15	43 14.4	. . 04.9	191 51.1	13.7	20 10.7	9.7	54.0
16	58 14.2	04.5	206 23.8	13.7	20 01.0	9.7	54.0
17	73 13.9	04.2	220 56.5	13.8	19 51.3	9.9	54.0
18	88 13.7	S22 03.8	235 29.3	13.9	N19 41.4	9.9	54.0
19	103 13.4	03.4	250 02.2	13.9	19 31.5	10.0	54.0
20	118 13.1	03.1	264 35.1	14.0	19 21.5	10.1	54.0
21	133 12.9	. . 02.7	279 08.1	14.0	19 11.4	10.2	54.1
22	148 12.6	02.4	293 41.1	14.1	19 01.2	10.2	54.1
23	163 12.4	02.0	308 14.2	14.1	N18 51.0	10.3	54.1
	SD 16.3	d 0.3	SD 14.7		14.7		14.7

Moonrise table:

Lat.	Twilight Naut.	Twilight Civil	Sunrise	Moonrise 7	8	9	10
°	h m	h m	h m	h m	h m	h m	h m
N 72	08 15	10 20	■■	□	□	□	17 06
N 70	07 58	09 37	■■	□	□	□	17 45
68	07 44	09 08	11 10	□	□	15 59	18 11
66	07 33	08 46	10 13	□	14 10	16 39	18 31
64	07 23	08 29	09 40	□	15 17	17 07	18 47
62	07 14	08 14	09 16	14 14	15 52	17 28	19 00
60	07 07	08 02	08 57	14 51	16 17	17 45	19 12
N 58	07 00	07 51	08 41	15 17	16 37	17 59	19 21
56	06 54	07 42	08 28	15 38	16 53	18 11	19 30
54	06 48	07 34	08 16	15 55	17 07	18 22	19 37
52	06 43	07 26	08 06	16 10	17 19	18 31	19 44
50	06 38	07 19	07 57	16 23	17 30	18 40	19 50
45	06 28	07 04	07 38	16 49	17 52	18 57	20 03
N 40	06 18	06 52	07 22	17 10	18 10	19 12	20 13
35	06 09	06 41	07 09	17 27	18 25	19 24	20 22
30	06 01	06 31	06 57	17 42	18 38	19 34	20 30
20	05 46	06 13	06 37	18 07	19 00	19 52	20 43
N 10	05 31	05 57	06 19	18 28	19 19	20 08	20 55
0	05 15	05 41	06 03	18 49	19 37	20 23	21 06
S 10	04 57	05 23	05 46	19 09	19 55	20 37	21 17
20	04 35	05 04	05 28	19 30	20 13	20 53	21 29
30	04 07	04 40	05 07	19 55	20 35	21 11	21 42
35	03 50	04 26	04 55	20 10	20 48	21 21	21 50
40	03 28	04 09	04 41	20 27	21 02	21 33	21 58
45	03 00	03 48	04 24	20 47	21 20	21 46	22 08
S 50	02 19	03 20	04 03	21 12	21 41	22 03	22 21
52	01 55	03 06	03 53	21 24	21 51	22 11	22 26
54	01 22	02 50	03 42	21 38	22 02	22 19	22 32
56	////	02 30	03 29	21 55	22 15	22 29	22 39
58	////	02 05	03 13	22 14	22 30	22 40	22 47
S 60	////	01 29	02 55	22 38	22 48	22 53	22 55

Moonset table:

Lat.	Sunset	Twilight Civil	Naut.	Moonset 7	8	9	10
°	h m	h m	h m	h m	h m	h m	h m
N 72	■■	13 54	15 59	□	□	□	13 06
N 70	■■	14 37	16 16	□	□	□	12 26
68	13 03	15 06	16 30	□	□	12 38	11 57
66	14 00	15 28	16 41	□	12 49	11 57	11 36
64	14 33	15 45	16 51	□	11 42	11 28	11 19
62	14 57	15 59	16 59	11 04	11 07	11 07	11 05
60	15 16	16 11	17 07	10 26	10 41	10 49	10 53
N 58	15 32	16 22	17 14	09 59	10 21	10 34	10 42
56	15 46	16 31	17 20	09 38	10 04	10 21	10 33
54	15 57	16 40	17 25	09 21	09 50	10 10	10 25
52	16 07	16 47	17 30	09 06	09 37	10 00	10 18
50	16 17	16 54	17 35	08 53	09 26	09 51	10 11
45	16 36	17 09	17 46	08 26	09 03	09 32	09 57
N 40	16 51	17 22	17 55	08 05	08 44	09 17	09 45
35	17 05	17 33	18 04	07 47	08 29	09 04	09 35
30	17 16	17 42	18 12	07 32	08 15	08 52	09 26
20	17 36	18 00	18 27	07 06	07 52	08 33	09 10
N 10	17 54	18 16	18 43	06 44	07 31	08 16	08 57
0	18 10	18 33	18 59	06 23	07 12	07 59	08 44
S 10	18 27	18 50	19 17	06 02	06 53	07 43	08 31
20	18 45	19 09	19 38	05 39	06 33	07 26	08 17
30	19 05	19 33	20 05	05 13	06 09	07 05	08 01
35	19 18	19 47	20 23	04 57	05 55	06 53	07 52
40	19 32	20 04	20 44	04 38	05 38	06 40	07 42
45	19 49	20 25	21 13	04 17	05 19	06 23	07 29
S 50	20 10	20 52	21 53	03 50	04 54	06 03	07 13
52	20 20	21 06	22 16	03 36	04 42	05 53	07 06
54	20 31	21 22	22 49	03 20	04 29	05 43	06 58
56	20 44	21 42	////	03 02	04 13	05 30	06 49
58	20 59	22 06	////	02 39	03 54	05 16	06 39
S 60	21 17	22 42	////	02 08	03 30	04 59	06 27

Day	SUN Eqn. of Time 00h	12h	Mer. Pass.	MOON Mer. Pass. Upper	Lower	Age	Phase
d	m s	m s	h m	h m	h m	d	%
7	05 55	06 08	12 06	12 36	00 11	15	100
8	06 21	06 34	12 07	01 00	13 25	16	98
9	06 46	06 59	12 07	01 48	14 11	17	94

© British Crown Copyright 2022. All rights reserved.

UT	ARIES GHA	VENUS −3.9 GHA	Dec	MARS −0.9 GHA	Dec	JUPITER −2.3 GHA	Dec	SATURN +0.8 GHA	Dec
d h	° ′	° ′	° ′	° ′	° ′	° ′	° ′	° ′	° ′
10 00	109 15.6	157 45.7	S19 34.5	43 19.7	N24 28.5	106 34.6	S 0 12.0	143 09.3	S14 54.4
01	124 18.0	172 45.0	33.7	58 22.3	28.5	121 36.7	11.9	158 11.5	54.4
02	139 20.5	187 44.2	32.9	73 24.9	28.5	136 38.9	11.7	173 13.7	54.3
03	154 23.0	202 43.5 ..	32.1	88 27.4 ..	28.5	151 41.0 ..	11.6	188 15.9 ..	54.2
04	169 25.4	217 42.7	31.3	103 30.0	28.5	166 43.1	11.4	203 18.1	54.1
05	184 27.9	232 42.0	30.5	118 32.6	28.5	181 45.3	11.3	218 20.3	54.0
06	199 30.4	247 41.3	S19 29.7	133 35.1	N24 28.4	196 47.4	S 0 11.1	233 22.5	S14 53.9
07	214 32.8	262 40.5	28.9	148 37.7	28.4	211 49.5	11.0	248 24.7	53.8
08	229 35.3	277 39.8	28.1	163 40.2	28.4	226 51.7	10.8	263 26.9	53.7
09	244 37.8	292 39.0 ..	27.3	178 42.8 ..	28.4	241 53.8 ..	10.7	278 29.1 ..	53.6
10	259 40.2	307 38.3	26.5	193 45.3	28.4	256 56.0	10.5	293 31.3	53.6
11	274 42.7	322 37.6	25.7	208 47.9	28.4	271 58.1	10.4	308 33.5	53.5
12	289 45.1	337 36.8	S19 24.9	223 50.4	N24 28.4	287 00.2	S 0 10.2	323 35.7	S14 53.4
13	304 47.6	352 36.1	24.1	238 53.0	28.3	302 02.4	10.1	338 37.9	53.3
14	319 50.1	7 35.3	23.3	253 55.5	28.3	317 04.5	09.9	353 40.1	53.2
15	334 52.5	22 34.6 ..	22.5	268 58.1 ..	28.3	332 06.6 ..	09.8	8 42.3 ..	53.1
16	349 55.0	37 33.9	21.6	284 00.6	28.3	347 08.8	09.6	23 44.5	53.0
17	4 57.5	52 33.1	20.8	299 03.1	28.3	2 10.9	09.5	38 46.7	52.9
18	19 59.9	67 32.4	S19 20.0	314 05.7	N24 28.3	17 13.0	S 0 09.3	53 48.9	S14 52.8
19	35 02.4	82 31.7	19.2	329 08.2	28.3	32 15.2	09.2	68 51.1	52.8
20	50 04.9	97 30.9	18.4	344 10.7	28.2	47 17.3	09.0	83 53.3	52.7
21	65 07.3	112 30.2 ..	17.6	359 13.3 ..	28.2	62 19.4 ..	08.9	98 55.5 ..	52.6
22	80 09.8	127 29.5	16.8	14 15.8	28.2	77 21.6	08.7	113 57.8	52.5
23	95 12.3	142 28.7	15.9	29 18.3	28.2	92 23.7	08.6	129 00.0	52.4
11 00	110 14.7	157 28.0	S19 15.1	44 20.9	N24 28.2	107 25.9	S 0 08.4	144 02.2	S14 52.3
01	125 17.2	172 27.3	14.3	59 23.4	28.2	122 28.0	08.2	159 04.4	52.2
02	140 19.6	187 26.6	13.5	74 25.9	28.2	137 30.1	08.1	174 06.6	52.1
03	155 22.1	202 25.8 ..	12.7	89 28.5 ..	28.1	152 32.3 ..	07.9	189 08.8 ..	52.0
04	170 24.6	217 25.1	11.8	104 31.0	28.1	167 34.4	07.8	204 11.0	52.0
05	185 27.0	232 24.4	11.0	119 33.5	28.1	182 36.5	07.6	219 13.2	51.9
06	200 29.5	247 23.6	S19 10.2	134 36.0	N24 28.1	197 38.7	S 0 07.5	234 15.4	S14 51.8
07	215 32.0	262 22.9	09.4	149 38.5	28.1	212 40.8	07.3	249 17.6	51.7
08	230 34.4	277 22.2	08.6	164 41.1	28.1	227 42.9	07.2	264 19.8	51.6
09	245 36.9	292 21.5 ..	07.7	179 43.6 ..	28.1	242 45.0 ..	07.0	279 22.0 ..	51.5
10	260 39.4	307 20.7	06.9	194 46.1	28.1	257 47.2	06.9	294 24.2	51.4
11	275 41.8	322 20.0	06.1	209 48.6	28.1	272 49.3	06.7	309 26.4	51.3
12	290 44.3	337 19.3	S19 05.2	224 51.1	N24 28.0	287 51.4	S 0 06.6	324 28.6	S14 51.2
13	305 46.8	352 18.6	04.4	239 53.6	28.0	302 53.6	06.4	339 30.8	51.1
14	320 49.2	7 17.9	03.6	254 56.1	28.0	317 55.7	06.2	354 33.0	51.1
15	335 51.7	22 17.1 ..	02.7	269 58.6 ..	28.0	332 57.8 ..	06.1	9 35.2 ..	51.0
16	350 54.1	37 16.4	01.9	285 01.2	28.0	348 00.0	05.9	24 37.4	50.9
17	5 56.6	52 15.7	01.1	300 03.7	28.0	3 02.1	05.8	39 39.6	50.8
18	20 59.1	67 15.0	S19 00.2	315 06.2	N24 28.0	18 04.2	S 0 05.6	54 41.8	S14 50.7
19	36 01.5	82 14.2	18 59.4	330 08.7	28.0	33 06.4	05.5	69 44.0	50.6
20	51 04.0	97 13.5	58.6	345 11.2	28.0	48 08.5	05.3	84 46.2	50.5
21	66 06.5	112 12.8 ..	57.7	0 13.7 ..	28.0	63 10.6 ..	05.2	99 48.4 ..	50.4
22	81 08.9	127 12.1	56.9	15 16.2	27.9	78 12.7	05.0	114 50.6	50.3
23	96 11.4	142 11.4	56.1	30 18.7	27.9	93 14.9	04.8	129 52.8	50.3
12 00	111 13.9	157 10.7	S18 55.2	45 21.1	N24 27.9	108 17.0	S 0 04.7	144 55.0	S14 50.2
01	126 16.3	172 09.9	54.4	60 23.6	27.9	123 19.1	04.5	159 57.2	50.1
02	141 18.8	187 09.2	53.5	75 26.1	27.9	138 21.3	04.4	174 59.4	50.0
03	156 21.2	202 08.5 ..	52.7	90 28.6 ..	27.9	153 23.4 ..	04.2	190 01.6 ..	49.9
04	171 23.7	217 07.8	51.8	105 31.1	27.9	168 25.5	04.1	205 03.8	49.8
05	186 26.2	232 07.1	51.0	120 33.6	27.9	183 27.6	03.9	220 06.0	49.7
06	201 28.6	247 06.4	S18 50.2	135 36.1	N24 27.9	198 29.8	S 0 03.8	235 08.2	S14 49.6
07	216 31.1	262 05.7	49.3	150 38.6	27.9	213 31.9	03.6	250 10.3	49.5
08	231 33.6	277 04.9	48.5	165 41.1	27.9	228 34.0	03.4	265 12.5	49.4
09	246 36.0	292 04.2 ..	47.6	180 43.5 ..	27.9	243 36.1 ..	03.3	280 14.7 ..	49.4
10	261 38.5	307 03.5	46.8	195 46.0	27.8	258 38.3	03.1	295 16.9	49.3
11	276 41.0	322 02.8	45.9	210 48.5	27.8	273 40.4	03.0	310 19.1	49.2
12	291 43.4	337 02.1	S18 45.1	225 51.0	N24 27.8	288 42.5	S 0 02.8	325 21.3	S14 49.1
13	306 45.9	352 01.4	44.2	240 53.4	27.8	303 44.7	02.7	340 23.5	49.0
14	321 48.4	7 00.7	43.3	255 55.9	27.8	318 46.8	02.5	355 25.7	48.9
15	336 50.8	22 00.0 ..	42.5	270 58.4 ..	27.8	333 48.9 ..	02.4	10 27.9 ..	48.8
16	351 53.3	36 59.3	41.6	286 00.9	27.8	348 51.0	02.2	25 30.1	48.7
17	6 55.7	51 58.6	40.8	301 03.3	27.8	3 53.2	02.0	40 32.3	48.6
18	21 58.2	66 57.9	S18 39.9	316 05.8	N24 27.8	18 55.3	S 0 01.9	55 34.5	S14 48.5
19	37 00.7	81 57.1	39.1	331 08.3	27.8	33 57.4	01.7	70 36.7	48.5
20	52 03.1	96 56.4	38.2	346 10.7	27.8	48 59.5	01.6	85 38.9	48.4
21	67 05.6	111 55.7 ..	37.3	1 13.2 ..	27.8	64 01.7 ..	01.4	100 41.1 ..	48.3
22	82 08.1	126 55.0	36.5	16 15.7	27.8	79 03.8	01.3	115 43.3	48.2
23	97 10.5	141 54.3	35.6	31 18.1	27.8	94 05.9	01.1	130 45.5	48.1
Mer. Pass.	h m 16 36.3	v −0.7	d 0.8	v 2.5	d 0.0	v 2.1	d 0.2	v 2.2	d 0.1

STARS

Name	SHA	Dec
Acamar	315 12.8	S40 13.0
Achernar	335 21.4	S57 07.6
Acrux	173 01.5	S63 13.3
Adhara	255 06.8	S29 00.2
Aldebaran	290 41.2	N16 33.3
Alioth	166 14.4	N55 49.8
Alkaid	152 53.4	N49 11.7
Alnair	27 35.3	S46 51.2
Alnilam	275 39.1	S 1 11.3
Alphard	217 49.1	S 8 45.5
Alphecca	126 05.4	N26 38.1
Alpheratz	357 36.6	N29 13.1
Altair	62 01.9	N 8 55.7
Ankaa	353 08.9	S42 11.2
Antares	112 18.1	S26 28.9
Arcturus	145 49.5	N19 03.6
Atria	107 14.3	S69 03.9
Avior	234 14.8	S59 34.9
Bellatrix	278 24.3	N 6 22.2
Betelgeuse	270 53.5	N 7 24.6
Canopus	263 52.6	S52 42.5
Capella	280 23.9	N46 01.3
Deneb	49 27.4	N45 21.7
Denebola	182 26.5	N14 26.5
Diphda	348 49.0	S17 51.8
Dubhe	193 42.6	N61 37.4
Elnath	278 03.6	N28 37.6
Eltanin	90 43.5	N51 29.0
Enif	33 40.7	N 9 58.8
Fomalhaut	15 16.6	S29 30.3
Gacrux	171 53.3	S57 14.2
Gienah	175 45.2	S17 40.1
Hadar	148 38.5	S60 28.7
Hamal	327 53.0	N23 34.3
Kaus Aust.	83 35.1	S34 22.4
Kochab	137 20.3	N74 03.3
Markab	13 31.7	N15 19.7
Menkar	314 07.7	N 4 10.7
Menkent	147 59.7	S36 28.8
Miaplacidus	221 37.7	S69 48.5
Mirfak	308 30.3	N49 56.7
Nunki	75 50.2	S26 16.1
Peacock	53 08.9	S56 39.8
Pollux	243 18.9	N27 58.2
Procyon	244 52.2	N 5 09.9
Rasalhague	96 00.4	N12 32.5
Regulus	207 35.9	N11 51.2
Rigel	281 05.2	S 8 10.6
Rigil Kent.	139 42.8	S60 55.5
Sabik	102 05.0	S15 45.2
Schedar	349 33.0	N56 40.0
Shaula	96 13.0	S37 07.2
Sirius	258 27.3	S16 44.9
Spica	158 24.0	S11 16.8
Suhail	222 47.1	S43 31.4
Vega	80 34.8	N38 48.2
Zuben'ubi	136 58.0	S16 08.2

	SHA	Mer. Pass.
	° ′	h m
Venus	47 13.3	13 31
Mars	294 06.2	20 59
Jupiter	357 11.1	16 48
Saturn	33 47.4	14 22

© British Crown Copyright 2022. All rights reserved.

UT	SUN GHA	SUN Dec	MOON GHA	v	MOON Dec	d	HP
d h	° ′	° ′	° ′	′	° ′	′	′
10 00	178 12.1	S22 01.6	322 47.3	14.2	N18 40.7	10.4	54.1
01	193 11.9	01.3	337 20.5	14.2	18 30.3	10.5	54.1
02	208 11.6	00.9	351 53.7	14.3	18 19.8	10.6	54.1
03	223 11.4 ..	00.5	6 27.0	14.4	18 09.2	10.6	54.1
04	238 11.1	22 00.2	21 00.4	14.4	17 58.6	10.7	54.1
05	253 10.8	21 59.8	35 33.8	14.4	17 47.9	10.8	54.1
06	268 10.6	S21 59.4	50 07.2	14.6	N17 37.1	10.8	54.1
07	283 10.3	59.1	64 40.8	14.5	17 26.3	11.0	54.1
08	298 10.1	58.7	79 14.3	14.6	17 15.3	10.9	54.1
09	313 09.8 ..	58.3	93 47.9	14.7	17 04.4	11.1	54.1
10	328 09.6	58.0	108 21.6	14.7	16 53.3	11.2	54.2
11	343 09.3	57.6	122 55.3	14.8	16 42.1	11.2	54.2
12	358 09.1	S21 57.2	137 29.1	14.8	N16 30.9	11.2	54.2
13	13 08.8	56.8	152 02.9	14.8	16 19.7	11.4	54.2
14	28 08.6	56.5	166 36.7	15.0	16 08.3	11.4	54.2
15	43 08.3 ..	56.1	181 10.7	14.9	15 56.9	11.5	54.2
16	58 08.1	55.7	195 44.6	15.0	15 45.4	11.5	54.2
17	73 07.8	55.3	210 18.6	15.0	15 33.9	11.6	54.2
18	88 07.6	S21 55.0	224 52.6	15.1	N15 22.3	11.7	54.2
19	103 07.3	54.6	239 26.7	15.2	15 10.6	11.7	54.2
20	118 07.1	54.2	254 00.9	15.1	14 58.9	11.8	54.3
21	133 06.8 ..	53.8	268 35.0	15.3	14 47.1	11.8	54.3
22	148 06.6	53.5	283 09.3	15.2	14 35.3	12.0	54.3
23	163 06.3	53.1	297 43.5	15.3	14 23.3	11.9	54.3
11 00	178 06.1	S21 52.7	312 17.8	15.4	N14 11.4	12.1	54.3
01	193 05.8	52.3	326 52.2	15.4	13 59.3	12.1	54.3
02	208 05.6	51.9	341 26.6	15.4	13 47.2	12.1	54.3
03	223 05.3 ..	51.5	356 01.0	15.5	13 35.1	12.2	54.3
04	238 05.1	51.2	10 35.4	15.5	13 22.9	12.3	54.4
05	253 04.8	50.8	25 09.9	15.6	13 10.6	12.3	54.4
06	268 04.6	S21 50.4	39 44.5	15.5	N12 58.3	12.4	54.4
07	283 04.3	50.0	54 19.0	15.6	12 45.9	12.4	54.4
08	298 04.1	49.6	68 53.6	15.7	12 33.5	12.5	54.4
09	313 03.8 ..	49.2	83 28.3	15.6	12 21.0	12.5	54.4
10	328 03.6	48.8	98 02.9	15.7	12 08.5	12.6	54.4
11	343 03.3	48.4	112 37.6	15.8	11 55.9	12.6	54.4
12	358 03.1	S21 48.1	127 12.4	15.7	N11 43.3	12.7	54.5
13	13 02.9	47.7	141 47.1	15.8	11 30.6	12.7	54.5
14	28 02.6	47.3	156 21.9	15.8	11 17.9	12.8	54.5
15	43 02.4 ..	46.9	170 56.7	15.9	11 05.1	12.9	54.5
16	58 02.1	46.5	185 31.6	15.9	10 52.2	12.8	54.5
17	73 01.9	46.1	200 06.5	15.9	10 39.4	13.0	54.5
18	88 01.6	S21 45.7	214 41.4	15.9	N10 26.4	12.9	54.5
19	103 01.4	45.3	229 16.3	15.9	10 13.5	13.1	54.6
20	118 01.1	44.9	243 51.2	16.0	10 00.4	13.0	54.6
21	133 00.9 ..	44.5	258 26.2	16.0	9 47.4	13.1	54.6
22	148 00.6	44.1	273 01.2	16.0	9 34.3	13.2	54.6
23	163 00.4	43.7	287 36.2	16.1	9 21.1	13.2	54.6
12 00	178 00.2	S21 43.3	302 11.3	16.0	N 9 07.9	13.2	54.6
01	192 59.9	42.9	316 46.3	16.1	8 54.7	13.3	54.7
02	207 59.7	42.5	331 21.4	16.1	8 41.4	13.3	54.7
03	222 59.4 ..	42.1	345 56.5	16.1	8 28.1	13.3	54.7
04	237 59.2	41.7	0 31.6	16.1	8 14.8	13.4	54.7
05	252 58.9	41.3	15 06.7	16.1	8 01.4	13.5	54.7
06	267 58.7	S21 40.9	29 41.8	16.2	N 7 47.9	13.4	54.7
07	282 58.5	40.5	44 17.0	16.1	7 34.5	13.5	54.8
08	297 58.2	40.1	58 52.1	16.2	7 21.0	13.6	54.8
09	312 58.0 ..	39.7	73 27.3	16.2	7 07.4	13.6	54.8
10	327 57.7	39.3	88 02.5	16.2	6 53.8	13.6	54.8
11	342 57.5	38.9	102 37.7	16.2	6 40.2	13.6	54.8
12	357 57.3	S21 38.5	117 12.9	16.2	N 6 26.6	13.7	54.9
13	12 57.0	38.1	131 48.1	16.2	6 12.9	13.7	54.9
14	27 56.8	37.7	146 23.3	16.2	5 59.2	13.7	54.9
15	42 56.5 ..	37.2	160 58.5	16.2	5 45.5	13.8	54.9
16	57 56.3	36.8	175 33.7	16.3	5 31.7	13.8	54.9
17	72 56.1	36.4	190 09.0	16.2	5 17.9	13.8	55.0
18	87 55.8	S21 36.0	204 44.2	16.2	N 5 04.1	13.9	55.0
19	102 55.6	35.6	219 19.4	16.2	4 50.2	13.9	55.0
20	117 55.3	35.2	233 54.6	16.2	4 36.3	13.9	55.0
21	132 55.1 ..	34.8	248 29.8	16.3	4 22.4	14.0	55.1
22	147 54.9	34.4	263 05.1	16.2	4 08.4	13.9	55.1
23	162 54.6	33.9	277 40.3	16.2	N 3 54.5	14.0	55.1
	SD 16.3	d 0.4	SD 14.8		14.8		14.9

Lat.	Twilight Naut.	Twilight Civil	Sunrise	Moonrise 10	Moonrise 11	Moonrise 12	Moonrise 13
°	h m	h m	h m	h m	h m	h m	h m
N 72	08 10	10 08	■	17 06	19 32	21 36	23 35
N 70	07 54	09 29	■	17 45	19 49	21 42	23 32
68	07 40	09 02	10 54	18 11	20 02	21 47	23 30
66	07 29	08 42	10 05	18 31	20 13	21 51	23 28
64	07 20	08 25	09 35	18 47	20 22	21 54	23 26
62	07 12	08 11	09 12	19 00	20 30	21 57	23 25
60	07 05	07 59	08 54	19 12	20 36	22 00	23 24
N 58	06 58	07 49	08 38	19 21	20 42	22 02	23 23
56	06 52	07 40	08 26	19 30	20 47	22 04	23 22
54	06 47	07 32	08 14	19 37	20 52	22 06	23 21
52	06 42	07 25	08 04	19 44	20 56	22 07	23 20
50	06 37	07 18	07 55	19 50	20 59	22 09	23 19
45	06 27	07 04	07 37	20 03	21 07	22 12	23 18
N 40	06 18	06 51	07 21	20 13	21 14	22 15	23 17
35	06 09	06 41	07 08	20 22	21 20	22 17	23 15
30	06 01	06 31	06 57	20 30	21 25	22 19	23 14
20	05 46	06 14	06 37	20 43	21 33	22 23	23 13
N 10	05 32	05 58	06 20	20 55	21 41	22 26	23 11
0	05 16	05 42	06 04	21 06	21 48	22 29	23 10
S 10	04 58	05 25	05 48	21 17	21 55	22 32	23 09
20	04 37	05 06	05 30	21 29	22 02	22 35	23 07
30	04 10	04 43	05 11	21 42	22 11	22 38	23 06
35	03 53	04 29	04 58	21 50	22 16	22 40	23 05
40	03 32	04 12	04 44	21 58	22 21	22 43	23 04
45	03 04	03 51	04 26	22 08	22 28	22 45	23 03
S 50	02 25	03 24	04 07	22 21	22 35	22 49	23 01
52	02 02	03 11	03 57	22 26	22 39	22 50	23 01
54	01 32	02 55	03 46	22 32	22 43	22 52	23 00
56	00 28	02 37	03 34	22 39	22 47	22 53	22 59
58	////	02 13	03 19	22 47	22 51	22 55	22 59
S 60	////	01 40	03 01	22 55	22 57	22 57	22 58

Lat.	Sunset	Twilight Civil	Twilight Naut.	Moonset 10	Moonset 11	Moonset 12	Moonset 13
°	h m	h m	h m	h m	h m	h m	h m
N 72	■	14 08	16 07	13 06	12 08	11 32	11 01
N 70	■	14 47	16 23	12 26	11 49	11 23	11 00
68	13 22	15 14	16 36	11 57	11 34	11 15	10 59
66	14 11	15 34	16 47	11 36	11 22	11 09	10 58
64	14 41	15 51	16 56	11 19	11 11	11 04	10 57
62	15 04	16 05	17 04	11 05	11 02	10 59	10 56
60	15 22	16 17	17 11	10 53	10 55	10 55	10 56
N 58	15 38	16 27	17 18	10 42	10 48	10 52	10 55
56	15 50	16 36	17 24	10 33	10 42	10 49	10 55
54	16 02	16 44	17 29	10 25	10 36	10 46	10 54
52	16 12	16 51	17 34	10 18	10 31	10 43	10 54
50	16 20	16 58	17 39	10 11	10 27	10 41	10 54
45	16 39	17 12	17 49	09 57	10 17	10 35	10 53
N 40	16 55	17 25	17 58	09 45	10 09	10 31	10 52
35	17 07	17 35	18 06	09 35	10 02	10 27	10 52
30	17 19	17 45	18 14	09 26	09 56	10 24	10 51
20	17 38	18 02	18 29	09 10	09 45	10 18	10 50
N 10	17 55	18 18	18 44	08 57	09 35	10 13	10 49
0	18 11	18 34	19 00	08 44	09 26	10 08	10 48
S 10	18 28	18 50	19 17	08 31	09 17	10 03	10 48
20	18 45	19 09	19 38	08 17	09 08	09 57	10 47
30	19 05	19 32	20 05	08 01	08 56	09 51	10 46
35	19 17	19 46	20 22	07 52	08 50	09 47	10 45
40	19 31	20 03	20 43	07 41	08 43	09 43	10 44
45	19 48	20 24	21 11	07 29	08 34	09 39	10 44
S 50	20 08	20 50	21 50	07 13	08 23	09 33	10 43
52	20 18	21 03	22 12	07 06	08 18	09 30	10 42
54	20 28	21 19	22 42	06 58	08 13	09 27	10 42
56	20 41	21 38	23 37	06 49	08 07	09 24	10 41
58	20 56	22 01	////	06 39	08 00	09 20	10 40
S 60	21 13	22 33	////	06 27	07 52	09 16	10 40

Day	SUN Eqn. of Time 00h	SUN Eqn. of Time 12h	SUN Mer. Pass.	MOON Mer. Pass. Upper	MOON Mer. Pass. Lower	Age	Phase
d	m s	m s	h m	h m	h m	d	%
10	07 11	07 23	12 07	02 33	14 55	18	89
11	07 35	07 47	12 08	03 16	15 37	19	83
12	07 59	08 10	12 08	03 58	16 18	20	75

© British Crown Copyright 2022. All rights reserved.

UT	ARIES GHA	VENUS −3.9 GHA	Dec	MARS −0.8 GHA	Dec	JUPITER −2.3 GHA	Dec	SATURN +0.8 GHA	Dec	STARS Name	SHA	Dec
13 00	112 13.0	156 53.6	S18 34.8	46 20.6	N24 27.8	109 08.0	S 0 00.9	145 47.7	S14 48.0	Acamar	315 12.9	S40 13.0
01	127 15.5	171 52.9	33.9	61 23.0	27.7	124 10.1	00.8	160 49.9	47.9	Achernar	335 21.4	S57 07.6
02	142 17.9	186 52.2	33.0	76 25.5	27.7	139 12.3	00.6	175 52.1	47.8	Acrux	173 01.7	S63 13.3
03	157 20.4	201 51.5	. . 32.2	91 27.9	. . 27.7	154 14.4	. . 00.5	190 54.3	. . 47.7	Adhara	255 06.8	S29 00.2
04	172 22.9	216 50.8	31.3	106 30.4	27.7	169 16.5	00.3	205 56.5	47.6	Aldebaran	290 41.2	N16 33.3
05	187 25.3	231 50.1	30.4	121 32.8	27.7	184 18.6	S 00.1	220 58.7	47.5			
06	202 27.8	246 49.4	S18 29.6	136 35.3	N24 27.7	199 20.8	0 00.0	236 00.9	S14 47.5	Alioth	166 14.3	N55 49.8
07	217 30.2	261 48.7	28.7	151 37.7	27.7	214 22.9	N 00.2	251 03.1	47.4	Alkaid	152 53.4	N49 11.6
08	232 32.7	276 48.0	27.8	166 40.2	27.7	229 25.0	00.3	266 05.3	47.3	Alnair	27 35.4	S46 51.2
F 09	247 35.2	291 47.3	. . 27.0	181 42.6	. . 27.7	244 27.1	. . 00.5	281 07.5	. . 47.2	Alnilam	275 39.1	S 1 11.3
R 10	262 37.6	306 46.6	26.1	196 45.1	27.7	259 29.2	00.6	296 09.7	47.1	Alphard	217 49.1	S 8 45.5
I 11	277 40.1	321 45.9	25.2	211 47.5	27.7	274 31.4	00.8	311 11.9	47.0			
D 12	292 42.6	336 45.2	S18 24.3	226 50.0	N24 27.7	289 33.5	S 0 01.0	326 14.1	S14 46.9	Alphecca	126 05.3	N26 38.1
A 13	307 45.0	351 44.5	23.5	241 52.4	27.7	304 35.6	01.1	341 16.3	46.8	Alpheratz	357 36.6	N29 13.1
Y 14	322 47.5	6 43.8	22.6	256 54.9	27.7	319 37.7	01.3	356 18.5	46.7	Altair	62 01.9	N 8 55.7
15	337 50.0	21 43.1	. . 21.7	271 57.3	. . 27.7	334 39.8	. . 01.4	11 20.7	. . 46.6	Ankaa	353 08.9	S42 11.2
16	352 52.4	36 42.5	20.8	286 59.7	27.7	349 42.0	01.6	26 22.9	46.6	Antares	112 18.1	S26 28.9
17	7 54.9	51 41.8	20.0	302 02.2	27.7	4 44.1	01.8	41 25.1	46.5			
18	22 57.3	66 41.1	S18 19.1	317 04.6	N24 27.7	19 46.2	N 0 01.9	56 27.3	S14 46.4	Arcturus	145 49.5	N19 03.6
19	37 59.8	81 40.4	18.2	332 07.0	27.7	34 48.3	02.1	71 29.5	46.3	Atria	107 14.3	S69 03.9
20	53 02.3	96 39.7	17.3	347 09.5	27.7	49 50.4	02.2	86 31.7	46.2	Avior	234 14.7	S59 34.9
21	68 04.7	111 39.0	. . 16.4	2 11.9	. . 27.7	64 52.6	. . 02.4	101 33.9	. . 46.1	Bellatrix	278 24.3	N 6 22.2
22	83 07.2	126 38.3	15.5	17 14.3	27.7	79 54.7	02.6	116 36.1	46.0	Betelgeuse	270 53.5	N 7 24.6
23	98 09.7	141 37.6	14.7	32 16.7	27.7	94 56.8	02.7	131 38.2	45.9			
14 00	113 12.1	156 36.9	S18 13.8	47 19.2	N24 27.7	109 58.9	N 0 02.9	146 40.4	S14 45.8	Canopus	263 52.6	S52 42.5
01	128 14.6	171 36.2	12.9	62 21.6	27.7	125 01.0	03.0	161 42.6	45.7	Capella	280 23.9	N46 01.3
02	143 17.1	186 35.5	12.0	77 24.0	27.7	140 03.1	03.2	176 44.8	45.6	Deneb	49 27.4	N45 21.7
03	158 19.5	201 34.9	. . 11.1	92 26.4	. . 27.7	155 05.3	. . 03.3	191 47.0	. . 45.6	Denebola	182 26.5	N14 26.5
04	173 22.0	216 34.2	10.2	107 28.8	27.7	170 07.4	03.5	206 49.2	45.5	Diphda	348 49.0	S17 51.8
05	188 24.5	231 33.5	09.3	122 31.3	27.7	185 09.5	03.7	221 51.4	45.4			
06	203 26.9	246 32.8	S18 08.5	137 33.7	N24 27.7	200 11.6	N 0 03.8	236 53.6	S14 45.3	Dubhe	193 42.6	N61 37.4
07	218 29.4	261 32.1	07.6	152 36.1	27.7	215 13.7	04.0	251 55.8	45.2	Elnath	278 03.6	N28 37.6
S 08	233 31.8	276 31.4	06.7	167 38.5	27.7	230 15.9	04.2	266 58.0	45.1	Eltanin	90 43.4	N51 29.0
A 09	248 34.3	291 30.7	. . 05.8	182 40.9	. . 27.7	245 18.0	. . 04.3	282 00.2	. . 45.0	Enif	33 40.7	N 9 58.8
T 10	263 36.8	306 30.1	04.9	197 43.3	27.7	260 20.1	04.5	297 02.4	44.9	Fomalhaut	15 16.6	S29 30.3
U 11	278 39.2	321 29.4	04.0	212 45.7	27.7	275 22.2	04.6	312 04.6	44.8			
R 12	293 41.7	336 28.7	S18 03.1	227 48.1	N24 27.7	290 24.3	N 0 04.8	327 06.8	S14 44.7	Gacrux	171 53.3	S57 14.2
D 13	308 44.2	351 28.0	02.2	242 50.6	27.7	305 26.4	05.0	342 09.0	44.6	Gienah	175 45.2	S17 40.1
A 14	323 46.6	6 27.3	01.3	257 53.0	27.7	320 28.5	05.1	357 11.2	44.5	Hadar	148 38.4	S60 28.7
Y 15	338 49.1	21 26.7	18 00.4	272 55.4	. . 27.7	335 30.7	. . 05.3	12 13.4	. . 44.5	Hamal	327 53.0	N23 34.3
16	353 51.6	36 26.0	17 59.5	287 57.8	27.7	350 32.8	05.4	27 15.6	44.4	Kaus Aust.	83 35.1	S34 22.4
17	8 54.0	51 25.3	58.6	303 00.2	27.7	5 34.9	05.6	42 17.8	44.3			
18	23 56.5	66 24.6	S17 57.7	318 02.6	N24 27.7	20 37.0	N 0 05.8	57 20.0	S14 44.2	Kochab	137 20.2	N74 03.3
19	38 59.0	81 23.9	56.8	333 05.0	27.7	35 39.1	05.9	72 22.2	44.1	Markab	13 31.7	N15 19.7
20	54 01.4	96 23.3	55.9	348 07.4	27.7	50 41.2	06.1	87 24.4	44.0	Menkar	314 07.7	N 4 10.7
21	69 03.9	111 22.6	. . 55.0	3 09.7	. . 27.7	65 43.3	. . 06.2	102 26.6	. . 43.9	Menkent	147 59.6	S36 28.8
22	84 06.3	126 21.9	54.1	18 12.1	27.7	80 45.5	06.4	117 28.7	43.8	Miaplacidus	221 37.7	S69 48.5
23	99 08.8	141 21.2	53.2	33 14.5	27.7	95 47.6	06.6	132 30.9	43.7			
15 00	114 11.3	156 20.6	S17 52.3	48 16.9	N24 27.7	110 49.7	N 0 06.7	147 33.1	S14 43.6	Mirfak	308 30.3	N49 56.7
01	129 13.7	171 19.9	51.4	63 19.3	27.7	125 51.8	06.9	162 35.3	43.5	Nunki	75 50.2	S26 16.1
02	144 16.2	186 19.2	50.5	78 21.7	27.7	140 53.9	07.1	177 37.5	43.5	Peacock	53 08.9	S56 39.8
03	159 18.7	201 18.5	. . 49.6	93 24.1	. . 27.7	155 56.0	. . 07.2	192 39.7	. . 43.4	Pollux	243 18.9	N27 58.2
04	174 21.1	216 17.9	48.7	108 26.5	27.7	170 58.1	07.4	207 41.9	43.3	Procyon	244 52.2	N 5 09.9
05	189 23.6	231 17.2	47.7	123 28.9	27.7	186 00.2	07.5	222 44.1	43.2			
06	204 26.1	246 16.5	S17 46.8	138 31.2	N24 27.7	201 02.4	N 0 07.7	237 46.3	S14 43.1	Rasalhague	96 00.4	N12 32.5
07	219 28.5	261 15.8	45.9	153 33.6	27.7	216 04.5	07.9	252 48.5	43.0	Regulus	207 35.9	N11 51.2
08	234 31.0	276 15.2	45.0	168 36.0	27.7	231 06.6	08.0	267 50.7	42.9	Rigel	281 05.2	S 8 10.6
S 09	249 33.4	291 14.5	. . 44.1	183 38.4	. . 27.7	246 08.7	. . 08.2	282 52.9	. . 42.8	Rigil Kent.	139 42.8	S60 55.5
U 10	264 35.9	306 13.8	43.2	198 40.7	27.7	261 10.8	08.4	297 55.1	42.7	Sabik	102 05.0	S15 45.2
N 11	279 38.4	321 13.2	42.3	213 43.1	27.7	276 12.9	08.5	312 57.3	42.6			
D 12	294 40.8	336 12.5	S17 41.4	228 45.5	N24 27.7	291 15.0	N 0 08.7	327 59.5	S14 42.5	Schedar	349 33.0	N56 40.0
A 13	309 43.3	351 11.8	40.4	243 47.9	27.7	306 17.1	08.8	343 01.7	42.4	Shaula	96 13.0	S37 07.2
Y 14	324 45.8	6 11.2	39.5	258 50.2	27.7	321 19.2	09.0	358 03.9	42.3	Sirius	258 27.3	S16 44.9
15	339 48.2	21 10.5	. . 38.6	273 52.6	. . 27.7	336 21.3	. . 09.2	13 06.0	. . 42.3	Spica	158 24.0	S11 16.8
16	354 50.7	36 09.8	37.7	288 55.0	27.7	351 23.5	09.3	28 08.2	42.2	Suhail	222 47.1	S43 31.4
17	9 53.2	51 09.2	36.8	303 57.3	27.7	6 25.6	09.5	43 10.4	42.1			
18	24 55.6	66 08.5	S17 35.8	318 59.7	N24 27.7	21 27.7	N 0 09.7	58 12.6	S14 42.0	Vega	80 34.8	N38 48.2
19	39 58.1	81 07.8	34.9	334 02.1	27.7	36 29.8	09.8	73 14.8	41.9	Zuben'ubi	136 58.0	S16 08.2
20	55 00.6	96 07.2	34.0	349 04.4	27.7	51 31.9	10.0	88 17.0	41.8		SHA	Mer. Pass.
21	70 03.0	111 06.5	. . 33.1	4 06.8	. . 27.7	66 34.0	. . 10.1	103 19.2	. . 41.7	Venus	43 24.8	13 34
22	85 05.5	126 05.8	32.1	19 09.1	27.7	81 36.1	10.3	118 21.4	41.6	Mars	294 07.0	20 47
23	100 07.9	141 05.2	31.2	34 11.5	27.8	96 38.2	10.5	133 23.6	41.5	Jupiter	356 46.8	16 38
Mer. Pass. 16 24.5		v −0.7	d 0.9	v 2.4	d 0.0	v 2.1	d 0.2	v 2.2	d 0.1	Saturn	33 28.3	14 11

© British Crown Copyright 2022. All rights reserved.

UT	SUN		MOON				Lat.	Twilight		Sunrise	Moonrise			
								Naut.	Civil		13	14	15	16
	GHA	Dec	GHA	v	Dec	d	HP							
	° '	° '	° '	'	° '	'	'	°	h m	h m	h m	h m	h m	h m	h m
d h								N 72	08 03	09 57	■■■	23 35	25 42	01 42	04 15
13 00	177 54.4	S21 33.5	292 15.5	16.2	N 3 40.5	14.1	55.1	N 70	07 48	09 21	■■■	23 32	25 29	01 29	03 42
01	192 54.2	33.1	306 50.7	16.2	3 26.4	14.0	55.1	68	07 36	08 56	10 39	23 30	25 18	01 18	03 19
02	207 53.9	32.7	321 25.9	16.1	3 12.4	14.1	55.2	66	07 26	08 37	09 57	23 28	25 10	01 10	03 01
03	222 53.7 ..	32.3	336 01.0	16.2	2 58.3	14.1	55.2	64	07 17	08 21	09 28	23 26	25 03	01 03	02 46
04	237 53.5	31.8	350 36.2	16.2	2 44.2	14.1	55.2	62	07 09	08 08	09 07	23 25	24 56	00 56	02 34
05	252 53.2	31.4	5 11.4	16.1	2 30.1	14.1	55.2	60	07 02	07 56	08 50	23 24	24 51	00 51	02 24
06	267 53.0	S21 31.0	19 45.5	16.2	N 2 16.0	14.2	55.3	N 58	06 56	07 46	08 35	23 23	24 46	00 46	02 15
07	282 52.7	30.6	34 21.7	16.1	2 01.8	14.1	55.3	56	06 50	07 38	08 23	23 22	24 42	00 42	02 07
08	297 52.5	30.2	48 56.8	16.1	1 47.7	14.2	55.3	54	06 45	07 30	08 12	23 21	24 38	00 38	02 00
F 09	312 52.3 ..	29.7	63 31.9	16.1	1 33.5	14.3	55.3	52	06 40	07 23	08 02	23 20	24 35	00 35	01 54
R 10	327 52.0	29.3	78 07.0	16.0	1 19.2	14.2	55.4	50	06 36	07 17	07 54	23 19	24 32	00 32	01 49
I 11	342 51.8	28.9	92 42.0	16.1	1 05.0	14.2	55.4	45	06 26	07 02	07 35	23 18	24 26	00 26	01 37
D 12	357 51.6	S21 28.5	107 17.1	16.0	N 0 50.8	14.3	55.4	N 40	06 17	06 51	07 20	23 17	24 20	00 20	01 27
A 13	12 51.3	28.0	121 52.1	16.0	0 36.5	14.3	55.4	35	06 09	06 40	07 08	23 15	24 15	00 15	01 19
Y 14	27 51.1	27.6	136 27.1	16.0	0 22.2	14.3	55.5	30	06 01	06 31	06 57	23 14	24 11	00 11	01 11
15	42 50.9 ..	27.2	151 02.1	16.0	N 0 07.9	14.3	55.5	20	05 47	06 14	06 38	23 13	24 04	00 04	00 59
16	57 50.6	26.8	165 37.1	15.9	S 0 06.4	14.3	55.5	N 10	05 33	05 59	06 21	23 11	23 58	24 48	00 48
17	72 50.4	26.3	180 12.0	15.9	0 20.7	14.5	55.6	0	05 17	05 43	06 05	23 10	23 53	24 38	00 38
18	87 50.2	S21 25.9	194 46.9	15.9	S 0 35.0	14.4	55.6	S 10	05 00	05 27	05 49	23 09	23 47	24 28	00 28
19	102 49.9	25.5	209 21.8	15.8	0 49.4	14.3	55.6	20	04 40	05 08	05 32	23 07	23 41	24 17	00 17
20	117 49.7	25.0	223 56.6	15.9	1 03.7	14.4	55.6	30	04 13	04 46	05 12	23 06	23 34	24 05	00 05
21	132 49.5 ..	24.6	238 31.5	15.7	1 18.1	14.3	55.7	35	03 56	04 32	05 01	23 05	23 30	23 59	24 31
22	147 49.2	24.2	253 06.2	15.8	1 32.4	14.3	55.7	40	03 36	04 15	04 47	23 04	23 26	23 51	24 20
23	162 49.0	23.7	267 41.0	15.7	1 46.8	14.4	55.7	45	03 09	03 55	04 31	23 03	23 21	23 42	24 07
14 00	177 48.8	S21 23.3	282 15.7	15.7	S 2 01.2	14.4	55.7	S 50	02 31	03 29	04 11	23 01	23 15	23 31	23 51
01	192 48.6	22.9	296 50.4	15.6	2 15.6	14.4	55.8	52	02 10	03 16	04 02	23 01	23 12	23 26	23 43
02	207 48.3	22.4	311 25.0	15.6	2 30.0	14.4	55.8	54	01 42	03 01	03 51	23 00	23 09	23 21	23 35
03	222 48.1 ..	22.0	325 59.6	15.6	2 44.4	14.4	55.8	56	00 55	02 43	03 39	22 59	23 06	23 14	23 26
04	237 47.9	21.6	340 34.2	15.5	2 58.8	14.4	55.9	58	////	02 21	03 25	22 59	23 03	23 08	23 15
05	252 47.6	21.1	355 08.7	15.5	3 13.2	14.4	55.9	S 60	////	01 51	03 08	22 58	22 59	23 00	23 03
06	267 47.4	S21 20.7	9 43.2	15.5	S 3 27.6	14.5	55.9								
07	282 47.2	20.3	24 17.7	15.3	3 42.1	14.4	56.0	Lat.	Sunset	Twilight		Moonset			
S 08	297 46.9	19.8	38 52.0	15.4	3 56.5	14.4	56.0			Civil	Naut.	13	14	15	16
A 09	312 46.7 ..	19.4	53 26.4	15.3	4 10.9	14.4	56.0								
T 10	327 46.5	18.9	68 00.7	15.2	4 25.3	14.4	56.0	°	h m	h m	h m	h m	h m	h m	h m
U 11	342 46.3	18.5	82 34.9	15.2	4 39.7	14.4	56.1	N 72	■■■	14 22	16 15	11 01	10 31	09 55	08 59
R 12	357 46.0	S21 18.0	97 09.1	15.2	S 4 54.1	14.4	56.1	N 70	■■■	14 57	16 30	11 00	10 37	10 11	09 34
D 13	12 45.8	17.6	111 43.3	15.1	5 08.5	14.4	56.1	68	13 40	15 22	16 43	10 59	10 42	10 23	09 59
A 14	27 45.6	17.2	126 17.4	15.0	5 22.9	14.4	56.2	66	14 22	15 42	16 53	10 58	10 46	10 34	10 18
Y 15	42 45.4 ..	16.7	140 51.4	15.0	5 37.3	14.4	56.2	64	14 50	15 58	17 02	10 57	10 50	10 43	10 34
16	57 45.1	16.3	155 25.4	14.9	5 51.7	14.4	56.2	62	15 12	16 11	17 10	10 56	10 53	10 50	10 48
17	72 44.9	15.8	169 59.3	14.9	6 06.1	14.4	56.3	60	15 29	16 22	17 16	10 56	10 56	10 57	10 59
18	87 44.7	S21 15.4	184 33.2	14.8	S 6 20.5	14.3	56.3	N 58	15 43	16 32	17 22	10 55	10 59	11 03	11 09
19	102 44.5	14.9	199 07.0	14.8	6 34.8	14.3	56.3	56	15 56	16 41	17 28	10 55	11 01	11 08	11 17
20	117 44.2	14.5	213 40.8	14.7	6 49.2	14.3	56.4	54	16 07	16 48	17 33	10 54	11 03	11 13	11 25
21	132 44.0 ..	14.0	228 14.5	14.6	7 03.5	14.4	56.4	52	16 16	16 55	17 38	10 54	11 05	11 17	11 32
22	147 43.8	13.6	242 48.1	14.5	7 17.9	14.3	56.4	50	16 25	17 02	17 42	10 54	11 07	11 21	11 38
23	162 43.6	13.1	257 21.6	14.5	7 32.2	14.3	56.5	45	16 43	17 16	17 52	10 53	11 10	11 30	11 52
15 00	177 43.3	S21 12.7	271 55.1	14.5	S 7 46.5	14.3	56.5	N 40	16 58	17 28	18 01	10 52	11 14	11 37	12 03
01	192 43.1	12.2	286 28.6	14.3	8 00.8	14.2	56.5	35	17 10	17 38	18 09	10 52	11 16	11 43	12 13
02	207 42.9	11.8	301 01.9	14.3	8 15.0	14.3	56.6	30	17 21	17 47	18 17	10 51	11 19	11 48	12 21
03	222 42.7 ..	11.3	315 35.2	14.2	8 29.3	14.2	56.6	20	17 40	18 04	18 31	10 50	11 23	11 58	12 36
04	237 42.4	10.9	330 08.4	14.1	8 43.5	14.2	56.6	N 10	17 57	18 19	18 45	10 49	11 27	12 06	12 49
05	252 42.2	10.4	344 41.5	14.1	8 57.7	14.2	56.7	0	18 13	18 35	19 01	10 48	11 30	12 14	13 01
06	267 42.0	S21 10.0	359 14.6	14.0	S 9 11.9	14.2	56.7	S 10	18 28	18 51	19 18	10 48	11 34	12 22	13 13
07	282 41.8	09.5	13 47.6	13.9	9 26.1	14.1	56.8	20	18 45	19 10	19 38	10 47	11 37	12 30	13 26
08	297 41.5	09.0	28 20.5	13.8	9 40.2	14.2	56.8	30	19 05	19 32	20 04	10 46	11 42	12 40	13 42
S 09	312 41.3 ..	08.6	42 53.3	13.8	9 54.4	14.1	56.8	35	19 17	19 46	20 21	10 45	11 44	12 45	13 50
U 10	327 41.1	08.1	57 26.1	13.7	10 08.5	14.0	56.9	40	19 30	20 02	20 42	10 44	11 47	12 52	14 00
N 11	342 40.9	07.7	71 58.8	13.5	10 22.5	14.1	56.9	45	19 46	20 22	21 08	10 44	11 50	12 59	14 12
D 12	357 40.7	S21 07.2	86 31.3	13.5	S10 36.6	14.0	56.9	S 50	20 06	20 47	21 45	10 43	11 54	13 08	14 27
A 13	12 40.4	06.8	101 03.8	13.5	10 50.6	14.0	57.0	52	20 15	21 00	22 06	10 42	11 56	13 12	14 33
Y 14	27 40.2	06.3	115 36.3	13.3	11 04.6	13.9	57.0	54	20 26	21 15	22 33	10 42	11 58	13 17	14 41
15	42 40.0 ..	05.8	130 08.6	13.2	11 18.5	14.0	57.0	56	20 38	21 33	23 17	10 41	12 00	13 22	14 49
16	57 39.8	05.4	144 40.8	13.2	11 32.5	13.8	57.1	58	20 52	21 55	////	10 40	12 02	13 28	14 59
17	72 39.6	04.9	159 13.0	13.0	11 46.3	13.9	57.1	S 60	21 08	22 24	////	10 40	12 05	13 34	15 10
18	87 39.3	S21 04.4	173 45.0	13.0	S12 00.2	13.8	57.2		SUN			MOON			
19	102 39.1	04.0	188 17.0	12.9	12 14.0	13.8	57.2								
20	117 38.9	03.5	202 48.9	12.7	12 27.8	13.7	57.2	Day	Eqn. of Time		Mer.	Mer. Pass.		Age	Phase
21	132 38.7 ..	03.0	217 20.6	12.7	12 41.5	13.7	57.3		00ʰ	12ʰ	Pass.	Upper	Lower		
22	147 38.5	02.6	231 52.3	12.6	12 55.2	13.7	57.3	d	m s	m s	h m	h m	h m	d %	
23	162 38.2	02.1	246 23.9	12.5	S13 08.9	13.6	57.3	13	08 22	08 33	12 09	04 39	16 59	21 66	
								14	08 44	08 55	12 09	05 20	17 41	22 56	
	SD 16.3	d 0.4	SD 15.1		15.3		15.5	15	09 06	09 17	12 09	06 03	18 26	23 46	

© British Crown Copyright 2022. All rights reserved.

UT	ARIES	VENUS −3·9		MARS −0·7		JUPITER −2·3		SATURN +0·8		STARS		
	GHA	GHA	Dec	GHA	Dec	GHA	Dec	GHA	Dec	Name	SHA	Dec
d h	° ′	° ′	° ′	° ′	° ′	° ′	° ′	° ′	° ′		° ′	° ′
16 00	115 10.4	156 04.5	S17 30.3	49 13.9	N24 27.8	111 40.3	N 0 10.6	148 25.8	S14 41.4	Acamar	315 12.9	S40 13.0
01	130 12.9	171 03.9	29.4	64 16.2	27.8	126 42.4	10.8	163 28.0	41.3	Achernar	335 21.4	S57 07.6
02	145 15.3	186 03.2	28.4	79 18.6	27.8	141 44.5	11.0	178 30.2	41.2	Acrux	173 01.6	S63 13.3
03	160 17.8	201 02.5 ..	27.5	94 20.9 ..	27.8	156 46.6 ..	11.1	193 32.4 ..	41.2	Adhara	255 06.8	S29 00.2
04	175 20.3	216 01.9	26.6	109 23.3	27.8	171 48.8	11.3	208 34.6	41.1	Aldebaran	290 41.2	N16 33.3
05	190 22.7	231 01.2	25.6	124 25.6	27.8	186 50.9	11.5	223 36.8	41.0			
06	205 25.2	246 00.6	S17 24.7	139 28.0	N24 27.8	201 53.0	N 0 11.6	238 38.9	S14 40.9	Alioth	166 14.3	N55 49.8
07	220 27.7	260 59.9	23.8	154 30.3	27.8	216 55.1	11.8	253 41.1	40.8	Alkaid	152 53.3	N49 11.6
08	235 30.1	275 59.2	22.9	169 32.7	27.8	231 57.2	12.0	268 43.3	40.7	Alnair	27 35.4	S46 51.2
M 09	250 32.6	290 58.6 ..	21.9	184 35.0 ..	27.8	246 59.3 ..	12.1	283 45.5 ..	40.6	Alnilam	275 39.1	S 1 11.3
O 10	265 35.1	305 57.9	21.0	199 37.3	27.8	262 01.4	12.3	298 47.7	40.5	Alphard	217 49.1	S 8 45.5
N 11	280 37.5	320 57.3	20.0	214 39.7	27.8	277 03.5	12.4	313 49.9	40.4			
D 12	295 40.0	335 56.6	S17 19.1	229 42.0	N24 27.8	292 05.6	N 0 12.6	328 52.1	S14 40.3	Alphecca	126 05.3	N26 38.1
A 13	310 42.4	350 56.0	18.2	244 44.4	27.8	307 07.7	12.8	343 54.3	40.2	Alpheratz	357 36.6	N29 13.1
Y 14	325 44.9	5 55.3	17.2	259 46.7	27.9	322 09.8	12.9	358 56.5	40.1	Altair	62 01.9	N 8 55.7
15	340 47.4	20 54.7 ..	16.3	274 49.0 ..	27.9	337 11.9 ..	13.1	13 58.7 ..	40.0	Ankaa	353 08.9	S42 11.2
16	355 49.8	35 54.0	15.4	289 51.4	27.9	352 14.0	13.3	29 00.9	40.0	Antares	112 18.1	S26 28.9
17	10 52.3	50 53.3	14.4	304 53.7	27.9	7 16.1	13.4	44 03.1	39.9			
18	25 54.8	65 52.7	S17 13.5	319 56.0	N24 27.9	22 18.2	N 0 13.6	59 05.3	S14 39.8	Arcturus	145 49.5	N19 03.6
19	40 57.2	80 52.0	12.5	334 58.4	27.9	37 20.3	13.8	74 07.4	39.7	Atria	107 14.2	S69 03.9
20	55 59.7	95 51.4	11.6	350 00.7	27.9	52 22.4	13.9	89 09.6	39.6	Avior	234 14.7	S59 34.9
21	71 02.2	110 50.7 ..	10.6	5 03.0 ..	27.9	67 24.5 ..	14.1	104 11.8 ..	39.5	Bellatrix	278 24.3	N 6 22.2
22	86 04.6	125 50.1	09.7	20 05.3	27.9	82 26.6	14.3	119 14.0	39.4	Betelgeuse	270 53.5	N 7 24.6
23	101 07.1	140 49.4	08.8	35 07.7	27.9	97 28.7	14.4	134 16.2	39.3			
17 00	116 09.5	155 48.8	S17 07.8	50 10.0	N24 27.9	112 30.8	N 0 14.6	149 18.4	S14 39.2	Canopus	263 52.6	S52 42.5
01	131 12.0	170 48.2	06.9	65 12.3	27.9	127 33.0	14.8	164 20.6	39.1	Capella	280 23.9	N46 01.3
02	146 14.5	185 47.5	05.9	80 14.6	28.0	142 35.1	14.9	179 22.8	39.0	Deneb	49 27.4	N45 21.7
03	161 16.9	200 46.9 ..	05.0	95 17.0 ..	28.0	157 37.2 ..	15.1	194 25.0 ..	38.9	Denebola	182 26.5	N14 26.5
04	176 19.4	215 46.2	04.0	110 19.3	28.0	172 39.3	15.3	209 27.2	38.8	Diphda	348 49.0	S17 51.8
05	191 21.9	230 45.6	03.1	125 21.6	28.0	187 41.4	15.4	224 29.4	38.7			
06	206 24.3	245 44.9	S17 02.1	140 23.9	N24 28.0	202 43.5	N 0 15.6	239 31.6	S14 38.7	Dubhe	193 42.6	N61 37.4
07	221 26.8	260 44.3	01.2	155 26.2	28.0	217 45.6	15.8	254 33.7	38.6	Elnath	278 03.6	N28 37.6
08	236 29.3	275 43.6	17 00.2	170 28.5	28.0	232 47.7	15.9	269 35.9	38.5	Eltanin	90 43.4	N51 29.0
T 09	251 31.7	290 43.0	16 59.3	185 30.8 ..	28.0	247 49.8 ..	16.1	284 38.1 ..	38.4	Enif	33 40.7	N 9 58.7
U 10	266 34.2	305 42.4	58.3	200 33.1	28.0	262 51.9	16.3	299 40.3	38.3	Fomalhaut	15 16.6	S29 30.3
E 11	281 36.7	320 41.7	57.3	215 35.5	28.0	277 54.0	16.4	314 42.5	38.2			
S 12	296 39.1	335 41.1	S16 56.4	230 37.8	N24 28.1	292 56.1	N 0 16.6	329 44.7	S14 38.1	Gacrux	171 53.3	S57 14.2
D 13	311 41.6	350 40.4	55.4	245 40.1	28.1	307 58.2	16.8	344 46.9	38.0	Gienah	175 45.1	S17 40.1
A 14	326 44.0	5 39.8	54.5	260 42.4	28.1	323 00.3	16.9	359 49.1	37.9	Hadar	148 38.4	S60 28.7
Y 15	341 46.5	20 39.1 ..	53.5	275 44.7 ..	28.1	338 02.4 ..	17.1	14 51.3 ..	37.8	Hamal	327 53.0	N23 34.3
16	356 49.0	35 38.5	52.6	290 47.0	28.1	353 04.5	17.3	29 53.5	37.7	Kaus Aust.	83 35.1	S34 22.4
17	11 51.4	50 37.9	51.6	305 49.3	28.1	8 06.6	17.4	44 55.7	37.6			
18	26 53.9	65 37.2	S16 50.6	320 51.6	N24 28.1	23 08.7	N 0 17.6	59 57.8	S14 37.5	Kochab	137 20.2	N74 03.3
19	41 56.4	80 36.6	49.7	335 53.9	28.1	38 10.8	17.8	75 00.0	37.4	Markab	13 31.7	N15 19.7
20	56 58.8	95 36.0	48.7	350 56.2	28.2	53 12.9	17.9	90 02.2	37.3	Menkar	314 07.7	N 4 10.7
21	72 01.3	110 35.3 ..	47.7	5 58.5 ..	28.2	68 15.0 ..	18.1	105 04.4 ..	37.3	Menkent	147 59.6	S36 28.8
22	87 03.8	125 34.7	46.8	21 00.8	28.2	83 17.1	18.3	120 06.6	37.2	Miaplacidus	221 37.7	S69 48.5
23	102 06.2	140 34.1	45.8	36 03.0	28.2	98 19.2	18.4	135 08.8	37.1			
18 00	117 08.7	155 33.4	S16 44.8	51 05.3	N24 28.2	113 21.3	N 0 18.6	150 11.0	S14 37.0	Mirfak	308 30.4	N49 56.7
01	132 11.2	170 32.8	43.9	66 07.6	28.2	128 23.3	18.8	165 13.2	36.9	Nunki	75 50.2	S26 16.1
02	147 13.6	185 32.1	42.9	81 09.9	28.2	143 25.4	18.9	180 15.4	36.8	Peacock	53 08.9	S56 39.8
03	162 16.1	200 31.5 ..	41.9	96 12.2 ..	28.2	158 27.5 ..	19.1	195 17.6 ..	36.7	Pollux	243 18.9	N27 58.2
04	177 18.5	215 30.9	41.0	111 14.5	28.3	173 29.6	19.3	210 19.7	36.6	Procyon	244 52.2	N 5 09.9
05	192 21.0	230 30.3	40.0	126 16.8	28.3	188 31.7	19.4	225 21.9	36.5			
06	207 23.5	245 29.6	S16 39.0	141 19.0	N24 28.3	203 33.8	N 0 19.6	240 24.1	S14 36.4	Rasalhague	96 00.4	N12 32.5
W 07	222 25.9	260 29.0	38.1	156 21.3	28.3	218 35.9	19.8	255 26.3	36.3	Regulus	207 35.9	N11 51.2
E 08	237 28.4	275 28.4	37.1	171 23.6	28.3	233 38.0	20.0	270 28.5	36.2	Rigel	281 05.2	S 8 10.6
D 09	252 30.9	290 27.7 ..	36.1	186 25.9 ..	28.3	248 40.1 ..	20.1	285 30.7 ..	36.1	Rigil Kent.	139 42.7	S60 55.5
N 10	267 33.3	305 27.1	35.1	201 28.2	28.3	263 42.2	20.3	300 32.9	36.0	Sabik	102 04.9	S15 45.2
E 11	282 35.8	320 26.5	34.2	216 30.4	28.4	278 44.3	20.5	315 35.1	35.9			
S 12	297 38.3	335 25.8	S16 33.2	231 32.7	N24 28.4	293 46.4	N 0 20.6	330 37.3	S14 35.9	Schedar	349 33.0	N56 40.0
D 13	312 40.7	350 25.2	32.2	246 35.0	28.4	308 48.5	20.8	345 39.5	35.8	Shaula	96 12.9	S37 07.1
A 14	327 43.2	5 24.6	31.2	261 37.2	28.4	323 50.6	21.0	0 41.6	35.7	Sirius	258 27.3	S16 44.9
Y 15	342 45.7	20 24.0 ..	30.3	276 39.5 ..	28.4	338 52.7 ..	21.1	15 43.8 ..	35.6	Spica	158 24.0	S11 16.8
16	357 48.1	35 23.3	29.3	291 41.8	28.4	353 54.8	21.3	30 46.0	35.5	Suhail	222 47.1	S43 31.4
17	12 50.6	50 22.7	28.3	306 44.1	28.4	8 56.9	21.5	45 48.2	35.4			
18	27 53.0	65 22.1	S16 27.3	321 46.3	N24 28.5	23 59.0	N 0 21.6	60 50.4	S14 35.3	Vega	80 34.7	N38 48.2
19	42 55.5	80 21.5	26.3	336 48.6	28.5	39 01.1	21.8	75 52.6	35.2	Zuben'ubi	136 57.9	S16 08.2
20	57 58.0	95 20.8	25.4	351 50.8	28.5	54 03.2	22.0	90 54.8	35.1		SHA	Mer. Pass.
21	73 00.4	110 20.2 ..	24.4	6 53.1 ..	28.5	69 05.3 ..	22.2	105 57.0 ..	35.0		° ′	h m
22	88 02.9	125 19.6	23.4	21 55.4	28.5	84 07.3	22.3	120 59.2	34.9	Venus	39 39.3	13 37
23	103 05.4	140 19.0	22.4	36 57.6	28.5	99 09.4	22.5	136 01.4	34.8	Mars	294 00.4	20 36
	h m									Jupiter	356 21.3	16 28
Mer. Pass. 16 12.7		v −0.6	d 1.0	v 2.3	d 0.0	v 2.1	d 0.2	v 2.2	d 0.1	Saturn	33 08.9	14 01

© British Crown Copyright 2022. All rights reserved.

UT	SUN		MOON				Lat.	Twilight		Sunrise	Moonrise			
	GHA	Dec	GHA	v	Dec	d	HP		Naut.	Civil		16	17	18	19
d h	° ′	° ′	° ′	′	° ′	′	′	°	h m	h m	h m	h m	h m	h m	h m
16 00	177 38.0	S21 01.6	260 55.4 12.3		S13 22.5	13.6	57.4	N 72	07 56	09 44	■■■	04 15	■■■	■■■	■■■
01	192 37.8	01.2	275 26.7 12.3		13 36.1	13.5	57.4	N 70	07 42	09 12	11 47	03 42	■■■	■■■	■■■
02	207 37.6	00.7	289 58.0 12.2		13 49.6	13.4	57.5	68	07 31	08 49	10 25	03 19	05 49	■■■	■■■
03	222 37.4	21 00.2	304 29.2 12.1		14 03.0	13.5	57.5	66	07 21	08 31	09 48	03 01	05 09	■■■	■■■
04	237 37.2	20 59.8	319 00.3 11.9		14 16.5	13.3	57.5	64	07 13	08 16	09 21	02 46	04 42	07 00	■■■
05	252 36.9	59.3	333 31.2 11.9		14 29.8	13.4	57.6	62	07 05	08 03	09 01	02 34	04 21	06 20	08 26
06	267 36.7	S20 58.8	348 02.1 11.7		S14 43.2	13.2	57.6	60	06 59	07 53	08 45	02 24	04 04	05 52	07 39
07	282 36.5	58.4	2 32.8 11.7		14 56.4	13.3	57.7	N 58	06 53	07 43	08 31	02 15	03 50	05 31	07 09
08	297 36.3	57.9	17 03.5 11.5		15 09.7	13.1	57.7	56	06 48	07 35	08 19	02 07	03 38	05 13	06 46
M 09	312 36.1 ··	57.4	31 34.0 11.4		15 22.8	13.1	57.7	54	06 43	07 27	08 09	02 00	03 27	04 58	06 27
O 10	327 35.9	56.9	46 04.4 11.3		15 35.9	13.1	57.8	52	06 39	07 21	08 00	01 54	03 18	04 46	06 11
N 11	342 35.7	56.5	60 34.7 11.2		15 49.0	12.9	57.8	50	06 34	07 15	07 51	01 49	03 10	04 34	05 57
D 12	357 35.4	S20 56.0	75 04.9 11.0		S16 01.9	13.0	57.9	45	06 25	07 01	07 34	01 37	02 52	04 11	05 30
A 13	12 35.2	55.5	89 34.9 11.0		16 14.9	12.8	57.9	N 40	06 16	06 50	07 19	01 27	02 38	03 52	05 08
Y 14	27 35.0	55.0	104 04.9 10.8		16 27.7	12.8	57.9	35	06 09	06 40	07 07	01 19	02 26	03 37	04 50
15	42 34.8 ··	54.5	118 34.7 10.7		16 40.5	12.7	58.0	30	06 01	06 31	06 56	01 11	02 15	03 24	04 34
16	57 34.6	54.1	133 04.4 10.6		16 53.2	12.7	58.0	20	05 47	06 14	06 38	00 59	01 58	03 01	04 08
17	72 34.4	53.6	147 34.0 10.5		17 05.9	12.6	58.1	N 10	05 33	05 59	06 22	00 48	01 42	02 41	03 45
18	87 34.2	S20 53.1	162 03.5 10.4		S17 18.5	12.5	58.1	0	05 18	05 44	06 06	00 38	01 28	02 23	03 24
19	102 34.0	52.6	176 32.9 10.2		17 31.0	12.4	58.1	S 10	05 02	05 28	05 51	00 28	01 14	02 05	03 03
20	117 33.7	52.1	191 02.1 10.1		17 43.4	12.4	58.2	20	04 42	05 10	05 34	00 17	00 58	01 46	02 41
21	132 33.5 ··	51.7	205 31.2 10.0		17 55.8	12.2	58.2	30	04 16	04 48	05 15	00 05	00 41	01 24	02 15
22	147 33.3	51.2	220 00.2 9.8		18 08.0	12.2	58.3	35	04 00	04 35	05 04	24 31	00 31	01 11	02 00
23	162 33.1	50.7	234 29.0 9.7		18 20.2	12.2	58.3	40	03 40	04 19	04 51	24 20	00 20	00 56	01 43
17 00	177 32.9	S20 50.2	248 57.7 9.6		S18 32.4	12.0	58.3	45	03 14	04 00	04 35	24 07	00 07	00 39	01 22
01	192 32.7	49.7	263 26.3 9.5		18 44.4	12.0	58.4	S 50	02 38	03 35	04 16	23 51	24 18	00 18	00 56
02	207 32.5	49.2	277 54.8 9.3		18 56.4	11.8	58.4	52	02 18	03 22	04 07	23 43	24 07	00 07	00 43
03	222 32.3 ··	48.8	292 23.1 9.2		19 08.2	11.8	58.5	54	01 52	03 08	03 57	23 35	23 56	24 28	00 28
04	237 32.1	48.3	306 51.3 9.1		19 20.0	11.7	58.5	56	01 13	02 51	03 45	23 26	23 43	24 12	00 12
05	252 31.9	47.8	321 19.4 8.9		19 31.7	11.6	58.5	58	////	02 30	03 31	23 15	23 28	23 51	24 37
06	267 31.6	S20 47.3	335 47.3 8.8		S19 43.3	11.5	58.6	S 60	////	02 02	03 16	23 03	23 10	23 26	24 05

UT	SUN		MOON				Lat.	Sunset	Twilight		Moonset			
	GHA	Dec	GHA	v	Dec	d	HP			Civil	Naut.	16	17	18	19
	° ′	° ′	° ′	′	° ′	′	′	°	h m	h m	h m	h m	h m	h m	h m
07	282 31.4	46.8	350 15.1 8.7		19 54.8	11.4	58.7	N 72	■■■	14 37	16 25	08 59	■■■	■■■	■■■
T 08	297 31.2	46.3	4 42.8 8.5		20 06.2	11.3	58.7	N 70	12 34	15 08	16 39	09 34	■■■	■■■	■■■
U 09	312 31.0 ··	45.8	19 10.3 8.4		20 17.5	11.2	58.7	68	13 56	15 32	16 50	09 59	09 13	■■■	■■■
E 10	327 30.8	45.3	33 37.7 8.3		20 28.7	11.1	58.7	66	14 33	15 50	17 00	10 18	09 55	■■■	■■■
S 11	342 30.6	44.8	48 05.0 8.1		20 39.8	11.0	58.8	64	14 59	16 05	17 08	10 34	10 23	10 03	■■■
D 12	357 30.4	S20 44.3	62 32.1 8.0		S20 50.8	10.9	58.8	62	15 19	16 17	17 15	10 48	10 45	10 44	10 47
A 13	12 30.2	43.8	76 59.1 7.9		21 01.7	10.8	58.9	60	15 36	16 28	17 22	10 59	11 03	11 12	11 35
Y 14	27 30.0	43.4	91 26.0 7.7		21 12.5	10.7	58.9	N 58	15 49	16 37	17 27	11 09	11 18	11 34	12 05
15	42 29.8 ··	42.9	105 52.7 7.6		21 23.2	10.6	58.9	56	16 01	16 46	17 33	11 17	11 31	11 52	12 29
16	57 29.6	42.4	120 19.3 7.4		21 33.8	10.4	59.0	54	16 12	16 53	17 37	11 25	11 42	12 07	12 48
17	72 29.4	41.9	134 45.7 7.3		21 44.2	10.3	59.0	52	16 21	17 00	17 42	11 32	11 52	12 20	13 04
18	87 29.2	S20 41.4	149 12.0 7.2		S21 54.5	10.3	59.1	50	16 29	17 06	17 46	11 38	12 01	12 32	13 18
19	102 29.0	40.9	163 38.2 7.0		22 04.8	10.1	59.1	45	16 47	17 19	17 56	11 52	12 20	12 57	13 46
20	117 28.8	40.4	178 04.2 6.9		22 14.9	9.9	59.1	N 40	17 01	17 31	18 04	12 03	12 35	13 16	14 08
21	132 28.5 ··	39.9	192 30.1 6.7		22 24.8	9.9	59.2	35	17 13	17 41	18 12	12 13	12 48	13 33	14 27
22	147 28.3	39.4	206 55.8 6.6		22 34.7	9.7	59.2	30	17 24	17 50	18 19	12 21	13 00	13 47	14 43
23	162 28.1	38.9	221 21.4 6.5		22 44.4	9.6	59.3	20	17 42	18 06	18 33	12 36	13 20	14 11	15 10
18 00	177 27.9	S20 38.4	235 46.9 6.3		S22 54.0	9.5	59.3	N 10	17 58	18 21	18 47	12 49	13 37	14 32	15 33
01	192 27.7	37.9	250 12.2 6.2		23 03.5	9.3	59.3	0	18 14	18 36	19 01	13 01	13 53	14 51	15 55
02	207 27.5	37.4	264 37.4 6.1		23 12.8	9.2	59.4	S 10	18 29	18 52	19 18	13 13	14 10	15 11	16 17
03	222 27.3 ··	36.9	279 02.5 5.9		23 22.0	9.1	59.4	20	18 45	19 09	19 38	13 26	14 27	15 32	16 40
04	237 27.1	36.4	293 27.4 5.8		23 31.1	8.9	59.5	30	19 05	19 31	20 03	13 42	14 47	15 57	17 07
05	252 26.9	35.9	307 52.2 5.6		23 40.0	8.8	59.5	35	19 16	19 45	20 20	13 50	14 59	16 11	17 23
06	267 26.7	S20 35.4	322 16.8 5.5		S23 48.8	8.7	59.5	40	19 29	20 00	20 39	14 00	15 13	16 28	17 42
W 07	282 26.5	34.8	336 41.3 5.4		23 57.5	8.5	59.6	45	19 44	20 20	21 05	14 12	15 29	16 48	18 04
E 08	297 26.3	34.3	351 05.7 5.2		24 06.0	8.3	59.6	S 50	20 03	20 44	21 41	14 27	15 49	17 14	18 33
D 09	312 26.1 ··	33.8	5 29.9 5.1		24 14.3	8.2	59.6	52	20 12	20 57	22 00	14 33	15 59	17 26	18 47
N 10	327 25.9	33.3	19 54.0 5.0		24 22.5	8.1	59.7	54	20 22	21 11	22 25	14 41	16 10	17 40	19 03
E 11	342 25.7	32.8	34 18.0 4.8		24 30.6	7.9	59.7	56	20 34	21 28	23 02	14 49	16 22	17 57	19 22
S 12	357 25.5	S20 32.3	48 41.8 4.7		S24 38.5	7.7	59.8	58	20 47	21 48	////	14 59	16 36	18 16	19 46
D 13	12 25.3	31.8	63 05.5 4.6		24 46.2	7.6	59.8	S 60	21 03	22 15	////	15 10	16 53	18 41	20 18
A 14	27 25.1	31.3	77 29.1 4.4		24 53.8	7.4	59.8								
Y 15	42 24.9 ··	30.8	91 52.5 4.3		25 01.2	7.3	59.9		SUN			MOON			
16	57 24.7	30.3	106 15.8 4.2		25 08.5	7.1	59.9	Day	Eqn. of Time		Mer.	Mer. Pass.		Age	Phase
17	72 24.5	29.8	120 39.0 4.1		25 15.6	6.9	59.9		00ʰ	12ʰ	Pass.	Upper	Lower		
18	87 24.3	S20 29.2	135 02.1 3.9		S25 22.5	6.8	60.0	d	m s	m s	h m	h m	h m	d	%
19	102 24.1	28.7	149 25.0 3.8		25 29.3	6.6	60.0	16	09 27	09 38	12 10	06 49	19 14	24	35
20	117 23.9	28.2	163 47.8 3.7		25 35.9	6.5	60.0	17	09 48	09 58	12 10	07 40	20 08	25	25
21	132 23.7 ··	27.7	178 10.5 3.5		25 42.4	6.2	60.1	18	10 08	10 18	12 10	08 37	21 08	26	16
22	147 23.5	27.2	192 33.0 3.5		25 48.6	6.1	60.1								
23	162 23.3	26.7	206 55.5 3.3		S25 54.7	5.9	60.2								
	SD 16.3	d 0.5	SD 15.8		16.0		16.3									

© British Crown Copyright 2022. All rights reserved.

UT	ARIES GHA	VENUS −3.9 GHA	Dec	MARS −0.6 GHA	Dec	JUPITER −2.2 GHA	Dec	SATURN +0.8 GHA	Dec	STARS Name	SHA	Dec
19 00	118 07.8	155 18.4	S16 21.4	51 59.9	N24 28.6	114 11.5	N 0 22.7	151 03.5	S14 34.7	Acamar	315 12.9	S40 13.0
01	133 10.3	170 17.7	20.4	67 02.1	28.6	129 13.6	22.8	166 05.7	34.6	Achernar	335 21.4	S57 07.5
02	148 12.8	185 17.1	19.5	82 04.4	28.6	144 15.7	23.0	181 07.9	34.5	Acrux	173 01.6	S63 13.3
03	163 15.2	200 16.5 ..	18.5	97 06.6 ..	28.6	159 17.8 ..	23.2	196 10.1 ..	34.4	Adhara	255 06.8	S29 00.3
04	178 17.7	215 15.9	17.5	112 08.9	28.6	174 19.9	23.3	211 12.3	34.4	Aldebaran	290 41.2	N16 33.3
05	193 20.2	230 15.3	16.5	127 11.1	28.6	189 22.0	23.5	226 14.5	34.3			
06	208 22.6	245 14.6	S16 15.5	142 13.4	N24 28.7	204 24.1	N 0 23.7	241 16.7	S14 34.2	Alioth	166 14.3	N55 49.8
07	223 25.1	260 14.0	14.5	157 15.6	28.7	219 26.2	23.9	256 18.9	34.1	Alkaid	152 53.3	N49 11.6
08	238 27.5	275 13.4	13.5	172 17.9	28.7	234 28.3	24.0	271 21.0	34.0	Alnair	27 35.4	S46 51.2
09	253 30.0	290 12.8 ..	12.5	187 20.1 ..	28.7	249 30.4 ..	24.2	286 23.2 ..	33.9	Alnilam	275 39.1	S 1 11.3
10	268 32.5	305 12.2	11.5	202 22.4	28.7	264 32.4	24.4	301 25.4	33.8	Alphard	217 49.0	S 8 45.5
11	283 34.9	320 11.6	10.5	217 24.6	28.8	279 34.5	24.5	316 27.6	33.7			
12	298 37.4	335 11.0	S16 09.5	232 26.9	N24 28.8	294 36.6	N 0 24.7	331 29.8	S14 33.6	Alphecca	126 05.3	N26 38.0
13	313 39.9	350 10.3	08.6	247 29.1	28.8	309 38.7	24.9	346 32.0	33.5	Alpheratz	357 36.6	N29 13.1
14	328 42.3	5 09.7	07.6	262 31.3	28.8	324 40.8	25.1	1 34.2	33.4	Altair	62 01.9	N 8 55.6
15	343 44.8	20 09.1 ..	06.6	277 33.6 ..	28.8	339 42.9 ..	25.2	16 36.4 ..	33.3	Ankaa	353 08.9	S42 11.2
16	358 47.3	35 08.5	05.6	292 35.8	28.8	354 45.0	25.4	31 38.6	33.2	Antares	112 18.1	S26 28.9
17	13 49.7	50 07.9	04.6	307 38.1	28.9	9 47.1	25.6	46 40.7	33.1			
18	28 52.2	65 07.3	S16 03.6	322 40.3	N24 28.9	24 49.2	N 0 25.7	61 42.9	S14 33.0	Arcturus	145 49.4	N19 03.6
19	43 54.7	80 06.7	02.6	337 42.5	28.9	39 51.3	25.9	76 45.1	32.9	Atria	107 14.2	S69 03.9
20	58 57.1	95 06.1	01.6	352 44.7	28.9	54 53.3	26.1	91 47.3	32.8	Avior	234 14.7	S59 34.9
21	73 59.6	110 05.4	16 00.6	7 47.0 ..	28.9	69 55.4 ..	26.3	106 49.5 ..	32.8	Bellatrix	278 24.3	N 6 22.2
22	89 02.0	125 04.8	15 59.6	22 49.2	29.0	84 57.5	26.4	121 51.7	32.7	Betelgeuse	270 53.5	N 7 24.6
23	104 04.5	140 04.2	58.6	37 51.4	29.0	99 59.6	26.6	136 53.9	32.6			
20 00	119 07.0	155 03.6	S15 57.6	52 53.7	N24 29.0	115 01.7	N 0 26.8	151 56.1	S14 32.5	Canopus	263 52.6	S52 42.6
01	134 09.4	170 03.0	56.6	67 55.9	29.0	130 03.8	26.9	166 58.2	32.4	Capella	280 23.9	N46 01.3
02	149 11.9	185 02.4	55.5	82 58.1	29.0	145 05.9	27.1	182 00.4	32.3	Deneb	49 27.4	N45 21.7
03	164 14.4	200 01.8 ..	54.5	98 00.3 ..	29.1	160 08.0 ..	27.3	197 02.6 ..	32.2	Denebola	182 26.4	N14 26.5
04	179 16.8	215 01.2	53.5	113 02.5	29.1	175 10.0	27.5	212 04.8	32.1	Diphda	348 49.0	S17 51.8
05	194 19.3	230 00.6	52.5	128 04.8	29.1	190 12.1	27.6	227 07.0	32.0			
06	209 21.8	245 00.0	S15 51.5	143 07.0	N24 29.1	205 14.2	N 0 27.8	242 09.2	S14 31.9	Dubhe	193 42.5	N61 37.4
07	224 24.2	259 59.4	50.5	158 09.2	29.1	220 16.3	28.0	257 11.4	31.8	Elnath	278 03.6	N28 37.6
08	239 26.7	274 58.8	49.5	173 11.4	29.2	235 18.4	28.2	272 13.6	31.7	Eltanin	90 43.4	N51 28.9
09	254 29.2	289 58.2 ..	48.5	188 13.6 ..	29.2	250 20.5 ..	28.3	287 15.7 ..	31.6	Enif	33 40.7	N 9 58.7
10	269 31.6	304 57.6	47.5	203 15.8	29.2	265 22.6	28.5	302 17.9	31.5	Fomalhaut	15 16.6	S29 30.2
11	284 34.1	319 57.0	46.5	218 18.0	29.2	280 24.7	28.7	317 20.1	31.4			
12	299 36.5	334 56.4	S15 45.5	233 20.3	N24 29.3	295 26.7	N 0 28.8	332 22.3	S14 31.3	Gacrux	171 53.2	S57 14.2
13	314 39.0	349 55.8	44.4	248 22.5	29.3	310 28.8	29.0	347 24.5	31.2	Gienah	175 45.1	S17 40.1
14	329 41.5	4 55.2	43.4	263 24.7	29.3	325 30.9	29.2	2 26.7	31.1	Hadar	148 38.3	S60 28.7
15	344 43.9	19 54.6 ..	42.4	278 26.9 ..	29.3	340 33.0 ..	29.4	17 28.9 ..	31.0	Hamal	327 53.0	N23 34.3
16	359 46.4	34 54.0	41.4	293 29.1	29.3	355 35.1	29.5	32 31.1	31.0	Kaus Aust.	83 35.0	S34 22.4
17	14 48.9	49 53.4	40.4	308 31.3	29.4	10 37.2	29.7	47 33.2	30.9			
18	29 51.3	64 52.8	S15 39.4	323 33.5	N24 29.4	25 39.2	N 0 29.9	62 35.4	S14 30.8	Kochab	137 20.1	N74 03.3
19	44 53.8	79 52.2	38.3	338 35.7	29.4	40 41.3	30.1	77 37.6	30.7	Markab	13 31.7	N15 19.7
20	59 56.3	94 51.6	37.3	353 37.9	29.4	55 43.4	30.2	92 39.8	30.6	Menkar	314 07.7	N 4 10.7
21	74 58.7	109 51.0 ..	36.3	8 40.1 ..	29.5	70 45.5 ..	30.4	107 42.0 ..	30.5	Menkent	147 59.6	S36 28.8
22	90 01.2	124 50.4	35.3	23 42.3	29.5	85 47.6	30.6	122 44.2	30.4	Miaplacidus	221 37.7	S69 48.5
23	105 03.6	139 49.8	34.3	38 44.5	29.5	100 49.7	30.7	137 46.4	30.3			
21 00	120 06.1	154 49.2	S15 33.2	53 46.7	N24 29.5	115 51.7	N 0 30.9	152 48.5	S14 30.2	Mirfak	308 30.4	N49 56.7
01	135 08.6	169 48.6	32.2	68 48.9	29.6	130 53.8	31.1	167 50.7	30.1	Nunki	75 50.1	S26 16.1
02	150 11.0	184 48.0	31.2	83 51.1	29.6	145 55.9	31.3	182 52.9	30.0	Peacock	53 08.9	S56 39.8
03	165 13.5	199 47.4 ..	30.2	98 53.2 ..	29.6	160 58.0 ..	31.4	197 55.1 ..	29.9	Pollux	243 18.9	N27 58.2
04	180 16.0	214 46.8	29.2	113 55.4	29.6	176 00.1	31.6	212 57.3	29.8	Procyon	244 52.2	N 5 09.9
05	195 18.4	229 46.3	28.1	128 57.6	29.6	191 02.2	31.8	227 59.5	29.7			
06	210 20.9	244 45.7	S15 27.1	143 59.8	N24 29.7	206 04.2	N 0 32.0	243 01.7	S14 29.6	Rasalhague	96 00.3	N12 32.5
07	225 23.4	259 45.1	26.1	159 02.0	29.7	221 06.3	32.1	258 03.9	29.5	Regulus	207 35.9	N11 51.2
08	240 25.8	274 44.5	25.1	174 04.2	29.7	236 08.4	32.3	273 06.0	29.4	Rigel	281 05.2	S 8 10.6
09	255 28.3	289 43.9 ..	24.0	189 06.4 ..	29.7	251 10.5 ..	32.5	288 08.2 ..	29.3	Rigil Kent.	139 42.6	S60 55.5
10	270 30.8	304 43.3	23.0	204 08.5	29.8	266 12.6	32.7	303 10.4	29.2	Sabik	102 04.9	S15 45.2
11	285 33.2	319 42.7	22.0	219 10.7	29.8	281 14.6	32.8	318 12.6	29.2			
12	300 35.7	334 42.1	S15 20.9	234 12.9	N24 29.8	296 16.7	N 0 33.0	333 14.8	S14 29.1	Schedar	349 33.1	N56 40.0
13	315 38.1	349 41.5	19.9	249 15.1	29.8	311 18.8	33.2	348 17.0	29.0	Shaula	96 12.9	S37 07.1
14	330 40.6	4 41.0	18.9	264 17.2	29.9	326 20.9	33.4	3 19.2	28.9	Sirius	258 27.3	S16 44.9
15	345 43.1	19 40.4 ..	17.8	279 19.4 ..	29.9	341 23.0 ..	33.5	18 21.3 ..	28.8	Spica	158 24.0	S11 16.8
16	0 45.5	34 39.8	16.8	294 21.6	29.9	356 25.0	33.7	33 23.5	28.7	Suhail	222 47.1	S43 31.4
17	15 48.0	49 39.2	15.8	309 23.8	30.0	11 27.1	33.9	48 25.7	28.6			
18	30 50.5	64 38.6	S15 14.7	324 25.9	N24 30.0	26 29.2	N 0 34.1	63 27.9	S14 28.5	Vega	80 34.7	N38 48.1
19	45 52.9	79 38.0	13.7	339 28.1	30.0	41 31.3	34.2	78 30.1	28.4	Zuben'ubi	136 57.9	S16 08.2
20	60 55.4	94 37.4	12.7	354 30.3	30.0	56 33.4	34.4	93 32.3	28.3		SHA	Mer. Pass.
21	75 57.9	109 36.9 ..	11.6	9 32.4 ..	30.1	71 35.4 ..	34.6	108 34.4 ..	28.2	Venus	35 56.7	13 40
22	91 00.3	124 36.3	10.6	24 34.6	30.1	86 37.5	34.8	123 36.6	28.1	Mars	293 46.7	20 25
23	106 02.8	139 35.7	09.6	39 36.8	30.1	101 39.6	34.9	138 38.8	28.0	Jupiter	355 54.7	16 18
Mer. Pass. 16 00.9		v −0.6	d 1.0	v 2.2	d 0.0	v 2.1	d 0.2	v 2.2	d 0.1	Saturn	32 49.1	13 50

© British Crown Copyright 2022. All rights reserved.

UT	SUN GHA	SUN Dec	MOON GHA	v	MOON Dec	d	HP
d h	° ′	° ′	° ′	′	° ′	′	′
19 00	177 23.1	S20 26.1	221 17.8	3.2	S26 00.6	5.7	60.2
01	192 22.9	25.6	235 40.0	3.1	26 06.3	5.6	60.2
02	207 22.8	25.1	250 02.1	3.0	26 11.9	5.3	60.3
03	222 22.6	.. 24.6	264 24.1	2.9	26 17.2	5.2	60.3
04	237 22.4	24.1	278 46.0	2.8	26 22.4	5.0	60.3
05	252 22.2	23.5	293 07.8	2.6	26 27.4	4.8	60.4
06	267 22.0	S20 23.0	307 29.4	2.6	S26 32.2	4.7	60.4
T 07	282 21.8	22.5	321 51.0	2.5	26 36.9	4.4	60.4
H 08	297 21.6	22.0	336 12.5	2.3	26 41.3	4.2	60.4
U 09	312 21.4	.. 21.5	350 33.8	2.3	26 45.5	4.1	60.5
R 10	327 21.2	20.9	4 55.1	2.2	26 49.6	3.8	60.5
S 11	342 21.0	20.4	19 16.3	2.1	26 53.4	3.7	60.5
D 12	357 20.8	S20 19.9	33 37.4	2.0	S26 57.1	3.4	60.6
A 13	12 20.6	19.4	47 58.4	1.9	27 00.5	3.3	60.6
Y 14	27 20.4	18.8	62 19.3	1.8	27 03.8	3.0	60.6
15	42 20.2	.. 18.3	76 40.1	1.8	27 06.8	2.9	60.7
16	57 20.0	17.8	91 00.9	1.6	27 09.7	2.6	60.7
17	72 19.9	17.2	105 21.5	1.6	27 12.3	2.5	60.7
18	87 19.7	S20 16.7	119 42.1	1.6	S27 14.8	2.2	60.7
19	102 19.5	16.2	134 02.7	1.4	27 17.0	2.0	60.8
20	117 19.3	15.7	148 23.1	1.4	27 19.0	1.9	60.8
21	132 19.1	.. 15.1	162 43.5	1.4	27 20.9	1.6	60.8
22	147 18.9	14.6	177 03.9	1.3	27 22.5	1.4	60.9
23	162 18.7	14.1	191 24.2	1.2	27 23.9	1.2	60.9
20 00	177 18.5	S20 13.5	205 44.4	1.2	S27 25.1	1.0	60.9
01	192 18.3	13.0	220 04.6	1.1	27 26.1	0.7	60.9
02	207 18.2	12.5	234 24.7	1.1	27 26.8	0.6	61.0
03	222 18.0	.. 11.9	248 44.8	1.0	27 27.4	0.3	61.0
04	237 17.8	11.4	263 04.8	1.0	27 27.7	0.1	61.0
05	252 17.6	10.9	277 24.8	1.0	27 27.8	0.1	61.0
06	267 17.4	S20 10.3	291 44.8	0.9	S27 27.7	0.3	61.0
F 07	282 17.2	09.8	306 04.7	0.9	27 27.4	0.5	61.1
R 08	297 17.0	09.2	320 24.6	0.9	27 26.9	0.7	61.1
I 09	312 16.8	.. 08.7	334 44.5	0.9	27 26.2	1.0	61.1
D 10	327 16.7	08.2	349 04.4	0.9	27 25.2	1.1	61.1
A 11	342 16.5	07.6	3 24.3	0.8	27 24.1	1.4	61.2
Y 12	357 16.3	S20 07.1	17 44.1	0.8	S27 22.7	1.6	61.2
13	12 16.1	06.5	32 03.9	0.8	27 21.1	1.9	61.2
14	27 15.9	06.0	46 23.7	0.9	27 19.2	2.0	61.2
15	42 15.7	.. 05.5	60 43.6	0.8	27 17.2	2.3	61.2
16	57 15.6	04.9	75 03.4	0.9	27 14.9	2.4	61.2
17	72 15.4	04.4	89 23.2	0.9	27 12.5	2.7	61.3
18	87 15.2	S20 03.8	103 43.1	0.8	S27 09.8	2.9	61.3
19	102 15.0	03.3	118 02.9	0.9	27 06.9	3.2	61.3
20	117 14.8	02.7	132 22.8	0.9	27 03.7	3.3	61.3
21	132 14.6	.. 02.2	146 42.6	1.0	27 00.4	3.6	61.3
22	147 14.5	01.6	161 02.6	0.9	26 56.8	3.7	61.3
23	162 14.3	01.1	175 22.5	0.9	26 53.1	4.0	61.4
21 00	177 14.1	S20 00.5	189 42.4	1.0	S26 49.1	4.2	61.4
01	192 13.9	20 00.0	204 02.4	1.1	26 44.9	4.4	61.4
02	207 13.7	19 59.4	218 22.5	1.0	26 40.5	4.7	61.4
03	222 13.6	.. 58.9	232 42.5	1.1	26 35.8	4.8	61.4
04	237 13.4	58.3	247 02.6	1.2	26 31.0	5.1	61.4
05	252 13.2	57.8	261 22.8	1.2	26 25.9	5.2	61.4
06	267 13.0	S19 57.2	275 43.0	1.3	S26 20.7	5.5	61.4
S 07	282 12.8	56.7	290 03.3	1.3	26 15.2	5.6	61.4
A 08	297 12.7	56.1	304 23.6	1.3	26 09.6	5.9	61.4
T 09	312 12.5	.. 55.6	318 43.9	1.5	26 03.7	6.1	61.5
U 10	327 12.3	55.0	333 04.4	1.5	25 57.6	6.3	61.5
R 11	342 12.1	54.5	347 24.9	1.5	25 51.3	6.5	61.5
D 12	357 12.0	S19 53.9	1 45.4	1.6	S25 44.8	6.7	61.5
A 13	12 11.8	53.3	16 06.0	1.7	25 38.1	6.9	61.5
Y 14	27 11.6	52.8	30 26.7	1.8	25 31.2	7.1	61.5
15	42 11.4	.. 52.2	44 47.5	1.9	25 24.1	7.2	61.5
16	57 11.3	51.7	59 08.4	1.9	25 16.9	7.5	61.5
17	72 11.1	51.1	73 29.3	2.0	25 09.4	7.7	61.5
18	87 10.9	S19 50.5	87 50.3	2.1	S25 01.7	7.9	61.5
19	102 10.7	50.0	102 11.4	2.2	24 53.8	8.0	61.5
20	117 10.6	49.4	116 32.6	2.3	24 45.8	8.3	61.5
21	132 10.4	.. 48.9	130 53.9	2.4	24 37.5	8.4	61.5
22	147 10.2	48.3	145 15.3	2.4	24 29.1	8.6	61.5
23	162 10.0	47.7	159 36.7	2.6	S24 20.5	8.8	61.5
	SD 16.3	d 0.5	SD 16.5		16.7		16.7

Lat.	Twilight Naut.	Twilight Civil	Sunrise	Moonrise 19	20	21	22
°	h m	h m	h m	h m	h m	h m	h m
N 72	07 48	09 32	■	■	■	■	■
N 70	07 36	09 03	11 07	■	■	■	■
68	07 25	08 41	10 11	■	■	■	■
66	07 16	08 24	09 38	■	■	■	11 27
64	07 08	08 10	09 14	■	■	11 39	10 46
62	07 01	07 59	08 55	08 26	10 01	10 17	10 18
60	06 55	07 48	08 40	07 39	09 01	09 40	09 56
N 58	06 50	07 40	08 27	07 09	08 27	09 14	09 38
56	06 45	07 32	08 15	06 46	08 02	08 53	09 23
54	06 40	07 25	08 05	06 27	07 42	08 35	09 10
52	06 36	07 18	07 56	06 11	07 25	08 21	08 58
50	06 32	07 12	07 49	05 57	07 11	08 08	08 48
45	06 23	06 59	07 32	05 30	06 41	07 41	08 26
N 40	06 15	06 48	07 18	05 08	06 18	07 19	08 09
35	06 08	06 39	07 06	04 50	05 59	07 02	07 54
30	06 01	06 30	06 56	04 34	05 43	06 46	07 41
20	05 47	06 14	06 38	04 08	05 16	06 20	07 19
N 10	05 34	06 00	06 22	03 45	04 52	05 58	07 00
0	05 20	05 45	06 07	03 24	04 30	05 37	06 42
S 10	05 03	05 30	05 52	03 03	04 08	05 16	06 24
20	04 44	05 12	05 36	02 41	03 44	04 53	06 04
30	04 19	04 51	05 18	02 15	03 17	04 27	05 42
35	04 03	04 38	05 07	02 00	03 01	04 12	05 29
40	03 44	04 23	04 54	01 43	02 42	03 54	05 13
45	03 19	04 04	04 39	01 22	02 19	03 32	04 55
S 50	02 45	03 40	04 21	00 56	01 51	03 04	04 32
52	02 26	03 28	04 12	00 43	01 36	02 51	04 21
54	02 02	03 14	04 02	00 28	01 20	02 35	04 09
56	01 29	02 58	03 51	00 12	01 01	02 17	03 55
58	////	02 39	03 38	24 37	00 37	01 55	03 38
S 60	////	02 13	03 23	24 05	00 05	01 26	03 17

Lat.	Sunset	Twilight Civil	Twilight Naut.	Moonset 19	20	21	22
°	h m	h m	h m	h m	h m	h m	h m
N 72	■	14 51	16 35	■	■	■	■
N 70	13 16	15 20	16 47	■	■	■	■
68	14 12	15 41	16 58	■	■	■	■
66	14 45	15 58	17 07	■	■	■	14 43
64	15 09	16 12	17 14	■	■	12 16	15 23
62	15 27	16 24	17 21	10 47	11 32	13 37	15 50
60	15 43	16 34	17 27	11 35	12 32	14 13	16 11
N 58	15 56	16 43	17 33	12 05	13 06	14 39	16 28
56	16 07	16 51	17 37	12 29	13 31	15 00	16 43
54	16 17	16 58	17 42	12 48	13 51	15 17	16 55
52	16 26	17 04	17 46	13 04	14 07	15 31	17 06
50	16 34	17 10	17 50	13 18	14 22	15 44	17 16
45	16 51	17 23	17 59	13 46	14 51	16 10	17 36
N 40	17 04	17 34	18 07	14 08	15 14	16 31	17 52
35	17 16	17 43	18 14	14 27	15 33	16 48	18 06
30	17 26	17 52	18 21	14 43	15 49	17 02	18 18
20	17 44	18 08	18 35	15 10	16 16	17 27	18 38
N 10	18 00	18 22	18 48	15 33	16 40	17 48	18 55
0	18 15	18 37	19 02	15 55	17 02	18 08	19 11
S 10	18 29	18 52	19 18	16 17	17 23	18 28	19 27
20	18 45	19 09	19 37	16 40	17 47	18 49	19 44
30	19 04	19 30	20 02	17 07	18 14	19 13	20 03
35	19 15	19 43	20 18	17 23	18 30	19 27	20 15
40	19 27	19 58	20 37	17 42	18 48	19 43	20 27
45	19 42	20 17	21 02	18 04	19 10	20 03	20 42
S 50	20 00	20 41	21 36	18 33	19 38	20 26	21 01
52	20 09	20 52	21 54	18 47	19 52	20 38	21 09
54	20 19	21 06	22 17	19 03	20 08	20 51	21 19
56	20 30	21 22	22 49	19 22	20 26	21 06	21 29
58	20 42	21 41	////	19 46	20 49	21 23	21 42
S 60	20 57	22 06	////	20 18	21 18	21 45	21 56

	SUN Eqn. of Time 00h	SUN Eqn. of Time 12h	SUN Mer. Pass.	MOON Mer. Pass. Upper	MOON Mer. Pass. Lower	Age	Phase
Day	m s	m s	h m	h m	h m	d	%
19	10 27	10 36	12 11	09 39	22 12	27	8
20	10 45	10 54	12 11	10 46	23 19	28	3
21	11 03	11 12	12 11	11 53	24 25	29	0

© British Crown Copyright 2022. All rights reserved.

UT	ARIES GHA	VENUS −3.9 GHA	VENUS Dec	MARS −0.5 GHA	MARS Dec	JUPITER −2.2 GHA	JUPITER Dec	SATURN +0.8 GHA	SATURN Dec	STARS Name	SHA	Dec
d h	° ′	° ′	° ′	° ′	° ′	° ′	° ′	° ′	° ′		° ′	° ′
22 00	121 05.3	154 35.1	S15 08.5	54 38.9	N24 30.1	116 41.7	N 0 35.1	153 41.0	S14 27.9	Acamar	315 12.9	S40 13.0
01	136 07.7	169 34.5	07.5	69 41.1	30.2	131 43.8	35.3	168 43.2	27.8	Achernar	335 21.5	S57 07.5
02	151 10.2	184 34.0	06.4	84 43.2	30.2	146 45.8	35.5	183 45.4	27.7	Acrux	173 01.6	S63 13.3
03	166 12.6	199 33.4 ..	05.4	99 45.4 ..	30.2	161 47.9 ..	35.6	198 47.6 ..	27.6	Adhara	255 06.8	S29 00.3
04	181 15.1	214 32.8	04.4	114 47.6	30.3	176 50.0	35.8	213 49.7	27.5	Aldebaran	290 41.2	N16 33.3
05	196 17.6	229 32.2	03.3	129 49.7	30.3	191 52.1	36.0	228 51.9	27.4			
06	211 20.0	244 31.6	S15 02.3	144 51.9	N24 30.3	206 54.1	N 0 36.2	243 54.1	S14 27.3	Alioth	166 14.2	N55 49.8
07	226 22.5	259 31.1	01.2	159 54.0	30.3	221 56.2	36.4	258 56.3	27.2	Alkaid	152 53.2	N49 11.6
08	241 25.0	274 30.5	15 00.2	174 56.2	30.4	236 58.3	36.5	273 58.5	27.2	Alnair	27 35.3	S46 51.2
S 09	256 27.4	289 29.9	14 59.1	189 58.3 ..	30.4	252 00.4 ..	36.7	289 00.7 ..	27.1	Alnilam	275 39.1	S 1 11.3
U 10	271 29.9	304 29.3	58.1	205 00.5	30.4	267 02.5	36.9	304 02.9	27.0	Alphard	217 49.0	S 8 45.5
N 11	286 32.4	319 28.8	57.0	220 02.6	30.4	282 04.5	37.1	319 05.0	26.9			
D 12	301 34.8	334 28.2	S14 56.0	235 04.8	N24 30.5	297 06.6	N 0 37.2	334 07.2	S14 26.8	Alphecca	126 05.3	N26 38.0
A 13	316 37.3	349 27.6	55.0	250 06.9	30.5	312 08.7	37.4	349 09.4	26.7	Alpheratz	357 36.6	N29 13.1
Y 14	331 39.8	4 27.0	53.9	265 09.1	30.5	327 10.8	37.6	4 11.6	26.6	Altair	62 01.9	N 8 55.6
15	346 42.2	19 26.5 ..	52.9	280 11.2 ..	30.6	342 12.8 ..	37.8	19 13.8 ..	26.5	Ankaa	353 08.9	S42 11.2
16	1 44.7	34 25.9	51.8	295 13.4	30.6	357 14.9	37.9	34 16.0	26.4	Antares	112 18.0	S26 28.9
17	16 47.1	49 25.3	50.8	310 15.5	30.6	12 17.0	38.1	49 18.1	26.3			
18	31 49.6	64 24.8	S14 49.7	325 17.6	N24 30.7	27 19.1	N 0 38.3	64 20.3	S14 26.2	Arcturus	145 49.4	N19 03.6
19	46 52.1	79 24.2	48.7	340 19.8	30.7	42 21.1	38.5	79 22.5	26.1	Atria	107 14.1	S69 03.9
20	61 54.5	94 23.6	47.6	355 21.9	30.7	57 23.2	38.7	94 24.7	26.0	Avior	234 14.7	S59 34.9
21	76 57.0	109 23.1 ..	46.5	10 24.0 ..	30.7	72 25.3 ..	38.8	109 26.9 ..	25.9	Bellatrix	278 24.3	N 6 22.2
22	91 59.5	124 22.5	45.5	25 26.2	30.8	87 27.4	39.0	124 29.1	25.8	Betelgeuse	270 53.5	N 7 24.6
23	107 01.9	139 21.9	44.4	40 28.3	30.8	102 29.4	39.2	139 31.3	25.7			
23 00	122 04.4	154 21.3	S14 43.4	55 30.4	N24 30.8	117 31.5	N 0 39.4	154 33.4	S14 25.6	Canopus	263 52.6	S52 42.6
01	137 06.9	169 20.8	42.3	70 32.6	30.9	132 33.6	39.5	169 35.6	25.5	Capella	280 23.9	N46 01.3
02	152 09.3	184 20.2	41.3	85 34.7	30.9	147 35.7	39.7	184 37.8	25.4	Deneb	49 27.4	N45 21.7
03	167 11.8	199 19.6 ..	40.2	100 36.8 ..	30.9	162 37.7 ..	39.9	199 40.0 ..	25.3	Denebola	182 26.4	N14 26.5
04	182 14.3	214 19.1	39.2	115 39.0	31.0	177 39.8	40.1	214 42.2	25.2	Diphda	348 49.0	S17 51.8
05	197 16.7	229 18.5	38.1	130 41.1	31.0	192 41.9	40.3	229 44.4	25.1			
06	212 19.2	244 18.0	S14 37.0	145 43.2	N24 31.0	207 43.9	N 0 40.4	244 46.5	S14 25.0	Dubhe	193 42.5	N61 37.4
07	227 21.6	259 17.4	36.0	160 45.3	31.1	222 46.0	40.6	259 48.7	24.9	Elnath	278 03.6	N28 37.6
08	242 24.1	274 16.8	34.9	175 47.5	31.1	237 48.1	40.8	274 50.9	24.9	Eltanin	90 43.4	N51 28.9
M 09	257 26.6	289 16.3 ..	33.8	190 49.6 ..	31.1	252 50.2 ..	41.0	289 53.1 ..	24.8	Enif	33 40.7	N 9 58.7
O 10	272 29.0	304 15.7	32.8	205 51.7	31.1	267 52.2	41.1	304 55.3	24.7	Fomalhaut	15 16.6	S29 30.2
N 11	287 31.5	319 15.1	31.7	220 53.8	31.2	282 54.3	41.3	319 57.5	24.6			
D 12	302 34.0	334 14.6	S14 30.7	235 55.9	N24 31.2	297 56.4	N 0 41.5	334 59.6	S14 24.5	Gacrux	171 53.2	S57 14.3
A 13	317 36.4	349 14.0	29.6	250 58.0	31.2	312 58.4	41.7	350 01.8	24.4	Gienah	175 45.1	S17 40.1
Y 14	332 38.9	4 13.5	28.5	266 00.2	31.3	328 00.5	41.9	5 04.0	24.3	Hadar	148 38.3	S60 28.7
15	347 41.4	19 12.9 ..	27.5	281 02.3 ..	31.3	343 02.6 ..	42.0	20 06.2 ..	24.2	Hamal	327 53.0	N23 34.3
16	2 43.8	34 12.3	26.4	296 04.4	31.3	358 04.7	42.2	35 08.4	24.1	Kaus Aust.	83 35.0	S34 22.4
17	17 46.3	49 11.8	25.3	311 06.5	31.4	13 06.7	42.4	50 10.6	24.0			
18	32 48.8	64 11.2	S14 24.3	326 08.6	N24 31.4	28 08.8	N 0 42.6	65 12.7	S14 23.9	Kochab	137 20.0	N74 03.3
19	47 51.2	79 10.7	23.2	341 10.7	31.4	43 10.9	42.8	80 14.9	23.8	Markab	13 31.7	N15 19.7
20	62 53.7	94 10.1	22.1	356 12.8	31.5	58 12.9	42.9	95 17.1	23.7	Menkar	314 07.7	N 4 10.7
21	77 56.1	109 09.6 ..	21.1	11 14.9 ..	31.5	73 15.0 ..	43.1	110 19.3 ..	23.6	Menkent	147 59.5	S36 28.8
22	92 58.6	124 09.0	20.0	26 17.0	31.5	88 17.1	43.3	125 21.5	23.5	Miaplacidus	221 37.7	S69 48.6
23	108 01.1	139 08.4	18.9	41 19.1	31.6	103 19.1	43.5	140 23.7	23.4			
24 00	123 03.5	154 07.9	S14 17.8	56 21.2	N24 31.6	118 21.2	N 0 43.7	155 25.8	S14 23.3	Mirfak	308 30.4	N49 56.7
01	138 06.0	169 07.3	16.8	71 23.3	31.6	133 23.3	43.8	170 28.0	23.2	Nunki	75 50.1	S26 16.1
02	153 08.5	184 06.8	15.7	86 25.4	31.7	148 25.4	44.0	185 30.2	23.1	Peacock	53 08.9	S56 39.7
03	168 10.9	199 06.2 ..	14.6	101 27.5 ..	31.7	163 27.4 ..	44.2	200 32.4 ..	23.0	Pollux	243 18.9	N27 58.2
04	183 13.4	214 05.7	13.5	116 29.6	31.7	178 29.5	44.4	215 34.6	22.9	Procyon	244 52.2	N 5 09.9
05	198 15.9	229 05.1	12.5	131 31.7	31.8	193 31.6	44.5	230 36.8	22.8			
06	213 18.3	244 04.6	S14 11.4	146 33.8	N24 31.8	208 33.6	N 0 44.7	245 38.9	S14 22.7	Rasalhague	96 00.3	N12 32.5
07	228 20.8	259 04.0	10.3	161 35.9	31.8	223 35.7	44.9	260 41.1	22.6	Regulus	207 35.9	N11 51.2
08	243 23.2	274 03.5	09.2	176 38.0	31.9	238 37.8	45.1	275 43.3	22.5	Rigel	281 05.2	S 8 10.6
T 09	258 25.7	289 02.9 ..	08.2	191 40.1 ..	31.9	253 39.8 ..	45.3	290 45.5 ..	22.4	Rigil Kent.	139 42.6	S60 55.5
U 10	273 28.2	304 02.4	07.1	206 42.2	32.0	268 41.9	45.4	305 47.7	22.4	Sabik	102 04.9	S15 45.2
E 11	288 30.6	319 01.8	06.0	221 44.3	32.0	283 44.0	45.6	320 49.9	22.3			
S 12	303 33.1	334 01.3	S14 04.9	236 46.4	N24 32.0	298 46.0	N 0 45.8	335 52.0	S14 22.2	Schedar	349 33.1	N56 40.0
D 13	318 35.6	349 00.7	03.9	251 48.4	32.1	313 48.1	46.0	350 54.2	22.1	Shaula	96 12.9	S37 07.1
A 14	333 38.0	4 00.2	02.8	266 50.5	32.1	328 50.2	46.2	5 56.4	22.0	Sirius	258 27.3	S16 44.9
Y 15	348 40.5	18 59.6 ..	01.7	281 52.6 ..	32.1	343 52.2 ..	46.4	20 58.6 ..	21.9	Spica	158 23.9	S11 16.9
16	3 43.0	33 59.1	14 00.6	296 54.7	32.2	358 54.3	46.5	36 00.8	21.8	Suhail	222 47.0	S43 31.5
17	18 45.4	48 58.5	13 59.5	311 56.8	32.2	13 56.4	46.7	51 02.9	21.7			
18	33 47.9	63 58.0	S13 58.4	326 58.9	N24 32.2	28 58.4	N 0 46.9	66 05.1	S14 21.6	Vega	80 34.7	N38 48.1
19	48 50.4	78 57.4	57.4	342 00.9	32.3	44 00.5	47.1	81 07.3	21.5	Zuben'ubi	136 57.9	S16 08.2
20	63 52.8	93 56.9	56.3	357 03.0	32.3	59 02.6	47.3	96 09.5	21.4		SHA	Mer. Pass.
21	78 55.3	108 56.4 ..	55.2	12 05.1 ..	32.3	74 04.6 ..	47.4	111 11.7 ..	21.3		° ′	h m
22	93 57.7	123 55.8	54.1	27 07.2	32.4	89 06.7	47.6	126 13.9	21.2	Venus	32 17.0	13 43
23	109 00.2	138 55.3	53.0	42 09.2	32.4	104 08.8	47.8	141 16.0	21.1	Mars	293 26.0	20 15
	h m									Jupiter	355 27.1	16 08
Mer. Pass. 15 49.1		v −0.6	d 1.1	v 2.1	d 0.0	v 2.1	d 0.2	v 2.2	d 0.1	Saturn	32 29.0	13 40

© British Crown Copyright 2022. All rights reserved.

UT	SUN GHA	SUN Dec	MOON GHA	v	MOON Dec	d	HP
d h	° ′	° ′	° ′	′	° ′	′	′
22 00	177 09.9	S19 47.2	173 58.3	2.7	S24 11.7	9.0	61.5
01	192 09.7	46.6	188 20.0	2.7	24 02.7	9.2	61.5
02	207 09.5	46.0	202 41.7	2.9	23 53.5	9.3	61.5
03	222 09.3 ..	45.5	217 03.6	2.9	23 44.2	9.5	61.5
04	237 09.2	44.9	231 25.5	3.1	23 34.7	9.7	61.5
05	252 09.0	44.3	245 47.6	3.2	23 25.0	9.9	61.5
06	267 08.8	S19 43.8	260 09.8	3.3	S23 15.1	10.0	61.5
07	282 08.7	43.2	274 32.1	3.3	23 05.1	10.2	61.5
08	297 08.5	42.6	288 54.4	3.5	22 54.9	10.4	61.5
S 09	312 08.3 ..	42.1	303 16.9	3.7	22 44.5	10.5	61.5
U 10	327 08.1	41.5	317 39.6	3.7	22 34.0	10.7	61.4
N 11	342 08.0	40.9	332 02.3	3.8	22 23.3	10.9	61.4
D 12	357 07.8	S19 40.3	346 25.1	4.0	S22 12.4	11.0	61.4
A 13	12 07.6	39.8	0 48.1	4.1	22 01.4	11.1	61.4
Y 14	27 07.5	39.2	15 11.2	4.1	21 50.3	11.3	61.4
15	42 07.3 ..	38.6	29 34.3	4.4	21 39.0	11.5	61.4
16	57 07.1	38.0	43 57.7	4.4	21 27.5	11.6	61.4
17	72 07.0	37.5	58 21.1	4.5	21 15.9	11.7	61.4
18	87 06.8	S19 36.9	72 44.6	4.7	S21 04.2	11.9	61.4
19	102 06.6	36.3	87 08.3	4.8	20 52.3	12.1	61.3
20	117 06.5	35.7	101 32.1	4.9	20 40.2	12.1	61.3
21	132 06.3 ..	35.2	115 56.0	5.0	20 28.1	12.3	61.3
22	147 06.1	34.6	130 20.0	5.2	20 15.8	12.5	61.3
23	162 06.0	34.0	144 44.2	5.3	20 03.3	12.5	61.3
23 00	177 05.8	S19 33.4	159 08.5	5.4	S19 50.8	12.7	61.3
01	192 05.6	32.8	173 32.9	5.5	19 38.1	12.9	61.3
02	207 05.5	32.3	187 57.4	5.6	19 25.2	12.9	61.2
03	222 05.3 ..	31.7	202 22.0	5.8	19 12.3	13.1	61.2
04	237 05.1	31.1	216 46.8	5.9	18 59.2	13.2	61.2
05	252 05.0	30.5	231 11.7	6.0	18 46.0	13.3	61.2
06	267 04.8	S19 29.9	245 36.7	6.1	S18 32.7	13.4	61.2
07	282 04.7	29.3	260 01.8	6.3	18 19.3	13.5	61.2
08	297 04.5	28.8	274 27.1	6.4	18 05.8	13.7	61.1
M 09	312 04.3 ..	28.2	288 52.5	6.5	17 52.1	13.7	61.1
O 10	327 04.2	27.6	303 18.0	6.6	17 38.4	13.8	61.1
N 11	342 04.0	27.0	317 43.6	6.8	17 24.6	14.0	61.1
D 12	357 03.9	S19 26.4	332 09.4	6.8	S17 10.6	14.1	61.0
A 13	12 03.7	25.8	346 35.2	7.0	16 56.5	14.1	61.0
Y 14	27 03.5	25.2	1 01.2	7.1	16 42.4	14.2	61.0
15	42 03.4 ..	24.6	15 27.3	7.3	16 28.2	14.4	61.0
16	57 03.2	24.1	29 53.6	7.3	16 13.8	14.4	61.0
17	72 03.1	23.5	44 19.9	7.5	15 59.4	14.5	60.9
18	87 02.9	S19 22.9	58 46.4	7.6	S15 44.9	14.6	60.9
19	102 02.7	22.3	73 13.0	7.7	15 30.3	14.7	60.9
20	117 02.6	21.7	87 39.7	7.8	15 15.6	14.8	60.9
21	132 02.4 ..	21.1	102 06.5	7.9	15 00.8	14.8	60.8
22	147 02.3	20.5	116 33.4	8.1	14 46.0	14.9	60.8
23	162 02.1	19.9	131 00.5	8.1	14 31.1	15.0	60.8
24 00	177 01.9	S19 19.3	145 27.6	8.3	S14 16.1	15.1	60.7
01	192 01.8	18.7	159 54.9	8.4	14 01.0	15.1	60.7
02	207 01.6	18.1	174 22.3	8.5	13 45.9	15.2	60.7
03	222 01.5 ..	17.5	188 49.8	8.6	13 30.7	15.3	60.7
04	237 01.3	16.9	203 17.4	8.7	13 15.4	15.3	60.6
05	252 01.2	16.3	217 45.1	8.8	13 00.1	15.4	60.6
06	267 01.0	S19 15.7	232 12.9	9.0	S12 44.7	15.5	60.6
07	282 00.9	15.1	246 40.9	9.0	12 29.2	15.5	60.5
T 08	297 00.7	14.5	261 08.9	9.2	12 13.7	15.6	60.5
U 09	312 00.6 ..	13.9	275 37.1	9.2	11 58.1	15.6	60.5
E 10	327 00.4	13.3	290 05.3	9.4	11 42.5	15.6	60.4
S 11	342 00.2	12.7	304 33.7	9.4	11 26.9	15.7	60.4
D 12	357 00.1	S19 12.1	319 02.1	9.6	S11 11.2	15.8	60.4
A 13	11 59.9	11.5	333 30.7	9.6	10 55.4	15.8	60.3
Y 14	26 59.8	10.9	347 59.3	9.8	10 39.6	15.9	60.3
15	41 59.6 ..	10.3	2 28.1	9.8	10 23.7	15.8	60.3
16	56 59.5	09.7	16 56.9	10.0	10 07.9	16.0	60.2
17	71 59.3	09.1	31 25.9	10.0	9 51.9	15.9	60.2
18	86 59.2	S19 08.5	45 54.9	10.1	S 9 36.0	16.0	60.2
19	101 59.0	07.9	60 24.0	10.3	9 20.0	16.1	60.1
20	116 58.9	07.3	74 53.3	10.3	9 03.9	16.0	60.1
21	131 58.7 ..	06.7	89 22.6	10.4	8 47.9	16.1	60.1
22	146 58.6	06.1	103 52.0	10.5	8 31.8	16.1	60.0
23	161 58.4	05.5	118 21.5	10.6	S 8 15.7	16.1	60.0
SD	16.3	d 0.6	16.7		16.6		16.5

Lat.	Twilight Naut.	Twilight Civil	Sunrise	Moonrise 22	23	24	25
°	h m	h m	h m	h m	h m	h m	h m
N 72	07 40	09 19	■	■	12 42	11 18	10 36
N 70	07 28	08 53	10 43	■	11 49	10 59	10 29
68	07 18	08 33	09 58	■	11 15	10 44	10 23
66	07 10	08 17	09 28	11 27	10 51	10 32	10 18
64	07 03	08 04	09 06	10 46	10 32	10 22	10 14
62	06 57	07 53	08 49	10 18	10 16	10 13	10 10
60	06 51	07 44	08 34	09 56	10 02	10 05	10 07
N 58	06 46	07 35	08 22	09 38	09 51	09 58	10 04
56	06 42	07 28	08 11	09 23	09 41	09 52	10 01
54	06 37	07 21	08 01	09 10	09 32	09 47	09 59
52	06 33	07 15	07 53	08 58	09 24	09 42	09 57
50	06 30	07 09	07 45	08 48	09 16	09 38	09 55
45	06 21	06 57	07 29	08 26	09 01	09 28	09 51
N 40	06 14	06 47	07 16	08 09	08 48	09 20	09 47
35	06 07	06 38	07 05	07 54	08 37	09 13	09 44
30	06 00	06 29	06 55	07 41	08 27	09 07	09 41
20	05 47	06 14	06 37	07 19	08 11	08 56	09 36
N 10	05 34	06 00	06 22	07 00	07 56	08 46	09 32
0	05 21	05 46	06 08	06 42	07 42	08 37	09 28
S 10	05 05	05 31	05 54	06 24	07 28	08 28	09 24
20	04 46	05 14	05 38	06 04	07 14	08 19	09 20
30	04 22	04 54	05 20	05 42	06 56	08 08	09 15
35	04 07	04 41	05 10	05 29	06 46	08 01	09 12
40	03 48	04 27	04 58	05 13	06 35	07 54	09 09
45	03 24	04 09	04 43	04 55	06 21	07 46	09 05
S 50	02 52	03 46	04 26	04 32	06 05	07 35	09 01
52	02 34	03 34	04 17	04 21	05 57	07 30	08 59
54	02 13	03 21	04 08	04 09	05 48	07 25	08 57
56	01 44	03 06	03 57	03 55	05 38	07 19	08 54
58	00 52	02 48	03 45	03 38	05 27	07 12	08 51
S 60	////	02 25	03 31	03 17	05 14	07 05	08 48

Lat.	Sunset	Twilight Civil	Twilight Naut.	Moonset 22	23	24	25
°	h m	h m	h m	h m	h m	h m	h m
N 72	■	15 06	16 45	■	15 37	18 54	21 22
N 70	13 42	15 31	16 57	■	16 28	19 10	21 25
68	14 27	15 51	17 06	■	16 59	19 22	21 28
66	14 56	16 07	17 14	14 43	17 22	19 33	21 30
64	15 18	16 20	17 21	15 23	17 40	19 41	21 32
62	15 36	16 31	17 27	15 50	17 55	19 48	21 34
60	15 50	16 40	17 33	16 11	18 07	19 55	21 35
N 58	16 03	16 49	17 38	16 28	18 17	20 00	21 36
56	16 13	16 56	17 43	16 43	18 26	20 05	21 37
54	16 23	17 03	17 47	16 55	18 34	20 09	21 39
52	16 31	17 09	17 51	17 06	18 42	20 13	21 39
50	16 39	17 15	17 54	17 16	18 48	20 16	21 40
45	16 55	17 27	18 03	17 36	19 02	20 24	21 42
N 40	17 08	17 37	18 10	17 52	19 13	20 30	21 44
35	17 19	17 46	18 17	18 06	19 23	20 36	21 45
30	17 29	17 55	18 24	18 18	19 31	20 40	21 46
20	17 46	18 09	18 36	18 38	19 45	20 48	21 48
N 10	18 01	18 23	18 49	18 55	19 58	20 55	21 50
0	18 15	18 37	19 03	19 11	20 09	21 02	21 51
S 10	18 30	18 52	19 18	19 27	20 20	21 08	21 53
20	18 45	19 09	19 37	19 44	20 32	21 15	21 54
30	19 03	19 29	20 01	20 03	20 46	21 23	21 56
35	19 13	19 41	20 16	20 15	20 54	21 27	21 57
40	19 25	19 56	20 34	20 27	21 03	21 32	21 58
45	19 39	20 14	20 58	20 42	21 13	21 38	21 59
S 50	19 57	20 37	21 30	21 01	21 25	21 45	22 01
52	20 05	20 48	21 47	21 09	21 31	21 48	22 01
54	20 14	21 01	22 08	21 19	21 37	21 51	22 02
56	20 25	21 16	22 36	21 29	21 44	21 55	22 03
58	20 37	21 34	23 23	21 42	21 52	21 59	22 04
S 60	20 51	21 56	////	21 56	22 01	22 03	22 05

Day	SUN Eqn. of Time 00ʰ	12ʰ	Mer. Pass.	MOON Mer. Pass. Upper	Lower	Age	Phase
d	m s	m s	h m	h m	h m	d	%
22	11 20	11 28	12 11	12 57	00 25	01	1
23	11 36	11 44	12 12	13 56	01 27	02	4
24	11 52	11 59	12 12	14 50	02 23	03	10

© British Crown Copyright 2022. All rights reserved.

UT	ARIES GHA	VENUS −3.9 GHA	Dec	MARS −0.4 GHA	Dec	JUPITER −2.2 GHA	Dec	SATURN +0.8 GHA	Dec	Name	SHA	Dec
25 00	124 02.7	153 54.7	S13 51.9	57 11.3	N24 32.5	119 10.8	N 0 48.0	156 18.2	S14 21.0	Acamar	315 12.9	S40 13.0
01	139 05.1	168 54.2	50.8	72 13.4	32.5	134 12.9	48.2	171 20.4	20.9	Achernar	335 21.5	S57 07.5
02	154 07.6	183 53.6	49.7	87 15.4	32.5	149 15.0	48.3	186 22.6	20.8	Acrux	173 01.5	S63 13.3
03	169 10.1	198 53.1 ..	48.7	102 17.5 ..	32.6	164 17.0 ..	48.5	201 24.8 ..	20.7	Adhara	255 06.8	S29 00.3
04	184 12.5	213 52.6	47.6	117 19.6	32.6	179 19.1	48.7	216 26.9	20.6	Aldebaran	290 41.3	N16 33.3
05	199 15.0	228 52.0	46.5	132 21.7	32.6	194 21.1	48.9	231 29.1	20.5			
06	214 17.5	243 51.5	S13 45.4	147 23.7	N24 32.7	209 23.2	N 0 49.1	246 31.3	S14 20.4	Alioth	166 14.2	N55 49.8
W 07	229 19.9	258 51.0	44.3	162 25.8	32.7	224 25.3	49.3	261 33.5	20.3	Alkaid	152 53.2	N49 11.6
E 08	244 22.4	273 50.4	43.2	177 27.8	32.8	239 27.3	49.4	276 35.7	20.2	Alnair	27 35.4	S46 51.2
D 09	259 24.8	288 49.9 ..	42.1	192 29.9 ..	32.8	254 29.4 ..	49.6	291 37.9 ..	20.1	Alnilam	275 39.1	S 1 11.3
N 10	274 27.3	303 49.3	41.0	207 32.0	32.8	269 31.5	49.8	306 40.0	20.0	Alphard	217 49.0	S 8 45.5
E 11	289 29.8	318 48.8	39.9	222 34.0	32.9	284 33.5	50.0	321 42.2	19.9			
S 12	304 32.2	333 48.3	S13 38.8	237 36.1	N24 32.9	299 35.6	N 0 50.2	336 44.4	S14 19.8	Alphecca	126 05.2	N26 38.0
D 13	319 34.7	348 47.7	37.7	252 38.1	32.9	314 37.6	50.3	351 46.6	19.7	Alpheratz	357 36.6	N29 13.1
A 14	334 37.2	3 47.2	36.6	267 40.2	33.0	329 39.7	50.5	6 48.8	19.6	Altair	62 01.9	N 8 55.6
Y 15	349 39.6	18 46.7 ..	35.5	282 42.2 ..	33.0	344 41.8 ..	50.7	21 50.9 ..	19.5	Ankaa	353 08.9	S42 11.2
16	4 42.1	33 46.1	34.4	297 44.3	33.1	359 43.8	50.9	36 53.1	19.5	Antares	112 18.0	S26 28.9
17	19 44.6	48 45.6	33.3	312 46.4	33.1	14 45.9	51.1	51 55.3	19.4			
18	34 47.0	63 45.1	S13 32.2	327 48.4	N24 33.1	29 48.0	N 0 51.3	66 57.5	S14 19.3	Arcturus	145 49.4	N19 03.6
19	49 49.5	78 44.5	31.1	342 50.5	33.2	44 50.0	51.4	81 59.7	19.2	Atria	107 14.1	S69 03.9
20	64 52.0	93 44.0	30.0	357 52.5	33.2	59 52.1	51.6	97 01.9	19.1	Avior	234 14.7	S59 35.0
21	79 54.4	108 43.5 ..	28.9	12 54.5 ..	33.3	74 54.1 ..	51.8	112 04.0 ..	19.0	Bellatrix	278 24.4	N 6 22.2
22	94 56.9	123 42.9	27.8	27 56.6	33.3	89 56.2	52.0	127 06.2	18.9	Betelgeuse	270 53.5	N 7 24.6
23	109 59.3	138 42.4	26.7	42 58.6	33.3	104 58.3	52.2	142 08.4	18.8			
26 00	125 01.8	153 41.9	S13 25.6	58 00.7	N24 33.4	120 00.3	N 0 52.4	157 10.6	S14 18.7	Canopus	263 52.6	S52 42.6
01	140 04.3	168 41.4	24.5	73 02.7	33.4	135 02.4	52.5	172 12.8	18.6	Capella	280 23.9	N46 01.4
02	155 06.7	183 40.8	23.4	88 04.8	33.5	150 04.4	52.7	187 14.9	18.5	Deneb	49 27.4	N45 21.7
03	170 09.2	198 40.3 ..	22.3	103 06.8 ..	33.5	165 06.5 ..	52.9	202 17.1 ..	18.4	Denebola	182 26.4	N14 26.5
04	185 11.7	213 39.8	21.2	118 08.8	33.5	180 08.6	53.1	217 19.3	18.3	Diphda	348 49.0	S17 51.8
05	200 14.1	228 39.2	20.1	133 10.9	33.6	195 10.6	53.3	232 21.5	18.2			
06	215 16.6	243 38.7	S13 19.0	148 12.9	N24 33.6	210 12.7	N 0 53.4	247 23.7	S14 18.1	Dubhe	193 42.5	N61 37.4
T 07	230 19.1	258 38.2	17.9	163 15.0	33.7	225 14.7	53.6	262 25.8	18.0	Elnath	278 03.6	N28 37.6
H 08	245 21.5	273 37.7	16.8	178 17.0	33.7	240 16.8	53.8	277 28.0	17.9	Eltanin	90 43.4	N51 28.9
U 09	260 24.0	288 37.1 ..	15.7	193 19.0 ..	33.7	255 18.9 ..	54.0	292 30.2 ..	17.8	Enif	33 40.7	N 9 58.7
R 10	275 26.5	303 36.6	14.6	208 21.1	33.8	270 20.9	54.2	307 32.4	17.7	Fomalhaut	15 16.6	S29 30.2
S 11	290 28.9	318 36.1	13.5	223 23.1	33.8	285 23.0	54.4	322 34.6	17.6			
D 12	305 31.4	333 35.6	S13 12.4	238 25.1	N24 33.9	300 25.0	N 0 54.6	337 36.7	S14 17.5	Gacrux	171 53.2	S57 14.3
A 13	320 33.8	348 35.0	11.2	253 27.1	33.9	315 27.1	54.7	352 38.9	17.4	Gienah	175 45.1	S17 40.1
Y 14	335 36.3	3 34.5	10.1	268 29.2	34.0	330 29.1	54.9	7 41.1	17.3	Hadar	148 38.3	S60 28.7
15	350 38.8	18 34.0 ..	09.0	283 31.2 ..	34.0	345 31.2 ..	55.1	22 43.3 ..	17.2	Hamal	327 53.0	N23 34.3
16	5 41.2	33 33.5	07.9	298 33.2	34.0	0 33.3	55.3	37 45.5	17.1	Kaus Aust.	83 35.0	S34 22.4
17	20 43.7	48 33.0	06.8	313 35.2	34.1	15 35.3	55.5	52 47.7	17.0			
18	35 46.2	63 32.4	S13 05.7	328 37.3	N24 34.1	30 37.4	N 0 55.7	67 49.8	S14 16.9	Kochab	137 20.0	N74 03.3
19	50 48.6	78 31.9	04.6	343 39.3	34.2	45 39.4	55.8	82 52.0	16.8	Markab	13 31.7	N15 19.7
20	65 51.1	93 31.4	03.5	358 41.3	34.2	60 41.5	56.0	97 54.2	16.7	Menkar	314 07.8	N 4 10.7
21	80 53.6	108 30.9 ..	02.3	13 43.3 ..	34.2	75 43.5 ..	56.2	112 56.4 ..	16.6	Menkent	147 59.5	S36 28.8
22	95 56.0	123 30.4	01.2	28 45.3	34.3	90 45.6	56.4	127 58.6	16.5	Miaplacidus	221 37.7	S69 48.6
23	110 58.5	138 29.9	13 00.1	43 47.4	34.3	105 47.7	56.6	143 00.7	16.4			
27 00	126 00.9	153 29.3	S12 59.0	58 49.4	N24 34.4	120 49.7	N 0 56.8	158 02.9	S14 16.3	Mirfak	308 30.4	N49 56.7
01	141 03.4	168 28.8	57.9	73 51.4	34.4	135 51.8	56.9	173 05.1	16.2	Nunki	75 50.1	S26 16.1
02	156 05.9	183 28.3	56.8	88 53.4	34.5	150 53.8	57.1	188 07.3	16.1	Peacock	53 08.9	S56 39.7
03	171 08.3	198 27.8 ..	55.6	103 55.4 ..	34.5	165 55.9 ..	57.3	203 09.5 ..	16.0	Pollux	243 18.9	N27 58.2
04	186 10.8	213 27.3	54.5	118 57.4	34.5	180 57.9	57.5	218 11.6	15.9	Procyon	244 52.2	N 5 09.9
05	201 13.3	228 26.8	53.4	133 59.4	34.6	196 00.0	57.7	233 13.8	15.9			
06	216 15.7	243 26.2	S12 52.3	149 01.4	N24 34.6	211 02.0	N 0 57.9	248 16.0	S14 15.8	Rasalhague	96 00.3	N12 32.5
07	231 18.2	258 25.7	51.2	164 03.4	34.7	226 04.1	58.1	263 18.2	15.7	Regulus	207 35.9	N11 51.2
08	246 20.7	273 25.2	50.0	179 05.4	34.7	241 06.2	58.2	278 20.4	15.6	Rigel	281 05.2	S 8 10.6
F 09	261 23.1	288 24.7 ..	48.9	194 07.5 ..	34.8	256 08.2 ..	58.4	293 22.5 ..	15.5	Rigil Kent.	139 42.6	S60 55.5
R 10	276 25.6	303 24.2	47.8	209 09.5	34.8	271 10.3	58.6	308 24.7	15.4	Sabik	102 04.9	S15 45.2
I 11	291 28.1	318 23.7	46.7	224 11.5	34.9	286 12.3	58.8	323 26.9	15.3			
D 12	306 30.5	333 23.2	S12 45.5	239 13.5	N24 34.9	301 14.4	N 0 59.0	338 29.1	S14 15.2	Schedar	349 33.1	N56 40.0
A 13	321 33.0	348 22.7	44.4	254 15.5	34.9	316 16.4	59.2	353 31.3	15.1	Shaula	96 12.9	S37 07.1
Y 14	336 35.4	3 22.1	43.3	269 17.5	35.0	331 18.5	59.4	8 33.4	15.0	Sirius	258 27.3	S16 45.0
15	351 37.9	18 21.6 ..	42.2	284 19.5 ..	35.0	346 20.5 ..	59.5	23 35.6 ..	14.9	Spica	158 23.9	S11 16.9
16	6 40.4	33 21.1	41.0	299 21.5	35.1	1 22.6	59.7	38 37.8	14.8	Suhail	222 47.0	S43 31.5
17	21 42.8	48 20.6	39.9	314 23.5	35.1	16 24.6	0 59.9	53 40.0	14.7			
18	36 45.3	63 20.1	S12 38.8	329 25.4	N24 35.2	31 26.7	N 1 00.1	68 42.1	S14 14.6	Vega	80 34.7	N38 48.1
19	51 47.8	78 19.6	37.7	344 27.4	35.2	46 28.7	00.3	83 44.3	14.5	Zuben'ubi	136 57.9	S16 08.2
20	66 50.2	93 19.1	36.5	359 29.4	35.3	61 30.8	00.5	98 46.5	14.4		SHA	Mer. Pass.
21	81 52.7	108 18.6 ..	35.4	14 31.4 ..	35.3	76 32.9 ..	00.7	113 48.7 ..	14.3	Venus	28 40.1	13 46
22	96 55.2	123 18.1	34.3	29 33.4	35.3	91 34.9	00.8	128 50.9	14.2	Mars	292 58.9	20 05
23	111 57.6	138 17.6	33.1	44 35.4	35.4	106 37.0	01.0	143 53.0	14.1	Jupiter	354 58.5	15 58
Mer. Pass. 15 37.3		v −0.5	d 1.1	v 2.0	d 0.0	v 2.1	d 0.2	v 2.2	d 0.1	Saturn	32 08.8	13 29

© British Crown Copyright 2022. All rights reserved.

UT	SUN		MOON					Lat.	Twilight		Sunrise	Moonrise			
									Naut.	Civil		25	26	27	28
	GHA	Dec	GHA	v	Dec	d	HP								
d h	° ′	° ′	° ′	′	° ′	′	′	°	h m	h m	h m	h m	h m	h m	h m
25 00	176 58.3	S19 04.9	132 51.1	10.6	S 7 59.6	16.2	60.0	N 72	07 31	09 06	11 45	10 36	10 02	09 28	08 46
01	191 58.1	04.3	147 20.7	10.8	7 43.4	16.2	59.9	N 70	07 20	08 43	10 22	10 29	10 03	09 38	09 08
02	206 58.0	03.6	161 50.5	10.8	7 27.2	16.2	59.9	68	07 11	08 25	09 44	10 23	10 04	09 46	09 25
03	221 57.8	.. 03.0	176 20.3	10.9	7 11.0	16.2	59.9	66	07 04	08 10	09 18	10 18	10 05	09 53	09 39
04	236 57.7	02.4	190 50.2	11.0	6 54.8	16.2	59.8	64	06 58	07 58	08 58	10 14	10 06	09 59	09 51
05	251 57.6	01.8	205 20.2	11.1	6 38.6	16.3	59.8	62	06 52	07 48	08 41	10 10	10 07	10 04	10 01
06	266 57.4	S19 01.2	219 50.3	11.1	S 6 22.3	16.3	59.8	60	06 47	07 39	08 28	10 07	10 08	10 08	10 10
W 07	281 57.3	00.6	234 20.4	11.2	6 06.0	16.2	59.7	N 58	06 42	07 31	08 16	10 04	10 08	10 12	10 17
E 08	296 57.1	19 00.0	248 50.6	11.3	5 49.8	16.3	59.7	56	06 38	07 24	08 06	10 01	10 09	10 16	10 24
D 09	311 57.0	18 59.3	263 20.9	11.4	5 33.5	16.3	59.7	54	06 34	07 17	07 57	09 59	10 09	10 19	10 30
N 10	326 56.8	58.7	277 51.3	11.5	5 17.2	16.3	59.6	52	06 30	07 12	07 49	09 57	10 10	10 22	10 36
E 11	341 56.7	58.1	292 21.8	11.5	5 00.9	16.3	59.6	50	06 27	07 06	07 42	09 55	10 10	10 25	10 41
S 12	356 56.5	S18 57.5	306 52.3	11.5	S 4 44.6	16.3	59.5	45	06 19	06 55	07 27	09 51	10 11	10 31	10 51
D 13	11 56.4	56.9	321 22.8	11.7	4 28.3	16.3	59.5	N 40	06 12	06 45	07 14	09 47	10 12	10 36	11 00
A 14	26 56.3	56.3	335 53.5	11.7	4 12.0	16.3	59.4	35	06 05	06 36	07 03	09 44	10 12	10 40	11 08
Y 15	41 56.1	.. 55.6	350 24.2	11.8	3 55.7	16.3	59.4	30	05 59	06 28	06 54	09 41	10 13	10 44	11 15
16	56 56.0	55.0	4 55.0	11.8	3 39.4	16.3	59.4	20	05 47	06 14	06 37	09 36	10 14	10 50	11 27
17	71 55.8	54.4	19 25.8	11.9	3 23.1	16.3	59.3	N 10	05 35	06 00	06 23	09 32	10 15	10 56	11 38
18	86 55.7	S18 53.8	33 56.7	12.0	S 3 06.8	16.3	59.3	0	05 22	05 47	06 09	09 28	10 16	11 02	11 48
19	101 55.5	53.2	48 27.7	12.0	2 50.5	16.2	59.3	S 10	05 07	05 33	05 55	09 24	10 17	11 08	11 58
20	116 55.4	52.5	62 58.7	12.1	2 34.3	16.3	59.2	20	04 49	05 17	05 40	09 20	10 18	11 14	12 09
21	131 55.3	.. 51.9	77 29.8	12.1	2 18.0	16.2	59.2	30	04 25	04 57	05 23	09 15	10 19	11 21	12 21
22	146 55.1	51.3	92 00.9	12.2	2 01.8	16.3	59.1	35	04 11	04 45	05 13	09 12	10 20	11 25	12 28
23	161 55.0	50.7	106 32.1	12.3	1 45.5	16.2	59.1	40	03 53	04 31	05 01	09 09	10 20	11 29	12 37
26 00	176 54.8	S18 50.1	121 03.4	12.3	S 1 29.3	16.2	59.1	45	03 30	04 13	04 48	09 05	10 21	11 35	12 46
01	191 54.7	49.4	135 34.7	12.3	1 13.1	16.2	59.0	S 50	02 59	03 51	04 31	09 01	10 23	11 41	12 58
02	206 54.6	48.8	150 06.0	12.4	0 56.9	16.2	59.0	52	02 43	03 41	04 23	08 59	10 23	11 44	13 04
03	221 54.4	.. 48.2	164 37.4	12.5	0 40.7	16.2	58.9	54	02 23	03 28	04 14	08 57	10 24	11 48	13 10
04	236 54.3	47.5	179 08.9	12.4	0 24.5	16.1	58.9	56	01 57	03 14	04 04	08 54	10 25	11 51	13 17
05	251 54.1	46.9	193 40.3	12.6	S 0 08.4	16.1	58.9	58	01 17	02 57	03 52	08 51	10 25	11 55	13 24
06	266 54.0	S18 46.3	208 11.9	12.6	N 0 07.7	16.1	58.8	S 60	////	02 36	03 39	08 48	10 26	12 00	13 33

UT	SUN		MOON					Lat.	Sunset	Twilight		Moonset			
										Civil	Naut.	25	26	27	28
d h	° ′	° ′	° ′	′	° ′	′	′	°	h m	h m	h m	h m	h m	h m	h m
07	281 53.9	45.7	222 43.5	12.6	0 23.8	16.1	58.8								
T 08	296 53.7	45.0	237 15.1	12.6	0 39.9	16.0	58.7	N 72	12 41	15 20	16 56	21 22	23 38	25 58	01 58
H 09	311 53.6	.. 44.4	251 46.7	12.8	0 55.9	16.0	58.7	N 70	14 04	15 43	17 06	21 25	23 31	25 38	01 38
U 10	326 53.5	43.8	266 18.5	12.7	1 11.9	16.0	58.7	68	14 42	16 01	17 15	21 28	23 26	25 23	01 23
R 11	341 53.3	43.1	280 50.2	12.8	1 27.9	15.9	58.6	66	15 08	16 16	17 22	21 30	23 21	25 11	01 11
S 12	356 53.2	S18 42.5	295 22.0	12.8	N 1 43.8	16.0	58.6	64	15 28	16 28	17 28	21 32	23 17	25 00	01 00
D 13	11 53.1	41.9	309 53.8	12.8	1 59.8	15.9	58.5	62	15 44	16 38	17 34	21 34	23 14	24 52	00 52
A 14	26 52.9	41.3	324 25.6	12.9	2 15.7	15.8	58.5	60	15 58	16 47	17 39	21 35	23 11	24 44	00 44
Y 15	41 52.8	.. 40.6	338 57.5	12.9	2 31.5	15.8	58.5	N 58	16 09	16 55	17 44	21 36	23 08	24 38	00 38
16	56 52.6	40.0	353 29.4	13.0	2 47.3	15.8	58.4	56	16 19	17 02	17 48	21 37	23 06	24 32	00 32
17	71 52.5	39.4	8 01.4	13.0	3 03.1	15.8	58.4	54	16 28	17 08	17 52	21 39	23 04	24 27	00 27
18	86 52.4	S18 38.7	22 33.4	13.0	N 3 18.9	15.7	58.3	52	16 36	17 14	17 55	21 39	23 02	24 22	00 22
19	101 52.2	38.1	37 05.4	13.0	3 34.6	15.7	58.3	50	16 44	17 19	17 58	21 40	23 00	24 18	00 18
20	116 52.1	37.4	51 37.4	13.0	3 50.3	15.6	58.3	45	16 59	17 31	18 06	21 42	22 57	24 09	00 09
21	131 52.0	.. 36.8	66 09.4	13.1	4 05.9	15.6	58.2	N 40	17 11	17 41	18 13	21 44	22 54	24 02	00 02
22	146 51.9	36.2	80 41.5	13.1	4 21.5	15.5	58.2	35	17 22	17 49	18 20	21 45	22 51	23 55	24 58
23	161 51.7	35.5	95 13.6	13.1	4 37.0	15.5	58.1	30	17 32	17 57	18 26	21 46	22 49	23 50	24 50
27 00	176 51.6	S18 34.9	109 45.7	13.2	N 4 52.5	15.5	58.1	20	17 48	18 11	18 38	21 48	22 45	23 40	24 35
01	191 51.5	34.3	124 17.9	13.1	5 08.0	15.4	58.0	N 10	18 02	18 25	18 50	21 50	22 41	23 32	24 22
02	206 51.3	33.6	138 50.0	13.2	5 23.4	15.4	58.0	0	18 16	18 38	19 03	21 51	22 38	23 24	24 10
03	221 51.2	.. 33.0	153 22.2	13.2	5 38.8	15.3	58.0	S 10	18 30	18 52	19 18	21 53	22 35	23 16	23 58
04	236 51.1	32.3	167 54.4	13.2	5 54.1	15.3	57.9	20	18 44	19 08	19 36	21 54	22 31	23 08	23 45
05	251 50.9	31.7	182 26.6	13.2	6 09.4	15.2	57.9	30	19 02	19 28	19 59	21 56	22 27	22 58	23 30
06	266 50.8	S18 31.1	196 58.8	13.3	N 6 24.6	15.1	57.9	35	19 12	19 40	20 14	21 57	22 25	22 53	23 22
07	281 50.7	30.4	211 31.1	13.2	6 39.7	15.2	57.8	40	19 23	19 54	20 31	21 58	22 22	22 47	23 12
08	296 50.5	29.8	226 03.3	13.3	6 54.9	15.0	57.8	45	19 37	20 11	20 54	21 59	22 19	22 39	23 01
F 09	311 50.4	.. 29.1	240 35.6	13.3	7 09.9	15.0	57.7	S 50	19 53	20 32	21 24	22 01	22 16	22 31	22 48
R 10	326 50.3	28.5	255 07.9	13.2	7 24.9	15.0	57.7	52	20 01	20 43	21 40	22 01	22 14	22 27	22 42
I 11	341 50.2	27.8	269 40.1	13.3	7 39.9	14.9	57.7	54	20 10	20 55	22 00	22 02	22 12	22 23	22 35
D 12	356 50.0	S18 27.2	284 12.4	13.3	N 7 54.8	14.8	57.6	56	20 20	21 09	22 25	22 03	22 10	22 18	22 27
A 13	11 49.9	26.6	298 44.7	13.3	8 09.6	14.8	57.6	58	20 31	21 26	23 01	22 04	22 08	22 13	22 18
Y 14	26 49.8	25.9	313 17.0	13.3	8 24.4	14.8	57.5	S 60	20 44	21 46	////	22 05	22 06	22 07	22 09
15	41 49.7	.. 25.3	327 49.3	13.3	8 39.2	14.6	57.5								
16	56 49.5	24.6	342 21.6	13.3	8 53.8	14.6	57.5								
17	71 49.4	24.0	356 53.9	13.3	9 08.4	14.6	57.4								
18	86 49.3	S18 23.3	11 26.2	13.3	N 9 23.0	14.5	57.4								
19	101 49.2	22.7	25 58.5	13.3	9 37.5	14.4	57.3								
20	116 49.0	22.0	40 30.8	13.3	9 51.9	14.3	57.3								
21	131 48.9	.. 21.4	55 03.1	13.3	10 06.2	14.3	57.3								
22	146 48.8	20.7	69 35.4	13.3	10 20.5	14.3	57.2								
23	161 48.7	20.1	84 07.7	13.3	N10 34.8	14.1	57.2								

	SUN				MOON			
Day	Eqn. of Time		Mer.	Mer. Pass.		Age	Phase	
	00h	12h	Pass.	Upper	Lower			
d	m s	m s	h m	h m	h m	d	%	
25	12 07	12 14	12 12	15 40	03 15	04	18	
26	12 20	12 27	12 12	16 27	04 04	05	28	
27	12 33	12 40	12 13	17 13	04 50	06	38	

SD 16.3　d 0.6　　SD 16.2　16.0　15.7

© British Crown Copyright 2022. All rights reserved.

UT	ARIES	VENUS −3·9		MARS −0·3		JUPITER −2·2		SATURN +0·8	
	GHA	GHA	Dec	GHA	Dec	GHA	Dec	GHA	Dec
d h	° ′	° ′	° ′	° ′	° ′	° ′	° ′	° ′	° ′
28 00	127 00.1	153 17.1	S12 32.0	59 37.4	N24 35.4	121 39.0	N 1 01.2	158 55.2	S14 14.0
01	142 02.5	168 16.6	30.9	74 39.4	35.5	136 41.1	01.4	173 57.4	13.9
02	157 05.0	183 16.1	29.7	89 41.4	35.5	151 43.1	01.6	188 59.6	13.8
03	172 07.5	198 15.6 ..	28.6	104 43.3 ..	35.6	166 45.2 ..	01.8	204 01.8 ..	13.7
04	187 09.9	213 15.1	27.5	119 45.3	35.6	181 47.2	02.0	219 03.9	13.6
05	202 12.4	228 14.6	26.3	134 47.3	35.7	196 49.3	02.1	234 06.1	13.5
S 06	217 14.9	243 14.1	S12 25.2	149 49.3	N24 35.7	211 51.3	N 1 02.3	249 08.3	S14 13.4
A 07	232 17.3	258 13.6	24.1	164 51.3	35.8	226 53.4	02.5	264 10.5	13.3
T 08	247 19.8	273 13.1	22.9	179 53.2	35.8	241 55.4	02.7	279 12.7	13.2
U 09	262 22.3	288 12.6 ..	21.8	194 55.2 ..	35.8	256 57.5 ..	02.9	294 14.8 ..	13.1
R 10	277 24.7	303 12.1	20.7	209 57.2	35.9	271 59.5	03.1	309 17.0	13.0
D 11	292 27.2	318 11.6	19.5	224 59.2	35.9	287 01.6	03.3	324 19.2	12.9
A 12	307 29.7	333 11.1	S12 18.4	240 01.1	N24 36.0	302 03.6	N 1 03.5	339 21.4	S14 12.8
Y 13	322 32.1	348 10.6	17.2	255 03.1	36.0	317 05.7	03.6	354 23.6	12.7
14	337 34.6	3 10.1	16.1	270 05.1	36.1	332 07.7	03.8	9 25.7	12.6
15	352 37.0	18 09.6 ..	15.0	285 07.1 ..	36.1	347 09.8 ..	04.0	24 27.9 ..	12.5
16	7 39.5	33 09.1	13.8	300 09.0	36.2	2 11.8	04.2	39 30.1	12.4
17	22 42.0	48 08.6	12.7	315 11.0	36.2	17 13.9	04.4	54 32.3	12.3
18	37 44.4	63 08.1	S12 11.5	330 13.0	N24 36.3	32 15.9	N 1 04.6	69 34.4	S14 12.2
19	52 46.9	78 07.6	10.4	345 14.9	36.3	47 18.0	04.8	84 36.6	12.1
20	67 49.4	93 07.1	09.3	0 16.9	36.4	62 20.0	05.0	99 38.8	12.0
21	82 51.8	108 06.6 ..	08.1	15 18.9 ..	36.4	77 22.1 ..	05.1	114 41.0 ..	11.9
22	97 54.3	123 06.1	07.0	30 20.8	36.5	92 24.1	05.3	129 43.2	11.8
23	112 56.8	138 05.6	05.8	45 22.8	36.5	107 26.1	05.5	144 45.3	11.7
29 00	127 59.2	153 05.1	S12 04.7	60 24.7	N24 36.6	122 28.2	N 1 05.7	159 47.5	S14 11.6
01	143 01.7	168 04.6	03.5	75 26.7	36.6	137 30.2	05.9	174 49.7	11.5
02	158 04.2	183 04.1	02.4	90 28.7	36.7	152 32.3	06.1	189 51.9	11.4
03	173 06.6	198 03.6 ..	01.2	105 30.6 ..	36.7	167 34.3 ..	06.3	204 54.1 ..	11.3
04	188 09.1	213 03.1	12 00.1	120 32.6	36.8	182 36.4	06.5	219 56.2	11.2
05	203 11.5	228 02.7	11 59.0	135 34.5	36.8	197 38.4	06.6	234 58.4	11.1
S 06	218 14.0	243 02.2	S11 57.8	150 36.5	N24 36.9	212 40.5	N 1 06.8	250 00.6	S14 11.0
U 07	233 16.5	258 01.7	56.7	165 38.4	36.9	227 42.5	07.0	265 02.8	11.0
N 08	248 18.9	273 01.2	55.5	180 40.4	36.9	242 44.6	07.2	280 04.9	10.9
D 09	263 21.4	288 00.7 ..	54.4	195 42.3 ..	37.0	257 46.6 ..	07.4	295 07.1 ..	10.8
A 10	278 23.9	303 00.2	53.2	210 44.3	37.0	272 48.7	07.6	310 09.3	10.7
Y 11	293 26.3	317 59.7	52.1	225 46.2	37.1	287 50.7	07.8	325 11.5	10.6
12	308 28.8	332 59.2	S11 50.9	240 48.2	N24 37.1	302 52.8	N 1 08.0	340 13.7	S14 10.5
13	323 31.3	347 58.7	49.8	255 50.1	37.2	317 54.8	08.2	355 15.8	10.4
14	338 33.7	2 58.3	48.6	270 52.1	37.2	332 56.8	08.3	10 18.0	10.3
15	353 36.2	17 57.8 ..	47.4	285 54.0 ..	37.3	347 58.9 ..	08.5	25 20.2 ..	10.2
16	8 38.7	32 57.3	46.3	300 56.0	37.3	3 00.9	08.7	40 22.4	10.1
17	23 41.1	47 56.8	45.1	315 57.9	37.4	18 03.0	08.9	55 24.5	10.0
18	38 43.6	62 56.3	S11 44.0	330 59.8	N24 37.4	33 05.0	N 1 09.1	70 26.7	S14 09.9
19	53 46.0	77 55.8	42.8	346 01.8	37.5	48 07.1	09.3	85 28.9	09.8
20	68 48.5	92 55.4	41.7	1 03.7	37.5	63 09.1	09.5	100 31.1	09.7
21	83 51.0	107 54.9 ..	40.5	16 05.7 ..	37.6	78 11.2 ..	09.7	115 33.3 ..	09.6
22	98 53.4	122 54.4	39.4	31 07.6	37.6	93 13.2	09.9	130 35.4	09.5
23	113 55.9	137 53.9	38.2	46 09.5	37.7	108 15.2	10.0	145 37.6	09.4
30 00	128 58.4	152 53.4	S11 37.0	61 11.5	N24 37.7	123 17.3	N 1 10.2	160 39.8	S14 09.3
01	144 00.8	167 52.9	35.9	76 13.4	37.8	138 19.3	10.4	175 42.0	09.2
02	159 03.3	182 52.5	34.7	91 15.3	37.8	153 21.4	10.6	190 44.1	09.1
03	174 05.8	197 52.0 ..	33.6	106 17.3 ..	37.9	168 23.4 ..	10.8	205 46.3 ..	09.0
04	189 08.2	212 51.5	32.4	121 19.2	37.9	183 25.5	11.0	220 48.5	08.9
05	204 10.7	227 51.0	31.3	136 21.1	38.0	198 27.5	11.2	235 50.7	08.8
06	219 13.1	242 50.5	S11 30.1	151 23.1	N24 38.1	213 29.5	N 1 11.4	250 52.9	S14 08.7
07	234 15.6	257 50.1	28.9	166 25.0	38.1	228 31.6	11.6	265 55.0	08.6
M 08	249 18.1	272 49.6	27.8	181 26.9	38.2	243 33.6	11.8	280 57.2	08.5
O 09	264 20.5	287 49.1 ..	26.6	196 28.8 ..	38.2	258 35.7 ..	11.9	295 59.4 ..	08.4
N 10	279 23.0	302 48.6	25.4	211 30.8	38.3	273 37.7	12.1	311 01.6	08.3
D 11	294 25.5	317 48.2	24.3	226 32.7	38.3	288 39.8	12.3	326 03.7	08.2
A 12	309 27.9	332 47.7	S11 23.1	241 34.6	N24 38.4	303 41.8	N 1 12.5	341 05.9	S14 08.1
Y 13	324 30.4	347 47.2	22.0	256 36.5	38.4	318 43.8	12.7	356 08.1	08.0
14	339 32.9	2 46.7	20.8	271 38.4	38.5	333 45.9	12.9	11 10.3	07.9
15	354 35.3	17 46.3 ..	19.6	286 40.4 ..	38.5	348 47.9 ..	13.1	26 12.5 ..	07.8
16	9 37.8	32 45.8	18.5	301 42.3	38.6	3 50.0	13.3	41 14.6	07.7
17	24 40.3	47 45.3	17.3	316 44.2	38.6	18 52.0	13.5	56 16.8	07.6
18	39 42.7	62 44.8	S11 16.1	331 46.1	N24 38.7	33 54.0	N 1 13.7	71 19.0	S14 07.5
19	54 45.2	77 44.4	15.0	346 48.0	38.7	48 56.1	13.9	86 21.2	07.4
20	69 47.6	92 43.9	13.8	1 49.9	38.8	63 58.1	14.0	101 23.3	07.3
21	84 50.1	107 43.4 ..	12.6	16 51.8 ..	38.8	79 00.2 ..	14.2	116 25.5 ..	07.2
22	99 52.6	122 43.0	11.5	31 53.7	38.9	94 02.2	14.4	131 27.7	07.1
23	114 55.0	137 42.5	10.3	46 55.7	38.9	109 04.2	14.6	146 29.9	07.0
Mer. Pass.	h m 15 25.5	v −0.5	d 1.2	v 1.9	d 0.0	v 2.0	d 0.2	v 2.2	d 0.1

STARS

Name	SHA	Dec
Acamar	315 12.9	S40 13.0
Achernar	335 21.5	S57 07.5
Acrux	173 01.5	S63 13.3
Adhara	255 06.8	S29 00.3
Aldebaran	290 41.3	N16 33.3
Alioth	166 14.1	N55 49.8
Alkaid	152 53.2	N49 11.6
Alnair	27 35.4	S46 51.2
Alnilam	275 39.1	S 1 11.3
Alphard	217 49.0	S 8 45.5
Alphecca	126 05.2	N26 38.0
Alpheratz	357 36.6	N29 13.1
Altair	62 01.8	N 8 55.6
Ankaa	353 08.9	S42 11.1
Antares	112 18.0	S26 28.9
Arcturus	145 49.4	N19 03.6
Atria	107 14.0	S69 03.9
Avior	234 14.7	S59 35.0
Bellatrix	278 24.4	N 6 22.2
Betelgeuse	270 53.6	N 7 24.6
Canopus	263 52.6	S52 42.6
Capella	280 23.9	N46 01.4
Deneb	49 27.4	N45 21.6
Denebola	182 26.4	N14 26.5
Diphda	348 49.1	S17 51.8
Dubhe	193 42.4	N61 37.4
Elnath	278 03.6	N28 37.6
Eltanin	90 43.3	N51 28.9
Enif	33 40.7	N 9 58.7
Fomalhaut	15 16.6	S29 30.2
Gacrux	171 53.1	S57 14.3
Gienah	175 45.0	S17 40.1
Hadar	148 38.2	S60 28.7
Hamal	327 53.0	N23 34.3
Kaus Aust.	83 35.0	S34 22.4
Kochab	137 19.9	N74 03.3
Markab	13 31.8	N15 19.7
Menkar	314 07.8	N 4 10.7
Menkent	147 59.5	S36 28.8
Miaplacidus	221 37.7	S69 48.6
Mirfak	308 30.4	N49 56.7
Nunki	75 50.1	S26 16.1
Peacock	53 08.8	S56 39.7
Pollux	243 18.9	N27 58.2
Procyon	244 52.2	N 5 09.9
Rasalhague	96 00.3	N12 32.4
Regulus	207 35.8	N11 51.2
Rigel	281 05.2	S 8 10.6
Rigil Kent.	139 42.5	S60 55.5
Sabik	102 04.8	S15 45.2
Schedar	349 33.1	N56 40.0
Shaula	96 12.8	S37 07.1
Sirius	258 27.3	S16 45.0
Spica	158 23.9	S11 16.9
Suhail	222 47.0	S43 31.5
Vega	80 34.7	N38 48.1
Zuben'ubi	136 57.8	S16 08.2

	SHA	Mer. Pass.
	° ′	h m
Venus	25 05.9	13 48
Mars	292 25.5	19 56
Jupiter	354 29.0	15 48
Saturn	31 48.3	13 19

© British Crown Copyright 2022. All rights reserved.

UT	SUN GHA	SUN Dec	MOON GHA	v	MOON Dec	d	HP
d h	° ′	° ′	° ′	′	° ′	′	′
28 00	176 48.5	S18 19.4	98 40.0	13.2	N10 48.9	14.1	57.2
01	191 48.4	18.8	113 12.2	13.3	11 03.0	14.0	57.1
02	206 48.3	18.1	127 44.5	13.2	11 17.0	14.0	57.1
03	221 48.2	.. 17.5	142 16.7	13.3	11 31.0	13.9	57.0
04	236 48.1	16.8	156 49.0	13.2	11 44.9	13.8	57.0
05	251 47.9	16.1	171 21.2	13.2	11 58.7	13.7	57.0
S 06	266 47.8	S18 15.5	185 53.4	13.3	N12 12.4	13.7	56.9
A 07	281 47.7	14.8	200 25.7	13.2	12 26.1	13.6	56.9
T 08	296 47.6	14.2	214 57.9	13.1	12 39.7	13.5	56.9
U 09	311 47.5	.. 13.5	229 30.0	13.2	12 53.2	13.4	56.8
R 10	326 47.3	12.9	244 02.2	13.2	13 06.6	13.4	56.8
D 11	341 47.2	12.2	258 34.4	13.1	13 20.0	13.3	56.8
A 12	356 47.1	S18 11.5	273 06.5	13.1	N13 33.3	13.2	56.7
Y 13	11 47.0	10.9	287 38.6	13.1	13 46.5	13.1	56.7
14	26 46.9	10.2	302 10.7	13.1	13 59.6	13.1	56.6
15	41 46.7	.. 09.6	316 42.8	13.0	14 12.7	13.0	56.6
16	56 46.6	08.9	331 14.8	13.0	14 25.7	12.9	56.6
17	71 46.5	08.2	345 46.8	13.1	14 38.6	12.8	56.5
18	86 46.4	S18 07.6	0 18.9	12.9	N14 51.4	12.7	56.5
19	101 46.3	06.9	14 50.8	13.0	15 04.1	12.7	56.5
20	116 46.2	06.2	29 22.8	12.9	15 16.8	12.5	56.4
21	131 46.0	.. 05.6	43 54.7	12.9	15 29.3	12.5	56.4
22	146 45.9	04.9	58 26.6	12.9	15 41.8	12.4	56.4
23	161 45.8	04.3	72 58.5	12.9	15 54.2	12.3	56.3
29 00	176 45.7	S18 03.6	87 30.4	12.8	N16 06.5	12.2	56.3
01	191 45.6	02.9	102 02.2	12.8	16 18.7	12.2	56.3
02	206 45.5	02.3	116 34.0	12.8	16 30.9	12.0	56.2
03	221 45.4	.. 01.6	131 05.8	12.7	16 42.9	12.0	56.2
04	236 45.3	00.9	145 37.5	12.7	16 54.9	11.8	56.2
05	251 45.1	18 00.3	160 09.2	12.7	17 06.7	11.8	56.1
S 06	266 45.0	S17 59.6	174 40.9	12.7	N17 18.5	11.7	56.1
U 07	281 44.9	58.9	189 12.6	12.6	17 30.2	11.6	56.1
N 08	296 44.8	58.2	203 44.2	12.6	17 41.8	11.5	56.0
D 09	311 44.7	.. 57.6	218 15.8	12.5	17 53.3	11.4	56.0
A 10	326 44.6	56.9	232 47.3	12.6	18 04.7	11.3	56.0
Y 11	341 44.5	56.2	247 18.9	12.4	18 16.0	11.2	56.0
12	356 44.4	S17 55.6	261 50.3	12.5	N18 27.2	11.1	55.9
13	11 44.3	54.9	276 21.8	12.4	18 38.3	11.1	55.9
14	26 44.1	54.2	290 53.2	12.4	18 49.4	10.9	55.9
15	41 44.0	.. 53.5	305 24.6	12.3	19 00.3	10.8	55.8
16	56 43.9	52.9	319 55.9	12.3	19 11.1	10.7	55.8
17	71 43.8	52.2	334 27.2	12.3	19 21.8	10.7	55.8
18	86 43.7	S17 51.5	348 58.5	12.2	N19 32.5	10.5	55.7
19	101 43.6	50.8	3 29.7	12.2	19 43.0	10.4	55.7
20	116 43.5	50.2	18 00.9	12.2	19 53.4	10.4	55.7
21	131 43.4	.. 49.5	32 32.1	12.1	20 03.8	10.2	55.7
22	146 43.3	48.8	47 03.2	12.1	20 14.0	10.1	55.6
23	161 43.2	48.1	61 34.3	12.0	20 24.1	10.0	55.6
30 00	176 43.1	S17 47.4	76 05.3	12.0	N20 34.1	9.9	55.6
01	191 43.0	46.8	90 36.3	12.0	20 44.0	9.9	55.6
02	206 42.9	46.1	105 07.3	11.9	20 53.9	9.7	55.5
03	221 42.8	.. 45.4	119 38.2	11.9	21 03.6	9.6	55.5
04	236 42.7	44.7	134 09.1	11.9	21 13.2	9.5	55.5
05	251 42.6	44.0	148 40.0	11.8	21 22.7	9.3	55.4
M 06	266 42.5	S17 43.4	163 10.8	11.7	N21 32.0	9.3	55.4
O 07	281 42.3	42.7	177 41.5	11.8	21 41.3	9.2	55.4
N 08	296 42.2	42.0	192 12.3	11.7	21 50.5	9.1	55.4
D 09	311 42.1	.. 41.3	206 43.0	11.6	21 59.6	8.9	55.3
A 10	326 42.0	40.6	221 13.6	11.6	22 08.5	8.8	55.3
Y 11	341 41.9	39.9	235 44.2	11.6	22 17.3	8.8	55.3
12	356 41.8	S17 39.3	250 14.8	11.5	N22 26.1	8.6	55.3
13	11 41.7	38.6	264 45.3	11.5	22 34.7	8.5	55.2
14	26 41.6	37.9	279 15.8	11.4	22 43.2	8.4	55.2
15	41 41.5	.. 37.2	293 46.2	11.4	22 51.6	8.3	55.2
16	56 41.4	36.5	308 16.6	11.4	22 59.9	8.1	55.2
17	71 41.3	35.8	322 47.0	11.3	23 08.0	8.1	55.1
18	86 41.2	S17 35.1	337 17.3	11.3	N23 16.1	7.9	55.1
19	101 41.1	34.4	351 47.6	11.3	23 24.0	7.8	55.1
20	116 41.0	33.8	6 17.9	11.2	23 31.8	7.7	55.1
21	131 40.9	.. 33.1	20 48.1	11.2	23 39.5	7.6	55.1
22	146 40.8	32.4	35 18.3	11.1	23 47.1	7.5	55.0
23	161 40.8	31.7	49 48.4	11.1	N23 54.6	7.3	55.0
	SD 16.3	d 0.7	SD 15.5		15.2		15.1

Twilight / Moonrise

Lat.	Naut.	Civil	Sunrise	Moonrise 28	29	30	31
°	h m	h m	h m	h m	h m	h m	h m
N 72	07 21	08 53	10 58	08 46	07 22	▭	▭
N 70	07 12	08 32	10 04	09 08	08 22	▭	▭
68	07 04	08 15	09 31	09 25	08 57	07 50	▭
66	06 57	08 02	09 08	09 39	09 22	08 55	▭
64	06 51	07 51	08 49	09 51	09 42	09 31	09 11
62	06 46	07 41	08 34	10 01	09 59	09 57	09 57
60	06 42	07 33	08 21	10 10	10 12	10 17	10 27
N 58	06 38	07 26	08 10	10 17	10 24	10 34	10 50
56	06 34	07 19	08 01	10 24	10 34	10 48	11 09
54	06 30	07 13	07 52	10 30	10 43	11 01	11 24
52	06 27	07 08	07 45	10 36	10 52	11 12	11 38
50	06 24	07 03	07 38	10 41	10 59	11 21	11 50
45	06 17	06 52	07 24	10 51	11 15	11 42	12 15
N 40	06 10	06 43	07 11	11 00	11 28	11 59	12 35
35	06 04	06 34	07 01	11 08	11 39	12 13	12 51
30	05 58	06 27	06 52	11 15	11 48	12 25	13 06
20	05 47	06 13	06 36	11 27	12 05	12 46	13 30
N 10	05 35	06 01	06 23	11 38	12 20	13 05	13 52
0	05 22	05 48	06 09	11 48	12 34	13 22	14 12
S 10	05 08	05 34	05 56	11 58	12 48	13 40	14 32
20	04 51	05 19	05 42	12 09	13 03	13 58	14 53
30	04 29	05 00	05 26	12 21	13 21	14 20	15 18
35	04 14	04 48	05 16	12 28	13 31	14 33	15 33
40	03 57	04 35	05 05	12 37	13 43	14 48	15 51
45	03 35	04 18	04 52	12 46	13 57	15 06	16 11
S 50	03 06	03 57	04 36	12 58	14 14	15 28	16 38
52	02 51	03 47	04 28	13 04	14 22	15 38	16 50
54	02 33	03 35	04 20	13 10	14 31	15 50	17 05
56	02 09	03 22	04 10	13 17	14 41	16 04	17 22
58	01 37	03 06	04 00	13 24	14 53	16 20	17 43
S 60	////	02 47	03 47	13 33	15 06	16 40	18 10

Sunset / Twilight / Moonset

Lat.	Sunset	Civil	Naut.	Moonset 28	29	30	31
°	h m	h m	h m	h m	h m	h m	h m
N 72	13 29	15 35	17 07	01 58	05 00	▭	▭
N 70	14 23	15 55	17 16	01 38	04 02	▭	▭
68	14 56	16 12	17 23	01 23	03 28	06 15	▭
66	15 19	16 25	17 30	01 11	03 04	05 10	▭
64	15 38	16 36	17 36	01 00	02 45	04 35	06 38
62	15 53	16 46	17 41	00 52	02 30	04 10	05 52
60	16 06	16 54	17 45	00 44	02 17	03 51	05 23
N 58	16 16	17 01	17 49	00 38	02 06	03 35	05 00
56	16 26	17 08	17 53	00 32	01 57	03 21	04 42
54	16 34	17 14	17 57	00 27	01 49	03 09	04 27
52	16 42	17 19	18 00	00 22	01 41	02 59	04 13
50	16 49	17 24	18 03	00 18	01 34	02 49	04 02
45	17 03	17 35	18 10	00 09	01 20	02 30	03 38
N 40	17 15	17 44	18 16	00 02	01 08	02 14	03 18
35	17 25	17 52	18 23	24 58	00 58	02 01	03 02
30	17 34	18 00	18 28	24 50	00 50	01 49	02 48
20	17 50	18 13	18 40	24 35	00 35	01 30	02 25
N 10	18 04	18 26	18 51	24 22	00 22	01 13	02 05
0	18 17	18 38	19 04	24 10	00 10	00 57	01 46
S 10	18 30	18 52	19 18	23 58	24 41	00 41	01 27
20	18 44	19 07	19 35	23 45	24 24	00 24	01 07
30	19 00	19 26	19 57	23 30	24 05	00 05	00 44
35	19 10	19 37	20 11	23 22	23 54	24 30	00 30
40	19 21	19 51	20 28	23 12	23 41	24 15	00 15
45	19 33	20 07	20 49	23 01	23 26	23 56	24 33
S 50	19 49	20 28	21 18	22 48	23 08	23 33	24 06
52	19 57	20 38	21 33	22 42	22 59	23 22	23 53
54	20 05	20 49	21 51	22 35	22 50	23 10	23 38
56	20 14	21 02	22 13	22 27	22 39	22 55	23 20
58	20 25	21 18	22 44	22 18	22 26	22 39	22 59
S 60	20 37	21 37	23 45	22 09	22 12	22 18	22 32

SUN / MOON

Day	Eqn. of Time 00ʰ	12ʰ	Mer. Pass.	Mer. Pass. Upper	Lower	Age	Phase
d	m s	m s	h m	h m	h m	d %	
28	12 46	12 51	12 13	17 59	05 36	07 49	
29	12 57	13 02	12 13	18 46	06 22	08 59	◑
30	13 07	13 12	12 13	19 34	07 10	09 68	

© British Crown Copyright 2022. All rights reserved.

UT	ARIES GHA	VENUS −3·9 GHA	Dec	MARS −0·3 GHA	Dec	JUPITER −2·2 GHA	Dec	SATURN +0·8 GHA	Dec	STARS Name	SHA	Dec
31 00	129 57.5	152 42.0	S11 09.1	61 57.6	N24 39.0	124 06.3	N 1 14.8	161 32.0	S14 06.9	Acamar	315 12.9	S40 13.0
01	145 00.0	167 41.5	07.9	76 59.5	39.0	139 08.3	15.0	176 34.2	06.8	Achernar	335 21.5	S57 07.5
02	160 02.4	182 41.1	06.8	92 01.4	39.1	154 10.4	15.2	191 36.4	06.7	Acrux	173 01.4	S63 13.4
03	175 04.9	197 40.6	.. 05.6	107 03.3	.. 39.1	169 12.4	.. 15.4	206 38.6	.. 06.6	Adhara	255 06.8	S29 00.3
04	190 07.4	212 40.1	04.4	122 05.2	39.2	184 14.4	15.6	221 40.8	06.5	Aldebaran	290 41.3	N16 33.3
05	205 09.8	227 39.7	03.3	137 07.1	39.3	199 16.5	15.8	236 42.9	06.4			
06	220 12.3	242 39.2	S11 02.1	152 09.0	N24 39.3	214 18.5	N 1 16.0	251 45.1	S14 06.3	Alioth	166 14.1	N55 49.8
07	235 14.8	257 38.7	11 00.9	167 10.9	39.4	229 20.6	16.1	266 47.3	06.2	Alkaid	152 53.2	N49 11.6
08	250 17.2	272 38.3	10 59.7	182 12.8	39.4	244 22.6	16.3	281 49.5	06.1	Alnair	27 35.4	S46 51.2
09	265 19.7	287 37.8	.. 58.6	197 14.7	.. 39.5	259 24.6	.. 16.5	296 51.6	.. 06.0	Alnilam	275 39.1	S 1 11.3
10	280 22.1	302 37.3	57.4	212 16.6	39.5	274 26.7	16.7	311 53.8	05.9	Alphard	217 49.0	S 8 45.5
11	295 24.6	317 36.9	56.2	227 18.5	39.6	289 28.7	16.9	326 56.0	05.8			
12	310 27.1	332 36.4	S10 55.0	242 20.4	N24 39.6	304 30.7	N 1 17.1	341 58.2	S14 05.7	Alphecca	126 05.2	N26 38.0
13	325 29.5	347 35.9	53.9	257 22.3	39.7	319 32.8	17.3	357 00.3	05.6	Alpheratz	357 36.6	N29 13.1
14	340 32.0	2 35.5	52.7	272 24.2	39.7	334 34.8	17.5	12 02.5	05.5	Altair	62 01.8	N 8 55.6
15	355 34.5	17 35.0	.. 51.5	287 26.1	.. 39.8	349 36.9	.. 17.7	27 04.7	.. 05.4	Ankaa	353 09.0	S42 11.1
16	10 36.9	32 34.6	50.3	302 28.0	39.8	4 38.9	17.9	42 06.9	05.3	Antares	112 18.0	S26 28.9
17	25 39.4	47 34.1	49.1	317 29.8	39.9	19 40.9	18.1	57 09.0	05.2			
18	40 41.9	62 33.6	S10 48.0	332 31.7	N24 40.0	34 43.0	N 1 18.3	72 11.2	S14 05.1	Arcturus	145 49.3	N19 03.6
19	55 44.3	77 33.2	46.8	347 33.6	40.0	49 45.0	18.4	87 13.4	05.0	Atria	107 14.0	S69 03.9
20	70 46.8	92 32.7	45.6	2 35.5	40.1	64 47.0	18.6	102 15.6	04.9	Avior	234 14.7	S59 35.0
21	85 49.3	107 32.3	.. 44.4	17 37.4	.. 40.1	79 49.1	.. 18.8	117 17.8	.. 04.8	Bellatrix	278 24.4	N 6 22.2
22	100 51.7	122 31.8	43.2	32 39.3	40.2	94 51.1	19.0	132 19.9	04.7	Betelgeuse	270 53.6	N 7 24.6
23	115 54.2	137 31.3	42.1	47 41.2	40.2	109 53.1	19.2	147 22.1	04.6			
1 00	130 56.6	152 30.9	S10 40.9	62 43.0	N24 40.3	124 55.2	N 1 19.4	162 24.3	S14 04.5	Canopus	263 52.6	S52 42.6
01	145 59.1	167 30.4	39.7	77 44.9	40.3	139 57.2	19.6	177 26.5	04.4	Capella	280 23.9	N46 01.4
02	161 01.6	182 30.0	38.5	92 46.8	40.4	154 59.3	19.8	192 28.6	04.3	Deneb	49 27.4	N45 21.6
03	176 04.0	197 29.5	.. 37.3	107 48.7	.. 40.5	170 01.3	.. 20.0	207 30.8	.. 04.2	Denebola	182 26.3	N14 26.5
04	191 06.5	212 29.0	36.2	122 50.6	40.5	185 03.3	20.2	222 33.0	04.1	Diphda	348 49.1	S17 51.8
05	206 09.0	227 28.6	35.0	137 52.4	40.6	200 05.4	20.4	237 35.2	04.0			
06	221 11.4	242 28.1	S10 33.8	152 54.3	N24 40.6	215 07.4	N 1 20.6	252 37.3	S14 03.9	Dubhe	193 42.4	N61 37.4
07	236 13.9	257 27.7	32.6	167 56.2	40.7	230 09.4	20.8	267 39.5	03.8	Elnath	278 03.6	N28 37.6
08	251 16.4	272 27.2	31.4	182 58.1	40.7	245 11.5	21.0	282 41.7	03.7	Eltanin	90 43.3	N51 28.9
09	266 18.8	287 26.8	.. 30.2	197 59.9	.. 40.8	260 13.5	.. 21.1	297 43.9	.. 03.6	Enif	33 40.7	N 9 58.7
10	281 21.3	302 26.3	29.0	213 01.8	40.8	275 15.5	21.3	312 46.0	03.5	Fomalhaut	15 16.6	S29 30.2
11	296 23.7	317 25.9	27.9	228 03.7	40.9	290 17.6	21.5	327 48.2	03.4			
12	311 26.2	332 25.4	S10 26.7	243 05.6	N24 41.0	305 19.6	N 1 21.7	342 50.4	S14 03.3	Gacrux	171 53.1	S57 14.3
13	326 28.7	347 24.9	25.5	258 07.4	41.0	320 21.6	21.9	357 52.6	03.2	Gienah	175 45.0	S17 40.2
14	341 31.1	2 24.5	24.3	273 09.3	41.1	335 23.7	22.1	12 54.7	03.1	Hadar	148 38.2	S60 28.8
15	356 33.6	17 24.0	.. 23.1	288 11.2	.. 41.1	350 25.7	.. 22.3	27 56.9	.. 03.0	Hamal	327 53.0	N23 34.3
16	11 36.1	32 23.6	21.9	303 13.0	41.2	5 27.7	22.5	42 59.1	02.9	Kaus Aust.	83 35.0	S34 22.4
17	26 38.5	47 23.1	20.7	318 14.9	41.2	20 29.8	22.7	58 01.3	02.8			
18	41 41.0	62 22.7	S10 19.5	333 16.8	N24 41.3	35 31.8	N 1 22.9	73 03.5	S14 02.7	Kochab	137 19.8	N74 03.3
19	56 43.5	77 22.2	18.3	348 18.6	41.4	50 33.8	23.1	88 05.6	02.6	Markab	13 31.8	N15 19.7
20	71 45.9	92 21.8	17.2	3 20.5	41.4	65 35.9	23.3	103 07.8	02.5	Menkar	314 07.8	N 4 10.7
21	86 48.4	107 21.3	.. 16.0	18 22.4	.. 41.5	80 37.9	.. 23.5	118 10.0	.. 02.4	Menkent	147 59.4	S36 28.8
22	101 50.9	122 20.9	14.8	33 24.2	41.5	95 39.9	23.7	133 12.2	02.3	Miaplacidus	221 37.7	S69 48.6
23	116 53.3	137 20.4	13.6	48 26.1	41.6	110 42.0	23.9	148 14.3	02.2			
2 00	131 55.8	152 20.0	S10 12.4	63 27.9	N24 41.6	125 44.0	N 1 24.1	163 16.5	S14 02.1	Mirfak	308 30.4	N49 56.7
01	146 58.2	167 19.5	11.2	78 29.8	41.7	140 46.0	24.2	178 18.7	02.0	Nunki	75 50.5	S26 16.1
02	162 00.7	182 19.1	10.0	93 31.6	41.7	155 48.0	24.4	193 20.9	01.9	Peacock	53 08.8	S56 39.7
03	177 03.2	197 18.6	.. 08.8	108 33.5	.. 41.8	170 50.1	.. 24.6	208 23.0	.. 01.8	Pollux	243 18.9	N27 58.2
04	192 05.6	212 18.2	07.6	123 35.4	41.9	185 52.1	24.8	223 25.2	01.7	Procyon	244 52.2	N 5 09.9
05	207 08.1	227 17.8	06.4	138 37.2	41.9	200 54.1	25.0	238 27.4	01.6			
06	222 10.6	242 17.3	S10 05.2	153 39.1	N24 42.0	215 56.2	N 1 25.2	253 29.6	S14 01.5	Rasalhague	96 00.3	N12 32.4
07	237 13.0	257 16.9	04.0	168 40.9	42.0	230 58.2	25.4	268 31.7	01.4	Regulus	207 35.8	N11 51.2
08	252 15.5	272 16.4	02.8	183 42.8	42.1	246 00.2	25.6	283 33.9	01.3	Rigel	281 05.2	S 8 10.6
09	267 18.0	287 16.0	.. 01.6	198 44.6	.. 42.2	261 02.3	.. 25.8	298 36.1	.. 01.2	Rigil Kent.	139 42.5	S60 55.5
10	282 20.4	302 15.5	10 00.4	213 46.5	42.2	276 04.3	26.0	313 38.3	01.1	Sabik	102 04.8	S15 45.2
11	297 22.9	317 15.1	9 59.2	228 48.3	42.3	291 06.3	26.2	328 40.4	01.0			
12	312 25.4	332 14.6	S 9 58.0	243 50.2	N24 42.3	306 08.4	N 1 26.4	343 42.6	S14 00.9	Schedar	349 33.1	N56 40.0
13	327 27.8	347 14.2	56.8	258 52.0	42.4	321 10.4	26.6	358 44.8	00.8	Shaula	96 12.8	S37 07.1
14	342 30.3	2 13.8	55.6	273 53.8	42.4	336 12.4	26.8	13 47.0	00.7	Sirius	258 27.3	S16 45.0
15	357 32.7	17 13.3	.. 54.4	288 55.7	.. 42.5	351 14.4	.. 27.0	28 49.1	.. 00.6	Spica	158 23.9	S11 16.9
16	12 35.2	32 12.9	53.2	303 57.5	42.6	6 16.5	27.2	43 51.3	00.5	Suhail	222 47.0	S43 31.5
17	27 37.7	47 12.4	52.0	318 59.4	42.6	21 18.5	27.4	58 53.5	00.4			
18	42 40.1	62 12.0	S 9 50.8	334 01.2	N24 42.7	36 20.5	N 1 27.6	73 55.7	S14 00.3	Vega	80 34.7	N38 48.1
19	57 42.6	77 11.6	49.6	349 03.0	42.7	51 22.6	27.8	88 57.8	00.2	Zuben'ubi	136 57.8	S16 08.2
20	72 45.1	92 11.1	48.4	4 04.9	42.8	66 24.6	27.9	104 00.0	00.1		SHA	Mer.Pass.
21	87 47.5	107 10.7	.. 47.2	19 06.7	.. 42.9	81 26.6	.. 28.1	119 02.2	14 00.0			h m
22	102 50.0	122 10.2	46.0	34 08.6	42.9	96 28.6	28.3	134 04.4	13 59.9	Venus	21 34.2	13 50
23	117 52.5	137 09.8	44.8	49 10.4	43.0	111 30.7	28.5	149 06.5	S13 59.8	Mars	291 46.4	19 47
	h m									Jupiter	353 58.5	15 38
Mer.Pass. 15 13.7		v −0.5	d 1.2	v 1.9	d 0.1	v 2.0	d 0.2	v 2.2	d 0.1	Saturn	31 27.6	13 08

© British Crown Copyright 2022. All rights reserved.

UT	SUN GHA	SUN Dec	MOON GHA	v	MOON Dec	d	HP
d h	° ′	° ′	° ′	′	° ′	′	′
31 00	176 40.7	S17 31.0	64 18.5	11.0	N24 01.9	7.2	55.0
01	191 40.6	30.3	78 48.5	11.0	24 09.1	7.1	55.0
02	206 40.5	29.6	93 18.5	11.0	24 16.2	7.0	54.9
03	221 40.4 ..	28.9	107 48.5	11.0	24 23.2	6.9	54.9
04	236 40.3	28.2	122 18.5	10.9	24 30.1	6.7	54.9
05	251 40.2	27.5	136 48.4	10.8	24 36.8	6.7	54.9
06	266 40.1	S17 26.8	151 18.2	10.9	N24 43.5	6.5	54.9
07	281 40.0	26.1	165 48.1	10.8	24 50.0	6.3	54.8
T 08	296 39.9	25.4	180 17.9	10.7	24 56.3	6.3	54.8
U 09	311 39.8 ..	24.7	194 47.6	10.7	25 02.6	6.1	54.8
E 10	326 39.7	24.0	209 17.3	10.7	25 08.7	6.0	54.8
S 11	341 39.6	23.3	223 47.0	10.7	25 14.7	5.9	54.8
D 12	356 39.5	S17 22.6	238 16.7	10.6	N25 20.6	5.8	54.8
A 13	11 39.4	21.9	252 46.3	10.6	25 26.4	5.6	54.7
Y 14	26 39.3	21.2	267 15.9	10.6	25 32.0	5.5	54.7
15	41 39.2 ..	20.5	281 45.5	10.5	25 37.5	5.4	54.7
16	56 39.2	19.8	296 15.0	10.5	25 42.9	5.3	54.7
17	71 39.1	19.1	310 44.5	10.5	25 48.2	5.1	54.7
18	86 39.0	S17 18.4	325 14.0	10.4	N25 53.3	5.0	54.6
19	101 38.9	17.7	339 43.4	10.4	25 58.3	4.9	54.6
20	116 38.8	17.0	354 12.8	10.4	26 03.2	4.7	54.6
21	131 38.7 ..	16.3	8 42.2	10.4	26 07.9	4.6	54.6
22	146 38.6	15.6	23 11.6	10.3	26 12.5	4.5	54.6
23	161 38.5	14.9	37 40.9	10.3	26 17.0	4.4	54.6
1 00	176 38.4	S17 14.2	52 10.2	10.3	N26 21.4	4.2	54.5
01	191 38.4	13.5	66 39.5	10.2	26 25.6	4.1	54.5
02	206 38.3	12.8	81 08.7	10.3	26 29.7	4.0	54.5
03	221 38.2 ..	12.1	95 38.0	10.2	26 33.7	3.8	54.5
04	236 38.1	11.4	110 07.2	10.2	26 37.5	3.7	54.5
05	251 38.0	10.7	124 37.4	10.1	26 41.2	3.6	54.5
06	266 37.9	S17 10.0	139 05.5	10.2	N26 44.8	3.4	54.5
W 07	281 37.8	09.3	153 34.7	10.1	26 48.2	3.3	54.4
E 08	296 37.7	08.6	168 03.8	10.1	26 51.5	3.2	54.4
D 09	311 37.7 ..	07.9	182 32.9	10.1	26 54.7	3.1	54.4
N 10	326 37.6	07.1	197 02.0	10.1	26 57.8	2.9	54.4
E 11	341 37.5	06.4	211 31.1	10.1	27 00.7	2.8	54.4
S 12	356 37.4	S17 05.7	226 00.2	10.0	N27 03.5	2.6	54.4
D 13	11 37.3	05.0	240 29.2	10.1	27 06.1	2.5	54.4
A 14	26 37.2	04.3	254 58.3	10.0	27 08.6	2.4	54.3
Y 15	41 37.2 ..	03.6	269 27.3	10.0	27 11.0	2.3	54.3
16	56 37.1	02.9	283 56.3	10.0	27 13.3	2.1	54.3
17	71 37.0	02.2	298 25.3	10.0	27 15.4	2.0	54.3
18	86 36.9	S17 01.4	312 54.3	10.0	N27 17.4	1.8	54.3
19	101 36.8	00.7	327 23.3	10.0	27 19.2	1.7	54.3
20	116 36.8	17 00.0	341 52.3	9.9	27 20.9	1.6	54.3
21	131 36.7	16 59.3	356 21.2	10.0	27 22.5	1.4	54.3
22	146 36.6	58.6	10 50.2	10.0	27 23.9	1.3	54.3
23	161 36.5	57.9	25 19.2	9.9	27 25.2	1.2	54.2
2 00	176 36.4	S16 57.2	39 48.1	10.0	N27 26.4	1.1	54.2
01	191 36.4	56.4	54 17.1	10.0	27 27.5	0.9	54.2
02	206 36.3	55.7	68 46.1	9.9	27 28.4	0.8	54.2
03	221 36.2 ..	55.0	83 15.0	10.0	27 29.2	0.6	54.2
04	236 36.1	54.3	97 44.0	10.0	27 29.8	0.5	54.2
05	251 36.0	53.6	112 13.0	9.9	27 30.3	0.4	54.2
06	266 36.0	S16 52.8	126 41.9	10.0	N27 30.7	0.2	54.2
07	281 35.9	52.1	141 10.9	10.0	27 30.9	0.1	54.2
T 08	296 35.8	51.4	155 39.9	10.0	27 31.0	0.0	54.2
H 09	311 35.7 ..	50.7	170 08.9	10.0	27 31.0	0.2	54.1
U 10	326 35.7	49.9	184 37.9	10.0	27 30.8	0.3	54.1
R 11	341 35.6	49.2	199 06.9	10.0	27 30.5	0.4	54.1
S 12	356 35.5	S16 48.5	213 35.9	10.1	N27 30.1	0.6	54.1
D 13	11 35.4	47.8	228 05.0	10.0	27 29.5	0.7	54.1
A 14	26 35.4	47.1	242 34.0	10.1	27 28.8	0.8	54.1
Y 15	41 35.3 ..	46.3	257 03.1	10.0	27 28.0	1.0	54.1
16	56 35.2	45.6	271 32.1	10.0	27 27.0	1.1	54.1
17	71 35.1	44.9	286 01.2	10.2	27 25.9	1.2	54.1
18	86 35.1	S16 44.2	300 30.4	10.1	N27 24.7	1.4	54.1
19	101 35.0	43.4	314 59.5	10.2	27 23.3	1.4	54.1
20	116 34.9	42.7	329 28.6	10.2	27 21.9	1.7	54.1
21	131 34.8 ..	42.0	343 57.8	10.2	27 20.2	1.7	54.1
22	146 34.8	41.2	358 27.0	10.2	27 18.5	1.9	54.0
23	161 34.7	40.5	12 56.2	10.2	N27 16.6	2.0	54.0
	SD 16.3	d 0.7	SD 14.9		14.8		14.7

Twilight / Sunrise / Moonrise

Lat.	Naut.	Civil	Sunrise	Moonrise 31	1	2	3
°	h m	h m	h m	h m	h m	h m	h m
N 72	07 10	08 40	10 29	□	□	□	□
N 70	07 02	08 21	09 47	□	□	□	□
68	06 56	08 06	09 18	□	□	□	□
66	06 50	07 54	08 57	□	□	□	□
64	06 45	07 44	08 40	09 11	□	□	□
62	06 40	07 35	08 26	09 57	10 03	10 33	11 53
60	06 36	07 27	08 14	10 27	10 47	11 29	12 36
N 58	06 33	07 20	08 04	10 50	11 17	12 01	13 05
56	06 29	07 14	07 55	11 09	11 40	12 26	13 27
54	06 26	07 09	07 47	11 24	11 58	12 45	13 45
52	06 23	07 04	07 40	11 38	12 14	13 02	14 01
50	06 20	06 59	07 34	11 50	12 28	13 16	14 14
45	06 14	06 49	07 20	12 15	12 55	13 44	14 41
N 40	06 08	06 40	07 09	12 35	13 17	14 07	15 03
35	06 02	06 32	06 59	12 51	13 36	14 26	15 20
30	05 57	06 25	06 50	13 06	13 51	14 42	15 36
20	05 46	06 13	06 36	13 30	14 18	15 09	16 02
N 10	05 35	06 00	06 22	13 52	14 41	15 32	16 24
0	05 23	05 48	06 10	14 12	15 03	15 54	16 45
S 10	05 10	05 35	05 57	14 32	15 24	16 16	17 05
20	04 53	05 21	05 44	14 53	15 47	16 39	17 28
30	04 32	05 02	05 28	15 18	16 14	17 06	17 53
35	04 18	04 52	05 19	15 33	16 30	17 22	18 08
40	04 02	04 39	05 09	15 51	16 49	17 41	18 26
45	03 41	04 23	04 56	16 11	17 11	18 04	18 47
S 50	03 13	04 03	04 41	16 38	17 40	18 32	19 14
52	02 59	03 53	04 34	16 50	17 54	18 47	19 26
54	02 42	03 43	04 26	17 05	18 11	19 03	19 41
56	02 21	03 30	04 17	17 22	18 30	19 23	19 58
58	01 53	03 15	04 07	17 43	18 55	19 47	20 19
S 60	01 08	02 57	03 55	18 10	19 27	20 19	20 45

Sunset / Twilight / Moonset

Lat.	Sunset	Civil	Naut.	Moonset 31	1	2	3
°	h m	h m	h m	h m	h m	h m	h m
N 72	13 59	15 49	17 18	□	□	□	□
N 70	14 41	16 07	17 26	□	□	□	□
68	15 10	16 22	17 33	□	□	□	□
66	15 31	16 34	17 38	□	□	□	□
64	15 48	16 44	17 43	06 38	□	□	□
62	16 02	16 53	17 48	05 52	07 32	08 49	09 15
60	16 13	17 01	17 53	05 23	06 48	07 53	08 31
N 58	16 23	17 08	17 55	05 00	06 18	07 21	08 02
56	16 32	17 14	17 59	04 42	05 56	06 56	07 40
54	16 40	17 19	18 02	04 27	05 37	06 37	07 22
52	16 47	17 24	18 05	04 13	05 22	06 20	07 06
50	16 54	17 29	18 07	04 02	05 08	06 06	06 53
45	17 07	17 39	18 14	03 38	04 41	05 37	06 25
N 40	17 19	17 47	18 20	03 18	04 19	05 15	06 03
35	17 28	17 55	18 25	03 02	04 01	04 56	05 45
30	17 37	18 02	18 31	02 48	03 46	04 40	05 30
20	17 52	18 15	18 41	02 25	03 20	04 13	05 03
N 10	18 05	18 27	18 52	02 05	02 57	03 49	04 40
0	18 17	18 39	19 04	01 46	02 36	03 28	04 19
S 10	18 29	18 52	19 18	01 27	02 15	03 06	03 57
20	18 43	19 06	19 34	01 07	01 53	02 42	03 34
30	18 58	19 24	19 55	00 44	01 27	02 15	03 07
35	19 07	19 35	20 08	00 30	01 12	01 59	02 52
40	19 18	19 48	20 23	00 15	00 54	01 39	02 33
45	19 30	20 03	20 45	24 33	00 33	01 18	02 11
S 50	19 45	20 21	21 12	24 06	00 06	00 49	01 42
52	19 52	20 32	21 26	23 53	24 34	00 34	01 28
54	20 00	20 43	21 42	23 38	24 18	00 18	01 12
56	20 08	20 55	22 03	23 20	23 58	24 52	00 52
58	20 18	21 10	22 29	22 59	23 34	24 28	00 28
S 60	20 30	21 27	23 11	22 32	23 01	23 56	25 14

SUN / MOON

Day	Eqn. of Time 00h	Eqn. of Time 12h	Mer. Pass.	Mer. Pass. Upper	Mer. Pass. Lower	Age	Phase
d	m s	m s	h m	h m	h m	d	%
31	13 17	13 22	12 13	20 24	07 59	10	77
1	13 26	13 30	12 14	21 15	08 49	11	84
2	13 34	13 38	12 14	22 06	09 41	12	91

© British Crown Copyright 2022. All rights reserved.

UT	ARIES	VENUS −3.9		MARS −0.2		JUPITER −2.2		SATURN +0.8		STARS		
	GHA	GHA	Dec	GHA	Dec	GHA	Dec	GHA	Dec	Name	SHA	Dec
d h	° ′	° ′	° ′	° ′	° ′	° ′	° ′	° ′	° ′		° ′	° ′
3 00	132 54.9	152 09.4	S 9 43.6	64 12.2	N24 43.0	126 32.7	N 1 28.7	164 08.7	S13 59.7	Acamar	315 13.0	S40 13.0
01	147 57.4	167 08.9	42.4	79 14.1	43.1	141 34.7	28.9	179 10.9	59.6	Achernar	335 21.6	S57 07.5
02	162 59.9	182 08.5	41.2	94 15.9	43.1	156 36.8	29.1	194 13.1	59.5	Acrux	173 01.4	S63 13.4
03	178 02.3	197 08.0	.. 40.0	109 17.7	.. 43.2	171 38.8	.. 29.3	209 15.2	.. 59.4	Adhara	255 06.8	S29 00.3
04	193 04.8	212 07.6	38.8	124 19.6	43.3	186 40.8	29.5	224 17.4	59.3	Aldebaran	290 41.3	N16 33.3
05	208 07.2	227 07.2	37.6	139 21.4	43.3	201 42.8	29.7	239 19.6	59.2			
06	223 09.7	242 06.7	S 9 36.4	154 23.2	N24 43.4	216 44.9	N 1 29.9	254 21.8	S13 59.1	Alioth	166 14.1	N55 49.8
07	238 12.2	257 06.3	35.2	169 25.0	43.4	231 46.9	30.1	269 23.9	59.0	Alkaid	152 53.1	N49 11.6
08	253 14.6	272 05.9	34.0	184 26.9	43.5	246 48.9	30.3	284 26.1	58.9	Alnair	27 35.3	S46 51.1
F 09	268 17.1	287 05.4	.. 32.8	199 28.7	.. 43.6	261 50.9	.. 30.5	299 28.3	.. 58.8	Alnilam	275 39.1	S 1 11.3
R 10	283 19.6	302 05.0	31.6	214 30.5	43.6	276 53.0	30.7	314 30.5	58.7	Alphard	217 49.0	S 8 45.6
I 11	298 22.0	317 04.6	30.3	229 32.3	43.7	291 55.0	30.9	329 32.6	58.6			
D 12	313 24.5	332 04.1	S 9 29.1	244 34.2	N24 43.7	306 57.0	N 1 31.1	344 34.8	S13 58.5	Alphecca	126 05.2	N26 38.0
A 13	328 27.0	347 03.7	27.9	259 36.0	43.8	321 59.0	31.3	359 37.0	58.4	Alpheratz	357 36.7	N29 13.1
Y 14	343 29.4	2 03.3	26.7	274 37.8	43.9	337 01.1	31.5	14 39.2	58.3	Altair	62 01.8	N 8 55.6
15	358 31.9	17 02.8	.. 25.5	289 39.6	.. 43.9	352 03.1	.. 31.7	29 41.3	.. 58.2	Ankaa	353 09.0	S42 11.1
16	13 34.4	32 02.4	24.3	304 41.4	44.0	7 05.1	31.9	44 43.5	58.1	Antares	112 17.9	S26 28.9
17	28 36.8	47 02.0	23.1	319 43.3	44.0	22 07.1	32.1	59 45.7	58.0			
18	43 39.3	62 01.5	S 9 21.9	334 45.1	N24 44.1	37 09.2	N 1 32.3	74 47.9	S13 57.9	Arcturus	145 49.3	N19 03.6
19	58 41.7	77 01.1	20.7	349 46.9	44.2	52 11.2	32.5	89 50.0	57.8	Atria	107 13.9	S69 03.9
20	73 44.2	92 00.7	19.5	4 48.7	44.2	67 13.2	32.7	104 52.2	57.7	Avior	234 14.7	S59 35.0
21	88 46.7	107 00.3	.. 18.2	19 50.5	.. 44.3	82 15.2	.. 32.9	119 54.4	.. 57.6	Bellatrix	278 24.4	N 6 22.2
22	103 49.1	121 59.8	17.0	34 52.3	44.3	97 17.3	33.0	134 56.6	57.5	Betelgeuse	270 53.6	N 7 24.6
23	118 51.6	136 59.4	15.8	49 54.1	44.4	112 19.3	33.2	149 58.7	57.4			
4 00	133 54.1	151 59.0	S 9 14.6	64 56.0	N24 44.5	127 21.3	N 1 33.4	165 00.9	S13 57.3	Canopus	263 52.7	S52 42.6
01	148 56.5	166 58.5	13.4	79 57.8	44.5	142 23.3	33.6	180 03.1	57.2	Capella	280 23.9	N46 01.4
02	163 59.0	181 58.1	12.2	94 59.6	44.6	157 25.4	33.8	195 05.3	57.1	Deneb	49 27.3	N45 21.6
03	179 01.5	196 57.7	.. 11.0	110 01.4	.. 44.6	172 27.4	.. 34.0	210 07.4	.. 57.0	Denebola	182 26.3	N14 26.5
04	194 03.9	211 57.3	09.7	125 03.2	44.7	187 29.4	34.2	225 09.6	56.9	Diphda	348 49.1	S17 51.8
05	209 06.4	226 56.8	08.5	140 05.0	44.8	202 31.4	34.4	240 11.8	56.8			
06	224 08.8	241 56.4	S 9 07.3	155 06.8	N24 44.8	217 33.5	N 1 34.6	255 14.0	S13 56.7	Dubhe	193 42.4	N61 37.4
07	239 11.3	256 56.0	06.1	170 08.6	44.9	232 35.5	34.8	270 16.1	56.6	Elnath	278 03.6	N28 37.6
S 08	254 13.8	271 55.6	04.9	185 10.4	45.0	247 37.5	35.0	285 18.3	56.5	Eltanin	90 43.3	N51 28.9
A 09	269 16.2	286 55.1	.. 03.7	200 12.2	.. 45.0	262 39.5	.. 35.2	300 20.5	.. 56.4	Enif	33 40.7	N 9 58.7
T 10	284 18.7	301 54.7	02.4	215 14.0	45.1	277 41.6	35.4	315 22.7	56.3	Fomalhaut	15 16.6	S29 30.2
U 11	299 21.2	316 54.3	01.2	230 15.8	45.1	292 43.6	35.6	330 24.8	56.2			
R 12	314 23.6	331 53.9	S 9 00.0	245 17.6	N24 45.2	307 45.6	N 1 35.8	345 27.0	S13 56.1	Gacrux	171 53.1	S57 14.3
D 13	329 26.1	346 53.4	8 58.8	260 19.4	45.3	322 47.6	36.0	0 29.2	56.0	Gienah	175 45.0	S17 40.2
A 14	344 28.6	1 53.0	57.6	275 21.2	45.3	337 49.6	36.2	15 31.3	55.9	Hadar	148 38.1	S60 28.8
Y 15	359 31.0	16 52.6	.. 56.3	290 23.0	.. 45.4	352 51.7	.. 36.4	30 33.5	.. 55.8	Hamal	327 53.0	N23 34.3
16	14 33.5	31 52.2	55.1	305 24.8	45.4	7 53.7	36.6	45 35.7	55.7	Kaus Aust.	83 34.9	S34 22.4
17	29 36.0	46 51.7	53.9	320 26.6	45.5	22 55.7	36.8	60 37.9	55.6			
18	44 38.4	61 51.3	S 8 52.7	335 28.4	N24 45.6	37 57.7	N 1 37.0	75 40.0	S13 55.5	Kochab	137 19.8	N74 03.3
19	59 40.9	76 50.9	51.5	350 30.2	45.6	52 59.8	37.2	90 42.2	55.4	Markab	13 31.8	N15 19.7
20	74 43.3	91 50.5	50.2	5 32.0	45.7	68 01.8	37.4	105 44.4	55.3	Menkar	314 07.8	N 4 10.7
21	89 45.8	106 50.1	.. 49.0	20 33.8	.. 45.8	83 03.8	.. 37.6	120 46.6	.. 55.2	Menkent	147 59.4	S36 28.8
22	104 48.3	121 49.6	47.8	35 35.6	45.8	98 05.8	37.8	135 48.7	55.1	Miaplacidus	221 37.7	S69 48.6
23	119 50.7	136 49.2	46.6	50 37.3	45.9	113 07.8	38.0	150 50.9	55.0			
5 00	134 53.2	151 48.8	S 8 45.3	65 39.1	N24 45.9	128 09.9	N 1 38.2	165 53.1	S13 54.9	Mirfak	308 30.4	N49 56.7
01	149 55.7	166 48.4	44.1	80 40.9	46.0	143 11.9	38.4	180 55.3	54.8	Nunki	75 50.0	S26 16.1
02	164 58.1	181 48.0	42.9	95 42.7	46.1	158 13.9	38.6	195 57.4	54.7	Peacock	53 08.8	S56 39.7
03	180 00.6	196 47.6	.. 41.7	110 44.5	.. 46.1	173 15.9	.. 38.8	210 59.6	.. 54.6	Pollux	243 18.9	N27 58.2
04	195 03.1	211 47.1	40.4	125 46.3	46.2	188 17.9	39.0	226 01.8	54.5	Procyon	244 52.2	N 5 09.9
05	210 05.5	226 46.7	39.2	140 48.1	46.3	203 20.0	39.2	241 04.0	54.4			
06	225 08.0	241 46.3	S 8 38.0	155 49.8	N24 46.3	218 22.0	N 1 39.4	256 06.1	S13 54.3	Rasalhague	96 00.2	N12 32.4
07	240 10.5	256 45.9	36.8	170 51.6	46.4	233 24.0	39.6	271 08.3	54.2	Regulus	207 35.8	N11 51.2
08	255 12.9	271 45.5	35.5	185 53.4	46.4	248 26.0	39.8	286 10.5	54.1	Rigel	281 05.2	S 8 10.6
S 09	270 15.4	286 45.1	.. 34.3	200 55.2	.. 46.5	263 28.0	.. 40.0	301 12.7	.. 54.0	Rigil Kent.	139 42.4	S60 55.5
U 10	285 17.8	301 44.6	33.1	215 57.0	46.6	278 30.1	40.2	316 14.8	53.9	Sabik	102 04.8	S15 45.2
N 11	300 20.3	316 44.2	31.9	230 58.7	46.6	293 32.1	40.4	331 17.0	53.8			
D 12	315 22.8	331 43.8	S 8 30.6	246 00.5	N24 46.7	308 34.1	N 1 40.6	346 19.2	S13 53.7	Schedar	349 33.2	N56 40.0
A 13	330 25.2	346 43.4	29.4	261 02.3	46.8	323 36.1	40.8	1 21.3	53.6	Shaula	96 12.8	S37 07.1
Y 14	345 27.7	1 43.0	28.2	276 04.1	46.8	338 38.1	41.0	16 23.5	53.5	Sirius	258 27.3	S16 45.0
15	0 30.2	16 42.6	.. 26.9	291 05.8	.. 46.9	353 40.1	.. 41.2	31 25.7	.. 53.4	Spica	158 23.8	S11 16.9
16	15 32.6	31 42.2	25.7	306 07.6	46.9	8 42.2	41.4	46 27.9	53.3	Suhail	222 47.0	S43 31.5
17	30 35.1	46 41.8	24.5	321 09.4	47.0	23 44.2	41.6	61 30.0	53.2			
18	45 37.6	61 41.3	S 8 23.3	336 11.2	N24 47.1	38 46.2	N 1 41.8	76 32.2	S13 53.1	Vega	80 34.6	N38 48.1
19	60 40.0	76 40.9	22.0	351 12.9	47.1	53 48.2	42.0	91 34.4	53.0	Zuben'ubi	136 57.8	S16 08.2
20	75 42.5	91 40.5	20.8	6 14.7	47.2	68 50.2	42.2	106 36.6	52.9		SHA	Mer. Pass.
21	90 45.0	106 40.1	.. 19.6	21 16.5	.. 47.3	83 52.2	.. 42.4	121 38.7	.. 52.8		° ′	h m
22	105 47.4	121 39.7	18.3	36 18.2	47.3	98 54.3	42.6	136 40.9	52.7	Venus	18 04.9	13 52
23	120 49.9	136 39.3	17.1	51 20.0	47.4	113 56.3	42.8	151 43.1	52.6	Mars	291 01.9	19 38
	h m									Jupiter	353 27.3	15 28
Mer. Pass. 15 01.9		v −0.4	d 1.2	v 1.8	d 0.1	v 2.0	d 0.2	v 2.2	d 0.1	Saturn	31 06.8	12 58

© British Crown Copyright 2022. All rights reserved.

SUN / MOON

UT	SUN GHA	SUN Dec	MOON GHA	v	MOON Dec	d	HP
d h	° ′	° ′	° ′	′	° ′	′	′
3 00	176 34.6	S16 39.8	27 25.4	10.3	N27 14.6	2.2	54.0
01	191 34.6	39.1	41 54.7	10.3	27 12.4	2.3	54.0
02	206 34.5	38.3	56 24.0	10.3	27 10.1	2.4	54.0
03	221 34.4 ..	37.6	70 53.3	10.4	27 07.7	2.5	54.0
04	236 34.4	36.9	85 22.7	10.3	27 05.2	2.7	54.0
05	251 34.3	36.1	99 52.0	10.4	27 02.5	2.8	54.0
06	266 34.2	S16 35.4	114 21.4	10.5	N26 59.7	2.9	54.0
07	281 34.1	34.7	128 50.9	10.4	26 56.8	3.1	54.0
08	296 34.1	33.9	143 20.3	10.6	26 53.7	3.2	54.0
F 09	311 34.0 ..	33.2	157 49.9	10.5	26 50.5	3.3	54.0
R 10	326 33.9	32.5	172 19.4	10.6	26 47.2	3.4	54.0
I 11	341 33.9	31.7	186 49.0	10.6	26 43.8	3.6	54.0
D 12	356 33.8	S16 31.0	201 18.6	10.6	N26 40.2	3.7	54.0
A 13	11 33.7	30.3	215 48.2	10.7	26 36.5	3.8	54.0
Y 14	26 33.7	29.5	230 17.9	10.7	26 32.7	3.9	54.0
15	41 33.6 ..	28.8	244 47.6	10.8	26 28.8	4.1	54.0
16	56 33.5	28.0	259 17.4	10.8	26 24.7	4.2	54.0
17	71 33.5	27.3	273 47.2	10.8	26 20.5	4.3	54.0
18	86 33.4	S16 26.6	288 17.0	10.9	N26 16.2	4.4	54.0
19	101 33.4	25.8	302 46.9	10.9	26 11.8	4.6	54.0
20	116 33.3	25.1	317 16.8	11.0	26 07.2	4.7	54.0
21	131 33.2 ..	24.3	331 46.8	11.0	26 02.5	4.8	54.0
22	146 33.2	23.6	346 16.8	11.1	25 57.7	4.9	54.0
23	161 33.1	22.9	0 46.9	11.1	25 52.8	5.0	54.0
4 00	176 33.0	S16 22.1	15 17.0	11.1	N25 47.8	5.2	54.0
01	191 33.0	21.4	29 47.1	11.2	25 42.6	5.3	53.9
02	206 32.9	20.6	44 17.3	11.3	25 37.3	5.4	53.9
03	221 32.9 ..	19.9	58 47.6	11.2	25 31.9	5.5	53.9
04	236 32.8	19.2	73 17.8	11.4	25 26.4	5.6	53.9
05	251 32.7	18.4	87 48.2	11.4	25 20.8	5.8	53.9
06	266 32.7	S16 17.7	102 18.6	11.4	N25 15.0	5.8	53.9
07	281 32.6	16.9	116 49.0	11.5	25 09.2	6.0	53.9
S 08	296 32.6	16.2	131 19.5	11.6	25 03.2	6.1	53.9
A 09	311 32.5 ..	15.4	145 50.1	11.6	24 57.1	6.2	53.9
T 10	326 32.4	14.7	160 20.7	11.6	24 50.9	6.4	53.9
U 11	341 32.4	13.9	174 51.3	11.7	24 44.5	6.4	53.9
R 12	356 32.3	S16 13.2	189 22.0	11.8	N24 38.1	6.6	53.9
D 13	11 32.3	12.4	203 52.8	11.8	24 31.5	6.6	53.9
A 14	26 32.2	11.7	218 23.6	11.8	24 24.9	6.8	53.9
Y 15	41 32.1 ..	10.9	232 54.4	11.9	24 18.1	6.9	53.9
16	56 32.1	10.2	247 25.3	12.0	24 11.2	7.0	53.9
17	71 32.0	09.4	261 56.3	12.0	24 04.2	7.1	54.0
18	86 32.0	S16 08.7	276 27.3	12.1	N23 57.1	7.2	54.0
19	101 31.9	07.9	290 58.4	12.2	23 49.9	7.3	54.0
20	116 31.9	07.2	305 29.6	12.1	23 42.6	7.4	54.0
21	131 31.8 ..	06.4	320 00.7	12.3	23 35.2	7.5	54.0
22	146 31.8	05.7	334 32.0	12.3	23 27.7	7.6	54.0
23	161 31.7	04.9	349 03.3	12.4	23 20.1	7.8	54.0
5 00	176 31.7	S16 04.2	3 34.7	12.4	N23 12.4	7.8	54.0
01	191 31.6	03.4	18 06.1	12.5	23 04.5	7.9	54.0
02	206 31.5	02.7	32 37.6	12.5	22 56.6	8.1	54.0
03	221 31.5 ..	01.9	47 09.1	12.6	22 48.5	8.1	54.0
04	236 31.4	01.2	61 40.7	12.6	22 40.4	8.3	54.0
05	251 31.4	16 00.4	76 12.3	12.7	22 32.1	8.3	54.0
06	266 31.3	S15 59.7	90 44.0	12.8	N22 23.8	8.4	54.0
07	281 31.3	58.9	105 15.8	12.8	22 15.4	8.6	54.0
S 08	296 31.2	58.1	119 47.6	12.9	22 06.8	8.6	54.0
U 09	311 31.2 ..	57.4	134 19.5	12.9	21 58.2	8.7	54.0
N 10	326 31.1	56.6	148 51.4	13.0	21 49.5	8.9	54.0
D 11	341 31.1	55.9	163 23.4	13.1	21 40.6	8.9	54.0
A 12	356 31.0	S15 55.1	177 55.5	13.1	N21 31.7	9.0	54.0
Y 13	11 31.0	54.4	192 27.6	13.2	21 22.7	9.1	54.0
14	26 30.9	53.6	206 59.8	13.2	21 13.6	9.2	54.0
15	41 30.9 ..	52.8	221 32.0	13.3	21 04.4	9.3	54.0
16	56 30.8	52.1	236 04.3	13.3	20 55.1	9.3	54.0
17	71 30.8	51.3	250 36.6	13.4	20 45.8	9.5	54.0
18	86 30.7	S15 50.6	265 09.0	13.5	N20 36.3	9.6	54.0
19	101 30.7	49.8	279 41.5	13.5	20 26.7	9.6	54.0
20	116 30.6	49.0	294 14.0	13.5	20 17.1	9.7	54.0
21	131 30.6 ..	48.3	308 46.5	13.7	20 07.4	9.9	54.0
22	146 30.6	47.5	323 19.2	13.6	19 57.5	9.9	54.0
23	161 30.5	46.7	337 51.9	13.7	N19 47.6	9.9	54.1
	SD 16.3	d 0.7	SD 14.7		14.7		14.7

Twilight / Moonrise

Lat.	Twilight Naut.	Twilight Civil	Sunrise	Moonrise 3	Moonrise 4	Moonrise 5	Moonrise 6
°	h m	h m	h m	h m	h m	h m	h m
N 72	07 00	08 26	10 06	▢	▢	▢	14 14
N 70	06 53	08 09	09 30	▢	▢	▢	15 12
68	06 47	07 56	09 06	▢	▢	13 13	15 46
66	06 42	07 45	08 46	▢	▢	14 12	16 10
64	06 38	07 36	08 31	▢	12 49	14 45	16 29
62	06 34	07 28	08 18	11 53	13 32	15 10	16 44
60	06 31	07 21	08 07	12 36	14 00	15 29	16 57
N 58	06 27	07 15	07 58	13 05	14 22	15 45	17 08
56	06 24	07 09	07 50	13 27	14 40	15 58	17 17
54	06 22	07 04	07 42	13 45	14 55	16 10	17 26
52	06 19	06 59	07 36	14 01	15 08	16 20	17 33
50	06 16	06 55	07 30	14 14	15 20	16 29	17 40
45	06 11	06 46	07 17	14 41	15 43	16 49	17 54
N 40	06 05	06 37	07 06	15 03	16 02	17 04	18 06
35	06 00	06 30	06 57	15 20	16 18	17 17	18 16
30	05 55	06 24	06 49	15 36	16 32	17 29	18 25
20	05 45	06 12	06 35	16 02	16 55	17 48	18 40
N 10	05 35	06 00	06 22	16 24	17 15	18 05	18 53
0	05 24	05 49	06 10	16 45	17 34	18 20	19 05
S 10	05 11	05 36	05 58	17 05	17 52	18 36	19 17
20	04 55	05 22	05 46	17 28	18 12	18 53	19 30
30	04 35	05 05	05 31	17 53	18 35	19 12	19 44
35	04 22	04 55	05 22	18 08	18 48	19 23	19 53
40	04 06	04 43	05 12	18 26	19 04	19 35	20 02
45	03 47	04 28	05 01	18 47	19 22	19 50	20 13
S 50	03 21	04 09	04 46	19 14	19 45	20 08	20 27
52	03 07	04 00	04 40	19 26	19 56	20 17	20 33
54	02 52	03 50	04 32	19 41	20 08	20 26	20 40
56	02 33	03 38	04 24	19 58	20 22	20 37	20 48
58	02 08	03 24	04 15	20 19	20 38	20 49	20 56
S 60	01 33	03 08	04 04	20 45	20 58	21 03	21 06

Sunset / Twilight / Moonset

Lat.	Sunset	Twilight Civil	Twilight Naut.	Moonset 3	Moonset 4	Moonset 5	Moonset 6
°	h m	h m	h m	h m	h m	h m	h m
N 72	14 23	16 03	17 30	▢	▢	▢	11 53
N 70	14 58	16 20	17 36	▢	▢	▢	10 53
68	15 23	16 33	17 42	▢	▢	11 18	10 18
66	15 42	16 44	17 47	▢	▢	10 03	09 53
64	15 58	16 53	17 51	▢	10 03	09 44	09 33
62	16 10	17 01	17 55	09 15	09 19	09 19	09 17
60	16 21	17 08	17 58	08 31	08 50	08 59	09 03
N 58	16 31	17 14	18 01	08 02	08 28	08 42	08 52
56	16 39	17 20	18 04	07 40	08 09	08 28	08 41
54	16 46	17 25	18 07	07 22	07 54	08 16	08 32
52	16 53	17 29	18 10	07 06	07 41	08 06	08 24
50	16 59	17 33	18 12	06 53	07 29	07 56	08 17
45	17 12	17 43	18 18	06 25	07 04	07 36	08 01
N 40	17 22	17 51	18 23	06 03	06 45	07 19	07 48
35	17 31	17 58	18 28	05 45	06 28	07 05	07 37
30	17 39	18 04	18 33	05 30	06 14	06 53	07 27
20	17 53	18 16	18 43	05 03	05 50	06 32	07 11
N 10	18 06	18 28	18 53	04 40	05 28	06 14	06 56
0	18 17	18 39	19 04	04 19	05 09	05 57	06 42
S 10	18 29	18 51	19 17	03 57	04 49	05 39	06 28
20	18 42	19 05	19 32	03 34	04 28	05 21	06 13
30	18 56	19 22	19 52	03 07	04 03	04 59	05 56
35	19 05	19 32	20 05	02 52	03 48	04 47	05 46
40	19 15	19 44	20 21	02 33	03 31	04 32	05 34
45	19 26	19 59	20 40	02 11	03 11	04 15	05 20
S 50	19 40	20 17	21 06	01 42	02 45	03 53	05 03
52	19 47	20 26	21 18	01 28	02 32	03 42	04 55
54	19 54	20 36	21 34	01 12	02 18	03 31	04 46
56	20 02	20 48	21 52	00 52	02 01	03 17	04 36
58	20 12	21 01	22 16	00 28	01 40	03 01	04 25
S 60	20 22	21 17	22 49	25 14	01 14	02 42	04 11

SUN / MOON

Day	SUN Eqn. of Time 00h	SUN Eqn. of Time 12h	SUN Mer. Pass.	MOON Mer. Pass. Upper	MOON Mer. Pass. Lower	Age	Phase
d	m s	m s	h m	h m	h m	d	%
3	13 41	13 45	12 14	22 57	10 32	13	95
4	13 48	13 51	12 14	23 45	11 21	14	98
5	13 53	13 56	12 14	24 31	12 09	15	100

© British Crown Copyright 2022. All rights reserved.

UT	ARIES	VENUS −3·9		MARS −0·1		JUPITER −2·2		SATURN +0·8		STARS		
	GHA	GHA	Dec	GHA	Dec	GHA	Dec	GHA	Dec	Name	SHA	Dec
d h	° ′	° ′	° ′	° ′	° ′	° ′	° ′	° ′	° ′		° ′	° ′
6 00	135 52.3	151 38.9	S 8 15.9	66 21.8	N24 47.5	128 58.3	N 1 43.0	166 45.3	S13 52.5	Acamar	315 13.0	S40 13.0
01	150 54.8	166 38.5	14.6	81 23.5	47.5	144 00.3	43.2	181 47.4	52.4	Achernar	335 21.6	S57 07.5
02	165 57.3	181 38.1	13.4	96 25.3	47.6	159 02.3	43.4	196 49.6	52.3	Acrux	173 01.4	S63 13.4
03	180 59.7	196 37.7 ..	12.2	111 27.1 ..	47.6	174 04.4 ..	43.6	211 51.8 ..	52.2	Adhara	255 06.8	S29 00.3
04	196 02.2	211 37.2	10.9	126 28.8	47.7	189 06.4	43.8	226 54.0	52.1	Aldebaran	290 41.3	N16 33.3
05	211 04.7	226 36.8	09.7	141 30.6	47.8	204 08.4	44.0	241 56.1	52.0			
06	226 07.1	241 36.4	S 8 08.5	156 32.3	N24 47.8	219 10.4	N 1 44.2	256 58.3	S13 51.9	Alioth	166 14.0	N55 49.8
07	241 09.6	256 36.0	07.2	171 34.1	47.9	234 12.4	44.4	272 00.5	51.8	Alkaid	152 53.1	N49 11.6
08	256 12.1	271 35.6	06.0	186 35.9	48.0	249 14.4	44.6	287 02.6	51.7	Alnair	27 35.3	S46 51.1
M 09	271 14.5	286 35.2 ..	04.8	201 37.6 ..	48.0	264 16.4 ..	44.8	302 04.8 ..	51.6	Alnilam	275 39.1	S 1 11.3
O 10	286 17.0	301 34.8	03.5	216 39.4	48.1	279 18.5	45.0	317 07.0	51.5	Alphard	217 49.0	S 8 45.6
N 11	301 19.4	316 34.4	02.3	231 41.1	48.2	294 20.5	45.2	332 09.2	51.4			
D 12	316 21.9	331 34.0	S 8 01.0	246 42.9	N24 48.2	309 22.5	N 1 45.4	347 11.3	S13 51.3	Alphecca	126 05.1	N26 38.0
A 13	331 24.4	346 33.6	7 59.8	261 44.6	48.3	324 24.5	45.6	2 13.5	51.2	Alpheratz	357 36.7	N29 13.0
Y 14	346 26.8	1 33.2	58.6	276 46.4	48.3	339 26.5	45.8	17 15.7	51.1	Altair	62 01.8	N 8 55.6
15	1 29.3	16 32.8 ..	57.3	291 48.1 ..	48.4	354 28.5 ..	46.0	32 17.9 ..	51.0	Ankaa	353 09.0	S42 11.1
16	16 31.8	31 32.4	56.1	306 49.9	48.5	9 30.6	46.2	47 20.0	50.9	Antares	112 17.9	S26 28.9
17	31 34.2	46 32.0	54.9	321 51.6	48.5	24 32.6	46.4	62 22.2	50.8			
18	46 36.7	61 31.6	S 7 53.6	336 53.4	N24 48.6	39 34.6	N 1 46.6	77 24.4	S13 50.7	Arcturus	145 49.3	N19 03.6
19	61 39.2	76 31.2	52.4	351 55.1	48.7	54 36.6	46.8	92 26.6	50.6	Atria	107 13.8	S69 03.9
20	76 41.6	91 30.8	51.1	6 56.9	48.7	69 38.6	47.0	107 28.7	50.5	Avior	234 14.7	S59 35.0
21	91 44.1	106 30.4 ..	49.9	21 58.6 ..	48.8	84 40.6 ..	47.2	122 30.9 ..	50.4	Bellatrix	278 24.4	N 6 22.2
22	106 46.6	121 30.0	48.7	37 00.4	48.9	99 42.6	47.4	137 33.1	50.3	Betelgeuse	270 53.6	N 7 24.6
23	121 49.0	136 29.6	47.4	52 02.1	48.9	114 44.6	47.6	152 35.2	50.2			
7 00	136 51.5	151 29.2	S 7 46.2	67 03.9	N24 49.0	129 46.7	N 1 47.8	167 37.4	S13 50.1	Canopus	263 52.7	S52 42.6
01	151 53.9	166 28.8	44.9	82 05.6	49.1	144 48.7	48.0	182 39.6	50.0	Capella	280 24.0	N46 01.4
02	166 56.4	181 28.4	43.7	97 07.3	49.1	159 50.7	48.2	197 41.8	49.9	Deneb	49 27.3	N45 21.6
03	181 58.9	196 28.0 ..	42.4	112 09.1 ..	49.2	174 52.7 ..	48.4	212 43.9 ..	49.8	Denebola	182 26.3	N14 26.5
04	197 01.3	211 27.6	41.2	127 10.8	49.3	189 54.7	48.6	227 46.1	49.7	Diphda	348 49.1	S17 51.8
05	212 03.8	226 27.2	40.0	142 12.6	49.3	204 56.7	48.8	242 48.3	49.6			
06	227 06.3	241 26.8	S 7 38.7	157 14.3	N24 49.4	219 58.7	N 1 49.0	257 50.5	S13 49.5	Dubhe	193 42.3	N61 37.4
07	242 08.7	256 26.4	37.5	172 16.0	49.4	235 00.7	49.2	272 52.6	49.4	Elnath	278 03.6	N28 37.6
T 08	257 11.2	271 26.0	36.2	187 17.8	49.5	250 02.8	49.4	287 54.8	49.3	Eltanin	90 43.3	N51 28.8
U 09	272 13.7	286 25.6 ..	35.0	202 19.5 ..	49.6	265 04.8 ..	49.6	302 57.0 ..	49.2	Enif	33 40.7	N 9 58.7
E 10	287 16.1	301 25.2	33.7	217 21.2	49.6	280 06.8	49.8	317 59.1	49.1	Fomalhaut	15 16.6	S29 30.2
S 11	302 18.6	316 24.8	32.5	232 23.0	49.7	295 08.8	50.0	333 01.3	49.0			
D 12	317 21.1	331 24.4	S 7 31.3	247 24.7	N24 49.8	310 10.8	N 1 50.2	348 03.5	S13 48.9	Gacrux	171 53.0	S57 14.3
A 13	332 23.5	346 24.0	30.0	262 26.4	49.8	325 12.8	50.4	3 05.7	48.8	Gienah	175 45.0	S17 40.2
Y 14	347 26.0	1 23.6	28.8	277 28.2	49.9	340 14.8	50.6	18 07.8	48.7	Hadar	148 38.1	S60 28.8
15	2 28.4	16 23.2 ..	27.5	292 29.9 ..	50.0	355 16.8 ..	50.8	33 10.0 ..	48.6	Hamal	327 53.1	N23 34.3
16	17 30.9	31 22.8	26.3	307 31.6	50.0	10 18.9	51.0	48 12.2	48.5	Kaus Aust.	83 34.9	S34 22.4
17	32 33.4	46 22.4	25.0	322 33.4	50.1	25 20.9	51.2	63 14.4	48.4			
18	47 35.8	61 22.0	S 7 23.8	337 35.1	N24 50.2	40 22.9	N 1 51.4	78 16.5	S13 48.3	Kochab	137 19.7	N74 03.3
19	62 38.3	76 21.6	22.5	352 36.8	50.2	55 24.9	51.6	93 18.7	48.2	Markab	13 31.8	N15 19.7
20	77 40.8	91 21.2	21.3	7 38.5	50.3	70 26.9	51.8	108 20.9	48.1	Menkar	314 07.8	N 4 10.7
21	92 43.2	106 20.8 ..	20.0	22 40.3 ..	50.4	85 28.9 ..	52.0	123 23.1 ..	48.0	Menkent	147 59.4	S36 28.9
22	107 45.7	121 20.4	18.8	37 42.0	50.4	100 30.9	52.2	138 25.2	47.9	Miaplacidus	221 37.7	S69 48.6
23	122 48.2	136 20.0	17.5	52 43.7	50.5	115 32.9	52.4	153 27.4	47.8			
8 00	137 50.6	151 19.7	S 7 16.3	67 45.4	N24 50.6	130 34.9	N 1 52.6	168 29.6	S13 47.7	Mirfak	308 30.5	N49 56.7
01	152 53.1	166 19.3	15.0	82 47.2	50.6	145 36.9	52.8	183 31.7	47.6	Nunki	75 50.0	S26 16.1
02	167 55.5	181 18.9	13.8	97 48.9	50.7	160 39.0	53.0	198 33.9	47.5	Peacock	53 08.8	S56 39.7
03	182 58.0	196 18.5 ..	12.5	112 50.6 ..	50.8	175 41.0 ..	53.2	213 36.1 ..	47.4	Pollux	243 18.9	N27 58.2
04	198 00.5	211 18.1	11.3	127 52.3	50.8	190 43.0	53.4	228 38.3	47.3	Procyon	244 52.2	N 5 09.9
05	213 02.9	226 17.7	10.0	142 54.0	50.9	205 45.0	53.6	243 40.4	47.2			
06	228 05.4	241 17.3	S 7 08.8	157 55.8	N24 51.0	220 47.0	N 1 53.8	258 42.6	S13 47.1	Rasalhague	96 00.2	N12 32.4
07	243 07.9	256 16.9	07.5	172 57.5	51.0	235 49.0	54.0	273 44.8	47.0	Regulus	207 35.8	N11 51.2
W 08	258 10.3	271 16.5	06.3	187 59.2	51.1	250 51.0	54.2	288 47.0	46.9	Rigel	281 05.2	S 8 10.6
E 09	273 12.8	286 16.1 ..	05.0	203 00.9 ..	51.2	265 53.0 ..	54.4	303 49.1 ..	46.8	Rigil Kent.	139 42.4	S60 55.5
D 10	288 15.3	301 15.8	03.8	218 02.6	51.2	280 55.0	54.6	318 51.3	46.7	Sabik	102 04.8	S15 45.2
N 11	303 17.7	316 15.4	02.5	233 04.3	51.3	295 57.0	54.8	333 53.5	46.6			
E 12	318 20.2	331 15.0	S 7 01.3	248 06.0	N24 51.4	310 59.0	N 1 55.0	348 55.6	S13 46.5	Schedar	349 33.2	N56 40.0
S 13	333 22.7	346 14.6	7 00.0	263 07.7	51.4	326 01.0	55.2	3 57.8	46.4	Shaula	96 12.8	S37 07.1
D 14	348 25.1	1 14.2	6 58.8	278 09.5	51.5	341 03.1	55.5	19 00.0	46.3	Sirius	258 27.3	S16 45.0
A 15	3 27.6	16 13.8 ..	57.5	293 11.2 ..	51.6	356 05.1 ..	55.7	34 02.2 ..	46.2	Spica	158 23.8	S11 16.9
Y 16	18 30.0	31 13.4	56.3	308 12.9	51.6	11 07.1	55.9	49 04.3	46.1	Suhail	222 47.0	S43 31.5
17	33 32.5	46 13.0	55.0	323 14.6	51.7	26 09.1	56.1	64 06.5	46.0			
18	48 35.0	61 12.7	S 6 53.7	338 16.3	N24 51.7	41 11.1	N 1 56.3	79 08.7	S13 45.9	Vega	80 34.6	N38 48.1
19	63 37.4	76 12.3	52.5	353 18.0	51.8	56 13.1	56.5	94 10.8	45.8	Zuben'ubi	136 57.7	S16 08.2
20	78 39.9	91 11.9	51.2	8 19.7	51.9	71 15.1	56.7	109 13.0	45.7		SHA	Mer. Pass.
21	93 42.4	106 11.5 ..	50.0	23 21.4 ..	51.9	86 17.1 ..	56.9	124 15.2 ..	45.6		° ′	h m
22	108 44.8	121 11.1	48.7	38 23.1	52.0	101 19.1	57.1	139 17.4	45.5	Venus	14 37.7	13 54
23	123 47.3	136 10.7	47.5	53 24.8	52.1	116 21.1	57.3	154 19.5	45.4	Mars	290 12.4	19 29
	h m									Jupiter	352 55.2	15 19
Mer. Pass. 14 50.1		v −0.4	d 1.2	v 1.7	d 0.1	v 2.0	d 0.2	v 2.2	d 0.1	Saturn	30 45.9	12 48

© British Crown Copyright 2022. All rights reserved.

UT	SUN GHA	SUN Dec	MOON GHA	MOON v	MOON Dec	MOON d	MOON HP	Lat.	Twilight Naut.	Twilight Civil	Sunrise	Moonrise 6	Moonrise 7	Moonrise 8	Moonrise 9
	° ′	° ′	° ′	′	° ′	′	′	°	h m	h m	h m	h m	h m	h m	h m
6 00	176 30.5	S15 46.0	352 24.6	13.8	N19 37.7	10.1	54.1	N 72	06 48	08 13	09 45	14 14	17 05	19 12	21 12
01	191 30.4	45.2	6 57.4	13.8	19 27.6	10.2	54.1	N 70	06 43	07 58	09 15	15 12	17 26	19 21	21 12
02	206 30.4	44.4	21 30.2	13.9	19 17.4	10.2	54.1	68	06 38	07 46	08 53	15 46	17 42	19 28	21 11
03	221 30.3 ..	43.7	36 03.1	14.0	19 07.2	10.3	54.1	66	06 34	07 36	08 36	16 10	17 55	19 34	21 11
04	236 30.3	42.9	50 36.1	14.0	18 56.9	10.4	54.1	64	06 31	07 28	08 22	16 29	18 06	19 39	21 11
05	251 30.2	42.1	65 09.1	14.1	18 46.5	10.5	54.1	62	06 27	07 20	08 10	16 44	18 15	19 43	21 11
06	266 30.2	S15 41.4	79 42.2	14.1	N18 36.0	10.5	54.1	60	06 24	07 14	08 00	16 57	18 23	19 47	21 10
07	281 30.2	40.6	94 15.3	14.2	18 25.5	10.7	54.1	N 58	06 22	07 08	07 51	17 08	18 30	19 50	21 10
08	296 30.1	39.8	108 48.5	14.2	18 14.8	10.7	54.1	56	06 19	07 03	07 43	17 17	18 36	19 53	21 10
M 09	311 30.1 ..	39.1	123 21.7	14.3	18 04.1	10.8	54.1	54	06 17	06 59	07 37	17 26	18 41	19 56	21 10
O 10	326 30.0	38.3	137 55.0	14.3	17 53.3	10.8	54.1	52	06 14	06 55	07 30	17 33	18 46	19 58	21 10
N 11	341 30.0	37.5	152 28.3	14.4	17 42.5	11.0	54.1	50	06 12	06 51	07 25	17 40	18 50	20 00	21 10
D 12	356 29.9	S15 36.8	167 01.7	14.4	N17 31.5	11.0	54.1	45	06 07	06 42	07 13	17 54	19 00	20 05	21 10
A 13	11 29.9	36.0	181 35.1	14.5	17 20.5	11.0	54.1	N 40	06 02	06 35	07 03	18 06	19 07	20 08	21 10
Y 14	26 29.9	35.2	196 08.6	14.6	17 09.5	11.2	54.2	35	05 58	06 28	06 54	18 16	19 14	20 12	21 09
15	41 29.8 ..	34.5	210 42.2	14.6	16 58.3	11.2	54.2	30	05 53	06 22	06 47	18 25	19 20	20 15	21 09
16	56 29.8	33.7	225 15.8	14.6	16 47.1	11.3	54.2	20	05 44	06 11	06 33	18 40	19 30	20 20	21 09
17	71 29.7	32.9	239 49.4	14.7	16 35.8	11.4	54.2	N 10	05 35	06 00	06 22	18 53	19 39	20 24	21 09
18	86 29.7	S15 32.1	254 23.1	14.7	N16 24.4	11.4	54.2	0	05 24	05 49	06 11	19 05	19 47	20 28	21 09
19	101 29.7	31.4	268 56.8	14.8	16 13.0	11.5	54.2	S 10	05 12	05 38	05 59	19 17	19 55	20 32	21 09
20	116 29.6	30.6	283 30.6	14.8	16 01.5	11.6	54.2	20	04 57	05 24	05 47	19 30	20 04	20 37	21 09
21	131 29.6 ..	29.8	298 04.4	14.9	15 49.9	11.6	54.2	30	04 38	05 08	05 33	19 44	20 14	20 42	21 09
22	146 29.6	29.0	312 38.3	14.9	15 38.3	11.7	54.2	35	04 25	04 58	05 25	19 53	20 20	20 44	21 09
23	161 29.5	28.3	327 12.2	15.0	15 26.6	11.8	54.2	40	04 11	04 47	05 16	20 02	20 26	20 48	21 09
7 00	176 29.5	S15 27.5	341 46.2	15.0	N15 14.8	11.8	54.2	45	03 52	04 32	05 05	20 13	20 33	20 51	21 08
01	191 29.4	26.7	356 20.2	15.1	15 03.0	11.9	54.3	S 50	03 28	04 15	04 52	20 27	20 42	20 56	21 08
02	206 29.4	25.9	10 54.3	15.1	14 51.1	12.0	54.3	52	03 15	04 06	04 45	20 33	20 46	20 58	21 08
03	221 29.4 ..	25.2	25 28.4	15.1	14 39.1	12.0	54.3	54	03 01	03 57	04 39	20 40	20 51	21 00	21 08
04	236 29.3	24.4	40 02.5	15.2	14 27.1	12.1	54.3	56	02 44	03 46	04 31	20 48	20 56	21 02	21 08
05	251 29.3	23.6	54 36.7	15.2	14 15.0	12.1	54.3	58	02 22	03 33	04 22	20 56	21 01	21 05	21 08
06	266 29.3	S15 22.8	69 10.9	15.3	N14 02.9	12.2	54.3	S 60	01 52	03 18	04 12	21 06	21 08	21 08	21 08
07	281 29.2	22.0	83 45.2	15.3	13 50.7	12.2	54.3								
T 08	296 29.2	21.3	98 19.5	15.4	13 38.5	12.3	54.3	Lat.	Sunset	Twilight Civil	Twilight Naut.	Moonset 6	Moonset 7	Moonset 8	Moonset 9
U 09	311 29.2 ..	20.5	112 53.9	15.3	13 26.2	12.4	54.3								
E 10	326 29.1	19.7	127 28.2	15.5	13 13.8	12.4	54.3	°	h m	h m	h m	h m	h m	h m	h m
S 11	341 29.1	18.9	142 02.7	15.4	13 01.4	12.5	54.4	N 72	14 45	16 17	17 42	11 53	10 33	09 52	09 20
D 12	356 29.1	S15 18.1	156 37.1	15.5	N12 48.9	12.5	54.4	N 70	15 15	16 32	17 47	10 53	10 09	09 41	09 17
A 13	11 29.0	17.4	171 11.6	15.6	12 36.4	12.6	54.4	68	15 36	16 43	17 51	10 18	09 51	09 32	09 14
Y 14	26 29.0	16.6	185 46.2	15.5	12 23.8	12.7	54.4	66	15 54	16 53	17 55	09 53	09 37	09 24	09 12
15	41 29.0 ..	15.8	200 20.7	15.7	12 11.1	12.6	54.4	64	16 08	17 02	17 59	09 33	09 25	09 17	09 10
16	56 28.9	15.0	214 55.4	15.6	11 58.5	12.8	54.4	62	16 19	17 09	18 02	09 17	09 14	09 11	09 08
17	71 28.9	14.2	229 30.0	15.7	11 45.7	12.8	54.4	60	16 29	17 15	18 05	09 03	09 05	09 06	09 07
18	86 28.9	S15 13.5	244 04.7	15.7	N11 32.9	12.8	54.4	N 58	16 38	17 21	18 07	08 52	08 58	09 02	09 05
19	101 28.8	12.7	258 39.4	15.7	11 20.1	12.9	54.4	56	16 45	17 26	18 10	08 41	08 51	08 58	09 04
20	116 28.8	11.9	273 14.1	15.8	11 07.2	12.9	54.5	54	16 52	17 30	18 12	08 32	08 44	08 54	09 03
21	131 28.8 ..	11.1	287 48.9	15.8	10 54.3	13.0	54.5	52	16 58	17 34	18 14	08 24	08 39	08 51	09 02
22	146 28.7	10.3	302 23.7	15.8	10 41.3	13.0	54.5	50	17 04	17 38	18 17	08 17	08 34	08 48	09 01
23	161 28.7	09.5	316 58.5	15.9	10 28.3	13.1	54.5	45	17 16	17 47	18 22	08 01	08 23	08 41	08 59
8 00	176 28.7	S15 08.7	331 33.4	15.8	N10 15.2	13.1	54.5	N 40	17 26	17 54	18 26	07 48	08 13	08 36	08 57
01	191 28.7	08.0	346 08.2	16.0	10 02.1	13.2	54.5	35	17 34	18 01	18 31	07 37	08 05	08 31	08 56
02	206 28.6	07.2	0 43.2	15.9	9 48.9	13.2	54.5	30	17 42	18 07	18 35	07 27	07 58	08 27	08 54
03	221 28.6 ..	06.4	15 18.1	15.9	9 35.7	13.2	54.5	20	17 55	18 18	18 44	07 11	07 46	08 20	08 52
04	236 28.6	05.6	29 53.0	16.0	9 22.5	13.3	54.6	N 10	18 07	18 28	18 53	06 56	07 35	08 13	08 50
05	251 28.5	04.8	44 28.0	16.0	9 09.2	13.3	54.6	0	18 18	18 39	19 04	06 42	07 25	08 07	08 48
06	266 28.5	S15 04.0	59 03.0	16.1	N 8 55.9	13.4	54.6	S 10	18 29	18 50	19 16	06 28	07 15	08 01	08 46
W 07	281 28.5	03.2	73 38.1	16.0	8 42.5	13.4	54.6	20	18 40	19 04	19 31	06 13	07 04	07 54	08 43
E 08	296 28.5	02.4	88 13.1	16.1	8 29.1	13.4	54.6	30	18 54	19 20	19 50	05 56	06 52	07 46	08 41
D 09	311 28.4 ..	01.6	102 48.2	16.1	8 15.7	13.5	54.6	35	19 02	19 29	20 02	05 46	06 44	07 42	08 40
N 10	326 28.4	00.9	117 23.3	16.1	8 02.2	13.5	54.6	40	19 11	19 41	20 17	05 34	06 36	07 37	08 38
E 11	341 28.4	15 00.1	131 58.4	16.1	7 48.7	13.6	54.7	45	19 22	19 55	20 35	05 20	06 26	07 31	08 36
S 12	356 28.4	S14 59.3	146 33.5	16.1	N 7 35.1	13.6	54.7	S 50	19 35	20 12	20 59	05 03	06 14	07 24	08 34
D 13	11 28.3	58.5	161 08.6	16.2	7 21.5	13.6	54.7	52	19 42	20 20	21 11	04 55	06 08	07 21	08 32
A 14	26 28.3	57.7	175 43.8	16.2	7 07.9	13.6	54.7	54	19 48	20 30	21 25	04 46	06 02	07 17	08 31
Y 15	41 28.3 ..	56.9	190 19.0	16.2	6 54.3	13.7	54.7	56	19 56	20 40	21 42	04 36	05 55	07 13	08 30
16	56 28.2	56.1	204 54.2	16.2	6 40.6	13.8	54.7	58	20 04	20 53	22 03	04 25	05 47	07 08	08 29
17	71 28.2	55.3	219 29.4	16.2	6 26.8	13.7	54.7	S 60	20 14	21 08	22 31	04 11	05 38	07 03	08 27
18	86 28.2	S14 54.5	234 04.6	16.2	N 6 13.1	13.8	54.8								
19	101 28.2	53.7	248 39.8	16.2	5 59.3	13.8	54.8			SUN			MOON		
20	116 28.2	52.9	263 15.0	16.3	5 45.5	13.8	54.8	Day	Eqn. of Time 00h	Eqn. of Time 12h	Mer. Pass.	Mer. Pass. Upper	Mer. Pass. Lower	Age	Phase
21	131 28.2 ..	52.1	277 50.3	16.2	5 31.7	13.9	54.8	d	m s	m s	h m	h m	h m	d %	
22	146 28.1	51.3	292 25.5	16.3	5 17.8	13.9	54.8	6	13 58	14 00	12 14	00 31	12 53	16 99	
23	161 28.1	50.5	307 00.8	16.2	N 5 03.9	13.9	54.8	7	14 02	14 04	12 14	01 15	13 36	17 97	
	SD 16.2	d 0.8	SD 14.8	14.8	14.9			8	14 05	14 06	12 14	01 57	14 18	18 93	

© British Crown Copyright 2022. All rights reserved.

UT	ARIES GHA	VENUS −3.9 GHA	Dec	MARS +0.0 GHA	Dec	JUPITER −2.1 GHA	Dec	SATURN +0.8 GHA	Dec	STARS Name	SHA	Dec
d h	° ′	° ′	° ′	° ′	° ′	° ′	° ′	° ′	° ′		° ′	° ′
9 00	138 49.8	151 10.3	S 6 46.2	68 26.5	N24 52.1	131 23.1	N 1 57.5	169 21.7	S13 45.3	Acamar	315 13.0	S40 13.0
01	153 52.2	166 10.0	45.0	83 28.2	52.2	146 25.1	57.7	184 23.9	45.2	Achernar	335 21.6	S57 07.5
02	168 54.7	181 09.6	43.7	98 29.9	52.3	161 27.1	57.9	199 26.1	45.1	Acrux	173 01.3	S63 13.4
03	183 57.1	196 09.2 ..	42.4	113 31.6 ..	52.3	176 29.1 ..	58.1	214 28.2 ..	45.0	Adhara	255 06.8	S29 00.3
04	198 59.6	211 08.8	41.2	128 33.3	52.4	191 31.2	58.3	229 30.4	44.9	Aldebaran	290 41.3	N16 33.3
05	214 02.1	226 08.4	39.9	143 35.0	52.5	206 33.2	58.5	244 32.6	44.8			
06	229 04.5	241 08.0	S 6 38.7	158 36.7	N24 52.6	221 35.2	N 1 58.7	259 34.7	S13 44.6	Alioth	166 14.0	N55 49.8
07	244 07.0	256 07.7	37.4	173 38.4	52.6	236 37.2	58.9	274 36.9	44.5	Alkaid	152 53.1	N49 11.6
08	259 09.5	271 07.3	36.1	188 40.1	52.7	251 39.2	59.1	289 39.1	44.4	Alnair	27 35.3	S46 51.1
09	274 11.9	286 06.9 ..	34.9	203 41.8 ..	52.8	266 41.2 ..	59.3	304 41.3 ..	44.3	Alnilam	275 39.1	S 1 11.3
10	289 14.4	301 06.5	33.6	218 43.5	52.8	281 43.2	59.5	319 43.4	44.2	Alphard	217 49.0	S 8 45.6
11	304 16.9	316 06.1	32.4	233 45.2	52.9	296 45.2	59.7	334 45.6	44.1			
12	319 19.3	331 05.8	S 6 31.1	248 46.9	N24 53.0	311 47.2	N 1 59.9	349 47.8	S13 44.0	Alphecca	126 05.1	N26 38.0
13	334 21.8	346 05.4	29.8	263 48.5	53.0	326 49.2	2 00.1	4 50.0	43.9	Alpheratz	357 36.7	N29 13.0
14	349 24.3	1 05.0	28.6	278 50.2	53.1	341 51.2	00.3	19 52.1	43.8	Altair	62 01.8	N 8 55.6
15	4 26.7	16 04.6 ..	27.3	293 51.9 ..	53.2	356 53.2 ..	00.5	34 54.3 ..	43.7	Ankaa	353 09.0	S42 11.1
16	19 29.2	31 04.2	26.1	308 53.6	53.2	11 55.2	00.7	49 56.5	43.6	Antares	112 17.9	S26 28.9
17	34 31.6	46 03.9	24.8	323 55.3	53.3	26 57.2	01.0	64 58.6	43.5			
18	49 34.1	61 03.5	S 6 23.5	338 57.0	N24 53.4	41 59.2	N 2 01.2	80 00.8	S13 43.4	Arcturus	145 49.3	N19 03.6
19	64 36.6	76 03.1	22.3	353 58.7	53.4	57 01.2	01.4	95 03.0	43.3	Atria	107 13.8	S69 03.9
20	79 39.0	91 02.7	21.0	9 00.4	53.5	72 03.2	01.6	110 05.2	43.2	Avior	234 14.8	S59 35.0
21	94 41.5	106 02.4 ..	19.7	24 02.0 ..	53.6	87 05.2 ..	01.8	125 07.3 ..	43.1	Bellatrix	278 24.4	N 6 22.2
22	109 44.0	121 02.0	18.5	39 03.7	53.6	102 07.2	02.0	140 09.5	43.0	Betelgeuse	270 53.6	N 7 24.6
23	124 46.4	136 01.6	17.2	54 05.4	53.7	117 09.2	02.2	155 11.7	42.9			
10 00	139 48.9	151 01.2	S 6 16.0	69 07.1	N24 53.8	132 11.2	N 2 02.4	170 13.8	S13 42.8	Canopus	263 52.7	S52 42.7
01	154 51.4	166 00.8	14.7	84 08.8	53.8	147 13.2	02.6	185 16.0	42.7	Capella	280 24.0	N46 01.4
02	169 53.8	181 00.5	13.4	99 10.4	53.9	162 15.2	02.8	200 18.2	42.6	Deneb	49 27.3	N45 21.6
03	184 56.3	196 00.1 ..	12.2	114 12.1 ..	54.0	177 17.2 ..	03.0	215 20.4 ..	42.5	Denebola	182 26.3	N14 26.5
04	199 58.7	210 59.7	10.9	129 13.8	54.0	192 19.2	03.2	230 22.5	42.4	Diphda	348 49.1	S17 51.8
05	215 01.2	225 59.3	09.6	144 15.5	54.1	207 21.2	03.4	245 24.7	42.3			
06	230 03.7	240 59.0	S 6 08.4	159 17.1	N24 54.2	222 23.3	N 2 03.6	260 26.9	S13 42.2	Dubhe	193 42.3	N61 37.5
07	245 06.1	255 58.6	07.1	174 18.8	54.2	237 25.3	03.8	275 29.1	42.1	Elnath	278 03.7	N28 37.6
08	260 08.6	270 58.2	05.8	189 20.5	54.3	252 27.3	04.0	290 31.2	42.0	Eltanin	90 43.3	N51 28.8
09	275 11.1	285 57.8 ..	04.6	204 22.2 ..	54.4	267 29.3 ..	04.2	305 33.4 ..	41.9	Enif	33 40.7	N 9 58.7
10	290 13.5	300 57.5	03.3	219 23.8	54.4	282 31.3	04.4	320 35.6	41.8	Fomalhaut	15 16.6	S29 30.2
11	305 16.0	315 57.1	02.0	234 25.5	54.5	297 33.3	04.6	335 37.7	41.7			
12	320 18.5	330 56.7	S 6 00.8	249 27.2	N24 54.6	312 35.3	N 2 04.8	350 39.9	S13 41.6	Gacrux	171 53.0	S57 14.3
13	335 20.9	345 56.4	5 59.5	264 28.9	54.6	327 37.3	05.1	5 42.1	41.5	Gienah	175 45.0	S17 40.2
14	350 23.4	0 56.0	58.2	279 30.5	54.7	342 39.3	05.3	20 44.3	41.4	Hadar	148 38.1	S60 28.8
15	5 25.9	15 55.6 ..	57.0	294 32.2 ..	54.8	357 41.3 ..	05.5	35 46.4 ..	41.3	Hamal	327 53.1	N23 34.3
16	20 28.3	30 55.2	55.7	309 33.9	54.8	12 43.3	05.7	50 48.6	41.2	Kaus Aust.	83 34.9	S34 22.4
17	35 30.8	45 54.9	54.4	324 35.5	54.9	27 45.3	05.9	65 50.8	41.1			
18	50 33.2	60 54.5	S 5 53.2	339 37.2	N24 55.0	42 47.3	N 2 06.1	80 52.9	S13 41.0	Kochab	137 19.6	N74 03.3
19	65 35.7	75 54.1	51.9	354 38.9	55.0	57 49.3	06.3	95 55.1	40.9	Markab	13 31.8	N15 19.6
20	80 38.2	90 53.8	50.6	9 40.5	55.1	72 51.3	06.5	110 57.3	40.8	Menkar	314 07.8	N 4 10.7
21	95 40.6	105 53.4 ..	49.4	24 42.2 ..	55.2	87 53.3 ..	06.7	125 59.5 ..	40.7	Menkent	147 59.4	S36 28.9
22	110 43.1	120 53.0	48.1	39 43.8	55.3	102 55.3	06.9	141 01.6	40.6	Miaplacidus	221 37.7	S69 48.7
23	125 45.6	135 52.6	46.8	54 45.5	55.3	117 57.3	07.1	156 03.8	40.5			
11 00	140 48.0	150 52.3	S 5 45.5	69 47.2	N24 55.4	132 59.3	N 2 07.3	171 06.0	S13 40.4	Mirfak	308 30.5	N49 56.7
01	155 50.5	165 51.9	44.3	84 48.8	55.5	148 01.3	07.5	186 08.1	40.3	Nunki	75 50.0	S26 16.1
02	170 53.0	180 51.5	43.0	99 50.5	55.5	163 03.3	07.7	201 10.3	40.2	Peacock	53 08.8	S56 39.7
03	185 55.4	195 51.2 ..	41.7	114 52.1 ..	55.6	178 05.3 ..	07.9	216 12.5 ..	40.1	Pollux	243 18.9	N27 58.2
04	200 57.9	210 50.8	40.5	129 53.8	55.7	193 07.3	08.1	231 14.7	40.0	Procyon	244 52.2	N 5 09.9
05	216 00.4	225 50.4	39.2	144 55.5	55.7	208 09.3	08.3	246 16.8	39.9			
06	231 02.8	240 50.1	S 5 37.9	159 57.1	N24 55.8	223 11.3	N 2 08.5	261 19.0	S13 39.8	Rasalhague	96 00.2	N12 32.4
07	246 05.3	255 49.7	36.6	174 58.8	55.9	238 13.3	08.8	276 21.2	39.7	Regulus	207 35.8	N11 51.2
08	261 07.7	270 49.3	35.4	190 00.4	55.9	253 15.3	09.0	291 23.3	39.6	Rigel	281 05.2	S 8 10.6
09	276 10.2	285 49.0 ..	34.1	205 02.1 ..	56.0	268 17.3 ..	09.2	306 25.5 ..	39.5	Rigil Kent.	139 42.4	S60 55.5
10	291 12.7	300 48.6	32.8	220 03.7	56.1	283 19.3	09.4	321 27.7	39.4	Sabik	102 04.8	S15 45.2
11	306 15.1	315 48.2	31.6	235 05.4	56.1	298 21.3	09.6	336 29.9	39.3			
12	321 17.6	330 47.9	S 5 30.3	250 07.0	N24 56.2	313 23.3	N 2 09.8	351 32.0	S13 39.2	Schedar	349 33.2	N56 39.9
13	336 20.1	345 47.5	29.0	265 08.7	56.3	328 25.2	10.0	6 34.2	39.1	Shaula	96 12.7	S37 07.1
14	351 22.5	0 47.1	27.7	280 10.3	56.3	343 27.2	10.2	21 36.4	39.0	Sirius	258 27.4	S16 45.0
15	6 25.0	15 46.8 ..	26.5	295 12.0 ..	56.4	358 29.2 ..	10.4	36 38.6 ..	38.9	Spica	158 23.8	S11 16.9
16	21 27.5	30 46.4	25.2	310 13.6	56.5	13 31.2	10.6	51 40.7	38.8	Suhail	222 47.0	S43 31.6
17	36 29.9	45 46.0	23.9	325 15.3	56.5	28 33.2	10.8	66 42.9	38.7			
18	51 32.4	60 45.7	S 5 22.6	340 16.9	N24 56.6	43 35.2	N 2 11.0	81 45.1	S13 38.6	Vega	80 34.6	N38 48.0
19	66 34.8	75 45.3	21.4	355 18.6	56.7	58 37.2	11.2	96 47.2	38.5	Zuben'ubi	136 57.7	S16 08.2
20	81 37.3	90 44.9	20.1	10 20.2	56.8	73 39.2	11.4	111 49.4	38.4			
21	96 39.8	105 44.6 ..	18.8	25 21.9 ..	56.8	88 41.2 ..	11.6	126 51.6 ..	38.3		SHA	Mer. Pass.
22	111 42.2	120 44.2	17.5	40 23.5	56.9	103 43.2	11.9	141 53.8	38.2	Venus	11 12.3	13 56
23	126 44.7	135 43.9	16.3	55 25.1	57.0	118 45.2	12.1	156 55.9	38.1	Mars	289 18.2	19 21
Mer. Pass.	h m 14 38.3	v −0.4	d 1.3	v 1.7	d 0.1	v 2.0	d 0.2	v 2.2	d 0.1	Jupiter	352 22.3	15 09
										Saturn	30 25.0	12 37

Day labels (left margin): THURSDAY (9), FRIDAY (10), SATURDAY (11)

© British Crown Copyright 2022. All rights reserved.

SUN / MOON

UT	SUN GHA	SUN Dec	MOON GHA	v	MOON Dec	d	HP
d h	° ′	° ′	° ′	′	° ′	′	′
9 00	176 28.1	S14 49.7	321 36.0	16.3	N 4 50.0	13.9	54.9
01	191 28.1	48.9	336 11.3	16.2	4 36.1	14.0	54.9
02	206 28.1	48.1	350 46.5	16.3	4 22.1	14.0	54.9
03	221 28.0	.. 47.3	5 21.8	16.3	4 08.1	14.0	54.9
04	236 28.0	46.5	19 57.1	16.3	3 54.1	14.1	54.9
05	251 28.0	45.7	34 32.4	16.2	3 40.0	14.0	54.9
06	266 28.0	S14 44.9	49 07.6	16.3	N 3 26.0	14.1	55.0
07	281 28.0	44.1	63 42.9	16.3	3 11.9	14.1	55.0
T 08	296 27.9	43.3	78 18.2	16.2	2 57.8	14.1	55.0
H 09	311 27.9	.. 42.5	92 53.4	16.3	2 43.7	14.2	55.0
U 10	326 27.9	41.7	107 28.7	16.3	2 29.5	14.1	55.0
R 11	341 27.9	40.9	122 04.0	16.2	2 15.4	14.2	55.0
S 12	356 27.9	S14 40.1	136 39.2	16.3	N 2 01.2	14.2	55.1
D 13	11 27.9	39.3	151 14.5	16.2	1 47.0	14.2	55.1
A 14	26 27.8	38.5	165 49.7	16.2	1 32.8	14.2	55.1
Y 15	41 27.8	.. 37.7	180 24.9	16.2	1 18.6	14.2	55.1
16	56 27.8	36.9	195 00.1	16.2	1 04.4	14.3	55.1
17	71 27.8	36.1	209 35.3	16.2	0 50.1	14.3	55.2
18	86 27.8	S14 35.3	224 10.5	16.2	N 0 35.8	14.2	55.2
19	101 27.8	34.5	238 45.7	16.1	0 21.6	14.3	55.2
20	116 27.7	33.7	253 20.8	16.2	N 0 07.3	14.3	55.2
21	131 27.7	.. 32.9	267 56.0	16.1	S 0 07.0	14.3	55.2
22	146 27.7	32.1	282 31.1	16.1	0 21.3	14.3	55.3
23	161 27.7	31.3	297 06.2	16.1	0 35.6	14.3	55.3
10 00	176 27.7	S14 30.5	311 41.3	16.1	S 0 49.9	14.3	55.3
01	191 27.7	29.7	326 16.4	16.0	1 04.2	14.4	55.3
02	206 27.7	28.9	340 51.4	16.0	1 18.6	14.3	55.3
03	221 27.7	.. 28.1	355 26.4	16.0	1 32.9	14.3	55.4
04	236 27.6	27.2	10 01.4	16.0	1 47.2	14.4	55.4
05	251 27.6	26.4	24 36.4	15.9	2 01.6	14.3	55.4
06	266 27.6	S14 25.6	39 11.3	16.0	S 2 15.9	14.3	55.4
07	281 27.6	24.8	53 46.3	15.8	2 30.2	14.4	55.4
08	296 27.6	24.0	68 21.1	15.9	2 44.6	14.3	55.5
F 09	311 27.6	.. 23.2	82 56.0	15.8	2 58.9	14.4	55.5
R 10	326 27.6	22.4	97 30.8	15.8	3 13.3	14.3	55.5
I 11	341 27.6	21.6	112 05.6	15.8	3 27.6	14.3	55.5
D 12	356 27.6	S14 20.8	126 40.4	15.7	S 3 41.9	14.4	55.5
A 13	11 27.6	20.0	141 15.1	15.7	3 56.3	14.3	55.6
Y 14	26 27.6	19.1	155 49.8	15.6	4 10.6	14.3	55.6
15	41 27.5	.. 18.3	170 24.4	15.7	4 24.9	14.3	55.6
16	56 27.5	17.5	184 59.1	15.5	4 39.2	14.3	55.6
17	71 27.5	16.7	199 33.6	15.6	4 53.5	14.3	55.7
18	86 27.5	S14 15.9	214 08.2	15.4	S 5 07.8	14.3	55.7
19	101 27.5	15.1	228 42.6	15.5	5 22.1	14.3	55.7
20	116 27.5	14.3	243 17.1	15.4	5 36.4	14.3	55.7
21	131 27.5	.. 13.4	257 51.5	15.4	5 50.7	14.2	55.8
22	146 27.5	12.6	272 25.9	15.3	6 04.9	14.3	55.8
23	161 27.5	11.8	287 00.2	15.2	6 19.2	14.2	55.8
11 00	176 27.5	S14 11.0	301 34.4	15.2	S 6 33.4	14.2	55.8
01	191 27.5	10.2	316 08.6	15.2	6 47.6	14.2	55.9
02	206 27.5	09.3	330 42.8	15.1	7 01.8	14.2	55.9
03	221 27.5	.. 08.5	345 16.9	15.1	7 16.0	14.2	55.9
04	236 27.5	07.7	359 51.0	15.0	7 30.2	14.1	55.9
05	251 27.5	06.9	14 25.0	14.9	7 44.3	14.2	56.0
06	266 27.5	S14 06.1	28 58.9	14.9	S 7 58.5	14.1	56.0
07	281 27.5	05.3	43 32.8	14.8	8 12.6	14.0	56.0
S 08	296 27.5	04.4	58 06.6	14.8	8 26.6	14.1	56.0
A 09	311 27.5	.. 03.6	72 40.4	14.7	8 40.7	14.1	56.1
T 10	326 27.5	02.8	87 14.1	14.7	8 54.8	14.0	56.1
U 11	341 27.5	02.0	101 47.8	14.6	9 08.8	14.0	56.1
R 12	356 27.5	S14 01.1	116 21.4	14.5	S 9 22.8	13.9	56.1
D 13	11 27.5	14 00.3	130 54.9	14.4	9 36.7	14.0	56.2
A 14	26 27.5	13 59.5	145 28.3	14.4	9 50.7	13.9	56.2
Y 15	41 27.5	.. 58.7	160 01.7	14.4	10 04.6	13.8	56.2
16	56 27.5	57.9	174 35.1	14.2	10 18.4	13.9	56.2
17	71 27.5	57.0	189 08.3	14.2	10 32.3	13.8	56.3
18	86 27.5	S13 56.2	203 41.5	14.1	S10 46.1	13.8	56.3
19	101 27.5	55.4	218 14.6	14.1	10 59.9	13.7	56.3
20	116 27.5	54.6	232 47.7	13.9	11 13.6	13.7	56.4
21	131 27.5	.. 53.7	247 20.6	13.9	11 27.3	13.7	56.4
22	146 27.5	52.9	261 53.5	13.8	11 41.0	13.7	56.4
23	161 27.5	52.1	276 26.3	13.8	S11 54.7	13.6	56.4
	SD 16.2	d 0.8	SD 15.0		15.1		15.3

Twilight / Sunrise / Moonrise

Lat.	Twilight Naut.	Twilight Civil	Sunrise	Moonrise 9	10	11	12
°	h m	h m	h m	h m	h m	h m	h m
N 72	06 36	07 59	09 25	21 12	23 14	25 33	01 33
N 70	06 32	07 46	09 00	21 12	23 05	25 09	01 09
68	06 29	07 36	08 40	21 11	22 57	24 50	00 50
66	06 26	07 27	08 25	21 11	22 50	24 35	00 35
64	06 23	07 19	08 12	21 11	22 45	24 24	00 24
62	06 20	07 13	08 01	21 11	22 40	24 13	00 13
60	06 18	07 07	07 52	21 10	22 36	24 05	00 05
N 58	06 16	07 02	07 44	21 10	22 32	23 57	25 28
56	06 14	06 58	07 37	21 10	22 29	23 51	25 17
54	06 12	06 53	07 31	21 10	22 26	23 45	25 08
52	06 10	06 50	07 25	21 10	22 24	23 40	25 00
50	06 08	06 46	07 20	21 10	22 21	23 35	24 52
45	06 04	06 38	07 09	21 10	22 16	23 25	24 37
N 40	05 59	06 31	06 59	21 10	22 12	23 16	24 24
35	05 55	06 25	06 51	21 09	22 08	23 09	24 13
30	05 51	06 20	06 44	21 09	22 05	23 03	24 04
20	05 43	06 09	06 32	21 09	22 00	22 52	23 48
N 10	05 34	05 59	06 21	21 09	21 55	22 43	23 34
0	05 25	05 49	06 11	21 09	21 50	22 34	23 21
S 10	05 13	05 38	06 00	21 09	21 46	22 25	23 08
20	04 59	05 26	05 49	21 09	21 41	22 16	22 54
30	04 41	05 11	05 36	21 09	21 36	22 06	22 39
35	04 29	05 01	05 28	21 09	21 33	22 00	22 30
40	04 15	04 50	05 20	21 09	21 30	21 53	22 19
45	03 58	04 37	05 09	21 08	21 26	21 45	22 08
S 50	03 35	04 21	04 57	21 08	21 21	21 36	21 53
52	03 23	04 13	04 51	21 08	21 19	21 32	21 47
54	03 10	04 04	04 45	21 08	21 17	21 27	21 39
56	02 54	03 54	04 38	21 08	21 15	21 22	21 31
58	02 35	03 42	04 30	21 08	21 12	21 16	21 22
S 60	02 09	03 28	04 20	21 08	21 09	21 09	21 12

Sunset / Twilight / Moonset

Lat.	Sunset	Twilight Civil	Twilight Naut.	Moonset 9	10	11	12
°	h m	h m	h m	h m	h m	h m	h m
N 72	15 05	16 31	17 54	09 20	08 50	08 17	07 31
N 70	15 30	16 44	17 58	09 17	08 54	08 29	07 57
68	15 49	16 54	18 01	09 14	08 58	08 39	08 17
66	16 05	17 03	18 04	09 12	09 00	08 48	08 34
64	16 17	17 10	18 07	09 10	09 03	08 55	08 47
62	16 28	17 17	18 09	09 08	09 05	09 02	08 58
60	16 37	17 22	18 12	09 07	09 07	09 07	09 08
N 58	16 45	17 27	18 14	09 05	09 08	09 12	09 17
56	16 52	17 32	18 16	09 04	09 10	09 16	09 24
54	16 58	17 36	18 18	09 03	09 11	09 20	09 31
52	17 04	17 40	18 19	09 02	09 12	09 24	09 37
50	17 09	17 43	18 21	09 01	09 13	09 27	09 42
45	17 20	17 51	18 25	08 59	09 16	09 34	09 54
N 40	17 29	17 58	18 29	08 57	09 18	09 40	10 04
35	17 37	18 04	18 33	08 56	09 20	09 45	10 13
30	17 44	18 09	18 37	08 54	09 21	09 50	10 20
20	17 57	18 19	18 45	08 52	09 24	09 57	10 33
N 10	18 07	18 29	18 54	08 50	09 26	10 04	10 45
0	18 18	18 39	19 04	08 48	09 29	10 11	10 56
S 10	18 28	18 50	19 15	08 46	09 31	10 17	11 07
20	18 39	19 02	19 29	08 43	09 33	10 25	11 18
30	18 52	19 17	19 47	08 41	09 36	10 33	11 32
35	18 59	19 26	19 58	08 40	09 38	10 37	11 39
40	19 08	19 37	20 12	08 38	09 39	10 43	11 48
45	19 18	19 50	20 30	08 36	09 41	10 49	11 59
S 50	19 30	20 06	20 52	08 34	09 44	10 56	12 11
52	19 36	20 14	21 03	08 32	09 45	11 00	12 17
54	19 42	20 23	21 16	08 31	09 46	11 03	12 24
56	19 49	20 33	21 32	08 30	09 48	11 08	12 31
58	19 57	20 44	21 51	08 29	09 49	11 12	12 40
S 60	20 06	20 58	22 15	08 27	09 51	11 18	12 49

SUN / MOON

Day	Eqn. of Time 00h	Eqn. of Time 12h	Mer. Pass.	Mer. Pass. Upper	Mer. Pass. Lower	Age	Phase
d	m s	m s	h m	h m	h m	d	%
9	14 08	14 08	12 14	02 38	14 58	19	88
10	14 09	14 10	12 14	03 19	15 39	20	80
11	14 10	14 10	12 14	04 01	16 22	21	72

© British Crown Copyright 2022. All rights reserved.

UT (d h)	ARIES GHA	VENUS −3.9 GHA	Dec	MARS +0.1 GHA	Dec	JUPITER −2.1 GHA	Dec	SATURN +0.7 GHA	Dec
12 00	141 47.2	150 43.5	S 5 15.0	70 26.8	N24 57.0	133 47.2	N 2 12.3	171 58.1	S13 37.9
01	156 49.6	165 43.1	13.7	85 28.4	57.1	148 49.2	12.5	187 00.3	37.8
02	171 52.1	180 42.8	12.4	100 30.1	57.2	163 51.2	12.7	202 02.4	37.7
03	186 54.6	195 42.4 ..	11.1	115 31.7 ..	57.2	178 53.2 ..	12.9	217 04.6 ..	37.6
04	201 57.0	210 42.0	09.9	130 33.3	57.3	193 55.2	13.1	232 06.8	37.5
05	216 59.5	225 41.7	08.6	145 35.0	57.4	208 57.2	13.3	247 09.0	37.4
S 06	232 02.0	240 41.3	S 5 07.3	160 36.6	N24 57.4	223 59.2	N 2 13.5	262 11.1	S13 37.3
U 07	247 04.4	255 41.0	06.0	175 38.2	57.5	239 01.2	13.7	277 13.3	37.2
N 08	262 06.9	270 40.6	04.8	190 39.9	57.6	254 03.2	13.9	292 15.5	37.1
D 09	277 09.3	285 40.2 ..	03.5	205 41.5 ..	57.6	269 05.2 ..	14.1	307 17.6 ..	37.0
A 10	292 11.8	300 39.9	02.2	220 43.1	57.7	284 07.2	14.3	322 19.8	36.9
Y 11	307 14.3	315 39.5	5 00.9	235 44.8	57.8	299 09.2	14.6	337 22.0	36.8
12	322 16.7	330 39.2	S 4 59.6	250 46.4	N24 57.9	314 11.2	N 2 14.8	352 24.2	S13 36.7
13	337 19.2	345 38.8	58.4	265 48.0	57.9	329 13.2	15.0	7 26.3	36.6
14	352 21.7	0 38.4	57.1	280 49.7	58.0	344 15.2	15.2	22 28.5	36.5
15	7 24.1	15 38.1 ..	55.8	295 51.3 ..	58.1	359 17.1 ..	15.4	37 30.7 ..	36.4
16	22 26.6	30 37.7	54.5	310 52.9	58.1	14 19.1	15.6	52 32.8	36.3
17	37 29.1	45 37.4	53.2	325 54.6	58.2	29 21.1	15.8	67 35.0	36.2
18	52 31.5	60 37.0	S 4 52.0	340 56.2	N24 58.3	44 23.1	N 2 16.0	82 37.2	S13 36.1
19	67 34.0	75 36.7	50.7	355 57.8	58.3	59 25.1	16.2	97 39.4	36.0
20	82 36.5	90 36.3	49.4	10 59.4	58.4	74 27.1	16.4	112 41.5	35.9
21	97 38.9	105 35.9 ..	48.1	26 01.1 ..	58.5	89 29.1 ..	16.6	127 43.7 ..	35.8
22	112 41.4	120 35.6	46.8	41 02.7	58.5	104 31.1	16.8	142 45.9	35.7
23	127 43.8	135 35.2	45.6	56 04.3	58.6	119 33.1	17.0	157 48.0	35.6
13 00	142 46.3	150 34.9	S 4 44.3	71 05.9	N24 58.7	134 35.1	N 2 17.3	172 50.2	S13 35.5
01	157 48.8	165 34.5	43.0	86 07.5	58.7	149 37.1	17.5	187 52.4	35.4
02	172 51.2	180 34.2	41.7	101 09.2	58.8	164 39.1	17.7	202 54.6	35.3
03	187 53.7	195 33.8 ..	40.4	116 10.8 ..	58.9	179 41.1 ..	17.9	217 56.7 ..	35.2
04	202 56.2	210 33.4	39.1	131 12.4	59.0	194 43.1	18.1	232 58.9	35.1
05	217 58.6	225 33.1	37.9	146 14.0	59.0	209 45.1	18.3	248 01.1	35.0
M 06	233 01.1	240 32.7	S 4 36.6	161 15.6	N24 59.1	224 47.0	N 2 18.5	263 03.2	S13 34.9
O 07	248 03.6	255 32.4	35.3	176 17.3	59.2	239 49.0	18.7	278 05.4	34.8
N 08	263 06.0	270 32.0	34.0	191 18.9	59.2	254 51.0	18.9	293 07.6	34.7
D 09	278 08.5	285 31.7 ..	32.7	206 20.5 ..	59.3	269 53.0 ..	19.1	308 09.8 ..	34.6
A 10	293 10.9	300 31.3	31.4	221 22.1	59.4	284 55.0	19.3	323 11.9	34.5
Y 11	308 13.4	315 31.0	30.2	236 23.7	59.4	299 57.0	19.6	338 14.1	34.4
12	323 15.9	330 30.6	S 4 28.9	251 25.3	N24 59.5	314 59.0	N 2 19.8	353 16.3	S13 34.3
13	338 18.3	345 30.3	27.6	266 26.9	59.6	330 01.0	20.0	8 18.4	34.2
14	353 20.8	0 29.9	26.3	281 28.5	59.6	345 03.0	20.2	23 20.6	34.1
15	8 23.3	15 29.6 ..	25.0	296 30.2 ..	59.7	0 05.0 ..	20.4	38 22.8 ..	34.0
16	23 25.7	30 29.2	23.7	311 31.8	59.8	15 07.0	20.6	53 25.0	33.9
17	38 28.2	45 28.8	22.5	326 33.4	59.8	30 09.0	20.8	68 27.1	33.8
18	53 30.7	60 28.5	S 4 21.2	341 35.0	N24 59.9	45 10.9	N 2 21.0	83 29.3	S13 33.7
19	68 33.1	75 28.1	19.9	356 36.6	25 00.0	60 12.9	21.2	98 31.5	33.6
20	83 35.6	90 27.8	18.6	11 38.2	00.1	75 14.9	21.4	113 33.6	33.5
21	98 38.1	105 27.4 ..	17.3	26 39.8 ..	00.1	90 16.9 ..	21.6	128 35.8 ..	33.4
22	113 40.5	120 27.1	16.0	41 41.4	00.2	105 18.9	21.9	143 38.0	33.3
23	128 43.0	135 26.7	14.7	56 43.0	00.3	120 20.9	22.1	158 40.2	33.2
14 00	143 45.4	150 26.4	S 4 13.5	71 44.6	N25 00.3	135 22.9	N 2 22.3	173 42.3	S13 33.1
01	158 47.9	165 26.0	12.2	86 46.2	00.4	150 24.9	22.5	188 44.5	33.0
02	173 50.4	180 25.7	10.9	101 47.8	00.5	165 26.9	22.7	203 46.7	32.9
03	188 52.8	195 25.3 ..	09.6	116 49.4 ..	00.5	180 28.9 ..	22.9	218 48.8 ..	32.8
04	203 55.3	210 25.0	08.3	131 51.0	00.6	195 30.8	23.1	233 51.0	32.6
05	218 57.8	225 24.6	07.0	146 52.6	00.7	210 32.8	23.3	248 53.2	32.5
T 06	234 00.2	240 24.3	S 4 05.7	161 54.2	N25 00.7	225 34.8	N 2 23.5	263 55.4	S13 32.4
U 07	249 02.7	255 23.9	04.4	176 55.8	00.8	240 36.8	23.7	278 57.5	32.3
E 08	264 05.2	270 23.6	03.1	191 57.4	00.9	255 38.8	23.9	293 59.7	32.2
S 09	279 07.6	285 23.2 ..	01.9	206 59.0 ..	01.0	270 40.8 ..	24.2	309 01.9 ..	32.1
D 10	294 10.1	300 22.9	4 00.6	222 00.6	01.0	285 42.8	24.4	324 04.0	32.0
A 11	309 12.6	315 22.6	3 59.3	237 02.2	01.1	300 44.8	24.6	339 06.2	31.9
Y 12	324 15.0	330 22.2	S 3 58.0	252 03.8	N25 01.2	315 46.8	N 2 24.8	354 08.4	S13 31.8
13	339 17.5	345 21.9	56.7	267 05.4	01.2	330 48.7	25.0	9 10.6	31.7
14	354 19.9	0 21.5	55.4	282 07.0	01.3	345 50.7	25.2	24 12.7	31.6
15	9 22.4	15 21.2 ..	54.1	297 08.6 ..	01.4	0 52.7 ..	25.4	39 14.9 ..	31.5
16	24 24.9	30 20.8	52.8	312 10.2	01.4	15 54.7	25.6	54 17.1	31.4
17	39 27.3	45 20.5	51.5	327 11.7	01.5	30 56.7	25.8	69 19.2	31.3
18	54 29.8	60 20.1	S 3 50.3	342 13.3	N25 01.6	45 58.7	N 2 26.1	84 21.4	S13 31.2
19	69 32.3	75 19.8	49.0	357 14.9	01.6	61 00.7	26.3	99 23.6	31.1
20	84 34.7	90 19.4	47.7	12 16.5	01.7	76 02.7	26.5	114 25.8	31.0
21	99 37.2	105 19.1 ..	46.4	27 18.1 ..	01.8	91 04.6 ..	26.7	129 27.9 ..	30.9
22	114 39.7	120 18.7	45.1	42 19.7	01.8	106 06.6	26.9	144 30.1	30.8
23	129 42.1	135 18.4	43.8	57 21.3	01.9	121 08.6	27.1	159 32.3	30.7
Mer. Pass. 14 26.5		v −0.4 d 1.3		v 1.6 d 0.1		v 2.0 d 0.2		v 2.2 d 0.1	

STARS

Name	SHA	Dec
Acamar	315 13.0	S40 13.0
Achernar	335 21.6	S57 07.5
Acrux	173 01.3	S63 13.4
Adhara	255 06.8	S29 00.3
Aldebaran	290 41.3	N16 33.3
Alioth	166 14.0	N55 49.8
Alkaid	152 53.0	N49 11.6
Alnair	27 35.3	S46 51.1
Alnilam	275 39.1	S 1 11.3
Alphard	217 49.0	S 8 45.6
Alphecca	126 05.1	N26 38.0
Alpheratz	357 36.7	N29 13.0
Altair	62 01.8	N 8 55.6
Ankaa	353 09.0	S42 11.1
Antares	112 17.9	S26 28.9
Arcturus	145 49.2	N19 03.6
Atria	107 13.7	S69 03.9
Avior	234 14.8	S59 35.1
Bellatrix	278 24.4	N 6 22.2
Betelgeuse	270 53.6	N 7 24.6
Canopus	263 52.7	S52 42.7
Capella	280 24.0	N46 01.4
Deneb	49 27.3	N45 21.6
Denebola	182 26.3	N14 26.5
Diphda	348 49.1	S17 51.8
Dubhe	193 42.3	N61 37.5
Elnath	278 03.7	N28 37.6
Eltanin	90 43.2	N51 28.8
Enif	33 40.7	N 9 58.7
Fomalhaut	15 16.6	S29 30.2
Gacrux	171 53.0	S57 14.4
Gienah	175 45.0	S17 40.2
Hadar	148 38.0	S60 28.8
Hamal	327 53.1	N23 34.3
Kaus Aust.	83 34.9	S34 22.4
Kochab	137 19.6	N74 03.3
Markab	13 31.8	N15 19.6
Menkar	314 07.8	N 4 10.7
Menkent	147 59.3	S36 28.9
Miaplacidus	221 37.7	S69 48.7
Mirfak	308 30.5	N49 56.7
Nunki	75 50.0	S26 16.1
Peacock	53 08.8	S56 39.7
Pollux	243 18.9	N27 58.2
Procyon	244 52.2	N 5 09.9
Rasalhague	96 00.2	N12 32.4
Regulus	207 35.8	N11 51.2
Rigel	281 05.2	S 8 10.6
Rigil Kent.	139 42.3	S60 55.5
Sabik	102 04.7	S15 45.2
Schedar	349 33.2	N56 39.9
Shaula	96 12.7	S37 07.1
Sirius	258 27.4	S16 45.0
Spica	158 23.8	S11 16.9
Suhail	222 47.0	S43 31.6
Vega	80 34.6	N38 48.0
Zuben'ubi	136 57.7	S16 08.2

	SHA	Mer. Pass.
Venus	7 48.6	13 58
Mars	288 19.6	19 14
Jupiter	351 48.8	15 00
Saturn	30 03.9	12 27

© British Crown Copyright 2022. All rights reserved.

SUN and MOON

UT (d h)	SUN GHA	SUN Dec	MOON GHA	v	MOON Dec	d	HP
12 00	176 27.5	S13 51.2	290 59.1	13.6	S12 08.3	13.5	56.5
01	191 27.5	50.4	305 31.7	13.6	12 21.8	13.5	56.5
02	206 27.5	49.6	320 04.3	13.5	12 35.3	13.5	56.5
03	221 27.5	.. 48.8	334 36.8	13.4	12 48.8	13.5	56.6
04	236 27.5	47.9	349 09.2	13.3	13 02.3	13.6	56.6
05	251 27.5	47.1	3 41.5	13.3	13 15.6	13.4	56.6
06 (SUNDAY)	266 27.5	S13 46.3	18 13.8	13.1	S13 29.0	13.3	56.6
07	281 27.5	45.4	32 45.9	13.1	13 42.3	13.2	56.7
08	296 27.5	44.6	47 18.0	13.0	13 55.5	13.2	56.7
09	311 27.5	.. 43.8	61 50.0	12.9	14 08.7	13.2	56.7
10	326 27.5	43.0	76 21.9	12.8	14 21.9	13.1	56.8
11	341 27.5	42.1	90 53.7	12.7	14 35.0	13.0	56.8
12	356 27.5	S13 41.3	105 25.4	12.6	S14 48.0	13.0	56.8
13	11 27.5	40.5	119 57.0	12.5	15 01.0	12.9	56.9
14	26 27.5	39.6	134 28.5	12.4	15 13.9	12.9	56.9
15	41 27.5	.. 38.8	148 59.9	12.4	15 26.8	12.8	56.9
16	56 27.6	38.0	163 31.3	12.2	15 39.6	12.8	56.9
17	71 27.6	37.1	178 02.5	12.1	15 52.4	12.7	57.0
18	86 27.6	S13 36.3	192 33.6	12.0	S16 05.1	12.6	57.0
19	101 27.6	35.5	207 04.6	12.0	16 17.7	12.6	57.0
20	116 27.6	34.6	221 35.6	11.8	16 30.3	12.5	57.1
21	131 27.6	.. 33.8	236 06.4	11.7	16 42.8	12.4	57.1
22	146 27.6	33.0	250 37.1	11.6	16 55.2	12.4	57.1
23	161 27.6	32.1	265 07.7	11.5	17 07.6	12.3	57.2
13 00	176 27.6	S13 31.3	279 38.2	11.5	S17 19.9	12.2	57.2
01	191 27.6	30.4	294 08.7	11.2	17 32.1	12.2	57.2
02	206 27.7	29.6	308 38.9	11.2	17 44.3	12.0	57.3
03	221 27.7	.. 28.8	323 09.1	11.1	17 56.3	12.0	57.3
04	236 27.7	27.9	337 39.2	11.0	18 08.3	12.0	57.3
05	251 27.7	27.1	352 09.2	10.8	18 20.3	11.8	57.4
06 (MONDAY)	266 27.7	S13 26.3	6 39.0	10.8	S18 32.1	11.8	57.4
07	281 27.7	25.4	21 08.8	10.7	18 43.9	11.7	57.4
08	296 27.7	24.6	35 38.4	10.5	18 55.6	11.6	57.5
09	311 27.7	.. 23.7	50 07.9	10.5	19 07.2	11.5	57.5
10	326 27.8	22.9	64 37.4	10.2	19 18.7	11.4	57.5
11	341 27.8	22.1	79 06.6	10.2	19 30.1	11.4	57.6
12	356 27.8	S13 21.2	93 35.8	10.1	S19 41.5	11.2	57.6
13	11 27.8	20.4	108 04.9	9.9	19 52.7	11.2	57.6
14	26 27.8	19.5	122 33.8	9.8	20 03.9	11.1	57.7
15	41 27.8	.. 18.7	137 02.6	9.7	20 15.0	10.9	57.7
16	56 27.8	17.8	151 31.3	9.6	20 25.9	10.9	57.7
17	71 27.9	17.0	165 59.9	9.5	20 36.8	10.8	57.8
18	86 27.9	S13 16.2	180 28.4	9.3	S20 47.6	10.7	57.8
19	101 27.9	15.3	194 56.7	9.2	20 58.3	10.6	57.8
20	116 27.9	14.5	209 24.9	9.1	21 08.9	10.5	57.9
21	131 27.9	.. 13.6	223 53.0	9.0	21 19.4	10.3	57.9
22	146 27.9	12.8	238 21.0	8.8	21 29.7	10.3	57.9
23	161 28.0	11.9	252 48.8	8.8	21 40.0	10.2	58.0
14 00	176 28.0	S13 11.1	267 16.6	8.6	S21 50.2	10.0	58.0
01	191 28.0	10.2	281 44.2	8.4	22 00.2	10.0	58.0
02	206 28.0	09.4	296 11.6	8.4	22 10.2	9.8	58.1
03	221 28.0	.. 08.6	310 39.0	8.2	22 20.0	9.7	58.1
04	236 28.1	07.7	325 06.2	8.1	22 29.7	9.6	58.1
05	251 28.1	06.9	339 33.3	8.0	22 39.3	9.5	58.2
06 (TUESDAY)	266 28.1	S13 06.0	354 00.3	7.8	S22 48.8	9.3	58.2
07	281 28.1	05.2	8 27.1	7.8	22 58.1	9.3	58.2
08	296 28.1	04.3	22 53.9	7.6	23 07.4	9.1	58.3
09	311 28.2	.. 03.5	37 20.5	7.4	23 16.5	9.0	58.3
10	326 28.2	02.6	51 46.9	7.4	23 25.5	8.8	58.4
11	341 28.2	01.8	66 13.3	7.2	23 34.3	8.8	58.4
12	356 28.2	S13 00.9	80 39.5	7.1	S23 43.1	8.6	58.4
13	11 28.2	13 00.1	95 05.6	7.0	23 51.7	8.4	58.5
14	26 28.3	12 59.2	109 31.6	6.8	24 00.1	8.4	58.5
15	41 28.3	.. 58.4	123 57.4	6.8	24 08.5	8.2	58.5
16	56 28.3	57.5	138 23.2	6.6	24 16.7	8.0	58.6
17	71 28.3	56.7	152 48.8	6.4	24 24.7	8.0	58.6
18	86 28.4	S12 55.8	167 14.2	6.4	S24 32.7	7.7	58.6
19	101 28.4	55.0	181 39.6	6.2	24 40.4	7.7	58.7
20	116 28.4	54.1	196 04.8	6.1	24 48.1	7.5	58.7
21	131 28.4	.. 53.3	210 29.9	6.0	24 55.6	7.3	58.7
22	146 28.5	52.4	224 54.9	5.9	25 02.9	7.2	58.8
23	161 28.5	51.5	239 19.8	5.8	S25 10.1	7.1	58.8
	SD 16.2	d 0.8	SD 15.5		15.7		15.9

Twilight / Sunrise / Moonrise

Lat.	Naut.	Civil	Sunrise	Moonrise 12	13	14	15
N 72	06 24	07 45	09 07	01 33	■	■	■
N 70	06 21	07 34	08 45	01 09	03 48	■	■
68	06 19	07 25	08 28	00 50	03 03	■	■
66	06 17	07 17	08 14	00 35	02 34	05 05	■
64	06 15	07 11	08 02	00 24	02 12	04 16	■
62	06 13	07 05	07 53	00 13	01 54	03 45	05 47
60	06 11	07 00	07 44	00 05	01 40	03 22	05 08
N 58	06 09	06 55	07 37	25 28	01 28	03 04	04 41
56	06 08	06 51	07 30	25 17	01 17	02 48	04 20
54	06 06	06 48	07 25	25 08	01 08	02 35	04 02
52	06 05	06 44	07 19	25 00	00 59	02 23	03 48
50	06 03	06 41	07 15	24 52	00 52	02 13	03 35
45	06 00	06 34	07 04	24 37	00 37	01 52	03 08
N 40	05 56	06 28	06 56	24 24	00 24	01 35	02 47
35	05 53	06 22	06 48	24 13	00 13	01 20	02 30
30	05 49	06 17	06 42	24 04	00 04	01 08	02 15
20	05 42	06 08	06 30	23 48	24 47	00 47	01 50
N 10	05 34	05 59	06 20	23 34	24 29	00 29	01 28
0	05 25	05 49	06 11	23 21	24 12	00 12	01 08
S 10	05 14	05 39	06 01	23 08	23 55	24 48	00 48
20	05 01	05 28	05 51	22 54	23 37	24 27	00 27
30	04 44	05 13	05 38	22 39	23 17	24 03	00 03
35	04 33	05 05	05 31	22 30	23 05	23 48	24 41
40	04 19	04 54	05 23	22 19	22 51	23 32	24 23
45	04 03	04 42	05 14	22 08	22 35	23 12	24 01
S 50	03 41	04 27	05 02	21 53	22 16	22 47	23 32
52	03 31	04 19	04 57	21 47	22 07	22 36	23 18
54	03 19	04 11	04 51	21 39	21 56	22 22	23 02
56	03 04	04 01	04 44	21 31	21 45	22 07	22 44
58	02 46	03 51	04 37	21 22	21 32	21 48	22 20
S 60	02 24	03 38	04 29	21 12	21 16	21 26	21 50

Sunset / Twilight / Moonset

Lat.	Sunset	Civil	Naut.	Moonset 12	13	14	15
N 72	15 23	16 45	18 06	07 31	■	■	■
N 70	15 45	16 56	18 09	07 57	06 56	■	■
68	16 02	17 05	18 11	08 17	07 43	■	■
66	16 16	17 12	18 13	08 34	08 14	07 31	■
64	16 27	17 19	18 15	08 47	08 37	08 21	■
62	16 37	17 24	18 17	08 58	08 55	08 52	08 51
60	16 45	17 29	18 18	09 08	09 10	09 16	09 30
N 58	16 52	17 34	18 20	09 17	09 24	09 35	09 57
56	16 59	17 38	18 22	09 24	09 35	09 51	10 19
54	17 04	17 41	18 23	09 31	09 45	10 05	10 37
52	17 10	17 45	18 25	09 37	09 54	10 17	10 52
50	17 14	17 48	18 26	09 42	10 02	10 28	11 05
45	17 25	17 55	18 29	09 54	10 19	10 50	11 32
N 40	17 33	18 01	18 33	10 04	10 33	11 09	11 54
35	17 40	18 06	18 36	10 13	10 45	11 24	12 12
30	17 47	18 11	18 40	10 20	10 56	11 37	12 27
20	17 58	18 21	18 47	10 33	11 14	12 00	12 53
N 10	18 08	18 30	18 55	10 45	11 30	12 20	13 16
0	18 18	18 39	19 03	10 56	11 45	12 38	13 37
S 10	18 27	18 49	19 14	11 07	11 59	12 57	13 58
20	18 37	19 00	19 27	11 18	12 16	13 17	14 21
30	18 49	19 14	19 44	11 32	12 34	13 40	14 47
35	18 56	19 23	19 55	11 39	12 45	13 53	15 03
40	19 04	19 33	20 08	11 48	12 57	14 09	15 21
45	19 14	19 45	20 24	11 59	13 12	14 28	15 43
S 50	19 25	20 00	20 45	12 11	13 30	14 52	16 11
52	19 30	20 08	20 56	12 17	13 39	15 03	16 25
54	19 36	20 16	21 08	12 24	13 49	15 16	16 40
56	19 42	20 25	21 22	12 31	14 00	15 31	16 59
58	19 50	20 36	21 39	12 40	14 12	15 49	17 22
S 60	19 58	20 48	22 00	12 49	14 27	16 11	17 52

SUN and MOON

Day	Eqn. of Time 00h	Eqn. of Time 12h	Mer. Pass.	Mer. Pass. Upper	Mer. Pass. Lower	Age	Phase
	m s	m s	h m	h m	h m	d	%
12	14 10	14 10	12 14	04 45	17 08	22	62
13	14 09	14 09	12 14	05 32	17 58	23	52
14	14 08	14 07	12 14	06 25	18 53	24	41

© British Crown Copyright 2022. All rights reserved.

UT	ARIES GHA	VENUS −3.9 GHA	VENUS Dec	MARS +0.1 GHA	MARS Dec	JUPITER −2.1 GHA	JUPITER Dec	SATURN +0.7 GHA	SATURN Dec	STARS Name	SHA	Dec
15 00	144 44.6	150 18.0	S 3 42.5	72 22.9	N25 02.0	136 10.6	N 2 27.3	174 34.4	S13 30.6	Acamar	315 13.0	S40 13.0
01	159 47.1	165 17.7	41.2	87 24.4	02.1	151 12.6	27.5	189 36.6	30.5	Achernar	335 21.6	S57 07.5
02	174 49.5	180 17.4	39.9	102 26.0	02.1	166 14.6	27.7	204 38.8	30.4	Acrux	173 01.3	S63 13.4
03	189 52.0	195 17.0	.. 38.6	117 27.6	.. 02.2	181 16.6	.. 27.9	219 41.0	.. 30.3	Adhara	255 06.8	S29 00.4
04	204 54.4	210 16.7	37.3	132 29.2	02.3	196 18.6	28.2	234 43.1	30.2	Aldebaran	290 41.3	N16 33.3
05	219 56.9	225 16.3	36.1	147 30.8	02.3	211 20.5	28.4	249 45.3	30.1			
W 06	234 59.4	240 16.0	S 3 34.8	162 32.3	N25 02.4	226 22.5	N 2 28.6	264 47.5	S13 30.0	Alioth	166 14.0	N55 49.8
E 07	250 01.8	255 15.6	33.5	177 33.9	02.5	241 24.5	28.8	279 49.6	29.9	Alkaid	152 53.0	N49 11.6
D 08	265 04.3	270 15.3	32.2	192 35.5	02.5	256 26.5	29.0	294 51.8	29.8	Alnair	27 35.3	S46 51.1
N 09	280 06.8	285 15.0	.. 30.9	207 37.1	.. 02.6	271 28.5	.. 29.2	309 54.0	.. 29.7	Alnilam	275 39.2	S 1 11.3
E 10	295 09.2	300 14.6	29.6	222 38.7	02.7	286 30.5	29.4	324 56.2	29.6	Alphard	217 49.0	S 8 45.6
S 11	310 11.7	315 14.3	28.3	237 40.2	02.7	301 32.5	29.6	339 58.3	29.5			
D 12	325 14.2	330 13.9	S 3 27.0	252 41.8	N25 02.8	316 34.4	N 2 29.8	355 00.5	S13 29.4	Alphecca	126 05.1	N26 38.0
A 13	340 16.6	345 13.6	25.7	267 43.4	02.9	331 36.4	30.1	10 02.7	29.3	Alpheratz	357 36.7	N29 13.0
Y 14	355 19.1	0 13.2	24.4	282 45.0	03.0	346 38.4	30.3	25 04.8	29.2	Altair	62 01.8	N 8 55.6
15	10 21.5	15 12.9	.. 23.1	297 46.5	.. 03.0	1 40.4	.. 30.5	40 07.0	.. 29.1	Ankaa	353 09.0	S42 11.1
16	25 24.0	30 12.6	21.8	312 48.1	03.1	16 42.4	30.7	55 09.2	29.0	Antares	112 17.8	S26 28.9
17	40 26.5	45 12.2	20.5	327 49.7	03.2	31 44.4	30.9	70 11.4	28.9			
18	55 28.9	60 11.9	S 3 19.2	342 51.2	N25 03.2	46 46.3	N 2 31.1	85 13.5	S13 28.8	Arcturus	145 49.2	N19 03.5
19	70 31.4	75 11.5	17.9	357 52.8	03.3	61 48.3	31.3	100 15.7	28.7	Atria	107 13.7	S69 03.9
20	85 33.9	90 11.2	16.6	12 54.4	03.4	76 50.3	31.5	115 17.9	28.6	Avior	234 14.8	S59 35.1
21	100 36.3	105 10.9	.. 15.4	27 56.0	.. 03.4	91 52.3	.. 31.7	130 20.0	.. 28.5	Bellatrix	278 24.4	N 6 22.2
22	115 38.8	120 10.5	14.1	42 57.5	03.5	106 54.3	32.0	145 22.2	28.4	Betelgeuse	270 53.6	N 7 24.6
23	130 41.3	135 10.2	12.8	57 59.1	03.6	121 56.3	32.2	160 24.4	28.3			
16 00	145 43.7	150 09.8	S 3 11.5	73 00.7	N25 03.6	136 58.3	N 2 32.4	175 26.6	S13 28.2	Canopus	263 52.7	S52 42.7
01	160 46.2	165 09.5	10.2	88 02.2	03.7	152 00.2	32.6	190 28.7	28.1	Capella	280 24.0	N46 01.4
02	175 48.7	180 09.2	08.9	103 03.8	03.8	167 02.2	32.8	205 30.9	28.0	Deneb	49 27.3	N45 21.6
03	190 51.1	195 08.8	.. 07.6	118 05.4	.. 03.9	182 04.2	.. 33.0	220 33.1	.. 27.9	Denebola	182 26.3	N14 26.5
04	205 53.6	210 08.5	06.3	133 06.9	03.9	197 06.2	33.2	235 35.2	27.7	Diphda	348 49.1	S17 51.8
05	220 56.0	225 08.1	05.0	148 08.5	04.0	212 08.2	33.4	250 37.4	27.6			
T 06	235 58.5	240 07.8	S 3 03.7	163 10.0	N25 04.1	227 10.2	N 2 33.7	265 39.6	S13 27.5	Dubhe	193 42.3	N61 37.5
H 07	251 01.0	255 07.5	02.4	178 11.6	04.1	242 12.1	33.9	280 41.8	27.4	Elnath	278 03.7	N28 37.6
U 08	266 03.4	270 07.1	3 01.1	193 13.2	04.2	257 14.1	34.1	295 43.9	27.3	Eltanin	90 43.2	N51 28.8
R 09	281 05.9	285 06.8	2 59.8	208 14.7	.. 04.3	272 16.1	.. 34.3	310 46.1	.. 27.2	Enif	33 40.7	N 9 58.7
S 10	296 08.4	300 06.4	58.5	223 16.3	04.3	287 18.1	34.5	325 48.3	27.1	Fomalhaut	15 16.6	S29 30.2
D 11	311 10.8	315 06.1	57.2	238 17.8	04.4	302 20.1	34.7	340 50.4	27.0			
A 12	326 13.3	330 05.8	S 2 55.9	253 19.4	N25 04.5	317 22.0	N 2 34.9	355 52.6	S13 26.9	Gacrux	171 53.0	S57 14.4
Y 13	341 15.8	345 05.5	54.6	268 21.0	04.5	332 24.0	35.1	10 54.8	26.8	Gienah	175 44.9	S17 40.2
14	356 18.2	0 05.1	53.3	283 22.5	04.6	347 26.0	35.3	25 57.0	26.7	Hadar	148 38.0	S60 28.8
15	11 20.7	15 04.8	.. 52.0	298 24.1	.. 04.7	2 28.0	.. 35.6	40 59.1	.. 26.6	Hamal	327 53.1	N23 34.3
16	26 23.2	30 04.4	50.7	313 25.6	04.7	17 30.0	35.8	56 01.3	26.5	Kaus Aust.	83 34.8	S34 22.4
17	41 25.6	45 04.1	49.4	328 27.2	04.8	32 32.0	36.0	71 03.5	26.4			
18	56 28.1	60 03.7	S 2 48.1	343 28.7	N25 04.9	47 33.9	N 2 36.2	86 05.6	S13 26.3	Kochab	137 19.5	N74 03.3
19	71 30.5	75 03.4	46.8	358 30.3	05.0	62 35.9	36.4	101 07.8	26.2	Markab	13 31.8	N15 19.6
20	86 33.0	90 03.1	45.5	13 31.8	05.0	77 37.9	36.6	116 10.0	26.1	Menkar	314 07.8	N 4 10.7
21	101 35.5	105 02.7	.. 44.2	28 33.4	.. 05.1	92 39.9	.. 36.8	131 12.2	.. 26.0	Menkent	147 59.3	S36 28.9
22	116 37.9	120 02.4	42.9	43 34.9	05.2	107 41.9	37.0	146 14.3	25.9	Miaplacidus	221 37.7	S69 48.7
23	131 40.4	135 02.1	41.6	58 36.5	05.2	122 43.8	37.3	161 16.5	25.8			
17 00	146 42.9	150 01.7	S 2 40.3	73 38.0	N25 05.3	137 45.8	N 2 37.5	176 18.7	S13 25.7	Mirfak	308 30.5	N49 56.7
01	161 45.3	165 01.4	39.0	88 39.6	05.4	152 47.8	37.7	191 20.8	25.6	Nunki	75 50.0	S26 16.1
02	176 47.8	180 01.1	37.7	103 41.1	05.4	167 49.8	37.9	206 23.0	25.5	Peacock	53 08.7	S56 39.6
03	191 50.3	195 00.7	.. 36.4	118 42.7	.. 05.5	182 51.8	.. 38.1	221 25.2	.. 25.4	Pollux	243 18.9	N27 58.2
04	206 52.7	210 00.4	35.1	133 44.2	05.6	197 53.7	38.3	236 27.4	25.3	Procyon	244 52.2	N 5 09.9
05	221 55.2	225 00.1	33.8	148 45.8	05.6	212 55.7	38.5	251 29.5	25.2			
F 06	236 57.7	239 59.7	S 2 32.5	163 47.3	N25 05.7	227 57.7	N 2 38.7	266 31.7	S13 25.1	Rasalhague	96 00.2	N12 32.4
R 07	252 00.1	254 59.4	31.2	178 48.9	05.8	242 59.7	39.0	281 33.9	25.0	Regulus	207 35.8	N11 51.2
I 08	267 02.6	269 59.1	29.9	193 50.4	05.8	258 01.7	39.2	296 36.0	24.9	Rigel	281 05.2	S 8 10.6
D 09	282 05.0	284 58.7	.. 28.6	208 51.9	.. 05.9	273 03.6	.. 39.4	311 38.2	.. 24.8	Rigil Kent.	139 42.3	S60 55.6
A 10	297 07.5	299 58.4	27.3	223 53.5	06.0	288 05.6	39.6	326 40.4	24.7	Sabik	102 04.7	S15 45.2
Y 11	312 10.0	314 58.1	26.0	238 55.0	06.1	303 07.6	39.8	341 42.6	24.6			
12	327 12.4	329 57.7	S 2 24.7	253 56.6	N25 06.1	318 09.6	N 2 40.0	356 44.7	S13 24.5	Schedar	349 33.2	N56 39.9
13	342 14.9	344 57.4	23.4	268 58.1	06.2	333 11.6	40.2	11 46.9	24.4	Shaula	96 12.7	S37 07.1
14	357 17.4	359 57.1	22.1	283 59.6	06.3	348 13.5	40.5	26 49.1	24.3	Sirius	258 27.4	S16 45.0
15	12 19.8	14 56.7	.. 20.8	299 01.2	.. 06.3	3 15.5	.. 40.7	41 51.3	.. 24.2	Spica	158 23.8	S11 16.9
16	27 22.3	29 56.4	19.5	314 02.7	06.4	18 17.5	40.9	56 53.4	24.1	Suhail	222 47.0	S43 31.6
17	42 24.8	44 56.1	18.2	329 04.2	06.5	33 19.5	41.1	71 55.6	24.0			
18	57 27.2	59 55.7	S 2 16.9	344 05.8	N25 06.5	48 21.5	N 2 41.3	86 57.8	S13 23.9	Vega	80 34.6	N38 48.0
19	72 29.7	74 55.4	15.6	359 07.3	06.6	63 23.4	41.5	101 59.9	23.8	Zuben'ubi	136 57.7	S16 08.3
20	87 32.2	89 55.1	14.3	14 08.9	06.7	78 25.4	41.7	117 02.1	23.7		SHA	Mer.Pass.
21	102 34.6	104 54.7	.. 13.0	29 10.4	.. 06.7	93 27.4	.. 41.9	132 04.3	.. 23.6	Venus	4 26.1	14 00
22	117 37.1	119 54.4	11.7	44 11.9	06.8	108 29.4	42.2	147 06.5	23.5	Mars	287 16.9	19 06
23	132 39.5	134 54.1	10.4	59 13.5	06.9	123 31.4	42.4	162 08.6	23.4	Jupiter	351 14.5	14 50
Mer.Pass. 14 14.7		v −0.3	d 1.3	v 1.6	d 0.1	v 2.0	d 0.2	v 2.2	d 0.1	Saturn	29 42.8	12 16

© British Crown Copyright 2022. All rights reserved.

UT	SUN GHA	SUN Dec	MOON GHA	v	MOON Dec	d	HP
d h	° ′	° ′	° ′	′	° ′	′	′
15 00	176 28.5	S12 50.7	253 44.6	5.6	S25 17.2	6.9	58.8
01	191 28.5	49.8	268 09.2	5.5	25 24.1	6.7	58.9
02	206 28.6	49.0	282 33.7	5.4	25 30.8	6.6	58.9
03	221 28.6	.. 48.1	296 58.1	5.3	25 37.4	6.4	58.9
04	236 28.6	47.3	311 22.4	5.1	25 43.8	6.3	59.0
05	251 28.6	46.4	325 46.5	5.1	25 50.1	6.1	59.0
06	266 28.7	S12 45.6	340 10.6	4.9	S25 56.2	6.0	59.1
W 07	281 28.7	44.7	354 34.5	4.9	26 02.2	5.7	59.1
E 08	296 28.7	43.8	8 58.4	4.7	26 07.9	5.7	59.1
D 09	311 28.8	.. 43.0	23 22.1	4.6	26 13.6	5.4	59.2
N 10	326 28.8	42.1	37 45.7	4.5	26 19.0	5.3	59.2
E 11	341 28.8	41.3	52 09.2	4.4	26 24.3	5.1	59.2
S 12	356 28.8	S12 40.4	66 32.6	4.3	S26 29.4	5.0	59.3
D 13	11 28.9	39.5	80 55.9	4.1	26 34.4	4.7	59.3
A 14	26 28.9	38.7	95 19.0	4.1	26 39.1	4.6	59.3
Y 15	41 28.9	.. 37.8	109 42.1	4.0	26 43.7	4.4	59.4
16	56 29.0	37.0	124 05.1	3.9	26 48.1	4.3	59.4
17	71 29.0	36.1	138 28.0	3.8	26 52.4	4.0	59.4
18	86 29.0	S12 35.2	152 50.8	3.7	S26 56.4	3.9	59.5
19	101 29.1	34.4	167 13.5	3.6	27 00.3	3.7	59.5
20	116 29.1	33.5	181 36.1	3.5	27 04.0	3.5	59.5
21	131 29.1	.. 32.7	195 58.6	3.5	27 07.5	3.4	59.6
22	146 29.2	31.8	210 21.1	3.3	27 10.9	3.1	59.6
23	161 29.2	30.9	224 43.4	3.3	27 14.0	3.0	59.6
16 00	176 29.2	S12 30.1	239 05.7	3.1	S27 17.0	2.7	59.7
01	191 29.2	29.2	253 27.8	3.1	27 19.7	2.6	59.7
02	206 29.3	28.3	267 49.9	3.1	27 22.3	2.4	59.7
03	221 29.3	.. 27.5	282 12.0	2.9	27 24.7	2.2	59.8
04	236 29.4	26.6	296 33.9	2.9	27 26.9	2.0	59.8
05	251 29.4	25.8	310 55.8	2.8	27 28.9	1.8	59.8
06	266 29.4	S12 24.9	325 17.6	2.8	S27 30.7	1.6	59.9
T 07	281 29.5	24.0	339 39.4	2.6	27 32.3	1.4	59.9
H 08	296 29.5	23.2	354 01.0	2.7	27 33.7	1.2	59.9
U 09	311 29.5	.. 22.3	8 22.7	2.5	27 34.9	1.0	59.9
R 10	326 29.6	21.4	22 44.2	2.5	27 35.9	0.9	60.0
S 11	341 29.6	20.6	37 05.7	2.5	27 36.8	0.6	60.0
D 12	356 29.6	S12 19.7	51 27.2	2.4	S27 37.4	0.4	60.0
A 13	11 29.7	18.8	65 48.6	2.3	27 37.8	0.2	60.1
Y 14	26 29.7	18.0	80 09.9	2.3	27 38.0	0.0	60.1
15	41 29.7	.. 17.1	94 31.2	2.3	27 38.0	0.2	60.1
16	56 29.8	16.2	108 52.5	2.2	27 37.8	0.4	60.2
17	71 29.8	15.3	123 13.7	2.2	27 37.4	0.6	60.2
18	86 29.9	S12 14.5	137 34.9	2.2	S27 36.8	0.8	60.2
19	101 29.9	13.6	151 56.1	2.1	27 36.0	1.0	60.2
20	116 29.9	12.7	166 17.2	2.1	27 35.0	1.2	60.3
21	131 30.0	.. 11.9	180 38.3	2.1	27 33.8	1.4	60.3
22	146 30.0	11.0	194 59.4	2.0	27 32.4	1.7	60.3
23	161 30.1	10.1	209 20.4	2.1	27 30.7	1.8	60.4
17 00	176 30.1	S12 09.3	223 41.5	2.0	S27 28.9	2.0	60.4
01	191 30.1	08.4	238 02.5	2.0	27 26.9	2.3	60.4
02	206 30.2	07.5	252 23.5	2.0	27 24.6	2.4	60.4
03	221 30.2	.. 06.6	266 44.5	2.0	27 22.2	2.7	60.5
04	236 30.3	05.8	281 05.5	2.0	27 19.5	2.9	60.5
05	251 30.3	04.9	295 26.5	2.0	27 16.6	3.0	60.5
06	266 30.3	S12 04.0	309 47.5	2.0	S27 13.6	3.3	60.5
07	281 30.4	03.1	324 08.5	2.0	27 10.3	3.5	60.6
08	296 30.4	02.3	338 29.5	2.0	27 06.8	3.7	60.6
F 09	311 30.5	.. 01.4	352 50.5	2.0	27 03.1	3.9	60.6
R 10	326 30.5	12 00.5	7 11.5	2.0	26 59.2	4.1	60.6
I 11	341 30.6	11 59.6	21 32.5	2.1	26 55.1	4.3	60.6
D 12	356 30.6	S11 58.8	35 53.6	2.1	S26 50.8	4.5	60.7
A 13	11 30.6	57.9	50 14.7	2.0	26 46.3	4.7	60.7
Y 14	26 30.7	57.0	64 35.7	2.2	26 41.6	5.0	60.7
15	41 30.7	.. 56.1	78 56.9	2.1	26 36.6	5.1	60.7
16	56 30.8	55.3	93 18.0	2.2	26 31.5	5.3	60.8
17	71 30.8	54.4	107 39.2	2.2	26 26.2	5.6	60.8
18	86 30.9	S11 53.5	122 00.4	2.3	S26 20.6	5.7	60.8
19	101 30.9	52.6	136 21.7	2.3	26 14.9	5.9	60.8
20	116 31.0	51.8	150 43.0	2.3	26 09.0	6.2	60.8
21	131 31.0	.. 50.9	165 04.3	2.4	26 02.8	6.3	60.9
22	146 31.1	50.0	179 25.7	2.4	25 56.5	6.5	60.9
23	161 31.1	49.1	193 47.1	2.5	S25 50.0	6.7	60.9
	SD 16.2	d 0.9	SD 16.1		16.4		16.5

Lat.	Twilight Naut.	Twilight Civil	Sunrise	Moonrise 15	Moonrise 16	Moonrise 17	Moonrise 18
°	h m	h m	h m	h m	h m	h m	h m
N 72	06 11	07 31	08 49	■■■■	■■■■	■■■■	■■■■
N 70	06 10	07 22	08 30	■■■■	■■■■	■■■■	■■■■
68	06 09	07 14	08 15	■■■■	■■■■	■■■■	■■■■
66	06 07	07 07	08 03	■■■■	■■■■	■■■■	■■■■
64	06 06	07 02	07 52	■■■■	■■■■	■■■■	09 13
62	06 05	06 57	07 44	05 47	07 48	08 30	08 31
60	06 04	06 52	07 36	05 08	06 42	07 39	08 02
N 58	06 03	06 49	07 30	04 41	06 08	07 07	07 39
56	06 02	06 45	07 24	04 20	05 42	06 43	07 21
54	06 00	06 42	07 18	04 02	05 22	06 24	07 05
52	05 59	06 39	07 14	03 48	05 05	06 07	06 52
50	05 58	06 36	07 09	03 35	04 51	05 53	06 40
45	05 55	06 30	07 00	03 08	04 21	05 25	06 16
N 40	05 53	06 24	06 52	02 47	03 58	05 02	05 56
35	05 50	06 19	06 45	02 30	03 39	04 43	05 39
30	05 47	06 15	06 39	02 15	03 23	04 27	05 25
20	05 40	06 06	06 29	01 50	02 55	04 00	05 00
N 10	05 33	05 58	06 19	01 28	02 32	03 36	04 39
0	05 25	05 49	06 11	01 08	02 10	03 14	04 19
S 10	05 15	05 40	06 02	00 48	01 48	02 53	03 59
20	05 03	05 29	05 52	00 27	01 25	02 29	03 38
30	04 46	05 16	05 41	00 03	00 57	02 02	03 13
35	04 36	05 08	05 34	24 41	00 41	01 46	02 58
40	04 24	04 58	05 27	24 23	00 23	01 27	02 41
45	04 08	04 47	05 18	24 01	00 01	01 04	02 21
S 50	03 48	04 32	05 08	23 32	24 35	00 35	01 55
52	03 38	04 25	05 03	23 18	24 21	00 21	01 43
54	03 27	04 18	04 57	23 02	24 04	00 04	01 28
56	03 14	04 09	04 51	22 44	23 45	25 12	01 12
58	02 58	03 59	04 44	22 20	23 20	24 51	00 51
S 60	02 38	03 48	04 37	21 50	22 48	24 26	00 26

Lat.	Sunset	Twilight Civil	Twilight Naut.	Moonset 15	Moonset 16	Moonset 17	Moonset 18
°	h m	h m	h m	h m	h m	h m	h m
N 72	15 40	16 59	18 19	■■■■	■■■■	■■■■	■■■■
N 70	15 59	17 08	18 20	■■■■	■■■■	■■■■	■■■■
68	16 14	17 16	18 21	■■■■	■■■■	■■■■	■■■■
66	16 27	17 22	18 22	■■■■	■■■■	■■■■	■■■■
64	16 37	17 28	18 23	■■■■	■■■■	■■■■	12 08
62	16 45	17 32	18 24	08 51	09 00	10 35	12 50
60	16 53	17 37	18 25	09 30	10 06	11 26	13 18
N 58	16 59	17 41	18 26	09 57	10 41	11 57	13 40
56	17 05	17 44	18 28	10 19	11 06	12 21	13 57
54	17 10	17 47	18 29	10 37	11 27	12 40	14 12
52	17 15	17 50	18 30	10 52	11 44	12 56	14 25
50	17 19	17 53	18 31	11 05	11 58	13 10	14 37
45	17 29	17 59	18 35	11 32	12 28	13 39	15 00
N 40	17 37	18 04	18 36	11 54	12 51	14 01	15 19
35	17 43	18 09	18 39	12 12	13 10	14 19	15 35
30	17 49	18 14	18 42	12 27	13 27	14 35	15 48
20	18 00	18 22	18 48	12 53	13 54	15 01	16 11
N 10	18 09	18 30	18 55	13 16	14 18	15 24	16 31
0	18 17	18 39	19 03	13 37	14 40	15 45	16 49
S 10	18 26	18 48	19 13	13 58	15 02	16 06	17 07
20	18 36	18 58	19 25	14 21	15 26	16 29	17 27
30	18 47	19 12	19 41	14 47	15 54	16 55	17 49
35	18 53	19 20	19 51	15 03	16 10	17 10	18 02
40	19 00	19 29	20 03	15 21	16 29	17 28	18 17
45	19 09	19 40	20 19	15 43	16 52	17 49	18 34
S 50	19 19	19 54	20 38	16 11	17 21	18 16	18 55
52	19 24	20 01	20 48	16 25	17 35	18 29	19 06
54	19 29	20 09	20 59	16 40	17 52	18 43	19 17
56	19 35	20 17	21 12	16 59	18 11	19 00	19 30
58	19 42	20 27	21 27	17 22	18 36	19 21	19 45
S 60	19 49	20 38	21 46	17 52	19 09	19 47	20 03

	SUN Eqn. of Time 00h	SUN Eqn. of Time 12h	SUN Mer. Pass.	MOON Mer. Pass. Upper	MOON Mer. Pass. Lower	Age	Phase
Day							
d	m s	m s	h m	h m	h m	d	%
15	14 06	14 05	12 14	07 23	19 53	25	30
16	14 03	14 02	12 14	08 25	20 57	26	20
17	14 00	13 58	12 14	09 30	22 02	27	12

© British Crown Copyright 2022. All rights reserved.

UT	ARIES GHA	VENUS −3.9 GHA	Dec	MARS +0.2 GHA	Dec	JUPITER −2.1 GHA	Dec	SATURN +0.7 GHA	Dec	STARS Name	SHA	Dec
18 00	147 42.0	149 53.7	S 2 09.1	74 15.0	N25 06.9	138 33.3	N 2 42.6	177 10.8	S13 23.2	Acamar	315 13.0	S40 13.0
01	162 44.5	164 53.4	07.8	89 16.5	07.0	153 35.3	42.8	192 13.0	23.1	Achernar	335 21.7	S57 07.5
02	177 46.9	179 53.1	06.5	104 18.0	07.1	168 37.3	43.0	207 15.1	23.0	Acrux	173 01.2	S63 13.5
03	192 49.4	194 52.7 ..	05.2	119 19.6 ..	07.1	183 39.3 ..	43.2	222 17.3 ..	22.9	Adhara	255 06.8	S29 00.4
04	207 51.9	209 52.4	03.9	134 21.1	07.2	198 41.2	43.4	237 19.5	22.8	Aldebaran	290 41.3	N16 33.3
05	222 54.3	224 52.1	02.6	149 22.6	07.3	213 43.2	43.7	252 21.7	22.7			
06	237 56.8	239 51.8	S 2 01.3	164 24.2	N25 07.4	228 45.2	N 2 43.9	267 23.8	S13 22.6	Alioth	166 13.9	N55 49.8
S 07	252 59.3	254 51.4	2 00.0	179 25.7	07.4	243 47.2	44.1	282 26.0	22.5	Alkaid	152 53.0	N49 11.6
A 08	268 01.7	269 51.1	1 58.7	194 27.2	07.5	258 49.1	44.3	297 28.2	22.4	Alnair	27 35.3	S46 51.1
T 09	283 04.2	284 50.8 ..	57.4	209 28.7 ..	07.6	273 51.1 ..	44.5	312 30.3 ..	22.3	Alnilam	275 39.2	S 1 11.3
U 10	298 06.7	299 50.5	56.1	224 30.3	07.6	288 53.1	44.7	327 32.5	22.2	Alphard	217 49.0	S 8 45.6
R 11	313 09.1	314 50.1	54.8	239 31.8	07.7	303 55.1	44.9	342 34.7	22.1			
D 12	328 11.6	329 49.8	S 1 53.5	254 33.3	N25 07.8	318 57.1	N 2 45.2	357 36.9	S13 22.0	Alphecca	126 05.0	N26 38.0
A 13	343 14.0	344 49.4	52.2	269 34.8	07.8	333 59.0	45.4	12 39.0	21.9	Alpheratz	357 36.7	N29 13.0
Y 14	358 16.5	359 49.1	50.9	284 36.3	07.9	349 01.0	45.6	27 41.2	21.8	Altair	62 01.7	N 8 55.6
15	13 19.0	14 48.8 ..	49.6	299 37.9 ..	08.0	4 03.0 ..	45.8	42 43.4 ..	21.7	Ankaa	353 09.0	S42 11.1
16	28 21.4	29 48.5	48.3	314 39.4	08.0	19 05.0	46.0	57 45.5	21.6	Antares	112 17.8	S26 28.9
17	43 23.9	44 48.1	47.0	329 40.9	08.1	34 06.9	46.2	72 47.7	21.5			
18	58 26.4	59 47.8	S 1 45.7	344 42.4	N25 08.2	49 08.9	N 2 46.4	87 49.9	S13 21.4	Arcturus	145 49.2	N19 03.5
19	73 28.8	74 47.5	44.4	359 43.9	08.2	64 10.9	46.7	102 52.1	21.3	Atria	107 13.6	S69 03.9
20	88 31.3	89 47.1	43.1	14 45.5	08.3	79 12.9	46.9	117 54.2	21.2	Avior	234 14.8	S59 35.1
21	103 33.8	104 46.8 ..	41.8	29 47.0 ..	08.4	94 14.8 ..	47.1	132 56.4 ..	21.1	Bellatrix	278 24.4	N 6 22.2
22	118 36.2	119 46.5	40.5	44 48.5	08.4	109 16.8	47.3	147 58.6	21.0	Betelgeuse	270 53.6	N 7 24.6
23	133 38.7	134 46.2	39.2	59 50.0	08.5	124 18.8	47.5	163 00.7	20.9			
19 00	148 41.1	149 45.8	S 1 37.9	74 51.5	N25 08.6	139 20.8	N 2 47.7	178 02.9	S13 20.8	Canopus	263 52.8	S52 42.7
01	163 43.6	164 45.5	36.6	89 53.0	08.6	154 22.7	47.9	193 05.1	20.7	Capella	280 24.0	N46 01.4
02	178 46.1	179 45.2	35.3	104 54.5	08.7	169 24.7	48.2	208 07.3	20.6	Deneb	49 27.3	N45 21.5
03	193 48.5	194 44.9 ..	34.0	119 56.1 ..	08.8	184 26.7 ..	48.4	223 09.4 ..	20.5	Denebola	182 26.2	N14 26.5
04	208 51.0	209 44.5	32.7	134 57.6	08.9	199 28.7	48.6	238 11.6	20.4	Diphda	348 49.1	S17 51.8
05	223 53.5	224 44.2	31.3	149 59.1	08.9	214 30.6	48.8	253 13.8	20.3			
06	238 55.9	239 43.9	S 1 30.0	165 00.6	N25 09.0	229 32.6	N 2 49.0	268 15.9	S13 20.2	Dubhe	193 42.2	N61 37.5
07	253 58.4	254 43.6	28.7	180 02.1	09.1	244 34.6	49.2	283 18.1	20.1	Elnath	278 03.7	N28 37.6
08	269 00.9	269 43.2	27.4	195 03.6	09.1	259 36.6	49.4	298 20.3	20.0	Eltanin	90 43.2	N51 28.8
S 09	284 03.3	284 42.9 ..	26.1	210 05.1 ..	09.2	274 38.5 ..	49.7	313 22.5 ..	19.9	Enif	33 40.6	N 9 58.7
U 10	299 05.8	299 42.6	24.8	225 06.6	09.3	289 40.5	49.9	328 24.6	19.8	Fomalhaut	15 16.6	S29 30.2
N 11	314 08.3	314 42.2	23.5	240 08.1	09.3	304 42.5	50.1	343 26.8	19.7			
D 12	329 10.7	329 41.9	S 1 22.2	255 09.6	N25 09.4	319 44.5	N 2 50.3	358 29.0	S13 19.6	Gacrux	171 52.9	S57 14.4
A 13	344 13.2	344 41.6	20.9	270 11.1	09.5	334 46.4	50.5	13 31.1	19.5	Gienah	175 44.9	S17 40.2
Y 14	359 15.6	359 41.3	19.6	285 12.7	09.5	349 48.4	50.7	28 33.3	19.4	Hadar	148 37.9	S60 28.8
15	14 18.1	14 40.9 ..	18.3	300 14.2 ..	09.6	4 50.4 ..	51.0	43 35.5 ..	19.3	Hamal	327 53.1	N23 34.3
16	29 20.6	29 40.6	17.0	315 15.7	09.7	19 52.3	51.2	58 37.7	19.2	Kaus Aust.	83 34.8	S34 22.4
17	44 23.0	44 40.3	15.7	330 17.2	09.7	34 54.3	51.4	73 39.8	19.1			
18	59 25.5	59 40.0	S 1 14.4	345 18.7	N25 09.8	49 56.3	N 2 51.6	88 42.0	S13 18.9	Kochab	137 19.4	N74 03.3
19	74 28.0	74 39.6	13.1	0 20.2	09.9	64 58.3	51.8	103 44.2	18.8	Markab	13 31.8	N15 19.6
20	89 30.4	89 39.3	11.8	15 21.7	09.9	80 00.2	52.0	118 46.3	18.7	Menkar	314 07.8	N 4 10.7
21	104 32.9	104 39.0 ..	10.5	30 23.2 ..	10.0	95 02.2 ..	52.2	133 48.5 ..	18.6	Menkent	147 59.3	S36 28.9
22	119 35.4	119 38.7	09.2	45 24.7	10.1	110 04.2	52.5	148 50.7	18.5	Miaplacidus	221 37.7	S69 48.7
23	134 37.8	134 38.4	07.9	60 26.2	10.1	125 06.2	52.7	163 52.9	18.4			
20 00	149 40.3	149 38.0	S 1 06.6	75 27.7	N25 10.2	140 08.1	N 2 52.9	178 55.0	S13 18.3	Mirfak	308 30.5	N49 56.7
01	164 42.8	164 37.7	05.2	90 29.2	10.3	155 10.1	53.1	193 57.2	18.2	Nunki	75 49.9	S26 16.1
02	179 45.2	179 37.4	03.9	105 30.7	10.3	170 12.1	53.3	208 59.4	18.1	Peacock	53 08.7	S56 39.6
03	194 47.7	194 37.1 ..	02.6	120 32.1 ..	10.4	185 14.0 ..	53.5	224 01.5 ..	18.0	Pollux	243 18.9	N27 58.2
04	209 50.1	209 36.7	01.3	135 33.6	10.5	200 16.0	53.8	239 03.7	17.9	Procyon	244 52.2	N 5 09.9
05	224 52.6	224 36.4	1 00.0	150 35.1	10.5	215 18.0	54.0	254 05.9	17.8			
06	239 55.1	239 36.1	S 0 58.7	165 36.6	N25 10.6	230 20.0	N 2 54.2	269 08.1	S13 17.7	Rasalhague	96 00.1	N12 32.4
07	254 57.5	254 35.8	57.4	180 38.1	10.7	245 21.9	54.4	284 10.2	17.6	Regulus	207 35.8	N11 51.2
08	270 00.0	269 35.4	56.1	195 39.6	10.7	260 23.9	54.6	299 12.4	17.5	Rigel	281 05.2	S 8 10.6
M 09	285 02.5	284 35.1 ..	54.8	210 41.1 ..	10.8	275 25.9 ..	54.8	314 14.6 ..	17.4	Rigil Kent.	139 42.2	S60 55.6
O 10	300 04.9	299 34.8	53.5	225 42.6	10.9	290 27.8	55.1	329 16.8	17.3	Sabik	102 04.7	S15 45.2
N 11	315 07.4	314 34.5	52.2	240 44.1	10.9	305 29.8	55.3	344 18.9	17.2			
D 12	330 09.9	329 34.1	S 0 50.9	255 45.6	N25 11.0	320 31.8	N 2 55.5	359 21.1	S13 17.1	Schedar	349 33.2	N56 39.9
A 13	345 12.3	344 33.8	49.6	270 47.1	11.1	335 33.8	55.7	14 23.3	17.0	Shaula	96 12.6	S37 07.1
Y 14	0 14.8	359 33.5	48.3	285 48.6	11.1	350 35.7	55.9	29 25.4	16.9	Sirius	258 27.4	S16 45.0
15	15 17.2	14 33.2 ..	47.0	300 50.0 ..	11.2	5 37.7 ..	56.1	44 27.6 ..	16.8	Spica	158 23.7	S11 16.9
16	30 19.7	29 32.9	45.7	315 51.5	11.3	20 39.7	56.3	59 29.8	16.7	Suhail	222 47.0	S43 31.6
17	45 22.2	44 32.5	44.3	330 53.0	11.3	35 41.6	56.6	74 32.0	16.6			
18	60 24.6	59 32.2	S 0 43.0	345 54.5	N25 11.4	50 43.6	N 2 56.8	89 34.1	S13 16.5	Vega	80 34.5	N38 48.0
19	75 27.1	74 31.9	41.7	0 56.0	11.5	65 45.6	57.0	104 36.3	16.4	Zuben'ubi	136 57.6	S16 08.3
20	90 29.6	89 31.6	40.4	15 57.5	11.5	80 47.5	57.2	119 38.5	16.3			
21	105 32.0	104 31.3 ..	39.1	30 59.0 ..	11.6	95 49.5 ..	57.4	134 40.6 ..	16.2		SHA	Mer. Pass.
22	120 34.5	119 30.9	37.8	46 00.4	11.7	110 51.5	57.6	149 42.8	16.1	Venus	1 04.7	14 01
23	135 37.0	134 30.6	36.5	61 01.9	11.7	125 53.5	57.9	164 45.0	16.0	Mars	286 10.4	18 59
Mer. Pass. 14 02.9		v −0.3	d 1.3	v 1.5	d 0.1	v 2.0	d 0.2	v 2.2	d 0.1	Jupiter	350 39.6	14 41
										Saturn	29 21.8	12 06

© British Crown Copyright 2022. All rights reserved.

UT	SUN GHA	SUN Dec	MOON GHA	v	MOON Dec	d	HP
d h	° ′	° ′	° ′	′	° ′	′	′
18 00	176 31.1	S11 48.2	208 08.6	2.5	S25 43.3	7.0	60.9
01	191 31.2	47.4	222 30.1	2.6	25 36.3	7.1	60.9
02	206 31.2	46.5	236 51.7	2.6	25 29.2	7.3	60.9
03	221 31.3	.. 45.6	251 13.3	2.7	25 21.9	7.5	61.0
04	236 31.3	44.7	265 35.0	2.8	25 14.4	7.7	61.0
05	251 31.4	43.8	279 56.8	2.8	25 06.7	7.8	61.0
06	266 31.4	S11 43.0	294 18.6	2.9	S24 58.9	8.1	61.0
07	281 31.5	42.1	308 40.5	3.0	24 50.8	8.3	61.0
S 08	296 31.5	41.2	323 02.5	3.0	24 42.5	8.4	61.0
A 09	311 31.6	.. 40.3	337 24.5	3.1	24 34.1	8.6	61.0
T 10	326 31.6	39.4	351 46.6	3.2	24 25.5	8.8	61.1
U 11	341 31.7	38.5	6 08.8	3.3	24 16.7	9.0	61.1
R 12	356 31.7	S11 37.7	20 31.1	3.3	S24 07.7	9.2	61.1
D 13	11 31.8	36.8	34 53.4	3.4	23 58.5	9.3	61.1
A 14	26 31.8	35.9	49 15.8	3.5	23 49.2	9.6	61.1
Y 15	41 31.9	.. 35.0	63 38.3	3.6	23 39.6	9.7	61.1
16	56 31.9	34.1	78 00.9	3.6	23 29.9	9.8	61.1
17	71 32.0	33.2	92 23.5	3.8	23 20.1	10.1	61.1
18	86 32.1	S11 32.4	106 46.3	3.8	S23 10.0	10.2	61.1
19	101 32.1	31.5	121 09.1	4.0	22 59.8	10.3	61.1
20	116 32.2	30.6	135 32.1	4.0	22 49.5	10.6	61.2
21	131 32.2	.. 29.7	149 55.1	4.1	22 38.9	10.7	61.2
22	146 32.3	28.8	164 18.2	4.2	22 28.2	10.9	61.2
23	161 32.3	27.9	178 41.4	4.3	22 17.3	11.0	61.2
19 00	176 32.4	S11 27.0	193 04.7	4.3	S22 06.3	11.2	61.2
01	191 32.4	26.1	207 28.0	4.5	21 55.1	11.3	61.2
02	206 32.5	25.3	221 51.5	4.6	21 43.8	11.5	61.2
03	221 32.5	.. 24.4	236 15.1	4.7	21 32.3	11.7	61.2
04	236 32.6	23.5	250 38.8	4.8	21 20.6	11.8	61.2
05	251 32.6	22.6	265 02.6	4.8	21 08.8	11.9	61.2
06	266 32.7	S11 21.7	279 26.4	5.0	S20 56.9	12.1	61.2
07	281 32.8	20.8	293 50.4	5.1	20 44.8	12.2	61.2
S 08	296 32.8	19.9	308 14.5	5.1	20 32.6	12.4	61.2
U 09	311 32.9	.. 19.0	322 38.6	5.3	20 20.2	12.5	61.2
N 10	326 32.9	18.1	337 02.9	5.4	20 07.7	12.7	61.2
D 11	341 33.0	17.3	351 27.3	5.5	19 55.0	12.8	61.2
A 12	356 33.0	S11 16.4	5 51.8	5.6	S19 42.2	12.9	61.2
Y 13	11 33.1	15.5	20 16.4	5.6	19 29.3	13.0	61.2
14	26 33.2	14.6	34 41.0	5.8	19 16.3	13.2	61.2
15	41 33.2	.. 13.7	49 05.8	5.9	19 03.1	13.3	61.2
16	56 33.3	12.8	63 30.7	6.0	18 49.8	13.4	61.2
17	71 33.3	11.9	77 55.7	6.1	18 36.4	13.6	61.2
18	86 33.4	S11 11.0	92 20.8	6.2	S18 22.8	13.7	61.2
19	101 33.5	10.1	106 46.0	6.3	18 09.1	13.8	61.2
20	116 33.5	09.2	121 11.3	6.4	17 55.3	13.9	61.2
21	131 33.6	.. 08.3	135 36.7	6.6	17 41.4	14.0	61.2
22	146 33.6	07.4	150 02.3	6.6	17 27.4	14.1	61.2
23	161 33.7	06.5	164 27.9	6.7	17 13.3	14.2	61.2
20 00	176 33.8	S11 05.7	178 53.6	6.8	S16 59.1	14.4	61.1
01	191 33.8	04.8	193 19.4	6.9	16 44.7	14.4	61.1
02	206 33.9	03.9	207 45.3	7.1	16 30.3	14.4	61.1
03	221 33.9	.. 03.0	222 11.4	7.1	16 15.7	14.6	61.1
04	236 34.0	02.1	236 37.5	7.2	16 01.1	14.8	61.1
05	251 34.1	01.2	251 03.7	7.4	15 46.3	14.8	61.1
06	266 34.1	S11 00.3	265 30.1	7.4	S15 31.5	14.9	61.1
07	281 34.2	10 59.4	279 56.5	7.5	15 16.6	15.1	61.1
08	296 34.3	58.5	294 23.0	7.7	15 01.5	15.1	61.1
M 09	311 34.3	.. 57.6	308 49.7	7.7	14 46.4	15.2	61.0
O 10	326 34.4	56.7	323 16.4	7.8	14 31.2	15.2	61.0
N 11	341 34.5	55.8	337 43.2	8.0	14 16.0	15.4	61.0
D 12	356 34.5	S10 54.9	352 10.2	8.0	S14 00.6	15.4	61.0
A 13	11 34.6	54.0	6 37.2	8.1	13 45.2	15.6	61.0
Y 14	26 34.7	53.1	21 04.3	8.2	13 29.6	15.5	61.0
15	41 34.7	.. 52.2	35 31.5	8.4	13 14.1	15.7	61.0
16	56 34.8	51.3	49 58.9	8.4	12 58.4	15.7	60.9
17	71 34.8	50.4	64 26.3	8.5	12 42.7	15.8	60.9
18	86 34.9	S10 49.5	78 53.8	8.6	S12 26.9	15.9	60.9
19	101 35.0	48.6	93 21.4	8.6	12 11.0	15.9	60.9
20	116 35.0	47.7	107 49.0	8.8	11 55.1	16.0	60.9
21	131 35.1	.. 46.8	122 16.8	8.9	11 39.1	16.0	60.8
22	146 35.2	45.9	136 44.7	8.9	11 23.0	16.1	60.8
23	161 35.3	45.0	151 12.6	9.1	S11 06.9	16.1	60.8
	SD 16.2	d 0.9	SD 16.6		16.7		16.6

Twilight / Sunrise / Moonrise

Lat.	Naut.	Civil	Sunrise	Moonrise 18	19	20	21
°	h m	h m	h m	h m	h m	h m	h m
N 72	05 58	07 17	08 32	■■	■■	10 02	09 06
N 70	05 58	07 09	08 16	■■	11 28	09 32	08 54
68	05 58	07 03	08 02	■■	09 57	09 10	08 44
66	05 58	06 57	07 52	■■	09 18	08 52	08 36
64	05 57	06 53	07 42	09 13	08 50	08 38	08 28
62	05 57	06 48	07 35	08 31	08 28	08 25	08 22
60	05 56	06 45	07 28	08 02	08 11	08 15	08 17
N 58	05 56	06 41	07 22	07 39	07 56	08 06	08 12
56	05 55	06 38	07 17	07 21	07 43	07 58	08 08
54	05 55	06 36	07 12	07 05	07 32	07 50	08 04
52	05 54	06 33	07 08	06 52	07 22	07 44	08 00
50	05 53	06 31	07 04	06 40	07 14	07 38	07 57
45	05 51	06 25	06 55	06 16	06 55	07 25	07 50
N 40	05 49	06 21	06 48	05 56	06 39	07 14	07 44
35	05 47	06 16	06 42	05 39	06 26	07 05	07 39
30	05 44	06 12	06 36	05 25	06 15	06 57	07 34
20	05 39	06 05	06 27	05 00	05 55	06 43	07 27
N 10	05 32	05 57	06 18	04 39	05 38	06 31	07 20
0	05 25	05 49	06 09	04 19	05 21	06 19	07 13
S 10	05 16	05 41	06 02	03 59	05 05	06 08	07 07
20	05 04	05 31	05 53	03 38	04 48	05 55	07 00
30	04 49	05 18	05 43	03 13	04 28	05 41	06 52
35	04 40	05 11	05 37	02 58	04 16	05 33	06 47
40	04 28	05 02	05 30	02 41	04 02	05 23	06 42
45	04 13	04 51	05 22	02 21	03 46	05 12	06 36
S 50	03 55	04 38	05 13	01 55	03 26	04 58	06 28
52	03 46	04 32	05 08	01 43	03 16	04 52	06 25
54	03 35	04 25	05 03	01 28	03 05	04 45	06 21
56	03 23	04 17	04 58	01 12	02 53	04 37	06 17
58	03 09	04 08	04 52	00 51	02 39	04 28	06 12
S 60	02 51	03 57	04 45	00 26	02 22	04 17	06 07

Sunset / Twilight / Moonset

Lat.	Sunset	Civil	Naut.	Moonset 18	19	20	21
°	h m	h m	h m	h m	h m	h m	h m
N 72	15 57	17 12	18 32	■■	■■	15 33	18 20
N 70	16 13	17 20	18 31	■■	12 05	16 00	18 29
68	16 27	17 26	18 31	■■	13 34	16 21	18 37
66	16 37	17 32	18 32	■■	14 13	16 36	18 43
64	16 46	17 36	18 32	12 08	14 39	16 49	18 48
62	16 54	17 40	18 32	12 50	14 59	17 00	18 52
60	17 01	17 44	18 33	13 18	15 16	17 09	18 56
N 58	17 07	17 47	18 33	13 40	15 30	17 17	18 59
56	17 12	17 50	18 34	13 57	15 42	17 24	19 02
54	17 17	17 53	18 34	14 12	15 51	17 31	19 05
52	17 21	17 55	18 35	14 25	16 01	17 36	19 07
50	17 25	17 58	18 35	14 37	16 09	17 41	19 09
45	17 33	18 03	18 37	15 00	16 27	17 52	19 14
N 40	17 40	18 08	18 39	15 19	16 41	18 01	19 18
35	17 46	18 12	18 41	15 35	16 52	18 08	19 21
30	17 51	18 16	18 44	15 48	17 03	18 15	19 24
20	18 01	18 23	18 49	16 11	17 20	18 26	19 29
N 10	18 09	18 31	18 55	16 31	17 35	18 36	19 33
0	18 17	18 38	19 03	16 49	17 49	18 45	19 37
S 10	18 25	18 47	19 12	17 07	18 03	18 54	19 41
20	18 34	18 56	19 23	17 27	18 18	19 04	19 45
30	18 44	19 09	19 38	17 49	18 35	19 15	19 50
35	18 50	19 16	19 47	18 02	18 45	19 21	19 53
40	18 56	19 25	19 59	18 17	18 56	19 28	19 56
45	19 04	19 35	20 13	18 34	19 09	19 36	19 59
S 50	19 14	19 48	20 31	18 55	19 24	19 46	20 03
52	19 18	19 54	20 40	19 06	19 31	19 50	20 05
54	19 23	20 01	20 50	19 17	19 39	19 55	20 07
56	19 28	20 09	21 02	19 30	19 48	20 00	20 09
58	19 34	20 18	21 16	19 45	19 58	20 06	20 12
S 60	19 41	20 28	21 33	20 03	20 10	20 13	20 15

SUN / MOON

Day	SUN Eqn. of Time 00h	12h	Mer. Pass.	MOON Mer. Pass. Upper	Lower	Age	Phase
d	m s	m s	h m	h m	h m	d	%
18	13 55	13 53	12 14	10 34	23 05	28	5
19	13 51	13 48	12 14	11 36	24 05	29	1
20	13 45	13 42	12 14	12 33	00 05	00	0 ●

© British Crown Copyright 2022. All rights reserved.

UT	ARIES	VENUS −3.9		MARS +0.3		JUPITER −2.1		SATURN +0.8		STARS		
	GHA	GHA	Dec	GHA	Dec	GHA	Dec	GHA	Dec	Name	SHA	Dec
d h	° ′	° ′	° ′	° ′	° ′	° ′	° ′	° ′	° ′		° ′	° ′
21 00	150 39.4	149 30.3	S 0 35.2	76 03.4	N25 11.8	140 55.4	N 2 58.1	179 47.2	S13 15.9	Acamar	315 13.1	S40 13.0
01	165 41.9	164 30.0	33.9	91 04.9	11.9	155 57.4	58.3	194 49.3	15.8	Achernar	335 21.7	S57 07.5
02	180 44.4	179 29.6	32.6	106 06.4	11.9	170 59.4	58.5	209 51.5	15.7	Acrux	173 01.2	S63 13.5
03	195 46.8	194 29.3 . .	31.3	121 07.8 . .	12.0	186 01.3 . .	58.7	224 53.7 . .	15.6	Adhara	255 06.8	S29 00.4
04	210 49.3	209 29.0	30.0	136 09.3	12.1	201 03.3	58.9	239 55.8	15.5	Aldebaran	290 41.3	N16 33.3
05	225 51.7	224 28.7	28.7	151 10.8	12.1	216 05.3	59.2	254 58.0	15.4			
06	240 54.2	239 28.4	S 0 27.4	166 12.3	N25 12.2	231 07.2	N 2 59.4	270 00.2	S13 15.3	Alioth	166 13.9	N55 49.9
07	255 56.7	254 28.0	26.0	181 13.8	12.3	246 09.2	59.6	285 02.4	15.2	Alkaid	152 52.9	N49 11.6
08	270 59.1	269 27.7	24.7	196 15.2	12.3	261 11.2	2 59.8	300 04.5	15.1	Alnair	27 35.3	S46 51.1
T 09	286 01.6	284 27.4 . .	23.4	211 16.7 . .	12.4	276 13.1	3 00.0	315 06.7 . .	15.0	Alnilam	275 39.2	S 1 11.3
U 10	301 04.1	299 27.1	22.1	226 18.2	12.5	291 15.1	00.2	330 08.9	14.9	Alphard	217 49.0	S 8 45.6
E 11	316 06.5	314 26.8	20.8	241 19.7	12.5	306 17.1	00.5	345 11.1	14.8			
S 12	331 09.0	329 26.4	S 0 19.5	256 21.1	N25 12.6	321 19.1	N 3 00.7	0 13.2	S13 14.7	Alphecca	126 05.0	N26 38.0
D 13	346 11.5	344 26.1	18.2	271 22.6	12.7	336 21.0	00.9	15 15.4	14.5	Alpheratz	357 36.7	N29 13.0
A 14	1 13.9	359 25.8	16.9	286 24.1	12.7	351 23.0	01.1	30 17.6	14.4	Altair	62 01.7	N 8 55.6
Y 15	16 16.4	14 25.5 . .	15.6	301 25.5 . .	12.8	6 25.0 . .	01.3	45 19.7 . .	14.3	Ankaa	353 09.0	S42 11.1
16	31 18.9	29 25.2	14.3	316 27.0	12.9	21 26.9	01.5	60 21.9	14.2	Antares	112 17.8	S26 28.9
17	46 21.3	44 24.9	13.0	331 28.5	12.9	36 28.9	01.8	75 24.1	14.1			
18	61 23.8	59 24.5	S 0 11.7	346 29.9	N25 13.0	51 30.9	N 3 02.0	90 26.3	S13 14.0	Arcturus	145 49.2	N19 03.5
19	76 26.2	74 24.2	10.4	1 31.4	13.1	66 32.8	02.2	105 28.4	13.9	Atria	107 13.5	S69 03.9
20	91 28.7	89 23.9	09.0	16 32.9	13.1	81 34.8	02.4	120 30.6	13.8	Avior	234 14.8	S59 35.1
21	106 31.2	104 23.6 . .	07.7	31 34.4 . .	13.2	96 36.8 . .	02.6	135 32.8 . .	13.7	Bellatrix	278 24.4	N 6 22.2
22	121 33.6	119 23.3	06.4	46 35.8	13.3	111 38.7	02.8	150 34.9	13.6	Betelgeuse	270 53.6	N 7 24.6
23	136 36.1	134 22.9	05.1	61 37.3	13.3	126 40.7	03.1	165 37.1	13.5			
22 00	151 38.6	149 22.6	S 0 03.8	76 38.8	N25 13.4	141 42.7	N 3 03.3	180 39.3	S13 13.4	Canopus	263 52.8	S52 42.7
01	166 41.0	164 22.3	02.5	91 40.2	13.5	156 44.6	03.5	195 41.5	13.3	Capella	280 24.0	N46 01.4
02	181 43.5	179 22.0	S 01.2	106 41.7	13.5	171 46.6	03.7	210 43.6	13.2	Deneb	49 27.3	N45 21.5
03	196 46.0	194 21.7	N 00.1	121 43.1 . .	13.6	186 48.6 . .	03.9	225 45.8 . .	13.1	Denebola	182 26.2	N14 26.5
04	211 48.4	209 21.3	01.4	136 44.6	13.6	201 50.5	04.2	240 48.0	13.0	Diphda	348 49.1	S17 51.8
05	226 50.9	224 21.0	02.7	151 46.1	13.7	216 52.5	04.4	255 50.2	12.9			
06	241 53.3	239 20.7	N 0 04.0	166 47.5	N25 13.8	231 54.5	N 3 04.6	270 52.3	S13 12.8	Dubhe	193 42.2	N61 37.5
W 07	256 55.8	254 20.4	05.3	181 49.0	13.8	246 56.4	04.8	285 54.5	12.7	Elnath	278 03.7	N28 37.6
E 08	271 58.3	269 20.1	06.6	196 50.5	13.9	261 58.4	05.0	300 56.7	12.6	Eltanin	90 43.1	N51 28.8
D 09	287 00.7	284 19.8 . .	08.0	211 51.9 . .	14.0	277 00.4 . .	05.2	315 58.8 . .	12.5	Enif	33 40.6	N 9 58.7
N 10	302 03.2	299 19.4	09.3	226 53.4	14.0	292 02.3	05.5	331 01.0	12.4	Fomalhaut	15 16.6	S29 30.2
E 11	317 05.7	314 19.1	10.6	241 54.8	14.1	307 04.3	05.7	346 03.2	12.3			
S 12	332 08.1	329 18.8	N 0 11.9	256 56.3	N25 14.2	322 06.3	N 3 05.9	1 05.4	S13 12.2	Gacrux	171 52.9	S57 14.4
D 13	347 10.6	344 18.5	13.2	271 57.7	14.2	337 08.2	06.1	16 07.5	12.1	Gienah	175 44.9	S17 40.2
A 14	2 13.1	359 18.2	14.5	286 59.2	14.3	352 10.2	06.3	31 09.7	12.0	Hadar	148 37.9	S60 28.8
Y 15	17 15.5	14 17.9 . .	15.8	302 00.7 . .	14.4	7 12.1 . .	06.5	46 11.9 . .	11.9	Hamal	327 53.1	N23 34.3
16	32 18.0	29 17.5	17.1	317 02.1	14.4	22 14.1	06.8	61 14.1	11.8	Kaus Aust.	83 34.8	S34 22.4
17	47 20.5	44 17.2	18.4	332 03.6	14.5	37 16.1	07.0	76 16.2	11.7			
18	62 22.9	59 16.9	N 0 19.7	347 05.0	N25 14.6	52 18.0	N 3 07.2	91 18.4	S13 11.6	Kochab	137 19.4	N74 03.3
19	77 25.4	74 16.6	21.0	2 06.5	14.6	67 20.0	07.4	106 20.6	11.5	Markab	13 31.8	N15 19.6
20	92 27.8	89 16.3	22.3	17 07.9	14.7	82 22.0	07.6	121 22.7	11.4	Menkar	314 07.9	N 4 10.7
21	107 30.3	104 16.0 . .	23.7	32 09.4 . .	14.7	97 23.9 . .	07.9	136 24.9 . .	11.3	Menkent	147 59.3	S36 28.9
22	122 32.8	119 15.6	25.0	47 10.8	14.8	112 25.9	08.1	151 27.1	11.2	Miaplacidus	221 37.7	S69 48.7
23	137 35.2	134 15.3	26.3	62 12.3	14.9	127 27.9	08.3	166 29.3	11.1			
23 00	152 37.7	149 15.0	N 0 27.6	77 13.7	N25 14.9	142 29.8	N 3 08.5	181 31.4	S13 11.0	Mirfak	308 30.6	N49 56.7
01	167 40.2	164 14.7	28.9	92 15.2	15.0	157 31.8	08.7	196 33.6	10.9	Nunki	75 49.9	S26 16.1
02	182 42.6	179 14.4	30.2	107 16.6	15.1	172 33.8	08.9	211 35.8	10.8	Peacock	53 08.7	S56 39.6
03	197 45.1	194 14.1 . .	31.5	122 18.1 . .	15.1	187 35.7 . .	09.2	226 38.0 . .	10.7	Pollux	243 18.9	N27 58.2
04	212 47.6	209 13.7	32.8	137 19.5	15.2	202 37.7	09.4	241 40.1	10.6	Procyon	244 52.2	N 5 09.9
05	227 50.0	224 13.4	34.1	152 21.0	15.3	217 39.6	09.6	256 42.3	10.5			
06	242 52.5	239 13.1	N 0 35.4	167 22.4	N25 15.3	232 41.6	N 3 09.8	271 44.5	S13 10.4	Rasalhague	96 00.1	N12 32.4
07	257 54.9	254 12.8	36.7	182 23.9	15.4	247 43.6	10.0	286 46.6	10.3	Regulus	207 35.8	N11 51.2
T 08	272 57.4	269 12.5	38.0	197 25.3	15.5	262 45.5	10.2	301 48.8	10.2	Rigel	281 05.3	S 8 10.6
H 09	287 59.9	284 12.2 . .	39.4	212 26.7 . .	15.5	277 47.5 . .	10.5	316 51.0 . .	10.1	Rigil Kent.	139 42.2	S60 55.6
U 10	303 02.3	299 11.8	40.7	227 28.2	15.6	292 49.5	10.7	331 53.2	09.9	Sabik	102 04.7	S15 45.2
R 11	318 04.8	314 11.5	42.0	242 29.6	15.6	307 51.4	10.9	346 55.3	09.8			
S 12	333 07.3	329 11.2	N 0 43.3	257 31.1	N25 15.7	322 53.4	N 3 11.1	1 57.5	S13 09.7	Schedar	349 33.3	N56 39.9
D 13	348 09.7	344 10.9	44.6	272 32.5	15.8	337 55.4	11.3	16 59.7	09.6	Shaula	96 12.6	S37 07.1
A 14	3 12.2	359 10.6	45.9	287 34.0	15.8	352 57.3	11.6	32 01.9	09.5	Sirius	258 27.4	S16 45.0
Y 15	18 14.7	14 10.3 . .	47.2	302 35.4 . .	15.9	7 59.3 . .	11.8	47 04.0 . .	09.4	Spica	158 23.7	S11 16.9
16	33 17.1	29 10.0	48.5	317 36.8	16.0	23 01.2	12.0	62 06.2	09.3	Suhail	222 47.0	S43 31.6
17	48 19.6	44 09.6	49.8	332 38.3	16.0	38 03.2	12.2	77 08.4	09.2			
18	63 22.1	59 09.3	N 0 51.1	347 39.7	N25 16.1	53 05.2	N 3 12.4	92 10.5	S13 09.1	Vega	80 34.5	N38 48.0
19	78 24.5	74 09.0	52.4	2 41.2	16.2	68 07.1	12.7	107 12.7	09.0	Zuben'ubi	136 57.6	S16 08.3
20	93 27.0	89 08.7	53.7	17 42.6	16.2	83 09.1	12.9	122 14.9	08.9		SHA	Mer. Pass.
21	108 29.4	104 08.4 . .	55.0	32 44.0 . .	16.3	98 11.1 . .	13.1	137 17.1 . .	08.8		° ′	h m
22	123 31.9	119 08.1	56.4	47 45.5	16.3	113 13.0	13.3	152 19.2	08.7	Venus	357 44.1	14 03
23	138 34.4	134 07.8	57.7	62 46.9	16.4	128 15.0	13.5	167 21.4	08.6	Mars	285 00.2	18 52
	h m									Jupiter	350 04.1	14 31
Mer. Pass. 13 51.2		v −0.3	d 1.3	v 1.5	d 0.1	v 2.0	d 0.2	v 2.2	d 0.1	Saturn	29 00.7	11 56

© British Crown Copyright 2022. All rights reserved.

INDEX TO SELECTED STARS, 2023

Name	No	Mag	SHA	Dec		No	Name	Mag	SHA	Dec
Acamar	7	3·2	315	S 40		1	Alpheratz	2·1	358	N 29
Achernar	5	0·5	335	S 57		2	Ankaa	2·4	353	S 42
Acrux	30	1·3	173	S 63		3	Schedar	2·2	350	N 57
Adhara	19	1·5	255	S 29		4	Diphda	2·0	349	S 18
Aldebaran	10	0·9	291	N 17		5	Achernar	0·5	335	S 57
Alioth	32	1·8	166	N 56		6	Hamal	2·0	328	N 24
Alkaid	34	1·9	153	N 49		7	Acamar	3·2	315	S 40
Alnair	55	1·7	28	S 47		8	Menkar	2·5	314	N 4
Alnilam	15	1·7	276	S 1		9	Mirfak	1·8	309	N 50
Alphard	25	2·0	218	S 9		10	Aldebaran	0·9	291	N 17
Alphecca	41	2·2	126	N 27		11	Rigel	0·1	281	S 8
Alpheratz	1	2·1	358	N 29		12	Capella	0·1	280	N 46
Altair	51	0·8	62	N 9		13	Bellatrix	1·6	278	N 6
Ankaa	2	2·4	353	S 42		14	Elnath	1·7	278	N 29
Antares	42	1·0	112	S 26		15	Alnilam	1·7	276	S 1
Arcturus	37	0·0	146	N 19		16	Betelgeuse	Var.*	271	N 7
Atria	43	1·9	107	S 69		17	Canopus	−0·7	264	S 53
Avior	22	1·9	234	S 60		18	Sirius	−1·5	258	S 17
Bellatrix	13	1·6	278	N 6		19	Adhara	1·5	255	S 29
Betelgeuse	16	Var.*	271	N 7		20	Procyon	0·4	245	N 5
Canopus	17	−0·7	264	S 53		21	Pollux	1·1	243	N 28
Capella	12	0·1	280	N 46		22	Avior	1·9	234	S 60
Deneb	53	1·3	49	N 45		23	Suhail	2·2	223	S 44
Denebola	28	2·1	182	N 14		24	Miaplacidus	1·7	222	S 70
Diphda	4	2·0	349	S 18		25	Alphard	2·0	218	S 9
Dubhe	27	1·8	194	N 62		26	Regulus	1·4	208	N 12
Elnath	14	1·7	278	N 29		27	Dubhe	1·8	194	N 62
Eltanin	47	2·2	91	N 51		28	Denebola	2·1	182	N 14
Enif	54	2·4	34	N 10		29	Gienah	2·6	176	S 18
Fomalhaut	56	1·2	15	S 29		30	Acrux	1·3	173	S 63
Gacrux	31	1·6	172	S 57		31	Gacrux	1·6	172	S 57
Gienah	29	2·6	176	S 18		32	Alioth	1·8	166	N 56
Hadar	35	0·6	149	S 60		33	Spica	1·0	158	S 11
Hamal	6	2·0	328	N 24		34	Alkaid	1·9	153	N 49
Kaus Australis	48	1·9	84	S 34		35	Hadar	0·6	149	S 60
Kochab	40	2·1	137	N 74		36	Menkent	2·1	148	S 36
Markab	57	2·5	14	N 15		37	Arcturus	0·0	146	N 19
Menkar	8	2·5	314	N 4		38	Rigil Kentaurus	−0·3	140	S 61
Menkent	36	2·1	148	S 36		39	Zubenelgenubi	2·8	137	S 16
Miaplacidus	24	1·7	222	S 70		40	Kochab	2·1	137	N 74
Mirfak	9	1·8	309	N 50		41	Alphecca	2·2	126	N 27
Nunki	50	2·0	76	S 26		42	Antares	1·0	112	S 26
Peacock	52	1·9	53	S 57		43	Atria	1·9	107	S 69
Pollux	21	1·1	243	N 28		44	Sabik	2·4	102	S 16
Procyon	20	0·4	245	N 5		45	Shaula	1·6	96	S 37
Rasalhague	46	2·1	96	N 13		46	Rasalhague	2·1	96	N 13
Regulus	26	1·4	208	N 12		47	Eltanin	2·2	91	N 51
Rigel	11	0·1	281	S 8		48	Kaus Australis	1·9	84	S 34
Rigil Kentaurus	38	−0·3	140	S 61		49	Vega	0·0	81	N 39
Sabik	44	2·4	102	S 16		50	Nunki	2·0	76	S 26
Schedar	3	2·2	350	N 57		51	Altair	0·8	62	N 9
Shaula	45	1·6	96	S 37		52	Peacock	1·9	53	S 57
Sirius	18	−1·5	258	S 17		53	Deneb	1·3	49	N 45
Spica	33	1·0	158	S 11		54	Enif	2·4	34	N 10
Suhail	23	2·2	223	S 44		55	Alnair	1·7	28	S 47
Vega	49	0·0	81	N 39		56	Fomalhaut	1·2	15	S 29
Zubenelgenubi	39	2·8	137	S 16		57	Markab	2·5	14	N 15

*0·1 — 1·2

ALTITUDE CORRECTION TABLES 10°–90°—SUN,STARS,PLANETS

OCT.—MAR. **SUN** APR.—SEPT.						**STARS AND PLANETS**				**DIP**				
App. Alt.	Lower Limb	Upper Limb	App. Alt.	Lower Limb	Upper Limb	App Alt.	Corrⁿ	App. Alt.	Additional Corrⁿ	Ht. of Eye	Corrⁿ	Ht. of Eye	Ht. of Eye	Corrⁿ
° ′	′	′	° ′	′	′	° ′	′		**2023**	m	′	ft.	m	′
9 33	+10·8	−21·5	9 39	+10·6	−21·2	9 55	−5·3		**VENUS**	2·4	−2·8	8·0	1·0	− 1·8
9 45	+10·9	−21·4	9 50	+10·7	−21·1	10 07	−5·2		Jan. 1–May 1	2·6	−2·9	8·6	1·5	− 2·2
9 56	+11·0	−21·3	10 02	+10·8	−21·0	10 20	−5·1		Dec. 2–Dec. 31	2·8	−3·0	9·2	2·0	− 2·5
10 08	+11·1	−21·2	10 14	+10·9	−20·9	10 32	−5·0		° ′	3·0	−3·1	9·8	2·5	− 2·8
10 20	+11·2	−21·1	10 27	+11·0	−20·8	10 46	−4·9		60 +0·1	3·2	−3·2	10·5	3·0	− 3·0
10 33	+11·3	−21·0	10 40	+11·1	−20·7	10 59	−4·8			3·4	−3·3	11·2		
10 46	+11·4	−20·9	10 53	+11·2	−20·6	11 14	−4·7		May 2–June 19	3·6	−3·4	11·9		See table
11 00	+11·5	−20·8	11 07	+11·3	−20·5	11 29	−4·6		Oct. 10–Dec. 1	3·8	−3·5	12·6		←
11 15	+11·6	−20·7	11 22	+11·4	−20·4	11 44	−4·5		° ′	4·0	−3·6	13·3	m	′
11 30	+11·7	−20·6	11 37	+11·5	−20·3	12 00	−4·4		41 +0·2	4·3	−3·7	14·1	20	− 7·9
11 45	+11·8	−20·5	11 53	+11·6	−20·2	12 17	−4·4		76 +0·1	4·5	−3·8	14·9	22	− 8·3
12 01	+11·9	−20·4	12 10	+11·7	−20·1	12 35	−4·3			4·7	−3·9	15·7	24	− 8·6
12 18	+12·0	−20·3	12 27	+11·8	−20·0	12 53	−4·2		June 20–July 12	5·0	−4·0	16·5	26	− 9·0
12 36	+12·1	−20·2	12 45	+11·9	−19·9	13 12	−4·1		Sept. 16–Oct. 9	5·2	−4·1	17·4	28	− 9·3
12 54	+12·2	−20·1	13 04	+12·0	−19·8	13 32	−4·0		° ′	5·5	−4·2	18·3		
13 14	+12·3	−20·0	13 24	+12·1	−19·7	13 53	−3·9		34 +0·3	5·8	−4·3	19·1	30	− 9·6
13 34	+12·4	−19·9	13 44	+12·2	−19·6	14 16	−3·8		60 +0·2	6·1	−4·4	20·1	32	−10·0
13 55	+12·5	−19·8	14 06	+12·3	−19·5	14 39	−3·7		80 +0·1	6·3	−4·5	21·0	34	−10·3
14 17	+12·6	−19·7	14 29	+12·4	−19·4	15 03	−3·6		July 13–July 28	6·6	−4·6	22·0	36	−10·6
14 41	+12·7	−19·6	14 53	+12·5	−19·3	15 29	−3·5		Aug. 31–Sept. 15	6·9	−4·7	22·9	38	−10·8
15 05	+12·8	−19·5	15 18	+12·6	−19·2	15 56	−3·4		° ′	7·2	−4·8	23·9		
15 31	+12·9	−19·4	15 45	+12·7	−19·1	16 25	−3·3		29 +0·4	7·5	−4·9	24·9	40	−11·1
15 59	+13·0	−19·3	16 13	+12·8	−19·0	16 55	−3·2		51 +0·3	7·9	−5·0	26·0	42	−11·4
16 27	+13·1	−19·2	16 43	+12·9	−18·9	17 27	−3·1		68 +0·2	8·2	−5·1	27·1	44	−11·7
16 58	+13·2	−19·1	17 14	+13·0	−18·8	18 01	−3·0		83 +0·1	8·5	−5·2	28·1	46	−11·9
17 30	+13·3	−19·0	17 47	+13·1	−18·7	18 37	−2·8		July 29–Aug. 30	8·8	−5·3	29·2	48	−12·2
18 05	+13·4	−18·9	18 23	+13·2	−18·6	19 16	−2·7		° ′	9·2	−5·4	30·4	ft.	
18 41	+13·5	−18·8	19 00	+13·3	−18·5	19 56	−2·6		26 +0·5	9·5	−5·5	31·5	2	− 1·4
19 20	+13·6	−18·7	19 41	+13·4	−18·4	20 40	−2·5		46 +0·4	9·9	−5·6	32·7	4	− 1·9
20 02	+13·7	−18·6	20 24	+13·5	−18·3	21 27	−2·4		60 +0·3	10·3	−5·7	33·9	6	− 2·4
20 46	+13·8	−18·5	21 10	+13·6	−18·2	22 17	−2·3		73 +0·2	10·6	−5·8	35·1	8	− 2·7
21 34	+13·9	−18·4	21 59	+13·7	−18·1	23 11	−2·2		84 +0·1	11·0	−5·9	36·3	10	− 3·1
22 25	+14·0	−18·3	22 52	+13·8	−18·0	24 09	−2·1		**MARS**	11·4	−6·0	37·6		See table
23 20	+14·1	−18·2	23 49	+13·9	−17·9	25 12	−2·0		Jan. 1–Feb. 11	11·8	−6·1	38·9		←
24 20	+14·2	−18·1	24 51	+14·0	−17·8	26 20	−1·9		° ′	12·2	−6·2	40·1	ft.	′
25 24	+14·3	−18·0	25 58	+14·1	−17·7	27 34	−1·8		41 +0·2	12·6	−6·3	41·5	70	− 8·1
26 34	+14·4	−17·9	27 11	+14·2	−17·6	28 54	−1·7		76 +0·1	13·0	−6·4	42·8	75	− 8·4
27 50	+14·5	−17·8	28 31	+14·3	−17·5	30 22	−1·6			13·4	−6·5	44·2	80	− 8·7
29 13	+14·6	−17·7	29 58	+14·4	−17·4	31 58	−1·5		Feb. 12–Dec. 31	13·8	−6·6	45·5	85	− 8·9
30 44	+14·7	−17·6	31 33	+14·5	−17·3	33 43	−1·4		° ′	14·2	−6·7	46·9	90	− 9·2
32 24	+14·8	−17·5	33 18	+14·6	−17·2	35 38	−1·3		60 +0·1	14·7	−6·8	48·4	95	− 9·5
34 15	+14·9	−17·4	35 15	+14·7	−17·1	37 45	−1·2			15·1	−6·9	49·8		
36 17	+15·0	−17·3	37 24	+14·8	−17·0	40 06	−1·1			15·5	−7·0	51·3	100	− 9·7
38 34	+15·1	−17·2	39 48	+14·9	−16·9	42 42	−1·0			16·0	−7·1	52·8	105	− 9·9
41 06	+15·2	−17·1	42 28	+15·0	−16·8	45 34	−0·9			16·5	−7·2	54·3	110	−10·2
43 56	+15·3	−17·0	45 29	+15·1	−16·7	48 45	−0·8			16·9	−7·3	55·8	115	−10·4
47 07	+15·4	−16·9	48 52	+15·2	−16·6	52 16	−0·7			17·4	−7·4	57·4	120	−10·6
50 43	+15·5	−16·8	52 41	+15·3	−16·5	56 09	−0·6			17·9	−7·5	58·9	125	−10·8
54 46	+15·6	−16·7	56 59	+15·4	−16·4	60 26	−0·5			18·4	−7·6	60·5		
59 21	+15·7	−16·6	61 50	+15·5	−16·3	65 06	−0·4			18·8	−7·7	62·1	130	−11·1
64 28	+15·8	−16·5	67 15	+15·6	−16·2	70 09	−0·3			19·3	−7·8	63·8	135	−11·3
70 10	+15·9	−16·4	73 14	+15·7	−16·1	75 32	−0·2			19·8	−7·9	65·4	140	−11·5
76 24	+16·0	−16·3	79 42	+15·8	−16·0	81 12	−0·1			20·4	−8·0	67·1	145	−11·7
83 05	+16·1	−16·2	86 31	+15·9	−15·9	87 03	0·0			20·9	−8·1	68·8	150	−11·9
90 00			90 00			90 00				21·4		70·5	155	−12·1

App. Alt. = Apparent altitude = Sextant altitude corrected for index error and dip.

UT	SUN		MOON					Twilight		Sunrise	Moonrise			
	GHA	Dec	GHA	v	Dec	d	HP	Lat.	Naut.	Civil		21	22	23	24

	GHA	Dec	GHA	v	Dec	d	HP
d h	° ′	° ′	° ′	′	° ′	′	′
21 00	176 35.3	S10 44.1	165 40.7	9.1	S10 50.8	16.2	60.8
01	191 35.4	43.2	180 08.8	9.2	10 34.6	16.3	60.8
02	206 35.5	42.3	194 37.0	9.3	10 18.3	16.3	60.7
03	221 35.5	.. 41.4	209 05.3	9.4	10 02.0	16.3	60.7
04	236 35.6	40.5	223 33.7	9.5	9 45.7	16.4	60.7
05	251 35.7	39.6	238 02.2	9.5	9 29.3	16.5	60.7
06	266 35.7	S10 38.7	252 30.7	9.6	S 9 12.8	16.5	60.7
07	281 35.8	37.8	266 59.3	9.7	8 56.3	16.5	60.6
08	296 35.9	36.9	281 28.0	9.8	8 39.8	16.5	60.6
09	311 35.9	.. 36.0	295 56.8	9.9	8 23.3	16.6	60.6
10	326 36.0	35.1	310 25.7	9.9	8 06.7	16.6	60.6
11	341 36.1	34.2	324 54.6	10.1	7 50.1	16.7	60.5
12	356 36.2	S10 33.3	339 23.7	10.0	S 7 33.4	16.7	60.5
13	11 36.2	32.3	353 52.7	10.2	7 16.7	16.7	60.5
14	26 36.3	31.4	8 21.9	10.2	7 00.0	16.7	60.4
15	41 36.4	.. 30.5	22 51.1	10.3	6 43.3	16.7	60.4
16	56 36.4	29.6	37 20.4	10.4	6 26.6	16.8	60.4
17	71 36.5	28.7	51 49.8	10.4	6 09.8	16.8	60.4
18	86 36.6	S10 27.8	66 19.2	10.6	S 5 53.0	16.8	60.3
19	101 36.7	26.9	80 48.8	10.5	5 36.2	16.8	60.3
20	116 36.7	26.0	95 18.3	10.7	5 19.4	16.8	60.3
21	131 36.8	.. 25.1	109 48.0	10.7	5 02.6	16.8	60.2
22	146 36.9	24.2	124 17.7	10.7	4 45.8	16.9	60.2
23	161 37.0	23.3	138 47.4	10.8	4 28.9	16.8	60.2
22 00	176 37.0	S10 22.4	153 17.2	10.9	S 4 12.1	16.9	60.2
01	191 37.1	21.5	167 47.1	11.0	3 55.2	16.8	60.1
02	206 37.2	20.6	182 17.1	11.0	3 38.4	16.9	60.1
03	221 37.3	.. 19.6	196 47.1	11.0	3 21.5	16.8	60.1
04	236 37.3	18.7	211 17.1	11.1	3 04.7	16.9	60.0
05	251 37.4	17.8	225 47.2	11.2	2 47.8	16.8	60.0
06	266 37.5	S10 16.9	240 17.4	11.2	S 2 31.0	16.9	60.0
07	281 37.6	16.0	254 47.6	11.2	2 14.1	16.8	59.9
08	296 37.6	15.1	269 17.8	11.3	1 57.3	16.8	59.9
09	311 37.7	.. 14.2	283 48.1	11.4	1 40.5	16.9	59.9
10	326 37.8	13.3	298 18.5	11.4	1 23.6	16.8	59.8
11	341 37.9	12.4	312 48.9	11.5	1 06.8	16.7	59.8
12	356 38.0	S10 11.4	327 19.4	11.4	S 0 50.1	16.8	59.8
13	11 38.0	10.5	341 49.8	11.6	0 33.3	16.8	59.7
14	26 38.1	09.6	356 20.4	11.6	S 0 16.5	16.7	59.7
15	41 38.2	.. 08.7	10 51.0	11.6	N 0 00.2	16.7	59.6
16	56 38.3	07.8	25 21.6	11.6	0 16.9	16.7	59.6
17	71 38.4	06.9	39 52.2	11.7	0 33.6	16.7	59.6
18	86 38.4	S10 06.0	54 22.9	11.8	N 0 50.3	16.6	59.5
19	101 38.5	05.1	68 53.7	11.7	1 06.9	16.6	59.5
20	116 38.6	04.1	83 24.4	11.8	1 23.5	16.6	59.5
21	131 38.7	.. 03.2	97 55.2	11.9	1 40.1	16.6	59.4
22	146 38.8	02.3	112 26.1	11.8	1 56.7	16.5	59.4
23	161 38.8	01.4	126 56.9	11.9	2 13.2	16.5	59.4
23 00	176 38.9	S10 00.5	141 27.8	12.0	N 2 29.7	16.4	59.3
01	191 39.0	9 59.6	155 58.8	11.9	2 46.1	16.5	59.3
02	206 39.1	58.7	170 29.7	12.0	3 02.6	16.3	59.2
03	221 39.2	.. 57.7	185 00.7	12.0	3 18.9	16.4	59.2
04	236 39.2	56.8	199 31.7	12.1	3 35.3	16.3	59.2
05	251 39.3	55.9	214 02.8	12.0	3 51.6	16.3	59.1
06	266 39.4	S 9 55.0	228 33.8	12.1	N 4 07.9	16.2	59.1
07	281 39.5	54.1	243 04.9	12.1	4 24.1	16.2	59.0
08	296 39.6	53.2	257 36.0	12.1	4 40.3	16.1	59.0
09	311 39.7	.. 52.2	272 07.1	12.2	4 56.4	16.1	59.0
10	326 39.8	51.3	286 38.3	12.1	5 12.5	16.0	58.9
11	341 39.8	50.4	301 09.4	12.2	5 28.5	16.0	58.9
12	356 39.9	S 9 49.5	315 40.6	12.2	N 5 44.5	15.9	58.9
13	11 40.0	48.6	330 11.8	12.2	6 00.4	15.9	58.8
14	26 40.1	47.7	344 43.0	12.2	6 16.3	15.8	58.8
15	41 40.2	.. 46.7	359 14.2	12.2	6 32.1	15.8	58.7
16	56 40.3	45.8	13 45.4	12.3	6 47.9	15.7	58.7
17	71 40.3	44.9	28 16.7	12.2	7 03.6	15.7	58.7
18	86 40.4	S 9 44.0	42 47.9	12.3	N 7 19.3	15.6	58.6
19	101 40.5	43.1	57 19.2	12.2	7 34.9	15.5	58.6
20	116 40.6	42.1	71 50.4	12.3	7 50.4	15.5	58.5
21	131 40.7	.. 41.2	86 21.7	12.3	8 05.9	15.4	58.5
22	146 40.8	40.3	100 53.0	12.3	8 21.3	15.4	58.5
23	161 40.9	39.4	115 24.3	12.2	N 8 36.7	15.3	58.4
	SD 16.2	d 0.9	SD 16.5		16.3		16.0

Lat.	Twilight		Sunrise	Moonrise			
	Naut.	Civil		21	22	23	24
°	h m	h m	h m	h m	h m	h m	h m
N 72	05 45	07 03	08 16	09 06	08 28	07 53	07 14
N 70	05 46	06 57	08 01	08 54	08 26	07 59	07 31
68	05 47	06 51	07 50	08 44	08 24	08 04	07 44
66	05 48	06 47	07 40	08 36	08 22	08 09	07 55
64	05 48	06 43	07 32	08 28	08 20	08 12	08 04
62	05 49	06 40	07 25	08 22	08 19	08 15	08 12
60	05 49	06 37	07 19	08 17	08 18	08 18	08 19
N 58	05 49	06 34	07 14	08 12	08 17	08 21	08 25
56	05 49	06 32	07 10	08 08	08 16	08 23	08 31
54	05 48	06 29	07 05	08 04	08 15	08 25	08 36
52	05 48	06 27	07 01	08 00	08 14	08 27	08 40
50	05 48	06 25	06 58	07 57	08 13	08 28	08 44
45	05 47	06 21	06 50	07 50	08 12	08 32	08 53
N 40	05 45	06 17	06 44	07 44	08 10	08 35	09 00
35	05 43	06 13	06 38	07 39	08 09	08 38	09 07
30	05 41	06 09	06 34	07 34	08 08	08 40	09 12
20	05 37	06 03	06 25	07 27	08 06	08 45	09 22
N 10	05 31	05 56	06 17	07 20	08 05	08 48	09 31
0	05 25	05 49	06 11	07 13	08 04	08 52	09 39
S 10	05 16	05 41	06 03	07 07	08 02	08 55	09 48
20	05 06	05 32	05 55	07 00	08 01	08 59	09 57
30	04 52	05 21	05 46	06 52	07 59	09 04	10 07
35	04 43	05 14	05 40	06 47	07 58	09 06	10 13
40	04 32	05 06	05 34	06 42	07 57	09 09	10 20
45	04 19	04 56	05 27	06 36	07 56	09 13	10 28
S 50	04 01	04 44	05 18	06 28	07 54	09 17	10 38
52	03 53	04 38	05 14	06 25	07 53	09 19	10 42
54	03 43	04 31	05 10	06 21	07 53	09 21	10 47
56	03 32	04 24	05 05	06 17	07 52	09 23	10 53
58	03 19	04 16	04 59	06 12	07 51	09 26	10 59
S 60	03 03	04 06	04 53	06 07	07 50	09 29	11 06

Lat.	Sunset	Twilight		Moonset			
		Civil	Naut.	21	22	23	24
°	h m	h m	h m	h m	h m	h m	h m
N 72	16 13	17 26	18 45	18 20	20 46	23 08	25 50
N 70	16 27	17 32	18 43	18 29	20 43	22 54	25 14
68	16 39	17 37	18 42	18 37	20 42	22 43	24 49
66	16 48	17 41	18 41	18 43	20 40	22 35	24 30
64	16 56	17 45	18 40	18 48	20 39	22 27	24 15
62	17 03	17 48	18 40	18 52	20 38	22 21	24 03
60	17 09	17 51	18 40	18 56	20 37	22 15	23 52
N 58	17 14	17 54	18 40	18 59	20 36	22 10	23 43
56	17 18	17 56	18 40	19 02	20 36	22 06	23 35
54	17 23	17 59	18 40	19 05	20 35	22 02	23 28
52	17 26	18 01	18 40	19 07	20 34	21 59	23 21
50	17 30	18 03	18 40	19 09	20 34	21 56	23 16
45	17 37	18 07	18 41	19 14	20 33	21 49	23 03
N 40	17 44	18 11	18 42	19 18	20 32	21 43	22 53
35	17 49	18 15	18 44	19 21	20 31	21 38	22 44
30	17 54	18 18	18 46	19 24	20 30	21 34	22 37
20	18 02	18 24	18 56	19 29	20 29	21 27	22 24
N 10	18 10	18 31	18 56	19 33	20 28	21 20	22 13
0	18 17	18 38	19 02	19 37	20 27	21 14	22 02
S 10	18 24	18 45	19 10	19 41	20 26	21 08	21 51
20	18 32	18 54	19 21	19 45	20 24	21 02	21 40
30	18 41	19 06	19 35	19 50	20 23	20 55	21 28
35	18 46	19 12	19 43	19 53	20 22	20 51	21 20
40	18 52	19 20	19 54	19 56	20 21	20 46	21 12
45	18 59	19 30	20 07	19 59	20 20	20 41	21 02
S 50	19 08	19 42	20 24	20 03	20 19	20 34	20 51
52	19 12	19 48	20 32	20 05	20 18	20 31	20 45
54	19 16	19 54	20 42	20 07	20 18	20 28	20 40
56	19 21	20 01	20 53	20 09	20 17	20 25	20 33
58	19 26	20 09	21 05	20 12	20 16	20 21	20 26
S 60	19 32	20 19	21 21	20 15	20 16	20 16	20 17

	SUN			MOON			
Day	Eqn. of Time		Mer.	Mer. Pass.		Age	Phase
	00h	12h	Pass.	Upper	Lower		
d	m s	m s	h m	h m	h m	d	%
21	13 39	13 36	12 14	13 25	00 59	01	2
22	13 32	13 28	12 13	14 15	01 51	02	7
23	13 24	13 20	12 13	15 03	02 39	03	14

© British Crown Copyright 2022. All rights reserved.

UT	ARIES	VENUS −3.9		MARS +0.3		JUPITER −2.1		SATURN +0.8		STARS		
d h	GHA	GHA	Dec	GHA	Dec	GHA	Dec	GHA	Dec	Name	SHA	Dec
24 00	153 36.8	149 07.4	N 0 59.0	77 48.3	N25 16.5	143 16.9	N 3 13.8	182 23.6	S13 08.5	Acamar	315 13.1	S40 13.0
01	168 39.3	164 07.1	1 00.3	92 49.8	16.5	158 18.9	14.0	197 25.8	08.4	Achernar	335 21.7	S57 07.5
02	183 41.8	179 06.8	01.6	107 51.2	16.6	173 20.9	14.2	212 27.9	08.3	Acrux	173 01.2	S63 13.5
03	198 44.2	194 06.5 ..	02.9	122 52.6 ..	16.7	188 22.8 ..	14.4	227 30.1 ..	08.2	Adhara	255 06.8	S29 00.4
04	213 46.7	209 06.2	04.2	137 54.1	16.7	203 24.8	14.6	242 32.3	08.1	Aldebaran	290 41.4	N16 33.3
05	228 49.2	224 05.9	05.5	152 55.5	16.8	218 26.7	14.8	257 34.4	08.0			
06	243 51.6	239 05.6	N 1 06.8	167 56.9	N25 16.8	233 28.7	N 3 15.1	272 36.6	S13 07.9	Alioth	166 13.9	N55 49.9
07	258 54.1	254 05.2	08.1	182 58.4	16.9	248 30.7	15.3	287 38.8	07.8	Alkaid	152 52.9	N49 11.6
08	273 56.5	269 04.9	09.4	197 59.8	17.0	263 32.6	15.5	302 41.0	07.7	Alnair	27 35.3	S46 51.1
F 09	288 59.0	284 04.6 ..	10.7	213 01.2 ..	17.0	278 34.6 ..	15.7	317 43.1 ..	07.6	Alnilam	275 39.2	S 1 11.3
R 10	304 01.5	299 04.3	12.1	228 02.6	17.1	293 36.5	15.9	332 45.3	07.5	Alphard	217 49.0	S 8 45.6
I 11	319 03.9	314 04.0	13.4	243 04.1	17.2	308 38.5	16.2	347 47.5	07.4			
D 12	334 06.4	329 03.7	N 1 14.7	258 05.5	N25 17.2	323 40.5	N 3 16.4	2 49.7	S13 07.3	Alphecca	126 05.0	N26 38.0
A 13	349 08.9	344 03.4	16.0	273 06.9	17.3	338 42.4	16.6	17 51.8	07.2	Alpheratz	357 36.7	N29 13.0
Y 14	4 11.3	359 03.0	17.3	288 08.4	17.3	353 44.4	16.8	32 54.0	07.1	Altair	62 01.7	N 8 55.6
15	19 13.8	14 02.7 ..	18.6	303 09.8 ..	17.4	8 46.3 ..	17.0	47 56.2 ..	07.0	Ankaa	353 09.0	S42 11.1
16	34 16.3	29 02.4	19.9	318 11.2	17.5	23 48.3	17.3	62 58.4	06.9	Antares	112 17.8	S26 28.9
17	49 18.7	44 02.1	21.2	333 12.6	17.5	38 50.3	17.5	78 00.5	06.8			
18	64 21.2	59 01.8	N 1 22.5	348 14.1	N25 17.6	53 52.2	N 3 17.7	93 02.7	S13 06.7	Arcturus	145 49.2	N19 03.5
19	79 23.7	74 01.5	23.8	3 15.5	17.7	68 54.2	17.9	108 04.9	06.6	Atria	107 13.5	S69 03.9
20	94 26.1	89 01.2	25.1	18 16.9	17.7	83 56.1	18.1	123 07.0	06.5	Avior	234 14.8	S59 35.1
21	109 28.6	104 00.9 ..	26.4	33 18.3 ..	17.8	98 58.1 ..	18.4	138 09.2 ..	06.4	Bellatrix	278 24.4	N 6 22.2
22	124 31.0	119 00.5	27.7	48 19.7	17.8	114 00.1	18.6	153 11.4	06.3	Betelgeuse	270 53.6	N 7 24.6
23	139 33.5	134 00.2	29.0	63 21.2	17.9	129 02.0	18.8	168 13.6	06.2			
25 00	154 36.0	148 59.9	N 1 30.4	78 22.6	N25 18.0	144 04.0	N 3 19.0	183 15.7	S13 06.1	Canopus	263 52.8	S52 42.7
01	169 38.4	163 59.6	31.7	93 24.0	18.0	159 05.9	19.2	198 17.9	06.0	Capella	280 24.1	N46 01.4
02	184 40.9	178 59.3	33.0	108 25.4	18.1	174 07.9	19.5	213 20.1	05.9	Deneb	49 27.3	N45 21.5
03	199 43.4	193 59.0 ..	34.3	123 26.8 ..	18.1	189 09.9 ..	19.7	228 22.3 ..	05.8	Denebola	182 26.2	N14 26.5
04	214 45.8	208 58.7	35.6	138 28.3	18.2	204 11.8	19.9	243 24.4	05.7	Diphda	348 49.1	S17 51.8
05	229 48.3	223 58.4	36.9	153 29.7	18.3	219 13.8	20.1	258 26.6	05.6			
06	244 50.8	238 58.0	N 1 38.2	168 31.1	N25 18.3	234 15.7	N 3 20.3	273 28.8	S13 05.5	Dubhe	193 42.2	N61 37.5
07	259 53.2	253 57.7	39.5	183 32.5	18.4	249 17.7	20.6	288 31.0	05.4	Elnath	278 03.7	N28 37.6
S 08	274 55.7	268 57.4	40.8	198 33.9	18.5	264 19.7	20.8	303 33.1	05.2	Eltanin	90 43.1	N51 28.8
A 09	289 58.2	283 57.1 ..	42.1	213 35.3 ..	18.5	279 21.6 ..	21.0	318 35.3 ..	05.1	Enif	33 40.6	N 9 58.7
T 10	305 00.6	298 56.8	43.4	228 36.8	18.6	294 23.6	21.2	333 37.5	05.0	Fomalhaut	15 16.6	S29 30.2
U 11	320 03.1	313 56.5	44.7	243 38.2	18.6	309 25.5	21.4	348 39.7	04.9			
R 12	335 05.5	328 56.2	N 1 46.0	258 39.6	N25 18.7	324 27.5	N 3 21.7	3 41.8	S13 04.8	Gacrux	171 52.9	S57 14.4
D 13	350 08.0	343 55.9	47.3	273 41.0	18.8	339 29.4	21.9	18 44.0	04.7	Gienah	175 44.9	S17 40.2
A 14	5 10.5	358 55.5	48.6	288 42.4	18.8	354 31.4	22.1	33 46.2	04.6	Hadar	148 37.9	S60 28.8
Y 15	20 12.9	13 55.2 ..	50.0	303 43.8 ..	18.9	9 33.4 ..	22.3	48 48.3 ..	04.5	Hamal	327 53.1	N23 34.3
16	35 15.4	28 54.9	51.3	318 45.2	18.9	24 35.3	22.5	63 50.5	04.4	Kaus Aust.	83 34.8	S34 22.4
17	50 17.9	43 54.6	52.6	333 46.6	19.0	39 37.3	22.8	78 52.7	04.3			
18	65 20.3	58 54.3	N 1 53.9	348 48.0	N25 19.1	54 39.2	N 3 23.0	93 54.9	S13 04.2	Kochab	137 19.3	N74 03.3
19	80 22.8	73 54.0	55.2	3 49.4	19.1	69 41.2	23.2	108 57.0	04.1	Markab	13 31.8	N15 19.6
20	95 25.3	88 53.7	56.5	18 50.9	19.2	84 43.1	23.4	123 59.2	04.0	Menkar	314 07.9	N 4 10.7
21	110 27.7	103 53.4 ..	57.8	33 52.3 ..	19.2	99 45.1 ..	23.6	139 01.4 ..	03.9	Menkent	147 59.2	S36 28.9
22	125 30.2	118 53.0	1 59.1	48 53.7	19.3	114 47.1	23.9	154 03.6	03.8	Miaplacidus	221 37.7	S69 48.8
23	140 32.6	133 52.7	2 00.4	63 55.1	19.4	129 49.0	24.1	169 05.7	03.7			
26 00	155 35.1	148 52.4	N 2 01.7	78 56.5	N25 19.4	144 51.0	N 3 24.3	184 07.9	S13 03.6	Mirfak	308 30.6	N49 56.7
01	170 37.6	163 52.1	03.0	93 57.9	19.5	159 52.9	24.5	199 10.1	03.5	Nunki	75 49.9	S26 16.1
02	185 40.0	178 51.8	04.3	108 59.3	19.5	174 54.9	24.7	214 12.3	03.4	Peacock	53 08.7	S56 39.6
03	200 42.5	193 51.5 ..	05.6	124 00.7 ..	19.6	189 56.8 ..	25.0	229 14.4 ..	03.3	Pollux	243 18.9	N27 58.2
04	215 45.0	208 51.2	06.9	139 02.1	19.7	204 58.8	25.2	244 16.6	03.2	Procyon	244 52.2	N 5 09.9
05	230 47.4	223 50.9	08.2	154 03.5	19.7	220 00.8	25.4	259 18.8	03.1			
06	245 49.9	238 50.5	N 2 09.5	169 04.9	N25 19.8	235 02.7	N 3 25.6	274 21.0	S13 03.0	Rasalhague	96 00.1	N12 32.4
07	260 52.4	253 50.2	10.9	184 06.3	19.8	250 04.7	25.8	289 23.1	02.9	Regulus	207 35.8	N11 51.2
08	275 54.8	268 49.9	12.2	199 07.7	19.9	265 06.6	26.1	304 25.3	02.8	Rigel	281 05.3	S 8 10.6
S 09	290 57.3	283 49.6 ..	13.5	214 09.1 ..	20.0	280 08.6 ..	26.3	319 27.5 ..	02.7	Rigil Kent.	139 42.2	S60 55.6
U 10	305 59.8	298 49.3	14.8	229 10.5	20.0	295 10.5	26.5	334 29.7	02.6	Sabik	102 04.6	S15 45.2
N 11	321 02.2	313 49.0	16.1	244 11.9	20.1	310 12.5	26.7	349 31.8	02.5			
D 12	336 04.7	328 48.7	N 2 17.4	259 13.3	N25 20.1	325 14.4	N 3 26.9	4 34.0	S13 02.4	Schedar	349 33.3	N56 39.9
A 13	351 07.1	343 48.4	18.7	274 14.7	20.2	340 16.4	27.2	19 36.2	02.3	Shaula	96 12.6	S37 07.1
Y 14	6 09.6	358 48.1	20.0	289 16.1	20.3	355 18.4	27.4	34 38.3	02.2	Sirius	258 27.4	S16 45.0
15	21 12.1	13 47.7 ..	21.3	304 17.5 ..	20.3	10 20.3 ..	27.6	49 40.5 ..	02.1	Spica	158 23.7	S11 17.0
16	36 14.5	28 47.4	22.6	319 18.9	20.4	25 22.3	27.8	64 42.7	02.0	Suhail	222 47.0	S43 31.6
17	51 17.0	43 47.1	23.9	334 20.3	20.4	40 24.2	28.1	79 44.9	01.9			
18	66 19.5	58 46.8	N 2 25.2	349 21.7	N25 20.5	55 26.2	N 3 28.3	94 47.0	S13 01.8	Vega	80 34.5	N38 48.0
19	81 21.9	73 46.5	26.5	4 23.1	20.6	70 28.1	28.5	109 49.2	01.7	Zuben'ubi	136 57.6	S16 08.3
20	96 24.4	88 46.2	27.8	19 24.5	20.6	85 30.1	28.7	124 51.4	01.6		SHA	Mer. Pass.
21	111 26.9	103 45.9 ..	29.1	34 25.9 ..	20.7	100 32.0 ..	28.9	139 53.6 ..	01.5	Venus	354 23.9	14 04
22	126 29.3	118 45.6	30.4	49 27.3	20.7	115 34.0	29.2	154 55.7	01.4	Mars	283 46.6	18 45
23	141 31.8	133 45.2	31.7	64 28.6	20.8	130 36.0	29.4	169 57.9	01.3	Jupiter	349 28.0	14 22
										Saturn	28 39.8	11 45
Mer. Pass. 13 39.4		v −0.3 d 1.3		v 1.4 d 0.1		v 2.0 d 0.2		v 2.2 d 0.1				

© British Crown Copyright 2022. All rights reserved.

UT	SUN GHA	SUN Dec	MOON GHA	v	Dec	d	HP
d h	° ′	° ′	° ′	′	° ′	′	′
24 00	176 41.0	S 9 38.5	129 55.5	12.3	N 8 52.0	15.2	58.4
01	191 41.0	37.5	144 26.8	12.3	9 07.2	15.2	58.3
02	206 41.1	36.6	158 58.1	12.3	9 22.4	15.1	58.3
03	221 41.2	.. 35.7	173 29.4	12.3	9 37.5	15.0	58.3
04	236 41.3	34.8	188 00.7	12.3	9 52.5	15.0	58.3
05	251 41.4	33.8	202 32.0	12.3	10 07.5	14.9	58.2
06	266 41.5	S 9 32.9	217 03.3	12.2	N10 22.4	14.8	58.1
07	281 41.6	32.0	231 34.5	12.3	10 37.2	14.7	58.1
08	296 41.7	31.1	246 05.8	12.3	10 51.9	14.7	58.1
F 09	311 41.8	.. 30.1	260 37.1	12.3	11 06.6	14.6	58.0
R 10	326 41.9	29.2	275 08.4	12.2	11 21.2	14.5	58.0
I 11	341 41.9	28.3	289 39.6	12.3	11 35.7	14.5	57.9
D 12	356 42.0	S 9 27.4	304 10.9	12.2	N11 50.2	14.3	57.9
A 13	11 42.1	26.5	318 42.1	12.2	12 04.5	14.3	57.8
Y 14	26 42.2	25.5	333 13.3	12.3	12 18.8	14.2	57.8
15	41 42.3	.. 24.6	347 44.6	12.2	12 33.0	14.2	57.8
16	56 42.4	23.7	2 15.8	12.2	12 47.2	14.0	57.7
17	71 42.5	22.8	16 47.0	12.1	13 01.2	14.0	57.7
18	86 42.6	S 9 21.8	31 18.1	12.2	N13 15.2	13.9	57.6
19	101 42.7	20.9	45 49.3	12.2	13 29.1	13.7	57.6
20	116 42.8	20.0	60 20.5	12.1	13 42.8	13.8	57.6
21	131 42.9	.. 19.0	74 51.6	12.1	13 56.6	13.6	57.5
22	146 43.0	18.1	89 22.7	12.1	14 10.2	13.5	57.5
23	161 43.1	17.2	103 53.8	12.1	14 23.7	13.5	57.5
25 00	176 43.2	S 9 16.3	118 24.9	12.1	N14 37.2	13.3	57.4
01	191 43.2	15.3	132 56.0	12.0	14 50.5	13.3	57.4
02	206 43.3	14.4	147 27.0	12.1	15 03.8	13.2	57.3
03	221 43.4	.. 13.5	161 58.1	12.0	15 17.0	13.0	57.3
04	236 43.5	12.6	176 29.1	12.0	15 30.0	13.0	57.3
05	251 43.6	11.6	191 00.1	11.9	15 43.0	12.9	57.2
06	266 43.7	S 9 10.7	205 31.0	12.0	N15 55.9	12.8	57.2
07	281 43.8	09.8	220 02.0	11.9	16 08.7	12.8	57.1
S 08	296 43.9	08.8	234 32.9	11.9	16 21.5	12.6	57.1
A 09	311 44.0	.. 07.9	249 03.8	11.9	16 34.1	12.5	57.1
T 10	326 44.1	07.0	263 34.7	11.8	16 46.6	12.4	57.0
U 11	341 44.2	06.1	278 05.5	11.8	16 59.0	12.3	57.0
R 12	356 44.3	S 9 05.1	292 36.3	11.8	N17 11.3	12.2	56.9
D 13	11 44.4	04.2	307 07.1	11.8	17 23.5	12.2	56.9
A 14	26 44.5	03.3	321 37.9	11.7	17 35.7	12.0	56.9
Y 15	41 44.6	.. 02.3	336 08.6	11.7	17 47.7	11.9	56.8
16	56 44.7	01.4	350 39.3	11.7	17 59.6	11.8	56.8
17	71 44.8	9 00.5	5 10.0	11.7	18 11.4	11.7	56.8
18	86 44.9	S 8 59.5	19 40.7	11.6	N18 23.1	11.7	56.7
19	101 45.0	58.6	34 11.3	11.6	18 34.8	11.5	56.7
20	116 45.1	57.7	48 41.9	11.6	18 46.3	11.4	56.6
21	131 45.2	.. 56.7	63 12.5	11.5	18 57.7	11.3	56.6
22	146 45.3	55.8	77 43.0	11.5	19 09.0	11.1	56.6
23	161 45.4	54.9	92 13.5	11.5	19 20.1	11.1	56.5
26 00	176 45.5	S 8 54.0	106 44.0	11.5	N19 31.2	11.0	56.5
01	191 45.6	53.0	121 14.5	11.4	19 42.2	10.9	56.5
02	206 45.7	52.1	135 44.9	11.4	19 53.1	10.7	56.4
03	221 45.8	.. 51.2	150 15.3	11.3	20 03.8	10.7	56.4
04	236 45.9	50.2	164 45.6	11.3	20 14.5	10.5	56.4
05	251 46.0	49.3	179 15.9	11.3	20 25.0	10.4	56.3
06	266 46.1	S 8 48.3	193 46.2	11.3	N20 35.4	10.3	56.3
07	281 46.2	47.4	208 16.5	11.2	20 45.7	10.2	56.3
08	296 46.3	46.5	222 46.7	11.2	20 55.9	10.1	56.2
S 09	311 46.4	.. 45.5	237 16.9	11.2	21 06.0	10.0	56.2
U 10	326 46.5	44.6	251 47.1	11.1	21 16.0	9.8	56.2
N 11	341 46.6	43.7	266 17.2	11.1	21 25.8	9.8	56.1
D 12	356 46.7	S 8 42.7	280 47.3	11.1	N21 35.6	9.6	56.1
A 13	11 46.8	41.8	295 17.4	11.0	21 45.2	9.5	56.1
Y 14	26 46.9	40.9	309 47.4	11.0	21 54.7	9.4	56.0
15	41 47.0	.. 39.9	324 17.4	11.0	22 04.1	9.2	56.0
16	56 47.1	39.0	338 47.4	10.9	22 13.3	9.2	56.0
17	71 47.2	38.1	353 17.3	10.9	22 22.5	9.0	55.9
18	86 47.3	S 8 37.1	7 47.2	10.9	N22 31.5	8.9	55.9
19	101 47.5	36.2	22 17.1	10.8	22 40.4	8.8	55.9
20	116 47.6	35.3	36 46.9	10.8	22 49.2	8.7	55.8
21	131 47.7	.. 34.3	51 16.7	10.8	22 57.9	8.6	55.8
22	146 47.8	33.4	65 46.5	10.7	23 06.5	8.4	55.8
23	161 47.9	32.4	80 16.2	10.7	N23 14.9	8.3	55.7
	SD 16.2	d 0.9	SD 15.8		15.5		15.3

Lat.	Twilight Naut.	Twilight Civil	Sunrise	Moonrise 24	Moonrise 25	Moonrise 26	Moonrise 27
°	h m	h m	h m	h m	h m	h m	h m
N 72	05 31	06 49	08 00	07 14	06 15	☐	☐
N 70	05 34	06 44	07 47	07 31	06 52	☐	☐
68	05 36	06 40	07 37	07 44	07 18	06 33	☐
66	05 38	06 37	07 29	07 55	07 39	07 15	☐
64	05 39	06 34	07 22	08 04	07 55	07 44	07 26
62	05 40	06 31	07 16	08 12	08 09	08 06	08 04
60	05 41	06 29	07 11	08 19	08 21	08 24	08 31
N 58	05 41	06 27	07 06	08 25	08 31	08 39	08 53
56	05 42	06 25	07 02	08 31	08 40	08 52	09 10
54	05 42	06 23	06 59	08 36	08 48	09 04	09 25
52	05 42	06 21	06 55	08 40	08 55	09 14	09 38
50	05 42	06 19	06 52	08 44	09 02	09 23	09 49
45	05 42	06 16	06 45	08 53	09 16	09 42	10 13
N 40	05 41	06 12	06 40	09 00	09 27	09 57	10 32
35	05 40	06 09	06 35	09 07	09 37	10 10	10 48
30	05 39	06 06	06 31	09 12	09 46	10 22	11 02
20	05 35	06 01	06 23	09 22	10 01	10 42	11 26
N 10	05 30	05 55	06 16	09 31	10 14	10 59	11 47
0	05 24	05 49	06 10	09 39	10 27	11 16	12 06
S 10	05 17	05 42	06 03	09 48	10 40	11 32	12 25
20	05 07	05 34	05 56	09 57	10 53	11 50	12 46
30	04 54	05 23	05 48	10 07	11 09	12 11	13 11
35	04 46	05 17	05 43	10 13	11 18	12 23	13 25
40	04 36	05 09	05 37	10 20	11 29	12 37	13 42
45	04 24	05 00	05 31	10 28	11 42	12 53	14 02
S 50	04 08	04 49	05 23	10 38	11 57	13 14	14 27
52	04 00	04 44	05 20	10 42	12 04	13 24	14 40
54	03 51	04 38	05 16	10 47	12 12	13 35	14 54
56	03 41	04 31	05 11	10 53	12 21	13 48	15 10
58	03 29	04 24	05 06	10 59	12 31	14 02	15 30
S 60	03 15	04 15	05 01	11 06	12 43	14 20	15 55

Lat.	Sunset	Twilight Civil	Twilight Naut.	Moonset 24	Moonset 25	Moonset 26	Moonset 27
°	h m	h m	h m	h m	h m	h m	h m
N 72	16 28	17 40	18 58	25 50	01 50	☐	☐
N 70	16 41	17 44	18 55	25 14	01 14	☐	☐
68	16 50	17 48	18 52	24 49	00 49	03 16	☐
66	16 58	17 51	18 50	24 30	00 30	02 35	☐
64	17 05	17 54	18 49	24 15	00 15	02 07	04 09
62	17 11	17 56	18 48	24 03	00 03	01 46	03 31
60	17 16	17 59	18 47	23 52	25 29	01 29	03 05
N 58	17 21	18 01	18 46	23 43	25 15	01 15	02 44
56	17 25	18 03	18 46	23 35	25 02	01 02	02 27
54	17 29	18 04	18 45	23 28	24 52	00 52	02 13
52	17 32	18 06	18 45	23 21	24 42	00 42	02 01
50	17 35	18 08	18 45	23 16	24 34	00 34	01 50
45	17 41	18 11	18 45	23 03	24 16	00 16	01 27
N 40	17 47	18 14	18 46	22 53	24 02	00 02	01 08
35	17 52	18 17	18 47	22 44	23 49	24 53	00 53
30	17 56	18 20	18 48	22 37	23 39	24 40	00 40
20	18 03	18 26	18 51	22 24	23 21	24 17	00 17
N 10	18 10	18 31	18 56	22 13	23 05	23 58	24 51
0	18 16	18 37	19 02	22 02	22 50	23 40	24 31
S 10	18 23	18 44	19 09	21 51	22 36	23 22	24 10
20	18 30	18 52	19 18	21 40	22 20	23 02	23 48
30	18 38	19 02	19 31	21 28	22 02	22 40	23 23
35	18 43	19 08	19 39	21 20	21 52	22 27	23 08
40	18 48	19 16	19 49	21 12	21 40	22 13	22 50
45	18 54	19 25	20 01	21 02	21 27	21 55	22 30
S 50	19 02	19 36	20 17	20 51	21 10	21 33	22 04
52	19 05	19 41	20 25	20 45	21 02	21 23	21 51
54	19 09	19 47	20 33	20 40	20 53	21 11	21 37
56	19 13	19 53	20 43	20 33	20 44	20 58	21 20
58	19 18	20 00	20 55	20 26	20 32	20 43	21 00
S 60	19 24	20 09	21 09	20 17	20 20	20 24	20 34

Day	SUN Eqn. of Time 00h	SUN Eqn. of Time 12h	SUN Mer. Pass.	MOON Mer. Pass. Upper	MOON Mer. Pass. Lower	Age	Phase
d	m s	m s	h m	h m	h m	d	%
24	13 16	13 12	12 13	15 51	03 27	04	22
25	13 08	13 03	12 13	16 39	04 15	05	32
26	12 58	12 53	12 13	17 28	05 03	06	42

© British Crown Copyright 2022. All rights reserved.

UT	ARIES GHA	VENUS −3.9 GHA	Dec	MARS +0.4 GHA	Dec	JUPITER −2.1 GHA	Dec	SATURN +0.8 GHA	Dec	Name	SHA	Dec
27 00	156 34.3	148 44.9	N 2 33.0	79 30.0	N25 20.8	145 37.9	N 3 29.6	185 00.1	S13 01.2	Acamar	315 13.1	S40 13.0
01	171 36.7	163 44.6	34.3	94 31.4	20.9	160 39.9	29.8	200 02.3	01.1	Achernar	335 21.7	S57 07.5
02	186 39.2	178 44.3	35.6	109 32.8	21.0	175 41.8	30.0	215 04.4	01.0	Acrux	173 01.2	S63 13.5
03	201 41.6	193 44.0 ..	36.9	124 34.2 ..	21.0	190 43.8 ..	30.3	230 06.6 ..	00.9	Adhara	255 06.9	S29 00.4
04	216 44.1	208 43.7	38.2	139 35.6	21.1	205 45.7	30.5	245 08.8	00.8	Aldebaran	290 41.4	N16 33.3
05	231 46.6	223 43.4	39.6	154 37.0	21.1	220 47.7	30.7	260 11.0	00.7			
06	246 49.0	238 43.1	N 2 40.9	169 38.4	N25 21.2	235 49.6	N 3 30.9	275 13.1	S13 00.6	Alioth	166 13.9	N55 49.9
07	261 51.5	253 42.8	42.2	184 39.8	21.3	250 51.6	31.2	290 15.3	00.5	Alkaid	152 52.9	N49 11.6
08	276 54.0	268 42.4	43.5	199 41.2	21.3	265 53.5	31.4	305 17.5	00.4	Alnair	27 35.3	S46 51.1
M 09	291 56.4	283 42.1 ..	44.8	214 42.5 ..	21.4	280 55.5 ..	31.6	320 19.7 ..	00.3	Alnilam	275 39.2	S 1 11.3
O 10	306 58.9	298 41.8	46.1	229 43.9	21.4	295 57.4	31.8	335 21.8	00.2	Alphard	217 49.0	S 8 45.6
N 11	322 01.4	313 41.5	47.4	244 45.3	21.5	310 59.4	32.0	350 24.0	13 00.0			
D 12	337 03.8	328 41.2	N 2 48.7	259 46.7	N25 21.5	326 01.4	N 3 32.3	5 26.2	S12 59.9	Alphecca	126 05.0	N26 38.0
A 13	352 06.3	343 40.9	50.0	274 48.1	21.6	341 03.3	32.5	20 28.4	59.8	Alpheratz	357 36.7	N29 13.0
Y 14	7 08.7	358 40.6	51.3	289 49.5	21.7	356 05.3	32.7	35 30.5	59.7	Altair	62 01.7	N 8 55.6
15	22 11.2	13 40.3 ..	52.6	304 50.8 ..	21.7	11 07.2 ..	32.9	50 32.7 ..	59.6	Ankaa	353 09.0	S42 11.1
16	37 13.7	28 40.0	53.9	319 52.2	21.8	26 09.2	33.1	65 34.9	59.5	Antares	112 17.7	S26 29.0
17	52 16.1	43 39.6	55.2	334 53.6	21.8	41 11.1	33.4	80 37.1	59.4			
18	67 18.6	58 39.3	N 2 56.5	349 55.0	N25 21.9	56 13.1	N 3 33.6	95 39.2	S12 59.3	Arcturus	145 49.1	N19 03.5
19	82 21.1	73 39.0	57.8	4 56.4	21.9	71 15.0	33.8	110 41.4	59.2	Atria	107 13.4	S69 03.9
20	97 23.5	88 38.7	2 59.1	19 57.8	22.0	86 17.0	34.0	125 43.6	59.1	Avior	234 14.8	S59 35.1
21	112 26.0	103 38.4	3 00.4	34 59.1 ..	22.1	101 18.9 ..	34.3	140 45.8 ..	59.0	Bellatrix	278 24.5	N 6 22.2
22	127 28.5	118 38.1	01.7	50 00.5	22.1	116 20.9	34.5	155 47.9	58.9	Betelgeuse	270 53.6	N 7 24.6
23	142 30.9	133 37.8	03.0	65 01.9	22.2	131 22.8	34.7	170 50.1	58.8			
28 00	157 33.4	148 37.5	N 3 04.3	80 03.3	N25 22.2	146 24.8	N 3 34.9	185 52.3	S12 58.7	Canopus	263 52.8	S52 42.7
01	172 35.9	163 37.2	05.6	95 04.6	22.3	161 26.7	35.1	200 54.5	58.6	Capella	280 24.1	N46 01.4
02	187 38.3	178 36.8	06.9	110 06.0	22.3	176 28.7	35.4	215 56.6	58.5	Deneb	49 27.3	N45 21.5
03	202 40.8	193 36.5 ..	08.2	125 07.4 ..	22.4	191 30.6 ..	35.6	230 58.8 ..	58.4	Denebola	182 26.2	N14 26.5
04	217 43.2	208 36.2	09.5	140 08.8	22.5	206 32.6	35.8	246 01.0	58.3	Diphda	348 49.1	S17 51.8
05	232 45.7	223 35.9	10.8	155 10.1	22.5	221 34.5	36.0	261 03.2	58.2			
06	247 48.2	238 35.6	N 3 12.1	170 11.5	N25 22.6	236 36.5	N 3 36.2	276 05.3	S12 58.1	Dubhe	193 42.2	N61 37.5
07	262 50.6	253 35.3	13.4	185 12.9	22.6	251 38.4	36.5	291 07.5	58.0	Elnath	278 03.7	N28 37.6
T 08	277 53.1	268 35.0	14.7	200 14.3	22.7	266 40.4	36.7	306 09.7	57.9	Eltanin	90 43.1	N51 28.8
U 09	292 55.6	283 34.7 ..	16.0	215 15.6 ..	22.7	281 42.3 ..	36.9	321 11.9 ..	57.8	Enif	33 40.6	N 9 58.7
E 10	307 58.0	298 34.4	17.3	230 17.0	22.8	296 44.3	37.1	336 14.0	57.7	Fomalhaut	15 16.6	S29 30.2
S 11	323 00.5	313 34.0	18.6	245 18.4	22.8	311 46.3	37.4	351 16.2	57.6			
D 12	338 03.0	328 33.7	N 3 19.9	260 19.8	N25 22.9	326 48.2	N 3 37.6	6 18.4	S12 57.5	Gacrux	171 52.9	S57 14.4
A 13	353 05.4	343 33.4	21.2	275 21.1	23.0	341 50.2	37.8	21 20.6	57.4	Gienah	175 44.9	S17 40.2
Y 14	8 07.9	358 33.1	22.5	290 22.5	23.0	356 52.1	38.0	36 22.7	57.3	Hadar	148 37.8	S60 28.9
15	23 10.4	13 32.8 ..	23.8	305 23.9 ..	23.1	11 54.1 ..	38.2	51 24.9 ..	57.2	Hamal	327 53.1	N23 34.3
16	38 12.8	28 32.5	25.1	320 25.2	23.1	26 56.0	38.5	66 27.1	57.1	Kaus Aust.	83 34.7	S34 22.4
17	53 15.3	43 32.2	26.4	335 26.6	23.2	41 58.0	38.7	81 29.3	57.0			
18	68 17.7	58 31.9	N 3 27.7	350 28.0	N25 23.2	56 59.9	N 3 38.9	96 31.4	S12 56.9	Kochab	137 19.3	N74 03.3
19	83 20.2	73 31.6	29.0	5 29.3	23.3	72 01.9	39.1	111 33.6	56.8	Markab	13 31.8	N15 19.6
20	98 22.7	88 31.2	30.3	20 30.7	23.3	87 03.8	39.4	126 35.8	56.7	Menkar	314 07.9	N 4 10.7
21	113 25.1	103 30.9 ..	31.6	35 32.1 ..	23.4	102 05.8 ..	39.6	141 38.0 ..	56.6	Menkent	147 59.2	S36 28.9
22	128 27.6	118 30.6	32.9	50 33.4	23.5	117 07.7	39.8	156 40.1	56.5	Miaplacidus	221 37.7	S69 48.8
23	143 30.1	133 30.3	34.2	65 34.8	23.5	132 09.7	40.0	171 42.3	56.4			
1 00	158 32.5	148 30.0	N 3 35.5	80 36.2	N25 23.6	147 11.6	N 3 40.2	186 44.5	S12 56.3	Mirfak	308 30.6	N49 56.7
01	173 35.0	163 29.7	36.8	95 37.5	23.6	162 13.6	40.5	201 46.7	56.2	Nunki	75 49.9	S26 16.1
02	188 37.5	178 29.4	38.1	110 38.9	23.7	177 15.5	40.7	216 48.9	56.1	Peacock	53 08.6	S56 39.6
03	203 39.9	193 29.1 ..	39.4	125 40.3 ..	23.7	192 17.5 ..	40.9	231 51.0 ..	56.0	Pollux	243 18.9	N27 58.2
04	218 42.4	208 28.8	40.7	140 41.6	23.8	207 19.4	41.1	246 53.2	55.9	Procyon	244 52.2	N 5 09.9
05	233 44.9	223 28.4	42.0	155 43.0	23.8	222 21.4	41.4	261 55.4	55.8			
06	248 47.3	238 28.1	N 3 43.3	170 44.3	N25 23.9	237 23.3	N 3 41.6	276 57.6	S12 55.7	Rasalhague	96 00.1	N12 32.4
W 07	263 49.8	253 27.8	44.6	185 45.7	23.9	252 25.3	41.8	291 59.7	55.6	Regulus	207 35.8	N11 51.2
E 08	278 52.2	268 27.5	45.9	200 47.1	24.0	267 27.2	42.0	307 01.9	55.5	Rigel	281 05.3	S 8 10.7
D 09	293 54.7	283 27.2 ..	47.2	215 48.4 ..	24.1	282 29.2 ..	42.3	322 04.1 ..	55.4	Rigil Kent.	139 42.1	S60 55.6
N 10	308 57.2	298 26.9	48.5	230 49.8	24.1	297 31.1	42.5	337 06.3	55.3	Sabik	102 04.6	S15 45.2
11	323 59.6	313 26.6	49.8	245 51.1	24.2	312 33.1	42.7	352 08.4	55.2			
E 12	339 02.1	328 26.3	N 3 51.1	260 52.5	N25 24.2	327 35.0	N 3 42.9	7 10.6	S12 55.1	Schedar	349 33.3	N56 39.9
S 13	354 04.6	343 25.9	52.4	275 53.9	24.3	342 36.9	43.1	22 12.8	55.0	Shaula	96 12.6	S37 07.1
D 14	9 07.0	358 25.6	53.7	290 55.2	24.3	357 38.9	43.4	37 15.0	54.9	Sirius	258 27.4	S16 45.0
A 15	24 09.5	13 25.3 ..	55.0	305 56.6 ..	24.4	12 40.8 ..	43.6	52 17.1 ..	54.8	Spica	158 23.7	S11 17.0
Y 16	39 12.0	28 25.0	56.3	320 57.9	24.4	27 42.8	43.8	67 19.3	54.7	Suhail	222 47.0	S43 31.7
17	54 14.4	43 24.7	57.6	335 59.3	24.5	42 44.7	44.0	82 21.5	54.6			
18	69 16.9	58 24.4	N 3 58.9	351 00.6	N25 24.5	57 46.7	N 3 44.3	97 23.7	S12 54.5	Vega	80 34.5	N38 48.0
19	84 19.4	73 24.1	4 00.2	6 02.0	24.6	72 48.6	44.5	112 25.8	54.4	Zuben'ubi	136 57.6	S16 08.3
20	99 21.8	88 23.8	01.5	21 03.4	24.6	87 50.6	44.7	127 28.0	54.3			
21	114 24.3	103 23.5 ..	02.8	36 04.7 ..	24.7	102 52.5 ..	44.9	142 30.2 ..	54.2		SHA	Mer. Pass.
22	129 26.7	118 23.1	04.1	51 06.1	24.7	117 54.5	45.2	157 32.4	54.1	Venus	351 04.1	14 06
23	144 29.2	133 22.8	05.3	66 07.4	24.8	132 56.4	45.4	172 34.5	54.0	Mars	282 29.9	18 38
Mer. Pass.	13 27.6	v −0.3	d 1.3	v 1.4	d 0.1	v 2.0	d 0.2	v 2.2	d 0.1	Jupiter	348 51.4	14 12
										Saturn	28 18.9	11 35

© British Crown Copyright 2022. All rights reserved.

UT	SUN GHA	SUN Dec	MOON GHA	v	MOON Dec	d	HP
d h	° ′	° ′	° ′	′	° ′	′	′
27 00	176 48.0	S 8 31.5	94 45.9	10.7	N23 23.2	8.2	55.7
01	191 48.1	30.6	109 15.6	10.6	23 31.4	8.0	55.7
02	206 48.2	29.6	123 45.2	10.6	23 39.4	8.0	55.6
03	221 48.3	. . 28.7	138 14.8	10.6	23 47.4	7.8	55.6
04	236 48.4	27.7	152 44.4	10.5	23 55.2	7.7	55.6
05	251 48.5	26.8	167 13.9	10.6	24 02.9	7.5	55.6
06	266 48.6	S 8 25.9	181 43.5	10.4	N24 10.4	7.5	55.5
M 07	281 48.7	24.9	196 12.9	10.5	24 17.9	7.3	55.5
O 08	296 48.8	24.0	210 42.4	10.4	24 25.2	7.2	55.5
N 09	311 49.0	. . 23.0	225 11.8	10.4	24 32.4	7.0	55.4
D 10	326 49.1	22.1	239 41.2	10.4	24 39.4	7.0	55.4
A 11	341 49.2	21.2	254 10.6	10.3	24 46.4	6.8	55.4
Y 12	356 49.3	S 8 20.2	268 39.9	10.3	N24 53.2	6.6	55.4
13	11 49.4	19.3	283 09.2	10.3	24 59.8	6.6	55.3
14	26 49.5	18.3	297 38.5	10.3	25 06.4	6.4	55.3
15	41 49.6	. . 17.4	312 07.8	10.2	25 12.8	6.3	55.3
16	56 49.7	16.5	326 37.0	10.2	25 19.1	6.1	55.3
17	71 49.8	15.5	341 06.2	10.2	25 25.2	6.0	55.2
18	86 49.9	S 8 14.6	355 35.4	10.2	N25 31.2	5.9	55.2
19	101 50.1	13.6	10 04.6	10.1	25 37.1	5.8	55.2
20	116 50.2	12.7	24 33.7	10.1	25 42.9	5.6	55.2
21	131 50.3	. . 11.8	39 02.8	10.1	25 48.5	5.5	55.1
22	146 50.4	10.8	53 31.9	10.0	25 54.0	5.4	55.1
23	161 50.5	09.9	68 00.9	10.1	25 59.4	5.2	55.1
28 00	176 50.6	S 8 08.9	82 30.0	10.0	N26 04.6	5.1	55.1
01	191 50.7	08.0	96 59.0	10.0	26 09.7	5.0	55.0
02	206 50.8	07.0	111 28.0	10.0	26 14.7	4.8	55.0
03	221 51.0	. . 06.1	125 57.0	9.9	26 19.5	4.7	55.0
04	236 51.1	05.2	140 25.9	10.0	26 24.2	4.6	55.0
05	251 51.2	04.2	154 54.9	9.9	26 28.8	4.4	54.9
06	266 51.3	S 8 03.3	169 23.8	9.9	N26 33.2	4.3	54.9
T 07	281 51.4	02.3	183 52.7	9.9	26 37.5	4.2	54.9
U 08	296 51.5	01.4	198 21.6	9.9	26 41.7	4.0	54.9
E 09	311 51.6	8 00.4	212 50.5	9.9	26 45.7	3.9	54.9
S 10	326 51.8	7 59.5	227 19.4	9.8	26 49.6	3.7	54.8
D 11	341 51.9	58.5	241 48.2	9.9	26 53.3	3.7	54.8
A 12	356 52.0	S 7 57.6	256 17.1	9.8	N26 57.0	3.5	54.8
Y 13	11 52.1	56.6	270 45.9	9.8	27 00.5	3.3	54.8
14	26 52.2	55.7	285 14.7	9.8	27 03.8	3.2	54.7
15	41 52.3	. . 54.8	299 43.5	9.8	27 07.0	3.1	54.7
16	56 52.4	53.8	314 12.3	9.8	27 10.1	2.9	54.7
17	71 52.6	52.9	328 41.1	9.8	27 13.0	2.9	54.7
18	86 52.7	S 7 51.9	343 09.9	9.8	N27 15.9	2.6	54.7
19	101 52.8	51.0	357 38.7	9.7	27 18.5	2.6	54.7
20	116 52.9	50.0	12 07.4	9.8	27 21.1	2.4	54.6
21	131 53.0	. . 49.1	26 36.2	9.8	27 23.5	2.2	54.6
22	146 53.2	48.1	41 05.0	9.7	27 25.7	2.1	54.6
23	161 53.3	47.2	55 33.7	9.8	27 27.8	2.0	54.6
1 00	176 53.4	S 7 46.2	70 02.5	9.7	N27 29.8	1.9	54.6
01	191 53.5	45.3	84 31.2	9.8	27 31.7	1.7	54.5
02	206 53.6	44.3	99 00.0	9.8	27 33.4	1.6	54.5
03	221 53.7	. . 43.4	113 28.8	9.7	27 35.0	1.4	54.5
04	236 53.9	42.4	127 57.5	9.8	27 36.4	1.3	54.5
05	251 54.0	41.5	142 26.3	9.8	27 37.7	1.2	54.5
06	266 54.1	S 7 40.5	156 55.1	9.8	N27 38.9	1.0	54.5
W 07	281 54.2	39.6	171 23.9	9.7	27 39.9	0.9	54.5
E 08	296 54.3	38.6	185 52.6	9.8	27 40.8	0.8	54.4
D 09	311 54.5	. . 37.7	200 21.4	9.8	27 41.6	0.6	54.4
N 10	326 54.6	36.7	214 50.2	9.9	27 42.2	0.5	54.4
E 11	341 54.7	35.8	229 19.1	9.8	27 42.7	0.4	54.4
S 12	356 54.8	S 7 34.8	243 47.9	9.8	N27 43.1	0.2	54.4
D 13	11 54.9	33.9	258 16.7	9.9	27 43.3	0.1	54.4
A 14	26 55.1	32.9	272 45.6	9.8	27 43.4	0.1	54.3
Y 15	41 55.2	. . 32.0	287 14.4	9.9	27 43.5	0.2	54.3
16	56 55.3	31.0	301 43.3	9.9	27 43.1	0.3	54.3
17	71 55.4	30.1	316 12.2	9.9	27 42.8	0.5	54.3
18	86 55.5	S 7 29.1	330 41.1	9.9	N27 42.3	0.6	54.3
19	101 55.7	28.2	345 10.0	10.0	27 41.7	0.7	54.3
20	116 55.8	27.2	359 39.0	9.9	27 41.0	0.9	54.3
21	131 55.9	. . 26.3	14 07.9	10.0	27 40.1	1.0	54.3
22	146 56.0	25.3	28 36.9	10.0	27 39.1	1.1	54.3
23	161 56.2	24.4	43 05.9	10.1	N27 38.0	1.3	54.2
	SD 16.2 d 0.9		SD 15.1		14.9		14.8

Twilight / Sunrise / Moonrise

Lat.	Twilight Naut.	Twilight Civil	Sunrise	Moonrise 27	28	1	2
°	h m	h m	h m	h m	h m	h m	h m
N 72	05 16	06 34	07 44	▢	▢	▢	▢
N 70	05 21	06 31	07 33	▢	▢	▢	▢
68	05 24	06 28	07 25	▢	▢	▢	▢
66	05 27	06 26	07 18	▢	▢	▢	▢
64	05 29	06 24	07 12	07 26	▢	▢	▢
62	05 31	06 22	07 07	08 04	08 05	08 20	09 28
60	05 32	06 20	07 02	08 31	08 47	09 20	10 20
N 58	05 34	06 19	06 58	08 53	09 15	09 53	10 51
56	05 34	06 17	06 55	09 10	09 37	10 18	11 15
54	05 35	06 16	06 52	09 25	09 55	10 38	11 34
52	05 36	06 15	06 49	09 38	10 11	10 54	11 50
50	05 36	06 14	06 46	09 49	10 24	11 09	12 04
45	05 37	06 11	06 40	10 13	10 51	11 38	12 33
N 40	05 37	06 08	06 35	10 32	11 13	12 01	12 55
35	05 36	06 06	06 31	10 48	11 31	12 20	13 13
30	05 36	06 03	06 27	11 02	11 47	12 36	13 29
20	05 33	05 59	06 21	11 26	12 13	13 03	13 56
N 10	05 29	05 54	06 15	11 47	12 36	13 27	14 19
0	05 24	05 48	06 09	12 06	12 57	13 49	14 40
S 10	05 17	05 42	06 03	12 25	13 19	14 11	15 02
20	05 09	05 35	05 57	12 46	13 42	14 35	15 24
30	04 57	05 26	05 50	13 11	14 08	15 02	15 51
35	04 49	05 20	05 46	13 25	14 24	15 19	16 07
40	04 40	05 13	05 41	13 42	14 43	15 38	16 25
45	04 28	05 05	05 35	14 02	15 05	16 01	16 47
S 50	04 14	04 55	05 28	14 27	15 34	16 30	17 15
52	04 06	04 50	05 25	14 40	15 48	16 45	17 28
54	03 58	04 45	05 22	14 54	16 04	17 01	17 44
56	03 49	04 38	05 18	15 10	16 24	17 22	18 02
58	03 38	04 32	05 14	15 30	16 48	17 47	18 25
S 60	03 25	04 24	05 09	15 55	17 20	18 22	18 54

Sunset / Twilight / Moonset

Lat.	Sunset	Twilight Civil	Twilight Naut.	Moonset 27	28	1	2
°	h m	h m	h m	h m	h m	h m	h m
N 72	16 43	17 53	19 12	▢	▢	▢	▢
N 70	16 54	17 56	19 07	▢	▢	▢	▢
68	17 02	17 59	19 03	▢	▢	▢	▢
66	17 09	18 01	19 00	▢	▢	▢	▢
64	17 15	18 03	18 58	04 09	▢	▢	▢
62	17 20	18 04	18 56	03 31	05 17	06 50	07 29
60	17 24	18 06	18 54	03 05	04 36	05 51	06 37
N 58	17 28	18 07	18 53	02 44	04 08	05 17	06 06
56	17 31	18 09	18 52	02 27	03 46	04 52	05 42
54	17 34	18 10	18 51	02 13	03 28	04 33	05 22
52	17 37	18 11	18 50	02 01	03 13	04 16	05 06
50	17 40	18 12	18 50	01 50	03 00	04 02	04 52
45	17 46	18 15	18 49	01 27	02 33	03 33	04 23
N 40	17 50	18 18	18 49	01 08	02 12	03 10	04 01
35	17 54	18 20	18 49	00 53	01 54	02 51	03 42
30	17 58	18 22	18 50	00 40	01 39	02 35	03 26
20	18 05	18 27	18 52	00 17	01 13	02 08	02 59
N 10	18 10	18 31	18 56	24 51	00 51	01 44	02 36
0	18 16	18 37	19 01	24 31	00 31	01 22	02 14
S 10	18 21	18 43	19 07	24 10	00 10	01 00	01 52
20	18 28	18 50	19 16	23 48	24 37	00 37	01 28
30	18 35	18 59	19 28	23 23	24 10	00 10	01 01
35	18 39	19 05	19 35	23 08	23 54	24 45	00 45
40	18 44	19 11	19 44	22 50	23 35	24 26	00 26
45	18 49	19 19	19 55	22 30	23 12	24 03	00 03
S 50	18 56	19 29	20 10	22 04	22 43	23 34	24 34
52	18 59	19 34	20 17	21 51	22 29	23 19	24 20
54	19 02	19 39	20 25	21 37	22 13	23 02	24 05
56	19 06	19 45	20 34	21 20	21 53	22 42	23 47
58	19 10	19 52	20 45	21 00	21 29	22 17	23 24
S 60	19 15	19 59	20 57	20 34	20 56	21 42	22 55

SUN / MOON

Day	SUN Eqn. of Time 00h	12h	Mer. Pass.	MOON Mer. Pass. Upper	Lower	Age	Phase
d	m s	m s	h m	h m	h m	d	%
27	12 48	12 43	12 13	18 18	05 53	07	52
28	12 38	12 32	12 13	19 10	06 44	08	61
1	12 27	12 21	12 12	20 01	07 36	09	70

© British Crown Copyright 2022. All rights reserved.

UT	ARIES	VENUS −3.9		MARS +0.5		JUPITER −2.1		SATURN +0.8		STARS		
	GHA	GHA	Dec	GHA	Dec	GHA	Dec	GHA	Dec	Name	SHA	Dec
d h	° ′	° ′	° ′	° ′	° ′	° ′	° ′	° ′	° ′		° ′	° ′
2 00	159 31.7	148 22.5 N 4 06.6		81 08.8 N25 24.8		147 58.4 N 3 45.6		187 36.7 S12 53.8		Acamar	315 13.1	S40 13.0
01	174 34.1	163 22.2	07.9	96 10.1	24.9	163 00.3	45.8	202 38.9	53.7	Achernar	335 21.7	S57 07.4
02	189 36.6	178 21.9	09.2	111 11.5	25.0	178 02.3	46.0	217 41.1	53.6	Acrux	173 01.2	S63 13.5
03	204 39.1	193 21.6 . .	10.5	126 12.8 . .	25.0	193 04.2 . .	46.3	232 43.3 . .	53.5	Adhara	255 06.9	S29 00.4
04	219 41.5	208 21.3	11.8	141 14.2	25.1	208 06.2	46.5	247 45.4	53.4	Aldebaran	290 41.4	N16 33.3
05	234 44.0	223 21.0	13.1	156 15.5	25.1	223 08.1	46.7	262 47.6	53.3			
06	249 46.5	238 20.6 N 4 14.4		171 16.9 N25 25.2		238 10.1 N 3 46.9		277 49.8 S12 53.2		Alioth	166 13.8	N55 49.9
07	264 48.9	253 20.3	15.7	186 18.2	25.2	253 12.0	47.2	292 52.0	53.1	Alkaid	152 52.9	N49 11.6
T 08	279 51.4	268 20.0	17.0	201 19.6	25.3	268 14.0	47.4	307 54.1	53.0	Alnair	27 35.3	S46 51.0
H 09	294 53.8	283 19.7 . .	18.3	216 20.9 . .	25.3	283 15.9 . .	47.6	322 56.3 . .	52.9	Alnilam	275 39.2	S 1 11.3
U 10	309 56.3	298 19.4	19.6	231 22.3	25.4	298 17.8	47.8	337 58.5	52.8	Alphard	217 49.0	S 8 45.6
R 11	324 58.8	313 19.1	20.9	246 23.6	25.4	313 19.8	48.1	353 00.7	52.7			
S 12	340 01.2	328 18.8 N 4 22.2		261 24.9 N25 25.5		328 21.7 N 3 48.3		8 02.8 S12 52.6		Alphecca	126 04.9	N26 38.0
D 13	355 03.7	343 18.5	23.5	276 26.3	25.5	343 23.7	48.5	23 05.0	52.5	Alpheratz	357 36.7	N29 13.0
A 14	10 06.2	358 18.1	24.8	291 27.6	25.6	358 25.6	48.7	38 07.2	52.4	Altair	62 01.7	N 8 55.6
Y 15	25 08.6	13 17.8 . .	26.1	306 29.0 . .	25.6	13 27.6 . .	48.9	53 09.4 . .	52.3	Ankaa	353 09.0	S42 11.0
16	40 11.1	28 17.5	27.4	321 30.3	25.7	28 29.5	49.2	68 11.5	52.2	Antares	112 17.7	S26 29.0
17	55 13.6	43 17.2	28.6	336 31.7	25.7	43 31.5	49.4	83 13.7	52.1			
18	70 16.0	58 16.9 N 4 29.9		351 33.0 N25 25.8		58 33.4 N 3 49.6		98 15.9 S12 52.0		Arcturus	145 49.1	N19 03.5
19	85 18.5	73 16.6	31.2	6 34.3	25.8	73 35.4	49.8	113 18.1	51.9	Atria	107 13.4	S69 03.9
20	100 21.0	88 16.3	32.5	21 35.7	25.9	88 37.3	50.1	128 20.3	51.8	Avior	234 14.9	S59 35.2
21	115 23.4	103 16.0 . .	33.8	36 37.0 . .	25.9	103 39.3 . .	50.3	143 22.4 . .	51.7	Bellatrix	278 24.5	N 6 22.2
22	130 25.9	118 15.6	35.1	51 38.4	26.0	118 41.2	50.5	158 24.6	51.6	Betelgeuse	270 53.6	N 7 24.6
23	145 28.3	133 15.3	36.4	66 39.7	26.0	133 43.1	50.7	173 26.8	51.5			
3 00	160 30.8	148 15.0 N 4 37.7		81 41.0 N25 26.1		148 45.1 N 3 51.0		188 29.0 S12 51.4		Canopus	263 52.9	S52 42.7
01	175 33.3	163 14.7	39.0	96 42.4	26.1	163 47.0	51.2	203 31.1	51.3	Capella	280 24.1	N46 01.4
02	190 35.7	178 14.4	40.3	111 43.7	26.2	178 49.0	51.4	218 33.3	51.2	Deneb	49 27.2	N45 21.5
03	205 38.2	193 14.1 . .	41.6	126 45.1 . .	26.2	193 50.9 . .	51.6	233 35.5 . .	51.1	Denebola	182 26.2	N14 26.5
04	220 40.7	208 13.8	42.9	141 46.4	26.3	208 52.9	51.9	248 37.7	51.0	Diphda	348 49.1	S17 51.8
05	235 43.1	223 13.5	44.2	156 47.7	26.3	223 54.8	52.1	263 39.8	50.9			
06	250 45.6	238 13.1 N 4 45.4		171 49.1 N25 26.4		238 56.8 N 3 52.3		278 42.0 S12 50.8		Dubhe	193 42.2	N61 37.5
07	265 48.1	253 12.8	46.7	186 50.4	26.4	253 58.7	52.5	293 44.2	50.7	Elnath	278 03.7	N28 37.6
08	280 50.5	268 12.5	48.0	201 51.7	26.5	269 00.7	52.7	308 46.4	50.6	Eltanin	90 43.1	N51 28.8
F 09	295 53.0	283 12.2 . .	49.3	216 53.1 . .	26.5	284 02.6 . .	53.0	323 48.6 . .	50.5	Enif	33 40.6	N 9 58.7
R 10	310 55.5	298 11.9	50.6	231 54.4	26.6	299 04.5	53.2	338 50.7	50.5	Fomalhaut	15 16.6	S29 30.2
I 11	325 57.9	313 11.6	51.9	246 55.7	26.6	314 06.5	53.4	353 52.9	50.3			
D 12	341 00.4	328 11.3 N 4 53.2		261 57.1 N25 26.7		329 08.4 N 3 53.6		8 55.1 S12 50.2		Gacrux	171 52.8	S57 14.5
A 13	356 02.8	343 10.9	54.5	276 58.4	26.7	344 10.4	53.9	23 57.3	50.1	Gienah	175 44.9	S17 40.3
Y 14	11 05.3	358 10.6	55.8	291 59.7	26.8	359 12.3	54.1	38 59.4	50.0	Hadar	148 37.8	S60 28.9
15	26 07.8	13 10.3 . .	57.1	307 01.1 . .	26.8	14 14.3 . .	54.3	54 01.6 . .	49.9	Hamal	327 53.1	N23 34.3
16	41 10.2	28 10.0	58.3	322 02.4	26.9	29 16.2	54.5	69 03.8	49.8	Kaus Aust.	83 34.7	S34 22.4
17	56 12.7	43 09.7	4 59.6	337 03.7	26.9	44 18.2	54.8	84 06.0	49.7			
18	71 15.2	58 09.4 N 5 00.9		352 05.1 N25 27.0		59 20.1 N 3 55.0		99 08.2 S12 49.6		Kochab	137 19.2	N74 03.3
19	86 17.6	73 09.1	02.2	7 06.4	27.0	74 22.0	55.2	114 10.3	49.5	Markab	13 31.7	N15 19.6
20	101 20.1	88 08.7	03.5	22 07.7	27.1	89 24.0	55.4	129 12.5	49.4	Menkar	314 07.9	N 4 10.7
21	116 22.6	103 08.4 . .	04.8	37 09.1 . .	27.1	104 25.9 . .	55.7	144 14.7 . .	49.3	Menkent	147 59.2	S36 28.9
22	131 25.0	118 08.1	06.1	52 10.4	27.2	119 27.9	55.9	159 16.9	49.2	Miaplacidus	221 37.8	S69 48.8
23	146 27.5	133 07.8	07.4	67 11.7	27.2	134 29.8	56.1	174 19.0	49.1			
4 00	161 29.9	148 07.5 N 5 08.6		82 13.0 N25 27.3		149 31.8 N 3 56.3		189 21.2 S12 49.0		Mirfak	308 30.6	N49 56.7
01	176 32.4	163 07.2	09.9	97 14.4	27.3	164 33.7	56.6	204 23.4	48.9	Nunki	75 49.8	S26 16.1
02	191 34.9	178 06.9	11.2	112 15.7	27.4	179 35.6	56.8	219 25.6	48.8	Peacock	53 08.6	S56 39.6
03	206 37.3	193 06.5 . .	12.5	127 17.0 . .	27.4	194 37.6 . .	57.0	234 27.8 . .	48.7	Pollux	243 18.9	N27 58.2
04	221 39.8	208 06.2	13.8	142 18.3	27.5	209 39.5	57.2	249 29.9	48.6	Procyon	244 52.2	N 5 09.9
05	236 42.3	223 05.9	15.1	157 19.7	27.5	224 41.5	57.5	264 32.1	48.5			
06	251 44.7	238 05.6 N 5 16.4		172 21.0 N25 27.6		239 43.4 N 3 57.7		279 34.3 S12 48.4		Rasalhague	96 00.0	N12 32.4
07	266 47.2	253 05.3	17.7	187 22.3	27.6	254 45.4	57.9	294 36.5	48.3	Regulus	207 35.7	N11 51.2
S 08	281 49.7	268 05.0	18.9	202 23.6	27.6	269 47.3	58.1	309 38.6	48.2	Rigel	281 05.3	S 8 10.7
A 09	296 52.1	283 04.7 . .	20.2	217 25.0 . .	27.7	284 49.3 . .	58.4	324 40.8 . .	48.1	Rigil Kent.	139 42.1	S60 55.6
T 10	311 54.6	298 04.3	21.5	232 26.3	27.7	299 51.2	58.6	339 43.0	48.0	Sabik	102 04.6	S15 45.3
U 11	326 57.1	313 04.0	22.8	247 27.6	27.8	314 53.1	58.8	354 45.2	47.9			
R 12	341 59.5	328 03.7 N 5 24.1		262 28.9 N25 27.8		329 55.1 N 3 59.0		9 47.4 S12 47.8		Schedar	349 33.3	N56 39.9
D 13	357 02.0	343 03.4	25.4	277 30.2	27.9	344 57.0	59.2	24 49.5	47.7	Shaula	96 12.5	S37 07.1
A 14	12 04.4	358 03.1	26.6	292 31.6	27.9	359 59.0	59.5	39 51.7	47.6	Sirius	258 27.4	S16 45.0
Y 15	27 06.9	13 02.8 . .	27.9	307 32.9 . .	28.0	15 00.9 . .	59.7	54 53.9 . .	47.5	Spica	158 23.7	S11 17.0
16	42 09.4	28 02.4	29.2	322 34.2	28.0	30 02.8	3 59.9	69 56.1	47.4	Suhail	222 47.0	S43 31.7
17	57 11.8	43 02.1	30.5	337 35.5	28.1	45 04.8	4 00.1	84 58.2	47.3			
18	72 14.3	58 01.8 N 5 31.8		352 36.8 N25 28.1		60 06.7 N 4 00.4		100 00.4 S12 47.2		Vega	80 34.4	N38 48.0
19	87 16.8	73 01.5	33.1	7 38.2	28.2	75 08.7	00.6	115 02.6	47.1	Zuben'ubi	136 57.6	S16 08.3
20	102 19.2	88 01.2	34.4	22 39.5	28.2	90 10.6	00.8	130 04.8	47.0			
21	117 21.7	103 00.9 . .	35.6	37 40.8 . .	28.3	105 12.6 . .	01.0	145 07.0 . .	46.9		SHA	Mer. Pass.
22	132 24.2	118 00.6	36.9	52 42.1	28.3	120 14.5	01.3	160 09.1	46.8		° ′	h m
23	147 26.7	133 00.2	38.2	67 43.4	28.3	135 16.4	01.5	175 11.3	46.7	Venus	347 44.2	14 07
	h m									Mars	281 10.2	18 32
Mer. Pass. 13 15.8		v −0.3 d 1.3		v 1.3 d 0.0		v 1.9 d 0.2		v 2.2 d 0.1		Jupiter	348 14.3	14 03
										Saturn	27 58.2	11 24

© British Crown Copyright 2022. All rights reserved.

SUN and MOON

UT (d h)	SUN GHA	SUN Dec	MOON GHA	v	MOON Dec	d	HP
2 00	176 56.3	S 7 23.4	57 35.0	10.0	N27 36.7	1.4	54.2
01	191 56.4	22.5	72 04.0	10.1	27 35.3	1.5	54.2
02	206 56.5	21.5	86 33.1	10.1	27 33.8	1.6	54.2
03	221 56.7	.. 20.6	101 02.2	10.1	27 32.2	1.8	54.2
04	236 56.8	19.6	115 31.3	10.2	27 30.4	2.0	54.2
05	251 56.9	18.7	130 00.5	10.2	27 28.4	2.0	54.2
T 06	266 57.0	S 7 17.7	144 29.7	10.2	N27 26.4	2.2	54.2
H 07	281 57.2	16.8	158 58.9	10.2	27 24.2	2.3	54.2
U 08	296 57.3	15.8	173 28.1	10.3	27 21.9	2.5	54.2
R 09	311 57.4	.. 14.9	187 57.4	10.3	27 19.4	2.6	54.2
S 10	326 57.5	13.9	202 26.7	10.4	27 16.8	2.7	54.1
D 11	341 57.7	12.9	216 56.1	10.4	27 14.1	2.8	54.1
A 12	356 57.8	S 7 12.0	231 25.5	10.4	N27 11.3	3.0	54.1
Y 13	11 57.9	11.0	245 54.9	10.4	27 08.3	3.1	54.1
14	26 58.0	10.1	260 24.3	10.5	27 05.2	3.2	54.1
15	41 58.2	.. 09.1	274 53.8	10.5	27 02.0	3.4	54.1
16	56 58.3	08.2	289 23.3	10.6	26 58.6	3.5	54.1
17	71 58.4	07.2	303 52.9	10.6	26 55.1	3.6	54.1
18	86 58.5	S 7 06.3	318 22.5	10.6	N26 51.5	3.7	54.1
19	101 58.7	05.3	332 52.1	10.7	26 47.8	3.9	54.1
20	116 58.8	04.4	347 21.8	10.7	26 43.9	4.0	54.1
21	131 58.9	.. 03.4	1 51.5	10.8	26 39.9	4.1	54.1
22	146 59.1	02.4	16 21.3	10.8	26 35.8	4.2	54.1
23	161 59.2	01.5	30 51.1	10.8	26 31.6	4.4	54.1
3 00	176 59.3	S 7 00.5	45 20.9	10.9	N26 27.2	4.4	54.1
01	191 59.4	6 59.6	59 50.8	11.0	26 22.8	4.6	54.1
02	206 59.6	58.6	74 20.8	10.9	26 18.2	4.8	54.1
03	221 59.7	.. 57.7	88 50.7	11.1	26 13.4	4.8	54.0
04	236 59.8	56.7	103 20.8	11.0	26 08.6	5.0	54.0
05	252 00.0	55.7	117 50.8	11.0	26 03.6	5.1	54.0
F 06	267 00.1	S 6 54.8	132 21.0	11.1	N25 58.5	5.2	54.0
R 07	282 00.2	53.8	146 51.1	11.2	25 53.3	5.3	54.0
I 08	297 00.4	52.9	161 21.3	11.3	25 48.0	5.5	54.0
D 09	312 00.5	.. 51.9	175 51.6	11.3	25 42.5	5.5	54.0
A 10	327 00.6	51.0	190 21.9	11.4	25 37.0	5.7	54.0
Y 11	342 00.7	50.0	204 52.3	11.4	25 31.3	5.8	54.0
12	357 00.9	S 6 49.0	219 22.7	11.5	N25 25.5	5.9	54.0
13	12 01.0	48.1	233 53.2	11.5	25 19.6	6.1	54.0
14	27 01.1	47.1	248 23.7	11.5	25 13.5	6.1	54.0
15	42 01.3	.. 46.2	262 54.2	11.7	25 07.4	6.3	54.0
16	57 01.4	45.2	277 24.9	11.6	25 01.1	6.4	54.0
17	72 01.5	44.2	291 55.5	11.8	24 54.7	6.4	54.0
18	87 01.7	S 6 43.3	306 26.3	11.7	N24 48.3	6.6	54.0
19	102 01.8	42.3	320 57.0	11.9	24 41.7	6.8	54.0
20	117 01.9	41.4	335 27.9	11.8	24 34.9	6.8	54.0
21	132 02.1	.. 40.4	349 58.7	12.0	24 28.1	6.9	54.0
22	147 02.2	39.4	4 29.7	12.0	24 21.2	7.0	54.0
23	162 02.3	38.5	19 00.7	12.0	24 14.2	7.2	54.0
4 00	177 02.5	S 6 37.5	33 31.7	12.1	N24 07.0	7.3	54.0
01	192 02.6	36.6	48 02.8	12.2	23 59.7	7.3	54.0
02	207 02.7	35.6	62 34.0	12.2	23 52.4	7.5	54.0
03	222 02.9	.. 34.6	77 05.2	12.3	23 44.9	7.6	54.0
04	237 03.0	33.7	91 36.5	12.3	23 37.3	7.7	54.0
05	252 03.1	32.7	106 07.8	12.4	23 29.6	7.8	54.0
S 06	267 03.3	S 6 31.8	120 39.2	12.4	N23 21.8	7.8	54.0
A 07	282 03.4	30.8	135 10.6	12.5	23 14.0	8.0	54.0
T 08	297 03.5	29.8	149 42.1	12.5	23 06.0	8.1	54.0
U 09	312 03.7	.. 28.9	164 13.6	12.6	22 57.9	8.2	54.0
R 10	327 03.8	27.9	178 45.2	12.7	22 49.7	8.3	54.1
D 11	342 04.0	26.9	193 16.9	12.7	22 41.4	8.4	54.1
A 12	357 04.1	S 6 26.0	207 48.6	12.8	N22 33.0	8.5	54.1
Y 13	12 04.2	25.0	222 20.4	12.8	22 24.5	8.6	54.1
14	27 04.4	24.1	236 52.2	12.9	22 15.9	8.7	54.1
15	42 04.5	.. 23.1	251 24.1	12.9	22 07.2	8.8	54.1
16	57 04.6	22.1	265 56.0	13.0	21 58.4	8.9	54.1
17	72 04.8	21.2	280 28.0	13.0	21 49.5	9.0	54.1
18	87 04.9	S 6 20.2	295 00.0	13.1	N21 40.5	9.1	54.1
19	102 05.0	19.2	309 32.1	13.2	21 31.4	9.2	54.1
20	117 05.2	18.3	324 04.3	13.2	21 22.2	9.2	54.1
21	132 05.3	.. 17.3	338 36.5	13.3	21 13.0	9.4	54.1
22	147 05.5	16.4	353 08.8	13.3	21 03.6	9.5	54.1
23	162 05.6	15.4	7 41.1	13.4	N20 54.1	9.5	54.1
SD	16.2	d 1.0	14.7		14.7		14.7

Twilight / Moonrise

Lat.	Naut.	Civil	Sunrise	Moonrise 2	3	4	5
N 72	05 01	06 19	07 28	▢	▢	▢	▢
N 70	05 07	06 18	07 19	▢	▢	▢	12 25
68	05 12	06 16	07 12	▢	▢	▢	13 13
66	05 16	06 15	07 06	▢	▢	11 33	13 44
64	05 19	06 14	07 02	▢	10 06	12 18	14 07
62	05 22	06 13	06 57	09 28	11 07	12 48	14 25
60	05 24	06 12	06 54	10 20	11 41	13 10	14 39
N 58	05 26	06 11	06 50	10 51	12 06	13 28	14 52
56	05 27	06 10	06 47	11 15	12 25	13 43	15 03
54	05 28	06 09	06 45	11 34	12 42	13 56	15 12
52	05 29	06 08	06 42	11 50	12 56	14 07	15 21
50	05 30	06 08	06 40	12 04	13 08	14 17	15 28
45	05 32	06 06	06 35	12 33	13 34	14 38	15 44
N 40	05 32	06 04	06 31	12 55	13 54	14 55	15 57
35	05 33	06 02	06 27	13 13	14 10	15 09	16 08
30	05 32	06 00	06 24	13 29	14 25	15 21	16 18
20	05 31	05 56	06 19	13 56	14 49	15 42	16 35
N 10	05 28	05 52	06 13	14 19	15 10	16 00	16 49
0	05 24	05 48	06 09	14 40	15 30	16 17	17 02
S 10	05 18	05 43	06 04	15 02	15 49	16 34	17 16
20	05 10	05 36	05 58	15 24	16 10	16 52	17 30
30	04 59	05 28	05 52	15 51	16 34	17 12	17 46
35	04 52	05 23	05 48	16 07	16 48	17 24	17 55
40	04 44	05 17	05 44	16 25	17 05	17 38	18 06
45	04 33	05 09	05 39	16 47	17 24	17 54	18 19
S 50	04 20	05 00	05 33	17 15	17 48	18 14	18 34
52	04 13	04 56	05 31	17 28	18 00	18 23	18 41
54	04 06	04 51	05 28	17 44	18 13	18 34	18 49
56	03 57	04 45	05 24	18 02	18 29	18 46	18 57
58	03 47	04 39	05 21	18 25	18 47	18 59	19 07
S 60	03 36	04 32	05 17	18 54	19 09	19 15	19 18

Sunset / Twilight / Moonset

Lat.	Sunset	Civil	Naut.	Moonset 2	3	4	5
N 72	16 58	18 07	19 26	▢	▢	▢	▢
N 70	17 06	18 08	19 19	▢	▢	▢	09 35
68	17 13	18 09	19 14	▢	▢	▢	08 45
66	17 19	18 11	19 10	▢	▢	08 49	08 13
64	17 24	18 12	19 07	▢	08 36	08 03	07 50
62	17 28	18 13	19 04	07 29	07 34	07 33	07 31
60	17 32	18 13	19 02	06 37	07 00	07 10	07 15
N 58	17 35	18 14	19 00	06 06	06 35	06 52	07 02
56	17 38	18 15	18 58	05 42	06 15	06 36	06 50
54	17 40	18 16	18 57	05 22	05 58	06 23	06 40
52	17 43	18 17	18 56	05 06	05 44	06 11	06 31
50	17 45	18 18	18 55	04 52	05 31	06 01	06 23
45	17 50	18 19	18 53	04 23	05 05	05 39	06 06
N 40	17 54	18 21	18 52	04 01	04 45	05 21	05 52
35	17 57	18 22	18 52	03 42	04 27	05 06	05 39
30	18 00	18 24	18 52	03 26	04 12	04 53	05 29
20	18 06	18 28	18 53	02 59	03 47	04 31	05 10
N 10	18 11	18 32	18 56	02 36	03 25	04 11	04 54
0	18 15	18 36	19 00	02 14	03 04	03 53	04 39
S 10	18 20	18 41	19 06	01 52	02 44	03 35	04 24
20	18 25	18 48	19 13	01 28	02 22	03 15	04 08
30	18 31	18 56	19 24	01 01	01 56	02 52	03 49
35	18 35	19 01	19 31	00 45	01 40	02 39	03 38
40	18 39	19 06	19 39	00 26	01 23	02 23	03 25
45	18 44	19 14	19 50	00 03	01 01	02 04	03 10
S 50	18 49	19 23	20 03	24 34	00 34	01 41	02 51
52	18 52	19 27	20 09	24 20	00 20	01 30	02 42
54	18 55	19 32	20 17	24 05	00 05	01 17	02 32
56	18 58	19 37	20 25	23 50	24 44	01 02	02 22
58	19 02	19 43	20 34	23 24	24 23	00 44	02 08
S 60	19 06	19 50	20 46	22 55	24 23	00 23	01 53

SUN and MOON

Day	Eqn. of Time 00ʰ	Eqn. of Time 12ʰ	Mer. Pass.	Mer. Pass. Upper	Mer. Pass. Lower	Age	Phase
2	12 15	12 09	12 12	20 52	08 27	10	79
3	12 03	11 57	12 12	21 41	09 17	11	86
4	11 50	11 44	12 12	22 28	10 05	12	92

© British Crown Copyright 2022. All rights reserved.

UT (d h)	ARIES GHA	VENUS −4.0 GHA	Dec	MARS +0.5 GHA	Dec	JUPITER −2.1 GHA	Dec	SATURN +0.8 GHA	Dec
5 00	162 29.1	147 59.9	N 5 39.5	82 44.7	N25 28.4	150 18.4	N 4 01.7	190 13.5	S12 46.6
01	177 31.6	162 59.6	40.8	97 46.0	28.4	165 20.3	01.9	205 15.7	46.5
02	192 34.0	177 59.3	42.0	112 47.4	28.5	180 22.3	02.2	220 17.9	46.4
03	207 36.5	192 59.0 ..	43.3	127 48.7 ..	28.5	195 24.2 ..	02.4	235 20.0 ..	46.3
04	222 38.9	207 58.7	44.6	142 50.0	28.6	210 26.1	02.6	250 22.2	46.2
05	237 41.4	222 58.3	45.9	157 51.3	28.6	225 28.1	02.8	265 24.4	46.1
06	252 43.9	237 58.0	N 5 47.2	172 52.6	N25 28.7	240 30.0	N 4 03.1	280 26.6	S12 46.0
07	267 46.3	252 57.7	48.5	187 53.9	28.7	255 32.0	03.3	295 28.7	45.9
08	282 48.8	267 57.4	49.7	202 55.2	28.7	270 33.9	03.5	310 30.9	45.8
S 09	297 51.3	282 57.1 ..	51.0	217 56.5 ..	28.8	285 35.9 ..	03.7	325 33.1 ..	45.7
U 10	312 53.7	297 56.8	52.3	232 57.9	28.8	300 37.8	04.0	340 35.3	45.6
N 11	327 56.2	312 56.4	53.6	247 59.2	28.9	315 39.7	04.2	355 37.5	45.5
D 12	342 58.7	327 56.1	N 5 54.9	263 00.5	N25 28.9	330 41.7	N 4 04.4	10 39.6	S12 45.4
A 13	358 01.1	342 55.8	56.1	278 01.8	29.0	345 43.6	04.6	25 41.8	45.3
Y 14	13 03.6	357 55.5	57.4	293 03.1	29.0	0 45.6	04.9	40 44.0	45.2
15	28 06.0	12 55.2	5 58.7	308 04.4 ..	29.1	15 47.5 ..	05.1	55 46.2 ..	45.1
16	43 08.5	27 54.8	6 00.0	323 05.7	29.1	30 49.4	05.3	70 48.4	45.0
17	58 11.0	42 54.5	01.3	338 07.0	29.1	45 51.4	05.5	85 50.5	44.9
18	73 13.4	57 54.2	N 6 02.5	353 08.3	N25 29.2	60 53.3	N 4 05.8	100 52.7	S12 44.8
19	88 15.9	72 53.9	03.8	8 09.6	29.2	75 55.3	06.0	115 54.9	44.7
20	103 18.4	87 53.6	05.1	23 10.9	29.3	90 57.2	06.2	130 57.1	44.6
21	118 20.8	102 53.3 ..	06.4	38 12.2 ..	29.3	105 59.1 ..	06.4	145 59.3 ..	44.5
22	133 23.3	117 52.9	07.6	53 13.5	29.4	121 01.1	06.7	161 01.4	44.4
23	148 25.8	132 52.6	08.9	68 14.8	29.4	136 03.0	06.9	176 03.6	44.3
6 00	163 28.2	147 52.3	N 6 10.2	83 16.2	N25 29.5	151 05.0	N 4 07.1	191 05.8	S12 44.2
01	178 30.7	162 52.0	11.5	98 17.5	29.5	166 06.9	07.3	206 08.0	44.1
02	193 33.2	177 51.7	12.8	113 18.8	29.5	181 08.8	07.6	221 10.2	44.0
03	208 35.6	192 51.3 ..	14.0	128 20.1 ..	29.6	196 10.8 ..	07.8	236 12.3 ..	43.9
04	223 38.1	207 51.0	15.3	143 21.4	29.6	211 12.7	08.0	251 14.5	43.8
05	238 40.5	222 50.7	16.6	158 22.7	29.7	226 14.6	08.2	266 16.7	43.7
06	253 43.0	237 50.4	N 6 17.9	173 24.0	N25 29.7	241 16.6	N 4 08.5	281 18.9	S12 43.6
07	268 45.5	252 50.1	19.1	188 25.3	29.8	256 18.5	08.7	296 21.0	43.5
08	283 47.9	267 49.7	20.4	203 26.6	29.8	271 20.5	08.9	311 23.2	43.4
M 09	298 50.4	282 49.4 ..	21.7	218 27.9 ..	29.8	286 22.4 ..	09.1	326 25.4 ..	43.3
O 10	313 52.9	297 49.1	23.0	233 29.2	29.9	301 24.3	09.4	341 27.6	43.1
N 11	328 55.3	312 48.8	24.2	248 30.5	29.9	316 26.3	09.6	356 29.8	43.0
D 12	343 57.8	327 48.5	N 6 25.5	263 31.8	N25 30.0	331 28.2	N 4 09.8	11 31.9	S12 42.9
A 13	359 00.3	342 48.2	26.8	278 33.1	30.0	346 30.2	10.0	26 34.1	42.8
Y 14	14 02.7	357 47.8	28.1	293 34.4	30.0	1 32.1	10.3	41 36.3	42.7
15	29 05.2	12 47.5 ..	29.3	308 35.6 ..	30.1	16 34.0 ..	10.5	56 38.5 ..	42.6
16	44 07.7	27 47.2	30.6	323 36.9	30.1	31 36.0	10.7	71 40.7	42.5
17	59 10.1	42 46.9	31.9	338 38.2	30.2	46 37.9	11.0	86 42.8	42.4
18	74 12.6	57 46.5	N 6 33.2	353 39.5	N25 30.2	61 39.8	N 4 11.2	101 45.0	S12 42.3
19	89 15.0	72 46.2	34.4	8 40.8	30.2	76 41.8	11.4	116 47.2	42.2
20	104 17.5	87 45.9	35.7	23 42.1	30.3	91 43.7	11.6	131 49.4	42.1
21	119 20.0	102 45.6 ..	37.0	38 43.4 ..	30.3	106 45.7 ..	11.9	146 51.6 ..	42.0
22	134 22.4	117 45.3	38.2	53 44.7	30.4	121 47.6	12.1	161 53.7	41.9
23	149 24.9	132 44.9	39.5	68 46.0	30.4	136 49.5	12.3	176 55.9	41.8
7 00	164 27.4	147 44.6	N 6 40.8	83 47.3	N25 30.5	151 51.5	N 4 12.5	191 58.1	S12 41.7
01	179 29.8	162 44.3	42.1	98 48.6	30.5	166 53.4	12.8	207 00.3	41.6
02	194 32.3	177 44.0	43.3	113 49.9	30.5	181 55.4	13.0	222 02.5	41.5
03	209 34.8	192 43.7 ..	44.6	128 51.2 ..	30.6	196 57.3 ..	13.2	237 04.6 ..	41.4
04	224 37.2	207 43.3	45.9	143 52.5	30.6	211 59.2	13.4	252 06.8	41.3
05	239 39.7	222 43.0	47.1	158 53.7	30.7	227 01.2	13.7	267 09.0	41.2
06	254 42.1	237 42.7	N 6 48.4	173 55.0	N25 30.7	242 03.1	N 4 13.9	282 11.2	S12 41.1
07	269 44.6	252 42.4	49.7	188 56.3	30.7	257 05.0	14.1	297 13.4	41.0
08	284 47.1	267 42.1	50.9	203 57.6	30.8	272 07.0	14.3	312 15.6	40.9
T 09	299 49.5	282 41.7 ..	52.2	218 58.9 ..	30.8	287 08.9 ..	14.6	327 17.7 ..	40.8
U 10	314 52.0	297 41.4	53.5	234 00.2	30.8	302 10.8	14.8	342 19.9	40.7
E 11	329 54.5	312 41.1	54.8	249 01.5	30.9	317 12.8	15.0	357 22.1	40.6
S 12	344 56.9	327 40.8	N 6 56.0	264 02.8	N25 30.9	332 14.7	N 4 15.2	12 24.3	S12 40.5
D 13	359 59.4	342 40.4	57.3	279 04.0	31.0	347 16.7	15.5	27 26.5	40.4
A 14	15 01.9	357 40.1	58.6	294 05.3	31.0	2 18.6	15.7	42 28.6	40.3
Y 15	30 04.3	12 39.8	6 59.8	309 06.6 ..	31.0	17 20.5 ..	15.9	57 30.8 ..	40.2
16	45 06.8	27 39.5	7 01.1	324 07.9	31.1	32 22.5	16.1	72 33.0	40.1
17	60 09.3	42 39.1	02.4	339 09.2	31.1	47 24.4	16.4	87 35.2	40.0
18	75 11.7	57 38.8	N 7 03.6	354 10.5	N25 31.2	62 26.3	N 4 16.6	102 37.4	S12 39.9
19	90 14.2	72 38.5	04.9	9 11.8	31.2	77 28.3	16.8	117 39.5	39.8
20	105 16.6	87 38.2	06.2	24 13.0	31.2	92 30.2	17.0	132 41.7	39.7
21	120 19.1	102 37.9 ..	07.4	39 14.3 ..	31.3	107 32.1 ..	17.3	147 43.9 ..	39.6
22	135 21.6	117 37.5	08.7	54 15.6	31.3	122 34.1	17.5	162 46.1	39.5
23	150 24.0	132 37.2	10.0	69 16.9	31.3	137 36.0	17.7	177 48.3	39.4
Mer.Pass.	13 04.0	v −0.3	d 1.3	v 1.3	d 0.0	v 1.9	d 0.2	v 2.2	d 0.1

STARS

Name	SHA	Dec
Acamar	315 13.1	S40 13.0
Achernar	335 21.7	S57 07.4
Acrux	173 01.1	S63 13.5
Adhara	255 06.9	S29 00.4
Aldebaran	290 41.4	N16 33.3
Alioth	166 13.8	N55 49.9
Alkaid	152 52.8	N49 11.6
Alnair	27 35.3	S46 51.0
Alnilam	275 39.2	S 1 11.3
Alphard	217 49.0	S 8 45.6
Alphecca	126 04.9	N26 38.0
Alpheratz	357 36.7	N29 13.0
Altair	62 01.7	N 8 55.6
Ankaa	353 09.0	S42 11.0
Antares	112 17.7	S26 29.0
Arcturus	145 49.1	N19 03.5
Atria	107 13.3	S69 03.9
Avior	234 14.9	S59 35.2
Bellatrix	278 24.5	N 6 22.2
Betelgeuse	270 53.7	N 7 24.6
Canopus	263 52.9	S52 42.7
Capella	280 24.1	N46 01.4
Deneb	49 27.2	N45 21.5
Denebola	182 26.2	N14 26.5
Diphda	348 49.1	S17 51.8
Dubhe	193 42.2	N61 37.5
Elnath	278 03.7	N28 37.6
Eltanin	90 43.0	N51 28.8
Enif	33 40.6	N 9 58.7
Fomalhaut	15 16.5	S29 30.1
Gacrux	171 52.8	S57 14.5
Gienah	175 44.9	S17 40.3
Hadar	148 37.8	S60 28.9
Hamal	327 53.2	N23 34.2
Kaus Aust.	83 34.7	S34 22.4
Kochab	137 19.1	N74 03.3
Markab	13 31.7	N15 19.6
Menkar	314 07.9	N 4 10.7
Menkent	147 59.2	S36 29.0
Miaplacidus	221 37.8	S69 48.8
Mirfak	308 30.6	N49 56.7
Nunki	75 49.8	S26 16.1
Peacock	53 08.6	S56 39.6
Pollux	243 18.9	N27 58.2
Procyon	244 52.2	N 5 09.9
Rasalhague	96 00.0	N12 32.4
Regulus	207 35.7	N11 51.2
Rigel	281 05.3	S 8 10.6
Rigil Kent.	139 42.0	S60 55.6
Sabik	102 04.6	S15 45.3
Schedar	349 33.3	N56 39.9
Shaula	96 12.5	S37 07.1
Sirius	258 27.4	S16 45.0
Spica	158 23.7	S11 17.0
Suhail	222 47.1	S43 31.7
Vega	80 34.4	N38 48.0
Zuben'ubi	136 57.5	S16 08.3

	SHA	Mer.Pass.
		h m
Venus	344 24.1	14 09
Mars	279 47.9	18 25
Jupiter	347 36.7	13 54
Saturn	27 37.6	11 14

© British Crown Copyright 2022. All rights reserved.

UT	SUN GHA	SUN Dec	MOON GHA	v	MOON Dec	d	HP
d h	° ′	° ′	° ′	′	° ′	′	′
5 00	177 05.7	S 6 14.4	22 13.5	13.4	N20 44.6	9.6	54.1
01	192 05.9	13.5	36 45.9	13.5	20 35.0	9.8	54.1
02	207 06.0	12.5	51 18.4	13.5	20 25.2	9.8	54.1
03	222 06.2	.. 11.5	65 50.9	13.6	20 15.4	9.9	54.1
04	237 06.3	10.6	80 23.5	13.7	20 05.5	10.0	54.1
05	252 06.4	09.6	94 56.2	13.7	19 55.5	10.0	54.1
06	267 06.6	S 6 08.6	109 28.9	13.7	N19 45.5	10.2	54.2
07	282 06.7	07.7	124 01.6	13.9	19 35.3	10.2	54.2
08	297 06.9	06.7	138 34.5	13.8	19 25.1	10.4	54.2
S 09	312 07.0	.. 05.7	153 07.3	13.9	19 14.7	10.4	54.2
U 10	327 07.1	04.8	167 40.2	14.0	19 04.3	10.5	54.2
N 11	342 07.3	03.8	182 13.2	14.0	18 53.8	10.6	54.2
D 12	357 07.4	S 6 02.8	196 46.2	14.1	N18 43.2	10.6	54.2
A 13	12 07.6	01.9	211 19.3	14.1	18 32.6	10.7	54.2
Y 14	27 07.7	00.9	225 52.4	14.2	18 21.9	10.9	54.2
15	42 07.8	6 00.0	240 25.6	14.2	18 11.0	10.8	54.2
16	57 08.0	5 59.0	254 58.8	14.3	18 00.2	11.0	54.2
17	72 08.1	58.0	269 32.1	14.3	17 49.2	11.1	54.2
18	87 08.3	S 5 57.1	284 05.4	14.3	N17 38.1	11.1	54.3
19	102 08.4	56.1	298 38.7	14.5	17 27.0	11.2	54.3
20	117 08.5	55.1	313 12.2	14.4	17 15.8	11.3	54.3
21	132 08.7	.. 54.2	327 45.6	14.5	17 04.5	11.3	54.3
22	147 08.8	53.2	342 19.1	14.6	16 53.2	11.4	54.3
23	162 09.0	52.2	356 52.7	14.6	16 41.8	11.5	54.3
6 00	177 09.1	S 5 51.2	11 26.3	14.6	N16 30.3	11.6	54.3
01	192 09.3	50.3	25 59.9	14.7	16 18.7	11.6	54.3
02	207 09.4	49.3	40 33.6	14.8	16 07.1	11.7	54.3
03	222 09.5	.. 48.3	55 07.4	14.7	15 55.4	11.8	54.3
04	237 09.7	47.4	69 41.1	14.9	15 43.6	11.8	54.3
05	252 09.8	46.4	84 15.0	14.8	15 31.8	11.9	54.4
06	267 10.0	S 5 45.4	98 48.8	14.9	N15 19.9	12.0	54.4
07	282 10.1	44.5	113 22.7	15.0	15 07.9	12.0	54.4
08	297 10.3	43.5	127 56.7	15.0	14 55.9	12.1	54.4
M 09	312 10.4	.. 42.5	142 30.7	15.0	14 43.8	12.2	54.4
O 10	327 10.6	41.6	157 04.7	15.1	14 31.6	12.2	54.4
N 11	342 10.7	40.6	171 38.8	15.1	14 19.4	12.3	54.4
D 12	357 10.8	S 5 39.6	186 12.9	15.1	N14 07.1	12.4	54.4
A 13	12 11.0	38.7	200 47.0	15.2	13 54.7	12.4	54.4
Y 14	27 11.1	37.7	215 21.2	15.2	13 42.3	12.4	54.5
15	42 11.3	.. 36.7	229 55.4	15.3	13 29.9	12.6	54.5
16	57 11.4	35.8	244 29.7	15.3	13 17.3	12.5	54.5
17	72 11.6	34.8	259 04.0	15.3	13 04.8	12.7	54.5
18	87 11.7	S 5 33.8	273 38.3	15.4	N12 52.1	12.7	54.5
19	102 11.9	32.8	288 12.7	15.4	12 39.4	12.7	54.5
20	117 12.0	31.9	302 47.1	15.4	12 26.7	12.9	54.5
21	132 12.2	.. 30.9	317 21.5	15.5	12 13.8	12.8	54.5
22	147 12.3	29.9	331 56.0	15.5	12 01.0	12.9	54.6
23	162 12.5	29.0	346 30.5	15.5	11 48.1	13.0	54.6
7 00	177 12.6	S 5 28.0	1 05.0	15.5	N11 35.1	13.0	54.6
01	192 12.8	27.0	15 39.5	15.6	11 22.1	13.1	54.6
02	207 12.9	26.1	30 14.1	15.6	11 09.0	13.1	54.6
03	222 13.0	.. 25.1	44 48.7	15.7	10 55.9	13.2	54.6
04	237 13.2	24.1	59 23.4	15.6	10 42.7	13.2	54.6
05	252 13.3	23.1	73 58.0	15.7	10 29.5	13.3	54.7
06	267 13.5	S 5 22.2	88 32.7	15.7	N10 16.2	13.3	54.7
07	282 13.6	21.2	103 07.4	15.7	10 02.9	13.4	54.7
08	297 13.8	20.2	117 42.1	15.8	9 49.6	13.4	54.7
T 09	312 13.9	.. 19.3	132 16.9	15.8	9 36.2	13.5	54.7
U 10	327 14.1	18.3	146 51.7	15.8	9 22.7	13.5	54.7
E 11	342 14.2	17.3	161 26.5	15.8	9 09.2	13.5	54.7
S 12	357 14.4	S 5 16.3	176 01.3	15.9	N 8 55.7	13.6	54.7
D 13	12 14.5	15.4	190 36.2	15.8	8 42.1	13.6	54.8
A 14	27 14.7	14.4	205 11.0	15.9	8 28.5	13.7	54.8
Y 15	42 14.8	.. 13.4	219 45.9	15.9	8 14.8	13.6	54.8
16	57 15.0	12.4	234 20.8	15.9	8 01.2	13.8	54.8
17	72 15.1	11.5	248 55.7	15.9	7 47.4	13.7	54.8
18	87 15.3	S 5 10.5	263 30.6	16.0	N 7 33.7	13.8	54.8
19	102 15.4	09.5	278 05.6	16.0	7 19.9	13.9	54.9
20	117 15.6	08.6	292 40.6	15.9	7 06.0	13.9	54.9
21	132 15.7	.. 07.6	307 15.5	16.0	6 52.1	13.9	54.9
22	147 15.9	06.6	321 50.5	16.0	6 38.2	13.9	54.9
23	162 16.0	05.6	336 25.5	16.0	N 6 24.3	14.0	54.9
	SD 16.1	d 1.0	SD 14.8		14.8		14.9

Lat.	Twilight Naut.	Twilight Civil	Sunrise	Moonrise 5	6	7	8
°	h m	h m	h m	h m	h m	h m	h m
N 72	04 46	06 05	07 12	▢	14 29	16 45	18 47
N 70	04 54	06 04	07 05	12 25	14 56	16 57	18 50
68	05 00	06 04	07 00	13 13	15 17	17 07	18 52
66	05 05	06 04	06 55	13 44	15 33	17 15	18 53
64	05 09	06 04	06 51	14 07	15 46	17 21	18 55
62	05 12	06 04	06 48	14 25	15 57	17 27	18 56
60	05 15	06 03	06 45	14 39	16 07	17 32	18 57
N 58	05 18	06 03	06 42	14 52	16 15	17 36	18 58
56	05 20	06 03	06 40	15 03	16 22	17 40	18 58
54	05 21	06 02	06 37	15 12	16 28	17 44	18 59
52	05 23	06 02	06 35	15 21	16 34	17 47	19 00
50	05 24	06 01	06 34	15 28	16 39	17 50	19 00
45	05 26	06 00	06 30	15 44	16 50	17 56	19 02
N 40	05 28	05 59	06 26	15 57	16 59	18 01	19 03
35	05 29	05 58	06 23	16 08	17 07	18 05	19 04
30	05 29	05 57	06 21	16 18	17 14	18 09	19 04
20	05 29	05 54	06 16	16 35	17 26	18 16	19 06
N 10	05 27	05 51	06 12	16 49	17 36	18 22	19 07
0	05 23	05 47	06 08	17 02	17 45	18 27	19 08
S 10	05 18	05 43	06 04	17 16	17 55	18 33	19 09
20	05 11	05 37	05 59	17 30	18 05	18 38	19 11
30	05 02	05 30	05 54	17 46	18 17	18 45	19 12
35	04 55	05 25	05 51	17 55	18 23	18 49	19 13
40	04 48	05 20	05 48	18 06	18 31	18 53	19 14
45	04 38	05 14	05 43	18 19	18 39	18 58	19 15
S 50	04 25	05 05	05 38	18 34	18 50	19 04	19 16
52	04 19	05 02	05 36	18 41	18 55	19 06	19 17
54	04 13	04 57	05 34	18 49	19 00	19 09	19 18
56	04 05	04 52	05 31	18 57	19 06	19 12	19 18
58	03 56	04 47	05 28	19 07	19 12	19 16	19 19
S 60	03 46	04 41	05 24	19 18	19 20	19 20	19 20

Lat.	Sunset	Twilight Civil	Twilight Naut.	Moonset 5	6	7	8
°	h m	h m	h m	h m	h m	h m	h m
N 72	17 13	18 20	19 40	▢	09 04	08 16	07 42
N 70	17 19	18 20	19 32	09 35	08 34	08 01	07 36
68	17 24	18 20	19 25	08 45	08 12	07 50	07 31
66	17 29	18 20	19 20	08 13	07 54	07 40	07 27
64	17 33	18 20	19 16	07 50	07 40	07 32	07 24
62	17 36	18 21	19 12	07 31	07 28	07 24	07 21
60	17 39	18 21	19 09	07 15	07 17	07 18	07 18
N 58	17 42	18 21	19 06	07 02	07 08	07 13	07 16
56	17 44	18 21	19 04	06 50	07 00	07 08	07 14
54	17 46	18 21	19 02	06 40	06 53	07 03	07 12
52	17 48	18 22	19 01	06 31	06 47	06 59	07 10
50	17 50	18 22	19 00	06 23	06 41	06 56	07 09
45	17 54	18 23	18 57	06 06	06 28	06 48	07 05
N 40	17 57	18 24	18 55	05 52	06 18	06 41	07 02
35	18 00	18 25	18 54	05 39	06 09	06 35	07 00
30	18 02	18 26	18 54	05 29	06 01	06 30	06 58
20	18 07	18 29	18 54	05 10	05 47	06 21	06 54
N 10	18 11	18 32	18 56	04 54	05 35	06 13	06 50
0	18 15	18 35	18 59	04 39	05 23	06 06	06 47
S 10	18 19	18 40	19 04	04 24	05 12	05 58	06 43
20	18 23	18 45	19 11	04 08	04 59	05 50	06 40
30	18 28	18 52	19 20	03 49	04 45	05 41	06 36
35	18 31	18 56	19 27	03 38	04 37	05 35	06 33
40	18 34	19 02	19 34	03 25	04 27	05 29	06 31
45	18 38	19 08	19 44	03 10	04 16	05 22	06 27
S 50	18 43	19 16	19 56	02 51	04 02	05 13	06 24
52	18 45	19 20	20 02	02 42	03 56	05 09	06 22
54	18 48	19 24	20 08	02 32	03 49	05 05	06 20
56	18 50	19 29	20 16	02 21	03 41	05 00	06 18
58	18 53	19 34	20 24	02 08	03 32	04 54	06 15
S 60	18 57	19 40	20 34	01 53	03 21	04 48	06 13

Day	SUN Eqn. of Time 00h	SUN Eqn. of Time 12h	SUN Mer. Pass.	MOON Mer. Pass. Upper	MOON Mer. Pass. Lower	Age	Phase
d	m s	m s	h m	h m	h m	d	%
5	11 37	11 31	12 12	23 13	10 51	13	96
6	11 24	11 17	12 11	23 56	11 34	14	99
7	11 10	11 03	12 11	24 37	12 16	15	100

© British Crown Copyright 2022. All rights reserved.

UT	ARIES	VENUS −4.0		MARS +0.6		JUPITER −2.1		SATURN +0.8		STARS		
	GHA	GHA	Dec	GHA	Dec	GHA	Dec	GHA	Dec	Name	SHA	Dec
d h	° ′	° ′	° ′	° ′	° ′	° ′	° ′	° ′	° ′		° ′	° ′
8 00	165 26.5	147 36.9	N 7 11.2	84 18.2	N25 31.4	152 38.0	N 4 18.0	192 50.4	S12 39.3	Acamar	315 13.1	S40 13.0
01	180 29.0	162 36.6	12.5	99 19.4	31.4	167 39.9	18.2	207 52.6	39.2	Achernar	335 21.8	S57 07.4
02	195 31.4	177 36.2	13.7	114 20.7	31.5	182 41.8	18.4	222 54.8	39.1	Acrux	173 01.1	S63 13.6
03	210 33.9	192 35.9 ..	15.0	129 22.0 ..	31.5	197 43.8 ..	18.6	237 57.0 ..	39.0	Adhara	255 06.9	S29 00.4
04	225 36.4	207 35.6	16.3	144 23.3	31.5	212 45.7	18.9	252 59.2	38.9	Aldebaran	290 41.4	N16 33.3
05	240 38.8	222 35.3	17.5	159 24.6	31.6	227 47.6	19.1	268 01.3	38.8			
06	255 41.3	237 34.9	N 7 18.8	174 25.8	N25 31.6	242 49.6	N 4 19.3	283 03.5	S12 38.7	Alioth	166 13.8	N55 49.9
W 07	270 43.7	252 34.6	20.1	189 27.1	31.6	257 51.5	19.5	298 05.7	38.6	Alkaid	152 52.8	N49 11.6
E 08	285 46.2	267 34.3	21.3	204 28.4	31.7	272 53.4	19.8	313 07.9	38.5	Alnair	27 35.3	S46 51.0
D 09	300 48.7	282 34.0 ..	22.6	219 29.7 ..	31.7	287 55.4 ..	20.0	328 10.1 ..	38.4	Alnilam	275 39.2	S 1 11.3
N 10	315 51.1	297 33.6	23.9	234 31.0	31.8	302 57.3	20.2	343 12.3	38.3	Alphard	217 49.0	S 8 45.6
E 11	330 53.6	312 33.3	25.1	249 32.2	31.8	317 59.2	20.4	358 14.4	38.2			
S 12	345 56.1	327 33.0	N 7 26.4	264 33.5	N25 31.8	333 01.2	N 4 20.7	13 16.6	S12 38.1	Alphecca	126 04.9	N26 38.0
D 13	0 58.5	342 32.7	27.6	279 34.8	31.9	348 03.1	20.9	28 18.8	38.0	Alpheratz	357 36.7	N29 13.0
A 14	16 01.0	357 32.3	28.9	294 36.1	31.9	3 05.0	21.1	43 21.0	37.9	Altair	62 01.6	N 8 55.5
Y 15	31 03.5	12 32.0 ..	30.2	309 37.3 ..	31.9	18 07.0 ..	21.3	58 23.2 ..	37.8	Ankaa	353 09.0	S42 11.0
16	46 05.9	27 31.7	31.4	324 38.6	32.0	33 08.9	21.6	73 25.3	37.7	Antares	112 17.7	S26 29.0
17	61 08.4	42 31.3	32.7	339 39.9	32.0	48 10.8	21.8	88 27.5	37.6			
18	76 10.9	57 31.0	N 7 33.9	354 41.2	N25 32.0	63 12.8	N 4 22.0	103 29.7	S12 37.5	Arcturus	145 49.1	N19 03.5
19	91 13.3	72 30.7	35.2	9 42.4	32.1	78 14.7	22.3	118 31.9	37.4	Atria	107 13.2	S69 03.9
20	106 15.8	87 30.4	36.5	24 43.7	32.1	93 16.7	22.5	133 34.1	37.3	Avior	234 14.9	S59 35.2
21	121 18.2	102 30.0 ..	37.7	39 45.0 ..	32.1	108 18.6 ..	22.7	148 36.3 ..	37.2	Bellatrix	278 24.5	N 6 22.2
22	136 20.7	117 29.7	39.0	54 46.2	32.2	123 20.5	22.9	163 38.4	37.1	Betelgeuse	270 53.7	N 7 24.6
23	151 23.2	132 29.4	40.2	69 47.5	32.2	138 22.5	23.2	178 40.6	37.0			
9 00	166 25.6	147 29.1	N 7 41.5	84 48.8	N25 32.2	153 24.4	N 4 23.4	193 42.8	S12 36.9	Canopus	263 52.9	S52 42.7
01	181 28.1	162 28.7	42.8	99 50.1	32.3	168 26.3	23.6	208 45.0	36.8	Capella	280 24.1	N46 01.4
02	196 30.6	177 28.4	44.0	114 51.3	32.3	183 28.3	23.8	223 47.2	36.7	Deneb	49 27.2	N45 21.5
03	211 33.0	192 28.1 ..	45.3	129 52.6 ..	32.4	198 30.2 ..	24.1	238 49.3 ..	36.6	Denebola	182 26.2	N14 26.5
04	226 35.5	207 27.7	46.5	144 53.9	32.4	213 32.1	24.3	253 51.5	36.5	Diphda	348 49.1	S17 51.8
05	241 38.0	222 27.4	47.8	159 55.1	32.4	228 34.1	24.5	268 53.7	36.4			
06	256 40.4	237 27.1	N 7 49.0	174 56.4	N25 32.5	243 36.0	N 4 24.7	283 55.9	S12 36.3	Dubhe	193 42.2	N61 37.6
T 07	271 42.9	252 26.8	50.3	189 57.7	32.5	258 37.9	25.0	298 58.1	36.2	Elnath	278 03.8	N28 37.6
H 08	286 45.3	267 26.4	51.6	204 58.9	32.5	273 39.9	25.2	314 00.3	36.1	Eltanin	90 43.0	N51 28.8
U 09	301 47.8	282 26.1 ..	52.8	220 00.2 ..	32.6	288 41.8 ..	25.4	329 02.4 ..	36.1	Enif	33 40.6	N 9 58.7
R 10	316 50.3	297 25.8	54.1	235 01.5	32.6	303 43.7	25.6	344 04.6	36.0	Fomalhaut	15 16.5	S29 30.1
S 11	331 52.7	312 25.4	55.3	250 02.7	32.6	318 45.7	25.9	359 06.8	35.9			
D 12	346 55.2	327 25.1	N 7 56.6	265 04.0	N25 32.7	333 47.6	N 4 26.1	14 09.0	S12 35.8	Gacrux	171 52.8	S57 14.5
A 13	1 57.7	342 24.8	57.8	280 05.3	32.7	348 49.5	26.3	29 11.2	35.7	Gienah	175 44.8	S17 40.3
Y 14	17 00.1	357 24.5	7 59.1	295 06.5	32.7	3 51.5	26.6	44 13.4	35.6	Hadar	148 37.7	S60 28.9
15	32 02.6	12 24.1	8 00.3	310 07.8 ..	32.8	18 53.4 ..	26.8	59 15.5 ..	35.5	Hamal	327 53.2	N23 34.2
16	47 05.1	27 23.8	01.6	325 09.0	32.8	33 55.3	27.0	74 17.7	35.4	Kaus Aust.	83 34.7	S34 22.4
17	62 07.5	42 23.5	02.8	340 10.3	32.8	48 57.3	27.2	89 19.9	35.3			
18	77 10.0	57 23.1	N 8 04.1	355 11.6	N25 32.9	63 59.2	N 4 27.5	104 22.1	S12 35.2	Kochab	137 19.1	N74 03.3
19	92 12.5	72 22.8	05.3	10 12.8	32.9	79 01.1	27.7	119 24.3	35.1	Markab	13 31.7	N15 19.6
20	107 14.9	87 22.5	06.6	25 14.1	32.9	94 03.0	27.9	134 26.5	35.0	Menkar	314 07.9	N 4 10.7
21	122 17.4	102 22.1 ..	07.9	40 15.4 ..	32.9	109 05.0 ..	28.1	149 28.6 ..	34.9	Menkent	147 59.2	S36 29.0
22	137 19.8	117 21.8	09.1	55 16.6	33.0	124 06.9	28.4	164 30.8	34.8	Miaplacidus	221 37.8	S69 48.8
23	152 22.3	132 21.5	10.4	70 17.9	33.0	139 08.8	28.6	179 33.0	34.7			
10 00	167 24.8	147 21.1	N 8 11.6	85 19.1	N25 33.0	154 10.8	N 4 28.8	194 35.2	S12 34.6	Mirfak	308 30.7	N49 56.7
01	182 27.2	162 20.8	12.9	100 20.4	33.1	169 12.7	29.1	209 37.4	34.5	Nunki	75 49.8	S26 16.1
02	197 29.7	177 20.5	14.1	115 21.7	33.1	184 14.6	29.3	224 39.5	34.4	Peacock	53 08.5	S56 39.6
03	212 32.2	192 20.2 ..	15.4	130 22.9 ..	33.1	199 16.6 ..	29.5	239 41.7 ..	34.3	Pollux	243 18.9	N27 58.2
04	227 34.6	207 19.8	16.6	145 24.2	33.2	214 18.5	29.7	254 43.9	34.2	Procyon	244 52.2	N 5 09.9
05	242 37.1	222 19.5	17.9	160 25.4	33.2	229 20.4	30.0	269 46.1	34.1			
06	257 39.6	237 19.2	N 8 19.1	175 26.7	N25 33.2	244 22.4	N 4 30.2	284 48.3	S12 34.0	Rasalhague	96 00.0	N12 32.4
07	272 42.0	252 18.8	20.4	190 27.9	33.3	259 24.3	30.4	299 50.5	33.9	Regulus	207 35.8	N11 51.2
08	287 44.5	267 18.5	21.6	205 29.2	33.3	274 26.2	30.6	314 52.6	33.8	Rigel	281 05.3	S 8 10.7
F 09	302 46.9	282 18.2 ..	22.8	220 30.5 ..	33.3	289 28.2 ..	30.9	329 54.8 ..	33.7	Rigil Kent.	139 42.0	S60 55.6
R 10	317 49.4	297 17.8	24.1	235 31.7	33.4	304 30.1	31.1	344 57.0	33.6	Sabik	102 04.5	S15 45.3
I 11	332 51.9	312 17.5	25.3	250 33.0	33.4	319 32.0	31.3	359 59.2	33.5			
D 12	347 54.3	327 17.2	N 8 26.6	265 34.2	N25 33.4	334 34.0	N 4 31.5	15 01.4	S12 33.4	Schedar	349 33.3	N56 39.8
A 13	2 56.8	342 16.8	27.8	280 35.5	33.4	349 35.9	31.8	30 03.6	33.3	Shaula	96 12.5	S37 07.1
Y 14	17 59.3	357 16.5	29.1	295 36.7	33.5	4 37.8	32.0	45 05.7	33.2	Sirius	258 27.5	S16 45.0
15	33 01.7	12 16.2 ..	30.3	310 38.0 ..	33.5	19 39.7 ..	32.2	60 07.9 ..	33.1	Spica	158 23.6	S11 17.0
16	48 04.2	27 15.8	31.6	325 39.2	33.5	34 41.7	32.5	75 10.1	33.0	Suhail	222 47.1	S43 31.7
17	63 06.7	42 15.5	32.8	340 40.5	33.6	49 43.6	32.7	90 12.3	32.9			
18	78 09.1	57 15.2	N 8 34.1	355 41.7	N25 33.6	64 45.5	N 4 32.9	105 14.5	S12 32.8	Vega	80 34.4	N38 48.0
19	93 11.6	72 14.8	35.3	10 43.0	33.6	79 47.5	33.1	120 16.7	32.7	Zuben'ubi	136 57.5	S16 08.3
20	108 14.1	87 14.5	36.6	25 44.2	33.6	94 49.4	33.4	135 18.9	32.6		SHA	Mer. Pass.
21	123 16.5	102 14.2 ..	37.8	40 45.5 ..	33.7	109 51.3 ..	33.6	150 21.0 ..	32.5		° ′	h m
22	138 19.0	117 13.8	39.0	55 46.7	33.7	124 53.3	33.8	165 23.2	32.4	Venus	341 03.4	14 10
23	153 21.4	132 13.5	40.3	70 48.0	33.7	139 55.2	34.0	180 25.4	32.3	Mars	278 23.1	18 19
	h m									Jupiter	346 58.7	13 45
Mer. Pass. 12 52.2	v −0.3 d 1.3			v 1.3 d 0.0		v 1.9 d 0.2		v 2.2 d 0.1		Saturn	27 17.2	11 04

© British Crown Copyright 2022. All rights reserved.

UT	SUN GHA	SUN Dec	MOON GHA	v	MOON Dec	d	HP
d h	° '	° '	° '	'	° '	'	'
8 00	177 16.2	S 5 04.7	351 00.5	16.0	N 6 10.3	14.0	54.9
01	192 16.3	03.7	5 35.5	16.0	5 56.3	14.0	54.9
02	207 16.5	02.7	20 10.5	16.1	5 42.3	14.1	55.0
03	222 16.6	.. 01.7	34 45.6	16.0	5 28.2	14.1	55.0
04	237 16.8	5 00.8	49 20.6	16.0	5 14.1	14.1	55.0
05	252 17.0	4 59.8	63 55.6	16.1	5 00.0	14.2	55.0
06	267 17.1	S 4 58.8	78 30.7	16.0	N 4 45.8	14.1	55.0
W 07	282 17.3	57.8	93 05.7	16.1	4 31.7	14.2	55.0
E 08	297 17.4	56.9	107 40.8	16.1	4 17.5	14.3	55.1
D 09	312 17.6	.. 55.9	122 15.8	16.1	4 03.2	14.3	55.1
N 10	327 17.7	54.9	136 50.9	16.1	3 49.0	14.3	55.1
E 11	342 17.9	53.9	151 26.0	16.0	3 34.7	14.3	55.1
S 12	357 18.0	S 4 53.0	166 01.0	16.1	N 3 20.4	14.3	55.1
D 13	12 18.2	52.0	180 36.1	16.0	3 06.1	14.3	55.1
A 14	27 18.3	51.0	195 11.1	16.1	2 51.8	14.4	55.2
Y 15	42 18.5	.. 50.0	209 46.2	16.0	2 37.4	14.4	55.2
16	57 18.6	49.1	224 21.2	16.0	2 23.0	14.4	55.2
17	72 18.8	48.1	238 56.2	16.0	2 08.6	14.4	55.2
18	87 18.9	S 4 47.1	253 31.2	16.1	N 1 54.2	14.4	55.2
19	102 19.1	46.1	268 06.3	16.0	1 39.8	14.4	55.2
20	117 19.3	45.2	282 41.3	16.0	1 25.4	14.5	55.3
21	132 19.4	.. 44.2	297 16.3	16.0	1 10.9	14.5	55.3
22	147 19.6	43.2	311 51.3	15.9	0 56.4	14.5	55.3
23	162 19.7	42.2	326 26.2	16.0	0 41.9	14.4	55.3
9 00	177 19.9	S 4 41.3	341 01.2	15.9	N 0 27.5	14.5	55.3
01	192 20.0	40.3	355 36.1	16.0	N 0 13.0	14.6	55.3
02	207 20.2	39.3	10 11.1	15.9	S 0 01.6	14.5	55.4
03	222 20.3	.. 38.3	24 46.0	15.9	0 16.1	14.5	55.4
04	237 20.5	37.4	39 20.9	15.9	0 30.6	14.5	55.4
05	252 20.7	36.4	53 55.8	15.8	0 45.1	14.6	55.4
06	267 20.8	S 4 35.4	68 30.6	15.9	S 0 59.7	14.5	55.4
T 07	282 21.0	34.4	83 05.5	15.8	1 14.2	14.6	55.5
H 08	297 21.1	33.5	97 40.3	15.8	1 28.8	14.5	55.5
U 09	312 21.3	.. 32.5	112 15.1	15.8	1 43.3	14.6	55.5
R 10	327 21.4	31.5	126 49.9	15.7	1 57.9	14.6	55.5
S 11	342 21.6	30.5	141 24.6	15.7	2 12.5	14.5	55.5
D 12	357 21.8	S 4 29.5	155 59.3	15.7	S 2 27.0	14.6	55.5
A 13	12 21.9	28.6	170 34.0	15.7	2 41.6	14.5	55.6
Y 14	27 22.1	27.6	185 08.7	15.6	2 56.1	14.6	55.6
15	42 22.2	.. 26.6	199 43.3	15.6	3 10.7	14.5	55.6
16	57 22.4	25.6	214 17.9	15.6	3 25.2	14.6	55.6
17	72 22.5	24.7	228 52.5	15.5	3 39.8	14.5	55.6
18	87 22.7	S 4 23.7	243 27.0	15.6	S 3 54.3	14.6	55.7
19	102 22.9	22.7	258 01.6	15.4	4 08.9	14.5	55.7
20	117 23.0	21.7	272 36.0	15.5	4 23.4	14.5	55.7
21	132 23.2	.. 20.7	287 10.5	15.4	4 37.9	14.5	55.7
22	147 23.3	19.8	301 44.9	15.3	4 52.4	14.5	55.7
23	162 23.5	18.8	316 19.2	15.4	5 06.9	14.5	55.8
10 00	177 23.7	S 4 17.8	330 53.6	15.3	S 5 21.4	14.5	55.8
01	192 23.8	16.8	345 27.9	15.2	5 35.9	14.5	55.8
02	207 24.0	15.8	0 02.1	15.2	5 50.4	14.4	55.8
03	222 24.1	.. 14.9	14 36.3	15.2	6 04.8	14.5	55.8
04	237 24.3	13.9	29 10.5	15.1	6 19.3	14.4	55.9
05	252 24.4	12.9	43 44.6	15.1	6 33.7	14.4	55.9
06	267 24.6	S 4 11.9	58 18.7	15.0	S 6 48.1	14.4	55.9
F 07	282 24.8	11.0	72 52.7	15.0	7 02.5	14.3	55.9
R 08	297 24.9	10.0	87 26.7	14.9	7 16.8	14.4	55.9
I 09	312 25.1	.. 09.0	102 00.6	14.9	7 31.2	14.3	56.0
D 10	327 25.2	08.0	116 34.5	14.8	7 45.5	14.3	56.0
A 11	342 25.4	07.0	131 08.3	14.8	7 59.8	14.3	56.0
Y 12	357 25.6	S 4 06.1	145 42.1	14.7	S 8 14.1	14.2	56.0
13	12 25.7	05.1	160 15.8	14.7	8 28.3	14.3	56.0
14	27 25.9	04.1	174 49.5	14.6	8 42.6	14.2	56.1
15	42 26.1	.. 03.1	189 23.1	14.6	8 56.8	14.2	56.1
16	57 26.2	02.1	203 56.7	14.5	9 11.0	14.1	56.1
17	72 26.4	01.2	218 30.2	14.4	9 25.1	14.1	56.1
18	87 26.5	S 4 00.2	233 03.6	14.4	S 9 39.2	14.1	56.1
19	102 26.7	3 59.2	247 37.0	14.3	9 53.3	14.1	56.2
20	117 26.9	58.2	262 10.3	14.3	10 07.4	14.0	56.2
21	132 27.0	.. 57.2	276 43.6	14.2	10 21.4	14.0	56.2
22	147 27.2	56.3	291 16.8	14.1	10 35.4	13.9	56.2
23	162 27.3	55.3	305 49.9	14.1	S10 49.3	13.9	56.2
	SD 16.1	d 1.0	SD 15.0	15.1	15.3		

Lat.	Twilight Naut.	Twilight Civil	Sunrise	Moonrise 8	9	10	11
°	h m	h m	h m	h m	h m	h m	h m
N 72	04 30	05 49	06 57	18 47	20 50	23 03	26 06
N 70	04 39	05 51	06 51	18 50	20 43	22 44	25 08
68	04 47	05 52	06 47	18 52	20 37	22 29	24 35
66	04 53	05 53	06 44	18 53	20 33	22 17	24 11
64	04 58	05 54	06 41	18 55	20 29	22 07	23 52
62	05 03	05 54	06 38	18 56	20 25	21 58	23 37
60	05 06	05 54	06 36	18 57	20 22	21 51	23 24
N 58	05 09	05 55	06 34	18 58	20 20	21 45	23 14
56	05 12	05 55	06 32	18 58	20 17	21 39	23 04
54	05 14	05 55	06 30	18 59	20 15	21 34	22 56
52	05 16	05 55	06 29	19 00	20 14	21 29	22 49
50	05 18	05 55	06 27	19 00	20 12	21 25	22 42
45	05 21	05 55	06 24	19 02	20 08	21 17	22 28
N 40	05 23	05 55	06 22	19 03	20 05	21 09	22 16
35	05 25	05 54	06 19	19 04	20 03	21 03	22 06
30	05 26	05 53	06 17	19 04	20 00	20 58	21 58
20	05 26	05 52	06 14	19 06	19 56	20 48	21 43
N 10	05 25	05 49	06 10	19 07	19 53	20 40	21 30
0	05 22	05 47	06 07	19 08	19 50	20 33	21 18
S 10	05 18	05 43	06 04	19 09	19 47	20 25	21 07
20	05 12	05 38	06 00	19 11	19 43	20 17	20 54
30	05 04	05 32	05 56	19 12	19 40	20 08	20 40
35	04 58	05 28	05 54	19 13	19 37	20 03	20 32
40	04 51	05 23	05 51	19 14	19 35	19 57	20 23
45	04 42	05 18	05 47	19 15	19 32	19 51	20 12
S 50	04 31	05 11	05 43	19 16	19 29	19 43	19 59
52	04 26	05 07	05 42	19 17	19 28	19 39	19 53
54	04 20	05 03	05 39	19 18	19 26	19 35	19 46
56	04 13	04 59	05 37	19 18	19 24	19 31	19 39
58	04 05	04 54	05 35	19 19	19 22	19 26	19 31
S 60	03 55	04 49	05 32	19 20	19 20	19 20	19 21

Lat.	Sunset	Twilight Civil	Twilight Naut.	Moonset 8	9	10	11
°	h m	h m	h m	h m	h m	h m	h m
N 72	17 27	18 34	19 55	07 42	07 11	06 38	05 56
N 70	17 32	18 32	19 45	07 36	07 13	06 48	06 18
68	17 36	18 31	19 37	07 31	07 14	06 56	06 35
66	17 39	18 30	19 30	07 27	07 15	07 03	06 49
64	17 42	18 29	19 25	07 24	07 16	07 09	07 00
62	17 44	18 29	19 20	07 21	07 17	07 14	07 10
60	17 47	18 28	19 17	07 18	07 18	07 18	07 19
N 58	17 49	18 28	19 14	07 16	07 19	07 22	07 26
56	17 50	18 27	19 11	07 14	07 20	07 26	07 33
54	17 52	18 27	19 08	07 12	07 20	07 29	07 39
52	17 53	18 27	19 06	07 10	07 21	07 32	07 44
50	17 55	18 27	19 04	07 09	07 21	07 34	07 49
45	17 58	18 27	19 01	07 05	07 22	07 40	07 59
N 40	18 00	18 27	18 58	07 02	07 23	07 45	08 08
35	18 02	18 28	18 57	07 00	07 24	07 49	08 16
30	18 04	18 28	18 56	06 58	07 25	07 53	08 23
20	18 08	18 30	18 55	06 54	07 26	07 59	08 34
N 10	18 11	18 32	18 56	06 50	07 27	08 05	08 44
0	18 14	18 35	18 59	06 47	07 28	08 10	08 54
S 10	18 17	18 38	19 03	06 43	07 29	08 15	09 04
20	18 20	18 43	19 09	06 40	07 30	08 21	09 14
30	18 25	18 49	19 17	06 36	07 31	08 28	09 26
35	18 27	18 52	19 22	06 33	07 32	08 31	09 33
40	18 30	18 57	19 28	06 29	07 33	08 36	09 41
45	18 33	19 02	19 38	06 27	07 33	08 41	09 50
S 50	18 37	19 09	19 49	06 24	07 35	08 47	10 02
52	18 38	19 13	19 54	06 22	07 35	08 50	10 07
54	18 40	19 16	20 00	06 20	07 36	08 53	10 13
56	18 43	19 21	20 07	06 18	07 36	08 56	10 19
58	18 45	19 25	20 15	06 15	07 37	09 00	10 26
S 60	18 48	19 30	20 24	06 13	07 37	09 04	10 35

Day	SUN Eqn. of Time 00h	12h	Mer. Pass.	MOON Mer. Pass. Upper	Lower	Age	Phase
d	m s	m s	h m	h m	h m	d	%
8	10 56	10 48	12 11	00 37	12 58	16	99
9	10 41	10 33	12 11	01 18	13 39	17	96
10	10 26	10 18	12 10	02 00	14 21	18	92

© British Crown Copyright 2022. All rights reserved.

UT	ARIES	VENUS −4.0		MARS +0.6		JUPITER −2.1		SATURN +0.8	
d h	GHA	GHA	Dec	GHA	Dec	GHA	Dec	GHA	Dec
11 00	168 23.9	147 13.1 N 8 41.5		85 49.2 N25 33.8		154 57.1 N 4 34.3		195 27.6 S12 32.2	
01	183 26.4	162 12.8	42.8	100 50.5	33.8	169 59.1	34.5	210 29.8	32.1
02	198 28.8	177 12.5	44.0	115 51.7	33.8	185 01.0	34.7	225 32.0	32.0
03	213 31.3	192 12.1 ..	45.3	130 53.0 ..	33.8	200 02.9 ..	35.0	240 34.1 ..	31.9
04	228 33.8	207 11.8	46.5	145 54.2	33.9	215 04.8	35.2	255 36.3	31.8
05	243 36.2	222 11.5	47.7	160 55.5	33.9	230 06.8	35.4	270 38.5	31.7
06	258 38.7	237 11.1 N 8 49.0		175 56.7 N25 33.9		245 08.7 N 4 35.6		285 40.7 S12 31.6	
07	273 41.2	252 10.8	50.2	190 58.0	34.0	260 10.6	35.9	300 42.9	31.5
08	288 43.6	267 10.5	51.5	205 59.2	34.0	275 12.6	36.1	315 45.1	31.4
09	303 46.1	282 10.1 ..	52.7	221 00.5 ..	34.0	290 14.5 ..	36.3	330 47.2 ..	31.3
10	318 48.6	297 09.8	53.9	236 01.7	34.0	305 16.4	36.5	345 49.4	31.2
11	333 51.0	312 09.4	55.2	251 03.0	34.1	320 18.4	36.8	0 51.6	31.1
12	348 53.5	327 09.1 N 8 56.4		266 04.2 N25 34.1		335 20.3 N 4 37.0		15 53.8 S12 31.0	
13	3 55.9	342 08.8	57.7	281 05.5	34.1	350 22.2	37.2	30 56.0	30.9
14	18 58.4	357 08.4 8 58.9		296 06.7	34.1	5 24.1	37.5	45 58.2	30.8
15	34 00.9	12 08.1 9 00.1		311 07.9 ..	34.2	20 26.1 ..	37.7	61 00.4 ..	30.7
16	49 03.3	27 07.8	01.4	326 09.2	34.2	35 28.0	37.9	76 02.5	30.6
17	64 05.8	42 07.4	02.6	341 10.4	34.2	50 29.9	38.1	91 04.7	30.5
18	79 08.3	57 07.1 N 9 03.8		356 11.7 N25 34.3		65 31.9 N 4 38.4		106 06.9 S12 30.4	
19	94 10.7	72 06.7	05.1	11 12.9	34.3	80 33.8	38.6	121 09.1	30.3
20	109 13.2	87 06.4	06.3	26 14.2	34.3	95 35.7	38.8	136 11.3	30.2
21	124 15.7	102 06.1 ..	07.6	41 15.4 ..	34.3	110 37.6 ..	39.1	151 13.5 ..	30.1
22	139 18.1	117 05.7	08.8	56 16.6	34.4	125 39.6	39.3	166 15.6	30.0
23	154 20.6	132 05.4	10.0	71 17.9	34.4	140 41.5	39.5	181 17.8	29.9
12 00	169 23.0	147 05.0 N 9 11.3		86 19.1 N25 34.4		155 43.4 N 4 39.7		196 20.0 S12 29.8	
01	184 25.5	162 04.7	12.5	101 20.4	34.4	170 45.4	40.0	211 22.2	29.7
02	199 28.0	177 04.4	13.7	116 21.6	34.5	185 47.3	40.2	226 24.4	29.6
03	214 30.4	192 04.0 ..	15.0	131 22.8 ..	34.5	200 49.2 ..	40.4	241 26.6 ..	29.5
04	229 32.9	207 03.7	16.2	146 24.1	34.5	215 51.1	40.6	256 28.8	29.4
05	244 35.4	222 03.3	17.4	161 25.3	34.5	230 53.1	40.9	271 30.9	29.3
06	259 37.8	237 03.0 N 9 18.7		176 26.5 N25 34.6		245 55.0 N 4 41.1		286 33.1 S12 29.2	
07	274 40.3	252 02.6	19.9	191 27.8	34.6	260 56.9	41.3	301 35.3	29.1
08	289 42.8	267 02.3	21.1	206 29.0	34.6	275 58.9	41.6	316 37.5	29.0
09	304 45.2	282 02.0 ..	22.4	221 30.3 ..	34.6	291 00.8 ..	41.8	331 39.7 ..	28.9
10	319 47.7	297 01.6	23.6	236 31.5	34.7	306 02.7	42.0	346 41.9	28.8
11	334 50.2	312 01.3	24.8	251 32.7	34.7	321 04.6	42.2	1 44.1	28.7
12	349 52.6	327 00.9 N 9 26.1		266 34.0 N25 34.7		336 06.6 N 4 42.5		16 46.2 S12 28.6	
13	4 55.1	342 00.6	27.3	281 35.2	34.7	351 08.5	42.7	31 48.4	28.5
14	19 57.5	357 00.3	28.5	296 36.4	34.7	6 10.4	42.9	46 50.6	28.4
15	35 00.0	11 59.9 ..	29.7	311 37.7 ..	34.8	21 12.4 ..	43.2	61 52.8 ..	28.3
16	50 02.5	26 59.6	31.0	326 38.9	34.8	36 14.3	43.4	76 55.0	28.2
17	65 04.9	41 59.2	32.2	341 40.1	34.8	51 16.2	43.6	91 57.2	28.1
18	80 07.4	56 58.9 N 9 33.4		356 41.4 N25 34.8		66 18.1 N 4 43.8		106 59.4 S12 28.0	
19	95 09.9	71 58.5	34.7	11 42.6	34.9	81 20.1	44.1	122 01.5	27.9
20	110 12.3	86 58.2	35.9	26 43.8	34.9	96 22.0	44.3	137 03.7	27.8
21	125 14.8	101 57.8 ..	37.1	41 45.1 ..	34.9	111 23.9 ..	44.5	152 05.9 ..	27.7
22	140 17.3	116 57.5	38.3	56 46.3	34.9	126 25.8	44.7	167 08.1	27.6
23	155 19.7	131 57.2	39.6	71 47.5	34.9	141 27.8	45.0	182 10.3	27.5
13 00	170 22.2	146 56.8 N 9 40.8		86 48.7 N25 35.0		156 29.7 N 4 45.2		197 12.5 S12 27.4	
01	185 24.7	161 56.5	42.0	101 50.0	35.0	171 31.6	45.4	212 14.7	27.3
02	200 27.1	176 56.1	43.2	116 51.2	35.0	186 33.5	45.7	227 16.8	27.2
03	215 29.6	191 55.8 ..	44.5	131 52.4 ..	35.0	201 35.5 ..	45.9	242 19.0 ..	27.1
04	230 32.0	206 55.4	45.7	146 53.7	35.1	216 37.4	46.1	257 21.2	27.0
05	245 34.5	221 55.1	46.9	161 54.9	35.1	231 39.3	46.3	272 23.4	26.9
06	260 37.0	236 54.7 N 9 48.1		176 56.1 N25 35.1		246 41.3 N 4 46.6		287 25.6 S12 26.8	
07	275 39.4	251 54.4	49.4	191 57.3	35.1	261 43.2	46.8	302 27.8	26.7
08	290 41.9	266 54.0	50.6	206 58.6	35.1	276 45.1	47.0	317 30.0	26.6
09	305 44.4	281 53.7 ..	51.8	221 59.8 ..	35.2	291 47.0 ..	47.3	332 32.2 ..	26.6
10	320 46.8	296 53.3	53.0	237 01.0	35.2	306 49.0	47.5	347 34.3	26.5
11	335 49.3	311 53.0	54.3	252 02.2	35.2	321 50.9	47.7	2 36.5	26.4
12	350 51.8	326 52.7 N 9 55.5		267 03.5 N25 35.2		336 52.8 N 4 47.9		17 38.7 S12 26.3	
13	5 54.2	341 52.3	56.7	282 04.7	35.2	351 54.7	48.2	32 40.9	26.2
14	20 56.7	356 52.0	57.9	297 05.9	35.3	6 56.7	48.4	47 43.1	26.1
15	35 59.1	11 51.6 9 59.1		312 07.1 ..	35.3	21 58.6 ..	48.6	62 45.3 ..	26.0
16	51 01.6	26 51.3 10 00.4		327 08.4	35.3	37 00.5	48.9	77 47.5	25.9
17	66 04.1	41 50.9	01.6	342 09.6	35.3	52 02.4	49.1	92 49.6	25.8
18	81 06.5	56 50.6 N10 02.8		357 10.8 N25 35.3		67 04.4 N 4 49.3		107 51.8 S12 25.7	
19	96 09.0	71 50.2	04.0	12 12.0	35.4	82 06.3	49.5	122 54.0	25.6
20	111 11.5	86 49.9	05.2	27 13.3	35.4	97 08.2	49.8	137 56.2	25.5
21	126 13.9	101 49.5 ..	06.5	42 14.5 ..	35.4	112 10.1 ..	50.0	152 58.4 ..	25.4
22	141 16.4	116 49.2	07.7	57 15.7	35.4	127 12.1	50.2	168 00.6	25.3
23	156 18.9	131 48.8	08.9	72 16.9	35.4	142 14.0	50.5	183 02.8	25.2
Mer. Pass.	h m 12 40.4	v −0.3	d 1.2	v 1.2	d 0.0	v 1.9	d 0.2	v 2.2	d 0.1

Day markers: SATURDAY (11), SUNDAY (12), MONDAY (13).

STARS

Name	SHA	Dec
Acamar	315 13.2	S40 13.0
Achernar	335 21.8	S57 07.4
Acrux	173 01.1	S63 13.6
Adhara	255 06.9	S29 00.4
Aldebaran	290 41.4	N16 33.3
Alioth	166 13.8	N55 49.9
Alkaid	152 52.8	N49 11.7
Alnair	27 35.2	S46 51.0
Alnilam	275 39.3	S 1 11.3
Alphard	217 49.0	S 8 45.6
Alphecca	126 04.9	N26 38.0
Alpheratz	357 36.7	N29 13.0
Altair	62 01.6	N 8 55.5
Ankaa	353 09.0	S42 11.0
Antares	112 17.6	S26 29.0
Arcturus	145 49.1	N19 03.5
Atria	107 13.2	S69 03.9
Avior	234 14.9	S59 35.2
Bellatrix	278 24.5	N 6 22.2
Betelgeuse	270 53.7	N 7 24.6
Canopus	263 52.9	S52 42.7
Capella	280 24.1	N46 01.4
Deneb	49 27.2	N45 21.5
Denebola	182 26.2	N14 26.5
Diphda	348 49.1	S17 51.8
Dubhe	193 42.2	N61 37.6
Elnath	278 03.8	N28 37.6
Eltanin	90 43.0	N51 28.8
Enif	33 40.6	N 9 58.7
Fomalhaut	15 16.5	S29 30.1
Gacrux	171 52.8	S57 14.5
Gienah	175 44.8	S17 40.3
Hadar	148 37.7	S60 28.9
Hamal	327 53.2	N23 34.2
Kaus Aust.	83 34.6	S34 22.4
Kochab	137 19.0	N74 03.3
Markab	13 31.7	N15 19.6
Menkar	314 07.9	N 4 10.7
Menkent	147 59.1	S36 29.0
Miaplacidus	221 37.8	S69 48.8
Mirfak	308 30.7	N49 56.7
Nunki	75 49.8	S26 16.1
Peacock	53 08.5	S56 39.6
Pollux	243 19.0	N27 58.2
Procyon	244 52.3	N 5 09.9
Rasalhague	96 00.0	N12 32.4
Regulus	207 35.8	N11 51.2
Rigel	281 05.3	S 8 10.7
Rigil Kent.	139 42.0	S60 55.6
Sabik	102 04.5	S15 45.3
Schedar	349 33.3	N56 39.8
Shaula	96 12.5	S37 07.1
Sirius	258 27.5	S16 45.0
Spica	158 23.6	S11 17.0
Suhail	222 47.1	S43 31.7
Vega	80 34.4	N38 48.0
Zuben'ubi	136 57.5	S16 08.3

	SHA	Mer. Pass.
	° '	h m
Venus	337 42.0	14 12
Mars	276 56.1	18 13
Jupiter	346 20.4	13 35
Saturn	26 57.0	10 53

© British Crown Copyright 2022. All rights reserved.

UT	SUN GHA	SUN Dec	MOON GHA	v	Dec	d	HP
d h	° ′	° ′	° ′	′	° ′	′	′
11 00	177 27.5	S 3 54.3	320 23.0	14.0	S11 03.2	13.9	56.3
01	192 27.7	53.3	334 56.0	13.9	11 17.1	13.8	56.3
02	207 27.8	52.3	349 28.9	13.9	11 30.9	13.8	56.3
03	222 28.0	.. 51.3	4 01.8	13.8	11 44.7	13.8	56.3
04	237 28.2	50.4	18 34.6	13.7	11 58.5	13.7	56.3
05	252 28.3	49.4	33 07.3	13.7	12 12.2	13.7	56.4
06	267 28.5	S 3 48.4	47 40.0	13.5	S12 25.9	13.6	56.4
S 07	282 28.6	47.4	62 12.5	13.5	12 39.5	13.6	56.4
A 08	297 28.8	46.4	76 45.0	13.5	12 53.1	13.5	56.4
T 09	312 29.0	.. 45.5	91 17.5	13.3	13 06.6	13.5	56.5
U 10	327 29.1	44.5	105 49.8	13.3	13 20.1	13.4	56.5
R 11	342 29.3	43.5	120 22.1	13.2	13 33.5	13.4	56.5
D 12	357 29.5	S 3 42.5	134 54.3	13.1	S13 46.9	13.3	56.5
A 13	12 29.6	41.5	149 26.4	13.1	14 00.2	13.3	56.5
Y 14	27 29.8	40.6	163 58.5	13.0	14 13.5	13.2	56.6
15	42 30.0	.. 39.6	178 30.5	12.8	14 26.7	13.2	56.6
16	57 30.1	38.6	193 02.3	12.8	14 39.9	13.1	56.6
17	72 30.3	37.6	207 34.1	12.8	14 53.0	13.1	56.6
18	87 30.5	S 3 36.6	222 05.9	12.6	S15 06.1	12.9	56.7
19	102 30.6	35.6	236 37.5	12.5	15 19.0	13.0	56.7
20	117 30.8	34.7	251 09.0	12.5	15 32.0	12.8	56.7
21	132 30.9	.. 33.7	265 40.5	12.4	15 44.8	12.8	56.7
22	147 31.1	32.7	280 11.9	12.2	15 57.6	12.8	56.7
23	162 31.3	31.7	294 43.1	12.2	16 10.4	12.6	56.8
12 00	177 31.4	S 3 30.7	309 14.3	12.1	S16 23.0	12.7	56.8
01	192 31.6	29.7	323 45.4	12.0	16 35.7	12.5	56.8
02	207 31.8	28.8	338 16.4	12.0	16 48.2	12.4	56.8
03	222 31.9	.. 27.8	352 47.4	11.8	17 00.6	12.4	56.9
04	237 32.1	26.8	7 18.2	11.7	17 13.0	12.4	56.9
05	252 32.3	25.8	21 48.9	11.6	17 25.4	12.2	56.9
06	267 32.4	S 3 24.8	36 19.5	11.6	S17 37.6	12.2	56.9
S 07	282 32.6	23.8	50 50.1	11.4	17 49.8	12.1	57.0
U 08	297 32.8	22.9	65 20.5	11.4	18 01.9	12.0	57.0
N 09	312 32.9	.. 21.9	79 50.9	11.2	18 13.9	11.9	57.0
D 10	327 33.1	20.9	94 21.1	11.2	18 25.8	11.9	57.0
A 11	342 33.3	19.9	108 51.3	11.0	18 37.7	11.7	57.1
Y 12	357 33.4	S 3 18.9	123 21.3	11.0	S18 49.4	11.7	57.1
13	12 33.6	17.9	137 51.3	10.8	19 01.1	11.6	57.1
14	27 33.8	17.0	152 21.1	10.8	19 12.7	11.5	57.1
15	42 33.9	.. 16.0	166 50.9	10.6	19 24.2	11.4	57.1
16	57 34.1	15.0	181 20.5	10.6	19 35.6	11.4	57.2
17	72 34.3	14.0	195 50.1	10.4	19 47.0	11.2	57.2
18	87 34.4	S 3 13.0	210 19.5	10.3	S19 58.2	11.1	57.2
19	102 34.6	12.0	224 48.8	10.3	20 09.3	11.1	57.2
20	117 34.8	11.1	239 18.1	10.1	20 20.4	10.9	57.3
21	132 34.9	.. 10.1	253 47.2	10.0	20 31.3	10.9	57.3
22	147 35.1	09.1	268 16.2	9.9	20 42.2	10.7	57.3
23	162 35.3	08.1	282 45.1	9.8	20 52.9	10.7	57.3
13 00	177 35.4	S 3 07.1	297 13.9	9.7	S21 03.6	10.6	57.4
01	192 35.6	06.1	311 42.6	9.6	21 14.2	10.4	57.4
02	207 35.8	05.2	326 11.2	9.5	21 24.6	10.3	57.4
03	222 36.0	.. 04.2	340 39.7	9.4	21 34.9	10.3	57.4
04	237 36.1	03.2	355 08.1	9.3	21 45.2	10.1	57.5
05	252 36.3	02.2	9 36.4	9.1	21 55.3	10.0	57.5
06	267 36.5	S 3 01.2	24 04.5	9.1	S22 05.3	9.9	57.5
07	282 36.6	3 00.2	38 32.6	8.9	22 15.2	9.8	57.5
08	297 36.8	2 59.2	53 00.5	8.9	22 25.0	9.7	57.6
M 09	312 37.0	.. 58.3	67 28.4	8.7	22 34.7	9.6	57.6
O 10	327 37.1	57.3	81 56.1	8.6	22 44.3	9.4	57.6
N 11	342 37.3	56.3	96 23.7	8.5	22 53.7	9.3	57.6
D 12	357 37.5	S 2 55.3	110 51.2	8.4	S23 03.0	9.2	57.7
A 13	12 37.6	54.3	125 18.6	8.3	23 12.2	9.1	57.7
Y 14	27 37.8	53.3	139 45.9	8.2	23 21.3	9.0	57.7
15	42 38.0	.. 52.4	154 13.1	8.1	23 30.3	8.8	57.7
16	57 38.2	51.4	168 40.2	8.0	23 39.1	8.7	57.8
17	72 38.3	50.4	183 07.2	7.8	23 47.8	8.6	57.8
18	87 38.5	S 2 49.4	197 34.0	7.8	S23 56.4	8.5	57.8
19	102 38.7	48.4	212 00.8	7.6	24 04.9	8.3	57.8
20	117 38.8	47.4	226 27.4	7.6	24 13.2	8.2	57.9
21	132 39.0	.. 46.4	240 54.0	7.4	24 21.4	8.0	57.9
22	147 39.2	45.5	255 20.4	7.3	24 29.4	7.9	57.9
23	162 39.4	44.5	269 46.7	7.2	S24 37.3	7.8	57.9
	SD 16.1	d 1.0	SD 15.4		15.6		15.7

Lat.	Twilight Naut.	Twilight Civil	Sunrise	Moonrise 11	Moonrise 12	Moonrise 13	Moonrise 14
°	h m	h m	h m	h m	h m	h m	h m
N 72	04 13	05 34	06 41	26 06	02 06	■■■	■■■
N 70	04 24	05 37	06 38	25 08	01 08	■■■	■■■
68	04 34	05 40	06 35	24 35	00 35	03 52	■■■
66	04 41	05 42	06 32	24 11	00 11	02 28	■■■
64	04 47	05 43	06 30	23 52	25 51	01 51	04 22
62	04 53	05 44	06 28	23 37	25 25	01 25	03 22
60	04 57	05 46	06 27	23 24	25 04	01 04	02 49
N 58	05 01	05 46	06 25	23 14	24 48	00 48	02 24
56	05 04	05 47	06 24	23 04	24 34	00 34	02 04
54	05 07	05 48	06 23	22 56	24 21	00 21	01 48
52	05 09	05 48	06 22	22 49	24 11	00 11	01 34
50	05 11	05 49	06 21	22 42	24 01	00 01	01 22
45	05 16	05 50	06 19	22 28	23 42	24 57	00 57
N 40	05 19	05 50	06 17	22 16	23 26	24 37	00 37
35	05 21	05 50	06 15	22 06	23 12	24 20	00 20
30	05 22	05 50	06 14	21 58	23 01	24 06	00 06
20	05 24	05 49	06 11	21 43	22 41	23 42	24 45
N 10	05 23	05 48	06 09	21 30	22 24	23 21	24 21
0	05 22	05 46	06 07	21 18	22 08	23 02	24 00
S 10	05 19	05 43	06 04	21 07	21 52	22 42	23 38
20	05 13	05 39	06 01	20 54	21 35	22 22	23 15
30	05 06	05 34	05 58	20 40	21 16	21 58	22 49
35	05 01	05 31	05 56	20 32	21 05	21 45	22 33
40	04 55	05 27	05 54	20 23	20 52	21 29	22 15
45	04 47	05 22	05 51	20 12	20 37	21 10	21 53
S 50	04 37	05 16	05 48	19 59	20 19	20 47	21 25
52	04 32	05 13	05 47	19 53	20 11	20 35	21 12
54	04 26	05 09	05 45	19 46	20 01	20 23	20 56
56	04 20	05 06	05 44	19 39	19 51	20 08	20 38
58	04 13	05 02	05 42	19 31	19 38	19 52	20 16
S 60	04 04	04 57	05 39	19 21	19 24	19 31	19 47

Lat.	Sunset	Twilight Civil	Twilight Naut.	Moonset 11	Moonset 12	Moonset 13	Moonset 14
°	h m	h m	h m	h m	h m	h m	h m
N 72	17 41	18 48	20 10	05 56	04 31	■■■	■■■
N 70	17 44	18 45	19 58	06 18	05 30	■■■	■■■
68	17 47	18 42	19 49	06 35	06 05	04 32	■■■
66	17 49	18 40	19 41	06 49	06 30	05 57	■■■
64	17 51	18 38	19 34	07 00	06 50	06 36	05 59
62	17 53	18 37	19 29	07 10	07 06	07 03	06 59
60	17 54	18 35	19 24	07 19	07 20	07 24	07 33
N 58	17 55	18 34	19 20	07 26	07 32	07 41	07 58
56	17 57	18 34	19 17	07 33	07 42	07 56	08 18
54	17 58	18 33	19 14	07 39	07 51	08 09	08 35
52	17 59	18 32	19 12	07 44	07 59	08 20	08 49
50	18 00	18 32	19 09	07 49	08 07	08 30	09 02
45	18 02	18 31	19 05	07 59	08 22	08 51	09 28
N 40	18 03	18 30	19 02	08 08	08 35	09 08	09 49
35	18 05	18 30	18 59	08 16	08 46	09 22	10 06
30	18 06	18 30	18 58	08 23	08 56	09 35	10 21
20	18 09	18 31	18 56	08 34	09 13	09 56	10 46
N 10	18 11	18 32	18 56	08 44	09 28	10 15	11 08
0	18 13	18 34	18 58	08 54	09 41	10 33	11 29
S 10	18 15	18 36	19 01	09 04	09 55	10 51	11 49
20	18 18	18 40	19 06	09 14	10 10	11 10	12 12
30	18 21	18 45	19 13	09 26	10 27	11 32	12 37
35	18 23	18 48	19 18	09 33	10 38	11 44	12 53
40	18 25	18 52	19 24	09 41	10 49	11 59	13 10
45	18 27	18 57	19 32	09 50	11 03	12 17	13 32
S 50	18 30	19 03	19 42	10 02	11 19	12 40	13 59
52	18 32	19 06	19 46	10 07	11 27	12 50	14 12
54	18 33	19 09	19 52	10 13	11 36	13 02	14 27
56	18 35	19 12	19 58	10 19	11 46	13 16	14 45
58	18 37	19 16	20 05	10 26	11 57	13 33	15 07
S 60	18 39	19 21	20 13	10 35	12 11	13 52	15 35

Day	SUN Eqn. of Time 00ʰ	SUN Eqn. of Time 12ʰ	SUN Mer. Pass.	MOON Mer. Pass. Upper	MOON Mer. Pass. Lower	Age	Phase
d	m s	m s	h m	h m	h m	d	%
11	10 10	10 02	12 10	02 43	15 06	19	85
12	09 55	09 47	12 10	03 30	15 54	20	77
13	09 39	09 30	12 10	04 20	16 47	21	67

© British Crown Copyright 2022. All rights reserved.

2023 MARCH 14, 15, 16 (TUES., WED., THURS.)

UT	ARIES GHA	VENUS −4.0 GHA	Dec	MARS +0.7 GHA	Dec	JUPITER −2.1 GHA	Dec	SATURN +0.9 GHA	Dec	Name	SHA	Dec
14 00	171 21.3	146 48.5	N10 10.1	87 18.1	N25 35.5	157 15.9	N 4 50.7	198 05.0	S12 25.1	Acamar	315 13.2	S40 13.0
01	186 23.8	161 48.1	11.3	102 19.4	35.5	172 17.8	50.9	213 07.1	25.0	Achernar	335 21.8	S57 07.4
02	201 26.3	176 47.8	12.5	117 20.6	35.5	187 19.8	51.1	228 09.3	24.9	Acrux	173 01.1	S63 13.6
03	216 28.7	191 47.4 ..	13.8	132 21.8 ..	35.5	202 21.7 ..	51.4	243 11.5 ..	24.8	Adhara	255 06.9	S29 00.4
04	231 31.2	206 47.1	15.0	147 23.0	35.5	217 23.6	51.6	258 13.7	24.7	Aldebaran	290 41.4	N16 33.3
05	246 33.6	221 46.7	16.2	162 24.2	35.5	232 25.5	51.8	273 15.9	24.6			
06	261 36.1	236 46.4	N10 17.4	177 25.5	N25 35.6	247 27.5	N 4 52.0	288 18.1	S12 24.5	Alioth	166 13.8	N55 49.9
07	276 38.6	251 46.0	18.6	192 26.7	35.6	262 29.4	52.3	303 20.3	24.4	Alkaid	152 52.8	N49 11.7
08	291 41.0	266 45.7	19.8	207 27.9	35.6	277 31.3	52.5	318 22.5	24.3	Alnair	27 35.2	S46 51.0
09	306 43.5	281 45.3 ..	21.0	222 29.1 ..	35.6	292 33.2 ..	52.7	333 24.6 ..	24.2	Alnilam	275 39.3	S 1 11.4
10	321 46.0	296 45.0	22.3	237 30.3	35.6	307 35.2	53.0	348 26.8	24.1	Alphard	217 49.0	S 8 45.6
11	336 48.4	311 44.6	23.5	252 31.5	35.7	322 37.1	53.2	3 29.0	24.0			
12	351 50.9	326 44.2	N10 24.7	267 32.8	N25 35.7	337 39.0	N 4 53.4	18 31.2	S12 23.9	Alphecca	126 04.8	N26 38.0
13	6 53.4	341 43.9	25.9	282 34.0	35.7	352 40.9	53.6	33 33.4	23.8	Alpheratz	357 36.7	N29 13.0
14	21 55.8	356 43.5	27.1	297 35.2	35.7	7 42.9	53.9	48 35.6	23.7	Altair	62 01.6	N 8 55.5
15	36 58.3	11 43.2 ..	28.3	312 36.4 ..	35.7	22 44.8 ..	54.1	63 37.8 ..	23.6	Ankaa	353 09.0	S42 11.0
16	52 00.8	26 42.8	29.5	327 37.6	35.7	37 46.7	54.3	78 40.0	23.5	Antares	112 17.6	S26 29.0
17	67 03.2	41 42.5	30.7	342 38.8	35.7	52 48.6	54.6	93 42.1	23.4			
18	82 05.7	56 42.1	N10 31.9	357 40.0	N25 35.8	67 50.6	N 4 54.8	108 44.3	S12 23.3	Arcturus	145 49.0	N19 03.5
19	97 08.1	71 41.8	33.1	12 41.3	35.8	82 52.5	55.0	123 46.5	23.2	Atria	107 13.1	S69 03.9
20	112 10.6	86 41.4	34.4	27 42.5	35.8	97 54.4	55.2	138 48.7	23.1	Avior	234 14.9	S59 35.2
21	127 13.1	101 41.1 ..	35.6	42 43.7 ..	35.8	112 56.3 ..	55.5	153 50.9 ..	23.0	Bellatrix	278 24.5	N 6 22.2
22	142 15.5	116 40.7	36.8	57 44.9	35.8	127 58.3	55.7	168 53.1	22.9	Betelgeuse	270 53.7	N 7 24.6
23	157 18.0	131 40.3	38.0	72 46.1	35.8	143 00.2	55.9	183 55.3	22.8			
15 00	172 20.5	146 40.0	N10 39.2	87 47.3	N25 35.9	158 02.1	N 4 56.2	198 57.5	S12 22.7	Canopus	263 53.0	S52 42.7
01	187 22.9	161 39.6	40.4	102 48.5	35.9	173 04.0	56.4	213 59.7	22.6	Capella	280 24.2	N46 01.4
02	202 25.4	176 39.3	41.6	117 49.7	35.9	188 06.0	56.6	229 01.8	22.5	Deneb	49 27.2	N45 21.5
03	217 27.9	191 38.9 ..	42.8	132 50.9 ..	35.9	203 07.9 ..	56.8	244 04.0 ..	22.4	Denebola	182 26.2	N14 26.5
04	232 30.3	206 38.6	44.0	147 52.2	35.9	218 09.8	57.1	259 06.2	22.3	Diphda	348 49.1	S17 51.8
05	247 32.8	221 38.2	45.2	162 53.4	35.9	233 11.7	57.3	274 08.4	22.2			
06	262 35.3	236 37.8	N10 46.4	177 54.6	N25 35.9	248 13.7	N 4 57.5	289 10.6	S12 22.1	Dubhe	193 42.2	N61 37.6
07	277 37.7	251 37.5	47.6	192 55.8	36.0	263 15.6	57.8	304 12.8	22.0	Elnath	278 03.8	N28 37.6
08	292 40.2	266 37.1	48.8	207 57.0	36.0	278 17.5	58.0	319 15.0	21.9	Eltanin	90 42.9	N51 28.8
09	307 42.6	281 36.8 ..	50.0	222 58.2 ..	36.0	293 19.4 ..	58.2	334 17.2 ..	21.9	Enif	33 40.6	N 9 58.7
10	322 45.1	296 36.4	51.2	237 59.4	36.0	308 21.3	58.4	349 19.4	21.8	Fomalhaut	15 16.5	S29 30.1
11	337 47.6	311 36.1	52.4	253 00.6	36.0	323 23.3	58.7	4 21.5	21.7			
12	352 50.0	326 35.7	N10 53.6	268 01.8	N25 36.0	338 25.2	N 4 58.9	19 23.7	S12 21.6	Gacrux	171 52.8	S57 14.5
13	7 52.5	341 35.3	54.8	283 03.0	36.0	353 27.1	59.1	34 25.9	21.5	Gienah	175 44.8	S17 40.3
14	22 55.0	356 35.0	56.0	298 04.2	36.1	8 29.0	59.4	49 28.1	21.4	Hadar	148 37.7	S60 28.9
15	37 57.4	11 34.6 ..	57.2	313 05.4 ..	36.1	23 31.0 ..	59.6	64 30.3 ..	21.3	Hamal	327 53.2	N23 34.2
16	52 59.9	26 34.3	58.4	328 06.6	36.1	38 32.9	4 59.8	79 32.5	21.2	Kaus Aust.	83 34.6	S34 22.4
17	68 02.4	41 33.9	10 59.6	343 07.8	36.1	53 34.8	5 00.0	94 34.7	21.1			
18	83 04.8	56 33.5	N11 00.8	358 09.0	N25 36.1	68 36.7	N 5 00.3	109 36.9	S12 21.0	Kochab	137 19.0	N74 03.3
19	98 07.3	71 33.2	02.0	13 10.3	36.1	83 38.6	00.5	124 39.1	20.9	Markab	13 31.7	N15 19.6
20	113 09.8	86 32.8	03.2	28 11.5	36.1	98 40.6	00.7	139 41.2	20.8	Menkar	314 07.9	N 4 10.7
21	128 12.2	101 32.5 ..	04.4	43 12.7 ..	36.1	113 42.5 ..	01.0	154 43.4 ..	20.7	Menkent	147 59.1	S36 29.0
22	143 14.7	116 32.1	05.6	58 13.9	36.2	128 44.4	01.2	169 45.6	20.6	Miaplacidus	221 37.9	S69 48.9
23	158 17.1	131 31.7	06.8	73 15.1	36.2	143 46.3	01.4	184 47.8	20.5			
16 00	173 19.6	146 31.4	N11 08.0	88 16.3	N25 36.2	158 48.3	N 5 01.7	199 50.0	S12 20.4	Mirfak	308 30.7	N49 56.7
01	188 22.1	161 31.0	09.2	103 17.5	36.2	173 50.2	01.9	214 52.2	20.3	Nunki	75 49.8	S26 16.1
02	203 24.5	176 30.6	10.4	118 18.7	36.2	188 52.1	02.1	229 54.4	20.2	Peacock	53 08.5	S56 39.5
03	218 27.0	191 30.3 ..	11.6	133 19.9 ..	36.2	203 54.0 ..	02.3	244 56.6 ..	20.1	Pollux	243 19.0	N27 58.2
04	233 29.5	206 29.9	12.8	148 21.1	36.2	218 55.9	02.6	259 58.8	20.0	Procyon	244 52.3	N 5 09.9
05	248 31.9	221 29.6	14.0	163 22.3	36.2	233 57.9	02.8	275 01.0	19.9			
06	263 34.4	236 29.2	N11 15.2	178 23.5	N25 36.2	248 59.8	N 5 03.0	290 03.1	S12 19.8	Rasalhague	96 00.0	N12 32.4
07	278 36.9	251 28.8	16.4	193 24.7	36.3	264 01.7	03.3	305 05.3	19.7	Regulus	207 35.8	N11 51.2
08	293 39.3	266 28.5	17.6	208 25.9	36.3	279 03.6	03.5	320 07.5	19.6	Rigel	281 05.3	S 8 10.7
09	308 41.8	281 28.1 ..	18.8	223 27.1 ..	36.3	294 05.6 ..	03.7	335 09.7 ..	19.5	Rigil Kent.	139 41.9	S60 55.7
10	323 44.2	296 27.7	20.0	238 28.3	36.3	309 07.5	03.9	350 11.9	19.4	Sabik	102 04.5	S15 45.3
11	338 46.7	311 27.4	21.3	253 29.5	36.3	324 09.4	04.2	5 14.1	19.3			
12	353 49.2	326 27.0	N11 22.4	268 30.7	N25 36.3	339 11.3	N 5 04.4	20 16.3	S12 19.2	Schedar	349 33.3	N56 39.8
13	8 51.6	341 26.6	23.5	283 31.9	36.3	354 13.2	04.6	35 18.5	19.1	Shaula	96 12.4	S37 07.1
14	23 54.1	356 26.3	24.7	298 33.0	36.3	9 15.2	04.9	50 20.7	19.0	Sirius	258 27.5	S16 45.0
15	38 56.6	11 25.9 ..	25.9	313 34.2 ..	36.3	24 17.1 ..	05.1	65 22.9 ..	18.9	Spica	158 23.6	S11 17.0
16	53 59.0	26 25.5	27.1	328 35.4	36.3	39 19.0	05.3	80 25.0	18.8	Suhail	222 47.1	S43 31.7
17	69 01.5	41 25.2	28.3	343 36.6	36.3	54 20.9	05.5	95 27.2	18.7			
18	84 04.0	56 24.8	N11 29.5	358 37.8	N25 36.4	69 22.9	N 5 05.8	110 29.4	S12 18.6	Vega	80 34.4	N38 48.0
19	99 06.4	71 24.5	30.7	13 39.0	36.4	84 24.8	06.0	125 31.6	18.5	Zuben'ubi	136 57.5	S16 08.3
20	114 08.9	86 24.1	31.9	28 40.2	36.4	99 26.7	06.2	140 33.8	18.4		SHA	Mer.Pass.
21	129 11.4	101 23.7 ..	33.1	43 41.4 ..	36.4	114 28.6 ..	06.5	155 36.0 ..	18.4			
22	144 13.8	116 23.3	34.2	58 42.6	36.4	129 30.5	06.7	170 38.2	18.3	Venus	334 19.5	14 14
23	159 16.3	131 23.0	35.4	73 43.8	36.4	144 32.5	06.9	185 40.4	18.2	Mars	275 26.8	18 07
Mer.Pass. 12 28.6		v −0.4	d 1.2	v 1.2	d 0.0	v 1.9	d 0.2	v 2.2	d 0.1	Jupiter	345 41.6	13 26
										Saturn	26 37.0	10 43

© British Crown Copyright 2022. All rights reserved.

SUN / MOON

UT	SUN GHA	SUN Dec	MOON GHA	v	MOON Dec	d	HP
d h	° ′	° ′	° ′	′	° ′	′	′
14 00	177 39.5	S 2 43.5	284 12.9	7.1	S24 45.1	7.6	58.0
01	192 39.7	42.5	298 39.0	7.0	24 52.7	7.5	58.0
02	207 39.9	41.5	313 05.0	6.9	25 00.2	7.4	58.0
03	222 40.0	.. 40.5	327 30.9	6.8	25 07.6	7.2	58.0
04	237 40.2	39.5	341 56.7	6.7	25 14.8	7.1	58.1
05	252 40.4	38.6	356 22.4	6.6	25 21.9	6.9	58.1
06	267 40.6	S 2 37.6	10 48.0	6.5	S25 28.8	6.8	58.1
07	282 40.7	36.6	25 13.5	6.4	25 35.6	6.6	58.1
T 08	297 40.9	35.6	39 38.9	6.3	25 42.2	6.4	58.2
U 09	312 41.1	.. 34.6	54 04.2	6.2	25 48.6	6.4	58.2
E 10	327 41.2	33.6	68 29.4	6.1	25 55.0	6.1	58.2
S 11	342 41.4	32.6	82 54.5	5.9	26 01.1	6.0	58.3
D 12	357 41.6	S 2 31.6	97 19.4	5.9	S26 07.1	5.9	58.3
A 13	12 41.8	30.7	111 44.3	5.9	26 13.0	5.7	58.3
Y 14	27 41.9	29.7	126 09.2	5.7	26 18.7	5.5	58.3
15	42 42.1	.. 28.7	140 33.9	5.6	26 24.2	5.4	58.4
16	57 42.3	27.7	154 58.5	5.5	26 29.6	5.2	58.4
17	72 42.4	26.7	169 23.0	5.4	26 34.8	5.0	58.4
18	87 42.6	S 2 25.7	183 47.4	5.4	S26 39.8	4.9	58.4
19	102 42.8	24.7	198 11.8	5.3	26 44.7	4.7	58.5
20	117 43.0	23.8	212 36.1	5.1	26 49.4	4.6	58.5
21	132 43.1	.. 22.8	227 00.2	5.1	26 54.0	4.4	58.5
22	147 43.3	21.8	241 24.3	5.0	26 58.4	4.2	58.5
23	162 43.5	20.8	255 48.3	5.0	27 02.6	4.0	58.6
15 00	177 43.7	S 2 19.8	270 12.3	4.8	S27 06.6	3.9	58.6
01	192 43.8	18.8	284 36.1	4.8	27 10.5	3.7	58.6
02	207 44.0	17.8	298 59.9	4.7	27 14.2	3.5	58.6
03	222 44.2	.. 16.8	313 23.6	4.6	27 17.7	3.3	58.7
04	237 44.4	15.9	327 47.2	4.6	27 21.0	3.2	58.7
05	252 44.5	14.9	342 10.8	4.4	27 24.2	3.0	58.7
06	267 44.7	S 2 13.9	356 34.2	4.5	S27 27.2	2.8	58.7
W 07	282 44.9	12.9	10 57.7	4.3	27 30.0	2.7	58.8
E 08	297 45.0	11.9	25 21.0	4.3	27 32.7	2.4	58.8
D 09	312 45.2	.. 10.9	39 44.3	4.2	27 35.1	2.3	58.8
N 10	327 45.4	09.9	54 07.5	4.2	27 37.4	2.1	58.8
E 11	342 45.6	08.9	68 30.7	4.1	27 39.5	1.9	58.9
S 12	357 45.7	S 2 08.0	82 53.8	4.0	S27 41.4	1.7	58.9
D 13	12 45.9	07.0	97 16.8	4.0	27 43.1	1.5	58.9
A 14	27 46.1	06.0	111 39.8	3.9	27 44.6	1.4	58.9
Y 15	42 46.3	.. 05.0	126 02.7	3.9	27 46.0	1.1	59.0
16	57 46.4	04.0	140 25.6	3.9	27 47.1	1.0	59.0
17	72 46.6	03.0	154 48.5	3.8	27 48.1	0.8	59.0
18	87 46.8	S 2 02.0	169 11.3	3.7	S27 48.9	0.6	59.0
19	102 47.0	01.0	183 34.0	3.7	27 49.5	0.4	59.1
20	117 47.1	2 00.1	197 56.7	3.7	27 49.9	0.2	59.1
21	132 47.3	1 59.1	212 19.4	3.7	27 50.1	0.1	59.1
22	147 47.5	58.1	226 42.1	3.6	27 50.2	0.2	59.1
23	162 47.7	57.1	241 04.7	3.6	27 50.0	0.4	59.2
16 00	177 47.8	S 1 56.1	255 27.3	3.5	S27 49.6	0.5	59.2
01	192 48.0	55.1	269 49.8	3.5	27 49.1	0.7	59.2
02	207 48.2	54.1	284 12.3	3.5	27 48.4	1.0	59.2
03	222 48.4	.. 53.1	298 34.8	3.5	27 47.4	1.1	59.3
04	237 48.6	52.2	312 57.3	3.5	27 46.3	1.3	59.3
05	252 48.7	51.2	327 19.8	3.4	27 45.0	1.5	59.3
06	267 48.9	S 1 50.2	341 42.2	3.5	S27 43.5	1.7	59.3
07	282 49.1	49.2	356 04.7	3.4	27 41.8	1.9	59.4
T 08	297 49.3	48.2	10 27.1	3.4	27 39.9	2.1	59.4
H 09	312 49.4	.. 47.2	24 49.5	3.4	27 37.8	2.3	59.4
U 10	327 49.6	46.2	39 11.9	3.4	27 35.5	2.4	59.4
R 11	342 49.8	45.2	53 34.3	3.4	27 33.1	2.7	59.4
S 12	357 50.0	S 1 44.2	67 56.7	3.4	S27 30.4	2.9	59.5
D 13	12 50.1	43.3	82 19.1	3.4	27 27.5	3.0	59.5
A 14	27 50.3	42.3	96 41.5	3.4	27 24.5	3.3	59.5
Y 15	42 50.5	.. 41.3	111 03.9	3.4	27 21.2	3.4	59.5
16	57 50.7	40.3	125 26.3	3.5	27 17.8	3.6	59.6
17	72 50.8	39.3	139 48.8	3.4	27 14.2	3.9	59.6
18	87 51.0	S 1 38.3	154 11.2	3.5	S27 10.3	4.0	59.6
19	102 51.2	37.3	168 33.7	3.5	27 06.3	4.2	59.6
20	117 51.4	36.3	182 56.2	3.5	27 02.1	4.4	59.6
21	132 51.6	.. 35.4	197 18.7	3.5	26 57.7	4.6	59.7
22	147 51.7	34.4	211 41.2	3.5	26 53.1	4.8	59.7
23	162 51.9	33.4	226 03.7	3.6	S26 48.3	4.9	59.7
	SD 16.1	d 1.0	SD 15.9		16.0		16.2

Twilight / Sunrise / Moonrise

Lat.	Twilight Naut.	Twilight Civil	Sunrise	Moonrise 14	15	16	17
°	h m	h m	h m	h m	h m	h m	h m
N 72	03 55	05 19	06 26	■■	■■	■■	■■
N 70	04 09	05 23	06 24	■■	■■	■■	■■
68	04 20	05 27	06 22	■■	■■	■■	■■
66	04 29	05 30	06 21	■■	■■	■■	■■
64	04 36	05 33	06 20	04 22	■■	■■	■■
62	04 42	05 35	06 19	03 22	05 29	06 50	06 47
60	04 48	05 36	06 18	02 49	04 28	05 38	06 09
N 58	04 52	05 38	06 17	02 24	03 54	05 03	05 42
56	04 56	05 39	06 16	02 04	03 29	04 37	05 21
54	04 59	05 40	06 16	01 48	03 10	04 16	05 04
52	05 02	05 41	06 15	01 34	02 53	03 59	04 49
50	05 05	05 42	06 14	01 22	02 39	03 44	04 35
45	05 10	05 44	06 13	00 57	02 09	03 15	04 08
N 40	05 14	05 45	06 12	00 37	01 47	02 51	03 47
35	05 17	05 46	06 11	00 20	01 28	02 32	03 29
30	05 19	05 46	06 10	00 06	01 12	02 16	03 14
20	05 21	05 47	06 09	24 45	00 45	01 48	02 48
N 10	05 22	05 46	06 07	24 21	00 21	01 24	02 25
0	05 21	05 45	06 06	24 00	00 00	01 01	02 04
S 10	05 19	05 43	06 04	23 38	24 39	00 39	01 43
20	05 15	05 40	06 02	23 15	24 15	00 15	01 20
30	05 08	05 36	06 00	22 49	23 48	24 54	00 54
35	05 04	05 33	05 59	22 33	23 31	24 38	00 38
40	04 58	05 30	05 57	22 15	23 12	24 20	00 20
45	04 51	05 26	05 55	21 53	22 49	23 58	25 18
S 50	04 42	05 21	05 53	21 25	22 19	23 31	24 55
52	04 38	05 18	05 52	21 12	22 05	23 17	24 44
54	04 33	05 15	05 51	20 56	21 48	23 01	24 31
56	04 27	05 12	05 50	20 38	21 28	22 43	24 16
58	04 21	05 09	05 48	20 16	21 02	22 20	23 59
S 60	04 13	05 05	05 47	19 47	20 28	21 50	23 38

Sunset / Twilight / Moonset

Lat.	Sunset	Twilight Civil	Twilight Naut.	Moonset 14	15	16	17
°	h m	h m	h m	h m	h m	h m	h m
N 72	17 55	19 02	20 27	■■	■■	■■	■■
N 70	17 56	18 57	20 12	■■	■■	■■	■■
68	17 58	18 53	20 01	■■	■■	■■	■■
66	17 59	18 50	19 51	■■	■■	■■	■■
64	18 00	18 47	19 44	05 59	■■	■■	■■
62	18 01	18 45	19 38	06 59	06 56	07 45	10 00
60	18 01	18 43	19 32	07 33	07 57	08 57	10 37
N 58	18 02	18 41	19 28	07 58	08 31	09 32	11 03
56	18 03	18 40	19 24	08 18	08 56	09 58	11 24
54	18 03	18 39	19 20	08 35	09 16	10 18	11 41
52	18 04	18 38	19 17	08 49	09 33	10 35	11 56
50	18 04	18 37	19 14	09 02	09 47	10 50	12 09
45	18 05	18 35	19 09	09 28	10 17	11 20	12 35
N 40	18 06	18 33	19 05	09 49	10 40	11 43	12 55
35	18 07	18 33	19 02	10 06	10 59	12 02	13 13
30	18 08	18 32	19 00	10 21	11 15	12 18	13 27
20	18 09	18 31	18 57	10 46	11 43	12 46	13 52
N 10	18 11	18 32	18 56	11 08	12 07	13 09	14 14
0	18 12	18 33	18 57	11 29	12 29	13 31	14 34
S 10	18 14	18 35	18 59	11 49	12 51	13 53	14 53
20	18 15	18 37	19 03	12 12	13 15	14 17	15 14
30	18 17	18 41	19 09	12 37	13 43	14 44	15 39
35	18 19	18 44	19 14	12 53	13 59	15 00	15 53
40	18 20	18 47	19 19	13 10	14 18	15 18	16 09
45	18 22	18 51	19 26	13 32	14 41	15 41	16 29
S 50	18 24	18 56	19 35	13 59	15 10	16 09	16 53
52	18 25	18 59	19 39	14 12	15 25	16 23	17 04
54	18 26	19 01	19 44	14 27	15 42	16 39	17 17
56	18 27	19 04	19 49	14 45	16 02	16 58	17 32
58	18 28	19 08	19 55	15 07	16 27	17 21	17 50
S 60	18 30	19 12	20 03	15 35	17 01	17 51	18 12

SUN / MOON

Day	SUN Eqn. of Time 00ʰ	SUN Eqn. of Time 12ʰ	SUN Mer. Pass.	MOON Mer. Pass. Upper	MOON Mer. Pass. Lower	Age	Phase
d	m s	m s	h m	h m	h m	d	%
14	09 22	09 14	12 09	05 15	17 44	22	57
15	09 06	08 57	12 09	06 14	18 45	23	46
16	08 49	08 40	12 09	07 16	19 48	24	34

© British Crown Copyright 2022. All rights reserved.

UT (d h)	ARIES GHA	VENUS −4.0 GHA	VENUS Dec	MARS +0.7 GHA	MARS Dec	JUPITER −2.1 GHA	JUPITER Dec	SATURN +0.9 GHA	SATURN Dec	STARS Name	SHA	Dec
17 00	174 18.7	146 22.6	N11 36.6	88 45.0	N25 36.4	159 34.4	N 5 07.1	200 42.6	S12 18.1	Acamar	315 13.2	S40 13.0
01	189 21.2	161 22.2	37.8	103 46.2	36.4	174 36.3	07.4	215 44.8	18.0	Achernar	335 21.8	S57 07.4
02	204 23.7	176 21.9	39.0	118 47.4	36.4	189 38.2	07.6	230 47.0	17.9	Acrux	173 01.1	S63 13.6
03	219 26.1	191 21.5 ..	40.2	133 48.6 ..	36.4	204 40.1 ..	07.8	245 49.1 ..	17.8	Adhara	255 06.9	S29 00.4
04	234 28.6	206 21.1	41.4	148 49.8	36.4	219 42.1	08.1	260 51.3	17.7	Aldebaran	290 41.4	N16 33.3
05	249 31.1	221 20.8	42.5	163 51.0	36.4	234 44.0	08.3	275 53.5	17.6			
06	264 33.5	236 20.4	N11 43.7	178 52.1	N25 36.5	249 45.9	N 5 08.5	290 55.7	S12 17.5	Alioth	166 13.7	N55 49.9
07	279 36.0	251 20.0	44.9	193 53.3	36.5	264 47.8	08.8	305 57.9	17.4	Alkaid	152 52.8	N49 11.7
08	294 38.5	266 19.7	46.1	208 54.5	36.5	279 49.7	09.0	321 00.1	17.3	Alnair	27 35.2	S46 51.0
F 09	309 40.9	281 19.3 ..	47.3	223 55.7 ..	36.5	294 51.7 ..	09.2	336 02.3 ..	17.2	Alnilam	275 39.3	S 1 11.3
R 10	324 43.4	296 18.9	48.5	238 56.9	36.5	309 53.6	09.4	351 04.5	17.1	Alphard	217 49.0	S 8 45.6
I 11	339 45.9	311 18.5	49.6	253 58.1	36.5	324 55.5	09.7	6 06.7	17.0			
D 12	354 48.3	326 18.2	N11 50.8	268 59.3	N25 36.5	339 57.4	N 5 09.9	21 08.9	S12 16.9	Alphecca	126 04.8	N26 38.0
A 13	9 50.8	341 17.8	52.0	284 00.5	36.5	354 59.3	10.1	36 11.1	16.8	Alpheratz	357 36.7	N29 12.9
Y 14	24 53.2	356 17.4	53.2	299 01.7	36.5	10 01.3	10.4	51 13.2	16.7	Altair	62 01.6	N 8 55.5
15	39 55.7	11 17.1 ..	54.4	314 02.8 ..	36.5	25 03.2 ..	10.6	66 15.4 ..	16.6	Ankaa	353 09.0	S42 11.0
16	54 58.2	26 16.7	55.5	329 04.0	36.5	40 05.1	10.8	81 17.6	16.5	Antares	112 17.6	S26 29.0
17	70 00.6	41 16.3	56.7	344 05.2	36.5	55 07.0	11.0	96 19.8	16.4			
18	85 03.1	56 15.9	N11 57.9	359 06.4	N25 36.5	70 08.9	N 5 11.3	111 22.0	S12 16.3	Arcturus	145 49.0	N19 03.5
19	100 05.6	71 15.6	11 59.1	14 07.6	36.5	85 10.9	11.5	126 24.2	16.2	Atria	107 13.1	S69 03.9
20	115 08.0	86 15.2	12 00.2	29 08.8	36.5	100 12.8	11.7	141 26.4	16.1	Avior	234 15.0	S59 35.2
21	130 10.5	101 14.8 ..	01.4	44 10.0 ..	36.5	115 14.7 ..	12.0	156 28.6 ..	16.0	Bellatrix	278 24.5	N 6 22.2
22	145 13.0	116 14.4	02.6	59 11.1	36.5	130 16.6	12.2	171 30.8	15.9	Betelgeuse	270 53.7	N 7 24.6
23	160 15.4	131 14.1	03.8	74 12.3	36.5	145 18.5	12.4	186 33.0	15.8			
18 00	175 17.9	146 13.7	N12 05.0	89 13.5	N25 36.6	160 20.5	N 5 12.6	201 35.2	S12 15.7	Canopus	263 53.0	S52 42.7
01	190 20.4	161 13.3	06.1	104 14.7	36.6	175 22.4	12.9	216 37.4	15.6	Capella	280 24.2	N46 01.4
02	205 22.8	176 12.9	07.3	119 15.9	36.6	190 24.3	13.1	231 39.6	15.5	Deneb	49 27.1	N45 21.5
03	220 25.3	191 12.6 ..	08.5	134 17.1 ..	36.6	205 26.2 ..	13.3	246 41.7 ..	15.5	Denebola	182 26.2	N14 26.5
04	235 27.7	206 12.2	09.6	149 18.2	36.6	220 28.1	13.6	261 43.9	15.4	Diphda	348 49.1	S17 51.8
05	250 30.2	221 11.8	10.8	164 19.4	36.6	235 30.1	13.8	276 46.1	15.3			
06	265 32.7	236 11.4	N12 12.0	179 20.6	N25 36.6	250 32.0	N 5 14.0	291 48.3	S12 15.2	Dubhe	193 42.2	N61 37.6
07	280 35.1	251 11.1	13.2	194 21.8	36.6	265 33.9	14.3	306 50.5	15.1	Elnath	278 03.8	N28 37.6
S 08	295 37.6	266 10.7	14.3	209 23.0	36.6	280 35.8	14.5	321 52.7	15.0	Eltanin	90 42.9	N51 28.8
A 09	310 40.1	281 10.3 ..	15.5	224 24.2 ..	36.6	295 37.7 ..	14.7	336 54.9 ..	14.9	Enif	33 40.5	N 9 58.7
T 10	325 42.5	296 09.9	16.7	239 25.3	36.6	310 39.6	14.9	351 57.1	14.8	Fomalhaut	15 16.5	S29 30.1
U 11	340 45.0	311 09.6	17.8	254 26.5	36.6	325 41.6	15.2	6 59.3	14.7			
R 12	355 47.5	326 09.2	N12 19.0	269 27.7	N25 36.6	340 43.5	N 5 15.4	22 01.5	S12 14.6	Gacrux	171 52.8	S57 14.5
D 13	10 49.9	341 08.8	20.2	284 28.9	36.6	355 45.4	15.6	37 03.7	14.5	Gienah	175 44.8	S17 40.3
A 14	25 52.4	356 08.4	21.3	299 30.0	36.6	10 47.3	15.9	52 05.9	14.4	Hadar	148 37.6	S60 29.0
Y 15	40 54.8	11 08.0 ..	22.5	314 31.2 ..	36.6	25 49.2 ..	16.1	67 08.1 ..	14.3	Hamal	327 53.2	N23 34.2
16	55 57.3	26 07.7	23.7	329 32.4	36.6	40 51.2	16.3	82 10.3	14.2	Kaus Aust.	83 34.6	S34 22.4
17	70 59.8	41 07.3	24.8	344 33.6	36.6	55 53.1	16.5	97 12.4	14.1			
18	86 02.3	56 06.9	N12 26.0	359 34.8	N25 36.6	70 55.0	N 5 16.8	112 14.6	S12 14.0	Kochab	137 18.9	N74 03.3
19	101 04.7	71 06.5	27.2	14 35.9	36.6	85 56.9	17.0	127 16.8	13.9	Markab	13 31.7	N15 19.6
20	116 07.2	86 06.1	28.3	29 37.1	36.6	100 58.8	17.2	142 19.0	13.8	Menkar	314 07.9	N 4 10.7
21	131 09.6	101 05.8 ..	29.5	44 38.3 ..	36.6	116 00.7 ..	17.5	157 21.2 ..	13.7	Menkent	147 59.1	S36 29.0
22	146 12.1	116 05.4	30.7	59 39.5	36.6	131 02.7	17.7	172 23.4	13.6	Miaplacidus	221 37.9	S69 48.9
23	161 14.6	131 05.0	31.8	74 40.6	36.6	146 04.6	17.9	187 25.6	13.5			
19 00	176 17.0	146 04.6	N12 33.0	89 41.8	N25 36.6	161 06.5	N 5 18.2	202 27.8	S12 13.4	Mirfak	308 30.7	N49 56.7
01	191 19.5	161 04.2	34.2	104 43.0	36.6	176 08.4	18.4	217 30.0	13.3	Nunki	75 49.7	S26 16.1
02	206 22.0	176 03.9	35.3	119 44.2	36.6	191 10.3	18.6	232 32.2	13.2	Peacock	53 08.4	S56 39.5
03	221 24.4	191 03.5 ..	36.5	134 45.3 ..	36.6	206 12.3 ..	18.8	247 34.4 ..	13.1	Pollux	243 19.0	N27 58.2
04	236 26.9	206 03.1	37.6	149 46.5	36.6	221 14.2	19.1	262 36.6	13.1	Procyon	244 52.3	N 5 09.9
05	251 29.3	221 02.7	38.8	164 47.7	36.6	236 16.1	19.3	277 38.8	13.0			
06	266 31.8	236 02.3	N12 40.0	179 48.9	N25 36.6	251 18.0	N 5 19.5	292 41.0	S12 12.9	Rasalhague	95 59.9	N12 32.4
07	281 34.3	251 01.9	41.1	194 50.0	36.6	266 19.9	19.8	307 43.2	12.8	Regulus	207 35.7	N11 51.2
08	296 36.7	266 01.6	42.3	209 51.2	36.6	281 21.8	20.0	322 45.4	12.7	Rigel	281 05.4	S 8 10.7
S 09	311 39.2	281 01.2 ..	43.4	224 52.4 ..	36.6	296 23.8 ..	20.2	337 47.5 ..	12.6	Rigil Kent.	139 41.9	S60 55.7
U 10	326 41.7	296 00.8	44.6	239 53.6	36.6	311 25.7	20.4	352 49.7	12.5	Sabik	102 04.5	S15 45.3
N 11	341 44.1	311 00.4	45.8	254 54.7	36.6	326 27.6	20.7	7 51.9	12.4			
D 12	356 46.6	326 00.0	N12 46.9	269 55.9	N25 36.6	341 29.5	N 5 20.9	22 54.1	S12 12.3	Schedar	349 33.3	N56 39.8
A 13	11 49.1	340 59.6	48.1	284 57.1	36.6	356 31.4	21.1	37 56.3	12.2	Shaula	96 12.4	S37 07.1
Y 14	26 51.5	355 59.2	49.2	299 58.2	36.6	11 33.3	21.4	52 58.5	12.1	Sirius	258 27.5	S16 45.1
15	41 54.0	10 58.9 ..	50.4	314 59.4 ..	36.6	26 35.3 ..	21.6	68 00.7 ..	12.0	Spica	158 23.6	S11 17.0
16	56 56.5	25 58.5	51.5	330 00.6	36.6	41 37.2	21.8	83 02.9	11.9	Suhail	222 47.1	S43 31.7
17	71 58.9	40 58.1	52.7	345 01.7	36.6	56 39.1	22.1	98 05.1	11.8			
18	87 01.4	55 57.7	N12 53.9	0 02.9	N25 36.6	71 41.0	N 5 22.3	113 07.3	S12 11.7	Vega	80 34.3	N38 47.9
19	102 03.8	70 57.3	55.0	15 04.1	36.6	86 42.9	22.5	128 09.5	11.6	Zuben'ubi	136 57.5	S16 08.3
20	117 06.3	85 56.9	56.2	30 05.3	36.6	101 44.9	22.7	143 11.7	11.5		SHA	Mer. Pass.
21	132 08.8	100 56.5 ..	57.3	45 06.4 ..	36.6	116 46.8 ..	23.0	158 13.9 ..	11.4			h m
22	147 11.2	115 56.2	58.5	60 07.6	36.6	131 48.7	23.2	173 16.1	11.3	Venus	330 55.8	14 15
23	162 13.7	130 55.8	59.6	75 08.8	36.6	146 50.6	23.4	188 18.3	11.2	Mars	273 55.6	18 02
Mer. Pass.	h m 12 16.8	v −0.4 d 1.2		v 1.2 d 0.0		v 1.9 d 0.2		v 2.2 d 0.1		Jupiter	345 02.6	13 17
										Saturn	26 17.3	10 32

© British Crown Copyright 2022. All rights reserved.

UT	SUN GHA	SUN Dec	MOON GHA	v	MOON Dec	d	HP
d h	° ′	° ′	° ′	′	° ′	′	′
17 00	177 52.1	S 1 32.4	240 26.3	3.6	S26 43.4	5.2	59.7
01	192 52.3	31.4	254 48.9	3.7	26 38.2	5.4	59.8
02	207 52.4	30.4	269 11.6	3.6	26 32.8	5.5	59.8
03	222 52.6	.. 29.4	283 34.2	3.7	26 27.3	5.7	59.8
04	237 52.8	28.4	297 56.9	3.8	26 21.6	6.0	59.8
05	252 53.0	27.4	312 19.7	3.8	26 15.6	6.1	59.8
06	267 53.2	S 1 26.5	326 42.5	3.8	S26 09.5	6.2	59.8
07	282 53.3	25.5	341 05.3	3.9	26 03.3	6.5	59.9
F 08	297 53.5	24.5	355 28.2	3.9	25 56.8	6.7	59.9
R 09	312 53.7	.. 23.5	9 51.1	3.9	25 50.1	6.8	59.9
I 10	327 53.9	22.5	24 14.0	4.0	25 43.3	7.0	59.9
D 11	342 54.1	21.5	38 37.0	4.1	25 36.3	7.2	59.9
A 12	357 54.2	S 1 20.5	53 00.1	4.1	S25 29.1	7.4	60.0
Y 13	12 54.4	19.5	67 23.2	4.2	25 21.7	7.6	60.0
14	27 54.6	18.5	81 46.4	4.2	25 14.1	7.7	60.0
15	42 54.8	.. 17.6	96 09.6	4.3	25 06.4	7.9	60.0
16	57 54.9	16.6	110 32.9	4.4	24 58.5	8.1	60.0
17	72 55.1	15.6	124 56.3	4.4	24 50.4	8.3	60.0
18	87 55.3	S 1 14.6	139 19.7	4.5	S24 42.1	8.4	60.1
19	102 55.5	13.6	153 43.2	4.5	24 33.7	8.7	60.1
20	117 55.7	12.6	168 06.7	4.6	24 25.0	8.7	60.1
21	132 55.8	.. 11.6	182 30.3	4.7	24 16.3	9.0	60.1
22	147 56.0	10.6	196 54.0	4.7	24 07.3	9.1	60.1
23	162 56.2	09.6	211 17.7	4.9	23 58.2	9.3	60.1
18 00	177 56.4	S 1 08.7	225 41.6	4.8	S23 48.9	9.5	60.2
01	192 56.6	07.7	240 05.4	5.0	23 39.4	9.6	60.2
02	207 56.7	06.7	254 29.4	5.0	23 29.8	9.8	60.2
03	222 56.9	.. 05.7	268 53.4	5.1	23 20.0	9.9	60.2
04	237 57.1	04.7	283 17.5	5.2	23 10.1	10.1	60.2
05	252 57.3	03.7	297 41.7	5.3	23 00.0	10.3	60.2
06	267 57.5	S 1 02.7	312 06.0	5.3	S22 49.7	10.4	60.2
S 07	282 57.6	01.7	326 30.3	5.4	22 39.3	10.6	60.3
A 08	297 57.8	1 00.7	340 54.7	5.5	22 28.7	10.7	60.3
T 09	312 58.0	0 59.8	355 19.2	5.6	22 18.0	10.9	60.3
U 10	327 58.2	58.8	9 43.8	5.7	22 07.1	11.0	60.3
R 11	342 58.4	57.8	24 08.5	5.7	21 56.1	11.2	60.3
D 12	357 58.5	S 0 56.8	38 33.2	5.8	S21 44.9	11.3	60.3
A 13	12 58.7	55.8	52 58.0	5.9	21 33.6	11.5	60.3
Y 14	27 58.9	54.8	67 22.9	6.0	21 22.1	11.6	60.3
15	42 59.1	.. 53.8	81 47.9	6.1	21 10.5	11.7	60.3
16	57 59.3	52.8	96 13.0	6.2	20 58.8	11.9	60.3
17	72 59.4	51.8	110 38.2	6.2	20 46.9	12.1	60.4
18	87 59.6	S 0 50.8	125 03.4	6.3	S20 34.8	12.2	60.4
19	102 59.8	49.9	139 28.7	6.5	20 22.6	12.3	60.4
20	118 00.0	48.9	153 54.2	6.5	20 10.3	12.4	60.4
21	133 00.2	.. 47.9	168 19.7	6.5	19 57.9	12.6	60.4
22	148 00.3	46.9	182 45.2	6.7	19 45.3	12.7	60.4
23	163 00.5	45.9	197 10.9	6.8	19 32.6	12.8	60.4
19 00	178 00.7	S 0 44.9	211 36.7	6.8	S19 19.8	13.0	60.4
01	193 00.9	43.9	226 02.5	6.9	19 06.8	13.0	60.4
02	208 01.1	42.9	240 28.4	7.1	18 53.8	13.2	60.4
03	223 01.3	.. 41.9	254 54.5	7.1	18 40.6	13.4	60.4
04	238 01.4	41.0	269 20.6	7.2	18 27.2	13.4	60.4
05	253 01.6	40.0	283 46.8	7.2	18 13.8	13.6	60.4
06	268 01.8	S 0 39.0	298 13.0	7.4	S18 00.2	13.6	60.4
07	283 02.0	38.0	312 39.4	7.4	17 46.6	13.8	60.4
08	298 02.2	37.0	327 05.8	7.6	17 32.8	13.9	60.4
S 09	313 02.3	.. 36.0	341 32.4	7.6	17 18.9	14.0	60.4
U 10	328 02.5	35.0	355 59.0	7.7	17 04.9	14.1	60.5
N 11	343 02.7	34.0	10 25.7	7.8	16 50.8	14.2	60.5
D 12	358 02.9	S 0 33.0	24 52.5	7.9	S16 36.6	14.4	60.5
A 13	13 03.1	32.1	39 19.4	7.9	16 22.2	14.4	60.5
Y 14	28 03.3	31.1	53 46.3	8.1	16 07.8	14.5	60.5
15	43 03.4	.. 30.1	68 13.4	8.1	15 53.3	14.6	60.5
16	58 03.6	29.1	82 40.5	8.2	15 38.7	14.7	60.5
17	73 03.8	28.1	97 07.7	8.3	15 24.0	14.8	60.5
18	88 04.0	S 0 27.1	111 35.0	8.4	S15 09.2	14.9	60.5
19	103 04.2	26.1	126 02.4	8.4	14 54.3	15.0	60.5
20	118 04.3	25.1	140 29.8	8.5	14 39.3	15.1	60.5
21	133 04.5	.. 24.1	154 57.3	8.7	14 24.2	15.1	60.4
22	148 04.7	23.2	169 25.0	8.6	14 09.1	15.3	60.4
23	163 04.9	22.2	183 52.6	8.8	S13 53.8	15.3	60.4
	SD 16.1	d 1.0	SD 16.3		16.4		16.5

Lat.	Twilight Naut.	Twilight Civil	Sunrise	Moonrise 17	18	19	20
°	h m	h m	h m	h m	h m	h m	h m
N 72	03 36	05 03	06 10	■	■	09 14	07 43
N 70	03 53	05 09	06 10	■	■	08 16	07 24
68	04 06	05 14	06 10	■	■	07 41	07 08
66	04 16	05 18	06 09	■	07 55	07 16	06 56
64	04 25	05 22	06 09	■	07 12	06 56	06 45
62	04 32	05 25	06 09	06 47	06 43	06 40	06 36
60	04 38	05 27	06 09	06 09	06 21	06 26	06 28
N 58	04 43	05 30	06 09	05 42	06 03	06 14	06 21
56	04 48	05 31	06 08	05 21	05 47	06 04	06 15
54	04 52	05 33	06 08	05 04	05 34	05 55	06 09
52	04 55	05 35	06 08	04 49	05 23	05 46	06 04
50	04 58	05 36	06 08	04 35	05 12	05 39	06 00
45	05 04	05 38	06 08	04 08	04 51	05 23	05 50
N 40	05 09	05 40	06 07	03 47	04 33	05 10	05 41
35	05 12	05 42	06 07	03 29	04 18	04 59	05 34
30	05 15	05 43	06 07	03 14	04 05	04 49	05 28
20	05 19	05 44	06 06	02 48	03 43	04 32	05 17
N 10	05 20	05 45	06 06	02 25	03 23	04 17	05 07
0	05 20	05 44	06 05	02 04	03 05	04 03	04 58
S 10	05 19	05 43	06 04	01 43	02 47	03 49	04 49
20	05 15	05 41	06 03	01 20	02 28	03 34	04 39
30	05 10	05 38	06 02	00 54	02 05	03 17	04 28
35	05 06	05 36	06 01	00 38	01 52	03 07	04 21
40	05 01	05 33	06 00	00 20	01 36	02 55	04 14
45	04 55	05 30	05 59	25 18	01 18	02 41	04 05
S 50	04 47	05 26	05 58	24 55	00 55	02 24	03 54
52	04 43	05 24	05 57	24 44	00 44	02 16	03 49
54	04 39	05 21	05 57	24 31	00 31	02 08	03 44
56	04 34	05 19	05 56	24 16	00 16	01 57	03 38
58	04 28	05 16	05 55	23 59	25 46	01 46	03 31
S 60	04 22	05 12	05 54	23 38	25 32	01 32	03 23

Lat.	Sunset	Twilight Civil	Twilight Naut.	Moonset 17	18	19	20
°	h m	h m	h m	h m	h m	h m	h m
N 72	18 08	19 16	20 44	■	■	11 45	15 10
N 70	18 08	19 10	20 27	■	■	12 42	15 27
68	18 09	19 04	20 13	■	■	13 15	15 40
66	18 09	19 00	20 03	■	11 00	13 39	15 50
64	18 09	18 56	19 54	■	11 42	13 57	15 59
62	18 09	18 53	19 46	10 00	12 10	14 12	16 07
60	18 09	18 50	19 40	10 37	12 31	14 25	16 13
N 58	18 09	18 48	19 35	11 03	12 49	14 36	16 19
56	18 09	18 46	19 30	11 24	13 03	14 45	16 24
54	18 09	18 44	19 26	11 41	13 16	14 53	16 28
52	18 09	18 43	19 23	11 56	13 27	15 00	16 32
50	18 09	18 41	19 19	12 09	13 37	15 07	16 36
45	18 09	18 39	19 13	12 35	13 57	15 21	16 44
N 40	18 10	18 37	19 08	12 55	14 14	15 33	16 50
35	18 10	18 35	19 04	13 13	14 27	15 42	16 56
30	18 10	18 34	19 02	13 27	14 39	15 51	17 00
20	18 10	18 32	18 59	13 52	15 00	16 05	17 09
N 10	18 11	18 32	18 56	14 14	15 17	16 18	17 16
0	18 11	18 32	18 56	14 34	15 33	16 30	17 23
S 10	18 12	18 33	18 57	14 53	15 50	16 41	17 29
20	18 13	18 35	19 00	15 14	16 07	16 54	17 36
30	18 14	18 38	19 06	15 39	16 26	17 07	17 44
35	18 14	18 40	19 09	15 53	16 38	17 15	17 48
40	18 15	18 42	19 14	16 09	16 51	17 25	17 54
45	18 16	18 45	19 20	16 29	17 06	17 35	17 59
S 50	18 17	18 49	19 28	16 53	17 24	17 48	18 06
52	18 18	18 51	19 31	17 04	17 33	17 54	18 09
54	18 18	18 54	19 36	17 17	17 43	18 00	18 13
56	18 19	18 56	19 41	17 32	17 54	18 07	18 17
58	18 20	18 59	19 46	17 50	18 06	18 15	18 21
S 60	18 21	19 02	19 53	18 12	18 20	18 24	18 26

Day	SUN Eqn. of Time 00h	12h	SUN Mer. Pass.	MOON Mer. Pass. Upper	Lower	Age	Phase
d	m s	m s	h m	h m	h m	d	%
17	08 32	08 23	12 08	20 50	08 19	25	24
18	08 15	08 06	12 08	21 49	09 19	26	14
19	07 58	07 49	12 08	22 44	10 17	27	7

© British Crown Copyright 2022. All rights reserved.

2023 MARCH 20, 21, 22 (MON., TUES., WED.)

UT	ARIES GHA	VENUS −4.0 GHA	Dec	MARS +0.8 GHA	Dec	JUPITER −2.1 GHA	Dec	SATURN +0.9 GHA	Dec
d h	° ′	° ′	° ′	° ′	° ′	° ′	° ′	° ′	° ′
20 00	177 16.2	145 55.4	N13 00.8	90 09.9	N25 36.6	161 52.5	N 5 23.7	203 20.5	S12 11.1
01	192 18.6	160 55.0	01.9	105 11.1	36.6	176 54.4	23.9	218 22.7	11.0
02	207 21.1	175 54.6	03.1	120 12.3	36.5	191 56.4	24.1	233 24.9	10.9
03	222 23.6	190 54.2 ..	04.2	135 13.4 ..	36.5	206 58.3 ..	24.3	248 27.1 ..	10.9
04	237 26.0	205 53.8	05.4	150 14.6	36.5	222 00.2	24.6	263 29.2	10.8
05	252 28.5	220 53.4	06.5	165 15.8	36.5	237 02.1	24.8	278 31.4	10.7
M 06	267 30.9	235 53.0	N13 07.7	180 16.9	N25 36.5	252 04.0	N 5 25.0	293 33.6	S12 10.6
O 07	282 33.4	250 52.6	08.8	195 18.1	36.5	267 05.9	25.3	308 35.8	10.5
N 08	297 35.9	265 52.3	10.0	210 19.3	36.5	282 07.8	25.5	323 38.0	10.4
D 09	312 38.3	280 51.9 ..	11.1	225 20.4 ..	36.5	297 09.8 ..	25.7	338 40.2 ..	10.3
A 10	327 40.8	295 51.5	12.2	240 21.6	36.5	312 11.7	26.0	353 42.4	10.2
Y 11	342 43.3	310 51.1	13.4	255 22.7	36.5	327 13.6	26.2	8 44.6	10.1
12	357 45.7	325 50.7	N13 14.5	270 23.9	N25 36.5	342 15.5	N 5 26.4	23 46.8	S12 10.0
13	12 48.2	340 50.3	15.7	285 25.1	36.5	357 17.4	26.6	38 49.0	09.9
14	27 50.7	355 49.9	16.8	300 26.2	36.5	12 19.3	26.9	53 51.2	09.8
15	42 53.1	10 49.5 ..	18.0	315 27.4 ..	36.5	27 21.3 ..	27.1	68 53.4 ..	09.7
16	57 55.6	25 49.1	19.1	330 28.6	36.5	42 23.2	27.3	83 55.6	09.6
17	72 58.1	40 48.7	20.2	345 29.7	36.5	57 25.1	27.6	98 57.8	09.5
18	88 00.5	55 48.3	N13 21.4	0 30.9	N25 36.5	72 27.0	N 5 27.8	114 00.0	S12 09.4
19	103 03.0	70 47.9	22.5	15 32.0	36.5	87 28.9	28.0	129 02.2	09.3
20	118 05.4	85 47.5	23.7	30 33.2	36.4	102 30.8	28.3	144 04.4	09.2
21	133 07.9	100 47.1 ..	24.8	45 34.4 ..	36.4	117 32.8 ..	28.5	159 06.6 ..	09.1
22	148 10.4	115 46.8	26.0	60 35.5	36.4	132 34.7	28.7	174 08.8	09.0
23	163 12.8	130 46.4	27.1	75 36.7	36.4	147 36.6	28.9	189 11.0	09.0
21 00	178 15.3	145 46.0	N13 28.2	90 37.8	N25 36.4	162 38.5	N 5 29.2	204 13.2	S12 08.9
01	193 17.8	160 45.6	29.4	105 39.0	36.4	177 40.4	29.4	219 15.4	08.8
02	208 20.2	175 45.2	30.5	120 40.1	36.4	192 42.3	29.6	234 17.6	08.7
03	223 22.7	190 44.8 ..	31.6	135 41.3 ..	36.4	207 44.2 ..	29.9	249 19.8 ..	08.6
04	238 25.2	205 44.4	32.8	150 42.5	36.4	222 46.2	30.1	264 22.0	08.5
05	253 27.6	220 44.0	33.9	165 43.6	36.4	237 48.1	30.3	279 24.1	08.4
T 06	268 30.1	235 43.6	N13 35.0	180 44.8	N25 36.4	252 50.0	N 5 30.5	294 26.3	S12 08.3
U 07	283 32.5	250 43.2	36.2	195 45.9	36.4	267 51.9	30.8	309 28.5	08.2
E 08	298 35.0	265 42.8	37.3	210 47.1	36.4	282 53.8	31.0	324 30.7	08.1
S 09	313 37.5	280 42.4 ..	38.4	225 48.2 ..	36.3	297 55.7 ..	31.2	339 32.9 ..	08.0
D 10	328 39.9	295 42.0	39.6	240 49.4	36.3	312 57.7	31.5	354 35.1	07.9
A 11	343 42.4	310 41.6	40.7	255 50.6	36.3	327 59.6	31.7	9 37.3	07.8
Y 12	358 44.9	325 41.2	N13 41.8	270 51.7	N25 36.3	343 01.5	N 5 31.9	24 39.5	S12 07.7
13	13 47.3	340 40.8	43.0	285 52.9	36.3	358 03.4	32.2	39 41.7	07.6
14	28 49.8	355 40.4	44.1	300 54.0	36.3	13 05.3	32.4	54 43.9	07.5
15	43 52.3	10 40.0 ..	45.2	315 55.2 ..	36.3	28 07.2 ..	32.6	69 46.1 ..	07.4
16	58 54.7	25 39.6	46.4	330 56.3	36.3	43 09.1	32.8	84 48.3	07.3
17	73 57.2	40 39.2	47.5	345 57.5	36.3	58 11.1	33.1	99 50.5	07.2
18	88 59.7	55 38.8	N13 48.6	0 58.6	N25 36.3	73 13.0	N 5 33.3	114 52.7	S12 07.2
19	104 02.1	70 38.4	49.7	15 59.8	36.2	88 14.9	33.5	129 54.9	07.1
20	119 04.6	85 38.0	50.9	31 00.9	36.2	103 16.8	33.8	144 57.1	07.0
21	134 07.0	100 37.6 ..	52.0	46 02.1 ..	36.2	118 18.7 ..	34.0	159 59.3 ..	06.9
22	149 09.5	115 37.2	53.1	61 03.2	36.2	133 20.6	34.2	175 01.5	06.8
23	164 12.0	130 36.8	54.3	76 04.4	36.2	148 22.5	34.5	190 03.7	06.7
22 00	179 14.4	145 36.4	N13 55.4	91 05.5	N25 36.2	163 24.5	N 5 34.7	205 05.9	S12 06.6
01	194 16.9	160 36.0	56.5	106 06.7	36.2	178 26.4	34.9	220 08.1	06.5
02	209 19.4	175 35.6	57.6	121 07.8	36.2	193 28.3	35.1	235 10.3	06.4
03	224 21.8	190 35.2 ..	58.7	136 09.0 ..	36.1	208 30.2 ..	35.4	250 12.5 ..	06.3
04	239 24.3	205 34.8	13 59.9	151 10.1	36.1	223 32.1	35.6	265 14.7	06.2
05	254 26.8	220 34.3	14 01.0	166 11.3	36.1	238 34.0	35.8	280 16.9	06.1
W 06	269 29.2	235 33.9	N14 02.1	181 12.4	N25 36.1	253 35.9	N 5 36.1	295 19.1	S12 06.0
E 07	284 31.7	250 33.5	03.2	196 13.6	36.1	268 37.9	36.3	310 21.3	05.9
D 08	299 34.1	265 33.1	04.4	211 14.7	36.1	283 39.8	36.5	325 23.5	05.8
N 09	314 36.6	280 32.7 ..	05.5	226 15.9 ..	36.1	298 41.7 ..	36.8	340 25.7 ..	05.7
E 10	329 39.1	295 32.3	06.6	241 17.0	36.1	313 43.6	37.0	355 27.9	05.6
S 11	344 41.5	310 31.9	07.7	256 18.2	36.0	328 45.5	37.2	10 30.1	05.5
D 12	359 44.0	325 31.5	N14 08.8	271 19.3	N25 36.0	343 47.4	N 5 37.4	25 32.3	S12 05.5
A 13	14 46.5	340 31.1	09.9	286 20.5	36.0	358 49.3	37.7	40 34.5	05.4
Y 14	29 48.9	355 30.7	11.1	301 21.6	36.0	13 51.2	37.9	55 36.7	05.3
15	44 51.4	10 30.3 ..	12.2	316 22.8 ..	36.0	28 53.2 ..	38.1	70 38.9 ..	05.2
16	59 53.9	25 29.9	13.3	331 23.9	36.0	43 55.1	38.4	85 41.1	05.1
17	74 56.3	40 29.5	14.4	346 25.1	36.0	58 57.0	38.6	100 43.3	05.0
18	89 58.8	55 29.1	N14 15.5	1 26.2	N25 35.9	73 58.9	N 5 38.8	115 45.5	S12 04.9
19	105 01.3	70 28.6	16.6	16 27.4	35.9	89 00.8	39.0	130 47.7	04.8
20	120 03.7	85 28.2	17.8	31 28.5	35.9	104 02.7	39.3	145 49.9	04.7
21	135 06.2	100 27.8 ..	18.9	46 29.6 ..	35.9	119 04.6 ..	39.5	160 52.1 ..	04.6
22	150 08.7	115 27.4	20.0	61 30.8	35.9	134 06.6	39.7	175 54.3	04.5
23	165 11.1	130 27.0	21.1	76 31.9	35.9	149 08.5	40.0	190 56.5	04.4
Mer. Pass. 12 05.0		v −0.4 d 1.1		v 1.2 d 0.0		v 1.9 d 0.2		v 2.2 d 0.1	

STARS

Name	SHA	Dec
Acamar	315 13.2	S40 13.0
Achernar	335 21.8	S57 07.4
Acrux	173 01.1	S63 13.6
Adhara	255 07.0	S29 00.4
Aldebaran	290 41.5	N16 33.3
Alioth	166 13.7	N55 49.9
Alkaid	152 52.7	N49 11.7
Alnair	27 35.2	S46 51.0
Alnilam	275 39.3	S 1 11.3
Alphard	217 49.0	S 8 45.6
Alphecca	126 04.8	N26 38.0
Alpheratz	357 36.7	N29 12.9
Altair	62 01.6	N 8 55.5
Ankaa	353 09.0	S42 11.0
Antares	112 17.5	S26 29.0
Arcturus	145 49.0	N19 03.5
Atria	107 13.0	S69 03.9
Avior	234 15.0	S59 35.2
Bellatrix	278 24.5	N 6 22.2
Betelgeuse	270 53.7	N 7 24.6
Canopus	263 53.0	S52 42.7
Capella	280 24.2	N46 01.4
Deneb	49 27.1	N45 21.4
Denebola	182 26.2	N14 26.5
Diphda	348 49.1	S17 51.8
Dubhe	193 42.2	N61 37.6
Elnath	278 03.8	N28 37.6
Eltanin	90 42.9	N51 28.8
Enif	33 40.5	N 9 58.7
Fomalhaut	15 16.5	S29 30.1
Gacrux	171 52.8	S57 14.6
Gienah	175 44.8	S17 40.3
Hadar	148 37.6	S60 29.0
Hamal	327 53.2	N23 34.2
Kaus Aust.	83 34.5	S34 22.4
Kochab	137 18.9	N74 03.3
Markab	13 31.7	N15 19.6
Menkar	314 07.9	N 4 10.7
Menkent	147 59.1	S36 29.0
Miaplacidus	221 37.9	S69 48.9
Mirfak	308 30.7	N49 56.7
Nunki	75 49.7	S26 16.1
Peacock	53 08.4	S56 39.5
Pollux	243 19.0	N27 58.3
Procyon	244 52.3	N 5 09.9
Rasalhague	95 59.9	N12 32.4
Regulus	207 35.8	N11 51.2
Rigel	281 05.4	S 8 10.6
Rigil Kent.	139 41.9	S60 55.7
Sabik	102 04.4	S15 45.3
Schedar	349 33.3	N56 39.8
Shaula	96 12.4	S37 07.2
Sirius	258 27.5	S16 45.0
Spica	158 23.6	S11 17.0
Suhail	222 47.1	S43 31.7
Vega	80 34.3	N38 47.9
Zuben'ubi	136 57.4	S16 08.3

	SHA	Mer. Pass.
	° ′	h m
Venus	327 30.7	14 17
Mars	272 22.5	17 56
Jupiter	344 23.2	13 08
Saturn	25 57.9	10 22

© British Crown Copyright 2022. All rights reserved.

SUN and MOON

UT	SUN GHA	SUN Dec	MOON GHA	v	MOON Dec	d	HP
d h	° ′	° ′	° ′	′	° ′	′	′
20 00	178 05.1	S 0 21.2	198 20.4	8.9	S13 38.5	15.4	60.4
01	193 05.3	20.2	212 48.3	8.9	13 23.1	15.5	60.4
02	208 05.4	19.2	227 16.2	9.0	13 07.6	15.5	60.4
03	223 05.6	.. 18.2	241 44.2	9.1	12 52.1	15.6	60.4
04	238 05.8	17.2	256 12.3	9.1	12 36.5	15.7	60.4
05	253 06.0	16.2	270 40.4	9.2	12 20.8	15.8	60.4
06	268 06.2	S 0 15.2	285 08.6	9.3	S12 05.0	15.8	60.4
07	283 06.4	14.3	299 36.9	9.4	11 49.2	15.9	60.4
08	298 06.5	13.3	314 05.3	9.5	11 33.3	16.0	60.4
M 09	313 06.7	.. 12.3	328 33.8	9.5	11 17.3	16.0	60.4
O 10	328 06.9	11.3	343 02.3	9.5	11 01.3	16.1	60.4
N 11	343 07.1	10.3	357 30.8	9.7	10 45.2	16.1	60.4
D 12	358 07.3	S 0 09.3	11 59.5	9.7	S10 29.1	16.2	60.4
A 13	13 07.5	08.3	26 28.2	9.8	10 12.9	16.3	60.4
Y 14	28 07.6	07.3	40 57.0	9.9	9 56.6	16.3	60.3
15	43 07.8	.. 06.3	55 25.9	9.9	9 40.3	16.3	60.3
16	58 08.0	05.4	69 54.8	9.9	9 24.0	16.4	60.3
17	73 08.2	04.4	84 23.7	10.1	9 07.6	16.5	60.3
18	88 08.4	S 0 03.4	98 52.8	10.1	S 8 51.1	16.5	60.3
19	103 08.6	02.4	113 21.9	10.2	8 34.6	16.5	60.3
20	118 08.7	01.4	127 51.1	10.2	8 18.1	16.6	60.3
21	133 08.9	S 00.4	142 20.3	10.3	8 01.5	16.6	60.3
22	148 09.1	N 00.5	156 49.6	10.3	7 44.9	16.6	60.3
23	163 09.3	01.6	171 18.9	10.4	7 28.3	16.7	60.2
21 00	178 09.5	N 0 02.6	185 48.3	10.4	S 7 11.6	16.7	60.2
01	193 09.7	03.5	200 17.7	10.6	6 54.9	16.7	60.2
02	208 09.8	04.5	214 47.3	10.5	6 38.2	16.8	60.2
03	223 10.0	.. 05.5	229 16.8	10.6	6 21.4	16.8	60.2
04	238 10.2	06.5	243 46.4	10.7	6 04.6	16.8	60.2
05	253 10.4	07.5	258 16.1	10.7	5 47.8	16.9	60.1
06	268 10.6	N 0 08.5	272 45.8	10.8	S 5 30.9	16.8	60.1
07	283 10.8	09.5	287 15.6	10.8	5 14.1	16.9	60.1
T 08	298 11.0	10.5	301 45.4	10.8	4 57.2	16.9	60.1
U 09	313 11.1	.. 11.5	316 15.2	10.9	4 40.3	16.9	60.1
E 10	328 11.3	12.4	330 45.1	11.0	4 23.4	16.9	60.1
S 11	343 11.5	13.4	345 15.1	11.0	4 06.5	17.0	60.0
D 12	358 11.7	N 0 14.4	359 45.1	11.0	S 3 49.5	16.9	60.0
A 13	13 11.9	15.4	14 15.1	11.1	3 32.6	17.0	60.0
Y 14	28 12.1	16.4	28 45.2	11.1	3 15.6	17.0	60.0
15	43 12.2	.. 17.4	43 15.3	11.1	2 58.6	16.9	60.0
16	58 12.4	18.4	57 45.4	11.2	2 41.7	17.0	59.9
17	73 12.6	19.4	72 15.6	11.2	2 24.7	17.0	59.9
18	88 12.8	N 0 20.3	86 45.8	11.3	S 2 07.7	16.9	59.9
19	103 13.0	21.3	101 16.1	11.3	1 50.8	17.0	59.9
20	118 13.2	22.3	115 46.4	11.3	1 33.8	17.0	59.9
21	133 13.4	.. 23.3	130 16.7	11.3	1 16.8	16.9	59.8
22	148 13.5	24.3	144 47.0	11.4	0 59.9	17.0	59.8
23	163 13.7	25.3	159 17.4	11.4	0 42.9	16.9	59.8
22 00	178 13.9	N 0 26.3	173 47.8	11.5	S 0 26.0	17.0	59.8
01	193 14.1	27.3	188 18.3	11.5	S 0 09.0	16.9	59.7
02	208 14.3	28.2	202 48.8	11.5	N 0 07.9	16.9	59.7
03	223 14.5	.. 29.2	217 19.3	11.5	0 24.8	16.9	59.7
04	238 14.6	30.2	231 49.8	11.5	0 41.7	16.9	59.7
05	253 14.8	31.2	246 20.3	11.6	0 58.6	16.8	59.6
06	268 15.0	N 0 32.2	260 50.9	11.6	N 1 15.4	16.8	59.6
W 07	283 15.2	33.2	275 21.5	11.6	1 32.2	16.8	59.6
E 08	298 15.4	34.2	289 52.1	11.6	1 49.0	16.8	59.6
D 09	313 15.6	.. 35.2	304 22.7	11.7	2 05.8	16.8	59.5
N 10	328 15.8	36.1	318 53.4	11.6	2 22.6	16.7	59.5
E 11	343 15.9	37.1	333 24.0	11.7	2 39.3	16.7	59.5
S 12	358 16.1	N 0 38.1	347 54.7	11.7	N 2 56.0	16.7	59.5
D 13	13 16.3	39.1	2 25.4	11.7	3 12.7	16.6	59.4
A 14	28 16.5	40.1	16 56.1	11.7	3 29.3	16.6	59.4
Y 15	43 16.7	.. 41.1	31 26.8	11.7	3 45.9	16.6	59.4
16	58 16.9	42.1	45 57.5	11.8	4 02.5	16.5	59.3
17	73 17.1	43.1	60 28.3	11.7	4 19.0	16.5	59.3
18	88 17.2	N 0 44.0	74 59.0	11.8	N 4 35.5	16.5	59.3
19	103 17.4	45.0	89 29.8	11.8	4 52.0	16.4	59.3
20	118 17.6	46.0	104 00.6	11.7	5 08.4	16.3	59.2
21	133 17.8	.. 47.0	118 31.3	11.8	5 24.7	16.4	59.2
22	148 18.0	48.0	133 02.1	11.8	5 41.1	16.2	59.2
23	163 18.2	49.0	147 32.9	11.8	N 5 57.3	16.3	59.1
	SD 16.1	d 1.0	SD 16.4		16.4		16.2

Twilight, Sunrise, Moonrise

Lat.	Twilight Naut.	Twilight Civil	Sunrise	Moonrise 20	Moonrise 21	Moonrise 22	Moonrise 23
°	h m	h m	h m	h m	h m	h m	h m
N 72	03 17	04 47	05 55	07 43	06 59	06 23	05 46
N 70	03 36	04 55	05 56	07 24	06 51	06 24	05 57
68	03 51	05 01	05 57	07 08	06 45	06 25	06 05
66	04 03	05 07	05 58	06 56	06 40	06 27	06 13
64	04 13	05 11	05 59	06 45	06 36	06 28	06 19
62	04 21	05 15	05 59	06 36	06 32	06 28	06 25
60	04 28	05 18	06 00	06 28	06 29	06 29	06 30
N 58	04 34	05 21	06 00	06 21	06 26	06 30	06 34
56	04 39	05 23	06 00	06 15	06 23	06 30	06 38
54	04 44	05 26	06 01	06 09	06 21	06 31	06 41
52	04 48	05 28	06 01	06 04	06 19	06 31	06 44
50	04 51	05 29	06 01	06 00	06 17	06 32	06 47
45	04 58	05 33	06 02	05 50	06 12	06 33	06 53
N 40	05 04	05 35	06 02	05 41	06 09	06 34	06 59
35	05 08	05 38	06 03	05 34	06 05	06 35	07 03
30	05 11	05 39	06 03	05 28	06 03	06 35	07 07
20	05 16	05 42	06 04	05 17	05 58	06 36	07 15
N 10	05 18	05 43	06 04	05 07	05 53	06 37	07 21
0	05 19	05 43	06 04	04 58	05 49	06 38	07 27
S 10	05 19	05 43	06 04	04 49	05 45	06 40	07 33
20	05 16	05 42	06 04	04 39	05 41	06 41	07 39
30	05 12	05 40	06 04	04 28	05 36	06 42	07 47
35	05 09	05 38	06 04	04 21	05 33	06 43	07 51
40	05 05	05 36	06 03	04 14	05 30	06 44	07 56
45	04 59	05 34	06 03	04 05	05 26	06 45	08 02
S 50	04 52	05 31	06 03	03 54	05 21	06 46	08 09
52	04 49	05 29	06 03	03 49	05 19	06 47	08 12
54	04 45	05 27	06 02	03 44	05 17	06 47	08 16
56	04 41	05 25	06 02	03 38	05 14	06 48	08 20
58	04 36	05 23	06 02	03 31	05 12	06 49	08 24
S 60	04 30	05 20	06 02	03 23	05 08	06 50	08 29

Sunset, Twilight, Moonset

Lat.	Sunset	Twilight Civil	Twilight Naut.	Moonset 20	Moonset 21	Moonset 22	Moonset 23
°	h m	h m	h m	h m	h m	h m	h m
N 72	18 22	19 31	21 03	15 10	17 43	20 07	22 38
N 70	18 21	19 23	20 42	15 27	17 46	19 59	22 16
68	18 19	19 16	20 27	15 40	17 49	19 53	21 59
66	18 18	19 10	20 14	15 50	17 52	19 48	21 45
64	18 18	19 05	20 04	15 59	17 54	19 44	21 34
62	18 17	19 01	19 55	16 07	17 55	19 40	21 25
60	18 16	18 58	19 48	16 13	17 57	19 37	21 16
N 58	18 16	18 55	19 42	16 19	17 58	19 34	21 09
56	18 15	18 52	19 37	16 24	17 59	19 32	21 03
54	18 15	18 50	19 32	16 28	18 00	19 30	20 58
52	18 14	18 48	19 28	16 32	18 01	19 28	20 53
50	18 14	18 46	19 24	16 36	18 02	19 26	20 48
45	18 13	18 43	19 17	16 44	18 04	19 22	20 39
N 40	18 13	18 40	19 11	16 50	18 05	19 18	20 31
35	18 12	18 37	19 07	16 56	18 07	19 16	20 24
30	18 12	18 36	19 04	17 00	18 08	19 13	20 18
20	18 11	18 33	18 59	17 09	18 10	19 09	20 07
N 10	18 11	18 32	18 56	17 16	18 11	19 05	19 58
0	18 10	18 31	18 55	17 23	18 13	19 01	19 50
S 10	18 10	18 31	18 56	17 29	18 14	18 58	19 41
20	18 10	18 32	18 58	17 36	18 16	18 54	19 33
30	18 10	18 34	19 02	17 44	18 18	18 50	19 22
35	18 10	18 35	19 05	17 48	18 19	18 47	19 17
40	18 10	18 37	19 09	17 54	18 20	18 45	19 10
45	18 10	18 40	19 14	17 59	18 21	18 41	19 02
S 50	18 11	18 43	19 21	18 06	18 22	18 38	18 53
52	18 11	18 44	19 24	18 09	18 23	18 36	18 49
54	18 11	18 46	19 28	18 13	18 24	18 34	18 45
56	18 11	18 48	19 32	18 17	18 25	18 32	18 39
58	18 11	18 50	19 37	18 21	18 25	18 29	18 34
S 60	18 11	18 53	19 43	18 26	18 26	18 27	18 27

SUN and MOON

	SUN Eqn. of Time 00ʰ	SUN Eqn. of Time 12ʰ	SUN Mer. Pass.	MOON Mer. Pass. Upper	MOON Mer. Pass. Lower	Age	Phase
Day							
d	m s	m s	h m	h m	h m	d	%
20	07 40	07 31	12 08	11 10	23 36	28	2
21	07 22	07 14	12 07	12 01	24 26	29	0
22	07 05	06 56	12 07	12 50	00 26	01	1

© British Crown Copyright 2022. All rights reserved.

2023 MARCH 23, 24, 25 (THURS., FRI., SAT.)

UT	ARIES GHA	VENUS −4.0 GHA	Dec	MARS +0.8 GHA	Dec	JUPITER −2.1 GHA	Dec	SATURN +0.9 GHA	Dec	Star Name	SHA	Dec
23 00	180 13.6	145 26.6	N14 22.2	91 33.1	N25 35.8	164 10.4	N 5 40.2	205 58.7	S12 04.3	Acamar	315 13.2	S40 12.9
01	195 16.0	160 26.2	23.3	106 34.2	35.8	179 12.3	40.4	221 00.9	04.2	Achernar	335 21.8	S57 07.3
02	210 18.5	175 25.8	24.4	121 35.4	35.8	194 14.2	40.7	236 03.1	04.1	Acrux	173 01.1	S63 13.7
03	225 21.0	190 25.4 ..	25.5	136 36.5 ..	35.8	209 16.1 ..	40.9	251 05.3 ..	04.0	Adhara	255 07.0	S29 00.4
04	240 23.4	205 24.9	26.6	151 37.6	35.8	224 18.0	41.1	266 07.5	04.0	Aldebaran	290 41.5	N16 33.3
05	255 25.9	220 24.5	27.7	166 38.8	35.8	239 19.9	41.3	281 09.7	03.9			
06	270 28.4	235 24.1	N14 28.9	181 39.9	N25 35.7	254 21.9	N 5 41.6	296 11.9	S12 03.8	Alioth	166 13.7	N55 50.0
07	285 30.8	250 23.7	30.0	196 41.1	35.7	269 23.8	41.8	311 14.1	03.7	Alkaid	152 52.7	N49 11.7
08	300 33.3	265 23.3	31.1	211 42.2	35.7	284 25.7	42.0	326 16.3	03.6	Alnair	27 35.2	S46 50.9
T 09	315 35.8	280 22.9 ..	32.2	226 43.3 ..	35.7	299 27.6 ..	42.3	341 18.5 ..	03.5	Alnilam	275 39.3	S 1 11.3
H 10	330 38.2	295 22.5	33.3	241 44.5	35.7	314 29.5	42.5	356 20.7	03.4	Alphard	217 49.0	S 8 45.7
U 11	345 40.7	310 22.1	34.4	256 45.6	35.7	329 31.4	42.7	11 22.9	03.3			
R 12	0 43.1	325 21.6	N14 35.5	271 46.8	N25 35.6	344 33.3	N 5 43.0	26 25.1	S12 03.2	Alphecca	126 04.8	N26 38.0
S 13	15 45.6	340 21.2	36.6	286 47.9	35.6	359 35.2	43.2	41 27.3	03.1	Alpheratz	357 36.7	N29 12.9
D 14	30 48.1	355 20.8	37.7	301 49.0	35.6	14 37.2	43.4	56 29.5	03.0	Altair	62 01.5	N 8 55.5
A 15	45 50.5	10 20.4 ..	38.8	316 50.2 ..	35.6	29 39.1 ..	43.6	71 31.7 ..	02.9	Ankaa	353 09.0	S42 11.0
Y 16	60 53.0	25 20.0	39.9	331 51.3	35.6	44 41.0	43.9	86 33.9	02.8	Antares	112 17.5	S26 29.0
17	75 55.5	40 19.6	41.0	346 52.5	35.5	59 42.9	44.1	101 36.1	02.7			
18	90 57.9	55 19.1	N14 42.1	1 53.6	N25 35.5	74 44.8	N 5 44.3	116 38.3	S12 02.6	Arcturus	145 49.0	N19 03.5
19	106 00.4	70 18.7	43.2	16 54.7	35.5	89 46.7	44.6	131 40.5	02.5	Atria	107 13.0	S69 03.9
20	121 02.9	85 18.3	44.3	31 55.9	35.5	104 48.6	44.8	146 42.7	02.5	Avior	234 15.0	S59 35.2
21	136 05.3	100 17.9 ..	45.4	46 57.0 ..	35.5	119 50.5 ..	45.0	161 44.9 ..	02.4	Bellatrix	278 24.6	N 6 22.2
22	151 07.8	115 17.5	46.5	61 58.1	35.4	134 52.5	45.3	176 47.1	02.3	Betelgeuse	270 53.7	N 7 24.6
23	166 10.2	130 17.1	47.6	76 59.3	35.4	149 54.4	45.5	191 49.3	02.2			
24 00	181 12.7	145 16.6	N14 48.7	92 00.4	N25 35.4	164 56.3	N 5 45.7	206 51.5	S12 02.1	Canopus	263 53.0	S52 42.7
01	196 15.2	160 16.2	49.8	107 01.5	35.4	179 58.2	45.9	221 53.7	02.0	Capella	280 24.2	N46 01.4
02	211 17.6	175 15.8	50.9	122 02.7	35.4	195 00.1	46.2	236 55.9	01.9	Deneb	49 27.1	N45 21.4
03	226 20.1	190 15.4 ..	52.0	137 03.8 ..	35.3	210 02.0 ..	46.4	251 58.1 ..	01.8	Denebola	182 26.2	N14 26.5
04	241 22.6	205 15.0	53.1	152 05.0	35.3	225 03.9	46.6	267 00.3	01.7	Diphda	348 49.1	S17 51.8
05	256 25.0	220 14.5	54.2	167 06.1	35.3	240 05.8	46.9	282 02.5	01.6			
06	271 27.5	235 14.1	N14 55.3	182 07.2	N25 35.3	255 07.7	N 5 47.1	297 04.7	S12 01.5	Dubhe	193 42.2	N61 37.6
07	286 30.0	250 13.7	56.3	197 08.4	35.3	270 09.7	47.3	312 06.9	01.4	Elnath	278 03.8	N28 37.6
08	301 32.4	265 13.3	57.4	212 09.5	35.2	285 11.6	47.6	327 09.1	01.3	Eltanin	90 42.8	N51 28.8
F 09	316 34.9	280 12.8 ..	58.5	227 10.6 ..	35.2	300 13.5 ..	47.8	342 11.3 ..	01.2	Enif	33 40.5	N 9 58.7
R 10	331 37.4	295 12.4	14 59.6	242 11.8	35.2	315 15.4	48.0	357 13.5	01.1	Fomalhaut	15 16.5	S29 30.1
I 11	346 39.8	310 12.0	15 00.7	257 12.9	35.2	330 17.3	48.2	12 15.7	01.1			
D 12	1 42.3	325 11.6	N15 01.8	272 14.0	N25 35.1	345 19.2	N 5 48.5	27 17.9	S12 01.0	Gacrux	171 52.8	S57 14.6
A 13	16 44.7	340 11.2	02.9	287 15.1	35.1	0 21.1	48.7	42 20.1	00.9	Gienah	175 44.8	S17 40.3
Y 14	31 47.2	355 10.7	04.0	302 16.3	35.1	15 23.0	48.9	57 22.3	00.8	Hadar	148 37.6	S60 29.0
15	46 49.7	10 10.3 ..	05.1	317 17.4 ..	35.1	30 24.9 ..	49.2	72 24.5 ..	00.7	Hamal	327 53.2	N23 34.2
16	61 52.1	25 09.9	06.2	332 18.5	35.1	45 26.9	49.4	87 26.7	00.6	Kaus Aust.	83 34.5	S34 22.4
17	76 54.6	40 09.5	07.2	347 19.7	35.0	60 28.8	49.6	102 28.9	00.5			
18	91 57.1	55 09.0	N15 08.3	2 20.8	N25 35.0	75 30.7	N 5 49.8	117 31.1	S12 00.4	Kochab	137 18.8	N74 03.4
19	106 59.5	70 08.6	09.4	17 21.9	35.0	90 32.6	50.1	132 33.3	00.3	Markab	13 31.7	N15 19.6
20	122 02.0	85 08.2	10.5	32 23.1	35.0	105 34.5	50.3	147 35.5	00.2	Menkar	314 08.0	N 4 10.7
21	137 04.5	100 07.8 ..	11.6	47 24.2 ..	34.9	120 36.4 ..	50.5	162 37.7 ..	00.1	Menkent	147 59.1	S36 29.0
22	152 06.9	115 07.3	12.7	62 25.3	34.9	135 38.3	50.8	177 39.9	12 00.0	Miaplacidus	221 38.0	S69 48.9
23	167 09.4	130 06.9	13.7	77 26.4	34.9	150 40.2	51.0	192 42.1	11 59.9			
25 00	182 11.8	145 06.5	N15 14.8	92 27.6	N25 34.9	165 42.1	N 5 51.2	207 44.3	S11 59.8	Mirfak	308 30.7	N49 56.7
01	197 14.3	160 06.1	15.9	107 28.7	34.8	180 44.1	51.5	222 46.5	59.8	Nunki	75 49.7	S26 16.1
02	212 16.8	175 05.6	17.0	122 29.8	34.8	195 46.0	51.7	237 48.7	59.7	Peacock	53 08.4	S56 39.5
03	227 19.2	190 05.2 ..	18.1	137 31.0 ..	34.8	210 47.9 ..	51.9	252 50.9 ..	59.6	Pollux	243 19.0	N27 58.3
04	242 21.7	205 04.8	19.1	152 32.1	34.8	225 49.8	52.1	267 53.1	59.5	Procyon	244 52.3	N 5 09.9
05	257 24.2	220 04.3	20.2	167 33.2	34.7	240 51.7	52.4	282 55.3	59.4			
06	272 26.6	235 03.9	N15 21.3	182 34.3	N25 34.7	255 53.6	N 5 52.6	297 57.5	S11 59.3	Rasalhague	95 59.9	N12 32.4
07	287 29.1	250 03.5	22.4	197 35.5	34.7	270 55.5	52.8	312 59.2	59.2	Regulus	207 35.8	N11 51.2
S 08	302 31.6	265 03.1	23.5	212 36.6	34.7	285 57.4	53.1	328 01.9	59.1	Rigel	281 05.4	S 8 10.6
A 09	317 34.0	280 02.6 ..	24.5	227 37.7 ..	34.6	300 59.3 ..	53.3	343 04.2 ..	59.0	Rigil Kent.	139 41.9	S60 55.7
T 10	332 36.5	295 02.2	25.6	242 38.8	34.6	316 01.3	53.5	358 06.4	58.9	Sabik	102 04.4	S15 43.3
U 11	347 39.0	310 01.8	26.7	257 40.0	34.6	331 03.2	53.8	13 08.6	58.8			
R 12	2 41.4	325 01.3	N15 27.8	272 41.1	N25 34.6	346 05.1	N 5 54.0	28 10.8	S11 58.7	Schedar	349 33.3	N56 39.8
D 13	17 43.9	340 00.9	28.8	287 42.2	34.5	1 07.0	54.2	43 13.0	58.6	Shaula	96 12.3	S37 07.2
A 14	32 46.3	355 00.5	29.9	302 43.3	34.5	16 08.9	54.4	58 15.2	58.6	Sirius	258 27.5	S16 45.1
Y 15	47 48.8	10 00.0 ..	31.0	317 44.5 ..	34.5	31 10.8 ..	54.7	73 17.4 ..	58.5	Spica	158 23.6	S11 17.0
16	62 51.3	24 59.6	32.1	332 45.6	34.4	46 12.7	54.9	88 19.6	58.4	Suhail	222 47.1	S43 31.7
17	77 53.7	39 59.2	33.1	347 46.7	34.4	61 14.6	55.1	103 21.8	58.3			
18	92 56.2	54 58.7	N15 34.2	2 47.8	N25 34.4	76 16.5	N 5 55.4	118 24.0	S11 58.2	Vega	80 34.3	N38 47.9
19	107 58.7	69 58.3	35.3	17 49.0	34.4	91 18.4	55.6	133 26.2	58.1	Zuben'ubi	136 57.4	S16 08.3
20	123 01.1	84 57.9	36.3	32 50.1	34.3	106 20.4	55.8	148 28.4	58.0		SHA	Mer. Pass.
21	138 03.6	99 57.4 ..	37.4	47 51.2 ..	34.3	121 22.3 ..	56.1	163 30.6 ..	57.9	Venus	324 03.9	14 19
22	153 06.1	114 57.0	38.5	62 52.3	34.3	136 24.2	56.3	178 32.8	57.8	Mars	270 47.7	17 51
23	168 08.5	129 56.6	39.5	77 53.4	34.2	151 26.1	56.5	193 35.0	57.7	Jupiter	343 43.6	12 59
Mer. Pass.	11 53.2	v −0.4	d 1.1	v 1.1	d 0.0	v 1.9	d 0.2	v 2.2	d 0.1	Saturn	25 38.8	10 11

© British Crown Copyright 2022. All rights reserved.

UT	SUN GHA	SUN Dec	MOON GHA	MOON v	MOON Dec	MOON d	MOON HP
d h	° ′	° ′	° ′	′	° ′	′	′
23 00	178 18.4	N 0 50.0	162 03.7	11.8	N 6 13.6	16.2	59.1
01	193 18.5	51.0	176 34.5	11.7	6 29.8	16.1	59.1
02	208 18.7	51.9	191 05.2	11.8	6 45.9	16.1	59.0
03	223 18.9 ..	52.9	205 36.0	11.8	7 02.0	16.0	59.0
04	238 19.1	53.9	220 06.8	11.8	7 18.0	16.0	59.0
05	253 19.3	54.9	234 37.6	11.8	7 34.0	15.9	58.9
06	268 19.5	N 0 55.9	249 08.4	11.8	N 7 49.9	15.8	58.9
07	283 19.7	56.9	263 39.2	11.7	8 05.7	15.8	58.9
T 08	298 19.9	57.9	278 09.9	11.8	8 21.5	15.8	58.9
H 09	313 20.0 ..	58.9	292 40.7	11.8	8 37.3	15.7	58.8
U 10	328 20.2	0 59.8	307 11.5	11.7	8 53.0	15.6	58.8
R 11	343 20.4	1 00.8	321 42.2	11.7	9 08.6	15.5	58.8
S 12	358 20.6	N 1 01.8	336 12.9	11.8	N 9 24.1	15.5	58.7
D 13	13 20.8	02.8	350 43.7	11.7	9 39.6	15.4	58.7
A 14	28 21.0	03.8	5 14.4	11.7	9 55.0	15.4	58.7
Y 15	43 21.2 ..	04.8	19 45.1	11.7	10 10.4	15.3	58.6
16	58 21.3	05.8	34 15.8	11.7	10 25.7	15.2	58.6
17	73 21.5	06.7	48 46.5	11.7	10 40.9	15.1	58.6
18	88 21.7	N 1 07.7	63 17.2	11.6	N10 56.0	15.1	58.5
19	103 21.9	08.7	77 47.8	11.7	11 11.1	15.0	58.5
20	118 22.1	09.7	92 18.5	11.6	11 26.1	14.9	58.4
21	133 22.3 ..	10.7	106 49.1	11.6	11 41.0	14.8	58.4
22	148 22.5	11.7	121 19.7	11.6	11 55.8	14.8	58.4
23	163 22.7	12.7	135 50.3	11.6	12 10.6	14.7	58.3
24 00	178 22.8	N 1 13.6	150 20.9	11.5	N12 25.3	14.6	58.3
01	193 23.0	14.6	164 51.4	11.6	12 39.9	14.5	58.3
02	208 23.2	15.6	179 22.0	11.5	12 54.4	14.4	58.2
03	223 23.4 ..	16.6	193 52.5	11.5	13 08.8	14.4	58.2
04	238 23.6	17.6	208 23.0	11.4	13 23.2	14.2	58.2
05	253 23.8	18.6	222 53.4	11.5	13 37.4	14.2	58.1
06	268 24.0	N 1 19.6	237 23.9	11.4	N13 51.6	14.1	58.1
07	283 24.1	20.5	251 54.3	11.4	14 05.7	14.0	58.1
08	298 24.3	21.5	266 24.7	11.4	14 19.7	13.9	58.0
F 09	313 24.5 ..	22.5	280 55.1	11.3	14 33.6	13.8	58.0
R 10	328 24.7	23.5	295 25.4	11.4	14 47.4	13.8	58.0
I 11	343 24.9	24.5	309 55.8	11.3	15 01.2	13.6	57.9
D 12	358 25.1	N 1 25.5	324 26.1	11.2	N15 14.8	13.5	57.9
A 13	13 25.3	26.5	338 56.3	11.3	15 28.3	13.5	57.8
Y 14	28 25.5	27.4	353 26.6	11.2	15 41.8	13.3	57.8
15	43 25.6 ..	28.4	7 56.8	11.2	15 55.1	13.3	57.8
16	58 25.8	29.4	22 27.0	11.1	16 08.4	13.2	57.7
17	73 26.0	30.4	36 57.1	11.2	16 21.6	13.0	57.7
18	88 26.2	N 1 31.4	51 27.3	11.1	N16 34.6	13.0	57.7
19	103 26.4	32.4	65 57.4	11.0	16 47.6	12.8	57.6
20	118 26.6	33.3	80 27.4	11.1	17 00.4	12.8	57.6
21	133 26.8 ..	34.3	94 57.5	11.0	17 13.2	12.6	57.6
22	148 27.0	35.3	109 27.5	11.0	17 25.8	12.6	57.5
23	163 27.1	36.3	123 57.5	10.9	17 38.4	12.4	57.5
25 00	178 27.3	N 1 37.3	138 27.4	10.9	N17 50.8	12.3	57.4
01	193 27.5	38.3	152 57.3	10.9	18 03.1	12.3	57.4
02	208 27.7	39.2	167 27.2	10.9	18 15.4	12.1	57.4
03	223 27.9 ..	40.2	181 57.1	10.8	18 27.5	12.0	57.3
04	238 28.1	41.2	196 26.9	10.8	18 39.5	11.9	57.3
05	253 28.3	42.2	210 56.7	10.7	18 51.4	11.8	57.3
06	268 28.5	N 1 43.2	225 26.4	10.7	N19 03.2	11.7	57.2
07	283 28.6	44.2	239 56.1	10.7	19 14.9	11.5	57.2
S 08	298 28.8	45.2	254 25.8	10.7	19 26.4	11.5	57.2
A 09	313 29.0 ..	46.1	268 55.5	10.6	19 37.9	11.3	57.1
T 10	328 29.2	47.1	283 25.1	10.6	19 49.2	11.2	57.1
U 11	343 29.4	48.1	297 54.7	10.5	20 00.4	11.1	57.1
R 12	358 29.6	N 1 49.1	312 24.2	10.5	N20 11.5	11.0	57.0
D 13	13 29.8	50.1	326 53.7	10.5	20 22.5	10.9	57.0
A 14	28 30.0	51.1	341 23.2	10.5	20 33.4	10.8	56.9
Y 15	43 30.1 ..	52.0	355 52.7	10.4	20 44.2	10.6	56.9
16	58 30.3	53.0	10 22.1	10.3	20 54.8	10.5	56.9
17	73 30.5	54.0	24 51.4	10.4	21 05.3	10.4	56.8
18	88 30.7	N 1 55.0	39 20.8	10.3	N21 15.7	10.3	56.8
19	103 30.9	56.0	53 50.1	10.3	21 26.0	10.1	56.8
20	118 31.1	57.0	68 19.4	10.2	21 36.1	10.0	56.7
21	133 31.3 ..	57.9	82 48.6	10.2	21 46.1	9.9	56.7
22	148 31.5	58.9	97 17.8	10.2	21 56.0	9.8	56.7
23	163 31.7	59.9	111 47.0	10.1	N22 05.8	9.7	56.6
	SD 16.1	d 1.0	SD 16.0		15.8		15.5

Lat.	Twilight Naut.	Twilight Civil	Sunrise	Moonrise 23	Moonrise 24	Moonrise 25	Moonrise 26
°	h m	h m	h m	h m	h m	h m	h m
N 72	02 55	04 30	05 39	05 46	04 58	▭	▭
N 70	03 18	04 40	05 42	05 57	05 23	04 24	▭
68	03 36	04 48	05 44	06 05	05 42	05 08	▭
66	03 50	04 55	05 46	06 13	05 57	05 37	04 59
64	04 01	05 00	05 48	06 19	06 10	06 00	05 44
62	04 10	05 05	05 49	06 25	06 21	06 18	06 15
60	04 18	05 09	05 51	06 30	06 30	06 33	06 38
N 58	04 25	05 12	05 52	06 34	06 39	06 45	06 56
56	04 31	05 15	05 53	06 38	06 46	06 57	07 12
54	04 36	05 18	05 53	06 41	06 52	07 06	07 25
52	04 40	05 20	05 54	06 44	06 58	07 15	07 37
50	04 44	05 23	05 55	06 47	07 04	07 23	07 48
45	04 53	05 27	05 56	06 53	07 15	07 40	08 10
N 40	04 59	05 31	05 58	06 59	07 25	07 54	08 27
35	05 04	05 33	05 59	07 03	07 33	08 06	08 42
30	05 08	05 36	05 59	07 07	07 41	08 16	08 56
20	05 13	05 39	06 01	07 15	07 53	08 34	09 18
N 10	05 17	05 41	06 02	07 21	08 05	08 50	09 38
0	05 18	05 42	06 03	07 27	08 15	09 05	09 56
S 10	05 19	05 43	06 04	07 33	08 26	09 20	10 14
20	05 17	05 43	06 05	07 39	08 38	09 36	10 34
30	05 14	05 42	06 06	07 47	08 51	09 55	10 57
35	05 11	05 41	06 06	07 51	08 59	10 06	11 11
40	05 08	05 40	06 07	07 56	09 08	10 18	11 27
45	05 03	05 38	06 07	08 02	09 18	10 33	11 46
S 50	04 57	05 35	06 08	08 09	09 31	10 52	12 10
52	04 55	05 34	06 08	08 12	09 37	11 00	12 21
54	04 51	05 33	06 08	08 16	09 44	11 10	12 34
56	04 47	05 31	06 08	08 20	09 51	11 21	12 49
58	04 43	05 29	06 09	08 24	09 59	11 34	13 07
S 60	04 38	05 27	06 09	08 29	10 09	11 49	13 29

Lat.	Sunset	Twilight Civil	Twilight Naut.	Moonset 23	Moonset 24	Moonset 25	Moonset 26
°	h m	h m	h m	h m	h m	h m	h m
N 72	18 36	19 46	21 23	22 38	▭	▭	▭
N 70	18 33	19 36	20 59	22 16	24 59	00 59	▭
68	18 30	19 27	20 40	21 59	24 17	00 17	▭
66	18 28	19 20	20 26	21 45	23 49	26 13	02 13
64	18 26	19 15	20 14	21 34	23 27	25 28	01 28
62	18 25	19 10	20 05	21 25	23 10	24 59	00 59
60	18 24	19 06	19 57	21 16	22 56	24 36	00 36
N 58	18 22	19 02	19 50	21 09	22 44	24 18	00 18
56	18 21	18 59	19 44	21 03	22 34	24 03	00 03
54	18 20	18 56	19 38	20 58	22 25	23 50	25 11
52	18 20	18 53	19 34	20 53	22 17	23 39	24 57
50	18 19	18 51	19 30	20 48	22 10	23 29	24 44
45	18 17	18 46	19 21	20 39	21 54	23 08	24 19
N 40	18 16	18 43	19 15	20 31	21 42	22 51	23 58
35	18 15	18 40	19 10	20 24	21 31	22 37	23 41
30	18 14	18 38	19 06	20 18	21 22	22 25	23 27
20	18 12	18 34	19 00	20 07	21 06	22 04	23 02
N 10	18 11	18 32	18 56	19 58	20 52	21 46	22 41
0	18 10	18 30	18 54	19 50	20 39	21 29	22 21
S 10	18 09	18 30	18 54	19 41	20 26	21 12	22 01
20	18 08	18 30	18 55	19 33	20 12	20 55	21 40
30	18 07	18 30	18 58	19 22	19 57	20 34	21 16
35	18 06	18 31	19 01	19 17	19 48	20 22	21 01
40	18 05	18 32	19 04	19 10	19 38	20 09	20 45
45	18 05	18 34	19 08	19 02	19 26	19 52	20 25
S 50	18 04	18 36	19 14	18 53	19 11	19 33	20 00
52	18 04	18 37	19 17	18 49	19 04	19 23	19 49
54	18 03	18 39	19 20	18 45	18 57	19 13	19 35
56	18 03	18 40	19 24	18 40	18 49	19 01	19 19
58	18 03	18 42	19 28	18 34	18 39	18 48	19 01
S 60	18 02	18 44	19 33	18 27	18 29	18 32	18 38

	SUN			MOON			
Day	Eqn. of Time 00h	Eqn. of Time 12h	Mer. Pass.	Mer. Pass. Upper	Mer. Pass. Lower	Age	Phase
d	m s	m s	h m	h m	h m	d	%
23	06 47	06 38	12 07	13 38	01 14	02	4
24	06 29	06 20	12 06	14 27	02 03	03	10
25	06 11	06 02	12 06	15 17	02 52	04	17

© British Crown Copyright 2022. All rights reserved.

UT	ARIES	VENUS −4.0		MARS +0.9		JUPITER −2.1		SATURN +0.9		STARS		
	GHA	GHA	Dec	GHA	Dec	GHA	Dec	GHA	Dec	Name	SHA	Dec
d h	° ′	° ′	° ′	° ′	° ′	° ′	° ′	° ′	° ′		° ′	° ′
26 00	183 11.0	144 56.1	N15 40.6	92 54.6	N25 34.2	166 28.0	N 5 56.7	208 37.2	S11 57.6	Acamar	315 13.2	S40 12.9
01	198 13.5	159 55.7	41.7	107 55.7	34.2	181 29.9	57.0	223 39.4	57.5	Achernar	335 21.8	S57 07.3
02	213 15.9	174 55.3	42.7	122 56.8	34.2	196 31.8	57.2	238 41.6	57.4	Acrux	173 01.1	S63 13.7
03	228 18.4	189 54.8 · ·	43.8	137 57.9 · ·	34.1	211 33.7 · ·	57.4	253 43.8 · ·	57.4	Adhara	255 07.0	S29 00.4
04	243 20.8	204 54.4	44.9	152 59.0	34.1	226 35.6	57.7	268 46.0	57.3	Aldebaran	290 41.5	N16 33.3
05	258 23.3	219 54.0	45.9	168 00.2	34.1	241 37.5	57.9	283 48.2	57.2			
06	273 25.8	234 53.5	N15 47.0	183 01.3	N25 34.0	256 39.5	N 5 58.1	298 50.4	S11 57.1	Alioth	166 13.7	N55 50.0
07	288 28.2	249 53.1	48.1	198 02.4	34.0	271 41.4	58.4	313 52.6	57.0	Alkaid	152 52.7	N49 11.7
08	303 30.7	264 52.6	49.1	213 03.5	34.0	286 43.3	58.6	328 54.8	56.9	Alnair	27 35.2	S46 50.9
S 09	318 33.2	279 52.2 · ·	50.2	228 04.6 · ·	33.9	301 45.2 · ·	58.8	343 57.1 · ·	56.8	Alnilam	275 39.3	S 1 11.3
U 10	333 35.6	294 51.8	51.2	243 05.8	33.9	316 47.1	59.0	358 59.3	56.7	Alphard	217 49.0	S 8 45.7
N 11	348 38.1	309 51.3	52.3	258 06.9	33.9	331 49.0	59.3	14 01.5	56.6			
D 12	3 40.6	324 50.9	N15 53.4	273 08.0	N25 33.9	346 50.9	N 5 59.5	29 03.7	S11 56.5	Alphecca	126 04.8	N26 38.0
A 13	18 43.0	339 50.5	54.4	288 09.1	33.8	1 52.8	5 59.7	44 05.9	56.4	Alpheratz	357 36.7	N29 12.9
Y 14	33 45.5	354 50.0	55.5	303 10.2	33.8	16 54.7	6 00.0	59 08.1	56.3	Altair	62 01.5	N 8 55.5
15	48 48.0	9 49.6 · ·	56.5	318 11.4 · ·	33.8	31 56.6 · ·	00.2	74 10.3 · ·	56.3	Ankaa	353 09.0	S42 10.9
16	63 50.4	24 49.1	57.6	333 12.5	33.7	46 58.5	00.4	89 12.5	56.2	Antares	112 17.5	S26 29.0
17	78 52.9	39 48.7	58.6	348 13.6	33.7	62 00.5	00.6	104 14.7	56.1			
18	93 55.3	54 48.3	N15 59.7	3 14.7	N25 33.7	77 02.4	N 6 00.9	119 16.9	S11 56.0	Arcturus	145 49.0	N19 03.5
19	108 57.8	69 47.8	16 00.7	18 15.8	33.6	92 04.3	01.1	134 19.1	55.9	Atria	107 12.9	S69 03.9
20	124 00.3	84 47.4	01.8	33 16.9	33.6	107 06.2	01.3	149 21.3	55.8	Avior	234 15.1	S59 35.2
21	139 02.7	99 46.9 · ·	02.9	48 18.0 · ·	33.6	122 08.1 · ·	01.6	164 23.5 · ·	55.7	Bellatrix	278 24.6	N 6 22.2
22	154 05.2	114 46.5	03.9	63 19.2	33.5	137 10.0	01.8	179 25.7	55.6	Betelgeuse	270 53.7	N 7 24.6
23	169 07.7	129 46.0	05.0	78 20.3	33.5	152 11.9	02.0	194 27.9	55.5			
27 00	184 10.1	144 45.6	N16 06.0	93 21.4	N25 33.5	167 13.8	N 6 02.3	209 30.1	S11 55.4	Canopus	263 53.1	S52 42.7
01	199 12.6	159 45.2	07.1	108 22.5	33.4	182 15.7	02.5	224 32.3	55.3	Capella	280 24.2	N46 01.4
02	214 15.1	174 44.7	08.1	123 23.6	33.4	197 17.6	02.7	239 34.6	55.2	Deneb	49 27.1	N45 21.4
03	229 17.5	189 44.3 · ·	09.2	138 24.7 · ·	33.4	212 19.5 · ·	02.9	254 36.8 · ·	55.2	Denebola	182 26.2	N14 26.5
04	244 20.0	204 43.8	10.2	153 25.8	33.3	227 21.5	03.2	269 39.0	55.1	Diphda	348 49.1	S17 51.7
05	259 22.4	219 43.4	11.3	168 27.0	33.3	242 23.4	03.4	284 41.2	55.0			
06	274 24.9	234 42.9	N16 12.3	183 28.1	N25 33.3	257 25.3	N 6 03.6	299 43.4	S11 54.9	Dubhe	193 42.2	N61 37.6
07	289 27.4	249 42.5	13.3	198 29.2	33.2	272 27.2	03.9	314 45.6	54.8	Elnath	278 03.8	N28 37.6
08	304 29.8	264 42.0	14.4	213 30.3	33.2	287 29.1	04.1	329 47.8	54.7	Eltanin	90 42.8	N51 28.8
M 09	319 32.3	279 41.6 · ·	15.4	228 31.4 · ·	33.2	302 31.0 · ·	04.3	344 50.0 · ·	54.6	Enif	33 40.5	N 9 58.7
O 10	334 34.8	294 41.1	16.5	243 32.5	33.1	317 32.9	04.6	359 52.2	54.5	Fomalhaut	15 16.5	S29 30.1
N 11	349 37.2	309 40.7	17.5	258 33.6	33.1	332 34.8	04.8	14 54.4	54.4			
D 12	4 39.7	324 40.3	N16 18.6	273 34.7	N25 33.0	347 36.7	N 6 05.0	29 56.6	S11 54.3	Gacrux	171 52.8	S57 14.6
A 13	19 42.2	339 39.8	19.6	288 35.9	33.0	2 38.6	05.2	44 58.8	54.2	Gienah	175 44.8	S17 40.3
Y 14	34 44.6	354 39.4	20.6	303 37.0	33.0	17 40.5	05.5	60 01.0	54.1	Hadar	148 37.6	S60 29.0
15	49 47.1	9 38.9 · ·	21.7	318 38.1 · ·	32.9	32 42.4 · ·	05.7	75 03.2 · ·	54.1	Hamal	327 53.2	N23 34.2
16	64 49.6	24 38.5	22.7	333 39.2	32.9	47 44.4	05.9	90 05.4	54.0	Kaus Aust.	83 34.5	S34 22.4
17	79 52.0	39 38.0	23.8	348 40.3	32.9	62 46.3	06.2	105 07.7	53.9			
18	94 54.5	54 37.6	N16 24.8	3 41.4	N25 32.8	77 48.2	N 6 06.4	120 09.9	S11 53.8	Kochab	137 18.8	N74 03.4
19	109 56.9	69 37.1	25.8	18 42.5	32.8	92 50.1	06.6	135 12.1	53.7	Markab	13 31.7	N15 19.6
20	124 59.4	84 36.7	26.9	33 43.6	32.8	107 52.0	06.9	150 14.3	53.6	Menkar	314 08.0	N 4 10.7
21	140 01.9	99 36.2 · ·	27.9	48 44.7 · ·	32.7	122 53.9 · ·	07.1	165 16.5 · ·	53.5	Menkent	147 59.0	S36 29.0
22	155 04.3	114 35.8	29.0	63 45.8	32.7	137 55.8	07.3	180 18.7	53.4	Miaplacidus	221 38.0	S69 48.9
23	170 06.8	129 35.3	30.0	78 46.9	32.6	152 57.7	07.5	195 20.9	53.3			
28 00	185 09.3	144 34.9	N16 31.0	93 48.1	N25 32.6	167 59.6	N 6 07.8	210 23.1	S11 53.2	Mirfak	308 30.7	N49 56.7
01	200 11.7	159 34.4	32.1	108 49.2	32.6	183 01.5	08.0	225 25.3	53.1	Nunki	75 49.7	S26 16.1
02	215 14.2	174 34.0	33.1	123 50.3	32.5	198 03.4	08.2	240 27.5	53.1	Peacock	53 08.3	S56 39.5
03	230 16.7	189 33.5 · ·	34.1	138 51.4 · ·	32.5	213 05.3 · ·	08.5	255 29.7 · ·	53.0	Pollux	243 19.0	N27 58.3
04	245 19.1	204 33.1	35.2	153 52.5	32.4	228 07.3	08.7	270 31.9	52.9	Procyon	244 52.3	N 5 09.9
05	260 21.6	219 32.6	36.2	168 53.6	32.4	243 09.2	08.9	285 34.1	52.8			
06	275 24.1	234 32.1	N16 37.2	183 54.7	N25 32.4	258 11.1	N 6 09.1	300 36.4	S11 52.7	Rasalhague	95 59.9	N12 32.4
07	290 26.5	249 31.7	38.2	198 55.8	32.3	273 13.0	09.4	315 38.6	52.6	Regulus	207 35.8	N11 51.2
T 08	305 29.0	264 31.2	39.3	213 56.9	32.3	288 14.9	09.6	330 40.8	52.5	Rigel	281 05.4	S 8 10.6
U 09	320 31.4	279 30.8 · ·	40.3	228 58.0 · ·	32.3	303 16.8 · ·	09.8	345 43.0 · ·	52.4	Rigil Kent.	139 41.8	S60 55.7
E 10	335 33.9	294 30.3	41.3	243 59.1	32.2	318 18.7	10.1	0 45.2	52.3	Sabik	102 04.4	S15 45.3
S 11	350 36.4	309 29.9	42.4	259 00.2	32.2	333 20.6	10.3	15 47.4	52.2			
D 12	5 38.8	324 29.4	N16 43.4	274 01.3	N25 32.1	348 22.5	N 6 10.5	30 49.6	S11 52.2	Schedar	349 33.3	N56 39.8
A 13	20 41.3	339 29.0	44.4	289 02.4	32.1	3 24.4	10.8	45 51.8	52.1	Shaula	96 12.3	S37 07.2
Y 14	35 43.8	354 28.5	45.4	304 03.5	32.0	18 26.3	11.0	60 54.0	52.0	Sirius	258 27.5	S16 45.1
15	50 46.2	9 28.0 · ·	46.5	319 04.6 · ·	32.0	33 28.2 · ·	11.2	75 56.2 · ·	51.9	Spica	158 23.6	S11 17.0
16	65 48.7	24 27.6	47.5	334 05.7	32.0	48 30.1	11.4	90 58.4	51.8	Suhail	222 47.1	S43 31.8
17	80 51.2	39 27.1	48.5	349 06.9	31.9	63 32.1	11.7	106 00.7	51.7			
18	95 53.6	54 26.7	N16 49.5	4 08.0	N25 31.9	78 34.0	N 6 11.9	121 02.9	S11 51.6	Vega	80 34.2	N38 47.9
19	110 56.1	69 26.2	50.6	19 09.1	31.8	93 35.9	12.1	136 05.1	51.5	Zuben'ubi	136 57.4	S16 08.3
20	125 58.6	84 25.8	51.6	34 10.2	31.8	108 37.8	12.4	151 07.3	51.4		SHA	Mer. Pass.
21	141 01.0	99 25.3 · ·	52.6	49 11.3 · ·	31.8	123 39.7 · ·	12.6	166 09.5 · ·	51.3		° ′	h m
22	156 03.5	114 24.8	53.6	64 12.4	31.7	138 41.6	12.8	181 11.7	51.2	Venus	320 35.5	14 21
23	171 05.9	129 24.4	54.6	79 13.5	31.7	153 43.5	13.1	196 13.9	51.2	Mars	269 11.3	17 45
	h m									Jupiter	343 03.7	12 49
Mer. Pass. 11 41.4		v −0.4	d 1.0	v 1.1	d 0.0	v 1.9	d 0.2	v 2.2	d 0.1	Saturn	25 20.0	10 01

© British Crown Copyright 2022. All rights reserved.

UT	SUN GHA	SUN Dec	MOON GHA	v	MOON Dec	d	HP
d h	° ′	° ′	° ′	′	° ′	′	′
26 00	178 31.8	N 2 00.9	126 16.1	10.1	N22 15.5	9.5	56.6
01	193 32.0	01.9	140 45.2	10.1	22 25.0	9.4	56.6
02	208 32.2	02.8	155 14.3	10.1	22 34.4	9.3	56.5
03	223 32.4	.. 03.8	169 43.4	10.0	22 43.7	9.1	56.5
04	238 32.6	04.8	184 12.4	9.9	22 52.8	9.1	56.5
05	253 32.8	05.8	198 41.3	10.0	23 01.9	8.9	56.4
06	268 33.0	N 2 06.8	213 10.3	9.9	N23 10.8	8.7	56.4
07	283 33.2	07.8	227 39.2	9.9	23 19.5	8.6	56.4
S 08	298 33.3	08.7	242 08.1	9.8	23 28.1	8.5	56.3
U 09	313 33.5	.. 09.7	256 36.9	9.9	23 36.6	8.4	56.3
N 10	328 33.7	10.7	271 05.8	9.8	23 45.0	8.3	56.3
D 11	343 33.9	11.7	285 34.6	9.7	23 53.3	8.1	56.2
A 12	358 34.1	N 2 12.7	300 03.3	9.8	N24 01.4	7.9	56.2
Y 13	13 34.3	13.6	314 32.1	9.7	24 09.3	7.9	56.2
14	28 34.5	14.6	329 00.8	9.6	24 17.2	7.7	56.1
15	43 34.7	.. 15.6	343 29.4	9.7	24 24.9	7.6	56.1
16	58 34.8	16.6	357 58.1	9.6	24 32.5	7.4	56.1
17	73 35.0	17.6	12 26.7	9.6	24 39.9	7.3	56.0
18	88 35.2	N 2 18.6	26 55.3	9.6	N24 47.2	7.2	56.0
19	103 35.4	19.5	41 23.9	9.5	24 54.4	7.0	56.0
20	118 35.6	20.5	55 52.4	9.5	25 01.4	6.9	55.9
21	133 35.8	.. 21.5	70 20.9	9.5	25 08.3	6.8	55.9
22	148 36.0	22.5	84 49.4	9.5	25 15.1	6.6	55.9
23	163 36.2	23.5	99 17.9	9.5	25 21.7	6.5	55.9
27 00	178 36.4	N 2 24.4	113 46.4	9.4	N25 28.2	6.3	55.8
01	193 36.5	25.4	128 14.8	9.4	25 34.5	6.2	55.8
02	208 36.7	26.4	142 43.2	9.4	25 40.7	6.1	55.8
03	223 36.9	.. 27.4	157 11.6	9.4	25 46.8	5.9	55.7
04	238 37.1	28.4	171 40.0	9.3	25 52.7	5.8	55.7
05	253 37.3	29.3	186 08.3	9.4	25 58.5	5.7	55.7
06	268 37.5	N 2 30.3	200 36.7	9.3	N26 04.2	5.5	55.6
07	283 37.7	31.3	215 05.0	9.3	26 09.7	5.3	55.6
08	298 37.9	32.3	229 33.3	9.3	26 15.0	5.3	55.6
M 09	313 38.0	.. 33.3	244 01.6	9.2	26 20.3	5.1	55.6
O 10	328 38.2	34.2	258 29.8	9.3	26 25.4	4.9	55.5
N 11	343 38.4	35.2	272 58.1	9.2	26 30.3	4.8	55.5
D 12	358 38.6	N 2 36.2	287 26.3	9.3	N26 35.1	4.7	55.5
A 13	13 38.8	37.2	301 54.6	9.2	26 39.8	4.5	55.5
Y 14	28 39.0	38.2	316 22.8	9.2	26 44.3	4.4	55.4
15	43 39.2	.. 39.1	330 51.0	9.2	26 48.7	4.2	55.4
16	58 39.4	40.1	345 19.2	9.2	26 52.9	4.1	55.4
17	73 39.6	41.1	359 47.4	9.2	26 57.0	4.0	55.3
18	88 39.7	N 2 42.1	14 15.6	9.2	N27 01.0	3.8	55.3
19	103 39.9	43.0	28 43.8	9.1	27 04.8	3.7	55.3
20	118 40.1	44.0	43 11.9	9.2	27 08.5	3.5	55.3
21	133 40.3	.. 45.0	57 40.1	9.2	27 12.0	3.4	55.2
22	148 40.5	46.0	72 08.3	9.2	27 15.4	3.3	55.2
23	163 40.7	47.0	86 36.5	9.1	27 18.7	3.1	55.2
28 00	178 40.9	N 2 47.9	101 04.6	9.2	N27 21.8	2.9	55.2
01	193 41.1	48.9	115 32.8	9.2	27 24.7	2.9	55.1
02	208 41.2	49.9	130 01.0	9.1	27 27.6	2.6	55.1
03	223 41.4	.. 50.9	144 29.1	9.2	27 30.2	2.6	55.1
04	238 41.6	51.8	158 57.3	9.2	27 32.8	2.4	55.1
05	253 41.8	52.8	173 25.5	9.2	27 35.2	2.2	55.0
06	268 42.0	N 2 53.8	187 53.7	9.1	N27 37.4	2.1	55.0
07	283 42.2	54.8	202 21.8	9.2	27 39.5	2.0	55.0
T 08	298 42.4	55.8	216 50.0	9.3	27 41.5	1.8	55.0
U 09	313 42.6	.. 56.7	231 18.3	9.2	27 43.3	1.7	55.0
E 10	328 42.8	57.7	245 46.5	9.2	27 45.0	1.5	54.9
S 11	343 42.9	58.7	260 14.7	9.2	27 46.5	1.4	54.9
D 12	358 43.1	N 2 59.7	274 42.9	9.3	N27 47.9	1.3	54.9
A 13	13 43.3	3 00.6	289 11.2	9.2	27 49.2	1.1	54.9
Y 14	28 43.5	01.6	303 39.4	9.3	27 50.3	1.0	54.9
15	43 43.7	.. 02.6	318 07.7	9.3	27 51.3	0.8	54.8
16	58 43.9	03.6	332 36.0	9.3	27 52.1	0.7	54.8
17	73 44.1	04.6	347 04.3	9.4	27 52.8	0.6	54.8
18	88 44.3	N 3 05.5	1 32.7	9.3	N27 53.4	0.4	54.8
19	103 44.4	06.5	16 01.0	9.4	27 53.8	0.3	54.8
20	118 44.6	07.5	30 29.4	9.4	27 54.1	0.1	54.7
21	133 44.8	.. 08.5	44 57.8	9.4	27 54.2	0.0	54.7
22	148 45.0	09.4	59 26.2	9.4	27 54.2	0.2	54.7
23	163 45.2	10.4	73 54.6	9.5	N27 54.0	0.3	54.7
	SD 16.1	d 1.0	SD 15.3		15.1		15.0

Lat.	Twilight Naut.	Twilight Civil	Sunrise	Moonrise 26	27	28	29
°	h m	h m	h m	h m	h m	h m	h m
N 72	02 31	04 13	05 24	□	□	□	□
N 70	02 59	04 25	05 28	□	□	□	□
68	03 20	04 35	05 32	□	□	□	□
66	03 36	04 42	05 35	04 59	□	□	□
64	03 48	04 49	05 37	05 44	05 00	□	□
62	03 59	04 55	05 40	06 15	06 12	06 14	06 57
60	04 08	04 59	05 41	06 38	06 48	07 12	08 02
N 58	04 15	05 04	05 43	06 56	07 14	07 45	08 36
56	04 22	05 07	05 45	07 12	07 35	08 10	09 02
54	04 28	05 10	05 46	07 25	07 52	08 30	09 22
52	04 33	05 13	05 47	07 37	08 06	08 46	09 38
50	04 37	05 16	05 48	07 48	08 19	09 01	09 53
45	04 47	05 21	05 51	08 10	08 46	09 30	10 22
N 40	04 54	05 26	05 53	08 27	09 07	09 53	10 45
35	04 59	05 29	05 54	08 42	09 24	10 11	11 04
30	05 04	05 32	05 56	08 56	09 39	10 28	11 20
20	05 11	05 36	05 58	09 18	10 05	10 55	11 48
N 10	05 15	05 39	06 00	09 38	10 27	11 19	12 11
0	05 17	05 41	06 02	09 56	10 48	11 41	12 33
S 10	05 19	05 43	06 04	10 14	11 09	12 03	12 55
20	05 18	05 44	06 06	10 34	11 32	12 27	13 19
30	05 16	05 44	06 07	10 57	11 58	12 55	13 46
35	05 14	05 43	06 08	11 11	12 13	13 11	14 02
40	05 11	05 43	06 10	11 27	12 32	13 30	14 21
45	05 07	05 42	06 11	11 46	12 53	13 53	14 44
S 50	05 02	05 40	06 12	12 10	13 21	14 23	15 13
52	05 00	05 39	06 13	12 21	13 35	14 38	15 27
54	04 57	05 38	06 14	12 34	13 51	14 55	15 44
56	04 54	05 37	06 14	12 49	14 10	15 16	16 03
58	04 50	05 36	06 15	13 07	14 33	15 42	16 28
S 60	04 46	05 35	06 16	13 29	15 03	16 18	17 01

Lat.	Sunset	Twilight Civil	Twilight Naut.	Moonset 26	27	28	29
°	h m	h m	h m	h m	h m	h m	h m
N 72	18 50	20 02	21 46	□	□	□	□
N 70	18 45	19 49	21 17	□	□	□	□
68	18 41	19 39	20 55	□	□	□	□
66	18 38	19 31	20 38	02 13	□	□	□
64	18 35	19 24	20 25	01 28	04 01	□	□
62	18 33	19 18	20 14	00 59	02 49	04 37	05 44
60	18 31	19 13	20 05	00 36	02 14	03 40	04 39
N 58	18 29	19 09	19 57	00 18	01 48	03 07	04 04
56	18 27	19 05	19 51	00 03	01 28	02 42	03 39
54	18 26	19 02	19 45	25 11	01 11	02 22	03 19
52	18 25	18 59	19 39	24 57	00 57	02 06	03 02
50	18 23	18 56	19 35	24 44	00 44	01 52	02 48
45	18 21	18 50	19 25	24 19	00 19	01 23	02 18
N 40	18 19	18 46	19 18	23 58	25 00	01 00	01 55
35	18 17	18 42	19 12	23 41	24 42	00 42	01 36
30	18 15	18 39	19 07	23 27	24 26	00 26	01 20
20	18 13	18 35	19 01	23 02	23 59	24 52	00 52
N 10	18 11	18 32	18 56	22 41	23 35	24 28	00 28
0	18 09	18 29	18 53	22 21	23 14	24 06	00 06
S 10	18 07	18 28	18 52	22 01	22 52	23 44	24 36
20	18 05	18 27	18 52	21 40	22 29	23 20	24 13
30	18 03	18 27	18 55	21 16	22 02	22 52	23 47
35	18 02	18 27	18 56	21 01	21 46	22 36	23 31
40	18 01	18 28	18 59	20 45	21 27	22 17	23 12
45	17 59	18 28	19 03	20 25	21 05	21 53	22 50
S 50	17 58	18 30	19 07	20 00	20 37	21 24	22 21
52	17 57	18 30	19 10	19 49	20 23	21 09	22 07
54	17 56	18 31	19 12	19 35	20 07	20 52	21 50
56	17 55	18 32	19 16	19 19	19 48	20 31	21 31
58	17 54	18 33	19 19	19 01	19 24	20 05	21 07
S 60	17 53	18 35	19 23	18 38	18 54	19 29	20 34

Day	SUN Eqn. of Time 00h	12h	Mer. Pass.	MOON Mer. Pass. Upper	Lower	Age	Phase
d	m s	m s	h m	h m	h m	d	%
26	05 53	05 44	12 06	16 08	03 43	05	25
27	05 35	05 26	12 05	17 01	04 35	06	35
28	05 17	05 08	12 05	17 54	05 27	07	44

© British Crown Copyright 2022. All rights reserved.

UT	ARIES GHA	VENUS −4.0 GHA	Dec	MARS +0.9 GHA	Dec	JUPITER −2.1 GHA	Dec	SATURN +0.9 GHA	Dec	STARS Name	SHA	Dec
d h	° ′	° ′	° ′	° ′	° ′	° ′	° ′	° ′	° ′		° ′	° ′
29 00	186 08.4	144 23.9	N16 55.6	94 14.6	N25 31.6	168 45.4	N 6 13.3	211 16.1	S11 51.1	Acamar	315 13.2	S40 12.9
01	201 10.9	159 23.5	56.7	109 15.7	31.6	183 47.3	13.5	226 18.3	51.0	Achernar	335 21.8	S57 07.3
02	216 13.3	174 23.0	57.7	124 16.8	31.5	198 49.2	13.7	241 20.5	50.9	Acrux	173 01.0	S63 13.7
03	231 15.8	189 22.5 ..	58.7	139 17.9 ..	31.5	213 51.1 ..	14.0	256 22.7 ..	50.8	Adhara	255 07.0	S29 00.4
04	246 18.3	204 22.1	16 59.7	154 19.0	31.5	228 53.0	14.2	271 25.0	50.7	Aldebaran	290 41.5	N16 33.3
05	261 20.7	219 21.6	17 00.7	169 20.1	31.4	243 54.9	14.4	286 27.2	50.6			
W 06	276 23.2	234 21.2	N17 01.7	184 21.2	N25 31.4	258 56.8	N 6 14.7	301 29.4	S11 50.5	Alioth	166 13.7	N55 50.0
E 07	291 25.7	249 20.7	02.8	199 22.3	31.3	273 58.8	14.9	316 31.6	50.4	Alkaid	152 52.7	N49 11.7
D 08	306 28.1	264 20.2	03.8	214 23.4	31.3	289 00.7	15.1	331 33.8	50.3	Alnair	27 35.1	S46 50.9
N 09	321 30.6	279 19.8 ..	04.8	229 24.5 ..	31.2	304 02.6 ..	15.3	346 36.0 ..	50.3	Alnilam	275 39.3	S 1 11.3
E 10	336 33.0	294 19.3	05.8	244 25.6	31.2	319 04.5	15.6	1 38.2	50.2	Alphard	217 49.0	S 8 45.7
S 11	351 35.5	309 18.8	06.8	259 26.7	31.1	334 06.4	15.8	16 40.4	50.1			
D 12	6 38.0	324 18.4	N17 07.8	274 27.8	N25 31.1	349 08.3	N 6 16.0	31 42.6	S11 50.0	Alphecca	126 04.7	N26 38.0
A 13	21 40.4	339 17.9	08.8	289 28.9	31.1	4 10.2	16.3	46 44.9	49.9	Alpheratz	357 36.7	N29 12.9
Y 14	36 42.9	354 17.4	09.8	304 30.0	31.0	19 12.1	16.5	61 47.1	49.8	Altair	62 01.5	N 8 55.5
15	51 45.4	9 17.0 ..	10.8	319 31.1 ..	31.0	34 14.0 ..	16.7	76 49.3 ..	49.7	Ankaa	353 09.0	S42 10.9
16	66 47.8	24 16.5	11.8	334 32.2	30.9	49 15.9	17.0	91 51.5	49.6	Antares	112 17.5	S26 29.0
17	81 50.3	39 16.1	12.8	349 33.3	30.9	64 17.8	17.2	106 53.7	49.5			
18	96 52.8	54 15.6	N17 13.8	4 34.4	N25 30.8	79 19.7	N 6 17.4	121 55.9	S11 49.4	Arcturus	145 49.0	N19 03.5
19	111 55.2	69 15.1	14.9	19 35.4	30.8	94 21.6	17.6	136 58.1	49.4	Atria	107 12.8	S69 03.9
20	126 57.7	84 14.7	15.9	34 36.5	30.7	109 23.5	17.9	152 00.3	49.3	Avior	234 15.1	S59 35.3
21	142 00.2	99 14.2 ..	16.9	49 37.6 ..	30.7	124 25.4 ..	18.1	167 02.5 ..	49.2	Bellatrix	278 24.6	N 6 22.2
22	157 02.6	114 13.7	17.9	64 38.7	30.6	139 27.4	18.3	182 04.8	49.1	Betelgeuse	270 53.8	N 7 24.6
23	172 05.1	129 13.2	18.9	79 39.8	30.6	154 29.3	18.6	197 07.0	49.0			
30 00	187 07.5	144 12.8	N17 19.9	94 40.9	N25 30.5	169 31.2	N 6 18.8	212 09.2	S11 48.9	Canopus	263 53.1	S52 42.7
01	202 10.0	159 12.3	20.9	109 42.0	30.5	184 33.1	19.0	227 11.4	48.8	Capella	280 24.2	N46 01.4
02	217 12.5	174 11.8	21.9	124 43.1	30.5	199 35.0	19.2	242 13.6	48.7	Deneb	49 27.0	N45 21.4
03	232 14.9	189 11.4 ..	22.9	139 44.2 ..	30.4	214 36.9 ..	19.5	257 15.8 ..	48.6	Denebola	182 26.1	N14 26.5
04	247 17.4	204 10.9	23.9	154 45.3	30.4	229 38.8	19.7	272 18.0	48.6	Diphda	348 49.1	S17 51.7
05	262 19.9	219 10.4	24.9	169 46.4	30.3	244 40.7	19.9	287 20.2	48.5			
T 06	277 22.3	234 10.0	N17 25.8	184 47.5	N25 30.3	259 42.6	N 6 20.2	302 22.4	S11 48.4	Dubhe	193 42.2	N61 37.7
H 07	292 24.8	249 09.5	26.8	199 48.6	30.2	274 44.5	20.4	317 24.7	48.3	Elnath	278 03.9	N28 37.6
U 08	307 27.3	264 09.0	27.8	214 49.7	30.2	289 46.4	20.6	332 26.9	48.2	Eltanin	90 42.8	N51 28.8
R 09	322 29.7	279 08.6 ..	28.8	229 50.8 ..	30.1	304 48.3 ..	20.9	347 29.1 ..	48.1	Enif	33 40.5	N 9 58.7
S 10	337 32.2	294 08.1	29.8	244 51.9	30.1	319 50.2	21.1	2 31.3	48.0	Fomalhaut	15 16.2	S29 30.1
D 11	352 34.7	309 07.6	30.8	259 53.0	30.0	334 52.1	21.3	17 33.5	47.9			
A 12	7 37.1	324 07.1	N17 31.8	274 54.1	N25 30.0	349 54.0	N 6 21.5	32 35.7	S11 47.8	Gacrux	171 52.7	S57 14.6
Y 13	22 39.6	339 06.7	32.8	289 55.1	29.9	4 55.9	21.8	47 37.9	47.7	Gienah	175 44.8	S17 40.3
14	37 42.0	354 06.2	33.8	304 56.2	29.9	19 57.9	22.0	62 40.1	47.7	Hadar	148 37.5	S60 29.0
15	52 44.5	9 05.7 ..	34.8	319 57.3 ..	29.8	34 59.8 ..	22.2	77 42.4 ..	47.6	Hamal	327 53.2	N23 34.2
16	67 47.0	24 05.2	35.8	334 58.4	29.8	50 01.7	22.5	92 44.6	47.5	Kaus Aust.	83 34.5	S34 22.4
17	82 49.4	39 04.8	36.8	349 59.5	29.7	65 03.6	22.7	107 46.8	47.4			
18	97 51.9	54 04.3	N17 37.7	5 00.6	N25 29.7	80 05.5	N 6 22.9	122 49.0	S11 47.3	Kochab	137 18.8	N74 03.4
19	112 54.4	69 03.8	38.7	20 01.7	29.6	95 07.4	23.1	137 51.2	47.2	Markab	13 31.7	N15 19.6
20	127 56.8	84 03.3	39.7	35 02.8	29.6	110 09.3	23.4	152 53.4	47.1	Menkar	314 08.0	N 4 10.7
21	142 59.3	99 02.9 ..	40.7	50 03.9 ..	29.5	125 11.2 ..	23.6	167 55.6 ..	47.0	Menkent	147 59.0	S36 29.0
22	158 01.8	114 02.4	41.7	65 05.0	29.5	140 13.1	23.8	182 57.8	46.9	Miaplacidus	221 38.0	S69 48.9
23	173 04.2	129 01.9	42.7	80 06.1	29.4	155 15.0	24.1	198 00.1	46.9			
31 00	188 06.7	144 01.4	N17 43.7	95 07.1	N25 29.4	170 16.9	N 6 24.3	213 02.3	S11 46.8	Mirfak	308 30.8	N49 56.7
01	203 09.1	159 01.0	44.6	110 08.2	29.3	185 18.8	24.5	228 04.5	46.7	Nunki	75 49.6	S26 16.1
02	218 11.6	174 00.5	45.6	125 09.3	29.2	200 20.7	24.8	243 06.7	46.6	Peacock	53 08.3	S56 39.5
03	233 14.1	189 00.0 ..	46.6	140 10.4 ..	29.2	215 22.6 ..	25.0	258 08.9 ..	46.5	Pollux	243 19.0	N27 58.3
04	248 16.5	203 59.5	47.6	155 11.5	29.1	230 24.5	25.2	273 11.1	46.4	Procyon	244 52.3	N 5 09.9
05	263 19.0	218 59.0	48.6	170 12.6	29.1	245 26.4	25.4	288 13.3	46.3			
F 06	278 21.5	233 58.6	N17 49.5	185 13.7	N25 29.0	260 28.3	N 6 25.7	303 15.6	S11 46.2	Rasalhague	95 59.8	N12 32.4
R 07	293 23.9	248 58.1	50.5	200 14.8	29.0	275 30.2	25.9	318 17.8	46.1	Regulus	207 35.8	N11 51.2
I 08	308 26.4	263 57.6	51.5	215 15.9	28.9	290 32.2	26.1	333 20.0	46.1	Rigel	281 05.4	S 8 10.6
D 09	323 28.9	278 57.1 ..	52.5	230 16.9 ..	28.9	305 34.1 ..	26.4	348 22.2 ..	46.0	Rigil Kent.	139 41.8	S60 55.7
A 10	338 31.3	293 56.7	53.4	245 18.0	28.8	320 36.0	26.6	3 24.4	45.9	Sabik	102 04.4	S15 45.3
Y 11	353 33.8	308 56.2	54.4	260 19.1	28.8	335 37.9	26.8	18 26.6	45.8			
12	8 36.3	323 55.7	N17 55.4	275 20.2	N25 28.7	350 39.8	N 6 27.0	33 28.8	S11 45.7	Schedar	349 33.3	N56 39.8
13	23 38.7	338 55.2	56.4	290 21.3	28.7	5 41.7	27.3	48 31.1	45.6	Shaula	96 12.3	S37 07.2
14	38 41.2	353 54.7	57.3	305 22.4	28.6	20 43.6	27.5	63 33.3	45.5	Sirius	258 27.5	S16 45.1
15	53 43.6	8 54.2 ..	58.3	320 23.5 ..	28.5	35 45.5 ..	27.7	78 35.5 ..	45.4	Spica	158 23.6	S11 17.0
16	68 46.1	23 53.8	17 59.3	335 24.5	28.5	50 47.4	28.0	93 37.7	45.4	Suhail	222 47.2	S43 31.8
17	83 48.6	38 53.3	18 00.2	350 25.6	28.4	65 49.3	28.2	108 39.9	45.3			
18	98 51.0	53 52.8	N18 01.2	5 26.7	N25 28.4	80 51.2	N 6 28.4	123 42.1	S11 45.2	Vega	80 34.2	N38 47.9
19	113 53.5	68 52.3	02.2	20 27.8	28.3	95 53.1	28.6	138 44.3	45.1	Zuben'ubi	136 57.4	S16 08.3
20	128 56.0	83 51.8	03.2	35 28.9	28.3	110 55.0	28.9	153 46.6	45.0		SHA	Mer. Pass.
21	143 58.4	98 51.3 ..	04.1	50 30.0 ..	28.2	125 56.9 ..	29.1	168 48.8 ..	44.9		° ′	h m
22	159 00.9	113 50.9	05.1	65 31.1	28.2	140 58.8	29.3	183 51.0	44.8	Venus	317 05.2	14 24
23	174 03.5	128 50.4	06.0	80 32.1	28.1	156 00.7	29.6	198 53.2	44.7	Mars	267 33.4	17 40
Mer. Pass. 11 29.6		v −0.5	d 1.0	v 1.1	d 0.0	v 1.9	d 0.2	v 2.2	d 0.1	Jupiter	342 23.6	12 40
										Saturn	25 01.6	9 50

© British Crown Copyright 2022. All rights reserved.

UT	SUN GHA	Dec	MOON GHA	v	Dec	d	HP
d h	° ′	° ′	° ′	′	° ′	′	′
29 00	178 45.4	N 3 11.4	88 23.1	9.5	N27 53.7	0.4	54.7
01	193 45.6	12.4	102 51.6	9.5	27 53.3	0.5	54.6
02	208 45.8	13.3	117 20.1	9.5	27 52.8	0.7	54.6
03	223 46.0	.. 14.3	131 48.6	9.6	27 52.1	0.9	54.6
04	238 46.1	15.3	146 17.2	9.6	27 51.2	1.0	54.6
05	253 46.3	16.3	160 45.8	9.6	27 50.2	1.1	54.6
06	268 46.5	N 3 17.2	175 14.4	9.7	N27 49.1	1.2	54.6
W 07	283 46.7	18.2	189 43.1	9.7	27 47.9	1.4	54.6
E 08	298 46.9	19.2	204 11.8	9.7	27 46.5	1.5	54.5
D 09	313 47.1	.. 20.2	218 40.5	9.8	27 45.0	1.7	54.5
N 10	328 47.3	21.1	233 09.3	9.8	27 43.3	1.8	54.5
E 11	343 47.5	22.1	247 38.1	9.8	27 41.5	1.9	54.5
S 12	358 47.6	N 3 23.1	262 06.9	9.9	N27 39.6	2.1	54.5
D 13	13 47.8	24.1	276 35.8	9.9	27 37.5	2.2	54.4
A 14	28 48.0	25.0	291 04.7	9.9	27 35.3	2.3	54.4
Y 15	43 48.2	.. 26.0	305 33.6	10.0	27 33.0	2.4	54.4
16	58 48.4	27.0	320 02.6	10.1	27 30.6	2.6	54.4
17	73 48.6	28.0	334 31.7	10.0	27 28.0	2.7	54.4
18	88 48.8	N 3 28.9	349 00.7	10.1	N27 25.2	2.8	54.4
19	103 49.0	29.9	3 29.8	10.2	27 22.4	3.0	54.4
20	118 49.1	30.9	17 59.0	10.2	27 19.4	3.1	54.4
21	133 49.3	.. 31.8	32 28.2	10.2	27 16.3	3.3	54.4
22	148 49.5	32.8	46 57.4	10.3	27 13.0	3.3	54.4
23	163 49.7	33.8	61 26.7	10.4	27 09.7	3.5	54.3
30 00	178 49.9	N 3 34.8	75 56.1	10.3	N27 06.2	3.7	54.3
01	193 50.1	35.7	90 25.4	10.5	27 02.5	3.7	54.3
02	208 50.3	36.7	104 54.9	10.5	26 58.8	3.9	54.3
03	223 50.5	.. 37.7	119 24.4	10.5	26 54.9	4.0	54.3
04	238 50.7	38.7	133 53.9	10.6	26 50.9	4.2	54.3
05	253 50.8	39.6	148 23.5	10.6	26 46.7	4.2	54.3
06	268 51.0	N 3 40.6	162 53.1	10.7	N26 42.5	4.4	54.3
T 07	283 51.2	41.6	177 22.8	10.7	26 38.1	4.5	54.3
H 08	298 51.4	42.5	191 52.5	10.8	26 33.6	4.7	54.3
U 09	313 51.6	.. 43.5	206 22.3	10.8	26 28.9	4.7	54.3
R 10	328 51.8	44.5	220 52.1	10.9	26 24.2	4.9	54.2
S 11	343 52.0	45.5	235 22.0	10.9	26 19.3	5.0	54.2
D 12	358 52.2	N 3 46.4	249 51.9	11.0	N26 14.3	5.1	54.2
A 13	13 52.3	47.4	264 21.9	11.1	26 09.2	5.3	54.2
Y 14	28 52.5	48.4	278 52.0	11.1	26 03.9	5.4	54.2
15	43 52.7	.. 49.3	293 22.1	11.1	25 58.5	5.4	54.2
16	58 52.9	50.3	307 52.2	11.2	25 53.1	5.6	54.2
17	73 53.1	51.3	322 22.4	11.3	25 47.5	5.8	54.2
18	88 53.3	N 3 52.3	336 52.7	11.3	N25 41.7	5.8	54.2
19	103 53.5	53.2	351 23.0	11.4	25 35.9	5.9	54.2
20	118 53.7	54.2	5 53.4	11.4	25 30.0	6.1	54.2
21	133 53.8	.. 55.2	20 23.8	11.5	25 23.9	6.2	54.2
22	148 54.0	56.1	34 54.3	11.6	25 17.7	6.3	54.2
23	163 54.2	57.1	49 24.9	11.6	25 11.4	6.4	54.2
31 00	178 54.4	N 3 58.1	63 55.5	11.6	N25 05.0	6.5	54.2
01	193 54.6	3 59.0	78 26.1	11.8	24 58.5	6.7	54.2
02	208 54.8	4 00.0	92 56.9	11.7	24 51.8	6.7	54.2
03	223 55.0	.. 01.0	107 27.6	11.9	24 45.1	6.9	54.2
04	238 55.1	02.0	121 58.5	11.9	24 38.2	6.9	54.2
05	253 55.3	02.9	136 29.4	11.9	24 31.3	7.1	54.2
06	268 55.5	N 4 03.9	151 00.3	12.1	N24 24.2	7.2	54.2
07	283 55.7	04.9	165 31.4	12.0	24 17.0	7.3	54.2
08	298 55.9	05.8	180 02.4	12.2	24 09.7	7.4	54.2
F 09	313 56.1	.. 06.8	194 33.6	12.2	24 02.3	7.5	54.2
R 10	328 56.3	07.8	209 04.8	12.2	23 54.8	7.6	54.2
I 11	343 56.5	08.7	223 36.0	12.3	23 47.2	7.7	54.2
D 12	358 56.6	N 4 09.7	238 07.3	12.4	N23 39.5	7.8	54.2
A 13	13 56.8	10.7	252 38.7	12.4	23 31.7	8.0	54.2
Y 14	28 57.0	11.6	267 10.1	12.5	23 23.7	8.0	54.2
15	43 57.2	.. 12.6	281 41.6	12.6	23 15.7	8.1	54.2
16	58 57.4	13.6	296 13.2	12.6	23 07.6	8.2	54.2
17	73 57.6	14.5	310 44.8	12.7	22 59.4	8.4	54.2
18	88 57.8	N 4 15.5	325 16.5	12.7	N22 51.0	8.4	54.2
19	103 57.9	16.5	339 48.2	12.8	22 42.6	8.5	54.2
20	118 58.1	17.4	354 20.0	12.8	22 34.1	8.7	54.2
21	133 58.3	.. 18.4	8 51.8	12.9	22 25.4	8.7	54.2
22	148 58.5	19.4	23 23.7	13.0	22 16.7	8.8	54.2
23	163 58.7	20.3	37 55.7	13.0	N22 07.9	8.9	54.2
	SD 16.0	d 1.0	SD 14.8		14.8		14.8

Twilight / Moonrise

Lat.	Twilight Naut.	Civil	Sunrise	Moonrise 29	30	31	1
°	h m	h m	h m	h m	h m	h m	h m
N 72	02 04	03 55	05 08	☐	☐	☐	☐
N 70	02 38	04 10	05 14	☐	☐	☐	☐
68	03 03	04 21	05 19	☐	☐	☐	10 26
66	03 21	04 30	05 23	☐	☐	☐	11 09
64	03 36	04 38	05 27	☐	☐	09 43	11 38
62	03 47	04 44	05 30	06 57	08 37	10 21	12 00
60	03 57	04 50	05 32	08 02	09 19	10 47	12 17
N 58	04 06	04 55	05 35	08 36	09 47	11 08	12 32
56	04 13	04 59	05 37	09 02	10 08	11 25	12 44
54	04 20	05 03	05 39	09 22	10 26	11 39	12 55
52	04 25	05 06	05 40	09 38	10 41	11 51	13 05
50	04 30	05 09	05 42	09 53	10 55	12 02	13 13
45	04 41	05 16	05 45	10 22	11 21	12 25	13 31
N 40	04 49	05 21	05 48	10 45	11 43	12 44	13 46
35	04 55	05 25	05 50	11 04	12 00	12 59	13 58
30	05 00	05 28	05 52	11 20	12 15	13 12	14 09
20	05 08	05 34	05 56	11 48	12 41	13 35	14 27
N 10	05 13	05 38	05 59	12 11	13 03	13 54	14 43
0	05 17	05 41	06 01	12 33	13 24	14 12	14 58
S 10	05 18	05 43	06 04	12 55	13 44	14 30	15 13
20	05 19	05 44	06 06	13 19	14 06	14 49	15 29
30	05 18	05 45	06 09	13 46	14 32	15 11	15 47
35	05 16	05 46	06 11	14 02	14 46	15 24	15 57
40	05 14	05 46	06 13	14 21	15 04	15 39	16 09
45	05 11	05 45	06 15	14 44	15 24	15 57	16 23
S 50	05 07	05 45	06 17	15 13	15 50	16 19	16 40
52	05 05	05 44	06 18	15 27	16 03	16 29	16 48
54	05 03	05 44	06 19	15 44	16 17	16 41	16 57
56	05 00	05 43	06 21	16 03	16 34	16 54	17 07
58	04 57	05 43	06 22	16 28	16 54	17 09	17 18
S 60	04 53	05 42	06 23	17 01	17 19	17 27	17 31

Sunset / Twilight / Moonset

Lat.	Sunset	Twilight Civil	Naut.	Moonset 29	30	31	1
°	h m	h m	h m	h m	h m	h m	h m
N 72	19 04	20 18	22 14	☐	☐	☐	☐
N 70	18 57	20 03	21 36	☐	☐	☐	☐
68	18 52	19 51	21 11	☐	☐	☐	07 22
66	18 48	19 41	20 52	☐	☐	☐	06 38
64	18 44	19 33	20 36	☐	☐	06 27	06 08
62	18 41	19 27	20 24	05 44	05 50	05 49	05 46
60	18 38	19 21	20 14	04 39	05 09	05 22	05 27
N 58	18 36	19 16	20 05	04 04	04 40	05 00	05 12
56	18 34	19 11	19 58	03 39	04 18	04 43	04 59
54	18 32	19 08	19 51	03 19	04 00	04 28	04 48
52	18 30	19 04	19 45	03 02	03 45	04 15	04 38
50	18 28	19 01	19 40	02 48	03 31	04 04	04 28
45	18 25	18 54	19 30	02 18	03 04	03 40	04 09
N 40	18 22	18 49	19 21	01 55	02 42	03 21	03 54
35	18 19	18 45	19 15	01 36	02 24	03 05	03 40
30	18 17	18 41	19 09	01 20	02 08	02 51	03 29
20	18 14	18 36	19 02	00 52	01 42	02 27	03 09
N 10	18 11	18 32	18 56	00 28	01 19	02 07	02 51
0	18 08	18 29	18 53	00 06	00 58	01 47	02 35
S 10	18 05	18 26	18 51	24 50	00 36	01 28	02 18
20	18 02	18 24	18 50	24 13	00 13	01 07	02 00
30	17 59	18 23	18 51	23 47	24 43	00 43	01 40
35	17 58	18 23	18 52	23 31	24 28	00 28	01 27
40	17 56	18 23	18 54	23 12	24 12	00 12	01 13
45	17 54	18 23	18 57	22 50	23 52	24 57	00 57
S 50	17 51	18 23	19 01	22 21	23 26	24 36	00 36
52	17 50	18 24	19 03	22 07	23 14	24 26	00 26
54	17 49	18 24	19 05	21 50	23 00	24 15	00 15
56	17 47	18 24	19 08	21 31	22 44	24 02	00 02
58	17 46	18 25	19 11	21 07	22 24	23 48	25 12
S 60	17 44	18 26	19 14	20 34	21 59	23 30	25 00

SUN / MOON

Day	Eqn. of Time 00ʰ	12ʰ	Mer. Pass.	Mer. Pass. Upper	Lower	Age	Phase
d	m s	m s	h m	h m	h m	d	%
29	04 59	04 50	12 05	18 46	06 20	08	54
30	04 41	04 32	12 05	19 36	07 11	09	63
31	04 23	04 14	12 04	20 23	08 00	10	72

© British Crown Copyright 2022. All rights reserved.

UT	ARIES GHA	VENUS −4.0 GHA	Dec	MARS +1.0 GHA	Dec	JUPITER −2.1 GHA	Dec	SATURN +0.9 GHA	Dec	STARS Name	SHA	Dec
d h	° ′	° ′	° ′	° ′	° ′	° ′	° ′	° ′	° ′		° ′	° ′
1 00	189 05.8	143 49.9	N18 07.0	95 33.2	N25 28.0	171 02.6	N 6 29.8	213 55.4	S11 44.6	Acamar	315 13.2	S40 12.9
01	204 08.3	158 49.4	08.0	110 34.3	28.0	186 04.5	30.0	228 57.6	44.6	Achernar	335 21.8	S57 07.3
02	219 10.8	173 48.9	08.9	125 35.4	27.9	201 06.4	30.3	243 59.8	44.5	Acrux	173 01.0	S63 13.7
03	234 13.2	188 48.4 ..	09.9	140 36.5 ..	27.9	216 08.3 ..	30.5	259 02.1 ..	44.4	Adhara	255 07.0	S29 00.4
04	249 15.7	203 47.9	10.9	155 37.6	27.8	231 10.3	30.7	274 04.3	44.3	Aldebaran	290 41.5	N16 33.3
05	264 18.1	218 47.5	11.8	170 38.6	27.8	246 12.2	30.9	289 06.5	44.2			
06	279 20.6	233 47.0	N18 12.8	185 39.7	N25 27.7	261 14.1	N 6 31.2	304 08.7	S11 44.1	Alioth	166 13.7	N55 50.0
07	294 23.1	248 46.5	13.7	200 40.8	27.6	276 16.0	31.4	319 10.9	44.0	Alkaid	152 52.7	N49 11.7
08	309 25.5	263 46.0	14.7	215 41.9	27.6	291 17.9	31.6	334 13.1	43.9	Alnair	27 35.1	S46 50.9
09	324 28.0	278 45.5 ..	15.7	230 43.0 ..	27.5	306 19.8 ..	31.9	349 15.4 ..	43.9	Alnilam	275 39.3	S 1 11.3
10	339 30.5	293 45.0	16.6	245 44.0	27.5	321 21.7	32.1	4 17.6	43.8	Alphard	217 49.0	S 8 45.7
11	354 32.9	308 44.5	17.6	260 45.1	27.4	336 23.6	32.3	19 19.8	43.7			
S 12	9 35.4	323 44.0	N18 18.5	275 46.2	N25 27.3	351 25.5	N 6 32.5	34 22.0	S11 43.6	Alphecca	126 04.7	N26 38.0
A 13	24 37.9	338 43.6	19.5	290 47.3	27.3	6 27.4	32.8	49 24.2	43.5	Alpheratz	357 36.7	N29 12.9
T 14	39 40.3	353 43.1	20.4	305 48.4	27.2	21 29.3	33.0	64 26.4	43.4	Altair	62 01.5	N 8 55.5
U 15	54 42.8	8 42.6 ..	21.4	320 49.5 ..	27.2	36 31.2 ..	33.2	79 28.7 ..	43.3	Ankaa	353 09.0	S42 10.9
R 16	69 45.2	23 42.1	22.3	335 50.5	27.1	51 33.1	33.5	94 30.9	43.2	Antares	112 17.5	S26 29.0
D 17	84 47.7	38 41.6	23.3	350 51.6	27.0	66 35.0	33.7	109 33.1	43.2			
A 18	99 50.2	53 41.1	N18 24.2	5 52.7	N25 27.0	81 36.9	N 6 33.9	124 35.3	S11 43.1	Arcturus	145 49.0	N19 03.6
Y 19	114 52.6	68 40.6	25.2	20 53.8	26.9	96 38.8	34.1	139 37.5	43.0	Atria	107 12.8	S69 03.9
20	129 55.1	83 40.1	26.1	35 54.9	26.9	111 40.7	34.4	154 39.7	42.9	Avior	234 15.1	S59 35.3
21	144 57.6	98 39.6 ..	27.1	50 55.9 ..	26.8	126 42.6 ..	34.6	169 42.0 ..	42.8	Bellatrix	278 24.6	N 6 22.2
22	160 00.0	113 39.1	28.0	65 57.0	26.7	141 44.5	34.8	184 44.2	42.7	Betelgeuse	270 53.8	N 7 24.6
23	175 02.5	128 38.6	29.0	80 58.1	26.7	156 46.4	35.1	199 46.4	42.6			
2 00	190 05.0	143 38.1	N18 29.9	95 59.2	N25 26.6	171 48.3	N 6 35.3	214 48.6	S11 42.5	Canopus	263 53.1	S52 42.7
01	205 07.4	158 37.6	30.9	111 00.2	26.5	186 50.2	35.5	229 50.8	42.5	Capella	280 24.3	N46 01.4
02	220 09.9	173 37.2	31.8	126 01.3	26.5	201 52.2	35.7	244 53.0	42.4	Deneb	49 27.0	N45 21.4
03	235 12.4	188 36.7 ..	32.8	141 02.4 ..	26.4	216 54.1 ..	36.0	259 55.3 ..	42.3	Denebola	182 26.1	N14 26.5
04	250 14.8	203 36.2	33.7	156 03.5	26.4	231 56.0	36.2	274 57.5	42.2	Diphda	348 49.1	S17 51.7
05	265 17.3	218 35.7	34.6	171 04.6	26.3	246 57.9	36.4	289 59.7	42.1			
06	280 19.7	233 35.2	N18 35.6	186 05.6	N25 26.2	261 59.8	N 6 36.7	305 01.9	S11 42.0	Dubhe	193 42.2	N61 37.7
07	295 22.2	248 34.7	36.5	201 06.7	26.2	277 01.7	36.9	320 04.1	41.9	Elnath	278 03.9	N28 37.6
08	310 24.7	263 34.2	37.5	216 07.8	26.1	292 03.6	37.1	335 06.3	41.8	Eltanin	90 42.7	N51 28.8
S 09	325 27.1	278 33.7 ..	38.4	231 08.9 ..	26.0	307 05.5 ..	37.3	350 08.6 ..	41.8	Enif	33 40.5	N 9 58.7
U 10	340 29.6	293 33.2	39.3	246 09.9	26.0	322 07.4	37.6	5 10.8	41.7	Fomalhaut	15 16.5	S29 30.1
N 11	355 32.1	308 32.7	40.3	261 11.0	25.9	337 09.3	37.8	20 13.0	41.6			
D 12	10 34.5	323 32.2	N18 41.2	276 12.1	N25 25.9	352 11.2	N 6 38.0	35 15.2	S11 41.5	Gacrux	171 52.7	S57 14.6
A 13	25 37.0	338 31.7	42.2	291 13.2	25.8	7 13.1	38.3	50 17.4	41.4	Gienah	175 44.8	S17 40.3
Y 14	40 39.5	353 31.2	43.1	306 14.2	25.7	22 15.0	38.5	65 19.7	41.3	Hadar	148 37.5	S60 29.0
15	55 41.9	8 30.7 ..	44.0	321 15.3 ..	25.7	37 16.9 ..	38.7	80 21.9 ..	41.2	Hamal	327 53.2	N23 34.2
16	70 44.4	23 30.2	45.0	336 16.4	25.6	52 18.8	38.9	95 24.1	41.1	Kaus Aust.	83 34.4	S34 22.4
17	85 46.9	38 29.7	45.9	351 17.5	25.5	67 20.7	39.2	110 26.3	41.1			
18	100 49.3	53 29.2	N18 46.8	6 18.5	N25 25.5	82 22.6	N 6 39.4	125 28.5	S11 41.0	Kochab	137 18.7	N74 03.4
19	115 51.8	68 28.7	47.8	21 19.6	25.4	97 24.5	39.6	140 30.8	40.9	Markab	13 31.7	N15 19.6
20	130 54.2	83 28.2	48.7	36 20.7	25.3	112 26.4	39.9	155 33.0	40.8	Menkar	314 08.0	N 4 10.7
21	145 56.7	98 27.7 ..	49.6	51 21.8 ..	25.3	127 28.3 ..	40.1	170 35.2 ..	40.7	Menkent	147 59.0	S36 29.1
22	160 59.2	113 27.2	50.5	66 22.8	25.2	142 30.2	40.3	185 37.4	40.6	Miaplacidus	221 38.1	S69 48.9
23	176 01.6	128 26.7	51.5	81 23.9	25.1	157 32.1	40.5	200 39.6	40.5			
3 00	191 04.1	143 26.2	N18 52.4	96 25.0	N25 25.1	172 34.0	N 6 40.8	215 41.8	S11 40.4	Mirfak	308 30.8	N49 56.6
01	206 06.6	158 25.7	53.3	111 26.1	25.0	187 35.9	41.0	230 44.1	40.4	Nunki	75 49.6	S26 16.1
02	221 09.0	173 25.2	54.2	126 27.1	24.9	202 37.8	41.2	245 46.3	40.3	Peacock	53 08.3	S56 39.5
03	236 11.5	188 24.7 ..	55.2	141 28.2 ..	24.9	217 39.7 ..	41.5	260 48.5 ..	40.2	Pollux	243 19.0	N27 58.3
04	251 14.0	203 24.2	56.1	156 29.3	24.8	232 41.7	41.7	275 50.7	40.1	Procyon	244 52.3	N 5 09.9
05	266 16.4	218 23.7	57.0	171 30.3	24.7	247 43.6	41.9	290 52.9	40.0			
06	281 18.9	233 23.2	N18 57.9	186 31.4	N25 24.7	262 45.5	N 6 42.1	305 55.2	S11 39.9	Rasalhague	96 59.8	N12 32.4
07	296 21.3	248 22.7	58.9	201 32.5	24.6	277 47.4	42.4	320 57.4	39.8	Regulus	207 35.8	N11 51.2
08	311 23.8	263 22.2	18 59.8	216 33.6	24.5	292 49.3	42.6	335 59.6	39.8	Rigel	281 05.4	S 8 10.6
M 09	326 26.3	278 21.7 ..	19 00.7	231 34.6 ..	24.5	307 51.2 ..	42.8	351 01.8 ..	39.7	Rigil Kent.	139 41.8	S60 55.7
O 10	341 28.7	293 21.1	01.6	246 35.7	24.4	322 53.1	43.1	6 04.0	39.6	Sabik	102 04.3	S15 45.3
N 11	356 31.2	308 20.6	02.5	261 36.8	24.3	337 55.0	43.3	21 06.3	39.5			
D 12	11 33.7	323 20.1	N19 03.5	276 37.8	N25 24.2	352 56.9	N 6 43.5	36 08.5	S11 39.4	Schedar	349 33.3	N56 39.7
A 13	26 36.1	338 19.6	04.4	291 38.9	24.2	7 58.8	43.7	51 10.7	39.3	Shaula	96 12.2	S37 07.2
Y 14	41 38.6	353 19.1	05.3	306 40.0	24.1	23 00.7	44.0	66 12.9	39.2	Sirius	258 27.6	S16 45.1
15	56 41.1	8 18.6 ..	06.2	321 41.1 ..	24.0	38 02.6 ..	44.2	81 15.1 ..	39.2	Spica	158 23.5	S11 17.0
16	71 43.5	23 18.1	07.1	336 42.1	24.0	53 04.5	44.4	96 17.4	39.1	Suhail	222 47.2	S43 31.8
17	86 46.0	38 17.6	08.0	351 43.2	23.9	68 06.4	44.7	111 19.6	39.0			
18	101 48.5	53 17.1	N19 08.9	6 44.3	N25 23.8	83 08.3	N 6 44.9	126 21.8	S11 38.9	Vega	80 34.2	N38 47.9
19	116 50.9	68 16.6	09.8	21 45.3	23.8	98 10.2	45.1	141 24.0	38.8	Zuben'ubi	136 57.4	S16 08.4
20	131 53.4	83 16.1	10.8	36 46.4	23.7	113 12.1	45.3	156 26.2	38.7		SHA	Mer. Pass.
21	146 55.8	98 15.6 ..	11.7	51 47.5 ..	23.6	128 14.0 ..	45.6	171 28.5 ..	38.6		° ′	h m
22	161 58.3	113 15.1	12.6	66 48.5	23.5	143 15.9	45.8	186 30.7	38.6	Venus	313 33.2	14 26
23	177 00.8	128 14.5	13.5	81 49.6	23.5	158 17.8	46.0	201 32.9	38.5	Mars	265 54.2	17 35
Mer. Pass.	h m 11 17.8	v −0.5	d 0.9	v 1.1	d 0.1	v 1.9	d 0.2	v 2.2	d 0.1	Jupiter	341 43.4	12 31
										Saturn	24 43.6	9 39

© British Crown Copyright 2022. All rights reserved.

UT	SUN GHA	SUN Dec	MOON GHA	v	Dec	d	HP
	° ′	° ′	° ′	′	° ′	′	′
d h							
1 00	178 58.9	N 4 21.3	52 27.7	13.1	N21 59.0	9.0	54.2
01	193 59.1	22.3	66 59.8	13.1	21 50.0	9.2	54.2
02	208 59.3	23.2	81 31.9	13.2	21 40.8	9.2	54.2
03	223 59.4	.. 24.2	96 04.1	13.2	21 31.6	9.3	54.2
04	238 59.6	25.2	110 36.3	13.4	21 22.3	9.3	54.2
05	253 59.8	26.1	125 08.7	13.3	21 13.0	9.5	54.2
06	269 00.0	N 4 27.1	139 41.0	13.4	N21 03.5	9.6	54.2
S 07	284 00.2	28.1	154 13.4	13.5	20 53.9	9.7	54.2
A 08	299 00.4	29.0	168 45.9	13.5	20 44.2	9.7	54.2
T 09	314 00.6	.. 30.0	183 18.4	13.6	20 34.5	9.8	54.2
U 10	329 00.7	31.0	197 51.0	13.7	20 24.7	10.0	54.2
R 11	344 00.9	31.9	212 23.7	13.7	20 14.7	10.0	54.2
D 12	359 01.1	N 4 32.9	226 56.4	13.7	N20 04.7	10.1	54.2
A 13	14 01.3	33.9	241 29.1	13.8	19 54.6	10.2	54.2
Y 14	29 01.5	34.8	256 01.9	13.9	19 44.4	10.2	54.2
15	44 01.7	.. 35.8	270 34.8	13.9	19 34.2	10.4	54.3
16	59 01.9	36.8	285 07.7	13.9	19 23.8	10.4	54.3
17	74 02.0	37.7	299 40.6	14.0	19 13.4	10.6	54.3
18	89 02.2	N 4 38.7	314 13.6	14.1	N19 02.8	10.6	54.3
19	104 02.4	39.6	328 46.7	14.1	18 52.2	10.6	54.3
20	119 02.6	40.6	343 19.8	14.2	18 41.6	10.8	54.3
21	134 02.8	.. 41.6	357 53.0	14.2	18 30.8	10.8	54.3
22	149 03.0	42.5	12 26.2	14.2	18 20.0	11.0	54.3
23	164 03.2	43.5	26 59.4	14.4	18 09.0	11.0	54.3
2 00	179 03.3	N 4 44.5	41 32.8	14.3	N17 58.0	11.0	54.3
01	194 03.5	45.4	56 06.1	14.4	17 47.0	11.2	54.3
02	209 03.7	46.4	70 39.5	14.5	17 35.8	11.2	54.3
03	224 03.9	.. 47.4	85 13.0	14.5	17 24.6	11.3	54.4
04	239 04.1	48.3	99 46.5	14.5	17 13.3	11.4	54.4
05	254 04.3	49.3	114 20.0	14.6	17 01.9	11.5	54.4
06	269 04.5	N 4 50.2	128 53.6	14.6	N16 50.4	11.5	54.4
S 07	284 04.6	51.2	143 27.2	14.7	16 38.9	11.6	54.4
U 08	299 04.8	52.2	158 00.9	14.7	16 27.3	11.7	54.4
N 09	314 05.0	.. 53.1	172 34.6	14.8	16 15.6	11.7	54.4
D 10	329 05.2	54.1	187 08.4	14.8	16 03.9	11.8	54.4
A 11	344 05.4	55.0	201 42.2	14.9	15 52.1	11.9	54.4
Y 12	359 05.6	N 4 56.0	216 16.1	14.9	N15 40.2	11.9	54.5
13	14 05.7	57.0	230 50.0	14.9	15 28.3	12.0	54.5
14	29 05.9	57.9	245 23.9	15.0	15 16.3	12.1	54.5
15	44 06.1	.. 58.9	259 57.9	15.0	15 04.2	12.2	54.5
16	59 06.3	4 59.9	274 31.9	15.0	14 52.0	12.2	54.5
17	74 06.5	5 00.8	289 05.9	15.1	14 39.8	12.3	54.5
18	89 06.7	N 5 01.8	303 40.0	15.1	N14 27.5	12.3	54.5
19	104 06.9	02.7	318 14.1	15.2	14 15.2	12.4	54.5
20	119 07.0	03.7	332 48.3	15.2	14 02.8	12.5	54.6
21	134 07.2	.. 04.7	347 22.5	15.2	13 50.3	12.5	54.6
22	149 07.4	05.6	1 56.7	15.2	13 37.8	12.6	54.6
23	164 07.6	06.6	16 30.9	15.3	13 25.2	12.6	54.6
3 00	179 07.8	N 5 07.5	31 05.2	15.4	N13 12.6	12.7	54.6
01	194 08.0	08.5	45 39.6	15.3	12 59.9	12.8	54.6
02	209 08.1	09.5	60 13.9	15.4	12 47.1	12.8	54.6
03	224 08.3	.. 10.4	74 48.3	15.4	12 34.3	12.9	54.7
04	239 08.5	11.4	89 22.7	15.4	12 21.4	12.9	54.7
05	254 08.7	12.3	103 57.1	15.5	12 08.5	13.0	54.7
06	269 08.9	N 5 13.3	118 31.6	15.5	N11 55.5	13.1	54.7
M 07	284 09.1	14.2	133 06.1	15.5	11 42.4	13.1	54.7
O 08	299 09.2	15.2	147 40.6	15.6	11 29.3	13.1	54.7
N 09	314 09.4	.. 16.2	162 15.2	15.5	11 16.2	13.2	54.7
D 10	329 09.6	17.1	176 49.7	15.6	11 03.0	13.3	54.8
A 11	344 09.8	18.1	191 24.3	15.7	10 49.7	13.3	54.8
Y 12	359 10.0	N 5 19.0	205 59.0	15.6	N10 36.4	13.3	54.8
13	14 10.2	20.0	220 33.6	15.7	10 23.1	13.4	54.8
14	29 10.3	20.9	235 08.3	15.6	10 09.7	13.5	54.8
15	44 10.5	.. 21.9	249 42.9	15.7	9 56.2	13.5	54.8
16	59 10.7	22.9	264 17.6	15.8	9 42.7	13.5	54.9
17	74 10.9	23.8	278 52.4	15.7	9 29.2	13.6	54.9
18	89 11.1	N 5 24.8	293 27.1	15.8	N 9 15.6	13.6	54.9
19	104 11.3	25.7	308 01.9	15.7	9 02.0	13.7	54.9
20	119 11.4	26.7	322 36.6	15.8	8 48.3	13.7	54.9
21	134 11.6	.. 27.6	337 11.4	15.8	8 34.6	13.8	54.9
22	149 11.8	28.6	351 46.2	15.8	8 20.8	13.8	55.0
23	164 12.0	29.6	6 21.0	15.8	N 8 07.0	13.9	55.0
	SD 16.0	d 1.0	SD 14.8		14.8		14.9

Lat.	Naut.	Civil	Sunrise	Moonrise 1	2	3	4
°	h m	h m	h m	h m	h m	h m	h m
N 72	01 29	03 37	04 52	▭	11 36	14 08	16 14
N 70	02 15	03 54	05 00	▭	12 17	14 25	16 20
68	02 44	04 07	05 06	10 26	12 44	14 38	16 25
66	03 06	04 18	05 12	11 09	13 04	14 49	16 29
64	03 22	04 26	05 16	11 38	13 21	14 58	16 32
62	03 36	04 34	05 20	12 00	13 34	15 05	16 35
60	03 47	04 40	05 23	12 17	13 46	15 12	16 37
N 58	03 56	04 46	05 26	12 32	13 55	15 18	16 40
56	04 04	04 51	05 29	12 44	14 04	15 23	16 42
54	04 11	04 55	05 31	12 55	14 11	15 27	16 43
52	04 18	04 59	05 33	13 05	14 18	15 31	16 45
50	04 23	05 03	05 35	13 13	14 24	15 35	16 46
45	04 35	05 10	05 40	13 31	14 37	15 43	16 49
N 40	04 43	05 16	05 43	13 46	14 48	15 50	16 52
35	04 51	05 21	05 46	13 58	14 57	15 56	16 54
30	04 56	05 25	05 49	14 09	15 05	16 01	16 56
20	05 05	05 31	05 53	14 27	15 19	16 09	17 00
N 10	05 11	05 36	05 57	14 43	15 31	16 17	17 03
0	05 16	05 40	06 00	14 58	15 42	16 24	17 05
S 10	05 18	05 43	06 04	15 13	15 53	16 31	17 08
20	05 20	05 45	06 07	15 29	16 05	16 38	17 11
30	05 19	05 47	06 11	15 47	16 18	16 47	17 14
35	05 19	05 48	06 13	15 57	16 26	16 52	17 16
40	05 17	05 49	06 16	16 09	16 34	16 57	17 19
45	05 15	05 49	06 18	16 23	16 45	17 04	17 21
S 50	05 12	05 49	06 22	16 40	16 57	17 11	17 24
52	05 10	05 49	06 23	16 48	17 03	17 15	17 25
54	05 08	05 49	06 25	16 57	17 09	17 19	17 27
56	05 06	05 49	06 27	17 07	17 16	17 23	17 29
58	05 04	05 49	06 29	17 18	17 24	17 27	17 30
S 60	05 01	05 49	06 31	17 31	17 32	17 33	17 33

Lat.	Sunset	Civil	Naut.	Moonset 1	2	3	4
°	h m	h m	h m	h m	h m	h m	h m
N 72	19 18	20 35	22 51	▭	07 47	06 45	06 07
N 70	19 10	20 17	21 59	▭	07 05	06 26	05 58
68	19 03	20 03	21 28	07 22	06 36	06 11	05 51
66	18 58	19 52	21 05	06 38	06 14	05 58	05 45
64	18 53	19 43	20 48	06 08	05 57	05 48	05 39
62	18 49	19 35	20 34	05 46	05 42	05 39	05 35
60	18 45	19 29	20 23	05 27	05 30	05 31	05 31
N 58	18 42	19 23	20 13	05 12	05 19	05 24	05 27
56	18 40	19 18	20 05	04 59	05 10	05 18	05 24
54	18 37	19 13	19 57	04 48	05 02	05 12	05 21
52	18 35	19 09	19 51	04 38	04 54	05 08	05 19
50	18 33	19 06	19 45	04 28	04 48	05 03	05 16
45	18 29	18 58	19 34	04 09	04 33	04 53	05 11
N 40	18 25	18 52	19 25	03 54	04 21	04 45	05 07
35	18 22	18 47	19 17	03 40	04 11	04 38	05 03
30	18 19	18 43	19 11	03 29	04 02	04 32	05 00
20	18 14	18 37	19 02	03 09	03 46	04 21	04 54
N 10	18 11	18 32	18 56	02 51	03 32	04 11	04 49
0	18 07	18 28	18 52	02 35	03 19	04 02	04 44
S 10	18 03	18 24	18 49	02 18	03 06	03 53	04 39
20	18 00	18 22	18 47	02 00	02 52	03 43	04 33
30	17 56	18 20	18 47	01 40	02 36	03 32	04 27
35	17 54	18 19	18 48	01 27	02 27	03 25	04 24
40	17 51	18 18	18 49	01 13	02 16	03 18	04 20
45	17 48	18 17	18 51	00 57	02 03	03 09	04 15
S 50	17 45	18 17	18 54	00 36	01 47	02 58	04 09
52	17 43	18 17	18 56	00 26	01 40	02 53	04 07
54	17 41	18 17	18 58	00 15	01 32	02 48	04 04
56	17 40	18 17	19 00	00 02	01 22	02 42	04 01
58	17 38	18 17	19 02	25 12	01 12	02 35	03 57
S 60	17 35	18 17	19 05	25 00	01 00	02 27	03 53

Day	SUN Eqn. of Time 00ʰ	12ʰ	Mer. Pass.	MOON Mer. Pass. Upper	Lower	Age	Phase
d	m s	m s	h m	h m	h m	d	%
1	04 05	03 56	12 04	21 09	08 46	11	80
2	03 47	03 38	12 04	21 52	09 31	12	87
3	03 29	03 20	12 03	22 34	10 13	13	93

© British Crown Copyright 2022. All rights reserved.

UT	ARIES GHA	VENUS −4.0 GHA	Dec	MARS +1.0 GHA	Dec	JUPITER −2.0 GHA	Dec	SATURN +0.9 GHA	Dec	STARS Name	SHA	Dec
d h	° ′	° ′	° ′	° ′	° ′	° ′	° ′	° ′	° ′		° ′	° ′
4 00	192 03.2	143 14.0	N19 14.4	96 50.7	N25 23.4	173 19.7	N 6 46.3	216 35.1	S11 38.4	Acamar	315 13.3	S40 12.9
01	207 05.7	158 13.5	15.3	111 51.7	23.3	188 21.6	46.5	231 37.4	38.3	Achernar	335 21.8	S57 07.3
02	222 08.2	173 13.0	16.2	126 52.8	23.3	203 23.5	46.7	246 39.6	38.2	Acrux	173 01.1	S63 13.7
03	237 10.6	188 12.5 ..	17.1	141 53.9 ..	23.2	218 25.4 ..	46.9	261 41.8 ..	38.1	Adhara	255 07.0	S29 00.4
04	252 13.1	203 12.0	18.0	156 54.9	23.1	233 27.3	47.2	276 44.0	38.0	Aldebaran	290 41.5	N16 33.3
05	267 15.6	218 11.5	18.9	171 56.0	23.0	248 29.2	47.4	291 46.2	37.9			
06	282 18.0	233 11.0	N19 19.8	186 57.1	N25 23.0	263 31.1	N 6 47.6	306 48.5	S11 37.9	Alioth	166 13.7	N55 50.0
07	297 20.5	248 10.4	20.7	201 58.1	22.9	278 33.0	47.9	321 50.7	37.8	Alkaid	152 52.7	N49 11.7
08	312 22.9	263 09.9	21.6	216 59.2	22.8	293 34.9	48.1	336 52.9	37.7	Alnair	27 35.1	S46 50.9
09	327 25.4	278 09.4 ..	22.5	232 00.3 ..	22.7	308 36.8 ..	48.3	351 55.1 ..	37.6	Alnilam	275 39.3	S 1 11.3
10	342 27.9	293 08.9	23.4	247 01.3	22.7	323 38.7	48.5	6 57.3	37.5	Alphard	217 49.0	S 8 45.7
11	357 30.3	308 08.4	24.3	262 02.4	22.6	338 40.6	48.8	21 59.6	37.4			
12	12 32.8	323 07.9	N19 25.2	277 03.5	N25 22.5	353 42.6	N 6 49.0	37 01.8	S11 37.4	Alphecca	126 04.7	N26 38.0
13	27 35.3	338 07.4	26.1	292 04.5	22.5	8 44.5	49.2	52 04.0	37.3	Alpheratz	357 36.7	N29 12.9
14	42 37.7	353 06.8	27.0	307 05.6	22.4	23 46.4	49.5	67 06.2	37.2	Altair	62 01.5	N 8 55.5
15	57 40.2	8 06.3 ..	27.9	322 06.7 ..	22.3	38 48.3 ..	49.7	82 08.5 ..	37.1	Ankaa	353 09.0	S42 10.9
16	72 42.7	23 05.8	28.8	337 07.7	22.2	53 50.2	49.9	97 10.7	37.0	Antares	112 17.4	S26 29.0
17	87 45.1	38 05.3	29.7	352 08.8	22.2	68 52.1	50.1	112 12.9	36.9			
18	102 47.6	53 04.8	N19 30.6	7 09.9	N25 22.1	83 54.0	N 6 50.4	127 15.1	S11 36.8	Arcturus	145 48.9	N19 03.6
19	117 50.1	68 04.3	31.5	22 10.9	22.0	98 55.9	50.6	142 17.4	36.8	Atria	107 12.7	S69 03.9
20	132 52.5	83 03.7	32.4	37 12.0	21.9	113 57.8	50.8	157 19.6	36.7	Avior	234 15.1	S59 35.3
21	147 55.0	98 03.2 ..	33.3	52 13.0 ..	21.8	128 59.7 ..	51.1	172 21.8 ..	36.6	Bellatrix	278 24.6	N 6 22.2
22	162 57.4	113 02.7	34.1	67 14.1	21.8	144 01.6	51.3	187 24.0	36.5	Betelgeuse	270 53.8	N 7 24.6
23	177 59.9	128 02.2	35.0	82 15.2	21.7	159 03.5	51.5	202 26.2	36.4			
5 00	193 02.4	143 01.7	N19 35.9	97 16.2	N25 21.6	174 05.4	N 6 51.7	217 28.5	S11 36.3	Canopus	263 53.1	S52 42.7
01	208 04.8	158 01.2	36.8	112 17.3	21.5	189 07.3	52.0	232 30.7	36.2	Capella	280 24.3	N46 01.4
02	223 07.3	173 00.6	37.7	127 18.4	21.5	204 09.2	52.2	247 32.9	36.2	Deneb	49 27.0	N45 21.4
03	238 09.8	188 00.1 ..	38.6	142 19.4 ..	21.4	219 11.1 ..	52.4	262 35.1 ..	36.1	Denebola	182 26.2	N14 26.5
04	253 12.2	202 59.6	39.5	157 20.5	21.3	234 13.0	52.6	277 37.4	36.0	Diphda	348 49.1	S17 51.7
05	268 14.7	217 59.1	40.3	172 21.6	21.2	249 14.9	52.9	292 39.6	35.9			
06	283 17.2	232 58.5	N19 41.2	187 22.6	N25 21.2	264 16.8	N 6 53.1	307 41.8	S11 35.8	Dubhe	193 42.2	N61 37.7
07	298 19.6	247 58.0	42.1	202 23.7	21.1	279 18.7	53.3	322 44.0	35.7	Elnath	278 03.9	N28 37.6
08	313 22.1	262 57.5	43.0	217 24.7	21.0	294 20.6	53.6	337 46.3	35.6	Eltanin	90 42.7	N51 28.8
09	328 24.5	277 57.0 ..	43.9	232 25.8 ..	20.9	309 22.5 ..	53.8	352 48.5 ..	35.5	Enif	33 40.5	N 9 58.7
10	343 27.0	292 56.5	44.7	247 26.9	20.8	324 24.4	54.0	7 50.7	35.5	Fomalhaut	15 16.4	S29 30.0
11	358 29.5	307 55.9	45.6	262 27.9	20.8	339 26.3	54.2	22 52.9	35.4			
12	13 31.9	322 55.4	N19 46.5	277 29.0	N25 20.7	354 28.2	N 6 54.5	37 55.2	S11 35.3	Gacrux	171 52.7	S57 14.6
13	28 34.4	337 54.9	47.4	292 30.0	20.6	9 30.1	54.7	52 57.4	35.2	Gienah	175 44.8	S17 40.3
14	43 36.9	352 54.4	48.2	307 31.1	20.5	24 32.0	54.9	67 59.6	35.1	Hadar	148 37.5	S60 29.0
15	58 39.3	7 53.8 ..	49.1	322 32.2 ..	20.4	39 33.9 ..	55.2	83 01.8 ..	35.1	Hamal	327 53.2	N23 34.2
16	73 41.8	22 53.3	50.0	337 33.2	20.4	54 35.8	55.4	98 04.0	35.0	Kaus Aust.	83 34.4	S34 22.4
17	88 44.3	37 52.8	50.9	352 34.3	20.3	69 37.7	55.6	113 06.3	34.9			
18	103 46.7	52 52.3	N19 51.7	7 35.3	N25 20.2	84 39.6	N 6 55.8	128 08.5	S11 34.8	Kochab	137 18.7	N74 03.4
19	118 49.2	67 51.7	52.6	22 36.4	20.1	99 41.5	56.1	143 10.7	34.7	Markab	13 31.7	N15 19.6
20	133 51.7	82 51.2	53.5	37 37.5	20.0	114 43.4	56.3	158 12.9	34.6	Menkar	314 08.0	N 4 10.7
21	148 54.1	97 50.7 ..	54.3	52 38.5 ..	20.0	129 45.3 ..	56.5	173 15.2 ..	34.5	Menkent	147 59.0	S36 29.1
22	163 56.6	112 50.2	55.2	67 39.6	19.9	144 47.2	56.8	188 17.4	34.5	Miaplacidus	221 38.1	S69 48.9
23	178 59.0	127 49.6	56.1	82 40.6	19.8	159 49.1	57.0	203 19.6	34.4			
6 00	194 01.5	142 49.1	N19 57.0	97 41.7	N25 19.7	174 51.0	N 6 57.2	218 21.8	S11 34.3	Mirfak	308 30.8	N49 56.6
01	209 04.0	157 48.6	57.8	112 42.7	19.6	189 52.9	57.4	233 24.1	34.2	Nunki	75 49.6	S26 16.1
02	224 06.4	172 48.1	58.7	127 43.8	19.5	204 54.8	57.7	248 26.3	34.1	Peacock	53 08.2	S56 39.5
03	239 08.9	187 47.5	19 59.5	142 44.9 ..	19.5	219 56.7 ..	57.9	263 28.5 ..	34.0	Pollux	243 19.1	N27 58.3
04	254 11.4	202 47.0	20 00.4	157 45.9	19.4	234 58.6	58.1	278 30.8	34.0	Procyon	244 52.3	N 5 09.9
05	269 13.8	217 46.5	01.3	172 47.0	19.3	250 00.5	58.3	293 33.0	33.9			
06	284 16.3	232 45.9	N20 02.1	187 48.0	N25 19.2	265 02.4	N 6 58.6	308 35.2	S11 33.8	Rasalhague	95 59.8	N12 32.4
07	299 18.8	247 45.4	03.0	202 49.1	19.1	280 04.4	58.8	323 37.4	33.7	Regulus	207 35.8	N11 51.2
08	314 21.2	262 44.9	03.9	217 50.2	19.1	295 06.3	59.0	338 39.7	33.6	Rigel	281 05.4	S 8 10.6
09	329 23.7	277 44.3 ..	04.7	232 51.2 ..	19.0	310 08.2 ..	59.3	353 41.9 ..	33.5	Rigil Kent.	139 41.8	S60 55.8
10	344 26.2	292 43.8	05.6	247 52.3	18.9	325 10.1	59.5	8 44.1	33.4	Sabik	102 04.3	S15 45.3
11	359 28.6	307 43.3	06.4	262 53.3	18.8	340 12.0	59.7	23 46.3	33.4			
12	14 31.1	322 42.8	N20 07.2	277 54.4	N25 18.7	355 13.9	N 6 59.9	38 48.6	S11 33.3	Schedar	349 33.3	N56 39.7
13	29 33.5	337 42.2	08.1	292 55.4	18.6	10 15.8	7 00.2	53 50.8	33.2	Shaula	96 12.2	S37 07.2
14	44 36.0	352 41.7	09.0	307 56.5	18.5	25 17.7	00.4	68 53.0	33.1	Sirius	258 27.6	S16 45.0
15	59 38.5	7 41.2 ..	09.8	322 57.5 ..	18.5	40 19.6 ..	00.6	83 55.2 ..	33.0	Spica	158 23.5	S11 17.0
16	74 40.9	22 40.6	10.7	337 58.6	18.4	55 21.5	00.9	98 57.5	32.9	Suhail	222 47.2	S43 31.8
17	89 43.4	37 40.1	11.6	352 59.7	18.3	70 23.4	01.1	113 59.7	32.9			
18	104 45.9	52 39.6	N20 12.4	8 00.7	N25 18.2	85 25.3	N 7 01.3	129 01.9	S11 32.8	Vega	80 34.2	N38 48.0
19	119 48.3	67 39.0	13.3	23 01.8	18.1	100 27.2	01.5	144 04.1	32.7	Zuben'ubi	136 57.4	S16 08.4
20	134 50.8	82 38.5	14.1	38 02.8	18.0	115 29.1	01.8	159 06.4	32.6		SHA	Mer. Pass.
21	149 53.3	97 38.0 ..	15.0	53 03.9 ..	17.9	130 31.0 ..	02.0	174 08.6 ..	32.5		° ′	h m
22	164 55.7	112 37.4	15.8	68 04.9	17.9	145 32.9	02.2	189 10.8	32.4	Venus	309 59.3	14 28
23	179 58.2	127 36.9	16.6	83 06.0	17.8	160 34.8	02.4	204 13.1	32.4	Mars	264 13.9	17 30
Mer. Pass.	h m 11 06.0	v −0.5	d 0.9	v 1.1	d 0.1	v 1.9	d 0.2	v 2.2	d 0.1	Jupiter	341 03.0	12 22
										Saturn	24 26.1	9 29

© British Crown Copyright 2022. All rights reserved.

UT	SUN		MOON				Lat.	Twilight		Sunrise	Moonrise			
								Naut.	Civil		4	5	6	7
	GHA	Dec	GHA	v	Dec	d	HP							
d h	° ′	° ′	° ′	′	° ′	′	′	N 72	00 27	03 18	04 36	16 14	18 17	20 27	23 06
4 00	179 12.2	N 5 30.5	20 55.8	15.9	N 7 53.1	13.9	55.0	N 70	01 48	03 37	04 46	16 20	18 14	20 13	22 29
01	194 12.4	31.5	35 30.7	15.8	7 39.2	13.9	55.0	68	02 25	03 53	04 54	16 25	18 11	20 02	22 04
02	209 12.5	32.4	50 05.5	15.9	7 25.3	14.0	55.0	66	02 49	04 05	05 00	16 29	18 09	19 52	21 45
03	224 12.7	. . 33.4	64 40.4	15.8	7 11.3	14.0	55.1	64	03 08	04 15	05 05	16 32	18 07	19 45	21 29
04	239 12.9	34.3	79 15.2	15.9	6 57.3	14.0	55.1	62	03 23	04 23	05 10	16 35	18 05	19 38	21 17
05	254 13.1	35.3	93 50.1	15.9	6 43.3	14.1	55.1	60	03 36	04 31	05 14	16 37	18 04	19 32	21 06
06	269 13.3	N 5 36.2	108 25.0	15.9	N 6 29.2	14.1	55.1	N 58	03 46	04 37	05 18	16 40	18 02	19 27	20 57
07	284 13.5	37.2	122 59.9	15.8	6 15.1	14.1	55.1	56	03 55	04 43	05 21	16 42	18 01	19 23	20 48
T 08	299 13.6	38.1	137 34.7	15.9	6 01.0	14.2	55.1	54	04 03	04 48	05 24	16 43	18 00	19 19	20 41
U 09	314 13.8	. . 39.1	152 09.6	15.9	5 46.8	14.2	55.2	52	04 10	04 52	05 27	16 45	17 59	19 15	20 35
E 10	329 14.0	40.1	166 44.5	15.9	5 32.6	14.3	55.2	50	04 16	04 56	05 29	16 46	17 58	19 12	20 29
S 11	344 14.2	41.0	181 19.4	15.9	5 18.3	14.3	55.2	45	04 29	05 04	05 34	16 49	17 56	19 05	20 17
D 12	359 14.4	N 5 42.0	195 54.3	15.9	N 5 04.0	14.3	55.2	N 40	04 38	05 11	05 38	16 52	17 55	18 59	20 06
A 13	14 14.5	42.9	210 29.2	15.9	4 49.7	14.3	55.2	35	04 46	05 16	05 42	16 54	17 53	18 54	19 58
Y 14	29 14.7	43.9	225 04.1	15.9	4 35.4	14.4	55.3	30	04 53	05 21	05 45	16 56	17 52	18 50	19 50
15	44 14.9	. . 44.8	239 39.0	15.9	4 21.0	14.4	55.3	20	05 02	05 28	05 51	17 00	17 50	18 43	19 37
16	59 15.1	45.8	254 13.9	15.9	4 06.6	14.4	55.3	N 10	05 09	05 34	05 55	17 03	17 49	18 36	19 26
17	74 15.3	46.7	268 48.8	15.9	3 52.2	14.4	55.3	0	05 15	05 39	05 59	17 05	17 47	18 30	19 15
18	89 15.5	N 5 47.7	283 23.7	15.8	N 3 37.8	14.5	55.3	S 10	05 18	05 43	06 04	17 08	17 45	18 24	19 05
19	104 15.6	48.6	297 58.5	15.9	3 23.3	14.5	55.4	20	05 20	05 46	06 08	17 11	17 44	18 18	18 54
20	119 15.8	49.6	312 33.4	15.8	3 08.8	14.5	55.4	30	05 21	05 49	06 13	17 14	17 42	18 10	18 41
21	134 16.0	. . 50.5	327 08.2	15.9	2 54.3	14.6	55.4	35	05 21	05 50	06 16	17 16	17 41	18 06	18 34
22	149 16.2	51.5	341 43.1	15.8	2 39.7	14.5	55.4	40	05 20	05 52	06 19	17 19	17 40	18 02	18 26
23	164 16.4	52.4	356 17.9	15.9	2 25.2	14.6	55.4	45	05 19	05 53	06 22	17 21	17 38	17 56	18 17
5 00	179 16.5	N 5 53.4	10 52.8	15.8	N 2 10.6	14.6	55.5	S 50	05 17	05 54	06 26	17 24	17 37	17 50	18 05
01	194 16.7	54.3	25 27.6	15.8	1 56.0	14.7	55.5	52	05 15	05 54	06 28	17 25	17 36	17 47	18 00
02	209 16.9	55.3	40 02.4	15.8	1 41.3	14.6	55.5	54	05 14	05 55	06 30	17 27	17 35	17 44	17 54
03	224 17.1	. . 56.2	54 37.2	15.7	1 26.7	14.7	55.5	56	05 12	05 55	06 33	17 29	17 34	17 40	17 48
04	239 17.3	57.2	69 11.9	15.8	1 12.0	14.6	55.5	58	05 10	05 56	06 35	17 30	17 33	17 37	17 41
05	254 17.4	58.1	83 46.7	15.7	0 57.4	14.7	55.6	S 60	05 08	05 56	06 38	17 33	17 32	17 32	17 33

UT	SUN		MOON				Lat.	Sunset	Twilight		Moonset			
									Civil	Naut.	4	5	6	7
06	269 17.6	N 5 59.1	98 21.4	15.7	N 0 42.7	14.7	55.6							
W 07	284 17.8	6 00.0	112 56.1	15.7	0 28.0	14.7	55.6	°	h m	h m	h m	h m	h m	h m	h m
E 08	299 18.0	01.0	127 30.8	15.7	N 0 13.3	14.8	55.6	N 72	19 32	20 53	////	06 07	05 34	05 02	04 24
D 09	314 18.2	. . 01.9	142 05.5	15.7	S 0 01.5	14.7	55.6	N 70	19 22	20 32	22 26	05 58	05 34	05 09	04 41
N 10	329 18.3	02.9	156 40.2	15.6	0 16.2	14.8	55.7	68	19 14	20 16	21 47	05 51	05 33	05 15	04 55
E 11	344 18.5	03.8	171 14.8	15.6	0 31.0	14.7	55.7	66	19 08	20 03	21 20	05 45	05 32	05 20	05 06
S 12	359 18.7	N 6 04.8	185 49.4	15.6	S 0 45.7	14.8	55.7	64	19 02	19 53	21 01	05 39	05 32	05 24	05 15
D 13	14 18.9	05.7	200 24.0	15.6	1 00.5	14.8	55.7	62	18 57	19 44	20 45	05 35	05 31	05 27	05 23
A 14	29 19.1	06.7	214 58.6	15.5	1 15.3	14.7	55.7	60	18 53	19 37	20 32	05 31	05 31	05 30	05 30
Y 15	44 19.2	. . 07.6	229 33.1	15.5	1 30.1	14.7	55.8	N 58	18 49	19 30	20 21	05 27	05 30	05 33	05 37
16	59 19.4	08.6	244 07.6	15.5	1 44.8	14.8	55.8	56	18 46	19 24	20 12	05 24	05 30	05 36	05 42
17	74 19.6	09.5	258 42.1	15.4	1 59.6	14.8	55.8	54	18 43	19 19	20 04	05 21	05 30	05 38	05 47
18	89 19.8	N 6 10.5	273 16.5	15.4	S 2 14.4	14.8	55.8	52	18 40	19 15	19 57	05 19	05 29	05 40	05 52
19	104 20.0	11.4	287 50.9	15.4	2 29.2	14.8	55.9	50	18 38	19 11	19 51	05 16	05 29	05 42	05 56
20	119 20.1	12.4	302 25.3	15.4	2 44.0	14.9	55.9	45	18 32	19 02	19 38	05 11	05 28	05 46	06 05
21	134 20.3	. . 13.3	316 59.7	15.3	2 58.9	14.8	55.9	N 40	18 28	18 55	19 28	05 07	05 28	05 49	06 12
22	149 20.5	14.3	331 34.0	15.3	3 13.7	14.8	55.9	35	18 24	18 50	19 20	05 03	05 27	05 52	06 19
23	164 20.7	15.2	346 08.3	15.2	3 28.5	14.8	55.9	30	18 21	18 45	19 13	05 00	05 27	05 55	06 24
6 00	179 20.9	N 6 16.2	0 42.5	15.2	S 3 43.3	14.8	56.0	20	18 15	18 37	19 03	04 54	05 26	05 59	06 34
01	194 21.0	17.1	15 16.7	15.2	3 58.1	14.7	56.0	N 10	18 10	18 32	18 56	04 49	05 26	06 03	06 43
02	209 21.2	18.1	29 50.9	15.1	4 12.8	14.8	56.0	0	18 06	18 27	18 51	04 44	05 25	06 07	06 51
03	224 21.4	. . 19.0	44 25.0	15.1	4 27.6	14.8	56.0	S 10	18 02	18 23	18 47	04 39	05 25	06 11	07 00
04	239 21.6	19.9	58 59.1	15.0	4 42.4	14.8	56.1	20	17 57	18 19	18 45	04 33	05 24	06 15	07 08
05	254 21.8	20.9	73 33.1	15.0	4 57.2	14.7	56.1	30	17 52	18 16	18 44	04 27	05 23	06 20	07 19
06	269 21.9	N 6 21.8	88 07.1	15.0	S 5 11.9	14.8	56.1	35	17 49	18 15	18 44	04 24	05 23	06 22	07 24
07	284 22.1	22.8	102 41.1	14.9	5 26.7	14.7	56.1	40	17 46	18 13	18 45	04 20	05 22	06 26	07 31
T 08	299 22.3	23.7	117 15.0	14.9	5 41.4	14.8	56.1	45	17 43	18 12	18 46	04 15	05 21	06 29	07 39
H 09	314 22.5	. . 24.7	131 48.9	14.8	5 56.2	14.7	56.2	S 50	17 38	18 11	18 48	04 09	05 21	06 33	07 49
U 10	329 22.7	25.6	146 22.7	14.8	6 10.9	14.7	56.2	52	17 36	18 10	18 49	04 07	05 20	06 35	07 53
R 11	344 22.8	26.6	160 56.5	14.7	6 25.6	14.7	56.2	54	17 34	18 10	18 50	04 04	05 20	06 37	07 58
S 12	359 23.0	N 6 27.5	175 30.2	14.6	S 6 40.3	14.7	56.2	56	17 32	18 09	18 52	04 01	05 19	06 40	08 03
D 13	14 23.2	28.5	190 03.8	14.7	6 55.0	14.6	56.2	58	17 29	18 08	18 54	03 57	05 19	06 43	08 09
A 14	29 23.4	29.4	204 37.5	14.5	7 09.6	14.6	56.3	S 60	17 26	18 08	18 56	03 53	05 18	06 46	08 16
Y 15	44 23.5	. . 30.3	219 11.0	14.5	7 24.2	14.7	56.3			SUN		MOON			
16	59 23.7	31.3	233 44.5	14.5	7 38.9	14.6	56.3								
17	74 23.9	32.2	248 18.0	14.4	7 53.4	14.6	56.3	Day	Eqn. of Time		Mer.	Mer. Pass.		Age	Phase
18	89 24.1	N 6 33.2	262 51.4	14.3	S 8 08.0	14.6	56.4		00ʰ	12ʰ	Pass.	Upper	Lower		
19	104 24.3	34.1	277 24.7	14.3	8 22.6	14.5	56.4	d	m s	m s	h m	h m	h m	d %	
20	119 24.4	35.1	291 58.0	14.3	8 37.1	14.5	56.4	4	03 12	03 03	12 03	23 15	10 55	14 97	
21	134 24.6	. . 36.0	306 31.3	14.1	8 51.6	14.5	56.4	5	02 54	02 46	12 03	23 57	11 36	15 99	
22	149 24.8	36.9	321 04.4	14.1	9 06.1	14.4	56.4	6	02 37	02 28	12 02	24 41	12 19	16 100	
23	164 25.0	37.9	335 37.5	14.1	S 9 20.5	14.4	56.5								
	SD 16.0	d 0.9	SD 15.0		15.2		15.3									

© British Crown Copyright 2022. All rights reserved.

UT	ARIES GHA	VENUS −4.0 GHA	VENUS Dec	MARS +1.1 GHA	MARS Dec	JUPITER −2.0 GHA	JUPITER Dec	SATURN +0.9 GHA	SATURN Dec
7 00	195 00.6	142 36.4	N20 17.5	98 07.0	N25 17.7	175 36.7	N 7 02.7	219 15.3	S11 32.3
01	210 03.1	157 35.8	18.3	113 08.1	17.6	190 38.6	02.9	234 17.5	32.2
02	225 05.6	172 35.3	19.2	128 09.1	17.5	205 40.5	03.1	249 19.7	32.1
03	240 08.0	187 34.7 ..	20.0	143 10.2 ..	17.4	220 42.4 ..	03.4	264 22.0 ..	32.0
04	255 10.5	202 34.2	20.9	158 11.2	17.3	235 44.3	03.6	279 24.2	31.9
05	270 13.0	217 33.7	21.7	173 12.3	17.2	250 46.2	03.8	294 26.4	31.9
F 06	285 15.4	232 33.1 N20	22.5	188 13.3 N25	17.2	265 48.1 N 7	04.0	309 28.7 S11	31.8
R 07	300 17.9	247 32.6	23.4	203 14.4	17.1	280 50.0	04.3	324 30.9	31.7
I 08	315 20.4	262 32.1	24.2	218 15.5	17.0	295 51.9	04.5	339 33.1	31.6
D 09	330 22.8	277 31.5 ..	25.1	233 16.5 ..	16.9	310 53.8 ..	04.7	354 35.3 ..	31.5
A 10	345 25.3	292 31.0	25.9	248 17.6	16.8	325 55.7	04.9	9 37.6	31.4
Y 11	0 27.8	307 30.4	26.7	263 18.6	16.7	340 57.6	05.2	24 39.8	31.4
12	15 30.2	322 29.9 N20	27.6	278 19.7 N25	16.6	355 59.5 N 7	05.4	39 42.0 S11	31.3
13	30 32.7	337 29.4	28.4	293 20.7	16.5	11 01.4	05.6	54 44.2	31.2
14	45 35.1	352 28.8	29.2	308 21.8	16.4	26 03.3	05.9	69 46.5	31.1
15	60 37.6	7 28.3 ..	30.1	323 22.8 ..	16.4	41 05.2 ..	06.1	84 48.7 ..	31.0
16	75 40.1	22 27.7	30.9	338 23.9	16.3	56 07.1	06.3	99 50.9	30.9
17	90 42.5	37 27.2	31.7	353 24.9	16.2	71 09.0	06.5	114 53.2	30.9
18	105 45.0	52 26.7 N20	32.6	8 26.0 N25	16.1	86 10.9 N 7	06.8	129 55.4 S11	30.8
19	120 47.5	67 26.1	33.4	23 27.0	16.0	101 12.8	07.0	144 57.6	30.7
20	135 49.9	82 25.6	34.2	38 28.1	15.9	116 14.7	07.2	159 59.9	30.6
21	150 52.4	97 25.0 ..	35.0	53 29.1 ..	15.8	131 16.6 ..	07.4	175 02.1 ..	30.5
22	165 54.9	112 24.5	35.9	68 30.2	15.7	146 18.5	07.7	190 04.3	30.4
23	180 57.3	127 23.9	36.7	83 31.2	15.6	161 20.4	07.9	205 06.5	30.4
8 00	195 59.8	142 23.4 N20	37.5	98 32.3 N25	15.5	176 22.3 N 7	08.1	220 08.8 S11	30.3
01	211 02.2	157 22.9	38.3	113 33.3	15.4	191 24.2	08.4	235 11.0	30.2
02	226 04.7	172 22.3	39.2	128 34.4	15.3	206 26.1	08.6	250 13.2	30.1
03	241 07.2	187 21.8 ..	40.0	143 35.4 ..	15.3	221 28.0 ..	08.8	265 15.5 ..	30.0
04	256 09.6	202 21.2	40.8	158 36.5	15.2	236 29.9	09.0	280 17.7	29.9
05	271 12.1	217 20.7	41.6	173 37.5	15.1	251 31.8	09.3	295 19.9	29.9
S 06	286 14.6	232 20.1 N20	42.5	188 38.6 N25	15.0	266 33.7 N 7	09.5	310 22.1 S11	29.8
A 07	301 17.0	247 19.6	43.3	203 39.6	14.9	281 35.6	09.7	325 24.4	29.7
T 08	316 19.5	262 19.0	44.1	218 40.7	14.8	296 37.5	09.9	340 26.6	29.6
U 09	331 22.0	277 18.5 ..	44.9	233 41.7 ..	14.7	311 39.4 ..	10.2	355 28.8 ..	29.5
R 10	346 24.4	292 17.9	45.7	248 42.7	14.6	326 41.3	10.4	10 31.1	29.5
D 11	1 26.9	307 17.4	46.5	263 43.8	14.5	341 43.2	10.6	25 33.3	29.4
A 12	16 29.4	322 16.8 N20	47.3	278 44.8 N25	14.4	356 45.1 N 7	10.8	40 35.5 S11	29.3
Y 13	31 31.8	337 16.3	48.2	293 45.9	14.3	11 47.0	11.1	55 37.8	29.2
14	46 34.3	352 15.8	49.0	308 46.9	14.2	26 48.9	11.3	70 40.0	29.1
15	61 36.7	7 15.2 ..	49.8	323 48.0 ..	14.1	41 50.8 ..	11.5	85 42.2 ..	29.0
16	76 39.2	22 14.7	50.6	338 49.0	14.0	56 52.7	11.8	100 44.5	29.0
17	91 41.7	37 14.1	51.4	353 50.1	13.9	71 54.6	12.0	115 46.7	28.9
18	106 44.1	52 13.6 N20	52.2	8 51.1 N25	13.8	86 56.5 N 7	12.2	130 48.9 S11	28.8
19	121 46.6	67 13.0	53.0	23 52.2	13.7	101 58.4	12.4	145 51.1	28.7
20	136 49.1	82 12.5	53.8	38 53.2	13.6	117 00.3	12.7	160 53.4	28.6
21	151 51.5	97 11.9 ..	54.6	53 54.3 ..	13.6	132 02.2 ..	12.9	175 55.6 ..	28.5
22	166 54.0	112 11.4	55.4	68 55.3	13.5	147 04.1	13.1	190 57.8	28.5
23	181 56.5	127 10.8	56.2	83 56.3	13.4	162 06.0	13.3	206 00.1	28.4
9 00	196 58.9	142 10.3 N20	57.0	98 57.4 N25	13.3	177 07.9 N 7	13.6	221 02.3 S11	28.3
01	212 01.4	157 09.7	57.8	113 58.4	13.2	192 09.8	13.8	236 04.5	28.2
02	227 03.9	172 09.1	58.6	128 59.5	13.1	207 11.7	14.0	251 06.8	28.1
03	242 06.3	187 08.6 20	59.4	144 00.5 ..	13.0	222 13.6 ..	14.3	266 09.0 ..	28.1
04	257 08.8	202 08.0 21	00.2	159 01.6	12.9	237 15.5	14.5	281 11.2	28.0
05	272 11.2	217 07.5	01.0	174 02.6	12.8	252 17.4	14.7	296 13.5	27.9
S 06	287 13.7	232 06.9 N21	01.8	189 03.7 N25	12.7	267 19.3 N 7	14.9	311 15.7 S11	27.8
U 07	302 16.2	247 06.4	02.6	204 04.7	12.6	282 21.2	15.2	326 17.9	27.7
N 08	317 18.6	262 05.8	03.4	219 05.7	12.5	297 23.1	15.4	341 20.2	27.6
D 09	332 21.1	277 05.3 ..	04.2	234 06.8 ..	12.4	312 25.0 ..	15.6	356 22.4 ..	27.6
A 10	347 23.6	292 04.7	05.0	249 07.8	12.3	327 26.9	15.8	11 24.6	27.5
Y 11	2 26.0	307 04.2	05.8	264 08.9	12.2	342 28.8	16.1	26 26.9	27.4
12	17 28.5	322 03.6 N21	06.6	279 09.9 N25	12.1	357 30.7 N 7	16.3	41 29.1 S11	27.3
13	32 31.0	337 03.1	07.4	294 11.0	12.0	12 32.6	16.5	56 31.3	27.2
14	47 33.4	352 02.5	08.2	309 12.0	11.9	27 34.5	16.7	71 33.6	27.2
15	62 35.9	7 01.9 ..	09.0	324 13.0 ..	11.8	42 36.4 ..	17.0	86 35.8 ..	27.1
16	77 38.3	22 01.4	09.8	339 14.1	11.7	57 38.3	17.2	101 38.0	27.0
17	92 40.8	37 00.8	10.5	354 15.1	11.6	72 40.2	17.4	116 40.3	26.9
18	107 43.3	52 00.3 N21	11.3	9 16.2 N25	11.5	87 42.1 N 7	17.7	131 42.5 S11	26.8
19	122 45.7	66 59.7	12.1	24 17.2	11.4	102 44.0	17.9	146 44.7	26.8
20	137 48.2	81 59.2	12.9	39 18.3	11.3	117 45.9	18.1	161 47.0	26.7
21	152 50.7	96 58.6 ..	13.7	54 19.3 ..	11.2	132 47.8 ..	18.3	176 49.2 ..	26.6
22	167 53.1	111 58.0	14.5	69 20.3	11.1	147 49.7	18.6	191 51.4	26.5
23	182 55.6	126 57.5	15.3	84 21.4	11.0	162 51.6	18.8	206 53.7	26.4
Mer. Pass.	10 54.2	v −0.5	d 0.8	v 1.0	d 0.1	v 1.9	d 0.2	v 2.2	d 0.1

STARS

Name	SHA	Dec
Acamar	315 13.3	S40 12.9
Achernar	335 21.9	S57 07.3
Acrux	173 01.1	S63 13.7
Adhara	255 07.1	S29 00.4
Aldebaran	290 41.5	N16 33.3
Alioth	166 13.7	N55 50.0
Alkaid	152 52.7	N49 11.7
Alnair	27 35.1	S46 50.9
Alnilam	275 39.4	S 1 11.3
Alphard	217 49.0	S 8 45.7
Alphecca	126 04.7	N26 38.0
Alpheratz	357 36.7	N29 12.9
Altair	62 01.4	N 8 55.6
Ankaa	353 09.0	S42 10.9
Antares	112 17.4	S26 29.0
Arcturus	145 48.9	N19 03.6
Atria	107 12.7	S69 03.9
Avior	234 15.2	S59 35.3
Bellatrix	278 24.6	N 6 22.2
Betelgeuse	270 53.8	N 7 24.6
Canopus	263 53.2	S52 42.7
Capella	280 24.3	N46 01.4
Deneb	49 27.0	N45 21.4
Denebola	182 26.2	N14 26.5
Diphda	348 49.1	S17 51.7
Dubhe	193 42.2	N61 37.7
Elnath	278 03.9	N28 37.6
Eltanin	90 42.7	N51 28.8
Enif	33 40.4	N 9 58.7
Fomalhaut	15 16.4	S29 30.0
Gacrux	171 52.7	S57 14.7
Gienah	175 44.8	S17 40.3
Hadar	148 37.5	S60 29.1
Hamal	327 53.2	N23 34.2
Kaus Aust.	83 34.4	S34 22.4
Kochab	137 18.7	N74 03.4
Markab	13 31.6	N15 19.6
Menkar	314 08.0	N 4 10.7
Menkent	147 59.0	S36 29.1
Miaplacidus	221 38.2	S69 49.0
Mirfak	308 30.8	N49 56.6
Nunki	75 49.6	S26 16.1
Peacock	53 08.2	S56 39.5
Pollux	243 19.1	N27 58.3
Procyon	244 52.4	N 5 09.9
Rasalhague	95 59.8	N12 32.4
Regulus	207 35.8	N11 51.2
Rigel	281 05.5	S 8 10.6
Rigil Kent.	139 41.7	S60 55.8
Sabik	102 04.3	S15 45.3
Schedar	349 33.3	N56 39.7
Shaula	96 12.2	S37 07.2
Sirius	258 27.6	S16 45.0
Spica	158 23.5	S11 17.0
Suhail	222 47.2	S43 31.8
Vega	80 34.1	N38 48.0
Zuben'ubi	136 57.4	S16 08.4

	SHA	Mer. Pass.
Venus	306 23.6	14 31
Mars	262 32.5	17 25
Jupiter	340 22.5	12 13
Saturn	24 09.0	9 18

© British Crown Copyright 2022. All rights reserved.

UT	SUN GHA	SUN Dec	MOON GHA	v	MOON Dec	d	HP
d h	° ′	° ′	° ′	′	° ′	′	′
7 00	179 25.1	N 6 38.8	350 10.6	13.9	S 9 34.9	14.4	56.5
01	194 25.3	39.8	4 43.5	14.0	9 49.3	14.4	56.5
02	209 25.5	40.7	19 16.5	13.8	10 03.7	14.3	56.5
03	224 25.7 ..	41.7	33 49.3	13.8	10 18.0	14.3	56.5
04	239 25.8	42.6	48 22.1	13.7	10 32.3	14.2	56.6
05	254 26.0	43.5	62 54.8	13.7	10 46.5	14.2	56.6
06	269 26.2	N 6 44.5	77 27.5	13.5	S11 00.7	14.2	56.6
07	284 26.4	45.4	92 00.0	13.5	11 14.9	14.1	56.6
F 08	299 26.6	46.4	106 32.5	13.5	11 29.0	14.1	56.7
R 09	314 26.7 ..	47.3	121 05.0	13.3	11 43.1	14.1	56.7
I 10	329 26.9	48.2	135 37.3	13.3	11 57.2	14.0	56.7
D 11	344 27.1	49.2	150 09.6	13.2	12 11.2	13.9	56.7
A 12	359 27.3	N 6 50.1	164 41.8	13.2	S12 25.1	13.9	56.7
Y 13	14 27.4	51.1	179 14.0	13.0	12 39.0	13.9	56.8
14	29 27.6	52.0	193 46.0	13.0	12 52.9	13.8	56.8
15	44 27.8 ..	52.9	208 18.0	12.9	13 06.7	13.8	56.8
16	59 28.0	53.9	222 49.9	12.9	13 20.5	13.7	56.8
17	74 28.1	54.8	237 21.8	12.7	13 34.2	13.7	56.8
18	89 28.3	N 6 55.8	251 53.5	12.7	S13 47.9	13.6	56.9
19	104 28.5	56.7	266 25.2	12.6	14 01.5	13.6	56.9
20	119 28.7	57.6	280 56.8	12.5	14 15.1	13.5	56.9
21	134 28.8 ..	58.6	295 28.3	12.4	14 28.6	13.4	56.9
22	149 29.0	6 59.5	309 59.7	12.3	14 42.0	13.4	57.0
23	164 29.2	7 00.4	324 31.0	12.2	14 55.4	13.3	57.0
8 00	179 29.4	N 7 01.4	339 02.2	12.2	S15 08.7	13.3	57.0
01	194 29.5	02.3	353 33.4	12.1	15 22.0	13.1	57.0
02	209 29.7	03.3	8 04.5	12.0	15 35.1	13.2	57.0
03	224 29.9 ..	04.2	22 35.5	11.8	15 48.3	13.0	57.1
04	239 30.1	05.1	37 06.3	11.8	16 01.3	13.0	57.1
05	254 30.2	06.1	51 37.1	11.8	16 14.3	13.0	57.1
06	269 30.4	N 7 07.0	66 07.9	11.6	S16 27.3	12.8	57.1
S 07	284 30.6	07.9	80 38.5	11.5	16 40.1	12.8	57.1
A 08	299 30.8	08.9	95 09.0	11.4	16 52.9	12.7	57.2
T 09	314 30.9 ..	09.8	109 39.4	11.4	17 05.6	12.6	57.2
U 10	329 31.1	10.7	124 09.8	11.2	17 18.2	12.6	57.2
R 11	344 31.3	11.7	138 40.0	11.2	17 30.8	12.5	57.2
D 12	359 31.4	N 7 12.6	153 10.2	11.0	S17 43.3	12.3	57.2
A 13	14 31.6	13.5	167 40.2	11.0	17 55.6	12.4	57.3
Y 14	29 31.8	14.5	182 10.2	10.9	18 08.0	12.2	57.3
15	44 32.0 ..	15.4	196 40.1	10.7	18 20.2	12.1	57.3
16	59 32.1	16.4	211 09.8	10.7	18 32.3	12.1	57.3
17	74 32.3	17.3	225 39.5	10.6	18 44.4	12.0	57.3
18	89 32.5	N 7 18.2	240 09.1	10.4	S18 56.4	11.8	57.4
19	104 32.7	19.2	254 38.5	10.4	19 08.2	11.8	57.4
20	119 32.8	20.1	269 07.9	10.3	19 20.0	11.7	57.4
21	134 33.0 ..	21.0	283 37.2	10.2	19 31.7	11.6	57.4
22	149 33.2	22.0	298 06.4	10.0	19 43.3	11.5	57.4
23	164 33.3	22.9	312 35.4	10.0	19 54.8	11.5	57.5
9 00	179 33.5	N 7 23.8	327 04.4	9.9	S20 06.3	11.3	57.5
01	194 33.7	24.7	341 33.3	9.7	20 17.6	11.2	57.5
02	209 33.9	25.7	356 02.0	9.7	20 28.8	11.1	57.5
03	224 34.0 ..	26.6	10 30.7	9.5	20 39.9	11.0	57.5
04	239 34.2	27.5	24 59.2	9.5	20 50.9	10.9	57.6
05	254 34.4	28.5	39 27.7	9.3	21 01.8	10.8	57.6
06	269 34.5	N 7 29.4	53 56.0	9.3	S21 12.6	10.7	57.6
07	284 34.7	30.3	68 24.3	9.1	21 23.3	10.6	57.6
08	299 34.9	31.3	82 52.4	9.1	21 33.9	10.4	57.6
S 09	314 35.1 ..	32.2	97 20.5	8.9	21 44.3	10.4	57.7
U 10	329 35.2	33.1	111 48.4	8.9	21 54.7	10.2	57.7
N 11	344 35.4	34.1	126 16.3	8.7	22 04.9	10.2	57.7
D 12	359 35.6	N 7 35.0	140 44.0	8.6	S22 15.1	10.0	57.7
A 13	14 35.7	35.9	155 11.6	8.5	22 25.1	9.9	57.7
Y 14	29 35.9	36.8	169 39.1	8.5	22 35.0	9.7	57.8
15	44 36.1 ..	37.8	184 06.6	8.3	22 44.7	9.7	57.8
16	59 36.3	38.7	198 33.9	8.2	22 54.4	9.5	57.8
17	74 36.4	39.6	213 01.1	8.1	23 03.9	9.4	57.8
18	89 36.6	N 7 40.6	227 28.2	8.0	S23 13.3	9.3	57.8
19	104 36.8	41.5	241 55.2	7.9	23 22.6	9.1	57.8
20	119 36.9	42.4	256 22.1	7.8	23 31.7	9.0	57.9
21	134 37.1 ..	43.3	270 48.9	7.7	23 40.7	8.9	57.9
22	149 37.3	44.3	285 15.6	7.6	23 49.6	8.7	57.9
23	164 37.4	45.2	299 42.2	7.5	S23 58.3	8.7	57.9
SD	16.0	d 0.9	SD 15.5		15.6		15.7

Twilight / Sunrise / Moonrise

Lat.	Twilight Naut.	Twilight Civil	Sunrise	Moonrise 7	8	9	10
°	h m	h m	h m	h m	h m	h m	h m
N 72	////	02 57	04 20	23 06	■■■■	■■■■	■■■■
N 70	01 13	03 20	04 31	22 29	■■■■	■■■■	■■■■
68	02 02	03 38	04 41	22 04	24 40	00 40	■■■■
66	02 32	03 52	04 48	21 45	23 55	■■■■	■■■■
64	02 54	04 03	04 55	21 29	23 25	25 44	01 44
62	03 11	04 13	04 59	21 17	23 03	25 00	01 00
60	03 25	04 21	05 05	21 06	22 46	24 31	00 31
N 58	03 36	04 28	05 09	20 57	22 31	24 09	00 09
56	03 46	04 34	05 13	20 48	22 18	23 51	25 19
54	03 55	04 40	05 17	20 41	22 07	23 35	25 00
52	04 02	04 45	05 20	20 35	21 58	23 22	24 44
50	04 09	04 49	05 23	20 29	21 49	23 11	24 30
45	04 22	04 58	05 29	20 17	21 31	22 47	24 02
N 40	04 33	05 06	05 34	20 06	21 16	22 28	23 39
35	04 42	05 12	05 38	19 58	21 04	22 12	23 21
30	04 49	05 17	05 42	19 50	20 53	21 59	23 05
20	05 00	05 26	05 48	19 37	20 35	21 36	22 39
N 10	05 08	05 32	05 54	19 26	20 19	21 16	22 16
0	05 14	05 38	05 59	19 15	20 04	20 57	21 55
S 10	05 18	05 42	06 04	19 05	19 50	20 39	21 33
20	05 21	05 47	06 09	18 54	19 34	20 19	21 11
30	05 23	05 51	06 15	18 41	19 16	19 57	20 45
35	05 23	05 53	06 18	18 34	19 06	19 44	20 30
40	05 23	05 54	06 22	18 26	18 54	19 29	20 12
45	05 22	05 56	06 26	18 17	18 41	19 11	19 51
S 50	05 21	05 59	06 31	18 05	18 24	18 49	19 24
52	05 20	05 59	06 33	18 00	18 16	18 39	19 11
54	05 19	06 00	06 36	17 54	18 08	18 27	18 56
56	05 18	06 01	06 39	17 48	17 58	18 14	18 39
58	05 17	06 02	06 42	17 41	17 47	17 58	18 18
S 60	05 15	06 03	06 45	17 33	17 35	17 40	17 52

Sunset / Twilight / Moonset

Lat.	Sunset	Twilight Civil	Twilight Naut.	Moonset 7	8	9	10
°	h m	h m	h m	h m	h m	h m	h m
N 72	19 47	21 12	////	04 24	03 22	■■■■	■■■■
N 70	19 35	20 48	23 05	04 41	04 01	■■■■	■■■■
68	19 26	20 29	22 08	05 06	04 28	03 35	■■■■
66	19 18	20 15	21 36	05 06	04 49	04 22	■■■■
64	19 11	20 03	21 14	05 15	05 05	04 52	04 26
62	19 05	19 53	20 56	05 23	05 19	05 15	05 11
60	19 00	19 45	20 42	05 30	05 31	05 34	05 40
N 58	18 56	19 37	20 30	05 37	05 41	05 49	06 03
56	18 52	19 31	20 20	05 42	05 50	06 03	06 22
54	18 48	19 25	20 11	05 47	05 59	06 14	06 37
52	18 45	19 20	20 03	05 52	06 06	06 24	06 51
50	18 42	19 16	19 56	05 56	06 12	06 34	07 03
45	18 36	19 06	19 42	06 05	06 26	06 53	07 27
N 40	18 31	18 59	19 32	06 12	06 39	07 09	07 47
35	18 27	18 52	19 23	06 19	06 48	07 23	08 04
30	18 23	18 47	19 16	06 27	06 57	07 34	08 18
20	18 16	18 38	19 04	06 34	07 12	07 55	08 43
N 10	18 10	18 32	18 56	06 43	07 26	08 12	09 04
0	18 05	18 26	18 50	06 51	07 38	08 29	09 24
S 10	18 00	18 21	18 46	07 00	07 51	08 46	09 44
20	17 55	18 17	18 42	07 08	08 04	09 04	10 06
30	17 49	18 13	18 41	07 19	08 20	09 24	10 30
35	17 45	18 11	18 40	07 24	08 29	09 36	10 45
40	17 42	18 09	18 40	07 31	08 40	09 50	11 02
45	17 37	18 07	18 41	07 39	08 52	10 07	11 23
S 50	17 32	18 04	18 42	07 49	09 07	10 28	11 49
52	17 30	18 03	18 42	07 53	09 14	10 38	12 01
54	17 27	18 02	18 43	07 58	09 22	10 49	12 16
56	17 24	18 01	18 44	08 03	09 31	11 02	12 33
58	17 21	18 00	18 46	08 09	09 41	11 16	12 53
S 60	17 17	17 59	18 47	08 16	09 52	11 34	13 19

SUN and MOON

Day	SUN Eqn. of Time 00h	12h	Mer. Pass.	MOON Mer. Pass. Upper	Lower	Age	Phase
d	m s	m s	h m	h m	h m	d	%
7	02 20	02 11	12 02	00 41	13 03	17	98
8	02 03	01 55	12 02	01 27	13 51	18	94
9	01 46	01 38	12 02	02 16	14 43	19	88

© British Crown Copyright 2022. All rights reserved.

UT	ARIES	VENUS −4.0		MARS +1.1		JUPITER −2.0		SATURN +0.9		STARS		
d h	GHA	GHA	Dec	GHA	Dec	GHA	Dec	GHA	Dec	Name	SHA	Dec
10 00	197 58.1	141 56.9	N21 16.0	99 22.4	N25 10.9	177 53.5	N 7 19.0	221 55.9	S11 26.3	Acamar	315 13.3	S40 12.9
01	213 00.5	156 56.4	16.8	114 23.5	10.8	192 55.4	19.2	236 58.1	26.3	Achernar	335 21.9	S57 07.2
02	228 03.0	171 55.8	17.6	129 24.5	10.7	207 57.3	19.5	252 00.4	26.2	Acrux	173 01.0	S63 13.8
03	243 05.5	186 55.2 ..	18.4	144 25.5 ..	10.6	222 59.2 ..	19.7	267 02.6 ..	26.1	Adhara	255 07.1	S29 00.4
04	258 07.9	201 54.7	19.1	159 26.6	10.4	238 01.1	19.9	282 04.8	26.0	Aldebaran	290 41.5	N16 33.3
05	273 10.4	216 54.1	19.9	174 27.6	10.3	253 03.0	20.1	297 07.1	25.9			
06	288 12.8	231 53.6	N21 20.7	189 28.7	N25 10.2	268 04.9	N 7 20.4	312 09.3	S11 25.9	Alioth	166 13.7	N55 50.0
07	303 15.3	246 53.0	21.5	204 29.7	10.1	283 06.8	20.6	327 11.5	25.8	Alkaid	152 52.7	N49 11.8
M 08	318 17.8	261 52.4	22.2	219 30.7	10.0	298 08.7	20.8	342 13.8	25.7	Alnair	27 35.0	S46 50.9
O 09	333 20.2	276 51.9 ..	23.0	234 31.8 ..	09.9	313 10.6 ..	21.0	357 16.0 ..	25.6	Alnilam	275 39.4	S 1 11.3
N 10	348 22.7	291 51.3	23.8	249 32.8	09.8	328 12.5	21.3	12 18.2	25.5	Alphard	217 49.0	S 8 45.7
D 11	3 25.2	306 50.7	24.6	264 33.9	09.7	343 14.4	21.5	27 20.5	25.5			
A 12	18 27.6	321 50.2	N21 25.3	279 34.9	N25 09.6	358 16.3	N 7 21.7	42 22.7	S11 25.4	Alphecca	126 04.7	N26 38.0
Y 13	33 30.1	336 49.6	26.1	294 35.9	09.5	13 18.2	22.0	57 24.9	25.3	Alpheratz	357 36.6	N29 12.9
14	48 32.6	351 49.1	26.9	309 37.0	09.4	28 20.1	22.2	72 27.2	25.2	Altair	62 01.4	N 8 55.6
15	63 35.0	6 48.5 ..	27.6	324 38.0 ..	09.3	43 22.0 ..	22.4	87 29.4 ..	25.1	Ankaa	353 09.0	S42 10.9
16	78 37.5	21 47.9	28.4	339 39.0	09.2	58 23.9	22.6	102 31.7	25.1	Antares	112 17.4	S26 29.0
17	93 40.0	36 47.4	29.2	354 40.1	09.1	73 25.8	22.9	117 33.9	25.0			
18	108 42.4	51 46.8	N21 29.9	9 41.1	N25 09.0	88 27.7	N 7 23.1	132 36.1	S11 24.9	Arcturus	145 48.9	N19 03.6
19	123 44.9	66 46.2	30.7	24 42.2	08.9	103 29.6	23.3	147 38.4	24.8	Atria	107 12.6	S69 03.9
20	138 47.3	81 45.7	31.4	39 43.2	08.8	118 31.5	23.5	162 40.6	24.7	Avior	234 15.2	S59 35.3
21	153 49.8	96 45.1 ..	32.2	54 44.2 ..	08.7	133 33.4 ..	23.8	177 42.8 ..	24.6	Bellatrix	278 24.6	N 6 22.2
22	168 52.3	111 44.5	33.0	69 45.3	08.5	148 35.3	24.0	192 45.1	24.6	Betelgeuse	270 53.8	N 7 24.6
23	183 54.7	126 44.0	33.7	84 46.3	08.4	163 37.2	24.2	207 47.3	24.5			
11 00	198 57.2	141 43.4	N21 34.5	99 47.3	N25 08.3	178 39.1	N 7 24.4	222 49.5	S11 24.4	Canopus	263 53.2	S52 42.7
01	213 59.7	156 42.8	35.2	114 48.4	08.2	193 41.0	24.7	237 51.8	24.3	Capella	280 24.3	N46 01.4
02	229 02.1	171 42.3	36.0	129 49.4	08.1	208 42.9	24.9	252 54.0	24.2	Deneb	49 26.9	N45 21.4
03	244 04.6	186 41.7 ..	36.8	144 50.4 ..	08.0	223 44.8 ..	25.1	267 56.2 ..	24.2	Denebola	182 26.2	N14 26.5
04	259 07.1	201 41.1	37.5	159 51.5	07.9	238 46.7	25.3	282 58.5	24.1	Diphda	348 49.1	S17 51.7
05	274 09.5	216 40.6	38.3	174 52.5	07.8	253 48.6	25.6	298 00.7	24.0			
06	289 12.0	231 40.0	N21 39.0	189 53.6	N25 07.7	268 50.5	N 7 25.8	313 03.0	S11 23.9	Dubhe	193 42.3	N61 37.7
07	304 14.5	246 39.4	39.8	204 54.6	07.6	283 52.4	26.0	328 05.2	23.8	Elnath	278 03.9	N28 37.6
T 08	319 16.9	261 38.8	40.5	219 55.6	07.5	298 54.3	26.2	343 07.4	23.8	Eltanin	90 42.7	N51 28.8
U 09	334 19.4	276 38.3 ..	41.3	234 56.7 ..	07.4	313 56.2 ..	26.5	358 09.7 ..	23.7	Enif	33 40.4	N 9 58.7
E 10	349 21.8	291 37.7	42.0	249 57.7	07.2	328 58.1	26.7	13 11.9	23.6	Fomalhaut	15 16.4	S29 30.0
S 11	4 24.3	306 37.1	42.8	264 58.7	07.1	344 00.0	26.9	28 14.1	23.5			
D 12	19 26.8	321 36.6	N21 43.5	279 59.8	N25 07.0	359 01.9	N 7 27.1	43 16.4	S11 23.4	Gacrux	171 52.7	S57 14.7
A 13	34 29.2	336 36.0	44.3	295 00.8	06.9	14 03.8	27.4	58 18.6	23.4	Gienah	175 44.8	S17 40.4
Y 14	49 31.7	351 35.4	45.0	310 01.8	06.8	29 05.7	27.6	73 20.9	23.3	Hadar	148 37.5	S60 29.1
15	64 34.2	6 34.9 ..	45.7	325 02.9 ..	06.7	44 07.6 ..	27.8	88 23.1 ..	23.2	Hamal	327 53.2	N23 34.2
16	79 36.6	21 34.3	46.5	340 03.9	06.6	59 09.5	28.1	103 25.3	23.1	Kaus Aust.	83 34.4	S34 22.4
17	94 39.1	36 33.7	47.2	355 04.9	06.5	74 11.4	28.3	118 27.6	23.0			
18	109 41.6	51 33.1	N21 48.0	10 06.0	N25 06.4	89 13.3	N 7 28.5	133 29.8	S11 23.0	Kochab	137 18.7	N74 03.4
19	124 44.0	66 32.6	48.7	25 07.0	06.2	104 15.2	28.7	148 32.0	22.9	Markab	13 31.6	N15 19.6
20	139 46.5	81 32.0	49.5	40 08.0	06.1	119 17.1	29.0	163 34.3	22.8	Menkar	314 08.0	N 4 10.7
21	154 49.0	96 31.4 ..	50.2	55 09.1 ..	06.0	134 19.0 ..	29.2	178 36.5 ..	22.7	Menkent	147 59.0	S36 29.1
22	169 51.4	111 30.8	50.9	70 10.1	05.9	149 20.9	29.4	193 38.8	22.6	Miaplacidus	221 38.2	S69 49.0
23	184 53.9	126 30.3	51.7	85 11.1	05.8	164 22.8	29.6	208 41.0	22.6			
12 00	199 56.3	141 29.7	N21 52.4	100 12.2	N25 05.7	179 24.7	N 7 29.9	223 43.2	S11 22.5	Mirfak	308 30.8	N49 56.6
01	214 58.8	156 29.1	53.1	115 13.2	05.6	194 26.6	30.1	238 45.5	22.4	Nunki	75 49.5	S26 16.1
02	230 01.3	171 28.5	53.9	130 14.2	05.5	209 28.5	30.3	253 47.7	22.3	Peacock	53 08.2	S56 39.5
03	245 03.7	186 28.0 ..	54.6	145 15.3 ..	05.3	224 30.4 ..	30.5	268 50.0 ..	22.3	Pollux	243 19.1	N27 58.3
04	260 06.2	201 27.4	55.3	160 16.3	05.2	239 32.3	30.8	283 52.2	22.2	Procyon	244 52.4	N 5 09.9
05	275 08.7	216 26.8	56.1	175 17.3	05.1	254 34.2	31.0	298 54.4	22.1			
06	290 11.1	231 26.2	N21 56.8	190 18.4	N25 05.0	269 36.1	N 7 31.2	313 56.7	S11 22.0	Rasalhague	95 59.8	N12 32.4
W 07	305 13.6	246 25.7	57.5	205 19.4	04.9	284 38.0	31.4	328 58.9	21.9	Regulus	207 35.8	N11 51.2
E 08	320 16.1	261 25.1	58.2	220 20.4	04.8	299 39.9	31.7	344 01.2	21.9	Rigel	281 05.5	S 8 10.6
D 09	335 18.5	276 24.5 ..	59.0	235 21.5 ..	04.7	314 41.8 ..	31.9	359 03.4 ..	21.8	Rigil Kent.	139 41.7	S60 55.8
N 10	350 21.0	291 23.9	21 59.7	250 22.5	04.5	329 43.7	32.1	14 05.6	21.7	Sabik	102 04.3	S15 45.3
E 11	5 23.4	306 23.4	22 00.4	265 23.5	04.4	344 45.6	32.3	29 07.9	21.6			
S 12	20 25.9	321 22.8	N22 01.1	280 24.6	N25 04.3	359 47.5	N 7 32.6	44 10.1	S11 21.5	Schedar	349 33.3	N56 39.7
D 13	35 28.4	336 22.2	01.9	295 25.6	04.2	14 49.4	32.8	59 12.3	21.5	Shaula	96 12.2	S37 07.2
A 14	50 30.8	351 21.6	02.6	310 26.6	04.1	29 51.3	33.0	74 14.6	21.4	Sirius	258 27.6	S16 45.0
Y 15	65 33.3	6 21.0 ..	03.3	325 27.6 ..	04.0	44 53.2 ..	33.2	89 16.8 ..	21.3	Spica	158 23.5	S11 17.0
16	80 35.8	21 20.5	04.0	340 28.7	03.8	59 55.1	33.5	104 19.1	21.2	Suhail	222 47.2	S43 31.8
17	95 38.2	36 19.9	04.8	355 29.7	03.7	74 57.0	33.7	119 21.3	21.1			
18	110 40.7	51 19.3	N22 05.5	10 30.7	N25 03.6	89 58.9	N 7 33.9	134 23.5	S11 21.1	Vega	80 34.1	N38 48.0
19	125 43.2	66 18.7	06.2	25 31.8	03.5	105 00.8	34.1	149 25.8	21.0	Zuben'ubi	136 57.3	S16 08.4
20	140 45.6	81 18.1	06.9	40 32.8	03.4	120 02.7	34.4	164 28.0	20.9		SHA	Mer. Pass.
21	155 48.1	96 17.6 ..	07.6	55 33.8 ..	03.3	135 04.6 ..	34.6	179 30.3 ..	20.8			
22	170 50.6	111 17.0	08.3	70 34.9	03.1	150 06.5	34.8	194 32.5	20.8	Venus	302 46.2	14 34
23	185 53.0	126 16.4	09.0	85 35.9	03.0	165 08.4	35.0	209 34.8	20.7	Mars	260 50.1	17 20
	h m									Jupiter	339 41.9	12 04
Mer. Pass. 10 42.4		v −0.6 d 0.7		v 1.0 d 0.1		v 1.9 d 0.2		v 2.2 d 0.1		Saturn	23 52.3	9 07

© British Crown Copyright 2022. All rights reserved.

SUN and MOON

UT	SUN GHA	SUN Dec	MOON GHA	v	MOON Dec	d	HP
d h	° ′	° ′	° ′	′	° ′	′	′
10 00	179 37.6	N 7 46.1	314 08.7	7.4	S24 07.0	8.4	57.9
01	194 37.8	47.1	328 35.1	7.3	24 15.4	8.4	58.0
02	209 38.0	48.0	343 01.4	7.2	24 23.8	8.2	58.0
03	224 38.1 ..	48.9	357 27.6	7.1	24 32.0	8.0	58.0
04	239 38.3	49.8	11 53.7	7.0	24 40.0	8.0	58.0
05	254 38.5	50.8	26 19.7	7.0	24 48.0	7.7	58.0
06	269 38.6	N 7 51.7	40 45.7	6.8	S24 55.7	7.7	58.0
07	284 38.8	52.6	55 11.5	6.7	25 03.4	7.4	58.1
08	299 39.0	53.5	69 37.2	6.6	25 10.8	7.4	58.1
M 09	314 39.1 ..	54.5	84 02.8	6.5	25 18.2	7.2	58.1
O 10	329 39.3	55.4	98 28.3	6.5	25 25.4	7.0	58.1
N 11	344 39.5	56.3	112 53.8	6.3	25 32.4	6.9	58.1
D 12	359 39.6	N 7 57.2	127 19.1	6.3	S25 39.3	6.7	58.2
A 13	14 39.8	58.2	141 44.4	6.2	25 46.0	6.6	58.2
Y 14	29 40.0	7 59.1	156 09.6	6.0	25 52.6	6.4	58.2
15	44 40.1	8 00.0	170 34.6	6.0	25 59.0	6.3	58.2
16	59 40.3	00.9	184 59.6	5.9	26 05.3	6.1	58.2
17	74 40.5	01.9	199 24.5	5.9	26 11.4	6.0	58.2
18	89 40.6	N 8 02.8	213 49.4	5.7	S26 17.4	5.7	58.3
19	104 40.8	03.7	228 14.1	5.7	26 23.1	5.7	58.3
20	119 41.0	04.6	242 38.8	5.5	26 28.8	5.4	58.3
21	134 41.1 ..	05.5	257 03.3	5.5	26 34.2	5.3	58.3
22	149 41.3	06.5	271 27.8	5.5	26 39.5	5.2	58.3
23	164 41.5	07.4	285 52.3	5.3	26 44.7	4.9	58.3
11 00	179 41.6	N 8 08.3	300 16.6	5.3	S26 49.6	4.8	58.4
01	194 41.8	09.2	314 40.9	5.2	26 54.4	4.7	58.4
02	209 42.0	10.2	329 05.1	5.1	26 59.1	4.4	58.4
03	224 42.1 ..	11.1	343 29.2	5.1	27 03.5	4.3	58.4
04	239 42.3	12.0	357 53.3	5.0	27 07.8	4.1	58.4
05	254 42.5	12.9	12 17.3	4.9	27 11.9	3.9	58.4
06	269 42.6	N 8 13.8	26 41.2	4.9	S27 15.8	3.8	58.5
07	284 42.8	14.8	41 05.1	4.8	27 19.6	3.6	58.5
T 08	299 43.0	15.7	55 28.9	4.7	27 23.2	3.4	58.5
U 09	314 43.1 ..	16.6	69 52.6	4.7	27 26.6	3.3	58.5
E 10	329 43.3	17.5	84 16.3	4.7	27 29.9	3.0	58.5
S 11	344 43.5	18.4	98 40.0	4.5	27 32.9	2.9	58.5
D 12	359 43.6	N 8 19.3	113 03.5	4.6	S27 35.8	2.7	58.6
A 13	14 43.8	20.3	127 27.1	4.4	27 38.5	2.5	58.6
Y 14	29 44.0	21.2	141 50.5	4.5	27 41.0	2.4	58.6
15	44 44.1 ..	22.1	156 14.0	4.4	27 43.4	2.1	58.6
16	59 44.3	23.0	170 37.4	4.3	27 45.5	2.0	58.6
17	74 44.5	23.9	185 00.7	4.3	27 47.5	1.8	58.6
18	89 44.6	N 8 24.9	199 24.0	4.3	S27 49.3	1.6	58.6
19	104 44.8	25.8	213 47.3	4.2	27 50.9	1.4	58.7
20	119 44.9	26.7	228 10.5	4.2	27 52.3	1.3	58.7
21	134 45.1 ..	27.6	242 33.7	4.1	27 53.6	1.0	58.7
22	149 45.3	28.5	256 56.8	4.2	27 54.6	1.0	58.7
23	164 45.4	29.4	271 20.0	4.1	27 55.5	0.7	58.7
12 00	179 45.6	N 8 30.4	285 43.1	4.0	S27 56.2	0.5	58.7
01	194 45.8	31.3	300 06.1	4.1	27 56.7	0.3	58.8
02	209 45.9	32.2	314 29.2	4.0	27 57.0	0.1	58.8
03	224 46.1 ..	33.1	328 52.2	4.0	27 57.1	0.0	58.8
04	239 46.2	34.0	343 15.2	4.0	27 57.1	0.3	58.8
05	254 46.4	34.9	357 38.2	4.0	27 56.8	0.4	58.8
06	269 46.6	N 8 35.8	12 01.2	4.0	S27 56.4	0.6	58.8
W 07	284 46.7	36.8	26 24.2	4.0	27 55.8	0.9	58.8
E 08	299 46.9	37.7	40 47.2	3.9	27 54.9	1.0	58.9
D 09	314 47.1 ..	38.6	55 10.1	4.0	27 53.9	1.2	58.9
N 10	329 47.2	39.5	69 33.1	3.9	27 52.7	1.3	58.9
E 11	344 47.4	40.4	83 56.0	4.0	27 51.4	1.6	58.9
S 12	359 47.5	N 8 41.3	98 19.0	3.9	S27 49.8	1.8	58.9
D 13	14 47.7	42.2	112 41.9	4.0	27 48.0	1.9	58.9
A 14	29 47.9	43.2	127 04.9	4.0	27 46.1	2.1	58.9
Y 15	44 48.0 ..	44.1	141 27.9	3.9	27 44.0	2.3	58.9
16	59 48.2	45.0	155 50.8	4.0	27 41.7	2.5	59.0
17	74 48.3	45.9	170 13.8	4.0	27 39.2	2.7	59.0
18	89 48.5	N 8 46.8	184 36.8	4.1	S27 36.5	2.9	59.0
19	104 48.7	47.7	198 59.9	4.0	27 33.6	3.1	59.0
20	119 48.8	48.6	213 22.9	4.1	27 30.5	3.2	59.0
21	134 49.0 ..	49.5	227 46.0	4.1	27 27.3	3.5	59.0
22	149 49.2	50.4	242 09.1	4.1	27 23.8	3.6	59.0
23	164 49.3	51.4	256 32.2	4.1	S27 20.2	3.8	59.1
	SD 16.0	d 0.9	SD 15.8		16.0		16.1

Twilight / Sunrise / Moonrise

Lat.	Naut.	Civil	Sunrise	Moonrise 10	Moonrise 11	Moonrise 12	Moonrise 13
°	h m	h m	h m	h m	h m	h m	h m
N 72	////	02 35	04 04	■■■■	■■■■	■■■■	■■■■
N 70	////	03 02	04 17	■■■■	■■■■	■■■■	■■■■
68	01 36	03 23	04 28	■■■■	■■■■	■■■■	■■■■
66	02 13	03 39	04 37	■■■■	■■■■	■■■■	■■■■
64	02 38	03 51	04 44	01 44	■■■■	■■■■	■■■■
62	02 58	04 02	04 51	01 00	03 07	■■■■	05 04
60	03 13	04 11	04 56	00 31	02 15	03 37	04 17
N 58	03 26	04 19	05 01	00 09	01 43	02 59	03 46
56	03 37	04 26	05 06	25 19	01 19	02 33	03 23
54	03 46	04 32	05 09	25 00	01 00	02 12	03 04
52	03 54	04 38	05 13	24 44	00 44	01 54	02 48
50	04 02	04 43	05 16	24 30	00 30	01 39	02 34
45	04 16	04 53	05 23	24 02	00 02	01 09	02 06
N 40	04 28	05 01	05 29	23 39	24 46	00 46	01 44
35	04 37	05 08	05 34	23 21	24 26	00 26	01 25
30	04 45	05 14	05 38	23 05	24 10	00 10	01 09
20	04 57	05 23	05 46	22 39	23 42	24 42	00 42
N 10	05 06	05 31	05 52	22 16	23 18	24 19	00 19
0	05 13	05 37	05 58	21 55	22 55	23 57	24 57
S 10	05 18	05 42	06 04	21 33	22 33	23 35	24 38
20	05 22	05 47	06 10	21 11	22 09	23 12	24 17
30	05 25	05 52	06 16	20 45	21 41	22 45	23 53
35	05 25	05 55	06 20	20 30	21 25	22 28	23 39
40	05 26	05 57	06 25	20 12	21 05	22 10	23 22
45	05 26	06 00	06 30	19 51	20 42	21 47	23 02
S 50	05 26	06 03	06 36	19 24	20 13	21 18	22 37
52	05 25	06 04	06 38	19 11	19 58	21 04	22 25
54	05 25	06 06	06 41	18 56	19 41	20 47	22 11
56	05 24	06 07	06 45	18 39	19 21	20 28	21 55
58	05 23	06 09	06 48	18 18	18 56	20 03	21 35
S 60	05 22	06 10	06 52	17 52	18 22	19 30	21 11

Twilight / Sunset / Moonset

Lat.	Sunset	Civil	Naut.	Moonset 10	Moonset 11	Moonset 12	Moonset 13
°	h m	h m	h m	h m	h m	h m	h m
N 72	20 02	21 34	////	■■■■	■■■■	■■■■	■■■■
N 70	19 48	21 04	////	■■■■	■■■■	■■■■	■■■■
68	19 37	20 43	22 35	■■■■	■■■■	■■■■	■■■■
66	19 28	20 27	21 54	■■■■	■■■■	■■■■	■■■■
64	19 20	20 13	21 28	04 26	■■■■	■■■■	07 26
62	19 13	20 02	21 08	05 11	05 05	■■■■	08 12
60	19 08	19 53	20 52	05 40	05 58	06 44	08 12
N 58	19 02	19 45	20 39	06 03	06 30	07 21	08 43
56	18 58	19 38	20 27	06 22	06 54	07 47	09 06
54	18 54	19 31	20 18	06 37	07 13	08 08	09 24
52	18 50	19 26	20 09	06 51	07 30	08 26	09 40
50	18 47	19 21	20 02	07 03	07 44	08 41	09 54
45	18 40	19 10	19 47	07 27	08 13	09 11	10 21
N 40	18 34	19 02	19 35	07 47	08 35	09 34	10 43
35	18 29	18 55	19 26	08 04	08 54	09 54	11 01
30	18 25	18 49	19 18	08 18	09 10	10 10	11 17
20	18 17	18 39	19 05	08 43	09 38	10 38	11 43
N 10	18 10	18 32	18 56	09 04	10 01	11 02	12 05
0	18 04	18 25	18 50	09 24	10 23	11 25	12 26
S 10	17 58	18 20	18 44	09 44	10 45	11 47	12 47
20	17 52	18 14	18 40	10 06	11 09	12 11	13 09
30	17 45	18 09	18 37	10 30	11 36	12 38	13 34
35	17 41	18 07	18 36	10 45	11 52	12 55	13 49
40	17 37	18 04	18 36	11 02	12 11	13 14	14 07
45	17 32	18 01	18 35	11 23	12 34	13 37	14 27
S 50	17 26	17 58	18 36	11 49	13 04	14 06	14 53
52	17 23	17 57	18 36	12 01	13 18	14 20	15 06
54	17 20	17 56	18 36	12 16	13 35	14 37	15 20
56	17 17	17 54	18 37	12 33	13 55	14 57	15 37
58	17 13	17 52	18 38	12 53	14 20	15 22	15 57
S 60	17 09	17 51	18 39	13 19	14 54	15 55	16 21

SUN and MOON

Day	Eqn. of Time 00h	Eqn. of Time 12h	Mer. Pass.	Mer. Pass. Upper	Mer. Pass. Lower	Age	Phase
d	m s	m s	h m	h m	h m	d	%
10	01 30	01 22	12 01	03 11	15 39	20	80
11	01 14	01 06	12 01	04 09	16 39	21	71
12	00 58	00 50	12 01	05 10	17 41	22	60

© British Crown Copyright 2022. All rights reserved.

UT	ARIES	VENUS −4.1		MARS +1.1		JUPITER −2.0		SATURN +0.9		STARS		
	GHA	GHA	Dec	GHA	Dec	GHA	Dec	GHA	Dec	Name	SHA	Dec
d h	° ′	° ′	° ′	° ′	° ′	° ′	° ′	° ′	° ′		° ′	° ′
13 00	200 55.5	141 15.8	N22 09.8	100 36.9	N25 02.9	180 10.3	N 7 35.3	224 37.0	S11 20.6	Acamar	315 13.3	S40 12.9
01	215 57.9	156 15.2	10.5	115 37.9	02.8	195 12.2	35.5	239 39.2	20.5	Achernar	335 21.8	S57 07.2
02	231 00.4	171 14.7	11.2	130 39.0	02.7	210 14.1	35.7	254 41.5	20.4	Acrux	173 01.0	S63 13.8
03	246 02.9	186 14.1 ..	11.9	145 40.0 ..	02.5	225 16.0 ..	35.9	269 43.7 ..	20.4	Adhara	255 07.1	S29 00.4
04	261 05.3	201 13.5	12.6	160 41.0	02.4	240 17.9	36.2	284 46.0	20.3	Aldebaran	290 41.5	N16 33.3
05	276 07.8	216 12.9	13.3	175 42.1	02.3	255 19.8	36.4	299 48.2	20.2			
06	291 10.3	231 12.3	N22 14.0	190 43.1	N25 02.2	270 21.7	N 7 36.6	314 50.4	S11 20.1	Alioth	166 13.7	N55 50.0
07	306 12.7	246 11.7	14.7	205 44.1	02.1	285 23.6	36.8	329 52.7	20.0	Alkaid	152 52.7	N49 11.8
T 08	321 15.2	261 11.2	15.4	220 45.1	01.9	300 25.5	37.1	344 54.9	20.0	Alnair	27 35.0	S46 50.9
H 09	336 17.7	276 10.6 ..	16.1	235 46.2 ..	01.8	315 27.4 ..	37.3	359 57.2 ..	19.9	Alnilam	275 39.4	S 1 11.3
U 10	351 20.1	291 10.0	16.8	250 47.2	01.7	330 29.3	37.5	14 59.4	19.8	Alphard	217 49.0	S 8 45.7
R 11	6 22.6	306 09.4	17.5	265 48.2	01.6	345 31.2	37.7	30 01.6	19.7			
S 12	21 25.1	321 08.8	N22 18.2	280 49.2	N25 01.5	0 33.1	N 7 38.0	45 03.9	S11 19.7	Alphecca	126 04.7	N26 38.0
D 13	36 27.5	336 08.2	18.9	295 50.3	01.3	15 35.0	38.2	60 06.1	19.6	Alpheratz	357 36.6	N29 12.9
A 14	51 30.0	351 07.7	19.6	310 51.3	01.2	30 36.9	38.4	75 08.4	19.5	Altair	62 01.4	N 8 55.6
Y 15	66 32.4	6 07.1 ..	20.3	325 52.3 ..	01.1	45 38.8 ..	38.6	90 10.6 ..	19.4	Ankaa	353 09.0	S42 10.8
16	81 34.9	21 06.5	21.0	340 53.3	01.0	60 40.7	38.9	105 12.9	19.3	Antares	112 17.4	S26 29.0
17	96 37.4	36 05.9	21.7	355 54.4	00.9	75 42.6	39.1	120 15.1	19.3			
18	111 39.8	51 05.3	N22 22.4	10 55.4	N25 00.7	90 44.5	N 7 39.3	135 17.3	S11 19.2	Arcturus	145 48.9	N19 03.6
19	126 42.3	66 04.7	23.1	25 56.4	00.6	105 46.4	39.5	150 19.6	19.1	Atria	107 12.6	S69 03.9
20	141 44.8	81 04.1	23.8	40 57.5	00.5	120 48.3	39.8	165 21.8	19.0	Avior	234 15.2	S59 35.3
21	156 47.2	96 03.5 ..	24.5	55 58.5 ..	00.4	135 50.2 ..	40.0	180 24.1 ..	19.0	Bellatrix	278 24.6	N 6 22.2
22	171 49.7	111 03.0	25.2	70 59.5	00.2	150 52.1	40.2	195 26.3	18.9	Betelgeuse	270 53.8	N 7 24.6
23	186 52.2	126 02.4	25.9	86 00.5	00.1	165 54.0	40.4	210 28.6	18.8			
14 00	201 54.6	141 01.8	N22 26.6	101 01.6	N25 00.0	180 55.9	N 7 40.7	225 30.8	S11 18.7	Canopus	263 53.2	S52 42.7
01	216 57.1	156 01.2	27.2	116 02.6	24 59.9	195 57.8	40.9	240 33.0	18.6	Capella	280 24.3	N46 01.4
02	231 59.6	171 00.6	27.9	131 03.6	59.7	210 59.7	41.1	255 35.3	18.6	Deneb	49 26.9	N45 21.4
03	247 02.0	186 00.0 ..	28.6	146 04.6 ..	59.6	226 01.6 ..	41.3	270 37.5 ..	18.5	Denebola	182 26.1	N14 26.5
04	262 04.5	200 59.4	29.3	161 05.7	59.5	241 03.5	41.6	285 39.8	18.4	Diphda	348 49.1	S17 51.7
05	277 06.9	215 58.8	30.0	176 06.7	59.4	256 05.4	41.8	300 42.0	18.3			
06	292 09.4	230 58.2	N22 30.7	191 07.7	N24 59.2	271 07.3	N 7 42.0	315 44.3	S11 18.3	Dubhe	193 42.3	N61 37.7
07	307 11.9	245 57.7	31.3	206 08.7	59.1	286 09.2	42.2	330 46.5	18.2	Elnath	278 03.9	N28 37.6
F 08	322 14.3	260 57.1	32.0	221 09.8	59.0	301 11.1	42.5	345 48.8	18.1	Eltanin	90 42.6	N51 28.8
R 09	337 16.8	275 56.5 ..	32.7	236 10.8 ..	58.9	316 13.0 ..	42.7	0 51.0 ..	18.0	Enif	33 40.4	N 9 58.7
I 10	352 19.3	290 55.9	33.4	251 11.8	58.7	331 14.9	42.9	15 53.2	17.9	Fomalhaut	15 16.4	S29 30.0
D 11	7 21.7	305 55.3	34.1	266 12.8	58.6	346 16.8	43.1	30 55.5	17.9			
A 12	22 24.2	320 54.7	N22 34.7	281 13.8	N24 58.5	1 18.7	N 7 43.4	45 57.7	S11 17.8	Gacrux	171 52.7	S57 14.7
Y 13	37 26.7	335 54.1	35.4	296 14.9	58.4	16 20.6	43.6	61 00.0	17.7	Gienah	175 44.8	S17 40.4
14	52 29.1	350 53.5	36.1	311 15.9	58.2	31 22.5	43.8	76 02.2	17.6	Hadar	148 37.5	S60 29.1
15	67 31.6	5 52.9 ..	36.8	326 16.9 ..	58.1	46 24.4 ..	44.0	91 04.5 ..	17.6	Hamal	327 53.2	N23 34.2
16	82 34.1	20 52.3	37.4	341 17.9	58.0	61 26.3	44.3	106 06.7	17.5	Kaus Aust.	83 34.3	S34 22.4
17	97 36.5	35 51.7	38.1	356 19.0	57.9	76 28.2	44.5	121 09.0	17.4			
18	112 39.0	50 51.1	N22 38.8	11 20.0	N24 57.7	91 30.1	N 7 44.7	136 11.2	S11 17.3	Kochab	137 18.6	N74 03.5
19	127 41.4	65 50.5	39.4	26 21.0	57.6	106 32.0	44.9	151 13.4	17.3	Markab	13 31.6	N15 19.6
20	142 43.9	80 50.0	40.1	41 22.0	57.5	121 33.9	45.2	166 15.7	17.2	Menkar	314 08.0	N 4 10.7
21	157 46.4	95 49.4 ..	40.8	56 23.1 ..	57.3	136 35.8 ..	45.4	181 17.9 ..	17.1	Menkent	147 59.0	S36 29.1
22	172 48.8	110 48.8	41.5	71 24.1	57.2	151 37.7	45.6	196 20.2	17.0	Miaplacidus	221 38.2	S69 49.0
23	187 51.3	125 48.2	42.1	86 25.1	57.1	166 39.6	45.8	211 22.4	16.9			
15 00	202 53.8	140 47.6	N22 42.8	101 26.1	N24 57.0	181 41.5	N 7 46.1	226 24.7	S11 16.9	Mirfak	308 30.8	N49 56.6
01	217 56.2	155 47.0	43.4	116 27.1	56.8	196 43.4	46.3	241 26.9	16.8	Nunki	75 49.5	S26 16.1
02	232 58.7	170 46.4	44.1	131 28.2	56.7	211 45.3	46.5	256 29.2	16.7	Peacock	53 08.1	S56 39.5
03	248 01.2	185 45.8 ..	44.8	146 29.2 ..	56.6	226 47.2 ..	46.7	271 31.4 ..	16.6	Pollux	243 19.1	N27 58.3
04	263 03.6	200 45.2	45.4	161 30.2	56.4	241 49.1	47.0	286 33.7	16.6	Procyon	244 52.4	N 5 09.9
05	278 06.1	215 44.6	46.1	176 31.2	56.3	256 51.0	47.2	301 35.9	16.5			
06	293 08.5	230 44.0	N22 46.7	191 32.2	N24 56.2	271 52.9	N 7 47.4	316 38.1	S11 16.4	Rasalhague	95 59.7	N12 32.4
07	308 11.0	245 43.4	47.4	206 33.3	56.1	286 54.8	47.6	331 40.4	16.3	Regulus	207 35.8	N11 51.2
S 08	323 13.5	260 42.8	48.1	221 34.3	55.9	301 56.7	47.9	346 42.6	16.3	Rigel	281 05.5	S 8 10.6
A 09	338 15.9	275 42.2 ..	48.7	236 35.3 ..	55.8	316 58.6 ..	48.1	1 44.9 ..	16.2	Rigil Kent.	139 41.7	S60 55.8
T 10	353 18.4	290 41.6	49.4	251 36.3	55.7	332 00.5	48.3	16 47.1	16.1	Sabik	102 04.3	S15 45.3
U 11	8 20.9	305 41.0	50.0	266 37.3	55.5	347 02.4	48.5	31 49.4	16.0			
R 12	23 23.3	320 40.4	N22 50.7	281 38.4	N24 55.4	2 04.3	N 7 48.8	46 51.6	S11 16.0	Schedar	349 33.3	N56 39.7
D 13	38 25.8	335 39.8	51.3	296 39.4	55.3	17 06.2	49.0	61 53.9	15.9	Shaula	96 12.1	S37 07.2
A 14	53 28.3	350 39.2	52.0	311 40.4	55.1	32 08.1	49.2	76 56.1	15.8	Sirius	258 27.6	S16 45.0
Y 15	68 30.7	5 38.6 ..	52.6	326 41.4 ..	54.9	47 10.0 ..	49.4	91 58.4 ..	15.7	Spica	158 23.5	S11 17.0
16	83 33.2	20 38.0	53.3	341 42.4	54.9	62 11.9	49.6	107 00.6	15.6	Suhail	222 47.2	S43 31.8
17	98 35.7	35 37.4	53.9	356 43.5	54.7	77 13.8	49.9	122 02.9	15.6			
18	113 38.1	50 36.8	N22 54.6	11 44.5	N24 54.6	92 15.7	N 7 50.1	137 05.1	S11 15.5	Vega	80 34.1	N38 48.0
19	128 40.6	65 36.2	55.2	26 45.5	54.5	107 17.6	50.3	152 07.4	15.4	Zuben'ubi	136 57.3	S16 08.4
20	143 43.0	80 35.6	55.9	41 46.5	54.3	122 19.5	50.5	167 09.6	15.3		SHA	Mer. Pass.
21	158 45.5	95 35.0 ..	56.5	56 47.5 ..	54.2	137 21.4 ..	50.8	182 11.9 ..	15.3		° ′	h m
22	173 48.0	110 34.4	57.1	71 48.6	54.1	152 23.3	51.0	197 14.1	15.2	Venus	299 07.2	14 36
23	188 50.4	125 33.8	57.8	86 49.6	53.9	167 25.2	51.2	212 16.3	15.1	Mars	259 06.9	17 15
	h m									Jupiter	339 01.3	11 55
Mer. Pass. 10 30.6		v −0.6	d 0.7	v 1.0	d 0.1	v 1.9	d 0.2	v 2.2	d 0.1	Saturn	23 36.2	8 57

© British Crown Copyright 2022. All rights reserved.

SUN and MOON

UT	SUN GHA	SUN Dec	MOON GHA	v	Dec	d	HP
d h	° ′	° ′	° ′	′	° ′	′	′
13 00	179 49.5	N 8 52.3	270 55.3	4.2	S27 16.4	4.0	59.1
01	194 49.6	53.2	285 18.5	4.2	27 12.4	4.2	59.1
02	209 49.8	54.1	299 41.7	4.2	27 08.2	4.4	59.1
03	224 50.0 ..	55.0	314 04.9	4.3	27 03.8	4.5	59.1
04	239 50.1	55.9	328 28.2	4.3	26 59.3	4.7	59.1
05	254 50.3	56.8	342 51.5	4.3	26 54.6	4.9	59.1
06	269 50.4	N 8 57.7	357 14.8	4.4	S26 49.7	5.1	59.1
07	284 50.6	58.6	11 38.2	4.5	26 44.6	5.3	59.1
T 08	299 50.7	8 59.5	26 01.7	4.5	26 39.3	5.4	59.2
H 09	314 50.9	9 00.4	40 25.2	4.5	26 33.9	5.7	59.2
U 10	329 51.1	01.4	54 48.7	4.6	26 28.2	5.8	59.2
R 11	344 51.2	02.3	69 12.3	4.6	26 22.4	6.0	59.2
S 12	359 51.4	N 9 03.2	83 35.9	4.7	S26 16.4	6.1	59.2
D 13	14 51.5	04.1	97 59.6	4.7	26 10.3	6.3	59.2
A 14	29 51.7	05.0	112 23.3	4.8	26 03.9	6.5	59.2
Y 15	44 51.9 ..	05.9	126 47.1	4.9	25 57.4	6.7	59.2
16	59 52.0	06.8	141 11.0	4.9	25 50.7	6.8	59.2
17	74 52.2	07.7	155 34.9	4.9	25 43.9	7.0	59.3
18	89 52.3	N 9 08.6	169 58.8	5.1	S25 36.9	7.2	59.3
19	104 52.5	09.5	184 22.9	5.1	25 29.7	7.4	59.3
20	119 52.6	10.4	198 47.0	5.1	25 22.3	7.5	59.3
21	134 52.8 ..	11.3	213 11.1	5.3	25 14.8	7.7	59.3
22	149 53.0	12.2	227 35.4	5.3	25 07.1	7.9	59.3
23	164 53.1	13.1	241 59.7	5.3	24 59.2	8.0	59.3
14 00	179 53.3	N 9 14.0	256 24.0	5.5	S24 51.2	8.2	59.3
01	194 53.4	14.9	270 48.5	5.5	24 43.0	8.4	59.3
02	209 53.6	15.8	285 13.0	5.6	24 34.6	8.5	59.3
03	224 53.7 ..	16.7	299 37.6	5.6	24 26.1	8.7	59.4
04	239 53.9	17.6	314 02.2	5.8	24 17.4	8.8	59.4
05	254 54.0	18.5	328 27.0	5.8	24 08.6	9.0	59.4
06	269 54.2	N 9 19.4	342 51.8	5.8	S23 59.6	9.2	59.4
07	284 54.4	20.3	357 16.6	6.0	23 50.4	9.3	59.4
08	299 54.5	21.2	11 41.6	6.0	23 41.1	9.4	59.4
F 09	314 54.7 ..	22.1	26 06.6	6.1	23 31.7	9.7	59.4
R 10	329 54.8	23.1	40 31.7	6.2	23 22.0	9.7	59.4
I 11	344 55.0	24.0	54 56.9	6.3	23 12.3	9.9	59.4
D 12	359 55.1	N 9 24.9	69 22.2	6.4	S23 02.4	10.1	59.4
A 13	14 55.3	25.8	83 47.6	6.4	22 52.3	10.2	59.4
Y 14	29 55.4	26.7	98 13.0	6.5	22 42.1	10.3	59.4
15	44 55.6 ..	27.6	112 38.5	6.6	22 31.8	10.5	59.5
16	59 55.7	28.5	127 04.1	6.7	22 21.3	10.7	59.5
17	74 55.9	29.4	141 29.8	6.8	22 10.6	10.7	59.5
18	89 56.0	N 9 30.3	155 55.6	6.8	S21 59.9	10.9	59.5
19	104 56.2	31.1	170 21.4	7.0	21 49.0	11.1	59.5
20	119 56.4	32.0	184 47.4	7.0	21 37.9	11.2	59.5
21	134 56.5 ..	32.9	199 13.4	7.1	21 26.7	11.3	59.5
22	149 56.7	33.8	213 39.5	7.2	21 15.4	11.4	59.5
23	164 56.8	34.7	228 05.7	7.2	21 04.0	11.6	59.5
15 00	179 57.0	N 9 35.6	242 31.9	7.4	S20 52.4	11.7	59.5
01	194 57.1	36.5	256 58.3	7.4	20 40.7	11.9	59.5
02	209 57.3	37.4	271 24.7	7.6	20 28.8	11.9	59.5
03	224 57.4 ..	38.3	285 51.3	7.6	20 16.9	12.1	59.5
04	239 57.6	39.2	300 17.9	7.7	20 04.8	12.2	59.5
05	254 57.7	40.1	314 44.6	7.8	19 52.6	12.4	59.5
06	269 57.9	N 9 41.0	329 11.4	7.8	S19 40.2	12.4	59.5
07	284 58.0	41.9	343 38.2	8.0	19 27.8	12.6	59.5
S 08	299 58.2	42.8	358 05.2	8.0	19 15.2	12.7	59.5
A 09	314 58.3 ..	43.7	12 32.2	8.1	19 02.5	12.8	59.6
T 10	329 58.5	44.6	26 59.3	8.2	18 49.7	12.9	59.6
U 11	344 58.6	45.5	41 26.5	8.3	18 36.8	13.0	59.6
R 12	359 58.8	N 9 46.4	55 53.8	8.4	S18 23.8	13.2	59.6
D 13	14 58.9	47.3	70 21.2	8.4	18 10.6	13.2	59.6
A 14	29 59.1	48.2	84 48.6	8.6	17 57.4	13.4	59.6
Y 15	44 59.2 ..	49.1	99 16.2	8.6	17 44.0	13.4	59.6
16	59 59.4	50.0	113 43.8	8.7	17 30.6	13.6	59.6
17	74 59.5	50.9	128 11.5	8.8	17 17.0	13.6	59.6
18	89 59.7	N 9 51.7	142 39.3	8.8	S17 03.4	13.8	59.6
19	104 59.8	52.6	157 07.1	8.9	16 49.6	13.9	59.6
20	120 00.0	53.5	171 35.0	9.1	16 35.7	13.9	59.6
21	135 00.2 ..	54.4	186 03.1	9.1	16 21.8	14.1	59.6
22	150 00.3	55.3	200 31.2	9.1	16 07.7	14.1	59.6
23	165 00.4	56.2	214 59.3	9.3	S15 53.6	14.2	59.6
	SD 16.0	d 0.9	SD 16.1		16.2		16.2

Twilight, Sunrise and Moonrise

Lat.	Twilight Naut.	Twilight Civil	Sunrise	Moonrise 13	14	15	16
°	h m	h m	h m	h m	h m	h m	h m
N 72	////	02 10	03 47	■	■	■	06 22
N 70	////	02 43	04 02	■	■	07 16	05 54
68	01 01	03 07	04 15	■	■	06 15	05 33
66	01 52	03 25	04 25	■	07 02	05 40	05 16
64	02 22	03 39	04 34	■	05 36	05 14	05 02
62	02 44	03 51	04 41	05 04	04 59	04 54	04 50
60	03 01	04 02	04 47	04 17	04 32	04 38	04 50
N 58	03 15	04 10	04 53	03 46	04 11	04 24	04 31
56	03 27	04 18	04 58	03 23	03 53	04 12	04 23
54	03 38	04 25	05 02	03 04	03 39	04 01	04 17
52	03 47	04 31	05 06	02 48	03 26	03 51	04 10
50	03 54	04 36	05 10	02 34	03 14	03 43	04 05
45	04 10	04 47	05 18	02 06	02 50	03 25	03 52
N 40	04 23	04 56	05 24	01 44	02 31	03 10	03 42
35	04 33	05 04	05 30	01 25	02 15	02 57	03 33
30	04 41	05 10	05 35	01 09	02 01	02 46	03 25
20	04 54	05 21	05 43	00 42	01 37	02 27	03 12
N 10	05 04	05 29	05 50	00 19	01 17	02 10	03 00
0	05 12	05 36	05 57	24 57	00 57	01 55	02 49
S 10	05 18	05 42	06 04	24 38	00 38	01 39	02 37
20	05 23	05 48	06 10	24 17	00 17	01 22	02 25
30	05 26	05 54	06 18	23 53	25 03	01 03	02 12
35	05 28	05 57	06 23	23 39	24 51	00 51	02 04
40	05 29	06 00	06 28	23 22	24 38	00 38	01 54
45	05 30	06 04	06 33	23 02	24 22	00 22	01 44
S 50	05 30	06 07	06 40	22 37	24 03	00 03	01 30
52	05 30	06 09	06 43	22 25	23 54	25 24	01 24
54	05 30	06 11	06 47	22 11	23 44	25 17	01 17
56	05 30	06 13	06 51	21 55	23 32	25 10	01 10
58	05 29	06 15	06 55	21 35	23 18	25 01	01 01
S 60	05 29	06 17	07 00	21 11	23 02	24 51	00 51

Sunset, Twilight and Moonset

Lat.	Sunset	Twilight Civil	Twilight Naut.	Moonset 13	14	15	16
°	h m	h m	h m	h m	h m	h m	h m
N 72	20 18	21 58	////	■	■	■	12 10
N 70	20 01	21 23	////	■	■	09 22	12 35
68	19 48	20 58	23 15	■	■	10 21	12 54
66	19 38	20 39	22 15	■	07 34	10 55	13 09
64	19 29	20 24	21 43	■	08 59	11 19	13 22
62	19 21	20 11	21 20	07 26	09 36	11 38	13 32
60	19 15	20 01	21 02	08 12	10 02	11 54	13 41
N 58	19 09	19 52	20 48	08 43	10 23	12 07	13 48
56	19 04	19 44	20 35	09 06	10 40	12 18	13 55
54	19 00	19 37	20 25	09 24	10 54	12 28	14 01
52	18 55	19 31	20 16	09 40	11 06	12 37	14 06
50	18 52	19 26	20 08	09 54	11 17	12 44	14 11
45	18 44	19 14	19 51	10 21	11 40	13 01	14 22
N 40	18 37	19 05	19 39	10 43	11 58	13 14	14 30
35	18 31	18 57	19 28	11 01	12 13	13 26	14 37
30	18 26	18 51	19 20	11 17	12 26	13 36	14 44
20	18 18	18 40	19 07	11 43	12 48	13 53	14 55
N 10	18 10	18 32	18 57	12 05	13 07	14 07	15 04
0	18 04	18 25	18 49	12 26	13 25	14 21	15 13
S 10	17 57	18 18	18 43	12 47	13 43	14 34	15 22
20	17 50	18 12	18 38	13 09	14 01	14 49	15 31
30	17 42	18 06	18 34	13 34	14 23	15 05	15 42
35	17 38	18 03	18 32	13 49	14 35	15 14	15 48
40	17 32	18 00	18 31	14 07	14 50	15 25	15 54
45	17 27	17 56	18 30	14 27	15 07	15 37	16 02
S 50	17 20	17 52	18 30	14 53	15 27	15 52	16 12
52	17 16	17 51	18 30	15 06	15 37	15 59	16 16
54	17 13	17 49	18 30	15 20	15 48	16 07	16 21
56	17 09	17 47	18 30	15 37	16 01	16 15	16 26
58	17 05	17 45	18 30	15 57	16 15	16 25	16 31
S 60	17 00	17 42	18 30	16 21	16 32	16 36	16 38

SUN and MOON

Day	SUN Eqn. of Time 00h	12h	Mer. Pass.	MOON Mer. Pass. Upper	Lower	Age	Phase
d	m s	m s	h m	h m	h m	d	%
13	00 42	00 35	12 01	06 11	18 42	23	49
14	00 27	00 20	12 00	07 11	19 40	24	37
15	00 12	00 05	12 00	08 08	20 35	25	27

© British Crown Copyright 2022. All rights reserved.

UT	ARIES GHA	VENUS −4.1 GHA	Dec	MARS +1.2 GHA	Dec	JUPITER −2.0 GHA	Dec	SATURN +0.9 GHA	Dec	STARS Name	SHA	Dec
16 00	203 52.9	140 33.2	N22 58.4	101 50.6	N24 53.8	182 27.1	N 7 51.4	227 18.6	S11 15.0	Acamar	315 13.3	S40 12.8
01	218 55.4	155 32.6	59.1	116 51.6	53.7	197 29.0	51.7	242 20.8	15.0	Achernar	335 21.8	S57 07.2
02	233 57.8	170 32.0	22 59.7	131 52.6	53.5	212 30.9	51.9	257 23.1	14.9	Acrux	173 01.1	S63 13.8
03	249 00.3	185 31.4	23 00.3	146 53.6 . .	53.4	227 32.8 . .	52.1	272 25.3 . .	14.8	Adhara	255 07.1	S29 00.4
04	264 02.8	200 30.8	01.0	161 54.7	53.3	242 34.7	52.3	287 27.6	14.7	Aldebaran	290 41.5	N16 33.3
05	279 05.2	215 30.2	01.6	176 55.7	53.1	257 36.6	52.6	302 29.8	14.7			
06	294 07.7	230 29.6	N23 02.2	191 56.7	N24 53.0	272 38.5	N 7 52.8	317 32.1	S11 14.6	Alioth	166 13.7	N55 50.1
07	309 10.2	245 29.0	02.9	206 57.7	52.8	287 40.4	53.0	332 34.3	14.5	Alkaid	152 52.7	N49 11.8
08	324 12.6	260 28.4	03.5	221 58.7	52.7	302 42.3	53.2	347 36.6	14.4	Alnair	27 35.0	S46 50.8
S 09	339 15.1	275 27.8 . .	04.1	236 59.7 . .	52.6	317 44.2 . .	53.5	2 38.8 . .	14.4	Alnilam	275 39.4	S 1 11.3
U 10	354 17.5	290 27.2	04.8	252 00.8	52.4	332 46.1	53.7	17 41.1	14.3	Alphard	217 49.1	S 8 45.7
N 11	9 20.0	305 26.6	05.4	267 01.8	52.3	347 48.0	53.9	32 43.3	14.2			
D 12	24 22.5	320 26.0	N23 06.0	282 02.8	N24 52.2	2 49.9	N 7 54.1	47 45.6	S11 14.1	Alphecca	126 04.6	N26 38.0
A 13	39 24.9	335 25.4	06.7	297 03.8	52.0	17 51.8	54.3	62 47.8	14.1	Alpheratz	357 36.6	N29 12.9
Y 14	54 27.4	350 24.8	07.3	312 04.8	51.9	32 53.7	54.6	77 50.1	14.0	Altair	62 01.4	N 8 55.6
15	69 29.9	5 24.2 . .	07.9	327 05.8 . .	51.8	47 55.6 . .	54.8	92 52.3 . .	13.9	Ankaa	353 09.0	S42 10.8
16	84 32.3	20 23.6	08.5	342 06.9	51.6	62 57.5	55.0	107 54.6	13.8	Antares	112 17.3	S26 29.0
17	99 34.8	35 23.0	09.2	357 07.9	51.5	77 59.4	55.2	122 56.8	13.8			
18	114 37.3	50 22.4	N23 09.8	12 08.9	N24 51.3	93 01.3	N 7 55.5	137 59.1	S11 13.7	Arcturus	145 48.9	N19 03.6
19	129 39.7	65 21.7	10.4	27 09.9	51.2	108 03.2	55.7	153 01.3	13.6	Atria	107 12.5	S69 04.0
20	144 42.2	80 21.1	11.0	42 10.9	51.1	123 05.1	55.9	168 03.6	13.5	Avior	234 15.3	S59 35.3
21	159 44.6	95 20.5 . .	11.6	57 11.9 . .	50.9	138 07.0 . .	56.1	183 05.8 . .	13.5	Bellatrix	278 24.6	N 6 22.2
22	174 47.1	110 19.9	12.3	72 13.0	50.8	153 08.9	56.4	198 08.1	13.4	Betelgeuse	270 53.8	N 7 24.6
23	189 49.6	125 19.3	12.9	87 14.0	50.6	168 10.8	56.6	213 10.3	13.3			
17 00	204 52.0	140 18.7	N23 13.5	102 15.0	N24 50.5	183 12.7	N 7 56.8	228 12.6	S11 13.2	Canopus	263 53.2	S52 42.7
01	219 54.5	155 18.1	14.1	117 16.0	50.4	198 14.6	57.0	243 14.8	13.2	Capella	280 24.3	N46 01.4
02	234 57.0	170 17.5	14.7	132 17.0	50.2	213 16.5	57.3	258 17.1	13.1	Deneb	49 26.9	N45 21.4
03	249 59.4	185 16.9 . .	15.3	147 18.0 . .	50.1	228 18.4 . .	57.5	273 19.3 . .	13.0	Denebola	182 26.2	N14 26.5
04	265 01.9	200 16.3	15.9	162 19.0	49.9	243 20.3	57.7	288 21.6	12.9	Diphda	348 49.1	S17 51.7
05	280 04.4	215 15.7	16.6	177 20.1	49.8	258 22.2	57.9	303 23.8	12.9			
06	295 06.8	230 15.1	N23 17.2	192 21.1	N24 49.7	273 24.1	N 7 58.1	318 26.1	S11 12.8	Dubhe	193 42.3	N61 37.7
07	310 09.3	245 14.5	17.8	207 22.1	49.5	288 26.0	58.4	333 28.3	12.7	Elnath	278 03.9	N28 37.6
08	325 11.8	260 13.9	18.4	222 23.1	49.4	303 27.9	58.6	348 30.6	12.6	Eltanin	90 42.6	N51 28.8
M 09	340 14.2	275 13.2 . .	19.0	237 24.1 . .	49.2	318 29.8 . .	58.8	3 32.8 . .	12.6	Enif	33 40.4	N 9 58.7
O 10	355 16.7	290 12.6	19.6	252 25.1	49.1	333 31.7	59.0	18 35.1	12.5	Fomalhaut	15 16.4	S29 30.0
N 11	10 19.1	305 12.0	20.2	267 26.1	48.9	348 33.6	59.3	33 37.3	12.4			
D 12	25 21.6	320 11.4	N23 20.8	282 27.2	N24 48.8	3 35.5	N 7 59.5	48 39.6	S11 12.3	Gacrux	171 52.7	S57 14.7
A 13	40 24.1	335 10.8	21.4	297 28.2	48.7	18 37.4	59.7	63 41.9	12.3	Gienah	175 44.8	S17 40.4
Y 14	55 26.5	350 10.2	22.0	312 29.2	48.5	33 39.3	7 59.9	78 44.1	12.2	Hadar	148 37.5	S60 29.1
15	70 29.0	5 09.6 . .	22.6	327 30.2 . .	48.4	48 41.2	8 00.2	93 46.4 . .	12.1	Hamal	327 53.2	N23 34.2
16	85 31.5	20 09.0	23.2	342 31.2	48.2	63 43.1	00.4	108 48.6	12.0	Kaus Aust.	83 34.3	S34 22.4
17	100 33.9	35 08.4	23.8	357 32.2	48.1	78 45.0	00.6	123 50.9	12.0			
18	115 36.4	50 07.8	N23 24.4	12 33.2	N24 47.9	93 46.9	N 8 00.8	138 53.1	S11 11.9	Kochab	137 18.6	N74 03.5
19	130 38.9	65 07.1	25.0	27 34.2	47.8	108 48.8	01.0	153 55.4	11.8	Markab	13 31.6	N15 19.6
20	145 41.3	80 06.5	25.6	42 35.3	47.7	123 50.7	01.3	168 57.6	11.8	Menkar	314 08.0	N 4 10.7
21	160 43.8	95 05.9 . .	26.2	57 36.3 . .	47.5	138 52.5 . .	01.5	183 59.9 . .	11.7	Menkent	147 59.0	S36 29.1
22	175 46.2	110 05.3	26.8	72 37.3	47.4	153 54.4	01.7	199 02.1	11.6	Miaplacidus	221 38.3	S69 49.0
23	190 48.7	125 04.7	27.4	87 38.3	47.2	168 56.3	01.9	214 04.4	11.5			
18 00	205 51.2	140 04.1	N23 28.0	102 39.3	N24 47.1	183 58.2	N 8 02.2	229 06.6	S11 11.5	Mirfak	308 30.8	N49 56.6
01	220 53.6	155 03.5	28.5	117 40.3	46.9	199 00.1	02.4	244 08.9	11.4	Nunki	75 49.5	S26 16.1
02	235 56.1	170 02.9	29.1	132 41.3	46.8	214 02.0	02.6	259 11.1	11.3	Peacock	53 08.1	S56 39.4
03	250 58.6	185 02.2 . .	29.7	147 42.3 . .	46.6	229 03.9 . .	02.8	274 13.4 . .	11.2	Pollux	243 19.1	N27 58.3
04	266 01.0	200 01.6	30.3	162 43.3	46.5	244 05.8	03.0	289 15.6	11.2	Procyon	244 52.4	N 5 09.9
05	281 03.5	215 01.0	30.9	177 44.4	46.3	259 07.7	03.3	304 17.9	11.1			
06	296 06.0	230 00.4	N23 31.5	192 45.4	N24 46.2	274 09.6	N 8 03.5	319 20.2	S11 11.0	Rasalhague	95 59.7	N12 32.4
07	311 08.4	244 59.8	32.1	207 46.4	46.0	289 11.5	03.7	334 22.4	10.9	Regulus	207 35.8	N11 51.2
08	326 10.9	259 59.2	32.6	222 47.4	45.9	304 13.4	03.9	349 24.7	10.9	Rigel	281 05.5	S 8 10.6
T 09	341 13.4	274 58.6 . .	33.2	237 48.4 . .	45.8	319 15.3 . .	04.2	4 26.9 . .	10.8	Rigil Kent.	139 41.7	S60 55.8
U 10	356 15.8	289 57.9	33.8	252 49.4	45.6	334 17.2	04.4	19 29.2	10.7	Sabik	102 04.2	S15 45.3
E 11	11 18.3	304 57.3	34.4	267 50.4	45.5	349 19.1	04.6	34 31.4	10.6			
S 12	26 20.7	319 56.7	N23 35.0	282 51.4	N24 45.3	4 21.0	N 8 04.8	49 33.7	S11 10.6	Schedar	349 33.3	N56 39.7
D 13	41 23.2	334 56.1	35.5	297 52.4	45.2	19 22.9	05.1	64 35.9	10.5	Shaula	96 12.1	S37 07.2
A 14	56 25.7	349 55.5	36.1	312 53.4	45.0	34 24.8	05.3	79 38.2	10.4	Sirius	258 27.6	S16 45.0
Y 15	71 28.1	4 54.9 . .	36.7	327 54.5 . .	44.9	49 26.7 . .	05.5	94 40.4 . .	10.4	Spica	158 23.5	S11 17.0
16	86 30.6	19 54.3	37.3	342 55.5	44.7	64 28.6	05.7	109 42.7	10.3	Suhail	222 47.3	S43 31.8
17	101 33.1	34 53.6	37.8	357 56.5	44.6	79 30.5	05.9	124 45.0	10.2			
18	116 35.5	49 53.0	N23 38.4	12 57.5	N24 44.4	94 32.4	N 8 06.2	139 47.2	S11 10.1	Vega	80 34.1	N38 48.0
19	131 38.0	64 52.4	39.0	27 58.5	44.3	109 34.3	06.4	154 49.5	10.1	Zuben'ubi	136 57.3	S16 08.4
20	146 40.5	79 51.8	39.5	42 59.5	44.1	124 36.2	06.6	169 51.7	10.0		SHA	Mer. Pass.
21	161 42.9	94 51.2 . .	40.1	58 00.5 . .	44.0	139 38.1 . .	06.8	184 54.0 . .	09.9	Venus	295 26.7	h m 14 39
22	176 45.4	109 50.6	40.7	73 01.5	43.8	154 40.0	07.1	199 56.2	09.8	Mars	257 22.9	17 10
23	191 47.8	124 49.9	41.3	88 02.5	43.7	169 41.9	07.3	214 58.5	09.8	Jupiter	338 20.6	11 46
Mer. Pass. 10 18.8		v −0.6	d 0.6	v 1.0	d 0.1	v 1.9	d 0.2	v 2.3	d 0.1	Saturn	23 20.5	8 46

© British Crown Copyright 2022. All rights reserved.

SUN / MOON

UT	SUN GHA	Dec	MOON GHA	v	Dec	d	HP
d h	° ′	° ′	° ′	′	° ′	′	′
16 00	180 00.6	N 9 57.1	229 27.6	9.3	S15 39.4	14.4	59.6
01	195 00.7	58.0	243 55.9	9.4	15 25.0	14.4	59.6
02	210 00.9	58.9	258 24.3	9.5	15 10.6	14.5	59.6
03	225 01.0	9 59.8	272 52.8	9.5	14 56.1	14.6	59.6
04	240 01.2	10 00.7	287 21.3	9.7	14 41.5	14.6	59.6
05	255 01.3	01.5	301 50.0	9.7	14 26.9	14.8	59.6
06	270 01.5	N10 02.4	316 18.7	9.7	S14 12.1	14.8	59.6
07	285 01.6	03.3	330 47.4	9.9	13 57.3	14.9	59.6
08	300 01.8	04.2	345 16.3	9.9	13 42.4	15.0	59.6
S 09	315 01.9	05.1	359 45.2	10.0	13 27.4	15.0	59.6
U 10	330 02.1	06.0	14 14.2	10.0	13 12.4	15.1	59.6
N 11	345 02.2	06.9	28 43.2	10.1	12 57.3	15.2	59.6
D 12	0 02.4	N10 07.8	43 12.3	10.2	S12 42.1	15.3	59.6
A 13	15 02.5	08.6	57 41.5	10.3	12 26.8	15.3	59.6
Y 14	30 02.6	09.5	72 10.8	10.3	12 11.5	15.4	59.6
15	45 02.8	10.4	86 40.1	10.4	11 56.1	15.5	59.6
16	60 02.9	11.3	101 09.5	10.4	11 40.6	15.5	59.6
17	75 03.1	12.2	115 38.9	10.5	11 25.1	15.6	59.6
18	90 03.2	N10 13.1	130 08.4	10.6	S11 09.5	15.7	59.6
19	105 03.4	14.0	144 38.0	10.6	10 53.8	15.7	59.6
20	120 03.5	14.8	159 07.6	10.7	10 38.1	15.7	59.6
21	135 03.7	15.7	173 37.3	10.7	10 22.4	15.8	59.5
22	150 03.8	16.6	188 07.0	10.8	10 06.6	15.9	59.5
23	165 04.0	17.5	202 36.8	10.9	9 50.7	15.9	59.5
17 00	180 04.1	N10 18.4	217 06.7	10.9	S 9 34.8	16.0	59.5
01	195 04.2	19.3	231 36.6	11.0	9 18.8	16.0	59.5
02	210 04.4	20.2	246 06.6	11.0	9 02.8	16.0	59.5
03	225 04.5	21.0	260 36.6	11.0	8 46.8	16.1	59.5
04	240 04.7	21.9	275 06.6	11.2	8 30.7	16.2	59.5
05	255 04.8	22.8	289 36.8	11.1	8 14.5	16.2	59.5
06	270 05.0	N10 23.7	304 06.9	11.2	S 7 58.3	16.2	59.5
07	285 05.1	24.6	318 37.1	11.3	7 42.1	16.3	59.5
08	300 05.3	25.4	333 07.4	11.3	7 25.8	16.3	59.5
M 09	315 05.4	26.3	347 37.7	11.3	7 09.5	16.3	59.5
O 10	330 05.5	27.2	2 08.0	11.4	6 53.2	16.3	59.5
N 11	345 05.7	28.1	16 38.4	11.5	6 36.9	16.4	59.5
D 12	0 05.8	N10 29.0	31 08.9	11.5	S 6 20.5	16.5	59.4
A 13	15 06.0	29.8	45 39.4	11.5	6 04.0	16.4	59.4
Y 14	30 06.1	30.7	60 09.9	11.5	5 47.6	16.5	59.4
15	45 06.3	31.6	74 40.4	11.6	5 31.1	16.5	59.4
16	60 06.4	32.5	89 11.0	11.7	5 14.6	16.5	59.4
17	75 06.5	33.4	103 41.7	11.6	4 58.1	16.5	59.4
18	90 06.7	N10 34.2	118 12.3	11.7	S 4 41.6	16.6	59.4
19	105 06.8	35.1	132 43.0	11.8	4 25.0	16.6	59.4
20	120 07.0	36.0	147 13.8	11.7	4 08.4	16.6	59.4
21	135 07.1	36.9	161 44.5	11.8	3 51.8	16.6	59.4
22	150 07.2	37.8	176 15.3	11.8	3 35.2	16.6	59.3
23	165 07.4	38.6	190 46.1	11.9	3 18.6	16.6	59.3
18 00	180 07.5	N10 39.5	205 17.0	11.9	S 3 02.0	16.7	59.3
01	195 07.7	40.4	219 47.9	11.9	2 45.3	16.6	59.3
02	210 07.8	41.3	234 18.8	11.9	2 28.7	16.7	59.3
03	225 07.9	42.1	248 49.7	12.0	2 12.0	16.7	59.3
04	240 08.1	43.0	263 20.7	12.0	1 55.3	16.6	59.3
05	255 08.2	43.9	277 51.7	12.0	1 38.7	16.7	59.3
06	270 08.4	N10 44.8	292 22.7	12.0	S 1 22.0	16.7	59.2
07	285 08.5	45.6	306 53.7	12.0	1 05.3	16.6	59.2
08	300 08.6	46.5	321 24.7	12.1	0 48.7	16.7	59.2
T 09	315 08.8	47.4	335 55.8	12.0	0 32.0	16.7	59.2
U 10	330 08.9	48.3	350 26.8	12.1	S 0 15.3	16.6	59.2
E 11	345 09.1	49.1	4 57.9	12.1	N 0 01.3	16.6	59.2
S 12	0 09.2	N10 50.0	19 29.0	12.2	N 0 17.9	16.7	59.2
D 13	15 09.3	50.9	34 00.2	12.1	0 34.6	16.6	59.1
A 14	30 09.5	51.7	48 31.3	12.1	0 51.2	16.6	59.1
Y 15	45 09.6	52.6	63 02.4	12.2	1 07.8	16.6	59.1
16	60 09.7	53.5	77 33.6	12.1	1 24.4	16.6	59.1
17	75 09.9	54.4	92 04.7	12.2	1 41.0	16.6	59.1
18	90 10.0	N10 55.2	106 35.9	12.2	N 1 57.6	16.5	59.1
19	105 10.2	56.1	121 07.1	12.1	2 14.1	16.5	59.0
20	120 10.3	57.0	135 38.2	12.2	2 30.6	16.5	59.0
21	135 10.4	57.8	150 09.4	12.2	2 47.1	16.5	59.0
22	150 10.6	58.7	164 40.6	12.2	3 03.6	16.5	59.0
23	165 10.7	59.6	179 11.8	12.2	N 3 20.1	16.4	59.0
	SD 16.0	d 0.9	SD 16.2		16.2		16.1

Twilight / Sunrise / Moonrise

Lat.	Naut.	Civil	Sunrise	16	17	18	19
°	h m	h m	h m	h m	h m	h m	h m
N 72	////	01 40	03 29	06 22	05 29	04 51	04 16
N 70	////	02 23	03 47	05 54	05 17	04 49	04 22
68	////	02 50	04 02	05 33	05 07	04 47	04 27
66	01 27	03 11	04 13	05 16	04 59	04 45	04 31
64	02 04	03 27	04 23	05 02	04 52	04 44	04 35
62	02 30	03 41	04 31	04 50	04 46	04 42	04 38
60	02 49	03 52	04 39	04 40	04 41	04 41	04 41
N 58	03 05	04 01	04 45	04 31	04 36	04 40	04 44
56	03 18	04 10	04 50	04 23	04 32	04 39	04 46
54	03 29	04 17	04 55	04 17	04 28	04 38	04 48
52	03 39	04 24	05 00	04 10	04 25	04 38	04 50
50	03 47	04 29	05 04	04 05	04 22	04 37	04 52
45	04 04	04 42	05 13	03 52	04 15	04 36	04 56
N 40	04 18	04 52	05 20	03 42	04 09	04 34	04 59
35	04 29	05 00	05 26	03 33	04 04	04 33	05 02
30	04 38	05 07	05 31	03 25	04 00	04 32	05 04
20	04 52	05 18	05 41	03 12	03 53	04 31	05 08
N 10	05 02	05 27	05 49	03 00	03 46	04 29	05 12
0	05 11	05 35	05 56	02 49	03 39	04 28	05 16
S 10	05 18	05 42	06 04	02 37	03 33	04 27	05 20
20	05 23	05 49	06 11	02 25	03 26	04 25	05 24
30	05 28	05 56	06 20	02 12	03 19	04 24	05 28
35	05 30	05 59	06 25	02 04	03 14	04 23	05 31
40	05 32	06 03	06 31	01 54	03 09	04 22	05 34
45	05 33	06 07	06 37	01 44	03 03	04 21	05 37
S 50	05 34	06 12	06 45	01 30	02 56	04 19	05 42
52	05 35	06 14	06 48	01 24	02 53	04 19	05 44
54	05 35	06 16	06 52	01 17	02 49	04 18	05 46
56	05 35	06 18	06 57	01 10	02 45	04 17	05 48
58	05 35	06 21	07 01	01 01	02 40	04 16	05 51
S 60	05 36	06 24	07 07	00 51	02 35	04 16	05 54

Sunset / Twilight / Moonset

Lat.	Sunset	Civil	Naut.	16	17	18	19
°	h m	h m	h m	h m	h m	h m	h m
N 72	20 34	22 28	////	12 10	14 49	17 11	19 35
N 70	20 15	21 42	////	12 35	14 58	17 09	19 21
68	20 00	21 13	////	12 54	15 05	17 07	19 10
66	19 48	20 52	22 41	13 09	15 10	17 06	19 01
64	19 38	20 35	22 00	13 22	15 15	17 04	18 53
62	19 30	20 21	21 33	13 32	15 19	17 03	18 46
60	19 22	20 09	21 13	13 41	15 23	17 02	18 41
N 58	19 16	20 00	20 57	13 48	15 26	17 01	18 36
56	19 10	19 51	20 44	13 55	15 29	17 01	18 31
54	19 05	19 44	20 32	14 01	15 32	17 00	18 27
52	19 01	19 37	20 22	14 06	15 34	16 59	18 24
50	18 56	19 31	20 14	14 11	15 36	16 59	18 21
45	18 48	19 18	19 56	14 22	15 40	16 57	18 14
N 40	18 40	19 08	19 42	14 30	15 44	16 56	18 08
35	18 34	19 00	19 31	14 37	15 47	16 55	18 03
30	18 28	18 53	19 22	14 44	15 50	16 55	17 59
20	18 19	18 41	19 08	14 55	15 55	16 53	17 51
N 10	18 11	18 32	18 57	15 04	15 59	16 52	17 45
0	18 03	18 24	18 48	15 13	16 03	16 51	17 39
S 10	17 55	18 17	18 41	15 22	16 07	16 50	17 32
20	17 48	18 10	18 36	15 31	16 11	16 48	17 26
30	17 39	18 03	18 31	15 42	16 15	16 47	17 19
35	17 34	17 59	18 29	15 48	16 18	16 46	17 14
40	17 28	17 55	18 27	15 54	16 20	16 45	17 10
45	17 21	17 51	18 25	16 02	16 24	16 44	17 04
S 50	17 14	17 47	18 24	16 12	16 28	16 43	16 57
52	17 10	17 44	18 24	16 16	16 30	16 42	16 54
54	17 06	17 42	18 23	16 21	16 31	16 41	16 51
56	17 02	17 40	18 23	16 26	16 34	16 41	16 48
58	16 57	17 37	18 23	16 31	16 36	16 40	16 44
S 60	16 51	17 34	18 22	16 38	16 39	16 39	16 39

SUN / MOON

Day	Eqn. of Time 00h	Eqn. of Time 12h	Mer. Pass.	Mer. Pass. Upper	Mer. Pass. Lower	Age	Phase
d	m s	m s	h m	h m	h m	d	%
16	00 02	00 09	12 00	09 01	21 26	26	17
17	00 16	00 23	12 00	09 51	22 15	27	9
18	00 30	00 37	11 59	10 39	23 03	28	4

© British Crown Copyright 2022. All rights reserved.

UT	ARIES	VENUS −4.1		MARS +1.2		JUPITER −2.0		SATURN +0.9		STARS		
	GHA	GHA	Dec	GHA	Dec	GHA	Dec	GHA	Dec	Name	SHA	Dec
d h	° ′	° ′	° ′	° ′	° ′	° ′	° ′	° ′	° ′		° ′	° ′
19 00	206 50.3	139 49.3	N23 41.8	103 03.5	N24 43.5	184 43.8	N 8 07.5	230 00.7	S11 09.7	Acamar	315 13.3	S40 12.8
01	221 52.8	154 48.7	.. 42.4	118 04.5	43.4	199 45.7	07.7	245 03.0	09.6	Achernar	335 21.8	S57 07.2
02	236 55.2	169 48.1	42.9	133 05.6	43.2	214 47.6	07.9	260 05.3	09.6	Acrux	173 01.1	S63 13.8
03	251 57.7	184 47.5	.. 43.5	148 06.6	.. 43.1	229 49.5	.. 08.2	275 07.5	.. 09.5	Adhara	255 07.1	S29 00.4
04	267 00.2	199 46.8	44.1	163 07.6	42.9	244 51.4	08.4	290 09.8	09.4	Aldebaran	290 41.6	N16 33.3
05	282 02.6	214 46.2	44.6	178 08.6	42.8	259 53.3	08.6	305 12.0	09.3			
W 06	297 05.1	229 45.6	N23 45.2	193 09.6	N24 42.6	274 55.2	N 8 08.8	320 14.3	S11 09.3	Alioth	166 13.7	N55 50.1
E 07	312 07.6	244 45.0	45.7	208 10.6	42.5	289 57.1	09.1	335 16.5	09.2	Alkaid	152 52.7	N49 11.8
D 08	327 10.0	259 44.4	46.3	223 11.6	42.3	304 59.0	09.3	350 18.8	09.1	Alnair	27 35.0	S46 50.8
N 09	342 12.5	274 43.8	.. 46.9	238 12.6	.. 42.1	320 00.9	.. 09.5	5 21.0	.. 09.0	Alnilam	275 39.4	S 1 11.3
E 10	357 15.0	289 43.1	47.4	253 13.6	42.0	335 02.8	09.7	20 23.3	09.0	Alphard	217 49.1	S 8 45.7
S 11	12 17.4	304 42.5	48.0	268 14.6	41.8	350 04.7	09.9	35 25.6	08.9			
D 12	27 19.9	319 41.9	N23 48.5	283 15.6	N24 41.7	5 06.6	N 8 10.2	50 27.8	S11 08.8	Alphecca	126 04.6	N26 38.0
A 13	42 22.3	334 41.3	49.1	298 16.6	41.5	20 08.5	10.4	65 30.1	08.8	Alpheratz	357 36.6	N29 12.9
Y 14	57 24.8	349 40.7	49.6	313 17.6	41.4	35 10.4	10.6	80 32.3	08.7	Altair	62 01.3	N 8 55.6
15	72 27.3	4 40.0	.. 50.2	328 18.6	.. 41.2	50 12.3	.. 10.8	95 34.6	.. 08.6	Ankaa	353 09.0	S42 10.8
16	87 29.7	19 39.4	50.7	343 19.7	41.1	65 14.2	11.0	110 36.8	08.5	Antares	112 17.3	S26 29.0
17	102 32.2	34 38.8	51.3	358 20.7	40.9	80 16.1	11.3	125 39.1	08.5			
18	117 34.7	49 38.2	N23 51.8	13 21.7	N24 40.8	95 18.0	N 8 11.5	140 41.4	S11 08.4	Arcturus	145 48.9	N19 03.6
19	132 37.1	64 37.6	52.4	28 22.7	40.6	110 19.9	11.7	155 43.6	08.3	Atria	107 12.5	S69 04.0
20	147 39.6	79 36.9	52.9	43 23.7	40.4	125 21.8	11.9	170 45.9	08.3	Avior	234 15.3	S59 35.3
21	162 42.1	94 36.3	.. 53.4	58 24.7	.. 40.3	140 23.7	.. 12.2	185 48.1	.. 08.2	Bellatrix	278 24.6	N 6 22.2
22	177 44.5	109 35.7	54.0	73 25.7	40.1	155 25.6	12.4	200 50.4	08.1	Betelgeuse	270 53.8	N 7 24.6
23	192 47.0	124 35.1	54.5	88 26.7	40.0	170 27.5	12.6	215 52.7	08.0			
20 00	207 49.5	139 34.4	N23 55.1	103 27.7	N24 39.8	185 29.4	N 8 12.8	230 54.9	S11 08.0	Canopus	263 53.3	S52 42.7
01	222 51.9	154 33.8	55.6	118 28.7	39.7	200 31.3	13.0	245 57.2	07.9	Capella	280 24.4	N46 01.4
02	237 54.4	169 33.2	56.1	133 29.7	39.5	215 33.2	13.3	260 59.4	07.8	Deneb	49 26.9	N45 21.4
03	252 56.8	184 32.6	.. 56.7	148 30.7	.. 39.3	230 35.1	.. 13.5	276 01.7	.. 07.8	Denebola	182 26.2	N14 26.5
04	267 59.3	199 32.0	57.2	163 31.7	39.2	245 37.0	13.7	291 03.9	07.7	Diphda	348 49.1	S17 51.7
05	283 01.8	214 31.3	57.8	178 32.7	39.0	260 38.9	13.9	306 06.2	07.6			
T 06	298 04.2	229 30.7	N23 58.3	193 33.7	N24 38.9	275 40.8	N 8 14.2	321 08.5	S11 07.5	Dubhe	193 42.3	N61 37.7
H 07	313 06.7	244 30.1	58.8	208 34.7	38.7	290 42.7	14.4	336 10.7	07.5	Elnath	278 03.9	N28 37.6
U 08	328 09.2	259 29.5	59.4	223 35.7	38.6	305 44.6	14.6	351 13.0	07.4	Eltanin	90 42.6	N51 28.8
R 09	343 11.6	274 28.8	23 59.9	238 36.7	.. 38.4	320 46.5	.. 14.8	6 15.2	.. 07.3	Enif	33 40.4	N 9 58.7
S 10	358 14.1	289 28.2	24 00.4	253 37.8	38.2	335 48.4	15.0	21 17.5	07.3	Fomalhaut	15 16.4	S29 30.0
D 11	13 16.6	304 27.6	00.9	268 38.8	38.1	350 50.3	15.3	36 19.8	07.2			
A 12	28 19.0	319 27.0	N24 01.5	283 39.8	N24 37.9	5 52.2	N 8 15.5	51 22.0	S11 07.1	Gacrux	171 52.7	S57 14.7
Y 13	43 21.5	334 26.4	02.0	298 40.8	37.8	20 54.1	15.7	66 24.3	07.0	Gienah	175 44.8	S17 40.4
14	58 23.9	349 25.9	02.5	313 41.8	37.6	35 56.0	15.9	81 26.5	07.0	Hadar	148 37.4	S60 29.1
15	73 26.4	4 25.1	.. 03.0	328 42.8	.. 37.4	50 57.9	.. 16.1	96 28.8	.. 06.9	Hamal	327 53.2	N23 34.2
16	88 28.9	19 24.5	03.6	343 43.8	37.3	65 59.8	16.4	111 31.1	06.8	Kaus Aust.	83 34.3	S34 22.4
17	103 31.3	34 23.9	04.1	358 44.8	37.1	81 01.7	16.6	126 33.3	06.8			
18	118 33.8	49 23.2	N24 04.6	13 45.8	N24 37.0	96 03.6	N 8 16.8	141 35.6	S11 06.7	Kochab	137 18.6	N74 03.5
19	133 36.3	64 22.6	05.1	28 46.8	36.8	111 05.5	17.0	156 37.8	06.6	Markab	13 31.6	N15 19.6
20	148 38.7	79 22.0	05.6	43 47.8	36.6	126 07.4	17.2	171 40.1	06.5	Menkar	314 08.0	N 4 10.7
21	163 41.2	94 21.4	.. 06.2	58 48.8	.. 36.5	141 09.3	.. 17.5	186 42.4	.. 06.5	Menkent	147 58.9	S36 29.1
22	178 43.7	109 20.7	06.7	73 49.8	36.3	156 11.2	17.7	201 44.6	06.4	Miaplacidus	221 38.3	S69 49.0
23	193 46.1	124 20.1	07.2	88 50.8	36.2	171 13.1	17.9	216 46.9	06.3			
21 00	208 48.6	139 19.5	N24 07.7	103 51.8	N24 36.0	186 15.0	N 8 18.1	231 49.1	S11 06.3	Mirfak	308 30.8	N49 56.6
01	223 51.1	154 18.9	08.2	118 52.8	35.8	201 16.9	18.4	246 51.4	06.2	Nunki	75 49.4	S26 16.1
02	238 53.5	169 18.2	08.7	133 53.8	35.7	216 18.8	18.6	261 53.7	06.1	Peacock	53 08.0	S56 39.4
03	253 56.0	184 17.6	.. 09.2	148 54.8	.. 35.5	231 20.7	.. 18.8	276 55.9	.. 06.0	Pollux	243 19.1	N27 58.3
04	268 58.4	199 17.0	09.8	163 55.8	35.3	246 22.6	19.0	291 58.2	06.0	Procyon	244 52.4	N 5 09.9
05	284 00.9	214 16.3	10.3	178 56.8	35.2	261 24.5	19.2	307 00.5	05.9			
F 06	299 03.4	229 15.7	N24 10.8	193 57.8	N24 35.0	276 26.4	N 8 19.5	322 02.7	S11 05.8	Rasalhague	95 59.7	N12 32.4
R 07	314 05.8	244 15.1	11.3	208 58.8	34.9	291 28.3	19.7	337 05.0	05.8	Regulus	207 35.8	N11 51.2
I 08	329 08.3	259 14.5	11.8	223 59.8	34.7	306 30.2	19.9	352 07.2	05.7	Rigel	281 05.5	S 8 10.6
D 09	344 10.8	274 13.8	.. 12.3	239 00.8	.. 34.5	321 32.1	.. 20.1	7 09.5	.. 05.6	Rigil Kent.	139 41.7	S60 55.8
A 10	359 13.2	289 13.2	12.8	254 01.8	34.4	336 34.0	20.3	22 11.8	05.6	Sabik	102 04.2	S15 45.3
Y 11	14 15.7	304 12.6	13.3	269 02.8	34.2	351 35.9	20.6	37 14.0	05.5			
12	29 18.2	319 12.0	N24 13.8	284 03.8	N24 34.0	6 37.8	N 8 20.8	52 16.3	S11 05.4	Schedar	349 33.3	N56 39.7
13	44 20.6	334 11.3	14.3	299 04.8	33.9	21 39.7	21.0	67 18.6	05.3	Shaula	96 12.1	S37 07.2
14	59 23.1	349 10.7	14.8	314 05.8	33.7	36 41.6	21.2	82 20.8	05.3	Sirius	258 27.6	S16 45.0
15	74 25.6	4 10.1	.. 15.3	329 06.8	.. 33.5	51 43.5	.. 21.4	97 23.1	.. 05.2	Spica	158 23.5	S11 17.0
16	89 28.0	19 09.4	15.8	344 07.8	33.4	66 45.4	21.7	112 25.3	05.1	Suhail	222 47.3	S43 31.8
17	104 30.5	34 08.8	16.3	359 08.8	33.2	81 47.3	21.9	127 27.6	05.1			
18	119 32.9	49 08.2	N24 16.8	14 09.8	N24 33.0	96 49.2	N 8 22.1	142 29.9	S11 05.0	Vega	80 34.0	N38 48.0
19	134 35.4	64 07.6	17.3	29 10.8	32.9	111 51.1	22.3	157 32.1	04.9	Zuben'ubi	136 57.3	S16 08.4
20	149 37.9	79 06.9	17.8	44 11.8	32.7	126 53.0	22.5	172 34.4	04.9		SHA	Mer. Pass.
21	164 40.3	94 06.3	.. 18.3	59 12.8	.. 32.5	141 54.9	.. 22.8	187 36.7	.. 04.8		° ′	h m
22	179 42.8	109 05.7	18.7	74 13.8	32.4	156 56.8	23.0	202 38.9	04.7	Venus	291 45.0	14 42
23	194 45.3	124 05.0	19.2	89 14.8	32.2	171 58.7	23.2	217 41.2	04.6	Mars	255 38.3	17 05
	h m									Jupiter	337 40.0	11 37
Mer. Pass. 10 07.0		v −0.6 d 0.5		v 1.0 d 0.2		v 1.9 d 0.2		v 2.3 d 0.1		Saturn	23 05.5	8 35

© British Crown Copyright 2022. All rights reserved.

UT	SUN GHA	SUN Dec	MOON GHA	v	MOON Dec	d	HP
d h	° ′	° ′	° ′	′	° ′	′	′
19 00	180 10.8	N11 00.5	193 43.0	12.2	N 3 36.5	16.4	59.0
01	195 11.0	01.3	208 14.2	12.2	3 52.9	16.4	58.9
02	210 11.1	02.2	222 45.4	12.1	4 09.3	16.3	58.9
03	225 11.3 ..	03.1	237 16.5	12.2	4 25.6	16.4	58.9
04	240 11.4	03.9	251 47.7	12.2	4 42.0	16.2	58.9
05	255 11.5	04.8	266 18.9	12.2	4 58.2	16.3	58.9
06	270 11.7	N11 05.7	280 50.1	12.1	N 5 14.5	16.2	58.8
W 07	285 11.8	06.5	295 21.2	12.2	5 30.7	16.2	58.8
E 08	300 11.9	07.4	309 52.4	12.1	5 46.9	16.1	58.8
D 09	315 12.1 ..	08.3	324 23.5	12.2	6 03.0	16.1	58.8
N 10	330 12.2	09.1	338 54.7	12.1	6 19.1	16.0	58.7
E 11	345 12.3	10.0	353 25.8	12.1	6 35.1	16.0	58.7
S 12	0 12.5	N11 10.9	7 56.9	12.1	N 6 51.1	16.0	58.7
D 13	15 12.6	11.7	22 28.0	12.1	7 07.1	15.9	58.7
A 14	30 12.7	12.6	36 59.1	12.1	7 23.0	15.9	58.7
Y 15	45 12.9 ..	13.5	51 30.2	12.0	7 38.9	15.8	58.6
16	60 13.0	14.3	66 01.2	12.1	7 54.7	15.7	58.6
17	75 13.1	15.2	80 32.3	12.0	8 10.4	15.7	58.6
18	90 13.3	N11 16.0	95 03.3	12.0	N 8 26.1	15.7	58.6
19	105 13.4	16.9	109 34.3	12.0	8 41.8	15.6	58.6
20	120 13.5	17.8	124 05.3	11.9	8 57.4	15.6	58.5
21	135 13.7 ..	18.6	138 36.2	12.0	9 13.0	15.4	58.5
22	150 13.8	19.5	153 07.2	11.9	9 28.4	15.5	58.5
23	165 13.9	20.4	167 38.1	11.9	N 9 43.9	15.3	58.5
20 00	180 14.1	N11 21.2					
01	195 14.2	22.1					
02	210 14.3	22.9	*An annular-total eclipse of*				
03	225 14.5 ..	23.8	*the Sun occurs on this*				
04	240 14.6	24.7	*date. See page 5.*				
05	255 14.7	25.5					
06	270 14.9	N11 26.4	269 13.9	11.7	N11 30.1	14.9	58.3
T 07	285 15.0	27.2	283 44.6	11.7	11 45.0	14.8	58.3
H 08	300 15.1	28.1	298 15.3	11.6	11 59.8	14.8	58.2
U 09	315 15.2 ..	29.0	312 45.9	11.7	12 14.6	14.7	58.2
R 10	330 15.4	29.8	327 16.6	11.6	12 29.3	14.6	58.2
S 11	345 15.5	30.7	341 47.2	11.5	12 43.9	14.5	58.2
D 12	0 15.6	N11 31.5	356 17.7	11.6	N12 58.4	14.5	58.1
A 13	15 15.8	32.4	10 48.3	11.5	13 12.9	14.3	58.1
Y 14	30 15.9	33.2	25 18.8	11.4	13 27.2	14.3	58.1
15	45 16.0 ..	34.1	39 49.2	11.5	13 41.5	14.2	58.1
16	60 16.2	35.0	54 19.7	11.3	13 55.7	14.2	58.0
17	75 16.3	35.8	68 50.0	11.4	14 09.9	14.0	58.0
18	90 16.4	N11 36.7	83 20.4	11.3	N14 23.9	14.0	58.0
19	105 16.5	37.5	97 50.7	11.3	14 37.9	13.9	57.9
20	120 16.6	38.4	112 21.0	11.3	14 51.8	13.7	57.9
21	135 16.8 ..	39.2	126 51.3	11.2	15 05.5	13.7	57.9
22	150 16.9	40.1	141 21.5	11.1	15 19.2	13.6	57.9
23	165 17.1	40.9	155 51.6	11.2	15 32.8	13.6	57.8
21 00	180 17.2	N11 41.8	170 21.8	11.1	N15 46.4	13.4	57.8
01	195 17.3	42.6	184 51.9	11.0	15 59.8	13.3	57.8
02	210 17.4	43.5	199 22.9	11.0	16 13.1	13.2	57.7
03	225 17.6 ..	44.4	213 51.9	11.0	16 26.3	13.2	57.7
04	240 17.7	45.2	228 21.9	10.9	16 39.5	13.0	57.7
05	255 17.8	46.1	242 52.8	10.9	16 52.5	12.9	57.7
06	270 17.9	N11 46.9	257 21.7	10.9	N17 05.4	12.9	57.6
07	285 18.1	47.8	271 51.6	10.8	17 18.3	12.7	57.6
08	300 18.2	48.6	286 21.4	10.7	17 31.0	12.6	57.6
F 09	315 18.3 ..	49.5	300 51.1	10.8	17 43.6	12.6	57.5
R 10	330 18.4	50.3	315 20.9	10.6	17 56.2	12.4	57.5
I 11	345 18.6	51.2	329 50.5	10.7	18 08.6	12.3	57.5
D 12	0 18.7	N11 52.0	344 20.2	10.6	N18 20.9	12.2	57.5
A 13	15 18.8	52.9	358 49.8	10.5	18 33.1	12.1	57.4
Y 14	30 18.9	53.7	13 19.3	10.5	18 45.2	12.0	57.4
15	45 19.1 ..	54.6	27 48.8	10.5	18 57.2	11.9	57.4
16	60 19.2	55.4	42 18.3	10.4	19 09.1	11.8	57.3
17	75 19.3	56.3	56 47.7	10.4	19 20.9	11.6	57.3
18	90 19.4	N11 57.1	71 17.1	10.3	N19 32.5	11.6	57.3
19	105 19.6	58.0	85 46.4	10.3	19 44.1	11.4	57.3
20	120 19.7	58.8	100 15.7	10.3	19 55.5	11.4	57.2
21	135 19.8	11 59.6	114 45.0	10.2	20 06.9	11.2	57.2
22	150 19.9	12 00.5	129 14.2	10.1	20 18.1	11.0	57.2
23	165 20.1	N12 01.3	143 43.3	10.1	N20 29.1	11.0	57.1
	SD 15.9	d 0.9	SD 16.0		15.8		15.7

Lat.	Twilight Naut.	Twilight Civil	Sunrise	Moonrise 19	20	21	22
°	h m	h m	h m	h m	h m	h m	h m
N 72	////	01 01	03 11	04 16	03 35	02 30	▭
N 70	////	02 00	03 32	04 22	03 52	03 10	▭
68	////	02 33	03 49	04 27	04 06	03 38	02 44
66	00 53	02 57	04 02	04 31	04 17	03 59	03 33
64	01 44	03 15	04 13	04 35	04 26	04 17	04 04
62	02 14	03 30	04 22	04 38	04 35	04 31	04 27
60	02 36	03 42	04 30	04 41	04 42	04 43	04 46
N 58	02 54	03 53	04 37	04 44	04 48	04 54	05 02
56	03 08	04 02	04 43	04 46	04 54	05 03	05 15
54	03 20	04 10	04 48	04 48	04 59	05 11	05 27
52	03 31	04 17	04 53	04 50	05 03	05 18	05 38
50	03 40	04 23	04 58	04 52	05 07	05 25	05 47
45	03 59	04 36	05 07	04 56	05 16	05 39	06 07
N 40	04 13	04 47	05 15	04 59	05 24	05 51	06 23
35	04 25	04 56	05 22	05 02	05 30	06 02	06 36
30	04 34	05 04	05 28	05 04	05 36	06 11	06 48
20	04 49	05 16	05 38	05 08	05 46	06 26	07 09
N 10	05 01	05 26	05 47	05 12	05 55	06 40	07 27
0	05 10	05 35	05 56	05 16	06 04	06 53	07 44
S 10	05 18	05 42	06 04	05 20	06 12	07 06	08 01
20	05 24	05 50	06 12	05 24	06 22	07 20	08 19
30	05 30	05 58	06 22	05 28	06 32	07 36	08 40
35	05 32	06 02	06 27	05 31	06 38	07 46	08 53
40	05 34	06 06	06 34	05 34	06 45	07 57	09 07
45	05 37	06 11	06 41	05 37	06 54	08 09	09 24
S 50	05 39	06 16	06 49	05 42	07 04	08 25	09 46
52	05 39	06 19	06 53	05 44	07 08	08 33	09 56
54	05 40	06 21	06 58	05 46	07 13	08 41	10 08
56	05 41	06 24	07 03	05 48	07 19	08 50	10 21
58	05 41	06 27	07 08	05 51	07 26	09 01	10 36
S 60	05 42	06 31	07 14	05 54	07 33	09 13	10 55

Lat.	Sunset	Twilight Civil	Twilight Naut.	Moonset 19	20	21	22
°	h m	h m	h m	h m	h m	h m	h m
N 72	20 51	23 15	////	19 35	22 24	▭	▭
N 70	20 29	22 05	////	19 21	21 46	▭	▭
68	20 12	21 30	////	19 10	21 20	23 59	▭
66	19 59	21 05	23 21	19 01	21 00	23 12	▭
64	19 47	20 46	22 46	18 53	20 44	22 42	24 54
62	19 38	20 31	21 48	18 46	20 31	22 19	24 11
60	19 30	20 18	21 25	18 41	20 20	22 01	23 42
N 58	19 23	20 07	21 07	18 36	20 11	21 46	23 20
56	19 16	19 58	20 52	18 31	20 02	21 33	23 02
54	19 11	19 50	20 40	18 27	19 55	21 22	22 47
52	19 06	19 43	20 29	18 24	19 48	21 12	22 34
50	19 01	19 36	20 20	18 21	19 42	21 04	22 23
45	18 51	19 23	20 01	18 14	19 30	20 45	21 59
N 40	18 43	19 12	19 46	18 08	19 19	20 30	21 40
35	18 36	19 03	19 34	18 03	19 11	20 18	21 24
30	18 30	18 55	19 24	17 59	19 03	20 07	21 11
20	18 20	18 42	19 09	17 51	18 49	19 48	20 47
N 10	18 11	18 32	18 57	17 45	18 38	19 32	20 27
0	18 02	18 23	18 48	17 39	18 27	19 17	20 09
S 10	17 54	18 15	18 40	17 32	18 16	19 02	19 50
20	17 45	18 08	18 34	17 26	18 05	18 46	19 30
30	17 36	18 00	18 28	17 19	17 52	18 28	19 08
35	17 30	17 56	18 25	17 14	17 44	18 17	18 54
40	17 24	17 51	18 23	17 10	17 36	18 05	18 39
45	17 16	17 46	18 21	17 04	17 26	17 51	18 21
S 50	17 08	17 41	18 18	16 57	17 14	17 33	17 58
52	17 04	17 38	18 18	16 54	17 08	17 25	17 47
54	16 59	17 36	18 17	16 51	17 02	17 16	17 35
56	16 54	17 33	18 16	16 48	16 56	17 06	17 21
58	16 49	17 30	18 15	16 44	16 48	16 55	17 05
S 60	16 43	17 26	18 15	16 39	16 40	16 42	16 46

Day	SUN Eqn. of Time 00ʰ	SUN Eqn. of Time 12ʰ	SUN Mer. Pass.	MOON Mer. Pass. Upper	MOON Mer. Pass. Lower	Age	Phase
d	m s	m s	h m	h m	h m	d	%
19	00 43	00 50	11 59	11 27	23 51	29	1
20	00 56	01 02	11 59	12 15	24 40	00	0
21	01 08	01 15	11 59	13 05	00 40	01	2

© British Crown Copyright 2022. All rights reserved.

UT	ARIES	VENUS −4.1		MARS +1.2		JUPITER −2.0		SATURN +0.9		STARS		
	GHA	GHA	Dec	GHA	Dec	GHA	Dec	GHA	Dec	Name	SHA	Dec
d h	° ′	° ′	° ′	° ′	° ′	° ′	° ′	° ′	° ′		° ′	° ′
22 00	209 47.7	139 04.4	N24 19.7	104 15.8	N24 32.0	187 00.6	N 8 23.4	232 43.4	S11 04.6	Acamar	315 13.3	S40 12.8
01	224 50.2	154 03.8	20.2	119 16.8	31.9	202 02.5	23.6	247 45.7	04.5	Achernar	335 21.8	S57 07.2
02	239 52.7	169 03.2	20.7	134 17.8	31.7	217 04.4	23.9	262 48.0	04.4	Acrux	173 01.1	S63 13.8
03	254 55.1	184 02.5	.. 21.2	149 18.8	.. 31.5	232 06.3	.. 24.1	277 50.2	.. 04.4	Adhara	255 07.1	S29 00.4
04	269 57.6	199 01.9	21.7	164 19.8	31.4	247 08.2	24.3	292 52.5	04.3	Aldebaran	290 41.6	N16 33.3
05	285 00.0	214 01.3	22.1	179 20.8	31.2	262 10.1	24.5	307 54.8	04.2			
06	300 02.5	229 00.6	N24 22.6	194 21.8	N24 31.0	277 12.0	N 8 24.7	322 57.0	S11 04.2	Alioth	166 13.7	N55 50.1
07	315 05.0	244 00.0	23.1	209 22.8	30.9	292 13.9	25.0	337 59.3	04.1	Alkaid	152 52.7	N49 11.8
S 08	330 07.4	258 59.4	23.6	224 23.8	30.7	307 15.8	25.2	353 01.6	04.0	Alnair	27 34.9	S46 50.8
A 09	345 09.9	273 58.8	.. 24.1	239 24.8	.. 30.5	322 17.7	.. 25.4	8 03.8	.. 03.9	Alnilam	275 39.4	S 1 11.3
T 10	0 12.4	288 58.1	24.5	254 25.8	30.3	337 19.6	25.6	23 06.1	03.9	Alphard	217 49.1	S 8 45.7
U 11	15 14.8	303 57.5	25.0	269 26.8	30.2	352 21.5	25.8	38 08.4	03.8			
R 12	30 17.3	318 56.9	N24 25.5	284 27.8	N24 30.0	7 23.4	N 8 26.1	53 10.6	S11 03.7	Alphecca	126 04.6	N26 38.0
D 13	45 19.8	333 56.2	26.0	299 28.8	29.8	22 25.3	26.3	68 12.9	03.7	Alpheratz	357 36.6	N29 12.9
A 14	60 22.2	348 55.6	26.4	314 29.8	29.7	37 27.2	26.5	83 15.2	03.6	Altair	62 01.3	N 8 55.6
Y 15	75 24.7	3 55.0	.. 26.9	329 30.8	.. 29.5	52 29.1	.. 26.7	98 17.4	.. 03.5	Ankaa	353 08.9	S42 10.8
16	90 27.2	18 54.3	27.4	344 31.8	29.3	67 31.0	26.9	113 19.7	03.5	Antares	112 17.3	S26 29.0
17	105 29.6	33 53.7	27.9	359 32.8	29.1	82 32.9	27.2	128 21.9	03.4			
18	120 32.1	48 53.1	N24 28.3	14 33.8	N24 29.0	97 34.8	N 8 27.4	143 24.2	S11 03.3	Arcturus	145 48.9	N19 03.6
19	135 34.5	63 52.4	28.8	29 34.8	28.8	112 36.7	27.6	158 26.5	03.3	Atria	107 12.4	S69 04.0
20	150 37.0	78 51.8	29.3	44 35.8	28.6	127 38.6	27.8	173 28.7	03.2	Avior	234 15.3	S59 35.3
21	165 39.5	93 51.2	.. 29.7	59 36.8	.. 28.5	142 40.5	.. 28.0	188 31.0	.. 03.1	Bellatrix	278 24.7	N 6 22.2
22	180 41.9	108 50.5	30.2	74 37.8	28.3	157 42.4	28.3	203 33.3	03.1	Betelgeuse	270 53.8	N 7 24.6
23	195 44.4	123 49.9	30.6	89 38.8	28.1	172 44.3	28.5	218 35.5	03.0			
23 00	210 46.9	138 49.3	N24 31.1	104 39.8	N24 27.9	187 46.2	N 8 28.7	233 37.8	S11 02.9	Canopus	263 53.3	S52 42.7
01	225 49.3	153 48.7	31.6	119 40.8	27.8	202 48.1	28.9	248 40.1	02.8	Capella	280 24.4	N46 01.3
02	240 51.8	168 48.0	32.0	134 41.8	27.6	217 50.0	29.1	263 42.3	02.8	Deneb	49 26.8	N45 21.4
03	255 54.3	183 47.4	.. 32.5	149 42.8	.. 27.4	232 51.9	.. 29.4	278 44.6	.. 02.7	Denebola	182 26.2	N14 26.5
04	270 56.7	198 46.8	32.9	164 43.8	27.2	247 53.8	29.6	293 46.9	02.6	Diphda	348 49.1	S17 51.7
05	285 59.2	213 46.1	33.4	179 44.8	27.1	262 55.7	29.8	308 49.1	02.6			
06	301 01.7	228 45.5	N24 33.9	194 45.8	N24 26.9	277 57.6	N 8 30.0	323 51.4	S11 02.5	Dubhe	193 42.3	N61 37.7
07	316 04.1	243 44.9	34.3	209 46.8	26.7	292 59.5	30.2	338 53.7	02.4	Elnath	278 03.9	N28 37.6
S 08	331 06.6	258 44.2	34.8	224 47.8	26.5	308 01.4	30.5	353 55.9	02.4	Eltanin	90 42.6	N51 28.8
U 09	346 09.0	273 43.6	.. 35.2	239 48.8	.. 26.4	323 03.3	.. 30.7	8 58.2	.. 02.3	Enif	33 40.3	N 9 58.7
N 10	1 11.5	288 43.0	35.7	254 49.8	26.2	338 05.2	30.9	24 00.5	02.2	Fomalhaut	15 16.3	S29 30.0
D 11	16 14.0	303 42.3	36.1	269 50.8	26.0	353 07.1	31.1	39 02.8	02.2			
A 12	31 16.4	318 41.7	N24 36.6	284 51.8	N24 25.8	8 09.0	N 8 31.3	54 05.0	S11 02.1	Gacrux	171 52.7	S57 14.7
Y 13	46 18.9	333 41.1	37.0	299 52.8	25.7	23 10.9	31.6	69 07.3	02.0	Gienah	175 44.8	S17 39.4
14	61 21.4	348 40.4	37.5	314 53.8	25.5	38 12.8	31.8	84 09.6	02.0	Hadar	148 37.4	S60 29.1
15	76 23.8	3 39.8	.. 37.9	329 54.7	.. 25.3	53 14.7	.. 32.0	99 11.8	.. 01.9	Hamal	327 53.2	N23 34.2
16	91 26.3	18 39.2	38.3	344 55.7	25.1	68 16.6	32.2	114 14.1	01.8	Kaus Aust.	83 34.2	S34 22.4
17	106 28.8	33 38.5	38.8	359 56.7	25.0	83 18.5	32.4	129 16.4	01.8			
18	121 31.2	48 37.9	N24 39.2	14 57.7	N24 24.8	98 20.4	N 8 32.7	144 18.6	S11 01.7	Kochab	137 18.6	N74 03.5
19	136 33.7	63 37.3	39.7	29 58.7	24.6	113 22.3	32.9	159 20.9	01.6	Markab	13 31.6	N15 19.6
20	151 36.2	78 36.6	40.1	44 59.7	24.4	128 24.2	33.1	174 23.2	01.6	Menkar	314 08.0	N 4 10.7
21	166 38.6	93 36.0	.. 40.6	60 00.7	.. 24.2	143 26.1	.. 33.3	189 25.4	.. 01.5	Menkent	147 58.9	S36 29.1
22	181 41.1	108 35.4	41.0	75 01.7	24.1	158 28.0	33.5	204 27.7	01.4	Miaplacidus	221 38.4	S69 49.0
23	196 43.5	123 34.7	41.4	90 02.7	23.9	173 29.9	33.8	219 30.0	01.3			
24 00	211 46.0	138 34.1	N24 41.9	105 03.7	N24 23.7	188 31.8	N 8 34.0	234 32.2	S11 01.3	Mirfak	308 30.8	N49 56.6
01	226 48.5	153 33.5	42.3	120 04.7	23.5	203 33.7	34.2	249 34.5	01.2	Nunki	75 49.4	S26 16.1
02	241 50.9	168 32.8	42.7	135 05.7	23.4	218 35.6	34.4	264 36.8	01.1	Peacock	53 08.0	S56 39.4
03	256 53.4	183 32.2	.. 43.2	150 06.7	.. 23.2	233 37.5	.. 34.6	279 39.1	.. 01.1	Pollux	243 19.1	N27 58.3
04	271 55.9	198 31.6	43.6	165 07.7	23.0	248 39.4	34.8	294 41.3	01.0	Procyon	244 52.4	N 5 09.9
05	286 58.3	213 30.9	44.0	180 08.7	22.8	263 41.3	35.1	309 43.6	00.9			
06	302 00.8	228 30.3	N24 44.4	195 09.7	N24 22.6	278 43.2	N 8 35.3	324 45.9	S11 00.9	Rasalhague	95 59.7	N12 32.4
07	317 03.3	243 29.7	44.9	210 10.7	22.5	293 45.1	35.5	339 48.1	00.8	Regulus	207 35.8	N11 51.2
08	332 05.7	258 29.0	45.3	225 11.7	22.3	308 47.0	35.7	354 50.4	00.7	Rigel	281 05.5	S 8 10.6
M 09	347 08.2	273 28.4	.. 45.7	240 12.7	.. 22.1	323 48.9	.. 35.9	9 52.7	.. 00.7	Rigil Kent.	139 41.7	S60 55.8
O 10	2 10.6	288 27.8	46.2	255 13.7	21.9	338 50.8	36.2	24 54.9	00.6	Sabik	102 04.2	S15 45.3
N 11	17 13.1	303 27.1	46.6	270 14.6	21.7	353 52.7	36.4	39 57.2	00.5			
D 12	32 15.6	318 26.5	N24 47.0	285 15.6	N24 21.5	8 54.6	N 8 36.6	54 59.5	S11 00.5	Schedar	349 33.2	N56 39.7
A 13	47 18.0	333 25.9	47.4	300 16.6	21.4	23 56.5	36.8	70 01.8	00.4	Shaula	96 12.1	S37 07.2
Y 14	62 20.5	348 25.2	47.8	315 17.6	21.2	38 58.4	37.0	85 04.0	00.3	Sirius	258 27.7	S16 45.0
15	77 23.0	3 24.6	.. 48.3	330 18.6	.. 21.0	54 00.3	.. 37.3	100 06.3	.. 00.3	Spica	158 23.5	S11 17.0
16	92 25.4	18 23.9	48.7	345 19.6	20.8	69 02.2	37.5	115 08.6	00.2	Suhail	222 47.3	S43 31.8
17	107 27.9	33 23.3	49.1	0 20.6	20.6	84 04.1	37.7	130 10.8	00.1			
18	122 30.4	48 22.7	N24 49.5	15 21.6	N24 20.5	99 06.0	N 8 37.9	145 13.1	S11 00.1	Vega	80 34.0	N38 48.0
19	137 32.8	63 22.0	49.9	30 22.6	20.3	114 07.9	38.1	160 15.4	11 00.0	Zuben'ubi	136 57.3	S16 08.4
20	152 35.3	78 21.4	50.3	45 23.6	20.1	129 09.8	38.3	175 17.7	10 59.9		SHA	Mer. Pass.
21	167 37.8	93 20.8	.. 50.7	60 24.6	.. 19.9	144 11.7	.. 38.6	190 19.9	.. 59.9		° ′	h m
22	182 40.2	108 20.1	51.2	75 25.6	19.7	159 13.6	38.8	205 22.2	59.8	Venus	288 02.4	14 45
23	197 42.7	123 19.5	51.6	90 26.6	19.5	174 15.5	39.0	220 24.5	59.7	Mars	253 52.9	17 00
	h m									Jupiter	336 59.3	11 27
Mer. Pass. 9 55.2		v −0.6	d 0.4	v 1.0	d 0.2	v 1.9	d 0.2	v 2.3	d 0.1	Saturn	22 50.9	8 24

© British Crown Copyright 2022. All rights reserved.

SUN and MOON

UT	SUN GHA	SUN Dec	MOON GHA	v	MOON Dec	d	HP
d h	° ′	° ′	° ′	′	° ′	′	′
22 00	180 20.2	N12 02.2	158 12.4	10.1	N20 40.1	10.9	57.1
01	195 20.3	03.0	172 41.5	10.0	20 51.0	10.7	57.1
02	210 20.4	03.9	187 10.5	10.0	21 01.7	10.6	57.0
03	225 20.6 ..	04.7	201 39.5	10.0	21 12.3	10.5	57.0
04	240 20.7	05.6	216 08.5	9.9	21 22.8	10.4	57.0
05	255 20.8	06.4	230 37.4	9.9	21 33.2	10.2	57.0
06	270 20.9	N12 07.2	245 06.2	9.9	N21 43.4	10.1	56.9
S 07	285 21.0	08.1	259 35.1	9.7	21 53.5	10.0	56.9
A 08	300 21.2	08.9	274 03.8	9.8	22 03.5	9.9	56.9
T 09	315 21.3 ..	09.8	288 32.6	9.7	22 13.4	9.7	56.8
U 10	330 21.4	10.6	303 01.3	9.6	22 23.1	9.6	56.8
R 11	345 21.5	11.5	317 29.9	9.6	22 32.7	9.5	56.8
D 12	0 21.7	N12 12.3	331 58.5	9.6	N22 42.2	9.4	56.8
A 13	15 21.8	13.1	346 27.1	9.5	22 51.6	9.2	56.7
Y 14	30 21.9	14.0	0 55.6	9.5	23 00.8	9.1	56.7
15	45 22.0 ..	14.8	15 24.1	9.5	23 09.9	9.0	56.7
16	60 22.1	15.7	29 52.6	9.4	23 18.9	8.8	56.6
17	75 22.3	16.5	44 21.0	9.4	23 27.7	8.7	56.6
18	90 22.4	N12 17.3	58 49.4	9.3	N23 36.4	8.5	56.5
19	105 22.5	18.2	73 17.7	9.3	23 44.9	8.5	56.5
20	120 22.6	19.0	87 46.0	9.3	23 53.4	8.3	56.5
21	135 22.7 ..	19.9	102 14.3	9.2	24 01.7	8.1	56.5
22	150 22.9	20.7	116 42.5	9.2	24 09.8	8.0	56.5
23	165 23.0	21.5	131 10.7	9.2	24 17.8	7.9	56.4
23 00	180 23.1	N12 22.4	145 38.9	9.1	N24 25.7	7.8	56.4
01	195 23.2	23.2	160 07.0	9.2	24 33.5	7.6	56.4
02	210 23.3	24.0	174 35.2	9.0	24 41.1	7.4	56.3
03	225 23.4 ..	24.9	189 03.2	9.1	24 48.5	7.4	56.3
04	240 23.6	25.7	203 31.3	9.0	24 55.9	7.2	56.3
05	255 23.7	26.5	217 59.3	9.0	25 03.1	7.0	56.3
06	270 23.8	N12 27.4	232 27.3	8.9	N25 10.1	6.9	56.2
07	285 23.9	28.2	246 55.2	9.0	25 17.0	6.8	56.2
08	300 24.0	29.1	261 23.2	8.9	25 23.8	6.6	56.2
S 09	315 24.1 ..	29.9	275 51.1	8.8	25 30.4	6.5	56.1
U 10	330 24.3	30.7	290 18.9	8.9	25 36.9	6.3	56.1
N 11	345 24.4	31.6	304 46.8	8.8	25 43.2	6.2	56.1
D 12	0 24.5	N12 32.4	319 14.6	8.8	N25 49.4	6.1	56.1
A 13	15 24.6	33.2	333 42.4	8.8	25 55.5	5.9	56.0
Y 14	30 24.7	34.1	348 10.2	8.8	26 01.4	5.8	56.0
15	45 24.8 ..	34.9	2 38.0	8.7	26 07.2	5.6	56.0
16	60 25.0	35.7	17 05.7	8.8	26 12.8	5.5	55.9
17	75 25.1	36.5	31 33.5	8.7	26 18.3	5.3	55.9
18	90 25.2	N12 37.4	46 01.2	8.7	N26 23.6	5.2	55.9
19	105 25.3	38.2	60 28.9	8.7	26 28.8	5.0	55.9
20	120 25.4	39.0	74 56.6	8.6	26 33.8	4.9	55.8
21	135 25.5 ..	39.9	89 24.2	8.7	26 38.7	4.8	55.8
22	150 25.6	40.7	103 51.9	8.6	26 43.5	4.6	55.8
23	165 25.8	41.5	118 19.5	8.7	26 48.1	4.4	55.8
24 00	180 25.9	N12 42.4	132 47.2	8.6	N26 52.5	4.3	55.7
01	195 26.0	43.2	147 14.8	8.6	26 56.8	4.2	55.7
02	210 26.1	44.0	161 42.4	8.6	27 01.0	4.0	55.7
03	225 26.2 ..	44.8	176 10.0	8.6	27 05.0	3.9	55.6
04	240 26.3	45.7	190 37.6	8.6	27 08.9	3.7	55.6
05	255 26.4	46.5	205 05.2	8.6	27 12.6	3.6	55.6
06	270 26.6	N12 47.3	219 32.8	8.6	N27 16.2	3.4	55.6
07	285 26.7	48.1	234 00.4	8.6	27 19.6	3.3	55.5
08	300 26.8	49.0	248 28.0	8.6	27 22.9	3.1	55.5
M 09	315 26.9 ..	49.8	262 55.6	8.6	27 26.0	3.0	55.5
O 10	330 27.0	50.6	277 23.2	8.6	27 29.0	2.8	55.5
N 11	345 27.1	51.4	291 50.8	8.6	27 31.8	2.7	55.4
D 12	0 27.2	N12 52.3	306 18.4	8.6	N27 34.5	2.5	55.4
A 13	15 27.3	53.1	320 46.0	8.7	27 37.0	2.4	55.4
Y 14	30 27.4	53.9	335 13.7	8.6	27 39.4	2.3	55.4
15	45 27.6 ..	54.7	349 41.3	8.6	27 41.7	2.1	55.3
16	60 27.7	55.6	4 08.9	8.7	27 43.8	1.9	55.3
17	75 27.8	56.4	18 36.6	8.6	27 45.7	1.8	55.3
18	90 27.9	N12 57.2	33 04.2	8.7	N27 47.5	1.7	55.3
19	105 28.0	58.0	47 31.9	8.7	27 49.2	1.5	55.2
20	120 28.1	58.8	61 59.6	8.7	27 50.7	1.3	55.2
21	135 28.2	12 59.7	76 27.3	8.7	27 52.0	1.2	55.2
22	150 28.3	13 00.5	90 55.0	8.8	27 53.2	1.1	55.2
23	165 28.4	N13 01.3	105 22.8	8.7	N27 54.3	0.9	55.2
	SD 15.9	d 0.8	SD 15.5		15.3		15.1

Twilight / Sunrise / Moonrise

Lat.	Twilight Naut.	Twilight Civil	Sunrise	Moonrise 22	Moonrise 23	Moonrise 24	Moonrise 25
°	h m	h m	h m	h m	h m	h m	h m
N 72	////	////	02 52	□	□	□	□
N 70	////	01 33	03 17	□	□	□	□
68	////	02 14	03 35	02 44	□	□	□
66	////	02 42	03 50	03 33	□	□	□
64	01 21	03 02	04 02	04 04	03 41	□	□
62	01 58	03 19	04 12	04 27	04 24	04 23	04 36
60	02 23	03 32	04 21	04 46	04 54	05 10	05 48
N 58	02 43	03 44	04 29	05 02	05 16	05 41	06 23
56	02 58	03 54	04 36	05 15	05 34	06 04	06 49
54	03 12	04 02	04 42	05 27	05 50	06 23	07 09
52	03 23	04 10	04 47	05 38	06 03	06 39	07 26
50	03 33	04 17	04 52	05 47	06 15	06 53	07 41
45	03 53	04 31	05 02	06 07	06 40	07 21	08 11
N 40	04 08	04 43	05 11	06 23	07 00	07 43	08 34
35	04 21	04 52	05 19	06 36	07 16	08 02	08 53
30	04 31	05 00	05 25	06 48	07 31	08 18	09 09
20	04 47	05 14	05 36	07 09	07 55	08 45	09 37
N 10	04 59	05 24	05 46	07 27	08 16	09 08	10 01
0	05 09	05 34	05 55	07 44	08 36	09 30	10 23
S 10	05 18	05 42	06 04	08 01	08 56	09 52	10 46
20	05 25	05 51	06 13	08 19	09 18	10 15	11 09
30	05 31	05 59	06 24	08 40	09 43	10 43	11 37
35	05 34	06 04	06 30	08 53	09 58	10 59	11 54
40	05 37	06 09	06 37	09 07	10 15	11 18	12 13
45	05 40	06 14	06 45	09 24	10 36	11 41	12 36
S 50	05 43	06 21	06 54	09 46	11 02	12 10	13 06
52	05 44	06 23	06 58	09 56	11 15	12 25	13 21
54	05 45	06 26	07 03	10 08	11 30	12 42	13 38
56	05 46	06 30	07 09	10 21	11 47	13 02	13 58
58	05 47	06 33	07 14	10 36	12 08	13 27	14 24
S 60	05 48	06 37	07 21	10 55	12 35	14 02	15 00

Sunset / Twilight / Moonset

Lat.	Sunset	Twilight Civil	Twilight Naut.	Moonset 22	Moonset 23	Moonset 24	Moonset 25
°	h m	h m	h m	h m	h m	h m	h m
N 72	21 09	////	////	□	□	□	□
N 70	20 44	22 33	////	□	□	□	□
68	20 25	21 48	////	□	□	□	□
66	20 09	21 19	////	□	□	□	□
64	19 57	20 58	22 44	24 54	00 54	□	□
62	19 46	20 41	22 03	24 11	00 11	02 04	03 43
60	19 37	20 27	21 37	23 42	25 17	01 17	02 31
N 58	19 29	20 15	21 17	23 20	24 47	00 47	01 55
56	19 23	20 05	21 01	23 02	24 24	00 24	01 30
54	19 16	19 56	20 47	22 47	24 05	00 05	01 09
52	19 11	19 48	20 36	22 34	23 49	24 52	00 52
50	19 06	19 41	20 26	22 23	23 35	24 38	00 38
45	18 55	19 27	20 05	21 59	23 08	24 08	00 08
N 40	18 46	19 15	19 50	21 40	22 46	23 45	24 36
35	18 39	19 05	19 37	21 24	22 28	23 26	24 17
30	18 32	18 57	19 27	21 11	22 12	23 09	24 01
20	18 21	18 43	19 10	20 47	21 44	22 42	23 34
N 10	18 11	18 32	18 58	20 27	21 23	22 18	23 11
0	18 02	18 23	18 48	20 09	21 02	21 56	22 49
S 10	17 53	18 14	18 39	19 50	20 41	21 33	22 27
20	17 43	18 06	18 32	19 30	20 18	21 10	22 03
30	17 33	17 57	18 25	19 08	19 52	20 42	21 36
35	17 26	17 52	18 22	18 54	19 37	20 25	21 19
40	17 20	17 47	18 19	18 39	19 19	20 06	21 00
45	17 12	17 42	18 16	18 21	18 58	19 43	20 37
S 50	17 02	17 35	18 13	17 58	18 31	19 14	20 07
52	16 58	17 32	18 12	17 47	18 18	18 59	19 53
54	16 53	17 29	18 11	17 35	18 02	18 42	19 36
56	16 47	17 26	18 10	17 21	17 45	18 21	19 15
58	16 41	17 22	18 08	17 05	17 23	17 56	18 50
S 60	16 35	17 18	18 07	16 46	16 56	17 21	18 14

SUN and MOON data

Day	SUN Eqn. of Time 00h	SUN Eqn. of Time 12h	SUN Mer. Pass.	MOON Mer. Pass. Upper	MOON Mer. Pass. Lower	Age	Phase
d	m s	m s	h m	h m	h m	d	%
22	01 21	01 26	11 59	13 56	01 30	02	6
23	01 32	01 38	11 58	14 49	02 22	03	12
24	01 43	01 49	11 58	15 43	03 16	04	20

© British Crown Copyright 2022. All rights reserved.

UT	ARIES GHA	VENUS −4.1 GHA	Dec	MARS +1.3 GHA	Dec	JUPITER −2.0 GHA	Dec	SATURN +0.9 GHA	Dec	STARS Name	SHA	Dec
d h	° ′	° ′	° ′	° ′	° ′	° ′	° ′	° ′	° ′		° ′	° ′
25 00	212 45.1	138 18.9	N24 52.0	105 27.6	N24 19.4	189 17.4	N 8 39.2	235 26.7	S10 59.7	Acamar	315 13.3	S40 12.8
01	227 47.6	153 18.2	52.4	120 28.6	19.2	204 19.3	39.4	250 29.0	59.6	Achernar	335 21.8	S57 07.1
02	242 50.1	168 17.6	52.8	135 29.5	19.0	219 21.2	39.7	265 31.3	59.5	Acrux	173 01.1	S63 13.8
03	257 52.5	183 17.0 ..	53.2	150 30.5 ..	18.8	234 23.1 ..	39.9	280 33.6 ..	59.5	Adhara	255 07.1	S29 00.4
04	272 55.0	198 16.3	53.6	165 31.5	18.6	249 25.0	40.1	295 35.8	59.4	Aldebaran	290 41.6	N16 33.3
05	287 57.5	213 15.7	54.0	180 32.5	18.4	264 26.9	40.3	310 38.1	59.3			
06	302 59.9	228 15.1	N24 54.4	195 33.5	N24 18.2	279 28.8	N 8 40.5	325 40.4	S10 59.3	Alioth	166 13.7	N55 50.1
07	318 02.4	243 14.4	54.8	210 34.5	18.1	294 30.7	40.7	340 42.6	59.2	Alkaid	152 52.6	N49 11.8
08	333 04.9	258 13.8	55.2	225 35.5	17.9	309 32.6	41.0	355 44.9	59.1	Alnair	27 34.9	S46 50.8
09	348 07.3	273 13.1 ..	55.6	240 36.5 ..	17.7	324 34.5 ..	41.2	10 47.2 ..	59.1	Alnilam	275 39.4	S 1 11.3
10	3 09.8	288 12.5	56.0	255 37.5	17.5	339 36.4	41.4	25 49.5	59.0	Alphard	217 49.1	S 8 45.7
11	18 12.3	303 11.9	56.4	270 38.5	17.3	354 38.3	41.6	40 51.7	58.9			
12	33 14.7	318 11.2	N24 56.8	285 39.5	N24 17.1	9 40.2	N 8 41.8	55 54.0	S10 58.8	Alphecca	126 04.6	N26 38.0
13	48 17.2	333 10.6	57.2	300 40.5	16.9	24 42.1	42.1	70 56.3	58.8	Alpheratz	357 36.6	N29 12.9
14	63 19.6	348 10.0	57.6	315 41.5	16.7	39 44.0	42.3	85 58.6	58.7	Altair	62 01.3	N 8 55.6
15	78 22.1	3 09.3 ..	58.0	330 42.4 ..	16.6	54 45.9 ..	42.5	101 00.8 ..	58.7	Ankaa	353 08.9	S42 10.8
16	93 24.6	18 08.7	58.4	345 43.4	16.4	69 47.8	42.7	116 03.1	58.6	Antares	112 17.3	S26 29.0
17	108 27.0	33 08.1	58.7	0 44.4	16.2	84 49.7	42.9	131 05.4	58.6			
18	123 29.5	48 07.4	N24 59.1	15 45.4	N24 16.0	99 51.6	N 8 43.1	146 07.7	S10 58.5	Arcturus	145 48.9	N19 03.6
19	138 32.0	63 06.8	59.5	30 46.4	15.8	114 53.5	43.4	161 09.9	58.4	Atria	107 12.4	S69 04.0
20	153 34.4	78 06.2	24 59.9	45 47.4	15.6	129 55.4	43.6	176 12.2	58.4	Avior	234 15.4	S59 35.3
21	168 36.9	93 05.5	25 00.3	60 48.4 ..	15.4	144 57.3 ..	43.8	191 14.5 ..	58.3	Bellatrix	278 24.7	N 6 22.2
22	183 39.4	108 04.9	00.7	75 49.4	15.2	159 59.2	44.0	206 16.8	58.2	Betelgeuse	270 53.8	N 7 24.6
23	198 41.8	123 04.2	01.1	90 50.4	15.0	175 01.1	44.2	221 19.0	58.2			
26 00	213 44.3	138 03.6	N25 01.4	105 51.4	N24 14.9	190 03.0	N 8 44.4	236 21.3	S10 58.1	Canopus	263 53.3	S52 42.7
01	228 46.8	153 03.0	01.8	120 52.4	14.7	205 04.9	44.7	251 23.6	58.0	Capella	280 24.4	N46 01.3
02	243 49.2	168 02.3	02.2	135 53.3	14.5	220 06.8	44.9	266 25.9	58.0	Deneb	49 26.8	N45 21.4
03	258 51.7	183 01.7 ..	02.6	150 54.3 ..	14.3	235 08.7 ..	45.1	281 28.1 ..	57.9	Denebola	182 26.2	N14 26.5
04	273 54.1	198 01.1	03.0	165 55.3	14.1	250 10.6	45.3	296 30.4	57.8	Diphda	348 49.0	S17 51.6
05	288 56.6	213 00.4	03.3	180 56.3	13.9	265 12.5	45.5	311 32.7	57.8			
06	303 59.1	227 59.8	N25 03.7	195 57.3	N24 13.7	280 14.4	N 8 45.8	326 35.0	S10 57.7	Dubhe	193 42.3	N61 37.8
07	319 01.5	242 59.2	04.1	210 58.3	13.5	295 16.3	46.0	341 37.2	57.6	Elnath	278 03.9	N28 37.6
08	334 04.0	257 58.5	04.5	225 59.3	13.3	310 18.2	46.2	356 39.5	57.6	Eltanin	90 42.5	N51 28.8
09	349 06.5	272 57.9 ..	04.8	241 00.3 ..	13.1	325 20.1 ..	46.4	11 41.8 ..	57.5	Enif	33 40.3	N 9 58.7
10	4 08.9	287 57.2	05.2	256 01.3	12.9	340 22.0	46.6	26 44.1	57.4	Fomalhaut	15 16.3	S29 30.0
11	19 11.4	302 56.6	05.6	271 02.3	12.7	355 23.9	46.8	41 46.3	57.4			
12	34 13.9	317 56.0	N25 05.9	286 03.3	N24 12.6	10 25.8	N 8 47.1	56 48.6	S10 57.3	Gacrux	171 52.7	S57 14.8
13	49 16.3	332 55.3	06.3	301 04.2	12.4	25 27.7	47.3	71 50.9	57.2	Gienah	175 44.8	S17 40.4
14	64 18.8	347 54.7	06.7	316 05.2	12.2	40 29.6	47.5	86 53.2	57.2	Hadar	148 37.4	S60 29.1
15	79 21.2	2 54.1 ..	07.0	331 06.2 ..	12.0	55 31.5 ..	47.7	101 55.4 ..	57.1	Hamal	327 58.3	N23 34.2
16	94 23.7	17 53.4	07.4	346 07.2	11.8	70 33.4	47.9	116 57.7	57.1	Kaus Aust.	83 34.2	S34 22.3
17	109 26.2	32 52.8	07.8	1 08.2	11.6	85 35.3	48.1	132 00.0	57.0			
18	124 28.6	47 52.2	N25 08.1	16 09.2	N24 11.4	100 37.2	N 8 48.4	147 02.3	S10 56.9	Kochab	137 18.6	N74 03.5
19	139 31.1	62 51.5	08.5	31 10.2	11.2	115 39.1	48.6	162 04.6	56.9	Markab	13 31.5	N15 19.6
20	154 33.6	77 50.9	08.8	46 11.2	11.0	130 41.0	48.8	177 06.8	56.8	Menkar	314 08.0	N 4 10.7
21	169 36.0	92 50.2 ..	09.2	61 12.2 ..	10.8	145 42.9 ..	49.0	192 09.1 ..	56.7	Menkent	147 58.9	S36 29.1
22	184 38.5	107 49.6	09.6	76 13.1	10.6	160 44.8	49.2	207 11.4	56.7	Miaplacidus	221 38.4	S69 49.0
23	199 41.0	122 49.0	09.9	91 14.1	10.4	175 46.7	49.4	222 13.7	56.6			
27 00	214 43.4	137 48.3	N25 10.3	106 15.1	N24 10.2	190 48.6	N 8 49.7	237 15.9	S10 56.5	Mirfak	308 30.8	N49 56.6
01	229 45.9	152 47.7	10.6	121 16.1	10.0	205 50.5	49.9	252 18.2	56.5	Nunki	75 49.4	S26 16.0
02	244 48.4	167 47.1	11.0	136 17.1	09.8	220 52.4	50.1	267 20.5	56.4	Peacock	53 08.0	S56 39.4
03	259 50.8	182 46.4 ..	11.3	151 18.1 ..	09.6	235 54.3 ..	50.3	282 22.8 ..	56.3	Pollux	243 19.1	N27 58.3
04	274 53.3	197 45.8	11.7	166 19.1	09.4	250 56.2	50.5	297 25.1	56.3	Procyon	244 52.4	N 5 09.9
05	289 55.7	212 45.2	12.0	181 20.1	09.2	265 58.1	50.7	312 27.3	56.2			
06	304 58.2	227 44.5	N25 12.4	196 21.1	N24 09.0	281 00.0	N 8 51.0	327 29.6	S10 56.2	Rasalhague	95 59.7	N12 32.4
07	320 00.7	242 43.9	12.7	211 22.0	08.8	296 01.9	51.2	342 31.9	56.1	Regulus	207 35.8	N11 51.2
08	335 03.1	257 43.2	13.1	226 23.0	08.6	311 03.8	51.4	357 34.2	56.0	Rigel	281 05.5	S 8 10.6
09	350 05.6	272 42.6 ..	13.4	241 24.0 ..	08.4	326 05.7 ..	51.6	12 36.4 ..	56.0	Rigil Kent.	139 41.6	S60 55.9
10	5 08.1	287 42.0	13.7	256 25.0	08.3	341 07.6	51.8	27 38.7	55.9	Sabik	102 04.2	S15 45.3
11	20 10.5	302 41.3	14.1	271 26.0	08.1	356 09.5	52.0	42 41.0	55.8			
12	35 13.0	317 40.7	N25 14.4	286 27.0	N24 07.9	11 11.4	N 8 52.3	57 43.3	S10 55.8	Schedar	349 33.2	N56 39.7
13	50 15.5	332 40.1	14.8	301 28.0	07.7	26 13.3	52.5	72 45.6	55.7	Shaula	96 12.0	S37 07.2
14	65 17.9	347 39.4	15.1	316 29.0	07.5	41 15.3	52.7	87 47.8	55.6	Sirius	258 27.7	S16 45.0
15	80 20.4	2 38.8 ..	15.4	331 29.9 ..	07.3	56 17.2 ..	52.9	102 50.1 ..	55.6	Spica	158 23.5	S11 17.0
16	95 22.9	17 38.2	15.8	346 30.9	07.1	71 19.1	53.1	117 52.4	55.5	Suhail	222 47.3	S43 31.8
17	110 25.3	32 37.5	16.1	1 31.9	06.9	86 21.0	53.3	132 54.7	55.5			
18	125 27.8	47 36.9	N25 16.5	16 32.9	N24 06.7	101 22.9	N 8 53.6	147 57.0	S10 55.4	Vega	80 34.0	N38 48.0
19	140 30.2	62 36.3	16.8	31 33.9	06.5	116 24.8	53.8	162 59.2	55.3	Zuben'ubi	136 57.3	S16 08.4
20	155 32.7	77 35.6	17.1	46 34.9	06.3	131 26.7	54.0	178 01.5	55.3		SHA	Mer. Pass.
21	170 35.2	92 35.0 ..	17.5	61 35.9 ..	06.1	146 28.6 ..	54.2	193 03.8 ..	55.2		° ′	h m
22	185 37.6	107 34.3	17.8	76 36.9	05.9	161 30.5	54.4	208 06.1	55.1	Venus	284 19.3	14 48
23	200 40.1	122 33.7	18.1	91 37.8	05.7	176 32.4	54.6	223 08.4	55.1	Mars	252 07.1	16 55
Mer. Pass.	h m 9 43.5	v −0.6	d 0.4	v 1.0	d 0.2	v 1.9	d 0.2	v 2.3	d 0.1	Jupiter	336 18.7	11 18
										Saturn	22 37.0	8 13

© British Crown Copyright 2022. All rights reserved.

UT	SUN GHA	SUN Dec	MOON GHA	v	MOON Dec	d	HP
d h	° ′	° ′	° ′	′	° ′	′	′
25 00	180 28.5	N13 02.1	119 50.5	8.8	N27 55.2	0.8	55.1
01	195 28.7	02.9	134 18.3	8.8	27 56.0	0.6	55.1
02	210 28.8	03.8	148 46.1	8.9	27 56.6	0.5	55.1
03	225 28.9	04.6	163 14.0	8.8	27 57.1	0.4	55.1
04	240 29.0	05.4	177 41.8	8.9	27 57.5	0.2	55.1
05	255 29.1	06.2	192 09.7	8.9	27 57.7	0.0	55.0
06	270 29.2	N13 07.0	206 37.6	8.9	N27 57.7	0.1	55.0
07	285 29.3	07.8	221 05.5	9.0	27 57.6	0.2	55.0
08	300 29.4	08.7	235 33.5	9.0	27 57.4	0.4	55.0
09	315 29.5	09.5	250 01.5	9.0	27 57.0	0.5	55.0
10	330 29.6	10.3	264 29.5	9.1	27 56.5	0.6	54.9
11	345 29.7	11.1	278 57.6	9.1	27 55.9	0.8	54.9
12	0 29.8	N13 11.9	293 25.7	9.1	N27 55.1	1.0	54.9
13	15 30.0	12.7	307 53.8	9.2	27 54.1	1.1	54.9
14	30 30.1	13.6	322 22.0	9.2	27 53.0	1.2	54.9
15	45 30.2	14.4	336 50.2	9.2	27 51.8	1.4	54.8
16	60 30.3	15.2	351 18.4	9.3	27 50.4	1.5	54.8
17	75 30.4	16.0	5 46.7	9.4	27 48.9	1.6	54.8
18	90 30.5	N13 16.8	20 15.1	9.3	N27 47.3	1.8	54.8
19	105 30.6	17.6	34 43.4	9.4	27 45.5	1.9	54.8
20	120 30.7	18.4	49 11.8	9.5	27 43.6	2.1	54.7
21	135 30.8	19.2	63 40.3	9.5	27 41.5	2.2	54.7
22	150 30.9	20.1	78 08.8	9.5	27 39.3	2.3	54.7
23	165 31.0	20.9	92 37.3	9.6	27 37.0	2.5	54.7
26 00	180 31.1	N13 21.7	107 05.9	9.7	N27 34.5	2.6	54.7
01	195 31.2	22.5	121 34.6	9.7	27 31.9	2.7	54.7
02	210 31.3	23.3	136 03.3	9.7	27 29.2	2.9	54.7
03	225 31.4	24.1	150 32.0	9.8	27 26.3	3.0	54.6
04	240 31.5	24.9	165 00.8	9.8	27 23.3	3.1	54.6
05	255 31.6	25.7	179 29.6	9.9	27 20.2	3.3	54.6
06	270 31.7	N13 26.5	193 58.5	10.0	N27 16.9	3.4	54.6
07	285 31.8	27.3	208 27.5	10.0	27 13.5	3.5	54.6
08	300 31.9	28.1	222 56.5	10.0	27 10.0	3.6	54.6
09	315 32.0	29.0	237 25.5	10.1	27 06.4	3.8	54.5
10	330 32.1	29.8	251 54.6	10.2	27 02.6	4.0	54.5
11	345 32.2	30.6	266 23.8	10.2	26 58.6	4.0	54.5
12	0 32.3	N13 31.4	280 53.0	10.3	N26 54.6	4.2	54.5
13	15 32.4	32.2	295 22.3	10.3	26 50.4	4.3	54.5
14	30 32.5	33.0	309 51.6	10.4	26 46.1	4.4	54.5
15	45 32.6	33.8	324 21.0	10.5	26 41.7	4.6	54.5
16	60 32.7	34.6	338 50.5	10.5	26 37.1	4.6	54.5
17	75 32.8	35.4	353 20.0	10.6	26 32.5	4.8	54.5
18	90 32.9	N13 36.2	7 49.6	10.6	N26 27.7	5.0	54.4
19	105 33.0	37.0	22 19.2	10.7	26 22.7	5.0	54.4
20	120 33.1	37.8	36 48.9	10.8	26 17.7	5.2	54.4
21	135 33.2	38.6	51 18.7	10.8	26 12.5	5.3	54.4
22	150 33.3	39.4	65 48.5	10.9	26 07.2	5.4	54.4
23	165 33.4	40.2	80 18.4	10.9	26 01.8	5.5	54.4
27 00	180 33.5	N13 41.0	94 48.3	11.0	N25 56.3	5.6	54.4
01	195 33.6	41.8	109 18.3	11.1	25 50.7	5.8	54.4
02	210 33.7	42.6	123 48.4	11.1	25 44.9	5.9	54.4
03	225 33.8	43.4	138 18.5	11.2	25 39.0	6.0	54.4
04	240 33.9	44.2	152 48.7	11.3	25 33.0	6.1	54.3
05	255 34.0	45.0	167 19.0	11.3	25 26.9	6.2	54.3
06	270 34.1	N13 45.8	181 49.3	11.4	N25 20.7	6.4	54.3
07	285 34.2	46.6	196 19.7	11.5	25 14.3	6.4	54.3
08	300 34.3	47.4	210 50.2	11.5	25 07.9	6.6	54.3
09	315 34.4	48.2	225 20.7	11.6	25 01.3	6.7	54.3
10	330 34.5	49.0	239 51.3	11.7	24 54.6	6.8	54.3
11	345 34.6	49.8	254 22.0	11.7	24 47.8	6.9	54.3
12	0 34.7	N13 50.6	268 52.7	11.8	N24 40.9	7.0	54.3
13	15 34.8	51.4	283 23.5	11.8	24 33.9	7.1	54.3
14	30 34.9	52.2	297 54.3	11.9	24 26.8	7.2	54.3
15	45 35.0	53.0	312 25.2	12.0	24 19.6	7.3	54.3
16	60 35.1	53.8	326 56.2	12.1	24 12.3	7.5	54.3
17	75 35.2	54.6	341 27.3	12.1	24 04.8	7.5	54.3
18	90 35.3	N13 55.4	355 58.4	12.2	N23 57.3	7.7	54.3
19	105 35.4	56.2	10 29.6	12.3	23 49.6	7.7	54.3
20	120 35.5	57.0	25 00.9	12.3	23 41.9	7.9	54.3
21	135 35.6	57.7	39 32.2	12.4	23 34.0	8.0	54.2
22	150 35.7	58.5	54 03.6	12.4	23 26.0	8.0	54.2
23	165 35.8	59.3	68 35.0	12.5	N23 18.0	8.2	54.2
	SD 15.9	d 0.8	SD 15.0		14.9		14.8

Lat.	Twilight Naut.	Twilight Civil	Sunrise	Moonrise 25	Moonrise 26	Moonrise 27	Moonrise 28
°	h m	h m	h m	h m	h m	h m	h m
N 72	////	////	02 32	▢	▢	▢	▢
N 70	////	00 57	03 01	▢	▢	▢	▢
68	////	01 53	03 22	▢	▢	▢	▢
66	////	02 26	03 38	▢	▢	▢	08 26
64	00 49	02 49	03 52	▢	▢	06 57	09 05
62	01 40	03 07	04 03	04 36	06 04	07 50	09 32
60	02 09	03 22	04 13	05 48	06 56	08 22	09 53
N 58	02 31	03 35	04 21	06 23	07 27	08 46	10 09
56	02 49	03 46	04 28	06 49	07 51	09 05	10 24
54	03 03	03 55	04 35	07 09	08 10	09 21	10 36
52	03 15	04 03	04 41	07 26	08 26	09 34	10 47
50	03 26	04 11	04 46	07 41	08 40	09 46	10 56
45	03 47	04 26	04 58	08 11	09 08	10 11	11 16
N 40	04 03	04 38	05 07	08 34	09 30	10 31	11 33
35	04 17	04 48	05 15	08 53	09 49	10 47	11 46
30	04 27	04 57	05 22	09 09	10 04	11 01	11 58
20	04 45	05 11	05 34	09 37	10 31	11 25	12 18
N 10	04 58	05 23	05 45	10 01	10 54	11 46	12 36
0	05 09	05 33	05 54	10 23	11 15	12 05	12 52
S 10	05 18	05 43	06 04	10 46	11 37	12 24	13 08
20	05 26	05 52	06 14	11 09	11 59	12 45	13 25
30	05 33	06 01	06 26	11 37	12 26	13 08	13 45
35	05 36	06 06	06 32	11 54	12 42	13 22	13 57
40	05 40	06 12	06 40	12 13	13 00	13 38	14 10
45	05 43	06 18	06 48	12 36	13 21	13 57	14 25
S 50	05 47	06 25	06 59	13 06	13 49	14 21	14 44
52	05 48	06 28	07 03	13 21	14 02	14 32	14 53
54	05 50	06 32	07 08	13 38	14 18	14 45	15 03
56	05 51	06 35	07 14	13 58	14 36	15 00	15 15
58	05 53	06 39	07 21	14 24	14 58	15 17	15 28
S 60	05 55	06 44	07 28	15 00	15 27	15 38	15 43

Lat.	Sunset	Twilight Civil	Twilight Naut.	Moonset 25	Moonset 26	Moonset 27	Moonset 28
°	h m	h m	h m	h m	h m	h m	h m
N 72	21 29	////	////	▢	▢	▢	▢
N 70	20 59	23 15	////	▢	▢	▢	▢
68	20 37	22 09	////	▢	▢	▢	05 07
66	20 20	21 34	////	▢	▢	▢	04 56
64	20 06	21 10	23 21	▢	▢	04 27
62	19 55	20 51	22 21	03 43	04 04	04 03	04 00
60	19 45	20 36	21 50	02 31	03 12	03 31	03 38
N 58	19 36	20 23	21 27	01 55	02 41	03 06	03 21
56	19 29	20 12	21 10	01 30	02 17	02 47	03 06
54	19 22	20 02	20 55	01 09	01 58	02 31	02 53
52	19 16	19 54	20 42	00 52	01 41	02 17	02 42
50	19 11	19 46	20 31	00 38	01 27	02 04	02 32
45	18 59	19 31	20 10	00 08	00 59	01 39	02 11
N 40	18 49	19 18	19 53	24 36	00 36	01 19	01 54
35	18 41	19 08	19 40	24 17	00 17	01 02	01 39
30	18 34	18 59	19 29	24 01	00 01	00 47	01 26
20	18 22	18 45	19 11	23 34	24 22	00 22	01 05
N 10	18 11	18 33	18 58	23 11	24 00	00 00	00 46
0	18 01	18 23	18 47	22 49	23 40	24 28	00 28
S 10	17 52	18 13	18 38	22 27	23 19	24 10	00 10
20	17 41	18 04	18 30	22 03	22 57	23 51	24 43
30	17 30	17 54	18 22	21 36	22 32	23 29	24 25
35	17 23	17 49	18 19	21 19	22 17	23 16	24 15
40	17 16	17 43	18 15	21 00	21 59	23 00	24 03
45	17 07	17 37	18 12	20 37	21 38	22 42	23 48
S 50	16 56	17 30	18 08	20 07	21 11	22 20	23 30
52	16 52	17 27	18 06	19 53	20 58	22 09	23 22
54	16 46	17 23	18 05	19 36	20 42	21 56	23 13
56	16 40	17 20	18 03	19 15	20 24	21 42	23 02
58	16 34	17 15	18 02	18 50	20 03	21 25	22 50
S 60	16 26	17 11	18 00	18 14	19 34	21 05	22 35

	SUN	SUN	SUN	MOON	MOON	MOON	MOON
Day	Eqn. of Time 00h	Eqn. of Time 12h	Mer. Pass.	Mer. Pass. Upper	Mer. Pass. Lower	Age	Phase
d	m s	m s	h m	h m	h m	d	%
25	01 54	01 59	11 58	16 36	04 10	05	28
26	02 04	02 09	11 58	17 28	05 02	06	37
27	02 14	02 19	11 58	18 17	05 52	07	46

© British Crown Copyright 2022. All rights reserved.

UT	ARIES GHA	VENUS −4.1 GHA	Dec	MARS +1.3 GHA	Dec	JUPITER −2.1 GHA	Dec	SATURN +0.9 GHA	Dec
28 00	215 42.6	137 33.1	N25 18.4	106 38.8	N24 05.5	191 34.3	N 8 54.9	238 10.6	S10 55.0
01	230 45.0	152 32.4	.. 18.8	121 39.8	05.3	206 36.2	55.1	253 12.9	55.0
02	245 47.5	167 31.8	19.1	136 40.8	05.1	221 38.1	55.3	268 15.2	54.9
03	260 50.0	182 31.2	.. 19.4	151 41.8	.. 04.8	236 40.0	.. 55.5	283 17.5	.. 54.8
04	275 52.4	197 30.5	19.7	166 42.8	04.6	251 41.9	55.7	298 19.8	54.8
05	290 54.9	212 29.9	20.1	181 43.8	04.4	266 43.8	55.9	313 22.0	54.7
06	305 57.4	227 29.3	N25 20.4	196 44.8	N24 04.2	281 45.7	N 8 56.1	328 24.3	S10 54.6
07	320 59.8	242 28.6	20.7	211 45.7	04.0	296 47.6	56.4	343 26.6	54.6
08	336 02.3	257 28.0	21.0	226 46.7	03.8	311 49.5	56.6	358 28.9	54.5
F 09	351 04.7	272 27.4	.. 21.3	241 47.7	.. 03.6	326 51.4	.. 56.8	13 31.2	.. 54.5
R 10	6 07.2	287 26.7	21.6	256 48.7	03.4	341 53.3	57.0	28 33.5	54.4
I 11	21 09.7	302 26.1	22.0	271 49.7	03.2	356 55.2	57.2	43 35.7	54.3
D 12	36 12.1	317 25.5	N25 22.3	286 50.7	N24 03.0	11 57.1	N 8 57.4	58 38.0	S10 54.3
A 13	51 14.6	332 24.8	22.6	301 51.7	02.8	26 59.0	57.7	73 40.3	54.2
Y 14	66 17.1	347 24.2	22.9	316 52.6	02.6	42 00.9	57.9	88 42.6	54.1
15	81 19.5	2 23.5	.. 23.2	331 53.6	.. 02.4	57 02.8	.. 58.1	103 44.9	.. 54.1
16	96 22.0	17 22.9	23.5	346 54.6	02.2	72 04.7	58.3	118 47.2	54.0
17	111 24.5	32 22.3	23.8	1 55.6	02.0	87 06.6	58.5	133 49.4	54.0
18	126 26.9	47 21.6	N25 24.1	16 56.6	N24 01.8	102 08.5	N 8 58.7	148 51.7	S10 53.9
19	141 29.4	62 21.0	24.4	31 57.6	01.6	117 10.4	59.0	163 54.0	53.8
20	156 31.8	77 20.4	24.7	46 58.6	01.4	132 12.3	59.2	178 56.3	53.8
21	171 34.3	92 19.7	.. 25.1	61 59.5	.. 01.2	147 14.2	.. 59.4	193 58.6	.. 53.7
22	186 36.8	107 19.1	25.4	77 00.5	01.0	162 16.1	59.6	209 00.9	53.6
23	201 39.2	122 18.5	25.7	92 01.5	00.8	177 18.0	8 59.8	224 03.1	53.6
29 00	216 41.7	137 17.8	N25 26.0	107 02.5	N24 00.6	192 19.9	N 9 00.0	239 05.4	S10 53.5
01	231 44.2	152 17.2	26.3	122 03.5	00.3	207 21.8	00.2	254 07.7	53.5
02	246 46.6	167 16.6	26.6	137 04.5	24 00.1	222 23.7	00.5	269 10.0	53.4
03	261 49.1	182 15.9	.. 26.8	152 05.5	23 59.9	237 25.6	.. 00.7	284 12.3	.. 53.3
04	276 51.6	197 15.3	27.1	167 06.4	59.7	252 27.5	00.9	299 14.6	53.3
05	291 54.0	212 14.7	27.4	182 07.4	59.5	267 29.4	01.1	314 16.8	53.2
06	306 56.5	227 14.0	N25 27.7	197 08.4	N23 59.3	282 31.3	N 9 01.3	329 19.1	S10 53.1
07	321 59.0	242 13.4	28.0	212 09.4	59.1	297 33.2	01.5	344 21.4	53.1
S 08	337 01.4	257 12.8	28.3	227 10.4	58.9	312 35.1	01.7	359 23.7	53.0
A 09	352 03.9	272 12.1	.. 28.6	242 11.4	.. 58.7	327 37.0	.. 02.0	14 26.0	.. 53.0
T 10	7 06.3	287 11.5	28.9	257 12.4	58.5	342 38.9	02.2	29 28.3	52.9
U 11	22 08.8	302 10.9	29.2	272 13.3	58.3	357 40.9	02.4	44 30.5	52.8
R 12	37 11.3	317 10.2	N25 29.5	287 14.3	N23 58.0	12 42.8	N 9 02.6	59 32.8	S10 52.8
D 13	52 13.7	332 09.6	29.8	302 15.3	57.8	27 44.7	02.8	74 35.1	52.7
A 14	67 16.2	347 09.0	30.0	317 16.3	57.6	42 46.6	03.0	89 37.4	52.7
Y 15	82 18.7	2 08.3	.. 30.3	332 17.3	.. 57.4	57 48.5	.. 03.3	104 39.7	.. 52.6
16	97 21.1	17 07.7	30.6	347 18.3	57.2	72 50.4	03.5	119 42.0	52.6
17	112 23.6	32 07.1	30.9	2 19.2	57.0	87 52.3	03.7	134 44.3	52.5
18	127 26.1	47 06.4	N25 31.2	17 20.2	N23 56.8	102 54.2	N 9 03.9	149 46.5	S10 52.4
19	142 28.5	62 05.8	31.4	32 21.2	56.6	117 56.1	04.1	164 48.8	52.4
20	157 31.0	77 05.2	31.7	47 22.2	56.4	132 58.0	04.3	179 51.1	52.3
21	172 33.5	92 04.5	.. 32.0	62 23.2	.. 56.2	147 59.9	.. 04.5	194 53.4	.. 52.2
22	187 35.9	107 03.9	32.3	77 24.2	55.9	163 01.8	04.8	209 55.7	52.2
23	202 38.4	122 03.3	32.5	92 25.2	55.7	178 03.7	05.0	224 58.0	52.1
30 00	217 40.8	137 02.6	N25 32.8	107 26.1	N23 55.5	193 05.6	N 9 05.2	240 00.3	S10 52.0
01	232 43.3	152 02.0	33.1	122 27.1	55.3	208 07.5	05.4	255 02.5	52.0
02	247 45.8	167 01.4	33.4	137 28.1	55.1	223 09.4	05.6	270 04.8	51.9
03	262 48.2	182 00.7	.. 33.6	152 29.1	.. 54.9	238 11.3	.. 05.8	285 07.1	.. 51.9
04	277 50.7	197 00.1	33.9	167 30.1	54.7	253 13.2	06.0	300 09.4	51.8
05	292 53.2	211 59.5	34.2	182 31.1	54.4	268 15.1	06.3	315 11.7	51.7
06	307 55.6	226 58.9	N25 34.4	197 32.0	N23 54.2	283 17.0	N 9 06.5	330 14.0	S10 51.7
07	322 58.1	241 58.2	34.7	212 33.0	54.0	298 18.9	06.7	345 16.3	51.6
08	338 00.6	256 57.6	35.0	227 34.0	53.8	313 20.8	06.9	0 18.6	51.6
S 09	353 03.0	271 57.0	.. 35.2	242 35.0	.. 53.6	328 22.7	.. 07.1	15 20.8	.. 51.5
U 10	8 05.5	286 56.3	35.5	257 36.0	53.4	343 24.6	07.3	30 23.1	51.4
N 11	23 07.9	301 55.7	35.7	272 37.0	53.2	358 26.5	07.5	45 25.4	51.4
D 12	38 10.4	316 55.1	N25 36.0	287 37.9	N23 52.9	13 28.4	N 9 07.8	60 27.7	S10 51.3
A 13	53 12.9	331 54.4	36.3	302 38.9	52.7	28 30.3	08.0	75 30.0	51.3
Y 14	68 15.3	346 53.8	36.5	317 39.9	52.5	43 32.2	08.2	90 32.3	51.2
15	83 17.8	1 53.2	.. 36.8	332 40.9	.. 52.3	58 34.1	.. 08.4	105 34.6	.. 51.1
16	98 20.3	16 52.5	37.0	347 41.9	52.1	73 36.0	08.6	120 36.9	51.1
17	113 22.7	31 51.9	37.3	2 42.9	51.9	88 37.9	08.8	135 39.2	51.0
18	128 25.2	46 51.3	N25 37.5	17 43.8	N23 51.6	103 39.9	N 9 09.0	150 41.4	S10 51.0
19	143 27.7	61 50.7	37.8	32 44.8	51.4	118 41.8	09.2	165 43.7	50.9
20	158 30.1	76 50.0	38.0	47 45.8	51.2	133 43.7	09.5	180 46.0	50.8
21	173 32.6	91 49.4	.. 38.3	62 46.8	.. 51.0	148 45.6	.. 09.7	195 48.3	.. 50.8
22	188 35.1	106 48.8	38.5	77 47.8	50.8	163 47.5	09.9	210 50.6	50.7
23	203 37.5	121 48.1	38.8	92 48.8	50.6	178 49.4	10.1	225 52.9	50.7
Mer. Pass.	h m 9 31.7	v −0.6	d 0.3	v 1.0	d 0.2	v 1.9	d 0.2	v 2.3	d 0.1

STARS

Name	SHA	Dec
Acamar	315 13.3	S40 12.8
Achernar	335 21.8	S57 07.1
Acrux	173 01.1	S63 13.8
Adhara	255 07.2	S29 00.4
Aldebaran	290 41.6	N16 33.3
Alioth	166 13.7	N55 50.1
Alkaid	152 52.6	N49 11.8
Alnair	27 34.9	S46 50.8
Alnilam	275 39.4	S 1 11.3
Alphard	217 49.1	S 8 45.7
Alphecca	126 04.6	N26 38.1
Alpheratz	357 36.5	N29 12.9
Altair	62 01.3	N 8 55.6
Ankaa	353 08.9	S42 10.8
Antares	112 17.3	S26 29.0
Arcturus	145 48.9	N19 03.6
Atria	107 12.3	S69 04.0
Avior	234 15.4	S59 35.3
Bellatrix	278 24.7	N 6 22.2
Betelgeuse	270 53.9	N 7 24.6
Canopus	263 53.3	S52 42.7
Capella	280 24.4	N46 01.3
Deneb	49 26.8	N45 21.4
Denebola	182 26.2	N14 26.5
Diphda	348 49.0	S17 51.6
Dubhe	193 42.4	N61 37.8
Elnath	278 04.0	N28 37.6
Eltanin	90 42.5	N51 28.8
Enif	33 40.3	N 9 58.7
Fomalhaut	15 16.3	S29 29.9
Gacrux	171 52.8	S57 14.8
Gienah	175 44.8	S17 40.4
Hadar	148 37.4	S60 29.2
Hamal	327 53.2	N23 34.2
Kaus Aust.	83 34.2	S34 22.4
Kochab	137 18.6	N74 03.5
Markab	13 31.5	N15 19.6
Menkar	314 08.0	N 4 10.7
Menkent	147 58.9	S36 29.1
Miaplacidus	221 38.5	S69 49.0
Mirfak	308 30.8	N49 56.6
Nunki	75 49.4	S26 16.0
Peacock	53 07.9	S56 39.4
Pollux	243 19.1	N27 58.3
Procyon	244 52.4	N 5 09.9
Rasalhague	95 59.6	N12 32.4
Regulus	207 35.8	N11 51.2
Rigel	281 05.5	S 8 10.6
Rigil Kent.	139 41.6	S60 55.9
Sabik	102 04.2	S15 45.3
Schedar	349 33.2	N56 39.7
Shaula	96 12.0	S37 07.2
Sirius	258 27.7	S16 45.0
Spica	158 23.5	S11 17.1
Suhail	222 47.3	S43 31.8
Vega	80 34.0	N38 48.0
Zuben'ubi	136 57.3	S16 08.4

	SHA	Mer. Pass.
	° '	h m
Venus	280 36.1	14 51
Mars	250 20.8	16 51
Jupiter	335 38.2	11 09
Saturn	22 23.7	8 02

© British Crown Copyright 2022. All rights reserved.

SUN and MOON

UT	SUN GHA	SUN Dec	MOON GHA	v	MOON Dec	d	HP
d h	° ′	° ′	° ′	′	° ′	′	′
28 00	180 35.9	N14 00.1	83 06.5	12.6	N23 09.8	8.2	54.2
01	195 36.0	00.9	97 38.1	12.7	23 01.6	8.4	54.2
02	210 36.1	01.7	112 09.8	12.7	22 53.2	8.5	54.2
03	225 36.1	02.5	126 41.5	12.7	22 44.7	8.5	54.2
04	240 36.2	03.3	141 13.2	12.9	22 36.2	8.7	54.2
05	255 36.3	04.1	155 45.1	12.9	22 27.5	8.7	54.2
06	270 36.4	N14 04.9	170 17.0	13.0	N22 18.8	8.9	54.2
07	285 36.5	05.6	184 49.0	13.0	22 09.9	8.9	54.2
08	300 36.6	06.4	199 21.0	13.1	22 01.0	9.0	54.2
F 09	315 36.7	07.2	213 53.1	13.1	21 52.0	9.2	54.2
R 10	330 36.8	08.0	228 25.2	13.3	21 42.8	9.2	54.2
I 11	345 36.9	08.8	242 57.5	13.2	21 33.6	9.3	54.2
D 12	0 37.0	N14 09.6	257 29.7	13.4	N21 24.3	9.4	54.2
A 13	15 37.1	10.4	272 02.1	13.4	21 14.9	9.5	54.2
Y 14	30 37.2	11.2	286 34.5	13.5	21 05.4	9.6	54.2
15	45 37.3	11.9	301 07.0	13.5	20 55.8	9.6	54.2
16	60 37.3	12.7	315 39.5	13.6	20 46.2	9.8	54.2
17	75 37.4	13.5	330 12.1	13.6	20 36.4	9.8	54.3
18	90 37.5	N14 14.3	344 44.7	13.7	N20 26.6	10.0	54.3
19	105 37.6	15.1	359 17.4	13.8	20 16.6	10.0	54.3
20	120 37.7	15.9	13 50.2	13.8	20 06.6	10.1	54.3
21	135 37.8	16.6	28 23.0	13.9	19 56.5	10.2	54.3
22	150 37.9	17.4	42 55.9	14.0	19 46.3	10.2	54.3
23	165 38.0	18.2	57 28.9	14.0	19 36.1	10.4	54.3
29 00	180 38.1	N14 19.0	72 01.9	14.0	N19 25.7	10.4	54.3
01	195 38.2	19.8	86 34.9	14.1	19 15.3	10.5	54.3
02	210 38.2	20.6	101 08.0	14.2	19 04.8	10.6	54.3
03	225 38.3	21.3	115 41.2	14.2	18 54.2	10.7	54.3
04	240 38.4	22.1	130 14.4	14.3	18 43.5	10.7	54.3
05	255 38.5	22.9	144 47.7	14.3	18 32.8	10.8	54.3
06	270 38.6	N14 23.7	159 21.0	14.4	N18 22.0	10.9	54.3
07	285 38.7	24.5	173 54.4	14.4	18 11.1	11.0	54.3
S 08	300 38.8	25.2	188 27.8	14.5	18 00.1	11.1	54.3
A 09	315 38.9	26.0	203 01.3	14.5	17 49.0	11.1	54.3
T 10	330 38.9	26.8	217 34.8	14.6	17 37.9	11.2	54.3
U 11	345 39.0	27.6	232 08.4	14.6	17 26.7	11.3	54.4
R 12	0 39.1	N14 28.3	246 42.0	14.7	N17 15.4	11.3	54.4
D 13	15 39.2	29.1	261 15.7	14.7	17 04.1	11.4	54.4
A 14	30 39.3	29.9	275 49.4	14.8	16 52.7	11.5	54.4
Y 15	45 39.4	30.7	290 23.2	14.8	16 41.2	11.6	54.4
16	60 39.5	31.4	304 57.0	14.9	16 29.6	11.6	54.4
17	75 39.5	32.2	319 30.9	14.9	16 18.0	11.7	54.4
18	90 39.6	N14 33.0	334 04.8	14.9	N16 06.3	11.8	54.4
19	105 39.7	33.8	348 38.7	15.0	15 54.5	11.8	54.4
20	120 39.8	34.5	3 12.7	15.1	15 42.7	11.9	54.4
21	135 39.9	35.3	17 46.8	15.0	15 30.8	12.0	54.5
22	150 40.0	36.1	32 20.8	15.2	15 18.8	12.0	54.5
23	165 40.1	36.9	46 55.0	15.1	15 06.8	12.1	54.5
30 00	180 40.1	N14 37.6	61 29.1	15.2	N14 54.7	12.2	54.5
01	195 40.2	38.4	76 03.3	15.3	14 42.5	12.2	54.5
02	210 40.3	39.2	90 37.6	15.2	14 30.3	12.3	54.5
03	225 40.4	39.9	105 11.8	15.3	14 18.0	12.3	54.5
04	240 40.5	40.7	119 46.1	15.4	14 05.7	12.4	54.5
05	255 40.6	41.5	134 20.5	15.4	13 53.3	12.5	54.6
06	270 40.6	N14 42.2	148 54.9	15.4	N13 40.8	12.5	54.6
07	285 40.7	43.0	163 29.3	15.4	13 28.3	12.6	54.6
08	300 40.8	43.8	178 03.7	15.5	13 15.7	12.7	54.6
S 09	315 40.9	44.6	192 38.2	15.5	13 03.0	12.7	54.6
U 10	330 41.0	45.3	207 12.7	15.5	12 50.3	12.8	54.6
N 11	345 41.0	46.1	221 47.2	15.6	12 37.5	12.8	54.6
D 12	0 41.1	N14 46.9	236 21.8	15.6	N12 24.7	12.8	54.7
A 13	15 41.2	47.6	250 56.4	15.6	12 11.9	13.0	54.7
Y 14	30 41.3	48.4	265 31.0	15.7	11 58.9	13.0	54.7
15	45 41.4	49.2	280 05.7	15.7	11 45.9	13.0	54.7
16	60 41.4	49.9	294 40.4	15.7	11 32.9	13.1	54.7
17	75 41.5	50.7	309 15.1	15.7	11 19.8	13.1	54.7
18	90 41.6	N14 51.4	323 49.8	15.7	N11 06.7	13.2	54.7
19	105 41.7	52.2	338 24.5	15.8	10 53.5	13.3	54.8
20	120 41.8	53.0	352 59.3	15.8	10 40.2	13.2	54.8
21	135 41.8	53.7	7 34.1	15.8	10 27.0	13.4	54.8
22	150 41.9	54.5	22 08.9	15.8	10 13.6	13.4	54.8
23	165 42.0	55.3	36 43.7	15.9	N10 00.2	13.4	54.8
	SD 15.9	d 0.8	SD 14.8		14.8		14.9

Twilight / Sunrise / Moonrise

Lat.	Twilight Naut.	Twilight Civil	Sunrise	Moonrise 28	29	30	1
°	h m	h m	h m	h m	h m	h m	h m
N 72	////	////	02 11	▭	07 38	11 22	13 35
N 70	////	////	02 44	▭	09 25	11 46	13 45
68	////	01 29	03 08	▭	10 04	12 04	13 53
66	////	02 09	03 27	08 26	10 31	12 18	13 59
64	////	02 36	03 41	09 05	10 52	12 30	14 05
62	01 19	02 56	03 54	09 32	11 08	12 40	14 10
60	01 55	03 13	04 04	09 53	11 22	12 48	14 14
N 58	02 19	03 26	04 13	10 09	11 33	12 56	14 17
56	02 39	03 38	04 21	10 24	11 43	13 02	14 21
54	02 54	03 48	04 29	10 36	11 52	13 08	14 24
52	03 07	03 57	04 35	10 47	12 00	13 13	14 26
50	03 19	04 04	04 41	10 56	12 07	13 18	14 29
45	03 41	04 21	04 53	11 16	12 22	13 28	14 34
N 40	03 59	04 34	05 03	11 33	12 35	13 36	14 38
35	04 13	04 45	05 12	11 46	12 45	13 44	14 42
30	04 24	04 54	05 19	11 58	12 54	13 50	14 45
20	04 42	05 09	05 32	12 18	13 10	14 01	14 51
N 10	04 56	05 22	05 44	12 36	13 24	14 10	14 56
0	05 08	05 33	05 54	12 52	13 36	14 19	15 00
S 10	05 18	05 43	06 04	13 08	13 49	14 28	15 05
20	05 26	05 53	06 15	13 25	14 03	14 37	15 10
30	05 35	06 03	06 28	13 45	14 18	14 47	15 15
35	05 39	06 08	06 35	13 57	14 27	14 54	15 18
40	05 43	06 15	06 43	14 10	14 37	15 00	15 22
45	05 47	06 21	06 52	14 25	14 49	15 08	15 26
S 50	05 51	06 29	07 03	14 44	15 03	15 18	15 31
52	05 53	06 33	07 08	14 53	15 09	15 22	15 33
54	05 55	06 37	07 14	15 03	15 17	15 27	15 36
56	05 57	06 41	07 20	15 15	15 25	15 32	15 39
58	05 59	06 45	07 27	15 28	15 34	15 38	15 42
S 60	06 01	06 50	07 36	15 43	15 45	15 45	15 45

Sunset / Twilight / Moonset

Lat.	Sunset	Twilight Civil	Twilight Naut.	Moonset 28	29	30	1
°	h m	h m	h m	h m	h m	h m	h m
N 72	21 50	////	////	▭	07 33	05 18	04 34
N 70	21 15	////	////	▭	05 44	04 52	04 21
68	20 50	22 33	////	▭	05 03	04 33	04 11
66	20 31	21 50	////	05 07	04 35	04 17	04 02
64	20 16	21 22	////	04 27	04 14	04 04	03 55
62	20 03	21 01	22 43	04 00	03 56	03 53	03 49
60	19 52	20 45	22 04	03 38	03 42	03 43	03 43
N 58	19 43	20 31	21 39	03 21	03 29	03 35	03 39
56	19 35	20 19	21 19	03 06	03 19	03 27	03 34
54	19 28	20 09	21 03	02 53	03 09	03 21	03 30
52	19 21	20 00	20 49	02 42	03 01	03 15	03 27
50	19 15	19 52	20 38	02 32	02 53	03 09	03 23
45	19 03	19 35	20 15	02 11	02 36	02 58	03 16
N 40	18 52	19 22	19 57	01 54	02 23	02 48	03 10
35	18 44	19 11	19 43	01 39	02 11	02 39	03 05
30	18 36	19 01	19 31	01 26	02 01	02 32	03 01
20	18 23	18 46	19 13	01 05	01 44	02 19	02 53
N 10	18 11	18 33	18 59	00 46	01 28	02 08	02 45
0	18 01	18 22	18 47	00 28	01 14	01 57	02 39
S 10	17 50	18 12	18 37	00 10	00 59	01 46	02 32
20	17 39	18 02	18 28	24 43	00 43	01 35	02 25
30	17 27	17 52	18 20	24 25	00 25	01 21	02 16
35	17 20	17 46	18 16	24 15	00 15	01 13	02 12
40	17 12	17 40	18 12	24 03	00 03	01 05	02 06
45	17 02	17 33	18 07	23 48	24 54	00 54	02 00
S 50	16 51	17 25	18 03	23 30	24 41	00 41	01 52
52	16 46	17 21	18 01	23 22	24 35	00 35	01 48
54	16 40	17 17	17 59	23 13	24 29	00 29	01 44
56	16 34	17 13	17 57	23 02	24 21	00 21	01 40
58	16 26	17 09	17 55	22 50	24 13	00 13	01 35
S 60	16 18	17 03	17 53	22 35	24 04	00 04	01 29

SUN and MOON

Day	SUN Eqn. of Time 00h	SUN Eqn. of Time 12h	SUN Mer. Pass.	MOON Mer. Pass. Upper	MOON Mer. Pass. Lower	Age	Phase
d	m s	m s	h m	h m	h m	d	%
28	02 23	02 28	11 58	19 03	06 40	08	56
29	02 32	02 36	11 57	19 47	07 25	09	65
30	02 40	02 44	11 57	20 29	08 08	10	74

© British Crown Copyright 2022. All rights reserved.

UT	ARIES GHA	VENUS −4.2 GHA	Dec	MARS +1.3 GHA	Dec	JUPITER −2.1 GHA	Dec	SATURN +0.9 GHA	Dec	STARS Name	SHA	Dec
d h ° '	° '	° '	° '	° '	° '	° '	° '	° '	° '		° '	° '
1 00	218 40.0	136 47.5	N25 39.0	107 49.7	N23 50.3	193 51.3	N 9 10.3	240 55.2	S10 50.6	Acamar	315 13.3	S40 12.8
01	233 42.4	151 46.9	39.3	122 50.7	50.1	208 53.2	10.5	255 57.5	50.5	Achernar	335 21.8	S57 07.1
02	248 44.9	166 46.2	39.5	137 51.7	49.9	223 55.1	10.7	270 59.8	50.5	Acrux	173 01.1	S63 13.9
03	263 47.4	181 45.6 . .	39.7	152 52.7 . .	49.7	238 57.0 . .	11.0	286 02.0 . .	50.4	Adhara	255 07.2	S29 00.4
04	278 49.8	196 45.0	40.0	167 53.7	49.5	253 58.9	11.2	301 04.3	50.4	Aldebaran	290 41.6	N16 33.3
05	293 52.3	211 44.4	40.2	182 54.6	49.2	269 00.8	11.4	316 06.6	50.3			
06	308 54.8	226 43.7	N25 40.5	197 55.6	N23 49.0	284 02.7	N 9 11.6	331 08.9	S10 50.3	Alioth	166 13.7	N55 50.1
07	323 57.2	241 43.1	40.7	212 56.6	48.8	299 04.6	11.8	346 11.2	50.2	Alkaid	152 52.6	N49 11.9
08	338 59.7	256 42.5	40.9	227 57.6	48.6	314 06.5	12.0	1 13.5	50.1	Alnair	27 34.8	S46 50.8
M 09	354 02.2	271 41.8 . .	41.2	242 58.6 . .	48.4	329 08.4 . .	12.2	16 15.8 . .	50.1	Alnilam	275 39.4	S 1 11.3
O 10	9 04.6	286 41.2	41.4	257 59.6	48.1	344 10.3	12.5	31 18.1	50.0	Alphard	217 49.1	S 8 45.7
N 11	24 07.1	301 40.6	41.6	273 00.5	47.9	359 12.2	12.7	46 20.4	50.0			
D 12	39 09.5	316 40.0	N25 41.9	288 01.5	N23 47.7	14 14.1	N 9 12.9	61 22.7	S10 49.9	Alphecca	126 04.6	N26 38.1
A 13	54 12.0	331 39.3	42.1	303 02.5	47.5	29 16.0	13.1	76 25.0	49.8	Alpheratz	357 36.5	N29 12.9
Y 14	69 14.5	346 38.7	42.3	318 03.5	47.3	44 17.9	13.3	91 27.2	49.8	Altair	62 01.3	N 8 55.6
15	84 16.9	1 38.1 . .	42.6	333 04.5 . .	47.0	59 19.8 . .	13.5	106 29.5 . .	49.7	Ankaa	353 08.9	S42 10.8
16	99 19.4	16 37.5	42.8	348 05.4	46.8	74 21.7	13.7	121 31.8	49.7	Antares	112 17.3	S26 29.0
17	114 21.9	31 36.8	43.0	3 06.4	46.6	89 23.6	13.9	136 34.1	49.6			
18	129 24.3	46 36.2	N25 43.2	18 07.4	N23 46.4	104 25.5	N 9 14.2	151 36.4	S10 49.5	Arcturus	145 48.9	N19 03.6
19	144 26.8	61 35.6	43.5	33 08.4	46.1	119 27.4	14.4	166 38.7	49.5	Atria	107 12.3	S69 04.0
20	159 29.3	76 34.9	43.7	48 09.4	45.9	134 29.4	14.6	181 41.0	49.4	Avior	234 15.6	S59 35.3
21	174 31.7	91 34.3 . .	43.9	63 10.4 . .	45.7	149 31.3 . .	14.8	196 43.3 . .	49.4	Bellatrix	278 24.7	N 6 22.2
22	189 34.2	106 33.7	44.1	78 11.3	45.5	164 33.2	15.0	211 45.6	49.3	Betelgeuse	270 53.9	N 7 24.6
23	204 36.7	121 33.1	44.3	93 12.3	45.3	179 35.1	15.2	226 47.9	49.3			
2 00	219 39.1	136 32.4	N25 44.6	108 13.3	N23 45.0	194 37.0	N 9 15.4	241 50.2	S10 49.2	Canopus	263 53.4	S52 42.7
01	234 41.6	151 31.8	44.8	123 14.3	44.8	209 38.9	15.6	256 52.5	49.1	Capella	280 24.4	N46 01.3
02	249 44.0	166 31.2	45.0	138 15.3	44.6	224 40.8	15.9	271 54.8	49.1	Deneb	49 26.8	N45 21.4
03	264 46.5	181 30.6 . .	45.2	153 16.2 . .	44.4	239 42.7 . .	16.1	286 57.0 . .	49.0	Denebola	182 26.2	N14 26.5
04	279 49.0	196 29.9	45.4	168 17.2	44.1	254 44.6	16.3	301 59.3	49.0	Diphda	348 49.0	S17 51.6
05	294 51.4	211 29.3	45.6	183 18.2	43.9	269 46.5	16.5	317 01.6	48.9			
06	309 53.9	226 28.7	N25 45.8	198 19.2	N23 43.7	284 48.4	N 9 16.7	332 03.9	S10 48.8	Dubhe	193 42.4	N61 37.8
07	324 56.4	241 28.1	46.1	213 20.2	43.5	299 50.3	16.9	347 06.2	48.8	Elnath	278 04.0	N28 37.6
08	339 58.8	256 27.4	46.3	228 21.2	43.2	314 52.2	17.1	2 08.5	48.7	Eltanin	90 42.5	N51 28.8
T 09	355 01.3	271 26.8 . .	46.5	243 22.1 . .	43.0	329 54.1 . .	17.3	17 10.8 . .	48.7	Enif	33 40.3	N 9 58.7
U 10	10 03.8	286 26.2	46.7	258 23.1	42.8	344 56.0	17.6	32 13.1	48.6	Fomalhaut	15 16.3	S29 29.9
E 11	25 06.2	301 25.6	46.9	273 24.1	42.6	359 57.9	17.8	47 15.4	48.6			
S 12	40 08.7	316 24.9	N25 47.1	288 25.1	N23 42.3	14 59.8	N 9 18.0	62 17.7	S10 48.5	Gacrux	171 52.8	S57 14.8
D 13	55 11.2	331 24.3	47.3	303 26.1	42.1	30 01.7	18.2	77 20.0	48.4	Gienah	175 44.8	S17 40.4
A 14	70 13.6	346 23.7	47.5	318 27.0	41.9	45 03.6	18.4	92 22.3	48.4	Hadar	148 37.4	S60 29.2
Y 15	85 16.1	1 23.1 . .	47.7	333 28.0 . .	41.6	60 05.5 . .	18.6	107 24.6 . .	48.3	Hamal	327 53.2	N23 34.2
16	100 18.5	16 22.5	47.9	348 29.0	41.4	75 07.4	18.8	122 26.9	48.3	Kaus Aust.	83 34.2	S34 22.4
17	115 21.0	31 21.8	48.1	3 30.0	41.2	90 09.3	19.0	137 29.2	48.2			
18	130 23.5	46 21.2	N25 48.3	18 31.0	N23 41.0	105 11.3	N 9 19.3	152 31.5	S10 48.2	Kochab	137 18.6	N74 03.5
19	145 25.9	61 20.6	48.5	33 31.9	40.7	120 13.2	19.5	167 33.7	48.1	Markab	13 31.5	N15 19.6
20	160 28.4	76 20.0	48.7	48 32.9	40.5	135 15.1	19.7	182 36.0	48.0	Menkar	314 08.0	N 4 10.7
21	175 30.9	91 19.3 . .	48.9	63 33.9 . .	40.3	150 17.0 . .	19.9	197 38.3 . .	48.0	Menkent	147 58.9	S36 29.1
22	190 33.3	106 18.7	49.1	78 34.9	40.0	165 18.9	20.1	212 40.6	47.9	Miaplacidus	221 38.5	S69 49.0
23	205 35.8	121 18.1	49.3	93 35.9	39.8	180 20.8	20.3	227 42.9	47.9			
3 00	220 38.3	136 17.5	N25 49.4	108 36.8	N23 39.6	195 22.7	N 9 20.5	242 45.2	S10 47.8	Mirfak	308 30.8	N49 56.6
01	235 40.7	151 16.9	49.6	123 37.8	39.4	210 24.6	20.7	257 47.5	47.8	Nunki	75 49.3	S26 16.0
02	250 43.2	166 16.2	49.8	138 38.8	39.1	225 26.5	20.9	272 49.8	47.7	Peacock	53 07.9	S56 39.4
03	265 45.6	181 15.6 . .	50.0	153 39.8 . .	38.9	240 28.4 . .	21.2	287 52.1 . .	47.6	Pollux	243 19.2	N27 58.3
04	280 48.1	196 15.0	50.2	168 40.8	38.7	255 30.3	21.4	302 54.4	47.6	Procyon	244 52.4	N 5 09.9
05	295 50.6	211 14.4	50.4	183 41.7	38.4	270 32.2	21.6	317 56.7	47.5			
06	310 53.0	226 13.8	N25 50.6	198 42.7	N23 38.2	285 34.1	N 9 21.8	332 59.0	S10 47.5	Rasalhague	95 59.6	N12 32.4
07	325 55.5	241 13.1	50.7	213 43.7	38.0	300 36.0	22.0	348 01.3	47.4	Regulus	207 35.9	N11 51.2
08	340 58.0	256 12.5	50.9	228 44.7	37.7	315 37.9	22.2	3 03.6	47.4	Rigel	281 05.5	S 8 10.6
W 09	356 00.4	271 11.9 . .	51.1	243 45.7 . .	37.5	330 39.8 . .	22.4	18 05.9 . .	47.3	Rigil Kent.	139 41.6	S60 55.9
E 10	11 02.9	286 11.3	51.3	258 46.6	37.3	345 41.7	22.6	33 08.2	47.2	Sabik	102 04.1	S15 45.3
D 11	26 05.4	301 10.7	51.5	273 47.6	37.0	0 43.6	22.9	48 10.5	47.2			
N 12	41 07.8	316 10.0	N25 51.6	288 48.6	N23 36.8	15 45.5	N 9 23.1	63 12.8	S10 47.1	Schedar	349 33.2	N56 39.6
E 13	56 10.3	331 09.4	51.8	303 49.6	36.6	30 47.5	23.3	78 15.1	47.1	Shaula	96 12.0	S37 07.2
S 14	71 12.8	346 08.8	52.0	318 50.6	36.4	45 49.4	23.5	93 17.4	47.0	Sirius	258 27.7	S16 45.0
D 15	86 15.2	1 08.2 . .	52.2	333 51.5 . .	36.1	60 51.3 . .	23.7	108 19.7 . .	47.0	Spica	158 23.5	S11 17.1
A 16	101 17.7	16 07.6	52.3	348 52.5	35.9	75 53.2	23.9	123 22.0	46.9	Suhail	222 47.3	S43 31.8
Y 17	116 20.1	31 06.9	52.5	3 53.5	35.7	90 55.1	24.1	138 24.3	46.9			
18	131 22.6	46 06.3	N25 52.7	18 54.5	N23 35.4	105 57.0	N 9 24.3	153 26.6	S10 46.8	Vega	80 33.9	N38 48.0
19	146 25.1	61 05.7	52.8	33 55.5	35.2	120 58.9	24.5	168 28.9	46.7	Zuben'ubi	136 57.3	S16 08.4
20	161 27.5	76 05.1	53.0	48 56.4	34.9	136 00.8	24.8	183 31.2	46.7			
21	176 30.0	91 04.5 . .	53.2	63 57.4 . .	34.7	151 02.7 . .	25.0	198 33.5 . .	46.6		SHA	Mer. Pass.
22	191 32.5	106 03.9	53.3	78 58.4	34.5	166 04.6	25.2	213 35.8	46.6	Venus	276 53.3	14 54
23	206 34.9	121 03.2	53.5	93 59.4	34.2	181 06.5	25.4	228 38.1	46.5	Mars	248 34.2	16 46
Mer. Pass.	h m 9 19.9	v −0.6	d 0.2	v 1.0	d 0.2	v 1.9	d 0.2	v 2.3	d 0.1	Jupiter	334 57.9	11 00
										Saturn	22 11.0	7 51

© British Crown Copyright 2022. All rights reserved.

UT	SUN GHA	SUN Dec	MOON GHA	v	Dec	d	HP
d h	° ′	° ′	° ′	′	° ′	′	′
1 00	180 42.1	N14 56.0	51 18.6	15.9	N 9 46.8	13.5	54.8
01	195 42.2	56.8	65 53.5	15.8	9 33.3	13.5	54.9
02	210 42.2	57.5	80 28.3	15.9	9 19.8	13.6	54.9
03	225 42.3 ..	58.3	95 03.2	15.9	9 06.2	13.6	54.9
04	240 42.4	59.1	109 38.1	16.0	8 52.6	13.7	54.9
05	255 42.5	14 59.8	124 13.1	15.9	8 38.9	13.7	54.9
06	270 42.5	N15 00.6	138 48.0	15.9	N 8 25.2	13.8	55.0
07	285 42.6	01.3	153 22.9	16.0	8 11.4	13.7	55.0
08	300 42.7	02.1	167 57.9	16.0	7 57.7	13.9	55.0
M 09	315 42.8 ..	02.9	182 32.9	15.9	7 43.8	13.9	55.0
O 10	330 42.9	03.6	197 07.8	16.0	7 29.9	13.9	55.0
N 11	345 42.9	04.4	211 42.8	16.0	7 16.0	13.9	55.1
D 12	0 43.0	N15 05.1	226 17.8	16.0	N 7 02.1	14.0	55.1
A 13	15 43.1	05.9	240 52.8	16.0	6 48.1	14.0	55.1
Y 14	30 43.2	06.6	255 27.8	16.0	6 34.1	14.1	55.1
15	45 43.2 ..	07.4	270 02.8	16.0	6 20.0	14.1	55.1
16	60 43.3	08.1	284 37.8	16.0	6 05.9	14.1	55.2
17	75 43.4	08.9	299 12.8	16.0	5 51.8	14.2	55.2
18	90 43.5	N15 09.7	313 47.8	16.0	N 5 37.6	14.2	55.2
19	105 43.5	10.4	328 22.8	16.0	5 23.4	14.3	55.2
20	120 43.6	11.2	342 57.8	16.0	5 09.1	14.2	55.3
21	135 43.7 ..	11.9	357 32.8	15.9	4 54.9	14.3	55.3
22	150 43.7	12.7	12 07.7	16.0	4 40.6	14.4	55.3
23	165 43.8	13.4	26 42.7	16.0	4 26.2	14.3	55.3
2 00	180 43.9	N15 14.2	41 17.7	16.0	N 4 11.9	14.4	55.3
01	195 44.0	14.9	55 52.7	15.9	3 57.5	14.4	55.4
02	210 44.0	15.7	70 27.6	16.0	3 43.1	14.5	55.4
03	225 44.1 ..	16.4	85 02.6	15.9	3 28.6	14.5	55.4
04	240 44.2	17.2	99 37.5	15.9	3 14.1	14.5	55.4
05	255 44.3	17.9	114 12.4	15.9	2 59.6	14.5	55.5
06	270 44.3	N15 18.7	128 47.3	15.9	N 2 45.1	14.5	55.5
07	285 44.4	19.4	143 22.2	15.9	2 30.6	14.6	55.5
T 08	300 44.5	20.2	157 57.1	15.9	2 16.0	14.6	55.5
U 09	315 44.5 ..	20.9	172 32.0	15.8	2 01.4	14.6	55.6
E 10	330 44.6	21.6	187 06.8	15.8	1 46.8	14.6	55.6
S 11	345 44.7	22.4	201 41.6	15.8	1 32.2	14.7	55.6
D 12	0 44.8	N15 23.1	216 16.4	15.8	N 1 17.5	14.7	55.6
A 13	15 44.8	23.9	230 51.2	15.8	1 02.8	14.7	55.6
Y 14	30 44.9	24.6	245 26.0	15.7	0 48.1	14.7	55.7
15	45 45.0 ..	25.4	260 00.7	15.7	0 33.4	14.7	55.7
16	60 45.0	26.1	274 35.4	15.7	0 18.7	14.8	55.7
17	75 45.1	26.9	289 10.1	15.7	N 0 03.9	14.7	55.7
18	90 45.2	N15 27.6	303 44.8	15.6	S 0 10.8	14.8	55.8
19	105 45.2	28.3	318 19.4	15.6	0 25.6	14.8	55.8
20	120 45.3	29.1	332 54.0	15.6	0 40.4	14.8	55.8
21	135 45.4 ..	29.8	347 28.6	15.5	0 55.2	14.8	55.8
22	150 45.4	30.6	2 03.1	15.5	1 10.0	14.8	55.9
23	165 45.5	31.3	16 37.6	15.5	1 24.8	14.8	55.9
3 00	180 45.6	N15 32.1	31 12.1	15.4	S 1 39.6	14.9	55.9
01	195 45.6	32.8	45 46.5	15.4	1 54.5	14.8	56.0
02	210 45.7	33.5	60 20.9	15.4	2 09.3	14.8	56.0
03	225 45.8 ..	34.3	74 55.3	15.3	2 24.1	14.9	56.0
04	240 45.8	35.0	89 29.6	15.3	2 39.0	14.9	56.0
05	255 45.9	35.7	104 03.9	15.2	2 53.9	14.8	56.1
06	270 46.0	N15 36.5	118 38.1	15.2	S 3 08.7	14.9	56.1
W 07	285 46.0	37.2	133 12.3	15.2	3 23.6	14.8	56.1
E 08	300 46.1	38.0	147 46.5	15.1	3 38.4	14.9	56.1
D 09	315 46.2 ..	38.7	162 20.6	15.1	3 53.3	14.9	56.2
N 10	330 46.2	39.4	176 54.7	15.0	4 08.2	14.8	56.2
E 11	345 46.3	40.2	191 28.7	15.0	4 23.0	14.9	56.2
S 12	0 46.4	N15 40.9	206 02.7	14.9	S 4 37.9	14.8	56.2
D 13	15 46.4	41.6	220 36.6	14.9	4 52.7	14.9	56.3
A 14	30 46.5	42.4	235 10.5	14.8	5 07.6	14.8	56.3
Y 15	45 46.6 ..	43.1	249 44.3	14.8	5 22.4	14.9	56.3
16	60 46.6	43.8	264 18.1	14.7	5 37.3	14.8	56.4
17	75 46.7	44.6	278 51.8	14.7	5 52.1	14.8	56.4
18	90 46.7	N15 45.3	293 25.5	14.6	S 6 06.9	14.8	56.4
19	105 46.8	46.0	307 59.1	14.5	6 21.7	14.8	56.4
20	120 46.9	46.8	322 32.6	14.5	6 36.5	14.8	56.5
21	135 46.9 ..	47.5	337 06.1	14.5	6 51.3	14.8	56.5
22	150 47.0	48.2	351 39.6	14.3	7 06.1	14.7	56.5
23	165 47.1	49.0	6 12.9	14.3	S 7 20.8	14.8	56.5
	SD 15.9	d 0.7	SD 15.0		15.2		15.3

Lat.	Twilight Naut.	Twilight Civil	Sunrise	Moonrise 1	Moonrise 2	Moonrise 3	Moonrise 4
°	h m	h m	h m	h m	h m	h m	h m
N 72	////	////	01 46	13 35	15 37	17 44	20 07
N 70	////	////	02 27	13 45	15 38	17 34	19 43
68	////	00 59	02 54	13 53	15 38	17 27	19 24
66	////	01 51	03 15	13 59	15 39	17 21	19 10
64	////	02 22	03 31	14 05	15 39	17 15	18 58
62	00 52	02 45	03 45	14 10	15 39	17 11	18 48
60	01 39	03 03	03 56	14 14	15 39	17 07	18 39
N 58	02 07	03 17	04 06	14 17	15 39	17 04	18 32
56	02 28	03 30	04 15	14 21	15 39	17 00	18 25
54	02 45	03 41	04 22	14 24	15 40	16 58	18 19
52	02 59	03 50	04 29	14 26	15 40	16 55	18 14
50	03 12	03 59	04 35	14 29	15 40	16 53	18 09
45	03 36	04 16	04 48	14 34	15 40	16 48	17 59
N 40	03 54	04 30	04 59	14 38	15 40	16 44	17 51
35	04 09	04 41	05 09	14 42	15 41	16 41	17 44
30	04 21	04 51	05 17	14 45	15 41	16 38	17 37
20	04 40	05 07	05 30	14 51	15 41	16 33	17 27
N 10	04 55	05 21	05 42	14 56	15 41	16 28	17 17
0	05 07	05 32	05 54	15 00	15 42	16 24	17 09
S 10	05 18	05 43	06 05	15 05	15 42	16 20	17 00
20	05 27	05 53	06 16	15 10	15 42	16 15	16 51
30	05 36	06 05	06 29	15 15	15 43	16 11	16 41
35	05 41	06 11	06 37	15 18	15 43	16 08	16 35
40	05 45	06 17	06 46	15 22	15 43	16 05	16 28
45	05 50	06 25	06 56	15 26	15 43	16 01	16 20
S 50	05 55	06 33	07 08	15 31	15 44	15 57	16 11
52	05 57	06 37	07 13	15 33	15 44	15 55	16 07
54	05 59	06 41	07 19	15 36	15 44	15 52	16 02
56	06 02	06 46	07 26	15 39	15 44	15 50	15 57
58	06 04	06 51	07 34	15 42	15 44	15 47	15 51
S 60	06 07	06 57	07 43	15 45	15 45	15 44	15 45

Lat.	Sunset	Twilight Civil	Twilight Naut.	Moonset 1	Moonset 2	Moonset 3	Moonset 4
°	h m	h m	h m	h m	h m	h m	h m
N 72	22 15	////	////	04 34	04 00	03 28	02 54
N 70	21 32	////	////	04 21	03 56	03 32	03 06
68	21 03	23 08	////	04 11	03 53	03 35	03 16
66	20 42	22 08	////	04 02	03 50	03 37	03 24
64	20 25	21 36	////	03 55	03 47	03 39	03 31
62	20 11	21 12	23 14	03 49	03 45	03 41	03 37
60	20 00	20 54	22 20	03 43	03 43	03 43	03 43
N 58	19 50	20 39	21 50	03 39	03 41	03 44	03 47
56	19 41	20 26	21 28	03 34	03 40	03 45	03 51
54	19 33	20 15	21 11	03 30	03 38	03 47	03 55
52	19 26	20 05	20 56	03 27	03 37	03 48	03 59
50	19 20	19 57	20 44	03 23	03 36	03 49	04 02
45	19 06	19 39	20 19	03 16	03 34	03 51	04 09
N 40	18 55	19 25	20 01	03 10	03 31	03 52	04 15
35	18 46	19 13	19 46	03 05	03 30	03 54	04 20
30	18 38	19 03	19 34	03 01	03 28	03 55	04 24
20	18 24	18 47	19 14	02 53	03 25	03 58	04 32
N 10	18 12	18 34	18 59	02 45	03 22	04 00	04 39
0	18 00	18 22	18 47	02 39	03 20	04 02	04 45
S 10	17 49	18 11	18 36	02 32	03 17	04 04	04 51
20	17 38	18 00	18 27	02 25	03 15	04 06	04 58
30	17 24	17 49	18 18	02 16	03 12	04 08	05 06
35	17 17	17 43	18 13	02 12	03 10	04 09	05 11
40	17 08	17 36	18 08	02 06	03 08	04 11	05 16
45	16 58	17 29	18 04	02 00	03 06	04 13	05 22
S 50	16 46	17 20	17 58	01 52	03 03	04 15	05 29
52	16 40	17 16	17 56	01 48	03 01	04 16	05 33
54	16 34	17 12	17 54	01 44	03 00	04 17	05 36
56	16 27	17 07	17 51	01 40	02 58	04 18	05 40
58	16 19	17 02	17 49	01 35	02 57	04 19	05 45
S 60	16 11	16 56	17 46	01 29	02 55	04 21	05 50

	SUN Eqn. of Time 00ʰ	SUN Eqn. of Time 12ʰ	SUN Mer. Pass.	MOON Mer. Pass. Upper	MOON Mer. Pass. Lower	Age	Phase
Day	m s	m s	h m	h m	h m	d %	
d							
1	02 48	02 52	11 57	21 10	08 50	11 82	
2	02 55	02 59	11 57	21 52	09 31	12 89	◐
3	03 02	03 05	11 57	22 34	10 13	13 95	

© British Crown Copyright 2022. All rights reserved.

UT	ARIES GHA	VENUS −4.2 GHA	Dec	MARS +1.4 GHA	Dec	JUPITER −2.1 GHA	Dec	SATURN +0.9 GHA	Dec	STARS Name	SHA	Dec
4 00	221 37.4	136 02.6	N25 53.7	109 00.3	N23 34.0	196 08.4	N 9 25.6	243 40.4	S10 46.5	Acamar	315 13.3	S40 12.8
01	236 39.9	151 02.0	53.8	124 01.3	33.8	211 10.3	25.8	258 42.7	46.4	Achernar	335 21.8	S57 07.1
02	251 42.3	166 01.4	54.0	139 02.3	33.5	226 12.2	26.0	273 45.0	46.3	Acrux	173 01.1	S63 13.9
03	266 44.8	181 00.8 ..	54.1	154 03.3 ..	33.3	241 14.1 ..	26.2	288 47.3 ..	46.3	Adhara	255 07.2	S29 00.4
04	281 47.2	196 00.2	54.3	169 04.3	33.1	256 16.0	26.4	303 49.6	46.2	Aldebaran	290 41.6	N16 33.3
05	296 49.7	210 59.5	54.5	184 05.2	32.8	271 17.9	26.7	318 51.9	46.2			
06	311 52.2	225 58.9	N25 54.6	199 06.2	N23 32.6	286 19.9	N 9 26.9	333 54.2	S10 46.1	Alioth	166 13.7	N55 50.1
07	326 54.6	240 58.3	54.8	214 07.2	32.4	301 21.8	27.1	348 56.5	46.1	Alkaid	152 52.7	N49 11.9
T 08	341 57.1	255 57.7	54.9	229 08.2	32.1	316 23.7	27.3	3 58.8	46.0	Alnair	27 34.8	S46 50.8
H 09	356 59.6	270 57.1 ..	55.1	244 09.2 ..	31.9	331 25.6 ..	27.5	19 01.1 ..	46.0	Alnilam	275 39.4	S 1 11.3
U 10	12 02.0	285 56.5	55.2	259 10.1	31.6	346 27.5	27.7	34 03.4	45.9	Alphard	217 49.1	S 8 45.7
R 11	27 04.5	300 55.9	55.4	274 11.1	31.4	1 29.4	27.9	49 05.7	45.8			
S 12	42 07.0	315 55.2	N25 55.5	289 12.1	N23 31.2	16 31.3	N 9 28.1	64 08.0	S10 45.8	Alphecca	126 04.6	N26 38.1
D 13	57 09.4	330 54.6	55.7	304 13.1	30.9	31 33.2	28.3	79 10.3	45.7	Alpheratz	357 36.5	N29 12.9
A 14	72 11.9	345 54.0	55.8	319 14.1	30.7	46 35.1	28.5	94 12.6	45.7	Altair	62 01.2	N 8 55.6
Y 15	87 14.4	0 53.4 ..	56.0	334 15.0 ..	30.5	61 37.0 ..	28.8	109 14.9 ..	45.6	Ankaa	353 08.9	S42 10.7
16	102 16.8	15 52.8	56.1	349 16.0	30.2	76 38.9	29.0	124 17.2	45.6	Antares	112 17.2	S26 29.0
17	117 19.3	30 52.2	56.3	4 17.0	30.0	91 40.8	29.2	139 19.5	45.5			
18	132 21.7	45 51.6	N25 56.4	19 18.0	N23 29.7	106 42.7	N 9 29.4	154 21.8	S10 45.5	Arcturus	145 48.9	N19 03.6
19	147 24.2	60 51.0	56.5	34 18.9	29.5	121 44.6	29.6	169 24.1	45.4	Atria	107 12.3	S69 04.0
20	162 26.7	75 50.3	56.7	49 19.9	29.3	136 46.5	29.8	184 26.4	45.4	Avior	234 15.4	S55 35.3
21	177 29.1	90 49.7 ..	56.8	64 20.9 ..	29.0	151 48.4 ..	30.0	199 28.7 ..	45.3	Bellatrix	278 24.7	N 6 22.2
22	192 31.6	105 49.1	57.0	79 21.9	28.8	166 50.4	30.2	214 31.0	45.2	Betelgeuse	270 53.9	N 7 24.6
23	207 34.1	120 48.5	57.1	94 22.9	28.5	181 52.3	30.4	229 33.3	45.2			
5 00	222 36.5	135 47.9	N25 57.2	109 23.8	N23 28.3	196 54.2	N 9 30.7	244 35.6	S10 45.1	Canopus	263 53.4	S52 42.7
01	237 39.0	150 47.3	57.4	124 24.8	28.1	211 56.1	30.9	259 37.9	45.1	Capella	280 24.4	N46 01.3
02	252 41.5	165 46.7	57.5	139 25.8	27.8	226 58.0	31.1	274 40.2	45.0	Deneb	49 26.7	N45 21.4
03	267 43.9	180 46.1 ..	57.6	154 26.8 ..	27.6	241 59.9 ..	31.3	289 42.5 ..	45.0	Denebola	182 26.2	N14 26.5
04	282 46.4	195 45.5	57.8	169 27.7	27.3	257 01.8	31.5	304 44.8	44.9	Diphda	348 49.0	S17 51.6
05	297 48.9	210 44.9	57.9	184 28.7	27.1	272 03.7	31.7	319 47.1	44.9			
06	312 51.3	225 44.2	N25 58.0	199 29.7	N23 26.8	287 05.6	N 9 31.9	334 49.4	S10 44.8	Dubhe	193 42.4	N61 37.8
07	327 53.8	240 43.6	58.1	214 30.7	26.6	302 07.5	32.1	349 51.7	44.8	Elnath	278 04.0	N28 37.6
F 08	342 56.2	255 43.0	58.3	229 31.7	26.4	317 09.4	32.3	4 54.0	44.7	Eltanin	90 42.5	N51 28.9
R 09	357 58.7	270 42.4 ..	58.4	244 32.6 ..	26.1	332 11.3 ..	32.5	19 56.3 ..	44.6	Enif	33 40.2	N 9 58.7
I 10	13 01.2	285 41.8	58.5	259 33.6	25.9	347 13.2	32.8	34 58.6	44.6	Fomalhaut	15 16.3	S29 29.9
D 11	28 03.6	300 41.2	58.6	274 34.6	25.6	2 15.1	33.0	50 00.9	44.5			
A 12	43 06.1	315 40.6	N25 58.8	289 35.6	N23 25.4	17 17.0	N 9 33.2	65 03.2	S10 44.5	Gacrux	171 52.8	S57 14.8
Y 13	58 08.6	330 40.0	58.9	304 36.5	25.1	32 19.0	33.4	80 05.5	44.4	Gienah	175 44.8	S17 40.4
14	73 11.0	345 39.4	59.0	319 37.5	24.9	47 20.9	33.6	95 07.8	44.4	Hadar	148 37.4	S60 29.2
15	88 13.5	0 38.8 ..	59.1	334 38.5 ..	24.7	62 22.8 ..	33.8	110 10.1 ..	44.3	Hamal	327 53.2	N23 34.2
16	103 16.0	15 38.2	59.2	349 39.5	24.4	77 24.7	34.0	125 12.4	44.3	Kaus Aust.	83 34.1	S34 22.4
17	118 18.4	30 37.6	59.3	4 40.5	24.2	92 26.6	34.2	140 14.7	44.2			
18	133 20.9	45 37.0	N25 59.5	19 41.4	N23 23.9	107 28.5	N 9 34.4	155 17.0	S10 44.2	Kochab	137 18.6	N74 03.6
19	148 23.3	60 36.4	59.6	34 42.4	23.7	122 30.4	34.6	170 19.3	44.1	Markab	13 31.5	N15 19.6
20	163 25.8	75 35.7	59.7	49 43.4	23.4	137 32.3	34.8	185 21.6	44.1	Menkar	314 08.0	N 4 10.7
21	178 28.3	90 35.1 ..	59.8	64 44.4 ..	23.2	152 34.2 ..	35.1	200 23.9 ..	44.0	Menkent	147 58.9	S36 29.2
22	193 30.7	105 34.5	25 59.9	79 45.3	22.9	167 36.1	35.3	215 26.2	43.9	Miaplacidus	221 38.6	S69 49.0
23	208 33.2	120 33.9	26 00.0	94 46.3	22.7	182 38.0	35.5	230 28.5	43.9			
6 00	223 35.7	135 33.3	N26 00.1	109 47.3	N23 22.4	197 39.9	N 9 35.7	245 30.9	S10 43.8	Mirfak	308 30.8	N49 56.6
01	238 38.1	150 32.7	00.2	124 48.3	22.2	212 41.8	35.9	260 33.2	43.8	Nunki	75 49.3	S26 16.0
02	253 40.6	165 32.1	00.3	139 49.3	21.9	227 43.8	36.1	275 35.5	43.7	Peacock	53 07.9	S56 39.4
03	268 43.1	180 31.5 ..	00.4	154 50.2 ..	21.7	242 45.7 ..	36.3	290 37.8 ..	43.7	Pollux	243 19.2	N27 58.3
04	283 45.5	195 30.9	00.5	169 51.2	21.5	257 47.6	36.5	305 40.1	43.6	Procyon	244 52.5	N 5 09.9
05	298 48.0	210 30.3	00.6	184 52.2	21.2	272 49.5	36.7	320 42.4	43.6			
06	313 50.5	225 29.7	N26 00.7	199 53.2	N23 21.0	287 51.4	N 9 36.9	335 44.7	S10 43.5	Rasalhague	95 59.6	N12 32.4
07	328 52.9	240 29.1	00.8	214 54.1	20.7	302 53.3	37.1	350 47.0	43.5	Regulus	207 35.9	N11 51.2
S 08	343 55.4	255 28.5	00.9	229 55.1	20.5	317 55.2	37.4	5 49.3	43.4	Rigel	281 05.5	S 8 10.8
A 09	358 57.8	270 27.9 ..	01.0	244 56.1 ..	20.2	332 57.1 ..	37.6	20 51.6 ..	43.4	Rigil Kent.	139 41.6	S60 55.9
T 10	14 00.3	285 27.3	01.1	259 57.1	20.0	347 59.0	37.8	35 53.9	43.3	Sabik	102 04.1	S15 45.3
U 11	29 02.8	300 26.7	01.2	274 58.0	19.7	3 00.9	38.0	50 56.2	43.3			
R 12	44 05.2	315 26.1	N26 01.3	289 59.0	N23 19.5	18 02.8	N 9 38.2	65 58.5	S10 43.2	Schedar	349 33.2	N56 39.6
D 13	59 07.7	330 25.5	01.4	305 00.0	19.2	33 04.7	38.4	81 00.8	43.1	Shaula	96 12.0	S37 07.2
A 14	74 10.2	345 24.9	01.5	320 01.0	19.0	48 06.6	38.6	96 03.1	43.1	Sirius	258 27.7	S16 45.0
Y 15	89 12.6	0 24.3 ..	01.6	335 02.0 ..	18.7	63 08.6 ..	38.8	111 05.4 ..	43.0	Spica	158 23.5	S11 17.0
16	104 15.1	15 23.7	01.7	350 02.9	18.5	78 10.5	39.0	126 07.7	43.0	Suhail	222 47.4	S43 31.8
17	119 17.6	30 23.1	01.8	5 03.9	18.2	93 12.4	39.2	141 10.1	42.9			
18	134 20.0	45 22.5	N26 01.9	20 04.9	N23 18.0	108 14.3	N 9 39.4	156 12.4	S10 42.9	Vega	80 33.9	N38 48.0
19	149 22.5	60 21.9	01.9	35 05.9	17.7	123 16.2	39.6	171 14.7	42.8	Zuben'ubi	136 57.3	S16 08.4
20	164 25.0	75 21.3	02.0	50 06.8	17.5	138 18.1	39.9	186 17.0	42.8			
21	179 27.4	90 20.7 ..	02.1	65 07.8 ..	17.2	153 20.0 ..	40.1	201 19.3 ..	42.7		SHA	Mer. Pass.
22	194 29.9	105 20.1	02.2	80 08.8	17.0	168 21.9	40.3	216 21.6	42.7	Venus	273 11.4	14 57
23	209 32.3	120 19.5	02.3	95 09.8	16.7	183 23.8	40.5	231 23.9	42.6	Mars	246 47.3	16 41
	h m									Jupiter	334 17.6	10 51
Mer. Pass. 9 08.1		v −0.6 d 0.1		v 1.0 d 0.2		v 1.9 d 0.2		v 2.3 d 0.1		Saturn	21 59.0	7 40

© British Crown Copyright 2022. All rights reserved.

SUN / MOON

UT	SUN GHA	Dec	MOON GHA	v	Dec	d	HP
d h	° ′	° ′	° ′	′	° ′	′	′
4 00	180 47.1	N15 49.7	20 46.2	14.3	S 7 35.6	14.7	56.6
01	195 47.2	50.4	35 19.5	14.2	7 50.3	14.7	56.6
02	210 47.2	51.1	49 52.7	14.1	8 05.0	14.7	56.6
03	225 47.3 . .	51.9	64 25.8	14.0	8 19.7	14.6	56.6
04	240 47.4	52.6	78 58.8	14.0	8 34.3	14.7	56.7
05	255 47.5	53.3	93 31.8	13.9	8 49.0	14.6	56.7
06	270 47.5	N15 54.1	108 04.7	13.9	S 9 03.6	14.6	56.7
07	285 47.5	54.8	122 37.6	13.8	9 18.2	14.6	56.7
08	300 47.6	55.5	137 10.4	13.7	9 32.8	14.5	56.8
09	315 47.7 . .	56.2	151 43.1	13.6	9 47.3	14.5	56.8
10	330 47.7	57.0	166 15.7	13.5	10 01.8	14.5	56.8
11	345 47.8	57.7	180 48.2	13.5	10 16.3	14.4	56.9
12	0 47.8	N15 58.4	195 20.7	13.4	S10 30.7	14.4	56.9
13	15 47.9	59.1	209 53.1	13.3	10 45.1	14.4	56.9
14	30 48.0	15 59.8	224 25.4	13.3	10 59.5	14.4	56.9
15	45 48.0	16 00.6	238 57.7	13.2	11 13.9	14.3	57.0
16	60 48.1	01.3	253 29.9	13.0	11 28.2	14.2	57.0
17	75 48.1	02.0	268 01.9	13.0	11 42.4	14.3	57.0
18	90 48.2	N16 02.7	282 33.9	13.0	S11 56.7	14.1	57.1
19	105 48.3	03.5	297 05.9	12.8	12 10.8	14.2	57.1
20	120 48.3	04.2	311 37.7	12.7	12 25.0	14.1	57.1
21	135 48.4 . .	04.9	326 09.4	12.7	12 39.1	14.1	57.1
22	150 48.4	05.6	340 41.1	12.6	12 53.2	14.0	57.2
23	165 48.5	06.3	355 12.7	12.5	13 07.2	13.9	57.2
5 00	180 48.5	N16 07.1	9 44.2	12.4	S13 21.1	13.9	57.2
01	195 48.6	07.8	24 15.6	12.3	13 35.0	13.9	57.2
02	210 48.6	08.5	38 46.9	12.2	13 48.9	13.8	57.3
03	225 48.7 . .	09.2	53 18.1	12.1	14 02.7	13.8	57.3
04	240 48.8	09.9	67 49.2	12.0	14 16.5	13.7	57.3
05	255 48.8	10.6	82 20.2	12.0	14 30.2	13.6	57.4
06	270 48.9	N16 11.4	96 51.2	11.8	S14 43.8	13.6	57.4
07	285 48.9	12.1	111 22.0	11.8	14 57.4	13.5	57.4
08	300 49.0	12.8	125 52.8	11.6	15 10.9	13.5	57.4
09	315 49.0 . .	13.5	140 23.4	11.6	15 24.4	13.4	57.5
10	330 49.1	14.2	154 54.0	11.4	15 37.8	13.3	57.5
11	345 49.1	14.9	169 24.4	11.4	15 51.1	13.3	57.5
12	0 49.2	N16 15.6	183 54.8	11.2	S16 04.4	13.1	57.5
13	15 49.2	16.3	198 25.0	11.2	16 17.5	13.2	57.6
14	30 49.3	17.1	212 55.2	11.0	16 30.7	13.0	57.6
15	45 49.4 . .	17.8	227 25.2	11.0	16 43.7	13.0	57.6
16	60 49.4	18.5	241 55.2	10.8	16 56.7	12.9	57.6
17	75 49.5	19.2	256 25.0	10.8	17 09.6	12.9	57.7
18	90 49.5	N16 19.9	270 54.8	10.6	S17 22.5	12.7	57.7
19	105 49.6	20.6	285 24.4	10.5	17 35.2	12.7	57.7
20	120 49.6	21.3	299 53.9	10.5	17 47.9	12.6	57.7
21	135 49.7 . .	22.0	314 23.4	10.3	18 00.5	12.5	57.8
22	150 49.7	22.7	328 52.7	10.2	18 13.0	12.4	57.8
23	165 49.8	23.4	343 21.9	10.1	18 25.4	12.3	57.8
6 00	180 49.8	N16 24.2	357 51.0	10.0	S18 37.7	12.3	57.8
01	195 49.9	24.9	12 20.0	9.9	18 50.0	12.1	57.9
02	210 49.9	25.6	26 48.9	9.7	19 02.1	12.1	57.9
03	225 50.0 . .	26.3	41 17.6	9.7	19 14.2	12.0	57.9
04	240 50.0	27.0	55 46.3	9.6	19 26.2	11.9	57.9
05	255 50.1	27.7	70 14.9	9.4	19 38.1	11.7	58.0
06	270 50.1	N16 28.4	84 43.3	9.3	S19 49.8	11.7	58.0
07	285 50.2	29.1	99 11.6	9.3	20 01.5	11.6	58.0
08	300 50.2	29.8	113 39.9	9.1	20 13.1	11.5	58.0
09	315 50.2 . .	30.5	128 08.0	9.0	20 24.6	11.4	58.0
10	330 50.3	31.2	142 36.0	8.9	20 36.0	11.2	58.1
11	345 50.3	31.9	157 03.9	8.7	20 47.2	11.2	58.1
12	0 50.4	N16 32.6	171 31.6	8.7	S20 58.4	11.1	58.1
13	15 50.4	33.3	185 59.3	8.6	21 09.5	10.9	58.1
14	30 50.5	34.0	200 26.9	8.4	21 20.4	10.8	58.2
15	45 50.5 . .	34.7	214 54.3	8.3	21 31.2	10.8	58.2
16	60 50.6	35.4	229 21.6	8.3	21 42.0	10.6	58.2
17	75 50.6	36.1	243 48.9	8.1	21 52.6	10.4	58.2
18	90 50.7	N16 36.8	258 16.0	8.0	S22 03.0	10.4	58.2
19	105 50.7	37.5	272 43.0	7.8	22 13.4	10.2	58.3
20	120 50.8	38.2	287 09.8	7.8	22 23.6	10.2	58.3
21	135 50.8 . .	38.9	301 36.6	7.7	22 33.8	10.0	58.3
22	150 50.9	39.6	316 03.3	7.5	22 43.8	9.8	58.3
23	165 50.9	40.3	330 29.8	7.5	S22 53.6	9.8	58.3
	SD 15.9	d 0.7	SD 15.5		15.7		15.8

Twilight / Moonrise

Lat.	Naut.	Civil	Sunrise	Moonrise 4	5	6	7
°	h m	h m	h m	h m	h m	h m	h m
N 72	////	////	01 17	20 07	■■■■	■■■■	■■■■
N 70	////	////	02 08	19 43	22 32	■■■■	■■■■
68	////	////	02 40	19 24	21 44	■■■■	■■■■
66	////	01 31	03 03	19 10	21 13	23 57	■■■■
64	////	02 07	03 21	18 58	20 51	23 01	■■■■
62	////	02 33	03 36	18 48	20 33	22 28	24 35
60	01 21	02 53	03 48	18 39	20 18	22 04	23 52
N 58	01 54	03 09	03 59	18 32	20 06	21 45	23 24
56	02 18	03 22	04 08	18 25	19 55	21 29	23 02
54	02 36	03 34	04 16	18 19	19 46	21 15	22 44
52	02 52	03 44	04 24	18 14	19 37	21 03	22 29
50	03 05	03 53	04 30	18 09	19 30	20 53	22 16
45	03 30	04 11	04 44	17 59	19 14	20 31	21 49
N 40	03 50	04 26	04 56	17 51	19 01	20 14	21 27
35	04 05	04 38	05 06	17 44	18 50	19 59	21 10
30	04 18	04 49	05 14	17 37	18 40	19 47	20 55
20	04 38	05 06	05 29	17 27	18 24	19 25	20 29
N 10	04 54	05 20	05 41	17 17	18 10	19 07	20 07
0	05 07	05 32	05 53	17 09	17 57	18 49	19 47
S 10	05 18	05 43	06 05	17 00	17 44	18 32	19 26
20	05 28	05 54	06 17	16 51	17 30	18 14	19 05
30	05 38	06 06	06 31	16 41	17 14	17 53	18 40
35	05 43	06 13	06 39	16 35	17 05	17 41	18 25
40	05 48	06 20	06 49	16 28	16 55	17 28	18 08
45	05 53	06 28	06 59	16 20	16 43	17 11	17 48
S 50	05 59	06 37	07 12	16 11	16 28	16 51	17 23
52	06 01	06 42	07 18	16 07	16 22	16 42	17 11
54	06 04	06 46	07 25	16 02	16 14	16 31	16 57
56	06 07	06 51	07 32	15 57	16 06	16 20	16 41
58	06 10	06 57	07 40	15 51	15 57	16 06	16 22
S 60	06 13	07 03	07 50	15 45	15 46	15 50	15 59

Twilight / Moonset

Lat.	Sunset	Civil	Naut.	Moonset 4	5	6	7
°	h m	h m	h m	h m	h m	h m	h m
N 72	22 47	////	////	02 54	02 05	■■■■	■■■■
N 70	21 50	////	////	03 06	02 32	01 25	■■■■
68	21 17	////	////	03 16	02 52	02 15	■■■■
66	20 53	22 29	////	03 24	03 08	02 46	01 54
64	20 35	21 50	////	03 31	03 22	03 10	02 51
62	20 20	21 23	////	03 37	03 33	03 29	03 25
60	20 07	21 03	22 39	03 43	03 43	03 45	03 50
N 58	19 56	20 47	22 03	03 47	03 51	03 58	04 09
56	19 47	20 33	21 38	03 51	03 59	04 10	04 26
54	19 38	20 21	21 19	03 55	04 06	04 20	04 40
52	19 31	20 11	21 04	03 59	04 12	04 29	04 52
50	19 24	20 02	20 50	04 02	04 17	04 37	05 03
45	19 10	19 43	20 24	04 09	04 29	04 54	05 26
N 40	18 58	19 28	20 04	04 15	04 39	05 09	05 45
35	18 48	19 16	19 49	04 20	04 48	05 21	06 00
30	18 40	19 05	19 36	04 24	04 56	05 32	06 14
20	18 25	18 48	19 16	04 32	05 09	05 50	06 37
N 10	18 12	18 34	19 00	04 39	05 20	06 06	06 57
0	18 00	18 22	18 47	04 45	05 31	06 21	07 16
S 10	17 48	18 10	18 35	04 51	05 42	06 36	07 35
20	17 36	17 59	18 25	04 58	05 54	06 53	07 55
30	17 22	17 47	18 15	05 06	06 07	07 12	08 19
35	17 14	17 40	18 10	05 11	06 15	07 23	08 33
40	17 04	17 33	18 05	05 16	06 24	07 35	08 49
45	16 54	17 25	18 00	05 22	06 34	07 50	09 08
S 50	16 41	17 15	17 54	05 29	06 47	08 09	09 32
52	16 35	17 11	17 51	05 33	06 53	08 18	09 44
54	16 28	17 06	17 49	05 36	07 00	08 28	09 57
56	16 21	17 01	17 46	05 40	07 07	08 39	10 13
58	16 12	16 56	17 43	05 45	07 16	08 52	10 31
S 60	16 03	16 49	17 40	05 50	07 25	09 07	10 54

SUN / MOON

Day	SUN Eqn. of Time 00h	12h	Mer. Pass.	MOON Mer. Pass. Upper	Lower	Age	Phase
d	m s	m s	h m	h m	h m	d	%
4	03 08	03 11	11 57	23 20	10 57	14	98
5	03 14	03 17	11 57	24 09	11 44	15	100
6	03 19	03 21	11 57	00 09	12 35	16	99

© British Crown Copyright 2022. All rights reserved.

UT	ARIES GHA	VENUS −4.2 GHA	Dec	MARS +1.4 GHA	Dec	JUPITER −2.1 GHA	Dec	SATURN +0.9 GHA	Dec	STARS Name	SHA	Dec
d h 7 00	224 34.8	135 18.9	N26 02.4	110 10.7	N23 16.5	198 25.7	N 9 40.7	246 26.2	S10 42.6	Acamar	315 13.3	S40 12.7
01	239 37.3	150 18.3	02.4	125 11.7	16.2	213 27.6	40.9	261 28.5	42.5	Achernar	335 21.8	S57 07.1
02	254 39.7	165 17.7	02.5	140 12.7	16.0	228 29.5	41.1	276 30.8	42.5	Acrux	173 01.1	S63 13.9
03	269 42.2	180 17.1 ..	02.6	155 13.7 ..	15.7	243 31.5 ..	41.3	291 33.1 ..	42.4	Adhara	255 07.2	S29 00.4
04	284 44.7	195 16.5	02.7	170 14.6	15.4	258 33.4	41.5	306 35.3	42.4	Aldebaran	290 41.6	N16 33.3
05	299 47.1	210 16.0	02.7	185 15.6	15.2	273 35.3	41.7	321 37.8	42.3			
06	314 49.6	225 15.4	N26 02.8	200 16.6	N23 14.9	288 37.2	N 9 41.9	336 40.1	S10 42.3	Alioth	166 13.7	N55 50.2
07	329 52.1	240 14.8	02.9	215 17.6	14.7	303 39.1	42.1	351 42.4	42.2	Alkaid	152 52.7	N49 11.9
08	344 54.5	255 14.2	03.0	230 18.6	14.4	318 41.0	42.4	6 44.7	42.2	Alnair	27 34.8	S46 50.8
09	359 57.0	270 13.6 ..	03.0	245 19.5 ..	14.2	333 42.9 ..	42.6	21 47.0 ..	42.1	Alnilam	275 39.4	S 1 11.3
10	14 59.5	285 13.0	03.1	260 20.5	13.9	348 44.8	42.8	36 49.3	42.1	Alphard	217 49.1	S 8 45.7
11	30 01.9	300 12.4	03.2	275 21.5	13.7	3 46.7	43.0	51 51.6	42.0			
12	45 04.4	315 11.8	N26 03.2	290 22.5	N23 13.4	18 48.6	N 9 43.2	66 53.9	S10 41.9	Alphecca	126 04.6	N26 38.1
13	60 06.8	330 11.2	03.3	305 23.4	13.2	33 50.5	43.4	81 56.2	41.9	Alpheratz	357 36.5	N29 12.9
14	75 09.3	345 10.6	03.4	320 24.4	12.9	48 52.4	43.6	96 58.5	41.8	Altair	62 01.2	N 8 55.6
15	90 11.8	0 10.0 ..	03.4	335 25.4 ..	12.6	63 54.4 ..	43.8	112 00.8 ..	41.8	Ankaa	353 08.9	S42 10.7
16	105 14.2	15 09.4	03.5	350 26.4	12.4	78 56.3	44.0	127 03.2	41.7	Antares	112 17.2	S26 29.0
17	120 16.7	30 08.8	03.6	5 27.3	12.1	93 58.2	44.2	142 05.5	41.7			
18	135 19.2	45 08.3	N26 03.6	20 28.3	N23 11.9	109 00.1	N 9 44.4	157 07.8	S10 41.6	Arcturus	145 48.9	N19 03.6
19	150 21.6	60 07.7	03.7	35 29.3	11.6	124 02.0	44.6	172 10.1	41.6	Atria	107 12.2	S69 04.0
20	165 24.1	75 07.1	03.7	50 30.3	11.4	139 03.9	44.8	187 12.4	41.5	Avior	234 15.5	S59 35.3
21	180 26.6	90 06.5 ..	03.8	65 31.2 ..	11.1	154 05.8 ..	45.1	202 14.7 ..	41.5	Bellatrix	278 24.7	N 6 22.2
22	195 29.0	105 05.9	03.8	80 32.2	10.9	169 07.7	45.3	217 17.0	41.4	Betelgeuse	270 53.9	N 7 24.6
23	210 31.5	120 05.3	03.9	95 33.2	10.6	184 09.6	45.5	232 19.3	41.4			
8 00	225 33.9	135 04.7	N26 03.9	110 34.2	N23 10.3	199 11.5	N 9 45.7	247 21.6	S10 41.3	Canopus	263 53.4	S52 42.7
01	240 36.4	150 04.1	04.0	125 35.1	10.1	214 13.4	45.9	262 24.0	41.3	Capella	280 24.4	N46 01.3
02	255 38.9	165 03.5	04.1	140 36.1	09.8	229 15.4	46.1	277 26.3	41.2	Deneb	49 26.7	N45 21.4
03	270 41.3	180 03.0 ..	04.1	155 37.1 ..	09.6	244 17.3 ..	46.3	292 28.6 ..	41.2	Denebola	182 26.2	N14 26.5
04	285 43.8	195 02.4	04.1	170 38.1	09.3	259 19.2	46.5	307 30.9	41.1	Diphda	348 49.0	S17 51.6
05	300 46.3	210 01.8	04.2	185 39.0	09.0	274 21.1	46.7	322 33.2	41.1			
06	315 48.7	225 01.2	N26 04.2	200 40.0	N23 08.8	289 23.0	N 9 46.9	337 35.5	S10 41.0	Dubhe	193 42.4	N61 37.8
07	330 51.2	240 00.6	04.3	215 41.0	08.5	304 24.9	47.1	352 37.8	41.0	Elnath	278 04.0	N28 37.6
08	345 53.7	255 00.0	04.3	230 42.0	08.3	319 26.8	47.3	7 40.1	40.9	Eltanin	90 42.4	N51 28.9
09	0 56.1	269 59.4 ..	04.4	245 42.9 ..	08.0	334 28.7 ..	47.5	22 42.5 ..	40.9	Enif	33 40.2	N 9 58.7
10	15 58.6	284 58.9	04.4	260 43.9	07.7	349 30.6	47.8	37 44.8	40.8	Fomalhaut	15 16.2	S29 29.9
11	31 01.1	299 58.3	04.5	275 44.9	07.5	4 32.5	48.0	52 47.1	40.8			
12	46 03.5	314 57.7	N26 04.5	290 45.9	N23 07.2	19 34.5	N 9 48.2	67 49.4	S10 40.7	Gacrux	171 52.8	S57 14.8
13	61 06.0	329 57.1	04.5	305 46.8	07.0	34 36.4	48.4	82 51.7	40.7	Gienah	175 44.8	S17 40.4
14	76 08.4	344 56.5	04.6	320 47.8	06.7	49 38.3	48.6	97 54.0	40.6	Hadar	148 37.4	S60 29.2
15	91 10.9	359 55.9 ..	04.6	335 48.8 ..	06.4	64 40.2 ..	48.8	112 56.3 ..	40.6	Hamal	327 53.1	N23 34.2
16	106 13.4	14 55.4	04.6	350 49.8	06.2	79 42.1	49.0	127 58.6	40.5	Kaus Aust.	83 34.1	S34 22.4
17	121 15.8	29 54.8	04.7	5 50.7	05.9	94 44.0	49.2	143 01.0	40.5			
18	136 18.3	44 54.2	N26 04.7	20 51.7	N23 05.7	109 45.9	N 9 49.4	158 03.3	S10 40.4	Kochab	137 18.6	N74 03.6
19	151 20.8	59 53.6	04.7	35 52.7	05.4	124 47.8	49.6	173 05.6	40.4	Markab	13 31.5	N15 19.6
20	166 23.2	74 53.0	04.8	50 53.7	05.1	139 49.7	49.8	188 07.9	40.3	Menkar	314 08.0	N 4 10.7
21	181 25.7	89 52.4 ..	04.8	65 54.6 ..	04.9	154 51.6 ..	50.0	203 10.2 ..	40.3	Menkent	147 58.9	S36 29.2
22	196 28.2	104 51.9	04.8	80 55.6	04.6	169 53.6	50.2	218 12.5	40.2	Miaplacidus	221 38.6	S69 49.0
23	211 30.6	119 51.3	04.9	95 56.6	04.3	184 55.5	50.4	233 14.8	40.2			
9 00	226 33.1	134 50.7	N26 04.9	110 57.6	N23 04.1	199 57.4	N 9 50.6	248 17.2	S10 40.1	Mirfak	308 30.8	N49 56.5
01	241 35.6	149 50.1	04.9	125 58.5	03.8	214 59.3	50.9	263 19.5	40.1	Nunki	75 49.3	S26 16.0
02	256 38.0	164 49.5	04.9	140 59.5	03.6	230 01.2	51.1	278 21.8	40.0	Peacock	53 07.8	S56 39.4
03	271 40.5	179 49.0 ..	04.9	156 00.5 ..	03.3	245 03.1 ..	51.3	293 24.1 ..	40.0	Pollux	243 19.2	N27 58.3
04	286 42.9	194 48.4	05.0	171 01.5	03.0	260 05.0	51.5	308 26.4	39.9	Procyon	244 52.5	N 5 09.9
05	301 45.4	209 47.8	05.0	186 02.4	02.8	275 06.9	51.7	323 28.7	39.9			
06	316 47.9	224 47.2	N26 05.0	201 03.4	N23 02.5	290 08.8	N 9 51.9	338 31.0	S10 39.8	Rasalhague	95 59.6	N12 32.4
07	331 50.3	239 46.7	05.0	216 04.4	02.2	305 10.7	52.1	353 33.4	39.8	Regulus	207 35.9	N11 51.2
08	346 52.8	254 46.1	05.0	231 05.4	02.0	320 12.7	52.3	8 35.7	39.7	Rigel	281 05.5	S 8 10.6
09	1 55.3	269 45.5 ..	05.1	246 06.3 ..	01.7	335 14.6 ..	52.5	23 38.0 ..	39.7	Rigil Kent.	139 41.6	S60 55.9
10	16 57.7	284 44.9	05.1	261 07.3	01.4	350 16.5	52.7	38 40.3	39.6	Sabik	102 04.1	S15 45.3
11	32 00.2	299 44.3	05.1	276 08.3	01.2	5 18.4	52.9	53 42.6	39.6			
12	47 02.7	314 43.8	N26 05.1	291 09.3	N23 00.9	20 20.3	N 9 53.1	68 44.9	S10 39.5	Schedar	349 33.1	N56 39.6
13	62 05.1	329 43.2	05.1	306 10.2	00.6	35 22.2	53.3	83 47.3	39.5	Shaula	96 11.9	S37 07.2
14	77 07.6	344 42.6	05.1	321 11.2	00.4	50 24.1	53.5	98 49.6	39.4	Sirius	258 27.7	S16 45.0
15	92 10.1	359 42.1 ..	05.1	336 12.2	23 00.1	65 26.0 ..	53.7	113 51.9 ..	39.4	Spica	158 23.5	S11 17.1
16	107 12.5	14 41.5	05.1	351 13.2	22 59.8	80 27.9	53.9	128 54.2	39.3	Suhail	222 47.4	S43 31.8
17	122 15.0	29 40.9	05.1	6 14.1	59.6	95 29.9	54.1	143 56.5	39.3			
18	137 17.4	44 40.3	N26 05.2	21 15.1	N22 59.3	110 31.8	N 9 54.3	158 58.8	S10 39.2	Vega	80 33.9	N38 48.0
19	152 19.9	59 39.8	05.2	36 16.1	59.0	125 33.7	54.6	174 01.2	39.2	Zuben'ubi	136 57.2	S16 08.4
20	167 22.4	74 39.2	05.2	51 17.1	58.8	140 35.6	54.8	189 03.5	39.1		SHA	Mer. Pass.
21	182 24.8	89 38.6 ..	05.2	66 18.0 ..	58.5	155 37.5 ..	55.0	204 05.8 ..	39.1	Venus	269 30.8	15 00
22	197 27.3	104 38.1	05.2	81 19.0	58.2	170 39.4	55.2	219 08.1	39.1	Mars	245 00.2	16 37
23	212 29.8	119 37.5	05.2	96 20.0	58.0	185 41.3	55.4	234 10.4	39.0	Jupiter	333 37.6	10 42
Mer. Pass. 8 56.3		v −0.6	d 0.0	v 1.0	d 0.3	v 1.9	d 0.2	v 2.3	d 0.1	Saturn	21 47.7	7 29

© British Crown Copyright 2022. All rights reserved.

SUN and MOON

UT	SUN GHA	SUN Dec	MOON GHA	v	MOON Dec	d	HP
d h	° ′	° ′	° ′	′	° ′	′	′
7 00	180 50.9	N16 41.0	344 56.3	7.3	S23 03.4	9.6	58.4
01	195 51.0	41.7	359 22.6	7.2	23 13.0	9.4	58.4
02	210 51.0	42.4	13 48.8	7.1	23 22.4	9.4	58.4
03	225 51.1	.. 43.1	28 14.9	7.0	23 31.8	9.2	58.4
04	240 51.1	43.8	42 40.9	6.9	23 41.0	9.1	58.4
05	255 51.2	44.5	57 06.8	6.8	23 50.1	8.9	58.5
06	270 51.2	N16 45.1	71 32.6	6.7	S23 59.0	8.8	58.5
07	285 51.2	45.8	85 58.3	6.5	24 07.8	8.6	58.5
08	300 51.3	46.5	100 23.8	6.5	24 16.4	8.5	58.5
S 09	315 51.3	.. 47.2	114 49.3	6.4	24 24.9	8.4	58.5
U 10	330 51.4	47.9	129 14.7	6.2	24 33.3	8.2	58.6
N 11	345 51.4	48.6	143 39.9	6.2	24 41.5	8.1	58.6
D 12	0 51.5	N16 49.3	158 05.1	6.0	S24 49.6	7.9	58.6
A 13	15 51.5	50.0	172 30.1	6.0	24 57.5	7.7	58.6
Y 14	30 51.5	50.7	186 55.1	5.9	25 05.2	7.7	58.6
15	45 51.6	.. 51.4	201 20.0	5.7	25 12.9	7.4	58.7
16	60 51.6	52.0	215 44.7	5.7	25 20.3	7.3	58.7
17	75 51.7	52.7	230 09.4	5.5	25 27.6	7.1	58.7
18	90 51.7	N16 53.4	244 33.9	5.5	S25 34.7	7.0	58.7
19	105 51.7	54.1	258 58.4	5.4	25 41.7	6.8	58.7
20	120 51.8	54.8	273 22.8	5.3	25 48.5	6.7	58.7
21	135 51.8	.. 55.5	287 47.1	5.2	25 55.2	6.5	58.8
22	150 51.9	56.2	302 11.3	5.1	26 01.7	6.3	58.8
23	165 51.9	56.8	316 35.4	5.0	26 08.0	6.2	58.8
8 00	180 51.9	N16 57.5	330 59.4	5.0	S26 14.2	6.0	58.8
01	195 52.0	58.2	345 23.4	4.8	26 20.2	5.8	58.8
02	210 52.0	58.9	359 47.2	4.8	26 26.0	5.6	58.8
03	225 52.0	16 59.6	14 11.0	4.7	26 31.6	5.5	58.9
04	240 52.1	17 00.3	28 34.7	4.6	26 37.1	5.3	58.9
05	255 52.1	00.9	42 58.3	4.5	26 42.4	5.1	58.9
06	270 52.2	N17 01.6	57 21.8	4.5	S26 47.5	5.0	58.9
07	285 52.2	02.3	71 45.3	4.4	26 52.5	4.8	58.9
08	300 52.2	03.0	86 08.7	4.3	26 57.3	4.6	58.9
M 09	315 52.3	.. 03.7	100 32.0	4.3	27 01.9	4.4	58.9
O 10	330 52.3	04.3	114 55.3	4.2	27 06.3	4.2	58.9
N 11	345 52.3	05.0	129 18.5	4.1	27 10.5	4.1	59.0
D 12	0 52.4	N17 05.7	143 41.6	4.1	S27 14.6	3.9	59.0
A 13	15 52.4	06.4	158 04.7	4.0	27 18.5	3.7	59.0
Y 14	30 52.4	07.1	172 27.7	4.0	27 22.2	3.5	59.0
15	45 52.5	.. 07.7	186 50.7	3.9	27 25.7	3.3	59.0
16	60 52.5	08.4	201 13.6	3.8	27 29.0	3.2	59.0
17	75 52.5	09.1	215 36.4	3.8	27 32.2	2.9	59.0
18	90 52.6	N17 09.8	229 59.2	3.7	S27 35.1	2.8	59.0
19	105 52.6	10.4	244 21.9	3.7	27 37.9	2.6	59.1
20	120 52.6	11.1	258 44.6	3.7	27 40.5	2.3	59.1
21	135 52.7	.. 11.8	273 07.3	3.6	27 42.8	2.2	59.1
22	150 52.7	12.5	287 29.9	3.6	27 45.0	2.1	59.1
23	165 52.7	13.1	301 52.5	3.6	27 47.1	1.8	59.1
9 00	180 52.8	N17 13.8	316 15.1	3.5	S27 48.9	1.6	59.1
01	195 52.8	14.5	330 37.6	3.5	27 50.5	1.4	59.1
02	210 52.8	15.1	345 00.1	3.4	27 51.9	1.3	59.1
03	225 52.9	.. 15.8	359 22.5	3.5	27 53.2	1.0	59.1
04	240 52.9	16.5	13 45.0	3.4	27 54.2	0.9	59.1
05	255 52.9	17.2	28 07.4	3.4	27 55.1	0.7	59.2
06	270 53.0	N17 17.8	42 29.8	3.4	S27 55.8	0.4	59.2
07	285 53.0	18.5	56 52.2	3.3	27 56.2	0.3	59.2
08	300 53.0	19.2	71 14.5	3.4	27 56.5	0.1	59.2
T 09	315 53.1	.. 19.8	85 36.9	3.3	27 56.6	0.1	59.2
U 10	330 53.1	20.5	99 59.2	3.4	27 56.5	0.3	59.2
E 11	345 53.1	21.2	114 21.6	3.3	27 56.2	0.5	59.2
S 12	0 53.1	N17 21.8	128 43.9	3.3	S27 55.7	0.7	59.2
D 13	15 53.2	22.5	143 06.2	3.4	27 55.0	0.9	59.2
A 14	30 53.2	23.2	157 28.6	3.3	27 54.1	1.0	59.2
Y 15	45 53.2	.. 23.8	171 50.9	3.4	27 53.1	1.3	59.2
16	60 53.3	24.5	186 13.3	3.3	27 51.8	1.5	59.2
17	75 53.3	25.2	200 35.6	3.4	27 50.3	1.6	59.3
18	90 53.3	N17 25.8	214 58.0	3.4	S27 48.7	1.9	59.3
19	105 53.3	26.5	229 20.4	3.4	27 46.8	2.0	59.3
20	120 53.4	27.1	243 42.8	3.5	27 44.8	2.3	59.3
21	135 53.4	.. 27.8	258 05.3	3.4	27 42.5	2.4	59.3
22	150 53.4	28.5	272 27.7	3.5	27 40.1	2.6	59.3
23	165 53.4	29.1	286 50.2	3.5	S27 37.5	2.8	59.3
	SD 15.9	d 0.7	SD 16.0		16.1		16.1

Twilight, Sunrise and Moonrise

Lat.	Twilight Naut.	Twilight Civil	Sunrise	Moonrise 7	8	9	10
°	h m	h m	h m	h m	h m	h m	h m
N 72	////	////	00 32	■	■	■	■
N 70	////	////	01 48	■	■	■	■
68	////	////	02 25	■	■	■	■
66	////	01 06	02 51	■	■	■	■
64	////	01 52	03 11	■	■	■	■
62	////	02 21	03 27	24 35	00 35	■	03 19
60	00 59	02 43	03 40	23 52	25 27	01 27	02 21
N 58	01 41	03 00	03 52	23 24	24 50	00 50	01 47
56	02 07	03 15	04 02	23 02	24 24	00 24	01 23
54	02 28	03 27	04 10	22 44	24 03	00 03	01 03
52	02 44	03 38	04 18	22 29	23 46	24 46	00 46
50	02 58	03 47	04 25	22 16	23 31	24 32	00 32
45	03 25	04 07	04 40	21 49	23 01	24 02	00 02
N 40	03 46	04 22	04 52	21 27	22 37	23 39	24 31
35	04 02	04 35	05 03	21 10	22 18	23 20	24 14
30	04 15	04 46	05 12	20 55	22 02	23 04	23 59
20	04 36	05 04	05 27	20 29	21 34	22 36	23 34
N 10	04 53	05 19	05 41	20 07	21 10	22 13	23 12
0	05 06	05 31	05 53	19 47	20 48	21 50	22 52
S 10	05 18	05 43	06 05	19 26	20 26	21 28	22 32
20	05 29	05 55	06 18	19 05	20 02	21 04	22 10
30	05 39	06 08	06 33	18 40	19 34	20 37	21 45
35	05 45	06 15	06 42	18 25	19 18	20 20	21 30
40	05 50	06 23	06 51	18 08	18 59	20 01	21 12
45	05 56	06 31	07 03	17 48	18 37	19 38	20 52
S 50	06 03	06 42	07 16	17 23	18 08	19 09	20 25
52	06 05	06 46	07 23	17 11	17 53	18 54	20 12
54	06 08	06 51	07 30	16 57	17 37	18 37	19 57
56	06 11	06 57	07 38	16 41	17 18	18 17	19 40
58	06 15	07 03	07 47	16 22	16 53	17 52	19 19
S 60	06 18	07 09	07 57	15 59	16 22	17 17	18 52

Sunset, Twilight and Moonset

Lat.	Sunset	Twilight Civil	Twilight Naut.	Moonset 7	8	9	10
°	h m	h m	h m	h m	h m	h m	h m
N 72	☐	☐	☐	■	■	■	■
N 70	22 11	////	////	■	■	■	■
68	21 32	////	////	■	■	■	■
66	21 05	22 56	////	01 54	■	■	■
64	20 44	22 05	////	02 51	■	■	■
62	20 28	21 35	////	03 25	03 20	■	04 57
60	20 14	21 13	23 02	03 50	04 02	04 37	05 55
N 58	20 03	20 55	22 17	04 09	04 31	05 14	06 28
56	19 53	20 40	21 49	04 26	04 53	05 40	06 52
54	19 44	20 27	21 28	04 40	05 12	06 01	07 12
52	19 36	20 17	21 11	04 52	05 27	06 18	07 28
50	19 29	20 08	20 57	05 03	05 41	06 33	07 43
45	19 14	19 47	20 29	05 26	06 08	07 03	08 11
N 40	19 01	19 31	20 08	05 45	06 30	07 27	08 34
35	18 51	19 18	19 52	06 00	06 49	07 46	08 53
30	18 42	19 07	19 38	06 14	07 04	08 03	09 09
20	18 26	18 49	19 17	06 37	07 31	08 31	09 36
N 10	18 13	18 35	19 00	06 57	07 54	08 55	09 59
0	18 00	18 22	18 47	07 16	08 15	09 18	10 20
S 10	17 48	18 09	18 35	07 35	08 37	09 40	10 42
20	17 34	17 57	18 24	07 55	09 00	10 04	11 04
30	17 20	17 45	18 13	08 19	09 27	10 32	11 31
35	17 11	17 38	18 08	08 33	09 43	10 48	11 46
40	17 01	17 30	18 02	08 49	10 01	11 08	12 04
45	16 50	17 21	17 56	09 08	10 23	11 31	12 26
S 50	16 36	17 11	17 50	09 32	10 52	12 00	12 53
52	16 30	17 06	17 47	09 44	11 06	12 15	13 06
54	16 23	17 01	17 44	09 57	11 22	12 32	13 21
56	16 15	16 56	17 41	10 13	11 41	12 52	13 39
58	16 06	16 50	17 37	10 31	12 05	13 18	14 01
S 60	15 56	16 43	17 34	10 54	12 37	13 52	14 28

SUN and MOON

Day	SUN Eqn. of Time 00h	SUN Eqn. of Time 12h	Mer. Pass.	MOON Mer. Pass. Upper	MOON Mer. Pass. Lower	Age	Phase
d	m s	m s	h m	h m	h m	d	%
7	03 24	03 26	11 57	01 03	13 31	17	96
8	03 28	03 29	11 57	02 01	14 31	18	91
9	03 31	03 33	11 56	03 03	15 34	19	83

© British Crown Copyright 2022. All rights reserved.

UT	ARIES GHA	VENUS −4.2 GHA	Dec	MARS +1.4 GHA	Dec	JUPITER −2.1 GHA	Dec	SATURN +0.9 GHA	Dec
10 00	227 32.2	134 36.9	N26 05.2	111 21.0	N22 57.7	200 43.2	N 9 55.6	249 12.7	S10 39.0
01	242 34.7	149 36.4	05.2	126 21.9	57.4	215 45.1	55.8	264 15.1	38.9
02	257 37.2	164 35.8	05.2	141 22.9	57.2	230 47.1	56.0	279 17.4	38.9
03	272 39.6	179 35.2 ..	05.1	156 23.9 ..	56.9	245 49.0 ..	56.2	294 19.7 ..	38.8
04	287 42.1	194 34.6	05.1	171 24.9	56.6	260 50.9	56.4	309 22.0	38.8
05	302 44.6	209 34.1	05.1	186 25.8	56.4	275 52.8	56.6	324 24.3	38.7
W 06	317 47.0	224 33.5	N26 05.1	201 26.8	N22 56.1	290 54.7	N 9 56.8	339 26.7	S10 38.7
E 07	332 49.5	239 32.9	05.1	216 27.8	55.8	305 56.6	57.0	354 29.0	38.6
D 08	347 51.9	254 32.4	05.1	231 28.8	55.5	320 58.5	57.2	9 31.3	38.6
N 09	2 54.4	269 31.8 ..	05.1	246 29.7 ..	55.3	336 00.4 ..	57.4	24 33.6 ..	38.5
E 10	17 56.9	284 31.2	05.1	261 30.7	55.0	351 02.3	57.6	39 35.9	38.5
S 11	32 59.3	299 30.7	05.1	276 31.7	54.7	6 04.3	57.8	54 38.2	38.4
D 12	48 01.8	314 30.1	N26 05.1	291 32.7	N22 54.5	21 06.2	N 9 58.0	69 40.6	S10 38.4
A 13	63 04.3	329 29.6	05.0	306 33.6	54.2	36 08.1	58.3	84 42.9	38.3
Y 14	78 06.7	344 29.0	05.0	321 34.6	53.9	51 10.0	58.5	99 45.2	38.3
15	93 09.2	359 28.4 ..	05.0	336 35.6 ..	53.6	66 11.9 ..	58.7	114 47.5 ..	38.2
16	108 11.7	14 27.9	05.0	351 36.6	53.4	81 13.8	58.9	129 49.8	38.2
17	123 14.1	29 27.3	05.0	6 37.5	53.1	96 15.7	59.1	144 52.2	38.1
18	138 16.6	44 26.7	N26 04.9	21 38.5	N22 52.8	111 17.6	N 9 59.3	159 54.5	S10 38.1
19	153 19.1	59 26.2	04.9	36 39.5	52.5	126 19.6	59.5	174 56.8	38.0
20	168 21.5	74 25.6	04.9	51 40.5	52.2	141 21.5	59.7	189 59.1	38.0
21	183 24.0	89 25.1 ..	04.9	66 41.4 ..	52.0	156 23.4	9 59.9	205 01.4 ..	38.0
22	198 26.4	104 24.5	04.8	81 42.4	51.7	171 25.3	10 00.1	220 03.8	37.9
23	213 28.9	119 23.9	04.8	96 43.4	51.5	186 27.2	00.3	235 06.1	37.9
11 00	228 31.4	134 23.4	N26 04.8	111 44.3	N22 51.2	201 29.1	N10 00.5	250 08.4	S10 37.8
01	243 33.8	149 22.8	04.7	126 45.3	50.9	216 31.0	00.7	265 10.7	37.8
02	258 36.3	164 22.3	04.7	141 46.3	50.6	231 32.9	00.9	280 13.1	37.7
03	273 38.8	179 21.7 ..	04.7	156 47.3 ..	50.4	246 34.8 ..	01.1	295 15.4 ..	37.7
04	288 41.2	194 21.1	04.7	171 48.2	50.1	261 36.8	01.3	310 17.7	37.6
05	303 43.7	209 20.6	04.6	186 49.2	49.8	276 38.7	01.5	325 20.0	37.6
T 06	318 46.2	224 20.0	N26 04.6	201 50.2	N22 49.5	291 40.6	N10 01.7	340 22.3	S10 37.5
H 07	333 48.6	239 19.5	04.6	216 51.2	49.2	306 42.5	01.9	355 24.7	37.5
U 08	348 51.1	254 18.9	04.5	231 52.1	49.0	321 44.4	02.1	10 27.0	37.4
R 09	3 53.6	269 18.4 ..	04.5	246 53.1 ..	48.7	336 46.3 ..	02.3	25 29.3 ..	37.4
S 10	18 56.0	284 17.8	04.5	261 54.1	48.4	351 48.2	02.5	40 31.6	37.3
D 11	33 58.5	299 17.3	04.4	276 55.1	48.1	6 50.2	02.8	55 33.9	37.3
A 12	49 00.9	314 16.7	N26 04.4	291 56.0	N22 47.9	21 52.1	N10 03.0	70 36.3	S10 37.3
Y 13	64 03.4	329 16.2	04.3	306 57.0	47.6	36 54.0	03.2	85 38.6	37.2
14	79 05.9	344 15.6	04.3	321 58.0	47.3	51 55.9	03.4	100 40.9	37.2
15	94 08.3	359 15.0 ..	04.2	336 59.0 ..	47.0	66 57.8 ..	03.6	115 43.2 ..	37.1
16	109 10.8	14 14.5	04.2	351 59.9	46.8	81 59.7	03.8	130 45.6	37.1
17	124 13.3	29 13.9	04.1	7 00.9	46.5	97 01.6	04.0	145 47.9	37.0
18	139 15.7	44 13.4	N26 04.1	22 01.9	N22 46.2	112 03.5	N10 04.2	160 50.2	S10 37.0
19	154 18.2	59 12.8	04.0	37 02.8	45.9	127 05.5	04.4	175 52.5	36.9
20	169 20.7	74 12.3	04.0	52 03.8	45.6	142 07.4	04.6	190 54.9	36.9
21	184 23.1	89 11.7 ..	03.9	67 04.8 ..	45.4	157 09.3 ..	04.8	205 57.2 ..	36.8
22	199 25.6	104 11.2	03.9	82 05.8	45.1	172 11.2	05.0	220 59.5	36.8
23	214 28.0	119 10.6	03.8	97 06.7	44.8	187 13.1	05.2	236 01.8	36.7
12 00	229 30.5	134 10.1	N26 03.8	112 07.7	N22 44.5	202 15.0	N10 05.4	251 04.2	S10 36.7
01	244 33.0	149 09.6	03.7	127 08.7	44.2	217 16.9	05.6	266 06.5	36.7
02	259 35.4	164 09.0	03.7	142 09.7	44.0	232 18.8	05.8	281 08.8	36.6
03	274 37.9	179 08.5 ..	03.6	157 10.6 ..	43.7	247 20.8 ..	06.0	296 11.1 ..	36.6
04	289 40.4	194 07.9	03.6	172 11.6	43.4	262 22.7	06.2	311 13.5	36.5
05	304 42.8	209 07.4	03.5	187 12.6	43.1	277 24.6	06.4	326 15.8	36.5
F 06	319 45.3	224 06.8	N26 03.4	202 13.6	N22 42.8	292 26.5	N10 06.6	341 18.1	S10 36.4
R 07	334 47.8	239 06.3	03.4	217 14.5	42.6	307 28.4	06.8	356 20.4	36.4
I 08	349 50.2	254 05.7	03.3	232 15.5	42.3	322 30.3	07.0	11 22.8	36.3
D 09	4 52.7	269 05.2 ..	03.2	247 16.5 ..	42.0	337 32.2 ..	07.2	26 25.1 ..	36.3
A 10	19 55.2	284 04.6	03.2	262 17.4	41.7	352 34.2	07.4	41 27.4	36.2
Y 11	34 57.6	299 04.1	03.1	277 18.4	41.4	7 36.1	07.6	56 29.7	36.2
12	50 00.1	314 03.6	N26 03.0	292 19.4	N22 41.1	22 38.0	N10 07.8	71 32.1	S10 36.1
13	65 02.5	329 03.0	03.0	307 20.4	40.9	37 39.9	08.0	86 34.4	36.1
14	80 05.0	344 02.5	02.9	322 21.3	40.6	52 41.8	08.2	101 36.7	36.1
15	95 07.5	359 01.9 ..	02.8	337 22.3 ..	40.3	67 43.7 ..	08.4	116 39.0 ..	36.0
16	110 09.9	14 01.4	02.8	352 23.3	40.0	82 45.6	08.6	131 41.4	36.0
17	125 12.4	29 00.9	02.7	7 24.3	39.7	97 47.6	08.9	146 43.7	35.9
18	140 14.9	44 00.3	N26 02.6	22 25.2	N22 39.4	112 49.5	N10 09.1	161 46.0	S10 35.9
19	155 17.3	58 59.8	02.5	37 26.2	39.2	127 51.4	09.3	176 48.3	35.8
20	170 19.8	73 59.2	02.5	52 27.2	38.9	142 53.3	09.5	191 50.7	35.8
21	185 22.3	88 58.7 ..	02.4	67 28.2 ..	38.6	157 55.2 ..	09.7	206 53.0 ..	35.8
22	200 24.7	103 58.2	02.3	82 29.1	38.3	172 57.1	09.9	221 55.3	35.7
23	215 27.2	118 57.6	02.2	97 30.1	38.0	187 59.0	10.1	236 57.7	35.7
Mer. Pass.	h m 8 44.5	v −0.6	d 0.0	v 1.0	d 0.3	v 1.9	d 0.2	v 2.3	d 0.0

STARS

Name	SHA	Dec
Acamar	315 13.3	S40 12.7
Achernar	335 21.8	S57 07.1
Acrux	173 01.1	S63 13.9
Adhara	255 07.2	S29 00.4
Aldebaran	290 41.6	N16 33.3
Alioth	166 13.7	N55 50.2
Alkaid	152 52.7	N49 11.9
Alnair	27 34.7	S46 50.8
Alnilam	275 39.4	S 1 11.3
Alphard	217 49.1	S 8 45.7
Alphecca	126 04.6	N26 38.1
Alpheratz	357 36.5	N29 12.9
Altair	62 01.2	N 8 55.6
Ankaa	353 08.8	S42 10.7
Antares	112 17.2	S26 29.0
Arcturus	145 48.9	N19 03.6
Atria	107 12.2	S69 04.0
Avior	234 15.5	S59 35.3
Bellatrix	278 24.7	N 6 22.2
Betelgeuse	270 53.9	N 7 24.6
Canopus	263 53.4	S52 42.7
Capella	280 24.4	N46 01.3
Deneb	49 26.7	N45 21.5
Denebola	182 26.2	N14 26.5
Diphda	348 49.0	S17 51.6
Dubhe	193 42.4	N61 37.8
Elnath	278 04.0	N28 37.6
Eltanin	90 42.4	N51 28.9
Enif	33 40.2	N 9 58.7
Fomalhaut	15 16.2	S29 29.9
Gacrux	171 52.8	S57 14.8
Gienah	175 44.8	S17 40.4
Hadar	148 37.4	S60 29.2
Hamal	327 53.1	N23 34.2
Kaus Aust.	83 34.1	S34 22.4
Kochab	137 18.6	N74 03.6
Markab	13 31.4	N15 19.6
Menkar	314 07.9	N 4 10.8
Menkent	147 58.9	S36 29.2
Miaplacidus	221 38.6	S69 49.0
Mirfak	308 30.8	N49 56.5
Nunki	75 49.3	S26 16.0
Peacock	53 07.8	S56 39.4
Pollux	243 19.2	N27 58.3
Procyon	244 52.5	N 5 09.9
Rasalhague	95 59.6	N12 32.4
Regulus	207 35.9	N11 51.2
Rigel	281 05.5	S 8 10.6
Rigil Kent.	139 41.6	S60 55.9
Sabik	102 04.1	S15 45.3
Schedar	349 33.1	N56 39.6
Shaula	96 11.9	S37 07.2
Sirius	258 27.7	S16 45.0
Spica	158 23.5	S11 17.1
Suhail	222 47.4	S43 31.8
Vega	80 33.9	N38 48.0
Zuben'ubi	136 57.2	S16 08.4

	SHA	Mer. Pass.
	° ′	h m
Venus	265 52.0	15 03
Mars	243 13.0	16 32
Jupiter	332 57.7	10 33
Saturn	21 37.0	7 18

© British Crown Copyright 2022. All rights reserved.

UT	SUN GHA	SUN Dec	MOON GHA	v	Dec	d	HP
d h	° ′	° ′	° ′	′	° ′	′	′
10 00	180 53.5	N17 29.8	301 12.7	3.5	S27 34.7	3.0	59.3
01	195 53.5	30.4	315 35.2	3.6	27 31.7	3.2	59.3
02	210 53.5	31.1	329 57.8	3.6	27 28.5	3.4	59.3
03	225 53.6	.. 31.8	344 20.4	3.7	27 25.1	3.6	59.3
04	240 53.6	32.4	358 43.1	3.7	27 21.5	3.7	59.3
05	255 53.6	33.1	13 05.8	3.7	27 17.8	4.0	59.3
06	270 53.6	N17 33.7	27 28.5	3.8	S27 13.8	4.1	59.3
W 07	285 53.7	34.4	41 51.3	3.8	27 09.7	4.3	59.3
E 08	300 53.7	35.1	56 14.1	3.8	27 05.4	4.5	59.3
D 09	315 53.7	.. 35.7	70 36.9	4.0	27 00.9	4.7	59.3
N 10	330 53.7	36.4	84 59.9	3.9	26 56.2	4.9	59.3
E 11	345 53.7	37.0	99 22.8	4.1	26 51.3	5.0	59.3
S 12	0 53.8	N17 37.7	113 45.9	4.1	S26 46.3	5.3	59.3
D 13	15 53.8	38.3	128 09.0	4.1	26 41.0	5.4	59.3
A 14	30 53.8	39.0	142 32.1	4.2	26 35.6	5.6	59.3
Y 15	45 53.8	.. 39.6	156 55.3	4.3	26 30.0	5.8	59.4
16	60 53.9	40.3	171 18.6	4.3	26 24.2	5.9	59.4
17	75 53.9	40.9	185 41.9	4.5	26 18.3	6.2	59.4
18	90 53.9	N17 41.6	200 05.4	4.4	S26 12.1	6.3	59.4
19	105 53.9	42.2	214 28.8	4.6	26 05.8	6.5	59.4
20	120 53.9	42.9	228 52.4	4.6	25 59.3	6.6	59.4
21	135 54.0	.. 43.5	243 16.0	4.7	25 52.7	6.8	59.4
22	150 54.0	44.2	257 39.7	4.8	25 45.9	7.0	59.4
23	165 54.0	44.8	272 03.5	4.8	25 38.9	7.2	59.4
11 00	180 54.0	N17 45.5	286 27.3	4.9	S25 31.7	7.3	59.4
01	195 54.0	46.1	300 51.2	5.1	25 24.4	7.6	59.4
02	210 54.1	46.8	315 15.3	5.0	25 16.8	7.6	59.4
03	225 54.1	.. 47.4	329 39.3	5.2	25 09.2	7.9	59.4
04	240 54.1	48.1	344 03.5	5.3	25 01.3	8.0	59.4
05	255 54.1	48.7	358 27.8	5.3	24 53.3	8.1	59.4
06	270 54.1	N17 49.4	12 52.1	5.4	S24 45.2	8.3	59.4
T 07	285 54.2	50.0	27 16.5	5.5	24 36.9	8.5	59.4
H 08	300 54.2	50.6	41 41.0	5.6	24 28.4	8.6	59.4
U 09	315 54.2	.. 51.3	56 05.6	5.7	24 19.8	8.8	59.4
R 10	330 54.2	51.9	70 30.3	5.8	24 11.0	9.0	59.4
S 11	345 54.2	52.6	84 55.1	5.9	24 02.0	9.1	59.4
D 12	0 54.2	N17 53.2	99 20.0	5.9	S23 52.9	9.2	59.4
A 13	15 54.3	53.9	113 44.9	6.1	23 43.7	9.4	59.4
Y 14	30 54.3	54.5	128 10.0	6.1	23 34.3	9.6	59.4
15	45 54.3	.. 55.1	142 35.1	6.3	23 24.7	9.7	59.4
16	60 54.3	55.8	157 00.4	6.3	23 15.0	9.8	59.4
17	75 54.3	56.4	171 25.7	6.4	23 05.2	10.0	59.4
18	90 54.3	N17 57.1	185 51.1	6.6	S22 55.2	10.1	59.4
19	105 54.4	57.7	200 16.7	6.6	22 45.1	10.3	59.4
20	120 54.4	58.3	214 42.3	6.7	22 34.8	10.4	59.4
21	135 54.4	.. 59.0	229 08.0	6.8	22 24.4	10.5	59.3
22	150 54.4	17 59.6	243 33.8	6.9	22 13.9	10.7	59.3
23	165 54.4	18 00.2	257 59.7	7.0	22 03.2	10.8	59.3
12 00	180 54.4	N18 00.9	272 25.7	7.1	S21 52.4	10.9	59.3
01	195 54.4	01.5	286 51.8	7.2	21 41.5	11.1	59.3
02	210 54.5	02.1	301 18.0	7.3	21 30.4	11.2	59.3
03	225 54.5	.. 02.8	315 44.3	7.4	21 19.2	11.3	59.3
04	240 54.5	03.4	330 10.7	7.5	21 07.9	11.5	59.3
05	255 54.5	04.0	344 37.2	7.6	20 56.4	11.5	59.3
06	270 54.5	N18 04.7	359 03.8	7.6	S20 44.9	11.7	59.3
F 07	285 54.5	05.3	13 30.4	7.8	20 33.2	11.8	59.3
R 08	300 54.5	05.9	27 57.2	7.9	20 21.4	12.0	59.3
I 09	315 54.5	.. 06.6	42 24.1	8.0	20 09.4	12.0	59.3
D 10	330 54.6	07.2	56 51.1	8.0	19 57.4	12.2	59.3
A 11	345 54.6	07.8	71 18.1	8.2	19 45.2	12.3	59.3
Y 12	0 54.6	N18 08.5	85 45.3	8.3	S19 32.9	12.4	59.3
13	15 54.6	09.1	100 12.6	8.3	19 20.5	12.5	59.3
14	30 54.6	09.7	114 39.9	8.5	19 08.0	12.6	59.3
15	45 54.6	.. 10.3	129 07.4	8.5	18 55.4	12.7	59.3
16	60 54.6	11.0	143 34.9	8.7	18 42.7	12.8	59.3
17	75 54.6	11.6	158 02.6	8.7	18 29.9	13.0	59.3
18	90 54.6	N18 12.2	172 30.3	8.8	S18 16.9	13.0	59.3
19	105 54.6	12.9	186 58.1	8.9	18 03.9	13.1	59.3
20	120 54.7	13.5	201 26.0	9.0	17 50.8	13.3	59.2
21	135 54.7	.. 14.1	215 54.0	9.1	17 37.6	13.4	59.2
22	150 54.7	14.7	230 22.1	9.2	17 24.2	13.4	59.2
23	165 54.7	15.4	244 50.3	9.3	S17 10.8	13.5	59.2
	SD 15.9	d 0.6	SD 16.2		16.2		16.2

Twilight / Sunrise / Moonrise

Lat.	Naut.	Civil	Sunrise	Moonrise 10	11	12	13
°	h m	h m	h m	h m	h m	h m	h m
N 72	▭	▭	▭	■■■	■■■	■■■	05 00
N 70	////	////	01 26	■■■	■■■	■■■	04 22
68	////	////	02 10	■■■	■■■	04 53	03 55
66	////	00 30	02 39	■■■	■■■	04 03	03 34
64	////	01 36	03 01	■■■	04 02	03 32	03 18
62	////	02 09	03 18	03 19	03 12	03 08	03 04
60	00 26	02 33	03 33	02 21	02 41	02 49	02 52
N 58	01 26	02 52	03 45	01 47	02 18	02 33	02 42
56	01 56	03 07	03 56	01 23	01 58	02 19	02 33
54	02 19	03 21	04 05	01 03	01 42	02 08	02 25
52	02 37	03 32	04 13	00 46	01 28	01 57	02 17
50	02 51	03 42	04 20	00 32	01 16	01 48	02 11
45	03 20	04 03	04 36	00 02	00 51	01 28	01 57
N 40	03 42	04 19	04 49	24 31	00 31	01 12	01 45
35	03 59	04 32	05 00	24 14	00 14	00 58	01 35
30	04 13	04 44	05 10	23 59	24 46	00 46	01 26
20	04 35	05 02	05 26	23 34	24 25	00 25	01 11
N 10	04 52	05 18	05 40	23 12	24 07	00 07	00 58
0	05 06	05 31	05 53	22 52	23 51	24 45	00 45
S 10	05 18	05 44	06 06	22 32	23 34	24 32	00 32
20	05 30	05 56	06 20	22 10	23 15	24 19	00 19
30	05 41	06 10	06 35	21 45	22 54	24 03	00 03
35	05 47	06 17	06 44	21 30	22 42	23 54	25 04
40	05 53	06 25	06 54	21 12	22 28	23 44	24 57
45	05 59	06 35	07 06	20 52	22 11	23 31	24 50
S 50	06 06	06 45	07 21	20 25	21 50	23 16	24 41
52	06 09	06 50	07 27	20 12	21 40	23 09	24 36
54	06 13	06 56	07 35	19 57	21 28	23 01	24 32
56	06 16	07 02	07 43	19 40	21 15	22 52	24 27
58	06 20	07 08	07 53	19 19	21 00	22 42	24 21
S 60	06 24	07 15	08 04	18 52	20 42	22 31	24 14

Sunset / Twilight / Moonset

Lat.	Sunset	Civil	Naut.	Moonset 10	11	12	13
°	h m	h m	h m	h m	h m	h m	h m
N 72	▭	▭	▭	■■■	■■■	■■■	09 22
N 70	22 35	////	////	■■■	■■■	■■■	09 58
68	21 47	////	////	■■■	■■■	07 33	10 23
66	21 17	////	////	■■■	■■■	08 22	10 42
64	20 54	22 22	////	■■■	06 22	08 52	10 57
62	20 36	21 47	////	04 57	07 11	09 15	11 09
60	20 20	21 22	////	05 55	07 42	09 33	11 20
N 58	20 09	21 03	22 32	06 28	08 05	09 48	11 29
56	19 59	20 47	21 59	06 52	08 23	10 01	11 37
54	19 49	20 34	21 36	07 12	08 39	10 12	11 44
52	19 41	20 22	21 18	07 28	08 52	10 22	11 51
50	19 33	20 12	21 03	07 43	09 04	10 31	11 57
45	19 17	19 51	20 34	08 11	09 29	10 49	12 09
N 40	19 04	19 35	20 12	08 34	09 48	11 04	12 19
35	18 53	19 21	19 55	08 53	10 04	11 17	12 28
30	18 44	19 10	19 41	09 09	10 18	11 27	12 35
20	18 27	18 51	19 18	09 36	10 41	11 46	12 48
N 10	18 13	18 35	19 01	09 59	11 02	12 02	12 59
0	18 00	18 22	18 47	10 20	11 20	12 17	13 09
S 10	17 47	18 09	18 34	10 42	11 39	12 32	13 20
20	17 33	17 56	18 23	11 04	11 59	12 47	13 31
30	17 17	17 43	18 11	11 31	12 22	13 05	13 43
35	17 08	17 35	18 06	11 46	12 35	13 16	13 50
40	16 58	17 27	17 59	12 04	12 50	13 27	13 58
45	16 46	17 18	17 53	12 26	13 08	13 41	14 07
S 50	16 31	17 07	17 46	12 53	13 31	13 58	14 18
52	16 25	17 02	17 43	13 06	13 41	14 06	14 23
54	16 17	16 56	17 39	13 21	13 53	14 14	14 29
56	16 09	16 51	17 36	13 39	14 07	14 24	14 35
58	15 59	16 44	17 32	14 01	14 23	14 35	14 42
S 60	15 48	16 37	17 28	14 28	14 42	14 48	14 50

SUN / MOON

Day	Eqn. of Time 00h	12h	Mer. Pass.	Mer. Pass. Upper	Lower	Age	Phase
d	m s	m s	h m	h m	h m	d	%
10	03 34	03 35	11 56	04 05	16 36	20	73
11	03 36	03 37	11 56	05 06	17 36	21	63
12	03 38	03 38	11 56	06 04	18 31	22	51

© British Crown Copyright 2022. All rights reserved.

UT (d h)	ARIES GHA	VENUS −4.2 GHA	Dec	MARS +1.5 GHA	Dec	JUPITER −2.1 GHA	Dec	SATURN +0.8 GHA	Dec	STARS Name	SHA	Dec
13 00	230 29.7	133 57.1	N26 02.1	112 31.1	N22 37.7	203 01.0	N10 10.3	252 00.0	S10 35.6	Acamar	315 13.3	S40 12.7
01	245 32.1	148 56.6	02.1	127 32.0	37.4	218 02.9	10.5	267 02.3	35.6	Achernar	335 21.7	S57 07.0
02	260 34.6	163 56.0	02.0	142 33.0	37.2	233 04.8	10.7	282 04.6	35.5	Acrux	173 01.1	S63 13.9
03	275 37.0	178 55.5 ..	01.9	157 34.0 ..	36.9	248 06.7 ..	10.9	297 07.0 ..	35.5	Adhara	255 07.2	S29 00.4
04	290 39.5	193 55.0	01.8	172 35.0	36.6	263 08.6	11.1	312 09.3	35.4	Aldebaran	290 41.6	N16 33.3
05	305 42.0	208 54.4	01.7	187 35.9	36.3	278 10.5	11.3	327 11.6	35.4			
06	320 44.4	223 53.9	N26 01.6	202 36.9	N22 36.0	293 12.4	N10 11.5	342 13.9	S10 35.4	Alioth	166 13.8	N55 50.2
07	335 46.9	238 53.4	01.5	217 37.9	35.7	308 14.4	11.7	357 16.3	35.3	Alkaid	152 52.7	N49 11.9
S 08	350 49.4	253 52.8	01.4	232 38.9	35.4	323 16.3	11.9	12 18.6	35.3	Alnair	27 34.7	S46 50.7
A 09	5 51.8	268 52.3 ..	01.4	247 39.8 ..	35.2	338 18.2 ..	12.1	27 20.9 ..	35.2	Alnilam	275 39.4	S 1 11.3
T 10	20 54.3	283 51.8	01.3	262 40.8	34.9	353 20.1	12.3	42 23.3	35.2	Alphard	217 49.1	S 8 45.7
U 11	35 56.8	298 51.2	01.2	277 41.8	34.6	8 22.0	12.5	57 25.6	35.1			
R 12	50 59.2	313 50.7	N26 01.1	292 42.7	N22 34.3	23 23.9	N10 12.7	72 27.9	S10 35.1	Alphecca	126 04.6	N26 38.1
D 13	66 01.7	328 50.2	01.0	307 43.7	34.0	38 25.8	12.9	87 30.3	35.0	Alpheratz	357 36.4	N29 12.9
A 14	81 04.1	343 49.6	00.9	322 44.7	33.7	53 27.8	13.1	102 32.6	35.0	Altair	62 01.2	N 8 55.6
Y 15	96 06.6	358 49.1 ..	00.8	337 45.7 ..	33.4	68 29.7 ..	13.3	117 34.9 ..	35.0	Ankaa	353 08.8	S42 10.7
16	111 09.1	13 48.6	00.7	352 46.6	33.1	83 31.6	13.5	132 37.2	34.9	Antares	112 17.2	S26 29.0
17	126 11.5	28 48.1	00.6	7 47.6	32.8	98 33.5	13.7	147 39.6	34.9			
18	141 14.0	43 47.5	N26 00.5	22 48.6	N22 32.6	113 35.4	N10 13.9	162 41.9	S10 34.8	Arcturus	145 48.9	N19 03.6
19	156 16.5	58 47.0	00.4	37 49.6	32.3	128 37.3	14.1	177 44.2	34.8	Atria	107 12.2	S69 04.1
20	171 18.9	73 46.5	00.3	52 50.5	32.0	143 39.3	14.3	192 46.6	34.7	Avior	234 15.5	S59 35.3
21	186 21.4	88 46.0 ..	00.2	67 51.5 ..	31.7	158 41.2 ..	14.5	207 48.9 ..	34.7	Bellatrix	278 24.7	N 6 22.2
22	201 23.9	103 45.4	00.1	82 52.5	31.4	173 43.1	14.7	222 51.2	34.7	Betelgeuse	270 53.9	N 7 24.6
23	216 26.3	118 44.9	26 00.0	97 53.4	31.1	188 45.0	14.9	237 53.6	34.6			
14 00	231 28.8	133 44.4	N25 59.9	112 54.4	N22 30.8	203 46.9	N10 15.1	252 55.9	S10 34.6	Canopus	263 53.4	S52 42.6
01	246 31.3	148 43.9	59.7	127 55.4	30.5	218 48.8	15.3	267 58.2	34.6	Capella	280 24.4	N46 01.3
02	261 33.7	163 43.3	59.6	142 56.4	30.2	233 50.7	15.5	283 00.6	34.5	Deneb	49 26.6	N45 21.5
03	276 36.2	178 42.8 ..	59.5	157 57.3 ..	29.9	248 52.7 ..	15.7	298 02.9 ..	34.4	Denebola	182 26.2	N14 26.5
04	291 38.6	193 42.3	59.4	172 58.3	29.6	263 54.6	15.9	313 05.2	34.4	Diphda	348 48.9	S17 51.6
05	306 41.1	208 41.8	59.3	187 59.3	29.4	278 56.5	16.1	328 07.5	34.4			
06	321 43.6	223 41.3	N25 59.2	203 00.3	N22 29.1	293 58.4	N10 16.3	343 09.9	S10 34.3	Dubhe	193 42.5	N61 37.8
07	336 46.0	238 40.7	59.1	218 01.2	28.8	309 00.3	16.5	358 12.2	34.3	Elnath	278 04.0	N28 37.6
S 08	351 48.5	253 40.2	58.9	233 02.2	28.5	324 02.2	16.7	13 14.5	34.2	Eltanin	90 42.4	N51 28.9
U 09	6 51.0	268 39.7 ..	58.8	248 03.2 ..	28.2	339 04.2 ..	16.9	28 16.9 ..	34.2	Enif	33 40.2	N 9 58.7
N 10	21 53.4	283 39.2	58.7	263 04.1	27.9	354 06.1	17.1	43 19.2	34.1	Fomalhaut	15 16.2	S29 29.9
D 11	36 55.9	298 38.7	58.6	278 05.1	27.6	9 08.0	17.3	58 21.5	34.1			
A 12	51 58.4	313 38.2	N25 58.5	293 06.1	N22 27.3	24 09.9	N10 17.5	73 23.9	S10 34.1	Gacrux	171 52.8	S57 14.8
Y 13	67 00.8	328 37.6	58.3	308 07.1	27.0	39 11.8	17.7	88 26.2	34.0	Gienah	175 44.8	S17 40.4
14	82 03.3	343 37.1	58.2	323 08.0	26.7	54 13.7	17.9	103 28.5	34.0	Hadar	148 37.4	S60 29.2
15	97 05.8	358 36.6 ..	58.1	338 09.0 ..	26.4	69 15.7 ..	18.1	118 30.9 ..	33.9	Hamal	327 53.1	N23 34.2
16	112 08.2	13 36.1	58.0	353 10.0	26.1	84 17.6	18.3	133 33.2	33.9	Kaus Aust.	83 34.1	S34 22.4
17	127 10.7	28 35.6	57.9	8 10.9	25.8	99 19.5	18.5	148 35.5	33.9			
18	142 13.1	43 35.1	N25 57.7	23 11.9	N22 25.5	114 21.4	N10 18.7	163 37.9	S10 33.8	Kochab	137 18.6	N74 03.6
19	157 15.6	58 34.6	57.6	38 12.9	25.2	129 23.3	18.9	178 40.2	33.8	Markab	13 31.4	N15 19.6
20	172 18.1	73 34.0	57.5	53 13.9	24.9	144 25.2	19.1	193 42.5	33.7	Menkar	314 07.9	N 4 10.8
21	187 20.5	88 33.5 ..	57.3	68 14.8 ..	24.6	159 27.2 ..	19.3	208 44.9 ..	33.7	Menkent	147 58.9	S36 29.2
22	202 23.0	103 33.0	57.2	83 15.8	24.4	174 29.1	19.5	223 47.2	33.6	Miaplacidus	221 38.7	S69 49.0
23	217 25.5	118 32.5	57.1	98 16.8	24.1	189 31.0	19.7	238 49.5	33.6			
15 00	232 27.9	133 32.0	N25 56.9	113 17.8	N22 23.8	204 32.9	N10 19.9	253 51.9	S10 33.6	Mirfak	308 30.8	N49 56.5
01	247 30.4	148 31.5	56.8	128 18.7	23.5	219 34.8	20.1	268 54.2	33.5	Nunki	75 49.2	S26 16.0
02	262 32.9	163 31.0	56.7	143 19.7	23.2	234 36.7	20.3	283 56.5	33.5	Peacock	53 07.7	S56 39.4
03	277 35.3	178 30.5 ..	56.5	158 20.7 ..	22.9	249 38.7 ..	20.5	298 58.9 ..	33.4	Pollux	243 19.2	N27 58.3
04	292 37.8	193 30.0	56.4	173 21.6	22.6	264 40.6	20.7	314 01.2	33.4	Procyon	244 52.5	N 5 09.9
05	307 40.2	208 29.5	56.3	188 22.6	22.3	279 42.5	20.9	329 03.6	33.4			
06	322 42.7	223 29.0	N25 56.1	203 23.6	N22 22.0	294 44.4	N10 21.1	344 05.9	S10 33.3	Rasalhague	95 59.5	N12 32.4
07	337 45.2	238 28.4	56.0	218 24.6	21.7	309 46.3	21.3	359 08.2	33.3	Regulus	207 35.9	N11 51.2
M 08	352 47.6	253 27.9	55.8	233 25.5	21.4	324 48.2	21.5	14 10.6	33.2	Rigel	281 05.5	S 8 10.6
O 09	7 50.1	268 27.4 ..	55.7	248 26.5 ..	21.1	339 50.2 ..	21.7	29 12.9 ..	33.2	Rigil Kent.	139 41.6	S60 55.9
N 10	22 52.6	283 26.9	55.5	263 27.5	20.8	354 52.1	21.9	44 15.2	33.1	Sabik	102 04.1	S15 45.3
D 11	37 55.0	298 26.4	55.4	278 28.4	20.5	9 54.0	22.1	59 17.6	33.1			
A 12	52 57.5	313 25.9	N25 55.2	293 29.4	N22 20.2	24 55.9	N10 22.3	74 19.9	S10 33.1	Schedar	349 33.1	N56 39.6
Y 13	68 00.0	328 25.4	55.1	308 30.4	19.9	39 57.8	22.5	89 22.2	33.0	Shaula	96 11.9	S37 07.2
14	83 02.4	343 24.9	54.9	323 31.4	19.6	54 59.7	22.7	104 24.6	33.0	Sirius	258 27.7	S16 45.0
15	98 04.9	358 24.4 ..	54.8	338 32.3 ..	19.3	70 01.7 ..	22.9	119 26.9 ..	32.9	Spica	158 23.5	S11 17.1
16	113 07.4	13 23.9	54.6	353 33.3	19.0	85 03.6	23.1	134 29.2	32.9	Suhail	222 47.4	S43 31.8
17	128 09.8	28 23.4	54.5	8 34.3	18.7	100 05.5	23.3	149 31.6	32.9			
18	143 12.3	43 22.9	N25 54.3	23 35.3	N22 18.4	115 07.4	N10 23.5	164 33.9	S10 32.8	Vega	80 33.9	N38 48.1
19	158 14.7	58 22.4	54.2	38 36.2	18.1	130 09.3	23.7	179 36.3	32.8	Zuben'ubi	136 57.2	S16 08.4
20	173 17.2	73 21.9	54.0	53 37.2	17.8	145 11.3	23.9	194 38.6	32.7			
21	188 19.7	88 21.4 ..	53.9	68 38.2 ..	17.5	160 13.2 ..	24.1	209 40.9 ..	32.7		SHA	Mer. Pass.
22	203 22.1	103 20.9	53.7	83 39.1	17.2	175 15.1	24.3	224 43.3	32.7	Venus	262 15.6	15 06
23	218 24.6	118 20.4	53.6	98 40.1	16.9	190 17.0	24.5	239 45.6	32.6	Mars	241 25.6	16 27
Mer. Pass. 8 32.7		v −0.5	d 0.1	v 1.0	d 0.3	v −1.9	d 0.2	v 2.3	d 0.0	Jupiter	332 18.1	10 24
										Saturn	21 27.1	7 07

© British Crown Copyright 2022. All rights reserved.

UT	SUN GHA	SUN Dec	MOON GHA	v	MOON Dec	d	HP
d h	° '	° '	° '	'	° '	'	'
13 00	180 54.7	N18 16.0	259 18.6	9.4	S16 57.3	13.6	59.2
01	195 54.7	16.6	273 47.0	9.4	16 43.7	13.7	59.2
02	210 54.7	17.2	288 15.4	9.6	16 30.0	13.8	59.2
03	225 54.7 ..	17.8	302 44.0	9.6	16 16.2	13.9	59.2
04	240 54.7	18.5	317 12.6	9.7	16 02.3	13.9	59.2
05	255 54.7	19.1	331 41.3	9.8	15 48.4	14.1	59.2
06	270 54.7	N18 19.7	346 10.1	9.9	S15 34.3	14.1	59.2
07	285 54.7	20.3	0 39.0	10.0	15 20.2	14.2	59.1
S 08	300 54.7	20.9	15 08.0	10.0	15 06.0	14.3	59.2
A 09	315 54.7 ..	21.6	29 37.0	10.2	14 51.7	14.3	59.2
T 10	330 54.8	22.2	44 06.2	10.2	14 37.4	14.5	59.2
U 11	345 54.8	22.8	58 35.4	10.3	14 22.9	14.5	59.2
R 12	0 54.8	N18 23.4	73 04.7	10.3	S14 08.4	14.6	59.1
D 13	15 54.8	24.0	87 34.0	10.5	13 53.8	14.6	59.1
A 14	30 54.8	24.6	102 03.5	10.5	13 39.2	14.7	59.1
Y 15	45 54.8 ..	25.3	116 33.0	10.6	13 24.5	14.8	59.1
16	60 54.8	25.9	131 02.6	10.7	13 09.7	14.9	59.1
17	75 54.8	26.5	145 32.3	10.7	12 54.8	14.9	59.1
18	90 54.8	N18 27.1	160 02.0	10.9	S12 39.9	15.0	59.1
19	105 54.8	27.7	174 31.9	10.9	12 24.9	15.0	59.1
20	120 54.8	28.3	189 01.8	10.9	12 09.9	15.1	59.1
21	135 54.8 ..	28.9	203 31.7	11.0	11 54.8	15.2	59.1
22	150 54.8	29.5	218 01.7	11.1	11 39.6	15.2	59.1
23	165 54.8	30.2	232 31.8	11.2	11 24.4	15.2	59.0
14 00	180 54.8	N18 30.8	247 02.0	11.2	S11 09.2	15.4	59.0
01	195 54.8	31.4	261 32.2	11.3	10 53.8	15.3	59.0
02	210 54.8	32.0	276 02.5	11.4	10 38.5	15.5	59.0
03	225 54.8 ..	32.6	290 32.9	11.4	10 23.0	15.4	59.0
04	240 54.8	33.2	305 03.3	11.5	10 07.6	15.5	59.0
05	255 54.8	33.8	319 33.8	11.5	9 52.1	15.6	59.0
06	270 54.8	N18 34.4	334 04.3	11.6	S 9 36.5	15.6	59.0
07	285 54.8	35.0	348 34.9	11.7	9 20.9	15.7	59.0
S 08	300 54.8	35.6	3 05.6	11.7	9 05.2	15.7	59.0
U 09	315 54.8 ..	36.2	17 36.3	11.8	8 49.5	15.7	58.9
N 10	330 54.8	36.8	32 07.1	11.8	8 33.8	15.8	58.9
D 11	345 54.8	37.4	46 37.9	11.9	8 18.0	15.8	58.9
A 12	0 54.8	N18 38.0	61 08.8	11.9	S 8 02.2	15.8	58.9
Y 13	15 54.8	38.6	75 39.7	11.9	7 46.4	15.9	58.9
14	30 54.8	39.2	90 10.6	12.1	7 30.5	15.9	58.9
15	45 54.8 ..	39.9	104 41.7	12.0	7 14.6	15.9	58.9
16	60 54.8	40.5	119 12.7	12.2	6 58.7	16.0	58.9
17	75 54.8	41.1	133 43.9	12.1	6 42.7	16.0	58.9
18	90 54.8	N18 41.7	148 15.0	12.2	S 6 26.7	16.0	58.8
19	105 54.8	42.3	162 46.2	12.3	6 10.7	16.1	58.8
20	120 54.8	42.9	177 17.5	12.2	5 54.6	16.0	58.8
21	135 54.8 ..	43.5	191 48.7	12.4	5 38.6	16.1	58.8
22	150 54.8	44.0	206 20.1	12.3	5 22.5	16.1	58.8
23	165 54.8	44.6	220 51.4	12.4	5 06.4	16.2	58.8
15 00	180 54.8	N18 45.2	235 22.8	12.5	S 4 50.2	16.1	58.8
01	195 54.8	45.8	249 54.3	12.4	4 34.1	16.2	58.8
02	210 54.8	46.4	264 25.7	12.5	4 17.9	16.2	58.8
03	225 54.7 ..	47.0	278 57.2	12.6	4 01.7	16.2	58.7
04	240 54.7	47.6	293 28.8	12.5	3 45.5	16.2	58.7
05	255 54.7	48.2	308 00.3	12.6	3 29.3	16.2	58.7
06	270 54.7	N18 48.8	322 31.9	12.6	S 3 13.1	16.2	58.7
07	285 54.7	49.4	337 03.5	12.7	2 56.9	16.2	58.7
08	300 54.7	50.0	351 35.2	12.7	2 40.7	16.3	58.7
M 09	315 54.7 ..	50.6	6 06.9	12.7	2 24.4	16.2	58.7
O 10	330 54.7	51.2	20 38.6	12.7	2 08.2	16.3	58.6
N 11	345 54.7	51.8	35 10.3	12.7	1 51.9	16.2	58.6
D 12	0 54.7	N18 52.4	49 42.0	12.8	S 1 35.7	16.3	58.6
A 13	15 54.7	53.0	64 13.8	12.8	1 19.4	16.2	58.6
Y 14	30 54.7	53.5	78 45.6	12.8	1 03.2	16.3	58.6
15	45 54.7 ..	54.1	93 17.4	12.8	0 46.9	16.2	58.6
16	60 54.7	54.7	107 49.2	12.8	0 30.7	16.3	58.6
17	75 54.6	55.3	122 21.0	12.9	S 0 14.4	16.2	58.5
18	90 54.6	N18 55.9	136 52.9	12.8	N 0 01.8	16.2	58.5
19	105 54.6	56.5	151 24.7	12.9	0 18.0	16.3	58.5
20	120 54.6	57.1	165 56.6	12.9	0 34.3	16.2	58.5
21	135 54.6 ..	57.7	180 28.5	12.9	0 50.5	16.2	58.5
22	150 54.6	58.2	195 00.4	12.9	1 06.7	16.2	58.5
23	165 54.6	58.8	209 32.3	12.9	N 1 22.9	16.1	58.5
	SD 15.9 d 0.6		SD 16.1		16.1		16.0

Moonrise

Lat.	Twilight Naut.	Twilight Civil	Sunrise	13	14	15	16
°	h m	h m	h m	h m	h m	h m	h m
N 72	☐	☐	☐	05 00	03 56	03 16	02 41
N 70	////	////	00 57	04 22	03 40	03 10	02 44
68	////	////	01 54	03 55	03 27	03 06	02 47
66	////	////	02 27	03 34	03 16	03 02	02 49
64	////	01 17	02 51	03 18	03 07	02 59	02 50
62	////	01 57	03 10	03 04	03 00	02 56	02 52
60	////	02 23	03 25	02 52	02 53	02 53	02 53
N 58	01 09	02 44	03 38	02 42	02 47	02 51	02 55
56	01 45	03 00	03 50	02 33	02 42	02 49	02 56
54	02 10	03 14	03 59	02 25	02 37	02 47	02 57
52	02 29	03 26	04 08	02 17	02 33	02 46	02 58
50	02 45	03 37	04 16	02 11	02 29	02 44	02 58
45	03 15	03 59	04 33	01 57	02 20	02 41	03 00
N 40	03 38	04 16	04 46	01 45	02 13	02 38	03 02
35	03 56	04 30	04 58	01 35	02 07	02 36	03 03
30	04 10	04 41	05 07	01 26	02 01	02 34	03 04
20	04 33	05 01	05 24	01 11	01 52	02 30	03 07
N 10	04 51	05 17	05 39	00 58	01 44	02 27	03 08
0	05 06	05 31	05 53	00 45	01 36	02 24	03 10
S 10	05 19	05 44	06 06	00 32	01 28	02 21	03 12
20	05 31	05 57	06 21	00 19	01 19	02 17	03 14
30	05 43	06 12	06 37	00 03	01 09	02 14	03 16
35	05 49	06 19	06 46	25 04	01 04	02 11	03 18
40	05 55	06 28	06 57	24 57	00 57	02 09	03 19
45	06 02	06 38	07 10	24 50	00 50	02 06	03 21
S 50	06 10	06 49	07 25	24 41	00 41	02 03	03 23
52	06 13	06 55	07 32	24 36	00 36	02 01	03 24
54	06 17	07 00	07 40	24 32	00 32	02 00	03 25
56	06 21	07 06	07 49	24 27	00 27	01 58	03 26
58	06 25	07 13	07 59	24 21	00 21	01 55	03 28
S 60	06 29	07 21	08 10	24 14	00 14	01 53	03 29

Moonset

Lat.	Sunset	Twilight Civil	Twilight Naut.	13	14	15	16
°	h m	h m	h m	h m	h m	h m	h m
N 72	☐	☐	☐	09 22	12 11	14 33	16 51
N 70	23 07	////	////	09 58	12 24	14 34	16 42
68	22 03	////	////	10 23	12 35	14 36	16 34
66	21 29	////	////	10 42	12 43	14 37	16 28
64	21 04	22 42	////	10 57	12 50	14 38	16 23
62	20 45	22 00	////	11 09	12 56	14 38	16 19
60	20 29	21 32	////	11 20	13 02	14 39	16 15
N 58	20 16	21 11	22 49	11 29	13 06	14 40	16 11
56	20 04	20 54	22 11	11 37	13 10	14 40	16 09
54	19 54	20 40	21 45	11 44	13 14	14 40	16 06
52	19 46	20 28	21 25	11 51	13 17	14 41	16 03
50	19 38	20 17	21 09	11 57	13 20	14 41	16 01
45	19 21	19 55	20 38	12 09	13 26	14 42	15 57
N 40	19 07	19 38	20 16	12 19	13 32	14 43	15 53
35	18 56	19 24	19 58	12 28	13 36	14 43	15 49
30	18 46	19 12	19 43	12 35	13 40	14 44	15 46
20	18 28	18 52	19 20	12 48	13 47	14 45	15 41
N 10	18 14	18 36	19 02	12 59	13 53	14 45	15 37
0	18 00	18 22	18 47	13 09	13 59	14 46	15 32
S 10	17 46	18 08	18 34	13 20	14 04	14 46	15 28
20	17 32	17 55	18 22	13 31	14 10	14 47	15 24
30	17 15	17 41	18 10	13 43	14 16	14 48	15 18
35	17 06	17 33	18 03	13 50	14 20	14 48	15 16
40	16 55	17 24	17 57	13 58	14 24	14 49	15 12
45	16 43	17 14	17 50	14 07	14 29	14 49	15 08
S 50	16 27	17 03	17 42	14 18	14 35	14 50	15 04
52	16 20	16 58	17 39	14 23	14 38	14 50	15 02
54	16 12	16 52	17 35	14 29	14 40	14 50	15 00
56	16 03	16 46	17 31	14 35	14 44	14 51	14 57
58	15 53	16 39	17 27	14 42	14 47	14 51	14 54
S 60	15 42	16 31	17 23	14 50	14 51	14 51	14 51

Day	SUN Eqn. of Time 00h	SUN Eqn. of Time 12h	Mer. Pass.	MOON Mer. Pass. Upper	MOON Mer. Pass. Lower	Age	Phase
d	m s	m s	h m	h m	h m	d	%
13	03 39	03 39	11 56	06 57	19 23	23	40
14	03 39	03 39	11 56	07 47	20 11	24	29
15	03 39	03 39	11 56	08 35	20 58	25	19

© British Crown Copyright 2022. All rights reserved.

2023 MAY 16, 17, 18 (TUES., WED., THURS.)

UT	ARIES GHA	VENUS −4.3 GHA	Dec	MARS +1.5 GHA	Dec	JUPITER −2.1 GHA	Dec	SATURN +0.8 GHA	Dec	STARS Name	SHA	Dec
16 00	233 27.1	133 19.9	N25 53.4	113 41.1	N22 16.6	205 18.9	N10 24.7	254 47.9	S10 32.6	Acamar	315 13.3	S40 12.7
01	248 29.5	148 19.5	53.2	128 42.1	16.3	220 20.8	24.9	269 50.3	32.5	Achernar	335 21.7	S57 07.0
02	263 32.0	163 19.0	53.1	143 43.0	16.0	235 22.8	25.1	284 52.6	32.5	Acrux	173 01.2	S63 13.9
03	278 34.5	178 18.5 . .	52.9	158 44.0 . .	15.7	250 24.7 . .	25.3	299 55.0 . .	32.5	Adhara	255 07.2	S29 00.4
04	293 36.9	193 18.0	52.7	173 45.0	15.4	265 26.6	25.5	314 57.3	32.4	Aldebaran	290 41.6	N16 33.3
05	308 39.4	208 17.5	52.6	188 45.9	15.1	280 28.5	25.7	329 59.6	32.4			
06	323 41.8	223 17.0	N25 52.4	203 46.9	N22 14.8	295 30.4	N10 25.9	345 02.0	S10 32.3	Alioth	166 13.8	N55 50.2
T 07	338 44.3	238 16.5	52.2	218 47.9	14.4	310 32.4	26.1	0 04.3	32.3	Alkaid	152 52.7	N49 11.9
U 08	353 46.8	253 16.0	52.1	233 48.9	14.1	325 34.3	26.3	15 06.7	32.3	Alnair	27 34.7	S46 50.7
E 09	8 49.2	268 15.5 . .	51.9	248 49.8 . .	13.8	340 36.2 . .	26.5	30 09.0 . .	32.2	Alnilam	275 39.4	S 1 11.3
S 10	23 51.7	283 15.0	51.7	263 50.8	13.5	355 38.1	26.7	45 11.3	32.2	Alphard	217 49.2	S 8 45.7
D 11	38 54.2	298 14.5	51.6	278 51.8	13.2	10 40.0	26.9	60 13.7	32.1			
A 12	53 56.6	313 14.1	N25 51.4	293 52.7	N22 12.9	25 42.0	N10 27.1	75 16.0	S10 32.1	Alphecca	126 04.6	N26 38.1
Y 13	68 59.1	328 13.6	51.2	308 53.7	12.6	40 43.9	27.3	90 18.4	32.1	Alpheratz	357 36.4	N29 12.9
14	84 01.6	343 13.1	51.0	323 54.7	12.3	55 45.8	27.5	105 20.7	32.0	Altair	62 01.1	N 8 55.6
15	99 04.0	358 12.6 . .	50.9	338 55.7 . .	12.0	70 47.7 . .	27.7	120 23.0 . .	32.0	Ankaa	353 08.8	S42 10.7
16	114 06.5	13 12.1	50.7	353 56.6	11.7	85 49.6	27.9	135 25.4	31.9	Antares	112 17.2	S26 29.0
17	129 09.0	28 11.6	50.5	8 57.6	11.4	100 51.5	28.1	150 27.7	31.9			
18	144 11.4	43 11.1	N25 50.3	23 58.6	N22 11.1	115 53.5	N10 28.3	165 30.1	S10 31.9	Arcturus	145 48.9	N19 03.7
19	159 13.9	58 10.7	50.2	38 59.5	10.8	130 55.4	28.5	180 32.4	31.8	Atria	107 12.1	S69 04.1
20	174 16.3	73 10.2	50.0	54 00.5	10.5	145 57.3	28.7	195 34.7	31.8	Avior	234 15.6	S59 35.3
21	189 18.8	88 09.7 . .	49.8	69 01.5 . .	10.2	160 59.2 . .	28.9	210 37.1 . .	31.7	Bellatrix	278 24.7	N 6 22.2
22	204 21.3	103 09.2	49.6	84 02.5	09.9	176 01.1	29.1	225 39.4	31.7	Betelgeuse	270 53.9	N 7 24.6
23	219 23.7	118 08.7	49.4	99 03.4	09.6	191 03.1	29.3	240 41.8	31.7			
17 00	234 26.2	133 08.2	N25 49.2	114 04.4	N22 09.2	206 05.0	N10 29.5	255 44.1	S10 31.6	Canopus	263 53.4	S52 42.6
01	249 28.7	148 07.8	49.1	129 05.4	08.9	221 06.9	29.7	270 46.4	31.6	Capella	280 24.4	N46 01.3
02	264 31.1	163 07.3	48.9	144 06.3	08.6	236 08.8	29.9	285 48.8	31.6	Deneb	49 26.6	N45 21.5
03	279 33.6	178 06.8 . .	48.7	159 07.3 . .	08.3	251 10.7 . .	30.1	300 51.1 . .	31.5	Denebola	182 26.2	N14 26.6
04	294 36.1	193 06.3	48.5	174 08.3	08.0	266 12.7	30.3	315 53.5	31.5	Diphda	348 48.9	S17 51.6
05	309 38.5	208 05.9	48.3	189 09.3	07.7	281 14.6	30.5	330 55.8	31.4			
06	324 41.0	223 05.4	N25 48.1	204 10.2	N22 07.4	296 16.5	N10 30.7	345 58.2	S10 31.4	Dubhe	193 42.5	N61 37.8
W 07	339 43.5	238 04.9	47.9	219 11.2	07.1	311 18.4	30.9	1 00.5	31.4	Elnath	278 04.0	N28 37.6
E 08	354 45.9	253 04.4	47.7	234 12.2	06.8	326 20.3	31.1	16 02.8	31.3	Eltanin	90 42.4	N51 28.9
D 09	9 48.4	268 04.0 . .	47.5	249 13.2 . .	06.5	341 22.3 . .	31.3	31 05.2 . .	31.3	Enif	33 40.2	N 9 58.7
N 10	24 50.8	283 03.5	47.3	264 14.1	06.2	356 24.2	31.5	46 07.5	31.2	Fomalhaut	15 16.2	S29 29.9
E 11	39 53.3	298 03.0	47.1	279 15.1	05.8	11 26.1	31.7	61 09.9	31.2			
S 12	54 55.8	313 02.5	N25 46.9	294 16.1	N22 05.5	26 28.0	N10 31.9	76 12.2	S10 31.2	Gacrux	171 52.8	S57 14.8
D 13	69 58.2	328 02.1	46.7	309 17.0	05.2	41 29.9	32.1	91 14.6	31.1	Gienah	175 44.8	S17 40.4
A 14	85 00.7	343 01.6	46.5	324 18.0	04.9	56 31.9	32.3	106 16.9	31.1	Hadar	148 37.4	S60 29.2
Y 15	100 03.2	358 01.1 . .	46.3	339 19.0 . .	04.6	71 33.8 . .	32.5	121 19.2 . .	31.1	Hamal	327 53.1	N23 34.2
16	115 05.6	13 00.7	46.1	354 20.0	04.3	86 35.7	32.7	136 21.6	31.0	Kaus Aust.	83 34.0	S34 22.4
17	130 08.1	28 00.2	45.9	9 20.9	04.0	101 37.6	32.9	151 23.9	31.0			
18	145 10.6	42 59.7	N25 45.7	24 21.9	N22 03.7	116 39.5	N10 33.1	166 26.3	S10 30.9	Kochab	137 18.6	N74 03.6
19	160 13.0	57 59.2	45.5	39 22.9	03.4	131 41.5	33.3	181 28.6	30.9	Markab	13 31.4	N15 19.6
20	175 15.5	72 58.8	45.3	54 23.8	03.0	146 43.4	33.4	196 31.0	30.9	Menkar	314 07.9	N 4 10.8
21	190 17.9	87 58.3 . .	45.1	69 24.8 . .	02.7	161 45.3 . .	33.6	211 33.3 . .	30.8	Menkent	147 58.9	S36 29.2
22	205 20.4	102 57.8	44.9	84 25.8	02.4	176 47.2	33.8	226 35.6	30.8	Miaplacidus	221 38.7	S69 49.0
23	220 22.9	117 57.4	44.7	99 26.8	02.1	191 49.1	34.0	241 38.0	30.8			
18 00	235 25.3	132 56.9	N25 44.5	114 27.7	N22 01.8	206 51.1	N10 34.2	256 40.3	S10 30.7	Mirfak	308 30.8	N49 56.5
01	250 27.8	147 56.5	44.3	129 28.7	01.5	221 53.0	34.4	271 42.7	30.7	Nunki	75 49.2	S26 16.0
02	265 30.3	162 56.0	44.0	144 29.7	01.2	236 54.9	34.6	286 45.0	30.6	Peacock	53 07.7	S56 39.4
03	280 32.7	177 55.5 . .	43.8	159 30.6 . .	00.9	251 56.8 . .	34.8	301 47.4 . .	30.6	Pollux	243 19.2	N27 58.3
04	295 35.2	192 55.1	43.6	174 31.6	00.5	266 58.8	35.0	316 49.7	30.6	Procyon	244 52.5	N 5 09.9
05	310 37.7	207 54.6	43.4	189 32.6	22 00.2	282 00.7	35.2	331 52.1	30.5			
06	325 40.1	222 54.1	N25 43.2	204 33.6	N21 59.9	297 02.6	N10 35.4	346 54.4	S10 30.5	Rasalhague	96 59.5	N12 32.5
T 07	340 42.6	237 53.7	43.0	219 34.5	59.6	312 04.5	35.6	1 56.8	30.5	Regulus	207 39.9	N11 51.2
H 08	355 45.1	252 53.2	42.8	234 35.5	59.3	327 06.4	35.8	16 59.1	30.4	Rigel	281 05.5	S 8 10.6
U 09	10 47.5	267 52.8 . .	42.5	249 36.5 . .	59.0	342 08.4 . .	36.0	32 01.4 . .	30.4	Rigil Kent.	139 41.6	S60 56.0
R 10	25 50.0	282 52.3	42.3	264 37.4	58.6	357 10.3	36.2	47 03.8	30.3	Sabik	102 04.1	S15 45.3
S 11	40 52.4	297 51.9	42.1	279 38.4	58.3	12 12.2	36.4	62 06.1	30.3			
D 12	55 54.9	312 51.4	N25 41.9	294 39.4	N21 58.0	27 14.1	N10 36.6	77 08.5	S10 30.3	Schedar	349 33.0	N56 39.6
A 13	70 57.4	327 50.9	41.6	309 40.4	57.7	42 16.0	36.8	92 10.8	30.2	Shaula	96 11.9	S37 07.2
Y 14	85 59.8	342 50.5	41.4	324 41.3	57.4	57 18.0	37.0	107 13.2	30.2	Sirius	258 27.7	S16 45.0
15	101 02.3	357 50.0 . .	41.2	339 42.3 . .	57.1	72 19.9 . .	37.2	122 15.5 . .	30.2	Spica	158 23.5	S11 17.1
16	116 04.8	12 49.6	41.0	354 43.3	56.8	87 21.8	37.4	137 17.9	30.1	Suhail	222 47.4	S43 31.8
17	131 07.2	27 49.1	40.7	9 44.2	56.4	102 23.7	37.6	152 20.2	30.1			
18	146 09.7	42 48.7	N25 40.5	24 45.2	N21 56.1	117 25.7	N10 37.8	167 22.6	S10 30.1	Vega	80 33.8	N38 48.1
19	161 12.2	57 48.2	40.3	39 46.2	55.8	132 27.6	38.0	182 24.9	30.0	Zuben'ubi	136 57.2	S16 08.4
20	176 14.6	72 47.8	40.0	54 47.2	55.5	147 29.5	38.2	197 27.3	30.0			
21	191 17.1	87 47.3 . .	39.8	69 48.1 . .	55.2	162 31.4 . .	38.4	212 29.6 . .	29.9		SHA	Mer. Pass.
22	206 19.6	102 46.9	39.6	84 49.1	54.8	177 33.3	38.6	227 32.0	29.9	Venus	258 42.0	15 08
23	221 22.0	117 46.4	39.3	99 50.1	54.5	192 35.3	38.8	242 34.3	29.9	Mars	239 38.2	16 23
										Jupiter	331 38.8	10 14
Mer. Pass. 8 20.9		v −0.5 d 0.2		v 1.0 d 0.3		v 1.9 d 0.2		v 2.3 d 0.0		Saturn	21 17.9	6 56

© British Crown Copyright 2022. All rights reserved.

SUN and MOON

UT (d h)	SUN GHA	Dec	MOON GHA	v	Dec	d	HP
16 00	180 54.6	N18 59.4	224 04.2	12.9	N 1 39.0	16.2	58.4
01	195 54.6	19 00.0	238 36.1	12.9	1 55.2	16.1	58.4
02	210 54.6	00.6	253 08.0	12.9	2 11.3	16.2	58.4
03	225 54.5	.. 01.2	267 39.9	13.0	2 27.5	16.1	58.4
04	240 54.5	01.7	282 11.9	12.9	2 43.6	16.1	58.4
05	255 54.5	02.3	296 43.8	12.9	2 59.7	16.0	58.4
06	270 54.5	N19 02.9	311 15.7	12.9	N 3 15.7	16.1	58.3
07	285 54.5	03.5	325 47.6	12.9	3 31.8	16.0	58.3
08	300 54.5	04.1	340 19.5	12.9	3 47.8	16.0	58.3
09	315 54.5	.. 04.6	354 51.4	13.0	4 03.8	15.9	58.3
10	330 54.5	05.2	9 23.4	12.9	4 19.7	16.0	58.3
11	345 54.4	05.8	23 55.3	12.8	4 35.7	15.9	58.3
12	0 54.4	N19 06.4	38 27.1	12.9	N 4 51.6	15.8	58.2
13	15 54.4	06.9	52 59.0	12.9	5 07.4	15.9	58.2
14	30 54.4	07.5	67 30.9	12.9	5 23.3	15.8	58.2
15	45 54.4	.. 08.1	82 02.8	12.8	5 39.1	15.7	58.2
16	60 54.4	08.7	96 34.6	12.9	5 54.8	15.8	58.2
17	75 54.4	09.2	111 06.5	12.8	6 10.6	15.7	58.2
18	90 54.3	N19 09.8	125 38.3	12.8	N 6 26.3	15.6	58.1
19	105 54.3	10.4	140 10.1	12.8	6 41.9	15.7	58.1
20	120 54.3	11.0	154 41.9	12.8	6 57.6	15.5	58.1
21	135 54.3	.. 11.5	169 13.7	12.7	7 13.1	15.6	58.1
22	150 54.3	12.1	183 45.4	12.8	7 28.7	15.5	58.1
23	165 54.3	12.7	198 17.2	12.7	7 44.2	15.4	58.1
17 00	180 54.2	N19 13.2	212 48.9	12.7	N 7 59.6	15.4	58.0
01	195 54.2	13.8	227 20.6	12.6	8 15.0	15.3	58.0
02	210 54.2	14.4	241 52.2	12.7	8 30.3	15.3	58.0
03	225 54.2	.. 15.0	256 23.9	12.6	8 45.6	15.3	58.0
04	240 54.2	15.5	270 55.5	12.6	9 00.9	15.2	58.0
05	255 54.2	16.1	285 27.1	12.6	9 16.1	15.1	57.9
06	270 54.1	N19 16.7	299 58.7	12.5	N 9 31.2	15.1	57.9
07	285 54.1	17.2	314 30.2	12.6	9 46.3	15.1	57.9
08	300 54.1	17.8	329 01.8	12.4	10 01.4	14.9	57.9
09	315 54.1	.. 18.4	343 33.2	12.5	10 16.3	15.0	57.9
10	330 54.1	18.9	358 04.7	12.4	10 31.3	14.8	57.8
11	345 54.0	19.5	12 36.1	12.4	10 46.1	14.8	57.8
12	0 54.0	N19 20.0	27 07.5	12.4	N11 00.9	14.8	57.8
13	15 54.0	20.6	41 38.9	12.3	11 15.7	14.6	57.8
14	30 54.0	21.2	56 10.2	12.3	11 30.3	14.6	57.8
15	45 54.0	.. 21.7	70 41.5	12.3	11 44.9	14.6	57.8
16	60 53.9	22.3	85 12.8	12.2	11 59.5	14.5	57.7
17	75 53.9	22.9	99 44.0	12.2	12 14.0	14.4	57.7
18	90 53.9	N19 23.4	114 15.2	12.1	N12 28.4	14.3	57.7
19	105 53.9	24.0	128 46.3	12.1	12 42.7	14.3	57.7
20	120 53.9	24.5	143 17.4	12.1	12 57.0	14.2	57.6
21	135 53.8	.. 25.1	157 48.5	12.0	13 11.2	14.1	57.6
22	150 53.8	25.7	172 19.5	12.0	13 25.3	14.0	57.6
23	165 53.8	26.2	186 50.5	12.0	13 39.3	14.0	57.6
18 00	180 53.8	N19 26.8	201 21.5	11.9	N13 53.3	13.9	57.6
01	195 53.8	27.3	215 52.4	11.9	14 07.2	13.8	57.5
02	210 53.7	27.9	230 23.3	11.8	14 21.0	13.8	57.5
03	225 53.7	.. 28.4	244 54.1	11.8	14 34.8	13.6	57.5
04	240 53.7	29.0	259 24.9	11.7	14 48.4	13.6	57.5
05	255 53.7	29.5	273 55.6	11.7	15 02.0	13.5	57.5
06	270 53.6	N19 30.1	288 26.3	11.6	N15 15.5	13.4	57.4
07	285 53.6	30.6	302 56.9	11.6	15 28.9	13.3	57.4
08	300 53.6	31.2	317 27.5	11.6	15 42.2	13.2	57.4
09	315 53.6	.. 31.8	331 58.1	11.5	15 55.4	13.2	57.4
10	330 53.5	32.3	346 28.6	11.4	16 08.6	13.1	57.4
11	345 53.5	32.9	0 59.0	11.4	16 21.7	12.9	57.3
12	0 53.5	N19 33.4	15 29.4	11.4	N16 34.6	12.9	57.3
13	15 53.5	34.0	29 59.8	11.3	16 47.5	12.8	57.3
14	30 53.4	34.5	44 30.1	11.3	17 00.3	12.7	57.3
15	45 53.4	.. 35.0	59 00.4	11.2	17 13.0	12.6	57.2
16	60 53.4	35.6	73 30.6	11.1	17 25.6	12.5	57.2
17	75 53.4	36.1	88 00.7	11.1	17 38.1	12.4	57.2
18	90 53.3	N19 36.7	102 30.8	11.1	N17 50.5	12.3	57.2
19	105 53.3	37.2	117 00.9	11.0	18 02.8	12.2	57.2
20	120 53.3	37.8	131 30.9	11.0	18 15.0	12.1	57.1
21	135 53.2	.. 38.3	146 00.9	10.9	18 27.1	12.0	57.1
22	150 53.2	38.9	160 30.8	10.8	18 39.1	11.9	57.1
23	165 53.2	39.4	175 00.6	10.8	N18 51.0	11.8	57.1
	SD 15.8	d 0.6	SD 15.9		15.8		15.6

Twilight, Sunrise and Moonrise

Lat.	Naut.	Civil	Sunrise	Moonrise 16	17	18	19
N 72	□	□	□	02 41	02 05	01 16	□
N 70	□	□	□	02 44	02 17	01 43	00 37
68	////	////	01 37	02 47	02 27	02 03	01 27
66	////	////	02 15	02 49	02 35	02 20	01 58
64	////	00 55	02 42	02 50	02 42	02 33	02 22
62	////	01 44	03 02	02 52	02 48	02 45	02 41
60	////	02 14	03 18	02 53	02 54	02 54	02 57
N 58	00 49	02 36	03 32	02 55	02 58	03 03	03 10
56	01 34	02 54	03 44	02 56	03 03	03 11	03 22
54	02 01	03 08	03 55	02 57	03 06	03 18	03 32
52	02 22	03 21	04 04	02 58	03 10	03 24	03 41
50	02 39	03 32	04 12	02 58	03 13	03 29	03 49
45	03 11	03 55	04 29	03 00	03 20	03 42	04 06
N 40	03 34	04 13	04 43	03 02	03 26	03 52	04 21
35	03 53	04 27	04 55	03 03	03 31	04 00	04 33
30	04 08	04 39	05 06	03 04	03 35	04 08	04 44
20	04 32	05 00	05 23	03 07	03 43	04 21	05 02
N 10	04 50	05 16	05 39	03 08	03 50	04 33	05 18
0	05 05	05 31	05 53	03 10	03 57	04 44	05 34
S 10	05 19	05 45	06 07	03 12	04 03	04 56	05 49
20	05 32	05 59	06 22	03 14	04 11	05 08	06 06
30	05 44	06 13	06 39	03 16	04 19	05 22	06 25
35	05 51	06 22	06 49	03 18	04 24	05 30	06 36
40	05 58	06 31	07 00	03 19	04 29	05 39	06 49
45	06 05	06 41	07 13	03 21	04 35	05 50	07 04
S 50	06 13	06 53	07 29	03 23	04 43	06 03	07 23
52	06 17	06 59	07 36	03 24	04 47	06 09	07 32
54	06 21	07 05	07 45	03 25	04 51	06 16	07 43
56	06 25	07 11	07 54	03 26	04 55	06 24	07 54
58	06 30	07 19	08 05	03 28	05 00	06 33	08 07
S 60	06 34	07 27	08 17	03 29	05 05	06 43	08 23

Sunset, Twilight and Moonset

Lat.	Sunset	Civil	Naut.	Moonset 16	17	18	19
N 72	□	□	□	16 51	19 20	□	□
N 70	□	□	□	16 42	18 56	21 44	□
68	22 21	////	////	16 34	18 37	20 56	□
66	21 41	////	////	16 28	18 22	20 25	22 56
64	21 14	23 07	////	16 23	18 10	20 03	22 05
62	20 53	22 13	////	16 19	18 00	19 45	21 34
60	20 36	21 42	////	16 15	17 51	19 30	21 10
N 58	20 22	21 19	23 11	16 11	17 44	19 18	20 52
56	20 10	21 01	22 23	16 09	17 37	19 07	20 36
54	19 59	20 46	21 54	16 06	17 31	18 57	20 23
52	19 50	20 33	21 33	16 03	17 26	18 49	20 11
50	19 42	20 22	21 16	16 01	17 21	18 41	20 01
45	19 24	19 59	20 43	15 57	17 11	18 25	19 39
N 40	19 10	19 41	20 19	15 53	17 02	18 12	19 22
35	18 58	19 26	20 01	15 49	16 55	18 01	19 08
30	18 48	19 14	19 45	15 46	16 49	17 52	18 55
20	18 30	18 53	19 21	15 41	16 38	17 35	18 34
N 10	18 14	18 37	19 03	15 37	16 28	17 21	18 15
0	18 00	18 22	18 47	15 32	16 19	17 08	17 58
S 10	17 46	18 08	18 34	15 28	16 10	16 54	17 41
20	17 31	17 54	18 21	15 24	16 01	16 40	17 23
30	17 14	17 39	18 08	15 18	15 50	16 24	17 02
35	17 04	17 31	18 02	15 16	15 44	16 15	16 50
40	16 53	17 22	17 55	15 12	15 37	16 04	16 36
45	16 39	17 11	17 47	15 08	15 29	15 52	16 19
S 50	16 23	16 59	17 39	15 04	15 19	15 37	15 59
52	16 16	16 54	17 35	15 02	15 15	15 30	15 49
54	16 07	16 48	17 31	15 00	15 10	15 22	15 39
56	15 58	16 41	17 27	14 57	15 04	15 14	15 26
58	15 47	16 34	17 23	14 54	14 58	15 04	15 12
S 60	15 35	16 25	17 18	14 51	14 52	14 53	14 56

SUN and MOON

Day	Eqn. of Time 00h	12h	Mer. Pass.	Mer. Pass. Upper	Lower	Age	Phase
	m s	m s	h m	h m	h m	d	%
16	03 38	03 38	11 56	09 21	21 44	26	11
17	03 37	03 36	11 56	10 08	22 32	27	5
18	03 35	03 34	11 56	10 56	23 21	28	2

© British Crown Copyright 2022. All rights reserved.

UT	ARIES	VENUS −4.3		MARS +1.5		JUPITER −2.1		SATURN +0.8		STARS		
	GHA	GHA	Dec	GHA	Dec	GHA	Dec	GHA	Dec	Name	SHA	Dec
d h	° ′	° ′	° ′	° ′	° ′	° ′	° ′	° ′	° ′		° ′	° ′
19 00	236 24.5	132 46.0 N25 39.1		114 51.0 N21 54.2		207 37.2 N10 39.0		257 36.7 S10 29.8		Acamar	315 13.2 S40 12.7	
01	251 26.9	147 45.5	38.9	129 52.0	53.9	222 39.1	39.1	272 39.0	29.8	Achernar	335 21.7 S57 07.0	
02	266 29.4	162 45.1	38.6	144 53.0	53.6	237 41.0	39.3	287 41.4	29.8	Acrux	173 01.2 S63 13.9	
03	281 31.9	177 44.6 . .	38.4	159 54.0 . .	53.3	252 43.0 . .	39.5	302 43.7 . .	29.7	Adhara	255 07.2 S29 00.4	
04	296 34.3	192 44.2	38.1	174 54.9	52.9	267 44.9	39.7	317 46.1	29.7	Aldebaran	290 41.6 N16 33.3	
05	311 36.8	207 43.8	37.9	189 55.9	52.6	282 46.8	39.9	332 48.4	29.7			
06	326 39.3	222 43.3 N25 37.7		204 56.9 N21 52.3		297 48.7 N10 40.1		347 50.8 S10 29.6		Alioth	166 13.8 N55 50.2	
07	341 41.7	237 42.9	37.4	219 57.8	52.0	312 50.7	40.3	2 53.1	29.6	Alkaid	152 52.7 N49 11.9	
08	356 44.2	252 42.4	37.2	234 58.8	51.7	327 52.6	40.5	17 55.5	29.5	Alnair	27 34.7 S46 50.7	
F 09	11 46.7	267 42.0 . .	36.9	249 59.8 . .	51.3	342 54.5 . .	40.7	32 57.8 . .	29.5	Alnilam	275 39.4 S 1 11.3	
R 10	26 49.1	282 41.5	36.7	265 00.8	51.0	357 56.4	40.9	48 00.2	29.5	Alphard	217 49.2 S 8 45.7	
I 11	41 51.6	297 41.1	36.4	280 01.7	50.7	12 58.3	41.1	63 02.5	29.4			
D 12	56 54.1	312 40.7 N25 36.2		295 02.7 N21 50.4		28 00.3 N10 41.3		78 04.9 S10 29.4		Alphecca	126 04.5 N26 38.1	
A 13	71 56.5	327 40.2	35.9	310 03.7	50.0	43 02.2	41.5	93 07.2	29.4	Alpheratz	357 36.4 N29 12.9	
Y 14	86 59.0	342 39.8	35.7	325 04.6	49.7	58 04.1	41.7	108 09.6	29.3	Altair	62 01.1 N 8 55.6	
15	102 01.4	357 39.4 . .	35.4	340 05.6 . .	49.4	73 06.0 . .	41.9	123 11.9 . .	29.3	Ankaa	353 08.8 S42 10.7	
16	117 03.9	12 38.9	35.2	355 06.6	49.1	88 08.0	42.1	138 14.3	29.3	Antares	112 17.2 S26 29.0	
17	132 06.4	27 38.5	34.9	10 07.6	48.8	103 09.9	42.3	153 16.6	29.2			
18	147 08.8	42 38.1 N25 34.7		25 08.5 N21 48.4		118 11.8 N10 42.5		168 19.0 S10 29.2		Arcturus	145 48.9 N19 03.7	
19	162 11.3	57 37.6	34.4	40 09.5	48.1	133 13.7	42.7	183 21.3	29.2	Atria	107 12.1 S69 04.1	
20	177 13.8	72 37.2	34.2	55 10.5	47.8	148 15.7	42.9	198 23.7	29.1	Avior	234 15.6 S59 35.3	
21	192 16.2	87 36.8 . .	33.9	70 11.4 . .	47.5	163 17.6 . .	43.1	213 26.0 . .	29.1	Bellatrix	278 24.7 N 6 22.2	
22	207 18.7	102 36.3	33.7	85 12.4	47.1	178 19.5	43.2	228 28.4	29.1	Betelgeuse	270 53.9 N 7 24.6	
23	222 21.2	117 35.9	33.4	100 13.4	46.8	193 21.4	43.4	243 30.7	29.0			
20 00	237 23.6	132 35.5 N25 33.1		115 14.4 N21 46.5		208 23.3 N10 43.6		258 33.1 S10 29.0		Canopus	263 53.5 S52 42.6	
01	252 26.1	147 35.0	32.9	130 15.3	46.2	223 25.3	43.8	273 35.4	29.0	Capella	280 24.4 N46 01.3	
02	267 28.5	162 34.6	32.6	145 16.3	45.8	238 27.2	44.0	288 37.8	28.9	Deneb	49 26.6 N45 21.5	
03	282 31.0	177 34.2 . .	32.3	160 17.3 . .	45.5	253 29.1 . .	44.2	303 40.1 . .	28.9	Denebola	182 26.2 N14 26.6	
04	297 33.5	192 33.8	32.1	175 18.2	45.2	268 31.0	44.4	318 42.5	28.9	Diphda	348 48.9 S17 51.6	
05	312 35.9	207 33.3	31.8	190 19.2	44.9	283 33.0	44.6	333 44.8	28.8			
06	327 38.4	222 32.9 N25 31.6		205 20.2 N21 44.5		298 34.9 N10 44.8		348 47.2 S10 28.8		Dubhe	193 42.5 N61 37.8	
S 07	342 40.9	237 32.5	31.3	220 21.2	44.2	313 36.8	45.0	3 49.5	28.7	Elnath	278 04.0 N28 37.6	
A 08	357 43.3	252 32.1	31.0	235 22.1	43.9	328 38.7	45.2	18 51.9	28.7	Eltanin	90 42.4 N51 28.9	
T 09	12 45.8	267 31.6 . .	30.7	250 23.1 . .	43.6	343 40.7 . .	45.4	33 54.2 . .	28.7	Enif	33 40.1 N 9 58.7	
U 10	27 48.3	282 31.2	30.5	265 24.1	43.2	358 42.6	45.6	48 56.6	28.6	Fomalhaut	15 16.1 S29 29.9	
R 11	42 50.7	297 30.8	30.2	280 25.0	42.9	13 44.5	45.8	63 58.9	28.6			
D 12	57 53.2	312 30.4 N25 29.9		295 26.0 N21 42.6		28 46.4 N10 46.0		79 01.3 S10 28.6		Gacrux	171 52.8 S57 14.8	
A 13	72 55.7	327 29.9	29.7	310 27.0	42.3	43 48.4	46.2	94 03.7	28.5	Gienah	175 44.8 S17 40.4	
Y 14	87 58.1	342 29.5	29.4	325 28.0	41.9	58 50.3	46.4	109 06.0	28.5	Hadar	148 37.4 S60 29.3	
15	103 00.6	357 29.1 . .	29.1	340 28.9 . .	41.6	73 52.2 . .	46.6	124 08.4 . .	28.5	Hamal	327 53.1 N23 34.2	
16	118 03.0	12 28.7	28.8	355 29.9	41.3	88 54.1	46.7	139 10.7	28.4	Kaus Aust.	83 34.0 S34 22.4	
17	133 05.5	27 28.3	28.6	10 30.9	40.9	103 56.1	46.9	154 13.1	28.4			
18	148 08.0	42 27.9 N25 28.3		25 31.8 N21 40.6		118 58.0 N10 47.1		169 15.4 S10 28.4		Kochab	137 18.6 N74 03.6	
19	163 10.4	57 27.4	28.0	40 32.8	40.3	133 59.9	47.3	184 17.8	28.3	Markab	13 31.4 N15 19.6	
20	178 12.9	72 27.0	27.7	55 33.8	40.0	149 01.8	47.5	199 20.1	28.3	Menkar	314 07.9 N 4 10.8	
21	193 15.4	87 26.6 . .	27.4	70 34.8 . .	39.6	164 03.8 . .	47.7	214 22.5 . .	28.3	Menkent	147 58.9 S36 29.2	
22	208 17.8	102 26.2	27.1	85 35.7	39.3	179 05.7	47.9	229 24.8	28.2	Miaplacidus	221 38.8 S69 49.0	
23	223 20.3	117 25.8	26.9	100 36.7	39.0	194 07.6	48.1	244 27.2	28.2			
21 00	238 22.8	132 25.4 N25 26.6		115 37.7 N21 38.6		209 09.5 N10 48.3		259 29.6 S10 28.2		Mirfak	308 30.7 N49 56.5	
01	253 25.2	147 25.0	26.3	130 38.6	38.3	224 11.5	48.5	274 31.9	28.1	Nunki	75 49.2 S26 16.0	
02	268 27.7	162 24.6	26.0	145 39.6	38.0	239 13.4	48.7	289 34.3	28.1	Peacock	53 07.7 S56 39.4	
03	283 30.2	177 24.1 . .	25.7	160 40.6 . .	37.7	254 15.3 . .	48.9	304 36.6 . .	28.1	Pollux	243 19.2 N27 58.3	
04	298 32.6	192 23.7	25.4	175 41.6	37.3	269 17.2	49.1	319 39.0	28.0	Procyon	244 52.5 N 5 09.9	
05	313 35.1	207 23.3	25.1	190 42.5	37.0	284 19.2	49.3	334 41.3	28.0			
06	328 37.5	222 22.9 N25 24.8		205 43.5 N21 36.7		299 21.1 N10 49.5		349 43.7 S10 28.0		Rasalhague	95 59.5 N12 32.5	
07	343 40.0	237 22.5	24.6	220 44.5	36.3	314 23.0	49.6	4 46.1	27.9	Regulus	207 35.9 N11 51.2	
08	358 42.5	252 22.1	24.3	235 45.4	36.0	329 25.0	49.8	19 48.4	27.9	Rigel	281 05.5 S 8 10.6	
S 09	13 44.9	267 21.7 . .	24.0	250 46.4 . .	35.7	344 26.9 . .	50.0	34 50.8 . .	27.9	Rigil Kent.	139 41.6 S60 56.0	
U 10	28 47.4	282 21.3	23.7	265 47.4	35.3	359 28.8	50.2	49 53.1	27.8	Sabik	102 04.0 S15 45.3	
N 11	43 49.9	297 20.9	23.4	280 48.4	35.0	14 30.7	50.4	64 55.5	27.8			
D 12	58 52.3	312 20.5 N25 23.1		295 49.3 N21 34.7		29 32.7 N10 50.6		79 57.8 S10 27.8		Schedar	349 33.0 N56 39.6	
A 13	73 54.8	327 20.1	22.8	310 50.3	34.3	44 34.6	50.8	95 00.2	27.7	Shaula	96 11.9 S37 07.2	
Y 14	88 57.3	342 19.7	22.5	325 51.3	34.0	59 36.5	51.0	110 02.6	27.7	Sirius	258 27.7 S16 45.0	
15	103 59.7	357 19.3 . .	22.2	340 52.2 . .	33.7	74 38.4 . .	51.2	125 04.9 . .	27.7	Spica	158 23.5 S11 17.1	
16	119 02.2	12 18.9	21.9	355 53.2	33.3	89 40.4	51.4	140 07.3	27.7	Suhail	222 47.4 S43 31.8	
17	134 04.7	27 18.5	21.6	10 54.2	33.0	104 42.3	51.6	155 09.6	27.6			
18	149 07.1	42 18.1 N25 21.3		25 55.2 N21 32.7		119 44.2 N10 51.8		170 12.0 S10 27.6		Vega	80 33.8 N38 48.1	
19	164 09.6	57 17.7	21.0	40 56.1	32.3	134 46.1	52.0	185 14.3	27.6	Zuben'ubi	136 57.2 S16 08.4	
20	179 12.0	72 17.3	20.7	55 57.1	32.0	149 48.1	52.2	200 16.7	27.5		SHA	Mer. Pass.
21	194 14.5	87 16.9 . .	20.4	70 58.1 . .	31.7	164 50.0 . .	52.3	215 19.1 . .	27.5		° ′	h m
22	209 17.0	102 16.5	20.1	85 59.1	31.3	179 51.9	52.5	230 21.4	27.5	Venus	255 11.8	15 10
23	224 21.2	117 16.1	19.8	101 00.0	31.0	194 53.9	52.7	245 23.8	27.4	Mars	237 50.7	16 18
	h m									Jupiter	330 59.7	10 05
Mer. Pass. 8 09.1		v −0.4 d 0.3		v 1.0 d 0.3		v 1.9 d 0.2		v 2.4 d 0.0		Saturn	21 09.4	6 45

© British Crown Copyright 2022. All rights reserved.

UT	SUN GHA	SUN Dec	MOON GHA	v	MOON Dec	d	HP
19 00	180 53.2	N19 40.0	189 30.4	10.8	N19 02.8	11.7	57.0
01	195 53.1	40.5	204 00.2	10.7	19 14.5	11.5	57.0
02	210 53.1	41.0	218 29.9	10.6	19 26.0	11.5	57.0
03	225 53.1	.. 41.6	232 59.5	10.6	19 37.5	11.4	57.0
04	240 53.0	42.1	247 29.1	10.6	19 48.9	11.2	56.9
05	255 53.0	42.7	261 58.7	10.5	20 00.1	11.2	56.9
06	270 53.0	N19 43.2	276 28.2	10.4	N20 11.3	11.0	56.9
07	285 53.0	43.7	290 57.6	10.4	20 22.3	11.0	56.9
F 08	300 52.9	44.3	305 27.0	10.3	20 33.3	10.8	56.9
R 09	315 52.9	.. 44.8	319 56.3	10.3	20 44.1	10.7	56.8
I 10	330 52.9	45.3	334 25.6	10.3	20 54.8	10.5	56.8
D 11	345 52.8	45.9	348 54.9	10.1	21 05.3	10.5	56.8
A 12	0 52.8	N19 46.4	3 24.0	10.2	N21 15.8	10.3	56.8
Y 13	15 52.8	47.0	17 53.2	10.0	21 26.1	10.3	56.7
14	30 52.7	47.5	32 22.2	10.1	21 36.4	10.1	56.7
15	45 52.7	.. 48.0	46 51.3	10.0	21 46.5	10.0	56.7
16	60 52.7	48.6	61 20.3	9.9	21 56.5	9.8	56.7
17	75 52.6	49.1	75 49.2	9.9	22 06.3	9.8	56.6
18	90 52.6	N19 49.6	90 18.1	9.8	N22 16.1	9.6	56.6
19	105 52.6	50.2	104 46.9	9.8	22 25.7	9.5	56.6
20	120 52.5	50.7	119 15.7	9.7	22 35.2	9.3	56.6
21	135 52.5	.. 51.2	133 44.4	9.7	22 44.5	9.3	56.6
22	150 52.5	51.7	148 13.1	9.6	22 53.8	9.1	56.5
23	165 52.4	52.3	162 41.7	9.6	23 02.9	9.0	56.5
20 00	180 52.4	N19 52.8	177 10.3	9.5	N23 11.9	8.8	56.5
01	195 52.4	53.3	191 38.8	9.5	23 20.7	8.8	56.5
02	210 52.3	53.9	206 07.3	9.5	23 29.5	8.6	56.4
03	225 52.3	.. 54.4	220 35.8	9.4	23 38.1	8.4	56.4
04	240 52.3	54.9	235 04.2	9.3	23 46.5	8.4	56.4
05	255 52.2	55.6	249 32.5	9.4	23 54.9	8.2	56.4
06	270 52.2	N19 56.0	264 00.9	9.2	N24 03.1	8.0	56.3
07	285 52.2	56.5	278 29.1	9.3	24 11.1	8.0	56.3
S 08	300 52.1	57.0	292 57.4	9.2	24 19.1	7.8	56.3
A 09	315 52.1	.. 57.5	307 25.6	9.1	24 26.9	7.6	56.3
T 10	330 52.1	58.1	321 53.7	9.1	24 34.5	7.5	56.2
U 11	345 52.0	58.6	336 21.8	9.1	24 42.0	7.4	56.2
R 12	0 52.0	N19 59.1	350 49.9	9.0	N24 49.4	7.3	56.2
D 13	15 51.9	19 59.6	5 17.9	9.0	24 56.7	7.1	56.2
A 14	30 51.9	20 00.1	19 45.9	9.0	25 03.8	7.0	56.2
Y 15	45 51.9	.. 00.7	34 13.9	8.9	25 10.8	6.8	56.1
16	60 51.8	01.2	48 41.8	8.9	25 17.6	6.7	56.1
17	75 51.8	01.7	63 09.7	8.8	25 24.3	6.6	56.1
18	90 51.8	N20 02.2	77 37.5	8.9	N25 30.9	6.4	56.1
19	105 51.7	02.7	92 05.4	8.8	25 37.3	6.2	56.0
20	120 51.7	03.3	106 33.2	8.7	25 43.5	6.2	56.0
21	135 51.6	.. 03.8	121 00.9	8.8	25 49.7	5.9	56.0
22	150 51.6	04.3	135 28.7	8.7	25 55.6	5.9	56.0
23	165 51.6	04.8	149 56.4	8.6	26 01.5	5.7	55.9
21 00	180 51.5	N20 05.3	164 24.0	8.7	N26 07.2	5.5	55.9
01	195 51.5	05.8	178 51.7	8.6	26 12.7	5.4	55.9
02	210 51.4	06.3	193 19.3	8.6	26 18.1	5.3	55.9
03	225 51.4	.. 06.9	207 46.9	8.6	26 23.4	5.1	55.8
04	240 51.4	07.4	222 14.5	8.6	26 28.5	5.0	55.8
05	255 51.3	07.9	236 42.1	8.5	26 33.5	4.8	55.8
06	270 51.3	N20 08.4	251 09.6	8.5	N26 38.3	4.7	55.8
07	285 51.2	08.9	265 37.1	8.6	26 43.0	4.5	55.8
S 08	300 51.2	09.4	280 04.7	8.4	26 47.5	4.4	55.7
U 09	315 51.2	.. 09.9	294 32.1	8.5	26 51.9	4.3	55.7
N 10	330 51.1	10.4	308 59.6	8.5	26 56.2	4.0	55.7
D 11	345 51.1	10.9	323 27.1	8.4	27 00.2	4.0	55.7
A 12	0 51.0	N20 11.4	337 54.5	8.5	N27 04.2	3.8	55.6
Y 13	15 51.0	11.9	352 22.0	8.4	27 08.0	3.6	55.6
14	30 50.9	12.5	6 49.4	8.4	27 11.6	3.5	55.6
15	45 50.9	.. 13.0	21 16.8	8.5	27 15.1	3.4	55.6
16	60 50.9	13.5	35 44.3	8.4	27 18.5	3.2	55.6
17	75 50.8	14.0	50 11.7	8.4	27 21.7	3.0	55.5
18	90 50.8	N20 14.5	64 39.1	8.4	N27 24.7	2.9	55.5
19	105 50.7	15.0	79 06.5	8.4	27 27.6	2.8	55.5
20	120 50.7	15.5	93 33.9	8.4	27 30.4	2.6	55.5
21	135 50.6	.. 16.0	108 01.3	8.4	27 33.0	2.4	55.4
22	150 50.6	16.5	122 28.7	8.5	27 35.4	2.3	55.4
23	165 50.5	17.0	136 56.2	8.4	N27 37.7	2.2	55.4
	SD 15.8	d 0.5	SD 15.5		15.3		15.2

Twilight / Sunrise / Moonrise

Lat.	Naut.	Civil	Sunrise	Moonrise 19	20	21	22
N 72	□	□	□	□	□	□	□
N 70	□	□	□	00 37	□	□	□
68	////	////	01 18	01 27	□	□	□
66	////	////	02 03	01 58	01 14	□	□
64	////	00 19	02 32	02 22	02 06	□	□
62	////	01 30	02 54	02 41	02 38	02 36	02 40
60	////	02 04	03 12	02 57	03 02	03 14	03 41
N 58	00 17	02 28	03 26	03 10	03 21	03 41	04 15
56	01 22	02 47	03 39	03 22	03 38	04 02	04 40
54	01 53	03 03	03 50	03 32	03 51	04 20	05 00
52	02 15	03 16	03 59	03 41	04 03	04 35	05 17
50	02 33	03 28	04 08	03 49	04 14	04 48	05 32
45	03 07	03 51	04 26	04 06	04 37	05 14	06 01
N 40	03 31	04 10	04 41	04 21	04 55	05 36	06 24
35	03 50	04 25	04 53	04 33	05 10	05 54	06 43
30	04 06	04 38	05 04	04 44	05 24	06 09	06 59
20	04 30	04 59	05 22	05 02	05 47	06 35	07 27
N 10	04 49	05 16	05 38	05 18	06 07	06 58	07 51
0	05 05	05 31	05 53	05 34	06 25	07 19	08 13
S 10	05 20	05 45	06 08	05 49	06 44	07 40	08 35
20	05 33	06 00	06 23	06 06	07 04	08 03	08 59
30	05 46	06 15	06 41	06 25	07 28	08 29	09 27
35	05 53	06 24	06 51	06 36	07 42	08 45	09 43
40	06 00	06 33	07 03	06 49	07 58	09 03	10 02
45	06 08	06 44	07 16	07 04	08 17	09 26	10 26
S 50	06 17	06 57	07 33	07 23	08 42	09 54	10 56
52	06 21	07 02	07 41	07 32	08 53	10 08	11 10
54	06 25	07 09	07 50	07 43	09 07	10 24	11 28
56	06 29	07 16	07 59	07 54	09 22	10 43	11 48
58	06 34	07 24	08 10	08 07	09 41	11 07	12 14
S 60	06 39	07 32	08 23	08 23	10 04	11 38	12 51

Sunset / Twilight / Moonset

Lat.	Sunset	Civil	Naut.	Moonset 19	20	21	22
N 72	□	□	□	□	□	□	□
N 70	□	□	□	□	□	□	□
68	22 41	////	////	□	□	□	□
66	21 53	////	////	22 56	□	□	□
64	21 23	////	////	22 05	□	□	□
62	21 01	22 27	////	21 34	23 26	25 15	01 15
60	20 43	21 52	////	21 10	22 49	24 14	00 14
N 58	20 28	21 27	////	20 52	22 22	23 40	24 36
56	20 15	21 08	22 35	20 36	22 01	23 15	24 11
54	20 04	20 52	22 03	20 23	21 44	22 55	23 51
52	19 55	20 38	21 40	20 11	21 29	22 39	23 34
50	19 46	20 26	21 21	20 01	21 17	22 24	23 20
45	19 28	20 03	20 47	19 39	20 50	21 55	22 50
N 40	19 13	19 44	20 23	19 22	20 30	21 32	22 27
35	19 00	19 29	20 03	19 08	20 13	21 14	22 08
30	18 49	19 16	19 48	18 55	19 58	20 57	21 52
20	18 31	18 55	19 23	18 34	19 33	20 30	21 24
N 10	18 15	18 37	19 04	18 15	19 11	20 07	21 01
0	18 00	18 22	18 48	17 58	18 51	19 45	20 39
S 10	17 45	18 08	18 33	17 41	18 31	19 23	20 16
20	17 30	17 53	18 20	17 23	18 09	18 59	19 52
30	17 12	17 38	18 07	17 02	17 44	18 32	19 25
35	17 02	17 29	18 00	16 50	17 30	18 16	19 08
40	16 50	17 20	17 53	16 36	17 13	17 57	18 49
45	16 36	17 09	17 45	16 19	16 53	17 35	18 26
S 50	16 20	16 56	17 36	15 59	16 28	17 06	17 56
52	16 12	16 50	17 32	15 49	16 16	16 52	17 41
54	16 03	16 44	17 28	15 39	16 02	16 36	17 24
56	15 53	16 37	17 23	15 26	15 46	16 16	17 03
58	15 42	16 29	17 18	15 12	15 27	15 52	16 37
S 60	15 29	16 20	17 13	14 56	15 03	15 21	16 01

SUN / MOON

Day	Eqn. of Time 00h	12h	Mer. Pass.	Mer. Pass. Upper	Lower	Age	Phase
	m s	m s	h m	h m	h m	d	%
19	03 33	03 31	11 56	11 46	24 12	29	0
20	03 30	03 28	11 57	12 38	00 12	01	1
21	03 26	03 24	11 57	13 32	01 05	02	4

© British Crown Copyright 2022. All rights reserved.

UT	ARIES GHA	VENUS −4.3 GHA	Dec	MARS +1.5 GHA	Dec	JUPITER −2.1 GHA	Dec	SATURN +0.8 GHA	Dec	Star Name	SHA	Dec
d h	° ′	° ′	° ′	° ′	° ′	° ′	° ′	° ′	° ′		° ′	° ′
22 00	239 21.9	132 15.7	N25 19.4	116 01.0	N21 30.7	209 55.8	N10 52.9	260 26.1	S10 27.4	Acamar	315 13.2	S40 12.7
01	254 24.4	147 15.3	19.1	131 02.0	30.3	224 57.7	53.1	275 28.5	27.4	Achernar	335 21.7	S57 07.0
02	269 26.8	162 15.0	18.8	146 02.9	30.0	239 59.6	53.3	290 30.9	27.3	Acrux	173 01.2	S63 13.9
03	284 29.3	177 14.6 ..	18.5	161 03.9 ..	29.7	255 01.6 ..	53.5	305 33.2 ..	27.3	Adhara	255 07.2	S29 00.3
04	299 31.8	192 14.2	18.2	176 04.9	29.3	270 03.5	53.7	320 35.6	27.3	Aldebaran	290 41.5	N16 33.3
05	314 34.2	207 13.8	17.9	191 05.9	29.0	285 05.4	53.9	335 37.9	27.2			
06	329 36.7	222 13.4	N25 17.6	206 06.8	N21 28.6	300 07.3	N10 54.1	350 40.3	S10 27.2	Alioth	166 13.8	N55 50.2
07	344 39.2	237 13.0	17.3	221 07.8	28.3	315 09.3	54.3	5 42.7	27.2	Alkaid	152 52.7	N49 11.9
08	359 41.6	252 12.6	16.9	236 08.8	28.0	330 11.2	54.5	20 45.0	27.1	Alnair	27 34.6	S46 50.7
09	14 44.1	267 12.2 ..	16.6	251 09.7 ..	27.6	345 13.1 ..	54.7	35 47.4 ..	27.1	Alnilam	275 39.4	S 1 11.3
10	29 46.5	282 11.9	16.3	266 10.7	27.3	0 15.1	54.8	50 49.7	27.1	Alphard	217 49.2	S 8 45.6
11	44 49.0	297 11.5	16.0	281 11.7	27.0	15 17.0	55.0	65 52.1	27.1			
12	59 51.5	312 11.1	N25 15.7	296 12.7	N21 26.6	30 18.9	N10 55.2	80 54.5	S10 27.0	Alphecca	126 04.5	N26 38.1
13	74 53.9	327 10.7	15.3	311 13.6	26.3	45 20.8	55.4	95 56.8	27.0	Alpheratz	357 36.4	N29 12.9
14	89 56.4	342 10.3	15.0	326 14.6	25.9	60 22.8	55.6	110 59.2	27.0	Altair	62 01.1	N 8 55.7
15	104 58.9	357 10.0 ..	14.7	341 15.6 ..	25.6	75 24.7 ..	55.8	126 01.5 ..	26.9	Ankaa	353 08.7	S42 10.7
16	120 01.3	12 09.6	14.4	356 16.5	25.3	90 26.6	56.0	141 03.9	26.9	Antares	112 17.2	S26 29.0
17	135 03.8	27 09.2	14.0	11 17.5	24.9	105 28.6	56.2	156 06.3	26.9			
18	150 06.3	42 08.8	N25 13.7	26 18.5	N21 24.6	120 30.5	N10 56.4	171 08.6	S10 26.8	Arcturus	145 48.9	N19 03.7
19	165 08.7	57 08.4	13.4	41 19.5	24.3	135 32.4	56.6	186 11.0	26.8	Atria	107 12.1	S69 04.1
20	180 11.2	72 08.1	13.1	56 20.4	23.9	150 34.3	56.8	201 13.4	26.8	Avior	234 15.6	S59 35.3
21	195 13.6	87 07.7 ..	12.7	71 21.4 ..	23.6	165 36.3 ..	57.0	216 15.7 ..	26.7	Bellatrix	278 24.7	N 6 22.2
22	210 16.1	102 07.3	12.4	86 22.4	23.2	180 38.2	57.1	231 18.1	26.7	Betelgeuse	270 53.9	N 7 24.6
23	225 18.6	117 06.9	12.1	101 23.3	22.9	195 40.1	57.3	246 20.4	26.7			
23 00	240 21.0	132 06.6	N25 11.7	116 24.3	N21 22.6	210 42.1	N10 57.5	261 22.8	S10 26.7	Canopus	263 53.5	S52 42.6
01	255 23.5	147 06.2	11.4	131 25.3	22.2	225 44.0	57.7	276 25.2	26.6	Capella	280 24.4	N46 01.3
02	270 26.0	162 05.8	11.1	146 26.3	21.9	240 45.9	57.9	291 27.5	26.6	Deneb	49 26.5	N45 21.5
03	285 28.4	177 05.5 ..	10.7	161 27.2 ..	21.5	255 47.8 ..	58.1	306 29.9 ..	26.6	Denebola	182 26.2	N14 26.6
04	300 30.9	192 05.1	10.4	176 28.2	21.2	270 49.8	58.3	321 32.3	26.5	Diphda	348 48.9	S17 51.5
05	315 33.4	207 04.7	10.1	191 29.2	20.8	285 51.7	58.5	336 34.6	26.5			
06	330 35.8	222 04.4	N25 09.7	206 30.2	N21 20.5	300 53.6	N10 58.7	351 37.0	S10 26.5	Dubhe	193 42.5	N61 37.8
07	345 38.3	237 04.0	09.4	221 31.1	20.2	315 55.6	58.9	6 39.3	26.4	Elnath	278 04.0	N28 37.6
08	0 40.8	252 03.6	09.0	236 32.1	19.8	330 57.5	59.1	21 41.7	26.4	Eltanin	90 42.3	N51 28.9
09	15 43.2	267 03.3 ..	08.7	251 33.1 ..	19.5	345 59.4 ..	59.2	36 44.1 ..	26.4	Enif	33 40.1	N 9 58.8
10	30 45.7	282 02.9	08.4	266 34.0	19.1	1 01.3	59.4	51 46.4	26.4	Fomalhaut	15 16.1	S29 29.9
11	45 48.1	297 02.5	08.0	281 35.0	18.8	16 03.3	59.6	66 48.8	26.3			
12	60 50.6	312 02.2	N25 07.7	296 36.0	N21 18.5	31 05.2	N10 59.8	81 51.2	S10 26.3	Gacrux	171 52.8	S57 14.8
13	75 53.1	327 01.8	07.3	311 37.0	18.1	46 07.1	11 00.0	96 53.5	26.3	Gienah	175 44.8	S17 40.4
14	90 55.5	342 01.5	07.0	326 37.9	17.8	61 09.1	00.2	111 55.9	26.2	Hadar	148 37.4	S60 29.3
15	105 58.0	357 01.1 ..	06.6	341 38.9 ..	17.4	76 11.0 ..	00.4	126 58.3 ..	26.2	Hamal	327 53.1	N23 34.2
16	121 00.5	12 00.7	06.3	356 39.9	17.1	91 12.9	00.6	142 00.6	26.2	Kaus Aust.	83 34.0	S34 22.4
17	136 02.9	27 00.4	05.9	11 40.8	16.7	106 14.9	00.8	157 03.0	26.1			
18	151 05.4	42 00.0	N25 05.6	26 41.8	N21 16.4	121 16.8	N11 01.0	172 05.4	S10 26.1	Kochab	137 18.6	N74 03.7
19	166 07.9	56 59.7	05.2	41 42.8	16.0	136 18.7	01.1	187 07.7	26.1	Markab	13 31.3	N15 19.7
20	181 10.3	71 59.3	04.9	56 43.8	15.7	151 20.6	01.3	202 10.1	26.1	Menkar	314 07.9	N 4 10.8
21	196 12.8	86 59.0 ..	04.5	71 44.7 ..	15.4	166 22.6 ..	01.5	217 12.5 ..	26.0	Menkent	147 58.9	S36 29.2
22	211 15.3	101 58.6	04.2	86 45.7	15.0	181 24.5	01.7	232 14.8	26.0	Miaplacidus	221 38.8	S69 49.0
23	226 17.7	116 58.2	03.8	101 46.7	14.7	196 26.4	01.9	247 17.2	26.0			
24 00	241 20.2	131 57.9	N25 03.5	116 47.6	N21 14.3	211 28.4	N11 02.1	262 19.6	S10 25.9	Mirfak	308 30.7	N49 56.5
01	256 22.6	146 57.5	03.1	131 48.6	14.0	226 30.3	02.3	277 21.9	25.9	Nunki	75 49.2	S26 16.0
02	271 25.1	161 57.2	02.8	146 49.6	13.6	241 32.2	02.5	292 24.3	25.9	Peacock	53 07.6	S56 39.4
03	286 27.6	176 56.8 ..	02.4	161 50.6 ..	13.3	256 34.2 ..	02.7	307 26.7 ..	25.9	Pollux	243 19.2	N27 58.3
04	301 30.0	191 56.5	02.0	176 51.5	12.9	271 36.1	02.9	322 29.0	25.8	Procyon	244 52.5	N 5 09.9
05	316 32.5	206 56.2	01.7	191 52.5	12.6	286 38.0	03.0	337 31.4	25.8			
06	331 35.0	221 55.8	N25 01.3	206 53.5	N21 12.2	301 40.0	N11 03.2	352 33.8	S10 25.8	Rasalhague	96 59.5	N12 32.5
07	346 37.4	236 55.5	01.0	221 54.5	11.9	316 41.9	03.4	7 36.1	25.7	Regulus	207 35.9	N11 51.2
08	1 39.9	251 55.1	00.6	236 55.4	11.5	331 43.8	03.6	22 38.5	25.7	Rigel	281 05.5	S 8 10.5
09	16 42.4	266 54.8	25 00.2	251 56.4 ..	11.2	346 45.7 ..	03.8	37 40.9 ..	25.7	Rigil Kent.	139 41.6	S60 56.0
10	31 44.8	281 54.4	24 59.9	266 57.4	10.8	1 47.7	04.0	52 43.2	25.7	Sabik	102 04.0	S15 45.3
11	46 47.3	296 54.1	59.5	281 58.3	10.5	16 49.6	04.2	67 45.6	25.6			
12	61 49.8	311 53.8	N24 59.1	296 59.3	N21 10.2	31 51.5	N11 04.4	82 48.0	S10 25.6	Schedar	349 33.0	N56 39.6
13	76 52.2	326 53.4	58.8	312 00.3	09.8	46 53.5	04.6	97 50.3	25.6	Shaula	96 11.8	S37 07.2
14	91 54.7	341 53.1	58.4	327 01.3	09.5	61 55.4	04.8	112 52.7	25.5	Sirius	258 27.7	S16 45.0
15	106 57.1	356 52.7 ..	58.0	342 02.2 ..	09.1	76 57.3 ..	05.0	127 55.1 ..	25.5	Spica	158 23.5	S11 17.1
16	121 59.6	11 52.4	57.7	357 03.2	08.8	91 59.3	05.1	142 57.4	25.5	Suhail	222 47.5	S43 31.8
17	137 02.1	26 52.1	57.3	12 04.2	08.4	107 01.2	05.3	157 59.8	25.5			
18	152 04.5	41 51.7	N24 56.9	27 05.2	N21 08.1	122 03.1	N11 05.5	173 02.2	S10 25.4	Vega	80 33.8	N38 48.1
19	167 07.0	56 51.4	56.5	42 06.1	07.7	137 05.1	05.7	188 04.5	25.4	Zuben'ubi	136 57.2	S16 08.4
20	182 09.5	71 51.1	56.2	57 07.1	07.4	152 07.0	05.9	203 06.9	25.4		SHA	Mer. Pass.
21	197 11.9	86 50.7 ..	55.8	72 08.1 ..	07.0	167 08.9 ..	06.1	218 09.3 ..	25.4		° ′	h m
22	212 14.4	101 50.4	55.4	87 09.0	06.7	182 10.9	06.3	233 11.7	25.3	Venus	251 45.5	15 12
23	227 16.9	116 50.1	55.0	102 10.0	06.4	197 12.8	06.5	248 14.0	25.3	Mars	236 03.3	16 13
Mer. Pass.	h m 7 57.3	v −0.4	d 0.3	v 1.0	d 0.3	v 1.9	d 0.2	v 2.4	d 0.0	Jupiter	330 21.0	9 56
										Saturn	21 01.8	6 33

© British Crown Copyright 2022. All rights reserved.

UT	SUN GHA	SUN Dec	MOON GHA	v	MOON Dec	d	HP
22 00	180 50.5	N20 17.5	151 23.6	8.4	N27 39.9	2.0	55.4
01	195 50.5	18.0	165 51.0	8.5	27 41.9	1.9	55.4
02	210 50.4	18.5	180 18.5	8.4	27 43.8	1.7	55.3
03	225 50.4 ..	19.0	194 45.9	8.5	27 45.5	1.6	55.3
04	240 50.3	19.5	209 13.4	8.4	27 47.1	1.4	55.3
05	255 50.3	20.0	223 40.8	8.5	27 48.5	1.2	55.3
06	270 50.2	N20 20.5	238 08.3	8.5	N27 49.7	1.2	55.3
M 07	285 50.2	21.0	252 35.8	8.6	27 50.9	0.9	55.2
O 08	300 50.1	21.5	267 03.4	8.5	27 51.8	0.9	55.2
N 09	315 50.1 ..	22.0	281 30.9	8.6	27 52.7	0.6	55.2
D 10	330 50.0	22.5	295 58.5	8.5	27 53.3	0.6	55.2
A 11	345 50.0	22.9	310 26.0	8.6	27 53.9	0.3	55.2
Y 12	0 49.9	N20 23.4	324 53.6	8.7	N27 54.2	0.3	55.1
13	15 49.9	23.9	339 21.3	8.6	27 54.5	0.1	55.1
14	30 49.8	24.4	353 48.9	8.7	27 54.6	0.1	55.1
15	45 49.8 ..	24.9	8 16.6	8.7	27 54.5	0.2	55.1
16	60 49.7	25.4	22 44.3	8.7	27 54.3	0.3	55.1
17	75 49.7	25.9	37 12.0	8.8	27 54.0	0.5	55.0
18	90 49.7	N20 26.4	51 39.8	8.8	N27 53.5	0.7	55.0
19	105 49.6	26.9	66 07.6	8.8	27 52.8	0.7	55.0
20	120 49.6	27.4	80 35.4	8.9	27 52.1	1.0	55.0
21	135 49.5 ..	27.8	95 03.3	8.9	27 51.1	1.0	55.0
22	150 49.5	28.3	109 31.2	9.0	27 50.1	1.2	54.9
23	165 49.4	28.8	123 59.2	8.9	27 48.9	1.4	54.9
23 00	180 49.4	N20 29.3	138 27.1	9.1	N27 47.5	1.5	54.9
01	195 49.3	29.8	152 55.2	9.0	27 46.0	1.6	54.9
02	210 49.3	30.3	167 23.2	9.1	27 44.4	1.8	54.9
03	225 49.2 ..	30.8	181 51.3	9.2	27 42.6	1.9	54.9
04	240 49.1	31.2	196 19.5	9.2	27 40.7	2.1	54.8
05	255 49.1	31.7	210 47.7	9.2	27 38.6	2.2	54.8
06	270 49.0	N20 32.2	225 15.9	9.3	N27 36.4	2.3	54.8
T 07	285 49.0	32.7	239 44.2	9.3	27 34.1	2.5	54.8
U 08	300 48.9	33.2	254 12.5	9.4	27 31.6	2.6	54.8
E 09	315 48.9 ..	33.6	268 40.9	9.5	27 29.0	2.7	54.8
S 10	330 48.8	34.1	283 09.4	9.4	27 26.3	2.9	54.7
D 11	345 48.8	34.6	297 37.8	9.6	27 23.4	3.0	54.7
A 12	0 48.7	N20 35.1	312 06.4	9.6	N27 20.4	3.1	54.7
Y 13	15 48.7	35.6	326 35.0	9.6	27 17.3	3.3	54.7
14	30 48.6	36.0	341 03.6	9.7	27 14.0	3.4	54.7
15	45 48.6 ..	36.5	355 32.3	9.8	27 10.6	3.6	54.7
16	60 48.5	37.0	10 01.1	9.8	27 07.0	3.7	54.7
17	75 48.5	37.5	24 29.9	9.9	27 03.3	3.8	54.6
18	90 48.4	N20 37.9	38 58.8	9.9	N26 59.5	3.9	54.6
19	105 48.4	38.4	53 27.7	10.0	26 55.6	4.1	54.6
20	120 48.3	38.9	67 56.7	10.1	26 51.5	4.2	54.6
21	135 48.2 ..	39.4	82 25.8	10.1	26 47.3	4.3	54.6
22	150 48.2	39.8	96 54.9	10.1	26 43.0	4.5	54.6
23	165 48.1	40.3	111 24.0	10.3	26 38.5	4.6	54.6
24 00	180 48.1	N20 40.8	125 53.3	10.3	N26 33.9	4.7	54.5
01	195 48.0	41.2	140 22.6	10.4	26 29.2	4.8	54.5
02	210 48.0	41.7	154 52.0	10.4	26 24.4	4.9	54.5
03	225 47.9 ..	42.2	169 21.4	10.5	26 19.5	5.1	54.5
04	240 47.9	42.6	183 50.9	10.6	26 14.4	5.2	54.5
05	255 47.8	43.1	198 20.5	10.6	26 09.2	5.4	54.5
06	270 47.7	N20 43.6	212 50.1	10.7	N26 03.8	5.4	54.5
W 07	285 47.7	44.0	227 19.8	10.7	25 58.4	5.6	54.5
E 08	300 47.6	44.5	241 49.5	10.9	25 52.8	5.6	54.4
D 09	315 47.6 ..	45.0	256 19.4	10.9	25 47.2	5.8	54.4
N 10	330 47.5	45.4	270 49.3	10.9	25 41.4	6.0	54.4
E 11	345 47.4	45.9	285 19.2	11.1	25 35.4	6.0	54.4
S 12	0 47.4	N20 46.4	299 49.3	11.1	N25 29.4	6.2	54.4
D 13	15 47.3	46.8	314 19.4	11.2	25 23.2	6.2	54.4
A 14	30 47.3	47.3	328 49.6	11.2	25 17.0	6.4	54.4
Y 15	45 47.2 ..	47.8	343 19.8	11.3	25 10.6	6.5	54.4
16	60 47.2	48.2	357 50.1	11.4	25 04.1	6.6	54.4
17	75 47.1	48.7	12 20.5	11.5	24 57.5	6.7	54.4
18	90 47.0	N20 49.1	26 51.0	11.5	N24 50.8	6.9	54.3
19	105 47.0	49.6	41 21.5	11.6	24 43.9	6.9	54.3
20	120 46.9	50.1	55 52.1	11.7	24 37.0	7.0	54.3
21	135 46.9 ..	50.5	70 22.8	11.7	24 30.0	7.2	54.3
22	150 46.8	51.0	84 53.5	11.8	24 22.8	7.3	54.3
23	165 46.7	51.4	99 24.3	11.9	N24 15.5	7.3	54.3
	SD 15.8	d 0.5	SD 15.0		14.9		14.8

Twilight / Sunrise / Moonrise

Lat.	Naut.	Civil	Sunrise	Moonrise 22	23	24	25
N 72	□	□	□	□	□	□	□
N 70	□	□	□	□	□	□	□
68	////	////	00 56	□	□	□	□
66	////	////	01 51	□	□	□	05 32
64	////	////	02 23	□	□	□	06 31
62	////	01 16	02 47	02 40	03 36	05 21	07 04
60	////	01 54	03 06	03 41	04 37	05 59	07 29
N 58	////	02 21	03 21	04 15	05 11	06 25	07 48
56	01 09	02 41	03 34	04 40	05 36	06 46	08 04
54	01 44	02 57	03 46	05 00	05 56	07 03	08 18
52	02 08	03 11	03 56	05 17	06 12	07 18	08 30
50	02 28	03 24	04 05	05 32	06 27	07 31	08 40
45	03 03	03 48	04 23	06 01	06 56	07 57	09 02
N 40	03 28	04 07	04 39	06 24	07 18	08 18	09 20
35	03 48	04 23	04 54	06 43	07 37	08 35	09 34
30	04 04	04 36	05 03	06 59	07 53	08 50	09 47
20	04 29	04 58	05 22	07 27	08 21	09 15	10 09
N 10	04 49	05 15	05 38	07 51	08 44	09 37	10 28
0	05 05	05 31	05 53	08 13	09 06	09 57	10 45
S 10	05 20	05 46	06 08	08 35	09 28	10 17	11 03
20	05 34	06 01	06 24	08 59	09 51	10 39	11 21
30	05 48	06 17	06 43	09 27	10 18	11 04	11 43
35	05 55	06 26	06 53	09 43	10 34	11 18	11 55
40	06 02	06 36	07 05	10 02	10 53	11 35	12 09
45	06 11	06 47	07 19	10 26	11 15	11 55	12 26
S 50	06 20	07 00	07 37	10 56	11 44	12 20	12 47
52	06 24	07 06	07 45	11 10	11 58	12 33	12 57
54	06 28	07 13	07 54	11 28	12 14	12 47	13 08
56	06 33	07 20	08 04	11 48	12 34	13 03	13 21
58	06 38	07 28	08 16	12 14	12 58	13 22	13 35
S 60	06 44	07 38	08 30	12 51	13 29	13 46	13 52

Sunset / Twilight / Moonset

Lat.	Sunset	Civil	Naut.	Moonset 22	23	24	25
N 72	□	□	□	□	□	□	□
N 70	□	□	□	□	□	□	□
68	23 06	////	////	□	□	□	□
66	22 06	////	////	□	□	□	03 45
64	21 33	////	////	□	□	□	02 46
62	21 08	22 42	////	01 15	02 11	02 14	02 12
60	20 49	22 02	////	00 14	01 09	01 36	01 47
N 58	20 34	21 35	22 49	24 36	00 36	01 09	01 27
56	20 20	21 14	22 49	24 11	00 11	00 48	01 11
54	20 09	20 57	22 12	23 51	24 30	00 30	00 57
52	19 59	20 43	21 47	23 34	24 15	00 15	00 44
50	19 50	20 31	21 27	23 20	24 02	00 02	00 33
45	19 31	20 06	20 52	22 50	23 35	24 10	00 10
N 40	19 15	19 47	20 26	22 27	23 14	23 52	24 23
35	19 02	19 31	20 06	22 08	22 56	23 36	24 11
30	18 51	19 18	19 50	21 52	22 41	23 23	23 59
20	18 32	18 56	19 25	21 24	22 15	23 00	23 40
N 10	18 16	18 38	19 05	21 01	21 52	22 40	23 23
0	18 00	18 22	18 48	20 39	21 31	22 21	23 07
S 10	17 45	18 08	18 33	20 16	21 10	22 02	22 52
20	17 29	17 53	18 20	19 52	20 47	21 44	22 34
30	17 11	17 36	18 06	19 25	20 20	21 18	22 15
35	17 00	17 28	17 59	19 08	20 05	21 04	22 03
40	16 48	17 18	17 51	18 49	19 46	20 47	21 50
45	16 34	17 06	17 42	18 26	19 24	20 28	21 34
S 50	16 16	16 53	17 33	17 56	18 56	20 04	21 14
52	16 08	16 47	17 29	17 41	18 42	19 52	21 05
54	15 59	16 40	17 25	17 24	18 26	19 38	20 54
56	15 49	16 33	17 20	17 03	18 07	19 22	20 42
58	15 37	16 25	17 15	16 37	17 43	19 04	20 28
S 60	15 23	16 15	17 09	16 01	17 12	18 40	20 12

SUN / MOON

Day	Eqn. of Time 00h	12h	Mer. Pass.	Mer. Pass. Upper	Lower	Age	Phase
d	m s	m s	h m	h m	h m	d	%
22	03 22	03 20	11 57	14 26	01 59	03	8
23	03 18	03 15	11 57	15 18	02 52	04	15
24	03 12	03 10	11 57	16 09	03 44	05	22

© British Crown Copyright 2022. All rights reserved.

UT (d h)	ARIES GHA	VENUS −4.3 GHA	Dec	MARS +1.5 GHA	Dec	JUPITER −2.1 GHA	Dec	SATURN +0.8 GHA	Dec	STARS Name	SHA	Dec
25 00	242 19.3	131 49.7	N24 54.7	117 11.0	N21 06.0	212 14.7	N11 06.6	263 16.4	S10 25.3	Acamar	315 13.2	S40 12.6
01	257 21.8	146 49.4	54.3	132 12.0	05.6	227 16.7	06.8	278 18.8	25.2	Achernar	335 21.7	S57 07.0
02	272 24.3	161 49.1	53.9	147 12.9	05.3	242 18.6	07.0	293 21.1	25.2	Acrux	173 01.2	S63 14.0
03	287 26.7	176 48.8 ..	53.5	162 13.9 ..	04.9	257 20.5 ..	07.2	308 23.5 ..	25.2	Adhara	255 07.2	S29 00.3
04	302 29.2	191 48.4	53.1	177 14.9	04.5	272 22.5	07.4	323 25.9	25.2	Aldebaran	290 41.5	N16 33.3
05	317 31.6	206 48.1	52.8	192 15.9	04.2	287 24.4	07.6	338 28.2	25.1			
06	332 34.1	221 47.8	N24 52.4	207 16.8	N21 03.8	302 26.3	N11 07.8	353 30.6	S10 25.1	Alioth	166 13.8	N55 50.2
T 07	347 36.6	236 47.5	52.0	222 17.8	03.5	317 28.3	08.0	8 33.0	25.1	Alkaid	152 52.7	N49 11.9
H 08	2 39.0	251 47.1	51.6	237 18.8	03.1	332 30.2	08.1	23 35.4	25.1	Alnair	27 34.6	S46 50.7
U 09	17 41.5	266 46.8 ..	51.2	252 19.7 ..	02.8	347 32.1 ..	08.3	38 37.7 ..	25.0	Alnilam	275 39.4	S 1 11.3
R 10	32 44.0	281 46.5	50.8	267 20.7	02.4	2 34.1	08.5	53 40.1	25.0	Alphard	217 49.2	S 8 45.6
S 11	47 46.4	296 46.2	50.4	282 21.7	02.1	17 36.0	08.7	68 42.5	25.0			
D 12	62 48.9	311 45.9	N24 50.0	297 22.7	N21 01.7	32 37.9	N11 08.9	83 44.8	S10 24.9	Alphecca	126 04.5	N26 38.2
A 13	77 51.4	326 45.5	49.7	312 23.6	01.4	47 39.9	09.1	98 47.2	24.9	Alpheratz	357 36.4	N29 12.9
Y 14	92 53.8	341 45.2	49.3	327 24.6	01.0	62 41.8	09.3	113 49.6	24.9	Altair	62 01.1	N 8 55.7
15	107 56.3	356 44.9 ..	48.9	342 25.6 ..	00.7	77 43.7 ..	09.5	128 52.0 ..	24.9	Ankaa	353 08.7	S42 10.6
16	122 58.7	11 44.6	48.5	357 26.6	00.3	92 45.7	09.6	143 54.3	24.8	Antares	112 17.1	S26 29.1
17	138 01.2	26 44.3	48.1	12 27.5	21 00.0	107 47.6	09.8	158 56.7	24.8			
18	153 03.7	41 44.0	N24 47.7	27 28.5	N20 59.6	122 49.5	N11 10.0	173 59.1	S10 24.8	Arcturus	145 48.9	N19 03.7
19	168 06.1	56 43.6	47.3	42 29.5	59.2	137 51.5	10.2	189 01.5	24.8	Atria	107 12.0	S69 04.1
20	183 08.6	71 43.3	46.9	57 30.4	58.9	152 53.4	10.4	204 03.8	24.7	Avior	234 15.6	S59 35.3
21	198 11.1	86 43.0 ..	46.5	72 31.4 ..	58.5	167 55.3 ..	10.6	219 06.2 ..	24.7	Bellatrix	278 24.7	N 6 22.2
22	213 13.5	101 42.7	46.1	87 32.4	58.2	182 57.3	10.8	234 08.6	24.7	Betelgeuse	270 53.9	N 7 24.7
23	228 16.0	116 42.4	45.7	102 33.4	57.8	197 59.2	11.0	249 10.9	24.7			
26 00	243 18.5	131 42.1	N24 45.3	117 34.3	N20 57.5	213 01.1	N11 11.2	264 13.3	S10 24.6	Canopus	263 53.5	S52 42.6
01	258 20.9	146 41.8	44.9	132 35.3	57.1	228 03.1	11.3	279 15.7	24.6	Capella	280 24.4	N46 01.3
02	273 23.4	161 41.5	44.5	147 36.3	56.7	243 05.0	11.5	294 18.1	24.6	Deneb	49 26.5	N45 21.5
03	288 25.9	176 41.2 ..	44.1	162 37.3 ..	56.4	258 06.9 ..	11.7	309 20.4 ..	24.6	Denebola	182 26.2	N14 26.6
04	303 28.3	191 40.9	43.7	177 38.2	56.0	273 08.9	11.9	324 22.8	24.5	Diphda	348 48.9	S17 51.5
05	318 30.8	206 40.6	43.3	192 39.2	55.7	288 10.8	12.1	339 25.2	24.5			
06	333 33.2	221 40.3	N24 42.9	207 40.2	N20 55.3	303 12.7	N11 12.3	354 27.6	S10 24.5	Dubhe	193 42.6	N61 37.8
07	348 35.7	236 40.0	42.5	222 41.2	55.0	318 14.7	12.5	9 29.9	24.5	Elnath	278 04.0	N28 37.6
08	3 38.2	251 39.7	42.1	237 42.1	54.6	333 16.6	12.6	24 32.3	24.4	Eltanin	90 42.3	N51 29.0
F 09	18 40.6	266 39.4 ..	41.7	252 43.1 ..	54.2	348 18.5 ..	12.8	39 34.7 ..	24.4	Enif	33 40.1	N 9 58.8
R 10	33 43.1	281 39.1	41.2	267 44.0	53.9	3 20.5	13.0	54 37.1	24.4	Fomalhaut	15 16.1	S29 29.8
I 11	48 45.6	296 38.8	40.8	282 45.0	53.5	18 22.4	13.2	69 39.4	24.4			
D 12	63 48.0	311 38.5	N24 40.4	297 46.0	N20 53.2	33 24.3	N11 13.4	84 41.8	S10 24.3	Gacrux	171 52.9	S57 14.9
A 13	78 50.5	326 38.2	40.0	312 47.0	52.8	48 26.3	13.6	99 44.2	24.3	Gienah	175 44.8	S17 40.4
Y 14	93 53.0	341 37.9	39.6	327 48.0	52.4	63 28.2	13.8	114 46.6	24.3	Hadar	148 37.4	S60 29.3
15	108 55.4	356 37.6 ..	39.2	342 48.9 ..	52.1	78 30.2 ..	14.0	129 48.9 ..	24.3	Hamal	327 53.0	N23 34.2
16	123 57.9	11 37.3	38.8	357 49.9	51.7	93 32.1	14.1	144 51.3	24.2	Kaus Aust.	83 34.0	S34 22.4
17	139 00.4	26 37.0	38.3	12 50.9	51.4	108 34.0	14.3	159 53.7	24.2			
18	154 02.8	41 36.7	N24 37.9	27 51.9	N20 51.0	123 36.0	N11 14.5	174 56.1	S10 24.2	Kochab	137 18.7	N74 03.7
19	169 05.3	56 36.4	37.5	42 52.8	50.6	138 37.9	14.7	189 58.5	24.2	Markab	13 31.3	N15 19.7
20	184 07.7	71 36.2	37.1	57 53.8	50.3	153 39.8	14.9	205 00.8	24.1	Menkar	314 07.9	N 4 10.8
21	199 10.2	86 35.9 ..	36.7	72 54.8 ..	49.9	168 41.8 ..	15.1	220 03.2 ..	24.1	Menkent	147 58.9	S36 29.2
22	214 12.7	101 35.6	36.3	87 55.8	49.6	183 43.7	15.3	235 05.6	24.1	Miaplacidus	221 38.9	S69 49.0
23	229 15.1	116 35.3	35.8	102 56.7	49.2	198 45.6	15.4	250 08.0	24.1			
27 00	244 17.6	131 35.0	N24 35.4	117 57.7	N20 48.8	213 47.6	N11 15.6	265 10.3	S10 24.0	Mirfak	308 30.7	N49 56.5
01	259 20.1	146 34.7	35.0	132 58.7	48.5	228 49.5	15.8	280 12.7	24.0	Nunki	75 49.2	S26 16.0
02	274 22.5	161 34.5	34.6	147 59.7	48.1	243 51.4	16.0	295 15.1	24.0	Peacock	53 07.6	S56 39.4
03	289 25.0	176 34.2 ..	34.1	163 00.6 ..	47.8	258 53.4 ..	16.2	310 17.5 ..	24.0	Pollux	243 19.2	N27 58.3
04	304 27.5	191 33.9	33.7	178 01.6	47.4	273 55.3	16.4	325 19.8	23.9	Procyon	244 52.5	N 5 09.9
05	319 29.9	206 33.6	33.3	193 02.6	47.0	288 57.3	16.6	340 22.2	23.9			
06	334 32.4	221 33.3	N24 32.9	208 03.5	N20 46.7	303 59.2	N11 16.7	355 24.6	S10 23.9	Rasalhague	96 59.5	N12 32.5
07	349 34.9	236 33.1	32.4	223 04.5	46.3	319 01.1	16.9	10 27.0	23.9	Regulus	207 35.9	N11 51.2
S 08	4 37.3	251 32.8	32.0	238 05.5	45.9	334 03.1	17.1	25 29.4	23.8	Rigel	281 05.5	S 8 10.5
A 09	19 39.8	266 32.5 ..	31.6	253 06.5 ..	45.6	349 05.0 ..	17.3	40 31.7 ..	23.8	Rigil Kent.	139 41.6	S60 56.0
T 10	34 42.2	281 32.2	31.1	268 07.4	45.2	4 06.9	17.5	55 34.1	23.8	Sabik	102 04.0	S15 45.3
U 11	49 44.7	296 32.0	30.7	283 08.4	44.9	19 08.9	17.7	70 36.5	23.8			
R 12	64 47.2	311 31.7	N24 30.3	298 09.4	N20 44.5	34 10.8	N11 17.9	85 38.9	S10 23.7	Schedar	349 32.9	N56 39.6
D 13	79 49.6	326 31.4	29.8	313 10.4	44.1	49 12.8	18.0	100 41.3	23.7	Shaula	96 11.8	S37 07.2
A 14	94 52.1	341 31.1	29.4	328 11.3	43.8	64 14.7	18.2	115 43.6	23.7	Sirius	258 27.7	S16 45.0
Y 15	109 54.6	356 30.9 ..	29.0	343 12.3 ..	43.4	79 16.6 ..	18.4	130 46.0 ..	23.7	Spica	158 23.5	S11 17.1
16	124 57.0	11 30.6	28.5	358 13.3	43.0	94 18.6	18.6	145 48.4	23.6	Suhail	222 47.5	S43 31.8
17	139 59.5	26 30.3	28.1	13 14.3	42.7	109 20.5	18.8	160 50.8	23.6			
18	155 02.0	41 30.1	N24 27.7	28 15.2	N20 42.3	124 22.4	N11 19.0	175 53.2	S10 23.6	Vega	80 33.8	N38 48.1
19	170 04.4	56 29.8	27.2	43 16.2	41.9	139 24.4	19.2	190 55.5	23.6	Zuben'ubi	136 57.2	S16 08.4
20	185 06.9	71 29.5	26.8	58 17.2	41.6	154 26.3	19.3	205 57.9	23.6			
21	200 09.3	86 29.3 ..	26.3	73 18.2 ..	41.2	169 28.3 ..	19.5	221 00.3 ..	23.5		SHA	Mer. Pass.
22	215 11.8	101 29.0	25.9	88 19.1	40.8	184 30.2	19.7	236 02.7	23.5	Venus	248 23.6	15 14
23	230 14.3	116 28.8	25.5	103 20.1	40.5	199 32.1	19.9	251 05.1	23.5	Mars	234 15.9	16 09
										Jupiter	329 42.7	9 47
Mer. Pass. 7 45.5		v −0.3	d 0.4	v 1.0	d 0.4	v 1.9	d 0.2	v 2.4	d 0.0	Saturn	20 54.9	6 22

© British Crown Copyright 2022. All rights reserved.

SUN / MOON

UT	SUN GHA	SUN Dec	MOON GHA	v	MOON Dec	d	HP
25 00	180 46.7	N20 51.9	113 55.2	12.0	N24 08.2	7.5	54.3
01	195 46.6	52.3	128 26.2	12.0	24 00.7	7.6	54.3
02	210 46.6	52.8	142 57.2	12.1	23 53.1	7.7	54.3
03	225 46.5	.. 53.2	157 28.3	12.2	23 45.4	7.8	54.3
04	240 46.4	53.7	171 59.5	12.2	23 37.6	7.9	54.3
05	255 46.4	54.2	186 30.7	12.4	23 29.7	8.0	54.3
06	270 46.3	N20 54.6	201 02.1	12.3	N23 21.7	8.0	54.3
T 07	285 46.2	55.1	215 33.4	12.5	23 13.7	8.2	54.3
H 08	300 46.2	55.5	230 04.9	12.5	23 05.5	8.3	54.3
U 09	315 46.1	.. 56.0	244 36.4	12.6	22 57.2	8.4	54.2
R 10	330 46.1	56.4	259 08.0	12.7	22 48.8	8.5	54.2
S 11	345 46.0	56.9	273 39.7	12.8	22 40.3	8.6	54.2
D 12	0 45.9	N20 57.3	288 11.5	12.8	N22 31.7	8.7	54.2
A 13	15 45.9	57.7	302 43.3	12.9	22 23.0	8.7	54.2
Y 14	30 45.8	58.2	317 15.2	12.9	22 14.3	8.9	54.2
15	45 45.7	.. 58.6	331 47.1	13.0	22 05.4	9.0	54.2
16	60 45.7	59.1	346 19.1	13.1	21 56.4	9.0	54.2
17	75 45.6	20 59.5	0 51.2	13.2	21 47.4	9.1	54.2
18	90 45.5	N21 00.0	15 23.4	13.2	N21 38.3	9.3	54.2
19	105 45.5	00.4	29 55.6	13.3	21 29.0	9.3	54.2
20	120 45.4	00.9	44 27.9	13.4	21 19.7	9.4	54.2
21	135 45.3	.. 01.3	59 00.3	13.4	21 10.3	9.5	54.2
22	150 45.3	01.7	73 32.7	13.5	21 00.8	9.6	54.2
23	165 45.2	02.2	88 05.2	13.6	20 51.2	9.6	54.2
26 00	180 45.2	N21 02.6	102 37.8	13.6	N20 41.6	9.8	54.2
01	195 45.1	03.1	117 10.4	13.7	20 31.8	9.8	54.2
02	210 45.0	03.5	131 43.1	13.7	20 22.0	10.0	54.2
03	225 45.0	.. 03.9	146 15.8	13.9	20 12.0	10.0	54.2
04	240 44.9	04.4	160 48.7	13.8	20 02.0	10.1	54.2
05	255 44.8	04.8	175 21.5	14.0	19 51.9	10.1	54.2
06	270 44.8	N21 05.3	189 54.5	14.0	N19 41.8	10.3	54.2
F 07	285 44.7	05.7	204 27.5	14.1	19 31.5	10.3	54.2
R 08	300 44.6	06.1	219 00.6	14.1	19 21.2	10.4	54.2
I 09	315 44.6	.. 06.6	233 33.7	14.2	19 10.8	10.5	54.2
D 10	330 44.5	07.0	248 06.9	14.3	19 00.3	10.5	54.2
A 11	345 44.4	07.4	262 40.2	14.3	18 49.8	10.7	54.2
Y 12	0 44.3	N21 07.9	277 13.5	14.4	N18 39.1	10.7	54.2
13	15 44.3	08.3	291 46.9	14.4	18 28.4	10.8	54.2
14	30 44.2	08.7	306 20.3	14.5	18 17.6	10.8	54.2
15	45 44.1	.. 09.2	320 53.8	14.5	18 06.8	11.0	54.2
16	60 44.1	09.6	335 27.3	14.6	17 55.8	11.0	54.2
17	75 44.0	10.0	350 00.9	14.7	17 44.8	11.1	54.2
18	90 43.9	N21 10.5	4 34.6	14.7	N17 33.7	11.1	54.2
19	105 43.9	10.9	19 08.3	14.8	17 22.6	11.2	54.3
20	120 43.8	11.3	33 42.1	14.8	17 11.4	11.3	54.3
21	135 43.7	.. 11.7	48 15.9	14.9	17 00.1	11.4	54.3
22	150 43.7	12.2	62 49.8	14.9	16 48.7	11.4	54.3
23	165 43.6	12.6	77 23.7	15.0	16 37.3	11.5	54.3
27 00	180 43.5	N21 13.0	91 57.7	15.0	N16 25.8	11.6	54.3
01	195 43.4	13.4	106 31.7	15.1	16 14.2	11.6	54.3
02	210 43.4	13.9	121 05.8	15.1	16 02.6	11.7	54.3
03	225 43.3	.. 14.3	135 39.9	15.2	15 50.9	11.7	54.3
04	240 43.2	14.7	150 14.1	15.2	15 39.2	11.9	54.3
05	255 43.2	15.1	164 48.3	15.3	15 27.3	11.9	54.3
06	270 43.1	N21 15.6	179 22.6	15.3	N15 15.4	11.9	54.3
S 07	285 43.0	16.0	193 56.9	15.3	15 03.5	12.0	54.3
A 08	300 42.9	16.4	208 31.2	15.4	14 51.5	12.1	54.3
T 09	315 42.9	.. 16.8	223 05.6	15.5	14 39.4	12.1	54.4
U 10	330 42.8	17.2	237 40.1	15.4	14 27.3	12.2	54.4
R 11	345 42.7	17.7	252 14.5	15.6	14 15.1	12.2	54.4
D 12	0 42.7	N21 18.1	266 49.1	15.5	N14 02.9	12.3	54.4
A 13	15 42.6	18.5	281 23.6	15.6	13 50.6	12.4	54.4
Y 14	30 42.5	18.9	295 58.2	15.6	13 38.2	12.4	54.4
15	45 42.4	.. 19.3	310 32.8	15.7	13 25.8	12.5	54.4
16	60 42.4	19.7	325 07.5	15.7	13 13.3	12.5	54.4
17	75 42.3	20.1	339 42.2	15.8	13 00.8	12.6	54.4
18	90 42.2	N21 20.6	354 17.0	15.7	N12 48.2	12.6	54.4
19	105 42.1	21.0	8 51.7	15.9	12 35.6	12.7	54.5
20	120 42.1	21.4	23 26.6	15.8	12 22.9	12.8	54.5
21	135 42.0	.. 21.8	38 01.4	15.9	12 10.1	12.8	54.5
22	150 41.9	22.2	52 36.3	15.9	11 57.3	12.8	54.5
23	165 41.8	22.6	67 11.2	15.9	N11 44.5	12.9	54.5
	SD 15.8	d 0.4	SD 14.8		14.8		14.8

Twilight / Sunrise / Moonrise

Lat.	Naut.	Civil	Sunrise	Moonrise 25	26	27	28
N 72	▢	▢	▢	▢	▢	08 32	10 54
N 70	▢	▢	▢	▢	06 10	09 06	11 09
68	////	////	00 22	▢	07 21	09 30	11 20
66	////	////	01 39	05 32	07 57	09 48	11 30
64	////	////	02 15	06 31	08 22	10 03	11 38
62	////	01 00	02 40	07 04	08 42	10 15	11 44
60	////	01 45	03 00	07 29	08 58	10 26	11 50
N 58	////	02 14	03 16	07 48	09 12	10 35	11 55
56	00 54	02 35	03 30	08 04	09 24	10 42	12 00
54	01 36	02 53	03 42	08 18	09 34	10 49	12 04
52	02 02	03 07	03 52	08 30	09 43	10 56	12 08
50	02 22	03 20	04 01	08 40	09 51	11 01	12 11
45	02 59	03 45	04 21	09 02	10 08	11 13	12 18
N 40	03 25	04 05	04 37	09 20	10 22	11 23	12 24
35	03 46	04 21	04 50	09 34	10 34	11 32	12 29
30	04 02	04 35	05 01	09 47	10 44	11 39	12 34
20	04 28	04 57	05 21	10 09	11 01	11 52	12 42
N 10	04 49	05 15	05 38	10 28	11 16	12 03	12 48
0	05 06	05 31	05 53	10 45	11 31	12 13	12 55
S 10	05 21	05 47	06 09	11 03	11 45	12 24	13 01
20	05 35	06 02	06 25	11 21	12 00	12 35	13 08
30	05 49	06 18	06 44	11 43	12 17	12 47	13 15
35	05 57	06 28	06 55	11 55	12 27	12 55	13 20
40	06 05	06 38	07 08	12 09	12 38	13 03	13 25
45	06 13	06 50	07 22	12 26	12 51	13 12	13 30
S 50	06 23	07 03	07 40	12 47	13 07	13 24	13 37
52	06 27	07 10	07 49	12 57	13 15	13 29	13 40
54	06 32	07 17	07 58	13 08	13 23	13 35	13 44
56	06 37	07 24	08 09	13 21	13 33	13 41	13 48
58	06 42	07 33	08 21	13 35	13 43	13 48	13 52
S 60	06 48	07 43	08 35	13 52	13 55	13 56	13 57

Sunset / Twilight / Moonset

Lat.	Sunset	Civil	Naut.	Moonset 25	26	27	28
N 72	▢	▢	▢	▢	▢	03 55	03 01
N 70	▢	▢	▢	▢	04 46	03 20	02 44
68	▢	▢	▢	▢	03 33	02 55	02 31
66	22 19	////	////	03 45	02 56	02 35	02 20
64	21 42	////	////	02 46	02 30	02 19	02 10
62	21 16	23 00	////	02 12	02 09	02 06	02 02
60	20 56	22 12	////	01 47	01 52	01 54	01 55
N 58	20 39	21 42	////	01 27	01 38	01 44	01 49
56	20 25	21 20	23 05	01 11	01 26	01 36	01 43
54	20 13	21 03	22 21	00 57	01 15	01 28	01 38
52	20 03	20 48	21 54	00 44	01 05	01 21	01 34
50	19 53	20 35	21 33	00 33	00 57	01 15	01 29
45	19 34	20 10	20 56	00 10	00 38	01 01	01 20
N 40	19 18	19 50	20 29	24 23	00 23	00 50	01 13
35	19 05	19 33	20 09	24 11	00 11	00 40	01 06
30	18 53	19 20	19 52	23 59	24 32	00 32	01 01
20	18 33	18 57	19 26	23 40	24 17	00 17	00 51
N 10	18 16	18 39	19 06	23 23	24 04	00 04	00 42
0	18 01	18 23	18 49	23 07	23 52	24 33	00 33
S 10	17 45	18 08	18 33	22 52	23 39	24 25	00 25
20	17 28	17 52	18 19	22 34	23 26	24 16	00 16
30	17 10	17 35	18 05	22 15	23 11	24 06	00 06
35	16 59	17 26	17 57	22 03	23 02	24 00	00 00
40	16 46	17 16	17 49	21 50	22 52	23 53	24 54
45	16 31	17 04	17 41	21 34	22 39	23 45	24 49
S 50	16 13	16 50	17 31	21 14	22 25	23 35	24 45
52	16 05	16 44	17 26	21 05	22 18	23 30	24 42
54	15 55	16 37	17 22	20 54	22 10	23 25	24 40
56	15 45	16 29	17 17	20 42	22 02	23 20	24 37
58	15 32	16 21	17 11	20 28	21 52	23 13	24 34
S 60	15 18	16 11	17 05	20 12	21 40	23 06	24 31

SUN / MOON

Day	Eqn. of Time 00h	12h	Mer. Pass.	Mer. Pass. Upper	Lower	Age	Phase
d	m s	m s	h m	h m	h m	d %	
25	03 07	03 04	11 57	16 56	04 33	06 30	
26	03 01	02 58	11 57	17 41	05 19	07 39	
27	02 54	02 51	11 57	18 24	06 03	08 49	

© British Crown Copyright 2022. All rights reserved.

UT	ARIES GHA	VENUS −4.3 GHA	Dec	MARS +1.6 GHA	Dec	JUPITER −2.1 GHA	Dec	SATURN +0.8 GHA	Dec
28 00	245 16.7	131 28.5	N24 25.0	118 21.1	N20 40.1	214 34.1	N11 20.1	266 07.4	S10 23.5
01	260 19.2	146 28.2	24.6	133 22.1	39.7	229 36.0	20.3	281 09.8	23.4
02	275 21.7	161 28.0	24.1	148 23.0	39.4	244 37.9	20.4	296 12.2	23.4
03	290 24.1	176 27.7 ..	23.7	163 24.0 ..	39.0	259 39.9 ..	20.6	311 14.6 ..	23.4
04	305 26.6	191 27.5	23.2	178 25.0	38.6	274 41.8	20.8	326 17.0	23.4
05	320 29.1	206 27.2	22.8	193 26.0	38.3	289 43.8	21.0	341 19.3	23.4
S 06	335 31.5	221 27.0	N24 22.3	208 26.9	N20 37.9	304 45.7	N11 21.2	356 21.7	S10 23.3
U 07	350 34.0	236 26.7	21.9	223 27.9	37.5	319 47.6	21.4	11 24.1	23.3
N 08	5 36.5	251 26.5	21.4	238 28.9	37.2	334 49.6	21.6	26 26.5	23.3
D 09	20 38.9	266 26.2 ..	21.0	253 29.9 ..	36.8	349 51.5 ..	21.7	41 28.9 ..	23.3
A 10	35 41.4	281 26.0	20.5	268 30.8	36.4	4 53.5	21.9	56 31.3	23.2
Y 11	50 43.8	296 25.7	20.1	283 31.8	36.0	19 55.4	22.1	71 33.6	23.2
12	65 46.3	311 25.5	N24 19.6	298 32.8	N20 35.7	34 57.3	N11 22.3	86 36.0	S10 23.2
13	80 48.8	326 25.2	19.2	313 33.7	35.3	49 59.3	22.5	101 38.4	23.2
14	95 51.2	341 25.0	18.7	328 34.7	34.9	65 01.2	22.7	116 40.8	23.2
15	110 53.7	356 24.7 ..	18.2	343 35.7 ..	34.6	80 03.2 ..	22.8	131 43.2 ..	23.1
16	125 56.2	11 24.5	17.8	358 36.7	34.2	95 05.1	23.0	146 45.6	23.1
17	140 58.6	26 24.2	17.3	13 37.6	33.8	110 07.0	23.2	161 47.9	23.1
18	156 01.1	41 24.0	N24 16.9	28 38.6	N20 33.5	125 09.0	N11 23.4	176 50.3	S10 23.1
19	171 03.6	56 23.8	16.4	43 39.6	33.1	140 10.9	23.6	191 52.7	23.0
20	186 06.0	71 23.5	15.9	58 40.6	32.7	155 12.9	23.8	206 55.1	23.0
21	201 08.5	86 23.3 ..	15.5	73 41.5 ..	32.3	170 14.8 ..	23.9	221 57.5 ..	23.0
22	216 10.9	101 23.0	15.0	88 42.5	32.0	185 16.7	24.1	236 59.9	23.0
23	231 13.4	116 22.8	14.6	103 43.5	31.6	200 18.7	24.3	252 02.3	23.0
29 00	246 15.9	131 22.6	N24 14.1	118 44.5	N20 31.2	215 20.6	N11 24.5	267 04.6	S10 22.9
01	261 18.3	146 22.3	13.6	133 45.4	30.9	230 22.6	24.7	282 07.0	22.9
02	276 20.8	161 22.1	13.2	148 46.4	30.5	245 24.5	24.9	297 09.4	22.9
03	291 23.3	176 21.9 ..	12.7	163 47.4 ..	30.1	260 26.4 ..	25.0	312 11.8 ..	22.9
04	306 25.7	191 21.6	12.2	178 48.4	29.7	275 28.4	25.2	327 14.2	22.9
05	321 28.2	206 21.4	11.8	193 49.3	29.4	290 30.3	25.4	342 16.6	22.8
M 06	336 30.7	221 21.2	N24 11.3	208 50.3	N20 29.0	305 32.3	N11 25.6	357 18.9	S10 22.8
O 07	351 33.1	236 20.9	10.8	223 51.3	28.6	320 34.2	25.8	12 21.3	22.8
N 08	6 35.6	251 20.7	10.3	238 52.3	28.2	335 36.1	26.0	27 23.7	22.8
D 09	21 38.1	266 20.5 ..	09.9	253 53.2 ..	27.9	350 38.1 ..	26.1	42 26.1 ..	22.7
A 10	36 40.5	281 20.3	09.4	268 54.2	27.5	5 40.0	26.3	57 28.5	22.7
Y 11	51 43.0	296 20.0	08.9	283 55.2	27.1	20 42.0	26.5	72 30.9	22.7
12	66 45.4	311 19.8	N24 08.5	298 56.2	N20 26.7	35 43.9	N11 26.7	87 33.3	S10 22.7
13	81 47.9	326 19.6	08.0	313 57.1	26.4	50 45.8	26.9	102 35.7	22.7
14	96 50.4	341 19.4	07.5	328 58.1	26.0	65 47.8	27.1	117 38.0	22.6
15	111 52.8	356 19.2 ..	07.0	343 59.1 ..	25.6	80 49.7 ..	27.2	132 40.4 ..	22.6
16	126 55.3	11 18.9	06.5	359 00.1	25.2	95 51.7	27.4	147 42.8	22.6
17	141 57.8	26 18.7	06.1	14 01.1	24.9	110 53.6	27.6	162 45.2	22.6
18	157 00.2	41 18.5	N24 05.6	29 02.0	N20 24.5	125 55.6	N11 27.8	177 47.6	S10 22.6
19	172 02.7	56 18.3	05.1	44 03.0	24.1	140 57.5	28.0	192 50.0	22.5
20	187 05.2	71 18.1	04.6	59 04.0	23.7	155 59.4	28.2	207 52.4	22.5
21	202 07.6	86 17.9 ..	04.1	74 05.0 ..	23.4	171 01.4 ..	28.3	222 54.8 ..	22.5
22	217 10.1	101 17.7	03.7	89 05.9	23.0	186 03.3	28.5	237 57.1	22.5
23	232 12.6	116 17.4	03.2	104 06.9	22.6	201 05.3	28.7	252 59.5	22.5
30 00	247 15.0	131 17.2	N24 02.7	119 07.9	N20 22.2	216 07.2	N11 28.9	268 01.9	S10 22.4
01	262 17.5	146 17.0	02.2	134 08.9	21.9	231 09.1	29.1	283 04.3	22.4
02	277 19.9	161 16.8	01.7	149 09.8	21.5	246 11.1	29.2	298 06.7	22.4
03	292 22.4	176 16.6 ..	01.2	164 10.8 ..	21.1	261 13.0 ..	29.4	313 09.1 ..	22.4
04	307 24.9	191 16.4	00.7	179 11.8	20.7	276 15.0	29.6	328 11.5	22.4
05	322 27.3	206 16.2	24 00.2	194 12.8	20.3	291 16.9	29.8	343 13.9	22.3
T 06	337 29.8	221 16.0	N23 59.8	209 13.7	N20 20.0	306 18.9	N11 30.0	358 16.3	S10 22.3
U 07	352 32.3	236 15.8	59.3	224 14.7	19.6	321 20.8	30.2	13 18.6	22.3
E 08	7 34.7	251 15.6	58.8	239 15.7	19.2	336 22.7	30.3	28 21.0	22.3
S 09	22 37.2	266 15.4 ..	58.3	254 16.7 ..	18.8	351 24.7 ..	30.5	43 23.4 ..	22.3
D 10	37 39.7	281 15.2	57.8	269 17.6	18.5	6 26.6	30.7	58 25.8	22.2
A 11	52 42.1	296 15.0	57.3	284 18.6	18.1	21 28.6	30.9	73 28.2	22.2
Y 12	67 44.6	311 14.8	N23 56.8	299 19.6	N20 17.7	36 30.5	N11 31.1	88 30.6	S10 22.2
13	82 47.0	326 14.6	56.3	314 20.6	17.3	51 32.5	31.2	103 33.0	22.2
14	97 49.5	341 14.4	55.8	329 21.5	16.9	66 34.4	31.4	118 35.4	22.2
15	112 52.0	356 14.2 ..	55.3	344 22.5 ..	16.5	81 36.3 ..	31.6	133 37.8 ..	22.1
16	127 54.4	11 14.0	54.8	359 23.5	16.2	96 38.3	31.8	148 40.2	22.1
17	142 56.9	26 13.8	54.3	14 24.5	15.8	111 40.2	32.0	163 42.5	22.1
18	157 59.4	41 13.6	N23 53.8	29 25.4	N20 15.4	126 42.2	N11 32.1	178 44.9	S10 22.1
19	173 01.8	56 13.5	53.3	44 26.4	15.0	141 44.1	32.3	193 47.3	22.1
20	188 04.3	71 13.3	52.8	59 27.4	14.6	156 46.1	32.5	208 49.7	22.1
21	203 06.8	86 13.1 ..	52.3	74 28.4 ..	14.3	171 48.0 ..	32.7	223 52.1 ..	22.0
22	218 09.2	101 12.9	51.8	89 29.4	13.9	186 50.0	32.9	238 54.5	22.0
23	233 11.7	116 12.7	51.3	104 30.3	13.5	201 51.9	33.1	253 56.9	22.0
Mer. Pass.	h m 7 33.7	v −0.2 d 0.5		v 1.0 d 0.4		v 1.9 d 0.2		v 2.4 d 0.0	

STARS

Name	SHA	Dec
Acamar	315 13.2	S40 12.6
Achernar	335 21.6	S57 06.9
Acrux	173 01.2	S63 14.0
Adhara	255 07.2	S29 00.3
Aldebaran	290 41.5	N16 33.3
Alioth	166 13.8	N55 50.2
Alkaid	152 52.7	N49 12.0
Alnair	27 34.6	S46 50.7
Alnilam	275 39.4	S 1 11.3
Alphard	217 49.2	S 8 45.6
Alphecca	126 04.5	N26 38.2
Alpheratz	357 36.3	N29 12.9
Altair	62 01.1	N 8 55.7
Ankaa	353 08.7	S42 10.6
Antares	112 17.1	S26 29.1
Arcturus	145 48.9	N19 03.7
Atria	107 12.0	S69 04.1
Avior	234 15.7	S59 35.2
Bellatrix	278 24.7	N 6 22.2
Betelgeuse	270 53.9	N 7 24.7
Canopus	263 53.5	S52 42.6
Capella	280 24.4	N46 01.3
Deneb	49 26.5	N45 21.5
Denebola	182 26.2	N14 26.6
Diphda	348 48.8	S17 51.5
Dubhe	193 42.6	N61 37.8
Elnath	278 04.0	N28 37.6
Eltanin	90 42.3	N51 29.0
Enif	33 40.1	N 9 58.8
Fomalhaut	15 16.0	S29 29.8
Gacrux	171 52.9	S57 14.9
Gienah	175 44.8	S17 40.4
Hadar	148 37.4	S60 29.3
Hamal	327 53.0	N23 34.2
Kaus Aust.	83 34.0	S34 22.4
Kochab	137 18.7	N74 03.7
Markab	13 31.3	N15 19.7
Menkar	314 07.9	N 4 10.8
Menkent	147 58.9	S36 29.2
Miaplacidus	221 38.9	S69 49.0
Mirfak	308 30.7	N49 56.5
Nunki	75 49.1	S26 16.0
Peacock	53 07.5	S56 39.4
Pollux	243 19.2	N27 58.3
Procyon	244 52.5	N 5 09.9
Rasalhague	95 59.5	N12 32.5
Regulus	207 35.9	N11 51.2
Rigel	281 05.5	S 8 10.5
Rigil Kent.	139 41.6	S60 56.0
Sabik	102 04.0	S15 43.3
Schedar	349 32.9	N56 39.6
Shaula	96 11.8	S37 07.2
Sirius	258 27.7	S16 45.0
Spica	158 23.5	S11 17.1
Suhail	222 47.5	S43 31.8
Vega	80 33.8	N38 48.1
Zuben'ubi	136 57.2	S16 08.4

	SHA	Mer. Pass.
	° ′	h m
Venus	245 06.7	15 15
Mars	232 28.6	16 04
Jupiter	329 04.7	9 37
Saturn	20 48.8	6 11

© British Crown Copyright 2022. All rights reserved.

UT	SUN		MOON					Lat.	Twilight		Sunrise	Moonrise			
	GHA	Dec	GHA	v	Dec	d	HP		Naut.	Civil		28	29	30	31
	° ′	° ′	° ′	′	° ′	′	′	°	h m	h m	h m	h m	h m	h m	h m
d h								N 72	☐	☐	☐	10 54	12 57	14 59	17 10
28 00	180 41.8	N21 23.0	81 46.1	16.0	N11 31.6	12.9	54.5	N 70	☐	☐	☐	11 09	13 01	14 54	16 54
01	195 41.7	23.4	96 21.1	15.9	11 18.7	13.0	54.5	68	☐	☐	☐	11 20	13 05	14 50	16 41
02	210 41.6	23.9	110 56.0	16.1	11 05.7	13.1	54.6	66	////	////	01 26	11 30	13 08	14 47	16 31
03	225 41.5 ..	24.3	125 31.1	16.0	10 52.6	13.1	54.6	64	////	////	02 06	11 38	13 10	14 44	16 22
04	240 41.5	24.7	140 06.1	16.1	10 39.5	13.1	54.6	62	////	00 41	02 34	11 44	13 12	14 42	16 15
05	255 41.4	25.1	154 41.2	16.0	10 26.4	13.2	54.6	60	////	01 36	02 55	11 50	13 14	14 40	16 09
06	270 41.3	N21 25.5	169 16.2	16.1	N10 13.2	13.2	54.6	N 58	////	02 07	03 12	11 55	13 16	14 38	16 03
07	285 41.2	25.9	183 51.3	16.2	10 00.0	13.3	54.6	56	00 37	02 30	03 26	12 00	13 17	14 36	15 58
08	300 41.2	26.3	198 26.5	16.1	9 46.7	13.3	54.6	54	01 27	02 48	03 38	12 04	13 19	14 35	15 54
S 09	315 41.1 ..	26.7	213 01.6	16.2	9 33.4	13.4	54.7	52	01 56	03 03	03 49	12 08	13 20	14 33	15 50
U 10	330 41.0	27.1	227 36.8	16.2	9 20.0	13.4	54.7	50	02 18	03 16	03 59	12 11	13 21	14 32	15 46
N 11	345 40.9	27.5	242 12.0	16.2	9 06.6	13.4	54.7	45	02 56	03 43	04 19	12 18	13 23	14 30	15 39
D 12	0 40.8	N21 27.9	256 47.2	16.2	N 8 53.2	13.5	54.7	N 40	03 23	04 03	04 35	12 24	13 25	14 28	15 32
A 13	15 40.8	28.3	271 22.4	16.2	8 39.7	13.6	54.7	35	03 44	04 20	04 48	12 29	13 26	14 26	15 27
Y 14	30 40.7	28.7	285 57.6	16.2	8 26.1	13.5	54.7	30	04 01	04 33	05 00	12 34	13 28	14 24	15 22
15	45 40.6 ..	29.1	300 32.8	16.3	8 12.6	13.6	54.8	20	04 28	04 56	05 20	12 42	13 31	14 21	15 14
16	60 40.5	29.5	315 08.1	16.3	7 59.0	13.7	54.8	N 10	04 48	05 15	05 38	12 48	13 33	14 19	15 07
17	75 40.5	29.9	329 43.4	16.2	7 45.3	13.7	54.8	0	05 06	05 32	05 54	12 55	13 35	14 17	15 00
18	90 40.4	N21 30.3	344 18.6	16.3	N 7 31.6	13.7	54.8	S 10	05 21	05 47	06 10	13 01	13 38	14 15	14 53
19	105 40.3	30.7	358 53.9	16.3	7 17.9	13.8	54.8	20	05 36	06 03	06 27	13 08	13 40	14 12	14 46
20	120 40.2	31.1	13 29.2	16.3	7 04.1	13.8	54.9	30	05 51	06 20	06 46	13 15	13 42	14 10	14 38
21	135 40.1 ..	31.5	28 04.5	16.3	6 50.3	13.8	54.9	35	05 58	06 30	06 57	13 20	13 44	14 08	14 34
22	150 40.1	31.9	42 39.8	16.3	6 36.5	13.9	54.9	40	06 07	06 40	07 10	13 25	13 46	14 06	14 29
23	165 40.0	32.3	57 15.1	16.3	6 22.6	13.9	54.9	45	06 16	06 52	07 25	13 30	13 48	14 05	14 23
29 00	180 39.9	N21 32.7	71 50.4	16.4	N 6 08.7	13.9	54.9	S 50	06 26	07 06	07 44	13 37	13 50	14 02	14 16
01	195 39.8	33.1	86 25.8	16.3	5 54.8	14.0	55.0	52	06 30	07 13	07 52	13 40	13 51	14 01	14 13
02	210 39.7	33.5	101 01.1	16.3	5 40.8	14.0	55.0	54	06 35	07 20	08 02	13 44	13 52	14 00	14 09
03	225 39.7 ..	33.9	115 36.4	16.3	5 26.8	14.1	55.0	56	06 40	07 28	08 13	13 48	13 53	13 59	14 05
04	240 39.6	34.2	130 11.7	16.3	5 12.7	14.0	55.0	58	06 46	07 37	08 26	13 52	13 55	13 58	14 01
05	255 39.5	34.6	144 47.0	16.3	4 58.7	14.1	55.0	S 60	06 52	07 47	08 41	13 57	13 56	13 56	13 56
06	270 39.4	N21 35.0	159 22.3	16.3	N 4 44.6	14.1	55.1	Lat.	Sunset	Twilight		Moonset			
07	285 39.3	35.4	173 57.6	16.3	4 30.5	14.2	55.1			Civil	Naut.	28	29	30	31
08	300 39.3	35.8	188 32.9	16.3	4 16.3	14.2	55.1								
M 09	315 39.2 ..	36.2	203 08.2	16.3	4 02.1	14.2	55.1	°	h m	h m	h m	h m	h m	h m	h m
O 10	330 39.1	36.6	217 43.5	16.3	3 47.9	14.2	55.2	N 72	☐	☐	☐	03 01	02 25	01 54	01 21
N 11	345 39.0	37.0	232 18.8	16.2	3 33.7	14.3	55.2	N 70	☐	☐	☐	02 44	02 18	01 54	01 29
D 12	0 38.9	N21 37.4	246 54.0	16.3	N 3 19.4	14.3	55.2	68	☐	☐	☐	02 31	02 12	01 54	01 36
A 13	15 38.8	37.7	261 29.3	16.2	3 05.1	14.3	55.2	66	22 32	////	////	02 20	02 06	01 54	01 42
Y 14	30 38.8	38.1	276 04.5	16.2	2 50.8	14.4	55.3	64	21 51	////	////	02 10	02 02	01 54	01 46
15	45 38.7 ..	38.5	290 39.7	16.3	2 36.4	14.3	55.3	62	21 23	23 22	////	02 02	01 58	01 54	01 51
16	60 38.6	38.9	305 15.0	16.1	2 22.1	14.4	55.3	60	21 02	22 22	////	01 55	01 55	01 54	01 54
17	75 38.5	39.3	319 50.1	16.2	2 07.7	14.4	55.3	N 58	20 44	21 50	////	01 49	01 52	01 54	01 57
18	90 38.4	N21 39.7	334 25.3	16.2	N 1 53.3	14.4	55.4	56	20 30	21 26	23 25	01 43	01 49	01 55	02 00
19	105 38.3	40.0	349 00.5	16.1	1 38.9	14.5	55.4	54	20 17	21 08	22 30	01 38	01 47	01 55	02 03
20	120 38.3	40.4	3 35.6	16.1	1 24.4	14.5	55.4	52	20 07	20 52	22 00	01 34	01 44	01 55	02 05
21	135 38.2 ..	40.8	18 10.7	16.1	1 09.9	14.4	55.4	50	19 57	20 39	21 39	01 29	01 42	01 55	02 07
22	150 38.1	41.2	32 45.8	16.1	0 55.5	14.5	55.5	45	19 37	20 13	21 00	01 20	01 38	01 55	02 12
23	165 38.0	41.6	47 20.9	16.0	0 40.9	14.5	55.5	N 40	19 20	19 52	20 32	01 13	01 34	01 55	02 16
30 00	180 37.9	N21 41.9	61 55.9	16.0	N 0 26.4	14.5	55.5	35	19 07	19 36	20 11	01 06	01 31	01 55	02 20
01	195 37.8	42.3	76 30.9	16.0	N 0 11.9	14.6	55.5	30	18 55	19 22	19 54	01 01	01 28	01 55	02 23
02	210 37.8	42.7	91 05.9	16.0	S 0 02.7	14.5	55.6	20	18 35	18 59	19 27	00 51	01 23	01 55	02 28
03	225 37.7 ..	43.1	105 40.9	15.9	0 17.2	14.6	55.6	N 10	18 17	18 40	19 07	00 42	01 19	01 55	02 33
04	240 37.6	43.5	120 15.8	15.9	0 31.8	14.6	55.6	0	18 01	18 23	18 49	00 33	01 14	01 55	02 37
05	255 37.5	43.8	134 50.7	15.9	0 46.4	14.6	55.6	S 10	17 45	18 08	18 34	00 25	01 10	01 55	02 41
06	270 37.4	N21 44.2	149 25.6	15.8	S 1 01.0	14.6	55.7	20	17 28	17 52	18 19	00 16	01 05	01 55	02 46
07	285 37.3	44.6	164 00.4	15.8	1 15.6	14.7	55.7	30	17 09	17 35	18 04	00 06	01 00	01 55	02 52
T 08	300 37.2	45.0	178 35.2	15.8	1 30.3	14.6	55.7	35	16 57	17 25	17 56	00 00	00 57	01 55	02 55
U 09	315 37.2 ..	45.3	193 10.0	15.7	1 44.9	14.7	55.8	40	16 45	17 14	17 48	24 54	00 54	01 55	02 58
E 10	330 37.1	45.7	207 44.7	15.7	1 59.6	14.6	55.8	45	16 29	17 02	17 39	24 49	00 49	01 55	03 02
S 11	345 37.0	46.1	222 19.4	15.7	2 14.2	14.7	55.8	S 50	16 11	16 48	17 29	24 45	00 45	01 55	03 07
D 12	0 36.9	N21 46.4	236 54.1	15.6	S 2 28.9	14.6	55.8	52	16 02	16 41	17 24	24 42	00 42	01 55	03 10
A 13	15 36.8	46.8	251 28.7	15.5	2 43.5	14.7	55.9	54	15 52	16 34	17 19	24 40	00 40	01 55	03 12
Y 14	30 36.7	47.2	266 03.2	15.6	2 58.2	14.7	55.9	56	15 41	16 26	17 14	24 37	00 37	01 55	03 15
15	45 36.6 ..	47.6	280 37.8	15.4	3 12.9	14.7	55.9	58	15 28	16 17	17 08	24 34	00 34	01 55	03 18
16	60 36.6	47.9	295 12.2	15.5	3 27.6	14.7	56.0	S 60	15 13	16 07	17 02	24 31	00 31	01 55	03 21
17	75 36.5	48.3	309 46.7	15.3	3 42.3	14.7	56.0			SUN			MOON		
18	90 36.4	N21 48.7	324 21.0	15.4	S 3 57.0	14.7	56.0	Day	Eqn. of Time		Mer.	Mer. Pass.		Age	Phase
19	105 36.3	49.0	338 55.4	15.3	4 11.7	14.6	56.0		00ʰ	12ʰ	Pass.	Upper	Lower		
20	120 36.2	49.4	353 29.7	15.2	4 26.3	14.7	56.1	d	m s	m s	h m	h m	h m	d	%
21	135 36.1 ..	49.8	8 03.9	15.2	4 41.0	14.7	56.1	28	02 47	02 44	11 57	19 05	06 44	09	58
22	150 36.0	50.1	22 38.1	15.1	4 55.7	14.7	56.1	29	02 40	02 36	11 57	19 45	07 25	10	68
23	165 35.9	50.5	37 12.2	15.1	S 5 10.4	14.7	56.2	30	02 32	02 28	11 58	20 27	08 06	11	77
	SD 15.8	d 0.4	SD 14.9		15.0		15.2									

© British Crown Copyright 2022. All rights reserved.

UT	ARIES GHA	VENUS −4.4 GHA	Dec	MARS +1.6 GHA	Dec	JUPITER −2.1 GHA	Dec	SATURN +0.8 GHA	Dec	Star Name	SHA	Dec
31 00	248 14.2	131 12.5	N23 50.8	119 31.3	N20 13.1	216 53.8	N11 33.2	268 59.3	S10 22.0	Acamar	315 13.2	S40 12.6
01	263 16.6	146 12.3	50.3	134 32.3	12.7	231 55.8	33.4	284 01.7	22.0	Achernar	335 21.6	S57 06.9
02	278 19.1	161 12.2	49.8	149 33.3	12.4	246 57.7	33.6	299 04.1	21.9	Acrux	173 01.3	S63 14.0
03	293 21.5	176 12.0 ..	49.3	164 34.2 ..	12.0	261 59.7 ..	33.8	314 06.5 ..	21.9	Adhara	255 07.3	S29 00.3
04	308 24.0	191 11.8	48.8	179 35.2	11.6	277 01.6	34.0	329 08.9	21.9	Aldebaran	290 41.5	N16 33.3
05	323 26.5	206 11.6	48.3	194 36.2	11.2	292 03.6	34.1	344 11.3	21.9			
W 06	338 28.9	221 11.4	N23 47.7	209 37.2	N20 10.8	307 05.5	N11 34.3	359 13.6	S10 21.9	Alioth	166 13.8	N55 50.2
E 07	353 31.4	236 11.3	47.2	224 38.1	10.4	322 07.5	34.5	14 16.0	21.9	Alkaid	152 52.7	N49 12.0
D 08	8 33.9	251 11.1	46.7	239 39.1	10.0	337 09.4	34.7	29 18.4	21.8	Alnair	27 34.5	S46 50.7
N 09	23 36.3	266 10.9 ..	46.2	254 40.1 ..	09.7	352 11.3 ..	34.9	44 20.8 ..	21.8	Alnilam	275 39.4	S 1 11.3
E 10	38 38.8	281 10.8	45.7	269 41.1	09.3	7 13.3	35.0	59 23.2	21.8	Alphard	217 49.2	S 8 45.6
S 11	53 41.3	296 10.6	45.2	284 42.1	08.9	22 15.2	35.2	74 25.6	21.8			
D 12	68 43.7	311 10.4	N23 44.7	299 43.0	N20 08.5	37 17.2	N11 35.4	89 28.0	S10 21.8	Alphecca	126 04.5	N26 38.2
A 13	83 46.2	326 10.2	44.2	314 44.0	08.1	52 19.1	35.6	104 30.4	21.7	Alpheratz	357 36.3	N29 12.9
Y 14	98 48.7	341 10.1	43.6	329 45.0	07.7	67 21.1	35.8	119 32.8	21.7	Altair	62 01.0	N 8 55.7
15	113 51.1	356 09.9 ..	43.1	344 46.0 ..	07.4	82 23.0 ..	35.9	134 35.2 ..	21.7	Ankaa	353 08.7	S42 10.6
16	128 53.6	11 09.7	42.6	359 46.9	07.0	97 25.0	36.1	149 37.6	21.7	Antares	112 17.1	S26 29.1
17	143 56.0	26 09.6	42.1	14 47.9	06.6	112 26.9	36.3	164 40.0	21.7			
18	158 58.5	41 09.4	N23 41.6	29 48.9	N20 06.2	127 28.9	N11 36.5	179 42.4	S10 21.7	Arcturus	145 48.9	N19 03.7
19	174 01.0	56 09.2	41.0	44 49.9	05.8	142 30.8	36.7	194 44.8	21.6	Atria	107 12.0	S69 04.1
20	189 03.4	71 09.1	40.5	59 50.8	05.4	157 32.8	36.8	209 47.2	21.6	Avior	234 15.7	S59 35.2
21	204 05.9	86 08.9 ..	40.0	74 51.8 ..	05.0	172 34.7 ..	37.0	224 49.6 ..	21.6	Bellatrix	278 24.7	N 6 22.2
22	219 08.4	101 08.8	39.5	89 52.8	04.7	187 36.6	37.2	239 52.0	21.6	Betelgeuse	270 53.9	N 7 24.7
23	234 10.8	116 08.6	39.0	104 53.8	04.3	202 38.6	37.4	254 54.4	21.6			
1 00	249 13.3	131 08.5	N23 38.4	119 54.8	N20 03.9	217 40.5	N11 37.6	269 56.8	S10 21.5	Canopus	263 53.5	S52 42.6
01	264 15.8	146 08.3	37.9	134 55.7	03.5	232 42.5	37.7	284 59.2	21.5	Capella	280 24.4	N46 01.3
02	279 18.2	161 08.1	37.4	149 56.7	03.1	247 44.4	37.9	300 01.5	21.5	Deneb	49 26.5	N45 21.5
03	294 20.7	176 08.0 ..	36.9	164 57.7 ..	02.7	262 46.4 ..	38.1	315 03.9 ..	21.5	Denebola	182 26.2	N14 26.6
04	309 23.1	191 07.8	36.3	179 58.7	02.3	277 48.3	38.3	330 06.3	21.5	Diphda	348 48.8	S17 51.5
05	324 25.6	206 07.7	35.8	194 59.6	01.9	292 50.3	38.5	345 08.7	21.5			
T 06	339 28.1	221 07.5	N23 35.3	210 00.6	N20 01.5	307 52.2	N11 38.6	0 11.1	S10 21.5	Dubhe	193 42.6	N61 37.8
H 07	354 30.5	236 07.4	34.7	225 01.6	01.2	322 54.2	38.8	15 13.5	21.4	Elnath	278 04.0	N28 37.6
U 08	9 33.0	251 07.2	34.2	240 02.6	00.8	337 56.1	39.0	30 15.9	21.4	Eltanin	90 42.3	N51 29.0
R 09	24 35.5	266 07.1 ..	33.7	255 03.6 ..	00.4	352 58.1 ..	39.2	45 18.3 ..	21.4	Enif	33 40.0	N 9 58.8
S 10	39 37.9	281 07.0	33.1	270 04.5	20 00.0	8 00.0	39.3	60 20.7	21.4	Fomalhaut	15 16.0	S29 29.8
D 11	54 40.4	296 06.8	32.6	285 05.5	19 59.6	23 02.0	39.5	75 23.1	21.4			
A 12	69 42.9	311 06.7	N23 32.1	300 06.5	N19 59.2	38 03.9	N11 39.7	90 25.5	S10 21.4	Gacrux	171 52.9	S57 14.9
Y 13	84 45.3	326 06.5	31.5	315 07.5	58.8	53 05.9	39.9	105 27.9	21.3	Gienah	175 44.9	S17 40.4
14	99 47.8	341 06.4	31.0	330 08.4	58.4	68 07.8	40.1	120 30.3	21.3	Hadar	148 37.4	S60 29.3
15	114 50.3	356 06.2 ..	30.5	345 09.4 ..	58.0	83 09.7 ..	40.2	135 32.7 ..	21.3	Hamal	327 53.0	N23 34.2
16	129 52.7	11 06.1	29.9	0 10.4	57.6	98 11.7	40.4	150 35.1	21.3	Kaus Aust.	83 33.9	S34 22.4
17	144 55.2	26 06.0	29.4	15 11.4	57.3	113 13.6	40.6	165 37.5	21.3			
18	159 57.6	41 05.8	N23 28.9	30 12.4	N19 56.9	128 15.6	N11 40.8	180 39.9	S10 21.3	Kochab	137 18.7	N74 03.7
19	175 00.1	56 05.7	28.3	45 13.3	56.5	143 17.5	41.0	195 42.3	21.2	Markab	13 31.3	N15 19.7
20	190 02.6	71 05.6	27.8	60 14.3	56.1	158 19.5	41.1	210 44.7	21.2	Menkar	314 07.9	N 4 10.8
21	205 05.0	86 05.4 ..	27.2	75 15.3 ..	55.7	173 21.4 ..	41.3	225 47.1 ..	21.2	Menkent	147 58.9	S36 29.2
22	220 07.5	101 05.3	26.7	90 16.3	55.3	188 23.4	41.5	240 49.5	21.2	Miaplacidus	221 39.0	S69 49.0
23	235 10.0	116 05.2	26.2	105 17.2	54.9	203 25.3	41.7	255 51.9	21.2			
2 00	250 12.4	131 05.0	N23 25.6	120 18.2	N19 54.5	218 27.3	N11 41.8	270 54.3	S10 21.2	Mirfak	308 30.7	N49 56.5
01	265 14.9	146 04.9	25.1	135 19.2	54.1	233 29.2	42.0	285 56.7	21.2	Nunki	75 49.1	S26 16.0
02	280 17.4	161 04.8	24.5	150 20.2	53.7	248 31.2	42.2	300 59.1	21.1	Peacock	53 07.5	S56 39.4
03	295 19.8	176 04.7 ..	24.0	165 21.2 ..	53.3	263 33.1 ..	42.4	316 01.5 ..	21.1	Pollux	243 19.2	N27 58.3
04	310 22.3	191 04.5	23.4	180 22.1	52.9	278 35.1	42.6	331 03.9	21.1	Procyon	244 52.5	N 5 09.9
05	325 24.8	206 04.4	22.9	195 23.1	52.5	293 37.0	42.8	346 06.3	21.1			
F 06	340 27.2	221 04.3	N23 22.3	210 24.1	N19 52.2	308 39.0	N11 42.9	1 08.7	S10 21.1	Rasalhague	95 59.5	N12 32.5
R 07	355 29.7	236 04.2	21.8	225 25.1	51.8	323 40.9	43.1	16 11.1	21.1	Regulus	207 35.9	N11 51.3
I 08	10 32.1	251 04.0	21.2	240 26.0	51.4	338 42.9	43.3	31 13.5	21.0	Rigel	281 05.5	S 8 10.5
D 09	25 34.6	266 03.9 ..	20.7	255 27.0 ..	51.0	353 44.8 ..	43.4	46 15.9 ..	21.0	Rigil Kent.	139 41.6	S60 56.0
A 10	40 37.1	281 03.8	20.1	270 28.0	50.6	8 46.8	43.6	61 18.3	21.0	Sabik	102 04.0	S15 45.3
Y 11	55 39.5	296 03.7	19.6	285 29.0	50.2	23 48.7	43.8	76 20.7	21.0			
12	70 42.0	311 03.6	N23 19.0	300 30.0	N19 49.8	38 50.7	N11 44.0	91 23.1	S10 21.0	Schedar	349 32.9	N56 39.6
13	85 44.5	326 03.5	18.5	315 30.9	49.4	53 52.6	44.2	106 25.5	21.0	Shaula	96 11.8	S37 07.2
14	100 46.9	341 03.4	17.9	330 31.9	49.0	68 54.6	44.3	121 27.9	21.0	Sirius	258 27.7	S16 44.9
15	115 49.4	356 03.2 ..	17.4	345 32.9 ..	48.6	83 56.5 ..	44.5	136 30.3 ..	20.9	Spica	158 23.5	S11 17.0
16	130 51.9	11 03.1	16.8	0 33.9	48.2	98 58.5	44.7	151 32.7	20.9	Suhail	222 47.5	S43 31.8
17	145 54.3	26 03.0	16.3	15 34.9	47.8	114 00.4	44.9	166 35.1	20.9			
18	160 56.8	41 02.9	N23 15.7	30 35.8	N19 47.4	129 02.4	N11 45.0	181 37.5	S10 20.9	Vega	80 33.8	N38 48.1
19	175 59.2	56 02.8	15.2	45 36.8	47.0	144 04.3	45.2	196 39.9	20.9	Zuben'ubi	136 57.2	S16 08.4
20	191 01.7	71 02.7	14.6	60 37.8	46.6	159 06.3	45.4	211 42.3	20.9		SHA	Mer. Pass.
21	206 04.2	86 02.6 ..	14.0	75 38.8 ..	46.2	174 08.2 ..	45.6	226 44.7 ..	20.9			
22	221 06.6	101 02.5	13.5	90 39.7	45.8	189 10.2	45.7	241 47.1	20.8	Venus	241 55.2	15 16
23	236 09.1	116 02.4	12.9	105 40.7	45.4	204 12.1	45.9	256 49.5	20.8	Mars	230 41.5	15 59
										Jupiter	328 27.2	9 28
Mer. Pass. 7 21.9		v −0.1	d 0.5	v 1.0	d 0.4	v 1.9	d 0.2	v 2.4	d 0.0	Saturn	20 43.5	5 59

© British Crown Copyright 2022. All rights reserved.

UT	SUN GHA	SUN Dec	MOON GHA	v	MOON Dec	d	HP
d h	° ′	° ′	° ′	′	° ′	′	′
31 00	180 35.8	N21 50.8	51 46.3	15.0	S 5 25.1	14.6	56.2
01	195 35.8	51.2	66 20.3	14.9	5 39.7	14.7	56.2
02	210 35.7	51.6	80 54.2	14.9	5 54.4	14.7	56.3
03	225 35.6 ..	51.9	95 28.1	14.9	6 09.1	14.6	56.3
04	240 35.5	52.3	110 02.0	14.7	6 23.7	14.7	56.3
05	255 35.4	52.6	124 35.7	14.8	6 38.4	14.6	56.3
06	270 35.3	N21 53.0	139 09.5	14.6	S 6 53.0	14.6	56.4
W 07	285 35.2	53.4	153 43.1	14.6	7 07.6	14.6	56.4
E 08	300 35.1	53.7	168 16.7	14.5	7 22.2	14.6	56.4
D 09	315 35.0 ..	54.1	182 50.2	14.5	7 36.8	14.6	56.5
N 10	330 35.0	54.4	197 23.7	14.3	7 51.4	14.6	56.5
E 11	345 34.9	54.8	211 57.0	14.3	8 06.0	14.5	56.5
S 12	0 34.8	N21 55.1	226 30.3	14.3	S 8 20.5	14.6	56.6
D 13	15 34.7	55.5	241 03.6	14.1	8 35.1	14.5	56.6
A 14	30 34.6	55.9	255 36.7	14.1	8 49.6	14.5	56.6
Y 15	45 34.5 ..	56.2	270 09.8	14.0	9 04.1	14.4	56.7
16	60 34.4	56.6	284 42.8	14.0	9 18.5	14.5	56.7
17	75 34.3	56.9	299 15.8	13.8	9 33.0	14.4	56.7
18	90 34.2	N21 57.3	313 48.6	13.8	S 9 47.4	14.4	56.8
19	105 34.1	57.6	328 21.4	13.7	10 01.8	14.4	56.8
20	120 34.0	58.0	342 54.1	13.6	10 16.2	14.3	56.8
21	135 33.9 ..	58.3	357 26.7	13.6	10 30.5	14.3	56.9
22	150 33.9	58.7	11 59.3	13.4	10 44.8	14.3	56.9
23	165 33.8	59.0	26 31.7	13.4	10 59.1	14.3	56.9
1 00	180 33.7	N21 59.4	41 04.1	13.3	S11 13.4	14.2	57.0
01	195 33.6	21 59.7	55 36.4	13.1	11 27.6	14.2	57.0
02	210 33.5	22 00.0	70 08.5	13.1	11 41.8	14.1	57.0
03	225 33.4 ..	00.4	84 40.6	13.0	11 55.9	14.1	57.1
04	240 33.3	00.7	99 12.6	13.0	12 10.0	14.1	57.1
05	255 33.2	01.1	113 44.6	12.8	12 24.1	14.0	57.1
06	270 33.1	N22 01.4	128 16.4	12.7	S12 38.1	14.0	57.2
T 07	285 33.0	01.8	142 48.1	12.6	12 52.1	14.0	57.2
H 08	300 32.9	02.1	157 19.7	12.6	13 06.1	13.9	57.2
U 09	315 32.8 ..	02.4	171 51.3	12.4	13 20.0	13.9	57.3
R 10	330 32.7	02.8	186 22.7	12.3	13 33.9	13.8	57.3
S 11	345 32.6	03.1	200 54.0	12.3	13 47.7	13.7	57.3
D 12	0 32.5	N22 03.5	215 25.3	12.1	S14 01.4	13.7	57.4
A 13	15 32.5	03.8	229 56.4	12.1	14 15.1	13.7	57.4
Y 14	30 32.4	04.1	244 27.5	11.9	14 28.8	13.6	57.4
15	45 32.3 ..	04.5	258 58.4	11.8	14 42.4	13.6	57.5
16	60 32.2	04.8	273 29.2	11.7	14 56.0	13.5	57.5
17	75 32.1	05.2	287 59.9	11.7	15 09.5	13.4	57.5
18	90 32.0	N22 05.5	302 30.6	11.5	S15 22.9	13.4	57.6
19	105 31.9	05.8	317 01.1	11.4	15 36.3	13.3	57.6
20	120 31.8	06.2	331 31.5	11.2	15 49.6	13.3	57.6
21	135 31.7 ..	06.5	346 01.7	11.2	16 02.9	13.2	57.7
22	150 31.6	06.8	0 31.9	11.1	16 16.1	13.1	57.7
23	165 31.5	07.2	15 02.0	10.9	16 29.2	13.0	57.7
2 00	180 31.4	N22 07.5	29 31.9	10.9	S16 42.2	13.0	57.8
01	195 31.3	07.8	44 01.8	10.7	16 55.2	13.0	57.8
02	210 31.2	08.1	58 31.5	10.6	17 08.2	12.8	57.8
03	225 31.1 ..	08.5	73 01.1	10.5	17 21.0	12.8	57.9
04	240 31.0	08.8	87 30.6	10.4	17 33.8	12.7	57.9
05	255 30.9	09.1	102 00.0	10.3	17 46.5	12.6	57.9
06	270 30.8	N22 09.5	116 29.3	10.1	S17 59.1	12.5	58.0
07	285 30.7	09.8	130 58.4	10.0	18 11.6	12.5	58.0
08	300 30.6	10.1	145 27.4	9.9	18 24.1	12.3	58.0
F 09	315 30.5 ..	10.4	159 56.3	9.8	18 36.4	12.3	58.1
R 10	330 30.4	10.8	174 25.1	9.7	18 48.7	12.2	58.1
I 11	345 30.3	11.1	188 53.8	9.5	19 00.9	12.1	58.1
D 12	0 30.2	N22 11.4	203 22.3	9.4	S19 13.0	12.1	58.2
A 13	15 30.1	11.7	217 50.7	9.3	19 25.1	11.9	58.2
Y 14	30 30.0	12.0	232 19.0	9.2	19 37.0	11.8	58.2
15	45 29.9 ..	12.4	246 47.2	9.0	19 48.8	11.7	58.3
16	60 29.8	12.7	261 15.2	9.0	20 00.5	11.7	58.3
17	75 29.7	13.0	275 43.2	8.8	20 12.1	11.5	58.3
18	90 29.6	N22 13.3	290 11.0	8.6	S20 23.7	11.5	58.3
19	105 29.5	13.6	304 38.6	8.6	20 35.2	11.3	58.4
20	120 29.4	14.0	319 06.2	8.4	20 46.5	11.2	58.4
21	135 29.3 ..	14.3	333 33.6	8.3	20 57.7	11.1	58.4
22	150 29.2	14.6	348 00.9	8.2	21 08.8	11.0	58.5
23	165 29.1	14.9	2 28.1	8.0	S21 19.8	10.9	58.5
	SD 15.8	d 0.3	SD 15.4		15.6		15.8

Lat.	Twilight Naut.	Twilight Civil	Sunrise	Moonrise 31	Moonrise 1	Moonrise 2	Moonrise 3
°	h m	h m	h m	h m	h m	h m	h m
N 72	▢	▢	▢	17 10	20 01	▬	▬
N 70	▢	▢	▢	16 54	19 17	▬	▬
68	▢	▢	▢	16 41	18 48	21 44	▬
66	////	////	01 14	16 31	18 26	20 45	▬
64	////	////	01 59	16 22	18 09	20 11	22 44
62	////	00 04	02 28	16 15	17 56	19 46	21 49
60	////	01 27	02 50	16 09	17 44	19 27	21 17
N 58	////	02 01	03 08	16 03	17 34	19 11	20 53
56	00 04	02 25	03 22	15 58	17 25	18 58	20 34
54	01 19	02 44	03 35	15 54	17 18	18 46	20 18
52	01 51	03 00	03 46	15 50	17 11	18 36	20 04
50	02 13	03 13	03 56	15 46	17 04	18 27	19 52
45	02 53	03 41	04 17	15 39	16 51	18 08	19 27
N 40	03 21	04 01	04 33	15 32	16 40	17 52	19 07
35	03 42	04 18	04 47	15 27	16 31	17 39	18 51
30	04 00	04 32	04 59	15 22	16 23	17 28	18 37
20	04 27	04 56	05 20	15 14	16 09	17 09	18 13
N 10	04 48	05 15	05 38	15 07	15 57	16 52	17 52
0	05 06	05 32	05 54	15 00	15 46	16 37	17 33
S 10	05 22	05 48	06 10	14 53	15 35	16 22	17 14
20	05 37	06 04	06 28	14 46	15 23	16 05	16 54
30	05 52	06 23	06 48	14 38	15 10	15 47	16 30
35	06 00	06 31	06 59	14 34	15 02	15 36	16 17
40	06 08	06 42	07 12	14 29	14 54	15 24	16 01
45	06 18	06 55	07 28	14 23	14 44	15 09	15 43
S 50	06 28	07 09	07 47	14 16	14 32	14 52	15 20
52	06 33	07 16	07 56	14 13	14 26	14 44	15 09
54	06 38	07 23	08 06	14 09	14 20	14 35	14 57
56	06 44	07 32	08 17	14 05	14 13	14 25	14 42
58	06 50	07 41	08 31	14 01	14 06	14 13	14 26
S 60	06 56	07 51	08 46	13 56	13 57	14 00	14 06

Lat.	Sunset	Twilight Civil	Twilight Naut.	Moonset 31	Moonset 1	Moonset 2	Moonset 3
°	h m	h m	h m	h m	h m	h m	h m
N 72	▢	▢	▢	01 21	(00 42 / 23 30)	▬	▬
N 70	▢	▢	▢	01 29	01 00	00 16	▬
68	▢	▢	▢	01 36	01 15	(00 47 / 23 38)	▬
66	22 46	////	////	01 42	01 28	01 09	00 39
64	21 59	////	////	01 46	01 38	01 28	01 13
62	21 29	////	////	01 51	01 47	01 43	01 39
60	21 07	22 31	////	01 54	01 54	01 55	01 59
N 58	20 49	21 57	////	01 57	02 01	02 06	02 15
56	20 34	21 32	////	02 00	02 07	02 16	02 30
54	20 21	21 13	22 39	02 03	02 12	02 25	02 42
52	20 10	20 57	22 07	02 05	02 17	02 32	02 53
50	20 00	20 43	21 44	02 07	02 22	02 39	03 02
45	19 39	20 16	21 03	02 12	02 31	02 54	03 23
N 40	19 23	19 55	20 35	02 16	02 39	03 06	03 40
35	19 09	19 38	20 14	02 20	02 46	03 17	03 54
30	18 56	19 23	19 56	02 23	02 52	03 26	04 06
20	18 36	19 00	19 29	02 28	03 03	03 42	04 27
N 10	18 18	18 41	19 08	02 33	03 13	03 56	04 46
0	18 01	18 24	18 50	02 37	03 21	04 10	05 03
S 10	17 45	18 08	18 34	02 41	03 30	04 23	05 20
20	17 28	17 52	18 19	02 46	03 40	04 37	05 39
30	17 08	17 34	18 04	02 52	03 51	04 54	06 00
35	16 56	17 24	17 56	02 55	03 57	05 03	06 13
40	16 43	17 13	17 47	02 58	04 04	05 14	06 28
45	16 28	17 01	17 38	03 02	04 13	05 27	06 45
S 50	16 09	16 46	17 27	03 07	04 23	05 43	07 07
52	16 00	16 39	17 22	03 10	04 28	05 51	07 17
54	15 49	16 32	17 17	03 12	04 33	05 59	07 29
56	15 38	16 24	17 12	03 15	04 39	06 08	07 43
58	15 25	16 14	17 06	03 18	04 46	06 19	07 59
S 60	15 09	16 04	16 59	03 21	04 53	06 32	08 18

	SUN Eqn. of Time 00h	SUN Eqn. of Time 12h	SUN Mer. Pass.	MOON Mer. Pass. Upper	MOON Mer. Pass. Lower	Age	Phase
Day							
d	m s	m s	h m	h m	h m	d %	
31	02 24	02 19	11 58	21 11	08 48	12 85	◗
1	02 15	02 10	11 58	21 58	09 34	13 91	
2	02 06	02 01	11 58	22 50	10 23	14 97	

© British Crown Copyright 2022. All rights reserved.

UT	ARIES	VENUS −4.4		MARS +1.6		JUPITER −2.1		SATURN +0.8		STARS		
	GHA	GHA	Dec	GHA	Dec	GHA	Dec	GHA	Dec	Name	SHA	Dec
d h	° ′	° ′	° ′	° ′	° ′	° ′	° ′	° ′	° ′		° ′	° ′
3 00	251 11.6	131 02.3	N23 12.4	120 41.7	N19 45.0	219 14.1	N11 46.1	271 52.0	S10 20.8	Acamar	315 13.2	S40 12.6
01	266 14.0	146 02.2	11.8	135 42.7	44.6	234 16.0	46.3	286 54.4	20.8	Achernar	335 21.6	S57 06.9
02	281 16.5	161 02.1	11.2	150 43.7	44.2	249 18.0	46.5	301 56.8	20.8	Acrux	173 01.3	S63 14.0
03	296 19.0	176 02.0 ..	10.7	165 44.6 ..	43.8	264 19.9 ..	46.6	316 59.2 ..	20.8	Adhara	255 07.3	S29 00.3
04	311 21.4	191 01.9	10.1	180 45.6	43.4	279 21.9	46.8	332 01.6	20.8	Aldebaran	290 41.5	N16 33.3
05	326 23.9	206 01.8	09.5	195 46.6	43.0	294 23.8	47.0	347 04.0	20.7			
06	341 26.4	221 01.7	N23 09.0	210 47.6	N19 42.6	309 25.8	N11 47.2	2 06.4	S10 20.7	Alioth	166 13.9	N55 50.2
S 07	356 28.8	236 01.6	08.4	225 48.6	42.2	324 27.7	47.3	17 08.8	20.7	Alkaid	152 52.7	N49 12.0
A 08	11 31.3	251 01.5	07.8	240 49.5	41.8	339 29.7	47.5	32 11.2	20.7	Alnair	27 34.5	S46 50.7
T 09	26 33.7	266 01.4 ..	07.3	255 50.5 ..	41.4	354 31.6 ..	47.7	47 13.6 ..	20.7	Alnilam	275 39.4	S 1 11.3
U 10	41 36.2	281 01.4	06.7	270 51.5	41.0	9 33.6	47.9	62 16.0	20.7	Alphard	217 49.2	S 8 45.6
R 11	56 38.7	296 01.3	06.1	285 52.5	40.6	24 35.5	48.0	77 18.4	20.7			
D 12	71 41.1	311 01.2	N23 05.6	300 53.5	N19 40.2	39 37.5	N11 48.2	92 20.8	S10 20.7	Alphecca	126 04.5	N26 38.2
A 13	86 43.6	326 01.1	05.0	315 54.4	39.8	54 39.5	48.4	107 23.2	20.6	Alpheratz	357 36.3	N29 12.9
Y 14	101 46.1	341 01.0	04.4	330 55.4	39.4	69 41.4	48.6	122 25.6	20.6	Altair	62 01.0	N 8 55.7
15	116 48.5	356 00.9 ..	03.8	345 56.4 ..	39.0	84 43.4 ..	48.7	137 28.0 ..	20.6	Ankaa	353 08.6	S42 10.6
16	131 51.0	11 00.8	03.3	0 57.4	38.6	99 45.3	48.9	152 30.4	20.6	Antares	112 17.1	S26 29.1
17	146 53.5	26 00.8	02.7	15 58.4	38.2	114 47.3	49.1	167 32.8	20.6			
18	161 55.9	41 00.7	N23 02.1	30 59.3	N19 37.8	129 49.2	N11 49.3	182 35.2	S10 20.6	Arcturus	145 48.9	N19 03.7
19	176 58.4	56 00.6	01.5	46 00.3	37.4	144 51.2	49.4	197 37.7	20.6	Atria	107 12.0	S69 04.1
20	192 00.9	71 00.5	01.0	61 01.3	37.0	159 53.1	49.6	212 40.1	20.6	Avior	234 15.7	S59 35.2
21	207 03.3	86 00.5	23 00.4	76 02.3 ..	36.6	174 55.1 ..	49.8	227 42.5 ..	20.5	Bellatrix	278 24.7	N 6 22.2
22	222 05.8	101 00.4	22 59.8	91 03.3	36.2	189 57.0	50.0	242 44.9	20.5	Betelgeuse	270 53.9	N 7 24.7
23	237 08.2	116 00.3	59.2	106 04.2	35.8	204 59.0	50.1	257 47.3	20.5			
4 00	252 10.7	131 00.2	N22 58.7	121 05.2	N19 35.4	220 00.9	N11 50.3	272 49.7	S10 20.5	Canopus	263 53.5	S52 42.6
01	267 13.2	146 00.2	58.1	136 06.2	35.0	235 02.9	50.5	287 52.1	20.5	Capella	280 24.4	N46 01.3
02	282 15.6	161 00.1	57.5	151 07.2	34.6	250 04.8	50.7	302 54.5	20.5	Deneb	49 26.4	N45 21.5
03	297 18.1	176 00.0 ..	56.9	166 08.2 ..	34.2	265 06.8 ..	50.8	317 56.9 ..	20.5	Denebola	182 26.3	N14 26.6
04	312 20.6	191 00.0	56.3	181 09.1	33.8	280 08.7	51.0	332 59.3	20.5	Diphda	348 48.8	S17 51.5
05	327 23.0	205 59.9	55.8	196 10.1	33.4	295 10.7	51.2	348 01.7	20.4			
06	342 25.5	220 59.8	N22 55.2	211 11.1	N19 33.0	310 12.7	N11 51.4	3 04.1	S10 20.4	Dubhe	193 42.6	N61 37.8
07	357 28.0	235 59.8	54.6	226 12.1	32.6	325 14.6	51.5	18 06.5	20.4	Elnath	278 04.0	N28 37.6
S 08	12 30.4	250 59.7	54.0	241 13.1	32.2	340 16.6	51.7	33 09.0	20.4	Eltanin	90 42.3	N51 29.0
U 09	27 32.9	265 59.7 ..	53.4	256 14.0 ..	31.8	355 18.5 ..	51.9	48 11.4 ..	20.4	Enif	33 40.0	N 9 58.8
N 10	42 35.4	280 59.6	52.8	271 15.0	31.4	10 20.5	52.1	63 13.8	20.4	Fomalhaut	15 16.0	S29 29.8
D 11	57 37.8	295 59.5	52.2	286 16.0	31.0	25 22.4	52.2	78 16.2	20.4			
A 12	72 40.3	310 59.5	N22 51.7	301 17.0	N19 30.6	40 24.4	N11 52.4	93 18.6	S10 20.4	Gacrux	171 52.9	S57 14.9
Y 13	87 42.7	325 59.4	51.1	316 18.0	30.2	55 26.3	52.6	108 21.0	20.3	Gienah	175 44.9	S17 40.4
14	102 45.2	340 59.4	50.5	331 18.9	29.8	70 28.3	52.8	123 23.4	20.3	Hadar	148 37.4	S60 29.3
15	117 47.7	355 59.3 ..	49.9	346 19.9 ..	29.4	85 30.2 ..	52.9	138 25.8 ..	20.3	Hamal	327 53.0	N23 34.2
16	132 50.1	10 59.3	49.3	1 20.9	29.0	100 32.2	53.1	153 28.2	20.3	Kaus Aust.	83 33.9	S34 22.4
17	147 52.6	25 59.2	48.7	16 21.9	28.6	115 34.2	53.3	168 30.6	20.3			
18	162 55.1	40 59.2	N22 48.1	31 22.9	N19 28.1	130 36.1	N11 53.5	183 33.0	S10 20.3	Kochab	137 18.7	N74 03.7
19	177 57.5	55 59.1	47.5	46 23.8	27.7	145 38.1	53.6	198 35.5	20.3	Markab	13 31.2	N15 19.7
20	193 00.0	70 59.1	46.9	61 24.8	27.3	160 40.0	53.8	213 37.9	20.3	Menkar	314 07.9	N 4 10.8
21	208 02.5	85 59.0 ..	46.3	76 25.8 ..	26.9	175 42.0 ..	54.0	228 40.3 ..	20.3	Menkent	147 58.9	S36 29.2
22	223 04.9	100 59.0	45.7	91 26.8	26.5	190 43.9	54.2	243 42.7	20.2	Miaplacidus	221 39.0	S69 49.0
23	238 07.4	115 58.9	45.1	106 27.8	26.1	205 45.9	54.3	258 45.1	20.2			
5 00	253 09.9	130 58.9	N22 44.5	121 28.7	N19 25.7	220 47.8	N11 54.5	273 47.5	S10 20.2	Mirfak	308 30.7	N49 56.5
01	268 12.3	145 58.9	43.9	136 29.7	25.3	235 49.8	54.7	288 49.9	20.2	Nunki	75 49.1	S26 16.0
02	283 14.8	160 58.8	43.3	151 30.7	24.9	250 51.8	54.9	303 52.3	20.2	Peacock	53 07.5	S56 39.4
03	298 17.2	175 58.8 ..	42.8	166 31.7 ..	24.5	265 53.7 ..	55.0	318 54.7 ..	20.2	Pollux	243 19.2	N27 58.3
04	313 19.7	190 58.7	42.2	181 32.7	24.1	280 55.7	55.2	333 57.2	20.2	Procyon	244 52.5	N 5 09.9
05	328 22.2	205 58.7	41.6	196 33.6	23.7	295 57.6	55.4	348 59.6	20.2			
06	343 24.6	220 58.7	N22 41.0	211 34.6	N19 23.3	310 59.6	N11 55.6	4 02.0	S10 20.2	Rasalhague	95 59.5	N12 32.5
07	358 27.1	235 58.6	40.4	226 35.6	22.8	326 01.5	55.7	19 04.4	20.1	Regulus	207 36.0	N11 51.3
08	13 29.6	250 58.6	39.7	241 36.6	22.4	341 03.5	55.9	34 06.8	20.1	Rigel	281 05.5	S 8 10.5
M 09	28 32.0	265 58.6 ..	39.1	256 37.6 ..	22.0	356 05.4 ..	56.1	49 09.2 ..	20.1	Rigil Kent.	139 41.6	S60 56.0
O 10	43 34.5	280 58.5	38.5	271 38.6	21.6	11 07.4	56.2	64 11.6	20.1	Sabik	102 04.0	S15 45.2
N 11	58 37.0	295 58.5	37.9	286 39.5	21.2	26 09.4	56.4	79 14.0	20.1			
D 12	73 39.4	310 58.5	N22 37.3	301 40.5	N19 20.8	41 11.3	N11 56.6	94 16.5	S10 20.1	Schedar	349 32.8	N56 39.6
A 13	88 41.9	325 58.5	36.7	316 41.5	20.4	56 13.3	56.8	109 18.9	20.1	Shaula	96 11.8	S37 07.2
Y 14	103 44.4	340 58.4	36.1	331 42.5	20.0	71 15.2	56.9	124 21.3	20.1	Sirius	258 27.7	S16 44.9
15	118 46.8	355 58.4 ..	35.5	346 43.5 ..	19.6	86 17.2 ..	57.1	139 23.7 ..	20.1	Spica	158 23.5	S11 17.0
16	133 49.3	10 58.4	34.9	1 44.4	19.2	101 19.1	57.3	154 26.1	20.1	Suhail	222 47.5	S43 31.8
17	148 51.7	25 58.4	34.3	16 45.4	18.7	116 21.1	57.5	169 28.5	20.0			
18	163 54.2	40 58.4	N22 33.7	31 46.4	N19 18.3	131 23.1	N11 57.6	184 30.9	S10 20.0	Vega	80 33.7	N38 48.2
19	178 56.7	55 58.3	33.1	46 47.4	17.9	146 25.0	57.8	199 33.4	20.0	Zuben'ubi	136 57.2	S16 08.4
20	193 59.1	70 58.3	32.5	61 48.4	17.5	161 27.0	58.0	214 35.8	20.0		SHA	Mer. Pass.
21	209 01.6	85 58.3 ..	31.9	76 49.4 ..	17.1	176 28.9 ..	58.2	229 38.2 ..	20.0		° ′	h m
22	224 04.1	100 58.3	31.3	91 50.3	16.7	191 30.9	58.3	244 40.6	20.0	Venus	238 49.5	15 16
23	239 06.5	115 58.3	30.6	106 51.3	16.3	206 32.8	58.5	259 43.0	20.0	Mars	228 54.5	15 55
Mer. Pass.	h m 7 10.1	v −0.1	d 0.6	v 1.0	d 0.4	v 2.0	d 0.2	v 2.4	d 0.0	Jupiter	327 50.2	9 19
										Saturn	20 39.0	5 48

© British Crown Copyright 2022. All rights reserved.

SUN / MOON

UT	SUN GHA	SUN Dec	MOON GHA	v	MOON Dec	d	HP
3 00	180 29.0	N22 15.2	16 55.1	8.0	S21 30.7	10.8	58.5
01	195 28.9	15.5	31 22.1	7.8	21 41.5	10.7	58.6
02	210 28.8	15.9	45 48.9	7.6	21 52.2	10.5	58.6
03	225 28.7	.. 16.2	60 15.5	7.6	22 02.7	10.5	58.6
04	240 28.6	16.5	74 42.1	7.4	22 13.2	10.3	58.6
05	255 28.5	16.8	89 08.5	7.3	22 23.5	10.1	58.7
06	270 28.4	N22 17.1	103 34.8	7.1	S22 33.6	10.1	58.7
07	285 28.3	17.4	118 00.9	7.1	22 43.7	9.9	58.7
S 08	300 28.2	17.7	132 27.0	6.9	22 53.6	9.8	58.8
A 09	315 28.1	.. 18.0	146 52.9	6.8	23 03.4	9.7	58.8
T 10	330 28.0	18.3	161 18.7	6.6	23 13.1	9.6	58.8
U 11	345 27.9	18.6	175 44.3	6.6	23 22.7	9.4	58.9
R 12	0 27.8	N22 19.0	190 09.9	6.4	S23 32.1	9.2	58.9
D 13	15 27.7	19.3	204 35.3	6.3	23 41.3	9.1	58.9
A 14	30 27.6	19.6	219 00.6	6.2	23 50.4	9.0	58.9
Y 15	45 27.5	.. 19.9	233 25.8	6.0	23 59.4	8.9	59.0
16	60 27.4	20.2	247 50.8	5.9	24 08.3	8.7	59.0
17	75 27.3	20.5	262 15.7	5.9	24 17.0	8.5	59.0
18	90 27.2	N22 20.8	276 40.6	5.7	S24 25.5	8.4	59.0
19	105 27.1	21.1	291 05.3	5.5	24 33.9	8.3	59.1
20	120 27.0	21.4	305 29.8	5.5	24 42.2	8.1	59.1
21	135 26.9	.. 21.7	319 54.3	5.3	24 50.3	7.9	59.1
22	150 26.8	22.0	334 18.6	5.3	24 58.2	7.8	59.1
23	165 26.7	22.3	348 42.9	5.1	25 06.0	7.7	59.2
4 00	180 26.6	N22 22.6	3 07.0	5.0	S25 13.7	7.4	59.2
01	195 26.5	22.9	17 31.0	4.9	25 21.1	7.4	59.2
02	210 26.4	23.2	31 54.9	4.8	25 28.5	7.1	59.2
03	225 26.3	.. 23.5	46 18.7	4.7	25 35.6	7.0	59.3
04	240 26.1	23.8	60 42.4	4.5	25 42.6	6.8	59.3
05	255 26.0	24.1	75 05.9	4.5	25 49.4	6.7	59.3
06	270 25.9	N22 24.4	89 29.4	4.4	S25 56.1	6.5	59.3
07	285 25.8	24.7	103 52.8	4.2	26 02.6	6.3	59.4
S 08	300 25.7	24.9	118 16.0	4.2	26 08.9	6.1	59.4
U 09	315 25.6	.. 25.2	132 39.2	4.1	26 15.0	6.0	59.4
N 10	330 25.5	25.5	147 02.3	3.9	26 21.0	5.8	59.4
D 11	345 25.4	25.8	161 25.2	3.9	26 26.8	5.6	59.4
A 12	0 25.3	N22 26.1	175 48.1	3.8	S26 32.4	5.4	59.5
Y 13	15 25.2	26.4	190 10.9	3.7	26 37.8	5.3	59.5
14	30 25.1	26.7	204 33.6	3.6	26 43.1	5.0	59.5
15	45 25.0	.. 27.0	218 56.2	3.5	26 48.1	4.9	59.5
16	60 24.9	27.3	233 18.7	3.5	26 53.0	4.7	59.5
17	75 24.8	27.6	247 41.2	3.4	26 57.7	4.5	59.6
18	90 24.7	N22 27.8	262 03.6	3.2	S27 02.2	4.4	59.6
19	105 24.6	28.1	276 25.8	3.3	27 06.6	4.1	59.6
20	120 24.5	28.4	290 48.1	3.1	27 10.7	3.9	59.6
21	135 24.3	.. 28.7	305 10.2	3.1	27 14.6	3.8	59.6
22	150 24.2	29.0	319 32.3	3.0	27 18.4	3.6	59.7
23	165 24.1	29.3	333 54.3	2.9	27 22.0	3.3	59.7
5 00	180 24.0	N22 29.5	348 16.2	2.9	S27 25.3	3.2	59.7
01	195 23.9	29.8	2 38.1	2.8	27 28.5	3.0	59.7
02	210 23.8	30.1	16 59.9	2.8	27 31.5	2.8	59.7
03	225 23.7	.. 30.4	31 21.7	2.7	27 34.3	2.6	59.7
04	240 23.6	30.7	45 43.4	2.6	27 36.9	2.4	59.8
05	255 23.5	30.9	60 05.0	2.6	27 39.3	2.2	59.8
06	270 23.4	N22 31.2	74 26.6	2.6	S27 41.5	2.0	59.8
07	285 23.3	31.5	88 48.2	2.5	27 43.5	1.8	59.8
M 08	300 23.2	31.8	103 09.7	2.5	27 45.3	1.6	59.8
O 09	315 23.0	.. 32.1	117 31.2	2.4	27 46.9	1.4	59.8
N 10	330 22.9	32.3	131 52.6	2.4	27 48.3	1.1	59.8
D 11	345 22.8	32.6	146 14.0	2.4	27 49.4	1.0	59.9
A 12	0 22.7	N22 32.9	160 35.4	2.4	S27 50.4	0.8	59.9
Y 13	15 22.6	33.2	174 56.8	2.3	27 51.2	0.6	59.9
14	30 22.5	33.4	189 18.1	2.3	27 51.8	0.4	59.9
15	45 22.4	.. 33.7	203 39.4	2.3	27 52.2	0.2	59.9
16	60 22.3	34.0	218 00.7	2.3	27 52.4	0.1	59.9
17	75 22.2	34.2	232 22.0	2.2	27 52.3	0.2	59.9
18	90 22.1	N22 34.5	246 43.2	2.3	S27 52.1	0.4	59.9
19	105 21.9	34.8	261 04.5	2.3	27 51.7	0.7	60.0
20	120 21.8	35.0	275 25.8	2.2	27 51.0	0.8	60.0
21	135 21.7	.. 35.3	289 47.0	2.3	27 50.2	1.1	60.0
22	150 21.6	35.6	304 08.3	2.2	27 49.1	1.2	60.0
23	165 21.5	35.8	318 29.5	2.3	S27 47.9	1.5	60.0
	SD 15.8	d 0.3	SD 16.0		16.2		16.3

Moonrise

Lat.	Twilight Naut.	Twilight Civil	Sunrise	Moonrise 3	4	5	6
N 72	□	□	□	■	■	■	■
N 70	□	□	□	■	■	■	■
68	////	////	□	■	■	■	■
66	////	////	01 00	■	■	■	■
64	////	////	01 51	22 44	■	■	■
62	////	////	02 23	21 49	24 04	00 04	01 31
60	////	01 18	02 46	21 17	23 03	24 16	00 16
N 58	////	01 55	03 04	20 53	22 29	23 40	24 20
56	////	02 21	03 19	20 34	22 04	23 14	23 59
54	01 11	02 41	03 33	20 18	21 44	22 54	23 42
52	01 46	02 57	03 44	20 04	21 27	22 36	23 27
50	02 09	03 11	03 54	19 52	21 13	22 22	23 13
45	02 51	03 39	04 15	19 27	20 44	21 52	22 47
N 40	03 19	04 00	04 32	19 07	20 21	21 28	22 25
35	03 41	04 17	04 47	18 51	20 02	21 09	22 07
30	03 59	04 32	04 59	18 37	19 46	20 52	21 52
20	04 27	04 56	05 20	18 13	19 19	20 24	21 26
N 10	04 48	05 15	05 38	17 52	18 55	20 00	21 03
0	05 06	05 32	05 55	17 33	18 34	19 38	20 42
S 10	05 22	05 49	06 11	17 14	18 12	19 16	20 21
20	05 38	06 05	06 29	16 54	17 49	18 52	19 59
30	05 53	06 23	06 49	16 30	17 23	18 24	19 32
35	06 02	06 33	07 01	16 17	17 07	18 07	19 17
40	06 10	06 44	07 14	16 01	16 49	17 48	18 59
45	06 20	06 57	07 30	15 43	16 27	17 25	18 37
S 50	06 31	07 12	07 50	15 20	15 59	16 55	18 09
52	06 36	07 19	07 59	15 09	15 46	16 41	17 55
54	06 41	07 26	08 09	14 57	15 31	16 24	17 40
56	06 47	07 35	08 21	14 42	15 12	16 04	17 21
58	06 53	07 44	08 35	14 26	14 50	15 38	16 58
S 60	07 00	07 55	08 51	14 06	14 22	15 04	16 28

Moonset

Lat.	Sunset	Twilight Civil	Twilight Naut.	Moonset 3	4	5	6
N 72	□	□	□	■	■	■	■
N 70	□	□	□	■	■	■	■
68	□	□	□	■	■	■	■
66	23 01	////	////	00 39	■	■	■
64	22 07	////	////	01 13	00 39	■	■
62	21 35	////	////	01 39	01 35	01 30	02 19
60	21 12	22 41	////	01 59	02 08	02 31	03 34
N 58	20 53	22 03	////	02 15	02 32	03 06	04 09
56	20 38	21 37	////	02 30	02 52	03 31	04 35
54	20 25	21 17	22 48	02 42	03 08	03 51	04 55
52	20 13	21 00	22 13	02 53	03 23	04 08	05 13
50	20 03	20 46	21 48	03 02	03 35	04 22	05 27
45	19 42	20 18	21 07	03 23	04 01	04 52	05 57
N 40	19 25	19 57	20 38	03 40	04 22	05 15	06 20
35	19 10	19 40	20 16	03 54	04 39	05 34	06 39
30	18 58	19 25	19 58	04 06	04 54	05 50	06 56
20	18 37	19 01	19 30	04 27	05 19	06 18	07 25
N 10	18 19	18 42	19 09	04 46	05 41	06 42	07 47
0	18 02	18 24	18 50	05 03	06 01	07 04	08 09
S 10	17 45	18 08	18 34	05 20	06 22	07 26	08 31
20	17 28	17 51	18 19	05 39	06 44	07 50	08 54
30	17 07	17 34	18 03	06 00	07 10	08 18	09 21
35	16 56	17 24	17 55	06 13	07 25	08 34	09 37
40	16 42	17 12	17 46	06 28	07 42	08 54	09 56
45	16 26	17 00	17 36	06 45	08 04	09 17	10 18
S 50	16 07	16 45	17 26	07 07	08 31	09 46	10 47
52	15 57	16 38	17 21	07 17	08 44	10 01	11 01
54	15 47	16 30	17 15	07 29	08 59	10 18	11 17
56	15 35	16 21	17 10	07 43	09 17	10 38	11 36
58	15 22	16 12	17 04	07 59	09 38	11 03	11 59
S 60	15 06	16 01	16 57	08 18	10 06	11 38	12 29

SUN / MOON

Day	Eqn. of Time 00h	Eqn. of Time 12h	Mer. Pass.	Mer. Pass. Upper	Mer. Pass. Lower	Age	Phase
d	m s	m s	h m	h m	h m	d	%
3	01 56	01 51	11 58	23 47	11 18	15	99
4	01 46	01 41	11 58	24 49	12 18	16	100
5	01 36	01 31	11 58	00 49	13 21	17	97

© British Crown Copyright 2022. All rights reserved.

UT	ARIES	VENUS −4·4		MARS +1·6		JUPITER −2·1		SATURN +0·8		STARS		
d h	GHA	GHA	Dec	GHA	Dec	GHA	Dec	GHA	Dec	Name	SHA	Dec
6 00	254 09.0	130 58.3	N22 30.0	121 52.3	N19 15.9	221 34.8	N11 58.7	274 45.4	S10 20.0	Acamar	315 13.2	S40 12.6
01	269 11.5	145 58.3	29.4	136 53.3	15.4	236 36.8	58.8	289 47.8	20.0	Achernar	335 21.6	S57 06.9
02	284 13.9	160 58.2	28.8	151 54.3	15.0	251 38.7	59.0	304 50.3	20.0	Acrux	173 01.3	S63 14.0
03	299 16.4	175 58.2 ..	28.2	166 55.2 ..	14.6	266 40.7 ..	59.2	319 52.7 ..	20.0	Adhara	255 07.3	S29 00.3
04	314 18.9	190 58.2	27.6	181 56.2	14.2	281 42.6	59.4	334 55.1	19.9	Aldebaran	290 41.5	N16 33.3
05	329 21.3	205 58.2	27.0	196 57.2	13.8	296 44.6	59.5	349 57.5	19.9			
06	344 23.8	220 58.2	N22 26.3	211 58.2	N19 13.4	311 46.6	N11 59.7	4 59.9	S10 19.9	Alioth	166 13.9	N55 50.2
07	359 26.2	235 58.2	25.7	226 59.2	13.0	326 48.5	11 59.9	20 02.3	19.9	Alkaid	152 52.7	N49 12.0
08	14 28.7	250 58.2	25.1	242 00.2	12.6	341 50.5	12 00.0	35 04.8	19.9	Alnair	27 34.5	S46 50.7
09	29 31.2	265 58.2 ..	24.5	257 01.1 ..	12.1	356 52.4 ..	00.2	50 07.2 ..	19.9	Alnilam	275 39.4	S 1 11.2
10	44 33.6	280 58.2	23.9	272 02.1	11.7	11 54.4	00.4	65 09.6	19.9	Alphard	217 49.2	S 8 45.6
11	59 36.1	295 58.2	23.2	287 03.1	11.3	26 56.4	00.6	80 12.0	19.9			
12	74 38.6	310 58.2	N22 22.6	302 04.1	N19 10.9	41 58.3	N12 00.7	95 14.4	S10 19.9	Alphecca	126 04.5	N26 38.2
13	89 41.0	325 58.2	22.0	317 05.1	10.5	57 00.3	00.9	110 16.8	19.9	Alpheratz	357 36.3	N29 12.9
14	104 43.5	340 58.2	21.4	332 06.0	10.1	72 02.2	01.1	125 19.3	19.9	Altair	62 01.0	N 8 55.7
15	119 46.0	355 58.2 ..	20.8	347 07.0 ..	09.7	87 04.2 ..	01.2	140 21.7 ..	19.8	Ankaa	353 08.6	S42 10.6
16	134 48.4	10 58.2	20.1	2 08.0	09.2	102 06.1	01.4	155 24.1	19.8	Antares	112 17.1	S26 29.1
17	149 50.9	25 58.3	19.5	17 09.0	08.8	117 08.1	01.6	170 26.5	19.8			
18	164 53.4	40 58.3	N22 18.9	32 10.0	N19 08.4	132 10.1	N12 01.8	185 28.9	S10 19.8	Arcturus	145 48.9	N19 03.7
19	179 55.8	55 58.3	18.3	47 11.0	08.0	147 12.0	01.9	200 31.3	19.8	Atria	107 12.0	S69 04.2
20	194 58.3	70 58.3	17.6	62 11.9	07.6	162 14.0	02.1	215 33.8	19.8	Avior	234 15.7	S59 35.2
21	210 00.7	85 58.3 ..	17.0	77 12.9 ..	07.2	177 15.9 ..	02.3	230 36.2 ..	19.8	Bellatrix	278 24.6	N 6 22.2
22	225 03.2	100 58.3	16.4	92 13.9	06.7	192 17.9	02.4	245 38.6	19.8	Betelgeuse	270 53.9	N 7 24.7
23	240 05.7	115 58.3	15.8	107 14.9	06.3	207 19.9	02.6	260 41.0	19.8			
7 00	255 08.1	130 58.4	N22 15.1	122 15.9	N19 05.9	222 21.8	N12 02.8	275 43.4	S10 19.8	Canopus	263 53.5	S52 42.5
01	270 10.6	145 58.4	14.5	137 16.9	05.5	237 23.8	03.0	290 45.9	19.8	Capella	280 24.3	N46 01.2
02	285 13.1	160 58.4	13.9	152 17.8	05.1	252 25.8	03.1	305 48.3	19.8	Deneb	49 26.4	N45 21.6
03	300 15.5	175 58.4 ..	13.2	167 18.8 ..	04.7	267 27.7 ..	03.3	320 50.7 ..	19.7	Denebola	182 26.3	N14 26.6
04	315 18.0	190 58.5	12.6	182 19.8	04.2	282 29.7	03.5	335 53.1	19.7	Diphda	348 48.8	S17 51.5
05	330 20.5	205 58.5	12.0	197 20.8	03.8	297 31.6	03.6	350 55.5	19.7			
06	345 22.9	220 58.5	N22 11.3	212 21.8	N19 03.4	312 33.6	N12 03.8	5 58.0	S10 19.7	Dubhe	193 42.7	N61 37.8
07	0 25.4	235 58.5	10.7	227 22.8	03.0	327 35.6	04.0	21 00.4	19.7	Elnath	278 03.9	N28 37.6
08	15 27.9	250 58.6	10.1	242 23.7	02.6	342 37.5	04.2	36 02.8	19.7	Eltanin	90 42.3	N51 29.0
09	30 30.3	265 58.6 ..	09.4	257 24.7 ..	02.1	357 39.5 ..	04.3	51 05.2 ..	19.7	Enif	33 40.0	N 9 58.8
10	45 32.8	280 58.6	08.8	272 25.7	01.7	12 41.4	04.5	66 07.6	19.7	Fomalhaut	15 16.0	S29 29.8
11	60 35.2	295 58.7	08.2	287 26.7	01.3	27 43.4	04.7	81 10.1	19.7			
12	75 37.7	310 58.7	N22 07.5	302 27.7	N19 00.9	42 45.4	N12 04.8	96 12.5	S10 19.7	Gacrux	171 52.9	S57 14.9
13	90 40.2	325 58.7	06.9	317 28.7	00.5	57 47.3	05.0	111 14.9	19.7	Gienah	175 44.9	S17 40.4
14	105 42.6	340 58.8	06.3	332 29.6	19 00.0	72 49.3	05.2	126 17.3	19.7	Hadar	148 37.4	S60 29.3
15	120 45.1	355 58.8 ..	05.6	347 30.6	18 59.6	87 51.3 ..	05.4	141 19.7 ..	19.7	Hamal	327 53.0	N23 34.2
16	135 47.6	10 58.9	05.0	2 31.6	59.2	102 53.2	05.5	156 22.2	19.7	Kaus Aust.	83 33.9	S34 22.4
17	150 50.0	25 58.9	04.3	17 32.6	58.8	117 55.2	05.7	171 24.6	19.6			
18	165 52.5	40 58.9	N22 03.7	32 33.6	N18 58.4	132 57.1	N12 05.9	186 27.0	S10 19.6	Kochab	137 18.8	N74 03.7
19	180 55.0	55 59.0	03.1	47 34.6	57.9	147 59.1	06.0	201 29.4	19.6	Markab	13 31.2	N15 19.7
20	195 57.4	70 59.0	02.4	62 35.5	57.5	163 01.1	06.2	216 31.8	19.6	Menkar	314 07.8	N 4 10.8
21	210 59.9	85 59.1 ..	01.8	77 36.5 ..	57.1	178 03.0 ..	06.4	231 34.3 ..	19.6	Menkent	147 58.9	S36 29.2
22	226 02.3	100 59.1	01.1	92 37.5	56.7	193 05.0	06.5	246 36.7	19.6	Miaplacidus	221 39.0	S69 49.0
23	241 04.8	115 59.2	22 00.5	107 38.5	56.3	208 07.0	06.7	261 39.1	19.6			
8 00	256 07.3	130 59.2	N21 59.8	122 39.5	N18 55.8	223 08.9	N12 06.9	276 41.5	S10 19.6	Mirfak	308 30.6	N49 56.5
01	271 09.7	145 59.3	59.2	137 40.5	55.4	238 10.9	07.0	291 44.0	19.6	Nunki	75 49.1	S26 16.0
02	286 12.2	160 59.4	58.5	152 41.4	55.0	253 12.8	07.2	306 46.4	19.6	Peacock	53 07.4	S56 39.4
03	301 14.7	175 59.4 ..	57.9	167 42.4 ..	54.6	268 14.8 ..	07.4	321 48.8 ..	19.6	Pollux	243 19.2	N27 58.3
04	316 17.1	190 59.4	57.3	182 43.4	54.1	283 16.8	07.6	336 51.2	19.6	Procyon	244 52.5	N 5 09.9
05	331 19.6	205 59.5	56.6	197 44.4	53.7	298 18.7	07.7	351 53.7	19.6			
06	346 22.1	220 59.6	N21 55.9	212 45.4	N18 53.3	313 20.7	N12 07.9	6 56.1	S10 19.6	Rasalhague	95 59.4	N12 32.5
07	1 24.5	235 59.6	55.3	227 46.4	52.9	328 22.7	08.1	21 58.5	19.6	Regulus	207 36.0	N11 51.3
08	16 27.0	250 59.7	54.7	242 47.3	52.4	343 24.6	08.2	37 00.9	19.6	Rigel	281 05.5	S 8 10.5
09	31 29.5	265 59.7 ..	54.0	257 48.3 ..	52.0	358 26.6 ..	08.4	52 03.3 ..	19.5	Rigil Kent.	139 41.6	S60 56.0
10	46 31.9	280 59.8	53.4	272 49.3	51.6	13 28.6	08.6	67 05.8	19.5	Sabik	102 04.0	S15 45.2
11	61 34.4	295 59.9	52.7	287 50.3	51.2	28 30.5	08.7	82 08.2	19.5			
12	76 36.8	310 59.9	N21 52.1	302 51.3	N18 50.7	43 32.5	N12 08.9	97 10.6	S10 19.5	Schedar	349 32.8	N56 39.6
13	91 39.3	326 00.0	51.4	317 52.3	50.3	58 34.4	09.1	112 13.0	19.5	Shaula	96 11.8	S37 07.2
14	106 41.8	341 00.1	50.8	332 53.2	49.9	73 36.4	09.2	127 15.5	19.5	Sirius	258 27.7	S16 44.9
15	121 44.2	356 00.1 ..	50.1	347 54.2 ..	49.5	88 38.4 ..	09.4	142 17.9 ..	19.5	Spica	158 23.5	S11 17.0
16	136 46.7	11 00.2	49.4	2 55.2	49.0	103 40.3	09.6	157 20.3	19.5	Suhail	222 47.5	S43 31.8
17	151 49.2	26 00.3	48.8	17 56.2	48.6	118 42.3	09.8	172 22.7	19.5			
18	166 51.6	41 00.4	N21 48.1	32 57.2	N18 48.2	133 44.3	N12 09.9	187 25.2	S10 19.5	Vega	80 33.7	N38 48.2
19	181 54.1	56 00.4	47.5	47 58.2	47.8	148 46.2	10.1	202 27.6	19.5	Zuben'ubi	136 57.2	S16 08.4
20	196 56.6	71 00.5	46.8	62 59.2	47.3	163 48.2	10.3	217 30.0	19.5			
21	211 59.0	86 00.6 ..	46.2	78 00.1 ..	46.9	178 50.2 ..	10.4	232 32.5 ..	19.5		SHA	Mer. Pass.
22	227 01.5	101 00.7	45.5	93 01.1	46.5	193 52.1	10.6	247 34.9	19.5	Venus	235 50.2	15 16
23	242 04.0	116 00.8	44.9	108 02.1	46.1	208 54.1	10.8	262 37.3	19.5	Mars	227 07.7	15 50
Mer. Pass. 6 58.3		v 0.0	d 0.6	v 1.0	d 0.4	v 2.0	d 0.2	v 2.4	d 0.0	Jupiter	327 13.7	9 09
										Saturn	20 35.3	5 36

© British Crown Copyright 2022. All rights reserved.

UT	SUN GHA	SUN Dec	MOON GHA	v	MOON Dec	d	HP
d h	° ′	° ′	° ′	′	° ′	′	′
6 00	180 21.4	N22 36.1	332 50.8	2.2	S27 46.4	1.7	60.0
01	195 21.3	36.4	347 12.0	2.3	27 44.7	1.8	60.0
02	210 21.2	36.6	1 33.3	2.3	27 42.9	2.1	60.0
03	225 21.1	36.9	15 54.6	2.4	27 40.8	2.3	60.0
04	240 20.9	37.2	30 16.0	2.3	27 38.5	2.4	60.0
05	255 20.8	37.4	44 37.3	2.4	27 36.1	2.7	60.0
06	270 20.7	N22 37.7	58 58.7	2.4	S27 33.4	2.9	60.0
07	285 20.6	38.0	73 20.1	2.4	27 30.5	3.1	60.1
08	300 20.5	38.2	87 41.5	2.5	27 27.4	3.3	60.1
09	315 20.4	38.5	102 03.0	2.5	27 24.1	3.5	60.1
10	330 20.3	38.7	116 24.5	2.5	27 20.6	3.6	60.1
11	345 20.2	39.0	130 46.0	2.6	27 17.0	3.9	60.1
12	0 20.0	N22 39.3	145 07.6	2.6	S27 13.1	4.1	60.1
13	15 19.9	39.5	159 29.2	2.7	27 09.0	4.3	60.1
14	30 19.8	39.8	173 50.9	2.7	27 04.7	4.5	60.1
15	45 19.7	40.0	188 12.6	2.8	27 00.2	4.6	60.1
16	60 19.6	40.3	202 34.4	2.9	26 55.6	4.9	60.1
17	75 19.5	40.5	216 56.3	2.9	26 50.7	5.1	60.1
18	90 19.4	N22 40.8	231 18.2	2.9	S26 45.6	5.2	60.1
19	105 19.2	41.0	245 40.1	3.1	26 40.4	5.4	60.1
20	120 19.1	41.3	260 02.2	3.0	26 35.0	5.7	60.1
21	135 19.0	41.5	274 24.2	3.2	26 29.3	5.8	60.1
22	150 18.9	41.8	288 46.4	3.2	26 23.5	6.0	60.1
23	165 18.8	42.0	303 08.6	3.3	26 17.5	6.2	60.1
7 00	180 18.7	N22 42.3	317 30.9	3.4	S26 11.3	6.4	60.1
01	195 18.6	42.5	331 53.3	3.5	26 04.9	6.5	60.1
02	210 18.4	42.8	346 15.8	3.5	25 58.4	6.8	60.1
03	225 18.3	43.0	0 38.3	3.6	25 51.6	6.9	60.1
04	240 18.2	43.3	15 00.9	3.7	25 44.7	7.1	60.1
05	255 18.1	43.5	29 23.6	3.8	25 37.6	7.3	60.1
06	270 18.0	N22 43.8	43 46.4	3.9	S25 30.3	7.5	60.1
07	285 17.9	44.0	58 09.3	4.0	25 22.8	7.6	60.1
08	300 17.8	44.3	72 32.3	4.0	25 15.2	7.8	60.1
09	315 17.6	44.5	86 55.3	4.2	25 07.4	8.0	60.1
10	330 17.5	44.7	101 18.5	4.2	24 59.4	8.1	60.1
11	345 17.4	45.0	115 41.7	4.3	24 51.3	8.4	60.1
12	0 17.3	N22 45.2	130 05.0	4.5	S24 42.9	8.5	60.1
13	15 17.2	45.5	144 28.5	4.5	24 34.4	8.6	60.1
14	30 17.1	45.7	158 52.0	4.6	24 25.8	8.8	60.1
15	45 16.9	46.0	173 15.6	4.8	24 17.0	9.0	60.1
16	60 16.8	46.2	187 39.4	4.8	24 08.0	9.2	60.1
17	75 16.7	46.4	202 03.2	4.9	23 58.8	9.3	60.0
18	90 16.6	N22 46.7	216 27.1	5.1	S23 49.5	9.4	60.0
19	105 16.5	46.9	230 51.2	5.1	23 40.1	9.6	60.0
20	120 16.4	47.1	245 15.3	5.2	23 30.5	9.8	60.0
21	135 16.2	47.4	259 39.5	5.4	23 20.7	9.9	60.0
22	150 16.1	47.6	274 03.9	5.4	23 10.8	10.1	60.0
23	165 16.0	47.8	288 28.3	5.6	23 00.7	10.2	60.0
8 00	180 15.9	N22 48.1	302 52.9	5.7	S22 50.5	10.3	60.0
01	195 15.8	48.3	317 17.6	5.8	22 40.2	10.5	60.0
02	210 15.6	48.5	331 42.4	5.8	22 29.7	10.7	60.0
03	225 15.5	48.8	346 07.2	6.0	22 19.0	10.8	60.0
04	240 15.4	49.0	0 32.2	6.2	22 08.2	10.9	60.0
05	255 15.3	49.2	14 57.4	6.2	21 57.3	11.1	60.0
06	270 15.2	N22 49.5	29 22.6	6.3	S21 46.2	11.1	59.9
07	285 15.1	49.7	43 47.9	6.4	21 35.1	11.4	59.9
08	300 14.9	49.9	58 13.3	6.6	21 23.7	11.4	59.9
09	315 14.8	50.1	72 38.9	6.7	21 12.3	11.6	59.9
10	330 14.7	50.4	87 04.6	6.7	21 00.7	11.7	59.9
11	345 14.6	50.6	101 30.3	6.9	20 49.0	11.9	59.9
12	0 14.5	N22 50.8	115 56.2	7.0	S20 37.1	11.9	59.9
13	15 14.3	51.0	130 22.2	7.1	20 25.2	12.1	59.9
14	30 14.2	51.3	144 48.3	7.2	20 13.1	12.2	59.9
15	45 14.1	51.5	159 14.5	7.4	20 00.9	12.3	59.9
16	60 14.0	51.7	173 40.9	7.4	19 48.6	12.5	59.8
17	75 13.9	51.9	188 07.3	7.6	19 36.1	12.5	59.8
18	90 13.7	N22 52.1	202 33.9	7.6	S19 23.6	12.7	59.8
19	105 13.6	52.4	217 00.5	7.8	19 10.9	12.7	59.8
20	120 13.5	52.6	231 27.3	7.9	18 58.2	12.9	59.8
21	135 13.4	52.8	245 54.2	7.9	18 45.3	13.0	59.8
22	150 13.3	53.0	260 21.1	8.1	18 32.3	13.1	59.8
23	165 13.1	53.2	274 48.2	8.2	S18 19.2	13.1	59.7
	SD 15.8	d 0.2	SD 16.4		16.4		16.3

Lat.	Twilight Naut.	Twilight Civil	Sunrise	Moonrise 6	Moonrise 7	Moonrise 8	Moonrise 9
°	h m	h m	h m	h m	h m	h m	h m
N 72	▨	▨	▨	▨	▨	▨	03 50
N 70	▨	▨	▨	▨	▨	▨	02 52
68	▨	▨	▨	▨	▨	▨	02 18
66	////	////	00 46	▨	▨	02 30	01 52
64	////	////	01 45	▨	01 49	01 33	01 32
62	////	////	02 18	01 31	01 24	01 20	01 16
60	////	01 10	02 42	00 16	00 47	00 58	01 03
N 58	////	01 50	03 01	24 20	00 20	00 40	00 51
56	////	02 17	03 17	23 59	24 25	00 25	00 41
54	01 04	02 38	03 30	23 42	24 12	00 12	00 32
52	01 41	02 55	03 42	23 27	24 00	00 00	00 23
50	02 06	03 09	03 52	23 13	23 50	24 16	00 16
45	02 49	03 37	04 14	22 47	23 28	24 00	00 00
N 40	03 18	03 59	04 31	22 25	23 11	23 47	24 17
35	03 40	04 17	04 46	22 07	22 56	23 36	24 10
30	03 58	04 31	04 59	21 52	22 43	23 26	24 03
20	04 26	04 55	05 20	21 26	22 21	23 09	23 52
N 10	04 48	05 15	05 38	21 03	22 02	22 55	23 42
0	05 07	05 33	05 55	20 42	21 44	22 41	23 33
S 10	05 23	05 49	06 12	20 21	21 26	22 27	23 24
20	05 39	06 06	06 30	19 59	21 06	22 12	23 14
30	05 55	06 24	06 51	19 32	20 44	21 54	23 02
35	06 03	06 34	07 02	19 17	20 30	21 44	22 56
40	06 12	06 46	07 16	18 59	20 15	21 33	22 48
45	06 22	06 59	07 32	18 37	19 57	21 19	22 39
S 50	06 33	07 14	07 52	18 09	19 34	21 02	22 29
52	06 38	07 21	08 02	17 55	19 23	20 54	22 24
54	06 43	07 29	08 12	17 40	19 10	20 45	22 18
56	06 49	07 38	08 24	17 21	18 56	20 35	22 12
58	06 56	07 48	08 38	16 58	18 39	20 24	22 05
S 60	07 03	07 59	08 55	16 28	18 18	20 10	21 57

Lat.	Sunset	Twilight Civil	Twilight Naut.	Moonset 6	Moonset 7	Moonset 8	Moonset 9
°	h m	h m	h m	h m	h m	h m	h m
N 72	▨	▨	▨	▨	▨	▨	06 23
N 70	▨	▨	▨	▨	▨	▨	07 19
68	▨	▨	▨	▨	▨	▨	07 52
66	23 16	////	////	▨	▨	05 41	08 15
64	22 14	////	////	▨	▨	06 22	08 34
62	21 41	////	////	02 19	04 39	06 50	08 49
60	21 17	22 50	////	03 34	05 16	07 11	09 01
N 58	20 57	22 09	////	04 09	05 43	07 28	09 12
56	20 41	21 42	////	04 35	06 03	07 42	09 21
54	20 28	21 21	22 56	04 55	06 20	07 55	09 30
52	20 16	21 04	22 18	05 13	06 35	08 06	09 37
50	20 06	20 49	21 52	05 27	06 48	08 15	09 44
45	19 44	20 21	21 10	05 57	07 14	08 36	09 58
N 40	19 27	19 59	20 40	06 20	07 34	08 52	10 09
35	19 12	19 41	20 18	06 39	07 51	09 06	10 19
30	18 59	19 27	20 00	06 56	08 06	09 18	10 27
20	18 38	19 02	19 31	07 23	08 31	09 38	10 42
N 10	18 20	18 43	19 09	07 47	08 52	09 55	10 54
0	18 03	18 25	18 51	08 09	09 12	10 11	11 06
S 10	17 46	18 08	18 35	08 31	09 32	10 28	11 18
20	17 28	17 52	18 19	08 54	09 53	10 45	11 30
30	17 07	17 33	18 03	09 21	10 17	11 04	11 44
35	16 55	17 23	17 55	09 37	10 31	11 15	11 52
40	16 41	17 12	17 46	09 56	10 47	11 28	12 01
45	16 25	16 59	17 36	10 18	11 07	11 43	12 12
S 50	16 05	16 43	17 24	10 47	11 31	12 02	12 24
52	15 56	16 36	17 19	11 01	11 42	12 10	12 30
54	15 45	16 28	17 14	11 17	11 55	12 20	12 37
56	15 33	16 20	17 08	11 36	12 10	12 31	12 44
58	15 19	16 10	17 02	11 59	12 28	12 43	12 52
S 60	15 03	15 59	16 55	12 29	12 49	12 57	13 01

	SUN Eqn. of Time 00h	SUN Eqn. of Time 12h	SUN Mer. Pass.	MOON Mer. Pass. Upper	MOON Mer. Pass. Lower	Age	Phase
Day	m s	m s	h m	h m	h m	d	%
6	01 26	01 20	11 59	01 54	14 26	18	92
7	01 15	01 09	11 59	02 57	15 28	19	85
8	01 04	00 58	11 59	03 58	16 26	20	76

© British Crown Copyright 2022. All rights reserved.

UT	ARIES	VENUS −4.5		MARS +1.6		JUPITER −2.1		SATURN +0.8		STARS		
	GHA	GHA	Dec	GHA	Dec	GHA	Dec	GHA	Dec	Name	SHA	Dec
d h	° ′	° ′	° ′	° ′	° ′	° ′	° ′	° ′	° ′		° ′	° ′
9 00	257 06.4	131 00.8 N21 44.2		123 03.1 N18 45.6		223 56.1 N12 10.9		277 39.7 S10 19.5		Acamar	315 13.1	S40 12.6
01	272 08.9	146 00.9	43.5	138 04.1	45.2	238 58.0	11.1	292 42.2	19.5	Achernar	335 21.5	S57 06.9
02	287 11.3	161 01.0	42.9	153 05.1	44.8	254 00.0	11.3	307 44.6	19.5	Acrux	173 01.3	S63 14.0
03	302 13.8	176 01.1 ..	42.2	168 06.0 ..	44.4	269 02.0 ..	11.4	322 47.0 ..	19.5	Adhara	255 07.3	S29 00.3
04	317 16.3	191 01.2	41.6	183 07.0	43.9	284 03.9	11.6	337 49.4	19.5	Aldebaran	290 41.5	N16 33.3
05	332 18.7	206 01.3	40.9	198 08.0	43.5	299 05.9	11.8	352 51.9	19.4			
06	347 21.2	221 01.4 N21 40.2		213 09.0 N18 43.1		314 07.9 N12 11.9		7 54.3 S10 19.4		Alioth	166 13.9	N55 50.2
07	2 23.7	236 01.5	39.6	228 10.0	42.6	329 09.8	12.1	22 56.7	19.4	Alkaid	152 52.7	N49 12.0
08	17 26.1	251 01.6	38.9	243 11.0	42.2	344 11.8	12.3	37 59.1	19.4	Alnair	27 34.4	S46 50.7
F 09	32 28.6	266 01.6 ..	38.2	258 12.0 ..	41.8	359 13.8 ..	12.4	53 01.6 ..	19.4	Alnilam	275 39.4	S 1 11.2
R 10	47 31.1	281 01.7	37.6	273 12.9	41.4	14 15.7	12.6	68 04.0	19.4	Alphard	217 49.2	S 8 45.6
I 11	62 33.5	296 01.8	36.9	288 13.9	40.9	29 17.7	12.8	83 06.4	19.4			
D 12	77 36.0	311 01.9 N21 36.2		303 14.9 N18 40.5		44 19.7 N12 12.9		98 08.9 S10 19.4		Alphecca	126 04.5	N26 38.2
A 13	92 38.5	326 02.0	35.6	318 15.9	40.1	59 21.6	13.1	113 11.3	19.4	Alpheratz	357 36.2	N29 12.9
Y 14	107 40.9	341 02.1	34.9	333 16.9	39.6	74 23.6	13.3	128 13.7	19.4	Altair	62 01.0	N 8 55.7
15	122 43.4	356 02.2 ..	34.2	348 17.9 ..	39.2	89 25.6 ..	13.4	143 16.1 ..	19.4	Ankaa	353 08.6	S42 10.6
16	137 45.8	11 02.4	33.6	3 18.8	38.8	104 27.5	13.6	158 18.6	19.4	Antares	112 17.1	S26 29.1
17	152 48.3	26 02.5	32.9	18 19.8	38.4	119 29.5	13.8	173 21.0	19.4			
18	167 50.8	41 02.6 N21 32.2		33 20.8 N18 37.9		134 31.5 N12 14.0		188 23.4 S10 19.4		Arcturus	145 48.9	N19 03.7
19	182 53.2	56 02.7	31.6	48 21.8	37.5	149 33.4	14.1	203 25.9	19.4	Atria	107 11.9	S69 04.2
20	197 55.7	71 02.8	30.9	63 22.8	37.1	164 35.4	14.3	218 28.3	19.4	Avior	234 15.7	S59 35.2
21	212 58.2	86 02.9 ..	30.2	78 23.8 ..	36.6	179 37.4 ..	14.5	233 30.7 ..	19.4	Bellatrix	278 24.6	N 6 22.2
22	228 00.6	101 03.0	29.5	93 24.8	36.2	194 39.3	14.6	248 33.2	19.4	Betelgeuse	270 53.9	N 7 24.7
23	243 03.1	116 03.1	28.9	108 25.7	35.8	209 41.3	14.8	263 35.6	19.4			
10 00	258 05.6	131 03.2 N21 28.2		123 26.7 N18 35.3		224 43.3 N12 15.0		278 38.0 S10 19.4		Canopus	263 53.5	S52 42.5
01	273 08.0	146 03.4	27.5	138 27.7	34.9	239 45.2	15.1	293 40.4	19.4	Capella	280 24.3	N46 01.2
02	288 10.5	161 03.5	26.9	153 28.7	34.5	254 47.2	15.3	308 42.9	19.4	Deneb	49 26.4	N45 21.6
03	303 12.9	176 03.6 ..	26.2	168 29.7 ..	34.2	269 49.2 ..	15.5	323 45.3 ..	19.4	Denebola	182 26.3	N14 26.6
04	318 15.4	191 03.7	25.5	183 30.7	33.6	284 51.1	15.6	338 47.7	19.4	Diphda	348 48.8	S17 51.5
05	333 17.9	206 03.8	24.8	198 31.7	33.2	299 53.1	15.8	353 50.2	19.4			
06	348 20.3	221 04.0 N21 24.2		213 32.6 N18 32.7		314 55.1 N12 16.0		8 52.6 S10 19.4		Dubhe	193 42.7	N61 37.8
S 07	3 22.8	236 04.1	23.5	228 33.6	32.3	329 57.0	16.1	23 55.0	19.4	Elnath	278 03.9	N28 37.6
A 08	18 25.3	251 04.2	22.8	243 34.6	31.9	344 59.0	16.3	38 57.5	19.4	Eltanin	90 42.3	N51 29.0
T 09	33 27.7	266 04.3 ..	22.1	258 35.6 ..	31.4	0 01.0 ..	16.4	53 59.9 ..	19.3	Enif	33 40.0	N 9 58.8
U 10	48 30.2	281 04.5	21.4	273 36.6	31.0	15 03.0	16.6	69 02.3	19.3	Fomalhaut	15 15.9	S29 29.8
R 11	63 32.7	296 04.6	20.8	288 37.6	30.6	30 04.9	16.8	84 04.8	19.3			
D 12	78 35.1	311 04.7 N21 20.1		303 38.6 N18 30.2		45 06.9 N12 16.9		99 07.2 S10 19.3		Gacrux	171 52.9	S57 14.9
A 13	93 37.6	326 04.9	19.4	318 39.5	29.7	60 08.9	17.1	114 09.6	19.3	Gienah	175 44.9	S17 40.4
Y 14	108 40.1	341 05.0	18.7	333 40.5	29.3	75 10.8	17.3	129 12.1	19.3	Hadar	148 37.4	S60 29.3
15	123 42.5	356 05.1 ..	18.0	348 41.5 ..	28.8	90 12.8 ..	17.4	144 14.5 ..	19.3	Hamal	327 52.9	N23 34.2
16	138 45.0	11 05.3	17.4	3 42.5	28.4	105 14.8	17.6	159 16.9	19.3	Kaus Aust.	83 33.9	S34 22.4
17	153 47.4	26 05.4	16.7	18 43.5	28.0	120 16.7	17.8	174 19.4	19.3			
18	168 49.9	41 05.6 N21 16.0		33 44.5 N18 27.5		135 18.7 N12 17.9		189 21.8 S10 19.3		Kochab	137 18.8	N74 03.7
19	183 52.4	56 05.7	15.3	48 45.5	27.1	150 20.7	18.1	204 24.2	19.3	Markab	13 31.2	N15 19.7
20	198 54.8	71 05.8	14.6	63 46.4	26.7	165 22.7	18.3	219 26.7	19.3	Menkar	314 07.8	N 4 10.8
21	213 57.3	86 06.0 ..	13.9	78 47.4 ..	26.2	180 24.6 ..	18.4	234 29.1 ..	19.3	Menkent	147 58.9	S36 29.2
22	228 59.8	101 06.1	13.2	93 48.4	25.8	195 26.6	18.6	249 31.5	19.3	Miaplacidus	221 39.1	S69 49.0
23	244 02.2	116 06.3	12.6	108 49.4	25.4	210 28.6	18.8	264 34.0	19.3			
11 00	259 04.7	131 06.4 N21 11.9		123 50.4 N18 24.9		225 30.5 N12 18.9		279 36.4 S10 19.3		Mirfak	308 30.6	N49 56.5
01	274 07.2	146 06.6	11.2	138 51.4	24.5	240 32.5	19.1	294 38.8	19.3	Nunki	75 49.1	S26 16.0
02	289 09.6	161 06.7	10.5	153 52.4	24.0	255 34.5	19.3	309 41.3	19.3	Peacock	53 07.4	S56 39.4
03	304 12.1	176 06.9 ..	09.8	168 53.4 ..	23.6	270 36.5 ..	19.4	324 43.7 ..	19.3	Pollux	243 19.2	N27 58.3
04	319 14.6	191 07.0	09.1	183 54.3	23.2	285 38.4	19.6	339 46.1	19.3	Procyon	244 52.5	N 5 09.9
05	334 17.0	206 07.2	08.4	198 55.3	22.7	300 40.4	19.8	354 48.6	19.3			
06	349 19.5	221 07.4 N21 07.7		213 56.3 N18 22.3		315 42.4 N12 19.9		9 51.0 S10 19.3		Rasalhague	96 59.4	N12 32.5
07	4 21.9	236 07.5	07.1	228 57.3	21.9	330 44.3	20.1	24 53.4	19.3	Regulus	207 36.0	N11 51.3
08	19 24.4	251 07.7	06.4	243 58.3	21.4	345 46.3	20.3	39 55.9	19.3	Rigel	281 05.5	S 8 10.5
S 09	34 26.9	266 07.8 ..	05.7	258 59.3 ..	21.0	0 48.3 ..	20.4	54 58.3 ..	19.3	Rigil Kent.	139 41.6	S60 56.0
U 10	49 29.3	281 08.0	05.0	274 00.3	20.5	15 50.3	20.6	70 00.7	19.3	Sabik	102 04.0	S15 45.3
N 11	64 31.8	296 08.2	04.3	289 01.2	20.1	30 52.2	20.7	85 03.2	19.3			
D 12	79 34.3	311 08.3 N21 03.6		304 02.2 N18 19.7		45 54.2 N12 20.9		100 05.6 S10 19.3		Schedar	349 32.8	N56 39.6
A 13	94 36.7	326 08.5	02.9	319 03.2	19.2	60 56.2	21.1	115 08.1	19.3	Shaula	96 11.7	S37 07.2
Y 14	109 39.2	341 08.7	02.2	334 04.2	18.8	75 58.1	21.2	130 10.5	19.3	Sirius	258 27.7	S16 44.9
15	124 41.7	356 08.8 ..	01.5	349 05.2 ..	18.3	91 00.1 ..	21.4	145 12.9 ..	19.3	Spica	158 23.5	S11 17.0
16	139 44.1	11 09.0	00.8	4 06.2	17.9	106 02.1	21.6	160 15.4	19.3	Suhail	222 47.5	S43 31.8
17	154 46.6	26 09.2 21 00.1		19 07.2	17.5	121 04.1	21.7	175 17.8	19.3			
18	169 49.0	41 09.4 N20 59.4		34 08.2 N18 17.0		136 06.0 N12 21.9		190 20.2 S10 19.3		Vega	80 33.7	N38 48.2
19	184 51.5	56 09.5	58.7	49 09.1	16.6	151 08.0	22.1	205 22.7	19.3	Zuben'ubi	136 57.2	S16 08.4
20	199 54.0	71 09.7	58.0	64 10.1	16.1	166 10.0	22.2	220 25.1	19.3		SHA	Mer. Pass.
21	214 56.4	86 09.9 ..	57.3	79 11.1 ..	15.7	181 12.0 ..	22.4	235 27.6 ..	19.3		° ′	h m
22	229 58.9	101 10.1	56.6	94 12.1	15.3	196 13.9	22.6	250 30.0	19.3	Venus	232 57.7	15 16
23	245 01.4	116 10.3	55.9	109 13.1	14.8	211 15.9	22.7	265 32.4	19.3	Mars	225 21.2	15 45
Mer. Pass.	h m 6 46.5	v 0.1	d 0.7	v 1.0	d 0.4	v 2.0	d 0.2	v 2.4	d 0.0	Jupiter	326 37.7	9 00
										Saturn	20 32.5	5 25

© British Crown Copyright 2022. All rights reserved.

SUN and MOON

UT	SUN GHA	SUN Dec	MOON GHA	v	MOON Dec	d	HP
d h	° ′	° ′	° ′	′	° ′	′	′
9 00	180 13.0	N22 53.5	289 15.4	8.4	S18 06.1	13.3	59.7
01	195 12.9	53.7	303 42.8	8.4	17 52.8	13.4	59.7
02	210 12.8	53.9	318 10.2	8.5	17 39.4	13.5	59.7
03	225 12.7 ..	54.1	332 37.7	8.6	17 25.9	13.6	59.7
04	240 12.5	54.3	347 05.3	8.7	17 12.3	13.6	59.7
05	255 12.4	54.5	1 33.0	8.9	16 58.7	13.8	59.7
06	270 12.3 N22	54.7	16 00.9	8.9	S16 44.9	13.8	59.6
07	285 12.2	54.9	30 28.8	9.1	16 31.1	13.9	59.6
F 08	300 12.1	55.2	44 56.9	9.1	16 17.2	14.1	59.6
R 09	315 11.9 ..	55.4	59 25.0	9.2	16 03.1	14.1	59.6
I 10	330 11.8	55.6	73 53.2	9.4	15 49.0	14.1	59.6
11	345 11.7	55.8	88 21.6	9.4	15 34.9	14.3	59.6
D 12	0 11.6 N22	56.0	102 50.0	9.5	S15 20.6	14.3	59.5
A 13	15 11.4	56.2	117 18.5	9.7	15 06.3	14.4	59.5
Y 14	30 11.3	56.4	131 47.2	9.7	14 51.9	14.5	59.5
15	45 11.2 ..	56.6	146 15.9	9.8	14 37.4	14.6	59.5
16	60 11.1	56.8	160 44.7	9.9	14 22.8	14.6	59.5
17	75 11.0	57.0	175 13.6	10.0	14 08.2	14.7	59.5
18	90 10.8 N22	57.2	189 42.6	10.1	S13 53.5	14.8	59.4
19	105 10.7	57.4	204 11.7	10.2	13 38.7	14.8	59.4
20	120 10.6	57.6	218 40.9	10.3	13 23.9	14.9	59.4
21	135 10.5 ..	57.8	233 10.2	10.4	13 09.0	14.9	59.4
22	150 10.3	58.0	247 39.6	10.4	12 54.1	15.0	59.4
23	165 10.2	58.2	262 09.0	10.6	12 39.1	15.1	59.4
10 00	180 10.1 N22	58.4	276 38.6	10.6	S12 24.0	15.1	59.3
01	195 10.0	58.6	291 08.2	10.7	12 08.9	15.2	59.3
02	210 09.8	58.8	305 37.9	10.8	11 53.7	15.2	59.3
03	225 09.7 ..	59.0	320 07.7	10.9	11 38.5	15.3	59.3
04	240 09.6	59.2	334 37.6	10.9	11 23.2	15.4	59.3
05	255 09.5	59.4	349 07.5	11.0	11 07.8	15.3	59.2
06	270 09.3 N22	59.6	3 37.5	11.1	S10 52.5	15.5	59.2
07	285 09.2	22 59.8	18 07.6	11.2	10 37.0	15.4	59.2
S 08	300 09.1	23 00.0	32 37.8	11.3	10 21.6	15.6	59.2
A 09	315 09.0 ..	00.2	47 08.1	11.3	10 06.0	15.5	59.2
T 10	330 08.9	00.4	61 38.4	11.4	9 50.5	15.6	59.2
U 11	345 08.7	00.6	76 08.8	11.5	9 34.9	15.6	59.1
R 12	0 08.6 N23	00.8	90 39.3	11.5	S 9 19.3	15.7	59.1
D 13	15 08.5	01.0	105 09.8	11.6	9 03.6	15.7	59.1
A 14	30 08.4	01.1	119 40.4	11.7	8 47.9	15.8	59.1
Y 15	45 08.2 ..	01.3	134 11.1	11.7	8 32.1	15.7	59.1
16	60 08.1	01.5	148 41.8	11.8	8 16.4	15.9	59.0
17	75 08.0	01.7	163 12.6	11.9	8 00.5	15.8	59.0
18	90 07.8 N23	01.9	177 43.5	11.9	S 7 44.7	15.9	59.0
19	105 07.7	02.1	192 14.4	12.0	7 28.8	15.8	59.0
20	120 07.6	02.3	206 45.4	12.1	7 13.0	16.0	59.0
21	135 07.5 ..	02.5	221 16.5	12.1	6 57.0	15.9	58.9
22	150 07.3	02.6	235 47.6	12.1	6 41.1	16.0	58.9
23	165 07.2	02.8	250 18.7	12.3	6 25.1	15.9	58.9
11 00	180 07.1 N23	03.0	264 50.0	12.2	S 6 09.2	16.0	58.9
01	195 07.0	03.2	279 21.2	12.3	5 53.2	16.1	58.9
02	210 06.8	03.4	293 52.5	12.4	5 37.1	16.0	58.8
03	225 06.7 ..	03.5	308 23.9	12.4	5 21.1	16.0	58.8
04	240 06.6	03.7	322 55.3	12.5	5 05.1	16.1	58.8
05	255 06.5	03.9	337 26.8	12.5	4 49.0	16.1	58.8
06	270 06.3 N23	04.1	351 58.3	12.5	S 4 32.9	16.1	58.7
07	285 06.2	04.3	6 29.8	12.6	4 16.8	16.1	58.7
S 08	300 06.1	04.4	21 01.4	12.7	4 00.7	16.1	58.7
U 09	315 06.0 ..	04.6	35 33.1	12.7	3 44.6	16.1	58.7
N 10	330 05.8	04.8	50 04.8	12.7	3 28.5	16.1	58.7
D 11	345 05.7	05.0	64 36.5	12.7	3 12.4	16.1	58.6
A 12	0 05.6 N23	05.1	79 08.2	12.8	S 2 56.3	16.1	58.6
Y 13	15 05.4	05.3	93 40.0	12.9	2 40.2	16.1	58.6
14	30 05.3	05.5	108 11.9	12.8	2 24.1	16.2	58.6
15	45 05.2 ..	05.7	122 43.7	12.9	2 07.9	16.1	58.6
16	60 05.1	05.8	137 15.6	13.0	1 51.8	16.1	58.5
17	75 04.9	06.0	151 47.6	12.9	1 35.7	16.1	58.5
18	90 04.8 N23	06.2	166 19.5	13.0	S 1 19.6	16.1	58.5
19	105 04.7	06.3	180 51.5	13.0	1 03.5	16.1	58.5
20	120 04.6	06.5	195 23.5	13.0	0 47.4	16.1	58.4
21	135 04.4 ..	06.7	209 55.5	13.1	0 31.3	16.1	58.4
22	150 04.3	06.8	224 27.6	13.1	S 0 15.2	16.1	58.4
23	165 04.2	07.0	238 59.7	13.1	N 0 00.9	16.0	58.4
	SD 15.8	d 0.2	SD 16.2		16.1		16.0

Twilight, Sunrise and Moonrise

Lat.	Twilight Naut.	Twilight Civil	Sunrise	Moonrise 9	10	11	12
°	h m	h m	h m	h m	h m	h m	h m
N 72	☐	☐	☐	03 50	02 21	01 38	01 03
N 70	☐	☐	☐	02 52	02 01	01 30	01 03
68	☐	☐	☐	02 18	01 45	01 23	01 04
66	////	////	00 30	01 52	01 32	01 17	01 04
64	////	////	01 40	01 32	01 22	01 13	01 04
62	////	////	02 14	01 16	01 12	01 09	01 05
60	////	01 03	02 39	01 03	01 04	01 05	01 05
N 58	////	01 46	02 59	00 51	00 57	01 02	01 05
56	////	02 14	03 15	00 41	00 51	00 59	01 06
54	00 58	02 35	03 29	00 32	00 45	00 56	01 06
52	01 38	02 53	03 41	00 23	00 40	00 54	01 06
50	02 04	03 07	03 51	00 16	00 36	00 52	01 06
45	02 47	03 36	04 13	00 00	00 26	00 47	01 06
N 40	03 17	03 58	04 31	24 11	00 17	00 43	01 07
35	03 40	04 16	04 46	24 10	00 10	00 39	01 07
30	03 58	04 31	04 58	24 03	00 03	00 36	01 07
20	04 26	04 55	05 20	23 52	24 31	00 31	01 08
N 10	04 49	05 16	05 39	23 42	24 26	00 26	01 08
0	05 07	05 33	05 56	23 33	24 22	00 22	01 09
S 10	05 24	05 50	06 13	23 24	24 18	00 18	01 09
20	05 40	06 07	06 31	23 14	24 13	00 13	01 09
30	05 56	06 26	06 52	23 02	24 07	00 07	01 10
35	06 04	06 36	07 04	22 56	24 04	00 04	01 10
40	06 13	06 47	07 18	22 48	24 01	00 01	01 11
45	06 23	07 01	07 34	22 39	23 57	25 11	01 11
S 50	06 35	07 16	07 54	22 29	23 52	25 12	01 12
52	06 40	07 23	08 04	22 24	23 49	25 12	01 12
54	06 45	07 31	08 15	22 18	23 47	25 12	01 13
56	06 51	07 40	08 27	22 12	23 44	25 13	01 13
58	06 58	07 50	08 41	22 05	23 41	25 13	01 13
S 60	07 05	08 02	08 58	21 57	23 37	25 14	01 14

Sunset, Twilight and Moonset

Lat.	Sunset	Twilight Civil	Twilight Naut.	Moonset 9	10	11	12
°	h m	h m	h m	h m	h m	h m	h m
N 72	☐	☐	☐	06 23	09 40	12 06	14 22
N 70	☐	☐	☐	07 19	09 57	12 10	14 16
68	☐	☐	☐	07 52	10 11	12 14	14 11
66	23 35	////	////	08 15	10 22	12 17	14 07
64	22 21	////	////	08 34	10 31	12 19	14 04
62	21 45	////	////	08 49	10 39	12 21	14 01
60	21 20	22 58	////	09 01	10 45	12 23	13 58
N 58	21 01	22 14	////	09 12	10 51	12 25	13 56
56	20 44	21 45	////	09 21	10 56	12 26	13 54
54	20 31	21 24	23 03	09 30	11 01	12 28	13 53
52	20 18	21 07	22 22	09 37	11 05	12 29	13 51
50	20 08	20 52	21 56	09 44	11 08	12 30	13 50
45	19 46	20 23	21 12	09 58	11 17	12 32	13 46
N 40	19 28	20 01	20 42	10 09	11 23	12 34	13 44
35	19 13	19 43	20 19	10 19	11 29	12 36	13 42
30	19 01	19 28	20 01	10 27	11 34	12 38	13 40
20	18 39	19 03	19 33	10 42	11 42	12 40	13 36
N 10	18 20	18 43	19 10	10 54	11 50	12 42	13 33
0	18 03	18 26	18 52	11 06	11 57	12 44	13 30
S 10	17 46	18 09	18 35	11 18	12 04	12 46	13 28
20	17 28	17 52	18 19	11 30	12 11	12 48	13 25
30	17 07	17 33	18 03	11 44	12 19	12 51	13 21
35	16 55	17 23	17 54	11 52	12 24	12 52	13 19
40	16 41	17 11	17 45	12 01	12 29	12 53	13 17
45	16 24	16 58	17 35	12 12	12 35	12 55	13 14
S 50	16 04	16 42	17 24	12 24	12 42	12 57	13 11
52	15 55	16 35	17 19	12 30	12 45	12 58	13 10
54	15 44	16 27	17 13	12 37	12 49	12 59	13 08
56	15 31	16 18	17 07	12 44	12 53	13 00	13 07
58	15 17	16 08	17 01	12 52	12 57	13 01	13 05
S 60	15 00	15 57	16 53	13 01	13 02	13 03	13 03

SUN and MOON — daily data

Day	SUN Eqn. of Time 00h	SUN Eqn. of Time 12h	SUN Mer. Pass.	MOON Mer. Pass. Upper	MOON Mer. Pass. Lower	Age	Phase
d	m s	m s	h m	h m	h m	d	%
9	00 52	00 47	11 59	04 54	17 20	21	65
10	00 41	00 35	11 59	05 45	18 09	22	54
11	00 29	00 23	12 00	06 33	18 56	23	42

© British Crown Copyright 2022. All rights reserved.

UT	ARIES	VENUS −4·5		MARS +1·7		JUPITER −2·1		SATURN +0·7		STARS		
	GHA	GHA	Dec	GHA	Dec	GHA	Dec	GHA	Dec	Name	SHA	Dec
d h	° ′	° ′	° ′	° ′	° ′	° ′	° ′	° ′	° ′		° ′	° ′
12 00	260 03.8	131 10.4	N20 55.2	124 14.1	N18 14.4	226 17.9	N12 22.9	280 34.9	S10 19.3	Acamar	315 13.1	S40 12.5
01	275 06.3	146 10.6	54.5	139 15.1	13.9	241 19.8	23.0	295 37.3	19.3	Achernar	335 21.5	S57 06.9
02	290 08.8	161 10.8	53.8	154 16.1	13.5	256 21.8	23.2	310 39.7	19.3	Acrux	173 01.4	S63 14.0
03	305 11.2	176 11.0 ..	53.1	169 17.0 ..	13.1	271 23.8 ..	23.4	325 42.2 ..	19.3	Adhara	255 07.3	S29 00.3
04	320 13.7	191 11.2	52.4	184 18.0	12.6	286 25.8	23.5	340 44.6	19.3	Aldebaran	290 41.5	N16 33.3
05	335 16.2	206 11.4	51.7	199 19.0	12.2	301 27.7	23.7	355 47.1	19.3			
06	350 18.6	221 11.6	N20 51.0	214 20.0	N18 11.7	316 29.7	N12 23.9	10 49.5	S10 19.3	Alioth	166 13.9	N55 50.3
07	5 21.1	236 11.8	50.3	229 21.0	11.3	331 31.7	24.0	25 51.9	19.3	Alkaid	152 52.8	N49 12.0
M 08	20 23.5	251 12.0	49.6	244 22.0	10.8	346 33.7	24.2	40 54.4	19.3	Alnair	27 34.4	S46 50.7
O 09	35 26.0	266 12.2 ..	48.9	259 23.0 ..	10.4	1 35.6 ..	24.3	55 56.8 ..	19.3	Alnilam	275 39.4	S 1 11.2
N 10	50 28.5	281 12.4	48.2	274 24.0	10.0	16 37.6	24.5	70 59.3	19.3	Alphard	217 49.2	S 8 45.6
D 11	65 30.9	296 12.6	47.5	289 24.9	09.5	31 39.6	24.7	86 01.7	19.3			
A 12	80 33.4	311 12.8	N20 46.8	304 25.9	N18 09.1	46 41.6	N12 24.8	101 04.1	S10 19.3	Alphecca	126 04.5	N26 38.2
Y 13	95 35.9	326 13.0	46.1	319 26.9	08.6	61 43.5	25.0	116 06.6	19.3	Alpheratz	357 36.2	N29 13.0
14	110 38.3	341 13.2	45.4	334 27.9	08.2	76 45.5	25.2	131 09.0	19.3	Altair	62 01.0	N 8 55.7
15	125 40.8	356 13.4 ..	44.7	349 28.9 ..	07.7	91 47.5 ..	25.3	146 11.5 ..	19.3	Ankaa	353 08.6	S42 10.6
16	140 43.3	11 13.6	44.0	4 29.9	07.3	106 49.5	25.5	161 13.9	19.3	Antares	112 17.1	S26 29.1
17	155 45.7	26 13.8	43.3	19 30.9	06.9	121 51.4	25.7	176 16.3	19.3			
18	170 48.2	41 14.0	N20 42.5	34 31.9	N18 06.4	136 53.4	N12 25.8	191 18.8	S10 19.3	Arcturus	145 48.9	N19 03.7
19	185 50.6	56 14.2	41.8	49 32.8	06.0	151 55.4	26.0	206 21.2	19.3	Atria	107 11.9	S69 04.2
20	200 53.1	71 14.4	41.1	64 33.8	05.5	166 57.4	26.1	221 23.7	19.3	Avior	234 15.8	S59 35.2
21	215 55.6	86 14.6 ..	40.4	79 34.8 ..	05.1	181 59.3 ..	26.3	236 26.1 ..	19.3	Bellatrix	278 24.6	N 6 22.2
22	230 58.0	101 14.8	39.7	94 35.8	04.6	197 01.3	26.5	251 28.5	19.3	Betelgeuse	270 53.9	N 7 24.7
23	246 00.5	116 15.1	39.0	109 36.8	04.2	212 03.3	26.6	266 31.0	19.3			
13 00	261 03.0	131 15.3	N20 38.3	124 37.8	N18 03.7	227 05.3	N12 26.8	281 33.4	S10 19.3	Canopus	263 53.5	S52 42.5
01	276 05.4	146 15.5	37.6	139 38.8	03.3	242 07.3	27.0	296 35.9	19.3	Capella	280 24.3	N46 01.2
02	291 07.9	161 15.7	36.9	154 39.8	02.8	257 09.2	27.1	311 38.3	19.3	Deneb	49 26.4	N45 21.6
03	306 10.4	176 15.9 ..	36.1	169 40.8 ..	02.4	272 11.2 ..	27.3	326 40.8 ..	19.3	Denebola	182 26.3	N14 26.6
04	321 12.8	191 16.2	35.4	184 41.7	01.9	287 13.2	27.4	341 43.2	19.3	Diphda	348 48.7	S17 51.5
05	336 15.3	206 16.4	34.7	199 42.7	01.5	302 15.2	27.6	356 45.6	19.3			
06	351 17.8	221 16.6	N20 34.0	214 43.7	N18 01.1	317 17.1	N12 27.8	11 48.1	S10 19.3	Dubhe	193 42.7	N61 37.8
07	6 20.2	236 16.9	33.3	229 44.7	00.6	332 19.1	27.9	26 50.5	19.3	Elnath	278 03.9	N28 37.6
T 08	21 22.7	251 17.1	32.6	244 45.7	18 00.2	347 21.1	28.1	41 53.0	19.3	Eltanin	90 42.3	N51 29.1
U 09	36 25.1	266 17.3 ..	31.8	259 46.7	17 59.7	2 23.1 ..	28.2	56 55.4 ..	19.3	Enif	33 39.9	N 9 58.8
E 10	51 27.6	281 17.5	31.1	274 47.7	59.3	17 25.0	28.4	71 57.9	19.3	Fomalhaut	15 15.9	S29 29.8
S 11	66 30.1	296 17.8	30.4	289 48.7	58.8	32 27.0	28.6	87 00.3	19.3			
D 12	81 32.5	311 18.0	N20 29.7	304 49.7	N17 58.4	47 29.0	N12 28.7	102 02.7	S10 19.3	Gacrux	171 53.0	S57 14.9
A 13	96 35.0	326 18.3	29.0	319 50.6	57.9	62 31.0	28.9	117 05.2	19.3	Gienah	175 44.9	S17 40.4
Y 14	111 37.5	341 18.5	28.3	334 51.6	57.5	77 33.0	29.1	132 07.6	19.3	Hadar	148 37.5	S60 29.3
15	126 39.9	356 18.7 ..	27.5	349 52.6 ..	57.0	92 34.9 ..	29.2	147 10.1 ..	19.3	Hamal	327 52.9	N23 34.2
16	141 42.4	11 19.0	26.8	4 53.6	56.6	107 36.9	29.4	162 12.5	19.3	Kaus Aust.	83 33.9	S34 22.4
17	156 44.9	26 19.2	26.1	19 54.6	56.1	122 38.9	29.5	177 15.0	19.3			
18	171 47.3	41 19.5	N20 25.4	34 55.6	N17 55.7	137 40.9	N12 29.7	192 17.4	S10 19.3	Kochab	137 18.8	N74 03.7
19	186 49.8	56 19.7	24.6	49 56.6	55.2	152 42.9	29.9	207 19.9	19.4	Markab	13 31.2	N15 19.7
20	201 52.3	71 20.0	23.9	64 57.6	54.8	167 44.8	30.0	222 22.3	19.4	Menkar	314 07.8	N 4 10.8
21	216 54.7	86 20.2 ..	23.2	79 58.6 ..	54.3	182 46.8 ..	30.2	237 24.8 ..	19.4	Menkent	147 58.9	S36 29.2
22	231 57.2	101 20.5	22.5	94 59.5	53.9	197 48.8	30.3	252 27.2	19.4	Miaplacidus	221 39.1	S69 49.0
23	246 59.6	116 20.7	21.8	110 00.5	53.4	212 50.8	30.5	267 29.6	19.4			
14 00	262 02.1	131 21.0	N20 21.0	125 01.5	N17 53.0	227 52.7	N12 30.7	282 32.1	S10 19.4	Mirfak	308 30.6	N49 56.5
01	277 04.6	146 21.2	20.3	140 02.5	52.5	242 54.7	30.8	297 34.5	19.4	Nunki	75 49.0	S26 16.0
02	292 07.0	161 21.5	19.6	155 03.5	52.1	257 56.7	31.0	312 37.0	19.4	Peacock	53 07.4	S56 39.4
03	307 09.5	176 21.7 ..	18.9	170 04.5 ..	51.6	272 58.7 ..	31.1	327 39.4 ..	19.4	Pollux	243 19.2	N27 58.3
04	322 12.0	191 22.0	18.1	185 05.5	51.2	288 00.7	31.3	342 41.9	19.4	Procyon	244 52.5	N 5 09.9
05	337 14.4	206 22.3	17.4	200 06.5	50.7	303 02.6	31.5	357 44.3	19.4			
06	352 16.9	221 22.5	N20 16.7	215 07.5	N17 50.3	318 04.6	N12 31.6	12 46.8	S10 19.4	Rasalhague	95 59.4	N12 32.5
W 07	7 19.4	236 22.8	16.0	230 08.4	49.8	333 06.6	31.8	27 49.2	19.4	Regulus	207 36.0	N11 51.3
E 08	22 21.8	251 23.1	15.2	245 09.4	49.4	348 08.6	31.9	42 51.7	19.4	Rigel	281 05.5	S 8 10.5
D 09	37 24.3	266 23.3 ..	14.5	260 10.4 ..	48.9	3 10.6 ..	32.1	57 54.1 ..	19.4	Rigil Kent.	139 41.6	S60 56.1
N 10	52 26.7	281 23.6	13.8	275 11.4	48.5	18 12.5	32.3	72 56.6	19.4	Sabik	102 03.9	S15 45.2
E 11	67 29.2	296 23.9	13.0	290 12.4	48.0	33 14.5	32.4	87 59.0	19.4			
S 12	82 31.7	311 24.1	N20 12.3	305 13.4	N17 47.6	48 16.5	N12 32.6	103 01.5	S10 19.4	Schedar	349 32.7	N56 39.6
D 13	97 34.1	326 24.4	11.6	320 14.4	47.1	63 18.5	32.7	118 03.9	19.4	Shaula	96 11.7	S37 07.2
A 14	112 36.6	341 24.7	10.8	335 15.4	46.6	78 20.5	32.9	133 06.4	19.4	Sirius	258 27.7	S16 44.9
Y 15	127 39.1	356 25.0 ..	10.1	350 16.4 ..	46.2	93 22.5 ..	33.1	148 08.8 ..	19.4	Spica	158 23.5	S11 17.0
16	142 41.5	11 25.2	09.4	5 17.4	45.7	108 24.4	33.2	163 11.2	19.4	Suhail	222 47.6	S43 31.8
17	157 44.0	26 25.5	08.7	20 18.3	45.3	123 26.4	33.4	178 13.7	19.4			
18	172 46.5	41 25.8	N20 07.9	35 19.3	N17 44.8	138 28.4	N12 33.5	193 16.1	S10 19.4	Vega	80 33.7	N38 48.2
19	187 48.9	56 26.1	07.2	50 20.3	44.4	153 30.4	33.7	208 18.6	19.4	Zuben'ubi	136 57.2	S16 08.4
20	202 51.4	71 26.4	06.5	65 21.3	43.9	168 32.4	33.9	223 21.0	19.4		SHA	Mer. Pass.
21	217 53.9	86 26.7 ..	05.7	80 22.3 ..	43.5	183 34.3 ..	34.0	238 23.5 ..	19.4		° ′	h m
22	232 56.3	101 26.9	05.0	95 23.3	43.0	198 36.3	34.2	253 25.9	19.4	Venus	230 12.3	15 15
23	247 58.8	116 27.2	04.3	110 24.3	42.6	213 38.3	34.3	268 28.4	19.4	Mars	223 34.8	15 40
	h m									Jupiter	326 02.3	8 50
Mer. Pass. 6 34.7		v 0.2	d 0.7	v 1.0	d 0.4	v 2.0	d 0.2	v 2.4	d 0.0	Saturn	20 30.5	5 13

© British Crown Copyright 2022. All rights reserved.

UT	SUN GHA	SUN Dec	MOON GHA	v	Dec	d	HP
d h	° ′	° ′	° ′	′	° ′	′	′
12 00	180 04.0	N23 07.2	253 31.8	13.1	N 0 16.9	16.1	58.4
01	195 03.9	07.3	268 03.9	13.2	0 33.0	16.0	58.3
02	210 03.8	07.5	282 36.1	13.1	0 49.0	16.1	58.3
03	225 03.7 ..	07.7	297 08.2	13.2	1 05.1	16.0	58.3
04	240 03.5	07.8	311 40.4	13.2	1 21.1	15.9	58.3
05	255 03.4	08.0	326 12.6	13.2	1 37.0	16.0	58.3
06	270 03.3	N23 08.2	340 44.8	13.2	N 1 53.0	16.0	58.2
07	285 03.1	08.3	355 17.0	13.2	2 09.0	15.9	58.2
M 08	300 03.0	08.5	9 49.2	13.3	2 24.9	15.9	58.2
O 09	315 02.9 ..	08.6	24 21.5	13.2	2 40.8	15.9	58.2
N 10	330 02.8	08.8	38 53.7	13.3	2 56.7	15.8	58.1
D 11	345 02.6	08.9	53 26.0	13.2	3 12.5	15.9	58.1
A 12	0 02.5	N23 09.1	67 58.2	13.3	N 3 28.4	15.8	58.1
Y 13	15 02.4	09.3	82 30.5	13.3	3 44.2	15.7	58.1
14	30 02.2	09.4	97 02.8	13.2	3 59.9	15.8	58.1
15	45 02.1 ..	09.6	111 35.0	13.3	4 15.7	15.7	58.0
16	60 02.0	09.7	126 07.3	13.3	4 31.4	15.7	58.0
17	75 01.8	09.9	140 39.6	13.2	4 47.1	15.6	58.0
18	90 01.7	N23 10.0	155 11.8	13.3	N 5 02.7	15.6	58.0
19	105 01.6	10.2	169 44.1	13.3	5 18.3	15.6	57.9
20	120 01.5	10.3	184 16.4	13.2	5 33.9	15.6	57.9
21	135 01.3 ..	10.5	198 48.6	13.3	5 49.5	15.5	57.9
22	150 01.2	10.6	213 20.9	13.2	6 05.0	15.4	57.9
23	165 01.1	10.8	227 53.1	13.2	6 20.4	15.4	57.9
13 00	180 00.9	N23 10.9	242 25.3	13.3	N 6 35.8	15.4	57.8
01	195 00.8	11.1	256 57.6	13.2	6 51.2	15.4	57.8
02	210 00.7	11.2	271 29.8	13.2	7 06.6	15.3	57.8
03	225 00.5 ..	11.4	286 02.0	13.1	7 21.9	15.2	57.8
04	240 00.4	11.5	300 34.1	13.2	7 37.1	15.2	57.7
05	255 00.3	11.7	315 06.3	13.2	7 52.3	15.2	57.7
06	270 00.1	N23 11.8	329 38.5	13.1	N 8 07.5	15.1	57.7
07	285 00.0	12.0	344 10.6	13.1	8 22.6	15.0	57.7
T 08	299 59.9	12.1	358 42.7	13.1	8 37.6	15.1	57.7
U 09	314 59.8 ..	12.2	13 14.8	13.1	8 52.7	14.9	57.6
E 10	329 59.6	12.4	27 46.9	13.1	9 07.6	14.9	57.6
S 11	344 59.5	12.5	42 19.0	13.0	9 22.5	14.9	57.6
D 12	359 59.4	N23 12.7	56 51.0	13.0	N 9 37.4	14.8	57.6
A 13	14 59.2	12.8	71 23.0	13.0	9 52.2	14.7	57.5
Y 14	29 59.1	12.9	85 55.0	12.9	10 06.9	14.7	57.5
15	44 59.0 ..	13.1	100 26.9	13.0	10 21.6	14.6	57.5
16	59 58.8	13.2	114 58.9	12.9	10 36.2	14.6	57.5
17	74 58.7	13.4	129 30.8	12.9	10 50.8	14.5	57.5
18	89 58.6	N23 13.5	144 02.7	12.8	N11 05.3	14.4	57.4
19	104 58.4	13.6	158 34.5	12.8	11 19.7	14.4	57.4
20	119 58.3	13.8	173 06.3	12.8	11 34.1	14.3	57.4
21	134 58.2 ..	13.9	187 38.1	12.8	11 48.4	14.3	57.4
22	149 58.0	14.0	202 09.9	12.7	12 02.7	14.2	57.3
23	164 57.9	14.2	216 41.6	12.7	12 16.9	14.1	57.3
14 00	179 57.8	N23 14.3	231 13.3	12.6	N12 31.0	14.1	57.3
01	194 57.6	14.4	245 44.9	12.7	12 45.1	13.9	57.3
02	209 57.5	14.5	260 16.6	12.6	12 59.0	14.0	57.3
03	224 57.4 ..	14.7	274 48.2	12.5	13 13.0	13.8	57.2
04	239 57.3	14.8	289 19.7	12.5	13 26.8	13.8	57.2
05	254 57.1	14.9	303 51.2	12.5	13 40.6	13.7	57.2
06	269 57.0	N23 15.1	318 22.7	12.4	N13 54.3	13.6	57.2
W 07	284 56.9	15.2	332 54.1	12.4	14 07.9	13.5	57.1
E 08	299 56.7	15.3	347 25.5	12.3	14 21.4	13.5	57.1
D 09	314 56.6 ..	15.4	1 56.8	12.3	14 34.9	13.4	57.1
N 10	329 56.5	15.6	16 28.1	12.3	14 48.3	13.3	57.1
E 11	344 56.3	15.7	30 59.4	12.2	15 01.6	13.2	57.1
S 12	359 56.2	N23 15.8	45 30.6	12.2	N15 14.8	13.2	57.0
D 13	14 56.1	15.9	60 01.8	12.1	15 28.0	13.0	57.0
A 14	29 55.9	16.1	74 32.9	12.1	15 41.0	13.0	57.0
Y 15	44 55.8 ..	16.2	89 04.0	12.0	15 54.0	12.9	57.0
16	59 55.7	16.3	103 35.0	12.0	16 06.9	12.8	57.0
17	74 55.5	16.4	118 06.0	12.0	16 19.7	12.7	56.9
18	89 55.4	N23 16.5	132 37.0	11.9	N16 32.4	12.7	56.9
19	104 55.3	16.7	147 07.9	11.8	16 45.1	12.5	56.9
20	119 55.1	16.8	161 38.7	11.8	16 57.6	12.5	56.9
21	134 55.0 ..	16.9	176 09.5	11.8	17 10.1	12.3	56.8
22	149 54.9	17.0	190 40.3	11.7	17 22.4	12.3	56.8
23	164 54.7	17.1	205 11.0	11.6	N17 34.7	12.2	56.8
	SD 15.8	d 0.1	SD 15.8		15.7		15.5

Lat.	Naut.	Civil	Sunrise	Moonrise 12	13	14	15
°	h m	h m	h m	h m	h m	h m	h m
N 72	□	□	□	01 03	(00 28 / 23 46)	22 23	□
N 70	□	□	□	01 03	00 37	(00 07 / 23 19)	□
68	□	□	□	01 04	00 45	(00 23 / 23 53)	22 38
66	□	□	□	01 04	00 51	00 37	(00 18 / 23 48)
64	////	////	01 36	01 04	00 56	00 48	00 38
62	////	////	02 12	01 05	01 01	00 57	00 54
60	////	00 57	02 37	01 05	01 05	01 06	01 08
N 58	////	01 43	02 57	01 05	01 09	01 13	01 19
56	////	02 12	03 14	01 06	01 12	01 20	01 29
54	00 52	02 34	03 28	01 06	01 15	01 26	01 38
52	01 35	02 51	03 40	01 06	01 18	01 31	01 46
50	02 02	03 06	03 51	01 06	01 20	01 36	01 54
45	02 46	03 36	04 13	01 06	01 26	01 46	02 09
N 40	03 16	03 58	04 31	01 07	01 30	01 55	02 22
35	03 39	04 16	04 45	01 07	01 34	02 02	02 33
30	03 58	04 31	04 58	01 07	01 38	02 09	02 43
20	04 26	04 56	05 20	01 08	01 44	02 21	03 00
N 10	04 49	05 16	05 39	01 08	01 49	02 31	03 15
0	05 08	05 34	05 56	01 09	01 54	02 41	03 29
S 10	05 25	05 51	06 14	01 09	02 00	02 50	03 43
20	05 41	06 08	06 32	01 09	02 05	03 01	03 58
30	05 57	06 27	06 53	01 10	02 12	03 13	04 15
35	06 05	06 37	07 05	01 10	02 15	03 20	04 25
40	06 15	06 49	07 19	01 11	02 20	03 28	04 37
45	06 25	07 02	07 36	01 11	02 25	03 38	04 51
S 50	06 37	07 18	07 56	01 12	02 31	03 49	05 08
52	06 42	07 25	08 06	01 12	02 33	03 55	05 16
54	06 47	07 33	08 17	01 12	02 37	04 01	05 25
56	06 53	07 42	08 30	01 13	02 40	04 07	05 35
58	07 00	07 52	08 44	01 13	02 44	04 15	05 47
S 60	07 07	08 04	09 01	01 14	02 48	04 23	06 00

Lat.	Sunset	Civil	Naut.	Moonset 12	13	14	15
°	h m	h m	h m	h m	h m	h m	h m
N 72	□	□	□	14 22	16 43	19 46	□
N 70	□	□	□	14 16	16 24	18 51	□
68	□	□	□	14 11	16 10	18 18	21 17
66	□	□	□	14 07	15 58	17 55	20 08
64	22 26	////	////	14 04	15 48	17 36	19 32
62	21 49	////	////	14 01	15 40	17 21	19 07
60	21 23	23 05	////	13 58	15 33	17 09	18 47
N 58	21 03	22 18	////	13 56	15 27	16 58	18 31
56	20 47	21 49	////	13 54	15 21	16 49	18 17
54	20 33	21 27	23 10	13 53	15 16	16 41	18 05
52	20 21	21 09	22 26	13 51	15 12	16 33	17 55
50	20 10	20 54	21 59	13 50	15 08	16 27	17 45
45	19 47	20 25	21 14	13 46	15 00	16 13	17 26
N 40	19 30	20 02	20 44	13 44	14 52	16 01	17 10
35	19 15	19 44	20 21	13 42	14 46	15 51	16 57
30	19 02	19 29	20 03	13 40	14 41	15 43	16 45
20	18 40	19 04	19 34	13 36	14 32	15 28	16 25
N 10	18 21	18 44	19 11	13 33	14 24	15 15	16 08
0	18 04	18 26	18 52	13 30	14 16	15 03	15 52
S 10	17 46	18 09	18 36	13 28	14 09	14 51	15 36
20	17 28	17 52	18 20	13 25	14 01	14 39	15 20
30	17 07	17 33	18 03	13 21	13 52	14 24	15 00
35	16 55	17 23	17 55	13 19	13 47	14 16	14 49
40	16 41	17 11	17 45	13 17	13 41	14 07	14 36
45	16 24	16 58	17 35	13 14	13 34	13 56	14 21
S 50	16 04	16 42	17 23	13 11	13 26	13 43	14 03
52	15 54	16 35	17 18	13 10	13 22	13 36	13 54
54	15 43	16 27	17 13	13 08	13 18	13 30	13 44
56	15 30	16 18	17 07	13 07	13 14	13 22	13 33
58	15 16	16 07	17 00	13 05	13 09	13 14	13 21
S 60	14 59	15 56	16 52	13 03	13 03	13 04	13 07

Day	SUN Eqn. of Time 00h	12h	Mer. Pass.	MOON Mer. Pass. Upper	Lower	Age	Phase
d	m s	m s	h m	h m	h m	d	%
12	00 16	00 10	12 00	07 19	19 42	24	32
13	00 04	00 02	12 00	08 05	20 28	25	22
14	00 09	00 15	12 00	08 52	21 16	26	14

© British Crown Copyright 2022. All rights reserved.

UT	ARIES GHA	VENUS −4.5 GHA	Dec	MARS +1.7 GHA	Dec	JUPITER −2.1 GHA	Dec	SATURN +0.7 GHA	Dec	STARS Name	SHA	Dec
d h	° ′	° ′	° ′	° ′	° ′	° ′	° ′	° ′	° ′		° ′	° ′
15 00	263 01.2	131 27.5	N20 03.5	125 25.3	N17 42.1	228 40.3	N12 34.5	283 30.8	S10 19.5	Acamar	315 13.1	S40 12.5
01	278 03.7	146 27.8	02.8	140 26.3	41.6	243 42.3	34.7	298 33.3	19.5	Achernar	335 21.5	S57 06.9
02	293 06.2	161 28.1	02.0	155 27.3	41.2	258 44.3	34.8	313 35.7	19.5	Acrux	173 01.4	S63 14.0
03	308 08.6	176 28.4 ..	01.3	170 28.2 ..	40.7	273 46.2 ..	35.0	328 38.2 ..	19.5	Adhara	255 07.3	S29 00.3
04	323 11.1	191 28.7	20 00.6	185 29.2	40.3	288 48.2	35.1	343 40.6	19.5	Aldebaran	290 41.5	N16 33.3
05	338 13.6	206 29.0	19 59.8	200 30.2	39.8	303 50.2	35.3	358 43.1	19.5			
06	353 16.0	221 29.3	N19 59.1	215 31.2	N17 39.4	318 52.2	N12 35.5	13 45.5	S10 19.5	Alioth	166 13.9	N55 50.3
07	8 18.5	236 29.6	58.4	230 32.2	38.9	333 54.2	35.6	28 48.0	19.5	Alkaid	152 52.8	N49 12.0
T 08	23 21.0	251 29.9	57.6	245 33.2	38.5	348 56.2	35.8	43 50.4	19.5	Alnair	27 34.4	S46 50.7
H 09	38 23.4	266 30.2 ..	56.9	260 34.2 ..	38.0	3 58.1 ..	35.9	58 52.9 ..	19.5	Alnilam	275 39.4	S 1 11.2
U 10	53 25.9	281 30.5	56.1	275 35.2	37.5	19 00.1	36.1	73 55.4	19.5	Alphard	217 49.2	S 8 45.6
R 11	68 28.4	296 30.8	55.4	290 36.2	37.1	34 02.1	36.2	88 57.8	19.5			
S 12	83 30.8	311 31.1	N19 54.7	305 37.2	N17 36.6	49 04.1	N12 36.4	104 00.3	S10 19.5	Alphecca	126 04.5	N26 38.2
D 13	98 33.3	326 31.4	53.9	320 38.1	36.2	64 06.1	36.6	119 02.7	19.5	Alpheratz	357 36.2	N29 13.0
A 14	113 35.7	341 31.7	53.2	335 39.1	35.7	79 08.1	36.7	134 05.2	19.5	Altair	62 00.9	N 8 55.7
Y 15	128 38.2	356 32.1 ..	52.4	350 40.1 ..	35.3	94 10.0 ..	36.9	149 07.6 ..	19.5	Ankaa	353 08.5	S42 10.6
16	143 40.7	11 32.4	51.7	5 41.1	34.8	109 12.0	37.0	164 10.1	19.5	Antares	112 17.1	S26 29.1
17	158 43.1	26 32.7	51.0	20 42.1	34.3	124 14.0	37.2	179 12.5	19.5			
18	173 45.6	41 33.0	N19 50.2	35 43.1	N17 33.9	139 16.0	N12 37.3	194 15.0	S10 19.5	Arcturus	145 48.9	N19 03.7
19	188 48.1	56 33.3	49.5	50 44.1	33.4	154 18.0	37.5	209 17.4	19.5	Atria	107 11.9	S69 04.2
20	203 50.5	71 33.6	48.7	65 45.1	33.0	169 20.0	37.7	224 19.9	19.6	Avior	234 15.8	S59 35.2
21	218 53.0	86 34.0 ..	48.0	80 46.1 ..	32.5	184 22.0 ..	37.8	239 22.3 ..	19.6	Bellatrix	278 24.6	N 6 22.2
22	233 55.5	101 34.3	47.2	95 47.1	32.0	199 23.9	38.0	254 24.8	19.6	Betelgeuse	270 53.8	N 7 24.7
23	248 57.9	116 34.6	46.5	110 48.1	31.6	214 25.9	38.1	269 27.2	19.6			
16 00	264 00.4	131 34.9	N19 45.7	125 49.0	N17 31.1	229 27.9	N12 38.3	284 29.7	S10 19.6	Canopus	263 53.5	S52 42.5
01	279 02.9	146 35.3	45.0	140 50.0	30.7	244 29.9	38.5	299 32.1	19.6	Capella	280 24.3	N46 01.2
02	294 05.3	161 35.6	44.2	155 51.0	30.2	259 31.9	38.6	314 34.6	19.6	Deneb	49 26.4	N45 21.6
03	309 07.8	176 35.9 ..	43.5	170 52.0 ..	29.7	274 33.9 ..	38.8	329 37.1 ..	19.6	Denebola	182 26.3	N14 26.6
04	324 10.2	191 36.3	42.8	185 53.0	29.3	289 35.8	38.8	344 39.5	19.6	Diphda	348 48.7	S17 51.4
05	339 12.7	206 36.6	42.0	200 54.0	28.8	304 37.8	39.1	359 42.0	19.6			
06	354 15.2	221 36.9	N19 41.3	215 55.0	N17 28.4	319 39.8	N12 39.2	14 44.4	S10 19.6	Dubhe	193 42.7	N61 37.8
07	9 17.6	236 37.3	40.5	230 56.0	27.9	334 41.8	39.4	29 46.9	19.6	Elnath	278 03.9	N28 37.6
F 08	24 20.1	251 37.6	39.8	245 57.0	27.4	349 43.8	39.6	44 49.3	19.6	Eltanin	90 42.2	N51 29.1
R 09	39 22.6	266 38.0 ..	39.0	260 58.0 ..	27.0	4 45.8 ..	39.7	59 51.8 ..	19.6	Enif	33 39.9	N 9 58.8
I 10	54 25.0	281 38.3	38.3	275 59.0	26.5	19 47.8	39.9	74 54.2	19.6	Fomalhaut	15 15.9	S29 29.8
D 11	69 27.5	296 38.7	37.5	291 00.0	26.0	34 49.8	40.0	89 56.7	19.6			
A 12	84 30.0	311 39.0	N19 36.8	306 00.9	N17 25.6	49 51.7	N12 40.2	104 59.2	S10 19.7	Gacrux	171 53.0	S57 14.9
Y 13	99 32.4	326 39.4	36.0	321 01.9	25.1	64 53.7	40.3	120 01.6	19.7	Gienah	175 44.9	S17 40.4
14	114 34.9	341 39.7	35.3	336 02.9	24.7	79 55.7	40.5	135 04.1	19.7	Hadar	148 37.5	S60 29.3
15	129 37.4	356 40.1 ..	34.5	351 03.9 ..	24.2	94 57.7 ..	40.7	150 06.5 ..	19.7	Hamal	327 52.9	N23 34.2
16	144 39.8	11 40.4	33.8	6 04.9	23.7	109 59.7	40.8	165 09.0	19.7	Kaus Aust.	83 33.9	S34 22.4
17	159 42.3	26 40.8	33.0	21 05.9	23.3	125 01.7	41.0	180 11.4	19.7			
18	174 44.7	41 41.1	N19 32.2	36 06.9	N17 22.8	140 03.7	N12 41.1	195 13.9	S10 19.7	Kochab	137 18.9	N74 03.8
19	189 47.2	56 41.5	31.5	51 07.9	22.3	155 05.7	41.3	210 16.3	19.7	Markab	13 31.1	N15 19.7
20	204 49.7	71 41.8	30.7	66 08.9	21.9	170 07.6	41.4	225 18.8	19.7	Menkar	314 07.8	N 4 10.8
21	219 52.1	86 42.2 ..	30.0	81 09.9 ..	21.4	185 09.6 ..	41.5	240 21.3 ..	19.7	Menkent	147 58.9	S36 29.2
22	234 54.6	101 42.6	29.2	96 10.9	21.0	200 11.6	41.7	255 23.7	19.7	Miaplacidus	221 39.1	S69 49.0
23	249 57.1	116 42.9	28.5	111 11.9	20.5	215 13.6	41.9	270 26.2	19.7			
17 00	264 59.5	131 43.3	N19 27.7	126 12.8	N17 20.0	230 15.6	N12 42.1	285 28.6	S10 19.7	Mirfak	308 30.6	N49 56.5
01	280 02.0	146 43.7	27.0	141 13.8	19.6	245 17.6	42.2	300 31.1	19.7	Nunki	75 49.0	S26 16.0
02	295 04.5	161 44.0	26.2	156 14.8	19.1	260 19.6	42.4	315 33.5	19.8	Peacock	53 07.3	S56 39.4
03	310 06.9	176 44.4 ..	25.5	171 15.8 ..	18.6	275 21.6 ..	42.5	330 36.0 ..	19.8	Pollux	243 19.2	N27 58.3
04	325 09.4	191 44.8	24.7	186 16.8	18.2	290 23.5	42.7	345 38.5	19.8	Procyon	244 52.5	N 5 09.9
05	340 11.8	206 45.1	23.9	201 17.8	17.7	305 25.5	42.8	0 40.9	19.8			
06	355 14.3	221 45.5	N19 23.2	216 18.8	N17 17.2	320 27.5	N12 43.0	15 43.4	S10 19.8	Rasalhague	95 59.4	N12 32.6
07	10 16.8	236 45.9	22.4	231 19.8	16.8	335 29.5	43.1	30 45.8	19.8	Regulus	207 36.0	N11 51.3
S 08	25 19.2	251 46.3	21.7	246 20.8	16.3	350 31.5	43.3	45 48.3	19.8	Rigel	281 05.5	S 8 10.5
A 09	40 21.7	266 46.6 ..	20.9	261 21.8 ..	15.8	5 33.5 ..	43.5	60 50.8 ..	19.8	Rigil Kent.	139 41.6	S60 56.1
T 10	55 24.2	281 47.0	20.1	276 22.8	15.4	20 35.5	43.6	75 53.2	19.8	Sabik	102 03.9	S15 45.2
U 11	70 26.6	296 47.4	19.4	291 23.8	14.9	35 37.5	43.8	90 55.7	19.8			
R 12	85 29.1	311 47.8	N19 18.6	306 24.8	N17 14.4	50 39.5	N12 43.9	105 58.1	S10 19.8	Schedar	349 32.7	N56 39.6
D 13	100 31.6	326 48.2	17.9	321 25.7	14.0	65 41.5	44.1	121 00.6	19.8	Shaula	96 11.7	S37 07.2
A 14	115 34.0	341 48.6	17.1	336 26.7	13.5	80 43.4	44.2	136 03.1	19.9	Sirius	258 27.7	S16 44.9
Y 15	130 36.5	356 49.0 ..	16.3	351 27.7 ..	13.0	95 45.4 ..	44.4	151 05.5 ..	19.9	Spica	158 23.5	S11 17.0
16	145 39.0	11 49.4	15.6	6 28.7	12.6	110 47.4	44.5	166 08.0	19.9	Suhail	222 47.6	S43 31.8
17	160 41.4	26 49.7	14.8	21 29.7	12.1	125 49.4	44.7	181 10.4	19.9			
18	175 43.9	41 50.1	N19 14.1	36 30.7	N17 11.6	140 51.4	N12 44.9	196 12.9	S10 19.9	Vega	80 33.7	N38 48.2
19	190 46.3	56 50.5	13.3	51 31.7	11.2	155 53.4	45.0	211 15.4	19.9	Zuben'ubi	136 57.2	S16 08.4
20	205 48.8	71 50.9	12.5	66 32.7	10.7	170 55.4	45.2	226 17.8	19.9			
21	220 51.3	86 51.3 ..	11.8	81 33.7 ..	10.2	185 57.4 ..	45.3	241 20.3 ..	19.9			
22	235 53.7	101 51.7	11.0	96 34.7	09.8	200 59.4	45.5	256 22.7	19.9			
23	250 56.2	116 52.1	10.2	111 35.7	09.3	216 01.4	45.6	271 25.2	19.9			

											SHA	Mer. Pass.
											° ′	h m
										Venus	227 34.6	15 13
										Mars	221 48.7	15 36
										Jupiter	325 27.5	8 41
										Saturn	20 29.3	5 01

	ARIES	VENUS	MARS	JUPITER	SATURN
Mer. Pass.	h m 6 22.9	v 0.3 d 0.8	v 1.0 d 0.5	v 2.0 d 0.2	v 2.5 d 0.0

© British Crown Copyright 2022. All rights reserved.

UT	SUN GHA	Dec	MOON GHA	v	Dec	d	HP
d h	° ′	° ′	° ′	′	° ′	′	′
15 00	179 54.6	N23 17.2	219 41.6	11.6	N17 46.9	12.1	56.8
01	194 54.5	17.3	234 12.2	11.6	17 59.0	12.0	56.8
02	209 54.3	17.5	248 42.8	11.5	18 11.0	11.8	56.7
03	224 54.2 ..	17.6	263 13.3	11.4	18 22.8	11.8	56.7
04	239 54.0	17.7	277 43.7	11.4	18 34.6	11.7	56.7
05	254 53.9	17.8	292 14.1	11.4	18 46.3	11.6	56.7
06	269 53.8	N23 17.9	306 44.5	11.3	N18 57.9	11.5	56.7
T 07	284 53.6	18.0	321 14.8	11.2	19 09.4	11.4	56.6
H 08	299 53.5	18.1	335 45.0	11.2	19 20.8	11.3	56.6
U 09	314 53.4 ..	18.2	350 15.2	11.1	19 32.1	11.2	56.6
R 10	329 53.2	18.3	4 45.3	11.1	19 43.3	11.1	56.6
S 11	344 53.1	18.4	19 15.4	11.0	19 54.4	11.0	56.5
D 12	359 53.0	N23 18.5	33 45.4	11.0	N20 05.4	10.9	56.5
A 13	14 52.8	18.7	48 15.4	10.9	20 16.3	10.7	56.5
Y 14	29 52.7	18.8	62 45.3	10.9	20 27.0	10.7	56.5
15	44 52.6 ..	18.9	77 15.2	10.8	20 37.7	10.5	56.5
16	59 52.4	19.0	91 45.0	10.7	20 48.2	10.5	56.4
17	74 52.3	19.1	106 14.7	10.7	20 58.7	10.3	56.4
18	89 52.2	N23 19.2	120 44.4	10.7	N21 09.0	10.2	56.4
19	104 52.0	19.3	135 14.1	10.6	21 19.2	10.1	56.4
20	119 51.9	19.4	149 43.7	10.5	21 29.3	10.0	56.4
21	134 51.8 ..	19.5	164 13.2	10.5	21 39.3	9.9	56.3
22	149 51.6	19.6	178 42.7	10.5	21 49.2	9.7	56.3
23	164 51.5	19.7	193 12.2	10.3	21 58.9	9.6	56.3
16 00	179 51.4	N23 19.8	207 41.5	10.4	N22 08.5	9.6	56.3
01	194 51.2	19.9	222 10.9	10.2	22 18.1	9.4	56.3
02	209 51.1	20.0	236 40.1	10.3	22 27.5	9.2	56.2
03	224 51.0 ..	20.0	251 09.4	10.1	22 36.7	9.2	56.2
04	239 50.8	20.1	265 38.5	10.2	22 45.9	9.0	56.2
05	254 50.7	20.2	280 07.7	10.0	22 54.9	8.9	56.2
06	269 50.5	N23 20.3	294 36.7	10.1	N23 03.8	8.8	56.1
07	284 50.4	20.4	309 05.8	9.9	23 12.6	8.7	56.1
08	299 50.3	20.5	323 34.7	10.0	23 21.3	8.5	56.1
F 09	314 50.1 ..	20.6	338 03.7	9.8	23 29.8	8.5	56.1
R 10	329 50.0	20.7	352 32.5	9.8	23 38.3	8.3	56.1
I 11	344 49.9	20.8	7 01.3	9.8	23 46.6	8.1	56.0
D 12	359 49.7	N23 20.9	21 30.1	9.7	N23 54.7	8.0	56.0
A 13	14 49.6	21.0	35 58.8	9.7	24 02.7	7.9	56.0
Y 14	29 49.5	21.0	50 27.5	9.7	24 10.6	7.8	56.0
15	44 49.3 ..	21.1	64 56.2	9.5	24 18.4	7.7	55.9
16	59 49.2	21.2	79 24.7	9.6	24 26.1	7.5	55.9
17	74 49.1	21.3	93 53.3	9.5	24 33.6	7.4	55.9
18	89 48.9	N23 21.4	108 21.8	9.4	N24 41.0	7.2	55.9
19	104 48.8	21.5	122 50.2	9.4	24 48.2	7.1	55.9
20	119 48.6	21.6	137 18.6	9.4	24 55.3	7.0	55.9
21	134 48.5 ..	21.6	151 47.0	9.3	25 02.3	6.8	55.8
22	149 48.4	21.7	166 15.3	9.3	25 09.1	6.8	55.8
23	164 48.2	21.8	180 43.6	9.3	25 15.9	6.5	55.8
17 00	179 48.1	N23 21.9	195 11.9	9.2	N25 22.4	6.5	55.8
01	194 48.0	22.0	209 40.1	9.2	25 28.9	6.3	55.8
02	209 47.8	22.0	224 08.3	9.1	25 35.2	6.1	55.7
03	224 47.7 ..	22.1	238 36.4	9.1	25 41.3	6.0	55.7
04	239 47.6	22.2	253 04.5	9.1	25 47.3	5.9	55.7
05	254 47.4	22.3	267 32.6	9.0	25 53.2	5.8	55.7
06	269 47.3	N23 22.3	282 00.6	9.0	N25 59.0	5.6	55.7
07	284 47.1	22.4	296 28.6	9.0	26 04.6	5.4	55.6
S 08	299 47.0	22.5	310 56.6	8.9	26 10.0	5.4	55.6
A 09	314 46.9 ..	22.6	325 24.5	8.9	26 15.4	5.1	55.6
T 10	329 46.7	22.6	339 52.4	8.9	26 20.5	5.1	55.6
U 11	344 46.6	22.7	354 20.3	8.8	26 25.6	4.9	55.6
R 12	359 46.5	N23 22.8	8 48.1	8.9	N26 30.5	4.7	55.6
D 13	14 46.3	22.9	23 16.0	8.8	26 35.2	4.6	55.5
A 14	29 46.2	22.9	37 43.8	8.7	26 39.8	4.5	55.5
Y 15	44 46.1 ..	23.0	52 11.5	8.8	26 44.3	4.3	55.5
16	59 45.9	23.1	66 39.3	8.7	26 48.6	4.2	55.5
17	74 45.8	23.1	81 07.0	8.8	26 52.8	4.0	55.5
18	89 45.6	N23 23.2	95 34.8	8.7	N26 56.8	3.9	55.4
19	104 45.5	23.3	110 02.5	8.7	27 00.7	3.8	55.4
20	119 45.4	23.3	124 30.2	8.6	27 04.5	3.6	55.4
21	134 45.2 ..	23.4	138 57.8	8.7	27 08.1	3.4	55.4
22	149 45.1	23.5	153 25.5	8.6	27 11.5	3.3	55.3
23	164 45.0	23.5	167 53.1	8.7	N27 14.8	3.2	55.3
	SD 15.8	d 0.1	SD 15.4		15.3		15.1

Moonrise

Lat.	Twilight Naut.	Civil	Sunrise	15	16	17	18
°	h m	h m	h m	h m	h m	h m	h m
N 72	□	□	□	□	□	□	□
N 70	□	□	□	22 38			
68	□	□	□	(00 18 / 23 48)			
66	□	□	□	(00 25 / 23 58)			
64	////	////	01 33	00 38			
62	////	////	02 10	00 54	00 51	00 49	
60	////	00 52	02 36	01 08	01 12	01 21	01 41
N 58	////	01 41	02 56	01 19	01 29	01 45	02 13
56	////	02 11	03 13	01 29	01 43	02 04	02 36
54	00 48	02 33	03 27	01 38	01 56	02 20	02 56
52	01 33	02 51	03 39	01 46	02 07	02 34	03 12
50	02 00	03 06	03 50	01 54	02 16	02 46	03 26
45	02 46	03 35	04 13	02 09	02 37	03 12	03 54
N 40	03 16	03 58	04 31	02 22	02 54	03 32	04 17
35	03 39	04 16	04 46	02 33	03 08	03 49	04 36
30	03 58	04 31	04 59	02 43	03 21	04 04	04 52
20	04 27	04 56	05 21	03 00	03 42	04 29	05 19
N 10	04 49	05 16	05 39	03 15	04 01	04 50	05 42
0	05 08	05 34	05 57	03 29	04 19	05 11	06 04
S 10	05 25	05 52	06 14	03 43	04 36	05 31	06 26
20	05 41	06 09	06 33	03 58	04 55	05 53	06 50
30	05 58	06 28	06 54	04 15	05 17	06 19	07 17
35	06 07	06 38	07 06	04 25	05 30	06 34	07 34
40	06 16	06 50	07 20	04 37	05 45	06 51	07 53
45	06 26	07 03	07 37	04 51	06 03	07 13	08 16
S 50	06 38	07 19	07 58	05 08	06 26	07 40	08 45
52	06 43	07 27	08 08	05 16	06 37	07 53	09 00
54	06 49	07 35	08 19	05 25	06 49	08 08	09 17
56	06 55	07 44	08 31	05 35	07 03	08 26	09 37
58	07 02	07 54	08 46	05 47	07 19	08 48	10 02
S 60	07 09	08 06	09 03	06 00	07 40	09 16	10 38

Moonset

Lat.	Sunset	Twilight Civil	Naut.	15	16	17	18
°	h m	h m	h m	h m	h m	h m	h m
N 72	□	□	□	□	□	□	□
N 70	□	□	□	21 17			
68	□	□	□	20 08			
66	□	□	□				
64	22 30	////	////	19 32	21 47		
62	21 52	////	////	19 07	20 56	22 46	24 08
60	21 26	23 10	////	18 47	20 25	21 55	23 03
N 58	21 05	22 21	////	18 31	20 02	21 24	22 28
56	20 49	21 51	////	18 17	19 43	21 01	22 03
54	20 34	21 29	23 15	18 05	19 27	20 42	21 43
52	20 22	21 11	22 29	17 55	19 13	20 26	21 26
50	20 11	20 56	22 01	17 45	19 01	20 12	21 11
45	19 49	20 26	21 16	17 26	18 37	19 43	20 42
N 40	19 31	20 04	20 45	17 10	18 17	19 21	20 19
35	19 16	19 46	20 22	16 57	18 01	19 03	20 00
30	19 03	19 30	20 04	16 45	17 47	18 47	19 44
20	18 41	19 05	19 34	16 25	17 23	18 21	19 16
N 10	18 22	18 45	19 12	16 08	17 03	17 58	18 52
0	18 04	18 27	18 53	15 52	16 43	17 36	18 30
S 10	17 47	18 10	18 36	15 36	16 24	17 15	18 08
20	17 28	17 52	18 20	15 20	16 04	16 52	17 44
30	17 07	17 34	18 04	15 00	15 40	16 26	17 16
35	16 55	17 23	17 55	14 49	15 27	16 10	17 00
40	16 41	17 11	17 45	14 36	15 11	15 52	16 41
45	16 24	16 58	17 35	14 21	14 52	15 30	16 18
S 50	16 03	16 42	17 23	14 03	14 28	15 03	15 48
52	15 54	16 34	17 18	13 54	14 17	14 49	15 33
54	15 42	16 26	17 12	13 44	14 05	14 34	15 16
56	15 30	16 17	17 06	13 33	13 50	14 16	14 56
58	15 15	16 07	17 00	13 21	13 33	13 54	14 30
S 60	14 58	15 55	16 52	13 07	13 12	13 25	13 55

Day	SUN Eqn. of Time 00h	12h	Mer. Pass.	MOON Mer. Pass. Upper	Lower	Age	Phase
d	m s	m s	h m	h m	h m	d	%
15	00 21	00 28	12 00	09 40	22 05	27	7
16	00 34	00 41	12 01	10 31	22 57	28	3
17	00 47	00 54	12 01	11 23	23 50	29	1

© British Crown Copyright 2022. All rights reserved.

UT	ARIES GHA	VENUS −4.6 GHA	Dec	MARS +1.7 GHA	Dec	JUPITER −2.2 GHA	Dec	SATURN +0.7 GHA	Dec	STARS Name	SHA	Dec
18 00	265 58.7	131 52.5	N19 09.5	126 36.7	N17 08.8	231 03.4	N12 45.8	286 27.7	S10 19.9	Acamar	315 13.1	S40 12.5
01	281 01.1	146 53.0	08.7	141 37.7	08.4	246 05.4	45.9	301 30.1	20.0	Achernar	335 21.4	S57 06.8
02	296 03.6	161 53.4	07.9	156 38.7	07.9	261 07.3	46.1	316 32.6	20.0	Acrux	173 01.4	S63 14.0
03	311 06.1	176 53.8 ..	07.2	171 39.6 ..	07.4	276 09.3 ..	46.2	331 35.1 ..	20.0	Adhara	255 07.3	S29 00.2
04	326 08.5	191 54.2	06.4	186 40.6	07.0	291 11.3	46.4	346 37.5	20.0	Aldebaran	290 41.4	N16 33.3
05	341 11.0	206 54.6	05.6	201 41.6	06.5	306 13.3	46.5	1 40.0	20.0			
06	356 13.5	221 55.0	N19 04.9	216 42.6	N17 06.0	321 15.3	N12 46.7	16 42.4	S10 20.0	Alioth	166 14.0	N55 50.3
07	11 15.9	236 55.4	04.1	231 43.6	05.5	336 17.3	46.9	31 44.9	20.0	Alkaid	152 52.8	N49 12.0
08	26 18.4	251 55.8	03.3	246 44.6	05.1	351 19.3	47.0	46 47.4	20.0	Al Na'ir	27 34.3	S46 50.7
S 09	41 20.8	266 56.3 ..	02.6	261 45.6 ..	04.6	6 21.3 ..	47.2	61 49.8 ..	20.0	Alnilam	275 39.4	S 1 11.2
U 10	56 23.3	281 56.7	01.8	276 46.6	04.1	21 23.3	47.3	76 52.3	20.0	Alphard	217 49.2	S 8 45.6
N 11	71 25.8	296 57.1	01.0	291 47.6	03.7	36 25.3	47.5	91 54.8	20.0			
D 12	86 28.2	311 57.5	N19 00.3	306 48.6	N17 03.2	51 27.3	N12 47.6	106 57.2	S10 20.1	Alphecca	126 04.5	N26 38.2
A 13	101 30.7	326 58.0	18 59.5	321 49.6	02.7	66 29.3	47.8	121 59.7	20.1	Alpheratz	357 36.1	N29 13.0
Y 14	116 33.2	341 58.4	58.7	336 50.6	02.2	81 31.3	47.9	137 02.1	20.1	Altair	62 00.9	N 8 55.7
15	131 35.6	356 58.8 ..	58.0	351 51.6 ..	01.8	96 33.3 ..	48.1	152 04.6 ..	20.1	Ankaa	353 08.5	S42 10.5
16	146 38.1	11 59.2	57.2	6 52.6	01.3	111 35.2	48.2	167 07.1	20.1	Antares	112 17.1	S26 29.1
17	161 40.6	26 59.7	56.4	21 53.6	00.8	126 37.2	48.4	182 09.5	20.1			
18	176 43.0	42 00.1	N18 55.7	36 54.6	N17 00.4	141 39.2	N12 48.5	197 12.0	S10 20.1	Arcturus	145 48.9	N19 03.7
19	191 45.5	57 00.6	54.9	51 55.5	16 59.9	156 41.2	48.7	212 14.5	20.1	Atria	107 11.9	S69 04.2
20	206 48.0	72 01.0	54.1	66 56.5	59.4	171 43.2	48.9	227 16.9	20.1	Avior	234 15.8	S59 35.2
21	221 50.4	87 01.4 ..	53.3	81 57.5 ..	58.9	186 45.2 ..	49.0	242 19.4 ..	20.1	Bellatrix	278 24.6	N 6 22.2
22	236 52.9	102 01.9	52.6	96 58.5	58.5	201 47.2	49.2	257 21.9	20.2	Betelgeuse	270 53.8	N 7 24.7
23	251 55.3	117 02.3	51.8	111 59.5	58.0	216 49.2	49.3	272 24.3	20.2			
19 00	266 57.8	132 02.8	N18 51.0	127 00.5	N16 57.5	231 51.2	N12 49.5	287 26.8	S10 20.2	Canopus	263 53.5	S52 42.5
01	282 00.3	147 03.2	50.2	142 01.5	57.0	246 53.2	49.6	302 29.3	20.2	Capella	280 24.4	N46 01.2
02	297 02.7	162 03.7	49.5	157 02.5	56.6	261 55.2	49.8	317 31.7	20.2	Deneb	49 26.3	N45 21.6
03	312 05.2	177 04.1 ..	48.7	172 03.5 ..	56.1	276 57.2 ..	49.9	332 34.2 ..	20.2	Denebola	182 26.3	N14 26.6
04	327 07.7	192 04.6	47.9	187 04.5	55.6	291 59.2	50.1	347 36.7	20.2	Diphda	348 48.7	S17 51.4
05	342 10.1	207 05.0	47.1	202 05.5	55.2	307 01.2	50.2	2 39.1	20.2			
06	357 12.6	222 05.5	N18 46.4	217 06.5	N16 54.7	322 03.2	N12 50.4	17 41.6	S10 20.2	Dubhe	193 42.8	N61 37.8
07	12 15.1	237 05.9	45.6	232 07.5	54.2	337 05.2	50.5	32 44.1	20.3	Elnath	278 03.9	N28 37.6
08	27 17.5	252 06.4	44.8	247 08.5	53.7	352 07.2	50.7	47 46.5	20.3	Eltanin	90 42.2	N51 29.1
M 09	42 20.0	267 06.8 ..	44.0	262 09.5 ..	53.3	7 09.2 ..	50.8	62 49.0 ..	20.3	Enif	33 39.9	N 9 58.8
O 10	57 22.5	282 07.3	43.3	277 10.5	52.8	22 11.2	51.0	77 51.5	20.3	Fomalhaut	15 15.9	S29 29.8
N 11	72 24.9	297 07.8	42.5	292 11.5	52.3	37 13.2	51.1	92 53.9	20.3			
D 12	87 27.4	312 08.2	N18 41.7	307 12.4	N16 51.8	52 15.2	N12 51.3	107 56.4	S10 20.3	Gacrux	171 53.0	S57 14.9
A 13	102 29.8	327 08.7	40.9	322 13.4	51.4	67 17.1	51.4	122 58.9	20.3	Gienah	175 44.9	S17 40.4
Y 14	117 32.3	342 09.2	40.2	337 14.4	50.9	82 19.1	51.6	138 01.3	20.3	Hadar	148 37.5	S60 29.4
15	132 34.8	357 09.6 ..	39.4	352 15.4 ..	50.4	97 21.1 ..	51.7	153 03.8 ..	20.3	Hamal	327 52.9	N23 34.2
16	147 37.2	12 10.1	38.6	7 16.4	49.9	112 23.1	51.9	168 06.3	20.4	Kaus Aust.	83 33.8	S34 22.4
17	162 39.7	27 10.6	37.8	22 17.4	49.4	127 25.1	52.0	183 08.7	20.4			
18	177 42.2	42 11.0	N18 37.0	37 18.4	N16 49.0	142 27.1	N12 52.2	198 11.2	S10 20.4	Kochab	137 18.9	N74 03.8
19	192 44.6	57 11.5	36.3	52 19.4	48.5	157 29.1	52.4	213 13.7	20.4	Markab	13 31.1	N15 19.7
20	207 47.1	72 12.0	35.5	67 20.4	48.0	172 31.1	52.5	228 16.1	20.4	Menkar	314 07.8	N 4 10.8
21	222 49.6	87 12.5 ..	34.7	82 21.4 ..	47.5	187 33.1 ..	52.7	243 18.6 ..	20.4	Menkent	147 58.9	S36 29.2
22	237 52.0	102 13.0	33.9	97 22.4	47.1	202 35.1	52.8	258 21.1	20.4	Miaplacidus	221 39.2	S69 49.0
23	252 54.5	117 13.5	33.2	112 23.4	46.6	217 37.1	53.0	273 23.5	20.4			
20 00	267 57.0	132 13.9	N18 32.4	127 24.4	N16 46.1	232 39.1	N12 53.1	288 26.0	S10 20.5	Mirfak	308 30.5	N49 56.5
01	282 59.4	147 14.4	31.6	142 25.4	45.6	247 41.1	53.3	303 28.5	20.5	Nunki	75 49.0	S26 16.0
02	298 01.9	162 14.9	30.8	157 26.4	45.2	262 43.1	53.4	318 31.0	20.5	Peacock	53 07.3	S56 39.4
03	313 04.3	177 15.4 ..	30.0	172 27.4 ..	44.7	277 45.1 ..	53.6	333 33.4 ..	20.5	Pollux	243 19.2	N27 58.3
04	328 06.8	192 15.9	29.2	187 28.4	44.2	292 47.1	53.7	348 35.9	20.5	Procyon	244 52.5	N 5 09.9
05	343 09.3	207 16.4	28.5	202 29.4	43.7	307 49.1	53.9	3 38.4	20.5			
06	358 11.7	222 16.9	N18 27.7	217 30.4	N16 43.2	322 51.1	N12 54.0	18 40.8	S10 20.5	Rasalhague	95 59.4	N12 32.6
07	13 14.2	237 17.4	26.9	232 31.4	42.8	337 53.1	54.2	33 43.3	20.5	Regulus	207 36.0	N11 51.3
08	28 16.7	252 17.9	26.1	247 32.3	42.3	352 55.1	54.3	48 45.8	20.6	Rigel	281 05.5	S 8 10.5
T 09	43 19.1	267 18.4 ..	25.3	262 33.3 ..	41.8	7 57.1 ..	54.5	63 48.3 ..	20.6	Rigil Kent.	139 41.6	S60 56.1
U 10	58 21.6	282 18.9	24.5	277 34.3	41.3	22 59.1	54.6	78 50.7	20.6	Sabik	102 03.9	S15 45.2
E 11	73 24.1	297 19.4	23.8	292 35.3	40.8	38 01.1	54.8	93 53.2	20.6			
S 12	88 26.5	312 19.9	N18 23.0	307 36.3	N16 40.4	53 03.1	N12 54.9	108 55.7	S10 20.6	Schedar	349 32.7	N56 39.6
D 13	103 29.0	327 20.4	22.2	322 37.3	39.9	68 05.1	55.1	123 58.1	20.6	Shaula	96 11.7	S37 07.2
A 14	118 31.4	342 20.9	21.4	337 38.3	39.4	83 07.1	55.2	139 00.6	20.6	Sirius	258 27.7	S16 44.9
Y 15	133 33.9	357 21.4 ..	20.6	352 39.3 ..	38.9	98 09.1 ..	55.4	154 03.1 ..	20.6	Spica	158 23.5	S11 17.0
16	148 36.4	12 21.9	19.8	7 40.3	38.4	113 11.1	55.5	169 05.6	20.7	Suhail	222 47.6	S43 31.7
17	163 38.8	27 22.5	19.1	22 41.3	38.0	128 13.1	55.7	184 08.0	20.7			
18	178 41.3	42 23.0	N18 18.3	37 42.3	N16 37.5	143 15.1	N12 55.8	199 10.5	S10 20.7	Vega	80 33.7	N38 48.2
19	193 43.8	57 23.5	17.5	52 43.3	37.0	158 17.1	56.0	214 13.0	20.7	Zuben'ubi	136 57.2	S16 08.4
20	208 46.2	72 24.0	16.7	67 44.3	36.5	173 19.1	56.1	229 15.4	20.7		SHA	Mer. Pass.
21	223 48.7	87 24.5 ..	15.9	82 45.3 ..	36.0	188 21.1 ..	56.3	244 17.9 ..	20.7		° ′	h m
22	238 51.2	102 25.1	15.1	97 46.3	35.6	203 23.1	56.4	259 20.4	20.7	Venus	225 04.9	15 11
23	253 53.6	117 25.6	14.3	112 47.3	35.1	218 25.1	56.6	274 22.9	20.7	Mars	220 02.7	15 31
	h m									Jupiter	324 53.4	8 31
Mer. Pass. 6 11.1		v 0.5	d 0.8	v 1.0	d 0.5	v 2.0	d 0.2	v 2.5	d 0.0	Saturn	20 29.0	4 49

© British Crown Copyright 2022. All rights reserved.

UT	SUN GHA	SUN Dec	MOON GHA	MOON v	MOON Dec	MOON d	MOON HP
d h	° ′	° ′	° ′	′	° ′	′	′
18 00	179 44.8	N23 23.6	182 20.8	8.6	N27 18.0	3.0	55.3
01	194 44.7	23.6	196 48.4	8.6	27 21.0	2.9	55.3
02	209 44.6	23.7	211 16.0	8.6	27 23.9	2.7	55.3
03	224 44.4	23.8	225 43.6	8.6	27 26.6	2.6	55.3
04	239 44.3	23.8	240 11.2	8.6	27 29.2	2.4	55.3
05	254 44.1	23.9	254 38.8	8.6	27 31.6	2.3	55.2
06	269 44.0	N23 23.9	269 06.4	8.6	N27 33.9	2.1	55.2
07	284 43.9	24.0	283 34.0	8.6	27 36.0	2.0	55.2
S 08	299 43.7	24.1	298 01.6	8.6	27 38.0	1.9	55.2
U 09	314 43.6	24.1	312 29.2	8.6	27 39.9	1.6	55.2
N 10	329 43.5	24.2	326 56.8	8.6	27 41.5	1.6	55.1
D 11	344 43.3	24.2	341 24.4	8.6	27 43.1	1.4	55.1
A 12	359 43.2	N23 24.3	355 52.0	8.6	N27 44.5	1.2	55.1
Y 13	14 43.0	24.3	10 19.6	8.7	27 45.7	1.2	55.1
14	29 42.9	24.4	24 47.3	8.6	27 46.9	0.9	55.1
15	44 42.8	24.4	39 14.9	8.7	27 47.8	0.8	55.1
16	59 42.6	24.5	53 42.6	8.6	27 48.6	0.7	55.0
17	74 42.5	24.5	68 10.2	8.7	27 49.3	0.5	55.0
18	89 42.4	N23 24.6	82 37.9	8.7	N27 49.8	0.4	55.0
19	104 42.2	24.6	97 05.6	8.7	27 50.2	0.2	55.0
20	119 42.1	24.7	111 33.3	8.8	27 50.4	0.1	55.0
21	134 41.9	24.7	126 01.1	8.7	27 50.5	0.1	55.0
22	149 41.8	24.8	140 28.8	8.8	27 50.4	0.2	54.9
23	164 41.7	24.8	154 56.6	8.8	27 50.2	0.3	54.9
19 00	179 41.5	N23 24.9	169 24.4	8.9	N27 49.9	0.5	54.9
01	194 41.4	24.9	183 52.3	8.8	27 49.4	0.6	54.9
02	209 41.3	25.0	198 20.1	8.9	27 48.8	0.8	54.9
03	224 41.1	25.0	212 48.0	8.9	27 48.0	0.9	54.9
04	239 41.0	25.1	227 15.9	9.0	27 47.1	1.1	54.9
05	254 40.9	25.1	241 43.9	9.0	27 46.0	1.2	54.8
06	269 40.7	N23 25.1	256 11.9	9.0	N27 44.8	1.4	54.8
07	284 40.6	25.2	270 39.9	9.1	27 43.4	1.5	54.8
08	299 40.4	25.2	285 08.0	9.0	27 41.9	1.6	54.8
M 09	314 40.3	25.3	299 36.0	9.2	27 40.3	1.8	54.8
O 10	329 40.2	25.3	314 04.2	9.1	27 38.5	1.9	54.8
N 11	344 40.0	25.3	328 32.3	9.2	27 36.6	2.0	54.7
D 12	359 39.9	N23 25.4	343 00.5	9.3	N27 34.6	2.2	54.7
A 13	14 39.8	25.4	357 28.8	9.3	27 32.4	2.4	54.7
Y 14	29 39.6	25.4	11 57.1	9.3	27 30.0	2.4	54.7
15	44 39.5	25.5	26 25.4	9.4	27 27.6	2.6	54.7
16	59 39.3	25.5	40 53.8	9.4	27 25.0	2.8	54.7
17	74 39.2	25.5	55 22.2	9.5	27 22.2	2.9	54.7
18	89 39.1	N23 25.6	69 50.7	9.5	N27 19.3	3.0	54.6
19	104 38.9	25.6	84 19.2	9.6	27 16.3	3.1	54.6
20	119 38.8	25.6	98 47.8	9.6	27 13.2	3.3	54.6
21	134 38.7	25.7	113 16.4	9.7	27 09.9	3.4	54.6
22	149 38.5	25.7	127 45.1	9.8	27 06.5	3.6	54.6
23	164 38.4	25.7	142 13.9	9.8	27 02.9	3.7	54.6
20 00	179 38.2	N23 25.8	156 42.7	9.8	N26 59.2	3.8	54.6
01	194 38.1	25.8	171 11.5	9.9	26 55.4	3.9	54.6
02	209 38.0	25.8	185 40.4	10.0	26 51.5	4.1	54.5
03	224 37.8	25.8	200 09.4	10.0	26 47.4	4.2	54.5
04	239 37.7	25.9	214 38.4	10.0	26 43.2	4.3	54.5
05	254 37.6	25.9	229 07.4	10.2	26 38.9	4.5	54.5
06	269 37.4	N23 25.9	243 36.6	10.2	N26 34.4	4.6	54.5
07	284 37.3	25.9	258 05.8	10.2	26 29.8	4.7	54.5
08	299 37.1	26.0	272 35.0	10.4	26 25.1	4.9	54.5
T 09	314 37.0	26.0	287 04.4	10.3	26 20.2	4.9	54.5
U 10	329 36.9	26.0	301 33.7	10.5	26 15.3	5.1	54.4
E 11	344 36.7	26.0	316 03.2	10.5	26 10.2	5.2	54.4
S 12	359 36.6	N23 26.0	330 32.7	10.6	N26 05.0	5.4	54.4
D 13	14 36.5	26.1	345 02.3	10.6	25 59.6	5.4	54.4
A 14	29 36.3	26.1	359 31.9	10.7	25 54.2	5.6	54.4
Y 15	44 36.2	26.1	14 01.6	10.8	25 48.6	5.7	54.4
16	59 36.0	26.1	28 31.4	10.8	25 42.9	5.8	54.4
17	74 35.9	26.1	43 01.2	11.0	25 37.1	5.9	54.4
18	89 35.8	N23 26.1	57 31.2	10.9	N25 31.2	6.1	54.4
19	104 35.6	26.2	72 01.1	11.1	25 25.1	6.2	54.3
20	119 35.5	26.2	86 31.2	11.1	25 18.9	6.2	54.3
21	134 35.4	26.2	101 01.3	11.2	25 12.7	6.4	54.3
22	149 35.2	26.2	115 31.5	11.3	25 06.3	6.5	54.3
23	164 35.1	26.2	130 01.8	11.3	N24 59.8	6.7	54.3
	SD 15.8	d 0.0	SD 15.0		14.9		14.8

Twilight / Moonrise

Lat.	Naut.	Civil	Sunrise	18	19	20	21
°	h m	h m	h m	h m	h m	h m	h m
N 72	▭	▭	▭	▭	▭	▭	▭
N 70	▭	▭	▭	▭	▭	▭	▭
68	▭	▭	▭	▭	▭	▭	▭
66	▭	▭	▭	▭	▭	▭	▭
64	////	////	01 31	▭	▭	▭	03 58
62	////	////	02 09	00 50	01 20	02 55	04 39
60	////	00 50	02 36	01 41	02 26	03 39	05 08
N 58	////	01 40	02 56	02 13	03 00	04 09	05 29
56	////	02 10	03 13	02 36	03 25	04 31	05 47
54	00 45	02 33	03 27	02 56	03 44	04 49	06 02
52	01 32	02 51	03 39	03 12	04 02	05 05	06 15
50	02 00	03 06	03 50	03 26	04 17	05 18	06 26
45	02 46	03 35	04 13	03 54	04 46	05 46	06 50
N 40	03 16	03 58	04 31	04 17	05 09	06 07	07 08
35	03 39	04 16	04 46	04 36	05 28	06 25	07 24
30	03 58	04 32	04 59	04 52	05 44	06 40	07 38
20	04 27	04 57	05 21	05 19	06 12	07 06	08 01
N 10	04 50	05 17	05 40	05 42	06 36	07 29	08 21
0	05 09	05 35	05 58	06 04	06 58	07 50	08 39
S 10	05 26	05 52	06 15	06 26	07 20	08 11	08 58
20	05 42	06 10	06 34	06 50	07 43	08 33	09 17
30	05 59	06 29	06 55	07 17	08 11	08 59	09 40
35	06 07	06 39	07 07	07 34	08 27	09 14	09 53
40	06 17	06 51	07 21	07 53	08 46	09 31	10 08
45	06 27	07 04	07 38	08 16	09 09	09 52	10 27
S 50	06 39	07 21	07 59	08 45	09 38	10 19	10 49
52	06 44	07 28	08 09	09 00	09 53	10 32	11 00
54	06 50	07 36	08 20	09 17	10 10	10 47	11 12
56	06 56	07 45	08 33	09 37	10 30	11 04	11 26
58	07 03	07 56	08 48	10 02	10 55	11 25	11 42
S 60	07 10	08 07	09 05	10 38	11 28	11 51	12 01

Sunset / Twilight / Moonset

Lat.	Sunset	Civil	Naut.	18	19	20	21
°	h m	h m	h m	h m	h m	h m	h m
N 72	▭	▭	▭	▭	▭	▭	▭
N 70	▭	▭	▭	▭	▭	▭	▭
68	▭	▭	▭	▭	▭	▭	▭
66	▭	▭	▭	▭	▭	▭	▭
64	22 32	////	////	▭	▭	▭	01 05
62	21 54	////	////	24 08	00 08	00 23	00 23
60	21 27	23 14	////	23 03	23 39	23 54	24 01
N 58	21 07	22 23	////	22 28	23 09	23 32	23 45
56	20 50	21 53	////	22 03	22 46	23 14	23 31
54	20 36	21 30	23 18	21 43	22 28	22 59	23 20
52	20 23	21 12	22 31	21 26	22 12	22 45	23 09
50	20 12	20 57	22 03	21 11	21 58	22 34	23 00
45	19 50	20 27	21 17	20 42	21 31	22 09	22 40
N 40	19 32	20 05	20 46	20 19	21 09	21 50	22 23
35	19 17	19 46	20 23	20 00	20 50	21 33	22 10
30	19 04	19 31	20 05	19 44	20 34	21 19	21 58
20	18 42	19 06	19 35	19 16	20 08	20 55	21 37
N 10	18 23	18 46	19 13	18 52	19 45	20 34	21 19
0	18 05	18 28	18 54	18 30	19 23	20 14	21 02
S 10	17 48	18 10	18 37	18 08	19 01	19 54	20 45
20	17 29	17 53	18 21	17 44	18 38	19 33	20 27
30	17 08	17 34	18 04	17 16	18 11	19 08	20 05
35	16 55	17 24	17 55	17 00	17 55	18 53	19 53
40	16 41	17 12	17 46	16 41	17 36	18 36	19 38
45	16 24	16 58	17 35	16 18	17 14	18 16	19 21
S 50	16 04	16 42	17 24	15 48	16 45	17 50	19 00
52	15 54	16 35	17 18	15 33	16 30	17 37	18 50
54	15 43	16 26	17 13	15 16	16 14	17 23	18 38
56	15 30	16 17	17 07	14 56	15 54	17 06	18 25
58	15 15	16 07	17 00	14 30	15 29	16 45	18 09
S 60	14 58	15 55	16 52	13 55	14 55	16 19	17 50

SUN / MOON

Day	Eqn. of Time 00ʰ	Eqn. of Time 12ʰ	Mer. Pass.	Mer. Pass. Upper	Mer. Pass. Lower	Age	Phase
d	m s	m s	h m	h m	h m	d	%
18	01 00	01 07	12 01	12 17	24 44	00	0
19	01 14	01 20	12 01	13 10	00 44	01	2
20	01 27	01 33	12 02	14 02	01 36	02	5

© British Crown Copyright 2022. All rights reserved.

UT	ARIES	VENUS −4.6		MARS +1.7		JUPITER −2.2		SATURN +0.7		STARS		
d h	GHA	GHA	Dec	GHA	Dec	GHA	Dec	GHA	Dec	Name	SHA	Dec
21 00	268 56.1	132 26.1	N18 13.5	127 48.3	N16 34.6	233 27.1	N12 56.7	289 25.3	S10 20.8	Acamar	315 13.1	S40 12.5
01	283 58.6	147 26.6	12.8	142 49.3	34.1	248 29.1	56.9	304 27.8	20.8	Achernar	335 21.4	S57 06.8
02	299 01.0	162 27.2	12.0	157 50.3	33.6	263 31.1	57.0	319 30.3	20.8	Acrux	173 01.4	S63 14.0
03	314 03.5	177 27.7 ..	11.2	172 51.3 ..	33.1	278 33.1 ..	57.2	334 32.8 ..	20.8	Adhara	255 07.3	S29 00.2
04	329 05.9	192 28.2	10.4	187 52.3	32.7	293 35.1	57.3	349 35.2	20.8	Aldebaran	290 41.4	N16 33.3
05	344 08.4	207 28.8	09.6	202 53.3	32.2	308 37.1	57.5	4 37.7	20.8			
W 06	359 10.9	222 29.3	N18 08.8	217 54.3	N16 31.7	323 39.1	N12 57.6	19 40.2	S10 20.8	Alioth	166 14.0	N55 50.3
E 07	14 13.3	237 29.9	08.0	232 55.3	31.2	338 41.1	57.8	34 42.7	20.9	Alkaid	152 52.8	N49 12.0
D 08	29 15.8	252 30.4	07.2	247 56.3	30.7	353 43.1	57.9	49 45.1	20.9	Alnair	27 34.3	S46 50.7
N 09	44 18.3	267 30.9 ..	06.4	262 57.2 ..	30.2	8 45.1 ..	58.1	64 47.6 ..	20.9	Alnilam	275 39.4	S 1 11.2
E 10	59 20.7	282 31.5	05.7	277 58.2	29.8	23 47.1	58.2	79 50.1	20.9	Alphard	217 49.2	S 8 45.6
S 11	74 23.2	297 32.0	04.9	292 59.2	29.3	38 49.1	58.4	94 52.6	20.9			
D 12	89 25.7	312 32.6	N18 04.1	308 00.2	N16 28.8	53 51.2	N12 58.5	109 55.0	S10 20.9	Alphecca	126 04.5	N26 38.2
A 13	104 28.1	327 33.1	03.3	323 01.2	28.3	68 53.2	58.6	124 57.5	20.9	Alpheratz	357 36.1	N29 13.0
Y 14	119 30.6	342 33.7	02.5	338 02.2	27.8	83 55.2	58.8	140 00.0	21.0	Altair	62 00.9	N 8 55.8
15	134 33.1	357 34.2 ..	01.7	353 03.2 ..	27.3	98 57.2 ..	58.9	155 02.5 ..	21.0	Ankaa	353 08.5	S42 10.5
16	149 35.5	12 34.8	00.9	8 04.2	26.9	113 59.2	59.1	170 04.9	21.0	Antares	112 17.1	S26 29.1
17	164 38.0	27 35.3	18 00.1	23 05.2	26.4	129 01.2	59.2	185 07.4	21.0			
18	179 40.4	42 35.9	N17 59.3	38 06.2	N16 25.9	144 03.2	N12 59.4	200 09.9	S10 21.0	Arcturus	145 48.9	N19 03.7
19	194 42.9	57 36.5	58.5	53 07.2	25.4	159 05.2	59.5	215 12.4	21.0	Atria	107 11.9	S69 04.2
20	209 45.4	72 37.0	57.7	68 08.2	24.9	174 07.2	59.7	230 14.8	21.0	Avior	234 15.8	S59 35.2
21	224 47.8	87 37.6 ..	56.9	83 09.2 ..	24.4	189 09.2	12 59.8	245 17.3 ..	21.1	Bellatrix	278 24.6	N 6 22.3
22	239 50.3	102 38.2	56.2	98 10.2	23.9	204 11.2	13 00.0	260 19.8	21.1	Betelgeuse	270 53.8	N 7 24.7
23	254 52.8	117 38.7	55.4	113 11.2	23.5	219 13.2	00.1	275 22.3	21.1			
22 00	269 55.2	132 39.3	N17 54.6	128 12.2	N16 23.0	234 15.2	N13 00.3	290 24.7	S10 21.1	Canopus	263 53.5	S52 42.5
01	284 57.7	147 39.9	53.8	143 13.2	22.5	249 17.2	00.4	305 27.2	21.1	Capella	280 24.3	N46 01.2
02	300 00.2	162 40.4	53.0	158 14.2	22.0	264 19.2	00.6	320 29.7	21.1	Deneb	49 26.3	N45 21.6
03	315 02.6	177 41.0 ..	52.2	173 15.2 ..	21.5	279 21.2 ..	00.7	335 32.2 ..	21.2	Denebola	182 26.3	N14 26.6
04	330 05.1	192 41.6	51.4	188 16.2	21.0	294 23.2	00.9	350 34.7	21.2	Diphda	348 48.7	S17 51.4
05	345 07.6	207 42.2	50.6	203 17.2	20.5	309 25.2	01.0	5 37.1	21.2			
T 06	0 10.0	222 42.8	N17 49.8	218 18.2	N16 20.0	324 27.2	N13 01.2	20 39.6	S10 21.2	Dubhe	193 42.8	N61 37.8
H 07	15 12.5	237 43.3	49.0	233 19.2	19.6	339 29.2	01.3	35 42.1	21.2	Elnath	278 03.9	N28 37.6
U 08	30 14.9	252 43.9	48.2	248 20.2	19.1	354 31.3	01.5	50 44.6	21.2	Eltanin	90 42.2	N51 29.1
R 09	45 17.4	267 44.5 ..	47.4	263 21.2 ..	18.6	9 33.3 ..	01.6	65 47.0 ..	21.2	Enif	33 39.9	N 9 58.9
S 10	60 19.9	282 45.1	46.6	278 22.2	18.1	24 35.3	01.8	80 49.5	21.3	Fomalhaut	15 15.8	S29 29.8
D 11	75 22.3	297 45.7	45.8	293 23.2	17.6	39 37.3	01.9	95 52.0	21.3			
A 12	90 24.8	312 46.3	N17 45.0	308 24.2	N16 17.1	54 39.3	N13 02.0	110 54.5	S10 21.3	Gacrux	171 53.0	S57 14.9
Y 13	105 27.3	327 46.9	44.2	323 25.2	16.6	69 41.3	02.2	125 57.0	21.3	Gienah	175 44.9	S17 40.4
14	120 29.7	342 47.5	43.4	338 26.2	16.1	84 43.3	02.3	140 59.4	21.3	Hadar	148 37.5	S60 29.4
15	135 32.2	357 48.1 ..	42.6	353 27.2 ..	15.7	99 45.3 ..	02.5	156 01.9 ..	21.3	Hamal	327 52.8	N23 34.2
16	150 34.7	12 48.7	41.8	8 28.2	15.2	114 47.3	02.6	171 04.4	21.4	Kaus Aust.	83 33.8	S34 22.4
17	165 37.1	27 49.3	41.0	23 29.2	14.7	129 49.3	02.8	186 06.9	21.4			
18	180 39.6	42 49.9	N17 40.2	38 30.2	N16 14.2	144 51.3	N13 02.9	201 09.4	S10 21.4	Kochab	137 18.9	N74 03.8
19	195 42.1	57 50.5	39.4	53 31.2	13.7	159 53.3	03.1	216 11.8	21.4	Markab	13 31.1	N15 19.7
20	210 44.5	72 51.1	38.6	68 32.2	13.2	174 55.3	03.2	231 14.3	21.4	Menkar	314 07.7	N 4 10.9
21	225 47.0	87 51.7 ..	37.8	83 33.2 ..	12.7	189 57.3 ..	03.4	246 16.8 ..	21.4	Menkent	147 58.9	S36 29.2
22	240 49.4	102 52.3	37.0	98 34.2	12.2	204 59.4	03.5	261 19.3	21.5	Miaplacidus	221 39.2	S69 49.0
23	255 51.9	117 52.9	36.2	113 35.2	11.7	220 01.4	03.7	276 21.8	21.5			
23 00	270 54.4	132 53.5	N17 35.4	128 36.1	N16 11.2	235 03.4	N13 03.8	291 24.2	S10 21.5	Mirfak	308 30.5	N49 56.5
01	285 56.8	147 54.2	34.6	143 37.1	10.8	250 05.4	03.9	306 26.7	21.5	Nunki	75 49.0	S26 16.0
02	300 59.3	162 54.8	33.8	158 38.1	10.3	265 07.4	04.1	321 29.2	21.5	Peacock	53 07.3	S56 39.4
03	316 01.8	177 55.4 ..	33.0	173 39.1 ..	09.8	280 09.4 ..	04.2	336 31.7 ..	21.5	Pollux	243 19.2	N27 58.3
04	331 04.2	192 56.0	32.2	188 40.1	09.3	295 11.4	04.4	351 34.2	21.6	Procyon	244 52.5	N 5 09.9
05	346 06.7	207 56.6	31.4	203 41.1	08.8	310 13.4	04.5	6 36.7	21.6			
06	1 09.2	222 57.3	N17 30.6	218 42.1	N16 08.3	325 15.4	N13 04.7	21 39.1	S10 21.6	Rasalhague	95 59.4	N12 32.6
07	16 11.6	237 57.9	29.8	233 43.1	07.8	340 17.4	04.8	36 41.6	21.6	Regulus	207 36.0	N11 51.3
08	31 14.1	252 58.5	29.0	248 44.1	07.3	355 19.4	05.0	51 44.1	21.6	Rigel	281 05.4	S 8 10.5
F 09	46 16.5	267 59.2 ..	28.2	263 45.1 ..	06.8	10 21.5 ..	05.1	66 46.6 ..	21.6	Rigil Kent.	139 41.7	S60 56.1
R 10	61 19.0	282 59.8	27.4	278 46.1	06.3	25 23.5	05.3	81 49.1	21.7	Sabik	102 03.9	S15 45.2
I 11	76 21.5	298 00.4	26.6	293 47.1	05.8	40 25.5	05.4	96 51.5	21.7			
D 12	91 23.9	313 01.1	N17 25.8	308 48.1	N16 05.3	55 27.5	N13 05.6	111 54.0	S10 21.7	Schedar	349 32.6	N56 39.6
A 13	106 26.4	328 01.7	25.0	323 49.1	04.9	70 29.5	05.7	126 56.5	21.7	Shaula	96 11.7	S37 07.3
Y 14	121 28.9	343 02.3	24.2	338 50.1	04.4	85 31.5	05.8	141 59.0	21.7	Sirius	258 27.7	S16 44.9
15	136 31.3	358 03.0 ..	23.4	353 51.1 ..	03.9	100 33.5 ..	06.0	157 01.5 ..	21.8	Spica	158 23.5	S11 17.0
16	151 33.8	13 03.6	22.6	8 52.1	03.4	115 35.5	06.1	172 04.0	21.8	Suhail	222 47.6	S43 31.7
17	166 36.3	28 04.3	21.8	23 53.1	02.9	130 37.5	06.3	187 06.4	21.8			
18	181 38.7	43 04.9	N17 21.0	38 54.1	N16 02.4	145 39.6	N13 06.4	202 08.9	S10 21.8	Vega	80 33.7	N38 48.2
19	196 41.2	58 05.6	20.2	53 55.1	01.9	160 41.6	06.6	217 11.4	21.8	Zuben'ubi	136 57.2	S16 08.4
20	211 43.7	73 06.2	19.4	68 56.1	01.4	175 43.6	06.7	232 13.9	21.8			
21	226 46.1	88 06.9 ..	18.6	83 57.1 ..	00.9	190 45.6 ..	06.9	247 16.4 ..	21.9		SHA	Mer. Pass.
22	241 48.6	103 07.5	17.8	98 58.1	16 00.4	205 47.6	07.0	262 18.9	21.9	Venus	222 44.1	15 09
23	256 51.0	118 08.2	17.0	113 59.1	N15 59.9	220 49.6	07.1	277 21.4	21.9	Mars	218 17.0	15 26
	h m									Jupiter	324 20.0	8 22
Mer. Pass. 5 59.3		v 0.6	d 0.8	v 1.0	d 0.5	v 2.0	d 0.1	v 2.5	d 0.0	Saturn	20 29.5	4 38

© British Crown Copyright 2022. All rights reserved.

SUN / MOON

UT	SUN GHA	SUN Dec	MOON GHA	v	MOON Dec	d	HP
21	° ′	° ′	° ′	′	° ′	′	′
00	179 34.9	N23 26.2	144 32.1	11.4	N24 53.1	6.7	54.3
01	194 34.8	26.2	159 02.5	11.5	24 46.4	6.8	54.3
02	209 34.7	26.2	173 33.0	11.5	24 39.6	7.0	54.3
03	224 34.5 ..	26.3	188 03.5	11.6	24 32.6	7.1	54.3
04	239 34.4	26.3	202 34.1	11.7	24 25.5	7.1	54.3
05	254 34.3	26.3	217 04.8	11.8	24 18.4	7.3	54.3
W 06	269 34.1	N23 26.3	231 35.6	11.8	N24 11.1	7.4	54.2
E 07	284 34.0	26.3	246 06.4	11.9	24 03.7	7.5	54.2
D 08	299 33.8	26.3	260 37.3	12.0	23 56.2	7.6	54.2
N 09	314 33.7 ..	26.3	275 08.3	12.1	23 48.6	7.7	54.2
E 10	329 33.6	26.3	289 39.4	12.1	23 40.9	7.8	54.2
S 11	344 33.4	26.3	304 10.5	12.2	23 33.1	7.9	54.2
D 12	359 33.3	N23 26.3	318 41.7	12.3	N23 25.2	8.0	54.2
A 13	14 33.2	26.3	333 13.0	12.3	23 17.2	8.1	54.2
Y 14	29 33.0	26.3	347 44.3	12.4	23 09.1	8.2	54.2
15	44 32.9 ..	26.3	2 15.7	12.5	23 00.9	8.4	54.2
16	59 32.8	26.3	16 47.2	12.6	22 52.5	8.4	54.2
17	74 32.6	26.3	31 18.8	12.6	22 44.1	8.5	54.2
18	89 32.5	N23 26.3	45 50.4	12.7	N22 35.6	8.6	54.2
19	104 32.3	26.3	60 22.1	12.8	22 27.0	8.6	54.2
20	119 32.2	26.3	74 53.9	12.9	22 18.4	8.8	54.1
21	134 32.1 ..	26.3	89 25.8	12.9	22 09.6	8.9	54.1
22	149 31.9	26.3	103 57.7	13.0	22 00.7	9.0	54.1
23	164 31.8	26.3	118 29.7	13.1	21 51.7	9.0	54.1
22 00	179 31.7	N23 26.3	133 01.8	13.1	N21 42.7	9.2	54.1
01	194 31.5	26.3	147 33.9	13.2	21 33.5	9.2	54.1
02	209 31.4	26.3	162 06.1	13.3	21 24.3	9.4	54.1
03	224 31.2 ..	26.3	176 38.4	13.4	21 14.9	9.4	54.1
04	239 31.1	26.2	191 10.8	13.4	21 05.5	9.5	54.1
05	254 31.0	26.2	205 43.2	13.5	20 56.0	9.6	54.1
T 06	269 30.8	N23 26.2	220 15.7	13.6	N20 46.4	9.6	54.1
H 07	284 30.7	26.2	234 48.3	13.6	20 36.8	9.8	54.1
U 08	299 30.6	26.2	249 20.9	13.7	20 27.0	9.8	54.1
R 09	314 30.4 ..	26.2	263 53.6	13.8	20 17.2	10.0	54.1
S 10	329 30.3	26.2	278 26.4	13.8	20 07.2	10.0	54.1
D 11	344 30.2	26.2	292 59.2	13.9	19 57.2	10.0	54.1
A 12	359 30.0	N23 26.1	307 32.1	14.0	N19 47.2	10.2	54.1
Y 13	14 29.9	26.1	322 05.1	14.1	19 37.0	10.2	54.1
14	29 29.7	26.1	336 38.2	14.1	19 26.8	10.4	54.1
15	44 29.6 ..	26.1	351 11.3	14.1	19 16.4	10.4	54.1
16	59 29.5	26.1	5 44.4	14.3	19 06.0	10.4	54.1
17	74 29.3	26.1	20 17.7	14.3	18 55.6	10.6	54.1
18	89 29.2	N23 26.0	34 51.0	14.3	N18 45.0	10.6	54.1
19	104 29.1	26.0	49 24.3	14.5	18 34.4	10.7	54.1
20	119 28.9	26.0	63 57.8	14.5	18 23.7	10.8	54.1
21	134 28.8 ..	26.0	78 31.3	14.5	18 12.9	10.8	54.1
22	149 28.7	26.0	93 04.8	14.6	18 02.1	11.0	54.1
23	164 28.5	25.9	107 38.4	14.7	17 51.2	11.0	54.1
23 00	179 28.4	N23 25.9	122 12.1	14.7	N17 40.2	11.1	54.1
01	194 28.2	25.9	136 45.8	14.8	17 29.1	11.1	54.1
02	209 28.1	25.9	151 19.6	14.9	17 18.0	11.2	54.1
03	224 28.0 ..	25.8	165 53.5	14.9	17 06.8	11.2	54.1
04	239 27.8	25.8	180 27.4	14.9	16 55.6	11.3	54.1
05	254 27.7	25.8	195 01.3	15.1	16 44.3	11.4	54.1
F 06	269 27.6	N23 25.8	209 35.4	15.0	N16 32.9	11.5	54.1
R 07	284 27.4	25.7	224 09.4	15.2	16 21.4	11.5	54.1
I 08	299 27.3	25.7	238 43.6	15.2	16 09.9	11.6	54.1
D 09	314 27.2 ..	25.7	253 17.8	15.2	15 58.3	11.6	54.1
A 10	329 27.0	25.6	267 52.0	15.3	15 46.7	11.7	54.1
Y 11	344 26.9	25.6	282 26.3	15.3	15 35.0	11.8	54.1
12	359 26.8	N23 25.6	297 00.6	15.4	N15 23.2	11.8	54.1
13	14 26.6	25.5	311 35.0	15.5	15 11.4	11.9	54.1
14	29 26.5	25.5	326 09.5	15.4	14 59.5	11.9	54.1
15	44 26.3 ..	25.5	340 43.9	15.6	14 47.6	12.0	54.1
16	59 26.2	25.4	355 18.5	15.6	14 35.6	12.1	54.1
17	74 26.1	25.4	9 53.1	15.6	14 23.5	12.1	54.2
18	89 25.9	N23 25.4	24 27.7	15.7	N14 11.4	12.2	54.2
19	104 25.8	25.3	39 02.4	15.7	13 59.2	12.2	54.2
20	119 25.6	25.3	53 37.1	15.8	13 47.0	12.2	54.2
21	134 25.5 ..	25.3	68 11.9	15.8	13 34.8	12.4	54.2
22	149 25.4	25.2	82 46.7	15.8	13 22.4	12.4	54.2
23	164 25.3	25.2	97 21.5	15.9	N13 10.0	12.4	54.2
SD	15.8	d 0.0	SD 14.8		14.7		14.7

Twilight / Moonrise

Lat.	Twilight Naut.	Twilight Civil	Sunrise	Moonrise 21	22	23	24
°	h m	h m	h m	h m	h m	h m	h m
N 72	☐	☐	☐	☐	☐	05 37	08 17
N 70	☐	☐	☐	☐	☐	06 27	08 37
68	☐	☐	☐	☐	04 32	06 58	08 52
66	☐	☐	☐	☐	05 24	07 21	09 04
64	////	////	01 31	03 58	05 56	07 39	09 15
62	////	////	02 09	04 39	06 19	07 54	09 23
60	////	00 49	02 36	05 08	06 38	08 06	09 31
N 58	////	01 41	02 56	05 29	06 53	08 16	09 37
56	////	02 11	03 13	05 47	07 06	08 25	09 43
54	00 45	02 33	03 28	06 02	07 18	08 33	09 48
52	01 32	02 51	03 40	06 15	07 28	08 41	09 52
50	02 00	03 06	03 51	06 26	07 37	08 47	09 57
45	02 46	03 36	04 13	06 50	07 55	09 01	10 05
N 40	03 17	03 59	04 31	07 08	08 11	09 12	10 13
35	03 40	04 17	04 47	07 24	08 23	09 22	10 19
30	03 59	04 32	05 00	07 38	08 35	09 30	10 25
20	04 28	04 57	05 22	08 01	08 54	09 45	10 34
N 10	04 51	05 18	05 41	08 21	09 10	09 57	10 43
0	05 10	05 36	05 58	08 39	09 26	10 09	10 51
S 10	05 27	05 53	06 16	08 58	09 41	10 21	10 58
20	05 43	06 10	06 34	09 17	09 57	10 33	11 07
30	05 59	06 29	06 56	09 40	10 16	10 47	11 16
35	06 08	06 40	07 08	09 53	10 27	10 56	11 22
40	06 18	06 52	07 22	10 08	10 39	11 05	11 28
45	06 28	07 05	07 39	10 27	10 54	11 16	11 35
S 50	06 40	07 21	08 00	10 49	11 11	11 29	11 43
52	06 45	07 29	08 10	11 00	11 20	11 35	11 47
54	06 51	07 37	08 21	11 12	11 29	11 42	11 51
56	06 57	07 46	08 34	11 26	11 39	11 49	11 56
58	07 04	07 56	08 48	11 42	11 51	11 57	12 01
S 60	07 11	08 08	09 06	12 01	12 05	12 07	12 07

Sunset / Twilight / Moonset

Lat.	Sunset	Twilight Civil	Twilight Naut.	Moonset 21	22	23	24
°	h m	h m	h m	h m	h m	h m	h m
N 72	☐	☐	☐	☐	☐	02 40	01 28
N 70	☐	☐	☐	☐	☐	01 48	01 06
68	☐	☐	☐	☐	02 10	01 16	00 49
66	☐	☐	☐	☐	01 17	00 52	00 35
64	22 33	////	////	01 05	00 45	00 33	00 24
62	21 54	////	////	00 23	00 21	00 17	00 14
60	21 28	23 15	////	24 01	00 01	00 04	00 05
N 58	21 07	22 23	////	23 45	23 53	23 58	24 01
56	20 51	21 53	////	23 31	23 43	23 51	23 58
54	20 36	21 31	23 19	23 20	23 34	23 45	23 54
52	20 24	21 13	22 31	23 09	23 26	23 40	23 51
50	20 13	20 58	22 03	23 00	23 19	23 35	23 48
45	19 51	20 28	21 18	22 40	23 04	23 24	23 42
N 40	19 32	20 05	20 47	22 23	22 52	23 16	23 37
35	19 17	19 47	20 24	22 10	22 41	23 08	23 33
30	19 04	19 32	20 05	21 58	22 31	23 01	23 29
20	18 42	19 07	19 36	21 37	22 15	22 49	23 22
N 10	18 23	18 46	19 13	21 19	22 00	22 39	23 16
0	18 06	18 28	18 54	21 02	21 47	22 29	23 10
S 10	17 48	18 11	18 37	20 45	21 33	22 19	23 04
20	17 30	17 54	18 21	20 27	21 19	22 09	22 58
30	17 08	17 35	18 05	20 05	21 02	21 57	22 51
35	16 56	17 24	17 56	19 53	20 52	21 50	22 47
40	16 42	17 12	17 46	19 38	20 40	21 42	22 42
45	16 25	16 59	17 36	19 21	20 27	21 32	22 36
S 50	16 04	16 43	17 24	19 00	20 11	21 21	22 30
52	15 54	16 35	17 19	18 50	20 03	21 15	22 27
54	15 43	16 27	17 13	18 38	19 54	21 09	22 23
56	15 30	16 18	17 07	18 25	19 44	21 03	22 19
58	15 16	16 08	17 00	18 09	19 33	20 55	22 15
S 60	14 58	15 56	16 53	17 50	19 20	20 47	22 10

SUN / MOON

Day	SUN Eqn. of Time 00h	12h	Mer. Pass.	MOON Mer. Pass. Upper	Lower	Age	Phase
d	m s	m s	h m	h m	h m	d	%
21	01 40	01 47	12 02	14 51	02 27	03	10
22	01 53	02 00	12 02	15 36	03 14	04	17
23	02 06	02 13	12 02	16 19	03 58	05	24

© British Crown Copyright 2022. All rights reserved.

2023 JUNE 24, 25, 26 (SAT., SUN., MON.)

UT	ARIES	VENUS −4.6		MARS +1.7		JUPITER −2.2		SATURN +0.7		STARS		
d h	GHA	GHA	Dec	GHA	Dec	GHA	Dec	GHA	Dec	Name	SHA	Dec
24 00	271 53.5	133 08.9	N17 16.2	129 00.1	N15 59.4	235 51.6	N13 07.3	292 23.8	S10 21.9	Acamar	315 13.0	S40 12.5
01	286 56.0	148 09.5	15.4	144 01.1	58.9	250 53.6	07.4	307 26.3	21.9	Achernar	335 21.4	S57 06.8
02	301 58.4	163 10.2	14.6	159 02.1	58.4	265 55.6	07.6	322 28.8	22.0	Acrux	173 01.5	S63 14.0
03	317 00.9	178 10.8 ..	13.8	174 03.1 ..	57.9	280 57.7 ..	07.7	337 31.3 ..	22.0	Adhara	255 07.3	S29 00.2
04	332 03.4	193 11.5	13.0	189 04.1	57.4	295 59.7	07.9	352 33.8	22.0	Aldebaran	290 41.4	N16 33.3
05	347 05.8	208 12.2	12.2	204 05.1	56.9	311 01.7	08.0	7 36.3	22.0			
06	2 08.3	223 12.8	N17 11.4	219 06.1	N15 56.4	326 03.7	N13 08.2	22 38.8	S10 22.0	Alioth	166 14.0	N55 50.3
07	17 10.8	238 13.5	10.6	234 07.1	55.9	341 05.7	08.3	37 41.2	22.0	Alkaid	152 52.8	N49 12.0
S 08	32 13.2	253 14.2	09.8	249 08.1	55.5	356 07.7	08.4	52 43.7	22.1	Alnair	27 34.3	S46 50.7
A 09	47 15.7	268 14.9 ..	09.0	264 09.1 ..	55.0	11 09.7 ..	08.6	67 46.2 ..	22.1	Alnilam	275 39.4	S 1 11.2
T 10	62 18.2	283 15.6	08.1	279 10.1	54.5	26 11.8	08.7	82 48.7	22.1	Alphard	217 49.2	S 8 45.6
U 11	77 20.6	298 16.2	07.3	294 11.1	54.0	41 13.8	08.9	97 51.2	22.1			
R 12	92 23.1	313 16.9	N17 06.5	309 12.1	N15 53.5	56 15.8	N13 09.0	112 53.7	S10 22.1	Alphecca	126 04.5	N26 38.3
D 13	107 25.5	328 17.6	05.7	324 13.1	53.0	71 17.8	09.2	127 56.2	22.2	Alpheratz	357 36.1	N29 13.0
A 14	122 28.0	343 18.3	04.9	339 14.1	52.5	86 19.8	09.3	142 58.6	22.2	Altair	62 00.9	N 8 55.8
Y 15	137 30.5	358 19.0 ..	04.1	354 15.1 ..	52.0	101 21.8 ..	09.4	158 01.1 ..	22.2	Ankaa	353 08.4	S42 10.5
16	152 32.9	13 19.7	03.3	9 16.1	51.5	116 23.8	09.6	173 03.6	22.2	Antares	112 17.1	S26 29.1
17	167 35.4	28 20.4	02.5	24 17.1	51.0	131 25.9	09.7	188 06.1	22.2			
18	182 37.9	43 21.1	N17 01.7	39 18.1	N15 50.5	146 27.9	N13 09.9	203 08.6	S10 22.3	Arcturus	145 48.9	N19 03.7
19	197 40.3	58 21.7	00.9	54 19.1	50.0	161 29.9	10.0	218 11.1	22.3	Atria	107 11.9	S69 04.2
20	212 42.8	73 22.4	17 00.1	69 20.1	49.5	176 31.9	10.2	233 13.6	22.3	Avior	234 15.8	S59 35.2
21	227 45.3	88 23.1	16 59.3	84 21.1 ..	49.0	191 33.9 ..	10.3	248 16.1 ..	22.3	Bellatrix	278 24.6	N 6 22.3
22	242 47.7	103 23.9	58.5	99 22.1	48.5	206 35.9	10.4	263 18.5	22.3	Betelgeuse	270 53.8	N 7 24.7
23	257 50.2	118 24.6	57.7	114 23.1	48.0	221 37.9	10.6	278 21.0	22.4			
25 00	272 52.6	133 25.3	N16 56.9	129 24.1	N15 47.5	236 40.0	N13 10.7	293 23.5	S10 22.4	Canopus	263 53.5	S52 42.4
01	287 55.1	148 26.0	56.0	144 25.1	47.0	251 42.0	10.9	308 26.0	22.4	Capella	280 24.3	N46 01.2
02	302 57.6	163 26.7	55.2	159 26.1	46.5	266 44.0	11.0	323 28.5	22.4	Deneb	49 26.3	N45 21.6
03	318 00.0	178 27.4 ..	54.4	174 27.1 ..	46.0	281 46.0 ..	11.2	338 31.0 ..	22.4	Denebola	182 26.3	N14 26.6
04	333 02.5	193 28.1	53.6	189 28.1	45.5	296 48.0	11.3	353 33.5	22.4	Diphda	348 48.6	S17 51.4
05	348 05.0	208 28.8	52.8	204 29.1	45.0	311 50.0	11.4	8 36.0	22.5			
06	3 07.4	223 29.5	N16 52.0	219 30.1	N15 44.5	326 52.1	N13 11.6	23 38.5	S10 22.5	Dubhe	193 42.8	N61 37.8
07	18 09.9	238 30.3	51.2	234 31.1	44.0	341 54.1	11.7	38 41.0	22.5	Elnath	278 03.9	N28 37.6
S 08	33 12.4	253 31.0	50.4	249 32.1	43.5	356 56.1	11.9	53 43.4	22.5	Eltanin	90 42.2	N51 29.1
U 09	48 14.8	268 31.7 ..	49.6	264 33.1 ..	43.0	11 58.1 ..	12.0	68 45.9 ..	22.6	Enif	33 39.8	N 9 58.9
N 10	63 17.3	283 32.4	48.8	279 34.1	42.5	27 00.1	12.2	83 48.4	22.6	Fomalhaut	15 15.8	S29 29.8
D 11	78 19.8	298 33.2	48.0	294 35.1	42.0	42 02.1	12.3	98 50.9	22.6			
A 12	93 22.2	313 33.9	N16 47.1	309 36.1	N15 41.5	57 04.2	N13 12.4	113 53.4	S10 22.6	Gacrux	171 53.0	S57 14.9
Y 13	108 24.7	328 34.6	46.3	324 37.1	41.0	72 06.2	12.6	128 55.9	22.6	Gienah	175 44.9	S17 40.4
14	123 27.1	343 35.4	45.5	339 38.1	40.5	87 08.2	12.7	143 58.4	22.7	Hadar	148 37.5	S60 29.4
15	138 29.6	358 36.1 ..	44.7	354 39.1 ..	40.0	102 10.2 ..	12.9	159 00.9 ..	22.7	Hamal	327 52.8	N23 34.2
16	153 32.1	13 36.8	43.9	9 40.1	39.5	117 12.2	13.0	174 03.4	22.7	Kaus Aust.	83 33.8	S34 22.4
17	168 34.5	28 37.6	43.1	24 41.1	39.0	132 14.3	13.1	189 05.9	22.7			
18	183 37.0	43 38.3	N16 42.3	39 42.1	N15 38.5	147 16.3	N13 13.3	204 08.4	S10 22.7	Kochab	137 19.0	N74 03.8
19	198 39.5	58 39.1	41.5	54 43.1	38.0	162 18.3	13.4	219 10.8	22.8	Markab	13 31.1	N15 19.8
20	213 41.9	73 39.8	40.7	69 44.1	37.5	177 20.3	13.6	234 13.3	22.8	Menkar	314 07.7	N 4 10.9
21	228 44.4	88 40.5 ..	39.9	84 45.1 ..	37.0	192 22.3 ..	13.7	249 15.8 ..	22.8	Menkent	147 58.9	S36 29.2
22	243 46.9	103 41.3	39.0	99 46.1	36.5	207 24.4	13.9	264 18.3	22.8	Miaplacidus	221 39.2	S69 48.9
23	258 49.3	118 42.0	38.2	114 47.1	36.0	222 26.4	14.0	279 20.8	22.8			
26 00	273 51.8	133 42.8	N16 37.4	129 48.1	N15 35.5	237 28.4	N13 14.1	294 23.3	S10 22.9	Mirfak	308 30.5	N49 56.5
01	288 54.2	148 43.5	36.6	144 49.1	35.0	252 30.4	14.3	309 25.8	22.9	Nunki	75 49.0	S26 16.0
02	303 56.7	163 44.3	35.8	159 50.2	34.5	267 32.4	14.4	324 28.3	22.9	Peacock	53 07.2	S56 39.4
03	318 59.2	178 45.1 ..	35.0	174 51.2 ..	34.0	282 34.5 ..	14.6	339 30.8 ..	22.9	Pollux	243 19.2	N27 58.3
04	334 01.6	193 45.8	34.2	189 52.2	33.5	297 36.5	14.7	354 33.3	22.9	Procyon	244 52.5	N 5 09.9
05	349 04.1	208 46.6	33.4	204 53.2	32.9	312 38.5	14.8	9 35.8	23.0			
06	4 06.6	223 47.4	N16 32.6	219 54.2	N15 32.4	327 40.5	N13 15.0	24 38.3	S10 23.0	Rasalhague	95 59.4	N12 32.6
07	19 09.0	238 48.1	31.7	234 55.2	31.9	342 42.5	15.1	39 40.8	23.0	Regulus	207 36.0	N11 51.3
08	34 11.5	253 48.9	30.9	249 56.2	31.4	357 44.6	15.3	54 43.3	23.0	Rigel	281 05.4	S 8 10.4
M 09	49 14.0	268 49.7 ..	30.1	264 57.2 ..	30.9	12 46.6 ..	15.4	69 45.7 ..	23.1	Rigil Kent.	139 41.7	S60 56.1
O 10	64 16.4	283 50.4	29.3	279 58.2	30.4	27 48.6	15.5	84 48.2	23.1	Sabik	102 03.9	S15 45.2
N 11	79 18.9	298 51.2	28.5	294 59.2	29.9	42 50.6	15.7	99 50.7	23.1			
D 12	94 21.4	313 52.0	N16 27.7	310 00.2	N15 29.4	57 52.6	N13 15.8	114 53.2	S10 23.1	Schedar	349 32.6	N56 39.6
A 13	109 23.8	328 52.8	26.9	325 01.2	28.9	72 54.7	16.0	129 55.7	23.1	Shaula	96 11.7	S37 07.3
Y 14	124 26.3	343 53.6	26.1	340 02.2	28.4	87 56.7	16.1	144 58.2	23.2	Sirius	258 27.7	S16 44.9
15	139 28.7	358 54.3 ..	25.2	355 03.2 ..	27.9	102 58.7 ..	16.2	160 00.7 ..	23.2	Spica	158 23.6	S11 17.0
16	154 31.2	13 55.1	24.4	10 04.2	27.4	118 00.7	16.4	175 03.2	23.2	Suhail	222 47.6	S43 31.7
17	169 33.7	28 55.9	23.6	25 05.2	26.9	133 02.7	16.5	190 05.7	23.2			
18	184 36.1	43 56.7	N16 22.8	40 06.2	N15 26.4	148 04.8	N13 16.7	205 08.2	S10 23.3	Vega	80 33.7	N38 48.3
19	199 38.6	58 57.5	22.0	55 07.2	25.9	163 06.8	16.8	220 10.7	23.3	Zuben'ubi	136 57.2	S16 08.4
20	214 41.1	73 58.3	21.2	70 08.2	25.4	178 08.8	16.9	235 13.2	23.3		SHA	Mer. Pass.
21	229 43.5	88 59.1 ..	20.4	85 09.2 ..	24.9	193 10.8 ..	17.1	250 15.7 ..	23.3		° ′	h m
22	244 46.0	103 59.9	19.6	100 10.2	24.4	208 12.9	17.2	265 18.2	23.3	Venus	220 32.6	15 06
23	259 48.5	119 00.7	18.7	115 11.2	23.9	223 14.9	17.4	280 20.7	23.4	Mars	216 31.5	15 21
	h m									Jupiter	323 47.3	8 12
Mer. Pass. 5 47.5		v 0.7 d 0.8		v 1.0 d 0.5		v 2.0 d 0.1		v 2.5 d 0.0		Saturn	20 30.9	4 26

© British Crown Copyright 2022. All rights reserved.

SUN / MOON

UT	SUN GHA	SUN Dec	MOON GHA	v	MOON Dec	d	HP
d h	° ′	° ′	° ′	′	° ′	′	′
24 00	179 25.1	N23 25.1	111 56.4	15.9	N12 57.6	12.5	54.2
01	194 25.0	25.1	126 31.3	16.0	12 45.1	12.5	54.2
02	209 24.9	25.1	141 06.3	16.0	12 32.6	12.6	54.2
03	224 24.7	.. 25.0	155 41.3	16.1	12 20.0	12.6	54.2
04	239 24.6	25.0	170 16.4	16.1	12 07.4	12.7	54.2
05	254 24.5	24.9	184 51.5	16.1	11 54.7	12.7	54.2
S 06	269 24.3	N23 24.9	199 26.6	16.1	N11 42.0	12.8	54.3
A 07	284 24.2	24.8	214 01.7	16.2	11 29.2	12.8	54.3
T 08	299 24.1	24.8	228 36.9	16.2	11 16.4	12.9	54.3
U 09	314 23.9	.. 24.7	243 12.1	16.3	11 03.5	12.9	54.3
R 10	329 23.8	24.7	257 47.4	16.2	10 50.6	13.0	54.3
D 11	344 23.7	24.6	272 22.6	16.4	10 37.6	13.0	54.3
A 12	359 23.5	N23 24.6	286 58.0	16.3	N10 24.6	13.0	54.3
Y 13	14 23.4	24.5	301 33.3	16.4	10 11.6	13.1	54.3
14	29 23.2	24.5	316 08.7	16.3	9 58.5	13.1	54.3
15	44 23.1	.. 24.4	330 44.0	16.5	9 45.4	13.2	54.3
16	59 23.0	24.4	345 19.5	16.4	9 32.2	13.2	54.4
17	74 22.8	24.3	359 54.9	16.5	9 19.0	13.3	54.4
18	89 22.7	N23 24.3	14 30.4	16.4	N 9 05.7	13.3	54.4
19	104 22.6	24.2	29 05.8	16.5	8 52.4	13.3	54.4
20	119 22.4	24.2	43 41.3	16.6	8 39.1	13.3	54.4
21	134 22.3	.. 24.1	58 16.9	16.5	8 25.8	13.4	54.4
22	149 22.2	24.1	72 52.4	16.6	8 12.4	13.5	54.4
23	164 22.0	24.0	87 28.0	16.5	7 58.9	13.5	54.5
25 00	179 21.9	N23 24.0	102 03.5	16.6	N 7 45.4	13.5	54.5
01	194 21.8	23.9	116 39.1	16.6	7 31.9	13.5	54.5
02	209 21.6	23.8	131 14.7	16.7	7 18.4	13.6	54.5
03	224 21.5	.. 23.8	145 50.4	16.6	7 04.8	13.6	54.5
04	239 21.4	23.7	160 26.0	16.6	6 51.2	13.6	54.5
05	254 21.2	23.7	175 01.6	16.7	6 37.6	13.7	54.5
S 06	269 21.1	N23 23.6	189 37.3	16.7	N 6 23.9	13.7	54.6
U 07	284 21.0	23.5	204 13.0	16.7	6 10.2	13.7	54.6
N 08	299 20.8	23.5	218 48.6	16.7	5 56.5	13.8	54.6
D 09	314 20.7	.. 23.4	233 24.3	16.7	5 42.7	13.8	54.6
A 10	329 20.6	23.3	248 00.0	16.7	5 28.9	13.8	54.6
Y 11	344 20.4	23.3	262 35.7	16.7	5 15.1	13.8	54.6
12	359 20.3	N23 23.2	277 11.4	16.7	N 5 01.3	13.9	54.7
13	14 20.2	23.1	291 47.1	16.7	4 47.4	13.9	54.7
14	29 20.0	23.1	306 22.8	16.6	4 33.5	13.9	54.7
15	44 19.9	.. 23.0	320 58.4	16.7	4 19.6	14.0	54.7
16	59 19.8	22.9	335 34.1	16.7	4 05.6	14.0	54.7
17	74 19.6	22.9	350 09.8	16.7	3 51.6	14.0	54.8
18	89 19.5	N23 22.8	4 45.5	16.7	N 3 37.6	14.0	54.8
19	104 19.4	22.7	19 21.2	16.7	3 23.6	14.0	54.8
20	119 19.2	22.6	33 56.9	16.6	3 09.6	14.1	54.8
21	134 19.1	.. 22.6	48 32.5	16.7	2 55.5	14.1	54.8
22	149 19.0	22.5	63 08.2	16.6	2 41.4	14.1	54.9
23	164 18.8	22.4	77 43.8	16.7	2 27.3	14.1	54.9
26 00	179 18.7	N23 22.3	92 19.5	16.6	N 2 13.2	14.1	54.9
01	194 18.6	22.3	106 55.1	16.6	1 59.1	14.2	54.9
02	209 18.4	22.2	121 30.7	16.6	1 44.9	14.2	54.9
03	224 18.3	.. 22.1	136 06.3	16.6	1 30.7	14.2	55.0
04	239 18.2	22.0	150 41.9	16.6	1 16.5	14.2	55.0
05	254 18.1	22.0	165 17.5	16.5	1 02.3	14.2	55.0
M 06	269 17.9	N23 21.9	179 53.0	16.5	N 0 48.1	14.3	55.0
O 07	284 17.8	21.8	194 28.5	16.5	0 33.8	14.2	55.1
N 08	299 17.7	21.7	209 04.0	16.5	N 0 19.6	14.3	55.1
D 09	314 17.5	.. 21.6	223 39.5	16.5	N 0 05.3	14.3	55.1
A 10	329 17.4	21.6	238 15.0	16.4	S 0 09.0	14.3	55.1
Y 11	344 17.3	21.5	252 50.4	16.4	0 23.3	14.3	55.2
12	359 17.1	N23 21.4	267 25.8	16.4	S 0 37.6	14.3	55.2
13	14 17.0	21.3	282 01.2	16.4	0 51.9	14.4	55.2
14	29 16.9	21.2	296 36.6	16.3	1 06.3	14.3	55.2
15	44 16.7	.. 21.1	311 11.9	16.3	1 20.6	14.3	55.3
16	59 16.6	21.1	325 47.2	16.3	1 34.9	14.4	55.3
17	74 16.5	21.0	340 22.5	16.2	1 49.3	14.3	55.3
18	89 16.3	N23 20.9	354 57.7	16.2	S 2 03.6	14.4	55.3
19	104 16.2	20.8	9 32.9	16.2	2 18.0	14.4	55.4
20	119 16.1	20.7	24 08.1	16.1	2 32.4	14.3	55.4
21	134 16.0	.. 20.6	38 43.2	16.1	2 46.8	14.3	55.4
22	149 15.8	20.5	53 18.3	16.0	3 01.1	14.4	55.4
23	164 15.7	20.4	67 53.3	16.0	S 3 15.5	14.4	55.5
SD	15.8	d 0.1	SD 14.8		14.9		15.0

Twilight / Sunrise / Moonrise

Lat.	Naut.	Civil	Sunrise	Moonrise 24	25	26	27
°	h m	h m	h m	h m	h m	h m	h m
N 72	□	□	□	08 17	10 22	12 21	14 24
N 70	□	□	□	08 37	10 30	12 20	14 13
68	□	□	□	08 52	10 37	12 19	14 05
66	□	□	□	09 04	10 42	12 18	13 57
64	////	////	01 33	09 15	10 46	12 17	13 51
62	////	////	02 11	09 23	10 50	12 17	13 46
60	////	00 52	02 37	09 31	10 53	12 16	13 42
N 58	////	01 42	02 58	09 37	10 56	12 16	13 38
56	////	02 12	03 14	09 43	10 59	12 16	13 34
54	00 47	02 34	03 29	09 48	11 01	12 15	13 31
52	01 34	02 52	03 41	09 52	11 03	12 15	13 28
50	02 02	03 07	03 52	09 57	11 05	12 15	13 26
45	02 47	03 37	04 14	10 05	11 09	12 14	13 20
N 40	03 18	03 59	04 32	10 13	11 13	12 13	13 16
35	03 41	04 18	04 47	10 19	11 16	12 13	13 12
30	04 00	04 33	05 00	10 25	11 19	12 13	13 08
20	04 29	04 58	05 22	10 34	11 23	12 12	13 02
N 10	04 51	05 18	05 41	10 43	11 27	12 11	12 57
0	05 10	05 36	05 59	10 51	11 31	12 11	12 52
S 10	05 27	05 54	06 16	10 58	11 35	12 11	12 48
20	05 43	06 11	06 35	11 07	11 39	12 10	12 42
30	06 00	06 30	06 56	11 16	11 43	12 09	12 37
35	06 09	06 40	07 08	11 22	11 46	12 09	12 34
40	06 18	06 52	07 23	11 28	11 48	12 09	12 30
45	06 28	07 06	07 39	11 35	11 52	12 08	12 26
S 50	06 40	07 22	08 00	11 43	11 56	12 08	12 21
52	06 45	07 29	08 10	11 47	11 58	12 08	12 18
54	06 51	07 37	08 21	11 51	12 00	12 08	12 13
56	06 57	07 46	08 34	11 56	12 02	12 07	12 13
58	07 04	07 57	08 49	12 01	12 04	12 07	12 10
S 60	07 12	08 08	09 06	12 07	12 07	12 07	12 07

Sunset / Twilight / Moonset

Lat.	Sunset	Civil	Naut.	Moonset 24	25	26	27
°	h m	h m	h m	h m	h m	h m	h m
N 72	□	□	□	01 28	00 48	(00 11 / 23 46)	23 11
N 70	□	□	□	01 06	00 38	(00 14 / 23 50)	23 24
68	□	□	□	00 49	00 29	(00 12 / 23 58)	23 35
66	□	□	□	00 35	00 22	(23 52 / 23 58)	23 44
64	22 32	////	////	00 24	00 16	00 08	(00 00)
62	21 54	////	////	00 14	00 10	00 07	(23 59)
60	21 28	23 13	////	00 05	00 06	00 05	00 05
N 58	21 07	22 23	////	24 01	23 58	00 04	00 07
56	20 51	21 53	////	23 58	24 03	00 03	00 09
54	20 37	21 31	23 17	23 54	24 02	00 02	00 10
52	20 24	21 13	22 31	23 51	24 01	00 01	00 12
50	20 13	20 58	22 03	23 48	24 01	00 01	00 13
45	19 51	20 28	21 18	23 42	23 59	24 16	00 16
N 40	19 33	20 06	20 47	23 37	23 58	24 18	00 18
35	19 18	19 48	20 24	23 33	23 56	24 20	00 20
30	19 05	19 32	20 06	23 29	23 55	24 22	00 22
20	18 43	19 07	19 37	23 22	23 53	24 25	00 25
N 10	18 24	18 47	19 14	23 16	23 52	24 28	00 28
0	18 06	18 29	18 55	23 10	23 50	24 31	00 31
S 10	17 49	18 12	18 38	23 04	23 48	24 33	00 33
20	17 30	17 54	18 22	22 58	23 47	24 36	00 36
30	17 09	17 36	18 05	22 51	23 45	24 39	00 39
35	16 57	17 25	17 57	22 47	23 43	24 41	00 41
40	16 43	17 13	17 47	22 42	23 42	24 43	00 43
45	16 26	17 00	17 37	22 36	23 40	24 46	00 46
S 50	16 05	16 44	17 25	22 30	23 39	24 48	00 48
52	15 55	16 36	17 20	22 27	23 38	24 50	00 50
54	15 44	16 28	17 14	22 23	23 37	24 51	00 51
56	15 32	16 20	17 08	22 19	23 36	24 53	00 53
58	15 17	16 09	17 01	22 15	23 34	24 55	00 55
S 60	14 59	15 57	16 54	22 10	23 33	24 57	00 57

SUN / MOON

Day	Eqn. of Time 00h	Eqn. of Time 12h	Mer. Pass.	Mer. Pass. Upper	Mer. Pass. Lower	Age	Phase
d	m s	m s	h m	h m	h m	d	%
24	02 19	02 26	12 02	17 00	04 40	06	33
25	02 32	02 39	12 03	17 40	05 20	07	42
26	02 45	02 51	12 03	18 21	06 00	08	52

© British Crown Copyright 2022. All rights reserved.

UT	ARIES GHA	VENUS −4.6 GHA	Dec	MARS +1.7 GHA	Dec	JUPITER −2.2 GHA	Dec	SATURN +0.7 GHA	Dec	STARS Name	SHA	Dec
27 00	274 50.9	134 01.5	N16 17.9	130 12.2	N15 23.3	238 16.9	N13 17.5	295 23.2	S10 23.4	Acamar	315 13.0	S40 12.5
01	289 53.4	149 02.3	17.1	145 13.2	22.8	253 18.9	17.6	310 25.7	23.4	Achernar	335 21.3	S57 06.8
02	304 55.9	164 03.1	16.3	160 14.2	22.3	268 21.0	17.8	325 28.2	23.4	Acrux	173 01.5	S63 14.0
03	319 58.3	179 03.9 ..	15.5	175 15.2 ..	21.8	283 23.0 ..	17.9	340 30.7 ..	23.5	Adhara	255 07.3	S29 00.2
04	335 00.8	194 04.7	14.7	190 16.2	21.3	298 25.0	18.1	355 33.2	23.5	Aldebaran	290 41.4	N16 33.3
05	350 03.2	209 05.5	13.9	205 17.2	20.8	313 27.0	18.2	10 35.7	23.5			
06	5 05.7	224 06.4	N16 13.0	220 18.2	N15 20.3	328 29.1	N13 18.3	25 38.2	S10 23.5	Alioth	166 14.0	N55 50.3
07	20 08.2	239 07.2	12.2	235 19.2	19.8	343 31.1	18.5	40 40.7	23.6	Alkaid	152 52.8	N49 12.0
T 08	35 10.6	254 08.0	11.4	250 20.2	19.3	358 33.1	18.6	55 43.2	23.6	Alnair	27 34.2	S46 50.7
U 09	50 13.1	269 08.8 ..	10.6	265 21.2 ..	18.8	13 35.1 ..	18.7	70 45.7 ..	23.6	Alnilam	275 39.4	S 1 11.2
E 10	65 15.6	284 09.6	09.8	280 22.2	18.3	28 37.2	18.9	85 48.1	23.6	Alphard	217 49.3	S 8 45.6
S 11	80 18.0	299 10.5	09.0	295 23.2	17.8	43 39.2	19.0	100 50.6	23.6			
D 12	95 20.5	314 11.3	N16 08.2	310 24.2	N15 17.2	58 41.2	N13 19.2	115 53.1	S10 23.7	Alphecca	126 04.5	N26 38.3
A 13	110 23.0	329 12.1	07.3	325 25.2	16.7	73 43.2	19.3	130 55.6	23.7	Alpheratz	357 36.1	N29 13.0
Y 14	125 25.4	344 13.0	06.5	340 26.2	16.2	88 45.3	19.4	145 58.1	23.7	Altair	62 00.9	N 8 55.8
15	140 27.9	359 13.8 ..	05.7	355 27.2 ..	15.7	103 47.3 ..	19.6	161 00.6 ..	23.7	Ankaa	353 08.4	S42 10.5
16	155 30.3	14 14.6	04.9	10 28.3	15.2	118 49.3	19.7	176 03.1	23.8	Antares	112 17.1	S26 29.1
17	170 32.8	29 15.5	04.1	25 29.3	14.7	133 51.3	19.8	191 05.6	23.8			
18	185 35.3	44 16.3	N16 03.3	40 30.3	N15 14.2	148 53.4	N13 20.0	206 08.1	S10 23.8	Arcturus	145 48.9	N19 03.8
19	200 37.7	59 17.1	02.5	55 31.3	13.7	163 55.4	20.1	221 10.6	23.8	Atria	107 11.9	S69 04.3
20	215 40.2	74 18.0	01.6	70 32.3	13.2	178 57.4	20.3	236 13.1	23.9	Avior	234 15.8	S59 35.1
21	230 42.7	89 18.8 ..	00.8	85 33.3 ..	12.7	193 59.4 ..	20.4	251 15.6 ..	23.9	Bellatrix	278 24.6	N 6 22.3
22	245 45.1	104 19.7	16 00.0	100 34.3	12.1	209 01.5	20.5	266 18.1	23.9	Betelgeuse	270 53.8	N 7 24.7
23	260 47.6	119 20.5	15 59.2	115 35.3	11.6	224 03.5	20.7	281 20.6	23.9			
28 00	275 50.1	134 21.4	N15 58.4	130 36.3	N15 11.1	239 05.5	N13 20.8	296 23.1	S10 24.0	Canopus	263 53.5	S52 42.4
01	290 52.5	149 22.2	57.6	145 37.3	10.6	254 07.5	21.0	311 25.6	24.0	Capella	280 24.3	N46 01.2
02	305 55.0	164 23.1	56.8	160 38.3	10.1	269 09.6	21.1	326 28.1	24.0	Deneb	49 26.3	N45 21.7
03	320 57.5	179 24.0 ..	55.9	175 39.3 ..	09.6	284 11.6 ..	21.2	341 30.6 ..	24.0	Denebola	182 26.3	N14 26.6
04	335 59.9	194 24.8	55.1	190 40.3	09.1	299 13.6	21.4	356 33.1	24.0	Diphda	348 48.6	S17 51.4
05	351 02.4	209 25.7	54.3	205 41.3	08.6	314 15.7	21.5	11 35.6	24.1			
06	6 04.8	224 26.5	N15 53.5	220 42.3	N15 08.1	329 17.7	N13 21.6	26 38.1	S10 24.1	Dubhe	193 42.8	N61 37.8
W 07	21 07.3	239 27.4	52.7	235 43.3	07.5	344 19.7	21.8	41 40.6	24.1	Elnath	278 03.9	N28 37.6
E 08	36 09.8	254 28.3	51.9	250 44.3	07.0	359 21.7	21.9	56 43.1	24.1	Eltanin	90 42.2	N51 29.1
D 09	51 12.2	269 29.2 ..	51.0	265 45.3 ..	06.5	14 23.8 ..	22.0	71 45.6 ..	24.2	Enif	33 39.8	N 9 58.9
N 10	66 14.7	284 30.0	50.2	280 46.3	06.0	29 25.8	22.2	86 48.1	24.2	Fomalhaut	15 15.8	S29 29.8
E 11	81 17.2	299 30.9	49.4	295 47.3	05.5	44 27.8	22.3	101 50.7	24.2			
S 12	96 19.6	314 31.8	N15 48.6	310 48.3	N15 05.0	59 29.9	N13 22.5	116 53.2	S10 24.2	Gacrux	171 53.1	S57 14.9
D 13	111 22.1	329 32.7	47.8	325 49.3	04.5	74 31.9	22.6	131 55.7	24.3	Gienah	175 44.9	S17 40.4
A 14	126 24.6	344 33.6	47.0	340 50.3	04.0	89 33.9	22.7	146 58.2	24.3	Hadar	148 37.5	S60 29.4
Y 15	141 27.0	359 34.4 ..	46.2	355 51.3 ..	03.4	104 35.9 ..	22.9	162 00.7 ..	24.3	Hamal	327 52.8	N23 34.3
16	156 29.5	14 35.3	45.3	10 52.3	02.9	119 38.0	23.0	177 03.2	24.3	Kaus Aust.	83 33.8	S34 22.4
17	171 32.0	29 36.2	44.5	25 53.4	02.4	134 40.0	23.1	192 05.7	24.4			
18	186 34.4	44 37.1	N15 43.7	40 54.4	N15 01.9	149 42.0	N13 23.3	207 08.2	S10 24.4	Kochab	137 19.0	N74 03.8
19	201 36.9	59 38.0	42.9	55 55.4	01.4	164 44.1	23.4	222 10.7	24.4	Markab	13 31.1	N15 19.8
20	216 39.3	74 38.9	42.1	70 56.4	00.9	179 46.1	23.5	237 13.2	24.4	Menkar	314 07.7	N 4 10.9
21	231 41.8	89 39.8 ..	41.3	85 57.4	15 00.4	194 48.1 ..	23.7	252 15.7 ..	24.5	Menkent	147 59.0	S36 29.2
22	246 44.3	104 40.7	40.5	100 58.4	14 59.8	209 50.2	23.8	267 18.2	24.5	Miaplacidus	221 39.3	S69 48.9
23	261 46.7	119 41.6	39.6	115 59.4	59.3	224 52.2	24.0	282 20.7	24.5			
29 00	276 49.2	134 42.5	N15 38.8	131 00.4	N14 58.8	239 54.2	N13 24.1	297 23.2	S10 24.5	Mirfak	308 30.5	N49 56.5
01	291 51.7	149 43.4	38.0	146 01.4	58.3	254 56.2	24.2	312 25.7	24.6	Nunki	75 49.0	S26 16.0
02	306 54.1	164 44.3	37.2	161 02.4	57.8	269 58.3	24.4	327 28.2	24.6	Peacock	53 07.2	S56 39.4
03	321 56.6	179 45.2 ..	36.4	176 03.4 ..	57.3	285 00.3 ..	24.5	342 30.7 ..	24.6	Pollux	243 19.2	N27 58.3
04	336 59.1	194 46.1	35.6	191 04.4	56.7	300 02.3	24.6	357 33.2	24.7	Procyon	244 52.5	N 5 09.9
05	352 01.5	209 47.1	34.7	206 05.4	56.2	315 04.4	24.8	12 35.7	24.7			
06	7 04.0	224 48.0	N15 33.9	221 06.4	N14 55.7	330 06.4	N13 24.9	27 38.2	S10 24.7	Rasalhague	95 59.4	N12 32.6
07	22 06.4	239 48.9	33.1	236 07.4	55.2	345 08.4	25.0	42 40.7	24.7	Regulus	207 36.0	N11 51.3
T 08	37 08.9	254 49.8	32.3	251 08.4	54.7	0 10.5	25.2	57 43.2	24.8	Rigel	281 05.4	S 8 10.4
H 09	52 11.4	269 50.7 ..	31.5	266 09.4 ..	54.2	15 12.5 ..	25.3	72 45.7 ..	24.8	Rigil Kent.	139 41.7	S60 56.1
U 10	67 13.8	284 51.7	30.7	281 10.4	53.7	30 14.5	25.4	87 48.2	24.8	Sabik	102 03.9	S15 45.2
R 11	82 16.3	299 52.6	29.8	296 11.4	53.1	45 16.6	25.6	102 50.7	24.8			
S 12	97 18.8	314 53.5	N15 29.0	311 12.4	N14 52.6	60 18.6	N13 25.7	117 53.3	S10 24.9	Schedar	349 32.6	N56 39.6
D 13	112 21.2	329 54.5	28.2	326 13.5	52.1	75 20.6	25.8	132 55.8	24.9	Shaula	96 11.7	S37 07.3
A 14	127 23.7	344 55.4	27.4	341 14.5	51.6	90 22.7	26.0	147 58.3	24.9	Sirius	258 27.7	S16 44.9
Y 15	142 26.2	359 56.3 ..	26.6	356 15.5 ..	51.1	105 24.7 ..	26.1	163 00.8 ..	24.9	Spica	158 23.6	S11 17.0
16	157 28.6	14 57.3	25.8	11 16.5	50.5	120 26.7	26.3	178 03.3	25.0	Suhail	222 47.6	S43 31.7
17	172 31.1	29 58.2	25.0	26 17.5	50.0	135 28.8	26.4	193 05.8	25.0			
18	187 33.6	44 59.2	N15 24.1	41 18.5	N14 49.5	150 30.8	N13 26.5	208 08.3	S10 25.0	Vega	80 33.7	N38 48.3
19	202 36.0	60 00.1	23.3	56 19.5	49.0	165 32.8	26.7	223 10.8	25.0	Zuben'ubi	136 57.2	S16 08.4
20	217 38.5	75 01.0	22.5	71 20.5	48.5	180 34.9	26.8	238 13.3	25.1		SHA	Mer. Pass.
21	232 40.9	90 02.0 ..	21.7	86 21.5 ..	48.0	195 36.9 ..	26.9	253 15.8 ..	25.1			
22	247 43.4	105 03.0	20.9	101 22.5	47.4	210 38.9	27.1	268 18.3	25.1	Venus	218 31.3	15 02
23	262 45.9	120 03.9	20.1	116 23.5	46.9	225 41.0	27.2	283 20.8	25.2	Mars	214 46.2	15 17
	h m									Jupiter	323 15.5	8 03
Mer. Pass. 5 35.7	v 0.9 d 0.8	v 1.0 d 0.5		v 2.0 d 0.1		v 2.5 d 0.0				Saturn	20 33.1	4 14

© British Crown Copyright 2022. All rights reserved.

UT	SUN GHA	SUN Dec	MOON GHA	v	MOON Dec	d	HP
d h	° ′	° ′	° ′	′	° ′	′	′
27 00	179 15.6	N23 20.3	82 28.3	16.0	S 3 29.9	14.4	55.5
01	194 15.4	20.2	97 03.3	15.9	3 44.3	14.4	55.5
02	209 15.3	20.2	111 38.2	15.9	3 58.7	14.4	55.5
03	224 15.2	.. 20.1	126 13.1	15.8	4 13.1	14.4	55.6
04	239 15.0	20.0	140 47.9	15.8	4 27.5	14.3	55.6
05	254 14.9	19.9	155 22.7	15.7	4 41.8	14.4	55.6
06	269 14.8	N23 19.8	169 57.4	15.7	S 4 56.2	14.4	55.7
07	284 14.6	19.7	184 32.1	15.6	5 10.6	14.4	55.7
08	299 14.5	19.6	199 06.7	15.6	5 25.0	14.3	55.7
09	314 14.4	.. 19.5	213 41.3	15.5	5 39.3	14.4	55.8
10	329 14.3	19.4	228 15.8	15.5	5 53.7	14.4	55.8
11	344 14.1	19.3	242 50.3	15.4	6 08.1	14.3	55.8
12	359 14.0	N23 19.2	257 24.7	15.4	S 6 22.4	14.3	55.8
13	14 13.9	19.1	271 59.1	15.2	6 36.7	14.3	55.9
14	29 13.7	19.0	286 33.3	15.3	6 51.1	14.3	55.9
15	44 13.6	.. 18.9	301 07.6	15.1	7 05.4	14.3	55.9
16	59 13.5	18.8	315 41.7	15.2	7 19.7	14.3	56.0
17	74 13.4	18.7	330 15.9	15.0	7 34.0	14.3	56.0
18	89 13.2	N23 18.6	344 49.9	15.0	S 7 48.3	14.2	56.0
19	104 13.1	18.5	359 23.9	14.9	8 02.5	14.3	56.1
20	119 13.0	18.3	13 57.8	14.8	8 16.8	14.2	56.1
21	134 12.8	.. 18.2	28 31.6	14.8	8 31.0	14.2	56.1
22	149 12.7	18.1	43 05.4	14.7	8 45.2	14.2	56.2
23	164 12.6	18.0	57 39.1	14.6	8 59.4	14.2	56.2
28 00	179 12.4	N23 17.9	72 12.7	14.6	S 9 13.6	14.1	56.2
01	194 12.3	17.8	86 46.3	14.4	9 27.7	14.2	56.3
02	209 12.2	17.7	101 19.7	14.4	9 41.9	14.1	56.3
03	224 12.1	.. 17.6	115 53.1	14.3	9 56.0	14.0	56.3
04	239 11.9	17.5	130 26.4	14.3	10 10.0	14.1	56.4
05	254 11.8	17.4	144 59.7	14.1	10 24.1	14.0	56.4
06	269 11.7	N23 17.2	159 32.8	14.1	S10 38.1	14.0	56.4
07	284 11.6	17.1	174 05.9	14.0	10 52.1	14.0	56.5
08	299 11.4	17.0	188 38.9	13.9	11 06.1	14.0	56.5
09	314 11.3	.. 16.9	203 11.8	13.8	11 20.1	13.9	56.5
10	329 11.2	16.8	217 44.6	13.8	11 34.0	13.8	56.6
11	344 11.0	16.7	232 17.4	13.6	11 47.8	13.9	56.6
12	359 10.9	N23 16.5	246 50.0	13.5	S12 01.7	13.8	56.6
13	14 10.8	16.4	261 22.5	13.5	12 15.5	13.8	56.7
14	29 10.7	16.3	275 55.0	13.4	12 29.3	13.7	56.7
15	44 10.5	.. 16.2	290 27.4	13.2	12 43.0	13.7	56.8
16	59 10.4	16.1	304 59.6	13.2	12 56.7	13.7	56.8
17	74 10.3	15.9	319 31.8	13.1	13 10.4	13.6	56.8
18	89 10.1	N23 15.8	334 03.9	13.0	S13 24.0	13.6	56.9
19	104 10.0	15.7	348 35.9	12.9	13 37.6	13.5	56.9
20	119 09.9	15.6	3 07.8	12.7	13 51.1	13.5	56.9
21	134 09.8	.. 15.5	17 39.5	12.7	14 04.6	13.4	57.0
22	149 09.6	15.3	32 11.2	12.6	14 18.0	13.4	57.0
23	164 09.5	15.2	46 42.8	12.5	14 31.4	13.3	57.0
29 00	179 09.4	N23 15.1	61 14.3	12.3	S14 44.8	13.2	57.1
01	194 09.3	15.0	75 45.6	12.3	14 58.0	13.3	57.1
02	209 09.1	14.8	90 16.9	12.1	15 11.3	13.2	57.2
03	224 09.0	.. 14.7	104 48.0	12.1	15 24.5	13.1	57.2
04	239 08.9	14.6	119 19.1	11.9	15 37.6	13.1	57.2
05	254 08.8	14.4	133 50.0	11.8	15 50.7	13.0	57.3
06	269 08.6	N23 14.3	148 20.8	11.7	S16 03.7	12.9	57.3
07	284 08.5	14.2	162 51.5	11.6	16 16.6	12.9	57.3
08	299 08.4	14.0	177 22.1	11.5	16 29.5	12.9	57.4
09	314 08.3	.. 13.9	191 52.6	11.4	16 42.4	12.7	57.4
10	329 08.1	13.8	206 23.0	11.2	16 55.1	12.7	57.5
11	344 08.0	13.6	220 53.2	11.1	17 07.8	12.7	57.5
12	359 07.9	N23 13.5	235 23.3	11.0	S17 20.5	12.5	57.5
13	14 07.8	13.4	249 53.3	10.9	17 33.0	12.5	57.6
14	29 07.6	13.2	264 23.2	10.8	17 45.5	12.4	57.6
15	44 07.5	.. 13.1	278 53.0	10.6	17 57.9	12.4	57.6
16	59 07.4	13.0	293 22.6	10.5	18 10.3	12.2	57.7
17	74 07.3	12.8	307 52.1	10.4	18 22.5	12.2	57.7
18	89 07.1	N23 12.7	322 21.5	10.3	S18 34.7	12.1	57.8
19	104 07.0	12.5	336 50.8	10.1	18 46.8	12.0	57.8
20	119 06.9	12.4	351 19.9	10.1	18 58.8	12.0	57.8
21	134 06.8	.. 12.3	5 49.0	9.8	19 10.8	11.8	57.9
22	149 06.6	12.1	20 17.8	9.8	19 22.6	11.8	57.9
23	164 06.5	12.0	34 46.6	9.6	S19 34.4	11.7	58.0
	SD 15.8	d 0.1	SD 15.2		15.4		15.7

Side annotations: **TUESDAY** (27), **WEDNESDAY** (28), **THURSDAY** (29)

Moonrise

Lat.	Twilight Naut.	Twilight Civil	Sunrise	27	28	29	30
°	h m	h m	h m	h m	h m	h m	h m
N 72	□	□	□	14 24	16 47	■■■■	■■■■
N 70	□	□	□	14 13	16 20	19 16	■■■■
68	□	□	□	14 05	16 00	18 21	■■■■
66	□	□	□	13 57	15 45	17 48	20 41
64	////	////	01 36	13 51	15 32	17 24	19 36
62	////	////	02 13	13 46	15 21	17 05	19 01
60	////	00 56	02 39	13 42	15 12	16 50	18 36
N 58	////	01 45	02 59	13 38	15 04	16 37	18 16
56	////	02 14	03 16	13 34	14 57	16 26	17 59
54	00 52	02 36	03 30	13 31	14 51	16 16	17 45
52	01 36	02 54	03 42	13 28	14 45	16 07	17 33
50	02 04	03 09	03 53	13 26	14 40	16 00	17 23
45	02 49	03 38	04 15	13 20	14 30	15 43	17 00
N 40	03 19	04 01	04 33	13 16	14 21	15 30	16 43
35	03 42	04 19	04 48	13 12	14 13	15 18	16 28
30	04 01	04 34	05 01	13 08	14 07	15 09	16 15
20	04 30	04 59	05 23	13 02	13 55	14 52	15 53
N 10	04 52	05 19	05 42	12 57	13 45	14 37	15 34
0	05 11	05 37	06 00	12 52	13 36	14 24	15 17
S 10	05 28	05 54	06 17	12 48	13 27	14 10	14 59
20	05 44	06 11	06 35	12 42	13 17	13 56	14 41
30	06 00	06 30	06 56	12 37	13 06	13 40	14 20
35	06 09	06 41	07 09	12 34	13 00	13 31	14 07
40	06 18	06 52	07 23	12 30	12 53	13 20	13 53
45	06 29	07 06	07 40	12 26	12 45	13 08	13 37
S 50	06 40	07 22	08 00	12 21	12 35	12 53	13 16
52	06 45	07 29	08 10	12 18	12 30	12 46	13 07
54	06 51	07 37	08 21	12 16	12 26	12 38	12 56
56	06 57	07 46	08 33	12 13	12 20	12 29	12 44
58	07 04	07 56	08 48	12 10	12 14	12 20	12 30
S 60	07 11	08 08	09 05	12 07	12 07	12 09	12 13

Moonset

Lat.	Sunset	Twilight Civil	Twilight Naut.	27	28	29	30
°	h m	h m	h m	h m	h m	h m	h m
N 72	□	□	□	23 11	22 21	■■■■	■■■■
N 70	□	□	□	23 24	22 50	21 35	■■■■
68	□	□	□	23 35	23 12	22 32	■■■■
66	□	□	□	23 44	23 29	23 06	22 05
64	22 29	////	////	{00 00 / 23 52}	23 43	23 31	23 12
62	21 53	////	////	{00 03 / 23 59}	23 55	23 51	23 47
60	21 27	23 09	////	00 05	00 05	00 05	00 08
N 58	21 07	22 21	////	00 07	00 10	00 14	00 21
56	20 50	21 52	////	00 09	00 15	00 22	00 33
54	20 36	21 30	23 13	00 10	00 19	00 29	00 44
52	20 24	21 13	22 30	00 12	00 23	00 36	00 53
50	20 13	20 58	22 03	00 13	00 26	00 42	01 01
45	19 51	20 28	21 18	00 16	00 34	00 54	01 19
N 40	19 33	20 06	20 47	00 18	00 40	01 04	01 34
35	19 18	19 48	20 24	00 20	00 45	01 13	01 47
30	19 05	19 33	20 06	00 22	00 50	01 21	01 57
20	18 43	19 08	19 37	00 25	00 58	01 35	02 12
N 10	18 24	18 47	19 15	00 28	01 06	01 47	02 33
0	18 07	18 29	18 56	00 31	01 13	01 58	02 48
S 10	17 50	18 12	18 39	00 33	01 20	02 10	03 04
20	17 31	17 55	18 23	00 36	01 27	02 22	03 21
30	17 10	17 36	18 06	00 39	01 36	02 36	03 40
35	16 58	17 26	17 58	00 41	01 41	02 44	03 51
40	16 44	17 14	17 48	00 43	01 46	02 53	04 04
45	16 27	17 01	17 38	00 46	01 53	03 04	04 20
S 50	16 07	16 45	17 26	00 48	02 01	03 18	04 39
52	15 57	16 38	17 21	00 50	02 05	03 24	04 48
54	15 46	16 29	17 16	00 51	02 09	03 31	04 58
56	15 33	16 20	17 09	00 53	02 13	03 38	05 09
58	15 19	16 10	17 03	00 55	02 18	03 47	05 23
S 60	15 01	15 59	16 55	00 57	02 24	03 57	05 38

	SUN			MOON			
Day	Eqn. of Time 00h	Eqn. of Time 12h	Mer. Pass.	Mer. Pass. Upper	Mer. Pass. Lower	Age	Phase
d	m s	m s	h m	h m	h m	d	%
27	02 58	03 04	12 03	19 02	06 41	09	62
28	03 10	03 16	12 03	19 47	07 24	10	71
29	03 22	03 28	12 03	20 36	08 11	11	80

© British Crown Copyright 2022. All rights reserved.

UT	ARIES GHA	VENUS −4.7 GHA	Dec	MARS +1.7 GHA	Dec	JUPITER −2.2 GHA	Dec	SATURN +0.7 GHA	Dec	STARS Name	SHA	Dec
30 00	277 48.3	135 04.9	N15 19.3	131 24.5	N14 46.4	240 43.0	N13 27.3	298 23.3	S10 25.2	Acamar	315 13.0	S40 12.5
01	292 50.8	150 05.8	18.4	146 25.5	45.9	255 45.0	27.5	313 25.8	25.2	Achernar	335 21.3	S57 06.8
02	307 53.3	165 06.8	17.6	161 26.5	45.4	270 47.1	27.6	328 28.4	25.2	Acrux	173 01.5	S63 14.0
03	322 55.7	180 07.8 ..	16.8	176 27.5 ..	44.8	285 49.1 ..	27.7	343 30.9 ..	25.3	Adhara	255 07.2	S29 00.2
04	337 58.2	195 08.7	16.0	191 28.5	44.3	300 51.2	27.9	358 33.4	25.3	Aldebaran	290 41.4	N16 33.3
05	353 00.7	210 09.7	15.2	206 29.6	43.8	315 53.2	28.0	13 35.9	25.3			
06	8 03.1	225 10.7	N15 14.4	221 30.6	N14 43.3	330 55.2	N13 28.1	28 38.4	S10 25.3	Alioth	166 14.0	N55 50.3
07	23 05.6	240 11.6	13.5	236 31.6	42.8	345 57.3	28.3	43 40.9	25.4	Alkaid	152 52.8	N49 12.0
08	38 08.1	255 12.6	12.7	251 32.6	42.2	0 59.3	28.4	58 43.4	25.4	Alnair	27 34.2	S46 50.7
F 09	53 10.5	270 13.6 ..	11.9	266 33.6 ..	41.7	16 01.3 ..	28.5	73 45.9 ..	25.4	Alnilam	275 39.3	S 1 11.2
R 10	68 13.0	285 14.6	11.1	281 34.6	41.2	31 03.4	28.7	88 48.4	25.5	Alphard	217 49.3	S 8 45.6
I 11	83 15.4	300 15.5	10.3	296 35.6	40.7	46 05.4	28.8	103 50.9	25.5			
D 12	98 17.9	315 16.5	N15 09.5	311 36.6	N14 40.2	61 07.4	N13 28.9	118 53.4	S10 25.5	Alphecca	126 04.6	N26 38.3
A 13	113 20.4	330 17.5	08.7	326 37.6	39.6	76 09.5	29.1	133 55.9	25.5	Alpheratz	357 36.0	N29 13.0
Y 14	128 22.8	345 18.5	07.8	341 38.6	39.1	91 11.5	29.2	148 58.5	25.6	Altair	62 00.9	N 8 55.8
15	143 25.3	0 19.5 ..	07.0	356 39.6 ..	38.6	106 13.6 ..	29.3	164 01.0 ..	25.6	Ankaa	353 08.4	S42 10.5
16	158 27.8	15 20.5	06.2	11 40.6	38.1	121 15.6	29.5	179 03.5	25.6	Antares	112 17.1	S26 29.1
17	173 30.2	30 21.5	05.4	26 41.6	37.6	136 17.6	29.6	194 06.0	25.6			
18	188 32.7	45 22.5	N15 04.6	41 42.6	N14 37.0	151 19.7	N13 29.7	209 08.5	S10 25.7	Arcturus	145 48.9	N19 03.8
19	203 35.2	60 23.5	03.8	56 43.6	36.5	166 21.7	29.9	224 11.0	25.7	Atria	107 11.9	S69 04.3
20	218 37.6	75 24.5	03.0	71 44.7	36.0	181 23.7	30.0	239 13.5	25.7	Avior	234 15.8	S59 35.1
21	233 40.1	90 25.5 ..	02.1	86 45.7 ..	35.5	196 25.8 ..	30.1	254 16.0 ..	25.8	Bellatrix	278 24.6	N 6 22.3
22	248 42.6	105 26.5	01.3	101 46.7	34.9	211 27.8	30.3	269 18.5	25.8	Betelgeuse	270 53.8	N 7 24.7
23	263 45.0	120 27.5	15 00.5	116 47.7	34.4	226 29.9	30.4	284 21.1	25.8			
1 00	278 47.5	135 28.5	N14 59.7	131 48.7	N14 33.9	241 31.9	N13 30.5	299 23.6	S10 25.8	Canopus	263 53.5	S52 42.4
01	293 49.9	150 29.5	58.9	146 49.7	33.4	256 33.9	30.7	314 26.1	25.9	Capella	280 24.2	N46 01.2
02	308 52.4	165 30.6	58.1	161 50.7	32.9	271 36.0	30.8	329 28.6	25.9	Deneb	49 26.3	N45 21.7
03	323 54.9	180 31.6 ..	57.3	176 51.7 ..	32.3	286 38.0 ..	30.9	344 31.1 ..	25.9	Denebola	182 26.3	N14 26.6
04	338 57.3	195 32.6	56.4	191 52.7	31.8	301 40.1	31.0	359 33.6	26.0	Diphda	348 48.6	S17 51.4
05	353 59.8	210 33.6	55.6	206 53.7	31.3	316 42.1	31.2	14 36.1	26.0			
06	9 02.3	225 34.6	N14 54.8	221 54.7	N14 30.8	331 44.1	N13 31.3	29 38.6	S10 26.0	Dubhe	193 42.8	N61 37.8
07	24 04.7	240 35.7	54.0	236 55.7	30.2	346 46.2	31.4	44 41.2	26.0	Elnath	278 03.8	N28 37.6
S 08	39 07.2	255 36.7	53.2	251 56.7	29.7	1 48.2	31.6	59 43.7	26.1	Eltanin	90 42.2	N51 29.2
A 09	54 09.7	270 37.7 ..	52.4	266 57.7 ..	29.2	16 50.3 ..	31.7	74 46.2 ..	26.1	Enif	33 39.8	N 9 58.9
T 10	69 12.1	285 38.8	51.6	281 58.8	28.7	31 52.3	31.8	89 48.7	26.1	Fomalhaut	15 15.8	S29 29.7
U 11	84 14.6	300 39.8	50.8	296 59.8	28.1	46 54.3	32.0	104 51.2	26.2			
R 12	99 17.1	315 40.9	N14 49.9	312 00.8	N14 27.6	61 56.4	N13 32.1	119 53.7	S10 26.2	Gacrux	171 53.1	S57 14.9
D 13	114 19.5	330 41.9	49.1	327 01.8	27.1	76 58.4	32.2	134 56.2	26.2	Gienah	175 44.9	S17 40.4
A 14	129 22.0	345 42.9	48.3	342 02.8	26.6	92 00.5	32.4	149 58.7	26.2	Hadar	148 37.6	S60 29.4
Y 15	144 24.4	0 44.0 ..	47.5	357 03.8 ..	26.0	107 02.5 ..	32.5	165 01.3 ..	26.3	Hamal	327 52.8	N23 34.3
16	159 26.9	15 45.0	46.7	12 04.8	25.5	122 04.6	32.6	180 03.8	26.3	Kaus Aust.	83 33.8	S34 22.4
17	174 29.4	30 46.1	45.9	27 05.8	25.0	137 06.6	32.8	195 06.3	26.3			
18	189 31.8	45 47.1	N14 45.1	42 06.8	N14 24.5	152 08.6	N13 32.9	210 08.8	S10 26.4	Kochab	137 19.1	N74 03.8
19	204 34.3	60 48.2	44.2	57 07.8	23.9	167 10.7	33.0	225 11.3	26.4	Markab	13 31.0	N15 19.8
20	219 36.8	75 49.3	43.4	72 08.8	23.4	182 12.7	33.1	240 13.8	26.4	Menkar	314 07.7	N 4 10.9
21	234 39.2	90 50.3 ..	42.6	87 09.8 ..	22.9	197 14.8 ..	33.3	255 16.3 ..	26.5	Menkent	147 59.0	S36 29.2
22	249 41.7	105 51.4	41.8	102 10.8	22.4	212 16.8	33.4	270 18.9	26.5	Miaplacidus	221 39.3	S69 48.9
23	264 44.2	120 52.4	41.0	117 11.9	21.8	227 18.9	33.5	285 21.4	26.5			
2 00	279 46.6	135 53.5	N14 40.2	132 12.9	N14 21.3	242 20.9	N13 33.7	300 23.9	S10 26.5	Mirfak	308 30.4	N49 56.5
01	294 49.1	150 54.6	39.4	147 13.9	20.8	257 22.9	33.8	315 26.4	26.6	Nunki	75 49.0	S26 16.0
02	309 51.6	165 55.7	38.6	162 14.9	20.3	272 25.0	33.9	330 28.9	26.6	Peacock	53 07.2	S56 39.4
03	324 54.0	180 56.7 ..	37.8	177 15.9 ..	19.7	287 27.0 ..	34.1	345 31.4 ..	26.6	Pollux	243 19.2	N27 58.3
04	339 56.5	195 57.8	36.9	192 16.9	19.2	302 29.1	34.2	0 34.0	26.7	Procyon	244 52.5	N 5 09.9
05	354 58.9	210 58.9	36.1	207 17.9	18.7	317 31.1	34.3	15 36.5	26.7			
06	10 01.4	226 00.0	N14 35.3	222 18.9	N14 18.1	332 33.2	N13 34.5	30 39.0	S10 26.7	Rasalhague	95 59.4	N12 32.6
07	25 03.9	241 01.1	34.5	237 19.9	17.6	347 35.2	34.6	45 41.5	26.8	Regulus	207 36.0	N11 51.3
08	40 06.3	256 02.1	33.7	252 20.9	17.1	2 37.2	34.7	60 44.0	26.8	Rigel	281 05.4	S 8 10.4
S 09	55 08.8	271 03.2 ..	32.9	267 21.9 ..	16.6	17 39.3 ..	34.8	75 46.5 ..	26.8	Rigil Kent.	139 41.7	S60 56.1
U 10	70 11.3	286 04.3	32.1	282 23.0	16.0	32 41.3	35.0	90 49.0	26.8	Sabik	102 03.9	S15 45.2
N 11	85 13.7	301 05.4	31.3	297 24.0	15.5	47 43.4	35.1	105 51.6	26.9			
D 12	100 16.2	316 06.5	N14 30.5	312 25.0	N14 15.0	62 45.4	N13 35.2	120 54.1	S10 26.9	Schedar	349 32.5	N56 39.6
A 13	115 18.7	331 07.6	29.6	327 26.0	14.4	77 47.5	35.4	135 56.6	26.9	Shaula	96 11.7	S37 07.3
Y 14	130 21.1	346 08.7	28.8	342 27.0	13.9	92 49.5	35.5	150 59.1	27.0	Sirius	258 27.7	S16 44.9
15	145 23.6	1 09.8 ..	28.0	357 28.0 ..	13.4	107 51.6 ..	35.6	166 01.6 ..	27.0	Spica	158 23.6	S11 17.0
16	160 26.0	16 10.9	27.2	12 29.0	12.9	122 53.6	35.7	181 04.2	27.0	Suhail	222 47.6	S43 31.7
17	175 28.5	31 12.0	26.4	27 30.0	12.3	137 55.7	35.9	196 06.7	27.1			
18	190 31.0	46 13.1	N14 25.6	42 31.0	N14 11.8	152 57.7	N13 36.0	211 09.2	S10 27.1	Vega	80 33.6	N38 48.3
19	205 33.4	61 14.3	24.8	57 32.0	11.3	167 59.7	36.1	226 11.7	27.1	Zuben'ubi	136 57.2	S16 08.4
20	220 35.9	76 15.4	24.0	72 33.0	10.7	183 01.8	36.3	241 14.2	27.2		SHA	Mer. Pass.
21	235 38.4	91 16.5 ..	23.2	87 34.1 ..	10.2	198 03.8 ..	36.4	256 16.7 ..	27.2	Venus	216 41.0	14 57
22	250 40.8	106 17.6	22.4	102 35.1	09.7	213 05.9	36.5	271 19.3	27.2	Mars	213 01.2	15 12
23	265 43.3	121 18.7	21.5	117 36.1	09.1	228 07.9	36.7	286 21.8	27.2	Jupiter	322 44.4	7 53
Mer. Pass.	5 23.9	v 1.0	d 0.8	v 1.0	d 0.5	v 2.0	d 0.1	v 2.5	d 0.0	Saturn	20 36.1	4 02

© British Crown Copyright 2022. All rights reserved.

UT	SUN GHA	SUN Dec	MOON GHA	v	Dec	d	HP
d h	° '	° '	° '	'	° '	'	'
30 00	179 06.4	N23 11.8	49 15.2	9.5	S19 46.1	11.6	58.0
01	194 06.3	11.7	63 43.7	9.4	19 57.7	11.5	58.0
02	209 06.1	11.6	78 12.1	9.2	20 09.2	11.4	58.1
03	224 06.0	.. 11.4	92 40.3	9.1	20 20.6	11.3	58.1
04	239 05.9	11.3	107 08.4	9.0	20 31.9	11.2	58.1
05	254 05.8	11.1	121 36.4	8.9	20 43.1	11.1	58.2
06	269 05.6	N23 11.0	136 04.3	8.7	S20 54.2	11.0	58.2
07	284 05.5	10.8	150 32.0	8.5	21 05.2	11.0	58.3
08	299 05.4	10.7	164 59.5	8.5	21 16.2	10.8	58.3
F 09	314 05.3	.. 10.5	179 27.0	8.3	21 27.0	10.6	58.3
R 10	329 05.2	10.4	193 54.3	8.1	21 37.6	10.6	58.4
I 11	344 05.0	10.2	208 21.4	8.1	21 48.2	10.5	58.4
D 12	359 04.9	N23 10.1	222 48.5	7.9	S21 58.7	10.4	58.4
A 13	14 04.8	09.9	237 15.4	7.7	22 09.1	10.2	58.5
Y 14	29 04.7	09.8	251 42.1	7.7	22 19.3	10.1	58.5
15	44 04.5	.. 09.6	266 08.8	7.5	22 29.4	10.0	58.6
16	59 04.4	09.5	280 35.3	7.3	22 39.4	9.9	58.6
17	74 04.3	09.3	295 01.6	7.2	22 49.3	9.8	58.6
18	89 04.2	N23 09.1	309 27.8	7.1	S22 59.1	9.6	58.7
19	104 04.1	09.0	323 53.9	7.0	23 08.7	9.6	58.7
20	119 03.9	08.8	338 19.9	6.8	23 18.3	9.3	58.7
21	134 03.8	.. 08.7	352 45.7	6.7	23 27.6	9.3	58.8
22	149 03.7	08.5	7 11.4	6.5	23 36.9	9.1	58.8
23	164 03.6	08.4	21 36.9	6.4	23 46.0	9.0	58.9
1 00	179 03.4	N23 08.2	36 02.3	6.3	S23 55.0	8.8	58.9
01	194 03.3	08.0	50 27.6	6.2	24 03.8	8.7	58.9
02	209 03.2	07.9	64 52.8	6.0	24 12.5	8.6	59.0
03	224 03.1	.. 07.7	79 17.8	5.8	24 21.1	8.4	59.0
04	239 03.0	07.5	93 42.6	5.8	24 29.5	8.3	59.0
05	254 02.8	07.4	108 07.4	5.6	24 37.8	8.1	59.1
06	269 02.7	N23 07.2	122 32.0	5.5	S24 45.9	8.0	59.1
S 07	284 02.6	07.1	136 56.5	5.4	24 53.9	7.8	59.1
A 08	299 02.5	06.9	151 20.9	5.2	25 01.7	7.7	59.2
T 09	314 02.4	.. 06.7	165 45.1	5.1	25 09.4	7.5	59.2
U 10	329 02.2	06.6	180 09.2	5.0	25 16.9	7.4	59.2
R 11	344 02.1	06.4	194 33.2	4.8	25 24.3	7.2	59.3
D 12	359 02.0	N23 06.2	208 57.0	4.8	S25 31.5	7.0	59.3
A 13	14 01.9	06.1	223 20.8	4.6	25 38.5	6.9	59.4
Y 14	29 01.8	05.9	237 44.4	4.4	25 45.4	6.7	59.4
15	44 01.6	.. 05.7	252 07.8	4.4	25 52.1	6.6	59.4
16	59 01.5	05.5	266 31.2	4.3	25 58.7	6.4	59.5
17	74 01.4	05.4	280 54.5	4.1	26 05.1	6.2	59.5
18	89 01.3	N23 05.2	295 17.6	4.0	S26 11.3	6.0	59.5
19	104 01.2	05.0	309 40.6	3.9	26 17.3	5.9	59.6
20	119 01.0	04.8	324 03.5	3.8	26 23.2	5.7	59.6
21	134 00.9	.. 04.7	338 26.3	3.7	26 28.9	5.5	59.6
22	149 00.8	04.5	352 49.0	3.6	26 34.4	5.3	59.6
23	164 00.7	04.3	7 11.6	3.5	26 39.7	5.2	59.7
2 00	179 00.6	N23 04.1	21 34.1	3.4	S26 44.9	4.9	59.7
01	194 00.4	04.0	35 56.5	3.2	26 49.8	4.8	59.7
02	209 00.3	03.8	50 18.7	3.2	26 54.6	4.6	59.8
03	224 00.2	.. 03.6	64 40.9	3.1	26 59.2	4.4	59.8
04	239 00.1	03.4	79 03.0	3.0	27 03.6	4.3	59.8
05	254 00.0	03.3	93 25.0	2.9	27 07.9	4.0	59.9
06	268 59.9	N23 03.1	107 46.9	2.8	S27 11.9	3.8	59.9
07	283 59.7	02.9	122 08.7	2.7	27 15.7	3.7	59.9
08	298 59.6	02.7	136 30.4	2.6	27 19.4	3.4	59.9
S 09	313 59.5	.. 02.5	150 52.0	2.6	27 22.8	3.3	60.0
U 10	328 59.4	02.3	165 13.6	2.4	27 26.1	3.1	60.0
N 11	343 59.3	02.2	179 35.0	2.4	27 29.2	2.8	60.0
D 12	358 59.2	N23 02.0	193 56.4	2.4	S27 32.0	2.7	60.1
A 13	13 59.0	01.8	208 17.8	2.2	27 34.7	2.5	60.1
Y 14	28 58.9	01.6	222 39.0	2.2	27 37.2	2.2	60.1
15	43 58.8	.. 01.4	237 00.2	2.1	27 39.4	2.1	60.1
16	58 58.7	01.2	251 21.3	2.1	27 41.5	1.9	60.2
17	73 58.6	01.0	265 42.4	2.0	27 43.4	1.6	60.2
18	88 58.5	N23 00.8	280 03.4	2.0	S27 45.0	1.5	60.2
19	103 58.3	00.7	294 24.4	1.9	27 46.5	1.2	60.2
20	118 58.2	00.5	308 45.3	1.8	27 47.7	1.0	60.3
21	133 58.1	.. 00.3	323 06.1	1.8	27 48.7	0.9	60.3
22	148 58.0	23 00.1	337 26.9	1.8	27 49.6	0.6	60.3
23	163 57.9	N22 59.9	351 47.7	1.7	S27 50.2	0.4	60.3
	SD 15.8	d 0.2	SD 15.9		16.2		16.4

Twilight / Sunrise / Moonrise

Lat.	Twilight Naut.	Twilight Civil	Sunrise	Moonrise 30	Moonrise 1	Moonrise 2	Moonrise 3
°	h m	h m	h m	h m	h m	h m	h m
N 72	▢	▢	▢	■■	■■	■■	■■
N 70	▢	▢	▢	■■	■■	■■	■■
68	▢	▢	▢	■■	■■	■■	■■
66	////	////	00 16	20 41	■■	■■	■■
64	////	////	01 41	19 36	■■	■■	■■
62	////	////	02 16	19 01	21 10	■■	23 36
60	////	01 03	02 42	18 36	20 25	21 58	22 47
N 58	////	01 48	03 02	18 16	19 56	21 22	22 16
56	////	02 17	03 18	17 59	19 33	20 55	21 53
54	00 57	02 38	03 32	17 45	19 15	20 34	21 33
52	01 40	02 56	03 44	17 33	19 00	20 17	21 17
50	02 06	03 11	03 55	17 23	18 46	20 02	21 03
45	02 51	03 40	04 17	17 00	18 19	19 32	20 34
N 40	03 21	04 02	04 35	16 43	17 57	19 09	20 12
35	03 43	04 20	04 50	16 28	17 39	18 49	19 53
30	04 02	04 35	05 02	16 15	17 24	18 33	19 37
20	04 30	05 00	05 24	15 53	16 58	18 05	19 10
N 10	04 53	05 20	05 43	15 34	16 36	17 41	18 46
0	05 12	05 38	06 00	15 17	16 15	17 19	18 25
S 10	05 28	05 55	06 17	14 59	15 55	16 56	18 03
20	05 44	06 12	06 36	14 41	15 33	16 33	17 39
30	06 00	06 30	06 57	14 20	15 08	16 05	17 12
35	06 09	06 41	07 09	14 07	14 53	15 49	16 56
40	06 18	06 52	07 23	13 53	14 36	15 30	16 37
45	06 28	07 06	07 39	13 37	14 15	15 07	16 14
S 50	06 40	07 21	08 00	13 16	13 50	14 38	15 45
52	06 45	07 29	08 09	13 07	13 37	14 24	15 31
54	06 51	07 37	08 20	12 56	13 23	14 07	15 14
56	06 57	07 46	08 33	12 44	13 07	13 48	14 54
58	07 03	07 56	08 47	12 30	12 48	13 23	14 30
S 60	07 11	08 07	09 04	12 13	12 24	12 51	13 57

Sunset / Twilight / Moonset

Lat.	Sunset	Twilight Civil	Twilight Naut.	Moonset 30	Moonset 1	Moonset 2	Moonset 3
°	h m	h m	h m	h m	h m	h m	h m
N 72	▢	▢	▢	■■	■■	■■	■■
N 70	▢	▢	▢	■■	■■	■■	■■
68	▢	▢	▢	■■	■■	■■	■■
66	23 42	////	////	22 05	■■	■■	■■
64	22 26	////	////	23 12	■■	■■	■■
62	21 50	////	////	23 47	23 43	■■	■■
60	21 25	23 03	////	00 08	00 13	00 28	01 10
N 58	21 05	22 19	////	00 21	00 34	00 58	01 47
56	20 49	21 50	////	00 33	00 51	01 21	02 13
54	20 35	21 29	23 08	00 44	01 05	01 39	02 34
52	20 23	21 11	22 27	00 53	01 18	01 55	02 51
50	20 13	20 57	22 01	01 01	01 29	02 09	03 06
45	19 51	20 28	21 17	01 19	01 52	02 37	03 36
N 40	19 33	20 05	20 47	01 34	02 11	02 59	04 00
35	19 18	19 48	20 24	01 47	02 27	03 17	04 19
30	19 05	19 33	20 06	01 57	02 41	03 33	04 36
20	18 44	19 08	19 37	02 16	03 04	04 00	05 04
N 10	18 25	18 48	19 15	02 33	03 25	04 23	05 28
0	18 08	18 30	18 56	02 48	03 44	04 45	05 50
S 10	17 50	18 13	18 39	03 04	04 03	05 07	06 12
20	17 32	17 56	18 24	03 21	04 24	05 30	06 36
30	17 11	17 38	18 07	03 40	04 48	05 57	07 04
35	16 59	17 27	17 59	03 51	05 02	06 13	07 20
40	16 45	17 16	17 50	04 04	05 18	06 32	07 39
45	16 29	17 02	17 39	04 20	05 38	06 54	08 02
S 50	16 08	16 47	17 28	04 39	06 02	07 23	08 32
52	15 59	16 39	17 23	04 48	06 14	07 37	08 46
54	15 48	16 31	17 17	04 58	06 28	07 53	09 03
56	15 35	16 22	17 11	05 09	06 44	08 13	09 23
58	15 21	16 12	17 05	05 23	07 02	08 37	09 48
S 60	15 04	16 01	16 57	05 38	07 26	09 09	10 21

SUN / MOON

Day	SUN Eqn. of Time 00h	SUN Eqn. of Time 12h	Mer. Pass.	MOON Mer. Pass. Upper	MOON Mer. Pass. Lower	Age	Phase
d	m s	m s	h m	h m	h m	d	%
30	03 34	03 40	12 04	21 30	09 02	12	88
1	03 46	03 52	12 04	22 30	09 59	13	94
2	03 57	04 03	12 04	23 34	11 02	14	98

© British Crown Copyright 2022. All rights reserved.

UT	ARIES GHA	VENUS −4.7 GHA	Dec	MARS +1.7 GHA	Dec	JUPITER −2.2 GHA	Dec	SATURN +0.6 GHA	Dec	STARS Name	SHA	Dec
3 00	280 45.8	136 19.9	N14 20.7	132 37.1	N14 08.6	243 10.0	N13 36.8	301 24.3	S10 27.3	Acamar	315 13.0	S40 12.4
01	295 48.2	151 21.0	19.9	147 38.1	08.1	258 12.0	36.9	316 26.8	27.3	Achernar	335 21.3	S57 06.8
02	310 50.7	166 22.1	19.1	162 39.1	07.6	273 14.1	37.0	331 29.3	27.3	Acrux	173 01.5	S63 14.0
03	325 53.2	181 23.3 ..	18.3	177 40.1 ..	07.0	288 16.1 ..	37.2	346 31.9 ..	27.4	Adhara	255 07.2	S29 00.2
04	340 55.6	196 24.4	17.5	192 41.1	06.5	303 18.2	37.3	1 34.4	27.4	Aldebaran	290 41.4	N16 33.4
05	355 58.1	211 25.5	16.7	207 42.1	06.0	318 20.2	37.4	16 36.9	27.4			
M 06	11 00.5	226 26.7	N14 15.9	222 43.1	N14 05.4	333 22.3	N13 37.6	31 39.4	S10 27.5	Alioth	166 14.1	N55 50.3
O 07	26 03.0	241 27.8	15.1	237 44.1	04.9	348 24.3	37.7	46 41.9	27.5	Alkaid	152 52.9	N49 12.0
N 08	41 05.5	256 29.0	14.3	252 45.2	04.4	3 26.4	37.8	61 44.5	27.5	Al Na'ir	27 34.2	S46 50.7
D 09	56 07.9	271 30.1 ..	13.5	267 46.2 ..	03.8	18 28.4 ..	37.9	76 47.0 ..	27.6	Alnilam	275 39.3	S 1 11.2
A 10	71 10.4	286 31.3	12.7	282 47.2	03.3	33 30.5	38.1	91 49.5	27.6	Alphard	217 49.3	S 8 45.6
Y 11	86 12.9	301 32.4	11.8	297 48.2	02.8	48 32.5	38.2	106 52.0	27.6			
12	101 15.3	316 33.6	N14 11.0	312 49.2	N14 02.2	63 34.6	N13 38.3	121 54.5	S10 27.7	Alphecca	126 04.6	N26 38.3
13	116 17.8	331 34.7	10.2	327 50.2	01.7	78 36.6	38.4	136 57.1	27.7	Alpheratz	357 36.0	N29 13.0
14	131 20.3	346 35.9	09.4	342 51.2	01.2	93 38.7	38.6	151 59.6	27.7	Altair	62 00.9	N 8 55.8
15	146 22.7	1 37.0 ..	08.6	357 52.2 ..	00.6	108 40.7 ..	38.7	167 02.1 ..	27.8	Ankaa	353 08.3	S42 10.5
16	161 25.2	16 38.2	07.8	12 53.2	14 00.1	123 42.8	38.8	182 04.6	27.8	Antares	112 17.1	S26 29.1
17	176 27.7	31 39.4	07.0	27 54.2	13 59.6	138 44.8	39.0	197 07.1	27.8			
18	191 30.1	46 40.5	N14 06.2	42 55.3	N13 59.0	153 46.9	N13 39.1	212 09.7	S10 27.8	Arcturus	145 48.9	N19 03.8
19	206 32.6	61 41.7	05.4	57 56.3	58.5	168 48.9	39.2	227 12.2	27.9	Atria	107 11.9	S69 04.3
20	221 35.0	76 42.9	04.6	72 57.3	58.0	183 51.0	39.3	242 14.7	27.9	Avior	234 15.9	S59 35.1
21	236 37.5	91 44.1 ..	03.8	87 58.3 ..	57.4	198 53.0 ..	39.5	257 17.2 ..	27.9	Bellatrix	278 24.5	N 6 22.3
22	251 40.0	106 45.2	03.0	102 59.3	56.9	213 55.1	39.6	272 19.8	28.0	Betelgeuse	270 53.8	N 7 24.7
23	266 42.4	121 46.4	02.2	118 00.3	56.4	228 57.1	39.7	287 22.3	28.0			
4 00	281 44.9	136 47.6	N14 01.4	133 01.3	N13 55.8	243 59.3	N13 39.8	302 24.8	S10 28.0	Canopus	263 53.5	S52 42.4
01	296 47.4	151 48.8	14 00.6	148 02.3	55.3	259 01.2	40.0	317 27.3	28.1	Capella	280 24.2	N46 01.2
02	311 49.8	166 50.0	13 59.8	163 03.3	54.8	274 03.3	40.1	332 29.8	28.1	Deneb	49 26.2	N45 21.7
03	326 52.3	181 51.2 ..	59.0	178 04.3 ..	54.2	289 05.3 ..	40.2	347 32.4 ..	28.1	Denebola	182 26.3	N14 26.6
04	341 54.8	196 52.4	58.1	193 05.4	53.7	304 07.4	40.4	2 34.9	28.2	Diphda	348 48.6	S17 51.4
05	356 57.2	211 53.6	57.3	208 06.4	53.2	319 09.4	40.5	17 37.4	28.2			
T 06	11 59.7	226 54.8	N13 56.5	223 07.4	N13 52.6	334 11.5	N13 40.6	32 39.9	S10 28.2	Dubhe	193 42.8	N61 37.8
U 07	27 02.2	241 56.0	55.7	238 08.4	52.1	349 13.5	40.7	47 42.5	28.3	Elnath	278 03.8	N28 37.6
E 08	42 04.6	256 57.2	54.9	253 09.4	51.6	4 15.6	40.9	62 45.0	28.3	Eltanin	90 42.2	N51 29.2
S 09	57 07.1	271 58.4 ..	54.1	268 10.4 ..	51.0	19 17.6 ..	41.0	77 47.5 ..	28.3	Enif	33 39.8	N 9 58.9
D 10	72 09.5	286 59.6	53.3	283 11.4	50.5	34 19.7	41.1	92 50.0	28.4	Fomalhaut	15 15.7	S29 29.7
A 11	87 12.0	302 00.8	52.5	298 12.4	50.0	49 21.7	41.2	107 52.6	28.4			
Y 12	102 14.5	317 02.0	N13 51.7	313 13.4	N13 49.4	64 23.8	N13 41.4	122 55.1	S10 28.4	Gacrux	171 53.1	S57 14.9
13	117 16.9	332 03.2	50.9	328 14.5	48.9	79 25.9	41.5	137 57.6	28.5	Gienah	175 44.9	S17 40.4
14	132 19.4	347 04.5	50.1	343 15.5	48.4	94 27.9	41.6	153 00.1	28.5	Hadar	148 37.6	S60 29.4
15	147 21.9	2 05.7 ..	49.3	358 16.5 ..	47.8	109 30.0 ..	41.7	168 02.7 ..	28.5	Hamal	327 52.7	N23 34.3
16	162 24.3	17 06.9	48.5	13 17.5	47.3	124 32.0	41.9	183 05.2	28.6	Kaus Aust.	83 33.8	S34 22.4
17	177 26.8	32 08.1	47.7	28 18.5	46.7	139 34.1	42.0	198 07.7	28.6			
18	192 29.3	47 09.4	N13 46.9	43 19.5	N13 46.2	154 36.1	N13 42.1	213 10.2	S10 28.6	Kochab	137 19.1	N74 03.8
19	207 31.7	62 10.6	46.1	58 20.5	45.7	169 38.2	42.2	228 12.8	28.7	Markab	13 31.0	N15 19.8
20	222 34.2	77 11.8	45.3	73 21.5	45.1	184 40.2	42.4	243 15.3	28.7	Menkar	314 07.7	N 4 10.9
21	237 36.7	92 13.1 ..	44.5	88 22.5 ..	44.6	199 42.3 ..	42.5	258 17.8 ..	28.7	Menkent	147 59.0	S36 29.3
22	252 39.1	107 14.3	43.7	103 23.6	44.1	214 44.3	42.6	273 20.3	28.8	Miaplacidus	221 39.3	S69 48.9
23	267 41.6	122 15.6	42.9	118 24.6	43.5	229 46.4	42.7	288 22.9	28.8			
5 00	282 44.0	137 16.8	N13 42.1	133 25.6	N13 43.0	244 48.5	N13 42.9	303 25.4	S10 28.8	Mirfak	308 30.4	N49 56.5
01	297 46.5	152 18.0	41.3	148 26.6	42.4	259 50.5	43.0	318 27.9	28.9	Nunki	75 48.9	S26 16.0
02	312 49.0	167 19.3	40.5	163 27.6	41.9	274 52.6	43.1	333 30.4	28.9	Peacock	53 07.1	S56 39.4
03	327 51.4	182 20.6 ..	39.7	178 28.6 ..	41.4	289 54.6 ..	43.2	348 33.0 ..	28.9	Pollux	243 19.2	N27 58.2
04	342 53.9	197 21.8	38.9	193 29.6	40.8	304 56.7	43.4	3 35.5	29.0	Procyon	244 52.5	N 5 09.9
05	357 56.4	212 23.1	38.1	208 30.6	40.3	319 58.7	43.5	18 38.0	29.0			
W 06	12 58.8	227 24.3	N13 37.3	223 31.6	N13 39.8	335 00.8	N13 43.6	33 40.5	S10 29.0	Rasalhague	96 59.4	N12 32.6
E 07	28 01.3	242 25.6	36.5	238 32.7	39.2	350 02.9	43.7	48 43.1	29.1	Regulus	207 36.0	N11 51.3
D 08	43 03.8	257 26.9	35.7	253 33.7	38.7	5 04.9	43.9	63 45.6	29.1	Rigel	281 05.4	S 8 10.4
N 09	58 06.2	272 28.1 ..	34.9	268 34.7 ..	38.1	20 07.0 ..	44.0	78 48.1 ..	29.2	Rigil Kent.	139 41.7	S60 56.1
E 10	73 08.7	287 29.4	34.1	283 35.7	37.6	35 09.0	44.1	93 50.7	29.2	Sabik	102 03.9	S15 45.2
S 11	88 11.2	302 30.7	33.3	298 36.7	37.1	50 11.1	44.2	108 53.2	29.2			
D 12	103 13.6	317 31.9	N13 32.5	313 37.7	N13 36.5	65 13.1	N13 44.4	123 55.7	S10 29.3	Schedar	349 32.5	N56 39.7
A 13	118 16.1	332 33.2	31.7	328 38.7	36.0	80 15.2	44.5	138 58.2	29.3	Shaula	96 11.7	S37 07.3
Y 14	133 18.5	347 34.5	30.9	343 39.7	35.4	95 17.3	44.6	154 00.8	29.3	Sirius	258 27.7	S16 44.8
15	148 21.0	2 35.8 ..	30.1	358 40.8 ..	34.9	110 19.3 ..	44.7	169 03.3 ..	29.4	Spica	158 23.6	S11 17.0
16	163 23.5	17 37.1	29.3	13 41.8	34.4	125 21.4	44.9	184 05.8	29.4	Suhail	222 47.6	S43 31.7
17	178 25.9	32 38.4	28.5	28 42.8	33.8	140 23.4	45.0	199 08.4	29.4			
18	193 28.4	47 39.7	N13 27.7	43 43.8	N13 33.3	155 25.5	N13 45.1	214 10.9	S10 29.5	Vega	80 33.6	N38 48.3
19	208 30.9	62 41.0	26.9	58 44.8	32.7	170 27.6	45.2	229 13.4	29.5	Zuben'ubi	136 57.2	S16 08.4
20	223 33.3	77 42.3	26.1	73 45.8	32.2	185 29.6	45.4	244 15.9	29.5		SHA	Mer. Pass.
21	238 35.8	92 43.6 ..	25.4	88 46.8 ..	31.7	200 31.7 ..	45.5	259 18.5 ..	29.6		° ′	h m
22	253 38.3	107 44.9	24.6	103 47.8	31.1	215 33.7	45.6	274 21.0	29.6	Venus	215 02.7	14 52
23	268 40.7	122 46.2	23.8	118 48.8	30.6	230 35.8	45.7	289 23.5	29.6	Mars	211 16.4	15 07
	h m									Jupiter	322 14.3	7 43
Mer. Pass.	5 12.2	v 1.2	d 0.8	v 1.0	d 0.5	v 2.1	d 0.1	v 2.5	d 0.0	Saturn	20 39.9	3 50

© British Crown Copyright 2022. All rights reserved.

SUN and MOON

UT	SUN GHA	SUN Dec	MOON GHA	v	MOON Dec	d	HP
3 00	178 57.8	N22 59.7	6 08.4	1.7	S27 50.6	0.2	60.4
01	193 57.6	59.5	20 29.1	1.7	27 50.8	0.0	60.4
02	208 57.5	59.3	34 49.8	1.6	27 50.8	0.2	60.4
03	223 57.4	.. 59.1	49 10.4	1.6	27 50.6	0.5	60.4
04	238 57.3	58.9	63 31.0	1.6	27 50.1	0.6	60.4
05	253 57.2	58.7	77 51.6	1.6	27 49.5	0.9	60.5
06	268 57.1	N22 58.5	92 12.2	1.5	S27 48.6	1.0	60.5
07	283 57.0	58.3	106 32.7	1.6	27 47.6	1.3	60.5
M 08	298 56.8	58.1	120 53.3	1.5	27 46.3	1.5	60.5
O 09	313 56.7	.. 57.9	135 13.8	1.5	27 44.8	1.7	60.5
N 10	328 56.6	57.7	149 34.3	1.5	27 43.1	1.9	60.6
D 11	343 56.5	57.5	163 54.8	1.6	27 41.2	2.1	60.6
A 12	358 56.4	N22 57.3	178 15.4	1.5	S27 39.1	2.4	60.6
Y 13	13 56.3	57.1	192 35.9	1.5	27 36.7	2.5	60.6
14	28 56.2	56.9	206 56.4	1.6	27 34.2	2.8	60.6
15	43 56.0	.. 56.7	221 17.0	1.5	27 31.4	3.0	60.6
16	58 55.9	56.5	235 37.5	1.6	27 28.4	3.1	60.7
17	73 55.8	56.3	249 58.1	1.6	27 25.3	3.4	60.7
18	88 55.7	N22 56.1	264 18.7	1.7	S27 21.9	3.6	60.7
19	103 55.6	55.9	278 39.4	1.6	27 18.3	3.9	60.7
20	118 55.5	55.7	293 00.0	1.7	27 14.4	4.0	60.7
21	133 55.4	.. 55.5	307 20.7	1.7	27 10.4	4.2	60.7
22	148 55.2	55.3	321 41.4	1.8	27 06.2	4.4	60.7
23	163 55.1	55.1	336 02.2	1.8	27 01.8	4.7	60.7
4 00	178 55.0	N22 54.8	350 23.0	1.9	S26 57.1	4.8	60.8
01	193 54.9	54.6	4 43.9	1.9	26 52.3	5.1	60.8
02	208 54.8	54.4	19 04.8	1.9	26 47.2	5.3	60.8
03	223 54.7	.. 54.2	33 25.7	2.0	26 41.9	5.4	60.8
04	238 54.6	54.0	47 46.7	2.1	26 36.5	5.7	60.8
05	253 54.5	53.8	62 07.8	2.1	26 30.8	5.9	60.8
06	268 54.4	N22 53.6	76 28.9	2.1	S26 24.9	6.0	60.8
07	283 54.2	53.4	90 50.0	2.3	26 18.9	6.3	60.8
T 08	298 54.1	53.1	105 11.3	2.3	26 12.6	6.4	60.8
U 09	313 54.0	.. 52.9	119 32.6	2.4	26 06.2	6.7	60.8
E 10	328 53.9	52.7	133 54.0	2.4	25 59.5	6.8	60.8
S 11	343 53.8	52.5	148 15.4	2.5	25 52.7	7.1	60.9
D 12	358 53.7	N22 52.3	162 36.9	2.6	S25 45.6	7.2	60.9
A 13	13 53.6	52.0	176 58.5	2.7	25 38.4	7.5	60.9
Y 14	28 53.5	51.8	191 20.2	2.7	25 30.9	7.6	60.9
15	43 53.4	.. 51.6	205 41.9	2.9	25 23.3	7.8	60.9
16	58 53.2	51.4	220 03.8	2.9	25 15.5	8.0	60.9
17	73 53.1	51.2	234 25.7	3.0	25 07.5	8.1	60.9
18	88 53.0	N22 50.9	248 47.7	3.1	S24 59.4	8.4	60.9
19	103 52.9	50.7	263 09.8	3.2	24 51.0	8.5	60.9
20	118 52.8	50.5	277 32.0	3.3	24 42.5	8.7	60.9
21	133 52.7	.. 50.3	291 54.3	3.4	24 33.8	8.9	60.9
22	148 52.6	50.0	306 16.7	3.4	24 24.9	9.1	60.9
23	163 52.5	49.8	320 39.1	3.6	24 15.8	9.3	60.9
5 00	178 52.4	N22 49.6	335 01.7	3.7	S24 06.5	9.4	60.9
01	193 52.3	49.4	349 24.4	3.8	23 57.1	9.6	60.9
02	208 52.1	49.1	3 47.2	3.8	23 47.5	9.7	60.9
03	223 52.0	.. 48.9	18 10.0	4.0	23 37.8	9.9	60.9
04	238 51.9	48.7	32 33.0	4.1	23 27.9	10.1	60.9
05	253 51.8	48.4	46 56.1	4.2	23 17.8	10.3	60.9
06	268 51.7	N22 48.2	61 19.3	4.3	S23 07.5	10.4	60.9
07	283 51.6	48.0	75 42.6	4.4	22 57.1	10.5	60.9
W 08	298 51.5	47.8	90 06.0	4.5	22 46.6	10.7	60.9
E 09	313 51.4	.. 47.5	104 29.5	4.7	22 35.9	10.9	60.9
D 10	328 51.3	47.3	118 53.2	4.7	22 25.0	11.0	60.9
N 11	343 51.2	47.1	133 16.9	4.8	22 14.0	11.2	60.8
E 12	358 51.1	N22 46.8	147 40.7	5.0	S22 02.8	11.3	60.8
S 13	13 51.0	46.6	162 04.7	5.1	21 51.5	11.5	60.8
D 14	28 50.9	46.3	176 28.8	5.2	21 40.0	11.6	60.8
A 15	43 50.7	.. 46.1	190 53.0	5.3	21 28.4	11.8	60.8
Y 16	58 50.6	45.9	205 17.3	5.4	21 16.6	11.9	60.8
17	73 50.5	45.6	219 41.7	5.5	21 04.7	12.0	60.8
18	88 50.4	N22 45.4	234 06.2	5.7	S20 52.7	12.2	60.8
19	103 50.3	45.2	248 30.9	5.8	20 40.5	12.3	60.8
20	118 50.2	44.9	262 55.7	5.8	20 28.2	12.4	60.8
21	133 50.1	.. 44.7	277 20.5	6.0	20 15.8	12.5	60.8
22	148 50.0	44.4	291 45.5	6.2	20 03.3	12.7	60.8
23	163 49.9	44.2	306 10.7	6.2	S19 50.6	12.8	60.7
	SD 15.8	d 0.2	SD 16.5		16.6		16.6

Twilight, Sunrise, Moonrise

Lat.	Twilight Naut.	Twilight Civil	Sunrise	Moonrise 3	4	5	6
N 72	☐	☐	☐	■	■	■	■
N 70	☐	☐	☐	■	■	■	01 44
68	☐	☐	☐	■	■	■	00 47
66	////	////	00 40	■	■	01 46	(00 13 / 23 44)
64	////	////	01 46	■	■	(00 10 / 23 48)	23 36
62	////	////	02 21	23 36	23 32	23 28	23 24
60	////	01 10	02 45	22 47	23 05	23 12	23 15
N 58	////	01 53	03 05	22 16	22 44	22 58	23 06
56	////	02 20	03 21	21 53	22 26	22 46	22 59
54	01 05	02 41	03 34	21 33	22 11	22 36	22 52
52	01 44	02 58	03 46	21 17	21 58	22 26	22 46
50	02 09	03 13	03 57	21 03	21 47	22 18	22 40
45	02 53	03 42	04 19	20 34	21 23	22 00	22 28
N 40	03 22	04 04	04 36	20 12	21 04	21 45	22 18
35	03 45	04 21	04 51	19 53	20 48	21 32	22 09
30	04 03	04 36	05 04	19 37	20 34	21 21	22 02
20	04 32	05 01	05 25	19 10	20 10	21 02	21 49
N 10	04 54	05 21	05 44	18 46	19 49	20 46	21 37
0	05 12	05 38	06 01	18 25	19 29	20 30	21 26
S 10	05 29	05 55	06 18	18 03	19 10	20 15	21 15
20	05 45	06 12	06 36	17 39	18 49	19 58	21 03
30	06 01	06 30	06 57	17 12	18 24	19 38	20 50
35	06 09	06 41	07 09	16 56	18 10	19 27	20 42
40	06 18	06 52	07 22	16 37	17 53	19 14	20 33
45	06 28	07 05	07 39	16 14	17 33	18 58	20 22
S 50	06 39	07 21	07 59	15 45	17 08	18 39	20 10
52	06 44	07 28	08 08	15 31	16 56	18 30	20 04
54	06 50	07 36	08 19	15 16	16 42	18 20	19 57
56	06 56	07 44	08 31	14 54	16 26	18 08	19 49
58	07 02	07 54	08 45	14 30	16 06	17 54	19 41
S 60	07 09	08 06	09 02	13 57	15 42	17 38	19 31

Sunset, Twilight, Moonset

Lat.	Sunset	Twilight Civil	Twilight Naut.	Moonset 3	4	5	6
N 72	☐	☐	☐	■	■	■	04 06
N 70	☐	☐	☐	■	■	■	05 02
68	☐	☐	☐	■	■	01 57	05 34
66	23 24	////	////	■	■	03 32	05 58
64	22 21	////	////	■	■	03 32	06 17
62	21 47	////	////	■	01 51	04 09	06 17
60	21 23	22 56	////	01 10	02 39	04 35	06 32
N 58	21 03	22 15	////	01 47	03 10	04 56	06 45
56	20 47	21 48	////	02 13	03 33	05 13	06 56
54	20 34	21 27	23 02	02 34	03 52	05 27	07 06
52	20 22	21 10	22 24	02 51	04 08	05 39	07 14
50	20 12	20 55	21 59	03 06	04 22	05 50	07 22
45	19 50	20 27	21 15	03 36	04 50	06 13	07 38
N 40	19 32	20 05	20 46	04 00	05 12	06 31	07 52
35	19 18	19 47	20 24	04 19	05 30	06 47	08 03
30	19 05	19 32	20 05	04 36	05 46	07 00	08 13
20	18 44	19 08	19 37	05 04	06 12	07 22	08 28
N 10	18 25	18 48	19 15	05 28	06 35	07 41	08 44
0	18 08	18 31	18 57	05 50	06 56	07 59	08 57
S 10	17 51	18 14	18 40	06 12	07 17	08 16	09 11
20	17 33	17 57	18 24	06 36	07 39	08 35	09 25
30	17 12	17 39	18 08	07 04	08 05	08 57	09 41
35	17 00	17 28	18 00	07 20	08 20	09 09	09 50
40	16 47	17 17	17 51	07 39	08 37	09 23	10 00
45	16 30	17 04	17 41	08 02	08 58	09 40	10 13
S 50	16 10	16 48	17 30	08 32	09 24	10 01	10 27
52	16 01	16 41	17 25	08 46	09 37	10 11	10 34
54	15 50	16 33	17 19	09 03	09 51	10 22	10 42
56	15 38	16 25	17 13	09 23	10 08	10 34	10 50
58	15 24	16 15	17 07	09 48	10 28	10 48	10 59
S 60	15 07	16 04	17 00	10 21	10 53	11 05	11 10

SUN and MOON

Day	Eqn. of Time 00h	Eqn. of Time 12h	Mer. Pass.	Mer. Pass. Upper	Mer. Pass. Lower	Age	Phase
d	m s	m s	h m	h m	h m	d	%
3	04 09	04 14	12 04	24 40	12 07	15	100
4	04 20	04 25	12 04	00 40	13 13	16	98
5	04 30	04 36	12 05	01 44	14 15	17	94

© British Crown Copyright 2022. All rights reserved.

UT	ARIES GHA	VENUS −4.7 GHA	Dec	MARS +1.7 GHA	Dec	JUPITER −2.2 GHA	Dec	SATURN +0.6 GHA	Dec
6 00	283 43.2	137 47.5	N13 23.0	133 49.9	N13 30.0	245 37.9	N13 45.9	304 26.1	S10 29.7
01	298 45.7	152 48.8	22.2	148 50.9	29.5	260 39.9	46.0	319 28.6	29.7
02	313 48.1	167 50.1	21.4	163 51.9	29.0	275 42.0	46.1	334 31.1	29.7
03	328 50.6	182 51.4	.. 20.6	178 52.9	.. 28.4	290 44.0	.. 46.2	349 33.6	.. 29.8
04	343 53.0	197 52.7	19.8	193 53.9	27.9	305 46.1	46.3	4 36.2	29.8
05	358 55.5	212 54.0	19.0	208 54.9	27.3	320 48.2	46.5	19 38.7	29.9
06	13 58.0	227 55.4	N13 18.2	223 55.9	N13 26.8	335 50.2	N13 46.6	34 41.2	S10 29.9
07	29 00.4	242 56.7	17.4	238 56.9	26.2	350 52.3	46.7	49 43.8	29.9
08	44 02.9	257 58.0	16.6	253 58.0	25.7	5 54.3	46.8	64 46.3	30.0
09	59 05.4	272 59.4	.. 15.8	268 59.0	.. 25.2	20 56.4	.. 47.0	79 48.8	.. 30.0
10	74 07.8	288 00.7	15.0	284 00.0	24.6	35 58.5	47.1	94 51.4	30.0
11	89 10.3	303 02.0	14.2	299 01.0	24.1	51 00.5	47.2	109 53.9	30.1
12	104 12.8	318 03.4	N13 13.5	314 02.0	N13 23.5	66 02.6	N13 47.3	124 56.4	S10 30.1
13	119 15.2	333 04.7	12.7	329 03.0	23.0	81 04.6	47.4	139 59.0	30.1
14	134 17.7	348 06.0	11.9	344 04.0	22.4	96 06.7	47.6	155 01.5	30.2
15	149 20.1	3 07.4	.. 11.1	359 05.0	.. 21.9	111 08.8	.. 47.7	170 04.0	.. 30.2
16	164 22.6	18 08.7	10.3	14 06.1	21.4	126 10.8	47.8	185 06.6	30.3
17	179 25.1	33 10.1	09.5	29 07.1	20.8	141 12.9	47.9	200 09.1	30.3
18	194 27.5	48 11.5	N13 08.7	44 08.1	N13 20.3	156 15.0	N13 48.1	215 11.6	S10 30.3
19	209 30.0	63 12.8	07.9	59 09.1	19.7	171 17.0	48.2	230 14.2	30.4
20	224 32.5	78 14.2	07.1	74 10.1	19.2	186 19.1	48.3	245 16.7	30.4
21	239 34.9	93 15.5	.. 06.3	89 11.1	.. 18.6	201 21.2	.. 48.4	260 19.2	.. 30.4
22	254 37.4	108 16.9	05.6	104 12.1	18.1	216 23.2	48.5	275 21.7	30.5
23	269 39.9	123 18.3	04.8	119 13.2	17.5	231 25.3	48.7	290 24.3	30.5
7 00	284 42.3	138 19.6	N13 04.0	134 14.2	N13 17.0	246 27.3	N13 48.8	305 26.8	S10 30.5
01	299 44.8	153 21.0	03.2	149 15.2	16.5	261 29.4	48.9	320 29.3	30.6
02	314 47.3	168 22.4	02.4	164 16.2	15.9	276 31.5	49.0	335 31.9	30.6
03	329 49.7	183 23.8	.. 01.6	179 17.2	.. 15.4	291 33.5	.. 49.2	350 34.4	.. 30.7
04	344 52.2	198 25.2	00.8	194 18.2	14.8	306 35.6	49.3	5 37.0	30.7
05	359 54.6	213 26.5	13 00.1	209 19.2	14.3	321 37.7	49.4	20 39.5	30.7
06	14 57.1	228 27.9	N12 59.3	224 20.2	N13 13.7	336 39.7	N13 49.5	35 42.0	S10 30.8
07	29 59.6	243 29.3	58.5	239 21.3	13.2	351 41.8	49.6	50 44.6	30.8
08	45 02.0	258 30.7	57.7	254 22.3	12.6	6 43.9	49.8	65 47.1	30.8
09	60 04.5	273 32.1	.. 56.9	269 23.3	.. 12.1	21 45.9	.. 49.9	80 49.6	.. 30.9
10	75 07.0	288 33.5	56.1	284 24.3	11.5	36 48.0	50.0	95 52.2	30.9
11	90 09.4	303 34.9	55.3	299 25.3	11.0	51 50.1	50.1	110 54.7	31.0
12	105 11.9	318 36.3	N12 54.6	314 26.3	N13 10.5	66 52.1	N13 50.2	125 57.2	S10 31.0
13	120 14.4	333 37.7	53.8	329 27.3	09.9	81 54.2	50.4	140 59.8	31.0
14	135 16.8	348 39.1	53.0	344 28.4	09.4	96 56.3	50.5	156 02.3	31.1
15	150 19.3	3 40.5	.. 52.2	359 29.4	.. 08.8	111 58.3	.. 50.6	171 04.8	.. 31.1
16	165 21.8	18 42.0	51.4	14 30.4	08.3	127 00.4	50.7	186 07.4	31.1
17	180 24.2	33 43.4	50.6	29 31.4	07.7	142 02.5	50.8	201 09.9	31.2
18	195 26.7	48 44.8	N12 49.9	44 32.4	N13 07.2	157 04.5	N13 51.0	216 12.4	S10 31.2
19	210 29.1	63 46.2	49.1	59 33.4	06.6	172 06.6	51.1	231 15.0	31.3
20	225 31.6	78 47.6	48.3	74 34.4	06.1	187 08.7	51.2	246 17.5	31.3
21	240 34.1	93 49.1	.. 47.5	89 35.4	.. 05.5	202 10.7	.. 51.3	261 20.1	.. 31.3
22	255 36.5	108 50.5	46.7	104 36.5	05.0	217 12.8	51.4	276 22.6	31.4
23	270 39.0	123 51.9	46.0	119 37.5	04.4	232 14.9	51.6	291 25.1	31.4
8 00	285 41.5	138 53.4	N12 45.2	134 38.5	N13 03.9	247 17.0	N13 51.7	306 27.7	S10 31.4
01	300 43.9	153 54.8	44.4	149 39.5	03.3	262 19.0	51.8	321 30.2	31.5
02	315 46.4	168 56.3	43.6	164 40.5	02.8	277 21.1	51.9	336 32.7	31.5
03	330 48.9	183 57.7	.. 42.8	179 41.5	.. 02.2	292 23.2	.. 52.0	351 35.3	.. 31.6
04	345 51.3	198 59.2	42.1	194 42.5	01.7	307 25.2	52.2	6 37.8	31.6
05	0 53.8	214 00.6	41.3	209 43.6	01.1	322 27.3	52.3	21 40.3	31.6
06	15 56.2	229 02.1	N12 40.5	224 44.6	N13 00.6	337 29.4	N13 52.4	36 42.9	S10 31.7
07	30 58.7	244 03.5	39.7	239 45.6	00.0	352 31.4	52.5	51 45.4	31.7
08	46 01.2	259 05.0	38.9	254 46.6	12 59.5	7 33.5	52.6	66 48.0	31.7
09	61 03.6	274 06.4	.. 38.2	269 47.6	.. 58.9	22 35.6	.. 52.8	81 50.5	.. 31.8
10	76 06.1	289 07.9	37.4	284 48.6	58.4	37 37.7	52.9	96 53.0	31.8
11	91 08.6	304 09.4	36.6	299 49.6	57.8	52 39.7	53.0	111 55.6	31.9
12	106 11.0	319 10.8	N12 35.8	314 50.7	N12 57.3	67 41.8	N13 53.1	126 58.1	S10 31.9
13	121 13.5	334 12.3	35.1	329 51.7	56.7	82 43.9	53.2	142 00.7	31.9
14	136 16.0	349 13.8	34.3	344 52.7	56.2	97 45.9	53.3	157 03.2	32.0
15	151 18.4	4 15.3	.. 33.5	359 53.7	.. 55.6	112 48.0	.. 53.5	172 05.7	.. 32.0
16	166 20.9	19 16.8	32.7	14 54.7	55.1	127 50.1	53.6	187 08.3	32.1
17	181 23.4	34 18.2	32.0	29 55.7	54.5	142 52.2	53.7	202 10.8	32.1
18	196 25.8	49 19.7	N12 31.2	44 56.7	N12 54.0	157 54.2	N13 53.8	217 13.4	S10 32.1
19	211 28.3	64 21.2	30.4	59 57.8	53.4	172 56.3	53.9	232 15.9	32.2
20	226 30.7	79 22.7	29.6	74 58.8	52.9	187 58.4	54.1	247 18.4	32.2
21	241 33.2	94 24.2	.. 28.9	89 59.8	.. 52.3	203 00.4	.. 54.2	262 21.0	.. 32.3
22	256 35.7	109 25.7	28.1	105 00.8	51.8	218 02.5	54.3	277 23.5	32.3
23	271 38.1	124 27.2	27.3	120 01.8	51.2	233 04.6	54.4	292 26.1	32.3
Mer. Pass.	h m 5 00.4	v 1.4 d 0.8		v 1.0 d 0.5		v 2.1 d 0.1		v 2.5 d 0.0	

STARS

Name	SHA	Dec
Acamar	315 12.9	S40 12.4
Achernar	335 21.2	S57 06.8
Acrux	173 01.6	S63 14.0
Adhara	255 07.2	S29 00.2
Aldebaran	290 41.3	N16 33.4
Alioth	166 14.1	N55 50.3
Alkaid	152 52.9	N49 12.0
Alnair	27 34.1	S46 50.7
Alnilam	275 39.3	S 1 11.2
Alphard	217 49.3	S 8 45.6
Alphecca	126 04.6	N26 38.3
Alpheratz	357 36.0	N29 13.0
Altair	62 00.8	N 8 55.8
Ankaa	353 08.3	S42 10.5
Antares	112 17.1	S26 29.1
Arcturus	145 48.9	N19 03.8
Atria	107 11.9	S69 04.3
Avior	234 15.9	S59 35.1
Bellatrix	278 24.5	N 6 22.3
Betelgeuse	270 53.8	N 7 24.7
Canopus	263 53.5	S52 42.4
Capella	280 24.2	N46 01.2
Deneb	49 26.2	N45 21.7
Denebola	182 26.3	N14 26.6
Diphda	348 48.5	S17 51.4
Dubhe	193 42.9	N61 37.8
Elnath	278 03.8	N28 37.6
Eltanin	90 42.2	N51 29.2
Enif	33 39.8	N 9 58.9
Fomalhaut	15 15.7	S29 29.7
Gacrux	171 53.1	S57 14.9
Gienah	175 44.9	S17 40.4
Hadar	148 37.6	S60 29.4
Hamal	327 52.7	N23 34.3
Kaus Aust.	83 33.8	S34 22.4
Kochab	137 19.2	N74 03.8
Markab	13 31.0	N15 19.8
Menkar	314 07.6	N 4 10.9
Menkent	147 59.0	S36 29.3
Miaplacidus	221 39.4	S69 48.9
Mirfak	308 30.4	N49 56.5
Nunki	75 48.9	S26 16.0
Peacock	53 07.1	S56 39.5
Pollux	243 19.2	N27 58.2
Procyon	244 52.5	N 5 10.0
Rasalhague	95 59.4	N12 32.6
Regulus	207 36.0	N11 51.3
Rigel	281 05.4	S 8 10.4
Rigil Kent.	139 41.7	S60 56.1
Sabik	102 03.9	S15 45.2
Schedar	349 32.4	N56 39.7
Shaula	96 11.7	S37 07.3
Sirius	258 27.7	S16 44.8
Spica	158 23.6	S11 17.0
Suhail	222 47.6	S43 31.7
Vega	80 33.6	N38 48.3
Zuben'ubi	136 57.2	S16 08.4

	SHA	Mer. Pass.
	° ′	h m
Venus	213 37.3	14 45
Mars	209 31.8	15 02
Jupiter	321 45.0	7 33
Saturn	20 44.5	3 38

© British Crown Copyright 2022. All rights reserved.

SUN / MOON

UT	SUN GHA	SUN Dec	MOON GHA	v	MOON Dec	d	HP
d h	° ′	° ′	° ′	′	° ′	′	′
6 00	178 49.8	N22 43.9	320 35.9	6.3	S19 37.8	13.0	60.7
01	193 49.7	43.7	335 01.2	6.5	19 24.8	13.0	60.7
02	208 49.6	43.5	349 26.7	6.6	19 11.8	13.2	60.7
03	223 49.5	. . 43.2	3 52.3	6.7	18 58.6	13.2	60.7
04	238 49.4	43.0	18 18.0	6.8	18 45.4	13.4	60.7
05	253 49.3	42.7	32 43.8	6.9	18 32.0	13.5	60.7
06	268 49.2	N22 42.5	47 09.7	7.1	S18 18.5	13.7	60.6
07	283 49.1	42.2	61 35.8	7.1	18 04.8	13.7	60.6
T 08	298 48.9	42.0	76 01.9	7.3	17 51.1	13.8	60.6
H 09	313 48.8	. . 41.7	90 28.2	7.4	17 37.3	13.9	60.6
U 10	328 48.7	41.5	104 54.6	7.5	17 23.4	14.0	60.6
R 11	343 48.6	41.2	119 21.1	7.6	17 09.4	14.2	60.6
S 12	358 48.5	N22 41.0	133 47.7	7.7	S16 55.2	14.2	60.5
D 13	13 48.4	40.7	148 14.4	7.9	16 41.0	14.3	60.5
A 14	28 48.3	40.5	162 41.3	7.9	16 26.7	14.4	60.5
Y 15	43 48.2	. . 40.2	177 08.2	8.1	16 12.3	14.5	60.5
16	58 48.1	40.0	191 35.3	8.1	15 57.8	14.5	60.5
17	73 48.0	39.7	206 02.4	8.3	15 43.3	14.7	60.5
18	88 47.9	N22 39.5	220 29.7	8.4	S15 28.6	14.7	60.4
19	103 47.8	39.2	234 57.1	8.5	15 13.9	14.9	60.4
20	118 47.7	38.9	249 24.6	8.6	14 59.0	14.9	60.4
21	133 47.6	. . 38.7	263 52.2	8.7	14 44.1	14.9	60.4
22	148 47.5	38.4	278 19.9	8.8	14 29.2	15.1	60.4
23	163 47.4	38.2	292 47.7	8.9	14 14.1	15.1	60.3
7 00	178 47.3	N22 37.9	307 15.6	9.0	S13 59.0	15.2	60.3
01	193 47.2	37.6	321 43.6	9.1	13 43.8	15.3	60.3
02	208 47.1	37.4	336 11.7	9.2	13 28.5	15.3	60.3
03	223 47.0	. . 37.1	350 39.9	9.3	13 13.2	15.4	60.3
04	238 46.9	36.9	5 08.2	9.5	12 57.8	15.4	60.2
05	253 46.8	36.6	19 36.7	9.5	12 42.4	15.5	60.2
06	268 46.7	N22 36.3	34 05.2	9.6	S12 26.9	15.6	60.2
07	283 46.6	36.1	48 33.8	9.7	12 11.3	15.6	60.2
F 08	298 46.5	35.8	63 02.5	9.7	11 55.7	15.7	60.2
R 09	313 46.4	. . 35.5	77 31.2	9.9	11 40.0	15.7	60.1
I 10	328 46.3	35.3	92 00.1	10.0	11 24.3	15.8	60.1
D 11	343 46.2	35.0	106 29.1	10.1	11 08.5	15.9	60.1
A 12	358 46.1	N22 34.7	120 58.2	10.1	S10 52.6	15.8	60.1
Y 13	13 46.0	34.5	135 27.3	10.3	10 36.8	15.9	60.0
14	28 45.9	34.2	149 56.6	10.3	10 20.9	16.0	60.0
15	43 45.8	. . 33.9	164 25.9	10.4	10 04.9	16.0	60.0
16	58 45.7	33.7	178 55.3	10.5	9 48.9	16.1	60.0
17	73 45.6	33.4	193 24.8	10.6	9 32.8	16.0	59.9
18	88 45.5	N22 33.1	207 54.4	10.6	S 9 16.8	16.1	59.9
19	103 45.4	32.8	222 24.0	10.7	9 00.7	16.2	59.9
20	118 45.3	32.6	236 53.7	10.9	8 44.5	16.2	59.9
21	133 45.2	. . 32.3	251 23.6	10.8	8 28.3	16.2	59.8
22	148 45.1	32.0	265 53.4	11.0	8 12.1	16.2	59.8
23	163 45.0	31.8	280 23.4	11.0	7 55.9	16.3	59.8
8 00	178 44.9	N22 31.5	294 53.4	11.2	S 7 39.6	16.3	59.7
01	193 44.8	31.2	309 23.6	11.1	7 23.3	16.3	59.7
02	208 44.7	30.9	323 53.7	11.3	7 07.0	16.3	59.7
03	223 44.6	. . 30.6	338 24.0	11.3	6 50.7	16.4	59.7
04	238 44.5	30.4	352 54.3	11.4	6 34.3	16.3	59.6
05	253 44.4	30.1	7 24.7	11.4	6 18.0	16.4	59.6
06	268 44.3	N22 29.8	21 55.1	11.6	S 6 01.6	16.4	59.6
07	283 44.2	29.5	36 25.7	11.5	5 45.2	16.4	59.5
S 08	298 44.1	29.2	50 56.2	11.7	5 28.8	16.5	59.5
A 09	313 44.0	. . 29.0	65 26.9	11.7	5 12.3	16.5	59.5
T 10	328 43.9	28.7	79 57.6	11.7	4 55.9	16.5	59.5
U 11	343 43.8	28.4	94 28.3	11.9	4 39.4	16.4	59.4
R 12	358 43.7	N22 28.1	108 59.2	11.8	S 4 23.0	16.5	59.4
D 13	13 43.6	27.8	123 30.0	12.0	4 06.5	16.4	59.4
A 14	28 43.5	27.5	138 01.0	11.9	3 50.1	16.5	59.3
Y 15	43 43.4	. . 27.3	152 31.9	12.1	3 33.6	16.5	59.3
16	58 43.3	27.0	167 03.0	12.1	3 17.1	16.4	59.3
17	73 43.2	26.7	181 34.1	12.1	3 00.7	16.5	59.3
18	88 43.2	N22 26.4	196 05.2	12.2	S 2 44.2	16.4	59.2
19	103 43.1	26.1	210 36.4	12.2	2 27.8	16.5	59.2
20	118 43.0	25.8	225 07.6	12.3	2 11.3	16.4	59.2
21	133 42.9	. . 25.5	239 38.9	12.3	1 54.9	16.5	59.1
22	148 42.8	25.2	254 10.2	12.3	1 38.4	16.4	59.1
23	163 42.7	24.9	268 41.5	12.4	S 1 22.0	16.4	59.1
	SD 15.8	d 0.3	SD 16.5		16.4		16.2

Twilight / Sunrise / Moonrise

Lat.	Twilight Naut.	Twilight Civil	Sunrise	Moonrise 6	Moonrise 7	Moonrise 8	Moonrise 9
°	h m	h m	h m	h m	h m	h m	h m
N 72	☐	☐	☐	■■■	00 52	(00 01 / 23 23)	22 49
N 70	☐	☐	☐	01 44	(00 26 / 23 49)	23 22	22 55
68	☐	☐	☐	00 47	(00 05 / 23 40)	23 20	23 01
66	////	////	00 56	(00 13 / 23 49)	23 33	23 19	23 06
64	////	////	01 53	23 36	23 26	23 18	23 10
62	////	////	02 26	23 28	23 21	23 17	23 13
60	////	01 19	02 49	23 15	23 16	23 16	23 16
N 58	////	01 58	03 08	23 06	23 11	23 15	23 19
56	////	02 24	03 24	22 59	23 07	23 14	23 21
54	01 12	02 45	03 37	22 52	23 04	23 14	23 23
52	01 49	03 02	03 49	22 46	23 01	23 13	23 25
50	02 13	03 16	03 59	22 40	22 58	23 13	23 27
45	02 56	03 44	04 21	22 28	22 51	23 12	23 31
N 40	03 25	04 06	04 38	22 18	22 46	23 11	23 35
35	03 47	04 23	04 52	22 09	22 41	23 10	23 38
30	04 05	04 38	05 05	22 02	22 37	23 09	23 40
20	04 33	05 02	05 26	21 49	22 30	23 08	23 45
N 10	04 55	05 21	05 44	21 37	22 24	23 07	23 49
0	05 13	05 39	06 01	21 26	22 18	23 06	23 53
S 10	05 29	05 55	06 18	21 15	22 12	23 05	23 57
20	05 45	06 12	06 36	21 03	22 05	23 04	24 01
30	06 00	06 30	06 56	20 50	21 58	23 03	24 06
35	06 09	06 40	07 08	20 42	21 54	23 02	24 08
40	06 18	06 51	07 22	20 33	21 49	23 01	24 12
45	06 27	07 04	07 38	20 22	21 43	23 01	24 15
S 50	06 38	07 20	07 57	20 10	21 37	23 00	24 20
52	06 43	07 27	08 07	20 04	21 33	22 59	24 22
54	06 49	07 34	08 17	19 57	21 30	22 59	24 24
56	06 54	07 43	08 29	19 49	21 26	22 58	24 27
58	07 01	07 52	08 43	19 41	21 22	22 57	24 30
S 60	07 08	08 03	08 59	19 31	21 17	22 57	24 33

Sunset / Twilight / Moonset

Lat.	Sunset	Twilight Civil	Twilight Naut.	Moonset 6	Moonset 7	Moonset 8	Moonset 9
°	h m	h m	h m	h m	h m	h m	h m
N 72	☐	☐	☐	■■■	06 56	09 34	11 54
N 70	☐	☐	☐	04 06	07 20	09 42	11 51
68	☐	☐	☐	05 02	07 38	09 48	11 49
66	23 09	////	////	05 34	07 52	09 53	11 47
64	22 15	////	////	05 58	08 04	09 58	11 45
62	21 43	////	////	06 17	08 14	10 02	11 44
60	21 19	22 49	·	06 32	08 22	10 05	11 43
N 58	21 01	22 10	////	06 45	08 29	10 08	11 42
56	20 45	21 44	////	06 56	08 36	10 10	11 41
54	20 32	21 24	22 55	07 06	08 42	10 13	11 40
52	20 20	21 08	22 20	07 14	08 47	10 15	11 39
50	20 10	20 53	21 56	07 22	08 51	10 16	11 38
45	19 49	20 25	21 14	07 38	09 01	10 21	11 37
N 40	19 32	20 04	20 45	07 52	09 10	10 24	11 35
35	19 17	19 47	20 23	08 03	09 17	10 27	11 34
30	19 05	19 32	20 05	08 13	09 23	10 29	11 33
20	18 44	19 08	19 37	08 29	09 33	10 34	11 31
N 10	18 25	18 48	19 15	08 44	09 43	10 37	11 30
0	18 09	18 31	18 57	08 57	09 51	10 41	11 28
S 10	17 52	18 15	18 41	09 11	09 59	10 44	11 27
20	17 34	17 58	18 25	09 25	10 08	10 48	11 25
30	17 14	17 40	18 10	09 41	10 18	10 52	11 23
35	17 02	17 30	18 01	09 50	10 24	10 54	11 22
40	16 48	17 19	17 52	10 00	10 31	10 57	11 21
45	16 32	17 06	17 43	10 13	10 38	11 00	11 20
S 50	16 13	16 51	17 32	10 27	10 47	11 03	11 18
52	16 03	16 44	17 27	10 34	10 51	11 05	11 17
54	15 53	16 36	17 21	10 42	10 56	11 07	11 17
56	15 41	16 27	17 16	10 50	11 01	11 09	11 16
58	15 27	16 18	17 09	10 59	11 06	11 11	11 15
S 60	15 11	16 07	17 02	11 10	11 12	11 13	11 14

SUN / MOON

Day	SUN Eqn. of Time 00ʰ	SUN Eqn. of Time 12ʰ	SUN Mer. Pass.	MOON Mer. Pass. Upper	MOON Mer. Pass. Lower	Age	Phase
d	m s	m s	h m	h m	h m	d	%
6	04 41	04 46	12 05	02 44	15 12	18	87
7	04 51	04 55	12 05	03 39	16 04	19	78
8	05 00	05 05	12 05	04 29	16 54	20	68

© British Crown Copyright 2022. All rights reserved.

ARIES · VENUS −4.7 · MARS +1.7 · JUPITER −2.2 · SATURN +0.6

UT	ARIES GHA	VENUS GHA	VENUS Dec	MARS GHA	MARS Dec	JUPITER GHA	JUPITER Dec	SATURN GHA	SATURN Dec
SUNDAY									
9 00	286 40.6	139 28.7	N12 26.6	135 02.8	N12 50.7	248 06.7	N13 54.5	307 28.6	S10 32.4
01	301 43.1	154 30.2	25.8	150 03.9	50.1	263 08.7	54.6	322 31.1	32.4
02	316 45.5	169 31.7	25.0	165 04.9	49.6	278 10.8	54.8	337 33.7	32.5
03	331 48.0	184 33.2	.. 24.3	180 05.9	.. 49.0	293 12.9	.. 54.9	352 36.2	.. 32.5
04	346 50.5	199 34.8	23.5	195 06.9	48.5	308 15.0	55.0	7 38.8	32.5
05	1 52.9	214 36.3	22.7	210 07.9	47.9	323 17.0	55.1	22 41.3	32.6
06	16 55.4	229 37.8	N12 21.9	225 08.9	N12 47.4	338 19.1	N13 55.2	37 43.8	S10 32.6
07	31 57.9	244 39.3	21.2	240 09.9	46.8	353 21.2	55.3	52 46.4	32.7
08	47 00.3	259 40.9	20.4	255 11.0	46.3	8 23.3	55.5	67 48.9	32.7
09	62 02.8	274 42.4	.. 19.6	270 12.0	.. 45.7	23 25.3	.. 55.6	82 51.5	.. 32.7
10	77 05.2	289 43.9	18.9	285 13.0	45.2	38 27.4	55.7	97 54.0	32.8
11	92 07.7	304 45.5	18.1	300 14.0	44.6	53 29.5	55.8	112 56.5	32.8
12	107 10.2	319 47.0	N12 17.3	315 15.0	N12 44.0	68 31.6	N13 55.9	127 59.1	S10 32.9
13	122 12.6	334 48.5	16.6	330 16.0	43.5	83 33.6	56.1	143 01.6	32.9
14	137 15.1	349 50.1	15.8	345 17.0	42.9	98 35.7	56.2	158 04.2	32.9
15	152 17.6	4 51.6	.. 15.0	0 18.1	.. 42.4	113 37.8	.. 56.3	173 06.7	.. 33.0
16	167 20.0	19 53.2	14.3	15 19.1	41.8	128 39.9	56.4	188 09.3	33.0
17	182 22.5	34 54.7	13.5	30 20.1	41.3	143 41.9	56.5	203 11.8	33.1
18	197 25.0	49 56.3	N12 12.7	45 21.1	N12 40.7	158 44.0	N13 56.6	218 14.3	S10 33.1
19	212 27.4	64 57.8	12.0	60 22.1	40.2	173 46.1	56.7	233 16.9	33.1
20	227 29.9	79 59.4	11.2	75 23.1	39.6	188 48.2	56.9	248 19.4	33.2
21	242 32.3	95 01.0	.. 10.5	90 24.2	.. 39.1	203 50.3	.. 57.0	263 22.0	.. 33.2
22	257 34.8	110 02.5	09.7	105 25.2	38.5	218 52.3	57.1	278 24.5	33.3
23	272 37.3	125 04.1	08.9	120 26.2	37.9	233 54.4	57.2	293 27.1	33.3
MONDAY									
10 00	287 39.7	140 05.7	N12 08.2	135 27.2	N12 37.4	248 56.5	N13 57.3	308 29.6	S10 33.3
01	302 42.2	155 07.3	07.4	150 28.2	36.8	263 58.6	57.4	323 32.2	33.4
02	317 44.7	170 08.8	06.7	165 29.2	36.3	279 00.7	57.6	338 34.7	33.4
03	332 47.1	185 10.4	.. 05.9	180 30.2	.. 35.7	294 02.7	.. 57.7	353 37.2	.. 33.5
04	347 49.6	200 12.0	05.1	195 31.3	35.2	309 04.8	57.8	8 39.8	33.5
05	2 52.1	215 13.6	04.4	210 32.3	34.6	324 06.9	57.9	23 42.3	33.5
06	17 54.5	230 15.2	N12 03.6	225 33.3	N12 34.1	339 09.0	N13 58.0	38 44.9	S10 33.6
07	32 57.0	245 16.8	02.9	240 34.3	33.5	354 11.0	58.1	53 47.4	33.6
08	47 59.5	260 18.4	02.1	255 35.3	32.9	9 13.1	58.3	68 50.0	33.7
09	63 01.9	275 20.0	.. 01.3	270 36.3	.. 32.4	24 15.2	.. 58.4	83 52.5	.. 33.7
10	78 04.4	290 21.6	12 00.6	285 37.4	31.8	39 17.3	58.5	98 55.1	33.7
11	93 06.8	305 23.2	11 59.8	300 38.4	31.3	54 19.4	58.6	113 57.6	33.8
12	108 09.3	320 24.8	N11 59.1	315 39.4	N12 30.7	69 21.4	N13 58.7	129 00.1	S10 33.8
13	123 11.8	335 26.4	58.3	330 40.4	30.2	84 23.5	58.8	144 02.7	33.9
14	138 14.2	350 28.0	57.6	345 41.4	29.6	99 25.6	58.9	159 05.2	33.9
15	153 16.7	5 29.6	.. 56.8	0 42.4	.. 29.0	114 27.7	.. 59.1	174 07.8	.. 34.0
16	168 19.2	20 31.3	56.0	15 43.5	28.5	129 29.8	59.2	189 10.3	34.0
17	183 21.6	35 32.9	55.3	30 44.5	27.9	144 31.9	59.3	204 12.9	34.0
18	198 24.1	50 34.5	N11 54.5	45 45.5	N12 27.4	159 33.9	N13 59.4	219 15.4	S10 34.1
19	213 26.6	65 36.1	53.8	60 46.5	26.8	174 36.0	59.5	234 18.0	34.1
20	228 29.0	80 37.8	53.0	75 47.5	26.3	189 38.1	59.6	249 20.5	34.2
21	243 31.5	95 39.4	.. 52.3	90 48.5	.. 25.7	204 40.2	.. 59.7	264 23.1	.. 34.2
22	258 34.0	110 41.1	51.5	105 49.6	25.1	219 42.3	13 59.9	279 25.6	34.2
23	273 36.4	125 42.7	50.8	120 50.6	24.6	234 44.3	14 00.0	294 28.2	34.3
TUESDAY									
11 00	288 38.9	140 44.3	N11 50.0	135 51.6	N12 24.0	249 46.4	N14 00.1	309 30.7	S10 34.3
01	303 41.3	155 46.0	49.3	150 52.6	23.5	264 48.5	00.2	324 33.3	34.4
02	318 43.8	170 47.6	48.5	165 53.6	22.9	279 50.6	00.3	339 35.8	34.4
03	333 46.3	185 49.3	.. 47.8	180 54.6	.. 22.3	294 52.7	.. 00.4	354 38.4	.. 34.5
04	348 48.7	200 51.0	47.0	195 55.6	21.8	309 54.8	00.5	9 40.9	34.5
05	3 51.2	215 52.6	46.3	210 56.7	21.2	324 56.8	00.7	24 43.4	34.5
06	18 53.7	230 54.3	N11 45.5	225 57.7	N12 20.7	339 58.9	N14 00.8	39 46.0	S10 34.6
07	33 56.1	245 55.9	44.8	240 58.7	20.1	355 01.0	00.9	54 48.5	34.6
08	48 58.6	260 57.6	44.0	255 59.7	19.5	10 03.1	01.0	69 51.1	34.7
09	64 01.1	275 59.3	.. 43.3	271 00.7	.. 19.0	25 05.2	.. 01.1	84 53.6	.. 34.7
10	79 03.5	291 01.0	42.5	286 01.7	18.4	40 07.3	01.2	99 56.2	34.8
11	94 06.0	306 02.6	41.8	301 02.8	17.9	55 09.4	01.3	114 58.7	34.8
12	109 08.4	321 04.3	N11 41.1	316 03.8	N12 17.3	70 11.4	N14 01.4	130 01.3	S10 34.8
13	124 10.9	336 06.0	40.3	331 04.8	16.7	85 13.5	01.6	145 03.8	34.9
14	139 13.4	351 07.7	39.6	346 05.8	16.2	100 15.6	01.7	160 06.4	34.9
15	154 15.8	6 09.4	.. 38.8	1 06.8	.. 15.6	115 17.7	.. 01.8	175 08.9	.. 35.0
16	169 18.3	21 11.1	38.1	16 07.8	15.1	130 19.8	01.9	190 11.5	35.0
17	184 20.8	36 12.8	37.3	31 08.9	14.5	145 21.9	02.0	205 14.0	35.1
18	199 23.2	51 14.5	N11 36.6	46 09.9	N12 13.9	160 24.0	N14 02.1	220 16.6	S10 35.1
19	214 25.7	66 16.2	35.9	61 10.9	13.4	175 26.0	02.2	235 19.1	35.1
20	229 28.2	81 17.9	35.1	76 11.9	12.8	190 28.1	02.3	250 21.7	35.2
21	244 30.6	96 19.6	.. 34.4	91 12.9	.. 12.3	205 30.2	.. 02.5	265 24.2	.. 35.2
22	259 33.1	111 21.3	33.6	106 13.9	11.7	220 32.3	02.6	280 26.8	35.3
23	274 35.6	126 23.0	32.9	121 15.0	11.1	235 34.4	02.7	295 29.3	35.3
Mer. Pass.	4 48.6	v 1.6	d 0.8	v 1.0	d 0.6	v 2.1	d 0.1	v 2.5	d 0.0

STARS

Name	SHA	Dec
Acamar	315 12.9	S40 12.4
Achernar	335 21.2	S57 06.8
Acrux	173 01.6	S63 14.0
Adhara	255 07.2	S29 00.2
Aldebaran	290 41.3	N16 33.4
Alioth	166 14.1	N55 50.3
Alkaid	152 52.9	N49 12.1
Al Na'ir	27 34.1	S46 50.7
Alnilam	275 39.3	S 1 11.2
Alphard	217 49.3	S 8 45.6
Alphecca	126 04.6	N26 38.3
Alpheratz	357 36.0	N29 13.0
Altair	62 00.8	N 8 55.8
Ankaa	353 08.3	S42 10.5
Antares	112 17.1	S26 29.1
Arcturus	145 48.9	N19 03.8
Atria	107 11.9	S69 04.3
Avior	234 15.9	S59 35.1
Bellatrix	278 24.5	N 6 22.3
Betelgeuse	270 53.8	N 7 24.7
Canopus	263 53.5	S52 42.4
Capella	280 24.2	N46 01.2
Deneb	49 26.2	N45 21.7
Denebola	182 26.3	N14 26.6
Diphda	348 48.5	S17 51.4
Dubhe	193 42.9	N61 37.8
Elnath	278 03.8	N28 37.6
Eltanin	90 42.2	N51 29.2
Enif	33 39.8	N 9 58.9
Fomalhaut	15 15.7	S29 29.7
Gacrux	171 53.1	S57 14.9
Gienah	175 44.9	S17 40.4
Hadar	148 37.6	S60 29.4
Hamal	327 52.7	N23 34.3
Kaus Aust.	83 33.8	S34 22.4
Kochab	137 19.2	N74 03.8
Markab	13 31.0	N15 19.8
Menkar	314 07.6	N 4 10.9
Menkent	147 59.0	S36 29.3
Miaplacidus	221 39.4	S69 48.9
Mirfak	308 30.3	N49 56.5
Nunki	75 48.9	S26 16.0
Peacock	53 07.1	S56 39.5
Pollux	243 19.2	N27 58.2
Procyon	244 52.5	N 5 10.0
Rasalhague	95 59.4	N12 32.6
Regulus	207 36.0	N11 51.3
Rigel	281 05.4	S 8 10.4
Rigil Kent.	139 41.8	S60 56.1
Sabik	102 03.9	S15 45.2
Schedar	349 32.4	N56 39.7
Shaula	96 11.7	S37 07.3
Sirius	258 27.7	S16 44.8
Spica	158 23.6	S11 17.0
Suhail	222 47.6	S43 31.7
Vega	80 33.6	N38 48.3
Zuben'ubi	136 57.2	S16 08.4

	SHA	Mer. Pass.
Venus	212 25.9	14 38
Mars	207 47.5	14 57
Jupiter	321 16.8	7 23
Saturn	20 49.9	3 25

© British Crown Copyright 2022. All rights reserved.

UT	SUN GHA	SUN Dec	MOON GHA	MOON v	MOON Dec	MOON d	MOON HP	Lat.	Twilight Naut.	Twilight Civil	Sunrise	Moonrise 9	Moonrise 10	Moonrise 11	Moonrise 12
d h	° ′	° ′	° ′	′	° ′	′	′	°	h m	h m	h m	h m	h m	h m	h m
9 00	178 42.6	N22 24.7	283 12.9	12.4	S 1 05.6	16.4	59.0	N 72	☐	☐	☐	22 49	22 09	21 07	☐
01	193 42.5	24.4	297 44.3	12.5	0 49.2	16.4	59.0	N 70	☐	☐	☐	22 55	22 26	21 46	☐
02	208 42.4	24.1	312 15.8	12.5	0 32.8	16.4	59.0	68	☐	☐	01 11	23 01	22 40	22 14	21 25
03	223 42.3 ..	23.8	326 47.3	12.5	S 0 16.4	16.4	59.0	66	////	////	02 01	23 06	22 52	22 35	22 10
04	238 42.2	23.5	341 18.8	12.6	0 00.0	16.3	58.9	64	////	////	02 31	23 10	23 01	22 52	22 40
05	253 42.1	23.2	355 50.4	12.6	N 0 16.3	16.4	58.9	62	////	////	02 51	23 13	23 09	23 06	23 03
06	268 42.0	N22 22.9	10 22.0	12.6	N 0 32.7	16.3	58.9	60	////	01 28	02 54	23 16	23 16	23 18	23 21
07	283 41.9	22.6	24 53.6	12.7	0 49.0	16.3	58.8	N 58	////	02 04	03 12	23 19	23 23	23 28	23 36
08	298 41.8	22.3	39 25.3	12.7	1 05.3	16.2	58.8	56	////	02 29	03 28	23 21	23 28	23 37	23 50
S 09	313 41.7 ..	22.0	53 57.0	12.7	1 21.5	16.3	58.8	54	01 21	02 49	03 41	23 23	23 33	23 45	24 01
U 10	328 41.6	21.7	68 28.7	12.8	1 37.8	16.2	58.7	52	01 54	03 05	03 52	23 25	23 38	23 53	24 11
N 11	343 41.6	21.4	83 00.5	12.7	1 54.0	16.2	58.7	50	02 18	03 19	04 02	23 27	23 42	23 59	24 20
D 12	358 41.5	N22 21.1	97 32.2	12.8	N 2 10.2	16.1	58.7	45	02 59	03 47	04 23	23 31	23 51	24 14	00 14
A 13	13 41.4	20.8	112 04.0	12.8	2 26.3	16.2	58.6	N 40	03 27	04 08	04 40	23 35	23 59	24 25	00 25
Y 14	28 41.3	20.5	126 35.8	12.8	2 42.5	16.1	58.6	35	03 49	04 25	04 54	23 38	24 06	00 06	00 36
15	43 41.2 ..	20.2	141 07.6	12.9	2 58.6	16.0	58.6	30	04 06	04 39	05 06	23 40	24 11	00 11	00 44
16	58 41.1	19.9	155 39.5	12.8	3 14.6	16.1	58.6	20	04 34	05 03	05 27	23 45	24 22	00 22	01 00
17	73 41.0	19.6	170 11.3	12.9	3 30.7	16.0	58.5	N 10	04 55	05 22	05 45	23 49	24 31	00 31	01 14
18	88 40.9	N22 19.3	184 43.2	12.9	N 3 46.7	15.9	58.5	0	05 13	05 39	06 02	23 53	24 39	00 39	01 26
19	103 40.8	19.0	199 15.1	12.9	4 02.6	16.0	58.5	S 10	05 29	05 56	06 18	23 57	24 48	00 48	01 39
20	118 40.7	18.7	213 47.0	12.9	4 18.6	15.9	58.4	20	05 45	06 12	06 36	24 01	00 01	00 57	01 53
21	133 40.6 ..	18.4	228 18.9	12.9	4 34.5	15.8	58.4	30	06 00	06 30	06 56	24 06	00 06	01 07	02 09
22	148 40.5	18.1	242 50.8	13.0	4 50.3	15.8	58.4	35	06 08	06 40	07 07	24 08	00 08	01 14	02 19
23	163 40.5	17.8	257 22.8	12.9	5 06.1	15.8	58.3	40	06 17	06 51	07 21	24 12	00 12	01 21	02 29
10 00	178 40.4	N22 17.4	271 54.7	13.0	N 5 21.9	15.8	58.3	45	06 26	07 03	07 36	24 15	00 15	01 29	02 42
01	193 40.3	17.1	286 26.7	12.9	5 37.7	15.6	58.3	S 50	06 37	07 18	07 56	24 20	00 20	01 39	02 58
02	208 40.2	16.8	300 58.6	13.0	5 53.3	15.7	58.2	52	06 42	07 25	08 05	24 22	00 22	01 44	03 05
03	223 40.1 ..	16.5	315 30.6	12.9	6 09.0	15.6	58.2	54	06 47	07 32	08 15	24 24	00 24	01 49	03 13
04	238 40.0	16.2	330 02.5	13.0	6 24.6	15.6	58.2	56	06 53	07 41	08 27	24 27	00 27	01 55	03 22
05	253 39.9	15.9	344 34.5	12.9	6 40.2	15.5	58.2	58	06 59	07 50	08 40	24 30	00 30	02 01	03 33
06	268 39.8	N22 15.6	359 06.4	13.0	N 6 55.7	15.4	58.1	S 60	07 05	08 01	08 56	24 33	00 33	02 08	03 45

UT	SUN GHA	SUN Dec	MOON GHA	MOON v	MOON Dec	MOON d	MOON HP	Lat.	Sunset	Twilight Civil	Twilight Naut.	Moonset 9	Moonset 10	Moonset 11	Moonset 12
								°	h m	h m	h m	h m	h m	h m	h m
07	283 39.7	15.3	13 38.4	12.9	7 11.1	15.4	58.1	N 72	☐	☐	☐	11 54	14 14	16 56	☐
08	298 39.7	15.0	28 10.4	12.9	7 26.5	15.4	58.1	N 70	☐	☐	☐	11 51	13 59	16 19	☐
M 09	313 39.6 ..	14.6	42 42.3	13.0	7 41.9	15.3	58.0	68	☐	☐	☐	11 49	13 48	15 53	18 23
O 10	328 39.5	14.3	57 14.3	12.9	7 57.2	15.2	58.0	66	22 56	////	////	11 47	13 39	15 33	17 39
N 11	343 39.4	14.0	71 46.2	12.9	8 12.4	15.2	58.0	64	22 08	////	////	11 45	13 31	15 18	17 10
D 12	358 39.3	N22 13.7	86 18.1	13.0	N 8 27.6	15.2	57.9	62	21 38	////	////	11 44	13 24	15 05	16 49
A 13	13 39.2	13.4	100 50.1	12.9	8 42.8	15.1	57.9	60	21 16	22 40	////	11 43	13 18	14 54	16 31
Y 14	28 39.1	13.1	115 22.0	12.9	8 57.9	15.0	57.9	N 58	20 57	22 05	////	11 42	13 13	14 44	16 16
15	43 39.0 ..	12.7	129 53.9	12.9	9 12.9	15.0	57.8	56	20 42	21 40	////	11 41	13 09	14 36	16 04
16	58 38.9	12.4	144 25.8	12.9	9 27.9	14.9	57.8	54	20 29	21 21	22 48	11 40	13 05	14 29	15 53
17	73 38.9	12.1	158 57.7	12.8	9 42.8	14.8	57.8	52	20 18	21 05	22 15	11 39	13 01	14 22	15 43
18	88 38.8	N22 11.8	173 29.5	12.9	N 9 57.6	14.8	57.8	50	20 08	20 51	21 52	11 38	12 58	14 17	15 35
19	103 38.7	11.5	188 01.4	12.8	10 12.4	14.7	57.7	45	19 47	20 24	21 11	11 37	12 51	14 04	15 17
20	118 38.6	11.1	202 33.2	12.8	10 27.1	14.7	57.7	N 40	19 30	20 03	20 43	11 35	12 45	13 54	15 02
21	133 38.5 ..	10.8	217 05.0	12.8	10 41.8	14.6	57.7	35	19 16	19 46	20 22	11 34	12 40	13 45	14 50
22	148 38.4	10.5	231 36.8	12.8	10 56.4	14.5	57.6	30	19 04	19 31	20 04	11 33	12 35	13 37	14 39
23	163 38.3	10.2	246 08.6	12.8	11 10.9	14.5	57.6	20	18 43	19 08	19 37	11 31	12 28	13 24	14 20
11 00	178 38.3	N22 09.9	260 40.4	12.7	N11 25.4	14.4	57.6	N 10	18 26	18 48	19 15	11 30	12 21	13 12	14 04
01	193 38.2	09.5	275 12.1	12.8	11 39.8	14.3	57.5	0	18 09	18 31	18 57	11 28	12 15	13 01	13 50
02	208 38.1	09.2	289 43.9	12.7	11 54.1	14.3	57.5	S 10	17 53	18 15	18 41	11 27	12 08	12 51	13 35
03	223 38.0 ..	08.9	304 15.6	12.6	12 08.4	14.2	57.5	20	17 35	17 59	18 26	11 25	12 02	12 39	13 19
04	238 37.9	08.5	318 47.2	12.7	12 22.6	14.1	57.5	30	17 15	17 41	18 11	11 23	11 54	12 26	13 01
05	253 37.8	08.2	333 18.9	12.6	12 36.7	14.0	57.4	35	17 04	17 31	18 03	11 22	11 50	12 19	12 50
06	268 37.7	N22 07.9	347 50.5	12.6	N12 50.7	14.0	57.4	40	16 50	17 20	17 54	11 21	11 45	12 10	12 39
07	283 37.7	07.6	2 22.1	12.6	13 04.7	13.9	57.4	45	16 35	17 08	17 45	11 20	11 40	12 01	12 25
08	298 37.6	07.2	16 53.7	12.5	13 18.6	13.8	57.3	S 50	16 15	16 53	17 34	11 18	11 33	11 49	12 08
T 09	313 37.5 ..	06.9	31 25.2	12.5	13 32.4	13.7	57.3	52	16 06	16 46	17 29	11 17	11 30	11 43	12 00
U 10	328 37.4	06.6	45 56.7	12.5	13 46.1	13.7	57.3	54	15 56	16 39	17 24	11 17	11 26	11 37	11 51
E 11	343 37.3	06.2	60 28.2	12.4	13 59.8	13.6	57.2	56	15 44	16 30	17 18	11 16	11 23	11 31	11 41
S 12	358 37.2	N22 05.9	74 59.6	12.4	N14 13.4	13.5	57.2	58	15 31	16 21	17 12	11 15	11 19	11 23	11 29
D 13	13 37.1	05.6	89 31.0	12.4	14 26.9	13.4	57.2	S 60	15 15	16 10	17 06	11 14	11 14	11 15	11 17
A 14	28 37.1	05.2	104 02.4	12.4	14 40.3	13.3	57.2								
Y 15	43 37.0 ..	04.9	118 33.8	12.3	14 53.6	13.3	57.1								
16	58 36.9	04.6	133 05.1	12.3	15 06.9	13.2	57.1								
17	73 36.8	04.2	147 36.4	12.2	15 20.1	13.1	57.1								
18	88 36.7	N22 03.9	162 07.6	12.2	N15 33.2	13.0	57.0								
19	103 36.7	03.6	176 38.8	12.2	15 46.2	12.9	57.0								
20	118 36.6	03.2	191 10.0	12.1	15 59.1	12.8	57.0								
21	133 36.5 ..	02.9	205 41.1	12.1	16 11.9	12.7	57.0								
22	148 36.4	02.6	220 12.2	12.1	16 24.6	12.7	56.9								
23	163 36.3	02.2	234 43.3	12.0	N16 37.3	12.6	56.9								
	SD 15.8	d 0.3	SD 16.0		15.8		15.6									

	SUN			MOON			
Day	Eqn. of Time 00h	Eqn. of Time 12h	Mer. Pass.	Mer. Pass. Upper	Mer. Pass. Lower	Age	Phase
d	m s	m s	h m	h m	h m	d	%
9	05 09	05 14	12 05	05 17	17 41	21	57
10	05 18	05 23	12 05	06 04	18 27	22	45
11	05 27	05 31	12 06	06 50	19 14	23	35

© British Crown Copyright 2022. All rights reserved.

UT (d h)	ARIES GHA	VENUS −4.7 GHA	Dec	MARS +1.8 GHA	Dec	JUPITER −2.3 GHA	Dec	SATURN +0.6 GHA	Dec
12 00	289 38.0	141 24.7	N11 32.2	136 16.0	N12 10.6	250 36.5	N14 02.8	310 31.9	S10 35.4
01	304 40.5	156 26.5	31.4	151 17.0	10.0	265 38.6	02.9	325 34.4	35.4
02	319 42.9	171 28.2	30.7	166 18.0	09.4	280 40.7	03.0	340 37.0	35.4
03	334 45.4	186 29.9	29.9	181 19.0	08.9	295 42.7	03.1	355 39.5	35.5
04	349 47.9	201 31.6	29.2	196 20.1	08.3	310 44.8	03.2	10 42.1	35.5
05	4 50.3	216 33.4	28.5	211 21.1	07.8	325 46.9	03.4	25 44.7	35.6
W 06	19 52.8	231 35.1	N11 27.7	226 22.1	N12 07.2	340 49.0	N14 03.5	40 47.2	S10 35.6
E 07	34 55.3	246 36.8	27.0	241 23.1	06.6	355 51.1	03.6	55 49.8	35.7
D 08	49 57.7	261 38.6	26.3	256 24.1	06.1	10 53.2	03.7	70 52.3	35.7
N 09	65 00.2	276 40.3	25.5	271 25.1	05.5	25 55.3	03.8	85 54.9	35.7
E 10	80 02.7	291 42.1	24.8	286 26.2	04.9	40 57.4	03.9	100 57.4	35.8
S 11	95 05.1	306 43.8	24.1	301 27.2	04.4	55 59.5	04.0	116 00.0	35.8
D 12	110 07.6	321 45.6	N11 23.3	316 28.2	N12 03.8	71 01.6	N14 04.1	131 02.5	S10 35.9
A 13	125 10.1	336 47.3	22.6	331 29.2	03.2	86 03.6	04.2	146 05.1	35.9
Y 14	140 12.5	351 49.1	21.9	346 30.2	02.7	101 05.7	04.4	161 07.6	36.0
15	155 15.0	6 50.9	21.1	1 31.2	02.1	116 07.8	04.5	176 10.2	36.0
16	170 17.4	21 52.6	20.4	16 32.3	01.6	131 09.9	04.6	191 12.7	36.1
17	185 19.9	36 54.4	19.7	31 33.3	01.0	146 12.0	04.7	206 15.3	36.1
18	200 22.4	51 56.2	N11 19.0	46 34.3	N12 00.4	161 14.1	N14 04.8	221 17.8	S10 36.1
19	215 24.8	66 58.0	18.2	61 35.3	11 59.9	176 16.2	04.9	236 20.4	36.2
20	230 27.3	81 59.7	17.5	76 36.3	59.3	191 18.3	05.0	251 22.9	36.2
21	245 29.8	97 01.5	16.8	91 37.3	58.7	206 20.4	05.1	266 25.5	36.3
22	260 32.2	112 03.3	16.0	106 38.4	58.2	221 22.5	05.2	281 28.1	36.3
23	275 34.7	127 05.1	15.3	121 39.4	57.6	236 24.6	05.4	296 30.6	36.4
13 00	290 37.2	142 06.9	N11 14.6	136 40.4	N11 57.0	251 26.7	N14 05.5	311 33.2	S10 36.4
01	305 39.6	157 08.7	13.9	151 41.4	56.5	266 28.7	05.6	326 35.7	36.5
02	320 42.1	172 10.5	13.1	166 42.4	55.9	281 30.8	05.7	341 38.3	36.5
03	335 44.5	187 12.3	12.4	181 43.5	55.3	296 32.9	05.8	356 40.8	36.5
04	350 47.0	202 14.1	11.7	196 44.5	54.8	311 35.0	05.9	11 43.4	36.6
05	5 49.5	217 15.9	11.0	211 45.5	54.2	326 37.1	06.0	26 45.9	36.6
T 06	20 51.9	232 17.7	N11 10.3	226 46.5	N11 53.6	341 39.2	N14 06.1	41 48.5	S10 36.7
H 07	35 54.4	247 19.5	09.5	241 47.5	53.1	356 41.3	06.2	56 51.0	36.7
U 08	50 56.9	262 21.4	08.8	256 48.5	52.5	11 43.4	06.3	71 53.6	36.8
R 09	65 59.3	277 23.2	08.1	271 49.6	51.9	26 45.5	06.5	86 56.2	36.8
S 10	81 01.8	292 25.0	07.4	286 50.6	51.4	41 47.6	06.6	101 58.7	36.9
D 11	96 04.3	307 26.8	06.6	301 51.6	50.8	56 49.7	06.7	117 01.3	36.9
A 12	111 06.7	322 28.7	N11 05.9	316 52.6	N11 50.2	71 51.8	N14 06.8	132 03.8	S10 36.9
Y 13	126 09.2	337 30.5	05.2	331 53.6	49.7	86 53.9	06.9	147 06.4	37.0
14	141 11.7	352 32.3	04.5	346 54.6	49.1	101 56.0	07.0	162 08.9	37.0
15	156 14.1	7 34.2	03.8	1 55.7	48.5	116 58.1	07.1	177 11.5	37.1
16	171 16.6	22 36.0	03.1	16 56.7	48.0	132 00.2	07.2	192 14.0	37.1
17	186 19.0	37 37.9	02.3	31 57.7	47.4	147 02.3	07.3	207 16.6	37.2
18	201 21.5	52 39.7	N11 01.6	46 58.7	N11 46.8	162 04.4	N14 07.4	222 19.2	S10 37.2
19	216 24.0	67 41.6	00.9	61 59.7	46.3	177 06.5	07.5	237 21.7	37.3
20	231 26.4	82 43.4	11 00.2	77 00.8	45.7	192 08.6	07.6	252 24.3	37.3
21	246 28.9	97 45.3	10 59.5	92 01.8	45.1	207 10.6	07.8	267 26.8	37.4
22	261 31.4	112 47.2	58.8	107 02.8	44.6	222 12.7	07.9	282 29.4	37.4
23	276 33.8	127 49.0	58.1	122 03.8	44.0	237 14.8	08.0	297 31.9	37.4
14 00	291 36.3	142 50.9	N10 57.4	137 04.8	N11 43.4	252 16.9	N14 08.1	312 34.5	S10 37.5
01	306 38.8	157 52.8	56.6	152 05.8	42.8	267 19.0	08.2	327 37.1	37.5
02	321 41.2	172 54.6	55.9	167 06.9	42.3	282 21.1	08.3	342 39.6	37.6
03	336 43.7	187 56.5	55.2	182 07.9	41.7	297 23.2	08.4	357 42.2	37.6
04	351 46.2	202 58.4	54.5	197 08.9	41.1	312 25.3	08.5	12 44.7	37.7
05	6 48.6	218 00.3	53.8	212 09.9	40.6	327 27.4	08.6	27 47.3	37.7
F 06	21 51.1	233 02.2	N10 53.1	227 10.9	N11 40.0	342 29.5	N14 08.7	42 49.9	S10 37.8
R 07	36 53.5	248 04.1	52.4	242 12.0	39.4	357 31.6	08.8	57 52.4	37.8
I 08	51 56.0	263 06.0	51.7	257 13.0	38.9	12 33.7	08.9	72 55.0	37.9
D 09	66 58.5	278 07.9	51.0	272 14.0	38.3	27 35.8	09.1	87 57.5	37.9
A 10	82 00.9	293 09.8	50.3	287 15.0	37.7	42 37.9	09.2	103 00.1	38.0
Y 11	97 03.4	308 11.7	49.6	302 16.0	37.2	57 40.0	09.3	118 02.7	38.0
12	112 05.9	323 13.6	N10 48.9	317 17.0	N11 36.6	72 42.1	N14 09.4	133 05.2	S10 38.0
13	127 08.3	338 15.5	48.2	332 18.1	36.0	87 44.2	09.5	148 07.8	38.1
14	142 10.8	353 17.4	47.5	347 19.1	35.4	102 46.3	09.6	163 10.3	38.1
15	157 13.3	8 19.3	46.8	2 20.1	34.9	117 48.4	09.7	178 12.9	38.2
16	172 15.7	23 21.3	46.1	17 21.1	34.3	132 50.5	09.8	193 15.5	38.2
17	187 18.2	38 23.2	45.4	32 22.1	33.7	147 52.6	09.9	208 18.0	38.3
18	202 20.7	53 25.1	N10 44.7	47 23.2	N11 33.2	162 54.7	N14 10.0	223 20.6	S10 38.3
19	217 23.1	68 27.0	44.0	62 24.2	32.6	177 56.8	10.1	238 23.1	38.4
20	232 25.6	83 29.0	43.3	77 25.2	32.0	192 58.9	10.2	253 25.7	38.4
21	247 28.0	98 30.9	42.6	92 26.2	31.4	208 01.0	10.3	268 28.3	38.5
22	262 30.5	113 32.9	41.9	107 27.2	30.9	223 03.1	10.4	283 30.8	38.5
23	277 33.0	128 34.8	41.2	122 28.3	30.3	238 05.2	10.5	298 33.4	38.6
Mer. Pass.	4 36.8	v 1.8	d 0.7	v 1.0	d 0.6	v 2.1	d 0.1	v 2.6	d 0.0

STARS

Name	SHA	Dec
Acamar	315 12.9	S40 12.4
Achernar	335 21.2	S57 06.8
Acrux	173 01.6	S63 14.0
Adhara	255 07.2	S29 00.1
Aldebaran	290 41.3	N16 33.4
Alioth	166 14.1	N55 50.3
Alkaid	152 52.9	N49 12.1
Alnair	27 34.1	S46 50.7
Alnilam	275 39.3	S 1 11.2
Alphard	217 49.3	S 8 45.6
Alphecca	126 04.6	N26 38.3
Alpheratz	357 35.9	N29 13.1
Altair	62 00.8	N 8 55.8
Ankaa	353 08.3	S42 10.5
Antares	112 17.1	S26 29.1
Arcturus	145 49.0	N19 03.8
Atria	107 11.9	S69 04.3
Avior	234 15.9	S59 35.1
Bellatrix	278 24.5	N 6 22.3
Betelgeuse	270 53.7	N 7 24.7
Canopus	263 53.5	S52 42.3
Capella	280 24.1	N46 01.2
Deneb	49 26.2	N45 21.7
Denebola	182 26.3	N14 26.6
Diphda	348 48.5	S17 51.3
Dubhe	193 42.9	N61 37.8
Elnath	278 03.8	N28 37.6
Eltanin	90 42.2	N51 29.2
Enif	33 39.7	N 9 58.9
Fomalhaut	15 15.7	S29 29.7
Gacrux	171 53.2	S57 14.9
Gienah	175 45.0	S17 40.4
Hadar	148 37.6	S60 29.4
Hamal	327 52.7	N23 34.3
Kaus Aust.	83 33.8	S34 22.4
Kochab	137 19.3	N74 03.8
Markab	13 30.9	N15 19.8
Menkar	314 07.6	N 4 10.9
Menkent	147 59.0	S36 29.3
Miaplacidus	221 39.4	S69 48.9
Mirfak	308 30.3	N49 56.5
Nunki	75 48.9	S26 16.0
Peacock	53 07.1	S56 39.5
Pollux	243 19.2	N27 58.2
Procyon	244 52.5	N 5 10.0
Rasalhague	95 59.4	N12 32.6
Regulus	207 36.0	N11 51.3
Rigel	281 05.3	S 8 10.4
Rigil Kent.	139 41.8	S60 56.1
Sabik	102 03.9	S15 45.2
Schedar	349 32.4	N56 39.7
Shaula	96 11.7	S37 07.3
Sirius	258 27.7	S16 44.8
Spica	158 23.6	S11 17.0
Suhail	222 47.6	S43 31.7
Vega	80 33.6	N38 48.4
Zuben'ubi	136 57.2	S16 08.4

	SHA	Mer. Pass.
Venus	211 29.7	14 30
Mars	206 03.2	14 52
Jupiter	320 49.5	7 13
Saturn	20 56.0	3 13

© British Crown Copyright 2022. All rights reserved.

SUN and MOON

UT (d h)	SUN GHA	SUN Dec	MOON GHA	v	MOON Dec	d	HP
12 00	178 36.2	N22 01.9	249 14.3	11.9	N16 49.9	12.4	56.9
01	193 36.2	01.5	263 45.2	12.0	17 02.3	12.4	56.9
02	208 36.1	01.2	278 16.2	11.9	17 14.7	12.3	56.8
03	223 36.0	.. 00.9	292 47.1	11.8	17 27.0	12.2	56.8
04	238 35.9	00.5	307 17.9	11.8	17 39.2	12.1	56.8
05	253 35.8	22 00.2	321 48.7	11.8	17 51.3	12.0	56.7
W 06	268 35.8	N21 59.8	336 19.5	11.7	N18 03.3	11.9	56.7
E 07	283 35.7	59.5	350 50.2	11.7	18 15.2	11.8	56.7
D 08	298 35.6	59.1	5 20.9	11.6	18 27.0	11.7	56.7
N 09	313 35.5	.. 58.8	19 51.5	11.6	18 38.7	11.6	56.6
E 10	328 35.4	58.4	34 22.1	11.5	18 50.3	11.5	56.6
S 11	343 35.4	58.1	48 52.6	11.5	19 01.8	11.4	56.6
D 12	358 35.3	N21 57.7	63 23.1	11.4	N19 13.2	11.3	56.6
A 13	13 35.2	57.4	77 53.5	11.4	19 24.5	11.2	56.5
Y 14	28 35.1	57.0	92 23.9	11.4	19 35.7	11.1	56.5
15	43 35.0	.. 56.7	106 54.3	11.3	19 46.8	10.9	56.5
16	58 35.0	56.3	121 24.6	11.2	19 57.7	10.9	56.5
17	73 34.9	56.0	135 54.8	11.3	20 08.6	10.8	56.4
18	88 34.8	N21 55.6	150 25.1	11.1	N20 19.4	10.7	56.4
19	103 34.7	55.3	164 55.2	11.1	20 30.1	10.5	56.4
20	118 34.6	54.9	179 25.3	11.1	20 40.6	10.5	56.4
21	133 34.6	.. 54.6	193 55.4	11.0	20 51.1	10.3	56.3
22	148 34.5	54.2	208 25.4	11.0	21 01.4	10.2	56.3
23	163 34.4	53.9	222 55.4	10.9	21 11.6	10.1	56.3
13 00	178 34.3	N21 53.5	237 25.3	10.9	N21 21.7	10.0	56.3
01	193 34.3	53.2	251 55.2	10.8	21 31.7	9.9	56.2
02	208 34.2	52.8	266 25.0	10.8	21 41.6	9.8	56.2
03	223 34.1	.. 52.5	280 54.8	10.7	21 51.4	9.7	56.2
04	238 34.0	52.1	295 24.5	10.7	22 01.1	9.5	56.2
05	253 34.0	51.7	309 54.2	10.6	22 10.6	9.4	56.1
T 06	268 33.9	N21 51.4	324 23.8	10.6	N22 20.0	9.3	56.1
H 07	283 33.8	51.0	338 53.4	10.5	22 29.3	9.2	56.1
U 08	298 33.7	50.7	353 22.9	10.5	22 38.5	9.1	56.1
R 09	313 33.7	.. 50.3	7 52.4	10.4	22 47.6	8.9	56.0
S 10	328 33.6	49.9	22 21.8	10.4	22 56.5	8.8	56.0
D 11	343 33.5	49.6	36 51.2	10.4	23 05.3	8.7	56.0
A 12	358 33.4	N21 49.2	51 20.6	10.3	N23 14.0	8.6	56.0
Y 13	13 33.4	48.8	65 49.9	10.2	23 22.6	8.5	55.9
14	28 33.3	48.5	80 19.1	10.2	23 31.1	8.3	55.9
15	43 33.2	.. 48.1	94 48.3	10.2	23 39.4	8.2	55.9
16	58 33.1	47.7	109 17.5	10.1	23 47.6	8.1	55.9
17	73 33.1	47.4	123 46.6	10.0	23 55.7	8.0	55.9
18	88 33.0	N21 47.0	138 15.6	10.1	N24 03.7	7.8	55.8
19	103 32.9	46.6	152 44.7	9.9	24 11.5	7.7	55.8
20	118 32.8	46.3	167 13.6	10.0	24 19.2	7.6	55.8
21	133 32.8	.. 45.9	181 42.6	9.9	24 26.8	7.4	55.8
22	148 32.7	45.5	196 11.5	9.8	24 34.2	7.3	55.7
23	163 32.6	45.2	210 40.3	9.8	24 41.5	7.2	55.7
14 00	178 32.6	N21 44.8	225 09.1	9.8	N24 48.7	7.1	55.7
01	193 32.5	44.4	239 37.9	9.7	24 55.8	6.9	55.7
02	208 32.4	44.0	254 06.6	9.7	25 02.7	6.8	55.7
03	223 32.3	.. 43.7	268 35.3	9.7	25 09.5	6.6	55.6
04	238 32.3	43.3	283 04.0	9.6	25 16.1	6.6	55.6
05	253 32.2	42.9	297 32.6	9.5	25 22.7	6.4	55.6
F 06	268 32.1	N21 42.5	312 01.1	9.6	N25 29.1	6.2	55.6
R 07	283 32.1	42.2	326 29.7	9.5	25 35.3	6.1	55.6
I 08	298 32.0	41.8	340 58.2	9.4	25 41.4	6.0	55.5
D 09	313 31.9	.. 41.4	355 26.6	9.5	25 47.4	5.9	55.5
A 10	328 31.8	41.0	9 55.1	9.3	25 53.3	5.7	55.5
Y 11	343 31.8	40.7	24 23.4	9.4	25 59.0	5.6	55.5
12	358 31.7	N21 40.3	38 51.8	9.3	N26 04.6	5.4	55.5
13	13 31.6	39.9	53 20.1	9.3	26 10.0	5.3	55.4
14	28 31.6	39.5	67 48.4	9.3	26 15.3	5.2	55.4
15	43 31.5	.. 39.1	82 16.7	9.3	26 20.5	5.0	55.4
16	58 31.4	38.8	96 45.0	9.2	26 25.5	4.9	55.4
17	73 31.4	38.4	111 13.2	9.2	26 30.4	4.7	55.4
18	88 31.3	N21 38.0	125 41.4	9.1	N26 35.1	4.6	55.3
19	103 31.2	37.6	140 09.5	9.2	26 39.7	4.5	55.3
20	118 31.2	37.2	154 37.7	9.1	26 44.2	4.3	55.3
21	133 31.1	.. 36.8	169 05.8	9.1	26 48.5	4.2	55.3
22	148 31.0	36.5	183 33.9	9.0	26 52.7	4.0	55.3
23	163 31.0	36.1	198 01.9	9.1	N26 56.7	3.9	55.2

SD 15.8   d 0.4 | SD 15.4   15.2   15.1

Twilight and Moonrise

Lat.	Naut.	Civil	Sunrise	Moonrise 12	13	14	15
N 72	□	□	□	□	□	□	□
N 70	□	□	□	□	□	□	□
68	□	□	□	21 25	□	□	□
66	////	////	01 25	22 10	□	□	□
64	////	////	02 09	22 40	22 19	□	□
62	////	00 27	02 38	23 03	23 00	22 59	23 13
60	////	01 37	02 59	23 21	23 28	23 44	24 19
N 58	////	02 11	03 17	23 36	23 50	24 13	00 13
56	00 25	02 34	03 32	23 50	24 08	00 08	00 36
54	01 29	02 53	03 44	24 01	00 01	00 23	00 54
52	02 00	03 09	03 55	24 11	00 11	00 36	01 10
50	02 23	03 22	04 05	24 20	00 20	00 48	01 24
45	03 02	03 49	04 26	00 14	00 40	01 12	01 51
N 40	03 30	04 10	04 42	00 25	00 56	01 31	02 13
35	03 51	04 27	04 56	00 36	01 09	01 47	02 32
30	04 08	04 41	05 08	00 44	01 21	02 02	02 48
20	04 35	05 04	05 28	01 00	01 41	02 26	03 14
N 10	04 56	05 23	05 46	01 14	01 59	02 47	03 37
0	05 14	05 40	06 02	01 26	02 15	03 06	03 59
S 10	05 30	05 56	06 18	01 39	02 32	03 26	04 21
20	05 45	06 12	06 35	01 53	02 50	03 47	04 44
30	06 00	06 29	06 55	02 09	03 11	04 12	05 11
35	06 07	06 39	07 06	02 19	03 23	04 27	05 27
40	06 16	06 49	07 19	02 29	03 37	04 44	05 46
45	06 25	07 02	07 35	02 42	03 54	05 04	06 09
S 50	06 35	07 16	07 54	02 58	04 15	05 30	06 38
52	06 40	07 23	08 02	03 05	04 25	05 42	06 52
54	06 45	07 30	08 12	03 13	04 37	05 57	07 08
56	06 50	07 38	08 24	03 22	04 50	06 14	07 28
58	06 56	07 47	08 37	03 33	05 05	06 34	07 53
S 60	07 03	07 58	08 52	03 45	05 23	07 00	08 27

Sunset, Twilight and Moonset

Lat.	Sunset	Civil	Naut.	Moonset 12	13	14	15
N 72	□	□	□	□	□	□	□
N 70	□	□	□	□	□	□	□
68	□	□	□	18 23	□	□	□
66	22 43	////	////	17 39	19 16	□	□
64	22 00	////	////	17 10	18 36	20 26	22 03
62	21 32	23 33	////	16 49	18 09	19 42	20 57
60	21 11	22 31	////	16 31	17 58	19 27	20 40
N 58	20 54	21 59	////	16 16	17 47	19 12	20 22
56	20 39	21 36	23 36	16 04	17 30	18 50	19 51
54	20 27	21 17	22 40	15 53	17 15	18 32	19 37
52	20 16	21 02	22 10	15 43	17 02	18 16	19 20
50	20 06	20 48	21 48	15 35	16 52	18 03	19 06
45	19 46	20 22	21 09	15 17	16 28	17 36	18 36
N 40	19 29	20 01	20 41	15 02	16 09	17 14	18 13
35	19 15	19 44	20 20	14 50	15 54	16 56	17 54
30	19 03	19 30	20 03	14 39	15 40	16 41	17 38
20	18 43	19 07	19 36	14 20	15 18	16 15	17 10
N 10	18 26	18 48	19 15	14 04	14 58	15 52	16 47
0	18 09	18 32	18 58	13 50	14 40	15 32	16 25
S 10	17 53	18 16	18 42	13 35	14 21	15 11	16 03
20	17 36	18 00	18 27	13 19	14 02	14 48	15 39
30	17 17	17 43	18 12	13 01	13 39	14 23	15 11
35	17 05	17 33	18 04	12 50	13 26	14 08	14 55
40	16 52	17 22	17 56	12 39	13 11	13 50	14 36
45	16 37	17 10	17 47	12 25	12 53	13 29	14 14
S 50	16 18	16 56	17 36	12 08	12 31	13 02	13 44
52	16 09	16 49	17 32	12 00	12 21	12 50	13 29
54	15 59	16 42	17 27	11 51	12 09	12 35	13 13
56	15 48	16 34	17 21	11 41	11 55	12 18	12 53
58	15 35	16 25	17 16	11 29	11 40	11 57	12 18
S 60	15 20	16 14	17 09	11 17	11 21	11 31	11 54

SUN and MOON

Day	SUN Eqn. of Time 00h	12h	Mer. Pass.	MOON Mer. Pass. Upper	Lower	Age	Phase
d	m s	m s	h m	h m	h m	d	%
12	05 35	05 39	12 06	07 38	20 02	24	25
13	05 42	05 46	12 06	08 27	20 53	25	17
14	05 50	05 53	12 06	09 19	21 45	26	10

© British Crown Copyright 2022. All rights reserved.

UT	ARIES	VENUS −4.7		MARS +1.8		JUPITER −2.3		SATURN +0.6	
d h	GHA	GHA	Dec	GHA	Dec	GHA	Dec	GHA	Dec
15 00	292 35.4	143 36.8	N10 40.5	137 29.3	N11 29.7	253 07.4	N14 10.7	313 35.9	S10 38.6
01	307 37.9	158 38.7	39.8	152 30.3	29.2	268 09.5	10.8	328 38.5	38.7
02	322 40.4	173 40.7	39.1	167 31.3	28.6	283 11.6	10.9	343 41.1	38.7
03	337 42.8	188 42.6 ..	38.4	182 32.3 ..	28.0	298 13.7 ..	11.0	358 43.6 ..	38.7
04	352 45.3	203 44.6	37.7	197 33.3	27.4	313 15.8	11.1	13 46.2	38.8
05	7 47.8	218 46.6	37.0	212 34.4	26.9	328 17.9	11.2	28 48.7	38.8
S 06	22 50.2	233 48.5	N10 36.3	227 35.4	N11 26.3	343 20.0	N14 11.3	43 51.3	S10 38.9
A 07	37 52.7	248 50.5	35.6	242 36.4	25.7	358 22.1	11.4	58 53.9	38.9
T 08	52 55.2	263 52.5	34.9	257 37.4	25.1	13 24.2	11.5	73 56.4	39.0
U 09	67 57.6	278 54.4 ..	34.2	272 38.4 ..	24.6	28 26.3 ..	11.6	88 59.0 ..	39.0
R 10	83 00.1	293 56.4	33.6	287 39.5	24.0	43 28.4	11.7	104 01.6	39.1
D 11	98 02.5	308 58.4	32.9	302 40.5	23.4	58 30.5	11.8	119 04.1	39.1
A 12	113 05.0	324 00.4	N10 32.2	317 41.5	N11 22.9	73 32.6	N14 11.9	134 06.7	S10 39.2
Y 13	128 07.5	339 02.4	31.5	332 42.5	22.3	88 34.7	12.0	149 09.2	39.2
14	143 09.9	354 04.4	30.8	347 43.5	21.7	103 36.8	12.1	164 11.8	39.3
15	158 12.4	9 06.4 ..	30.1	2 44.6 ..	21.1	118 38.9 ..	12.2	179 14.4 ..	39.3
16	173 14.9	24 08.4	29.4	17 45.6	20.6	133 41.0	12.3	194 16.9	39.4
17	188 17.3	39 10.4	28.7	32 46.6	20.0	148 43.1	12.5	209 19.5	39.4
18	203 19.8	54 12.4	N10 28.1	47 47.6	N11 19.4	163 45.2	N14 12.6	224 22.1	S10 39.5
19	218 22.3	69 14.4	27.4	62 48.6	18.8	178 47.3	12.7	239 24.6	39.5
20	233 24.7	84 16.4	26.7	77 49.7	18.3	193 49.5	12.8	254 27.2	39.6
21	248 27.2	99 18.5 ..	26.0	92 50.7 ..	17.7	208 51.6 ..	12.9	269 29.8 ..	39.6
22	263 29.7	114 20.5	25.3	107 51.7	17.1	223 53.7	13.0	284 32.3	39.7
23	278 32.1	129 22.5	24.7	122 52.7	16.5	238 55.8	13.1	299 34.9	39.7
16 00	293 34.6	144 24.5	N10 24.0	137 53.7	N11 16.0	253 57.9	N14 13.2	314 37.4	S10 39.7
01	308 37.0	159 26.6	23.3	152 54.8	15.4	269 00.0	13.3	329 40.0	39.8
02	323 39.5	174 28.6	22.6	167 55.8	14.8	284 02.1	13.4	344 42.6	39.8
03	338 42.0	189 30.7 ..	21.9	182 56.8 ..	14.2	299 04.2 ..	13.5	359 45.1 ..	39.9
04	353 44.4	204 32.7	21.3	197 57.8	13.7	314 06.3	13.6	14 47.7	39.9
05	8 46.9	219 34.7	20.6	212 58.8	13.1	329 08.4	13.7	29 50.3	40.0
S 06	23 49.4	234 36.8	N10 19.9	227 59.8	N11 12.5	344 10.5	N14 13.8	44 52.8	S10 40.0
U 07	38 51.8	249 38.9	19.2	243 00.9	11.9	359 12.6	13.9	59 55.4	40.1
N 08	53 54.3	264 40.9	18.6	258 01.9	11.4	14 14.8	14.0	74 58.0	40.1
D 09	68 56.8	279 43.0 ..	17.9	273 02.9 ..	10.8	29 16.9 ..	14.1	90 00.5 ..	40.2
A 10	83 59.2	294 45.0	17.2	288 03.9	10.2	44 19.0	14.2	105 03.1	40.2
Y 11	99 01.7	309 47.1	16.6	303 04.9	09.6	59 21.1	14.3	120 05.7	40.3
12	114 04.1	324 49.2	N10 15.9	318 06.0	N11 09.0	74 23.2	N14 14.4	135 08.2	S10 40.3
13	129 06.6	339 51.3	15.2	333 07.0	08.5	89 25.3	14.5	150 10.8	40.4
14	144 09.1	354 53.3	14.6	348 08.0	07.9	104 27.4	14.6	165 13.4	40.4
15	159 11.5	9 55.4 ..	13.9	3 09.0 ..	07.3	119 29.5 ..	14.7	180 15.9 ..	40.5
16	174 14.0	24 57.5	13.2	18 10.0	06.7	134 31.6	14.8	195 18.5	40.5
17	189 16.5	39 59.6	12.6	33 11.1	06.2	149 33.8	14.9	210 21.1	40.6
18	204 18.9	55 01.7	N10 11.9	48 12.1	N11 05.6	164 35.9	N14 15.0	225 23.6	S10 40.6
19	219 21.4	70 03.8	11.2	63 13.1	05.0	179 38.0	15.1	240 26.2	40.7
20	234 23.9	85 05.9	10.6	78 14.1	04.4	194 40.1	15.3	255 28.8	40.7
21	249 26.3	100 08.0 ..	09.9	93 15.1 ..	03.9	209 42.2 ..	15.4	270 31.3 ..	40.8
22	264 28.8	115 10.1	09.2	108 16.2	03.3	224 44.3	15.5	285 33.9	40.8
23	279 31.3	130 12.2	08.6	123 17.2	02.7	239 46.4	15.6	300 36.5	40.9
17 00	294 33.7	145 14.3	N10 07.9	138 18.2	N11 02.1	254 48.5	N14 15.7	315 39.0	S10 40.9
01	309 36.2	160 16.4	07.2	153 19.2	01.5	269 50.7	15.8	330 41.6	41.0
02	324 38.6	175 18.5	06.6	168 20.2	01.0	284 52.8	15.9	345 44.2	41.0
03	339 41.1	190 20.7 ..	05.9	183 21.3	11 00.4	299 54.9 ..	16.0	0 46.7 ..	41.1
04	354 43.6	205 22.8	05.3	198 22.3	10 59.8	314 57.0	16.1	15 49.3	41.1
05	9 46.0	220 24.9	04.6	213 23.3	59.2	329 59.1	16.2	30 51.9	41.2
M 06	24 48.5	235 27.1	N10 04.0	228 24.3	N10 58.6	345 01.2	N14 16.3	45 54.4	S10 41.2
O 07	39 51.0	250 29.2	03.3	243 25.3	58.1	0 03.3	16.4	60 57.0	41.3
N 08	54 53.4	265 31.3	02.7	258 26.4	57.5	15 05.5	16.5	75 59.6	41.3
D 09	69 55.9	280 33.5 ..	02.0	273 27.4 ..	56.9	30 07.6 ..	16.6	91 02.1 ..	41.4
A 10	84 58.4	295 35.6	01.3	288 28.4	56.3	45 09.7	16.7	106 04.7	41.4
Y 11	100 00.8	310 37.8	00.7	303 29.4	55.7	60 11.8	16.8	121 07.3	41.5
12	115 03.3	325 39.9	N10 00.0	318 30.4	N10 55.0	75 13.9	N14 16.9	136 09.9	S10 41.5
13	130 05.8	340 42.1	9 59.4	333 31.5	54.6	90 16.0	17.0	151 12.4	41.6
14	145 08.2	355 44.3	58.7	348 32.5	54.0	105 18.2	17.1	166 15.0	41.6
15	160 10.7	10 46.4 ..	58.1	3 33.5 ..	53.4	120 20.3 ..	17.2	181 17.6 ..	41.7
16	175 13.1	25 48.6	57.4	18 34.5	52.8	135 22.4	17.3	196 20.1	41.7
17	190 15.6	40 50.8	56.8	33 35.5	52.3	150 24.5	17.4	211 22.7	41.8
18	205 18.1	55 53.0	N 9 56.2	48 36.6	N10 51.7	165 26.6	N14 17.5	226 25.3	S10 41.8
19	220 20.5	70 55.1	55.5	63 37.6	51.1	180 28.7	17.6	241 27.8	41.9
20	235 23.0	85 57.3	54.9	78 38.6	50.5	195 30.9	17.7	256 30.4	41.9
21	250 25.5	100 59.5 ..	54.2	93 39.6 ..	49.9	210 33.0 ..	17.8	271 33.0 ..	42.0
22	265 27.9	116 01.7	53.6	108 40.6	49.4	225 35.1	17.9	286 35.6	42.0
23	280 30.4	131 03.9	52.9	123 41.7	48.8	240 37.2	18.0	301 38.1	42.1
Mer.Pass.	h m 4 25.0	v 2.1	d 0.7	v 1.0	d 0.6	v 2.1	d 0.1	v 2.6	d 0.0

STARS

Name	SHA	Dec
Acamar	315 12.9	S40 12.4
Achernar	335 21.1	S57 06.8
Acrux	173 01.6	S63 14.0
Adhara	255 07.2	S29 00.1
Aldebaran	290 41.3	N16 33.4
Alioth	166 14.1	N55 50.3
Alkaid	152 52.9	N49 12.1
Alnair	27 34.1	S46 50.7
Alnilam	275 39.3	S 1 11.1
Alphard	217 49.3	S 8 45.6
Alphecca	126 04.6	N26 38.3
Alpheratz	357 35.9	N29 13.1
Altair	62 00.8	N 8 55.8
Ankaa	353 08.2	S42 10.5
Antares	112 17.1	S26 29.1
Arcturus	145 49.0	N19 03.8
Atria	107 11.9	S69 04.3
Avior	234 15.9	S59 35.1
Bellatrix	278 24.5	N 6 22.3
Betelgeuse	270 53.7	N 7 24.7
Canopus	263 53.5	S52 42.3
Capella	280 24.1	N46 01.2
Deneb	49 26.3	N45 21.8
Denebola	182 26.3	N14 26.6
Diphda	348 48.5	S17 51.3
Dubhe	193 42.9	N61 37.8
Elnath	278 03.7	N28 37.6
Eltanin	90 42.3	N51 29.2
Enif	33 39.7	N 9 58.9
Fomalhaut	15 15.6	S29 29.7
Gacrux	171 53.2	S57 14.9
Gienah	175 45.0	S17 40.4
Hadar	148 37.6	S60 29.4
Hamal	327 56.2	N23 34.3
Kaus Aust.	83 33.7	S34 22.4
Kochab	137 19.3	N74 03.8
Markab	13 30.9	N15 19.8
Menkar	314 07.6	N 4 10.9
Menkent	147 59.0	S36 29.3
Miaplacidus	221 39.4	S69 48.9
Mirfak	308 30.3	N49 56.5
Nunki	75 48.9	S26 16.0
Peacock	53 07.1	S56 39.5
Pollux	243 19.2	N27 58.2
Procyon	244 52.5	N 5 10.0
Rasalhague	95 59.4	N12 32.6
Regulus	207 36.0	N11 51.3
Rigel	281 05.3	S 8 10.4
Rigil Kent.	139 41.8	S60 56.1
Sabik	102 03.9	S15 45.2
Schedar	349 32.3	N56 39.7
Shaula	96 11.7	S37 07.3
Sirius	258 27.7	S16 44.8
Spica	158 23.6	S11 17.0
Suhail	222 47.6	S43 31.6
Vega	80 33.6	N38 48.4
Zuben'ubi	136 57.3	S16 08.4

	SHA	Mer.Pass.
	° ′	h m
Venus	210 50.0	14 20
Mars	204 19.2	14 47
Jupiter	320 23.3	7 03
Saturn	21 02.9	3 01

© British Crown Copyright 2022. All rights reserved.

UT	SUN GHA	SUN Dec	MOON GHA	v	MOON Dec	d	HP
d h	° ′	° ′	° ′	′	° ′	′	′
15 00	178 30.9	N21 35.7	212 30.0	9.0	N27 00.6	3.8	55.2
01	193 30.8	35.3	226 58.0	9.0	27 04.4	3.6	55.2
02	208 30.7	34.9	241 26.0	9.0	27 08.0	3.4	55.2
03	223 30.7 ..	34.5	255 54.0	9.0	27 11.4	3.4	55.2
04	238 30.6	34.1	270 22.0	9.0	27 14.8	3.2	55.1
05	253 30.6	33.7	284 50.0	8.9	27 18.0	3.0	55.1
06	268 30.5	N21 33.4	299 17.9	9.0	N27 21.0	2.9	55.1
S 07	283 30.4	33.0	313 45.9	8.9	27 23.9	2.8	55.1
A 08	298 30.4	32.6	328 13.8	8.9	27 26.7	2.6	55.1
T 09	313 30.3 ..	32.2	342 41.7	9.0	27 29.3	2.4	55.1
U 10	328 30.2	31.8	357 09.7	8.9	27 31.7	2.3	55.0
R 11	343 30.2	31.4	11 37.6	8.9	27 34.0	2.2	55.0
D 12	358 30.1	N21 31.0	26 05.5	8.9	N27 36.2	2.1	55.0
A 13	13 30.0	30.6	40 33.4	8.9	27 38.3	1.9	55.0
Y 14	28 30.0	30.2	55 01.3	8.9	27 40.2	1.7	55.0
15	43 29.9 ..	29.8	69 29.2	8.9	27 41.9	1.6	55.0
16	58 29.8	29.4	83 57.1	8.9	27 43.5	1.5	54.9
17	73 29.8	29.0	98 25.0	8.9	27 45.0	1.3	54.9
18	88 29.7	N21 28.6	112 52.9	9.0	N27 46.3	1.1	54.9
19	103 29.6	28.2	127 20.9	8.9	27 47.4	1.1	54.9
20	118 29.6	27.8	141 48.8	8.9	27 48.5	0.8	54.9
21	133 29.5 ..	27.4	156 16.7	9.0	27 49.3	0.8	54.9
22	148 29.5	27.0	170 44.7	8.9	27 50.1	0.6	54.8
23	163 29.4	26.6	185 12.6	9.0	27 50.7	0.4	54.8
16 00	178 29.3	N21 26.2	199 40.6	9.0	N27 51.1	0.3	54.8
01	193 29.3	25.8	214 08.6	8.9	27 51.4	0.2	54.8
02	208 29.2	25.4	228 36.5	9.1	27 51.6	0.0	54.8
03	223 29.2 ..	25.0	243 04.6	9.0	27 51.6	0.1	54.8
04	238 29.1	24.6	257 32.6	9.0	27 51.5	0.3	54.8
05	253 29.0	24.2	272 00.6	9.1	27 51.2	0.4	54.7
06	268 29.0	N21 23.8	286 28.7	9.1	N27 50.8	0.6	54.7
S 07	283 28.9	23.4	300 56.8	9.1	27 50.2	0.6	54.7
U 08	298 28.8	23.0	315 24.9	9.1	27 49.6	0.9	54.7
N 09	313 28.8 ..	22.6	329 53.0	9.2	27 48.7	1.0	54.7
D 10	328 28.7	22.2	344 21.2	9.2	27 47.7	1.1	54.7
A 11	343 28.7	21.8	358 49.4	9.2	27 46.6	1.2	54.7
Y 12	358 28.6	N21 21.3	13 17.6	9.2	N27 45.4	1.4	54.6
13	13 28.6	20.9	27 45.8	9.3	27 44.0	1.6	54.6
14	28 28.5	20.5	42 14.1	9.3	27 42.4	1.7	54.6
15	43 28.4 ..	20.1	56 42.4	9.4	27 40.7	1.8	54.6
16	58 28.4	19.7	71 10.8	9.4	27 38.9	1.9	54.6
17	73 28.3	19.3	85 39.2	9.4	27 37.0	2.1	54.6
18	88 28.3	N21 18.9	100 07.6	9.4	N27 34.9	2.2	54.6
19	103 28.2	18.5	114 36.0	9.5	27 32.7	2.4	54.5
20	118 28.1	18.0	129 04.5	9.5	27 30.3	2.5	54.5
21	133 28.1 ..	17.6	143 33.0	9.6	27 27.8	2.7	54.5
22	148 28.0	17.2	158 01.6	9.6	27 25.1	2.7	54.5
23	163 28.0	16.8	172 30.2	9.7	27 22.4	3.0	54.5
17 00	178 27.9	N21 16.4	186 58.9	9.7	N27 19.4	3.0	54.5
01	193 27.9	16.0	201 27.6	9.7	27 16.4	3.2	54.5
02	208 27.8	15.5	215 56.3	9.8	27 13.2	3.3	54.5
03	223 27.7 ..	15.1	230 25.1	9.9	27 09.9	3.4	54.4
04	238 27.7	14.7	244 54.0	9.9	27 06.5	3.6	54.4
05	253 27.6	14.3	259 22.9	9.9	27 02.9	3.7	54.4
06	268 27.6	N21 13.9	273 51.8	10.0	N26 59.2	3.9	54.4
07	283 27.5	13.4	288 20.8	10.1	26 55.3	4.0	54.4
08	298 27.5	13.0	302 49.9	10.1	26 51.3	4.1	54.4
M 09	313 27.4 ..	12.6	317 19.0	10.1	26 47.2	4.2	54.4
O 10	328 27.4	12.2	331 48.1	10.2	26 43.0	4.3	54.4
N 11	343 27.3	11.8	346 17.3	10.3	26 38.7	4.5	54.4
D 12	358 27.3	N21 11.3	0 46.6	10.3	N26 34.2	4.6	54.3
A 13	13 27.2	10.9	15 15.9	10.4	26 29.6	4.8	54.3
Y 14	28 27.1	10.5	29 45.3	10.4	26 24.8	4.8	54.3
15	43 27.1 ..	10.0	44 14.7	10.5	26 20.0	5.0	54.3
16	58 27.0	09.6	58 44.2	10.6	26 15.0	5.1	54.3
17	73 27.0	09.2	73 13.8	10.6	26 09.9	5.3	54.3
18	88 26.9	N21 08.8	87 43.4	10.7	N26 04.6	5.3	54.3
19	103 26.9	08.3	102 13.1	10.7	25 59.3	5.5	54.3
20	118 26.8	07.9	116 42.8	10.8	25 53.8	5.6	54.3
21	133 26.8 ..	07.5	131 12.6	10.9	25 48.2	5.7	54.3
22	148 26.7	07.0	145 42.5	10.9	25 42.5	5.9	54.2
23	163 26.7	06.6	160 12.4	11.0	N25 36.6	5.9	54.2
	SD 15.8	d 0.4	SD 15.0		14.9		14.8

Lat.	Twilight Naut.	Twilight Civil	Sunrise	Moonrise 15	Moonrise 16	Moonrise 17	Moonrise 18
°	h m	h m	h m	h m	h m	h m	h m
N 72	▭	▭	▭	▭	▭	▭	▭
N 70	▭	▭	▭	▭	▭	▭	▭
68	▭	▭	▭	▭	▭	▭	▭
66	////	////	01 38	▭	▭	▭	▭
64	////	////	02 17	▭	▭	▭	01 22
62	////	00 55	02 44	23 13	24 33	00 33	02 17
60	////	01 47	03 05	24 19	00 19	01 24	02 50
N 58	////	02 18	03 22	00 13	00 54	01 56	03 14
56	00 50	02 40	03 36	00 36	01 19	02 20	03 33
54	01 38	02 58	03 48	00 54	01 39	02 39	03 49
52	02 07	03 13	03 59	01 10	01 56	02 55	04 03
50	02 28	03 26	04 08	01 24	02 11	03 09	04 15
45	03 06	03 52	04 28	01 51	02 40	03 37	04 40
N 40	03 33	04 12	04 44	02 13	03 03	03 59	05 00
35	03 53	04 29	04 58	02 32	03 22	04 18	05 16
30	04 10	04 43	05 09	02 48	03 39	04 33	05 30
20	04 37	05 05	05 29	03 14	04 06	05 00	05 54
N 10	04 57	05 24	05 47	03 37	04 30	05 23	06 15
0	05 14	05 40	06 02	03 59	04 52	05 44	06 35
S 10	05 30	05 56	06 18	04 21	05 14	06 06	06 54
20	05 44	06 11	06 35	04 44	05 38	06 29	07 15
30	05 59	06 28	06 54	05 11	06 06	06 55	07 38
35	06 06	06 38	07 05	05 27	06 22	07 11	07 52
40	06 15	06 48	07 18	05 46	06 41	07 29	08 08
45	06 23	07 00	07 33	06 09	07 05	07 51	08 28
S 50	06 34	07 14	07 51	06 38	07 34	08 18	08 51
52	06 38	07 20	08 00	06 52	07 49	08 32	09 03
54	06 43	07 28	08 09	07 08	08 06	08 47	09 16
56	06 48	07 35	08 20	07 28	08 26	09 06	09 31
58	06 54	07 44	08 33	07 53	08 52	09 28	09 48
S 60	07 00	07 54	08 47	08 27	09 28	09 57	10 10

Lat.	Sunset	Twilight Civil	Twilight Naut.	Moonset 15	Moonset 16	Moonset 17	Moonset 18
°	h m	h m	h m	h m	h m	h m	h m
N 72	▭	▭	▭	▭	▭	▭	▭
N 70	▭	▭	▭	▭	▭	▭	▭
68	▭	▭	▭	▭	▭	▭	▭
66	22 30	////	////	▭	▭	▭	23 42
64	21 52	////	////	▭	▭	23 30	23 01
62	21 26	23 11	////	22 03	22 33	22 35	22 32
60	21 06	22 22	////	20 57	21 41	22 02	22 11
N 58	20 49	21 53	////	20 22	21 10	21 37	21 53
56	20 35	21 31	23 16	19 57	20 46	21 18	21 38
54	20 23	21 13	22 31	19 37	20 27	21 01	21 25
52	20 13	20 58	22 04	19 20	20 10	20 47	21 13
50	20 03	20 45	21 43	19 06	19 56	20 35	21 03
45	19 43	20 19	21 06	18 36	19 27	20 09	20 42
N 40	19 27	19 59	20 39	18 13	19 05	19 48	20 24
35	19 14	19 43	20 18	17 54	18 46	19 31	20 10
30	19 02	19 29	20 02	17 38	18 30	19 17	19 57
20	18 43	19 07	19 35	17 10	18 03	18 51	19 35
N 10	18 26	18 48	19 15	16 47	17 39	18 29	19 16
0	18 10	18 32	18 58	16 25	17 18	18 09	18 58
S 10	17 54	18 16	18 42	16 03	16 56	17 48	18 40
20	17 37	18 01	18 28	15 39	16 32	17 26	18 20
30	17 18	17 44	18 14	15 11	16 04	17 01	17 58
35	17 07	17 35	18 06	14 55	15 48	16 45	17 45
40	16 55	17 24	17 58	14 36	15 29	16 28	17 29
45	16 40	17 13	17 49	14 13	15 06	16 06	17 11
S 50	16 21	16 59	17 39	13 44	14 37	15 39	16 48
52	16 13	16 52	17 35	13 29	14 22	15 26	16 37
54	16 03	16 45	17 30	13 13	14 05	15 11	16 25
56	15 52	16 37	17 25	12 53	13 45	14 53	16 10
58	15 40	16 29	17 19	12 28	13 19	14 31	15 53
S 60	15 25	16 19	17 13	11 54	12 44	14 02	15 32

Day	SUN Eqn. of Time 00ʰ	SUN Eqn. of Time 12ʰ	SUN Mer. Pass.	MOON Mer. Pass. Upper	MOON Mer. Pass. Lower	Age	Phase
d	m s	m s	h m	h m	h m	d	%
15	05 56	05 59	12 06	10 12	22 38	27	5
16	06 03	06 05	12 06	11 05	23 31	28	2
17	06 08	06 11	12 06	11 57	24 22	29	0

© British Crown Copyright 2022. All rights reserved.

UT	ARIES GHA	VENUS −4.7 GHA	Dec	MARS +1.8 GHA	Dec	JUPITER −2.3 GHA	Dec	SATURN +0.6 GHA	Dec	STARS Name	SHA	Dec
d h	° ′	° ′	° ′	° ′	° ′	° ′	° ′	° ′	° ′		° ′	° ′
18 00	295 32.9	146 06.1 N 9	52.3	138 42.7 N10	48.2	255 39.3 N14	18.1	316 40.7 S10	42.1	Acamar	315 12.8	S40 12.4
01	310 35.3	161 08.3	51.6	153 43.7	47.6	270 41.4	18.2	331 43.3	42.2	Achernar	335 21.1	S57 06.7
02	325 37.8	176 10.5	51.0	168 44.7	47.0	285 43.6	18.3	346 45.8	42.2	Acrux	173 01.7	S63 14.0
03	340 40.3	191 12.7 ..	50.4	183 45.8 ..	46.5	300 45.7 ..	18.4	1 48.4 ..	42.3	Adhara	255 07.2	S29 00.1
04	355 42.7	206 14.9	49.7	198 46.8	45.9	315 47.8	18.5	16 51.0	42.3	Aldebaran	290 41.3	N16 33.4
05	10 45.2	221 17.1	49.1	213 47.8	45.3	330 49.9	18.6	31 53.6	42.4			
T 06	25 47.6	236 19.4 N 9	48.5	228 48.8 N10	44.7	345 52.0 N14	18.7	46 56.1 S10	42.4	Alioth	166 14.1	N55 50.3
U 07	40 50.1	251 21.6	47.8	243 49.8	44.1	0 54.2	18.8	61 58.7	42.5	Alkaid	152 52.9	N49 12.1
E 08	55 52.6	266 23.8	47.2	258 50.9	43.5	15 56.3	18.9	77 01.3	42.5	Alnair	27 34.0	S46 50.7
S 09	70 55.0	281 26.0 ..	46.6	273 51.9 ..	43.0	30 58.4 ..	19.0	92 03.8 ..	42.6	Alnilam	275 39.3	S 1 11.1
D 10	85 57.5	296 28.3	45.9	288 52.9	42.4	46 00.5	19.1	107 06.4	42.6	Alphard	217 49.3	S 8 45.6
A 11	101 00.0	311 30.5	45.3	303 53.9	41.8	61 02.6	19.2	122 09.0	42.7			
Y 12	116 02.4	326 32.8 N 9	44.7	318 54.9 N10	41.2	76 04.8 N14	19.3	137 11.6 S10	42.7	Alphecca	126 04.6	N26 38.3
13	131 04.9	341 35.0	44.0	333 56.0	40.6	91 06.9	19.4	152 14.1	42.8	Alpheratz	357 35.9	N29 13.1
14	146 07.4	356 37.2	43.4	348 57.0	40.0	106 09.0	19.5	167 16.7	42.8	Altair	62 00.8	N 8 55.8
15	161 09.8	11 39.5 ..	42.8	3 58.0 ..	39.5	121 11.1 ..	19.6	182 19.3 ..	42.9	Ankaa	353 08.2	S42 10.5
16	176 12.3	26 41.8	42.1	18 59.0	38.9	136 13.3	19.7	197 21.8	42.9	Antares	112 17.1	S26 29.1
17	191 14.8	41 44.0	41.5	34 00.0	38.3	151 15.4	19.8	212 24.4	43.0			
18	206 17.2	56 46.3 N 9	40.9	49 01.1 N10	37.7	166 17.5 N14	19.9	227 27.0 S10	43.0	Arcturus	145 49.0	N19 03.8
19	221 19.7	71 48.5	40.3	64 02.1	37.1	181 19.6	20.0	242 29.6	43.1	Atria	107 12.0	S69 04.3
20	236 22.1	86 50.8	39.6	79 03.1	36.5	196 21.7	20.1	257 32.1	43.1	Avior	234 15.9	S59 35.0
21	251 24.6	101 53.1 ..	39.0	94 04.1 ..	36.0	211 23.9 ..	20.2	272 34.7 ..	43.2	Bellatrix	278 24.5	N 6 22.3
22	266 27.1	116 55.4	38.4	109 05.1	35.4	226 26.0	20.3	287 37.3	43.2	Betelgeuse	270 53.7	N 7 24.7
23	281 29.5	131 57.6	37.8	124 06.2	34.8	241 28.1	20.4	302 39.9	43.3			
19 00	296 32.0	146 59.9 N 9	37.2	139 07.2 N10	34.2	256 30.2 N14	20.5	317 42.4 S10	43.3	Canopus	263 53.5	S52 42.3
01	311 34.5	162 02.2	36.5	154 08.2	33.6	271 32.4	20.6	332 45.0	43.4	Capella	280 24.1	N46 01.2
02	326 36.9	177 04.5	35.9	169 09.2	33.0	286 34.5	20.7	347 47.6	43.4	Deneb	49 26.2	N45 21.8
03	341 39.4	192 06.8 ..	35.3	184 10.2 ..	32.5	301 36.6 ..	20.8	2 50.2 ..	43.5	Denebola	182 26.3	N14 26.6
04	356 41.9	207 09.1	34.7	199 11.3	31.9	316 38.7	20.9	17 52.7	43.5	Diphda	348 48.4	S17 51.3
05	11 44.3	222 11.4	34.1	214 12.3	31.3	331 40.9	21.0	32 55.3	43.6			
W 06	26 46.8	237 13.7 N 9	33.4	229 13.3 N10	30.7	346 43.0 N14	21.1	47 57.9 S10	43.7	Dubhe	193 42.9	N61 37.7
E 07	41 49.2	252 16.0	32.8	244 14.3	30.1	1 45.1	21.2	63 00.5	43.7	Elnath	278 03.7	N28 37.6
D 08	56 51.7	267 18.3	32.2	259 15.4	29.5	16 47.2	21.3	78 03.0	43.8	Eltanin	90 42.3	N51 29.2
N 09	71 54.2	282 20.7 ..	31.6	274 16.4 ..	28.9	31 49.4 ..	21.4	93 05.6 ..	43.8	Enif	33 39.7	N 9 59.0
E 10	86 56.6	297 23.0	31.0	289 17.4	28.4	46 51.5	21.5	108 08.2	43.9	Fomalhaut	15 15.6	S29 29.7
S 11	101 59.1	312 25.3	30.4	304 18.4	27.8	61 53.6	21.6	123 10.8	43.9			
D 12	117 01.6	327 27.6 N 9	29.8	319 19.4 N10	27.2	76 55.7 N14	21.7	138 13.3 S10	44.0	Gacrux	171 53.2	S57 14.9
A 13	132 04.0	342 30.0	29.2	334 20.5	26.6	91 57.9	21.7	153 15.9	44.0	Gienah	175 45.0	S17 40.4
Y 14	147 06.5	357 32.3	28.6	349 21.5	26.0	107 00.0	21.8	168 18.5	44.1	Hadar	148 37.7	S60 29.4
15	162 09.0	12 34.7 ..	28.0	4 22.5 ..	25.4	122 02.1 ..	21.9	183 21.1 ..	44.1	Hamal	327 52.6	N23 34.3
16	177 11.4	27 37.0	27.3	19 23.5	24.8	137 04.3	22.0	198 23.6	44.2	Kaus Aust.	83 33.7	S34 22.4
17	192 13.9	42 39.3	26.7	34 24.5	24.3	152 06.4	22.1	213 26.2	44.2			
18	207 16.4	57 41.7 N 9	26.1	49 25.6 N10	23.7	167 08.5 N14	22.2	228 28.8 S10	44.3	Kochab	137 19.4	N74 03.8
19	222 18.8	72 44.1	25.5	64 26.6	23.1	182 10.6	22.3	243 31.4	44.3	Markab	13 30.9	N15 19.9
20	237 21.3	87 46.4	24.9	79 27.6	22.5	197 12.8	22.4	258 33.9	44.4	Menkar	314 07.5	N 4 10.9
21	252 23.7	102 48.8 ..	24.3	94 28.6 ..	21.9	212 14.9 ..	22.5	273 36.5 ..	44.4	Menkent	147 59.0	S36 29.3
22	267 26.2	117 51.1	23.7	109 29.7	21.3	227 17.0	22.6	288 39.1	44.5	Miaplacidus	221 39.4	S69 48.8
23	282 28.7	132 53.5	23.1	124 30.7	20.7	242 19.2	22.7	303 41.7	44.5			
20 00	297 31.1	147 55.9 N 9	22.5	139 31.7 N10	20.1	257 21.3 N14	22.8	318 44.2 S10	44.6	Mirfak	308 30.2	N49 56.5
01	312 33.6	162 58.3	21.9	154 32.7	19.6	272 23.4	22.9	333 46.8	44.7	Nunki	75 48.9	S26 16.0
02	327 36.1	178 00.6	21.3	169 33.7	19.0	287 25.5	23.0	348 49.4	44.7	Peacock	53 07.0	S56 39.5
03	342 38.5	193 03.0 ..	20.7	184 34.8 ..	18.4	302 27.7 ..	23.1	3 52.0 ..	44.8	Pollux	243 19.2	N27 58.2
04	357 41.0	208 05.4	20.1	199 35.8	17.8	317 29.8	23.2	18 54.6	44.8	Procyon	244 52.4	N 5 10.0
05	12 43.5	223 07.8	19.6	214 36.8	17.2	332 31.9	23.3	33 57.1	44.9			
T 06	27 45.9	238 10.2 N 9	19.0	229 37.8 N10	16.6	347 34.1 N14	23.4	48 59.7 S10	44.9	Rasalhague	95 59.4	N12 32.7
H 07	42 48.4	253 12.6	18.4	244 38.8	16.0	2 36.2	23.5	64 02.3	45.0	Regulus	207 36.0	N11 51.3
U 08	57 50.9	268 15.0	17.8	259 39.9	15.4	17 38.3	23.6	79 04.9	45.0	Rigel	281 05.3	S 8 10.4
R 09	72 53.3	283 17.4 ..	17.2	274 40.9 ..	14.9	32 40.5 ..	23.7	94 07.4 ..	45.1	Rigil Kent.	139 41.8	S60 56.1
S 10	87 55.8	298 19.8	16.6	289 41.9	14.3	47 42.6	23.8	109 10.0	45.1	Sabik	102 03.9	S15 45.2
D 11	102 58.2	313 22.2	16.0	304 42.9	13.7	62 44.7	23.9	124 12.6	45.2			
A 12	118 00.7	328 24.7 N 9	15.4	319 44.0 N10	13.1	77 46.9 N14	24.0	139 15.2 S10	45.2	Schedar	349 32.3	N56 39.7
Y 13	133 03.2	343 27.1	14.8	334 45.0	12.5	92 49.0	24.1	154 17.8	45.3	Shaula	96 11.7	S37 07.3
14	148 05.6	358 29.5	14.3	349 46.0	11.9	107 51.1	24.2	169 20.3	45.3	Sirius	258 27.6	S16 44.8
15	163 08.1	13 31.9 ..	13.7	4 47.0 ..	11.3	122 53.3 ..	24.2	184 22.9 ..	45.4	Spica	158 23.6	S11 17.0
16	178 10.6	28 34.4	13.1	19 48.0	10.7	137 55.4	24.3	199 25.5	45.4	Suhail	222 47.6	S43 31.6
17	193 13.0	43 36.8	12.5	34 49.1	10.1	152 57.5	24.4	214 28.1	45.5			
18	208 15.5	58 39.3 N 9	11.9	49 50.1 N10	09.6	167 59.7 N14	24.5	229 30.7 S10	45.6	Vega	80 33.6	N38 48.4
19	223 18.0	73 41.7	11.3	64 51.1	09.0	183 01.8	24.6	244 33.2	45.6	Zuben'ubi	136 57.3	S16 08.4
20	238 20.4	88 44.2	10.8	79 52.1	08.4	198 03.9	24.7	259 35.8	45.7		SHA	Mer. Pass.
21	253 22.9	103 46.6 ..	10.2	94 53.1 ..	07.8	213 06.1 ..	24.8	274 38.4 ..	45.7	Venus	210 27.9	14 10
22	268 25.3	118 49.1	09.6	109 54.2	07.2	228 08.2	24.9	289 41.0	45.8	Mars	202 35.2	14 43
23	283 27.8	133 51.5	09.0	124 55.2	06.6	243 10.3	25.0	304 43.6	45.8	Jupiter	319 58.2	6 53
Mer. Pass. 4 13.2		v 2.3 d 0.6		v 1.0 d 0.6		v 2.1 d 0.1		v 2.6 d 0.1		Saturn	21 10.4	2 49

© British Crown Copyright 2022. All rights reserved.

UT	SUN GHA	Dec	MOON GHA	v	Dec	d	HP
d h	° ′	° ′	° ′	′	° ′	′	′
18 00	178 26.6	N21 06.2	174 42.4	11.1	N25 30.7	6.1	54.2
01	193 26.6	05.8	189 12.5	11.1	25 24.6	6.2	54.2
02	208 26.5	05.3	203 42.6	11.2	25 18.4	6.3	54.2
03	223 26.5	.. 04.9	218 12.8	11.3	25 12.1	6.4	54.2
04	238 26.4	04.4	232 43.1	11.3	25 05.7	6.6	54.2
05	253 26.4	04.0	247 13.4	11.4	24 59.1	6.6	54.2
06	268 26.3	N21 03.6	261 43.8	11.4	N24 52.5	6.8	54.2
07	283 26.3	03.1	276 14.2	11.6	24 45.7	6.8	54.2
08	298 26.2	02.7	290 44.8	11.6	24 38.9	7.0	54.2
T 09	313 26.2	.. 02.3	305 15.4	11.7	24 31.9	7.1	54.2
U 10	328 26.1	01.8	319 46.1	11.7	24 24.8	7.2	54.1
E 11	343 26.1	01.4	334 16.8	11.8	24 17.6	7.3	54.1
S 12	358 26.0	N21 00.9	348 47.6	11.9	N24 10.3	7.4	54.1
D 13	13 26.0	00.5	3 18.5	11.9	24 02.9	7.6	54.1
A 14	28 25.9	21 00.1	17 49.4	12.0	23 55.3	7.6	54.1
Y 15	43 25.9	20 59.6	32 20.4	12.1	23 47.7	7.7	54.1
16	58 25.8	59.2	46 51.5	12.2	23 40.0	7.8	54.1
17	73 25.8	58.7	61 22.7	12.2	23 32.2	8.0	54.1
18	88 25.7	N20 58.3	75 53.9	12.3	N23 24.2	8.0	54.1
19	103 25.7	57.9	90 25.2	12.4	23 16.2	8.2	54.1
20	118 25.7	57.4	104 56.6	12.5	23 08.0	8.2	54.1
21	133 25.6	.. 57.0	119 28.1	12.5	22 59.8	8.3	54.1
22	148 25.6	56.5	133 59.6	12.6	22 51.5	8.5	54.1
23	163 25.5	56.1	148 31.2	12.6	22 43.0	8.5	54.1
19 00	178 25.5	N20 55.6	163 02.8	12.8	N22 34.5	8.6	54.1
01	193 25.4	55.2	177 34.6	12.8	22 25.9	8.8	54.1
02	208 25.4	54.7	192 06.4	12.8	22 17.1	8.8	54.0
03	223 25.3	.. 54.3	206 38.2	13.0	22 08.3	8.9	54.0
04	238 25.3	53.8	221 10.2	13.0	21 59.4	9.0	54.0
05	253 25.2	53.4	235 42.2	13.1	21 50.4	9.1	54.0
06	268 25.2	N20 52.9	250 14.3	13.1	N21 41.3	9.2	54.0
W 07	283 25.2	52.5	264 46.4	13.3	21 32.1	9.2	54.0
E 08	298 25.1	52.0	279 18.7	13.3	21 22.9	9.4	54.0
D 09	313 25.1	.. 51.6	293 51.0	13.3	21 13.5	9.4	54.0
N 10	328 25.0	51.1	308 23.3	13.5	21 04.1	9.6	54.0
E 11	343 25.0	50.7	322 55.8	13.5	20 54.5	9.6	54.0
S 12	358 24.9	N20 50.2	337 28.3	13.5	N20 44.9	9.7	54.0
D 13	13 24.9	49.8	352 00.8	13.7	20 35.2	9.8	54.0
A 14	28 24.9	49.3	6 33.5	13.7	20 25.4	9.9	54.0
Y 15	43 24.8	.. 48.9	21 06.2	13.8	20 15.5	9.9	54.0
16	58 24.8	48.4	35 39.0	13.8	20 05.6	10.1	54.0
17	73 24.7	47.9	50 11.8	14.0	19 55.5	10.1	54.0
18	88 24.7	N20 47.5	64 44.8	13.9	N19 45.4	10.2	54.0
19	103 24.7	47.0	79 17.7	14.1	19 35.2	10.3	54.0
20	118 24.6	46.6	93 50.8	14.1	19 24.9	10.3	54.0
21	133 24.6	.. 46.1	108 23.9	14.2	19 14.6	10.5	54.0
22	148 24.5	45.6	122 57.1	14.2	19 04.1	10.5	54.0
23	163 24.5	45.2	137 30.3	14.4	18 53.6	10.5	54.0
20 00	178 24.5	N20 44.7	152 03.7	14.3	N18 43.1	10.7	54.0
01	193 24.4	44.3	166 37.0	14.5	18 32.4	10.7	54.0
02	208 24.4	43.8	181 10.5	14.5	18 21.7	10.8	54.0
03	223 24.3	.. 43.3	195 44.0	14.6	18 10.9	10.9	54.0
04	238 24.3	42.9	210 17.6	14.6	18 00.0	10.9	54.0
05	253 24.3	42.4	224 51.2	14.7	17 49.1	11.1	54.0
06	268 24.2	N20 41.9	239 24.9	14.7	N17 38.0	11.0	54.0
T 07	283 24.2	41.5	253 58.6	14.8	17 27.0	11.2	54.0
H 08	298 24.1	41.0	268 32.4	14.9	17 15.8	11.2	54.0
U 09	313 24.1	.. 40.5	283 06.3	14.9	17 04.6	11.3	54.0
R 10	328 24.1	40.1	297 40.2	15.0	16 53.3	11.3	54.0
S 11	343 24.0	39.6	312 14.2	15.1	16 42.0	11.4	54.0
D 12	358 24.0	N20 39.1	326 48.3	15.1	N16 30.5	11.4	54.0
A 13	13 24.0	38.7	341 22.4	15.2	16 19.1	11.6	54.0
Y 14	28 23.9	38.2	355 56.6	15.2	16 07.5	11.6	54.0
15	43 23.9	.. 37.7	10 30.8	15.2	15 55.9	11.7	54.0
16	58 23.8	37.3	25 05.0	15.4	15 44.2	11.7	54.0
17	73 23.8	36.8	39 39.4	15.4	15 32.5	11.8	54.0
18	88 23.8	N20 36.3	54 13.8	15.4	N15 20.7	11.8	54.0
19	103 23.7	35.8	68 48.2	15.5	15 08.9	11.9	54.0
20	118 23.7	35.4	83 22.7	15.5	14 57.0	12.0	54.0
21	133 23.7	.. 34.9	97 57.2	15.6	14 45.0	12.0	54.0
22	148 23.6	34.4	112 31.8	15.6	14 33.0	12.1	54.0
23	163 23.6	33.9	127 06.4	15.7	N14 20.9	12.1	54.0
	SD 15.8	d 0.5	SD 14.7		14.7		14.7

Moonrise

Lat.	Twilight Naut.	Civil	Sunrise	18	19	20	21
°	h m	h m	h m	h m	h m	h m	h m
N 72	□	□	□	□	□	□	05 44
N 70	□	□	□	□	□	03 47	06 09
68	////	////	00 42	□	□	04 29	06 28
66	////	////	01 51	□	02 51	04 57	06 43
64	////	////	02 26	01 22	03 31	05 18	06 55
62	////	01 14	02 51	02 17	03 59	05 35	07 06
60	////	01 57	03 11	02 50	04 20	05 49	07 15
N 58	////	02 25	03 27	03 14	04 37	06 01	07 22
56	01 07	02 46	03 41	03 33	04 52	06 11	07 29
54	01 47	03 03	03 52	03 49	05 04	06 20	07 35
52	02 13	03 18	04 03	04 03	05 15	06 28	07 40
50	02 33	03 30	04 12	04 15	05 25	06 36	07 45
45	03 10	03 56	04 31	04 40	05 45	06 51	07 56
N 40	03 36	04 15	04 47	05 00	06 02	07 04	08 04
35	03 56	04 31	05 00	05 16	06 15	07 14	08 12
30	04 12	04 44	05 11	05 30	06 27	07 24	08 18
20	04 38	05 07	05 31	05 54	06 48	07 40	08 29
N 10	04 58	05 25	05 47	06 15	07 06	07 53	08 39
0	05 15	05 41	06 03	06 35	07 22	08 06	08 48
S 10	05 30	05 56	06 18	06 54	07 38	08 19	08 57
20	05 44	06 11	06 34	07 15	07 56	08 33	09 07
30	05 58	06 27	06 53	07 38	08 16	08 49	09 18
35	06 05	06 36	07 04	07 52	08 27	08 58	09 24
40	06 13	06 46	07 16	08 08	08 41	09 08	09 31
45	06 22	06 58	07 31	08 28	08 57	09 20	09 40
S 50	06 31	07 11	07 48	08 51	09 16	09 34	09 50
52	06 35	07 18	07 57	09 03	09 25	09 41	09 54
54	06 40	07 24	08 06	09 16	09 35	09 49	09 59
56	06 45	07 32	08 16	09 31	09 46	09 57	10 05
58	06 50	07 40	08 28	09 48	10 00	10 06	10 11
S 60	06 56	07 50	08 42	10 10	10 15	10 17	10 18

Moonset

Lat.	Sunset	Twilight Civil	Naut.	18	19	20	21
°	h m	h m	h m	h m	h m	h m	h m
N 72	□	□	□	□	□	23 55	23 10
N 70	□	□	□	□	□	(00 22 / 23 28)	22 57
68	23 20	////	////	□	23 39	23 07	22 46
66	22 18	////	////	23 42	23 09	22 51	22 37
64	21 44	////	////	23 01	22 47	22 37	22 29
62	21 19	22 54	////	22 32	22 29	22 26	22 22
60	21 00	22 13	////	22 11	22 14	22 16	22 16
N 58	20 44	21 46	////	21 53	22 02	22 07	22 11
56	20 31	21 25	23 01	21 38	21 51	22 00	22 06
54	20 19	21 08	22 23	21 25	21 41	21 53	22 02
52	20 09	20 54	21 58	21 13	21 32	21 47	21 55
50	20 00	20 41	21 38	21 03	21 24	21 41	21 55
45	19 41	20 16	21 02	20 42	21 08	21 29	21 48
N 40	19 26	19 57	20 36	20 24	20 54	21 19	21 41
35	19 13	19 41	20 16	20 10	20 42	21 10	21 36
30	19 01	19 28	20 00	19 57	20 32	21 03	21 31
20	18 42	19 06	19 34	19 35	20 14	20 50	21 22
N 10	18 25	18 48	19 14	19 16	19 58	20 38	21 15
0	18 10	18 32	18 58	18 58	19 44	20 27	21 08
S 10	17 55	18 17	18 43	18 40	19 29	20 16	21 01
20	17 38	18 02	18 29	18 20	19 13	20 04	20 53
30	17 20	17 46	18 15	17 58	18 55	19 50	20 44
35	17 09	17 37	18 08	17 45	18 44	19 42	20 39
40	16 57	17 27	18 00	17 29	18 32	19 33	20 33
45	16 42	17 11	17 51	17 11	18 17	19 22	20 27
S 50	16 25	17 02	17 42	16 48	17 59	19 09	20 18
52	16 17	16 55	17 38	16 37	17 50	19 03	20 15
54	16 07	16 49	17 33	16 25	17 41	18 56	20 10
56	15 57	16 41	17 28	16 10	17 30	18 49	20 06
58	15 45	16 33	17 23	15 53	17 17	18 40	20 01
S 60	15 31	16 23	17 17	15 32	17 03	18 30	19 55

Day	SUN Eqn. of Time 00h	12h	Mer. Pass.	MOON Mer. Pass. Upper	Lower	Age	Phase
d	m s	m s	h m	h m	h m	d	%
18	06 13	06 16	12 06	12 46	00 22	01	1
19	06 18	06 20	12 06	13 33	01 10	02	3
20	06 22	06 24	12 06	14 17	01 55	03	7

© British Crown Copyright 2022. All rights reserved.

UT (d h)	ARIES GHA	VENUS −4.6 GHA	Dec	MARS +1.8 GHA	Dec	JUPITER −2.3 GHA	Dec	SATURN +0.6 GHA	Dec	STARS Name	SHA	Dec
21 00	298 30.3	148 54.0 N 9	08.5	139 56.2 N10	06.0	258 12.5 N14	25.1	319 46.1 S10	45.9	Acamar	315 12.8	S40 12.4
01	313 32.7	163 56.5	07.9	154 57.2	05.4	273 14.6	25.2	334 48.7	45.9	Achernar	335 21.0	S57 06.7
02	328 35.2	178 58.9	07.3	169 58.3	04.8	288 16.7	25.3	349 51.3	46.0	Acrux	173 01.7	S63 14.0
03	343 37.7	194 01.4 ..	06.7	184 59.3 ..	04.2	303 18.9 ..	25.4	4 53.9 ..	46.0	Adhara	255 07.2	S29 00.1
04	358 40.1	209 03.9	06.2	200 00.3	03.7	318 21.0	25.5	19 56.5	46.1	Aldebaran	290 41.2	N16 33.4
05	13 42.6	224 06.4	05.6	215 01.3	03.1	333 23.1	25.6	34 59.0	46.1			
F 06	28 45.1	239 08.9 N 9	05.0	230 02.3 N10	02.5	348 25.3 N14	25.7	50 01.6 S10	46.2	Alioth	166 14.2	N55 50.3
R 07	43 47.5	254 11.3	04.5	245 03.4	01.9	3 27.4	25.8	65 04.2	46.3	Alkaid	152 53.0	N49 12.1
I 08	58 50.0	269 13.8	03.9	260 04.4	01.3	18 29.5	25.9	80 06.8	46.3	Alnair	27 34.0	S46 50.7
D 09	73 52.5	284 16.3 ..	03.3	275 05.4 ..	00.7	33 31.7 ..	25.9	95 09.4 ..	46.4	Alnilam	275 39.2	S 1 11.1
A 10	88 54.9	299 18.8	02.8	290 06.4 10	00.1	48 33.8	26.0	110 11.9	46.4	Alphard	217 49.3	S 8 45.5
Y 11	103 57.4	314 21.3	02.2	305 07.5 9	59.5	63 36.0	26.1	125 14.5	46.5			
12	118 59.8	329 23.9 N 9	01.6	320 08.5 N 9	58.9	78 38.1 N14	26.2	140 17.1 S10	46.5	Alphecca	126 04.6	N26 38.3
13	134 02.3	344 26.4	01.1	335 09.5	58.3	93 40.2	26.3	155 19.7	46.6	Alpheratz	357 35.9	N29 13.1
14	149 04.8	359 28.9	00.5	350 10.5	57.7	108 42.4	26.4	170 22.3	46.6	Altair	62 00.8	N 8 55.9
15	164 07.2	14 31.4 9	00.0	5 11.5 ..	57.2	123 44.5 ..	26.5	185 24.9 ..	46.7	Ankaa	353 08.2	S42 10.5
16	179 09.7	29 33.9 8	59.4	20 12.6	56.6	138 46.7	26.6	200 27.4	46.7	Antares	112 17.1	S26 29.1
17	194 12.2	44 36.5	58.9	35 13.6	56.0	153 48.8	26.7	215 30.0	46.8			
18	209 14.6	59 39.0 N 8	58.3	50 14.6 N 9	55.4	168 50.9 N14	26.8	230 32.6 S10	46.9	Arcturus	145 49.0	N19 03.8
19	224 17.1	74 41.5	57.7	65 15.6	54.8	183 53.1	26.9	245 35.2	46.9	Atria	107 12.0	S69 04.3
20	239 19.6	89 44.1	57.2	80 16.7	54.2	198 55.2	27.0	260 37.8	47.0	Avior	234 15.9	S59 35.0
21	254 22.0	104 46.6 ..	56.6	95 17.7 ..	53.6	213 57.4 ..	27.1	275 40.4 ..	47.0	Bellatrix	278 24.4	N 6 22.3
22	269 24.5	119 49.2	56.1	110 18.7	53.0	228 59.5	27.2	290 42.9	47.1	Betelgeuse	270 53.7	N 7 24.7
23	284 27.0	134 51.7	55.5	125 19.7	52.4	244 01.6	27.2	305 45.5	47.1			
22 00	299 29.4	149 54.3 N 8	55.0	140 20.7 N 9	51.8	259 03.8 N14	27.3	320 48.1 S10	47.2	Canopus	263 53.4	S52 42.3
01	314 31.9	164 56.8	54.4	155 21.8	51.2	274 05.9	27.4	335 50.7	47.2	Capella	280 24.1	N46 01.2
02	329 34.3	179 59.4	53.9	170 22.8	50.6	289 08.1	27.5	350 53.3	47.3	Deneb	49 26.2	N45 21.8
03	344 36.8	195 02.0 ..	53.3	185 23.8 ..	50.0	304 10.2 ..	27.6	5 55.8 ..	47.4	Denebola	182 26.4	N14 26.6
04	359 39.3	210 04.5	52.8	200 24.8	49.4	319 12.3	27.7	20 58.4	47.4	Diphda	348 48.4	S17 51.3
05	14 41.7	225 07.1	52.2	215 25.9	48.9	334 14.5	27.8	36 01.0	47.5			
S 06	29 44.2	240 09.7 N 8	51.7	230 26.9 N 9	48.3	349 16.6 N14	27.9	51 03.6 S10	47.5	Dubhe	193 42.9	N61 37.7
A 07	44 46.7	255 12.3	51.2	245 27.9	47.7	4 18.8	28.0	66 06.2	47.6	Elnath	278 03.7	N28 37.6
T 08	59 49.1	270 14.9	50.6	260 28.9	47.1	19 20.9	28.1	81 08.8	47.6	Eltanin	90 42.3	N51 29.3
U 09	74 51.6	285 17.5 ..	50.1	275 29.9 ..	46.5	34 23.0 ..	28.2	96 11.4 ..	47.7	Enif	33 39.7	N 9 59.0
R 10	89 54.1	300 20.1	49.5	290 31.0	45.9	49 25.2	28.3	111 13.9	47.7	Fomalhaut	15 15.6	S29 29.7
D 11	104 56.5	315 22.7	49.0	305 32.0	45.3	64 27.3	28.3	126 16.5	47.8			
A 12	119 59.0	330 25.3 N 8	48.5	320 33.0 N 9	44.7	79 29.5 N14	28.4	141 19.1 S10	47.8	Gacrux	171 53.2	S57 14.9
Y 13	135 01.4	345 27.9	47.9	335 34.0	44.1	94 31.6	28.5	156 21.7	47.9	Gienah	175 45.0	S17 40.3
14	150 03.9	0 30.5	47.4	350 35.1	43.5	109 33.8	28.6	171 24.3	48.0	Hadar	148 37.7	S60 29.4
15	165 06.4	15 33.1 ..	46.9	5 36.1 ..	42.9	124 35.9 ..	28.7	186 26.9 ..	48.0	Hamal	327 52.6	N23 34.3
16	180 08.8	30 35.7	46.3	20 37.1	42.3	139 38.1	28.8	201 29.4	48.1	Kaus Aust.	83 33.7	S34 22.4
17	195 11.3	45 38.3	45.8	35 38.1	41.7	154 40.2	28.9	216 32.0	48.1			
18	210 13.8	60 41.0 N 8	45.3	50 39.1 N 9	41.1	169 42.3 N14	29.0	231 34.6 S10	48.2	Kochab	137 19.4	N74 03.8
19	225 16.2	75 43.6	44.7	65 40.2	40.5	184 44.5	29.1	246 37.2	48.2	Markab	13 30.9	N15 19.9
20	240 18.7	90 46.2	44.2	80 41.2	39.9	199 46.6	29.2	261 39.8	48.3	Menkar	314 07.5	N 4 10.9
21	255 21.2	105 48.9 ..	43.7	95 42.2 ..	39.3	214 48.8 ..	29.3	276 42.4 ..	48.3	Menkent	147 59.0	S36 29.3
22	270 23.6	120 51.5	43.2	110 43.2	38.7	229 50.9	29.3	291 45.0	48.4	Miaplacidus	221 39.4	S69 48.8
23	285 26.1	135 54.1	42.6	125 44.3	38.1	244 53.1	29.4	306 47.5	48.5			
23 00	300 28.6	150 56.8 N 8	42.1	140 45.3 N 9	37.6	259 55.2 N14	29.5	321 50.1 S10	48.5	Mirfak	308 30.2	N49 56.5
01	315 31.0	165 59.4	41.6	155 46.3	37.0	274 57.4	29.6	336 52.7	48.6	Nunki	75 48.9	S26 16.0
02	330 33.5	181 02.1	41.1	170 47.3	36.4	289 59.5	29.7	351 55.3	48.6	Peacock	53 07.0	S56 39.5
03	345 35.9	196 04.8 ..	40.6	185 48.4 ..	35.8	305 01.7 ..	29.8	6 57.9 ..	48.7	Pollux	243 19.2	N27 58.2
04	0 38.4	211 07.4	40.0	200 49.4	35.2	320 03.8	29.9	22 00.5	48.7	Procyon	244 52.4	N 5 10.0
05	15 40.9	226 10.1	39.5	215 50.4	34.6	335 06.0	30.0	37 03.1	48.8			
S 06	30 43.3	241 12.8 N 8	39.0	230 51.4 N 9	34.0	350 08.1 N14	30.1	52 05.6 S10	48.9	Rasalhague	96 59.4	N12 32.7
U 07	45 45.8	256 15.4	38.5	245 52.4	33.4	5 10.3	30.2	67 08.2	48.9	Regulus	207 36.0	N11 51.3
N 08	60 48.3	271 18.1	38.0	260 53.5	32.8	20 12.4	30.2	82 10.8	49.0	Rigel	281 05.3	S 8 10.4
D 09	75 50.7	286 20.8 ..	37.5	275 54.5 ..	32.2	35 14.5 ..	30.3	97 13.4 ..	49.0	Rigil Kent.	139 41.9	S60 56.1
A 10	90 53.2	301 23.5	36.9	290 55.5	31.6	50 16.7	30.4	112 16.0	49.1	Sabik	102 03.9	S15 45.2
Y 11	105 55.7	316 26.2	36.4	305 56.5	31.0	65 18.8	30.5	127 18.6	49.1			
12	120 58.1	331 28.9 N 8	35.9	320 57.6 N 9	30.4	80 21.0 N14	30.6	142 21.2 S10	49.2	Schedar	349 32.3	N56 39.7
13	136 00.6	346 31.6	35.4	335 58.6	29.8	95 23.1	30.7	157 23.8	49.2	Shaula	96 11.7	S37 07.3
14	151 03.1	1 34.3	34.9	350 59.6	29.2	110 25.3	30.8	172 26.3	49.3	Sirius	258 27.6	S16 44.8
15	166 05.5	16 37.0 ..	34.4	6 00.6 ..	28.6	125 27.4 ..	30.9	187 28.9 ..	49.4	Spica	158 23.6	S11 17.0
16	181 08.0	31 39.7	33.9	21 01.7	28.0	140 29.6	31.0	202 31.5	49.4	Suhail	222 47.6	S43 31.6
17	196 10.4	46 42.4	33.4	36 02.7	27.4	155 31.7	31.0	217 34.1	49.5			
18	211 12.9	61 45.1 N 8	32.9	51 03.7 N 9	26.8	170 33.9 N14	31.1	232 36.7 S10	49.5	Vega	80 33.6	N38 48.4
19	226 15.4	76 47.9	32.4	66 04.7	26.2	185 36.0	31.2	247 39.3	49.6	Zuben'ubi	136 57.3	S16 08.4
20	241 17.8	91 50.6	31.9	81 05.7	25.6	200 38.2	31.3	262 41.9	49.6			
21	256 20.3	106 53.3 ..	31.4	96 06.8 ..	25.0	215 40.3 ..	31.4	277 44.5 ..	49.7			
22	271 22.8	121 56.1	30.9	111 07.8	24.4	230 42.5	31.5	292 47.1	49.8			
23	286 25.2	136 58.8	30.4	126 08.8	23.8	245 44.7	31.6	307 49.6	49.8			
Mer. Pass.	h m 4 01.4	v 2.6 d 0.5		v 1.0 d 0.6		v 2.1 d 0.1		v 2.6 d 0.1				

	SHA	Mer. Pass.
	° ′	h m
Venus	210 24.9	13 58
Mars	200 51.3	14 38
Jupiter	319 34.4	6 43
Saturn	21 18.7	2 36

© British Crown Copyright 2022. All rights reserved.

SUN and MOON

UT	SUN GHA	SUN Dec	MOON GHA	v	Dec	d	HP
d h	° ′	° ′	° ′	′	° ′	′	′
21 00	178 23.6	N20 33.5	141 41.1	15.8	N14 08.8	12.2	54.0
01	193 23.5	33.0	156 15.9	15.8	13 56.6	12.2	54.0
02	208 23.5	32.5	170 50.7	15.8	13 44.4	12.3	54.0
03	223 23.5 ..	32.0	185 25.5	15.9	13 32.1	12.3	54.0
04	238 23.4	31.6	200 00.4	15.9	13 19.8	12.4	54.0
05	253 23.4	31.1	214 35.3	15.9	13 07.4	12.4	54.0
06	268 23.4	N20 30.6	229 10.2	16.1	N12 55.0	12.5	54.0
07	283 23.3	30.1	243 45.3	16.0	12 42.5	12.6	54.0
08	298 23.3	29.6	258 20.3	16.1	12 29.9	12.5	54.0
F 09	313 23.3 ..	29.2	272 55.4	16.1	12 17.4	12.7	54.0
R 10	328 23.2	28.7	287 30.5	16.2	12 04.7	12.6	54.0
I 11	343 23.2	28.2	302 05.7	16.2	11 52.1	12.8	54.0
D 12	358 23.2	N20 27.7	316 40.9	16.3	N11 39.3	12.7	54.1
A 13	13 23.2	27.2	331 16.2	16.3	11 26.6	12.8	54.1
Y 14	28 23.1	26.7	345 51.5	16.3	11 13.8	12.9	54.1
15	43 23.1 ..	26.3	0 26.8	16.4	11 00.9	12.9	54.1
16	58 23.1	25.8	15 02.2	16.3	10 48.0	12.9	54.1
17	73 23.0	25.3	29 37.5	16.5	10 35.1	13.0	54.1
18	88 23.0	N20 24.8	44 13.0	16.4	N10 22.1	13.0	54.1
19	103 23.0	24.3	58 48.4	16.5	10 09.1	13.1	54.1
20	118 23.0	23.8	73 23.9	16.5	9 56.0	13.1	54.1
21	133 22.9 ..	23.3	87 59.4	16.6	9 42.9	13.1	54.1
22	148 22.9	22.8	102 35.0	16.6	9 29.8	13.2	54.1
23	163 22.9	22.3	117 10.6	16.6	9 16.6	13.2	54.1
22 00	178 22.8	N20 21.9	131 46.2	16.6	N 9 03.4	13.2	54.1
01	193 22.8	21.4	146 21.8	16.7	8 50.2	13.3	54.2
02	208 22.8	20.9	160 57.5	16.7	8 36.9	13.3	54.2
03	223 22.8 ..	20.4	175 33.2	16.7	8 23.6	13.4	54.2
04	238 22.7	19.9	190 08.9	16.7	8 10.2	13.4	54.2
05	253 22.7	19.4	204 44.6	16.8	7 56.8	13.4	54.2
06	268 22.7	N20 18.9	219 20.4	16.7	N 7 43.4	13.4	54.2
07	283 22.7	18.4	233 56.1	16.8	7 30.0	13.5	54.2
S 08	298 22.6	17.9	248 31.9	16.9	7 16.5	13.5	54.2
A 09	313 22.6 ..	17.4	263 07.8	16.8	7 03.0	13.6	54.2
T 10	328 22.6	16.9	277 43.6	16.8	6 49.4	13.5	54.2
U 11	343 22.6	16.4	292 19.4	16.9	6 35.9	13.6	54.3
R 12	358 22.5	N20 15.9	306 55.3	16.9	N 6 22.3	13.6	54.3
D 13	13 22.5	15.4	321 31.2	16.9	6 08.7	13.7	54.3
A 14	28 22.5	14.9	336 07.1	16.9	5 55.0	13.7	54.3
Y 15	43 22.5 ..	14.4	350 43.0	16.9	5 41.3	13.7	54.3
16	58 22.4	13.9	5 18.9	16.9	5 27.6	13.7	54.3
17	73 22.4	13.4	19 54.8	16.9	5 13.9	13.8	54.3
18	88 22.4	N20 12.9	34 30.7	17.0	N 5 00.1	13.8	54.3
19	103 22.4	12.4	49 06.7	16.9	4 46.4	13.8	54.4
20	118 22.3	11.9	63 42.6	17.0	4 32.6	13.8	54.4
21	133 22.3 ..	11.4	78 18.6	16.9	4 18.8	13.9	54.4
22	148 22.3	10.9	92 54.5	17.0	4 04.9	13.8	54.4
23	163 22.3	10.4	107 30.5	17.0	3 51.1	13.9	54.4
23 00	178 22.3	N20 09.9	122 06.5	16.9	N 3 37.2	13.9	54.4
01	193 22.2	09.4	136 42.4	17.0	3 23.3	13.9	54.4
02	208 22.2	08.9	151 18.4	17.0	3 09.4	14.0	54.4
03	223 22.2 ..	08.4	165 54.4	16.9	2 55.4	13.9	54.5
04	238 22.2	07.9	180 30.3	17.0	2 41.5	14.0	54.5
05	253 22.1	07.4	195 06.3	17.0	2 27.5	14.0	54.5
06	268 22.1	N20 06.9	209 42.3	16.9	N 2 13.5	14.0	54.5
07	283 22.1	06.4	224 18.2	17.0	1 59.5	14.0	54.5
08	298 22.1	05.9	238 54.2	16.9	1 45.5	14.1	54.5
S 09	313 22.1 ..	05.3	253 30.1	16.9	1 31.4	14.0	54.6
U 10	328 22.1	04.8	268 06.0	17.0	1 17.4	14.1	54.6
N 11	343 22.0	04.3	282 42.0	16.9	1 03.3	14.0	54.6
D 12	358 22.0	N20 03.8	297 17.9	16.9	N 0 49.3	14.1	54.6
A 13	13 22.0	03.3	311 53.8	16.9	0 35.2	14.1	54.6
Y 14	28 22.0	02.8	326 29.7	16.8	0 21.1	14.1	54.6
15	43 22.0 ..	02.3	341 05.5	16.9	N 0 07.0	14.1	54.7
16	58 21.9	01.8	355 41.4	16.8	S 0 07.1	14.1	54.7
17	73 21.9	01.3	10 17.2	16.8	0 21.2	14.2	54.7
18	88 21.9	N20 00.7	24 53.0	16.8	S 0 35.4	14.1	54.7
19	103 21.9	20 00.2	39 28.8	16.8	0 49.5	14.1	54.7
20	118 21.9	19 59.7	54 04.6	16.8	1 03.6	14.2	54.8
21	133 21.9 ..	59.2	68 40.4	16.7	1 17.8	14.1	54.8
22	148 21.8	58.7	83 16.1	16.7	1 31.9	14.2	54.8
23	163 21.8	58.2	97 51.8	16.7	S 1 46.1	14.1	54.8
SD	15.8	d 0.5	SD 14.7		14.8		14.9

Twilight, Sunrise, Moonrise

Lat.	Twilight Naut.	Twilight Civil	Sunrise	Moonrise 21	Moonrise 22	Moonrise 23	Moonrise 24
°	h m	h m	h m	h m	h m	h m	h m
N 72	☐	☐	☐	05 44	07 54	09 52	11 51
N 70	☐	☐	☐	06 09	08 05	09 54	11 44
68	////	////	01 12	06 28	08 14	09 56	11 38
66	////	////	02 04	06 43	08 22	09 57	11 33
64	////	////	02 36	06 55	08 28	09 58	11 29
62	////	01 29	02 59	07 06	08 33	09 59	11 25
60	////	02 07	03 17	07 15	08 38	09 59	11 22
N 58	////	02 33	03 33	07 22	08 42	10 00	11 20
56	01 22	02 52	03 45	07 29	08 45	10 01	11 17
54	01 56	03 09	03 57	07 35	08 48	10 01	11 15
52	02 20	03 23	04 07	07 40	08 51	10 02	11 13
50	02 39	03 35	04 15	07 45	08 54	10 02	11 11
45	03 14	03 59	04 34	07 56	09 00	10 03	11 07
N 40	03 39	04 18	04 49	08 04	09 04	10 04	11 04
35	03 58	04 33	05 02	08 12	09 08	10 05	11 02
30	04 14	04 46	05 13	08 18	09 12	10 05	10 59
20	04 39	05 08	05 32	08 29	09 18	10 06	10 55
N 10	04 59	05 25	05 48	08 39	09 24	10 07	10 52
0	05 15	05 41	06 03	08 48	09 29	10 08	10 48
S 10	05 30	05 56	06 18	08 57	09 34	10 09	10 45
20	05 43	06 10	06 34	09 07	09 39	10 10	10 41
30	05 57	06 26	06 52	09 18	09 45	10 11	10 38
35	06 04	06 35	07 02	09 24	09 49	10 12	10 35
40	06 11	06 44	07 14	09 31	09 53	10 13	10 33
45	06 19	06 56	07 28	09 40	09 57	10 13	10 30
S 50	06 29	07 09	07 45	09 50	10 02	10 14	10 26
52	06 33	07 15	07 53	09 54	10 05	10 15	10 25
54	06 37	07 21	08 02	09 59	10 08	10 15	10 23
56	06 42	07 28	08 12	10 05	10 11	10 16	10 21
58	06 47	07 36	08 23	10 11	10 14	10 17	10 19
S 60	06 52	07 45	08 37	10 18	10 18	10 17	10 17

Sunset, Twilight, Moonset

Lat.	Sunset	Twilight Civil	Twilight Naut.	Moonset 21	Moonset 22	Moonset 23	Moonset 24
°	h m	h m	h m	h m	h m	h m	h m
N 72	☐	☐	☐	23 10	22 37	22 07	21 34
N 70	☐	☐	☐	22 57	22 32	22 09	21 44
68	22 54	////	////	22 46	22 28	22 11	21 53
66	22 05	////	////	22 37	22 24	22 12	22 00
64	21 35	////	////	22 29	22 21	22 13	22 05
62	21 12	22 39	////	22 22	22 18	22 15	22 11
60	20 54	22 03	////	22 16	22 16	22 16	22 15
N 58	20 39	21 38	////	22 11	22 14	22 16	22 19
56	20 26	21 19	22 47	22 06	22 12	22 17	22 23
54	20 15	21 03	22 14	22 02	22 10	22 18	22 26
52	20 05	20 49	21 51	21 59	22 09	22 19	22 29
50	19 57	20 37	21 33	21 55	22 07	22 19	22 31
45	19 38	20 13	20 58	21 48	22 04	22 20	22 37
N 40	19 23	19 55	20 33	21 41	22 02	22 22	22 42
35	19 11	19 39	20 14	21 36	21 59	22 23	22 46
30	19 00	19 24	19 58	21 31	21 57	22 23	22 50
20	18 41	19 05	19 33	21 22	21 54	22 25	22 57
N 10	18 25	18 48	19 14	21 15	21 51	22 26	23 02
0	18 10	18 32	18 58	21 08	21 48	22 27	23 08
S 10	17 55	18 18	18 43	21 01	21 45	22 28	23 13
20	17 40	18 03	18 30	20 53	21 41	22 30	23 19
30	17 22	17 47	18 16	20 44	21 38	22 31	23 26
35	17 11	17 38	18 09	20 39	21 36	22 32	23 30
40	16 59	17 29	18 02	20 33	21 33	22 33	23 34
45	16 45	17 18	17 54	20 27	21 30	22 34	23 39
S 50	16 28	17 05	17 45	20 18	21 27	22 35	23 45
52	16 20	16 59	17 41	20 15	21 25	22 36	23 48
54	16 12	16 52	17 37	20 10	21 23	22 36	23 51
56	16 02	16 45	17 32	20 06	21 21	22 37	23 55
58	15 50	16 37	17 27	20 01	21 19	22 38	23 59
S 60	15 37	16 28	17 22	19 55	21 17	22 39	24 03

SUN and MOON data

Day	SUN Eqn. of Time 00h	SUN Eqn. of Time 12h	SUN Mer. Pass.	MOON Mer. Pass. Upper	MOON Mer. Pass. Lower	Age	Phase
d	m s	m s	h m	h m	h m	d	%
21	06 26	06 27	12 06	14 58	02 38	04	12
22	06 29	06 30	12 06	15 38	03 18	05	19
23	06 31	06 32	12 07	16 18	03 58	06	27

© British Crown Copyright 2022. All rights reserved.

UT	ARIES GHA	VENUS −4.6 GHA	Dec	MARS +1.8 GHA	Dec	JUPITER −2.3 GHA	Dec	SATURN +0.5 GHA	Dec	STARS Name	SHA	Dec
24 MON												
00	301 27.7	152 01.5	N 8 29.9	141 09.8	N 9 23.2	260 46.8	N14 31.7	322 52.2	S10 49.9	Acamar	315 12.8	S40 12.4
01	316 30.2	167 04.3	29.4	156 10.9	22.6	275 49.0	31.8	337 54.8	49.9	Achernar	335 21.0	S57 06.7
02	331 32.6	182 07.0	28.9	171 11.9	22.0	290 51.1	31.8	352 57.4	50.0	Acrux	173 01.7	S63 14.0
03	346 35.1	197 09.8	28.4	186 12.9	21.4	305 53.3	31.9	8 00.0	50.0	Adhara	255 07.2	S29 00.1
04	1 37.5	212 12.5	27.9	201 13.9	20.8	320 55.4	32.0	23 02.6	50.1	Aldebaran	290 41.2	N16 33.4
05	16 40.0	227 15.3	27.4	216 15.0	20.2	335 57.6	32.1	38 05.2	50.2			
06	31 42.5	242 18.1	N 8 27.0	231 16.0	N 9 19.6	350 59.7	N14 32.2	53 07.8	S10 50.2	Alioth	166 14.2	N55 50.3
07	46 44.9	257 20.9	26.5	246 17.0	19.0	6 01.9	32.3	68 10.4	50.3	Alkaid	152 53.0	N49 12.1
08	61 47.4	272 23.6	26.0	261 18.0	18.4	21 04.0	32.4	83 12.9	50.3	Alnair	27 34.0	S46 50.7
09	76 49.9	287 26.4	25.5	276 19.0	17.8	36 06.2	32.5	98 15.5	50.4	Alnilam	275 39.2	S 1 11.1
10	91 52.3	302 29.2	25.0	291 20.1	17.2	51 08.3	32.5	113 18.1	50.4	Alphard	217 49.3	S 8 45.5
11	106 54.8	317 32.0	24.5	306 21.1	16.6	66 10.5	32.6	128 20.7	50.5			
12	121 57.3	332 34.8	N 8 24.1	321 22.1	N 9 16.0	81 12.7	N14 32.7	143 23.3	S10 50.6	Alphecca	126 04.6	N26 38.3
13	136 59.7	347 37.6	23.6	336 23.1	15.4	96 14.8	32.8	158 25.9	50.6	Alpheratz	357 35.8	N29 13.1
14	152 02.2	2 40.4	23.1	351 24.2	14.8	111 17.0	32.9	173 28.5	50.7	Altair	62 00.8	N 8 55.9
15	167 04.7	17 43.2	22.6	6 25.2	14.2	126 19.1	33.0	188 31.1	50.7	Ankaa	353 08.1	S42 10.5
16	182 07.1	32 46.0	22.1	21 26.2	13.6	141 21.3	33.1	203 33.7	50.8	Antares	112 17.1	S26 29.1
17	197 09.6	47 48.8	21.7	36 27.2	13.0	156 23.4	33.1	218 36.3	50.8			
18	212 12.0	62 51.6	N 8 21.2	51 28.3	N 9 12.4	171 25.6	N14 33.2	233 38.9	S10 50.9	Arcturus	145 49.0	N19 03.8
19	227 14.5	77 54.4	20.7	66 29.3	11.8	186 27.7	33.3	248 41.4	51.0	Atria	107 12.0	S69 04.4
20	242 17.0	92 57.2	20.2	81 30.3	11.2	201 29.9	33.4	263 44.0	51.0	Avior	234 15.9	S59 35.0
21	257 19.4	108 00.1	19.8	96 31.3	10.6	216 32.1	33.5	278 46.6	51.1	Bellatrix	278 24.4	N 6 22.3
22	272 21.9	123 02.9	19.3	111 32.3	10.0	231 34.2	33.6	293 49.2	51.1	Betelgeuse	270 53.7	N 7 24.8
23	287 24.4	138 05.7	18.8	126 33.4	09.4	246 36.4	33.7	308 51.8	51.2			
25 TUE												
00	302 26.8	153 08.6	N 8 18.4	141 34.4	N 9 08.8	261 38.5	N14 33.8	323 54.4	S10 51.2	Canopus	263 53.4	S52 42.3
01	317 29.3	168 11.4	17.9	156 35.4	08.2	276 40.7	33.8	338 57.0	51.3	Capella	280 24.0	N46 01.2
02	332 31.8	183 14.2	17.4	171 36.4	07.6	291 42.8	33.9	353 59.6	51.4	Deneb	49 26.2	N45 21.8
03	347 34.2	198 17.1	17.0	186 37.5	07.0	306 45.0	34.0	9 02.2	51.4	Denebola	182 26.4	N14 26.6
04	2 36.7	213 19.9	16.5	201 38.5	06.4	321 47.2	34.1	24 04.8	51.5	Diphda	348 48.4	S17 51.3
05	17 39.1	228 22.8	16.1	216 39.5	05.8	336 49.3	34.2	39 07.4	51.5			
06	32 41.6	243 25.7	N 8 15.6	231 40.5	N 9 05.2	351 51.5	N14 34.3	54 10.0	S10 51.6	Dubhe	193 43.0	N61 37.7
07	47 44.1	258 28.5	15.1	246 41.6	04.6	6 53.6	34.4	69 12.5	51.7	Elnath	278 03.7	N28 37.6
08	62 46.5	273 31.4	14.7	261 42.6	04.0	21 55.8	34.4	84 15.1	51.7	Eltanin	90 42.3	N51 29.3
09	77 49.0	288 34.3	14.2	276 43.6	03.4	36 58.0	34.5	99 17.7	51.8	Enif	33 39.7	N 9 59.0
10	92 51.5	303 37.1	13.8	291 44.6	02.8	52 00.1	34.6	114 20.3	51.8	Fomalhaut	15 15.6	S29 29.7
11	107 53.9	318 40.0	13.3	306 45.7	02.2	67 02.3	34.7	129 22.9	51.9			
12	122 56.4	333 42.9	N 8 12.9	321 46.7	N 9 01.6	82 04.4	N14 34.8	144 25.5	S10 51.9	Gacrux	171 53.2	S57 14.9
13	137 58.9	348 45.8	12.4	336 47.7	01.0	97 06.6	34.9	159 28.1	52.0	Gienah	175 45.0	S17 40.3
14	153 01.3	3 48.7	12.0	351 48.7	9 00.4	112 08.8	34.9	174 30.7	52.1	Hadar	148 37.7	S60 29.4
15	168 03.8	18 51.6	11.5	6 49.7	8 59.8	127 10.9	35.0	189 33.3	52.1	Hamal	327 52.6	N23 34.3
16	183 06.3	33 54.5	11.1	21 50.8	59.2	142 13.1	35.1	204 35.9	52.2	Kaus Aust.	83 33.7	S34 22.4
17	198 08.7	48 57.4	10.6	36 51.8	58.6	157 15.3	35.2	219 38.5	52.2			
18	213 11.2	64 00.3	N 8 10.2	51 52.8	N 8 58.0	172 17.4	N14 35.3	234 41.1	S10 52.3	Kochab	137 19.5	N74 03.8
19	228 13.6	79 03.2	09.8	66 53.8	57.4	187 19.6	35.4	249 43.7	52.4	Markab	13 30.9	N15 19.9
20	243 16.1	94 06.1	09.3	81 54.9	56.8	202 21.7	35.5	264 46.3	52.4	Menkar	314 07.5	N 4 11.0
21	258 18.6	109 09.1	08.9	96 55.9	56.2	217 23.9	35.5	279 48.9	52.5	Menkent	147 59.0	S36 29.2
22	273 21.0	124 12.0	08.4	111 56.9	55.6	232 26.1	35.6	294 51.4	52.5	Miaplacidus	221 39.5	S69 48.8
23	288 23.5	139 14.9	08.0	126 57.9	55.0	247 28.2	35.7	309 54.0	52.6			
26 WED												
00	303 26.0	154 17.8	N 8 07.6	141 59.0	N 8 54.4	262 30.4	N14 35.8	324 56.6	S10 52.7	Mirfak	308 30.2	N49 56.5
01	318 28.4	169 20.8	07.1	157 00.0	53.8	277 32.6	35.9	339 59.2	52.7	Nunki	75 48.9	S26 16.0
02	333 30.9	184 23.7	06.7	172 01.0	53.2	292 34.7	36.0	355 01.8	52.8	Peacock	53 07.0	S56 39.5
03	348 33.4	199 26.7	06.3	187 02.0	52.6	307 36.9	36.0	10 04.4	52.8	Pollux	243 19.2	N27 58.2
04	3 35.8	214 29.6	05.8	202 03.1	51.9	322 39.1	36.1	25 07.0	52.9	Procyon	244 52.4	N 5 10.0
05	18 38.3	229 32.6	05.4	217 04.1	51.3	337 41.2	36.2	40 09.6	52.9			
06	33 40.8	244 35.5	N 8 05.0	232 05.1	N 8 50.7	352 43.4	N14 36.3	55 12.2	S10 53.0	Rasalhague	96 59.4	N12 32.7
07	48 43.2	259 38.5	04.6	247 06.1	50.1	7 45.6	36.4	70 14.8	53.1	Regulus	207 36.0	N11 51.3
08	63 45.7	274 41.4	04.1	262 07.2	49.5	22 47.7	36.5	85 17.4	53.1	Rigel	281 05.3	S 8 10.3
09	78 48.1	289 44.4	03.7	277 08.2	48.9	37 49.9	36.5	100 20.0	53.2	Rigil Kent.	139 41.9	S60 56.1
10	93 50.6	304 47.4	03.3	292 09.2	48.3	52 52.1	36.6	115 22.6	53.2	Sabik	102 03.9	S15 45.2
11	108 53.1	319 50.4	02.9	307 10.2	47.7	67 54.2	36.7	130 25.2	53.3			
12	123 55.5	334 53.3	N 8 02.4	322 11.2	N 8 47.1	82 56.4	N14 36.8	145 27.8	S10 53.4	Schedar	349 32.2	N56 39.7
13	138 58.0	349 56.3	02.0	337 12.3	46.5	97 58.6	36.9	160 30.4	53.4	Shaula	96 11.7	S37 07.3
14	154 00.5	4 59.3	01.6	352 13.3	45.9	113 00.7	37.0	175 33.0	53.5	Sirius	258 27.6	S16 44.8
15	169 02.9	20 02.3	01.2	7 14.3	45.3	128 02.9	37.0	190 35.6	53.5	Spica	158 23.6	S11 17.0
16	184 05.4	35 05.3	00.8	22 15.3	44.7	143 05.1	37.1	205 38.2	53.6	Suhail	222 47.6	S43 31.6
17	199 07.9	50 08.3	00.4	37 16.4	44.1	158 07.2	37.2	220 40.8	53.7			
18	214 10.3	65 11.3	N 8 00.0	52 17.4	N 8 43.5	173 09.4	N14 37.3	235 43.4	S10 53.7	Vega	80 33.6	N38 48.4
19	229 12.8	80 14.3	7 59.5	67 18.4	42.9	188 11.6	37.4	250 46.0	53.8	Zuben'ubi	136 57.3	S16 08.4
20	244 15.2	95 17.3	59.1	82 19.4	42.3	203 13.7	37.5	265 48.5	53.8			
21	259 17.7	110 20.3	58.7	97 20.5	41.7	218 15.9	37.5	280 51.1	53.9		SHA	Mer. Pass.
22	274 20.2	125 23.4	58.3	112 21.5	41.1	233 18.1	37.6	295 53.7	54.0	Venus	210 41.7	13 45
23	289 22.3	140 26.4	57.9	127 22.5	40.4	248 20.2	37.7	310 56.3	54.0	Mars	199 07.6	14 33
										Jupiter	319 11.7	6 32
Mer. Pass.	h m 3 49.6	v 2.9	d 0.5	v 1.0	d 0.6	v 2.2	d 0.1	v 2.6	d 0.1	Saturn	21 27.6	2 24

© British Crown Copyright 2022. All rights reserved.

UT	SUN		MOON					Lat.	Twilight		Sunrise	Moonrise			
									Naut.	Civil		24	25	26	27
	GHA	Dec	GHA	v	Dec	d	HP		h m	h m	h m	h m	h m	h m	h m
d h	° ′	° ′	° ′	′	° ′	′	′	N 72	▭	▭	▭	11 51	14 01	17 01	■■
24 00	178 21.8	N19 57.6	112 27.5	16.7	S 2 00.2	14.2	54.8	N 70	▭	▭	▭	11 44	13 41	16 04	■■
01	193 21.8	57.1	127 03.2	16.6	2 14.4	14.2	54.9	68	////	////	01 33	11 38	13 26	15 31	18 51
02	208 21.8	56.6	141 38.8	16.6	2 28.6	14.1	54.9	66	////	////	02 17	11 33	13 14	15 07	17 24
03	223 21.8 ..	56.1	156 14.4	16.6	2 42.7	14.2	54.9	64	////	00 40	02 45	11 29	13 04	14 48	16 47
04	238 21.8	55.6	170 50.0	16.5	2 56.9	14.2	54.9	62	////	01 44	03 07	11 25	12 56	14 33	16 21
05	253 21.7	55.0	185 25.5	16.5	3 11.1	14.1	54.9	60	////	02 17	03 24	11 22	12 48	14 20	16 00
06	268 21.7	N19 54.5	200 01.0	16.5	S 3 25.2	14.2	55.0	N 58	00 37	02 40	03 38	11 20	12 42	14 10	15 44
07	283 21.7	54.0	214 36.5	16.5	3 39.4	14.1	55.0	56	01 35	02 59	03 51	11 17	12 36	14 00	15 30
08	298 21.7	53.5	229 12.0	16.4	3 53.5	14.2	55.0	54	02 05	03 14	04 01	11 15	12 31	13 52	15 17
M 09	313 21.7 ..	52.9	243 47.4	16.3	4 07.7	14.1	55.0	52	02 27	03 28	04 11	11 13	12 27	13 45	15 07
O 10	328 21.7	52.4	258 22.7	16.4	4 21.8	14.1	55.1	50	02 45	03 39	04 19	11 11	12 23	13 38	14 57
N 11	343 21.7	51.9	272 58.1	16.3	4 36.0	14.1	55.1	45	03 18	04 02	04 37	11 07	12 14	13 24	14 38
D 12	358 21.7	N19 51.4	287 33.4	16.2	S 4 50.1	14.2	55.1	N 40	03 42	04 21	04 52	11 04	12 07	13 12	14 22
A 13	13 21.6	50.8	302 08.6	16.2	5 04.3	14.1	55.1	35	04 01	04 36	05 04	11 02	12 01	13 02	14 08
Y 14	28 21.6	50.3	316 43.8	16.2	5 18.4	14.1	55.2	30	04 17	04 48	05 15	10 59	11 55	12 54	13 57
15	43 21.6 ..	49.8	331 19.0	16.1	5 32.5	14.1	55.2	20	04 41	05 09	05 33	10 55	11 46	12 39	13 37
16	58 21.6	49.3	345 54.1	16.1	5 46.6	14.1	55.2	N 10	05 00	05 26	05 48	10 52	11 38	12 26	13 20
17	73 21.6	48.7	0 29.2	16.0	6 00.7	14.1	55.2	0	05 16	05 41	06 03	10 48	11 30	12 15	13 04
18	88 21.6	N19 48.2	15 04.2	16.0	S 6 14.8	14.1	55.3	S 10	05 29	05 55	06 17	10 45	11 22	12 03	12 48
19	103 21.6	47.7	29 39.2	15.9	6 28.9	14.1	55.3	20	05 43	06 09	06 33	10 41	11 14	11 50	12 31
20	118 21.6	47.1	44 14.1	15.9	6 43.0	14.0	55.3	30	05 55	06 25	06 50	10 38	11 05	11 36	12 12
21	133 21.6 ..	46.6	58 49.0	15.8	6 57.0	14.1	55.3	35	06 02	06 33	07 00	10 35	11 00	11 28	12 01
22	148 21.5	46.1	73 23.8	15.8	7 11.1	14.0	55.4	40	06 09	06 42	07 12	10 33	10 54	11 19	11 48
23	163 21.5	45.6	87 58.6	15.7	7 25.1	14.0	55.4	45	06 17	06 53	07 25	10 30	10 48	11 08	11 33
25 00	178 21.5	N19 45.0	102 33.3	15.6	S 7 39.1	14.0	55.4	S 50	06 26	07 05	07 41	10 26	10 40	10 55	11 15
01	193 21.5	44.5	117 07.9	15.6	7 53.1	14.0	55.4	52	06 29	07 11	07 49	10 25	10 36	10 49	11 07
02	208 21.5	44.0	131 42.5	15.6	8 07.1	13.9	55.5	54	06 33	07 17	07 58	10 23	10 32	10 43	10 57
03	223 21.5 ..	43.4	146 17.1	15.4	8 21.0	14.0	55.5	56	06 38	07 24	08 07	10 21	10 27	10 35	10 46
04	238 21.5	42.9	160 51.5	15.4	8 35.0	13.9	55.5	58	06 42	07 32	08 18	10 19	10 22	10 27	10 34
05	253 21.5	42.4	175 25.9	15.4	8 48.9	13.9	55.6	S 60	06 48	07 40	08 31	10 17	10 17	10 18	10 20

UT	SUN		MOON					Lat.	Sunset	Twilight		Moonset			
										Civil	Naut.	24	25	26	27
	GHA	Dec	GHA	v	Dec	d	HP		h m	h m	h m	h m	h m	h m	h m
06	268 21.5	N19 41.8	190 00.3	15.3	S 9 02.8	13.9	55.6	°							
07	283 21.5	41.3	204 34.6	15.2	9 16.7	13.8	55.6	N 72	▭	▭	▭	21 34	20 53	19 28	■■
T 08	298 21.5	40.7	219 08.8	15.2	9 30.5	13.9	55.6	N 70	▭	▭	▭	21 44	21 15	20 26	■■
U 09	313 21.5 ..	40.2	233 43.0	15.0	9 44.4	13.8	55.7	68	22 34	////	////	21 53	21 31	21 01	19 25
E 10	328 21.5	39.7	248 17.0	15.1	9 58.2	13.8	55.7	66	21 53	////	////	22 00	21 45	21 27	20 53
S 11	343 21.4	39.1	262 51.1	14.9	10 12.0	13.7	55.7	64	21 26	23 21	////	22 05	21 57	21 46	21 31
D 12	358 21.4	N19 38.6	277 25.0	14.9	S10 25.7	13.7	55.8	62	21 05	22 25	////	22 11	22 07	22 03	21 58
A 13	13 21.4	38.1	291 58.9	14.8	10 39.4	13.7	55.8	60	20 48	21 54	////	22 15	22 15	22 16	22 20
Y 14	28 21.4	37.5	306 32.7	14.7	10 53.1	13.7	55.8	N 58	20 33	21 31	23 26	22 19	22 23	22 28	22 37
15	43 21.4 ..	37.0	321 06.4	14.7	11 06.8	13.7	55.8	56	20 21	21 12	22 35	22 23	22 29	22 38	22 52
16	58 21.4	36.4	335 40.1	14.5	11 20.5	13.6	55.9	54	20 11	20 57	22 06	22 26	22 35	22 47	23 04
17	73 21.4	35.9	350 13.6	14.5	11 34.1	13.5	55.9	52	20 01	20 44	21 44	22 29	22 41	22 55	23 16
18	88 21.4	N19 35.3	4 47.1	14.4	S11 47.6	13.6	55.9	50	19 53	20 33	21 26	22 31	22 45	23 03	23 26
19	103 21.4	34.8	19 20.5	14.4	12 01.2	13.5	56.0	45	19 35	20 10	20 54	22 37	22 56	23 18	23 47
20	118 21.4	34.3	33 53.9	14.2	12 14.7	13.5	56.0	N 40	19 21	19 52	20 30	22 42	23 05	23 31	24 04
21	133 21.4 ..	33.7	48 27.1	14.2	12 28.2	13.4	56.0	35	19 09	19 37	20 11	22 46	23 12	23 42	24 18
22	148 21.4	33.2	63 00.3	14.1	12 41.6	13.4	56.1	30	18 58	19 24	19 56	22 50	23 19	23 52	24 31
23	163 21.4	32.6	77 33.4	14.0	12 55.0	13.3	56.1	20	18 40	19 04	19 32	22 57	23 31	24 09	00 09
26 00	178 21.4	N19 32.1	92 06.4	13.9	S13 08.3	13.3	56.1	N 10	18 25	18 47	19 13	23 02	23 41	24 24	00 24
01	193 21.4	31.5	106 39.3	13.8	13 21.6	13.3	56.2	0	18 10	18 32	18 58	23 08	23 51	24 37	00 37
02	208 21.4	31.0	121 12.1	13.7	13 34.9	13.2	56.2	S 10	17 56	18 18	18 44	23 13	24 01	00 01	00 51
03	223 21.4 ..	30.4	135 44.8	13.6	13 48.1	13.2	56.3	20	17 41	18 04	18 31	23 19	24 11	00 11	01 06
04	238 21.4	29.9	150 17.4	13.6	14 01.3	13.2	56.3	30	17 23	17 49	18 18	23 26	24 23	00 23	01 23
05	253 21.4	29.3	164 50.0	13.4	14 14.5	13.1	56.3	35	17 13	17 40	18 11	23 30	24 30	00 30	01 33
06	268 21.4	N19 28.8	179 22.4	13.4	S14 27.6	13.0	56.3	40	17 02	17 31	18 04	23 34	24 38	00 38	01 45
W 07	283 21.4	28.2	193 54.8	13.2	14 40.6	13.0	56.4	45	16 48	17 21	17 57	23 39	24 47	00 47	01 59
E 08	298 21.4	27.7	208 27.0	13.2	14 53.6	13.0	56.4	S 50	16 32	17 08	17 48	23 45	24 58	00 58	02 15
D 09	313 21.4 ..	27.1	222 59.2	13.0	15 06.6	12.9	56.4	52	16 25	17 03	17 44	23 48	25 04	01 04	02 23
N 10	328 21.4	26.6	237 31.2	13.0	15 19.5	12.8	56.5	54	16 16	16 56	17 40	23 51	25 09	01 09	02 32
E 11	343 21.4	26.0	252 03.2	12.8	15 32.3	12.8	56.5	56	16 06	16 50	17 36	23 55	25 16	01 16	02 42
S 12	358 21.4	N19 25.5	266 35.0	12.8	S15 45.1	12.7	56.5	58	15 56	16 42	17 31	23 59	25 23	01 23	02 53
D 13	13 21.4	24.9	281 06.8	12.6	15 57.8	12.7	56.6	S 60	15 43	16 34	17 26	24 03	00 03	01 31	03 07
A 14	28 21.4	24.4	295 38.4	12.6	16 10.5	12.6	56.6								
Y 15	43 21.4 ..	23.8	310 10.0	12.4	16 23.1	12.6	56.6								
16	58 21.4	23.3	324 41.4	12.3	16 35.7	12.5	56.7								
17	73 21.4	22.7	339 12.7	12.2	16 48.2	12.4	56.7								

Day	SUN			MOON			
18	88 21.4 N19 22.2						
19	103 21.4 21.6						
		Eqn. of Time	Mer.	Mer. Pass.		Age	Phase
20	118 21.4 21.1	00ʰ	12ʰ Pass.	Upper	Lower		
21	133 21.4 .. 20.5						
22	148 21.4 19.9	d	m s	m s	h m	h m	h m	d %
23	163 21.4 19.4	24	06 33	06 33	12 07	16 58	04 38	07 36
		25	06 34	06 34	12 07	17 40	05 19	08 46
	SD 15.8 d 0.5	26	06 34	06 34	12 07	18 26	06 03	09 56
	SD 15.0 15.2 15.4						

© British Crown Copyright 2022. All rights reserved.

UT	ARIES GHA	VENUS −4.5 GHA	Dec	MARS +1.8 GHA	Dec	JUPITER −2.3 GHA	Dec	SATURN +0.5 GHA	Dec	STARS Name	SHA	Dec
27 00	304 25.1	155 29.4 N 7 57.5		142 23.5 N 8 39.8		263 22.4 N14 37.8		325 58.9 S10 54.1		Acamar	315 12.8	S40 12.3
01	319 27.6	170 32.4	57.1	157 24.6	39.2	278 24.6	37.9	341 01.5	54.1	Achernar	335 21.0	S57 06.7
02	334 30.0	185 35.5	56.7	172 25.6	38.6	293 26.7	37.9	356 04.1	54.2	Acrux	173 01.7	S63 14.0
03	349 32.5	200 38.5 . .	56.3	187 26.6 . .	38.0	308 28.9 . .	38.0	11 06.7 . .	54.3	Adhara	255 07.2	S29 00.1
04	4 35.0	215 41.6	55.9	202 27.6	37.4	323 31.1	38.1	26 09.3	54.3	Aldebaran	290 41.2	N16 33.4
05	19 37.4	230 44.6	55.5	217 28.7	36.8	338 33.3	38.2	41 11.9	54.4			
06	34 39.9	245 47.7 N 7 55.1		232 29.7 N 8 36.2		353 35.4 N14 38.3		56 14.5 S10 54.4		Alioth	166 14.2	N55 50.3
T 07	49 42.4	260 50.7	54.7	247 30.7	35.6	8 37.6	38.4	71 17.1	54.5	Alkaid	152 53.0	N49 12.1
H 08	64 44.8	275 53.8	54.3	262 31.7	35.0	23 39.8	38.4	86 19.7	54.6	Alnair	27 34.0	S46 50.7
U 09	79 47.3	290 56.8 . .	54.0	277 32.8 . .	34.4	38 41.9 . .	38.5	101 22.3 . .	54.6	Alnilam	275 39.2	S 1 11.1
R 10	94 49.7	305 59.9	53.6	292 33.8	33.8	53 44.1	38.6	116 24.9	54.7	Alphard	217 49.3	S 8 45.5
S 11	109 52.2	321 03.0	53.2	307 34.8	33.2	68 46.3	38.7	131 27.5	54.7			
D 12	124 54.7	336 06.0 N 7 52.8		322 35.8 N 8 32.6		83 48.5 N14 38.8		146 30.1 S10 54.8		Alphecca	126 04.6	N26 38.3
A 13	139 57.1	351 09.1	52.4	337 36.8	32.0	98 50.6	38.8	161 32.7	54.9	Alpheratz	357 35.8	N29 13.1
Y 14	154 59.6	6 12.2	52.0	352 37.9	31.3	113 52.8	38.9	176 35.3	54.9	Altair	62 00.8	N 8 55.9
15	170 02.1	21 15.3 . .	51.6	7 38.9 . .	30.7	128 55.0 . .	39.0	191 37.9 . .	55.0	Ankaa	353 08.1	S42 10.5
16	185 04.5	36 18.4	51.3	22 39.9	30.1	143 57.2	39.1	206 40.5	55.0	Antares	112 17.1	S26 29.1
17	200 07.0	51 21.5	50.9	37 40.9	29.5	158 59.3	39.2	221 43.1	55.1			
18	215 09.5	66 24.6 N 7 50.5		52 42.0 N 8 28.9		174 01.5 N14 39.2		236 45.7 S10 55.2		Arcturus	145 49.0	N19 03.8
19	230 11.9	81 27.7	50.1	67 43.0	28.3	189 03.7	39.3	251 48.3	55.2	Atria	107 12.0	S69 04.4
20	245 14.4	96 30.8	49.7	82 44.0	27.7	204 05.9	39.4	266 50.9	55.3	Avior	234 15.9	S59 35.0
21	260 16.9	111 33.9 . .	49.4	97 45.0 . .	27.1	219 08.0 . .	39.5	281 53.5 . .	55.3	Bellatrix	278 24.4	N 6 22.3
22	275 19.3	126 37.0	49.0	112 46.1	26.5	234 10.2	39.6	296 56.1	55.4	Betelgeuse	270 53.7	N 7 24.8
23	290 21.8	141 40.1	48.6	127 47.1	25.9	249 12.4	39.6	311 58.7	55.5			
28 00	305 24.2	156 43.2 N 7 48.3		142 48.1 N 8 25.3		264 14.6 N14 39.7		327 01.3 S10 55.5		Canopus	263 53.4	S52 42.3
01	320 26.7	171 46.4	47.9	157 49.1	24.7	279 16.7	39.8	342 03.9	55.6	Capella	280 24.0	N46 01.2
02	335 29.2	186 49.5	47.5	172 50.2	24.0	294 18.9	39.9	357 06.5	55.6	Deneb	49 26.2	N45 21.8
03	350 31.6	201 52.6 . .	47.2	187 51.2 . .	23.4	309 21.1 . .	40.0	12 09.1 . .	55.7	Denebola	182 26.4	N14 26.6
04	5 34.1	216 55.8	46.8	202 52.2	22.8	324 23.3	40.0	27 11.7	55.8	Diphda	348 48.4	S17 51.3
05	20 36.6	231 58.9	46.4	217 53.2	22.2	339 25.4	40.1	42 14.3	55.8			
06	35 39.0	247 02.1 N 7 46.1		232 54.3 N 8 21.6		354 27.6 N14 40.2		57 16.9 S10 55.9		Dubhe	193 43.0	N61 37.7
07	50 41.5	262 05.2	45.7	247 55.3	21.0	9 29.8	40.3	72 19.5	55.9	Elnath	278 03.7	N28 37.6
08	65 44.0	277 08.4	45.3	262 56.3	20.4	24 32.0	40.4	87 22.1	56.0	Eltanin	90 42.3	N51 29.3
F 09	80 46.4	292 11.5 . .	45.0	277 57.3 . .	19.8	39 34.2 . .	40.4	102 24.7 . .	56.1	Enif	33 39.7	N 9 59.0
R 10	95 48.9	307 14.7	44.6	292 58.4	19.2	54 36.3	40.5	117 27.3	56.1	Fomalhaut	15 15.5	S29 29.7
I 11	110 51.4	322 17.8	44.3	307 59.4	18.6	69 38.5	40.6	132 29.9	56.2			
D 12	125 53.8	337 21.0 N 7 43.9		323 00.4 N 8 17.9		84 40.7 N14 40.7		147 32.5 S10 56.2		Gacrux	171 53.3	S57 14.9
A 13	140 56.3	352 24.2	43.6	338 01.4	17.3	99 42.9	40.8	162 35.1	56.3	Gienah	175 45.0	S17 40.3
Y 14	155 58.7	7 27.4	43.2	353 02.5	16.7	114 45.1	40.9	177 37.7	56.4	Hadar	148 37.7	S60 29.4
15	171 01.2	22 30.5 . .	42.9	8 03.5 . .	16.1	129 47.2 . .	40.9	192 40.3 . .	56.4	Hamal	327 52.5	N23 34.3
16	186 03.7	37 33.7	42.5	23 04.5	15.5	144 49.4	41.0	207 42.9	56.5	Kaus Aust.	83 33.7	S34 22.4
17	201 06.1	52 36.9	42.2	38 05.5	14.9	159 51.6	41.1	222 45.5	56.6			
18	216 08.6	67 40.1 N 7 41.8		53 06.6 N 8 14.3		174 53.8 N14 41.1		237 48.1 S10 56.6		Kochab	137 19.6	N74 03.8
19	231 11.1	82 43.3	41.5	68 07.6	13.7	189 56.0	41.2	252 50.7	56.7	Markab	13 30.8	N15 19.9
20	246 13.5	97 46.5	41.2	83 08.6	13.1	204 58.1	41.3	267 53.3	56.7	Menkar	314 07.5	N 4 11.0
21	261 16.0	112 49.7 . .	40.8	98 09.6 . .	12.5	220 00.3 . .	41.4	282 55.9 . .	56.8	Menkent	147 59.1	S36 29.2
22	276 18.5	127 52.9	40.5	113 10.7	11.8	235 02.5	41.5	297 58.5	56.9	Miaplacidus	221 39.5	S69 48.8
23	291 20.9	142 56.1	40.1	128 11.7	11.2	250 04.7	41.5	313 01.1	56.9			
29 00	306 23.4	157 59.3 N 7 39.8		143 12.7 N 8 10.6		265 06.9 N14 41.6		328 03.7 S10 57.0		Mirfak	308 30.1	N49 56.5
01	321 25.9	173 02.6	39.5	158 13.7	10.0	280 09.0	41.7	343 06.3	57.0	Nunki	75 48.9	S26 16.0
02	336 28.3	188 05.8	39.1	173 14.7	09.4	295 11.2	41.8	358 08.9	57.1	Peacock	53 07.0	S56 39.5
03	351 30.8	203 09.0 . .	38.8	188 15.8 . .	08.8	310 13.4 . .	41.8	13 11.5 . .	57.2	Pollux	243 19.1	N27 58.2
04	6 33.2	218 12.2	38.5	203 16.8	08.2	325 15.6	41.9	28 14.1	57.2	Procyon	244 52.4	N 5 10.0
05	21 35.7	233 15.5	38.1	218 17.8	07.6	340 17.8	42.0	43 16.7	57.3			
06	36 38.2	248 18.7 N 7 37.8		233 18.8 N 8 06.9		355 20.0 N14 42.1		58 19.3 S10 57.4		Rasalhague	95 59.4	N12 32.7
07	51 40.6	263 21.9	37.5	248 19.9	06.3	10 22.1	42.2	73 21.9	57.4	Regulus	207 36.0	N11 51.3
S 08	66 43.1	278 25.2	37.2	263 20.9	05.7	25 24.3	42.2	88 24.5	57.5	Rigel	281 05.3	S 8 10.3
A 09	81 45.6	293 28.4 . .	36.8	278 21.9 . .	05.1	40 26.5 . .	42.3	103 27.2 . .	57.5	Rigil Kent.	139 41.9	S60 56.1
T 10	96 48.0	308 31.7	36.5	293 22.9	04.5	55 28.7	42.4	118 29.8	57.6	Sabik	102 03.9	S15 45.2
U 11	111 50.5	323 34.9	36.2	308 24.0	03.9	70 30.9	42.5	133 32.4	57.7			
R 12	126 53.0	338 38.2 N 7 35.9		323 25.0 N 8 03.3		85 33.1 N14 42.5		148 35.0 S10 57.7		Schedar	349 32.2	N56 39.7
D 13	141 55.4	353 41.5	35.6	338 26.0	02.7	100 35.3	42.6	163 37.6	57.8	Shaula	96 11.7	S37 07.3
A 14	156 57.9	8 44.7	35.3	353 27.0	02.1	115 37.4	42.7	178 40.2	57.8	Sirius	258 27.6	S16 44.8
Y 15	172 00.3	23 48.0 . .	34.9	8 28.1 . .	01.4	130 39.6 . .	42.8	193 42.8 . .	57.9	Spica	158 23.6	S11 17.0
16	187 02.8	38 51.3	34.6	23 29.1	00.8	145 41.8	42.8	208 45.4	58.0	Suhail	222 47.6	S43 31.6
17	202 05.3	53 54.6	34.3	38 30.1	8 00.2	160 44.0	42.9	223 48.0	58.0			
18	217 07.7	68 57.8 N 7 34.0		53 31.1 N 7 59.6		175 46.2 N14 43.0		238 50.6 S10 58.1		Vega	80 33.6	N38 48.4
19	232 10.2	84 01.1	33.7	68 32.2	59.0	190 48.4	43.1	253 53.2	58.2	Zuben'ubi	136 57.3	S16 08.4
20	247 12.7	99 04.4	33.4	83 33.2	58.4	205 50.6	43.2	268 55.8	58.2			
21	262 15.1	114 07.7 . .	33.1	98 34.2 . .	57.8	220 52.7 . .	43.2	283 58.4 . .	58.3		SHA	Mer. Pass.
22	277 17.6	129 11.0	32.8	113 35.2	57.1	235 54.9	43.3	299 01.0	58.3	Venus	211 19.0	13 30
23	292 20.1	144 14.3	32.5	128 36.3	56.5	250 57.1	43.4	314 03.6	58.4	Mars	197 23.9	14 28
Mer. Pass. 3 37.8		v 3.2 d 0.4		v 1.0 d 0.6		v 2.2 d 0.1		v 2.6 d 0.1		Jupiter	318 50.3	6 22
										Saturn	21 37.1	2 12

© British Crown Copyright 2022. All rights reserved.

UT	SUN GHA	SUN Dec	MOON GHA	v	MOON Dec	d	HP
d h	° ′	° ′	° ′	′	° ′	′	′
27 00	178 21.4	N19 18.8	80 48.9	11.4	S18 13.8	12.0	57.0
01	193 21.4	18.3	95 19.3	11.3	18 25.8	11.9	57.0
02	208 21.4	17.7	109 49.6	11.2	18 37.7	11.8	57.1
03	223 21.4 ..	17.1	124 19.8	11.1	18 49.5	11.7	57.1
04	238 21.4	16.6	138 49.9	10.9	19 01.2	11.7	57.1
05	253 21.4	16.0	153 19.8	10.9	19 12.9	11.6	57.2
06	268 21.4	N19 15.5	167 49.7	10.7	S19 24.5	11.5	57.2
07	283 21.4	14.9	182 19.4	10.5	19 36.0	11.4	57.2
T 08	298 21.4	14.3	196 48.9	10.5	19 47.4	11.3	57.3
H 09	313 21.5 ..	13.8	211 18.4	10.3	19 58.7	11.2	57.3
U 10	328 21.5	13.2	225 47.7	10.2	20 09.9	11.2	57.4
R 11	343 21.5	12.6	240 16.9	10.1	20 21.1	11.1	57.4
S 12	358 21.5	N19 12.1	254 46.0	10.0	S20 32.2	10.9	57.4
D 13	13 21.5	11.5	269 15.0	9.8	20 43.1	10.9	57.5
A 14	28 21.5	10.9	283 43.8	9.7	20 54.0	10.8	57.5
Y 15	43 21.5 ..	10.4	298 12.5	9.6	21 04.8	10.7	57.6
16	58 21.5	09.8	312 41.1	9.4	21 15.5	10.5	57.6
17	73 21.5	09.2	327 09.5	9.3	21 26.0	10.5	57.6
18	88 21.5	N19 08.7	341 37.8	9.2	S21 36.5	10.4	57.7
19	103 21.5	08.1	356 06.0	9.0	21 46.9	10.3	57.7
20	118 21.5	07.5	10 34.0	8.9	21 57.2	10.2	57.8
21	133 21.6 ..	07.0	25 01.9	8.8	22 07.4	10.0	57.8
22	148 21.6	06.4	39 29.7	8.7	22 17.4	10.0	57.8
23	163 21.6	05.8	53 57.4	8.5	22 27.4	9.8	57.9
28 00	178 21.6	N19 05.2	68 24.9	8.3	S22 37.2	9.8	57.9
01	193 21.6	04.7	82 52.2	8.3	22 47.0	9.6	57.9
02	208 21.6	04.1	97 19.5	8.1	22 56.6	9.5	58.0
03	223 21.6 ..	03.5	111 46.6	8.0	23 06.1	9.4	58.0
04	238 21.6	02.9	126 13.6	7.8	23 15.5	9.3	58.1
05	253 21.6	02.4	140 40.4	7.7	23 24.8	9.1	58.1
06	268 21.6	N19 01.8	155 07.1	7.6	S23 33.9	9.0	58.2
07	283 21.7	01.2	169 33.7	7.4	23 42.9	8.9	58.2
08	298 21.7	00.6	184 00.1	7.3	23 51.8	8.8	58.2
F 09	313 21.7	19 00.1	198 26.4	7.2	24 00.6	8.6	58.3
R 10	328 21.7	18 59.5	212 52.6	7.0	24 09.2	8.5	58.3
I 11	343 21.7	58.9	227 18.6	7.0	24 17.7	8.4	58.4
D 12	358 21.7	N18 58.3	241 44.6	6.7	S24 26.1	8.2	58.4
A 13	13 21.7	57.8	256 10.3	6.7	24 34.3	8.1	58.4
Y 14	28 21.8	57.2	270 36.0	6.5	24 42.4	8.0	58.5
15	43 21.8 ..	56.6	285 01.5	6.3	24 50.4	7.8	58.5
16	58 21.8	56.0	299 26.8	6.3	24 58.2	7.7	58.6
17	73 21.8	55.4	313 52.1	6.1	25 05.9	7.5	58.6
18	88 21.8	N18 54.8	328 17.2	6.0	S25 13.4	7.4	58.6
19	103 21.8	54.3	342 42.4	5.8	25 20.8	7.2	58.7
20	118 21.8	53.7	357 07.0	5.7	25 28.0	7.1	58.7
21	133 21.9 ..	53.1	11 31.7	5.6	25 35.1	7.0	58.8
22	148 21.9	52.5	25 56.3	5.5	25 42.1	6.7	58.8
23	163 21.9	51.9	40 20.8	5.3	25 48.8	6.7	58.8
29 00	178 21.9	N18 51.3	54 45.1	5.2	S25 55.5	6.4	58.9
01	193 21.9	50.8	69 09.3	5.1	26 01.9	6.3	58.9
02	208 21.9	50.2	83 33.4	5.0	26 08.2	6.2	59.0
03	223 22.0 ..	49.6	97 57.4	4.9	26 14.4	6.0	59.0
04	238 22.0	49.0	112 21.3	4.7	26 20.4	5.8	59.0
05	253 22.0	48.4	126 45.0	4.6	26 26.2	5.6	59.1
06	268 22.0	N18 47.8	141 08.6	4.5	S26 31.8	5.5	59.1
07	283 22.0	47.2	155 32.1	4.4	26 37.3	5.3	59.1
S 08	298 22.1	46.6	169 55.5	4.2	26 42.6	5.2	59.2
A 09	313 22.1 ..	46.1	184 18.7	4.2	26 47.8	4.9	59.2
T 10	328 22.1	45.5	198 41.9	4.0	26 52.7	4.8	59.3
U 11	343 22.1	44.9	213 04.9	3.9	26 57.5	4.6	59.3
R 12	358 22.1	N18 44.3	227 27.8	3.8	S27 02.1	4.5	59.3
D 13	13 22.2	43.7	241 50.6	3.8	27 06.6	4.2	59.4
A 14	28 22.2	43.1	256 13.4	3.6	27 10.8	4.1	59.4
Y 15	43 22.2 ..	42.5	270 36.0	3.5	27 14.9	3.9	59.5
16	58 22.2	41.9	284 58.5	3.4	27 18.8	3.7	59.5
17	73 22.2	41.3	299 20.9	3.3	27 22.5	3.5	59.5
18	88 22.3	N18 40.7	313 43.2	3.2	S27 26.0	3.3	59.6
19	103 22.3	40.1	328 05.4	3.2	27 29.3	3.2	59.6
20	118 22.3	39.5	342 27.6	3.0	27 32.5	2.9	59.6
21	133 22.3 ..	38.9	356 49.6	3.0	27 35.4	2.8	59.7
22	148 22.3	38.3	11 11.6	2.8	27 38.2	2.6	59.7
23	163 22.4	37.7	25 33.4	2.8	S27 40.8	2.3	59.8
	SD 15.8	d 0.6	SD 15.6		15.9		16.2

Twilight / Sunrise / Moonrise

Lat.	Naut.	Civil	Sunrise	27	28	29	30
°	h m	h m	h m	h m	h m	h m	h m
N 72	▭	▭	▭	■	■	■	■
N 70	////	////	00 28	■	■	■	■
68	////	////	01 52	18 51	■	■	■
66	////	////	02 29	17 24	■	■	■
64	////	01 11	02 54	16 47	19 24	■	■
62	////	01 57	03 14	16 21	18 21	20 37	21 56
60	////	02 26	03 31	16 00	17 47	19 30	20 41
N 58	01 04	02 48	03 44	15 44	17 22	18 55	20 05
56	01 47	03 06	03 56	15 30	17 02	18 30	19 39
54	02 14	03 20	04 06	15 17	16 46	18 10	19 18
52	02 34	03 33	04 15	15 07	16 32	17 53	19 01
50	02 51	03 44	04 23	14 57	16 19	17 38	18 46
45	03 22	04 06	04 40	14 38	15 54	17 09	18 16
N 40	03 46	04 24	04 54	14 22	15 34	16 46	17 53
35	04 04	04 38	05 06	14 08	15 17	16 27	17 34
30	04 19	04 50	05 16	13 57	15 03	16 11	17 17
20	04 42	05 10	05 34	13 37	14 38	15 43	16 49
N 10	05 01	05 27	05 49	13 20	14 18	15 20	16 25
0	05 16	05 41	06 03	13 04	13 58	14 58	16 03
S 10	05 29	05 55	06 17	12 48	13 39	14 37	15 40
20	05 42	06 08	06 32	12 31	13 18	14 13	15 16
30	05 54	06 23	06 48	12 12	12 55	13 46	14 48
35	06 00	06 31	06 58	12 01	12 41	13 31	14 32
40	06 07	06 40	07 09	11 48	12 25	13 12	14 12
45	06 14	06 50	07 22	11 33	12 06	12 50	13 49
S 50	06 22	07 02	07 38	11 15	11 43	12 22	13 19
52	06 26	07 07	07 45	11 07	11 31	12 09	13 05
54	06 30	07 13	07 53	10 57	11 19	11 53	12 48
56	06 34	07 20	08 02	10 46	11 04	11 35	12 27
58	06 38	07 27	08 12	10 34	10 47	11 12	12 02
S 60	06 43	07 35	08 24	10 20	10 27	10 43	11 27

Sunset / Twilight / Moonset

Lat.	Sunset	Civil	Naut.	27	28	29	30
°	h m	h m	h m	h m	h m	h m	h m
N 72	▭	▭	▭	■	■	■	■
N 70	23 25	////	////	■	■	■	■
68	22 17	////	////	19 25	■	■	■
66	21 41	////	////	20 53	■	■	■
64	21 16	22 56	////	21 31	20 50	■	■
62	20 57	22 12	////	21 58	21 54	21 46	22 43
60	20 41	21 44	////	22 20	22 28	22 53	23 58
N 58	20 27	21 23	23 03	22 37	22 54	23 28	24 34
56	20 16	21 06	22 23	22 52	23 14	23 53	25 00
54	20 06	20 51	21 57	23 04	23 31	24 14	00 14
52	19 57	20 39	21 37	23 16	23 45	24 31	00 31
50	19 49	20 28	21 21	23 26	23 58	24 46	00 46
45	19 32	20 06	20 50	23 47	24 24	00 24	01 15
N 40	19 18	19 49	20 27	24 04	00 04	00 45	01 39
35	19 06	19 35	20 09	24 18	00 18	01 03	01 58
30	18 56	19 22	19 54	24 31	00 31	01 18	02 14
20	18 39	19 03	19 31	00 09	00 52	01 43	02 42
N 10	18 24	18 46	19 12	00 24	01 11	02 05	03 06
0	18 10	18 32	18 57	00 37	01 29	02 26	03 29
S 10	17 56	18 18	18 44	00 51	01 47	02 47	03 51
20	17 42	18 05	18 32	01 06	02 06	03 09	04 15
30	17 25	17 50	18 19	01 23	02 28	03 35	04 43
35	17 15	17 42	18 13	01 33	02 41	03 50	04 59
40	17 04	17 34	18 07	01 45	02 56	04 08	05 18
45	16 52	17 24	17 59	01 59	03 14	04 30	05 42
S 50	16 36	17 12	17 51	02 15	03 36	04 57	06 11
52	16 29	17 06	17 48	02 23	03 47	05 10	06 26
54	16 21	17 01	17 44	02 32	03 59	05 26	06 43
56	16 12	16 54	17 40	02 42	04 13	05 44	07 03
58	16 01	16 47	17 36	02 53	04 29	06 06	07 29
S 60	15 49	16 39	17 31	03 07	04 49	06 35	08 04

SUN / MOON

Day	Eqn. of Time 00h	Eqn. of Time 12h	Mer. Pass.	Mer. Pass. Upper	Mer. Pass. Lower	Age	Phase
d	m s	m s	h m	h m	h m	d	%
27	06 34	06 34	12 07	19 16	06 50	10	66
28	06 34	06 33	12 07	20 12	07 43	11	76
29	06 32	06 32	12 07	21 13	08 42	12	85

© British Crown Copyright 2022. All rights reserved.

UT	ARIES GHA	VENUS −4.4 GHA	Dec	MARS +1.8 GHA	Dec	JUPITER −2.4 GHA	Dec	SATURN +0.5 GHA	Dec
30 00	307 22.5	159 17.6	N 7 32.2	143 37.3	N 7 55.9	265 59.3	N14 43.5	329 06.2	S10 58.5
01	322 25.0	174 20.9	31.9	158 38.3	55.3	281 01.5	43.5	344 08.8	58.5
02	337 27.5	189 24.2	31.6	173 39.3	54.7	296 03.7	43.6	359 11.4	58.6
03	352 29.9	204 27.6 ..	31.3	188 40.4 ..	54.1	311 05.9 ..	43.7	14 14.0 ..	58.7
04	7 32.4	219 30.9	31.0	203 41.4	53.5	326 08.1	43.7	29 16.6	58.7
05	22 34.8	234 34.2	30.7	218 42.4	52.9	341 10.3	43.8	44 19.2	58.8
06	37 37.3	249 37.5	N 7 30.4	233 43.4	N 7 52.2	356 12.4	N14 43.9	59 21.8	S10 58.8
07	52 39.8	264 40.9	30.1	248 44.5	51.6	11 14.6	44.0	74 24.4	58.9
08	67 42.2	279 44.2	29.8	263 45.5	51.0	26 16.8	44.1	89 27.1	59.0
S 09	82 44.7	294 47.5 ..	29.6	278 46.5 ..	50.4	41 19.0 ..	44.1	104 29.7 ..	59.0
U 10	97 47.2	309 50.9	29.3	293 47.5	49.8	56 21.2	44.2	119 32.3	59.1
N 11	112 49.6	324 54.2	29.0	308 48.6	49.2	71 23.4	44.3	134 34.9	59.2
D 12	127 52.1	339 57.6	N 7 28.7	323 49.6	N 7 48.6	86 25.6	N14 44.4	149 37.5	S10 59.2
A 13	142 54.6	355 00.9	28.4	338 50.6	47.9	101 27.8	44.4	164 40.1	59.3
Y 14	157 57.0	10 04.3	28.1	353 51.6	47.3	116 30.0	44.5	179 42.7	59.3
15	172 59.5	25 07.7 ..	27.9	8 52.7 ..	46.7	131 32.2 ..	44.6	194 45.3 ..	59.4
16	188 02.0	40 11.0	27.6	23 53.7	46.1	146 34.4	44.7	209 47.9	59.5
17	203 04.4	55 14.4	27.3	38 54.7	45.5	161 36.6	44.7	224 50.5	59.5
18	218 06.9	70 17.8	N 7 27.1	53 55.7	N 7 44.9	176 38.7	N14 44.8	239 53.1	S10 59.6
19	233 09.3	85 21.1	26.8	68 56.8	44.2	191 40.9	44.9	254 55.7	59.7
20	248 11.8	100 24.5	26.5	83 57.8	43.6	206 43.1	44.9	269 58.3	59.7
21	263 14.3	115 27.9 ..	26.2	98 58.8 ..	43.0	221 45.3 ..	45.0	285 00.9 ..	59.8
22	278 16.7	130 31.3	26.0	113 59.8	42.4	236 47.5	45.1	300 03.5	59.8
23	293 19.2	145 34.7	25.7	129 00.9	41.8	251 49.7	45.2	315 06.1	10 59.9
31 00	308 21.7	160 38.1	N 7 25.4	144 01.9	N 7 41.2	266 51.9	N14 45.2	330 08.8	S11 00.0
01	323 24.1	175 41.5	25.2	159 02.9	40.6	281 54.1	45.3	345 11.4	00.0
02	338 26.6	190 44.9	24.9	174 03.9	39.9	296 56.3	45.4	0 14.0	00.1
03	353 29.1	205 48.3 ..	24.7	189 05.0 ..	39.3	311 58.5 ..	45.5	15 16.6 ..	00.2
04	8 31.5	220 51.7	24.4	204 06.0	38.7	327 00.7	45.5	30 19.2	00.2
05	23 34.0	235 55.1	24.2	219 07.0	38.1	342 02.9	45.6	45 21.8	00.3
06	38 36.5	250 58.5	N 7 23.9	234 08.0	N 7 37.5	357 05.1	N14 45.7	60 24.4	S11 00.3
07	53 38.9	266 01.9	23.6	249 09.1	36.9	12 07.3	45.8	75 27.0	00.4
08	68 41.4	281 05.4	23.4	264 10.1	36.2	27 09.5	45.8	90 29.6	00.5
M 09	83 43.8	296 08.8 ..	23.1	279 11.1 ..	35.6	42 11.7 ..	45.9	105 32.2 ..	00.5
O 10	98 46.3	311 12.2	22.9	294 12.1	35.0	57 13.9	46.0	120 34.8	00.6
N 11	113 48.8	326 15.7	22.7	309 13.2	34.4	72 16.1	46.0	135 37.4	00.7
D 12	128 51.2	341 19.1	N 7 22.4	324 14.2	N 7 33.8	87 18.3	N14 46.1	150 40.0	S11 00.7
A 13	143 53.7	356 22.5	22.2	339 15.2	33.2	102 20.5	46.2	165 42.7	00.8
Y 14	158 56.2	11 26.0	21.9	354 16.2	32.5	117 22.7	46.3	180 45.3	00.9
15	173 58.6	26 29.4 ..	21.7	9 17.3 ..	31.9	132 24.9 ..	46.3	195 47.9 ..	00.9
16	189 01.1	41 32.9	21.4	24 18.3	31.3	147 27.1	46.4	210 50.5	01.0
17	204 03.6	56 36.3	21.2	39 19.3	30.7	162 29.3	46.5	225 53.1	01.0
18	219 06.0	71 39.8	N 7 21.0	54 20.3	N 7 30.1	177 31.5	N14 46.6	240 55.7	S11 01.1
19	234 08.5	86 43.3	20.7	69 21.4	29.4	192 33.7	46.6	255 58.3	01.2
20	249 11.0	101 46.7	20.5	84 22.4	28.8	207 35.9	46.7	271 00.9	01.2
21	264 13.4	116 50.2 ..	20.3	99 23.4 ..	28.2	222 38.1 ..	46.8	286 03.5 ..	01.3
22	279 15.9	131 53.7	20.0	114 24.4	27.6	237 40.3	46.8	301 06.1	01.4
23	294 18.3	146 57.2	19.8	129 25.5	27.0	252 42.5	46.9	316 08.7	01.4
1 00	309 20.8	162 00.6	N 7 19.6	144 26.5	N 7 26.4	267 44.7	N14 47.0	331 11.4	S11 01.5
01	324 23.3	177 04.1	19.4	159 27.5	25.7	282 46.9	47.1	346 14.0	01.6
02	339 25.7	192 07.6	19.1	174 28.5	25.1	297 49.1	47.1	1 16.6	01.6
03	354 28.2	207 11.1 ..	18.9	189 29.6 ..	24.5	312 51.3 ..	47.2	16 19.2 ..	01.7
04	9 30.7	222 14.6	18.7	204 30.6	23.9	327 53.5	47.3	31 21.8	01.7
05	24 33.1	237 18.1	18.5	219 31.6	23.3	342 55.7	47.3	46 24.4	01.8
06	39 35.6	252 21.6	N 7 18.3	234 32.6	N 7 22.6	357 57.9	N14 47.4	61 27.0	S11 01.9
07	54 38.1	267 25.1	18.1	249 33.7	22.0	13 00.1	47.5	76 29.6	01.9
T 08	69 40.5	282 28.6	17.8	264 34.7	21.4	28 02.3	47.6	91 32.2	02.0
U 09	84 43.0	297 32.1 ..	17.6	279 35.7 ..	20.8	43 04.5 ..	47.6	106 34.8 ..	02.1
E 10	99 45.5	312 35.6	17.4	294 36.7	20.2	58 06.7	47.7	121 37.5	02.1
S 11	114 47.9	327 39.1	17.2	309 37.8	19.6	73 08.9	47.8	136 40.1	02.2
D 12	129 50.4	342 42.7	N 7 17.0	324 38.8	N 7 18.9	88 11.1	N14 47.8	151 42.7	S11 02.3
A 13	144 52.8	357 46.2	16.8	339 39.8	18.3	103 13.3	47.9	166 45.3	02.3
Y 14	159 55.3	12 49.7	16.6	354 40.8	17.7	118 15.5	48.0	181 47.9	02.4
15	174 57.8	27 53.3 ..	16.4	9 41.9 ..	17.1	133 17.7 ..	48.0	196 50.5 ..	02.5
16	190 00.2	42 56.8	16.2	24 42.9	16.5	148 19.9	48.1	211 53.1	02.5
17	205 02.7	58 00.3	16.0	39 43.9	15.8	163 22.1	48.2	226 55.7	02.6
18	220 05.2	73 03.9	N 7 15.8	54 44.9	N 7 15.2	178 24.3	N14 48.3	241 58.3	S11 02.6
19	235 07.6	88 07.4	15.6	69 46.0	14.6	193 26.5	48.3	257 01.0	02.7
20	250 10.1	103 11.0	15.4	84 47.0	14.0	208 28.7	48.4	272 03.6	02.8
21	265 12.6	118 14.5 ..	15.2	99 48.0 ..	13.4	223 30.9 ..	48.5	287 06.2 ..	02.8
22	280 15.0	133 18.1	15.0	114 49.0	12.7	238 33.1	48.5	302 08.8	02.9
23	295 17.5	148 21.6	14.8	129 50.1	12.1	253 35.4	48.6	317 11.4	03.0
Mer. Pass.	h m 3 26.0	v 3.4	d 0.2	v 1.0	d 0.6	v 2.2	d 0.1	v 2.6	d 0.1

STARS

Name	SHA	Dec
Acamar	315 12.7	S40 12.3
Achernar	335 20.9	S57 06.7
Acrux	173 01.8	S63 14.0
Adhara	255 07.2	S29 00.1
Aldebaran	290 41.2	N16 33.4
Alioth	166 14.2	N55 50.2
Alkaid	152 53.0	N49 12.1
Alnair	27 34.0	S46 50.7
Alnilam	275 39.2	S 1 11.1
Alphard	217 49.2	S 8 45.5
Alphecca	126 04.6	N26 38.3
Alpheratz	357 35.8	N29 13.1
Altair	62 00.8	N 8 55.9
Ankaa	353 08.1	S42 10.5
Antares	112 17.1	S26 29.1
Arcturus	145 49.0	N19 03.8
Atria	107 12.0	S69 04.4
Avior	234 15.9	S59 35.0
Bellatrix	278 24.4	N 6 22.3
Betelgeuse	270 53.6	N 7 24.8
Canopus	263 53.4	S52 42.2
Capella	280 24.0	N46 01.2
Deneb	49 26.1	N45 21.8
Denebola	182 26.4	N14 26.6
Diphda	348 48.3	S17 51.3
Dubhe	193 43.0	N61 37.7
Elnath	278 03.6	N28 37.6
Eltanin	90 42.3	N51 29.3
Enif	33 39.6	N 9 59.0
Fomalhaut	15 15.5	S29 29.7
Gacrux	171 53.3	S57 14.9
Gienah	175 45.0	S17 40.3
Hadar	148 37.8	S60 29.4
Hamal	327 52.5	N23 34.3
Kaus Aust.	83 33.7	S34 22.4
Kochab	137 19.6	N74 03.8
Markab	13 30.8	N15 19.9
Menkar	314 07.4	N 4 11.0
Menkent	147 59.1	S36 29.2
Miaplacidus	221 39.5	S69 48.8
Mirfak	308 30.1	N49 56.5
Nunki	75 48.9	S26 16.0
Peacock	53 07.0	S56 39.5
Pollux	243 19.1	N27 58.2
Procyon	244 52.4	N 5 10.0
Rasalhague	95 59.4	N12 32.7
Regulus	207 36.0	N11 51.3
Rigel	281 05.2	S 8 10.3
Rigil Kent.	139 41.9	S60 56.1
Sabik	102 03.9	S15 45.2
Schedar	349 32.1	N56 39.8
Shaula	96 11.7	S37 07.3
Sirius	258 27.6	S16 44.7
Spica	158 23.6	S11 17.0
Suhail	222 47.6	S43 31.6
Vega	80 33.6	N38 48.4
Zuben'ubi	136 57.3	S16 08.4

	SHA	Mer. Pass.
	° ′	h m
Venus	212 16.4	13 14
Mars	195 40.2	14 23
Jupiter	318 30.2	6 12
Saturn	21 47.1	1 59

© British Crown Copyright 2022. All rights reserved.

UT	SUN GHA	SUN Dec	MOON GHA	v	MOON Dec	d	HP
30 00	178 22.4	N18 37.1	39 55.2	2.7	S27 43.1	2.2	59.8
01	193 22.4	36.5	54 16.9	2.6	27 45.3	2.0	59.8
02	208 22.4	35.9	68 38.5	2.6	27 47.3	1.8	59.9
03	223 22.5	.. 35.3	83 00.1	2.5	27 49.1	1.5	59.9
04	238 22.5	34.7	97 21.6	2.4	27 50.6	1.4	59.9
05	253 22.5	34.1	111 43.0	2.3	27 52.0	1.2	60.0
S 06	268 22.5	N18 33.5	126 04.3	2.3	S27 53.2	1.0	60.0
U 07	283 22.6	32.9	140 25.6	2.2	27 54.2	0.7	60.0
N 08	298 22.6	32.3	154 46.8	2.2	27 54.9	0.6	60.1
D 09	313 22.6	.. 31.7	169 08.0	2.1	27 55.5	0.3	60.1
A 10	328 22.6	31.1	183 29.1	2.0	27 55.8	0.2	60.1
Y 11	343 22.7	30.5	197 50.1	2.0	27 56.0	0.1	60.2
12	358 22.7	N18 29.9	212 11.1	2.0	S27 55.9	0.2	60.2
13	13 22.7	29.3	226 32.1	1.9	27 55.7	0.5	60.2
14	28 22.7	28.7	240 53.0	1.9	27 55.2	0.7	60.3
15	43 22.8	.. 28.1	255 13.9	1.9	27 54.5	0.9	60.3
16	58 22.8	27.5	269 34.8	1.8	27 53.6	1.1	60.3
17	73 22.8	26.9	283 55.6	1.8	27 52.5	1.3	60.4
18	88 22.9	N18 26.3	298 16.4	1.7	S27 51.2	1.5	60.4
19	103 22.9	25.7	312 37.1	1.7	27 49.7	1.7	60.4
20	118 22.9	25.1	326 57.8	1.8	27 48.0	2.0	60.5
21	133 22.9	.. 24.5	341 18.6	1.7	27 46.0	2.1	60.5
22	148 23.0	23.9	355 39.3	1.6	27 43.9	2.4	60.5
23	163 23.0	23.2	9 59.9	1.7	27 41.5	2.6	60.5
31 00	178 23.0	N18 22.6	24 20.6	1.7	S27 38.9	2.7	60.6
01	193 23.1	22.0	38 41.3	1.6	27 36.2	3.0	60.6
02	208 23.1	21.4	53 01.9	1.7	27 33.2	3.3	60.6
03	223 23.1	.. 20.8	67 22.6	1.7	27 29.9	3.4	60.6
04	238 23.2	20.2	81 43.3	1.7	27 26.5	3.6	60.7
05	253 23.2	19.6	96 04.0	1.6	27 22.9	3.9	60.7
06	268 23.2	N18 19.0	110 24.6	1.7	S27 19.0	4.0	60.7
07	283 23.2	18.3	124 45.3	1.7	27 15.0	4.3	60.7
M 08	298 23.3	17.7	139 06.0	1.8	27 10.7	4.5	60.8
O 09	313 23.3	.. 17.1	153 26.8	1.7	27 06.2	4.7	60.8
N 10	328 23.3	16.5	167 47.5	1.8	27 01.5	4.9	60.8
D 11	343 23.4	15.9	182 08.3	1.8	26 56.6	5.1	60.9
A 12	358 23.4	N18 15.3	196 29.1	1.8	S26 51.5	5.3	60.9
Y 13	13 23.4	14.7	210 49.9	1.9	26 46.2	5.5	60.9
14	28 23.5	14.0	225 10.8	1.9	26 40.7	5.7	60.9
15	43 23.5	.. 13.4	239 31.7	2.0	26 35.0	6.0	61.0
16	58 23.5	12.8	253 52.7	1.9	26 29.0	6.1	61.0
17	73 23.6	12.2	268 13.6	2.1	26 22.9	6.3	61.0
18	88 23.6	N18 11.6	282 34.7	2.1	S26 16.6	6.6	61.0
19	103 23.6	10.9	296 55.8	2.1	26 10.0	6.7	61.0
20	118 23.7	10.3	311 16.9	2.2	26 03.3	7.0	61.0
21	133 23.7	.. 09.7	325 38.1	2.2	25 56.3	7.1	61.1
22	148 23.8	09.1	339 59.3	2.3	25 49.2	7.4	61.1
23	163 23.8	08.5	354 20.6	2.4	25 41.8	7.5	61.1
1 00	178 23.8	N18 07.8	8 42.0	2.4	S25 34.3	7.7	61.1
01	193 23.9	07.2	23 03.4	2.5	25 26.6	8.0	61.1
02	208 23.9	06.6	37 24.9	2.6	25 18.6	8.1	61.1
03	223 23.9	.. 06.0	51 46.5	2.6	25 10.5	8.3	61.2
04	238 24.0	05.3	66 08.1	2.7	25 02.2	8.5	61.2
05	253 24.0	04.7	80 29.8	2.8	24 53.7	8.7	61.2
06	268 24.0	N18 04.1	94 51.6	2.8	S24 45.0	8.9	61.2
07	283 24.1	03.5	109 13.4	3.0	24 36.1	9.1	61.2
T 08	298 24.1	02.8	123 35.4	3.0	24 27.0	9.2	61.2
U 09	313 24.2	.. 02.2	137 57.4	3.1	24 17.8	9.5	61.2
E 10	328 24.2	01.6	152 19.5	3.2	24 08.3	9.6	61.3
S 11	343 24.2	00.9	166 41.7	3.3	23 58.7	9.8	61.3
D 12	358 24.3	N18 00.3	181 04.0	3.3	S23 48.9	10.0	61.3
A 13	13 24.3	17 59.7	195 26.3	3.5	23 38.9	10.1	61.3
Y 14	28 24.4	59.1	209 48.8	3.5	23 28.8	10.3	61.3
15	43 24.4	.. 58.4	224 11.3	3.6	23 18.5	10.5	61.3
16	58 24.4	57.8	238 33.9	3.8	23 08.0	10.7	61.3
17	73 24.5	57.2	252 56.7	3.8	22 57.3	10.8	61.3
18	88 24.5	N17 56.5	267 19.5	3.9	S22 46.5	11.0	61.3
19	103 24.6	55.9	281 42.4	4.0	22 35.5	11.2	61.3
20	118 24.6	55.3	296 05.4	4.1	22 24.3	11.3	61.3
21	133 24.6	.. 54.6	310 28.5	4.3	22 13.0	11.5	61.3
22	148 24.7	54.0	324 51.8	4.3	22 01.5	11.6	61.4
23	163 24.7	53.4	339 15.1	4.4	S21 49.9	11.8	61.4
	SD 15.8	d 0.6	SD 16.4		16.6		16.7

Twilight / Sunrise / Moonrise

Lat.	Twilight Naut.	Twilight Civil	Sunrise	Moonrise 30	31	1	2
N 72	□	□	□	■	■	■	23 44
N 70	////	////	01 14	■	■	■	23 01
68	////	////	02 08	■	■	23 55	22 32
66	////	////	02 40	■	■	22 45	22 10
64	////	01 32	03 04	■	22 58	22 08	21 52
62	////	02 10	03 22	21 56	21 10	21 41	21 37
60	////	02 36	03 38	20 41	21 10	21 20	21 25
N 58	01 23	02 56	03 50	20 05	20 44	21 03	21 14
56	01 58	03 12	04 01	19 39	20 23	20 49	21 04
54	02 22	03 26	04 11	19 18	20 06	20 36	20 56
52	02 41	03 38	04 20	19 01	19 51	20 25	20 48
50	02 57	03 48	04 27	18 46	19 38	20 15	20 41
45	03 27	04 10	04 44	18 16	19 12	19 54	20 27
N 40	03 49	04 27	04 57	17 53	18 50	19 37	20 14
35	04 07	04 40	05 08	17 34	18 33	19 23	20 04
30	04 21	04 52	05 18	17 17	18 18	19 10	19 55
20	04 44	05 11	05 35	16 49	17 52	18 48	19 39
N 10	05 01	05 27	05 49	16 25	17 29	18 30	19 25
0	05 16	05 41	06 03	16 03	17 08	18 12	19 12
S 10	05 29	05 54	06 16	15 40	16 47	17 54	18 58
20	05 41	06 07	06 30	15 16	16 25	17 35	18 44
30	05 52	06 21	06 46	14 48	15 58	17 13	18 28
35	05 58	06 29	06 56	14 32	15 43	17 00	18 18
40	06 05	06 37	07 06	14 12	15 25	16 45	18 07
45	06 11	06 47	07 18	13 49	15 03	16 27	17 54
S 50	06 19	06 58	07 33	13 19	14 36	16 05	17 39
52	06 22	07 03	07 40	13 05	14 22	15 54	17 31
54	06 25	07 09	07 48	12 48	14 06	15 42	17 23
56	06 29	07 15	07 57	12 27	13 48	15 28	17 14
58	06 33	07 21	08 06	12 02	13 25	15 12	17 03
S 60	06 38	07 29	08 18	11 27	12 56	14 52	16 50

Sunset / Twilight / Moonset

Lat.	Sunset	Twilight Civil	Twilight Naut.	Moonset 30	31	1	2
N 72	□	□	□	■	■	■	■
N 70	22 50	////	////	■	■	■	01 17
68	22 00	////	////	■	■	■	02 26
66	21 29	////	////	■	■	■	03 02
64	21 07	22 36	////	■	23 59	27 02	03 02
62	20 48	22 00	////	22 43	25 11	01 11	03 27
60	20 34	21 34	////	23 58	25 47	01 47	03 47
N 58	20 21	21 15	22 45	24 34	00 34	02 12	04 04
56	20 10	20 57	22 12	25 00	01 00	02 32	04 17
54	20 01	20 45	21 48	00 14	01 20	02 49	04 29
52	19 52	20 34	21 30	00 31	01 37	03 04	04 40
50	19 45	20 23	21 14	00 46	01 52	03 16	04 49
45	19 28	20 02	20 45	01 15	02 22	03 42	05 08
N 40	19 15	19 46	20 23	01 39	02 45	04 02	05 24
35	19 04	19 32	20 06	01 58	03 04	04 19	05 37
30	18 54	19 20	19 51	02 14	03 21	04 34	05 49
20	18 38	19 01	19 29	02 42	03 48	04 58	06 08
N 10	18 23	18 45	19 11	03 06	04 12	05 19	06 25
0	18 10	18 32	18 57	03 29	04 34	05 39	06 41
S 10	17 57	18 19	18 44	03 51	04 56	05 58	06 56
20	17 43	18 06	18 32	04 15	05 19	06 19	07 13
30	17 27	17 52	18 21	04 43	05 46	06 43	07 31
35	17 18	17 44	18 15	04 59	06 02	06 57	07 42
40	17 07	17 36	18 09	05 18	06 21	07 13	07 55
45	16 55	17 27	18 02	05 42	06 43	07 32	08 09
S 50	16 40	17 15	17 55	06 11	07 11	07 55	08 27
52	16 33	17 10	17 51	06 26	07 25	08 07	08 35
54	16 25	17 05	17 48	06 43	07 41	08 19	08 44
56	16 17	16 59	17 44	07 03	08 00	08 34	08 54
58	16 07	16 52	17 40	07 29	08 23	08 51	09 06
S 60	15 56	16 45	17 36	08 04	08 53	09 12	09 19

SUN and MOON

Day	SUN Eqn. of Time 00h	12h	Mer. Pass.	MOON Mer. Pass. Upper	Lower	Age	Phase
d	m s	m s	h m	h m	h m	d	%
30	06 30	06 29	12 06	22 18	09 45	13	92
31	06 28	06 26	12 06	23 24	10 51	14	97
1	06 25	06 23	12 06	24 27	11 56	15	100

© British Crown Copyright 2022. All rights reserved.

UT	ARIES GHA	VENUS −4.2 GHA	Dec	MARS +1.8 GHA	Dec	JUPITER −2.4 GHA	Dec	SATURN +0.5 GHA	Dec	STARS Name	SHA	Dec
2 00	310 20.0	163 25.2	N 7 14.6	144 51.1	N 7 11.5	268 37.6	N14 48.7	332 14.0	S11 03.0	Acamar	315 12.7	S40 12.3
01	325 22.4	178 28.8	14.5	159 52.1	10.9	283 39.8	48.7	347 16.6	03.1	Achernar	335 20.9	S57 06.7
02	340 24.9	193 32.3	14.3	174 53.1	10.3	298 42.0	48.8	2 19.2	03.2	Acrux	173 01.8	S63 14.0
03	355 27.3	208 35.9 ..	14.1	189 54.2 ..	09.6	313 44.2 ..	48.9	17 21.8 ..	03.2	Adhara	255 07.1	S29 00.1
04	10 29.8	223 39.5	13.9	204 55.2	09.0	328 46.4	48.9	32 24.5	03.3	Aldebaran	290 41.1	N16 33.4
05	25 32.3	238 43.1	13.7	219 56.2	08.4	343 48.6	49.0	47 27.1	03.4			
W 06	40 34.7	253 46.6	N 7 13.5	234 57.2	N 7 07.8	358 50.8	N14 49.1	62 29.7	S11 03.4	Alioth	166 14.2	N55 50.2
E 07	55 37.2	268 50.2	13.4	249 58.2	07.2	13 53.0	49.2	77 32.3	03.5	Alkaid	152 53.0	N49 12.0
D 08	70 39.7	283 53.8	13.2	264 59.3	06.5	28 55.2	49.2	92 34.9	03.5	Alnair	27 33.9	S46 50.7
N 09	85 42.1	298 57.4 ..	13.0	280 00.3 ..	05.9	43 57.4 ..	49.3	107 37.5 ..	03.6	Alnilam	275 39.2	S 1 11.1
E 10	100 44.6	314 01.0	12.9	295 01.3	05.3	58 59.7	49.4	122 40.1	03.7	Alphard	217 49.2	S 8 45.5
S 11	115 47.1	329 04.6	12.7	310 02.3	04.7	74 01.9	49.4	137 42.7	03.7			
D 12	130 49.5	344 08.2	N 7 12.5	325 03.4	N 7 04.0	89 04.1	N14 49.5	152 45.4	S11 03.8	Alphecca	126 04.6	N26 38.3
A 13	145 52.0	359 11.8	12.3	340 04.4	03.4	104 06.3	49.6	167 48.0	03.9	Alpheratz	357 35.8	N29 13.1
Y 14	160 54.4	14 15.4	12.2	355 05.4	02.8	119 08.5	49.6	182 50.6	03.9	Altair	62 00.8	N 8 55.9
15	175 56.9	29 19.0 ..	12.0	10 06.4 ..	02.2	134 10.7 ..	49.7	197 53.2 ..	04.0	Ankaa	353 08.1	S42 10.5
16	190 59.4	44 22.6	11.9	25 07.5	01.6	149 12.9	49.8	212 55.8	04.1	Antares	112 17.1	S26 29.1
17	206 01.8	59 26.3	11.7	40 08.5	00.9	164 15.1	49.8	227 58.4	04.1			
18	221 04.3	74 29.9	N 7 11.5	55 09.5	N 7 00.3	179 17.3	N14 49.9	243 01.0	S11 04.2	Arcturus	145 49.0	N19 03.8
19	236 06.8	89 33.5	11.4	70 10.5	6 59.7	194 19.6	50.0	258 03.7	04.3	Atria	107 12.1	S69 04.4
20	251 09.2	104 37.1	11.2	85 11.6	59.1	209 21.8	50.0	273 06.3	04.3	Avior	234 15.9	S59 35.0
21	266 11.7	119 40.8 ..	11.1	100 12.6 ..	58.5	224 24.0 ..	50.1	288 08.9 ..	04.4	Bellatrix	278 24.4	N 6 22.3
22	281 14.2	134 44.4	10.9	115 13.6	57.8	239 26.2	50.2	303 11.5	04.5	Betelgeuse	270 53.6	N 7 24.8
23	296 16.6	149 48.0	10.8	130 14.6	57.2	254 28.4	50.2	318 14.1	04.5			
3 00	311 19.1	164 51.7	N 7 10.6	145 15.7	N 6 56.6	269 30.6	N14 50.3	333 16.7	S11 04.6	Canopus	263 53.4	S52 42.2
01	326 21.6	179 55.3	10.5	160 16.7	56.0	284 32.8	50.4	348 19.3	04.7	Capella	280 23.9	N46 01.2
02	341 24.0	194 59.0	10.3	175 17.7	55.3	299 35.0	50.4	3 22.0	04.7	Deneb	49 26.1	N45 21.9
03	356 26.5	210 02.6 ..	10.2	190 18.7 ..	54.7	314 37.3 ..	50.5	18 24.6 ..	04.8	Denebola	182 26.4	N14 26.6
04	11 28.9	225 06.3	10.0	205 19.8	54.1	329 39.5	50.6	33 27.2	04.8	Diphda	348 48.3	S17 51.3
05	26 31.4	240 09.9	09.9	220 20.8	53.5	344 41.7	50.6	48 29.8	04.9			
T 06	41 33.9	255 13.6	N 7 09.8	235 21.8	N 6 52.8	359 43.9	N14 50.7	63 32.4	S11 05.0	Dubhe	193 43.0	N61 37.7
H 07	56 36.3	270 17.2	09.6	250 22.8	52.2	14 46.1	50.8	78 35.0	05.0	Elnath	278 03.6	N28 37.6
U 08	71 38.8	285 20.9	09.5	265 23.9	51.6	29 48.3	50.8	93 37.6	05.1	Eltanin	90 42.3	N51 29.3
R 09	86 41.3	300 24.6 ..	09.3	280 24.9 ..	51.0	44 50.6 ..	50.9	108 40.3 ..	05.2	Enif	33 39.6	N 9 59.0
S 10	101 43.7	315 28.2	09.2	295 25.9	50.4	59 52.8	51.0	123 42.9	05.2	Fomalhaut	15 15.5	S29 29.7
D 11	116 46.2	330 31.9	09.1	310 26.9	49.7	74 55.0	51.0	138 45.5	05.3			
A 12	131 48.7	345 35.6	N 7 08.9	325 28.0	N 6 49.1	89 57.2	N14 51.1	153 48.1	S11 05.4	Gacrux	171 53.3	S57 14.9
Y 13	146 51.1	0 39.3	08.8	340 29.0	48.5	104 59.4	51.2	168 50.7	05.4	Gienah	175 45.0	S17 40.3
14	161 53.6	15 42.9	08.7	355 30.0	47.9	120 01.6	51.2	183 53.3	05.5	Hadar	148 37.8	S60 29.4
15	176 56.1	30 46.6 ..	08.6	10 31.0 ..	47.2	135 03.9 ..	51.3	198 55.9 ..	05.6	Hamal	327 52.5	N23 34.4
16	191 58.5	45 50.3	08.4	25 32.1	46.6	150 06.1	51.4	213 58.6	05.6	Kaus Aust.	83 33.7	S34 22.4
17	207 01.0	60 54.0	08.3	40 33.1	46.0	165 08.3	51.4	229 01.2	05.7			
18	222 03.4	75 57.7	N 7 08.2	55 34.1	N 6 45.4	180 10.5	N14 51.5	244 03.8	S11 05.8	Kochab	137 19.7	N74 03.8
19	237 05.9	91 01.4	08.1	70 35.1	44.7	195 12.7	51.6	259 06.4	05.8	Markab	13 30.8	N15 19.9
20	252 08.4	106 05.1	08.0	85 36.2	44.1	210 15.0	51.6	274 09.0	05.9	Menkar	314 07.4	N 4 11.0
21	267 10.8	121 08.8 ..	07.8	100 37.2 ..	43.5	225 17.2 ..	51.7	289 11.6 ..	06.0	Menkent	147 59.1	S36 29.2
22	282 13.3	136 12.5	07.7	115 38.2	42.9	240 19.4	51.8	304 14.3	06.0	Miaplacidus	221 39.5	S69 48.8
23	297 15.8	151 16.2	07.6	130 39.2	42.2	255 21.6	51.8	319 16.9	06.1			
4 00	312 18.2	166 19.9	N 7 07.5	145 40.3	N 6 41.6	270 23.8	N14 51.9	334 19.5	S11 06.2	Mirfak	308 30.1	N49 56.5
01	327 20.7	181 23.6	07.4	160 41.3	41.0	285 26.1	52.0	349 22.1	06.2	Nunki	75 48.9	S26 16.0
02	342 23.2	196 27.4	07.3	175 42.3	40.4	300 28.3	52.0	4 24.7	06.3	Peacock	53 07.0	S56 39.5
03	357 25.6	211 31.1 ..	07.2	190 43.3 ..	39.7	315 30.5 ..	52.1	19 27.3 ..	06.4	Pollux	243 19.1	N27 58.2
04	12 28.1	226 34.8	07.1	205 44.4	39.1	330 32.7	52.2	34 30.0	06.4	Procyon	244 52.4	N 5 10.0
05	27 30.5	241 38.5	07.0	220 45.4	38.5	345 34.9	52.2	49 32.6	06.5			
F 06	42 33.0	256 42.3	N 7 06.9	235 46.4	N 6 37.9	0 37.2	N14 52.3	64 35.2	S11 06.6	Rasalhague	95 59.4	N12 32.7
R 07	57 35.5	271 46.0	06.8	250 47.4	37.2	15 39.4	52.3	79 37.8	06.6	Regulus	207 36.0	N11 51.3
I 08	72 37.9	286 49.7	06.7	265 48.5	36.6	30 41.6	52.4	94 40.4	06.7	Rigel	281 05.2	S 8 10.3
D 09	87 40.4	301 53.5 ..	06.6	280 49.5 ..	36.0	45 43.8 ..	52.5	109 43.0 ..	06.8	Rigil Kent.	139 41.9	S60 56.1
A 10	102 42.9	316 57.2	06.5	295 50.5	35.4	60 46.1	52.5	124 45.7	06.8	Sabik	102 03.9	S15 45.2
Y 11	117 45.3	332 00.9	06.4	310 51.5	34.7	75 48.3	52.6	139 48.3	06.9			
12	132 47.8	347 04.7	N 7 06.3	325 52.6	N 6 34.1	90 50.5	N14 52.7	154 50.9	S11 07.0	Schedar	349 32.1	N56 39.8
13	147 50.3	2 08.4	06.2	340 53.6	33.5	105 52.7	52.7	169 53.5	07.0	Shaula	96 11.7	S37 07.3
14	162 52.7	17 12.2	06.1	355 54.6	32.9	120 54.9	52.8	184 56.1	07.1	Sirius	258 27.6	S16 44.7
15	177 55.2	32 15.9 ..	06.0	10 55.6 ..	32.2	135 57.2 ..	52.9	199 58.7 ..	07.2	Spica	158 23.6	S11 17.0
16	192 57.7	47 19.7	06.0	25 56.7	31.6	150 59.4	52.9	215 01.4	07.2	Suhail	222 47.6	S43 31.6
17	208 00.1	62 23.5	05.9	40 57.7	31.0	166 01.6	53.0	230 04.0	07.3			
18	223 02.6	77 27.2	N 7 05.8	55 58.7	N 6 30.4	181 03.8	N14 53.1	245 06.6	S11 07.4	Vega	80 33.7	N38 48.4
19	238 05.0	92 31.0	05.7	70 59.7	29.7	196 06.1	53.1	260 09.2	07.4	Zuben'ubi	136 57.3	S16 08.4
20	253 07.5	107 34.8	05.6	86 00.8	29.1	211 08.3	53.2	275 11.8	07.5			
21	268 10.0	122 38.5 ..	05.6	101 01.8 ..	28.5	226 10.5 ..	53.2	290 14.4 ..	07.6		SHA	Mer. Pass.
22	283 12.4	137 42.3	05.5	116 02.8	27.9	241 12.8	53.3	305 17.1	07.6	Venus	213 32.6	12 57
23	298 14.9	152 46.1	05.4	131 03.8	27.2	256 15.0	53.4	320 19.7	07.7	Mars	193 56.6	14 18
Mer. Pass.	3 14.2	v 3.7	d 0.1	v 1.0	d 0.6	v 2.2	d 0.1	v 2.6	d 0.1	Jupiter	318 11.5	6 01
										Saturn	21 57.6	1 47

© British Crown Copyright 2022. All rights reserved.

UT	SUN GHA	SUN Dec	MOON GHA	MOON v	MOON Dec	MOON d	MOON HP
d h	° ′	° ′	° ′	′	° ′	′	′
2 00	178 24.8	N17 52.7	353 38.5	4.5	S21 38.1	11.9	61.4
01	193 24.8	52.1	8 02.0	4.7	21 26.2	12.1	61.4
02	208 24.9	51.5	22 25.7	4.7	21 14.1	12.3	61.4
03	223 24.9	50.8	36 49.4	4.8	21 01.8	12.4	61.4
04	238 24.9	50.2	51 13.2	5.0	20 49.4	12.5	61.4
05	253 25.0	49.5	65 37.2	5.0	20 36.9	12.7	61.4
W 06	268 25.0	N17 48.9	80 01.2	5.2	S20 24.2	12.8	61.4
E 07	283 25.1	48.3	94 25.4	5.2	20 11.4	13.0	61.4
D 08	298 25.1	47.6	108 49.6	5.4	19 58.4	13.0	61.4
N 09	313 25.2	47.0	123 14.0	5.5	19 45.4	13.3	61.4
E 10	328 25.2	46.4	137 38.5	5.6	19 32.1	13.3	61.4
S 11	343 25.3	45.7	152 03.1	5.7	19 18.8	13.5	61.4
D 12	358 25.3	N17 45.1	166 27.8	5.8	S19 05.3	13.6	61.4
A 13	13 25.3	44.4	180 52.6	5.9	18 51.7	13.8	61.4
Y 14	28 25.4	43.8	195 17.5	6.0	18 37.9	13.8	61.3
15	43 25.4	43.1	209 42.5	6.1	18 24.1	14.0	61.3
16	58 25.5	42.5	224 07.6	6.2	18 10.1	14.1	61.3
17	73 25.5	41.9	238 32.8	6.4	17 56.0	14.2	61.3
18	88 25.6	N17 41.2	252 58.2	6.4	S17 41.8	14.3	61.3
19	103 25.6	40.6	267 23.6	6.6	17 27.5	14.4	61.3
20	118 25.7	39.9	281 49.2	6.7	17 13.1	14.6	61.3
21	133 25.7	39.3	296 14.9	6.7	16 58.5	14.6	61.3
22	148 25.8	38.6	310 40.6	6.9	16 43.9	14.8	61.3
23	163 25.8	38.0	325 06.5	7.0	16 29.1	14.8	61.3
3 00	178 25.9	N17 37.3	339 32.5	7.1	S16 14.3	15.0	61.3
01	193 25.9	36.7	353 58.6	7.2	15 59.3	15.0	61.3
02	208 26.0	36.0	8 24.8	7.3	15 44.3	15.2	61.3
03	223 26.0	35.4	22 51.1	7.4	15 29.1	15.2	61.2
04	238 26.1	34.7	37 17.5	7.5	15 13.9	15.3	61.2
05	253 26.1	34.1	51 44.0	7.6	14 58.6	15.4	61.2
06	268 26.2	N17 33.4	66 10.6	7.7	S14 43.2	15.5	61.2
T 07	283 26.2	32.8	80 37.3	7.8	14 27.7	15.6	61.2
H 08	298 26.3	32.1	95 04.1	8.0	14 12.1	15.6	61.2
U 09	313 26.3	31.5	109 31.1	8.0	13 56.5	15.7	61.2
R 10	328 26.4	30.8	123 58.1	8.1	13 40.8	15.8	61.1
S 11	343 26.4	30.2	138 25.2	8.2	13 25.0	15.9	61.1
D 12	358 26.5	N17 29.5	152 52.4	8.3	S13 09.1	16.0	61.1
A 13	13 26.5	28.9	167 19.7	8.4	12 53.1	16.0	61.1
Y 14	28 26.6	28.2	181 47.1	8.5	12 37.1	16.1	61.1
15	43 26.6	27.6	196 14.6	8.6	12 21.0	16.1	61.1
16	58 26.7	26.9	210 42.2	8.7	12 04.9	16.2	61.0
17	73 26.7	26.3	225 09.9	8.8	11 48.7	16.3	61.0
18	88 26.8	N17 25.6	239 37.7	8.9	S11 32.4	16.3	61.0
19	103 26.8	25.0	254 05.6	8.9	11 16.1	16.4	61.0
20	118 26.9	24.3	268 33.5	9.1	10 59.7	16.4	61.0
21	133 27.0	23.6	283 01.6	9.1	10 43.3	16.5	60.9
22	148 27.0	23.0	297 29.7	9.2	10 26.8	16.5	60.9
23	163 27.1	22.3	311 57.9	9.3	10 10.3	16.6	60.9
4 00	178 27.1	N17 21.7	326 26.2	9.4	S 9 53.7	16.6	60.9
01	193 27.2	21.0	340 54.6	9.5	9 37.1	16.7	60.9
02	208 27.2	20.3	355 23.1	9.6	9 20.4	16.7	60.8
03	223 27.3	19.7	9 51.7	9.6	9 03.7	16.8	60.8
04	238 27.3	19.0	24 20.3	9.8	8 46.9	16.7	60.8
05	253 27.4	18.4	38 49.1	9.8	8 30.2	16.9	60.8
06	268 27.5	N17 17.7	53 17.9	9.8	S 8 13.3	16.8	60.7
07	283 27.5	17.0	67 46.7	10.0	7 56.5	16.9	60.7
F 08	298 27.6	16.4	82 15.7	10.0	7 39.6	16.9	60.7
R 09	313 27.6	15.7	96 44.7	10.1	7 22.7	16.9	60.7
I 10	328 27.7	15.0	111 13.8	10.2	7 05.8	17.0	60.6
D 11	343 27.7	14.4	125 43.0	10.3	6 48.8	16.9	60.6
A 12	358 27.8	N17 13.7	140 12.3	10.3	S 6 31.9	17.0	60.6
Y 13	13 27.9	13.1	154 41.6	10.4	6 14.9	17.1	60.6
14	28 27.9	12.4	169 11.0	10.4	5 57.8	17.0	60.5
15	43 28.0	11.7	183 40.4	10.5	5 40.8	17.0	60.5
16	58 28.0	11.1	198 09.9	10.6	5 23.8	17.1	60.5
17	73 28.1	10.4	212 39.5	10.7	5 06.7	17.1	60.4
18	88 28.2	N17 09.7	227 09.2	10.7	S 4 49.6	17.0	60.4
19	103 28.2	09.1	241 38.9	10.7	4 32.6	17.1	60.4
20	118 28.3	08.4	256 08.6	10.9	4 15.5	17.1	60.4
21	133 28.3	07.7	270 38.5	10.9	3 58.4	17.1	60.3
22	148 28.4	07.0	285 08.4	10.9	3 41.3	17.1	60.3
23	163 28.5	06.4	299 38.3	11.0	S 3 24.2	17.1	60.3
	SD 15.8	d 0.7	SD 16.7		16.7		16.5

Lat.	Twilight Naut.	Twilight Civil	Sunrise	Moonrise 2	Moonrise 3	Moonrise 4	Moonrise 5
°	h m	h m	h m	h m	h m	h m	h m
N 72	▱	▱	▱	23 44	22 30	21 48	21 12
N 70	////	////	01 41	23 01	22 14	21 43	21 15
68	////	////	02 24	22 32	22 01	21 38	21 18
66	////	00 49	02 52	22 10	21 50	21 35	21 21
64	////	01 49	03 13	21 52	21 41	21 32	21 23
62	////	02 22	03 30	21 37	21 33	21 29	21 25
60	00 44	02 45	03 45	21 25	21 26	21 26	21 26
N 58	01 39	03 04	03 57	21 14	21 20	21 24	21 28
56	02 09	03 19	04 07	21 04	21 15	21 22	21 29
54	02 31	03 32	04 16	20 56	21 10	21 21	21 31
52	02 48	03 43	04 24	20 48	21 05	21 19	21 32
50	03 03	03 53	04 32	20 41	21 01	21 18	21 33
45	03 31	04 14	04 47	20 27	20 52	21 15	21 35
N 40	03 53	04 30	05 00	20 14	20 45	21 12	21 37
35	04 09	04 43	05 11	20 04	20 39	21 10	21 38
30	04 23	04 54	05 20	19 55	20 33	21 08	21 40
20	04 45	05 13	05 36	19 39	20 23	21 04	21 42
N 10	05 02	05 28	05 50	19 25	20 13	21 01	21 45
0	05 16	05 41	06 03	19 12	20 07	20 58	21 47
S 10	05 28	05 54	06 15	18 58	19 59	20 55	21 49
20	05 39	06 06	06 29	18 44	19 50	20 52	21 52
30	05 50	06 19	06 44	18 28	19 40	20 48	21 54
35	05 56	06 26	06 53	18 18	19 34	20 46	21 56
40	06 02	06 34	07 03	18 07	19 27	20 44	21 58
45	06 08	06 43	07 15	17 54	19 20	20 41	22 00
S 50	06 15	06 54	07 29	17 39	19 10	20 38	22 03
52	06 18	06 59	07 36	17 31	19 06	20 37	22 04
54	06 21	07 04	07 43	17 23	19 01	20 35	22 05
56	06 24	07 10	07 51	17 14	18 56	20 33	22 07
58	06 28	07 16	08 00	17 03	18 50	20 31	22 08
S 60	06 32	07 23	08 11	16 50	18 43	20 29	22 10

Lat.	Sunset	Twilight Civil	Twilight Naut.	Moonset 2	Moonset 3	Moonset 4	Moonset 5
°	h m	h m	h m	h m	h m	h m	h m
N 72	▱	▱	▱	▰	03 35	06 43	09 14
N 70	22 25	////	////	▰	04 16	06 56	09 15
68	21 45	////	////	01 17	04 43	07 07	09 15
66	21 17	23 12	////	02 26	05 03	07 15	09 16
64	20 57	22 18	////	03 02	05 22	07 22	09 16
62	20 40	21 47	////	03 27	05 33	07 29	09 17
60	20 26	21 25	23 17	03 47	05 44	07 34	09 17
N 58	20 14	21 06	22 29	04 04	05 54	07 39	09 18
56	20 04	20 52	22 01	04 17	06 02	07 43	09 18
54	19 55	20 39	21 39	04 29	06 10	07 46	09 18
52	19 47	20 28	21 22	04 40	06 16	07 50	09 19
50	19 40	20 18	21 08	04 49	06 22	07 53	09 19
45	19 25	19 58	20 40	05 08	06 35	07 59	09 19
N 40	19 12	19 42	20 19	05 24	06 46	08 04	09 20
35	19 01	19 29	20 02	05 37	06 55	08 09	09 20
30	18 52	19 18	19 49	05 49	07 03	08 13	09 20
20	18 36	19 00	19 27	06 08	07 16	08 20	09 21
N 10	18 22	18 45	19 10	06 25	07 27	08 26	09 21
0	18 10	18 31	18 57	06 41	07 38	08 31	09 21
S 10	17 57	18 19	18 44	06 56	07 49	08 37	09 22
20	17 44	18 07	18 33	07 13	08 00	08 43	09 22
30	17 29	17 54	18 22	07 31	08 13	08 49	09 22
35	17 20	17 46	18 17	07 42	08 20	08 53	09 23
40	17 10	17 39	18 11	07 55	08 28	08 57	09 23
45	16 58	17 30	18 05	08 09	08 38	09 02	09 23
S 50	16 44	17 19	17 58	08 27	08 49	09 08	09 23
52	16 38	17 14	17 55	08 35	08 55	09 10	09 23
54	16 30	17 09	17 52	08 44	09 01	09 13	09 23
56	16 22	17 04	17 49	08 54	09 07	09 16	09 24
58	16 13	16 57	17 45	09 06	09 14	09 20	09 24
S 60	16 03	16 50	17 41	09 19	09 22	09 23	09 24

Day	SUN Eqn. of Time 00h	SUN Eqn. of Time 12h	SUN Mer. Pass.	MOON Mer. Pass. Upper	MOON Mer. Pass. Lower	MOON Age	MOON Phase
d	m s	m s	h m	h m	h m	d	%
2	06 21	06 19	12 06	00 27	12 56	16	99
3	06 17	06 14	12 06	01 25	13 53	17	95
4	06 12	06 09	12 06	02 19	14 45	18	89

© British Crown Copyright 2022. All rights reserved.

UT (d h)	ARIES GHA	VENUS −4.0 GHA	Dec	MARS +1.8 GHA	Dec	JUPITER −2.4 GHA	Dec	SATURN +0.5 GHA	Dec	Name	SHA	Dec
5 00	313 17.4	167 49.9	N 7 05.3	146 04.8	N 6 26.6	271 17.2	N14 53.4	335 22.3	S11 07.8	Acamar	315 12.7	S40 12.3
01	328 19.8	182 53.6	05.3	161 05.9	26.0	286 19.4	53.5	350 24.9	07.8	Achernar	335 20.9	S57 06.7
02	343 22.3	197 57.4	05.2	176 06.9	25.4	301 21.7	53.6	5 27.5	07.9	Acrux	173 01.8	S63 14.0
03	358 24.8	213 01.2 ..	05.1	191 07.9 ..	24.7	316 23.9 ..	53.6	20 30.2 ..	08.0	Adhara	255 07.1	S29 00.0
04	13 27.2	228 05.0	05.1	206 08.9	24.1	331 26.1	53.7	35 32.8	08.0	Aldebaran	290 41.1	N16 33.4
05	28 29.7	243 08.8	05.0	221 10.0	23.5	346 28.3	53.7	50 35.4	08.1			
06	43 32.1	258 12.6	N 7 04.9	236 11.0	N 6 22.8	1 30.6	N14 53.8	65 38.0	S11 08.2	Alioth	166 14.3	N55 50.2
07	58 34.6	273 16.4	04.9	251 12.0	22.2	16 32.8	53.9	80 40.6	08.2	Alkaid	152 53.0	N49 12.0
S 08	73 37.1	288 20.2	04.8	266 13.0	21.6	31 35.0	53.9	95 43.3	08.3	Alnair	27 33.9	S46 50.7
A 09	88 39.5	303 24.0 ..	04.8	281 14.1 ..	21.0	46 37.3 ..	54.0	110 45.9 ..	08.4	Alnilam	275 39.1	S 1 11.1
T 10	103 42.0	318 27.8	04.7	296 15.1	20.3	61 39.5	54.1	125 48.5	08.4	Alphard	217 49.2	S 8 45.5
U 11	118 44.5	333 31.6	04.6	311 16.1	19.7	76 41.7	54.1	140 51.1	08.5			
R 12	133 46.9	348 35.4	N 7 04.6	326 17.1	N 6 19.1	91 44.0	N14 54.2	155 53.7	S11 08.6	Alphecca	126 04.7	N26 38.3
D 13	148 49.4	3 39.2	04.5	341 18.2	18.5	106 46.2	54.2	170 56.3	08.6	Alpheratz	357 35.8	N29 13.2
A 14	163 51.9	18 43.0	04.5	356 19.2	17.8	121 48.4	54.3	185 59.0	08.7	Altair	62 00.8	N 8 55.9
Y 15	178 54.3	33 46.8 ..	04.4	11 20.2 ..	17.2	136 50.6 ..	54.4	201 01.6 ..	08.8	Ankaa	353 08.0	S42 10.5
16	193 56.8	48 50.6	04.4	26 21.2	16.6	151 52.9	54.4	216 04.2	08.8	Antares	112 17.1	S26 29.1
17	208 59.3	63 54.5	04.3	41 22.3	15.9	166 55.1	54.5	231 06.8	08.9			
18	224 01.7	78 58.3	N 7 04.3	56 23.3	N 6 15.3	181 57.3	N14 54.5	246 09.4	S11 09.0	Arcturus	145 49.0	N19 03.8
19	239 04.2	94 02.1	04.3	71 24.3	14.7	196 59.6	54.6	261 12.1	09.0	Atria	107 12.1	S69 04.4
20	254 06.6	109 05.9	04.2	86 25.3	14.1	212 01.8	54.7	276 14.7	09.1	Avior	234 15.9	S59 34.9
21	269 09.1	124 09.8 ..	04.2	101 26.4 ..	13.4	227 04.0 ..	54.7	291 17.3 ..	09.2	Bellatrix	278 24.4	N 6 22.3
22	284 11.6	139 13.6	04.1	116 27.4	12.8	242 06.3	54.8	306 19.9	09.2	Betelgeuse	270 53.6	N 7 24.8
23	299 14.0	154 17.4	04.1	131 28.4	12.2	257 08.5	54.9	321 22.5	09.3			
6 00	314 16.5	169 21.3	N 7 04.1	146 29.4	N 6 11.5	272 10.7	N14 54.9	336 25.2	S11 09.4	Canopus	263 53.4	S52 42.2
01	329 19.0	184 25.1	04.0	161 30.5	10.9	287 13.0	55.0	351 27.8	09.4	Capella	280 23.9	N46 01.2
02	344 21.4	199 29.0	04.0	176 31.5	10.3	302 15.2	55.0	6 30.4	09.5	Deneb	49 26.1	N45 21.9
03	359 23.9	214 32.8 ..	04.0	191 32.5 ..	09.7	317 17.4 ..	55.1	21 33.0 ..	09.6	Denebola	182 26.4	N14 26.6
04	14 26.4	229 36.6	04.0	206 33.5	09.0	332 19.7	55.2	36 35.6	09.6	Diphda	348 48.3	S17 51.3
05	29 28.8	244 40.5	03.9	221 34.6	08.4	347 21.9	55.2	51 38.3	09.7			
06	44 31.3	259 44.3	N 7 03.9	236 35.6	N 6 07.8	2 24.1	N14 55.3	66 40.9	S11 09.8	Dubhe	193 43.0	N61 37.7
07	59 33.8	274 48.2	03.9	251 36.6	07.1	17 26.4	55.3	81 43.5	09.8	Elnath	278 03.6	N28 37.6
S 08	74 36.2	289 52.1	03.9	266 37.6	06.5	32 28.6	55.4	96 46.1	09.9	Eltanin	90 42.3	N51 29.3
U 09	89 38.7	304 55.9 ..	03.8	281 38.6 ..	05.9	47 30.9 ..	55.5	111 48.8 ..	10.0	Enif	33 39.6	N 9 59.0
N 10	104 41.1	319 59.8	03.8	296 39.7	05.3	62 33.1	55.5	126 51.4	10.0	Fomalhaut	15 15.5	S29 29.7
D 11	119 43.6	335 03.6	03.8	311 40.7	04.6	77 35.3	55.6	141 54.0	10.1			
A 12	134 46.1	350 07.5	N 7 03.8	326 41.7	N 6 04.0	92 37.6	N14 55.6	156 56.6	S11 10.2	Gacrux	171 53.3	S57 14.9
Y 13	149 48.5	5 11.4	03.8	341 42.7	03.4	107 39.8	55.7	171 59.2	10.2	Gienah	175 45.0	S17 40.3
14	164 51.0	20 15.2	03.8	356 43.8	02.7	122 42.0	55.8	187 01.9	10.3	Hadar	148 37.8	S60 29.4
15	179 53.5	35 19.1 ..	03.8	11 44.8 ..	02.1	137 44.3 ..	55.8	202 04.5 ..	10.4	Hamal	327 52.5	N23 34.4
16	194 55.9	50 23.0	03.8	26 45.8	01.5	152 46.5	55.9	217 07.1	10.4	Kaus Aust.	83 33.7	S34 22.4
17	209 58.4	65 26.9	03.7	41 46.8	00.8	167 48.8	55.9	232 09.7	10.5			
18	225 00.9	80 30.7	N 7 03.7	56 47.9	N 6 00.2	182 51.0	N14 56.0	247 12.3	S11 10.6	Kochab	137 19.7	N74 03.8
19	240 03.3	95 34.6	03.7	71 48.9	5 59.6	197 53.2	56.0	262 15.0	10.6	Markab	13 30.8	N15 19.9
20	255 05.8	110 38.5	03.7	86 49.9	59.0	212 55.5	56.1	277 17.6	10.7	Menkar	314 07.4	N 4 11.0
21	270 08.2	125 42.4 ..	03.7	101 50.9 ..	58.3	227 57.7 ..	56.2	292 20.2 ..	10.8	Menkent	147 59.1	S36 29.2
22	285 10.7	140 46.3	03.7	116 52.0	57.7	243 00.0	56.2	307 22.8	10.8	Miaplacidus	221 39.5	S69 48.8
23	300 13.2	155 50.1	03.7	131 53.0	57.1	258 02.2	56.3	322 25.5	10.9			
7 00	315 15.6	170 54.0	N 7 03.7	146 54.0	N 5 56.4	273 04.4	N14 56.3	337 28.1	S11 11.0	Mirfak	308 30.0	N49 56.5
01	330 18.1	185 57.9	03.7	161 55.0	55.8	288 06.7	56.4	352 30.7	11.0	Nunki	75 48.9	S26 16.0
02	345 20.6	201 01.8	03.8	176 56.1	55.2	303 08.9	56.5	7 33.3	11.1	Peacock	53 07.0	S56 39.5
03	0 23.0	216 05.7 ..	03.8	191 57.1 ..	54.5	318 11.2 ..	56.5	22 35.9 ..	11.2	Pollux	243 19.1	N27 58.2
04	15 25.5	231 09.6	03.8	206 58.1	53.9	333 13.4	56.6	37 38.6	11.2	Procyon	244 52.4	N 5 10.0
05	30 28.0	246 13.5	03.8	221 59.1	53.3	348 15.6	56.6	52 41.2	11.3			
06	45 30.4	261 17.4	N 7 03.8	237 00.1	N 5 52.6	3 17.9	N14 56.7	67 43.8	S11 11.4	Rasalhague	96 59.4	N12 32.7
07	60 32.9	276 21.3	03.8	252 01.2	52.0	18 20.1	56.7	82 46.4	11.5	Regulus	207 36.0	N11 51.3
08	75 35.4	291 25.2	03.8	267 02.2	51.4	33 22.4	56.8	97 49.1	11.5	Rigel	281 05.2	S 8 10.3
M 09	90 37.8	306 29.1 ..	03.8	282 03.2 ..	50.8	48 24.6 ..	56.9	112 51.7 ..	11.6	Rigil Kent.	139 42.0	S60 56.1
O 10	105 40.3	321 33.0	03.9	297 04.2	50.1	63 26.9	56.9	127 54.3	11.7	Sabik	102 03.9	S15 45.2
N 11	120 42.7	336 36.9	03.9	312 05.3	49.5	78 29.1	57.0	142 56.9	11.7			
D 12	135 45.2	351 40.9	N 7 03.9	327 06.3	N 5 48.9	93 31.3	N14 57.0	157 59.5	S11 11.8	Schedar	349 32.1	N56 39.8
A 13	150 47.7	6 44.8	03.9	342 07.3	48.2	108 33.6	57.1	173 02.2	11.9	Shaula	96 11.7	S37 07.3
Y 14	165 50.1	21 48.7	04.0	357 08.3	47.6	123 35.8	57.2	188 04.8	11.9	Sirius	258 27.6	S16 44.7
15	180 52.6	36 52.6 ..	04.0	12 09.4 ..	47.0	138 38.1 ..	57.2	203 07.4 ..	12.0	Spica	158 23.7	S11 17.0
16	195 55.1	51 56.5	04.0	27 10.4	46.3	153 40.3	57.3	218 10.0	12.1	Suhail	222 47.6	S43 31.6
17	210 57.5	67 00.4	04.0	42 11.4	45.7	168 42.6	57.3	233 12.7	12.1			
18	226 00.0	82 04.4	N 7 04.1	57 12.4	N 5 45.1	183 44.8	N14 57.4	248 15.3	S11 12.2	Vega	80 33.7	N38 48.5
19	241 02.5	97 08.3	04.1	72 13.4	44.4	198 47.1	57.4	263 17.9	12.3	Zuben'ubi	136 57.3	S16 08.4
20	256 04.9	112 12.2	04.1	87 14.5	43.8	213 49.3	57.5	278 20.5	12.3			
21	271 07.4	127 16.2 ..	04.2	102 15.5 ..	43.2	228 51.6 ..	57.5	293 23.2 ..	12.4		SHA	Mer. Pass.
22	286 09.9	142 20.1	04.2	117 16.5	42.5	243 53.8	57.6	308 25.8	12.5	Venus	215 04.8	12 39
23	301 12.3	157 24.0	04.3	132 17.5	41.9	258 56.0	57.7	323 28.4	12.5	Mars	192 12.9	14 13
Mer. Pass.	h m 3 02.4	v 3.9	d 0.0	v 1.0	d 0.6	v 2.2	d 0.1	v 2.6	d 0.1	Jupiter	317 54.2	5 50
										Saturn	22 08.7	1 34

© British Crown Copyright 2022. All rights reserved.

UT	SUN GHA	SUN Dec	MOON GHA	v	Dec	d	HP
5 00	178 28.5	N17 05.7	314 08.3	11.0	S 3 07.1	17.1	60.2
01	193 28.6	05.0	328 38.3	11.1	2 50.0	17.1	60.2
02	208 28.6	04.4	343 08.4	11.2	2 32.9	17.1	60.2
03	223 28.7	.. 03.7	357 38.6	11.2	2 15.8	17.0	60.1
04	238 28.8	03.0	12 08.8	11.3	1 58.8	17.1	60.1
05	253 28.8	02.3	26 39.1	11.3	1 41.7	17.1	60.1
SATURDAY 06	268 28.9	N17 01.7	41 09.4	11.3	S 1 24.6	17.0	60.0
07	283 28.9	01.0	55 39.7	11.4	1 07.6	17.0	60.0
08	298 29.0	17 00.3	70 10.1	11.4	0 50.6	17.1	60.0
09	313 29.1	16 59.6	84 40.5	11.5	0 33.5	17.0	59.9
10	328 29.1	59.0	99 11.0	11.5	S 0 16.5	16.9	59.9
11	343 29.2	58.3	113 41.5	11.5	N 0 00.4	17.0	59.9
12	358 29.3	N16 57.6	128 12.0	11.6	N 0 17.4	16.9	59.8
13	13 29.3	56.9	142 42.6	11.6	0 34.3	17.0	59.8
14	28 29.4	56.3	157 13.2	11.7	0 51.3	16.8	59.8
15	43 29.5	.. 55.6	171 43.9	11.7	1 08.1	16.9	59.7
16	58 29.5	54.9	186 14.6	11.7	1 25.0	16.8	59.7
17	73 29.6	54.2	200 45.3	11.8	1 41.8	16.8	59.7
18	88 29.7	N16 53.6	215 16.1	11.7	N 1 58.6	16.8	59.6
19	103 29.7	52.9	229 46.8	11.8	2 15.4	16.8	59.6
20	118 29.8	52.2	244 17.6	11.9	2 32.2	16.7	59.6
21	133 29.9	.. 51.5	258 48.5	11.8	2 48.9	16.6	59.5
22	148 29.9	50.8	273 19.3	11.9	3 05.5	16.7	59.5
23	163 30.0	50.2	287 50.2	11.9	3 22.2	16.6	59.4
6 00	178 30.1	N16 49.5	302 21.1	11.9	N 3 38.8	16.5	59.4
01	193 30.1	48.8	316 52.0	12.0	3 55.3	16.6	59.4
02	208 30.2	48.1	331 23.0	12.0	4 11.9	16.4	59.3
03	223 30.3	.. 47.4	345 54.0	11.9	4 28.3	16.5	59.3
04	238 30.3	46.7	0 24.9	12.0	4 44.8	16.4	59.3
05	253 30.4	46.1	14 55.9	12.0	5 01.2	16.3	59.2
SUNDAY 06	268 30.5	N16 45.4	29 26.9	12.1	N 5 17.5	16.3	59.2
07	283 30.5	44.7	43 58.0	12.0	5 33.8	16.2	59.2
08	298 30.6	44.0	58 29.0	12.1	5 50.0	16.2	59.1
09	313 30.7	.. 43.3	73 00.1	12.0	6 06.2	16.2	59.1
10	328 30.7	42.6	87 31.1	12.1	6 22.4	16.1	59.0
11	343 30.8	41.9	102 02.2	12.1	6 38.5	16.0	59.0
12	358 30.9	N16 41.2	116 33.3	12.0	N 6 54.5	16.0	59.0
13	13 31.0	40.6	131 04.3	12.1	7 10.5	15.9	58.9
14	28 31.0	39.9	145 35.4	12.1	7 26.4	15.9	58.9
15	43 31.1	.. 39.2	160 06.5	12.1	7 42.3	15.8	58.9
16	58 31.2	38.5	174 37.6	12.1	7 58.1	15.7	58.8
17	73 31.2	37.8	189 08.7	12.1	8 13.8	15.7	58.8
18	88 31.3	N16 37.1	203 39.8	12.1	N 8 29.5	15.7	58.7
19	103 31.4	36.4	218 10.9	12.1	8 45.2	15.5	58.7
20	118 31.5	35.7	232 42.0	12.1	9 00.7	15.5	58.7
21	133 31.5	.. 35.0	247 13.1	12.1	9 16.2	15.4	58.6
22	148 31.6	34.3	261 44.2	12.0	9 31.6	15.4	58.6
23	163 31.7	33.7	276 15.2	12.1	9 47.0	15.3	58.6
7 00	178 31.7	N16 33.0	290 46.3	12.1	N10 02.3	15.2	58.5
01	193 31.8	32.3	305 17.4	12.0	10 17.5	15.2	58.5
02	208 31.9	31.6	319 48.4	12.1	10 32.7	15.1	58.4
03	223 32.0	.. 30.9	334 19.5	12.0	10 47.8	15.0	58.4
04	238 32.0	30.2	348 50.5	12.1	11 02.8	14.9	58.4
05	253 32.1	29.5	3 21.6	12.0	11 17.7	14.9	58.3
MONDAY 06	268 32.2	N16 28.8	17 52.6	12.0	N11 32.6	14.8	58.3
07	283 32.3	28.1	32 23.6	12.0	11 47.4	14.7	58.3
08	298 32.3	27.4	46 54.6	11.9	12 02.1	14.6	58.2
09	313 32.4	.. 26.7	61 25.5	12.0	12 16.7	14.6	58.2
10	328 32.5	26.0	75 56.5	11.9	12 31.3	14.4	58.1
11	343 32.6	25.3	90 27.4	11.9	12 45.7	14.4	58.1
12	358 32.6	N16 24.6	104 58.3	11.9	N13 00.1	14.3	58.1
13	13 32.7	23.9	119 29.2	11.9	13 14.4	14.2	58.0
14	28 32.8	23.2	134 00.1	11.9	13 28.6	14.2	58.0
15	43 32.9	.. 22.5	148 31.0	11.8	13 42.8	14.0	58.0
16	58 32.9	21.8	163 01.8	11.8	13 56.8	14.0	57.9
17	73 33.0	21.1	177 32.6	11.8	14 10.8	13.9	57.9
18	88 33.1	N16 20.4	192 03.4	11.8	N14 24.7	13.8	57.8
19	103 33.2	19.7	206 34.2	11.7	14 38.5	13.7	57.8
20	118 33.3	19.0	221 04.9	11.7	14 52.2	13.6	57.8
21	133 33.3	.. 18.3	235 35.6	11.7	15 05.8	13.5	57.7
22	148 33.4	17.6	250 06.3	11.7	15 19.3	13.4	57.7
23	163 33.5	16.9	264 37.0	11.6	N15 32.7	13.4	57.7
SD	15.8	d 0.7	16.3		16.1		15.8

Lat.	Twilight Naut.	Twilight Civil	Sunrise	Moonrise 5	6	7	8
N 72	////	////	00 53	21 12	20 34	19 41	▭
N 70	////	////	02 02	21 15	20 47	20 10	18 53
68	////	////	02 38	21 18	20 58	20 33	19 53
66	////	01 21	03 03	21 21	21 07	20 50	20 28
64	////	02 05	03 23	21 23	21 14	21 05	20 53
62	////	02 33	03 39	21 25	21 21	21 17	21 13
60	01 13	02 55	03 52	21 26	21 27	21 27	21 30
N 58	01 53	03 12	04 03	21 28	21 32	21 37	21 44
56	02 19	03 26	04 13	21 29	21 36	21 45	21 56
54	02 39	03 38	04 21	21 31	21 41	21 52	22 06
52	02 55	03 49	04 29	21 32	21 44	21 58	22 16
50	03 09	03 58	04 36	21 33	21 48	22 04	22 24
45	03 36	04 18	04 51	21 35	21 55	22 17	22 42
N 40	03 56	04 35	05 03	21 37	22 01	22 28	22 57
35	04 12	04 45	05 13	21 38	22 07	22 37	23 09
30	04 25	04 56	05 22	21 40	22 12	22 45	23 21
20	04 46	05 14	05 37	21 42	22 20	22 59	23 40
N 10	05 02	05 28	05 50	21 45	22 28	23 11	23 56
0	05 16	05 41	06 02	21 47	22 35	23 23	24 12
S 10	05 27	05 53	06 15	21 49	22 42	23 35	24 28
20	05 38	06 04	06 27	21 52	22 50	23 47	24 45
30	05 48	06 17	06 42	21 54	22 58	24 02	00 02
35	05 54	06 24	06 50	21 56	23 04	24 10	00 10
40	05 59	06 31	07 00	21 58	23 09	24 20	00 20
45	06 05	06 40	07 11	22 00	23 16	24 31	00 31
S 50	06 11	06 49	07 24	22 03	23 25	24 45	00 45
52	06 13	06 54	07 30	22 04	23 29	24 52	00 52
54	06 16	06 59	07 37	22 05	23 33	24 59	00 59
56	06 19	07 04	07 45	22 07	23 38	25 08	01 08
58	06 22	07 10	07 54	22 08	23 43	25 17	01 17
S 60	06 26	07 16	08 03	22 10	23 49	25 28	01 28

Lat.	Sunset	Twilight Civil	Twilight Naut.	Moonset 5	6	7	8
N 72	23 04	////	////	09 14	11 37	14 13	▭
N 70	22 04	////	////	09 15	11 27	13 45	16 46
68	21 30	////	////	09 15	11 19	13 25	15 47
66	21 06	22 44	////	09 16	11 12	13 09	15 13
64	20 47	22 03	////	09 16	11 06	12 56	14 49
62	20 31	21 35	////	09 17	11 01	12 45	14 30
60	20 18	21 15	22 52	09 17	10 57	12 35	14 14
N 58	20 07	20 58	22 15	09 18	10 53	12 27	14 01
56	19 58	20 44	21 50	09 18	10 50	12 20	13 50
54	19 49	20 32	21 31	09 18	10 47	12 14	13 40
52	19 42	20 22	21 15	09 19	10 44	12 08	13 31
50	19 35	20 13	21 01	09 19	10 42	12 03	13 24
45	19 20	19 53	20 35	09 19	10 37	11 52	13 07
N 40	19 09	19 38	20 15	09 20	10 32	11 43	12 53
35	18 58	19 26	19 59	09 20	10 28	11 36	12 42
30	18 50	19 15	19 46	09 20	10 25	11 29	12 32
20	18 35	18 58	19 25	09 21	10 19	11 17	12 15
N 10	18 22	18 44	19 09	09 21	10 14	11 07	12 00
0	18 09	18 31	18 56	09 21	10 10	10 58	11 46
S 10	17 57	18 19	18 45	09 22	10 05	10 48	11 32
20	17 45	18 08	18 34	09 22	10 00	10 38	11 18
30	17 30	17 55	18 24	09 22	09 54	10 27	11 01
35	17 22	17 49	18 19	09 23	09 51	10 20	10 51
40	17 13	17 41	18 13	09 23	09 47	10 13	10 40
45	17 02	17 33	18 08	09 23	09 43	10 04	10 27
S 50	16 48	17 23	18 02	09 23	09 38	09 54	10 12
52	16 42	17 19	17 59	09 23	09 36	09 49	10 05
54	16 35	17 14	17 56	09 23	09 33	09 44	09 57
56	16 28	17 09	17 53	09 24	09 31	09 38	09 48
58	16 19	17 03	17 50	09 24	09 27	09 32	09 37
S 60	16 09	16 56	17 47	09 24	09 24	09 24	09 26

	SUN			MOON			
Day	Eqn. of Time 00h	Eqn. of Time 12h	Mer. Pass.	Mer. Pass. Upper	Mer. Pass. Lower	Age	Phase
d	m s	m s	h m	h m	h m	d	%
5	06 06	06 03	12 06	03 10	15 34	19	81
6	06 00	05 57	12 06	03 58	16 22	20	71
7	05 53	05 50	12 06	04 46	17 10	21	60

© British Crown Copyright 2022. All rights reserved.

UT	ARIES GHA	VENUS −4.1 GHA	Dec	MARS +1.8 GHA	Dec	JUPITER −2.4 GHA	Dec	SATURN +0.5 GHA	Dec	STARS Name	SHA	Dec
8 00	316 14.8	172 27.9	N 7 04.3	147 18.6	N 5 41.3	273 58.3	N14 57.7	338 31.0	S11 12.6	Acamar	315 12.7	S40 12.3
01	331 17.2	187 31.9	04.3	162 19.6	40.6	289 00.5	57.8	353 33.7	12.7	Achernar	335 20.8	S57 06.7
02	346 19.7	202 35.8	04.4	177 20.6	40.0	304 02.8	57.8	8 36.3	12.7	Acrux	173 01.8	S63 13.9
03	1 22.2	217 39.8 ..	04.4	192 21.6 ..	39.4	319 05.0 ..	57.9	23 38.9 ..	12.8	Adhara	255 07.1	S29 00.0
04	16 24.6	232 43.7	04.5	207 22.7	38.7	334 07.3	57.9	38 41.5	12.9	Aldebaran	290 41.1	N16 33.4
05	31 27.1	247 47.6	04.5	222 23.7	38.1	349 09.5	58.0	53 44.2	13.0			
06	46 29.6	262 51.6	N 7 04.6	237 24.7	N 5 37.5	4 11.8	N14 58.1	68 46.8	S11 13.0	Alioth	166 14.3	N55 50.2
07	61 32.0	277 55.5	04.6	252 25.7	36.8	19 14.0	58.1	83 49.4	13.1	Alkaid	152 53.1	N49 12.0
08	76 34.5	292 59.5	04.7	267 26.8	36.2	34 16.3	58.2	98 52.0	13.2	Alnair	27 33.9	S46 50.7
09	91 37.0	308 03.4 ..	04.7	282 27.8 ..	35.6	49 18.5 ..	58.2	113 54.7 ..	13.2	Alnilam	275 39.1	S 1 11.1
10	106 39.4	323 07.4	04.8	297 28.8	34.9	64 20.8	58.3	128 57.3	13.3	Alphard	217 49.2	S 8 45.5
11	121 41.9	338 11.3	04.9	312 29.8	34.3	79 23.0	58.3	143 59.9	13.4			
12	136 44.3	353 15.3	N 7 04.9	327 30.8	N 5 33.7	94 25.3	N14 58.4	159 02.5	S11 13.4	Alphecca	126 04.7	N26 38.3
13	151 46.8	8 19.2	05.0	342 31.9	33.0	109 27.5	58.4	174 05.2	13.5	Alpheratz	357 35.7	N29 13.2
14	166 49.3	23 23.2	05.0	357 32.9	32.4	124 29.8	58.5	189 07.8	13.6	Altair	62 00.8	N 8 55.9
15	181 51.7	38 27.1 ..	05.1	12 33.9 ..	31.8	139 32.0 ..	58.6	204 10.4 ..	13.6	Ankaa	353 08.0	S42 10.5
16	196 54.2	53 31.1	05.2	27 34.9	31.1	154 34.3	58.6	219 13.0	13.7	Antares	112 17.1	S26 29.1
17	211 56.7	68 35.1	05.2	42 36.0	30.5	169 36.5	58.7	234 15.7	13.8			
18	226 59.1	83 39.0	N 7 05.3	57 37.0	N 5 29.9	184 38.8	N14 58.7	249 18.3	S11 13.8	Arcturus	145 49.0	N19 03.8
19	242 01.6	98 43.0	05.4	72 38.0	29.2	199 41.0	58.8	264 20.9	13.9	Atria	107 12.1	S69 04.4
20	257 04.1	113 47.0	05.4	87 39.0	28.6	214 43.3	58.8	279 23.5	14.0	Avior	234 15.9	S59 34.9
21	272 06.5	128 50.9 ..	05.5	102 40.0 ..	28.0	229 45.6 ..	58.9	294 26.2 ..	14.0	Bellatrix	278 24.3	N 6 22.3
22	287 09.0	143 54.9	05.6	117 41.1	27.3	244 47.8	58.9	309 28.8	14.1	Betelgeuse	270 53.6	N 7 24.8
23	302 11.5	158 58.9	05.7	132 42.1	26.7	259 50.1	59.0	324 31.4	14.2			
9 00	317 13.9	174 02.8	N 7 05.8	147 43.1	N 5 26.1	274 52.3	N14 59.0	339 34.0	S11 14.3	Canopus	263 53.3	S52 42.2
01	332 16.4	189 06.8	05.8	162 44.1	25.4	289 54.6	59.1	354 36.7	14.3	Capella	280 23.9	N46 01.2
02	347 18.8	204 10.8	05.9	177 45.2	24.8	304 56.8	59.1	9 39.3	14.4	Deneb	49 26.1	N45 21.9
03	2 21.3	219 14.7 ..	06.0	192 46.2 ..	24.2	319 59.1 ..	59.2	24 41.9 ..	14.5	Denebola	182 26.4	N14 26.6
04	17 23.8	234 18.7	06.1	207 47.2	23.5	335 01.3	59.3	39 44.5	14.5	Diphda	348 48.3	S17 51.3
05	32 26.2	249 22.7	06.2	222 48.2	22.9	350 03.6	59.3	54 47.2	14.6			
06	47 28.7	264 26.7	N 7 06.2	237 49.3	N 5 22.3	5 05.9	N14 59.4	69 49.8	S11 14.7	Dubhe	193 43.0	N61 37.7
07	62 31.2	279 30.6	06.3	252 50.3	21.6	20 08.1	59.4	84 52.4	14.7	Elnath	278 03.6	N28 37.6
08	77 33.6	294 34.6	06.4	267 51.3	21.0	35 10.4	59.5	99 55.0	14.8	Eltanin	90 42.4	N51 29.3
09	92 36.1	309 38.6 ..	06.5	282 52.3 ..	20.4	50 12.6 ..	59.5	114 57.7 ..	14.9	Enif	33 39.6	N 9 59.0
10	107 38.6	324 42.6	06.6	297 53.3	19.7	65 14.9	59.6	130 00.3	14.9	Fomalhaut	15 15.5	S29 29.7
11	122 41.0	339 46.6	06.7	312 54.4	19.1	80 17.1	59.6	145 02.9	15.0			
12	137 43.5	354 50.6	N 7 06.8	327 55.4	N 5 18.4	95 19.4	N14 59.7	160 05.5	S11 15.1	Gacrux	171 53.3	S57 14.8
13	152 46.0	9 54.5	06.9	342 56.4	17.8	110 21.7	59.7	175 08.2	15.2	Gienah	175 45.0	S17 40.3
14	167 48.4	24 58.5	07.0	357 57.4	17.2	125 23.9	59.8	190 10.8	15.2	Hadar	148 37.8	S60 29.4
15	182 50.9	40 02.5 ..	07.1	12 58.5 ..	16.5	140 26.2 ..	59.8	205 13.4 ..	15.3	Hamal	327 52.4	N23 34.4
16	197 53.3	55 06.5	07.2	27 59.5	15.9	155 28.4	59.9	220 16.1	15.4	Kaus Aust.	83 33.8	S34 22.4
17	212 55.8	70 10.5	07.3	43 00.5	15.3	170 30.7 14	59.9	235 18.7	15.4			
18	227 58.3	85 14.5	N 7 07.4	58 01.5	N 5 14.6	185 32.9	N15 00.0	250 21.3	S11 15.5	Kochab	137 19.8	N74 03.8
19	243 00.7	100 18.5	07.5	73 02.5	14.0	200 35.2	00.1	265 23.9	15.6	Markab	13 30.8	N15 19.9
20	258 03.2	115 22.5	07.6	88 03.6	13.4	215 37.5	00.1	280 26.6	15.6	Menkar	314 07.4	N 4 11.0
21	273 05.7	130 26.5 ..	07.7	103 04.6 ..	12.7	230 39.7 ..	00.2	295 29.2 ..	15.7	Menkent	147 59.1	S36 29.2
22	288 08.1	145 30.5	07.8	118 05.6	12.1	245 42.0	00.2	310 31.8	15.8	Miaplacidus	221 39.5	S69 48.7
23	303 10.6	160 34.5	07.9	133 06.6	11.5	260 44.3	00.3	325 34.4	15.8			
10 00	318 13.1	175 38.5	N 7 08.1	148 07.7	N 5 10.8	275 46.5	N15 00.3	340 37.1	S11 15.9	Mirfak	308 30.0	N49 56.5
01	333 15.5	190 42.5	08.2	163 08.7	10.2	290 48.8	00.4	355 39.7	16.0	Nunki	75 48.9	S26 16.0
02	348 18.0	205 46.5	08.3	178 09.7	09.5	305 51.0	00.5	10 42.3	16.0	Peacock	53 07.0	S56 39.6
03	3 20.4	220 50.5 ..	08.4	193 10.7 ..	08.9	320 53.3 ..	00.5	25 45.0 ..	16.1	Pollux	243 19.1	N27 58.2
04	18 22.9	235 54.5	08.5	208 11.7	08.3	335 55.6	00.5	40 47.6	16.2	Procyon	244 52.4	N 5 10.0
05	33 25.4	250 58.5	08.6	223 12.8	07.6	350 57.8	00.6	55 50.2	16.3			
06	48 27.8	266 02.5	N 7 08.8	238 13.8	N 5 07.0	6 00.1	N15 00.6	70 52.8	S11 16.3	Rasalhague	96 59.4	N12 32.7
07	63 30.3	281 06.5	08.9	253 14.8	06.4	21 02.4	00.7	85 55.5	16.4	Regulus	207 36.0	N11 51.3
08	78 32.8	296 10.5	09.0	268 15.8	05.7	36 04.6	00.7	100 58.1	16.5	Rigel	281 05.2	S 8 10.3
09	93 35.2	311 14.5 ..	09.1	283 16.9 ..	05.1	51 06.9 ..	00.8	116 00.7 ..	16.5	Rigil Kent.	139 42.0	S60 56.1
10	108 37.7	326 18.5	09.3	298 17.9	04.4	66 09.1	00.8	131 03.4	16.6	Sabik	102 03.9	S15 45.2
11	123 40.2	341 22.5	09.4	313 18.9	03.8	81 11.4	00.9	146 06.0	16.7			
12	138 42.6	356 26.5	N 7 09.5	328 19.9	N 5 03.2	96 13.7	N15 00.9	161 08.6	S11 16.7	Schedar	349 32.1	N56 39.8
13	153 45.1	11 30.5	09.6	343 20.9	02.5	111 15.9	01.0	176 11.2	16.8	Shaula	96 11.7	S37 07.3
14	168 47.6	26 34.5	09.8	358 22.0	01.9	126 18.2	01.0	191 13.9	16.9	Sirius	258 27.6	S16 44.7
15	183 50.0	41 38.5 ..	09.9	13 23.0 ..	01.3	141 20.5 ..	01.1	206 16.5 ..	17.0	Spica	158 23.7	S11 17.0
16	198 52.5	56 42.5	10.0	28 24.0	00.6	156 22.7	01.1	221 19.1	17.0	Suhail	222 47.6	S43 31.5
17	213 54.9	71 46.5	10.2	43 25.0	5 00.0	171 25.0	01.2	236 21.8	17.1			
18	228 57.4	86 50.5	N 7 10.3	58 26.1	N 4 59.4	186 27.3	N15 01.2	251 24.4	S11 17.2	Vega	80 33.7	N38 48.5
19	243 59.9	101 54.6	10.5	73 27.1	58.7	201 29.5	01.3	266 27.0	17.2	Zuben'ubi	136 57.3	S16 08.4
20	259 02.3	116 58.6	10.6	88 28.1	58.1	216 31.8	01.3	281 29.6	17.3		SHA	Mer. Pass.
21	274 04.8	132 02.6 ..	10.7	103 29.1 ..	57.4	231 34.1 ..	01.4	296 32.3 ..	17.4	Venus	216 48.9	12 21
22	289 07.3	147 06.6	10.9	118 30.1	56.8	246 36.3	01.4	311 34.9	17.4	Mars	190 29.2	14 08
23	304 09.7	162 10.6	11.0	133 31.2	56.2	261 38.6	01.5	326 37.5	17.5	Jupiter	317 38.4	5 40
Mer. Pass. 2 50.6		v 4.0	d 0.1	v 1.0	d 0.6	v 2.3	d 0.1	v 2.6	d 0.1	Saturn	22 20.1	1 21

© British Crown Copyright 2022. All rights reserved.

UT	SUN GHA	SUN Dec	MOON GHA	v	Dec	d	HP
8 00	178 33.6	N16 16.2	279 07.6	11.6	N15 46.1	13.2	57.6
01	193 33.7	15.5	293 38.2	11.6	15 59.3	13.2	57.6
02	208 33.7	14.8	308 08.8	11.6	16 12.5	13.0	57.5
03	223 33.8	.. 14.1	322 39.4	11.5	16 25.5	13.0	57.5
04	238 33.9	13.4	337 09.9	11.5	16 38.5	12.8	57.5
05	253 34.0	12.7	351 40.4	11.4	16 51.3	12.8	57.4
06	268 34.1	N16 11.9	6 10.8	11.4	N17 04.1	12.6	57.4
07	283 34.1	11.2	20 41.2	11.4	17 16.7	12.6	57.4
08	298 34.2	10.5	35 11.6	11.4	17 29.3	12.4	57.3
09	313 34.3	.. 09.8	49 42.0	11.3	17 41.7	12.4	57.3
10	328 34.4	09.1	64 12.3	11.3	17 54.1	12.2	57.3
11	343 34.5	08.4	78 42.6	11.2	18 06.3	12.2	57.2
12	358 34.5	N16 07.7	93 12.8	11.2	N18 18.5	12.0	57.2
13	13 34.6	07.0	107 43.0	11.2	18 30.5	12.0	57.2
14	28 34.7	06.3	122 13.2	11.1	18 42.5	11.8	57.1
15	43 34.8	.. 05.6	136 43.3	11.1	18 54.3	11.7	57.1
16	58 34.9	04.9	151 13.4	11.1	19 06.0	11.6	57.1
17	73 35.0	04.1	165 43.5	11.0	19 17.6	11.5	57.0
18	88 35.0	N16 03.4	180 13.5	11.0	N19 29.1	11.4	57.0
19	103 35.1	02.7	194 43.5	11.0	19 40.5	11.3	56.9
20	118 35.2	02.0	209 13.5	10.9	19 51.8	11.2	56.9
21	133 35.3	.. 01.3	223 43.4	10.9	20 03.0	11.0	56.9
22	148 35.4	16 00.6	238 13.3	10.8	20 14.0	11.0	56.8
23	163 35.5	15 59.9	252 43.1	10.8	20 25.0	10.8	56.8
9 00	178 35.5	N15 59.1	267 12.9	10.8	N20 35.8	10.7	56.8
01	193 35.6	58.4	281 42.7	10.7	20 46.5	10.6	56.7
02	208 35.7	57.7	296 12.4	10.7	20 57.1	10.5	56.7
03	223 35.8	.. 57.0	310 42.1	10.6	21 07.6	10.4	56.7
04	238 35.9	56.3	325 11.7	10.6	21 18.0	10.2	56.6
05	253 36.0	55.6	339 41.3	10.6	21 28.2	10.2	56.6
06	268 36.1	N15 54.8	354 10.9	10.5	N21 38.4	10.0	56.6
07	283 36.1	54.1	8 40.4	10.5	21 48.4	9.9	56.5
08	298 36.2	53.4	23 09.9	10.4	21 58.3	9.7	56.5
09	313 36.3	.. 52.7	37 39.3	10.4	22 08.0	9.7	56.5
10	328 36.4	52.0	52 08.7	10.4	22 17.7	9.5	56.5
11	343 36.5	51.2	66 38.1	10.3	22 27.2	9.4	56.4
12	358 36.6	N15 50.5	81 07.4	10.3	N22 36.6	9.3	56.4
13	13 36.7	49.8	95 36.7	10.2	22 45.9	9.1	56.4
14	28 36.8	49.1	110 05.9	10.2	22 55.0	9.1	56.3
15	43 36.8	.. 48.4	124 35.1	10.2	23 04.1	8.9	56.3
16	58 36.9	47.6	139 04.3	10.1	23 13.0	8.8	56.3
17	73 37.0	46.9	153 33.4	10.1	23 21.8	8.6	56.2
18	88 37.1	N15 46.2	168 02.5	10.0	N23 30.4	8.5	56.2
19	103 37.2	45.5	182 31.5	10.0	23 38.9	8.4	56.2
20	118 37.3	44.7	197 00.5	10.0	23 47.3	8.3	56.2
21	133 37.4	.. 44.0	211 29.5	10.0	23 55.6	8.1	56.1
22	148 37.5	43.3	225 58.5	9.8	24 03.7	8.0	56.1
23	163 37.6	42.6	240 27.3	9.9	24 11.7	7.9	56.1
10 00	178 37.7	N15 41.8	254 56.2	9.8	N24 19.6	7.8	56.0
01	193 37.7	41.1	269 25.0	9.8	24 27.4	7.6	56.0
02	208 37.8	40.4	283 53.8	9.8	24 35.0	7.5	56.0
03	223 37.9	.. 39.7	298 22.6	9.7	24 42.5	7.3	55.9
04	238 38.0	38.9	312 51.3	9.7	24 49.8	7.2	55.9
05	253 38.1	38.2	327 20.0	9.6	24 57.0	7.1	55.9
06	268 38.2	N15 37.5	341 48.6	9.6	N25 04.1	7.0	55.9
07	283 38.3	36.8	356 17.2	9.6	25 11.1	6.8	55.8
08	298 38.4	36.0	10 45.8	9.6	25 17.9	6.6	55.8
09	313 38.5	.. 35.3	25 14.4	9.5	25 24.5	6.6	55.8
10	328 38.6	34.6	39 42.9	9.5	25 31.1	6.4	55.8
11	343 38.7	33.8	54 11.4	9.5	25 37.5	6.3	55.7
12	358 38.8	N15 33.1	68 39.9	9.4	N25 43.8	6.1	55.7
13	13 38.9	32.4	83 08.3	9.4	25 49.9	6.0	55.7
14	28 39.0	31.6	97 36.7	9.4	25 55.9	5.8	55.7
15	43 39.1	.. 30.9	112 05.1	9.3	26 01.7	5.7	55.6
16	58 39.1	30.2	126 33.4	9.3	26 07.4	5.6	55.6
17	73 39.2	29.4	141 01.7	9.3	26 13.0	5.5	55.6
18	88 39.3	N15 28.7	155 30.0	9.3	N26 18.5	5.3	55.5
19	103 39.4	28.0	169 58.3	9.3	26 23.8	5.1	55.5
20	118 39.5	27.2	184 26.6	9.2	26 28.9	5.0	55.5
21	133 39.6	.. 26.5	198 54.8	9.2	26 33.9	4.9	55.5
22	148 39.7	25.8	213 23.0	9.2	26 38.8	4.7	55.5
23	163 39.8	25.0	227 51.2	9.2	N26 43.5	4.6	55.4
	SD 15.8	d 0.7	SD 15.6		15.4		15.2

Left day labels: **TUESDAY** (8), **WEDNESDAY** (9), **THURSDAY** (10)

Lat.	Twilight Naut.	Twilight Civil	Sunrise	Moonrise 8	9	10	11
°	h m	h m	h m	h m	h m	h m	h m
N 72	////	////	01 32	▭	▭	▭	▭
N 70	////	////	02 21	18 53	▭	▭	▭
68	////	00 15	02 52	19 53	▭	▭	▭
66	////	01 44	03 15	20 28	19 35	▭	▭
64	////	02 19	03 32	20 53	20 35	▭	▭
62	00 14	02 44	03 47	21 13	21 10	21 07	▭
60	01 33	03 04	03 59	21 30	21 35	21 47	22 15
N 58	02 06	03 20	04 09	21 44	21 55	22 15	22 49
56	02 29	03 33	04 19	21 56	22 12	22 36	23 15
54	02 47	03 44	04 27	22 06	22 26	22 54	23 35
52	03 02	03 54	04 34	22 16	22 38	23 09	23 52
50	03 15	04 03	04 40	22 24	22 49	23 23	24 06
45	03 41	04 21	04 54	22 42	23 12	23 50	24 36
N 40	04 00	04 36	05 06	22 57	23 31	24 11	00 11
35	04 15	04 48	05 15	23 10	23 47	24 29	00 29
30	04 28	04 58	05 24	23 21	24 00	00 00	00 45
20	04 48	05 15	05 38	23 40	24 24	00 24	01 11
N 10	05 03	05 29	05 51	23 56	24 44	00 44	01 34
0	05 16	05 41	06 02	24 12	00 12	01 03	01 55
S 10	05 27	05 52	06 14	24 28	00 28	01 22	02 17
20	05 37	06 03	06 26	24 45	00 45	01 43	02 40
30	05 46	06 15	06 39	00 02	01 05	02 07	03 06
35	05 51	06 21	06 47	00 10	01 16	02 21	03 22
40	05 56	06 28	06 56	00 20	01 29	02 37	03 41
45	06 01	06 36	07 07	00 31	01 45	02 57	04 03
S 50	06 06	06 45	07 19	00 45	02 05	03 21	04 32
52	06 09	06 49	07 25	00 52	02 14	03 34	04 46
54	06 11	06 53	07 32	00 59	02 25	03 47	05 02
56	06 14	06 58	07 39	01 08	02 37	04 03	05 22
58	06 17	07 04	07 47	01 17	02 51	04 22	05 46
S 60	06 20	07 10	07 56	01 28	03 07	04 46	06 18

Lat.	Sunset	Twilight Civil	Twilight Naut.	Moonset 8	9	10	11
°	h m	h m	h m	h m	h m	h m	h m
N 72	22 30	////	////	▭	▭	▭	▭
N 70	21 45	////	////	16 46	▭	▭	▭
68	21 16	23 27	////	15 47	▭	▭	▭
66	20 54	22 22	////	15 13	17 52	▭	▭
64	20 37	21 48	////	14 49	16 52	▭	▭
62	20 22	21 24	23 31	14 30	16 18	18 10	19 59
60	20 10	21 05	22 33	14 14	15 54	17 39	18 53
N 58	20 00	20 49	22 02	14 01	15 34	17 03	18 18
56	19 51	20 36	21 39	13 50	15 18	16 41	17 53
54	19 43	20 25	21 22	13 40	15 04	16 24	17 33
52	19 36	20 15	21 08	13 31	14 52	16 09	17 16
50	19 30	20 07	20 54	13 24	14 42	15 56	17 01
45	19 16	19 49	20 29	13 07	14 20	15 29	16 32
N 40	19 05	19 34	20 10	12 53	14 02	15 08	16 09
35	18 55	19 23	19 55	12 42	13 47	14 51	15 50
30	18 47	19 13	19 43	12 32	13 34	14 36	15 34
20	18 33	18 56	19 23	12 15	13 13	14 10	15 06
N 10	18 20	18 42	19 08	12 00	12 54	13 48	14 43
0	18 09	18 30	18 55	11 46	12 36	13 28	14 21
S 10	17 58	18 19	18 45	11 32	12 19	13 08	13 59
20	17 46	18 08	18 35	11 18	12 00	12 46	13 35
30	17 32	17 57	18 25	11 01	11 39	12 21	13 08
35	17 24	17 51	18 21	10 51	11 26	12 06	12 52
40	17 15	17 44	18 11	10 40	11 12	11 49	12 33
45	17 05	17 36	18 11	10 27	10 55	11 29	12 10
S 50	16 52	17 27	18 05	10 12	10 34	11 03	11 41
52	16 47	17 23	18 03	10 05	10 24	10 51	11 27
54	16 40	17 18	18 01	09 57	10 13	10 36	11 10
56	16 33	17 14	17 58	09 48	10 01	10 20	10 51
58	16 25	17 08	17 55	09 37	09 46	10 00	10 26
S 60	16 16	17 02	17 52	09 26	09 29	09 36	09 53

Day	SUN Eqn. of Time 00h	12h	Mer. Pass.	MOON Mer. Pass. Upper	Lower	Age	Phase
d	m s	m s	h m	h m	h m	d	%
8	05 46	05 42	12 06	05 34	17 59	22	49
9	05 38	05 34	12 06	06 24	18 50	23	39
10	05 30	05 25	12 05	07 15	19 42	24	29

© British Crown Copyright 2022. All rights reserved.

UT	ARIES	VENUS −4.1		MARS +1.8		JUPITER −2.4		SATURN +0.5		STARS		
	GHA	GHA	Dec	GHA	Dec	GHA	Dec	GHA	Dec	Name	SHA	Dec
d h	° ′	° ′	° ′	° ′	° ′	° ′	° ′	° ′	° ′		° ′	° ′
11 00	319 12.2	177 14.6 N 7 11.2		148 32.2 N 4 55.5		276 40.9 N15 01.5		341 40.2 S11 17.6		Acamar	315 12.6	S40 12.3
01	334 14.7	192 18.6	11.3	163 33.2	54.9	291 43.1	01.6	356 42.8	17.6	Achernar	335 20.8	S57 06.7
02	349 17.1	207 22.7	11.5	178 34.2	54.2	306 45.4	01.6	11 45.4	17.7	Acrux	173 01.8	S63 13.9
03	4 19.6	222 26.7 . .	11.6	193 35.2 . .	53.6	321 47.7 . .	01.7	26 48.0 . .	17.8	Adhara	255 07.1	S29 00.0
04	19 22.1	237 30.7	11.8	208 36.3	53.0	336 50.0	01.7	41 50.7	17.9	Aldebaran	290 41.1	N16 33.4
05	34 24.5	252 34.7	11.9	223 37.3	52.3	351 52.2	01.8	56 53.3	17.9			
06	49 27.0	267 38.7 N 7 12.1		238 38.3 N 4 51.7		6 54.5 N15 01.8		71 55.9 S11 18.0		Alioth	166 14.3	N55 50.2
07	64 29.4	282 42.7	12.2	253 39.3	51.1	21 56.8	01.9	86 58.6	18.1	Alkaid	152 53.1	N49 12.0
08	79 31.9	297 46.8	12.4	268 40.4	50.4	36 59.0	01.9	102 01.2	18.1	Alnair	27 33.9	S46 50.7
F 09	94 34.4	312 50.8 . .	12.5	283 41.4 . .	49.8	52 01.3 . .	02.0	117 03.8 . .	18.2	Alnilam	275 39.1	S 1 11.1
R 10	109 36.8	327 54.8	12.7	298 42.4	49.1	67 03.6	02.0	132 06.5	18.3	Alphard	217 49.2	S 8 45.5
I 11	124 39.3	342 58.8	12.9	313 43.4	48.5	82 05.9	02.1	147 09.1	18.3			
D 12	139 41.8	358 02.8 N 7 13.0		328 44.4 N 4 47.9		97 08.1 N15 02.1		162 11.7 S11 18.4		Alphecca	126 04.7	N26 38.3
A 13	154 44.2	13 06.9	13.2	343 45.5	47.2	112 10.4	02.2	177 14.3	18.5	Alpheratz	357 35.7	N29 13.2
Y 14	169 46.7	28 10.9	13.4	358 46.5	46.6	127 12.7	02.2	192 17.0	18.6	Altair	62 00.8	N 8 55.9
15	184 49.2	43 14.9 . .	13.5	13 47.5 . .	45.9	142 14.9 . .	02.3	207 19.6 . .	18.6	Ankaa	353 08.0	S42 10.5
16	199 51.6	58 18.9	13.7	28 48.5	45.3	157 17.2	02.3	222 22.2	18.7	Antares	112 17.1	S26 29.1
17	214 54.1	73 23.0	13.9	43 49.5	44.7	172 19.5	02.4	237 24.9	18.8			
18	229 56.6	88 27.0 N 7 14.0		58 50.6 N 4 44.0		187 21.8 N15 02.4		252 27.5 S11 18.8		Arcturus	145 49.1	N19 03.8
19	244 59.0	103 31.0	14.2	73 51.6	43.4	202 24.0	02.5	267 30.1	18.9	Atria	107 12.2	S69 04.4
20	260 01.5	118 35.0	14.4	88 52.6	42.7	217 26.3	02.5	282 32.8	19.0	Avior	234 15.8	S59 34.9
21	275 03.9	133 39.0 . .	14.5	103 53.6 . .	42.1	232 28.6 . .	02.5	297 35.4 . .	19.0	Bellatrix	278 24.3	N 6 22.3
22	290 06.4	148 43.1	14.7	118 54.6	41.5	247 30.9	02.6	312 38.0	19.1	Betelgeuse	270 53.6	N 7 24.8
23	305 08.9	163 47.1	14.9	133 55.7	40.8	262 33.1	02.6	327 40.6	19.2			
12 00	320 11.3	178 51.1 N 7 15.1		148 56.7 N 4 40.2		277 35.4 N15 02.7		342 43.3 S11 19.3		Canopus	263 53.3	S52 42.2
01	335 13.8	193 55.1	15.3	163 57.7	39.5	292 37.7	02.7	357 45.9	19.3	Capella	280 23.9	N46 01.2
02	350 16.3	208 59.2	15.4	178 58.7	38.9	307 40.0	02.8	12 48.5	19.4	Deneb	49 26.1	N45 21.9
03	5 18.7	224 03.2 . .	15.6	193 59.8 . .	38.3	322 42.2 . .	02.8	27 51.2 . .	19.5	Denebola	182 26.4	N14 26.6
04	20 21.2	239 07.2	15.8	209 00.8	37.6	337 44.5	02.9	42 53.8	19.5	Diphda	348 48.3	S17 51.3
05	35 23.7	254 11.2	16.0	224 01.8	37.0	352 46.8	02.9	57 56.4	19.6			
06	50 26.1	269 15.3 N 7 16.2		239 02.8 N 4 36.3		7 49.1 N15 03.0		72 59.1 S11 19.7		Dubhe	193 43.0	N61 37.7
07	65 28.6	284 19.3	16.4	254 03.8	35.7	22 51.4	03.0	88 01.7	19.7	Elnath	278 03.5	N28 37.6
S 08	80 31.1	299 23.3	16.5	269 04.9	35.1	37 53.6	03.1	103 04.3	19.8	Eltanin	90 42.4	N51 29.3
A 09	95 33.5	314 27.3 . .	16.7	284 05.9 . .	34.4	52 55.9 . .	03.1	118 07.0 . .	19.9	Enif	33 39.6	N 9 59.0
T 10	110 36.0	329 31.4	16.9	299 06.9	33.8	67 58.2	03.2	133 09.6	20.0	Fomalhaut	15 15.5	S29 29.7
U 11	125 38.4	344 35.4	17.1	314 07.9	33.1	83 00.5	03.2	148 12.2	20.0			
R 12	140 40.9	359 39.4 N 7 17.3		329 08.9 N 4 32.5		98 02.7 N15 03.3		163 14.9 S11 20.1		Gacrux	171 53.3	S57 14.8
D 13	155 43.4	14 43.4	17.5	344 10.0	31.9	113 05.0	03.3	178 17.5	20.2	Gienah	175 45.0	S17 40.3
A 14	170 45.8	29 47.5	17.7	359 11.0	31.2	128 07.3	03.3	193 20.1	20.2	Hadar	148 37.9	S60 29.4
Y 15	185 48.3	44 51.5 . .	17.9	14 12.0 . .	30.6	143 09.6 . .	03.4	208 22.7 . .	20.3	Hamal	327 52.4	N23 34.4
16	200 50.8	59 55.5	18.1	29 13.0	29.9	158 11.9	03.4	223 25.4	20.4	Kaus Aust.	83 33.8	S34 22.4
17	215 53.2	74 59.5	18.3	44 14.0	29.3	173 14.2	03.5	238 28.0	20.4			
18	230 55.7	90 03.6 N 7 18.5		59 15.1 N 4 28.7		188 16.4 N15 03.5		253 30.6 S11 20.5		Kochab	137 19.8	N74 03.8
19	245 58.2	105 07.6	18.7	74 16.1	28.0	203 18.7	03.6	268 33.3	20.6	Markab	13 30.8	N15 19.9
20	261 00.6	120 11.6	18.9	89 17.1	27.4	218 21.0	03.6	283 35.9	20.7	Menkar	314 07.4	N 4 11.0
21	276 03.1	135 15.6 . .	19.1	104 18.1 . .	26.7	233 23.3 . .	03.7	298 38.5 . .	20.7	Menkent	147 59.1	S36 29.2
22	291 05.5	150 19.7	19.3	119 19.1	26.1	248 25.6	03.7	313 41.2	20.8	Miaplacidus	221 39.5	S69 48.7
23	306 08.0	165 23.7	19.5	134 20.2	25.5	263 27.8	03.8	328 43.8	20.9			
13 00	321 10.5	180 27.7 N 7 19.7		149 21.2 N 4 24.8		278 30.1 N15 03.8		343 46.4 S11 20.9		Mirfak	308 30.0	N49 56.5
01	336 12.9	195 31.7	19.9	164 22.2	24.2	293 32.4	03.8	358 49.1	21.0	Nunki	75 48.9	S26 16.0
02	351 15.4	210 35.8	20.1	179 23.2	23.5	308 34.7	03.9	13 51.7	21.1	Peacock	53 07.0	S56 39.6
03	6 17.9	225 39.8 . .	20.3	194 24.2 . .	22.9	323 37.0 . .	03.9	28 54.3 . .	21.2	Pollux	243 19.1	N27 58.2
04	21 20.3	240 43.8	20.6	209 25.3	22.2	338 39.3	04.0	43 57.0	21.2	Procyon	244 52.4	N 5 10.0
05	36 22.8	255 47.8	20.8	224 26.3	21.6	353 41.5	04.0	58 59.6	21.3			
06	51 25.3	270 51.8 N 7 21.0		239 27.3 N 4 21.0		8 43.8 N15 04.1		74 02.2 S11 21.4		Rasalhague	95 59.4	N12 32.7
07	66 27.7	285 55.9	21.2	254 28.3	20.3	23 46.1	04.1	89 04.9	21.4	Regulus	207 36.0	N11 51.3
08	81 30.2	300 59.9	21.4	269 29.3	19.7	38 48.4	04.2	104 07.5	21.5	Rigel	281 05.2	S 8 10.3
S 09	96 32.7	316 03.9 . .	21.6	284 30.4 . .	19.0	53 50.7 . .	04.2	119 10.1 . .	21.6	Rigil Kent.	139 42.0	S60 56.1
U 10	111 35.1	331 07.9	21.8	299 31.4	18.4	68 53.0	04.2	134 12.8	21.6	Sabik	102 03.9	S15 45.2
N 11	126 37.6	346 12.0	22.1	314 32.4	17.8	83 55.3	04.3	149 15.4	21.7			
D 12	141 40.0	1 16.0 N 7 22.3		329 33.4 N 4 17.1		98 57.5 N15 04.3		164 18.0 S11 21.8		Schedar	349 32.0	N56 39.8
A 13	156 42.5	16 20.0	22.5	344 34.4	16.5	113 59.8	04.4	179 20.7	21.9	Shaula	96 11.7	S37 07.3
Y 14	171 45.0	31 24.0	22.7	359 35.5	15.8	129 02.1	04.4	194 23.3	21.9	Sirius	258 27.5	S16 44.7
15	186 47.4	46 28.0 . .	23.0	14 36.5 . .	15.2	144 04.4 . .	04.5	209 25.9 . .	22.0	Spica	158 23.7	S11 17.0
16	201 49.9	61 32.1	23.2	29 37.5	14.5	159 06.7	04.5	224 28.6	22.1	Suhail	222 47.6	S43 31.5
17	216 52.4	76 36.1	23.4	44 38.5	13.9	174 09.0	04.6	239 31.2	22.1			
18	231 54.8	91 40.1 N 7 23.6		59 39.5 N 4 13.3		189 11.3 N15 04.6		254 33.8 S11 22.2		Vega	80 33.7	N38 48.5
19	246 57.3	106 44.1	23.9	74 40.6	12.6	204 13.6	04.6	269 36.5	22.3	Zuben'ubi	136 57.3	S16 08.4
20	261 59.8	121 48.1	24.1	89 41.6	12.0	219 15.9	04.7	284 39.1	22.4		SHA	Mer. Pass.
21	277 02.2	136 52.1 . .	24.3	104 42.6 . .	11.3	234 18.1 . .	04.7	299 41.7 . .	22.4		° ′	h m
22	292 04.7	151 56.2	24.6	119 43.6	10.7	249 20.4	04.8	314 44.4	22.5	Venus	218 39.8	12 01
23	307 07.2	167 00.2	24.8	134 44.6	10.0	264 22.7	04.8	329 47.0	22.6	Mars	188 45.4	14 03
	h m									Jupiter	317 24.1	5 29
Mer. Pass. 2 38.8		v 4.0 d 0.2		v 1.0 d 0.6		v 2.3 d 0.0		v 2.6 d 0.1		Saturn	22 31.9	1 09

© British Crown Copyright 2022. All rights reserved.

UT	SUN GHA	SUN Dec	MOON GHA	v	MOON Dec	d	HP
d h	° '	° '	° '	'	° '	'	'
11 00	178 39.9	N15 24.3	242 19.4	9.1	N26 48.1	4.5	55.4
01	193 40.0	23.6	256 47.5	9.1	26 52.6	4.3	55.4
02	208 40.1	22.8	271 15.6	9.2	26 56.9	4.2	55.4
03	223 40.2 ..	22.1	285 43.8	9.1	27 01.1	4.0	55.3
04	238 40.3	21.3	300 11.9	9.0	27 05.1	3.9	55.3
05	253 40.4	20.6	314 39.9	9.1	27 09.0	3.7	55.3
06	268 40.5	N15 19.9	329 08.0	9.1	N27 12.7	3.6	55.3
07	283 40.6	19.1	343 36.1	9.0	27 16.3	3.5	55.2
08	298 40.7	18.4	358 04.1	9.1	27 19.8	3.3	55.2
F 09	313 40.8 ..	17.7	12 32.2	9.0	27 23.1	3.2	55.2
R 10	328 40.9	16.9	27 00.2	9.0	27 26.3	3.0	55.2
I 11	343 41.0	16.2	41 28.2	9.0	27 29.3	2.9	55.2
D 12	358 41.1	N15 15.4	55 56.2	9.0	N27 32.2	2.7	55.1
A 13	13 41.2	14.7	70 24.2	9.0	27 34.9	2.6	55.1
Y 14	28 41.3	13.9	84 52.2	9.0	27 37.5	2.4	55.1
15	43 41.4 ..	13.2	99 20.2	9.0	27 39.9	2.4	55.1
16	58 41.5	12.5	113 48.2	9.0	27 42.3	2.1	55.0
17	73 41.6	11.7	128 16.2	9.1	27 44.4	2.0	55.0
18	88 41.7	N15 11.0	142 44.3	9.0	N27 46.4	1.9	55.0
19	103 41.8	10.2	157 12.3	9.0	27 48.3	1.7	55.0
20	118 41.9	09.5	171 40.3	9.0	27 50.0	1.6	55.0
21	133 42.0 ..	08.7	186 08.3	9.0	27 51.6	1.5	54.9
22	148 42.1	08.0	200 36.3	9.0	27 53.1	1.3	54.9
23	163 42.2	07.2	215 04.3	9.0	27 54.4	1.1	54.9
12 00	178 42.3	N15 06.5	229 32.3	9.1	N27 55.5	1.0	54.9
01	193 42.4	05.8	244 00.4	9.0	27 56.5	0.9	54.9
02	208 42.5	05.0	258 28.4	9.1	27 57.4	0.7	54.9
03	223 42.6 ..	04.3	272 56.5	9.1	27 58.1	0.6	54.8
04	238 42.7	03.5	287 24.6	9.1	27 58.7	0.4	54.8
05	253 42.8	02.8	301 52.7	9.1	27 59.1	0.3	54.8
06	268 42.9	N15 02.0	316 20.8	9.1	N27 59.4	0.2	54.8
07	283 43.0	01.3	330 48.9	9.1	27 59.6	0.0	54.8
S 08	298 43.1	15 00.5	345 17.0	9.2	27 59.6	0.1	54.7
A 09	313 43.2	14 59.8	359 45.2	9.2	27 59.5	0.3	54.7
T 10	328 43.3	59.0	14 13.4	9.2	27 59.2	0.4	54.7
U 11	343 43.4	58.3	28 41.6	9.2	27 58.8	0.6	54.7
R 12	358 43.6	N14 57.5	43 09.8	9.2	N27 58.2	0.7	54.7
D 13	13 43.7	56.8	57 38.0	9.3	27 57.5	0.8	54.7
A 14	28 43.8	56.0	72 06.3	9.3	27 56.7	1.0	54.6
Y 15	43 43.9 ..	55.3	86 34.6	9.3	27 55.7	1.1	54.6
16	58 44.0	54.5	101 02.9	9.4	27 54.6	1.3	54.6
17	73 44.1	53.7	115 31.3	9.4	27 53.3	1.4	54.6
18	88 44.2	N14 53.0	129 59.7	9.4	N27 51.9	1.5	54.6
19	103 44.3	52.2	144 28.1	9.5	27 50.4	1.7	54.6
20	118 44.4	51.5	158 56.6	9.5	27 48.7	1.8	54.5
21	133 44.5 ..	50.7	173 25.1	9.5	27 46.9	1.9	54.5
22	148 44.6	50.0	187 53.6	9.5	27 45.0	2.1	54.5
23	163 44.7	49.2	202 22.1	9.6	27 42.9	2.3	54.5
13 00	178 44.8	N14 48.5	216 50.7	9.7	N27 40.6	2.3	54.5
01	193 44.9	47.7	231 19.4	9.6	27 38.3	2.5	54.5
02	208 45.1	46.9	245 48.0	9.8	27 35.8	2.7	54.5
03	223 45.2 ..	46.2	260 16.8	9.7	27 33.1	2.7	54.5
04	238 45.3	45.4	274 45.5	9.8	27 30.4	2.9	54.4
05	253 45.4	44.7	289 14.3	9.9	27 27.5	3.1	54.4
06	268 45.5	N14 43.9	303 43.2	9.9	N27 24.4	3.1	54.4
07	283 45.6	43.2	318 12.1	9.9	27 21.3	3.3	54.4
08	298 45.7	42.4	332 41.0	10.0	27 18.0	3.5	54.4
S 09	313 45.8 ..	41.6	347 10.0	10.0	27 14.5	3.5	54.4
U 10	328 45.9	40.9	1 39.0	10.1	27 11.0	3.7	54.4
N 11	343 46.0	40.1	16 08.1	10.1	27 07.3	3.9	54.4
D 12	358 46.1	N14 39.4	30 37.2	10.2	N27 03.4	3.9	54.3
A 13	13 46.3	38.6	45 06.4	10.2	26 59.5	4.1	54.3
Y 14	28 46.4	37.8	59 35.6	10.3	26 55.4	4.2	54.3
15	43 46.5 ..	37.1	74 04.9	10.3	26 51.2	4.4	54.3
16	58 46.6	36.3	88 34.2	10.4	26 46.8	4.4	54.3
17	73 46.7	35.5	103 03.6	10.5	26 42.4	4.6	54.3
18	88 46.8	N14 34.8	117 33.1	10.5	N26 37.8	4.8	54.3
19	103 46.9	34.0	132 02.6	10.5	26 33.0	4.8	54.3
20	118 47.0	33.2	146 32.1	10.6	26 28.2	5.0	54.2
21	133 47.2 ..	32.5	161 01.7	10.7	26 23.2	5.1	54.2
22	148 47.3	31.7	175 31.4	10.7	26 18.1	5.2	54.2
23	163 47.4	30.9	190 01.1	10.8	N26 12.9	5.3	54.2
	SD 15.8	d 0.8	SD 15.0		14.9		14.8

Lat.	Twilight Naut.	Twilight Civil	Sunrise	Moonrise 11	Moonrise 12	Moonrise 13	Moonrise 14
°	h m	h m	h m	h m	h m	h m	h m
N 72	////	////	01 59	▭	▭	▭	▭
N 70	////	////	02 39	▭	▭	▭	▭
68	////	01 13	03 05	▭	▭	▭	▭
66	////	02 03	03 26	▭	▭	▭	▭
64	////	02 33	03 42	▭	▭	▭	▭
62	01 05	02 55	03 55	21 08	22 08	23 55	25 39
60	01 50	03 13	04 06	22 15	23 11	24 33	00 33
N 58	02 18	03 27	04 16	22 49	23 45	24 59	00 59
56	02 39	03 40	04 24	23 15	24 10	00 10	01 20
54	02 55	03 50	04 32	23 35	24 35	00 30	01 38
52	03 09	04 00	04 39	23 52	24 47	00 47	01 52
50	03 21	04 08	04 45	24 06	00 06	01 01	02 05
45	03 45	04 25	04 58	24 36	00 36	01 30	02 32
N 40	04 03	04 39	05 08	00 11	00 59	01 53	02 52
35	04 18	04 51	05 17	00 29	01 18	02 12	03 10
30	04 30	05 00	05 25	00 45	01 34	02 28	03 24
20	04 49	05 16	05 39	01 11	02 02	02 55	03 50
N 10	05 03	05 29	05 51	01 34	02 26	03 19	04 11
0	05 15	05 40	06 02	01 55	02 48	03 41	04 31
S 10	05 26	05 51	06 12	02 17	03 11	04 03	04 52
20	05 35	06 01	06 24	02 40	03 35	04 26	05 13
30	05 44	06 12	06 37	03 06	04 02	04 53	05 38
35	05 48	06 18	06 44	03 22	04 19	05 09	05 52
40	05 52	06 24	06 53	03 41	04 38	05 28	06 09
45	05 57	06 32	07 02	04 03	05 02	05 50	06 30
S 50	06 02	06 40	07 14	04 32	05 32	06 19	06 55
52	06 04	06 44	07 20	04 46	05 47	06 33	07 07
54	06 06	06 48	07 26	05 02	06 04	06 50	07 21
56	06 08	06 52	07 32	05 22	06 25	07 09	07 37
58	06 11	06 57	07 40	05 46	06 51	07 33	07 56
S 60	06 13	07 03	07 48	06 18	07 28	08 05	08 20

Lat.	Sunset	Twilight Civil	Twilight Naut.	Moonset 11	Moonset 12	Moonset 13	Moonset 14
°	h m	h m	h m	h m	h m	h m	h m
N 72	22 04	////	////	▭	▭	▭	▭
N 70	21 27	////	////	▭	▭	▭	▭
68	21 02	22 48	////	▭	▭	▭	▭
66	20 42	22 03	////	▭	▭	▭	22 19
64	20 26	21 34	////	▭	▭	▭	21 20
62	20 13	21 12	22 57	19 59	20 49	20 49	20 46
60	20 02	20 55	22 16	18 53	19 46	20 11	20 21
N 58	19 53	20 41	21 49	18 18	19 12	19 44	20 01
56	19 44	20 29	21 29	17 53	18 47	19 22	19 45
54	19 37	20 18	21 13	17 33	18 27	19 05	19 31
52	19 30	20 09	20 59	17 16	18 10	18 50	19 18
50	19 24	20 01	20 47	17 01	17 55	18 37	19 07
45	19 12	19 44	20 24	16 32	17 26	18 10	18 45
N 40	19 01	19 30	20 06	16 09	17 03	17 48	18 26
35	18 52	19 19	19 52	15 50	16 44	17 31	18 11
30	18 44	19 10	19 40	15 34	16 27	17 15	17 57
20	18 31	18 54	19 21	15 06	16 00	16 49	17 34
N 10	18 19	18 41	19 07	14 43	15 36	16 27	17 14
0	18 09	18 30	18 55	14 21	15 14	16 05	16 55
S 10	17 58	18 19	18 45	13 59	14 51	15 44	16 36
20	17 47	18 09	18 35	13 35	14 28	15 22	16 16
30	17 34	17 59	18 27	13 08	14 00	14 55	15 52
35	17 26	17 53	18 23	12 52	13 43	14 39	15 38
40	17 18	17 46	18 18	12 33	13 24	14 21	15 22
45	17 08	17 39	18 14	12 10	13 01	13 59	15 02
S 50	16 57	17 31	18 09	11 41	12 31	13 31	14 38
52	16 51	17 27	18 07	11 27	12 16	13 17	14 26
54	16 45	17 23	18 05	11 10	11 58	13 01	14 13
56	16 39	17 19	18 03	10 51	11 37	12 41	13 57
58	16 31	17 14	18 01	10 26	11 11	12 18	13 38
S 60	16 23	17 08	17 58	09 53	10 34	11 46	13 15

	SUN Eqn. of Time 00ʰ	SUN Eqn. of Time 12ʰ	SUN Mer. Pass.	MOON Mer. Pass. Upper	MOON Mer. Pass. Lower	Age	Phase
Day	m s	m s	h m	h m	h m	d	%
11	05 21	05 16	12 05	08 08	20 35	25	21
12	05 11	05 06	12 05	09 01	21 27	26	14
13	05 01	04 56	12 05	09 53	22 19	27	8

© British Crown Copyright 2022. All rights reserved.

UT	ARIES GHA	VENUS −4.1 GHA	Dec	MARS +1.8 GHA	Dec	JUPITER −2.5 GHA	Dec	SATURN +0.4 GHA	Dec	STARS Name	SHA	Dec
14 00	322 09.6	182 04.2	N 7 25.0	149 45.7	N 4 09.4	279 25.0	N15 04.9	344 49.6	S11 22.6	Acamar	315 12.6	S40 12.3
01	337 12.1	197 08.2	25.3	164 46.7	08.8	294 27.3	04.9	359 52.3	22.7	Achernar	335 20.8	S57 06.7
02	352 14.5	212 12.2	25.5	179 47.7	08.1	309 29.6	04.9	14 54.9	22.8	Acrux	173 01.9	S63 13.9
03	7 17.0	227 16.2 ..	25.7	194 48.7 ..	07.5	324 31.9 ..	05.0	29 57.5 ..	22.9	Adhara	255 07.1	S29 00.0
04	22 19.5	242 20.2	26.0	209 49.7	06.8	339 34.2	05.0	45 00.2	22.9	Aldebaran	290 41.1	N16 33.4
05	37 21.9	257 24.3	26.2	224 50.8	06.2	354 36.5	05.1	60 02.8	23.0			
06	52 24.4	272 28.3	N 7 26.5	239 51.8	N 4 05.5	9 38.8	N15 05.1	75 05.4	S11 23.1	Alioth	166 14.3	N55 50.2
M 07	67 26.9	287 32.3	26.7	254 52.8	04.9	24 41.1	05.2	90 08.1	23.1	Alkaid	152 53.1	N49 12.0
O 08	82 29.3	302 36.3	27.0	269 53.8	04.3	39 43.3	05.2	105 10.7	23.2	Alnair	27 33.9	S46 50.7
N 09	97 31.8	317 40.3 ..	27.2	284 54.8 ..	03.6	54 45.6 ..	05.2	120 13.3 ..	23.3	Alnilam	275 39.1	S 1 11.1
D 10	112 34.3	332 44.3	27.4	299 55.8	03.0	69 47.9	05.3	135 16.0	23.3	Alphard	217 49.2	S 8 45.5
A 11	127 36.7	347 48.3	27.7	314 56.9	02.3	84 50.2	05.3	150 18.6	23.4			
Y 12	142 39.2	2 52.3	N 7 27.9	329 57.9	N 4 01.7	99 52.5	N15 05.4	165 21.2	S11 23.5	Alphecca	126 04.7	N26 38.3
13	157 41.7	17 56.3	28.2	344 58.9	01.0	114 54.8	05.4	180 23.9	23.6	Alpheratz	357 35.7	N29 13.2
14	172 44.1	33 00.3	28.4	359 59.9	4 00.4	129 57.1	05.4	195 26.5	23.6	Altair	62 00.8	N 8 55.9
15	187 46.6	48 04.3 ..	28.7	15 00.9	3 59.7	144 59.4 ..	05.5	210 29.1 ..	23.7	Ankaa	353 08.0	S42 10.5
16	202 49.0	63 08.3	28.9	30 02.0	59.1	160 01.7	05.5	225 31.8	23.8	Antares	112 17.1	S26 29.1
17	217 51.5	78 12.3	29.2	45 03.0	58.5	175 04.0	05.6	240 34.4	23.8			
18	232 54.0	93 16.3	N 7 29.5	60 04.0	N 3 57.8	190 06.3	N15 05.6	255 37.0	S11 23.9	Arcturus	145 49.1	N19 03.8
19	247 56.4	108 20.3	29.7	75 05.0	57.2	205 08.6	05.7	270 39.7	24.0	Atria	107 12.2	S69 04.4
20	262 58.9	123 24.3	30.0	90 06.0	56.5	220 10.9	05.7	285 42.3	24.1	Avior	234 15.8	S59 34.9
21	278 01.4	138 28.3 ..	30.2	105 07.1 ..	55.9	235 13.2 ..	05.7	300 44.9 ..	24.1	Bellatrix	278 24.3	N 6 22.4
22	293 03.8	153 32.3	30.5	120 08.1	55.2	250 15.5	05.8	315 47.6	24.2	Betelgeuse	270 53.5	N 7 24.8
23	308 06.3	168 36.3	30.7	135 09.1	54.6	265 17.8	05.8	330 50.2	24.3			
15 00	323 08.8	183 40.3	N 7 31.0	150 10.1	N 3 53.9	280 20.1	N15 05.9	345 52.8	S11 24.3	Canopus	263 53.3	S52 42.2
01	338 11.2	198 44.3	31.3	165 11.1	53.3	295 22.4	05.9	0 55.5	24.4	Capella	280 23.8	N46 01.2
02	353 13.7	213 48.3	31.5	180 12.1	52.7	310 24.7	05.9	15 58.1	24.5	Deneb	49 26.1	N45 21.9
03	8 16.1	228 52.3 ..	31.8	195 13.2 ..	52.0	325 27.0 ..	06.0	31 00.8 ..	24.6	Denebola	182 26.4	N14 26.6
04	23 18.6	243 56.3	32.1	210 14.2	51.4	340 29.3	06.0	46 03.4	24.6	Diphda	348 48.2	S17 51.3
05	38 21.1	259 00.3	32.3	225 15.2	50.7	355 31.6	06.1	61 06.0	24.7			
06	53 23.5	274 04.3	N 7 32.6	240 16.2	N 3 50.1	10 33.9	N15 06.1	76 08.7	S11 24.8	Dubhe	193 43.0	N61 37.6
T 07	68 26.0	289 08.3	32.9	255 17.2	49.4	25 36.2	06.1	91 11.3	24.8	Elnath	278 03.5	N28 37.6
U 08	83 28.5	304 12.3	33.1	270 18.3	48.8	40 38.5	06.2	106 13.9	24.9	Eltanin	90 42.4	N51 29.3
E 09	98 30.9	319 16.3 ..	33.4	285 19.3 ..	48.1	55 40.8 ..	06.2	121 16.6 ..	25.0	Enif	33 39.6	N 9 59.0
S 10	113 33.4	334 20.2	33.7	300 20.3	47.5	70 43.1	06.3	136 19.2	25.1	Fomalhaut	15 15.4	S29 29.7
D 11	128 35.9	349 24.2	33.9	315 21.3	46.9	85 45.4	06.3	151 21.8	25.1			
A 12	143 38.3	4 28.2	N 7 34.2	330 22.3	N 3 46.2	100 47.7	N15 06.3	166 24.5	S11 25.2	Gacrux	171 53.4	S57 14.8
Y 13	158 40.8	19 32.2	34.5	345 23.3	45.6	115 50.0	06.4	181 27.1	25.3	Gienah	175 45.0	S17 40.3
14	173 43.3	34 36.2	34.8	0 24.4	44.9	130 52.3	06.4	196 29.7	25.3	Hadar	148 37.9	S60 29.4
15	188 45.7	49 40.2 ..	35.0	15 25.4 ..	44.3	145 54.6 ..	06.5	211 32.4 ..	25.4	Hamal	327 52.4	N23 34.4
16	203 48.2	64 44.1	35.3	30 26.4	43.6	160 56.9	06.5	226 35.0	25.5	Kaus Aust.	83 33.8	S34 22.4
17	218 50.6	79 48.1	35.6	45 27.4	43.0	175 59.2	06.5	241 37.7	25.6			
18	233 53.1	94 52.1	N 7 35.9	60 28.4	N 3 42.3	191 01.5	N15 06.6	256 40.3	S11 25.6	Kochab	137 19.9	N74 03.8
19	248 55.6	109 56.1	36.2	75 29.5	41.7	206 03.8	06.6	271 42.9	25.7	Markab	13 30.7	N15 20.0
20	263 58.0	125 00.0	36.4	90 30.5	41.0	221 06.1	06.6	286 45.6	25.8	Menkar	314 07.3	N 4 11.0
21	279 00.5	140 04.0 ..	36.7	105 31.5 ..	40.4	236 08.4 ..	06.7	301 48.2 ..	25.8	Menkent	147 59.1	S36 29.2
22	294 03.0	155 08.0	37.0	120 32.5	39.8	251 10.7	06.7	316 50.8	25.9	Miaplacidus	221 39.5	S69 48.7
23	309 05.4	170 12.0	37.3	135 33.5	39.1	266 13.0	06.8	331 53.5	26.0			
16 00	324 07.9	185 15.9	N 7 37.6	150 34.5	N 3 38.5	281 15.3	N15 06.8	346 56.1	S11 26.1	Mirfak	308 29.9	N49 56.5
01	339 10.4	200 19.9	37.9	165 35.6	37.8	296 17.6	06.8	1 58.7	26.1	Nunki	75 48.9	S26 16.0
02	354 12.8	215 23.9	38.1	180 36.6	37.2	311 19.9	06.9	17 01.4	26.2	Peacock	53 07.0	S56 39.6
03	9 15.3	230 27.8 ..	38.4	195 37.6 ..	36.5	326 22.2 ..	06.9	32 04.0 ..	26.3	Pollux	243 19.0	N27 58.2
04	24 17.8	245 31.8	38.7	210 38.6	35.9	341 24.5	07.0	47 06.6	26.3	Procyon	244 52.3	N 5 10.0
05	39 20.2	260 35.8	39.0	225 39.6	35.2	356 26.9	07.0	62 09.3	26.4			
06	54 22.7	275 39.7	N 7 39.3	240 40.7	N 3 34.6	11 29.2	N15 07.0	77 11.9	S11 26.5	Rasalhague	95 59.4	N12 32.7
W 07	69 25.1	290 43.7	39.6	255 41.7	33.9	26 31.5	07.1	92 14.6	26.6	Regulus	207 36.0	N11 51.3
E 08	84 27.6	305 47.6	39.9	270 42.7	33.3	41 33.8	07.1	107 17.2	26.6	Rigel	281 05.1	S 8 10.3
D 09	99 30.1	320 51.6 ..	40.2	285 43.7 ..	32.6	56 36.1 ..	07.1	122 19.8 ..	26.7	Rigil Kent.	139 42.0	S60 56.1
N 10	114 32.5	335 55.6	40.5	300 44.7	32.0	71 38.4	07.2	137 22.5	26.8	Sabik	102 03.9	S15 45.2
E 11	129 35.0	350 59.5	40.8	315 45.7	31.4	86 40.7	07.2	152 25.1	26.8			
S 12	144 37.5	6 03.5	N 7 41.1	330 46.8	N 3 30.7	101 43.0	N15 07.3	167 27.7	S11 26.9	Schedar	349 32.0	N56 39.8
D 13	159 39.9	21 07.4	41.4	345 47.8	30.1	116 45.3	07.3	182 30.4	27.0	Shaula	96 11.7	S37 07.3
A 14	174 42.4	36 11.4	41.7	0 48.8	29.4	131 47.6	07.3	197 33.0	27.1	Sirius	258 27.5	S16 44.7
Y 15	189 44.9	51 15.3 ..	42.0	15 49.8 ..	28.8	146 49.9 ..	07.4	212 35.6 ..	27.1	Spica	158 23.7	S11 17.0
16	204 47.3	66 19.3	42.3	30 50.8	28.1	161 52.3	07.4	227 38.3	27.2	Suhail	222 47.6	S43 31.5
17	219 49.8	81 23.2	42.6	45 51.8	27.5	176 54.6	07.4	242 40.9	27.3			
18	234 52.2	96 27.1	N 7 42.9	60 52.9	N 3 26.8	191 56.9	N15 07.5	257 43.6	S11 27.3	Vega	80 33.7	N38 48.5
19	249 54.7	111 31.1	43.2	75 53.9	26.2	206 59.2	07.5	272 46.2	27.4	Zuben'ubi	136 57.3	S16 08.4
20	264 57.2	126 35.0	43.5	90 54.9	25.5	222 01.5	07.5	287 48.8	27.5			
21	279 59.6	141 39.0 ..	43.8	105 55.9 ..	24.9	237 03.8 ..	07.6	302 51.5 ..	27.6		SHA	Mer. Pass.
22	295 02.1	156 42.9	44.1	120 56.9	24.2	252 06.1	07.6	317 54.1	27.6	Venus	220 31.6	11 42
23	310 04.6	171 46.8	44.4	135 57.9	23.6	267 08.4	07.7	332 56.7	27.7	Mars	187 01.4	13 58
Mer. Pass.	h m 2 27.0	v 4.0 d 0.3		v 1.0 d 0.6		v 2.3 d 0.0		v 2.6 d 0.1		Jupiter	317 11.3	5 18
										Saturn	22 44.1	0 56

© British Crown Copyright 2022. All rights reserved.

SUN / MOON

UT	SUN GHA	SUN Dec	MOON GHA	v	MOON Dec	d	HP
d h	° ′	° ′	° ′	′	° ′	′	′
14 00	178 47.5	N14 30.2	204 30.9	10.9	N26 07.6	5.5	54.2
01	193 47.6	29.4	219 00.8	10.9	26 02.1	5.6	54.2
02	208 47.7	28.6	233 30.7	11.0	25 56.5	5.7	54.2
03	223 47.8	.. 27.9	248 00.7	11.0	25 50.8	5.8	54.2
04	238 48.0	27.1	262 30.7	11.1	25 45.0	5.9	54.2
05	253 48.1	26.3	277 00.8	11.2	25 39.1	6.1	54.2
06	268 48.2	N14 25.6	291 31.0	11.2	N25 33.0	6.2	54.2
07	283 48.3	24.8	306 01.2	11.3	25 26.8	6.3	54.1
08	298 48.4	24.0	320 31.5	11.3	25 20.5	6.4	54.1
M 09	313 48.5	.. 23.3	335 01.8	11.4	25 14.1	6.5	54.1
O 10	328 48.7	22.5	349 32.2	11.5	25 07.6	6.6	54.1
N 11	343 48.8	21.7	4 02.7	11.5	25 01.0	6.8	54.1
D 12	358 48.9	N14 21.0	18 33.2	11.7	N24 54.2	6.8	54.1
A 13	13 49.0	20.2	33 03.9	11.6	24 47.4	7.0	54.1
Y 14	28 49.1	19.4	47 34.5	11.8	24 40.4	7.1	54.1
15	43 49.2	.. 18.6	62 05.3	11.8	24 33.3	7.2	54.1
16	58 49.4	17.9	76 36.1	11.9	24 26.1	7.3	54.1
17	73 49.5	17.1	91 07.0	11.9	24 18.8	7.4	54.1
18	88 49.6	N14 16.3	105 37.9	12.0	N24 11.4	7.5	54.1
19	103 49.7	15.5	120 08.9	12.1	24 03.9	7.6	54.1
20	118 49.8	14.8	134 40.0	12.2	23 56.3	7.7	54.0
21	133 49.9	.. 14.0	149 11.2	12.2	23 48.6	7.8	54.0
22	148 50.1	13.2	163 42.4	12.3	23 40.8	8.0	54.0
23	163 50.2	12.4	178 13.7	12.3	23 32.8	8.0	54.0
15 00	178 50.3	N14 11.7	192 45.0	12.4	N23 24.8	8.1	54.0
01	193 50.4	10.9	207 16.4	12.5	23 16.7	8.2	54.0
02	208 50.5	10.1	221 47.9	12.6	23 08.5	8.4	54.0
03	223 50.7	.. 09.3	236 19.5	12.6	23 00.1	8.4	54.0
04	238 50.8	08.6	250 51.1	12.7	22 51.7	8.5	54.0
05	253 50.9	07.8	265 22.8	12.8	22 43.2	8.7	54.0
06	268 51.0	N14 07.0	279 54.6	12.8	N22 34.5	8.7	54.0
07	283 51.1	06.2	294 26.4	12.9	22 25.8	8.8	54.0
T 08	298 51.3	05.5	308 58.3	13.0	22 17.0	8.9	54.0
U 09	313 51.4	.. 04.7	323 30.3	13.0	22 08.1	9.0	54.0
E 10	328 51.5	03.9	338 02.3	13.1	21 59.1	9.1	54.0
S 11	343 51.6	03.1	352 34.4	13.2	21 50.0	9.2	54.0
D 12	358 51.8	N14 02.3	7 06.6	13.2	N21 40.8	9.3	54.0
A 13	13 51.9	01.6	21 38.8	13.4	21 31.5	9.4	54.0
Y 14	28 52.0	00.8	36 11.2	13.3	21 22.1	9.4	54.0
15	43 52.1	14 00.0	50 43.5	13.5	21 12.7	9.6	54.0
16	58 52.2	13 59.2	65 16.0	13.5	21 03.1	9.6	54.0
17	73 52.4	58.4	79 48.5	13.6	20 53.5	9.7	54.0
18	88 52.5	N13 57.6	94 21.1	13.6	N20 43.8	9.8	53.9
19	103 52.6	56.9	108 53.7	13.7	20 34.0	9.9	53.9
20	118 52.7	56.1	123 26.4	13.8	20 24.1	10.0	53.9
21	133 52.9	.. 55.3	137 59.2	13.9	20 14.1	10.0	53.9
22	148 53.0	54.5	152 32.1	13.9	20 04.1	10.2	53.9
23	163 53.1	53.7	167 05.0	14.0	19 53.9	10.2	53.9
16 00	178 53.2	N13 52.9	181 38.0	14.0	N19 43.7	10.3	53.9
01	193 53.4	52.2	196 11.0	14.1	19 33.4	10.4	53.9
02	208 53.5	51.4	210 44.1	14.2	19 23.0	10.4	53.9
03	223 53.6	.. 50.6	225 17.3	14.2	19 12.6	10.6	53.9
04	238 53.7	49.8	239 50.5	14.3	19 02.0	10.6	53.9
05	253 53.9	49.0	254 23.8	14.4	18 51.4	10.7	53.9
06	268 54.0	N13 48.2	268 57.2	14.4	N18 40.7	10.7	53.9
W 07	283 54.1	47.4	283 30.6	14.5	18 30.0	10.9	53.9
E 08	298 54.2	46.6	298 04.1	14.5	18 19.1	10.9	53.9
D 09	313 54.4	.. 45.9	312 37.6	14.6	18 08.2	10.9	53.9
N 10	328 54.5	45.1	327 11.2	14.7	17 57.3	11.1	53.9
E 11	343 54.6	44.3	341 44.9	14.7	17 46.2	11.1	53.9
S 12	358 54.8	N13 43.5	356 18.6	14.8	N17 35.1	11.2	53.9
D 13	13 54.9	42.7	10 52.4	14.9	17 23.9	11.3	53.9
A 14	28 55.0	41.9	25 26.3	14.9	17 12.6	11.3	53.9
Y 15	43 55.1	.. 41.1	40 00.2	14.9	17 01.3	11.4	53.9
16	58 55.3	40.3	54 34.1	15.0	16 49.9	11.4	53.9
17	73 55.4	39.5	69 08.1	15.1	16 38.5	11.6	53.9
18	88 55.5	N13 38.7	83 42.2	15.1	N16 26.9	11.6	53.9
19	103 55.7	38.0	98 16.3	15.2	16 15.3	11.6	53.9
20	118 55.8	37.2	112 50.5	15.3	16 03.7	11.7	53.9
21	133 55.9	.. 36.4	127 24.8	15.3	15 52.0	11.8	53.9
22	148 56.0	35.6	141 59.1	15.3	15 40.2	11.8	53.9
23	163 56.2	34.8	156 33.4	15.4	N15 28.4	11.9	53.9
	SD 15.8	d 0.8	SD 14.7		14.7		14.7

Twilight / Sunrise / Moonrise

Lat.	Naut.	Civil	Sunrise	Moonrise 14	15	16	17
°	h m	h m	h m	h m	h m	h m	h m
N 72	////	////	02 22	▢	▢	▢	03 09
N 70	////	////	02 55	▢	▢	00 48	03 42
68	////	01 41	03 18	▢	▢	01 57	04 05
66	////	02 19	03 36	▢	00 08	02 32	04 23
64	////	02 46	03 51	▢	01 06	02 58	04 38
62	01 30	03 06	04 03	25 39	01 39	03 17	04 50
60	02 05	03 22	04 13	00 33	02 03	03 33	05 00
N 58	02 29	03 35	04 22	00 59	02 22	03 47	05 09
56	02 48	03 47	04 30	01 20	02 38	03 58	05 17
54	03 03	03 57	04 37	01 38	02 52	04 08	05 24
52	03 16	04 05	04 43	01 52	03 04	04 17	05 30
50	03 27	04 13	04 49	02 05	03 15	04 25	05 36
45	03 50	04 29	05 01	02 32	03 36	04 42	05 48
N 40	04 07	04 42	05 11	02 52	03 54	04 56	05 57
35	04 21	04 53	05 20	03 10	04 09	05 08	06 06
30	04 32	05 02	05 27	03 24	04 22	05 18	06 13
20	04 50	05 17	05 40	03 50	04 43	05 35	06 26
N 10	05 04	05 29	05 51	04 11	05 02	05 51	06 37
0	05 15	05 40	06 01	04 31	05 19	06 05	06 47
S 10	05 25	05 50	06 11	04 52	05 37	06 19	06 58
20	05 33	05 59	06 22	05 13	05 55	06 34	07 09
30	05 41	06 09	06 34	05 38	06 17	06 51	07 21
35	05 45	06 15	06 41	05 52	06 29	07 01	07 28
40	05 49	06 21	06 49	06 09	06 43	07 12	07 36
45	05 53	06 27	06 58	06 30	07 00	07 25	07 46
S 50	05 57	06 35	07 09	06 55	07 21	07 41	07 57
52	05 59	06 38	07 14	07 07	07 31	07 49	08 02
54	06 00	06 42	07 19	07 21	07 42	07 57	08 08
56	06 02	06 46	07 25	07 37	07 55	08 06	08 14
58	06 04	06 50	07 32	07 56	08 09	08 17	08 21
S 60	06 06	06 55	07 40	08 20	08 26	08 29	08 29

Sunset / Twilight / Moonset

Lat.	Sunset	Civil	Naut.	Moonset 14	15	16	17
°	h m	h m	h m	h m	h m	h m	h m
N 72	21 41	////	////	▢	▢	22 27	21 34
N 70	21 10	23 40	////	▢	23 16	21 52	21 17
68	20 48	22 21	////	▢	22 06	21 27	21 03
66	20 30	21 45	////	22 19	21 29	21 08	20 52
64	20 16	21 20	23 43	21 20	21 03	20 52	20 43
62	20 04	21 01	22 33	20 46	20 43	20 39	20 35
60	19 54	20 45	22 01	20 21	20 26	20 27	20 28
N 58	19 45	20 32	21 37	20 01	20 12	20 18	20 22
56	19 38	20 21	21 19	19 45	19 59	20 09	20 16
54	19 31	20 11	21 04	19 31	19 49	20 01	20 11
52	19 25	20 03	20 51	19 18	19 39	19 54	20 07
50	19 19	19 55	20 40	19 07	19 30	19 48	20 03
45	19 07	19 39	20 18	18 45	19 12	19 35	19 54
N 40	18 57	19 26	20 01	18 26	18 57	19 23	19 46
35	18 49	19 16	19 48	18 11	18 45	19 13	19 40
30	18 41	19 07	19 36	17 57	18 33	19 05	19 34
20	18 29	18 52	19 19	17 34	18 14	18 51	19 24
N 10	18 18	18 40	19 05	17 14	17 57	18 38	19 15
0	18 08	18 29	18 54	16 55	17 42	18 26	19 07
S 10	17 58	18 20	18 45	16 36	17 26	18 13	18 59
20	17 47	18 10	18 36	16 16	17 09	18 00	18 50
30	17 35	18 00	18 28	15 52	16 49	17 45	18 40
35	17 29	17 55	18 25	15 38	16 37	17 36	18 34
40	17 21	17 49	18 21	15 22	16 24	17 26	18 27
45	17 12	17 42	18 17	15 02	16 08	17 14	18 19
S 50	17 01	17 35	18 13	14 38	15 49	16 59	18 09
52	16 56	17 32	18 11	14 26	15 39	16 52	18 05
54	16 51	17 28	18 10	14 13	15 29	16 45	18 00
56	16 44	17 24	18 08	13 57	15 17	16 36	17 54
58	16 38	17 20	18 06	13 38	15 03	16 27	17 48
S 60	16 30	17 15	18 04	13 15	14 46	16 15	17 41

SUN / MOON

Day	Eqn. of Time 00ʰ	12ʰ	Mer. Pass.	Mer. Pass. Upper	Lower	Age	Phase
d	m s	m s	h m	h m	h m	d	%
14	04 50	04 45	12 05	10 43	23 07	28	3
15	04 39	04 33	12 05	11 31	23 53	29	1
16	04 27	04 21	12 04	12 15	24 37	00	0

© British Crown Copyright 2022. All rights reserved.

UT	ARIES	VENUS −4·0		MARS +1·8		JUPITER −2·5		SATURN +0·4		STARS		
	GHA	GHA	Dec	GHA	Dec	GHA	Dec	GHA	Dec	Name	SHA	Dec
d h	° ′	° ′	° ′	° ′	° ′	° ′	° ′	° ′	° ′		° ′	° ′
17 00	325 07.0	186 50.8 N 7 44.7		150 59.0 N 3 22.9		282 10.7 N15 07.7		347 59.4 S11 27.8		Acamar	315 12.6	S40 12.3
01	340 09.5	201 54.7	45.0	166 00.0	22.3	297 13.1	07.7	3 02.0	27.8	Achernar	335 20.7	S57 06.7
02	355 12.0	216 58.6	45.3	181 01.0	21.6	312 15.4	07.8	18 04.7	27.9	Acrux	173 01.9	S63 13.9
03	10 14.4	232 02.6 ..	45.6	196 02.0 ..	21.0	327 17.7 ..	07.8	33 07.3 ..	28.0	Adhara	255 07.1	S29 00.0
04	25 16.9	247 06.5	45.9	211 03.0	20.4	342 20.0	07.8	48 09.9	28.1	Aldebaran	290 41.0	N16 33.4
05	40 19.4	262 10.4	46.2	226 04.0	19.7	357 22.3	07.9	63 12.6	28.1			
06	55 21.8	277 14.3 N 7 46.6		241 05.1 N 3 19.1		12 24.6 N15 07.9		78 15.2 S11 28.2		Alioth	166 14.3	N55 50.2
07	70 24.3	292 18.2	46.9	256 06.1	18.4	27 26.9	07.9	93 17.8	28.3	Alkaid	152 53.1	N49 12.0
T 08	85 26.7	307 22.2	47.2	271 07.1	17.8	42 29.3	08.0	108 20.5	28.3	Alnair	27 33.9	S46 50.7
H 09	100 29.2	322 26.1 ..	47.5	286 08.1 ..	17.1	57 31.6 ..	08.0	123 23.1 ..	28.4	Alnilam	275 39.1	S 1 11.1
U 10	115 31.7	337 30.0	47.8	301 09.1	16.5	72 33.9	08.0	138 25.8	28.5	Alphard	217 49.2	S 8 45.5
R 11	130 34.1	352 33.9	48.1	316 10.1	15.8	87 36.2	08.1	153 28.4	28.6			
S 12	145 36.6	7 37.8 N 7 48.4		331 11.2 N 3 15.2		102 38.5 N15 08.1		168 31.0 S11 28.6		Alphecca	126 04.7	N26 38.3
D 13	160 39.1	22 41.7	48.8	346 12.2	14.5	117 40.8	08.1	183 33.7	28.7	Alpheratz	357 35.7	N29 13.2
A 14	175 41.5	37 45.6	49.1	1 13.2	13.9	132 43.2	08.2	198 36.3	28.8	Altair	62 00.8	N 8 55.9
Y 15	190 44.0	52 49.5 ..	49.4	16 14.2 ..	13.2	147 45.5 ..	08.2	213 38.9 ..	28.8	Ankaa	353 07.9	S42 10.5
16	205 46.5	67 53.4	49.7	31 15.2	12.6	162 47.8	08.3	228 41.6	28.9	Antares	112 17.2	S26 29.1
17	220 48.9	82 57.4	50.0	46 16.2	11.9	177 50.1	08.3	243 44.2	29.0			
18	235 51.4	98 01.3 N 7 50.4		61 17.3 N 3 11.3		192 52.4 N15 08.3		258 46.9 S11 29.1		Arcturus	145 49.1	N19 03.8
19	250 53.9	113 05.1	50.7	76 18.3	10.6	207 54.8	08.4	273 49.5	29.1	Atria	107 12.2	S69 04.4
20	265 56.3	128 09.0	51.0	91 19.3	10.0	222 57.1	08.4	288 52.1	29.2	Avior	234 15.8	S59 34.9
21	280 58.8	143 12.9 ..	51.3	106 20.3 ..	09.3	237 59.4 ..	08.4	303 54.8 ..	29.3	Bellatrix	278 24.3	N 6 22.4
22	296 01.2	158 16.8	51.7	121 21.3	08.7	253 01.7	08.5	318 57.4	29.3	Betelgeuse	270 53.5	N 7 24.8
23	311 03.7	173 20.7	52.0	136 22.3	08.0	268 04.0	08.5	334 00.0	29.4			
18 00	326 06.2	188 24.6 N 7 52.3		151 23.3 N 3 07.4		283 06.4 N15 08.5		349 02.7 S11 29.5		Canopus	263 53.3	S52 42.2
01	341 08.6	203 28.5	52.6	166 24.4	06.7	298 08.7	08.6	4 05.3	29.6	Capella	280 23.8	N46 01.2
02	356 11.1	218 32.4	53.0	181 25.4	06.1	313 11.0	08.6	19 08.0	29.6	Deneb	49 26.1	N45 21.9
03	11 13.6	233 36.3 ..	53.3	196 26.4 ..	05.4	328 13.3 ..	08.6	34 10.6 ..	29.7	Denebola	182 26.4	N14 26.6
04	26 16.0	248 40.1	53.6	211 27.4	04.8	343 15.6	08.7	49 13.2	29.8	Diphda	348 48.2	S17 51.3
05	41 18.5	263 44.0	54.0	226 28.4	04.1	358 18.0	08.7	64 15.9	29.9			
06	56 21.0	278 47.9 N 7 54.3		241 29.4 N 3 03.5		13 20.3 N15 08.7		79 18.5 S11 29.9		Dubhe	193 43.0	N61 37.6
07	71 23.4	293 51.8	54.6	256 30.5	02.8	28 22.6	08.8	94 21.2	30.0	Elnath	278 03.5	N28 37.6
08	86 25.9	308 55.6	54.9	271 31.5	02.2	43 24.9	08.8	109 23.8	30.1	Eltanin	90 42.4	N51 29.4
F 09	101 28.3	323 59.5 ..	55.3	286 32.5 ..	01.5	58 27.3 ..	08.8	124 26.4 ..	30.1	Enif	33 39.6	N 9 59.1
R 10	116 30.8	339 03.4	55.6	301 33.5	00.9	73 29.6	08.9	139 29.1	30.2	Fomalhaut	15 15.4	S29 29.7
I 11	131 33.3	354 07.2	56.0	316 34.5	3 00.3	88 31.9	08.9	154 31.7	30.3			
D 12	146 35.7	9 11.1 N 7 56.3		331 35.5 N 2 59.6		103 34.2 N15 08.9		169 34.3 S11 30.4		Gacrux	171 53.4	S57 14.8
A 13	161 38.2	24 15.0	56.6	346 36.6	59.0	118 36.6	09.0	184 37.0	30.4	Gienah	175 45.0	S17 40.3
Y 14	176 40.7	39 18.8	57.0	1 37.6	58.3	133 38.9	09.0	199 39.6	30.5	Hadar	148 37.9	S60 29.4
15	191 43.1	54 22.7 ..	57.3	16 38.6 ..	57.7	148 41.2 ..	09.0	214 42.3 ..	30.6	Hamal	327 52.4	N23 34.4
16	206 45.6	69 26.5	57.6	31 39.6	57.0	163 43.5	09.0	229 44.9	30.6	Kaus Aust.	83 33.8	S34 22.5
17	221 48.1	84 30.4	58.0	46 40.6	56.4	178 45.9	09.1	244 47.5	30.7			
18	236 50.5	99 34.2 N 7 58.3		61 41.6 N 2 55.7		193 48.2 N15 09.1		259 50.2 S11 30.8		Kochab	137 19.9	N74 03.8
19	251 53.0	114 38.1	58.7	76 42.6	55.1	208 50.5	09.1	274 52.8	30.9	Markab	13 30.7	N15 20.0
20	266 55.5	129 41.9	59.0	91 43.7	54.4	223 52.8	09.2	289 55.5	30.9	Menkar	314 07.3	N 4 11.0
21	281 57.9	144 45.8 ..	59.3	106 44.7 ..	53.8	238 55.2 ..	09.2	304 58.1 ..	31.0	Menkent	147 59.1	S36 29.2
22	297 00.4	159 49.6	7 59.7	121 45.7	53.1	253 57.5	09.2	320 00.7	31.1	Miaplacidus	221 39.5	S69 48.7
23	312 02.8	174 53.4	8 00.0	136 46.7	52.5	268 59.8	09.3	335 03.4	31.1			
19 00	327 05.3	189 57.3 N 8 00.4		151 47.7 N 2 51.8		284 02.1 N15 09.3		350 06.0 S11 31.2		Mirfak	308 29.9	N49 56.5
01	342 07.8	205 01.1	00.7	166 48.7	51.2	299 04.5	09.3	5 08.7	31.3	Nunki	75 48.9	S26 16.1
02	357 10.2	220 04.9	01.1	181 49.7	50.5	314 06.8	09.4	20 11.3	31.4	Peacock	53 07.0	S56 39.6
03	12 12.7	235 08.8 ..	01.4	196 50.8 ..	49.9	329 09.1 ..	09.4	35 13.9 ..	31.4	Pollux	243 19.0	N27 58.2
04	27 15.2	250 12.6	01.7	211 51.8	49.2	344 11.5	09.4	50 16.6	31.5	Procyon	244 52.3	N 5 10.0
05	42 17.6	265 16.4	02.1	226 52.8	48.6	359 13.8	09.5	65 19.2	31.6			
06	57 20.1	280 20.2 N 8 02.4		241 53.8 N 2 47.9		14 16.1 N15 09.5		80 21.8 S11 31.7		Rasalhague	95 59.4	N12 32.7
07	72 22.6	295 24.0	02.8	256 54.8	47.3	29 18.5	09.5	95 24.5	31.7	Regulus	207 36.0	N11 51.3
S 08	87 25.0	310 27.9	03.1	271 55.8	46.6	44 20.8	09.5	110 27.1	31.8	Rigel	281 05.1	S 8 10.3
A 09	102 27.5	325 31.7 ..	03.5	286 56.8 ..	46.0	59 23.1 ..	09.6	125 29.8 ..	31.9	Rigil Kent.	139 42.1	S60 56.1
T 10	117 29.9	340 35.5	03.8	301 57.9	45.3	74 25.4	09.6	140 32.4	31.9	Sabik	102 04.0	S15 45.2
U 11	132 32.4	355 39.3	04.2	316 58.9	44.7	89 27.8	09.6	155 35.0	32.0			
R 12	147 34.9	10 43.1 N 8 04.5		331 59.9 N 2 44.0		104 30.1 N15 09.7		170 37.7 S11 32.1		Schedar	349 32.0	N56 39.8
D 13	162 37.3	25 46.9	04.9	347 00.9	43.4	119 32.4	09.7	185 40.3	32.2	Shaula	96 11.7	S37 07.3
A 14	177 39.8	40 50.7	05.2	2 01.9	42.7	134 34.8	09.7	200 43.0	32.2	Sirius	258 27.5	S16 44.7
Y 15	192 42.3	55 54.5 ..	05.6	17 02.9 ..	42.0	149 37.1 ..	09.8	215 45.6 ..	32.3	Spica	158 23.7	S11 17.0
16	207 44.7	70 58.3	05.9	32 03.9	41.4	164 39.4	09.8	230 48.2	32.4	Suhail	222 47.6	S43 31.5
17	222 47.2	86 02.1	06.3	47 05.0	40.7	179 41.8	09.8	245 50.9	32.4			
18	237 49.7	101 05.9 N 8 06.7		62 06.0 N 2 40.1		194 44.1 N15 09.8		260 53.5 S11 32.5		Vega	80 33.7	N38 48.5
19	252 52.1	116 09.7	07.0	77 07.0	39.4	209 46.4	09.9	275 56.2	32.6	Zuben'ubi	136 57.4	S16 08.4
20	267 54.6	131 13.4	07.4	92 08.0	38.8	224 48.8	09.9	290 58.8	32.7			
21	282 57.1	146 17.2 ..	07.7	107 09.0 ..	38.1	239 51.1 ..	09.9	306 01.4 ..	32.7		SHA	Mer. Pass.
22	297 59.5	161 21.0	08.1	122 10.0	37.5	254 53.5	10.0	321 04.1	32.8	Venus	222 18.4	11 23
23	313 02.0	176 24.8	08.4	137 11.0	36.8	269 55.8	10.0	336 06.7	32.9	Mars	185 17.2	13 54
	h m									Jupiter	317 00.2	5 07
Mer. Pass. 2 15.2		v 3.9 d 0.3		v 1.0 d 0.6		v 2.3 d 0.0		v 2.6 d 0.1		Saturn	22 56.5	0 44

© British Crown Copyright 2022. All rights reserved.

SUN and MOON

UT	SUN GHA	SUN Dec	MOON GHA	v	MOON Dec	d	HP
d h	° ′	° ′	° ′	′	° ′	′	′
17 00	178 56.3	N13 34.0	171 07.8	15.5	N15 16.5	12.0	53.9
01	193 56.4	33.2	185 42.3	15.5	15 04.5	12.0	53.9
02	208 56.6	32.4	200 16.8	15.5	14 52.5	12.1	53.9
03	223 56.7	.. 31.6	214 51.3	15.6	14 40.4	12.1	53.9
04	238 56.8	30.8	229 25.9	15.7	14 28.3	12.2	53.9
05	253 57.0	30.0	244 00.6	15.7	14 16.1	12.2	53.9
06	268 57.1	N13 29.2	258 35.3	15.7	N14 03.9	12.3	53.9
T 07	283 57.2	28.4	273 10.0	15.8	13 51.6	12.3	54.0
H 08	298 57.4	27.6	287 44.8	15.9	13 39.3	12.4	54.0
U 09	313 57.5	.. 26.8	302 19.7	15.8	13 26.9	12.5	54.0
R 10	328 57.6	26.0	316 54.5	16.0	13 14.4	12.5	54.0
S 11	343 57.7	25.2	331 29.5	15.9	13 01.9	12.5	54.0
D 12	358 57.9	N13 24.4	346 04.4	16.1	N12 49.4	12.6	54.0
A 13	13 58.0	23.6	0 39.5	16.0	12 36.8	12.7	54.0
Y 14	28 58.1	22.8	15 14.5	16.1	12 24.1	12.7	54.0
15	43 58.3	.. 22.0	29 49.6	16.2	12 11.4	12.7	54.0
16	58 58.4	21.2	44 24.8	16.1	11 58.7	12.8	54.0
17	73 58.6	20.4	58 59.9	16.3	11 45.9	12.9	54.0
18	88 58.7	N13 19.6	73 35.2	16.2	N11 33.0	12.8	54.0
19	103 58.8	18.8	88 10.4	16.3	11 20.2	13.0	54.0
20	118 59.0	18.0	102 45.7	16.3	11 07.2	12.9	54.0
21	133 59.1	.. 17.2	117 21.0	16.4	10 54.3	13.0	54.0
22	148 59.2	16.4	131 56.4	16.4	10 41.3	13.1	54.0
23	163 59.4	15.6	146 31.8	16.4	10 28.2	13.1	54.0
18 00	178 59.5	N13 14.8	161 07.2	16.5	N10 15.1	13.1	54.0
01	193 59.6	14.0	175 42.7	16.5	10 02.0	13.2	54.0
02	208 59.8	13.2	190 18.2	16.5	9 48.8	13.2	54.0
03	223 59.9	.. 12.4	204 53.7	16.6	9 35.6	13.2	54.0
04	239 00.0	11.6	219 29.3	16.6	9 22.4	13.3	54.1
05	254 00.2	10.8	234 04.9	16.6	9 09.1	13.3	54.1
06	269 00.3	N13 10.0	248 40.5	16.7	N 8 55.8	13.3	54.1
F 07	284 00.5	09.2	263 16.2	16.6	8 42.5	13.4	54.1
R 08	299 00.6	08.4	277 51.8	16.7	8 29.1	13.4	54.1
I 09	314 00.7	.. 07.6	292 27.5	16.8	8 15.7	13.5	54.1
D 10	329 00.9	06.8	307 03.3	16.7	8 02.2	13.5	54.1
A 11	344 01.0	06.0	321 39.0	16.8	7 48.7	13.5	54.1
Y 12	359 01.1	N13 05.1	336 14.8	16.8	N 7 35.2	13.5	54.1
13	14 01.3	04.3	350 50.6	16.8	7 21.7	13.6	54.1
14	29 01.4	03.5	5 26.4	16.8	7 08.1	13.6	54.1
15	44 01.6	.. 02.7	20 02.2	16.9	6 54.5	13.6	54.1
16	59 01.7	01.9	34 38.1	16.9	6 40.9	13.7	54.1
17	74 01.8	01.1	49 14.0	16.9	6 27.2	13.7	54.1
18	89 02.0	N13 00.3	63 49.9	16.9	N 6 13.5	13.7	54.2
19	104 02.1	12 59.5	78 25.8	16.9	5 59.8	13.7	54.2
20	119 02.3	58.7	93 01.7	16.9	5 46.1	13.8	54.2
21	134 02.4	.. 57.9	107 37.6	17.0	5 32.3	13.8	54.2
22	149 02.5	57.1	122 13.6	16.9	5 18.5	13.8	54.2
23	164 02.7	56.2	136 49.5	17.0	5 04.7	13.8	54.2
19 00	179 02.8	N12 55.4	151 25.5	17.0	N 4 50.9	13.9	54.2
01	194 03.0	54.6	166 01.5	17.0	4 37.0	13.8	54.2
02	209 03.1	53.8	180 37.5	17.0	4 23.2	13.9	54.2
03	224 03.2	.. 53.0	195 13.5	17.0	4 09.3	13.9	54.2
04	239 03.4	52.2	209 49.5	17.0	3 55.4	14.0	54.3
05	254 03.5	51.4	224 25.5	17.0	3 41.4	13.9	54.3
06	269 03.7	N12 50.6	239 01.5	17.1	N 3 27.5	14.0	54.3
S 07	284 03.9	49.7	253 37.6	17.0	3 13.5	14.0	54.3
A 08	299 04.0	48.9	268 13.6	17.0	2 59.5	14.0	54.3
T 09	314 04.1	.. 48.1	282 49.6	17.1	2 45.5	14.0	54.3
U 10	329 04.2	47.3	297 25.7	17.0	2 31.5	14.0	54.3
R 11	344 04.4	46.5	312 01.7	17.0	2 17.5	14.0	54.3
D 12	359 04.5	N12 45.7	326 37.7	17.1	N 2 03.5	14.1	54.3
A 13	14 04.7	44.8	341 13.8	17.0	1 49.4	14.1	54.4
Y 14	29 04.8	44.0	355 49.8	17.1	1 35.3	14.0	54.4
15	44 05.0	.. 43.2	10 25.8	17.0	1 21.3	14.1	54.4
16	59 05.1	42.4	25 01.8	17.0	1 07.2	14.1	54.4
17	74 05.3	41.6	39 37.8	17.1	0 53.1	14.1	54.4
18	89 05.4	N12 40.8	54 13.9	16.9	N 0 39.0	14.1	54.4
19	104 05.5	39.9	68 49.8	17.0	0 24.9	14.2	54.4
20	119 05.7	39.1	83 25.8	17.0	N 0 10.7	14.1	54.5
21	134 05.8	.. 38.3	98 01.8	17.0	S 0 03.4	14.1	54.5
22	149 06.0	37.5	112 37.8	16.9	0 17.5	14.2	54.5
23	164 06.1	36.7	127 13.7	17.0	S 0 31.7	14.1	54.5
	SD 15.8	d 0.8	SD 14.7		14.7		14.8

Twilight, Sunrise and Moonrise

Lat.	Naut.	Civil	Sunrise	Moonrise 17	18	19	20
°	h m	h m	h m	h m	h m	h m	h m
N 72	////	////	02 42	03 09	05 28	07 29	09 26
N 70	////	01 09	03 10	03 42	05 43	07 33	09 22
68	////	02 03	03 31	04 05	05 54	07 37	09 18
66	////	02 35	03 47	04 23	06 04	07 40	09 15
64	01 01	02 58	04 00	04 38	06 12	07 42	09 13
62	01 49	03 16	04 11	04 50	06 18	07 44	09 10
60	02 18	03 30	04 21	05 00	06 24	07 46	09 08
N 58	02 39	03 43	04 29	05 09	06 29	07 48	09 07
56	02 57	03 53	04 36	05 17	06 34	07 49	09 05
54	03 11	04 03	04 43	05 24	06 38	07 51	09 04
52	03 23	04 11	04 48	05 30	06 41	07 52	09 03
50	03 33	04 18	04 54	05 36	06 45	07 53	09 02
45	03 54	04 33	05 05	05 48	06 52	07 55	08 59
N 40	04 10	04 45	05 14	05 57	06 58	07 57	08 57
35	04 23	04 55	05 22	06 06	07 03	07 59	08 56
30	04 34	05 04	05 29	06 13	07 07	08 01	08 54
20	04 51	05 18	05 41	06 26	07 15	08 03	08 52
N 10	05 04	05 29	05 51	06 37	07 22	08 06	08 49
0	05 15	05 39	06 01	06 47	07 28	08 08	08 47
S 10	05 24	05 48	06 10	06 58	07 34	08 10	08 45
20	05 31	05 57	06 20	07 09	07 41	08 12	08 43
30	05 38	06 07	06 31	07 21	07 49	08 15	08 41
35	05 42	06 11	06 37	07 28	07 53	08 16	08 39
40	05 45	06 17	06 45	07 36	07 58	08 18	08 38
45	05 48	06 23	06 53	07 46	08 03	08 20	08 36
S 50	05 52	06 30	07 03	07 57	08 10	08 22	08 34
52	05 53	06 33	07 08	08 02	08 13	08 23	08 33
54	05 55	06 36	07 13	08 08	08 17	08 24	08 32
56	05 56	06 40	07 19	08 14	08 20	08 26	08 31
58	05 57	06 43	07 25	08 21	08 25	08 27	08 29
S 60	05 59	06 48	07 32	08 29	08 29	08 29	08 28

Sunset, Twilight and Moonset

Lat.	Sunset	Civil	Naut.	Moonset 17	18	19	20
°	h m	h m	h m	h m	h m	h m	h m
N 72	21 20	////	////	21 34	20 58	20 27	19 55
N 70	20 54	22 47	////	21 17	20 50	20 27	20 03
68	20 34	21 59	////	21 03	20 44	20 27	20 09
66	20 18	21 29	////	20 52	20 39	20 27	20 14
64	20 06	21 07	22 57	20 43	20 35	20 27	20 19
62	19 55	20 50	22 14	20 35	20 31	20 27	20 23
60	19 46	20 35	21 46	20 28	20 27	20 27	20 26
N 58	19 37	20 23	21 26	20 22	20 24	20 27	20 29
56	19 30	20 13	21 09	20 16	20 22	20 27	20 32
54	19 24	20 04	20 55	20 11	20 19	20 27	20 34
52	19 18	19 56	20 43	20 07	20 17	20 27	20 37
50	19 13	19 49	20 33	20 03	20 15	20 27	20 39
45	19 02	19 34	20 12	19 54	20 11	20 27	20 43
N 40	18 53	19 22	19 56	19 46	20 07	20 27	20 47
35	18 45	19 12	19 44	19 40	20 04	20 27	20 50
30	18 38	19 03	19 33	19 34	20 01	20 27	20 53
20	18 27	18 50	19 16	19 24	19 56	20 27	20 58
N 10	18 17	18 38	19 04	19 15	19 51	20 27	21 02
0	18 07	18 29	18 53	19 07	19 47	20 27	21 06
S 10	17 58	18 20	18 44	18 59	19 43	20 27	21 11
20	17 48	18 11	18 37	18 50	19 38	20 26	21 15
30	17 37	18 02	18 30	18 40	19 33	20 26	21 20
35	17 31	17 57	18 27	18 34	19 30	20 26	21 23
40	17 24	17 52	18 23	18 27	19 27	20 26	21 27
45	17 15	17 46	18 20	18 19	19 23	20 26	21 30
S 50	17 05	17 39	18 17	18 09	19 18	20 26	21 35
52	17 01	17 36	18 16	18 05	19 16	20 26	21 37
54	16 56	17 33	18 14	18 00	19 13	20 26	21 40
56	16 50	17 29	18 13	17 54	19 10	20 26	21 42
58	16 44	17 25	18 11	17 48	19 07	20 26	21 45
S 60	16 37	17 21	18 10	17 41	19 04	20 26	21 48

SUN and MOON (Eqn. of Time etc.)

Day	SUN Eqn. of Time 00h	12h	Mer. Pass.	MOON Mer. Pass. Upper	Lower	Age	Phase
d	m s	m s	h m	h m	h m	d	%
17	04 15	04 09	12 04	12 57	00 37	01	1
18	04 02	03 56	12 04	13 38	01 18	02	4
19	03 49	03 42	12 04	14 17	01 57	03	9

© British Crown Copyright 2022. All rights reserved.

UT	ARIES	VENUS −4.1		MARS +1.8		JUPITER −2.5		SATURN +0.4		STARS		
	GHA	GHA	Dec	GHA	Dec	GHA	Dec	GHA	Dec	Name	SHA	Dec
d h	° ′	° ′	° ′	° ′	° ′	° ′	° ′	° ′	° ′		° ′	° ′
20 00	328 04.4	191 28.6 N 8 08.8		152 12.1 N 2 36.2		284 58.1 N15 10.0		351 09.4 S11 32.9		Acamar	315 12.5	S40 12.3
01	343 06.9	206 32.3	09.2	167 13.1	35.5	300 00.5	10.1	6 12.0	33.0	Achernar	335 20.7	S57 06.7
02	358 09.4	221 36.1	09.5	182 14.1	34.9	315 02.8	10.1	21 14.6	33.1	Acrux	173 01.9	S63 13.9
03	13 11.8	236 39.9 ..	09.9	197 15.1 ..	34.2	330 05.1 ..	10.1	36 17.3 ..	33.2	Adhara	255 07.0	S29 00.0
04	28 14.3	251 43.6	10.2	212 16.1	33.6	345 07.5	10.1	51 19.9	33.2	Aldebaran	290 41.0	N16 33.4
05	43 16.8	266 47.4	10.6	227 17.1	32.9	0 09.8	10.2	66 22.6	33.3			
06	58 19.2	281 51.1 N 8 11.0		242 18.1 N 2 32.3		15 12.1 N15 10.2		81 25.2 S11 33.4		Alioth	166 14.3	N55 50.2
07	73 21.7	296 54.9	11.3	257 19.2	31.6	30 14.5	10.2	96 27.8	33.5	Alkaid	152 53.1	N49 12.0
08	88 24.2	311 58.7	11.7	272 20.2	31.0	45 16.8	10.3	111 30.5	33.5	Alnair	27 33.9	S46 50.7
S 09	103 26.6	327 02.4 ..	12.0	287 21.2 ..	30.3	60 19.2 ..	10.3	126 33.1 ..	33.6	Alnilam	275 39.0	S 1 11.1
U 10	118 29.1	342 06.1	12.4	302 22.2	29.7	75 21.5	10.3	141 35.8	33.7	Alphard	217 49.2	S 8 45.5
N 11	133 31.6	357 09.9	12.8	317 23.2	29.0	90 23.8	10.3	156 38.4	33.7			
D 12	148 34.0	12 13.6 N 8 13.1		332 24.2 N 2 28.4		105 26.2 N15 10.4		171 41.0 S11 33.8		Alphecca	126 04.7	N26 38.3
A 13	163 36.5	27 17.4	13.5	347 25.2	27.7	120 28.5	10.4	186 43.7	33.9	Alpheratz	357 35.7	N29 13.2
Y 14	178 38.9	42 21.1	13.9	2 26.2	27.1	135 30.9	10.4	201 46.3	34.0	Altair	62 00.8	N 8 55.9
15	193 41.4	57 24.8 ..	14.2	17 27.3 ..	26.4	150 33.2 ..	10.4	216 49.0 ..	34.0	Ankaa	353 07.9	S42 10.5
16	208 43.9	72 28.6	14.6	32 28.3	25.8	165 35.5	10.5	231 51.6	34.1	Antares	112 17.2	S26 29.1
17	223 46.3	87 32.3	15.0	47 29.3	25.1	180 37.9	10.5	246 54.2	34.2			
18	238 48.8	102 36.0 N 8 15.3		62 30.3 N 2 24.5		195 40.2 N15 10.5		261 56.9 S11 34.2		Arcturus	145 49.1	N19 03.8
19	253 51.3	117 39.7	15.7	77 31.3	23.8	210 42.6	10.6	276 59.5	34.3	Atria	107 12.3	S69 04.4
20	268 53.7	132 43.5	16.1	92 32.3	23.2	225 44.9	10.6	292 02.2	34.4	Avior	234 15.8	S59 34.9
21	283 56.2	147 47.2 ..	16.4	107 33.3 ..	22.5	240 47.3 ..	10.6	307 04.8 ..	34.5	Bellatrix	278 24.2	N 6 22.4
22	298 58.7	162 50.9	16.8	122 34.3	21.9	255 49.6	10.6	322 07.4	34.5	Betelgeuse	270 53.5	N 7 24.8
23	314 01.1	177 54.6	17.2	137 35.4	21.2	270 51.9	10.7	337 10.1	34.6			
21 00	329 03.6	192 58.3 N 8 17.5		152 36.4 N 2 20.5		285 54.3 N15 10.7		352 12.7 S11 34.7		Canopus	263 53.2	S52 42.2
01	344 06.0	208 02.0	17.9	167 37.4	19.9	300 56.6	10.7	7 15.4	34.8	Capella	280 23.8	N46 01.2
02	359 08.5	223 05.7	18.3	182 38.4	19.2	315 59.0	10.7	22 18.0	34.8	Deneb	49 26.2	N45 21.9
03	14 11.0	238 09.4 ..	18.7	197 39.4 ..	18.6	331 01.3 ..	10.8	37 20.7 ..	34.9	Denebola	182 26.4	N14 26.6
04	29 13.4	253 13.1	19.0	212 40.4	17.9	346 03.7	10.8	52 23.3	35.0	Diphda	348 48.2	S17 51.3
05	44 15.9	268 16.8	19.4	227 41.4	17.3	1 06.0	10.8	67 25.9	35.0			
06	59 18.4	283 20.5 N 8 19.8		242 42.4 N 2 16.6		16 08.4 N15 10.8		82 28.6 S11 35.1		Dubhe	193 43.0	N61 37.6
07	74 20.8	298 24.2	20.2	257 43.5	16.0	31 10.7	10.9	97 31.2	35.2	Elnath	278 03.5	N28 37.6
08	89 23.3	313 27.8	20.5	272 44.5	15.3	46 13.0	10.9	112 33.9	35.3	Eltanin	90 42.4	N51 29.4
M 09	104 25.8	328 31.5 ..	20.9	287 45.5 ..	14.7	61 15.4 ..	10.9	127 36.5 ..	35.3	Enif	33 39.6	N 9 59.1
O 10	119 28.2	343 35.2	21.3	302 46.5	14.0	76 17.7	10.9	142 39.1	35.4	Fomalhaut	15 15.4	S29 29.7
N 11	134 30.7	358 38.9	21.6	317 47.5	13.4	91 20.1	11.0	157 41.8	35.5			
D 12	149 33.2	13 42.5 N 8 22.0		332 48.5 N 2 12.7		106 22.4 N15 11.0		172 44.4 S11 35.5		Gacrux	171 53.4	S57 14.8
A 13	164 35.6	28 46.2	22.4	347 49.5	12.1	121 24.8	11.0	187 47.1	35.6	Gienah	175 45.0	S17 40.3
Y 14	179 38.1	43 49.9	22.8	2 50.5	11.4	136 27.1	11.1	202 49.7	35.7	Hadar	148 37.9	S60 29.4
15	194 40.5	58 53.5 ..	23.2	17 51.6 ..	10.8	151 29.5 ..	11.1	217 52.3 ..	35.8	Hamal	327 52.4	N23 34.4
16	209 43.0	73 57.2	23.5	32 52.6	10.1	166 31.8	11.1	232 55.0	35.8	Kaus Aust.	83 33.8	S34 22.5
17	224 45.5	89 00.8	23.9	47 53.6	09.5	181 34.2	11.1	247 57.6	35.9			
18	239 47.9	104 04.5 N 8 24.3		62 54.6 N 2 08.8		196 36.5 N15 11.2		263 00.3 S11 36.0		Kochab	137 20.0	N74 03.8
19	254 50.4	119 08.1	24.7	77 55.6	08.1	211 38.9	11.2	278 02.9	36.0	Markab	13 30.7	N15 20.0
20	269 52.9	134 11.8	25.0	92 56.6	07.5	226 41.2	11.2	293 05.5	36.1	Menkar	314 07.3	N 4 11.0
21	284 55.3	149 15.4 ..	25.4	107 57.6 ..	06.8	241 43.6 ..	11.2	308 08.2 ..	36.2	Menkent	147 59.2	S36 29.2
22	299 57.8	164 19.1	25.8	122 58.6	06.2	256 45.9	11.3	323 10.8	36.3	Miaplacidus	221 39.5	S69 48.7
23	315 00.3	179 22.7	26.2	137 59.7	05.5	271 48.3	11.3	338 13.5	36.3			
22 00	330 02.7	194 26.3 N 8 26.6		153 00.7 N 2 04.9		286 50.6 N15 11.3		353 16.1 S11 36.4		Mirfak	308 29.9	N49 56.5
01	345 05.2	209 29.9	26.9	168 01.7	04.2	301 53.0	11.3	8 18.8	36.5	Nunki	75 48.9	S26 16.1
02	0 07.6	224 33.6	27.3	183 02.7	03.6	316 55.3	11.3	23 21.4	36.6	Peacock	53 07.0	S56 39.6
03	15 10.1	239 37.2 ..	27.7	198 03.7 ..	02.9	331 57.7 ..	11.4	38 24.0 ..	36.6	Pollux	243 19.0	N27 58.2
04	30 12.6	254 40.8	28.1	213 04.7	02.3	347 00.0	11.4	53 26.7	36.7	Procyon	244 52.3	N 5 10.0
05	45 15.0	269 44.4	28.5	228 05.7	01.6	2 02.4	11.4	68 29.3	36.8			
06	60 17.5	284 48.0 N 8 28.8		243 06.7 N 2 01.0		17 04.8 N15 11.4		83 32.0 S11 36.8		Rasalhague	95 59.5	N12 32.7
07	75 20.0	299 51.7	29.2	258 07.7	2 00.3	32 07.1	11.5	98 34.6	36.9	Regulus	207 36.0	N11 51.3
T 08	90 22.4	314 55.3	29.6	273 08.8	1 59.7	47 09.5	11.5	113 37.2	37.0	Rigel	281 05.1	S 8 10.3
U 09	105 24.9	329 58.9 ..	30.0	288 09.8 ..	59.0	62 11.8 ..	11.5	128 39.9 ..	37.1	Rigil Kent.	139 42.1	S60 56.1
E 10	120 27.4	345 02.5	30.4	303 10.8	58.3	77 14.2	11.5	143 42.5	37.1	Sabik	102 04.0	S15 45.2
S 11	135 29.8	0 06.1	30.8	318 11.8	57.7	92 16.5	11.6	158 45.2	37.2			
D 12	150 32.3	15 09.6 N 8 31.1		333 12.8 N 1 57.0		107 18.9 N15 11.6		173 47.8 S11 37.3		Schedar	349 32.0	N56 39.9
A 13	165 34.8	30 13.2	31.5	348 13.8	56.4	122 21.2	11.6	188 50.5	37.3	Shaula	96 11.7	S37 07.3
Y 14	180 37.2	45 16.8	31.9	3 14.8	55.7	137 23.6	11.6	203 53.1	37.4	Sirius	258 27.5	S16 44.7
15	195 39.7	60 20.4 ..	32.3	18 15.8 ..	55.1	152 25.9 ..	11.7	218 55.7 ..	37.5	Spica	158 23.7	S11 17.0
16	210 42.1	75 24.0	32.7	33 16.8	54.4	167 28.3	11.7	233 58.4	37.6	Suhail	222 47.6	S43 31.5
17	225 44.6	90 27.6	33.1	48 17.8	53.8	182 30.7	11.7	249 01.0	37.6			
18	240 47.1	105 31.1 N 8 33.4		63 18.9 N 1 53.1		197 33.0 N15 11.7		264 03.7 S11 37.7		Vega	80 33.7	N38 48.5
19	255 49.5	120 34.7	33.8	78 19.9	52.5	212 35.4	11.7	279 06.3	37.8	Zuben'ubi	136 57.4	S16 08.4
20	270 52.0	135 38.3	34.2	93 20.9	51.8	227 37.7	11.8	294 08.9	37.9		SHA	Mer.Pass.
21	285 54.5	150 41.8 ..	34.6	108 21.9 ..	51.2	242 40.1 ..	11.8	309 11.6 ..	37.9		° ′	h m
22	300 56.9	165 45.4	35.0	123 22.9	50.5	257 42.5	11.8	324 14.2	38.0	Venus	223 54.7	11 05
23	315 59.4	180 48.9	35.4	138 23.9	49.8	272 44.8	11.8	339 16.9	38.1	Mars	183 32.8	13 49
	h m									Jupiter	316 50.7	4 56
Mer.Pass.	2 03.4	v 3.7	d 0.4	v 1.0	d 0.7	v 2.3	d 0.0	v 2.6	d 0.1	Saturn	23 09.1	0 31

© British Crown Copyright 2022. All rights reserved.

SUN / MOON

UT	SUN GHA	SUN Dec	MOON GHA	v	MOON Dec	d	HP
d h	° ′	° ′	° ′	′	° ′	′	′
20 00	179 06.3	N12 35.8	141 49.7	16.9	S 0 45.8	14.1	54.5
01	194 06.4	35.0	156 25.6	16.9	0 59.9	14.2	54.5
02	209 06.6	34.2	171 01.5	16.9	1 14.1	14.2	54.5
03	224 06.7 ..	33.4	185 37.4	16.9	1 28.3	14.1	54.5
04	239 06.9	32.6	200 13.3	16.9	1 42.4	14.2	54.6
05	254 07.0	31.7	214 49.2	16.8	1 56.6	14.1	54.6
06	269 07.2	N12 30.9	229 25.0	16.8	S 2 10.7	14.2	54.6
07	284 07.3	30.1	244 00.8	16.8	2 24.9	14.1	54.6
08	299 07.4	29.3	258 36.6	16.8	2 39.0	14.2	54.6
S 09	314 07.6 ..	28.5	273 12.4	16.7	2 53.2	14.1	54.6
U 10	329 07.7	27.6	287 48.1	16.7	3 07.3	14.2	54.7
N 11	344 07.9	26.8	302 23.8	16.7	3 21.5	14.1	54.7
D 12	359 08.0	N12 26.0	316 59.5	16.7	S 3 35.6	14.1	54.7
A 13	14 08.2	25.2	331 35.2	16.6	3 49.7	14.2	54.7
Y 14	29 08.3	24.3	346 10.8	16.6	4 03.9	14.1	54.7
15	44 08.5 ..	23.5	0 46.4	16.6	4 18.0	14.1	54.7
16	59 08.6	22.7	15 22.0	16.6	4 32.1	14.1	54.8
17	74 08.8	21.9	29 57.6	16.5	4 46.2	14.1	54.8
18	89 08.9	N12 21.0	44 33.1	16.4	S 5 00.3	14.1	54.8
19	104 09.1	20.2	59 08.5	16.5	5 14.4	14.1	54.8
20	119 09.2	19.4	73 44.0	16.4	5 28.5	14.0	54.8
21	134 09.4 ..	18.5	88 19.4	16.4	5 42.5	14.1	54.9
22	149 09.5	17.7	102 54.8	16.3	5 56.6	14.0	54.9
23	164 09.7	16.9	117 30.1	16.3	6 10.6	14.0	54.9
21 00	179 09.8	N12 16.1	132 05.4	16.2	S 6 24.6	14.1	54.9
01	194 10.0	15.2	146 40.6	16.2	6 38.7	14.0	54.9
02	209 10.1	14.4	161 15.8	16.2	6 52.7	13.9	54.9
03	224 10.3 ..	13.6	175 51.0	16.1	7 06.6	14.0	55.0
04	239 10.5	12.7	190 26.1	16.1	7 20.6	13.9	55.0
05	254 10.6	11.9	205 01.1	16.1	7 34.5	13.9	55.0
06	269 10.8	N12 11.1	219 36.2	15.9	S 7 48.4	13.9	55.0
07	284 10.9	10.3	234 11.1	15.9	8 02.3	13.9	55.0
08	299 11.1	09.4	248 46.0	15.9	8 16.2	13.9	55.1
M 09	314 11.2 ..	08.6	263 20.9	15.8	8 30.1	13.8	55.1
O 10	329 11.4	07.8	277 55.7	15.8	8 43.9	13.8	55.1
N 11	344 11.5	06.9	292 30.5	15.7	8 57.7	13.8	55.1
D 12	359 11.7	N12 06.1	307 05.2	15.6	S 9 11.5	13.8	55.2
A 13	14 11.8	05.3	321 39.8	15.6	9 25.3	13.7	55.2
Y 14	29 12.0	04.4	336 14.4	15.6	9 39.0	13.7	55.2
15	44 12.1 ..	03.6	350 49.0	15.5	9 52.7	13.7	55.2
16	59 12.3	02.8	5 23.5	15.4	10 06.4	13.7	55.2
17	74 12.4	01.9	19 57.9	15.3	10 20.1	13.6	55.3
18	89 12.6	N12 01.1	34 32.2	15.3	S10 33.7	13.6	55.3
19	104 12.8	12 00.3	49 06.5	15.2	10 47.3	13.5	55.3
20	119 12.9	11 59.4	63 40.7	15.2	11 00.8	13.6	55.3
21	134 13.1 ..	58.6	78 14.9	15.1	11 14.4	13.4	55.4
22	149 13.2	57.8	92 49.0	15.0	11 27.8	13.5	55.4
23	164 13.4	56.9	107 23.0	15.0	11 41.3	13.4	55.4
22 00	179 13.5	N11 56.1	121 57.0	14.9	S11 54.7	13.4	55.4
01	194 13.7	55.3	136 30.9	14.8	12 08.1	13.3	55.5
02	209 13.8	54.4	151 04.7	14.8	12 21.4	13.4	55.5
03	224 14.0 ..	53.6	165 38.5	14.6	12 34.8	13.2	55.5
04	239 14.2	52.7	180 12.1	14.6	12 48.0	13.3	55.5
05	254 14.3	51.9	194 45.7	14.6	13 01.3	13.1	55.6
06	269 14.5	N11 51.1	209 19.3	14.4	S13 14.4	13.2	55.6
07	284 14.6	50.2	223 52.7	14.4	13 27.6	13.1	55.6
08	299 14.8	49.4	238 26.1	14.3	13 40.7	13.0	55.6
T 09	314 15.0 ..	48.5	252 59.4	14.2	13 53.7	13.0	55.7
U 10	329 15.1	47.7	267 32.6	14.1	14 06.7	13.0	55.7
E 11	344 15.3	46.9	282 05.7	14.0	14 19.7	12.9	55.7
S 12	359 15.4	N11 46.0	296 38.7	14.0	S14 32.6	12.9	55.7
D 13	14 15.6	45.2	311 11.7	13.9	14 45.5	12.8	55.8
A 14	29 15.7	44.3	325 44.6	13.8	14 58.3	12.7	55.8
Y 15	44 15.9 ..	43.5	340 17.4	13.7	15 11.0	12.7	55.8
16	59 16.1	42.7	354 50.1	13.6	15 23.7	12.7	55.8
17	74 16.2	41.8	9 22.7	13.5	15 36.4	12.6	55.9
18	89 16.4	N11 41.0	23 55.2	13.4	S15 49.0	12.5	55.9
19	104 16.5	40.1	38 27.6	13.4	16 01.5	12.5	55.9
20	119 16.7	39.3	53 00.0	13.2	16 14.0	12.4	56.0
21	134 16.9 ..	38.5	67 32.2	13.2	16 26.4	12.4	56.0
22	149 17.0	37.6	82 04.4	13.0	16 38.8	12.3	56.0
23	164 17.2	36.8	96 36.4	13.0	S16 51.1	12.2	56.0
	SD 15.8	d 0.8	SD 14.9		15.0		15.2

Twilight / Sunrise / Moonrise

Lat.	Twilight Naut.	Twilight Civil	Sunrise	Moonrise 20	21	22	23
°	h m	h m	h m	h m	h m	h m	h m
N 72	////	////	03 01	09 26	11 30	14 01	■■■
N 70	////	01 42	03 25	09 22	11 15	13 25	■■■
68	////	02 22	03 43	09 18	11 03	13 00	15 27
66	////	02 49	03 57	09 15	10 54	12 40	14 44
64	01 29	03 09	04 09	09 13	10 46	12 25	14 15
62	02 06	03 26	04 19	09 10	10 39	12 12	13 54
60	02 30	03 39	04 28	09 08	10 33	12 01	13 36
N 58	02 50	03 50	04 35	09 07	10 27	11 52	13 22
56	03 05	04 00	04 42	09 05	10 23	11 44	13 09
54	03 18	04 09	04 48	09 04	10 19	11 37	12 59
52	03 29	04 16	04 53	09 03	10 15	11 30	12 49
50	03 39	04 23	04 58	09 02	10 12	11 24	12 41
45	03 59	04 37	05 08	08 59	10 04	11 12	12 23
N 40	04 14	04 48	05 17	08 57	09 58	11 02	12 08
35	04 26	04 58	05 24	08 56	09 53	10 53	11 56
30	04 36	05 06	05 31	08 54	09 49	10 46	11 45
20	04 52	05 19	05 42	08 52	09 41	10 32	11 27
N 10	05 04	05 30	05 51	08 49	09 34	10 21	11 11
0	05 14	05 39	06 00	08 47	09 28	10 11	10 57
S 10	05 22	05 47	06 09	08 45	09 22	10 00	10 42
20	05 29	05 55	06 18	08 43	09 15	09 49	10 27
30	05 36	06 04	06 28	08 41	09 07	09 36	10 09
35	05 38	06 08	06 34	08 39	09 03	09 29	09 59
40	05 41	06 13	06 40	08 38	08 58	09 21	09 48
45	05 44	06 18	06 48	08 36	08 53	09 12	09 34
S 50	05 46	06 24	06 57	08 34	08 46	09 00	09 18
52	05 47	06 27	07 02	08 33	08 43	08 55	09 10
54	05 48	06 30	07 06	08 32	08 40	08 49	09 01
56	05 49	06 33	07 11	08 31	08 36	08 43	08 52
58	05 51	06 36	07 17	08 29	08 32	08 36	08 41
S 60	05 52	06 40	07 24	08 28	08 27	08 28	08 29

Sunset / Twilight / Moonset

Lat.	Sunset	Twilight Civil	Twilight Naut.	Moonset 20	21	22	23
°	h m	h m	h m	h m	h m	h m	h m
N 72	21 01	23 44	////	19 55	19 18	18 17	■■■
N 70	20 38	22 17	////	20 03	19 35	18 56	■■■
68	20 21	21 39	////	20 09	19 49	19 23	18 33
66	20 07	21 14	23 46	20 14	20 00	19 43	19 17
64	19 55	20 54	22 30	20 19	20 10	20 00	19 47
62	19 45	20 38	21 56	20 23	20 18	20 14	20 09
60	19 37	20 25	21 33	20 26	20 26	20 26	20 28
N 58	19 30	20 14	21 14	20 29	20 32	20 36	20 43
56	19 23	20 05	20 59	20 32	20 38	20 45	20 56
54	19 17	19 56	20 46	20 34	20 43	20 53	21 07
52	19 12	19 49	20 35	20 37	20 47	21 00	21 17
50	19 07	19 42	20 26	20 39	20 51	21 07	21 27
45	18 57	19 28	20 07	20 43	21 01	21 21	21 46
N 40	18 49	19 17	19 52	20 47	21 09	21 32	22 02
35	18 42	19 08	19 40	20 50	21 15	21 42	22 15
30	18 35	19 00	19 30	20 53	21 21	21 51	22 27
20	18 25	18 47	19 14	20 58	21 31	22 06	22 47
N 10	18 15	18 37	19 02	21 02	21 40	22 20	23 04
0	18 07	18 28	18 52	21 06	21 48	22 32	23 21
S 10	17 58	18 19	18 44	21 11	21 56	22 45	23 37
20	17 49	18 11	18 37	21 15	22 05	22 58	23 55
30	17 39	18 03	18 31	21 20	22 16	23 14	24 15
35	17 33	17 59	18 29	21 23	22 22	23 23	24 27
40	17 26	17 54	18 26	21 27	22 29	23 33	24 41
45	17 19	17 49	18 23	21 30	22 37	23 46	24 58
S 50	17 10	17 43	18 21	21 35	22 46	24 00	00 00
52	17 06	17 40	18 20	21 37	22 51	24 07	00 07
54	17 01	17 38	18 19	21 40	22 56	24 15	00 15
56	16 56	17 35	18 18	21 42	23 01	24 24	00 24
58	16 50	17 31	18 17	21 45	23 07	24 34	00 34
S 60	16 44	17 27	18 16	21 48	23 14	24 46	00 46

SUN / MOON

Day	Eqn. of Time 00ʰ	Eqn. of Time 12ʰ	Mer. Pass.	Moon Mer. Pass. Upper	Moon Mer. Pass. Lower	Age	Phase
d	m s	m s	h m	h m	h m	d %	
20	03 35	03 28	12 03	14 57	02 37	04 15	
21	03 21	03 14	12 03	15 38	03 17	05 22	◐
22	03 06	02 59	12 03	16 21	03 59	06 31	

© British Crown Copyright 2022. All rights reserved.

2023 AUGUST 23, 24, 25 (WED., THURS., FRI.)

UT	ARIES GHA	VENUS −4.3 GHA	Dec	MARS +1.8 GHA	Dec	JUPITER −2.5 GHA	Dec	SATURN +0.4 GHA	Dec
23 00	331 01.9	195 52.5 N 8	35.8	153 24.9 N 1	49.2	287 47.2 N15	11.9	354 19.5 S11	38.1
01	346 04.3	210 56.0	36.2	168 25.9	48.5	302 49.5	11.9	9 22.2	38.2
02	1 06.8	225 59.6	36.5	183 26.9	47.9	317 51.9	11.9	24 24.8	38.3
03	16 09.3	241 03.1 ..	36.9	198 28.0 ..	47.2	332 54.3 ..	11.9	39 27.4 ..	38.4
04	31 11.7	256 06.7	37.3	213 29.0	46.6	347 56.6	11.9	54 30.1	38.4
05	46 14.2	271 10.2	37.7	228 30.0	45.9	2 59.0	12.0	69 32.7	38.5
06	61 16.6	286 13.7 N 8	38.1	243 31.0 N 1	45.3	18 01.3 N15	12.0	84 35.4 S11	38.6
W 07	76 19.1	301 17.3	38.5	258 32.0	44.6	33 03.7	12.0	99 38.0	38.6
E 08	91 21.6	316 20.8	38.9	273 33.0	44.0	48 06.1	12.0	114 40.6	38.7
D 09	106 24.0	331 24.3 ..	39.3	288 34.0 ..	43.3	63 08.4 ..	12.0	129 43.3 ..	38.8
N 10	121 26.5	346 27.8	39.6	303 35.0	42.6	78 10.8	12.1	144 45.9	38.9
E 11	136 29.0	1 31.3	40.0	318 36.0	42.0	93 13.1	12.1	159 48.6	38.9
S 12	151 31.4	16 34.8 N 8	40.4	333 37.0 N 1	41.3	108 15.5 N15	12.1	174 51.2 S11	39.0
D 13	166 33.9	31 38.3	40.8	348 38.1	40.7	123 17.9	12.1	189 53.9	39.1
A 14	181 36.4	46 41.8	41.2	3 39.1	40.0	138 20.2	12.2	204 56.5	39.2
Y 15	196 38.8	61 45.3 ..	41.6	18 40.1 ..	39.4	153 22.6 ..	12.2	219 59.1 ..	39.2
16	211 41.3	76 48.8	42.0	33 41.1	38.7	168 25.0	12.2	235 01.8	39.3
17	226 43.7	91 52.3	42.4	48 42.1	38.1	183 27.3	12.2	250 04.4	39.4
18	241 46.2	106 55.8 N 8	42.8	63 43.1 N 1	37.4	198 29.7 N15	12.2	265 07.1 S11	39.4
19	256 48.7	121 59.3	43.2	78 44.1	36.7	213 32.1	12.3	280 09.7	39.5
20	271 51.1	137 02.8	43.6	93 45.1	36.1	228 34.4	12.3	295 12.3	39.6
21	286 53.6	152 06.3 ..	43.9	108 46.1 ..	35.4	243 36.8 ..	12.3	310 15.0 ..	39.7
22	301 56.1	167 09.7	44.3	123 47.1	34.8	258 39.2	12.3	325 17.6	39.7
23	316 58.5	182 13.2	44.7	138 48.1	34.1	273 41.5	12.3	340 20.3	39.8
24 00	332 01.0	197 16.7 N 8	45.1	153 49.2 N 1	33.5	288 43.9 N15	12.4	355 22.9 S11	39.9
01	347 03.5	212 20.1	45.5	168 50.2	32.8	303 46.3	12.4	10 25.6	39.9
02	2 05.9	227 23.6	45.9	183 51.2	32.2	318 48.6	12.4	25 28.2	40.0
03	17 08.4	242 27.1 ..	46.3	198 52.2 ..	31.5	333 51.0 ..	12.4	40 30.8 ..	40.1
04	32 10.9	257 30.5	46.7	213 53.2	30.8	348 53.4	12.4	55 33.5	40.2
05	47 13.3	272 34.0	47.1	228 54.2	30.2	3 55.7	12.4	70 36.1	40.2
06	62 15.8	287 37.4 N 8	47.5	243 55.2 N 1	29.5	18 58.1 N15	12.5	85 38.8 S11	40.3
T 07	77 18.2	302 40.8	47.9	258 56.2	28.9	34 00.5	12.5	100 41.4	40.4
H 08	92 20.7	317 44.3	48.3	273 57.2	28.2	49 02.9	12.5	115 44.1	40.4
U 09	107 23.2	332 47.7 ..	48.6	288 58.2 ..	27.6	64 05.2 ..	12.5	130 46.7 ..	40.5
R 10	122 25.6	347 51.1	49.0	303 59.2	26.9	79 07.6	12.5	145 49.3	40.6
S 11	137 28.1	2 54.6	49.4	319 00.2	26.3	94 10.0	12.6	160 52.0	40.7
D 12	152 30.6	17 58.0 N 8	49.8	334 01.3 N 1	25.6	109 12.3 N15	12.6	175 54.6 S11	40.7
A 13	167 33.0	33 01.4	50.2	349 02.3	24.9	124 14.7	12.6	190 57.3	40.8
Y 14	182 35.5	48 04.8	50.6	4 03.3	24.3	139 17.1	12.6	205 59.9	40.9
15	197 38.0	63 08.2 ..	51.0	19 04.3 ..	23.6	154 19.5 ..	12.6	221 02.6 ..	41.0
16	212 40.4	78 11.6	51.4	34 05.3	23.0	169 21.8	12.7	236 05.2	41.0
17	227 42.9	93 15.0	51.8	49 06.3	22.3	184 24.2	12.7	251 07.8	41.1
18	242 45.4	108 18.4 N 8	52.2	64 07.3 N 1	21.7	199 26.6 N15	12.7	266 10.5 S11	41.2
19	257 47.8	123 21.8	52.6	79 08.3	21.0	214 28.9	12.7	281 13.1	41.2
20	272 50.3	138 25.2	53.0	94 09.3	20.4	229 31.3	12.7	296 15.8	41.3
21	287 52.7	153 28.6 ..	53.4	109 10.3 ..	19.7	244 33.7 ..	12.7	311 18.4 ..	41.4
22	302 55.2	168 32.0	53.8	124 11.3	19.0	259 36.1	12.8	326 21.1	41.5
23	317 57.7	183 35.4	54.2	139 12.3	18.4	274 38.4	12.8	341 23.7	41.5
25 00	333 00.1	198 38.8 N 8	54.6	154 13.4 N 1	17.7	289 40.8 N15	12.8	356 26.3 S11	41.6
01	348 02.6	213 42.1	54.9	169 14.4	17.1	304 43.2	12.8	11 29.0	41.7
02	3 05.1	228 45.5	55.3	184 15.4	16.4	319 45.6	12.8	26 31.6	41.7
03	18 07.5	243 48.9 ..	55.7	199 16.4 ..	15.8	334 47.9 ..	12.8	41 34.3 ..	41.8
04	33 10.0	258 52.2	56.1	214 17.4	15.1	349 50.3	12.9	56 36.9	41.9
05	48 12.5	273 55.6	56.5	229 18.4	14.5	4 52.7	12.9	71 39.5	42.0
06	63 14.9	288 58.9 N 8	56.9	244 19.4 N 1	13.8	19 55.1 N15	12.9	86 42.2 S11	42.0
07	78 17.4	304 02.3	57.3	259 20.4	13.1	34 57.5	12.9	101 44.8	42.1
08	93 19.9	319 05.6	57.7	274 21.4	12.5	49 59.8	12.9	116 47.5	42.2
F 09	108 22.3	334 09.0 ..	58.1	289 22.4 ..	11.8	65 02.2 ..	12.9	131 50.1 ..	42.2
R 10	123 24.8	349 12.3	58.5	304 23.4	11.2	80 04.6	13.0	146 52.8	42.3
I 11	138 27.2	4 15.7	58.9	319 24.4	10.5	95 07.0	13.0	161 55.4	42.4
D 12	153 29.7	19 19.0 N 8	59.3	334 25.4 N 1	09.9	110 09.3 N15	13.0	176 58.0 S11	42.5
A 13	168 32.2	34 22.3 8	59.7	349 26.4	09.2	125 11.7	13.0	192 00.7	42.5
Y 14	183 34.6	49 25.6 9	00.1	4 27.5	08.5	140 14.1	13.0	207 03.3	42.6
15	198 37.1	64 29.0 ..	00.5	19 28.5 ..	07.9	155 16.5 ..	13.0	222 06.0 ..	42.7
16	213 39.6	79 32.3	00.9	34 29.5	07.2	170 18.9	13.1	237 08.6	42.8
17	228 42.0	94 35.6	01.3	49 30.5	06.6	185 21.2	13.1	252 11.3	42.8
18	243 44.5	109 38.9 N 9	01.7	64 31.5 N 1	05.9	200 23.6 N15	13.1	267 13.9 S11	42.9
19	258 47.0	124 42.2	02.1	79 32.5	05.3	215 26.0	13.1	282 16.5	43.0
20	273 49.4	139 45.5	02.4	94 33.5	04.6	230 28.4	13.1	297 19.2	43.0
21	288 51.9	154 48.8 ..	02.8	109 34.5 ..	03.9	245 30.8 ..	13.1	312 21.8 ..	43.1
22	303 54.3	169 52.1	03.2	124 35.5	03.3	260 33.2	13.2	327 24.5	43.2
23	318 56.8	184 55.4	03.6	139 36.5	02.6	275 35.5	13.2	342 27.1	43.3
Mer. Pass.	h m 1 51.6	v 3.4	d 0.4	v 1.0	d 0.7	v 2.4	d 0.0	v 2.6	d 0.1

STARS

Name	SHA	Dec
Acamar	315 12.5	S40 12.3
Achernar	335 20.7	S57 06.7
Acrux	173 01.9	S63 13.9
Adhara	255 07.0	S29 00.0
Aldebaran	290 41.0	N16 33.4
Alioth	166 14.4	N55 50.2
Alkaid	152 53.2	N49 12.0
Alnair	27 33.9	S46 50.7
Alnilam	275 39.0	S 1 11.1
Alphard	217 49.2	S 8 45.5
Alphecca	126 04.7	N26 38.3
Alpheratz	357 35.7	N29 13.2
Altair	62 00.8	N 8 55.9
Ankaa	353 07.9	S42 10.5
Antares	112 17.2	S26 29.1
Arcturus	145 49.1	N19 03.8
Atria	107 12.3	S69 04.4
Avior	234 15.8	S59 34.9
Bellatrix	278 24.2	N 6 22.4
Betelgeuse	270 53.5	N 7 24.8
Canopus	263 53.2	S52 42.1
Capella	280 23.7	N46 01.2
Deneb	49 26.2	N45 22.0
Denebola	182 26.4	N14 26.6
Diphda	348 48.2	S17 51.3
Dubhe	193 43.0	N61 37.6
Elnath	278 03.5	N28 37.6
Eltanin	90 42.5	N51 29.4
Enif	33 39.6	N 9 59.1
Fomalhaut	15 15.4	S29 29.7
Gacrux	171 53.4	S57 14.8
Gienah	175 45.0	S17 40.3
Hadar	148 38.0	S60 29.4
Hamal	327 52.3	N23 34.4
Kaus Aust.	83 33.8	S34 22.5
Kochab	137 20.1	N74 03.8
Markab	13 30.7	N15 20.0
Menkar	314 07.3	N 4 11.0
Menkent	147 59.2	S36 29.2
Miaplacidus	221 39.5	S69 48.7
Mirfak	308 29.8	N49 56.5
Nunki	75 48.9	S26 16.1
Peacock	53 07.0	S56 39.6
Pollux	243 19.0	N27 58.2
Procyon	244 52.3	N 5 10.0
Rasalhague	95 59.5	N12 32.7
Regulus	207 36.0	N11 51.3
Rigel	281 05.1	S 8 10.3
Rigil Kent.	139 42.1	S60 56.1
Sabik	102 04.0	S15 45.2
Schedar	349 31.9	N56 39.9
Shaula	96 11.8	S37 07.3
Sirius	258 27.5	S16 44.7
Spica	158 23.7	S11 17.0
Suhail	222 47.6	S43 31.5
Vega	80 33.7	N38 48.5
Zuben'ubi	136 57.4	S16 08.4

	SHA	Mer. Pass.
	° ′	h m
Venus	225 15.7	10 48
Mars	181 48.2	13 44
Jupiter	316 42.9	4 44
Saturn	23 21.9	0 18

© British Crown Copyright 2022. All rights reserved.

UT	SUN GHA	SUN Dec	MOON GHA	v	MOON Dec	d	HP
d h	° ′	° ′	° ′	′	° ′	′	′
23 00	179 17.3	N11 35.9	111 08.4	12.8	S17 03.3	12.2	56.1
01	194 17.5	35.1	125 40.2	12.8	17 15.5	12.1	56.1
02	209 17.7	34.2	140 12.0	12.7	17 27.6	12.1	56.1
03	224 17.8	. . 33.4	154 43.7	12.6	17 39.7	11.9	56.2
04	239 18.0	32.5	169 15.3	12.4	17 51.6	11.9	56.2
05	254 18.2	31.7	183 46.7	12.4	18 03.5	11.9	56.2
06	269 18.3	N11 30.9	198 18.1	12.2	S18 15.4	11.7	56.3
W 07	284 18.5	30.0	212 49.3	12.2	18 27.1	11.7	56.3
E 08	299 18.6	29.2	227 20.5	12.1	18 38.8	11.7	56.3
D 09	314 18.8	. . 28.3	241 51.6	11.9	18 50.5	11.5	56.3
N 10	329 19.0	27.5	256 22.5	11.8	19 02.0	11.5	56.4
E 11	344 19.1	26.6	270 53.3	11.8	19 13.5	11.3	56.4
S 12	359 19.3	N11 25.8	285 24.1	11.6	S19 24.8	11.4	56.4
D 13	14 19.5	24.9	299 54.7	11.5	19 36.2	11.2	56.5
A 14	29 19.6	24.1	314 25.2	11.4	19 47.4	11.1	56.5
Y 15	44 19.8	. . 23.2	328 55.6	11.3	19 58.5	11.1	56.5
16	59 20.0	22.4	343 25.9	11.2	20 09.6	11.0	56.6
17	74 20.1	21.5	357 56.1	11.0	20 20.6	10.9	56.6
18	89 20.3	N11 20.7	12 26.1	11.0	S20 31.5	10.8	56.6
19	104 20.4	19.8	26 56.1	10.8	20 42.3	10.7	56.7
20	119 20.6	19.0	41 25.9	10.8	20 53.0	10.6	56.7
21	134 20.8	. . 18.1	55 55.7	10.6	21 03.6	10.5	56.7
22	149 20.9	17.3	70 25.3	10.5	21 14.1	10.4	56.8
23	164 21.1	16.4	84 54.8	10.3	21 24.5	10.4	56.8
24 00	179 21.3	N11 15.6	99 24.1	10.3	S21 34.9	10.2	56.8
01	194 21.4	14.7	113 53.4	10.1	21 45.1	10.2	56.9
02	209 21.6	13.9	128 22.5	10.1	21 55.3	10.0	56.9
03	224 21.8	. . 13.0	142 51.6	9.9	22 05.3	9.9	56.9
04	239 21.9	12.2	157 20.5	9.7	22 15.2	9.9	57.0
05	254 22.1	11.3	171 49.2	9.7	22 25.1	9.7	57.0
06	269 22.3	N11 10.5	186 17.9	9.5	S22 34.8	9.6	57.0
T 07	284 22.4	09.6	200 46.4	9.5	22 44.4	9.5	57.1
H 08	299 22.6	08.8	215 14.9	9.3	22 53.9	9.5	57.1
U 09	314 22.8	. . 07.9	229 43.2	9.1	23 03.4	9.2	57.1
R 10	329 22.9	07.0	244 11.3	9.1	23 12.6	9.2	57.2
S 11	344 23.1	06.2	258 39.4	8.9	23 21.8	9.1	57.2
D 12	359 23.3	N11 05.3	273 07.3	8.8	S23 30.9	8.9	57.3
A 13	14 23.4	04.5	287 35.1	8.7	23 39.8	8.9	57.3
Y 14	29 23.6	03.6	302 02.8	8.6	23 48.7	8.7	57.3
15	44 23.8	. . 02.8	316 30.4	8.5	23 57.4	8.6	57.4
16	59 24.0	01.9	330 57.9	8.3	24 06.0	8.5	57.4
17	74 24.1	01.1	345 25.2	8.2	24 14.5	8.3	57.4
18	89 24.3	N11 00.2	359 52.4	8.1	S24 22.8	8.2	57.5
19	104 24.5	10 59.3	14 19.5	7.9	24 31.0	8.1	57.5
20	119 24.6	58.5	28 46.4	7.9	24 39.1	8.0	57.5
21	134 24.8	. . 57.6	43 13.3	7.7	24 47.1	7.8	57.6
22	149 25.0	56.8	57 40.0	7.6	24 54.9	7.7	57.6
23	164 25.1	55.9	72 06.6	7.4	25 02.6	7.6	57.7
25 00	179 25.3	N10 55.1	86 33.0	7.4	S25 10.2	7.4	57.7
01	194 25.5	54.2	100 59.4	7.2	25 17.6	7.3	57.7
02	209 25.7	53.3	115 25.6	7.1	25 24.9	7.2	57.8
03	224 25.8	. . 52.5	129 51.7	7.0	25 32.1	7.0	57.8
04	239 26.0	51.6	144 17.7	6.9	25 39.1	6.8	57.8
05	254 26.2	50.8	158 43.6	6.7	25 45.9	6.8	57.9
06	269 26.3	N10 49.9	173 09.3	6.7	S25 52.7	6.6	57.9
F 07	284 26.5	49.0	187 35.0	6.5	25 59.3	6.4	58.0
R 08	299 26.7	48.2	202 00.5	6.4	26 05.7	6.3	58.0
I 09	314 26.9	. . 47.3	216 25.9	6.3	26 12.0	6.1	58.0
D 10	329 27.0	46.5	230 51.2	6.1	26 18.1	6.0	58.1
A 11	344 27.2	45.6	245 16.3	6.1	26 24.1	5.8	58.1
Y 12	359 27.4	N10 44.7	259 41.4	5.9	S26 29.9	5.7	58.1
13	14 27.5	43.9	274 06.3	5.9	26 35.6	5.5	58.2
14	29 27.7	43.0	288 31.2	5.7	26 41.1	5.4	58.2
15	44 27.9	. . 42.1	302 55.9	5.6	26 46.5	5.2	58.3
16	59 28.1	41.3	317 20.5	5.5	26 51.7	5.0	58.3
17	74 28.2	40.4	331 45.0	5.4	26 56.7	4.9	58.3
18	89 28.4	N10 39.6	346 09.4	5.3	S27 01.6	4.7	58.4
19	104 28.6	38.7	0 33.7	5.2	27 06.3	4.5	58.4
20	119 28.8	37.8	14 57.9	5.1	27 10.8	4.4	58.4
21	134 28.9	. . 37.0	29 22.0	5.0	27 15.2	4.2	58.5
22	149 29.1	36.1	43 46.0	4.9	27 19.4	4.0	58.5
23	164 29.3	35.2	58 09.9	4.8	S27 23.4	3.9	58.6
	SD 15.8	d 0.9	SD 15.4		15.6		15.8

Lat.	Twilight Naut.	Twilight Civil	Sunrise	Moonrise 23	Moonrise 24	Moonrise 25	Moonrise 26
°	h m	h m	h m	h m	h m	h m	h m
N 72	////	01 10	03 18	■■■	■■■	■■■	■■■
N 70	////	02 07	03 39	■■■	■■■	■■■	■■■
68	////	02 39	03 55	15 27	■■■	■■■	■■■
66	01 01	03 02	04 07	14 44	■■■	■■■	■■■
64	01 51	03 21	04 18	14 15	16 28	■■■	■■■
62	02 20	03 35	04 27	13 54	15 46	17 54	■■■
60	02 42	03 47	04 35	13 36	15 18	17 03	18 30
N 58	02 59	03 58	04 42	13 22	14 57	16 31	17 51
56	03 13	04 07	04 48	13 09	14 39	16 07	17 24
54	03 25	04 15	04 53	12 59	14 24	15 48	17 03
52	03 36	04 22	04 58	12 49	14 11	15 32	16 45
50	03 45	04 28	05 03	12 41	14 00	15 18	16 30
45	04 03	04 41	05 12	12 23	13 36	14 50	15 59
N 40	04 17	04 51	05 20	12 08	13 18	14 28	15 35
35	04 29	05 00	05 27	11 56	13 02	14 10	15 16
30	04 38	05 08	05 32	11 45	12 48	13 54	14 59
20	04 53	05 20	05 42	11 27	12 26	13 27	14 31
N 10	05 05	05 30	05 51	11 11	12 06	13 05	14 07
0	05 14	05 38	05 59	10 57	11 48	12 44	13 45
S 10	05 21	05 46	06 07	10 42	11 29	12 23	13 22
20	05 27	05 53	06 15	10 27	11 10	12 00	12 58
30	05 33	06 00	06 25	10 09	10 48	11 34	12 30
35	05 35	06 04	06 30	09 59	10 35	11 19	12 13
40	05 37	06 09	06 36	09 48	10 20	11 01	11 54
45	05 39	06 13	06 43	09 34	10 03	10 40	11 31
S 50	05 41	06 18	06 51	09 18	09 41	10 14	11 01
52	05 42	06 21	06 55	09 10	09 31	10 01	10 46
54	05 42	06 23	07 00	09 01	09 19	09 46	10 29
56	05 43	06 26	07 04	08 52	09 06	09 29	10 09
58	05 43	06 29	07 09	08 41	08 51	09 08	09 44
S 60	05 44	06 32	07 15	08 29	08 33	08 43	09 09

Lat.	Sunset	Twilight Civil	Twilight Naut.	Moonset 23	Moonset 24	Moonset 25	Moonset 26
°	h m	h m	h m	h m	h m	h m	h m
N 72	20 43	22 42	////	■■■	■■■	■■■	■■■
N 70	20 23	21 52	////	■■■	■■■	■■■	■■■
68	20 08	21 21	////	18 33	■■■	■■■	■■■
66	19 55	20 59	22 53	19 17	■■■	■■■	■■■
64	19 45	20 42	22 09	19 47	19 21	■■■	■■■
62	19 36	20 27	21 41	20 09	20 04	19 55	■■■
60	19 28	20 15	21 20	20 28	20 33	20 47	21 29
N 58	19 22	20 05	21 03	20 43	20 55	21 19	22 07
56	19 16	19 57	20 49	20 56	21 13	21 43	22 34
54	19 10	19 49	20 38	21 07	21 29	22 02	22 56
52	19 06	19 42	20 28	21 17	21 42	22 19	23 13
50	19 01	19 36	20 19	21 27	21 54	22 33	23 23
45	18 52	19 23	20 01	21 46	22 18	23 01	23 59
N 40	18 44	19 13	19 47	22 02	22 38	23 24	24 23
35	18 38	19 04	19 35	22 15	22 54	23 43	24 42
30	18 32	18 57	19 26	22 27	23 09	23 59	24 59
20	18 22	18 45	19 11	22 47	23 33	24 26	00 26
N 10	18 14	18 35	19 00	23 04	23 54	24 50	00 50
0	18 06	18 27	18 51	23 21	24 14	00 14	01 12
S 10	17 58	18 19	18 44	23 37	24 34	00 34	01 34
20	17 50	18 12	18 38	23 55	24 55	00 55	01 58
30	17 41	18 05	18 33	24 15	00 15	01 20	02 25
35	17 35	18 01	18 31	24 27	00 27	01 34	02 41
40	17 29	17 57	18 28	24 41	00 41	01 51	03 00
45	17 22	17 52	18 27	24 58	00 58	02 11	03 23
S 50	17 14	17 47	18 25	00 00	01 18	02 37	03 53
52	17 10	17 45	18 24	00 07	01 28	02 50	04 07
54	17 06	17 43	18 24	00 15	01 39	03 04	04 24
56	17 02	17 40	18 23	00 24	01 51	03 21	04 44
58	16 56	17 37	18 23	00 34	02 06	03 41	05 09
S 60	16 51	17 34	18 22	00 46	02 23	04 06	05 44

Day	SUN Eqn. of Time 00h	SUN Eqn. of Time 12h	SUN Mer. Pass.	MOON Mer. Pass. Upper	MOON Mer. Pass. Lower	Age	Phase
d	m s	m s	h m	h m	h m	d	%
23	02 51	02 43	12 03	17 09	04 44	07	41
24	02 35	02 27	12 03	18 01	05 34	08	51
25	02 19	02 11	12 02	18 58	06 28	09	62

© British Crown Copyright 2022. All rights reserved.

UT	ARIES GHA	VENUS −4.5 GHA	Dec	MARS +1.8 GHA	Dec	JUPITER −2.6 GHA	Dec	SATURN +0.4 GHA	Dec	STARS Name	SHA	Dec
26 00	333 59.3	199 58.7	N 9 04.0	154 37.5	N 1 02.0	290 37.9	N15 13.2	357 29.8	S11 43.3	Acamar	315 12.5	S40 12.3
01	349 01.7	215 01.9	04.4	169 38.5	01.3	305 40.3	13.2	12 32.4	43.4	Achernar	335 20.6	S57 06.7
02	4 04.2	230 05.2	04.8	184 39.5	00.7	320 42.7	13.2	27 35.0	43.5	Acrux	173 01.9	S63 13.9
03	19 06.7	245 08.5 ..	05.2	199 40.5	1 00.0	335 45.1 ..	13.2	42 37.7 ..	43.5	Adhara	255 07.0	S29 00.0
04	34 09.1	260 11.8	05.6	214 41.5	0 59.3	350 47.5	13.2	57 40.3	43.6	Aldebaran	290 41.0	N16 33.4
05	49 11.6	275 15.0	06.0	229 42.6	58.7	5 49.8	13.3	72 43.0	43.7			
S 06	64 14.1	290 18.3	N 9 06.4	244 43.6	N 0 58.0	20 52.2	N15 13.3	87 45.6	S11 43.8	Alioth	166 14.4	N55 50.2
A 07	79 16.5	305 21.5	06.8	259 44.6	57.4	35 54.6	13.3	102 48.3	43.8	Alkaid	152 53.2	N49 12.0
T 08	94 19.0	320 24.8	07.2	274 45.6	56.7	50 57.0	13.3	117 50.9	43.9	Alnair	27 33.9	S46 50.7
U 09	109 21.5	335 28.0 ..	07.6	289 46.6 ..	56.1	65 59.4 ..	13.3	132 53.5 ..	44.0	Alnilam	275 39.0	S 1 11.1
R 10	124 23.9	350 31.3	08.0	304 47.6	55.4	81 01.8	13.3	147 56.2	44.0	Alphard	217 49.2	S 8 45.5
D 11	139 26.4	5 34.5	08.4	319 48.6	54.7	96 04.2	13.3	162 58.8	44.1			
A 12	154 28.8	20 37.8	N 9 08.8	334 49.6	N 0 54.1	111 06.6	N15 13.4	178 01.5	S11 44.2	Alphecca	126 04.7	N26 38.3
Y 13	169 31.3	35 41.0	09.1	349 50.6	53.4	126 08.9	13.4	193 04.1	44.3	Alpheratz	357 35.6	N29 13.2
14	184 33.8	50 44.2	09.5	4 51.6	52.8	141 11.3	13.4	208 06.8	44.3	Altair	62 00.8	N 8 55.9
15	199 36.2	65 47.4 ..	09.9	19 52.6 ..	52.1	156 13.7 ..	13.4	223 09.4 ..	44.4	Ankaa	353 07.9	S42 10.5
16	214 38.7	80 50.7	10.3	34 53.6	51.5	171 16.1	13.4	238 12.0	44.4	Antares	112 17.2	S26 29.1
17	229 41.2	95 53.9	10.7	49 54.6	50.8	186 18.5	13.4	253 14.7	44.5			
18	244 43.6	110 57.1	N 9 11.1	64 55.6	N 0 50.1	201 20.9	N15 13.4	268 17.3	S11 44.6	Arcturus	145 49.1	N19 03.8
19	259 46.1	126 00.3	11.5	79 56.6	49.5	216 23.3	13.5	283 20.0	44.7	Atria	107 12.3	S69 04.4
20	274 48.6	141 03.5	11.9	94 57.6	48.8	231 25.7	13.5	298 22.6	44.8	Avior	234 15.8	S59 34.8
21	289 51.0	156 06.7 ..	12.3	109 58.6 ..	48.2	246 28.1 ..	13.5	313 25.3 ..	44.8	Bellatrix	278 24.2	N 6 22.4
22	304 53.5	171 09.9	12.7	124 59.6	47.5	261 30.4	13.5	328 27.9	44.9	Betelgeuse	270 53.5	N 7 24.8
23	319 56.0	186 13.1	13.1	140 00.6	46.9	276 32.8	13.5	343 30.5	45.0			
27 00	334 58.4	201 16.3	N 9 13.5	155 01.7	N 0 46.2	291 35.2	N15 13.5	358 33.2	S11 45.1	Canopus	263 53.2	S52 42.1
01	350 00.9	216 19.5	13.9	170 02.7	45.5	306 37.6	13.5	13 35.8	45.1	Capella	280 23.7	N46 01.2
02	5 03.3	231 22.7	14.3	185 03.7	44.9	321 40.0	13.5	28 38.5	45.2	Deneb	49 26.2	N45 22.0
03	20 05.8	246 25.8 ..	14.7	200 04.7 ..	44.2	336 42.4 ..	13.6	43 41.1 ..	45.3	Denebola	182 26.4	N14 26.6
04	35 08.3	261 29.0	15.0	215 05.7	43.6	351 44.8	13.6	58 43.8	45.3	Diphda	348 48.2	S17 51.3
05	50 10.7	276 32.2	15.4	230 06.7	42.9	6 47.2	13.6	73 46.4	45.4			
06	65 13.2	291 35.3	N 9 15.8	245 07.7	N 0 42.3	21 49.6	N15 13.6	88 49.0	S11 45.5	Dubhe	193 43.0	N61 37.6
07	80 15.7	306 38.5	16.2	260 08.7	41.6	36 52.0	13.6	103 51.7	45.6	Elnath	278 03.4	N28 37.6
S 08	95 18.1	321 41.6	16.6	275 09.7	40.9	51 54.4	13.6	118 54.3	45.6	Eltanin	90 42.5	N51 29.4
U 09	110 20.6	336 44.8 ..	17.0	290 10.7 ..	40.3	66 56.8 ..	13.6	133 57.0 ..	45.7	Enif	33 39.6	N 9 59.1
N 10	125 23.1	351 47.9	17.4	305 11.7	39.6	81 59.2	13.6	148 59.6	45.8	Fomalhaut	15 15.4	S29 29.7
D 11	140 25.5	6 51.1	17.8	320 12.7	39.0	97 01.6	13.6	164 02.3	45.8			
A 12	155 28.0	21 54.2	N 9 18.2	335 13.7	N 0 38.3	112 04.0	N15 13.7	179 04.9	S11 45.9	Gacrux	171 53.4	S57 14.8
Y 13	170 30.5	36 57.4	18.6	350 14.7	37.6	127 06.3	13.7	194 07.5	46.0	Gienah	175 45.0	S17 40.3
14	185 32.9	52 00.5	19.0	5 15.7	37.0	142 08.7	13.7	209 10.2	46.1	Hadar	148 38.0	S60 29.4
15	200 35.4	67 03.6 ..	19.3	20 16.7 ..	36.3	157 11.1 ..	13.7	224 12.8 ..	46.1	Hamal	327 52.3	N23 34.4
16	215 37.8	82 06.7	19.7	35 17.7	35.7	172 13.5	13.7	239 15.5	46.2	Kaus Aust.	83 33.8	S34 22.5
17	230 40.3	97 09.9	20.1	50 18.7	35.0	187 15.9	13.7	254 18.1	46.3			
18	245 42.8	112 13.0	N 9 20.5	65 19.7	N 0 34.4	202 18.3	N15 13.7	269 20.8	S11 46.3	Kochab	137 20.1	N74 03.8
19	260 45.2	127 16.1	20.9	80 20.7	33.7	217 20.7	13.7	284 23.4	46.4	Markab	13 30.7	N15 20.0
20	275 47.7	142 19.2	21.3	95 21.7	33.0	232 23.1	13.8	299 26.1	46.5	Menkar	314 07.2	N 4 11.0
21	290 50.2	157 22.3 ..	21.7	110 22.7 ..	32.4	247 25.5 ..	13.8	314 28.7 ..	46.6	Menkent	147 59.2	S36 29.2
22	305 52.6	172 25.4	22.1	125 23.7	31.7	262 27.9	13.8	329 31.3	46.6	Miaplacidus	221 39.4	S69 48.6
23	320 55.1	187 28.5	22.5	140 24.8	31.1	277 30.3	13.8	344 34.0	46.7			
28 00	335 57.6	202 31.6	N 9 22.9	155 25.8	N 0 30.4	292 32.7	N15 13.8	359 36.6	S11 46.8	Mirfak	308 29.8	N49 56.5
01	351 00.0	217 34.7	23.2	170 26.8	29.7	307 35.1	13.8	14 39.3	46.8	Nunki	75 48.9	S26 16.1
02	6 02.5	232 37.7	23.6	185 27.8	29.1	322 37.5	13.8	29 41.9	46.9	Peacock	53 07.0	S56 39.6
03	21 05.0	247 40.8 ..	24.0	200 28.8 ..	28.4	337 39.9 ..	13.8	44 44.6 ..	47.0	Pollux	243 19.0	N27 58.2
04	36 07.4	262 43.9	24.4	215 29.8	27.8	352 42.3	13.8	59 47.2	47.1	Procyon	244 52.3	N 5 10.0
05	51 09.9	277 47.0	24.8	230 30.8	27.1	7 44.7	13.8	74 49.8	47.1			
06	66 12.3	292 50.0	N 9 25.2	245 31.8	N 0 26.5	22 47.1	N15 13.9	89 52.5	S11 47.2	Rasalhague	95 59.5	N12 32.7
07	81 14.8	307 53.1	25.6	260 32.8	25.8	37 49.5	13.9	104 55.1	47.3	Regulus	207 36.0	N11 51.3
08	96 17.3	322 56.1	26.0	275 33.8	25.1	52 51.9	13.9	119 57.8	47.3	Rigel	281 05.0	S 8 10.3
M 09	111 19.7	337 59.2 ..	26.3	290 34.8 ..	24.5	67 54.3 ..	13.9	135 00.4 ..	47.4	Rigil Kent.	139 42.2	S60 56.1
O 10	126 22.2	353 02.2	26.7	305 35.8	23.8	82 56.7	13.9	150 03.1	47.5	Sabik	102 04.0	S15 45.2
N 11	141 24.7	8 05.3	27.1	320 36.8	23.2	97 59.1	13.9	165 05.7	47.6			
D 12	156 27.1	23 08.3	N 9 27.5	335 37.8	N 0 22.5	113 01.5	N15 13.9	180 08.3	S11 47.6	Schedar	349 31.9	N56 39.9
A 13	171 29.6	38 11.4	27.9	350 38.8	21.8	128 03.9	13.9	195 11.0	47.7	Shaula	96 11.8	S37 07.3
Y 14	186 32.1	53 14.4	28.3	5 39.8	21.2	143 06.3	13.9	210 13.6	47.8	Sirius	258 27.4	S16 44.7
15	201 34.5	68 17.4 ..	28.7	20 40.8 ..	20.5	158 08.8 ..	13.9	225 16.3 ..	47.8	Spica	158 23.7	S11 17.0
16	216 37.0	83 20.4	29.1	35 41.8	19.9	173 11.2	13.9	240 18.9	47.9	Suhail	222 47.6	S43 31.5
17	231 39.5	98 23.5	29.4	50 42.8	19.2	188 13.6	14.0	255 21.6	48.0			
18	246 41.9	113 26.5	N 9 29.8	65 43.8	N 0 18.5	203 16.0	N15 14.0	270 24.2	S11 48.1	Vega	80 33.7	N38 48.5
19	261 44.4	128 29.5	30.2	80 44.8	17.9	218 18.4	14.0	285 26.8	48.1	Zuben'ubi	136 57.4	S16 08.3
20	276 46.8	143 32.5	30.6	95 45.8	17.2	233 20.8	14.0	300 29.5	48.2			
21	291 49.3	158 35.5 ..	31.0	110 46.8 ..	16.6	248 23.2 ..	14.0	315 32.1 ..	48.3		SHA	Mer. Pass.
22	306 51.8	173 38.5	31.4	125 47.8	15.9	263 25.6	14.0	330 34.8	48.3	Venus	226 17.9	10 33
23	321 54.2	188 41.5	31.7	140 48.8	15.3	278 28.0	14.0	345 37.4	48.4	Mars	180 03.2	13 39
Mer. Pass. 1 39.8		v 3.1	d 0.4	v 1.0	d 0.7	v 2.4	d 0.0	v 2.6	d 0.1	Jupiter	316 36.8	4 33
										Saturn	23 34.8	0 06

© British Crown Copyright 2022. All rights reserved.

UT	SUN GHA	Dec	MOON GHA	v	Dec	d	HP
d h	° ′	° ′	° ′	′	° ′	′	′
26 00	179 29.5	N10 34.4	72 33.7	4.6	S27 27.3	3.7	58.6
01	194 29.6	33.5	86 57.3	4.6	27 31.0	3.5	58.6
02	209 29.8	32.6	101 20.9	4.5	27 34.5	3.3	58.7
03	224 30.0 ..	31.8	115 44.4	4.5	27 37.8	3.2	58.7
04	239 30.2	30.9	130 07.9	4.3	27 41.0	3.0	58.7
05	254 30.3	30.0	144 31.2	4.2	27 44.0	2.8	58.8
06	269 30.5	N10 29.2	158 54.4	4.2	S27 46.8	2.6	58.8
07	284 30.7	28.3	173 17.6	4.0	27 49.4	2.4	58.9
S 08	299 30.9	27.4	187 40.6	4.0	27 51.8	2.3	58.9
A 09	314 31.0 ..	26.6	202 03.6	3.9	27 54.1	2.0	58.9
T 10	329 31.2	25.7	216 26.5	3.9	27 56.1	1.9	59.0
U 11	344 31.4	24.8	230 49.4	3.7	27 58.0	1.7	59.0
R 12	359 31.6	N10 24.0	245 12.1	3.7	S27 59.7	1.5	59.1
D 13	14 31.8	23.1	259 34.8	3.6	28 01.2	1.3	59.1
A 14	29 31.9	22.2	273 57.4	3.5	28 02.5	1.2	59.1
Y 15	44 32.1 ..	21.3	288 19.9	3.5	28 03.7	0.9	59.2
16	59 32.3	20.5	302 42.4	3.4	28 04.6	0.7	59.2
17	74 32.5	19.6	317 04.8	3.4	28 05.3	0.6	59.2
18	89 32.6	N10 18.7	331 27.2	3.3	S28 05.9	0.3	59.3
19	104 32.8	17.9	345 49.5	3.2	28 06.2	0.2	59.3
20	119 33.0	17.0	0 11.7	3.2	28 06.4	0.0	59.3
21	134 33.2 ..	16.1	14 33.9	3.1	28 06.4	0.3	59.4
22	149 33.4	15.3	28 56.0	3.1	28 06.1	0.4	59.4
23	164 33.5	14.4	43 18.1	3.1	28 05.7	0.6	59.5
27 00	179 33.7	N10 13.5	57 40.2	3.0	S28 05.1	0.9	59.5
01	194 33.9	12.6	72 02.2	2.9	28 04.2	1.0	59.5
02	209 34.1	11.8	86 24.1	3.0	28 03.2	1.2	59.6
03	224 34.3 ..	10.9	100 46.1	2.8	28 02.0	1.5	59.6
04	239 34.4	10.0	115 07.9	2.9	28 00.5	1.6	59.6
05	254 34.6	09.1	129 29.8	2.8	27 58.9	1.8	59.7
06	269 34.8	N10 08.3	143 51.6	2.8	S27 57.1	2.1	59.7
07	284 35.0	07.4	158 13.4	2.8	27 55.0	2.2	59.7
S 08	299 35.2	06.5	172 35.2	2.8	27 52.8	2.4	59.8
U 09	314 35.3 ..	05.6	186 57.0	2.7	27 50.4	2.7	59.8
N 10	329 35.5	04.8	201 18.7	2.7	27 47.7	2.8	59.9
D 11	344 35.7	03.9	215 40.4	2.7	27 44.9	3.1	59.9
A 12	359 35.9	N10 03.0	230 02.1	2.7	S27 41.8	3.2	59.9
Y 13	14 36.1	02.1	244 23.8	2.7	27 38.6	3.5	60.0
14	29 36.2	01.3	258 45.5	2.7	27 35.1	3.6	60.0
15	44 36.4	N10 00.4	273 07.2	2.7	27 31.5	3.9	60.0
16	59 36.6	9 59.5	287 28.9	2.7	27 27.6	4.0	60.1
17	74 36.8	58.6	301 50.6	2.7	27 23.6	4.3	60.1
18	89 37.0	N 9 57.8	316 12.3	2.7	S27 19.3	4.4	60.1
19	104 37.2	56.9	330 34.0	2.7	27 14.9	4.7	60.2
20	119 37.3	56.0	344 55.7	2.7	27 10.2	4.9	60.2
21	134 37.5 ..	55.1	359 17.4	2.7	27 05.3	5.1	60.2
22	149 37.7	54.2	13 39.1	2.8	27 00.2	5.2	60.2
23	164 37.9	53.4	28 00.9	2.8	S26 55.0	5.5	60.3
28 00	179 38.1	N 9 52.5	42 22.6	2.8	S26 49.5	5.7	60.3
01	194 38.2	51.6	56 44.4	2.8	26 43.8	5.8	60.3
02	209 38.4	50.7	71 06.2	2.9	26 38.0	6.1	60.4
03	224 38.6 ..	49.9	85 28.1	2.8	26 31.9	6.3	60.4
04	239 38.8	49.0	99 49.9	3.0	26 25.6	6.5	60.4
05	254 39.0	48.1	114 11.9	2.9	26 19.1	6.6	60.5
06	269 39.2	N 9 47.2	128 33.8	3.0	S26 12.5	6.9	60.5
07	284 39.4	46.3	142 55.8	3.0	26 05.6	7.0	60.5
M 08	299 39.5	45.4	157 17.8	3.1	25 58.6	7.3	60.5
O 09	314 39.7 ..	44.6	171 39.9	3.1	25 51.3	7.4	60.6
N 10	329 39.9	43.7	186 02.0	3.1	25 43.9	7.7	60.6
11	344 40.1	42.8	200 24.1	3.2	25 36.2	7.8	60.6
D 12	359 40.3	N 9 41.9	214 46.3	3.2	S25 28.4	8.0	60.7
A 13	14 40.5	41.0	229 08.5	3.4	25 20.4	8.2	60.7
Y 14	29 40.6	40.2	243 30.9	3.3	25 12.2	8.4	60.7
15	44 40.8 ..	39.3	257 53.2	3.4	25 03.8	8.6	60.7
16	59 41.0	38.4	272 15.6	3.5	24 55.2	8.8	60.8
17	74 41.2	37.5	286 38.1	3.5	24 46.4	8.9	60.8
18	89 41.4	N 9 36.6	301 00.6	3.6	S24 37.5	9.2	60.8
19	104 41.6	35.7	315 23.2	3.7	24 28.3	9.3	60.8
20	119 41.8	34.9	329 45.9	3.7	24 19.0	9.5	60.9
21	134 42.0 ..	34.0	344 08.6	3.8	24 09.5	9.7	60.9
22	149 42.1	33.1	358 31.4	3.8	23 59.8	9.8	60.9
23	164 42.3	32.2	12 54.2	4.0	S23 50.0	10.1	60.9
	SD 15.9	d 0.9	SD 16.1		16.3		16.5

Lat.	Twilight Naut.	Civil	Sunrise	Moonrise 26	27	28	29
°	h m	h m	h m	h m	h m	h m	h m
N 72	////	01 46	03 34	■■■	■■■	■■■	■■■
N 70	////	02 28	03 52	■■■	■■■	■■■	22 08
68	////	02 55	04 06	■■■	■■■	■■■	21 11
66	01 32	03 15	04 18	■■■	■■■	■■■	20 36
64	02 09	03 31	04 27	■■■	■■■	20 36	20 11
62	02 34	03 44	04 35	■■■	20 06	19 57	19 51
60	02 53	03 56	04 42	18 30	19 14	19 29	19 35
N 58	03 08	04 05	04 48	17 51	18 42	19 08	19 21
56	03 21	04 13	04 54	17 24	18 18	18 50	19 09
54	03 32	04 21	04 59	17 03	17 58	18 35	18 58
52	03 42	04 27	05 03	16 45	17 42	18 22	18 49
50	03 50	04 33	05 07	16 30	17 28	18 10	18 40
45	04 07	04 45	05 16	15 59	16 59	17 46	18 22
N 40	04 21	04 55	05 23	15 35	16 36	17 26	18 08
35	04 32	05 03	05 29	15 16	16 17	17 10	17 55
30	04 40	05 09	05 34	14 59	16 01	16 56	17 44
20	04 54	05 21	05 43	14 31	15 33	16 32	17 25
N 10	05 05	05 30	05 51	14 07	15 10	16 11	17 08
0	05 13	05 37	05 58	13 44	14 48	15 51	16 53
S 10	05 20	05 44	06 05	13 22	14 26	15 32	16 37
20	05 25	05 51	06 13	12 58	14 02	15 11	16 20
30	05 29	05 57	06 21	12 30	13 34	14 46	16 00
35	05 31	06 01	06 26	12 13	13 18	14 32	15 49
40	05 33	06 04	06 32	11 54	12 59	14 15	15 36
45	05 34	06 08	06 38	11 31	12 36	13 55	15 20
S 50	05 35	06 13	06 45	11 01	12 07	13 29	15 01
52	05 35	06 15	06 49	10 46	11 52	13 17	14 52
54	05 36	06 17	06 53	10 29	11 35	13 03	14 41
56	05 36	06 19	06 57	10 09	11 15	12 46	14 30
58	05 36	06 21	07 01	09 44	10 50	12 26	14 16
S 60	05 36	06 24	07 07	09 09	10 15	12 01	14 00

Lat.	Sunset	Twilight Civil	Naut.	Moonset 26	27	28	29
°	h m	h m	h m	h m	h m	h m	h m
N 72	20 25	22 08	////	■■■	■■■	■■■	■■■
N 70	20 08	21 30	////	■■■	■■■	■■■	■■■
68	19 54	21 04	23 37	■■■	■■■	■■■	■■■
66	19 43	20 45	22 24	■■■	■■■	■■■	■■■
64	19 34	20 29	21 50	■■■	■■■	23 50	26 21
62	19 26	20 16	21 26	■■■	22 07	24 28	00 28
60	19 19	20 06	21 07	21 29	22 58	24 55	00 55
N 58	19 13	19 56	20 52	22 07	23 30	25 16	01 16
56	19 08	19 48	20 40	22 34	23 54	25 33	01 33
54	19 03	19 41	20 29	22 56	24 13	00 13	01 48
52	18 59	19 35	20 20	23 13	24 29	00 29	02 00
50	18 55	19 29	20 11	23 29	24 43	00 43	02 11
45	18 47	19 17	19 55	23 59	25 11	01 11	02 33
N 40	18 40	19 08	19 42	24 23	00 23	01 34	02 53
35	18 34	19 00	19 31	24 42	00 42	01 52	03 08
30	18 29	18 53	19 22	24 59	00 59	02 08	03 21
20	18 20	18 42	19 09	00 26	01 28	02 34	03 44
N 10	18 12	18 33	18 58	00 50	01 52	02 57	04 03
0	18 05	18 26	18 50	01 12	02 14	03 18	04 21
S 10	17 58	18 19	18 44	01 34	02 37	03 39	04 39
20	17 50	18 13	18 39	01 58	03 01	04 02	04 57
30	17 42	18 06	18 34	02 25	03 29	04 28	05 19
35	17 37	18 03	18 33	02 41	03 45	04 43	05 32
40	17 32	18 00	18 31	03 00	04 05	05 00	05 46
45	17 26	17 56	18 30	03 23	04 28	05 21	06 03
S 50	17 19	17 51	18 29	03 53	04 58	05 48	06 24
52	17 15	17 50	18 29	04 07	05 12	06 00	06 34
54	17 11	17 47	18 29	04 24	05 29	06 15	06 45
56	17 07	17 43	18 28	04 44	05 49	06 32	06 57
58	17 03	17 43	18 29	05 09	06 15	06 52	07 11
S 60	16 58	17 40	18 29	05 44	06 50	07 18	07 28

	SUN Eqn. of Time 00ʰ	12ʰ	Mer. Pass.	MOON Mer. Pass. Upper	Lower	Age	Phase
Day	m s	m s	h m	h m	h m	d	%
26	02 03	01 54	12 02	19 59	07 28	10	72
27	01 46	01 37	12 02	21 03	08 31	11	82
28	01 28	01 19	12 01	22 06	09 35	12	90

© British Crown Copyright 2022. All rights reserved.

UT	ARIES GHA	VENUS −4.6 GHA	Dec	MARS +1.7 GHA	Dec	JUPITER −2.6 GHA	Dec	SATURN +0.4 GHA	Dec	STARS Name	SHA	Dec
29 00	336 56.7	203 44.5 N 9	32.1	155 49.8 N 0	14.6	293 30.4 N15	14.0	0 40.1 S11	48.5	Acamar	315 12.5	S40 12.3
01	351 59.2	218 47.5	32.5	170 50.8	13.9	308 32.8	14.0	15 42.7	48.6	Achernar	335 20.6	S57 06.7
02	7 01.6	233 50.4	32.9	185 51.8	13.3	323 35.2	14.0	30 45.3	48.6	Acrux	173 02.0	S63 13.9
03	22 04.1	248 53.4 ..	33.3	200 52.8 ..	12.6	338 37.6 ..	14.0	45 48.0 ..	48.7	Adhara	255 07.0	S29 00.0
04	37 06.6	263 56.4	33.7	215 53.8	12.0	353 40.0	14.0	60 50.6	48.8	Aldebaran	290 40.9	N16 33.4
05	52 09.0	278 59.4	34.0	230 54.8	11.3	8 42.5	14.1	75 53.3	48.8			
06	67 11.5	294 02.3 N 9	34.4	245 55.8 N 0	10.6	23 44.9 N15	14.1	90 55.9 S11	48.9	Alioth	166 14.4	N55 50.1
07	82 13.9	309 05.3	34.8	260 56.8	10.0	38 47.3	14.1	105 58.6	49.0	Alkaid	152 53.2	N49 12.0
T 08	97 16.4	324 08.2	35.2	275 57.8	09.3	53 49.7	14.1	121 01.2	49.1	Alnair	27 33.8	S46 50.8
U 09	112 18.9	339 11.2 ..	35.6	290 58.8 ..	08.7	68 52.1 ..	14.1	136 03.8 ..	49.1	Alnilam	275 39.0	S 1 11.0
E 10	127 21.3	354 14.1	35.9	305 59.8	08.0	83 54.5	14.1	151 06.5	49.2	Alphard	217 49.2	S 8 45.5
S 11	142 23.8	9 17.1	36.3	321 00.8	07.3	98 56.9	14.1	166 09.1	49.3			
D 12	157 26.3	24 20.0 N 9	36.7	336 01.8 N 0	06.7	113 59.3 N15	14.1	181 11.8 S11	49.3	Alphecca	126 04.8	N26 38.3
A 13	172 28.7	39 23.0	37.1	351 02.8	06.0	129 01.7	14.1	196 14.4	49.4	Alpheratz	357 35.6	N29 13.3
Y 14	187 31.2	54 25.9	37.5	6 03.8	05.4	144 04.1	14.1	211 17.1	49.5	Altair	62 00.8	N 8 55.9
15	202 33.7	69 28.8 ..	37.8	21 04.8 ..	04.7	159 06.6 ..	14.1	226 19.7 ..	49.6	Ankaa	353 07.9	S42 10.5
16	217 36.1	84 31.7	38.2	36 05.8	04.0	174 09.0	14.1	241 22.3	49.6	Antares	112 17.2	S26 29.1
17	232 38.6	99 34.7	38.6	51 06.8	03.4	189 11.4	14.1	256 25.0	49.7			
18	247 41.1	114 37.6 N 9	39.0	66 07.8 N 0	02.7	204 13.8 N15	14.1	271 27.6 S11	49.8	Arcturus	145 49.1	N19 03.8
19	262 43.5	129 40.5	39.4	81 08.8	02.1	219 16.2	14.1	286 30.3	49.8	Atria	107 12.4	S69 04.4
20	277 46.0	144 43.4	39.7	96 09.8	01.4	234 18.6	14.2	301 32.9	49.9	Avior	234 15.8	S59 34.8
21	292 48.4	159 46.3 ..	40.1	111 10.8 ..	00.8	249 21.0 ..	14.2	316 35.6 ..	50.0	Bellatrix	278 24.2	N 6 22.4
22	307 50.9	174 49.2	40.5	126 11.8 N	00.1	264 23.5	14.2	331 38.2	50.0	Betelgeuse	270 53.4	N 7 24.8
23	322 53.4	189 52.1	40.9	141 12.8 S	00.6	279 25.9	14.2	346 40.8	50.1			
30 00	337 55.8	204 55.0 N 9	41.2	156 13.8 S 0	01.2	294 28.3 N15	14.2	1 43.5 S11	50.2	Canopus	263 53.2	S52 42.1
01	352 58.3	219 57.9	41.6	171 14.8	01.9	309 30.7	14.2	16 46.1	50.3	Capella	280 23.7	N46 01.2
02	8 00.8	235 00.7	42.0	186 15.8	02.5	324 33.1	14.2	31 48.8	50.3	Deneb	49 26.2	N45 22.0
03	23 03.2	250 03.6 ..	42.4	201 16.8 ..	03.2	339 35.5 ..	14.2	46 51.4 ..	50.4	Denebola	182 26.4	N14 26.6
04	38 05.7	265 06.5	42.7	216 17.8	03.9	354 38.0	14.2	61 54.1	50.5	Diphda	348 48.1	S17 51.3
05	53 08.2	280 09.3	43.1	231 18.8	04.5	9 40.4	14.2	76 56.7	50.5			
06	68 10.6	295 12.2 N 9	43.5	246 19.8 S 0	05.2	24 42.8 N15	14.2	91 59.3 S11	50.6	Dubhe	193 43.0	N61 37.6
W 07	83 13.1	310 15.1	43.9	261 20.8	05.8	39 45.2	14.2	107 02.0	50.7	Elnath	278 03.4	N28 37.6
E 08	98 15.6	325 17.9	44.2	276 21.8	06.5	54 47.6	14.2	122 04.6	50.8	Eltanin	90 42.5	N51 29.4
D 09	113 18.0	340 20.8 ..	44.6	291 22.8 ..	07.2	69 50.0 ..	14.2	137 07.3 ..	50.8	Enif	33 39.6	N 9 59.1
N 10	128 20.5	355 23.6	45.0	306 23.8	07.8	84 52.5	14.2	152 09.9	50.9	Fomalhaut	15 15.4	S29 29.7
E 11	143 22.9	10 26.5	45.3	321 24.8	08.5	99 54.9	14.2	167 12.6	51.0			
S 12	158 25.4	25 29.3 N 9	45.7	336 25.8 S 0	09.1	114 57.3 N15	14.2	182 15.2 S11	51.0	Gacrux	171 53.4	S57 14.8
D 13	173 27.9	40 32.1	46.1	351 26.8	09.8	129 59.7	14.2	197 17.8	51.1	Gienah	175 45.0	S17 40.3
A 14	188 30.3	55 35.0	46.5	6 27.8	10.5	145 02.1	14.2	212 20.5	51.2	Hadar	148 38.0	S60 29.4
Y 15	203 32.8	70 37.8 ..	46.8	21 28.8 ..	11.1	160 04.6 ..	14.3	227 23.1 ..	51.3	Hamal	327 52.3	N23 34.4
16	218 35.3	85 40.6	47.2	36 29.8	11.8	175 07.0	14.3	242 25.8	51.3	Kaus Aust.	83 33.8	S34 22.5
17	233 37.7	100 43.4	47.6	51 30.8	12.4	190 09.4	14.3	257 28.4	51.4			
18	248 40.2	115 46.2 N 9	47.9	66 31.8 S 0	13.1	205 11.8 N15	14.3	272 31.1 S11	51.5	Kochab	137 20.2	N74 03.8
19	263 42.7	130 49.0	48.3	81 32.8	13.8	220 14.3	14.3	287 33.7	51.5	Markab	13 30.7	N15 20.0
20	278 45.1	145 51.8	48.7	96 33.8	14.4	235 16.7	14.3	302 36.3	51.6	Menkar	314 07.2	N 4 11.0
21	293 47.6	160 54.6 ..	49.0	111 34.8 ..	15.1	250 19.1 ..	14.3	317 39.0 ..	51.7	Menkent	147 59.2	S36 29.2
22	308 50.0	175 57.4	49.4	126 35.8	15.7	265 21.5	14.3	332 41.6	51.7	Miaplacidus	221 39.4	S69 48.6
23	323 52.5	191 00.2	49.8	141 36.8	16.4	280 23.9	14.3	347 44.3	51.8			
31 00	338 55.0	206 03.0 N 9	50.1	156 37.8 S 0	17.1	295 26.4 N15	14.3	2 46.9 S11	51.9	Mirfak	308 29.8	N49 56.5
01	353 57.4	221 05.8	50.5	171 38.8	17.7	310 28.8	14.3	17 49.6	52.0	Nunki	75 48.9	S26 16.1
02	8 59.9	236 08.6	50.9	186 39.8	18.4	325 31.2	14.3	32 52.2	52.0	Peacock	53 07.0	S56 39.6
03	24 02.4	251 11.3 ..	51.2	201 40.8 ..	19.0	340 33.6 ..	14.3	47 54.8 ..	52.1	Pollux	243 19.0	N27 58.2
04	39 04.8	266 14.1	51.6	216 41.8	19.7	355 36.1	14.3	62 57.5	52.2	Procyon	244 52.3	N 5 10.0
05	54 07.3	281 16.9	52.0	231 42.8	20.4	10 38.5	14.3	78 00.1	52.2			
06	69 09.8	296 19.6 N 9	52.3	246 43.8 S 0	21.0	25 40.9 N15	14.3	93 02.8 S11	52.3	Rasalhague	95 59.5	N12 32.7
T 07	84 12.2	311 22.4	52.7	261 44.8	21.7	40 43.3	14.3	108 05.4	52.4	Regulus	207 36.0	N11 51.3
H 08	99 14.7	326 25.1	53.1	276 45.8	22.3	55 45.8	14.3	123 08.1	52.5	Rigel	281 05.0	S 8 10.3
U 09	114 17.2	341 27.9 ..	53.4	291 46.8 ..	23.0	70 48.2 ..	14.3	138 10.7 ..	52.5	Rigil Kent.	139 42.2	S60 56.1
R 10	129 19.6	356 30.6	53.8	306 47.8	23.7	85 50.6	14.3	153 13.3	52.6	Sabik	102 04.0	S15 45.2
S 11	144 22.1	11 33.4	54.2	321 48.8	24.3	100 53.1	14.3	168 16.0	52.7			
D 12	159 24.5	26 36.1 N 9	54.5	336 49.8 S 0	25.0	115 55.5 N15	14.3	183 18.6 S11	52.7	Schedar	349 31.9	N56 39.9
A 13	174 27.0	41 38.8	54.9	351 50.8	25.6	130 57.9	14.3	198 21.3	52.8	Shaula	96 11.8	S37 07.3
Y 14	189 29.5	56 41.6	55.2	6 51.8	26.3	146 00.3	14.3	213 23.9	52.9	Sirius	258 27.4	S16 44.7
15	204 31.9	71 44.3 ..	55.6	21 52.8 ..	27.0	161 02.8 ..	14.3	228 26.6 ..	53.0	Spica	158 23.7	S11 17.0
16	219 34.4	86 47.0	56.0	36 53.8	27.6	176 05.2	14.3	243 29.2	53.0	Suhail	222 47.6	S43 31.5
17	234 36.9	101 49.7	56.3	51 54.8	28.3	191 07.6	14.3	258 31.8	53.1			
18	249 39.3	116 52.4 N 9	56.7	66 55.8 S 0	28.9	206 10.1 N15	14.3	273 34.5 S11	53.2	Vega	80 33.8	N38 48.5
19	264 41.8	131 55.1	57.0	81 56.8	29.6	221 12.5	14.3	288 37.1	53.2	Zuben'ubi	136 57.4	S16 08.4
20	279 44.3	146 57.8	57.4	96 57.8	30.3	236 14.9	14.3	303 39.8	53.3			
21	294 46.7	162 00.5 ..	57.7	111 58.8 ..	30.9	251 17.3 ..	14.3	318 42.4 ..	53.4			
22	309 49.2	177 03.2	58.1	126 59.8	31.6	266 19.8	14.3	333 45.0	53.4			
23	324 52.5	192 05.9	58.5	142 00.8	32.2	281 22.2	14.3	348 47.7	53.5			

		SHA	Mer. Pass.
		° ′	h m
Venus		226 59.1	10 18
Mars		178 18.0	13 34
Jupiter		316 32.5	4 21
Saturn		23 47.6	23 49

	ARIES	VENUS	MARS	JUPITER	SATURN
Mer. Pass.	1 28.0	v 2.8 d 0.4	v 1.0 d 0.7	v 2.4 d 0.0	v 2.6 d 0.1

© British Crown Copyright 2022. All rights reserved.

UT	SUN GHA	Dec	MOON GHA	v	Dec	d	HP
d h	° '	° '	° '	'	° '	'	'
29 00	179 42.5	N 9 31.3	27 17.2	4.0	S23 39.9	10.2	60.9
01	194 42.7	30.4	41 40.2	4.0	23 29.7	10.4	61.0
02	209 42.9	29.5	56 03.2	4.2	23 19.3	10.5	61.0
03	224 43.1	28.7	70 26.4	4.2	23 08.8	10.7	61.0
04	239 43.3	27.8	84 49.6	4.3	22 58.1	10.9	61.0
05	254 43.5	26.9	99 12.9	4.4	22 47.2	11.1	61.0
06	269 43.6	N 9 26.0	113 36.3	4.5	S22 36.1	11.2	61.1
07	284 43.8	25.1	127 59.8	4.5	22 24.9	11.4	61.1
T 08	299 44.0	24.2	142 23.3	4.6	22 13.5	11.6	61.1
U 09	314 44.2	23.3	156 46.9	4.7	22 01.9	11.7	61.1
E 10	329 44.4	22.5	171 10.6	4.8	21 50.2	11.9	61.1
S 11	344 44.6	21.6	185 34.4	4.9	21 38.3	12.0	61.2
D 12	359 44.8	N 9 20.7	199 58.3	4.9	S21 26.3	12.2	61.2
A 13	14 45.0	19.8	214 22.2	5.1	21 14.1	12.3	61.2
Y 14	29 45.1	18.9	228 46.3	5.1	21 01.8	12.5	61.2
15	44 45.3	18.0	243 10.4	5.2	20 49.3	12.6	61.2
16	59 45.5	17.1	257 34.6	5.3	20 36.7	12.8	61.2
17	74 45.7	16.2	271 58.9	5.4	20 23.9	12.9	61.2
18	89 45.9	N 9 15.3	286 23.3	5.5	S20 11.0	13.1	61.3
19	104 46.1	14.4	300 47.8	5.6	19 57.9	13.2	61.3
20	119 46.3	13.6	315 12.4	5.6	19 44.7	13.3	61.3
21	134 46.5	12.7	329 37.0	5.8	19 31.4	13.5	61.3
22	149 46.7	11.8	344 01.8	5.8	19 17.9	13.6	61.3
23	164 46.9	10.9	358 26.6	6.0	19 04.3	13.7	61.3
30 00	179 47.1	N 9 10.0	12 51.6	6.0	S18 50.6	13.9	61.3
01	194 47.2	09.1	27 16.6	6.1	18 36.7	14.0	61.3
02	209 47.4	08.2	41 41.7	6.2	18 22.7	14.1	61.3
03	224 47.6	07.3	56 06.9	6.3	18 08.6	14.3	61.3
04	239 47.8	06.4	70 32.2	6.4	17 54.3	14.4	61.3
05	254 48.0	05.5	84 57.6	6.4	17 39.9	14.4	61.4
06	269 48.2	N 9 04.6	99 23.0	6.6	S17 25.5	14.7	61.4
W 07	284 48.4	03.7	113 48.6	6.6	17 10.8	14.7	61.4
E 08	299 48.6	02.9	128 14.2	6.8	16 56.1	14.8	61.4
D 09	314 48.8	02.0	142 40.0	6.8	16 41.3	15.0	61.4
N 10	329 49.0	01.1	157 05.8	6.9	16 26.3	15.0	61.4
E 11	344 49.2	9 00.2	171 31.7	7.1	16 11.3	15.2	61.4
S 12	359 49.4	N 8 59.3	185 57.8	7.1	S15 56.1	15.2	61.4
D 13	14 49.6	58.4	200 23.9	7.1	15 40.9	15.4	61.4
A 14	29 49.7	57.5	214 50.0	7.3	15 25.5	15.5	61.4
Y 15	44 49.9	56.6	229 16.3	7.4	15 10.0	15.5	61.4
16	59 50.1	55.7	243 42.7	7.4	14 54.5	15.7	61.4
17	74 50.3	54.8	258 09.1	7.6	14 38.8	15.7	61.4
18	89 50.5	N 8 53.9	272 35.7	7.7	S14 23.1	15.8	61.4
19	104 50.7	53.0	287 02.3	7.7	14 07.3	16.0	61.4
20	119 50.9	52.1	301 29.0	7.8	13 51.3	16.0	61.4
21	134 51.1	51.2	315 55.8	7.9	13 35.3	16.1	61.4
22	149 51.3	50.3	330 22.7	7.9	13 19.2	16.1	61.4
23	164 51.5	49.4	344 49.6	8.1	13 03.1	16.3	61.4
31 00	179 51.7	N 8 48.5	359 16.7	8.1	S12 46.8	16.3	61.4
01	194 51.9	47.6	13 43.8	8.2	12 30.5	16.4	61.4
02	209 52.1	46.7	28 11.0	8.3	12 14.1	16.5	61.4
03	224 52.3	45.8	42 38.3	8.4	11 57.6	16.6	61.4
04	239 52.5	44.9	57 05.7	8.4	11 41.0	16.6	61.3
05	254 52.7	44.0	71 33.1	8.5	11 24.4	16.6	61.3
06	269 52.8	N 8 43.1	86 00.6	8.6	S11 07.8	16.8	61.3
07	284 53.0	42.2	100 28.2	8.7	10 51.0	16.8	61.3
T 08	299 53.2	41.3	114 55.9	8.7	10 34.2	16.8	61.3
H 09	314 53.4	40.4	129 23.6	8.8	10 17.4	16.9	61.3
U 10	329 53.6	39.5	143 51.4	8.9	10 00.5	17.0	61.3
R 11	344 53.8	38.6	158 19.3	9.0	9 43.5	17.0	61.3
S 12	359 54.0	N 8 37.7	172 47.3	9.0	S 9 26.5	17.1	61.3
D 13	14 54.2	36.8	187 15.3	9.1	9 09.4	17.1	61.3
A 14	29 54.4	35.9	201 43.4	9.2	8 52.3	17.2	61.2
Y 15	44 54.6	35.0	216 11.6	9.2	8 35.1	17.2	61.2
16	59 54.8	34.1	230 39.8	9.3	8 17.9	17.2	61.2
17	74 55.0	33.2	245 08.1	9.4	8 00.7	17.3	61.2
18	89 55.2	N 8 32.3	259 36.5	9.5	S 7 43.4	17.3	61.2
19	104 55.4	31.4	274 05.0	9.5	7 26.1	17.4	61.2
20	119 55.6	30.5	288 33.5	9.5	7 08.7	17.4	61.1
21	134 55.8	29.6	303 02.0	9.6	6 51.3	17.4	61.1
22	149 56.0	28.7	317 30.6	9.7	6 33.9	17.4	61.1
23	164 56.2	27.8	331 59.3	9.7	S 6 16.5	17.5	61.1
	SD 15.9	d 0.9	SD 16.7	16.7	16.7		

Twilight and Moonrise

Lat.	Naut.	Civil	Sunrise	Moonrise 29	30	31	1
°	h m	h m	h m	h m	h m	h m	h m
N 72	////	02 13	03 50	■■■	21 12	20 19	19 39
N 70	////	02 46	04 05	22 08	20 46	20 08	19 39
68	01 05	03 09	04 17	21 11	20 27	20 00	19 38
66	01 55	03 27	04 28	20 36	20 11	19 53	19 38
64	02 24	03 42	04 36	20 11	19 58	19 47	19 38
62	02 46	03 54	04 43	19 51	19 46	19 42	19 38
60	03 03	04 04	04 49	19 35	19 37	19 37	19 37
N 58	03 17	04 12	04 55	19 21	19 28	19 33	19 37
56	03 29	04 20	05 00	19 09	19 21	19 30	19 37
54	03 39	04 26	05 04	18 58	19 14	19 27	19 37
52	03 48	04 32	05 08	18 49	19 08	19 24	19 37
50	03 56	04 38	05 11	18 40	19 03	19 21	19 37
45	04 12	04 49	05 19	18 22	18 51	19 15	19 36
N 40	04 24	04 58	05 26	18 08	18 41	19 10	19 36
35	04 34	05 05	05 31	17 55	18 33	19 06	19 36
30	04 42	05 11	05 36	17 44	18 25	19 02	19 36
20	04 55	05 21	05 44	17 25	18 12	18 55	19 35
N 10	05 05	05 30	05 51	17 08	18 01	18 49	19 35
0	05 12	05 36	05 57	16 53	17 50	18 44	19 35
S 10	05 18	05 43	06 04	16 37	17 39	18 38	19 35
20	05 23	05 48	06 11	16 20	17 28	18 32	19 35
30	05 26	05 54	06 18	16 00	17 14	18 26	19 34
35	05 27	05 57	06 22	15 49	17 06	18 22	19 34
40	05 28	06 00	06 27	15 36	16 58	18 17	19 34
45	05 29	06 03	06 33	15 20	16 47	18 12	19 34
S 50	05 29	06 07	06 39	15 01	16 34	18 06	19 34
52	05 29	06 08	06 42	14 52	16 28	18 03	19 34
54	05 29	06 10	06 46	14 41	16 22	18 00	19 34
56	05 29	06 12	06 49	14 30	16 15	17 56	19 34
58	05 28	06 14	06 53	14 16	16 06	17 52	19 34
S 60	05 28	06 16	06 58	14 00	15 57	17 48	19 34

Sunset, Twilight and Moonset

Lat.	Sunset	Civil	Naut.	Moonset 29	30	31	1
°	h m	h m	h m	h m	h m	h m	h m
N 72	20 08	21 41	////	■■■	■■■	03 27	06 13
N 70	19 53	21 11	////	■■■	00 29	03 50	06 19
68	19 41	20 48	22 45	■■■	01 24	04 07	06 25
66	19 32	20 31	22 01	■■■	01 57	04 21	06 29
64	19 24	20 17	21 33	26 21	02 21	04 32	06 33
62	19 17	20 06	21 12	00 28	02 40	04 42	06 36
60	19 10	19 56	20 55	00 55	02 55	04 50	06 38
N 58	19 05	19 47	20 42	01 16	03 08	04 57	06 41
56	19 00	19 40	20 30	01 33	03 19	05 03	06 43
54	18 56	19 34	20 20	01 48	03 29	05 09	06 45
52	18 52	19 28	20 12	02 00	03 37	05 14	06 46
50	18 49	19 23	20 04	02 11	03 45	05 18	06 48
45	18 41	19 12	19 49	02 34	04 01	05 28	06 51
N 40	18 35	19 03	19 36	02 53	04 15	05 36	06 54
35	18 30	18 56	19 27	03 08	04 26	05 45	06 57
30	18 25	18 50	19 18	03 21	04 36	05 48	06 59
20	18 17	18 40	19 06	03 44	04 52	05 59	07 02
N 10	18 10	18 32	18 56	04 03	05 07	06 08	07 05
0	18 04	18 25	18 49	04 21	05 20	06 16	07 08
S 10	17 58	18 19	18 44	04 39	05 33	06 24	07 11
20	17 51	18 13	18 39	04 57	05 47	06 33	07 14
30	17 44	18 08	18 36	05 19	06 03	06 42	07 17
35	17 40	18 05	18 35	05 32	06 13	06 48	07 19
40	17 35	18 02	18 34	05 46	06 23	06 54	07 21
45	17 29	17 59	18 33	06 03	06 35	07 01	07 24
S 50	17 23	17 56	18 33	06 24	06 50	07 10	07 27
52	17 20	17 54	18 33	06 34	06 57	07 14	07 28
54	17 17	17 52	18 34	06 45	07 04	07 18	07 29
56	17 13	17 51	18 34	06 57	07 12	07 23	07 31
58	17 09	17 49	18 34	07 11	07 22	07 28	07 33
S 60	17 05	17 47	18 35	07 28	07 33	07 34	07 35

SUN and MOON

Day	Eqn. of Time 00h	12h	Mer. Pass.	Mer. Pass. Upper	Lower	Age	Phase
d	m s	m s	h m	h m	h m	d	%
29	01 10	01 01	12 01	23 06	10 37	13	96
30	00 52	00 43	12 01	24 03	11 35	14	99
31	00 34	00 24	12 00	00 03	12 30	15	100

© British Crown Copyright 2022. All rights reserved.

UT	ARIES	VENUS −4·7		MARS +1·7		JUPITER −2·6		SATURN +0·4		STARS		
	GHA	GHA	Dec	GHA	Dec	GHA	Dec	GHA	Dec	Name	SHA	Dec
d h	° ′	° ′	° ′	° ′	° ′	° ′	° ′	° ′	° ′		° ′	° ′
1 00	339 54.1	207 08.6	N 9 58.8	157 01.8	S 0 32.9	296 24.6	N15 14.3	3 50.3	S11 53.6	Acamar	315 12.4	S40 12.3
01	354 56.6	222 11.3	59.2	172 02.8	33.6	311 27.1	14.3	18 53.0	53.7	Achernar	335 20.6	S57 06.8
02	9 59.0	237 14.0	59.5	187 03.8	34.2	326 29.5	14.3	33 55.6	53.7	Acrux	173 02.0	S63 13.9
03	25 01.5	252 16.6	9 59.9	202 04.8 . .	34.9	341 31.9 . .	14.3	48 58.3 . .	53.8	Adhara	255 07.0	S29 00.0
04	40 04.0	267 19.3	10 00.2	217 05.8	35.5	356 34.4	14.3	64 00.9	53.9	Aldebaran	290 40.9	N16 33.4
05	55 06.4	282 22.0	00.6	232 06.7	36.2	11 36.8	14.3	79 03.5	53.9			
06	70 08.9	297 24.6	N10 00.9	247 07.7	S 0 36.9	26 39.2	N15 14.3	94 06.2	S11 54.0	Alioth	166 14.4	N55 50.1
07	85 11.4	312 27.3	01.3	262 08.7	37.5	41 41.7	14.3	109 08.8	54.1	Alkaid	152 53.2	N49 12.0
08	100 13.8	327 29.9	01.6	277 09.7	38.2	56 44.1	14.3	124 11.5	54.2	Alnair	27 33.8	S46 50.8
F 09	115 16.3	342 32.6 . .	02.0	292 10.7 . .	38.8	71 46.5 . .	14.3	139 14.1 . .	54.2	Alnilam	275 39.0	S 1 11.0
R 10	130 18.8	357 35.2	02.4	307 11.7	39.5	86 49.0	14.3	154 16.8	54.3	Alphard	217 49.2	S 8 45.5
I 11	145 21.2	12 37.8	02.7	322 12.7	40.2	101 51.4	14.3	169 19.4	54.4			
D 12	160 23.7	27 40.5	N10 03.1	337 13.7	S 0 40.8	116 53.9	N15 14.3	184 22.0	S11 54.4	Alphecca	126 04.8	N26 38.3
A 13	175 26.1	42 43.1	03.4	352 14.7	41.5	131 56.3	14.3	199 24.7	54.5	Alpheratz	357 35.6	N29 13.3
Y 14	190 28.6	57 45.7	03.8	7 15.7	42.2	146 58.7	14.3	214 27.3	54.6	Altair	62 00.8	N 8 56.0
15	205 31.1	72 48.4 . .	04.1	22 16.7 . .	42.8	162 01.2 . .	14.3	229 30.0 . .	54.6	Ankaa	353 07.9	S42 10.5
16	220 33.5	87 51.0	04.4	37 17.7	43.5	177 03.6	14.3	244 32.6	54.7	Antares	112 17.2	S26 29.1
17	235 36.0	102 53.6	04.8	52 18.7	44.1	192 06.0	14.3	259 35.3	54.8			
18	250 38.5	117 56.2	N10 05.1	67 19.7	S 0 44.8	207 08.5	N15 14.3	274 37.9	S11 54.9	Arcturus	145 49.1	N19 03.8
19	265 40.9	132 58.8	05.5	82 20.7	45.5	222 10.9	14.3	289 40.5	54.9	Atria	107 12.4	S69 04.4
20	280 43.4	148 01.4	05.8	97 21.7	46.1	237 13.4	14.3	304 43.2	55.0	Avior	234 15.7	S59 34.8
21	295 45.9	163 04.0 . .	06.2	112 22.7 . .	46.8	252 15.8 . .	14.3	319 45.8 . .	55.1	Bellatrix	278 24.2	N 6 22.4
22	310 48.3	178 06.6	06.5	127 23.7	47.4	267 18.2	14.3	334 48.5	55.1	Betelgeuse	270 53.4	N 7 24.8
23	325 50.8	193 09.2	06.9	142 24.7	48.1	282 20.7	14.3	349 51.1	55.2			
2 00	340 53.3	208 11.7	N10 07.2	157 25.7	S 0 48.8	297 23.1	N15 14.3	4 53.7	S11 55.3	Canopus	263 53.1	S52 42.1
01	355 55.7	223 14.3	07.6	172 26.7	49.4	312 25.6	14.3	19 56.4	55.3	Capella	280 23.6	N46 01.2
02	10 58.2	238 16.9	07.9	187 27.6	50.1	327 28.0	14.3	34 59.0	55.4	Deneb	49 26.2	N45 22.0
03	26 00.6	253 19.5 . .	08.2	202 28.6 . .	50.7	342 30.4 . .	14.3	50 01.7 . .	55.5	Denebola	182 26.4	N14 26.6
04	41 03.1	268 22.0	08.6	217 29.6	51.4	357 32.9	14.3	65 04.3	55.6	Diphda	348 48.1	S17 51.3
05	56 05.6	283 24.6	08.9	232 30.6	52.1	12 35.3	14.3	80 07.0	55.6			
06	71 08.0	298 27.2	N10 09.3	247 31.6	S 0 52.7	27 37.8	N15 14.3	95 09.6	S11 55.7	Dubhe	193 43.0	N61 37.5
07	86 10.5	313 29.7	09.6	262 32.6	53.4	42 40.2	14.3	110 12.2	55.8	Elnath	278 03.4	N28 37.6
S 08	101 13.0	328 32.3	09.9	277 33.6	54.0	57 42.6	14.3	125 14.9	55.8	Eltanin	90 42.5	N51 29.4
A 09	116 15.4	343 34.8 . .	10.3	292 34.6 . .	54.7	72 45.1 . .	14.3	140 17.5 . .	55.9	Enif	33 39.6	N 9 59.1
T 10	131 17.9	358 37.3	10.6	307 35.6	55.4	87 47.5	14.3	155 20.2	56.0	Fomalhaut	15 15.4	S29 29.7
U 11	146 20.4	13 39.9	11.0	322 36.6	56.0	102 50.0	14.3	170 22.8	56.0			
R 12	161 22.8	28 42.4	N10 11.3	337 37.6	S 0 56.7	117 52.4	N15 14.3	185 25.5	S11 56.1	Gacrux	171 53.4	S57 14.8
D 13	176 25.3	43 44.9	11.6	352 38.6	57.3	132 54.9	14.3	200 28.1	56.2	Gienah	175 45.1	S17 40.3
A 14	191 27.7	58 47.5	12.0	7 39.6	58.0	147 57.3	14.3	215 30.7	56.3	Hadar	148 38.0	S60 29.3
Y 15	206 30.2	73 50.0 . .	12.3	22 40.6 . .	58.7	162 59.8 . .	14.3	230 33.4 . .	56.3	Hamal	327 52.3	N23 34.4
16	221 32.7	88 52.5	12.6	37 41.6	0 59.3	178 02.2	14.3	245 36.0	56.4	Kaus Aust.	83 33.8	S34 22.5
17	236 35.1	103 55.0	13.0	52 42.6	1 00.0	193 04.6	14.3	260 38.7	56.5			
18	251 37.6	118 57.5	N10 13.3	67 43.6	S 1 00.7	208 07.1	N15 14.3	275 41.3	S11 56.5	Kochab	137 20.2	N74 03.8
19	266 40.1	134 00.0	13.6	82 44.5	01.3	223 09.5	14.3	290 43.9	56.6	Markab	13 30.7	N15 20.0
20	281 42.5	149 02.5	14.0	97 45.5	02.0	238 12.0	14.3	305 46.6	56.7	Menkar	314 07.2	N 4 11.0
21	296 45.0	164 05.0 . .	14.3	112 46.5 . .	02.6	253 14.4 . .	14.3	320 49.2 . .	56.7	Menkent	147 59.2	S36 29.2
22	311 47.5	179 07.5	14.6	127 47.5	03.3	268 16.9	14.3	335 51.9	56.8	Miaplacidus	221 39.4	S69 48.6
23	326 49.9	194 10.0	15.0	142 48.5	04.0	283 19.3	14.3	350 54.5	56.9			
3 00	341 52.4	209 12.5	N10 15.3	157 49.5	S 1 04.6	298 21.8	N15 14.3	5 57.2	S11 57.0	Mirfak	308 29.7	N49 56.5
01	356 54.9	224 14.9	15.6	172 50.5	05.3	313 24.2	14.3	20 59.8	57.0	Nunki	75 48.9	S26 16.1
02	11 57.3	239 17.4	16.0	187 51.5	05.9	328 26.7	14.3	36 02.4	57.1	Peacock	53 07.0	S56 39.6
03	26 59.8	254 19.9 . .	16.3	202 52.5 . .	06.6	343 29.1 . .	14.3	51 05.1 . .	57.2	Pollux	243 18.9	N27 58.2
04	42 02.2	269 22.3	16.6	217 53.5	07.3	358 31.6	14.3	66 07.7	57.2	Procyon	244 52.2	N 5 10.0
05	57 04.7	284 24.8	16.9	232 54.5	07.9	13 34.0	14.2	81 10.4	57.3			
06	72 07.2	299 27.3	N10 17.3	247 55.5	S 1 08.6	28 36.5	N15 14.2	96 13.0	S11 57.4	Rasalhague	95 59.5	N12 32.7
07	87 09.6	314 29.7	17.6	262 56.5	09.2	43 38.9	14.2	111 15.6	57.4	Regulus	207 36.0	N11 51.3
08	102 12.1	329 32.2	17.9	277 57.4	09.9	58 41.4	14.2	126 18.3	57.5	Rigel	281 05.0	S 8 10.3
S 09	117 14.6	344 34.6 . .	18.2	292 58.4 . .	10.6	73 43.8 . .	14.2	141 20.9 . .	57.6	Rigil Kent.	139 42.2	S60 56.1
U 10	132 17.0	359 37.0	18.6	307 59.4	11.2	88 46.3	14.2	156 23.6	57.6	Sabik	102 04.0	S15 45.2
N 11	147 19.5	14 39.5	18.9	323 00.4	11.9	103 48.7	14.2	171 26.2	57.7			
D 12	162 22.0	29 41.9	N10 19.2	338 01.4	S 1 12.6	118 51.2	N15 14.2	186 28.8	S11 57.8	Schedar	349 31.9	N56 39.9
A 13	177 24.4	44 44.3	19.5	353 02.4	13.2	133 53.6	14.2	201 31.5	57.9	Shaula	96 11.8	S37 07.3
Y. 14	192 26.9	59 46.8	19.9	8 03.4	13.9	148 56.1	14.2	216 34.1	57.9	Sirius	258 27.4	S16 44.7
15	207 29.3	74 49.2 . .	20.2	23 04.4 . .	14.5	163 58.5 . .	14.2	231 36.8 . .	58.0	Spica	158 23.7	S11 17.0
16	222 31.8	89 51.6	20.5	38 05.4	15.2	179 01.0	14.2	246 39.4	58.1	Suhail	222 47.6	S43 31.4
17	237 34.3	104 54.0	20.8	53 06.4	15.9	194 03.5	14.2	261 42.1	58.1			
18	252 36.7	119 56.4	N10 21.1	68 07.4	S 1 16.5	209 05.9	N15 14.2	276 44.7	S11 58.2	Vega	80 33.8	N38 48.5
19	267 39.2	134 58.8	21.5	83 08.4	17.2	224 08.4	14.2	291 47.3	58.3	Zuben'ubi	136 57.4	S16 08.3
20	282 41.7	150 01.2	21.8	98 09.3	17.8	239 10.8	14.2	306 50.0	58.3			
21	297 44.1	165 03.6 . .	22.1	113 10.3 . .	18.5	254 13.3 . .	14.2	321 52.6 . .	58.4		SHA	Mer. Pass.
22	312 46.6	180 06.0	22.4	128 11.3	19.2	269 15.7	14.2	336 55.3	58.5	Venus	° ′ 227 18.5	h m 10 05
23	327 49.1	195 08.4	22.7	143 12.3	19.8	284 18.2	14.2	351 57.9	58.6	Mars	176 32.4	13 29
Mer. Pass.	h m 1 16.2	v 2.5	d 0.3	v 1.0	d 0.7	v 2.4	d 0.0	v 2.6	d 0.1	Jupiter Saturn	316 29.9 24 00.5	4 10 23 36

© British Crown Copyright 2022. All rights reserved.

UT	SUN GHA	SUN Dec	MOON GHA	v	Dec	d	HP
1 00	179 56.4	N 8 26.9	346 28.0	9.8	S 5 59.0	17.5	61.1
01	194 56.6	26.0	0 56.8	9.9	5 41.5	17.5	61.1
02	209 56.8	25.1	15 25.7	9.9	5 24.0	17.6	61.1
03	224 57.0	.. 24.2	29 54.6	10.0	5 06.4	17.5	61.0
04	239 57.2	23.3	44 23.6	10.0	4 48.9	17.6	61.0
05	254 57.4	22.4	58 52.6	10.0	4 31.3	17.6	61.0
06	269 57.6	N 8 21.5	73 21.6	10.1	S 4 13.7	17.6	61.0
07	284 57.8	20.6	87 50.7	10.2	3 56.1	17.6	61.0
F 08	299 58.0	19.7	102 19.9	10.2	3 38.5	17.6	60.9
R 09	314 58.2	.. 18.8	116 49.1	10.3	3 20.9	17.6	60.9
I 10	329 58.4	17.9	131 18.4	10.3	3 03.3	17.6	60.9
D 11	344 58.6	17.0	145 47.7	10.3	2 45.7	17.6	60.9
A 12	359 58.8	N 8 16.1	160 17.0	10.4	S 2 28.1	17.6	60.8
Y 13	14 59.0	15.2	174 46.4	10.4	2 10.5	17.6	60.8
14	29 59.2	14.3	189 15.8	10.5	1 52.9	17.7	60.8
15	44 59.4	.. 13.4	203 45.3	10.5	1 35.2	17.6	60.8
16	59 59.6	12.4	218 14.8	10.5	1 17.6	17.6	60.7
17	74 59.8	11.5	232 44.3	10.6	1 00.0	17.5	60.7
18	90 00.0	N 8 10.6	247 13.9	10.6	S 0 42.5	17.5	60.7
19	105 00.2	09.7	261 43.5	10.7	0 24.9	17.5	60.7
20	120 00.4	08.8	276 13.2	10.7	S 0 07.3	17.5	60.6
21	135 00.6	.. 07.9	290 42.9	10.7	N 0 10.2	17.5	60.6
22	150 00.8	07.0	305 12.6	10.7	0 27.7	17.5	60.6
23	165 01.0	06.1	319 42.3	10.8	0 45.2	17.5	60.5
2 00	180 01.2	N 8 05.2	334 12.1	10.8	N 1 02.7	17.5	60.5
01	195 01.4	04.3	348 41.9	10.8	1 20.2	17.4	60.5
02	210 01.6	03.4	3 11.7	10.9	1 37.6	17.4	60.5
03	225 01.8	.. 02.5	17 41.6	10.8	1 55.0	17.4	60.4
04	240 02.0	01.5	32 11.4	10.9	2 12.4	17.4	60.4
05	255 02.2	8 00.6	46 41.3	10.9	2 29.8	17.3	60.4
06	270 02.4	N 7 59.7	61 11.2	11.0	N 2 47.1	17.3	60.3
S 07	285 02.6	58.8	75 41.2	10.9	3 04.4	17.2	60.3
A 08	300 02.8	57.9	90 11.1	11.0	3 21.6	17.2	60.3
T 09	315 03.0	.. 57.0	104 41.1	11.0	3 38.8	17.2	60.2
U 10	330 03.2	56.1	119 11.1	11.0	3 56.0	17.1	60.2
R 11	345 03.4	55.2	133 41.1	11.0	4 13.1	17.1	60.2
D 12	0 03.6	N 7 54.3	148 11.1	11.1	N 4 30.2	17.1	60.1
A 13	15 03.8	53.4	162 41.2	11.0	4 47.3	17.0	60.1
Y 14	30 04.0	52.4	177 11.2	11.1	5 04.3	16.9	60.1
15	45 04.2	.. 51.5	191 41.3	11.0	5 21.2	16.9	60.0
16	60 04.4	50.6	206 11.3	11.1	5 38.1	16.9	60.0
17	75 04.6	49.7	220 41.4	11.1	5 55.0	16.8	60.0
18	90 04.8	N 7 48.8	235 11.5	11.1	N 6 11.8	16.7	59.9
19	105 05.0	47.9	249 41.6	11.0	6 28.5	16.7	59.9
20	120 05.2	47.0	264 11.6	11.1	6 45.2	16.6	59.9
21	135 05.4	.. 46.1	278 41.7	11.1	7 01.8	16.6	59.8
22	150 05.6	45.1	293 11.8	11.1	7 18.4	16.5	59.8
23	165 05.8	44.2	307 41.9	11.1	7 34.9	16.5	59.8
3 00	180 06.0	N 7 43.3	322 12.0	11.1	N 7 51.4	16.4	59.7
01	195 06.2	42.4	336 42.1	11.1	8 07.8	16.3	59.7
02	210 06.4	41.5	351 12.2	11.1	8 24.1	16.3	59.6
03	225 06.6	.. 40.6	5 42.3	11.1	8 40.4	16.2	59.6
04	240 06.8	39.7	20 12.4	11.1	8 56.6	16.1	59.6
05	255 07.0	38.7	34 42.5	11.1	9 12.7	16.1	59.5
06	270 07.2	N 7 37.8	49 12.6	11.1	N 9 28.8	16.0	59.5
07	285 07.4	36.9	63 42.7	11.0	9 44.8	15.9	59.5
08	300 07.6	36.0	78 12.7	11.0	10 00.7	15.9	59.4
S 09	315 07.8	.. 35.1	92 42.8	11.0	10 16.6	15.7	59.4
U 10	330 08.1	34.2	107 12.8	11.1	10 32.3	15.7	59.3
N 11	345 08.3	33.2	121 42.9	11.0	10 48.0	15.7	59.3
D 12	0 08.5	N 7 32.3	136 12.9	11.0	N11 03.7	15.5	59.3
A 13	15 08.7	31.4	150 42.9	11.0	11 19.2	15.5	59.2
Y 14	30 08.9	30.5	165 12.9	11.0	11 34.7	15.3	59.2
15	45 09.1	.. 29.6	179 42.9	10.9	11 50.0	15.3	59.1
16	60 09.3	28.7	194 12.8	10.9	12 05.3	15.2	59.1
17	75 09.5	27.7	208 42.8	10.9	12 20.5	15.2	59.1
18	90 09.7	N 7 26.8	223 12.7	11.0	N12 35.7	15.0	59.0
19	105 09.9	25.9	237 42.7	10.9	12 50.7	14.9	59.0
20	120 10.1	25.0	252 12.6	10.8	13 05.6	14.9	59.0
21	135 10.3	.. 24.1	266 42.4	10.9	13 20.5	14.8	58.9
22	150 10.5	23.2	281 12.3	10.8	13 35.3	14.7	58.9
23	165 10.7	22.2	295 42.1	10.9	N13 50.0	14.5	58.8
	SD 15.9	d 0.9	SD 16.6		16.4		16.1

Lat.	Twilight Naut.	Twilight Civil	Sunrise	Moonrise 1	2	3	4
°	h m	h m	h m	h m	h m	h m	h m
N 72	////	02 36	04 05	19 39	19 02	18 16	16 34
N 70	////	03 03	04 18	19 39	19 10	18 37	17 43
68	01 37	03 23	04 29	19 38	19 18	18 54	18 21
66	02 14	03 39	04 37	19 38	19 24	19 08	18 47
64	02 39	03 52	04 45	19 38	19 29	19 19	19 08
62	02 58	04 03	04 51	19 38	19 33	19 29	19 25
60	03 13	04 12	04 56	19 37	19 37	19 37	19 39
N 58	03 26	04 19	05 01	19 37	19 41	19 45	19 51
56	03 37	04 26	05 06	19 37	19 44	19 52	20 01
54	03 46	04 32	05 09	19 37	19 47	19 58	20 11
52	03 54	04 37	05 13	19 37	19 49	20 03	20 19
50	04 01	04 42	05 16	19 37	19 52	20 08	20 27
45	04 16	04 52	05 23	19 36	19 57	20 19	20 43
N 40	04 27	05 01	05 28	19 36	20 01	20 27	20 56
35	04 37	05 07	05 33	19 36	20 05	20 35	21 08
30	04 44	05 13	05 37	19 36	20 08	20 42	21 18
20	04 56	05 22	05 45	19 35	20 14	20 54	21 35
N 10	05 05	05 30	05 51	19 35	20 20	21 04	21 51
0	05 11	05 36	05 56	19 35	20 25	21 14	22 05
S 10	05 16	05 41	06 02	19 35	20 30	21 24	22 19
20	05 20	05 46	06 08	19 35	20 35	21 35	22 35
30	05 23	05 51	06 15	19 34	20 41	21 47	22 53
35	05 24	05 53	06 18	19 34	20 45	21 55	23 03
40	05 24	05 55	06 22	19 34	20 49	22 03	23 15
45	05 24	05 58	06 27	19 34	20 54	22 13	23 30
S 50	05 23	06 01	06 33	19 34	21 00	22 24	23 48
52	05 23	06 02	06 36	19 34	21 03	22 30	23 56
54	05 22	06 03	06 39	19 34	21 06	22 36	24 05
56	05 21	06 04	06 42	19 34	21 09	22 43	24 16
58	05 20	06 06	06 45	19 34	21 13	22 51	24 28
S 60	05 19	06 07	06 49	19 34	21 17	22 59	24 43

Lat.	Sunset	Twilight Civil	Twilight Naut.	Moonset 1	2	3	4
°	h m	h m	h m	h m	h m	h m	h m
N 72	19 51	21 18	////	06 13	08 43	11 16	14 44
N 70	19 39	20 52	23 22	06 19	08 38	10 57	13 37
68	19 28	20 33	22 15	06 25	08 34	10 43	13 01
66	19 20	20 18	21 41	06 29	08 30	10 31	12 36
64	19 13	20 05	21 17	06 33	08 27	10 21	12 17
62	19 07	19 55	20 58	06 36	08 25	10 13	12 01
60	19 02	19 46	20 44	06 38	08 23	10 05	11 48
N 58	18 57	19 38	20 31	06 41	08 21	09 59	11 37
56	18 53	19 32	20 21	06 43	08 19	09 54	11 27
54	18 49	19 26	20 12	06 45	08 18	09 49	11 19
52	18 46	19 21	20 04	06 46	08 16	09 44	11 11
50	18 43	19 16	19 57	06 48	08 15	09 40	11 04
45	18 36	19 06	19 42	06 51	08 12	09 32	10 50
N 40	18 31	18 58	19 31	06 54	08 10	09 25	10 38
35	18 26	18 52	19 22	06 57	08 08	09 18	10 28
30	18 22	18 46	19 15	06 59	08 07	09 13	10 19
20	18 15	18 37	19 03	07 02	08 04	09 04	10 04
N 10	18 09	18 30	18 55	07 05	08 01	08 56	09 50
0	18 03	18 24	18 48	07 08	07 59	08 48	09 38
S 10	17 58	18 19	18 43	07 11	07 56	08 41	09 26
20	17 52	18 14	18 40	07 14	07 53	08 33	09 13
30	17 45	18 09	18 37	07 17	07 51	08 24	08 58
35	17 42	18 07	18 37	07 19	07 49	08 18	08 49
40	17 38	18 05	18 36	07 21	07 47	08 12	08 40
45	17 33	18 02	18 36	07 24	07 45	08 06	08 28
S 50	17 27	18 00	18 37	07 27	07 42	07 58	08 15
52	17 25	17 59	18 38	07 28	07 41	07 54	08 09
54	17 22	17 58	18 39	07 29	07 39	07 50	08 02
56	17 19	17 56	18 39	07 31	07 38	07 45	07 54
58	17 15	17 55	18 40	07 33	07 36	07 40	07 45
S 60	17 12	17 54	18 42	07 35	07 35	07 35	07 35

	SUN Eqn. of Time 00h	SUN Eqn. of Time 12h	SUN Mer. Pass.	MOON Mer. Pass. Upper	MOON Mer. Pass. Lower	Age	Phase
Day	m s	m s	h m	h m	h m	d	%
1	00 15	00 05	12 00	00 56	13 22	16	97
2	00 04	00 14	12 00	01 47	14 12	17	91
3	00 24	00 33	11 59	02 36	15 01	18	84

© British Crown Copyright 2022. All rights reserved.

UT (d h)	ARIES GHA	VENUS −4.7 GHA	Dec	MARS +1.7 GHA	Dec	JUPITER −2.6 GHA	Dec	SATURN +0.4 GHA	Dec	STARS Name	SHA	Dec
4 00	342 51.5	210 10.8	N10 23.1	158 13.3	S 1 20.5	299 20.6	N15 14.1	7 00.5	S11 58.6	Acamar	315 12.4	S40 12.3
01	357 54.0	225 13.1	23.4	173 14.3	21.2	314 23.1	14.1	22 03.2	58.7	Achernar	335 20.6	S57 06.8
02	12 56.5	240 15.5	23.7	188 15.3	21.8	329 25.6	14.1	37 05.8	58.8	Acrux	173 02.0	S63 13.8
03	27 58.9	255 17.9 ..	24.0	203 16.3 ..	22.5	344 28.0 ..	14.1	52 08.5 ..	58.8	Adhara	255 06.9	S28 59.9
04	43 01.4	270 20.2	24.3	218 17.3	23.1	359 30.5	14.1	67 11.1	58.9	Aldebaran	290 40.9	N16 33.4
05	58 03.8	285 22.6	24.6	233 18.3	23.8	14 32.9	14.1	82 13.7	59.0			
06	73 06.3	300 25.0	N10 24.9	248 19.3	S 1 24.5	29 35.4	N15 14.1	97 16.4	S11 59.0	Alioth	166 14.4	N55 50.1
07	88 08.8	315 27.3	25.2	263 20.2	25.1	44 37.8	14.1	112 19.0	59.1	Alkaid	152 53.2	N49 12.0
M 08	103 11.2	330 29.7	25.6	278 21.2	25.8	59 40.3	14.1	127 21.7	59.2	Alnair	27 33.8	S46 50.8
O 09	118 13.7	345 32.0 ..	25.9	293 22.2 ..	26.4	74 42.8 ..	14.1	142 24.3 ..	59.2	Alnilam	275 38.9	S 1 11.0
N 10	133 16.2	0 34.4	26.2	308 23.2	27.1	89 45.2	14.1	157 27.0	59.3	Alphard	217 49.2	S 8 45.5
D 11	148 18.6	15 36.7	26.5	323 24.2	27.8	104 47.7	14.1	172 29.6	59.4			
A 12	163 21.1	30 39.0	N10 26.8	338 25.2	S 1 28.4	119 50.1	N15 14.1	187 32.2	S11 59.4	Alphecca	126 04.8	N26 38.3
Y 13	178 23.6	45 41.3	27.1	353 26.2	29.1	134 52.6	14.1	202 34.9	59.5	Alpheratz	357 35.6	N29 13.3
14	193 26.0	60 43.7	27.4	8 27.2	29.7	149 55.1	14.1	217 37.5	59.6	Altair	62 00.8	N 8 56.0
15	208 28.5	75 46.0 ..	27.7	23 28.2 ..	30.4	164 57.5 ..	14.1	232 40.2 ..	59.7	Ankaa	353 07.8	S42 10.5
16	223 31.0	90 48.3	28.0	38 29.2	31.1	180 00.0	14.0	247 42.8	59.7	Antares	112 17.2	S26 29.1
17	238 33.4	105 50.6	28.3	53 30.1	31.7	195 02.5	14.0	262 45.4	59.8			
18	253 35.9	120 52.9	N10 28.6	68 31.1	S 1 32.4	210 04.9	N15 14.0	277 48.1	S11 59.9	Arcturus	145 49.1	N19 03.8
19	268 38.3	135 55.2	28.9	83 32.1	33.1	225 07.4	14.0	292 50.7	11 59.9	Atria	107 12.4	S69 04.4
20	283 40.8	150 57.5	29.2	98 33.1	33.7	240 09.8	14.0	307 53.4	12 00.0	Avior	234 15.7	S59 34.8
21	298 43.3	165 59.8 ..	29.5	113 34.1 ..	34.4	255 12.3 ..	14.0	322 56.0 ..	00.1	Bellatrix	278 24.1	N 6 22.4
22	313 45.7	181 02.1	29.8	128 35.1	35.0	270 14.8	14.0	337 58.6	00.1	Betelgeuse	270 53.4	N 7 24.8
23	328 48.2	196 04.4	30.1	143 36.1	35.7	285 17.2	14.0	353 01.3	00.2			
5 00	343 50.7	211 06.7	N10 30.4	158 37.1	S 1 36.4	300 19.7	N15 14.0	8 03.9	S12 00.3	Canopus	263 53.1	S52 42.1
01	358 53.1	226 09.0	30.7	173 38.0	37.0	315 22.2	14.0	23 06.6	00.3	Capella	280 23.6	N46 01.2
02	13 55.6	241 11.2	31.0	188 39.0	37.7	330 24.6	14.0	38 09.2	00.4	Deneb	49 26.2	N45 22.0
03	28 58.1	256 13.5 ..	31.3	203 40.0 ..	38.3	345 27.1 ..	13.9	53 11.8 ..	00.5	Denebola	182 26.4	N14 26.6
04	44 00.5	271 15.8	31.6	218 41.0	39.0	0 29.6	13.9	68 14.5	00.6	Diphda	348 48.1	S17 51.3
05	59 03.0	286 18.0	31.9	233 42.0	39.7	15 32.0	13.9	83 17.1	00.6			
06	74 05.4	301 20.3	N10 32.2	248 43.0	S 1 40.3	30 34.5	N15 13.9	98 19.8	S12 00.7	Dubhe	193 43.0	N61 37.5
07	89 07.9	316 22.6	32.5	263 44.0	41.0	45 37.0	13.9	113 22.4	00.8	Elnath	278 03.3	N28 37.6
T 08	104 10.4	331 24.8	32.8	278 45.0	41.7	60 39.4	13.9	128 25.0	00.8	Eltanin	90 42.5	N51 29.4
U 09	119 12.8	346 27.1 ..	33.1	293 46.0 ..	42.3	75 41.9 ..	13.9	143 27.7 ..	00.9	Enif	33 39.6	N 9 59.1
E 10	134 15.3	1 29.3	33.4	308 46.9	43.0	90 44.4	13.9	158 30.3	01.0	Fomalhaut	15 15.4	S29 29.7
S 11	149 17.8	16 31.5	33.7	323 47.9	43.6	105 46.8	13.9	173 33.0	01.0			
D 12	164 20.2	31 33.8	N10 34.0	338 48.9	S 1 44.3	120 49.3	N15 13.9	188 35.6	S12 01.1	Gacrux	171 53.5	S57 14.7
A 13	179 22.7	46 36.0	34.3	353 49.9	45.0	135 51.8	13.9	203 38.2	01.2	Gienah	175 45.1	S17 40.3
Y 14	194 25.2	61 38.2	34.6	8 50.9	45.6	150 54.3	13.8	218 40.9	01.2	Hadar	148 38.0	S60 29.3
15	209 27.6	76 40.5 ..	34.9	23 51.9 ..	46.3	165 56.7 ..	13.8	233 43.5 ..	01.3	Hamal	327 52.2	N23 34.5
16	224 30.1	91 42.7	35.1	38 52.9	47.0	180 59.2	13.8	248 46.2	01.4	Kaus Aust.	83 33.8	S34 22.5
17	239 32.6	106 44.9	35.4	53 53.9	47.6	196 01.7	13.8	263 48.8	01.4			
18	254 35.0	121 47.1	N10 35.7	68 54.8	S 1 48.3	211 04.1	N15 13.8	278 51.4	S12 01.5	Kochab	137 20.3	N74 03.8
19	269 37.5	136 49.3	36.0	83 55.8	48.9	226 06.6	13.8	293 54.1	01.6	Markab	13 30.7	N15 20.0
20	284 39.9	151 51.5	36.3	98 56.8	49.6	241 09.1	13.8	308 56.7	01.6	Menkar	314 07.2	N 4 11.1
21	299 42.4	166 53.7 ..	36.6	113 57.8 ..	50.3	256 11.6 ..	13.8	323 59.4 ..	01.7	Menkent	147 59.2	S36 29.2
22	314 44.9	181 55.9	36.9	128 58.8	50.9	271 14.0	13.8	339 02.0	01.8	Miaplacidus	221 39.4	S69 48.6
23	329 47.3	196 58.1	37.2	143 59.8	51.6	286 16.5	13.7	354 04.6	01.9			
6 00	344 49.8	212 00.3	N10 37.4	159 00.8	S 1 52.2	301 19.0	N15 13.7	9 07.3	S12 01.9	Mirfak	308 29.7	N49 56.5
01	359 52.3	227 02.5	37.7	174 01.7	52.9	316 21.4	13.7	24 09.9	02.0	Nunki	75 49.0	S26 16.1
02	14 54.7	242 04.6	38.0	189 02.7	53.6	331 23.9	13.7	39 12.6	02.1	Peacock	53 07.0	S56 39.6
03	29 57.2	257 06.8 ..	38.3	204 03.7 ..	54.2	346 26.4 ..	13.7	54 15.2 ..	02.1	Pollux	243 18.9	N27 58.2
04	44 59.7	272 09.0	38.6	219 04.7	54.9	1 28.9	13.7	69 17.8	02.2	Procyon	244 52.2	N 5 10.0
05	60 02.1	287 11.2	38.8	234 05.7	55.6	16 31.3	13.7	84 20.5	02.3			
06	75 04.6	302 13.3	N10 39.1	249 06.7	S 1 56.2	31 33.8	N15 13.7	99 23.1	S12 02.3	Rasalhague	95 59.5	N12 32.7
W 07	90 07.1	317 15.5	39.4	264 07.7	56.9	46 36.3	13.7	114 25.8	02.4	Regulus	207 35.9	N11 51.3
E 08	105 09.5	332 17.6	39.7	279 08.6	57.5	61 38.8	13.6	129 28.4	02.5	Rigel	281 05.0	S 8 10.3
D 09	120 12.0	347 19.8 ..	40.0	294 09.6 ..	58.2	76 41.2 ..	13.6	144 31.0 ..	02.5	Rigil Kent.	139 42.2	S60 56.1
N 10	135 14.4	2 21.9	40.2	309 10.6	58.9	91 43.7	13.6	159 33.7	02.6	Sabik	102 04.0	S15 45.2
E 11	150 16.9	17 24.1	40.5	324 11.6	1 59.5	106 46.2	13.6	174 36.3	02.7			
S 12	165 19.4	32 26.2	N10 40.8	339 12.6	S 2 00.2	121 48.7	N15 13.6	189 39.0	S12 02.7	Schedar	349 31.8	N56 39.9
D 13	180 21.8	47 28.4	41.1	354 13.6	00.8	136 51.2	13.6	204 41.6	02.8	Shaula	96 11.8	S37 07.3
A 14	195 24.3	62 30.5	41.3	9 14.6	01.5	151 53.6	13.6	219 44.2	02.9	Sirius	258 27.4	S16 44.7
Y 15	210 26.8	77 32.6 ..	41.6	24 15.5 ..	02.2	166 56.1 ..	13.6	234 46.9 ..	02.9	Spica	158 23.7	S11 17.0
16	225 29.2	92 34.7	41.9	39 16.5	02.8	181 58.6	13.6	249 49.5	03.0	Suhail	222 47.5	S43 31.4
17	240 31.7	107 36.9	42.1	54 17.5	03.5	197 01.1	13.5	264 52.1	03.1			
18	255 34.2	122 39.0	N10 42.4	69 18.5	S 2 04.2	212 03.5	N15 13.5	279 54.8	S12 03.1	Vega	80 33.8	N38 48.5
19	270 36.6	137 41.1	42.7	84 19.5	04.8	227 06.0	13.5	294 57.4	03.2	Zuben'ubi	136 57.4	S16 08.3
20	285 39.1	152 43.2	43.0	99 20.5	05.5	242 08.5	13.5	310 00.1	03.3			
21	300 41.5	167 45.3 ..	43.2	114 21.4 ..	06.1	257 11.0 ..	13.5	325 02.7 ..	03.3		SHA	Mer. Pass.
22	315 44.0	182 47.4	43.5	129 22.4	06.8	272 13.5	13.5	340 05.3	03.4	Venus	227 16.0	9 54
23	330 46.5	197 49.5	43.8	144 23.4	07.5	287 16.0	13.5	355 08.0	03.5	Mars	174 46.4	13 25
Mer. Pass.	1 04.4	v 2.2	d 0.3	v 1.0	d 0.7	v 2.5	d 0.0	v 2.6	d 0.1	Jupiter	316 29.0	3 58
										Saturn	24 13.3	23 24

© British Crown Copyright 2022. All rights reserved.

UT	SUN GHA	SUN Dec	MOON GHA	MOON v	MOON Dec	MOON d	MOON HP
d h	° '	° '	° '	'	° '	'	'
4 00	180 10.9	N 7 21.3	310 12.0	10.7	N14 04.5	14.5	58.8
01	195 11.1	20.4	324 41.7	10.8	14 19.0	14.4	58.8
02	210 11.3	19.5	339 11.5	10.8	14 33.4	14.3	58.7
03	225 11.5 ..	18.6	353 41.3	10.7	14 47.7	14.2	58.7
04	240 11.8	17.6	8 11.0	10.7	15 01.9	14.1	58.6
05	255 12.0	16.7	22 40.7	10.7	15 16.0	14.0	58.6
06	270 12.2	N 7 15.8	37 10.4	10.6	N15 30.0	14.0	58.5
07	285 12.4	14.9	51 40.0	10.6	15 44.0	13.8	58.5
M 08	300 12.6	14.0	66 09.6	10.6	15 57.8	13.7	58.5
O 09	315 12.8 ..	13.0	80 39.2	10.6	16 11.5	13.6	58.4
N 10	330 13.0	12.1	95 08.8	10.5	16 25.1	13.4	58.4
D 11	345 13.2	11.2	109 38.3	10.5	16 38.5	13.4	58.3
A 12	0 13.4	N 7 10.3	124 07.8	10.5	N16 51.9	13.3	58.3
Y 13	15 13.6	09.3	138 37.3	10.5	17 05.2	13.2	58.3
14	30 13.8	08.4	153 06.8	10.4	17 18.4	13.0	58.2
15	45 14.0 ..	07.5	167 36.2	10.4	17 31.4	13.0	58.2
16	60 14.2	06.6	182 05.6	10.3	17 44.4	12.8	58.1
17	75 14.4	05.7	196 34.9	10.3	17 57.2	12.8	58.1
18	90 14.7	N 7 04.7	211 04.2	10.3	N18 10.0	12.6	58.1
19	105 14.9	03.8	225 33.5	10.3	18 22.6	12.5	58.0
20	120 15.1	02.9	240 02.8	10.2	18 35.1	12.4	58.0
21	135 15.3 ..	02.0	254 32.0	10.2	18 47.5	12.2	57.9
22	150 15.5	01.0	269 01.2	10.2	18 59.7	12.2	57.9
23	165 15.7	7 00.1	283 30.4	10.1	19 11.9	12.0	57.9
5 00	180 15.9	N 6 59.2	297 59.5	10.1	N19 23.9	12.0	57.8
01	195 16.1	58.3	312 28.6	10.0	19 35.9	11.8	57.8
02	210 16.3	57.3	326 57.6	10.1	19 47.7	11.6	57.7
03	225 16.5 ..	56.4	341 26.7	10.0	19 59.3	11.6	57.7
04	240 16.7	55.5	355 55.7	9.9	20 10.9	11.4	57.7
05	255 16.9	54.6	10 24.6	9.9	20 22.3	11.3	57.6
06	270 17.2	N 6 53.6	24 53.5	9.9	N20 33.6	11.2	57.6
07	285 17.4	52.7	39 22.4	9.9	20 44.8	11.1	57.5
T 08	300 17.6	51.8	53 51.3	9.8	20 55.9	10.9	57.5
U 09	315 17.8 ..	50.9	68 20.1	9.8	21 06.8	10.9	57.5
E 10	330 18.0	49.9	82 48.9	9.7	21 17.7	10.6	57.4
S 11	345 18.2	49.0	97 17.6	9.7	21 28.3	10.6	57.4
D 12	0 18.4	N 6 48.1	111 46.3	9.7	N21 38.9	10.4	57.4
A 13	15 18.6	47.2	126 15.0	9.6	21 49.3	10.3	57.3
Y 14	30 18.8	46.2	140 43.6	9.6	21 59.6	10.2	57.3
15	45 19.0 ..	45.3	155 12.2	9.6	22 09.8	10.0	57.2
16	60 19.2	44.4	169 40.8	9.5	22 19.8	10.0	57.2
17	75 19.5	43.5	184 09.3	9.6	22 29.8	9.7	57.2
18	90 19.7	N 6 42.5	198 37.9	9.4	N22 39.5	9.7	57.1
19	105 19.9	41.6	213 06.3	9.5	22 49.2	9.5	57.1
20	120 20.1	40.7	227 34.8	9.4	22 58.7	9.4	57.0
21	135 20.3 ..	39.7	242 03.2	9.3	23 08.1	9.2	57.0
22	150 20.5	38.8	256 31.5	9.4	23 17.3	9.1	57.0
23	165 20.7	37.9	270 59.9	9.3	23 26.4	9.0	56.9
6 00	180 20.9	N 6 37.0	285 28.2	9.3	N23 35.4	8.8	56.9
01	195 21.1	36.0	299 56.5	9.2	23 44.2	8.7	56.9
02	210 21.4	35.1	314 24.7	9.2	23 52.9	8.6	56.8
03	225 21.6 ..	34.2	328 52.9	9.2	24 01.5	8.4	56.8
04	240 21.8	33.2	343 21.1	9.2	24 09.9	8.3	56.7
05	255 22.0	32.3	357 49.3	9.1	24 18.2	8.2	56.7
06	270 22.2	N 6 31.4	12 17.4	9.1	N24 26.4	8.0	56.7
07	285 22.4	30.5	26 45.5	9.0	24 34.4	7.8	56.6
W 08	300 22.6	29.5	41 13.5	9.1	24 42.2	7.8	56.6
E 09	315 22.8 ..	28.6	55 41.6	9.0	24 50.0	7.5	56.6
D 10	330 23.0	27.7	70 09.6	9.0	24 57.5	7.5	56.5
N 11	345 23.3	26.7	84 37.6	8.9	25 05.0	7.3	56.5
E 12	0 23.5	N 6 25.8	99 05.5	9.0	N25 12.3	7.2	56.5
S 13	15 23.7	24.9	113 33.5	8.9	25 19.5	7.0	56.4
D 14	30 23.9	23.9	128 01.4	8.8	25 26.5	6.8	56.4
A 15	45 24.1 ..	23.0	142 29.2	8.9	25 33.3	6.8	56.4
Y 16	60 24.3	22.1	156 57.1	8.8	25 40.1	6.6	56.3
17	75 24.5	21.1	171 24.9	8.9	25 46.7	6.4	56.3
18	90 24.7	N 6 20.2	185 52.8	8.8	N25 53.1	6.3	56.3
19	105 24.9	19.3	200 20.6	8.7	25 59.4	6.1	56.2
20	120 25.2	18.3	214 48.3	8.8	26 05.5	6.0	56.2
21	135 25.4 ..	17.4	229 16.1	8.7	26 11.5	5.9	56.2
22	150 25.6	16.5	243 43.8	8.8	26 17.4	5.7	56.1
23	165 25.8	15.5	258 11.6	8.7	N26 23.1	5.6	56.1
	SD 15.9	d 0.9	SD 15.9		15.6		15.4

Lat.	Twilight Naut.	Twilight Civil	Sunrise	Moonrise 4	5	6	7
°	h m	h m	h m	h m	h m	h m	h m
N 72	////	02 56	04 19	16 34	□	□	□
N 70	01 13	03 19	04 31	17 43	□	□	□
68	02 01	03 37	04 40	18 21	□	□	□
66	02 31	03 50	04 47	18 47	18 10	□	□
64	02 52	04 02	04 53	19 08	18 52	18 09	□
62	03 09	04 11	04 59	19 25	19 20	19 15	19 09
60	03 23	04 19	05 04	19 39	19 42	19 51	20 11
N 58	03 34	04 26	05 08	19 51	20 00	20 16	20 45
56	03 44	04 32	05 11	20 01	20 15	20 37	21 10
54	03 53	04 38	05 15	20 11	20 28	20 54	21 30
52	04 00	04 43	05 18	20 19	20 40	21 08	21 47
50	04 07	04 47	05 20	20 27	20 50	21 21	22 01
45	04 20	04 56	05 26	20 43	21 12	21 47	22 31
N 40	04 31	05 04	05 31	20 56	21 29	22 08	22 54
35	04 39	05 10	05 35	21 08	21 44	22 26	23 13
30	04 46	05 15	05 39	21 18	21 57	22 41	23 29
20	04 57	05 23	05 45	21 35	22 19	23 06	23 57
N 10	05 05	05 29	05 51	21 50	22 38	23 29	24 21
0	05 11	05 35	05 56	22 05	22 56	23 50	24 43
S 10	05 15	05 39	06 00	22 19	23 15	24 10	00 10
20	05 18	05 43	06 05	22 35	23 34	24 33	00 33
30	05 19	05 47	06 11	22 53	23 57	24 59	00 59
35	05 20	05 49	06 14	23 03	24 10	00 10	01 15
40	05 19	05 51	06 18	23 15	24 26	00 26	01 33
45	05 19	05 52	06 22	23 30	24 45	00 45	01 55
S 50	05 17	05 54	06 27	23 48	25 08	01 08	02 23
52	05 16	05 55	06 29	23 56	25 19	01 19	02 36
54	05 15	05 56	06 31	24 05	00 05	01 32	02 53
56	05 14	05 57	06 34	24 16	00 16	01 47	03 11
58	05 12	05 58	06 37	24 28	00 28	02 05	03 34
S 60	05 11	05 59	06 40	24 43	00 43	02 26	04 05

Lat.	Sunset	Twilight Civil	Twilight Naut.	Moonset 4	5	6	7
°	h m	h m	h m	h m	h m	h m	h m
N 72	19 35	20 56	////	14 44	□	□	□
N 70	19 24	20 35	22 33	13 37	□	□	□
68	19 16	20 18	21 50	13 01	□	□	□
66	19 08	20 04	21 23	12 36	15 01	□	□
64	19 02	19 53	21 02	12 17	14 20	16 54	□
62	18 57	19 44	20 46	12 01	13 52	15 47	17 46
60	18 52	19 36	20 32	11 48	13 31	15 13	16 44
N 58	18 48	19 30	20 21	11 37	13 14	14 48	16 10
56	18 45	19 24	20 12	11 27	12 59	14 28	15 45
54	18 42	19 18	20 03	11 19	12 47	14 11	15 26
52	18 39	19 14	19 56	11 11	12 36	13 57	15 09
50	18 36	19 09	19 50	11 04	12 26	13 44	14 55
45	18 30	19 00	19 36	10 50	12 06	13 19	14 25
N 40	18 26	18 53	19 26	10 38	11 49	12 59	14 03
35	18 22	18 47	19 18	10 28	11 36	12 42	13 44
30	18 18	18 42	19 11	10 19	11 24	12 27	13 28
20	18 12	18 34	19 00	10 04	11 03	12 03	13 01
N 10	18 07	18 28	18 53	09 50	10 46	11 41	12 37
0	18 02	18 23	18 47	09 38	10 29	11 22	12 15
S 10	17 57	18 18	18 43	09 26	10 13	11 02	11 54
20	17 52	18 15	18 40	09 13	09 55	10 41	11 30
30	17 47	18 11	18 39	08 58	09 35	10 17	11 03
35	17 44	18 09	18 39	08 49	09 24	10 03	10 47
40	17 40	18 08	18 39	08 40	09 10	09 46	10 29
45	17 36	18 06	18 40	08 29	08 55	09 27	10 06
S 50	17 32	18 04	18 41	08 15	08 36	09 02	09 38
52	17 30	18 03	18 42	08 09	08 27	08 51	09 24
54	17 27	18 03	18 44	08 02	08 17	08 37	09 08
56	17 25	18 02	18 45	07 54	08 05	08 22	08 49
58	17 22	18 01	18 47	07 45	07 52	08 04	08 25
S 60	17 18	18 00	18 48	07 35	07 37	07 42	07 54

Day	SUN Eqn. of Time 00h	SUN Eqn. of Time 12h	SUN Mer. Pass.	MOON Mer. Pass. Upper	MOON Mer. Pass. Lower	Age	Phase
d	m s	m s	h m	h m	h m	d	%
4	00 43	00 53	11 59	03 26	15 51	19	75
5	01 03	01 13	11 59	04 17	16 43	20	65
6	01 23	01 33	11 58	05 09	17 36	21	55

© British Crown Copyright 2022. All rights reserved.

UT	ARIES GHA	VENUS −4.8 GHA	Dec	MARS +1.7 GHA	Dec	JUPITER −2.6 GHA	Dec	SATURN +0.4 GHA	Dec	STARS Name	SHA	Dec
7 00	345 48.9	212 51.6	N10 44.0	159 24.4	S 2 08.1	302 18.4	N15 13.4	10 10.6	S12 03.6	Acamar	315 12.4	S40 12.3
01	0 51.4	227 53.7	44.3	174 25.4	08.8	317 20.9	13.4	25 13.3	03.6	Achernar	335 20.5	S57 06.8
02	15 53.9	242 55.8	44.6	189 26.4	09.5	332 23.4	13.4	40 15.9	03.7	Acrux	173 02.0	S63 13.8
03	30 56.3	257 57.8	.. 44.8	204 27.4	.. 10.1	347 25.9	.. 13.4	55 18.5	.. 03.8	Adhara	255 06.9	S28 59.9
04	45 58.8	272 59.9	45.1	219 28.3	10.8	2 28.4	13.4	70 21.2	03.8	Aldebaran	290 40.9	N16 33.5
05	61 01.3	288 02.0	45.3	234 29.3	11.4	17 30.8	13.4	85 23.8	03.9			
06	76 03.7	303 04.1	N10 45.6	249 30.3	S 2 12.1	32 33.3	N15 13.4	100 26.5	S12 04.0	Alioth	166 14.4	N55 50.1
07	91 06.2	318 06.1	45.9	264 31.3	12.8	47 35.8	13.4	115 29.1	04.0	Alkaid	152 53.2	N49 12.0
T 08	106 08.7	333 08.2	46.1	279 32.3	13.4	62 38.3	13.3	130 31.7	04.1	Alnair	27 33.8	S46 50.8
H 09	121 11.1	348 10.3	.. 46.4	294 33.3	.. 14.1	77 40.8	.. 13.3	145 34.4	.. 04.2	Alnilam	275 38.9	S 1 11.0
U 10	136 13.6	3 12.3	46.6	309 34.2	14.7	92 43.3	13.3	160 37.0	04.2	Alphard	217 49.1	S 8 45.5
R 11	151 16.0	18 14.4	46.9	324 35.2	15.4	107 45.8	13.3	175 39.6	04.3			
S 12	166 18.5	33 16.4	N10 47.2	339 36.2	S 2 16.1	122 48.2	N15 13.3	190 42.3	S12 04.3	Alphecca	126 04.8	N26 38.3
D 13	181 21.0	48 18.5	47.4	354 37.2	16.7	137 50.7	13.3	205 44.9	04.4	Alpheratz	357 35.6	N29 13.3
A 14	196 23.4	63 20.5	47.7	9 38.2	17.4	152 53.2	13.3	220 47.6	04.5	Altair	62 00.8	N 8 56.0
Y 15	211 25.9	78 22.5	.. 47.9	24 39.1	.. 18.1	167 55.7	.. 13.2	235 50.2	.. 04.6	Ankaa	353 07.8	S42 10.5
16	226 28.4	93 24.6	48.2	39 40.1	18.7	182 58.2	13.2	250 52.8	04.6	Antares	112 17.2	S26 29.1
17	241 30.8	108 26.6	48.4	54 41.1	19.4	198 00.7	13.2	265 55.5	04.7			
18	256 33.3	123 28.6	N10 48.7	69 42.1	S 2 20.0	213 03.2	N15 13.2	280 58.1	S12 04.8	Arcturus	145 49.1	N19 03.8
19	271 35.8	138 30.6	48.9	84 43.1	20.7	228 05.6	13.2	296 00.8	04.8	Atria	107 12.5	S69 04.4
20	286 38.2	153 32.6	49.2	99 44.1	21.4	243 08.1	13.2	311 03.4	04.9	Avior	234 15.7	S59 34.8
21	301 40.7	168 34.7	.. 49.4	114 45.0	.. 22.0	258 10.6	.. 13.1	326 06.0	.. 05.0	Bellatrix	278 24.1	N 6 22.4
22	316 43.2	183 36.7	49.7	129 46.0	22.7	273 13.1	13.1	341 08.7	05.0	Betelgeuse	270 53.4	N 7 24.8
23	331 45.6	198 38.7	49.9	144 47.0	23.4	288 15.6	13.1	356 11.3	05.1			
8 00	346 48.1	213 40.7	N10 50.2	159 48.0	S 2 24.0	303 18.1	N15 13.1	11 13.9	S12 05.2	Canopus	263 53.1	S52 42.1
01	1 50.5	228 42.7	50.4	174 49.0	24.7	318 20.6	13.1	26 16.6	05.2	Capella	280 23.6	N46 01.2
02	16 53.0	243 44.7	50.7	189 50.0	25.3	333 23.1	13.1	41 19.2	05.3	Deneb	49 26.2	N45 22.0
03	31 55.5	258 46.7	.. 50.9	204 50.9	.. 26.0	348 25.6	.. 13.1	56 21.9	.. 05.4	Denebola	182 26.4	N14 26.6
04	46 57.9	273 48.6	51.2	219 51.9	26.7	3 28.1	13.0	71 24.5	05.4	Diphda	348 48.1	S17 51.3
05	62 00.4	288 50.6	51.4	234 52.9	27.3	18 30.6	13.0	86 27.1	05.5			
06	77 02.9	303 52.6	N10 51.7	249 53.9	S 2 28.0	33 33.0	N15 13.0	101 29.8	S12 05.6	Dubhe	193 43.0	N61 37.5
07	92 05.3	318 54.6	51.9	264 54.9	28.6	48 35.5	13.0	116 32.4	05.6	Elnath	278 03.3	N28 37.6
F 08	107 07.8	333 56.5	52.1	279 55.8	29.3	63 38.0	13.0	131 35.0	05.7	Eltanin	90 42.6	N51 29.4
R 09	122 10.3	348 58.5	.. 52.4	294 56.8	.. 30.0	78 40.5	.. 13.0	146 37.7	.. 05.8	Enif	33 39.6	N 9 59.1
I 10	137 12.7	4 00.5	52.6	309 57.8	30.6	93 43.0	12.9	161 40.3	05.8	Fomalhaut	15 15.4	S29 29.7
D 11	152 15.2	19 02.4	52.9	324 58.8	31.3	108 45.5	12.9	176 43.0	05.9			
A 12	167 17.7	34 04.4	N10 53.1	339 59.8	S 2 32.0	123 48.0	N15 12.9	191 45.6	S12 06.0	Gacrux	171 53.5	S57 14.7
Y 13	182 20.1	49 06.3	53.3	355 00.7	32.6	138 50.5	12.9	206 48.2	06.0	Gienah	175 45.0	S17 40.3
14	197 22.6	64 08.3	53.6	10 01.7	33.3	153 53.0	12.9	221 50.9	06.1	Hadar	148 38.1	S60 29.3
15	212 25.0	79 10.2	.. 53.8	25 02.7	.. 33.9	168 55.5	.. 12.9	236 53.5	.. 06.2	Hamal	327 52.2	N23 34.5
16	227 27.5	94 12.2	54.0	40 03.7	34.6	183 58.0	12.8	251 56.1	06.2	Kaus Aust.	83 33.8	S34 22.5
17	242 30.0	109 14.1	54.3	55 04.7	35.3	199 00.5	12.8	266 58.8	06.3			
18	257 32.4	124 16.0	N10 54.5	70 05.6	S 2 35.9	214 03.0	N15 12.8	282 01.4	S12 06.4	Kochab	137 20.3	N74 03.7
19	272 34.9	139 18.0	54.7	85 06.6	36.6	229 05.5	12.8	297 04.1	06.4	Markab	13 30.7	N15 20.0
20	287 37.4	154 19.9	55.0	100 07.6	37.3	244 08.0	12.8	312 06.7	06.5	Menkar	314 07.2	N 4 11.1
21	302 39.8	169 21.8	.. 55.2	115 08.6	.. 37.9	259 10.5	.. 12.8	327 09.3	.. 06.6	Menkent	147 59.2	S36 29.2
22	317 42.3	184 23.7	55.4	130 09.6	38.6	274 13.0	12.7	342 12.0	06.6	Miaplacidus	221 39.4	S69 48.6
23	332 44.8	199 25.7	55.7	145 10.5	39.2	289 15.5	12.7	357 14.6	06.7			
9 00	347 47.2	214 27.6	N10 55.9	160 11.5	S 2 39.9	304 18.0	N15 12.7	12 17.2	S12 06.8	Mirfak	308 29.7	N49 56.6
01	2 49.7	229 29.5	56.1	175 12.5	40.6	319 20.5	12.7	27 19.9	06.8	Nunki	75 49.0	S26 16.1
02	17 52.1	244 31.4	56.4	190 13.5	41.2	334 23.0	12.7	42 22.5	06.9	Peacock	53 07.0	S56 39.6
03	32 54.6	259 33.3	.. 56.6	205 14.5	.. 41.9	349 25.5	.. 12.6	57 25.1	.. 07.0	Pollux	243 18.9	N27 58.2
04	47 57.1	274 35.2	56.8	220 15.4	42.5	4 28.0	12.6	72 27.8	07.0	Procyon	244 52.2	N 5 10.0
05	62 59.5	289 37.1	57.0	235 16.4	43.2	19 30.5	12.6	87 30.4	07.1			
06	78 02.0	304 39.0	N10 57.3	250 17.4	S 2 43.9	34 33.0	N15 12.6	102 33.1	S12 07.2	Rasalhague	95 59.5	N12 32.7
07	93 04.5	319 40.8	57.5	265 18.4	44.5	49 35.5	12.6	117 35.7	07.2	Regulus	207 35.9	N11 51.3
S 08	108 06.9	334 42.7	57.7	280 19.3	45.2	64 38.0	12.6	132 38.3	07.3	Rigel	281 05.0	S 8 10.3
A 09	123 09.4	349 44.6	.. 57.9	295 20.3	.. 45.9	79 40.5	.. 12.5	147 41.0	.. 07.4	Rigil Kent.	139 42.2	S60 56.1
T 10	138 11.9	4 46.5	58.1	310 21.3	46.5	94 43.0	12.5	162 43.6	07.4	Sabik	102 04.0	S15 45.2
U 11	153 14.3	19 48.4	58.4	325 22.3	47.2	109 45.5	12.5	177 46.2	07.5			
R 12	168 16.8	34 50.2	N10 58.6	340 23.3	S 2 47.8	124 48.0	N15 12.5	192 48.9	S12 07.6	Schedar	349 31.8	N56 40.0
D 13	183 19.3	49 52.1	58.8	355 24.2	48.5	139 50.5	12.5	207 51.5	07.6	Shaula	96 11.8	S37 07.3
A 14	198 21.7	64 53.9	59.0	10 25.2	49.2	154 53.0	12.4	222 54.1	07.7	Sirius	258 27.4	S16 44.7
Y 15	213 24.2	79 55.8	.. 59.2	25 26.2	.. 49.8	169 55.5	.. 12.4	237 56.8	.. 07.8	Spica	158 23.7	S11 17.0
16	228 26.6	94 57.7	59.5	40 27.2	50.5	184 58.0	12.4	252 59.4	07.8	Suhail	222 47.5	S43 31.4
17	243 29.1	109 59.5	59.7	55 28.1	51.1	200 00.5	12.4	268 02.1	07.9			
18	258 31.6	125 01.4	N10 59.9	70 29.1	S 2 51.8	215 03.0	N15 12.4	283 04.7	S12 08.0	Vega	80 33.8	N38 48.6
19	273 34.0	140 03.2	11 00.1	85 30.1	52.5	230 05.5	12.3	298 07.3	08.0	Zuben'ubi	136 57.4	S16 08.3
20	288 36.5	155 05.0	00.3	100 31.1	53.1	245 08.0	12.3	313 10.0	08.1			
21	303 39.0	170 06.9	.. 00.5	115 32.1	.. 53.8	260 10.5	.. 12.3	328 12.6	.. 08.2		SHA	Mer. Pass.
22	318 41.4	185 08.7	00.7	130 33.0	54.5	275 13.0	12.3	343 15.2	08.2	Venus	226 52.6	9 44
23	333 43.9	200 10.5	00.9	145 34.0	55.1	290 15.5	12.3	358 17.9	08.3	Mars	172 59.9	13 20
Mer. Pass.	0 52.7	v 2.0	d 0.2	v 1.0	d 0.7	v 2.5	d 0.0	v 2.6	d 0.1	Jupiter	316 30.0	3 46
										Saturn	24 25.9	23 11

© British Crown Copyright 2022. All rights reserved.

UT	SUN GHA	SUN Dec	MOON GHA	v	MOON Dec	d	HP
7 00	180 26.0	N 6 14.6	272 39.3	8.6	N26 28.7	5.4	56.1
01	195 26.2	13.7	287 06.9	8.7	26 34.1	5.3	56.0
02	210 26.4	12.7	301 34.6	8.7	26 39.4	5.1	56.0
03	225 26.6	.. 11.8	316 02.3	8.6	26 44.5	5.0	56.0
04	240 26.9	10.9	330 29.9	8.7	26 49.5	4.8	55.9
05	255 27.1	09.9	344 57.6	8.6	26 54.3	4.7	55.9
06	270 27.3	N 6 09.0	359 25.2	8.6	N26 59.0	4.5	55.9
T 07	285 27.5	08.1	13 52.8	8.6	27 03.5	4.4	55.8
H 08	300 27.7	07.1	28 20.4	8.6	27 07.9	4.3	55.8
U 09	315 27.9	.. 06.2	42 48.0	8.6	27 12.2	4.0	55.8
R 10	330 28.1	05.3	57 15.6	8.6	27 16.2	4.0	55.8
S 11	345 28.4	04.3	71 43.2	8.6	27 20.2	3.8	55.7
D 12	0 28.6	N 6 03.4	86 10.8	8.6	N27 24.0	3.6	55.7
A 13	15 28.8	02.5	100 38.4	8.6	27 27.6	3.5	55.7
Y 14	30 29.0	01.5	115 06.0	8.5	27 31.1	3.4	55.6
15	45 29.2	6 00.6	129 33.5	8.6	27 34.5	3.2	55.6
16	60 29.4	5 59.7	144 01.1	8.6	27 37.7	3.0	55.6
17	75 29.6	58.7	158 28.7	8.6	27 40.7	2.9	55.5
18	90 29.9	N 5 57.8	172 56.3	8.6	N27 43.6	2.8	55.5
19	105 30.1	56.8	187 23.9	8.6	27 46.4	2.6	55.5
20	120 30.3	55.9	201 51.5	8.6	27 49.0	2.4	55.5
21	135 30.5	.. 55.0	216 19.1	8.6	27 51.4	2.4	55.4
22	150 30.7	54.0	230 46.7	8.6	27 53.8	2.1	55.4
23	165 30.9	53.1	245 14.3	8.6	27 55.9	2.0	55.4
8 00	180 31.1	N 5 52.2	259 41.9	8.7	N27 57.9	1.9	55.4
01	195 31.4	51.2	274 09.6	8.6	27 59.8	1.7	55.3
02	210 31.6	50.3	288 37.2	8.7	28 01.5	1.6	55.3
03	225 31.8	.. 49.3	303 04.9	8.6	28 03.1	1.4	55.3
04	240 32.0	48.4	317 32.5	8.7	28 04.5	1.3	55.3
05	255 32.2	47.5	332 00.2	8.8	28 05.8	1.1	55.2
06	270 32.4	N 5 46.5	346 28.0	8.7	N28 06.9	1.0	55.2
F 07	285 32.6	45.6	0 55.7	8.7	28 07.9	0.8	55.2
R 08	300 32.9	44.7	15 23.4	8.8	28 08.7	0.7	55.2
I 09	315 33.1	.. 43.7	29 51.2	8.8	28 09.4	0.5	55.1
D 10	330 33.3	42.8	44 19.0	8.8	28 09.9	0.4	55.1
A 11	345 33.5	41.8	58 46.8	8.8	28 10.3	0.3	55.1
Y 12	0 33.7	N 5 40.9	73 14.6	8.9	N28 10.6	0.1	55.1
13	15 33.9	40.0	87 42.5	8.9	28 10.7	0.0	55.0
14	30 34.1	39.0	102 10.4	8.9	28 10.7	0.2	55.0
15	45 34.4	.. 38.1	116 38.3	9.0	28 10.5	0.4	55.0
16	60 34.6	37.1	131 06.3	9.0	28 10.1	0.4	55.0
17	75 34.8	36.2	145 34.3	9.0	28 09.7	0.7	54.9
18	90 35.0	N 5 35.3	160 02.3	9.0	N28 09.0	0.7	54.9
19	105 35.2	34.3	174 30.3	9.1	28 08.3	0.9	54.9
20	120 35.4	33.4	188 58.4	9.1	28 07.4	1.1	54.9
21	135 35.7	.. 32.4	203 26.5	9.1	28 06.3	1.1	54.9
22	150 35.9	31.5	217 54.6	9.2	28 05.2	1.4	54.8
23	165 36.1	30.6	232 22.8	9.3	28 03.8	1.4	54.8
9 00	180 36.3	N 5 29.6	246 51.1	9.2	N28 02.4	1.7	54.8
01	195 36.5	28.7	261 19.3	9.3	28 00.7	1.7	54.8
02	210 36.7	27.7	275 47.6	9.4	27 59.0	1.9	54.8
03	225 37.0	.. 26.8	290 16.0	9.4	27 57.1	2.0	54.7
04	240 37.2	25.8	304 44.4	9.4	27 55.1	2.2	54.7
05	255 37.4	24.9	319 12.8	9.5	27 52.9	2.3	54.7
06	270 37.6	N 5 24.0	333 41.3	9.5	N27 50.6	2.4	54.7
S 07	285 37.8	23.0	348 09.8	9.5	27 48.2	2.6	54.7
A 08	300 38.0	22.1	2 38.3	9.7	27 45.6	2.7	54.7
T 09	315 38.2	.. 21.1	17 07.0	9.6	27 42.9	2.9	54.6
U 10	330 38.5	20.2	31 35.6	9.7	27 40.0	3.0	54.6
R 11	345 38.7	19.2	46 04.3	9.8	27 37.0	3.1	54.6
D 12	0 38.9	N 5 18.3	60 33.1	9.8	N27 33.9	3.2	54.6
A 13	15 39.1	17.4	75 01.9	9.9	27 30.7	3.4	54.6
Y 14	30 39.3	16.4	89 30.8	9.9	27 27.3	3.5	54.5
15	45 39.6	.. 15.5	103 59.7	10.0	27 23.8	3.7	54.5
16	60 39.8	14.5	118 28.7	10.0	27 20.1	3.8	54.5
17	75 40.0	13.6	132 57.7	10.1	27 16.3	3.9	54.5
18	90 40.2	N 5 12.6	147 26.8	10.1	N27 12.4	4.0	54.5
19	105 40.4	11.7	161 55.9	10.2	27 08.4	4.2	54.5
20	120 40.6	10.7	176 25.1	10.3	27 04.2	4.3	54.4
21	135 40.9	.. 09.8	190 54.4	10.3	26 59.9	4.4	54.4
22	150 41.1	08.9	205 23.7	10.3	26 55.5	4.6	54.4
23	165 41.3	07.9	219 53.0	10.5	N26 50.9	4.7	54.4
	SD 15.9	d 0.9	SD 15.2		15.0		14.9

Twilight / Sunrise / Moonrise

Lat.	Naut.	Civil	Sunrise	Moonrise 7	8	9	10
°	h m	h m	h m	h m	h m	h m	h m
N 72	00 26	03 15	04 34	▭	▭	▭	▭
N 70	01 45	03 34	04 43	▭	▭	▭	▭
68	02 21	03 49	04 50	▭	▭	▭	▭
66	02 46	04 01	04 57	▭	▭	▭	▭
64	03 05	04 11	05 02	▭	▭	▭	22 34
62	03 20	04 20	05 07	19 09	▭	21 28	23 16
60	03 32	04 27	05 11	20 11	20 58	22 15	23 45
N 58	03 42	04 33	05 14	20 45	21 34	22 45	24 06
56	03 51	04 39	05 17	21 10	22 00	23 07	24 24
54	03 59	04 44	05 20	21 30	22 21	23 26	24 39
52	04 06	04 48	05 23	21 47	22 39	23 42	24 52
50	04 12	04 52	05 25	22 01	22 53	23 55	25 04
45	04 24	05 00	05 30	22 31	23 23	24 23	00 23
N 40	04 34	05 06	05 34	22 54	23 47	24 45	00 45
35	04 42	05 12	05 37	23 13	24 06	00 06	01 03
30	04 48	05 16	05 41	23 29	24 22	00 22	01 18
20	04 58	05 24	05 46	23 57	24 50	00 50	01 44
N 10	05 05	05 29	05 50	24 21	00 21	01 14	02 07
0	05 10	05 34	05 54	24 43	00 43	01 36	02 28
S 10	05 13	05 37	05 59	00 10	01 06	01 59	02 49
20	05 15	05 41	06 03	00 33	01 30	02 23	03 11
30	05 16	05 43	06 07	00 59	01 58	02 51	03 37
35	05 15	05 45	06 10	01 15	02 14	03 07	03 52
40	05 15	05 46	06 13	01 33	02 34	03 26	04 10
45	05 13	05 47	06 16	01 55	02 57	03 49	04 31
S 50	05 11	05 48	06 20	02 23	03 27	04 19	04 58
52	05 09	05 48	06 22	02 36	03 42	04 34	05 11
54	05 08	05 49	06 24	02 52	04 00	04 51	05 26
56	05 06	05 49	06 26	03 11	04 21	05 11	05 43
58	05 04	05 50	06 29	03 34	04 48	05 37	06 05
S 60	05 02	05 50	06 31	04 05	05 26	06 12	06 31

Sunset / Twilight / Moonset

Lat.	Sunset	Civil	Naut.	Moonset 7	8	9	10
°	h m	h m	h m	h m	h m	h m	h m
N 72	19 19	20 36	23 04	▭	▭	▭	▭
N 70	19 10	20 18	22 02	▭	▭	▭	▭
68	19 03	20 03	21 29	▭	▭	▭	▭
66	18 57	19 52	21 06	▭	▭	▭	▭
64	18 52	19 42	20 48	▭	▭	▭	19 45
62	18 47	19 34	20 33	17 46	▭	19 07	19 02
60	18 43	19 27	20 21	16 44	17 49	18 20	18 33
N 58	18 40	19 21	20 11	16 10	17 12	17 50	18 11
56	18 37	19 15	20 02	15 45	16 46	17 27	17 53
54	18 34	19 11	19 55	15 26	16 25	17 08	17 37
52	18 32	19 06	19 48	15 10	16 08	16 52	17 24
50	18 30	19 03	19 42	14 55	15 53	16 38	17 12
45	18 25	18 55	19 30	14 25	15 23	16 10	16 48
N 40	18 21	18 48	19 21	14 03	15 00	15 48	16 28
35	18 17	18 43	19 13	13 44	14 40	15 29	16 11
30	18 14	18 39	19 07	13 28	14 24	15 14	15 57
20	18 09	18 32	18 57	13 01	13 56	14 47	15 33
N 10	18 05	18 26	18 51	12 37	13 32	14 23	15 12
0	18 01	18 22	18 46	12 15	13 09	14 02	14 52
S 10	17 57	18 18	18 43	11 54	12 47	13 40	14 32
20	17 53	18 15	18 41	11 30	12 22	13 16	14 11
30	17 49	18 13	18 40	11 03	11 54	12 49	13 46
35	17 46	18 11	18 41	10 47	11 38	12 33	13 31
40	17 43	18 10	18 42	10 29	11 18	12 14	13 14
45	17 40	18 09	18 43	10 06	10 54	11 51	12 53
S 50	17 36	18 08	18 46	09 38	10 24	11 21	12 27
52	17 34	18 08	18 47	09 24	10 09	11 07	12 15
54	17 32	18 08	18 49	09 08	09 51	10 50	12 00
56	17 30	18 07	18 51	08 49	09 30	10 30	11 43
58	17 28	18 07	18 53	08 25	09 03	10 04	11 22
S 60	17 25	18 07	18 55	07 54	08 25	09 29	10 56

Day	SUN Eqn. of Time 00h	12h	Mer. Pass.	MOON Mer. Pass. Upper	Lower	Age	Phase
d	m s	m s	h m	h m	h m	d %	
7	01 44	01 54	11 58	06 02	18 29	22 44	
8	02 04	02 14	11 58	06 56	19 23	23 35	
9	02 25	02 35	11 57	07 49	20 15	24 26	

© British Crown Copyright 2022. All rights reserved.

2023 SEPTEMBER 10, 11, 12 (SUN., MON., TUES.)

UT	ARIES GHA	VENUS −4.8 GHA	Dec	MARS +1.7 GHA	Dec	JUPITER −2.7 GHA	Dec	SATURN +0.4 GHA	Dec	STARS Name	SHA	Dec
10 00	348 46.4	215 12.4	N11 01.1	160 35.0	S 2 55.8	305 18.0	N15 12.2	13 20.5	S12 08.4	Acamar	315 12.4	S40 12.3
01	3 48.8	230 14.2	01.4	175 36.0	56.4	320 20.5	12.2	28 23.1	08.4	Achernar	335 20.5	S57 06.8
02	18 51.3	245 16.0	01.6	190 36.9	57.1	335 23.0	12.2	43 25.8	08.5	Acrux	173 02.0	S63 13.8
03	33 53.8	260 17.8 ..	01.8	205 37.9 ..	57.8	350 25.5 ..	12.2	58 28.4 ..	08.6	Adhara	255 06.9	S28 59.9
04	48 56.2	275 19.6	02.0	220 38.9	58.4	5 28.1	12.2	73 31.1	08.6	Aldebaran	290 40.8	N16 33.5
05	63 58.7	290 21.4	02.2	235 39.9	59.1	20 30.6	12.1	88 33.7	08.7			
06	79 01.1	305 23.2	N11 02.4	250 40.8	S 2 59.7	35 33.1	N15 12.1	103 36.3	S12 08.8	Alioth	166 14.4	N55 50.1
07	94 03.6	320 25.0	02.6	265 41.8	3 00.4	50 35.6	12.1	118 39.0	08.8	Alkaid	152 53.2	N49 11.9
08	109 06.1	335 26.8	02.8	280 42.8	01.1	65 38.1	12.1	133 41.6	08.9	Alnair	27 33.8	S46 50.8
S 09	124 08.5	350 28.6 ..	03.0	295 43.8 ..	01.7	80 40.6 ..	12.1	148 44.2 ..	09.0	Alnilam	275 38.9	S 1 11.0
U 10	139 11.0	5 30.4	03.2	310 44.7	02.4	95 43.1	12.0	163 46.9	09.0	Alphard	217 49.1	S 8 45.5
N 11	154 13.5	20 32.2	03.4	325 45.7	03.1	110 45.6	12.0	178 49.5	09.1			
D 12	169 15.9	35 34.0	N11 03.6	340 46.7	S 3 03.7	125 48.1	N15 12.0	193 52.1	S12 09.2	Alphecca	126 04.8	N26 38.3
A 13	184 18.4	50 35.8	03.8	355 47.7	04.4	140 50.6	12.0	208 54.8	09.2	Alpheratz	357 35.6	N29 13.3
Y 14	199 20.9	65 37.5	04.0	10 48.6	05.0	155 53.2	11.9	223 57.4	09.3	Altair	62 00.8	N 8 56.0
15	214 23.3	80 39.3 ..	04.2	25 49.6 ..	05.7	170 55.7 ..	11.9	239 00.0 ..	09.4	Ankaa	353 07.8	S42 10.5
16	229 25.8	95 41.1	04.4	40 50.6	06.4	185 58.2	11.9	254 02.7	09.4	Antares	112 17.3	S26 29.1
17	244 28.3	110 42.8	04.6	55 51.6	07.0	201 00.7	11.9	269 05.3	09.5			
18	259 30.7	125 44.6	N11 04.8	70 52.5	S 3 07.7	216 03.2	N15 11.9	284 07.9	S12 09.5	Arcturus	145 49.1	N19 03.8
19	274 33.2	140 46.3	05.0	85 53.5	08.4	231 05.7	11.8	299 10.6	09.6	Atria	107 12.5	S69 04.4
20	289 35.6	155 48.1	05.2	100 54.5	09.0	246 08.2	11.8	314 13.2	09.7	Avior	234 15.7	S59 34.8
21	304 38.1	170 49.9 ..	05.4	115 55.5 ..	09.7	261 10.7 ..	11.8	329 15.8 ..	09.7	Bellatrix	278 24.1	N 6 22.4
22	319 40.6	185 51.6	05.5	130 56.4	10.3	276 13.3	11.8	344 18.5	09.8	Betelgeuse	270 53.3	N 7 24.8
23	334 43.0	200 53.3	05.7	145 57.4	11.0	291 15.8	11.7	359 21.1	09.9			
11 00	349 45.5	215 55.1	N11 05.9	160 58.4	S 3 11.7	306 18.3	N15 11.7	14 23.8	S12 09.9	Canopus	263 53.0	S52 42.1
01	4 48.0	230 56.8	06.1	175 59.4	12.3	321 20.8	11.7	29 26.4	10.0	Capella	280 23.5	N46 01.2
02	19 50.4	245 58.6	06.3	191 00.3	13.0	336 23.3	11.7	44 29.0	10.1	Deneb	49 26.2	N45 22.0
03	34 52.9	261 00.3 ..	06.5	206 01.3 ..	13.6	351 25.8 ..	11.7	59 31.7 ..	10.1	Denebola	182 26.4	N14 26.6
04	49 55.4	276 02.0	06.7	221 02.3	14.3	6 28.4	11.6	74 34.3	10.2	Diphda	348 48.1	S17 51.3
05	64 57.8	291 03.7	06.9	236 03.3	15.0	21 30.9	11.6	89 36.9	10.3			
06	80 00.3	306 05.5	N11 07.0	251 04.2	S 3 15.6	36 33.4	N15 11.6	104 39.6	S12 10.3	Dubhe	193 43.0	N61 37.5
07	95 02.7	321 07.2	07.2	266 05.2	16.3	51 35.9	11.6	119 42.2	10.4	Elnath	278 03.3	N28 37.6
08	110 05.2	336 08.9	07.4	281 06.2	16.9	66 38.4	11.5	134 44.8	10.5	Eltanin	90 42.6	N51 29.4
M 09	125 07.7	351 10.6 ..	07.6	296 07.2 ..	17.6	81 40.9 ..	11.5	149 47.5 ..	10.5	Enif	33 39.6	N 9 59.1
O 10	140 10.1	6 12.3	07.8	311 08.1	18.3	96 43.5	11.5	164 50.1	10.6	Fomalhaut	15 15.4	S29 29.7
N 11	155 12.6	21 14.0	08.0	326 09.1	18.9	111 46.0	11.5	179 52.7	10.7			
D 12	170 15.1	36 15.7	N11 08.1	341 10.1	S 3 19.6	126 48.5	N15 11.4	194 55.4	S12 10.7	Gacrux	171 53.5	S57 14.7
A 13	185 17.5	51 17.4	08.3	356 11.0	20.3	141 51.0	11.4	209 58.0	10.8	Gienah	175 45.0	S17 40.3
Y 14	200 20.0	66 19.1	08.5	11 12.0	20.9	156 53.5	11.4	225 00.6	10.9	Hadar	148 38.1	S60 29.3
15	215 22.5	81 20.8 ..	08.7	26 13.0 ..	21.6	171 56.1 ..	11.4	240 03.3 ..	10.9	Hamal	327 52.2	N23 34.5
16	230 24.9	96 22.5	08.8	41 14.0	22.2	186 58.6	11.3	255 05.9	11.0	Kaus Aust.	83 33.9	S34 22.5
17	245 27.4	111 24.1	09.0	56 14.9	22.9	202 01.1	11.3	270 08.5	11.0			
18	260 29.9	126 25.8	N11 09.2	71 15.9	S 3 23.6	217 03.6	N15 11.3	285 11.2	S12 11.1	Kochab	137 20.4	N74 03.7
19	275 32.3	141 27.5	09.4	86 16.9	24.2	232 06.1	11.3	300 13.8	11.2	Markab	13 30.7	N15 20.0
20	290 34.8	156 29.2	09.5	101 17.8	24.9	247 08.7	11.3	315 16.4	11.2	Menkar	314 07.1	N 4 11.1
21	305 37.2	171 30.8 ..	09.7	116 18.8 ..	25.5	262 11.2 ..	11.2	330 19.1 ..	11.3	Menkent	147 59.2	S36 29.2
22	320 39.7	186 32.5	09.9	131 19.8	26.2	277 13.7	11.2	345 21.7	11.4	Miaplacidus	221 39.3	S69 48.6
23	335 42.2	201 34.2	10.0	146 20.8	26.9	292 16.2	11.2	0 24.3	11.4			
12 00	350 44.6	216 35.8	N11 10.2	161 21.7	S 3 27.5	307 18.8	N15 11.2	15 27.0	S12 11.5	Mirfak	308 29.6	N49 56.6
01	5 47.1	231 37.5	10.4	176 22.7	28.2	322 21.3	11.1	30 29.6	11.6	Nunki	75 49.0	S26 16.1
02	20 49.6	246 39.1	10.6	191 23.7	28.9	337 23.8	11.1	45 32.2	11.6	Peacock	53 07.0	S56 39.7
03	35 52.0	261 40.8 ..	10.7	206 24.6 ..	29.5	352 26.3 ..	11.1	60 34.9 ..	11.7	Pollux	243 18.9	N27 58.2
04	50 54.5	276 42.4	10.9	221 25.6	30.2	7 28.9	11.1	75 37.5	11.8	Procyon	244 52.2	N 5 10.0
05	65 57.0	291 44.1	11.1	236 26.6	30.8	22 31.4	11.0	90 40.1	11.8			
06	80 59.4	306 45.7	N11 11.2	251 27.6	S 3 31.5	37 33.9	N15 11.0	105 42.8	S12 11.9	Rasalhague	95 59.5	N12 32.7
07	96 01.9	321 47.3	11.4	266 28.5	32.2	52 36.4	11.0	120 45.4	12.0	Regulus	207 35.9	N11 51.3
08	111 04.4	336 49.0	11.5	281 29.5	32.8	67 39.0	10.9	135 48.0	12.0	Rigel	281 04.9	S 8 10.3
T 09	126 06.8	351 50.6 ..	11.7	296 30.5 ..	33.5	82 41.5 ..	10.9	150 50.7 ..	12.1	Rigil Kent.	139 42.3	S60 56.1
U 10	141 09.3	6 52.2	11.9	311 31.4	34.1	97 44.0	10.9	165 53.3	12.1	Sabik	102 04.0	S15 45.2
E 11	156 11.7	21 53.8	12.0	326 32.4	34.8	112 46.5	10.9	180 55.9	12.2			
S 12	171 14.2	36 55.5	N11 12.2	341 33.4	S 3 35.5	127 49.1	N15 10.8	195 58.6	S12 12.3	Schedar	349 31.8	N56 40.0
D 13	186 16.7	51 57.1	12.3	356 34.4	36.1	142 51.6	10.8	211 01.2	12.3	Shaula	96 11.8	S37 07.3
A 14	201 19.1	66 58.7	12.5	11 35.3	36.8	157 54.1	10.8	226 03.8	12.4	Sirius	258 27.3	S16 44.7
Y 15	216 21.6	82 00.3 ..	12.6	26 36.3 ..	37.4	172 56.6 ..	10.8	241 06.5 ..	12.5	Spica	158 23.7	S11 17.0
16	231 24.1	97 01.9	12.8	41 37.3	38.1	187 59.2	10.7	256 09.1	12.5	Suhail	222 47.5	S43 31.4
17	246 26.5	112 03.5	13.0	56 38.2	38.8	203 01.7	10.7	271 11.7	12.6			
18	261 29.0	127 05.1	N11 13.1	71 39.2	S 3 39.4	218 04.2	N15 10.7	286 14.4	S12 12.7	Vega	80 33.8	N38 48.6
19	276 31.5	142 06.7	13.3	86 40.2	40.1	233 06.8	10.7	301 17.0	12.7	Zuben'ubi	136 57.4	S16 08.3
20	291 33.9	157 08.3	13.4	101 41.1	40.8	248 09.3	10.6	316 19.6	12.8		SHA	Mer. Pass.
21	306 36.4	172 09.9 ..	13.6	116 42.1 ..	41.4	263 11.8 ..	10.6	331 22.2 ..	12.8		° ′	h m
22	321 38.8	187 11.5	13.7	131 43.1	42.1	278 14.4	10.6	346 24.9	12.9	Venus	226 09.6	9 35
23	336 41.3	202 13.1	13.9	146 44.0	42.7	293 16.9	10.5	1 27.5	13.0	Mars	171 12.9	13 15
	h m									Jupiter	316 32.8	3 34
Mer. Pass. 0 40.9		v 1.7	d 0.2	v 1.0	d 0.7	v 2.5	d 0.0	v 2.6	d 0.1	Saturn	24 38.3	22 58

© British Crown Copyright 2022. All rights reserved.

SUN and MOON

UT	SUN GHA	SUN Dec	MOON GHA	v	MOON Dec	d	HP
d h	° ′	° ′	° ′	′	° ′	′	′
10 00	180 41.5	N 5 07.0	234 22.5	10.5	N26 46.2	4.8	54.4
01	195 41.7	06.0	248 52.0	10.5	26 41.4	4.9	54.4
02	210 41.9	05.1	263 21.5	10.6	26 36.5	5.0	54.4
03	225 42.2	.. 04.1	277 51.1	10.7	26 31.5	5.2	54.4
04	240 42.4	03.2	292 20.8	10.7	26 26.3	5.4	54.3
05	255 42.6	02.2	306 50.5	10.8	26 21.0	5.4	54.3
06	270 42.8	N 5 01.3	321 20.3	10.9	N26 15.6	5.6	54.3
07	285 43.0	5 00.3	335 50.2	10.9	26 10.0	5.7	54.3
S 08	300 43.2	4 59.4	350 20.1	11.0	26 04.3	5.7	54.3
U 09	315 43.5	.. 58.4	4 50.1	11.1	25 58.6	5.9	54.3
N 10	330 43.7	57.5	19 20.2	11.1	25 52.7	6.1	54.3
D 11	345 43.9	56.6	33 50.3	11.2	25 46.6	6.1	54.3
A 12	0 44.1	N 4 55.6	48 20.5	11.2	N25 40.5	6.2	54.2
Y 13	15 44.3	54.7	62 50.7	11.3	25 34.3	6.4	54.2
14	30 44.6	53.7	77 21.0	11.4	25 27.9	6.5	54.2
15	45 44.8	.. 52.8	91 51.4	11.5	25 21.4	6.6	54.2
16	60 45.0	51.8	106 21.9	11.5	25 14.8	6.7	54.2
17	75 45.2	50.9	120 52.4	11.6	25 08.1	6.8	54.2
18	90 45.4	N 4 49.9	135 23.0	11.7	N25 01.3	7.0	54.2
19	105 45.6	49.0	149 53.7	11.7	24 54.3	7.0	54.2
20	120 45.9	48.0	164 24.4	11.8	24 47.3	7.2	54.2
21	135 46.1	.. 47.1	178 55.2	11.8	24 40.1	7.2	54.2
22	150 46.3	46.1	193 26.0	12.0	24 32.9	7.4	54.1
23	165 46.5	45.2	207 57.0	12.0	24 25.5	7.5	54.1
11 00	180 46.7	N 4 44.2	222 28.0	12.0	N24 18.0	7.6	54.1
01	195 47.0	43.3	236 59.0	12.2	24 10.4	7.6	54.1
02	210 47.2	42.3	251 30.2	12.2	24 02.8	7.8	54.1
03	225 47.4	.. 41.4	266 01.4	12.3	23 55.0	7.9	54.1
04	240 47.6	40.4	280 32.7	12.3	23 47.1	8.0	54.1
05	255 47.8	39.5	295 04.0	12.4	23 39.1	8.1	54.1
06	270 48.1	N 4 38.5	309 35.4	12.5	N23 31.0	8.2	54.1
07	285 48.3	37.6	324 06.9	12.6	23 22.8	8.3	54.1
M 08	300 48.5	36.6	338 38.5	12.6	23 14.5	8.5	54.1
O 09	315 48.7	.. 35.7	353 10.1	12.7	23 06.0	8.5	54.1
N 10	330 48.9	34.7	7 41.8	12.7	22 57.5	8.6	54.1
D 11	345 49.2	33.8	22 13.5	12.9	22 48.9	8.7	54.1
A 12	0 49.4	N 4 32.8	36 45.4	12.9	N22 40.2	8.7	54.0
Y 13	15 49.6	31.9	51 17.3	12.9	22 31.5	8.9	54.0
14	30 49.8	30.9	65 49.2	13.1	22 22.6	9.0	54.0
15	45 50.0	.. 30.0	80 21.3	13.1	22 13.6	9.1	54.0
16	60 50.3	29.0	94 53.4	13.2	22 04.5	9.2	54.0
17	75 50.5	28.1	109 25.6	13.2	21 55.3	9.2	54.0
18	90 50.7	N 4 27.1	123 57.8	13.3	N21 46.1	9.4	54.0
19	105 50.9	26.2	138 30.1	13.4	21 36.7	9.4	54.0
20	120 51.1	25.2	153 02.5	13.4	21 27.3	9.5	54.0
21	135 51.3	.. 24.3	167 34.9	13.5	21 17.8	9.7	54.0
22	150 51.6	23.3	182 07.4	13.6	21 08.1	9.7	54.0
23	165 51.8	22.4	196 40.0	13.6	20 58.4	9.8	54.0
12 00	180 52.0	N 4 21.4	211 12.6	13.8	N20 48.6	9.8	54.0
01	195 52.2	20.5	225 45.4	13.7	20 38.8	10.0	54.0
02	210 52.4	19.5	240 18.1	13.9	20 28.8	10.1	54.0
03	225 52.7	.. 18.6	254 51.0	13.9	20 18.7	10.1	54.0
04	240 52.9	17.6	269 23.9	13.9	20 08.6	10.2	54.0
05	255 53.1	16.7	283 56.8	14.1	19 58.4	10.3	54.0
06	270 53.3	N 4 15.7	298 29.9	14.1	N19 48.1	10.4	54.0
07	285 53.5	14.7	313 03.0	14.1	19 37.7	10.4	54.0
T 08	300 53.8	13.8	327 36.1	14.2	19 27.3	10.5	54.0
U 09	315 54.0	.. 12.8	342 09.3	14.3	19 16.8	10.7	54.0
E 10	330 54.2	11.9	356 42.6	14.4	19 06.1	10.6	54.0
S 11	345 54.4	10.9	11 16.0	14.4	18 55.5	10.8	54.0
D 12	0 54.7	N 4 10.0	25 49.4	14.4	N18 44.7	10.8	54.0
A 13	15 54.9	09.0	40 22.8	14.6	18 33.9	11.0	54.0
Y 14	30 55.1	08.1	54 56.4	14.5	18 22.9	10.9	54.0
15	45 55.3	.. 07.1	69 29.9	14.7	18 12.0	11.1	54.0
16	60 55.5	06.2	84 03.6	14.7	18 00.9	11.1	54.0
17	75 55.8	05.2	98 37.3	14.8	17 49.8	11.2	54.0
18	90 56.0	N 4 04.3	113 11.1	14.8	N17 38.6	11.3	54.0
19	105 56.2	03.3	127 44.9	14.8	17 27.3	11.4	54.0
20	120 56.4	02.3	142 18.7	15.0	17 15.9	11.4	54.0
21	135 56.6	.. 01.4	156 52.7	15.0	17 04.5	11.4	54.0
22	150 56.9	4 00.4	171 26.7	15.0	16 53.1	11.6	54.0
23	165 57.1	N 3 59.5	186 00.7	15.1	N16 41.5	11.6	54.0
	SD 15.9	d 1.0	SD 14.8		14.7		14.7

Twilight, Sunrise and Moonrise

Lat.	Naut.	Civil	Sunrise	Moonrise 10	11	12	13
°	h m	h m	h m	h m	h m	h m	h m
N 72	01 24	03 32	04 47	☐	☐	☐	00 20
N 70	02 10	03 48	04 55	☐	☐	☐	01 08
68	02 39	04 01	05 01	☐	23 12	25 38	01 38
66	03 00	04 12	05 06	☐	☐	00 03	02 01
64	03 17	04 21	05 11	22 34	24 34	00 34	02 18
62	03 30	04 28	05 14	23 16	24 57	00 57	02 32
60	03 41	04 35	05 18	23 45	25 16	01 16	02 44
N 58	03 50	04 40	05 21	24 06	00 06	01 31	02 55
56	03 58	04 45	05 23	24 24	00 24	01 44	03 04
54	04 05	04 49	05 25	24 39	00 39	01 56	03 12
52	04 12	04 53	05 27	24 52	00 52	02 06	03 19
50	04 17	04 56	05 29	25 04	01 04	02 14	03 25
45	04 28	05 04	05 33	00 23	01 27	02 33	03 39
N 40	04 37	05 09	05 37	00 45	01 46	02 48	03 50
35	04 44	05 14	05 40	01 03	02 02	03 01	04 00
30	04 50	05 18	05 42	01 18	02 15	03 12	04 08
20	04 59	05 24	05 46	01 44	02 38	03 31	04 22
N 10	05 05	05 29	05 50	02 07	02 58	03 48	04 35
0	05 09	05 33	05 53	02 28	03 17	04 03	04 46
S 10	05 11	05 36	05 57	02 49	03 35	04 18	04 58
20	05 12	05 38	06 00	03 11	03 55	04 34	05 10
30	05 12	05 40	06 04	03 37	04 18	04 53	05 24
35	05 11	05 40	06 06	03 52	04 31	05 04	05 32
40	05 10	05 41	06 08	04 10	04 46	05 16	05 41
45	05 07	05 41	06 11	04 31	05 04	05 31	05 52
S 50	05 04	05 42	06 14	04 58	05 27	05 48	06 05
52	05 03	05 42	06 15	05 11	05 37	05 56	06 11
54	05 01	05 42	06 17	05 26	05 49	06 06	06 17
56	04 58	05 41	06 18	05 43	06 03	06 16	06 25
58	04 56	05 41	06 20	06 05	06 19	06 28	06 33
S 60	04 53	05 41	06 22	06 31	06 39	06 41	06 42

Sunset, Twilight and Moonset

Lat.	Sunset	Civil	Naut.	Moonset 10	11	12	13
°	h m	h m	h m	h m	h m	h m	h m
N 72	19 03	20 18	22 19	☐	☐	21 12	20 01
N 70	18 56	20 02	21 37	☐	☐	20 22	19 40
68	18 50	19 49	21 10	☐	20 46	19 51	19 23
66	18 45	19 39	20 50	☐	19 54	19 27	19 10
64	18 41	19 30	20 34	19 45	19 22	19 08	18 58
62	18 37	19 23	20 21	19 02	18 57	18 53	18 49
60	18 34	19 17	20 10	18 33	18 38	18 40	18 40
N 58	18 32	19 12	20 01	18 11	18 22	18 29	18 33
56	18 29	19 07	19 53	17 53	18 09	18 19	18 27
54	18 27	19 03	19 46	17 37	17 57	18 11	18 21
52	18 25	18 59	19 40	17 24	17 46	18 03	18 16
50	18 23	18 56	19 35	17 12	17 37	17 56	18 11
45	18 19	18 49	19 24	16 48	17 17	17 41	18 00
N 40	18 16	18 43	19 15	16 28	17 01	17 28	17 52
35	18 13	18 39	19 09	16 11	16 47	17 17	17 44
30	18 11	18 35	19 03	15 57	16 35	17 08	17 38
20	18 07	18 29	18 55	15 33	16 14	16 52	17 26
N 10	18 03	18 24	18 49	15 12	15 56	16 38	17 16
0	18 00	18 21	18 45	14 52	15 39	16 24	17 06
S 10	17 57	18 18	18 42	14 32	15 22	16 11	16 57
20	17 54	18 16	18 41	14 11	15 04	15 56	16 46
30	17 50	18 14	18 42	13 46	14 43	15 39	16 34
35	17 48	18 13	18 43	13 31	14 30	15 29	16 27
40	17 46	18 13	18 44	13 14	14 16	15 18	16 20
45	17 43	18 13	18 47	12 53	13 59	15 05	16 10
S 50	17 41	18 13	18 50	12 27	13 37	14 49	15 59
52	17 39	18 13	18 52	12 15	13 27	14 41	15 54
54	17 38	18 13	18 54	12 00	13 16	14 32	15 48
56	17 36	18 13	18 56	11 43	13 02	14 23	15 41
58	17 34	18 13	18 59	11 22	12 47	14 12	15 34
S 60	17 32	18 14	19 02	10 56	12 28	13 59	15 26

SUN and MOON

Day	Eqn. of Time 00h	12h	Mer. Pass.	Mer. Pass. Upper	Lower	Age	Phase
d	m s	m s	h m	h m	h m	d	%
10	02 46	02 56	11 57	08 40	21 04	25	18
11	03 07	03 17	11 57	09 28	21 51	26	11
12	03 28	03 38	11 56	10 14	22 35	27	6

© British Crown Copyright 2022. All rights reserved.

UT	ARIES	VENUS −4·8		MARS +1·7		JUPITER −2·7		SATURN +0·5		STARS		
	GHA	GHA	Dec	GHA	Dec	GHA	Dec	GHA	Dec	Name	SHA	Dec
d h	° ′	° ′	° ′	° ′	° ′	° ′	° ′	° ′	° ′		° ′	° ′
13 00	351 43.8	217 14.6 N11 14.0		161 45.0 S 3 43.4		308 19.4 N15 10.5		16 30.1 S12 13.0		Acamar	315 12.4	S40 12.3
01	6 46.2	232 16.2	14.2	176 46.0	44.1	323 22.0	10.5	31 32.8	13.1	Achernar	335 20.5	S57 06.8
02	21 48.7	247 17.8	14.3	191 47.0	44.7	338 24.5	10.5	46 35.4	13.2	Acrux	173 02.0	S63 13.8
03	36 51.2	262 19.4 . .	14.5	206 47.9	45.4	353 27.0 . .	10.4	61 38.0 . .	13.2	Adhara	255 06.9	S28 59.9
04	51 53.6	277 20.9	14.6	221 48.9	46.0	8 29.6	10.4	76 40.7	13.3	Aldebaran	290 40.8	N16 33.5
05	66 56.1	292 22.5	14.7	236 49.9	46.7	23 32.1	10.4	91 43.3	13.4			
06	81 58.6	307 24.0 N11 14.9		251 50.8 S 3 47.4		38 34.6 N15 10.4		106 45.9 S12 13.4		Alioth	166 14.4	N55 50.1
W 07	97 01.0	322 25.6	15.0	266 51.8	48.0	53 37.2	10.3	121 48.6	13.5	Alkaid	152 53.2	N49 11.9
E 08	112 03.5	337 27.2	15.2	281 52.8	48.7	68 39.7	10.3	136 51.2	13.6	Alnair	27 33.8	S46 50.8
D 09	127 06.0	352 28.7 . .	15.3	296 53.7 . .	49.3	83 42.2 . .	10.3	151 53.8 . .	13.6	Alnilam	275 38.9	S 1 11.0
N 10	142 08.4	7 30.3	15.4	311 54.7	50.0	98 44.8	10.2	166 56.5	13.7	Alphard	217 49.1	S 8 45.5
E 11	157 10.9	22 31.8	15.6	326 55.7	50.7	113 47.3	10.2	181 59.1	13.7			
S 12	172 13.3	37 33.3 N11 15.7		341 56.6 S 3 51.3		128 49.8 N15 10.2		197 01.7 S12 13.8		Alphecca	126 04.8	N26 38.3
D 13	187 15.8	52 34.9	15.9	356 57.6	52.0	143 52.4	10.2	212 04.4	13.9	Alpheratz	357 35.6	N29 13.3
A 14	202 18.3	67 36.4	16.0	11 58.6	52.6	158 54.9	10.1	227 07.0	13.9	Altair	62 00.8	N 8 56.0
Y 15	217 20.7	82 37.9 . .	16.1	26 59.5 . .	53.3	173 57.4 . .	10.1	242 09.6 . .	14.0	Ankaa	353 07.8	S42 10.5
16	232 23.2	97 39.5	16.3	42 00.5	54.0	189 00.0	10.1	257 12.2	14.1	Antares	112 17.3	S26 29.1
17	247 25.7	112 41.0	16.4	57 01.5	54.6	204 02.5	10.0	272 14.9	14.1			
18	262 28.1	127 42.5 N11 16.5		72 02.4 S 3 55.3		219 05.1 N15 10.0		287 17.5 S12 14.2		Arcturus	145 49.2	N19 03.7
19	277 30.6	142 44.0	16.7	87 03.4	55.9	234 07.6	10.0	302 20.1	14.2	Atria	107 12.5	S69 04.4
20	292 33.1	157 45.6	16.8	102 04.4	56.6	249 10.1	10.0	317 22.8	14.3	Avior	234 15.6	S59 34.8
21	307 35.5	172 47.1 . .	16.9	117 05.3 . .	57.3	264 12.7 . .	09.9	332 25.4 . .	14.4	Bellatrix	278 24.1	N 6 22.4
22	322 38.0	187 48.6	17.0	132 06.3	57.9	279 15.2	09.9	347 28.0	14.4	Betelgeuse	270 53.3	N 7 24.8
23	337 40.4	202 50.1	17.2	147 07.3	58.6	294 17.7	09.9	2 30.7	14.5			
14 00	352 42.9	217 51.6 N11 17.3		162 08.2 S 3 59.3		309 20.3 N15 09.8		17 33.3 S12 14.6		Canopus	263 53.0	S52 42.1
01	7 45.4	232 53.1	17.4	177 09.2	3 59.9	324 22.8	09.8	32 35.9	14.6	Capella	280 23.5	N46 01.2
02	22 47.8	247 54.6	17.6	192 10.2	4 00.6	339 25.4	09.8	47 38.6	14.7	Deneb	49 26.2	N45 22.1
03	37 50.3	262 56.1 . .	17.7	207 11.1 . .	01.2	354 27.9 . .	09.7	62 41.2 . .	14.8	Denebola	182 26.4	N14 26.6
04	52 52.8	277 57.6	17.8	222 12.1	01.9	9 30.5	09.7	77 43.8	14.8	Diphda	348 48.1	S17 51.3
05	67 55.2	292 59.1	17.9	237 13.1	02.6	24 33.0	09.7	92 46.4	14.9			
06	82 57.7	308 00.5 N11 18.0		252 14.0 S 4 03.2		39 35.5 N15 09.7		107 49.1 S12 14.9		Dubhe	193 43.0	N61 37.5
T 07	98 00.2	323 02.0	18.2	267 15.0	03.9	54 38.1	09.6	122 51.7	15.0	Elnath	278 03.3	N28 37.6
H 08	113 02.6	338 03.5	18.3	282 16.0	04.5	69 40.6	09.6	137 54.3	15.1	Eltanin	90 42.6	N51 29.4
U 09	128 05.1	353 05.0 . .	18.4	297 16.9 . .	05.2	84 43.2 . .	09.6	152 57.0 . .	15.1	Enif	33 39.6	N 9 59.1
R 10	143 07.6	8 06.4	18.5	312 17.9	05.9	99 45.7	09.5	167 59.6	15.2	Fomalhaut	15 15.4	S29 29.8
S 11	158 10.0	23 07.9	18.6	327 18.8	06.5	114 48.3	09.5	183 02.2	15.3			
D 12	173 12.5	38 09.4 N11 18.8		342 19.8 S 4 07.2		129 50.8 N15 09.5		198 04.8 S12 15.3		Gacrux	171 53.5	S57 14.7
A 13	188 14.9	53 10.8	18.9	357 20.8	07.8	144 53.3	09.4	213 07.5	15.4	Gienah	175 45.1	S17 40.3
Y 14	203 17.4	68 12.3	19.0	12 21.7	08.5	159 55.9	09.4	228 10.1	15.4	Hadar	148 38.1	S60 29.3
15	218 19.9	83 13.8 . .	19.1	27 22.7 . .	09.2	174 58.4 . .	09.4	243 12.7 . .	15.5	Hamal	327 52.2	N23 34.5
16	233 22.3	98 15.2	19.2	42 23.7	09.8	190 01.0	09.3	258 15.4	15.6	Kaus Aust.	83 33.9	S34 22.5
17	248 24.8	113 16.7	19.3	57 24.6	10.5	205 03.5	09.3	273 18.0	15.6			
18	263 27.3	128 18.1 N11 19.4		72 25.6 S 4 11.1		220 06.1 N15 09.3		288 20.6 S12 15.7		Kochab	137 20.4	N74 03.7
19	278 29.7	143 19.6	19.5	87 26.6	11.8	235 08.6	09.3	303 23.3	15.8	Markab	13 30.7	N15 20.0
20	293 32.2	158 21.0	19.6	102 27.5	12.5	250 11.2	09.2	318 25.9	15.8	Menkar	314 07.1	N 4 11.1
21	308 34.7	173 22.4 . .	19.8	117 28.5 . .	13.1	265 13.7 . .	09.2	333 28.5 . .	15.9	Menkent	147 59.2	S36 29.2
22	323 37.1	188 23.9	19.9	132 29.5	13.8	280 16.3	09.2	348 31.1	15.9	Miaplacidus	221 39.3	S69 48.6
23	338 39.6	203 25.3	20.0	147 30.4	14.4	295 18.8	09.1	3 33.8	16.0			
15 00	353 42.1	218 26.7 N11 20.1		162 31.4 S 4 15.1		310 21.4 N15 09.1		18 36.4 S12 16.1		Mirfak	308 29.6	N49 56.6
01	8 44.5	233 28.2	20.2	177 32.3	15.8	325 23.9	09.1	33 39.0	16.1	Nunki	75 49.0	S26 16.1
02	23 47.0	248 29.6	20.3	192 33.3	16.4	340 26.5	09.0	48 41.7	16.2	Peacock	53 07.0	S56 39.7
03	38 49.4	263 31.0 . .	20.4	207 34.3 . .	17.1	355 29.0 . .	09.0	63 44.3 . .	16.3	Pollux	243 18.9	N27 58.2
04	53 51.9	278 32.4	20.5	222 35.2	17.7	10 31.5	09.0	78 46.9	16.3	Procyon	244 52.2	N 5 10.0
05	68 54.4	293 33.8	20.6	237 36.2	18.4	25 34.1	08.9	93 49.5	16.4			
06	83 56.8	308 35.3 N11 20.7		252 37.2 S 4 19.1		40 36.7 N15 08.9		108 52.2 S12 16.4		Rasalhague	95 59.6	N12 32.7
07	98 59.3	323 36.7	20.8	267 38.1	19.7	55 39.2	08.9	123 54.8	16.5	Regulus	207 35.9	N11 51.2
F 08	114 01.8	338 38.1	20.9	282 39.1	20.4	70 41.8	08.8	138 57.4	16.6	Rigel	281 04.9	S 8 10.2
R 09	129 04.2	353 39.5 . .	21.0	297 40.0 . .	21.0	85 44.3 . .	08.8	154 00.1 . .	16.6	Rigil Kent.	139 42.3	S60 56.1
I 10	144 06.7	8 40.9	21.1	312 41.0	21.7	100 46.9	08.8	169 02.7	16.7	Sabik	102 04.1	S15 45.2
D 11	159 09.2	23 42.3	21.2	327 42.0	22.4	115 49.4	08.7	184 05.3	16.8			
A 12	174 11.6	38 43.7 N11 21.3		342 42.9 S 4 23.0		130 52.0 N15 08.7		199 07.9 S12 16.8		Schedar	349 31.8	N56 40.0
Y 13	189 14.1	53 45.1	21.4	357 43.9	23.7	145 54.5	08.7	214 10.6	16.9	Shaula	96 11.8	S37 07.3
14	204 16.5	68 46.4	21.5	12 44.8	24.3	160 57.1	08.6	229 13.2	16.9	Sirius	258 27.3	S16 44.7
15	219 19.0	83 47.8 . .	21.5	27 45.8 . .	25.0	175 59.6 . .	08.6	244 15.8 . .	17.0	Spica	158 23.7	S11 17.0
16	234 21.5	98 49.2	21.6	42 46.8	25.7	191 02.2	08.6	259 18.4	17.1	Suhail	222 47.5	S43 31.4
17	249 23.9	113 50.6	21.7	57 47.7	26.3	206 04.7	08.5	274 21.1	17.1			
18	264 26.4	128 52.0 N11 21.8		72 48.7 S 4 27.0		221 07.3 N15 08.5		289 23.7 S12 17.2		Vega	80 33.8	N38 48.6
19	279 28.9	143 53.3	21.9	87 49.7	27.6	236 09.8	08.5	304 26.3	17.2	Zuben'ubi	136 57.4	S16 08.3
20	294 31.3	158 54.7	22.0	102 50.6	28.3	251 12.4	08.4	319 29.0	17.3			
21	309 33.8	173 56.1 . .	22.1	117 51.6 . .	28.9	266 14.9 . .	08.4	334 31.6 . .	17.4		SHA	Mer. Pass.
22	324 36.3	188 57.4	22.2	132 52.5	29.6	281 17.5	08.4	349 34.2	17.4	Venus	° ′ 225 08.7	h m 9 28
23	339 38.7	203 58.8	22.2	147 53.5	30.3	296 20.1	08.3	4 36.8	17.5	Mars	169 25.3	13 11
	h m									Jupiter	316 37.4	3 22
Mer. Pass. 0 29.1		v 1.5	d 0.1	v 1.0	d 0.7	v 2.5	d 0.0	v 2.6	d 0.1	Saturn	24 50.4	22 46

© British Crown Copyright 2022. All rights reserved.

SUN / MOON

UT	SUN GHA	SUN Dec	MOON GHA	v	MOON Dec	d	HP
d h	° ′	° ′	° ′	′	° ′	′	′
13 00	180 57.3	N 3 58.5	200 34.8	15.1	N16 29.9	11.7	54.0
01	195 57.5	57.6	215 08.9	15.2	16 18.2	11.7	54.0
02	210 57.7	56.6	229 43.1	15.3	16 06.5	11.8	54.0
03	225 58.0	.. 55.7	244 17.4	15.3	15 54.7	11.9	54.0
04	240 58.2	54.7	258 51.7	15.4	15 42.8	11.9	54.0
05	255 58.4	53.7	273 26.1	15.4	15 30.9	12.0	54.0
06	270 58.6	N 3 52.8	288 00.5	15.4	N15 18.9	12.1	54.0
W 07	285 58.8	51.8	302 34.9	15.5	15 06.8	12.1	54.0
E 08	300 59.1	50.9	317 09.4	15.6	14 54.7	12.1	54.0
D 09	315 59.3	.. 49.9	331 44.0	15.6	14 42.6	12.3	54.0
N 10	330 59.5	49.0	346 18.6	15.6	14 30.3	12.3	54.0
E 11	345 59.7	48.0	0 53.2	15.7	14 18.0	12.3	54.0
S 12	1 00.0	N 3 47.0	15 27.9	15.8	N14 05.7	12.4	54.0
D 13	16 00.2	46.1	30 02.7	15.8	13 53.3	12.4	54.0
A 14	31 00.4	45.1	44 37.5	15.8	13 40.9	12.5	54.0
Y 15	46 00.6	.. 44.2	59 12.3	15.8	13 28.4	12.6	54.0
16	61 00.8	43.2	73 47.1	16.0	13 15.8	12.6	54.0
17	76 01.1	42.3	88 22.1	15.9	13 03.2	12.7	54.0
18	91 01.3	N 3 41.3	102 57.0	16.0	N12 50.5	12.7	54.0
19	106 01.5	40.3	117 32.0	16.0	12 37.8	12.7	54.0
20	121 01.7	39.4	132 07.0	16.1	12 25.1	12.9	54.0
21	136 01.9	.. 38.4	146 42.1	16.1	12 12.2	12.8	54.0
22	151 02.2	37.5	161 17.2	16.2	11 59.4	12.9	54.0
23	166 02.4	36.5	175 52.4	16.2	11 46.5	13.0	54.1
14 00	181 02.6	N 3 35.6	190 27.6	16.2	N11 33.5	13.0	54.1
01	196 02.8	34.6	205 02.8	16.2	11 20.5	13.0	54.1
02	211 03.1	33.6	219 38.0	16.3	11 07.5	13.1	54.1
03	226 03.3	.. 32.7	234 13.3	16.3	10 54.4	13.1	54.1
04	241 03.5	31.7	248 48.6	16.4	10 41.3	13.2	54.1
05	256 03.7	30.8	263 24.0	16.4	10 28.1	13.2	54.1
06	271 03.9	N 3 29.8	277 59.4	16.4	N10 14.9	13.3	54.1
T 07	286 04.2	28.8	292 34.8	16.5	10 01.6	13.3	54.1
H 08	301 04.4	27.9	307 10.3	16.4	9 48.3	13.3	54.1
U 09	316 04.6	.. 26.9	321 45.7	16.5	9 35.0	13.4	54.1
R 10	331 04.8	26.0	336 21.2	16.6	9 21.6	13.4	54.1
S 11	346 05.0	25.0	350 56.8	16.5	9 08.2	13.4	54.1
D 12	1 05.3	N 3 24.1	5 32.3	16.6	N 8 54.8	13.5	54.1
A 13	16 05.5	23.1	20 07.9	16.6	8 41.3	13.5	54.1
Y 14	31 05.7	22.1	34 43.5	16.7	8 27.8	13.6	54.2
15	46 05.9	.. 21.2	49 19.2	16.6	8 14.2	13.6	54.2
16	61 06.2	20.2	63 54.8	16.7	8 00.6	13.6	54.2
17	76 06.4	19.3	78 30.5	16.7	7 47.0	13.7	54.2
18	91 06.6	N 3 18.3	93 06.2	16.7	N 7 33.3	13.6	54.2
19	106 06.8	17.3	107 41.9	16.7	7 19.7	13.8	54.2
20	121 07.0	16.4	122 17.6	16.8	7 05.9	13.7	54.2
21	136 07.3	.. 15.4	136 53.4	16.8	6 52.2	13.8	54.2
22	151 07.5	14.5	151 29.2	16.7	6 38.4	13.8	54.2
23	166 07.7	13.5	166 04.9	16.9	6 24.6	13.8	54.2
15 00	181 07.9	N 3 12.5	180 40.8	16.8	N 6 10.8	13.9	54.2
01	196 08.2	11.6	195 16.6	16.8	5 56.9	13.9	54.2
02	211 08.4	10.6	209 52.4	16.8	5 43.0	13.9	54.3
03	226 08.6	.. 09.6	224 28.2	16.9	5 29.1	13.9	54.3
04	241 08.8	08.7	239 04.1	16.9	5 15.2	14.0	54.3
05	256 09.0	07.7	253 40.0	16.8	5 01.2	13.9	54.3
06	271 09.3	N 3 06.8	268 15.8	16.9	N 4 47.3	14.0	54.3
07	286 09.5	05.8	282 51.7	16.9	4 33.3	14.1	54.3
08	301 09.7	04.8	297 27.6	16.9	4 19.2	14.0	54.3
F 09	316 09.9	.. 03.9	312 03.5	16.9	4 05.2	14.1	54.3
R 10	331 10.2	02.9	326 39.4	16.9	3 51.1	14.1	54.3
I 11	346 10.4	02.0	341 15.3	17.0	3 37.0	14.1	54.3
D 12	1 10.6	N 3 01.0	355 51.3	16.9	N 3 22.9	14.1	54.3
A 13	16 10.8	3 00.0	10 27.2	16.9	3 08.8	14.1	54.4
Y 14	31 11.0	2 59.1	25 03.1	16.9	2 54.7	14.2	54.4
15	46 11.3	.. 58.1	39 39.0	16.9	2 40.5	14.2	54.4
16	61 11.5	57.1	54 14.9	17.0	2 26.3	14.1	54.4
17	76 11.7	56.2	68 50.9	16.9	2 12.2	14.2	54.4
18	91 11.9	N 2 55.2	83 26.8	16.9	N 1 58.0	14.3	54.4
19	106 12.2	54.3	98 02.7	16.9	1 43.7	14.2	54.4
20	121 12.4	53.3	112 38.6	16.9	1 29.5	14.2	54.4
21	136 12.6	.. 52.3	127 14.5	16.9	1 15.3	14.3	54.4
22	151 12.8	51.4	141 50.4	16.9	1 01.0	14.2	54.5
23	166 13.0	50.4	156 26.3	16.9	N 0 46.8	14.3	54.5
	SD 15.9	d 1.0	SD 14.7		14.8		14.8

Twilight / Sunrise / Moonrise

Lat.	Twilight Naut.	Twilight Civil	Sunrise	Moonrise 13	14	15	16
°	h m	h m	h m	h m	h m	h m	h m
N 72	01 56	03 48	05 01	00 20	02 59	05 04	07 02
N 70	02 31	04 02	05 07	01 08	03 18	05 11	07 01
68	02 55	04 13	05 12	01 38	03 33	05 17	06 59
66	03 13	04 23	05 16	02 01	03 44	05 22	06 58
64	03 28	04 30	05 19	02 18	03 54	05 26	06 57
62	03 40	04 37	05 22	02 32	04 03	05 30	06 56
60	03 50	04 42	05 25	02 44	04 10	05 33	06 55
N 58	03 58	04 47	05 27	02 55	04 16	05 36	06 55
56	04 05	04 51	05 29	03 04	04 22	05 38	06 54
54	04 12	04 55	05 31	03 12	04 26	05 40	06 54
52	04 17	04 58	05 32	03 19	04 31	05 42	06 53
50	04 22	05 01	05 34	03 25	04 35	05 44	06 53
45	04 32	05 07	05 37	03 39	04 44	05 48	06 52
N 40	04 40	05 12	05 40	03 50	04 51	05 51	06 51
35	04 47	05 16	05 42	04 00	04 57	05 54	06 50
30	04 52	05 20	05 44	04 08	05 02	05 56	06 50
20	04 59	05 25	05 47	04 22	05 12	06 00	06 49
N 10	05 04	05 29	05 50	04 35	05 20	06 04	06 48
0	05 08	05 32	05 52	04 46	05 28	06 08	06 47
S 10	05 09	05 34	05 55	04 58	05 35	06 11	06 46
20	05 10	05 35	05 57	05 10	05 43	06 15	06 46
30	05 08	05 36	06 00	05 24	05 52	06 19	06 45
35	05 07	05 36	06 01	05 32	05 58	06 21	06 44
40	05 05	05 36	06 03	05 41	06 03	06 24	06 44
45	05 02	05 36	06 05	05 52	06 10	06 27	06 43
S 50	04 58	05 35	06 07	06 05	06 19	06 31	06 42
52	04 56	05 35	06 08	06 11	06 22	06 32	06 42
54	04 53	05 34	06 09	06 17	06 26	06 34	06 41
56	04 50	05 34	06 11	06 25	06 31	06 36	06 41
58	04 47	05 33	06 12	06 33	06 36	06 38	06 41
S 60	04 43	05 32	06 13	06 42	06 42	06 41	06 40

Sunset / Twilight / Moonset

Lat.	Sunset	Twilight Civil	Twilight Naut.	Moonset 13	14	15	16
°	h m	h m	h m	h m	h m	h m	h m
N 72	18 47	19 59	21 48	20 01	19 21	18 48	18 17
N 70	18 42	19 46	21 15	19 40	19 11	18 46	18 22
68	18 37	19 35	20 52	19 23	19 02	18 44	18 26
66	18 34	19 26	20 35	19 10	18 55	18 43	18 30
64	18 30	19 19	20 21	18 58	18 50	18 41	18 33
62	18 28	19 13	20 09	18 49	18 44	18 40	18 36
60	18 25	19 08	20 00	18 40	18 40	18 39	18 38
N 58	18 23	19 03	19 51	18 33	18 36	18 38	18 40
56	18 21	18 59	19 44	18 27	18 32	18 37	18 42
54	18 19	18 55	19 38	18 21	18 29	18 37	18 44
52	18 18	18 52	19 33	18 16	18 26	18 36	18 45
50	18 16	18 49	19 28	18 11	18 24	18 35	18 47
45	18 14	18 43	19 18	18 00	18 18	18 34	18 50
N 40	18 11	18 38	19 10	17 52	18 13	18 33	18 53
35	18 09	18 34	19 04	17 44	18 09	18 32	18 55
30	18 07	18 31	18 59	17 38	18 05	18 31	18 57
20	18 04	18 26	18 52	17 26	17 58	18 29	19 00
N 10	18 01	18 22	18 47	17 16	17 52	18 28	19 03
0	17 59	18 20	18 44	17 06	17 47	18 27	19 06
S 10	17 57	18 18	18 42	16 57	17 41	18 25	19 09
20	17 54	18 16	18 42	16 46	17 35	18 24	19 12
30	17 52	18 16	18 43	16 34	17 28	18 22	19 16
35	17 50	18 16	18 45	16 27	17 24	18 21	19 18
40	17 49	18 16	18 47	16 20	17 20	18 20	19 20
45	17 47	18 16	18 50	16 11	17 15	18 19	19 23
S 50	17 45	18 17	18 55	15 59	17 08	18 17	19 26
52	17 44	18 18	18 57	15 54	17 05	18 16	19 28
54	17 43	18 18	18 59	15 48	17 02	18 15	19 29
56	17 42	18 19	19 02	15 41	16 58	18 15	19 31
58	17 41	18 20	19 06	15 34	16 54	18 14	19 33
S 60	17 39	18 21	19 09	15 26	16 50	18 13	19 35

SUN / MOON

Day	SUN Eqn. of Time 00h	SUN Eqn. of Time 12h	SUN Mer. Pass.	MOON Mer. Pass. Upper	MOON Mer. Pass. Lower	Age	Phase
d	m s	m s	h m	h m	h m	d	%
13	03 49	03 59	11 56	10 56	23 17	28	2
14	04 10	04 21	11 56	11 37	23 57	29	0
15	04 31	04 42	11 55	12 17	24 37	00	0

© British Crown Copyright 2022. All rights reserved.

UT	ARIES GHA	VENUS −4.8 GHA	Dec	MARS +1.7 GHA	Dec	JUPITER −2.7 GHA	Dec	SATURN +0.5 GHA	Dec	STARS Name	SHA	Dec
d h	° ′	° ′	° ′	° ′	° ′	° ′	° ′	° ′	° ′		° ′	° ′
16 00	354 41.2	219 00.2	N11 22.3	162 54.5	S 4 30.9	311 22.6	N15 08.3	19 39.5	S12 17.6	Acamar	315 12.3	S40 12.3
01	9 43.7	234 01.5	22.4	177 55.4	31.6	326 25.2	08.3	34 42.1	17.6	Achernar	335 20.5	S57 06.8
02	24 46.1	249 02.9	22.5	192 56.4	32.2	341 27.7	08.2	49 44.7	17.7	Acrux	173 02.0	S63 13.8
03	39 48.6	264 04.2 ..	22.6	207 57.3 ..	32.9	356 30.3 ..	08.2	64 47.3 ..	17.7	Adhara	255 06.9	S28 59.9
04	54 51.0	279 05.6	22.7	222 58.3	33.6	11 32.8	08.2	79 50.0	17.8	Aldebaran	290 40.8	N16 33.5
05	69 53.5	294 06.9	22.7	237 59.3	34.2	26 35.4	08.1	94 52.6	17.9			
06	84 56.0	309 08.3	N11 22.8	253 00.2	S 4 34.9	41 38.0	N15 08.1	109 55.2	S12 17.9	Alioth	166 14.4	N55 50.1
07	99 58.4	324 09.6	22.9	268 01.2	35.5	56 40.5	08.1	124 57.9	18.0	Alkaid	152 53.3	N49 11.9
S 08	115 00.9	339 10.9	23.0	283 02.1	36.2	71 43.1	08.0	140 00.5	18.0	Alnair	27 33.8	S46 50.8
A 09	130 03.4	354 12.3 ..	23.0	298 03.1 ..	36.9	86 45.6 ..	08.0	155 03.1 ..	18.1	Alnilam	275 38.8	S 1 11.0
T 10	145 05.8	9 13.6	23.1	313 04.1	37.5	101 48.2	07.9	170 05.7	18.2	Alphard	217 49.1	S 8 45.5
U 11	160 08.3	24 14.9	23.2	328 05.0	38.2	116 50.8	07.9	185 08.4	18.2			
R 12	175 10.8	39 16.2	N11 23.3	343 06.0	S 4 38.8	131 53.3	N15 07.9	200 11.0	S12 18.3	Alphecca	126 04.8	N26 38.3
D 13	190 13.2	54 17.6	23.3	358 06.9	39.5	146 55.9	07.8	215 13.6	18.4	Alpheratz	357 35.6	N29 13.3
A 14	205 15.7	69 18.9	23.4	13 07.9	40.2	161 58.4	07.8	230 16.2	18.4	Altair	62 00.9	N 8 56.0
Y 15	220 18.1	84 20.2 ..	23.5	28 08.8 ..	40.8	177 01.0 ..	07.8	245 18.9 ..	18.5	Ankaa	353 07.8	S42 10.5
16	235 20.6	99 21.5	23.5	43 09.8	41.5	192 03.6	07.7	260 21.5	18.5	Antares	112 17.3	S26 29.1
17	250 23.1	114 22.8	23.6	58 10.8	42.1	207 06.1	07.7	275 24.1	18.6			
18	265 25.5	129 24.1	N11 23.7	73 11.7	S 4 42.8	222 08.7	N15 07.7	290 26.7	S12 18.7	Arcturus	145 49.2	N19 03.7
19	280 28.0	144 25.4	23.7	88 12.7	43.4	237 11.3	07.6	305 29.4	18.7	Atria	107 12.6	S69 04.4
20	295 30.5	159 26.7	23.8	103 13.6	44.1	252 13.8	07.6	320 32.0	18.8	Avior	234 15.6	S59 34.8
21	310 32.9	174 28.0 ..	23.9	118 14.6 ..	44.8	267 16.4 ..	07.5	335 34.6 ..	18.8	Bellatrix	278 24.0	N 6 22.4
22	325 35.4	189 29.3	23.9	133 15.5	45.4	282 18.9	07.5	350 37.2	18.9	Betelgeuse	270 53.3	N 7 24.8
23	340 37.9	204 30.6	24.0	148 16.5	46.1	297 21.5	07.5	5 39.9	19.0			
17 00	355 40.3	219 31.9	N11 24.1	163 17.5	S 4 46.7	312 24.1	N15 07.4	20 42.5	S12 19.0	Canopus	263 53.0	S52 42.1
01	10 42.8	234 33.2	24.1	178 18.4	47.4	327 26.6	07.4	35 45.1	19.1	Capella	280 23.5	N46 01.2
02	25 45.3	249 34.5	24.2	193 19.4	48.1	342 29.2	07.4	50 47.7	19.1	Deneb	49 26.2	N45 22.1
03	40 47.7	264 35.8 ..	24.2	208 20.3 ..	48.7	357 31.8 ..	07.3	65 50.4 ..	19.2	Denebola	182 26.4	N14 26.6
04	55 50.2	279 37.1	24.3	223 21.3	49.4	12 34.3	07.3	80 53.0	19.3	Diphda	348 48.1	S17 51.3
05	70 52.6	294 38.3	24.3	238 22.2	50.0	27 36.9	07.3	95 55.6	19.3			
06	85 55.1	309 39.6	N11 24.4	253 23.2	S 4 50.7	42 39.5	N15 07.2	110 58.2	S12 19.4	Dubhe	193 43.0	N61 37.5
07	100 57.6	324 40.9	24.5	268 24.2	51.4	57 42.0	07.2	126 00.9	19.4	Elnath	278 03.2	N28 37.6
08	116 00.0	339 42.1	24.5	283 25.1	52.0	72 44.6	07.1	141 03.5	19.5	Eltanin	90 42.6	N51 29.4
S 09	131 02.5	354 43.4 ..	24.6	298 26.1 ..	52.7	87 47.2 ..	07.1	156 06.1 ..	19.6	Enif	33 39.6	N 9 59.1
U 10	146 05.0	9 44.7	24.6	313 27.0	53.3	102 49.7	07.1	171 08.7	19.6	Fomalhaut	15 15.4	S29 29.8
N 11	161 07.4	24 45.9	24.7	328 28.0	54.0	117 52.3	07.0	186 11.4	19.7			
D 12	176 09.9	39 47.2	N11 24.7	343 28.9	S 4 54.6	132 54.9	N15 07.0	201 14.0	S12 19.7	Gacrux	171 53.5	S57 14.7
A 13	191 12.4	54 48.4	24.8	358 29.9	55.3	147 57.4	07.0	216 16.6	19.8	Gienah	175 45.1	S17 40.3
Y 14	206 14.8	69 49.7	24.8	13 30.9	56.0	163 00.0	06.9	231 19.2	19.9	Hadar	148 38.1	S60 29.3
15	221 17.3	84 50.9 ..	24.9	28 31.8 ..	56.6	178 02.6 ..	06.9	246 21.9 ..	19.9	Hamal	327 52.2	N23 34.5
16	236 19.7	99 52.2	24.9	43 32.8	57.3	193 05.2	06.8	261 24.5	20.0	Kaus Aust.	83 33.9	S34 22.5
17	251 22.2	114 53.4	25.0	58 33.7	57.9	208 07.7	06.8	276 27.1	20.0			
18	266 24.7	129 54.7	N11 25.0	73 34.7	S 4 58.6	223 10.3	N15 06.8	291 29.7	S12 20.1	Kochab	137 20.5	N74 03.7
19	281 27.1	144 55.9	25.0	88 35.6	59.3	238 12.9	06.7	306 32.4	20.2	Markab	13 30.7	N15 20.1
20	296 29.6	159 57.2	25.1	103 36.6	4 59.9	253 15.4	06.7	321 35.0	20.2	Menkar	314 07.1	N 4 11.1
21	311 32.1	174 58.4 ..	25.1	118 37.5	5 00.6	268 18.0 ..	06.6	336 37.6 ..	20.3	Menkent	147 59.2	S36 29.2
22	326 34.5	189 59.6	25.2	133 38.5	01.2	283 20.6	06.6	351 40.2	20.3	Miaplacidus	221 39.3	S69 48.5
23	341 37.0	205 00.8	25.2	148 39.4	01.9	298 23.2	06.6	6 42.9	20.4			
18 00	356 39.5	220 02.1	N11 25.2	163 40.4	S 5 02.5	313 25.7	N15 06.5	21 45.5	S12 20.5	Mirfak	308 29.6	N49 56.6
01	11 41.9	235 03.3	25.3	178 41.4	03.2	328 28.3	06.5	36 48.1	20.5	Nunki	75 49.0	S26 16.1
02	26 44.4	250 04.5	25.3	193 42.3	03.9	343 30.9	06.5	51 50.7	20.6	Peacock	53 07.0	S56 39.7
03	41 46.9	265 05.7 ..	25.4	208 43.3 ..	04.5	358 33.4 ..	06.4	66 53.4 ..	20.6	Pollux	243 18.8	N27 58.2
04	56 49.3	280 06.9	25.4	223 44.2	05.2	13 36.0	06.4	81 56.0	20.7	Procyon	244 52.1	N 5 10.0
05	71 51.8	295 08.2	25.4	238 45.2	05.8	28 38.6	06.3	96 58.6	20.8			
06	86 54.2	310 09.4	N11 25.5	253 46.1	S 5 06.5	43 41.2	N15 06.3	112 01.2	S12 20.8	Rasalhague	95 59.6	N12 32.7
07	101 56.7	325 10.6	25.5	268 47.1	07.1	58 43.7	06.3	127 03.8	20.9	Regulus	207 35.9	N11 51.2
08	116 59.2	340 11.8	25.5	283 48.0	07.8	73 46.3	06.2	142 06.5	20.9	Rigel	281 04.9	S 8 10.2
M 09	132 01.6	355 13.0 ..	25.6	298 49.0 ..	08.5	88 48.9 ..	06.2	157 09.1 ..	21.0	Rigil Kent.	139 42.3	S60 56.1
O 10	147 04.1	10 14.2	25.6	313 49.9	09.1	103 51.5	06.1	172 11.7	21.1	Sabik	102 04.1	S15 45.2
N 11	162 06.6	25 15.4	25.6	328 50.9	09.8	118 54.1	06.1	187 14.3	21.1			
D 12	177 09.0	40 16.6	N11 25.6	343 51.8	S 5 10.4	133 56.6	N15 06.1	202 17.0	S12 21.2	Schedar	349 31.8	N56 40.0
A 13	192 11.5	55 17.7	25.7	358 52.8	11.1	148 59.2	06.0	217 19.6	21.2	Shaula	96 11.9	S37 07.3
Y 14	207 14.0	70 18.9	25.7	13 53.7	11.8	164 01.8	06.0	232 22.2	21.3	Sirius	258 27.3	S16 44.6
15	222 16.4	85 20.1 ..	25.7	28 54.7 ..	12.4	179 04.4 ..	05.9	247 24.8 ..	21.4	Spica	158 23.8	S11 17.0
16	237 18.9	100 21.3	25.7	43 55.7	13.1	194 06.9	05.9	262 27.4	21.4	Suhail	222 47.5	S43 31.4
17	252 21.3	115 22.5	25.8	58 56.6	13.7	209 09.5	05.9	277 30.1	21.5			
18	267 23.8	130 23.7	N11 25.8	73 57.6	S 5 14.4	224 12.1	N15 05.8	292 32.7	S12 21.5	Vega	80 33.9	N38 48.6
19	282 26.3	145 24.8	25.8	88 58.5	15.0	239 14.7	05.8	307 35.3	21.6	Zuben'ubi	136 57.5	S16 08.3
20	297 28.7	160 26.0	25.8	103 59.5	15.7	254 17.3	05.7	322 37.9	21.7		SHA	Mer. Pass.
21	312 31.2	175 27.2 ..	25.8	119 00.4 ..	16.4	269 19.8 ..	05.7	337 40.6 ..	21.7		° ′	h m
22	327 33.7	190 28.3	25.9	134 01.4	17.0	284 22.4	05.6	352 43.2	21.8	Venus	223 51.6	9 21
23	342 36.1	205 29.5	25.9	149 02.3	17.7	299 25.0	05.6	7 45.8	21.8	Mars	167 37.1	13 06
Mer. Pass.	h m 0 17.3	v 1.3	d 0.0	v 1.0	d 0.7	v 2.6	d 0.0	v 2.6	d 0.1	Jupiter	316 43.8	3 10
										Saturn	25 02.2	22 33

© British Crown Copyright 2022. All rights reserved.

UT	SUN GHA	SUN Dec	MOON GHA	v	Dec	d	HP
d h	° ′	° ′	° ′	′	° ′	′	′
16 00	181 13.3	N 2 49.4	171 02.2	16.9	N 0 32.5	14.2	54.5
01	196 13.5	48.5	185 38.1	16.9	0 18.3	14.3	54.5
02	211 13.7	47.5	200 14.0	16.8	N 0 04.0	14.3	54.5
03	226 13.9	.. 46.6	214 49.8	16.9	S 0 10.3	14.3	54.5
04	241 14.2	45.6	229 25.7	16.8	0 24.6	14.3	54.5
05	256 14.4	44.6	244 01.5	16.8	0 38.9	14.3	54.5
06	271 14.6	N 2 43.7	258 37.3	16.8	S 0 53.2	14.3	54.6
07	286 14.8	42.7	273 13.1	16.8	1 07.5	14.3	54.6
S 08	301 15.1	41.7	287 48.9	16.8	1 21.8	14.3	54.6
A 09	316 15.3	.. 40.8	302 24.7	16.7	1 36.1	14.3	54.6
T 10	331 15.5	39.8	317 00.4	16.8	1 50.4	14.3	54.6
U 11	346 15.7	38.8	331 36.2	16.7	2 04.7	14.3	54.6
R 12	1 15.9	N 2 37.9	346 11.9	16.7	S 2 19.0	14.3	54.6
D 13	16 16.2	36.9	0 47.6	16.7	2 33.3	14.3	54.7
A 14	31 16.4	35.9	15 23.3	16.6	2 47.6	14.3	54.7
Y 15	46 16.6	.. 35.0	29 58.9	16.6	3 01.9	14.3	54.7
16	61 16.8	34.0	44 34.5	16.6	3 16.2	14.3	54.7
17	76 17.1	33.1	59 10.1	16.6	3 30.5	14.3	54.7
18	91 17.3	N 2 32.1	73 45.7	16.6	S 3 44.8	14.3	54.7
19	106 17.5	31.1	88 21.3	16.5	3 59.1	14.2	54.7
20	121 17.7	30.2	102 56.8	16.5	4 13.3	14.3	54.8
21	136 17.9	.. 29.2	117 32.3	16.4	4 27.6	14.3	54.8
22	151 18.2	28.2	132 07.7	16.4	4 41.9	14.2	54.8
23	166 18.4	27.3	146 43.1	16.4	4 56.1	14.2	54.8
17 00	181 18.6	N 2 26.3	161 18.5	16.4	S 5 10.3	14.2	54.8
01	196 18.8	25.3	175 53.9	16.3	5 24.5	14.2	54.8
02	211 19.1	24.4	190 29.2	16.3	5 38.7	14.2	54.9
03	226 19.3	.. 23.4	205 04.5	16.3	5 52.9	14.2	54.9
04	241 19.5	22.4	219 39.8	16.2	6 07.1	14.2	54.9
05	256 19.7	21.5	234 15.0	16.2	6 21.3	14.1	54.9
06	271 20.0	N 2 20.5	248 50.2	16.1	S 6 35.4	14.2	54.9
07	286 20.2	19.5	263 25.3	16.1	6 49.6	14.1	54.9
S 08	301 20.4	18.6	278 00.4	16.0	7 03.7	14.1	54.9
U 09	316 20.6	.. 17.6	292 35.4	16.1	7 17.8	14.0	55.0
N 10	331 20.8	16.6	307 10.5	15.9	7 31.8	14.1	55.0
D 11	346 21.1	15.7	321 45.4	15.9	7 45.9	14.0	55.0
A 12	1 21.3	N 2 14.7	336 20.3	15.9	S 7 59.9	14.0	55.0
Y 13	16 21.5	13.7	350 55.2	15.8	8 13.9	14.0	55.0
14	31 21.7	12.8	5 30.0	15.8	8 27.9	13.9	55.0
15	46 22.0	.. 11.8	20 04.8	15.7	8 41.8	14.0	55.1
16	61 22.2	10.8	34 39.5	15.7	8 55.8	13.9	55.1
17	76 22.4	09.9	49 14.2	15.7	9 09.7	13.9	55.1
18	91 22.6	N 2 08.9	63 48.9	15.5	S 9 23.6	13.8	55.1
19	106 22.8	07.9	78 23.4	15.5	9 37.4	13.8	55.1
20	121 23.1	07.0	92 57.9	15.5	9 51.2	13.8	55.1
21	136 23.3	.. 06.0	107 32.4	15.4	10 05.0	13.8	55.2
22	151 23.5	05.0	122 06.8	15.4	10 18.8	13.7	55.2
23	166 23.7	04.1	136 41.2	15.3	10 32.5	13.7	55.2
18 00	181 24.0	N 2 03.1	151 15.5	15.2	S10 46.2	13.7	55.2
01	196 24.2	02.1	165 49.7	15.2	10 59.9	13.6	55.2
02	211 24.4	01.2	180 23.9	15.1	11 13.5	13.6	55.3
03	226 24.6	2 00.2	194 58.0	15.0	11 27.1	13.5	55.3
04	241 24.9	1 59.2	209 32.0	15.0	11 40.6	13.5	55.3
05	256 25.1	58.3	224 06.0	15.0	11 54.1	13.5	55.3
06	271 25.3	N 1 57.3	238 40.0	14.8	S12 07.6	13.4	55.3
07	286 25.5	56.3	253 13.8	14.8	12 21.0	13.4	55.3
M 08	301 25.7	55.4	267 47.6	14.7	12 34.4	13.4	55.4
O 09	316 26.0	.. 54.4	282 21.3	14.7	12 47.8	13.3	55.4
N 10	331 26.2	53.4	296 55.0	14.6	13 01.1	13.2	55.4
D 11	346 26.4	52.5	311 28.6	14.5	13 14.3	13.3	55.4
A 12	1 26.6	N 1 51.5	326 02.1	14.4	S13 27.6	13.1	55.4
Y 13	16 26.9	50.5	340 35.5	14.4	13 40.7	13.1	55.5
14	31 27.1	49.6	355 08.9	14.3	13 53.8	13.1	55.5
15	46 27.3	.. 48.6	9 42.2	14.2	14 06.9	13.0	55.5
16	61 27.5	47.6	24 15.4	14.2	14 19.9	13.0	55.5
17	76 27.8	46.7	38 48.6	14.1	14 32.9	12.9	55.5
18	91 28.0	N 1 45.7	53 21.7	14.0	S14 45.8	12.9	55.6
19	106 28.2	44.7	67 54.7	13.9	14 58.7	12.8	55.6
20	121 28.4	43.8	82 27.6	13.8	15 11.5	12.7	55.6
21	136 28.6	.. 42.8	97 00.4	13.8	15 24.2	12.7	55.6
22	151 28.9	41.8	111 33.2	13.6	15 36.9	12.7	55.6
23	166 29.1	40.8	126 05.8	13.6	S15 49.6	12.6	55.7
	SD 15.9	d 1.0	SD 14.9		15.0		15.1

Lat.	Twilight Naut.	Twilight Civil	Sunrise	Moonrise 16	17	18	19
°	h m	h m	h m	h m	h m	h m	h m
N 72	02 21	04 04	05 15	07 02	09 04	11 24	▬▬
N 70	02 49	04 15	05 19	07 01	08 53	10 57	13 44
68	03 10	04 25	05 22	06 59	08 44	10 36	12 50
66	03 26	04 33	05 25	06 58	08 36	10 20	12 17
64	03 39	04 39	05 28	06 57	08 30	10 07	11 54
62	03 49	04 45	05 30	06 56	08 24	09 56	11 35
60	03 58	04 50	05 32	06 55	08 19	09 47	11 20
N 58	04 05	04 54	05 33	06 55	08 15	09 39	11 07
56	04 12	04 57	05 35	06 54	08 12	09 32	10 56
54	04 18	05 00	05 36	06 54	08 08	09 26	10 46
52	04 23	05 03	05 37	06 53	08 05	09 21	10 38
50	04 27	05 06	05 38	06 53	08 03	09 15	10 30
45	04 36	05 11	05 41	06 52	07 57	09 04	10 14
N 40	04 43	05 15	05 42	06 51	07 52	08 55	10 00
35	04 49	05 19	05 44	06 50	07 48	08 47	09 49
30	04 53	05 21	05 45	06 50	07 44	08 40	09 39
20	05 00	05 26	05 48	06 49	07 38	08 29	09 22
N 10	05 05	05 29	05 50	06 48	07 33	08 19	09 08
0	05 07	05 31	05 51	06 47	07 27	08 10	08 54
S 10	05 08	05 32	05 53	06 46	07 22	08 00	08 41
20	05 07	05 33	05 55	06 46	07 17	07 50	08 27
30	05 05	05 32	05 56	06 45	07 11	07 39	08 11
35	05 03	05 32	05 57	06 44	07 08	07 33	08 01
40	05 00	05 31	05 58	06 44	07 04	07 26	07 51
45	04 56	05 30	05 59	06 43	06 59	07 17	07 38
S 50	04 51	05 29	06 01	06 42	06 54	07 07	07 23
52	04 48	05 28	06 01	06 42	06 52	07 03	07 16
54	04 46	05 27	06 02	06 41	06 49	06 58	07 09
56	04 42	05 26	06 03	06 41	06 46	06 52	07 00
58	04 38	05 24	06 03	06 41	06 43	06 46	06 50
S 60	04 34	05 23	06 04	06 40	06 39	06 39	06 39

Lat.	Sunset	Twilight Civil	Twilight Naut.	Moonset 16	17	18	19
°	h m	h m	h m	h m	h m	h m	h m
N 72	18 32	19 42	21 22	18 17	17 41	16 51	▬▬
N 70	18 28	19 31	20 55	18 22	17 55	17 20	16 07
68	18 25	19 22	20 36	18 26	18 07	17 43	17 03
66	18 22	19 14	20 20	18 30	18 16	18 00	17 37
64	18 20	19 08	20 08	18 33	18 24	18 14	18 02
62	18 18	19 03	19 58	18 36	18 31	18 27	18 22
60	18 16	18 58	19 49	18 38	18 37	18 37	18 38
N 58	18 15	18 54	19 42	18 40	18 43	18 46	18 51
56	18 13	18 51	19 36	18 42	18 47	18 54	19 03
54	18 12	18 48	19 30	18 44	18 52	19 01	19 14
52	18 11	18 45	19 25	18 45	18 56	19 08	19 23
50	18 10	18 42	19 21	18 47	18 59	19 13	19 31
45	18 08	18 37	19 12	18 50	19 07	19 26	19 49
N 40	18 06	18 33	19 05	18 53	19 13	19 36	20 04
35	18 05	18 30	19 00	18 55	19 19	19 45	20 16
30	18 03	18 27	18 55	18 57	19 24	19 53	20 27
20	18 01	18 23	18 49	19 00	19 33	20 07	20 46
N 10	17 59	18 20	18 45	19 03	19 40	20 19	21 02
0	17 58	18 19	18 43	19 06	19 47	20 31	21 17
S 10	17 56	18 17	18 42	19 09	19 55	20 42	21 33
20	17 55	18 17	18 42	19 12	20 02	20 54	21 49
30	17 53	18 17	18 45	19 16	20 11	21 08	22 08
35	17 53	18 18	18 47	19 18	20 16	21 17	22 20
40	17 52	18 19	18 50	19 20	20 22	21 26	22 32
45	17 51	18 20	18 54	19 23	20 29	21 37	22 48
S 50	17 49	18 22	18 59	19 26	20 37	21 50	23 07
52	17 49	18 23	19 02	19 28	20 41	21 57	23 16
54	17 48	18 24	19 05	19 29	20 45	22 04	23 26
56	17 48	18 25	19 08	19 31	20 50	22 11	23 37
58	17 47	18 26	19 12	19 33	20 55	22 20	23 50
S 60	17 46	18 28	19 17	19 35	21 01	22 30	24 06

	SUN Eqn. of Time 00h	12h	SUN Mer. Pass.	MOON Mer. Pass. Upper	Lower	Age	Phase
Day	m s	m s	h m	h m	h m	d	%
16	04 53	05 03	11 55	12 57	00 37	01	2
17	05 14	05 25	11 55	13 37	01 17	02	5
18	05 35	05 46	11 54	14 20	01 58	03	11

© British Crown Copyright 2022. All rights reserved.

UT	ARIES	VENUS −4.8		MARS +1.7		JUPITER −2.7		SATURN +0.5		STARS		
d h	GHA	GHA	Dec	GHA	Dec	GHA	Dec	GHA	Dec	Name	SHA	Dec
19 00	357 38.6	220 30.7 N11 25.9		164 03.3 S 5 18.3		314 27.6 N15 05.6		22 48.4 S12 21.9		Acamar	315 12.3	S40 12.3
01	12 41.1	235 31.8 . . 25.9		179 04.2 . . 19.0		329 30.2 . . 05.5		37 51.0 . . 21.9		Achernar	335 20.5	S57 06.8
02	27 43.5	250 33.0 25.9		194 05.2 19.6		344 32.7 05.5		52 53.7 22.0		Acrux	173 02.0	S63 13.8
03	42 46.0	265 34.1 . . 25.9		209 06.1 . . 20.3		359 35.3 . . 05.4		67 56.3 . . 22.1		Adhara	255 06.8	S28 59.9
04	57 48.5	280 35.3 26.0		224 07.1 21.0		14 37.9 05.4		82 58.9 22.1		Aldebaran	290 40.8	N16 33.5
05	72 50.9	295 36.4 26.0		239 08.0 21.6		29 40.5 05.4		98 01.5 22.2				
06	87 53.4	330 37.6 N11 26.0		254 09.0 S 5 22.3		44 43.1 N15 05.3		113 04.1 S12 22.2		Alioth	166 14.4	N55 50.0
07	102 55.8	325 38.7 26.0		269 09.9 22.9		59 45.7 05.3		128 06.8 22.3		Alkaid	152 53.3	N49 11.9
08	117 58.3	340 39.9 26.0		284 10.9 23.6		74 48.2 05.2		143 09.4 22.4		Alnair	27 33.9	S46 50.8
09	133 00.8	355 41.0 . . 26.0		299 11.8 . . 24.2		89 50.8 . . 05.2		158 12.0 . . 22.4		Alnilam	275 38.8	S 1 11.0
10	148 03.2	10 42.1 26.0		314 12.8 24.9		104 53.4 05.1		173 14.6 22.5		Alphard	217 49.1	S 8 45.5
11	163 05.7	25 43.3 26.0		329 13.7 25.6		119 56.0 05.1		188 17.3 22.5				
12	178 08.2	40 44.4 N11 26.0		344 14.7 S 5 26.2		134 58.6 N15 05.1		203 19.9 S12 22.6		Alphecca	126 04.9	N26 38.3
13	193 10.6	55 45.5 26.0		359 15.6 26.9		150 01.2 05.0		218 22.5 22.6		Alpheratz	357 35.6	N29 13.3
14	208 13.1	70 46.7 26.0		14 16.6 27.5		165 03.7 05.0		233 25.1 22.7		Altair	62 00.9	N 8 56.0
15	223 15.6	85 47.8 . . 26.0		29 17.5 . . 28.2		180 06.3 . . 04.9		248 27.7 . . 22.8		Ankaa	353 07.8	S42 10.5
16	238 18.0	100 48.9 26.0		44 18.5 28.8		195 08.9 04.9		263 30.4 22.8		Antares	112 17.3	S26 29.1
17	253 20.5	115 50.0 26.0		59 19.4 29.5		210 11.5 04.8		278 33.0 22.9				
18	268 23.0	130 51.1 N11 26.0		74 20.4 S 5 30.1		225 14.1 N15 04.8		293 35.6 S12 22.9		Arcturus	145 49.2	N19 03.7
19	283 25.4	145 52.3 26.0		89 21.3 30.8		240 16.7 04.8		308 38.2 23.0		Atria	107 12.6	S69 04.4
20	298 27.9	160 53.4 26.0		104 22.3 31.5		255 19.3 04.7		323 40.8 23.1		Avior	234 15.6	S59 34.8
21	313 30.3	175 54.5 . . 26.0		119 23.2 . . 32.1		270 21.9 . . 04.7		338 43.5 . . 23.1		Bellatrix	278 24.0	N 6 22.4
22	328 32.8	190 55.6 26.0		134 24.2 32.8		285 24.4 04.6		353 46.1 23.2		Betelgeuse	270 53.3	N 7 24.8
23	343 35.3	205 56.7 26.0		149 25.1 33.4		300 27.0 04.6		8 48.7 23.2				
20 00	358 37.7	220 57.8 N11 26.0		164 26.1 S 5 34.1		315 29.6 N15 04.5		23 51.3 S12 23.3		Canopus	263 53.0	S52 42.1
01	13 40.2	235 58.9 26.0		179 27.0 34.7		330 32.2 04.5		38 53.9 23.3		Capella	280 23.5	N46 01.2
02	28 42.7	251 00.0 26.0		194 28.0 35.4		345 34.8 04.5		53 56.6 23.4		Deneb	49 26.3	N45 22.1
03	43 45.1	266 01.1 . . 26.0		209 28.9 . . 36.1		0 37.4 . . 04.4		68 59.2 . . 23.5		Denebola	182 26.4	N14 26.6
04	58 47.6	281 02.2 26.0		224 29.8 36.7		15 40.0 · 04.4		84 01.8 23.5		Diphda	348 48.1	S17 51.3
05	73 50.1	296 03.3 26.0		239 30.8 37.4		30 42.6 04.3		99 04.4 23.6				
06	88 52.5	311 04.3 N11 26.0		254 31.7 S 5 38.0		45 45.2 N15 04.3		114 07.0 S12 23.6		Dubhe	193 43.0	N61 37.5
07	103 55.0	326 05.4 25.9		269 32.7 38.7		60 47.8 04.2		129 09.6 23.7		Elnath	278 03.2	N28 37.6
08	118 57.4	341 06.5 25.9		284 33.6 39.3		75 50.3 04.2		144 12.3 23.7		Eltanin	90 42.7	N51 29.4
09	133 59.9	356 07.6 . . 25.9		299 34.6 . . 40.0		90 52.9 . . 04.2		159 14.9 . . 23.8		Enif	33 39.6	N 9 59.1
10	149 02.4	11 08.7 25.9		314 35.5 40.6		105 55.5 04.1		174 17.5 23.9		Fomalhaut	15 15.4	S29 29.8
11	164 04.8	26 09.7 25.9		329 36.5 41.3		120 58.1 04.1		189 20.1 23.9				
12	179 07.3	41 10.8 N11 25.9		344 37.4 S 5 42.0		136 00.7 N15 04.0		204 22.7 S12 24.0		Gacrux	171 53.5	S57 14.7
13	194 09.8	56 11.9 25.8		359 38.4 42.6		151 03.3 04.0		219 25.4 24.0		Gienah	175 45.1	S17 40.2
14	209 12.2	71 13.0 25.8		14 39.3 43.3		166 05.9 03.9		234 28.0 24.1		Hadar	148 38.1	S60 29.3
15	224 14.7	86 14.0 . . 25.8		29 40.3 . . 43.9		181 08.5 . . 03.9		249 30.6 . . 24.1		Hamal	327 52.2	N23 34.5
16	239 17.2	101 15.1 25.8		44 41.2 44.6		196 11.1 03.8		264 33.2 24.2		Kaus Aust.	83 33.9	S34 22.5
17	254 19.6	116 16.1 25.8		59 42.2 45.2		211 13.7 03.8		279 35.8 24.3				
18	269 22.1	131 17.2 N11 25.7		74 43.1 S 5 45.9		226 16.3 N15 03.7		294 38.4 S12 24.3		Kochab	137 20.5	N74 03.7
19	284 24.6	146 18.3 25.7		89 44.0 46.5		241 18.9 03.7		309 41.1 24.4		Markab	13 30.7	N15 20.1
20	299 27.0	161 19.3 25.7		104 45.0 47.2		256 21.5 03.7		324 43.7 24.4		Menkar	314 07.1	N 4 11.1
21	314 29.5	176 20.4 . . 25.7		119 45.9 . . 47.9		271 24.1 . . 03.6		339 46.3 . . 24.5		Menkent	147 59.3	S36 29.2
22	329 31.9	191 21.4 25.6		134 46.9 48.5		286 26.7 03.6		354 48.9 24.5		Miaplacidus	221 39.3	S69 48.5
23	344 34.4	206 22.4 25.6		149 47.8 49.2		301 29.3 03.5		9 51.5 24.6				
21 00	359 36.9	221 23.5 N11 25.6		164 48.8 S 5 49.8		316 31.9 N15 03.5		24 54.2 S12 24.7		Mirfak	308 29.6	N49 56.6
01	14 39.3	236 24.5 25.5		179 49.7 50.5		331 34.4 03.4		39 56.8 24.7		Nunki	75 49.0	S26 16.1
02	29 41.8	251 25.6 25.5		194 50.7 51.1		346 37.0 03.4		54 59.4 24.8		Peacock	53 07.1	S56 39.7
03	44 44.3	266 26.6 . . 25.5		209 51.6 . . 51.8		1 39.6 . . 03.3		70 02.0 . . 24.8		Pollux	243 18.8	N27 58.2
04	59 46.7	281 27.6 25.4		224 52.5 52.4		16 42.2 03.3		85 04.6 24.9		Procyon	244 52.1	N 5 10.0
05	74 49.2	296 28.7 25.4		239 53.5 53.1		31 44.8 03.2		100 07.2 24.9				
06	89 51.7	311 29.7 N11 25.4		254 54.4 S 5 53.8		46 47.4 N15 03.2		115 09.9 S12 25.0		Rasalhague	95 59.6	N12 32.7
07	104 54.1	326 30.7 25.3		269 55.4 54.4		61 50.0 03.2		130 12.5 25.1		Regulus	207 35.9	N11 51.2
08	119 56.6	341 31.7 25.3		284 56.3 55.1		76 52.6 03.1		145 15.1 25.1		Rigel	281 04.9	S 8 10.2
09	134 59.1	356 32.8 . . 25.3		299 57.3 . . 55.7		91 55.2 . . 03.1		160 17.7 . . 25.2		Rigil Kent.	139 42.3	S60 56.0
10	150 01.5	11 33.8 25.2		314 58.2 56.4		106 57.8 03.0		175 20.3 25.2		Sabik	102 04.1	S15 45.2
11	165 04.0	26 34.8 25.2		329 59.2 57.0		122 00.4 03.0		190 22.9 25.3				
12	180 06.4	41 35.8 N11 25.2		345 00.1 S 5 57.7		137 03.0 N15 02.9		205 25.6 S12 25.3		Schedar	349 31.8	N56 40.0
13	195 08.9	56 36.8 25.1		0 01.0 58.3		152 05.6 02.9		220 28.2 25.4		Shaula	96 11.9	S37 07.3
14	210 11.4	71 37.8 25.1		15 02.0 59.0		167 08.2 02.8		235 30.8 25.5		Sirius	258 27.3	S16 44.6
15	225 13.8	86 38.8 . . 25.0		30 02.9 5 59.6		182 10.8 . . 02.8		250 33.4 . . 25.5		Spica	158 23.8	S11 17.0
16	240 16.3	101 39.9 25.0		45 03.9 6 00.3		197 13.4 02.7		265 36.0 25.6		Suhail	222 47.5	S43 31.4
17	255 18.8	116 40.9 24.9		60 04.8 01.0		212 16.0 02.7		280 38.6 25.6				
18	270 21.2	131 41.9 N11 24.9		75 05.8 S 6 01.6		227 18.7 N15 02.6		295 41.3 S12 25.7		Vega	80 33.9	N38 48.6
19	285 23.7	146 42.9 24.8		90 06.7 02.3		242 21.3 02.6		310 43.9 25.7		Zuben'ubi	136 57.5	S16 08.3
20	300 26.2	161 43.9 24.8		105 07.6 02.9		257 23.9 02.5		325 46.5 25.8				
21	315 28.6	176 44.8 . . 24.7		120 08.6 . . 03.6		272 26.5 . . 02.5		340 49.1 . . 25.8			SHA	Mer. Pass.
22	330 31.1	191 45.8 24.7		135 09.5 04.2		287 29.1 02.4		355 51.7 25.9		Venus	222 20.1	9 15
23	345 33.6	206 46.8 24.6		150 10.5 04.9		302 31.7 02.4		10 54.3 26.0		Mars	165 48.3	13 01
										Jupiter	316 51.9	2 58
Mer. Pass. 0 05.5		v 1.1 d 0.0		v 0.9 d 0.7		v 2.6 d 0.0		v 2.6 d 0.1		Saturn	25 13.6	22 21

© British Crown Copyright 2022. All rights reserved.

UT	SUN GHA	SUN Dec	MOON GHA	v	MOON Dec	d	HP
d h	° ′	° ′	° ′	′	° ′	′	′
25 00	182 01.1	S 0 40.1	59 49.6	4.7	S25 10.7	8.4	59.8
01	197 01.3	41.0	74 13.3	4.8	25 02.3	8.5	59.8
02	212 01.6	42.0	88 37.1	4.9	24 53.8	8.7	59.8
03	227 01.8	. . 43.0	103 01.0	4.9	24 45.1	8.9	59.9
04	242 02.0	44.0	117 24.9	4.9	24 36.2	9.1	59.9
05	257 02.2	44.9	131 48.8	5.0	24 27.1	9.2	59.9
06	272 02.4	S 0 45.9	146 12.8	5.1	S24 17.9	9.4	59.9
07	287 02.6	46.9	160 36.9	5.1	24 08.5	9.6	60.0
08	302 02.9	47.9	175 01.0	5.2	23 58.9	9.8	60.0
M 09	317 03.1	. . 48.8	189 25.2	5.3	23 49.1	9.9	60.0
O 10	332 03.3	49.8	203 49.5	5.3	23 39.2	10.0	60.0
N 11	347 03.5	50.8	218 13.8	5.4	23 29.2	10.3	60.1
D 12	2 03.7	S 0 51.7	232 38.2	5.4	S23 18.9	10.4	60.1
A 13	17 03.9	52.7	247 02.6	5.5	23 08.5	10.5	60.1
Y 14	32 04.2	53.7	261 27.1	5.6	22 58.0	10.8	60.1
15	47 04.4	. . 54.7	275 51.7	5.6	22 47.2	10.8	60.2
16	62 04.6	55.6	290 16.3	5.8	22 36.4	11.1	60.2
17	77 04.8	56.6	304 41.1	5.7	22 25.3	11.2	60.2
18	92 05.0	S 0 57.6	319 05.8	5.9	S22 14.1	11.3	60.2
19	107 05.2	58.6	333 30.7	5.9	22 02.8	11.5	60.3
20	122 05.5	0 59.5	347 55.6	6.0	21 51.3	11.7	60.3
21	137 05.7	1 00.5	2 20.6	6.1	21 39.6	11.8	60.3
22	152 05.9	01.5	16 45.7	6.1	21 27.8	11.9	60.3
23	167 06.1	02.5	31 10.8	6.2	21 15.9	12.1	60.3
26 00	182 06.3	S 1 03.4	45 36.0	6.3	S21 03.8	12.2	60.4
01	197 06.5	04.4	60 01.3	6.3	20 51.6	12.4	60.4
02	212 06.8	05.4	74 26.6	6.4	20 39.2	12.5	60.4
03	227 07.0	. . 06.3	88 52.0	6.5	20 26.7	12.7	60.4
04	242 07.2	07.3	103 17.5	6.6	20 14.0	12.8	60.4
05	257 07.4	08.3	117 43.1	6.7	20 01.2	12.9	60.5
06	272 07.6	S 1 09.3	132 08.8	6.7	S19 48.3	13.1	60.5
07	287 07.8	10.2	146 34.5	6.8	19 35.2	13.2	60.5
T 08	302 08.1	11.2	161 00.3	6.8	19 22.0	13.4	60.5
U 09	317 08.3	. . 12.2	175 26.1	7.0	19 08.6	13.4	60.5
E 10	332 08.5	13.2	189 52.1	7.0	18 55.2	13.6	60.6
S 11	347 08.7	14.1	204 18.1	7.1	18 41.6	13.7	60.6
D 12	2 08.9	S 1 15.1	218 44.2	7.2	S18 27.9	13.9	60.6
A 13	17 09.1	16.1	233 10.4	7.2	18 14.0	13.9	60.6
Y 14	32 09.3	17.1	247 36.6	7.3	18 00.1	14.1	60.6
15	47 09.6	. . 18.0	262 02.9	7.4	17 46.0	14.2	60.6
16	62 09.8	19.0	276 29.3	7.5	17 31.8	14.3	60.7
17	77 10.0	20.0	290 55.8	7.5	17 17.5	14.5	60.7
18	92 10.2	S 1 20.9	305 22.3	7.6	S17 03.0	14.5	60.7
19	107 10.4	21.9	319 48.9	7.7	16 48.5	14.7	60.7
20	122 10.6	22.9	334 15.6	7.7	16 33.8	14.8	60.7
21	137 10.9	. . 23.9	348 42.3	7.9	16 19.0	14.8	60.7
22	152 11.1	24.8	3 09.2	7.9	16 04.2	15.0	60.7
23	167 11.3	25.8	17 36.1	7.9	15 49.2	15.1	60.8
27 00	182 11.5	S 1 26.8	32 03.0	8.1	S15 34.1	15.2	60.8
01	197 11.7	27.8	46 30.1	8.1	15 18.9	15.3	60.8
02	212 11.9	28.7	60 57.2	8.2	15 03.6	15.4	60.8
03	227 12.1	. . 29.7	75 24.4	8.3	14 48.2	15.5	60.8
04	242 12.4	30.7	89 51.6	8.3	14 32.7	15.5	60.8
05	257 12.6	31.6	104 18.9	8.4	14 17.2	15.7	60.8
06	272 12.8	S 1 32.6	118 46.3	8.5	S14 01.5	15.8	60.8
W 07	287 13.0	33.6	133 13.8	8.5	13 45.7	15.8	60.8
E 08	302 13.2	34.6	147 41.3	8.6	13 29.9	15.9	60.9
D 09	317 13.4	. . 35.5	162 08.9	8.6	13 14.0	16.0	60.9
N 10	332 13.6	36.5	176 36.5	8.8	12 58.0	16.1	60.9
E 11	347 13.9	37.5	191 04.3	8.7	12 41.9	16.2	60.9
S 12	2 14.1	S 1 38.5	205 32.0	8.9	S12 25.7	16.3	60.9
D 13	17 14.3	39.4	219 59.9	8.9	12 09.4	16.3	60.9
A 14	32 14.5	40.4	234 27.8	9.0	11 53.1	16.4	60.9
Y 15	47 14.7	. . 41.4	248 55.8	9.0	11 36.7	16.5	60.9
16	62 14.9	42.3	263 23.8	9.1	11 20.2	16.5	60.9
17	77 15.1	43.3	277 51.9	9.1	11 03.7	16.6	60.9
18	92 15.3	S 1 44.3	292 20.0	9.2	S10 47.1	16.7	60.9
19	107 15.6	45.3	306 48.2	9.3	10 30.4	16.8	60.9
20	122 15.8	46.2	321 16.5	9.3	10 13.6	16.8	60.9
21	137 16.0	. . 47.2	335 44.8	9.4	9 56.8	16.8	60.9
22	152 16.2	48.2	350 13.2	9.4	9 40.0	17.0	60.9
23	167 16.4	49.2	4 41.6	9.4	S 9 23.0	16.9	60.9
	SD 16.0	d 1.0	SD 16.4		16.5		16.6

Twilight / Moonrise

Lat.	Naut.	Civil	Sunrise	Moonrise 25	26	27	28
°	h m	h m	h m	h m	h m	h m	h m
N 72	03 20	04 47	05 55	▬▬	20 13	18 55	18 11
N 70	03 37	04 53	05 54	▬▬	19 28	18 38	18 06
68	03 50	04 58	05 54	20 30	18 57	18 25	18 01
66	04 00	05 02	05 54	19 12	18 35	18 14	17 58
64	04 09	05 06	05 53	18 34	18 16	18 04	17 54
62	04 16	05 09	05 53	18 07	18 01	17 56	17 52
60	04 22	05 11	05 53	17 46	17 49	17 49	17 49
N 58	04 27	05 13	05 53	17 29	17 38	17 43	17 47
56	04 31	05 15	05 52	17 14	17 28	17 37	17 45
54	04 35	05 17	05 52	17 01	17 19	17 33	17 43
52	04 39	05 18	05 52	16 50	17 12	17 28	17 42
50	04 42	05 20	05 52	16 40	17 05	17 24	17 40
45	04 48	05 22	05 51	16 19	16 50	17 15	17 37
N 40	04 52	05 24	05 51	16 02	16 37	17 07	17 34
35	04 56	05 25	05 51	15 47	16 27	17 01	17 32
30	04 59	05 26	05 50	15 35	16 17	16 55	17 30
20	05 02	05 28	05 50	15 13	16 01	16 45	17 26
N 10	05 04	05 28	05 49	14 54	15 47	16 36	17 23
0	05 04	05 28	05 48	14 36	15 34	16 28	17 20
S 10	05 02	05 26	05 47	14 19	15 20	16 20	17 17
20	04 59	05 24	05 46	13 59	15 06	16 11	17 14
30	04 53	05 21	05 45	13 37	14 49	16 01	17 10
35	04 49	05 19	05 44	13 24	14 40	15 55	17 08
40	04 45	05 16	05 43	13 09	14 29	15 48	17 06
45	04 38	05 13	05 42	12 51	14 16	15 40	17 03
S 50	04 30	05 09	05 41	12 29	14 00	15 30	17 00
52	04 26	05 06	05 40	12 18	13 52	15 26	16 58
54	04 22	05 04	05 40	12 06	13 44	15 21	16 56
56	04 17	05 02	05 39	11 52	13 34	15 16	16 55
58	04 11	04 59	05 38	11 35	13 23	15 10	16 53
S 60	04 05	04 55	05 37	11 15	13 11	15 03	16 50

Twilight / Moonset

Lat.	Sunset	Civil	Naut.	Moonset 25	26	27	28
°	h m	h m	h m	h m	h m	h m	h m
N 72	17 46	18 53	20 18	▬▬	23 50	27 01	03 01
N 70	17 46	18 47	20 03	▬▬	▬▬	00 33	03 15
68	17 47	18 42	19 50	21 29	25 01	01 01	03 26
66	17 47	18 38	19 40	22 46	25 22	01 22	03 35
64	17 48	18 35	19 32	23 23	25 39	01 39	03 42
62	17 48	18 32	19 25	23 49	25 52	01 52	03 48
60	17 49	18 30	19 19	24 09	00 09	02 04	03 54
N 58	17 49	18 28	19 14	24 25	00 25	02 14	03 59
56	17 49	18 26	19 10	24 39	00 39	02 22	04 03
54	17 50	18 25	19 06	24 51	00 51	02 30	04 07
52	17 50	18 23	19 03	25 02	01 02	02 37	04 10
50	17 50	18 22	19 00	25 11	01 11	02 43	04 13
45	17 51	18 20	18 54	00 08	01 31	02 56	04 20
N 40	17 51	18 18	18 50	00 28	01 47	03 07	04 25
35	17 52	18 17	18 46	00 45	02 00	03 16	04 30
30	17 52	18 16	18 44	01 00	02 12	03 24	04 34
20	17 53	18 15	18 40	01 24	02 31	03 37	04 41
N 10	17 54	18 15	18 39	01 45	02 48	03 49	04 47
0	17 55	18 15	18 39	02 05	03 04	04 00	04 53
S 10	17 56	18 17	18 41	02 25	03 20	04 11	04 58
20	17 57	18 19	18 44	02 45	03 36	04 22	05 04
30	17 58	18 22	18 50	03 09	03 55	04 35	05 11
35	17 59	18 24	18 54	03 23	04 06	04 43	05 15
40	18 00	18 27	18 59	03 39	04 18	04 51	05 19
45	18 01	18 31	19 05	03 58	04 33	05 01	05 24
S 50	18 03	18 35	19 14	04 22	04 51	05 12	05 30
52	18 04	18 38	19 18	04 33	04 59	05 18	05 33
54	18 04	18 40	19 22	04 46	05 08	05 24	05 36
56	18 05	18 43	19 27	05 01	05 19	05 30	05 39
58	18 06	18 46	19 33	05 18	05 30	05 38	05 42
S 60	18 07	18 49	19 40	05 39	05 44	05 46	05 46

SUN / MOON

Day	Eqn. of Time 00ʰ	12ʰ	Mer. Pass.	Mer. Pass. Upper	Lower	Age	Phase
d	m s	m s	h m	h m	h m	d %	
25	08 04	08 14	11 52	20 50	08 21	10 79	
26	08 25	08 35	11 51	21 47	09 19	11 88	
27	08 46	08 56	11 51	22 41	10 14	12 95	◗

© British Crown Copyright 2022. All rights reserved.

UT	ARIES GHA	VENUS −4.7 GHA	VENUS Dec	MARS +1.6 GHA	MARS Dec	JUPITER −2.8 GHA	JUPITER Dec	SATURN +0.5 GHA	SATURN Dec	STARS Name	SHA	Dec
28 00	6 30.9	223 48.0	N11 07.1	167 25.5	S 7 39.2	323 52.7	N14 54.5	32 12.5	S12 33.6	Acamar	315 12.3	S40 12.3
01	21 33.3	238 48.6	06.9	182 26.5	39.8	338 55.3	54.5	47 15.1	33.6	Achernar	335 20.4	S57 06.8
02	36 35.8	253 49.3	06.7	197 27.4	40.5	353 58.0	54.4	62 17.7	33.7	Acrux	173 02.0	S63 13.7
03	51 38.2	268 50.0 ..	06.6	212 28.3 ..	41.1	9 00.6 ..	54.3	77 20.3 ..	33.7	Adhara	255 06.8	S28 59.9
04	66 40.7	283 50.7	06.4	227 29.2	41.8	24 03.3	54.3	92 22.9	33.8	Aldebaran	290 40.7	N16 33.5
05	81 43.2	298 51.4	06.2	242 30.1	42.4	39 05.9	54.2	107 25.5	33.8			
06	96 45.6	313 52.1	N11 06.0	257 31.1	S 7 43.1	54 08.6	N14 54.2	122 28.1	S12 33.9	Alioth	166 14.4	N55 50.0
T 07	111 48.1	328 52.8	05.8	272 32.0	43.7	69 11.2	54.1	137 30.7	33.9	Alkaid	152 53.3	N49 11.9
H 08	126 50.6	343 53.5	05.6	287 32.9	44.4	84 13.9	54.0	152 33.3	34.0	Al Na'ir	27 33.9	S46 50.9
U 09	141 53.0	358 54.1 ..	05.4	302 33.8 ..	45.0	99 16.5 ..	54.0	167 35.9 ..	34.0	Alnilam	275 38.8	S 1 11.0
R 10	156 55.5	13 54.8	05.2	317 34.7	45.7	114 19.2	53.9	182 38.5	34.1	Alphard	217 49.0	S 8 45.5
S 11	171 58.0	28 55.5	05.0	332 35.7	46.3	129 21.8	53.9	197 41.1	34.1			
D 12	187 00.4	43 56.2	N11 04.8	347 36.6	S 7 46.9	144 24.5	N14 53.8	212 43.7	S12 34.2	Alphecca	126 04.9	N26 38.3
A 13	202 02.9	58 56.8	04.6	2 37.5	47.6	159 27.1	53.7	227 46.3	34.2	Alpheratz	357 35.5	N29 13.4
Y 14	217 05.3	73 57.5	04.4	17 38.4	48.2	174 29.8	53.7	242 48.9	34.3	Altair	62 00.9	N 8 56.0
15	232 07.8	88 58.2 ..	04.2	32 39.3 ..	48.9	189 32.4 ..	53.6	257 51.5 ..	34.3	Ankaa	353 07.8	S42 10.6
16	247 10.3	103 58.8	04.0	47 40.2	49.5	204 35.1	53.5	272 54.1	34.4	Antares	112 17.3	S26 29.1
17	262 12.7	118 59.5	03.8	62 41.2	50.2	219 37.8	53.5	287 56.7	34.4			
18	277 15.2	134 00.2	N11 03.5	77 42.1	S 7 50.8	234 40.4	N14 53.4	302 59.3	S12 34.5	Arcturus	145 49.2	N19 03.7
19	292 17.7	149 00.8	03.3	92 43.0	51.5	249 43.1	53.4	318 01.9	34.5	Atria	107 12.7	S69 04.4
20	307 20.1	164 01.5	03.1	107 43.9	52.1	264 45.7	53.3	333 04.5	34.6	Avior	234 15.5	S59 34.7
21	322 22.6	179 02.2 ..	02.9	122 44.8 ..	52.8	279 48.4 ..	53.2	348 07.1 ..	34.6	Bellatrix	278 24.0	N 6 22.4
22	337 25.1	194 02.8	02.7	137 45.8	53.4	294 51.0	53.2	3 09.7	34.7	Betelgeuse	270 53.2	N 7 24.8
23	352 27.5	209 03.5	02.5	152 46.7	54.0	309 53.7	53.1	18 12.3	34.7			
29 00	7 30.0	224 04.1	N11 02.3	167 47.6	S 7 54.7	324 56.3	N14 53.0	33 14.9	S12 34.7	Canopus	263 52.9	S52 42.1
01	22 32.5	239 04.8	02.1	182 48.5	55.3	339 59.0	53.0	48 17.5	34.8	Capella	280 23.3	N46 01.2
02	37 34.9	254 05.4	01.9	197 49.4	56.0	355 01.7	52.9	63 20.1	34.8	Deneb	49 26.3	N45 22.1
03	52 37.4	269 06.1 ..	01.6	212 50.3 ..	56.6	10 04.3 ..	52.9	78 22.7 ..	34.9	Denebola	182 26.4	N14 26.5
04	67 39.8	284 06.7	01.4	227 51.3	57.3	25 07.0	52.8	93 25.3	34.9	Diphda	348 48.0	S17 51.3
05	82 42.3	299 07.4	01.2	242 52.2	57.9	40 09.6	52.7	108 27.9	35.0			
06	97 44.8	314 08.0	N11 01.0	257 53.1	S 7 58.6	55 12.3	N14 52.7	123 30.4	S12 35.0	Dubhe	193 42.9	N61 37.4
07	112 47.2	329 08.7	00.8	272 54.0	59.2	70 15.0	52.6	138 33.0	35.1	Elnath	278 03.1	N28 37.6
08	127 49.7	344 09.3	00.5	287 54.9	7 59.8	85 17.6	52.5	153 35.6	35.1	Eltanin	90 42.8	N51 29.4
F 09	142 52.2	359 09.9 ..	00.3	302 55.8	8 00.5	100 20.3 ..	52.5	168 38.2 ..	35.2	Enif	33 39.6	N 9 59.1
R 10	157 54.6	14 10.6	11 00.1	317 56.8	01.1	115 22.9	52.4	183 40.8	35.2	Fomalhaut	15 15.4	S29 29.8
I 11	172 57.1	29 11.2	10 59.9	332 57.7	01.8	130 25.6	52.4	198 43.4	35.3			
D 12	187 59.6	44 11.8	N10 59.6	347 58.6	S 8 02.4	145 28.3	N14 52.3	213 46.0	S12 35.3	Gacrux	171 53.5	S57 14.6
A 13	203 02.0	59 12.5	59.4	2 59.5	03.1	160 30.9	52.2	228 48.6	35.4	Gienah	175 45.0	S17 40.2
Y 14	218 04.5	74 13.1	59.2	18 00.4	03.7	175 33.6	52.2	243 51.2	35.4	Hadar	148 38.2	S60 29.3
15	233 06.9	89 13.7 ..	59.0	33 01.3 ..	04.3	190 36.2 ..	52.1	258 53.8 ..	35.5	Hamal	327 52.1	N23 34.5
16	248 09.4	104 14.4	58.7	48 02.2	05.0	205 38.9	52.0	273 56.4	35.5	Kaus Aust.	83 33.9	S34 22.5
17	263 11.9	119 15.0	58.5	63 03.2	05.6	220 41.6	52.0	288 59.0	35.6			
18	278 14.3	134 15.6	N10 58.3	78 04.1	S 8 06.3	235 44.2	N14 51.9	304 01.6	S12 35.6	Kochab	137 20.6	N74 03.7
19	293 16.8	149 16.2	58.0	93 05.0	06.9	250 46.9	51.8	319 04.2	35.7	Markab	13 30.7	N15 20.1
20	308 19.3	164 16.8	57.8	108 05.9	07.6	265 49.6	51.8	334 06.8	35.7	Menkar	314 07.0	N 4 11.1
21	323 21.7	179 17.5 ..	57.6	123 06.8 ..	08.2	280 52.2 ..	51.7	349 09.4 ..	35.7	Menkent	147 59.3	S36 29.1
22	338 24.2	194 18.1	57.3	138 07.7	08.8	295 54.9	51.6	4 12.0	35.8	Miaplacidus	221 39.2	S69 48.5
23	353 26.7	209 18.7	57.1	153 08.6	09.5	310 57.5	51.6	19 14.6	35.8			
30 00	8 29.1	224 19.3	N10 56.9	168 09.6	S 8 10.1	326 00.2	N14 51.5	34 17.2	S12 35.9	Mirfak	308 29.5	N49 56.6
01	23 31.6	239 19.9	56.6	183 10.5	10.8	341 02.9	51.5	49 19.8	35.9	Nunki	75 49.0	S26 16.1
02	38 34.1	254 20.5	56.4	198 11.4	11.4	356 05.5	51.4	64 22.4	36.0	Peacock	53 07.1	S56 39.7
03	53 36.5	269 21.1 ..	56.2	213 12.3 ..	12.1	11 08.2 ..	51.3	79 25.0 ..	36.0	Pollux	243 18.7	N27 58.1
04	68 39.0	284 21.7	55.9	228 13.2	12.7	26 10.9	51.3	94 27.6	36.1	Procyon	244 52.1	N 5 10.0
05	83 41.4	299 22.4	55.7	243 14.1	13.3	41 13.5	51.2	109 30.2	36.1			
06	98 43.9	314 23.0	N10 55.4	258 15.0	S 8 14.0	56 16.2	N14 51.1	124 32.7	S12 36.2	Rasalhague	95 59.6	N12 32.7
07	113 46.4	329 23.6	55.2	273 15.9	14.6	71 18.9	51.1	139 35.3	36.2	Regulus	207 35.8	N11 51.2
S 08	128 48.8	344 24.2	54.9	288 16.9	15.3	86 21.5	51.0	154 37.9	36.3	Rigel	281 04.8	S 8 10.2
A 09	143 51.3	359 24.8 ..	54.7	303 17.8 ..	15.9	101 24.2 ..	50.9	169 40.5 ..	36.3	Rigil Kent.	139 42.4	S60 56.0
T 10	158 53.8	14 25.4	54.5	318 18.7	16.6	116 26.9	50.9	184 43.1	36.4	Sabik	102 04.1	S15 45.2
U 11	173 56.2	29 26.0	54.2	333 19.6	17.2	131 29.5	50.8	199 45.7	36.4			
R 12	188 58.7	44 26.5	N10 54.0	348 20.5	S 8 17.8	146 32.2	N14 50.7	214 48.3	S12 36.4	Schedar	349 31.7	N56 40.1
D 13	204 01.2	59 27.1	53.7	3 21.4	18.5	161 34.9	50.7	229 50.9	36.5	Shaula	96 11.9	S37 07.3
A 14	219 03.6	74 27.7	53.5	18 22.3	19.1	176 37.5	50.6	244 53.5	36.5	Sirius	258 27.2	S16 44.6
Y 15	234 06.1	89 28.3 ..	53.2	33 23.2 ..	19.8	191 40.2 ..	50.5	259 56.1 ..	36.6	Spica	158 23.8	S11 17.0
16	249 08.5	104 28.9	53.0	48 24.1	20.4	206 42.9	50.5	274 58.7	36.6	Suhail	222 47.4	S43 31.4
17	264 11.0	119 29.5	52.7	63 25.1	21.0	221 45.5	50.4	290 01.3	36.7			
18	279 13.5	134 30.1	N10 52.5	78 26.0	S 8 21.7	236 48.2	N14 50.3	305 03.9	S12 36.7	Vega	80 33.9	N38 48.6
19	294 15.9	149 30.7	52.2	93 26.9	22.3	251 50.9	50.3	320 06.5	36.8	Zuben'ubi	136 57.5	S16 08.3
20	309 18.4	164 31.2	51.9	108 27.8	23.0	266 53.5	50.2	335 09.1	36.8			
21	324 20.9	179 31.8 ..	51.7	123 28.7 ..	23.6	281 56.2 ..	50.1	350 11.6 ..	36.9		SHA	Mer. Pass.
22	339 23.3	194 32.4	51.4	138 29.6	24.3	296 58.9	50.1	5 14.2	36.9	Venus	216 34.1	9 03
23	354 25.8	209 33.0	51.2	153 30.5	24.9	312 01.6	50.0	20 16.8	36.9	Mars	160 17.6	12 48
Mer. Pass. 23 26.2		v 0.6	d 0.2	v 0.9	d 0.6	v 2.7	d 0.1	v 2.6	d 0.0	Jupiter	317 26.4	2 20
										Saturn	25 44.9	21 43

© British Crown Copyright 2022. All rights reserved.

UT	SUN GHA	SUN Dec	MOON GHA	v	Dec	d	HP
	° ′	° ′	° ′	′	° ′	′	′
28 00	182 16.6	S 1 50.1	19 10.0	9.6	S 9 06.1	17.1	60.9
01	197 16.8	51.1	33 38.6	9.6	8 49.0	17.1	60.9
02	212 17.0	52.1	48 07.2	9.6	8 31.9	17.1	60.9
03	227 17.3	.. 53.0	62 35.8	9.7	8 14.8	17.2	60.9
04	242 17.5	54.0	77 04.5	9.7	7 57.6	17.2	60.9
05	257 17.7	55.0	91 33.2	9.8	7 40.4	17.3	60.9
06	272 17.9	S 1 56.0	106 02.0	9.8	S 7 23.1	17.3	60.9
07	287 18.1	56.9	120 30.8	9.8	7 05.8	17.3	60.9
08	302 18.3	57.9	134 59.6	9.9	6 48.5	17.4	60.9
09	317 18.5	.. 58.9	149 28.5	10.0	6 31.1	17.4	60.9
10	332 18.7	1 59.8	163 57.5	10.0	6 13.7	17.5	60.9
11	347 18.9	2 00.8	178 26.5	10.0	5 56.2	17.5	60.9
12	2 19.2	S 2 01.8	192 55.5	10.1	S 5 38.7	17.5	60.9
13	17 19.4	02.8	207 24.6	10.1	5 21.2	17.5	60.9
14	32 19.6	03.7	221 53.7	10.1	5 03.7	17.6	60.9
15	47 19.8	.. 04.7	236 22.8	10.2	4 46.1	17.6	60.9
16	62 20.0	05.7	250 52.0	10.2	4 28.5	17.6	60.9
17	77 20.2	06.7	265 21.2	10.2	4 10.9	17.6	60.9
18	92 20.4	S 2 07.6	279 50.4	10.3	S 3 53.3	17.7	60.9
19	107 20.6	08.6	294 19.7	10.3	3 35.6	17.6	60.8
20	122 20.8	09.6	308 49.0	10.4	3 18.0	17.7	60.8
21	137 21.1	.. 10.5	323 18.4	10.3	3 00.3	17.7	60.8
22	152 21.3	11.5	337 47.7	10.4	2 42.6	17.7	60.8
23	167 21.5	12.5	352 17.1	10.4	2 24.9	17.7	60.8
29 00	182 21.7	S 2 13.5	6 46.5	10.5	S 2 07.2	17.7	60.8
01	197 21.9	14.4	21 16.0	10.4	1 49.5	17.7	60.8
02	212 22.1	15.4	35 45.4	10.5	1 31.8	17.8	60.8
03	227 22.3	.. 16.4	50 14.9	10.5	1 14.0	17.7	60.8
04	242 22.5	17.3	64 44.4	10.6	0 56.3	17.7	60.7
05	257 22.7	18.3	79 14.0	10.5	0 38.6	17.7	60.7
06	272 22.9	S 2 19.3	93 43.5	10.6	S 0 20.9	17.7	60.7
07	287 23.2	20.3	108 13.1	10.6	S 0 03.2	17.7	60.7
08	302 23.4	21.2	122 42.7	10.6	N 0 14.5	17.7	60.7
09	317 23.6	.. 22.2	137 12.3	10.6	0 32.2	17.6	60.7
10	332 23.8	23.2	151 41.9	10.6	0 49.8	17.7	60.6
11	347 24.0	24.1	166 11.5	10.7	1 07.5	17.6	60.6
12	2 24.2	S 2 25.1	180 41.2	10.6	N 1 25.1	17.7	60.6
13	17 24.4	26.1	195 10.8	10.7	1 42.8	17.6	60.6
14	32 24.6	27.1	209 40.5	10.6	2 00.4	17.5	60.6
15	47 24.8	.. 28.0	224 10.1	10.7	2 17.9	17.6	60.6
16	62 25.0	29.0	238 39.8	10.7	2 35.5	17.5	60.5
17	77 25.2	30.0	253 09.5	10.7	2 53.0	17.5	60.5
18	92 25.5	S 2 30.9	267 39.2	10.7	N 3 10.5	17.5	60.5
19	107 25.7	31.9	282 08.9	10.7	3 28.0	17.5	60.5
20	122 25.9	32.9	296 38.6	10.7	3 45.5	17.4	60.5
21	137 26.1	.. 33.9	311 08.3	10.7	4 02.9	17.3	60.4
22	152 26.3	34.8	325 38.0	10.7	4 20.2	17.4	60.4
23	167 26.5	35.8	340 07.7	10.6	4 37.6	17.3	60.4
30 00	182 26.7	S 2 36.8	354 37.3	10.7	N 4 54.9	17.2	60.4
01	197 26.9	37.7	9 07.0	10.7	5 12.1	17.3	60.3
02	212 27.1	38.7	23 36.7	10.7	5 29.4	17.1	60.3
03	227 27.3	.. 39.7	38 06.4	10.7	5 46.5	17.2	60.3
04	242 27.5	40.6	52 36.1	10.7	6 03.7	17.1	60.3
05	257 27.7	41.6	67 05.8	10.6	6 20.8	17.0	60.2
06	272 27.9	S 2 42.6	81 35.4	10.7	N 6 37.8	17.0	60.2
07	287 28.1	43.6	96 05.1	10.6	6 54.8	16.9	60.2
08	302 28.4	44.5	110 34.7	10.7	7 11.7	16.9	60.2
09	317 28.6	.. 45.5	125 04.4	10.6	7 28.6	16.8	60.1
10	332 28.8	46.5	139 34.0	10.6	7 45.4	16.8	60.1
11	347 29.0	47.4	154 03.6	10.6	8 02.2	16.7	60.1
12	2 29.2	S 2 48.4	168 33.2	10.6	N 8 18.9	16.6	60.1
13	17 29.4	49.4	183 02.8	10.5	8 35.5	16.6	60.0
14	32 29.6	50.4	197 32.3	10.6	8 52.1	16.5	60.0
15	47 29.8	.. 51.3	212 01.9	10.5	9 08.6	16.5	60.0
16	62 30.0	52.3	226 31.4	10.5	9 25.1	16.4	60.0
17	77 30.2	53.3	241 00.9	10.5	9 41.5	16.3	59.9
18	92 30.4	S 2 54.2	255 30.4	10.5	N 9 57.8	16.2	59.9
19	107 30.6	55.2	269 59.9	10.4	10 14.0	16.2	59.9
20	122 30.8	56.2	284 29.3	10.4	10 30.2	16.1	59.8
21	137 31.0	.. 57.1	298 58.7	10.4	10 46.3	16.0	59.8
22	152 31.2	58.1	313 28.1	10.4	11 02.3	16.0	59.8
23	167 31.4	59.1	327 57.5	10.4	N11 18.3	15.8	59.7
	SD 16.0	d 1.0	SD 16.6		16.5		16.4

Columns marked for THURSDAY (28), FRIDAY (29), SATURDAY (30).

Twilight / Sunrise / Moonrise

Lat.	Twilight Naut.	Twilight Civil	Sunrise	Moonrise 28	29	30	1
°	h m	h m	h m	h m	h m	h m	h m
N 72	03 37	05 01	06 08	18 11	17 33	16 52	15 51
N 70	03 51	05 05	06 06	18 06	17 37	17 06	16 25
68	04 02	05 09	06 05	18 01	17 40	17 18	16 49
66	04 11	05 12	06 03	17 58	17 43	17 27	17 09
64	04 18	05 15	06 02	17 54	17 45	17 35	17 25
62	04 24	05 17	06 01	17 52	17 47	17 42	17 38
60	04 29	05 18	06 00	17 49	17 49	17 49	17 49
N 58	04 34	05 20	05 59	17 47	17 50	17 54	17 59
56	04 38	05 21	05 58	17 45	17 52	17 59	18 07
54	04 41	05 22	05 58	17 43	17 53	18 03	18 15
52	04 44	05 23	05 57	17 42	17 54	18 07	18 22
50	04 46	05 24	05 56	17 40	17 55	18 11	18 28
45	04 52	05 26	05 55	17 37	17 58	18 19	18 42
N 40	04 55	05 27	05 54	17 34	18 00	18 25	18 53
35	04 58	05 28	05 53	17 32	18 01	18 31	19 03
30	05 00	05 28	05 52	17 30	18 03	18 36	19 12
20	05 03	05 28	05 50	17 26	18 06	18 45	19 26
N 10	05 03	05 28	05 49	17 23	18 08	18 53	19 39
0	05 02	05 26	05 47	17 20	18 10	19 01	19 52
S 10	05 00	05 24	05 45	17 17	18 13	19 08	20 04
20	04 56	05 22	05 44	17 14	18 15	19 16	20 18
30	04 49	05 17	05 41	17 10	18 18	19 26	20 33
35	04 45	05 15	05 40	17 08	18 20	19 31	20 42
40	04 39	05 11	05 38	17 06	18 22	19 38	20 53
45	04 32	05 07	05 36	17 03	18 24	19 45	21 05
S 50	04 23	05 02	05 34	17 00	18 27	19 54	21 20
52	04 19	04 59	05 33	16 58	18 28	19 58	21 27
54	04 14	04 57	05 32	16 56	18 30	20 02	21 35
56	04 08	04 53	05 31	16 55	18 31	20 08	21 44
58	04 02	04 50	05 29	16 53	18 33	20 13	21 54
S 60	03 54	04 46	05 28	16 50	18 35	20 20	22 05

Sunset / Twilight / Moonset

Lat.	Sunset	Twilight Civil	Twilight Naut.	Moonset 28	29	30	1
°	h m	h m	h m	h m	h m	h m	h m
N 72	17 30	18 37	20 00	03 01	05 36	08 08	10 58
N 70	17 32	18 33	19 47	03 15	05 37	07 57	10 26
68	17 34	18 30	19 36	03 26	05 38	07 48	10 03
66	17 36	18 27	19 28	03 35	05 39	07 40	09 45
64	17 37	18 24	19 21	03 42	05 39	07 34	09 31
62	17 39	18 23	19 15	03 48	05 40	07 29	09 19
60	17 40	18 21	19 10	03 54	05 40	07 24	09 09
N 58	17 41	18 19	19 05	03 59	05 40	07 20	09 01
56	17 41	18 18	19 02	04 03	05 41	07 17	08 53
54	17 42	18 17	18 58	04 07	05 41	07 14	08 46
52	17 43	18 16	18 56	04 10	05 41	07 11	08 40
50	17 44	18 16	18 53	04 13	05 41	07 08	08 35
45	17 45	18 14	18 48	04 20	05 42	07 03	08 23
N 40	17 46	18 13	18 45	04 25	05 42	06 58	08 13
35	17 47	18 13	18 42	04 30	05 42	06 54	08 05
30	17 48	18 12	18 40	04 34	05 43	06 51	07 58
20	17 50	18 12	18 38	04 41	05 43	06 44	07 46
N 10	17 52	18 13	18 37	04 47	05 44	06 39	07 35
0	17 54	18 14	18 38	04 53	05 44	06 34	07 25
S 10	17 55	18 16	18 41	04 58	05 44	06 29	07 15
20	17 58	18 20	18 45	05 04	05 44	06 24	07 04
30	18 00	18 24	18 52	05 11	05 45	06 18	06 52
35	18 01	18 27	18 57	05 15	05 45	06 14	06 45
40	18 03	18 30	19 02	05 19	05 45	06 11	06 37
45	18 05	18 35	19 09	05 24	05 45	06 06	06 28
S 50	18 08	18 40	19 19	05 30	05 46	06 01	06 17
52	18 09	18 43	19 23	05 33	05 46	05 58	06 12
54	18 10	18 46	19 28	05 36	05 46	05 56	06 07
56	18 11	18 49	19 34	05 39	05 46	05 53	06 00
58	18 13	18 53	19 41	05 42	05 46	05 49	05 54
S 60	18 14	18 57	19 48	05 46	05 46	05 46	05 46

SUN and MOON

Day	SUN Eqn. of Time 00h	12h	Mer. Pass.	MOON Mer. Pass. Upper	Lower	Age	Phase
d	m s	m s	h m	h m	h m	d	%
28	09 06	09 16	11 51	23 32	11 06	13	99
29	09 26	09 36	11 50	24 22	11 57	14	100
30	09 46	09 56	11 50	00 22	12 47	15	98

○

© British Crown Copyright 2022. All rights reserved.

UT	ARIES GHA	VENUS −4.7 GHA	Dec	MARS +1.6 GHA	Dec	JUPITER −2.8 GHA	Dec	SATURN +0.5 GHA	Dec	STARS Name	SHA	Dec
1 00	9 28.3	224 33.6	N10 50.9	168 31.4	S 8 25.5	327 04.2	N14 49.9	35 19.4	S12 37.0	Acamar	315 12.2	S40 12.3
01	24 30.7	239 34.1	50.7	183 32.3	26.2	342 06.9	49.9	50 22.0	37.0	Achernar	335 20.4	S57 06.9
02	39 33.2	254 34.7	50.4	198 33.2	26.8	357 09.6	49.8	65 24.6	37.1	Acrux	173 02.0	S63 13.7
03	54 35.7	269 35.3 ..	50.1	213 34.1 ..	27.5	12 12.2 ..	49.7	80 27.2 ..	37.1	Adhara	255 06.7	S28 59.9
04	69 38.1	284 35.8	49.9	228 35.1	28.1	27 14.9	49.7	95 29.8	37.2	Aldebaran	290 40.7	N16 33.5
05	84 40.6	299 36.4	49.6	243 36.0	28.7	42 17.6	49.6	110 32.4	37.2			
06	99 43.0	314 37.0	N10 49.3	258 36.9	S 8 29.4	57 20.3	N14 49.5	125 35.0	S12 37.3	Alioth	166 14.4	N55 50.0
07	114 45.5	329 37.5	49.1	273 37.8	30.0	72 22.9	49.5	140 37.6	37.3	Alkaid	152 53.3	N49 11.9
08	129 48.0	344 38.1	48.8	288 38.7	30.7	87 25.6	49.4	155 40.2	37.4	Alnair	27 33.9	S46 50.5
09	144 50.4	359 38.7 ..	48.5	303 39.6 ..	31.3	102 28.3 ..	49.3	170 42.7 ..	37.4	Alnilam	275 38.7	S 1 11.0
10	159 52.9	14 39.2	48.3	318 40.5	31.9	117 31.0	49.3	185 45.3	37.4	Alphard	217 49.0	S 8 45.5
11	174 55.4	29 39.8	48.0	333 41.4	32.6	132 33.6	49.2	200 47.9	37.5			
12	189 57.8	44 40.3	N10 47.7	348 42.3	S 8 33.2	147 36.3	N14 49.1	215 50.5	S12 37.5	Alphecca	126 04.9	N26 38.3
13	205 00.3	59 40.9	47.5	3 43.2	33.9	162 39.0	49.1	230 53.1	37.6	Alpheratz	357 35.5	N29 13.4
14	220 02.8	74 41.5	47.2	18 44.1	34.5	177 41.7	49.0	245 55.7	37.6	Altair	62 00.9	N 8 56.0
15	235 05.2	89 42.0 ..	46.9	33 45.0 ..	35.1	192 44.3 ..	48.9	260 58.3 ..	37.7	Ankaa	353 07.8	S42 10.6
16	250 07.7	104 42.6	46.6	48 46.0	35.8	207 47.0	48.9	276 00.9	37.7	Antares	112 17.3	S26 29.1
17	265 10.2	119 43.1	46.4	63 46.9	36.4	222 49.7	48.8	291 03.5	37.8			
18	280 12.6	134 43.7	N10 46.1	78 47.8	S 8 37.1	237 52.4	N14 48.7	306 06.1	S12 37.8	Arcturus	145 49.2	N19 03.7
19	295 15.1	149 44.2	45.8	93 48.7	37.7	252 55.0	48.7	321 08.7	37.9	Atria	107 12.8	S69 04.4
20	310 17.5	164 44.7	45.5	108 49.6	38.3	267 57.7	48.6	336 11.2	37.9	Avior	234 15.5	S59 34.7
21	325 20.0	179 45.3 ..	45.2	123 50.5 ..	39.0	283 00.4 ..	48.5	351 13.8 ..	37.9	Bellatrix	278 23.9	N 6 22.4
22	340 22.5	194 45.8	45.0	138 51.4	39.6	298 03.1	48.5	6 16.4	38.0	Betelgeuse	270 53.2	N 7 24.8
23	355 24.9	209 46.4	44.7	153 52.3	40.3	313 05.7	48.4	21 19.0	38.0			
2 00	10 27.4	224 46.9	N10 44.4	168 53.2	S 8 40.9	328 08.4	N14 48.3	36 21.6	S12 38.1	Canopus	263 52.8	S52 42.1
01	25 29.9	239 47.4	44.1	183 54.1	41.5	343 11.1	48.2	51 24.2	38.1	Capella	280 23.5	N46 01.2
02	40 32.3	254 48.0	43.8	198 55.0	42.2	358 13.8	48.2	66 26.8	38.2	Deneb	49 26.3	N45 22.1
03	55 34.8	269 48.5 ..	43.5	213 55.9 ..	42.8	13 16.5 ..	48.1	81 29.4 ..	38.2	Denebola	182 26.4	N14 26.5
04	70 37.3	284 49.0	43.3	228 56.8	43.5	28 19.1	48.0	96 32.0	38.3	Diphda	348 48.0	S17 51.3
05	85 39.7	299 49.6	43.0	243 57.7	44.1	43 21.8	48.0	111 34.5	38.3			
06	100 42.2	314 50.1	N10 42.7	258 58.6	S 8 44.7	58 24.5	N14 47.9	126 37.1	S12 38.3	Dubhe	193 42.9	N61 37.4
07	115 44.6	329 50.6	42.4	273 59.5	45.4	73 27.2	47.8	141 39.7	38.4	Elnath	278 03.1	N28 37.6
08	130 47.1	344 51.2	42.1	289 00.4	46.0	88 29.9	47.8	156 42.3	38.4	Eltanin	90 42.8	N51 29.4
09	145 49.6	359 51.7 ..	41.8	304 01.3 ..	46.7	103 32.5 ..	47.7	171 44.9 ..	38.5	Enif	33 39.6	N 9 59.1
10	160 52.0	14 52.2	41.5	319 02.2	47.3	118 35.2	47.6	186 47.5	38.5	Fomalhaut	15 15.4	S29 29.8
11	175 54.5	29 52.7	41.2	334 03.1	47.9	133 37.9	47.6	201 50.1	38.6			
12	190 57.0	44 53.3	N10 40.9	349 04.0	S 8 48.6	148 40.6	N14 47.5	216 52.7	S12 38.6	Gacrux	171 53.5	S57 14.6
13	205 59.4	59 53.8	40.6	4 05.0	49.2	163 43.3	47.4	231 55.2	38.6	Gienah	175 45.0	S17 40.2
14	221 01.9	74 54.3	40.3	19 05.9	49.9	178 45.9	47.3	246 57.8	38.7	Hadar	148 38.2	S60 29.2
15	236 04.4	89 54.8 ..	40.1	34 06.8 ..	50.5	193 48.6 ..	47.3	262 00.4 ..	38.7	Hamal	327 52.1	N23 34.5
16	251 06.8	104 55.3	39.8	49 07.7	51.1	208 51.3	47.2	277 03.0	38.8	Kaus Aust.	83 34.0	S34 22.5
17	266 09.3	119 55.8	39.5	64 08.6	51.8	223 54.0	47.1	292 05.6	38.8			
18	281 11.8	134 56.4	N10 39.2	79 09.5	S 8 52.4	238 56.7	N14 47.1	307 08.2	S12 38.9	Kochab	137 20.7	N74 03.6
19	296 14.2	149 56.9	38.9	94 10.4	53.0	253 59.4	47.0	322 10.8	38.9	Markab	13 30.7	N15 20.1
20	311 16.7	164 57.4	38.6	109 11.3	53.7	269 02.0	46.9	337 13.4	39.0	Menkar	314 07.0	N 4 11.1
21	326 19.1	179 57.9 ..	38.3	124 12.2 ..	54.3	284 04.7 ..	46.9	352 15.9 ..	39.0	Menkent	147 59.3	S36 29.1
22	341 21.6	194 58.4	37.9	139 13.1	54.9	299 07.4	46.8	7 18.5	39.0	Miaplacidus	221 39.1	S69 48.5
23	356 24.1	209 58.9	37.6	154 14.0	55.6	314 10.1	46.7	22 21.1	39.1			
3 00	11 26.5	224 59.4	N10 37.3	169 14.9	S 8 56.2	329 12.8	N14 46.6	37 23.7	S12 39.1	Mirfak	308 29.4	N49 56.6
01	26 29.0	239 59.9	37.0	184 15.8	56.9	344 15.5	46.6	52 26.3	39.2	Nunki	75 49.1	S26 16.1
02	41 31.5	255 00.4	36.7	199 16.7	57.5	359 18.1	46.5	67 28.9	39.2	Peacock	53 07.1	S56 39.7
03	56 33.9	270 00.9 ..	36.4	214 17.6 ..	58.1	14 20.8 ..	46.4	82 31.5 ..	39.3	Pollux	243 18.7	N27 58.1
04	71 36.4	285 01.4	36.1	229 18.5	58.8	29 23.5	46.4	97 34.0	39.3	Procyon	244 52.0	N 5 10.0
05	86 38.9	300 01.9	35.8	244 19.4	8 59.4	44 26.2	46.3	112 36.6	39.3			
06	101 41.3	315 02.4	N10 35.5	259 20.3	S 9 00.0	59 28.9	N14 46.2	127 39.2	S12 39.4	Rasalhague	95 59.6	N12 32.7
07	116 43.8	330 02.9	35.2	274 21.2	00.7	74 31.6	46.2	142 41.8	39.4	Regulus	207 35.8	N11 51.2
08	131 46.3	345 03.4	34.9	289 22.1	01.3	89 34.3	46.1	157 44.4	39.5	Rigel	281 04.8	S 8 10.2
09	146 48.7	0 03.9 ..	34.5	304 23.0 ..	02.0	104 37.0 ..	46.0	172 47.0 ..	39.5	Rigil Kent.	139 42.4	S60 56.0
10	161 51.2	15 04.4	34.2	319 23.9	02.6	119 39.6	45.9	187 49.6	39.6	Sabik	102 04.1	S15 45.2
11	176 53.6	30 04.8	33.9	334 24.8	03.2	134 42.3	45.9	202 52.1	39.6			
12	191 56.1	45 05.3	N10 33.6	349 25.7	S 9 03.9	149 45.0	N14 45.8	217 54.7	S12 39.6	Schedar	349 31.7	N56 40.1
13	206 58.6	60 05.8	33.3	4 26.6	04.5	164 47.7	45.7	232 57.3	39.7	Shaula	96 11.9	S37 07.3
14	222 01.0	75 06.3	33.0	19 27.5	05.1	179 50.4	45.7	247 59.9	39.7	Sirius	258 27.2	S16 44.6
15	237 03.5	90 06.8 ..	32.6	34 28.4 ..	05.8	194 53.1 ..	45.6	263 02.5 ..	39.8	Spica	158 23.8	S11 17.0
16	252 06.0	105 07.3	32.3	49 29.3	06.4	209 55.8	45.5	278 05.1	39.8	Suhail	222 47.4	S43 31.4
17	267 08.4	120 07.8	32.0	64 30.2	07.0	224 58.5	45.4	293 07.7	39.9			
18	282 10.9	135 08.2	N10 31.7	79 31.1	S 9 07.7	240 01.1	N14 45.4	308 10.2	S12 39.9	Vega	80 34.0	N38 48.6
19	297 13.4	150 08.7	31.4	94 32.0	08.3	255 03.8	45.3	323 12.8	39.9	Zuben'ubi	136 57.5	S16 08.3
20	312 15.8	165 09.2	31.0	109 32.9	09.0	270 06.5	45.2	338 15.4	40.0			
21	327 18.3	180 09.7 ..	30.7	124 33.8 ..	09.6	285 09.2 ..	45.1	353 18.0 ..	40.0		SHA	Mer. Pass.
22	342 20.7	195 10.1	30.4	139 34.7	10.2	300 11.9	45.1	8 20.6	40.1	Venus	214 19.5	9 01
23	357 23.2	210 10.6	30.1	154 35.6	10.9	315 14.6	45.0	23 23.2	40.1	Mars	158 25.8	12 44
Mer. Pass. 23 14.4		v 0.5	d 0.3	v 0.9	d 0.6	v 2.7	d 0.1	v 2.6	d 0.0	Jupiter	317 41.0	2 07
										Saturn	25 54.2	21 31

© British Crown Copyright 2022. All rights reserved.

UT	SUN GHA	SUN Dec	MOON GHA	v	MOON Dec	d	HP
d h	° ′	° ′	° ′	′	° ′	′	′
1 00	182 31.6	S 3 00.0	342 26.9	10.3	N11 34.1	15.8	59.7
01	197 31.8	01.0	356 56.2	10.3	11 49.9	15.7	59.7
02	212 32.1	02.0	11 25.5	10.3	12 05.6	15.7	59.6
03	227 32.3 ..	03.0	25 54.8	10.2	12 21.3	15.5	59.6
04	242 32.5	03.9	40 24.0	10.2	12 36.8	15.5	59.6
05	257 32.7	04.9	54 53.2	10.2	12 52.3	15.3	59.5
06	272 32.9	S 3 05.9	69 22.4	10.2	N13 07.6	15.3	59.5
07	287 33.1	06.8	83 51.6	10.1	13 22.9	15.2	59.5
08	302 33.3	07.8	98 20.7	10.1	13 38.1	15.1	59.4
S 09	317 33.5 ..	08.8	112 49.8	10.1	13 53.2	15.0	59.4
U 10	332 33.7	09.7	127 18.9	10.0	14 08.2	14.9	59.4
N 11	347 33.9	10.7	141 47.9	10.0	14 23.1	14.8	59.3
D 12	2 34.1	S 3 11.7	156 16.9	10.0	N14 37.9	14.7	59.3
A 13	17 34.3	12.6	170 45.9	9.9	14 52.6	14.6	59.3
Y 14	32 34.5	13.6	185 14.8	9.9	15 07.2	14.5	59.2
15	47 34.7 ..	14.6	199 43.7	9.9	15 21.7	14.4	59.2
16	62 34.9	15.6	214 12.6	9.8	15 36.1	14.3	59.2
17	77 35.1	16.5	228 41.4	9.8	15 50.4	14.2	59.1
18	92 35.3	S 3 17.5	243 10.2	9.7	N16 04.6	14.1	59.1
19	107 35.5	18.5	257 38.9	9.7	16 18.7	14.0	59.1
20	122 35.7	19.4	272 07.6	9.7	16 32.7	13.9	59.0
21	137 35.9 ..	20.4	286 36.3	9.7	16 46.6	13.7	59.0
22	152 36.1	21.4	301 05.0	9.6	17 00.3	13.7	58.9
23	167 36.3	22.3	315 33.6	9.5	17 14.0	13.5	58.9
2 00	182 36.5	S 3 23.3	330 02.1	9.6	N17 27.5	13.5	58.9
01	197 36.7	24.3	344 30.7	9.5	17 41.0	13.3	58.8
02	212 36.9	25.2	358 59.2	9.4	17 54.3	13.2	58.8
03	227 37.1 ..	26.2	13 27.6	9.4	18 07.5	13.1	58.8
04	242 37.3	27.2	27 56.0	9.4	18 20.6	12.9	58.7
05	257 37.5	28.1	42 24.4	9.3	18 33.5	12.9	58.7
06	272 37.7	S 3 29.1	56 52.7	9.3	N18 46.4	12.7	58.6
07	287 37.9	30.1	71 21.0	9.3	18 59.1	12.6	58.6
08	302 38.1	31.0	85 49.3	9.2	19 11.7	12.5	58.6
M 09	317 38.3 ..	32.0	100 17.5	9.2	19 24.2	12.3	58.5
O 10	332 38.5	33.0	114 45.7	9.1	19 36.5	12.3	58.5
N 11	347 38.7	33.9	129 13.8	9.1	19 48.8	12.1	58.5
D 12	2 38.9	S 3 34.9	143 41.9	9.0	N20 00.9	11.9	58.4
A 13	17 39.1	35.9	158 09.9	9.0	20 12.8	11.9	58.4
Y 14	32 39.3	36.9	172 37.9	9.0	20 24.7	11.7	58.3
15	47 39.5 ..	37.8	187 05.9	8.9	20 36.4	11.6	58.3
16	62 39.7	38.8	201 33.8	8.9	20 48.0	11.5	58.3
17	77 39.9	39.8	216 01.7	8.9	20 59.5	11.3	58.2
18	92 40.1	S 3 40.7	230 29.6	8.8	N21 10.8	11.2	58.2
19	107 40.3	41.7	244 57.4	8.8	21 22.0	11.0	58.1
20	122 40.5	42.7	259 25.2	8.7	21 33.0	11.0	58.1
21	137 40.7 ..	43.6	273 52.9	8.7	21 44.0	10.7	58.1
22	152 40.9	44.6	288 20.6	8.7	21 54.7	10.7	58.0
23	167 41.1	45.6	302 48.3	8.6	22 05.4	10.5	58.0
3 00	182 41.3	S 3 46.5	317 15.9	8.6	N22 15.9	10.4	58.0
01	197 41.5	47.5	331 43.5	8.5	22 26.3	10.2	57.9
02	212 41.7	48.5	346 11.0	8.6	22 36.5	10.1	57.9
03	227 41.9 ..	49.4	0 38.6	8.4	22 46.6	9.9	57.8
04	242 42.1	50.4	15 06.0	8.5	22 56.5	9.9	57.8
05	257 42.3	51.4	29 33.5	8.4	23 06.4	9.6	57.8
06	272 42.5	S 3 52.3	44 00.9	8.4	N23 16.0	9.5	57.7
07	287 42.7	53.3	58 28.3	8.3	23 25.5	9.4	57.7
08	302 42.9	54.3	72 55.6	8.3	23 34.9	9.3	57.6
T 09	317 43.1 ..	55.2	87 22.9	8.3	23 44.2	9.1	57.6
U 10	332 43.3	56.2	101 50.2	8.2	23 53.3	8.9	57.6
E 11	347 43.5	57.1	116 17.4	8.2	24 02.2	8.8	57.5
S 12	2 43.7	S 3 58.1	130 44.6	8.2	N24 11.0	8.6	57.5
D 13	17 43.9	3 59.1	145 11.8	8.1	24 19.6	8.5	57.5
A 14	32 44.1	4 00.0	159 38.9	8.2	24 28.1	8.4	57.4
Y 15	47 44.3 ..	01.0	174 06.1	8.1	24 36.5	8.2	57.4
16	62 44.5	02.0	188 34.2	8.1	24 44.7	8.0	57.3
17	77 44.7	02.9	203 00.2	8.1	24 52.7	8.0	57.3
18	92 44.9	S 4 03.9	217 27.3	8.0	N25 00.7	7.7	57.3
19	107 45.1	04.9	231 54.3	8.0	25 08.4	7.6	57.2
20	122 45.2	05.8	246 21.3	7.9	25 16.0	7.5	57.2
21	137 45.4 ..	06.8	260 48.2	8.0	25 23.5	7.2	57.1
22	152 45.6	07.8	275 15.2	7.9	25 30.7	7.2	57.1
23	167 45.8	08.7	289 42.1	7.9	N25 37.9	7.0	57.1
	SD 16.0	d 1.0	SD 16.2		15.9		15.7

Lat.	Twilight Naut.	Twilight Civil	Sunrise	Moonrise 1	2	3	4
°	h m	h m	h m	h m	h m	h m	h m
N 72	03 53	05 15	06 22	15 51	□	□	□
N 70	04 04	05 17	06 18	16 25	□	□	□
68	04 14	05 20	06 15	16 49	15 58	□	□
66	04 21	05 22	06 13	17 09	16 41	□	□
64	04 27	05 23	06 11	17 25	17 10	16 45	□
62	04 32	05 25	06 09	17 38	17 33	17 27	17 20
60	04 37	05 26	06 07	17 49	17 51	17 56	18 10
N 58	04 41	05 26	06 06	17 59	18 06	18 19	18 42
56	04 44	05 27	06 04	18 07	18 19	18 37	19 05
54	04 47	05 28	06 03	18 15	18 31	18 53	19 25
52	04 49	05 28	06 02	18 22	18 41	19 06	19 41
50	04 51	05 29	06 01	18 28	18 50	19 18	19 55
45	04 55	05 29	05 59	18 42	19 09	19 42	20 24
N 40	04 58	05 30	05 57	18 53	19 25	20 02	20 46
35	05 01	05 30	05 55	19 03	19 38	20 19	21 05
30	05 02	05 30	05 54	19 12	19 50	20 33	21 21
20	05 03	05 29	05 51	19 26	20 10	20 58	21 48
N 10	05 03	05 28	05 49	19 39	20 28	21 19	22 12
0	05 01	05 25	05 46	19 52	20 45	21 39	22 34
S 10	04 58	05 23	05 44	20 04	21 01	21 59	22 55
20	04 53	05 19	05 41	20 18	21 19	22 20	23 20
30	04 46	05 14	05 38	20 33	21 40	22 46	23 48
35	04 40	05 10	05 36	20 42	21 52	23 00	24 04
40	04 34	05 06	05 33	20 53	22 07	23 18	24 23
45	04 26	05 01	05 31	21 05	22 24	23 39	24 46
S 50	04 16	04 55	05 28	21 20	22 45	24 05	00 05
52	04 11	04 52	05 26	21 27	22 55	24 18	00 18
54	04 06	04 49	05 25	21 35	23 06	24 33	00 33
56	03 59	04 45	05 23	21 44	23 19	24 50	00 50
58	03 52	04 41	05 21	21 54	23 34	25 11	01 11
S 60	03 44	04 36	05 19	22 05	23 53	25 39	01 39

Lat.	Sunset	Twilight Civil	Twilight Naut.	Moonset 1	2	3	4
°	h m	h m	h m	h m	h m	h m	h m
N 72	17 15	18 22	19 43	10 58	□	□	□
N 70	17 19	18 19	19 32	10 26	□	□	□
68	17 22	18 17	19 23	10 03	12 44	□	□
66	17 24	18 15	19 15	09 45	12 02	□	□
64	17 27	18 14	19 10	09 31	11 34	13 53	□
62	17 29	18 13	19 05	09 19	11 13	13 11	15 13
60	17 31	18 12	19 00	09 09	10 56	12 42	14 23
N 58	17 32	18 11	18 57	09 01	10 41	12 21	13 52
56	17 33	18 10	18 54	08 53	10 29	12 03	13 29
54	17 35	18 10	18 51	08 46	10 18	11 48	13 10
52	17 36	18 09	18 49	08 40	10 09	11 35	12 54
50	17 37	18 09	18 47	08 35	10 00	11 23	12 40
45	17 39	18 09	18 43	08 23	09 43	11 00	12 12
N 40	17 41	18 08	18 40	08 13	09 28	10 41	11 50
35	17 43	18 08	18 38	08 05	09 16	10 25	11 31
30	17 45	18 09	18 36	07 58	09 05	10 12	11 16
20	17 48	18 10	18 35	07 46	08 47	09 49	10 49
N 10	17 50	18 11	18 36	07 35	08 31	09 29	10 26
0	17 53	18 13	18 37	07 25	08 17	09 10	10 05
S 10	17 55	18 16	18 41	07 15	08 02	08 52	09 44
20	17 58	18 20	18 46	07 04	07 47	08 32	09 21
30	18 02	18 26	18 54	06 52	07 29	08 09	08 55
35	18 04	18 29	18 59	06 45	07 19	07 56	08 40
40	18 06	18 33	19 05	06 37	07 07	07 41	08 22
45	18 09	18 38	19 14	06 28	06 54	07 23	08 00
S 50	18 12	18 45	19 24	06 17	06 36	07 01	07 33
52	18 14	18 48	19 29	06 12	06 29	06 50	07 20
54	18 15	18 51	19 35	06 07	06 20	06 38	07 04
56	18 17	18 55	19 41	06 00	06 10	06 24	06 47
58	18 19	18 59	19 48	05 54	05 59	06 09	06 25
S 60	18 22	19 04	19 57	05 46	05 47	05 50	05 57

	SUN Eqn. of Time 00h	SUN Eqn. of Time 12h	SUN Mer. Pass.	MOON Mer. Pass. Upper	MOON Mer. Pass. Lower	Age	Phase
Day	m s	m s	h m	h m	h m	d	%
1	10 06	10 16	11 50	01 13	13 38	16	94
2	10 26	10 35	11 49	02 04	14 31	17	88
3	10 45	10 54	11 49	02 57	15 24	18	80

© British Crown Copyright 2022. All rights reserved.

Planets

UT	ARIES GHA	VENUS −4.7 GHA	Dec	MARS +1.6 GHA	Dec	JUPITER −2.8 GHA	Dec	SATURN +0.5 GHA	Dec
4 00 (W)	12 25.7	225 11.1	N10 29.7	169 36.5	S 9 11.5	330 17.3	N14 44.9	38 25.7	S12 40.1
01	27 28.1	240 11.5	29.4	184 37.4	12.1	345 20.0	44.9	53 28.3	40.2
02	42 30.6	255 12.0	29.1	199 38.2	12.8	0 22.7	44.8	68 30.9	40.2
03	57 33.1	270 12.5 . .	28.7	214 39.1 . .	13.4	15 25.4 . .	44.7	83 33.5 . .	40.3
04	72 35.5	285 12.9	28.4	229 40.0	14.0	30 28.1	44.6	98 36.1	40.3
05	87 38.0	300 13.4	28.1	244 40.9	14.7	45 30.8	44.6	113 38.7	40.4
06 (E)	102 40.5	315 13.9 N10	27.7	259 41.8 S 9	15.3	60 33.4 N14	44.5	128 41.2 S12	40.4
07 (D)	117 42.9	330 14.3	27.4	274 42.7	15.9	75 36.1	44.4	143 43.8	40.4
08 (N)	132 45.4	345 14.8	27.1	289 43.6	16.6	90 38.8	44.4	158 46.4	40.5
09 (E)	147 47.9	0 15.2 . .	26.7	304 44.5 . .	17.2	105 41.5 . .	44.3	173 49.0 . .	40.5
10 (S)	162 50.3	15 15.7	26.4	319 45.4	17.8	120 44.2	44.2	188 51.6	40.6
11 (D)	177 52.8	30 16.2	26.1	334 46.3	18.5	135 46.9	44.1	203 54.1	40.6
12 (A)	192 55.2	45 16.6 N10	25.7	349 47.2 S 9	19.1	150 49.6 N14	44.1	218 56.7 S12	40.6
13 (Y)	207 57.7	60 17.1	25.4	4 48.1	19.7	165 52.3	44.0	233 59.3	40.7
14	223 00.2	75 17.5	25.0	19 49.0	20.4	180 55.0	43.9	249 01.9	40.7
15	238 02.6	90 18.0 . .	24.7	34 49.9 . .	21.0	195 57.7 . .	43.8	264 04.5 . .	40.8
16	253 05.1	105 18.4	24.4	49 50.8	21.6	211 00.4	43.8	279 07.1	40.8
17	268 07.6	120 18.9	24.0	64 51.7	22.3	226 03.1	43.7	294 09.6	40.8
18	283 10.0	135 19.3 N10	23.7	79 52.6 S 9	22.9	241 05.8 N14	43.6	309 12.2 S12	40.9
19	298 12.5	150 19.8	23.3	94 53.5	23.5	256 08.5	43.5	324 14.8	40.9
20	313 15.0	165 20.2	23.0	109 54.4	24.2	271 11.2	43.5	339 17.4	41.0
21	328 17.4	180 20.6 . .	22.6	124 55.3 . .	24.8	286 13.9 . .	43.4	354 20.0 . .	41.0
22	343 19.9	195 21.1	22.3	139 56.1	25.4	301 16.6	43.3	9 22.5	41.1
23	358 22.4	210 21.5	21.9	154 57.0	26.1	316 19.3	43.2	24 25.1	41.1
5 00	13 24.8	225 22.0 N10	21.6	169 57.9 S 9	26.7	331 22.0 N14	43.2	39 27.7 S12	41.1
01	28 27.3	240 22.4	21.2	184 58.8	27.3	346 24.7	43.1	54 30.3	41.2
02	43 29.7	255 22.8	20.9	199 59.7	28.0	1 27.4	43.0	69 32.9	41.2
03	58 32.2	270 23.3 . .	20.5	215 00.6 . .	28.6	16 30.1 . .	42.9	84 35.4 . .	41.3
04	73 34.7	285 23.7	20.2	230 01.5	29.2	31 32.8	42.9	99 38.0	41.3
05	88 37.1	300 24.1	19.8	245 02.4	29.9	46 35.5	42.8	114 40.6	41.3
06 (T)	103 39.6	315 24.6 N10	19.5	260 03.3 S 9	30.5	61 38.2 N14	42.7	129 43.2 S12	41.4
07 (H)	118 42.1	330 25.0	19.1	275 04.2	31.1	76 40.9	42.7	144 45.8	41.4
08 (U)	133 44.5	345 25.4	18.7	290 05.1	31.8	91 43.6	42.6	159 48.3	41.5
09 (R)	148 47.0	0 25.9 . .	18.4	305 06.0 . .	32.4	106 46.3 . .	42.5	174 50.9 . .	41.5
10 (S)	163 49.5	15 26.3	18.0	320 06.9	33.0	121 49.0	42.4	189 53.5	41.5
11 (D)	178 51.9	30 26.7	17.7	335 07.7	33.7	136 51.7	42.4	204 56.1	41.6
12 (A)	193 54.4	45 27.1 N10	17.3	350 08.6 S 9	34.3	151 54.4 N14	42.3	219 58.7 S12	41.6
13 (Y)	208 56.9	60 27.6	16.9	5 09.5	34.9	166 57.1	42.2	235 01.2	41.7
14	223 59.3	75 28.0	16.6	20 10.4	35.6	181 59.8	42.1	250 03.8	41.7
15	239 01.8	90 28.4 . .	16.2	35 11.3 . .	36.2	197 02.5 . .	42.1	265 06.4 . .	41.7
16	254 04.2	105 28.8	15.8	50 12.2	36.8	212 05.2	42.0	280 09.0	41.8
17	269 06.7	120 29.2	15.5	65 13.1	37.5	227 07.9	41.9	295 11.5	41.8
18	284 09.2	135 29.6 N10	15.1	80 14.0 S 9	38.1	242 10.6 N14	41.8	310 14.1 S12	41.9
19	299 11.6	150 30.1	14.7	95 14.9	38.7	257 13.3	41.7	325 16.7	41.9
20	314 14.1	165 30.5	14.4	110 15.8	39.4	272 16.0	41.7	340 19.3	41.9
21	329 16.6	180 30.9 . .	14.0	125 16.6 . .	40.0	287 18.7 . .	41.6	355 21.9 . .	42.0
22	344 19.0	195 31.3	13.6	140 17.5	40.6	302 21.4	41.5	10 24.4	42.0
23	359 21.5	210 31.7	13.3	155 18.4	41.3	317 24.1	41.4	25 27.0	42.1
6 00	14 24.0	225 32.1 N10	12.9	170 19.3 S 9	41.9	332 26.8 N14	41.4	40 29.6 S12	42.1
01	29 26.4	240 32.5	12.5	185 20.2	42.5	347 29.5	41.3	55 32.2	42.1
02	44 28.9	255 32.9	12.1	200 21.1	43.2	2 32.2	41.2	70 34.7	42.2
03	59 31.4	270 33.3 . .	11.8	215 22.0 . .	43.8	17 34.9 . .	41.1	85 37.3 . .	42.2
04	74 33.8	285 33.7	11.4	230 22.9	44.4	32 37.6	41.1	100 39.9	42.2
05	89 36.3	300 34.1	11.0	245 23.7	45.0	47 40.3	41.0	115 42.5	42.3
06 (F)	104 38.7	315 34.5 N10	10.6	260 24.6 S 9	45.7	62 43.0 N14	40.9	130 45.0 S12	42.3
07 (R)	119 41.2	330 34.9	10.3	275 25.5	46.3	77 45.7	40.8	145 47.6	42.4
08 (I)	134 43.7	345 35.3	09.9	290 26.4	46.9	92 48.4	40.8	160 50.2	42.4
09 (D)	149 46.1	0 35.7 . .	09.5	305 27.3 . .	47.6	107 51.1 . .	40.7	175 52.8 . .	42.4
10 (A)	164 48.6	15 36.1	09.1	320 28.2	48.2	122 53.8	40.6	190 55.4	42.5
11 (Y)	179 51.1	30 36.5	08.7	335 29.1	48.8	137 56.6	40.5	205 57.9	42.5
12	194 53.5	45 36.9 N10	08.3	350 30.0 S 9	49.5	152 59.3 N14	40.5	221 00.5 S12	42.6
13	209 56.0	60 37.3	08.0	5 30.8	50.1	168 02.0	40.4	236 03.1	42.6
14	224 58.5	75 37.7	07.6	20 31.7	50.7	183 04.7	40.3	251 05.7	42.6
15	240 00.9	90 38.1 . .	07.2	35 32.6 . .	51.3	198 07.4 . .	40.2	266 08.2 . .	42.7
16	255 03.4	105 38.5	06.8	50 33.5	52.0	213 10.1	40.1	281 10.8	42.7
17	270 05.8	120 38.9	06.4	65 34.4	52.6	228 12.8	40.1	296 13.4	42.8
18	285 08.3	135 39.3 N10	06.0	80 35.3 S 9	53.2	243 15.5 N14	40.0	311 16.0 S12	42.8
19	300 10.8	150 39.6	05.6	95 36.2	53.9	258 18.2	39.9	326 18.5	42.8
20	315 13.2	165 40.0	05.2	110 37.0	54.5	273 20.9	39.8	341 21.1	42.9
21	330 15.7	180 40.4 . .	04.9	125 37.9 . .	55.1	288 23.6 . .	39.8	356 23.7 . .	42.9
22	345 18.2	195 40.8	04.5	140 38.8	55.8	303 26.3	39.7	11 26.2	42.9
23	0 20.6	210 41.2	04.1	155 39.7	56.4	318 29.1	39.6	26 28.8	43.0
Mer. Pass.	23 02.6	v 0.4 d 0.4		v 0.9 d 0.6		v 2.7 d 0.1		v 2.6 d 0.0	

Stars

Name	SHA	Dec
Acamar	315 12.2	S40 12.4
Achernar	335 20.4	S57 06.9
Acrux	173 02.0	S63 13.7
Adhara	255 06.7	S28 59.9
Aldebaran	290 40.7	N16 33.5
Alioth	166 14.4	N55 50.0
Alkaid	152 53.3	N49 11.8
Alnair	27 33.9	S46 50.9
Alnilam	275 38.7	S 1 11.0
Alphard	217 49.0	S 8 45.5
Alphecca	126 04.9	N26 38.3
Alpheratz	357 35.5	N29 13.4
Altair	62 00.9	N 8 56.0
Ankaa	353 07.8	S42 10.6
Antares	112 17.4	S26 29.1
Arcturus	145 49.2	N19 03.7
Atria	107 12.8	S69 04.4
Avior	234 15.4	S59 34.7
Bellatrix	278 23.9	N 6 22.4
Betelgeuse	270 53.2	N 7 24.8
Canopus	263 52.8	S52 42.1
Capella	280 23.3	N46 01.2
Deneb	49 26.3	N45 22.1
Denebola	182 26.3	N14 26.5
Diphda	348 48.0	S17 51.3
Dubhe	193 42.9	N61 37.4
Elnath	278 03.1	N28 37.6
Eltanin	90 42.8	N51 29.4
Enif	33 39.6	N 9 59.1
Fomalhaut	15 15.4	S29 29.8
Gacrux	171 53.5	S57 14.6
Gienah	175 45.0	S17 40.2
Hadar	148 38.2	S60 29.2
Hamal	327 52.1	N23 34.5
Kaus Aust.	83 34.0	S34 22.5
Kochab	137 20.7	N74 03.6
Markab	13 30.7	N15 20.1
Menkar	314 07.0	N 4 11.1
Menkent	147 59.3	S36 29.1
Miaplacidus	221 39.1	S69 48.5
Mirfak	308 29.4	N49 56.6
Nunki	75 49.1	S26 16.1
Peacock	53 07.2	S56 39.7
Pollux	243 18.7	N27 58.1
Procyon	244 52.0	N 5 10.0
Rasalhague	95 59.6	N12 32.7
Regulus	207 35.8	N11 51.2
Rigel	281 04.8	S 8 10.3
Rigil Kent.	139 42.4	S60 56.0
Sabik	102 04.1	S15 45.2
Schedar	349 31.7	N56 40.1
Shaula	96 12.0	S37 07.3
Sirius	258 27.2	S16 44.7
Spica	158 23.8	S11 17.0
Suhail	222 47.4	S43 31.4
Vega	80 34.0	N38 48.6
Zuben'ubi	136 57.5	S16 08.3

	SHA	Mer. Pass.
	° ′	h m
Venus	211 57.1	8 58
Mars	156 33.1	12 39
Jupiter	317 57.1	1 54
Saturn	26 02.9	21 18

© British Crown Copyright 2022. All rights reserved.

UT	SUN GHA	SUN Dec	MOON GHA	v	Dec	d	HP
d h	° ′	° ′	° ′	′	° ′	′	′
4 00	182 46.0	S 4 09.7	304 09.0	7.9	N25 44.9	6.8	57.0
01	197 46.2	10.7	318 35.9	7.9	25 51.7	6.7	57.0
02	212 46.4	11.6	333 02.7	7.9	25 58.4	6.5	57.0
03	227 46.6	.. 12.6	347 29.6	7.8	26 04.9	6.4	56.9
04	242 46.8	13.6	1 56.4	7.8	26 11.3	6.2	56.9
05	257 47.0	14.5	16 23.2	7.8	26 17.5	6.1	56.9
06	272 47.2	S 4 15.5	30 50.0	7.8	N26 23.6	5.9	56.8
W 07	287 47.4	16.4	45 16.8	7.7	26 29.5	5.7	56.8
E 08	302 47.6	17.4	59 43.5	7.8	26 35.2	5.6	56.7
D 09	317 47.8	.. 18.3	74 10.3	7.7	26 40.8	5.5	56.7
N 10	332 48.0	19.3	88 37.0	7.8	26 46.3	5.3	56.7
E 11	347 48.2	20.3	103 03.8	7.7	26 51.6	5.1	56.6
S 12	2 48.4	S 4 21.3	117 30.5	7.7	N26 56.7	5.0	56.6
D 13	17 48.5	22.2	131 57.2	7.7	27 01.7	4.8	56.6
A 14	32 48.7	23.2	146 23.9	7.8	27 06.5	4.6	56.5
Y 15	47 48.9	.. 24.2	160 50.7	7.7	27 11.1	4.5	56.5
16	62 49.1	25.1	175 17.4	7.7	27 15.6	4.4	56.5
17	77 49.3	26.1	189 44.1	7.7	27 20.0	4.2	56.4
18	92 49.5	S 4 27.0	204 10.8	7.7	N27 24.2	4.0	56.4
19	107 49.7	28.0	218 37.5	7.7	27 28.2	3.9	56.4
20	122 49.9	29.0	233 04.2	7.8	27 32.1	3.7	56.3
21	137 50.1	.. 29.9	247 31.0	7.7	27 35.8	3.5	56.3
22	152 50.3	30.9	261 57.7	7.7	27 39.3	3.4	56.3
23	167 50.5	31.9	276 24.4	7.8	27 42.7	3.3	56.2
5 00	182 50.7	S 4 32.8	290 51.2	7.7	N27 46.0	3.1	56.2
01	197 50.8	33.8	305 17.9	7.8	27 49.1	2.9	56.2
02	212 51.0	34.8	319 44.7	7.7	27 52.0	2.8	56.1
03	227 51.2	.. 35.7	334 11.4	7.8	27 54.8	2.6	56.1
04	242 51.4	36.7	348 38.2	7.8	27 57.4	2.5	56.1
05	257 51.6	37.6	3 05.0	7.9	27 59.9	2.3	56.0
06	272 51.8	S 4 38.6	17 31.9	7.8	N28 02.2	2.1	56.0
T 07	287 52.0	39.6	31 58.7	7.8	28 04.3	2.0	56.0
H 08	302 52.2	40.5	46 25.5	7.9	28 06.3	1.8	55.9
U 09	317 52.4	.. 41.5	60 52.4	7.9	28 08.1	1.7	55.9
R 10	332 52.6	42.4	75 19.3	7.9	28 09.8	1.5	55.9
S 11	347 52.7	43.4	89 46.2	8.0	28 11.3	1.4	55.8
D 12	2 52.9	S 4 44.4	104 13.2	8.0	N28 12.7	1.2	55.8
A 13	17 53.1	45.3	118 40.2	8.0	28 13.9	1.1	55.8
Y 14	32 53.3	46.3	133 07.2	8.0	28 15.0	0.9	55.7
15	47 53.5	.. 47.3	147 34.2	8.0	28 15.9	0.8	55.7
16	62 53.7	48.2	162 01.2	8.1	28 16.7	0.6	55.7
17	77 53.9	49.2	176 28.3	8.2	28 17.3	0.4	55.6
18	92 54.1	S 4 50.1	190 55.5	8.1	N28 17.7	0.3	55.6
19	107 54.2	51.1	205 22.6	8.2	28 18.0	0.0	55.6
20	122 54.4	52.1	219 49.8	8.2	28 18.2	0.0	55.6
21	137 54.6	.. 53.0	234 17.0	8.3	28 18.2	0.2	55.5
22	152 54.8	54.0	248 44.3	8.3	28 18.0	0.3	55.5
23	167 55.0	54.9	263 11.6	8.4	28 17.7	0.4	55.5
6 00	182 55.2	S 4 55.9	277 39.0	8.3	N28 17.3	0.6	55.4
01	197 55.4	56.9	292 06.3	8.5	28 16.7	0.8	55.4
02	212 55.6	57.8	306 33.8	8.4	28 15.9	0.9	55.4
03	227 55.7	.. 58.8	321 01.2	8.6	28 15.0	1.0	55.4
04	242 55.9	4 59.7	335 28.8	8.5	28 14.0	1.2	55.3
05	257 56.1	5 00.7	349 56.3	8.6	28 12.8	1.3	55.3
06	272 56.3	S 5 01.7	4 23.9	8.7	N28 11.5	1.5	55.3
F 07	287 56.5	02.6	18 51.6	8.7	28 10.0	1.6	55.3
R 08	302 56.7	03.6	33 19.3	8.8	28 08.4	1.8	55.2
I 09	317 56.9	.. 04.5	47 47.1	8.8	28 06.6	1.9	55.2
D 10	332 57.0	05.5	62 14.9	8.8	28 04.7	2.1	55.2
A 11	347 57.2	06.5	76 42.7	9.0	28 02.6	2.2	55.2
Y 12	2 57.4	S 5 07.4	91 10.7	8.9	N28 00.4	2.3	55.1
13	17 57.6	08.4	105 38.6	9.1	27 58.1	2.5	55.1
14	32 57.8	09.3	120 06.7	9.1	27 55.6	2.6	55.1
15	47 58.0	.. 10.3	134 34.8	9.1	27 53.0	2.8	55.1
16	62 58.1	11.3	149 02.9	9.2	27 50.2	2.9	55.0
17	77 58.3	12.2	163 31.1	9.3	27 47.3	3.0	55.0
18	92 58.5	S 5 13.2	177 59.4	9.3	N27 44.3	3.2	55.0
19	107 58.7	14.1	192 27.7	9.4	27 41.1	3.3	55.0
20	122 58.9	15.1	206 56.1	9.4	27 37.8	3.5	54.9
21	137 59.1	.. 16.0	221 24.5	9.5	27 34.3	3.6	54.9
22	152 59.3	17.0	235 53.0	9.6	27 30.7	3.7	54.9
23	167 59.4	18.0	250 21.6	9.7	N27 27.0	3.8	54.9
	SD 16.0	d 1.0	SD 15.4		15.2		15.0

Lat.	Naut. Twilight	Civil Twilight	Sunrise	Moonrise 4	5	6	7
°	h m	h m	h m	h m	h m	h m	h m
N 72	04 08	05 28	06 35	▢	▢	▢	▢
N 70	04 17	05 29	06 30	▢	▢	▢	▢
68	04 25	05 30	06 26	▢	▢	▢	▢
66	04 31	05 31	06 22	▢	▢	▢	▢
64	04 36	05 32	06 19	▢	▢	▢	19 45
62	04 41	05 32	06 17	17 20	▢	18 52	20 49
60	04 44	05 33	06 14	18 10	18 45	19 54	21 23
N 58	04 47	05 33	06 12	18 42	19 23	20 28	21 48
56	04 50	05 33	06 10	19 05	19 50	20 52	22 08
54	04 52	05 33	06 09	19 25	20 11	21 12	22 24
52	04 54	05 33	06 07	19 41	20 28	21 29	22 38
50	04 56	05 33	06 06	19 55	20 44	21 43	22 50
45	04 59	05 33	06 02	20 24	21 14	22 12	23 16
N 40	05 01	05 33	06 00	20 46	21 37	22 35	23 36
35	05 03	05 32	05 58	21 05	21 57	22 54	23 53
30	05 04	05 32	05 55	21 21	22 14	23 10	24 07
20	05 04	05 30	05 52	21 48	22 42	23 37	24 32
N 10	05 03	05 27	05 48	22 12	23 06	24 00	00 00
0	05 00	05 24	05 45	22 34	23 29	24 22	00 22
S 10	04 56	05 21	05 42	22 56	23 51	24 44	00 44
20	04 50	05 16	05 38	23 20	24 16	00 16	01 07
30	04 42	05 10	05 34	23 48	24 44	00 44	01 34
35	04 36	05 06	05 31	24 04	00 04	01 01	01 50
40	04 29	05 01	05 29	24 23	00 23	01 20	02 08
45	04 20	04 56	05 25	24 46	00 46	01 44	02 30
S 50	04 09	04 48	05 21	00 05	01 16	02 15	02 59
52	04 04	04 45	05 19	00 18	01 31	02 30	03 12
54	03 58	04 41	05 17	00 33	01 49	02 47	03 28
56	03 51	04 37	05 15	00 50	02 09	03 09	03 47
58	03 43	04 32	05 12	01 11	02 36	03 36	04 11
S 60	03 33	04 27	05 10	01 39	03 13	04 15	04 41

Lat.	Sunset	Civil Twilight	Naut. Twilight	Moonset 4	5	6	7
°	h m	h m	h m	h m	h m	h m	h m
N 72	16 59	18 07	19 26	▢	▢	▢	▢
N 70	17 05	18 05	19 17	▢	▢	▢	▢
68	17 09	18 05	19 10	▢	▢	▢	▢
66	17 13	18 04	19 04	▢	▢	▢	▢
64	17 16	18 03	18 59	▢	▢	▢	18 23
62	17 19	18 03	18 55	15 13	▢	17 28	17 19
60	17 22	18 03	18 51	14 23	15 43	16 27	16 44
N 58	17 24	18 03	18 48	13 52	15 06	15 53	16 19
56	17 26	18 03	18 46	13 29	14 39	15 28	15 58
54	17 27	18 03	18 44	13 10	14 18	15 08	15 41
52	17 29	18 03	18 42	12 54	14 00	14 51	15 27
50	17 31	18 03	18 40	12 40	13 45	14 36	15 14
45	17 34	18 03	18 37	12 12	13 15	14 07	14 48
N 40	17 37	18 04	18 35	11 50	12 51	13 44	14 27
35	17 39	18 04	18 33	11 31	12 32	13 25	14 10
30	17 41	18 05	18 33	11 16	12 15	13 09	13 55
20	17 45	18 07	18 32	10 49	11 47	12 41	13 29
N 10	17 48	18 09	18 34	10 26	11 23	12 17	13 07
0	17 52	18 12	18 37	10 05	11 00	11 55	12 47
S 10	17 55	18 16	18 41	09 44	10 38	11 32	12 26
20	17 59	18 21	18 47	09 21	10 14	11 08	12 03
30	18 03	18 28	18 56	08 55	09 46	10 40	11 37
35	18 06	18 32	19 02	08 40	09 29	10 24	11 22
40	18 09	18 36	19 09	08 22	09 09	10 04	11 04
45	18 13	18 42	19 18	08 00	08 46	09 41	10 42
S 50	18 17	18 50	19 29	07 33	08 16	09 10	10 14
52	18 19	18 53	19 35	07 20	08 01	08 55	10 01
54	18 21	18 57	19 41	07 04	07 43	08 37	09 45
56	18 23	19 01	19 48	06 47	07 22	08 16	09 26
58	18 26	19 06	19 56	06 25	06 56	07 49	09 04
S 60	18 29	19 12	20 06	05 57	06 19	07 10	08 33

	SUN			MOON			
Day	Eqn. of Time 00h	12h	Mer. Pass.	Mer. Pass. Upper	Lower	Age	Phase
d	m s	m s	h m	h m	h m	d	%
4	11 04	11 13	11 49	03 52	16 20	19	70
5	11 22	11 31	11 48	04 47	17 15	20	61
6	11 40	11 49	11 48	05 42	18 08	21	51

© British Crown Copyright 2022. All rights reserved.

UT	ARIES GHA	VENUS GHA	VENUS Dec	MARS GHA	MARS Dec	JUPITER GHA	JUPITER Dec	SATURN GHA	SATURN Dec	STARS Name	SHA	Dec
7 00	15 23.1	225 41.6	N10 03.7	170 40.6	S 9 57.0	333 31.8	N14 39.5	41 31.4	S12 43.0	Acamar	315 12.2	S40 12.4
01	30 25.6	240 41.9	03.3	185 41.5	57.6	348 34.5	39.4	56 34.0	43.1	Achernar	335 20.4	S57 06.9
02	45 28.0	255 42.3	02.9	200 42.3	58.3	3 37.2	39.4	71 36.5	43.1	Acrux	173 02.0	S63 13.7
03	60 30.5	270 42.7	.. 02.5	215 43.2	.. 58.9	18 39.9	.. 39.3	86 39.1	.. 43.1	Adhara	255 06.7	S28 59.9
04	75 33.0	285 43.1	02.1	230 44.1	9 59.5	33 42.6	39.2	101 41.7	43.2	Aldebaran	290 40.6	N16 33.5
05	90 35.4	300 43.4	01.7	245 45.0	10 00.2	48 45.3	39.1	116 44.3	43.2			
06	105 37.9	315 43.8	N10 01.3	260 45.9	S10 00.8	63 48.0	N14 39.1	131 46.8	S12 43.2	Alioth	166 14.4	N55 49.9
07	120 40.3	330 44.2	00.9	275 46.8	01.4	78 50.7	39.0	146 49.4	43.3	Alkaid	152 53.3	N49 11.8
S 08	135 42.8	345 44.5	00.5	290 47.6	02.0	93 53.5	38.9	161 52.0	43.3	Alnair	27 33.9	S46 50.9
A 09	150 45.3	0 44.9	10 00.1	305 48.5	.. 02.7	108 56.2	.. 38.8	176 54.6	.. 43.4	Alnilam	275 38.7	S 1 11.0
T 10	165 47.7	15 45.3	9 59.7	320 49.4	03.3	123 58.9	38.7	191 57.1	43.4	Alphard	217 49.0	S 8 45.5
U 11	180 50.2	30 45.7	59.3	335 50.3	03.9	139 01.6	38.7	206 59.7	43.4			
R 12	195 52.7	45 46.0	N 9 58.9	350 51.2	S10 04.6	154 04.3	N14 38.6	222 02.3	S12 43.5	Alphecca	126 04.9	N26 38.3
D 13	210 55.1	60 46.4	58.5	5 52.1	05.2	169 07.0	38.5	237 04.8	43.5	Alpheratz	357 35.5	N29 13.4
A 14	225 57.6	75 46.7	58.0	20 52.9	05.8	184 09.7	38.4	252 07.4	43.5	Altair	62 00.9	N 8 56.0
Y 15	241 00.1	90 47.1	.. 57.6	35 53.8	.. 06.4	199 12.5	.. 38.3	267 10.0	.. 43.6	Ankaa	353 07.7	S42 10.6
16	256 02.5	105 47.5	57.2	50 54.7	07.1	214 15.2	38.3	282 12.6	43.6	Antares	112 17.4	S26 29.1
17	271 05.0	120 47.8	56.8	65 55.6	07.7	229 17.9	38.2	297 15.1	43.7			
18	286 07.5	135 48.2	N 9 56.4	80 56.5	S10 08.3	244 20.6	N14 38.1	312 17.7	S12 43.7	Arcturus	145 49.2	N19 03.7
19	301 09.9	150 48.5	56.0	95 57.3	08.9	259 23.3	38.0	327 20.3	43.7	Atria	107 12.8	S69 04.4
20	316 12.4	165 48.9	55.6	110 58.2	09.6	274 26.0	38.0	342 22.8	43.8	Avior	234 15.4	S59 34.7
21	331 14.8	180 49.3	.. 55.2	125 59.1	.. 10.2	289 28.7	.. 37.9	357 25.4	.. 43.8	Bellatrix	278 23.9	N 6 22.4
22	346 17.3	195 49.6	54.8	141 00.0	10.8	304 31.5	37.8	12 28.0	43.8	Betelgeuse	270 53.1	N 7 24.8
23	1 19.8	210 50.0	54.3	156 00.9	11.5	319 34.2	37.7	27 30.6	43.9			
8 00	16 22.2	225 50.3	N 9 53.9	171 01.7	S10 12.1	334 36.9	N14 37.6	42 33.1	S12 43.9	Canopus	263 52.8	S52 42.1
01	31 24.7	240 50.7	53.5	186 02.6	12.7	349 39.6	37.6	57 35.7	43.9	Capella	280 23.2	N46 01.2
02	46 27.2	255 51.0	53.1	201 03.5	13.3	4 42.3	37.5	72 38.3	44.0	Deneb	49 26.4	N45 22.1
03	61 29.6	270 51.4	.. 52.7	216 04.4	.. 14.0	19 45.0	.. 37.4	87 40.8	.. 44.0	Denebola	182 26.3	N14 26.5
04	76 32.1	285 51.7	52.2	231 05.3	14.6	34 47.8	37.3	102 43.4	44.1	Diphda	348 48.0	S17 51.3
05	91 34.6	300 52.1	51.8	246 06.1	15.2	49 50.5	37.2	117 46.0	44.1			
06	106 37.0	315 52.4	N 9 51.4	261 07.0	S10 15.8	64 53.2	N14 37.2	132 48.6	S12 44.1	Dubhe	193 42.8	N61 37.3
07	121 39.5	330 52.8	51.0	276 07.9	16.5	79 55.9	37.1	147 51.1	44.2	Elnath	278 03.1	N28 37.6
S 08	136 41.9	345 53.1	50.6	291 08.8	17.1	94 58.6	37.0	162 53.7	44.2	Eltanin	90 42.8	N51 29.4
U 09	151 44.4	0 53.4	.. 50.1	306 09.6	.. 17.7	110 01.3	.. 36.9	177 56.3	.. 44.2	Enif	33 39.6	N 9 59.1
N 10	166 46.9	15 53.8	49.7	321 10.5	18.3	125 04.1	36.8	192 58.8	44.3	Fomalhaut	15 15.4	S29 29.8
D 11	181 49.3	30 54.1	49.3	336 11.4	19.0	140 06.8	36.8	208 01.4	44.3			
A 12	196 51.8	45 54.5	N 9 48.9	351 12.3	S10 19.6	155 09.5	N14 36.7	223 04.0	S12 44.3	Gacrux	171 53.4	S57 14.6
Y 13	211 54.3	60 54.8	48.4	6 13.2	20.2	170 12.2	36.6	238 06.5	44.4	Gienah	175 45.0	S17 40.2
14	226 56.7	75 55.1	48.0	21 14.0	20.8	185 14.9	36.5	253 09.1	44.4	Hadar	148 38.2	S60 29.2
15	241 59.2	90 55.5	.. 47.6	36 14.9	.. 21.5	200 17.7	.. 36.4	268 11.7	.. 44.5	Hamal	327 52.1	N23 34.5
16	257 01.7	105 55.8	47.1	51 15.8	22.1	215 20.4	36.4	283 14.2	44.5	Kaus Aust.	83 34.0	S34 22.5
17	272 04.1	120 56.1	46.7	66 16.7	22.7	230 23.1	36.3	298 16.8	44.5			
18	287 06.6	135 56.5	N 9 46.3	81 17.5	S10 23.3	245 25.8	N14 36.2	313 19.4	S12 44.6	Kochab	137 20.8	N74 03.6
19	302 09.1	150 56.8	45.8	96 18.4	24.0	260 28.5	36.1	328 21.9	44.6	Markab	13 30.7	N15 20.1
20	317 11.5	165 57.1	45.4	111 19.3	24.6	275 31.3	36.0	343 24.5	44.6	Menkar	314 07.0	N 4 11.1
21	332 14.0	180 57.5	.. 45.0	126 20.2	.. 25.2	290 34.0	.. 35.9	358 27.1	.. 44.7	Menkent	147 59.3	S36 29.1
22	347 16.4	195 57.8	44.5	141 21.0	25.8	305 36.7	35.9	13 29.6	44.7	Miaplacidus	221 39.0	S69 48.5
23	2 18.9	210 58.1	44.1	156 21.9	26.5	320 39.4	35.8	28 32.2	44.7			
9 00	17 21.4	225 58.4	N 9 43.7	171 22.8	S10 27.1	335 42.2	N14 35.7	43 34.8	S12 44.8	Mirfak	308 29.4	N49 56.7
01	32 23.8	240 58.8	43.2	186 23.7	27.7	350 44.9	35.6	58 37.4	44.8	Nunki	75 49.1	S26 16.1
02	47 26.3	255 59.1	42.8	201 24.5	28.3	5 47.6	35.5	73 39.9	44.8	Peacock	53 07.2	S56 39.7
03	62 28.8	270 59.4	.. 42.3	216 25.4	.. 29.0	20 50.3	.. 35.5	88 42.5	.. 44.9	Pollux	243 18.7	N27 58.1
04	77 31.2	285 59.7	41.9	231 26.3	29.6	35 53.0	35.4	103 45.1	44.9	Procyon	244 52.0	N 5 10.0
05	92 33.7	301 00.1	41.4	246 27.2	30.2	50 55.8	35.3	118 47.6	44.9			
06	107 36.2	316 00.4	N 9 41.0	261 28.0	S10 30.8	65 58.5	N14 35.2	133 50.2	S12 45.0	Rasalhague	95 59.7	N12 32.7
07	122 38.6	331 00.7	40.6	276 28.9	31.5	81 01.2	35.1	148 52.8	45.0	Regulus	207 35.8	N11 51.2
M 08	137 41.1	346 01.0	40.1	291 29.8	32.1	96 03.9	35.1	163 55.3	45.1	Rigel	281 04.7	S 8 10.3
O 09	152 43.6	1 01.3	.. 39.7	306 30.7	.. 32.7	111 06.7	.. 35.0	178 57.9	.. 45.1	Rigil Kent.	139 42.4	S60 56.0
N 10	167 46.0	16 01.7	39.2	321 31.5	33.3	126 09.4	34.9	194 00.4	45.1	Sabik	102 04.2	S15 45.2
D 11	182 48.5	31 02.0	38.8	336 32.4	33.9	141 12.1	34.8	209 03.0	45.2			
A 12	197 50.9	46 02.3	N 9 38.3	351 33.3	S10 34.6	156 14.8	N14 34.6	224 05.6	S12 45.2	Schedar	349 31.7	N56 40.1
Y 13	212 53.4	61 02.6	37.9	6 34.2	35.2	171 17.6	34.6	239 08.1	45.2	Shaula	96 12.0	S37 07.3
14	227 55.9	76 02.9	37.4	21 35.0	35.8	186 20.3	34.6	254 10.7	45.3	Sirius	258 27.1	S16 44.7
15	242 58.3	91 03.2	.. 37.0	36 35.9	.. 36.4	201 23.0	.. 34.5	269 13.3	.. 45.3	Spica	158 23.7	S11 17.0
16	258 00.8	106 03.5	36.5	51 36.8	37.1	216 25.7	34.4	284 15.8	45.3	Suhail	222 47.3	S43 31.3
17	273 03.3	121 03.8	36.1	66 37.6	37.7	231 28.5	34.3	299 18.4	45.4			
18	288 05.7	136 04.1	N 9 35.6	81 38.5	S10 38.3	246 31.2	N14 34.2	314 21.0	S12 45.4	Vega	80 34.0	N38 48.6
19	303 08.2	151 04.4	35.2	96 39.4	38.9	261 33.9	34.2	329 23.5	45.4	Zuben'ubi	136 57.5	S16 08.3
20	318 10.7	166 04.8	34.7	111 40.3	39.6	276 36.6	34.1	344 26.1	45.5			
21	333 13.1	181 05.1	.. 34.2	126 41.1	.. 40.2	291 39.4	.. 34.0	359 28.7	.. 45.5		SHA	Mer.Pass.
22	348 15.6	196 05.4	33.8	141 42.0	40.8	306 42.1	33.9	14 31.2	45.5	Venus	209 28.1	8 56
23	3 18.0	211 05.7	33.3	156 42.9	41.4	321 44.8	33.8	29 33.8	45.6	Mars	154 39.5	12 35
Mer.Pass.	22 50.8	v 0.3	d 0.4	v 0.9	d 0.6	v 2.7	d 0.1	v 2.6	d 0.0	Jupiter	318 14.7	1 41
										Saturn	26 10.9	21 06

© British Crown Copyright 2022. All rights reserved.

UT	SUN GHA	SUN Dec	MOON GHA	MOON v	MOON Dec	MOON d	MOON HP
d h	° ′	° ′	° ′	′	° ′	′	′
7 00	182 59.6	S 5 18.9	264 50.3	9.7	N27 23.2	4.0	54.9
01	197 59.8	19.9	279 19.0	9.7	27 19.2	4.1	54.8
02	213 00.0	20.8	293 47.7	9.9	27 15.1	4.3	54.8
03	228 00.2 · ·	21.8	308 16.6	9.9	27 10.8	4.4	54.8
04	243 00.3	22.8	322 45.5	10.0	27 06.4	4.5	54.8
05	258 00.5	23.7	337 14.5	10.0	27 01.9	4.6	54.8
06	273 00.7	S 5 24.7	351 43.5	10.1	N26 57.3	4.8	54.7
07	288 00.9	25.6	6 12.6	10.2	26 52.5	4.9	54.7
S 08	303 01.1	26.6	20 41.8	10.3	26 47.6	5.0	54.7
A 09	318 01.3 · ·	27.5	35 11.1	10.3	26 42.6	5.1	54.7
T 10	333 01.4	28.5	49 40.4	10.4	26 37.5	5.3	54.7
U 11	348 01.6	29.5	64 09.8	10.4	26 32.2	5.4	54.6
R 12	3 01.8	S 5 30.4	78 39.2	10.6	N26 26.8	5.5	54.6
D 13	18 02.0	31.4	93 08.8	10.6	26 21.3	5.6	54.6
A 14	33 02.2	32.3	107 38.4	10.7	26 15.7	5.8	54.6
Y 15	48 02.3 · ·	33.3	122 08.1	10.7	26 09.9	5.9	54.6
16	63 02.5	34.2	136 37.8	10.9	26 04.0	6.0	54.5
17	78 02.7	35.2	151 07.7	10.9	25 58.0	6.1	54.5
18	93 02.9	S 5 36.1	165 37.6	10.9	N25 51.9	6.2	54.5
19	108 03.1	37.1	180 07.5	11.1	25 45.7	6.3	54.5
20	123 03.2	38.1	194 37.6	11.1	25 39.4	6.5	54.5
21	138 03.4 · ·	39.0	209 07.7	11.2	25 32.9	6.6	54.5
22	153 03.6	40.0	223 37.9	11.3	25 26.3	6.7	54.5
23	168 03.8	40.9	238 08.2	11.4	25 19.6	6.8	54.5
8 00	183 03.9	S 5 41.9	252 38.6	11.4	N25 12.8	6.9	54.4
01	198 04.1	42.8	267 09.0	11.5	25 05.9	7.0	54.4
02	213 04.3	43.8	281 39.5	11.6	24 58.9	7.2	54.4
03	228 04.5 · ·	44.7	296 10.1	11.6	24 51.7	7.2	54.4
04	243 04.7	45.7	310 40.7	11.8	24 44.5	7.4	54.4
05	258 04.8	46.6	325 11.5	11.8	24 37.1	7.4	54.4
06	273 05.0	S 5 47.6	339 42.3	11.9	N24 29.7	7.6	54.4
07	288 05.2	48.6	354 13.2	11.9	24 22.1	7.7	54.3
S 08	303 05.4	49.5	8 44.1	12.1	24 14.4	7.8	54.3
U 09	318 05.5 · ·	50.5	23 15.2	12.1	24 06.6	7.8	54.3
N 10	333 05.7	51.4	37 46.3	12.2	23 58.8	8.0	54.3
D 11	348 05.9	52.4	52 17.5	12.2	23 50.8	8.1	54.3
A 12	3 06.1	S 5 53.3	66 48.7	12.4	N23 42.7	8.2	54.3
Y 13	18 06.2	54.3	81 20.1	12.4	23 34.5	8.3	54.3
14	33 06.4	55.2	95 51.5	12.4	23 26.2	8.4	54.3
15	48 06.6 · ·	56.2	110 22.9	12.6	23 17.8	8.5	54.3
16	63 06.8	57.1	124 54.5	12.6	23 09.3	8.6	54.3
17	78 06.9	58.1	139 26.1	12.8	23 00.7	8.7	54.2
18	93 07.1	S 5 59.0	153 57.9	12.7	N22 52.0	8.8	54.2
19	108 07.3	6 00.0	168 29.6	12.9	22 43.2	8.8	54.2
20	123 07.5	00.9	183 01.5	12.9	22 34.4	9.0	54.2
21	138 07.6 · ·	01.9	197 33.4	13.0	22 25.4	9.1	54.2
22	153 07.8	02.9	212 05.4	13.1	22 16.3	9.1	54.2
23	168 08.0	03.8	226 37.5	13.2	22 07.2	9.3	54.2
9 00	183 08.2	S 6 04.8	241 09.7	13.2	N21 57.9	9.3	54.2
01	198 08.3	05.7	255 41.9	13.3	21 48.6	9.4	54.2
02	213 08.5	06.7	270 14.2	13.3	21 39.2	9.6	54.2
03	228 08.7 · ·	07.6	284 46.5	13.5	21 29.6	9.6	54.2
04	243 08.9	08.6	299 19.0	13.5	21 20.0	9.7	54.2
05	258 09.0	09.5	313 51.5	13.5	21 10.3	9.7	54.2
06	273 09.2	S 6 10.5	328 24.0	13.7	N21 00.6	9.9	54.1
07	288 09.4	11.4	342 56.7	13.7	20 50.7	10.0	54.1
08	303 09.5	12.4	357 29.4	13.8	20 40.7	10.0	54.1
M 09	318 09.7 · ·	13.3	12 02.2	13.8	20 30.7	10.1	54.1
O 10	333 09.9	14.3	26 35.0	14.0	20 20.6	10.2	54.1
N 11	348 10.1	15.2	41 08.0	13.9	20 10.4	10.3	54.1
D 12	3 10.2	S 6 16.2	55 40.9	14.1	N20 00.1	10.3	54.1
A 13	18 10.4	17.1	70 14.0	14.1	19 49.8	10.5	54.1
Y 14	33 10.6	18.1	84 47.1	14.2	19 39.3	10.5	54.1
15	48 10.7 · ·	19.0	99 20.3	14.2	19 28.8	10.6	54.1
16	63 10.9	20.0	113 53.5	14.3	19 18.2	10.7	54.1
17	78 11.1	20.9	128 26.8	14.4	19 07.5	10.7	54.1
18	93 11.3	S 6 21.9	143 00.2	14.4	N18 56.8	10.8	54.1
19	108 11.4	22.8	157 33.6	14.5	18 46.0	10.9	54.1
20	123 11.6	23.8	172 07.1	14.6	18 35.1	11.0	54.1
21	138 11.8 · ·	24.7	186 40.7	14.6	18 24.1	11.1	54.1
22	153 11.9	25.7	201 14.3	14.7	18 13.0	11.1	54.1
23	168 12.1	26.6	215 48.0	14.7	N18 01.9	11.2	54.1
	SD 16.0	d 1.0	SD 14.9		14.8		14.7

Lat.	Twilight Naut.	Twilight Civil	Sunrise	Moonrise 7	Moonrise 8	Moonrise 9	Moonrise 10
°	h m	h m	h m	h m	h m	h m	h m
N 72	04 22	05 41	06 49	□	□	□	
N 70	04 30	05 41	06 42	□	□	22 21	24 46
68	04 36	05 41	06 37	□	□	23 04	25 05
66	04 41	05 41	06 32	□	21 23	23 33	25 20
64	04 45	05 40	06 28	19 45	22 05	23 54	25 33
62	04 49	05 40	06 24	20 49	22 34	24 11	00 11
60	04 51	05 40	06 21	21 23	22 55	24 25	00 25
N 58	04 54	05 39	06 19	21 48	23 13	24 37	00 37
56	04 56	05 39	06 16	22 08	23 28	24 48	00 48
54	04 58	05 39	06 14	22 24	23 40	24 57	00 57
52	04 59	05 38	06 12	22 38	23 51	25 05	01 05
50	05 00	05 38	06 10	22 50	24 01	00 01	01 12
45	05 03	05 37	06 06	23 16	24 22	00 22	01 28
N 40	05 04	05 36	06 03	23 36	24 38	00 38	01 41
35	05 05	05 35	06 00	23 53	24 52	00 52	01 53
30	05 06	05 33	05 57	24 07	00 07	01 04	02 01
20	05 05	05 30	05 53	24 32	00 32	01 25	02 17
N 10	05 03	05 27	05 48	00 00	00 53	01 43	02 31
0	04 59	05 24	05 44	00 22	01 12	01 59	02 44
S 10	04 54	05 19	05 40	00 44	01 32	02 16	02 57
20	04 48	05 13	05 36	01 07	01 53	02 34	03 10
30	04 38	05 06	05 30	01 34	02 17	02 54	03 26
35	04 32	05 02	05 27	01 50	02 31	03 06	03 35
40	04 24	04 56	05 24	02 08	02 47	03 19	03 46
45	04 14	04 50	05 20	02 30	03 07	03 35	03 58
S 50	04 02	04 42	05 15	02 59	03 31	03 54	04 12
52	03 56	04 38	05 12	03 12	03 42	04 03	04 19
54	03 49	04 34	05 10	03 28	03 56	04 14	04 27
56	03 42	04 29	05 07	03 47	04 11	04 25	04 35
58	03 33	04 23	05 04	04 11	04 29	04 39	04 44
S 60	03 22	04 17	05 00	04 41	04 51	04 54	04 55

Lat.	Sunset	Twilight Civil	Twilight Naut.	Moonset 7	Moonset 8	Moonset 9	Moonset 10
°	h m	h m	h m	h m	h m	h m	h m
N 72	16 44	17 52	19 10	▭	▭	▭	18 33
N 70	16 51	17 52	19 03	▭	▭	19 03	18 06
68	16 57	17 52	18 57	▭	▭	18 18	17 45
66	17 02	17 53	18 52	▭	18 25	17 49	17 28
64	17 06	17 53	18 48	18 23	17 42	17 26	17 15
62	17 09	17 54	18 45	17 19	17 13	17 08	17 03
60	17 13	17 54	18 42	16 44	16 51	16 53	16 53
N 58	17 15	17 55	18 40	16 19	16 32	16 40	16 45
56	17 18	17 55	18 38	15 58	16 17	16 29	16 37
54	17 20	17 55	18 36	15 41	16 04	16 19	16 30
52	17 22	17 56	18 35	15 27	15 52	16 10	16 24
50	17 24	17 56	18 34	15 14	15 42	16 03	16 19
45	17 28	17 58	18 31	14 48	15 20	15 46	16 06
N 40	17 32	17 59	18 30	14 27	15 03	15 32	15 56
35	17 35	18 00	18 29	14 10	14 48	15 20	15 48
30	17 38	18 01	18 29	13 55	14 35	15 10	15 40
20	17 42	18 04	18 30	13 29	14 13	14 52	15 27
N 10	17 47	18 08	18 32	13 07	13 54	14 36	15 15
0	17 51	18 12	18 36	12 47	13 35	14 21	15 04
S 10	17 55	18 16	18 41	12 26	13 17	14 06	14 53
20	18 00	18 22	18 48	12 03	12 58	13 50	14 41
30	18 05	18 29	18 58	11 37	12 35	13 32	14 27
35	18 08	18 34	19 04	11 22	12 21	13 21	14 19
40	18 12	18 40	19 12	11 04	12 06	13 08	14 10
45	18 16	18 46	19 22	10 42	11 47	12 54	13 59
S 50	18 22	18 55	19 35	10 14	11 24	12 35	13 46
52	18 24	18 59	19 41	10 01	11 13	12 27	13 40
54	18 27	19 03	19 48	09 45	11 00	12 17	13 33
56	18 29	19 08	19 56	09 26	10 45	12 06	13 26
58	18 33	19 14	20 05	09 04	10 28	11 54	13 17
S 60	18 36	19 20	20 15	08 33	10 06	11 39	13 07

	SUN Eqn. of Time 00h	SUN Eqn. of Time 12h	SUN Mer. Pass.	MOON Mer. Pass. Upper	MOON Mer. Pass. Lower	Age	Phase
Day							
d	m s	m s	h m	h m	h m	d %	
7	11 58	12 07	11 48	06 34	18 59	22 41	
8	12 15	12 24	11 48	07 24	19 48	23 32	
9	12 32	12 41	11 47	08 10	20 32	24 24	

© British Crown Copyright 2022. All rights reserved.

UT	ARIES GHA	VENUS −4.6 GHA	Dec	MARS +1.6 GHA	Dec	JUPITER −2.9 GHA	Dec	SATURN +0.6 GHA	Dec	STARS Name	SHA	Dec
10 00	18 20.5	226 06.0 N 9 32.9		171 43.7 S10 42.0		336 47.6 N14 33.7		44 36.4 S12 45.6		Acamar	315 12.2	S40 12.4
01	33 23.0	241 06.3	32.4	186 44.6	42.7	351 50.3	33.7	59 38.9	45.6	Achernar	335 20.4	S57 06.9
02	48 25.4	256 06.6	31.9	201 45.5	43.3	6 53.0	33.6	74 41.5	45.7	Acrux	173 02.0	S63 13.7
03	63 27.9	271 06.9 . .	31.5	216 46.3 . .	43.9	21 55.7 . .	33.5	89 44.0 . .	45.7	Adhara	255 06.7	S28 59.9
04	78 30.4	286 07.2	31.0	231 47.2	44.5	36 58.5	33.4	104 46.6	45.7	Aldebaran	290 40.6	N16 33.5
05	93 32.8	301 07.5	30.6	246 48.1	45.1	52 01.2	33.3	119 49.2	45.8			
06	108 35.3	316 07.7 N 9 30.1		261 49.0 S10 45.8		67 03.9 N14 33.2		134 51.7 S12 45.8		Alioth	166 14.4	N55 49.9
07	123 37.8	331 08.0	29.6	276 49.8	46.4	82 06.7	33.2	149 54.3	45.8	Alkaid	152 53.3	N49 11.8
T 08	138 40.2	346 08.3	29.2	291 50.7	47.0	97 09.4	33.1	164 56.9	45.9	Alnair	27 33.9	S46 50.9
U 09	153 42.7	1 08.6 . .	28.7	306 51.6 . .	47.6	112 12.1 . .	33.0	179 59.4 . .	45.9	Alnilam	275 38.7	S 1 11.0
E 10	168 45.2	16 08.9	28.2	321 52.4	48.3	127 14.8	32.9	195 02.0	45.9	Alphard	217 49.0	S 8 45.5
S 11	183 47.6	31 09.2	27.8	336 53.3	48.9	142 17.6	32.8	210 04.6	46.0			
D 12	198 50.1	46 09.5 N 9 27.3		351 54.2 S10 49.5		157 20.3 N14 32.7		225 07.1 S12 46.0		Alphecca	126 04.9	N26 38.3
A 13	213 52.5	61 09.8	26.8	6 55.0	50.1	172 23.0	32.7	240 09.7	46.0	Alpheratz	357 35.5	N29 13.4
Y 14	228 55.0	76 10.1	26.3	21 55.9	50.7	187 25.8	32.6	255 12.2	46.1	Altair	62 00.9	N 8 56.0
15	243 57.5	91 10.4 . .	25.9	36 56.8 . .	51.4	202 28.5 . .	32.5	270 14.8 . .	46.1	Ankaa	353 07.7	S42 10.6
16	258 59.9	106 10.6	25.4	51 57.6	52.0	217 31.2	32.4	285 17.4	46.1	Antares	112 17.4	S26 29.1
17	274 02.4	121 10.9	24.9	66 58.5	52.6	232 34.0	32.3	300 19.9	46.2			
18	289 04.9	136 11.2 N 9 24.4		81 59.4 S10 53.2		247 36.7 N14 32.2		315 22.5 S12 46.2		Arcturus	145 49.2	N19 03.7
19	304 07.3	151 11.5	24.0	97 00.2	53.8	262 39.4	32.2	330 25.0	46.2	Atria	107 12.9	S69 04.4
20	319 09.8	166 11.8	23.5	112 01.1	54.5	277 42.2	32.1	345 27.6	46.3	Avior	234 15.4	S59 34.7
21	334 12.3	181 12.1 . .	23.0	127 02.0 . .	55.1	292 44.9 . .	32.0	0 30.2 . .	46.3	Bellatrix	278 23.9	N 6 22.4
22	349 14.7	196 12.3	22.5	142 02.8	55.7	307 47.6	31.9	15 32.7	46.3	Betelgeuse	270 53.1	N 7 24.8
23	4 17.2	211 12.6	22.1	157 03.7	56.3	322 50.4	31.8	30 35.5	46.4			
11 00	19 19.7	226 12.9 N 9 21.6		172 04.6 S10 56.9		337 53.1 N14 31.7		45 37.8 S12 46.4		Canopus	263 52.7	S52 42.1
01	34 22.1	241 13.2	21.1	187 05.4	57.5	352 55.8	31.6	60 40.4	46.4	Capella	280 23.2	N46 01.2
02	49 24.6	256 13.4	20.6	202 06.3	58.2	7 58.6	31.6	75 43.0	46.5	Deneb	49 26.4	N45 22.1
03	64 27.0	271 13.7 . .	20.1	217 07.2 . .	58.8	23 01.3 . .	31.5	90 45.5 . .	46.5	Denebola	182 26.3	N14 26.5
04	79 29.5	286 14.0	19.6	232 08.0	10 59.4	38 04.0	31.4	105 48.1	46.5	Diphda	348 48.0	S17 51.3
05	94 32.0	301 14.3	19.2	247 08.9	11 00.0	53 06.8	31.3	120 50.6	46.6			
06	109 34.4	316 14.5 N 9 18.7		262 09.8 S11 00.6		68 09.5 N14 31.2		135 53.2 S12 46.6		Dubhe	193 42.8	N61 37.3
W 07	124 36.9	331 14.8	18.2	277 10.6	01.3	83 12.2	31.1	150 55.8	46.6	Elnath	278 03.0	N28 37.6
E 08	139 39.4	346 15.1	17.7	292 11.5	01.9	98 15.0	31.1	165 58.3	46.7	Eltanin	90 42.9	N51 29.4
D 09	154 41.8	1 15.4 . .	17.2	307 12.4 . .	02.5	113 17.7 . .	31.0	181 00.9 . .	46.7	Enif	33 39.6	N 9 59.1
N 10	169 44.3	16 15.6	16.7	322 13.2	03.1	128 20.4	30.9	196 03.4	46.7	Fomalhaut	15 15.4	S29 29.8
E 11	184 46.8	31 15.9	16.2	337 14.1	03.7	143 23.2	30.8	211 06.0	46.8			
S 12	199 49.2	46 16.2 N 9 15.7		352 14.9 S11 04.4		158 25.9 N14 30.7		226 08.6 S12 46.8		Gacrux	171 53.4	S57 14.6
D 13	214 51.7	61 16.4	15.2	7 15.8	05.0	173 28.6	30.6	241 11.1	46.8	Gienah	175 45.0	S17 40.2
A 14	229 54.1	76 16.7	14.8	22 16.7	05.6	188 31.4	30.5	256 13.7	46.8	Hadar	148 38.2	S60 29.2
Y 15	244 56.6	91 16.9 . .	14.3	37 17.5 . .	06.2	203 34.1 . .	30.5	271 16.2 . .	46.9	Hamal	327 52.1	N23 34.6
16	259 59.1	106 17.2	13.8	52 18.4	06.8	218 36.9	30.4	286 18.8	46.9	Kaus Aust.	83 34.0	S34 22.5
17	275 01.5	121 17.5	13.3	67 19.3	07.4	233 39.6	30.3	301 21.4	46.9			
18	290 04.0	136 17.7 N 9 12.8		82 20.1 S11 08.1		248 42.3 N14 30.2		316 23.9 S12 47.0		Kochab	137 20.8	N74 03.6
19	305 06.5	151 18.0	12.3	97 21.0	08.7	263 45.1	30.1	331 26.5	47.0	Markab	13 30.7	N15 20.1
20	320 08.9	166 18.3	11.8	112 21.8	09.3	278 47.8	30.0	346 29.0	47.0	Menkar	314 07.0	N 4 11.1
21	335 11.4	181 18.5 . .	11.3	127 22.7 . .	09.9	293 50.5 . .	29.9	1 31.6 . .	47.1	Menkent	147 59.3	S36 29.1
22	350 13.9	196 18.8	10.8	142 23.6	10.5	308 53.3	29.9	16 34.1	47.1	Miaplacidus	221 39.0	S69 48.5
23	5 16.3	211 19.0	10.3	157 24.4	11.1	323 56.0	29.8	31 36.7	47.1			
12 00	20 18.8	226 19.3 N 9 09.8		172 25.3 S11 11.8		338 58.8 N14 29.7		46 39.3 S12 47.2		Mirfak	308 29.4	N49 56.7
01	35 21.3	241 19.5	09.3	187 26.2	12.4	354 01.5	29.6	61 41.8	47.2	Nunki	75 49.1	S26 16.1
02	50 23.7	256 19.8	08.8	202 27.0	13.0	9 04.2	29.5	76 44.4	47.2	Peacock	53 07.2	S56 39.7
03	65 26.2	271 20.0 . .	08.3	217 27.9 . .	13.6	24 07.0 . .	29.4	91 46.9 . .	47.3	Pollux	243 18.6	N27 58.1
04	80 28.6	286 20.3	07.8	232 28.7	14.2	39 09.7	29.3	106 49.5	47.3	Procyon	244 52.0	N 5 10.0
05	95 31.1	301 20.5	07.3	247 29.6	14.8	54 12.5	29.3	121 52.0	47.3			
06	110 33.6	316 20.8 N 9 06.8		262 30.5 S11 15.5		69 15.2 N14 29.2		136 54.6 S12 47.3		Rasalhague	96 59.7	N12 32.7
T 07	125 36.0	331 21.0	06.2	277 31.3	16.1	84 17.9	29.1	151 57.2	47.4	Regulus	207 35.8	N11 51.2
H 08	140 38.5	346 21.3	05.7	292 32.2	16.7	99 20.7	29.0	166 59.7	47.4	Rigel	281 04.7	S 8 10.3
U 09	155 41.0	1 21.5 . .	05.2	307 33.0 . .	17.3	114 23.4 . .	28.9	182 02.3 . .	47.4	Rigil Kent.	139 42.4	S60 56.0
R 10	170 43.4	16 21.8	04.7	322 33.9	17.9	129 26.2	28.8	197 04.8	47.5	Sabik	102 04.2	S15 45.2
S 11	185 45.9	31 22.0	04.2	337 34.8	18.5	144 28.9	28.7	212 07.4	47.5			
D 12	200 48.4	46 22.3 N 9 03.7		352 35.6 S11 19.1		159 31.6 N14 28.6		227 09.9 S12 47.5		Schedar	349 31.7	N56 40.1
A 13	215 50.8	61 22.5	03.2	7 36.5	19.8	174 34.4	28.6	242 12.5	47.6	Shaula	96 12.0	S37 07.3
Y 14	230 53.3	76 22.8	02.7	22 37.3	20.4	189 37.1	28.5	257 15.0	47.6	Sirius	258 27.1	S16 44.7
15	245 55.7	91 23.0 . .	02.2	37 38.2 . .	21.0	204 39.9 . .	28.4	272 17.6 . .	47.6	Spica	158 23.7	S11 17.0
16	260 58.2	106 23.2	01.6	52 39.0	21.6	219 42.6	28.3	287 20.2	47.7	Suhail	222 47.3	S43 31.3
17	276 00.7	121 23.5	01.1	67 39.9	22.2	234 45.4	28.2	302 22.7	47.7			
18	291 03.1	136 23.7 N 9 00.6		82 40.8 S11 22.8		249 48.1 N14 28.1		317 25.3 S12 47.7		Vega	80 34.0	N38 48.6
19	306 05.6	151 24.0	9 00.1	97 41.6	23.4	264 50.8	28.0	332 27.8	47.7	Zuben'ubi	136 57.5	S16 08.3
20	321 08.1	166 24.2	8 59.6	112 42.5	24.1	279 53.6	28.0	347 30.4	47.8		SHA	Mer. Pass.
21	336 10.5	181 24.4 . .	59.1	127 43.3 . .	24.7	294 56.3 . .	27.9	2 32.9 . .	47.8	Venus	206 53.2	8 55
22	351 13.0	196 24.7	58.5	142 44.2	25.3	309 59.1	27.8	17 35.5	47.8	Mars	152 44.9	12 31
23	6 15.5	211 24.9	58.0	157 45.0	25.9	325 01.8	27.7	32 38.0	47.9	Jupiter	318 33.4	1 28
Mer. Pass.	h m 22 39.0	v 0.3 d 0.5		v 0.9 d 0.6		v 2.7 d 0.1		v 2.6 d 0.0		Saturn	26 18.2	20 54

© British Crown Copyright 2022. All rights reserved.

SUN / MOON

UT	SUN GHA	SUN Dec	MOON GHA	v	MOON Dec	d	HP
d h	° ′	° ′	° ′	′	° ′	′	′
10 00	183 12.3	S 6 27.6	230 21.7	14.8	N17 50.7	11.2	54.1
01	198 12.4	28.5	244 55.5	14.9	17 39.5	11.4	54.1
02	213 12.6	29.5	259 29.4	14.9	17 28.1	11.4	54.1
03	228 12.8 ..	30.4	274 03.3	15.0	17 16.7	11.4	54.1
04	243 12.9	31.4	288 37.3	15.0	17 05.3	11.6	54.1
05	258 13.1	32.3	303 11.3	15.1	16 53.7	11.6	54.1
06	273 13.3	S 6 33.2	317 45.4	15.1	N16 42.1	11.6	54.1
07	288 13.4	34.2	332 19.5	15.2	16 30.5	11.8	54.1
08	303 13.6	35.1	346 53.7	15.3	16 18.7	11.8	54.1
09	318 13.8 ..	36.1	1 28.0	15.3	16 06.9	11.8	54.1
10	333 13.9	37.0	16 02.3	15.3	15 55.1	11.9	54.1
11	348 14.1	38.0	30 36.6	15.4	15 43.2	12.0	54.1
12	3 14.3	S 6 38.9	45 11.0	15.5	N15 31.2	12.1	54.1
13	18 14.4	39.9	59 45.5	15.5	15 19.1	12.1	54.1
14	33 14.6	40.8	74 20.0	15.5	15 07.0	12.1	54.1
15	48 14.8 ..	41.8	88 54.5	15.6	14 54.9	12.3	54.1
16	63 14.9	42.7	103 29.1	15.6	14 42.6	12.2	54.1
17	78 15.1	43.7	118 03.7	15.7	14 30.4	12.4	54.1
18	93 15.3	S 6 44.6	132 38.4	15.7	N14 18.0	12.4	54.1
19	108 15.4	45.6	147 13.1	15.8	14 05.6	12.4	54.1
20	123 15.6	46.5	161 47.9	15.8	13 53.2	12.5	54.1
21	138 15.8 ..	47.4	176 22.7	15.9	13 40.7	12.6	54.1
22	153 15.9	48.4	190 57.6	15.9	13 28.1	12.6	54.1
23	168 16.1	49.3	205 32.5	15.9	13 15.5	12.7	54.1
11 00	183 16.3	S 6 50.3	220 07.4	16.0	N13 02.8	12.7	54.1
01	198 16.4	51.2	234 42.4	16.0	12 50.1	12.8	54.1
02	213 16.6	52.2	249 17.4	16.1	12 37.3	12.8	54.1
03	228 16.8 ..	53.1	263 52.5	16.1	12 24.5	12.8	54.1
04	243 16.9	54.1	278 27.6	16.1	12 11.7	13.0	54.2
05	258 17.1	55.0	293 02.7	16.2	11 58.7	12.9	54.2
06	273 17.2	S 6 55.9	307 37.9	16.2	N11 45.8	13.0	54.2
07	288 17.4	56.9	322 13.1	16.2	11 32.8	13.1	54.2
08	303 17.6	57.8	336 48.3	16.3	11 19.7	13.1	54.2
09	318 17.7 ..	58.8	351 23.6	16.3	11 06.6	13.1	54.2
10	333 17.9	6 59.7	5 58.9	16.3	10 53.5	13.2	54.2
11	348 18.0	7 00.7	20 34.2	16.4	10 40.3	13.3	54.2
12	3 18.2	S 7 01.6	35 09.6	16.4	N10 27.0	13.2	54.2
13	18 18.4	02.5	49 45.0	16.4	10 13.8	13.4	54.2
14	33 18.5	03.5	64 20.4	16.5	10 00.4	13.3	54.2
15	48 18.7 ..	04.4	78 55.9	16.4	9 47.1	13.4	54.2
16	63 18.9	05.4	93 31.3	16.5	9 33.7	13.5	54.2
17	78 19.0	06.3	108 06.8	16.5	9 20.2	13.5	54.2
18	93 19.2	S 7 07.3	122 42.3	16.6	N 9 06.7	13.5	54.3
19	108 19.3	08.2	137 17.9	16.6	8 53.2	13.5	54.3
20	123 19.5	09.1	151 53.5	16.5	8 39.7	13.6	54.3
21	138 19.7 ..	10.1	166 29.0	16.7	8 26.1	13.7	54.3
22	153 19.8	11.0	181 04.7	16.6	8 12.4	13.6	54.3
23	168 20.0	12.0	195 40.3	16.6	7 58.8	13.7	54.3
12 00	183 20.1	S 7 12.9	210 15.9	16.7	N 7 45.1	13.8	54.3
01	198 20.3	13.9	224 51.6	16.7	7 31.3	13.7	54.3
02	213 20.4	14.8	239 27.3	16.7	7 17.6	13.8	54.3
03	228 20.6 ..	15.7	254 03.0	16.7	7 03.8	13.8	54.3
04	243 20.8	16.7	268 38.7	16.7	6 50.0	13.9	54.3
05	258 20.9	17.6	283 14.4	16.8	6 36.1	13.9	54.4
06	273 21.1	S 7 18.6	297 50.2	16.7	N 6 22.2	13.9	54.4
07	288 21.2	19.5	312 25.9	16.8	6 08.3	14.0	54.4
08	303 21.4	20.4	327 01.7	16.8	5 54.3	13.9	54.4
09	318 21.5 ..	21.4	341 37.5	16.7	5 40.4	14.1	54.4
10	333 21.7	22.3	356 13.2	16.8	5 26.3	14.0	54.4
11	348 21.9	23.2	10 49.0	16.8	5 12.3	14.0	54.4
12	3 22.0	S 7 24.2	25 24.8	16.8	N 4 58.3	14.1	54.4
13	18 22.2	25.1	40 00.6	16.8	4 44.2	14.1	54.4
14	33 22.3	26.1	54 36.4	16.9	4 30.1	14.2	54.5
15	48 22.5 ..	27.0	69 12.3	16.8	4 15.9	14.1	54.5
16	63 22.6	27.9	83 48.1	16.8	4 01.8	14.2	54.5
17	78 22.8	28.9	98 23.9	16.8	3 47.6	14.2	54.5
18	93 22.9	S 7 29.8	112 59.7	16.8	N 3 33.4	14.2	54.5
19	108 23.1	30.8	127 35.5	16.8	3 19.2	14.2	54.5
20	123 23.3	31.7	142 11.3	16.9	3 05.0	14.3	54.5
21	138 23.4 ..	32.6	156 47.2	16.8	2 50.7	14.2	54.5
22	153 23.6	33.6	171 23.0	16.8	2 36.5	14.3	54.6
23	168 23.7	34.5	185 58.8	16.8	N 2 22.2	14.3	54.6
	SD 16.0	d 0.9	SD 14.7		14.8		14.8

Twilight / Sunrise / Moonrise

Lat.	Twilight Naut.	Twilight Civil	Sunrise	Moonrise 10	11	12	13
°	h m	h m	h m	h m	h m	h m	h m
N 72	04 36	05 55	07 03	▭	00 21	02 33	04 33
N 70	04 42	05 53	06 55	24 46	00 46	02 44	04 35
68	04 47	05 51	06 48	25 05	01 05	02 53	04 36
66	04 51	05 50	06 42	25 20	01 20	03 00	04 37
64	04 54	05 49	06 37	25 33	01 33	03 06	04 38
62	04 57	05 48	06 32	00 11	01 43	03 11	04 38
60	04 59	05 47	06 29	00 25	01 52	03 16	04 39
N 58	05 00	05 46	06 25	00 37	02 00	03 20	04 39
56	05 02	05 45	06 22	00 48	02 06	03 23	04 40
54	05 03	05 44	06 20	00 57	02 12	03 26	04 40
52	05 04	05 43	06 17	01 05	02 18	03 29	04 41
50	05 05	05 43	06 15	01 12	02 23	03 32	04 41
45	05 07	05 41	06 10	01 28	02 33	03 37	04 42
N 40	05 07	05 39	06 06	01 41	02 42	03 42	04 42
35	05 08	05 37	06 02	01 51	02 49	03 46	04 43
30	05 07	05 35	05 59	02 01	02 56	03 50	04 43
20	05 06	05 31	05 53	02 17	03 07	03 56	04 44
N 10	05 03	05 27	05 48	02 31	03 16	04 01	04 45
0	04 59	05 23	05 44	02 44	03 26	04 06	04 46
S 10	04 53	05 17	05 39	02 57	03 35	04 11	04 46
20	04 45	05 11	05 33	03 10	03 44	04 16	04 47
30	04 34	05 03	05 27	03 26	03 55	04 22	04 48
35	04 27	04 58	05 23	03 35	04 01	04 26	04 49
40	04 19	04 52	05 19	03 46	04 09	04 29	04 49
45	04 08	04 44	05 14	03 58	04 17	04 34	04 50
S 50	03 55	04 35	05 08	04 12	04 27	04 39	04 51
52	03 48	04 31	05 06	04 19	04 31	04 42	04 51
54	03 41	04 26	05 03	04 27	04 36	04 44	04 52
56	03 32	04 21	04 59	04 35	04 42	04 47	04 52
58	03 23	04 14	04 56	04 44	04 48	04 50	04 52
S 60	03 11	04 07	04 51	04 55	04 55	04 54	04 53

Sunset / Twilight / Moonset

Lat.	Sunset	Twilight Civil	Twilight Naut.	Moonset 10	11	12	13
°	h m	h m	h m	h m	h m	h m	h m
N 72	16 28	17 37	18 55	18 33	17 47	17 12	16 40
N 70	16 37	17 39	18 49	18 06	17 33	17 07	16 43
68	16 44	17 40	18 45	17 45	17 22	17 03	16 45
66	16 50	17 42	18 41	17 28	17 13	17 00	16 47
64	16 55	17 43	18 38	17 15	17 05	16 57	16 48
62	17 00	17 44	18 35	17 03	16 59	16 54	16 50
60	17 04	17 45	18 33	16 53	16 53	16 52	16 51
N 58	17 07	17 46	18 32	16 45	16 48	16 50	16 52
56	17 10	17 47	18 30	16 37	16 43	16 48	16 53
54	17 13	17 48	18 29	16 30	16 39	16 47	16 54
52	17 16	17 49	18 28	16 24	16 35	16 45	16 55
50	17 18	17 50	18 27	16 19	16 32	16 44	16 55
45	17 23	17 52	18 26	16 06	16 24	16 41	16 57
N 40	17 27	17 54	18 26	15 56	16 18	16 38	16 58
35	17 31	17 56	18 25	15 48	16 13	16 36	16 59
30	17 34	17 58	18 26	15 40	16 08	16 34	17 00
20	17 40	18 02	18 28	15 27	16 00	16 31	17 02
N 10	17 45	18 06	18 31	15 15	15 52	16 28	17 04
0	17 50	18 11	18 35	15 04	15 45	16 25	17 05
S 10	17 55	18 16	18 41	14 53	15 38	16 22	17 06
20	18 01	18 23	18 49	14 41	15 30	16 19	17 08
30	18 07	18 31	19 00	14 27	15 22	16 16	17 10
35	18 11	18 37	19 07	14 19	15 17	16 14	17 11
40	18 15	18 43	19 16	14 11	15 11	16 11	17 12
45	18 20	18 50	19 26	13 59	15 04	16 08	17 13
S 50	18 26	19 00	19 40	13 46	14 56	16 05	17 15
52	18 29	19 04	19 47	13 40	14 52	16 04	17 15
54	18 32	19 09	19 55	13 33	14 48	16 02	17 16
56	18 36	19 15	20 03	13 26	14 44	16 00	17 17
58	18 39	19 21	20 13	13 17	14 38	15 58	17 18
S 60	18 44	19 28	20 25	13 07	14 32	15 56	17 19

SUN / MOON

	SUN Eqn. of Time 00h	SUN Eqn. of Time 12h	SUN Mer. Pass.	MOON Mer. Pass. Upper	MOON Mer. Pass. Lower	Age	Phase
Day							
d	m s	m s	h m	h m	h m	d	%
10	12 49	12 57	11 47	08 54	21 15	25	16
11	13 05	13 13	11 47	09 35	21 56	26	10
12	13 20	13 28	11 47	10 16	22 35	27	5

© British Crown Copyright 2022. All rights reserved.

UT	ARIES	VENUS −4.6		MARS +1.6		JUPITER −2.9		SATURN +0.6		STARS		
	GHA	GHA	Dec	GHA	Dec	GHA	Dec	GHA	Dec	Name	SHA	Dec
d h	° ′	° ′	° ′	° ′	° ′	° ′	° ′	° ′	° ′		° ′	° ′
13 00	21 17.9	226 25.1	N 8 57.5	172 45.9	S11 26.5	340 04.6	N14 27.6	47 40.6	S12 47.9	Acamar	315 12.2	S40 12.4
01	36 20.4	241 25.4	57.0	187 46.8	27.1	355 07.3	27.5	62 43.1	47.9	Achernar	335 20.4	S57 06.9
02	51 22.9	256 25.6	56.4	202 47.6	27.7	10 10.0	27.4	77 45.7	48.0	Acrux	173 02.0	S63 13.7
03	66 25.3	271 25.8 ..	55.9	217 48.5 ..	28.4	25 12.8 ..	27.3	92 48.2 ..	48.0	Adhara	255 06.6	S28 59.9
04	81 27.8	286 26.1	55.4	232 49.3	29.0	40 15.5	27.3	107 50.8	48.0	Aldebaran	290 40.6	N16 33.5
05	96 30.2	301 26.3	54.9	247 50.2	29.6	55 18.3	27.2	122 53.3	48.0			
06	111 32.7	316 26.5	N 8 54.3	262 51.0	S11 30.2	70 21.0	N14 27.1	137 55.9	S12 48.1	Alioth	166 14.4	N55 49.9
07	126 35.2	331 26.8	53.8	277 51.9	30.8	85 23.8	27.0	152 58.5	48.1	Alkaid	152 53.3	N49 11.8
08	141 37.6	346 27.0	53.3	292 52.7	31.4	100 26.5	26.9	168 01.0	48.1	Alnair	27 33.9	S46 50.9
F 09	156 40.1	1 27.2 ..	52.8	307 53.6 ..	32.0	115 29.3 ..	26.8	183 03.6 ..	48.2	Alnilam	275 38.6	S 1 11.0
R 10	171 42.6	16 27.4	52.2	322 54.5	32.6	130 32.0	26.7	198 06.1	48.2	Alphard	217 49.0	S 8 45.5
I 11	186 45.0	31 27.7	51.7	337 55.3	33.3	145 34.7	26.6	213 08.7	48.2			
D 12	201 47.5	46 27.9	N 8 51.2	352 56.2	S11 33.9	160 37.5	N14 26.6	228 11.2	S12 48.2	Alphecca	126 04.9	N26 38.3
A 13	216 50.0	61 28.1	50.6	7 57.0	34.5	175 40.2	26.5	243 13.8	48.3	Alpheratz	357 35.5	N29 13.4
Y 14	231 52.4	76 28.3	50.1	22 57.9	35.1	190 43.0	26.4	258 16.3	48.3	Altair	62 01.0	N 8 56.0
15	246 54.9	91 28.5 ..	49.6	37 58.7 ..	35.7	205 45.7 ..	26.3	273 18.9 ..	48.3	Ankaa	353 07.8	S42 10.6
16	261 57.3	106 28.8	49.0	52 59.6	36.3	220 48.5	26.2	288 21.4	48.4	Antares	112 17.4	S26 29.1
17	276 59.8	121 29.0	48.5	68 00.4	36.9	235 51.2	26.1	303 24.0	48.4			
18	292 02.3	136 29.2	N 8 48.0	83 01.3	S11 37.5	250 54.0	N14 26.0	318 26.5	S12 48.4	Arcturus	145 49.2	N19 03.7
19	307 04.7	151 29.4	47.4	98 02.1	38.2	265 56.7	25.9	333 29.1	48.4	Atria	107 12.9	S69 04.4
20	322 07.2	166 29.6	46.9	113 03.0	38.8	280 59.5	25.8	348 31.6	48.5	Avior	234 15.3	S59 34.7
21	337 09.7	181 29.9 ..	46.3	128 03.8 ..	39.4	296 02.2 ..	25.8	3 34.2 ..	48.5	Bellatrix	278 23.8	N 6 22.4
22	352 12.1	196 30.1	45.8	143 04.7	40.0	311 05.0	25.7	18 36.7	48.5	Betelgeuse	270 53.1	N 7 24.8
23	7 14.6	211 30.3	45.3	158 05.5	40.6	326 07.7	25.6	33 39.3	48.6			
14 00	22 17.1	226 30.5	N 8 44.7	173 06.4	S11 41.2	341 10.5	N14 25.5	48 41.8	S12 48.6	Canopus	263 52.7	S52 42.1
01	37 19.5	241 30.7	44.2	188 07.2	41.8	356 13.2	25.4	63 44.4	48.6	Capella	280 23.2	N46 01.2
02	52 22.0	256 30.9	43.6	203 08.1	42.4	11 16.0	25.3	78 46.9	48.6	Deneb	49 26.4	N45 22.1
03	67 24.5	271 31.1 ..	43.1	218 09.0 ..	43.0	26 18.7 ..	25.2	93 49.5 ..	48.7	Denebola	182 26.3	N14 26.5
04	82 26.9	286 31.3	42.5	233 09.8	43.6	41 21.5	25.1	108 52.0	48.7	Diphda	348 48.0	S17 51.3
05	97 29.4	301 31.6	42.0	248 10.7	44.3	56 24.2	25.0	123 54.6	48.7			
06	112 31.8	316 31.8	N 8 41.4	263 11.5	S11 44.9	71 27.0	N14 25.0	138 57.1	S12 48.8	Dubhe	193 42.8	N61 37.3
07	127 34.3	331 32.0	40.9	278 12.4	45.5	86 29.7	24.9	153 59.7	48.8	Elnath	278 03.0	N28 37.6
S 08	142 36.8	346 32.2	40.3	293 13.2	46.1	101 32.5	24.8	169 02.2	48.8	Eltanin	90 42.9	N51 29.4
A 09	157 39.2	1 32.4 ..	39.8	308 14.1 ..	46.7	116 35.2 ..	24.7	184 04.8 ..	48.8	Enif	33 39.7	N 9 59.1
T 10	172 41.7	16 32.6	39.2	323 14.9	47.3	131 38.0	24.6	199 07.3	48.9	Fomalhaut	15 15.4	S29 29.8
U 11	187 44.2	31 32.8	38.7	338 15.8	47.9	146 40.7	24.5	214 09.9	48.9			
R 12	202 46.6	46 33.0	N 8 38.1	353 16.6	S11 48.5	161 43.5	N14 24.4	229 12.4	S12 48.9	Gacrux	171 53.4	S57 14.6
D 13	217 49.1	61 33.2	37.6	8 17.4	49.1	176 46.2	24.3	244 15.0	48.9	Gienah	175 45.0	S17 40.2
A 14	232 51.6	76 33.4	37.0	23 18.3	49.7	191 49.0	24.2	259 17.5	49.0	Hadar	148 38.2	S60 29.2
Y 15	247 54.0	91 33.6 ..	36.5	38 19.1 ..	50.4	206 51.7 ..	24.1	274 20.1 ..	49.0	Hamal	327 52.1	N23 34.6
16	262 56.5	106 33.8	35.9	53 20.0	51.0	221 54.5	24.1	289 22.6	49.0	Kaus Aust.	83 34.0	S34 22.5
17	277 59.0	121 34.0	35.4	68 20.8	51.6	236 57.2	24.0	304 25.1	49.1			
18	293 01.4	136 34.2	N 8 34.8	83 21.7	S11 52.2	252 00.0	N14 23.9	319 27.7	S12 49.1	Kochab	137 20.8	N74 03.6
19	308 03.9	151 34.4	34.3	98 22.5	52.8	267 02.7	23.8	334 30.2	49.1	Markab	13 30.7	N15 20.1
20	323 06.3	166 34.6	33.7	113 23.4	53.4	282 05.5	23.7	349 32.8	49.1	Menkar	314 07.0	N 4 11.1
21	338 08.8	181 34.8 ..	33.1	128 24.2 ..	54.0	297 08.2 ..	23.6	4 35.3 ..	49.2	Menkent	147 59.3	S36 29.1
22	353 11.3	196 35.0	32.6	143 25.1	54.6	312 11.0	23.5	19 37.9	49.2	Miaplacidus	221 38.9	S69 48.5
23	8 13.7	211 35.2	32.0	158 25.9	55.2	327 13.7	23.4	34 40.4	49.2			
15 00	23 16.2	226 35.4	N 8 31.5	173 26.8	S11 55.8	342 16.5	N14 23.3	49 43.0	S12 49.2	Mirfak	308 29.3	N49 56.7
01	38 18.7	241 35.6	30.9	188 27.6	56.4	357 19.2	23.2	64 45.5	49.3	Nunki	75 49.1	S26 16.1
02	53 21.1	256 35.8	30.3	203 28.5	57.0	12 22.0	23.2	79 48.1	49.3	Peacock	53 07.2	S56 39.7
03	68 23.6	271 36.0 ..	29.8	218 29.3 ..	57.7	27 24.8 ..	23.1	94 50.6 ..	49.3	Pollux	243 18.6	N27 58.1
04	83 26.1	286 36.2	29.2	233 30.2	58.3	42 27.5	23.0	109 53.2	49.4	Procyon	244 51.9	N 5 10.0
05	98 28.5	301 36.3	28.6	248 31.0	58.9	57 30.3	22.9	124 55.7	49.4			
06	113 31.0	316 36.5	N 8 28.1	263 31.9	S11 59.5	72 33.0	N14 22.8	139 58.2	S12 49.4	Rasalhague	95 59.7	N12 32.7
07	128 33.4	331 36.7	27.5	278 32.7	12 00.1	87 35.8	22.7	155 00.8	49.4	Regulus	207 35.8	N11 51.2
08	143 35.9	346 36.9	26.9	293 33.5	00.7	102 38.5	22.6	170 03.3	49.5	Rigel	281 04.7	S 8 10.3
S 09	158 38.4	1 37.1 ..	26.4	308 34.4 ..	01.3	117 41.3 ..	22.5	185 05.9 ..	49.5	Rigil Kent.	139 42.4	S60 56.0
U 10	173 40.8	16 37.3	25.8	323 35.2	01.9	132 44.0	22.4	200 08.4	49.5	Sabik	102 04.2	S15 45.2
N 11	188 43.3	31 37.5	25.2	338 36.1	02.5	147 46.8	22.3	215 11.0	49.5			
D 12	203 45.8	46 37.7	N 8 24.7	353 36.9	S12 03.1	162 49.5	N14 22.3	230 13.5	S12 49.6	Schedar	349 31.7	N56 40.1
A 13	218 48.2	61 37.8	24.1	8 37.8	03.7	177 52.3	22.2	245 16.1	49.6	Shaula	96 12.0	S37 07.3
Y 14	233 50.7	76 38.0	23.5	23 38.6	04.3	192 55.1	22.1	260 18.6	49.6	Sirius	258 27.1	S16 44.7
15	248 53.2	91 38.2 ..	22.9	38 39.5 ..	04.9	207 57.8 ..	22.0	275 21.1 ..	49.6	Spica	158 23.7	S11 17.0
16	263 55.6	106 38.4	22.4	53 40.3	05.5	223 00.6	21.9	290 23.7	49.7	Suhail	222 47.3	S43 31.3
17	278 58.1	121 38.6	21.8	68 41.1	06.1	238 03.3	21.8	305 26.2	49.7			
18	294 00.6	136 38.8	N 8 21.2	83 42.0	S12 06.7	253 06.1	N14 21.7	320 28.8	S12 49.7	Vega	80 34.0	N38 48.6
19	309 03.0	151 38.9	20.6	98 42.8	07.4	268 08.8	21.6	335 31.3	49.7	Zuben'ubi	136 57.5	S16 08.3
20	324 05.5	166 39.1	20.1	113 43.7	08.0	283 11.6	21.5	350 33.9	49.8			
21	339 07.9	181 39.3 ..	19.5	128 44.5 ..	08.6	298 14.4 ..	21.4	5 36.4 ..	49.8			SHA Mer. Pass.
22	354 10.4	196 39.5	18.9	143 45.3	09.2	313 17.1	21.3	20 39.0	49.8	Venus	204 13.4	° ′ h m
23	9 12.9	211 39.6	18.3	158 46.2	09.8	328 19.9	21.2	35 41.5	49.8	Mars	150 49.3	12 27
	h m									Jupiter	318 53.4	1 15
Mer. Pass. 22 27.2		v 0.2	d 0.6	v 0.8	d 0.6	v 2.8	d 0.1	v 2.5	d 0.0	Saturn	26 24.8	20 42

(Venus row: SHA 204 13.4, Mer. Pass. 8 54)

© British Crown Copyright 2022. All rights reserved.

UT	SUN		MOON					Lat.	Twilight		Sunrise	Moonrise			
									Naut.	Civil		13	14	15	16
	GHA	Dec	GHA	v	Dec	d	HP	°	h m	h m	h m	h m	h m	h m	h m
d h	° ′	° ′	° ′	′	° ′	′	′	N 72	04 49	06 08	07 18	04 33	06 34	08 47	12 04
13 00	183 23.9	S 7 35.4	200 34.6	16.8	N 2 07.9	14.3	54.6	N 70	04 54	06 05	07 07	04 35	06 26	08 26	10 53
01	198 24.0	36.4	215 10.4	16.8	1 53.6	14.3	54.6	68	04 57	06 02	06 59	04 36	06 20	08 10	10 17
02	213 24.2	37.3	229 46.2	16.7	1 39.2	14.3	54.6	66	05 00	06 00	06 52	04 37	06 15	07 57	09 51
03	228 24.3 ··	38.3	244 21.9	16.8	1 24.9	14.4	54.6	64	05 02	05 57	06 46	04 38	06 10	07 47	09 31
04	243 24.5	39.2	258 57.7	16.8	1 10.5	14.3	54.6	62	05 04	05 56	06 41	04 38	06 06	07 38	09 16
05	258 24.6	40.1	273 33.5	16.7	0 56.2	14.4	54.6	60	05 06	05 54	06 36	04 39	06 03	07 30	09 02
06	273 24.8	S 7 41.1	288 09.2	16.8	N 0 41.8	14.4	54.7	N 58	05 07	05 52	06 32	04 39	06 00	07 23	08 51
07	288 24.9	42.0	302 45.0	16.7	0 27.4	14.4	54.7	56	05 08	05 51	06 28	04 40	05 57	07 18	08 41
08	303 25.1	42.9	317 20.7	16.7	N 0 13.0	14.4	54.7	54	05 09	05 50	06 25	04 40	05 55	07 12	08 33
F 09	318 25.2 ··	43.9	331 56.4	16.7	S 0 01.4	14.5	54.7	52	05 09	05 48	06 22	04 41	05 53	07 08	08 25
R 10	333 25.4	44.8	346 32.1	16.7	0 15.9	14.4	54.7	50	05 10	05 47	06 20	04 41	05 51	07 03	08 18
I 11	348 25.5	45.7	1 07.8	16.7	0 30.3	14.4	54.7	45	05 10	05 44	06 14	04 42	05 47	06 54	08 04
D 12	3 25.7	S 7 46.7	15 43.5	16.6	S 0 44.7	14.5	54.7	N 40	05 10	05 42	06 09	04 42	05 44	06 46	07 52
A 13	18 25.8	47.6	30 19.1	16.6	0 59.2	14.4	54.8	35	05 10	05 39	06 05	04 43	05 41	06 40	07 42
Y 14	33 26.0	48.5	44 54.7	16.6	1 13.6	14.4	54.8	30	05 09	05 37	06 01	04 43	05 38	06 34	07 33
15	48 26.1 ··	49.5	59 30.3	16.6	1 28.0	14.5	54.8	20	05 07	05 32	05 54	04 44	05 34	06 24	07 18
16	63 26.3	50.4	74 05.9	16.6	1 42.5	14.5	54.8	N 10	05 03	05 27	05 48	04 45	05 30	06 16	07 05
17	78 26.4	51.3	88 41.5	16.5	1 57.0	14.4	54.8	0	04 58	05 22	05 43	04 46	05 26	06 08	06 52
18	93 26.6	S 7 52.3	103 17.0	16.5	S 2 11.4	14.5	54.8	S 10	04 51	05 16	05 37	04 46	05 22	06 00	06 40
19	108 26.7	53.2	117 52.5	16.5	2 25.9	14.4	54.8	20	04 42	05 08	05 31	04 47	05 19	05 52	06 27
20	123 26.9	54.1	132 28.0	16.5	2 40.3	14.5	54.9	30	04 31	04 59	05 23	04 48	05 14	05 42	06 13
21	138 27.0 ··	55.1	147 03.5	16.4	2 54.8	14.4	54.9	35	04 23	04 53	05 19	04 49	05 12	05 37	06 04
22	153 27.2	56.0	161 38.9	16.4	3 09.2	14.5	54.9	40	04 14	04 47	05 14	04 49	05 09	05 31	05 55
23	168 27.3	56.9	176 14.3	16.4	3 23.7	14.4	54.9	45	04 02	04 39	05 09	04 50	05 06	05 24	05 44
14 00	183 27.5	S 7 57.9	190 49.7	16.3	S 3 38.1	14.5	54.9	S 50	03 48	04 28	05 02	04 51	05 02	05 15	05 30
01	198 27.6	58.8	205 25.0	16.3	3 52.6	14.4	54.9	52	03 40	04 24	04 59	04 51	05 01	05 11	05 24
02	213 27.8	7 59.7	220 00.3	16.4	4 07.0	14.4	55.0	54	03 32	04 18	04 55	04 52	04 59	05 07	05 17
03	228 27.9	8 00.7	234 35.6	16.3	4 21.4	14.4	55.0	56	03 23	04 12	04 52	04 52	04 57	05 02	05 10
04	243 28.1	01.6	249 10.9	16.2	4 35.8	14.4	55.0	58	03 12	04 06	04 47	04 52	04 55	04 57	05 01
05	258 28.2	02.5	263 46.1	16.1	4 50.3	14.4	55.0	S 60	03 00	03 58	04 43	04 53	04 52	04 51	04 51

UT	SUN		MOON					Lat.	Sunset	Twilight		Moonset			
										Civil	Naut.	13	14	15	16
d h	° ′	° ′	° ′	′	° ′	′	′	°	h m	h m	h m	h m	h m	h m	h m
06	273 28.4	S 8 03.5	278 21.2	16.2	S 5 04.7	14.4	55.0	N 72	16 12	17 22	18 40	16 40	16 07	15 23	13 40
07	288 28.5	04.4	292 56.4	16.1	5 19.1	14.3	55.0	N 70	16 23	17 26	18 36	16 43	16 17	15 46	14 53
S 08	303 28.7	05.3	307 31.5	16.0	5 33.4	14.4	55.1	68	16 32	17 29	18 33	16 45	16 26	16 04	15 31
A 09	318 28.8 ··	06.3	322 06.5	16.0	5 47.8	14.4	55.1	66	16 39	17 31	18 30	16 47	16 33	16 18	15 58
T 10	333 28.9	07.2	336 41.5	16.0	6 02.2	14.3	55.1	64	16 45	17 33	18 28	16 48	16 40	16 30	16 18
U 11	348 29.1	08.1	351 16.5	15.9	6 16.5	14.3	55.1	62	16 50	17 35	18 26	16 50	16 45	16 40	16 35
R 12	3 29.2	S 8 09.0	5 51.4	15.9	S 6 30.8	14.3	55.1	60	16 55	17 37	18 25	16 51	16 50	16 49	16 49
D 13	18 29.4	10.0	20 26.3	15.9	6 45.1	14.3	55.1	N 58	16 59	17 39	18 24	16 52	16 54	16 57	17 02
A 14	33 29.5	10.9	35 01.2	15.8	6 59.4	14.3	55.2	56	17 03	17 40	18 23	16 53	16 58	17 04	17 12
Y 15	48 29.7 ··	11.8	49 36.0	15.7	7 13.7	14.3	55.2	54	17 06	17 42	18 22	16 54	17 01	17 10	17 22
16	63 29.8	12.8	64 10.7	15.7	7 28.0	14.2	55.2	52	17 09	17 43	18 22	16 55	17 04	17 16	17 30
17	78 30.0	13.7	78 45.4	15.7	S 7 42.2	14.2	55.2	50	17 12	17 44	18 21	16 55	17 07	17 21	17 37
18	93 30.1	S 8 14.6						45	17 18	17 47	18 21	16 57	17 13	17 32	17 54
19	108 30.3	15.5	An annular eclipse of					N 40	17 23	17 50	18 21	16 58	17 19	17 41	18 07
20	123 30.4	16.5	the Sun occurs on this					35	17 27	17 52	18 22	16 59	17 23	17 49	18 18
21	138 30.5 ··	17.4	date. See page 5.					30	17 31	17 55	18 23	17 00	17 27	17 56	18 28
22	153 30.7	18.3						20	17 38	18 00	18 25	17 02	17 34	18 08	18 46
23	168 30.8	19.3						N 10	17 44	18 05	18 29	17 04	17 40	18 19	19 01
15 00	183 31.0	S 8 20.2	180 47.0	15.3	S 9 21.2	14.1	55.3	0	17 49	18 10	18 35	17 05	17 46	18 29	19 15
01	198 31.1	21.1	195 21.3	15.2	9 35.3	14.0	55.4	S 10	17 55	18 17	18 41	17 06	17 52	18 39	19 29
02	213 31.2	22.0	209 55.5	15.2	9 49.3	14.0	55.4	20	18 02	18 24	18 50	17 08	17 58	18 50	19 44
03	228 31.4 ··	23.0	224 29.7	15.1	10 03.3	13.9	55.4	30	18 09	18 33	19 02	17 10	18 05	19 02	20 02
04	243 31.5	23.9	239 03.8	15.0	10 17.2	14.0	55.4	35	18 13	18 39	19 10	17 11	18 09	19 09	20 12
05	258 31.7	24.8	253 37.8	15.0	10 31.2	13.9	55.4	40	18 18	18 46	19 19	17 12	18 14	19 18	20 24
06	273 31.8	S 8 25.7	268 11.8	14.9	S10 45.1	13.8	55.4	45	18 24	18 55	19 31	17 13	18 19	19 27	20 38
07	288 32.0	26.7	282 45.7	14.9	10 58.9	13.8	55.5	S 50	18 31	19 05	19 46	17 15	18 25	19 39	20 55
08	303 32.1	27.6	297 19.6	14.8	11 12.7	13.8	55.5	52	18 34	19 10	19 53	17 15	18 29	19 44	21 03
S 09	318 32.2 ··	28.5	311 53.4	14.8	11 26.5	13.8	55.5	54	18 38	19 15	20 02	17 16	18 32	19 50	21 13
U 10	333 32.4	29.5	326 27.2	14.6	11 40.3	13.7	55.5	56	18 42	19 21	20 11	17 17	18 35	19 57	21 23
N 11	348 32.5	30.4	341 00.8	14.6	11 54.0	13.6	55.5	58	18 46	19 28	20 22	17 18	18 40	20 05	21 35
D 12	3 32.6	S 8 31.3	355 34.4	14.6	S12 07.6	13.7	55.6	S 60	18 51	19 36	20 35	17 19	18 44	20 13	21 48
A 13	18 32.8	32.2	10 08.0	14.4	12 21.3	13.5	55.6								
Y 14	33 32.9	33.2	24 41.4	14.4	12 34.8	13.6	55.6								
15	48 33.1 ··	34.1	39 14.8	14.4	12 48.4	13.5	55.6								
16	63 33.2	35.0	53 48.2	14.2	13 01.9	13.4	55.6								
17	78 33.3	35.9	68 21.4	14.2	13 15.3	13.4	55.7								
18	93 33.5	S 8 36.9	82 54.6	14.1	S13 28.7	13.4	55.7		SUN			MOON			
19	108 33.6	37.8	97 27.7	14.0	13 42.1	13.3	55.7	Day	Eqn. of Time		Mer.	Mer. Pass.		Age	Phase
20	123 33.8	38.7	112 00.7	14.0	13 55.4	13.2	55.7		00ʰ	12ʰ	Pass.	Upper	Lower		
21	138 33.9 ··	39.6	126 33.7	13.9	14 08.6	13.2	55.7	d	m s	m s	h m	h m	h m	d	%
22	153 34.0	40.5	141 06.6	13.8	14 21.8	13.2	55.7	13	13 35	13 42	11 46	10 55	23 15	28	2
23	168 34.2	41.5	155 39.4	13.7	S14 35.0	13.1	55.8	14	13 50	13 57	11 46	11 36	23 57	29	0
	SD 16.1	d 0.9	SD 14.9		15.0		15.1	15	14 04	14 10	11 46	12 18	24 40	01	1

© British Crown Copyright 2022. All rights reserved.

UT	ARIES GHA	VENUS −4.5 GHA	Dec	MARS +1.6 GHA	Dec	JUPITER −2.9 GHA	Dec	SATURN +0.6 GHA	Dec
16 00	24 15.3	226 39.8	N 8 17.7	173 47.0	S12 10.4	343 22.6	N14 21.2	50 44.0	S12 49.9
01	39 17.8	241 40.0	17.1	188 47.9	11.0	358 25.4	21.1	65 46.6	49.9
02	54 20.3	256 40.2	16.6	203 48.7	11.6	13 28.1	21.0	80 49.1	49.9
03	69 22.7	271 40.3 ..	16.0	218 49.6 ..	12.2	28 30.9 ..	20.9	95 51.7 ..	49.9
04	84 25.2	286 40.5	15.4	233 50.4	12.8	43 33.7	20.8	110 54.2	50.0
05	99 27.7	301 40.7	14.8	248 51.2	13.4	58 36.4	20.7	125 56.7	50.0
06	114 30.1	316 40.9	N 8 14.2	263 52.1	S12 14.0	73 39.2	N14 20.6	140 59.3	S12 50.0
07	129 32.6	331 41.0	13.6	278 52.9	14.6	88 41.9	20.5	156 01.8	50.0
08	144 35.0	346 41.2	13.1	293 53.8	15.2	103 44.7	20.4	171 04.4	50.1
09	159 37.5	1 41.4 ..	12.5	308 54.6 ..	15.8	118 47.5 ..	20.3	186 06.9 ..	50.1
10	174 40.0	16 41.5	11.9	323 55.4	16.4	133 50.2	20.2	201 09.5	50.1
11	189 42.4	31 41.7	11.3	338 56.3	17.0	148 53.0	20.1	216 12.0	50.1
12	204 44.9	46 41.9	N 8 10.7	353 57.1	S12 17.6	163 55.7	N14 20.0	231 14.5	S12 50.2
13	219 47.4	61 42.0	10.1	8 58.0	18.2	178 58.5	20.0	246 17.1	50.2
14	234 49.8	76 42.2	09.5	23 58.8	18.8	194 01.3	19.9	261 19.6	50.2
15	249 52.3	91 42.4 ..	08.9	38 59.6 ..	19.4	209 04.0 ..	19.8	276 22.2 ..	50.2
16	264 54.8	106 42.5	08.3	54 00.5	20.0	224 06.8	19.7	291 24.7	50.3
17	279 57.2	121 42.7	07.7	69 01.3	20.6	239 09.5	19.6	306 27.2	50.3
18	294 59.7	136 42.9	N 8 07.1	84 02.2	S12 21.2	254 12.3	N14 19.5	321 29.8	S12 50.3
19	310 02.2	151 43.0	06.5	99 03.0	21.8	269 15.1	19.4	336 32.3	50.3
20	325 04.6	166 43.2	05.9	114 03.8	22.4	284 17.8	19.3	351 34.9	50.4
21	340 07.1	181 43.3 ..	05.3	129 04.7 ..	23.0	299 20.6 ..	19.2	6 37.4 ..	50.4
22	355 09.5	196 43.5	04.7	144 05.5	23.6	314 23.3	19.1	21 39.9	50.4
23	10 12.0	211 43.7	04.1	159 06.3	24.2	329 26.1	19.0	36 42.5	50.4
17 00	25 14.5	226 43.8	N 8 03.5	174 07.2	S12 24.8	344 28.9	N14 18.9	51 45.0	S12 50.5
01	40 16.9	241 44.0	02.9	189 08.0	25.5	359 31.6	18.9	66 47.6	50.5
02	55 19.4	256 44.1	02.3	204 08.8	26.1	14 34.4	18.8	81 50.1	50.5
03	70 21.9	271 44.3 ..	01.7	219 09.7 ..	26.7	29 37.2 ..	18.7	96 52.6 ..	50.5
04	85 24.3	286 44.5	01.1	234 10.5	27.3	44 39.9	18.6	111 55.2	50.6
05	100 26.8	301 44.6	8 00.5	249 11.4	27.9	59 42.7	18.5	126 57.7	50.6
06	115 29.3	316 44.8	N 7 59.9	264 12.2	S12 28.5	74 45.4	N14 18.4	142 00.2	S12 50.6
07	130 31.7	331 44.9	59.3	279 13.0	29.1	89 48.2	18.3	157 02.8	50.6
08	145 34.2	346 45.1	58.7	294 13.9	29.7	104 51.0	18.2	172 05.3	50.6
09	160 36.7	1 45.2 ..	58.1	309 14.7 ..	30.3	119 53.7 ..	18.1	187 07.9 ..	50.7
10	175 39.1	16 45.4	57.5	324 15.5	30.9	134 56.5	18.0	202 10.4	50.7
11	190 41.6	31 45.5	56.9	339 16.4	31.5	149 59.3	17.9	217 12.9	50.7
12	205 44.0	46 45.7	N 7 56.3	354 17.2	S12 32.1	165 02.0	N14 17.8	232 15.5	S12 50.7
13	220 46.5	61 45.8	55.7	9 18.0	32.7	180 04.8	17.7	247 18.0	50.8
14	235 49.0	76 46.0	55.1	24 18.9	33.3	195 07.6	17.6	262 20.5	50.8
15	250 51.4	91 46.1 ..	54.4	39 19.7 ..	33.9	210 10.3 ..	17.6	277 23.1 ..	50.8
16	265 53.9	106 46.3	53.8	54 20.5	34.5	225 13.1	17.5	292 25.6	50.8
17	280 56.4	121 46.4	53.2	69 21.4	35.1	240 15.9	17.4	307 28.1	50.9
18	295 58.8	136 46.6	N 7 52.6	84 22.2	S12 35.7	255 18.6	N14 17.3	322 30.7	S12 50.9
19	311 01.3	151 46.7	52.0	99 23.0	36.3	270 21.4	17.2	337 33.2	50.9
20	326 03.8	166 46.9	51.4	114 23.9	36.9	285 24.1	17.1	352 35.8	50.9
21	341 06.2	181 47.0 ..	50.8	129 24.7 ..	37.5	300 26.9 ..	17.0	7 38.3 ..	50.9
22	356 08.7	196 47.1	50.1	144 25.5	38.0	315 29.7	16.9	22 40.8	51.0
23	11 11.1	211 47.3	49.5	159 26.4	38.6	330 32.4	16.8	37 43.4	51.0
18 00	26 13.6	226 47.4	N 7 48.9	174 27.2	S12 39.2	345 35.2	N14 16.7	52 45.9	S12 51.0
01	41 16.1	241 47.6	48.3	189 28.0	39.8	0 38.0	16.6	67 48.4	51.0
02	56 18.5	256 47.7	47.7	204 28.9	40.4	15 40.7	16.5	82 51.0	51.1
03	71 21.0	271 47.8 ..	47.0	219 29.7 ..	41.0	30 43.5 ..	16.4	97 53.5 ..	51.1
04	86 23.5	286 48.0	46.4	234 30.5	41.6	45 46.3	16.3	112 56.0	51.1
05	101 25.9	301 48.1	45.8	249 31.4	42.2	60 49.0	16.2	127 58.6	51.1
06	116 28.4	316 48.3	N 7 45.2	264 32.2	S12 42.8	75 51.8	N14 16.1	143 01.1	S12 51.1
07	131 30.9	331 48.4	44.5	279 33.0	43.4	90 54.6	16.1	158 03.6	51.2
08	146 33.3	346 48.5	43.9	294 33.8	44.0	105 57.3	16.0	173 06.2	51.2
09	161 35.8	1 48.7 ..	43.3	309 34.7 ..	44.6	121 00.1 ..	15.9	188 08.7 ..	51.2
10	176 38.3	16 48.8	42.7	324 35.5	45.2	136 02.9	15.8	203 11.2	51.2
11	191 40.7	31 48.9	42.0	339 36.3	45.8	151 05.6	15.7	218 13.8	51.2
12	206 43.2	46 49.1	N 7 41.4	354 37.2	S12 46.4	166 08.4	N14 15.6	233 16.3	S12 51.3
13	221 45.6	61 49.2	40.8	9 38.0	47.0	181 11.2	15.5	248 18.8	51.3
14	236 48.1	76 49.3	40.1	24 38.8	47.6	196 14.0	15.4	263 21.4	51.3
15	251 50.6	91 49.5 ..	39.5	39 39.6 ..	48.2	211 16.7 ..	15.3	278 23.9 ..	51.3
16	266 53.0	106 49.6	38.9	54 40.5	48.8	226 19.5	15.2	293 26.4	51.4
17	281 55.5	121 49.7	38.3	69 41.3	49.4	241 22.3	15.1	308 29.0	51.4
18	296 58.0	136 49.9	N 7 37.6	84 42.1	S12 50.0	256 25.0	N14 15.0	323 31.5	S12 51.4
19	312 00.4	151 50.0	37.0	99 43.0	50.6	271 27.8	14.9	338 34.0	51.4
20	327 02.9	166 50.1	36.4	114 43.8	51.2	286 30.6	14.8	353 36.6	51.4
21	342 05.4	181 50.2 ..	35.7	129 44.6 ..	51.8	301 33.3 ..	14.7	8 39.1 ..	51.5
22	357 07.8	196 50.4	35.1	144 45.4	52.4	316 36.1	14.6	23 41.6	51.5
23	12 10.3	211 50.5	34.4	159 46.3	53.0	331 38.9	14.5	38 44.2	51.5
Mer. Pass. 22 15.4	v 0.1 d 0.6			v 0.8 d 0.6		v 2.8 d 0.1		v 2.5 d 0.0	

STARS

Name	SHA	Dec
Acamar	315 12.2	S40 12.4
Achernar	335 20.4	S57 06.9
Acrux	173 01.9	S63 13.7
Adhara	255 06.6	S28 59.9
Aldebaran	290 40.6	N16 33.5
Alioth	166 14.4	N55 49.9
Alkaid	152 53.3	N49 11.8
Alnair	27 33.9	S46 50.9
Alnilam	275 38.6	S 1 11.0
Alphard	217 48.9	S 8 45.5
Alphecca	126 04.9	N26 38.2
Alpheratz	357 35.5	N29 13.4
Altair	62 01.0	N 8 56.0
Ankaa	353 07.8	S42 10.6
Antares	112 17.4	S26 29.1
Arcturus	145 49.2	N19 03.7
Atria	107 12.9	S69 04.4
Avior	234 15.3	S59 34.7
Bellatrix	278 23.8	N 6 22.4
Betelgeuse	270 53.1	N 7 24.8
Canopus	263 52.7	S52 42.1
Capella	280 23.2	N46 01.2
Deneb	49 26.4	N45 22.1
Denebola	182 26.3	N14 26.5
Diphda	348 48.0	S17 51.3
Dubhe	193 42.8	N61 37.3
Elnath	278 03.0	N28 37.6
Eltanin	90 42.9	N51 29.4
Enif	33 39.7	N 9 59.1
Fomalhaut	15 15.4	S29 29.8
Gacrux	171 53.4	S57 14.6
Gienah	175 45.0	S17 40.2
Hadar	148 38.2	S60 29.2
Hamal	327 52.0	N23 34.6
Kaus Aust.	83 34.0	S34 22.5
Kochab	137 20.8	N74 03.6
Markab	13 30.7	N15 20.1
Menkar	314 06.9	N 4 11.1
Menkent	147 59.3	S36 29.1
Miaplacidus	221 38.9	S69 48.5
Mirfak	308 29.3	N49 56.7
Nunki	75 49.1	S26 16.1
Peacock	53 07.3	S56 39.7
Pollux	243 18.6	N27 58.1
Procyon	244 51.9	N 5 10.0
Rasalhague	95 59.7	N12 32.7
Regulus	207 35.8	N11 51.2
Rigel	281 04.7	S 8 10.3
Rigil Kent.	139 42.4	S60 55.9
Sabik	102 04.2	S15 45.2
Schedar	349 31.7	N56 40.2
Shaula	96 12.0	S37 07.3
Sirius	258 27.1	S16 44.7
Spica	158 23.7	S11 17.0
Suhail	222 47.3	S43 31.3
Vega	80 34.1	N38 48.6
Zuben'ubi	136 57.5	S16 08.3

	SHA	Mer. Pass.
Venus	201 29.4	8 53
Mars	148 52.7	12 23
Jupiter	319 14.4	1 02
Saturn	26 30.5	20 30

© British Crown Copyright 2022. All rights reserved.

UT	SUN GHA	SUN Dec	MOON GHA	v	MOON Dec	d	HP
d h	° ′	° ′	° ′	′	° ′	′	′
16 00	183 34.3	S 8 42.4	170 12.1	13.7	S14 48.1	13.0	55.8
01	198 34.4	43.3	184 44.8	13.5	15 01.1	13.0	55.8
02	213 34.6	44.2	199 17.3	13.5	15 14.1	12.9	55.8
03	228 34.7	.. 45.2	213 49.8	13.4	15 27.0	12.9	55.8
04	243 34.8	46.1	228 22.2	13.4	15 39.9	12.8	55.9
05	258 35.0	47.0	242 54.6	13.2	15 52.7	12.8	55.9
06	273 35.1	S 8 47.9	257 26.8	13.1	S16 05.5	12.6	55.9
07	288 35.3	48.8	271 58.9	13.1	16 18.1	12.7	55.9
08	303 35.4	49.8	286 31.0	13.0	16 30.8	12.5	55.9
M 09	318 35.5	.. 50.7	301 03.0	12.9	16 43.3	12.5	56.0
O 10	333 35.7	51.6	315 34.9	12.8	16 55.8	12.4	56.0
N 11	348 35.8	52.5	330 06.7	12.7	17 08.2	12.4	56.0
D 12	3 35.9	S 8 53.4	344 38.4	12.7	S17 20.6	12.3	56.0
A 13	18 36.1	54.4	359 10.1	12.5	17 32.9	12.2	56.0
Y 14	33 36.2	55.3	13 41.6	12.5	17 45.1	12.1	56.1
15	48 36.3	.. 56.2	28 13.1	12.3	17 57.2	12.1	56.1
16	63 36.5	57.1	42 44.4	12.3	18 09.3	12.0	56.1
17	78 36.6	58.0	57 15.7	12.2	18 21.3	11.9	56.1
18	93 36.7	S 8 59.0	71 46.9	12.0	S18 33.2	11.8	56.1
19	108 36.8	8 59.9	86 17.9	12.0	18 45.0	11.8	56.2
20	123 37.0	9 00.8	100 48.9	11.9	18 56.8	11.6	56.2
21	138 37.1	.. 01.7	115 19.8	11.8	19 08.4	11.6	56.2
22	153 37.2	02.6	129 50.6	11.7	19 20.0	11.5	56.2
23	168 37.4	03.6	144 21.3	11.7	19 31.5	11.4	56.2
17 00	183 37.5	S 9 04.5	158 52.0	11.5	S19 42.9	11.4	56.3
01	198 37.6	05.4	173 22.5	11.4	19 54.3	11.2	56.3
02	213 37.8	06.3	187 52.9	11.3	20 05.5	11.2	56.3
03	228 37.9	.. 07.2	202 23.2	11.2	20 16.7	11.0	56.3
04	243 38.0	08.1	216 53.4	11.1	20 27.7	11.0	56.3
05	258 38.2	09.1	231 23.5	11.1	20 38.7	10.9	56.4
06	273 38.3	S 9 10.0	245 53.6	10.9	S20 49.6	10.8	56.4
07	288 38.4	10.9	260 23.5	10.8	21 00.4	10.7	56.4
T 08	303 38.5	11.8	274 53.3	10.7	21 11.1	10.5	56.4
U 09	318 38.7	.. 12.7	289 23.0	10.7	21 21.6	10.5	56.4
E 10	333 38.8	13.6	303 52.7	10.5	21 32.1	10.4	56.5
S 11	348 38.9	14.5	318 22.2	10.4	21 42.5	10.3	56.5
D 12	3 39.0	S 9 15.5	332 51.6	10.3	S21 52.8	10.2	56.5
A 13	18 39.2	16.4	347 20.9	10.3	22 03.0	10.1	56.5
Y 14	33 39.3	17.3	1 50.2	10.1	22 13.1	9.9	56.5
15	48 39.4	.. 18.2	16 19.3	10.0	22 23.0	9.9	56.6
16	63 39.6	19.1	30 48.3	9.9	22 32.9	9.8	56.6
17	78 39.7	20.0	45 17.2	9.9	22 42.7	9.6	56.6
18	93 39.8	S 9 20.9	59 46.1	9.7	S22 52.3	9.5	56.6
19	108 39.9	21.9	74 14.8	9.6	23 01.8	9.5	56.6
20	123 40.1	22.8	88 43.4	9.5	23 11.3	9.3	56.7
21	138 40.2	.. 23.7	103 11.9	9.4	23 20.6	9.2	56.7
22	153 40.3	24.6	117 40.3	9.3	23 29.8	9.0	56.7
23	168 40.4	25.5	132 08.6	9.2	23 38.8	9.0	56.7
18 00	183 40.6	S 9 26.4	146 36.8	9.1	S23 47.8	8.8	56.8
01	198 40.7	27.3	161 04.9	9.1	23 56.6	8.7	56.8
02	213 40.8	28.2	175 33.0	8.9	24 05.3	8.6	56.8
03	228 40.9	.. 29.1	190 00.9	8.8	24 13.9	8.5	56.8
04	243 41.1	30.1	204 28.7	8.7	24 22.4	8.3	56.8
05	258 41.2	31.0	218 56.4	8.6	24 30.7	8.2	56.9
06	273 41.3	S 9 31.9	233 24.0	8.5	S24 38.9	8.1	56.9
07	288 41.4	32.8	247 51.5	8.4	24 47.0	7.9	56.9
W 08	303 41.5	33.7	262 18.9	8.3	24 54.9	7.9	56.9
E 09	318 41.7	.. 34.6	276 46.2	8.3	25 02.8	7.6	56.9
D 10	333 41.8	35.5	291 13.5	8.1	25 10.4	7.6	57.0
N 11	348 41.9	36.4	305 40.6	8.0	25 18.0	7.4	57.0
E 12	3 42.0	S 9 37.3	320 07.6	7.9	S25 25.4	7.3	57.0
S 13	18 42.2	38.2	334 34.5	7.9	25 32.7	7.1	57.0
D 14	33 42.3	39.2	349 01.4	7.7	25 39.8	7.0	57.0
A 15	48 42.4	.. 40.1	3 28.1	7.7	25 46.8	6.9	57.1
Y 16	63 42.5	41.0	17 54.8	7.5	25 53.7	6.7	57.1
17	78 42.6	41.9	32 21.3	7.5	26 00.4	6.6	57.1
18	93 42.8	S 9 42.8	46 47.8	7.3	S26 07.0	6.4	57.1
19	108 42.9	43.7	61 14.1	7.3	26 13.4	6.3	57.2
20	123 43.0	44.6	75 40.4	7.2	26 19.7	6.1	57.2
21	138 43.1	.. 45.5	90 06.6	7.1	26 25.8	6.0	57.2
22	153 43.2	46.4	104 32.7	7.0	26 31.8	5.8	57.2
23	168 43.3	47.3	118 58.7	7.0	S26 37.6	5.7	57.2
	SD 16.1	d 0.9	SD 15.3		15.4		15.5

Moonrise

Lat.	Twilight Naut.	Twilight Civil	Sunrise	Moonrise 16	17	18	19
°	h m	h m	h m	h m	h m	h m	h m
N 72	05 03	06 21	07 32	12 04	■	■	■
N 70	05 06	06 16	07 20	10 53	■	■	■
68	05 08	06 12	07 10	10 17	■	■	■
66	05 10	06 09	07 02	09 51	12 10	■	■
64	05 11	06 06	06 55	09 31	11 30	14 15	■
62	05 12	06 03	06 49	09 16	11 02	13 00	15 35
60	05 13	06 01	06 43	09 02	10 41	12 25	14 05
N 58	05 13	05 59	06 39	08 51	10 24	11 59	13 29
56	05 14	05 57	06 35	08 41	10 09	11 39	13 03
54	05 14	05 55	06 31	08 33	09 57	11 22	12 42
52	05 14	05 53	06 28	08 25	09 46	11 08	12 25
50	05 14	05 52	06 24	08 18	09 36	10 55	12 10
45	05 14	05 48	06 18	08 04	09 16	10 30	11 41
N 40	05 13	05 45	06 12	07 52	09 00	10 09	11 17
35	05 12	05 42	06 07	07 42	08 46	09 52	10 58
30	05 11	05 39	06 03	07 33	08 34	09 38	10 42
20	05 07	05 33	05 55	07 18	08 14	09 13	10 14
N 10	05 03	05 27	05 49	07 05	07 57	08 52	09 51
0	04 57	05 21	05 42	06 52	07 40	08 32	09 29
S 10	04 49	05 14	05 36	06 40	07 24	08 13	09 07
20	04 40	05 06	05 28	06 27	07 07	07 52	08 43
30	04 27	04 56	05 20	06 13	06 47	07 28	08 16
35	04 19	04 49	05 15	06 04	06 36	07 14	08 00
40	04 09	04 42	05 10	05 55	06 23	06 58	07 42
45	03 56	04 33	05 04	05 44	06 08	06 39	07 20
S 50	03 40	04 22	04 56	05 30	05 49	06 15	06 51
52	03 33	04 17	04 52	05 24	05 41	06 04	06 38
54	03 24	04 11	04 48	05 17	05 31	05 51	06 22
56	03 14	04 04	04 44	05 10	05 20	05 36	06 03
58	03 02	03 57	04 39	05 01	05 07	05 18	05 40
S 60	02 48	03 48	04 34	04 51	04 53	04 57	05 10

Moonset

Lat.	Sunset	Twilight Civil	Twilight Naut.	Moonset 16	17	18	19
°	h m	h m	h m	h m	h m	h m	h m
N 72	15 57	17 08	18 26	13 40	■	■	■
N 70	16 09	17 13	18 23	14 53	■	■	■
68	16 19	17 17	18 21	15 31	■	■	■
66	16 28	17 20	18 19	15 58	15 20	■	■
64	16 35	17 23	18 18	16 18	16 01	15 06	■
62	16 41	17 26	18 17	16 35	16 30	16 22	15 46
60	16 46	17 29	18 17	16 49	16 51	16 58	17 16
N 58	16 51	17 31	18 16	17 02	17 09	17 24	17 53
56	16 55	17 33	18 16	17 12	17 25	17 45	18 19
54	16 59	17 35	18 16	17 22	17 38	18 02	18 40
52	17 02	17 37	18 16	17 30	17 49	18 17	18 57
50	17 06	17 38	18 16	17 37	17 59	18 29	19 12
45	17 12	17 42	18 16	17 54	18 21	18 56	19 42
N 40	17 18	17 45	18 17	18 07	18 38	19 17	20 06
35	17 23	17 49	18 18	18 18	18 53	19 35	20 25
30	17 27	17 52	18 19	18 28	19 06	19 50	20 42
20	17 35	17 57	18 23	18 46	19 28	20 16	21 10
N 10	17 42	18 03	18 28	19 01	19 47	20 38	21 34
0	17 49	18 10	18 34	19 15	20 05	20 59	21 57
S 10	17 55	18 17	18 42	19 29	20 23	21 20	22 19
20	18 03	18 25	18 51	19 44	20 42	21 42	22 44
30	18 11	18 36	19 04	20 02	21 04	22 08	23 12
35	18 16	18 42	19 13	20 12	21 18	22 24	23 28
40	18 22	18 50	19 23	20 24	21 33	22 42	23 48
45	18 28	18 59	19 36	20 38	21 51	23 04	24 11
S 50	18 36	19 10	19 52	20 55	22 14	23 31	24 42
52	18 40	19 15	20 00	21 03	22 25	23 45	24 57
54	18 44	19 21	20 09	21 13	22 37	24 00	00 00
56	18 48	19 29	20 19	21 23	22 52	24 19	00 19
58	18 53	19 36	20 31	21 35	23 08	24 42	00 42
S 60	18 59	19 45	20 46	21 48	23 29	25 11	01 11

	SUN Eqn. of Time 00h	12h	Mer. Pass.	MOON Mer. Pass. Upper	Lower	Age	Phase
Day	m s	m s	h m	h m	h m	d	%
16	14 17	14 23	11 46	13 03	00 40	02	3
17	14 30	14 36	11 45	13 52	01 27	03	8
18	14 42	14 48	11 45	14 46	02 18	04	14

© British Crown Copyright 2022. All rights reserved.

UT	ARIES GHA	VENUS −4.5 GHA	Dec	MARS +1.5 GHA	Dec	JUPITER −2.9 GHA	Dec	SATURN +0.6 GHA	Dec	STARS Name	SHA	Dec
19 00	27 12.8	226 50.6	N 7 33.8	174 47.1	S12 53.6	346 41.6	N14 14.4	53 46.7	S12 51.5	Acamar	315 12.1	S40 12.4
01	42 15.2	241 50.8	33.2	189 47.9	54.2	1 44.4	14.3	68 49.2	51.5	Achernar	335 20.3	S57 06.9
02	57 17.7	256 50.9	32.5	204 48.8	54.8	16 47.2	14.3	83 51.8	51.6	Acrux	173 01.9	S63 13.6
03	72 20.1	271 51.0	.. 31.9	219 49.6	.. 55.3	31 50.0	.. 14.2	98 54.3	.. 51.6	Adhara	255 06.6	S28 59.9
04	87 22.6	286 51.1	31.3	234 50.4	55.9	46 52.7	14.1	113 56.8	51.6	Aldebaran	290 40.6	N16 33.5
05	102 25.1	301 51.3	30.6	249 51.2	56.5	61 55.5	14.0	128 59.3	51.6			
06	117 27.5	316 51.4	N 7 30.0	264 52.1	S12 57.1	76 58.3	N14 13.9	144 01.9	S12 51.6	Alioth	166 14.4	N55 49.9
07	132 30.0	331 51.5	29.3	279 52.9	57.7	92 01.0	13.8	159 04.4	51.7	Alkaid	152 53.3	N49 11.8
T 08	147 32.5	346 51.6	28.7	294 53.7	58.3	107 03.8	13.7	174 06.9	51.7	Alnair	27 33.9	S46 50.9
H 09	162 34.9	1 51.7	.. 28.0	309 54.5	.. 58.9	122 06.6	.. 13.6	189 09.5	.. 51.7	Alnilam	275 38.6	S 1 11.1
U 10	177 37.4	16 51.9	27.4	324 55.4	12 59.5	137 09.3	13.5	204 12.0	51.7	Alphard	217 48.9	S 8 45.5
R 11	192 39.9	31 52.0	26.7	339 56.2	13 00.1	152 12.1	13.4	219 14.5	51.7			
S 12	207 42.3	46 52.1	N 7 26.1	354 57.0	S13 00.7	167 14.9	N14 13.3	234 17.1	S12 51.8	Alphecca	126 04.9	N26 38.2
D 13	222 44.8	61 52.2	25.5	9 57.8	01.3	182 17.7	13.2	249 19.6	51.8	Alpheratz	357 35.5	N29 13.4
A 14	237 47.3	76 52.3	24.8	24 58.7	01.9	197 20.4	13.1	264 22.1	51.8	Altair	62 01.0	N 8 56.0
Y 15	252 49.7	91 52.4	.. 24.2	39 59.5	.. 02.5	212 23.2	.. 13.0	279 24.6	.. 51.8	Ankaa	353 07.8	S42 10.6
16	267 52.2	106 52.6	23.5	55 00.3	03.1	227 26.0	12.9	294 27.2	51.8	Antares	112 17.4	S26 29.1
17	282 54.6	121 52.7	22.9	70 01.1	03.7	242 28.8	12.8	309 29.7	51.9			
18	297 57.1	136 52.8	N 7 22.2	85 01.9	S13 04.2	257 31.5	N14 12.7	324 32.2	S12 51.9	Arcturus	145 49.2	N19 03.7
19	312 59.6	151 52.9	21.6	100 02.8	04.8	272 34.3	12.6	339 34.8	51.9	Atria	107 12.9	S69 04.3
20	328 02.0	166 53.0	20.9	115 03.6	05.4	287 37.1	12.5	354 37.3	51.9	Avior	234 15.3	S59 34.7
21	343 04.5	181 53.1	.. 20.2	130 04.4	.. 06.0	302 39.8	.. 12.4	9 39.8	.. 51.9	Bellatrix	278 23.8	N 6 22.4
22	358 07.0	196 53.2	19.6	145 05.2	06.6	317 42.6	12.3	24 42.3	52.0	Betelgeuse	270 53.1	N 7 24.8
23	13 09.4	211 53.4	18.9	160 06.1	07.2	332 45.4	12.2	39 44.9	52.0			
20 00	28 11.9	226 53.5	N 7 18.3	175 06.9	S13 07.8	347 48.2	N14 12.2	54 47.4	S12 52.0	Canopus	263 52.7	S52 42.1
01	43 14.4	241 53.6	17.6	190 07.7	08.4	2 50.9	12.1	69 49.9	52.0	Capella	280 23.1	N46 01.2
02	58 16.8	256 53.7	17.0	205 08.5	09.0	17 53.7	12.0	84 52.4	52.0	Deneb	49 26.4	N45 22.1
03	73 19.3	271 53.8	.. 16.3	220 09.3	.. 09.6	32 56.5	.. 11.9	99 55.0	.. 52.1	Denebola	182 26.3	N14 26.5
04	88 21.8	286 53.9	15.7	235 10.2	10.2	47 59.3	11.8	114 57.5	52.1	Diphda	348 48.0	S17 51.3
05	103 24.2	301 54.0	15.0	250 11.0	10.8	63 02.0	11.7	130 00.0	52.1			
06	118 26.7	316 54.1	N 7 14.3	265 11.8	S13 11.3	78 04.8	N14 11.6	145 02.6	S12 52.1	Dubhe	193 42.7	N61 37.3
07	133 29.1	331 54.2	13.7	280 12.6	11.9	93 07.6	11.5	160 05.1	52.1	Elnath	278 03.0	N28 37.6
08	148 31.6	346 54.3	13.0	295 13.4	12.5	108 10.4	11.4	175 07.6	52.2	Eltanin	90 42.9	N51 29.4
F 09	163 34.1	1 54.4	.. 12.3	310 14.3	.. 13.1	123 13.1	.. 11.3	190 10.1	.. 52.2	Enif	33 39.7	N 9 59.2
R 10	178 36.5	16 54.5	11.7	325 15.1	13.7	138 15.9	11.2	205 12.7	52.2	Fomalhaut	15 15.4	S29 29.8
I 11	193 39.0	31 54.6	11.0	340 15.9	14.3	153 18.7	11.1	220 15.2	52.2			
D 12	208 41.5	46 54.7	N 7 10.4	355 16.7	S13 14.9	168 21.5	N14 11.0	235 17.7	S12 52.2	Gacrux	171 53.4	S57 14.6
A 13	223 43.9	61 54.8	09.7	10 17.5	15.5	183 24.2	10.9	250 20.2	52.2	Gienah	175 45.0	S17 40.2
Y 14	238 46.4	76 55.0	09.0	25 18.4	16.1	198 27.0	10.8	265 22.8	52.3	Hadar	148 38.2	S60 29.2
15	253 48.9	91 55.1	.. 08.4	40 19.2	.. 16.6	213 29.8	.. 10.7	280 25.3	.. 52.3	Hamal	327 52.0	N23 34.6
16	268 51.3	106 55.2	07.7	55 20.0	17.2	228 32.6	10.6	295 27.8	52.3	Kaus Aust.	83 34.0	S34 22.5
17	283 53.8	121 55.3	07.0	70 20.8	17.8	243 35.3	10.5	310 30.3	52.3			
18	298 56.2	136 55.4	N 7 06.4	85 21.6	S13 18.4	258 38.1	N14 10.4	325 32.9	S12 52.4	Kochab	137 20.9	N74 03.5
19	313 58.7	151 55.5	05.7	100 22.4	19.0	273 40.9	10.3	340 35.4	52.4	Markab	13 30.7	N15 20.1
20	329 01.2	166 55.6	05.0	115 23.3	19.6	288 43.7	10.2	355 37.9	52.4	Menkar	314 06.9	N 4 11.1
21	344 03.6	181 55.6	.. 04.3	130 24.1	.. 20.2	303 46.4	.. 10.1	10 40.4	.. 52.4	Menkent	147 59.3	S36 29.1
22	359 06.1	196 55.7	03.7	145 24.9	20.8	318 49.2	10.0	25 43.0	52.4	Miaplacidus	221 38.8	S69 48.5
23	14 08.6	211 55.8	03.0	160 25.7	21.4	333 52.0	09.9	40 45.5	52.4			
21 00	29 11.0	226 55.9	N 7 02.3	175 26.5	S13 21.9	348 54.8	N14 09.8	55 48.0	S12 52.4	Mirfak	308 29.3	N49 56.7
01	44 13.5	241 56.0	01.7	190 27.4	22.5	3 57.5	09.7	70 50.5	52.5	Nunki	75 49.1	S26 16.1
02	59 16.0	256 56.1	01.0	205 28.2	23.1	19 00.3	09.6	85 53.0	52.5	Peacock	53 07.3	S56 39.7
03	74 18.4	271 56.2	7 00.3	220 29.0	.. 23.7	34 03.1	.. 09.6	100 55.6	.. 52.5	Pollux	243 18.6	N27 58.1
04	89 20.9	286 56.3	6 59.6	235 29.8	24.3	49 05.9	09.5	115 58.1	52.5	Procyon	244 51.9	N 5 10.0
05	104 23.4	301 56.4	58.9	250 30.6	24.9	64 08.7	09.4	131 00.6	52.5			
06	119 25.8	316 56.5	N 6 58.3	265 31.4	S13 25.5	79 11.4	N14 09.3	146 03.1	S12 52.6	Rasalhague	95 59.7	N12 32.7
07	134 28.3	331 56.6	57.6	280 32.2	26.1	94 14.2	09.2	161 05.7	52.6	Regulus	207 35.7	N11 51.2
S 08	149 30.7	346 56.7	56.9	295 33.1	26.6	109 17.0	09.1	176 08.2	52.6	Rigel	281 04.7	S 8 10.3
A 09	164 33.2	1 56.8	.. 56.2	310 33.9	.. 27.2	124 19.8	.. 09.0	191 10.7	.. 52.6	Rigil Kent.	139 42.4	S60 55.9
T 10	179 35.7	16 56.9	55.6	325 34.7	27.8	139 22.5	08.9	206 13.2	52.6	Sabik	102 04.2	S15 45.2
U 11	194 38.1	31 57.0	54.9	340 35.5	28.4	154 25.3	08.8	221 15.7	52.6			
R 12	209 40.6	46 57.0	N 6 54.2	355 36.3	S13 29.0	169 28.1	N14 08.7	236 18.3	S12 52.7	Schedar	349 31.7	N56 40.2
D 13	224 43.1	61 57.1	53.5	10 37.1	29.6	184 30.9	08.6	251 20.8	52.7	Shaula	96 12.0	S37 07.3
A 14	239 45.5	76 57.2	52.8	25 37.9	30.2	199 33.7	08.5	266 23.3	52.7	Sirius	258 27.1	S16 44.7
Y 15	254 48.0	91 57.3	.. 52.1	40 38.8	.. 30.7	214 36.4	.. 08.4	281 25.8	.. 52.7	Spica	158 23.7	S11 17.0
16	269 50.5	106 57.4	51.5	55 39.6	31.3	229 39.2	08.3	296 28.4	52.7	Suhail	222 47.2	S43 31.3
17	284 52.9	121 57.5	50.8	70 40.4	31.9	244 42.0	08.2	311 30.9	52.7			
18	299 55.4	136 57.6	N 6 50.1	85 41.2	S13 32.5	259 44.8	N14 08.1	326 33.4	S12 52.8	Vega	80 34.1	N38 48.6
19	314 57.9	151 57.7	49.4	100 42.0	33.1	274 47.5	08.0	341 35.9	52.8	Zuben'ubi	136 57.5	S16 08.3
20	330 00.3	166 57.7	48.7	115 42.8	33.7	289 50.3	07.9	356 38.4	52.8			
21	345 02.8	181 57.8	.. 48.0	130 43.6	.. 34.3	304 53.1	.. 07.8	11 41.0	.. 52.8		SHA	Mer. Pass.
22	0 05.2	196 57.9	47.3	145 44.4	34.8	319 55.9	07.7	26 43.5	52.8	Venus	198 41.6	8 52
23	15 07.7	211 58.0	46.6	160 45.3	35.4	334 58.7	07.6	41 46.0	52.8	Mars	146 55.0	12 19
Mer. Pass.	22 03.6	v 0.1	d 0.7	v 0.8	d 0.6	v 2.8	d 0.1	v 2.5	d 0.0	Jupiter	319 36.3	0 49
										Saturn	26 35.5	20 17

© British Crown Copyright 2022. All rights reserved.

SUN and MOON

UT (d h)	SUN GHA	SUN Dec	MOON GHA	v	Dec	d	HP
19 00	183 43.5	S 9 48.2	133 24.7	6.8	S26 43.3	5.5	57.3
01	198 43.6	49.1	147 50.5	6.8	26 48.8	5.4	57.3
02	213 43.7	50.0	162 16.3	6.7	26 54.2	5.2	57.3
03	228 43.8	.. 50.9	176 42.0	6.6	26 59.4	5.1	57.3
04	243 43.9	51.8	191 07.6	6.5	27 04.5	4.9	57.3
05	258 44.1	52.8	205 33.1	6.5	27 09.4	4.7	57.4
THURSDAY 06	273 44.2	S 9 53.7	219 58.6	6.3	S27 14.1	4.6	57.4
07	288 44.3	54.6	234 23.9	6.3	27 18.7	4.4	57.4
08	303 44.4	55.5	248 49.2	6.2	27 23.1	4.3	57.4
09	318 44.5	.. 56.4	263 14.4	6.2	27 27.4	4.1	57.5
10	333 44.6	57.3	277 39.6	6.1	27 31.5	4.0	57.5
11	348 44.7	58.2	292 04.7	6.0	27 35.5	3.7	57.5
12	3 44.9	S 9 59.1	306 29.7	5.9	S27 39.2	3.6	57.5
13	18 45.0	10 00.0	320 54.6	5.9	27 42.8	3.5	57.5
14	33 45.1	00.9	335 19.5	5.8	27 46.3	3.3	57.6
15	48 45.2	.. 01.8	349 44.3	5.7	27 49.6	3.1	57.6
16	63 45.3	02.7	4 09.0	5.7	27 52.7	2.9	57.6
17	78 45.4	03.6	18 33.7	5.6	27 55.6	2.8	57.6
18	93 45.5	S10 04.5	32 58.3	5.6	S27 58.4	2.6	57.6
19	108 45.7	05.4	47 22.9	5.5	28 01.0	2.4	57.7
20	123 45.8	06.3	61 47.4	5.5	28 03.4	2.3	57.7
21	138 45.9	.. 07.2	76 11.9	5.4	28 05.7	2.0	57.7
22	153 46.0	08.1	90 36.3	5.3	28 07.7	1.9	57.7
23	168 46.1	09.0	105 00.6	5.4	28 09.6	1.8	57.8
20 00	183 46.2	S10 09.9	119 25.0	5.2	S28 11.4	1.5	57.8
01	198 46.3	10.8	133 49.2	5.2	28 12.9	1.4	57.8
02	213 46.4	11.7	148 13.4	5.2	28 14.3	1.2	57.8
03	228 46.6	.. 12.6	162 37.6	5.2	28 15.5	1.0	57.8
04	243 46.7	13.5	177 01.8	5.1	28 16.5	0.9	57.9
05	258 46.8	14.4	191 25.9	5.0	28 17.4	0.7	57.9
FRIDAY 06	273 46.9	S10 15.3	205 49.9	5.1	S28 18.1	0.5	57.9
07	288 47.0	16.2	220 14.0	5.0	28 18.6	0.3	57.9
08	303 47.1	17.1	234 38.0	4.9	28 18.9	0.1	58.0
09	318 47.2	.. 18.0	249 01.9	5.0	28 19.0	0.1	58.0
10	333 47.3	18.9	263 25.9	4.9	28 18.9	0.2	58.0
11	348 47.4	19.8	277 49.8	4.9	28 18.7	0.4	58.0
12	3 47.5	S10 20.7	292 13.7	4.9	S28 18.3	0.6	58.0
13	18 47.6	21.6	306 37.6	4.8	28 17.7	0.7	58.1
14	33 47.8	22.5	321 01.4	4.9	28 17.0	1.0	58.1
15	48 47.9	.. 23.4	335 25.3	4.8	28 16.0	1.1	58.1
16	63 48.0	24.3	349 49.1	4.8	28 14.9	1.4	58.1
17	78 48.1	25.1	4 12.9	4.8	28 13.5	1.5	58.2
18	93 48.2	S10 26.0	18 36.7	4.8	S28 12.0	1.6	58.2
19	108 48.3	26.9	33 00.5	4.8	28 10.4	1.9	58.2
20	123 48.4	27.8	47 24.3	4.8	28 08.5	2.0	58.2
21	138 48.5	.. 28.7	61 48.1	4.8	28 06.5	2.3	58.2
22	153 48.6	29.6	76 11.9	4.7	28 04.2	2.4	58.3
23	168 48.7	30.5	90 35.6	4.8	28 01.8	2.6	58.3
21 00	183 48.8	S10 31.4	104 59.4	4.8	S27 59.2	2.8	58.3
01	198 48.9	32.3	119 23.2	4.8	27 56.4	2.9	58.3
02	213 49.0	33.2	133 47.0	4.8	27 53.5	3.1	58.3
03	228 49.1	.. 34.1	148 10.8	4.9	27 50.4	3.4	58.4
04	243 49.2	35.0	162 34.6	4.9	27 47.0	3.5	58.4
05	258 49.3	35.9	176 58.5	4.8	27 43.5	3.7	58.4
SATURDAY 06	273 49.4	S10 36.8	191 22.3	4.9	S27 39.8	3.8	58.4
07	288 49.5	37.7	205 46.2	4.9	27 36.0	4.1	58.5
08	303 49.7	38.5	220 10.1	4.9	27 31.9	4.2	58.5
09	318 49.8	.. 39.4	234 34.0	4.9	27 27.7	4.4	58.5
10	333 49.9	40.3	248 57.9	5.0	27 23.3	4.6	58.5
11	348 50.0	41.2	263 21.9	4.9	27 18.7	4.7	58.5
12	3 50.1	S10 42.1	277 45.8	5.0	S27 14.0	5.0	58.6
13	18 50.2	43.0	292 09.8	5.1	27 09.0	5.1	58.6
14	33 50.3	43.9	306 33.9	5.1	27 03.9	5.3	58.6
15	48 50.4	.. 44.8	320 58.0	5.1	26 58.6	5.5	58.6
16	63 50.5	45.7	335 22.1	5.1	26 53.1	5.6	58.6
17	78 50.6	46.6	349 46.2	5.2	26 47.5	5.9	58.7
18	93 50.7	S10 47.4	4 10.4	5.2	S26 41.6	6.0	58.7
19	108 50.8	48.3	18 34.6	5.3	26 35.6	6.1	58.7
20	123 50.9	49.2	32 58.9	5.3	26 29.5	6.4	58.7
21	138 51.0	.. 50.1	47 23.2	5.3	26 23.1	6.5	58.8
22	153 51.1	51.0	61 47.5	5.4	26 16.6	6.7	58.8
23	168 51.2	51.9	76 11.9	5.4	S26 09.9	6.9	58.8
	SD 16.1	d 0.9	SD 15.7		15.8		16.0

Twilight, Sunrise and Moonrise

Lat.	Twilight Naut.	Twilight Civil	Sunrise	Moonrise 19	20	21	22
N 72	05 16	06 34	07 48	■■	■■	■■	■■
N 70	05 17	06 28	07 33	■■	■■	■■	■■
68	05 18	06 23	07 21	■■	■■	■■	■■
66	05 19	06 18	07 12	■■	■■	■■	17 59
64	05 19	06 14	07 04	■■	■■	■■	16 57
62	05 20	06 11	06 57	15 35	■■	16 33	16 22
60	05 20	06 08	06 51	14 05	15 17	15 47	15 57
N 58	05 20	06 05	06 46	13 29	14 37	15 17	15 37
56	05 20	06 03	06 41	13 03	14 10	14 54	15 20
54	05 19	06 01	06 37	12 42	13 48	14 35	15 05
52	05 19	05 58	06 33	12 25	13 30	14 19	14 53
50	05 19	05 56	06 29	12 10	13 15	14 05	14 42
45	05 18	05 52	06 22	11 41	12 44	13 37	14 18
N 40	05 16	05 48	06 15	11 17	12 20	13 15	14 00
35	05 15	05 44	06 10	10 58	12 01	12 56	13 44
30	05 13	05 41	06 05	10 42	11 44	12 40	13 30
20	05 08	05 34	05 56	10 14	11 15	12 13	13 07
N 10	05 03	05 27	05 49	09 51	10 51	11 50	12 47
0	04 56	05 20	05 41	09 29	10 28	11 28	12 27
S 10	04 48	05 13	05 34	09 07	10 05	11 07	12 08
20	04 37	05 04	05 26	08 43	09 41	10 43	11 48
30	04 23	04 52	05 17	08 16	09 13	10 16	11 24
35	04 15	04 46	05 12	08 00	08 56	10 00	11 10
40	04 04	04 37	05 06	07 42	08 36	09 41	10 54
45	03 50	04 28	04 58	07 20	08 13	09 18	10 34
S 50	03 33	04 15	04 50	06 51	07 42	08 49	10 10
52	03 25	04 10	04 46	06 38	07 27	08 35	09 58
54	03 15	04 03	04 41	06 22	07 10	08 18	09 44
56	03 04	03 56	04 36	06 03	06 48	07 59	09 28
58	02 51	03 48	04 31	05 40	06 22	07 34	09 09
S 60	02 36	03 38	04 25	05 10	05 44	07 00	08 46

Sunset, Twilight and Moonset

Lat.	Sunset	Twilight Civil	Twilight Naut.	Moonset 19	20	21	22
N 72	15 40	16 54	18 12	■■	■■	■■	■■
N 70	15 55	17 00	18 11	■■	■■	■■	■■
68	16 07	17 05	18 10	■■	■■	■■	19 38
66	16 16	17 10	18 09	■■	■■	■■	20 39
64	16 25	17 14	18 09	■■	■■	19 00	21 13
62	16 32	17 17	18 09	15 46	■■	19 46	21 57
60	16 38	17 20	18 09	17 16	18 10	19 46	21 57
N 58	16 43	17 23	18 09	17 53	18 49	20 15	21 57
56	16 48	17 26	18 09	18 19	19 17	20 38	22 14
54	16 52	17 28	18 09	18 40	19 38	20 56	22 27
52	16 56	17 30	18 10	18 57	19 56	21 12	22 39
50	17 00	17 32	18 10	19 12	20 11	21 26	22 50
45	17 07	17 37	18 11	19 42	20 42	21 53	23 12
N 40	17 14	17 41	18 13	20 06	21 06	22 15	23 30
35	17 19	17 45	18 14	20 25	21 25	22 33	23 44
30	17 24	17 49	18 16	20 42	21 42	22 48	23 57
20	17 33	17 55	18 21	21 10	22 10	23 14	24 19
N 10	17 41	18 02	18 27	21 34	22 34	23 36	24 37
0	17 48	18 09	18 34	21 57	22 57	23 57	24 55
S 10	17 56	18 17	18 42	22 19	23 19	24 17	00 17
20	18 04	18 26	18 53	22 44	23 43	24 39	00 39
30	18 13	18 38	19 07	23 12	24 11	00 11	01 05
35	18 19	18 45	19 16	23 28	24 28	00 28	01 19
40	18 25	18 53	19 27	23 48	24 47	00 47	01 36
45	18 32	19 03	19 40	24 11	00 11	01 10	01 57
S 50	18 41	19 15	19 58	24 42	00 42	01 39	02 22
52	18 45	19 21	20 07	24 57	00 57	01 54	02 35
54	18 50	19 28	20 16	00 00	01 14	02 11	02 49
56	18 55	19 35	20 28	00 19	01 35	02 31	03 05
58	19 00	19 44	20 41	00 42	02 02	02 56	03 24
S 60	19 07	19 53	20 57	01 11	02 40	03 29	03 48

SUN and MOON data

Day	SUN Eqn. of Time 00h	12h	Mer. Pass.	MOON Mer. Pass. Upper	Lower	Age	Phase
	m s	m s	h m	h m	h m	d	%
19	14 54	14 59	11 45	15 43	03 14	05	22
20	15 05	15 10	11 45	16 42	04 12	06	32
21	15 15	15 20	11 45	17 43	05 13	07	43

© British Crown Copyright 2022. All rights reserved.

UT	ARIES	VENUS −4.5		MARS +1.5		JUPITER −2.9		SATURN +0.6		STARS		
	GHA	GHA	Dec	GHA	Dec	GHA	Dec	GHA	Dec	Name	SHA	Dec
d h	° ′	° ′	° ′	° ′	° ′	° ′	° ′	° ′	° ′		° ′	° ′
22 00	30 10.2	226 58.1 N 6 46.0		175 46.1 S13 36.0		350 01.4 N14 07.5		56 48.5 S12 52.9		Acamar	315 12.1	S40 12.4
01	45 12.6	241 58.2	45.3	190 46.9	36.6	5 04.2	07.4	71 51.0	52.9	Achernar	335 20.3	S57 07.0
02	60 15.1	256 58.2	44.6	205 47.7	37.2	20 07.0	07.3	86 53.6	52.9	Acrux	173 01.9	S63 13.6
03	75 17.6	271 58.3 . .	43.9	220 48.5 . .	37.8	35 09.8 . .	07.2	101 56.1 . .	52.9	Adhara	255 06.6	S28 59.9
04	90 20.0	286 58.4	43.2	235 49.3	38.3	50 12.6	07.1	116 58.6	52.9	Aldebaran	290 40.5	N16 33.5
05	105 22.5	301 58.5	42.5	250 50.1	38.9	65 15.3	07.0	132 01.1	52.9			
06	120 25.0	316 58.6 N 6 41.8		265 50.9 S13 39.5		80 18.1 N14 06.9		147 03.6 S12 52.9		Alioth	166 14.4	N55 49.9
07	135 27.4	331 58.6	41.1	280 51.7	40.1	95 20.9	06.8	162 06.1	53.0	Alkaid	152 53.3	N49 11.7
08	150 29.9	346 58.7	40.4	295 52.6	40.7	110 23.7	06.7	177 08.7	53.0	Alnair	27 34.0	S46 50.9
S 09	165 32.4	1 58.8 . .	39.7	310 53.4 . .	41.3	125 26.5 . .	06.6	192 11.2 . .	53.0	Alnilam	275 38.6	S 1 11.1
U 10	180 34.8	16 58.9	39.0	325 54.2	41.8	140 29.3	06.5	207 13.7	53.0	Alphard	217 48.9	S 8 45.5
N 11	195 37.3	31 58.9	38.3	340 55.0	42.4	155 32.0	06.4	222 16.2	53.0			
D 12	210 39.7	46 59.0 N 6 37.6		355 55.8 S13 43.0		170 34.8 N14 06.3		237 18.7 S12 53.0		Alphecca	126 04.9	N26 38.2
A 13	225 42.2	61 59.1	36.9	10 56.6	43.6	185 37.6	06.2	252 21.3	53.1	Alpheratz	357 35.5	N29 13.4
Y 14	240 44.7	76 59.2	36.2	25 57.4	44.2	200 40.4	06.1	267 23.8	53.1	Altair	62 01.0	N 8 56.0
15	255 47.1	91 59.2 . .	35.5	40 58.2 . .	44.8	215 43.2 . .	06.0	282 26.3 . .	53.1	Ankaa	353 07.8	S42 10.6
16	270 49.6	106 59.3	34.8	55 59.0	45.3	230 45.9	05.9	297 28.8	53.1	Antares	112 17.4	S26 29.1
17	285 52.1	121 59.4	34.1	70 59.8	45.9	245 48.7	05.8	312 31.3	53.1			
18	300 54.5	136 59.5 N 6 33.4		86 00.6 S13 46.5		260 51.5 N14 05.7		327 33.8 S12 53.1		Arcturus	145 49.2	N19 03.6
19	315 57.0	151 59.5	32.7	101 01.4	47.1	275 54.3	05.6	342 36.4	53.1	Atria	107 13.0	S69 04.3
20	330 59.5	166 59.6	32.0	116 02.2	47.7	290 57.1	05.5	357 38.9	53.2	Avior	234 15.2	S59 34.7
21	346 01.9	181 59.7 . .	31.3	131 03.1 . .	48.2	305 59.8 . .	05.4	12 41.4 . .	53.2	Bellatrix	278 23.8	N 6 22.4
22	1 04.4	196 59.7	30.6	146 03.9	48.8	321 02.6	05.3	27 43.9	53.2	Betelgeuse	270 53.0	N 7 24.8
23	16 06.9	211 59.8	29.9	161 04.7	49.4	336 05.4	05.3	42 46.4	53.2			
23 00	31 09.3	226 59.9 N 6 29.2		176 05.5 S13 50.0		351 08.2 N14 05.2		57 48.9 S12 53.2		Canopus	263 52.6	S52 42.1
01	46 11.8	242 00.0	28.5	191 06.3	50.6	6 11.0	05.1	72 51.5	53.2	Capella	280 23.1	N46 01.2
02	61 14.2	257 00.0	27.8	206 07.1	51.1	21 13.8	05.0	87 54.0	53.3	Deneb	49 26.5	N45 22.1
03	76 16.7	272 00.1 . .	27.0	221 07.9 . .	51.7	36 16.5 . .	04.9	102 56.5 . .	53.3	Denebola	182 26.3	N14 26.5
04	91 19.2	287 00.2	26.3	236 08.7	52.3	51 19.3	04.8	117 59.0	53.3	Diphda	348 48.0	S17 51.3
05	106 21.6	302 00.2	25.6	251 09.5	52.9	66 22.1	04.7	133 01.5	53.3			
06	121 24.1	317 00.3 N 6 24.9		266 10.3 S13 53.5		81 24.9 N14 04.6		148 04.0 S12 53.3		Dubhe	193 42.7	N61 37.3
07	136 26.6	332 00.4	24.2	281 11.1	54.0	96 27.7	04.5	163 06.5	53.3	Elnath	278 02.9	N28 37.6
08	151 29.0	347 00.4	23.5	296 11.9	54.6	111 30.5	04.4	178 09.1	53.3	Eltanin	90 42.9	N51 29.4
M 09	166 31.5	2 00.5 . .	22.8	311 12.7 . .	55.2	126 33.2 . .	04.3	193 11.6 . .	53.4	Enif	33 39.7	N 9 59.2
O 10	181 34.0	17 00.5	22.1	326 13.5	55.8	141 36.0	04.2	208 14.1	53.4	Fomalhaut	15 15.4	S29 29.8
N 11	196 36.4	32 00.6	21.3	341 14.3	56.4	156 38.8	04.1	223 16.6	53.4			
D 12	211 38.9	47 00.7 N 6 20.6		356 15.1 S13 56.9		171 41.6 N14 04.0		238 19.1 S12 53.4		Gacrux	171 53.4	S57 14.6
A 13	226 41.3	62 00.7	19.9	11 15.9	57.5	186 44.4	03.9	253 21.6	53.4	Gienah	175 45.5	S17 40.2
Y 14	241 43.8	77 00.8	19.2	26 16.7	58.1	201 47.2	03.8	268 24.1	53.4	Hadar	148 38.2	S60 29.2
15	256 46.3	92 00.9 . .	18.5	41 17.5 . .	58.7	216 49.9 . .	03.7	283 26.7 . .	53.4	Hamal	327 52.0	N23 34.6
16	271 48.7	107 00.9	17.8	56 18.3	59.2	231 52.7	03.6	298 29.2	53.5	Kaus Aust.	83 34.1	S34 22.5
17	286 51.2	122 01.0	17.0	71 19.1	13 59.8	246 55.5	03.5	313 31.7	53.5			
18	301 53.7	137 01.0 N 6 16.3		86 20.0 S14 00.4		261 58.3 N14 03.4		328 34.2 S12 53.5		Kochab	137 20.9	N74 03.5
19	316 56.1	152 01.1	15.6	101 20.8	01.0	277 01.1	03.3	343 36.7	53.5	Markab	13 30.7	N15 20.1
20	331 58.6	167 01.2	14.9	116 21.6	01.6	292 03.9	03.2	358 39.2	53.5	Menkar	314 06.9	N 4 11.1
21	347 01.1	182 01.2 . .	14.2	131 22.4 . .	02.1	307 06.7 . .	03.1	13 41.7 . .	53.5	Menkent	147 59.3	S36 29.1
22	2 03.5	197 01.3	13.4	146 23.2	02.7	322 09.4	03.0	28 44.2	53.5	Miaplacidus	221 38.8	S69 48.5
23	17 06.0	212 01.3	12.7	161 24.0	03.3	337 12.2	02.9	43 46.8	53.5			
24 00	32 08.5	227 01.4 N 6 12.0		176 24.8 S14 03.9		352 15.0 N14 02.8		58 49.3 S12 53.6		Mirfak	308 29.3	N49 56.7
01	47 10.9	242 01.4	11.3	191 25.6	04.4	7 17.8	02.7	73 51.8	53.6	Nunki	75 49.1	S26 16.1
02	62 13.4	257 01.5	10.5	206 26.4	05.0	22 20.6	02.6	88 54.3	53.6	Peacock	53 07.3	S56 39.7
03	77 15.8	272 01.5 . .	09.8	221 27.2 . .	05.6	37 23.4 . .	02.5	103 56.8 . .	53.6	Pollux	243 18.5	N27 58.1
04	92 18.3	287 01.6	09.1	236 28.0	06.2	52 26.2	02.4	118 59.3	53.6	Procyon	244 51.9	N 5 10.0
05	107 20.8	302 01.7	08.4	251 28.8	06.7	67 28.9	02.3	134 01.8	53.6			
06	122 23.2	317 01.7 N 6 07.6		266 29.6 S14 07.3		82 31.7 N14 02.2		149 04.3 S12 53.6		Rasalhague	95 59.7	N12 32.7
07	137 25.7	332 01.8	06.9	281 30.4	07.9	97 34.5	02.1	164 06.8	53.6	Regulus	207 35.7	N11 51.2
T 08	152 28.2	347 01.8	06.2	296 31.2	08.5	112 37.3	02.0	179 09.4	53.7	Rigel	281 04.6	S 8 10.3
U 09	167 30.6	2 01.9 . .	05.4	311 32.0 . .	09.0	127 40.1 . .	01.9	194 11.9 . .	53.7	Rigil Kent.	139 42.4	S60 55.9
E 10	182 33.1	17 01.9	04.7	326 32.8	09.6	142 42.9	01.8	209 14.4	53.7	Sabik	102 04.2	S15 45.2
S 11	197 35.6	32 02.0	04.0	341 33.6	10.2	157 45.7	01.7	224 16.9	53.7			
D 12	212 38.0	47 02.0 N 6 03.2		356 34.4 S14 10.8		172 48.4 N14 01.6		239 19.4 S12 53.7		Schedar	349 31.7	N56 40.2
A 13	227 40.5	62 02.1	02.5	11 35.2	11.3	187 51.2	01.5	254 21.9	53.7	Shaula	96 12.0	S37 07.3
Y 14	242 43.0	77 02.1	01.8	26 35.9	11.9	202 54.0	01.4	269 24.4	53.7	Sirius	258 27.0	S16 44.7
15	257 45.4	92 02.2 . .	01.0	41 36.7 . .	12.5	217 56.8 . .	01.3	284 26.9 . .	53.7	Spica	158 23.7	S11 17.0
16	272 47.9	107 02.2	6 00.3	56 37.5	13.1	232 59.6	01.2	299 29.4	53.8	Suhail	222 47.2	S43 31.3
17	287 50.3	122 02.3	5 59.6	71 38.3	13.6	248 02.4	01.1	314 31.9	53.8			
18	302 52.8	137 02.3 N 5 58.8		86 39.1 S14 14.2		263 05.2 N14 01.0		329 34.4 S12 53.8		Vega	80 34.1	N38 48.6
19	317 55.3	152 02.3	58.1	101 39.9	14.8	278 07.9	00.9	344 37.0	53.8	Zuben'ubi	136 57.5	S16 08.3
20	332 57.7	167 02.4	57.4	116 40.7	15.4	293 10.7	00.8	359 39.5	53.8			
21	348 00.2	182 02.4 . .	56.6	131 41.5 . .	15.9	308 13.5 . .	00.7	14 42.0 . .	53.8		SHA	Mer. Pass.
22	3 02.7	197 02.5	55.9	146 42.3	16.5	323 16.3	00.6	29 44.5	53.8	Venus	195 50.6	8 52
23	18 05.1	212 02.5	55.1	161 43.1	17.1	338 19.1	00.5	44 47.0	53.8	Mars	144 56.2	12 15
	h m									Jupiter	319 58.9	0 35
Mer. Pass. 21 51.8		v 0.1 d 0.7		v 0.8 d 0.6		v 2.8 d 0.1		v 2.5 d 0.0		Saturn	26 39.6	20 05

© British Crown Copyright 2022. All rights reserved.

SUN / MOON

UT	SUN GHA	SUN Dec	MOON GHA	v	Dec	d	HP
d h	° ′	° ′	° ′	′	° ′	′	′
22 00	183 51.3	S10 52.8	90 36.3	5.5	S26 03.0	7.0	58.8
01	198 51.4	53.7	105 00.8	5.6	25 56.0	7.2	58.8
02	213 51.5	54.5	119 25.4	5.5	25 48.8	7.4	58.9
03	228 51.6	.. 55.4	133 49.9	5.7	25 41.4	7.5	58.9
04	243 51.7	56.3	148 14.6	5.7	25 33.9	7.8	58.9
05	258 51.8	57.2	162 39.3	5.7	25 26.1	7.8	58.9
06	273 51.8	S10 58.1	177 04.0	5.8	S25 18.3	8.1	58.9
07	288 51.9	59.0	191 28.8	5.9	25 10.2	8.2	59.0
S 08	303 52.0	10 59.8	205 53.7	5.9	25 02.0	8.4	59.0
U 09	318 52.1	11 00.7	220 18.6	6.0	24 53.6	8.5	59.0
N 10	333 52.2	01.6	234 43.6	6.0	24 45.1	8.7	59.0
D 11	348 52.3	02.5	249 08.6	6.1	24 36.4	8.8	59.0
A 12	3 52.4	S11 03.4	263 33.7	6.2	S24 27.6	9.0	59.1
Y 13	18 52.5	04.3	277 58.9	6.2	24 18.6	9.2	59.1
14	33 52.6	05.2	292 24.1	6.3	24 09.4	9.3	59.1
15	48 52.7	.. 06.0	306 49.4	6.4	24 00.1	9.5	59.1
16	63 52.8	06.9	321 14.8	6.4	23 50.6	9.7	59.1
17	78 52.9	07.8	335 40.2	6.5	23 40.9	9.8	59.2
18	93 53.0	S11 08.7	350 05.7	6.6	S23 31.1	9.9	59.2
19	108 53.1	09.6	4 31.3	6.6	23 21.2	10.1	59.2
20	123 53.2	10.4	18 56.9	6.7	23 11.1	10.2	59.2
21	138 53.3	.. 11.3	33 22.6	6.8	23 00.9	10.4	59.2
22	153 53.4	12.2	47 48.4	6.8	22 50.5	10.6	59.3
23	168 53.5	13.1	62 14.2	6.9	22 39.9	10.6	59.3
23 00	183 53.5	S11 14.0	76 40.1	7.0	S22 29.3	10.9	59.3
01	198 53.6	14.8	91 06.1	7.0	22 18.4	10.9	59.3
02	213 53.7	15.7	105 32.1	7.1	22 07.5	11.1	59.3
03	228 53.8	.. 16.6	119 58.2	7.2	21 56.4	11.3	59.3
04	243 53.9	17.5	134 24.4	7.3	21 45.1	11.4	59.4
05	258 54.0	18.4	148 50.7	7.3	21 33.7	11.5	59.4
06	273 54.1	S11 19.2	163 17.0	7.4	S21 22.2	11.7	59.4
07	288 54.2	20.1	177 43.4	7.5	21 10.5	11.8	59.4
08	303 54.3	21.0	192 09.9	7.6	20 58.7	11.9	59.4
M 09	318 54.4	.. 21.9	206 36.5	7.6	20 46.8	12.1	59.4
O 10	333 54.4	22.7	221 03.1	7.7	20 34.7	12.1	59.5
N 11	348 54.5	23.6	235 29.8	7.8	20 22.6	12.4	59.5
D 12	3 54.6	S11 24.5	249 56.6	7.8	S20 10.2	12.4	59.5
A 13	18 54.7	25.4	264 23.4	7.9	19 57.8	12.6	59.5
Y 14	33 54.8	26.2	278 50.3	8.0	19 45.2	12.7	59.5
15	48 54.9	.. 27.1	293 17.3	8.1	19 32.5	12.8	59.6
16	63 55.0	28.0	307 44.4	8.1	19 19.7	12.9	59.6
17	78 55.1	28.9	322 11.5	8.2	19 06.8	13.1	59.6
18	93 55.1	S11 29.7	336 38.7	8.3	S18 53.7	13.2	59.6
19	108 55.2	30.6	351 06.0	8.3	18 40.5	13.3	59.6
20	123 55.3	31.5	5 33.3	8.5	18 27.2	13.4	59.6
21	138 55.4	.. 32.4	20 00.8	8.4	18 13.8	13.5	59.6
22	153 55.5	33.2	34 28.2	8.6	18 00.3	13.7	59.7
23	168 55.6	34.1	48 55.8	8.6	17 46.6	13.7	59.7
24 00	183 55.7	S11 35.0	63 23.4	8.7	S17 32.9	13.9	59.7
01	198 55.7	35.9	77 51.1	8.8	17 19.0	13.9	59.7
02	213 55.8	36.7	92 18.9	8.8	17 05.1	14.1	59.7
03	228 55.9	.. 37.6	106 46.7	8.9	16 51.0	14.2	59.7
04	243 56.0	38.5	121 14.6	9.0	16 36.8	14.2	59.7
05	258 56.1	39.3	135 42.6	9.1	16 22.6	14.4	59.8
06	273 56.2	S11 40.2	150 10.7	9.1	S16 08.2	14.5	59.8
07	288 56.2	41.1	164 38.8	9.1	15 53.7	14.6	59.8
T 08	303 56.3	42.0	179 06.9	9.3	15 39.1	14.6	59.8
U 09	318 56.4	.. 42.8	193 35.2	9.3	15 24.5	14.8	59.8
E 10	333 56.5	43.7	208 03.5	9.3	15 09.7	14.9	59.8
S 11	348 56.6	44.6	222 31.8	9.4	14 54.8	14.9	59.8
D 12	3 56.7	S11 45.4	237 00.2	9.5	S14 39.9	15.0	59.8
A 13	18 56.7	46.3	251 28.7	9.6	14 24.9	15.2	59.9
Y 14	33 56.8	47.2	265 57.3	9.6	14 09.7	15.2	59.9
15	48 56.9	.. 48.0	280 25.9	9.6	13 54.5	15.3	59.9
16	63 57.0	48.9	294 54.5	9.8	13 39.2	15.3	59.9
17	78 57.1	49.8	309 23.3	9.8	13 23.9	15.5	59.9
18	93 57.1	S11 50.6	323 52.1	9.8	S13 08.4	15.5	59.9
19	108 57.2	51.5	338 20.9	9.9	12 52.9	15.6	59.9
20	123 57.3	52.4	352 49.8	9.9	12 37.3	15.7	59.9
21	138 57.4	.. 53.2	7 18.7	10.0	12 21.6	15.8	59.9
22	153 57.4	54.1	21 47.7	10.1	12 05.8	15.8	60.0
23	168 57.5	55.0	36 16.8	10.1	S11 50.0	15.9	60.0
	SD 16.1	d 0.9	SD 16.1		16.2		16.3

Twilight / Moonrise

Lat.	Naut.	Civil	Sunrise	22	23	24	25
°	h m	h m	h m	h m	h m	h m	h m
N 72	05 28	06 47	08 03	■■■	■■■	17 33	16 42
N 70	05 28	06 40	07 46	■■■	18 18	17 08	16 32
68	05 28	06 33	07 33	■■■	17 30	16 49	16 24
66	05 28	06 28	07 22	17 59	16 58	16 34	16 17
64	05 28	06 23	07 13	16 57	16 35	16 21	16 11
62	05 27	06 19	07 05	16 22	16 16	16 11	16 06
60	05 27	06 15	06 58	15 57	16 00	16 01	16 01
N 58	05 26	06 12	06 52	15 37	15 47	15 53	15 57
56	05 25	06 09	06 47	15 20	15 36	15 46	15 54
54	05 25	06 06	06 42	15 05	15 25	15 40	15 51
52	05 24	06 03	06 38	14 53	15 16	15 34	15 48
50	05 23	06 01	06 34	14 42	15 08	15 28	15 45
45	05 21	05 56	06 26	14 18	14 51	15 17	15 39
N 40	05 19	05 51	06 19	14 00	14 37	15 07	15 34
35	05 17	05 47	06 12	13 44	14 24	14 59	15 30
30	05 15	05 43	06 07	13 30	14 14	14 52	15 26
20	05 09	05 35	05 57	13 07	13 55	14 39	15 20
N 10	05 03	05 28	05 49	12 47	13 39	14 28	15 14
0	04 55	05 20	05 41	12 27	13 24	14 17	15 08
S 10	04 46	05 11	05 33	12 08	13 09	14 07	15 03
20	04 35	05 01	05 24	11 48	12 52	13 56	14 57
30	04 20	04 49	05 14	11 24	12 34	13 43	14 50
35	04 10	04 42	05 08	11 10	12 23	13 35	14 47
40	03 59	04 33	05 01	10 54	12 10	13 26	14 42
45	03 45	04 22	04 53	10 34	11 55	13 16	14 37
S 50	03 26	04 09	04 44	10 10	11 36	13 04	14 31
52	03 17	04 03	04 39	09 58	11 27	12 58	14 28
54	03 07	03 56	04 35	09 44	11 17	12 52	14 25
56	02 55	03 48	04 29	09 28	11 06	12 45	14 21
58	02 41	03 39	04 23	09 09	10 53	12 37	14 18
S 60	02 23	03 29	04 16	08 46	10 38	12 28	14 13

Moonset / Twilight

Lat.	Sunset	Civil	Naut.	22	23	24	25
°	h m	h m	h m	h m	h m	h m	h m
N 72	15 24	16 39	17 58	■■■	■■■	23 58	26 37
N 70	15 41	16 47	17 58	■■■	21 19	24 20	00 20
68	15 54	16 54	17 59	■■■	22 05	24 36	00 36
66	16 05	17 00	17 59	19 38	22 35	24 50	00 50
64	16 14	17 04	18 00	20 39	22 58	25 01	01 01
62	16 22	17 09	18 00	21 13	23 15	25 10	01 10
60	16 29	17 12	18 01	21 38	23 30	25 18	01 18
N 58	16 35	17 16	18 02	21 57	23 42	25 25	01 25
56	16 41	17 19	18 02	22 14	23 53	25 31	01 31
54	16 45	17 22	18 03	22 27	24 02	00 02	01 36
52	16 50	17 24	18 04	22 39	24 10	00 10	01 41
50	16 54	17 27	18 04	22 50	24 18	00 18	01 45
45	17 02	17 32	18 07	23 12	24 34	00 34	01 55
N 40	17 10	17 37	18 09	23 30	24 46	00 46	02 03
35	17 16	17 42	18 11	23 44	24 57	00 57	02 09
30	17 21	17 46	18 14	23 57	25 07	01 07	02 15
20	17 31	17 53	18 19	24 19	00 19	01 23	02 25
N 10	17 40	18 01	18 26	24 37	00 37	01 37	02 34
0	17 48	18 09	18 33	24 55	00 55	01 50	02 42
S 10	17 56	18 17	18 44	00 17	01 12	02 03	02 50
20	18 05	18 28	18 54	00 39	01 30	02 16	02 58
30	18 15	18 40	19 09	01 05	01 51	02 32	03 08
35	18 21	18 48	19 19	01 19	02 03	02 41	03 13
40	18 28	18 57	19 32	01 36	02 17	02 51	03 19
45	18 36	19 07	19 45	01 57	02 34	03 02	03 26
S 50	18 46	19 21	20 04	02 22	02 54	03 17	03 35
52	18 50	19 27	20 13	02 35	03 03	03 23	03 39
54	18 55	19 34	20 24	02 49	03 14	03 30	03 43
56	19 01	19 42	20 36	03 05	03 26	03 39	03 48
58	19 07	19 52	20 51	03 24	03 39	03 48	03 53
S 60	19 14	20 02	21 09	03 48	03 55	03 58	03 59

SUN / MOON

Day	Eqn. of Time 00h	Eqn. of Time 12h	Mer. Pass.	Mer. Pass. Upper	Mer. Pass. Lower	Age	Phase
d	m s	m s	h m	h m	h m	d	%
22	15 25	15 30	11 45	18 41	06 12	08	54
23	15 34	15 38	11 44	19 37	07 09	09	65
24	15 42	15 46	11 44	20 30	08 04	10	76

© British Crown Copyright 2022. All rights reserved.

UT	ARIES	VENUS −4·5		MARS +1·5		JUPITER −2·9		SATURN +0·6		STARS		
d h	GHA	GHA	Dec	GHA	Dec	GHA	Dec	GHA	Dec	Name	SHA	Dec
25 00	33 07.6	227 02.6 N 5 54.4		176 43.9 S14 17.6		353 21.9 N14 00.4		59 49.5 S12 53.9		Acamar	315 12.1	S40 12.4
01	48 10.1	242 02.6	53.7	191 44.7	18.2	8 24.7	00.3	74 52.0	53.9	Achernar	335 20.3	S57 07.0
02	63 12.5	257 02.7	52.9	206 45.5	18.8	23 27.5	00.2	89 54.5	53.9	Acrux	173 01.9	S63 13.6
03	78 15.0	272 02.7 ..	52.2	221 46.3 ..	19.4	38 30.2 ..	00.1	104 57.0 ..	53.9	Adhara	255 06.5	S29 00.0
04	93 17.4	287 02.7	51.4	236 47.1	19.9	53 33.0 14 00.0		119 59.5	53.9	Aldebaran	290 40.5	N16 33.5
05	108 19.9	302 02.8	50.7	251 47.9	20.5	68 35.8 13 59.9		135 02.0	53.9			
06	123 22.4	317 02.8 N 5 49.9		266 48.7 S14 21.1		83 38.6 N13 59.8		150 04.5 S12 53.9		Alioth	166 14.4	N55 49.8
W 07	138 24.8	332 02.9	49.2	281 49.5	21.6	98 41.4	59.7	165 07.0	53.9	Alkaid	152 53.3	N49 11.7
E 08	153 27.3	347 02.9	48.5	296 50.3	22.2	113 44.2	59.6	180 09.6	53.9	Alnair	27 34.0	S46 50.9
D 09	168 29.8	2 02.9 ..	47.7	311 51.1 ..	22.8	128 47.0 ..	59.5	195 12.1 ..	54.0	Alnilam	275 38.6	S 1 11.1
N 10	183 32.2	17 03.0	47.0	326 51.9	23.4	143 49.8	59.4	210 14.6	54.0	Alphard	217 48.9	S 8 45.5
E 11	198 34.7	32 03.0	46.2	341 52.7	23.9	158 52.6	59.3	225 17.1	54.0			
S 12	213 37.2	47 03.1 N 5 45.5		356 53.4 S14 24.5		173 55.3 N13 59.2		240 19.6 S12 54.0		Alphecca	126 05.0	N26 38.2
D 13	228 39.6	62 03.1	44.7	11 54.2	25.1	188 58.1	59.1	255 22.1	54.0	Alpheratz	357 35.5	N29 13.4
A 14	243 42.1	77 03.1	44.0	26 55.0	25.6	204 00.9	59.0	270 24.6	54.0	Altair	62 01.0	N 8 56.0
Y 15	258 44.6	92 03.2 ..	43.2	41 55.8 ..	26.2	219 03.7 ..	58.9	285 27.1 ..	54.0	Ankaa	353 07.8	S42 10.7
16	273 47.0	107 03.2	42.5	56 56.6	26.8	234 06.5	58.8	300 29.6	54.0	Antares	112 17.4	S26 29.1
17	288 49.5	122 03.2	41.7	71 57.4	27.3	249 09.3	58.7	315 32.1	54.0			
18	303 51.9	137 03.3 N 5 41.0		86 58.2 S14 27.9		264 12.1 N13 58.6		330 34.6 S12 54.1		Arcturus	145 49.2	N19 03.6
19	318 54.4	152 03.3	40.2	101 59.0	28.5	279 14.9	58.5	345 37.1	54.1	Atria	107 13.0	S69 04.3
20	333 56.9	167 03.3	39.5	116 59.8	29.1	294 17.7	58.4	0 39.6	54.1	Avior	234 15.2	S59 34.7
21	348 59.3	182 03.4 ..	38.7	132 00.6 ..	29.6	309 20.4 ..	58.3	15 42.1 ..	54.1	Bellatrix	278 23.8	N 6 22.4
22	4 01.8	197 03.4	38.0	147 01.4	30.2	324 23.2	58.2	30 44.6	54.1	Betelgeuse	270 53.0	N 7 24.8
23	19 04.3	212 03.4	37.2	162 02.2	30.8	339 26.0	58.1	45 47.1	54.1			
26 00	34 06.7	227 03.5 N 5 36.4		177 02.9 S14 31.3		354 28.8 N13 58.0		60 49.6 S12 54.1		Canopus	263 52.6	S52 42.1
01	49 09.2	242 03.5	35.7	192 03.7	31.9	9 31.6	57.9	75 52.1	54.1	Capella	280 23.1	N46 01.2
02	64 11.7	257 03.5	34.9	207 04.5	32.5	24 34.4	57.8	90 54.6	54.1	Deneb	49 26.5	N45 22.1
03	79 14.1	272 03.6 ..	34.2	222 05.3 ..	33.0	39 37.2 ..	57.7	105 57.1 ..	54.1	Denebola	182 26.3	N14 26.5
04	94 16.6	287 03.6	33.4	237 06.1	33.6	54 40.0	57.6	120 59.6	54.2	Diphda	348 48.0	S17 51.3
05	109 19.0	302 03.6	32.7	252 06.9	34.2	69 42.8	57.5	136 02.1	54.2			
06	124 21.5	317 03.6 N 5 31.9		267 07.7 S14 34.7		84 45.5 N13 57.4		151 04.7 S12 54.2		Dubhe	193 42.7	N61 37.2
T 07	139 24.0	332 03.7	31.1	282 08.5	35.3	99 48.3	57.3	166 07.2	54.2	Elnath	278 02.9	N28 37.6
H 08	154 26.4	347 03.7	30.4	297 09.3	35.9	114 51.1	57.2	181 09.7	54.2	Eltanin	90 43.0	N51 29.3
U 09	169 28.9	2 03.7 ..	29.6	312 10.0 ..	36.4	129 53.9 ..	57.1	196 12.2 ..	54.2	Enif	33 39.7	N 9 59.1
R 10	184 31.4	17 03.8	28.8	327 10.8	37.0	144 56.7	57.0	211 14.7	54.2	Fomalhaut	15 15.4	S29 29.8
S 11	199 33.8	32 03.8	28.1	342 11.6	37.6	159 59.5	56.9	226 17.2	54.2			
D 12	214 36.3	47 03.8 N 5 27.3		357 12.4 S14 38.1		175 02.3 N13 56.8		241 19.7 S12 54.2		Gacrux	171 53.4	S57 14.6
A 13	229 38.8	62 03.8	26.6	12 13.2	38.7	190 05.1	56.7	256 22.2	54.2	Gienah	175 44.9	S17 40.2
Y 14	244 41.2	77 03.9	25.8	27 14.0	39.3	205 07.9	56.6	271 24.7	54.3	Hadar	148 38.2	S60 29.1
15	259 43.7	92 03.9 ..	25.0	42 14.8 ..	39.8	220 10.7 ..	56.5	286 27.2 ..	54.3	Hamal	327 52.0	N23 34.6
16	274 46.2	107 03.9	24.3	57 15.6	40.4	235 13.5	56.4	301 29.7	54.3	Kaus Aust.	83 34.1	S34 22.5
17	289 48.6	122 03.9	23.5	72 16.3	41.0	250 16.2	56.3	316 32.2	54.3			
18	304 51.1	137 04.0 N 5 22.7		87 17.1 S14 41.5		265 19.0 N13 56.2		331 34.7 S12 54.2		Kochab	137 20.9	N74 03.5
19	319 53.5	152 04.0	22.0	102 17.9	42.1	280 21.8	56.1	346 37.2	54.3	Markab	13 30.7	N15 20.1
20	334 56.0	167 04.0	21.2	117 18.7	42.7	295 24.6	56.0	1 39.7	54.3	Menkar	314 06.9	N 4 11.1
21	349 58.5	182 04.0 ..	20.4	132 19.5 ..	43.2	310 27.4 ..	55.9	16 42.2 ..	54.3	Menkent	147 59.3	S36 29.1
22	5 00.9	197 04.0	19.6	147 20.3	43.8	325 30.2	55.8	31 44.7	54.3	Miaplacidus	221 38.7	S69 48.5
23	20 03.4	212 04.1	18.9	162 21.1	44.4	340 33.0	55.7	46 47.2	54.3			
27 00	35 05.9	227 04.1 N 5 18.1		177 21.8 S14 44.9		355 35.8 N13 55.6		61 49.7 S12 54.3		Mirfak	308 29.3	N49 56.7
01	50 08.3	242 04.1	17.3	192 22.6	45.5	10 38.6	55.5	76 52.2	54.3	Nunki	75 49.2	S26 16.1
02	65 10.8	257 04.1	16.6	207 23.4	46.0	25 41.4	55.4	91 54.7	54.4	Peacock	53 07.3	S56 39.7
03	80 13.3	272 04.1 ..	15.8	222 24.2 ..	46.6	40 44.2 ..	55.3	106 57.2 ..	54.4	Pollux	243 18.5	N27 58.1
04	95 15.7	287 04.2	15.0	237 25.0	47.2	55 46.9	55.2	121 59.7	54.4	Procyon	244 51.9	N 5 10.0
05	110 18.2	302 04.2	14.2	252 25.8	47.7	70 49.7	55.1	137 02.2	54.4			
06	125 20.7	317 04.2 N 5 13.5		267 26.5 S14 48.3		85 52.5 N13 55.0		152 04.7 S12 54.4		Rasalhague	96 59.7	N12 32.7
F 07	140 23.1	332 04.2	12.7	282 27.3	48.9	100 55.3	54.9	167 07.2	54.4	Regulus	207 35.7	N11 51.2
R 08	155 25.6	347 04.2	11.9	297 28.1	49.4	115 58.1	54.8	182 09.7	54.4	Rigel	281 04.6	S 8 10.3
I 09	170 28.0	2 04.2 ..	11.1	312 28.9 ..	50.0	131 00.9 ..	54.7	197 12.2 ..	54.4	Rigil Kent.	139 42.4	S60 55.9
D 10	185 30.5	17 04.3	10.4	327 29.7	50.5	146 03.7	54.6	212 14.7	54.4	Sabik	102 04.2	S15 45.2
A 11	200 33.0	32 04.3	09.6	342 30.5	51.1	161 06.5	54.5	227 17.2	54.4			
Y 12	215 35.4	47 04.3 N 5 08.8		357 31.2 S14 51.7		176 09.3 N13 54.4		242 19.7 S12 54.4		Schedar	349 31.7	N56 40.2
13	230 37.9	62 04.3	08.0	12 32.0	52.2	191 12.1	54.3	257 22.2	54.4	Shaula	96 12.0	S37 07.3
14	245 40.4	77 04.3	07.2	27 32.8	52.8	206 14.9	54.2	272 24.7	54.5	Sirius	258 27.0	S16 44.7
15	260 42.8	92 04.3 ..	06.5	42 33.6 ..	53.4	221 17.7 ..	54.0	287 27.1 ..	54.5	Spica	158 23.7	S11 17.0
16	275 45.3	107 04.3	05.7	57 34.4	53.9	236 20.5	53.9	302 29.6	54.5	Suhail	222 47.2	S43 31.3
17	290 47.8	122 04.4	04.9	72 35.1	54.5	251 23.2	53.8	317 32.1	54.5			
18	305 50.2	137 04.4 N 5 04.1		87 35.9 S14 55.0		266 26.0 N13 53.7		332 34.6 S12 54.5		Vega	80 34.1	N38 48.5
19	320 52.7	152 04.4	03.3	102 36.7	55.6	281 28.8	53.6	347 37.1	54.5	Zuben'ubi	136 57.5	S16 08.3
20	335 55.1	167 04.4	02.5	117 37.5	56.2	296 31.6	53.5	2 39.6	54.5		SHA	Mer. Pass.
21	350 57.6	182 04.4 ..	01.8	132 38.3 ..	56.7	311 34.4 ..	53.4	17 42.1 ..	54.5			
22	6 00.1	197 04.4	01.0	147 39.0	57.3	326 37.2	53.3	32 44.6	54.5	Venus	192 56.7	8 52
23	21 02.5	212 04.4	00.2	162 39.8	57.8	341 40.0	53.2	47 47.1	54.5	Mars	142 56.2	12 11
	h m									Jupiter	320 22.1	0 22
Mer. Pass. 21 40.0		v 0.0 d 0.8		v 0.8 d 0.6		v 2.8 d 0.1		v 2.5 d 0.0		Saturn	26 42.9	19 53

© British Crown Copyright 2022. All rights reserved.

UT	SUN GHA	SUN Dec	MOON GHA	v	MOON Dec	d	HP
	° ′	° ′	° ′	′	° ′	′	′
25 00	183 57.6	S11 55.8	50 45.9	10.2	S11 34.1	16.0	60.0
01	198 57.7	56.7	65 15.1	10.2	11 18.1	16.1	60.0
02	213 57.8	57.6	79 44.3	10.2	11 02.0	16.1	60.0
03	228 57.8	.. 58.4	94 13.5	10.3	10 45.9	16.2	60.0
04	243 57.9	11 59.3	108 42.8	10.4	10 29.7	16.2	60.0
05	258 58.0	12 00.1	123 12.2	10.4	10 13.5	16.3	60.0
W 06	273 58.1	S12 01.0	137 41.6	10.4	S 9 57.2	16.3	60.0
E 07	288 58.1	01.9	152 11.0	10.5	9 40.9	16.5	60.0
D 08	303 58.2	02.7	166 40.5	10.6	9 24.4	16.4	60.0
N 09	318 58.3	.. 03.6	181 10.1	10.5	9 08.0	16.6	60.0
E 10	333 58.4	04.5	195 39.6	10.7	8 51.4	16.5	60.0
S 11	348 58.4	05.3	210 09.3	10.6	8 34.9	16.7	60.1
D 12	3 58.5	S12 06.2	224 38.9	10.7	S 8 18.2	16.6	60.1
A 13	18 58.6	07.0	239 08.6	10.7	8 01.6	16.8	60.1
Y 14	33 58.7	07.9	253 38.3	10.8	7 44.8	16.7	60.1
15	48 58.7	.. 08.8	268 08.1	10.8	7 28.1	16.8	60.1
16	63 58.8	09.6	282 37.9	10.8	7 11.3	16.9	60.1
17	78 58.9	10.5	297 07.7	10.9	6 54.4	16.9	60.1
18	93 58.9	S12 11.3	311 37.6	10.9	S 6 37.5	16.9	60.1
19	108 59.0	12.2	326 07.5	10.9	6 20.6	17.0	60.1
20	123 59.1	13.1	340 37.4	11.0	6 03.6	17.0	60.1
21	138 59.2	.. 13.9	355 07.4	11.0	5 46.6	17.0	60.1
22	153 59.2	14.8	9 37.4	11.0	5 29.6	17.1	60.1
23	168 59.3	15.6	24 07.4	11.0	5 12.5	17.1	60.1
26 00	183 59.4	S12 16.5	38 37.4	11.1	S 4 55.4	17.1	60.1
01	198 59.4	17.3	53 07.5	11.1	4 38.3	17.2	60.1
02	213 59.5	18.2	67 37.6	11.1	4 21.1	17.1	60.1
03	228 59.6	.. 19.1	82 07.7	11.1	4 04.0	17.2	60.1
04	243 59.7	19.9	96 37.8	11.2	3 46.8	17.3	60.1
05	258 59.7	20.8	111 08.0	11.1	3 29.5	17.2	60.1
T 06	273 59.8	S12 21.6	125 38.1	11.2	S 3 12.3	17.2	60.1
H 07	288 59.9	22.5	140 08.3	11.2	2 55.1	17.3	60.1
U 08	303 59.9	23.3	154 38.5	11.2	2 37.8	17.3	60.1
R 09	319 00.0	.. 24.2	169 08.7	11.3	2 20.5	17.3	60.1
S 10	334 00.1	25.0	183 39.0	11.2	2 03.2	17.3	60.1
D 11	349 00.1	25.9	198 09.2	11.2	1 45.9	17.3	60.1
A 12	4 00.2	S12 26.8	212 39.4	11.3	S 1 28.6	17.3	60.1
Y 13	19 00.3	27.6	227 09.7	11.3	1 11.3	17.4	60.1
14	34 00.3	28.5	241 40.0	11.3	0 53.9	17.3	60.1
15	49 00.4	.. 29.3	256 10.3	11.2	0 36.6	17.3	60.1
16	64 00.5	30.2	270 40.5	11.3	0 19.3	17.4	60.1
17	79 00.5	31.0	285 10.8	11.3	S 0 01.9	17.3	60.1
18	94 00.6	S12 31.9	299 41.1	11.3	N 0 15.4	17.3	60.1
19	109 00.6	32.7	314 11.4	11.3	0 32.7	17.4	60.1
20	124 00.7	33.6	328 41.7	11.3	0 50.1	17.3	60.0
21	139 00.8	.. 34.4	343 12.0	11.3	1 07.4	17.3	60.0
22	154 00.8	35.3	357 42.3	11.3	1 24.7	17.3	60.0
23	169 00.9	36.1	12 12.6	11.3	1 42.0	17.3	60.0
27 00	184 01.0	S12 37.0	26 42.9	11.2	N 1 59.3	17.2	60.0
01	199 01.0	37.8	41 13.1	11.3	2 16.5	17.3	60.0
02	214 01.1	38.7	55 43.4	11.3	2 33.8	17.2	60.0
03	229 01.2	.. 39.5	70 13.7	11.2	2 51.0	17.3	60.0
04	244 01.2	40.4	84 43.9	11.3	3 08.3	17.2	60.0
05	259 01.3	41.2	99 14.2	11.2	3 25.5	17.1	60.0
F 06	274 01.3	S12 42.0	113 44.4	11.3	N 3 42.6	17.2	60.0
R 07	289 01.4	42.9	128 14.7	11.2	3 59.8	17.1	60.0
I 08	304 01.5	43.7	142 44.9	11.2	4 16.9	17.1	59.9
D 09	319 01.5	.. 44.6	157 15.1	11.2	4 34.0	17.1	59.9
A 10	334 01.6	45.4	171 45.3	11.1	4 51.1	17.0	59.9
Y 11	349 01.6	46.3	186 15.4	11.2	5 08.1	17.0	59.9
12	4 01.7	S12 47.1	200 45.6	11.1	N 5 25.1	17.0	59.9
13	19 01.8	48.0	215 15.7	11.1	5 42.1	16.9	59.9
14	34 01.8	48.8	229 45.8	11.1	5 59.0	16.9	59.9
15	49 01.9	.. 49.7	244 15.9	11.1	6 15.9	16.9	59.9
16	64 01.9	50.5	258 46.0	11.1	6 32.8	16.8	59.8
17	79 02.0	51.3	273 16.1	11.0	6 49.6	16.7	59.8
18	94 02.0	S12 52.2	287 46.1	11.0	N 7 06.3	16.8	59.8
19	109 02.1	53.0	302 16.1	11.0	7 23.1	16.6	59.8
20	124 02.2	53.9	316 46.1	10.9	7 39.7	16.7	59.8
21	139 02.2	.. 54.7	331 16.0	10.9	7 56.4	16.5	59.8
22	154 02.3	55.6	345 45.9	10.9	8 12.9	16.6	59.8
23	169 02.3	56.4	0 15.8	10.9	N 8 29.5	16.4	59.7
	SD 16.1	d 0.9	SD 16.4		16.4		16.3

Lat.	Twilight Naut.	Civil	Sunrise	Moonrise 25	26	27	28
°	h m	h m	h m	h m	h m	h m	h m
N 72	05 41	07 01	08 20	16 42	16 03	15 25	14 38
N 70	05 39	06 51	08 00	16 32	16 03	15 34	15 00
68	05 38	06 44	07 45	16 24	16 02	15 41	15 17
66	05 37	06 37	07 33	16 17	16 02	15 47	15 31
64	05 36	06 31	07 22	16 11	16 01	15 52	15 42
62	05 35	06 27	07 14	16 06	16 01	15 57	15 52
60	05 33	06 22	07 06	16 01	16 01	16 00	16 00
N 58	05 32	06 18	06 59	15 57	16 01	16 04	16 08
56	05 31	06 15	06 54	15 54	16 00	16 07	16 15
54	05 30	06 11	06 48	15 51	16 00	16 10	16 21
52	05 29	06 09	06 43	15 48	16 00	16 12	16 26
50	05 28	06 06	06 39	15 45	16 00	16 15	16 31
45	05 25	06 00	06 30	15 39	16 00	16 20	16 42
N 40	05 22	05 54	06 22	15 34	15 59	16 24	16 51
35	05 20	05 49	06 15	15 30	15 59	16 28	16 58
30	05 17	05 45	06 09	15 26	15 59	16 31	17 05
20	05 10	05 36	05 59	15 20	15 58	16 37	17 17
N 10	05 03	05 28	05 49	15 14	15 58	16 42	17 27
0	04 55	05 19	05 41	15 08	15 58	16 47	17 37
S 10	04 45	05 10	05 32	15 03	15 58	16 52	17 47
20	04 33	04 59	05 22	14 57	15 57	16 58	17 58
30	04 17	04 46	05 11	14 50	15 57	17 04	18 11
35	04 06	04 38	05 05	14 47	15 57	17 07	18 18
40	03 54	04 29	04 57	14 42	15 57	17 11	18 26
45	03 39	04 17	04 49	14 37	15 57	17 16	18 36
S 50	03 19	04 03	04 38	14 31	15 57	17 22	18 48
52	03 09	03 56	04 33	14 28	15 56	17 25	18 53
54	02 58	03 49	04 28	14 25	15 56	17 28	19 00
56	02 45	03 40	04 22	14 21	15 56	17 31	19 06
58	02 29	03 30	04 15	14 18	15 56	17 35	19 14
S 60	02 10	03 19	04 08	14 13	15 56	17 39	19 23

Lat.	Sunset	Twilight Civil	Naut.	Moonset 25	26	27	28
°	h m	h m	h m	h m	h m	h m	h m
N 72	15 07	16 25	17 45	26 37	02 37	05 04	07 38
N 70	15 26	16 35	17 47	00 20	02 43	04 59	07 19
68	15 42	16 43	17 48	00 36	02 48	04 55	07 05
66	15 54	16 50	17 50	00 50	02 53	04 52	06 53
64	16 04	16 55	17 51	01 01	02 56	04 49	06 43
62	16 13	17 00	17 52	01 10	02 59	04 47	06 35
60	16 21	17 05	17 53	01 18	03 02	04 45	06 28
N 58	16 28	17 09	17 55	01 25	03 04	04 43	06 21
56	16 34	17 12	17 56	01 31	03 07	04 41	06 16
54	16 39	17 16	17 57	01 36	03 08	04 40	06 11
52	16 44	17 19	17 58	01 41	03 10	04 38	06 07
50	16 48	17 21	17 59	01 45	03 12	04 37	06 03
45	16 58	17 28	18 02	01 55	03 15	04 35	05 54
N 40	17 06	17 33	18 05	02 03	03 18	04 32	05 47
35	17 12	17 38	18 08	02 09	03 20	04 31	05 41
30	17 18	17 43	18 11	02 15	03 22	04 29	05 36
20	17 29	17 52	18 17	02 25	03 26	04 26	05 26
N 10	17 38	18 00	18 25	02 34	03 29	04 23	05 18
0	17 47	18 09	18 33	02 42	03 32	04 21	05 11
S 10	17 56	18 18	18 43	02 50	03 35	04 19	05 03
20	18 06	18 29	18 56	02 58	03 38	04 16	04 55
30	18 17	18 42	19 12	03 08	03 41	04 13	04 46
35	18 24	18 51	19 22	03 13	03 43	04 12	04 41
40	18 32	19 00	19 34	03 19	03 45	04 10	04 35
45	18 40	19 12	19 50	03 26	03 48	04 08	04 28
S 50	18 51	19 26	20 11	03 35	03 50	04 05	04 20
52	18 56	19 33	20 21	03 39	03 52	04 04	04 17
54	19 01	19 41	20 32	03 43	03 53	04 03	04 13
56	19 08	19 50	20 45	03 48	03 55	04 01	04 08
58	19 14	20 00	21 01	03 53	03 56	04 00	04 03
S 60	19 22	20 11	21 21	03 59	03 58	03 58	03 58

	SUN Eqn. of Time 00h	12h	Mer. Pass.	MOON Mer. Pass. Upper	Lower	Age	Phase
Day	m s	m s	h m	h m	h m	d	%
25	15 50	15 54	11 44	21 20	08 55	11	85
26	15 57	16 01	11 44	22 10	09 45	12	93
27	16 04	16 07	11 44	22 59	10 34	13	98

© British Crown Copyright 2022. All rights reserved.

UT	ARIES GHA	VENUS −4.4 GHA	Dec	MARS +1.5 GHA	Dec	JUPITER −2.9 GHA	Dec	SATURN +0.7 GHA	Dec
28 00	36 05.0	227 04.4	N 4 59.4	177 40.6	S14 58.4	356 42.8	N13 53.1	62 49.6	S12 54.5
01	51 07.5	242 04.4	58.6	192 41.4	59.0	11 45.6	53.0	77 52.1	54.5
02	66 09.9	257 04.4	57.8	207 42.2	14 59.5	26 48.4	52.9	92 54.4	54.5
03	81 12.4	272 04.4 ..	57.0	222 42.9	15 00.1	41 51.2 ..	52.8	107 57.1 ..	54.5
04	96 14.9	287 04.5	56.2	237 43.7	00.6	56 54.0	52.7	122 59.6	54.6
05	111 17.3	302 04.5	55.5	252 44.5	01.2	71 56.8	52.6	138 02.1	54.6
S 06	126 19.8	317 04.5	N 4 54.7	267 45.3	S15 01.8	86 59.6	N13 52.5	153 04.6	S12 54.6
A 07	141 22.3	332 04.5	53.9	282 46.1	02.3	102 02.3	52.4	168 07.1	54.6
T 08	156 24.7	347 04.5	53.1	297 46.8	02.9	117 05.1	52.3	183 09.6	54.6
U 09	171 27.2	2 04.5 ..	52.3	312 47.6 ..	03.4	132 07.9 ..	52.2	198 12.1 ..	54.6
R 10	186 29.6	17 04.5	51.5	327 48.4	04.0	147 10.7	52.1	213 14.6	54.6
D 11	201 32.1	32 04.5	50.7	342 49.2	04.5	162 13.5	52.0	228 17.1	54.6
A 12	216 34.6	47 04.5	N 4 49.9	357 49.9	S15 05.1	177 16.3	N13 51.9	243 19.6	S12 54.6
Y 13	231 37.0	62 04.5	49.1	12 50.7	05.7	192 19.1	51.8	258 22.0	54.6
14	246 39.5	77 04.5	48.3	27 51.5	06.2	207 21.9	51.7	273 24.5	54.6
15	261 42.0	92 04.5 ..	47.5	42 52.3 ..	06.8	222 24.7 ..	51.6	288 27.0 ..	54.6
16	276 44.4	107 04.5	46.7	57 53.0	07.3	237 27.5	51.5	303 29.5	54.6
17	291 46.9	122 04.5	45.9	72 53.8	07.9	252 30.3	51.4	318 32.0	54.6
18	306 49.4	137 04.5	N 4 45.1	87 54.6	S15 08.4	267 33.1	N13 51.3	333 34.5	S12 54.6
19	321 51.8	152 04.5	44.3	102 55.4	09.0	282 35.9	51.2	348 37.0	54.6
20	336 54.3	167 04.5	43.5	117 56.1	09.6	297 38.7	51.1	3 39.5	54.7
21	351 56.7	182 04.5 ..	42.7	132 56.9 ..	10.1	312 41.5 ..	51.0	18 42.0 ..	54.7
22	6 59.2	197 04.5	41.9	147 57.7	10.7	327 44.3	50.9	33 44.5	54.7
23	22 01.7	212 04.5	41.1	162 58.5	11.2	342 47.1	50.8	48 47.0	54.7
29 00	37 04.1	227 04.5	N 4 40.3	177 59.2	S15 11.8	357 49.8	N13 50.7	63 49.5	S12 54.7
01	52 06.6	242 04.5	39.5	193 00.0	12.3	12 52.6	50.6	78 52.0	54.7
02	67 09.1	257 04.5	38.7	208 00.8	12.9	27 55.4	50.5	93 54.4	54.7
03	82 11.5	272 04.5 ..	37.9	223 01.6 ..	13.5	42 58.2 ..	50.4	108 56.9 ..	54.7
04	97 14.0	287 04.5	37.1	238 02.3	14.0	58 01.0	50.3	123 59.4	54.7
05	112 16.5	302 04.5	36.3	253 03.1	14.6	73 03.8	50.2	139 01.9	54.7
S 06	127 18.9	317 04.5	N 4 35.5	268 03.9	S15 15.1	88 06.6	N13 50.1	154 04.4	S12 54.7
U 07	142 21.4	332 04.5	34.7	283 04.6	15.7	103 09.4	50.0	169 06.9	54.7
N 08	157 23.9	347 04.5	33.9	298 05.4	16.2	118 12.2	49.9	184 09.4	54.7
D 09	172 26.3	2 04.5 ..	33.1	313 06.2 ..	16.8	133 15.0 ..	49.8	199 11.9 ..	54.7
A 10	187 28.8	17 04.5	32.3	328 07.0	17.3	148 17.8	49.7	214 14.4	54.7
Y 11	202 31.2	32 04.4	31.5	343 07.7	17.9	163 20.6	49.6	229 16.9	54.7
12	217 33.7	47 04.4	N 4 30.7	358 08.5	S15 18.4	178 23.4	N13 49.5	244 19.4	S12 54.7
13	232 36.2	62 04.4	29.9	13 09.3	19.0	193 26.2	49.4	259 21.8	54.7
14	247 38.6	77 04.4	29.1	28 10.0	19.5	208 29.0	49.3	274 24.3	54.7
15	262 41.1	92 04.4 ..	28.3	43 10.8 ..	20.1	223 31.8 ..	49.2	289 26.8 ..	54.7
16	277 43.6	107 04.4	27.4	58 11.6	20.6	238 34.6	49.1	304 29.3	54.8
17	292 46.0	122 04.4	26.6	73 12.4	21.2	253 37.4	49.0	319 31.8	54.8
18	307 48.5	137 04.4	N 4 25.8	88 13.1	S15 21.8	268 40.2	N13 48.9	334 34.3	S12 54.8
19	322 51.0	152 04.4	25.0	103 13.9	22.3	283 42.9	48.8	349 36.8	54.8
20	337 53.4	167 04.4	24.2	118 14.7	22.9	298 45.7	48.7	4 39.3	54.8
21	352 55.9	182 04.4 ..	23.4	133 15.4 ..	23.4	313 48.5 ..	48.6	19 41.8 ..	54.8
22	7 58.4	197 04.3	22.6	148 16.2	24.0	328 51.3	48.5	34 44.2	54.8
23	23 00.8	212 04.3	21.8	163 17.0	24.5	343 54.1	48.4	49 46.7	54.8
30 00	38 03.3	227 04.3	N 4 20.9	178 17.7	S15 25.1	358 56.9	N13 48.3	64 49.2	S12 54.8
01	53 05.7	242 04.3	20.1	193 18.5	25.6	13 59.7	48.1	79 51.7	54.8
02	68 08.2	257 04.3	19.3	208 19.3	26.2	29 02.5	48.0	94 54.2	54.8
03	83 10.7	272 04.3 ..	18.5	223 20.0 ..	26.7	44 05.3 ..	47.9	109 56.7 ..	54.8
04	98 13.1	287 04.3	17.7	238 20.8	27.3	59 08.1	47.8	124 59.2	54.8
05	113 15.6	302 04.2	16.8	253 21.6	27.8	74 10.9	47.7	140 01.7	54.8
M 06	128 18.1	317 04.2	N 4 16.0	268 22.3	S15 28.4	89 13.7	N13 47.6	155 04.1	S12 54.8
O 07	143 20.5	332 04.2	15.2	283 23.1	28.9	104 16.5	47.5	170 06.6	54.8
N 08	158 23.0	347 04.2	14.4	298 23.9	29.5	119 19.3	47.4	185 09.1	54.8
D 09	173 25.5	2 04.2 ..	13.6	313 24.6 ..	30.0	134 22.1 ..	47.3	200 11.6 ..	54.8
A 10	188 27.9	17 04.2	12.7	328 25.4	30.6	149 24.9	47.2	215 14.1	54.8
Y 11	203 30.4	32 04.1	11.9	343 26.2	31.1	164 27.7	47.1	230 16.6	54.8
12	218 32.8	47 04.1	N 4 11.1	358 26.9	S15 31.7	179 30.5	N13 47.0	245 19.1	S12 54.8
13	233 35.3	62 04.1	10.3	13 27.7	32.2	194 33.3	46.9	260 21.5	54.8
14	248 37.8	77 04.1	09.5	28 28.5	32.8	209 36.1	46.8	275 24.0	54.8
15	263 40.2	92 04.1 ..	08.6	43 29.2 ..	33.3	224 38.9 ..	46.7	290 26.5 ..	54.8
16	278 42.7	107 04.1	07.8	58 30.0	33.9	239 41.7	46.6	305 29.0	54.8
17	293 45.2	122 04.0	07.0	73 30.8	34.4	254 44.5	46.5	320 31.5	54.8
18	308 47.6	137 04.0	N 4 06.2	88 31.5	S15 34.9	269 47.2	N13 46.4	335 34.0	S12 54.8
19	323 50.1	152 04.0	05.3	103 32.3	35.5	284 50.0	46.3	350 36.4	54.8
20	338 52.6	167 04.0	04.5	118 33.0	36.0	299 52.8	46.2	5 38.9	54.8
21	353 55.0	182 04.0 ..	03.7	133 33.8 ..	36.6	314 55.6 ..	46.1	20 41.4 ..	54.9
22	8 57.5	197 03.9	02.9	148 34.6	37.1	329 58.4	46.0	35 43.9	54.9
23	24 00.0	212 03.9	02.0	163 35.3	37.7	345 01.2	45.9	50 46.4	54.9
Mer. Pass.	21 28.2	v 0.0	d 0.8	v 0.8	d 0.6	v 2.8	d 0.1	v 2.5	d 0.0

STARS

Name	SHA	Dec
Acamar	315 12.1	S40 12.4
Achernar	335 20.3	S57 07.0
Acrux	173 01.9	S63 13.6
Adhara	255 06.5	S29 00.0
Aldebaran	290 40.5	N16 33.5
Alioth	166 14.4	N55 49.8
Alkaid	152 53.3	N49 11.7
Alnair	27 34.0	S46 50.9
Alnilam	275 38.5	S 1 11.1
Alphard	217 48.8	S 8 45.5
Alphecca	126 05.0	N26 38.2
Alpheratz	357 35.5	N29 13.5
Altair	62 01.0	N 8 56.0
Ankaa	353 07.8	S42 10.7
Antares	112 17.4	S26 29.1
Arcturus	145 49.2	N19 03.6
Atria	107 13.0	S69 04.3
Avior	234 15.1	S59 34.7
Bellatrix	278 23.7	N 6 22.4
Betelgeuse	270 53.0	N 7 24.8
Canopus	263 52.6	S52 42.1
Capella	280 23.1	N46 01.2
Deneb	49 26.5	N45 22.1
Denebola	182 26.2	N14 26.4
Diphda	348 48.0	S17 51.3
Dubhe	193 42.6	N61 37.2
Elnath	278 02.9	N28 37.6
Eltanin	90 43.0	N51 29.3
Enif	33 39.7	N 9 59.1
Fomalhaut	15 15.4	S29 29.9
Gacrux	171 53.3	S57 14.5
Gienah	175 44.9	S17 40.2
Hadar	148 38.2	S60 29.1
Hamal	327 52.0	N23 34.6
Kaus Aust.	83 34.1	S34 22.5
Kochab	137 20.9	N74 03.5
Markab	13 30.7	N15 20.1
Menkar	314 06.9	N 4 11.1
Menkent	147 59.2	S36 29.1
Miaplacidus	221 38.7	S69 48.5
Mirfak	308 29.2	N49 56.7
Nunki	75 49.2	S26 16.1
Peacock	53 07.3	S56 39.7
Pollux	243 18.5	N27 58.1
Procyon	244 51.8	N 5 10.0
Rasalhague	95 59.7	N12 32.7
Regulus	207 35.7	N11 51.2
Rigel	281 04.6	S 8 10.3
Rigil Kent.	139 42.4	S60 55.9
Sabik	102 04.2	S15 45.2
Schedar	349 31.7	N56 40.2
Shaula	96 12.0	S37 07.3
Sirius	258 27.0	S16 44.7
Spica	158 23.7	S11 17.0
Suhail	222 47.2	S43 31.3
Vega	80 34.1	N38 48.5
Zuben'ubi	136 57.5	S16 08.3

	SHA	Mer. Pass.
Venus	190 00.4	8 52
Mars	140 55.1	12 07
Jupiter	320 45.7	0 09
Saturn	26 45.3	19 41

© British Crown Copyright 2022. All rights reserved.

SUN / MOON

UT	SUN GHA	SUN Dec	MOON GHA	v	MOON Dec	d	HP
d h	° ′	° ′	° ′	′	° ′	′	′
28 00	184 02.4	S12 57.2	14 45.7	10.8	N 8 45.9	16.4	59.7
01	199 02.4	58.1	29 15.5	10.8	9 02.3	16.4	59.7
02	214 02.5	58.9	43 45.3	10.8	9 18.7	16.3	59.7
03	229 02.5	12 59.8	58 15.1	10.7	9 35.0	16.2	59.7
04	244 02.6	13 00.6	72 44.8	10.7	9 51.2	16.2	59.7
05	259 02.6	01.4	87 14.5	10.7	10 07.4	16.1	59.6
06	274 02.7	S13 02.3	101 44.2	10.6	N10 23.5	16.1	59.6
07	289 02.8	03.1	116 13.8	10.6	10 39.6	16.0	59.6
S 08	304 02.8	04.0	130 43.4	10.5	10 55.6	15.9	59.6
A 09	319 02.9	04.8	145 12.9	10.5	11 11.5	15.8	59.6
T 10	334 02.9	05.6	159 42.4	10.5	11 27.3	15.8	59.5
U 11	349 03.0	06.5	174 11.9	10.4	11 43.1	15.7	59.5
R 12	4 03.0	S13 07.3	188 41.3	10.4	N11 58.8	15.6	59.5
D 13	19 03.1	08.1	203 10.7	10.4	12 14.4	15.5	59.5
A 14	34 03.1	09.0	217 40.1	10.3	12 29.9	15.5	59.5
Y 15	49 03.2	09.8	232 09.4	10.2	12 45.4	15.4	59.4
16	64 03.2	10.6	246 38.6	10.3	13 00.8	15.3	59.4
17	79 03.3	11.5	261 07.9	10.1	13 16.1	15.2	59.4
18	94 03.3	S13 12.3	275 37.0	10.2	N13 31.3	15.2	59.4
19	109 03.4	13.1	290 06.2	10.0	13 46.5	15.0	59.3
20	124 03.4	14.0	304 35.2	10.1	14 01.5	15.0	59.3
21	139 03.5	14.8	319 04.3	10.0	14 16.5	14.8	59.3
22	154 03.5	15.6	333 33.3	9.9	14 31.3	14.8	59.3
23	169 03.6	16.5	348 02.2	9.9	14 46.1	14.7	59.2
29 00	184 03.6	S13 17.3	2 31.1	9.8	N15 00.8	14.6	59.2
01	199 03.6	18.1	16 59.9	9.8	15 15.4	14.5	59.2
02	214 03.7	19.0	31 28.7	9.8	15 29.9	14.4	59.2
03	229 03.7	19.8	45 57.5	9.7	15 44.3	14.3	59.2
04	244 03.8	20.6	60 26.2	9.6	15 58.6	14.2	59.1
05	259 03.8	21.5	74 54.8	9.6	16 12.8	14.1	59.1
06	274 03.9	S13 22.3	89 23.4	9.6	N16 26.9	14.0	59.1
07	289 03.9	23.1	103 52.0	9.4	16 40.9	13.8	59.0
08	304 04.0	24.0	118 20.4	9.5	16 54.7	13.8	59.0
S 09	319 04.0	24.8	132 48.9	9.4	17 08.5	13.7	59.0
U 10	334 04.1	25.6	147 17.3	9.3	17 22.2	13.6	59.0
N 11	349 04.1	26.4	161 45.6	9.3	17 35.8	13.4	58.9
D 12	4 04.1	S13 27.3	176 13.9	9.2	N17 49.2	13.4	58.9
A 13	19 04.2	28.1	190 42.1	9.2	18 02.6	13.2	58.9
Y 14	34 04.2	28.9	205 10.3	9.1	18 15.8	13.1	58.9
15	49 04.3	29.8	219 38.4	9.1	18 28.9	13.0	58.8
16	64 04.3	30.6	234 06.5	9.0	18 41.9	12.9	58.8
17	79 04.4	31.4	248 34.5	9.0	18 54.8	12.7	58.8
18	94 04.4	S13 32.2	263 02.5	8.9	N19 07.5	12.7	58.7
19	109 04.4	33.1	277 30.4	8.8	19 20.2	12.5	58.7
20	124 04.5	33.9	291 58.2	8.8	19 32.7	12.4	58.7
21	139 04.5	34.7	306 26.0	8.8	19 45.1	12.3	58.7
22	154 04.6	35.5	320 53.8	8.7	19 57.4	12.1	58.6
23	169 04.6	36.4	335 21.5	8.6	20 09.5	12.0	58.6
30 00	184 04.6	S13 37.2	349 49.1	8.6	N20 21.5	11.9	58.6
01	199 04.7	38.0	4 16.7	8.5	20 33.4	11.8	58.5
02	214 04.7	38.8	18 44.2	8.5	20 45.2	11.6	58.5
03	229 04.7	39.6	33 11.7	8.5	20 56.8	11.5	58.5
04	244 04.8	40.5	47 39.2	8.3	21 08.3	11.4	58.4
05	259 04.8	41.3	62 06.5	8.4	21 19.7	11.2	58.4
06	274 04.9	S13 42.1	76 33.9	8.3	N21 30.9	11.1	58.4
07	289 04.9	42.9	91 01.2	8.2	21 42.0	10.9	58.3
08	304 04.9	43.8	105 28.4	8.2	21 52.9	10.9	58.3
M 09	319 05.0	44.6	119 55.6	8.1	22 03.8	10.6	58.3
O 10	334 05.0	45.4	134 22.7	8.1	22 14.4	10.6	58.3
N 11	349 05.0	46.2	148 49.8	8.0	22 25.0	10.4	58.2
D 12	4 05.1	S13 47.0	163 16.8	8.0	N22 35.4	10.3	58.2
A 13	19 05.1	47.8	177 43.8	8.0	22 45.7	10.1	58.2
Y 14	34 05.1	48.7	192 10.8	7.9	22 55.8	9.9	58.1
15	49 05.2	49.5	206 37.7	7.8	23 05.7	9.9	58.1
16	64 05.2	50.3	221 04.5	7.8	23 15.6	9.7	58.1
17	79 05.2	51.1	235 31.3	7.8	23 25.3	9.5	58.0
18	94 05.3	S13 51.9	249 58.1	7.7	N23 34.8	9.4	58.0
19	109 05.3	52.8	264 24.8	7.7	23 44.2	9.2	58.0
20	124 05.3	53.6	278 51.5	7.6	23 53.4	9.1	57.9
21	139 05.4	54.4	293 18.1	7.6	24 02.5	9.0	57.9
22	154 05.4	55.2	307 44.7	7.5	24 11.5	8.8	57.9
23	169 05.4	56.0	322 11.2	7.5	N24 20.3	8.6	57.8
	SD 16.1	d 0.8	SD 16.2		16.1		15.9

Twilight / Sunrise / Moonrise

Lat.	Naut.	Civil	Sunrise	Moonrise 28	29	30	31
°	h m	h m	h m	h m	h m	h m	h m
N 72	05 53	07 14	08 37	14 38	12 47	☐	☐
N 70	05 50	07 03	08 14	15 00	14 03	☐	☐
68	05 48	06 54	07 57	15 17	14 42	☐	☐
66	05 46	06 46	07 43	15 31	15 09	14 27	☐
64	05 44	06 40	07 32	15 42	15 30	15 12	☐
62	05 42	06 34	07 22	15 52	15 47	15 42	15 36
60	05 40	06 29	07 14	16 00	16 02	16 05	16 14
N 58	05 38	06 25	07 06	16 08	16 14	16 24	16 41
56	05 37	06 21	07 00	16 15	16 25	16 39	17 02
54	05 35	06 17	06 54	16 21	16 34	16 53	17 20
52	05 34	06 14	06 49	16 26	16 43	17 04	17 35
50	05 32	06 10	06 44	16 31	16 50	17 15	17 48
45	05 29	06 03	06 34	16 42	17 07	17 37	18 15
N 40	05 25	05 57	06 25	16 51	17 20	17 55	18 36
35	05 22	05 52	06 18	16 58	17 32	18 10	18 54
30	05 19	05 47	06 11	17 05	17 42	18 23	19 10
20	05 11	05 37	06 00	17 17	17 59	18 46	19 36
N 10	05 03	05 28	05 50	17 27	18 15	19 05	19 59
0	04 54	05 19	05 40	17 37	18 30	19 24	20 20
S 10	04 44	05 09	05 31	17 47	18 44	19 42	20 41
20	04 31	04 57	05 20	17 58	19 00	20 02	21 04
30	04 13	04 43	05 08	18 11	19 18	20 26	21 31
35	04 03	04 35	05 01	18 18	19 29	20 39	21 47
40	03 50	04 24	04 53	18 26	19 41	20 55	22 05
45	03 33	04 12	04 44	18 36	19 56	21 14	22 28
S 50	03 12	03 57	04 32	18 48	20 14	21 38	22 56
52	03 01	03 50	04 27	18 53	20 23	21 50	23 11
54	02 49	03 41	04 21	19 00	20 32	22 03	23 27
56	02 35	03 32	04 15	19 06	20 43	22 19	23 46
58	02 18	03 21	04 07	19 14	20 56	22 37	24 11
S 60	01 56	03 09	03 59	19 23	21 10	22 59	24 43

Sunset / Twilight / Moonset

Lat.	Sunset	Civil	Naut.	Moonset 28	29	30	31
°	h m	h m	h m	h m	h m	h m	h m
N 72	14 49	16 11	17 33	07 38	11 19	☐	☐
N 70	15 12	16 23	17 35	07 19	10 05	☐	☐
68	15 29	16 32	17 38	07 05	09 28	☐	☐
66	15 43	16 40	17 40	06 53	09 02	11 37	☐
64	15 55	16 46	17 42	06 43	08 42	10 52	☐
62	16 04	16 52	17 44	06 35	08 27	10 23	12 26
60	16 13	16 57	17 46	06 28	08 13	10 01	11 48
N 58	16 20	17 02	17 48	06 21	08 02	09 43	11 22
56	16 27	17 06	17 50	06 16	07 52	09 28	11 01
54	16 33	17 10	17 51	06 11	07 43	09 16	10 44
52	16 38	17 13	17 53	06 07	07 36	09 04	10 29
50	16 43	17 16	17 54	06 03	07 29	08 54	10 16
45	16 53	17 23	17 58	05 54	07 14	08 34	09 50
N 40	17 02	17 30	18 01	05 47	07 02	08 17	09 29
35	17 09	17 35	18 05	05 41	06 52	08 03	09 12
30	17 16	17 40	18 08	05 36	06 43	07 51	08 57
20	17 27	17 50	18 16	05 26	06 28	07 30	08 32
N 10	17 37	17 59	18 24	05 18	06 14	07 12	08 11
0	17 47	18 08	18 33	05 11	06 02	06 55	07 50
S 10	17 57	18 19	18 44	05 03	05 50	06 38	07 30
20	18 07	18 30	18 57	04 55	05 36	06 21	07 09
30	18 20	18 45	19 15	04 46	05 21	06 00	06 44
35	18 27	18 54	19 26	04 41	05 13	05 49	06 30
40	18 35	19 04	19 39	04 35	05 03	05 35	06 13
45	18 44	19 16	19 55	04 28	04 52	05 19	05 53
S 50	18 56	19 32	20 17	04 20	04 38	05 00	05 28
52	19 01	19 39	20 28	04 17	04 32	04 50	05 16
54	19 07	19 48	20 40	04 13	04 24	04 40	05 02
56	19 14	19 57	20 55	04 08	04 17	04 28	04 46
58	19 22	20 08	21 13	04 03	04 08	04 15	04 28
S 60	19 30	20 21	21 35	03 58	03 58	04 00	04 05

SUN / MOON

Day	SUN Eqn. of Time 00h	12h	Mer. Pass.	MOON Mer. Pass. Upper	Lower	Age	Phase
d	m s	m s	h m	h m	h m	d	%
28	16 09	16 12	11 44	23 50	11 24	14	100
29	16 14	16 16	11 44	24 42	12 16	15	99
30	16 18	16 20	11 44	00 42	13 09	16	97 ◯

© British Crown Copyright 2022. All rights reserved.

UT	ARIES GHA	VENUS −4.4 GHA	VENUS Dec	MARS +1.5 GHA	MARS Dec	JUPITER −2.9 GHA	JUPITER Dec	SATURN +0.7 GHA	SATURN Dec	STARS Name	SHA	Dec
31 00	39 02.4	227 03.9	N 4 01.2	178 36.1	S15 38.2	0 04.0	N13 45.8	65 48.9	S12 54.9	Acamar	315 12.1	S40 12.5
01	54 04.9	242 03.9	4 00.4	193 36.9	38.8	15 06.8	45.7	80 51.4	54.9	Achernar	335 20.3	S57 07.0
02	69 07.3	257 03.8	3 59.5	208 37.6	39.3	30 09.6	45.6	95 53.8	54.9	Acrux	173 01.8	S63 13.6
03	84 09.8	272 03.8	.. 58.7	223 38.4	.. 39.9	45 12.4	.. 45.5	110 56.3	.. 54.9	Adhara	255 06.5	S29 00.0
04	99 12.3	287 03.8	57.9	238 39.1	40.4	60 15.2	45.4	125 58.8	54.9	Aldebaran	290 40.5	N16 33.5
05	114 14.7	302 03.8	57.0	253 39.9	41.0	75 18.0	45.3	141 01.3	54.9			
06	129 17.2	317 03.7	N 3 56.2	268 40.7	S15 41.5	90 20.8	N13 45.2	156 03.8	S12 54.9	Alioth	166 14.4	N55 49.8
07	144 19.7	332 03.7	55.4	283 41.4	42.1	105 23.6	45.1	171 06.2	54.9	Alkaid	152 53.3	N49 11.7
08	159 22.1	347 03.7	54.5	298 42.2	42.6	120 26.4	45.0	186 08.7	54.9	Alnair	27 34.0	S46 50.9
09	174 24.6	2 03.7	.. 53.7	313 42.9	.. 43.1	135 29.2	.. 44.9	201 11.2	.. 54.9	Alnilam	275 38.5	S 1 11.1
10	189 27.1	17 03.6	52.9	328 43.7	43.7	150 32.0	44.8	216 13.7	54.9	Alphard	217 48.8	S 8 45.5
11	204 29.5	32 03.6	52.0	343 44.5	44.2	165 34.8	44.7	231 16.2	54.9			
12	219 32.0	47 03.6	N 3 51.2	358 45.2	S15 44.8	180 37.6	N13 44.6	246 18.7	S12 54.9	Alphecca	126 05.0	N26 38.2
13	234 34.5	62 03.5	50.4	13 46.0	45.3	195 40.4	44.5	261 21.1	54.9	Alpheratz	357 35.5	N29 13.5
14	249 36.9	77 03.5	49.5	28 46.7	45.9	210 43.2	44.4	276 23.6	54.9	Altair	62 01.0	N 8 56.0
15	264 39.4	92 03.5	.. 48.7	43 47.5	.. 46.4	225 46.0	.. 44.3	291 26.1	.. 54.9	Ankaa	353 07.8	S42 10.7
16	279 41.8	107 03.5	47.8	58 48.3	46.9	240 48.8	44.2	306 28.6	54.9	Antares	112 17.4	S26 29.0
17	294 44.3	122 03.4	47.0	73 49.0	47.5	255 51.6	44.1	321 31.1	54.9			
18	309 46.8	137 03.4	N 3 46.2	88 49.8	S15 48.0	270 54.4	N13 44.0	336 33.5	S12 54.9	Arcturus	145 49.2	N19 03.6
19	324 49.2	152 03.4	45.3	103 50.5	48.6	285 57.2	43.9	351 36.0	54.9	Atria	107 13.0	S69 04.3
20	339 51.7	167 03.3	44.5	118 51.3	49.1	301 00.0	43.8	6 38.5	54.9	Avior	234 15.1	S59 34.7
21	354 54.2	182 03.3	.. 43.7	133 52.0	.. 49.7	316 02.8	.. 43.6	21 41.0	.. 54.9	Bellatrix	278 23.7	N 6 22.4
22	9 56.6	197 03.3	42.8	148 52.8	50.2	331 05.6	43.5	36 43.5	54.9	Betelgeuse	270 53.0	N 7 24.8
23	24 59.1	212 03.2	42.0	163 53.6	50.7	346 08.4	43.4	51 45.9	54.9			
1 00	40 01.6	227 03.2	N 3 41.1	178 54.3	S15 51.3	1 11.1	N13 43.3	66 48.4	S12 54.9	Canopus	263 52.5	S52 42.2
01	55 04.0	242 03.2	40.3	193 55.1	51.8	16 13.9	43.2	81 50.9	54.9	Capella	280 23.0	N46 01.2
02	70 06.5	257 03.1	39.4	208 55.8	52.4	31 16.7	43.1	96 53.4	54.9	Deneb	49 26.5	N45 22.2
03	85 09.0	272 03.1	.. 38.6	223 56.6	.. 52.9	46 19.5	.. 43.0	111 55.9	.. 54.9	Denebola	182 26.2	N14 26.4
04	100 11.4	287 03.1	37.7	238 57.3	53.5	61 22.3	42.9	126 58.3	54.9	Diphda	348 48.0	S17 51.3
05	115 13.9	302 03.0	36.9	253 58.1	54.0	76 25.1	42.8	142 00.8	54.9			
06	130 16.3	317 03.0	N 3 36.1	268 58.9	S15 54.5	91 27.9	N13 42.7	157 03.3	S12 54.9	Dubhe	193 42.6	N61 37.2
07	145 18.8	332 03.0	35.2	283 59.6	55.1	106 30.7	42.6	172 05.8	54.9	Elnath	278 02.9	N28 37.6
08	160 21.3	347 02.9	34.4	299 00.4	55.6	121 33.5	42.5	187 08.3	54.9	Eltanin	90 43.0	N51 29.3
09	175 23.7	2 02.9	.. 33.5	314 01.1	.. 56.2	136 36.3	.. 42.4	202 10.7	.. 54.9	Enif	33 39.7	N 9 59.2
10	190 26.2	17 02.9	32.7	329 01.9	56.7	151 39.1	42.3	217 13.2	54.9	Fomalhaut	15 15.4	S29 29.9
11	205 28.7	32 02.8	31.8	344 02.6	57.2	166 41.9	42.2	232 15.7	54.9			
12	220 31.1	47 02.8	N 3 31.0	359 03.4	S15 57.8	181 44.7	N13 42.1	247 18.2	S12 54.9	Gacrux	171 53.3	S57 14.5
13	235 33.6	62 02.7	30.1	14 04.1	58.3	196 47.5	42.0	262 20.6	54.9	Gienah	175 44.9	S17 40.2
14	250 36.1	77 02.7	29.3	29 04.9	58.9	211 50.3	41.9	277 23.1	54.9	Hadar	148 38.1	S60 29.1
15	265 38.5	92 02.7	.. 28.4	44 05.6	.. 59.4	226 53.1	.. 41.8	292 25.6	.. 54.9	Hamal	327 52.0	N23 34.6
16	280 41.0	107 02.6	27.6	59 06.4	15 59.9	241 55.9	41.7	307 28.1	54.9	Kaus Aust.	83 34.1	S34 22.5
17	295 43.5	122 02.6	26.7	74 07.1	16 00.5	256 58.7	41.6	322 30.5	54.9			
18	310 45.9	137 02.5	N 3 25.9	89 07.9	S16 01.0	272 01.5	N13 41.5	337 33.0	S12 54.9	Kochab	137 20.9	N74 03.5
19	325 48.4	152 02.5	25.0	104 08.6	01.5	287 04.3	41.4	352 35.5	54.9	Markab	13 30.7	N15 20.1
20	340 50.8	167 02.5	24.2	119 09.4	02.1	302 07.1	41.3	7 38.0	54.9	Menkar	314 06.9	N 4 11.1
21	355 53.3	182 02.4	.. 23.3	134 10.2	.. 02.6	317 09.9	.. 41.2	22 40.5	.. 54.9	Menkent	147 59.2	S36 29.1
22	10 55.8	197 02.4	22.5	149 10.9	03.2	332 12.7	41.1	37 42.9	54.9	Miaplacidus	221 38.6	S69 48.5
23	25 58.2	212 02.3	21.6	164 11.7	03.7	347 15.5	41.0	52 45.4	54.9			
2 00	41 00.7	227 02.3	N 3 20.7	179 12.4	S16 04.2	2 18.3	N13 40.9	67 47.9	S12 54.9	Mirfak	308 29.2	N49 56.7
01	56 03.2	242 02.3	19.9	194 13.2	04.8	17 21.1	40.8	82 50.4	54.9	Nunki	75 49.2	S26 16.1
02	71 05.6	257 02.2	19.0	209 13.9	05.3	32 23.9	40.7	97 52.8	54.9	Peacock	53 07.4	S56 39.7
03	86 08.1	272 02.2	.. 18.2	224 14.7	.. 05.8	47 26.7	.. 40.6	112 55.3	.. 54.9	Pollux	243 18.5	N27 58.1
04	101 10.6	287 02.1	17.3	239 15.4	06.4	62 29.5	40.5	127 57.8	54.9	Procyon	244 51.8	N 5 10.0
05	116 13.0	302 02.1	16.5	254 16.2	06.9	77 32.3	40.4	143 00.3	54.9			
06	131 15.5	317 02.0	N 3 15.6	269 16.9	S16 07.5	92 35.1	N13 40.3	158 02.7	S12 54.9	Rasalhague	95 59.7	N12 32.7
07	146 17.9	332 02.0	14.7	284 17.7	08.0	107 37.9	40.2	173 05.2	54.9	Regulus	207 35.6	N11 51.1
08	161 20.4	347 01.9	13.9	299 18.4	08.5	122 40.7	40.1	188 07.7	54.9	Rigel	281 04.6	S 8 10.3
09	176 22.9	2 01.9	.. 13.0	314 19.2	.. 09.1	137 43.5	.. 40.0	203 10.2	.. 54.9	Rigil Kent.	139 42.4	S60 55.9
10	191 25.3	17 01.9	12.2	329 19.9	09.6	152 46.3	39.9	218 12.6	54.9	Sabik	102 04.2	S15 45.2
11	206 27.8	32 01.8	11.3	344 20.6	10.1	167 49.1	39.8	233 15.1	54.9			
12	221 30.3	47 01.8	N 3 10.4	359 21.4	S16 10.7	182 51.9	N13 39.7	248 17.6	S12 54.9	Schedar	349 31.7	N56 40.2
13	236 32.7	62 01.7	09.6	14 22.1	11.2	197 54.6	39.5	263 20.0	54.9	Shaula	96 12.1	S37 07.3
14	251 35.2	77 01.7	08.7	29 22.9	11.7	212 57.4	39.4	278 22.5	54.9	Sirius	258 27.0	S16 44.7
15	266 37.7	92 01.6	.. 07.8	44 23.6	.. 12.3	228 00.2	.. 39.3	293 25.0	.. 54.9	Spica	158 23.7	S11 17.0
16	281 40.1	107 01.6	07.0	59 24.4	12.8	243 03.0	39.2	308 27.5	54.9	Suhail	222 47.1	S43 31.3
17	296 42.6	122 01.5	06.1	74 25.1	13.3	258 05.8	39.1	323 29.9	54.9			
18	311 45.1	137 01.5	N 3 05.3	89 25.9	S16 13.9	273 08.6	N13 39.0	338 32.4	S12 54.9	Vega	80 34.1	N38 48.5
19	326 47.5	152 01.4	04.4	104 26.6	14.4	288 11.4	38.9	353 34.9	54.9	Zuben'ubi	136 57.5	S16 08.3
20	341 50.0	167 01.4	03.5	119 27.4	14.9	303 14.2	38.8	8 37.4	54.9		SHA	Mer. Pass.
21	356 52.4	182 01.3	.. 02.7	134 28.1	.. 15.5	318 17.0	.. 38.7	23 39.8	.. 54.9			h m
22	11 54.9	197 01.3	01.8	149 28.9	16.0	333 19.8	38.6	38 42.3	54.9	Venus	187 01.6	8 52
23	26 57.4	212 01.2	00.9	164 29.6	16.5	348 22.6	38.5	53 44.8	54.9	Mars	138 52.8	12 04
Mer. Pass.	21 16.4	v 0.0	d 0.8	v 0.8	d 0.5	v 2.8	d 0.1	v 2.5	d 0.0	Jupiter	321 09.6	23 51
										Saturn	26 46.9	19 30

© British Crown Copyright 2022. All rights reserved.

UT	SUN GHA	SUN Dec	MOON GHA	v	MOON Dec	d	HP
d h	° ′	° ′	° ′	′	° ′	′	′
31 00	184 05.5	S13 56.8	336 37.7	7.5	N24 28.9	8.5	57.8
01	199 05.5	57.6	351 04.2	7.5	24 37.4	8.3	57.8
02	214 05.5	58.5	5 30.7	7.4	24 45.7	8.2	57.7
03	229 05.6	13 59.3	19 57.1	7.3	24 53.9	8.0	57.7
04	244 05.6	14 00.1	34 23.4	7.4	25 01.9	7.9	57.7
05	259 05.6	00.9	48 49.8	7.3	25 09.8	7.7	57.6
06	274 05.7	S14 01.7	63 16.1	7.3	N25 17.5	7.6	57.6
07	289 05.7	02.5	77 42.4	7.2	25 25.1	7.4	57.6
08	304 05.7	03.3	92 08.6	7.2	25 32.5	7.2	57.5
09	319 05.7	04.1	106 34.8	7.2	25 39.7	7.1	57.5
10	334 05.8	05.0	121 01.0	7.2	25 46.8	6.9	57.5
11	349 05.8	05.8	135 27.2	7.1	25 53.7	6.8	57.4
12	4 05.8	S14 06.6	149 53.3	7.1	N26 00.5	6.6	57.4
13	19 05.8	07.4	164 19.4	7.1	26 07.1	6.4	57.4
14	34 05.9	08.2	178 45.5	7.1	26 13.5	6.3	57.3
15	49 05.9	09.0	193 11.6	7.0	26 19.8	6.1	57.3
16	64 05.9	09.8	207 37.6	7.0	26 25.9	6.0	57.3
17	79 05.9	10.6	222 03.6	7.1	26 31.9	5.8	57.2
18	94 06.0	S14 11.4	236 29.7	7.0	N26 37.7	5.6	57.2
19	109 06.0	12.2	250 55.7	6.9	26 43.3	5.5	57.2
20	124 06.0	13.0	265 21.6	7.0	26 48.8	5.3	57.1
21	139 06.0	13.8	279 47.6	7.0	26 54.1	5.2	57.1
22	154 06.1	14.6	294 13.6	6.9	26 59.3	5.0	57.1
23	169 06.1	15.5	308 39.5	7.0	27 04.3	4.8	57.0
1 00	184 06.1	S14 16.3	323 05.5	6.9	N27 09.1	4.6	57.0
01	199 06.1	17.1	337 31.4	7.0	27 13.7	4.5	57.0
02	214 06.2	17.9	351 57.4	6.9	27 18.2	4.4	56.9
03	229 06.2	18.7	6 23.3	7.0	27 22.6	4.1	56.9
04	244 06.2	19.5	20 49.3	6.9	27 26.7	4.0	56.9
05	259 06.2	20.3	35 15.2	6.9	27 30.7	3.9	56.8
06	274 06.2	S14 21.1	49 41.1	7.0	N27 34.6	3.7	56.8
07	289 06.3	21.9	64 07.1	6.9	27 38.3	3.5	56.8
08	304 06.3	22.7	78 33.0	7.0	27 41.8	3.3	56.7
09	319 06.3	23.5	92 59.0	6.9	27 45.1	3.2	56.7
10	334 06.3	24.3	107 24.9	7.0	27 48.3	3.0	56.7
11	349 06.3	25.1	121 50.9	7.0	27 51.3	2.9	56.6
12	4 06.4	S14 25.9	136 16.9	7.0	N27 54.2	2.7	56.6
13	19 06.4	26.7	150 42.9	7.0	27 56.9	2.5	56.6
14	34 06.4	27.5	165 08.9	7.1	27 59.4	2.4	56.5
15	49 06.4	28.3	179 35.0	7.0	28 01.8	2.2	56.5
16	64 06.4	29.1	194 01.0	7.1	28 04.0	2.0	56.5
17	79 06.4	29.9	208 27.1	7.1	28 06.0	1.9	56.4
18	94 06.5	S14 30.7	222 53.2	7.1	N28 07.9	1.7	56.4
19	109 06.5	31.5	237 19.3	7.1	28 09.6	1.6	56.4
20	124 06.5	32.3	251 45.4	7.2	28 11.2	1.4	56.3
21	139 06.5	33.1	266 11.6	7.2	28 12.6	1.2	56.3
22	154 06.5	33.9	280 37.8	7.3	28 13.8	1.1	56.3
23	169 06.5	34.7	295 04.1	7.2	28 14.9	0.9	56.2
2 00	184 06.6	S14 35.5	309 30.3	7.3	N28 15.8	0.7	56.2
01	199 06.6	36.3	323 56.6	7.4	28 16.5	0.6	56.2
02	214 06.6	37.1	338 23.0	7.3	28 17.1	0.5	56.1
03	229 06.6	37.8	352 49.3	7.4	28 17.6	0.2	56.1
04	244 06.6	38.6	7 15.7	7.5	28 17.8	0.1	56.1
05	259 06.6	39.4	21 42.2	7.5	28 17.9	0.0	56.0
06	274 06.6	S14 40.2	36 08.7	7.5	N28 17.9	0.2	56.0
07	289 06.6	41.0	50 35.2	7.6	28 17.7	0.3	56.0
08	304 06.7	41.8	65 01.8	7.6	28 17.4	0.6	56.0
09	319 06.7	42.6	79 28.4	7.7	28 16.8	0.6	55.9
10	334 06.7	43.4	93 55.1	7.7	28 16.2	0.8	55.9
11	349 06.7	44.2	108 21.8	7.8	28 15.4	1.0	55.9
12	4 06.7	S14 45.0	122 48.6	7.8	N28 14.4	1.1	55.8
13	19 06.7	45.8	137 15.4	7.9	28 13.3	1.3	55.8
14	34 06.7	46.6	151 42.3	7.9	28 12.0	1.5	55.8
15	49 06.7	47.4	166 09.2	8.0	28 10.5	1.5	55.8
16	64 06.7	48.1	180 36.2	8.0	28 09.0	1.8	55.7
17	79 06.7	48.9	195 03.2	8.1	28 07.2	1.8	55.7
18	94 06.7	S14 49.7	209 30.3	8.2	N28 05.4	2.1	55.7
19	109 06.8	50.5	223 57.5	8.2	28 03.3	2.2	55.6
20	124 06.8	51.3	238 24.7	8.3	28 01.1	2.3	55.6
21	139 06.8	52.1	252 52.0	8.4	27 58.8	2.5	55.6
22	154 06.8	52.9	267 19.4	8.4	27 56.3	2.6	55.6
23	169 06.8	53.7	281 46.8	8.4	N27 53.7	2.7	55.5
SD	16.1	d 0.8	SD 15.6		15.4		15.2

Day labels: TUESDAY (31), WEDNESDAY (1), THURSDAY (2)

Lat.	Twilight Naut.	Twilight Civil	Sunrise	Moonrise 31	1	2	3
°	h m	h m	h m	h m	h m	h m	h m
N 72	06 05	07 28	08 55	▭	▭	▭	▭
N 70	06 01	07 15	08 29	▭	▭	▭	▭
68	05 57	07 05	08 09	▭	▭	▭	▭
66	05 54	06 56	07 54	▭	▭	▭	▭
64	05 52	06 48	07 41			▭	
62	05 49	06 42	07 31	15 36	15 21	▭	18 15
60	05 47	06 36	07 21	16 14	16 38	17 33	18 57
N 58	05 45	06 31	07 13	16 41	17 14	18 10	19 26
56	05 43	06 27	07 06	17 02	17 40	18 36	19 48
54	05 41	06 22	07 00	17 20	18 00	18 56	20 06
52	05 39	06 19	06 54	17 35	18 17	19 14	20 21
50	05 37	06 15	06 49	17 48	18 32	19 29	20 34
45	05 33	06 07	06 38	18 15	19 02	19 58	21 01
N 40	05 29	06 01	06 29	18 36	19 26	20 22	21 23
35	05 25	05 54	06 21	18 54	19 45	20 41	21 40
30	05 21	05 49	06 14	19 10	20 02	20 58	21 56
20	05 12	05 39	06 01	19 36	20 30	21 25	22 21
N 10	05 04	05 29	05 50	19 59	20 54	21 49	22 44
0	04 54	05 19	05 40	20 20	21 16	22 12	23 04
S 10	04 43	05 08	05 30	20 41	21 39	22 34	23 25
20	04 29	04 56	05 19	21 04	22 03	22 58	23 47
30	04 10	04 40	05 06	21 31	22 32	23 26	24 12
35	03 59	04 31	04 58	21 47	22 48	23 42	24 27
40	03 45	04 20	04 49	22 05	23 08	24 01	00 01
45	03 28	04 07	04 39	22 28	23 32	24 24	00 24
S 50	03 05	03 51	04 27	22 56	24 03	00 03	00 54
52	02 54	03 43	04 21	23 11	24 18	00 18	01 08
54	02 41	03 34	04 15	23 27	24 36	00 36	01 25
56	02 25	03 24	04 08	23 46	24 57	00 57	01 45
58	02 06	03 13	04 00	24 11	00 11	01 25	02 11
S 60	01 42	02 59	03 51	24 43	00 43	02 05	02 45

Lat.	Sunset	Twilight Civil	Twilight Naut.	Moonset 31	1	2	3
°	h m	h m	h m	h m	h m	h m	h m
N 72	14 31	15 58	17 20	▭	▭	▭	▭
N 70	14 57	16 11	17 25	▭	▭	▭	▭
68	15 16	16 21	17 28	▭	▭	▭	▭
66	15 32	16 30	17 31	▭	▭	▭	▭
64	15 45	16 38	17 34	▭		▭	▭
62	15 56	16 44	17 37	12 26	14 40	▭	15 33
60	16 05	16 50	17 39	11 48	13 23	14 24	14 51
N 58	16 13	16 55	17 42	11 22	12 47	13 47	14 22
56	16 20	17 00	17 44	11 01	12 21	13 21	13 59
54	16 26	17 04	17 46	10 44	12 01	13 00	13 41
52	16 32	17 08	17 48	10 29	11 44	12 43	13 26
50	16 37	17 11	17 49	10 16	11 29	12 28	13 12
45	16 49	17 19	17 54	09 50	10 59	11 58	12 44
N 40	16 58	17 26	17 58	09 29	10 36	11 34	12 22
35	17 06	17 32	18 02	09 12	10 17	11 15	12 04
30	17 13	17 38	18 06	08 57	10 01	10 58	11 49
20	17 26	17 48	18 14	08 32	09 33	10 30	11 22
N 10	17 37	17 58	18 23	08 11	09 09	10 06	10 59
0	17 47	18 08	18 33	07 50	08 47	09 43	10 37
S 10	17 58	18 19	18 45	07 30	08 25	09 21	10 16
20	18 09	18 32	18 59	07 09	08 01	08 56	09 52
30	18 22	18 47	19 17	06 44	07 34	08 28	09 25
35	18 30	18 57	19 29	06 30	07 17	08 11	09 09
40	18 38	19 08	19 43	06 13	06 58	07 51	08 51
45	18 49	19 21	20 01	05 53	06 36	07 28	08 28
S 50	19 01	19 38	20 24	05 28	06 06	06 57	07 59
52	19 07	19 45	20 35	05 16	05 52	06 42	07 44
54	19 13	19 54	20 49	05 02	05 35	06 24	07 28
56	19 21	20 05	21 05	04 46	05 16	06 02	07 08
58	19 29	20 17	21 24	04 28	04 51	05 35	06 43
S 60	19 38	20 30	21 50	04 05	04 18	04 55	06 08

Day	SUN Eqn. of Time 00h	12h	Mer. Pass.	MOON Mer. Pass. Upper	Lower	Age	Phase
d	m s	m s	h m	h m	h m	d	%
31	16 22	16 23	11 44	01 37	14 05	17	91
1	16 24	16 25	11 44	02 33	15 02	18	85
2	16 26	16 27	11 44	03 30	15 57	19	77

© British Crown Copyright 2022. All rights reserved.

2023 NOVEMBER 3, 4, 5 (FRI., SAT., SUN.)

UT	ARIES GHA	VENUS −4.4 GHA	Dec	MARS +1.4 GHA	Dec	JUPITER −2.9 GHA	Dec	SATURN +0.7 GHA	Dec	STARS Name	SHA	Dec
3 00	41 59.8	227 01.2	N 3 00.1	179 30.3	S16 17.1	3 25.4	N13 38.4	68 47.2	S12 54.9	Acamar	315 12.1	S40 12.5
01	57 02.3	242 01.1	2 59.2	194 31.1	17.6	18 28.2	38.3	83 49.7	54.9	Achernar	335 20.3	S57 07.0
02	72 04.8	257 01.1	58.3	209 31.8	18.1	33 31.0	38.2	98 52.2	54.8	Acrux	173 01.8	S63 13.6
03	87 07.2	272 01.0 ..	57.4	224 32.6 ..	18.7	48 33.8 ..	38.1	113 54.7 ..	54.8	Adhara	255 06.5	S29 00.0
04	102 09.7	287 00.9	56.6	239 33.3	19.2	63 36.6	38.0	128 57.1	54.8	Aldebaran	290 40.5	N16 33.5
05	117 12.2	302 00.9	55.7	254 34.1	19.7	78 39.4	37.9	143 59.6	54.8			
06	132 14.6	317 00.8	N 2 54.8	269 34.8	S16 20.3	93 42.2	N13 37.8	159 02.1	S12 54.8	Alioth	166 14.3	N55 49.8
07	147 17.1	332 00.8	54.0	284 35.6	20.8	108 45.0	37.7	174 04.5	54.8	Alkaid	152 53.3	N49 11.7
08	162 19.6	347 00.7	53.1	299 36.3	21.3	123 47.8	37.6	189 07.0	54.8	Alnair	27 34.0	S46 50.9
09	177 22.0	2 00.7 ..	52.2	314 37.0 ..	21.8	138 50.6 ..	37.5	204 09.5 ..	54.8	Alnilam	275 38.5	S 1 11.1
10	192 24.5	17 00.6	51.3	329 37.8	22.4	153 53.4	37.4	219 11.9	54.8	Alphard	217 48.8	S 8 45.5
11	207 26.9	32 00.6	50.5	344 38.5	22.9	168 56.2	37.3	234 14.4	54.8			
12	222 29.4	47 00.5	N 2 49.6	359 39.3	S16 23.4	183 59.0	N13 37.2	249 16.9	S12 54.8	Alphecca	126 05.0	N26 38.2
13	237 31.9	62 00.4	48.7	14 40.0	24.0	199 01.8	37.1	264 19.4	54.8	Alpheratz	357 35.5	N29 13.5
14	252 34.3	77 00.4	47.9	29 40.8	24.5	214 04.6	37.0	279 21.8	54.8	Altair	62 01.0	N 8 56.0
15	267 36.8	92 00.3 ..	47.0	44 41.5 ..	25.0	229 07.4 ..	36.9	294 24.3 ..	54.8	Ankaa	353 07.8	S42 10.7
16	282 39.3	107 00.3	46.1	59 42.2	25.6	244 10.2	36.8	309 26.8	54.8	Antares	112 17.4	S26 29.0
17	297 41.7	122 00.2	45.2	74 43.0	26.1	259 13.0	36.7	324 29.2	54.8			
18	312 44.2	137 00.2	N 2 44.3	89 43.7	S16 26.6	274 15.8	N13 36.6	339 31.7	S12 54.8	Arcturus	145 49.2	N19 03.6
19	327 46.7	152 00.1	43.5	104 44.5	27.1	289 18.6	36.5	354 34.2	54.8	Atria	107 13.0	S69 04.3
20	342 49.1	167 00.0	42.6	119 45.2	27.7	304 21.4	36.4	9 36.6	54.8	Avior	234 15.1	S59 34.7
21	357 51.6	182 00.0 ..	41.7	134 45.9 ..	28.2	319 24.2 ..	36.3	24 39.1 ..	54.8	Bellatrix	278 23.7	N 6 22.4
22	12 54.1	196 59.9	40.8	149 46.7	28.7	334 27.0	36.2	39 41.6	54.8	Betelgeuse	270 52.9	N 7 24.8
23	27 56.5	211 59.9	40.0	164 47.4	29.3	349 29.8	36.1	54 44.0	54.8			
4 00	42 59.0	226 59.8	N 2 39.1	179 48.2	S16 29.8	4 32.6	N13 36.0	69 46.5	S12 54.8	Canopus	263 52.5	S52 42.2
01	58 01.4	241 59.7	38.2	194 48.9	30.3	19 35.4	35.9	84 49.0	54.8	Capella	280 23.0	N46 01.2
02	73 03.9	256 59.7	37.3	209 49.6	30.8	34 38.2	35.8	99 51.4	54.8	Deneb	49 26.5	N45 22.2
03	88 06.4	271 59.6 ..	36.4	224 50.4 ..	31.4	49 41.0 ..	35.7	114 53.9 ..	54.8	Denebola	182 26.2	N14 26.4
04	103 08.8	286 59.5	35.6	239 51.1	31.9	64 43.8	35.6	129 56.4	54.8	Diphda	348 48.0	S17 51.4
05	118 11.3	301 59.5	34.7	254 51.8	32.4	79 46.5	35.5	144 58.8	54.8			
06	133 13.8	316 59.4	N 2 33.8	269 52.6	S16 32.9	94 49.3	N13 35.4	160 01.3	S12 54.8	Dubhe	193 42.6	N61 37.2
07	148 16.2	331 59.4	32.9	284 53.3	33.5	109 52.1	35.2	175 03.8	54.7	Elnath	278 02.8	N28 37.6
08	163 18.7	346 59.3	32.0	299 54.1	34.0	124 54.9	35.1	190 06.2	54.7	Eltanin	90 43.0	N51 29.3
09	178 21.2	1 59.2 ..	31.1	314 54.8 ..	34.5	139 57.7 ..	35.0	205 08.7 ..	54.7	Enif	33 39.7	N 9 59.2
10	193 23.6	16 59.2	30.3	329 55.5	35.0	155 00.5	34.9	220 11.2	54.7	Fomalhaut	15 15.4	S29 29.9
11	208 26.1	31 59.1	29.4	344 56.3	35.6	170 03.3	34.8	235 13.6	54.7			
12	223 28.6	46 59.0	N 2 28.5	359 57.0	S16 36.1	185 06.1	N13 34.7	250 16.1	S12 54.7	Gacrux	171 53.3	S57 14.5
13	238 31.0	61 59.0	27.6	14 57.7	36.6	200 08.9	34.6	265 18.6	54.7	Gienah	175 44.9	S17 40.2
14	253 33.5	76 58.9	26.7	29 58.5	37.1	215 11.7	34.5	280 21.0	54.7	Hadar	148 38.1	S60 29.1
15	268 35.9	91 58.8 ..	25.8	44 59.2 ..	37.7	230 14.5 ..	34.4	295 23.5 ..	54.7	Hamal	327 52.0	N23 34.6
16	283 38.4	106 58.8	24.9	59 59.9	38.2	245 17.3	34.3	310 26.0	54.7	Kaus Aust.	83 34.1	S34 22.5
17	298 40.9	121 58.7	24.0	75 00.7	38.7	260 20.1	34.2	325 28.4	54.7			
18	313 43.3	136 58.6	N 2 23.2	90 01.4	S16 39.2	275 22.9	N13 34.1	340 30.9	S12 54.7	Kochab	137 20.9	N74 03.4
19	328 45.8	151 58.6	22.3	105 02.1	39.8	290 25.7	34.0	355 33.3	54.7	Markab	13 30.7	N15 20.1
20	343 48.3	166 58.5	21.4	120 02.9	40.3	305 28.5	33.9	10 35.8	54.7	Menkar	314 06.9	N 4 11.1
21	358 50.7	181 58.4 ..	20.5	135 03.6 ..	40.8	320 31.3 ..	33.8	25 38.3 ..	54.7	Menkent	147 59.2	S36 29.1
22	13 53.2	196 58.4	19.6	150 04.3	41.3	335 34.1	33.7	40 40.7	54.7	Miaplacidus	221 38.6	S69 48.5
23	28 55.7	211 58.3	18.7	165 05.1	41.9	350 36.9	33.6	55 43.2	54.7			
5 00	43 58.1	226 58.2	N 2 17.8	180 05.8	S16 42.4	5 39.7	N13 33.5	70 45.7	S12 54.7	Mirfak	308 29.2	N49 56.8
01	59 00.6	241 58.1	16.9	195 06.5	42.9	20 42.5	33.4	85 48.1	54.7	Nunki	75 49.2	S26 16.1
02	74 03.0	256 58.1	16.0	210 07.3	43.4	35 45.3	33.3	100 50.6	54.7	Peacock	53 07.4	S56 39.7
03	89 05.5	271 58.0 ..	15.1	225 08.0 ..	43.9	50 48.1 ..	33.2	115 53.0 ..	54.6	Pollux	243 18.4	N27 58.1
04	104 08.0	286 57.9	14.2	240 08.7	44.5	65 50.9	33.1	130 55.5	54.6	Procyon	244 51.8	N 5 09.9
05	119 10.4	301 57.9	13.4	255 09.5	45.0	80 53.7	33.0	145 58.0	54.6			
06	134 12.9	316 57.8	N 2 12.5	270 10.2	S16 45.5	95 56.5	N13 32.9	161 00.4	S12 54.6	Rasalhague	96 59.7	N12 32.7
07	149 15.4	331 57.7	11.6	285 10.9	46.0	110 59.3	32.8	176 02.9	54.6	Regulus	207 35.6	N11 51.1
08	164 17.8	346 57.6	10.7	300 11.7	46.5	126 02.1	32.7	191 05.4	54.6	Rigel	281 04.6	S 8 10.3
09	179 20.3	1 57.6 ..	09.8	315 12.4 ..	47.1	141 04.9 ..	32.6	206 07.8 ..	54.6	Rigil Kent.	139 42.4	S60 55.9
10	194 22.8	16 57.5	08.9	330 13.1	47.6	156 07.7	32.5	221 10.3	54.6	Sabik	102 04.2	S15 45.2
11	209 25.2	31 57.4	08.0	345 13.9	48.1	171 10.5	32.4	236 12.7	54.6			
12	224 27.7	46 57.3	N 2 07.1	0 14.6	S16 48.6	186 13.3	N13 32.3	251 15.2	S12 54.6	Schedar	349 31.7	N56 40.2
13	239 30.2	61 57.3	06.2	15 15.3	49.1	201 16.1	32.2	266 17.7	54.6	Shaula	96 12.1	S37 07.3
14	254 32.6	76 57.2	05.3	30 16.1	49.7	216 18.9	32.1	281 20.1	54.6	Sirius	258 26.9	S16 44.7
15	269 35.1	91 57.1 ..	04.4	45 16.8 ..	50.2	231 21.6 ..	32.0	296 22.6 ..	54.6	Spica	158 23.7	S11 17.0
16	284 37.5	106 57.0	03.5	60 17.5	50.7	246 24.4	31.9	311 25.0	54.6	Suhail	222 47.1	S43 31.4
17	299 40.0	121 57.0	02.6	75 18.2	51.2	261 27.2	31.8	326 27.5	54.6			
18	314 42.5	136 56.9	N 2 01.7	90 19.0	S16 51.7	276 30.0	N13 31.7	341 30.0	S12 54.6	Vega	80 34.1	N38 48.5
19	329 44.9	151 56.8	2 00.8	105 19.7	52.3	291 32.8	31.6	356 32.4	54.6	Zuben'ubi	136 57.5	S16 08.3
20	344 47.4	166 56.7	1 59.9	120 20.4	52.8	306 35.6	31.5	11 34.9	54.5			
21	359 49.9	181 56.7 ..	59.0	135 21.2 ..	53.3	321 38.4 ..	31.4	26 37.3 ..	54.5		SHA	Mer. Pass.
22	14 52.3	196 56.6	58.1	150 21.9	53.8	336 41.2	31.3	41 39.8	54.5	Venus	184 00.8	8 52
23	29 54.8	211 56.5	57.2	165 22.6	54.3	351 44.0	31.2	56 42.3	54.5	Mars	136 49.2	12 00
Mer. Pass.	21 04.6	v −0.1	d 0.9	v 0.7	d 0.5	v 2.8	d 0.1	v 2.5	d 0.0	Jupiter	321 33.6	23 37
										Saturn	26 47.5	19 18

Mer. Pass. (Venus): h m ; SHA Mer. Pass. columns for Venus 184 00.8 / 8 52; Mars 136 49.2 / 12 00; Jupiter 321 33.6 / 23 37; Saturn 26 47.5 / 19 18

© British Crown Copyright 2022. All rights reserved.

UT	SUN GHA	SUN Dec	MOON GHA	v	MOON Dec	d	HP
d h	° ′	° ′	° ′	′	° ′	′	′
3 00	184 06.8	S14 54.4	296 14.2	8.6	N27 51.0	2.9	55.5
01	199 06.8	55.2	310 41.8	8.6	27 48.1	3.1	55.5
02	214 06.8	56.0	325 09.4	8.7	27 45.0	3.2	55.5
03	229 06.8	.. 56.8	339 37.1	8.7	27 41.8	3.3	55.4
04	244 06.8	57.6	354 04.8	8.8	27 38.5	3.5	55.4
05	259 06.8	58.4	8 32.6	8.9	27 35.0	3.6	55.4
06	274 06.8	S14 59.1	23 00.5	9.0	N27 31.4	3.7	55.3
07	289 06.8	14 59.9	37 28.5	9.0	27 27.7	3.9	55.3
08	304 06.8	15 00.7	51 56.5	9.1	27 23.8	4.1	55.3
F 09	319 06.8	.. 01.5	66 24.6	9.2	27 19.7	4.1	55.3
R 10	334 06.8	02.3	80 52.8	9.3	27 15.6	4.3	55.2
I 11	349 06.8	03.1	95 21.1	9.3	27 11.3	4.5	55.2
D 12	4 06.8	S15 03.8	109 49.4	9.4	N27 06.8	4.5	55.2
A 13	19 06.8	04.6	124 17.8	9.5	27 02.3	4.7	55.2
Y 14	34 06.8	05.4	138 46.3	9.6	26 57.6	4.8	55.2
15	49 06.8	.. 06.2	153 14.9	9.7	26 52.8	5.0	55.1
16	64 06.8	07.0	167 43.6	9.7	26 47.8	5.1	55.1
17	79 06.8	07.7	182 12.3	9.8	26 42.7	5.2	55.1
18	94 06.8	S15 08.5	196 41.1	9.9	N26 37.5	5.3	55.1
19	109 06.8	09.3	211 10.0	10.0	26 32.2	5.5	55.0
20	124 06.8	10.1	225 39.0	10.0	26 26.7	5.6	55.0
21	139 06.8	.. 10.8	240 08.0	10.2	26 21.1	5.7	55.0
22	154 06.8	11.6	254 37.2	10.2	26 15.4	5.9	55.0
23	169 06.8	12.4	269 06.4	10.3	26 09.5	5.9	55.0
4 00	184 06.8	S15 13.2	283 35.7	10.4	N26 03.6	6.1	54.9
01	199 06.8	13.9	298 05.1	10.4	25 57.5	6.2	54.9
02	214 06.8	14.7	312 34.5	10.6	25 51.3	6.3	54.9
03	229 06.8	.. 15.5	327 04.1	10.6	25 45.0	6.5	54.9
04	244 06.8	16.3	341 33.7	10.7	25 38.5	6.5	54.9
05	259 06.8	17.0	356 03.4	10.9	25 32.0	6.7	54.8
06	274 06.8	S15 17.8	10 33.3	10.8	N25 25.3	6.8	54.8
S 07	289 06.8	18.6	25 03.1	11.0	25 18.5	6.9	54.8
A 08	304 06.8	19.4	39 33.1	11.1	25 11.6	7.0	54.8
T 09	319 06.8	.. 20.1	54 03.2	11.1	25 04.6	7.1	54.8
U 10	334 06.8	20.9	68 33.3	11.3	24 57.5	7.3	54.7
R 11	349 06.8	21.7	83 03.6	11.3	24 50.2	7.3	54.7
D 12	4 06.8	S15 22.4	97 33.9	11.4	N24 42.9	7.5	54.7
A 13	19 06.7	23.2	112 04.3	11.5	24 35.4	7.5	54.7
Y 14	34 06.7	24.0	126 34.8	11.5	24 27.9	7.7	54.7
15	49 06.7	.. 24.8	141 05.3	11.7	24 20.2	7.8	54.7
16	64 06.7	25.5	155 36.0	11.7	24 12.4	7.9	54.6
17	79 06.7	26.3	170 06.7	11.8	24 04.5	8.0	54.6
18	94 06.7	S15 27.1	184 37.5	11.9	N23 56.5	8.1	54.6
19	109 06.7	27.8	199 08.4	12.0	23 48.4	8.2	54.6
20	124 06.7	28.6	213 39.4	12.1	23 40.2	8.2	54.6
21	139 06.7	.. 29.4	228 10.5	12.2	23 32.0	8.4	54.6
22	154 06.7	30.1	242 41.7	12.2	23 23.6	8.5	54.5
23	169 06.6	30.9	257 12.9	12.3	23 15.1	8.6	54.5
5 00	184 06.6	S15 31.7	271 44.2	12.5	N23 06.5	8.7	54.5
01	199 06.6	32.4	286 15.7	12.4	22 57.8	8.8	54.5
02	214 06.6	33.2	300 47.1	12.6	22 49.0	8.9	54.5
03	229 06.6	.. 33.9	315 18.7	12.7	22 40.1	8.9	54.5
04	244 06.6	34.7	329 50.4	12.7	22 31.2	9.1	54.5
05	259 06.6	35.5	344 22.1	12.8	22 22.1	9.2	54.5
06	274 06.6	S15 36.2	358 53.9	12.9	N22 12.9	9.2	54.4
07	289 06.5	37.0	13 25.8	13.0	22 03.7	9.4	54.4
08	304 06.5	37.8	27 57.8	13.1	21 54.3	9.4	54.4
S 09	319 06.5	.. 38.5	42 29.9	13.1	21 44.9	9.5	54.4
U 10	334 06.5	39.3	57 02.0	13.2	21 35.4	9.6	54.4
N 11	349 06.5	40.0	71 34.2	13.3	21 25.8	9.7	54.4
D 12	4 06.5	S15 40.8	86 06.5	13.4	N21 16.1	9.8	54.4
A 13	19 06.5	41.6	100 38.9	13.4	21 06.3	9.8	54.4
Y 14	34 06.4	42.3	115 11.3	13.6	20 56.5	10.0	54.4
15	49 06.4	.. 43.1	129 43.9	13.6	20 46.5	10.0	54.3
16	64 06.4	43.8	144 16.5	13.7	20 36.5	10.1	54.3
17	79 06.4	44.6	158 49.2	13.7	20 26.4	10.2	54.3
18	94 06.4	S15 45.3	173 21.9	13.8	N20 16.2	10.3	54.3
19	109 06.3	46.1	187 54.7	13.9	20 05.9	10.4	54.3
20	124 06.3	46.9	202 27.6	14.0	19 55.5	10.4	54.3
21	139 06.3	.. 47.6	217 00.6	14.0	19 45.1	10.5	54.3
22	154 06.3	48.4	231 33.6	14.2	19 34.6	10.6	54.3
23	169 06.3	49.1	246 06.8	14.2	N19 24.0	10.6	54.3
	SD 16.2	d 0.8	SD 15.0		14.9		14.8

Lat.	Naut.	Civil	Sunrise	Moonrise 3	4	5	6
°	h m	h m	h m	h m	h m	h m	h m
N 72	06 17	07 42	09 14	□	□	□	21 32
N 70	06 11	07 27	08 44	□	□	□	22 08
68	06 07	07 15	08 22	□	□	20 19	22 33
66	06 03	07 05	08 05	□	18 11	20 58	22 52
64	05 59	06 57	07 51	□	19 29	21 25	23 07
62	05 56	06 50	07 39	18 15	20 05	21 46	23 20
60	05 53	06 43	07 29	18 57	20 31	22 03	23 31
N 58	05 51	06 38	07 20	19 26	20 51	22 17	23 40
56	05 48	06 32	07 13	19 48	21 08	22 29	23 48
54	05 46	06 28	07 06	20 06	21 22	22 39	23 55
52	05 44	06 24	07 00	20 21	21 34	22 49	24 02
50	05 41	06 20	06 54	20 34	21 45	22 57	24 07
45	05 36	06 11	06 42	21 01	22 08	23 14	24 20
N 40	05 32	06 04	06 32	21 23	22 26	23 29	24 30
35	05 27	05 57	06 23	21 40	22 41	23 41	24 39
30	05 23	05 51	06 16	21 56	22 54	23 51	24 46
20	05 14	05 40	06 03	22 21	23 16	24 09	00 09
N 10	05 04	05 29	05 51	22 44	23 35	24 24	00 24
0	04 54	05 19	05 40	23 04	23 53	24 39	00 39
S 10	04 42	05 07	05 29	23 25	24 11	00 11	00 53
20	04 27	04 54	05 17	23 47	24 30	00 30	01 09
30	04 08	04 38	05 03	24 12	00 12	00 52	01 26
35	03 55	04 28	04 55	24 27	00 27	01 05	01 36
40	03 41	04 17	04 46	00 01	00 44	01 19	01 48
45	03 22	04 03	04 35	00 24	01 05	01 37	02 01
S 50	02 58	03 45	04 22	00 54	01 31	01 58	02 18
52	02 46	03 37	04 16	01 08	01 44	02 08	02 26
54	02 32	03 27	04 09	01 25	01 58	02 19	02 34
56	02 15	03 17	04 01	01 45	02 15	02 32	02 44
58	01 54	03 04	03 53	02 11	02 35	02 47	02 55
S 60	01 25	02 49	03 43	02 45	03 00	03 05	03 07

Lat.	Sunset	Civil	Naut.	Moonset 3	4	5	6
°	h m	h m	h m	h m	h m	h m	h m
N 72	14 11	15 44	17 09	□	□	□	17 12
N 70	14 42	15 59	17 14	□	□	□	16 35
68	15 04	16 11	17 19	□	□	16 52	16 08
66	15 21	16 21	17 23	□	17 22	16 11	15 47
64	15 35	16 29	17 26	□	16 04	15 43	15 31
62	15 47	16 37	17 30	15 33	15 27	15 22	15 17
60	15 57	16 43	17 33	14 51	15 01	15 04	15 05
N 58	16 06	16 49	17 35	14 22	14 40	14 50	14 55
56	16 14	16 54	17 38	13 59	14 23	14 37	14 46
54	16 21	16 58	17 40	13 41	14 08	14 26	14 38
52	16 27	17 03	17 43	13 26	13 55	14 16	14 31
50	16 32	17 07	17 45	13 12	13 44	14 07	14 25
45	16 45	17 15	17 50	12 44	13 20	13 48	14 11
N 40	16 55	17 23	17 55	12 22	13 01	13 33	13 59
35	17 03	17 30	18 00	12 04	12 46	13 20	13 49
30	17 11	17 36	18 04	11 49	12 32	13 09	13 41
20	17 24	17 47	18 13	11 22	12 08	12 49	13 26
N 10	17 36	17 58	18 23	10 59	11 48	12 32	13 12
0	17 47	18 08	18 33	10 37	11 28	12 16	13 00
S 10	17 58	18 20	18 46	10 16	11 09	11 59	12 47
20	18 10	18 33	19 01	09 52	10 48	11 42	12 34
30	18 24	18 50	19 20	09 25	10 24	11 22	12 18
35	18 33	19 00	19 32	09 09	10 10	11 10	12 09
40	18 42	19 11	19 47	08 51	09 53	10 56	11 58
45	18 53	19 25	20 06	08 28	09 33	10 40	11 46
S 50	19 06	19 43	20 31	07 59	09 08	10 20	11 31
52	19 13	19 52	20 43	07 44	08 56	10 10	11 24
54	19 20	20 01	20 57	07 28	08 42	09 59	11 16
56	19 27	20 12	21 15	07 08	08 25	09 47	11 07
58	19 36	20 25	21 37	06 43	08 06	09 32	10 57
S 60	19 46	20 40	22 07	06 08	07 41	09 15	10 45

Day	SUN Eqn. of Time 00h	SUN Eqn. of Time 12h	SUN Mer. Pass.	MOON Mer. Pass. Upper	MOON Mer. Pass. Lower	Age	Phase
d	m s	m s	h m	h m	h m	d	%
3	16 27	16 27	11 44	04 25	16 51	20	68
4	16 27	16 27	11 44	05 16	17 41	21	58
5	16 27	16 26	11 44	06 05	18 27	22	49

© British Crown Copyright 2022. All rights reserved.

UT	ARIES GHA	VENUS −4·4 GHA	Dec	MARS +1·4 GHA	Dec	JUPITER −2·9 GHA	Dec	SATURN +0·7 GHA	Dec	STARS Name	SHA	Dec
MONDAY												
6 00	44 57.3	226 56.4	N 1 56.3	180 23.3	S16 54.8	6 46.8	N13 31.1	71 44.7	S12 54.5	Acamar	315 12.1	S40 12.5
01	59 59.7	241 56.3	55.4	195 24.1	55.4	21 49.6	31.0	86 47.2	54.5	Achernar	335 20.4	S57 07.0
02	75 02.2	256 56.3	54.5	210 24.8	55.9	36 52.4	30.9	101 49.6	54.5	Acrux	173 01.8	S63 13.6
03	90 04.7	271 56.2 ..	53.6	225 25.5 ..	56.4	51 55.2 ..	30.8	116 52.1 ..	54.5	Adhara	255 06.5	S29 00.0
04	105 07.1	286 56.1	52.7	240 26.2	56.9	66 58.0	30.7	131 54.6	54.5	Aldebaran	290 40.5	N16 33.5
05	120 09.6	301 56.0	51.8	255 27.0	57.4	82 00.8	30.6	146 57.0	54.5			
06	135 12.0	316 55.9	N 1 50.9	270 27.7	S16 57.9	97 03.6	N13 30.4	161 59.5	S12 54.5	Alioth	166 14.3	N55 49.8
07	150 14.5	331 55.9	50.0	285 28.4	58.5	112 06.4	30.3	177 01.9	54.5	Alkaid	152 53.3	N49 11.6
08	165 17.0	346 55.8	49.1	300 29.1	59.0	127 09.2	30.2	192 04.4	54.5	Alnair	27 34.0	S46 50.9
09	180 19.4	1 55.7 ..	48.2	315 29.9	16 59.5	142 12.0 ..	30.1	207 06.8 ..	54.5	Alnilam	275 38.5	S 1 11.1
10	195 21.9	16 55.6	47.2	330 30.6	17 00.0	157 14.8	30.0	222 09.3	54.4	Alphard	217 48.8	S 8 45.5
11	210 24.4	31 55.5	46.3	345 31.3	00.5	172 17.6	29.9	237 11.8	54.4			
12	225 26.8	46 55.4	N 1 45.4	0 32.0	S17 01.0	187 20.4	N13 29.8	252 14.2	S12 54.4	Alphecca	126 05.0	N26 38.2
13	240 29.3	61 55.4	44.5	15 32.8	01.5	202 23.2	29.7	267 16.7	54.4	Alpheratz	357 35.6	N29 13.5
14	255 31.8	76 55.3	43.6	30 33.5	02.1	217 26.0	29.6	282 19.1	54.4	Altair	62 01.0	N 8 56.0
15	270 34.2	91 55.2 ..	42.7	45 34.2 ..	02.6	232 28.8 ..	29.5	297 21.6 ..	54.4	Ankaa	353 07.8	S42 10.7
16	285 36.7	106 55.1	41.8	60 34.9	03.1	247 31.6	29.4	312 24.0	54.4	Antares	112 17.4	S26 29.0
17	300 39.1	121 55.0	40.9	75 35.7	03.6	262 34.4	29.3	327 26.5	54.4			
18	315 41.6	136 54.9	N 1 40.0	90 36.4	S17 04.1	277 37.1	N13 29.2	342 29.0	S12 54.4	Arcturus	145 49.2	N19 03.6
19	330 44.1	151 54.9	39.1	105 37.1	04.6	292 39.9	29.1	357 31.4	54.4	Atria	107 13.0	S69 04.3
20	345 46.5	166 54.8	38.2	120 37.8	05.1	307 42.7	29.0	12 33.9	54.4	Avior	234 15.0	S59 34.7
21	0 49.0	181 54.7 ..	37.2	135 38.5 ..	05.7	322 45.5 ..	28.9	27 36.3 ..	54.3	Bellatrix	278 23.7	N 6 22.4
22	15 51.5	196 54.6	36.3	150 39.3	06.2	337 48.3	28.8	42 38.8	54.3	Betelgeuse	270 52.9	N 7 24.8
23	30 53.9	211 54.5	35.4	165 40.0	06.7	352 51.1	28.7	57 41.2	54.3			
TUESDAY												
7 00	45 56.4	226 54.4	N 1 34.5	180 40.7	S17 07.2	7 53.9	N13 28.6	72 43.7	S12 54.3	Canopus	263 52.5	S52 42.2
01	60 58.9	241 54.3	33.6	195 41.4	07.7	22 56.7	28.5	87 46.1	54.3	Capella	280 23.0	N46 01.2
02	76 01.3	256 54.2	32.7	210 42.2	08.2	37 59.5	28.4	102 48.6	54.3	Deneb	49 26.6	N45 22.1
03	91 03.8	271 54.2 ..	31.8	225 42.9 ..	08.7	53 02.3 ..	28.3	117 51.0 ..	54.3	Denebola	182 26.2	N14 26.4
04	106 06.3	286 54.1	30.9	240 43.6	09.2	68 05.1	28.2	132 53.5	54.3	Diphda	348 48.0	S17 51.4
05	121 08.7	301 54.0	29.9	255 44.3	09.7	83 07.9	28.1	147 56.0	54.3			
06	136 11.2	316 53.9	N 1 29.0	270 45.0	S17 10.3	98 10.7	N13 28.0	162 58.4	S12 54.3	Dubhe	193 42.5	N61 37.2
07	151 13.6	331 53.8	28.1	285 45.8	10.8	113 13.5	27.9	178 00.9	54.3	Elnath	278 02.8	N28 37.6
08	166 16.1	346 53.7	27.2	300 46.5	11.3	128 16.3	27.8	193 03.3	54.3	Eltanin	90 43.0	N51 29.3
09	181 18.6	1 53.6 ..	26.3	315 47.2 ..	11.8	143 19.1 ..	27.7	208 05.8 ..	54.2	Enif	33 39.7	N 9 59.1
10	196 21.0	16 53.5	25.4	330 47.9	12.3	158 21.9	27.6	223 08.2	54.2	Fomalhaut	15 15.4	S29 29.9
11	211 23.5	31 53.4	24.4	345 48.6	12.8	173 24.7	27.5	238 10.7	54.2			
12	226 26.0	46 53.3	N 1 23.5	0 49.3	S17 13.3	188 27.5	N13 27.4	253 13.1	S12 54.2	Gacrux	171 53.3	S57 14.5
13	241 28.4	61 53.2	22.6	15 50.1	13.8	203 30.3	27.3	268 15.6	54.2	Gienah	175 44.9	S17 40.2
14	256 30.9	76 53.2	21.7	30 50.8	14.3	218 33.1	27.2	283 18.0	54.2	Hadar	148 38.1	S60 29.1
15	271 33.4	91 53.1 ..	20.8	45 51.5 ..	14.8	233 35.8 ..	27.1	298 20.5 ..	54.2	Hamal	327 52.0	N23 34.6
16	286 35.8	106 53.0	19.9	60 52.2	15.3	248 38.6	27.0	313 22.9	54.2	Kaus Aust.	83 34.1	S34 22.5
17	301 38.3	121 52.9	18.9	75 52.9	15.9	263 41.4	26.9	328 25.4	54.2			
18	316 40.8	136 52.8	N 1 18.0	90 53.6	S17 16.4	278 44.2	N13 26.8	343 27.8	S12 54.2	Kochab	137 20.9	N74 03.4
19	331 43.2	151 52.7	17.1	105 54.4	16.9	293 47.0	26.7	358 30.3	54.2	Markab	13 30.7	N15 20.1
20	346 45.7	166 52.6	16.2	120 55.1	17.4	308 49.8	26.6	13 32.7	54.1	Menkar	314 06.9	N 4 11.1
21	1 48.1	181 52.5 ..	15.2	135 55.8 ..	17.9	323 52.6 ..	26.5	28 35.2 ..	54.1	Menkent	147 59.2	S36 29.1
22	16 50.6	196 52.4	14.3	150 56.5	18.4	338 55.4	26.4	43 37.6	54.1	Miaplacidus	221 38.5	S69 48.5
23	31 53.1	211 52.3	13.4	165 57.2	18.9	353 58.2	26.3	58 40.1	54.1			
WEDNESDAY												
8 00	46 55.5	226 52.2	N 1 12.5	180 57.9	S17 19.4	9 01.0	N13 26.2	73 42.5	S12 54.1	Mirfak	308 29.2	N49 56.8
01	61 58.0	241 52.1	11.6	195 58.7	19.9	24 03.8	26.1	88 45.0	54.1	Nunki	75 49.2	S26 16.1
02	77 00.5	256 52.0	10.6	210 59.4	20.4	39 06.6	26.0	103 47.4	54.1	Peacock	53 07.4	S56 39.7
03	92 02.9	271 51.9 ..	09.7	226 00.1 ..	20.9	54 09.4 ..	25.9	118 49.9 ..	54.1	Pollux	243 18.4	N27 58.1
04	107 05.4	286 51.8	08.8	241 00.8	21.4	69 12.2	25.8	133 52.3	54.1	Procyon	244 51.8	N 5 09.9
05	122 07.9	301 51.7	07.9	256 01.5	21.9	84 15.0	25.7	148 54.8	54.1			
06	137 10.3	316 51.6	N 1 06.9	271 02.2	S17 22.4	99 17.8	N13 25.6	163 57.2	S12 54.0	Rasalhague	95 59.7	N12 32.7
07	152 12.8	331 51.5	06.0	286 02.9	22.9	114 20.6	25.5	178 59.7	54.0	Regulus	207 35.6	N11 51.1
08	167 15.2	346 51.4	05.1	301 03.7	23.4	129 23.4	25.4	194 02.1	54.0	Rigel	281 04.5	S 8 10.3
09	182 17.7	1 51.3 ..	04.2	316 04.4 ..	24.0	144 26.1 ..	25.3	209 04.6 ..	54.0	Rigil Kent.	139 42.4	S60 55.9
10	197 20.2	16 51.2	03.2	331 05.1	24.5	159 28.9	25.2	224 07.0	54.0	Sabik	102 04.2	S15 45.2
11	212 22.6	31 51.1	02.3	346 05.8	25.0	174 31.7	25.1	239 09.5	54.0			
12	227 25.1	46 51.0	N 1 01.4	1 06.5	S17 25.5	189 34.5	N13 25.0	254 11.9	S12 54.0	Schedar	349 31.7	N56 40.3
13	242 27.6	61 50.9	1 00.5	16 07.2	26.0	204 37.3	24.9	269 14.4	54.0	Shaula	96 12.1	S37 07.3
14	257 30.0	76 50.8	0 59.5	31 07.9	26.5	219 40.1	24.8	284 16.8	54.0	Sirius	258 26.9	S16 44.7
15	272 32.5	91 50.7 ..	58.6	46 08.6 ..	27.0	234 42.9 ..	24.7	299 19.3 ..	53.9	Spica	158 23.7	S11 17.0
16	287 35.0	106 50.6	57.7	61 09.3	27.5	249 45.7	24.6	314 21.7	53.9	Suhail	222 47.1	S43 31.4
17	302 37.4	121 50.5	56.7	76 10.1	28.0	264 48.5	24.5	329 24.2	53.9			
18	317 39.9	136 50.4	N 0 55.8	91 10.8	S17 28.5	279 51.3	N13 24.4	344 26.6	S12 53.9	Vega	80 34.2	N38 48.5
19	332 42.4	151 50.3	54.9	106 11.5	29.0	294 54.1	24.3	359 29.1	53.9	Zuben'ubi	136 57.5	S16 08.3
20	347 44.8	166 50.2	53.9	121 12.2	29.5	309 56.9	24.2	14 31.5	53.9			
21	2 47.3	181 50.1 ..	53.0	136 12.9 ..	30.0	324 59.7 ..	24.1	29 34.0 ..	53.9		SHA	Mer. Pass.
22	17 49.7	196 50.0	52.1	151 13.6	30.5	340 02.5	24.0	44 36.4	53.9	Venus	180 58.0	8 52
23	32 52.2	211 49.9	51.2	166 14.3	31.0	355 05.3	23.9	59 38.9	53.9	Mars	134 44.3	11 57
Mer. Pass. 20 52.8		v −0.1 d 0.9		v 0.7 d 0.5		v 2.8 d 0.1		v 2.5 d 0.0		Jupiter	321 57.5	23 24
										Saturn	26 47.3	19 06

© British Crown Copyright 2022. All rights reserved.

SUN and MOON — GHA / Dec

UT	SUN GHA	SUN Dec	MOON GHA	v	MOON Dec	d	HP
6 MONDAY	° '	° '	° '	'	° '	'	'
00	184 06.2	S15 49.9	260 40.0	14.2	N19 13.4	10.8	54.3
01	199 06.2	50.6	275 13.2	14.3	19 02.6	10.8	54.3
02	214 06.2	51.4	289 46.5	14.4	18 51.8	10.9	54.3
03	229 06.2	.. 52.1	304 19.9	14.5	18 40.9	10.9	54.3
04	244 06.2	52.9	318 53.4	14.5	18 30.0	11.0	54.3
05	259 06.1	53.6	333 26.9	14.6	18 19.0	11.1	54.2
06	274 06.1	S15 54.4	348 00.5	14.7	N18 07.9	11.2	54.2
07	289 06.1	55.2	2 34.2	14.7	17 56.7	11.2	54.2
08	304 06.1	55.9	17 07.9	14.8	17 45.5	11.3	54.2
09	319 06.0	.. 56.7	31 41.7	14.8	17 34.2	11.4	54.2
10	334 06.0	57.4	46 15.5	14.9	17 22.8	11.5	54.2
11	349 06.0	58.2	60 49.4	15.0	17 11.3	11.5	54.2
12	4 06.0	S15 58.9	75 23.4	15.1	N16 59.8	11.5	54.2
13	19 05.9	15 59.6	89 57.5	15.0	16 48.3	11.7	54.2
14	34 05.9	16 00.4	104 31.5	15.2	16 36.6	11.7	54.2
15	49 05.9	.. 01.1	119 05.7	15.2	16 24.9	11.7	54.2
16	64 05.9	01.9	133 39.9	15.3	16 13.2	11.8	54.2
17	79 05.8	02.6	148 14.2	15.3	16 01.4	11.9	54.2
18	94 05.8	S16 03.4	162 48.5	15.4	N15 49.5	12.0	54.2
19	109 05.8	04.1	177 22.9	15.4	15 37.5	12.0	54.2
20	124 05.8	04.9	191 57.3	15.5	15 25.5	12.0	54.2
21	139 05.7	.. 05.6	206 31.8	15.5	15 13.5	12.2	54.2
22	154 05.7	06.4	221 06.3	15.6	15 01.3	12.1	54.2
23	169 05.7	07.1	235 40.9	15.7	14 49.2	12.3	54.2
7 TUESDAY							
00	184 05.6	S16 07.9	250 15.6	15.7	N14 36.9	12.3	54.2
01	199 05.6	08.6	264 50.3	15.7	14 24.6	12.3	54.2
02	214 05.6	09.3	279 25.0	15.8	14 12.3	12.4	54.2
03	229 05.6	.. 10.1	293 59.8	15.8	13 59.9	12.4	54.2
04	244 05.5	10.8	308 34.6	15.9	13 47.5	12.6	54.2
05	259 05.5	11.6	323 09.5	15.9	13 34.9	12.5	54.2
06	274 05.5	S16 12.3	337 44.4	16.0	N13 22.4	12.6	54.2
07	289 05.4	13.0	352 19.4	16.0	13 09.8	12.7	54.2
08	304 05.4	13.8	6 54.4	16.0	12 57.1	12.7	54.2
09	319 05.4	.. 14.5	21 29.4	16.1	12 44.4	12.7	54.2
10	334 05.3	15.3	36 04.5	16.2	12 31.7	12.8	54.2
11	349 05.3	16.0	50 39.7	16.1	12 18.9	12.9	54.2
12	4 05.3	S16 16.7	65 14.8	16.2	N12 06.0	12.9	54.2
13	19 05.2	17.5	79 50.0	16.3	11 53.1	13.0	54.2
14	34 05.2	18.2	94 25.3	16.3	11 40.1	12.9	54.2
15	49 05.2	.. 18.9	109 00.6	16.3	11 27.2	13.1	54.2
16	64 05.1	19.7	123 35.9	16.3	11 14.1	13.1	54.2
17	79 05.1	20.4	138 11.2	16.4	11 01.0	13.1	54.3
18	94 05.1	S16 21.2	152 46.6	16.4	N10 47.9	13.2	54.3
19	109 05.0	21.9	167 22.0	16.5	10 34.7	13.2	54.3
20	124 05.0	22.6	181 57.5	16.5	10 21.5	13.2	54.3
21	139 04.9	.. 23.4	196 33.0	16.5	10 08.3	13.3	54.3
22	154 04.9	24.1	211 08.5	16.5	9 55.0	13.4	54.3
23	169 04.9	24.8	225 44.0	16.5	9 41.6	13.3	54.3
8 WEDNESDAY							
00	184 04.8	S16 25.6	240 19.5	16.6	N 9 28.3	13.4	54.3
01	199 04.8	26.3	254 55.1	16.6	9 14.9	13.5	54.3
02	214 04.8	27.0	269 30.7	16.7	9 01.4	13.5	54.3
03	229 04.7	.. 27.7	284 06.4	16.6	8 47.9	13.5	54.3
04	244 04.7	28.5	298 42.0	16.7	8 34.4	13.6	54.3
05	259 04.6	29.2	313 17.7	16.7	8 20.8	13.6	54.3
06	274 04.6	S16 29.9	327 53.4	16.7	N 8 07.2	13.6	54.3
07	289 04.5	30.7	342 29.1	16.7	7 53.6	13.7	54.4
08	304 04.5	31.4	357 04.8	16.8	7 39.9	13.6	54.4
09	319 04.5	.. 32.1	11 40.6	16.8	7 26.3	13.8	54.4
10	334 04.4	32.8	26 16.4	16.7	7 12.5	13.7	54.4
11	349 04.4	33.6	40 52.1	16.8	6 58.8	13.8	54.4
12	4 04.3	S16 34.3	55 27.9	16.8	N 6 45.0	13.9	54.4
13	19 04.3	35.0	70 03.7	16.9	6 31.1	13.8	54.4
14	34 04.3	35.8	84 39.6	16.8	6 17.3	13.9	54.4
15	49 04.2	.. 36.5	99 15.4	16.8	6 03.4	13.9	54.4
16	64 04.2	37.2	113 51.2	16.9	5 49.5	13.9	54.4
17	79 04.1	37.9	128 27.1	16.8	5 35.6	14.0	54.5
18	94 04.1	S16 38.6	143 02.9	16.9	N 5 21.6	14.0	54.5
19	109 04.0	39.4	157 38.8	16.9	5 07.6	14.0	54.5
20	124 04.0	40.1	172 14.7	16.8	4 53.6	14.1	54.5
21	139 03.9	.. 40.8	186 50.5	16.9	4 39.5	14.0	54.5
22	154 03.9	41.5	201 26.4	16.9	4 25.5	14.1	54.5
23	169 03.8	42.3	216 02.3	16.9	N 4 11.4	14.1	54.5
SD	16.2	d 0.7	SD 14.8		14.8		14.8

Twilight / Sunrise / Moonrise

Lat.	Twilight Naut.	Civil	Sunrise	Moonrise 6	7	8	9
°	h m	h m	h m	h m	h m	h m	h m
N 72	06 28	07 55	09 36	21 32	23 56	25 59	01 59
N 70	06 22	07 39	09 00	22 08	24 12	00 12	02 04
68	06 16	07 25	08 35	22 33	24 24	00 24	02 08
66	06 11	07 14	08 16	22 52	24 34	00 34	02 11
64	06 07	07 05	08 00	23 07	24 42	00 42	02 14
62	06 03	06 57	07 48	23 19	24 49	00 49	02 16
60	06 00	06 50	07 37	23 31	24 55	00 55	02 18
N 58	05 57	06 44	07 27	23 40	25 01	01 01	02 20
56	05 54	06 38	07 19	23 48	25 05	01 05	02 22
54	05 51	06 33	07 12	23 55	25 10	01 10	02 23
52	05 48	06 29	07 05	24 02	00 02	01 13	02 25
50	05 46	06 24	06 59	24 07	00 07	01 17	02 26
45	05 40	06 15	06 46	24 20	00 20	01 24	02 28
N 40	05 35	06 07	06 35	24 30	00 30	01 31	02 31
35	05 30	06 00	06 26	24 39	00 39	01 36	02 33
30	05 25	05 53	06 18	24 46	00 46	01 41	02 34
20	05 15	05 41	06 04	00 09	01 00	01 49	02 37
N 10	05 05	05 30	05 52	00 24	01 11	01 56	02 40
0	04 54	05 19	05 40	00 39	01 22	02 02	02 42
S 10	04 41	05 06	05 28	00 53	01 32	02 09	02 45
20	04 25	04 52	05 16	01 09	01 43	02 16	02 47
30	04 05	04 35	05 01	01 26	01 56	02 24	02 50
35	03 52	04 25	04 52	01 36	02 04	02 28	02 52
40	03 37	04 13	04 43	01 48	02 12	02 34	02 54
45	03 17	03 58	04 31	02 01	02 22	02 39	02 56
S 50	02 52	03 40	04 17	02 18	02 33	02 47	02 58
52	02 39	03 31	04 10	02 26	02 39	02 50	03 00
54	02 23	03 21	04 03	02 34	02 45	02 53	03 01
56	02 05	03 09	03 55	02 44	02 51	02 57	03 02
58	01 41	02 56	03 46	02 55	02 59	03 02	03 04
S 60	01 07	02 40	03 35	03 07	03 07	03 07	03 06

Sunset / Twilight / Moonset

Lat.	Sunset	Twilight Civil	Naut.	Moonset 6	7	8	9
°	h m	h m	h m	h m	h m	h m	h m
N 72	13 50	15 31	16 57	17 12	16 14	15 37	15 05
N 70	14 26	15 47	17 04	16 35	15 57	15 29	15 05
68	14 51	16 01	17 10	16 08	15 43	15 23	15 04
66	15 10	16 12	17 15	15 47	15 31	15 17	15 04
64	15 26	16 21	17 19	15 31	15 21	15 12	15 04
62	15 39	16 29	17 23	15 17	15 13	15 08	15 04
60	15 50	16 36	17 27	15 05	15 05	15 05	15 04
N 58	15 59	16 43	17 30	14 55	14 59	15 01	15 03
56	16 08	16 48	17 33	14 46	14 53	14 58	15 03
54	16 15	16 53	17 36	14 38	14 48	14 56	15 03
52	16 22	16 58	17 38	14 31	14 43	14 54	15 03
50	16 28	17 02	17 41	14 25	14 39	14 51	15 03
45	16 41	17 12	17 47	14 11	14 30	14 47	15 03
N 40	16 51	17 20	17 52	13 59	14 22	14 43	15 02
35	17 01	17 27	17 57	13 49	14 15	14 39	15 02
30	17 09	17 34	18 02	13 41	14 09	14 36	15 02
20	17 23	17 46	18 12	13 26	13 59	14 31	15 02
N 10	17 35	17 57	18 22	13 12	13 50	14 26	15 02
0	17 47	18 09	18 34	13 00	13 41	14 22	15 01
S 10	17 59	18 21	18 47	12 47	13 33	14 17	15 01
20	18 12	18 35	19 03	12 34	13 23	14 12	15 01
30	18 27	18 52	19 23	12 18	13 13	14 07	15 00
35	18 35	19 03	19 36	12 09	13 07	14 03	15 00
40	18 45	19 15	19 52	11 58	12 59	14 00	15 00
45	18 57	19 30	20 11	11 46	12 51	13 55	14 59
S 50	19 11	19 49	20 37	11 31	12 41	13 50	14 59
52	19 18	19 58	20 51	11 24	12 36	13 48	14 59
54	19 26	20 08	21 06	11 16	12 31	13 45	14 59
56	19 34	20 20	21 26	11 07	12 25	13 42	14 59
58	19 43	20 34	21 50	10 57	12 19	13 39	14 58
S 60	19 54	20 50	22 26	10 45	12 12	13 35	14 58

SUN and MOON — daily

Day	SUN Eqn. of Time 00h	12h	Mer. Pass.	MOON Mer. Pass. Upper	Lower	Age	Phase
d	m s	m s	h m	h m	h m	d	%
6	16 25	16 24	11 44	06 49	19 11	23	39
7	16 23	16 21	11 44	07 32	19 52	24	30
8	16 19	16 17	11 44	08 12	20 32	25	22

© British Crown Copyright 2022. All rights reserved.

UT	ARIES	VENUS −4.3		MARS +1.4		JUPITER −2.9		SATURN +0.7		STARS		
	GHA	GHA	Dec	GHA	Dec	GHA	Dec	GHA	Dec	Name	SHA	Dec
d h	° ′	° ′	° ′	° ′	° ′	° ′	° ′	° ′	° ′		° ′	° ′
9 00	47 54.7	226 49.8	N 0 50.2	181 15.0	S17 31.5	10 08.0	N13 23.8	74 41.3	S12 53.8	Acamar	315 12.1	S40 12.5
01	62 57.1	241 49.7	49.3	196 15.7	32.0	25 10.8	23.7	89 43.7	53.8	Achernar	335 20.4	S57 07.0
02	77 59.6	256 49.6	48.4	211 16.4	32.5	40 13.6	23.6	104 46.2	53.8	Acrux	173 01.7	S63 13.6
03	93 02.1	271 49.5	.. 47.4	226 17.2	.. 33.0	55 16.4	.. 23.5	119 48.6	.. 53.8	Adhara	255 06.4	S29 00.0
04	108 04.5	286 49.4	46.5	241 17.9	33.5	70 19.2	23.4	134 51.1	53.8	Aldebaran	290 40.4	N16 33.5
05	123 07.0	301 49.3	45.6	256 18.6	34.0	85 22.0	23.3	149 53.5	53.8			
06	138 09.5	316 49.2	N 0 44.6	271 19.3	S17 34.5	100 24.8	N13 23.2	164 56.0	S12 53.8	Alioth	166 14.3	N55 49.7
07	153 11.9	331 49.1	43.7	286 20.0	35.0	115 27.6	23.1	179 58.4	53.8	Alkaid	152 53.2	N49 11.6
T 08	168 14.4	346 49.0	42.8	301 20.7	35.5	130 30.4	23.0	195 00.9	53.7	Alnair	27 34.0	S46 51.0
H 09	183 16.8	1 48.8	.. 41.8	316 21.4	.. 36.0	145 33.2	.. 22.9	210 03.3	.. 53.7	Alnilam	275 38.5	S 1 11.1
U 10	198 19.3	16 48.7	40.9	331 22.1	36.5	160 36.0	22.8	225 05.8	53.7	Alphard	217 48.8	S 8 45.5
R 11	213 21.8	31 48.6	39.9	346 22.8	37.0	175 38.8	22.7	240 08.2	53.7			
S 12	228 24.2	46 48.5	N 0 39.0	1 23.5	S17 37.5	190 41.6	N13 22.6	255 10.6	S12 53.7	Alphecca	126 05.0	N26 38.1
D 13	243 26.7	61 48.4	38.1	16 24.2	38.0	205 44.4	22.5	270 13.1	53.7	Alpheratz	357 35.6	N29 13.5
A 14	258 29.2	76 48.3	37.1	31 24.9	38.5	220 47.1	22.4	285 15.5	53.7	Altair	62 01.1	N 8 56.0
Y 15	273 31.6	91 48.2	.. 36.2	46 25.6	.. 39.0	235 49.9	.. 22.3	300 18.0	.. 53.7	Ankaa	353 07.8	S42 10.7
16	288 34.1	106 48.1	35.3	61 26.3	39.5	250 52.7	22.2	315 20.4	53.6	Antares	112 17.4	S26 29.0
17	303 36.6	121 48.0	34.3	76 27.0	40.0	265 55.5	22.1	330 22.9	53.6			
18	318 39.0	136 47.9	N 0 33.4	91 27.7	S17 40.5	280 58.3	N13 22.0	345 25.3	S12 53.6	Arcturus	145 49.2	N19 03.6
19	333 41.5	151 47.8	32.4	106 28.5	41.0	296 01.1	21.9	0 27.8	53.6	Atria	107 13.1	S69 04.3
20	348 44.0	166 47.6	31.5	121 29.2	41.5	311 03.9	21.8	15 30.2	53.6	Avior	234 15.0	S59 34.7
21	3 46.4	181 47.5	.. 30.6	136 29.9	.. 42.0	326 06.7	.. 21.7	30 32.6	.. 53.6	Bellatrix	278 23.7	N 6 22.4
22	18 48.9	196 47.4	29.6	151 30.6	42.4	341 09.5	21.6	45 35.1	53.6	Betelgeuse	270 52.9	N 7 24.8
23	33 51.3	211 47.3	28.7	166 31.3	42.9	356 12.3	21.5	60 37.5	53.6			
10 00	48 53.8	226 47.2	N 0 27.7	181 32.0	S17 43.4	11 15.1	N13 21.4	75 40.0	S12 53.5	Canopus	263 52.5	S52 42.2
01	63 56.3	241 47.1	26.8	196 32.7	43.9	26 17.9	21.3	90 42.4	53.5	Capella	280 23.0	N46 01.3
02	78 58.7	256 47.0	25.9	211 33.4	44.4	41 20.6	21.2	105 44.8	53.5	Deneb	49 26.6	N45 22.1
03	94 01.2	271 46.9	.. 24.9	226 34.1	.. 44.9	56 23.4	.. 21.1	120 47.3	.. 53.5	Denebola	182 26.2	N14 26.4
04	109 03.7	286 46.7	24.0	241 34.8	45.4	71 26.2	21.0	135 49.7	53.5	Diphda	348 48.0	S17 51.4
05	124 06.1	301 46.6	23.0	256 35.5	45.9	86 29.0	20.9	150 52.2	53.5			
06	139 08.6	316 46.5	N 0 22.1	271 36.2	S17 46.4	101 31.8	N13 20.8	165 54.6	S12 53.5	Dubhe	193 42.5	N61 37.2
07	154 11.1	331 46.4	21.1	286 36.9	46.9	116 34.6	20.7	180 57.1	53.4	Elnath	278 02.8	N28 37.6
08	169 13.5	346 46.3	20.2	301 37.6	47.4	131 37.4	20.6	195 59.5	53.4	Eltanin	90 43.1	N51 29.3
F 09	184 16.0	1 46.2	.. 19.3	316 38.3	.. 47.9	146 40.2	.. 20.5	211 01.9	.. 53.4	Enif	33 39.7	N 9 59.1
R 10	199 18.5	16 46.1	18.3	331 39.0	48.4	161 43.0	20.4	226 04.4	53.4	Fomalhaut	15 15.5	S29 29.9
I 11	214 20.9	31 45.9	17.4	346 39.7	48.9	176 45.8	20.3	241 06.8	53.4			
D 12	229 23.4	46 45.8	N 0 16.4	1 40.4	S17 49.4	191 48.5	N13 20.2	256 09.3	S12 53.4	Gacrux	171 53.2	S57 14.5
A 13	244 25.8	61 45.7	15.5	16 41.1	49.9	206 51.3	20.1	271 11.7	53.3	Gienah	175 44.9	S17 40.3
Y 14	259 28.3	76 45.6	14.5	31 41.8	50.3	221 54.1	20.0	286 14.1	53.3	Hadar	148 38.1	S60 29.1
15	274 30.8	91 45.5	.. 13.6	46 42.5	.. 50.8	236 56.9	.. 19.9	301 16.6	.. 53.3	Hamal	327 52.0	N23 34.6
16	289 33.2	106 45.3	12.6	61 43.2	51.3	251 59.7	19.8	316 19.0	53.3	Kaus Aust.	83 34.1	S34 22.5
17	304 35.7	121 45.2	11.7	76 43.9	51.8	267 02.5	19.7	331 21.5	53.3			
18	319 38.2	136 45.1	N 0 10.7	91 44.6	S17 52.3	282 05.3	N13 19.6	346 23.9	S12 53.3	Kochab	137 20.9	N74 03.4
19	334 40.6	151 45.0	09.8	106 45.3	52.8	297 08.1	19.5	1 26.3	53.3	Markab	13 30.7	N15 20.1
20	349 43.1	166 44.9	08.9	121 46.0	53.3	312 10.9	19.4	16 28.8	53.3	Menkar	314 06.9	N 4 11.1
21	4 45.6	181 44.8	.. 07.9	136 46.7	.. 53.8	327 13.7	.. 19.3	31 31.2	.. 53.2	Menkent	147 59.2	S36 29.1
22	19 48.0	196 44.6	07.0	151 47.4	54.3	342 16.4	19.2	46 33.6	53.2	Miaplacidus	221 38.5	S69 48.5
23	34 50.5	211 44.5	06.0	166 48.1	54.8	357 19.2	19.1	61 36.1	53.2			
11 00	49 52.9	226 44.4	N 0 05.1	181 48.8	S17 55.3	12 22.0	N13 19.0	76 38.5	S12 53.2	Mirfak	308 29.2	N49 56.8
01	64 55.4	241 44.3	04.1	196 49.5	55.7	27 24.8	18.9	91 41.0	53.2	Nunki	75 49.2	S26 16.1
02	79 57.9	256 44.1	03.2	211 50.2	56.2	42 27.6	18.8	106 43.4	53.2	Peacock	53 07.4	S56 39.7
03	95 00.3	271 44.0	.. 02.2	226 50.9	.. 56.7	57 30.4	.. 18.7	121 45.8	.. 53.2	Pollux	243 18.4	N27 58.1
04	110 02.8	286 43.9	01.3	241 51.6	57.2	72 33.2	18.6	136 48.3	53.1	Procyon	244 51.7	N 5 09.9
05	125 05.3	301 43.8	N 00.3	256 52.2	57.7	87 36.0	18.5	151 50.7	53.1			
06	140 07.7	316 43.7	S 0 00.6	271 52.9	S17 58.2	102 38.8	N13 18.4	166 53.2	S12 53.1	Rasalhague	95 59.8	N12 32.7
07	155 10.2	331 43.5	01.6	286 53.6	58.7	117 41.5	18.3	181 55.6	53.1	Regulus	207 35.6	N11 51.1
S 08	170 12.7	346 43.4	02.5	301 54.3	59.2	132 44.3	18.2	196 58.0	53.1	Rigel	281 04.5	S 8 10.3
A 09	185 15.1	1 43.3	.. 03.5	316 55.0	17 59.7	147 47.1	.. 18.1	212 00.5	.. 53.1	Rigil Kent.	139 42.4	S60 55.9
T 10	200 17.6	16 43.2	04.5	331 55.7	18 00.1	162 49.9	18.0	227 02.9	53.1	Sabik	102 04.2	S15 45.2
U 11	215 20.1	31 43.0	05.4	346 56.4	00.6	177 52.7	17.9	242 05.3	53.0			
R 12	230 22.5	46 42.9	S 0 06.4	1 57.1	S18 01.1	192 55.5	N13 17.8	257 07.8	S12 53.0	Schedar	349 31.7	N56 40.3
D 13	245 25.0	61 42.8	07.3	16 57.8	01.6	207 58.3	17.7	272 10.2	53.0	Shaula	96 12.1	S37 07.3
A 14	260 27.4	76 42.7	08.3	31 58.5	02.1	223 01.1	17.6	287 12.6	53.0	Sirius	258 26.9	S16 44.7
Y 15	275 29.9	91 42.5	.. 09.2	46 59.2	.. 02.6	238 03.9	.. 17.5	302 15.1	.. 53.0	Spica	158 23.7	S11 17.0
16	290 32.4	106 42.4	10.2	61 59.9	03.1	253 06.6	17.4	317 17.5	53.0	Suhail	222 47.0	S43 31.4
17	305 34.8	121 42.3	11.1	77 00.6	03.5	268 09.4	17.3	332 19.9	52.9			
18	320 37.3	136 42.2	S 0 12.1	92 01.3	S18 04.0	283 12.2	N13 17.2	347 22.4	S12 52.9	Vega	80 34.2	N38 48.5
19	335 39.8	151 42.0	13.0	107 02.0	04.5	298 15.0	17.1	2 24.8	52.9	Zuben'ubi	136 57.5	S16 08.3
20	350 42.2	166 41.9	14.0	122 02.7	05.0	313 17.8	17.0	17 27.3	52.9			
21	5 44.7	181 41.8	.. 15.0	137 03.3	.. 05.5	328 20.6	.. 16.9	32 29.7	.. 52.9		SHA	Mer. Pass.
22	20 47.2	196 41.7	15.9	152 04.0	06.0	343 23.4	16.8	47 32.1	52.9		° ′	h m
23	35 49.6	211 41.5	16.9	167 04.7	06.4	358 26.2	16.7	62 34.6	52.8	Venus	177 53.4	8 53
	h m									Mars	132 38.2	11 53
Mer. Pass. 20 41.0		v −0.1	d 0.9	v 0.7	d 0.5	v 2.8	d 0.1	v 2.4	d 0.0	Jupiter	322 21.2	23 11
										Saturn	26 46.2	18 54

© British Crown Copyright 2022. All rights reserved.

UT	SUN GHA	SUN Dec	MOON GHA	v	Dec	d	HP
d h	° '	° '	° '	'	° '	'	'
9 00	184 03.8	S16 43.0	230 38.2	16.8	N 3 57.3	14.2	54.5
01	199 03.8	43.7	245 14.0	16.9	3 43.1	14.1	54.6
02	214 03.7	44.4	259 49.9	16.9	3 29.0	14.2	54.6
03	229 03.7 ..	45.1	274 25.8	16.9	3 14.8	14.2	54.6
04	244 03.6	45.9	289 01.7	16.8	3 00.6	14.2	54.6
05	259 03.6	46.6	303 37.5	16.9	2 46.4	14.3	54.6
06	274 03.5	S16 47.3	318 13.4	16.8	N 2 32.1	14.2	54.6
07	289 03.5	48.0	332 49.2	16.9	2 17.9	14.3	54.6
08	304 03.4	48.7	347 25.1	16.8	2 03.6	14.3	54.7
09	319 03.4 ..	49.4	2 00.9	16.8	1 49.3	14.3	54.7
10	334 03.3	50.2	16 36.7	16.8	1 35.0	14.3	54.7
11	349 03.3	50.9	31 12.5	16.8	1 20.7	14.3	54.7
12	4 03.2	S16 51.6	45 48.3	16.8	N 1 06.4	14.4	54.7
13	19 03.2	52.3	60 24.1	16.8	0 52.0	14.3	54.7
14	34 03.1	53.0	74 59.9	16.8	0 37.7	14.4	54.8
15	49 03.0 ..	53.7	89 35.7	16.7	0 23.3	14.4	54.8
16	64 03.0	54.4	104 11.4	16.7	N 0 08.9	14.4	54.8
17	79 02.9	55.2	118 47.1	16.7	S 0 05.5	14.4	54.8
18	94 02.9	S16 55.9	133 22.8	16.7	S 0 19.9	14.4	54.8
19	109 02.8	56.6	147 58.5	16.7	0 34.3	14.4	54.8
20	124 02.8	57.3	162 34.2	16.6	0 48.7	14.4	54.9
21	139 02.7 ..	58.0	177 09.8	16.6	1 03.1	14.5	54.9
22	154 02.7	58.7	191 45.4	16.6	1 17.6	14.4	54.9
23	169 02.6	16 59.4	206 21.0	16.6	1 32.0	14.4	54.9
10 00	184 02.6	S17 00.1	220 56.6	16.5	S 1 46.4	14.5	54.9
01	199 02.5	00.8	235 32.1	16.5	2 00.9	14.4	54.9
02	214 02.4	01.5	250 07.6	16.5	2 15.3	14.5	55.0
03	229 02.4 ..	02.2	264 43.1	16.4	2 29.8	14.4	55.0
04	244 02.3	03.0	279 18.5	16.5	2 44.2	14.5	55.0
05	259 02.3	03.7	293 54.0	16.3	2 58.7	14.5	55.0
06	274 02.2	S17 04.4	308 29.3	16.4	S 3 13.2	14.4	55.0
07	289 02.1	05.1	323 04.7	16.3	3 27.6	14.5	55.1
08	304 02.1	05.8	337 40.0	16.3	3 42.1	14.4	55.1
09	319 02.0 ..	06.5	352 15.3	16.2	3 56.5	14.5	55.1
10	334 02.0	07.2	6 50.5	16.2	4 11.0	14.4	55.1
11	349 01.9	07.9	21 25.7	16.2	4 25.4	14.4	55.1
12	4 01.8	S17 08.6	36 00.9	16.1	S 4 39.8	14.5	55.2
13	19 01.8	09.3	50 36.0	16.1	4 54.3	14.4	55.2
14	34 01.7	10.0	65 11.1	16.0	5 08.7	14.4	55.2
15	49 01.7 ..	10.7	79 46.1	16.0	5 23.1	14.4	55.2
16	64 01.6	11.4	94 21.1	16.0	5 37.5	14.4	55.2
17	79 01.5	12.1	108 56.1	15.9	5 51.9	14.4	55.3
18	94 01.5	S17 12.8	123 31.0	15.8	S 6 06.3	14.4	55.3
19	109 01.4	13.5	138 05.8	15.8	6 20.7	14.3	55.3
20	124 01.4	14.2	152 40.6	15.8	6 35.0	14.4	55.3
21	139 01.3 ..	14.9	167 15.4	15.7	6 49.4	14.3	55.3
22	154 01.2	15.6	181 50.1	15.7	7 03.7	14.3	55.4
23	169 01.2	16.3	196 24.8	15.6	7 18.0	14.3	55.4
11 00	184 01.1	S17 17.0	210 59.4	15.5	S 7 32.3	14.3	55.4
01	199 01.0	17.7	225 33.9	15.5	7 46.6	14.3	55.4
02	214 01.0	18.4	240 08.4	15.4	8 00.9	14.2	55.4
03	229 00.9 ..	19.1	254 42.8	15.4	8 15.1	14.2	55.5
04	244 00.8	19.8	269 17.2	15.3	8 29.3	14.3	55.5
05	259 00.8	20.5	283 51.5	15.3	8 43.6	14.1	55.5
06	274 00.7	S17 21.2	298 25.8	15.2	S 8 57.7	14.2	55.5
07	289 00.6	21.8	313 00.0	15.1	9 11.9	14.1	55.6
08	304 00.6	22.5	327 34.1	15.1	9 26.0	14.1	55.6
09	319 00.5 ..	23.2	342 08.2	15.0	9 40.1	14.1	55.6
10	334 00.4	23.9	356 42.2	14.9	9 54.2	14.1	55.6
11	349 00.4	24.6	11 16.1	14.9	10 08.3	14.0	55.6
12	4 00.3	S17 25.3	25 50.0	14.8	S10 22.3	14.0	55.7
13	19 00.2	26.0	40 23.8	14.8	10 36.3	13.9	55.7
14	34 00.1	26.7	54 57.6	14.6	10 50.2	14.0	55.7
15	49 00.1 ..	27.4	69 31.2	14.6	11 04.2	13.9	55.7
16	64 00.0	28.1	84 04.8	14.5	11 18.1	13.8	55.8
17	78 59.9	28.7	98 38.3	14.5	11 31.9	13.8	55.8
18	93 59.9	S17 29.4	113 11.8	14.4	S11 45.7	13.8	55.8
19	108 59.8	30.1	127 45.2	14.3	11 59.5	13.8	55.8
20	123 59.7	30.8	142 18.5	14.2	12 13.3	13.7	55.8
21	138 59.6 ..	31.5	156 51.7	14.2	12 27.0	13.7	55.9
22	153 59.6	32.2	171 24.9	14.0	12 40.7	13.6	55.9
23	168 59.5	32.9	185 57.9	14.0	S12 54.3	13.6	55.9
	SD 16.2	d 0.7	SD 14.9		15.0		15.2

Twilight / Sunrise / Moonrise

Lat.	Naut.	Civil	Sunrise	9	10	11	12
°	h m	h m	h m	h m	h m	h m	h m
N 72	06 40	08 09	10 00	01 59	03 58	06 04	08 40
N 70	06 32	07 51	09 17	02 04	03 54	05 50	08 03
68	06 25	07 36	08 48	02 08	03 50	05 38	07 37
66	06 20	07 24	08 27	02 11	03 48	05 28	07 18
64	06 15	07 13	08 10	02 14	03 45	05 20	07 02
62	06 10	07 05	07 56	02 16	03 43	05 13	06 49
60	06 06	06 57	07 44	02 18	03 42	05 08	06 39
N 58	06 02	06 50	07 34	02 20	03 40	05 02	06 29
56	05 59	06 44	07 25	02 22	03 39	04 58	06 21
54	05 56	06 39	07 17	02 23	03 37	04 54	06 14
52	05 53	06 34	07 10	02 25	03 36	04 50	06 07
50	05 50	06 29	07 04	02 26	03 35	04 47	06 01
45	05 44	06 19	06 50	02 28	03 33	04 40	05 49
N 40	05 38	06 10	06 39	02 31	03 31	04 34	05 39
35	05 32	06 03	06 29	02 33	03 30	04 29	05 30
30	05 27	05 56	06 21	02 34	03 28	04 24	05 22
20	05 16	05 43	06 06	02 37	03 26	04 16	05 09
N 10	05 05	05 31	05 53	02 40	03 24	04 10	04 58
0	04 54	05 19	05 40	02 42	03 22	04 03	04 47
S 10	04 40	05 06	05 28	02 45	03 20	03 57	04 37
20	04 24	04 51	05 14	02 47	03 18	03 51	04 25
30	04 02	04 33	04 59	02 50	03 16	03 43	04 13
35	03 49	04 22	04 50	02 52	03 15	03 39	04 06
40	03 33	04 10	04 39	02 54	03 13	03 34	03 57
45	03 12	03 54	04 27	02 56	03 12	03 29	03 48
S 50	02 45	03 34	04 12	02 58	03 10	03 22	03 36
52	02 31	03 25	04 05	02 59	03 09	03 19	03 31
54	02 15	03 14	03 57	03 01	03 08	03 16	03 25
56	01 54	03 02	03 49	03 02	03 07	03 12	03 19
58	01 27	02 47	03 39	03 04	03 06	03 08	03 12
S 60	00 45	02 30	03 27	03 06	03 05	03 04	03 04

Sunset / Twilight / Moonset

Lat.	Sunset	Civil	Naut.	9	10	11	12
°	h m	h m	h m	h m	h m	h m	h m
N 72	13 27	15 17	16 46	15 05	14 33	13 54	12 51
N 70	14 10	15 36	16 54	15 05	14 40	14 11	13 30
68	14 38	15 51	17 01	15 04	14 46	14 25	13 58
66	15 00	16 03	17 07	15 04	14 51	14 37	14 19
64	15 17	16 13	17 12	15 04	14 55	14 46	14 36
62	15 31	16 22	17 17	15 04	14 59	14 55	14 50
60	15 42	16 30	17 21	15 04	15 03	15 02	15 02
N 58	15 53	16 37	17 24	15 03	15 05	15 08	15 12
56	16 02	16 43	17 28	15 03	15 08	15 14	15 21
54	16 10	16 48	17 31	15 03	15 10	15 19	15 29
52	16 17	16 53	17 34	15 03	15 13	15 23	15 37
50	16 23	16 58	17 37	15 03	15 15	15 28	15 43
45	16 37	17 08	17 43	15 03	15 19	15 37	15 57
N 40	16 48	17 17	17 49	15 02	15 23	15 44	16 09
35	16 58	17 25	17 55	15 02	15 26	15 51	16 19
30	17 07	17 32	18 01	15 02	15 28	15 57	16 28
20	17 22	17 45	18 11	15 02	15 33	16 07	16 43
N 10	17 35	17 57	18 22	15 02	15 38	16 16	16 57
0	17 47	18 09	18 34	15 01	15 42	16 24	17 09
S 10	18 00	18 22	18 48	15 01	15 46	16 32	17 22
20	18 14	18 37	19 05	15 01	15 50	16 41	17 36
30	18 29	18 55	19 26	15 00	15 55	16 52	17 51
35	18 38	19 06	19 39	15 00	15 58	16 58	18 00
40	18 48	19 19	19 56	15 00	16 01	17 04	18 11
45	19 01	19 35	20 17	14 59	16 05	17 12	18 23
S 50	19 17	19 55	20 44	14 59	16 09	17 22	18 38
52	19 24	20 04	20 59	14 59	16 11	17 27	18 45
54	19 32	20 15	21 16	14 59	16 14	17 32	18 53
56	19 41	20 28	21 37	14 59	16 16	17 37	19 02
58	19 51	20 43	22 05	14 58	16 19	17 43	19 12
S 60	20 02	21 01	22 51	14 58	16 22	17 50	19 24

Day	SUN Eqn. of Time 00h	12h	Mer. Pass.	MOON Mer. Pass. Upper	Lower	Age	Phase
d	m s	m s	h m	h m	h m	d	%
9	16 15	16 13	11 44	08 52	21 12	26	15
10	16 10	16 08	11 44	09 32	21 52	27	8
11	16 05	16 01	11 44	10 14	22 35	28	4

© British Crown Copyright 2022. All rights reserved.

UT	ARIES GHA	VENUS −4.3 GHA	Dec	MARS +1.4 GHA	Dec	JUPITER −2.9 GHA	Dec	SATURN +0.7 GHA	Dec	STARS Name	SHA	Dec
12 SUNDAY												
00	50 52.1	226 41.4	S 0 17.8	182 05.4	S18 06.9	13 28.9	N13 16.6	77 37.0	S12 52.8	Acamar	315 12.1	S40 12.5
01	65 54.6	241 41.3	18.8	197 06.1	07.4	28 31.7	16.5	92 39.4	52.8	Achernar	335 20.4	S57 07.1
02	80 57.0	256 41.1	19.7	212 06.8	07.9	43 34.5	16.4	107 41.9	52.8	Acrux	173 01.7	S63 13.6
03	95 59.5	271 41.0 ..	20.7	227 07.5 ..	08.4	58 37.3 ..	16.3	122 44.3 ..	52.8	Adhara	255 06.4	S29 00.0
04	111 01.9	286 40.9	21.7	242 08.2	08.9	73 40.1	16.2	137 46.7	52.8	Aldebaran	290 40.4	N16 33.5
05	126 04.4	301 40.7	22.6	257 08.9	09.3	88 42.9	16.1	152 49.2	52.7			
06	141 06.9	316 40.6	S 0 23.6	272 09.6	S18 09.8	103 45.7	N13 16.0	167 51.6	S12 52.7	Alioth	166 14.3	N55 49.7
07	156 09.3	331 40.5	24.5	287 10.2	10.3	118 48.4	15.9	182 54.0	52.7	Alkaid	152 53.2	N49 11.6
08	171 11.8	346 40.4	25.5	302 10.9	10.8	133 51.2	15.8	197 56.5	52.7	Alnair	27 34.1	S46 51.0
09	186 14.3	1 40.2 ..	26.4	317 11.6 ..	11.3	148 54.0 ..	15.7	212 58.9 ..	52.7	Alnilam	275 38.5	S 1 11.1
10	201 16.7	16 40.1	27.4	332 12.3	11.8	163 56.8	15.6	228 01.3	52.7	Alphard	217 48.7	S 8 45.5
11	216 19.2	31 40.0	28.4	347 13.0	12.2	178 59.6	15.5	243 03.7	52.6			
12	231 21.7	46 39.8	S 0 29.3	2 13.7	S18 12.7	194 02.4	N13 15.4	258 06.2	S12 52.6	Alphecca	126 05.0	N26 38.1
13	246 24.1	61 39.7	30.3	17 14.4	13.2	209 05.2	15.3	273 08.6	52.6	Alpheratz	357 35.6	N29 13.5
14	261 26.6	76 39.6	31.3	32 15.1	13.7	224 08.0	15.2	288 11.0	52.6	Altair	62 01.1	N 8 56.0
15	276 29.0	91 39.4 ..	32.2	47 15.8 ..	14.2	239 10.7 ..	15.1	303 13.5 ..	52.6	Ankaa	353 07.8	S42 10.7
16	291 31.5	106 39.3	33.2	62 16.4	14.6	254 13.5	15.0	318 15.9	52.6	Antares	112 17.4	S26 29.0
17	306 34.0	121 39.2	34.1	77 17.1	15.1	269 16.3	14.9	333 18.3	52.5			
18	321 36.4	136 39.0	S 0 35.1	92 17.8	S18 15.6	284 19.1	N13 14.8	348 20.8	S12 52.5	Arcturus	145 49.2	N19 03.6
19	336 38.9	151 38.9	36.1	107 18.5	16.1	299 21.9	14.7	3 23.2	52.5	Atria	107 13.1	S69 04.3
20	351 41.4	166 38.7	37.0	122 19.2	16.6	314 24.7	14.6	18 25.6	52.5	Avior	234 15.0	S59 34.7
21	6 43.8	181 38.6 ..	38.0	137 19.9 ..	17.0	329 27.4 ..	14.5	33 28.1 ..	52.5	Bellatrix	278 23.7	N 6 22.4
22	21 46.3	196 38.5	39.0	152 20.6	17.5	344 30.2	14.4	48 30.5	52.5	Betelgeuse	270 52.9	N 7 24.8
23	36 48.8	211 38.3	39.9	167 21.2	18.0	359 33.0	14.3	63 32.9	52.4			
13 MONDAY												
00	51 51.2	226 38.2	S 0 40.9	182 21.9	S18 18.5	14 35.8	N13 14.2	78 35.3	S12 52.4	Canopus	263 52.4	S52 42.2
01	66 53.7	241 38.1	41.8	197 22.6	18.9	29 38.6	14.1	93 37.8	52.4	Capella	280 22.9	N46 01.3
02	81 56.2	256 37.9	42.8	212 23.3	19.4	44 41.4	14.0	108 40.2	52.4	Deneb	49 26.6	N45 22.1
03	96 58.6	271 37.8 ..	43.8	227 24.0 ..	19.9	59 44.2 ..	13.9	123 42.6 ..	52.4	Denebola	182 26.2	N14 26.4
04	112 01.1	286 37.6	44.7	242 24.7	20.4	74 46.9	13.8	138 45.1	52.3	Diphda	348 48.0	S17 51.4
05	127 03.5	301 37.5	45.7	257 25.3	20.9	89 49.7	13.7	153 47.5	52.3			
06	142 06.0	316 37.4	S 0 46.7	272 26.0	S18 21.3	104 52.5	N13 13.6	168 49.9	S12 52.3	Dubhe	193 42.5	N61 37.2
07	157 08.5	331 37.2	47.6	287 26.7	21.8	119 55.3	13.5	183 52.4	52.3	Elnath	278 02.8	N28 37.6
08	172 10.9	346 37.1	48.6	302 27.4	22.3	134 58.1	13.4	198 54.8	52.3	Eltanin	90 43.1	N51 29.3
09	187 13.4	1 37.0 ..	49.6	317 28.1 ..	22.8	150 00.9 ..	13.3	213 57.2 ..	52.3	Enif	33 39.8	N 9 59.1
10	202 15.9	16 36.8	50.5	332 28.8	23.2	165 03.6	13.3	228 59.6	52.2	Fomalhaut	15 15.5	S29 29.9
11	217 18.3	31 36.7	51.5	347 29.4	23.7	180 06.4	13.2	244 02.1	52.2			
12	232 20.8	46 36.5	S 0 52.5	2 30.1	S18 24.2	195 09.2	N13 13.1	259 04.5	S12 52.2	Gacrux	171 53.2	S57 14.5
13	247 23.3	61 36.4	53.4	17 30.8	24.7	210 12.0	13.0	274 06.9	52.2	Gienah	175 44.8	S17 40.3
14	262 25.7	76 36.2	54.4	32 31.5	25.1	225 14.8	12.9	289 09.3	52.2	Hadar	148 38.1	S60 29.1
15	277 28.2	91 36.1 ..	55.4	47 32.2 ..	25.6	240 17.6 ..	12.8	304 11.8 ..	52.1	Hamal	327 52.0	N23 34.6
16	292 30.7	106 36.0	56.4	62 32.8	26.1	255 20.3	12.7	319 14.2	52.1	Kaus Aust.	83 34.1	S34 22.5
17	307 33.1	121 35.8	57.3	77 33.5	26.5	270 23.1	12.6	334 16.6	52.1			
18	322 35.6	136 35.7	S 0 58.3	92 34.2	S18 27.0	285 25.9	N13 12.5	349 19.1	S12 52.1	Kochab	137 20.9	N74 03.4
19	337 38.0	151 35.5	0 59.3	107 34.9	27.5	300 28.7	12.4	4 21.5	52.1	Markab	13 30.8	N15 20.1
20	352 40.5	166 35.4	1 00.2	122 35.6	28.0	315 31.5	12.3	19 23.9	52.0	Menkar	314 06.9	N 4 11.1
21	7 43.0	181 35.2 ..	01.2	137 36.2 ..	28.4	330 34.3 ..	12.2	34 26.3 ..	52.0	Menkent	147 59.2	S36 29.1
22	22 45.4	196 35.1	02.2	152 36.9	28.9	345 37.0	12.1	49 28.8	52.0	Miaplacidus	221 38.4	S69 48.5
23	37 47.9	211 35.0	03.1	167 37.6	29.4	0 39.8	12.0	64 31.2	52.0			
14 TUESDAY												
00	52 50.4	226 34.8	S 1 04.1	182 38.3	S18 29.9	15 42.6	N13 11.9	79 33.6	S12 52.0	Mirfak	308 29.2	N49 56.8
01	67 52.8	241 34.7	05.1	197 39.0	30.3	30 45.4	11.8	94 36.0	51.9	Nunki	75 49.2	S26 16.1
02	82 55.3	256 34.5	06.1	212 39.6	30.8	45 48.2	11.7	109 38.5	51.9	Peacock	53 07.4	S56 39.7
03	97 57.8	271 34.4 ..	07.0	227 40.3 ..	31.3	60 50.9 ..	11.6	124 40.9 ..	51.9	Pollux	243 18.4	N27 58.1
04	113 00.2	286 34.2	08.0	242 41.0	31.7	75 53.7	11.5	139 43.3	51.9	Procyon	244 51.7	N 5 09.9
05	128 02.7	301 34.1	09.0	257 41.7	32.2	90 56.5	11.4	154 45.7	51.9			
06	143 05.1	316 33.9	S 1 10.0	272 42.3	S18 32.7	105 59.3	N13 11.3	169 48.2	S12 51.8	Rasalhague	95 59.8	N12 32.7
07	158 07.6	331 33.8	10.9	287 43.0	33.2	121 02.1	11.2	184 50.6	51.8	Regulus	207 35.6	N11 51.1
08	173 10.1	346 33.6	11.9	302 43.7	33.6	136 04.9	11.1	199 53.0	51.8	Rigel	281 04.5	S 8 10.3
09	188 12.5	1 33.5 ..	12.9	317 44.4 ..	34.1	151 07.6 ..	11.0	214 55.4 ..	51.8	Rigil Kent.	139 42.4	S60 55.8
10	203 15.0	16 33.3	13.8	332 45.1	34.6	166 10.4	10.9	229 57.9	51.8	Sabik	102 04.2	S15 45.2
11	218 17.5	31 33.2	14.8	347 45.7	35.0	181 13.2	10.8	245 00.3	51.7			
12	233 19.9	46 33.1	S 1 15.8	2 46.4	S18 35.5	196 16.0	N13 10.7	260 02.7	S12 51.7	Schedar	349 31.8	N56 40.3
13	248 22.4	61 32.9	16.8	17 47.1	36.0	211 18.8	10.6	275 05.1	51.7	Shaula	96 12.1	S37 07.3
14	263 24.9	76 32.8	17.7	32 47.8	36.4	226 21.5	10.5	290 07.5	51.7	Sirius	258 26.9	S16 44.7
15	278 27.3	91 32.6 ..	18.7	47 48.4 ..	36.9	241 24.3 ..	10.4	305 10.0 ..	51.7	Spica	158 23.6	S11 17.0
16	293 29.8	106 32.5	19.7	62 49.1	37.4	256 27.1	10.3	320 12.4	51.6	Suhail	222 47.0	S43 31.4
17	308 32.3	121 32.3	20.7	77 49.8	37.8	271 29.9	10.3	335 14.8	51.6			
18	323 34.7	136 32.2	S 1 21.6	92 50.5	S18 38.3	286 32.7	N13 10.2	350 17.2	S12 51.6	Vega	80 34.2	N38 48.5
19	338 37.2	151 32.0	22.6	107 51.1	38.8	301 35.4	10.1	5 19.7	51.6	Zuben'ubi	136 57.5	S16 08.3
20	353 39.6	166 31.8	23.6	122 51.8	39.2	316 38.2	10.0	20 22.1	51.6		SHA	Mer. Pass.
21	8 42.1	181 31.7 ..	24.6	137 52.5 ..	39.7	331 41.0 ..	09.9	35 24.5 ..	51.5			
22	23 44.6	196 31.5	25.6	152 53.1	40.2	346 43.8	09.8	50 26.9	51.5	Venus	174 47.0	8 54
23	38 47.0	211 31.4	26.5	167 53.8	40.6	1 46.6	09.7	65 29.3	51.5	Mars	130 30.7	11 50
Mer. Pass. 20 29.2		v −0.1 d 1.0		v 0.7 d 0.5		v 2.8 d 0.1		v 2.4 d 0.0		Jupiter	322 44.6	22 57
										Saturn	26 44.1	18 43

© British Crown Copyright 2022. All rights reserved.

SUN / MOON

UT	SUN GHA	SUN Dec	MOON GHA	v	MOON Dec	d	HP
12 00	183 59.4	S17 33.5	200 30.9	13.9	S13 07.9	13.5	55.9
01	198 59.3	34.2	215 03.8	13.9	13 21.4	13.5	56.0
02	213 59.3	34.9	229 36.7	13.7	13 34.9	13.5	56.0
03	228 59.2 ..	35.6	244 09.4	13.7	13 48.4	13.3	56.0
04	243 59.1	36.3	258 42.1	13.6	14 01.7	13.4	56.0
05	258 59.0	37.0	273 14.7	13.5	14 15.1	13.3	56.1
06	273 59.0	S17 37.6	287 47.2	13.4	S14 28.4	13.2	56.1
07	288 58.9	38.3	302 19.6	13.3	14 41.6	13.2	56.1
S 08	303 58.8	39.0	316 51.9	13.2	14 54.8	13.2	56.1
U 09	318 58.7 ..	39.7	331 24.1	13.2	15 08.0	13.1	56.1
N 10	333 58.7	40.4	345 56.3	13.0	15 21.1	13.0	56.2
D 11	348 58.6	41.0	0 28.3	13.0	15 34.1	13.0	56.2
A 12	3 58.5	S17 41.7	15 00.3	12.9	S15 47.1	12.9	56.2
Y 13	18 58.4	42.4	29 32.2	12.8	16 00.0	12.8	56.2
14	33 58.3	43.1	44 04.0	12.6	16 12.8	12.8	56.3
15	48 58.3 ..	43.7	58 35.6	12.6	16 25.6	12.7	56.3
16	63 58.2	44.4	73 07.2	12.5	16 38.3	12.7	56.3
17	78 58.1	45.1	87 38.7	12.4	16 51.0	12.5	56.3
18	93 58.0	S17 45.8	102 10.1	12.4	S17 03.5	12.6	56.4
19	108 57.9	46.4	116 41.5	12.2	17 16.1	12.4	56.4
20	123 57.8	47.1	131 12.7	12.1	17 28.5	12.4	56.4
21	138 57.8 ..	47.8	145 43.8	12.0	17 40.9	12.3	56.4
22	153 57.7	48.5	160 14.8	11.9	17 53.2	12.2	56.5
23	168 57.6	49.1	174 45.7	11.8	18 05.4	12.2	56.5
13 00	183 57.5	S17 49.8	189 16.5	11.7	S18 17.6	12.1	56.5
01	198 57.4	50.5	203 47.2	11.6	18 29.7	12.0	56.5
02	213 57.4	51.1	218 17.8	11.6	18 41.7	11.9	56.5
03	228 57.3 ..	51.8	232 48.4	11.4	18 53.6	11.8	56.6
04	243 57.2	52.5	247 18.8	11.3	19 05.4	11.8	56.6
05	258 57.1	53.2	261 49.1	11.2	19 17.2	11.6	56.6
06	273 57.0	S17 53.8	276 19.3	11.1	S19 28.8	11.6	56.6
07	288 56.9	54.5	290 49.4	11.0	19 40.4	11.5	56.7
M 08	303 56.9	55.2	305 19.4	10.8	19 51.9	11.4	56.7
O 09	318 56.8 ..	55.8	319 49.2	10.8	20 03.3	11.3	56.7
N 10	333 56.7	56.5	334 19.0	10.7	20 14.6	11.3	56.7
D 11	348 56.6	57.2	348 48.7	10.6	20 25.9	11.1	56.8
A 12	3 56.5	S17 57.8	3 18.3	10.4	S20 37.0	11.0	56.8
Y 13	18 56.4	58.5	17 47.7	10.4	20 48.0	11.0	56.8
14	33 56.3	59.1	32 17.1	10.2	20 59.0	10.8	56.8
15	48 56.2	17 59.8	46 46.3	10.2	21 09.8	10.7	56.9
16	63 56.2	18 00.5	61 15.5	10.0	21 20.5	10.7	56.9
17	78 56.1	01.1	75 44.5	9.9	21 31.2	10.5	56.9
18	93 56.0	S18 01.8	90 13.4	9.9	S21 41.7	10.4	56.9
19	108 55.9	02.5	104 42.3	9.7	21 52.1	10.4	56.9
20	123 55.8	03.1	119 11.0	9.6	22 02.5	10.2	57.0
21	138 55.7 ..	03.8	133 39.6	9.5	22 12.7	10.1	57.0
22	153 55.6	04.4	148 08.1	9.3	22 22.8	10.0	57.0
23	168 55.5	05.1	162 36.4	9.3	22 32.8	9.9	57.0
14 00	183 55.4	S18 05.8	177 04.7	9.2	S22 42.7	9.7	57.1
01	198 55.3	06.4	191 32.9	9.1	22 52.4	9.7	57.1
02	213 55.2	07.1	206 01.0	8.9	23 02.1	9.5	57.1
03	228 55.1 ..	07.7	220 28.9	8.8	23 11.6	9.4	57.1
04	243 55.1	08.4	234 56.7	8.8	23 21.0	9.3	57.1
05	258 55.0	09.0	249 24.5	8.6	23 30.3	9.2	57.2
06	273 54.9	S18 09.7	263 52.1	8.5	S23 39.5	9.1	57.2
07	288 54.8	10.3	278 19.6	8.5	23 48.6	8.9	57.2
T 08	303 54.7	11.0	292 47.1	8.3	23 57.5	8.8	57.2
U 09	318 54.6 ..	11.7	307 14.4	8.2	24 06.3	8.7	57.3
E 10	333 54.5	12.3	321 41.6	8.1	24 15.0	8.5	57.3
S 11	348 54.4	13.0	336 08.7	8.0	24 23.5	8.4	57.3
D 12	3 54.3	S18 13.6	350 35.7	7.9	S24 31.9	8.3	57.3
A 13	18 54.2	14.3	5 02.6	7.7	24 40.2	8.1	57.3
Y 14	33 54.1	14.9	19 29.3	7.7	24 48.3	8.0	57.4
15	48 54.0 ..	15.6	33 56.0	7.6	24 56.3	7.9	57.4
16	63 53.9	16.2	48 22.6	7.5	25 04.2	7.7	57.4
17	78 53.8	16.9	62 49.1	7.4	25 11.9	7.6	57.4
18	93 53.7	S18 17.5	77 15.5	7.3	S25 19.5	7.5	57.4
19	108 53.6	18.2	91 41.8	7.1	25 27.0	7.3	57.5
20	123 53.5	18.8	106 07.9	7.1	25 34.3	7.1	57.5
21	138 53.4 ..	19.4	120 34.0	7.0	25 41.4	7.0	57.5
22	153 53.3	20.1	135 00.0	6.9	25 48.4	6.9	57.5
23	168 53.2	20.7	149 25.9	6.8	S25 55.3	6.7	57.5
	SD 16.2	d 0.7	SD 15.3		15.5		15.6

Twilight / Sunrise / Moonrise

Lat.	Naut.	Civil	Sunrise	Moonrise 12	13	14	15
N 72	06 51	08 23	10 30	08 40	■■	■■	■■
N 70	06 42	08 02	09 35	08 03	■■	■■	■■
68	06 34	07 46	09 02	07 37	10 11	■■	■■
66	06 28	07 33	08 38	07 18	09 26	■■	■■
64	06 22	07 22	08 20	07 02	08 56	11 14	■■
62	06 17	07 12	08 05	06 49	08 34	10 29	12 41
60	06 12	07 04	07 52	06 39	08 16	10 00	11 45
N 58	06 08	06 56	07 41	06 29	08 01	09 38	11 13
56	06 04	06 50	07 32	06 21	07 49	09 20	10 48
54	06 01	06 44	07 23	06 14	07 38	09 05	10 29
52	05 58	06 39	07 16	06 07	07 28	08 51	10 13
50	05 54	06 34	07 09	06 01	07 20	08 40	09 58
45	05 47	06 23	06 54	05 49	07 01	08 16	09 30
N 40	05 41	06 14	06 42	05 39	06 47	07 57	09 07
35	05 35	06 05	06 32	05 30	06 34	07 41	08 49
30	05 29	05 58	06 23	05 22	06 23	07 28	08 33
20	05 18	05 44	06 07	05 09	06 05	07 04	08 06
N 10	05 05	05 32	05 54	04 58	05 49	06 45	07 43
0	04 54	05 19	05 41	04 47	05 34	06 26	07 22
S 10	04 39	05 05	05 28	04 37	05 20	06 08	07 01
20	04 22	04 50	05 13	04 25	05 04	05 48	06 38
30	04 02	04 31	04 57	04 13	04 46	05 26	06 12
35	03 46	04 20	04 48	04 06	04 36	05 12	05 57
40	03 29	04 06	04 37	03 57	04 24	04 57	05 39
45	03 08	03 50	04 24	03 48	04 11	04 40	05 18
S 50	02 39	03 29	04 08	03 36	03 54	04 18	04 51
52	02 24	03 19	04 00	03 31	03 46	04 07	04 38
54	02 06	03 08	03 52	03 25	03 38	03 55	04 23
56	01 43	02 55	03 43	03 19	03 28	03 42	04 05
58	01 12	02 39	03 32	03 12	03 17	03 27	03 44
S 60	00 09	02 20	03 20	03 04	03 05	03 08	03 17

Sunset / Twilight / Moonset

Lat.	Sunset	Civil	Naut.	Moonset 12	13	14	15
N 72	12 58	15 04	16 36	12 51	■■	■■	■■
N 70	13 53	15 25	16 45	13 30	■■	■■	■■
68	14 25	15 41	16 53	13 58	13 04	■■	■■
66	14 49	15 55	17 00	14 19	13 51	■■	■■
64	15 08	16 06	17 06	14 36	14 21	13 53	■■
62	15 23	16 16	17 11	14 50	14 44	14 38	14 25
60	15 36	16 24	17 15	15 02	15 03	15 08	15 22
N 58	15 47	16 31	17 19	15 12	15 19	15 31	15 54
56	15 56	16 38	17 23	15 21	15 32	15 49	16 19
54	16 05	16 44	17 27	15 29	15 44	16 05	16 39
52	16 12	16 54	17 30	15 36	15 54	16 19	16 55
50	16 19	16 54	17 33	15 43	16 03	16 31	17 10
45	16 34	17 05	17 41	15 57	16 23	16 55	17 39
N 40	16 46	17 14	17 47	16 09	16 39	17 15	18 02
35	16 56	17 23	17 53	16 19	16 52	17 32	18 21
30	17 05	17 30	17 59	16 28	17 04	17 46	18 37
20	17 21	17 44	18 10	16 43	17 24	18 11	19 04
N 10	17 35	17 57	18 22	16 57	17 42	18 32	19 28
0	17 48	18 10	18 35	17 09	17 59	18 52	19 50
S 10	18 01	18 23	18 49	17 22	18 15	19 12	20 12
20	18 15	18 39	19 07	17 36	18 33	19 34	20 36
30	18 32	18 58	19 29	17 51	18 54	19 59	21 04
35	18 41	19 09	19 43	18 00	19 06	20 14	21 20
40	18 52	19 22	20 00	18 11	19 20	20 31	21 39
45	19 06	19 39	20 22	18 23	19 37	20 51	22 03
S 50	19 22	20 00	20 51	18 38	19 58	21 17	22 32
52	19 29	20 11	21 07	18 45	20 07	21 30	22 47
54	19 38	20 22	21 25	18 53	20 19	21 45	23 04
56	19 47	20 36	21 48	19 02	20 31	22 02	23 24
58	19 58	20 52	22 21	19 12	20 46	22 22	23 50
S 60	20 10	21 11	////	19 24	21 04	22 49	24 26

SUN / MOON

Day	SUN Eqn. of Time 00h	SUN Eqn. of Time 12h	Mer. Pass.	MOON Mer. Pass. Upper	MOON Mer. Pass. Lower	Age	Phase
d	m s	m s	h m	h m	h m	d	%
12	15 58	15 54	11 44	10 58	23 22	29	1
13	15 50	15 46	11 44	11 46	24 12	00	0
14	15 42	15 37	11 44	12 39	00 12	01	1

© British Crown Copyright 2022. All rights reserved.

UT	ARIES GHA	VENUS −4.3 GHA	Dec	MARS +1.4 GHA	Dec	JUPITER −2.9 GHA	Dec	SATURN +0.7 GHA	Dec
15 00	53 49.5	226 31.2	S 1 27.5	182 54.5	S18 41.1	16 49.3	N13 09.6	80 31.8	S12 51.5
01	68 52.0	241 31.1	28.5	197 55.2	41.6	31 52.1	09.5	95 34.2	51.5
02	83 54.4	256 30.9	29.5	212 55.8	42.0	46 54.9	09.4	110 36.6	51.4
03	98 56.9	271 30.8 ..	30.4	227 56.5 ..	42.5	61 57.7 ..	09.3	125 39.0 ..	51.4
04	113 59.4	286 30.6	31.4	242 57.2	43.0	77 00.4	09.2	140 41.5	51.4
05	129 01.8	301 30.5	32.4	257 57.9	43.4	92 03.2	09.1	155 43.9	51.4
06	144 04.3	316 30.3	S 1 33.4	272 58.5	S18 43.9	107 06.0	N13 09.0	170 46.3	S12 51.3
07	159 06.8	331 30.2	34.4	287 59.2	44.4	122 08.8	08.9	185 48.7	51.3
08	174 09.2	346 30.0	35.3	302 59.9	44.8	137 11.6	08.8	200 51.1	51.3
09	189 11.7	1 29.8 ..	36.3	318 00.5 ..	45.3	152 14.3 ..	08.7	215 53.6 ..	51.3
10	204 14.1	16 29.7	37.3	333 01.2	45.7	167 17.1	08.6	230 56.0	51.3
11	219 16.6	31 29.5	38.3	348 01.9	46.2	182 19.9	08.5	245 58.4	51.2
12	234 19.1	46 29.4	S 1 39.3	3 02.5	S18 46.7	197 22.7	N13 08.4	261 00.8	S12 51.2
13	249 21.5	61 29.2	40.2	18 03.2	47.1	212 25.4	08.3	276 03.2	51.2
14	264 24.0	76 29.1	41.2	33 03.9	47.6	227 28.2	08.2	291 05.6	51.2
15	279 26.5	91 28.9 ..	42.2	48 04.6 ..	48.1	242 31.0 ..	08.2	306 08.1 ..	51.2
16	294 28.9	106 28.7	43.2	63 05.2	48.5	257 33.8	08.1	321 10.5	51.1
17	309 31.4	121 28.6	44.2	78 05.9	49.0	272 36.6	08.0	336 12.9	51.1
18	324 33.9	136 28.4	S 1 45.1	93 06.6	S18 49.4	287 39.3	N13 07.9	351 15.3	S12 51.1
19	339 36.3	151 28.3	46.1	108 07.2	49.9	302 42.1	07.8	6 17.7	51.1
20	354 38.8	166 28.1	47.1	123 07.9	50.4	317 44.9	07.7	21 20.2	51.0
21	9 41.3	181 28.0 ..	48.1	138 08.6 ..	50.8	332 47.7 ..	07.6	36 22.6 ..	51.0
22	24 43.7	196 27.8	49.1	153 09.2	51.3	347 50.4	07.5	51 25.0	51.0
23	39 46.2	211 27.6	50.1	168 09.9	51.7	2 53.2	07.4	66 27.4	51.0
16 00	54 48.6	226 27.5	S 1 51.0	183 10.6	S18 52.2	17 56.0	N13 07.3	81 29.8	S12 51.0
01	69 51.1	241 27.3	52.0	198 11.2	52.7	32 58.8	07.2	96 32.2	50.9
02	84 53.6	256 27.1	53.0	213 11.9	53.1	48 01.5	07.1	111 34.7	50.9
03	99 56.0	271 27.0 ..	54.0	228 12.6 ..	53.6	63 04.3 ..	07.0	126 37.1 ..	50.9
04	114 58.5	286 26.8	55.0	243 13.2	54.0	78 07.1	06.9	141 39.5	50.9
05	130 01.0	301 26.7	56.0	258 13.9	54.5	93 09.9	06.8	156 41.9	50.8
06	145 03.4	316 26.5	S 1 56.9	273 14.6	S18 54.9	108 12.6	N13 06.7	171 44.3	S12 50.8
07	160 05.9	331 26.3	57.9	288 15.2	55.4	123 15.4	06.6	186 46.7	50.8
08	175 08.4	346 26.2	58.9	303 15.9	55.9	138 18.2	06.5	201 49.2	50.8
09	190 10.8	1 26.0	1 59.9	318 16.6 ..	56.3	153 21.0 ..	06.4	216 51.6 ..	50.7
10	205 13.3	16 25.8	2 00.9	333 17.2	56.8	168 23.7	06.4	231 54.0	50.7
11	220 15.8	31 25.7	01.9	348 17.9	57.2	183 26.5	06.3	246 56.4	50.7
12	235 18.2	46 25.5	S 2 02.9	3 18.5	S18 57.7	198 29.3	N13 06.2	261 58.8	S12 50.7
13	250 20.7	61 25.3	03.8	18 19.2	58.1	213 32.1	06.1	277 01.2	50.7
14	265 23.1	76 25.2	04.8	33 19.9	58.6	228 34.8	06.0	292 03.7	50.6
15	280 25.6	91 25.0 ..	05.8	48 20.5 ..	59.1	243 37.6 ..	05.9	307 06.1 ..	50.6
16	295 28.1	106 24.9	06.8	63 21.2	18 59.5	258 40.4	05.8	322 08.5	50.6
17	310 30.5	121 24.7	07.8	78 21.9	19 00.0	273 43.2	05.7	337 10.9	50.6
18	325 33.0	136 24.5	S 2 08.8	93 22.5	S19 00.4	288 45.9	N13 05.6	352 13.3	S12 50.6
19	340 35.5	151 24.4	09.8	108 23.2	00.9	303 48.7	05.5	7 15.7	50.5
20	355 37.9	166 24.2	10.8	123 23.8	01.3	318 51.5	05.4	22 18.1	50.5
21	10 40.4	181 24.0 ..	11.7	138 24.5 ..	01.8	333 54.2 ..	05.3	37 20.6 ..	50.5
22	25 42.9	196 23.8	12.7	153 25.2	02.2	348 57.0	05.2	52 23.0	50.4
23	40 45.3	211 23.7	13.7	168 25.8	02.7	3 59.8	05.1	67 25.4	50.4
17 00	55 47.8	226 23.5	S 2 14.7	183 26.5	S19 03.1	19 02.6	N13 05.0	82 27.8	S12 50.4
01	70 50.3	241 23.3	15.7	198 27.1	03.6	34 05.3	05.0	97 30.2	50.4
02	85 52.7	256 23.2	16.7	213 27.8	04.0	49 08.1	04.9	112 32.6	50.3
03	100 55.2	271 23.0 ..	17.7	228 28.5 ..	04.5	64 10.9 ..	04.8	127 35.0 ..	50.3
04	115 57.6	286 22.8	18.7	243 29.1	05.0	79 13.7	04.7	142 37.4	50.3
05	131 00.1	301 22.7	19.7	258 29.8	05.4	94 16.4	04.6	157 39.9	50.3
06	146 02.6	316 22.5	S 2 20.6	273 30.4	S19 05.9	109 19.2	N13 04.5	172 42.3	S12 50.2
07	161 05.0	331 22.3	21.6	288 31.1	06.3	124 22.0	04.4	187 44.7	50.2
08	176 07.5	346 22.1	22.6	303 31.8	06.8	139 24.7	04.3	202 47.1	50.2
09	191 10.0	1 22.0 ..	23.6	318 32.4 ..	07.2	154 27.5 ..	04.2	217 49.5 ..	50.2
10	206 12.4	16 21.8	24.6	333 33.1	07.7	169 30.3	04.1	232 51.9	50.1
11	221 14.9	31 21.6	25.6	348 33.7	08.1	184 33.0	04.0	247 54.3	50.1
12	236 17.4	46 21.5	S 2 26.6	3 34.4	S19 08.6	199 35.8	N13 03.9	262 56.7	S12 50.1
13	251 19.8	61 21.3	27.6	18 35.0	09.0	214 38.6	03.8	277 59.1	50.1
14	266 22.3	76 21.1	28.6	33 35.7	09.5	229 41.4	03.7	293 01.6	50.0
15	281 24.8	91 20.9 ..	29.6	48 36.4 ..	09.9	244 44.1 ..	03.7	308 04.0 ..	50.0
16	296 27.2	106 20.8	30.6	63 37.0	10.4	259 46.9	03.6	323 06.4	50.0
17	311 29.7	121 20.6	31.5	78 37.7	10.8	274 49.7	03.5	338 08.8	50.0
18	326 32.1	136 20.4	S 2 32.5	93 38.3	S19 11.3	289 52.4	N13 03.4	353 11.2	S12 49.9
19	341 34.6	151 20.2	33.5	108 39.0	11.7	304 55.2	03.3	8 13.6	49.9
20	356 37.1	166 20.1	34.5	123 39.6	12.2	319 58.0	03.2	23 16.0	49.9
21	11 39.5	181 19.9 ..	35.5	138 40.3 ..	12.6	335 00.7 ..	03.1	38 18.4 ..	49.9
22	26 42.0	196 19.7	36.5	153 41.0	13.1	350 03.5	03.0	53 20.8	49.8
23	41 44.5	211 19.5	37.5	168 41.6	13.5	5 06.3	02.9	68 23.2	49.8
Mer. Pass. 20 17.4		v −0.2	d 1.0	v 0.7	d 0.5	v 2.8	d 0.1	v 2.4	d 0.0

STARS

Name	SHA	Dec
Acamar	315 12.1	S40 12.5
Achernar	335 20.4	S57 07.1
Acrux	173 01.7	S63 13.6
Adhara	255 06.4	S29 00.0
Aldebaran	290 40.4	N16 33.5
Alioth	166 14.3	N55 49.7
Alkaid	152 53.2	N49 11.6
Alnair	27 34.1	S46 51.0
Alnilam	275 38.4	S 1 11.1
Alphard	217 48.7	S 8 45.5
Alphecca	126 04.9	N26 38.1
Alpheratz	357 35.6	N29 13.5
Altair	62 01.1	N 8 56.0
Ankaa	353 07.8	S42 10.7
Antares	112 17.4	S26 29.0
Arcturus	145 49.1	N19 03.5
Atria	107 13.1	S69 04.2
Avior	234 14.9	S59 34.8
Bellatrix	278 23.6	N 6 22.4
Betelgeuse	270 52.9	N 7 24.8
Canopus	263 52.4	S52 42.2
Capella	280 22.9	N46 01.3
Deneb	49 26.6	N45 22.1
Denebola	182 26.1	N14 26.4
Diphda	348 48.0	S17 51.4
Dubhe	193 42.4	N61 37.1
Elnath	278 02.8	N28 37.6
Eltanin	90 43.1	N51 29.3
Enif	33 39.8	N 9 59.1
Fomalhaut	15 15.5	S29 29.9
Gacrux	171 53.2	S57 14.5
Gienah	175 44.8	S17 40.3
Hadar	148 38.0	S60 29.1
Hamal	327 52.0	N23 34.6
Kaus Aust.	83 34.1	S34 22.5
Kochab	137 20.9	N74 03.4
Markab	13 30.8	N15 20.1
Menkar	314 06.8	N 4 11.1
Menkent	147 59.2	S36 29.1
Miaplacidus	221 38.4	S69 48.5
Mirfak	308 29.2	N49 56.8
Nunki	75 49.2	S26 16.1
Peacock	53 07.5	S56 39.7
Pollux	243 18.3	N27 58.1
Procyon	244 51.7	N 5 09.9
Rasalhague	95 59.8	N12 32.6
Regulus	207 35.5	N11 51.1
Rigel	281 04.5	S 8 10.3
Rigil Kent.	139 42.3	S60 55.8
Sabik	102 04.2	S15 45.2
Schedar	349 31.8	N56 40.3
Shaula	96 12.1	S37 07.3
Sirius	258 26.9	S16 44.7
Spica	158 23.6	S11 17.0
Suhail	222 47.0	S43 31.4
Vega	80 34.2	N38 48.5
Zuben'ubi	136 57.4	S16 08.3

	SHA	Mer. Pass.
		h m
Venus	171 38.8	8 54
Mars	128 21.9	11 47
Jupiter	323 07.3	22 44
Saturn	26 41.2	18 31

© British Crown Copyright 2022. All rights reserved.

UT	SUN GHA	SUN Dec	MOON GHA	v	Dec	d	HP
15 00	183 53.1	S18 21.4	163 51.7	6.7	S26 02.0	6.6	57.6
01	198 53.0	22.0	178 17.4	6.6	26 08.6	6.4	57.6
02	213 52.9	22.7	192 43.0	6.5	26 15.0	6.3	57.6
03	228 52.8	.. 23.3	207 08.5	6.5	26 21.3	6.1	57.6
04	243 52.7	24.0	221 34.0	6.3	26 27.4	5.9	57.6
05	258 52.6	24.6	235 59.3	6.3	26 33.3	5.8	57.7
06	273 52.5	S18 25.2	250 24.6	6.1	S26 39.1	5.6	57.7
W 07	288 52.4	25.9	264 49.7	6.1	26 44.7	5.5	57.7
E 08	303 52.3	26.5	279 14.8	6.0	26 50.2	5.3	57.7
D 09	318 52.2	.. 27.2	293 39.8	6.0	26 55.5	5.2	57.7
N 10	333 52.1	27.8	308 04.8	5.8	27 00.7	5.0	57.8
E 11	348 52.0	28.4	322 29.6	5.8	27 05.7	4.8	57.8
S 12	3 51.9	S18 29.1	336 54.4	5.7	S27 10.5	4.6	57.8
D 13	18 51.8	29.7	351 19.1	5.6	27 15.1	4.5	57.8
A 14	33 51.7	30.4	5 43.7	5.5	27 19.6	4.4	57.8
Y 15	48 51.6	.. 31.0	20 08.2	5.5	27 24.0	4.1	57.9
16	63 51.5	31.6	34 32.7	5.4	27 28.1	4.0	57.9
17	78 51.3	32.3	48 57.1	5.4	27 32.3	3.9	57.9
18	93 51.2	S18 32.9	63 21.5	5.2	S27 35.9	3.7	57.9
19	108 51.1	33.5	77 45.7	5.2	27 39.6	3.4	57.9
20	123 51.0	34.2	92 09.9	5.2	27 43.0	3.3	58.0
21	138 50.9	.. 34.8	106 34.1	5.1	27 46.3	3.1	58.0
22	153 50.8	35.4	120 58.2	5.0	27 49.4	3.0	58.0
23	168 50.7	36.1	135 22.2	5.0	27 52.4	2.7	58.0
16 00	183 50.6	S18 36.7	149 46.2	4.9	S27 55.1	2.6	58.0
01	198 50.5	37.3	164 10.1	4.9	27 57.7	2.5	58.0
02	213 50.4	38.0	178 34.0	4.8	28 00.2	2.2	58.1
03	228 50.3	.. 38.6	192 57.8	4.8	28 02.4	2.0	58.1
04	243 50.1	39.2	207 21.6	4.8	28 04.4	1.9	58.1
05	258 50.0	39.8	221 45.4	4.7	28 06.3	1.7	58.1
06	273 49.9	S18 40.5	236 09.1	4.6	S28 08.0	1.5	58.1
T 07	288 49.8	41.1	250 32.7	4.7	28 09.5	1.3	58.1
H 08	303 49.7	41.7	264 56.4	4.6	28 10.8	1.2	58.2
U 09	318 49.6	.. 42.4	279 20.0	4.5	28 12.0	1.0	58.2
R 10	333 49.5	43.0	293 43.5	4.5	28 13.0	0.7	58.2
S 11	348 49.4	43.6	308 07.0	4.5	28 13.7	0.5	58.2
D 12	3 49.2	S18 44.2	322 30.5	4.5	S28 14.3	0.5	58.2
A 13	18 49.1	44.9	336 54.0	4.5	28 14.8	0.2	58.2
Y 14	33 49.0	45.5	351 17.5	4.4	28 15.0	0.0	58.3
15	48 48.9	.. 46.1	5 40.9	4.4	28 15.0	0.1	58.3
16	63 48.8	46.7	20 04.3	4.4	28 14.9	0.3	58.3
17	78 48.7	47.3	34 27.7	4.4	28 14.6	0.6	58.3
18	93 48.6	S18 48.0	48 51.1	4.4	S28 14.0	0.6	58.3
19	108 48.4	48.6	63 14.5	4.4	28 13.4	0.9	58.3
20	123 48.3	49.2	77 37.9	4.4	28 12.5	1.1	58.4
21	138 48.2	.. 49.8	92 01.3	4.3	28 11.4	1.3	58.4
22	153 48.1	50.4	106 24.6	4.4	28 10.1	1.4	58.4
23	168 48.0	51.1	120 48.0	4.4	28 08.7	1.6	58.4
17 00	183 47.9	S18 51.7	135 11.4	4.3	S28 07.1	1.8	58.4
01	198 47.7	52.3	149 34.7	4.4	28 05.3	2.0	58.4
02	213 47.6	52.9	163 58.1	4.4	28 03.3	2.2	58.4
03	228 47.5	.. 53.5	178 21.5	4.4	28 01.1	2.4	58.5
04	243 47.4	54.1	192 44.9	4.4	27 58.7	2.5	58.5
05	258 47.3	54.8	207 08.3	4.4	27 56.2	2.8	58.5
06	273 47.1	S18 55.4	221 31.7	4.5	S27 53.4	2.9	58.5
07	288 47.0	56.0	235 55.2	4.4	27 50.5	3.1	58.5
08	303 46.9	56.6	250 18.6	4.5	27 47.4	3.3	58.5
F 09	318 46.8	.. 57.2	264 42.1	4.6	27 44.1	3.5	58.5
R 10	333 46.7	57.8	279 05.7	4.5	27 40.6	3.6	58.6
I 11	348 46.5	58.4	293 29.2	4.6	27 37.0	3.9	58.6
D 12	3 46.4	S18 59.0	307 52.8	4.6	S27 33.1	4.0	58.6
A 13	18 46.3	18 59.7	322 16.4	4.6	27 29.1	4.2	58.6
Y 14	33 46.2	19 00.3	336 40.0	4.7	27 24.9	4.4	58.6
15	48 46.0	.. 00.9	351 03.7	4.7	27 20.5	4.5	58.6
16	63 45.9	01.5	5 27.4	4.8	27 16.0	4.8	58.6
17	78 45.8	02.1	19 51.2	4.8	27 11.2	4.9	58.6
18	93 45.7	S19 02.7	34 15.0	4.8	S27 06.3	5.1	58.7
19	108 45.5	03.3	48 38.8	4.9	27 01.2	5.3	58.7
20	123 45.4	03.9	63 02.7	4.9	26 55.9	5.4	58.7
21	138 45.3	.. 04.5	77 26.6	5.0	26 50.5	5.6	58.7
22	153 45.2	05.1	91 50.6	5.1	26 44.9	5.8	58.7
23	168 45.0	05.7	106 14.7	5.1	S26 39.1	6.0	58.7
SD	16.2	d 0.6	SD 15.8		15.9		16.0

Twilight / Sunrise / Moonrise

Lat.	Naut.	Civil	Sunrise	15	16	17	18
N 72	07 02	08 38	11 19	■	■	■	■
N 70	06 51	08 14	09 54	■	■	■	■
68	06 43	07 56	09 16	■	■	■	■
66	06 35	07 42	08 50	■	■	■	■
64	06 29	07 30	08 30	■	■	■	15 20
62	06 23	07 19	08 13	12 41	■	14 48	14 36
60	06 18	07 10	08 00	11 45	13 10	13 52	14 06
N 58	06 14	07 02	07 48	11 13	12 31	13 19	13 44
56	06 10	06 55	07 38	10 48	12 03	12 54	13 25
54	06 06	06 49	07 29	10 29	11 41	12 35	13 09
52	06 02	06 43	07 21	10 13	11 24	12 18	12 56
50	05 59	06 38	07 14	09 58	11 08	12 04	12 44
45	05 51	06 27	06 58	09 30	10 38	11 34	12 19
N 40	05 44	06 17	06 46	09 07	10 14	11 12	11 59
35	05 37	06 08	06 35	08 49	09 54	10 53	11 43
30	05 31	06 00	06 26	08 33	09 37	10 36	11 28
20	05 19	05 46	06 09	08 06	09 09	10 09	11 04
N 10	05 07	05 33	05 55	07 43	08 44	09 45	10 43
0	04 54	05 19	05 41	07 22	08 22	09 23	10 23
S 10	04 39	05 05	05 27	07 01	07 59	09 01	10 03
20	04 21	04 49	05 13	06 38	07 35	08 37	09 41
30	03 58	04 29	04 56	06 12	07 07	08 09	09 16
35	03 44	04 18	04 46	05 57	06 50	07 53	09 02
40	03 26	04 03	04 34	05 39	06 31	07 34	08 44
45	03 03	03 46	04 20	05 18	06 07	07 10	08 24
S 50	02 33	03 25	04 04	04 51	05 37	06 41	07 58
52	02 17	03 14	03 56	04 38	05 23	06 26	07 45
54	01 57	03 02	03 47	04 23	05 05	06 09	07 31
56	01 32	02 48	03 37	04 05	04 45	05 48	07 14
58	00 55	02 31	03 26	03 44	04 19	05 23	06 53
S 60	////	02 10	03 13	03 17	03 43	04 47	06 27

Sunset / Twilight / Moonset

Lat.	Sunset	Civil	Naut.	15	16	17	18
N 72	12 09	14 51	16 26	■	■	■	■
N 70	13 34	15 14	16 37	■	■	■	■
68	14 12	15 32	16 45	■	■	■	■
66	14 39	15 47	16 53	■	■	■	■
64	14 59	15 59	16 59	■	■	■	18 06
62	15 15	16 09	17 05	14 25	■	16 32	18 49
60	15 29	16 18	17 10	15 22	16 02	17 28	19 18
N 58	15 41	16 26	17 15	15 54	16 42	18 01	19 40
56	15 51	16 33	17 19	16 19	17 10	18 25	19 58
54	16 00	16 40	17 23	16 39	17 31	18 45	20 13
52	16 08	16 45	17 27	16 55	17 49	19 01	20 26
50	16 15	16 51	17 30	17 10	18 04	19 15	20 37
45	16 30	17 02	17 38	17 39	18 35	19 44	21 01
N 40	16 43	17 12	17 45	18 02	18 59	20 06	21 20
35	16 54	17 21	17 52	18 21	19 19	20 25	21 36
30	17 04	17 29	17 58	18 37	19 36	20 41	21 49
20	17 20	17 43	18 10	19 04	20 04	21 07	22 12
N 10	17 35	17 57	18 22	19 28	20 28	21 30	22 32
0	17 48	18 10	18 36	19 50	20 51	21 52	22 50
S 10	18 02	18 24	18 51	20 12	21 13	22 13	23 09
20	18 17	18 41	19 09	20 36	21 38	22 34	23 28
30	18 34	19 00	19 32	21 04	22 06	23 02	23 50
35	18 44	19 12	19 47	21 20	22 22	23 17	24 03
40	18 56	19 27	20 05	21 39	22 42	23 35	24 18
45	19 10	19 44	20 27	22 03	23 05	23 56	24 36
S 50	19 27	20 06	20 59	22 32	23 35	24 23	00 23
52	19 35	20 17	21 15	22 47	23 50	24 36	00 36
54	19 43	20 29	21 35	23 04	24 07	00 07	00 51
56	19 54	20 43	22 01	23 24	24 28	00 28	01 08
58	20 05	21 01	22 40	23 50	24 54	00 54	01 29
S 60	20 18	21 22	////	24 26	00 26	01 29	01 56

SUN / MOON

Day	SUN Eqn. of Time 00h	12h	Mer. Pass.	MOON Mer. Pass. Upper	Lower	Age	Phase
15	15 33	15 28	11 45	13 36	01 07	02	5
16	15 23	15 17	11 45	14 36	02 06	03	11
17	15 12	15 06	11 45	15 37	03 07	04	19

© British Crown Copyright 2022. All rights reserved.

UT	ARIES GHA	VENUS −4.3 GHA	Dec	MARS +1.3 GHA	Dec	JUPITER −2.9 GHA	Dec	SATURN +0.8 GHA	Dec	Name	SHA	Dec
d h	° ′	° ′	° ′	° ′	° ′	° ′	° ′	° ′	° ′		° ′	° ′
18 00	56 46.9	226 19.4	S 2 38.5	183 42.3	S19 14.0	20 09.1	N13 02.8	83 25.7	S12 49.8	Acamar	315 12.1	S40 12.5
01	71 49.4	241 19.2	39.5	198 42.9	14.4	35 11.8	02.7	98 28.1	49.8	Achernar	335 20.4	S57 07.1
02	86 51.9	256 19.0	40.5	213 43.6	14.9	50 14.6	02.6	113 30.5	49.7	Acrux	173 01.6	S63 13.6
03	101 54.3	271 18.8 ..	41.5	228 44.2 ..	15.3	65 17.4 ..	02.5	128 32.9 ..	49.7	Adhara	255 06.4	S29 00.0
04	116 56.8	286 18.6	42.5	243 44.9	15.7	80 20.1	02.5	143 35.3	49.7	Aldebaran	290 40.4	N16 33.5
05	131 59.2	301 18.5	43.5	258 45.6	16.2	95 22.9	02.4	158 37.7	49.7			
S 06	147 01.7	316 18.3	S 2 44.5	273 46.2	S19 16.6	110 25.7	N13 02.3	173 40.1	S12 49.6	Alioth	166 14.2	N55 49.7
A 07	162 04.2	331 18.1	45.5	288 46.9	17.1	125 28.4	02.2	188 42.5	49.6	Alkaid	152 53.2	N49 11.6
T 08	177 06.6	346 17.9	46.4	303 47.5	17.5	140 31.2	02.1	203 44.9	49.6	Alnair	27 34.1	S46 51.0
U 09	192 09.1	1 17.7 ..	47.4	318 48.2 ..	18.0	155 34.0 ..	02.0	218 47.3 ..	49.6	Alnilam	275 38.4	S 1 11.1
R 10	207 11.6	16 17.6	48.4	333 48.8	18.4	170 36.7	01.9	233 49.7	49.5	Alphard	217 48.7	S 8 45.5
D 11	222 14.0	31 17.4	49.4	348 49.5	18.8	185 39.5	01.8	248 52.1	49.5			
A 12	237 16.5	46 17.2	S 2 50.4	3 50.1	S19 19.3	200 42.3	N13 01.7	263 54.5	S12 49.5	Alphecca	126 04.9	N26 38.1
Y 13	252 19.0	61 17.0	51.4	18 50.8	19.7	215 45.0	01.6	278 57.0	49.4	Alpheratz	357 35.6	N29 13.5
14	267 21.4	76 16.8	52.4	33 51.4	20.2	230 47.8	01.5	293 59.4	49.4	Altair	62 01.1	N 8 56.0
15	282 23.9	91 16.7 ..	53.4	48 52.1 ..	20.6	245 50.6 ..	01.4	309 01.8 ..	49.4	Ankaa	353 07.8	S42 10.7
16	297 26.4	106 16.5	54.4	63 52.7	21.0	260 53.3	01.4	324 04.2	49.4	Antares	112 17.4	S26 29.0
17	312 28.8	121 16.3	55.4	78 53.4	21.5	275 56.1	01.3	339 06.6	49.3			
18	327 31.3	136 16.1	S 2 56.4	93 54.0	S19 21.9	290 58.9	N13 01.2	354 09.0	S12 49.3	Arcturus	145 49.1	N19 03.5
19	342 33.7	151 15.9	57.4	108 54.7	22.4	306 01.6	01.1	9 11.4	49.3	Atria	107 13.1	S69 04.2
20	357 36.2	166 15.7	58.4	123 55.3	22.8	321 04.4	01.0	24 13.8	49.3	Avior	234 14.9	S59 34.8
21	12 38.7	181 15.6	2 59.4	138 56.0 ..	23.2	336 07.2 ..	00.9	39 16.2 ..	49.2	Bellatrix	278 23.6	N 6 22.3
22	27 41.1	196 15.4	3 00.4	153 56.6	23.7	351 09.9	00.8	54 18.6	49.2	Betelgeuse	270 52.8	N 7 24.8
23	42 43.6	211 15.2	01.4	168 57.3	24.1	6 12.7	00.7	69 21.0	49.2			
19 00	57 46.1	226 15.0	S 3 02.4	183 57.9	S19 24.6	21 15.5	N13 00.6	84 23.4	S12 49.2	Canopus	263 52.4	S52 42.2
01	72 48.5	241 14.8	03.4	198 58.6	25.0	36 18.2	00.5	99 25.8	49.1	Capella	280 22.9	N46 01.3
02	87 51.0	256 14.6	04.4	213 59.2	25.4	51 21.0	00.4	114 28.2	49.1	Deneb	49 26.6	N45 22.1
03	102 53.5	271 14.4 ..	05.4	228 59.9 ..	25.9	66 23.7 ..	00.4	129 30.6 ..	49.1	Denebola	182 26.1	N14 26.4
04	117 55.9	286 14.3	06.4	244 00.5	26.3	81 26.5	00.3	144 33.0	49.0	Diphda	348 48.0	S17 51.4
05	132 58.4	301 14.1	07.4	259 01.2	26.7	96 29.3	00.2	159 35.4	49.0			
S 06	148 00.9	316 13.9	S 3 08.4	274 01.8	S19 27.2	111 32.0	N13 00.1	174 37.8	S12 49.0	Dubhe	193 42.4	N61 37.1
U 07	163 03.3	331 13.7	09.4	289 02.5	27.6	126 34.8	13 00.0	189 40.2	49.0	Elnath	278 02.7	N28 37.7
N 08	178 05.8	346 13.5	10.4	304 03.1	28.1	141 37.6	12 59.9	204 42.6	48.9	Eltanin	90 43.1	N51 29.3
D 09	193 08.2	1 13.3 ..	11.4	319 03.8 ..	28.5	156 40.3 ..	59.8	219 45.1 ..	48.9	Enif	33 39.8	N 9 59.1
A 10	208 10.7	16 13.1	12.4	334 04.4	28.9	171 43.1	59.7	234 47.5	48.9	Fomalhaut	15 15.5	S29 29.9
Y 11	223 13.2	31 12.9	13.4	349 05.0	29.4	186 45.9	59.6	249 49.9	48.8			
12	238 15.6	46 12.8	S 3 14.4	4 05.7	S19 29.8	201 48.6	N12 59.5	264 52.3	S12 48.8	Gacrux	171 53.1	S57 14.5
13	253 18.1	61 12.6	15.4	19 06.3	30.2	216 51.4	59.5	279 54.7	48.8	Gienah	175 44.8	S17 40.3
14	268 20.6	76 12.4	16.4	34 07.0	30.7	231 54.1	59.4	294 57.1	48.8	Hadar	148 38.0	S60 29.1
15	283 23.0	91 12.2 ..	17.4	49 07.6 ..	31.1	246 56.9 ..	59.3	309 59.5 ..	48.7	Hamal	327 52.0	N23 34.6
16	298 25.5	106 12.0	18.4	64 08.3	31.6	261 59.7	59.2	325 01.9	48.7	Kaus Aust.	83 34.1	S34 22.5
17	313 28.0	121 11.8	19.4	79 08.9	32.0	277 02.4	59.1	340 04.3	48.7			
18	328 30.4	136 11.6	S 3 20.4	94 09.6	S19 32.4	292 05.2	N12 59.0	355 06.7	S12 48.7	Kochab	137 20.9	N74 03.3
19	343 32.9	151 11.4	21.4	109 10.2	32.9	307 07.9	58.9	10 09.1	48.6	Markab	13 30.8	N15 20.1
20	358 35.4	166 11.2	22.4	124 10.8	33.3	322 10.7	58.8	25 11.5	48.6	Menkar	314 06.8	N 4 11.1
21	13 37.8	181 11.0 ..	23.4	139 11.5 ..	33.7	337 13.5 ..	58.7	40 13.9 ..	48.6	Menkent	147 59.1	S36 29.1
22	28 40.3	196 10.8	24.4	154 12.1	34.2	352 16.2	58.6	55 16.3	48.5	Miaplacidus	221 38.3	S69 48.5
23	43 42.7	211 10.6	25.4	169 12.8	34.6	7 19.0	58.6	70 18.7	48.5			
20 00	58 45.2	226 10.5	S 3 26.4	184 13.4	S19 35.0	22 21.8	N12 58.5	85 21.1	S12 48.5	Mirfak	308 29.1	N49 56.8
01	73 47.7	241 10.3	27.4	199 14.1	35.5	37 24.5	58.4	100 23.5	48.5	Nunki	75 49.2	S26 16.1
02	88 50.1	256 10.1	28.4	214 14.7	35.9	52 27.3	58.3	115 25.9	48.4	Peacock	53 07.5	S56 39.7
03	103 52.6	271 09.9 ..	29.4	229 15.3 ..	36.3	67 30.0 ..	58.2	130 28.3 ..	48.4	Pollux	243 18.3	N27 58.1
04	118 55.1	286 09.7	30.4	244 16.0	36.8	82 32.8	58.1	145 30.7	48.4	Procyon	244 51.7	N 5 09.9
05	133 57.5	301 09.5	31.4	259 16.6	37.2	97 35.6	58.0	160 33.1	48.3			
M 06	149 00.0	316 09.3	S 3 32.4	274 17.3	S19 37.6	112 38.3	N12 57.9	175 35.5	S12 48.3	Rasalhague	96 59.8	N12 32.6
O 07	164 02.5	331 09.1	33.4	289 17.9	38.0	127 41.1	57.8	190 37.9	48.3	Regulus	207 35.5	N11 51.1
N 08	179 04.9	346 08.9	34.4	304 18.5	38.5	142 43.8	57.8	205 40.3	48.2	Rigel	281 04.5	S 8 10.3
D 09	194 07.4	1 08.7 ..	35.4	319 19.2 ..	38.9	157 46.6 ..	57.7	220 42.7 ..	48.2	Rigil Kent.	139 42.3	S60 55.8
A 10	209 09.8	16 08.5	36.4	334 19.8	39.3	172 49.3	57.6	235 45.1	48.2	Sabik	102 04.2	S15 45.2
Y 11	224 12.3	31 08.3	37.4	349 20.5	39.8	187 52.1	57.5	250 47.5	48.2			
12	239 14.8	46 08.1	S 3 38.4	4 21.1	S19 40.2	202 54.9	N12 57.4	265 49.9	S12 48.1	Schedar	349 31.8	N56 40.3
13	254 17.2	61 07.9	39.4	19 21.7	40.6	217 57.6	57.3	280 52.3	48.1	Shaula	96 12.1	S37 07.3
14	269 19.7	76 07.7	40.4	34 22.4	41.1	233 00.4	57.2	295 54.7	48.1	Sirius	258 26.8	S16 44.8
15	284 22.2	91 07.5 ..	41.4	49 23.0 ..	41.5	248 03.1 ..	57.1	310 57.1 ..	48.0	Spica	158 23.6	S11 17.0
16	299 24.6	106 07.3	42.4	64 23.7	41.9	263 05.9	57.0	325 59.5	48.0	Suhail	222 46.9	S43 31.4
17	314 27.1	121 07.1	43.4	79 24.3	42.3	278 08.7	57.0	341 01.9	48.0			
18	329 29.6	136 06.9	S 3 44.4	94 24.9	S19 42.8	293 11.4	N12 56.9	356 04.3	S12 48.0	Vega	80 34.2	N38 48.5
19	344 32.0	151 06.7	45.4	109 25.6	43.2	308 14.2	56.8	11 06.7	47.9	Zuben'ubi	136 57.4	S16 08.3
20	359 34.5	166 06.5	46.4	124 26.2	43.6	323 16.9	56.7	26 09.1	47.9		SHA	Mer. Pass.
21	14 37.0	181 06.3 ..	47.4	139 26.9 ..	44.0	338 19.7 ..	56.6	41 11.5 ..	47.9		° ′	h m
22	29 39.4	196 06.1	48.4	154 27.5	44.5	353 22.4	56.5	56 13.9	47.8	Venus	168 28.9	8 55
23	44 41.9	211 05.9	49.4	169 28.1	44.9	8 25.2	56.4	71 16.2	47.8	Mars	126 11.9	11 44
	h m									Jupiter	323 29.4	22 31
Mer. Pass. 20 05.6		v −0.2	d 1.0	v 0.6	d 0.4	v 2.8	d 0.1	v 2.4	d 0.0	Saturn	26 37.3	18 20

© British Crown Copyright 2022. All rights reserved.

UT	SUN GHA	SUN Dec	MOON GHA	v	MOON Dec	d	HP
d h	° '	° '	° '	'	° '	'	'
18 00	183 44.9	S19 06.3	120 38.8	5.1	S26 33.1	6.2	58.7
01	198 44.8	06.9	135 02.9	5.2	26 26.9	6.3	58.7
02	213 44.7	07.5	149 27.1	5.3	26 20.6	6.5	58.7
03	228 44.5	08.1	163 51.4	5.3	26 14.1	6.7	58.8
04	243 44.4	08.7	178 15.7	5.4	26 07.4	6.8	58.8
05	258 44.3	09.3	192 40.1	5.4	26 00.6	7.0	58.8
06	273 44.2	S19 09.9	207 04.5	5.5	S25 53.6	7.2	58.8
07	288 44.0	10.5	221 29.0	5.6	25 46.4	7.3	58.8
08	303 43.9	11.1	235 53.6	5.6	25 39.1	7.5	58.8
09	318 43.8	11.7	250 18.2	5.8	25 31.6	7.7	58.8
10	333 43.6	12.3	264 43.0	5.7	25 23.9	7.8	58.8
11	348 43.5	12.9	279 07.7	5.9	25 16.1	8.0	58.8
12	3 43.4	S19 13.5	293 32.6	5.9	S25 08.1	8.1	58.9
13	18 43.2	14.1	307 57.5	6.0	25 00.0	8.3	58.9
14	33 43.1	14.7	322 22.5	6.1	24 51.7	8.5	58.9
15	48 43.0	15.3	336 47.6	6.1	24 43.2	8.6	58.9
16	63 42.8	15.9	351 12.7	6.2	24 34.6	8.8	58.9
17	78 42.7	16.5	5 37.9	6.3	24 25.8	8.9	58.9
18	93 42.6	S19 17.1	20 03.2	6.4	S24 16.9	9.1	58.9
19	108 42.4	17.7	34 28.6	6.5	24 07.8	9.2	58.9
20	123 42.3	18.3	48 54.1	6.5	23 58.6	9.4	58.9
21	138 42.2	18.9	63 19.6	6.6	23 49.2	9.6	58.9
22	153 42.0	19.4	77 45.2	6.7	23 39.6	9.7	59.0
23	168 41.9	20.0	92 10.9	6.8	23 29.9	9.8	59.0
19 00	183 41.8	S19 20.6	106 36.7	6.9	S23 20.1	10.0	59.0
01	198 41.6	21.2	121 02.6	6.9	23 10.1	10.1	59.0
02	213 41.5	21.8	135 28.5	7.0	23 00.0	10.2	59.0
03	228 41.4	22.4	149 54.5	7.1	22 49.8	10.4	59.0
04	243 41.2	23.0	164 20.6	7.2	22 39.4	10.6	59.0
05	258 41.1	23.6	178 46.8	7.3	22 28.8	10.6	59.0
06	273 41.0	S19 24.1	193 13.1	7.4	S22 18.2	10.9	59.0
07	288 40.8	24.7	207 39.5	7.4	22 07.3	10.9	59.0
08	303 40.7	25.3	222 05.9	7.5	21 56.4	11.1	59.0
09	318 40.5	25.9	236 32.4	7.7	21 45.3	11.2	59.0
10	333 40.4	26.5	250 59.1	7.6	21 34.1	11.3	59.1
11	348 40.3	27.1	265 25.7	7.8	21 22.8	11.5	59.1
12	3 40.1	S19 27.6	279 52.5	7.9	S21 11.3	11.6	59.1
13	18 40.0	28.2	294 19.4	8.0	20 59.7	11.7	59.1
14	33 39.9	28.8	308 46.4	8.0	20 48.0	11.9	59.1
15	48 39.7	29.4	323 13.4	8.1	20 36.1	11.9	59.1
16	63 39.6	30.0	337 40.5	8.2	20 24.2	12.1	59.1
17	78 39.4	30.5	352 07.7	8.3	20 12.1	12.2	59.1
18	93 39.3	S19 31.1	6 35.0	8.4	S19 59.9	12.4	59.1
19	108 39.1	31.7	21 02.4	8.4	19 47.5	12.4	59.1
20	123 39.0	32.3	35 29.8	8.6	19 35.1	12.6	59.1
21	138 38.9	32.8	49 57.4	8.6	19 22.5	12.6	59.1
22	153 38.7	33.4	64 25.0	8.7	19 09.9	12.8	59.1
23	168 38.6	34.0	78 52.7	8.8	18 57.1	12.9	59.1
20 00	183 38.4	S19 34.6	93 20.5	8.9	S18 44.2	13.0	59.2
01	198 38.3	35.1	107 48.4	8.9	18 31.2	13.1	59.2
02	213 38.1	35.7	122 16.3	9.1	18 18.1	13.2	59.2
03	228 38.0	36.3	136 44.4	9.1	18 04.9	13.3	59.2
04	243 37.9	36.9	151 12.5	9.2	17 51.6	13.5	59.2
05	258 37.7	37.4	165 40.7	9.3	17 38.1	13.5	59.2
06	273 37.6	S19 38.0	180 09.0	9.3	S17 24.6	13.6	59.2
07	288 37.4	38.6	194 37.3	9.4	17 11.0	13.7	59.2
08	303 37.3	39.1	209 05.7	9.6	16 57.3	13.8	59.2
09	318 37.1	39.7	223 34.3	9.5	16 43.5	13.9	59.2
10	333 37.0	40.3	238 02.8	9.7	16 29.6	14.0	59.2
11	348 36.8	40.8	252 31.5	9.7	16 15.6	14.1	59.2
12	3 36.7	S19 41.4	267 00.2	9.8	S16 01.5	14.2	59.2
13	18 36.5	42.0	281 29.0	9.9	15 47.3	14.3	59.2
14	33 36.4	42.5	295 57.9	10.0	15 33.0	14.4	59.2
15	48 36.2	43.1	310 26.9	10.0	15 18.6	14.4	59.2
16	63 36.1	43.7	324 55.9	10.1	15 04.2	14.5	59.2
17	78 35.9	44.2	339 25.0	10.2	14 49.7	14.6	59.2
18	93 35.8	S19 44.8	353 54.2	10.2	S14 35.1	14.7	59.2
19	108 35.6	45.4	8 23.4	10.3	14 20.4	14.8	59.2
20	123 35.5	45.9	22 52.7	10.4	14 05.6	14.8	59.3
21	138 35.3	46.5	37 22.1	10.4	13 50.8	15.0	59.3
22	153 35.2	47.1	51 51.5	10.6	13 35.8	14.9	59.3
23	168 35.0	47.6	66 21.1	10.5	S13 20.9	15.1	59.3
	SD 16.2 d 0.6		SD 16.0		16.1		16.1

Lat.	Twilight Naut.	Twilight Civil	Sunrise	Moonrise 18	Moonrise 19	Moonrise 20	Moonrise 21
°	h m	h m	h m	h m	h m	h m	h m
N 72	07 12	08 52	■■■	■■■	■■■	16 07	15 08
N 70	07 01	08 26	10 16	■■■	■■■	15 35	14 54
68	06 51	08 06	09 31	■■■	16 02	15 11	14 43
66	06 43	07 50	09 01	■■■	15 20	14 52	14 34
64	06 36	07 37	08 39	15 20	14 51	14 37	14 26
62	06 30	07 26	08 22	14 36	14 29	14 24	14 19
60	06 24	07 17	08 07	14 06	14 11	14 13	14 13
N 58	06 19	07 08	07 55	13 44	13 56	14 03	14 08
56	06 15	07 01	07 44	13 25	13 43	13 55	14 03
54	06 10	06 54	07 35	13 09	13 32	13 47	13 59
52	06 07	06 48	07 26	12 56	13 22	13 40	13 55
50	06 03	06 43	07 19	12 44	13 13	13 34	13 51
45	05 55	06 30	07 02	12 19	12 54	13 21	13 44
N 40	05 47	06 20	06 49	11 59	12 38	13 10	13 37
35	05 40	06 11	06 38	11 43	12 25	13 01	13 32
30	05 34	06 03	06 28	11 28	12 13	12 52	13 27
20	05 21	05 48	06 11	11 04	11 53	12 38	13 18
N 10	05 08	05 34	05 56	10 43	11 36	12 25	13 11
0	04 54	05 20	05 42	10 23	11 20	12 13	13 03
S 10	04 39	05 05	05 27	10 03	11 03	12 01	12 56
20	04 20	04 48	05 12	09 41	10 46	11 48	12 49
30	03 56	04 28	04 54	09 16	10 25	11 33	12 40
35	03 41	04 16	04 44	09 02	10 13	11 25	12 35
40	03 23	04 01	04 32	08 44	09 59	11 15	12 29
45	02 59	03 43	04 17	08 24	09 43	11 03	12 22
S 50	02 27	03 20	04 00	07 58	09 23	10 49	12 14
52	02 10	03 09	03 52	07 45	09 13	10 42	12 10
54	01 49	02 56	03 42	07 31	09 02	10 35	12 06
56	01 20	02 41	03 32	07 14	08 50	10 27	12 01
58	00 34	02 23	03 20	06 53	08 35	10 17	11 56
S 60	////	02 01	03 06	06 27	08 18	10 06	11 50

Lat.	Sunset	Twilight Civil	Twilight Naut.	Moonset 18	Moonset 19	Moonset 20	Moonset 21
°	h m	h m	h m	h m	h m	h m	h m
N 72	■■■	14 38	16 17	■■■	■■■	21 11	23 56
N 70	13 14	15 04	16 29	■■■	■■■	21 42	24 07
68	13 59	15 24	16 38	■■■	19 23	22 04	24 15
66	14 29	15 39	16 47	■■■	20 03	22 21	24 23
64	14 51	15 52	16 54	18 06	20 31	22 35	24 28
62	15 08	16 04	17 00	18 49	20 52	22 46	24 34
60	15 23	16 13	17 06	19 18	21 09	22 56	24 38
N 58	15 35	16 22	17 11	19 40	21 23	23 04	24 42
56	15 46	16 29	17 15	19 58	21 35	23 12	24 45
54	15 56	16 36	17 20	20 13	21 46	23 18	24 48
52	16 04	16 42	17 23	20 26	21 55	23 24	24 51
50	16 12	16 48	17 27	20 37	22 04	23 30	24 54
45	16 28	17 00	17 36	21 01	22 21	23 41	24 59
N 40	16 41	17 10	17 43	21 20	22 35	23 50	25 04
35	16 52	17 19	17 50	21 36	22 47	23 58	25 07
30	17 02	17 28	17 57	21 49	22 58	24 05	00 05
20	17 20	17 43	18 10	22 12	23 16	24 17	00 17
N 10	17 35	17 57	18 23	22 32	23 31	24 28	00 28
0	17 49	18 11	18 36	22 50	23 45	24 37	00 37
S 10	18 03	18 26	18 52	23 09	24 00	00 00	00 47
20	18 19	18 43	19 11	23 28	24 15	00 15	00 57
30	18 37	19 03	19 35	23 50	24 32	00 32	01 08
35	18 47	19 16	19 50	24 03	00 03	00 42	01 15
40	18 59	19 30	20 09	24 18	00 18	00 53	01 23
45	19 14	19 48	20 33	24 36	00 36	01 06	01 31
S 50	19 32	20 12	21 06	00 23	00 57	01 22	01 41
52	19 40	20 23	21 23	00 36	01 08	01 30	01 46
54	19 49	20 36	21 45	00 51	01 19	01 38	01 51
56	20 00	20 51	22 14	01 08	01 32	01 47	01 57
58	20 12	21 10	23 06	01 29	01 47	01 57	02 03
S 60	20 26	21 33	////	01 56	02 06	02 09	02 10

	SUN Eqn. of Time 00h	SUN Eqn. of Time 12h	SUN Mer. Pass.	MOON Mer. Pass. Upper	MOON Mer. Pass. Lower	Age	Phase
Day							
d	m s	m s	h m	h m	h m	d	%
18	15 00	14 54	11 45	16 37	04 07	05	29
19	14 47	14 41	11 45	17 33	05 05	06	39
20	14 34	14 27	11 46	18 25	05 59	07	51

© British Crown Copyright 2022. All rights reserved.

UT (d h)	ARIES GHA	VENUS −4.2 GHA	Dec	MARS +1.4 GHA	Dec	JUPITER −2.9 GHA	Dec	SATURN +0.8 GHA	Dec	STARS Name	SHA	Dec
21 00	59 44.3	226 05.7	S 3 50.4	184 28.8	S19 45.3	23 28.0	N12 56.3	86 18.6	S12 47.8	Acamar	315 12.1	S40 12.6
01	74 46.8	241 05.5	51.4	199 29.4	45.8	38 30.7	56.3	101 21.0	47.7	Achernar	335 20.4	S57 07.1
02	89 49.3	256 05.3	52.4	214 30.0	46.2	53 33.5	56.2	116 23.4	47.7	Acrux	173 01.6	S63 13.6
03	104 51.7	271 05.1	.. 53.4	229 30.7	.. 46.6	68 36.2	.. 56.1	131 25.8	.. 47.7	Adhara	255 06.3	S29 00.0
04	119 54.2	286 04.9	54.5	244 31.3	47.0	83 39.0	56.0	146 28.2	47.7	Aldebaran	290 40.4	N16 33.5
05	134 56.7	301 04.7	55.5	259 31.9	47.5	98 41.7	55.9	161 30.6	47.6			
06	149 59.1	316 04.5	S 3 56.5	274 32.6	S19 47.9	113 44.5	N12 55.8	176 33.0	S12 47.6	Alioth	166 14.2	N55 49.7
07	165 01.6	331 04.3	57.5	289 33.2	48.3	128 47.2	55.7	191 35.4	47.6	Alkaid	152 53.2	N49 11.6
08	180 04.1	346 04.1	58.5	304 33.8	48.7	143 50.0	55.6	206 37.8	47.5	Alnair	27 34.1	S46 51.0
09	195 06.5	1 03.9	3 59.5	319 34.5	.. 49.1	158 52.7	.. 55.6	221 40.2	.. 47.5	Alnilam	275 38.4	S 1 11.1
10	210 09.0	16 03.7	4 00.5	334 35.1	49.6	173 55.5	55.5	236 42.6	47.5	Alphard	217 48.6	S 8 45.6
11	225 11.5	31 03.5	01.5	349 35.7	50.0	188 58.3	55.4	251 45.0	47.4			
12	240 13.9	46 03.3	S 4 02.5	4 36.4	S19 50.4	204 01.0	N12 55.3	266 47.4	S12 47.4	Alphecca	126 04.9	N26 38.1
13	255 16.4	61 03.0	03.5	19 37.0	50.8	219 03.8	55.2	281 49.8	47.4	Alpheratz	357 35.6	N29 13.5
14	270 18.8	76 02.8	04.5	34 37.7	51.3	234 06.5	55.1	296 52.2	47.3	Altair	62 01.1	N 8 55.9
15	285 21.3	91 02.6	.. 05.5	49 38.3	.. 51.7	249 09.3	.. 55.0	311 54.6	.. 47.3	Ankaa	353 07.8	S42 10.7
16	300 23.8	106 02.4	06.5	64 38.9	52.1	264 12.0	54.9	326 57.0	47.3	Antares	112 17.4	S26 29.0
17	315 26.2	121 02.2	07.5	79 39.5	52.5	279 14.8	54.9	341 59.4	47.2			
18	330 28.7	136 02.0	S 4 08.5	94 40.2	S19 52.9	294 17.5	N12 54.8	357 01.8	S12 47.2	Arcturus	145 49.1	N19 03.5
19	345 31.2	151 01.8	09.5	109 40.8	53.4	309 20.3	54.7	12 04.2	47.2	Atria	107 13.1	S69 04.2
20	0 33.6	166 01.6	10.5	124 41.4	53.8	324 23.0	54.6	27 06.5	47.2	Avior	234 14.8	S59 34.8
21	15 36.1	181 01.4	.. 11.5	139 42.1	.. 54.2	339 25.8	.. 54.5	42 08.9	.. 47.1	Bellatrix	278 23.6	N 6 22.3
22	30 38.6	196 01.2	12.6	154 42.7	54.6	354 28.5	54.4	57 11.3	47.1	Betelgeuse	270 52.8	N 7 24.8
23	45 41.0	211 01.0	13.6	169 43.3	55.0	9 31.3	54.3	72 13.7	47.1			
22 00	60 43.5	226 00.7	S 4 14.6	184 44.0	S19 55.5	24 34.0	N12 54.3	87 16.1	S12 47.0	Canopus	263 52.4	S52 42.2
01	75 45.9	241 00.5	15.6	199 44.6	55.9	39 36.8	54.2	102 18.5	47.0	Capella	280 22.9	N46 01.3
02	90 48.4	256 00.3	16.6	214 45.2	56.3	54 39.5	54.1	117 20.9	47.0	Deneb	49 26.6	N45 22.1
03	105 50.9	271 00.1	.. 17.6	229 45.9	.. 56.7	69 42.3	.. 54.0	132 23.3	.. 46.9	Denebola	182 26.1	N14 26.4
04	120 53.3	285 59.9	18.6	244 46.5	57.1	84 45.0	53.9	147 25.7	46.9	Diphda	348 48.0	S17 51.4
05	135 55.8	300 59.7	19.6	259 47.1	57.6	99 47.8	53.8	162 28.1	46.9			
06	150 58.3	315 59.5	S 4 20.6	274 47.7	S19 58.0	114 50.5	N12 53.7	177 30.5	S12 46.8	Dubhe	193 42.3	N61 37.1
07	166 00.7	330 59.3	21.6	289 48.4	58.4	129 53.3	53.7	192 32.9	46.8	Elnath	278 02.7	N28 37.7
08	181 03.2	345 59.1	22.6	304 49.0	58.8	144 56.0	53.6	207 35.2	46.8	Eltanin	90 43.1	N51 29.2
09	196 05.7	0 58.8	.. 23.6	319 49.6	.. 59.2	159 58.8	.. 53.5	222 37.6	.. 46.7	Enif	33 39.8	N 9 59.1
10	211 08.1	15 58.6	24.6	334 50.3	19 59.6	175 01.5	53.4	237 40.0	46.7	Fomalhaut	15 15.5	S29 29.9
11	226 10.6	30 58.4	25.7	349 50.9	20 00.1	190 04.3	53.3	252 42.4	46.7			
12	241 13.1	45 58.2	S 4 26.7	4 51.5	S20 00.5	205 07.0	N12 53.2	267 44.8	S12 46.6	Gacrux	171 53.1	S57 14.5
13	256 15.5	60 58.0	27.7	19 52.1	00.9	220 09.8	53.1	282 47.2	46.6	Gienah	175 44.8	S17 40.3
14	271 18.0	75 57.8	28.7	34 52.8	01.3	235 12.5	53.1	297 49.6	46.6	Hadar	148 38.0	S60 29.1
15	286 20.4	90 57.5	.. 29.7	49 53.4	.. 01.7	250 15.3	.. 53.0	312 52.0	.. 46.5	Hamal	327 52.0	N23 34.6
16	301 22.9	105 57.3	30.7	64 54.0	02.1	265 18.0	52.9	327 54.4	46.5	Kaus Aust.	83 34.1	S34 22.5
17	316 25.4	120 57.1	31.7	79 54.7	02.5	280 20.8	52.8	342 56.8	46.5			
18	331 27.8	135 56.9	S 4 32.7	94 55.3	S20 03.0	295 23.5	N12 52.7	357 59.2	S12 46.4	Kochab	137 20.9	N74 03.3
19	346 30.3	150 56.7	33.7	109 55.9	03.4	310 26.3	52.6	13 01.5	46.4	Markab	13 30.8	N15 20.1
20	1 32.8	165 56.5	34.7	124 56.5	03.8	325 29.0	52.5	28 03.9	46.4	Menkar	314 06.8	N 4 11.1
21	16 35.2	180 56.2	.. 35.7	139 57.2	.. 04.2	340 31.8	.. 52.5	43 06.3	.. 46.3	Menkent	147 59.1	S36 29.1
22	31 37.7	195 56.0	36.7	154 57.8	04.6	355 34.5	52.4	58 08.7	46.3	Miaplacidus	221 38.3	S69 48.5
23	46 40.2	210 55.8	37.8	169 58.4	05.0	10 37.3	52.3	73 11.1	46.3			
23 00	61 42.6	225 55.6	S 4 38.8	184 59.0	S20 05.4	25 40.0	N12 52.2	88 13.5	S12 46.2	Mirfak	308 29.1	N49 56.8
01	76 45.1	240 55.4	39.8	199 59.7	05.8	40 42.8	52.1	103 15.9	46.2	Nunki	75 49.2	S26 16.1
02	91 47.6	255 55.1	40.8	215 00.3	06.3	55 45.5	52.0	118 18.3	46.2	Peacock	53 07.5	S56 39.7
03	106 50.0	270 54.9	.. 41.8	230 00.9	.. 06.7	70 48.3	.. 52.0	133 20.7	.. 46.1	Pollux	243 18.3	N27 58.1
04	121 52.5	285 54.7	42.8	245 01.5	07.1	85 51.0	51.9	148 23.0	46.1	Procyon	244 51.6	N 5 09.9
05	136 54.9	300 54.5	43.8	260 02.2	07.5	100 53.8	51.8	163 25.4	46.1			
06	151 57.4	315 54.3	S 4 44.8	275 02.8	S20 07.9	115 56.5	N12 51.7	178 27.8	S12 46.0	Rasalhague	95 59.8	N12 32.6
07	166 59.9	330 54.0	45.8	290 03.4	08.3	130 59.2	51.6	193 30.2	46.0	Regulus	207 35.5	N11 51.1
08	182 02.3	345 53.8	46.8	305 04.0	08.7	146 02.0	51.5	208 32.6	46.0	Rigel	281 04.5	S 8 10.3
09	197 04.8	0 53.6	.. 47.8	320 04.6	.. 09.1	161 04.7	.. 51.5	223 35.0	.. 45.9	Rigil Kent.	139 42.3	S60 55.8
10	212 07.3	15 53.4	48.9	335 05.3	09.5	176 07.5	51.4	238 37.4	45.9	Sabik	102 04.2	S15 45.2
11	227 09.7	30 53.1	49.9	350 05.9	09.9	191 10.2	51.3	253 39.8	45.9			
12	242 12.2	45 52.9	S 4 50.9	5 06.5	S20 10.4	206 13.0	N12 51.2	268 42.1	S12 45.8	Schedar	349 31.8	N56 40.3
13	257 14.7	60 52.7	51.9	20 07.1	10.8	221 15.7	51.1	283 44.5	45.8	Shaula	96 12.1	S37 07.3
14	272 17.1	75 52.5	52.9	35 07.8	11.2	236 18.5	51.0	298 46.9	45.8	Sirius	258 26.8	S16 44.8
15	287 19.6	90 52.3	.. 53.9	50 08.4	.. 11.6	251 21.2	.. 50.9	313 49.3	.. 45.7	Spica	158 23.6	S11 17.0
16	302 22.0	105 52.0	54.9	65 09.0	12.0	266 23.9	50.9	328 51.7	45.7	Suhail	222 46.9	S43 31.4
17	317 24.5	120 51.8	55.9	80 09.6	12.4	281 26.7	50.8	343 54.1	45.7			
18	332 27.0	135 51.6	S 4 56.9	95 10.2	S20 12.8	296 29.4	N12 50.7	358 56.5	S12 45.6	Vega	80 34.2	N38 48.5
19	347 29.4	150 51.3	57.9	110 10.9	13.2	311 32.2	50.6	13 58.8	45.6	Zuben'ubi	136 57.4	S16 08.3
20	2 31.9	165 51.1	4 59.0	125 11.5	13.6	326 34.9	50.5	29 01.2	45.6			
21	17 34.4	180 50.9	5 00.0	140 12.1	.. 14.0	341 37.7	.. 50.4	44 03.6	.. 45.5		SHA	Mer.Pass.
22	32 36.8	195 50.7	01.0	155 12.7	14.4	356 40.4	50.4	59 06.0	45.5	Venus	165 17.3	8 56
23	47 39.3	210 50.4	02.0	170 13.3	14.8	11 43.1	50.3	74 08.4	45.5	Mars	124 00.5	11 41
Mer. Pass.	19 53.8	v −0.2	d 1.0	v 0.6	d 0.4	v 2.7	d 0.1	v 2.4	d 0.0	Jupiter	323 50.6	22 18
										Saturn	26 32.6	18 08

© British Crown Copyright 2022. All rights reserved.

SUN / MOON

UT	SUN GHA	SUN Dec	MOON GHA	v	MOON Dec	d	HP
d h	° ′	° ′	° ′	′	° ′	′	′
21 00	183 34.9	S19 48.2	80 50.6 10.7		S13 05.8	15.2	59.3
01	198 34.7	48.7	95 20.3 10.7		12 50.6	15.2	59.3
02	213 34.6	49.3	109 50.0 10.7		12 35.4	15.2	59.3
03	228 34.4 ..	49.8	124 19.7 10.8		12 20.2	15.4	59.3
04	243 34.3	50.4	138 49.5 10.9		12 04.8	15.4	59.3
05	258 34.1	51.0	153 19.4 10.9		11 49.4	15.5	59.3
06	273 34.0	S19 51.5	167 49.3 11.0		S11 33.9	15.5	59.3
07	288 33.8	52.1	182 19.3 11.1		11 18.4	15.6	59.3
08	303 33.7	52.6	196 49.4 11.1		11 02.8	15.6	59.3
09	318 33.5 ..	53.2	211 19.5 11.1		10 47.2	15.8	59.3
10	333 33.4	53.7	225 49.6 11.2		10 31.4	15.7	59.3
11	348 33.2	54.3	240 19.8 11.3		10 15.7	15.8	59.3
12	3 33.0	S19 54.8	254 50.1 11.3		S 9 59.9	15.9	59.3
13	18 32.9	55.4	269 20.4 11.3		9 44.0	15.9	59.3
14	33 32.7	55.9	283 50.7 11.4		9 28.1	16.0	59.3
15	48 32.6 ..	56.5	298 21.1 11.5		9 12.1	16.0	59.3
16	63 32.4	57.0	312 51.6 11.5		8 56.1	16.1	59.3
17	78 32.3	57.6	327 22.1 11.5		8 40.0	16.1	59.3
18	93 32.1	S19 58.1	341 52.6 11.6		S 8 23.9	16.2	59.3
19	108 31.9	58.7	356 23.2 11.6		8 07.7	16.2	59.3
20	123 31.8	59.2	10 53.8 11.7		7 51.5	16.2	59.3
21	138 31.6	19 59.8	25 24.5 11.7		7 35.3	16.3	59.3
22	153 31.5	20 00.3	39 55.2 11.7		7 19.0	16.3	59.3
23	168 31.3	00.9	54 25.9 11.8		7 02.7	16.4	59.3
22 00	183 31.2	S20 01.4	68 56.7 11.8		S 6 46.3	16.3	59.3
01	198 31.0	01.9	83 27.5 11.8		6 30.0	16.5	59.3
02	213 30.8	02.5	97 58.3 11.9		6 13.5	16.4	59.3
03	228 30.7 ..	03.0	112 29.2 11.9		5 57.1	16.5	59.3
04	243 30.5	03.6	127 00.1 11.9		5 40.6	16.5	59.3
05	258 30.4	04.1	141 31.0 12.0		5 24.1	16.6	59.3
06	273 30.2	S20 04.7	156 02.0 11.9		S 5 07.5	16.5	59.3
07	288 30.0	05.2	170 32.9 12.1		4 51.0	16.6	59.3
08	303 29.9	05.7	185 04.0 12.0		4 34.4	16.6	59.3
09	318 29.7 ..	06.3	199 35.0 12.1		4 17.8	16.7	59.3
10	333 29.5	06.8	214 06.1 12.0		4 01.1	16.6	59.3
11	348 29.4	07.3	228 37.1 12.1		3 44.5	16.7	59.3
12	3 29.2	S20 07.9	243 08.2 12.2		S 3 27.8	16.7	59.3
13	18 29.0	08.4	257 39.4 12.1		3 11.1	16.7	59.3
14	33 28.9	09.0	272 10.5 12.1		2 54.4	16.7	59.3
15	48 28.7 ..	09.5	286 41.6 12.2		2 37.7	16.7	59.3
16	63 28.6	10.0	301 12.8 12.2		2 21.0	16.7	59.3
17	78 28.4	10.6	315 44.0 12.2		2 04.3	16.8	59.3
18	93 28.2	S20 11.1	330 15.2 12.2		S 1 47.5	16.8	59.3
19	108 28.1	11.6	344 46.4 12.2		1 30.7	16.7	59.3
20	123 27.9	12.2	359 17.6 12.2		1 14.0	16.8	59.2
21	138 27.7 ..	12.7	13 48.8 12.3		0 57.2	16.8	59.2
22	153 27.6	13.2	28 20.1 12.2		0 40.4	16.7	59.2
23	168 27.4	13.7	42 51.3 12.2		0 23.7	16.8	59.2
23 00	183 27.2	S20 14.3	57 22.5 12.3		S 0 06.9	16.8	59.2
01	198 27.1	14.8	71 53.8 12.2		N 0 09.9	16.8	59.2
02	213 26.9	15.3	86 25.0 12.3		0 26.7	16.7	59.2
03	228 26.7 ..	15.9	100 56.3 12.2		0 43.4	16.8	59.2
04	243 26.5	16.4	115 27.5 12.3		1 00.2	16.7	59.2
05	258 26.4	16.9	129 58.8 12.2		1 16.9	16.8	59.2
06	273 26.2	S20 17.4	144 30.0 12.2		N 1 33.7	16.7	59.2
07	288 26.0	18.0	159 01.2 12.3		1 50.4	16.7	59.2
08	303 25.9	18.5	173 32.5 12.2		2 07.1	16.8	59.2
09	318 25.7 ..	19.0	188 03.7 12.2		2 23.9	16.6	59.2
10	333 25.5	19.5	202 34.9 12.2		2 40.6	16.6	59.2
11	348 25.4	20.0	217 06.1 12.2		2 57.2	16.7	59.2
12	3 25.2	S20 20.6	231 37.3 12.2		N 3 13.9	16.6	59.2
13	18 25.0	21.1	246 08.5 12.2		3 30.5	16.7	59.2
14	33 24.8	21.6	260 39.7 12.1		3 47.2	16.6	59.1
15	48 24.7 ..	22.1	275 10.8 12.1		4 03.8	16.6	59.1
16	63 24.5	22.6	289 41.9 12.2		4 20.4	16.5	59.1
17	78 24.3	23.2	304 13.1 12.1		4 36.9	16.5	59.1
18	93 24.1	S20 23.7	318 44.2 12.0		N 4 53.4	16.5	59.1
19	108 24.0	24.2	333 15.2 12.1		5 09.9	16.5	59.1
20	123 23.8	24.7	347 46.3 12.0		5 26.4	16.5	59.1
21	138 23.6 ..	25.2	2 17.3 12.1		5 42.9	16.4	59.1
22	153 23.4	25.7	16 48.4 12.0		5 59.3	16.3	59.1
23	168 23.3	26.3	31 19.4 11.9		N 6 15.6	16.4	59.1
	SD 16.2	d 0.5	SD 16.2	16.2			16.1

Twilight / Sunrise / Moonrise

Lat.	Naut.	Civil	Sunrise	21	22	23	24
°	h m	h m	h m	h m	h m	h m	h m
N 72	07 23	09 06	■■■	15 08	14 29	13 53	13 12
N 70	07 10	08 37	10 42	14 54	14 25	13 57	13 27
68	06 59	08 16	09 46	14 43	14 22	14 01	13 40
66	06 50	07 59	09 13	14 34	14 19	14 05	13 50
64	06 43	07 45	08 49	14 26	14 17	14 08	13 58
62	06 36	07 33	08 30	14 19	14 14	14 11	14 06
60	06 30	07 23	08 14	14 13	14 13	14 12	14 12
N 58	06 25	07 14	08 01	14 08	14 11	14 14	14 18
56	06 20	07 06	07 50	14 03	14 10	14 16	14 23
54	06 15	06 59	07 40	13 59	14 08	14 18	14 27
52	06 11	06 53	07 31	13 55	14 07	14 19	14 32
50	06 07	06 47	07 23	13 51	14 06	14 20	14 35
45	05 58	06 34	07 06	13 44	14 04	14 23	14 44
N 40	05 50	06 23	06 53	13 37	14 02	14 26	14 51
35	05 43	06 14	06 41	13 32	14 00	14 28	14 57
30	05 36	06 05	06 31	13 27	13 59	14 30	15 02
20	05 22	05 49	06 13	13 18	13 56	14 33	15 11
N 10	05 09	05 35	05 57	13 11	13 54	14 36	15 20
0	04 55	05 20	05 42	13 03	13 52	14 39	15 27
S 10	04 39	05 05	05 28	12 56	13 49	14 42	15 35
20	04 19	04 48	05 12	12 49	13 47	14 45	15 44
30	03 55	04 27	04 53	12 40	13 45	14 49	15 54
35	03 39	04 14	04 42	12 35	13 43	14 51	15 59
40	03 20	03 59	04 30	12 29	13 41	14 53	16 06
45	02 55	03 40	04 15	12 22	13 39	14 56	16 13
S 50	02 21	03 16	03 57	12 14	13 37	15 00	16 23
52	02 03	03 04	03 48	12 10	13 36	15 01	16 27
54	01 40	02 51	03 38	12 06	13 35	15 03	16 32
56	01 08	02 35	03 27	12 01	13 34	15 05	16 37
58	////	02 16	03 15	11 56	13 32	15 07	16 43
S 60	////	01 51	03 00	11 50	13 30	15 09	16 50

Sunset / Twilight / Moonset

Lat.	Sunset	Civil	Naut.	21	22	23	24
°	h m	h m	h m	h m	h m	h m	h m
N 72	■■■	14 25	16 08	23 56	26 20	02 20	04 44
N 70	12 49	14 54	16 21	24 07	00 07	02 19	04 31
68	13 46	15 15	16 32	24 15	00 15	02 19	04 22
66	14 19	15 32	16 41	24 22	00 22	02 18	04 14
64	14 43	15 46	16 49	24 28	00 28	02 18	04 07
62	15 02	15 58	16 55	24 34	00 34	02 18	04 01
60	15 17	16 08	17 01	24 38	00 38	02 17	03 57
N 58	15 30	16 17	17 07	24 42	00 42	02 17	03 52
56	15 42	16 25	17 12	24 45	00 45	02 17	03 48
54	15 52	16 32	17 16	24 48	00 48	02 17	03 45
52	16 00	16 39	17 21	24 51	00 51	02 17	03 42
50	16 08	16 45	17 25	24 54	00 54	02 16	03 39
45	16 25	16 58	17 34	24 59	00 59	02 16	03 33
N 40	16 39	17 09	17 42	25 04	01 04	02 16	03 28
35	16 51	17 18	17 49	25 07	01 07	02 16	03 24
30	17 01	17 27	17 56	00 05	01 11	02 15	03 20
20	17 19	17 43	18 10	00 17	01 17	02 15	03 13
N 10	17 35	17 57	18 23	00 28	01 22	02 15	03 07
0	17 50	18 12	18 37	00 37	01 26	02 14	03 02
S 10	18 05	18 27	18 54	00 47	01 31	02 14	02 57
20	18 21	18 45	19 13	00 57	01 36	02 13	02 51
30	18 39	19 06	19 38	01 08	01 41	02 13	02 44
35	18 50	19 19	19 54	01 15	01 45	02 13	02 41
40	19 03	19 34	20 13	01 22	01 48	02 12	02 36
45	19 18	19 53	20 38	01 31	01 52	02 12	02 32
S 50	19 36	20 17	21 12	01 41	01 57	02 11	02 26
52	19 45	20 29	21 31	01 46	01 59	02 11	02 23
54	19 55	20 43	21 55	01 51	02 02	02 11	02 20
56	20 06	20 59	22 28	01 57	02 04	02 11	02 17
58	20 19	21 18	////	02 03	02 07	02 10	02 14
S 60	20 34	21 44	////	02 10	02 10	02 10	02 10

SUN / MOON

	SUN Eqn. of Time 00h	SUN Eqn. of Time 12h	Mer. Pass.	MOON Mer. Pass. Upper	MOON Mer. Pass. Lower	Age	Phase
Day	m s	m s	h m	h m	h m	d	%
21	14 20	14 13	11 46	19 15	06 50	08	62
22	14 05	13 57	11 46	20 03	07 39	09	73
23	13 49	13 41	11 46	20 51	08 27	10	82

© British Crown Copyright 2022. All rights reserved.

UT	ARIES GHA	VENUS −4.2 GHA	Dec	MARS +1.4 GHA	Dec	JUPITER −2.8 GHA	Dec	SATURN +0.8 GHA	Dec	STARS Name	SHA	Dec
24 00	62 41.8	225 50.2	S 5 03.0	185 14.0	S20 15.2	26 45.9	N12 50.2	89 10.8	S12 45.4	Acamar	315 12.1	S40 12.6
01	77 44.2	240 50.0	04.0	200 14.6	15.6	41 48.6	50.1	104 13.1	45.4	Achernar	335 20.4	S57 07.1
02	92 46.7	255 49.8	05.0	215 15.2	16.0	56 51.4	50.0	119 15.5	45.4	Acrux	173 01.6	S63 13.6
03	107 49.2	270 49.5	.. 06.0	230 15.8	.. 16.4	71 54.1	.. 50.0	134 17.9	.. 45.3	Adhara	255 06.3	S29 00.1
04	122 51.6	285 49.3	07.0	245 16.4	16.8	86 56.8	49.9	149 20.3	45.3	Aldebaran	290 40.4	N16 33.5
05	137 54.1	300 49.1	08.1	260 17.0	17.3	101 59.6	49.8	164 22.7	45.3			
06	152 56.5	315 48.8	S 5 09.1	275 17.7	S20 17.7	117 02.3	N12 49.7	179 25.1	S12 45.2	Alioth	166 14.2	N55 49.7
F 07	167 59.0	330 48.6	10.1	290 18.3	18.1	132 05.1	49.6	194 27.5	45.2	Alkaid	152 53.2	N49 11.5
R 08	183 01.5	345 48.4	11.1	305 18.9	18.5	147 07.8	49.5	209 29.8	45.2	Alnair	27 34.1	S46 51.0
I 09	198 03.9	0 48.1	.. 12.1	320 19.5	.. 18.9	162 10.5	.. 49.5	224 32.2	.. 45.1	Alnilam	275 38.4	S 1 11.1
10	213 06.4	15 47.9	13.1	335 20.1	19.3	177 13.3	49.4	239 34.6	45.1	Alphard	217 48.6	S 8 45.6
11	228 08.9	30 47.7	14.1	350 20.7	19.7	192 16.0	49.3	254 37.0	45.0			
D 12	243 11.3	45 47.4	S 5 15.1	5 21.4	S20 20.1	207 18.8	N12 49.2	269 39.4	S12 45.0	Alphecca	126 04.9	N26 38.1
A 13	258 13.8	60 47.2	16.1	20 22.0	20.5	222 21.5	49.1	284 41.7	45.0	Alpheratz	357 35.6	N29 13.5
Y 14	273 16.3	75 47.0	17.2	35 22.6	20.9	237 24.2	49.0	299 44.1	44.9	Altair	62 01.1	N 8 55.9
15	288 18.7	90 46.7	.. 18.2	50 23.2	.. 21.3	252 27.0	.. 49.0	314 46.5	.. 44.9	Ankaa	353 07.8	S42 10.8
16	303 21.2	105 46.5	19.2	65 23.8	21.7	267 29.7	48.9	329 48.9	44.9	Antares	112 17.4	S26 29.0
17	318 23.7	120 46.3	20.2	80 24.4	22.1	282 32.5	48.8	344 51.3	44.8			
18	333 26.1	135 46.0	S 5 21.2	95 25.1	S20 22.5	297 35.2	N12 48.7	359 53.7	S12 44.8	Arcturus	145 49.1	N19 03.5
19	348 28.6	150 45.8	22.2	110 25.7	22.9	312 37.9	48.6	14 56.0	44.8	Atria	107 13.1	S69 04.2
20	3 31.0	165 45.6	23.2	125 26.3	23.3	327 40.7	48.6	29 58.4	44.7	Avior	234 14.8	S59 34.8
21	18 33.5	180 45.3	.. 24.2	140 26.9	.. 23.7	342 43.4	.. 48.5	45 00.8	.. 44.7	Bellatrix	278 23.6	N 6 22.3
22	33 36.0	195 45.1	25.2	155 27.5	24.1	357 46.1	48.4	60 03.2	44.7	Betelgeuse	270 52.8	N 7 24.8
23	48 38.4	210 44.9	26.3	170 28.1	24.5	12 48.9	48.3	75 05.6	44.6			
25 00	63 40.9	225 44.6	S 5 27.3	185 28.7	S20 24.9	27 51.6	N12 48.2	90 07.9	S12 44.6	Canopus	263 52.3	S52 42.3
01	78 43.4	240 44.4	28.3	200 29.3	25.3	42 54.4	48.2	105 10.3	44.5	Capella	280 22.8	N46 01.3
02	93 45.8	255 44.1	29.3	215 30.0	25.7	57 57.1	48.1	120 12.7	44.5	Deneb	49 26.7	N45 22.1
03	108 48.3	270 43.9	.. 30.3	230 30.6	.. 26.0	72 59.8	.. 48.0	135 15.1	.. 44.5	Denebola	182 26.1	N14 26.3
04	123 50.8	285 43.7	31.3	245 31.2	26.4	88 02.6	47.9	150 17.5	44.4	Diphda	348 48.0	S17 51.4
05	138 53.2	300 43.4	32.3	260 31.8	26.8	103 05.3	47.8	165 19.8	44.4			
06	153 55.7	315 43.2	S 5 33.3	275 32.4	S20 27.2	118 08.0	N12 47.7	180 22.2	S12 44.4	Dubhe	193 42.3	N61 37.1
S 07	168 58.1	330 42.9	34.3	290 33.0	27.6	133 10.8	47.7	195 24.6	44.3	Elnath	278 02.7	N28 37.7
A 08	184 00.6	345 42.7	35.4	305 33.6	28.0	148 13.5	47.6	210 27.0	44.3	Eltanin	90 43.1	N51 29.2
T 09	199 03.1	0 42.5	.. 36.4	320 34.2	.. 28.4	163 16.2	.. 47.5	225 29.4	.. 44.3	Enif	33 39.8	N 9 59.1
U 10	214 05.5	15 42.2	37.4	335 34.8	28.8	178 19.0	47.4	240 31.7	44.2	Fomalhaut	15 15.5	S29 29.9
R 11	229 08.0	30 42.0	38.4	350 35.5	29.2	193 21.7	47.3	255 34.1	44.2			
D 12	244 10.5	45 41.7	S 5 39.4	5 36.1	S20 29.6	208 24.4	N12 47.3	270 36.5	S12 44.1	Gacrux	171 53.1	S57 14.5
A 13	259 12.9	60 41.5	40.4	20 36.7	30.0	223 27.2	47.2	285 38.9	44.1	Gienah	175 44.8	S17 40.3
Y 14	274 15.4	75 41.3	41.4	35 37.3	30.4	238 29.9	47.1	300 41.3	44.1	Hadar	148 38.0	S60 29.1
15	289 17.9	90 41.0	.. 42.4	50 37.9	.. 30.8	253 32.6	.. 47.0	315 43.6	.. 44.0	Hamal	327 52.0	N23 34.6
16	304 20.3	105 40.8	43.5	65 38.5	31.2	268 35.4	46.9	330 46.0	44.0	Kaus Aust.	83 34.1	S34 22.4
17	319 22.8	120 40.5	44.5	80 39.1	31.6	283 38.1	46.9	345 48.4	44.0			
18	334 25.3	135 40.3	S 5 45.5	95 39.7	S20 32.0	298 40.8	N12 46.8	0 50.8	S12 43.9	Kochab	137 20.9	N74 03.3
19	349 27.7	150 40.0	46.5	110 40.3	32.4	313 43.6	46.7	15 53.1	43.9	Markab	13 30.8	N15 20.1
20	4 30.2	165 39.8	47.5	125 40.9	32.7	328 46.3	46.6	30 55.5	43.8	Menkar	314 06.8	N 4 11.1
21	19 32.6	180 39.5	.. 48.5	140 41.5	.. 33.1	343 49.0	.. 46.5	45 57.9	.. 43.8	Menkent	147 59.1	S36 29.1
22	34 35.1	195 39.3	49.5	155 42.2	33.5	358 51.8	46.5	61 00.3	43.8	Miaplacidus	221 38.2	S69 48.5
23	49 37.6	210 39.1	50.5	170 42.8	33.9	13 54.5	46.4	76 02.7	43.7			
26 00	64 40.0	225 38.8	S 5 51.6	185 43.4	S20 34.3	28 57.2	N12 46.3	91 05.0	S12 43.7	Mirfak	308 29.1	N49 56.8
01	79 42.5	240 38.6	52.6	200 44.0	34.7	44 00.0	46.2	106 07.4	43.7	Nunki	75 49.2	S26 16.1
02	94 45.0	255 38.3	53.6	215 44.6	35.1	59 02.7	46.2	121 09.8	43.6	Peacock	53 07.5	S56 39.7
03	109 47.4	270 38.1	.. 54.6	230 45.2	.. 35.5	74 05.4	.. 46.1	136 12.2	.. 43.6	Pollux	243 28.2	N27 58.1
04	124 49.9	285 37.8	55.6	245 45.8	35.9	89 08.2	46.0	151 14.5	43.5	Procyon	244 51.6	N 5 09.9
05	139 52.4	300 37.6	56.6	260 46.4	36.3	104 10.9	45.9	166 16.9	43.5			
06	154 54.8	315 37.3	S 5 57.6	275 47.0	S20 36.6	119 13.6	N12 45.8	181 19.3	S12 43.5	Rasalhague	96 59.8	N12 32.6
07	169 57.3	330 37.1	58.6	290 47.6	37.0	134 16.3	45.8	196 21.7	43.4	Regulus	207 35.4	N11 51.1
S 08	184 59.8	345 36.8	5 59.7	305 48.2	37.4	149 19.1	45.7	211 24.0	43.4	Rigel	281 04.5	S 8 10.4
U 09	200 02.2	0 36.6	6 00.7	320 48.8	.. 37.8	164 21.8	.. 45.6	226 26.4	.. 43.4	Rigil Kent.	139 42.3	S60 55.8
N 10	215 04.7	15 36.3	01.7	335 49.4	38.2	179 24.5	45.5	241 28.8	43.3	Sabik	102 04.2	S15 45.2
D 11	230 07.1	30 36.1	02.7	350 50.0	38.6	194 27.3	45.4	256 31.2	43.3			
A 12	245 09.6	45 35.8	S 6 03.7	5 50.6	S20 39.0	209 30.0	N12 45.4	271 33.5	S12 43.2	Schedar	349 31.8	N56 40.3
Y 13	260 12.1	60 35.6	04.7	20 51.2	39.4	224 32.7	45.3	286 35.9	43.2	Shaula	96 12.1	S37 07.3
14	275 14.5	75 35.3	05.7	35 51.8	39.7	239 35.5	45.2	301 38.3	43.2	Sirius	258 26.8	S16 44.8
15	290 17.0	90 35.1	.. 06.7	50 52.4	.. 40.1	254 38.2	.. 45.1	316 40.7	.. 43.1	Spica	158 23.6	S11 17.0
16	305 19.5	105 34.8	07.8	65 53.0	40.5	269 40.9	45.1	331 43.0	43.1	Suhail	222 46.9	S43 31.4
17	320 21.9	120 34.6	08.8	80 53.7	40.9	284 43.6	45.0	346 45.4	43.0			
18	335 24.4	135 34.3	S 6 09.8	95 54.3	S20 41.3	299 46.4	N12 44.9	1 47.8	S12 43.0	Vega	80 34.2	N38 48.5
19	350 26.9	150 34.0	10.8	110 54.9	41.7	314 49.1	44.8	16 50.2	43.0	Zuben'ubi	136 57.4	S16 08.3
20	5 29.3	165 33.8	11.8	125 55.5	42.0	329 51.8	44.7	31 52.5	42.9			
21	20 31.8	180 33.5	.. 12.8	140 56.1	.. 42.4	344 54.5	.. 44.7	46 54.9	.. 42.9		SHA	Mer. Pass.
22	35 34.2	195 33.3	13.8	155 56.7	42.8	359 57.3	44.6	61 57.3	42.8	Venus	162 03.7	8 57
23	50 36.7	210 33.0	14.8	170 57.3	43.2	15 00.0	44.5	76 59.6	42.8	Mars	121 47.8	11 38
Mer. Pass. 19 42.0		v −0.2	d 1.0	v 0.6	d 0.4	v 2.7	d 0.1	v 2.4	d 0.0	Jupiter	324 10.7	22 05
										Saturn	26 27.0	17 57

© British Crown Copyright 2022. All rights reserved.

UT	SUN GHA	SUN Dec	MOON GHA	v	MOON Dec	d	HP
d h	° ′	° ′	° ′	′	° ′	′	′
24 00	183 23.1	S20 26.8	45 50.3	12.0	N 6 32.0	16.3	59.1
01	198 22.9	27.3	60 21.3	11.9	6 48.3	16.2	59.1
02	213 22.7	27.8	74 52.2	11.8	7 04.5	16.3	59.0
03	228 22.6	.. 28.3	89 23.0	11.9	7 20.8	16.2	59.0
04	243 22.4	28.8	103 53.9	11.8	7 37.0	16.1	59.0
05	258 22.2	29.3	118 24.7	11.8	7 53.1	16.1	59.0
06	273 22.0	S20 29.8	132 55.5	11.8	N 8 09.2	16.0	59.0
07	288 21.9	30.3	147 26.3	11.7	8 25.2	16.0	59.0
08	303 21.7	30.8	161 57.0	11.7	8 41.2	16.0	59.0
F 09	318 21.5	.. 31.4	176 27.7	11.6	8 57.2	15.9	59.0
R 10	333 21.3	31.9	190 58.3	11.6	9 13.1	15.9	59.0
I 11	348 21.1	32.4	205 28.9	11.6	9 29.0	15.8	58.9
D 12	3 21.0	S20 32.9	219 59.5	11.5	N 9 44.8	15.7	58.9
A 13	18 20.8	33.4	234 30.0	11.5	10 00.5	15.7	58.9
Y 14	33 20.6	33.9	249 00.5	11.5	10 16.2	15.6	58.9
15	48 20.4	.. 34.4	263 31.0	11.4	10 31.8	15.6	58.9
16	63 20.2	34.9	278 01.4	11.3	10 47.4	15.5	58.9
17	78 20.1	35.4	292 31.7	11.3	11 02.9	15.4	58.9
18	93 19.9	S20 35.9	307 02.0	11.3	N11 18.3	15.4	58.9
19	108 19.7	36.4	321 32.3	11.2	11 33.7	15.4	58.8
20	123 19.5	36.9	336 02.5	11.2	11 49.1	15.2	58.8
21	138 19.3	.. 37.4	350 32.7	11.1	12 04.3	15.2	58.8
22	153 19.1	37.9	5 02.8	11.1	12 19.5	15.1	58.8
23	168 19.0	38.4	19 32.9	11.0	12 34.6	15.0	58.8
25 00	183 18.8	S20 38.9	34 02.9	11.0	N12 49.6	15.0	58.8
01	198 18.6	39.4	48 32.9	11.0	13 04.6	14.9	58.8
02	213 18.4	39.9	63 02.9	10.8	13 19.5	14.8	58.7
03	228 18.2	.. 40.4	77 32.7	10.8	13 34.3	14.8	58.7
04	243 18.0	40.9	92 02.5	10.8	13 49.1	14.6	58.7
05	258 17.9	41.4	106 32.3	10.7	14 03.7	14.6	58.7
06	273 17.7	S20 41.8	121 02.0	10.7	N14 18.3	14.5	58.7
07	288 17.5	42.3	135 31.7	10.6	14 32.8	14.4	58.7
08	303 17.3	42.8	150 01.3	10.5	14 47.2	14.4	58.7
S 09	318 17.1	.. 43.3	164 30.8	10.5	15 01.6	14.2	58.6
A 10	333 16.9	43.8	179 00.3	10.4	15 15.8	14.2	58.6
T 11	348 16.7	44.3	193 29.7	10.4	15 30.0	14.0	58.6
U 12	3 16.6	S20 44.8	207 59.1	10.3	N15 44.0	14.0	58.6
R 13	18 16.4	45.3	222 28.4	10.3	15 58.0	13.9	58.6
D 14	33 16.2	45.8	236 57.7	10.2	16 11.9	13.8	58.6
A 15	48 16.0	.. 46.3	251 26.9	10.1	16 25.7	13.7	58.5
Y 16	63 15.8	46.7	265 56.0	10.1	16 39.4	13.6	58.5
17	78 15.6	47.2	280 25.1	10.0	16 53.0	13.5	58.5
18	93 15.4	S20 47.7	294 54.1	9.9	N17 06.5	13.4	58.5
19	108 15.2	48.2	309 23.0	9.9	17 19.9	13.3	58.5
20	123 15.0	48.7	323 51.9	9.8	17 33.2	13.2	58.4
21	138 14.9	.. 49.2	338 20.7	9.8	17 46.4	13.0	58.4
22	153 14.7	49.6	352 49.5	9.7	17 59.4	13.0	58.4
23	168 14.5	50.1	7 18.2	9.6	18 12.4	12.9	58.4
26 00	183 14.3	S20 50.6	21 46.8	9.6	N18 25.3	12.8	58.4
01	198 14.1	51.1	36 15.4	9.5	18 38.1	12.7	58.4
02	213 13.9	51.6	50 43.9	9.5	18 50.8	12.5	58.3
03	228 13.7	.. 52.0	65 12.4	9.4	19 03.3	12.4	58.3
04	243 13.5	52.5	79 40.8	9.3	19 15.7	12.4	58.3
05	258 13.3	53.0	94 09.1	9.2	19 28.1	12.2	58.3
06	273 13.1	S20 53.5	108 37.3	9.2	N19 40.3	12.1	58.3
07	288 12.9	54.0	123 05.5	9.1	19 52.4	11.9	58.2
08	303 12.7	54.4	137 33.6	9.1	20 04.3	11.9	58.2
S 09	318 12.5	.. 54.9	152 01.7	9.0	20 16.2	11.7	58.2
U 10	333 12.3	55.4	166 29.7	8.9	20 27.9	11.7	58.2
N 11	348 12.2	55.9	180 57.6	8.9	20 39.6	11.4	58.1
D 12	3 12.0	S20 56.3	195 25.5	8.8	N20 51.0	11.4	58.1
A 13	18 11.8	56.8	209 53.3	8.8	21 02.4	11.3	58.1
Y 14	33 11.6	57.3	224 21.1	8.7	21 13.7	11.1	58.1
15	48 11.4	.. 57.7	238 48.8	8.6	21 24.8	11.0	58.1
16	63 11.2	58.2	253 16.4	8.5	21 35.8	10.8	58.0
17	78 11.0	58.7	267 43.9	8.5	21 46.6	10.7	58.0
18	93 10.8	S20 59.2	282 11.4	8.5	N21 57.3	10.6	58.0
19	108 10.6	20 59.6	296 38.9	8.4	22 07.9	10.5	58.0
20	123 10.4	21 00.1	311 06.3	8.3	22 18.4	10.3	57.9
21	138 10.2	.. 00.6	325 33.6	8.2	22 28.7	10.2	57.9
22	153 10.0	01.0	340 00.8	8.2	22 38.9	10.1	57.9
23	168 09.8	01.5	354 28.0	8.2	N22 49.0	9.9	57.9
	SD 16.2	d 0.5	SD 16.1		16.0		15.8

Twilight / Sunrise / Moonrise

Lat.	Naut.	Civil	Sunrise	Moonrise 24	25	26	27
°	h m	h m	h m	h m	h m	h m	h m
N 72	07 32	09 20	■	13 12	12 11	☐	☐
N 70	07 18	08 49	11 24	13 27	12 46	☐	☐
68	07 07	08 25	10 01	13 40	13 12	12 20	☐
66	06 57	08 07	09 24	13 50	13 32	13 04	☐
64	06 49	07 52	08 58	13 58	13 48	13 34	13 08
62	06 42	07 40	08 38	14 06	14 01	13 57	13 52
60	06 35	07 29	08 21	14 12	14 13	14 15	14 21
N 58	06 30	07 20	08 07	14 18	14 23	14 30	14 44
56	06 24	07 11	07 56	14 23	14 32	14 44	15 02
54	06 19	07 04	07 45	14 27	14 39	14 55	15 18
52	06 15	06 57	07 36	14 32	14 46	15 05	15 32
50	06 11	06 51	07 28	14 35	14 53	15 15	15 43
45	06 01	06 38	07 10	14 44	15 07	15 34	16 08
N 40	05 53	06 26	06 56	14 51	15 18	15 50	16 28
35	05 45	06 16	06 44	14 57	15 28	16 03	16 45
30	05 38	06 07	06 33	15 02	15 37	16 15	16 59
20	05 24	05 51	06 15	15 11	15 52	16 36	17 24
N 10	05 10	05 36	05 58	15 20	16 05	16 53	17 45
0	04 55	05 21	05 43	15 27	16 17	17 10	18 05
S 10	04 39	05 05	05 28	15 35	16 30	17 27	18 25
20	04 19	04 47	05 11	15 44	16 44	17 45	18 47
30	03 53	04 26	04 52	15 54	16 59	18 06	19 12
35	03 37	04 12	04 41	15 59	17 09	18 18	19 27
40	03 17	03 57	04 28	16 06	17 19	18 33	19 45
45	02 52	03 37	04 13	16 13	17 32	18 50	20 06
S 50	02 16	03 12	03 54	16 23	17 47	19 11	20 32
52	01 57	03 00	03 45	16 27	17 54	19 21	20 45
54	01 32	02 46	03 34	16 32	18 02	19 33	21 00
56	00 55	02 29	03 23	16 37	18 11	19 46	21 18
58	////	02 09	03 10	16 43	18 21	20 01	21 39
S 60	////	01 42	02 54	16 50	18 33	20 20	22 07

Sunset / Twilight / Moonset

Lat.	Sunset	Civil	Naut.	Moonset 24	25	26	27
°	h m	h m	h m	h m	h m	h m	h m
N 72	■	14 12	16 00	04 44	07 30	☐	☐
N 70	12 09	14 44	16 15	04 31	06 57	☐	☐
68	13 32	15 08	16 26	04 22	06 33	09 14	☐
66	14 09	15 26	16 36	04 14	06 15	08 31	☐
64	14 35	15 41	16 44	04 07	06 00	08 02	10 22
62	14 55	15 53	16 51	04 01	05 48	07 40	09 38
60	15 12	16 04	16 58	03 57	05 38	07 23	09 10
N 58	15 26	16 14	17 04	03 52	05 29	07 08	08 48
56	15 38	16 22	17 09	03 48	05 21	06 56	08 30
54	15 48	16 29	17 14	03 45	05 14	06 45	08 15
52	15 57	16 36	17 18	03 42	05 08	06 35	08 02
50	16 06	16 42	17 23	03 39	05 02	06 27	07 50
45	16 23	16 56	17 32	03 33	04 51	06 09	07 26
N 40	16 38	17 07	17 40	03 28	04 41	05 54	07 07
35	16 50	17 17	17 56	03 24	04 32	05 42	06 52
30	17 01	17 26	17 56	03 20	04 25	05 31	06 38
20	17 19	17 43	18 10	03 13	04 12	05 13	06 15
N 10	17 35	17 58	18 24	03 07	04 01	04 57	05 55
0	17 51	18 13	18 38	03 02	03 51	04 42	05 36
S 10	18 06	18 29	18 55	02 57	03 41	04 27	05 18
20	18 20	18 47	19 15	02 51	03 30	04 12	04 58
30	18 42	19 09	19 41	02 44	03 17	03 54	04 35
35	18 53	19 22	19 57	02 41	03 10	03 43	04 22
40	19 06	19 38	20 17	02 36	03 02	03 32	04 06
45	19 22	19 57	20 43	02 32	02 53	03 18	03 48
S 50	19 41	20 22	21 19	02 26	02 42	03 01	03 26
52	19 50	20 35	21 39	02 23	02 37	02 53	03 15
54	20 00	20 49	22 05	02 20	02 31	02 44	03 03
56	20 12	21 06	22 44	02 17	02 25	02 35	02 49
58	20 25	21 27	////	02 14	02 18	02 23	02 33
S 60	20 41	21 55	////	02 10	02 10	02 11	02 14

SUN / MOON

Day	SUN Eqn. of Time 00h	12h	Mer. Pass.	MOON Mer. Pass. Upper	Lower	Age	Phase
d	m s	m s	h m	h m	h m	d	%
24	13 33	13 24	11 47	21 39	09 15	11	90
25	13 15	13 07	11 47	22 30	10 04	12	96
26	12 57	12 48	11 47	23 23	10 56	13	99

© British Crown Copyright 2022. All rights reserved.

UT	ARIES GHA	VENUS −4.2 GHA	Dec	MARS +1.4 GHA	Dec	JUPITER −2.8 GHA	Dec	SATURN +0.8 GHA	Dec	STARS Name	SHA	Dec
d h	° ′	° ′	° ′	° ′	° ′	° ′	° ′	° ′	° ′		° ′	° ′
27 00	65 39.2	225 32.8	S 6 15.9	185 57.9	S20 43.6	30 02.7	N12 44.4	92 02.0	S12 42.8	Acamar	315 12.1	S40 12.6
01	80 41.6	240 32.5	16.9	200 58.5	44.0	45 05.4	44.4	107 04.4	42.7	Achernar	335 20.4	S57 07.1
02	95 44.1	255 32.3	17.9	215 59.1	44.3	60 08.2	44.3	122 06.8	42.7	Acrux	173 01.5	S63 13.6
03	110 46.6	270 32.0	.. 18.9	230 59.7	.. 44.7	75 10.9	.. 44.2	137 09.1	.. 42.7	Adhara	255 06.3	S29 00.1
04	125 49.0	285 31.7	19.9	246 00.3	45.1	90 13.6	44.1	152 11.5	42.6	Aldebaran	290 40.4	N16 33.5
05	140 51.5	300 31.5	20.9	261 00.9	45.5	105 16.3	44.0	167 13.9	42.6			
06	155 54.0	315 31.2	S 6 21.9	276 01.5	S20 45.9	120 19.1	N12 44.0	182 16.3	S12 42.5	Alioth	166 14.1	N55 49.6
07	170 56.4	330 31.0	22.9	291 02.1	46.3	135 21.8	43.9	197 18.6	42.5	Alkaid	152 53.1	N49 11.5
M 08	185 58.9	345 30.7	24.0	306 02.7	46.6	150 24.5	43.8	212 21.0	42.5	Alnair	27 34.1	S46 51.0
O 09	201 01.4	0 30.4	.. 25.0	321 03.3	.. 47.0	165 27.2	.. 43.7	227 23.4	.. 42.4	Alnilam	275 38.4	S 1 11.1
N 10	216 03.8	15 30.2	26.0	336 03.9	47.4	180 30.0	43.7	242 25.7	42.4	Alphard	217 48.6	S 8 45.6
D 11	231 06.3	30 29.9	27.0	351 04.5	47.8	195 32.7	43.6	257 28.1	42.3			
A 12	246 08.7	45 29.7	S 6 28.0	6 05.1	S20 48.1	210 35.4	N12 43.5	272 30.5	S12 42.3	Alphecca	126 04.9	N26 38.1
Y 13	261 11.2	60 29.4	29.0	21 05.7	48.5	225 38.1	43.4	287 32.9	42.3	Alpheratz	357 35.6	N29 13.5
14	276 13.7	75 29.1	30.0	36 06.3	48.9	240 40.9	43.4	302 35.2	42.2	Altair	62 01.1	N 8 55.9
15	291 16.1	90 28.9	.. 31.0	51 06.9	.. 49.3	255 43.6	.. 43.3	317 37.6	.. 42.2	Ankaa	353 07.9	S42 10.8
16	306 18.6	105 28.6	32.0	66 07.4	49.7	270 46.3	43.2	332 40.0	42.1	Antares	112 17.4	S26 29.0
17	321 21.1	120 28.4	33.1	81 08.0	50.0	285 49.0	43.1	347 42.3	42.1			
18	336 23.5	135 28.1	S 6 34.1	96 08.6	S20 50.4	300 51.7	N12 43.1	2 44.7	S12 42.1	Arcturus	145 49.1	N19 03.5
19	351 26.0	150 27.8	35.1	111 09.2	50.8	315 54.5	43.0	17 47.1	42.0	Atria	107 13.0	S69 04.2
20	6 28.5	165 27.6	36.1	126 09.8	51.2	330 57.2	42.9	32 49.4	42.0	Avior	234 14.8	S59 34.8
21	21 30.9	180 27.3	.. 37.1	141 10.4	.. 51.5	345 59.9	.. 42.8	47 51.8	.. 41.9	Bellatrix	278 23.6	N 6 22.3
22	36 33.4	195 27.0	38.1	156 11.0	51.9	1 02.6	42.8	62 54.2	41.9	Betelgeuse	270 52.8	N 7 24.7
23	51 35.9	210 26.8	39.1	171 11.6	52.3	16 05.3	42.7	77 56.6	41.9			
28 00	66 38.3	225 26.5	S 6 40.1	186 12.2	S20 52.7	31 08.1	N12 42.6	92 58.9	S12 41.8	Canopus	263 52.3	S52 42.3
01	81 40.8	240 26.2	41.2	201 12.8	53.0	46 10.8	42.5	108 01.3	41.8	Capella	280 22.8	N46 01.3
02	96 43.2	255 26.0	42.2	216 13.4	53.4	61 13.5	42.5	123 03.7	41.7	Deneb	49 26.7	N45 22.1
03	111 45.7	270 25.7	.. 43.2	231 14.0	.. 53.8	76 16.2	.. 42.4	138 06.0	.. 41.7	Denebola	182 26.0	N14 26.3
04	126 48.2	285 25.4	44.2	246 14.6	54.2	91 18.9	42.3	153 08.4	41.6	Diphda	348 48.1	S17 51.4
05	141 50.6	300 25.2	45.2	261 15.2	54.5	106 21.7	42.2	168 10.8	41.6			
06	156 53.1	315 24.9	S 6 46.2	276 15.8	S20 54.9	121 24.4	N12 42.2	183 13.1	S12 41.6	Dubhe	193 42.3	N61 37.1
07	171 55.6	330 24.6	47.2	291 16.4	55.3	136 27.1	42.1	198 15.5	41.5	Elnath	278 02.7	N28 37.7
T 08	186 58.0	345 24.4	48.2	306 17.0	55.7	151 29.8	42.0	213 17.9	41.5	Eltanin	90 43.1	N51 29.2
U 09	202 00.5	0 24.1	.. 49.3	321 17.6	.. 56.0	166 32.5	.. 41.9	228 20.2	.. 41.4	Enif	33 39.8	N 9 59.1
E 10	217 03.0	15 23.8	50.3	336 18.2	56.4	181 35.3	41.9	243 22.6	41.4	Fomalhaut	15 15.5	S29 29.9
S 11	232 05.4	30 23.6	51.3	351 18.7	56.8	196 38.0	41.8	258 25.0	41.4			
D 12	247 07.9	45 23.3	S 6 52.3	6 19.3	S20 57.1	211 40.7	N12 41.7	273 27.3	S12 41.3	Gacrux	171 53.0	S57 14.5
A 13	262 10.4	60 23.0	53.3	21 19.9	57.5	226 43.4	41.6	288 29.7	41.3	Gienah	175 44.7	S17 40.3
Y 14	277 12.8	75 22.7	54.3	36 20.5	57.9	241 46.1	41.6	303 32.1	41.2	Hadar	148 37.9	S60 29.0
15	292 15.3	90 22.5	.. 55.3	51 21.1	.. 58.3	256 48.8	.. 41.5	318 34.4	.. 41.2	Hamal	327 52.0	N23 34.6
16	307 17.7	105 22.2	56.3	66 21.7	58.6	271 51.6	41.4	333 36.8	41.2	Kaus Aust.	83 34.1	S34 22.4
17	322 20.2	120 21.9	57.3	81 22.3	59.0	286 54.3	41.3	348 39.2	41.1			
18	337 22.7	135 21.6	S 6 58.4	96 22.9	S20 59.4	301 57.0	N12 41.3	3 41.5	S12 41.1	Kochab	137 20.9	N74 03.3
19	352 25.1	150 21.4	6 59.4	111 23.5	20 59.7	316 59.7	41.2	18 43.9	41.0	Markab	13 30.8	N15 20.1
20	7 27.6	165 21.1	7 00.4	126 24.1	21 00.1	332 02.4	41.1	33 46.3	41.0	Menkar	314 06.8	N 4 11.1
21	22 30.1	180 20.8	.. 01.4	141 24.7	.. 00.5	347 05.1	.. 41.0	48 48.6	.. 40.9	Menkent	147 59.1	S36 29.0
22	37 32.5	195 20.6	02.4	156 25.2	00.8	2 07.9	41.0	63 51.0	40.9	Miaplacidus	221 38.2	S69 48.5
23	52 35.0	210 20.3	03.4	171 25.8	01.2	17 10.6	40.9	78 53.4	40.9			
29 00	67 37.5	225 20.0	S 7 04.4	186 26.4	S21 01.6	32 13.3	N12 40.8	93 55.7	S12 40.8	Mirfak	308 29.1	N49 56.8
01	82 39.9	240 19.7	05.4	201 27.0	01.9	47 16.0	40.7	108 58.1	40.7	Nunki	75 49.2	S26 16.1
02	97 42.4	255 19.4	06.4	216 27.6	02.3	62 18.7	40.7	124 00.5	40.7	Peacock	53 07.5	S56 39.7
03	112 44.9	270 19.2	.. 07.5	231 28.2	.. 02.7	77 21.4	.. 40.6	139 02.8	.. 40.7	Pollux	243 18.2	N27 58.1
04	127 47.3	285 18.9	08.5	246 28.8	03.0	92 24.1	40.5	154 05.2	40.7	Procyon	244 51.6	N 5 09.9
05	142 49.8	300 18.6	09.5	261 29.4	03.4	107 26.9	40.5	169 07.5	40.6			
06	157 52.2	315 18.3	S 7 10.5	276 30.0	S21 03.8	122 29.6	N12 40.4	184 09.9	S12 40.6	Rasalhague	95 59.8	N12 32.6
W 07	172 54.7	330 18.1	11.5	291 30.5	04.1	137 32.3	40.3	199 12.3	40.5	Regulus	207 35.4	N11 51.1
E 08	187 57.2	345 17.8	12.5	306 31.1	04.5	152 35.0	40.2	214 14.6	40.5	Rigel	281 04.4	S 8 10.4
D 09	202 59.6	0 17.5	.. 13.5	321 31.7	.. 04.9	167 37.7	.. 40.2	229 17.0	.. 40.4	Rigil Kent.	139 42.2	S60 55.8
N 10	218 02.1	15 17.2	14.5	336 32.3	05.2	182 40.4	40.1	244 19.4	40.4	Sabik	102 04.2	S15 45.2
E 11	233 04.6	30 16.9	15.5	351 32.9	05.6	197 43.1	40.0	259 21.7	40.4			
S 12	248 07.0	45 16.7	S 7 16.5	6 33.5	S21 06.0	212 45.8	N12 39.9	274 24.1	S12 40.3	Schedar	349 31.8	N56 40.3
D 13	263 09.5	60 16.4	17.6	21 34.1	06.3	227 48.5	39.9	289 26.5	40.3	Shaula	96 12.1	S37 07.3
A 14	278 12.0	75 16.1	18.6	36 34.7	06.7	242 51.3	39.8	304 28.8	40.2	Sirius	258 26.8	S16 44.8
Y 15	293 14.4	90 15.8	.. 19.6	51 35.2	.. 07.1	257 54.0	.. 39.7	319 31.2	.. 40.2	Spica	158 23.5	S11 17.0
16	308 16.9	105 15.5	20.6	66 35.8	07.4	272 56.7	39.7	334 33.5	40.1	Suhail	222 46.9	S43 31.4
17	323 19.4	120 15.3	21.6	81 36.4	07.8	287 59.4	39.6	349 35.9	40.1			
18	338 21.8	135 15.0	S 7 22.6	96 37.0	S21 08.1	303 02.1	N12 39.5	4 38.3	S12 40.1	Vega	80 34.2	N38 48.4
19	353 24.3	150 14.7	23.6	111 37.6	08.5	318 04.8	39.4	19 40.6	40.0	Zuben'ubi	136 57.4	S16 08.3
20	8 26.7	165 14.4	24.6	126 38.2	08.9	333 07.5	39.4	34 43.0	40.0		SHA	Mer. Pass.
21	23 29.2	180 14.1	.. 25.6	141 38.7	.. 09.2	348 10.2	.. 39.3	49 45.3	.. 39.9		° ′	h m
22	38 31.7	195 13.8	26.6	156 39.3	09.6	3 12.9	39.2	64 47.7	39.9	Venus	158 48.2	8 58
23	53 34.1	210 13.5	27.7	171 39.9	09.9	18 15.6	39.2	79 50.1	39.8	Mars	119 33.9	11 35
	h m									Jupiter	324 29.8	21 52
Mer. Pass. 19 30.2		v −0.3	d 1.0	v 0.6	d 0.4	v 2.7	d 0.1	v 2.4	d 0.0	Saturn	26 20.6	17 45

© British Crown Copyright 2022. All rights reserved.

UT	SUN GHA	SUN Dec	MOON GHA	v	MOON Dec	d	HP
d h	° ′	° ′	° ′	′	° ′	′	′
27 00	183 09.6	S21 02.0	8 55.2	8.0	N22 58.9	9.8	57.9
01	198 09.4	02.4	23 22.2	8.1	23 08.7	9.6	57.8
02	213 09.2	02.9	37 49.3	7.9	23 18.3	9.5	57.8
03	228 09.0 ..	03.3	52 16.2	8.0	23 27.8	9.3	57.8
04	243 08.8	03.8	66 43.2	7.8	23 37.1	9.3	57.8
05	258 08.6	04.3	81 10.0	7.8	23 46.4	9.0	57.7
06	273 08.4	S21 04.7	95 36.8	7.8	N23 55.4	8.9	57.7
07	288 08.2	05.2	110 03.6	7.7	24 04.3	8.8	57.7
08	303 08.0	05.6	124 30.3	7.6	24 13.1	8.6	57.7
M 09	318 07.8 ..	06.1	138 56.9	7.6	24 21.7	8.5	57.6
O 10	333 07.6	06.6	153 23.5	7.6	24 30.2	8.4	57.6
N 11	348 07.4	07.0	167 50.1	7.5	24 38.6	8.1	57.6
D 12	3 07.2	S21 07.5	182 16.6	7.4	N24 46.7	8.1	57.6
A 13	18 07.0	07.9	196 43.0	7.4	24 54.8	7.9	57.5
Y 14	33 06.8	08.4	211 09.4	7.4	25 02.7	7.7	57.5
15	48 06.6 ..	08.8	225 35.8	7.3	25 10.4	7.6	57.5
16	63 06.4	09.3	240 02.1	7.3	25 18.0	7.4	57.5
17	78 06.2	09.8	254 28.4	7.2	25 25.4	7.2	57.4
18	93 06.0	S21 10.2	268 54.6	7.2	N25 32.6	7.1	57.4
19	108 05.7	10.7	283 20.8	7.2	25 39.7	7.0	57.4
20	123 05.5	11.1	297 47.0	7.1	25 46.7	6.8	57.3
21	138 05.3 ..	11.6	312 13.1	7.1	25 53.5	6.6	57.3
22	153 05.1	12.0	326 39.2	7.0	26 00.1	6.5	57.3
23	168 04.9	12.5	341 05.2	7.1	26 06.6	6.3	57.3
28 00	183 04.7	S21 12.9	355 31.3	7.0	N26 12.9	6.2	57.3
01	198 04.5	13.4	9 57.3	6.9	26 19.1	6.0	57.2
02	213 04.3	13.8	24 23.2	6.9	26 25.1	5.8	57.2
03	228 04.1 ..	14.2	38 49.1	7.0	26 30.9	5.7	57.2
04	243 03.9	14.7	53 15.1	6.8	26 36.6	5.5	57.1
05	258 03.7	15.1	67 40.9	6.9	26 42.1	5.4	57.1
06	273 03.5	S21 15.6	82 06.8	6.8	N26 47.5	5.2	57.1
07	288 03.3	16.0	96 32.6	6.8	26 52.7	5.0	57.1
T 08	303 03.1	16.5	110 58.4	6.8	26 57.7	4.9	57.0
U 09	318 02.8 ..	16.9	125 24.2	6.8	27 02.6	4.7	57.0
E 10	333 02.6	17.3	139 50.0	6.8	27 07.3	4.5	57.0
S 11	348 02.4	17.8	154 15.8	6.7	27 11.8	4.4	57.0
D 12	3 02.2	S21 18.2	168 41.5	6.8	N27 16.2	4.2	56.9
A 13	18 02.0	18.7	183 07.3	6.7	27 20.4	4.1	56.9
Y 14	33 01.8	19.1	197 33.0	6.7	27 24.5	3.9	56.9
15	48 01.6 ..	19.5	211 58.7	6.8	27 28.4	3.6	56.9
16	63 01.4	20.0	226 24.5	6.7	27 32.1	3.6	56.8
17	78 01.2	20.4	240 50.2	6.7	27 35.7	3.3	56.8
18	93 01.0	S21 20.9	255 15.9	6.7	N27 39.0	3.3	56.8
19	108 00.7	21.3	269 41.6	6.7	27 42.3	3.0	56.7
20	123 00.5	21.7	284 07.3	6.7	27 45.3	2.9	56.7
21	138 00.3 ..	22.2	298 33.0	6.8	27 48.2	2.7	56.7
22	153 00.1	22.6	312 58.8	6.7	27 50.9	2.6	56.7
23	167 59.9	23.0	327 24.5	6.7	27 53.5	2.4	56.6
29 00	182 59.7	S21 23.5	341 50.2	6.8	N27 55.9	2.2	56.6
01	197 59.5	23.9	356 16.0	6.7	27 58.1	2.1	56.6
02	212 59.2	24.3	10 41.7	6.8	28 00.2	1.9	56.6
03	227 59.0 ..	24.7	25 07.5	6.8	28 02.1	1.8	56.5
04	242 58.8	25.2	39 33.3	6.8	28 03.9	1.5	56.5
05	257 58.6	25.6	53 59.1	6.9	28 05.4	1.4	56.5
06	272 58.4	S21 26.0	68 25.0	6.8	N28 06.8	1.3	56.4
W 07	287 58.2	26.5	82 50.8	6.9	28 08.1	1.1	56.4
E 08	302 57.9	26.9	97 16.7	6.9	28 09.2	0.9	56.4
D 09	317 57.7 ..	27.3	111 42.6	6.9	28 10.1	0.8	56.4
N 10	332 57.5	27.7	126 08.5	7.0	28 10.9	0.6	56.3
E 11	347 57.3	28.2	140 34.5	7.0	28 11.5	0.4	56.3
S 12	2 57.1	S21 28.6	155 00.5	7.0	N28 11.9	0.3	56.3
D 13	17 56.9	29.0	169 26.5	7.1	28 12.2	0.1	56.3
A 14	32 56.6	29.4	183 52.6	7.1	28 12.3	0.1	56.2
Y 15	47 56.4 ..	29.8	198 18.7	7.1	28 12.2	0.2	56.2
16	62 56.2	30.3	212 44.8	7.2	28 12.0	0.4	56.2
17	77 56.0	30.7	227 11.0	7.2	28 11.6	0.5	56.2
18	92 55.8	S21 31.1	241 37.2	7.3	N28 11.1	0.7	56.1
19	107 55.5	31.5	256 03.5	7.3	28 10.4	0.8	56.1
20	122 55.3	31.9	270 29.8	7.3	28 09.6	1.0	56.1
21	137 55.1 ..	32.4	284 56.1	7.4	28 08.6	1.2	56.0
22	152 54.9	32.8	299 22.5	7.5	28 07.4	1.3	56.0
23	167 54.7	33.2	313 49.0	7.5	N28 06.1	1.5	56.0
	SD 16.2	d 0.4	SD 15.7		15.5		15.3

Moonrise

Lat.	Twilight Naut.	Twilight Civil	Sunrise	27	28	29	30
°	h m	h m	h m	h m	h m	h m	h m
N 72	07 42	09 35	■	□	□	□	
N 70	07 26	08 59	■	□	□	□	
68	07 14	08 34	10 17	□	□	□	
66	07 04	08 15	09 35	□	□	□	
64	06 55	07 59	09 07	13 08	□	□	
62	06 47	07 46	08 45	13 52	13 46	□	15 39
60	06 40	07 35	08 28	14 21	14 37	15 17	16 32
N 58	06 34	07 25	08 13	14 44	15 09	15 54	17 04
56	06 29	07 16	08 01	15 02	15 33	16 21	17 28
54	06 24	07 08	07 50	15 18	15 52	16 42	17 47
52	06 19	07 01	07 41	15 32	16 08	16 59	18 03
50	06 15	06 55	07 32	15 43	16 22	17 14	18 17
45	06 05	06 41	07 14	16 08	16 51	17 44	18 45
N 40	05 56	06 29	06 59	16 28	17 14	18 08	19 08
35	05 48	06 19	06 47	16 45	17 33	18 27	19 26
30	05 40	06 10	06 35	16 59	17 49	18 44	19 42
20	05 26	05 53	06 16	17 24	18 16	19 12	20 09
N 10	05 11	05 37	06 00	17 45	18 40	19 36	20 32
0	04 56	05 22	05 44	18 05	19 02	19 58	20 53
S 10	04 39	05 06	05 28	18 25	19 24	20 21	21 14
20	04 19	04 47	05 11	18 47	19 48	20 45	21 37
30	03 52	04 25	04 52	19 12	20 16	21 13	22 04
35	03 36	04 11	04 40	19 27	20 32	21 30	22 20
40	03 15	03 55	04 27	19 45	20 51	21 49	22 38
45	02 49	03 35	04 11	20 06	21 15	22 13	22 59
S 50	02 11	03 09	03 51	20 32	21 45	22 43	23 27
52	01 51	02 56	03 42	20 45	21 59	22 58	23 40
54	01 23	02 42	03 31	21 00	22 17	23 16	23 56
56	00 40	02 24	03 19	21 18	22 38	23 37	24 14
58	////	02 02	03 05	21 39	23 04	24 03	00 03
S 60	////	01 33	02 49	22 07	23 41	24 41	00 41

Moonset

Lat.	Sunset	Twilight Civil	Twilight Naut.	27	28	29	30
°	h m	h m	h m	h m	h m	h m	h m
N 72	■	14 00	15 53	□	□	□	□
N 70	■	14 35	16 08	□	□	□	□
68	13 18	15 01	16 21	□	□	□	□
66	14 00	15 20	16 31	□	□	□	□
64	14 28	15 36	16 40	10 22	□	□	□
62	14 50	15 49	16 48	09 38	11 42	□	13 45
60	15 07	16 00	16 55	09 10	10 52	12 10	12 51
N 58	15 22	16 10	17 01	08 48	10 20	11 33	12 19
56	15 34	16 19	17 06	08 30	09 57	11 07	11 55
54	15 45	16 27	17 12	08 15	09 38	10 46	11 36
52	15 55	16 34	17 16	08 02	09 21	10 29	11 19
50	16 03	16 40	17 21	07 50	09 08	10 14	11 05
45	16 21	16 54	17 31	07 26	08 39	09 43	10 36
N 40	16 36	17 06	17 40	07 07	08 17	09 20	10 13
35	16 49	17 17	17 50	06 52	07 59	09 01	09 55
30	17 00	17 26	17 55	06 38	07 43	08 44	09 38
20	17 19	17 43	18 10	06 15	07 16	08 16	09 11
N 10	17 36	17 58	18 24	05 55	06 54	07 52	08 47
0	17 52	18 14	18 40	05 36	06 32	07 29	08 25
S 10	18 07	18 30	18 57	05 18	06 11	07 07	08 03
20	18 25	18 49	19 17	04 58	05 48	06 43	07 39
30	18 44	19 11	19 44	04 35	05 22	06 14	07 11
35	18 56	19 25	20 00	04 22	05 06	05 58	06 55
40	19 10	19 41	20 21	04 06	04 48	05 38	06 35
45	19 26	20 01	20 48	03 48	04 27	05 15	06 12
S 50	19 45	20 27	21 26	03 26	03 59	04 44	05 42
52	19 55	20 40	21 47	03 15	03 46	04 29	05 27
54	20 06	20 55	22 15	03 03	03 31	04 12	05 10
56	20 18	21 13	23 02	02 49	03 13	03 51	04 49
58	20 32	21 36	////	02 33	02 51	03 25	04 23
S 60	20 49	22 06	////	02 14	02 23	02 47	03 45

	SUN			MOON			
Day	Eqn. of Time 00h	12h	Mer. Pass.	Mer. Pass. Upper	Lower	Age	Phase
d	m s	m s	h m	h m	h m	d %	
27	12 39	12 29	11 48	24 19	11 51	14 100	
28	12 19	12 09	11 48	00 19	12 47	15 98	◯
29	11 59	11 49	11 48	01 16	13 44	16 95	

© British Crown Copyright 2022. All rights reserved.

UT	ARIES GHA	VENUS −4.2 GHA	Dec	MARS +1.4 GHA	Dec	JUPITER −2.8 GHA	Dec	SATURN +0.8 GHA	Dec	Name	SHA	Dec
30 00	68 36.6	225 13.3	S 7 28.7	186 40.5	S21 10.3	33 18.4	N12 39.1	94 52.4	S12 39.8	Acamar	315 12.1	S40 12.6
01	83 39.1	240 13.0	29.7	201 41.1	10.7	48 21.1	39.0	109 54.8	39.8	Achernar	335 20.4	S57 07.1
02	98 41.5	255 12.7	30.7	216 41.7	11.0	63 23.8	38.9	124 57.2	39.7	Acrux	173 01.5	S63 13.6
03	113 44.0	270 12.4	.. 31.7	231 42.2	.. 11.4	78 26.5	.. 38.9	139 59.5	.. 39.7	Adhara	255 06.3	S29 00.1
04	128 46.5	285 12.1	32.7	246 42.8	11.7	93 29.2	38.8	155 01.9	39.7	Aldebaran	290 40.3	N16 33.5
05	143 48.9	300 11.8	33.7	261 43.4	12.1	108 31.9	38.7	170 04.2	39.6			
T 06	158 51.4	315 11.5	S 7 34.7	276 44.0	S21 12.5	123 34.6	N12 38.7	185 06.6	S12 39.5	Alioth	166 14.1	N55 49.6
H 07	173 53.9	330 11.2	35.7	291 44.6	12.8	138 37.3	38.6	200 09.0	39.5	Alkaid	152 53.1	N49 11.5
U 08	188 56.3	345 11.0	36.7	306 45.2	13.2	153 40.0	38.5	215 11.3	39.4	Alnair	27 34.2	S46 51.0
R 09	203 58.8	0 10.7	.. 37.7	321 45.7	.. 13.5	168 42.7	.. 38.5	230 13.7	.. 39.4	Alnilam	275 38.4	S 1 11.1
S 10	219 01.2	15 10.4	38.8	336 46.3	13.9	183 45.4	38.4	245 16.0	39.4	Alphard	217 48.6	S 8 45.6
D 11	234 03.7	30 10.1	39.8	351 46.9	14.2	198 48.1	38.3	260 18.4	39.3			
A 12	249 06.2	45 09.8	S 7 40.8	6 47.5	S21 14.6	213 50.8	N12 38.2	275 20.8	S12 39.2	Alphecca	126 04.9	N26 38.0
Y 13	264 08.6	60 09.5	41.8	21 48.1	15.0	228 53.5	38.2	290 23.1	39.2	Alpheratz	357 35.6	N29 13.5
14	279 11.1	75 09.2	42.8	36 48.6	15.3	243 56.2	38.1	305 25.5	39.2	Altair	62 01.1	N 8 55.9
15	294 13.6	90 08.9	.. 43.8	51 49.2	.. 15.7	258 58.9	.. 38.0	320 27.8	.. 39.1	Ankaa	353 07.9	S42 10.8
16	309 16.0	105 08.6	44.8	66 49.8	16.0	274 01.7	38.0	335 30.2	39.1	Antares	112 17.4	S26 29.0
17	324 18.5	120 08.3	45.8	81 50.4	16.4	289 04.4	37.9	350 32.5	39.0			
18	339 21.0	135 08.0	S 7 46.8	96 51.0	S21 16.7	304 07.1	N12 37.8	5 34.9	S12 39.0	Arcturus	145 49.1	N19 03.5
19	354 23.4	150 07.8	47.8	111 51.5	17.1	319 09.8	37.8	20 37.3	39.0	Atria	107 13.0	S69 04.2
20	9 25.9	165 07.5	48.8	126 52.1	17.4	334 12.5	37.7	35 39.6	38.9	Avior	234 14.7	S59 34.8
21	24 28.3	180 07.2	.. 49.8	141 52.7	.. 17.8	349 15.2	.. 37.6	50 42.0	.. 38.9	Bellatrix	278 23.6	N 6 22.3
22	39 30.8	195 06.9	50.8	156 53.3	18.1	4 17.9	37.5	65 44.3	38.8	Betelgeuse	270 52.8	N 7 24.7
23	54 33.3	210 06.6	51.9	171 53.8	18.5	19 20.6	37.5	80 46.7	38.8			
1 00	69 35.7	225 06.3	S 7 52.9	186 54.4	S21 18.8	34 23.3	N12 37.4	95 49.1	S12 38.7	Canopus	263 52.3	S52 42.3
01	84 38.2	240 06.0	53.9	201 55.0	19.2	49 26.0	37.3	110 51.4	38.7	Capella	280 22.8	N46 01.3
02	99 40.7	255 05.7	54.9	216 55.6	19.5	64 28.7	37.3	125 53.8	38.6	Deneb	49 26.7	N45 22.1
03	114 43.1	270 05.4	.. 55.9	231 56.2	.. 19.9	79 31.4	.. 37.2	140 56.1	.. 38.6	Denebola	182 26.0	N14 26.3
04	129 45.6	285 05.1	56.9	246 56.7	20.2	94 34.1	37.1	155 58.5	38.6	Diphda	348 48.1	S17 51.4
05	144 48.1	300 04.8	57.9	261 57.3	20.6	109 36.8	37.1	171 00.8	38.5			
F 06	159 50.5	315 04.5	S 7 58.9	276 57.9	S21 20.9	124 39.5	N12 37.0	186 03.2	S12 38.5	Dubhe	193 42.2	N61 37.1
R 07	174 53.0	330 04.2	7 59.9	291 58.5	21.3	139 42.2	36.9	201 05.5	38.4	Elnath	278 02.7	N28 37.7
I 08	189 55.5	345 03.9	8 00.9	306 59.0	21.6	154 44.9	36.9	216 07.9	38.4	Eltanin	90 43.1	N51 29.2
D 09	204 57.9	0 03.6	.. 01.9	321 59.6	.. 22.0	169 47.6	.. 36.8	231 10.3	.. 38.3	Enif	33 39.8	N 9 59.1
A 10	220 00.4	15 03.3	02.9	337 00.2	22.3	184 50.3	36.7	246 12.6	38.3	Fomalhaut	15 15.5	S29 29.9
Y 11	235 02.8	30 03.0	03.9	352 00.8	22.7	199 53.0	36.7	261 15.0	38.2			
12	250 05.3	45 02.7	S 8 04.9	7 01.3	S21 23.0	214 55.7	N12 36.6	276 17.3	S12 38.2	Gacrux	171 53.0	S57 14.5
13	265 07.8	60 02.4	05.9	22 01.9	23.4	229 58.4	36.5	291 19.7	38.1	Gienah	175 44.7	S17 40.3
14	280 10.2	75 02.1	07.0	37 02.5	23.7	245 01.1	36.4	306 22.0	38.1	Hadar	148 37.9	S60 29.0
15	295 12.7	90 01.8	.. 08.0	52 03.1	.. 24.1	260 03.8	.. 36.4	321 24.4	.. 38.1	Hamal	327 52.0	N23 34.6
16	310 15.2	105 01.5	09.0	67 03.6	24.4	275 06.5	36.3	336 26.7	38.0	Kaus Aust.	83 34.1	S34 22.4
17	325 17.6	120 01.2	10.0	82 04.2	24.8	290 09.2	36.2	351 29.1	38.0			
18	340 20.1	135 00.9	S 8 11.0	97 04.8	S21 25.1	305 11.9	N12 36.2	6 31.5	S12 37.9	Kochab	137 20.8	N74 03.3
19	355 22.6	150 00.6	12.0	112 05.4	25.5	320 14.6	36.1	21 33.8	37.9	Markab	13 30.8	N15 20.1
20	10 25.0	165 00.3	13.0	127 05.9	25.8	335 17.3	36.0	36 36.2	37.8	Menkar	314 06.8	N 4 11.0
21	25 27.5	180 00.0	.. 14.0	142 06.5	.. 26.2	350 20.0	.. 36.0	51 38.5	.. 37.8	Menkent	147 59.1	S36 29.1
22	40 30.0	194 59.7	15.0	157 07.1	26.5	5 22.7	35.9	66 40.9	37.7	Miaplacidus	221 38.1	S69 48.5
23	55 32.4	209 59.4	16.0	172 07.6	26.8	20 25.4	35.8	81 43.2	37.7			
2 00	70 34.9	224 59.0	S 8 17.0	187 08.2	S21 27.2	35 28.1	N12 35.8	96 45.6	S12 37.6	Mirfak	308 29.1	N49 56.8
01	85 37.3	239 58.7	18.0	202 08.8	27.5	50 30.7	35.7	111 47.9	37.6	Nunki	75 49.2	S26 16.1
02	100 39.8	254 58.4	19.0	217 09.4	27.9	65 33.4	35.6	126 50.3	37.5	Peacock	53 07.5	S56 39.7
03	115 42.3	269 58.1	.. 20.0	232 09.9	.. 28.2	80 36.1	.. 35.6	141 52.6	.. 37.5	Pollux	243 18.2	N27 58.1
04	130 44.7	284 57.8	21.0	247 10.5	28.6	95 38.8	35.5	156 55.0	37.5	Procyon	244 51.6	N 5 09.9
05	145 47.2	299 57.5	22.0	262 11.1	28.9	110 41.5	35.4	171 57.3	37.4			
S 06	160 49.7	314 57.2	S 8 23.0	277 11.6	S21 29.2	125 44.2	N12 35.4	186 59.7	S12 37.4	Rasalhague	96 59.8	N12 32.6
A 07	175 52.1	329 56.9	24.0	292 12.2	29.6	140 46.9	35.3	202 02.0	37.3	Regulus	207 35.4	N11 51.0
T 08	190 54.6	344 56.6	25.0	307 12.8	29.9	155 49.6	35.2	217 04.4	37.3	Rigel	281 04.4	S 8 10.4
U 09	205 57.1	359 56.3	.. 26.0	322 13.4	.. 30.3	170 52.3	.. 35.2	232 06.8	.. 37.2	Rigil Kent.	139 42.2	S60 55.8
R 10	220 59.6	14 56.0	27.0	337 13.9	30.6	185 55.0	35.1	247 09.1	37.2	Sabik	102 04.2	S15 45.2
D 11	236 02.0	29 55.7	28.0	352 14.5	30.9	200 57.7	35.0	262 11.5	37.1			
A 12	251 04.5	44 55.3	S 8 29.0	7 15.1	S21 31.3	216 00.4	N12 35.0	277 13.8	S12 37.1	Schedar	349 31.8	N56 40.3
Y 13	266 06.9	59 55.0	30.0	22 15.6	31.6	231 03.1	34.9	292 16.2	37.0	Shaula	96 12.1	S37 07.3
14	281 09.4	74 54.7	31.1	37 16.2	32.0	246 05.8	34.8	307 18.5	37.0	Sirius	258 26.8	S16 44.8
15	296 11.8	89 54.4	.. 32.1	52 16.8	.. 32.3	261 08.5	.. 34.8	322 20.9	.. 36.9	Spica	158 23.5	S11 17.0
16	311 14.3	104 54.1	33.1	67 17.3	32.6	276 11.1	34.7	337 23.2	36.9	Suhail	222 46.8	S43 31.4
17	326 16.8	119 53.8	34.1	82 17.9	33.0	291 13.8	34.7	352 25.6	36.8			
18	341 19.2	134 53.5	S 8 35.1	97 18.5	S21 33.3	306 16.5	N12 34.6	7 27.9	S12 36.8	Vega	80 34.2	N38 48.4
19	356 21.7	149 53.1	36.1	112 19.0	33.7	321 19.2	34.5	22 30.3	36.8	Zuben'ubi	136 57.4	S16 08.4
20	11 24.2	164 52.8	37.1	127 19.6	34.0	336 21.9	34.5	37 32.6	36.7			
21	26 26.6	179 52.5	.. 38.1	142 20.2	.. 34.3	351 24.6	.. 34.4	52 35.0	.. 36.7		SHA	Mer. Pass.
22	41 29.1	194 52.2	39.1	157 20.7	34.7	6 27.3	34.3	67 37.3	36.6	Venus	155 30.5	9 00
23	56 31.6	209 51.9	40.1	172 21.3	35.0	21 30.0	34.3	82 39.7	36.6	Mars	117 18.7	11 32
Mer. Pass. 19 18.4		v −0.3	d 1.0	v 0.6	d 0.3	v 2.7	d 0.1	v 2.4	d 0.0	Jupiter	324 47.5	21 39
										Saturn	26 13.3	17 34

© British Crown Copyright 2022. All rights reserved.

SUN and MOON

UT	SUN GHA	SUN Dec	MOON GHA	v	MOON Dec	d	HP
30 00	182 54.4	S21 33.6	328 15.5	7.6	N28 04.6	1.6	56.0
01	197 54.2	34.0	342 42.1	7.6	28 03.0	1.8	55.9
02	212 54.0	34.4	357 08.7	7.6	28 01.2	1.9	55.9
03	227 53.8 ..	34.8	11 35.3	7.8	27 59.3	2.1	55.9
04	242 53.6	35.3	26 02.1	7.8	27 57.2	2.2	55.9
05	257 53.3	35.7	40 28.9	7.8	27 55.0	2.4	55.8
06	272 53.1	S21 36.1	54 55.7	7.9	N27 52.6	2.6	55.8
07	287 52.9	36.5	69 22.6	8.0	27 50.0	2.6	55.8
08	302 52.7	36.9	83 49.6	8.0	27 47.4	2.9	55.8
09	317 52.4 ..	37.3	98 16.6	8.1	27 44.5	3.0	55.7
10	332 52.2	37.7	112 43.7	8.2	27 41.5	3.1	55.7
11	347 52.0	38.1	127 10.9	8.3	27 38.4	3.3	55.7
12	2 51.8	S21 38.5	141 38.2	8.3	N27 35.1	3.4	55.7
13	17 51.5	38.9	156 05.5	8.4	27 31.7	3.5	55.6
14	32 51.3	39.3	170 32.9	8.4	27 28.2	3.8	55.6
15	47 51.1 ..	39.7	185 00.3	8.5	27 24.4	3.8	55.6
16	62 50.9	40.1	199 27.8	8.6	27 20.6	4.0	55.6
17	77 50.6	40.5	213 55.4	8.7	27 16.6	4.1	55.5
18	92 50.4	S21 40.9	228 23.1	8.8	N27 12.5	4.3	55.5
19	107 50.2	41.3	242 50.9	8.8	27 08.2	4.4	55.5
20	122 50.0	41.7	257 18.7	8.9	27 03.8	4.5	55.5
21	137 49.7 ..	42.1	271 46.6	9.0	26 59.3	4.7	55.4
22	152 49.5	42.5	286 14.6	9.1	26 54.6	4.8	55.4
23	167 49.3	42.9	300 42.7	9.2	26 49.8	5.0	55.4
1 00	182 49.1	S21 43.3	315 10.9	9.2	N26 44.8	5.1	55.4
01	197 48.8	43.7	329 39.1	9.3	26 39.7	5.2	55.4
02	212 48.6	44.1	344 07.4	9.4	26 34.5	5.3	55.3
03	227 48.4 ..	44.5	358 35.8	9.5	26 29.2	5.5	55.3
04	242 48.1	44.9	13 04.3	9.6	26 23.7	5.6	55.3
05	257 47.9	45.3	27 32.9	9.6	26 18.1	5.7	55.3
06	272 47.7	S21 45.7	42 01.5	9.8	N26 12.4	5.9	55.2
07	287 47.4	46.1	56 30.3	9.8	26 06.5	6.1	55.2
08	302 47.2	46.5	70 59.1	9.9	26 00.5	6.1	55.2
09	317 47.0 ..	46.9	85 28.0	10.0	25 54.4	6.2	55.2
10	332 46.8	47.3	99 57.0	10.1	25 48.2	6.4	55.2
11	347 46.5	47.7	114 26.1	10.2	25 41.8	6.4	55.1
12	2 46.3	S21 48.1	128 55.3	10.3	N25 35.4	6.6	55.1
13	17 46.1	48.4	143 24.6	10.3	25 28.8	6.7	55.1
14	32 45.8	48.8	157 53.9	10.5	25 22.1	6.9	55.1
15	47 45.6 ..	49.2	172 23.4	10.5	25 15.2	6.9	55.1
16	62 45.4	49.6	186 52.9	10.7	25 08.3	7.1	55.0
17	77 45.1	50.0	201 22.6	10.7	25 01.2	7.2	55.0
18	92 44.9	S21 50.4	215 52.3	10.8	N24 54.0	7.2	55.0
19	107 44.7	50.8	230 22.1	10.9	24 46.8	7.4	55.0
20	122 44.4	51.1	244 52.0	11.0	24 39.4	7.6	55.0
21	137 44.2 ..	51.5	259 22.0	11.0	24 31.8	7.6	54.9
22	152 44.0	51.9	273 52.0	11.2	24 24.2	7.7	54.9
23	167 43.7	52.3	288 22.2	11.3	24 16.5	7.8	54.9
2 00	182 43.5	S21 52.7	302 52.5	11.3	N24 08.7	8.0	54.9
01	197 43.3	53.0	317 22.8	11.5	24 00.7	8.0	54.9
02	212 43.0	53.4	331 53.3	11.5	23 52.7	8.2	54.8
03	227 42.8 ..	53.8	346 23.8	11.6	23 44.5	8.3	54.8
04	242 42.5	54.2	0 54.4	11.7	23 36.2	8.3	54.8
05	257 42.3	54.6	15 25.1	11.8	23 27.9	8.5	54.8
06	272 42.1	S21 54.9	29 55.9	11.9	N23 19.4	8.5	54.8
07	287 41.8	55.3	44 26.8	12.0	23 10.9	8.7	54.8
08	302 41.6	55.7	58 57.8	12.1	23 02.2	8.7	54.7
09	317 41.4 ..	56.1	73 28.9	12.2	22 53.5	8.9	54.7
10	332 41.1	56.4	88 00.1	12.2	22 44.6	9.0	54.7
11	347 40.9	56.8	102 31.3	12.3	22 35.6	9.0	54.7
12	2 40.6	S21 57.2	117 02.6	12.5	N22 26.6	9.1	54.7
13	17 40.4	57.5	131 34.1	12.5	22 17.5	9.3	54.7
14	32 40.2	57.9	146 05.6	12.6	22 08.2	9.3	54.6
15	47 39.9 ..	58.3	160 37.2	12.7	21 58.9	9.4	54.6
16	62 39.7	58.7	175 08.9	12.7	21 49.5	9.5	54.6
17	77 39.4	59.0	189 40.6	12.9	21 40.0	9.6	54.6
18	92 39.2	S21 59.4	204 12.5	13.0	N21 30.4	9.7	54.6
19	107 39.0	21 59.8	218 44.5	13.0	21 20.7	9.7	54.6
20	122 38.7	22 00.1	233 16.5	13.1	21 11.0	9.9	54.6
21	137 38.5 ..	00.5	247 48.6	13.2	21 01.1	9.9	54.5
22	152 38.2	00.8	262 20.8	13.3	20 51.2	10.0	54.5
23	167 38.0	01.2	276 53.1	13.4	N20 41.2	10.1	54.5
	SD 16.2	d 0.4	SD 15.2		15.0		14.9

Twilight / Sunrise / Moonrise

Lat.	Naut.	Civil	Sunrise	30	1	2	3
N 72	07 50	09 49	■	□	□	□	18 22
N 70	07 34	09 10	■	□	□	□	19 22
68	07 21	08 43	10 34	□	□	17 11	19 56
66	07 10	08 22	09 46	□	□	18 18	20 21
64	07 01	08 06	09 15	□	16 44	18 53	20 40
62	06 52	07 52	08 52	15 39	17 33	19 18	20 55
60	06 45	07 40	08 34	16 32	18 04	19 38	21 08
N 58	06 39	07 30	08 19	17 04	18 27	19 54	21 19
56	06 33	07 21	08 06	17 28	18 46	20 08	21 28
54	06 28	07 13	07 55	17 47	19 02	20 20	21 37
52	06 23	07 05	07 45	18 03	19 15	20 30	21 44
50	06 18	06 59	07 36	18 17	19 27	20 39	21 51
45	06 08	06 44	07 17	18 45	19 52	20 59	22 05
N 40	05 59	06 32	07 02	19 08	20 11	21 15	22 17
35	05 50	06 22	06 49	19 26	20 27	21 28	22 27
30	05 42	06 12	06 38	19 42	20 41	21 39	22 36
20	05 27	05 55	06 18	20 09	21 05	21 59	22 51
N 10	05 13	05 39	06 01	20 32	21 25	22 16	23 04
0	04 57	05 23	05 45	20 53	21 44	22 32	23 16
S 10	04 40	05 06	05 29	21 14	22 03	22 48	23 28
20	04 19	04 47	05 12	21 37	22 24	23 05	23 41
30	03 52	04 24	04 51	22 04	22 47	23 24	23 56
35	03 35	04 10	04 39	22 20	23 01	23 35	24 04
40	03 13	03 54	04 26	22 38	23 16	23 48	24 14
45	02 46	03 33	04 09	22 59	23 35	24 03	00 03
S 50	02 07	03 06	03 49	23 27	23 58	24 21	00 21
52	01 45	02 53	03 39	23 40	24 10	00 10	00 30
54	01 15	02 38	03 28	23 56	24 22	00 22	00 40
56	00 20	02 19	03 16	24 14	00 14	00 37	00 50
58	////	01 56	03 01	00 03	00 36	00 53	01 03
S 60	////	01 24	02 44	00 41	01 05	01 14	01 17

Sunset / Twilight / Moonset

Lat.	Sunset	Civil	Naut.	30	1	2	3
N 72	■	13 48	15 47	□	□	□	16 09
N 70	■	14 27	16 03	□	□	□	15 07
68	13 03	14 54	16 16	□	□	15 44	14 32
66	13 51	15 15	16 27	□	□	□	14 06
64	14 22	15 32	16 37	□	14 29	14 00	13 46
62	14 45	15 45	16 45	13 45	13 39	13 34	13 30
60	15 03	15 57	16 52	12 51	13 07	13 14	13 16
N 58	15 18	16 07	16 59	12 19	12 44	12 57	13 04
56	15 31	16 17	17 04	11 55	12 24	12 42	12 54
54	15 42	16 25	17 10	11 36	12 08	12 30	12 45
52	15 52	16 32	17 15	11 19	11 54	12 19	12 36
50	16 01	16 39	17 19	11 05	11 42	12 09	12 29
45	16 20	16 53	17 30	10 36	11 17	11 49	12 13
N 40	16 35	17 05	17 39	10 13	10 57	11 32	12 00
35	16 48	17 16	17 47	09 55	10 40	11 18	11 49
30	17 00	17 26	17 55	09 38	10 25	11 05	11 39
20	17 19	17 43	18 10	09 11	10 00	10 44	11 22
N 10	17 36	17 59	18 25	08 47	09 39	10 25	11 08
0	17 53	18 15	18 41	08 25	09 18	10 08	10 54
S 10	18 09	18 32	18 58	08 03	08 58	09 50	10 40
20	18 26	18 51	19 19	07 39	08 36	09 31	10 24
30	18 47	19 14	19 46	07 11	08 10	09 10	10 07
35	18 59	19 28	20 04	06 55	07 55	08 57	09 57
40	19 13	19 45	20 25	06 36	07 38	08 42	09 45
45	19 29	20 05	20 53	06 12	07 17	08 24	09 31
S 50	19 50	20 32	21 32	05 42	06 50	08 02	09 14
52	19 59	20 46	21 54	05 27	06 37	07 51	09 06
54	20 10	21 01	22 25	05 10	06 21	07 39	08 57
56	20 23	21 20	23 28	04 49	06 03	07 25	08 47
58	20 38	21 44	////	04 23	05 42	07 09	08 35
S 60	20 55	22 17	////	03 45	05 13	06 49	08 21

SUN and MOON data

Day	Eqn. of Time 00h	Eqn. of Time 12h	Mer. Pass.	Mer. Pass. Upper	Mer. Pass. Lower	Age	Phase
d	m s	m s	h m	h m	h m	d	%
30	11 38	11 28	11 49	02 12	14 39	17	90
1	11 17	11 06	11 49	03 06	15 32	18	83
2	10 54	10 43	11 49	03 56	16 20	19	75

© British Crown Copyright 2022. All rights reserved.

UT (d h)	ARIES GHA	VENUS −4.2 GHA	Dec	MARS +1.4 GHA	Dec	JUPITER −2.8 GHA	Dec	SATURN +0.8 GHA	Dec
3 00	71 34.0	224 51.6	S 8 41.1	187 21.9	S21 35.3	36 32.7	N12 34.2	97 42.0	S12 36.5
01	86 36.5	239 51.3	42.1	202 22.4	35.7	51 35.4	34.1	112 44.4	36.5
02	101 39.0	254 50.9	43.1	217 23.0	36.0	66 38.1	34.1	127 46.7	36.4
03	116 41.4	269 50.6	.. 44.1	232 23.6	.. 36.3	81 40.7	.. 34.0	142 49.1	.. 36.4
04	131 43.9	284 50.3	45.1	247 24.1	36.7	96 43.4	33.9	157 51.4	36.3
05	146 46.3	299 50.0	46.1	262 24.7	37.0	111 46.1	33.9	172 53.8	36.3
06	161 48.8	314 49.7	S 8 47.1	277 25.3	S21 37.3	126 48.8	N12 33.8	187 56.1	S12 36.2
07	176 51.3	329 49.3	48.1	292 25.8	37.7	141 51.5	33.7	202 58.5	36.2
08	191 53.7	344 49.0	49.1	307 26.4	38.0	156 54.2	33.7	218 00.8	36.1
S 09	206 56.2	359 48.7	.. 50.1	322 27.0	.. 38.3	171 56.9	.. 33.6	233 03.2	.. 36.1
U 10	221 58.7	14 48.4	51.1	337 27.5	38.7	186 59.6	33.6	248 05.5	36.0
N 11	237 01.1	29 48.1	52.1	352 28.1	39.0	202 02.2	33.5	263 07.8	36.0
D 12	252 03.6	44 47.7	S 8 53.1	7 28.6	S21 39.3	217 04.9	N12 33.4	278 10.2	S12 35.9
A 13	267 06.1	59 47.4	54.1	22 29.2	39.7	232 07.6	33.4	293 12.5	35.9
Y 14	282 08.5	74 47.1	55.1	37 29.8	40.0	247 10.3	33.3	308 14.9	35.8
15	297 11.0	89 46.8	.. 56.1	52 30.3	.. 40.3	262 13.0	.. 33.2	323 17.2	.. 35.8
16	312 13.4	104 46.4	57.1	67 30.9	40.7	277 15.7	33.2	338 19.6	35.7
17	327 15.9	119 46.1	58.1	82 31.5	41.0	292 18.4	33.1	353 21.9	35.7
18	342 18.4	134 45.8	S 8 59.1	97 32.0	S21 41.3	307 21.0	N12 33.0	8 24.3	S12 35.6
19	357 20.8	149 45.5	S 9 00.1	112 32.6	41.7	322 23.7	33.0	23 26.6	35.6
20	12 23.3	164 45.1	01.1	127 33.1	42.0	337 26.4	32.9	38 29.0	35.5
21	27 25.8	179 44.8	.. 02.1	142 33.7	.. 42.3	352 29.1	.. 32.9	53 31.3	.. 35.5
22	42 28.2	194 44.5	03.1	157 34.3	42.6	7 31.8	32.8	68 33.7	35.5
23	57 30.7	209 44.2	04.1	172 34.8	43.0	22 34.5	32.7	83 36.0	35.4
4 00	72 33.2	224 43.8	S 9 05.1	187 35.4	S21 43.3	37 37.1	N12 32.7	98 38.4	S12 35.4
01	87 35.6	239 43.5	06.1	202 35.9	43.6	52 39.8	32.6	113 40.7	35.3
02	102 38.1	254 43.2	07.0	217 36.5	44.0	67 42.5	32.5	128 43.0	35.3
03	117 40.6	269 42.8	.. 08.0	232 37.1	.. 44.3	82 45.2	.. 32.5	143 45.4	.. 35.2
04	132 43.0	284 42.5	09.0	247 37.6	44.6	97 47.9	32.4	158 47.7	35.2
05	147 45.5	299 42.2	10.0	262 38.2	44.9	112 50.5	32.4	173 50.1	35.1
06	162 47.9	314 41.9	S 9 11.0	277 38.7	S21 45.3	127 53.2	N12 32.3	188 52.4	S12 35.1
07	177 50.4	329 41.5	12.0	292 39.3	45.6	142 55.9	32.2	203 54.8	35.0
08	192 52.9	344 41.2	13.0	307 39.9	45.9	157 58.6	32.2	218 57.1	35.0
M 09	207 55.3	359 40.9	.. 14.0	322 40.4	.. 46.2	173 01.3	.. 32.1	233 59.5	.. 34.9
O 10	222 57.8	14 40.5	15.0	337 41.0	46.6	188 04.0	32.1	249 01.8	34.9
N 11	238 00.3	29 40.2	16.0	352 41.5	46.9	203 06.6	32.0	264 04.2	34.8
D 12	253 02.7	44 39.9	S 9 17.0	7 42.1	S21 47.2	218 09.3	N12 31.9	279 06.5	S12 34.8
A 13	268 05.2	59 39.5	18.0	22 42.6	47.5	233 12.0	31.9	294 08.8	34.7
Y 14	283 07.7	74 39.2	19.0	37 43.2	47.8	248 14.7	31.8	309 11.2	34.7
15	298 10.1	89 38.9	.. 20.0	52 43.8	.. 48.2	263 17.3	.. 31.7	324 13.5	.. 34.6
16	313 12.6	104 38.5	21.0	67 44.3	48.5	278 20.0	31.7	339 15.9	34.6
17	328 15.1	119 38.2	22.0	82 44.9	48.8	293 22.7	31.6	354 18.2	34.5
18	343 17.5	134 37.9	S 9 23.0	97 45.4	S21 49.1	308 25.4	N12 31.6	9 20.6	S12 34.5
19	358 20.0	149 37.5	24.0	112 46.0	49.5	323 28.1	31.5	24 22.9	34.4
20	13 22.4	164 37.2	25.0	127 46.5	49.8	338 30.7	31.4	39 25.2	34.4
21	28 24.9	179 36.9	.. 26.0	142 47.1	.. 50.1	353 33.4	.. 31.4	54 27.6	.. 34.3
22	43 27.4	194 36.5	27.0	157 47.6	50.4	8 36.1	31.3	69 29.9	34.3
23	58 29.8	209 36.2	27.9	172 48.2	50.7	23 38.8	31.3	84 32.3	34.2
5 00	73 32.3	224 35.8	S 9 28.9	187 48.8	S21 51.1	38 41.4	N12 31.2	99 34.6	S12 34.2
01	88 34.8	239 35.5	29.9	202 49.3	51.4	53 44.1	31.1	114 37.0	34.1
02	103 37.2	254 35.2	30.9	217 49.9	51.7	68 46.8	31.1	129 39.3	34.1
03	118 39.7	269 34.8	.. 31.9	232 50.4	.. 52.0	83 49.5	.. 31.0	144 41.6	.. 34.0
04	133 42.2	284 34.5	32.9	247 51.0	52.3	98 52.1	31.0	159 44.0	34.0
05	148 44.6	299 34.1	33.9	262 51.5	52.7	113 54.8	30.9	174 46.3	33.9
06	163 47.1	314 33.8	S 9 34.9	277 52.1	S21 53.0	128 57.5	N12 30.8	189 48.7	S12 33.9
07	178 49.5	329 33.5	35.9	292 52.6	53.3	144 00.2	30.8	204 51.0	33.8
08	193 52.0	344 33.1	36.9	307 53.2	53.6	159 02.8	30.7	219 53.3	33.8
T 09	208 54.5	359 32.8	.. 37.9	322 53.7	.. 53.9	174 05.5	.. 30.7	234 55.7	.. 33.7
U 10	223 56.9	14 32.4	38.9	337 54.3	54.2	189 08.2	30.6	249 58.0	33.7
E 11	238 59.4	29 32.1	39.8	352 54.8	54.5	204 10.9	30.6	265 00.4	33.6
S 12	254 01.9	44 31.7	S 9 40.8	7 55.4	S21 54.9	219 13.5	N12 30.5	280 02.7	S12 33.5
D 13	269 04.3	59 31.4	41.8	22 55.9	55.2	234 16.2	30.4	295 05.0	33.5
A 14	284 06.8	74 31.1	42.8	37 56.5	55.5	249 18.9	30.4	310 07.4	33.4
Y 15	299 09.3	89 30.7	.. 43.8	52 57.0	.. 55.8	264 21.5	.. 30.3	325 09.7	.. 33.4
16	314 11.7	104 30.4	44.8	67 57.6	56.1	279 24.2	30.3	340 12.1	33.3
17	329 14.2	119 30.0	45.8	82 58.1	56.4	294 26.9	30.2	355 14.4	33.3
18	344 16.7	134 29.7	S 9 46.8	97 58.7	S21 56.7	309 29.6	N12 30.1	10 16.7	S12 33.2
19	359 19.1	149 29.3	47.8	112 59.2	57.1	324 32.2	30.1	25 19.1	33.2
20	14 21.6	164 29.0	48.8	127 59.8	57.4	339 34.9	30.0	40 21.4	33.1
21	29 24.0	179 28.6	.. 49.7	143 00.3	.. 57.7	354 37.6	.. 30.0	55 23.8	.. 33.1
22	44 26.5	194 28.3	50.7	158 00.9	58.0	9 40.2	29.9	70 26.1	33.0
23	59 29.0	209 27.9	51.7	173 01.4	58.3	24 42.9	29.9	85 28.4	33.0
Mer. Pass. 19ʰ 06.6ᵐ		v −0.3	d 1.0	v 0.6	d 0.3	v 2.7	d 0.1	v 2.3	d 0.0

STARS

Name	SHA	Dec
Acamar	315 12.1	S40 12.6
Achernar	335 20.5	S57 07.1
Acrux	173 01.4	S63 13.6
Adhara	255 06.3	S29 00.1
Aldebaran	290 40.3	N16 33.5
Alioth	166 14.1	N55 49.6
Alkaid	152 53.1	N49 11.5
Al Na'ir	27 34.2	S46 51.0
Alnilam	275 38.3	S 1 11.1
Alphard	217 48.5	S 8 45.6
Alphecca	126 04.9	N26 38.0
Alpheratz	357 35.6	N29 13.5
Altair	62 01.1	N 8 55.9
Ankaa	353 07.9	S42 10.8
Antares	112 17.4	S26 29.0
Arcturus	145 49.0	N19 03.5
Atria	107 13.0	S69 04.2
Avior	234 14.7	S59 34.8
Bellatrix	278 23.5	N 6 22.3
Betelgeuse	270 52.8	N 7 24.7
Canopus	263 52.3	S52 42.3
Capella	280 22.8	N46 01.3
Deneb	49 26.7	N45 22.1
Denebola	182 26.0	N14 26.3
Diphda	348 48.1	S17 51.4
Dubhe	193 42.2	N61 37.1
Elnath	278 02.7	N28 37.7
Eltanin	90 43.1	N51 29.2
Enif	33 39.8	N 9 59.1
Fomalhaut	15 15.5	S29 29.9
Gacrux	171 53.0	S57 14.5
Gienah	175 44.7	S17 40.3
Hadar	148 37.9	S60 29.0
Hamal	327 52.0	N23 34.6
Kaus Aust.	83 34.1	S34 22.4
Kochab	137 20.8	N74 03.2
Markab	13 30.8	N15 20.1
Menkar	314 06.8	N 4 11.0
Menkent	147 59.0	S36 29.1
Miaplacidus	221 38.1	S69 48.5
Mirfak	308 29.1	N49 56.9
Nunki	75 49.2	S26 16.1
Peacock	53 07.5	S56 39.7
Pollux	243 18.2	N27 58.1
Procyon	244 51.6	N 5 09.9
Rasalhague	95 59.8	N12 32.6
Regulus	207 35.4	N11 51.0
Rigel	281 04.4	S 8 10.4
Rigil Kent.	139 42.2	S60 55.8
Sabik	102 04.2	S15 45.2
Schedar	349 31.8	N56 40.3
Shaula	96 12.1	S37 07.3
Sirius	258 26.7	S16 44.8
Spica	158 23.5	S11 17.0
Suhail	222 46.8	S43 31.4
Vega	80 34.2	N38 48.4
Zuben'ubi	136 57.4	S16 08.4

	SHA	Mer. Pass.
Venus	152 10.7	9ʰ 01ᵐ
Mars	115 02.2	11 29
Jupiter	325 04.0	21 26
Saturn	26 05.2	17 23

© British Crown Copyright 2022. All rights reserved.

UT	SUN GHA	Dec	MOON GHA	v	Dec	d	HP
3 00	182 37.8	S22 01.6	291 25.5	13.4	N20 31.1	10.2	54.5
01	197 37.5	01.9	305 57.9	13.5	20 20.9	10.2	54.5
02	212 37.3	02.3	320 30.4	13.6	20 10.7	10.4	54.5
03	227 37.0 ..	02.7	335 03.0	13.7	20 00.3	10.4	54.5
04	242 36.8	03.0	349 35.7	13.8	19 49.9	10.5	54.5
05	257 36.5	03.4	4 08.5	13.9	19 39.4	10.5	54.4
06	272 36.3	S22 03.7	18 41.4	13.9	N19 28.9	10.7	54.4
07	287 36.1	04.1	33 14.3	14.0	19 18.2	10.7	54.4
08	302 35.8	04.5	47 47.3	14.1	19 07.5	10.8	54.4
S 09	317 35.6 ..	04.8	62 20.4	14.1	18 56.7	10.9	54.4
U 10	332 35.3	05.2	76 53.5	14.3	18 45.8	10.9	54.4
N 11	347 35.1	05.5	91 26.8	14.3	18 34.9	11.0	54.4
D 12	2 34.8	S22 05.9	106 00.1	14.4	N18 23.9	11.1	54.4
A 13	17 34.6	06.2	120 33.5	14.4	18 12.8	11.1	54.4
Y 14	32 34.3	06.6	135 06.9	14.6	18 01.7	11.2	54.4
15	47 34.1 ..	06.9	149 40.5	14.6	17 50.5	11.3	54.3
16	62 33.9	07.3	164 14.1	14.6	17 39.2	11.3	54.3
17	77 33.6	07.6	178 47.7	14.8	17 27.9	11.5	54.3
18	92 33.4	S22 08.0	193 21.5	14.8	N17 16.4	11.4	54.3
19	107 33.1	08.3	207 55.3	14.8	17 05.0	11.6	54.3
20	122 32.9	08.7	222 29.1	15.0	16 53.4	11.6	54.3
21	137 32.6 ..	09.0	237 03.1	15.0	16 41.8	11.6	54.3
22	152 32.4	09.4	251 37.1	15.1	16 30.2	11.7	54.3
23	167 32.1	09.7	266 12.2	15.1	16 18.5	11.8	54.3
4 00	182 31.9	S22 10.1	280 45.3	15.2	N16 06.7	11.9	54.3
01	197 31.6	10.4	295 19.5	15.3	15 54.8	11.9	54.3
02	212 31.4	10.7	309 53.8	15.3	15 42.9	11.9	54.3
03	227 31.1 ..	11.1	324 28.1	15.4	15 31.0	12.0	54.3
04	242 30.9	11.4	339 02.5	15.4	15 19.0	12.1	54.3
05	257 30.6	11.8	353 36.9	15.5	15 06.9	12.1	54.3
06	272 30.4	S22 12.1	8 11.4	15.6	N14 54.8	12.2	54.3
07	287 30.1	12.5	22 46.0	15.6	14 42.6	12.2	54.3
08	302 29.9	12.8	37 20.6	15.7	14 30.4	12.3	54.2
M 09	317 29.6 ..	13.1	51 55.3	15.7	14 18.1	12.4	54.2
O 10	332 29.4	13.5	66 30.0	15.8	14 05.7	12.4	54.2
N 11	347 29.1	13.8	81 04.8	15.8	13 53.3	12.4	54.2
D 12	2 28.9	S22 14.1	95 39.6	15.9	N13 40.9	12.5	54.2
A 13	17 28.6	14.5	110 14.5	16.0	13 28.4	12.5	54.2
Y 14	32 28.4	14.8	124 49.5	15.9	13 15.9	12.6	54.2
15	47 28.1 ..	15.1	139 24.4	16.1	13 03.3	12.6	54.2
16	62 27.9	15.5	153 59.5	16.1	12 50.7	12.7	54.2
17	77 27.6	15.8	168 34.6	16.1	12 38.0	12.7	54.2
18	92 27.4	S22 16.1	183 09.7	16.2	N12 25.3	12.8	54.2
19	107 27.1	16.5	197 44.9	16.2	12 12.5	12.8	54.2
20	122 26.9	16.8	212 20.1	16.2	11 59.7	12.9	54.2
21	137 26.6 ..	17.1	226 55.3	16.3	11 46.8	12.9	54.2
22	152 26.4	17.5	241 30.6	16.4	11 33.9	12.9	54.2
23	167 26.1	17.8	256 06.0	16.4	11 21.0	13.0	54.2
5 00	182 25.8	S22 18.1	270 41.4	16.4	N11 08.0	13.1	54.2
01	197 25.6	18.4	285 16.8	16.4	10 54.9	13.0	54.2
02	212 25.3	18.8	299 52.2	16.5	10 41.9	13.1	54.2
03	227 25.1 ..	19.1	314 27.7	16.6	10 28.8	13.2	54.2
04	242 24.8	19.4	329 03.3	16.5	10 15.6	13.2	54.2
05	257 24.6	19.7	343 38.8	16.6	10 02.4	13.2	54.2
06	272 24.3	S22 20.1	358 14.4	16.7	N 9 49.2	13.2	54.2
07	287 24.1	20.4	12 50.1	16.6	9 36.0	13.3	54.3
08	302 23.8	20.7	27 25.7	16.7	9 22.7	13.4	54.3
T 09	317 23.5 ..	21.0	42 01.4	16.8	9 09.3	13.3	54.3
U 10	332 23.3	21.3	56 37.2	16.7	8 56.0	13.4	54.3
E 11	347 23.0	21.7	71 12.9	16.8	8 42.6	13.5	54.3
S 12	2 22.8	S22 22.0	85 48.7	16.8	N 8 29.1	13.4	54.3
D 13	17 22.5	22.3	100 24.5	16.8	8 15.7	13.5	54.3
A 14	32 22.3	22.6	115 00.3	16.9	8 02.2	13.6	54.3
Y 15	47 22.0 ..	22.9	129 36.2	16.9	7 48.6	13.5	54.3
16	62 21.7	23.3	144 12.1	16.9	7 35.1	13.6	54.3
17	77 21.5	23.6	158 48.0	16.9	7 21.5	13.7	54.3
18	92 21.2	S22 23.9	173 23.9	16.9	N 7 07.8	13.6	54.3
19	107 21.0	24.2	187 59.8	17.0	6 54.2	13.7	54.3
20	122 20.7	24.5	202 35.8	16.9	6 40.5	13.7	54.3
21	137 20.4 ..	24.8	217 11.7	17.0	6 26.8	13.7	54.3
22	152 20.2	25.1	231 47.7	17.0	6 13.1	13.8	54.3
23	167 19.9	25.4	246 23.7	17.0	N 5 59.3	13.8	54.4
	SD 16.3	d 0.3	SD 14.8		14.8		14.8

Lat.	Twilight Naut.	Civil	Sunrise	Moonrise 3	4	5	6
°	h m	h m	h m	h m	h m	h m	h m
N 72	07 58	10 03	■■	18 22	21 15	23 22	25 20
N 70	07 41	09 20		19 22	21 37	23 31	25 19
68	07 27	08 51	10 53	19 56	21 53	23 38	25 19
66	07 16	08 29	09 56	20 21	22 06	23 44	25 19
64	07 06	08 12	09 23	20 40	22 17	23 48	25 19
62	06 57	07 57	08 59	20 55	22 26	23 53	25 18
60	06 50	07 45	08 40	21 08	22 34	23 56	25 18
N 58	06 43	07 35	08 24	21 19	22 40	24 00	00 00
56	06 37	07 25	08 11	21 28	22 46	24 02	00 02
54	06 31	07 17	07 59	21 37	22 52	24 05	00 05
52	06 26	07 09	07 49	21 44	22 57	24 07	00 07
50	06 21	07 02	07 40	21 51	23 01	24 09	00 09
45	06 11	06 48	07 21	22 05	23 10	24 14	00 14
N 40	06 01	06 35	07 05	22 17	23 18	24 18	00 18
35	05 53	06 24	06 52	22 27	23 25	24 21	00 21
30	05 45	06 14	06 40	22 36	23 31	24 24	00 24
20	05 29	05 56	06 20	22 51	23 41	24 29	00 29
N 10	05 14	05 40	06 03	23 04	23 49	24 33	00 33
0	04 58	05 24	05 46	23 16	23 58	24 37	00 37
S 10	04 40	05 07	05 30	23 28	24 06	00 06	00 41
20	04 19	04 48	05 12	23 41	24 14	00 14	00 46
30	03 51	04 24	04 51	23 56	24 24	00 24	00 51
35	03 34	04 10	04 39	24 06	00 06	00 30	00 54
40	03 12	03 53	04 25	24 14	00 14	00 36	00 57
45	02 44	03 32	04 08	00 03	00 25	00 44	01 00
S 50	02 03	03 04	03 47	00 21	00 39	00 53	01 05
52	01 40	02 51	03 37	00 30	00 45	00 57	01 07
54	01 08	02 34	03 26	00 40	00 52	01 01	01 09
56	////	02 15	03 13	00 50	00 59	01 06	01 11
58	////	01 50	02 58	01 03	01 08	01 12	01 14
S 60	////	01 15	02 40	01 17	01 18	01 18	01 17

Lat.	Sunset	Twilight Civil	Naut.	Moonset 3	4	5	6
°	h m	h m	h m	h m	h m	h m	h m
N 72	■■	13 37	15 41	16 09	14 43	14 02	13 29
N 70	■■	14 20	15 59	15 07	14 20	13 50	13 25
68	12 46	14 49	16 12	14 32	14 02	13 41	13 23
66	13 44	15 11	16 24	14 06	13 48	13 33	13 20
64	14 16	15 28	16 34	13 46	13 36	13 27	13 18
62	14 41	15 42	16 42	13 30	13 25	13 21	13 17
60	15 00	15 55	16 50	13 16	13 16	13 16	13 15
N 58	15 15	16 05	16 57	13 04	13 08	13 11	13 14
56	15 29	16 15	17 03	12 54	13 02	13 07	13 12
54	15 40	16 23	17 08	12 45	12 55	13 04	13 11
52	15 51	16 31	17 14	12 36	12 50	13 01	13 10
50	16 00	16 37	17 18	12 29	12 45	12 58	13 09
45	16 19	16 52	17 29	12 13	12 34	12 51	13 07
N 40	16 35	17 05	17 39	12 00	12 24	12 46	13 06
35	16 48	17 16	17 47	11 49	12 16	12 41	13 04
30	17 00	17 26	17 55	11 39	12 09	12 37	13 03
20	17 20	17 44	18 11	11 22	11 57	12 29	13 00
N 10	17 37	18 00	18 26	11 08	11 46	12 23	12 58
0	17 54	18 18	18 42	10 54	11 36	12 17	12 56
S 10	18 10	18 33	19 00	10 40	11 26	12 11	12 54
20	18 28	18 53	19 22	10 24	11 15	12 04	12 52
30	18 49	19 16	19 49	10 07	11 03	11 56	12 50
35	19 01	19 31	20 07	09 57	10 55	11 52	12 48
40	19 16	19 48	20 29	09 45	10 47	11 47	12 47
45	19 33	20 09	20 57	09 31	10 37	11 41	12 45
S 50	19 54	20 37	21 38	09 14	10 25	11 34	12 42
52	20 04	20 51	22 02	09 06	10 19	11 31	12 41
54	20 15	21 07	22 35	08 57	10 13	11 27	12 40
56	20 28	21 26	////	08 47	10 06	11 23	12 39
58	20 43	21 52	////	08 35	09 58	11 19	12 37
S 60	21 02	22 28	////	08 21	09 49	11 14	12 36

	SUN Eqn. of Time 00h	12h	Mer. Pass.	MOON Mer. Pass. Upper	Lower	Age	Phase
d	m s	m s	h m	h m	h m	d	%
3	10 32	10 20	11 50	04 43	17 05	20	66
4	10 08	09 56	11 50	05 26	17 47	21	57
5	09 44	09 32	11 50	06 07	18 27	22	48

© British Crown Copyright 2022. All rights reserved.

2023 DECEMBER 6, 7, 8 (WED., THURS., FRI.)

UT	ARIES GHA	VENUS −4.2 GHA	VENUS Dec	MARS +1.4 GHA	MARS Dec	JUPITER −2.8 GHA	JUPITER Dec	SATURN +0.8 GHA	SATURN Dec
d h	° ′	° ′	° ′	° ′	° ′	° ′	° ′	° ′	° ′
6 00	74 31.4	224 27.6	S 9 52.7	188 02.0	S21 58.6	39 45.6	N12 29.8	100 30.8	S12 32.9
01	89 33.9	239 27.2	53.7	203 02.5	58.9	54 48.3	29.7	115 33.1	32.9
02	104 36.4	254 26.9	54.7	218 03.1	59.2	69 50.9	29.7	130 35.5	32.8
03	119 38.8	269 26.5	.. 55.7	233 03.6	.. 59.5	84 53.6	.. 29.6	145 37.8	.. 32.8
04	134 41.3	284 26.2	56.7	248 04.2	21 59.9	99 56.3	29.6	160 40.1	32.7
05	149 43.8	299 25.8	57.6	263 04.7	22 00.2	114 58.9	29.5	175 42.5	32.7
W 06	164 46.2	314 25.5	S 9 58.6	278 05.3	S22 00.5	130 01.6	N12 29.5	190 44.8	S12 32.6
E 07	179 48.7	329 25.1	9 59.6	293 05.8	00.8	145 04.3	29.4	205 47.1	32.6
D 08	194 51.2	344 24.8	10 00.6	308 06.4	01.1	160 06.9	29.3	220 49.5	32.5
N 09	209 53.6	359 24.4	.. 01.6	323 06.9	.. 01.4	175 09.6	.. 29.3	235 51.8	.. 32.5
E 10	224 56.1	14 24.1	02.6	338 07.5	01.7	190 12.3	29.2	250 54.2	32.4
S 11	239 58.5	29 23.7	03.6	353 08.0	02.0	205 14.9	29.2	265 56.5	32.4
D 12	255 01.0	44 23.4	S10 04.5	8 08.6	S22 02.3	220 17.6	N12 29.1	280 58.8	S12 32.3
A 13	270 03.5	59 23.0	05.5	23 09.1	02.6	235 20.3	29.1	296 01.2	32.3
Y 14	285 05.9	74 22.6	06.5	38 09.7	02.9	250 22.9	29.0	311 03.5	32.2
15	300 08.4	89 22.3	.. 07.5	53 10.2	.. 03.2	265 25.6	.. 28.9	326 05.8	.. 32.1
16	315 10.9	104 21.9	08.5	68 10.7	03.5	280 28.2	28.9	341 08.2	32.1
17	330 13.3	119 21.6	09.5	83 11.3	03.9	295 30.9	28.8	356 10.5	32.0
18	345 15.8	134 21.2	S10 10.5	98 11.8	S22 04.2	310 33.6	N12 28.8	11 12.8	S12 32.0
19	0 18.3	149 20.9	11.4	113 12.4	04.5	325 36.2	28.7	26 15.2	31.9
20	15 20.7	164 20.5	12.4	128 12.9	04.8	340 38.9	28.7	41 17.5	31.9
21	30 23.2	179 20.1	.. 13.4	143 13.5	.. 05.1	355 41.6	.. 28.6	56 19.8	.. 31.8
22	45 25.6	194 19.8	14.4	158 14.0	05.4	10 44.2	28.6	71 22.2	31.8
23	60 28.1	209 19.4	15.4	173 14.6	05.7	25 46.9	28.5	86 24.5	31.7
7 00	75 30.6	224 19.1	S10 16.4	188 15.1	S22 06.0	40 49.6	N12 28.4	101 26.9	S12 31.7
01	90 33.0	239 18.7	17.3	203 15.6	06.3	55 52.2	28.4	116 29.2	31.6
02	105 35.5	254 18.3	18.3	218 16.2	06.6	70 54.9	28.3	131 31.5	31.6
03	120 38.0	269 18.0	.. 19.3	233 16.7	.. 06.9	85 57.5	.. 28.3	146 33.9	.. 31.5
04	135 40.4	284 17.6	20.3	248 17.3	07.2	101 00.2	28.2	161 36.2	31.5
05	150 42.9	299 17.3	21.3	263 17.8	07.5	116 02.9	28.2	176 38.5	31.4
T 06	165 45.4	314 16.9	S10 22.2	278 18.4	S22 07.8	131 05.5	N12 28.1	191 40.9	S12 31.4
H 07	180 47.8	329 16.5	23.2	293 18.9	08.1	146 08.2	28.1	206 43.2	31.3
U 08	195 50.3	344 16.2	24.2	308 19.4	08.4	161 10.8	28.0	221 45.5	31.2
R 09	210 52.8	359 15.8	.. 25.2	323 20.0	.. 08.7	176 13.5	.. 27.9	236 47.9	.. 31.2
S 10	225 55.2	14 15.4	26.2	338 20.5	09.0	191 16.2	27.9	251 50.2	31.1
D 11	240 57.7	29 15.1	27.1	353 21.1	09.3	206 18.8	27.8	266 52.5	31.1
A 12	256 00.1	44 14.7	S10 28.1	8 21.6	S22 09.6	221 21.5	N12 27.8	281 54.9	S12 31.0
Y 13	271 02.6	59 14.3	29.1	23 22.1	09.9	236 24.1	27.7	296 57.2	31.0
14	286 05.1	74 14.0	30.1	38 22.7	10.2	251 26.8	27.7	311 59.5	30.9
15	301 07.5	89 13.6	.. 31.1	53 23.2	.. 10.5	266 29.5	.. 27.6	327 01.9	.. 30.9
16	316 10.0	104 13.2	32.0	68 23.8	10.8	281 32.1	27.6	342 04.2	30.8
17	331 12.5	119 12.9	33.0	83 24.3	11.1	296 34.8	27.5	357 06.5	30.8
18	346 14.9	134 12.5	S10 34.0	98 24.8	S22 11.4	311 37.4	N12 27.4	12 08.8	S12 30.7
19	1 17.4	149 12.1	35.0	113 25.4	11.7	326 40.1	27.4	27 11.2	30.7
20	16 19.9	164 11.8	35.9	128 25.9	12.0	341 42.7	27.4	42 13.5	30.6
21	31 22.3	179 11.4	.. 36.9	143 26.5	.. 12.2	356 45.4	.. 27.3	57 15.8	.. 30.5
22	46 24.8	194 11.0	37.9	158 27.0	12.5	11 48.0	27.3	72 18.2	30.5
23	61 27.3	209 10.6	38.9	173 27.5	12.8	26 50.7	27.2	87 20.5	30.4
8 00	76 29.7	224 10.3	S10 39.9	188 28.1	S22 13.1	41 53.4	N12 27.1	102 22.8	S12 30.4
01	91 32.2	239 09.9	40.8	203 28.6	13.4	56 56.0	27.1	117 25.2	30.3
02	106 34.6	254 09.5	41.8	218 29.2	13.7	71 58.7	27.0	132 27.5	30.3
03	121 37.1	269 09.2	.. 42.8	233 29.7	.. 14.0	87 01.3	.. 27.0	147 29.8	.. 30.2
04	136 39.6	284 08.8	43.8	248 30.2	14.3	102 04.0	26.9	162 32.2	30.2
05	151 42.0	299 08.4	44.7	263 30.8	14.6	117 06.6	26.9	177 34.5	30.1
F 06	166 44.5	314 08.0	S10 45.7	278 31.3	S22 14.9	132 09.3	N12 26.8	192 36.8	S12 30.1
R 07	181 47.0	329 07.7	46.7	293 31.8	15.2	147 11.9	26.8	207 39.2	30.0
I 08	196 49.4	344 07.3	47.7	308 32.4	15.5	162 14.6	26.7	222 41.5	29.9
D 09	211 51.9	359 06.9	.. 48.6	323 32.9	.. 15.8	177 17.2	.. 26.7	237 43.8	.. 29.9
A 10	226 54.4	14 06.6	49.6	338 33.4	16.0	192 19.9	26.6	252 46.1	29.8
Y 11	241 56.8	29 06.2	50.6	353 34.0	16.3	207 22.5	26.6	267 48.5	29.8
12	256 59.3	44 05.8	S10 51.5	8 34.5	S22 16.6	222 25.2	N12 26.5	282 50.8	S12 29.7
13	272 01.7	59 05.4	52.5	23 35.0	16.9	237 27.8	26.5	297 53.1	29.7
14	287 04.2	74 05.0	53.5	38 35.6	17.2	252 30.5	26.4	312 55.5	29.6
15	302 06.7	89 04.6	.. 54.5	53 36.1	.. 17.5	267 33.1	.. 26.4	327 57.8	.. 29.6
16	317 09.1	104 04.3	55.4	68 36.7	17.8	282 35.8	26.3	343 00.1	29.5
17	332 11.6	119 03.9	56.4	83 37.2	18.1	297 38.4	26.3	358 02.4	29.4
18	347 14.1	134 03.5	S10 57.4	98 37.7	S22 18.4	312 41.1	N12 26.2	13 04.8	S12 29.4
19	2 16.5	149 03.1	58.4	113 38.3	18.6	327 43.7	26.2	28 07.1	29.3
20	17 19.0	164 02.7	10 59.3	128 38.8	18.9	342 46.4	26.1	43 09.4	29.3
21	32 21.5	179 02.4	11 00.3	143 39.3	.. 19.2	357 49.0	.. 26.1	58 11.8	.. 29.2
22	47 23.9	194 02.0	01.3	158 39.9	19.5	12 51.7	26.0	73 14.1	29.2
23	62 26.4	209 01.6	02.2	173 40.4	19.8	27 54.3	26.0	88 16.4	29.1
Mer. Pass.	18ʰ 54.9ᵐ	v −0.4	d 1.0	v 0.5	d 0.3	v 2.7	d 0.1	v 2.3	d 0.1

STARS

Name	SHA	Dec
Acamar	315 12.1	S40 12.6
Achernar	335 20.5	S57 07.1
Acrux	173 01.4	S63 13.6
Adhara	255 06.3	S29 00.1
Aldebaran	290 40.3	N16 33.5
Alioth	166 14.0	N55 49.6
Alkaid	152 53.1	N49 11.5
Alnair	27 34.2	S46 51.0
Alnilam	275 38.3	S 1 11.1
Alphard	217 48.5	S 8 45.6
Alphecca	126 04.9	N26 38.0
Alpheratz	357 35.6	N29 13.5
Altair	62 01.1	N 8 55.9
Ankaa	353 07.9	S42 10.8
Antares	112 17.4	S26 29.0
Arcturus	145 49.0	N19 03.4
Atria	107 13.0	S69 04.2
Avior	234 14.7	S59 34.8
Bellatrix	278 23.5	N 6 22.3
Betelgeuse	270 52.8	N 7 24.7
Canopus	263 52.3	S52 42.3
Capella	280 22.8	N46 01.3
Deneb	49 26.7	N45 22.1
Denebola	182 26.0	N14 26.3
Diphda	348 48.1	S17 51.4
Dubhe	193 42.1	N61 37.1
Elnath	278 02.7	N28 37.7
Eltanin	90 43.1	N51 29.2
Enif	33 39.8	N 9 59.1
Fomalhaut	15 15.5	S29 29.9
Gacrux	171 52.9	S57 14.5
Gienah	175 44.7	S17 40.3
Hadar	148 37.8	S60 29.0
Hamal	327 52.0	N23 34.6
Kaus Aust.	83 34.1	S34 22.4
Kochab	137 20.8	N74 03.2
Markab	13 30.8	N15 20.1
Menkar	314 06.8	N 4 11.0
Menkent	147 59.0	S36 29.1
Miaplacidus	221 38.0	S69 48.5
Mirfak	308 29.1	N49 56.9
Nunki	75 49.2	S26 16.1
Peacock	53 07.6	S56 39.7
Pollux	243 18.1	N27 58.1
Procyon	244 51.5	N 5 09.9
Rasalhague	95 59.8	N12 32.6
Regulus	207 35.3	N11 51.0
Rigel	281 04.4	S 8 10.4
Rigil Kent.	139 42.2	S60 55.8
Sabik	102 04.2	S15 45.2
Schedar	349 31.9	N56 40.4
Shaula	96 12.1	S37 07.3
Sirius	258 26.7	S16 44.8
Spica	158 23.5	S11 17.0
Suhail	222 46.8	S43 31.4
Vega	80 34.3	N38 48.4
Zuben'ubi	136 57.3	S16 08.4

	SHA	Mer. Pass.
Venus	148 48.5	9ʰ 03ᵐ
Mars	112 44.5	11 27
Jupiter	325 19.0	21 13
Saturn	25 56.3	17 12

© British Crown Copyright 2022. All rights reserved.

SUN and MOON

UT	SUN GHA	SUN Dec	MOON GHA	v	Dec	d	HP
d h	° ′	° ′	° ′	′	° ′	′	′
6 00	182 19.7	S22 25.7	260 59.7	17.0	N 5 45.5	13.8	54.4
01	197 19.4	26.1	275 35.7	17.1	5 31.7	13.8	54.4
02	212 19.1	26.4	290 11.8	17.0	5 17.9	13.9	54.4
03	227 18.9 ..	26.7	304 47.8	17.1	5 04.0	13.9	54.4
04	242 18.6	27.0	319 23.9	17.0	4 50.1	13.9	54.4
05	257 18.4	27.3	333 59.9	17.1	4 36.2	13.9	54.4
06	272 18.1	S22 27.6	348 36.0	17.1	N 4 22.3	14.0	54.4
07	287 17.8	27.9	3 12.1	17.0	4 08.3	13.9	54.4
W 08	302 17.6	28.2	17 48.1	17.1	3 54.4	14.0	54.4
E 09	317 17.3 ..	28.5	32 24.2	17.1	3 40.4	14.0	54.5
D 10	332 17.0	28.8	47 00.3	17.1	3 26.4	14.1	54.5
N 11	347 16.8	29.1	61 36.4	17.1	3 12.3	14.0	54.5
E 12	2 16.5	S22 29.4	76 12.5	17.0	N 2 58.3	14.1	54.5
S 13	17 16.3	29.7	90 48.5	17.1	2 44.2	14.1	54.5
D 14	32 16.0	30.0	105 24.6	17.1	2 30.1	14.0	54.5
A 15	47 15.7 ..	30.3	120 00.7	17.0	2 16.1	14.2	54.5
Y 16	62 15.5	30.6	134 36.7	17.1	2 01.9	14.1	54.5
17	77 15.2	30.9	149 12.8	17.0	1 47.8	14.1	54.6
18	92 14.9	S22 31.2	163 48.8	17.1	N 1 33.7	14.2	54.6
19	107 14.7	31.5	178 24.9	17.0	1 19.5	14.2	54.6
20	122 14.4	31.8	193 00.9	17.0	1 05.3	14.1	54.6
21	137 14.1 ..	32.1	207 36.9	17.0	0 51.2	14.2	54.6
22	152 13.9	32.4	222 12.9	17.0	0 37.0	14.2	54.6
23	167 13.6	32.6	236 48.9	17.0	0 22.8	14.2	54.6
7 00	182 13.3	S22 32.9	251 24.9	16.9	N 0 08.6	14.3	54.7
01	197 13.1	33.2	266 00.8	17.0	S 0 05.7	14.2	54.7
02	212 12.8	33.5	280 36.8	16.9	0 19.9	14.2	54.7
03	227 12.5 ..	33.8	295 12.7	16.9	0 34.1	14.3	54.7
04	242 12.3	34.1	309 48.6	16.9	0 48.4	14.2	54.7
05	257 12.0	34.4	324 24.5	16.8	1 02.6	14.3	54.7
06	272 11.7	S22 34.7	339 00.3	16.9	S 1 16.9	14.3	54.8
07	287 11.5	34.9	353 36.2	16.8	1 31.2	14.2	54.8
T 08	302 11.2	35.2	8 12.0	16.8	1 45.4	14.3	54.8
H 09	317 10.9 ..	35.5	22 47.8	16.7	1 59.7	14.3	54.8
U 10	332 10.7	35.8	37 23.5	16.8	2 14.0	14.3	54.8
R 11	347 10.4	36.1	51 59.3	16.6	2 28.3	14.2	54.9
S 12	2 10.1	S22 36.4	66 34.9	16.7	S 2 42.5	14.3	54.9
D 13	17 09.9	36.6	81 10.6	16.6	2 56.8	14.3	54.9
A 14	32 09.6	36.9	95 46.2	16.6	3 11.1	14.3	54.9
Y 15	47 09.3 ..	37.2	110 21.8	16.6	3 25.4	14.3	54.9
16	62 09.0	37.5	124 57.4	16.5	3 39.7	14.2	55.0
17	77 08.8	37.8	139 32.9	16.5	3 53.9	14.3	55.0
18	92 08.5	S22 38.0	154 08.4	16.5	S 4 08.2	14.3	55.0
19	107 08.2	38.3	168 43.9	16.4	4 22.5	14.3	55.0
20	122 08.0	38.6	183 19.3	16.4	4 36.8	14.2	55.0
21	137 07.7 ..	38.9	197 54.7	16.3	4 51.0	14.3	55.1
22	152 07.4	39.1	212 30.0	16.3	5 05.3	14.2	55.1
23	167 07.2	39.4	227 05.3	16.2	5 19.5	14.3	55.1
8 00	182 06.9	S22 39.7	241 40.5	16.2	S 5 33.8	14.2	55.1
01	197 06.6	40.0	256 15.7	16.2	5 48.0	14.2	55.1
02	212 06.3	40.2	270 50.9	16.1	6 02.2	14.2	55.2
03	227 06.1 ..	40.5	285 26.0	16.0	6 16.4	14.2	55.2
04	242 05.8	40.8	300 01.0	16.0	6 30.6	14.2	55.2
05	257 05.5	41.0	314 36.0	16.0	6 44.8	14.2	55.2
06	272 05.3	S22 41.3	329 11.0	15.9	S 6 59.0	14.2	55.3
07	287 05.0	41.6	343 45.9	15.8	7 13.2	14.1	55.3
08	302 04.7	41.8	358 20.7	15.8	7 27.3	14.2	55.3
F 09	317 04.4 ..	42.1	12 55.5	15.7	7 41.5	14.1	55.3
R 10	332 04.2	42.4	27 30.2	15.7	7 55.6	14.1	55.4
I 11	347 03.9	42.6	42 04.9	15.6	8 09.7	14.1	55.4
D 12	2 03.6	S22 42.9	56 39.5	15.5	S 8 23.8	14.0	55.4
A 13	17 03.3	43.2	71 14.0	15.5	8 37.8	14.1	55.4
Y 14	32 03.1	43.4	85 48.5	15.4	8 51.9	14.0	55.4
15	47 02.8 ..	43.7	100 22.9	15.4	9 05.9	14.0	55.5
16	62 02.5	43.9	114 57.3	15.3	9 19.9	14.0	55.5
17	77 02.2	44.2	129 31.6	15.2	9 33.9	13.9	55.5
18	92 02.0	S22 44.5	144 05.8	15.1	S 9 47.8	13.9	55.6
19	107 01.7	44.7	158 39.9	15.1	10 01.7	13.9	55.6
20	122 01.4	45.0	173 14.0	15.0	10 15.6	13.9	55.6
21	137 01.1 ..	45.2	187 48.0	15.0	10 29.5	13.9	55.6
22	152 00.9	45.5	202 22.0	14.9	10 43.4	13.8	55.7
23	167 00.6	45.7	216 55.9	14.8	S10 57.2	13.8	55.7
	SD 16.3	d 0.3	SD 14.8		15.0		15.1

Twilight, Sunrise and Moonrise

Lat.	Twilight Naut.	Twilight Civil	Sunrise	Moonrise 6	7	8	9
°	h m	h m	h m	h m	h m	h m	h m
N 72	08 05	10 16	▮	25 20	01 20	03 20	05 37
N 70	07 47	09 29	▮	25 19	01 19	03 11	05 13
68	07 33	08 58	11 16	25 19	01 19	03 03	04 55
66	07 21	08 35	10 06	25 19	01 19	02 56	04 40
64	07 11	08 17	09 31	25 19	01 19	02 51	04 28
62	07 02	08 02	09 05	25 19	01 19	02 46	04 18
60	06 54	07 50	08 46	25 18	01 18	02 42	04 10
N 58	06 47	07 39	08 29	00 00	01 18	02 38	04 02
56	06 41	07 29	08 15	00 02	01 18	02 35	03 56
54	06 35	07 21	08 04	00 05	01 18	02 32	03 50
52	06 30	07 13	07 53	00 07	01 18	02 30	03 45
50	06 25	07 06	07 44	00 09	01 18	02 28	03 40
45	06 14	06 51	07 24	00 14	01 18	02 22	03 30
N 40	06 04	06 38	07 08	00 18	01 17	02 18	03 21
35	05 55	06 26	06 54	00 21	01 17	02 15	03 14
30	05 47	06 16	06 43	00 24	01 17	02 12	03 08
20	05 31	05 58	06 22	00 29	01 17	02 06	02 57
N 10	05 15	05 42	06 04	00 33	01 17	02 01	02 48
0	04 59	05 25	05 48	00 37	01 17	01 57	02 39
S 10	04 41	05 08	05 31	00 41	01 17	01 53	02 30
20	04 19	04 48	05 12	00 46	01 17	01 48	02 21
30	03 51	04 24	04 51	00 51	01 16	01 43	02 11
35	03 33	04 10	04 39	00 54	01 16	01 40	02 05
40	03 11	03 52	04 24	00 57	01 16	01 36	01 58
45	02 42	03 31	04 07	01 00	01 16	01 33	01 50
S 50	02 00	03 02	03 46	01 05	01 16	01 28	01 41
52	01 36	02 48	03 36	01 07	01 16	01 26	01 37
54	01 00	02 32	03 24	01 09	01 16	01 24	01 32
56	////	02 11	03 11	01 11	01 16	01 21	01 27
58	////	01 45	02 55	01 14	01 16	01 18	01 21
S 60	////	01 07	02 36	01 17	01 16	01 15	01 15

Sunset, Twilight and Moonset

Lat.	Sunset	Twilight Civil	Twilight Naut.	Moonset 6	7	8	9
°	h m	h m	h m	h m	h m	h m	h m
N 72	▮	13 26	15 37	13 29	12 58	12 23	11 36
N 70	▮	14 14	15 55	13 25	13 02	12 36	12 02
68	12 26	14 44	16 09	13 23	13 05	12 46	12 22
66	13 36	15 07	16 21	13 20	13 08	12 54	12 39
64	14 12	15 25	16 32	13 18	13 10	13 02	12 52
62	14 37	15 40	16 41	13 17	13 12	13 08	13 03
60	14 57	15 53	16 48	13 15	13 14	13 13	13 13
N 58	15 13	16 04	16 55	13 14	13 16	13 18	13 21
56	15 27	16 13	17 02	13 12	13 17	13 22	13 29
54	15 39	16 22	17 07	13 11	13 18	13 26	13 36
52	15 49	16 30	17 13	13 10	13 20	13 30	13 42
50	15 59	16 37	17 18	13 09	13 21	13 33	13 47
45	16 18	16 52	17 29	13 07	13 23	13 38	13 59
N 40	16 35	17 05	17 39	13 06	13 25	13 46	14 09
35	16 48	17 16	17 48	13 04	13 27	13 51	14 18
30	17 00	17 26	17 56	13 03	13 29	13 56	14 25
20	17 20	17 44	18 12	13 00	13 31	14 03	14 38
N 10	17 38	18 01	18 27	12 58	13 34	14 10	14 50
0	17 55	18 17	18 44	12 56	13 36	14 17	15 00
S 10	18 12	18 35	19 02	12 54	13 38	14 23	15 11
20	18 30	18 55	19 24	12 52	13 40	14 30	15 23
30	18 51	19 19	19 52	12 50	13 43	14 38	15 36
35	19 04	19 33	20 10	12 48	13 45	14 43	15 44
40	19 18	19 51	20 32	12 47	13 47	14 48	15 53
45	19 36	20 13	21 01	12 45	13 49	14 54	16 03
S 50	19 59	20 41	21 43	12 42	13 51	15 02	16 16
52	20 08	20 55	22 08	12 41	13 52	15 05	16 22
54	20 19	21 12	22 45	12 40	13 53	15 09	16 29
56	20 33	21 32	////	12 39	13 55	15 13	16 36
58	20 48	21 59	////	12 37	13 56	15 18	16 44
S 60	21 07	22 38	////	12 36	13 58	15 23	16 54

SUN and MOON

Day	SUN Eqn. of Time 00h	SUN Eqn. of Time 12h	SUN Mer. Pass.	MOON Mer. Pass. Upper	MOON Mer. Pass. Lower	Age	Phase
d	m s	m s	h m	h m	h m	d	%
6	09 19	09 07	11 51	06 47	19 07	23	38
7	08 54	08 41	11 51	07 26	19 46	24	29
8	08 28	08 15	11 52	08 07	20 28	25	21

© British Crown Copyright 2022. All rights reserved.

UT	ARIES GHA	VENUS −4.1 GHA	Dec	MARS +1.4 GHA	Dec	JUPITER −2.8 GHA	Dec	SATURN +0.8 GHA	Dec	STARS Name	SHA	Dec
9 00	77 28.9	224 01.2	S11 03.2	188 40.9	S22 20.1	42 57.0	N12 25.9	103 18.7	S12 29.1	Acamar	315 12.1	S40 12.6
01	92 31.3	239 00.8	04.2	203 41.5	20.4	57 59.6	25.9	118 21.1	29.0	Achernar	335 20.5	S57 07.2
02	107 33.8	254 00.4	05.1	218 42.0	20.6	73 02.3	25.8	133 23.4	28.9	Acrux	173 01.3	S63 13.6
03	122 36.2	269 00.1 ..	06.1	233 42.5 ..	20.9	88 04.9 ..	25.8	148 25.7 ..	28.9	Adhara	255 06.2	S29 00.1
04	137 38.7	283 59.7	07.1	248 43.0	21.2	103 07.6	25.7	163 28.0	28.9	Aldebaran	290 40.3	N16 33.5
05	152 41.2	298 59.3	08.0	263 43.6	21.5	118 10.2	25.7	178 30.4	28.8			
S 06	167 43.6	313 58.9	S11 09.0	278 44.1	S22 21.8	133 12.9	N12 25.6	193 32.7	S12 28.7	Alioth	166 14.0	N55 49.6
A 07	182 46.1	328 58.5	10.0	293 44.6	22.1	148 15.5	25.6	208 35.0	28.7	Alkaid	152 53.0	N49 11.5
T 08	197 48.6	343 58.1	11.0	308 45.2	22.3	163 18.2	25.5	223 37.4	28.6	Alnair	27 34.2	S46 51.0
U 09	212 51.0	358 57.7 ..	11.9	323 45.7 ..	22.6	178 20.8 ..	25.5	238 39.7 ..	28.6	Alnilam	275 38.3	S 1 11.2
R 10	227 53.5	13 57.4	12.9	338 46.2	22.9	193 23.4	25.4	253 42.0	28.5	Alphard	217 48.5	S 8 45.6
D 11	242 56.0	28 57.0	13.9	353 46.8	23.2	208 26.1	25.4	268 44.3	28.4			
A 12	257 58.4	43 56.6	S11 14.8	8 47.3	S22 23.5	223 28.7	N12 25.3	283 46.7	S12 28.4	Alphecca	126 04.9	N26 38.0
Y 13	273 00.9	58 56.2	15.8	23 47.8	23.7	238 31.4	25.3	298 49.0	28.3	Alpheratz	357 35.6	N29 13.5
14	288 03.4	73 55.8	16.7	38 48.4	24.0	253 34.0	25.2	313 51.3	28.3	Altair	62 01.1	N 8 55.9
15	303 05.8	88 55.4 ..	17.7	53 48.9 ..	24.3	268 36.7 ..	25.2	328 53.6 ..	28.2	Ankaa	353 07.9	S42 10.8
16	318 08.3	103 55.0	18.7	68 49.4	24.6	283 39.3	25.1	343 56.0	28.2	Antares	112 17.3	S26 29.0
17	333 10.7	118 54.6	19.6	83 49.9	24.9	298 42.0	25.1	358 58.3	28.1			
18	348 13.2	133 54.2	S11 20.6	98 50.5	S22 25.1	313 44.6	N12 25.0	14 00.6	S12 28.0	Arcturus	145 49.0	N19 03.4
19	3 15.7	148 53.8	21.6	113 51.0	25.4	328 47.2	25.0	29 02.9	28.0	Atria	107 13.0	S69 04.1
20	18 18.1	163 53.5	22.5	128 51.5	25.7	343 49.9	24.9	44 05.3	27.9	Avior	234 14.7	S59 34.9
21	33 20.6	178 53.1 ..	23.5	143 52.1 ..	26.0	358 52.5 ..	24.9	59 07.6 ..	27.9	Bellatrix	278 23.5	N 6 22.3
22	48 23.1	193 52.7	24.5	158 52.6	26.3	13 55.2	24.8	74 09.9	27.8	Betelgeuse	270 52.7	N 7 24.7
23	63 25.5	208 52.3	25.4	173 53.1	26.5	28 57.8	24.8	89 12.2	27.8			
10 00	78 28.0	223 51.9	S11 26.4	188 53.6	S22 26.8	44 00.4	N12 24.7	104 14.6	S12 27.7	Canopus	263 52.3	S52 42.3
01	93 30.5	238 51.5	27.3	203 54.2	27.1	59 03.1	24.7	119 16.9	27.6	Capella	280 22.8	N46 01.3
02	108 32.9	253 51.1	28.3	218 54.7	27.4	74 05.7	24.6	134 19.2	27.6	Deneb	49 26.7	N45 22.1
03	123 35.4	268 50.7 ..	29.3	233 55.2 ..	27.6	89 08.4 ..	24.6	149 21.5 ..	27.5	Denebola	182 25.9	N14 26.3
04	138 37.8	283 50.3	30.2	248 55.7	27.9	104 11.0	24.6	164 23.8	27.5	Diphda	348 48.1	S17 51.4
05	153 40.3	298 49.9	31.2	263 56.3	28.2	119 13.6	24.5	179 26.2	27.4			
S 06	168 42.8	313 49.5	S11 32.2	278 56.8	S22 28.5	134 16.3	N12 24.5	194 28.5	S12 27.4	Dubhe	193 42.1	N61 37.1
U 07	183 45.2	328 49.1	33.1	293 57.3	28.7	149 18.9	24.4	209 30.8	27.3	Elnath	278 02.6	N28 37.7
N 08	198 47.7	343 48.7	34.1	308 57.8	29.0	164 21.6	24.4	224 33.1	27.2	Eltanin	90 43.2	N51 29.1
D 09	213 50.2	358 48.3 ..	35.0	323 58.4 ..	29.3	179 24.2 ..	24.3	239 35.5 ..	27.2	Enif	33 39.8	N 9 59.1
A 10	228 52.6	13 47.9	36.0	338 58.9	29.5	194 26.8	24.3	254 37.8	27.1	Fomalhaut	15 15.6	S29 29.9
Y 11	243 55.1	28 47.5	36.9	353 59.4	29.8	209 29.5	24.2	269 40.1	27.1			
12	258 57.6	43 47.1	S11 37.9	8 59.9	S22 30.1	224 32.1	N12 24.2	284 42.4	S12 27.0	Gacrux	171 52.9	S57 14.5
13	274 00.0	58 46.7	38.9	24 00.5	30.4	239 34.7	24.1	299 44.7	26.9	Gienah	175 44.6	S17 40.3
14	289 02.5	73 46.3	39.8	39 01.0	30.6	254 37.4	24.1	314 47.1	26.9	Hadar	148 37.8	S60 29.0
15	304 05.0	88 45.9 ..	40.8	54 01.5 ..	30.9	269 40.0 ..	24.0	329 49.4 ..	26.8	Hamal	327 52.0	N23 34.6
16	319 07.4	103 45.5	41.7	69 02.0	31.2	284 42.6	24.0	344 51.7	26.8	Kaus Aust.	83 34.1	S34 22.4
17	334 09.9	118 45.1	42.7	84 02.6	31.4	299 45.3	23.9	359 54.0	26.7			
18	349 12.3	133 44.7	S11 43.7	99 03.1	S22 31.7	314 47.9	N12 23.9	14 56.4	S12 26.7	Kochab	137 20.8	N74 03.2
19	4 14.8	148 44.3	44.6	114 03.6	32.0	329 50.5	23.9	29 58.7	26.6	Markab	13 30.8	N15 20.1
20	19 17.3	163 43.9	45.6	129 04.1	32.3	344 53.2	23.8	45 01.0	26.5	Menkar	314 06.8	N 4 11.0
21	34 19.7	178 43.5 ..	46.5	144 04.7 ..	32.5	359 55.8 ..	23.8	60 03.3 ..	26.5	Menkent	147 59.0	S36 29.1
22	49 22.2	193 43.1	47.5	159 05.2	32.8	14 58.4	23.7	75 05.6	26.4	Miaplacidus	221 38.0	S69 48.6
23	64 24.7	208 42.7	48.4	174 05.7	33.1	30 01.1	23.7	90 08.0	26.4			
11 00	79 27.1	223 42.3	S11 49.4	189 06.2	S22 33.3	45 03.7	N12 23.6	105 10.3	S12 26.3	Mirfak	308 29.1	N49 56.9
01	94 29.6	238 41.9	50.3	204 06.7	33.6	60 06.3	23.6	120 12.6	26.2	Nunki	75 49.2	S26 16.1
02	109 32.1	253 41.4	51.3	219 07.3	33.9	75 09.0	23.5	135 14.9	26.2	Peacock	53 07.6	S56 39.7
03	124 34.5	268 41.0 ..	52.2	234 07.8 ..	34.1	90 11.6 ..	23.5	150 17.2 ..	26.1	Pollux	243 18.1	N27 58.1
04	139 37.0	283 40.6	53.2	249 08.3	34.4	105 14.2	23.5	165 19.6	26.1	Procyon	244 51.5	N 5 09.9
05	154 39.5	298 40.2	54.1	264 08.8	34.7	120 16.9	23.4	180 21.9	26.0			
M 06	169 41.9	313 39.8	S11 55.1	279 09.3	S22 34.9	135 19.5	N12 23.4	195 24.2	S12 26.0	Rasalhague	95 59.8	N12 32.6
O 07	184 44.4	328 39.4	56.1	294 09.9	35.2	150 22.1	23.3	210 26.5	25.9	Regulus	207 35.3	N11 51.0
N 08	199 46.8	343 39.0	57.0	309 10.4	35.5	165 24.8	23.3	225 28.8	25.8	Rigel	281 04.4	S 8 10.4
D 09	214 49.3	358 38.6 ..	58.0	324 10.9 ..	35.7	180 27.4 ..	23.2	240 31.2 ..	25.8	Rigil Kent.	139 42.1	S60 55.8
A 10	229 51.8	13 38.2	58.9	339 11.4	36.0	195 30.0	23.2	255 33.5	25.7	Sabik	102 04.2	S15 45.2
Y 11	244 54.2	28 37.8	11 59.9	354 11.9	36.2	210 32.7	23.1	270 35.8	25.7			
12	259 56.7	43 37.3	S12 00.8	12 12.5	S22 36.5	225 35.3	N12 23.1	285 38.1	S12 25.6	Schedar	349 31.9	N56 40.4
13	274 59.2	58 36.9	01.8	24 13.0	36.8	240 37.9	23.1	300 40.4	25.5	Shaula	96 12.0	S37 07.3
14	290 01.6	73 36.5	02.7	39 13.5	37.0	255 40.5	23.0	315 42.7	25.5	Sirius	258 26.7	S16 44.8
15	305 04.1	88 36.1 ..	03.7	54 14.0 ..	37.3	270 43.2 ..	23.0	330 45.1 ..	25.4	Spica	158 23.5	S11 17.1
16	320 06.6	103 35.7	04.6	69 14.5	37.6	285 45.8	22.9	345 47.4	25.4	Suhail	222 46.7	S43 31.5
17	335 09.0	118 35.3	05.6	84 15.1	37.8	300 48.4	22.9	0 49.7	25.3			
18	350 11.5	133 34.9	S12 06.5	99 15.6	S22 38.1	315 51.1	N12 22.8	15 52.0	S12 25.2	Vega	80 34.3	N38 48.4
19	5 14.0	148 34.5	07.5	114 16.1	38.3	330 53.7	22.8	30 54.3	25.2	Zuben'ubi	136 57.3	S16 08.4
20	20 16.4	163 34.0	08.4	129 16.6	38.6	345 56.3	22.8	45 56.7	25.1			
21	35 18.9	178 33.6 ..	09.3	144 17.1 ..	38.9	0 58.9 ..	22.7	60 59.0 ..	25.1		SHA	Mer. Pass.
22	50 21.3	193 33.2	10.3	159 17.7	39.1	16 01.6	22.7	76 01.3	25.0	Venus	145 23.9	9 05
23	65 23.8	208 32.8	11.2	174 18.2	39.4	31 04.2	22.6	91 03.6	24.9	Mars	110 25.6	11 24
Mer. Pass. 18 43.1		v −0.4 d 1.0		v 0.5 d 0.3		v 2.6 d 0.0		v 2.3 d 0.1		Jupiter	325 32.4	21 00
										Saturn	25 46.6	17 00

© British Crown Copyright 2022. All rights reserved.

SUN and MOON

UT (d h)	SUN GHA	SUN Dec	MOON GHA	v	MOON Dec	d	HP
9 00	182 00.3	S22 46.0	231 29.7	14.7	S11 11.0	13.7	55.7
01	197 00.0	46.2	246 03.4	14.6	11 24.7	13.7	55.7
02	211 59.7	46.5	260 37.0	14.6	11 38.4	13.7	55.8
03	226 59.5	. . 46.7	275 10.6	14.5	11 52.1	13.7	55.8
04	241 59.2	47.0	289 44.1	14.4	12 05.8	13.6	55.8
05	256 58.9	47.2	304 17.5	14.3	12 19.4	13.6	55.8
S 06	271 58.6	S22 47.5	318 50.8	14.2	S12 33.0	13.5	55.9
A 07	286 58.4	47.7	333 24.0	14.2	12 46.5	13.5	55.9
T 08	301 58.1	48.0	347 57.2	14.1	13 00.0	13.5	55.9
U 09	316 57.8	. . 48.2	2 30.3	13.9	13 13.5	13.4	56.0
R 10	331 57.5	48.5	17 03.2	13.9	13 26.9	13.4	56.0
D 11	346 57.2	48.7	31 36.1	13.9	13 40.3	13.3	56.0
A 12	1 57.0	S22 49.0	46 09.0	13.7	S13 53.6	13.3	56.0
Y 13	16 56.7	49.2	60 41.7	13.6	14 06.9	13.2	56.1
14	31 56.4	49.5	75 14.3	13.5	14 20.1	13.2	56.1
15	46 56.1	. . 49.7	89 46.8	13.5	14 33.3	13.2	56.1
16	61 55.8	49.9	104 19.3	13.3	14 46.5	13.1	56.2
17	76 55.6	50.2	118 51.6	13.3	14 59.6	13.0	56.2
18	91 55.3	S22 50.4	133 23.9	13.1	S15 12.6	13.0	56.2
19	106 55.0	50.7	147 56.0	13.1	15 25.6	12.9	56.2
20	121 54.7	50.9	162 28.1	13.0	15 38.5	12.9	56.3
21	136 54.4	. . 51.1	177 00.1	12.8	15 51.4	12.8	56.3
22	151 54.2	51.4	191 31.9	12.8	16 04.2	12.8	56.3
23	166 53.9	51.6	206 03.7	12.6	16 17.0	12.7	56.4
10 00	181 53.6	S22 51.8	220 35.3	12.6	S16 29.7	12.6	56.4
01	196 53.3	52.1	235 06.9	12.5	16 42.3	12.6	56.4
02	211 53.0	52.3	249 38.4	12.3	16 54.9	12.5	56.4
03	226 52.8	. . 52.6	264 09.7	12.2	17 07.4	12.5	56.5
04	241 52.5	52.8	278 40.9	12.2	17 19.9	12.4	56.5
05	256 52.2	53.0	293 12.1	12.0	17 32.3	12.3	56.5
S 06	271 51.9	S22 53.2	307 43.1	11.9	S17 44.6	12.2	56.6
U 07	286 51.6	53.5	322 14.0	11.9	17 56.8	12.2	56.6
N 08	301 51.3	53.7	336 44.9	11.7	18 09.0	12.1	56.6
D 09	316 51.1	. . 53.9	351 15.6	11.6	18 21.1	12.0	56.7
A 10	331 50.8	54.2	5 46.2	11.4	18 33.1	12.0	56.7
Y 11	346 50.5	54.4	20 16.6	11.4	18 45.1	11.8	56.7
12	1 50.2	S22 54.6	34 47.0	11.3	S18 56.9	11.8	56.7
13	16 49.9	54.8	49 17.3	11.1	19 08.7	11.7	56.8
14	31 49.6	55.1	63 47.4	11.0	19 20.4	11.7	56.8
15	46 49.4	. . 55.3	78 17.4	11.0	19 32.1	11.5	56.8
16	61 49.1	55.5	92 47.4	10.8	19 43.6	11.5	56.9
17	76 48.8	55.7	107 17.2	10.6	19 55.1	11.3	56.9
18	91 48.5	S22 55.9	121 46.8	10.6	S20 06.4	11.3	56.9
19	106 48.2	56.2	136 16.4	10.5	20 17.7	11.2	57.0
20	121 47.9	56.4	150 45.9	10.3	20 28.9	11.1	57.0
21	136 47.7	. . 56.6	165 15.2	10.2	20 40.0	11.0	57.0
22	151 47.4	56.8	179 44.4	10.1	20 51.0	10.9	57.1
23	166 47.1	57.0	194 13.5	10.0	21 01.9	10.9	57.1
11 00	181 46.8	S22 57.3	208 42.5	9.8	S21 12.8	10.7	57.1
01	196 46.5	57.5	223 11.3	9.8	21 23.5	10.6	57.1
02	211 46.2	57.7	237 40.1	9.6	21 34.1	10.5	57.2
03	226 45.9	. . 57.9	252 08.7	9.5	21 44.6	10.4	57.2
04	241 45.6	58.1	266 37.2	9.4	21 55.0	10.3	57.2
05	256 45.4	58.3	281 05.6	9.2	22 05.3	10.2	57.3
M 06	271 45.1	S22 58.5	295 33.8	9.2	S22 15.5	10.1	57.3
O 07	286 44.8	58.8	310 02.0	9.0	22 25.6	10.0	57.3
N 08	301 44.5	59.0	324 30.0	8.9	22 35.6	9.8	57.4
D 09	316 44.2	. . 59.2	338 57.9	8.8	22 45.4	9.8	57.4
A 10	331 43.9	59.4	353 25.7	8.6	22 55.2	9.6	57.4
Y 11	346 43.6	59.6	7 53.3	8.5	23 04.8	9.5	57.4
12	1 43.3	S22 59.8	22 20.8	8.5	S23 14.3	9.4	57.5
13	16 43.1	23 00.0	36 48.3	8.2	23 23.7	9.3	57.5
14	31 42.8	00.2	51 15.5	8.2	23 33.0	9.2	57.5
15	46 42.5	. . 00.4	65 42.7	8.1	23 42.2	9.0	57.6
16	61 42.2	00.6	80 09.8	7.9	23 51.2	8.9	57.6
17	76 41.9	00.8	94 36.7	7.8	24 00.1	8.8	57.6
18	91 41.6	S23 01.0	109 03.5	7.7	S24 08.9	8.6	57.6
19	106 41.3	01.2	123 30.2	7.6	24 17.5	8.6	57.7
20	121 41.0	01.4	137 56.8	7.4	24 26.1	8.3	57.7
21	136 40.8	. . 01.6	152 23.2	7.4	24 34.4	8.3	57.7
22	151 40.5	01.8	166 49.6	7.2	24 42.7	8.1	57.8
23	166 40.2	02.0	181 15.8	7.1	S24 50.8	8.0	57.8
	SD 16.3	d 0.2	SD 15.3		15.5		15.7

Twilight, Sunrise and Moonrise

Lat.	Naut.	Civil	Sunrise	Moonrise 9	10	11	12
N 72	08 11	10 28	■	05 37	■	■	■
N 70	07 53	09 37	■	05 13	07 53	■	■
68	07 38	09 04	■	04 55	07 07	■	■
66	07 25	08 41	10 15	04 40	06 38	09 12	■
64	07 15	08 22	09 37	04 28	06 16	08 21	■
62	07 06	08 07	09 11	04 18	05 58	07 49	09 54
60	06 58	07 54	08 50	04 10	05 44	07 26	09 13
N 58	06 50	07 43	08 34	04 02	05 32	07 07	08 45
56	06 44	07 33	08 19	03 56	05 21	06 52	08 23
54	06 38	07 24	08 07	03 50	05 12	06 38	08 06
52	06 33	07 16	07 57	03 45	05 04	06 27	07 50
50	06 28	07 09	07 47	03 40	04 56	06 16	07 37
45	06 16	06 53	07 27	03 30	04 41	05 55	07 11
N 40	06 06	06 40	07 11	03 21	04 28	05 38	06 50
35	05 57	06 29	06 57	03 14	04 17	05 24	06 32
30	05 49	06 18	06 45	03 08	04 08	05 11	06 17
20	05 33	06 00	06 24	02 57	03 52	04 50	05 52
N 10	05 17	05 43	06 06	02 48	03 38	04 32	05 30
0	05 00	05 26	05 49	02 39	03 25	04 15	05 10
S 10	04 42	05 09	05 32	02 30	03 12	03 58	04 49
20	04 20	04 49	05 13	02 21	02 58	03 40	04 28
30	03 51	04 24	04 52	02 11	02 43	03 19	04 03
35	03 33	04 10	04 39	02 05	02 34	03 07	03 49
40	03 11	03 52	04 24	01 58	02 23	02 54	03 32
45	02 41	03 30	04 07	01 50	02 12	02 38	03 12
S 50	01 58	03 01	03 45	01 41	01 57	02 18	02 47
52	01 32	02 47	03 35	01 37	01 51	02 09	02 35
54	00 54	02 30	03 23	01 32	01 43	01 59	02 22
56	////	02 09	03 09	01 27	01 35	01 47	02 06
58	////	01 41	02 53	01 21	01 26	01 33	01 47
S 60	////	01 00	02 34	01 15	01 15	01 18	01 25

Sunset, Twilight and Moonset

Lat.	Sunset	Civil	Naut.	Moonset 9	10	11	12
N 72	■	13 17	15 33	11 36	■	■	■
N 70	■	14 08	15 52	12 02	10 59	■	■
68	■	14 41	16 07	12 22	11 46	■	■
66	13 30	15 04	16 20	12 39	12 17	11 29	■
64	14 08	15 23	16 30	12 52	12 40	12 21	■
62	14 34	15 38	16 39	13 03	12 58	12 53	12 45
60	14 55	15 51	16 47	13 13	13 14	13 17	13 26
N 58	15 11	16 02	16 55	13 21	13 27	13 36	13 55
56	15 26	16 12	17 01	13 29	13 38	13 53	14 17
54	15 38	16 21	17 07	13 36	13 48	14 06	14 35
52	15 49	16 29	17 12	13 42	13 57	14 19	14 50
50	15 58	16 36	17 18	13 47	14 05	14 29	15 04
45	16 18	16 52	17 29	13 59	14 22	14 52	15 31
N 40	16 35	17 05	17 39	14 09	14 36	15 10	15 53
35	16 48	17 16	17 48	14 18	14 48	15 26	16 11
30	17 00	17 27	17 57	14 25	14 59	15 39	16 27
20	17 21	17 45	18 13	14 38	15 17	16 02	16 53
N 10	17 39	18 02	18 31	14 50	15 33	16 22	17 16
0	17 56	18 19	18 45	15 00	15 48	16 40	17 38
S 10	18 14	18 37	19 04	15 11	16 03	16 59	17 59
20	18 32	18 57	19 26	15 23	16 19	17 19	18 22
30	18 54	19 21	19 54	15 36	16 38	17 42	18 49
35	19 06	19 36	20 12	15 44	16 48	17 56	19 05
40	19 21	19 54	20 35	15 53	17 01	18 12	19 23
45	19 39	20 16	21 05	16 03	17 16	18 31	19 45
S 50	20 01	20 45	21 48	16 16	17 34	18 55	20 14
52	20 11	20 59	22 14	16 22	17 43	19 06	20 28
54	20 23	21 16	22 54	16 29	17 52	19 19	20 44
56	20 37	21 37	////	16 36	18 03	19 35	21 03
58	20 53	22 05	////	16 44	18 16	19 53	21 27
S 60	21 12	22 48	////	16 54	18 31	20 15	21 59

SUN and MOON data

Day	Eqn. of Time 00h	12h	Mer. Pass.	Mer. Pass. Upper	Lower	Age	Phase
	m s	m s	h m	h m	h m	d	%
9	08 02	07 48	11 52	08 50	21 12	26	13
10	07 35	07 21	11 53	09 36	22 01	27	7
11	07 08	06 54	11 53	10 27	22 55	28	3

© British Crown Copyright 2022. All rights reserved.

UT	ARIES GHA	VENUS −4.1 GHA	Dec	MARS +1.4 GHA	Dec	JUPITER −2.7 GHA	Dec	SATURN +0.8 GHA	Dec	STARS Name	SHA	Dec
12 00	80 26.3	223 32.4	S12 12.2	189 18.7	S22 39.6	46 06.8	N12 22.6	106 05.9	S12 24.9	Acamar	315 12.1	S40 12.6
01	95 28.7	238 31.9	13.1	204 19.2	39.9	61 09.4	22.5	121 08.2	24.8	Achernar	335 20.5	S57 07.2
02	110 31.2	253 31.5	14.1	219 19.7	40.2	76 12.1	22.5	136 10.6	24.8	Acrux	173 01.3	S63 13.6
03	125 33.7	268 31.1 ..	15.0	234 20.2 ..	40.4	91 14.7 ..	22.5	151 12.9 ..	24.7	Adhara	255 06.2	S29 00.1
04	140 36.1	283 30.7	16.0	249 20.7	40.7	106 17.3	22.4	166 15.2	24.6	Aldebaran	290 40.3	N16 33.5
05	155 38.6	298 30.3	16.9	264 21.3	40.9	121 19.9	22.4	181 17.5	24.6			
06	170 41.1	313 29.8	S12 17.9	279 21.8	S22 41.2	136 22.6	N12 22.3	196 19.8	S12 24.5	Alioth	166 14.0	N55 49.6
07	185 43.5	328 29.4	18.8	294 22.3	41.4	151 25.2	22.3	211 22.1	24.5	Alkaid	152 53.0	N49 11.4
08	200 46.0	343 29.0	19.7	309 22.8	41.7	166 27.8	22.2	226 24.5	24.4	Alnair	27 34.2	S46 51.0
09	215 48.4	358 28.6 ..	20.7	324 23.3 ..	41.9	181 30.4 ..	22.2	241 26.8 ..	24.3	Alnilam	275 38.3	S 1 11.2
10	230 50.9	13 28.2	21.6	339 23.8	42.2	196 33.0	22.2	256 29.1	24.3	Alphard	217 48.5	S 8 45.6
11	245 53.4	28 27.7	22.6	354 24.4	42.5	211 35.7	22.1	271 31.4	24.2			
12	260 55.8	43 27.3	S12 23.5	9 24.9	S22 42.7	226 38.3	N12 22.1	286 33.7	S12 24.2	Alphecca	126 04.8	N26 38.0
13	275 58.3	58 26.9	24.4	24 25.4	43.0	241 40.9	22.0	301 36.0	24.1	Alpheratz	357 35.6	N29 13.5
14	291 00.8	73 26.5	25.4	39 25.9	43.2	256 43.5	22.0	316 38.3	24.0	Altair	62 01.1	N 8 55.9
15	306 03.2	88 26.0 ..	26.3	54 26.4 ..	43.5	271 46.1 ..	22.0	331 40.7 ..	24.0	Ankaa	353 07.9	S42 10.8
16	321 05.7	103 25.6	27.3	69 26.9	43.7	286 48.8	21.9	346 43.0	23.9	Antares	112 17.3	S26 29.0
17	336 08.2	118 25.2	28.2	84 27.4	44.0	301 51.4	21.9	1 45.3	23.9			
18	351 10.6	133 24.8	S12 29.1	99 28.0	S22 44.2	316 54.0	N12 21.8	16 47.6	S12 23.8	Arcturus	145 49.0	N19 03.4
19	6 13.1	148 24.3	30.1	114 28.5	44.5	331 56.6	21.8	31 49.9	23.7	Atria	107 12.9	S69 04.1
20	21 15.6	163 23.9	31.0	129 29.0	44.7	346 59.2	21.8	46 52.2	23.7	Avior	234 14.6	S59 34.9
21	36 18.0	178 23.5 ..	32.0	144 29.5 ..	45.0	2 01.9 ..	21.7	61 54.5 ..	23.6	Bellatrix	278 23.5	N 6 22.3
22	51 20.5	193 23.0	32.9	159 30.0	45.2	17 04.5	21.7	76 56.9	23.6	Betelgeuse	270 52.7	N 7 24.7
23	66 22.9	208 22.6	33.8	174 30.5	45.5	32 07.1	21.6	91 59.2	23.5			
13 00	81 25.4	223 22.2	S12 34.8	189 31.0	S22 45.7	47 09.7	N12 21.6	107 01.5	S12 23.4	Canopus	263 52.2	S52 42.4
01	96 27.9	238 21.8	35.7	204 31.5	46.0	62 12.3	21.6	122 03.8	23.4	Capella	280 22.7	N46 01.3
02	111 30.3	253 21.3	36.6	219 32.0	46.2	77 14.9	21.5	137 06.1	23.3	Deneb	49 26.7	N45 22.1
03	126 32.8	268 20.9 ..	37.6	234 32.6 ..	46.5	92 17.6 ..	21.5	152 08.4 ..	23.2	Denebola	182 25.9	N14 26.3
04	141 35.3	283 20.5	38.5	249 33.1	46.7	107 20.2	21.4	167 10.7	23.2	Diphda	348 48.1	S17 51.4
05	156 37.7	298 20.0	39.5	264 33.6	47.0	122 22.8	21.4	182 13.0	23.1			
06	171 40.2	313 19.6	S12 40.4	279 34.1	S22 47.2	137 25.4	N12 21.3	197 15.4	S12 23.1	Dubhe	193 42.0	N61 37.1
07	186 42.7	328 19.2	41.3	294 34.6	47.5	152 28.0	21.3	212 17.7	23.0	Elnath	278 02.6	N28 37.7
08	201 45.1	343 18.7	42.3	309 35.1	47.7	167 30.6	21.3	227 20.0	22.9	Eltanin	90 43.2	N51 29.1
09	216 47.6	358 18.3 ..	43.2	324 35.6 ..	48.0	182 33.3 ..	21.3	242 22.3 ..	22.9	Enif	33 39.8	N 9 59.1
10	231 50.1	13 17.9	44.1	339 36.1	48.2	197 35.9	21.2	257 24.6	22.8	Fomalhaut	15 15.6	S29 29.9
11	246 52.5	28 17.4	45.1	354 36.6	48.4	212 38.5	21.2	272 26.9	22.8			
12	261 55.0	43 17.0	S12 46.0	9 37.2	S22 48.7	227 41.1	N12 21.1	287 29.2	S12 22.7	Gacrux	171 52.8	S57 14.5
13	276 57.4	58 16.5	46.9	24 37.7	48.9	242 43.7	21.1	302 31.5	22.6	Gienah	175 44.6	S17 40.3
14	291 59.9	73 16.1	47.9	39 38.2	49.2	257 46.3	21.1	317 33.9	22.6	Hadar	148 37.8	S60 29.0
15	307 02.4	88 15.7 ..	48.8	54 38.7 ..	49.4	272 48.9 ..	21.0	332 36.2 ..	22.5	Hamal	327 52.0	N23 34.6
16	322 04.8	103 15.2	49.7	69 39.2	49.7	287 51.5	21.0	347 38.5	22.4	Kaus Aust.	83 34.1	S34 22.4
17	337 07.3	118 14.8	50.6	84 39.7	49.9	302 54.2	20.9	2 40.8	22.4			
18	352 09.8	133 14.4	S12 51.6	99 40.2	S22 50.2	317 56.8	N12 20.9	17 43.1	S12 22.3	Kochab	137 20.7	N74 03.2
19	7 12.2	148 13.9	52.5	114 40.7	50.4	332 59.4	20.9	32 45.4	22.3	Markab	13 30.8	N15 20.1
20	22 14.7	163 13.5	53.4	129 41.2	50.6	348 02.0	20.8	47 47.7	22.2	Menkar	314 06.8	N 4 11.0
21	37 17.2	178 13.0 ..	54.4	144 41.7 ..	50.9	3 04.6 ..	20.8	62 50.0 ..	22.1	Menkent	147 59.0	S36 29.1
22	52 19.6	193 12.6	55.3	159 42.2	51.1	18 07.2	20.8	77 52.3	22.1	Miaplacidus	221 37.9	S69 48.6
23	67 22.1	208 12.2	56.2	174 42.7	51.4	33 09.8	20.7	92 54.6	22.0			
14 00	82 24.6	223 11.7	S12 57.1	189 43.2	S22 51.6	48 12.4	N12 20.7	107 57.0	S12 21.9	Mirfak	308 29.1	N49 56.9
01	97 27.0	238 11.3	58.1	204 43.8	51.8	63 15.0	20.7	122 59.3	21.9	Nunki	75 49.2	S26 16.1
02	112 29.5	253 10.8	59.0	219 44.3	52.1	78 17.7	20.6	138 01.6	21.8	Peacock	53 07.6	S56 39.7
03	127 31.9	268 10.4	12 59.9	234 44.8 ..	52.3	93 20.3 ..	20.5	153 03.9 ..	21.8	Pollux	243 18.1	N27 58.0
04	142 34.4	283 09.9	13 00.8	249 45.3	52.6	108 22.9	20.5	168 06.2	21.7	Procyon	244 51.5	N 5 09.8
05	157 36.9	298 09.5	01.8	264 45.8	52.8	123 25.5	20.5	183 08.5	21.6			
06	172 39.3	313 09.1	S13 02.7	279 46.3	S22 53.0	138 28.1	N12 20.5	198 10.8	S12 21.6	Rasalhague	95 59.7	N12 32.6
07	187 41.8	328 08.6	03.6	294 46.8	53.3	153 30.7	20.4	213 13.1	21.5	Regulus	207 35.3	N11 51.0
08	202 44.3	343 08.2	04.5	309 47.3	53.5	168 33.3	20.4	228 15.4	21.4	Rigel	281 04.4	S 8 10.4
09	217 46.7	358 07.7 ..	05.5	324 47.8 ..	53.7	183 35.9 ..	20.4	243 17.7 ..	21.4	Rigil Kent.	139 42.1	S60 55.8
10	232 49.2	13 07.3	06.4	339 48.3	54.0	198 38.5	20.3	258 20.0	21.3	Sabik	102 04.2	S15 45.2
11	247 51.7	28 06.8	07.3	354 48.8	54.2	213 41.1	20.3	273 22.4	21.3			
12	262 54.1	43 06.4	S13 08.2	9 49.3	S22 54.5	228 43.7	N12 20.3	288 24.7	S12 21.2	Schedar	349 31.9	N56 40.4
13	277 56.6	58 05.9	09.2	24 49.8	54.7	243 46.3	20.2	303 27.0	21.1	Shaula	96 12.0	S37 07.2
14	292 59.1	73 05.5	10.1	39 50.3	54.9	258 48.9	20.2	318 29.3	21.1	Sirius	258 26.7	S16 44.9
15	308 01.5	88 05.0 ..	11.0	54 50.8 ..	55.2	273 51.5 ..	20.1	333 31.6 ..	21.0	Spica	158 23.4	S11 17.1
16	323 04.0	103 04.6	11.9	69 51.3	55.4	288 54.1	20.1	348 33.9	20.9	Suhail	222 46.7	S43 31.5
17	338 06.4	118 04.1	12.8	84 51.8	55.6	303 56.7	20.1	3 36.2	20.9			
18	353 08.9	133 03.7	S13 13.8	99 52.3	S22 55.9	318 59.4	N12 20.0	18 38.5	S12 20.8	Vega	80 34.3	N38 48.4
19	8 11.4	148 03.2	14.7	114 52.8	56.1	334 02.0	20.0	33 40.8	20.8	Zuben'ubi	136 57.3	S16 08.4
20	23 13.8	163 02.8	15.6	129 53.3	56.3	349 04.6	20.0	48 43.1	20.7			
21	38 16.3	178 02.3 ..	16.5	144 53.8 ..	56.6	4 07.2 ..	19.9	63 45.4 ..	20.6			
22	53 18.8	193 01.9	17.4	159 54.3	56.8	19 09.8	19.9	78 47.7	20.6		SHA	Mer. Pass.
23	68 21.2	208 01.4	18.4	174 54.8	57.0	34 12.4	19.9	93 50.0	20.5	Venus	141 56.8	9 07
Mer. Pass. 18 31.3		v −0.4	d 0.9	v 0.5	d 0.2	v 2.6	d 0.0	v 2.3	d 0.1	Mars	108 05.6	11 22
										Jupiter	325 44.3	20 48
										Saturn	25 36.1	16 49

© British Crown Copyright 2022. All rights reserved.

SUN and MOON

UT (d h)	SUN GHA	SUN Dec	MOON GHA	v	MOON Dec	d	HP
12 00	181 39.9	S23 02.2	195 41.9	7.0	S24 58.8	7.8	57.8
01	196 39.6	02.4	210 07.9	6.9	25 06.6	7.7	57.8
02	211 39.3	02.6	224 33.8	6.7	25 14.3	7.5	57.9
03	226 39.0	.. 02.8	238 59.5	6.7	25 21.8	7.4	57.9
04	241 38.7	03.0	253 25.2	6.5	25 29.2	7.3	57.9
05	256 38.4	03.2	267 50.7	6.4	25 36.5	7.1	58.0
06	271 38.1	S23 03.4	282 16.1	6.4	S25 43.6	7.0	58.0
07	286 37.8	03.6	296 41.5	6.2	25 50.6	6.8	58.0
T 08	301 37.6	03.8	311 06.7	6.1	25 57.4	6.6	58.0
U 09	316 37.3	.. 04.0	325 31.8	6.0	26 04.0	6.5	58.1
E 10	331 37.0	04.1	339 56.8	5.9	26 10.5	6.4	58.1
S 11	346 36.7	04.3	354 21.7	5.8	26 16.9	6.1	58.1
D 12	1 36.4	S23 04.5	8 46.5	5.6	S26 23.0	6.1	58.2
A 13	16 36.1	04.7	23 11.1	5.6	26 29.1	5.8	58.2
Y 14	31 35.8	04.9	37 35.7	5.5	26 34.9	5.7	58.2
15	46 35.5	.. 05.1	52 00.2	5.4	26 40.6	5.6	58.2
16	61 35.2	05.3	66 24.6	5.3	26 46.2	5.3	58.3
17	76 34.9	05.4	80 48.9	5.2	26 51.5	5.2	58.3
18	91 34.6	S23 05.6	95 13.1	5.1	S26 56.7	5.1	58.3
19	106 34.3	05.8	109 37.2	5.0	27 01.8	4.8	58.3
20	121 34.0	06.0	124 01.2	5.0	27 06.6	4.7	58.4
21	136 33.8	.. 06.2	138 25.2	4.8	27 11.3	4.5	58.4
22	151 33.5	06.4	152 49.0	4.8	27 15.8	4.4	58.4
23	166 33.2	06.5	167 12.8	4.6	27 20.2	4.2	58.4
13 00	181 32.9	S23 06.7	181 36.4	4.6	S27 24.4	4.0	58.5
01	196 32.6	06.9	196 00.0	4.5	27 28.4	3.8	58.5
02	211 32.3	07.1	210 23.5	4.5	27 32.2	3.6	58.5
03	226 32.0	.. 07.2	224 47.0	4.4	27 35.8	3.5	58.5
04	241 31.7	07.4	239 10.4	4.3	27 39.3	3.3	58.6
05	256 31.4	07.6	253 33.7	4.2	27 42.6	3.1	58.6
06	271 31.1	S23 07.8	267 56.9	4.1	S27 45.7	2.9	58.6
W 07	286 30.8	07.9	282 20.0	4.1	27 48.6	2.7	58.6
E 08	301 30.5	08.1	296 43.1	4.1	27 51.3	2.6	58.7
D 09	316 30.2	.. 08.3	311 06.2	3.9	27 53.9	2.3	58.7
N 10	331 29.9	08.4	325 29.1	4.0	27 56.2	2.0	58.7
E 11	346 29.6	08.6	339 52.1	3.8	27 58.4	2.0	58.7
S 12	1 29.3	S23 08.8	354 14.9	3.8	S28 00.4	1.8	58.7
D 13	16 29.0	09.0	8 37.7	3.8	28 02.2	1.6	58.8
A 14	31 28.7	09.1	23 00.5	3.7	28 03.8	1.4	58.8
Y 15	46 28.5	.. 09.3	37 23.2	3.7	28 05.2	1.2	58.8
16	61 28.2	09.5	51 45.9	3.6	28 06.4	1.1	58.8
17	76 27.9	09.6	66 08.5	3.6	28 07.5	0.8	58.8
18	91 27.6	S23 09.8	80 31.1	3.5	S28 08.3	0.7	58.9
19	106 27.3	09.9	94 53.6	3.6	28 09.0	0.4	58.9
20	121 27.0	10.1	109 16.2	3.4	28 09.4	0.3	58.9
21	136 26.7	.. 10.3	123 38.7	3.4	28 09.7	0.1	58.9
22	151 26.4	10.4	138 01.1	3.5	28 09.8	0.1	58.9
23	166 26.1	10.6	152 23.6	3.4	28 09.7	0.4	59.0
14 00	181 25.8	S23 10.7	166 46.0	3.4	S28 09.3	0.5	59.0
01	196 25.5	10.9	181 08.4	3.4	28 08.8	0.7	59.0
02	211 25.2	11.1	195 30.8	3.3	28 08.1	0.9	59.0
03	226 24.9	.. 11.2	209 53.1	3.4	28 07.2	1.1	59.0
04	241 24.6	11.4	224 15.5	3.4	28 06.1	1.3	59.1
05	256 24.3	11.5	238 37.9	3.3	28 04.8	1.4	59.1
06	271 24.0	S23 11.7	253 00.2	3.3	S28 03.4	1.7	59.1
T 07	286 23.7	11.8	267 22.5	3.4	28 01.7	1.9	59.1
H 08	301 23.4	12.0	281 44.9	3.3	27 59.8	2.1	59.1
U 09	316 23.1	.. 12.1	296 07.2	3.4	27 57.7	2.3	59.1
R 10	331 22.8	12.3	310 29.6	3.4	27 55.4	2.4	59.2
S 11	346 22.5	12.4	324 52.0	3.4	27 53.0	2.7	59.2
D 12	1 22.2	S23 12.6	339 14.4	3.3	S27 50.3	2.8	59.2
A 13	16 21.9	12.7	353 36.7	3.5	27 47.5	3.1	59.2
Y 14	31 21.6	12.9	7 59.2	3.4	27 44.4	3.2	59.2
15	46 21.3	.. 13.0	22 21.6	3.5	27 41.2	3.5	59.2
16	61 21.0	13.2	36 44.1	3.4	27 37.7	3.6	59.2
17	76 20.7	13.3	51 06.5	3.5	27 34.1	3.8	59.3
18	91 20.4	S23 13.5	65 29.0	3.6	S27 30.3	4.0	59.3
19	106 20.1	13.6	79 51.6	3.6	27 26.3	4.2	59.3
20	121 19.8	13.8	94 14.2	3.6	27 22.1	4.4	59.3
21	136 19.5	.. 13.9	108 36.8	3.6	27 17.7	4.6	59.3
22	151 19.2	14.0	122 59.4	3.7	27 13.1	4.8	59.3
23	166 18.9	14.2	137 22.1	3.8	S27 08.3	4.9	59.3
	SD 16.3	d 0.2	SD 15.8		16.0		16.1

Twilight, Sunrise and Moonrise

Lat.	Naut.	Civil	Sunrise	Moonrise 12	13	14	15
N 72	08 17	10 39	■	■	■	■	■
N 70	07 57	09 43	■	■	■	■	■
68	07 42	09 10	■	■	■	■	■
66	07 29	08 45	10 22	■	■	■	■
64	07 18	08 26	09 43	■	■	■	13 53
62	07 09	08 11	09 15	09 54	■	13 09	12 48
60	07 01	07 57	08 54	09 13	10 51	11 51	12 13
N 58	06 54	07 46	08 37	08 45	10 13	11 15	11 47
56	06 47	07 36	08 23	08 23	09 47	10 49	11 27
54	06 41	07 27	08 11	08 06	09 26	10 28	11 10
52	06 35	07 19	08 00	07 50	09 08	10 11	10 55
50	06 30	07 12	07 50	07 37	08 53	09 56	10 43
45	06 19	06 56	07 29	07 11	08 23	09 26	10 16
N 40	06 08	06 42	07 13	06 50	07 59	09 13	09 55
35	05 59	06 31	06 59	06 32	07 40	08 43	09 38
30	05 51	06 20	06 47	06 17	07 23	08 26	09 23
20	05 34	06 02	06 26	05 52	06 55	07 58	08 57
N 10	05 18	05 45	06 08	05 30	06 32	07 34	08 35
0	05 02	05 28	05 50	05 10	06 09	07 12	08 14
S 10	04 43	05 10	05 33	04 49	05 47	06 49	07 53
20	04 21	04 50	05 14	04 28	05 23	06 25	07 31
30	03 52	04 25	04 52	04 03	04 56	05 57	07 05
35	03 33	04 10	04 40	03 49	04 40	05 40	06 49
40	03 11	03 52	04 25	03 32	04 21	05 21	06 31
45	02 41	03 30	04 07	03 12	03 58	04 58	06 10
S 50	01 56	03 01	03 45	02 47	03 29	04 27	05 42
52	01 30	02 46	03 34	02 35	03 15	04 13	05 29
54	00 48	02 28	03 22	02 22	02 58	03 55	05 14
56	////	02 07	03 08	02 06	02 39	03 34	04 55
58	////	01 38	02 52	01 47	02 15	03 08	04 33
S 60	////	00 53	02 32	01 25	01 43	02 32	04 04

Sunset, Twilight and Moonset

Lat.	Sunset	Civil	Naut.	Moonset 12	13	14	15
N 72	■	13 08	15 31	■	■	■	■
N 70	■	14 04	15 50	■	■	■	■
68	■	14 38	16 06	■	■	■	■
66	13 25	15 02	16 19	■	■	■	■
64	14 05	15 22	16 29	■	■	■	15 15
62	14 32	15 37	16 39	12 45	■	13 48	16 19
60	14 53	15 51	16 47	13 26	13 55	15 06	16 54
N 58	15 11	16 02	17 01	13 55	14 32	15 42	17 19
56	15 25	16 12	17 01	14 17	14 59	16 08	17 39
54	15 37	16 21	17 07	14 35	15 20	16 28	17 55
52	15 48	16 29	17 13	14 50	15 38	16 46	18 09
50	15 58	16 36	17 18	15 04	15 53	17 00	18 22
45	16 18	16 52	17 29	15 31	16 24	17 30	18 47
N 40	16 35	17 06	17 40	15 53	16 47	17 53	19 07
35	16 49	17 17	17 49	16 11	17 07	18 12	19 24
30	17 01	17 28	17 57	16 27	17 24	18 29	19 38
20	17 22	17 46	18 18	16 53	17 52	18 56	20 03
N 10	17 41	18 03	18 30	17 16	18 16	19 20	20 23
0	17 58	18 20	18 46	17 38	18 39	19 42	20 43
S 10	18 15	18 38	19 05	17 59	19 01	20 03	21 02
20	18 34	18 58	19 28	18 22	19 26	20 27	21 23
30	18 56	19 23	19 56	18 49	19 54	20 54	21 46
35	19 09	19 38	20 15	19 05	20 11	21 10	22 00
40	19 23	19 56	20 38	19 23	20 30	21 28	22 16
45	19 41	20 18	21 08	19 45	20 53	21 50	22 35
S 50	20 03	20 48	21 52	20 14	21 24	22 18	22 58
52	20 14	21 03	22 19	20 28	21 39	22 32	23 09
54	20 26	21 20	23 02	20 44	21 56	22 48	23 22
56	20 40	21 42	////	21 03	22 17	23 07	23 36
58	20 57	22 11	////	21 27	22 43	23 29	23 53
S 60	21 17	22 57	////	21 59	23 20	23 59	24 13

SUN and MOON

Day	Eqn. of Time 00h	12h	Mer. Pass.	Mer. Pass. Upper	Lower	Age	Phase
	m s	m s	h m	h m	h m	d	%
12	06 40	06 26	11 54	11 23	23 53	29	0
13	06 12	05 58	11 54	12 24	24 55	01	1
14	05 44	05 29	11 55	13 27	00 55	02	3

Phase: ● (New Moon)

© British Crown Copyright 2022. All rights reserved.

2023 DECEMBER 15, 16, 17 (FRI., SAT., SUN.)

UT	ARIES	VENUS −4·1		MARS +1·4		JUPITER −2·7		SATURN +0·9		STARS		
	GHA	GHA	Dec	GHA	Dec	GHA	Dec	GHA	Dec	Name	SHA	Dec
d h	° ′	° ′	° ′	° ′	° ′	° ′	° ′	° ′	° ′		° ′	° ′
15 00	83 23.7	223 01.0	S13 19.3	189 55.4	S22 57.3	49 15.0	N12 19.8	108 52.3	S12 20.4	Acamar	315 12.1	S40 12.7
01	98 26.2	238 00.5	20.2	204 55.9	57.5	64 17.6	19.8	123 54.7	20.4	Achernar	335 20.5	S57 07.2
02	113 28.6	253 00.0	21.1	219 56.4	57.7	79 20.2	19.8	138 57.0	20.3	Acrux	173 01.2	S63 13.6
03	128 31.1	267 59.6 ..	22.0	234 56.9 ..	57.9	94 22.8 ..	19.7	153 59.3 ..	20.2	Adhara	255 06.2	S29 00.2
04	143 33.6	282 59.1	22.9	249 57.4	58.2	109 25.4	19.7	169 01.6	20.2	Aldebaran	290 40.3	N16 33.5
05	158 36.0	297 58.7	23.9	264 57.9	58.4	124 28.0	19.7	184 03.9	20.1			
06	173 38.5	312 58.2	S13 24.8	279 58.4	S22 58.6	139 30.6	N12 19.6	199 06.2	S12 20.1	Alioth	166 13.9	N55 49.6
07	188 40.9	327 57.8	25.7	294 58.9	58.9	154 33.2	19.6	214 08.5	20.0	Alkaid	152 53.0	N49 11.4
08	203 43.4	342 57.3	26.6	309 59.4	59.1	169 35.8	19.6	229 10.8	19.9	Al Na'ir	27 34.2	S46 51.0
F 09	218 45.9	357 56.9 ..	27.5	324 59.9 ..	59.3	184 38.4 ..	19.5	244 13.1 ..	19.9	Alnilam	275 38.3	S 1 11.2
R 10	233 48.3	12 56.4	28.4	340 00.4	59.5	199 41.0	19.5	259 15.4	19.8	Alphard	217 48.4	S 8 45.6
I 11	248 50.8	27 55.9	29.3	355 00.9	22 59.8	214 43.6	19.5	274 17.7	19.7			
D 12	263 53.3	42 55.5	S13 30.2	10 01.4	S23 00.0	229 46.2	N12 19.4	289 20.0	S12 19.7	Alphecca	126 04.8	N26 38.0
A 13	278 55.7	57 55.0	31.2	25 01.9	00.2	244 48.8	19.4	304 22.3	19.6	Alpheratz	357 35.7	N29 13.5
Y 14	293 58.2	72 54.6	32.1	40 02.4	00.4	259 51.4	19.4	319 24.6	19.5	Altair	62 01.1	N 8 55.9
15	309 00.7	87 54.1 ..	33.0	55 02.9 ..	00.7	274 54.0 ..	19.3	334 26.9 ..	19.5	Ankaa	353 07.9	S42 10.8
16	324 03.1	102 53.6	33.9	70 03.4	00.9	289 56.5	19.3	349 29.2	19.4	Antares	112 17.3	S26 29.0
17	339 05.6	117 53.2	34.8	85 03.9	01.1	304 59.1	19.3	4 31.5	19.3			
18	354 08.1	132 52.7	S13 35.7	100 04.4	S23 01.3	320 01.7	N12 19.2	19 33.8	S12 19.3	Arcturus	145 49.0	N19 03.4
19	9 10.5	147 52.2	36.6	115 04.9	01.6	335 04.3	19.2	34 36.1	19.2	Atria	107 12.9	S69 04.1
20	24 13.0	162 51.8	37.5	130 05.4	01.8	350 06.9	19.2	49 38.4	19.1	Avior	234 14.6	S59 34.9
21	39 15.4	177 51.3 ..	38.4	145 05.8 ..	02.0	5 09.5 ..	19.1	64 40.7 ..	19.1	Bellatrix	278 23.5	N 6 22.3
22	54 17.9	192 50.8	39.3	160 06.3	02.2	20 12.1	19.1	79 43.0	19.0	Betelgeuse	270 52.7	N 7 24.7
23	69 20.4	207 50.4	40.2	175 06.8	02.5	35 14.7	19.1	94 45.4	19.0			
16 00	84 22.8	222 49.9	S13 41.2	190 07.3	S23 02.7	50 17.3	N12 19.1	109 47.7	S12 18.9	Canopus	263 52.2	S52 42.4
01	99 25.3	237 49.4	42.1	205 07.8	02.9	65 19.9	19.0	124 50.0	18.9	Capella	280 22.7	N46 01.3
02	114 27.8	252 49.0	43.0	220 08.3	03.1	80 22.5	19.0	139 52.3	18.8	Deneb	49 26.8	N45 22.1
03	129 30.2	267 48.5 ..	43.9	235 08.8 ..	03.3	95 25.1 ..	19.0	154 54.6 ..	18.7	Denebola	182 25.9	N14 26.3
04	144 32.7	282 48.0	44.8	250 09.3	03.6	110 27.7	18.9	169 56.9	18.6	Diphda	348 48.1	S17 51.4
05	159 35.2	297 47.6	45.7	265 09.8	03.8	125 30.3	18.9	184 59.2	18.6			
06	174 37.6	312 47.1	S13 46.6	280 10.3	S23 04.0	140 32.9	N12 18.9	200 01.5	S12 18.5	Dubhe	193 42.0	N61 37.1
07	189 40.1	327 46.6	47.5	295 10.8	04.2	155 35.5	18.8	215 03.8	18.4	Elnath	278 02.6	N28 37.7
08	204 42.6	342 46.2	48.4	310 11.3	04.4	170 38.0	18.8	230 06.1	18.4	Eltanin	90 43.1	N51 29.1
S 09	219 45.0	357 45.7 ..	49.3	325 11.8 ..	04.7	185 40.6 ..	18.8	245 08.4 ..	18.3	Enif	33 39.8	N 9 59.1
A 10	234 47.5	12 45.2	50.2	340 12.3	04.9	200 43.2	18.7	260 10.7	18.2	Fomalhaut	15 15.6	S29 29.9
T 11	249 49.9	27 44.7	51.1	355 12.8	05.1	215 45.8	18.7	275 13.0	18.2			
U 12	264 52.4	42 44.3	S13 52.0	10 13.3	S23 05.3	230 48.4	N12 18.7	290 15.3	S12 18.1	Gacrux	171 52.8	S57 14.5
R 13	279 54.9	57 43.8	52.9	25 13.8	05.5	245 51.0	18.7	305 17.6	18.0	Gienah	175 44.6	S17 40.3
D 14	294 57.3	72 43.3	53.8	40 14.3	05.7	260 53.6	18.6	320 19.9	18.0	Hadar	148 37.7	S60 29.0
A 15	309 59.8	87 42.9 ..	54.7	55 14.8 ..	06.0	275 56.2 ..	18.6	335 22.2 ..	17.9	Hamal	327 52.0	N23 34.6
Y 16	325 02.3	102 42.4	55.6	70 15.3	06.2	290 58.8	18.6	350 24.5	17.8	Kaus Aust.	83 34.1	S34 22.4
17	340 04.7	117 41.9	56.5	85 15.8	06.4	306 01.4	18.5	5 26.8	17.8			
18	355 07.2	132 41.4	S13 57.4	100 16.3	S23 06.6	321 03.9	N12 18.5	20 29.1	S12 17.7	Kochab	137 20.7	N74 03.2
19	10 09.7	147 41.0	58.3	115 16.8	06.8	336 06.5	18.5	35 31.4	17.6	Markab	13 30.8	N15 20.1
20	25 12.1	162 40.5	13 59.2	130 17.2	07.0	351 09.1	18.5	50 33.7	17.6	Menkar	314 06.8	N 4 11.0
21	40 14.6	177 40.0	14 00.1	145 17.7 ..	07.2	6 11.7 ..	18.4	65 36.0 ..	17.5	Menkent	147 58.9	S36 29.1
22	55 17.1	192 39.5	01.0	160 18.2	07.5	21 14.3	18.4	80 38.3	17.4	Miaplacidus	221 37.9	S69 48.6
23	70 19.5	207 39.0	01.9	175 18.7	07.7	36 16.9	18.4	95 40.6	17.4			
17 00	85 22.0	222 38.6	S14 02.8	190 19.2	S23 07.9	51 19.5	N12 18.3	110 42.9	S12 17.3	Mirfak	308 29.1	N49 56.9
01	100 24.4	237 38.1	03.7	205 19.7	08.1	66 22.0	18.3	125 45.2	17.2	Nunki	75 49.2	S26 16.1
02	115 26.9	252 37.6	04.6	220 20.2	08.3	81 24.6	18.3	140 47.5	17.2	Peacock	53 07.6	S56 39.7
03	130 29.4	267 37.1 ..	05.4	235 20.7 ..	08.5	96 27.2 ..	18.3	155 49.8 ..	17.1	Pollux	243 18.1	N27 58.0
04	145 31.8	282 36.7	06.3	250 21.2	08.7	111 29.8	18.2	170 52.1	17.0	Procyon	244 51.5	N 5 09.8
05	160 34.3	297 36.2	07.2	265 21.7	08.9	126 32.4	18.2	185 54.4	17.0			
06	175 36.8	312 35.7	S14 08.1	280 22.3	S23 09.2	141 35.0	N12 18.2	200 56.7	S12 16.9	Rasalhague	95 59.7	N12 32.5
07	190 39.2	327 35.2	09.0	295 22.7	09.4	156 37.5	18.1	215 59.0	16.8	Regulus	207 35.3	N11 51.0
08	205 41.7	342 34.7	09.9	310 23.2	09.6	171 40.1	18.1	231 01.3	16.8	Rigel	281 04.4	S 8 10.4
S 09	220 44.2	357 34.2 ..	10.8	325 23.6 ..	09.8	186 42.7 ..	18.1	246 03.6 ..	16.7	Rigil Kent.	139 42.0	S60 55.8
U 10	235 46.6	12 33.8	11.7	340 24.1	10.0	201 45.3	18.1	261 05.9	16.6	Sabik	102 04.2	S15 45.2
N 11	250 49.1	27 33.3	12.6	355 24.6	10.2	216 47.9	18.0	276 08.2	16.6			
D 12	265 51.5	42 32.8	S14 13.5	10 25.1	S23 10.4	231 50.5	N12 18.0	291 10.5	S12 16.5	Schedar	349 31.9	N56 40.4
A 13	280 54.0	57 32.3	14.4	25 25.6	10.6	246 53.0	18.0	306 12.8	16.4	Shaula	96 12.0	S37 07.2
Y 14	295 56.5	72 31.8	15.2	40 26.1	10.8	261 55.6	18.0	321 15.1	16.4	Sirius	258 26.7	S16 44.9
15	310 58.9	87 31.3 ..	16.1	55 26.6 ..	11.0	276 58.2 ..	17.9	336 17.4 ..	16.3	Spica	158 23.4	S11 17.1
16	326 01.4	102 30.8	17.0	70 27.1	11.2	292 00.8	17.9	351 19.7	16.2	Suhail	222 46.7	S43 31.5
17	341 03.9	117 30.4	17.9	85 27.6	11.4	307 03.4	17.9	6 22.0	16.2			
18	356 06.3	132 29.9	S14 18.8	100 28.1	S23 11.6	322 05.9	N12 17.8	21 24.3	S12 16.1	Vega	80 34.3	N38 48.4
19	11 08.8	147 29.4	19.7	115 28.5	11.8	337 08.5	17.8	36 26.6	16.0	Zuben'ubi	136 57.3	S16 08.4
20	26 11.3	162 28.9	20.6	130 29.0	12.0	352 11.1	17.8	51 28.8	16.0		SHA	Mer. Pass.
21	41 13.7	177 28.4 ..	21.4	145 29.5 ..	12.3	7 13.7 ..	17.8	66 31.1 ..	15.9		° ′	h m
22	56 16.2	192 27.9	22.3	160 30.0	12.5	22 16.3	17.7	81 33.4	15.8	Venus	138 27.1	9 09
23	71 18.7	207 27.4	23.2	175 30.5	12.7	37 18.8	17.7	96 35.7	15.8	Mars	105 44.5	11 19
	h m									Jupiter	325 54.5	20 35
Mer. Pass. 18 19.5		v −0.5	d 0.9	v 0.5	d 0.2	v 2.6	d 0.0	v 2.3	d 0.1	Saturn	25 24.8	16 38

© British Crown Copyright 2022. All rights reserved.

UT	SUN GHA	SUN Dec	MOON GHA	v	MOON Dec	d	HP
d h	° ′	° ′	° ′	′	° ′	′	′
15 00	181 18.6	S23 14.3	151 44.9	3.7	S27 03.4	5.2	59.4
01	196 18.3	14.5	166 07.6	3.9	26 58.2	5.3	59.4
02	211 18.0	14.6	180 30.5	3.9	26 52.9	5.6	59.4
03	226 17.7	.. 14.7	194 53.4	3.9	26 47.3	5.7	59.4
04	241 17.4	14.9	209 16.3	4.0	26 41.6	5.9	59.4
05	256 17.1	15.0	223 39.3	4.0	26 35.7	6.0	59.4
06	271 16.8	S23 15.1	238 02.3	4.1	S26 29.7	6.3	59.4
07	286 16.5	15.3	252 25.4	4.2	26 23.4	6.4	59.4
F 08	301 16.2	15.4	266 48.6	4.3	26 17.0	6.7	59.4
R 09	316 15.9	.. 15.5	281 11.9	4.3	26 10.3	6.8	59.4
I 10	331 15.6	15.7	295 35.2	4.3	26 03.5	6.9	59.5
D 11	346 15.3	15.8	309 58.5	4.5	25 56.6	7.2	59.5
A 12	1 15.0	S23 15.9	324 22.0	4.5	S25 49.4	7.3	59.5
Y 13	16 14.7	16.1	338 45.5	4.6	25 42.1	7.5	59.5
14	31 14.4	16.2	353 09.1	4.6	25 34.6	7.7	59.5
15	46 14.1	.. 16.3	7 32.7	4.7	25 26.9	7.8	59.5
16	61 13.8	16.5	21 56.4	4.8	25 19.1	8.1	59.5
17	76 13.5	16.6	36 20.2	4.9	25 11.0	8.1	59.5
18	91 13.2	S23 16.7	50 44.1	5.0	S25 02.9	8.4	59.5
19	106 12.9	16.8	65 08.1	5.1	24 54.5	8.5	59.5
20	121 12.6	17.0	79 32.2	5.1	24 46.0	8.7	59.5
21	136 12.3	.. 17.1	93 56.3	5.2	24 37.3	8.9	59.5
22	151 12.0	17.2	108 20.5	5.3	24 28.4	9.0	59.5
23	166 11.7	17.3	122 44.8	5.4	24 19.4	9.1	59.6
16 00	181 11.4	S23 17.4	137 09.2	5.5	S24 10.3	9.4	59.6
01	196 11.1	17.6	151 33.7	5.6	24 00.9	9.4	59.6
02	211 10.8	17.7	165 58.3	5.6	23 51.5	9.7	59.6
03	226 10.5	.. 17.8	180 22.9	5.8	23 41.8	9.8	59.6
04	241 10.2	17.9	194 47.7	5.8	23 32.0	9.9	59.6
05	256 09.9	18.0	209 12.5	6.0	23 22.1	10.1	59.6
06	271 09.6	S23 18.1	223 37.5	6.0	S23 12.0	10.2	59.6
07	286 09.3	18.3	238 02.5	6.1	23 01.8	10.4	59.6
S 08	301 09.0	18.4	252 27.6	6.3	22 51.4	10.6	59.6
A 09	316 08.7	.. 18.5	266 52.9	6.3	22 40.8	10.6	59.6
T 10	331 08.4	18.6	281 18.2	6.4	22 30.2	10.9	59.6
U 11	346 08.1	18.7	295 43.6	6.5	22 19.3	10.9	59.6
R 12	1 07.7	S23 18.8	310 09.1	6.6	S22 08.4	11.1	59.6
D 13	16 07.4	18.9	324 34.7	6.7	21 57.3	11.3	59.6
A 14	31 07.1	19.0	339 00.4	6.8	21 46.0	11.3	59.6
Y 15	46 06.8	.. 19.2	353 26.2	6.9	21 34.7	11.5	59.6
16	61 06.5	19.3	7 52.1	7.0	21 23.2	11.7	59.6
17	76 06.2	19.4	22 18.1	7.1	21 11.5	11.7	59.6
18	91 05.9	S23 19.5	36 44.2	7.2	S20 59.8	11.9	59.6
19	106 05.6	19.6	51 10.4	7.3	20 47.9	12.0	59.6
20	121 05.3	19.7	65 36.7	7.4	20 35.9	12.2	59.6
21	136 05.0	.. 19.8	80 03.1	7.5	20 23.7	12.2	59.6
22	151 04.7	19.9	94 29.6	7.6	20 11.5	12.4	59.6
23	166 04.4	20.0	108 56.2	7.7	19 59.1	12.5	59.6
17 00	181 04.1	S23 20.1	123 22.9	7.8	S19 46.6	12.6	59.6
01	196 03.8	20.2	137 49.7	7.9	19 34.0	12.8	59.6
02	211 03.5	20.3	152 16.6	8.0	19 21.2	12.8	59.6
03	226 03.2	.. 20.4	166 43.6	8.0	19 08.4	13.0	59.6
04	241 02.9	20.5	181 10.6	8.2	18 55.4	13.1	59.6
05	256 02.6	20.6	195 37.8	8.3	18 42.3	13.1	59.6
06	271 02.3	S23 20.7	210 05.1	8.4	S18 29.2	13.3	59.6
07	286 02.0	20.8	224 32.5	8.4	18 15.9	13.4	59.6
08	301 01.7	20.9	238 59.9	8.6	18 02.5	13.5	59.6
S 09	316 01.3	.. 21.0	253 27.5	8.6	17 49.0	13.6	59.6
U 10	331 01.0	21.1	267 55.1	8.8	17 35.4	13.7	59.6
N 11	346 00.7	21.1	282 22.9	8.8	17 21.7	13.8	59.6
D 12	1 00.4	S23 21.2	296 50.7	9.0	S17 07.9	13.9	59.6
A 13	16 00.1	21.3	311 18.7	9.0	16 54.0	13.9	59.6
Y 14	30 59.8	21.4	325 46.7	9.1	16 40.1	14.1	59.6
15	45 59.5	.. 21.5	340 14.8	9.2	16 26.0	14.2	59.5
16	60 59.2	21.6	354 43.0	9.3	16 11.8	14.2	59.5
17	75 58.9	21.7	9 11.3	9.4	15 57.6	14.3	59.5
18	90 58.6	S23 21.8	23 39.7	9.5	S15 43.3	14.5	59.5
19	105 58.3	21.9	38 08.2	9.6	15 28.8	14.5	59.5
20	120 58.0	21.9	52 36.8	9.6	15 14.3	14.5	59.5
21	135 57.7	.. 22.0	67 05.4	9.8	14 59.8	14.7	59.5
22	150 57.4	22.1	81 34.2	9.8	14 45.1	14.7	59.5
23	165 57.1	22.2	96 03.0	9.9	S14 30.4	14.8	59.5
	SD 16.3	d 0.1	SD 16.2		16.2		16.2

Lat.	Twilight Naut.	Twilight Civil	Sunrise	Moonrise 15	16	17	18
°	h m	h m	h m	h m	h m	h m	h m
N 72	08 21	10 49	■	■	■	14 46	13 32
N 70	08 01	09 49	■	■	■	14 02	13 15
68	07 45	09 14	■	■	14 51	13 32	13 01
66	07 32	08 49	10 28	■	13 43	13 09	12 49
64	07 21	08 30	09 47	13 53	13 07	12 51	12 40
62	07 12	08 14	09 19	12 48	12 41	12 36	12 31
60	07 04	08 00	08 58	12 13	12 21	12 23	12 24
N 58	06 56	07 49	08 40	11 47	12 04	12 12	12 18
56	06 49	07 39	08 26	11 27	11 49	12 03	12 12
54	06 43	07 30	08 13	11 10	11 37	11 54	12 07
52	06 38	07 21	08 02	10 55	11 26	11 47	12 02
50	06 32	07 14	07 52	10 43	11 16	11 40	11 58
45	06 21	06 58	07 32	10 16	10 55	11 25	11 49
N 40	06 10	06 45	07 15	09 55	10 38	11 12	11 41
35	06 01	06 33	07 01	09 38	10 24	11 02	11 34
30	05 52	06 22	06 49	09 23	10 11	10 53	11 29
20	05 36	06 04	06 28	08 57	09 50	10 37	11 18
N 10	05 20	05 46	06 09	08 35	09 31	10 23	11 09
0	05 03	05 29	05 52	08 14	09 14	10 09	11 01
S 10	04 44	05 11	05 34	07 53	08 56	09 56	10 52
20	04 22	04 51	05 15	07 31	08 37	09 42	10 43
30	03 53	04 26	04 53	07 05	08 15	09 25	10 33
35	03 34	04 11	04 40	06 49	08 02	09 16	10 27
40	03 11	03 53	04 25	06 31	07 48	09 05	10 20
45	02 41	03 30	04 08	06 10	07 30	08 52	10 12
S 50	01 56	03 01	03 45	05 42	07 08	08 36	10 02
52	01 28	02 46	03 34	05 29	06 57	08 28	09 58
54	00 44	02 28	03 22	05 15	06 45	08 20	09 53
56	////	02 06	03 08	04 55	06 31	08 11	09 47
58	////	01 37	02 51	04 33	06 15	08 00	09 41
S 60	////	00 48	02 31	04 04	05 55	07 47	09 34

Lat.	Sunset	Twilight Civil	Twilight Naut.	Moonset 15	16	17	18
°	h m	h m	h m	h m	h m	h m	h m
N 72	■	13 02	15 30	■	■	18 24	21 26
N 70	■	14 02	15 50	■	■	19 07	21 41
68	■	14 37	16 05	■	16 22	19 35	21 52
66	13 22	15 02	16 18	■	17 28	19 56	22 02
64	14 04	15 21	16 29	15 15	18 03	20 13	22 09
62	14 32	15 37	16 39	16 19	18 28	20 27	22 16
60	14 53	15 50	16 47	16 54	18 48	20 38	22 22
N 58	15 10	16 02	16 55	17 19	19 04	20 48	22 27
56	15 25	16 12	17 01	17 39	19 18	20 57	22 31
54	15 38	16 21	17 08	17 55	19 30	21 04	22 35
52	15 49	16 29	17 13	18 09	19 40	21 11	22 39
50	15 58	16 37	17 18	18 22	19 49	21 17	22 42
45	16 16	16 53	17 30	18 47	20 09	21 30	22 49
N 40	16 36	17 06	17 40	19 07	20 24	21 41	22 55
35	16 50	17 18	17 50	19 24	20 37	21 50	23 00
30	17 02	17 29	17 58	19 38	20 49	21 58	23 04
20	17 23	17 47	18 15	20 03	21 08	22 12	23 13
N 10	17 42	18 05	18 31	20 23	21 25	22 23	23 18
0	17 59	18 22	18 48	20 43	21 41	22 34	23 24
S 10	18 17	18 40	19 07	21 02	21 56	22 45	23 30
20	18 36	19 00	19 29	21 23	22 12	22 57	23 37
30	18 58	19 25	19 58	21 46	22 31	23 10	23 44
35	19 11	19 40	20 17	22 00	22 42	23 17	23 48
40	19 26	19 58	20 40	22 16	22 54	23 26	23 52
45	19 44	20 21	21 11	22 35	23 09	23 35	23 58
S 50	20 06	20 51	21 56	22 58	23 26	23 47	24 04
52	20 17	21 06	22 23	23 09	23 35	23 53	24 07
54	20 29	21 23	23 09	23 22	23 44	23 59	24 10
56	20 43	21 46	////	23 36	23 54	24 05	00 05
58	21 00	22 15	////	23 53	24 05	00 05	00 13
S 60	21 20	23 04	////	24 13	00 13	00 19	00 21

	SUN			MOON			
Day	Eqn. of Time 00h	12h	Mer. Pass.	Mer. Pass. Upper	Lower	Age	Phase
d	m s	m s	h m	h m	h m	d	%
15	05 15	05 01	11 55	14 29	01 58	03	8
16	04 46	04 32	11 55	15 27	02 58	04	16
17	04 17	04 02	11 56	16 22	03 55	05	25

© British Crown Copyright 2022. All rights reserved.

2023 DECEMBER 18, 19, 20 (MON., TUES., WED.)

UT	ARIES GHA	VENUS −4.1 GHA	VENUS Dec	MARS +1.4 GHA	MARS Dec	JUPITER −2.7 GHA	JUPITER Dec	SATURN +0.9 GHA	SATURN Dec	STARS Name	SHA	Dec
18 MONDAY												
00	86 21.1	222 26.9	S14 24.1	190 31.0	S23 12.9	52 21.4	N12 17.7	111 38.0	S12 15.7	Acamar	315 12.1	S40 12.7
01	101 23.6	237 26.4	25.0	205 31.5	13.1	67 24.0	17.7	126 40.3	15.6	Achernar	335 20.5	S57 07.2
02	116 26.0	252 25.9	25.9	220 32.0	13.3	82 26.6	17.6	141 42.6	15.6	Acrux	173 01.2	S63 13.6
03	131 28.5	267 25.5 ..	26.7	235 32.5 ..	13.5	97 29.1 ..	17.6	156 44.9 ..	15.5	Adhara	255 06.2	S29 00.2
04	146 31.0	282 25.0	27.6	250 32.9	13.7	112 31.7	17.6	171 47.2	15.4	Aldebaran	290 40.3	N16 33.5
05	161 33.4	297 24.5	28.5	265 33.4	13.9	127 34.3	17.6	186 49.5	15.4			
06	176 35.9	312 24.0	S14 29.4	280 33.9	S23 14.1	142 36.9	N12 17.5	201 51.8	S12 15.3	Alioth	166 13.9	N55 49.5
07	191 38.4	327 23.5	30.3	295 34.4	14.3	157 39.4	17.5	216 54.1	15.2	Alkaid	152 53.0	N49 11.4
08	206 40.8	342 23.0	31.1	310 34.9	14.5	172 42.0	17.5	231 56.4	15.2	Alnair	27 34.2	S46 51.0
09	221 43.3	357 22.5 ..	32.0	325 35.4 ..	14.7	187 44.6 ..	17.5	246 58.7 ..	15.1	Alnilam	275 38.3	S 1 11.2
10	236 45.8	12 22.0	32.9	340 35.9	14.9	202 47.2	17.4	262 01.0	15.0	Alphard	217 48.4	S 8 45.7
11	251 48.2	27 21.5	33.8	355 36.4	15.1	217 49.7	17.4	277 03.3	15.0			
12	266 50.7	42 21.0	S14 34.7	10 36.8	S23 15.3	232 52.3	N12 17.4	292 05.6	S12 14.9	Alphecca	126 04.8	N26 38.0
13	281 53.2	57 20.5	35.5	25 37.3	15.5	247 54.9	17.4	307 07.9	14.8	Alpheratz	357 35.7	N29 13.5
14	296 55.6	72 20.0	36.4	40 37.8	15.7	262 57.5	17.3	322 10.2	14.8	Altair	62 01.1	N 8 55.9
15	311 58.1	87 19.5 ..	37.3	55 38.3 ..	15.9	278 00.0 ..	17.3	337 12.5 ..	14.7	Ankaa	353 07.9	S42 10.8
16	327 00.5	102 19.0	38.2	70 38.8	16.1	293 02.6	17.3	352 14.8	14.6	Antares	112 17.3	S26 29.0
17	342 03.0	117 18.5	39.0	85 39.3	16.2	308 05.2	17.3	7 17.1	14.6			
18	357 05.5	132 18.0	S14 39.9	100 39.8	S23 16.4	323 07.8	N12 17.2	22 19.3	S12 14.5	Arcturus	145 48.9	N19 03.4
19	12 07.9	147 17.5	40.8	115 40.2	16.6	338 10.3	17.2	37 21.6	14.4	Atria	107 12.9	S69 04.1
20	27 10.4	162 17.0	41.6	130 40.7	16.8	353 12.9	17.2	52 23.9	14.4	Avior	234 14.6	S59 34.9
21	42 12.9	177 16.5 ..	42.5	145 41.2 ..	17.0	8 15.5 ..	17.2	67 26.2 ..	14.3	Bellatrix	278 23.5	N 6 22.3
22	57 15.3	192 16.0	43.4	160 41.7	17.2	23 18.0	17.2	82 28.5	14.2	Betelgeuse	270 52.7	N 7 24.7
23	72 17.8	207 15.5	44.3	175 42.2	17.4	38 20.6	17.1	97 30.8	14.1			
19 TUESDAY												
00	87 20.3	222 15.0	S14 45.1	190 42.7	S23 17.6	53 23.2	N12 17.1	112 33.1	S12 14.1	Canopus	263 52.2	S52 42.4
01	102 22.7	237 14.5	46.0	205 43.1	17.8	68 25.7	17.1	127 35.4	14.0	Capella	280 22.7	N46 01.3
02	117 25.2	252 14.0	46.9	220 43.6	18.0	83 28.3	17.1	142 37.7	13.9	Deneb	49 26.8	N45 22.1
03	132 27.6	267 13.5 ..	47.7	235 44.1 ..	18.2	98 30.9 ..	17.0	157 40.0 ..	13.9	Denebola	182 05.9	N14 26.2
04	147 30.1	282 13.0	48.6	250 44.6	18.4	113 33.4	17.0	172 42.3	13.8	Diphda	348 48.1	S17 51.4
05	162 32.6	297 12.5	49.5	265 45.1	18.6	128 36.0	17.0	187 44.6	13.7			
06	177 35.0	312 12.0	S14 50.3	280 45.6	S23 18.8	143 38.6	N12 17.0	202 46.9	S12 13.7	Dubhe	193 41.9	N61 37.1
07	192 37.5	327 11.5	51.2	295 46.0	18.9	158 41.1	17.0	217 49.2	13.6	Elnath	278 02.6	N28 37.7
08	207 40.0	342 11.0	52.1	310 46.5	19.1	173 43.7	16.9	232 51.4	13.5	Eltanin	90 43.1	N51 29.1
09	222 42.4	357 10.4 ..	52.9	325 47.0 ..	19.3	188 46.3 ..	16.9	247 53.7 ..	13.5	Enif	33 39.8	N 9 59.1
10	237 44.9	12 09.9	53.8	340 47.5	19.5	203 48.8	16.9	262 56.0	13.4	Fomalhaut	15 15.6	S29 29.9
11	252 47.4	27 09.4	54.7	355 48.0	19.7	218 51.4	16.9	277 58.3	13.3			
12	267 49.8	42 08.9	S14 55.5	10 48.5	S23 19.9	233 54.0	N12 16.8	293 00.6	S12 13.3	Gacrux	171 52.8	S57 14.5
13	282 52.3	57 08.4	56.4	25 48.9	20.1	248 56.5	16.8	308 02.9	13.2	Gienah	175 44.5	S17 40.3
14	297 54.8	72 07.9	57.3	40 49.4	20.3	263 59.1	16.8	323 05.2	13.1	Hadar	148 37.7	S60 29.0
15	312 57.2	87 07.4 ..	58.1	55 49.9 ..	20.5	279 01.7 ..	16.8	338 07.5 ..	13.0	Hamal	327 52.0	N23 34.6
16	327 59.7	102 06.9	59.0	70 50.4	20.6	294 04.2	16.8	353 09.8	13.0	Kaus Aust.	83 34.1	S34 22.4
17	343 02.1	117 06.4	14 59.9	85 50.9	20.8	309 06.8	16.7	8 12.1	12.9			
18	358 04.6	132 05.8	S15 00.7	100 51.3	S23 21.0	324 09.4	N12 16.7	23 14.4	S12 12.8	Kochab	137 20.6	N74 03.2
19	13 07.1	147 05.3	01.6	115 51.8	21.2	339 11.9	16.7	38 16.7	12.8	Markab	13 30.9	N15 20.1
20	28 09.5	162 04.8	02.4	130 52.3	21.4	354 14.5	16.7	53 18.9	12.7	Menkar	314 06.8	N 4 11.0
21	43 12.0	177 04.3 ..	03.3	145 52.8 ..	21.6	9 17.1 ..	16.7	68 21.2 ..	12.6	Menkent	147 58.9	S36 29.1
22	58 14.5	192 03.8	04.2	160 53.3	21.8	24 19.6	16.6	83 23.5	12.6	Miaplacidus	221 37.9	S69 48.6
23	73 16.9	207 03.3	05.0	175 53.7	21.9	39 22.2	16.6	98 25.8	12.5			
20 WEDNESDAY												
00	88 19.4	222 02.8	S15 05.9	190 54.2	S23 22.1	54 24.7	N12 16.6	113 28.1	S12 12.4	Mirfak	308 29.1	N49 56.9
01	103 21.9	237 02.2	06.7	205 54.7	22.3	69 27.3	16.6	128 30.4	12.3	Nunki	75 49.2	S26 16.1
02	118 24.3	252 01.7	07.6	220 55.2	22.5	84 29.9	16.6	143 32.7	12.3	Peacock	53 07.6	S56 39.7
03	133 26.8	267 01.2 ..	08.4	235 55.7 ..	22.7	99 32.4 ..	16.5	158 35.0 ..	12.2	Pollux	243 18.1	N27 58.0
04	148 29.3	282 00.7	09.3	250 56.1	22.9	114 35.0	16.5	173 37.3	12.1	Procyon	244 51.5	N 5 09.8
05	163 31.7	297 00.2	10.1	265 56.6	23.0	129 37.5	16.5	188 39.5	12.1			
06	178 34.2	311 59.7	S15 11.0	280 57.1	S23 23.2	144 40.1	N12 16.5	203 41.8	S12 12.0	Rasalhague	95 59.7	N12 32.5
07	193 36.6	326 59.1	11.9	295 57.6	23.4	159 42.7	16.5	218 44.1	11.9	Regulus	207 35.2	N11 51.0
08	208 39.1	341 58.6	12.7	310 58.1	23.6	174 45.2	16.4	233 46.4	11.9	Rigel	281 04.4	S 8 10.4
09	223 41.6	356 58.1 ..	13.6	325 58.5 ..	23.8	189 47.8 ..	16.4	248 48.7 ..	11.8	Rigil Kent.	139 42.0	S60 55.8
10	238 44.0	11 57.6	14.4	340 59.0	23.9	204 50.3	16.4	263 51.0	11.7	Sabik	102 04.2	S15 45.3
11	253 46.5	26 57.1	15.3	355 59.5	24.1	219 52.9	16.4	278 53.3	11.6			
12	268 49.0	41 56.5	S15 16.1	11 00.0	S23 24.3	234 55.4	N12 16.4	293 55.6	S12 11.6	Schedar	349 31.9	N56 40.4
13	283 51.4	56 56.0	17.0	26 00.4	24.5	249 58.0	16.3	308 57.9	11.5	Shaula	96 12.0	S37 07.2
14	298 53.9	71 55.5	17.8	41 00.9	24.6	265 00.6	16.3	324 00.1	11.4	Sirius	258 26.7	S16 44.9
15	313 56.4	86 55.0 ..	18.7	56 01.4 ..	24.8	280 03.1 ..	16.3	339 02.4 ..	11.4	Spica	158 23.4	S11 17.1
16	328 58.8	101 54.4	19.5	71 01.9	25.0	295 05.7	16.3	354 04.7	11.3	Suhail	222 46.7	S43 31.5
17	344 01.3	116 53.9	20.4	86 02.3	25.2	310 08.2	16.3	9 07.0	11.2			
18	359 03.7	131 53.4	S15 21.2	101 02.8	S23 25.4	325 10.8	N12 16.3	24 09.3	S12 11.2	Vega	80 34.3	N38 48.3
19	14 06.2	146 52.9	22.1	116 03.3	25.5	340 13.3	16.2	39 11.6	11.1	Zuben'ubi	136 57.3	S16 08.4
20	29 08.7	161 52.3	22.9	131 03.8	25.7	355 15.9	16.2	54 13.9	11.0		SHA	Mer.Pass.
21	44 11.1	176 51.8 ..	23.8	146 04.3 ..	25.9	10 18.4 ..	16.2	69 16.2 ..	10.9	Venus	134 54.7	9 11
22	59 13.6	191 51.3	24.6	161 04.7	26.1	25 21.0	16.2	84 18.4	10.9	Mars	103 22.4	11 17
23	74 16.1	206 50.8	25.4	176 05.2	26.2	40 23.5	16.2	99 20.7	10.8	Jupiter	326 02.9	20 23
Mer. Pass.	18 07.7	v −0.5	d 0.9	v 0.5	d 0.2	v 2.6	d 0.0	v 2.3	d 0.1	Saturn	25 12.8	16 27

© British Crown Copyright 2022. All rights reserved.

UT	SUN GHA	SUN Dec	MOON GHA	v	MOON Dec	d	HP
d h	° ′	° ′	° ′	′	° ′	′	′
18 00	180 56.8	S23 22.3	110 31.9	10.0	S14 15.6	14.9	59.5
01	195 56.4	22.3	125 00.9	10.0	14 00.7	15.0	59.5
02	210 56.1	22.4	139 29.9	10.2	13 45.7	15.0	59.5
03	225 55.8 ..	22.5	153 59.1	10.2	13 30.7	15.1	59.5
04	240 55.5	22.6	168 28.3	10.3	13 15.6	15.2	59.5
05	255 55.2	22.7	182 57.6	10.4	13 00.4	15.2	59.5
06	270 54.9	S23 22.7	197 27.0	10.5	S12 45.2	15.3	59.5
07	285 54.6	22.8	211 56.5	10.5	12 29.9	15.4	59.5
08	300 54.3	22.9	226 26.0	10.6	12 14.5	15.4	59.4
M 09	315 54.0 ..	23.0	240 55.6	10.7	11 59.1	15.5	59.4
O 10	330 53.7	23.0	255 25.3	10.8	11 43.6	15.5	59.4
N 11	345 53.4	23.1	269 55.1	10.8	11 28.1	15.6	59.4
D 12	0 53.1	S23 23.2	284 24.9	10.9	S11 12.5	15.7	59.4
A 13	15 52.8	23.3	298 54.8	11.0	10 56.8	15.7	59.4
Y 14	30 52.5	23.3	313 24.8	11.0	10 41.1	15.7	59.4
15	45 52.1 ..	23.4	327 54.8	11.1	10 25.4	15.8	59.4
16	60 51.8	23.5	342 24.9	11.2	10 09.6	15.9	59.4
17	75 51.5	23.5	356 55.1	11.2	9 53.7	15.8	59.4
18	90 51.2	S23 23.6	11 25.3	11.3	S 9 37.9	16.0	59.4
19	105 50.9	23.7	25 55.6	11.3	9 21.9	16.0	59.4
20	120 50.6	23.7	40 25.9	11.4	9 05.9	16.0	59.3
21	135 50.3 ..	23.8	54 56.3	11.5	8 49.9	16.0	59.3
22	150 50.0	23.9	69 26.8	11.5	8 33.9	16.1	59.3
23	165 49.7	23.9	83 57.3	11.6	8 17.8	16.2	59.3
19 00	180 49.4	S23 24.0	98 27.9	11.6	S 8 01.6	16.1	59.3
01	195 49.1	24.0	112 58.5	11.7	7 45.5	16.2	59.3
02	210 48.8	24.1	127 29.2	11.7	7 29.3	16.3	59.3
03	225 48.5 ..	24.2	141 59.9	11.8	7 13.0	16.2	59.3
04	240 48.1	24.2	156 30.7	11.9	6 56.8	16.3	59.3
05	255 47.8	24.3	171 01.6	11.9	6 40.5	16.3	59.2
06	270 47.5	S23 24.3	185 32.5	11.9	S 6 24.2	16.4	59.2
07	285 47.2	24.4	200 03.4	12.0	6 07.8	16.4	59.2
T 08	300 46.9	24.4	214 34.4	12.0	5 51.4	16.4	59.2
U 09	315 46.6 ..	24.5	229 05.4	12.0	5 35.0	16.4	59.2
E 10	330 46.3	24.6	243 36.4	12.1	5 18.6	16.4	59.2
S 11	345 46.0	24.6	258 07.5	12.2	5 02.2	16.4	59.2
D 12	0 45.7	S23 24.7	272 38.7	12.1	S 4 45.8	16.5	59.2
A 13	15 45.4	24.7	287 09.8	12.3	4 29.3	16.5	59.2
Y 14	30 45.1	24.8	301 41.1	12.2	4 12.8	16.5	59.1
15	45 44.8 ..	24.8	316 12.3	12.3	3 56.3	16.5	59.1
16	60 44.4	24.9	330 43.6	12.3	3 39.8	16.5	59.1
17	75 44.1	24.9	345 14.9	12.3	3 23.3	16.6	59.1
18	90 43.8	S23 25.0	359 46.2	12.4	S 3 06.7	16.5	59.1
19	105 43.5	25.0	14 17.6	12.4	2 50.2	16.6	59.1
20	120 43.2	25.0	28 49.0	12.4	2 33.6	16.5	59.1
21	135 42.9 ..	25.1	43 20.4	12.5	2 17.1	16.6	59.1
22	150 42.6	25.1	57 51.9	12.5	2 00.5	16.5	59.0
23	165 42.3	25.2	72 23.4	12.5	1 44.0	16.6	59.0
20 00	180 42.0	S23 25.2	86 54.9	12.5	S 1 27.4	16.5	59.0
01	195 41.7	25.3	101 26.4	12.5	1 10.9	16.6	59.0
02	210 41.4	25.3	115 57.9	12.6	0 54.3	16.6	59.0
03	225 41.0 ..	25.3	130 29.5	12.6	0 37.7	16.5	59.0
04	240 40.7	25.4	145 01.1	12.5	0 21.2	16.6	59.0
05	255 40.4	25.4	159 32.6	12.6	S 0 04.6	16.5	59.0
06	270 40.1	S23 25.5	174 04.2	12.7	N 0 11.9	16.5	58.9
07	285 39.8	25.5	188 35.9	12.6	0 28.4	16.6	58.9
W 08	300 39.5	25.5	203 07.5	12.6	0 45.0	16.5	58.9
E 09	315 39.2 ..	25.6	217 39.1	12.7	1 01.5	16.5	58.9
D 10	330 38.9	25.6	232 10.8	12.6	1 18.0	16.4	58.9
N 11	345 38.6	25.6	246 42.4	12.7	1 34.4	16.5	58.9
E 12	0 38.3	S23 25.7	261 14.1	12.6	N 1 50.9	16.5	58.9
S 13	15 38.0	25.7	275 45.7	12.7	2 07.4	16.4	58.8
D 14	30 37.6	25.7	290 17.4	12.7	2 23.8	16.4	58.8
A 15	45 37.3 ..	25.8	304 49.1	12.6	2 40.2	16.4	58.8
Y 16	60 37.0	25.8	319 20.7	12.7	2 56.6	16.4	58.8
17	75 36.7	25.8	333 52.4	12.7	3 13.0	16.3	58.8
18	90 36.4	S23 25.8	348 24.1	12.6	N 3 29.3	16.4	58.8
19	105 36.1	25.9	2 55.7	12.7	3 45.7	16.3	58.8
20	120 35.8	25.9	17 27.4	12.6	4 02.0	16.2	58.7
21	135 35.5 ..	25.9	31 59.0	12.7	4 18.2	16.3	58.7
22	150 35.2	25.9	46 30.7	12.6	4 34.5	16.2	58.7
23	165 34.9	26.0	61 02.3	12.6	N 4 50.7	16.2	58.7
	SD 16.3 d 0.1		SD 16.2		16.1		16.0

Lat.	Twilight Naut.	Twilight Civil	Sunrise	Moonrise 18	19	20	21
°	h m	h m	h m	h m	h m	h m	h m
N 72	08 24	10 55	■	13 32	12 50	12 14	11 37
N 70	08 04	09 53	■	13 15	12 43	12 16	11 48
68	07 48	09 17	■	13 01	12 38	12 18	11 58
66	07 35	08 52	10 33	12 49	12 34	12 20	12 05
64	07 24	08 32	09 50	12 40	12 30	12 21	12 12
62	07 14	08 16	09 22	12 31	12 27	12 22	12 18
60	07 06	08 03	09 00	12 24	12 24	12 23	12 23
N 58	06 58	07 51	08 43	12 18	12 21	12 24	12 28
56	06 52	07 41	08 28	12 12	12 19	12 25	12 32
54	06 45	07 32	08 16	12 07	12 17	12 26	12 35
52	06 40	07 23	08 04	12 02	12 15	12 27	12 39
50	06 34	07 16	07 55	11 58	12 13	12 27	12 42
45	06 23	07 00	07 34	11 49	12 10	12 29	12 48
N 40	06 12	06 46	07 17	11 41	12 06	12 30	12 54
35	06 03	06 35	07 03	11 34	12 04	12 31	12 59
30	05 54	06 24	06 50	11 29	12 01	12 32	13 03
20	05 38	06 05	06 29	11 18	11 57	12 34	13 11
N 10	05 21	05 48	06 11	11 09	11 53	12 35	13 17
0	05 04	05 31	05 53	11 01	11 50	12 37	13 24
S 10	04 45	05 13	05 36	10 52	11 46	12 38	13 30
20	04 23	04 52	05 17	10 43	11 42	12 40	13 37
30	03 54	04 27	04 55	10 33	11 38	12 42	13 45
35	03 35	04 12	04 42	10 27	11 36	12 43	13 50
40	03 12	03 54	04 26	10 20	11 33	12 44	13 55
45	02 41	03 31	04 08	10 12	11 30	12 46	14 01
S 50	01 56	03 01	03 46	10 02	11 26	12 47	14 08
52	01 28	02 46	03 35	09 58	11 24	12 48	14 12
54	00 41	02 28	03 23	09 53	11 22	12 49	14 16
56	////	02 06	03 08	09 47	11 20	12 50	14 20
58	////	01 36	02 52	09 41	11 17	12 51	14 25
S 60	////	00 46	02 31	09 34	11 15	12 52	14 30

Lat.	Sunset	Twilight Civil	Twilight Naut.	Moonset 18	19	20	21
°	h m	h m	h m	h m	h m	h m	h m
N 72	■	12 59	15 30	21 26	23 52	26 12	02 12
N 70	■	14 01	15 50	21 41	23 54	26 03	02 03
68	■	14 36	16 06	21 52	23 56	25 56	01 56
66	13 21	15 02	16 19	22 02	23 58	25 51	01 51
64	14 03	15 21	16 30	22 09	23 59	25 46	01 46
62	14 32	15 38	16 40	22 16	24 00	00 00	01 42
60	14 53	15 51	16 48	22 22	24 01	00 01	01 38
N 58	15 11	16 03	16 55	22 27	24 02	00 02	01 35
56	15 26	16 13	17 02	22 31	24 03	00 03	01 33
54	15 38	16 22	17 08	22 35	24 04	00 04	01 30
52	15 49	16 30	17 14	22 39	24 04	00 04	01 28
50	15 59	16 38	17 19	22 42	24 05	00 05	01 26
45	16 20	16 54	17 31	22 49	24 06	00 06	01 22
N 40	16 37	17 07	17 42	22 55	24 07	00 07	01 18
35	16 51	17 19	17 51	23 00	24 08	00 08	01 15
30	17 03	17 30	18 00	23 04	24 09	00 09	01 12
20	17 25	17 49	18 16	23 12	24 10	00 10	01 07
N 10	17 43	18 06	18 32	23 18	24 11	00 11	01 03
0	18 01	18 23	18 49	23 24	24 12	00 12	00 59
S 10	18 18	18 41	19 08	23 30	24 13	00 13	00 55
20	18 37	19 02	19 31	23 37	24 14	00 14	00 51
30	18 59	19 27	20 00	23 44	24 15	00 15	00 46
35	19 12	19 42	20 19	23 48	24 16	00 16	00 43
40	19 27	20 00	20 42	23 52	24 17	00 17	00 40
45	19 45	20 23	21 13	23 58	24 18	00 18	00 37
S 50	20 08	20 53	21 58	24 04	00 04	00 19	00 33
52	20 19	21 08	22 26	24 07	00 07	00 19	00 31
54	20 31	21 26	23 13	24 10	00 10	00 19	00 29
56	20 46	21 48	////	00 05	00 13	00 20	00 24
58	21 02	22 18	////	00 13	00 17	00 21	00 24
S 60	21 23	23 09	////	00 21	00 21	00 21	00 21

	SUN Eqn. of Time 00h	SUN Eqn. of Time 12h	SUN Mer. Pass.	MOON Mer. Pass. Upper	MOON Mer. Pass. Lower	Age	Phase
Day	m s	m s	h m	h m	h m	d	%
18	03 48	03 33	11 56	17 13	04 48	06	36
19	03 18	03 03	11 57	18 01	05 37	07	47
20	02 49	02 34	11 57	18 48	06 24	08	58

© British Crown Copyright 2022. All rights reserved.

2023 DECEMBER 21, 22, 23 (THURS., FRI., SAT.)

UT	ARIES GHA	VENUS −4.1 GHA	Dec	MARS +1.4 GHA	Dec	JUPITER −2.7 GHA	Dec	SATURN +0.9 GHA	Dec	STARS Name	SHA	Dec
d h	° ′	° ′	° ′	° ′	° ′	° ′	° ′	° ′	° ′		° ′	° ′
21 00	89 18.5	221 50.2	S15 26.3	191 05.7	S23 26.4	55 26.1	N12 16.2	114 23.0	S12 10.7	Acamar	315 12.1	S40 12.7
01	104 21.0	236 49.7	27.1	206 06.2	26.6	70 28.7	16.1	129 25.3	10.7	Achernar	335 20.6	S57 07.2
02	119 23.5	251 49.2	28.0	221 06.6	26.8	85 31.2	16.1	144 27.6	10.6	Acrux	173 01.2	S63 13.6
03	134 25.9	266 48.6 . .	28.8	236 07.1 . .	26.9	100 33.8 . .	16.1	159 29.9 . .	10.5	Adhara	255 06.2	S29 00.2
04	149 28.4	281 48.1	29.7	251 07.6	27.1	115 36.3	16.1	174 32.2	10.4	Aldebaran	290 40.3	N16 33.5
05	164 30.9	296 47.6	30.5	266 08.1	27.3	130 38.9	16.1	189 34.5	10.4			
T 06	179 33.3	311 47.0	S15 31.3	281 08.5	S23 27.4	145 41.4	N12 16.1	204 36.7	S12 10.3	Alioth	166 13.9	N55 49.5
H 07	194 35.8	326 46.5	32.2	296 09.0	27.6	160 44.0	16.0	219 39.0	10.2	Alkaid	152 52.9	N49 11.4
U 08	209 38.2	341 46.0	33.0	311 09.5	27.8	175 46.5	16.0	234 41.3	10.2	Alnair	27 34.2	S46 51.0
R 09	224 40.7	356 45.4 . .	33.9	326 10.0 . .	27.9	190 49.1 . .	16.0	249 43.6 . .	10.1	Alnilam	275 38.3	S 1 11.2
S 10	239 43.2	11 44.9	34.7	341 10.4	28.1	205 51.6	16.0	264 45.9	10.0	Alphard	217 48.4	S 8 45.7
D 11	254 45.6	26 44.4	35.5	356 10.9	28.3	220 54.2	16.0	279 48.2	09.9			
A 12	269 48.1	41 43.8	S15 36.4	11 11.4	S23 28.5	235 56.7	N12 16.0	294 50.5	S12 09.9	Alphecca	126 04.8	N26 37.9
Y 13	284 50.6	56 43.3	37.2	26 11.8	28.6	250 59.3	15.9	309 52.7	09.8	Alpheratz	357 35.7	N29 13.5
14	299 53.0	71 42.8	38.0	41 12.3	28.8	266 01.8	15.9	324 55.0	09.7	Altair	62 01.1	N 8 55.9
15	314 55.5	86 42.2 . .	38.9	56 12.8 . .	29.0	281 04.4 . .	15.9	339 57.3 . .	09.7	Ankaa	353 08.0	S42 10.8
16	329 58.0	101 41.7	39.7	71 13.3	29.1	296 06.9	15.9	354 59.6	09.6	Antares	112 17.3	S26 29.0
17	345 00.4	116 41.2	40.5	86 13.7	29.3	311 09.4	15.9	10 01.9	09.5			
18	0 02.9	131 40.6	S15 41.4	101 14.2	S23 29.5	326 12.0	N12 15.9	25 04.2	S12 09.4	Arcturus	145 48.9	N19 03.4
19	15 05.4	146 40.1	42.2	116 14.7	29.6	341 14.5	15.9	40 06.4	09.4	Atria	107 12.9	S69 04.1
20	30 07.8	161 39.5	43.0	131 15.2	29.8	356 17.1	15.8	55 08.7	09.3	Avior	234 14.6	S59 34.9
21	45 10.3	176 39.0 . .	43.9	146 15.6 . .	30.0	11 19.6 . .	15.8	70 11.0 . .	09.2	Bellatrix	278 23.5	N 6 22.3
22	60 12.7	191 38.5	44.7	161 16.1	30.1	26 22.2	15.8	85 13.3	09.2	Betelgeuse	270 52.7	N 7 24.7
23	75 15.2	206 37.9	45.5	176 16.6	30.3	41 24.7	15.8	100 15.6	09.1			
22 00	90 17.7	221 37.4	S15 46.4	191 17.0	S23 30.5	56 27.3	N12 15.8	115 17.9	S12 09.0	Canopus	263 52.2	S52 42.4
01	105 20.1	236 36.8	47.2	206 17.5	30.6	71 29.8	15.8	130 20.1	08.9	Capella	280 22.7	N46 01.4
02	120 22.6	251 36.3	48.0	221 18.0	30.8	86 32.4	15.8	145 22.4	08.9	Deneb	49 26.8	N45 22.0
03	135 25.1	266 35.8 . .	48.9	236 18.5 . .	30.9	101 34.9 . .	15.7	160 24.7 . .	08.8	Denebola	182 25.8	N14 26.2
04	150 27.5	281 35.2	49.7	251 18.9	31.1	116 37.4	15.7	175 27.0	08.7	Diphda	348 48.1	S17 51.4
05	165 30.0	296 34.7	50.5	266 19.4	31.3	131 40.0	15.7	190 29.3	08.6			
F 06	180 32.5	311 34.1	S15 51.3	281 19.9	S23 31.4	146 42.5	N12 15.7	205 31.6	S12 08.6	Dubhe	193 41.9	N61 37.1
R 07	195 34.9	326 33.6	52.2	296 20.3	31.6	161 45.1	15.7	220 33.8	08.5	Elnath	278 02.6	N28 37.7
I 08	210 37.4	341 33.0	53.0	311 20.8	31.7	176 47.6	15.7	235 36.1	08.4	Eltanin	90 43.1	N51 29.1
D 09	225 39.8	356 32.5 . .	53.8	326 21.3 . .	31.9	191 50.2 . .	15.7	250 38.4 . .	08.4	Enif	33 39.9	N 9 59.1
A 10	240 42.3	11 31.9	54.6	341 21.7	32.1	206 52.7	15.6	265 40.7	08.3	Fomalhaut	15 15.6	S29 29.9
Y 11	255 44.8	26 31.4	55.5	356 22.2	32.2	221 55.2	15.6	280 43.0	08.2			
12	270 47.2	41 30.8	S15 56.3	11 22.7	S23 32.4	236 57.8	N12 15.6	295 45.3	S12 08.1	Gacrux	171 52.7	S57 14.5
13	285 49.7	56 30.3	57.1	26 23.2	32.5	252 00.3	15.6	310 47.5	08.1	Gienah	175 44.5	S17 40.4
14	300 52.2	71 29.7	57.9	41 23.6	32.7	267 02.9	15.6	325 49.8	08.0	Hadar	148 37.6	S60 29.0
15	315 54.6	86 29.2 . .	58.7	56 24.1 . .	32.9	282 05.4 . .	15.6	340 52.1 . .	07.9	Hamal	327 52.0	N23 34.6
16	330 57.1	101 28.6	15 59.6	71 24.6	33.0	297 07.9	15.6	355 54.4	07.8	Kaus Aust.	83 34.1	S34 22.4
17	345 59.6	116 28.1	16 00.4	86 25.0	33.2	312 10.5	15.6	10 56.7	07.8			
18	1 02.0	131 27.5	S16 01.2	101 25.5	S23 33.3	327 13.0	N12 15.5	25 58.9	S12 07.7	Kochab	137 20.6	N74 03.1
19	16 04.5	146 27.0	02.0	116 26.0	33.5	342 15.6	15.5	41 01.2	07.6	Markab	13 30.9	N15 20.1
20	31 07.0	161 26.4	02.8	131 26.4	33.6	357 18.1	15.5	56 03.5	07.6	Menkar	314 06.8	N 4 11.0
21	46 09.4	176 25.9 . .	03.7	146 26.9 . .	33.8	12 20.6 . .	15.5	71 05.8 . .	07.5	Menkent	147 58.9	S36 29.1
22	61 11.9	191 25.3	04.5	161 27.4	34.0	27 23.2	15.5	86 08.1	07.4	Miaplacidus	221 37.8	S69 48.6
23	76 14.3	206 24.8	05.3	176 27.8	34.1	42 25.7	15.5	101 10.4	07.3			
23 00	91 16.8	221 24.2	S16 06.1	191 28.3	S23 34.3	57 28.2	N12 15.5	116 12.6	S12 07.3	Mirfak	308 29.1	N49 56.9
01	106 19.3	236 23.7	06.9	206 28.8	34.4	72 30.8	15.5	131 14.9	07.2	Nunki	75 49.2	S26 16.1
02	121 21.7	251 23.1	07.7	221 29.2	34.6	87 33.3	15.5	146 17.2	07.1	Peacock	53 07.6	S56 39.7
03	136 24.2	266 22.6 . .	08.6	236 29.7 . .	34.7	102 35.8 . .	15.4	161 19.5 . .	07.0	Pollux	243 18.0	N27 58.0
04	151 26.7	281 22.0	09.4	251 30.2	34.9	117 38.4	15.4	176 21.8	07.0	Procyon	244 51.4	N 5 09.8
05	166 29.1	296 21.4	10.2	266 30.6	35.0	132 40.9	15.4	191 24.0	06.9			
S 06	181 31.6	311 20.9	S16 11.0	281 31.1	S23 35.2	147 43.4	N12 15.4	206 26.3	S12 06.8	Rasalhague	95 59.7	N12 32.5
A 07	196 34.1	326 20.3	11.8	296 31.6	35.3	162 46.0	15.4	221 28.6	06.7	Regulus	207 35.2	N11 51.0
T 08	211 36.5	341 19.8	12.6	311 32.0	35.5	177 48.5	15.4	236 30.9	06.7	Rigel	281 04.4	S 8 10.4
U 09	226 39.0	356 19.2 . .	13.4	326 32.5 . .	35.6	192 51.0 . .	15.4	251 33.2 . .	06.6	Rigil Kent.	139 42.0	S60 55.8
R 10	241 41.5	11 18.7	14.2	341 33.0	35.8	207 53.6	15.4	266 35.4	06.5	Sabik	102 04.1	S15 45.3
D 11	256 43.9	26 18.1	15.0	356 33.4	35.9	222 56.1	15.4	281 37.7	06.5			
A 12	271 46.4	41 17.5	S16 15.8	11 33.9	S23 36.1	237 58.6	N12 15.3	296 40.0	S12 06.4	Schedar	349 32.0	N56 40.4
Y 13	286 48.8	56 17.0	16.7	26 34.4	36.2	253 01.2	15.3	311 42.3	06.3	Shaula	96 12.0	S37 07.2
14	301 51.3	71 16.4	17.5	41 34.8	36.4	268 03.7	15.3	326 44.5	06.2	Sirius	258 26.7	S16 44.9
15	316 53.8	86 15.9 . .	18.3	56 35.3 . .	36.5	283 06.2 . .	15.3	341 46.8 . .	06.2	Spica	158 23.4	S11 17.1
16	331 56.2	101 15.3	19.1	71 35.8	36.7	298 08.8	15.3	356 49.1	06.1	Suhail	222 46.6	S43 31.5
17	346 58.7	116 14.7	19.9	86 36.2	36.8	313 11.3	15.3	11 51.4	06.0			
18	2 01.2	131 14.2	S16 20.7	101 36.7	S23 37.0	328 13.8	N12 15.3	26 53.7	S12 05.9	Vega	80 34.3	N38 48.3
19	17 03.6	146 13.6	21.5	116 37.2	37.1	343 16.4	15.3	41 55.9	05.9	Zuben'ubi	136 57.2	S16 08.4
20	32 06.1	161 13.0	22.3	131 37.6	37.3	358 18.9	15.3	56 58.2	05.8			
21	47 08.6	176 12.5 . .	23.1	146 38.1 . .	37.4	13 21.4 . .	15.3	72 00.5 . .	05.7		SHA	Mer. Pass.
22	62 11.0	191 11.9	23.9	161 38.6	37.5	28 23.9	15.3	87 02.8	05.6	Venus	131 19.7	9 14
23	77 13.5	206 11.3	24.7	176 39.0	37.7	43 26.5	15.2	102 05.0	05.6	Mars	100 59.4	11 15
	h m									Jupiter	326 09.6	20 11
Mer. Pass. 17 55.9	v −0.5	d 0.8		v 0.5	d 0.2	v 2.5	d 0.0	v 2.3	d 0.1	Saturn	25 00.2	16 16

© British Crown Copyright 2022. All rights reserved.

UT	SUN		MOON					Lat.	Twilight		Sunrise	Moonrise			
									Naut.	Civil		21	22	23	24
	GHA	Dec	GHA	v	Dec	d	HP	°	h m	h m	h m	h m	h m	h m	h m
d h	° ′	° ′	° ′	′	° ′	′	′	N 72	08 26	10 58	■■■	11 37	10 47	☐	
21 00	180 34.5	S23 26.0	75 33.9	12.6	N 5 06.9	16.1	58.7	N 70	08 06	09 55	■■■	11 48	11 13	10 06	☐
01	195 34.2	26.0	90 05.5	12.6	5 23.0	16.2	58.7	68	07 50	09 19	■■■	11 58	11 33	10 55	☐
02	210 33.9	26.0	104 37.1	12.6	5 39.2	16.0	58.7	66	07 37	08 54	10 35	12 05	11 49	11 27	10 38
03	225 33.6	.. 26.1	119 08.7	12.6	5 55.2	16.1	58.6	64	07 26	08 34	09 52	12 12	12 02	11 51	11 32
04	240 33.3	26.1	133 40.3	12.6	6 11.3	16.0	58.6	62	07 16	08 18	09 24	12 18	12 14	12 09	12 05
05	255 33.0	26.1	148 11.8	12.6	6 27.3	16.0	58.6	60	07 08	08 04	09 02	12 23	12 23	12 25	12 30
06	270 32.7	S23 26.1	162 43.4	12.5	N 6 43.3	15.9	58.6	N 58	07 00	07 53	08 45	12 28	12 32	12 38	12 49
07	285 32.4	26.1	177 14.9	12.5	6 59.2	15.9	58.6	56	06 53	07 43	08 30	12 32	12 40	12 50	13 06
08	300 32.1	26.1	191 46.4	12.4	7 15.1	15.9	58.6	54	06 47	07 33	08 17	12 35	12 46	13 00	13 20
09	315 31.8	.. 26.2	206 17.8	12.5	7 31.0	15.8	58.5	52	06 41	07 25	08 06	12 39	12 52	13 09	13 32
10	330 31.4	26.2	220 49.3	12.4	7 46.8	15.7	58.5	50	06 36	07 18	07 56	12 42	12 58	13 17	13 43
11	345 31.1	26.2	235 20.7	12.4	8 02.5	15.7	58.5	45	06 24	07 02	07 35	12 48	13 10	13 35	14 06
12	0 30.8	S23 26.2	249 52.1	12.4	N 8 18.2	15.7	58.5	N 40	06 14	06 48	07 19	12 54	13 20	13 49	14 25
13	15 30.5	26.2	264 23.5	12.3	8 33.9	15.6	58.5	35	06 04	06 36	07 04	12 59	13 28	14 01	14 40
14	30 30.2	26.2	278 54.8	12.4	8 49.5	15.6	58.5	30	05 56	06 26	06 52	13 03	13 36	14 12	14 53
15	45 29.9	.. 26.2	293 26.2	12.2	9 05.1	15.5	58.5	20	05 39	06 07	06 31	13 11	13 49	14 31	15 16
16	60 29.6	26.2	307 57.4	12.3	9 20.6	15.4	58.4	N 10	05 23	05 49	06 12	13 17	14 01	14 47	15 36
17	75 29.3	26.3	322 28.7	12.2	9 36.0	15.4	58.4	0	05 06	05 32	05 55	13 24	14 12	15 02	15 55
18	90 29.0	S23 26.3	336 59.9	12.2	N 9 51.4	15.4	58.4	S 10	04 47	05 14	05 37	13 30	14 23	15 18	16 14
19	105 28.7	26.3	351 31.1	12.2	10 06.8	15.3	58.4	20	04 24	04 53	05 18	13 37	14 35	15 34	16 35
20	120 28.3	26.3	6 02.3	12.1	10 22.1	15.2	58.4	30	03 55	04 28	04 56	13 45	14 49	15 53	16 58
21	135 28.0	.. 26.3	20 33.4	12.1	10 37.3	15.2	58.4	35	03 36	04 13	04 43	13 50	14 57	16 05	17 12
22	150 27.7	26.3	35 04.5	12.0	10 52.5	15.1	58.3	40	03 13	03 55	04 28	13 55	15 06	16 18	17 29
23	165 27.4	26.3	49 35.5	12.0	11 07.6	15.1	58.3	45	02 42	03 32	04 10	14 01	15 17	16 33	17 48
22 00	180 27.1	S23 26.3	64 06.5	12.0	N11 22.7	15.0	58.3	S 50	01 57	03 02	03 47	14 08	15 30	16 52	18 13
01	195 26.8	26.3	78 37.5	11.9	11 37.7	14.9	58.3	52	01 29	02 47	03 36	14 12	15 36	17 01	18 25
02	210 26.5	26.3	93 08.4	11.9	11 52.6	14.8	58.3	54	00 41	02 29	03 24	14 16	15 43	17 11	18 39
03	225 26.2	.. 26.3	107 39.3	11.8	12 07.4	14.8	58.3	56	////	02 07	03 10	14 20	15 51	17 23	18 54
04	240 25.9	26.3	122 10.1	11.8	12 22.2	14.8	58.2	58	////	01 37	02 53	14 25	15 59	17 36	19 13
05	255 25.6	26.3	136 40.9	11.8	12 37.0	14.6	58.2	S 60	////	00 46	02 32	14 30	16 09	17 52	19 37
06	270 25.2	S23 26.3	151 11.7	11.7	N12 51.6	14.6	58.2	Lat.	Sunset	Twilight		Moonset			
07	285 24.9	26.3	165 42.4	11.6	13 06.2	14.5	58.2			Civil	Naut.	21	22	23	24
08	300 24.6	26.3	180 13.0	11.7	13 20.7	14.4	58.2	°	h m	h m	h m	h m	h m	h m	h m
09	315 24.3	.. 26.3	194 43.7	11.5	13 35.1	14.4	58.2	N 72	■■■	12 59	15 31	02 12	04 43	☐	☐
10	330 24.0	26.3	209 14.2	11.5	13 49.5	14.3	58.1	N 70	■■■	14 02	15 51	02 03	04 19	07 11	☐
11	345 23.7	26.3	223 44.7	11.5	14 03.8	14.2	58.1	68	■■■	14 37	16 07	01 56	04 01	06 23	☐
12	0 23.4	S23 26.3	238 15.2	11.4	N14 18.0	14.1	58.1	66	13 22	15 03	16 20	01 51	03 47	05 52	08 31
13	15 23.1	26.3	252 45.6	11.4	14 32.1	14.1	58.1	64	14 04	15 23	16 31	01 46	03 35	05 30	07 37
14	30 22.8	26.3	267 16.0	11.3	14 46.2	13.9	58.1	62	14 33	15 39	16 41	01 42	03 25	05 12	07 05
15	45 22.5	.. 26.2	281 46.3	11.2	15 00.1	13.9	58.1	60	14 55	15 52	16 49	01 38	03 17	04 57	06 41
16	60 22.1	26.2	296 16.5	11.3	15 14.0	13.8	58.0	N 58	15 12	16 04	16 57	01 35	03 09	04 45	06 22
17	75 21.8	26.2	310 46.8	11.1	15 27.8	13.7	58.0	56	15 27	16 14	17 04	01 33	03 03	04 34	06 06
18	90 21.5	S23 26.2	325 16.9	11.1	N15 41.5	13.6	58.0	54	15 40	16 23	17 10	01 30	02 57	04 25	05 53
19	105 21.2	26.2	339 47.0	11.0	15 55.1	13.6	58.0	52	15 51	16 32	17 15	01 28	02 52	04 17	05 41
20	120 20.9	26.2	354 17.0	11.0	16 08.7	13.4	58.0	50	16 01	16 39	17 21	01 26	02 47	04 09	05 31
21	135 20.6	.. 26.2	8 47.0	10.9	16 22.1	13.4	57.9	45	16 21	16 55	17 33	01 22	02 37	03 53	05 09
22	150 20.3	26.2	23 16.9	10.9	16 35.5	13.3	57.9	N 40	16 38	17 09	17 43	01 18	02 29	03 40	04 52
23	165 20.0	26.1	37 46.8	10.8	16 48.8	13.1	57.9	35	16 52	17 21	17 52	01 15	02 22	03 29	04 37
23 00	180 19.7	S23 26.1	52 16.6	10.8	N17 01.9	13.1	57.9	30	17 05	17 31	18 01	01 12	02 15	03 20	04 25
01	195 19.3	26.1	66 46.4	10.6	17 15.0	13.0	57.9	20	17 26	17 50	18 18	01 07	02 05	03 03	04 03
02	210 19.0	26.1	81 16.0	10.7	17 28.0	12.9	57.9	N 10	17 45	18 08	18 34	01 03	01 55	02 49	03 45
03	225 18.7	.. 26.1	95 45.7	10.5	17 40.9	12.8	57.8	0	18 02	18 25	18 51	00 59	01 46	02 36	03 27
04	240 18.4	26.0	110 15.2	10.5	17 53.7	12.7	57.8	S 10	18 20	18 43	19 10	00 55	01 38	02 22	03 10
05	255 18.1	26.0	124 44.7	10.5	18 06.4	12.5	57.8	20	18 39	19 03	19 33	00 51	01 28	02 08	02 52
06	270 17.8	S23 26.0	139 14.2	10.4	N18 18.9	12.5	57.8	30	19 01	19 28	20 02	00 46	01 18	01 52	02 31
07	285 17.5	26.0	153 43.6	10.3	18 31.4	12.4	57.8	35	19 14	19 44	20 20	00 43	01 12	01 43	02 18
08	300 17.2	26.0	168 12.9	10.2	18 43.8	12.3	57.8	40	19 29	20 02	20 44	00 40	01 05	01 32	02 04
09	315 16.9	.. 25.9	182 42.1	10.2	18 56.1	12.2	57.7	45	19 47	20 25	21 14	00 37	00 57	01 20	01 48
10	330 16.6	25.9	197 11.3	10.2	19 08.3	12.0	57.7	S 50	20 10	20 54	22 00	00 33	00 48	01 05	01 27
11	345 16.2	25.9	211 40.5	10.0	19 20.3	12.0	57.7	52	20 21	21 10	22 28	00 31	00 43	00 58	01 18
12	0 15.9	S23 25.9	226 09.5	10.0	N19 32.3	11.8	57.7	54	20 33	21 28	23 15	00 29	00 39	00 51	01 07
13	15 15.6	25.8	240 38.5	10.0	19 44.1	11.8	57.7	56	20 47	21 50	////	00 26	00 33	00 42	00 54
14	30 15.3	25.8	255 07.5	9.9	19 55.9	11.6	57.6	58	21 04	22 20	////	00 24	00 27	00 32	00 40
15	45 15.0	.. 25.8	269 36.4	9.8	20 07.5	11.5	57.6	S 60	21 25	23 11	////	00 21	00 21	00 21	00 24
16	60 14.7	25.7	284 05.2	9.7	20 19.0	11.4	57.6								
17	75 14.4	25.7	298 33.9	9.7	20 30.4	11.3	57.6			SUN			MOON		
18	90 14.1	S23 25.7	313 02.6	9.6	N20 41.7	11.2	57.6	Day	Eqn. of Time		Mer.	Mer. Pass.		Age	Phase
19	105 13.8	25.7	327 31.2	9.6	20 52.9	11.0	57.5		00ʰ	12ʰ	Pass.	Upper	Lower		
20	120 13.5	25.6	341 59.8	9.5	21 03.9	10.9	57.5	d	m s	m s	h m	h m	h m	d	%
21	135 13.1	.. 25.6	356 28.3	9.4	21 14.8	10.8	57.5	21	02 19	02 04	11 58	19 35	07 11	09	69
22	150 12.8	25.6	10 56.7	9.4	21 25.6	10.7	57.5	22	01 49	01 34	11 58	20 24	07 59	10	79
23	165 12.5	25.5	25 25.1	9.3	N21 36.3	10.6	57.5	23	01 19	01 04	11 59	21 15	08 49	11	87
	SD 16.3	d 0.0	SD 15.9		15.8		15.7									

© British Crown Copyright 2022. All rights reserved.

UT	ARIES	VENUS −4.1		MARS +1.4		JUPITER −2.6		SATURN +0.9		STARS		
	GHA	GHA	Dec	GHA	Dec	GHA	Dec	GHA	Dec	Name	SHA	Dec
d h	° ′	° ′	° ′	° ′	° ′	° ′	° ′	° ′	° ′		° ′	° ′
24 00	92 16.0	221 10.8	S16 25.5	191 39.5	S23 37.8	58 29.0	N12 15.2	117 07.3	S12 05.5	Acamar	315 12.1	S40 12.7
01	107 18.4	236 10.2	26.3	206 39.9	38.0	73 31.5	15.2	132 09.6	05.4	Achernar	335 20.6	S57 07.2
02	122 20.9	251 09.6	27.1	221 40.4	38.1	88 34.1	15.2	147 11.9	05.3	Acrux	173 01.1	S63 13.6
03	137 23.3	266 09.1 . .	27.9	236 40.9 . .	38.3	103 36.6 . .	15.2	162 14.2 . .	05.3	Adhara	255 06.2	S29 00.2
04	152 25.8	281 08.5	28.7	251 41.3	38.4	118 39.1	15.2	177 16.4	05.2	Aldebaran	290 40.3	N16 33.5
05	167 28.3	296 07.9	29.5	266 41.8	38.5	133 41.6	15.2	192 18.7	05.1			
06	182 30.7	311 07.4	S16 30.3	281 42.3	S23 38.7	148 44.2	N12 15.2	207 21.0	S12 05.0	Alioth	166 13.8	N55 49.5
07	197 33.2	326 06.8	31.1	296 42.7	38.8	163 46.7	15.2	222 23.3	05.0	Alkaid	152 52.9	N49 11.4
08	212 35.7	341 06.2	31.9	311 43.2	39.0	178 49.2	15.2	237 25.5	04.9	Alnair	27 34.3	S46 50.9
S 09	227 38.1	356 05.6 . .	32.7	326 43.7 . .	39.1	193 51.7 . .	15.2	252 27.8 . .	04.8	Alnilam	275 38.3	S 1 11.2
U 10	242 40.6	11 05.1	33.5	341 44.1	39.3	208 54.3	15.2	267 30.1	04.7	Alphard	217 48.4	S 8 45.7
N 11	257 43.1	26 04.5	34.3	356 44.6	39.4	223 56.8	15.2	282 32.4	04.7			
D 12	272 45.5	41 03.9	S16 35.0	11 45.0	S23 39.5	238 59.3	N12 15.1	297 34.6	S12 04.6	Alphecca	126 04.8	N26 37.9
A 13	287 48.0	56 03.4	35.8	26 45.5	39.7	254 01.8	15.1	312 36.9	04.5	Alpheratz	357 35.7	N29 13.5
Y 14	302 50.4	71 02.8	36.6	41 46.0	39.8	269 04.4	15.1	327 39.2	04.4	Altair	62 01.1	N 8 55.9
15	317 52.9	86 02.2 . .	37.4	56 46.4 . .	39.9	284 06.9 . .	15.1	342 41.5 . .	04.3	Ankaa	353 08.0	S42 10.8
16	332 55.4	101 01.6	38.2	71 46.9	40.1	299 09.4	15.1	357 43.8	04.3	Antares	112 17.3	S26 29.0
17	347 57.8	116 01.1	39.0	86 47.3	40.2	314 11.9	15.1	12 46.0	04.2			
18	3 00.3	131 00.5	S16 39.8	101 47.8	S23 40.4	329 14.5	N12 15.1	27 48.3	S12 04.1	Arcturus	145 48.9	N19 03.4
19	18 02.8	145 59.9	40.6	116 48.3	40.5	344 17.0	15.1	42 50.6	04.1	Atria	107 12.8	S69 04.1
20	33 05.2	160 59.3	41.4	131 48.7	40.6	359 19.5	15.1	57 52.9	04.0	Avior	234 14.5	S59 34.9
21	48 07.7	175 58.7 . .	42.1	146 49.2 . .	40.8	14 22.0 . .	15.1	72 55.1 . .	03.9	Bellatrix	278 23.5	N 6 22.3
22	63 10.2	190 58.2	42.9	161 49.6	40.9	29 24.5	15.1	87 57.4	03.8	Betelgeuse	270 52.7	N 7 24.7
23	78 12.6	205 57.6	43.7	176 50.1	41.0	44 27.1	15.1	102 59.7	03.8			
25 00	93 15.1	220 57.0	S16 44.5	191 50.6	S23 41.2	59 29.6	N12 15.1	118 02.0	S12 03.7	Canopus	263 52.2	S52 42.4
01	108 17.6	235 56.4	45.3	206 51.0	41.3	74 32.1	15.1	133 04.2	03.6	Capella	280 22.7	N46 01.4
02	123 20.0	250 55.8	46.1	221 51.5	41.4	89 34.6	15.1	148 06.5	03.5	Deneb	49 26.8	N45 22.0
03	138 22.5	265 55.3 . .	46.9	236 51.9 . .	41.6	104 37.1 . .	15.1	163 08.8 . .	03.5	Denebola	182 25.8	N14 26.2
04	153 24.9	280 54.7	47.6	251 52.4	41.7	119 39.6	15.0	178 11.0	03.4	Diphda	348 48.1	S17 51.4
05	168 27.4	295 54.1	48.4	266 52.9	41.8	134 42.2	15.0	193 13.3	03.3			
06	183 29.9	310 53.5	S16 49.2	281 53.3	S23 42.0	149 44.7	N12 15.0	208 15.6	S12 03.2	Dubhe	193 41.9	N61 37.0
07	198 32.3	325 52.9	50.0	296 53.8	42.1	164 47.2	15.0	223 17.9	03.2	Elnath	278 02.6	N28 37.7
08	213 34.8	340 52.3	50.8	311 54.2	42.2	179 49.7	15.0	238 20.1	03.1	Eltanin	90 43.1	N51 29.1
M 09	228 37.3	355 51.8 . .	51.5	326 54.7 . .	42.4	194 52.2 . .	15.0	253 22.4 . .	03.0	Enif	33 39.9	N 9 59.1
O 10	243 39.7	10 51.2	52.3	341 55.2	42.5	209 54.8	15.0	268 24.7	02.9	Fomalhaut	15 15.6	S29 29.9
N 11	258 42.2	25 50.6	53.1	356 55.6	42.6	224 57.3	15.0	283 27.0	02.8			
D 12	273 44.7	40 50.0	S16 53.9	11 56.1	S23 42.7	239 59.8	N12 15.0	298 29.2	S12 02.8	Gacrux	171 52.7	S57 14.5
A 13	288 47.1	55 49.4	54.6	26 56.5	42.9	255 02.3	15.0	313 31.5	02.7	Gienah	175 44.5	S17 40.4
Y 14	303 49.6	70 48.8	55.4	41 57.0	43.0	270 04.8	15.0	328 33.8	02.6	Hadar	148 37.6	S60 29.0
15	318 52.1	85 48.2 . .	56.2	56 57.4 . .	43.1	285 07.3 . .	15.0	343 36.1 . .	02.5	Hamal	327 52.0	N23 34.6
16	333 54.5	100 47.7	57.0	71 57.9	43.3	300 09.8	15.0	358 38.3	02.5	Kaus Aust.	83 34.1	S34 22.4
17	348 57.0	115 47.1	57.7	86 58.4	43.4	315 12.4	15.0	13 40.6	02.4			
18	3 59.4	130 46.5	S16 58.5	101 58.8	S23 43.5	330 14.9	N12 15.0	28 42.9	S12 02.3	Kochab	137 20.6	N74 03.1
19	19 01.9	145 45.9	16 59.3	116 59.3	43.6	345 17.4	15.0	43 45.1	02.2	Markab	13 30.9	N15 20.1
20	34 04.4	160 45.3	17 00.1	131 59.7	43.8	0 19.9	15.0	58 47.4	02.2	Menkar	314 06.8	N 4 11.0
21	49 06.8	175 44.7 . .	00.8	147 00.2 . .	43.9	15 22.4 . .	15.0	73 49.7 . .	02.1	Menkent	147 58.9	S36 29.1
22	64 09.3	190 44.1	01.6	162 00.6	44.0	30 24.9	15.0	88 52.0	02.0	Miaplacidus	221 37.8	S69 48.6
23	79 11.8	205 43.5	02.4	177 01.1	44.1	45 27.4	15.0	103 54.2	01.9			
26 00	94 14.2	220 42.9	S17 03.1	192 01.6	S23 44.3	60 29.9	N12 15.0	118 56.5	S12 01.9	Mirfak	308 29.1	N49 56.9
01	109 16.7	235 42.3	03.9	207 02.0	44.4	75 32.5	15.0	133 58.8	01.8	Nunki	75 49.2	S26 16.1
02	124 19.2	250 41.7	04.7	222 02.5	44.5	90 35.0	15.0	149 01.0	01.7	Peacock	53 07.6	S56 39.7
03	139 21.6	265 41.1 . .	05.4	237 02.9 . .	44.6	105 37.5 . .	15.0	164 03.3 . .	01.6	Pollux	243 18.0	N27 58.0
04	154 24.1	280 40.6	06.2	252 03.4	44.8	120 40.0	15.0	179 05.6	01.5	Procyon	244 51.4	N 5 09.8
05	169 26.6	295 40.0	07.0	267 03.8	44.9	135 42.5	15.0	194 07.9	01.5			
06	184 29.0	310 39.4	S17 07.8	282 04.3	S23 45.0	150 45.0	N12 15.0	209 10.1	S12 01.4	Rasalhague	95 59.7	N12 32.5
07	199 31.5	325 38.8	08.5	297 04.7	45.1	165 47.5	15.0	224 12.4	01.3	Regulus	207 35.2	N11 51.0
08	214 33.9	340 38.2	09.3	312 05.2	45.2	180 50.0	15.0	239 14.7	01.2	Rigel	281 04.4	S 8 10.4
T 09	229 36.4	355 37.6 . .	10.0	327 05.7 . .	45.4	195 52.5 . .	15.0	254 16.9 . .	01.2	Rigil Kent.	139 41.9	S60 55.8
U 10	244 38.9	10 37.0	10.8	342 06.1	45.5	210 55.0	15.0	269 19.2	01.1	Sabik	102 04.1	S15 45.3
E 11	259 41.3	25 36.4	11.5	357 06.6	45.6	225 57.5	14.9	284 21.5	01.0			
S 12	274 43.8	40 35.8	S17 12.3	12 07.0	S23 45.7	241 00.1	N12 14.9	299 23.8	S12 00.9	Schedar	349 32.0	N56 40.4
D 13	289 46.3	55 35.2	13.1	27 07.5	45.8	256 02.6	14.9	314 26.0	00.9	Shaula	96 12.0	S37 07.2
A 14	304 48.7	70 34.6	13.8	42 07.9	46.0	271 05.1	14.9	329 28.3	00.8	Sirius	258 26.7	S16 44.9
Y 15	319 51.2	85 34.0 . .	14.6	57 08.4 . .	46.1	286 07.6 . .	14.9	344 30.6 . .	00.7	Spica	158 23.3	S11 17.1
16	334 53.7	100 33.4	15.3	72 08.8	46.2	301 10.1	14.9	359 32.8	00.6	Suhail	222 46.6	S43 31.5
17	349 56.1	115 32.8	16.1	87 09.3	46.3	316 12.6	14.9	14 35.1	00.5			
18	4 58.6	130 32.2	S17 16.8	102 09.7	S23 46.4	331 15.1	N12 14.9	29 37.4	S12 00.5	Vega	80 34.3	N38 48.3
19	20 01.1	145 31.6	17.6	117 10.2	46.5	346 17.6	14.9	44 39.6	00.4	Zuben'ubi	136 57.2	S16 08.4
20	35 03.5	160 31.0	18.4	132 10.7	46.7	1 20.1	14.9	59 41.9	00.3		SHA	Mer. Pass.
21	50 06.0	175 30.4 . .	19.1	147 11.1 . .	46.8	16 22.6 . .	14.9	74 44.2 . .	00.2		° ′	h m
22	65 08.4	190 29.8	19.9	162 11.6	46.9	31 25.1	14.9	89 46.4	00.2	Venus	127 41.9	9 17
23	80 10.9	205 29.1	20.6	177 12.0	47.0	46 27.6	14.9	104 48.7	00.1	Mars	98 35.5	11 12
	h m									Jupiter	326 14.5	19 59
Mer. Pass. 17 44.1		v −0.6	d 0.8	v 0.5	d 0.1	v 2.5	d 0.0	v 2.3	d 0.1	Saturn	24 46.9	16 05

© British Crown Copyright 2022. All rights reserved.

UT	SUN GHA	SUN Dec	MOON GHA	v	MOON Dec	d	HP
d h	° ′	° ′	° ′	′	° ′	′	′
24 00	180 12.2	S23 25.5	39 53.4	9.2	N21 46.9	10.4	57.5
01	195 11.9	25.4	54 21.6	9.2	21 57.3	10.4	57.4
02	210 11.6	25.4	68 49.8	9.1	22 07.7	10.2	57.4
03	225 11.3	.. 25.4	83 17.9	9.1	22 17.9	10.0	57.4
04	240 11.0	25.3	97 46.0	8.9	22 27.9	9.9	57.4
05	255 10.7	25.3	112 13.9	9.0	22 37.8	9.9	57.4
06	270 10.4	S23 25.2	126 41.9	8.8	N22 47.7	9.6	57.3
07	285 10.0	25.2	141 09.7	8.8	22 57.3	9.6	57.3
S 08	300 09.7	25.2	155 37.5	8.8	23 06.9	9.4	57.3
U 09	315 09.4	.. 25.1	170 05.3	8.7	23 16.3	9.3	57.3
N 10	330 09.1	25.1	184 33.0	8.6	23 25.6	9.1	57.3
D 11	345 08.8	25.0	199 00.6	8.5	23 34.7	9.0	57.2
A 12	0 08.5	S23 25.0	213 28.1	8.5	N23 43.7	8.9	57.2
Y 13	15 08.2	24.9	227 55.6	8.5	23 52.6	8.7	57.2
14	30 07.9	24.9	242 23.1	8.4	24 01.3	8.6	57.2
15	45 07.6	.. 24.8	256 50.5	8.3	24 09.9	8.5	57.2
16	60 07.3	24.8	271 17.8	8.3	24 18.4	8.3	57.1
17	75 06.9	24.7	285 45.1	8.2	24 26.7	8.2	57.1
18	90 06.6	S23 24.7	300 12.3	8.2	N24 34.9	8.0	57.1
19	105 06.3	24.6	314 39.5	8.1	24 42.9	7.9	57.1
20	120 06.0	24.6	329 06.6	8.0	24 50.8	7.7	57.1
21	135 05.7	.. 24.5	343 33.6	8.1	24 58.5	7.6	57.0
22	150 05.4	24.5	358 00.7	7.9	25 06.1	7.5	57.0
23	165 05.1	24.4	12 27.6	7.9	25 13.6	7.3	57.0
25 00	180 04.8	S23 24.4	26 54.5	7.9	N25 20.9	7.1	57.0
01	195 04.5	24.3	41 21.4	7.8	25 28.0	7.0	57.0
02	210 04.2	24.3	55 48.2	7.8	25 35.0	6.9	56.9
03	225 03.9	.. 24.2	70 15.0	7.7	25 41.9	6.7	56.9
04	240 03.5	24.1	84 41.7	7.7	25 48.6	6.6	56.9
05	255 03.2	24.1	99 08.4	7.6	25 55.2	6.4	56.9
06	270 02.9	S23 24.0	113 35.0	7.6	N26 01.6	6.2	56.9
07	285 02.6	24.0	128 01.6	7.6	26 07.8	6.2	56.8
M 08	300 02.3	23.9	142 28.2	7.5	26 14.0	5.9	56.8
O 09	315 02.0	.. 23.8	156 54.7	7.5	26 19.9	5.8	56.8
N 10	330 01.7	23.8	171 21.2	7.5	26 25.7	5.6	56.8
D 11	345 01.4	23.7	185 47.7	7.4	26 31.3	5.5	56.8
A 12	0 01.1	S23 23.6	200 14.1	7.4	N26 36.8	5.4	56.7
Y 13	15 00.8	23.6	214 40.5	7.3	26 42.2	5.1	56.7
14	30 00.5	23.5	229 06.8	7.3	26 47.3	5.1	56.7
15	45 00.1	.. 23.4	243 33.1	7.3	26 52.4	4.8	56.7
16	59 59.8	23.4	257 59.4	7.3	26 57.2	4.7	56.7
17	74 59.5	23.3	272 25.7	7.3	27 01.9	4.6	56.6
18	89 59.2	S23 23.2	286 52.0	7.2	N27 06.5	4.4	56.6
19	104 58.9	23.2	301 18.2	7.2	27 10.9	4.2	56.6
20	119 58.6	23.1	315 44.4	7.2	27 15.1	4.1	56.6
21	134 58.3	.. 23.0	330 10.6	7.1	27 19.2	3.9	56.5
22	149 58.0	22.9	344 36.7	7.2	27 23.1	3.7	56.5
23	164 57.7	22.9	359 02.9	7.1	27 26.8	3.6	56.5
26 00	179 57.4	S23 22.8	13 29.0	7.1	N27 30.4	3.5	56.5
01	194 57.1	22.7	27 55.1	7.1	27 33.9	3.2	56.5
02	209 56.8	22.6	42 21.2	7.1	27 37.1	3.1	56.4
03	224 56.4	.. 22.6	56 47.3	7.1	27 40.2	3.0	56.4
04	239 56.1	22.5	71 13.4	7.1	27 43.2	2.8	56.4
05	254 55.8	22.4	85 39.5	7.1	27 46.0	2.6	56.4
06	269 55.5	S23 22.3	100 05.6	7.0	N27 48.6	2.5	56.4
07	284 55.2	22.2	114 31.6	7.1	27 51.1	2.3	56.3
T 08	299 54.9	22.2	128 57.7	7.1	27 53.4	2.1	56.3
U 09	314 54.6	.. 22.1	143 23.8	7.1	27 55.5	2.0	56.3
E 10	329 54.3	22.0	157 49.9	7.1	27 57.5	1.8	56.3
S 11	344 54.0	21.9	172 16.0	7.0	27 59.3	1.7	56.3
D 12	359 53.7	S23 21.8	186 42.0	7.1	N28 01.0	1.5	56.2
A 13	14 53.4	21.7	201 08.1	7.2	28 02.5	1.3	56.2
Y 14	29 53.1	21.7	215 34.3	7.1	28 03.8	1.2	56.2
15	44 52.7	.. 21.6	230 00.4	7.1	28 05.0	1.0	56.2
16	59 52.4	21.5	244 26.5	7.2	28 06.0	0.9	56.1
17	74 52.1	21.4	258 52.7	7.1	28 06.9	0.6	56.1
18	89 51.8	S23 21.3	273 18.8	7.2	N28 07.5	0.6	56.1
19	104 51.5	21.2	287 45.0	7.3	28 08.1	0.4	56.1
20	119 51.2	21.1	302 11.3	7.2	28 08.5	0.2	56.1
21	134 50.9	.. 21.0	316 37.5	7.3	28 08.7	0.0	56.0
22	149 50.6	20.9	331 03.8	7.2	28 08.7	0.0	56.0
23	164 50.3	20.8	345 30.0	7.4	N28 08.6	0.2	56.0
	SD 16.3	d 0.1	SD 15.6		15.5		15.3

Twilight / Sunrise / Moonrise

Lat.	Naut.	Civil	Sunrise	Moonrise 24	25	26	27
°	h m	h m	h m	h m	h m	h m	h m
N 72	08 27	10 57	■	□	□	□	□
N 70	08 07	09 55	■	□	□	□	□
68	07 51	09 20	■	□	□	□	□
66	07 38	08 55	10 35	10 38	□	□	□
64	07 27	08 35	09 53	11 32	□	□	□
62	07 17	08 19	09 25	12 05	12 01	11 54	13 04
60	07 09	08 06	09 03	12 30	12 41	13 09	14 10
N 58	07 01	07 54	08 46	12 49	13 09	13 45	14 45
56	06 55	07 44	08 31	13 06	13 31	14 11	15 10
54	06 48	07 35	08 18	13 20	13 48	14 31	15 30
52	06 43	07 26	08 07	13 32	14 04	14 48	15 47
50	06 37	07 19	07 57	13 43	14 17	15 03	16 02
45	06 26	07 03	07 37	14 06	14 44	15 33	16 31
N 40	06 15	06 49	07 20	14 24	15 06	15 56	16 54
35	06 06	06 38	07 06	14 40	15 24	16 16	17 13
30	05 57	06 27	06 53	14 53	15 40	16 32	17 29
20	05 41	06 08	06 32	15 16	16 06	17 00	17 57
N 10	05 24	05 51	06 14	15 36	16 29	17 24	18 20
0	05 07	05 34	05 56	15 55	16 50	17 47	18 42
S 10	04 48	05 16	05 39	16 14	17 12	18 09	19 04
20	04 26	04 55	05 20	16 35	17 35	18 33	19 28
30	03 57	04 30	04 58	16 58	18 02	19 02	19 55
35	03 38	04 15	04 45	17 12	18 18	19 18	20 11
40	03 15	03 57	04 31	17 29	18 37	19 38	20 30
45	02 44	03 34	04 11	17 48	18 59	20 01	20 53
S 50	01 59	03 04	03 49	18 13	19 28	20 32	21 21
52	01 31	02 49	03 38	18 25	19 42	20 47	21 35
54	00 44	02 31	03 26	18 39	19 59	21 05	21 52
56	////	02 09	03 11	18 54	20 19	21 26	22 11
58	////	01 39	02 55	19 13	20 43	21 53	22 35
S 60	////	00 48	02 34	19 37	21 17	22 31	23 07

Sunset / Twilight / Moonset

Lat.	Sunset	Civil	Naut.	Moonset 24	25	26	27
°	h m	h m	h m	h m	h m	h m	h m
N 72	■	13 03	15 33	□	□	□	□
N 70	■	14 05	15 53	□	□	□	□
68	■	14 40	16 09	□	□	□	□
66	13 25	15 05	16 22	08 31	□	□	□
64	14 07	15 25	16 33	07 37	□	□	□
62	14 35	15 41	16 43	07 05	09 04	11 08	11 55
60	14 57	15 54	16 51	06 41	08 24	09 53	10 48
N 58	15 14	16 06	16 59	06 22	07 56	09 17	10 14
56	15 29	16 16	17 05	06 06	07 35	08 52	09 48
54	15 41	16 25	17 12	05 53	07 17	08 31	09 28
52	15 53	16 33	17 17	05 41	07 02	08 14	09 11
50	16 02	16 41	17 23	05 31	06 49	08 00	08 58
45	16 23	16 57	17 34	05 09	06 23	07 30	08 27
N 40	16 40	17 11	17 45	04 52	06 02	07 07	08 04
35	16 54	17 22	17 54	04 37	05 44	06 48	07 44
30	17 07	17 33	18 03	04 25	05 29	06 31	07 28
20	17 28	17 52	18 19	04 05	05 04	06 03	07 00
N 10	17 46	18 09	18 35	03 45	04 42	05 40	06 36
0	18 04	18 26	18 52	03 27	04 21	05 18	06 14
S 10	18 21	18 44	19 11	03 10	04 01	04 55	05 51
20	18 40	19 05	19 34	02 52	03 39	04 32	05 27
30	19 02	19 30	20 03	02 31	03 14	04 04	04 59
35	19 15	19 45	20 22	02 18	03 00	03 48	04 42
40	19 30	20 03	20 45	02 04	02 42	03 29	04 23
45	19 48	20 26	21 15	01 48	02 22	03 06	03 59
S 50	20 11	20 55	22 01	01 27	01 56	02 36	03 29
52	20 22	21 10	22 29	01 18	01 44	02 22	03 14
54	20 34	21 28	23 15	01 07	01 30	02 05	02 56
56	20 48	21 51	////	00 54	01 14	01 45	02 35
58	21 05	22 20	////	00 40	00 54	01 20	02 08
S 60	21 25	23 10	////	00 24	00 30	00 47	01 30

SUN and MOON

Day	Eqn. of Time 00h	Eqn. of Time 12h	Mer. Pass.	Mer. Pass. Upper	Mer. Pass. Lower	Age	Phase
d	m s	m s	h m	h m	h m	d	%
24	00 49	00 35	11 59	22 08	09 41	12	93
25	00 20	00 05	12 00	23 04	10 36	13	97
26	00 10	00 25	12 00	24 00	11 32	14	100

© British Crown Copyright 2022. All rights reserved.

UT	ARIES GHA	VENUS −4.1 GHA	Dec	MARS +1.4 GHA	Dec	JUPITER −2.6 GHA	Dec	SATURN +0.9 GHA	Dec
d h	° ′	° ′	° ′	° ′	° ′	° ′	° ′	° ′	° ′
27 00	95 13.4	220 28.5	S17 21.4	192 12.5	S23 47.1	61 30.1	N12 14.9	119 51.0	S12 00.0
01	110 15.8	235 27.9	22.1	207 12.9	47.2	76 32.6	14.9	134 53.3	11 59.9
02	125 18.3	250 27.3	22.9	222 13.4	47.3	91 35.1	14.9	149 55.5	59.8
03	140 20.8	265 26.7 ..	23.6	237 13.8 ..	47.4	106 37.6 ..	14.9	164 57.8 ..	59.8
04	155 23.2	280 26.1	24.4	252 14.3	47.6	121 40.1	14.9	180 00.1	59.7
05	170 25.7	295 25.5	25.1	267 14.7	47.7	136 42.6	14.9	195 02.3	59.6
W 06	185 28.2	310 24.9	S17 25.9	282 15.2	S23 47.8	151 45.1	N12 14.9	210 04.6	S11 59.5
E 07	200 30.6	325 24.3	26.6	297 15.6	47.9	166 47.6	14.9	225 06.9	59.5
D 08	215 33.1	340 23.7	27.4	312 16.1	48.0	181 50.1	14.9	240 09.1	59.4
N 09	230 35.6	355 23.1 ..	28.1	327 16.5 ..	48.1	196 52.6 ..	14.9	255 11.4 ..	59.3
E 10	245 38.0	10 22.5	28.8	342 17.0	48.2	211 55.1	15.0	270 13.7	59.2
S 11	260 40.5	25 21.8	29.6	357 17.4	48.3	226 57.6	15.0	285 15.9	59.1
D 12	275 42.9	40 21.2	S17 30.3	12 17.9	S23 48.4	242 00.1	N12 15.0	300 18.2	S11 59.1
A 13	290 45.4	55 20.6	31.1	27 18.3	48.6	257 02.6	15.0	315 20.5	59.0
Y 14	305 47.9	70 20.0	31.8	42 18.8	48.7	272 05.1	15.0	330 22.7	58.9
15	320 50.3	85 19.4 ..	32.6	57 19.2 ..	48.8	287 07.6 ..	15.0	345 25.0 ..	58.8
16	335 52.8	100 18.8	33.3	72 19.7	48.9	302 10.1	15.0	0 27.3	58.7
17	350 55.3	115 18.2	34.0	87 20.1	49.0	317 12.6	15.0	15 29.5	58.7
18	5 57.7	130 17.5	S17 34.8	102 20.6	S23 49.1	332 15.1	N12 15.0	30 31.8	S11 58.6
19	21 00.2	145 16.9	35.5	117 21.0	49.2	347 17.6	15.0	45 34.1	58.5
20	36 02.7	160 16.3	36.3	132 21.5	49.3	2 20.1	15.0	60 36.3	58.4
21	51 05.1	175 15.7 ..	37.0	147 21.9 ..	49.4	17 22.6 ..	15.0	75 38.6 ..	58.4
22	66 07.6	190 15.1	37.7	162 22.4	49.5	32 25.1	15.0	90 40.9	58.3
23	81 10.1	205 14.5	38.5	177 22.8	49.6	47 27.6	15.0	105 43.1	58.2
28 00	96 12.5	220 13.8	S17 39.2	192 23.3	S23 49.7	62 30.1	N12 15.0	120 45.4	S11 58.1
01	111 15.0	235 13.2	39.9	207 23.7	49.8	77 32.6	15.0	135 47.7	58.0
02	126 17.4	250 12.6	40.7	222 24.2	49.9	92 35.1	15.0	150 49.9	58.0
03	141 19.9	265 12.0 ..	41.4	237 24.6 ..	50.0	107 37.6 ..	15.0	165 52.2 ..	57.9
04	156 22.4	280 11.4	42.1	252 25.1	50.1	122 40.1	15.0	180 54.5	57.8
05	171 24.8	295 10.7	42.9	267 25.5	50.2	137 42.5	15.0	195 56.7	57.7
T 06	186 27.3	310 10.1	S17 43.6	282 26.0	S23 50.3	152 45.0	N12 15.0	210 59.0	S11 57.6
H 07	201 29.8	325 09.5	44.3	297 26.4	50.4	167 47.5	15.0	226 01.3	57.6
U 08	216 32.2	340 08.9	45.0	312 26.9	50.5	182 50.0	15.0	241 03.5	57.5
R 09	231 34.7	355 08.3 ..	45.8	327 27.3 ..	50.6	197 52.5 ..	15.0	256 05.8 ..	57.4
S 10	246 37.2	10 07.6	46.5	342 27.8	50.7	212 55.0	15.0	271 08.1	57.3
D 11	261 39.6	25 07.0	47.2	357 28.2	50.8	227 57.5	15.0	286 10.3	57.2
A 12	276 42.1	40 06.4	S17 47.9	12 28.7	S23 50.9	243 00.0	N12 15.0	301 12.6	S11 57.2
Y 13	291 44.6	55 05.8	48.7	27 29.1	51.0	258 02.5	15.0	316 14.8	57.1
14	306 47.0	70 05.1	49.4	42 29.6	51.1	273 05.0	15.0	331 17.1	57.0
15	321 49.5	85 04.5 ..	50.1	57 30.0 ..	51.2	288 07.5 ..	15.0	346 19.4 ..	56.9
16	336 51.9	100 03.9	50.8	72 30.5	51.3	303 09.9	15.0	1 21.6	56.9
17	351 54.4	115 03.3	51.6	87 30.9	51.4	318 12.4	15.1	16 23.9	56.8
18	6 56.9	130 02.6	S17 52.3	102 31.4	S23 51.5	333 14.9	N12 15.1	31 26.2	S11 56.7
19	21 59.3	145 02.0	53.0	117 31.8	51.6	348 17.4	15.1	46 28.4	56.6
20	37 01.8	160 01.4	53.7	132 32.2	51.7	3 19.9	15.1	61 30.7	56.5
21	52 04.3	175 00.7 ..	54.4	147 32.7 ..	51.8	18 22.4 ..	15.1	76 33.0 ..	56.5
22	67 06.7	190 00.1	55.2	162 33.1	51.9	33 24.9	15.1	91 35.2	56.4
23	82 09.2	204 59.5	55.9	177 33.6	52.0	48 27.4	15.1	106 37.5	56.3
29 00	97 11.7	219 58.8	S17 56.6	192 34.0	S23 52.1	63 29.8	N12 15.1	121 39.7	S11 56.2
01	112 14.1	234 58.2	57.3	207 34.5	52.2	78 32.3	15.1	136 42.0	56.1
02	127 16.6	249 57.6	58.0	222 34.9	52.3	93 34.8	15.1	151 44.3	56.1
03	142 19.0	264 56.9 ..	58.7	237 35.4 ..	52.4	108 37.3 ..	15.1	166 46.5 ..	56.0
04	157 21.5	279 56.3	17 59.5	252 35.8	52.4	123 39.8	15.1	181 48.8	55.9
05	172 24.0	294 55.7	18 00.2	267 36.3	52.5	138 42.3	15.1	196 51.1	55.8
F 06	187 26.4	309 55.0	S18 00.9	282 36.7	S23 52.6	153 44.8	N12 15.1	211 53.3	S11 55.7
R 07	202 28.9	324 54.4	01.6	297 37.2	52.7	168 47.2	15.1	226 55.6	55.7
I 08	217 31.4	339 53.8	02.3	312 37.6	52.8	183 49.7	15.1	241 57.8	55.6
D 09	232 33.8	354 53.1 ..	03.0	327 38.0 ..	52.9	198 52.2 ..	15.2	257 00.1 ..	55.5
A 10	247 36.3	9 52.5	03.7	342 38.5	53.0	213 54.7	15.2	272 02.4	55.4
Y 11	262 38.8	24 51.9	04.4	357 38.9	53.1	228 57.2	15.2	287 04.6	55.3
12	277 41.2	39 51.2	S18 05.1	12 39.4	S23 53.2	243 59.7	N12 15.2	302 06.9	S11 55.3
13	292 43.7	54 50.6	05.8	27 39.8	53.3	259 02.1	15.2	317 09.2	55.2
14	307 46.2	69 50.0	06.6	42 40.3	53.3	274 04.6	15.2	332 11.4	55.1
15	322 48.6	84 49.3 ..	07.3	57 40.7 ..	53.4	289 07.1 ..	15.2	347 13.7 ..	55.0
16	337 51.1	99 48.7	08.0	72 41.2	53.5	304 09.6	15.2	2 15.9	54.9
17	352 53.5	114 48.0	08.7	87 41.6	53.6	319 12.1	15.2	17 18.2	54.8
18	7 56.0	129 47.4	S18 09.4	102 42.0	S23 53.7	334 14.5	N12 15.2	32 20.5	S11 54.8
19	22 58.5	144 46.8	10.1	117 42.5	53.8	349 17.0	15.2	47 22.7	54.7
20	38 00.9	159 46.1	10.8	132 42.9	53.9	4 19.5	15.2	62 25.0	54.6
21	53 03.4	174 45.5 ..	11.5	147 43.4 ..	53.9	19 22.0 ..	15.2	77 27.2 ..	54.5
22	68 05.9	189 44.8	12.2	162 43.8	54.0	34 24.5	15.3	92 29.5	54.4
23	83 08.3	204 44.2	12.9	177 44.3	54.1	49 26.9	15.3	107 31.8	54.4
Mer. Pass. 17 32.3		v −0.6 d 0.7		v 0.4 d 0.1		v 2.5 d 0.0		v 2.3 d 0.1	

STARS

Name	SHA	Dec
	° ′	° ′
Acamar	315 12.1	S40 12.7
Achernar	335 20.6	S57 07.2
Acrux	173 01.1	S63 13.6
Adhara	255 06.2	S29 00.2
Aldebaran	290 40.3	N16 33.5
Alioth	166 13.8	N55 49.5
Alkaid	152 52.9	N49 11.4
Alnair	27 34.3	S46 50.9
Alnilam	275 38.3	S 1 11.2
Alphard	217 48.4	S 8 45.7
Alphecca	126 04.8	N26 37.9
Alpheratz	357 35.7	N29 13.5
Altair	62 01.1	N 8 55.9
Ankaa	353 08.0	S42 10.8
Antares	112 17.2	S26 29.0
Arcturus	145 48.9	N19 03.3
Atria	107 12.8	S69 04.1
Avior	234 14.5	S59 35.0
Bellatrix	278 23.5	N 6 22.3
Betelgeuse	270 52.7	N 7 24.7
Canopus	263 52.2	S52 42.5
Capella	280 22.7	N46 01.4
Deneb	49 26.8	N45 22.0
Denebola	182 25.8	N14 26.2
Diphda	348 48.1	S17 51.5
Dubhe	193 41.8	N61 37.0
Elnath	278 02.6	N28 37.7
Eltanin	90 43.1	N51 29.0
Enif	33 39.9	N 9 59.1
Fomalhaut	15 15.6	S29 29.9
Gacrux	171 52.6	S57 14.5
Gienah	175 44.5	S17 40.4
Hadar	148 37.5	S60 29.0
Hamal	327 52.0	N23 34.6
Kaus Aust.	83 34.1	S34 22.4
Kochab	137 20.5	N74 03.1
Markab	13 30.9	N15 20.1
Menkar	314 06.8	N 4 11.0
Menkent	147 58.8	S36 29.1
Miaplacidus	221 37.7	S69 48.6
Mirfak	308 29.1	N49 56.9
Nunki	75 49.2	S26 16.1
Peacock	53 07.6	S56 39.6
Pollux	243 18.0	N27 58.0
Procyon	244 51.4	N 5 09.8
Rasalhague	95 59.7	N12 32.5
Regulus	207 35.2	N11 51.0
Rigel	281 04.4	S 8 10.4
Rigil Kent.	139 41.9	S60 55.8
Sabik	102 04.1	S15 45.3
Schedar	349 32.0	N56 40.4
Shaula	96 12.0	S37 07.2
Sirius	258 26.6	S16 44.9
Spica	158 23.3	S11 17.1
Suhail	222 46.6	S43 31.6
Vega	80 34.2	N38 48.3
Zuben'ubi	136 57.2	S16 08.4

	SHA	Mer. Pass.
	° ′	h m
Venus	124 01.3	9 19
Mars	96 10.8	11 10
Jupiter	326 17.6	19 47
Saturn	24 32.9	15 55

© British Crown Copyright 2022. All rights reserved.

UT	SUN GHA	SUN Dec	MOON GHA	v	MOON Dec	d	HP
d h	° ′	° ′	° ′	′	° ′	′	′
27 00	179 50.0	S23 20.7	359 56.4	7.3	N28 08.4	0.5	56.0
01	194 49.7	20.6	14 22.7	7.4	28 07.9	0.5	56.0
02	209 49.4	20.6	28 49.1	7.4	28 07.4	0.8	55.9
03	224 49.1	.. 20.5	43 15.5	7.5	28 06.6	0.9	55.9
04	239 48.8	20.4	57 42.0	7.4	28 05.7	1.0	55.9
05	254 48.4	20.3	72 08.4	7.6	28 04.7	1.2	55.9
06	269 48.1	S23 20.2	86 35.0	7.6	N28 03.5	1.4	55.9
07	284 47.8	20.1	101 01.6	7.6	28 02.1	1.5	55.8
08	299 47.5	20.0	115 28.2	7.6	28 00.6	1.7	55.8
09	314 47.2	.. 19.9	129 54.8	7.7	27 58.9	1.8	55.8
10	329 46.9	19.8	144 21.5	7.8	27 57.1	2.0	55.8
11	344 46.6	19.6	158 48.3	7.8	27 55.1	2.1	55.8
12	359 46.3	S23 19.5	173 15.1	7.8	N27 53.0	2.3	55.7
13	14 46.0	19.4	187 41.9	7.9	27 50.7	2.4	55.7
14	29 45.7	19.3	202 08.8	8.0	27 48.3	2.6	55.7
15	44 45.4	.. 19.2	216 35.8	8.0	27 45.7	2.7	55.7
16	59 45.1	19.1	231 02.8	8.1	27 43.0	2.9	55.7
17	74 44.8	19.0	245 29.9	8.1	27 40.1	3.0	55.6
18	89 44.5	S23 18.9	259 57.0	8.2	N27 37.1	3.2	55.6
19	104 44.2	18.8	274 24.2	8.3	27 33.9	3.3	55.6
20	119 43.8	18.7	288 51.5	8.3	27 30.6	3.4	55.6
21	134 43.5	.. 18.6	303 18.8	8.4	27 27.2	3.6	55.6
22	149 43.2	18.5	317 46.2	8.4	27 23.6	3.8	55.5
23	164 42.9	18.3	332 13.6	8.5	27 19.8	3.9	55.5
28 00	179 42.6	S23 18.2	346 41.1	8.6	N27 15.9	4.0	55.5
01	194 42.3	18.1	1 08.7	8.6	27 11.9	4.2	55.5
02	209 42.0	18.0	15 36.3	8.8	27 07.7	4.3	55.5
03	224 41.7	.. 17.9	30 04.1	8.8	27 03.4	4.5	55.4
04	239 41.4	17.8	44 31.9	8.8	26 58.9	4.6	55.4
05	254 41.1	17.6	58 59.7	8.9	26 54.3	4.7	55.4
06	269 40.8	S23 17.5	73 27.6	9.1	N26 49.6	4.9	55.4
07	284 40.5	17.4	87 55.7	9.0	26 44.7	5.0	55.4
08	299 40.2	17.3	102 23.7	9.2	26 39.7	5.1	55.3
09	314 39.9	.. 17.2	116 51.9	9.2	26 34.6	5.3	55.3
10	329 39.6	17.0	131 20.1	9.4	26 29.3	5.4	55.3
11	344 39.3	16.9	145 48.5	9.4	26 23.9	5.5	55.3
12	359 39.0	S23 16.8	160 16.9	9.4	N26 18.4	5.7	55.3
13	14 38.7	16.7	174 45.3	9.6	26 12.7	5.8	55.2
14	29 38.3	16.5	189 13.9	9.6	26 06.9	5.9	55.2
15	44 38.0	.. 16.4	203 42.5	9.8	26 01.0	6.0	55.2
16	59 37.7	16.3	218 11.3	9.8	25 55.0	6.2	55.2
17	74 37.4	16.2	232 40.1	9.8	25 48.8	6.3	55.2
18	89 37.1	S23 16.0	247 08.9	10.0	N25 42.5	6.4	55.1
19	104 36.8	15.9	261 37.9	10.1	25 36.1	6.6	55.1
20	119 36.5	15.8	276 07.0	10.1	25 29.5	6.7	55.1
21	134 36.2	.. 15.6	290 36.1	10.2	25 22.8	6.7	55.1
22	149 35.9	15.5	305 05.3	10.4	25 16.1	6.9	55.1
23	164 35.6	15.4	319 34.7	10.4	25 09.2	7.1	55.1
29 00	179 35.3	S23 15.2	334 04.1	10.4	N25 02.1	7.1	55.0
01	194 35.0	15.1	348 33.5	10.6	24 55.0	7.3	55.0
02	209 34.7	15.0	3 03.1	10.7	24 47.7	7.3	55.0
03	224 34.4	.. 14.8	17 32.8	10.7	24 40.4	7.5	55.0
04	239 34.1	14.7	32 02.5	10.9	24 32.9	7.6	55.0
05	254 33.8	14.6	46 32.4	10.9	24 25.3	7.7	54.9
06	269 33.5	S23 14.4	61 02.3	11.0	N24 17.6	7.8	54.9
07	284 33.2	14.3	75 32.3	11.1	24 09.8	8.0	54.9
08	299 32.9	14.1	90 02.4	11.2	24 01.8	8.0	54.9
09	314 32.6	.. 14.0	104 32.6	11.3	23 53.8	8.2	54.9
10	329 32.3	13.9	119 02.9	11.4	23 45.6	8.2	54.9
11	344 32.0	13.7	133 33.3	11.4	23 37.4	8.4	54.8
12	359 31.7	S23 13.6	148 03.7	11.6	N23 29.0	8.4	54.8
13	14 31.4	13.4	162 34.3	11.6	23 20.6	8.6	54.8
14	29 31.1	13.3	177 04.9	11.8	23 12.0	8.6	54.8
15	44 30.8	.. 13.1	191 35.7	11.8	23 03.4	8.8	54.8
16	59 30.5	13.0	206 06.5	11.9	22 54.6	8.8	54.8
17	74 30.2	12.8	220 37.4	12.0	22 45.8	9.0	54.8
18	89 29.8	S23 12.7	235 08.4	12.1	N22 36.8	9.1	54.7
19	104 29.5	12.6	249 39.5	12.2	22 27.7	9.1	54.7
20	119 29.2	12.4	264 10.7	12.2	22 18.6	9.2	54.7
21	134 28.9	.. 12.3	278 41.9	12.4	22 09.4	9.4	54.7
22	149 28.6	12.1	293 13.3	12.4	22 00.0	9.4	54.7
23	164 28.3	11.9	307 44.7	12.5	N21 50.6	9.5	54.7
	SD 16.3	d 0.1	SD 15.2		15.1		14.9

Twilight / Moonrise

Lat.	Naut.	Civil	Sunrise	Moonrise 27	28	29	30
°	h m	h m	h m	h m	h m	h m	h m
N 72	08 27	10 53	■	□	□	□	□
N 70	08 07	09 54	■	□	□	□	16 25
68	07 51	09 20	■	□	□	□	17 17
66	07 38	08 55	10 34	□	□	15 29	17 48
64	07 27	08 35	09 53	□	□	16 19	18 12
62	07 18	08 20	09 25	13 04	15 01	16 50	18 30
60	07 09	08 06	09 04	14 10	15 38	17 13	18 45
N 58	07 02	07 55	08 46	14 45	16 05	17 32	18 58
56	06 55	07 44	08 32	15 10	16 25	17 47	19 09
54	06 49	07 35	08 19	15 30	16 43	18 00	19 19
52	06 44	07 27	08 08	15 47	16 57	18 12	19 27
50	06 38	07 20	07 58	16 02	17 10	18 22	19 35
45	06 27	07 04	07 38	16 31	17 36	18 44	19 51
N 40	06 16	06 50	07 21	16 54	17 57	19 01	20 04
35	06 07	06 39	07 07	17 13	18 14	19 15	20 15
30	05 58	06 28	06 55	17 29	18 29	19 28	20 25
20	05 42	06 09	06 33	17 57	18 54	19 49	20 42
N 10	05 26	05 52	06 15	18 20	19 15	20 07	20 57
0	05 09	05 35	05 58	18 42	19 35	20 24	21 10
S 10	04 50	05 17	05 40	19 04	19 55	20 42	21 24
20	04 28	04 57	05 21	19 28	20 17	21 00	21 38
30	03 59	04 32	04 59	19 55	20 41	21 21	21 54
35	03 40	04 17	04 46	20 11	20 56	21 33	22 04
40	03 17	03 59	04 31	20 30	21 12	21 47	22 15
45	02 47	03 36	04 13	20 53	21 32	22 03	22 27
S 50	02 01	03 07	03 51	21 21	21 57	22 23	22 43
52	01 34	02 52	03 40	21 35	22 09	22 33	22 50
54	00 49	02 34	03 28	21 52	22 23	22 44	22 58
56	////	02 12	03 14	22 11	22 39	22 56	23 07
58	////	01 42	02 57	22 35	22 58	23 10	23 16
S 60	////	00 54	02 37	23 07	23 21	23 26	23 28

Sunset / Twilight / Moonset

Lat.	Sunset	Civil	Naut.	Moonset 27	28	29	30
°	h m	h m	h m	h m	h m	h m	h m
N 72	■	13 10	15 36	□	□	□	□
N 70	■	14 09	15 56	□	□	□	13 51
68	■	14 43	16 12	□	□	□	12 58
66	13 29	15 08	16 25	□	□	13 08	12 25
64	14 10	15 28	16 36	□	□	12 17	12 00
62	14 38	15 43	16 45	11 55	11 50	11 45	11 41
60	14 59	15 57	16 54	10 48	11 12	11 22	11 25
N 58	15 17	16 08	17 01	10 14	10 45	11 02	11 12
56	15 31	16 19	17 08	09 48	10 24	10 46	11 00
54	15 44	16 28	17 14	09 28	10 07	10 33	10 50
52	15 55	16 36	17 19	09 10	09 52	10 20	10 41
50	16 05	16 43	17 25	08 56	09 39	10 10	10 32
45	16 25	16 59	17 36	08 27	09 12	09 47	10 15
N 40	16 42	17 12	17 47	08 04	08 51	09 29	10 00
35	16 56	17 24	17 56	07 44	08 33	09 14	09 48
30	17 08	17 35	18 05	07 28	08 18	09 01	09 37
20	17 29	17 53	18 21	07 00	07 52	08 38	09 19
N 10	17 48	18 11	18 37	06 36	07 29	08 18	09 02
0	18 05	18 28	18 54	06 14	07 08	07 59	08 47
S 10	18 23	18 46	19 13	05 51	06 47	07 41	08 31
20	18 41	19 06	19 35	05 27	06 24	07 21	08 15
30	19 03	19 31	20 04	04 59	05 58	06 57	07 56
35	19 16	19 46	20 23	04 42	05 42	06 43	07 45
40	19 30	20 04	20 46	04 23	05 24	06 27	07 32
45	19 49	20 26	21 16	03 59	05 01	06 08	07 16
S 50	20 11	20 56	22 01	03 29	04 33	05 44	06 57
52	20 22	21 11	22 28	03 14	04 19	05 32	06 48
54	20 34	21 29	23 12	02 56	04 03	05 19	06 38
56	20 48	21 50	////	02 35	03 44	05 04	06 26
58	21 05	22 20	////	02 08	03 20	04 45	06 13
S 60	21 25	23 07	////	01 30	02 48	04 23	05 57

SUN / MOON

Day	Eqn. of Time 00h	Eqn. of Time 12h	Mer. Pass.	Mer. Pass. Upper	Mer. Pass. Lower	Age	Phase
d	m s	m s	h m	h m	h m	d	%
27	00 39	00 54	12 01	00 00	12 28	15	100
28	01 09	01 24	12 01	00 55	13 22	16	98
29	01 38	01 53	12 02	01 47	14 12	17	94

© British Crown Copyright 2022. All rights reserved.

UT	ARIES GHA	VENUS −4.0 GHA	Dec	MARS +1.4 GHA	Dec	JUPITER −2.6 GHA	Dec	SATURN +0.9 GHA	Dec	STARS Name	SHA	Dec
30 00	98 10.8	219 43.5	S18 13.6	192 44.7	S23 54.2	64 29.4	N12 15.3	122 34.0	S11 54.3	Acamar	315 12.1	S40 12.7
01	113 13.3	234 42.9	14.3	207 45.1	54.3	79 31.9	15.3	137 36.3	54.2	Achernar	335 20.6	S57 07.2
02	128 15.7	249 42.2	15.0	222 45.6	54.3	94 34.4	15.3	152 38.5	54.1	Acrux	173 01.0	S63 13.6
03	143 18.2	264 41.6	.. 15.7	237 46.0	.. 54.4	109 36.8	.. 15.3	167 40.8	.. 54.0	Adhara	255 06.1	S29 00.2
04	158 20.7	279 41.0	16.4	252 46.5	54.5	124 39.3	15.3	182 43.1	54.0	Aldebaran	290 40.3	N16 33.5
05	173 23.1	294 40.3	17.1	267 46.9	54.6	139 41.8	15.3	197 45.3	53.9			
S 06	188 25.6	309 39.7	S18 17.7	282 47.4	S23 54.7	154 44.3	N12 15.3	212 47.6	S11 53.8	Alioth	166 13.8	N55 49.5
A 07	203 28.0	324 39.0	18.4	297 47.8	54.8	169 46.7	15.3	227 49.8	53.7	Alkaid	152 52.8	N49 11.4
T 08	218 30.5	339 38.4	19.1	312 48.2	54.8	184 49.2	15.3	242 52.1	53.6	Alnair	27 34.3	S46 50.9
U 09	233 33.0	354 37.7	.. 19.8	327 48.7	.. 54.9	199 51.7	.. 15.4	257 54.4	.. 53.6	Alnilam	275 38.3	S 1 11.2
R 10	248 35.4	9 37.1	20.5	342 49.1	55.0	214 54.2	15.4	272 56.6	53.5	Alphard	217 48.3	S 8 45.7
D 11	263 37.9	24 36.4	21.2	357 49.6	55.1	229 56.6	15.4	287 58.9	53.4			
A 12	278 40.4	39 35.8	S18 21.9	12 50.0	S23 55.2	244 59.1	N12 15.4	303 01.1	S11 53.3	Alphecca	126 04.7	N26 37.9
Y 13	293 42.8	54 35.1	22.6	27 50.4	55.2	260 01.6	15.4	318 03.4	53.2	Alpheratz	357 35.7	N29 13.5
14	308 45.3	69 34.5	23.3	42 50.9	55.3	275 04.1	15.4	333 05.7	53.1	Altair	62 01.1	N 8 55.9
15	323 47.8	84 33.8	.. 24.0	57 51.3	.. 55.4	290 06.5	.. 15.4	348 07.9	.. 53.1	Ankaa	353 08.0	S42 10.8
16	338 50.2	99 33.2	24.6	72 51.8	55.5	305 09.0	15.4	3 10.2	53.0	Antares	112 17.2	S26 29.0
17	353 52.7	114 32.5	25.3	87 52.2	55.5	320 11.5	15.4	18 12.4	52.9			
18	8 55.2	129 31.9	S18 26.0	102 52.6	S23 55.6	335 14.0	N12 15.5	33 14.7	S11 52.8	Arcturus	145 48.8	N19 03.3
19	23 57.6	144 31.2	26.7	117 53.1	55.7	350 16.4	15.5	48 16.9	52.7	Atria	107 12.7	S69 04.1
20	39 00.1	159 30.6	27.4	132 53.5	55.8	5 18.9	15.5	63 19.2	52.7	Avior	234 14.5	S59 35.0
21	54 02.5	174 29.9	.. 28.1	147 54.0	.. 55.8	20 21.4	.. 15.5	78 21.5	.. 52.6	Bellatrix	278 23.5	N 6 22.3
22	69 05.0	189 29.2	28.7	162 54.4	55.9	35 23.8	15.5	93 23.7	52.5	Betelgeuse	270 52.7	N 7 24.7
23	84 07.5	204 28.6	29.4	177 54.9	56.0	50 26.3	15.5	108 26.0	52.4			
31 00	99 09.9	219 27.9	S18 30.1	192 55.3	S23 56.1	65 28.8	N12 15.5	123 28.2	S11 52.3	Canopus	263 52.2	S52 42.5
01	114 12.4	234 27.3	30.8	207 55.7	56.1	80 31.2	15.5	138 30.5	52.2	Capella	280 22.7	N46 01.4
02	129 14.9	249 26.6	31.5	222 56.2	56.2	95 33.7	15.5	153 32.7	52.2	Deneb	49 26.8	N45 22.0
03	144 17.3	264 26.0	.. 32.1	237 56.6	.. 56.3	110 36.2	.. 15.6	168 35.0	.. 52.1	Denebola	182 25.7	N14 26.2
04	159 19.8	279 25.3	32.8	252 57.0	56.4	125 38.7	15.6	183 37.3	52.0	Diphda	348 48.1	S17 51.5
05	174 22.3	294 24.6	33.5	267 57.5	56.4	140 41.1	15.6	198 39.5	51.9			
S 06	189 24.7	309 24.0	S18 34.2	282 57.9	S23 56.5	155 43.6	N12 15.6	213 41.8	S11 51.8	Dubhe	193 41.8	N61 37.0
U 07	204 27.2	324 23.3	34.8	297 58.4	56.6	170 46.1	15.6	228 44.0	51.8	Elnath	278 02.6	N28 37.7
N 08	219 29.6	339 22.7	35.5	312 58.8	56.6	185 48.5	15.6	243 46.3	51.7	Eltanin	90 43.1	N51 29.0
D 09	234 32.1	354 22.0	.. 36.2	327 59.2	.. 56.7	200 51.0	.. 15.6	258 48.5	.. 51.6	Enif	33 39.9	N 9 59.1
A 10	249 34.6	9 21.3	36.8	342 59.7	56.8	215 53.5	15.6	273 50.8	51.5	Fomalhaut	15 15.6	S29 29.9
Y 11	264 37.0	24 20.7	37.5	358 00.1	56.8	230 55.9	15.7	288 53.1	51.4			
12	279 39.5	39 20.0	S18 38.2	13 00.6	S23 56.9	245 58.4	N12 15.7	303 55.3	S11 51.3	Gacrux	171 52.6	S57 14.5
13	294 42.0	54 19.3	38.9	28 01.0	57.0	261 00.9	15.7	318 57.6	51.3	Gienah	175 44.4	S17 40.4
14	309 44.4	69 18.7	39.5	43 01.4	57.0	276 03.3	15.7	333 59.8	51.2	Hadar	148 37.5	S60 29.0
15	324 46.9	84 18.0	.. 40.2	58 01.9	.. 57.1	291 05.8	.. 15.7	349 02.1	.. 51.1	Hamal	327 52.0	N23 34.6
16	339 49.4	99 17.4	40.9	73 02.3	57.2	306 08.2	15.7	4 04.3	51.0	Kaus Aust.	83 34.1	S34 22.4
17	354 51.8	114 16.7	41.5	88 02.7	57.2	321 10.7	15.7	19 06.6	50.9			
18	9 54.3	129 16.0	S18 42.2	103 03.2	S23 57.3	336 13.2	N12 15.8	34 08.8	S11 50.8	Kochab	137 20.5	N74 03.1
19	24 56.8	144 15.4	42.9	118 03.6	57.4	351 15.6	15.8	49 11.1	50.8	Markab	13 30.9	N15 20.1
20	39 59.2	159 14.7	43.5	133 04.1	57.4	6 18.1	15.8	64 13.4	50.7	Menkar	314 06.8	N 4 11.0
21	55 01.7	174 14.0	.. 44.2	148 04.5	.. 57.5	21 20.6	.. 15.8	79 15.6	.. 50.6	Menkent	147 58.8	S36 29.1
22	70 04.1	189 13.4	44.8	163 04.9	57.6	36 23.0	15.8	94 17.9	50.5	Miaplacidus	221 37.7	S69 48.7
23	85 06.6	204 12.7	45.5	178 05.4	57.6	51 25.5	15.8	109 20.1	50.4			
1 00	100 09.1	219 12.0	S18 46.2	193 05.8	S23 57.7	66 27.9	N12 15.8	124 22.4	S11 50.3	Mirfak	308 29.1	N49 56.9
01	115 11.5	234 11.3	46.8	208 06.2	57.7	81 30.4	15.9	139 24.6	50.3	Nunki	75 49.2	S26 16.1
02	130 14.0	249 10.7	47.5	223 06.7	57.8	96 32.9	15.9	154 26.9	50.2	Peacock	53 07.6	S56 39.6
03	145 16.5	264 10.0	.. 48.1	238 07.1	.. 57.9	111 35.3	.. 15.9	169 29.1	.. 50.1	Pollux	243 18.0	N27 58.0
04	160 18.9	279 09.3	48.8	253 07.6	57.9	126 37.8	15.9	184 31.4	50.0	Procyon	244 51.4	N 5 09.8
05	175 21.4	294 08.7	49.5	268 08.0	58.0	141 40.2	15.9	199 33.6	49.9			
M 06	190 23.9	309 08.0	S18 50.1	283 08.4	S23 58.0	156 42.7	N12 15.9	214 35.9	S11 49.8	Rasalhague	95 59.7	N12 32.5
O 07	205 26.3	324 07.3	50.8	298 08.9	58.1	171 45.2	15.9	229 38.2	49.8	Regulus	207 35.1	N11 51.0
N 08	220 28.8	339 06.6	51.4	313 09.3	58.2	186 47.6	16.0	244 40.4	49.7	Rigel	281 04.4	S 8 10.5
D 09	235 31.3	354 06.0	.. 52.1	328 09.7	.. 58.2	201 50.1	.. 16.0	259 42.7	.. 49.6	Rigil Kent.	139 41.8	S60 55.8
A 10	250 33.7	9 05.3	52.7	343 10.2	58.3	216 52.5	16.0	274 44.9	49.5	Sabik	102 04.1	S15 45.3
Y 11	265 36.2	24 04.6	53.4	358 10.6	58.3	231 55.0	16.0	289 47.2	49.4			
12	280 38.6	39 04.0	S18 54.0	13 11.0	S23 58.4	246 57.5	N12 16.0	304 49.4	S11 49.3	Schedar	349 32.0	N56 40.4
13	295 41.1	54 03.3	54.7	28 11.5	58.5	261 59.9	16.0	319 51.7	49.3	Shaula	96 11.9	S37 07.2
14	310 43.6	69 02.6	55.3	43 11.9	58.5	277 02.4	16.1	334 53.9	49.2	Sirius	258 26.6	S16 44.9
15	325 46.0	84 01.9	.. 56.0	58 12.3	.. 58.6	292 04.8	.. 16.1	349 56.2	.. 49.1	Spica	158 23.3	S11 17.1
16	340 48.5	99 01.2	56.6	73 12.8	58.6	307 07.3	16.1	4 58.4	49.0	Suhail	222 46.6	S43 31.6
17	355 51.0	114 00.6	57.3	88 13.2	58.7	322 09.7	16.1	20 00.7	48.9			
18	10 53.4	128 59.9	S18 57.9	103 13.7	S23 58.7	337 12.2	N12 16.1	35 02.9	S11 48.8	Vega	80 34.2	N38 48.3
19	25 55.9	143 59.2	58.5	118 14.1	58.8	352 14.6	16.1	50 05.2	48.8	Zuben'ubi	136 57.2	S16 08.4
20	40 58.4	158 58.5	59.2	133 14.5	58.8	7 17.1	16.2	65 07.4	48.7		SHA	Mer.Pass.
21	56 00.8	173 57.9	18 59.8	148 15.0	.. 58.9	22 19.5	.. 16.2	80 09.7	.. 48.6	Venus	120 18.0	9 23
22	71 03.3	188 57.2	19 00.5	163 15.4	58.9	37 22.0	16.2	95 12.0	48.5	Mars	93 45.4	11 08
23	86 05.7	203 56.5	S19 01.1	178 15.8	59.0	52 24.5	16.2	110 14.2	48.4	Jupiter	326 18.8	19 35
Mer.Pass.	17 20.5	v −0.7	d 0.7	v 0.4	d 0.1	v 2.5	d 0.0	v 2.3	d 0.1	Saturn	24 18.3	15 44

© British Crown Copyright 2022. All rights reserved.

UT	SUN GHA	SUN Dec	MOON GHA	v	Dec	d	HP
30 00	179 28.0	S23 11.8	322 16.2	12.7	N21 41.1	9.6	54.6
01	194 27.7	11.6	336 47.9	12.7	21 31.5	9.7	54.6
02	209 27.4	11.5	351 19.6	12.7	21 21.8	9.8	54.6
03	224 27.1 ..	11.3	5 51.3	12.9	21 12.0	9.9	54.6
04	239 26.8	11.2	20 23.2	13.0	21 02.1	9.9	54.6
05	254 26.5	11.0	34 55.2	13.0	20 52.2	10.1	54.6
S 06	269 26.2 S23 10.9		49 27.2	13.2	N20 42.1	10.1	54.6
A 07	284 25.9	10.7	63 59.4	13.2	20 32.0	10.2	54.6
T 08	299 25.6	10.5	78 31.6	13.3	20 21.8	10.3	54.5
U 09	314 25.3 ..	10.4	93 03.9	13.4	20 11.5	10.4	54.5
R 10	329 25.0	10.2	107 36.3	13.4	20 01.1	10.4	54.5
D 11	344 24.7	10.1	122 08.7	13.6	19 50.7	10.5	54.5
A 12	359 24.4 S23 09.9		136 41.3	13.6	N19 40.2	10.6	54.5
Y 13	14 24.1	09.7	151 13.9	13.7	19 29.6	10.7	54.5
14	29 23.8	09.6	165 46.6	13.8	19 18.9	10.8	54.5
15	44 23.5 ..	09.4	180 19.4	13.9	19 08.1	10.8	54.5
16	59 23.2	09.2	194 52.3	13.9	18 57.3	10.9	54.4
17	74 22.9	09.1	209 25.2	14.1	18 46.4	11.0	54.4
18	89 22.6 S23 08.9		223 58.3	14.1	N18 35.4	11.0	54.4
19	104 22.3	08.7	238 31.4	14.2	18 24.4	11.1	54.4
20	119 22.0	08.6	253 04.6	14.2	18 13.3	11.2	54.4
21	134 21.7 ..	08.4	267 37.8	14.4	18 02.1	11.3	54.4
22	149 21.4	08.2	282 11.2	14.4	17 50.8	11.3	54.4
23	164 21.1	08.1	296 44.6	14.5	17 39.5	11.4	54.4
31 00	179 20.8 S23 07.9		311 18.1	14.5	N17 28.1	11.4	54.4
01	194 20.5	07.7	325 51.6	14.7	17 16.7	11.5	54.3
02	209 20.2	07.5	340 25.3	14.7	17 05.2	11.6	54.3
03	224 19.9 ..	07.4	354 59.0	14.7	16 53.6	11.6	54.3
04	239 19.6	07.2	9 32.7	14.9	16 42.0	11.7	54.3
05	254 19.3	07.0	24 06.6	14.9	16 30.3	11.8	54.3
S 06	269 19.0 S23 06.8		38 40.5	15.0	N16 18.5	11.8	54.3
U 07	284 18.7	06.7	53 14.5	15.1	16 06.7	11.9	54.3
N 08	299 18.4	06.5	67 48.6	15.1	15 54.8	11.9	54.3
D 09	314 18.1 ..	06.3	82 22.7	15.2	15 42.9	12.0	54.3
A 10	329 17.8	06.1	96 56.9	15.2	15 30.9	12.0	54.3
Y 11	344 17.5	05.9	111 31.1	15.3	15 18.9	12.1	54.3
12	359 17.2 S23 05.8		126 05.4	15.4	N15 06.8	12.2	54.3
13	14 16.9	05.6	140 39.8	15.5	14 54.6	12.2	54.2
14	29 16.6	05.4	155 14.3	15.5	14 42.4	12.2	54.2
15	44 16.3 ..	05.2	169 48.8	15.5	14 30.2	12.3	54.2
16	59 16.0	05.0	184 23.3	15.7	14 17.9	12.4	54.2
17	74 15.7	04.8	198 58.0	15.7	14 05.5	12.4	54.2
18	89 15.5 S23 04.6		213 32.7	15.7	N13 53.1	12.5	54.2
19	104 15.2	04.5	228 07.4	15.8	13 40.6	12.5	54.2
20	119 14.9	04.3	242 42.2	15.9	13 28.1	12.5	54.2
21	134 14.6 ..	04.1	257 17.1	15.9	13 15.6	12.6	54.2
22	149 14.3	03.9	271 52.0	15.9	13 03.0	12.7	54.2
23	164 14.0	03.7	286 26.9	16.1	12 50.3	12.7	54.2
1 00	179 13.7 S23 03.5		301 02.0	16.0	N12 37.6	12.7	54.2
01	194 13.4	03.3	315 37.0	16.2	12 24.9	12.8	54.2
02	209 13.1	03.1	330 12.2	16.1	12 12.1	12.8	54.2
03	224 12.8 ..	02.9	344 47.3	16.3	11 59.3	12.8	54.2
04	239 12.5	02.7	359 22.6	16.2	11 46.5	12.9	54.2
05	254 12.2	02.5	13 57.8	16.3	11 33.6	13.0	54.2
M 06	269 11.9 S23 02.3		28 33.1	16.4	N11 20.6	13.0	54.2
O 07	284 11.6	02.1	43 08.5	16.4	11 07.6	13.0	54.2
N 08	299 11.3	01.9	57 43.9	16.5	10 54.6	13.0	54.2
D 09	314 11.0 ..	01.7	72 19.4	16.5	10 41.6	13.1	54.2
A 10	329 10.7	01.5	86 54.9	16.5	10 28.5	13.2	54.2
Y 11	344 10.4	01.3	101 30.4	16.6	10 15.3	13.1	54.2
12	359 10.1 S23 01.1		116 06.0	16.6	N10 02.2	13.2	54.2
13	14 09.8	00.9	130 41.6	16.6	9 49.0	13.2	54.2
14	29 09.5	00.7	145 17.2	16.7	9 35.8	13.3	54.2
15	44 09.2 ..	00.5	159 52.9	16.8	9 22.5	13.3	54.2
16	59 08.9	00.3	174 28.7	16.7	9 09.2	13.3	54.2
17	74 08.6	23 00.1	189 04.4	16.8	8 55.9	13.4	54.2
18	89 08.3 S22 59.9		203 40.2	16.9	N 8 42.5	13.4	54.2
19	104 08.1	59.7	218 16.1	16.8	8 29.1	13.4	54.2
20	119 07.8	59.5	232 51.9	16.9	8 15.7	13.5	54.2
21	134 07.5 ..	59.3	247 27.8	16.9	8 02.2	13.4	54.2
22	149 07.2	59.1	262 03.7	17.0	7 48.8	13.6	54.2
23	164 06.9	58.9	276 39.7	17.0	N 7 35.2	13.5	54.2
	SD 16.3	d 0.2	SD 14.8		14.8		14.8

Twilight / Moonrise

Lat.	Naut.	Civil	Sunrise	30	31	1	2
N 72	08 25	10 46	■	☐	18 33	20 47	22 46
N 70	08 06	09 51	■	16 25	19 01	21 00	22 49
68	07 50	09 18	■	17 17	19 22	21 10	22 51
66	07 38	08 54	10 30	17 48	19 39	21 18	22 53
64	07 27	08 35	09 51	18 12	19 52	21 25	22 55
62	07 18	08 19	09 24	18 30	20 03	21 31	22 56
60	07 09	08 06	09 03	18 45	20 13	21 36	22 58
N 58	07 02	07 54	08 46	18 58	20 21	21 41	22 59
56	06 56	07 44	08 31	19 09	20 28	21 45	23 00
54	06 50	07 36	08 19	19 19	20 35	21 48	23 01
52	06 44	07 28	08 08	19 27	20 40	21 51	23 01
50	06 39	07 20	07 59	19 35	20 46	21 54	23 02
45	06 27	07 04	07 38	19 51	20 57	22 01	23 04
N 40	06 17	06 51	07 22	20 04	21 06	22 06	23 05
35	06 08	06 40	07 08	20 15	21 14	22 11	23 06
30	05 59	06 29	06 55	20 25	21 21	22 15	23 07
20	05 43	06 11	06 35	20 42	21 33	22 21	23 09
N 10	05 27	05 54	06 16	20 57	21 43	22 27	23 11
0	05 10	05 37	05 59	21 10	21 53	22 33	23 12
S 10	04 52	05 19	05 42	21 24	22 02	22 39	23 14
20	04 29	04 59	05 23	21 38	22 13	22 45	23 15
30	04 01	04 34	05 01	21 54	22 24	22 51	23 17
35	03 42	04 19	04 48	22 04	22 31	22 55	23 18
40	03 19	04 01	04 34	22 15	22 38	22 59	23 19
45	02 49	03 39	04 16	22 27	22 47	23 05	23 20
S 50	02 05	03 10	03 54	22 43	22 58	23 11	23 22
52	01 38	02 55	03 43	22 50	23 03	23 13	23 23
54	00 56	02 37	03 31	22 58	23 08	23 16	23 24
56	////	02 16	03 17	23 07	23 14	23 20	23 25
58	////	01 47	03 01	23 16	23 21	23 23	23 25
S 60	////	01 02	02 41	23 28	23 28	23 27	23 27

Twilight / Moonset

Lat.	Sunset	Civil	Naut.	30	31	1	2
N 72	■	13 20	15 41	☐	13 15	12 25	11 51
N 70	■	14 15	16 00	13 51	12 44	12 11	11 45
68	■	14 48	16 16	12 25	12 22	11 58	11 40
66	13 36	15 12	16 28	12 25	12 04	11 48	11 35
64	14 15	15 31	16 39	12 00	11 49	11 40	11 32
62	14 42	15 47	16 48	11 41	11 37	11 33	11 28
60	15 03	16 00	16 56	11 25	11 26	11 26	11 26
N 58	15 20	16 11	17 04	11 12	11 17	11 21	11 23
56	15 34	16 21	17 10	11 00	11 09	11 16	11 21
54	15 47	16 30	17 16	10 50	11 02	11 11	11 19
52	15 58	16 38	17 22	10 41	10 55	11 07	11 17
50	16 07	16 46	17 27	10 32	10 49	11 03	11 15
45	16 28	17 01	17 39	10 15	10 37	10 55	11 12
N 40	16 44	17 15	17 49	10 00	10 26	10 48	11 08
35	16 58	17 26	17 58	09 48	10 17	10 42	11 06
30	17 10	17 37	18 06	09 37	10 09	10 37	11 03
20	17 31	17 55	18 23	09 19	09 55	10 28	10 59
N 10	17 49	18 12	18 38	09 02	09 43	10 20	10 55
0	18 07	18 29	18 55	08 47	09 31	10 12	10 52
S 10	18 24	18 47	19 14	08 32	09 19	10 05	10 48
20	18 43	19 07	19 36	08 15	09 07	09 56	10 44
30	19 04	19 32	20 05	07 56	08 52	09 47	10 40
35	19 17	19 47	20 23	07 45	08 44	09 41	10 38
40	19 32	20 05	20 46	07 32	08 34	09 35	10 35
45	19 50	20 27	21 16	07 16	08 23	09 28	10 31
S 50	20 12	20 56	22 00	06 57	08 09	09 19	10 27
52	20 22	21 10	22 26	06 48	08 03	09 15	10 25
54	20 34	21 28	23 07	06 38	07 55	09 10	10 23
56	20 48	21 49	////	06 26	07 47	09 05	10 21
58	21 04	22 17	////	06 13	07 38	09 00	10 18
S 60	21 24	23 02	////	05 57	07 28	08 53	10 16

SUN and MOON

Day	Eqn. of Time 00h	Eqn. of Time 12h	Mer. Pass.	Mer. Pass. Upper	Mer. Pass. Lower	Age	Phase
	m s	m s	h m	h m	h m	d	%
30	02 07	02 22	12 02	14 59		18	88
31	02 36	02 50	12 03	03 21	15 42	19	82
1	03 05	03 19	12 03	04 03	16 23	20	74

© British Crown Copyright 2022. All rights reserved.

EXPLANATION

PRINCIPLE AND ARRANGEMENT

1. *Object.* The object of this Almanac is to provide, in a convenient form, the data required for the practice of astronomical navigation at sea.

2. *Principle.* The main contents of the Almanac consist of data from which the *Greenwich Hour Angle* (GHA) and the *Declination* (Dec) of all the bodies used for navigation can be obtained for any instant of *Universal Time* (UT, specifically UT1, or previously Greenwich Mean Time (GMT)).

The *Local Hour Angle* (LHA) can then be obtained by means of the formula:

$$\text{LHA} = \text{GHA} \; {- \text{ west} \atop + \text{ east}} \; \text{longitude}$$

The remaining data consist of: times of rising and setting of the Sun and Moon, and times of twilight; miscellaneous calendarial and planning data and auxiliary tables, including a list of Standard Times; corrections to be applied to observed altitude.

For the Sun, Moon, and planets, the GHA and Dec are tabulated directly for each hour of UT throughout the year. For the stars, the *Sidereal Hour Angle* (SHA) is given, and the GHA is obtained from:

$$\text{GHA Star} = \text{GHA Aries} + \text{SHA Star}$$

The SHA and Dec of the stars change slowly and may be regarded as constant over periods of several days. GHA Aries, or the Greenwich Hour Angle of the first point of Aries (the Vernal Equinox), is tabulated for each hour. Permanent tables give the appropriate increments and corrections to the tabulated hourly values of GHA and Dec for the minutes and seconds of UT.

The six-volume series of *Sight Reduction Tables for Marine Navigation* (published in U.S.A. as Pub. No. 229) has been designed for the solution of the navigational triangle and is intended for use with *The Nautical Almanac*.

Two alternative procedures for sight reduction are described on pages 277–318. The first requires the use of programmable calculators or computers, while the second uses a set of concise tables that is given on pages 286–317.

The tabular accuracy is $0\overset{\prime}{.}1$ throughout. The time argument on the daily pages of this Almanac is UT1 denoted throughout by UT. This scale may differ from the broadcast time signals (UTC) by an amount which, if ignored, will introduce an error of up to $0\overset{\prime}{.}2$ in longitude determined from astronomical observations. The difference arises because the time argument depends on the variable rate of rotation of the Earth while the broadcast time signals are based on an atomic time-scale. Step adjustments of exactly one second are made to the time signals as required (normally at 24^h on December 31 and June 30) so that the difference between the time signals and UT, as used in this Almanac, may not exceed $0\overset{s}{.}9$. Those who require to reduce observations to a precision of better than 1^s must therefore obtain the correction (DUT1) to the time signals from coding in the signal, or from other sources; the required time is given by UT1=UTC+DUT1 to a precision of $0\overset{s}{.}1$. Alternatively, the longitude, when determined from astronomical observations, may be corrected by the corresponding amount shown in the following table:

Correction to time signals	Correction to longitude
$-0\overset{s}{.}9$ to $-0\overset{s}{.}7$	$0\overset{\prime}{.}2$ to east
$-0\overset{s}{.}6$ to $-0\overset{s}{.}3$	$0\overset{\prime}{.}1$ to east
$-0\overset{s}{.}2$ to $+0\overset{s}{.}2$	no correction
$+0\overset{s}{.}3$ to $+0\overset{s}{.}6$	$0\overset{\prime}{.}1$ to west
$+0\overset{s}{.}7$ to $+0\overset{s}{.}9$	$0\overset{\prime}{.}2$ to west

© British Crown Copyright 2022. All rights reserved.

3. *Lay-out.* The ephemeral data for three days are presented on an opening of two pages: the left-hand page contains the data for the planets and stars; the right-hand page contains the data for the Sun and Moon, together with times of twilight, sunrise, sunset, moonrise and moonset.

The remaining contents are arranged as follows: for ease of reference the altitude-correction tables are given on pages A2, A3, A4, xxxiv and xxxv; calendar, Moon's phases, eclipses, and planet notes (i.e. data of general interest) precede the main tabulations. The Explanation is followed by information on standard times, star charts and list of star positions, sight reduction procedures and concise sight reduction tables, polar phenomena information and graphs, tables of increments and corrections and other auxiliary tables that are frequently used.

MAIN DATA

4. *Daily pages.* The daily pages give the GHA of Aries, the GHA and Dec of the Sun, Moon, and the four navigational planets, for each hour of UT. For the Moon, values of v and d are also tabulated for each hour to facilitate the correction of GHA and Dec to intermediate times; v and d for the Sun and planets change so slowly that they are given, at the foot of the appropriate columns, once only on the page; v is zero for Aries and negligible for the Sun, and is omitted. The SHA and Dec of the 57 selected stars, arranged in alphabetical order of proper name, are also given.

5. *Stars.* The SHA and Dec of 173 stars, including the 57 selected stars, are tabulated for each month on pages 268–273; no interpolation is required and the data can be used in precisely the same way as those for the selected stars on the daily pages. The stars are arranged in order of SHA.

The list of 173 includes all stars down to magnitude 3·0, together with a few fainter ones to fill the larger gaps. The 57 selected stars have been chosen from amongst these on account of brightness and distribution in the sky; they will suffice for the majority of observations.

The 57 selected stars are known by their proper names, but they are also numbered in descending order of SHA. In the list of 173 stars, the constellation names are always given on the left-hand page; on the facing page proper names are given where well-known names exist. Numbers for the selected stars are given in both columns.

An index to the selected stars, containing lists in both alphabetical and numerical order, is given on page xxxiii and is also reprinted on the bookmark.

6. *Increments and corrections.* The tables printed on tinted paper (pages ii–xxxi) at the back of the Almanac provide the increments and corrections for minutes and seconds to be applied to the hourly values of GHA and Dec. They consist of sixty tables, one for each minute, separated into two parts: increments to GHA for Sun and planets, Aries, and Moon for every minute and second; and, for each minute, corrections to be applied to GHA and Dec corresponding to the values of v and d given on the daily pages.

The increments are based on the following adopted hourly rates of increase of the GHA: Sun and planets, 15° precisely; Aries, 15° 02ʹ46; Moon, 14° 19ʹ0. The values of v on the daily pages are the excesses of the actual hourly motions over the adopted values; they are generally positive, except for Venus. The tabulated hourly values of the Sun's GHA have been adjusted to reduce to a minimum the error caused by treating v as negligible. The values of d on the daily pages are the hourly differences of the Dec. For the Moon, the true values of v and d are given for each hour; otherwise mean values are given for the three days on the page.

7. *Method of entry.* The UT of an observation is expressed as a day and hour, followed by a number of minutes and seconds. The tabular values of GHA and Dec, and, where necessary, the corresponding values of v and d, are taken directly from the daily pages for the day and hour of UT; this hour is always *before* the time of observation. SHA and Dec of the selected stars are also taken from the daily pages.

© British Crown Copyright 2022. All rights reserved.

The table of Increments and Corrections for the minute of UT is then selected. For the GHA, the increment for minutes and seconds is taken from the appropriate column opposite the seconds of UT; the v-correction is taken from the second part of the same table opposite the value of v as given on the daily pages. Both increment and v-correction are to be added to the GHA, except for Venus when v is prefixed by a minus sign and the v-correction is to be subtracted. For the Dec there is no increment, but a d-correction is applied in the same way as the v-correction; d is given without sign on the daily pages and the sign of the correction is to be supplied by inspection of the Dec column. In many cases the correction may be applied mentally.

8. *Examples.* (a) Sun and Moon. Required the GHA and Dec of the Sun and Moon on 2023 March 27 at $15^h\ 47^m\ 13^s$ UT.

	SUN			MOON			
	GHA	Dec	d	GHA	v	Dec	d
	° ′	° ′	′	° ′	′	° ′	′
Daily page, March 27ᵈ 15ʰ	43 39·2	N 2 39·1	1·0	330 51·0	9·2	N 26 48·7	4·2
Increments for 47ᵐ 13ˢ	11 48·3			11 16·0			
v or d corrections for 47ᵐ		+0·8			+7·3	+3·3	
Sum for March 27ᵈ 15ʰ 47ᵐ 13ˢ	55 27·5	N 2 39·9		342 14·3		N 26 52·0	

(b) Planets. Required the LHA and Dec of (i) Venus on 2023 March 27 at $13^h\ 20^m\ 58^s$ UT in longitude E $82°\ 32'$; (ii) Saturn on 2023 March 27 at $11^h\ 01^m\ 59^s$ UT in longitude W $84°\ 53'$.

	VENUS				SATURN			
	GHA	v	Dec	d	GHA	v	Dec	d
	° ′	′	° ′	′	° ′	′	° ′	′
Daily page, Mar. 27ᵈ (13ʰ)	339 39·8	−0·4	N 16 19·6	1·0 (11ʰ)	14 54·4	2·2	S 11 54·4	0·1
Increments (planets) (20ᵐ 58ˢ)	5 14·5			(01ᵐ 59ˢ)	0 29·8			
v or d corrections (20ᵐ)	−0·1		+0·3	(01ᵐ)	+0·1		+0·0	
Sum = GHA and Dec.	344 54·2		N 16 19·9		15 24·3		S 11 54·4	
Longitude (east)	+ 82 32·0			(west)	− 84 53·0			
Multiples of 360°	−360				+360			
LHA planet	67 26·2				290 31·3			

(c) Stars. Required the GHA and Dec of (i) *Aldebaran* on 2023 March 27 at $16^h\ 20^m\ 38^s$ UT; (ii) *Vega* on 2023 March 27 at $2^h\ 40^m\ 39^s$ UT.

	Aldebaran			Vega		
	GHA	Dec		GHA	Dec	
	° ′	° ′		° ′	° ′	
Daily page (SHA and Dec)	290 41·5	N 16 33·3		80 34·2	N 38 47·9	
Daily page (GHA Aries) (16ʰ)	64 49·6		(2ʰ)	214 15·1		
Increments (Aries) (20ᵐ 38ˢ)	5 10·3		(40ᵐ 39ˢ)	10 11·4		
Sum = GHA star	360 41·4			305 00·7		
Multiples of 360°	−360					
GHA star	0 41·4			305 00·7		

9. *Polaris (Pole Star) tables.* The tables on pages 274–276 provide means by which the latitude can be deduced from an observed altitude of *Polaris*, and they also give its azimuth; their use is explained and illustrated on those pages. They are based on the following formula:

$$\text{Latitude} - H_O = -p \cos h + \tfrac{1}{2}p \sin p \sin^2 h \tan(\text{latitude})$$

where

$H_O = $ Apparent altitude (corrected for refraction)

$p = $ polar distance of *Polaris* $= 90° - \text{Dec}$

$h = $ local hour angle of *Polaris* $= \text{LHA Aries} + \text{SHA}$

a_0, which is a function of LHA Aries only, is the value of both terms of the above formula calculated for mean values of the SHA ($314°\ 37'$) and Dec (N $89°\ 21'.8$) of *Polaris*, for a mean latitude of $50°$, and adjusted by the addition of a constant ($58'.8$).

© British Crown Copyright 2022. All rights reserved.

a_1, which is a function of LHA Aries and latitude, is the excess of the value of the second term over its mean value for latitude 50°, increased by a constant (0′.6) to make it always positive. a_2, which is a function of LHA Aries and date, is the correction to the first term for the variation of *Polaris* from its adopted mean position; it is increased by a constant (0′.6) to make it positive. The sum of the added constants is 1°, so that:

$$\text{Latitude} = \text{Apparent altitude (corrected for refraction)} - 1° + a_0 + a_1 + a_2$$

RISING AND SETTING PHENOMENA

10. *General.*   On the right-hand daily pages are given the times of sunrise and sunset, of the beginning and end of civil and nautical twilights, and of moonrise and moonset for a range of latitudes from N 72° to S 60°. These times, which are given to the nearest minute, are strictly the UT of the phenomena on the Greenwich meridian; they are given for every day for moonrise and moonset, but only for the middle day of the three on each page for the solar phenomena.

They are approximately the Local Mean Times (LMT) of the corresponding phenomena on other meridians; they can be formally interpolated if desired. The UT of a phenomenon is obtained from the LMT by:

$$\text{UT} = \text{LMT} \, {}^{+\ \text{west}}_{-\ \text{east}} \, \text{longitude}$$

in which the longitude must first be converted to time by the table on page i or otherwise. Interpolation for latitude can be done mentally or with the aid of Table I on page xxxii.

The following symbols are used to indicate the conditions under which, in high latitudes, some of the phenomena do not occur:

☐ Sun or Moon remains continuously above the horizon;

■ Sun or Moon remains continuously below the horizon;

//// twilight lasts all night.

Basis of the tabulations. At sunrise and sunset 16′ is allowed for semi-diameter and 34′ for horizontal refraction, so that at the times given the Sun's upper limb is on the visible horizon; all times refer to phenomena as seen from sea level with a clear horizon.

At the times given for the beginning and end of twilight, the Sun's zenith distance is 96° for civil, and 102° for nautical twilight. The degree of illumination at the times given for civil twilight (in good conditions and in the absence of other illumination) is such that the brightest stars are visible and the horizon is clearly defined. At the times given for nautical twilight, the horizon is in general not visible, and it is too dark for observation with a marine sextant.

Times corresponding to other depressions of the Sun may be obtained by interpolation or, for depressions of more than 12°, less reliably, by extrapolation; times so obtained will be subject to considerable uncertainty near extreme conditions.

At moonrise and moonset, allowance is made for semi-diameter, parallax, and refraction (34′), so that at the times given the Moon's upper limb is on the visible horizon as seen from sea level.

Polar phenomena. Information and graphs concerning the rising and setting of the Sun and Moon and the duration of civil twilight for high latitudes are given on pages 320–325.

11. *Sunrise, sunset, twilight.*   The tabulated times may be regarded, without serious error, as the LMT of the phenomena on any of the three days on the page and in any longitude. Precise times may normally be obtained by interpolating the tabular values for latitude and to the correct day and longitude, the latter being expressed as a fraction of a day by dividing it by 360°, positive for west and negative for east longitudes. In the extreme conditions near ☐, ■ or //// interpolation may not be possible in one direction, but accurate times are of little value in these circumstances.

Examples. Required the UT of (a) the beginning of morning twilights and sunrise on 2023 January 13 for latitude S 48° 55′, longitude E 75° 18′; (b) sunset and the end of evening twilights on 2023 January 15 for latitude N 67° 10′, longitude W 168° 05′.

© British Crown Copyright 2022. All rights reserved.

(a)	Twilight Nautical	Civil	Sunrise	(b)	Sunset	Twilight Civil	Nautical
From p. 19	d h m	d h m	d h m		d h m	d h m	d h m
LMT for Lat S 45°	13 03 09	13 03 55	13 04 31	N 66°	15 14 22	15 15 42	15 16 53
Corr. to S 48° 55'	−30	−20	−16	N 67° 10'	−22	−12	−6
(p. xxxii, Table I)							
Long (p. i) E 75° 18'	−5 01	−5 01	−5 01	W 168° 05'	+11 12	+11 12	+11 12
UT	12 21 38	12 22 34	12 23 14		16 01 12	16 02 42	16 03 59

The LMT are strictly for January 14 (middle date on page) and 0° longitude; for more precise times it is necessary to interpolate, but rounding errors may accumulate to about 2^m.

(a) to January $13^d − 75°/360° =$ Jan. $12^d{\cdot}8$, i.e. $\frac{1}{3}(1{\cdot}2) = 0{\cdot}4$ backwards towards the data for the same latitude interpolated similarly from page 17; the corrections are $−2^m$ to nautical twilight, $−2^m$ to civil twilight and $−1^m$ to sunrise.

(b) to January $15^d + 168°/360° =$ Jan. $15^d{\cdot}5$, i.e. $\frac{1}{3}(1{\cdot}5) = 0{\cdot}5$ forwards towards the data for the same latitude interpolated similarly from page 21; the corrections are $+7^m$ to sunset, $+4^m$ to civil twilight, and $+4^m$ to nautical twilight.

12. *Moonrise, moonset.* Precise times of moonrise and moonset are rarely needed; a glance at the tables will generally give sufficient indication of whether the Moon is available for observation and of the hours of rising and setting. If needed, precise times may be obtained as follows. Interpolate for latitude, using Table I on page xxxii, on the day wanted and also on the preceding day in east longitudes or the following day in west longitudes; take the difference between these times and interpolate for longitude by applying to the time for the day wanted the correction from Table II on page xxxii, so that the resulting time is between the two times used. In extreme conditions near □ or ■ interpolation for latitude or longitude may be possible only in one direction; accurate times are of little value in these circumstances.

To facilitate this interpolation, the times of moonrise and moonset are given for four days on each page; where no phenomenon occurs during a particular day (as happens once a month) the time of the phenomenon on the following day, increased by 24^h, is given; extra care must be taken when interpolating between two values, when one of those values exceeds 24^h. In practice it suffices to use the daily difference between the times for the nearest tabular latitude, and generally, to enter Table II with the nearest tabular arguments as in the examples below.

Examples. Required the UT of moonrise and moonset in latitude S 47° 10', longitudes E 124° 00' and W 78° 31' on 2023 January 8.

	Longitude E 124° 00' Moonrise	Moonset	Longitude W 78° 31' Moonrise	Moonset
	d h m	d h m	d h m	d h m
LMT for Lat. S 45°	8 21 20	8 05 19	8 21 20	8 05 19
Lat correction (p. xxxii, Table I)	+09	−11	+09	−11
Long correction (p. xxxii, Table II)	−10	−20	+04	+16
Correct LMT	8 21 19	8 04 48	8 21 33	8 05 24
Longitude (p. i)	−8 16	−8 16	+5 14	+5 14
UT	8 13 03	7 20 32	9 02 47	8 10 38

ALTITUDE CORRECTION TABLES

13. *General.* In general, two corrections are given for application to altitudes observed with a marine sextant; additional corrections are required for Venus and Mars and also for very low altitudes.

Tables of the correction for dip of the horizon, due to height of eye above sea level, are given on pages A2 and xxxiv. Strictly this correction should be applied first and subtracted from the sextant altitude to give apparent altitude, which is the correct argument for the other tables.

© British Crown Copyright 2022. All rights reserved.

Separate tables are given of the second correction for the Sun, for stars and planets (on pages A2 and A3), and for the Moon (on pages xxxiv and xxxv). For the Sun, values are given for both lower and upper limbs, for two periods of the year. The star tables are used for the planets, but additional corrections for parallax (page A2) are required for Venus and Mars. The Moon tables are in two parts: the main correction is a function of apparent altitude only and is tabulated for the lower limb (30′ must be subtracted to obtain the correction for the upper limb); the other, which is given for both lower and upper limbs, depends also on the horizontal parallax, which has to be taken from the daily pages.

An additional correction, given on page A4, is required for the change in the refraction, due to variations of pressure and temperature from the adopted standard conditions; it may generally be ignored for altitudes greater than 10°, except possibly in extreme conditions. The correction tables for the Sun, stars, and planets are in two parts; only those for altitudes greater than 10° are reprinted on the bookmark.

14. *Critical tables.* Some of the altitude correction tables are arranged as critical tables. In these, an interval of apparent altitude (or height of eye) corresponds to a single value of the correction; no interpolation is required. At a "critical" entry the upper of the two possible values of the correction is to be taken. For example, in the table of dip, a correction of −4′1 corresponds to all values of the height of eye from 5·3 to 5·5 metres (17·5 to 18·3 feet) inclusive.

15. *Examples.* The following examples illustrate the use of the altitude correction tables; the sextant altitudes given are assumed to be taken on 2023 August 9 with a marine sextant at height 5·4 metres (18 feet), temperature −3°C and pressure 982 mb, the Moon sights being taken at about 10^h UT.

	SUN lower limb	SUN upper limb	MOON lower limb	MOON upper limb	VENUS	*Polaris*
	° ′	° ′	° ′	° ′	° ′	° ′
Sextant altitude	21 19·7	3 20·2	33 27·6	26 06·7	4 32·6	49 36·5
Dip, height 5·4 metres (18 feet)	−4·1	−4·1	−4·1	−4·1	−4·1	−4·1
Main correction	+13·6	−29·3	+57·4	+60·5	−10·8	−0·8
−30′ for upper limb (Moon)	—	—	—	−30·0	—	—
L, U correction for Moon	—	—	+3·6	+2·9	—	—
Additional correction for Venus	—	—	—	—	+0·5	—
Additional refraction correction	−0·1	−0·6	−0·1	−0·1	−0·5	0·0
Corrected sextant altitude	21 29·1	2 46·2	34 24·4	26 35·9	4 17·7	49 31·6

The main corrections have been taken out with apparent altitude (sextant altitude corrected for index error and dip) as argument, interpolating where possible. These refinements are rarely necessary.

16. *Composition of the Corrections.* The table for the dip of the sea horizon is based on the formula:

Correction for dip $= -1\!\cdot\!76\sqrt{\text{(height of eye in metres)}} = -0\!\cdot\!97\sqrt{\text{(height of eye in feet)}}$

The correction table for the Sun includes the effects of semi-diameter, parallax and mean refraction.

The correction tables for the stars and planets allow for the effect of mean refraction.

The phase correction for Venus has been incorporated in the tabulations for GHA and Dec, and no correction for phase is required. The additional corrections for Venus and Mars allow for parallax. Alternatively, the correction for parallax may be calculated from $p \cos H$, where p is the parallax and H is the altitude. In 2023 the values for p are:

Venus	Jan. 1 0′1	May 1 0′2	June 19 0′3	July 12 0′4	July 28 0′5	Aug. 30 0′4	Sept. 15 0′3	Oct. 9 0′2	Dec. 1 0′1	Dec. 31

Mars	Jan. 1 0′2	Feb. 11 0′1	Dec. 31

The correction table for the Moon includes the effect of semi-diameter, parallax, augmentation and mean refraction.

© British Crown Copyright 2022. All rights reserved.

Mean refraction is calculated for a temperature of 10°C (50°F), a pressure of 1010 mb (29·83 inches), humidity of 80% and wavelength 0·50169 μm.

17. *Bubble sextant observations.* When observing with a bubble sextant, no correction is necessary for dip, semi-diameter, or augmentation. The altitude corrections for the stars and planets on page A2 and on the bookmark should be used for the Sun as well as for the stars and planets; for the Moon, it is easiest to take the mean of the corrections for lower and upper limbs and subtract 15′ from the altitude; the correction for dip must not be applied.

AUXILIARY AND PLANNING DATA

18. *Sun and Moon.* On the daily pages are given: hourly values of the horizontal parallax of the Moon; the semi-diameters and the times of meridian passage of both Sun and Moon over the Greenwich meridian; the equation of time; the age of the Moon, the percent (%) illuminated and a symbol indicating the phase. The times of the phases of the Moon are given in UT on page 4. For the Moon, the semi-diameters for each of the three days are given at the foot of the column; for the Sun a single value is sufficient. Table II on page xxxii may be used for interpolating the time of the Moon's meridian passage for longitude. The equation of time is given daily at 00^h and 12^h UT. The sign is *positive* for unshaded values and *negative* for shaded values. To obtain apparent time add the equation of time to mean time when the sign is *positive*. Subtract the equation of time from mean time when the sign is *negative*. At 12^h UT, when the sign is *positive*, meridian passage of the Sun occurs *before* 12^h UT, otherwise it occurs *after* 12^h UT.

19. *Planets.* The magnitudes of the planets are given immediately following their names in the headings on the daily pages; also given, for the middle day of the three on the page, are their SHA at 00^h UT and their times of meridian passage.

The planet notes and diagram on pages 8 and 9 provide descriptive information as to the suitability of the planets for observation during the year, and of their positions and movements.

20. *Stars.* The time of meridian passage of the first point of Aries over the Greenwich meridian is given on the daily pages, for the middle day of the three on the page, to 0^m1. The interval between successive meridian passages is $23^h\ 56^m1\ (24^h$ less $3^m9)$, so that times for intermediate days and other meridians can readily be derived. If a precise time is required, it may be obtained by finding the UT at which LHA Aries is zero.

The meridian passage of a star occurs when its LHA is zero, that is when LHA Aries + SHA = 360°. An approximate time can be obtained from the planet diagram on page 9.

The star charts on pages 266 and 267 are intended to assist identification. They show the relative positions of the stars in the sky as seen from the Earth and include all 173 stars used in the Almanac, together with a few others to complete the main constellation configurations. The local meridian at any time may be located on the chart by means of its SHA which is 360° − LHA Aries, or west longitude − GHA Aries.

21. *Star globe.* To set a star globe on which is printed a scale of LHA Aries, first set the globe for latitude and then rotate about the polar axis until the scale under the edge of the meridian circle reads LHA Aries.

To mark the positions of the Sun, Moon, and planets on the star globe, take the difference GHA Aries − GHA body and use this along the LHA Aries scale, in conjunction with the declination, to plot the position. GHA Aries − GHA body is most conveniently found by taking the difference when the GHA of the body is small (less than 15°), which happens once a day.

22. *Calendar.* On page 4 are given lists of ecclesiastical festivals, and of the principal anniversaries and holidays in the United Kingdom and the United States of America. The calendar on page 5 includes the day of the year as well as the day of the week.

© British Crown Copyright 2022. All rights reserved.

Brief particulars are given, at the foot of page 5, of the solar and lunar eclipses occurring during the year; the times given are in UT. The principal features of the more important solar eclipses are shown on the maps on pages 6 and 7.

23. *Standard times.* The lists on pages 262–265 give the standard times used in most countries. In general no attempt is made to give details of the beginning and end of summer time, since they are liable to frequent changes at short notice. For the latest information consult Admiralty List of Radio Signals Volume 2 (NP 282) corrected by Section VI of the weekly edition of Admiralty Notices to Mariners.

The Date or Calendar Line is an arbitrary line, on either side of which the date differs by one day; when crossing this line on a westerly course, the date must be advanced one day; when crossing it on an easterly course, the date must be put back one day. The line is a modification of the line of the 180th meridian, and is drawn so as to include, as far as possible, islands of any one group, etc., on the same side of the line. It may be traced by starting at the South Pole and joining up to the following positions:

Lat	S 51·0	S 45·0	S 15·0	S 5·0	N 48·0	N 53·0	N 65·5
Long	180·0	W 172·5	W 172·5	180·0	180·0	E 170·0	W 169·0

thence through the middle of the Diomede Islands to Lat N 68°·0, Long W 169°·0, passing east of Ostrov Vrangelya (Wrangel Island) to Lat N 75°·0, Long 180°·0, and thence to the North Pole.

ACCURACY

24. *Main data.* The quantities tabulated in this Almanac are generally correct to the nearest 0′·1; the exception is the Sun's GHA which is deliberately adjusted by up to 0′·15 to reduce the error due to ignoring the v-correction. The GHA and Dec at intermediate times cannot be obtained to this precision, since at least two quantities must be added; moreover, the v- and d-corrections are based on mean values of v and d and are taken from tables for the whole minute only. The largest error that can occur in the GHA or Dec of any body other than the Sun or Moon is less than 0′·2; it may reach 0′·25 for the GHA of the Sun and 0′·3 for that of the Moon.

In practice, it may be expected that only one third of the values of GHA and Dec taken out will have errors larger than 0′·05 and less than one tenth will have errors larger than 0′·1.

25. *Altitude corrections.* The errors in the altitude corrections are nominally of the same order as those in GHA and Dec, as they result from the addition of several quantities each correctly rounded off to 0′·1. But the actual values of the dip and of the refraction at low altitudes may, in extreme atmospheric conditions, differ considerably from the mean values used in the tables.

USE OF THIS ALMANAC IN 2024

This Almanac may be used for the Sun and stars in 2024 in the following manner.

For the Sun, take out the GHA and Dec for the same date but, for January and February (for February 29 use March 1), for a time $5^h 48^m 00^s$ *earlier* and, for March to December, for a time $18^h 12^m 00^s$ *later* than the UT of observation; in both cases *add* 87° 00′ to the GHA so obtained. The error, mainly due to planetary perturbations of the Earth, is unlikely to exceed 0′·4.

For the stars, calculate the GHA and Dec for the same date and the same time, but for January and February (for February 29 use March 1) *subtract* 15′·1 and for March to December *add* 44′·0 to the GHA so found. The error due to incomplete correction for precession and nutation is unlikely to exceed 0′·4. If preferred, the same result can be obtained by using a time $5^h 48^m 00^s$ earlier for January and February (for February 29 use March 1) and $18^h 12^m 00^s$ later for March to December, than the UT of observation (as for the Sun) and adding 86° 59′·2 to the GHA (or adding 87° as for the Sun and subtracting 0′·8, for precession, from the SHA of the star).

The Almanac cannot be so used for the Moon or planets.

© British Crown Copyright 2022. All rights reserved.

LIST I — PLACES FAST ON UTC (mainly those EAST OF GREENWICH)

The times given should be } *added* to UTC to give Standard Time
below should be } *subtracted* from Standard Time to give UTC.

	h	m		h	m
Admiralty Islands	10		Denmark*†	01	
Afghanistan	04	30	Djibouti	03	
Albania*	01		Egypt, Arab Republic of	02	
Algeria	01		Equatorial Guinea, Republic of	01	
Amirante Islands	04		Bioko	01	
Andaman Islands	05	30	Eritrea	03	
Angola	01		Estonia*†	02	
Armenia	04		Eswatini	02	
Australia			Ethiopia	03	
Australian Capital Territory*	10		Fiji*	12	
New South Wales*[1]	10		Finland*†	02	
Northern Territory	09	30	France*†	01	
Queensland	10		Gabon	01	
South Australia*	09	30	Georgia	04	
Tasmania*	10		Germany*†	01	
Victoria*	10		Gibraltar*	01	
Western Australia	08		Greece*†	02	
Whitsunday Islands	10		Guam	10	
Austria*†	01		Hong Kong	08	
Azerbaijan	04		Hungary*†	01	
Bahrain	03		India	05	30
Balearic Islands*†	01		Indonesia, Republic of		
Bangladesh	06		Bangka, Billiton, Java, West and		
Belarus	03		Central Kalimantan, Madura, Sumatra	07	
Belgium*†	01		Bali, Flores, South, North and East		
Benin	01		Kalimantan, Lombok, Sulawesi,		
Bosnia and Herzegovina*	01		Sumba, Sumbawa, West Timor ...	08	
Botswana, Republic of	02		Aru, Irian Jaya, Kai, Moluccas		
Brunei	08		Tanimbar	09	
Bulgaria*†	02		Iran*	03	30
Burma (Myanmar)	06	30	Iraq	03	
Burundi	02		Israel*	02	
Cambodia	07		Italy*†	01	
Cameroon Republic	01		Jan Mayen Island*	01	
Caroline Islands[2]	10		Japan	09	
Central African Republic	01		Jordan*	02	
Chad	01		Kazakhstan		
Chagos Archipelago & Diego Garcia	06		Western: Aktau, Uralsk, Atyrau ...	05	
Chatham Islands*	12	45	Eastern & Central: Astana	06	
China, People's Republic of	08		Kenya	03	
Christmas Island, Indian Ocean ...	07		Kerguelen Islands	05	
Cocos (Keeling) Islands	06	30	Kiribati Republic		
Comoro Islands (Comoros)	03		Gilbert Islands	12	
Congo, Democratic Republic			Phoenix Islands[3]	13	
West: Kinshasa, Equateur	01		Line Islands[3]	14	
East: Orientale, Kasai, Kivu, Shaba	02		Korea, North	09	
Congo Republic	01		Korea, South	09	
Corsica*†	01		Kuwait	03	
Crete*†	02		Kyrgyzstan	06	
Croatia*†	01		Laccadive Islands	05	30
Cyprus†: Ercan*, Larnaca*	02		Laos	07	
Czech Republic*†	01				

---

* Daylight-saving time may be kept in these places.   † For Summer time dates see List II footnotes.
[1] Except Broken Hill Area* which keeps $09^h 30^m$.
[2] Except Pohnpei, Pingelap and Kosrae which keep 11^h and Palau which keeps 09^h.
[3] The Line and Phoenix Is. not part of the Kiribati Republic may keep other time zones.

© British Crown Copyright 2022. All rights reserved.

LIST I — (*continued*)

	h	m		h	m
Latvia*†	02		Norilsk, Krasnoyarsk, Dikson,		
Lebanon*	02		Novosibirsk, Tomsk	07	
Lesotho	02		Irkutsk, Bratsk, Ulan-Ude	08	
Libya	02		Tiksi, Yakutsk, Chita	09	
Liechtenstein*	01		Vladivostok, Khabarovsk, Okhotsk	10	
Lithuania*†	02		Severo-Kurilsk, Magadan,		
Lord Howe Island*	10	30	Sakhalin Island	11	
Luxembourg*†	01		Petropavlovsk-K., Anadyr	12	
Macau	08		Rwanda	02	
Macedonia*, former Yugoslav Republic	01		Ryukyu Islands	09	
Madagascar, Democratic Republic of	03				
Malawi	02		Samoa*	13	
Malaysia, Malaya, Sabah, Sarawak ...	08		Santa Cruz Islands	11	
Maldives, Republic of The	05		Sardinia*†	01	
Malta*†	01		Saudi Arabia	03	
Mariana Islands	10		Schouten Islands	09	
Marshall Islands	12		Serbia*	01	
Mauritius	04		Seychelles	04	
Moldova*	02		Sicily*†	01	
Monaco*	01		Singapore	08	
Mongolia[4]	08		Slovakia*†	01	
Montenegro*	01		Slovenia*†	01	
Morocco	01		Socotra	03	
Mozambique	02		Solomon Islands	11	
Namibia	02		Somalia Republic	03	
Nauru	12		South Africa, Republic of	02	
Nepal	05	45	South Sudan	03	
Netherlands, The*†	01		Spain*†	01	
New Caledonia	11		Spanish Possessions in North Africa*	01	
New Zealand*	12		Spitsbergen (Svalbard)*	01	
Nicobar Islands	05	30	Sri Lanka	05	30
Niger	01		Sudan, Republic of	02	
Nigeria, Republic of	01		Sweden*†	01	
Norfolk Island*	11		Switzerland*	01	
Norway*	01		Syria (Syrian Arab Republic)*	02	
Novaya Zemlya	03				
Okinawa	09		Taiwan	08	
Oman	04		Tajikistan	05	
			Tanzania	03	
Pagalu (Annobon Islands)	01		Thailand	07	
Pakistan	05		Timor-Leste	09	
Palau Islands	09		Tonga	13	
Papua New Guinea[5]	10		Tunisia	01	
Pescadores Islands	08		Turkey	03	
Philippine Republic	08		Turkmenistan	05	
Poland*†	01		Tuvalu	12	
Qatar	03		Uganda	03	
Reunion	04		Ukraine*	02	
Romania*†	02		United Arab Emirates	04	
Russia[6]			Uzbekistan	05	
Kaliningrad	02		Vanuatu, Republic of	11	
Moscow, St. Petersburg, Arkhangelsk	03		Vietnam, Socialist Republic of	07	
Samara, Astrakhan, Saratov, ...					
Volgograd	04		Yemen	03	
Ekaterinburg, Ufa, Perm, Novyy Port	05		Zambia, Republic of	02	
Omsk	06		Zimbabwe	02	

* Daylight-saving time may be kept in these places.   † For Summer time dates see List II footnotes.
[4] Western regions of Mongolia keep 07[h].
[5] Excluding the Autonomous Region of Bougainville which keeps 11[h].
[6] The boundaries between the zones are irregular; listed are chief towns in each zone.

© British Crown Copyright 2022. All rights reserved.

LIST II — PLACES NORMALLY KEEPING UTC

Ascension Island	Ghana	Irish Republic*†	Portugal*†	Togo Republic
Burkina-Faso	Great Britain†	Ivory Coast	Principe	Tristan da Cunha
Canary Islands*†	Guinea-Bissau	Liberia	St. Helena	
Channel Islands†	Guinea Republic	Madeira*†	São Tomé	
Faeroes*, The	Iceland	Mali	Senegal	
Gambia, The	Ireland, Northern†	Mauritania	Sierra Leone	

* Daylight-saving time may be kept in these places.

† Summer time (daylight-saving time), one hour in advance of UTC, will be kept from 2023 March 26^d 01^h to October 29^d 01^h UTC (Ninth Summer Time Directive of the European Union). Ratification by member countries has not been verified.

LIST III — PLACES SLOW ON UTC (WEST OF GREENWICH)

The times given ⎱ *subtracted* from UTC to give Standard Time
below should be ⎰ *added* to Standard Time to give UTC.

	h	m		h	m
American Samoa	11		Canada (*continued*)		
Argentina	03		Prince Edward Island*	04	
Austral (Tubuai) Islands[1]	10		Quebec, east of long. W. 63°	04	
Azores*†	01		west of long. W. 63°* ...	05	
			Saskatchewan	06	
Bahamas*	05		Yukon	07	
Barbados	04		Cape Verde Islands	01	
Belize	06		Cayman Islands	05	
Bermuda*	04		Chile		
Bolivia	04		General*	04	
Brazil			Chilean Antarctic	03	
Fernando de Noronha I., Trindade I.,			Colombia	05	
Oceanic Is.	02		Cook Islands	10	
N and NE coastal states, Tocantins,			Costa Rica	06	
Minas Gerais, Goiás, Brasilia,			Cuba*	05	
S and E coastal states	03		Curaçao Island	04	
Amazonas[2], Mato Grosso do Sul,					
Mato Grosso, Rondônia, Roraima	04		Dominican Republic	04	
Acre	05				
British Antarctic Territory[3,4]	03		Easter Island (I. de Pascua)*	06	
			Ecuador	05	
Canada[4]‡			El Salvador	06	
Alberta*	07				
British Columbia*[4]	08		Falkland Islands	03	
Labrador*	04		Fernando de Noronha Island	02	
Manitoba*	06		French Guiana	03	
New Brunswick*	04				
Newfoundland*	03	30	Galápagos Islands	06	
Nunavut*			Greenland		
east of long. W. 85°	05		Danmarkshavn, Mesters Vig	00	
long. W. 85° to W. 102°	06		General*	03	
west of long. W. 102°	07		Scoresby Sound*	01	
Northwest Territories*	07		Thule*, Pituffik*	04	
Nova Scotia*	04		Grenada	04	
Ontario, east of long. W. 90°*	05		Guadeloupe	04	
Ontario, west of long. W. 90°* ...	06		Guatemala	06	
			Guyana, Republic of	04	

* Daylight-saving time may be kept in these places.   ‡ Dates for DST are given at the end of List III.

[1] This is the legal standard time, but local mean time is generally used.

[2] Except the cities of Eirunepe, Benjamin Constant and Tabatinga which keep 05^h.

[3] Stations may use UTC.

[4] Some areas may keep another time zone.

© British Crown Copyright 2022. All rights reserved.

	h	m
Haiti*	05	
Honduras	06	
Jamaica	05	
Johnston Island	10	
Juan Fernandez Islands*	04	
Leeward Islands	04	
Marquesas Islands	09	30
Martinique	04	
Mexico		
General*	06	
Quintana Roo	05	
Baja California Sur*, Chihuahua*		
Nayarit*, Sinaloa* and Sonara ...	07	
Baja California Norte*	08	
Midway Islands	11	
Nicaragua	06	
Niue	11	
Panama, Republic of	05	
Paraguay*	04	
Peru	05	
Pitcairn Island	08	
Puerto Rico	04	
St. Pierre and Miquelon*	03	
Society Islands	10	
South Georgia	02	
Suriname	03	
Trindade Island, South Atlantic ...	02	
Trinidad and Tobago	04	
Tuamotu Archipelago	10	
Tubuai (Austral) Islands	10	
Turks and Caicos Islands*	05	
United States of America ‡		
Alabama	06	
Alaska	09	
Aleutian Islands, east of W. 169° 30′	09	
Aleutian Islands, west of W. 169° 30′	10	
Arizona [5]	07	
Arkansas	06	
California	08	
Colorado	07	
Connecticut	05	
Delaware	05	
District of Columbia	05	
Florida [6]	05	
Georgia	05	
Hawaii [5]	10	

	h	m
United States of America ‡(continued)		
Idaho, southern part	07	
northern part	08	
Illinois	06	
Indiana [6]	05	
Iowa	06	
Kansas [6]	06	
Kentucky, eastern part	05	
western part	06	
Louisiana	06	
Maine	05	
Maryland	05	
Massachusetts	05	
Michigan [6]	05	
Minnesota	06	
Mississippi	06	
Missouri	06	
Montana	07	
Nebraska, eastern part	06	
western part	07	
Nevada	08	
New Hampshire	05	
New Jersey	05	
New Mexico	07	
New York	05	
North Carolina	05	
North Dakota, eastern part	06	
western part	07	
Ohio	05	
Oklahoma	06	
Oregon [6]	08	
Pennsylvania	05	
Rhode Island	05	
South Carolina	05	
South Dakota, eastern part	06	
western part	07	
Tennessee, eastern part	05	
western part	06	
Texas [6]	06	
Utah	07	
Vermont	05	
Virginia	05	
Washington D.C.	05	
Washington	08	
West Virginia	05	
Wisconsin	06	
Wyoming	07	
Uruguay	03	
Venezuela	04	
Virgin Islands	04	
Windward Islands	04	

* Daylight-saving time may be kept in these places.

‡ Daylight-saving (Summer) time, one hour fast on the time given, is kept during 2023 from March 12 (second Sunday) to November 5 (first Sunday), changing at 02^{h} 00^{m} local clock time.

[5] Exempt from keeping daylight-saving time, except for a portion of Arizona.

[6] A small portion of the state is in another time zone.

© British Crown Copyright 2022. All rights reserved.

STAR CHARTS

NORTHERN STARS

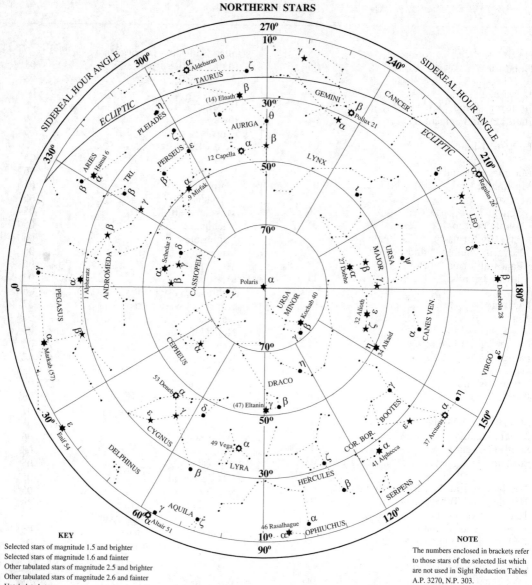

KEY

✿ Selected stars of magnitude 1.5 and brighter
★ Selected stars of magnitude 1.6 and fainter
★ Other tabulated stars of magnitude 2.5 and brighter
● Other tabulated stars of magnitude 2.6 and fainter
· Untabulated stars

NOTE

The numbers enclosed in brackets refer to those stars of the selected list which are not used in Sight Reduction Tables A.P. 3270, N.P. 303.

EQUATORIAL STARS (SHA 0° to 180°)

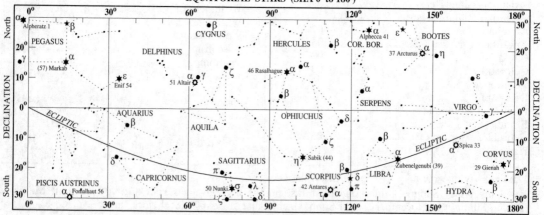

© British Crown Copyright 2022. All rights reserved.

SOUTHERN STARS

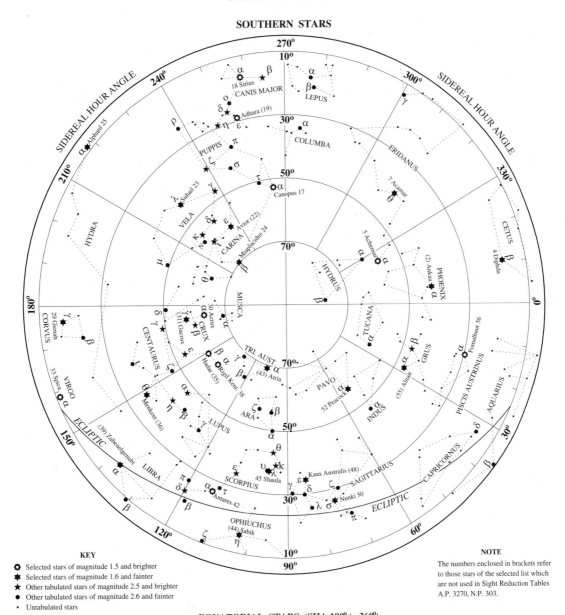

KEY

✪ Selected stars of magnitude 1.5 and brighter
★ Selected stars of magnitude 1.6 and fainter
★ Other tabulated stars of magnitude 2.5 and brighter
● Other tabulated stars of magnitude 2.6 and fainter
· Untabulated stars

NOTE

The numbers enclosed in brackets refer to those stars of the selected list which are not used in Sight Reduction Tables A.P. 3270, N.P. 303.

EQUATORIAL STARS (SHA 180° to 360°)

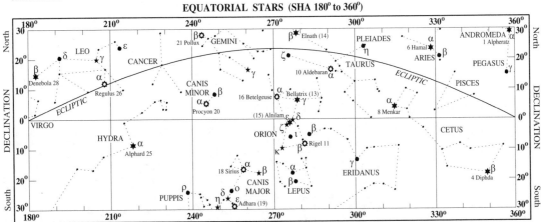

SIDEREAL HOUR ANGLE

© British Crown Copyright 2022. All rights reserved.

Mag.	Name and Number		SHA °	SHA JAN.	FEB.	MAR.	APR.	MAY	JUNE	Dec.	Dec. JAN.	FEB.	MAR.	APR.	MAY	JUNE
3·2	γ Cephei		4	56·7	57·2	57·4	57·1	56·5	55·7	N 77	45·9	45·8	45·6	45·5	45·4	45·4
2·5	α Pegasi	57	13	31·7	31·8	31·7	31·6	31·4	31·2	N 15	19·7	19·6	19·6	19·6	19·6	19·7
2·4	β Pegasi		13	47·0	47·1	47·0	46·9	46·7	46·4	N 28	12·5	12·4	12·3	12·3	12·3	12·4
1·2	α Piscis Aust.	56	15	16·6	16·6	16·5	16·4	16·2	15·9	S 29	30·3	30·2	30·1	30·0	29·9	29·8
2·1	β Gruis		18	59·9	59·9	59·9	59·7	59·4	59·1	S 46	46·1	46·0	45·9	45·8	45·6	45·5
2·9	α Tucanæ		24	59·6	59·7	59·5	59·3	58·9	58·5	S 60	09·0	08·8	08·7	08·5	08·4	08·3
1·7	α Gruis	55	27	35·4	35·3	35·2	35·0	34·7	34·4	S 46	51·2	51·1	51·0	50·9	50·7	50·7
2·9	δ Capricorni		32	55·8	55·8	55·7	55·5	55·2	55·0	S 16	01·5	01·5	01·5	01·4	01·3	01·2
2·4	ε Pegasi	54	33	40·7	40·7	40·6	40·4	40·2	39·9	N 9	58·8	58·7	58·7	58·7	58·7	58·8
2·9	β Aquarii		36	48·9	48·9	48·7	48·6	48·3	48·1	S 5	28·3	28·3	28·3	28·3	28·2	28·1
2·4	α Cephei		40	14·0	14·0	13·9	13·5	13·2	12·8	N 62	41·0	40·9	40·7	40·6	40·6	40·7
2·5	ε Cygni		48	13·4	13·3	13·2	13·0	12·7	12·5	N 34	03·3	03·2	03·1	03·1	03·1	03·3
1·3	α Cygni	53	49	27·4	27·3	27·2	26·9	26·6	26·4	N 45	21·7	21·6	21·5	21·4	21·5	21·6
3·1	α Indi		50	13·0	12·8	12·6	12·3	12·0	11·7	S 47	12·8	12·7	12·6	12·5	12·5	12·4
1·9	α Pavonis	52	53	08·9	08·8	08·5	08·1	07·7	07·3	S 56	39·8	39·7	39·5	39·5	39·4	39·4
2·2	γ Cygni		54	14·8	14·7	14·5	14·3	14·0	13·8	N 40	19·8	19·6	19·5	19·5	19·5	19·7
0·8	α Aquilæ	51	62	01·9	01·8	01·6	01·4	01·2	01·0	N 8	55·7	55·6	55·5	55·6	55·6	55·7
2·7	γ Aquilæ		63	10·2	10·1	09·9	09·7	09·4	09·2	N 10	40·1	40·0	39·9	40·0	40·0	40·1
2·9	δ Cygni		63	35·2	35·1	34·9	34·6	34·4	34·1	N 45	11·1	11·0	10·9	10·9	10·9	11·1
3·1	β Cygni		67	05·8	05·7	05·5	05·2	05·0	04·8	N 28	00·4	00·3	00·2	00·2	00·3	00·4
2·9	π Sagittarii		72	13·5	13·4	13·2	12·9	12·7	12·5	S 20	59·3	59·3	59·3	59·2	59·2	59·2
3·0	ζ Aquilæ		73	23·5	23·3	23·1	22·9	22·7	22·5	N 13	53·8	53·7	53·6	53·6	53·7	53·8
2·6	ζ Sagittarii		73	59·4	59·3	59·0	58·7	58·5	58·3	S 29	50·9	50·8	50·8	50·8	50·8	50·8
2·0	σ Sagittarii	50	75	50·2	50·0	49·8	49·5	49·2	49·0	S 26	16·1	16·1	16·1	16·1	16·0	16·0
0·0	α Lyræ	49	80	34·8	34·6	34·4	34·1	33·9	33·7	N 38	48·2	48·0	48·0	48·0	48·1	48·2
2·8	λ Sagittarii		82	39·7	39·5	39·2	39·0	38·7	38·5	S 25	24·5	24·5	24·5	24·5	24·5	24·5
1·9	ε Sagittarii	48	83	35·1	34·9	34·6	34·3	34·1	33·9	S 34	22·4	22·4	22·4	22·4	22·4	22·4
2·7	δ Sagittarii		84	23·5	23·3	23·1	22·8	22·6	22·4	S 29	49·1	49·1	49·1	49·1	49·1	49·1
3·0	γ Sagittarii		88	11·2	11·0	10·8	10·5	10·2	10·1	S 30	25·4	25·4	25·4	25·4	25·4	25·4
2·2	γ Draconis	47	90	43·4	43·2	42·9	42·6	42·4	42·3	N 51	29·0	28·8	28·8	28·8	28·9	29·1
2·8	β Ophiuchi		93	51·3	51·1	50·9	50·6	50·5	50·3	N 4	33·4	33·3	33·3	33·3	33·3	33·4
2·4	κ Scorpii		93	59·4	59·1	58·8	58·5	58·3	58·1	S 39	02·4	02·4	02·4	02·4	02·5	02·5
1·9	θ Scorpii		95	16·0	15·7	15·4	15·1	14·8	14·7	S 43	00·6	00·6	00·6	00·6	00·7	00·7
2·1	α Ophiuchi	46	95	60·4	60·2	60·0	59·7	59·5	59·4	N 12	32·5	32·4	32·4	32·4	32·5	32·5
1·6	λ Scorpii	45	96	13·0	12·7	12·4	12·1	11·9	11·7	S 37	07·2	07·1	07·1	07·2	07·2	07·2
3·0	α Aræ		96	36·3	36·0	35·7	35·3	35·0	34·8	S 49	53·5	53·5	53·5	53·5	53·6	53·6
2·7	υ Scorpii		96	55·6	55·3	55·1	54·8	54·5	54·4	S 37	18·8	18·7	18·8	18·8	18·8	18·9
2·8	β Draconis		97	16·2	16·0	15·7	15·4	15·1	15·0	N 52	16·8	16·7	16·6	16·7	16·8	17·0
2·8	β Aræ		98	12·5	12·1	11·8	11·4	11·1	10·9	S 55	32·9	32·9	32·9	32·9	33·0	33·1
Var.‡	α Herculis		101	04·9	04·7	04·5	04·3	04·1	04·0	N 14	21·7	21·6	21·6	21·6	21·7	21·8
2·4	η Ophiuchi	44	102	05·0	04·7	04·5	04·2	04·1	03·9	S 15	45·2	45·2	45·3	45·3	45·3	45·2
3·1	ζ Aræ		104	52·8	52·4	52·0	51·6	51·3	51·1	S 56	01·4	01·4	01·4	01·4	01·5	01·6
2·3	ε Scorpii		107	05·6	05·4	05·1	04·8	04·6	04·5	S 34	20·0	20·0	20·0	20·1	20·1	20·2
1·9	α Triang. Aust.	43	107	14·3	13·7	13·1	12·6	12·2	11·9	S 69	03·9	03·9	03·9	04·0	04·1	04·2
2·8	ζ Herculis		109	28·1	27·8	27·6	27·4	27·2	27·1	N 31	33·5	33·4	33·3	33·4	33·5	33·6
2·6	ζ Ophiuchi		110	24·0	23·7	23·5	23·3	23·1	23·0	S 10	36·8	36·9	36·9	36·9	36·9	36·9
2·8	τ Scorpii		110	40·7	40·4	40·2	39·9	39·7	39·6	S 28	15·7	15·8	15·8	15·8	15·9	15·9
2·8	β Herculis		112	12·2	12·0	11·7	11·5	11·4	11·3	N 21	26·2	26·1	26·1	26·1	26·2	26·3
1·0	α Scorpii	42	112	18·1	17·9	17·6	17·4	17·2	17·1	S 26	28·9	28·9	29·0	29·0	29·0	29·1
2·7	η Draconis		113	55·8	55·5	55·1	54·8	54·6	54·6	N 61	27·4	27·3	27·3	27·4	27·5	27·7
2·7	δ Ophiuchi		116	07·1	06·8	06·6	06·4	06·3	06·2	S 3	45·2	45·3	45·3	45·4	45·3	45·3
2·6	β Scorpii		118	18·7	18·5	18·2	18·0	17·9	17·8	S 19	52·0	52·1	52·1	52·2	52·2	52·2
2·3	δ Scorpii		119	34·9	34·7	34·4	34·2	34·1	34·0	S 22	41·2	41·2	41·3	41·3	41·3	41·3
2·9	π Scorpii		119	56·7	56·4	56·2	55·9	55·8	55·7	S 26	10·7	10·8	10·8	10·9	10·9	10·9
2·8	β Trianguli Aust.		120	42·9	42·5	42·0	41·6	41·3	41·2	S 63	29·8	29·8	29·9	30·0	30·1	30·2
2·6	α Serpentis		123	39·3	39·0	38·8	38·6	38·5	38·5	N 6	21·1	21·0	21·0	21·0	21·1	21·1
2·8	γ Lupi		125	50·2	49·9	49·7	49·4	49·3	49·2	S 41	14·4	14·5	14·6	14·6	14·7	14·8
2·2	α Coronæ Bor.	41	126	05·3	05·1	04·9	04·7	04·6	04·5	N 26	38·1	38·0	38·0	38·0	38·1	38·2

‡ 2·9 — 3·6

© British Crown Copyright 2022. All rights reserved.

Mag.	Name and Number	SHA °	JULY '	AUG. '	SEPT. '	OCT. '	NOV. '	DEC. '	Decl.	JULY '	AUG. '	SEPT. '	OCT. '	NOV. '	DEC. '
3·2	Errai	4	54·9	54·4	54·1	54·3	54·7	55·3	N 77	45·5	45·6	45·8	46·0	46·2	46·2
2·5	Markab 57	13	30·9	30·8	30·7	30·7	30·8	30·8	N 15	19·8	20·0	20·0	20·1	20·1	20·1
2·4	Scheat	13	46·2	46·0	45·9	46·0	46·0	46·1	N 28	12·5	12·6	12·8	12·8	12·9	12·9
1·2	Fomalhaut 56	15	15·6	15·4	15·4	15·4	15·5	15·6	S 29	29·7	29·7	29·8	29·8	29·9	29·9
2·1	Tiaki	18	58·8	58·5	58·5	58·5	58·6	58·8	S 46	45·5	45·6	45·6	45·7	45·8	45·8
2·9	α Tucanæ	24	58·1	57·8	57·7	57·9	58·1	58·3	S 60	08·3	08·4	08·5	08·7	08·7	08·7
1·7	Alnair 55	27	34·1	33·9	33·8	33·9	34·1	34·2	S 46	50·7	50·7	50·8	50·9	51·0	51·0
2·9	Deneb Algedi	32	54·8	54·6	54·6	54·7	54·8	54·8	S 16	01·2	01·1	01·1	01·2	01·2	01·2
2·4	Enif 54	33	39·7	39·6	39·6	39·7	39·8	39·8	N 9	58·9	59·0	59·1	59·1	59·1	59·1
2·9	Sadalsuud	36	47·9	47·8	47·8	47·8	47·9	48·0	S 5	28·0	28·0	28·0	28·0	28·0	28·0
2·4	Alderamin	40	12·5	12·4	12·5	12·8	13·1	13·4	N 62	40·9	41·1	41·3	41·4	41·4	41·3
2·5	Aljanah	48	12·3	12·2	12·3	12·4	12·6	12·7	N 34	03·4	03·6	03·7	03·8	03·8	03·7
1·3	Deneb 53	49	26·2	26·1	26·2	26·4	26·6	26·8	N 45	21·8	21·9	22·1	22·1	22·1	22·1
3·1	α Indi	50	11·4	11·3	11·4	11·5	11·7	11·8	S 47	12·5	12·5	12·6	12·7	12·7	12·7
1·9	Peacock 52	53	07·1	07·0	07·0	07·2	07·5	07·6	S 56	39·5	39·6	39·7	39·7	39·7	39·7
2·2	Sadr	54	13·6	13·6	13·7	13·8	14·0	14·1	N 40	19·8	20·0	20·1	20·2	20·2	20·1
0·8	Altair 51	62	00·8	00·8	00·8	01·0	01·1	01·1	N 8	55·8	55·9	56·0	56·0	56·0	55·9
2·7	γ Aquilæ	63	09·1	09·1	09·1	09·3	09·4	09·4	N 10	40·2	40·3	40·4	40·4	40·4	40·3
2·9	Fawaris	63	34·0	34·0	34·2	34·4	34·6	34·7	N 45	11·2	11·4	11·5	11·6	11·5	11·4
3·1	Albireo	67	04·7	04·7	04·8	04·9	05·1	05·1	N 28	00·5	00·7	00·7	00·8	00·7	00·6
2·9	Albaldah	72	12·3	12·3	12·4	12·5	12·6	12·6	S 20	59·1	59·1	59·2	59·2	59·2	59·1
3·0	ζ Aquilæ	73	22·4	22·4	22·5	22·6	22·7	22·8	N 13	53·9	54·0	54·1	54·1	54·0	54·0
2·6	Ascella	73	58·1	58·1	58·2	58·3	58·5	58·5	S 29	50·8	50·8	50·8	50·8	50·8	50·8
2·0	Nunki 50	75	48·9	48·9	49·0	49·1	49·2	49·2	S 26	16·0	16·0	16·1	16·1	16·1	16·1
0·0	Vega 49	80	33·6	33·7	33·8	34·0	34·2	34·3	N 38	48·4	48·5	48·6	48·6	48·5	48·4
2·8	Kaus Borealis	82	38·4	38·4	38·5	38·7	38·8	38·8	S 25	24·5	24·5	24·5	24·6	24·5	24·5
1·9	Kaus Australis 48	83	33·8	33·8	33·9	34·0	34·1	34·1	S 34	22·4	22·4	22·5	22·5	22·5	22·4
2·7	Kaus Media	84	22·3	22·3	22·4	22·5	22·6	22·6	S 29	49·1	49·1	49·1	49·1	49·1	49·1
3·0	Alnasl	88	10·0	10·0	10·1	10·3	10·3	10·3	S 30	25·4	25·5	25·5	25·5	25·5	25·4
2·2	Eltanin 47	90	42·3	42·4	42·6	42·9	43·1	43·1	N 51	29·2	29·3	29·4	29·4	29·3	29·1
2·8	Cebalrai	93	50·3	50·3	50·4	50·5	50·6	50·6	N 4	33·5	33·5	33·6	33·6	33·5	33·4
2·4	κ Scorpii	93	58·0	58·1	58·2	58·4	58·4	58·4	S 39	02·5	02·6	02·6	02·6	02·6	02·5
1·9	Sargas	95	14·6	14·6	14·8	15·0	15·1	15·0	S 43	00·8	00·9	00·9	00·9	00·8	00·7
2·1	Rasalhague 46	95	59·4	59·4	59·6	59·7	59·8	59·7	N 12	32·6	32·7	32·7	32·7	32·6	32·6
1·6	Shaula 45	96	11·7	11·7	11·8	12·0	12·1	12·0	S 37	07·3	07·3	07·3	07·3	07·3	07·2
3·0	α Aræ	96	34·8	34·8	35·0	35·2	35·3	35·3	S 49	53·7	53·8	53·8	53·8	53·7	53·7
2·7	Lesath	96	54·3	54·3	54·5	54·6	54·7	54·7	S 37	18·9	18·9	19·0	18·9	18·9	18·9
2·8	Rastaban	97	15·1	15·2	15·5	15·7	15·9	16·0	N 52	17·1	17·2	17·3	17·2	17·1	16·9
2·8	β Aræ	98	10·8	10·9	11·1	11·3	11·4	11·4	S 55	33·2	33·3	33·3	33·3	33·2	33·1
Var.‡	Rasalgethi	101	04·0	04·0	04·2	04·3	04·4	04·3	N 14	21·9	21·9	22·0	21·9	21·9	21·8
2·4	Sabik 44	102	03·9	03·9	04·1	04·2	04·2	04·2	S 15	45·2	45·2	45·2	45·2	45·2	45·2
3·1	ζ Aræ	104	51·1	51·2	51·5	51·7	51·8	51·7	S 56	01·7	01·8	01·8	01·8	01·7	01·6
2·3	Larawag	107	04·5	04·5	04·7	04·8	04·9	04·8	S 34	20·2	20·2	20·2	20·2	20·2	20·1
1·9	Atria 43	107	11·9	12·2	12·6	12·9	13·1	12·9	S 69	04·3	04·4	04·4	04·4	04·3	04·1
2·8	ζ Herculis	109	27·1	27·3	27·4	27·6	27·6	27·6	N 31	33·7	33·8	33·8	33·7	33·6	33·5
2·6	ζ Ophiuchi	110	23·0	23·1	23·2	23·3	23·3	23·3	S 10	36·9	36·8	36·8	36·8	36·9	36·9
2·8	Paikauhale	110	39·6	39·7	39·8	39·9	40·0	39·9	S 28	15·9	15·9	15·9	15·9	15·9	15·9
2·8	Kornephoros	112	11·3	11·4	11·6	11·7	11·7	11·7	N 21	26·4	26·5	26·5	26·4	26·3	26·2
1·0	Antares 42	112	17·1	17·1	17·3	17·4	17·4	17·3	S 26	29·1	29·1	29·1	29·1	29·0	29·0
2·7	Athebyne	113	54·7	55·0	55·3	55·6	55·8	55·8	N 61	27·8	27·9	27·9	27·8	27·6	27·4
2·7	Yed Prior	116	06·2	06·2	06·4	06·5	06·5	06·4	S 3	45·2	45·2	45·2	45·2	45·3	45·3
2·6	Acrab	118	17·8	17·9	18·0	18·1	18·1	18·0	S 19	52·2	52·2	52·2	52·2	52·2	52·2
2·3	Dschubba	119	34·0	34·1	34·2	34·3	34·3	34·2	S 22	41·4	41·4	41·3	41·3	41·3	41·3
2·9	Fang	119	55·7	55·8	55·9	56·0	56·0	55·9	S 26	10·9	11·0	10·9	10·9	10·9	10·9
2·8	β Trianguli Aust.	120	41·3	41·5	41·8	42·1	42·1	41·9	S 63	30·3	30·4	30·4	30·3	30·2	30·1
2·6	Unukalhai	123	38·5	38·6	38·7	38·8	38·8	38·7	N 6	21·2	21·2	21·2	21·2	21·1	21·0
2·8	γ Lupi	125	49·2	49·3	49·5	49·6	49·6	49·4	S 41	14·9	14·9	14·8	14·8	14·7	14·7
2·2	Alphecca 41	126	04·6	04·7	04·8	04·9	05·0	04·8	N 26	38·3	38·3	38·3	38·3	38·1	38·0

‡ 2·9 — 3·6

© British Crown Copyright 2022. All rights reserved.

Mag.	Name and Number			SHA							Declination						
				JAN.	FEB.	MAR.	APR.	MAY	JUNE			JAN.	FEB.	MAR.	APR.	MAY	JUNE
			°	′	′	′	′	′	′		°	′	′	′	′	′	′
2·9	γ	Trianguli Aust.	129	44·5	43·9	43·4	42·9	42·7	42·7	S	68	45·5	45·5	45·6	45·8	45·9	46·1
3·1	γ	Ursæ Minoris	129	49·6	49·1	48·6	48·2	48·1	48·2	N	71	44·8	44·7	44·7	44·8	45·0	45·2
2·6	β	Libræ	130	26·6	26·3	26·1	25·9	25·8	25·8	S	9	28·0	28·1	28·2	28·2	28·2	28·2
2·7	β	Lupi	134	59·7	59·4	59·1	58·9	58·8	58·7	S	43	13·4	13·4	13·5	13·6	13·7	13·8
2·8	α	Libræ 39	136	58·0	57·7	57·5	57·3	57·2	57·2	S	16	08·2	08·2	08·3	08·4	08·4	08·4
2·1	β	Ursæ Minoris 40	137	20·2	19·6	19·0	18·6	18·6	18·8	N	74	03·3	03·3	03·3	03·5	03·6	03·7
2·4	ε	Bootis	138	30·3	30·1	29·9	29·7	29·6	29·6	N	26	58·5	58·4	58·4	58·5	58·6	58·7
2·3	α	Lupi	139	08·4	08·0	07·7	07·5	07·4	07·4	S	47	29·0	29·0	29·1	29·3	29·4	29·5
−0·3	α	Centauri 38	139	42·7	42·3	41·9	41·7	41·6	41·6	S	60	55·5	55·5	55·7	55·8	55·9	56·1
2·3	η	Centauri	140	45·7	45·4	45·1	44·9	44·8	44·8	S	42	15·3	15·4	15·5	15·6	15·7	15·8
3·0	γ	Bootis	141	45·1	44·8	44·6	44·4	44·4	44·4	N	38	12·2	12·2	12·2	12·3	12·4	12·5
0·0	α	Bootis 37	145	49·5	49·2	49·0	48·9	48·9	48·9	N	19	03·6	03·6	03·5	03·6	03·6	03·7
2·1	θ	Centauri 36	147	59·6	59·3	59·1	59·0	58·9	58·9	S	36	28·8	28·9	29·0	29·1	29·2	29·2
0·6	β	Centauri 35	148	38·4	38·0	37·7	37·5	37·4	37·5	S	60	28·7	28·8	28·9	29·1	29·2	29·3
2·6	ζ	Centauri	150	45·5	45·2	44·9	44·8	44·7	44·8	S	47	23·8	23·9	24·1	24·2	24·3	24·4
2·7	η	Bootis	151	03·4	03·2	03·0	02·9	02·8	02·9	N	18	16·8	16·8	16·7	16·8	16·9	16·9
1·9	η	Ursæ Majoris 34	152	53·3	53·0	52·8	52·7	52·7	52·8	N	49	11·6	11·6	11·7	11·8	11·9	12·0
2·3	ε	Centauri	154	39·9	39·6	39·3	39·1	39·1	39·2	S	53	34·7	34·8	34·9	35·1	35·2	35·3
1·0	α	Virginis 33	158	24·0	23·8	23·6	23·5	23·5	23·5	S	11	16·8	16·9	17·0	17·0	17·1	17·0
2·3	ζ	Ursæ Majoris	158	47·2	46·9	46·6	46·5	46·5	46·7	N	54	48·0	48·0	48·1	48·2	48·4	48·5
2·8	ι	Centauri	159	31·7	31·5	31·3	31·2	31·2	31·2	S	36	49·8	49·9	50·0	50·2	50·2	50·3
2·8	ε	Virginis	164	10·2	10·0	09·9	09·8	09·8	09·8	N	10	50·1	50·0	50·0	50·0	50·0	50·1
2·9	α	Canum Venat.	165	43·5	43·2	43·0	42·9	43·0	43·1	N	38	11·4	11·4	11·5	11·6	11·7	11·7
1·8	ε	Ursæ Majoris 32	166	14·3	14·0	13·8	13·7	13·8	13·9	N	55	49·8	49·8	49·9	50·0	50·2	50·3
1·3	β	Crucis	167	44·0	43·6	43·4	43·3	43·4	43·5	S	59	48·6	48·7	48·8	49·0	49·2	49·2
2·9	γ	Virginis	169	17·7	17·4	17·3	17·2	17·3	17·3	S	1	34·5	34·6	34·7	34·7	34·7	34·7
2·2	γ	Centauri	169	18·2	17·9	17·7	17·7	17·7	17·8	S	49	04·9	05·0	05·2	05·3	05·5	05·5
2·7	α	Muscæ	170	21·5	21·0	20·8	20·7	20·8	21·1	S	69	15·4	15·5	15·7	15·9	16·0	16·1
2·7	β	Corvi	171	06·1	05·9	05·7	05·7	05·7	05·7	S	23	31·3	31·4	31·5	31·6	31·7	31·7
1·6	γ	Crucis 31	171	53·3	53·0	52·8	52·7	52·8	53·0	S	57	14·2	14·4	14·5	14·7	14·8	14·9
1·3	α	Crucis 30	173	01·7	01·3	01·1	01·0	01·2	01·4	S	63	13·3	13·4	13·6	13·8	13·9	14·0
2·6	γ	Corvi 29	175	45·2	45·0	44·8	44·8	44·8	44·9	S	17	40·1	40·2	40·3	40·4	40·4	40·4
2·6	δ	Centauri	177	36·7	36·4	36·3	36·2	36·3	36·5	S	50	50·8	50·9	51·1	51·2	51·3	51·4
2·4	γ	Ursæ Majoris	181	14·3	14·0	13·8	13·8	13·9	14·1	N	53	33·8	33·8	33·9	34·0	34·1	34·2
2·1	β	Leonis 28	182	26·5	26·3	26·2	26·1	26·2	26·3	N	14	26·5	26·5	26·5	26·5	26·5	26·6
2·6	δ	Leonis	191	10·0	09·8	09·7	09·7	09·8	09·8	N	20	23·8	23·7	23·7	23·8	23·8	23·9
3·0	ψ	Ursæ Majoris	192	15·5	15·3	15·2	15·2	15·3	15·5	N	44	22·2	22·3	22·3	22·4	22·5	22·6
1·8	α	Ursæ Majoris 27	193	42·6	42·3	42·2	42·3	42·5	42·7	N	61	37·4	37·5	37·6	37·7	37·8	37·8
2·4	β	Ursæ Majoris	194	11·4	11·1	11·0	11·1	11·2	11·5	N	56	15·3	15·4	15·5	15·6	15·7	15·7
2·7	μ	Velorum	198	03·4	03·2	03·2	03·3	03·4	03·6	S	49	32·3	32·5	32·6	32·8	32·8	32·8
2·8	θ	Carinæ	199	03·0	02·8	02·8	03·0	03·2	03·5	S	64	30·6	30·8	31·0	31·2	31·2	31·3
2·3	γ	Leonis	204	41·3	41·1	41·1	41·1	41·2	41·3	N	19	43·4	43·4	43·4	43·5	43·5	43·5
1·4	α	Leonis 26	207	35·9	35·8	35·8	35·8	35·9	36·0	N	11	51·2	51·2	51·2	51·2	51·2	51·3
3·0	ε	Leonis	213	12·5	12·4	12·4	12·4	12·5	12·6	N	23	40·0	40·0	40·0	40·1	40·1	40·1
3·1	N	Velorum	217	00·8	00·8	00·8	01·0	01·3	01·5	S	57	08·0	08·2	08·3	08·4	08·5	08·4
2·0	α	Hydræ 25	217	49·1	49·0	49·0	49·1	49·2	49·2	S	8	45·5	45·6	45·6	45·7	45·7	45·6
2·5	κ	Velorum	219	17·3	17·2	17·3	17·5	17·7	17·9	S	55	06·4	06·5	06·7	06·8	06·8	06·8
2·2	ι	Carinæ	220	34·0	34·0	34·1	34·3	34·6	34·8	S	59	22·1	22·3	22·5	22·6	22·6	22·6
1·7	β	Carinæ 24	221	37·7	37·7	37·9	38·3	38·7	39·1	S	69	48·5	48·7	48·9	49·0	49·0	49·0
2·2	λ	Velorum 23	222	47·1	47·0	47·1	47·2	47·4	47·6	S	43	31·4	31·6	31·7	31·8	31·8	31·8
3·1	ι	Ursæ Majoris	224	48·0	47·9	47·9	48·1	48·3	48·4	N	47	57·0	57·1	57·1	57·2	57·2	57·2
2·0	δ	Velorum	228	39·5	39·5	39·6	39·9	40·1	40·3	S	54	47·5	47·6	47·8	47·9	47·9	47·8
1·9	ε	Carinæ 22	234	14·7	14·8	14·9	15·2	15·5	15·8	S	59	34·9	35·1	35·2	35·3	35·3	35·2
1·8	γ	Velorum	237	26·0	26·0	26·1	26·4	26·6	26·7	S	47	24·2	24·4	24·5	24·5	24·5	24·4
2·8	ρ	Puppis	237	51·9	51·9	51·9	52·1	52·2	52·3	S	24	22·2	22·3	22·4	22·5	22·4	22·4
2·3	ζ	Puppis	238	53·8	53·8	53·9	54·1	54·3	54·4	S	40	04·0	04·2	04·3	04·3	04·3	04·2
1·1	β	Geminorum 21	243	18·9	18·9	19·0	19·1	19·2	19·2	N	27	58·2	58·2	58·2	58·3	58·3	58·3
0·4	α	Canis Minoris 20	244	52·2	52·2	52·3	52·4	52·5	52·5	N	5	09·9	09·9	09·9	09·9	09·9	09·9

© British Crown Copyright 2022. All rights reserved.

Mag.	Name and Number	SHA °	JULY	AUG.	SEPT.	OCT.	NOV.	DEC.	Declination	JULY	AUG.	SEPT.	OCT.	NOV.	DEC.
2·9	γ Trianguli Aust.	129	42·8	43·2	43·5	43·8	43·8	43·5	S 68	46·2	46·2	46·2	46·1	45·9	45·8
3·1	Pherkad	129	48·6	49·1	49·6	50·0	50·2	50·0	N 71	45·2	45·3	45·2	45·1	44·9	44·7
2·6	Zubeneschamali	130	25·8	25·9	26·0	26·1	26·1	25·9	S 9	28·2	28·1	28·1	28·1	28·2	28·2
2·7	β Lupi	134	58·8	58·9	59·1	59·2	59·1	58·9	S 43	13·8	13·9	13·8	13·7	13·7	13·6
2·8	Zubenelgenubi 39	136	57·3	57·3	57·4	57·5	57·5	57·3	S 16	08·4	08·4	08·3	08·3	08·3	08·4
2·1	Kochab 40	137	19·3	19·9	20·4	20·8	20·9	20·7	N 74	03·8	03·8	03·7	03·6	03·4	03·2
2·4	Izar	138	29·7	29·8	30·0	30·0	30·0	29·8	N 26	58·7	58·8	58·7	58·6	58·5	58·4
2·3	α Lupi	139	07·5	07·6	07·8	07·9	07·8	07·6	S 47	29·5	29·5	29·4	29·4	29·3	29·2
−0·3	Rigil Kent. 38	139	41·8	42·0	42·3	42·4	42·3	42·1	S 60	56·1	56·1	56·1	56·0	55·8	55·8
2·3	η Centauri	140	44·9	45·0	45·2	45·3	45·2	45·0	S 42	15·8	15·8	15·7	15·7	15·6	15·6
3·0	Seginus	141	44·5	44·7	44·8	44·9	44·8	44·7	N 38	12·6	12·6	12·5	12·4	12·2	12·1
0·0	Arcturus 37	145	49·0	49·1	49·2	49·2	49·1	49·0	N 19	03·8	03·8	03·7	03·7	03·6	03·4
2·1	Menkent 36	147	59·0	59·1	59·2	59·3	59·2	59·0	S 36	29·3	29·2	29·2	29·1	29·1	29·1
0·6	Hadar 35	148	37·6	37·9	38·1	38·2	38·1	37·7	S 60	29·4	29·4	29·3	29·2	29·1	29·0
2·6	ζ Centauri	150	44·9	45·0	45·2	45·2	45·1	44·8	S 47	24·4	24·4	24·3	24·2	24·1	24·1
2·7	Muphrid	151	02·9	03·0	03·1	03·2	03·1	02·9	N 18	17·0	17·0	16·9	16·9	16·7	16·6
1·9	Alkaid 34	152	52·9	53·1	53·2	53·3	53·2	53·0	N 49	12·1	12·0	11·9	11·8	11·6	11·4
2·3	ε Centauri	154	39·3	39·5	39·7	39·7	39·6	39·3	S 53	35·3	35·3	35·2	35·1	35·0	35·0
1·0	Spica 33	158	23·6	23·7	23·7	23·7	23·6	23·4	S 11	17·0	17·0	17·0	17·0	17·0	17·1
2·3	Mizar	158	46·9	47·1	47·2	47·3	47·2	46·9	N 54	48·5	48·4	48·3	48·2	48·0	47·8
2·8	ι Centauri	159	31·3	31·4	31·5	31·5	31·4	31·1	S 36	50·3	50·3	50·2	50·1	50·1	50·1
2·8	Vindemiatrix	164	09·9	10·0	10·0	10·0	09·9	09·7	N 10	50·1	50·1	50·1	50·0	49·9	49·8
2·9	Cor Caroli	165	43·2	43·3	43·4	43·4	43·2	43·0	N 38	11·8	11·7	11·6	11·5	11·3	11·2
1·8	Alioth 32	166	14·1	14·3	14·4	14·4	14·3	14·0	N 55	50·3	50·2	50·1	49·9	49·7	49·6
1·3	Mimosa	167	43·7	44·0	44·1	44·1	43·9	43·5	S 59	49·3	49·2	49·1	49·0	48·9	48·8
2·9	Porrima	169	17·4	17·4	17·5	17·4	17·3	17·1	S 1	34·6	34·6	34·6	34·6	34·7	34·8
2·2	Muhlifain	169	18·0	18·1	18·2	18·2	18·0	17·7	S 49	05·5	05·4	05·3	05·2	05·2	05·2
2·7	α Muscæ	170	21·4	21·8	22·0	22·0	21·6	21·1	S 69	16·1	16·1	16·0	15·8	15·7	15·7
2·7	Kraz	171	05·8	05·9	05·9	05·9	05·8	05·5	S 23	31·6	31·6	31·5	31·5	31·5	31·6
1·6	Gacrux 31	171	53·2	53·4	53·5	53·4	53·2	52·8	S 57	14·9	14·8	14·7	14·6	14·5	14·5
1·3	Acrux 30	173	01·6	01·9	02·0	02·0	01·7	01·3	S 63	14·0	13·9	13·8	13·7	13·6	13·6
2·6	Gienah 29	175	45·0	45·0	45·1	45·0	44·8	44·6	S 17	40·4	40·3	40·3	40·2	40·3	40·3
2·6	δ Centauri	177	36·6	36·8	36·8	36·8	36·5	36·2	S 50	51·4	51·3	51·2	51·1	51·0	51·0
2·4	Phecda	181	14·3	14·4	14·4	14·3	14·1	13·8	N 53	34·2	34·1	33·9	33·8	33·6	33·5
2·1	Denebola 28	182	26·3	26·4	26·4	26·3	26·1	25·9	N 14	26·6	26·6	26·6	26·5	26·4	26·3
2·6	Zosma	191	09·9	09·9	09·9	09·8	09·6	09·3	N 20	23·9	23·9	23·8	23·7	23·6	23·5
3·0	ψ Ursæ Majoris	192	15·6	15·6	15·6	15·5	15·2	14·9	N 44	22·5	22·4	22·3	22·2	22·0	21·9
1·8	Dubhe 27	193	42·9	43·0	43·0	42·8	42·5	42·0	N 61	37·8	37·6	37·5	37·3	37·2	37·1
2·4	Merak	194	11·6	11·7	11·6	11·5	11·2	10·8	N 56	15·7	15·6	15·4	15·3	15·1	15·0
2·7	μ Velorum	198	03·8	03·8	03·8	03·7	03·4	03·0	S 49	32·8	32·7	32·5	32·4	32·4	32·5
2·8	θ Carinæ	199	03·8	04·0	04·0	03·8	03·4	02·9	S 64	31·2	31·1	30·9	30·8	30·8	30·8
2·3	Algieba	204	41·3	41·3	41·3	41·1	40·9	40·6	N 19	43·5	43·5	43·4	43·4	43·3	43·2
1·4	Regulus 26	207	36·0	36·0	35·9	35·8	35·5	35·3	N 11	51·3	51·3	51·2	51·2	51·1	51·0
3·0	ε Leonis	213	12·6	12·6	12·5	12·3	12·1	11·8	N 23	40·1	40·1	40·0	40·0	39·9	39·8
3·1	N Velorum	217	01·7	01·7	01·6	01·4	01·0	00·6	S 57	08·3	08·2	08·0	08·0	08·0	08·1
2·0	Alphard 25	217	49·3	49·2	49·1	49·0	48·7	48·5	S 8	45·6	45·5	45·5	45·5	45·5	45·6
2·5	Markeb	219	18·1	18·1	18·0	17·7	17·4	17·0	S 55	06·7	06·6	06·4	06·3	06·3	06·5
2·2	Aspidiske	220	35·0	35·0	34·9	34·4	34·2	33·9	S 59	22·5	22·3	22·2	22·1	22·1	22·2
1·7	Miaplacidus 24	221	39·4	39·5	39·3	38·9	38·4	37·9	S 69	48·9	48·7	48·6	48·5	48·5	48·6
2·2	Suhail 23	222	47·6	47·6	47·5	47·3	47·0	46·7	S 43	31·7	31·5	31·4	31·3	31·4	31·5
3·1	Talitha	224	48·4	48·3	48·1	47·9	47·5	47·2	N 47	57·1	57·0	56·9	56·8	56·7	56·7
2·0	Alsephina	228	40·4	40·4	40·2	40·0	39·6	39·3	S 54	47·7	47·5	47·4	47·3	47·4	47·5
1·9	Avior 22	234	15·9	15·8	15·6	15·3	14·9	14·6	S 59	35·1	34·9	34·8	34·7	34·8	34·9
1·8	γ Velorum	237	26·8	26·7	26·5	26·2	25·9	25·7	S 47	24·3	24·1	24·0	24·0	24·0	24·2
2·8	Tureis	237	52·3	52·2	52·0	51·8	51·6	51·3	S 24	22·3	22·1	22·1	22·1	22·1	22·2
2·3	Naos	238	54·4	54·3	54·1	53·9	53·6	53·4	S 40	04·1	04·0	03·9	03·8	03·9	04·0
1·1	Pollux 21	243	19·2	19·1	18·9	18·6	18·3	18·1	N 27	58·2	58·2	58·2	58·1	58·1	58·0
0·4	Procyon 20	244	52·5	52·3	52·2	51·9	51·7	51·5	N 5	10·0	10·0	10·0	10·0	09·9	09·8

© British Crown Copyright 2022. All rights reserved.

Mag.	Name and Number			SHA						Declination						
			°	JAN.	FEB.	MAR.	APR.	MAY	JUNE	°	JAN.	FEB.	MAR.	APR.	MAY	JUNE
1·6	α Geminorum		245	58·8	58·8	58·8	59·0	59·1	59·1	N 31	50·2	50·2	50·3	50·3	50·3	50·3
3·3	σ Puppis		247	30·2	30·3	30·4	30·6	30·8	30·9	S 43	20·9	21·0	21·1	21·1	21·1	21·0
2·9	β Canis Minoris		247	53·8	53·8	53·9	54·0	54·1	54·1	N 8	14·5	14·5	14·5	14·5	14·5	14·6
2·4	η Canis Majoris		248	44·6	44·7	44·8	44·9	45·1	45·1	S 29	20·9	21·0	21·1	21·1	21·1	21·0
2·7	π Puppis		250	30·4	30·4	30·5	30·7	30·9	30·9	S 37	08·3	08·5	08·6	08·6	08·5	08·4
1·8	δ Canis Majoris		252	39·8	39·9	40·0	40·1	40·2	40·3	S 26	25·8	25·9	26·0	26·0	25·9	25·8
3·0	o Canis Majoris		254	00·0	00·0	00·1	00·2	00·4	00·4	S 23	52·0	52·2	52·2	52·2	52·2	52·1
1·5	ε Canis Majoris	19	255	06·8	06·8	06·9	07·1	07·2	07·3	S 29	00·2	00·4	00·4	00·4	00·4	00·3
2·9	τ Puppis		257	22·0	22·1	22·3	22·5	22·7	22·8	S 50	38·5	38·7	38·8	38·8	38·7	38·6
−1·5	α Canis Majoris	18	258	27·3	27·4	27·5	27·6	27·7	27·7	S 16	44·9	45·0	45·0	45·0	45·0	44·9
1·9	γ Geminorum		260	14·2	14·2	14·3	14·4	14·5	14·5	N 16	22·7	22·7	22·7	22·7	22·8	22·8
−0·7	α Carinæ	17	263	52·6	52·7	53·0	53·2	53·4	53·5	S 52	42·5	42·7	42·7	42·7	42·6	42·5
2·0	β Canis Majoris		264	04·1	04·1	04·2	04·4	04·5	04·5	S 17	58·1	58·2	58·2	58·2	58·2	58·1
2·6	θ Aurigæ		269	40·4	40·5	40·6	40·7	40·8	40·8	N 37	12·9	12·9	12·9	12·9	12·9	12·8
1·9	β Aurigæ		269	41·5	41·5	41·7	41·9	42·0	41·9	N 44	57·0	57·1	57·1	57·1	57·0	57·0
Var.‡	α Orionis	16	270	53·5	53·6	53·7	53·8	53·9	53·9	N 7	24·6	24·6	24·6	24·6	24·6	24·7
2·1	κ Orionis		272	47·1	47·1	47·2	47·4	47·4	47·4	S 9	39·8	39·8	39·8	39·8	39·8	39·7
1·9	ζ Orionis		274	31·0	31·1	31·2	31·3	31·4	31·3	S 1	55·9	55·9	55·9	55·9	55·9	55·8
2·6	α Columbæ		274	52·5	52·6	52·7	52·9	53·0	53·0	S 34	03·8	03·9	03·9	03·9	03·8	03·7
3·0	ζ Tauri		275	14·5	14·6	14·7	14·8	14·9	14·8	N 21	09·4	09·4	09·4	09·4	09·4	09·4
1·7	ε Orionis	15	275	39·1	39·1	39·3	39·4	39·4	39·4	S 1	11·3	11·3	11·4	11·3	11·3	11·2
2·8	ι Orionis		275	51·4	51·5	51·6	51·7	51·8	51·8	S 5	53·8	53·8	53·8	53·8	53·8	53·7
2·6	α Leporis		276	33·6	33·7	33·8	33·9	34·0	34·0	S 17	48·4	48·5	48·5	48·5	48·4	48·3
2·2	δ Orionis		276	42·1	42·1	42·2	42·4	42·4	42·4	S 0	17·0	17·0	17·0	17·0	17·0	16·9
2·8	β Leporis		277	41·3	41·4	41·5	41·7	41·7	41·7	S 20	44·6	44·6	44·7	44·6	44·6	44·4
1·7	β Tauri	14	278	03·6	03·7	03·8	03·9	04·0	03·9	N 28	37·6	37·6	37·6	37·6	37·6	37·6
1·6	γ Orionis	13	278	24·3	24·4	24·5	24·6	24·7	24·6	N 6	22·2	22·2	22·2	22·2	22·2	22·2
0·1	α Aurigæ	12	280	23·9	24·0	24·2	24·3	24·4	24·3	N 46	01·3	01·4	01·4	01·4	01·3	01·2
0·1	β Orionis	11	281	05·2	05·2	05·3	05·5	05·5	05·5	S 8	10·6	10·6	10·7	10·6	10·6	10·5
2·8	β Eridani		282	45·1	45·2	45·3	45·4	45·5	45·4	S 5	03·5	03·5	03·5	03·5	03·5	03·4
2·7	ι Aurigæ		285	22·4	22·5	22·6	22·8	22·8	22·7	N 33	12·2	12·2	12·2	12·2	12·1	12·1
0·9	α Tauri	10	290	41·2	41·3	41·4	41·5	41·6	41·5	N 16	33·3	33·3	33·3	33·3	33·3	33·3
2·9	ε Persei		300	08·9	09·0	09·1	09·2	09·2	09·1	N 40	04·7	04·7	04·7	04·6	04·6	04·5
3·0	γ Eridani		300	13·3	13·4	13·5	13·6	13·6	13·6	S 13	26·7	26·8	26·8	26·7	26·6	26·5
2·9	ζ Persei		301	06·2	06·3	06·4	06·5	06·5	06·4	N 31	57·2	57·2	57·2	57·1	57·1	57·1
2·9	η Tauri		302	47·1	47·2	47·3	47·4	47·4	47·3	N 24	10·6	10·6	10·6	10·6	10·5	10·5
1·8	α Persei	9	308	30·3	30·5	30·7	30·8	30·8	30·6	N 49	56·7	56·7	56·7	56·6	56·5	56·5
Var.§	β Persei		312	34·9	35·1	35·2	35·3	35·2	35·0	N 41	02·8	02·8	02·7	02·7	02·6	02·6
2·5	α Ceti	8	314	07·7	07·8	07·9	08·0	07·9	07·8	N 4	10·7	10·7	10·7	10·7	10·8	10·8
2·0	α Ursæ Minoris		314	38·0	51·1	63·3	70·7	70·3	62·3	N 89	21·9	22·0	21·9	21·8	21·7	21·5
3·2	θ Eridani	7	315	12·9	13·0	13·2	13·3	13·3	13·1	S 40	13·0	13·0	13·0	12·9	12·7	12·5
3·0	β Trianguli		327	16·3	16·5	16·6	16·6	16·5	16·3	N 35	05·9	05·8	05·8	05·7	05·7	05·7
2·0	α Arietis	6	327	53·0	53·1	53·2	53·2	53·1	52·9	N 23	34·3	34·3	34·2	34·2	34·2	34·2
2·3	γ Andromedæ		328	40·3	40·5	40·6	40·6	40·5	40·3	N 42	26·5	26·5	26·4	26·4	26·3	26·3
2·9	α Hydri		330	07·4	07·7	07·9	08·0	07·9	07·7	S 61	27·8	27·8	27·7	27·5	27·3	27·1
2·6	β Arietis		331	01·4	01·5	01·6	01·6	01·5	01·3	N 20	55·2	55·2	55·2	55·1	55·2	55·2
0·5	α Eridani	5	335	21·4	21·6	21·8	21·8	21·7	21·5	S 57	07·6	07·5	07·4	07·2	07·0	06·9
2·7	δ Cassiopeiæ		338	10·2	10·5	10·6	10·7	10·5	10·1	N 60	21·5	21·5	21·4	21·2	21·1	21·1
2·1	β Andromedæ		342	14·8	15·0	15·0	15·0	14·9	14·6	N 35	44·6	44·6	44·5	44·5	44·4	44·4
Var.‖	γ Cassiopeiæ		345	28·7	28·9	29·1	29·1	28·8	28·5	N 60	50·7	50·6	50·5	50·4	50·3	50·3
2·0	β Ceti	4	348	49·0	49·1	49·1	49·1	48·9	48·7	S 17	51·8	51·8	51·8	51·7	51·6	51·4
2·2	α Cassiopeiæ	3	349	33·0	33·2	33·3	33·3	33·1	32·7	N 56	40·0	39·9	39·8	39·7	39·6	39·6
2·4	α Phœnicis	2	353	08·9	09·0	09·0	09·0	08·8	08·5	S 42	11·2	11·1	11·0	10·8	10·7	10·6
2·8	β Hydri		353	16·1	16·6	16·9	16·8	16·3	15·7	S 77	07·9	07·8	07·6	07·4	07·2	07·1
2·8	γ Pegasi		356	23·9	24·0	24·0	23·9	23·8	23·5	N 15	18·7	18·6	18·6	18·6	18·6	18·7
2·3	β Cassiopeiæ		357	24·3	24·4	24·5	24·4	24·2	23·8	N 59	16·8	16·7	16·6	16·5	16·4	16·4
2·1	α Andromedæ	1	357	36·6	36·7	36·7	36·6	36·4	36·2	N 29	13·1	13·0	13·0	12·9	12·9	13·0

‡ 0·1 — 1·2   § 2·1 — 3·4   ‖ Irregular variable; 2021 mag. 2·2

© British Crown Copyright 2022. All rights reserved.

Mag.	Name and Number		SHA °	JULY	AUG.	SEPT.	OCT.	NOV.	DEC.	Declination	JULY	AUG.	SEPT.	OCT.	NOV.	DEC.
1·6	Castor		245	59·1	58·9	58·7	58·5	58·2	57·9	N 31	50·2	50·2	50·2	50·1	50·1	50·1
3·3	σ Puppis		247	30·9	30·8	30·6	30·3	30·1	29·8	S 43	20·8	20·7	20·6	20·6	20·7	20·8
2·9	Gomeisa		247	54·1	53·9	53·7	53·5	53·3	53·1	N 8	14·6	14·6	14·6	14·6	14·6	14·5
2·4	Aludra		248	45·1	45·0	44·8	44·6	44·3	44·1	S 29	20·8	20·7	20·6	20·6	20·7	20·8
2·7	π Puppis		250	30·9	30·8	30·6	30·3	30·1	29·9	S 37	08·3	08·1	08·0	08·0	08·1	08·3
1·8	Wezen		252	40·2	40·1	39·9	39·7	39·5	39·3	S 26	25·7	25·6	25·5	25·5	25·6	25·7
3·0	o Canis Majoris		253	60·4	60·2	60·0	59·8	59·6	59·4	S 23	52·0	51·8	51·8	51·8	51·9	52·0
1·5	Adhara	19	255	07·2	07·1	06·9	06·6	06·4	06·2	S 28	60·1	60·0	59·9	59·9	60·0	60·2
2·9	τ Puppis		257	22·8	22·6	22·4	22·1	21·8	21·6	S 50	38·4	38·3	38·2	38·2	38·2	38·4
−1·5	Sirius	18	258	27·7	27·5	27·3	27·1	26·9	26·7	S 16	44·8	44·7	44·6	44·7	44·7	44·9
1·9	Alhena		260	14·4	14·2	14·0	13·8	13·5	13·4	N 16	22·8	22·8	22·8	22·8	22·8	22·7
−0·7	Canopus	17	263	53·5	53·3	53·0	52·7	52·4	52·2	S 52	42·3	42·2	42·1	42·1	42·2	42·4
2·0	Mirzam		264	04·4	04·2	04·0	03·8	03·6	03·4	S 17	57·9	57·8	57·8	57·8	57·9	58·0
2·6	Mahasim		269	40·6	40·4	40·1	39·9	39·6	39·4	N 37	12·8	12·8	12·8	12·8	12·8	12·8
1·9	Menkalinan		269	41·8	41·5	41·2	40·9	40·6	40·4	N 44	56·9	56·9	56·9	56·9	56·9	56·9
Var.‡	Betelgeuse	16	270	53·7	53·5	53·3	53·1	52·9	52·7	N 7	24·7	24·8	24·8	24·8	24·8	24·7
2·1	Saiph		272	47·3	47·1	46·9	46·7	46·5	46·3	S 9	39·6	39·5	39·4	39·5	39·5	39·6
1·9	Alnitak		274	31·2	31·0	30·8	30·6	30·4	30·2	S 1	55·7	55·7	55·6	55·6	55·7	55·8
2·6	Phact		274	52·9	52·7	52·5	52·2	52·0	51·9	S 34	03·5	03·4	03·3	03·4	03·5	03·6
3·0	Tianguan		275	14·7	14·5	14·2	14·0	13·7	13·6	N 21	09·4	09·4	09·4	09·5	09·4	09·4
1·7	Alnilam	15	275	39·3	39·1	38·9	38·6	38·4	38·3	S 1	11·1	11·1	11·0	11·0	11·1	11·1
2·8	Hatysa		275	51·6	51·4	51·2	51·0	50·8	50·7	S 5	53·6	53·5	53·5	53·5	53·5	53·6
2·6	Arneb		276	33·9	33·7	33·4	33·2	33·0	32·9	S 17	48·2	48·1	48·1	48·1	48·2	48·3
2·2	Mintaka		276	42·3	42·1	41·8	41·6	41·4	41·3	S 0	16·8	16·8	16·7	16·7	16·8	16·9
2·8	Nihal		277	41·6	41·4	41·2	40·9	40·7	40·6	S 20	44·3	44·2	44·1	44·2	44·3	44·4
1·7	Elnath	14	278	03·8	03·5	03·3	03·0	02·8	02·6	N 28	37·6	37·6	37·6	37·6	37·6	37·7
1·6	Bellatrix	13	278	24·5	24·3	24·1	23·8	23·6	23·5	N 6	22·3	22·4	22·4	22·4	22·4	22·3
0·1	Capella	12	280	24·1	23·8	23·5	23·2	22·9	22·7	N 46	01·2	01·2	01·2	01·2	01·3	01·3
0·1	Rigel	11	281	05·3	05·1	04·9	04·7	04·5	04·4	S 8	10·4	10·3	10·2	10·3	10·3	10·4
2·8	Cursa		282	45·3	45·1	44·8	44·6	44·4	44·3	S 5	03·3	03·2	03·2	03·2	03·2	03·3
2·7	Hassaleh		285	22·5	22·3	22·0	21·8	21·5	21·4	N 33	12·1	12·1	12·2	12·2	12·2	12·3
0·9	Aldebaran	10	290	41·3	41·1	40·8	40·6	40·4	40·3	N 16	33·4	33·4	33·5	33·5	33·5	33·5
2·9	ε Persei		300	08·9	08·6	08·3	08·0	07·8	07·7	N 40	04·5	04·6	04·6	04·7	04·8	04·8
3·0	Zaurak		300	13·4	13·1	12·9	12·7	12·6	12·5	S 13	26·4	26·3	26·3	26·3	26·4	26·4
2·9	ζ Persei		301	06·2	05·9	05·6	05·4	05·2	05·1	N 31	57·1	57·1	57·2	57·2	57·3	57·3
2·9	Alcyone		302	47·1	46·8	46·5	46·3	46·2	46·1	N 24	10·6	10·6	10·7	10·7	10·8	10·8
1·8	Mirfak	9	308	30·3	29·9	29·6	29·3	29·2	29·1	N 49	56·5	56·5	56·6	56·7	56·8	56·9
Var.§	Algol		312	34·8	34·5	34·2	34·0	33·8	33·8	N 41	02·6	02·6	02·7	02·8	02·9	03·0
2·5	Menkar	8	314	07·6	07·3	07·1	07·0	06·9	06·8	N 4	10·9	11·0	11·1	11·1	11·1	11·0
2·0	Polaris		314	48·8	33·0	18·4	07·3	01·9	04·8	N 89	21·5	21·5	21·6	21·7	21·9	22·1
3·2	Acamar	7	315	12·9	12·6	12·3	12·2	12·1	12·1	S 40	12·4	12·3	12·3	12·4	12·5	12·6
3·0	β Trianguli		327	16·0	15·7	15·5	15·3	15·3	15·3	N 35	05·7	05·8	05·9	06·0	06·1	06·2
2·0	Hamal	6	327	52·7	52·4	52·2	52·1	52·0	52·0	N 23	34·3	34·4	34·5	34·6	34·6	34·6
2·3	Almach		328	40·0	39·7	39·4	39·3	39·2	39·2	N 42	26·3	26·4	26·5	26·7	26·8	26·8
2·9	α Hydri		330	07·3	06·9	06·6	06·4	06·4	06·6	S 61	27·0	27·0	27·0	27·2	27·3	27·4
2·6	Sheratan		331	01·0	00·8	00·6	00·5	00·4	00·4	N 20	55·3	55·4	55·5	55·5	55·6	55·6
0·5	Achernar	5	335	21·1	20·8	20·5	20·4	20·4	20·5	S 57	06·8	06·7	06·8	06·9	07·1	07·2
2·7	Ruchbah		338	09·7	09·3	09·0	08·9	08·8	08·9	N 60	21·1	21·2	21·4	21·6	21·7	21·8
2·1	Mirach		342	14·3	14·1	13·9	13·8	13·8	13·8	N 35	44·5	44·6	44·8	44·9	45·0	45·0
Var.‖	γ Cassiopeiæ		345	28·0	27·7	27·4	27·3	27·3	27·5	N 60	50·3	50·5	50·6	50·8	50·9	51·0
2·0	Diphda	4	348	48·5	48·2	48·1	48·0	48·0	48·1	S 17	51·3	51·3	51·3	51·3	51·4	51·4
2·2	Schedar	3	349	32·3	32·0	31·8	31·7	31·8	31·9	N 56	39·7	39·8	40·0	40·1	40·3	40·4
2·4	Ankaa	2	353	08·2	08·0	07·8	07·8	07·8	07·9	S 42	10·5	10·5	10·5	10·6	10·7	10·8
2·8	β Hydri		353	14·9	14·1	13·6	13·6	13·9	14·5	S 77	07·0	07·1	07·2	07·3	07·5	07·5
2·8	Algenib		356	23·3	23·1	22·9	22·9	22·9	23·0	N 15	18·8	18·9	19·0	19·0	19·1	19·1
2·3	Caph		357	23·4	23·1	22·9	22·9	23·0	23·1	N 59	16·5	16·6	16·8	17·0	17·1	17·2
2·1	Alpheratz	1	357	35·9	35·7	35·6	35·5	35·6	35·6	N 29	13·1	13·2	13·3	13·4	13·5	13·5

‡ 0·1 — 1·2   § 2·1 — 3·4   ‖ Irregular variable; 2021 mag. 2·2

© British Crown Copyright 2022. All rights reserved.

POLARIS (POLE STAR) TABLES, 2023
FOR DETERMINING LATITUDE FROM SEXTANT ALTITUDE AND FOR AZIMUTH

LHA ARIES	0°–9°	10°–19°	20°–29°	30°–39°	40°–49°	50°–59°	60°–69°	70°–79°	80°–89°	90°–99°	100°–109°	110°–119°
	a_0	a_0	a_0	a_0	a_0	a_0	a_0	a_0	a_0	a_0	a_0	a_0
0	0 32·1	0 27·7	0 24·3	0 22·0	0 20·8	0 20·7	0 21·9	0 24·1	0 27·4	0 31·7	0 36·8	0 42·6
1	31·6	27·4	24·1	21·8	20·7	20·8	22·0	24·4	27·8	32·2	37·4	43·2
2	31·2	27·0	23·8	21·7	20·7	20·9	22·2	24·7	28·2	32·7	38·0	43·9
3	30·7	26·6	23·5	21·5	20·6	20·9	22·4	25·0	28·6	33·2	38·5	44·5
4	30·2	26·3	23·3	21·4	20·6	21·0	22·6	25·3	29·1	33·7	39·1	45·1
5	0 29·8	0 25·9	0 23·0	0 21·2	0 20·6	0 21·1	0 22·8	0 25·7	0 29·5	0 34·2	0 39·7	0 45·7
6	29·4	25·6	22·8	21·1	20·6	21·3	23·1	26·0	29·9	34·7	40·2	46·3
7	29·0	25·2	22·6	21·0	20·6	21·4	23·3	26·3	30·4	35·2	40·8	47·0
8	28·5	24·9	22·4	20·9	20·6	21·5	23·6	26·7	30·8	35·8	41·4	47·6
9	28·1	24·6	22·2	20·8	20·7	21·7	23·8	27·1	31·3	36·3	42·0	48·3
10	0 27·7	0 24·3	0 22·0	0 20·8	0 20·7	0 21·9	0 24·1	0 27·4	0 31·7	0 36·8	0 42·6	0 48·9

Lat.	a_1	a_1	a_1	a_1	a_1	a_1	a_1	a_1	a_1	a_1	a_1	a_1
0	0·5	0·5	0·6	0·6	0·6	0·6	0·6	0·5	0·5	0·5	0·4	0·4
10	·5	·5	·6	·6	·6	·6	·6	·5	·5	·5	·4	·4
20	·5	·6	·6	·6	·6	·6	·6	·6	·5	·5	·4	·4
30	·5	·6	·6	·6	·6	·6	·6	·6	·5	·5	·5	·4
40	0·6	0·6	0·6	0·6	0·6	0·6	0·6	0·6	0·6	0·6	0·5	0·5
45	·6	·6	·6	·6	·6	·6	·6	·6	·6	·6	·6	·6
50	·6	·6	·6	·6	·6	·6	·6	·6	·6	·6	·6	·6
55	·6	·6	·6	·6	·6	·6	·6	·6	·6	·6	·6	·6
60	·6	·6	·6	·6	·6	·6	·6	·6	·6	·7	·7	·7
62	0·7	0·6	0·6	0·6	0·6	0·6	0·6	0·6	0·7	0·7	0·7	·7
64	·7	·6	·6	·6	·6	·6	·6	·6	·7	·7	·7	·8
66	·7	·7	·6	·6	·6	·6	·6	·7	·7	·7	·8	·8
68	0·7	0·7	0·6	0·6	0·6	0·6	0·6	0·7	0·7	0·8	0·8	0·8

Month	a_2	a_2	a_2	a_2	a_2	a_2	a_2	a_2	a_2	a_2	a_2	a_2
Jan.	0·7	0·7	0·7	0·7	0·7	0·7	0·7	0·7	0·7	0·7	0·7	0·7
Feb.	·6	·7	·7	·7	·8	·8	·8	·8	·8	·8	·8	·8
Mar.	·5	·6	·6	·7	·7	·8	·8	·8	·9	·9	·9	·9
Apr.	0·4	0·4	0·5	0·5	0·6	0·7	0·7	0·8	0·8	0·9	0·9	1·0
May	·2	·3	·3	·4	·5	·5	·6	·7	·7	·8	·8	0·9
June	·2	·2	·3	·3	·3	·4	·4	·5	·6	·6	·7	·8
July	0·3	0·3	0·3	0·3	0·3	0·3	0·3	0·4	0·4	0·5	0·5	0·6
Aug.	·4	·4	·3	·3	·3	·3	·3	·3	·3	·4	·4	·5
Sept.	·6	·5	·5	·4	·4	·4	·3	·3	·3	·3	·3	·3
Oct.	0·8	0·7	0·7	0·6	0·5	0·5	0·4	0·4	0·3	0·3	0·3	0·3
Nov.	0·9	0·9	0·8	0·8	·7	·7	·6	·5	·4	·4	·3	·3
Dec.	1·1	1·0	1·0	1·0	0·9	0·8	0·8	0·7	0·6	0·5	0·4	0·4

Lat.	AZIMUTH											
0	0·4	0·3	0·2	0·1	0·0	359·9	359·8	359·7	359·6	359·5	359·5	359·4
20	0·4	0·3	0·2	0·1	0·0	359·9	359·8	359·7	359·6	359·5	359·4	359·4
40	0·5	0·4	0·3	0·2	0·0	359·9	359·7	359·6	359·5	359·4	359·3	359·2
50	0·6	0·5	0·3	0·2	0·0	359·8	359·7	359·5	359·4	359·2	359·1	359·1
55	0·7	0·6	0·4	0·2	0·0	359·8	359·6	359·5	359·4	359·2	359·1	359·1
60	0·8	0·7	0·5	0·2	0·0	359·8	359·6	359·4	359·3	359·1	359·0	359·0
65	1·0	0·8	0·5	0·3	0·0	359·7	359·5	359·2	359·0	358·8	358·7	358·6

Latitude = Apparent altitude (corrected for refraction) $-1° + a_0 + a_1 + a_2$

The table is entered with LHA Aries to determine the column to be used; each column refers to a range of 10°. a_0 is taken, with mental interpolation, from the upper table with the units of LHA Aries in degrees as argument; a_1, a_2 are taken, without interpolation, from the second and third tables with arguments latitude and month respectively. a_0, a_1, a_2, are always positive. The final table gives the azimuth of *Polaris*.

© British Crown Copyright 2022. All rights reserved.

POLARIS (POLE STAR) TABLES, 2023
FOR DETERMINING LATITUDE FROM SEXTANT ALTITUDE AND FOR AZIMUTH

LHA ARIES	120° – 129°	130° – 139°	140° – 149°	150° – 159°	160° – 169°	170° – 179°	180° – 189°	190° – 199°	200° – 209°	210° – 219°	220° – 229°	230° – 239°
°	a_0	a_0	a_0	a_0	a_0	a_0	a_0	a_0	a_0	a_0	a_0	a_0
	° ′	° ′	° ′	° ′	° ′	° ′	° ′	° ′	° ′	° ′	° ′	° ′
0	0 48·9	0 55·5	1 02·1	1 08·7	1 14·9	1 20·7	1 25·8	1 30·0	1 33·4	1 35·6	1 36·8	1 36·9
1	49·5	56·1	02·8	09·3	15·5	21·2	26·2	30·4	33·6	35·8	36·9	36·8
2	50·2	56·8	03·5	10·0	16·1	21·7	26·7	30·8	33·9	36·0	36·9	36·7
3	50·8	57·5	04·1	10·6	16·7	22·3	27·1	31·1	34·2	36·1	37·0	36·7
4	51·5	58·1	04·8	11·2	17·3	22·8	27·6	31·5	34·4	36·3	37·0	36·6
5	0 52·2	0 58·8	1 05·4	1 11·8	1 17·9	1 23·3	1 28·0	1 31·8	1 34·6	1 36·4	1 37·0	1 36·5
6	52·8	0 59·5	06·1	12·5	18·4	23·8	28·4	32·1	34·9	36·5	37·0	36·4
7	53·5	1 00·1	06·7	13·1	19·0	24·3	28·8	32·5	35·1	36·6	37·0	36·2
8	54·1	00·8	07·4	13·7	19·6	24·8	29·2	32·8	35·3	36·7	37·0	36·1
9	54·8	01·5	08·0	14·3	20·1	25·3	29·6	33·1	35·5	36·8	36·9	35·9
10	0 55·5	1 02·1	1 08·7	1 14·9	1 20·7	1 25·8	1 30·0	1 33·4	1 35·6	1 36·8	1 36·9	1 35·8

Lat.	a_1	a_1	a_1	a_1	a_1	a_1	a_1	a_1	a_1	a_1	a_1	a_1
°	′	′	′	′	′	′	′	′	′	′	′	′
0	0·4	0·3	0·4	0·4	0·4	0·4	0·5	0·5	0·6	0·6	0·6	0·6
10	·4	·4	·4	·4	·4	·5	·5	·5	·6	·6	·6	·6
20	·4	·4	·4	·4	·5	·5	·5	·6	·6	·6	·6	·6
30	·5	·5	·5	·5	·5	·5	·5	·6	·6	·6	·6	·6
40	0·5	0·5	0·5	0·5	0·5	0·6	0·6	0·6	0·6	0·6	0·6	0·6
45	·6	·6	·6	·6	·6	·6	·6	·6	·6	·6	·6	·6
50	·6	·6	·6	·6	·6	·6	·6	·6	·6	·6	·6	·6
55	·6	·7	·6	·6	·6	·6	·6	·6	·6	·6	·6	·6
60	·7	·7	·7	·7	·7	·7	·6	·6	·6	·6	·6	·6
62	0·7	0·7	0·7	0·7	0·7	0·7	0·7	0·6	0·6	0·6	0·6	0·6
64	·8	·8	·8	·8	·7	·7	·7	·6	·6	·6	·6	·6
66	·8	·8	·8	·8	·8	·7	·7	·7	·6	·6	·6	·6
68	0·9	0·9	0·9	0·8	0·8	0·8	0·7	0·7	0·6	0·6	0·6	0·6

Month	a_2	a_2	a_2	a_2	a_2	a_2	a_2	a_2	a_2	a_2	a_2	a_2
	′	′	′	′	′	′	′	′	′	′	′	′
Jan.	0·6	0·6	0·6	0·6	0·5	0·5	0·5	0·5	0·5	0·5	0·5	0·5
Feb.	·8	·8	·7	·7	·6	·6	·6	·5	·5	·5	·4	·4
Mar.	0·9	0·9	0·9	0·8	·8	·7	·7	·6	·6	·5	·5	·4
Apr.	1·0	1·0	1·0	1·0	0·9	0·9	0·8	0·8	0·7	0·7	0·6	0·5
May	0·9	1·0	1·0	1·0	1·0	1·0	1·0	0·9	·9	·8	·7	·7
June	·8	0·9	0·9	1·0	1·0	1·0	1·0	1·0	·9	·9	·9	·8
July	0·7	0·7	0·8	0·8	0·9	0·9	0·9	0·9	0·9	0·9	0·9	0·9
Aug.	·5	·6	·6	·7	·7	·8	·8	·8	·9	·9	·9	·9
Sept.	·4	·4	·4	·5	·5	·6	·6	·7	·7	·8	·8	·8
Oct.	0·3	0·3	0·3	0·3	0·3	0·4	0·4	0·5	0·5	0·6	0·7	0·7
Nov.	·2	·2	·2	·2	·2	·2	·3	·3	·4	·4	·5	·5
Dec.	0·3	0·2	0·2	0·2	0·1	0·1	0·1	0·2	0·2	0·2	0·3	0·4

Lat.	AZIMUTH											
°	°	°	°	°	°	°	°	°	°	°	°	°
0	359·4	359·4	359·4	359·4	359·4	359·5	359·6	359·7	359·8	359·9	0·0	0·1
20	359·3	359·3	359·3	359·4	359·4	359·5	359·6	359·7	359·8	359·9	0·0	0·1
40	359·2	359·2	359·2	359·2	359·3	359·4	359·5	359·6	359·7	359·9	0·0	0·1
50	359·0	359·0	359·0	359·1	359·1	359·2	359·4	359·5	359·7	359·8	0·0	0·2
55	358·9	358·9	358·9	359·0	359·0	359·2	359·3	359·4	359·6	359·8	0·0	0·2
60	358·7	358·7	358·7	358·8	358·9	359·0	359·2	359·4	359·6	359·8	0·0	0·2
65	358·5	358·5	358·5	358·6	358·7	358·9	359·0	359·3	359·5	359·7	0·0	0·2

ILLUSTRATION	From the daily pages:	° ′		H_O	° ′
On 2023 April 21 at 23ʰ 18ᵐ 56ˢ UT in longitude W 37° 14′, the apparent altitude (corrected for refraction), H_O, of Polaris was 49° 31′·6	GHA Aries (23ʰ)	194 45·3		H_O	49 31·6
	Increment (18ᵐ 56ˢ)	4 44·8		a_0 (argument 162° 16′)	1 16·3
	Longitude (west)	−37 14		a_1 (Lat 50° approx.)	0·6
				a_2 (April)	0·9
	LHA Aries	162 16		Sum − 1° = Lat =	49 49·4

© British Crown Copyright 2022. All rights reserved.

POLARIS (POLE STAR) TABLES, 2023
FOR DETERMINING LATITUDE FROM SEXTANT ALTITUDE AND FOR AZIMUTH

LHA ARIES	240°–249°	250°–259°	260°–269°	270°–279°	280°–289°	290°–299°	300°–309°	310°–319°	320°–329°	330°–339°	340°–349°	350°–359°
°	a_0	a_0	a_0	a_0	a_0	a_0	a_0	a_0	a_0	a_0	a_0	a_0
0	1 35·8	1 33·6	1 30·3	1 26·1	1 21·1	1 15·4	1 09·2	1 02·6	0 56·0	0 49·4	0 43·1	0 37·3
1	35·6	33·3	29·9	25·6	20·5	14·8	08·5	02·0	55·3	48·8	42·5	36·7
2	35·4	33·0	29·6	25·2	20·0	14·2	07·9	01·3	54·6	48·1	41·9	36·2
3	35·2	32·7	29·2	24·7	19·4	13·6	07·2	00·6	54·0	47·5	41·3	35·6
4	35·0	32·4	28·7	24·2	18·9	12·9	06·6	1 00·0	53·3	46·8	40·7	35·1
5	1 34·8	1 32·1	1 28·3	1 23·7	1 18·3	1 12·3	1 05·9	0 59·3	0 52·7	0 46·2	0 40·1	0 34·6
6	34·6	31·7	27·9	23·2	17·7	11·7	05·3	58·6	52·0	45·6	39·5	34·1
7	34·3	31·4	27·5	22·7	17·2	11·1	04·6	58·0	51·4	44·9	39·0	33·6
8	34·1	31·0	27·0	22·2	16·6	10·4	04·0	57·3	50·7	44·3	38·4	33·1
9	33·8	30·7	26·6	21·6	16·0	09·8	03·3	56·6	50·0	43·7	37·8	32·6
10	1 33·6	1 30·3	1 26·1	1 21·1	1 15·4	1 09·2	1 02·6	0 56·0	0 49·4	0 43·1	0 37·3	0 32·1
Lat. °	a_1	a_1	a_1	a_1	a_1	a_1	a_1	a_1	a_1	a_1	a_1	a_1
0	0·6	0·5	0·5	0·5	0·4	0·4	0·4	0·3	0·4	0·4	0·4	0·4
10	·6	·5	·5	·5	·4	·4	·4	·4	·4	·4	·4	·5
20	·6	·6	·5	·5	·5	·4	·4	·4	·4	·4	·5	·5
30	·6	·6	·5	·5	·5	·5	·5	·5	·5	·5	·5	·5
40	0·6	0·6	0·6	0·6	0·5	0·5	0·5	0·5	0·5	0·5	0·5	0·6
45	·6	·6	·6	·6	·6	·6	·6	·6	·6	·6	·6	·6
50	·6	·6	·6	·6	·6	·6	·6	·6	·6	·6	·6	·6
55	·6	·6	·6	·6	·6	·6	·6	·7	·6	·6	·6	·6
60	·6	·6	·6	·7	·7	·7	·7	·7	·7	·7	·7	·7
62	0·6	0·6	0·7	0·7	0·7	0·7	0·7	0·7	0·7	0·7	0·7	0·7
64	·6	·6	·7	·7	·7	·8	·8	·8	·8	·8	·7	·7
66	·6	·7	·7	·7	·8	·8	·8	·8	·8	·8	·8	·7
68	0·6	0·7	0·7	0·8	0·8	0·8	0·9	0·9	0·9	0·8	0·8	0·8
Month	a_2	a_2	a_2	a_2	a_2	a_2	a_2	a_2	a_2	a_2	a_2	a_2
Jan.	0·5	0·5	0·5	0·5	0·5	0·5	0·6	0·6	0·6	0·6	0·7	0·7
Feb.	·4	·4	·4	·4	·4	·4	·4	·4	·5	·5	·6	·6
Mar.	·4	·3	·3	·3	·3	·3	·3	·3	·3	·4	·4	·5
Apr.	0·5	0·4	0·4	0·3	0·3	0·2	0·2	0·2	0·2	0·2	0·3	0·3
May	·6	·5	·5	·4	·4	·3	·3	·2	·2	·2	·2	·2
June	·8	·7	·6	·6	·5	·4	·4	·3	·3	·2	·2	·2
July	0·9	0·8	0·8	0·7	0·7	0·6	0·5	0·5	0·4	0·4	0·3	0·3
Aug.	·9	·9	·9	·8	·8	·7	·7	·6	·6	·5	·5	·4
Sept.	·9	·9	·9	·9	·9	·9	·8	·8	·8	·7	·7	·6
Oct.	0·8	0·8	0·9	0·9	0·9	0·9	0·9	0·9	0·9	0·9	0·9	0·8
Nov.	·6	·7	·8	·8	·9	·9	1·0	1·0	1·0	1·0	1·0	1·0
Dec.	0·4	0·5	0·6	0·7	0·8	0·8	0·9	1·0	1·0	1·0	1·1	1·1
Lat. °	AZIMUTH											
0	0·2	0·3	0·4	0·5	0·5	0·6	0·6	0·6	0·6	0·6	0·6	0·5
20	0·2	0·3	0·4	0·5	0·6	0·6	0·7	0·7	0·7	0·6	0·6	0·5
40	0·3	0·4	0·5	0·6	0·7	0·8	0·8	0·8	0·8	0·8	0·7	0·6
50	0·3	0·5	0·6	0·7	0·8	0·9	1·0	1·0	1·0	0·9	0·9	0·8
55	0·4	0·5	0·7	0·8	0·9	1·0	1·1	1·1	1·1	1·1	1·0	0·9
60	0·4	0·6	0·8	1·0	1·1	1·2	1·2	1·3	1·3	1·2	1·1	1·0
65	0·5	0·7	0·9	1·1	1·3	1·4	1·5	1·5	1·5	1·4	1·3	1·2

Latitude = Apparent altitude (corrected for refraction) $-1° + a_0 + a_1 + a_2$

The table is entered with LHA Aries to determine the column to be used; each column refers to a range of 10°. a_0 is taken, with mental interpolation, from the upper table with the units of LHA Aries in degrees as argument; a_1, a_2 are taken, without interpolation, from the second and third tables with arguments latitude and month respectively. a_0, a_1, a_2, are always positive. The final table gives the azimuth of *Polaris*.

© British Crown Copyright 2022. All rights reserved.

SIGHT REDUCTION PROCEDURES

METHODS AND FORMULAE FOR DIRECT COMPUTATION

1. *Introduction.* In this section, formulae and methods are provided for *calculating* position at sea from observed altitudes taken with a marine sextant using a computer or programmable calculator.

The method uses analogous concepts and similar terminology as that used in *manual* methods of astro-navigation, where position is found by plotting position lines from their intercept and azimuth on a marine chart.

The algorithms are presented in standard algebra suitable for translating into the programming language of the user's computer. The basic ephemeris data may be taken directly from the main tabular pages of a current version of *The Nautical Almanac*. Formulae are given for calculating altitude and azimuth from the *GHA* and *Dec* of a body, and the estimated position of the observer. Formulae are also given for reducing sextant observations to observed altitudes by applying the corrections for dip, refraction, parallax and semi-diameter.

The intercept and azimuth obtained from each observation determine a position line, and the observer should lie on or close to each position line. The method of least squares is used to calculate the fix by finding the position where the sum of the squares of the distances from the position lines is a minimum. The use of least squares has other advantages. For example, it is possible to improve the estimated position at the time of fix by repeating the calculation. It is also possible to include more observations in the solution and to reject doubtful ones.

2. *Notation.*

GHA = Greenwich hour angle. The range of GHA is from $0°$ to $360°$ starting at $0°$ on the Greenwich meridian increasing to the west, back to $360°$ on the Greenwich meridian.

SHA = sidereal hour angle. The range is $0°$ to $360°$.

Dec = declination. The sign convention for declination is north is positive, south is negative. The range is from $-90°$ at the south celestial pole to $+90°$ at the north celestial pole.

$Long$ = longitude. The sign convention is east is positive, west is negative. The range is $-180°$ to $+180°$.

Lat = latitude. The sign convention is north is positive, south is negative. The range is from $-90°$ to $+90°$.

LHA = $GHA + Long$ = local hour angle. The LHA increases to the west from $0°$ on the local meridian to $360°$.

H_c = calculated altitude. Above the horizon is positive, below the horizon is negative. The range is from $-90°$ in the nadir to $+90°$ in the zenith.

H_s = sextant altitude.

H = apparent altitude = sextant altitude corrected for instrumental error and dip.

H_o = observed altitude = apparent altitude corrected for refraction and, in appropriate cases, corrected for parallax and semi-diameter.

Z = Z_n = true azimuth. Z is measured from true north through east, south, west and back to north. The range is from $0°$ to $360°$.

I = sextant index error.

D = dip of horizon.

R = atmospheric refraction.

© British Crown Copyright 2022. All rights reserved.

HP = horizontal parallax of the Sun, Moon, Venus or Mars.
PA = parallax in altitude of the Sun, Moon, Venus or Mars.
SD = semi-diameter of the Sun or Moon.
p = intercept = $H_O - H_C$. Towards is positive, away is negative.
T = course or track, measured as for azimuth from the north.
V = speed in knots.

3. *Entering Basic Data.* When quantities such as GHA are entered, which in *The Nautical Almanac* are given in degrees and minutes, convert them to degrees and decimals of a degree by dividing the minutes by 60 and adding to the degrees; for example, if $GHA = 123°\ 45'\!.6$, enter the two numbers 123 and 45·6 into the memory and set $GHA = 123 + 45·6/60 = 123°\!.7600$. Although four decimal places of a degree are shown in the examples, it is assumed that full precision is maintained in the calculations.

When using a computer or programmable calculator, write a subroutine to convert degrees and minutes to degrees and decimals. Scientific calculators usually have a special key for this purpose. For quantities like *Dec* which require a minus sign for southern declination, change the sign from plus to minus after the value has been converted to degrees and decimals, *e.g.* $Dec = S\,0°\ 12'\!.3 = S\,0°\!.2050 = -0°\!.2050$. Other quantities which require conversion are semi-diameter, horizontal parallax, longitude and latitude.

4. *Interpolation of GHA and Dec* The GHA and Dec of the Sun, Moon and planets are interpolated to the time of observation by direct calculation as follows: If the universal time is $a^h\ b^m\ c^s$, form the interpolation factor $x = b/60 + c/3600$. Enter the tabular value GHA_0 for the preceding hour (a) and the tabular value GHA_1 for the following hour $(a + 1)$ then the interpolated value GHA is given by

$$GHA = GHA_0 + x(GHA_1 - GHA_0)$$

If the GHA passes through 360° between tabular values, add 360° to GHA_1 before interpolation. If the interpolated value exceeds 360°, subtract 360° from GHA.

Similarly for declination, enter the tabular value Dec_0 for the preceding hour (a) and the tabular value Dec_1 for the following hour $(a + 1)$, then the interpolated value Dec is given by

$$Dec = Dec_0 + x(Dec_1 - Dec_0)$$

5. *Example.* (a) Find the GHA and Dec of the Sun on 2023 January 27 at $10^h\ 47^m\ 13^s$ UT.

The interpolation factor $x = 47/60 + 13/3600 = 0^h\!.7869$

page 27 $10^h\ GHA_0 = 326°\ 50'\!.3 = 326°\!.8383$

             $11^h\ GHA_1 = 341°\ 50'\!.2 = 341°\!.8367$

$10^h\!.7869\ GHA = 326·8383 + 0·7869(341·8367 - 326·8383) = 338°\!.6412$

           $10^h\ Dec_0 = S\,18°\ 28'\!.5 = -18°\!.4750$

           $11^h\ Dec_1 = S\,18°\ 27'\!.8 = -18°\!.4633$

$10^h\!.7869\ Dec = -18·4750 + 0·7869(-18·4633 + 18·4750) = -18°\!.4658$

GHA Aries is interpolated in the same way as GHA of a body. For a star the SHA and *Dec* are taken from the tabular page and do not require interpolation, then

$$GHA = GHA\ \text{Aries} + SHA$$

where GHA Aries is interpolated to the time of observation.

© British Crown Copyright 2022. All rights reserved.

(b) Find the *GHA* and *Dec* of *Vega* on 2023 August 13 at 2^h 47^m 13^s UT.

The interpolation factor $x = 0^h\!.7869$ as in the previous example

page 158 2^h *GHA* $\text{Aries}_0 = 351°$ $15'\!.4 = 351°\!.2567$

3^h *GHA* $\text{Aries}_1 = 6°$ $17'\!.9 = 366°\!.2983$ (360° added)

$2^h\!.7869$ *GHA* Aries $= 351\!\cdot\!2567 + 0\!\cdot\!7869(366\!\cdot\!2983 - 351\!\cdot\!2567) = 363°\!.0936$

$SHA = 80°$ $33'\!.7 = 80°\!.5617$

$GHA = GHA$ Aries $+ SHA = 83°\!.6553$ (multiple of 360° removed)

$Dec = \text{N} 38°$ $48'\!.5 = +38°\!.8083$

6. *The calculated altitude and azimuth.* The calculated altitude H_C and true azimuth Z are determined from the *GHA* and *Dec* interpolated to the time of observation and from the *Long* and *Lat* estimated at the time of observation as follows:

Step 1.   Calculate the local hour angle

$$LHA = GHA + Long$$

Add or subtract multiples of 360° to set *LHA* in the range 0° to 360°.

Step 2.   Calculate S, C and the altitude H_C from

$$S = \sin Dec$$
$$C = \cos Dec \cos LHA$$
$$H_C = \sin^{-1}(S \sin Lat + C \cos Lat)$$

where $\sin^{-1}$ is the inverse function of sine.

Step 3.   Calculate X and A from

$$X = (S \cos Lat - C \sin Lat)/\cos H_C$$
$$\text{If } X > +1 \quad \text{set} \quad X = +1$$
$$\text{If } X < -1 \quad \text{set} \quad X = -1$$
$$A = \cos^{-1} X$$

where $\cos^{-1}$ is the inverse function of cosine.

Step 4.   Determine the azimuth Z

$$\text{If } LHA > 180° \quad \text{then} \quad Z = A$$
$$\text{Otherwise} \quad Z = 360° - A$$

7. *Example.* Find the calculated altitude H_C and azimuth Z when

$$GHA = 53° \quad Dec = \text{S} 15° \quad Lat = \text{N} 32° \quad Long = \text{W} 16°$$

For the calculation

$$GHA = 53°\!.0000 \quad Dec = -15°\!.0000 \quad Lat = +32°\!.0000 \quad Long = -16°\!.0000$$

Step 1. $LHA = 53\!\cdot\!0000 - 16\!\cdot\!0000 = 37\!\cdot\!0000$

Step 2. $S = -0\!\cdot\!2588$

$C = +0\!\cdot\!9659 \times 0\!\cdot\!7986 = 0\!\cdot\!7714$

$\sin H_C = -0\!\cdot\!2588 \times 0\!\cdot\!5299 + 0\!\cdot\!7714 \times 0\!\cdot\!8480 = 0\!\cdot\!5171$

$H_C = 31°\!.1346$

© British Crown Copyright 2022. All rights reserved.

Step 3.
$$X = (-0.2588 \times 0.8480 - 0.7714 \times 0.5299)/0.8560 = -0.7340$$
$$A = 137°2239$$

Step 4. Since $LHA \leq 180°$ then $Z = 360° - A = 222°7761$

8. *Reduction from sextant altitude to observed altitude.* The sextant altitude H_S is corrected for both dip and index error to produce the apparent altitude. The observed altitude H_O is calculated by applying a correction for refraction. For the Sun, Moon, Venus and Mars a correction for parallax is also applied to H, and for the Sun and Moon a further correction for semi-diameter is required. The corrections are calculated as follows:

Step 1. Calculate dip
$$D = 0°0293\sqrt{h}$$
where h is the height of eye above the horizon in metres.

Step 2. Calculate apparent altitude
$$H = H_S + I - D$$
where I is the sextant index error.

Step 3. Calculate refraction (R) at a standard temperature of $10°$ Celsius (C) and pressure of 1010 millibars (mb)
$$R_0 = 0°0167/\tan(H + 7.32/(H + 4.32))$$

If the temperature $T°C$ and pressure P mb are known calculate the refraction from
$$R = fR_0 \qquad \text{where} \qquad f = 0.28P/(T + 273)$$
otherwise set $\qquad R = R_0$

Step 4. Calculate the parallax in altitude (PA) from the horizontal parallax (HP) and the apparent altitude (H) for the Sun, Moon, Venus and Mars as follows:
$$PA = HP\cos H$$

For the Sun $HP = 0°0024$. This correction is very small and could be ignored.

For the Moon HP is taken for the nearest hour from the main tabular page and converted to degrees.

For Venus and Mars the HP is taken from the critical table at the bottom of page 259 and converted to degrees.

For the navigational stars and the remaining planets, Jupiter and Saturn, set $PA = 0$.

If an error of $0'2$ is significant the expression for the parallax in altitude for the Moon should include a small correction OB for the oblateness of the Earth as follows:

$$PA = HP\cos H + OB$$
where $\quad OB = -0°0032\sin^2 Lat \cos H + 0°0032\sin(2Lat)\cos Z \sin H$

At mid-latitudes and for altitudes of the Moon below $60°$ a simple approximation to OB is

$$OB = -0°0017\cos H$$

© British Crown Copyright 2022. All rights reserved.

Step 5. Calculate the semi-diameter for the Sun and Moon as follows:

Sun: *SD* is taken from the main tabular page and converted to degrees.

Moon: $SD = 0°2724HP$ where *HP* is taken for the nearest hour from the main tabular page and converted to degrees.

Step 6. Calculate the observed altitude

$$H_O = H - R + PA \pm SD$$

where the plus sign is used if the lower limb of the Sun or Moon was observed and the minus sign if the upper limb was observed.

9. *Example.* The following example illustrates how to use a calculator to reduce the sextant altitude (H_S) to observed altitude (H_O); the sextant altitudes given are assumed to be taken on 2023 August 9 with a marine sextant, zero index error, at height 5·4 m, temperature $-3°$ C and pressure 982 mb, the Moon sights are assumed to be taken at 10^h UT.

Body limb	Sun lower	Sun upper	Moon lower	Moon upper	Venus —	*Polaris* —
Sextant altitude: H_S	21·3283	3·3367	33·4600	26·1117	4·5433	49·6083
Step 1. Dip: $D = 0·0293\sqrt{h}$	0·0681	0·0681	0·0681	0·0681	0·0681	0·0681
Step 2. Apparent altitude: $H = H_S + I - D$	21·2602	3·2686	33·3919	26·0436	4·4752	49·5402
Step 3. Refraction: R_0	0·0423	0·2256	0·0251	0·0338	0·1798	0·0142
f	1·0184	1·0184	1·0184	1·0184	1·0184	1·0184
$R = f R_0$	0·0431	0·2298	0·0256	0·0344	0·1831	0·0144
Step 4. Parallax: HP	0·0024	0·0024	(56′·5) 0·9417	(56′·5) 0·9417	(0′·5) 0·0083	—
Parallax in altitude: $PA = HP \cos H$	0·0022	0·0024	0·7862	0·8460	0·0083	—
Step 5. Semi-diameter: Sun : $SD = 15·8/60$	0·2633	0·2633	—	—	—	—
Moon : $SD = 0·2724HP$	—	—	0·2565	0·2565	—	—
Step 6. Observed altitude: $H_O = H - R + PA \pm SD$	21·4827	2·7779	34·4090	26·5987	4·3005	49·5258

Note that for the Moon the correction for the oblateness of the Earth of about $-0°0017 \cos H$, which equals $-0°0014$ for the lower limb and $-0°0015$ for the upper limb, has been ignored in the above calculation.

10. *Position from intercept and azimuth using a chart.* An estimate is made of the position at the adopted time of fix. The position at the time of observation is then calculated by dead reckoning from the time of fix. For example, if the course (track) *T* and the speed *V* (in knots) of the observer are constant, then *Long* and *Lat* at the time of observation are calculated from

© British Crown Copyright 2022. All rights reserved.

$$Long = L_F + t\,(V/60)\sin T / \cos B_F$$
$$Lat = B_F + t\,(V/60)\cos T$$

where L_F and B_F are the estimated longitude and latitude at the time of fix and t is the time interval in hours from the time of fix to the time of observation, t is positive if the time of observation is after the time of fix and negative if it was before.

The position line of an observation is plotted on a chart using the intercept

$$p = H_O - H_C$$

and azimuth Z with origin at the calculated position ($Long$, Lat) at the time of observation, where H_C and Z are calculated using the method in section 6, page 279. Starting from this calculated position a line is drawn on the chart along the direction of the azimuth to the body. Convert p to nautical miles by multiplying by 60. The position line is drawn at right angles to the azimuth line, distance p from ($Long$, Lat) towards the body if p is positive and distance p away from the body if p is negative. Provided there are no gross errors, the navigator should be somewhere on or near the position line at the time of observation. Two or more position lines are required to determine a fix.

11. *Position from intercept and azimuth by calculation.* The position of the fix may be calculated from two or more sextant observations as follows.

If p_1, Z_1, are the intercept and azimuth of the first observation, p_2, Z_2, of the second observation and so on, form the summations

$$A = \cos^2 Z_1 + \cos^2 Z_2 + \cdots$$
$$B = \cos Z_1 \sin Z_1 + \cos Z_2 \sin Z_2 + \cdots$$
$$C = \sin^2 Z_1 + \sin^2 Z_2 + \cdots$$
$$D = p_1 \cos Z_1 + p_2 \cos Z_2 + \cdots$$
$$E = p_1 \sin Z_1 + p_2 \sin Z_2 + \cdots$$

where the number of terms in each summation is equal to the number of observations.

With $G = A\,C - B^2$, an improved estimate of the position at the time of fix (L_I, B_I) is given by

$$L_I = L_F + (A\,E - B\,D)/(G\cos B_F), \qquad B_I = B_F + (C\,D - B\,E)/G$$

Calculate the distance d between the initial estimated position (L_F, B_F) at the time of fix and the improved estimated position (L_I, B_I) in nautical miles from

$$d = 60\,\sqrt{((L_I - L_F)^2 \cos^2 B_F + (B_I - B_F)^2)}$$

If d exceeds about 20 nautical miles set $L_F = L_I$, $B_F = B_I$ and repeat the calculation until d, the distance between the position at the previous estimate and the improved estimate, is less than about 20 nautical miles.

12. *Example of direct computation.* Using the method described above, calculate the position of a ship on 2023 July 4 at $21^h\ 00^m\ 00^s$ UT from the marine sextant observations of the three stars *Regulus* (No. 26) at $20^h\ 39^m\ 23^s$ UT, *Antares* (No. 42) at $20^h\ 45^m\ 47^s$ UT and *Kochab* (No. 40) at $21^h\ 10^m\ 34^s$ UT, where the observed altitudes of the three stars corrected for the effects of refraction, dip and instrumental error, are $27°.2881$, $25°.8314$ and $47°.5651$ respectively. The ship was travelling at a constant speed of 20 knots on a course of 325° during the period of observation, and the position of the ship at the time of fix $21^h\ 00^m\ 00^s$ UT is only known to the nearest whole degree W 15°, N 32°.

© British Crown Copyright 2022. All rights reserved.

Intermediate values for the first iteration are shown in the table. *GHA* Aries was interpolated from the nearest tabular values on page 132. For the first iteration set $L_F = -15°0000$, $B_F = +32°0000$ at the time of fix at $21^h\ 00^m\ 00^s$ UT.

First Iteration

Body	Regulus	Antares	Kochab
No.	26	42	40
time of observation	$20^h\ 39^m\ 23^s$	$20^h\ 45^m\ 47^s$	$21^h\ 10^m\ 34^s$
H_O	27·2881	25·8314	47·5651
interpolation factor	0·6564	0·7631	0·1761
GHA Aries	232·4432	234·0476	240·2604
SHA (page 132)	207·6000	112·2850	137·3183
GHA	80·0432	346·3326	17·5787
Dec (page 132)	+11·8550	−26·4850	+74·0633
t	−0·3436	−0·2369	+0·1761
Long	−14·9225	−14·9466	−15·0397
Lat	+31·9062	+31·9353	+32·0481
Z	267·2132	151·6401	358·9591
H_C	27·2650	25·5256	47·9652
p	+0·0231	+0·3058	−0·4001

$$A = 1·7764 \quad B = -0·3876 \quad C = 1·2236 \quad D = -0·6703 \quad E = 0·1295 \quad G = 2·0234$$
$$(A\,E - B\,D)/(G \cos B_F) = -0·0174, \qquad (C\,D - B\,E)/G = -0·3805$$

An improved estimate of the position at the time of fix is

$$L_I = L_F - 0·0174 = -15·0174 \quad \text{and} \quad B_I = B_F - 0·3805 = +31·6195$$

Since the distance between the previous estimated position and the improved estimate is $d = 22·8$ nautical miles, set $L_F = -15·0174$, and $B_F = +31·6195$ and repeat the calculation. The table shows the intermediate values of the calculation for the second iteration. In each iteration the quantities H_O, *GHA*, *Dec* and t do not change.

Second Iteration

Body	Regulus	Antares	Kochab
No.	26	42	40
Long	−14·9402	−14·9642	−15·0569
Lat	+31·5256	+31·5548	+31·6676
Z	267·3996	151·5374	358·9737
H_C	27·2980	25·8531	47·5850
p	−0·0098	−0·0218	−0·0199

$$A = 1·7746 \quad B = -0·3916 \quad C = 1·2254 \quad D = -0·0003 \quad E = -0·0002 \quad G = 2·0213$$
$$(A\,E - B\,D)/(G \cos B_F) = -0·0003, \qquad (C\,D - B\,E)/G = -0·0002$$

An improved estimate of the position at the time of fix is

$$L_I = L_F - 0·0003 = -15·0177 \quad \text{and} \quad B_I = B_F - 0·0002 = +31·6192$$

The distance between the previous estimated position and the improved estimated position, $d = 0·02$ nautical miles, is so small that a third iteration would produce a negligible improvement to the estimate of the position.

© British Crown Copyright 2022. All rights reserved.

USE OF CONCISE SIGHT REDUCTION TABLES

1. *Introduction.*   The concise sight reduction tables given on pages 286 to 317 are intended for use when neither more extensive tables nor electronic computing aids are available. These "NAO sight reduction tables" provide for the reduction of the local hour angle and declination of a celestial object to azimuth and altitude, referred to an assumed position on the Earth, for use in the intercept method of celestial navigation which is now standard practice.

2. *Form of tables.*   Entries in the reduction table are at a fixed interval of one degree for all latitudes and hour angles. A compact arrangement results from division of the navigational triangle into two right spherical triangles, so that the table has to be entered twice. Assumed latitude and local hour angle are the arguments for the first entry. The reduction table responds with the intermediate arguments A, B, and Z_1, where A is used as one of the arguments for the second entry to the table, B has to be incremented by the declination to produce the quantity F, and Z_1 is a component of the azimuth angle. The reduction table is then reentered with A and F and yields H, P, and Z_2 where H is the altitude, P is the complement of the parallactic angle, and Z_2 is the second component of the azimuth angle. It is usually necessary to adjust the tabular altitude for the fractional parts of the intermediate entering arguments to derive computed altitude, and an auxiliary table is provided for the purpose. Rules governing signs of the quantities which must be added or subtracted are given in the instructions and summarized on each tabular page. Azimuth angle is the sum of two components and is converted to true azimuth by familiar rules, repeated at the bottom of the tabular pages.

Tabular altitude and intermediate quantities are given to the nearest minute of arc, although errors of 2′ in computed altitude may accrue during adjustment for the minutes parts of entering arguments. Components of azimuth angle are stated to 0°·1; for derived true azimuth, only whole degrees are warranted. Since objects near the zenith are difficult to observe with a marine sextant, they should be avoided; altitudes greater than about 80° are not suited to reduction by this method.

In many circumstances, the accuracy provided by these tables is sufficient. However, to maintain the full accuracy (0′·1) of the ephemeral data in the almanac throughout their reduction to altitude and azimuth, more extensive tables or a calculator should be used.

3. *Use of Tables.*

Step 1.   Determine the Greenwich hour angle (*GHA*) and Declination (*Dec*) of the body from the almanac. Select an assumed latitude (*Lat*) of integral degrees nearest to the estimated latitude. Choose an assumed longitude nearest to the estimated longitude such that the local hour angle

$$LHA = GHA \begin{array}{c} - \text{ west} \\ + \text{ east} \end{array} \text{ longitude}$$

has integral degrees.

Step 2.   Enter the reduction table with *Lat* and *LHA* as arguments. Record the quantities A, B and Z_1. Apply the rules for the sign of B and Z_1: B is minus if $90° < LHA < 270°$: Z_1 has the same sign as B. Set $A° =$ nearest whole degree of A and $A' =$ minutes part of A. This step may be repeated for all reductions before leaving the latitude opening of the table.

Step 3.   Record the declination *Dec*. Apply the rules for the sign of *Dec*: *Dec* is minus if the name of *Dec* (*i.e.* N or S) is contrary to latitude. Add B and *Dec* algebraically to produce F. If F is negative, the object is below the horizon (in sight reduction, this can occur when the objects are close to the horizon). Regard F as positive until step 7. Set $F° =$ nearest whole degree of F and $F' =$ minutes part of F.

© British Crown Copyright 2022. All rights reserved.

Step 4. Enter the reduction table a second time with $A°$ and $F°$ as arguments and record H, P, and Z_2. Set $P° = $ nearest whole degree of P and $Z_2° = $ nearest whole degree of Z_2.

Step 5. Enter the auxiliary table with F' and $P°$ as arguments to obtain $corr_1$ to H for F'. Apply the rule for the sign of $corr_1$: $corr_1$ is minus if $F < 90°$ and $F' > 29'$ or if $F > 90°$ and $F' < 30'$, otherwise $corr_1$ is plus.

Step 6. Enter the auxiliary table with A' and $Z_2°$ as arguments to obtain $corr_2$ to H for A'. Apply the rule for the sign of $corr_2$: $corr_2$ is minus if $A' < 30'$, otherwise $corr_2$ is plus.

Step 7. Calculate the computed altitude H_C as the sum of H, $corr_1$ and $corr_2$. Apply the rule for the sign of H_C: H_C is minus if F is negative.

Step 8. Apply the rule for the sign of Z_2: Z_2 is minus if $F > 90°$. If F is negative, replace Z_2 by $180° - Z_2$. Set the azimuth angle Z equal to the algebraic sum of Z_1 and Z_2 and ignore the resulting sign. Obtain the true azimuth Z_n from the rules

$$\text{For N latitude, if} \quad LHA > 180° \quad Z_n = Z$$
$$\text{if} \quad LHA < 180° \quad Z_n = 360° - Z$$

$$\text{For S latitude, if} \quad LHA > 180° \quad Z_n = 180° - Z$$
$$\text{if} \quad LHA < 180° \quad Z_n = 180° + Z$$

Observed altitude H_O is compared with H_C to obtain the altitude difference, which, with Z_n, is used to plot the position line.

4. *Example.* (a) Required the altitude and azimuth of *Schedar* on 2023 February 4 at UT $06^h 33^m$ from the estimated position N 53°, E 5°.

1. Assumed latitude $Lat = \quad 53°$ N
   From the almanac $GHA = 221° \ 58'$
   Assumed longitude $5° \ 02'$ E
   Local hour angle $LHA = 227$

2. Reduction table, 1st entry
   $(Lat, LHA) = (53, 227)$ $A = \quad 26 \quad 07$ $A° = 26, A' = 7$
                                 $B = -27 \quad 12$ $Z_1 = -49\cdot4,$ $90° < LHA < 270°$
3. From the almanac $Dec = +56 \quad 40$ Lat and Dec same
   Sum $= B + Dec$ $F = +29 \quad 28$ $F° = 29, F' = 28$

4. Reduction table, 2nd entry
   $(A°, F°) = (26, 29)$ $H = \quad 25 \quad 50$ $P° = 61$
                                                     $Z_2 = 76\cdot3, Z_2° = 76$

5. Auxiliary table, 1st entry
   $(F', P°) = (28, 61)$ $corr_1 = \quad \underline{+24}$ $F < 90°, F' < 29'$
   Sum $26 \quad 14$

6. Auxiliary table, 2nd entry
   $(A', Z_2°) = (7, 76)$ $corr_2 = \quad \underline{-2}$ $A' < 30'$
7. Sum $=$ computed altitude $H_C = +26° \ 12'$ $F > 0°$

8. Azimuth, first component $Z_1 = -49\cdot4$ same sign as B
   second component $Z_2 = \underline{+76\cdot3}$ $F < 90°, F > 0°$
   Sum $=$ azimuth angle $Z = \quad 26\cdot9$

   True azimuth $Z_n = \quad 027°$ N Lat, $LHA > 180°$

continued on page 318

© British Crown Copyright 2022. All rights reserved.

SIGHT REDUCTION TABLE

B: (−) for 90° < LHA < 270°
Dec:(−) for Lat. contrary name

Z₁: same sign as B
Z₂: (−) for F > 90°

Lat./A LHA/F	0° A/H	0° B/P	0° Z₁/Z₂	1° A/H	1° B/P	1° Z₁/Z₂	2° A/H	2° B/P	2° Z₁/Z₂	3° A/H	3° B/P	3° Z₁/Z₂	4° A/H	4° B/P	4° Z₁/Z₂	5° A/H	5° B/P	5° Z₁/Z₂	Lat./A LHA
0	0 00	90 00	90·0	0 00	89 00	90·0	0 00	88 00	90·0	0 00	87 00	90·0	0 00	86 00	90·0	0 00	85 00	90·0	180 / 360
1	1 00	90 00	90·0	1 00	89 00	90·0	1 00	88 00	90·0	1 00	87 00	89·9	1 00	86 00	89·9	1 00	85 00	89·9	181 / 359
2	2 00	90 00	90·0	2 00	89 00	90·0	2 00	88 00	89·9	2 00	87 00	89·9	2 00	86 00	89·9	2 00	85 00	89·9	182 / 358
3	3 00	90 00	90·0	3 00	89 00	90·0	3 00	88 00	89·9	3 00	87 00	89·8	3 00	86 00	89·8	3 00	85 00	89·7	183 / 357
4	4 00	90 00	90·0	4 00	89 00	89·9	4 00	88 00	89·9	4 00	87 00	89·8	4 00	86 00	89·7	4 59	84 59	89·7	184 / 356
5	5 00	90 00	90·0	5 00	89 00	89·9	5 00	88 00	89·8	5 00	86 59	89·7	4 59	85 59	89·7	4 59	84 59	89·6	185 / 355
6	6 00	90 00	90·0	6 00	89 00	89·9	6 00	87 59	89·8	6 00	86 59	89·7	5 59	85 59	89·6	5 59	84 58	89·5	186 / 354
7	7 00	90 00	90·0	7 00	89 00	89·9	7 00	87 59	89·8	6 59	86 59	89·6	6 59	85 58	89·5	6 58	84 58	89·4	187 / 353
8	8 00	90 00	90·0	8 00	89 00	89·9	8 00	87 59	89·7	7 59	86 58	89·6	7 59	85 58	89·4	7 58	84 57	89·3	188 / 352
9	9 00	90 00	90·0	9 00	88 59	89·8	9 00	87 59	89·7	8 59	86 58	89·5	8 59	85 57	89·4	8 58	84 56	89·2	189 / 351
10	10 00	90 00	90·0	10 00	88 59	89·8	10 00	87 58	89·6	9 59	86 57	89·5	9 59	85 56	89·3	9 58	84 55	89·2	190 / 350
11	11 00	90 00	90·0	11 00	88 59	89·8	11 00	87 58	89·6	10 59	86 57	89·4	10 58	85 56	89·2	10 57	84 54	89·0	191 / 349
12	12 00	90 00	90·0	12 00	88 58	89·8	12 00	87 57	89·6	11 59	86 56	89·4	11 58	85 55	89·2	11 57	84 53	88·9	192 / 348
13	13 00	90 00	90·0	13 00	88 58	89·8	13 00	87 57	89·5	12 59	86 56	89·3	12 58	85 54	89·1	12 57	84 52	88·8	193 / 347
14	14 00	90 00	90·0	14 00	88 58	89·8	14 00	87 56	89·5	13 59	86 55	89·3	13 58	85 53	89·0	13 57	84 51	88·8	194 / 346
15	15 00	90 00	90·0	15 00	88 58	89·7	15 00	87 56	89·5	14 59	86 54	89·2	14 58	85 52	88·9	14 56	84 49	88·7	195 / 345
16	16 00	90 00	90·0	16 00	88 58	89·7	16 00	87 55	89·4	15 59	86 53	89·2	15 58	85 51	88·9	15 56	84 48	88·6	196 / 344
17	17 00	90 00	90·0	17 00	88 57	89·7	17 00	87 55	89·4	16 59	86 52	89·1	16 57	85 50	88·8	16 56	84 46	88·5	197 / 343
18	18 00	90 00	90·0	18 00	88 57	89·7	18 00	87 54	89·4	17 58	86 51	89·0	17 57	85 48	88·7	17 56	84 45	88·4	198 / 342
19	19 00	90 00	90·0	19 00	88 57	89·6	19 00	87 53	89·3	18 58	86 50	89·0	18 57	85 46	88·6	18 55	84 43	88·3	199 / 341
20	20 00	90 00	90·0	20 00	88 56	89·6	20 00	87 52	89·3	19 58	86 48	88·9	19 57	85 45	88·5	19 55	84 41	88·2	200 / 340
21	21 00	90 00	90·0	21 00	88 56	89·6	21 00	87 51	89·2	20 58	86 47	88·8	20 57	85 43	88·4	20 55	84 39	88·1	201 / 339
22	22 00	90 00	90·0	22 00	88 55	89·6	22 00	87 51	89·2	21 58	86 46	88·8	21 57	85 41	88·4	21 54	84 37	88·0	202 / 338
23	23 00	90 00	90·0	23 00	88 55	89·5	23 00	87 50	89·1	22 58	86 44	88·7	22 56	85 39	88·3	22 54	84 34	87·9	203 / 337
24	24 00	90 00	90·0	24 00	88 54	89·5	24 00	87 49	89·1	23 58	86 43	88·7	23 56	85 37	88·2	23 54	84 32	87·8	204 / 336
25	25 00	90 00	90·0	25 00	88 54	89·5	25 00	87 48	89·1	24 58	86 41	88·6	24 56	85 35	88·1	24 54	84 29	87·7	205 / 335
26	26 00	90 00	90·0	26 00	88 53	89·5	26 00	87 47	89·0	25 58	86 40	88·5	25 56	85 33	88·1	25 53	84 26	87·6	206 / 334
27	27 00	90 00	90·0	27 00	88 53	89·4	27 00	87 45	89·0	26 58	86 38	88·5	26 56	85 31	88·0	26 53	84 24	87·5	207 / 333
28	28 00	90 00	90·0	28 00	88 52	89·4	28 00	87 44	88·9	27 57	86 36	88·4	27 56	85 28	87·9	27 53	84 20	87·3	208 / 332
29	29 00	90 00	90·0	29 00	88 51	89·4	29 00	87 43	88·9	28 57	86 34	88·3	28 55	85 26	87·8	28 53	84 17	87·2	209 / 331
30	30 00	90 00	90·0	30 00	88 51	89·4	30 00	87 41	88·8	29 57	86 32	88·3	29 55	85 23	87·7	29 52	84 14	87·1	210 / 330
31	31 00	90 00	90·0	31 00	88 50	89·4	31 00	87 40	88·8	30 57	86 30	88·2	30 55	85 21	87·6	30 52	84 10	87·0	211 / 329
32	32 00	90 00	90·0	32 00	88 49	89·4	32 00	87 39	88·8	31 57	86 28	88·1	31 55	85 17	87·5	31 52	84 07	86·9	212 / 328
33	33 00	90 00	90·0	33 00	88 48	89·3	33 00	87 37	88·7	32 57	86 25	88·1	32 55	85 14	87·4	32 51	84 03	86·8	213 / 327
34	34 00	90 00	90·0	34 00	88 48	89·3	34 00	87 35	88·7	33 57	86 23	88·0	33 54	85 11	87·3	33 51	83 59	86·6	214 / 326
35	35 00	90 00	90·0	35 00	88 47	89·3	35 00	87 34	88·6	34 57	86 20	87·9	34 54	85 07	87·2	34 51	83 54	86·5	215 / 325
36	36 00	90 00	90·0	36 00	88 46	89·3	36 00	87 32	88·5	35 57	86 18	87·8	35 54	85 04	87·1	35 51	83 50	86·4	216 / 324
37	37 00	90 00	90·0	37 00	88 45	89·2	37 00	87 30	88·5	36 56	86 15	87·7	36 54	85 00	87·0	36 50	83 45	86·2	217 / 323
38	38 00	90 00	90·0	38 00	88 44	89·2	38 00	87 28	88·4	37 56	86 12	87·7	37 53	84 56	86·9	37 50	83 40	86·1	218 / 322
39	39 00	90 00	90·0	39 00	88 43	89·2	39 00	87 26	88·4	38 56	86 09	87·6	38 53	84 52	86·8	38 49	83 35	86·0	219 / 321
40	40 00	90 00	90·0	40 00	88 42	89·2	40 00	87 23	88·3	39 56	86 05	87·5	39 53	84 47	86·7	39 49	83 29	85·8	220 / 320
41	41 00	90 00	90·0	41 00	88 41	89·1	41 00	87 21	88·3	40 56	86 02	87·4	40 53	84 42	86·5	40 49	83 23	85·7	221 / 319
42	42 00	90 00	90·0	42 00	88 39	89·1	42 00	87 19	88·2	41 56	85 58	87·3	41 52	84 37	86·4	41 48	83 17	85·5	222 / 318
43	43 00	90 00	90·0	43 00	88 38	89·1	43 00	87 16	88·1	42 56	85 54	87·2	42 52	84 32	86·3	42 48	83 11	85·4	223 / 317
44	44 00	90 00	90·0	43 59	88 37	89·0	43 59	87 13	88·1	43 55	85 50	87·1	43 52	84 27	86·1	43 47	83 04	85·2	224 / 316
45	45 00	90 00	90·0	44 59	88 35	89·0	44 59	87 10	88·0	44 55	85 46	87·0	44 52	84 21	86·0	44 47	82 57	85·0	225 / 315

© British Crown Copyright 2022. All rights reserved.

Lat / A	LHA / F	0° A/H	0° B/P	0° Z_1/Z_2	1° A/H	1° B/P	1° Z_1/Z_2	2° A/H	2° B/P	2° Z_1/Z_2	3° A/H	3° B/P	3° Z_1/Z_2	4° A/H	4° B/P	4° Z_1/Z_2	5° A/H	5° B/P	5° Z_1/Z_2	A	LHA
45	135	45 00	90 00	90·0	44 59	88 35	89·0	44 58	87 10	88·0	44 55	85 46	87·0	44 52	84 21	86·0	44 47	82 57	85·0	315	225
46	134	46 00	90 00	90·0	45 59	88 34	89·0	45 58	87 07	87·9	45 55	85 41	86·9	45 51	84 15	85·9	45 46	82 49	84·8	314	226
47	133	47 00	90 00	90·0	46 59	88 32	88·9	46 58	87 04	87·9	46 55	85 36	86·8	46 51	84 09	85·7	46 46	82 41	84·7	313	227
48	132	48 00	90 00	90·0	47 59	88 30	88·9	47 58	87 01	87·8	47 55	85 31	86·7	47 51	84 02	85·6	47 46	82 33	84·5	312	228
49	131	49 00	90 00	90·0	48 59	88 29	88·8	48 58	86 57	87·8	48 55	85 26	86·7	48 50	83 55	85·4	48 45	82 24	84·3	311	229
50	130	50 00	90 00	90·0	49 59	88 27	88·8	49 58	86 53	87·6	49 54	85 20	86·4	49 50	83 47	85·2	49 44	82 15	84·1	310	230
51	129	51 00	90 00	90·0	50 59	88 25	88·8	50 57	86 49	87·5	50 54	85 14	86·3	50 50	83 40	85·1	50 44	82 05	83·9	309	231
52	128	52 00	90 00	90·0	51 59	88 23	88·7	51 57	86 45	87·4	51 54	85 08	86·2	51 49	83 31	84·9	51 43	81 55	83·6	308	232
53	127	53 00	90 00	90·0	52 59	88 20	88·7	52 57	86 41	87·3	52 54	85 01	86·0	52 49	83 22	84·7	52 43	81 44	83·4	307	233
54	126	54 00	90 00	90·0	53 59	88 18	88·6	53 57	86 36	87·2	53 53	84 54	85·9	53 49	83 13	84·5	53 42	81 32	83·2	306	234
55	125	55 00	90 00	90·0	54 59	88 15	88·6	54 57	86 31	87·1	54 53	84 47	85·7	54 48	83 03	84·3	54 41	81 20	82·9	305	235
56	124	56 00	90 00	90·0	55 59	88 13	88·5	55 57	86 26	87·0	55 53	84 39	85·6	55 48	82 52	84·1	55 41	81 06	82·6	304	236
57	123	57 00	90 00	90·0	56 59	88 10	88·5	56 57	86 20	86·9	56 53	84 30	85·4	56 47	82 41	83·9	56 40	80 52	82·4	303	237
58	122	58 00	90 00	90·0	57 59	88 07	88·4	57 57	86 14	86·8	57 52	84 21	85·2	57 47	82 29	83·6	57 38	80 38	82·1	302	238
59	121	59 00	90 00	90·0	58 59	88 04	88·3	58 56	86 07	86·7	58 52	84 11	85·0	58 46	82 16	83·4	58 37	80 22	81·7	301	239
60	120	60 00	90 00	90·0	59 59	88 00	88·3	59 56	86 00	86·5	59 52	84 01	84·8	59 46	82 02	83·1	59 37	80 05	81·4	300	240
61	119	61 00	90 00	90·0	60 59	87 56	88·2	60 56	85 53	86·4	60 52	83 50	84·6	60 45	81 48	82·8	60 36	79 48	81·1	299	241
62	118	62 00	90 00	90·0	61 59	87 52	88·1	61 56	85 45	86·2	61 51	83 38	84·4	61 44	81 32	82·5	61 36	79 27	80·7	298	242
63	117	63 00	90 00	90·0	62 59	87 48	88·0	62 56	85 36	86·1	62 51	83 25	84·1	62 44	81 15	82·2	62 35	79 06	80·3	297	243
64	116	64 00	90 00	90·0	63 59	87 43	88·0	63 56	85 27	85·9	63 50	83 11	83·9	63 43	80 56	81·9	63 33	78 43	79·9	296	244
65	115	65 00	90 00	90·0	64 59	87 38	87·9	64 56	85 17	85·7	64 50	82 56	83·6	64 42	80 36	81·5	64 32	78 18	79·4	295	245
66	114	66 00	90 00	90·0	65 59	87 33	87·8	65 55	85 06	85·5	65 49	82 39	83·3	65 41	80 15	81·1	65 31	77 52	78·9	294	246
67	113	67 00	90 00	90·0	66 59	87 27	87·6	66 55	84 54	85·3	66 49	82 20	83·0	66 40	79 51	80·7	66 29	77 23	78·4	293	247
68	112	68 00	90 00	90·0	67 59	87 20	87·5	67 55	84 40	85·1	67 48	82 02	82·6	67 39	79 26	80·2	67 28	76 51	77·8	292	248
69	111	69 00	90 00	90·0	68 59	87 13	87·4	68 55	84 26	84·8	68 48	81 41	82·2	68 38	78 58	79·7	68 26	76 17	77·2	291	249
70	110	70 00	90 00	90·0	69 59	87 05	87·3	69 54	84 10	84·5	69 47	81 17	81·8	69 37	78 27	79·2	69 25	75 39	76·5	290	250
71	109	71 00	90 00	90·0	70 58	86 56	87·1	70 54	83 53	84·2	70 46	80 51	81·4	70 36	77 53	78·5	70 23	74 58	75·8	289	251
72	108	72 00	90 00	90·0	71 58	86 46	86·9	71 54	83 33	83·9	71 46	80 22	80·8	71 35	77 15	77·9	71 20	74 12	75·0	288	252
73	107	73 00	90 00	90·0	72 58	86 35	86·7	72 53	83 11	83·5	72 45	79 50	80·3	72 33	76 33	77·1	72 18	73 20	74·1	287	253
74	106	74 00	90 00	90·0	73 58	86 23	86·5	73 53	82 47	83·1	73 44	79 14	79·7	73 31	75 46	76·3	73 15	72 23	73·1	286	254
75	105	75 00	90 00	90·0	74 58	86 09	86·3	74 52	82 19	82·6	74 43	78 33	78·9	74 29	74 53	75·4	74 12	71 19	72·0	285	255
76	104	76 00	90 00	90·0	75 58	85 52	86·0	75 52	81 47	82·0	75 42	77 47	78·1	75 27	73 53	74·4	75 09	70 07	70·7	284	256
77	103	77 00	90 00	90·0	76 58	85 34	85·7	76 51	81 11	81·4	76 40	76 53	77·2	76 25	72 44	73·2	76 05	68 45	69·3	283	257
78	102	78 00	90 00	90·0	77 58	85 12	85·3	77 50	80 28	80·7	77 38	75 51	76·2	77 22	71 25	71·8	77 01	67 11	67·7	282	258
79	101	79 00	90 00	90·0	78 57	84 46	84·9	78 49	79 38	79·8	78 36	74 37	74·9	78 18	69 52	70·3	77 56	65 23	65·7	281	259
80	100	80 00	90 00	90·0	79 57	84 16	84·3	79 48	78 38	78·8	79 34	73 12	73·5	79 14	68 04	68·4	78 50	63 16	63·7	280	260
81	99	81 00	90 00	90·0	80 57	83 38	83·7	80 47	77 25	77·6	80 31	71 29	71·7	80 09	65 55	66·2	79 43	60 47	61·2	279	261
82	98	82 00	90 00	90·0	81 56	82 51	82·9	81 45	75 55	76·1	81 28	69 22	69·6	81 04	63 19	63·6	80 34	57 51	58·2	278	262
83	97	83 00	90 00	90·0	82 56	81 51	81·9	82 43	74 01	74·1	82 23	66 44	66·9	81 57	60 09	60·4	81 24	54 20	54·6	277	263
84	96	84 00	90 00	90·0	83 55	80 31	80·6	83 41	71 32	71·6	83 18	63 29	63·5	82 48	56 13	56·4	82 12	50 04	50·3	276	264
85	95	85 00	90 00	90·0	84 54	78 40	78·7	84 37	68 10	68·3	84 10	58 59	59·1	83 36	51 16	51·4	82 56	44 53	45·1	275	265
86	94	86 00	90 00	90·0	85 53	75 57	76·0	85 32	63 24	63·5	85 00	53 05	53·2	84 21	44 56	45·1	83 36	38 34	38·7	274	266
87	93	87 00	90 00	90·0	86 50	71 33	71·6	86 24	56 17	56·3	85 45	44 58	45·0	85 00	36 49	36·9	84 10	30 53	31·0	273	267
88	92	88 00	90 00	90·0	87 46	63 26	63·4	87 10	44 59	45·0	86 24	33 40	33·7	85 32	26 31	26·6	84 37	21 45	21·8	272	268
89	91	89 00	90 00	90·0	88 35	45 00	45·0	87 46	26 33	26·6	86 52	18 25	18·4	85 53	14 01	14·0	84 54	11 17	11·3	271	269
90	90	90 00	0 00	0·0	89 00	0 00		88 00	0 00	0·0	87 00	0 00	0·0	86 00	0 00	0·0	85 00	0 00	0·0	270	270

N. Lat.: for LHA > 180° ... $Z_n = Z$
for LHA < 180° ... $Z_n = 360° - Z$

S. Lat.: for LHA > 180° ... $Z_n = 180° - Z$
for LHA < 180° ... $Z_n = 180° + Z$

© British Crown Copyright 2022. All rights reserved.

SIGHT REDUCTION TABLE

B: (−) for 90° < LHA < 270°
Dec:(−) for Lat. contrary name

Z₁: same sign as B
Z₂: (−) for F > 90°

Lat./A LHA/F	F	6° A/H	6° B/P	6° Z₁/Z₂	7° A/H	7° B/P	7° Z₁/Z₂	8° A/H	8° B/P	8° Z₁/Z₂	9° A/H	9° B/P	9° Z₁/Z₂	10° A/H	10° B/P	10° Z₁/Z₂	11° A/H	11° B/P	11° Z₁/Z₂	A	LHA
0	180	0 00	84 00	90·0	0 00	83 00	90·0	0 00	82 00	90·0	0 00	81 00	90·0	0 00	80 00	90·0	0 00	79 00	90·0	180	360
1	179	1 00	84 00	89·9	1 00	83 00	89·9	0 59	82 00	89·9	0 59	81 00	89·8	0 59	80 00	89·8	0 59	79 00	89·8	181	359
2	178	1 59	84 00	89·8	1 59	83 00	89·8	1 59	82 00	89·7	1 59	81 00	89·7	1 58	80 00	89·7	1 58	79 00	89·6	182	358
3	177	2 59	84 00	89·7	2 59	82 59	89·6	2 58	81 59	89·6	2 58	80 59	89·5	2 57	79 59	89·5	2 57	78 59	89·4	183	357
4	176	3 59	83 59	89·6	3 58	82 59	89·5	3 58	81 59	89·4	3 57	80 59	89·4	3 56	79 59	89·3	3 56	78 58	89·2	184	356
5	175	4 58	83 59	89·5	4 58	82 58	89·4	4 57	81 58	89·3	4 56	80 58	89·2	4 55	79 58	89·1	4 54	78 57	89·0	185	355
6	174	5 58	83 58	89·4	5 57	82 58	89·3	5 56	81 57	89·2	5 56	80 57	89·1	5 55	79 57	89·0	5 53	78 56	88·9	186	354
7	173	6 58	83 57	89·3	6 57	82 57	89·2	6 56	81 56	89·0	6 55	80 56	88·9	6 54	79 56	88·8	6 52	78 55	88·7	187	353
8	172	7 57	83 57	89·2	7 56	82 56	89·0	7 55	81 55	88·9	7 54	80 55	88·7	7 53	79 54	88·6	7 51	78 54	88·5	188	352
9	171	8 57	83 56	89·1	8 56	82 55	88·9	8 55	81 54	88·7	8 53	80 54	88·6	8 52	79 53	88·4	8 50	78 52	88·3	189	351
10	170	9 57	83 54	88·9	9 55	82 54	88·7	9 54	81 53	88·6	9 53	80 52	88·4	9 51	79 51	88·2	9 49	78 50	88·1	190	350
11	169	10 56	83 53	88·8	10 55	82 52	88·6	10 53	81 51	88·5	10 52	80 50	88·3	10 50	79 49	88·1	10 48	78 48	87·9	191	349
12	168	11 56	83 52	88·7	11 55	82 51	88·5	11 53	81 49	88·3	11 51	80 48	88·1	11 49	79 47	87·9	11 47	78 46	87·7	192	348
13	167	12 55	83 51	88·6	12 54	82 49	88·4	12 52	81 48	88·2	12 50	80 46	87·9	12 48	79 45	87·7	12 45	78 43	87·5	193	347
14	166	13 55	83 49	88·5	13 54	82 47	88·3	13 52	81 46	88·0	13 49	80 44	87·7	13 47	79 42	87·5	13 44	78 40	87·3	194	346
15	165	14 55	83 47	88·4	14 53	82 45	88·1	14 51	81 43	87·9	14 49	80 41	87·6	14 46	79 39	87·3	14 43	78 37	87·1	195	345
16	164	15 54	83 46	88·2	15 53	82 43	88·0	15 50	81 41	87·7	15 48	80 39	87·4	15 45	79 36	87·1	15 42	78 34	86·9	196	344
17	163	16 54	83 44	88·1	16 52	82 41	87·9	16 50	81 38	87·6	16 47	80 36	87·3	16 44	79 33	87·0	16 41	78 31	86·7	197	343
18	162	17 54	83 42	88·0	17 52	82 39	87·7	17 49	81 36	87·4	17 46	80 33	87·1	17 43	79 30	86·8	17 39	78 27	86·5	198	342
19	161	18 54	83 39	87·9	18 51	82 36	87·6	18 48	81 33	87·3	18 45	80 29	86·9	18 42	79 26	86·6	18 38	78 23	86·2	199	341
20	160	19 53	83 37	87·8	19 51	82 33	87·5	19 48	81 30	87·1	19 45	80 26	86·7	19 41	79 22	86·4	19 37	78 19	86·0	200	340
21	159	20 53	83 35	87·7	20 50	82 30	87·3	20 47	81 26	86·9	20 44	80 22	86·6	20 40	79 18	86·2	20 36	78 14	85·8	201	339
22	158	21 52	83 32	87·6	21 50	82 27	87·2	21 47	81 23	86·8	21 43	80 18	86·4	21 39	79 14	86·0	21 35	78 10	85·6	202	338
23	157	22 52	83 29	87·5	22 49	82 24	87·1	22 46	81 19	86·6	22 42	80 14	86·2	22 38	79 09	85·8	22 33	78 05	85·4	203	337
24	156	23 52	83 26	87·3	23 49	82 21	86·9	23 45	81 15	86·5	23 41	80 10	86·0	23 37	79 05	85·6	23 32	77 59	85·1	204	336
25	155	24 51	83 23	87·2	24 48	82 17	86·8	24 44	81 11	86·3	24 40	80 05	85·8	24 36	78 59	85·4	24 31	77 54	84·9	205	335
26	154	25 51	83 20	87·1	25 48	82 13	86·6	25 44	81 07	86·1	25 39	80 00	85·6	25 35	78 54	85·2	25 29	77 48	84·7	206	334
27	153	26 50	83 16	87·0	26 47	82 09	86·5	26 43	81 02	85·9	26 38	79 55	85·4	26 33	78 48	85·0	26 28	77 42	84·4	207	333
28	152	27 50	83 13	86·8	27 46	82 05	86·3	27 42	80 57	85·8	27 37	79 50	85·2	27 32	78 42	84·7	27 27	77 35	84·2	208	332
29	151	28 50	83 09	86·7	28 46	82 01	86·1	28 41	80 52	85·6	28 37	79 44	85·0	28 31	78 36	84·5	28 25	77 28	84·0	209	331
30	150	29 49	83 05	86·5	29 45	81 56	86·0	29 41	80 47	85·4	29 36	79 38	84·8	29 30	78 29	84·3	29 24	77 21	83·7	210	330
31	149	30 49	83 01	86·4	30 45	81 51	85·8	30 40	80 41	85·2	30 35	79 32	84·6	30 29	78 23	84·0	30 22	77 13	83·5	211	329
32	148	31 48	82 56	86·3	31 44	81 46	85·6	31 39	80 35	85·0	31 34	79 25	84·4	31 27	78 15	83·8	31 21	77 05	83·2	212	328
33	147	32 48	82 51	86·1	32 43	81 40	85·5	32 38	80 29	84·8	32 33	79 18	84·2	32 26	78 08	83·6	32 19	76 57	82·9	213	327
34	146	33 47	82 46	86·0	33 43	81 35	85·3	33 37	80 23	84·6	33 32	79 11	84·0	33 25	78 00	83·3	33 18	76 48	82·7	214	326
35	145	34 47	82 41	85·8	34 42	81 29	85·1	34 37	80 16	84·4	34 30	79 03	83·8	34 24	77 51	83·1	34 16	76 39	82·4	215	325
36	144	35 46	82 36	85·7	35 41	81 22	84·9	35 36	80 09	84·2	35 29	78 55	83·5	35 22	77 42	82·8	35 14	76 29	82·1	216	324
37	143	36 46	82 30	85·5	36 41	81 16	84·8	36 35	80 01	84·0	36 28	78 47	83·2	36 21	77 33	82·5	36 13	76 19	81·8	217	323
38	142	37 45	82 24	85·3	37 40	81 09	84·6	37 34	79 53	83·8	37 27	78 38	83·0	37 19	77 23	82·3	37 11	76 09	81·5	218	322
39	141	38 45	82 18	85·2	38 39	81 01	84·4	38 33	79 45	83·6	38 26	78 29	82·8	38 18	77 13	82·0	38 09	75 57	81·2	219	321
40	140	39 44	82 11	85·0	39 39	80 54	84·2	39 32	79 36	83·3	39 24	78 19	82·5	39 16	77 02	81·7	39 08	75 45	80·9	220	320
41	139	40 44	82 04	84·8	40 38	80 46	84·0	40 31	79 27	83·1	40 23	78 09	82·3	40 15	76 51	81·4	40 05	75 33	80·6	221	319
42	138	41 43	81 57	84·6	41 37	80 37	83·7	41 30	79 17	82·9	41 22	77 58	82·0	41 13	76 39	81·1	41 04	75 21	80·3	222	318
43	137	42 42	81 49	84·4	42 36	80 28	83·5	42 29	79 07	82·6	42 21	77 47	81·7	42 12	76 27	80·8	42 02	75 07	79·9	223	317
44	136	43 42	81 41	84·2	43 35	80 19	83·3	43 28	78 57	82·3	43 19	77 35	81·4	43 10	76 14	80·5	43 00	74 53	79·6	224	316
45	135	44 41	81 33	84·0	44 34	80 09	83·1	44 27	78 46	82·1	44 18	77 22	81·1	44 08	76 00	80·1	43 57	74 38	79·2	225	315

© British Crown Copyright 2022. All rights reserved.

Lat./A (A)	LHA/F	6° A/H	6° B/P	6° Z₁/Z₂	7° A/H	7° B/P	7° Z₁/Z₂	8° A/H	8° B/P	8° Z₁/Z₂	9° A/H	9° B/P	9° Z₁/Z₂	10° A/H	10° B/P	10° Z₁/Z₂	11° A/H	11° B/P	11° Z₁/Z₂	LHA	Lat./A (A)
135	45	44 41	81 33	84·0	44 34	80 09	83·1	44 27	78 46	82·1	44 18	77 22	81·1	44 08	76 00	80·1	43 57	74 38	79·2	225	315
134	46	45 41	81 24	83·8	45 34	79 59	82·8	45 26	78 34	81·8	45 16	77 09	80·8	45 06	75 45	79·8	44 55	74 22	78·8	226	314
133	47	46 40	81 14	83·6	46 33	79 48	82·6	46 24	78 21	81·5	46 14	76 56	80·5	46 04	75 30	79·5	45 53	74 05	78·4	227	313
132	48	47 39	81 04	83·4	47 32	79 36	82·3	47 23	78 08	81·2	47 13	76 41	80·1	47 03	75 14	79·1	46 51	73 48	78·0	228	312
131	49	48 38	80 54	83·1	48 31	79 24	82·0	48 22	77 55	80·9	48 12	76 26	79·8	48 01	74 57	78·7	47 48	73 30	77·6	229	311
130	50	49 38	80 43	82·9	49 30	79 11	81·7	49 20	77 40	80·6	49 10	76 09	79·4	48 58	74 40	78·3	48 46	73 10	77·2	230	310
129	51	50 37	80 31	82·6	50 29	78 58	81·4	50 19	77 25	80·2	50 08	75 52	79·1	49 56	74 21	77·9	49 43	72 50	76·7	231	309
128	52	51 36	80 19	82·4	51 27	78 43	81·1	51 18	77 08	79·9	51 06	75 34	78·7	50 54	74 01	77·5	50 40	72 29	76·3	232	308
127	53	52 35	80 06	82·1	52 26	78 28	80·8	52 16	76 51	79·5	52 04	75 15	78·3	51 52	73 40	77·0	51 37	72 06	75·8	233	307
126	54	53 34	79 52	81·8	53 25	78 12	80·5	53 14	76 33	79·2	53 02	74 55	77·8	52 49	73 18	76·6	52 35	71 42	75·3	234	306
125	55	54 33	79 37	81·5	54 24	77 55	80·1	54 13	76 14	78·8	54 00	74 34	77·4	53 47	72 55	76·1	53 31	71 17	74·8	235	305
124	56	55 32	79 21	81·2	55 22	77 37	79·7	55 11	75 54	78·3	54 58	74 11	76·9	54 44	72 30	75·6	54 28	70 50	74·2	236	304
123	57	56 31	79 05	80·9	56 21	77 18	79·4	56 09	75 32	77·7	55 56	73 47	76·5	55 41	72 04	75·0	55 25	70 22	73·6	237	303
122	58	57 30	78 47	80·5	57 19	76 57	79·0	57 07	75 09	77·4	56 53	73 22	75·9	56 38	71 36	74·5	56 21	69 51	73·0	238	302
121	59	58 29	78 28	80·1	58 18	76 35	78·5	58 05	74 44	77·0	57 51	72 54	75·4	57 35	71 06	73·9	57 17	69 19	72·4	239	301
120	60	59 28	78 08	79·7	59 16	76 12	78·1	59 03	74 18	76·4	58 48	72 25	74·8	58 32	70 34	73·3	58 13	68 45	71·7	240	300
119	61	60 26	77 46	79·3	60 14	75 47	77·6	60 01	73 50	75·9	59 45	71 54	74·2	59 28	70 01	72·6	59 08	68 09	71·0	241	299
118	62	61 25	77 23	78·9	61 12	75 21	77·1	60 58	73 20	75·3	60 42	71 21	73·6	60 24	69 25	71·9	60 05	67 31	70·3	242	298
117	63	62 23	76 58	78·4	62 10	74 52	76·5	61 56	72 48	74·7	61 39	70 46	72·9	61 20	68 46	71·2	61 00	66 49	69·5	243	297
116	64	63 22	76 31	77·9	63 08	74 21	76·0	62 53	72 13	74·1	62 35	70 08	72·2	62 16	68 05	70·4	61 55	66 05	68·6	244	296
115	65	64 20	76 02	77·4	64 06	73 48	75·4	63 50	71 36	73·4	63 32	69 27	71·5	63 12	67 21	69·6	62 50	65 18	67·7	245	295
114	66	65 18	75 31	76·8	65 03	73 12	74·7	64 47	70 56	72·6	64 28	68 43	70·6	64 07	66 34	68·7	63 44	64 27	66·8	246	294
113	67	66 16	74 57	76·2	66 01	72 33	74·0	65 43	70 13	71·8	65 23	67 56	69·8	65 02	65 43	67·8	64 38	63 33	65·8	247	293
112	68	67 14	74 20	75·5	66 58	71 51	73·2	66 40	69 26	71·0	66 19	67 05	68·8	65 56	64 48	66·7	65 32	62 35	64·7	248	292
111	69	68 12	73 39	74·8	67 55	71 05	72·4	67 36	68 35	70·1	67 14	66 09	67·8	66 50	63 48	65·7	66 25	61 31	63·6	249	291
110	70	69 09	72 55	74·0	68 51	70 15	71·5	68 31	67 40	69·1	68 08	65 09	66·7	67 44	62 44	64·5	67 17	60 23	62·3	250	290
109	71	70 07	72 06	73·1	69 48	69 20	70·5	69 27	66 39	68·0	69 03	64 03	65·6	68 37	61 34	63·2	68 09	59 10	61·0	251	289
108	72	71 03	71 13	72·2	70 44	68 20	69·4	70 21	65 33	66·8	69 57	62 52	64·3	69 29	60 17	61·9	69 00	57 50	59·6	252	288
107	73	72 00	70 14	71·1	71 39	67 13	68·3	71 16	64 20	65·5	70 50	61 33	62·9	70 21	58 54	60·4	69 50	56 23	58·0	253	287
106	74	72 56	69 08	70·0	72 34	65 59	67·0	72 09	62 59	64·1	71 41	60 07	61·4	71 12	57 24	58·8	70 40	54 49	56·4	254	286
105	75	73 52	67 54	68·7	73 29	64 37	65·5	73 03	61 30	62·6	72 34	58 32	59·7	72 02	55 44	57·1	71 28	53 06	54·5	255	285
104	76	74 48	66 31	67·3	74 23	63 05	64·0	73 55	59 51	60·8	73 24	56 47	57·9	72 51	53 55	55·1	72 16	51 13	52·6	256	284
103	77	75 42	64 57	65·6	75 16	61 22	62·2	74 46	58 00	58·9	74 14	54 51	55·9	73 39	51 55	53·1	73 02	49 10	50·4	257	283
102	78	76 36	63 11	63·8	76 08	59 26	60·2	75 37	55 57	56·8	75 02	52 42	53·6	74 26	49 42	50·8	73 47	46 56	48·1	258	282
101	79	77 29	61 09	61·7	76 59	57 14	57·9	76 26	53 38	54·4	75 49	50 18	51·2	75 11	47 16	48·2	74 30	44 28	45·5	259	281
100	80	78 21	58 49	59·3	77 49	54 44	55·3	77 13	51 01	51·7	76 35	47 38	48·4	75 54	44 34	45·4	75 11	41 47	42·7	260	280
99	81	79 12	56 06	56·6	78 37	51 52	52·4	77 59	48 04	48·7	77 18	44 39	45·4	76 35	41 35	42·4	75 49	38 50	39·7	261	279
98	82	80 01	52 56	53·4	79 23	48 35	49·1	78 42	44 43	45·3	77 59	41 18	41·9	77 13	38 17	39·0	76 26	35 36	36·4	262	278
97	83	80 47	49 13	49·6	80 07	44 47	45·2	79 23	40 56	41·4	78 37	37 37	38·1	77 49	34 39	35·3	77 02	32 05	32·8	263	277
96	84	81 31	44 51	45·2	80 47	40 22	40·8	80 01	36 38	37·1	79 12	33 25	33·9	78 21	30 40	31·2	77 35	28 16	28·8	264	276
95	85	82 12	39 40	39·9	81 24	35 22	35·7	80 34	31 48	32·2	79 43	28 49	29·2	78 50	26 18	26·7	78 04	24 09	24·6	265	275
94	86	82 48	33 34	33·8	81 57	29 36	29·8	81 04	26 24	26·7	80 09	23 46	24·1	79 14	21 35	21·9	78 29	19 44	20·1	266	274
93	87	83 18	26 28	26·6	82 23	23 05	23·3	81 28	20 25	20·6	80 31	18 17	18·5	79 34	16 32	16·8	78 36	15 04	15·4	267	273
92	88	83 41	18 22	18·5	82 45	15 52	16·0	81 45	13 57	14·0	80 47	12 26	12·6	79 48	11 12	11·4	78 49	10 11	10·4	268	272
91	89	83 55	9 26	9·5	82 56	8 05	8·2	81 56	7 05	7·1	80 57	6 17	6·4	79 57	5 39	5·7	78 57	5 08	5·2	269	271
90	90	84 00	0 00	0·0	83 00	0 00	0·0	82 00	0 00	0·0	81 00	0 00	0·0	80 00	0 00	0·0	79 00	0 00	0·0	270	270

N. Lat: for LHA > 180° .... Z_n = Z
for LHA < 180° .... Z_n = 360° − Z

S. Lat.: for LHA > 180° .... Z_n = 180° − Z
for LHA < 180° .... Z_n = 180° + Z

© British Crown Copyright 2022. All rights reserved.

SIGHT REDUCTION TABLE

B: (−) for 90° < LHA < 270°
Dec: (−) for Lat. contrary name

Z₁: same sign as B
Z₂: (−) for F > 90°

Lat. / A		12°			13°			14°			15°			16°			17°			Lat. / A	
LHA/F	A	A/H	B/P	Z₁/Z₂	A/H	B/P	Z₁/Z₂	A/H	B/P	Z₁/Z₂	A/H	B/P	Z₁/Z₂	A/H	B/P	Z₁/Z₂	A/H	B/P	Z₁/Z₂	LHA	A
0	180	0 00	78 00	90·0	0 00	77 00	90·0	0 00	76 00	90·0	0 00	75 00	90·0	0 00	74 00	90·0	0 00	73 00	90·0	180	360
1	179	0 59	78 00	89·8	0 58	77 00	89·8	0 58	76 00	89·8	0 58	75 00	89·7	0 58	74 00	89·7	0 57	73 00	89·7	181	359
2	178	1 57	78 00	89·6	1 57	77 00	89·5	1 56	76 00	89·5	1 56	74 59	89·5	1 55	73 59	89·4	1 55	72 59	89·4	182	358
3	177	2 56	77 59	89·4	2 55	76 59	89·3	2 55	75 59	89·3	2 55	74 59	89·2	2 53	73 59	89·2	2 52	72 59	89·1	183	357
4	176	3 55	77 58	89·2	3 54	76 58	89·1	3 53	75 58	89·0	3 52	74 58	89·0	3 51	73 58	88·9	3 49	72 58	88·8	184	356
5	175	4 53	77 57	89·0	4 52	76 57	88·9	4 51	75 57	88·8	4 50	74 57	88·7	4 48	73 57	88·6	4 47	72 56	88·5	185	355
6	174	5 52	77 56	88·7	5 51	76 56	88·6	5 49	75 56	88·5	5 48	74 55	88·4	5 46	73 55	88·3	5 44	72 55	88·2	186	354
7	173	6 51	77 55	88·5	6 49	76 54	88·4	6 47	75 54	88·3	6 46	74 54	88·2	6 44	73 53	88·1	6 42	72 53	87·9	187	353
8	172	7 49	77 53	88·3	7 48	76 53	88·2	7 46	75 52	88·1	7 44	74 52	87·9	7 41	73 51	87·8	7 39	72 51	87·6	188	352
9	171	8 48	77 51	88·1	8 46	76 51	88·0	8 44	75 50	87·8	8 41	74 49	87·7	8 39	73 49	87·5	8 36	72 48	87·3	189	351
10	170	9 47	77 49	87·9	9 44	76 48	87·7	9 42	75 48	87·6	9 39	74 47	87·4	9 37	73 46	87·2	9 34	72 45	87·0	190	350
11	169	10 45	77 47	87·7	10 43	76 46	87·5	10 40	75 45	87·3	10 37	74 44	87·1	10 34	73 43	86·9	10 31	72 42	86·7	191	349
12	168	11 44	77 44	87·5	11 41	76 43	87·3	11 38	75 42	87·1	11 35	74 41	86·9	11 32	73 40	86·6	11 28	72 39	86·4	192	348
13	167	12 43	77 42	87·3	12 40	76 40	87·0	12 36	75 39	86·8	12 33	74 37	86·6	12 29	73 36	86·4	12 25	72 35	86·1	193	347
14	166	13 41	77 39	87·0	13 38	76 37	86·8	13 35	75 35	86·5	13 31	74 34	86·3	13 27	73 32	86·1	13 23	72 31	85·8	194	346
15	165	14 40	77 35	86·8	14 36	76 33	86·6	14 33	75 32	86·3	14 29	74 30	86·0	14 24	73 28	85·8	14 20	72 26	85·5	195	345
16	164	15 38	77 32	86·6	15 35	76 30	86·3	15 31	75 28	86·0	15 26	74 25	85·8	15 22	73 23	85·5	15 17	72 21	85·2	196	344
17	163	16 37	77 28	86·4	16 33	76 26	86·1	16 29	75 23	85·8	16 24	74 21	85·5	16 19	73 19	85·2	16 14	72 16	84·9	197	343
18	162	17 36	77 24	86·1	17 31	76 21	85·8	17 27	75 19	85·5	17 22	74 16	85·2	17 17	73 13	84·9	17 11	72 11	84·6	198	342
19	161	18 34	77 20	85·9	18 30	76 17	85·6	18 25	75 14	85·2	18 20	74 11	84·9	18 14	73 08	84·6	18 08	72 05	84·3	199	341
20	160	19 33	77 15	85·7	19 28	76 12	85·3	19 23	75 08	85·0	19 17	74 05	84·6	19 12	73 02	84·3	19 05	71 59	83·9	200	340
21	159	20 31	77 10	85·4	20 26	76 07	85·1	20 21	75 03	84·7	20 15	73 59	84·3	20 09	72 56	84·0	20 03	71 52	83·6	201	339
22	158	21 30	77 05	85·2	21 24	76 01	84·8	21 19	74 57	84·4	21 13	73 53	84·0	21 06	72 49	83·6	21 00	71 45	83·3	202	338
23	157	22 28	77 00	85·0	22 23	75 55	84·5	22 17	74 51	84·1	22 10	73 46	83·7	22 04	72 42	83·3	21 56	71 38	82·9	203	337
24	156	23 27	76 54	84·7	23 21	75 49	84·3	23 15	74 44	83·9	23 08	73 39	83·4	23 01	72 34	83·0	22 53	71 30	82·6	204	336
25	155	24 25	76 48	84·5	24 19	75 43	84·0	24 13	74 37	83·6	24 06	73 32	83·1	23 58	72 27	82·7	23 50	71 21	82·2	205	335
26	154	25 23	76 42	84·2	25 17	75 36	83·7	25 10	74 30	83·3	25 03	73 24	82·8	24 55	72 18	82·3	24 47	71 13	81·9	206	334
27	153	26 22	76 35	84·0	26 15	75 28	83·5	26 08	74 22	83·0	26 01	73 16	82·5	25 52	72 10	82·0	25 44	71 04	81·5	207	333
28	152	27 20	76 28	83·7	27 13	75 21	83·2	27 06	74 14	82·7	26 58	73 07	82·2	26 50	72 00	81·7	26 41	70 54	81·2	208	332
29	151	28 18	76 20	83·4	28 11	75 13	82·9	28 04	74 05	82·4	27 55	72 58	81·8	27 47	71 51	81·3	27 37	70 44	80·8	209	331
30	150	29 17	76 13	83·2	29 09	75 04	82·6	29 01	73 56	82·0	28 53	72 48	81·5	28 44	71 41	81·0	28 34	70 33	80·4	210	330
31	149	30 15	76 04	82·9	30 07	74 56	82·3	29 59	73 47	81·7	29 50	72 38	81·2	29 41	71 30	80·6	29 30	70 22	80·0	211	329
32	148	31 13	75 56	82·6	31 05	74 46	82·0	30 57	73 37	81·4	30 47	72 28	80·8	30 37	71 19	80·2	30 27	70 11	79·6	212	328
33	147	32 11	75 47	82·3	32 03	74 37	81·7	31 54	73 27	81·1	31 44	72 17	80·5	31 34	71 07	79·9	31 23	69 58	79·2	213	327
34	146	33 10	75 37	82·0	33 01	74 26	81·4	32 52	73 16	80·7	32 41	72 05	80·1	32 31	70 55	79·5	32 20	69 45	78·8	214	326
35	145	34 08	75 27	81·7	33 59	74 16	81·0	33 49	73 04	80·4	33 39	71 53	79·7	33 28	70 42	79·1	33 16	69 32	78·4	215	325
36	144	35 06	75 17	81·4	34 56	74 04	80·7	34 46	72 52	80·0	34 36	71 40	79·4	34 24	70 29	78·7	34 12	69 18	78·0	216	324
37	143	36 04	75 06	81·1	35 54	73 53	80·4	35 44	72 40	79·7	35 33	71 27	79·0	35 21	70 15	78·3	35 08	69 03	77·6	217	323
38	142	37 02	74 54	80·8	36 52	73 40	80·0	36 41	72 27	79·3	36 29	71 13	78·6	36 17	70 00	77·8	36 04	68 48	77·1	218	322
39	141	38 00	74 42	80·4	37 49	73 27	79·7	37 38	72 13	78·9	37 26	70 59	78·2	37 13	69 45	77·4	37 00	68 33	76·7	219	321
40	140	38 57	74 30	80·1	38 47	73 14	79·3	38 35	71 58	78·5	38 23	70 43	77·7	38 10	69 29	77·0	37 56	68 15	76·2	220	320
41	139	39 55	74 16	79·8	39 44	72 59	78·9	39 32	71 43	78·1	39 19	70 27	77·3	39 06	69 12	76·5	38 51	67 57	75·7	221	319
42	138	40 53	74 02	79·4	40 41	72 45	78·5	40 29	71 27	77·7	40 16	70 10	76·9	40 02	68 54	76·1	39 47	67 38	75·3	222	318
43	137	41 51	73 48	79·0	41 39	72 30	78·2	41 26	71 11	77·3	41 12	69 53	76·4	40 58	68 35	75·6	40 42	67 19	74·7	223	317
44	136	42 48	73 32	78·6	42 36	72 12	77·7	42 23	70 53	76·9	42 09	69 34	76·0	41 54	68 16	75·1	41 38	66 58	74·2	224	316
45	135	43 46	73 16	78·3	43 33	71 55	77·3	43 19	70 35	76·4	43 05	69 15	75·5	42 49	67 56	74·6	42 33	66 37	73·7	225	315

© British Crown Copyright 2022. All rights reserved.

Lat. / A																			Lat. / A	
	12°			13°			14°			15°			16°			17°			LHA	
LHA/F	A/H	B/P	Z₁/Z₂	A/H	B/P	Z₁/Z₂	A/H	B/P	Z₁/Z₂	A/H	B/P	Z₁/Z₂	A/H	B/P	Z₁/Z₂	A/H	B/P	Z₁/Z₂		
135	43 46	73 16	78.3	43 33	71 55	77.3	43 19	70 35	76.4	43 05	69 15	75.5	42 49	67 56	74.6	42 33	66 37	73.7	225	315
134	44 43	72 59	77.8	44 30	71 37	76.9	44 16	70 15	75.9	44 01	68 54	75.0	43 45	67 34	74.1	43 28	66 15	73.2	226	314
133	45 40	72 41	77.4	45 27	71 18	76.4	45 12	69 55	75.5	44 57	68 33	74.5	44 40	67 12	73.5	44 23	65 51	72.6	227	313
132	46 38	72 23	77.0	46 24	70 58	76.0	46 09	69 35	75.0	45 53	68 11	74.0	45 35	66 48	73.0	45 17	65 27	72.0	228	312
131	47 35	72 03	76.5	47 20	70 37	75.5	47 05	69 11	74.4	46 48	67 47	73.4	46 30	66 23	72.4	46 12	65 01	71.4	229	311
130	48 32	71 42	76.1	48 17	70 15	75.0	48 01	68 48	73.9	47 44	67 22	72.9	47 25	65 58	71.8	47 06	64 34	70.8	230	310
129	49 29	71 20	75.6	49 13	69 51	74.5	48 57	68 23	73.4	48 39	66 56	72.3	48 20	65 30	71.2	48 00	64 05	70.1	231	309
128	50 25	70 57	75.1	50 09	69 27	73.9	49 52	67 57	72.8	49 34	66 29	71.7	49 15	65 02	70.6	48 54	63 35	69.5	232	308
127	51 22	70 33	74.6	51 06	69 01	73.4	50 48	67 31	72.2	50 29	66 00	71.0	50 09	64 31	69.9	49 48	63 04	68.8	233	307
126	52 19	70 07	74.0	52 02	68 33	72.8	51 43	67 01	71.6	51 24	65 30	70.4	51 03	64 00	69.2	50 41	62 31	68.1	234	306
125	53 15	69 40	73.5	52 57	68 04	72.2	52 38	66 30	70.9	52 18	64 58	69.7	51 57	63 26	68.5	51 34	61 56	67.3	235	305
124	54 11	69 11	72.9	53 53	67 34	71.6	53 33	65 58	70.3	53 12	64 24	69.0	52 50	62 51	67.8	52 27	61 20	66.6	236	304
123	55 07	68 41	72.2	54 48	67 02	70.9	54 28	65 24	69.6	54 06	63 48	68.3	53 43	62 14	67.0	53 19	60 42	65.8	237	303
122	56 03	68 08	71.6	55 43	66 28	70.2	55 22	64 48	68.8	55 00	63 11	67.5	54 36	61 35	66.2	54 12	60 01	64.9	238	302
121	56 59	67 34	70.9	56 38	65 51	69.5	56 16	64 10	68.1	55 53	62 31	66.7	55 29	60 54	65.4	55 03	59 18	64.1	239	301
120	57 54	66 58	70.2	57 33	65 13	68.7	57 10	63 30	67.3	56 46	61 50	65.9	56 21	60 10	64.6	55 55	58 33	63.1	240	300
119	58 49	66 20	69.4	58 27	64 32	67.9	58 03	62 47	66.4	57 39	61 04	65.0	57 13	59 24	63.6	56 46	57 46	62.2	241	299
118	59 44	65 38	68.6	59 21	63 49	67.1	58 57	62 02	65.5	58 31	60 17	64.0	58 05	58 35	62.6	57 36	56 56	61.2	242	298
117	60 38	64 55	67.8	60 15	63 03	66.2	59 50	61 13	64.6	59 23	59 27	63.1	58 55	57 43	61.6	58 26	56 03	60.2	243	297
116	61 32	64 08	66.9	61 08	62 14	65.2	60 42	60 22	63.6	60 15	58 34	62.0	59 46	56 49	60.5	59 16	55 06	59.1	244	296
115	62 26	63 18	66.0	62 01	61 21	64.2	61 34	59 28	62.6	61 06	57 37	61.0	60 36	55 51	59.4	60 05	54 07	57.9	245	295
114	63 20	62 25	65.0	62 53	60 25	63.2	62 26	58 30	61.5	61 56	56 37	59.8	61 25	54 49	58.2	60 53	53 07	56.7	246	294
113	64 13	61 27	63.9	63 45	59 25	62.1	63 16	57 27	60.3	62 46	55 34	58.6	62 14	53 44	57.0	61 41	51 57	55.4	247	293
112	65 05	60 26	62.8	64 37	58 21	60.9	64 07	56 21	59.1	63 35	54 25	57.4	63 02	52 34	55.7	62 27	50 47	54.1	248	292
111	65 57	59 20	61.6	65 27	57 13	59.6	64 56	55 10	57.8	64 23	53 13	56.0	63 49	51 20	54.3	63 14	49 32	52.7	249	291
110	66 48	58 08	60.3	66 18	55 59	58.3	65 45	53 55	56.4	65 11	51 55	54.6	64 36	50 01	52.9	63 59	48 12	51.2	250	290
109	67 39	56 52	58.9	67 07	54 40	56.9	66 33	52 35	54.9	65 58	50 34	53.1	65 21	48 38	51.3	64 43	46 48	49.7	251	289
108	68 29	55 29	57.4	67 55	53 14	55.3	67 20	51 06	53.3	66 44	49 04	51.5	66 06	47 08	49.7	65 26	45 18	48.0	252	288
107	69 18	53 59	55.8	68 43	51 42	53.7	68 07	49 33	51.6	67 29	47 30	49.8	66 49	45 33	48.0	66 08	43 43	46.3	253	287
106	70 06	52 22	54.1	69 30	50 03	51.9	68 52	47 52	49.8	68 12	45 49	47.9	67 31	43 52	46.1	66 49	42 02	44.4	254	286
105	70 53	50 36	52.2	70 15	48 16	50.0	69 36	46 04	47.9	68 55	44 00	46.0	68 12	42 04	44.2	67 29	40 15	42.5	255	285
104	71 38	48 42	50.2	70 59	46 20	47.9	70 18	44 08	45.9	69 36	42 02	43.9	68 52	40 09	42.1	68 07	38 21	40.5	256	284
103	72 23	46 37	48.0	71 42	44 15	45.7	70 59	42 03	43.7	70 15	40 01	41.7	69 30	38 07	39.9	68 43	36 21	38.3	257	283
102	73 06	44 22	45.6	72 23	42 00	43.4	71 38	39 49	41.3	70 53	37 49	39.4	70 06	35 57	37.6	69 18	34 13	36.0	258	282
101	73 47	41 55	43.1	73 02	39 34	40.8	72 16	37 26	38.8	71 30	35 38	36.9	70 40	33 37	35.2	69 50	31 58	33.6	259	281
100	74 26	39 16	40.3	73 39	36 57	38.1	72 51	34 51	36.1	72 02	32 57	34.3	71 12	31 12	32.6	70 21	29 36	31.1	260	280
99	75 02	36 21	37.3	74 14	34 07	35.1	73 24	32 06	33.2	72 34	30 17	31.5	71 42	28 37	29.9	70 50	27 06	28.4	261	279
98	75 37	33 13	34.1	74 46	31 05	32.0	73 55	29 10	30.2	73 03	27 27	28.5	72 09	25 53	27.0	71 16	24 29	25.7	262	278
97	76 08	29 50	30.6	75 16	27 50	28.6	74 23	26 03	26.9	73 29	24 27	25.4	72 34	23 02	24.0	71 39	21 44	22.8	263	277
96	76 36	26 16	26.8	75 42	24 22	25.0	74 48	22 45	23.5	73 52	21 19	22.1	72 56	20 02	20.9	72 00	18 55	19.8	264	276
95	77 01	22 18	22.8	76 05	20 41	21.3	75 09	19 16	19.9	74 12	18 01	18.7	73 15	16 54	17.6	72 18	15 55	16.7	265	275
94	77 22	18 10	18.6	76 25	16 49	17.3	75 27	15 38	16.1	74 29	14 36	15.1	73 31	13 40	14.2	72 33	12 51	13.5	266	274
93	77 38	13 50	14.1	76 40	12 46	13.1	75 41	11 51	12.2	74 43	11 03	11.4	73 44	10 21	10.8	72 45	9 43	10.2	267	273
92	77 50	9 19	9.5	76 51	8 36	8.8	75 52	7 58	8.2	74 52	7 25	7.7	73 53	6 56	7.2	72 53	6 31	6.8	268	272
91	77 58	4 42	4.8	76 58	4 19	4.4	75 58	4 00	4.1	74 58	3 44	3.9	73 58	3 29	3.6	72 58	3 16	3.4	269	271
90	78 00	0 00	0.0	77 00	0 00	0.0	76 00	0 00	0.0	75 00	0 00	0.0	74 00	0 00	0.0	73 00	0 00	0.0	270	270

N. Lat.: for LHA > 180° ... Z_n = Z
for LHA < 180° ... Z_n = 360° − Z

S. Lat.: for LHA > 180° ... Z_n = 180° − Z
for LHA < 180° ... Z_n = 180° + Z

© British Crown Copyright 2022. All rights reserved.

SIGHT REDUCTION TABLE

B: (−) for 90° < LHA < 270°
Dec:(−) for Lat. contrary name

Z1: same sign as B
Z2: (−) for F > 90°

Z_1: same sign as B
Z_2: (−) for F > 90°

Lat./A LHA/F	F	18° A/H	18° B/P	18° Z_1/Z_2	19° A/H	19° B/P	19° Z_1/Z_2	20° A/H	20° B/P	20° Z_1/Z_2	21° A/H	21° B/P	21° Z_1/Z_2	22° A/H	22° B/P	22° Z_1/Z_2	23° A/H	23° B/P	23° Z_1/Z_2	Lat./A LHA	LHA
0	180	0 00	72 00	90·0	0 00	71 00	90·0	0 00	70 00	90·0	0 00	69 00	90·0	0 00	68 00	90·0	0 00	67 00	90·0	180	360
1	179	0 57	72 00	89·7	0 57	71 00	89·7	0 56	70 00	89·7	0 56	69 00	89·6	0 56	68 00	89·6	0 55	67 00	89·6	181	359
2	178	1 54	71 59	89·4	1 53	70 59	89·3	1 53	69 59	89·3	1 52	68 59	89·3	1 51	67 59	89·3	1 50	66 59	89·2	182	358
3	177	2 51	71 59	89·1	2 50	70 59	89·0	2 49	69 58	89·0	2 48	68 58	88·9	2 47	67 58	88·9	2 46	66 58	88·8	183	357
4	176	3 48	71 58	88·8	3 47	70 57	88·7	3 46	69 57	88·7	3 44	68 57	88·6	3 42	67 57	88·6	3 41	66 58	88·4	184	356
5	175	4 45	71 56	88·5	4 44	70 56	88·4	4 42	69 56	88·3	4 40	68 56	88·2	4 38	67 55	88·1	4 36	66 55	88·0	185	355
6	174	5 42	71 54	88·1	5 40	70 54	88·0	5 38	69 54	87·9	5 36	68 54	87·8	5 34	67 53	87·7	5 31	66 53	87·6	186	354
7	173	6 39	71 52	87·8	6 37	70 52	87·7	6 35	69 52	87·6	6 32	68 51	87·5	6 29	67 51	87·4	6 26	66 51	87·3	187	353
8	172	7 36	71 50	87·5	7 34	70 50	87·4	7 31	69 49	87·2	7 28	68 49	87·1	7 25	67 48	87·0	7 22	66 48	86·9	188	352
9	171	8 33	71 47	87·2	8 30	70 47	87·0	8 27	69 46	86·9	8 24	68 46	86·8	8 20	67 45	86·6	8 17	66 45	86·5	189	351
10	170	9 30	71 44	86·9	9 27	70 44	86·7	9 23	69 43	86·5	9 20	68 42	86·4	9 16	67 42	86·2	9 12	66 41	86·1	190	350
11	169	10 27	71 41	86·6	10 24	70 40	86·4	10 20	69 39	86·2	10 16	68 39	86·0	10 11	67 38	85·8	10 07	66 37	85·7	191	349
12	168	11 24	71 37	86·2	11 20	70 36	86·0	11 16	69 35	85·8	11 12	68 34	85·6	11 07	67 33	85·4	11 02	66 32	85·3	192	348
13	167	12 21	71 33	85·9	12 17	70 32	85·7	12 12	69 31	85·5	12 08	68 30	85·3	12 02	67 29	85·1	11 57	66 28	84·8	193	347
14	166	13 18	71 29	85·6	13 13	70 28	85·4	13 08	69 26	85·1	13 03	68 25	84·9	12 58	67 24	84·7	12 52	66 22	84·4	194	346
15	165	14 15	71 24	85·3	14 10	70 23	85·0	14 05	69 21	84·8	13 59	68 20	84·5	13 53	67 18	84·3	13 47	66 17	84·0	195	345
16	164	15 12	71 19	84·9	15 06	70 18	84·7	15 01	69 16	84·4	14 55	68 14	84·1	14 48	67 12	83·9	14 42	66 10	83·6	196	344
17	163	16 09	71 14	84·6	16 03	70 12	84·3	15 57	69 10	84·0	15 50	68 08	83·7	15 44	67 06	83·5	15 37	66 04	83·2	197	343
18	162	17 05	71 08	84·3	16 59	70 06	84·0	16 53	69 03	83·7	16 46	68 01	83·4	16 39	66 59	83·0	16 32	65 57	82·8	198	342
19	161	18 02	71 02	83·9	17 56	69 59	83·6	17 49	68 57	83·3	17 42	67 54	83·0	17 34	66 52	82·7	17 26	65 49	82·3	199	341
20	160	18 59	70 56	83·6	18 52	69 53	83·2	18 45	68 50	82·9	18 37	67 47	82·6	18 29	66 44	82·2	18 21	65 41	81·9	200	340
21	159	19 56	70 49	83·2	19 48	69 45	82·9	19 41	68 42	82·5	19 33	67 39	82·2	19 24	66 36	81·8	19 16	65 33	81·5	201	339
22	158	20 52	70 41	82·9	20 45	69 38	82·5	20 37	68 34	82·1	20 28	67 31	81·8	20 19	66 27	81·4	20 10	65 24	81·0	202	338
23	157	21 49	70 33	82·5	21 41	69 29	82·1	21 32	68 26	81·7	21 24	67 22	81·4	21 14	66 18	81·0	21 05	65 15	80·6	203	337
24	156	22 45	70 25	82·2	22 37	69 21	81·8	22 28	68 17	81·3	22 19	67 12	80·9	22 09	66 09	80·5	21 59	65 05	80·1	204	336
25	155	23 42	70 17	81·8	23 33	69 12	81·4	23 24	68 07	80·9	23 14	67 03	80·5	23 04	65 58	80·1	22 54	64 54	79·7	205	335
26	154	24 38	70 07	81·4	24 29	69 02	81·0	24 20	67 57	80·5	24 09	66 52	80·1	23 58	65 48	79·6	23 48	64 43	79·2	206	334
27	153	25 35	69 58	81·1	25 25	68 52	80·6	25 15	67 47	80·1	25 05	66 42	79·7	24 54	65 36	79·2	24 42	64 31	78·7	207	333
28	152	26 31	69 48	80·7	26 21	68 42	80·2	26 11	67 36	79·7	26 00	66 30	79·2	25 48	65 25	78·7	25 36	64 19	78·3	208	332
29	151	27 27	69 37	80·3	27 17	68 31	79·8	27 06	67 24	79·3	26 55	66 18	78·8	26 43	65 12	78·3	26 30	64 07	77·8	209	331
30	150	28 24	69 26	79·9	28 13	68 19	79·4	28 01	67 12	78·8	27 50	66 06	78·3	27 37	64 59	77·8	27 24	63 53	77·3	210	330
31	149	29 20	69 14	79·5	29 09	68 07	79·0	28 56	67 00	78·4	28 44	65 53	77·8	28 31	64 46	77·3	28 18	63 39	76·8	211	329
32	148	30 16	69 02	79·1	30 04	67 54	78·5	29 52	66 46	77·9	29 39	65 39	77·4	29 26	64 32	76·8	29 12	63 25	76·3	212	328
33	147	31 12	68 49	78·7	31 00	67 41	78·1	30 47	66 32	77·5	30 34	65 24	76·9	30 20	64 17	76·3	30 05	63 09	75·8	213	327
34	146	32 08	68 36	78·2	31 55	67 27	77·6	31 42	66 18	77·0	31 28	65 09	76·4	31 14	64 01	75·8	30 59	62 53	75·2	214	326
35	145	33 04	68 22	77·8	32 51	67 12	77·2	32 37	66 03	76·5	32 23	64 54	75·9	32 08	63 45	75·2	31 52	62 36	74·7	215	325
36	144	33 59	68 07	77·3	33 46	66 57	76·7	33 32	65 47	76·0	33 17	64 37	75·4	33 01	63 28	74·8	32 45	62 19	74·2	216	324
37	143	34 55	67 52	76·9	34 41	66 41	76·2	34 26	65 30	75·5	34 11	64 20	74·9	33 55	63 10	74·2	33 38	62 01	73·6	217	323
38	142	35 50	67 36	76·4	35 36	66 24	75·7	35 21	65 13	75·0	35 05	64 02	74·4	34 48	62 51	73·7	34 31	61 41	73·0	218	322
39	141	36 46	67 20	76·0	36 31	66 06	75·2	36 15	64 55	74·5	35 59	63 43	73·8	35 42	62 32	73·1	35 24	61 21	72·4	219	321
40	140	37 41	67 01	75·5	37 26	65 48	74·7	37 10	64 35	74·0	36 53	63 23	73·3	36 35	62 12	72·6	36 17	61 01	71·8	220	320
41	139	38 36	66 42	75·0	38 20	65 29	74·2	38 04	64 15	73·4	37 46	63 02	72·7	37 28	61 50	72·0	37 09	60 39	71·2	221	319
42	138	39 31	66 23	74·5	39 15	65 08	73·7	38 58	63 54	72·9	38 40	62 41	72·1	38 21	61 28	71·4	38 01	60 16	70·6	222	318
43	137	40 26	66 03	73·9	40 09	64 47	73·1	39 51	63 33	72·3	39 33	62 18	71·5	39 13	61 05	70·7	38 53	59 52	70·0	223	317
44	136	41 21	65 42	73·4	41 03	64 25	72·5	40 45	63 10	71·7	40 26	61 55	70·9	40 06	60 41	70·1	39 45	59 27	69·3	224	316
45	135	42 16	65 19	72·8	41 57	64 02	72·0	41 38	62 46	71·1	41 19	61 30	70·3	40 58	60 15	69·5	40 37	59 01	68·7	225	315

© British Crown Copyright 2022. All rights reserved.

Lat./A	Lat./A	18° A/H	18° B/P	18° Z_1/Z_2	19° A/H	19° B/P	19° Z_1/Z_2	20° A/H	20° B/P	20° Z_1/Z_2	21° A/H	21° B/P	21° Z_1/Z_2	22° A/H	22° B/P	22° Z_1/Z_2	23° A/H	23° B/P	23° Z_1/Z_2	Lat./A	Lat./A
LHA/F																				LHA	
135	45	42 16	65 19	72.8	41 57	64 02	72.0	41 38	62 46	71.1	41 19	61 30	70.3	40 58	60 15	69.5	40 37	59 01	68.7	225	315
134	46	43 10	64 56	72.3	42 51	63 38	71.4	42 32	62 21	70.5	42 11	61 05	69.6	41 50	59 49	68.8	41 28	58 34	68.0	226	314
133	47	44 04	64 32	71.7	43 45	63 13	70.8	43 25	61 55	69.9	43 04	60 38	69.0	42 42	59 21	68.1	42 19	58 06	67.3	227	313
132	48	44 58	64 06	71.1	44 38	62 46	70.1	44 18	61 27	69.2	43 56	60 09	68.3	43 33	58 53	67.4	43 10	57 37	66.5	228	312
131	49	45 52	63 39	70.4	45 32	62 18	69.5	45 10	60 59	68.5	44 48	59 40	67.6	44 24	58 22	66.7	44 00	57 06	65.8	229	311
130	50	46 46	63 11	69.8	46 25	61 49	68.8	46 03	60 29	67.8	45 39	59 09	66.9	45 15	57 51	65.9	44 50	56 34	65.0	230	310
129	51	47 39	62 42	69.1	47 17	61 19	68.1	46 55	59 57	67.1	46 31	58 37	66.1	46 06	57 18	65.2	45 40	56 00	64.2	231	309
128	52	48 33	62 11	68.4	48 10	60 47	67.4	47 46	59 25	66.4	47 22	58 03	65.4	46 56	56 44	64.4	46 30	55 25	63.4	232	308
127	53	49 25	61 38	67.7	49 02	60 13	66.6	48 38	58 50	65.6	48 13	57 28	64.6	47 46	56 07	63.6	47 19	54 48	62.6	233	307
126	54	50 18	61 04	67.0	49 54	59 38	65.9	49 29	58 14	64.8	49 03	56 51	63.7	48 36	55 30	62.7	48 08	54 10	61.7	234	306
125	55	51 10	60 28	66.2	50 46	59 01	65.1	50 20	57 36	64.0	49 53	56 12	62.9	49 25	54 50	61.9	48 56	53 30	60.8	235	305
124	56	52 03	59 50	65.4	51 37	58 23	64.2	51 10	56 56	63.1	50 43	55 32	62.0	50 14	54 09	61.0	49 44	52 48	59.9	236	304
123	57	52 54	59 11	64.6	52 28	57 42	63.4	52 00	56 15	62.2	51 32	54 49	61.1	51 02	53 26	60.0	50 32	52 04	59.0	237	303
122	58	53 46	58 29	63.7	53 18	56 59	62.5	52 50	55 31	61.3	52 22	54 05	60.2	51 50	52 41	59.1	51 19	51 18	58.0	238	302
121	59	54 37	57 45	62.8	54 08	56 14	61.5	53 39	54 45	60.4	53 09	53 18	59.2	52 38	51 53	58.1	52 06	50 30	57.0	239	301
120	60	55 27	56 59	61.8	54 58	55 27	60.6	54 28	53 57	59.4	53 57	52 29	58.2	53 25	51 04	57.0	52 52	49 40	55.9	240	300
119	61	56 17	56 10	60.9	55 47	54 37	59.6	55 16	53 06	58.3	54 43	51 38	57.1	54 11	50 12	55.9	53 37	48 48	54.8	241	299
118	62	57 07	55 19	59.8	56 36	53 45	58.5	56 04	52 13	57.2	55 31	50 44	56.0	54 57	49 17	54.8	54 22	47 53	53.7	242	298
117	63	57 56	54 25	58.8	57 24	52 49	57.4	56 51	51 17	56.1	56 17	49 47	54.9	55 42	48 20	53.7	55 06	46 55	52.5	243	297
116	64	58 44	53 27	57.6	58 12	51 51	56.3	57 38	50 18	55.0	57 03	48 48	53.7	56 27	47 20	52.5	55 50	45 55	51.3	244	296
115	65	59 32	52 27	56.5	58 58	50 50	55.1	58 24	49 16	53.7	57 47	47 45	52.5	57 10	46 17	51.2	56 32	44 52	50.0	245	295
114	66	60 19	51 23	55.2	59 45	49 45	53.8	59 09	48 11	52.5	58 32	46 39	51.2	57 53	45 11	49.9	57 14	43 47	48.7	246	294
113	67	61 06	50 15	53.9	60 30	48 37	52.5	59 53	47 02	51.2	59 15	45 30	49.8	58 36	44 02	48.6	57 55	42 38	47.4	247	293
112	68	61 52	49 04	52.6	61 15	47 25	51.1	60 36	45 50	49.8	59 57	44 18	48.4	59 17	42 50	47.2	58 36	41 26	46.0	248	292
111	69	62 37	47 48	51.2	61 58	46 09	49.7	61 19	44 33	48.3	60 39	43 02	47.0	59 57	41 34	45.7	59 15	40 10	44.5	249	291
110	70	63 21	46 28	49.7	62 41	44 48	48.2	62 01	43 13	46.8	61 19	41 42	45.4	60 36	40 15	44.2	59 53	38 52	43.0	250	290
109	71	64 04	45 03	48.1	63 23	43 24	46.6	62 41	41 49	45.2	61 58	40 18	43.9	61 15	38 52	42.6	60 30	37 29	41.4	251	289
108	72	64 45	43 34	46.4	64 04	41 54	44.9	63 21	40 20	43.5	62 37	38 50	42.2	61 52	37 25	40.9	61 06	36 03	39.7	252	288
107	73	65 26	41 59	44.7	64 43	40 20	43.2	63 59	38 46	41.8	63 14	37 18	40.5	62 27	35 53	39.2	61 41	34 34	38.0	253	287
106	74	66 06	40 19	42.9	65 21	38 41	41.4	64 36	37 08	40.0	63 49	35 41	38.7	63 02	34 18	37.4	62 14	33 00	36.3	254	286
105	75	66 44	38 32	40.9	65 58	36 56	39.5	65 11	35 25	38.1	64 23	33 59	36.8	63 35	32 39	35.6	62 46	31 22	34.4	255	285
104	76	67 20	36 40	38.9	66 33	35 05	37.4	65 45	33 37	36.1	64 56	32 13	34.8	64 07	30 55	33.6	63 16	29 41	32.5	256	284
103	77	67 55	34 42	36.8	67 07	33 07	35.3	66 18	31 43	34.0	65 27	30 23	32.8	64 37	29 06	31.6	63 45	27 55	30.6	257	283
102	78	68 29	32 37	34.5	67 39	31 07	33.1	66 48	29 44	31.9	65 57	28 26	30.7	65 05	27 14	29.6	64 13	26 06	28.5	258	282
101	79	69 00	30 25	32.2	68 09	29 00	30.8	67 17	27 40	29.6	66 25	26 26	28.5	65 32	25 17	27.4	64 38	24 12	26.4	259	281
100	80	69 30	28 07	29.7	68 38	26 47	28.4	67 44	25 30	27.3	66 50	24 20	26.2	65 56	23 15	25.2	65 02	22 15	24.3	260	280
99	81	69 57	25 43	27.1	69 03	24 26	25.9	68 09	23 15	24.8	67 14	22 10	23.8	66 19	21 10	22.9	65 23	20 14	22.1	261	279
98	82	70 21	23 11	24.5	69 27	22 00	23.3	68 31	20 56	22.3	67 36	19 56	21.4	66 40	19 00	20.6	65 43	18 09	19.8	262	278
97	83	70 44	20 34	21.7	69 48	19 29	20.7	68 51	18 31	19.7	67 55	17 37	18.9	66 58	16 47	18.1	66 01	16 01	17.4	263	277
96	84	71 03	17 50	18.8	70 07	16 53	17.9	69 09	16 01	17.1	68 12	15 14	16.3	67 14	14 30	15.7	66 16	13 50	15.1	264	276
95	85	71 21	15 01	15.8	70 23	14 12	15.0	69 25	13 28	14.3	68 26	12 48	13.7	67 28	12 10	13.1	66 29	11 36	12.6	265	275
94	86	71 35	12 07	12.8	70 36	11 27	12.1	69 37	10 51	11.6	68 38	10 18	11.0	67 39	9 48	10.6	66 40	9 20	10.1	266	274
93	87	71 46	09 09	9.6	70 46	08 39	9.1	69 47	08 11	8.7	68 48	7 46	8.3	67 48	7 23	8.0	66 49	7 02	7.6	267	273
92	88	71 54	06 08	6.4	70 54	05 47	6.1	69 54	05 29	5.8	68 55	5 12	5.6	67 55	4 56	5.3	66 55	4 42	5.3	268	272
91	89	71 58	03 04	3.2	70 58	02 54	3.1	69 59	02 45	2.9	68 59	2 36	2.8	67 59	2 28	2.7	66 59	2 21	2.6	269	271
90	90	72 00	00 00	0.0	71 00	00 00	0.0	70 00	00 00	0.0	69 00	0 00	0.0	68 00	0 00	0.0	67 00	0 00	0.0	270	270

N. Lat.: for LHA > 180° ... $Z_n = Z$
for LHA < 180° ... $Z_n = 360° - Z$

S. Lat.: for LHA > 180° ... $Z_n = 180° - Z$
for LHA < 180° ... $Z_n = 180° + Z$

© British Crown Copyright 2022. All rights reserved.

SIGHT REDUCTION TABLE

Z1: same sign as B
Z2: (−) for F > 90°

B: (−) for 90° < LHA < 270°
Dec:(−) for Lat. contrary name

Lat./A	24°			25°			26°			27°			28°			29°			Lat./A
LHA/F	A/H	B/P	Z1/Z2	A/H	B/P	Z1/Z2	A/H	B/P	Z1/Z2	A/H	B/P	Z1/Z2	A/H	B/P	Z1/Z2	A/H	B/P	Z1/Z2	LHA
0	0 00	66 00	90·0	0 00	65 00	90·0	0 00	64 00	90·0	0 00	63 00	90·0	0 00	62 00	90·0	0 00	61 00	90·0	180
1	0 55	66 00	89·6	0 54	65 00	89·6	0 54	64 00	89·6	0 53	63 00	89·5	0 53	62 00	89·5	0 52	61 00	89·5	179
2	1 50	65 59	89·2	1 49	64 59	89·2	1 48	63 59	89·1	1 47	62 59	89·1	1 46	61 59	89·1	1 45	60 59	89·0	178
3	2 44	65 58	88·8	2 43	64 58	88·7	2 42	63 58	88·7	2 40	62 58	88·6	2 39	61 58	88·6	2 37	60 58	88·5	177
4	3 39	65 57	88·4	3 37	64 57	88·3	3 36	63 57	88·2	3 34	62 57	88·2	3 32	61 57	88·1	3 30	60 56	88·1	176
5	4 34	65 55	88·0	4 32	64 55	87·9	4 30	63 55	87·8	4 27	62 55	87·7	4 25	61 55	87·6	4 22	60 54	87·6	175
6	5 29	65 53	87·6	5 26	64 53	87·5	5 23	63 53	87·4	5 21	62 52	87·3	5 18	61 52	87·2	5 15	60 52	87·1	174
7	6 24	65 50	87·1	6 20	64 50	87·0	6 17	63 50	86·9	6 14	62 50	86·8	6 11	61 49	86·7	6 07	60 49	86·6	173
8	7 18	65 47	86·7	7 15	64 47	86·6	7 11	63 47	86·5	7 08	62 46	86·3	7 04	61 46	86·2	6 59	60 46	86·1	172
9	8 13	65 44	86·3	8 09	64 44	86·2	8 05	63 43	86·0	8 01	62 43	85·9	7 56	61 42	85·7	7 52	60 42	85·6	171
10	9 08	65 40	85·9	9 03	64 40	85·7	8 59	63 39	85·6	8 54	62 39	85·4	8 49	61 38	85·3	8 44	60 38	85·1	170
11	10 02	65 36	85·5	9 57	64 35	85·3	9 52	63 35	85·1	9 47	62 34	85·0	9 42	61 33	84·8	9 36	60 33	84·6	169
12	10 57	65 32	85·1	10 52	64 31	84·9	10 46	63 30	84·7	10 41	62 29	84·5	10 35	61 28	84·3	10 29	60 28	84·1	168
13	11 52	65 27	84·6	11 46	64 26	84·4	11 40	63 25	84·2	11 34	62 24	84·0	11 27	61 23	83·8	11 21	60 23	83·6	167
14	12 46	65 21	84·2	12 40	64 20	84·0	12 34	63 19	83·8	12 27	62 18	83·5	12 20	61 17	83·3	12 13	60 16	83·1	166
15	13 41	65 15	83·8	13 34	64 14	83·5	13 27	63 13	83·3	13 20	62 11	83·1	13 13	61 10	82·8	13 05	60 09	82·6	165
16	14 35	65 09	83·3	14 28	64 07	83·1	14 21	63 06	82·8	14 13	62 04	82·6	14 05	61 03	82·3	13 57	60 02	82·1	164
17	15 29	65 02	82·9	15 22	64 00	82·6	15 14	62 59	82·4	15 06	61 57	82·1	14 58	60 56	81·8	14 49	59 54	81·6	163
18	16 24	64 55	82·5	16 16	63 53	82·2	16 08	62 51	81·9	15 59	61 49	81·6	15 50	60 47	81·3	15 41	59 46	81·0	162
19	17 18	64 47	82·0	17 10	63 45	81·7	17 01	62 43	81·4	16 52	61 41	81·1	16 42	60 39	80·8	16 33	59 37	80·5	161
20	18 12	64 39	81·6	18 03	63 36	81·3	17 54	62 34	80·9	17 45	61 32	80·6	17 35	60 30	80·3	17 24	59 28	80·0	160
21	19 07	64 30	81·1	18 57	63 28	80·8	18 47	62 25	80·4	18 37	61 23	80·1	18 27	60 20	79·8	18 16	59 18	79·5	159
22	20 01	64 21	80·7	19 51	63 18	80·3	19 41	62 15	80·0	19 30	61 13	79·6	19 19	60 10	79·3	19 08	59 08	78·9	158
23	20 55	64 11	80·2	20 44	63 08	79·8	20 34	62 05	79·5	20 22	61 02	79·1	20 11	59 59	78·7	19 59	58 57	78·4	157
24	21 49	64 01	79·7	21 38	62 58	79·3	21 27	61 54	79·0	21 15	60 51	78·6	21 03	59 48	78·2	20 50	58 45	77·8	156
25	22 43	63 50	79·3	22 31	62 46	78·9	22 19	61 43	78·4	22 07	60 39	78·0	21 55	59 36	77·7	21 42	58 33	77·3	155
26	23 36	63 39	78·8	23 25	62 35	78·4	23 12	61 31	77·9	22 59	60 27	77·5	22 46	59 24	77·1	22 33	58 20	76·7	154
27	24 30	63 27	78·3	24 18	62 22	77·8	24 05	61 18	77·4	23 52	60 14	77·0	23 38	59 10	76·5	23 24	58 07	76·1	153
28	25 24	63 14	77·8	25 11	62 10	77·3	24 57	61 05	76·9	24 44	60 01	76·4	24 29	58 57	76·0	24 15	57 53	75·5	152
29	26 17	63 01	77·3	26 04	61 56	76·8	25 50	60 51	76·3	25 36	59 47	75·9	25 21	58 42	75·4	25 05	57 38	75·0	151
30	27 11	62 48	76·8	26 57	61 42	76·3	26 42	60 37	75·8	26 27	59 32	75·3	26 12	58 27	74·8	25 56	57 23	74·4	150
31	28 04	62 33	76·3	27 50	61 27	75·8	27 35	60 22	75·2	27 19	59 16	74·7	27 03	58 11	74·2	26 46	57 07	73·8	149
32	28 57	62 18	75·7	28 42	61 12	75·2	28 27	60 06	74·7	28 10	59 00	74·2	27 54	57 55	73·7	27 37	56 50	73·1	148
33	29 50	62 02	75·2	29 35	60 56	74·7	29 19	59 49	74·1	29 02	58 43	73·6	28 45	57 38	73·0	28 27	56 32	72·5	147
34	30 43	61 46	74·7	30 27	60 39	74·1	30 10	59 32	73·5	29 53	58 26	73·0	29 36	57 20	72·4	29 17	56 14	71·9	146
35	31 36	61 28	74·1	31 19	60 21	73·5	31 02	59 14	72·9	30 44	58 07	72·4	30 26	57 01	71·8	30 07	55 55	71·2	145
36	32 29	61 10	73·5	32 11	60 02	72·9	31 53	58 55	72·3	31 35	57 48	71·7	31 16	56 41	71·2	30 56	55 35	70·6	144
37	33 21	60 52	73·0	33 03	59 43	72·3	32 45	58 35	71·7	32 26	57 28	71·1	32 06	56 21	70·5	31 46	55 14	69·9	143
38	34 13	60 32	72·4	33 55	59 23	71·7	33 36	58 15	71·1	33 16	57 07	70·5	32 56	55 59	69·9	32 35	54 53	69·3	142
39	35 06	60 11	71·8	34 47	59 02	71·1	34 27	57 54	70·5	34 06	56 45	69·9	33 45	55 37	69·2	33 24	54 30	68·6	141
40	35 58	59 50	71·2	35 38	58 40	70·5	35 17	57 31	69·8	34 56	56 22	69·2	34 35	55 14	68·5	34 12	54 07	67·9	140
41	36 49	59 28	70·5	36 29	58 17	69·8	36 08	57 08	69·1	35 46	55 59	68·5	35 24	54 50	67·8	35 01	53 42	67·1	139
42	37 41	59 04	69·9	37 20	57 54	69·2	36 58	56 43	68·5	36 36	55 34	67·8	36 13	54 25	67·1	35 49	53 17	66·4	138
43	38 32	58 40	69·2	38 11	57 29	68·5	37 48	56 18	67·8	37 25	55 08	67·1	37 02	53 59	66·4	36 37	52 50	65·7	137
44	39 23	58 15	68·6	39 01	57 03	67·8	38 38	55 52	67·1	38 14	54 41	66·3	37 50	53 32	65·6	37 25	52 23	64·9	136
45	40 14	57 48	67·9	39 51	56 36	67·1	39 28	55 24	66·3	39 03	54 13	65·6	38 38	53 04	64·9	38 12	51 54	64·1	135

Lat. / A   LHA (right column):
24°	25°	26°	27°	28°	29°	LHA
						180 – 225

© British Crown Copyright 2022. All rights reserved.

Lat. / A		24°			25°			26°			27°			28°			29°			Lat. / A	
LHA/F		A/H	B/P	Z_1/Z_2	A/H	B/P	Z_1/Z_2	A/H	B/P	Z_1/Z_2	A/H	B/P	Z_1/Z_2	A/H	B/P	Z_1/Z_2	A/H	B/P	Z_1/Z_2		LHA
45	135	40 14	57 48	67·9	39 51	56 36	67·1	39 28	55 24	66·3	39 03	54 13	65·6	38 38	53 04	64·9	38 12	51 54	64·1	225	315
46	134	41 05	57 21	67·2	40 41	56 08	66·4	40 17	54 56	65·6	39 52	53 44	64·8	39 26	52 34	64·1	38 59	51 25	63·3	226	314
47	133	41 55	56 52	66·4	41 31	55 38	65·6	41 06	54 26	64·8	40 40	53 14	64·0	40 13	52 04	63·3	39 46	50 54	62·5	227	313
48	132	42 45	56 22	65·7	42 20	55 08	64·9	41 54	53 55	64·0	41 28	52 43	63·2	41 00	51 32	62·5	40 32	50 22	61·7	228	312
49	131	43 35	55 50	64·9	43 09	54 36	64·1	42 43	53 22	63·2	42 15	52 10	62·4	41 47	50 59	61·6	41 18	49 48	60·9	229	311
50	130	44 25	55 17	64·1	43 58	54 02	63·3	43 31	52 49	62·4	43 03	51 36	61·6	42 34	50 24	60·8	42 04	49 14	60·0	230	310
51	129	45 14	54 43	63·3	44 47	53 28	62·4	44 18	52 13	61·6	43 49	51 00	60·7	43 20	49 48	59·9	42 49	48 38	59·1	231	309
52	128	46 03	54 08	62·5	45 35	52 52	61·6	45 06	51 37	60·7	44 36	50 23	59·8	44 05	49 11	59·0	43 34	48 00	58·2	232	308
53	127	46 51	53 30	61·6	46 22	52 14	60·7	45 52	50 59	59·8	45 22	49 45	58·9	44 51	48 32	58·1	44 18	47 21	57·2	233	307
54	126	47 39	52 51	60·8	47 09	51 34	59·8	46 39	50 19	58·8	46 07	49 05	58·0	45 35	47 52	57·1	45 02	46 41	56·3	234	306
55	125	48 27	52 11	59·8	47 56	50 53	58·9	47 25	49 37	58·0	46 52	48 23	57·0	46 19	47 10	56·2	45 46	45 59	55·3	235	305
56	124	49 14	51 28	58·9	48 43	50 11	57·9	48 10	48 54	57·0	47 37	47 40	56·1	47 03	46 27	55·2	46 29	45 15	54·3	236	304
57	123	50 01	50 44	57·9	49 28	49 26	56·9	48 55	48 09	56·0	48 21	46 54	55·0	47 46	45 41	54·1	47 11	44 30	53·3	237	303
58	122	50 47	49 58	56·9	50 14	48 39	55·9	49 40	47 22	54·9	49 05	46 07	54·0	48 29	44 54	53·1	47 53	43 43	52·2	238	302
59	121	51 33	49 09	55·9	50 58	47 51	54·9	50 23	46 34	53·9	49 48	45 18	52·9	49 11	44 05	52·0	48 34	42 54	51·1	239	301
60	120	52 18	48 19	54·8	51 43	47 00	53·8	51 07	45 43	52·8	50 30	44 28	51·8	49 53	43 14	50·9	49 14	42 03	50·0	240	300
61	119	53 02	47 26	53·7	52 26	46 07	52·7	51 49	44 50	51·7	51 12	43 35	50·7	50 33	42 22	49·7	49 54	41 10	48·8	241	299
62	118	53 46	46 31	52·6	53 09	45 12	51·5	52 31	43 54	50·5	51 53	42 39	49·5	51 13	41 27	48·6	50 33	40 16	47·6	242	298
63	117	54 29	45 33	51·4	53 51	44 14	50·3	53 13	42 57	49·3	52 33	41 42	48·3	51 53	40 30	47·3	51 12	39 19	46·4	243	297
64	116	55 12	44 30	50·2	54 33	43 14	49·1	53 53	41 57	48·1	53 13	40 42	47·1	52 31	39 30	46·1	51 49	38 20	45·2	244	296
65	115	55 53	43 30	48·9	55 13	42 11	47·8	54 33	40 55	46·8	53 51	39 40	45·8	53 09	38 29	44·8	52 26	37 19	43·9	245	295
66	114	56 34	42 25	47·6	55 53	41 06	46·5	55 12	39 50	45·4	54 29	38 36	44·4	53 46	37 25	43·5	53 02	36 16	42·6	246	294
67	113	57 14	41 16	46·2	56 32	39 58	45·1	55 50	38 42	44·1	55 06	37 29	43·1	54 22	36 19	42·1	53 37	35 11	41·2	247	293
68	112	57 53	40 05	44·8	57 10	38 47	43·7	56 27	37 32	42·7	55 42	36 19	41·7	54 57	35 10	40·7	54 11	34 03	39·8	248	292
69	111	58 32	38 50	43·3	57 47	37 33	42·2	57 03	36 18	41·2	56 17	35 07	40·2	55 31	33 59	39·3	54 44	32 53	38·4	249	291
70	110	59 09	37 32	41·8	58 24	36 16	40·7	57 38	35 02	39·7	56 51	33 52	38·7	56 04	32 45	37·8	55 16	31 41	36·9	250	290
71	109	59 45	36 11	40·2	58 58	34 55	39·2	58 12	33 43	38·1	57 24	32 35	37·2	56 36	31 29	36·3	55 47	30 26	35·4	251	289
72	108	60 19	34 46	38·6	59 32	33 32	37·6	58 44	32 21	36·5	57 56	31 14	35·6	57 07	30 10	34·7	56 17	29 08	33·8	252	288
73	107	60 53	33 18	36·9	60 05	32 05	35·9	59 16	30 56	34·9	58 26	29 51	34·0	57 36	28 48	33·1	56 46	27 49	32·2	253	287
74	106	61 25	31 46	35·2	60 36	30 35	34·2	59 46	29 28	33·2	58 55	28 25	32·3	58 05	27 24	31·4	57 13	26 26	30·6	254	286
75	105	61 56	30 10	33·4	61 06	29 02	32·4	60 15	27 57	31·4	59 23	26 56	30·5	58 31	25 57	29·7	57 39	25 02	28·9	255	285
76	104	62 26	28 31	31·5	61 34	27 25	30·5	60 42	26 23	29·6	59 50	25 24	28·8	58 57	24 28	28·0	58 04	23 35	27·2	256	284
77	103	62 53	26 48	29·6	62 01	25 45	28·6	61 08	24 46	27·8	60 15	23 49	27·0	59 21	22 56	26·2	58 27	22 05	25·5	257	283
78	102	63 20	25 02	27·6	62 26	24 02	26·7	61 32	23 05	25·9	60 38	22 12	25·1	59 44	21 21	24·4	58 49	20 34	23·7	258	282
79	101	63 44	23 12	25·5	62 50	22 15	24·7	61 55	21 22	23·9	61 00	20 32	23·2	60 05	19 44	22·5	59 09	19 00	21·8	259	281
80	100	64 07	21 18	23·4	63 12	20 25	22·6	62 16	19 36	21·9	61 20	18 49	21·2	60 24	18 05	20·6	59 28	17 24	20·0	260	280
81	99	64 28	19 22	21·3	63 32	18 33	20·5	62 35	17 47	19·9	61 39	17 04	19·2	60 42	16 24	18·6	59 45	15 46	18·1	261	279
82	98	64 47	17 22	19·1	63 50	16 37	18·4	62 53	15 56	17·8	61 56	15 17	17·2	60 58	14 40	16·7	60 01	14 06	16·2	262	278
83	97	65 03	15 18	16·8	64 06	14 39	16·2	63 08	14 02	15·6	62 10	13 27	15·1	61 12	12 55	14·7	60 14	12 24	14·2	263	277
84	96	65 18	13 13	14·5	64 20	12 38	14·0	63 22	12 06	13·5	62 23	11 36	13·0	61 25	11 07	12·6	60 26	10 41	12·2	264	276
85	95	65 31	11 05	12·1	64 32	10 35	11·7	63 33	10 08	11·3	62 35	9 42	10·9	61 36	9 19	10·6	60 37	8 56	10·2	265	275
86	94	65 41	8 54	9·8	64 42	8 30	9·4	63 43	8 08	9·1	62 44	7 48	8·8	61 44	7 28	8·5	60 45	7 10	8·2	266	274
87	93	65 49	6 42	7·3	64 50	6 24	7·1	63 50	6 07	6·8	62 51	5 52	6·6	61 51	5 37	6·4	60 52	5 24	6·2	267	273
88	92	65 55	4 29	4·9	64 56	4 17	4·7	63 56	4 06	4·6	62 56	3 55	4·4	61 56	3 45	4·3	60 56	3 36	4·1	268	272
89	91	65 59	2 15	2·5	64 59	2 09	2·4	63 59	2 03	2·3	62 59	1 58	2·2	61 59	1 53	2·1	60 59	1 48	2·1	269	271
90	90	66 00	0 00	0·0	65 00	0 00	0·0	64 00	0 00	0·0	63 00	0 00	0·0	62 00	0 00	0·0	61 00	0 00	0·0	270	270

N. Lat.: for LHA > 180° ... $Z_n = Z$
for LHA < 180° ... $Z_n = 360° − Z$

S. Lat.: for LHA > 180° ... $Z_n = 180° − Z$
for LHA < 180° ... $Z_n = 180° + Z$

© British Crown Copyright 2022. All rights reserved.

B: (−) for 90° < LHA < 270°
Dec:(−) for Lat. contrary name

Z₁: same sign as B
Z₂: (−) for F > 90°

SIGHT REDUCTION TABLE

LHA/F		30° A/H	30° B/P	30° Z₁/Z₂	31° A/H	31° B/P	31° Z₁/Z₂	32° A/H	32° B/P	32° Z₁/Z₂	33° A/H	33° B/P	33° Z₁/Z₂	34° A/H	34° B/P	34° Z₁/Z₂	35° A/H	35° B/P	35° Z₁/Z₂	LHA	
0	180	0 00	60 00	90.0	0 00	59 00	90.0	0 00	58 00	90.0	0 00	57 00	90.0	0 00	56 00	90.0	0 00	55 00	90.0	180	360
1	179	0 52	60 00	89.5	0 51	59 00	89.5	0 51	58 00	89.5	0 50	57 00	89.5	0 50	56 00	89.4	0 49	55 00	89.4	181	359
2	178	1 44	59 59	89.0	1 43	58 59	89.0	1 42	57 59	89.0	1 41	56 59	88.9	1 39	55 59	88.9	1 38	54 59	88.9	182	358
3	177	2 36	59 58	88.5	2 34	58 58	88.5	2 33	57 58	88.4	2 31	56 58	88.4	2 29	55 58	88.3	2 27	54 58	88.3	183	357
4	176	3 28	59 56	88.0	3 26	58 56	88.0	3 23	57 56	87.9	3 21	56 56	87.9	3 19	55 56	87.8	3 17	54 56	87.8	184	356
5	175	4 20	59 54	87.5	4 17	58 54	87.4	4 14	57 54	87.4	4 12	56 54	87.3	4 09	55 54	87.2	4 06	54 54	87.1	185	355
6	174	5 12	59 52	87.0	5 08	58 52	86.9	5 05	57 52	86.8	5 02	56 51	86.7	4 58	55 51	86.6	4 55	54 51	86.6	186	354
7	173	6 04	59 49	86.5	6 00	58 49	86.4	5 56	57 48	86.3	5 52	56 48	86.2	5 48	55 48	86.1	5 44	54 48	86.0	187	353
8	172	6 55	59 45	86.0	6 51	58 45	85.9	6 47	57 45	85.7	6 42	56 45	85.7	6 38	55 44	85.5	6 33	54 44	85.4	188	352
9	171	7 47	59 42	85.5	7 42	58 41	85.3	7 37	57 41	85.2	7 32	56 40	85.1	7 27	55 40	84.9	7 22	54 40	84.8	189	351
10	170	8 39	59 37	85.0	8 34	58 37	84.8	8 28	57 36	84.7	8 22	56 36	84.5	8 17	55 36	84.4	8 11	54 35	84.2	190	350
11	169	9 31	59 32	84.4	9 25	58 32	84.3	9 19	57 31	84.1	9 13	56 31	84.0	9 06	55 30	83.8	9 00	54 30	83.6	191	349
12	168	10 22	59 27	83.9	10 16	58 26	83.8	10 09	57 26	83.6	10 03	56 25	83.4	9 56	55 25	83.2	9 48	54 24	83.0	192	348
13	167	11 14	59 21	83.4	11 07	58 20	83.2	11 00	57 20	83.0	10 53	56 19	82.8	10 45	55 18	82.6	10 37	54 18	82.5	193	347
14	166	12 06	59 15	82.9	11 58	58 14	82.7	11 50	57 13	82.5	11 42	56 12	82.3	11 34	55 12	82.1	11 26	54 11	81.9	194	346
15	165	12 57	59 08	82.4	12 49	58 07	82.1	12 41	57 06	81.9	12 32	56 05	81.7	12 23	55 04	81.5	12 14	54 04	81.3	195	345
16	164	13 49	59 01	81.8	13 40	57 59	81.6	13 31	56 58	81.4	13 22	55 57	81.1	13 13	54 57	80.9	13 03	53 56	80.7	196	344
17	163	14 40	58 53	81.3	14 31	57 51	81.1	14 21	56 50	80.8	14 12	55 49	80.5	14 02	54 48	80.3	13 51	53 47	80.1	197	343
18	162	15 31	58 44	80.8	15 22	57 43	80.5	15 12	56 42	80.2	15 01	55 40	80.0	14 51	54 39	79.7	14 40	53 38	79.4	198	342
19	161	16 23	58 35	80.2	16 12	57 34	79.9	16 02	56 32	79.7	15 51	55 31	79.4	15 40	54 30	79.1	15 28	53 29	78.8	199	341
20	160	17 14	58 26	79.7	17 03	57 24	79.4	16 52	56 23	79.1	16 40	55 21	78.8	16 28	54 20	78.5	16 16	53 19	78.2	200	340
21	159	18 05	58 16	79.1	17 53	57 14	78.8	17 42	56 12	78.5	17 29	55 11	78.2	17 17	54 09	77.9	17 04	53 08	77.6	201	339
22	158	18 56	58 05	78.6	18 44	57 03	78.2	18 31	56 01	77.9	18 19	55 00	77.6	18 06	53 58	77.3	17 52	52 56	77.0	202	338
23	157	19 47	57 54	78.0	19 34	56 52	77.7	19 21	55 50	77.3	19 08	54 48	77.0	18 54	53 46	76.6	18 40	52 44	76.3	203	337
24	156	20 37	57 42	77.4	20 24	56 40	77.1	20 11	55 38	76.7	19 57	54 36	76.4	19 42	53 34	76.0	19 28	52 32	75.7	204	336
25	155	21 28	57 30	76.9	21 14	56 27	76.5	21 00	55 25	76.1	20 46	54 23	75.7	20 31	53 21	75.4	20 15	52 19	75.0	205	335
26	154	22 19	57 17	76.3	22 04	56 14	75.9	21 49	55 12	75.5	21 34	54 09	75.1	21 19	53 07	74.7	21 03	52 05	74.4	206	334
27	153	23 09	57 03	75.7	22 54	56 00	75.3	22 39	54 57	74.9	22 23	53 55	74.5	22 07	52 52	74.1	21 50	51 51	73.7	207	333
28	152	23 59	56 49	75.1	23 44	55 46	74.7	23 28	54 43	74.3	23 11	53 40	73.8	22 54	52 37	73.4	22 37	51 35	73.0	208	332
29	151	24 50	56 34	74.5	24 33	55 31	74.1	24 17	54 27	73.6	23 59	53 24	73.2	23 42	52 22	72.8	23 24	51 19	72.4	209	331
30	150	25 40	56 19	73.9	25 23	55 15	73.4	25 05	54 11	73.0	24 48	53 08	72.5	24 29	52 05	72.1	24 11	51 03	71.7	210	330
31	149	26 29	56 02	73.3	26 12	54 58	72.8	25 54	53 54	72.3	25 35	52 51	71.9	25 17	51 48	71.4	24 57	50 45	71.0	211	329
32	148	27 19	55 45	72.6	27 01	54 41	72.2	26 42	53 37	71.7	26 23	52 33	71.2	26 04	51 30	70.7	25 44	50 27	70.3	212	328
33	147	28 08	55 27	72.0	27 50	54 23	71.5	27 31	53 19	71.0	27 11	52 15	70.5	26 50	51 12	70.0	26 30	50 08	69.6	213	327
34	146	28 58	55 09	71.4	28 38	54 04	70.8	28 19	53 00	70.3	27 58	51 56	69.8	27 37	50 53	69.3	27 16	49 49	68.8	214	326
35	145	29 47	54 49	70.7	29 27	53 44	70.2	29 06	52 40	69.6	28 45	51 36	69.1	28 24	50 32	68.6	28 01	49 29	68.1	215	325
36	144	30 36	54 29	70.0	30 15	53 24	69.5	29 54	52 19	68.9	29 32	51 15	68.4	29 10	50 11	67.9	28 47	49 07	67.4	216	324
37	143	31 25	54 08	69.4	31 03	53 03	68.8	30 41	51 58	68.2	30 19	50 53	67.7	29 56	49 49	67.2	29 32	48 45	66.6	217	323
38	142	32 13	53 46	68.7	31 51	52 40	68.1	31 28	51 35	67.5	31 05	50 30	66.9	30 41	49 26	66.4	30 17	48 23	65.9	218	322
39	141	33 02	53 23	68.0	32 39	52 17	67.4	32 15	51 12	66.8	31 51	50 07	66.2	31 27	49 03	65.6	31 02	47 59	65.1	219	321
40	140	33 50	53 00	67.2	33 26	51 53	66.6	33 02	50 48	66.0	32 37	49 43	65.4	32 12	48 38	64.9	31 46	47 34	64.3	220	320
41	139	34 37	52 35	66.5	34 13	51 29	65.9	33 48	50 23	65.3	33 23	49 17	64.7	32 57	48 13	64.1	32 30	47 09	63.5	221	319
42	138	35 25	52 09	65.8	35 00	51 03	65.1	34 34	49 56	64.5	34 08	48 51	63.9	33 42	47 46	63.3	33 14	46 42	62.7	222	318
43	137	36 12	51 43	65.0	35 46	50 36	64.3	35 19	49 29	63.7	34 53	48 24	63.1	34 26	47 19	62.5	33 58	46 15	61.9	223	317
44	136	36 59	51 15	64.2	36 33	50 08	63.6	36 06	49 01	62.9	35 38	47 55	62.3	35 10	46 51	61.6	34 41	45 46	61.0	224	316
45	135	37 46	50 46	63.4	37 19	49 39	62.7	36 51	48 32	62.1	36 22	47 26	61.4	35 53	46 21	60.8	35 24	45 17	60.2	225	315

© British Crown Copyright 2022. All rights reserved.

Lat./A LHA/F	30° A/H	30° B/P	30° Z_1/Z_2	31° A/H	31° B/P	31° Z_1/Z_2	32° A/H	32° B/P	32° Z_1/Z_2	33° A/H	33° B/P	33° Z_1/Z_2	34° A/H	34° B/P	34° Z_1/Z_2	35° A/H	35° B/P	35° Z_1/Z_2	Lat./A LHA
135 / 45	37 46	50 46	63.4	37 19	49 39	62.7	36 51	48 32	62.1	36 22	47 26	61.4	35 53	46 21	60.8	35 24	45 17	60.2	315 / 225
134 / 46	38 32	50 16	62.6	38 04	49 08	61.9	37 36	48 02	61.2	37 06	46 56	60.6	36 37	45 51	59.9	36 06	44 46	59.3	314 / 226
133 / 47	39 18	49 45	61.8	38 49	48 37	61.1	38 20	47 30	60.4	37 50	46 24	59.7	37 19	45 19	59.1	36 48	44 15	58.4	313 / 227
132 / 48	40 04	49 13	61.0	39 34	48 05	60.2	39 04	46 58	59.5	38 33	45 51	58.8	38 02	44 46	58.2	37 30	43 42	57.5	312 / 228
131 / 49	40 49	48 39	60.1	40 19	47 31	59.4	39 48	46 24	58.6	39 16	45 18	57.9	38 44	44 12	57.2	38 11	43 08	56.6	311 / 229
130 / 50	41 34	48 04	59.2	41 03	46 56	58.5	40 31	45 49	57.7	39 59	44 42	57.0	39 26	43 37	56.3	38 52	42 33	55.6	310 / 230
129 / 51	42 18	47 28	58.3	41 46	46 20	57.5	41 14	45 12	56.8	40 41	44 06	56.1	40 07	43 01	55.4	39 32	41 57	54.7	309 / 231
128 / 52	43 02	46 50	57.4	42 29	45 42	56.6	41 56	44 34	55.9	41 22	43 28	55.1	40 47	42 23	54.4	40 12	41 19	53.7	308 / 232
127 / 53	43 46	46 11	56.4	43 12	45 03	55.6	42 38	43 55	54.9	42 03	42 49	54.1	41 28	41 44	53.4	40 52	40 41	52.7	307 / 233
126 / 54	44 29	45 31	55.5	43 54	44 22	54.7	43 19	43 15	53.9	42 44	42 09	53.1	42 07	41 04	52.4	41 30	40 01	51.7	306 / 234
125 / 55	45 11	44 49	54.5	44 36	43 40	53.7	44 00	42 33	52.9	43 24	41 27	52.1	42 46	40 23	51.4	42 09	39 19	50.7	305 / 235
124 / 56	45 53	44 05	53.5	45 17	42 57	52.6	44 40	41 50	51.8	44 03	40 44	51.1	43 25	39 40	50.3	42 46	38 37	49.6	304 / 236
123 / 57	46 35	43 20	52.4	45 58	42 11	51.6	45 20	41 05	50.8	44 42	39 59	50.0	44 03	38 55	49.3	43 24	37 53	48.5	303 / 237
122 / 58	47 16	42 33	51.3	46 38	41 25	50.4	45 59	40 18	49.7	45 20	39 13	48.9	44 40	38 09	48.2	44 00	37 07	47.5	302 / 238
121 / 59	47 57	41 44	50.2	47 17	40 36	49.4	46 38	39 30	48.6	45 58	38 25	47.8	45 17	37 22	47.1	44 36	36 20	46.3	301 / 239
120 / 60	48 35	40 54	49.1	47 56	39 46	48.3	47 16	38 40	47.5	46 35	37 36	46.7	45 53	36 33	45.9	45 11	35 32	45.2	300 / 240
119 / 61	49 14	40 01	47.9	48 34	38 54	47.1	47 53	37 48	46.3	47 11	36 45	45.5	46 29	35 42	44.8	45 46	34 42	44.0	299 / 241
118 / 62	49 53	39 07	46.8	49 11	38 00	45.9	48 29	36 55	45.1	47 46	35 52	44.3	47 03	34 50	43.6	46 19	33 50	42.8	298 / 242
117 / 63	50 30	38 11	45.5	49 48	37 04	44.7	49 05	36 00	43.9	48 21	34 57	43.1	47 37	33 57	42.3	46 53	32 57	41.6	297 / 243
116 / 64	51 07	37 13	44.3	50 23	36 07	43.4	49 40	35 03	42.6	48 55	34 01	41.8	48 10	33 01	41.1	47 25	32 03	40.4	296 / 244
115 / 65	51 43	36 12	43.0	50 58	35 07	42.2	50 14	34 04	41.3	49 28	33 03	40.6	48 43	32 05	39.8	47 56	31 07	39.1	295 / 245
114 / 66	52 18	35 10	41.7	51 33	34 06	40.8	50 47	33 04	40.0	50 00	32 04	39.3	49 14	31 05	38.5	48 26	30 10	37.8	294 / 246
113 / 67	52 52	34 05	40.3	52 06	33 02	39.5	51 19	32 01	38.7	50 32	31 02	37.9	49 44	30 05	37.2	48 56	29 10	36.5	293 / 247
112 / 68	53 25	32 59	38.9	52 38	31 56	38.1	51 50	30 57	37.3	51 02	29 59	36.6	50 14	29 03	35.8	49 25	28 09	35.2	292 / 248
111 / 69	53 57	31 50	37.5	53 09	30 49	36.7	52 21	29 50	35.9	51 32	28 53	35.2	50 43	27 59	34.5	49 53	27 06	33.8	291 / 249
110 / 70	54 28	30 39	36.1	53 39	29 39	35.2	52 50	28 42	34.5	52 00	27 46	33.8	51 10	26 53	33.1	50 20	26 02	32.4	290 / 250
109 / 71	54 58	29 25	34.6	54 08	28 27	33.8	53 18	27 31	33.0	52 28	26 36	32.3	51 37	25 46	31.6	50 46	24 56	31.0	289 / 251
108 / 72	55 27	28 09	33.0	54 37	27 13	32.2	53 46	26 19	31.5	52 54	25 27	30.8	52 03	24 37	30.2	51 10	23 49	29.5	288 / 252
107 / 73	55 55	26 51	31.4	55 03	25 57	30.7	54 12	25 04	30.0	53 19	24 14	29.3	52 27	23 26	28.7	51 34	22 40	28.1	287 / 253
106 / 74	56 21	25 31	29.8	55 29	24 39	29.1	54 36	23 48	28.4	53 43	23 00	27.8	52 50	22 14	27.1	51 57	21 29	26.6	286 / 254
105 / 75	56 46	24 09	28.2	55 53	23 18	27.5	55 00	22 30	26.8	54 06	21 44	26.2	53 12	21 00	25.6	52 18	20 17	25.0	285 / 255
104 / 76	57 10	22 44	26.5	56 16	21 56	25.8	55 23	21 10	25.2	54 28	20 26	24.6	53 33	19 44	24.0	52 38	19 04	23.5	284 / 256
103 / 77	57 33	21 17	24.8	56 38	20 31	24.1	55 43	19 48	23.5	54 48	19 06	23.0	53 53	18 27	22.4	52 57	17 49	21.9	283 / 257
102 / 78	57 54	19 48	23.0	56 59	19 05	22.4	56 03	18 24	21.9	55 07	17 45	21.3	54 11	17 08	20.8	53 15	16 32	20.3	282 / 258
101 / 79	58 13	18 17	21.2	57 17	17 37	20.7	56 21	16 58	20.1	55 25	16 22	19.6	54 28	15 48	19.2	53 31	15 15	18.7	281 / 259
100 / 80	58 32	16 44	19.4	57 35	16 07	18.9	56 38	15 32	18.4	55 41	14 58	17.9	54 44	14 26	17.5	53 47	13 56	17.1	280 / 260
99 / 81	58 48	15 10	17.6	57 51	14 36	17.1	56 53	14 03	16.6	55 56	13 33	16.2	54 58	13 03	15.8	54 00	12 36	15.4	279 / 261
98 / 82	59 03	13 33	15.7	58 05	13 02	15.3	57 07	12 33	14.9	56 09	12 06	14.5	55 11	11 40	14.1	54 13	11 14	13.8	278 / 262
97 / 83	59 16	11 55	13.8	58 18	11 28	13.4	57 19	11 02	13.0	56 21	10 38	12.7	55 22	10 14	12.7	54 24	9 52	12.1	277 / 263
96 / 84	59 28	10 16	11.9	58 29	9 52	11.5	57 30	9 30	11.2	56 31	9 09	10.9	55 32	8 49	10.6	54 33	8 29	10.4	276 / 264
95 / 85	59 37	8 35	9.9	58 38	8 15	9.6	57 39	7 56	9.4	56 40	7 39	9.1	55 41	7 22	8.9	54 41	7 06	8.7	275 / 265
94 / 86	59 46	6 53	8.0	58 46	6 37	7.7	57 47	6 22	7.5	56 47	6 08	7.3	55 48	5 54	7.1	54 48	5 41	7.0	274 / 266
93 / 87	59 52	5 11	6.0	58 52	4 59	5.8	57 52	4 47	5.6	56 53	4 36	5.5	55 53	4 26	5.4	54 53	4 16	5.2	273 / 267
92 / 88	59 56	3 28	4.0	58 57	3 19	3.9	57 57	3 12	3.8	56 57	3 05	3.7	55 57	2 58	3.6	54 57	2 51	3.5	272 / 268
91 / 89	59 59	1 44	2.0	58 59	1 40	1.9	57 59	1 36	1.9	56 59	1 32	1.8	55 59	1 29	1.8	54 59	1 26	1.7	271 / 269
90 / 90	60 00	0 00	0.0	59 00	0 00	0.0	58 00	0 00	0.0	57 00	0 00	0.0	56 00	0 00	0.0	55 00	0 00	0.0	270 / 270

N. Lat.: for LHA > 180° .... $Z_n = Z$
for LHA < 180° .... $Z_n = 360° - Z$

S. Lat.: for LHA > 180° .... $Z_n = 180° - Z$
for LHA < 180° .... $Z_n = 180° + Z$

© British Crown Copyright 2022. All rights reserved.

SIGHT REDUCTION TABLE

Z₁: same sign as B
Z₂: (−) for F > 90°
Lat. / A   LHA

B: (−) for 90° < LHA < 270°
Dec:(−) for Lat. contrary name
Lat. / A   LHA/F

LHA/F	36° A/H	36° B/P	36° Z₁/Z₂	37° A/H	37° B/P	37° Z₁/Z₂	38° A/H	38° B/P	38° Z₁/Z₂	39° A/H	39° B/P	39° Z₁/Z₂	40° A/H	40° B/P	40° Z₁/Z₂	41° A/H	41° B/P	41° Z₁/Z₂	LHA
0 / 180	0 00	54 00	90·0	0 00	53 00	90·0	0 00	52 00	90·0	0 00	51 00	90·0	0 00	50 00	90·0	0 00	49 00	90·0	180 / 360
1 / 179	0 49	54 00	89·4	0 48	53 00	89·4	0 47	52 00	89·4	0 47	51 00	89·4	0 46	50 00	89·4	0 45	49 00	89·3	181 / 359
2 / 178	1 37	53 59	88·8	1 36	52 59	88·8	1 35	51 59	88·8	1 33	50 59	88·7	1 32	49 59	88·7	1 31	48 59	88·7	182 / 358
3 / 177	2 26	53 58	88·2	2 24	52 58	88·2	2 22	51 58	88·2	2 20	50 58	88·1	2 18	49 58	88·1	2 16	48 58	88·0	183 / 357
4 / 176	3 14	53 56	87·6	3 12	52 56	87·6	3 09	51 56	87·5	3 06	50 56	87·5	3 04	49 56	87·4	3 01	48 56	87·4	184 / 356
5 / 175	4 03	53 54	87·1	3 59	52 54	87·0	3 56	51 54	86·9	3 53	50 54	86·8	3 50	49 54	86·8	3 46	48 54	86·7	185 / 355
6 / 174	4 51	53 51	86·5	4 47	52 51	86·4	4 43	51 51	86·3	4 40	50 51	86·2	4 36	49 51	86·1	4 31	48 51	86·1	186 / 354
7 / 173	5 39	53 48	85·9	5 35	52 48	85·8	5 31	51 48	85·7	5 26	50 47	85·6	5 21	49 47	85·5	5 17	48 47	85·4	187 / 353
8 / 172	6 28	53 44	85·3	6 23	52 44	85·2	6 18	51 44	85·1	6 13	50 44	84·9	6 07	49 43	84·8	6 02	48 43	84·7	188 / 352
9 / 171	7 16	53 40	84·7	7 11	52 39	84·6	7 05	51 39	84·4	6 59	50 39	84·3	6 53	49 39	84·2	6 47	48 39	84·1	189 / 351
10 / 170	8 05	53 35	84·1	7 58	52 35	83·9	7 52	51 34	83·8	7 45	50 34	83·7	7 39	49 34	83·5	7 32	48 34	83·4	190 / 350
11 / 169	8 53	53 30	83·5	8 46	52 29	83·3	8 39	51 29	83·2	8 32	50 29	83·0	8 24	49 29	82·9	8 17	48 28	82·7	191 / 349
12 / 168	9 41	53 24	82·9	9 33	52 23	82·7	9 26	51 23	82·5	9 18	50 23	82·4	9 10	49 23	82·2	9 02	48 22	82·1	192 / 348
13 / 167	10 29	53 17	82·3	10 21	52 17	82·1	10 13	51 17	81·9	10 04	50 16	81·7	9 55	49 16	81·6	9 46	48 16	81·4	193 / 347
14 / 166	11 17	53 10	81·7	11 08	52 10	81·5	10 59	51 10	81·3	10 50	50 09	81·1	10 41	49 09	80·9	10 31	48 09	80·7	194 / 346
15 / 165	12 05	53 03	81·1	11 56	52 02	80·8	11 46	51 02	80·6	11 36	50 02	80·4	11 26	49 01	80·2	11 16	48 01	80·0	195 / 345
16 / 164	12 53	52 55	80·4	12 43	51 54	80·2	12 33	50 54	80·0	12 22	49 53	79·8	12 11	48 53	79·6	12 00	47 53	79·3	196 / 344
17 / 163	13 41	52 46	79·8	13 30	51 46	79·6	13 19	50 45	79·3	13 08	49 45	79·1	12 57	48 44	78·9	12 45	47 44	78·7	197 / 343
18 / 162	14 29	52 37	79·2	14 17	51 37	78·9	14 06	50 36	78·7	13 54	49 35	78·4	13 42	48 35	78·2	13 29	47 34	78·0	198 / 342
19 / 161	15 16	52 28	78·6	15 04	51 27	78·3	14 52	50 26	78·0	14 39	49 25	77·8	14 27	48 25	77·5	14 13	47 24	77·3	199 / 341
20 / 160	16 04	52 17	77·9	15 51	51 16	77·6	15 38	50 16	77·4	15 25	49 15	77·1	15 12	48 14	76·8	14 58	47 14	76·6	200 / 340
21 / 159	16 51	52 07	77·3	16 38	51 05	77·0	16 24	50 05	76·7	16 10	49 04	76·4	15 56	48 03	76·1	15 42	47 03	75·9	201 / 339
22 / 158	17 39	51 55	76·6	17 24	50 54	76·3	17 10	49 53	76·0	16 56	48 52	75·7	16 41	47 51	75·4	16 25	46 51	75·2	202 / 338
23 / 157	18 26	51 43	76·0	18 11	50 42	75·7	17 56	49 41	75·4	17 41	48 40	75·0	17 25	47 39	74·7	17 09	46 38	74·4	203 / 337
24 / 156	19 13	51 30	75·3	18 57	50 29	75·0	18 42	49 28	74·7	18 26	48 27	74·3	18 09	47 26	74·0	17 53	46 25	73·7	204 / 336
25 / 155	20 00	51 17	74·7	19 44	50 15	74·3	19 27	49 14	74·0	19 10	48 13	73·6	18 53	47 12	73·3	18 36	46 12	73·0	205 / 335
26 / 154	20 46	51 03	74·0	20 30	50 01	73·6	20 13	49 00	73·3	19 55	47 59	72·9	19 37	46 58	72·6	19 19	45 57	72·3	206 / 334
27 / 153	21 33	50 48	73·3	21 15	49 47	73·0	20 58	48 45	72·6	20 40	47 44	72·2	20 21	46 43	71·9	20 02	45 42	71·5	207 / 333
28 / 152	22 19	50 33	72·6	22 01	49 31	72·3	21 43	48 30	71·9	21 24	47 28	71·5	21 05	46 28	71·1	20 45	45 27	70·8	208 / 332
29 / 151	23 06	50 17	72·0	22 47	49 15	71·6	22 28	48 14	71·2	22 08	47 12	70·8	21 48	46 11	70·4	21 28	45 11	70·0	209 / 331
30 / 150	23 52	50 00	71·3	23 32	48 58	70·8	23 12	47 57	70·4	22 52	46 55	70·0	22 31	45 54	69·6	22 10	44 54	69·3	210 / 330
31 / 149	24 37	49 43	70·5	24 17	48 41	70·1	23 57	47 39	69·7	23 36	46 38	69·3	23 14	45 37	68·9	22 52	44 37	68·5	211 / 329
32 / 148	25 23	49 25	69·8	25 02	48 23	69·4	24 41	47 21	69·0	24 19	46 19	68·5	23 57	45 18	68·1	23 34	44 17	67·7	212 / 328
33 / 147	26 09	49 06	69·1	25 47	48 04	68·7	25 25	47 02	68·2	25 02	46 00	67·8	24 40	44 59	67·3	24 16	43 58	66·9	213 / 327
34 / 146	26 54	48 46	68·4	26 32	47 44	67·9	26 09	46 42	67·4	25 45	45 41	67·0	25 22	44 39	66·6	24 58	43 38	66·1	214 / 326
35 / 145	27 39	48 26	67·6	27 16	47 23	67·1	26 52	46 21	66·7	26 28	45 20	66·2	26 04	44 19	65·8	25 39	43 18	65·3	215 / 325
36 / 144	28 24	48 04	66·9	28 00	47 02	66·4	27 36	46 00	65·9	27 11	44 58	65·4	26 46	43 57	65·0	26 20	42 57	64·5	216 / 324
37 / 143	29 08	47 42	66·1	28 44	46 40	65·6	28 19	45 38	65·1	27 53	44 36	64·6	27 27	43 35	64·2	27 01	42 34	63·7	217 / 323
38 / 142	29 52	47 19	65·3	29 27	46 17	64·8	29 02	45 15	64·3	28 35	44 13	63·8	28 08	43 12	63·3	27 41	42 12	62·9	218 / 322
39 / 141	30 36	46 56	64·5	30 10	45 53	64·0	29 44	44 51	63·5	29 17	43 49	63·0	28 49	42 48	62·5	28 21	41 48	62·0	219 / 321
40 / 140	31 20	46 31	63·7	30 53	45 28	63·2	30 26	44 26	62·7	29 58	43 25	62·2	29 30	42 24	61·7	29 01	41 23	61·2	220 / 320
41 / 139	32 03	46 05	62·9	31 36	45 03	62·4	31 08	44 01	61·8	30 39	42 59	61·3	30 10	41 58	60·8	29 41	40 58	60·3	221 / 319
42 / 138	32 46	45 39	62·1	32 18	44 36	61·5	31 49	43 34	61·0	31 20	42 33	60·5	30 50	41 32	59·9	30 20	40 32	59·4	222 / 318
43 / 137	33 29	45 11	61·3	33 00	44 09	60·7	32 30	43 07	60·1	32 00	42 05	59·6	31 30	41 05	59·1	30 59	40 04	58·5	223 / 317
44 / 136	34 12	44 43	60·4	33 42	43 40	59·8	33 11	42 38	59·3	32 40	41 37	58·7	32 09	40 36	58·2	31 37	39 36	57·6	224 / 316
45 / 135	34 54	44 13	59·6	34 23	43 11	59·0	33 52	42 09	58·4	33 20	41 08	57·8	32 48	40 07	57·3	32 15	39 08	56·7	225 / 315

© British Crown Copyright 2022. All rights reserved.

Lat./A	LHA/F	36° A/H	36° B/P	36° Z_1/Z_2	37° A/H	37° B/P	37° Z_1/Z_2	38° A/H	38° B/P	38° Z_1/Z_2	39° A/H	39° B/P	39° Z_1/Z_2	40° A/H	40° B/P	40° Z_1/Z_2	41° A/H	41° B/P	41° Z_1/Z_2	Lat./A	LHA
45	135	34 54	44 13	59·6	34 23	43 11	59·0	33 52	42 09	58·4	33 20	41 08	57·8	32 48	40 07	57·3	32 15	39 08	56·7	315	225
46	134	35 35	43 43	58·7	35 05	42 40	58·1	34 32	41 38	57·5	33 59	40 37	56·9	33 26	39 37	56·4	32 53	38 38	55·8	314	226
47	133	36 17	43 11	57·8	35 44	42 09	57·2	35 12	41 07	56·6	34 38	40 06	56·0	34 04	39 06	55·4	33 30	38 07	54·9	313	227
48	132	36 57	42 39	56·9	36 24	41 36	56·2	35 51	40 35	55·6	35 17	39 34	55·0	34 42	38 34	54·5	34 07	37 35	53·9	312	228
49	131	37 38	42 05	55·9	37 04	41 03	55·3	36 30	40 01	54·7	35 55	39 00	54·1	35 19	38 01	53·5	34 43	37 03	53·0	311	229
50	130	38 18	41 30	55·0	37 43	40 28	54·4	37 08	39 27	53·7	36 32	38 27	53·1	35 56	37 27	52·5	35 19	36 29	52·0	310	230
51	129	38 57	40 54	54·0	38 22	39 52	53·4	37 46	38 51	52·8	37 09	37 51	52·1	36 32	36 52	51·6	35 54	35 54	51·0	309	231
52	128	39 36	40 17	53·0	39 00	39 15	52·4	38 23	38 14	51·8	37 46	37 15	51·1	37 08	36 16	50·6	36 30	35 18	50·0	308	232
53	127	40 15	39 38	52·0	39 38	38 37	51·4	39 00	37 36	50·8	38 22	36 37	50·1	37 43	35 39	49·5	37 04	34 42	49·0	307	233
54	126	40 53	38 58	51·0	40 15	37 57	50·4	39 36	36 57	49·7	38 58	35 58	49·1	38 18	35 01	48·5	37 38	34 04	47·9	306	234
55	125	41 30	38 17	50·0	40 52	37 17	49·3	40 12	36 17	48·7	39 32	35 19	48·1	38 52	34 21	47·4	38 11	33 25	46·9	305	235
56	124	42 07	37 35	48·9	41 28	36 35	48·3	40 47	35 36	47·6	40 07	34 38	47·0	39 26	33 41	46·4	38 44	32 45	45·8	304	236
57	123	42 44	36 51	47·9	42 03	35 51	47·2	41 22	34 53	46·5	40 41	33 55	45·9	39 59	32 59	45·3	39 16	32 04	44·7	303	237
58	122	43 19	36 06	46·8	42 38	35 07	46·1	41 56	34 09	45·4	41 14	33 12	44·8	40 31	32 16	44·2	39 48	31 22	43·6	302	238
59	121	43 54	35 20	45·6	43 12	34 21	45·0	42 29	33 24	44·3	41 47	32 27	43·7	41 03	31 32	43·1	40 19	30 39	42·5	301	239
60	120	44 29	34 32	44·5	43 46	33 34	43·8	43 02	32 37	43·2	42 18	31 42	42·5	41 34	30 47	41·9	40 49	29 54	41·3	300	240
61	119	45 02	33 43	43·3	44 18	32 45	42·6	43 34	31 49	42·0	42 49	30 55	41·4	42 04	30 01	40·8	41 18	29 09	40·2	299	241
62	118	45 35	32 52	42·1	44 51	31 55	41·5	44 05	31 00	40·8	43 20	30 06	40·2	42 34	29 14	39·6	41 47	28 22	39·0	298	242
63	117	46 07	32 00	40·9	45 22	31 04	40·3	44 36	30 10	39·6	43 49	29 17	39·0	43 03	28 25	38·4	42 15	27 35	37·8	297	243
64	116	46 39	31 06	39·7	45 52	30 11	39·0	45 06	29 18	38·4	44 18	28 26	37·8	43 31	27 35	37·2	42 43	26 46	36·6	296	244
65	115	47 09	30 11	38·4	46 22	29 17	37·8	45 35	28 25	37·1	44 47	27 34	36·5	43 58	26 44	36·0	43 09	25 56	35·4	295	245
66	114	47 39	29 14	37·1	46 51	28 21	36·5	46 03	27 30	35·9	45 14	26 40	35·3	44 25	25 52	34·7	43 35	25 04	34·2	294	246
67	113	48 08	28 17	35·8	47 19	27 24	35·2	46 30	26 34	34·6	45 40	25 45	34·0	44 50	24 58	33·4	44 00	24 12	32·9	293	247
68	112	48 36	27 17	34·5	47 46	26 26	33·9	46 56	25 37	33·3	46 06	24 50	32·7	45 15	24 03	32·2	44 24	23 19	31·6	292	248
69	111	49 03	26 15	33·1	48 13	25 26	32·5	47 22	24 38	31·9	46 31	23 52	31·4	45 39	23 08	30·8	44 48	22 24	30·3	291	249
70	110	49 29	25 13	31·8	48 38	24 25	31·2	47 46	23 39	30·6	46 55	22 54	30·0	46 03	22 11	29·5	45 10	21 29	29·0	290	250
71	109	49 54	24 08	30·4	49 02	23 22	29·8	48 10	22 37	29·2	47 17	21 54	28·7	46 25	21 13	28·1	45 32	20 32	27·7	289	251
72	108	50 18	23 02	28·9	49 25	22 18	28·4	48 33	21 35	27·8	47 40	20 53	27·3	46 46	20 13	26·8	45 52	19 34	26·3	288	252
73	107	50 41	21 55	27·5	49 48	21 12	26·9	48 54	20 31	26·4	48 00	19 51	25·9	47 06	19 13	25·4	46 12	18 35	25·0	287	253
74	106	51 03	20 47	26·0	50 09	20 06	25·5	49 15	19 26	25·0	48 20	18 48	24·5	47 25	18 11	24·0	46 30	17 36	23·6	286	254
75	105	51 24	19 36	24·5	50 29	18 57	24·0	49 34	18 20	23·5	48 39	17 43	23·1	47 44	17 09	22·6	46 48	16 35	22·2	285	255
76	104	51 43	18 25	23·0	50 48	17 48	22·5	49 52	17 12	22·0	48 57	16 38	21·6	48 01	16 05	21·2	47 05	15 33	20·8	284	256
77	103	52 02	17 12	21·4	51 06	16 37	21·0	50 09	16 04	20·6	49 13	15 31	20·1	48 17	15 00	19·8	47 20	14 31	19·4	283	257
78	102	52 19	15 58	19·9	51 22	15 25	19·5	50 25	14 54	19·0	49 29	14 24	18·7	48 32	13 55	18·3	47 35	13 27	18·0	282	258
79	101	52 35	14 43	18·3	51 37	14 13	17·9	50 40	13 43	17·5	49 43	13 16	17·2	48 46	12 49	16·8	47 48	12 23	16·5	281	259
80	100	52 49	13 27	16·7	51 52	12 59	16·3	50 54	12 32	16·0	49 56	12 06	15·7	48 58	11 42	15·3	48 01	11 18	15·0	280	260
81	99	53 02	12 09	15·1	52 04	11 44	14·7	51 06	11 19	14·4	50 08	10 56	14·1	49 10	10 34	13·8	48 12	10 12	13·6	279	261
82	98	53 14	10 51	13·4	52 16	10 28	13·1	51 18	10 06	12·9	50 19	9 45	12·6	49 20	9 25	12·3	48 22	9 06	12·1	278	262
83	97	53 25	9 31	11·8	52 26	9 11	11·5	51 27	8 52	11·3	50 29	8 34	11·0	49 30	8 16	10·8	48 31	7 59	10·6	277	263
84	96	53 34	8 11	10·1	52 35	7 54	9·9	51 36	7 37	9·7	50 37	7 21	9·5	49 38	7 06	9·3	48 38	6 51	9·1	276	264
85	95	53 42	6 50	8·5	52 43	6 36	8·3	51 43	6 22	8·1	50 44	6 09	7·9	49 44	5 56	7·8	48 45	5 44	7·6	275	265
86	94	53 49	5 29	6·8	52 49	5 17	6·6	51 49	5 06	6·5	50 50	4 55	6·3	49 50	4 45	6·2	48 50	4 35	6·1	274	266
87	93	53 54	4 07	5·1	52 54	3 58	5·0	51 54	3 50	4·9	50 54	3 42	4·8	49 54	3 34	4·7	48 55	3 27	4·6	273	267
88	92	53 57	2 45	3·4	52 57	2 39	3·3	51 57	2 33	3·2	50 57	2 28	3·2	49 58	2 23	3·1	48 58	2 18	3·0	272	268
89	91	53 59	1 23	1·7	52 59	1 20	1·7	51 59	1 17	1·6	50 59	1 14	1·6	49 59	1 11	1·6	48 59	1 09	1·5	271	269
90	90	54 00	0 00	0·0	53 00	0 00	0·0	52 00	0 00	0·0	51 00	0 00	0·0	50 00	0 00	0·0	49 00	0 00	0·0	270	270

N. Lat: for LHA > 180° ... $Z_n = Z$
for LHA < 180° ... $Z_n = 360° - Z$

S. Lat.: for LHA > 180° ... $Z_n = 180° - Z$
for LHA < 180° ... $Z_n = 180° + Z$

© British Crown Copyright 2022. All rights reserved.

SIGHT REDUCTION TABLE

B: (−) for 90° < LHA < 270°
Dec:(−) for Lat. contrary name

Z₁: same sign as B
Z₂:: (−) for F > 90°

Lat./A	LHA/F	42° A/H	42° B/P	42° Z_1/Z_2	43° A/H	43° B/P	43° Z_1/Z_2	44° A/H	44° B/P	44° Z_1/Z_2	45° A/H	45° B/P	45° Z_1/Z_2	46° A/H	46° B/P	46° Z_1/Z_2	47° A/H	47° B/P	47° Z_1/Z_2	Lat./A	LHA
0	180	0 00	48 00	90.0	0 00	47 00	90.0	0 00	46 00	90.0	0 00	45 00	90.0	0 00	44 00	90.0	0 00	43 00	90.0	180	360
1	179	0 45	48 00	89.3	0 44	47 00	89.3	0 43	46 00	89.3	0 42	45 00	89.3	0 42	44 00	89.3	0 41	43 00	89.3	181	359
2	178	1 29	47 59	88.7	1 28	46 59	88.6	1 26	45 59	88.6	1 25	44 59	88.6	1 23	43 59	88.6	1 22	42 59	88.5	182	358
3	177	2 14	47 58	88.0	2 12	46 58	88.0	2 09	45 58	87.9	2 07	44 58	87.9	2 05	43 58	87.8	2 03	42 58	87.8	183	357
4	176	2 58	47 56	87.3	2 55	46 56	87.3	2 53	45 56	87.2	2 50	44 56	87.2	2 47	43 56	87.1	2 44	42 56	87.1	184	356
5	175	3 43	47 53	86.6	3 39	46 53	86.6	3 36	45 53	86.5	3 32	44 53	86.5	3 28	43 53	86.4	3 24	42 53	86.3	185	355
6	174	4 27	47 51	86.0	4 23	46 51	86.0	4 19	45 51	85.8	4 14	44 51	85.7	4 10	43 51	85.7	4 05	42 51	85.6	186	354
7	173	5 12	47 47	85.3	5 07	46 47	85.3	5 02	45 47	85.1	4 57	44 47	85.0	4 51	43 47	85.0	4 46	42 47	84.9	187	353
8	172	5 56	47 43	84.6	5 51	46 43	84.6	5 45	45 43	84.4	5 39	44 43	84.3	5 33	43 43	84.2	5 27	42 43	84.1	188	352
9	171	6 41	47 39	84.0	6 34	46 39	83.8	6 28	45 39	83.7	6 21	44 39	83.6	6 14	43 39	83.5	6 07	42 39	83.4	189	351
10	170	7 25	47 34	83.3	7 18	46 34	83.1	7 11	45 34	83.0	7 03	44 34	82.9	6 56	43 34	82.8	6 48	42 34	82.7	190	350
11	169	8 09	47 28	82.6	8 01	46 28	82.4	7 53	45 28	82.3	7 45	44 28	82.2	7 37	43 28	82.0	7 29	42 28	81.9	191	349
12	168	8 53	47 22	81.9	8 45	46 22	81.8	8 36	45 22	81.6	8 27	44 22	81.5	8 18	43 22	81.3	8 09	42 22	81.2	192	348
13	167	9 37	47 16	81.2	9 28	46 15	81.1	9 19	45 15	80.9	9 09	44 15	80.7	8 59	43 15	80.6	8 49	42 16	80.4	193	347
14	166	10 21	47 08	80.5	10 11	46 08	80.3	10 01	45 08	80.3	9 51	44 08	80.0	9 40	43 08	79.8	9 30	42 08	79.7	194	346
15	165	11 05	47 01	79.8	10 55	46 00	79.6	10 44	45 00	79.6	10 33	44 00	79.3	10 21	43 00	79.1	10 10	42 01	78.9	195	345
16	164	11 49	46 52	79.1	11 38	45 52	78.9	11 26	44 52	78.9	11 14	43 52	78.5	11 02	42 52	78.3	10 50	41 52	78.2	196	344
17	163	12 33	46 43	78.4	12 21	45 43	78.2	12 08	44 43	78.2	11 56	43 43	77.8	11 43	42 43	77.6	11 30	41 44	77.4	197	343
18	162	13 17	46 34	77.7	13 04	45 34	77.5	12 51	44 34	77.5	12 37	43 34	77.1	12 24	42 34	76.8	12 10	41 34	76.6	198	342
19	161	14 00	46 24	77.0	13 46	45 24	76.8	13 33	44 24	76.8	13 19	43 24	76.3	13 04	42 24	76.1	12 50	41 24	75.9	199	341
20	160	14 43	46 13	76.3	14 29	45 13	76.1	14 15	44 13	76.1	14 00	43 13	75.6	13 45	42 13	75.3	13 29	41 14	75.1	200	340
21	159	15 27	46 02	75.6	15 12	45 02	75.3	14 56	44 02	75.3	14 41	43 02	74.8	14 25	42 02	74.6	14 09	41 03	74.3	201	339
22	158	16 10	45 50	74.9	15 54	44 50	74.6	15 38	43 50	74.6	15 22	42 50	74.1	15 05	41 50	73.8	14 48	40 51	73.5	202	338
23	157	16 53	45 38	74.1	16 36	44 38	73.9	16 19	43 38	73.6	16 02	42 38	73.3	15 45	41 38	73.0	15 27	40 39	72.8	203	337
24	156	17 36	45 25	73.4	17 18	44 25	73.1	17 01	43 25	73.1	16 43	42 25	72.5	16 25	41 25	72.2	16 06	40 26	72.0	204	336
25	155	18 18	45 11	72.7	18 00	44 11	72.4	17 42	43 11	72.1	17 23	42 11	71.8	17 04	41 12	71.5	16 45	40 12	71.2	205	335
26	154	19 01	44 57	71.9	18 42	43 57	71.6	18 23	42 57	71.6	18 03	41 57	71.0	17 44	40 57	70.7	17 24	39 58	70.4	206	334
27	153	19 43	44 42	71.2	19 24	43 42	70.8	19 04	42 42	70.8	18 43	41 42	70.2	18 23	40 43	69.9	18 02	39 43	69.6	207	333
28	152	20 25	44 26	70.4	20 05	43 26	70.1	19 44	42 26	70.1	19 23	41 26	69.4	19 02	40 27	69.1	18 41	39 28	68.8	208	332
29	151	21 07	44 10	69.6	20 46	43 10	69.3	20 25	42 10	69.3	20 03	41 10	68.6	19 41	40 11	68.3	19 18	39 12	67.9	209	331
30	150	21 49	43 53	68.9	21 27	42 53	68.5	21 05	41 53	68.5	20 42	40 54	67.8	20 19	39 54	67.4	19 56	38 55	67.1	210	330
31	149	22 30	43 35	68.1	22 08	42 35	67.7	21 45	41 36	67.3	21 21	40 36	67.0	20 58	39 37	66.6	20 34	38 38	66.3	211	329
32	148	23 11	43 17	67.3	22 48	42 17	66.9	22 24	41 17	66.9	22 00	40 18	66.2	21 36	39 19	65.8	21 11	38 20	65.4	212	328
33	147	23 53	42 58	66.5	23 28	41 58	66.1	23 04	40 58	66.1	22 39	39 59	65.3	22 14	39 00	65.0	21 48	38 00	64.6	213	327
34	146	24 33	42 38	65.7	24 08	41 38	65.3	23 43	40 39	65.3	23 17	39 40	64.5	22 51	38 41	64.1	22 25	37 42	63.7	214	326
35	145	25 14	42 18	64.9	24 48	41 18	64.5	24 22	40 18	64.5	23 56	39 19	63.7	23 29	38 21	63.3	23 02	37 23	62.9	215	325
36	144	25 54	41 56	64.1	25 28	40 57	63.6	25 01	39 57	63.6	24 34	38 58	62.8	24 06	38 00	62.4	23 38	37 02	62.0	216	324
37	143	26 34	41 34	63.2	26 07	40 35	62.8	25 39	39 35	62.8	25 11	38 37	61.9	24 43	37 38	61.5	24 14	36 41	61.1	217	323
38	142	27 14	41 11	62.4	26 46	40 12	61.9	26 17	39 13	61.9	25 48	38 14	61.1	25 19	37 16	60.7	24 50	36 19	60.3	218	322
39	141	27 53	40 48	61.5	27 24	39 48	61.1	26 55	38 50	61.1	26 25	37 51	60.2	25 55	36 53	59.8	25 25	35 56	59.4	219	321
40	140	28 32	40 23	60.7	28 02	39 24	60.2	27 32	38 25	60.2	27 02	37 27	59.3	26 31	36 30	58.9	26 00	35 32	58.5	220	320
41	139	29 11	39 58	59.8	28 40	38 59	59.3	28 10	38 01	59.3	27 38	37 03	58.4	27 07	36 05	58.0	26 35	35 08	57.6	221	319
42	138	29 49	39 32	58.9	29 18	38 33	58.4	28 46	37 35	58.4	28 14	36 37	57.5	27 42	35 40	57.1	27 09	34 43	56.6	222	318
43	137	30 27	39 05	58.0	29 55	38 06	57.5	29 23	37 08	57.5	28 50	36 11	56.6	28 17	35 14	56.1	27 43	34 18	55.7	223	317
44	136	31 05	38 37	57.1	30 32	37 39	56.6	29 59	36 41	56.6	29 25	35 44	55.7	28 51	34 47	55.2	28 17	33 51	54.8	224	316
45	135	31 42	38 09	56.2	31 08	37 10	55.7	30 34	36 13	55.7	30 00	35 16	54.7	29 25	34 20	54.3	28 50	33 24	53.8	225	315

© British Crown Copyright 2022. All rights reserved.

Lat. / A		42°			43°			44°			45°			46°			47°			Lat. / A	
LHA/F		A/H	B/P	Z₁/Z₂	A/H	B/P	Z₁/Z₂	A/H	B/P	Z₁/Z₂	A/H	B/P	Z₁/Z₂	A/H	B/P	Z₁/Z₂	A/H	B/P	Z₁/Z₂	LHA	
45	135	31 42	38 09	56.2	31 08	37 10	55.7	30 34	36 13	55.2	30 00	35 16	54.7	29 25	34 20	54.3	28 50	33 24	53.8	225	315
46	134	32 19	37 39	55.3	31 45	36 41	54.8	31 10	35 44	54.2	30 34	34 47	53.8	29 59	33 51	53.3	29 23	32 56	52.9	226	314
47	133	32 55	37 08	54.3	32 20	36 11	53.8	31 45	35 14	53.3	31 08	34 18	52.8	30 32	33 22	52.4	29 55	32 27	51.9	227	313
48	132	33 31	36 37	53.4	32 55	35 40	52.9	32 19	34 43	52.3	31 42	33 47	51.9	31 05	32 52	51.4	30 27	31 58	50.9	228	312
49	131	34 07	36 05	52.4	33 30	35 08	51.9	32 53	34 11	51.4	32 15	33 16	50.9	31 37	32 21	50.4	30 59	31 28	49.9	229	311
50	130	34 42	35 31	51.4	34 04	34 35	50.9	33 26	33 39	50.4	32 48	32 44	49.9	32 09	31 50	49.4	31 30	30 56	48.9	230	310
51	129	35 17	34 57	50.4	34 38	34 01	49.9	33 59	33 05	49.4	33 20	32 11	48.9	32 40	31 17	48.4	32 00	30 24	47.9	231	309
52	128	35 51	34 22	49.4	35 12	33 26	48.9	34 32	32 31	48.4	33 52	31 37	47.9	33 11	30 44	47.4	32 30	29 52	46.9	232	308
53	127	36 24	33 45	48.4	35 44	32 50	47.9	35 04	31 56	47.3	34 23	31 02	46.8	33 42	30 10	46.3	33 00	29 18	45.9	233	307
54	126	36 57	33 08	47.4	36 17	32 13	46.8	35 35	31 20	46.3	34 54	30 27	45.8	34 12	29 35	45.3	33 30	28 44	44.8	234	306
55	125	37 30	32 30	46.3	36 48	31 36	45.8	36 06	30 43	45.2	35 24	29 50	44.7	34 41	28 59	44.2	33 58	28 08	43.8	235	305
56	124	38 02	31 51	45.2	37 19	30 57	44.7	36 37	30 04	44.2	35 53	29 13	43.6	35 10	28 22	43.2	34 26	27 32	42.7	236	304
57	123	38 33	31 10	44.1	37 50	30 17	43.6	37 06	29 25	43.1	36 22	28 34	42.6	35 38	27 45	42.1	34 53	26 56	41.6	237	303
58	122	39 04	30 29	43.0	38 20	29 36	42.5	37 36	28 45	42.0	36 51	27 55	41.5	36 06	27 06	41.0	35 20	26 18	40.5	238	302
59	121	39 34	29 47	41.9	38 50	28 55	41.4	38 04	28 04	40.9	37 19	27 15	40.4	36 33	26 27	39.9	35 46	25 39	39.4	239	301
60	120	40 04	29 03	40.8	39 18	28 12	40.2	38 32	27 22	39.7	37 46	26 34	39.2	36 59	25 46	38.8	36 12	25 00	38.3	240	300
61	119	40 32	28 18	39.6	39 46	27 28	39.1	38 59	26 39	38.6	38 12	25 52	38.1	37 25	25 05	37.6	36 37	24 20	37.2	241	299
62	118	41 00	27 32	38.5	40 13	26 43	37.9	39 26	25 56	37.4	38 38	25 09	36.9	37 50	24 23	36.5	37 02	23 39	36.0	242	298
63	117	41 28	26 45	37.3	40 40	25 58	36.8	39 52	25 11	36.3	39 03	24 25	35.8	38 14	23 40	35.3	37 25	22 57	34.9	243	297
64	116	41 54	25 58	36.1	41 06	25 11	35.6	40 17	24 25	35.1	39 28	23 41	34.6	38 38	22 57	34.1	37 48	22 14	33.7	244	296
65	115	42 20	25 09	34.9	41 31	24 23	34.4	40 41	23 38	33.9	39 51	22 55	33.4	39 01	22 12	33.0	38 11	21 31	32.5	245	295
66	114	42 45	24 19	33.6	41 55	23 34	33.1	41 05	22 50	32.7	40 14	22 08	32.2	39 23	21 27	31.8	38 32	20 46	31.3	246	294
67	113	43 10	23 28	32.4	42 19	22 44	31.9	41 28	22 02	31.4	40 36	21 21	31.0	39 45	20 40	30.5	38 53	20 01	30.1	247	293
68	112	43 33	22 35	31.1	42 42	21 53	30.6	41 50	21 12	30.2	40 58	20 32	29.7	40 06	19 53	29.3	39 13	19 15	28.9	248	292
69	111	43 56	21 42	29.8	43 04	21 01	29.4	42 11	20 22	28.9	41 19	19 43	28.5	40 26	19 05	28.1	39 33	18 29	27.7	249	291
70	110	44 18	20 48	28.5	43 25	20 08	28.1	42 32	19 30	27.7	41 38	18 53	27.2	40 45	18 17	26.8	39 51	17 41	26.5	250	290
71	109	44 38	19 53	27.2	43 45	19 15	26.8	42 51	18 38	26.4	41 57	18 02	26.0	41 03	17 27	25.6	40 09	16 53	25.2	251	289
72	108	44 58	18 57	25.9	44 04	18 20	25.5	43 10	17 45	25.1	42 16	17 10	24.7	41 21	16 37	24.3	40 26	16 05	24.0	252	288
73	107	45 17	17 59	24.6	44 24	17 24	24.1	43 28	16 51	23.8	42 33	16 18	23.4	41 38	15 46	23.0	40 42	15 15	22.7	253	287
74	106	45 35	17 01	23.2	44 40	16 28	22.8	43 45	15 56	22.4	42 49	15 25	22.1	41 54	14 54	21.7	40 58	14 25	21.4	254	286
75	105	45 53	16 02	21.8	44 57	15 31	21.4	44 01	15 00	21.1	43 05	14 31	20.8	42 09	14 02	20.4	41 12	13 34	20.1	255	285
76	104	46 09	15 02	20.4	45 12	14 33	20.1	44 16	14 04	19.7	43 19	13 36	19.4	42 23	13 09	19.1	41 26	12 43	18.8	256	284
77	103	46 24	14 02	19.0	45 27	13 34	18.7	44 30	13 07	18.4	43 33	12 41	18.1	42 36	12 15	17.8	41 39	11 51	17.5	257	283
78	102	46 38	13 00	17.6	45 40	12 34	17.3	44 43	12 09	17.0	43 46	11 45	16.7	42 48	11 21	16.5	41 51	10 58	16.2	258	282
79	101	46 51	11 58	16.2	45 53	11 34	15.9	44 55	11 11	15.6	43 57	10 48	15.4	43 00	10 26	15.1	42 02	10 05	14.9	259	281
80	100	47 03	10 55	14.8	46 04	10 33	14.5	45 06	10 12	14.2	44 08	9 51	14.0	43 10	9 31	13.8	42 12	9 12	13.6	260	280
81	99	47 13	9 51	13.3	46 15	9 31	13.1	45 16	9 12	12.8	44 18	8 53	12.6	43 19	8 35	12.4	42 21	8 18	12.2	261	279
82	98	47 23	8 47	11.9	46 24	8 29	11.6	45 26	8 12	11.4	44 27	7 55	11.2	43 28	7 39	11.1	42 29	7 24	10.9	262	278
83	97	47 32	7 42	10.4	46 33	7 27	10.2	45 34	7 12	10.0	44 34	6 57	9.9	43 35	6 43	9.7	42 36	6 29	9.5	263	277
84	96	47 39	6 37	8.9	46 40	6 24	8.8	45 41	6 11	8.6	44 41	5 58	8.5	43 42	5 46	8.3	42 42	5 34	8.2	264	276
85	95	47 46	5 32	7.4	46 46	5 20	7.3	45 46	5 09	7.2	44 47	4 59	7.1	43 47	4 49	6.9	42 48	4 39	6.8	265	275
86	94	47 51	4 26	6.0	46 51	4 17	5.9	45 51	4 08	5.7	44 52	3 59	5.6	43 52	3 51	5.6	42 52	3 43	5.5	266	274
87	93	47 55	3 20	4.5	46 55	3 13	4.4	45 55	3 06	4.3	44 55	3 00	4.2	43 55	2 54	4.2	42 56	2 48	4.1	267	273
88	92	47 58	2 13	3.0	46 58	2 09	2.9	45 58	2 04	2.9	44 58	2 00	2.8	43 58	1 56	2.8	42 58	1 52	2.7	268	272
89	91	47 59	1 07	1.5	46 59	1 04	1.5	45 59	1 02	1.4	44 59	1 00	1.4	43 59	0 58	1.4	42 59	0 56	1.4	269	271
90	90	48 00	0 00	0.0	47 00	0 00	0.0	46 00	0 00	0.0	45 00	0 00	0.0	44 00	0 00	0.0	43 00	0 00	0.0	270	270

N. Lat.: for LHA > 180° ... Zₙ = Z
for LHA < 180° ... Zₙ = 360° − Z

S. Lat.: for LHA > 180° ... Zₙ = 180° − Z
for LHA < 180° ... Zₙ = 180° + Z

© British Crown Copyright 2022. All rights reserved.

SIGHT REDUCTION TABLE

B: (−) for 90° < LHA < 270°
Dec:(−) for Lat. contrary name

Z_1: same sign as B
Z_2: (−) for F > 90°

Lat. / A LHA/F	48° A/H	48° B/P	48° Z_1/Z_2	49° A/H	49° B/P	49° Z_1/Z_2	50° A/H	50° B/P	50° Z_1/Z_2	51° A/H	51° B/P	51° Z_1/Z_2	52° A/H	52° B/P	52° Z_1/Z_2	53° A/H	53° B/P	53° Z_1/Z_2	Lat. / A LHA
0 / 180	0 00	42 00	90·0	0 00	41 00	90·0	0 00	40 00	90·0	0 00	39 00	90·0	0 00	38 00	90·0	0 00	37 00	90·0	180
1 / 179	0 40	42 00	89·3	0 39	41 00	89·2	0 39	40 00	89·2	0 38	39 00	89·2	0 37	38 00	89·2	0 36	37 00	89·2	181
2 / 178	1 20	41 59	88·5	1 19	40 59	88·5	1 17	39 59	88·5	1 16	38 59	88·4	1 14	37 59	88·4	1 12	36 59	88·4	182
3 / 177	2 00	41 58	87·8	1 58	40 58	87·8	1 56	39 58	87·7	1 53	38 58	87·7	1 51	37 58	87·6	1 48	36 58	87·6	183
4 / 176	2 41	41 56	87·0	2 37	40 56	87·0	2 34	39 56	86·9	2 31	38 56	86·9	2 28	37 56	86·8	2 24	36 56	86·8	184
5 / 175	3 21	41 53	86·3	3 17	40 54	86·2	3 13	39 54	86·2	3 09	38 54	86·1	3 05	37 54	86·1	3 00	36 54	86·0	185
6 / 174	4 01	41 51	85·5	3 56	40 51	85·5	3 51	39 51	85·4	3 46	38 51	85·3	3 41	37 51	85·3	3 36	36 51	85·2	186
7 / 173	4 41	41 47	84·8	4 35	40 47	84·7	4 30	39 47	84·6	4 24	38 47	84·5	4 18	37 47	84·5	4 12	36 48	84·4	187
8 / 172	5 21	41 43	84·0	5 14	40 43	83·9	5 08	39 43	83·9	5 01	38 44	83·8	4 55	37 44	83·7	4 48	36 44	83·6	188
9 / 171	6 01	41 39	83·3	5 53	40 39	83·2	5 46	39 39	83·1	5 39	38 39	83·0	5 32	37 39	82·9	5 24	36 40	82·8	189
10 / 170	6 40	41 34	82·5	6 32	40 34	82·4	6 25	39 34	82·3	6 16	38 34	82·2	6 08	37 35	82·1	6 00	36 35	82·0	190
11 / 169	7 20	41 28	81·8	7 11	40 28	81·7	7 03	39 29	81·5	6 54	38 29	81·4	6 45	37 29	81·3	6 36	36 29	81·2	191
12 / 168	8 00	41 22	81·0	7 50	40 22	80·9	7 41	39 23	80·8	7 31	38 23	80·6	7 21	37 23	80·5	7 11	36 24	80·4	192
13 / 167	8 39	41 16	80·3	8 29	40 16	80·1	8 19	39 16	80·0	8 08	38 16	79·8	7 58	37 17	79·7	7 47	36 17	79·6	193
14 / 166	9 19	41 09	79·5	9 08	40 09	79·3	8 57	39 09	79·2	8 45	38 09	79·0	8 34	37 10	78·9	8 22	36 10	78·7	194
15 / 165	9 58	41 01	78·7	9 47	40 01	78·6	9 35	39 02	78·4	9 22	38 02	78·2	9 10	37 02	78·1	8 58	36 03	77·9	195
16 / 164	10 38	40 53	78·0	10 25	39 53	77·8	10 12	38 53	77·6	9 59	37 54	77·4	9 46	36 54	77·3	9 33	35 55	77·1	196
17 / 163	11 17	40 44	77·2	11 04	39 44	77·0	10 50	38 45	76·8	10 36	37 45	76·6	10 22	36 46	76·5	10 08	35 47	76·3	197
18 / 162	11 56	40 34	76·4	11 42	39 35	76·2	11 27	38 35	76·0	11 13	37 36	75·8	10 58	36 37	75·6	10 43	35 38	75·5	198
19 / 161	12 35	40 25	75·6	12 20	39 25	75·4	12 05	38 26	75·2	11 49	37 26	75·0	11 34	36 27	74·8	11 18	35 28	74·6	199
20 / 160	13 14	40 14	74·9	12 58	39 15	74·6	12 42	38 15	74·4	12 26	37 16	74·2	12 09	36 17	74·0	11 53	35 18	73·8	200
21 / 159	13 52	40 03	74·1	13 36	39 04	73·8	13 19	38 04	73·6	13 02	37 05	73·4	12 45	36 06	73·2	12 27	35 08	73·0	201
22 / 158	14 31	39 51	73·3	14 14	38 52	73·0	13 56	37 53	72·8	13 38	36 54	72·6	13 20	35 55	72·3	13 02	34 56	72·1	202
23 / 157	15 09	39 39	72·5	14 51	38 40	72·2	14 33	37 41	72·0	14 14	36 42	71·7	13 55	35 43	71·5	13 36	34 45	71·3	203
24 / 156	15 48	39 26	71·7	15 29	38 27	71·4	15 09	37 28	71·2	14 50	36 31	70·9	14 30	35 31	70·7	14 10	34 33	70·4	204
25 / 155	16 26	39 13	70·9	16 06	38 14	70·6	15 46	37 15	70·3	15 25	36 17	70·1	15 05	35 17	69·8	14 44	34 20	69·6	205
26 / 154	17 03	38 59	70·1	16 43	38 00	69·8	16 22	37 01	69·5	16 01	36 03	69·2	15 39	35 05	69·0	15 18	34 07	68·7	206
27 / 153	17 41	38 44	69·3	17 20	37 45	69·0	16 58	36 47	68·7	16 36	35 49	68·4	16 14	34 51	68·1	15 51	33 53	67·9	207
28 / 152	18 19	38 29	68·4	17 56	37 30	68·1	17 34	36 32	67·8	17 11	35 34	67·5	16 48	34 34	67·3	16 25	33 39	67·0	208
29 / 151	18 56	38 13	67·6	18 33	37 15	67·3	18 09	36 16	67·0	17 46	35 18	66·7	17 22	34 21	66·4	16 58	33 23	66·1	209
30 / 150	19 33	37 57	66·8	19 09	36 58	66·5	18 45	36 00	66·1	18 20	35 03	65·8	17 56	34 05	65·5	17 31	33 08	65·2	210
31 / 149	20 10	37 40	65·9	19 45	36 41	65·6	19 20	35 44	65·3	18 55	34 46	65·0	18 29	33 49	64·7	18 03	32 52	64·4	211
32 / 148	20 46	37 22	65·1	20 21	36 24	64·8	19 55	35 26	64·4	19 29	34 29	64·1	19 02	33 32	63·8	18 36	32 35	63·5	212
33 / 147	21 22	37 03	64·2	20 56	36 06	63·9	20 30	35 08	63·6	20 03	34 11	63·2	19 35	33 14	62·9	19 08	32 17	62·6	213
34 / 146	21 58	36 44	63·4	21 31	35 47	63·0	21 04	34 49	62·7	20 36	33 53	62·3	20 08	32 56	62·0	19 40	32 00	61·7	214
35 / 145	22 34	36 25	62·5	22 06	35 27	62·1	21 38	34 30	61·8	21 10	33 33	61·4	20 41	32 37	61·1	20 12	31 41	60·8	215
36 / 144	23 10	36 04	61·6	22 41	35 07	61·3	22 12	34 10	60·9	21 43	33 14	60·5	21 13	32 18	60·2	20 43	31 22	59·9	216
37 / 143	23 45	35 43	60·8	23 15	34 46	60·4	22 45	33 50	60·0	22 15	32 53	59·6	21 45	31 58	59·3	21 14	31 02	59·0	217
38 / 142	24 20	35 21	59·9	23 49	34 25	59·5	23 19	33 28	59·1	22 48	32 32	58·7	22 16	31 37	58·4	21 45	30 42	58·0	218
39 / 141	24 54	34 59	59·0	24 23	34 02	58·6	23 52	33 07	58·2	23 20	32 11	57·8	22 48	31 16	57·5	22 15	30 21	57·1	219
40 / 140	25 28	34 36	58·1	24 57	33 39	57·7	24 24	32 44	57·3	23 52	31 49	56·9	23 19	30 54	56·5	22 45	30 00	56·2	220
41 / 139	26 02	34 12	57·1	25 30	33 16	56·7	24 57	32 21	56·3	24 23	31 26	56·0	23 49	30 32	55·6	23 15	29 38	55·2	221
42 / 138	26 36	33 47	56·2	26 02	32 52	55·8	25 28	31 57	55·4	24 54	31 02	55·0	24 20	30 08	54·6	23 45	29 15	54·3	222
43 / 137	27 09	33 22	55·3	26 35	32 27	54·9	26 00	31 32	54·5	25 25	30 38	54·1	24 50	29 45	53·7	24 14	28 53	53·3	223
44 / 136	27 42	32 56	54·3	27 07	32 01	53·9	26 31	31 07	53·5	25 55	30 13	53·1	25 19	29 20	52·7	24 43	28 28	52·4	224
45 / 135	28 14	32 29	53·4	27 38	31 35	53·0	27 02	30 41	52·5	26 25	29 48	52·1	25 48	28 55	51·8	25 11	28 03	51·4	225

© British Crown Copyright 2022. All rights reserved.

Lat./A LHA/F	48° A/H	48° B/P	48° Z1/Z2	49° A/H	49° B/P	49° Z1/Z2	50° A/H	50° B/P	50° Z1/Z2	51° A/H	51° B/P	51° Z1/Z2	52° A/H	52° B/P	52° Z1/Z2	53° A/H	53° B/P	53° Z1/Z2	Lat./A LHA
135	28 14	32 29	53·4	27 38	31 35	53·0	27 02	30 41	52·5	26 25	29 48	52·1	25 48	28 55	51·8	25 11	28 03	51·4	225
134	28 46	32 01	52·4	28 10	31 08	52·0	27 32	30 14	51·6	26 55	29 22	51·2	26 17	28 29	50·8	25 39	27 38	50·4	226
133	29 18	31 33	51·4	28 40	30 40	51·0	28 02	29 47	50·6	27 24	28 55	50·2	26 46	28 03	49·8	26 07	27 12	49·4	227
132	29 49	31 04	50·5	29 11	30 11	50·0	28 32	29 19	49·6	27 53	28 27	49·2	27 14	27 36	48·8	26 34	26 46	48·4	228
131	30 20	30 34	49·5	29 41	29 42	49·0	29 01	28 50	48·6	28 21	27 59	48·2	27 41	27 08	47·8	27 01	26 18	47·4	229
130	30 50	30 04	48·5	30 10	29 12	48·0	29 30	28 20	47·6	28 49	27 30	47·2	28 08	26 40	46·8	27 27	25 51	46·4	230
129	31 19	29 32	47·5	30 39	28 41	47·0	29 58	27 50	46·6	29 17	27 00	46·2	28 35	26 11	45·8	27 53	25 22	45·4	231
128	31 49	29 00	46·4	31 08	28 09	46·0	30 26	27 19	45·6	29 44	26 30	45·2	29 01	25 41	44·8	28 19	24 53	44·4	232
127	32 18	28 27	45·4	31 36	27 37	45·0	30 53	26 48	44·5	30 10	25 59	44·1	29 27	25 11	43·7	28 44	24 23	43·3	233
126	32 46	27 53	44·4	32 03	27 04	43·9	31 20	26 15	43·5	30 36	25 27	43·1	29 52	24 40	42·7	29 08	23 53	42·3	234
125	33 14	27 19	43·3	32 30	26 30	42·9	31 46	25 42	42·4	31 02	24 55	42·0	30 17	24 08	41·6	29 32	23 23	41·2	235
124	33 42	26 44	42·2	32 57	25 55	41·8	32 12	25 08	41·4	31 27	24 22	41·0	30 41	23 36	40·6	29 56	22 51	40·2	236
123	34 08	26 07	41·1	33 23	25 20	40·7	32 37	24 34	40·3	31 51	23 48	39·9	31 05	23 03	39·5	30 19	22 19	39·1	237
122	34 34	25 30	40·1	33 48	24 44	39·6	33 02	23 58	39·2	32 15	23 14	38·8	31 28	22 29	38·4	30 41	21 46	38·0	238
121	35 00	24 53	39·0	34 13	24 07	38·5	33 26	23 22	38·1	32 39	22 38	37·7	31 51	21 55	37·3	31 03	21 13	37·0	239
120	35 25	24 14	37·8	34 37	23 30	37·4	33 50	22 46	37·0	33 02	22 03	36·6	32 13	21 20	36·2	31 25	20 39	35·9	240
119	35 49	23 35	36·7	35 01	22 51	36·3	34 12	22 08	35·9	33 24	21 26	35·5	32 35	20 45	35·1	31 46	20 04	34·8	241
118	36 13	22 55	35·6	35 24	22 12	35·2	34 35	21 30	34·8	33 45	20 49	34·4	32 56	20 09	34·0	32 06	19 29	33·7	242
117	36 36	22 14	34·4	35 46	21 32	34·0	34 56	20 51	33·6	34 06	20 11	33·3	33 16	19 32	32·9	32 25	18 53	32·5	243
116	36 58	21 32	33·3	36 08	20 52	32·9	35 17	20 12	32·5	34 26	19 33	32·1	33 36	18 54	31·8	32 45	18 17	31·4	244
115	37 20	20 50	32·1	36 29	20 10	31·7	35 38	19 32	31·3	34 47	18 54	31·0	33 55	18 16	30·6	33 03	17 40	30·3	245
114	37 41	20 07	30·9	36 49	19 28	30·5	35 58	18 51	30·2	35 06	18 14	29·8	34 13	17 38	29·5	33 21	17 02	29·1	246
113	38 01	19 23	29·7	37 09	18 46	29·4	36 17	18 09	29·0	35 25	17 33	28·6	34 31	16 59	28·3	33 38	16 24	28·0	247
112	38 21	18 38	28·5	37 28	18 02	28·2	36 35	17 27	27·8	35 42	16 53	27·5	34 48	16 19	27·1	33 55	15 46	26·8	248
111	38 40	17 53	27·3	37 46	17 18	27·0	36 53	16 44	26·6	35 59	16 11	26·3	35 05	15 38	26·0	34 11	15 07	25·7	249
110	38 58	17 07	26·1	38 04	16 33	25·7	37 10	16 01	25·4	36 15	15 29	25·1	35 21	14 58	24·8	34 26	14 27	24·5	250
109	39 15	16 20	24·9	38 20	15 48	24·5	37 26	15 17	24·2	36 31	14 46	23·9	35 36	14 16	23·6	34 41	13 47	23·3	251
108	39 32	15 33	23·6	38 36	15 02	23·3	37 41	14 32	23·0	36 46	14 03	22·7	35 50	13 34	22·4	34 55	13 07	22·1	252
107	39 47	14 45	22·4	38 51	14 16	22·1	37 56	13 47	21·8	37 00	13 19	21·5	36 04	12 52	21·2	35 08	12 25	20·9	253
106	40 02	13 56	21·1	39 06	13 28	20·8	38 10	13 01	20·5	37 13	12 35	20·3	36 17	12 09	20·0	35 21	11 44	19·8	254
105	40 16	13 07	19·8	39 19	12 41	19·5	38 23	12 15	19·3	37 26	11 50	19·0	36 29	11 26	18·8	35 33	11 02	18·5	255
104	40 29	12 17	18·5	39 32	11 53	18·3	38 35	11 28	18·0	37 38	11 05	17·8	36 41	10 42	17·6	35 44	10 20	17·3	256
103	40 41	11 27	17·3	39 44	11 04	17·0	38 47	10 41	16·8	37 49	10 19	16·5	36 52	9 58	16·3	35 54	9 37	16·1	257
102	40 53	10 36	16·0	39 55	10 15	15·7	38 57	9 54	15·5	38 00	9 33	15·3	37 02	9 14	15·1	36 04	8 54	14·9	258
101	41 04	9 45	14·7	40 05	9 25	14·4	39 07	9 06	14·2	38 09	8 47	14·0	37 11	8 29	13·9	36 13	8 11	13·7	259
100	41 13	8 53	13·3	40 15	8 35	13·2	39 16	8 17	13·0	38 18	8 00	12·8	37 19	7 44	12·6	36 21	7 27	12·5	260
99	41 22	8 01	12·0	40 23	7 45	11·9	39 25	7 29	11·7	38 26	7 13	11·5	37 27	6 58	11·4	36 28	6 43	11·2	261
98	41 30	7 09	10·7	40 31	6 54	10·5	39 32	6 40	10·4	38 33	6 26	10·3	37 34	6 12	10·1	36 35	5 59	10·0	262
97	41 37	6 16	9·4	40 38	6 03	9·2	39 39	5 50	9·1	38 39	5 38	9·0	37 40	5 26	8·9	36 41	5 15	8·7	263
96	41 43	5 23	8·1	40 44	5 12	7·9	39 44	5 01	7·8	38 45	4 50	7·7	37 45	4 40	7·6	36 46	4 30	7·5	264
95	41 48	4 29	6·8	40 49	4 20	6·6	39 49	4 11	6·5	38 49	4 02	6·4	37 50	3 54	6·3	36 50	3 45	6·3	265
94	41 52	3 36	5·4	40 53	3 28	5·3	39 53	3 21	5·2	38 53	3 14	5·1	37 53	3 07	5·1	36 54	3 01	5·0	266
93	41 56	2 42	4·0	40 56	2 36	4·0	39 56	2 31	3·9	38 56	2 26	3·9	37 56	2 20	3·8	36 56	2 16	3·8	267
92	41 58	1 48	2·7	40 58	1 44	2·6	39 58	1 41	2·6	38 58	1 37	2·6	37 58	1 34	2·5	36 58	1 30	2·5	268
91	42 00	0 54	1·3	41 00	0 52	1·3	40 00	0 50	1·3	39 00	0 49	1·3	38 00	0 47	1·3	37 00	0 45	1·3	269
90	42 00	0 00	0·0	41 00	0 00	0·0	40 00	0 00	0·0	39 00	0 00	0·0	38 00	0 00	0·0	37 00	0 00	0·0	270

N. Lat: for LHA > 180° ... $Z_n = Z$
for LHA < 180° ... $Z_n = 360° - Z$

S. Lat.: for LHA > 180° ... $Z_n = 180° - Z$
for LHA < 180° ... $Z_n = 180° + Z$

© British Crown Copyright 2022. All rights reserved.

LATITUDE / A: 54° – 59°

SIGHT REDUCTION TABLE

B: (−) for 90° < LHA < 270°
Dec:(−) for Lat. contrary name

Z₁: same sign as B
Z₂: (−) for F > 90°

LHA/F	54° A/H	54° B/P	54° Z₁/Z₂	55° A/H	55° B/P	55° Z₁/Z₂	56° A/H	56° B/P	56° Z₁/Z₂	57° A/H	57° B/P	57° Z₁/Z₂	58° A/H	58° B/P	58° Z₁/Z₂	59° A/H	59° B/P	59° Z₁/Z₂	LHA/A
0 180	0 00	36 00	90·0	0 00	35 00	90·0	0 00	34 00	90·0	0 00	33 00	90·0	0 00	32 00	90·0	0 00	31 00	90·0	180 360
1 179	0 35	36 00	89·2	0 34	35 00	89·2	0 34	34 00	89·2	0 33	33 00	89·2	0 32	32 00	89·2	0 31	31 00	89·1	181 359
2 178	1 11	35 59	88·4	1 09	34 59	88·4	1 07	33 59	88·4	1 05	32 59	88·3	1 04	31 59	88·3	1 02	30 59	88·3	182 358
3 177	1 46	35 58	87·6	1 43	34 58	87·5	1 41	33 58	87·5	1 38	32 58	87·5	1 35	31 58	87·5	1 33	30 58	87·4	183 357
4 176	2 21	35 56	86·8	2 18	34 56	86·7	2 14	33 56	86·7	2 11	32 56	86·6	2 07	31 56	86·6	2 04	30 56	86·6	184 356
5 175	2 56	35 54	86·0	2 52	34 54	85·9	2 48	33 54	85·9	2 43	32 54	85·8	2 39	31 54	85·8	2 34	30 54	85·7	185 355
6 174	3 31	35 51	85·1	3 26	34 51	85·1	3 21	33 51	85·0	3 16	32 51	85·0	3 11	31 52	84·9	3 05	30 52	84·9	186 354
7 173	4 06	35 48	84·3	4 00	34 48	84·3	3 54	33 48	84·2	3 48	32 48	84·1	3 42	31 48	84·1	3 36	30 49	84·0	187 353
8 172	4 42	35 45	83·5	4 35	34 44	83·4	4 28	33 44	83·4	4 21	32 45	83·3	4 14	31 45	83·2	4 07	30 45	83·1	188 352
9 171	5 17	35 40	82·7	5 09	34 40	82·6	5 01	33 40	82·5	4 53	32 41	82·4	4 45	31 41	82·3	4 37	30 41	82·3	189 351
10 170	5 51	35 35	81·9	5 43	34 35	81·8	5 34	33 36	81·7	5 26	32 36	81·6	5 17	31 36	81·5	5 08	30 37	81·4	190 350
11 169	6 26	35 30	81·1	6 17	34 30	81·0	6 08	33 31	80·8	5 58	32 31	80·7	5 48	31 31	80·6	5 38	30 32	80·5	191 349
12 168	7 01	35 24	80·2	6 51	34 24	80·1	6 41	33 25	80·0	6 30	32 25	79·9	6 20	31 26	79·8	6 09	30 27	79·7	192 348
13 167	7 36	35 18	79·4	7 25	34 18	79·3	7 14	33 19	79·2	7 02	32 19	79·0	6 51	31 20	78·9	6 39	30 21	78·8	193 347
14 166	8 11	35 11	78·6	7 59	34 12	78·5	7 46	33 12	78·3	7 34	32 13	78·2	7 22	31 14	78·1	7 09	30 15	77·9	194 346
15 165	8 45	35 04	77·8	8 32	34 04	77·6	8 19	33 05	77·5	8 06	32 06	77·3	7 53	31 07	77·2	7 40	30 08	77·1	195 345
16 164	9 19	34 56	76·9	9 06	33 57	76·8	8 52	32 58	76·8	8 38	31 58	76·5	8 24	31 00	76·3	8 10	30 01	76·2	196 344
17 163	9 54	34 47	76·1	9 39	33 48	75·9	9 25	32 49	75·9	9 10	31 50	75·6	8 55	30 52	75·5	8 40	29 53	75·3	197 343
18 162	10 28	34 39	75·3	10 13	33 40	75·1	9 57	32 41	75·1	9 41	31 42	74·8	9 25	30 43	74·6	9 09	29 45	74·4	198 342
19 161	11 02	34 29	74·4	10 46	33 30	74·2	10 29	32 32	74·1	10 13	31 33	73·9	9 56	30 35	73·7	9 39	29 36	73·6	199 341
20 160	11 36	34 19	73·6	11 19	33 21	73·4	11 02	32 22	73·2	10 44	31 24	73·0	10 27	30 25	72·8	10 09	29 27	72·7	200 340
21 159	12 10	34 09	72·7	11 52	33 10	72·5	11 34	32 12	72·3	11 15	31 14	72·2	10 57	30 15	72·0	10 38	29 17	71·8	201 339
22 158	12 43	33 58	71·9	12 24	33 00	71·7	12 06	32 01	71·5	11 46	31 03	71·3	11 27	30 05	71·1	11 07	29 07	70·9	202 338
23 157	13 17	33 46	71·0	12 57	32 48	70·8	12 37	31 50	70·6	12 17	30 52	70·4	11 57	29 54	70·2	11 37	28 57	70·0	203 337
24 156	13 50	33 34	70·2	13 29	32 36	70·0	13 09	31 38	69·7	12 48	30 41	69·5	12 27	29 43	69·3	12 06	28 46	69·1	204 336
25 155	14 24	33 22	69·3	14 02	32 24	69·1	13 40	31 26	68·9	13 18	30 29	68·6	12 56	29 31	68·4	12 34	28 34	68·2	205 335
26 154	14 56	33 09	68·5	14 34	32 11	68·2	14 11	31 14	68·0	13 49	30 16	67·8	13 26	29 19	67·5	13 03	28 22	67·3	206 334
27 153	15 29	32 55	67·6	15 06	31 58	67·3	14 42	31 00	67·1	14 19	30 03	66·9	13 55	29 06	66·6	13 31	28 10	66·4	207 333
28 152	16 01	32 41	66·7	15 37	31 44	66·5	15 13	30 47	66·2	14 49	29 50	66·0	14 24	28 53	65·7	14 00	27 57	65·5	208 332
29 151	16 33	32 26	65·8	16 09	31 29	65·6	15 44	30 32	65·3	15 19	29 36	65·1	14 53	28 39	64·8	14 28	27 43	64·6	209 331
30 150	17 05	32 11	65·0	16 40	31 14	64·7	16 14	30 17	64·4	15 48	29 21	64·2	15 22	28 25	63·9	14 55	27 29	63·7	210 330
31 149	17 37	31 55	64·1	17 11	30 58	63·8	16 44	30 02	63·5	16 17	29 06	63·3	15 50	28 10	63·0	15 23	27 15	62·7	211 329
32 148	18 09	31 38	63·2	17 42	30 42	62·9	17 14	29 46	62·6	16 47	28 51	62·3	16 19	27 55	62·1	15 50	27 00	61·8	212 328
33 147	18 40	31 21	62·3	18 12	30 25	62·0	17 44	29 30	61·7	17 15	28 34	61·4	16 47	27 39	61·2	16 17	26 45	60·9	213 327
34 146	19 11	31 04	61·4	18 42	30 08	61·1	18 13	29 13	60·8	17 44	28 18	60·5	17 14	27 23	60·2	16 44	26 29	60·0	214 326
35 145	19 42	30 46	60·5	19 12	29 50	60·2	18 42	28 55	59·9	18 12	28 01	59·6	17 42	27 06	59·3	17 11	26 12	59·0	215 325
36 144	20 13	30 27	59·6	19 42	29 32	59·2	19 11	28 37	58·9	18 40	27 43	58·6	18 09	26 49	58·4	17 37	25 55	58·1	216 324
37 143	20 43	30 07	58·6	20 12	29 13	58·3	19 40	28 19	58·0	19 08	27 25	57·7	18 36	26 31	57·4	18 03	25 38	57·1	217 323
38 142	21 13	29 48	57·7	20 41	28 53	57·4	20 08	28 00	57·1	19 35	27 06	56·8	19 02	26 13	56·5	18 29	25 20	56·2	218 322
39 141	21 43	29 28	56·8	21 10	28 33	56·4	20 36	27 40	56·1	20 03	26 47	55·8	19 29	25 54	55·5	18 55	25 02	55·2	219 321
40 140	22 12	29 06	55·8	21 38	28 13	55·5	21 04	27 20	55·5	20 30	26 27	54·9	19 55	25 35	54·6	19 20	24 43	54·3	220 320
41 139	22 41	28 44	54·9	22 06	27 51	54·5	21 31	26 59	54·5	20 56	26 07	53·9	20 21	25 15	53·6	19 45	24 24	53·3	221 319
42 138	23 10	28 22	53·9	22 34	27 29	53·6	21 58	26 37	53·6	21 22	25 46	52·9	20 46	24 55	52·6	20 10	24 04	52·3	222 318
43 137	23 38	27 59	53·0	23 02	27 07	52·7	22 25	26 15	52·7	21 48	25 24	52·0	21 11	24 34	51·7	20 34	23 43	51·4	223 317
44 136	24 06	27 36	52·0	23 30	26 44	51·7	22 51	25 53	51·7	22 14	25 02	51·0	21 36	24 12	50·7	20 58	23 23	50·4	224 316
45 135	24 34	27 11	51·0	23 56	26 20	50·7	23 17	25 30	50·7	22 39	24 40	50·0	22 00	23 50	49·7	21 21	23 01	49·4	225 315

© British Crown Copyright 2022. All rights reserved.

Lat. / A		54°			55°			56°			57°			58°			59°				Lat. / A
LHA/F		A/H	B/P	Z_1/Z_2	A/H	B/P	Z_1/Z_2	A/H	B/P	Z_1/Z_2	A/H	B/P	Z_1/Z_2	A/H	B/P	Z_1/Z_2	A/H	B/P	Z_1/Z_2	LHA	
135	45	24 34	27 11	51·0	23 56	26 20	50·7	23 17	25 30	50·3	22 39	24 40	50·0	22 00	23 50	49·7	21 21	23 01	49·4	225	315
134	46	25 01	26 47	50·0	24 24	25 56	49·7	23 43	25 06	49·3	23 04	24 17	49·0	22 24	23 28	48·7	21 45	22 39	48·4	226	314
133	47	25 28	26 22	49·1	24 48	25 32	48·7	24 08	24 42	48·4	23 28	23 53	48·0	22 48	23 05	47·7	22 08	22 17	47·4	227	313
132	48	25 54	25 56	48·1	25 14	25 06	47·7	24 33	24 17	47·4	23 52	23 29	47·0	23 11	22 41	46·7	22 30	21 54	46·4	228	312
131	49	26 20	25 29	47·1	25 39	24 40	46·7	24 58	23 52	46·4	24 16	23 05	46·0	23 34	22 17	45·7	22 52	21 31	45·4	229	311
130	50	26 46	25 02	46·0	26 04	24 14	45·7	25 22	23 26	45·3	24 40	22 39	45·0	23 57	21 53	44·7	23 14	21 07	44·4	230	310
129	51	27 11	24 34	45·0	26 28	23 47	44·7	25 45	23 00	44·3	25 02	22 14	44·0	24 19	21 28	43·7	23 36	20 43	43·4	231	309
128	52	27 36	24 06	44·0	26 52	23 19	43·6	26 09	22 33	43·3	25 25	21 48	43·0	24 41	21 03	42·7	23 57	20 18	42·3	232	308
127	53	28 00	23 37	43·0	27 16	22 51	42·6	26 32	22 06	42·3	25 47	21 21	41·9	25 02	20 37	41·6	24 17	19 53	41·3	233	307
126	54	28 24	23 07	41·9	27 39	22 22	41·6	26 54	21 38	41·2	26 09	20 54	40·9	25 23	20 10	40·6	24 37	19 27	40·3	234	306
125	55	28 47	22 37	40·9	28 01	21 53	40·5	27 16	21 09	40·2	26 30	20 26	39·9	25 44	19 43	39·5	24 57	19 01	39·2	235	305
124	56	29 10	22 07	39·8	28 24	21 23	39·5	27 37	20 40	39·1	26 50	19 57	38·8	26 04	19 16	38·5	25 17	18 34	38·2	236	304
123	57	29 32	21 35	38·8	28 45	20 52	38·4	27 58	20 10	38·1	27 11	19 29	37·8	26 23	18 48	37·4	25 35	18 07	37·1	237	303
122	58	29 54	21 03	37·7	29 06	20 21	37·3	28 19	19 40	37·0	27 31	18 59	36·7	26 42	18 19	36·4	25 54	17 40	36·1	238	302
121	59	30 15	20 31	36·6	29 27	19 50	36·3	28 38	19 09	35·9	27 50	18 30	35·6	27 01	17 50	35·3	26 12	17 12	35·0	239	301
120	60	30 36	19 58	35·5	29 47	19 18	35·2	28 58	18 38	34·9	28 09	17 59	34·5	27 19	17 21	34·2	26 29	16 43	34·0	240	300
119	61	30 56	19 24	34·4	30 07	18 45	34·1	29 17	18 06	33·8	28 27	17 29	33·5	27 37	16 51	33·2	26 46	16 14	32·9	241	299
118	62	31 16	18 50	33·3	30 26	18 12	33·0	29 35	17 34	32·7	28 45	16 57	32·4	27 54	16 21	32·1	27 03	15 45	31·8	242	298
117	63	31 35	18 15	32·2	30 44	17 38	31·9	29 53	17 02	31·6	29 02	16 26	31·3	28 10	15 50	31·0	27 19	15 15	30·7	243	297
116	64	31 53	17 40	31·1	31 02	17 04	30·8	30 10	16 28	30·5	29 19	15 53	30·2	28 27	15 19	29·9	27 35	14 45	29·6	244	296
115	65	32 11	17 04	30·0	31 19	16 29	29·7	30 27	15 55	29·4	29 35	15 21	29·1	28 42	14 48	28·8	27 50	14 15	28·5	245	295
114	66	32 29	16 28	28·8	31 36	15 54	28·5	30 43	15 20	28·2	29 50	14 48	28·0	28 57	14 16	27·7	28 04	13 44	27·4	246	294
113	67	32 45	15 51	27·7	31 52	15 18	27·4	30 59	14 46	27·1	30 05	14 14	26·8	29 12	13 43	26·6	28 18	13 13	26·3	247	293
112	68	33 01	15 14	26·5	32 08	14 42	26·3	31 14	14 11	26·0	30 20	13 40	25·7	29 26	13 10	25·5	28 31	12 41	25·2	248	292
111	69	33 17	14 36	25·4	32 23	14 05	25·1	31 28	13 35	24·8	30 34	13 06	24·6	29 39	12 37	24·4	28 44	12 09	24·1	249	291
110	70	33 32	13 57	24·2	32 37	13 28	24·0	31 42	12 59	23·7	30 47	12 31	23·5	29 52	12 04	23·2	28 57	11 37	23·0	250	290
109	71	33 46	13 18	23·1	32 51	12 51	22·8	31 55	12 23	22·6	31 00	11 56	22·3	30 04	11 30	22·1	29 09	11 04	21·9	251	289
108	72	33 59	12 39	21·9	33 04	12 13	21·6	32 08	11 46	21·4	31 12	11 21	21·2	30 16	10 56	21·0	29 20	10 31	20·8	252	288
107	73	34 12	12 00	20·7	33 16	11 34	20·5	32 20	11 09	20·2	31 23	10 45	20·0	30 27	10 21	19·8	29 30	9 58	19·6	253	287
106	74	34 24	11 19	19·5	33 28	10 55	19·3	32 31	10 32	19·1	31 34	10 09	18·9	30 37	9 46	18·7	29 41	9 24	18·5	254	286
105	75	34 36	10 39	18·3	33 39	10 16	18·1	32 42	9 54	17·9	31 44	9 32	17·7	30 47	9 11	17·5	29 50	8 50	17·4	255	285
104	76	34 46	9 58	17·1	33 49	9 37	16·9	32 52	9 16	16·7	31 54	8 56	16·6	30 57	8 36	16·4	29 59	8 16	16·2	256	284
103	77	34 56	9 17	15·9	33 59	8 57	15·7	33 01	8 38	15·6	32 03	8 19	15·4	31 05	8 00	15·2	30 07	7 42	15·1	257	283
102	78	35 06	8 35	14·7	34 08	8 17	14·5	33 10	7 59	14·4	32 11	7 41	14·2	31 13	7 24	14·1	30 15	7 07	13·9	258	282
101	79	35 14	7 54	13·5	34 16	7 37	13·3	33 18	7 20	13·2	32 19	7 04	13·0	31 21	6 48	12·9	30 22	6 32	12·8	259	281
100	80	35 22	7 11	12·3	34 24	6 56	12·1	33 25	6 41	12·0	32 26	6 26	11·9	31 27	6 12	11·7	30 29	5 57	11·6	260	280
99	81	35 29	6 29	11·1	34 30	6 15	10·9	33 32	6 01	10·8	32 33	5 48	10·7	31 34	5 35	10·6	30 35	5 22	10·5	261	279
98	82	35 36	5 46	9·9	34 37	5 34	9·7	33 37	5 22	9·6	32 38	5 10	9·5	31 39	4 58	9·4	30 40	4 47	9·3	262	278
97	83	35 41	5 04	8·6	34 42	4 53	8·5	33 43	4 42	8·4	32 43	4 32	8·3	31 44	4 21	8·2	30 45	4 11	8·2	263	277
96	84	35 46	4 21	7·4	34 47	4 11	7·3	33 47	4 02	7·2	32 48	3 53	7·1	31 48	3 44	7·1	30 49	3 36	7·0	264	276
95	85	35 51	3 37	6·2	34 51	3 30	6·1	33 51	3 22	6·0	32 52	3 14	6·0	31 52	3 07	5·9	30 52	3 00	5·8	265	275
94	86	35 54	2 54	4·9	34 54	2 48	4·9	33 54	2 42	4·8	32 55	2 36	4·8	31 55	2 30	4·7	30 55	2 24	4·7	266	274
93	87	35 57	2 11	3·7	34 57	2 06	3·7	33 57	2 01	3·6	32 57	1 57	3·6	31 57	1 52	3·5	30 57	1 48	3·5	267	273
92	88	35 58	1 27	2·5	34 59	1 24	2·4	33 59	1 21	2·4	32 59	1 18	2·4	31 59	1 15	2·4	30 59	1 12	2·3	268	272
91	89	36 00	0 44	1·2	35 00	0 42	1·2	34 00	0 40	1·2	33 00	0 39	1·2	32 00	0 37	1·2	31 00	0 36	1·2	269	271
90	90	36 00	0 00	0·0	35 00	0 00	0·0	34 00	0 00	0·0	33 00	0 00	0·0	32 00	0 00	0·0	31 00	0 00	0·0	270	270

N. Lat.: for LHA > 180° ... $Z_n = Z$
for LHA < 180° ... $Z_n = 360° - Z$

S. Lat.: for LHA > 180° ... $Z_n = 180° - Z$
for LHA < 180° ... $Z_n = 180° + Z$

© British Crown Copyright 2022. All rights reserved.

SIGHT REDUCTION TABLE

B: (−) for 90° < LHA < 270°
Dec:(−) for Lat. contrary name

Z₁: same sign as B — Z_1: same sign as B
Z₂: (−) for F > 90° — Z_2: (−) for F > 90°

Lat./A	LHA/F	60° A/H	60° B/P	60° Z₁/Z₂	61° A/H	61° B/P	61° Z₁/Z₂	62° A/H	62° B/P	62° Z₁/Z₂	63° A/H	63° B/P	63° Z₁/Z₂	64° A/H	64° B/P	64° Z₁/Z₂	65° A/H	65° B/P	65° Z₁/Z₂	Lat./A	LHA
0	180	0 00	30 00	90·0	0 00	29 00	90·0	0 00	28 00	90·0	0 00	27 00	90·0	0 00	26 00	90·0	0 00	25 00	90·0	180	360
1	179	0 30	30 00	89·1	0 29	29 00	89·1	0 28	28 00	89·1	0 27	27 00	89·1	0 26	26 00	89·1	0 25	25 00	89·1	181	359
2	178	1 00	29 59	88·3	0 58	28 59	88·3	0 56	27 59	88·2	0 54	26 59	88·2	0 53	25 59	88·2	0 51	24 59	88·2	182	358
3	177	1 30	29 58	87·4	1 27	28 58	87·4	1 24	27 58	87·4	1 22	26 59	87·3	1 19	25 58	87·3	1 16	24 58	87·3	183	357
4	176	2 00	29 56	86·5	1 56	28 56	86·5	1 53	27 57	86·5	1 49	26 57	86·4	1 45	25 57	86·4	1 41	24 57	86·4	184	356
5	175	2 30	29 54	85·7	2 25	28 54	85·7	2 21	27 55	85·6	2 16	26 55	85·5	2 11	25 55	85·5	2 07	24 55	85·5	185	355
6	174	3 00	29 52	84·8	2 54	28 52	84·8	2 49	27 52	84·7	2 43	26 52	84·6	2 38	25 53	84·6	2 32	24 53	84·6	186	354
7	173	3 30	29 49	83·9	3 23	28 49	83·9	3 17	27 49	83·8	3 10	26 50	83·8	3 04	25 50	83·7	2 57	24 50	83·7	187	353
8	172	3 59	29 45	83·1	3 52	28 46	83·1	3 45	27 46	82·9	3 37	26 46	82·9	3 30	25 47	82·8	3 22	24 47	82·8	188	352
9	171	4 29	29 42	82·2	4 21	28 42	82·2	4 13	27 42	82·0	4 04	26 43	82·0	3 56	25 43	81·9	3 47	24 44	81·9	189	351
10	170	4 59	29 37	81·3	4 50	28 38	81·3	4 41	27 38	81·2	4 31	26 39	81·1	4 22	25 39	81·0	4 13	24 40	80·9	190	350
11	169	5 28	29 33	80·4	5 18	28 33	80·4	5 08	27 34	80·3	4 58	26 34	80·2	4 48	25 35	80·1	4 38	24 36	80·0	191	349
12	168	5 58	29 27	79·6	5 47	28 28	79·6	5 36	27 29	79·4	5 25	26 29	79·3	5 14	25 30	79·2	5 02	24 31	79·1	192	348
13	167	6 27	29 22	78·7	6 16	28 22	78·7	6 04	27 23	78·5	5 52	26 24	78·4	5 40	25 25	78·3	5 27	24 26	78·2	193	347
14	166	6 57	29 15	77·9	6 44	28 16	77·7	6 31	27 17	77·6	6 18	26 18	77·5	6 05	25 20	77·4	5 52	24 21	77·3	194	346
15	165	7 26	29 09	76·9	7 13	28 10	76·9	6 59	27 11	76·7	6 45	26 12	76·6	6 31	25 14	76·5	6 17	24 15	76·4	195	345
16	164	7 55	29 02	76·1	7 41	28 03	76·1	7 26	27 04	75·8	7 11	26 06	75·7	6 56	25 07	75·5	6 41	24 09	75·4	196	344
17	163	8 24	28 54	75·2	8 09	27 56	75·2	7 53	26 57	74·9	7 38	25 59	74·8	7 22	25 00	74·6	7 06	24 02	74·5	197	343
18	162	8 53	28 46	74·3	8 37	27 48	74·3	8 20	26 50	74·0	8 04	25 51	73·9	7 47	24 53	73·7	7 30	23 55	73·6	198	342
19	161	9 22	28 38	73·4	9 05	27 39	73·4	8 48	26 41	73·1	8 30	25 43	72·9	8 12	24 45	72·8	7 55	23 48	72·7	199	341
20	160	9 51	28 29	72·5	9 33	27 31	72·5	9 14	26 33	72·2	8 56	25 35	72·0	8 37	24 37	71·9	8 19	23 40	71·7	200	340
21	159	10 19	28 19	71·6	10 00	27 22	71·6	9 41	26 24	71·3	9 22	25 26	71·1	9 02	24 29	71·0	8 43	23 32	70·8	201	339
22	158	10 48	28 10	70·7	10 28	27 12	70·7	10 08	26 15	70·4	9 48	25 17	70·2	9 27	24 20	70·2	9 07	23 23	69·9	202	338
23	157	11 16	27 59	69·8	10 55	27 02	69·8	10 34	26 05	69·6	10 13	25 08	69·3	9 52	24 11	69·1	9 30	23 14	69·0	203	337
24	156	11 44	27 49	68·9	11 22	26 51	68·7	11 00	25 54	68·7	10 38	24 58	68·4	10 16	24 01	68·2	9 54	23 04	68·0	204	336
25	155	12 12	27 37	68·0	11 49	26 40	68·0	11 27	25 44	67·8	11 04	24 47	67·4	10 41	23 51	67·3	10 17	22 53	67·1	205	335
26	154	12 40	27 26	67·1	12 16	26 29	67·1	11 53	25 33	66·9	11 29	24 36	66·5	11 05	23 40	66·3	10 41	22 44	66·2	206	334
27	153	13 07	27 13	66·2	12 43	26 17	66·2	12 18	25 21	66·0	11 54	24 25	65·6	11 29	23 29	65·4	11 04	22 34	65·2	207	333
28	152	13 35	27 01	65·3	13 09	26 05	65·3	12 44	25 09	65·1	12 18	24 13	64·7	11 53	23 18	64·5	11 27	22 23	64·3	208	332
29	151	14 02	26 48	64·4	13 36	25 52	64·4	13 09	24 56	64·1	12 43	24 01	63·7	12 16	23 06	63·5	11 49	22 11	63·3	209	331
30	150	14 29	26 34	63·4	14 02	25 39	63·4	13 35	24 43	63·2	13 07	23 49	62·8	12 40	22 54	62·6	12 12	21 59	62·4	210	330
31	149	14 55	26 20	62·5	14 28	25 25	62·5	14 00	24 30	62·3	13 31	23 36	61·8	13 03	22 41	61·6	12 34	21 47	61·4	211	329
32	148	15 22	26 05	61·6	14 53	25 11	61·6	14 24	24 16	61·3	13 55	23 22	60·9	13 26	22 28	60·7	12 56	21 35	60·5	212	328
33	147	15 48	25 50	60·6	15 19	24 56	60·6	14 49	24 02	60·4	14 19	23 09	59·9	13 49	22 15	59·7	13 18	21 22	59·5	213	327
34	146	16 14	25 35	59·7	15 44	24 41	59·7	15 13	23 47	59·5	14 42	22 54	59·0	14 11	22 01	58·8	13 40	21 08	58·6	214	326
35	145	16 40	25 19	58·8	16 09	24 25	58·8	15 37	23 32	58·5	15 06	22 39	58·0	14 34	21 47	57·8	14 02	20 54	57·6	215	325
36	144	17 05	25 02	57·8	16 33	24 09	57·8	16 01	23 17	57·6	15 29	22 24	57·1	14 56	21 32	56·9	14 23	20 40	56·6	216	324
37	143	17 31	24 45	56·9	16 58	23 53	56·9	16 25	23 00	56·6	15 51	22 09	56·1	15 18	21 17	55·9	14 44	20 25	55·7	217	323
38	142	17 56	24 28	55·9	17 22	23 36	55·9	16 48	22 44	55·7	16 14	21 53	55·2	15 39	21 01	54·9	15 05	20 11	54·7	218	322
39	141	18 20	24 10	55·0	17 46	23 18	55·0	17 11	22 27	54·7	16 36	21 36	54·2	16 01	20 46	54·0	15 25	19 55	53·7	219	321
40	140	18 45	23 51	54·0	18 09	23 00	54·0	17 34	22 10	53·7	16 58	21 19	53·2	16 22	20 29	53·0	15 46	19 39	52·7	220	320
41	139	19 09	23 33	53·0	18 33	22 42	53·0	17 56	21 52	52·8	17 20	21 02	52·2	16 43	20 13	52·0	16 06	19 23	51·8	221	319
42	138	19 33	23 13	52·1	18 56	22 23	52·1	18 19	21 34	51·8	17 41	20 44	51·3	17 03	19 55	51·0	16 26	19 07	50·8	222	318
43	137	19 56	22 54	51·1	19 18	22 04	51·1	18 40	21 15	50·8	18 02	20 26	50·3	17 24	19 38	50·0	16 45	18 50	49·8	223	317
44	136	20 19	22 33	50·1	19 41	21 44	50·1	19 02	20 56	49·8	18 23	20 08	49·3	17 44	19 20	49·0	17 04	18 33	48·8	224	316
45	135	20 42	22 12	49·1	20 03	21 24	49·1	19 23	20 36	48·8	18 43	19 49	48·3	18 03	19 02	48·1	17 23	18 15	47·8	225	315

© British Crown Copyright 2022. All rights reserved.

Lat. / A		60°			61°			62°			63°			64°			65°			Lat. / A	
LHA/F		A/H	B/P	Z_1/Z_2	A/H	B/P	Z_1/Z_2	A/H	B/P	Z_1/Z_2	A/H	B/P	Z_1/Z_2	A/H	B/P	Z_1/Z_2	A/H	B/P	Z_1/Z_2	LHA	
45	135	20 42	22 12	49·1	20 03	21 24	48·8	19 23	20 36	48·6	18 43	19 49	48·3	18 03	19 02	48·1	17 23	18 15	47·8	225	315
46	134	21 05	21 51	48·1	20 25	21 04	47·8	19 44	20 16	47·6	19 04	19 29	47·3	18 23	18 43	47·1	17 42	17 57	46·8	226	314
47	133	21 27	21 30	47·1	20 46	20 43	46·8	20 05	19 56	46·6	19 24	19 10	46·3	18 42	18 24	46·1	18 00	17 39	45·8	227	313
48	132	21 49	21 07	46·1	21 07	20 21	45·8	20 25	19 35	45·6	19 43	18 50	45·3	19 01	18 04	45·1	18 18	17 20	44·8	228	312
49	131	22 10	20 45	45·1	21 28	19 59	44·8	20 45	19 14	44·6	20 02	18 29	44·3	19 19	17 45	44·0	18 36	17 01	43·8	229	311
50	130	22 31	20 22	44·1	21 48	19 37	43·8	21 05	18 52	43·5	20 21	18 08	43·3	19 37	17 24	43·0	18 53	16 41	42·8	230	310
51	129	22 52	19 58	43·1	22 08	19 14	42·8	21 24	18 30	42·5	20 40	17 47	42·3	19 55	17 04	42·0	19 10	16 21	41·8	231	309
52	128	23 12	19 34	42·1	22 28	18 51	41·8	21 43	18 08	41·5	20 58	17 25	41·2	20 13	16 43	41·0	19 27	16 01	40·8	232	308
53	127	23 32	19 10	41·0	22 47	18 27	40·7	22 01	17 45	40·5	21 15	17 03	40·2	20 30	16 21	40·0	19 44	15 41	39·7	233	307
54	126	23 52	18 45	40·0	23 06	18 03	39·7	22 19	17 21	39·4	21 33	16 40	39·2	20 46	16 00	39·0	20 00	15 20	38·7	234	306
55	125	24 11	18 19	39·0	23 24	17 38	38·7	22 37	16 58	38·4	21 50	16 17	38·2	21 03	15 38	37·9	20 15	14 58	37·7	235	305
56	124	24 29	17 54	37·9	23 42	17 13	37·6	22 54	16 34	37·4	22 07	15 54	37·1	21 19	15 15	36·9	20 31	14 37	36·7	236	304
57	123	24 48	17 27	36·9	23 59	16 48	36·6	23 11	16 09	36·3	22 23	15 31	36·1	21 34	14 53	35·8	20 46	14 15	35·6	237	303
58	122	25 05	17 01	35·8	24 17	16 22	35·5	23 28	15 44	35·3	22 39	15 07	35·0	21 49	14 29	34·8	21 00	13 53	34·6	238	302
59	121	25 23	16 34	34·8	24 33	15 56	34·5	23 44	15 19	34·2	22 54	14 43	34·0	22 04	14 06	33·8	21 14	13 30	33·5	239	301
60	120	25 40	16 06	33·7	24 50	15 29	33·4	23 59	14 53	33·2	23 09	14 18	32·9	22 19	13 42	32·7	21 28	13 07	32·5	240	300
61	119	25 56	15 38	32·6	25 05	15 03	32·4	24 15	14 27	32·1	23 24	13 53	31·9	22 33	13 18	31·7	21 42	12 44	31·5	241	299
62	118	26 12	15 10	31·5	25 21	14 35	31·3	24 29	14 01	31·1	23 38	13 27	30·8	22 46	12 54	30·6	21 55	12 21	30·4	242	298
63	117	26 27	14 41	30·5	25 36	14 08	30·2	24 44	13 34	30·0	23 52	13 01	29·8	22 59	12 29	29·5	22 07	11 57	29·3	243	297
64	116	26 42	14 12	29·4	25 50	13 39	29·1	24 57	13 07	28·9	24 06	12 35	28·7	23 12	12 04	28·5	22 19	11 33	28·3	244	296
65	115	26 57	13 43	28·3	26 04	13 11	28·1	25 11	12 40	27·8	24 18	12 09	27·6	23 25	11 39	27·4	22 31	11 09	27·2	245	295
66	114	27 11	13 13	27·2	26 17	12 42	27·0	25 24	12 12	26·8	24 30	11 43	26·6	23 36	11 13	26·4	22 43	10 44	26·2	246	294
67	113	27 24	12 43	26·1	26 30	12 13	25·9	25 36	11 44	25·7	24 42	11 16	25·5	23 48	10 47	25·3	22 54	10 20	25·1	247	293
68	112	27 37	12 12	25·0	26 43	11 44	24·8	25 48	11 16	24·6	24 54	10 48	24·4	23 59	10 21	24·2	23 04	9 55	24·0	248	292
69	111	27 50	11 41	23·9	26 55	11 14	23·7	26 00	10 47	23·5	25 05	10 21	23·3	24 09	9 55	23·1	23 14	9 29	23·0	249	291
70	110	28 01	11 10	22·8	27 06	10 44	22·6	26 11	10 18	22·4	25 15	9 53	22·2	24 20	9 28	22·0	23 24	9 04	21·9	250	290
71	109	28 13	10 39	21·7	27 17	10 14	21·5	26 21	9 49	21·3	25 25	9 25	21·1	24 29	9 01	21·0	23 33	8 38	20·8	251	289
72	108	28 24	10 07	20·6	27 27	9 43	20·4	26 31	9 20	20·2	25 35	8 57	20·0	24 38	8 34	19·9	23 42	8 12	19·7	252	288
73	107	28 34	9 35	19·4	27 37	9 12	19·3	26 41	8 50	19·1	25 44	8 28	18·9	24 47	8 07	18·8	23 50	7 46	18·6	253	287
74	106	28 44	9 03	18·3	27 47	8 41	18·2	26 50	8 20	18·0	25 52	8 00	17·8	24 55	7 39	17·7	23 58	7 19	17·6	254	286
75	105	28 53	8 30	17·2	27 55	8 10	17·0	26 58	7 50	16·9	26 01	7 31	16·7	25 03	7 12	16·6	24 06	6 53	16·5	255	285
76	104	29 01	7 57	16·1	28 04	7 38	15·9	27 06	7 20	15·8	26 08	7 02	15·6	25 10	6 44	15·5	24 13	6 26	15·4	256	284
77	103	29 09	7 24	14·9	28 11	7 06	14·8	27 13	6 49	14·7	26 15	6 32	14·5	25 17	6 16	14·4	24 19	5 59	14·3	257	283
78	102	29 17	6 51	13·8	28 18	6 34	13·7	27 20	6 19	13·5	26 22	6 03	13·4	25 23	5 47	13·3	24 25	5 32	13·2	258	282
79	101	29 24	6 17	12·7	28 25	6 02	12·5	27 27	5 48	12·4	26 28	5 33	12·3	25 29	5 19	12·2	24 31	5 05	12·1	259	281
80	100	29 30	5 44	11·5	28 31	5 30	11·4	27 32	5 17	11·3	26 33	5 03	11·2	25 35	4 50	11·1	24 36	4 38	11·0	260	280
81	99	29 36	5 10	10·4	28 37	4 57	10·3	27 38	4 45	10·2	26 38	4 33	10·1	25 39	4 22	10·0	24 40	4 10	9·9	261	279
82	98	29 41	4 36	9·2	28 41	4 25	9·1	27 42	4 14	9·0	26 43	4 03	9·0	25 44	3 53	8·9	24 44	3 43	8·8	262	278
83	97	29 45	4 01	8·1	28 46	3 52	8·0	27 46	3 42	7·9	26 47	3 33	7·8	25 48	3 24	7·8	24 48	3 15	7·7	263	277
84	96	29 49	3 27	6·9	28 50	3 19	6·9	27 50	3 11	6·8	26 50	3 03	6·7	25 51	2 55	6·7	24 51	2 47	6·6	264	276
85	95	29 52	2 53	5·8	28 53	2 46	5·7	27 53	2 39	5·6	26 53	2 33	5·6	25 54	2 26	5·6	24 54	2 19	5·5	265	275
86	94	29 55	2 18	4·6	28 55	2 13	4·6	27 56	2 07	4·5	26 56	2 02	4·5	25 56	1 57	4·4	24 56	1 52	4·4	266	274
87	93	29 57	1 44	3·5	28 57	1 40	3·4	27 57	1 36	3·4	26 58	1 32	3·4	25 58	1 28	3·3	24 58	1 24	3·3	267	273
88	92	29 59	1 09	2·3	28 59	1 06	2·3	27 59	1 04	2·3	26 59	1 01	2·2	25 59	0 59	2·2	24 59	0 56	2·2	268	272
89	91	30 00	0 35	1·2	29 00	0 33	1·1	28 00	0 32	1·1	27 00	0 31	1·1	26 00	0 29	1·1	25 00	0 28	1·1	269	271
90	90	30 00	0 00	0·0	29 00	0 00	0·0	28 00	0 00	0·0	27 00	0 00	0·0	26 00	0 00	0·0	25 00	0 00	0·0	270	270

N. Lat.: for LHA > 180° ... $Z_n = Z$
for LHA < 180° ... $Z_n = 360° − Z$

S. Lat.: for LHA > 180° ... $Z_n = 180° − Z$
for LHA < 180° ... $Z_n = 180° + Z$

© British Crown Copyright 2022. All rights reserved.

SIGHT REDUCTION TABLE

B: (−) for 90° < LHA < 270°
Dec:(−) for Lat. contrary name

Z1: same sign as B
Z2: (−) for F > 90°

Lat./A	LHA/F	66° A/H	66° B/P	66° Z1/Z2	67° A/H	67° B/P	67° Z1/Z2	68° A/H	68° B/P	68° Z1/Z2	69° A/H	69° B/P	69° Z1/Z2	70° A/H	70° B/P	70° Z1/Z2	71° A/H	71° B/P	71° Z1/Z2	Lat./A	LHA
180	0	0 00	24 00	90·0	0 00	23 00	90·0	0 00	22 00	90·0	0 00	21 00	90·0	0 00	20 00	90·0	0 00	19 00	90·0	360	180
179	1	0 24	24 00	89·1	0 23	23 00	89·1	0 22	22 00	89·1	0 22	21 00	89·1	0 21	20 00	89·1	0 20	19 00	89·1	359	181
178	2	0 49	23 59	88·2	0 47	22 59	88·2	0 45	21 59	88·1	0 43	20 59	88·1	0 41	19 59	88·1	0 39	18 59	88·1	358	182
177	3	1 13	23 58	87·3	1 10	22 58	87·3	1 07	21 58	87·2	1 04	20 58	87·2	1 02	19 58	87·2	0 59	18 59	87·2	357	183
176	4	1 38	23 57	86·3	1 34	22 57	86·3	1 30	21 57	86·3	1 26	20 57	86·3	1 22	19 57	86·2	1 18	18 57	86·2	356	184
175	5	2 02	23 55	85·4	1 57	22 55	85·4	1 52	21 55	85·4	1 47	20 56	85·3	1 42	19 56	85·3	1 38	18 56	85·3	355	185
174	6	2 26	23 53	84·5	2 20	22 53	84·5	2 15	21 53	84·4	2 09	20 54	84·4	2 03	19 54	84·4	1 57	18 54	84·3	354	186
173	7	2 50	23 50	83·6	2 44	22 50	83·6	2 37	21 51	83·5	2 30	20 51	83·5	2 23	19 52	83·4	2 16	18 52	83·4	353	187
172	8	3 15	23 48	82·7	3 07	22 48	82·7	2 59	21 48	82·6	2 52	20 49	82·5	2 44	19 49	82·5	2 36	18 50	82·4	352	188
171	9	3 39	23 44	81·8	3 30	22 45	81·8	3 22	21 45	81·6	3 13	20 46	81·6	3 04	19 46	81·5	2 55	18 47	81·5	351	189
170	10	4 03	23 41	80·8	3 53	22 41	80·8	3 44	21 42	80·7	3 34	20 42	80·7	3 24	19 43	80·6	3 14	18 44	80·5	350	190
169	11	4 27	23 36	79·9	4 17	22 37	79·9	4 06	21 38	79·8	3 55	20 39	79·7	3 45	19 40	79·6	3 34	18 41	79·6	349	191
168	12	4 51	23 32	79·0	4 40	22 33	79·0	4 28	21 34	78·9	4 16	20 35	78·8	4 05	19 36	78·7	3 53	18 37	78·6	348	192
167	13	5 15	23 27	78·1	5 03	22 28	78·1	4 50	21 29	77·9	4 37	20 30	77·8	4 25	19 32	77·8	4 12	18 33	77·7	347	193
166	14	5 39	23 22	77·2	5 25	22 23	77·2	5 12	21 24	77·0	4 58	20 26	76·9	4 45	19 27	76·8	4 31	18 28	76·7	346	194
165	15	6 03	23 16	76·2	5 48	22 18	76·1	5 34	21 19	76·0	5 19	20 21	76·0	5 05	19 22	75·9	4 50	18 24	75·8	345	195
164	16	6 26	23 10	75·3	6 11	22 12	75·2	5 56	21 13	75·1	5 40	20 15	75·0	5 25	19 17	74·9	5 09	18 19	74·8	344	196
163	17	6 50	23 04	74·4	6 34	22 06	74·3	6 17	21 08	74·2	6 01	20 09	74·1	5 44	19 11	74·0	5 28	18 14	73·9	343	197
162	18	7 13	22 57	73·5	6 56	21 59	73·3	6 39	21 01	73·2	6 21	20 03	73·1	6 04	19 06	73·0	5 46	18 08	72·9	342	198
161	19	7 37	22 50	72·5	7 19	21 52	72·4	7 00	20 54	72·3	6 42	19 57	72·2	6 24	18 59	72·1	6 05	18 02	72·0	341	199
160	20	8 00	22 42	71·6	7 41	21 45	71·5	7 22	20 47	71·4	7 02	19 50	71·2	6 43	18 53	71·1	6 24	17 56	71·0	340	200
159	21	8 23	22 34	70·7	8 03	21 37	70·5	7 43	20 40	70·4	7 23	19 43	70·3	7 02	18 46	70·2	6 42	17 49	70·1	339	201
158	22	8 46	22 26	69·7	8 25	21 29	69·6	8 04	20 32	69·5	7 43	19 35	69·3	7 22	18 39	69·2	7 00	17 42	69·1	338	202
157	23	9 09	22 17	68·8	8 47	21 21	68·7	8 25	20 24	68·5	8 03	19 28	68·4	7 41	18 31	68·3	7 19	17 35	68·1	337	203
156	24	9 31	22 08	67·9	9 09	21 12	67·7	8 46	20 16	67·6	8 23	19 19	67·4	8 00	18 24	67·3	7 37	17 28	67·2	336	204
155	25	9 54	21 58	66·9	9 30	21 03	66·8	9 07	20 07	66·6	8 43	19 11	66·5	8 19	18 15	66·3	7 55	17 20	66·2	335	205
154	26	10 16	21 49	66·0	9 52	20 53	65·8	9 27	19 57	65·7	9 02	19 02	65·5	8 37	18 07	65·4	8 12	17 12	65·2	334	206
153	27	10 38	21 38	65·0	10 13	20 43	64·9	9 48	19 48	64·7	9 22	18 53	64·6	8 56	17 58	64·4	8 30	17 03	64·3	333	207
152	28	11 00	21 28	64·1	10 34	20 33	63·9	10 08	19 38	63·8	9 41	18 43	63·6	9 14	17 49	63·5	8 48	16 55	63·3	332	208
151	29	11 22	21 17	63·1	10 55	20 22	63·0	10 28	19 28	62·8	10 00	18 34	62·6	9 33	17 39	62·5	9 05	16 46	62·3	331	209
150	30	11 44	21 05	62·2	11 16	20 11	62·0	10 48	19 17	61·8	10 19	18 23	61·7	9 51	17 30	61·5	9 22	16 36	61·4	330	210
149	31	12 06	20 53	61·2	11 37	20 00	61·1	11 07	19 06	60·9	10 38	18 13	60·7	10 09	17 20	60·5	9 39	16 27	60·4	329	211
148	32	12 27	20 41	60·3	11 57	19 48	60·1	11 27	18 55	59·9	10 57	18 02	59·7	10 27	17 09	59·6	9 56	16 17	59·4	328	212
147	33	12 48	20 29	59·3	12 17	19 36	59·1	11 46	18 43	58·9	11 15	17 51	58·8	10 44	16 58	58·6	10 13	16 06	58·4	327	213
146	34	13 09	20 16	58·4	12 37	19 23	58·2	12 06	18 31	58·0	11 34	17 39	57·8	11 02	16 47	57·6	10 30	15 56	57·5	326	214
145	35	13 29	20 02	57·4	12 57	19 10	57·2	12 24	18 19	57·0	11 52	17 27	56·8	11 19	16 36	56·7	10 46	15 45	56·5	325	215
144	36	13 50	19 49	56·4	13 17	18 57	56·2	12 43	18 06	56·0	12 10	17 15	55·9	11 36	16 24	55·7	11 02	15 34	55·5	324	216
143	37	14 10	19 34	55·5	13 36	18 44	55·3	13 02	17 53	55·1	12 27	17 03	54·9	11 53	16 12	54·7	11 18	15 23	54·5	323	217
142	38	14 30	19 20	54·5	13 55	18 30	54·3	13 20	17 40	54·1	12 45	16 50	53·9	12 09	16 00	53·7	11 34	15 11	53·5	322	218
141	39	14 50	19 05	53·5	14 14	18 15	53·3	13 38	17 26	53·1	13 02	16 37	52·9	12 26	15 48	52·7	11 49	14 59	52·5	321	219
140	40	15 09	18 50	52·5	14 33	18 01	52·3	13 56	17 12	52·1	13 19	16 23	51·9	12 42	15 35	51·7	12 05	14 47	51·6	320	220
139	41	15 29	18 34	51·5	14 51	17 46	51·3	14 14	16 57	51·1	13 36	16 09	50·9	12 58	15 22	50·8	12 20	14 34	50·6	319	221
138	42	15 48	18 18	50·6	15 09	17 30	50·3	14 31	16 43	50·1	13 52	15 55	49·9	13 14	15 08	49·8	12 35	14 21	49·6	318	222
137	43	16 06	18 02	49·6	15 27	17 15	49·4	14 48	16 28	49·1	14 09	15 41	49·0	13 29	14 54	48·8	12 50	14 08	48·6	317	223
136	44	16 25	17 46	48·6	15 45	16 59	48·4	15 05	16 12	48·2	14 25	15 26	48·0	13 45	14 40	47·8	13 04	13 55	47·6	316	224
135	45	16 43	17 29	47·6	16 02	16 42	47·4	15 22	15 57	47·2	14 41	15 11	47·0	14 00	14 26	46·8	13 19	13 41	46·6	315	225

© British Crown Copyright 2022. All rights reserved.

Lat. / A LHA/F	66° A/H	66° B/P	66° Z₁/Z₂	67° A/H	67° B/P	67° Z₁/Z₂	68° A/H	68° B/P	68° Z₁/Z₂	69° A/H	69° B/P	69° Z₁/Z₂	70° A/H	70° B/P	70° Z₁/Z₂	71° A/H	71° B/P	71° Z₁/Z₂	Lat. / A LHA
45 / 135	16 43	17 29	47·6	16 02	16 42	47·4	15 22	15 57	47·2	14 41	15 11	47·0	14 00	14 26	46·8	13 19	13 41	46·6	315 / 225
46 / 134	17 01	17 11	46·6	16 19	16 26	46·4	15 38	15 41	46·2	14 56	14 56	46·0	14 15	14 11	45·8	13 33	13 27	45·6	314 / 226
47 / 133	17 18	16 53	45·6	16 36	16 09	45·4	15 54	15 24	45·2	15 12	14 40	45·0	14 29	13 56	44·8	13 46	13 13	44·6	313 / 227
48 / 132	17 36	16 35	44·6	16 53	15 51	44·4	16 10	15 08	44·2	15 27	14 24	44·0	14 43	13 41	43·8	14 00	12 58	43·6	312 / 228
49 / 131	17 53	16 17	43·6	17 09	15 34	43·4	16 25	14 51	43·2	15 42	14 08	43·0	14 58	13 26	42·8	14 13	12 44	42·6	311 / 229
50 / 130	18 09	15 58	42·6	17 25	15 15	42·4	16 41	14 33	42·1	15 56	13 52	41·9	15 11	13 10	41·8	14 27	12 29	41·6	310 / 230
51 / 129	18 26	15 39	41·6	17 41	14 57	41·3	16 56	14 16	41·1	16 10	13 35	40·9	15 25	12 54	40·8	14 39	12 14	40·6	309 / 231
52 / 128	18 42	15 20	40·5	17 56	14 39	40·3	17 10	13 58	40·1	16 24	13 18	39·9	15 38	12 38	39·7	14 52	11 58	39·6	308 / 232
53 / 127	18 57	15 00	39·5	18 11	14 20	39·3	17 24	13 40	39·1	16 38	13 00	38·9	15 51	12 21	38·7	15 04	11 42	38·6	307 / 233
54 / 126	19 13	14 40	38·5	18 26	14 01	38·3	17 39	13 22	38·1	16 51	12 43	37·9	16 04	12 05	37·7	15 16	11 26	37·5	306 / 234
55 / 125	19 28	14 20	37·5	18 40	13 41	37·3	17 52	13 03	37·1	17 04	12 25	36·9	16 16	11 48	36·7	15 28	11 10	36·5	305 / 235
56 / 124	19 42	13 59	36·4	18 54	13 21	36·2	18 06	12 44	36·0	17 17	12 07	35·8	16 28	11 30	35·7	15 40	10 54	35·5	304 / 236
57 / 123	19 57	13 38	35·4	19 08	13 01	35·2	18 19	12 25	35·0	17 29	11 49	34·8	16 40	11 13	34·6	15 51	10 37	34·5	303 / 237
58 / 122	20 11	13 17	34·4	19 21	12 41	34·2	18 31	12 05	34·0	17 42	11 30	33·8	16 52	10 55	33·6	16 02	10 20	33·5	302 / 238
59 / 121	20 24	12 55	33·3	19 34	12 20	33·1	18 44	11 45	32·9	17 54	11 11	32·8	17 03	10 37	32·6	16 12	10 03	32·4	301 / 239
60 / 120	20 37	12 33	32·3	19 47	11 59	32·1	18 56	11 25	31·9	18 05	10 52	31·7	17 14	10 19	31·6	16 23	9 46	31·4	300 / 240
61 / 119	20 50	12 11	31·2	19 59	11 38	31·1	19 08	11 05	30·9	18 16	10 33	30·7	17 24	10 00	30·5	16 33	9 29	30·4	299 / 241
62 / 118	21 03	11 48	30·2	20 11	11 16	30·0	19 19	10 44	29·8	18 27	10 13	29·7	17 35	9 42	29·5	16 42	9 11	29·4	298 / 242
63 / 117	21 15	11 26	29·2	20 22	10 54	29·0	19 30	10 24	28·8	18 37	9 53	28·6	17 45	9 23	28·5	16 52	8 53	28·3	297 / 243
64 / 116	21 27	11 03	28·1	20 34	10 32	27·9	19 41	10 03	27·8	18 47	9 33	27·6	17 54	9 04	27·4	17 01	8 35	27·3	296 / 244
65 / 115	21 38	10 39	27·0	20 44	10 10	26·9	19 51	9 41	26·7	18 57	9 13	26·5	18 03	8 45	26·4	17 10	8 17	26·3	295 / 245
66 / 114	21 49	10 16	26·0	20 55	9 48	25·8	20 01	9 20	25·7	19 07	8 52	25·5	18 12	8 25	25·4	17 18	7 58	25·2	294 / 246
67 / 113	21 59	9 52	24·9	21 05	9 25	24·8	20 10	8 58	24·6	19 16	8 32	24·4	18 21	8 06	24·3	17 26	7 40	24·2	293 / 247
68 / 112	22 09	9 28	23·9	21 14	9 02	23·7	20 19	8 36	23·5	19 24	8 11	23·4	18 29	7 46	23·3	17 34	7 21	23·1	292 / 248
69 / 111	22 19	9 04	22·8	21 24	8 39	22·6	20 28	8 14	22·5	19 33	7 50	22·4	18 37	7 26	22·2	17 42	7 02	22·1	291 / 249
70 / 110	22 28	8 39	21·7	21 32	8 16	21·6	20 37	7 52	21·4	19 41	7 29	21·3	18 45	7 06	21·2	17 49	6 43	21·1	290 / 250
71 / 109	22 37	8 15	20·7	21 41	7 52	20·5	20 45	7 30	20·4	19 48	7 07	20·2	18 52	6 45	20·1	17 56	6 24	20·0	289 / 251
72 / 108	22 45	7 50	19·6	21 49	7 28	19·4	20 52	7 07	19·3	19 56	6 46	19·2	18 59	6 25	19·1	18 02	6 04	19·0	288 / 252
73 / 107	22 53	7 25	18·5	21 56	7 04	18·4	21 00	6 44	18·2	20 03	6 24	18·1	19 05	6 04	18·0	18 08	5 45	17·9	287 / 253
74 / 106	23 01	7 00	17·4	22 04	6 40	17·3	21 06	6 21	17·2	20 09	6 02	17·1	19 12	5 44	17·0	18 14	5 25	16·9	286 / 254
75 / 105	23 08	6 34	16·3	22 10	6 16	16·2	21 13	5 58	16·1	20 15	5 40	16·0	19 17	5 23	15·9	18 20	5 06	15·8	285 / 255
76 / 104	23 15	6 09	15·3	22 17	5 52	15·2	21 19	5 35	15·1	20 21	5 18	15·0	19 23	5 02	14·9	18 25	4 46	14·8	284 / 256
77 / 103	23 21	5 43	14·2	22 23	5 27	14·1	21 24	5 12	14·0	20 26	4 56	13·9	19 28	4 41	13·8	18 30	4 26	13·7	283 / 257
78 / 102	23 27	5 17	13·1	22 28	5 03	13·0	21 30	4 48	12·9	20 31	4 34	12·8	19 33	4 20	12·7	18 34	4 06	12·7	282 / 258
79 / 101	23 32	4 51	12·0	22 33	4 38	11·9	21 35	4 24	11·8	20 36	4 11	11·8	19 37	3 58	11·7	18 38	3 46	11·6	281 / 259
80 / 100	23 37	4 25	10·9	22 38	4 13	10·8	21 39	4 01	10·8	20 40	3 49	10·7	19 41	3 37	10·6	18 42	3 25	10·6	280 / 260
81 / 99	23 41	3 59	9·8	22 42	3 48	9·8	21 43	3 37	9·7	20 44	3 26	9·6	19 45	3 16	9·6	18 45	3 05	9·5	279 / 261
82 / 98	23 45	3 33	8·7	22 46	3 23	8·7	21 46	3 13	8·6	20 47	3 03	8·6	19 48	2 54	8·5	18 48	2 45	8·5	278 / 262
83 / 97	23 49	3 06	7·7	22 49	2 58	7·6	21 50	2 49	7·5	20 50	2 41	7·5	19 51	2 32	7·4	18 51	2 24	7·4	277 / 263
84 / 96	23 52	2 40	6·6	22 52	2 32	6·5	21 52	2 25	6·5	20 53	2 18	6·4	19 53	2 11	6·4	18 54	2 04	6·3	276 / 264
85 / 95	23 54	2 13	5·5	22 54	2 07	5·4	21 55	2 01	5·4	20 55	1 55	5·4	19 55	1 49	5·3	18 55	1 43	5·3	275 / 265
86 / 94	23 56	1 47	4·4	22 56	1 42	4·3	21 57	1 37	4·3	20 57	1 32	4·3	19 57	1 27	4·3	18 57	1 23	4·2	274 / 266
87 / 93	23 58	1 20	3·3	22 58	1 16	3·3	21 58	1 13	3·2	20 58	1 09	3·2	19 58	1 05	3·2	18 58	1 02	3·2	273 / 267
88 / 92	23 59	0 53	2·2	22 59	0 51	2·2	21 59	0 48	2·2	20 59	0 46	2·1	19 59	0 44	2·1	18 59	0 41	2·1	272 / 268
89 / 91	24 00	0 27	1·1	23 00	0 25	1·1	22 00	0 24	1·1	21 00	0 23	1·1	20 00	0 22	1·1	19 00	0 21	1·1	271 / 269
90 / 90	24 00	0 00	0·0	23 00	0 00	0·0	22 00	0 00	0·0	21 00	0 00	0·0	20 00	0 00	0·0	19 00	0 00	0·0	270 / 270

N. Lat.: for LHA > 180° ... $Z_n = Z$
for LHA < 180° ... $Z_n = 360° − Z$

S. Lat.: for LHA > 180° ... $Z_n = 180° − Z$
for LHA < 180° ... $Z_n = 180° + Z$

© British Crown Copyright 2022. All rights reserved.

SIGHT REDUCTION TABLE

B: (–) for 90° < LHA < 270°
Dec:(–) for Lat. contrary name

Z₁: same sign as B
Z₂: (–) for F > 90°

LHA/F	72° A/H	72° B/P	72° Z₁/Z₂	73° A/H	73° B/P	73° Z₁/Z₂	74° A/H	74° B/P	74° Z₁/Z₂	75° A/H	75° B/P	75° Z₁/Z₂	76° A/H	76° B/P	76° Z₁/Z₂	77° A/H	77° B/P	77° Z₁/Z₂	LHA
0 / 180	0 00	18 00	90·0	0 00	17 00	90·0	0 00	16 00	90·0	0 00	15 00	90·0	0 00	14 00	90·0	0 00	13 00	90·0	180 / 360
1 / 179	0 19	18 00	89·0	0 18	17 00	89·0	0 17	16 00	89·0	0 16	15 00	89·0	0 15	14 00	89·0	0 13	13 00	89·0	181 / 359
2 / 178	0 37	17 59	88·1	0 35	16 59	88·1	0 33	15 59	88·1	0 31	14 59	88·1	0 29	14 00	88·1	0 27	13 00	88·1	182 / 358
3 / 177	0 56	17 59	87·1	0 53	16 59	87·1	0 50	15 59	87·1	0 47	14 59	87·1	0 44	13 59	87·1	0 40	12 59	87·1	183 / 357
4 / 176	1 14	17 58	86·2	1 10	16 58	86·2	1 06	15 58	86·1	1 02	14 58	86·1	0 58	13 58	86·1	0 54	12 58	86·1	184 / 356
5 / 175	1 33	17 56	85·2	1 28	16 56	85·2	1 23	15 57	85·2	1 18	14 57	85·2	1 12	13 57	85·1	1 07	12 57	85·1	185 / 355
6 / 174	1 51	17 54	84·3	1 45	16 55	84·3	1 39	15 55	84·2	1 33	14 55	84·2	1 27	13 56	84·2	1 21	12 56	84·2	186 / 354
7 / 173	2 09	17 52	83·3	2 03	16 53	83·3	1 56	15 53	83·3	1 48	14 53	83·2	1 41	13 54	83·2	1 34	12 54	83·2	187 / 353
8 / 172	2 28	17 50	82·4	2 20	16 51	82·4	2 12	15 51	82·3	2 04	14 52	82·3	1 56	13 52	82·2	1 48	12 53	82·2	188 / 352
9 / 171	2 46	17 48	81·4	2 37	16 48	81·4	2 28	15 49	81·3	2 19	14 49	81·3	2 10	13 50	81·3	2 01	12 51	81·3	189 / 351
10 / 170	3 05	17 45	80·5	2 55	16 45	80·4	2 45	15 46	80·4	2 35	14 47	80·4	2 24	13 48	80·3	2 14	12 49	80·3	190 / 350
11 / 169	3 23	17 41	79·5	3 12	16 42	79·5	3 01	15 43	79·4	2 50	14 44	79·4	2 39	13 45	79·4	2 28	12 46	79·3	191 / 349
12 / 168	3 41	17 38	78·6	3 29	16 39	78·5	3 17	15 40	78·5	3 05	14 41	78·4	2 53	13 42	78·4	2 41	12 44	78·3	192 / 348
13 / 167	3 59	17 34	77·6	3 46	16 35	77·5	3 33	15 37	77·5	3 20	14 38	77·5	3 07	13 39	77·4	2 54	12 41	77·3	193 / 347
14 / 166	4 17	17 30	76·7	4 03	16 31	76·6	3 49	15 33	76·5	3 35	14 34	76·5	3 21	13 36	76·4	3 07	12 38	76·3	194 / 346
15 / 165	4 35	17 25	75·7	4 20	16 27	75·6	4 05	15 29	75·6	3 50	14 31	75·5	3 35	13 32	75·4	3 20	12 34	75·4	195 / 345
16 / 164	4 53	17 21	74·7	4 37	16 23	74·7	4 21	15 25	74·6	4 05	14 27	74·6	3 49	13 29	74·5	3 33	12 31	74·4	196 / 344
17 / 163	5 11	17 16	73·8	4 54	16 18	73·7	4 37	15 20	73·6	4 20	14 22	73·6	4 03	13 25	73·5	3 46	12 27	73·4	197 / 343
18 / 162	5 29	17 10	72·8	5 11	16 13	72·7	4 53	15 15	72·7	4 35	14 18	72·6	4 17	13 20	72·5	3 59	12 23	72·4	198 / 342
19 / 161	5 46	17 05	71·9	5 28	16 07	71·8	5 09	15 10	71·7	4 50	14 13	71·6	4 31	13 16	71·5	4 12	12 19	71·5	199 / 341
20 / 160	6 04	16 59	70·9	5 44	16 02	70·8	5 25	15 05	70·7	5 05	14 08	70·7	4 45	13 11	70·6	4 25	12 14	70·5	200 / 340
21 / 159	6 21	16 52	69·9	6 01	15 56	69·8	5 40	14 59	69·7	5 19	14 03	69·7	4 58	13 06	69·6	4 37	12 10	69·5	201 / 339
22 / 158	6 39	16 46	69·0	6 18	15 50	68·9	5 56	14 53	68·8	5 34	13 57	68·7	5 12	13 01	68·6	4 50	12 05	68·5	202 / 338
23 / 157	6 56	16 39	68·0	6 34	15 43	67·9	6 11	14 47	67·8	5 48	13 51	67·8	5 25	12 56	67·6	5 03	12 00	67·5	203 / 337
24 / 156	7 13	16 32	67·1	6 50	15 36	66·9	6 26	14 41	66·8	6 03	13 45	66·8	5 39	12 50	66·6	5 15	11 55	66·6	204 / 336
25 / 155	7 30	16 25	66·1	7 06	15 29	66·0	6 41	14 34	65·9	6 17	13 39	65·8	5 52	12 44	65·7	5 27	11 49	65·6	205 / 335
26 / 154	7 47	16 17	65·1	7 22	15 22	65·0	6 56	14 27	64·9	6 31	13 32	64·8	6 05	12 38	64·7	5 40	11 43	64·6	206 / 334
27 / 153	8 04	16 09	64·1	7 38	15 14	64·0	7 11	14 20	63·9	6 45	13 26	63·8	6 18	12 32	63·7	5 52	11 37	63·6	207 / 333
28 / 152	8 20	16 00	63·2	7 53	15 06	63·0	7 26	14 12	62·9	6 59	13 19	62·9	6 31	12 25	62·7	6 04	11 31	62·6	208 / 332
29 / 151	8 37	15 52	62·2	8 09	14 58	62·1	7 41	14 05	61·9	7 13	13 11	61·9	6 44	12 18	61·7	6 16	11 25	61·6	209 / 331
30 / 150	8 53	15 43	61·2	8 24	14 50	61·1	7 55	13 57	61·0	7 26	13 04	60·9	6 57	12 11	60·7	6 27	11 18	60·6	210 / 330
31 / 149	9 09	15 34	60·3	8 40	14 41	60·1	8 10	13 49	60·0	7 40	12 56	59·9	7 09	12 04	59·8	6 39	11 12	59·7	211 / 329
32 / 148	9 25	15 24	59·3	8 55	14 32	59·1	8 24	13 40	59·0	7 53	12 48	58·9	7 22	11 56	58·8	6 51	11 05	58·7	212 / 328
33 / 147	9 41	15 15	58·3	9 10	14 23	58·2	8 38	13 31	58·0	8 06	12 40	57·9	7 34	11 49	57·8	7 02	10 57	57·7	213 / 327
34 / 146	9 57	15 05	57·3	9 25	14 13	57·2	8 52	13 22	57·0	8 19	12 31	56·9	7 46	11 41	56·8	7 14	10 50	56·7	214 / 326
35 / 145	10 13	14 54	56·3	9 39	14 04	56·2	9 06	13 13	56·1	8 32	12 23	56·0	7 59	11 33	55·8	7 25	10 43	55·7	215 / 325
36 / 144	10 28	14 44	55·4	9 54	13 54	55·2	9 19	13 04	55·1	8 45	12 14	55·0	8 11	11 24	54·8	7 36	10 35	54·7	216 / 324
37 / 143	10 43	14 33	54·4	10 08	13 43	54·2	9 33	12 54	54·1	8 58	12 05	54·0	8 22	11 16	53·8	7 47	10 27	53·7	217 / 323
38 / 142	10 58	14 22	53·4	10 22	13 33	53·3	9 46	12 44	53·1	9 10	11 55	53·0	8 34	11 07	52·8	7 58	10 19	52·7	218 / 322
39 / 141	11 13	14 10	52·4	10 36	13 22	52·3	9 59	12 34	52·1	9 22	11 46	52·0	8 45	10 58	51·8	8 08	10 10	51·7	219 / 321
40 / 140	11 27	13 59	51·4	10 50	13 11	51·3	10 12	12 23	51·1	9 35	11 36	51·0	8 57	10 49	50·8	8 19	10 01	50·7	220 / 320
41 / 139	11 42	13 47	50·4	11 04	13 00	50·3	10 25	12 13	50·1	9 47	11 26	50·0	9 08	10 39	49·9	8 29	9 53	49·7	221 / 319
42 / 138	11 56	13 34	49·4	11 17	12 48	49·3	10 38	12 02	49·1	9 58	11 16	49·0	9 19	10 30	48·9	8 39	9 44	48·7	222 / 318
43 / 137	12 10	13 22	48·4	11 30	12 36	48·3	10 50	11 51	48·1	10 10	11 05	48·0	9 30	10 20	47·9	8 49	9 35	47·7	223 / 317
44 / 136	12 24	13 09	47·4	11 43	12 24	47·3	11 02	11 39	47·1	10 21	10 55	47·0	9 40	10 10	46·9	8 59	9 26	46·7	224 / 316
45 / 135	12 37	12 56	46·4	11 56	12 12	46·3	11 14	11 28	46·1	10 33	10 44	46·0	9 51	10 00	45·9	9 09	9 16	45·7	225 / 315

© British Crown Copyright 2022. All rights reserved.

Lat./A (A)	(F)	72° A/H	72° B/P	72° Z_1/Z_2	73° A/H	73° B/P	73° Z_1/Z_2	74° A/H	74° B/P	74° Z_1/Z_2	75° A/H	75° B/P	75° Z_1/Z_2	76° A/H	76° B/P	76° Z_1/Z_2	77° A/H	77° B/P	77° Z_1/Z_2	Lat./A LHA	LHA
45	135	12 37	12 56	46·4	11 56	12 12	46·3	11 14	11 28	46·1	10 33	10 44	46·0	9 51	10 00	45·9	9 09	9 16	45·7	315	225
46	134	12 51	12 43	45·4	12 08	11 59	45·3	11 26	11 16	45·1	10 44	10 33	45·0	10 01	9 50	44·9	9 19	9 07	44·7	314	226
47	133	13 04	12 30	44·4	12 21	11 47	44·3	11 38	11 04	44·1	10 55	10 21	44·0	10 11	9 39	43·9	9 28	8 57	43·7	313	227
48	132	13 17	12 16	43·4	12 33	11 34	43·3	11 49	10 52	43·1	11 05	10 10	43·0	10 21	9 28	42·9	9 37	8 47	42·7	312	228
49	131	13 29	12 02	42·4	12 45	11 21	42·3	12 00	10 39	42·1	11 16	9 58	42·0	10 31	9 17	41·9	9 46	8 37	41·7	311	229
50	130	13 42	11 48	41·4	12 57	11 07	41·3	12 11	10 27	41·1	11 26	9 46	41·0	10 41	9 06	40·9	9 55	8 26	40·7	310	230
51	129	13 54	11 33	40·4	13 08	10 53	40·3	12 22	10 14	40·1	11 36	9 34	40·0	10 50	8 55	39·8	10 04	8 16	39·7	309	231
52	128	14 06	11 19	39·4	13 19	10 40	39·2	12 33	10 01	39·1	11 46	9 22	39·0	10 59	8 44	38·8	10 13	8 05	38·7	308	232
53	127	14 17	11 04	38·4	13 30	10 26	38·2	12 43	9 47	38·1	11 56	9 10	38·0	11 08	8 32	37·8	10 21	7 55	37·7	307	233
54	126	14 29	10 49	37·4	13 41	10 11	37·2	12 53	9 34	37·1	12 05	8 57	36·9	11 17	8 20	36·8	10 29	7 44	36·7	306	234
55	125	14 40	10 33	36·4	13 51	9 57	36·2	13 03	9 20	36·1	12 14	8 44	35·9	11 26	8 08	35·8	10 37	7 33	35·7	305	235
56	124	14 51	10 18	35·3	14 02	9 42	35·2	13 13	9 07	35·1	12 23	8 31	34·9	11 34	7 56	34·8	10 45	7 21	34·7	304	236
57	123	15 01	10 02	34·3	14 12	9 27	34·2	13 22	8 53	34·0	12 32	8 18	33·9	11 42	7 44	33·8	10 52	7 10	33·7	303	237
58	122	15 12	9 46	33·3	14 21	9 12	33·2	13 31	8 38	33·0	12 41	8 05	32·9	11 50	7 32	32·8	11 00	6 58	32·7	302	238
59	121	15 22	9 30	32·3	14 31	8 57	32·1	13 40	8 24	32·0	12 49	7 51	31·9	11 58	7 19	31·8	11 07	6 47	31·7	301	239
60	120	15 31	9 14	31·3	14 40	8 41	31·1	13 49	8 10	31·0	12 57	7 38	30·9	12 06	7 06	30·8	11 14	6 35	30·6	300	240
61	119	15 41	8 57	30·2	14 49	8 26	30·1	13 57	7 55	30·0	13 05	7 24	29·8	12 13	6 54	29·7	11 21	6 23	29·6	299	241
62	118	15 50	8 40	29·2	14 58	8 10	29·1	14 05	7 40	28·9	13 13	7 10	28·8	12 20	6 41	28·7	11 27	6 11	28·6	298	242
63	117	15 59	8 23	28·2	15 06	7 54	28·0	14 13	7 25	27·9	13 20	6 56	27·8	12 27	6 27	27·7	11 34	5 59	27·6	297	243
64	116	16 08	8 06	27·2	15 14	7 38	27·0	14 21	7 10	26·9	13 27	6 42	26·8	12 34	6 14	26·7	11 40	5 47	26·6	296	244
65	115	16 16	7 49	26·1	15 22	7 22	26·0	14 28	6 55	25·9	13 34	6 28	25·8	12 40	6 01	25·7	11 46	5 34	25·6	295	245
66	114	16 24	7 32	25·1	15 29	7 05	25·0	14 35	6 39	24·9	13 41	6 13	24·7	12 46	5 47	24·6	11 52	5 22	24·6	294	246
67	113	16 32	7 14	24·1	15 37	6 49	23·9	14 42	6 24	23·8	13 47	5 59	23·7	12 52	5 34	23·6	11 57	5 09	23·5	293	247
68	112	16 39	6 56	23·0	15 44	6 32	22·9	14 48	6 08	22·8	13 53	5 44	22·7	12 58	5 20	22·6	12 02	4 57	22·5	292	248
69	111	16 46	6 38	22·0	15 50	6 15	21·9	14 55	5 52	21·8	13 59	5 29	21·7	13 03	5 06	21·6	12 07	4 44	21·5	291	249
70	110	16 53	6 20	20·9	15 57	5 58	20·8	15 01	5 36	20·7	14 05	5 14	20·6	13 08	4 52	20·6	12 12	4 31	20·5	290	250
71	109	16 59	6 02	19·9	16 03	5 41	19·8	15 06	5 20	19·7	14 10	4 59	19·6	13 13	4 38	19·5	12 17	4 18	19·5	289	251
72	108	17 05	5 44	18·9	16 09	5 24	18·8	15 12	5 04	18·7	14 15	4 44	18·6	13 18	4 24	18·5	12 21	4 05	18·4	288	252
73	107	17 11	5 26	17·8	16 14	5 06	17·7	15 17	4 48	17·6	14 20	4 29	17·6	13 23	4 10	17·5	12 25	3 52	17·4	287	253
74	106	17 17	5 07	16·8	16 19	4 49	16·7	15 22	4 31	16·6	14 24	4 13	16·5	13 27	3 56	16·5	12 29	3 38	16·4	286	254
75	105	17 22	4 48	15·7	16 24	4 31	15·7	15 26	4 15	15·6	14 29	3 58	15·5	13 31	3 42	15·4	12 33	3 25	15·4	285	255
76	104	17 27	4 30	14·7	16 29	4 14	14·6	15 31	3 58	14·6	14 33	3 43	14·5	13 35	3 27	14·4	12 36	3 12	14·4	284	256
77	103	17 31	4 11	13·6	16 33	3 56	13·6	15 35	3 41	13·5	14 36	3 27	13·4	13 38	3 13	13·4	12 40	2 58	13·3	283	257
78	102	17 36	3 52	12·6	16 37	3 38	12·5	15 38	3 25	12·5	14 40	3 11	12·4	13 41	2 58	12·4	12 43	2 45	12·3	282	258
79	101	17 39	3 33	11·6	16 41	3 20	11·5	15 42	3 08	11·4	14 43	2 56	11·4	13 44	2 43	11·3	12 45	2 31	11·3	281	259
80	100	17 43	3 14	10·5	16 44	3 02	10·4	15 45	2 51	10·4	14 46	2 40	10·3	13 47	2 29	10·3	12 48	2 18	10·3	280	260
81	99	17 46	2 55	9·5	16 47	2 44	9·4	15 48	2 34	9·4	14 49	2 24	9·3	13 49	2 14	9·3	12 50	2 04	9·2	279	261
82	98	17 49	2 35	8·4	16 50	2 26	8·4	15 50	2 17	8·3	14 51	2 08	8·3	13 52	1 59	8·2	12 52	1 50	8·2	278	262
83	97	17 52	2 16	7·4	16 52	2 08	7·3	15 53	2 00	7·3	14 53	1 52	7·2	13 54	1 44	7·2	12 54	1 37	7·2	277	263
84	96	17 54	1 57	6·3	16 54	1 50	6·3	15 55	1 43	6·2	14 55	1 36	6·2	13 55	1 30	6·2	12 56	1 23	6·1	276	264
85	95	17 56	1 37	5·3	16 56	1 32	5·2	15 56	1 26	5·2	14 56	1 20	5·2	13 57	1 15	5·2	12 57	1 09	5·1	275	265
86	94	17 57	1 18	4·2	16 57	1 13	4·2	15 58	1 09	4·2	14 58	1 04	4·1	13 58	1 00	4·1	12 58	0 55	4·1	274	266
87	93	17 58	0 58	3·2	16 59	0 55	3·1	15 59	0 52	3·1	14 59	0 48	3·1	13 59	0 45	3·1	12 59	0 42	3·1	273	267
88	92	17 59	0 39	2·1	16 59	0 37	2·1	15 59	0 34	2·1	14 59	0 32	2·1	13 59	0 30	2·1	13 00	0 28	2·1	272	268
89	91	18 00	0 19	1·1	17 00	0 18	1·0	16 00	0 17	1·0	15 00	0 16	1·0	14 00	0 15	1·0	13 00	0 14	1·0	271	269
90	90	18 00	0 00	0·0	17 00	0 00	0·0	16 00	0 00	0·0	15 00	0 00	0·0	14 00	0 00	0·0	13 00	0 00	0·0	270	270

N. Lat.: for LHA $> 180°$ ... $Z_n = Z$
for LHA $< 180°$ ... $Z_n = 360° - Z$

S. Lat.: for LHA $> 180°$ ... $Z_n = 180° - Z$
for LHA $< 180°$ ... $Z_n = 180° + Z$

© British Crown Copyright 2022. All rights reserved.

SIGHT REDUCTION TABLE

B: (−) for 90° < LHA < 270°
Dec:(−) for Lat. contrary name

Z_1: same sign as B
Z_2: (−) for F > 90°

Lat./A → LHA/F	78° A/H	78° B/P	78° Z_1/Z_2	79° A/H	79° B/P	79° Z_1/Z_2	80° A/H	80° B/P	80° Z_1/Z_2	81° A/H	81° B/P	81° Z_1/Z_2	82° A/H	82° B/P	82° Z_1/Z_2	83° A/H	83° B/P	83° Z_1/Z_2	Lat./A → LHA
0 / 180	0 00	12 00	90·0	0 00	11 00	90·0	0 00	10 00	90·0	0 00	9 00	90·0	0 00	8 00	90·0	0 00	7 00	90·0	180 / 360
1 / 179	0 12	12 00	89·0	0 11	11 00	89·0	0 10	10 00	89·0	0 09	9 00	89·0	0 08	8 00	89·0	0 07	7 00	89·0	181 / 359
2 / 178	0 25	12 00	88·0	0 23	11 00	88·0	0 21	10 00	88·0	0 19	9 00	88·0	0 17	8 00	88·0	0 15	7 00	88·0	182 / 358
3 / 177	0 37	11 59	87·1	0 34	10 59	87·1	0 31	9 59	87·0	0 28	8 59	87·0	0 25	7 59	87·0	0 22	6 59	87·0	183 / 357
4 / 176	0 50	11 58	86·1	0 46	10 58	86·1	0 42	9 58	86·0	0 38	8 59	86·0	0 33	7 59	86·0	0 29	6 59	86·0	184 / 356
5 / 175	1 02	11 57	85·1	0 57	10 58	85·1	0 52	9 58	85·1	0 47	8 58	85·1	0 42	7 58	85·0	0 37	6 58	85·0	185 / 355
6 / 174	1 15	11 56	84·1	1 09	10 56	84·1	1 02	9 57	84·1	0 56	8 57	84·1	0 50	7 57	84·1	0 44	6 58	84·0	186 / 354
7 / 173	1 27	11 55	83·2	1 20	10 55	83·1	1 13	9 56	83·1	1 06	8 56	83·1	0 58	7 56	83·1	0 51	6 57	83·1	187 / 353
8 / 172	1 39	11 53	82·2	1 31	10 54	82·1	1 23	9 54	82·1	1 15	8 55	82·1	1 07	7 55	82·1	0 58	6 56	82·1	188 / 352
9 / 171	1 52	11 51	81·2	1 43	10 52	81·2	1 33	9 53	81·2	1 24	8 53	81·1	1 15	7 54	81·1	1 06	6 55	81·1	189 / 351
10 / 170	2 04	11 49	80·2	1 54	10 50	80·2	1 44	9 51	80·1	1 33	8 52	80·1	1 23	7 53	80·1	1 13	6 54	80·1	190 / 350
11 / 169	2 16	11 47	79·2	2 05	10 48	79·2	1 54	9 49	79·2	1 43	8 50	79·1	1 31	7 51	79·1	1 20	6 52	79·1	191 / 349
12 / 168	2 29	11 45	78·3	2 16	10 46	78·2	2 04	9 47	78·2	1 52	8 48	78·1	1 39	7 50	78·1	1 27	6 51	78·1	192 / 348
13 / 167	2 41	11 42	77·3	2 28	10 43	77·2	2 14	9 45	77·2	2 01	8 46	77·2	1 48	7 48	77·1	1 34	6 49	77·1	193 / 347
14 / 166	2 53	11 39	76·3	2 39	10 41	76·2	2 24	9 43	76·2	2 10	8 44	76·2	1 56	7 46	76·1	1 41	6 48	76·1	194 / 346
15 / 165	3 05	11 36	75·3	2 50	10 38	75·3	2 35	9 40	75·2	2 19	8 42	75·2	2 04	7 44	75·1	1 48	6 46	75·1	195 / 345
16 / 164	3 17	11 33	74·3	3 01	10 35	74·3	2 45	9 37	74·2	2 28	8 39	74·2	2 12	7 42	74·1	1 56	6 44	74·1	196 / 344
17 / 163	3 29	11 29	73·4	3 12	10 32	73·3	2 55	9 34	73·2	2 37	8 37	73·2	2 20	7 39	73·1	2 03	6 42	73·1	197 / 343
18 / 162	3 41	11 26	72·4	3 23	10 28	72·3	3 05	9 31	72·3	2 46	8 34	72·2	2 28	7 37	72·1	2 09	6 40	72·1	198 / 342
19 / 161	3 53	11 22	71·4	3 34	10 25	71·3	3 14	9 28	71·3	2 55	8 31	71·2	2 36	7 34	71·1	2 16	6 37	71·1	199 / 341
20 / 160	4 05	11 18	70·4	3 45	10 21	70·3	3 24	9 24	70·3	3 04	8 28	70·2	2 44	7 31	70·1	2 23	6 35	70·1	200 / 340
21 / 159	4 16	11 13	69·4	3 55	10 17	69·4	3 34	9 21	69·3	3 13	8 25	69·2	2 52	7 28	69·2	2 30	6 32	69·1	201 / 339
22 / 158	4 28	11 09	68·4	4 06	10 13	68·4	3 44	9 17	68·3	3 22	8 21	68·2	2 59	7 25	68·2	2 37	6 30	68·1	202 / 338
23 / 157	4 40	11 04	67·5	4 17	10 09	67·4	3 53	9 13	67·3	3 30	8 18	67·3	3 07	7 22	67·2	2 44	6 27	67·2	203 / 337
24 / 156	4 51	10 59	66·5	4 27	10 04	66·4	4 03	9 09	66·4	3 39	8 14	66·3	3 15	7 19	66·2	2 50	6 24	66·2	204 / 336
25 / 155	5 02	10 54	65·5	4 38	9 59	65·5	4 13	9 05	65·4	3 47	8 10	65·3	3 22	7 16	65·2	2 57	6 21	65·2	205 / 335
26 / 154	5 14	10 49	64·5	4 48	9 55	64·5	4 22	9 00	64·4	3 56	8 06	64·3	3 30	7 12	64·2	3 04	6 18	64·2	206 / 334
27 / 153	5 25	10 43	63·5	4 58	9 50	63·5	4 31	8 56	63·4	4 04	8 02	63·3	3 37	7 08	63·2	3 10	6 15	63·2	207 / 333
28 / 152	5 36	10 38	62·5	5 08	9 44	62·5	4 41	8 51	62·4	4 13	7 58	62·3	3 45	7 04	62·2	3 17	6 11	62·2	208 / 332
29 / 151	5 47	10 32	61·5	5 18	9 39	61·5	4 50	8 46	61·4	4 21	7 53	61·3	3 52	7 00	61·2	3 23	6 08	61·2	209 / 331
30 / 150	5 58	10 26	60·5	5 28	9 33	60·5	4 59	8 41	60·4	4 29	7 49	60·3	3 59	6 56	60·2	3 30	6 04	60·2	210 / 330
31 / 149	6 09	10 20	59·6	5 38	9 28	59·5	5 08	8 36	59·4	4 37	7 44	59·3	4 07	6 52	59·2	3 36	6 00	59·2	211 / 329
32 / 148	6 20	10 13	58·6	5 48	9 22	58·5	5 17	8 30	58·4	4 45	7 39	58·3	4 14	6 48	58·3	3 42	5 57	58·2	212 / 328
33 / 147	6 30	10 06	57·6	5 58	9 16	57·5	5 26	8 25	57·4	4 53	7 34	57·3	4 21	6 43	57·3	3 48	5 53	57·2	213 / 327
34 / 146	6 41	10 00	56·6	6 08	9 09	56·5	5 34	8 19	56·4	5 01	7 29	56·3	4 28	6 39	56·3	3 54	5 49	56·2	214 / 326
35 / 145	6 51	9 53	55·6	6 17	9 03	55·5	5 43	8 13	55·4	5 09	7 24	55·3	4 35	6 34	55·3	4 00	5 45	55·2	215 / 325
36 / 144	7 01	9 45	54·6	6 26	8 56	54·5	5 51	8 07	54·4	5 17	7 18	54·3	4 42	6 29	54·3	4 06	5 40	54·3	216 / 324
37 / 143	7 11	9 38	53·6	6 36	8 49	53·5	6 00	8 01	53·4	5 24	7 13	53·3	4 48	6 24	53·3	4 12	5 36	53·2	217 / 323
38 / 142	7 21	9 31	52·6	6 45	8 43	52·6	6 08	7 55	52·5	5 32	7 07	52·3	4 55	6 19	52·3	4 18	5 32	52·2	218 / 322
39 / 141	7 31	9 23	51·6	6 54	8 35	51·6	6 16	7 48	51·5	5 39	7 01	51·4	5 01	6 14	51·3	4 24	5 27	51·2	219 / 321
40 / 140	7 41	9 15	50·6	7 03	8 28	50·6	6 25	7 42	50·4	5 46	6 55	50·3	5 08	6 09	50·3	4 30	5 22	50·2	220 / 320
41 / 139	7 50	9 07	49·6	7 11	8 21	49·5	6 32	7 35	49·4	5 53	6 49	49·4	5 14	6 03	49·3	4 35	5 18	49·2	221 / 319
42 / 138	8 00	8 59	48·6	7 20	8 13	48·5	6 40	7 28	48·4	6 01	6 43	48·4	5 21	5 58	48·3	4 41	5 13	48·2	222 / 318
43 / 137	8 09	8 50	47·6	7 29	8 05	47·5	6 48	7 21	47·4	6 07	6 36	47·3	5 27	5 52	47·3	4 46	5 08	47·2	223 / 317
44 / 136	8 18	8 42	46·6	7 37	7 58	46·5	6 56	7 14	46·4	6 14	6 30	46·4	5 33	5 46	46·3	4 51	5 03	46·2	224 / 316
45 / 135	8 27	8 33	45·6	7 45	7 50	45·5	7 03	7 06	45·4	6 21	6 23	45·4	5 39	5 41	45·3	4 58	4 58	45·2	225 / 315

© British Crown Copyright 2022. All rights reserved.

Lat./A LHA	/ A	83° A/H	83° B/P	83° Z₁/Z₂	82° A/H	82° B/P	82° Z₁/Z₂	81° A/H	81° B/P	81° Z₁/Z₂	80° A/H	80° B/P	80° Z₁/Z₂	79° A/H	79° B/P	79° Z₁/Z₂	78° A/H	78° B/P	78° Z₁/Z₂	Lat./A LHA/F	/ A
225	315	4 57	4 58	45.2	5 39	5 41	45.3	6 21	6 23	45.4	7 03	7 06	45.4	7 45	7 50	45.5	8 27	8 33	45.6	45	135
226	314	5 02	4 53	44.2	5 45	5 35	44.3	6 28	6 17	44.4	7 11	6 59	44.4	7 53	7 41	44.5	8 36	8 24	44.6	46	134
227	313	5 07	4 47	43.2	5 51	5 28	43.3	6 34	6 10	43.4	7 18	6 51	43.4	8 01	7 33	43.5	8 45	8 15	43.6	47	133
228	312	5 12	4 42	42.2	5 56	5 22	42.3	6 41	6 03	42.4	7 25	6 44	42.4	8 09	7 25	42.5	8 53	8 06	42.6	48	132
229	311	5 17	4 36	41.2	6 02	5 16	41.3	6 47	5 56	41.4	7 32	6 36	41.4	8 17	7 16	41.5	9 02	7 56	41.6	49	131
230	310	5 21	4 31	40.2	6 07	5 10	40.3	6 53	5 49	40.3	7 39	6 28	40.4	8 24	7 07	40.5	9 10	7 47	40.6	50	130
231	309	5 26	4 25	39.2	6 13	5 03	39.3	6 59	5 42	39.3	7 45	6 20	39.4	8 32	6 58	39.5	9 18	7 37	39.6	51	129
232	308	5 31	4 19	38.2	6 18	4 57	38.3	7 05	5 34	38.3	7 52	6 12	38.4	8 39	6 49	38.5	9 26	7 27	38.6	52	128
233	307	5 35	4 14	37.2	6 23	4 50	37.3	7 11	5 27	37.3	7 58	6 03	37.4	8 46	6 40	37.5	9 33	7 17	37.6	53	127
234	306	5 39	4 08	36.2	6 28	4 43	36.3	7 16	5 19	36.3	8 05	5 55	36.4	8 53	6 31	36.5	9 41	7 07	36.6	54	126
235	305	5 44	4 02	35.2	6 33	4 37	35.3	7 22	5 11	35.3	8 11	5 47	35.4	9 00	6 22	35.5	9 48	6 57	35.6	55	125
236	304	5 48	3 56	34.2	6 38	4 30	34.3	7 27	5 04	34.3	8 17	5 38	34.4	9 06	6 12	34.5	9 56	6 47	34.6	56	124
237	303	5 52	3 50	33.2	6 42	4 23	33.3	7 32	4 56	33.3	8 22	5 29	33.4	9 13	6 03	33.5	10 03	6 36	33.6	57	123
238	302	5 56	3 43	32.2	6 47	4 16	32.3	7 37	4 48	32.3	8 28	5 20	32.4	9 19	5 53	32.5	10 09	6 26	32.6	58	122
239	301	6 00	3 37	31.2	6 51	4 08	31.2	7 42	4 40	31.3	8 34	5 11	31.4	9 25	5 43	31.5	10 16	6 15	31.6	59	121
240	300	6 04	3 31	30.2	6 55	4 01	30.2	7 47	4 32	30.3	8 39	5 02	30.4	9 31	5 33	30.5	10 22	6 04	30.6	60	120
241	299	6 07	3 24	29.2	6 59	3 54	29.2	7 52	4 23	29.3	8 44	4 53	29.4	9 36	5 23	29.5	10 29	5 53	29.5	61	119
242	298	6 11	3 18	28.2	7 04	3 46	28.2	7 56	4 15	28.3	8 49	4 44	28.4	9 42	5 13	28.4	10 35	5 42	28.5	62	118
243	297	6 14	3 11	27.2	7 07	3 39	27.2	8 01	4 07	27.3	8 54	4 35	27.4	9 47	5 03	27.4	10 41	5 31	27.5	63	117
244	296	6 17	3 05	26.2	7 11	3 32	26.2	8 05	3 58	26.3	8 59	4 25	26.3	9 52	4 52	26.4	10 46	5 19	26.5	64	116
245	295	6 20	2 58	25.2	7 15	3 24	25.2	8 09	3 50	25.3	9 03	4 16	25.3	9 57	4 42	25.4	10 52	5 08	25.5	65	115
246	294	6 24	2 52	24.2	7 18	3 16	24.2	8 13	3 41	24.3	9 08	4 06	24.3	10 02	4 31	24.4	10 57	4 56	24.5	66	114
247	293	6 26	2 45	23.2	7 22	3 09	23.2	8 17	3 32	23.3	9 12	3 56	23.3	10 07	4 21	23.4	11 02	4 45	23.5	67	113
248	292	6 29	2 38	22.1	7 25	3 01	22.2	8 20	3 24	22.2	9 16	3 47	22.3	10 11	4 10	22.4	11 07	4 33	22.4	68	112
249	291	6 32	2 31	21.1	7 28	2 53	21.2	8 24	3 15	21.3	9 20	3 37	21.3	10 16	3 59	21.4	11 12	4 21	21.4	69	111
250	290	6 35	2 24	20.1	7 31	2 45	20.2	8 27	3 06	20.2	9 23	3 27	20.3	10 20	3 48	20.3	11 16	4 09	20.4	70	110
251	289	6 37	2 17	19.1	7 34	2 37	19.2	8 30	2 57	19.2	9 27	3 17	19.3	10 24	3 37	19.3	11 20	3 58	19.4	71	109
252	288	6 39	2 10	18.1	7 36	2 29	18.2	8 33	2 48	18.2	9 30	3 07	18.3	10 27	3 26	18.3	11 24	3 45	18.4	72	108
253	287	6 42	2 03	17.1	7 39	2 21	17.2	8 36	2 39	17.2	9 34	2 57	17.2	10 31	3 15	17.3	11 28	3 33	17.4	73	107
254	286	6 44	1 56	16.1	7 41	2 13	16.1	8 39	2 30	16.2	9 37	2 47	16.2	10 34	3 04	16.3	11 32	3 21	16.3	74	106
255	285	6 46	1 49	15.1	7 44	2 05	15.1	8 41	2 21	15.2	9 39	2 37	15.2	10 37	2 53	15.3	11 35	3 09	15.3	75	105
256	284	6 47	1 42	14.1	7 46	1 57	14.1	8 44	2 12	14.2	9 42	2 27	14.2	10 40	2 42	14.3	11 38	2 57	14.3	76	104
257	283	6 49	1 35	13.1	7 48	1 49	13.1	8 46	2 02	13.2	9 44	2 16	13.2	10 43	2 30	13.2	11 41	2 44	13.3	77	103
258	282	6 51	1 28	12.1	7 49	1 40	12.1	8 48	1 53	12.1	9 47	2 06	12.2	10 45	2 19	12.2	11 44	2 32	12.3	78	102
259	281	6 52	1 21	11.1	7 51	1 32	11.1	8 50	1 44	11.1	9 49	1 56	11.2	10 48	2 07	11.2	11 47	2 19	11.2	79	101
260	280	6 54	1 13	10.1	7 53	1 24	10.1	8 52	1 35	10.1	9 51	1 45	10.2	10 50	1 56	10.2	11 49	2 07	10.2	80	100
261	279	6 55	1 06	9.1	7 54	1 16	9.1	8 53	1 25	9.1	9 53	1 35	9.1	10 52	1 45	9.2	11 51	1 54	9.2	81	99
262	278	6 56	0 59	8.1	7 55	1 07	8.1	8 55	1 16	8.1	9 54	1 24	8.1	10 53	1 33	8.1	11 53	1 42	8.2	82	98
263	277	6 57	0 51	7.1	7 56	0 59	7.1	8 56	1 06	7.1	9 55	1 14	7.1	10 55	1 21	7.1	11 55	1 29	7.2	83	97
264	276	6 57	0 44	6.0	7 57	0 50	6.1	8 57	0 57	6.1	9 57	1 03	6.1	10 56	1 10	6.1	11 56	1 16	6.1	84	96
265	275	6 58	0 37	5.0	7 58	0 42	5.0	8 58	0 47	5.1	9 58	0 53	5.1	10 57	0 58	5.1	11 57	1 04	5.1	85	95
266	274	6 59	0 29	4.0	7 59	0 34	4.0	8 59	0 38	4.0	9 59	0 42	4.1	10 58	0 47	4.1	11 58	0 51	4.1	86	94
267	273	6 59	0 22	3.0	7 59	0 25	3.0	8 59	0 28	3.0	9 59	0 32	3.0	10 59	0 35	3.1	11 59	0 38	3.1	87	93
268	272	6 59	0 15	2.0	8 00	0 17	2.0	9 00	0 19	2.0	10 00	0 21	2.0	11 00	0 23	2.0	12 00	0 26	2.0	88	92
269	271	7 00	0 07	1.0	8 00	0 08	1.0	9 00	0 10	1.0	10 00	0 11	1.0	11 00	0 12	1.0	12 00	0 13	1.0	89	91
270	270	7 00	0 00	0.0	8 00	0 00	0.0	9 00	0 00	0.0	10 00	0 00	0.0	11 00	0 00	0.0	12 00	0 00	0.0	90	90

S. Lat.: for LHA > 180° ... $Z_n = 180° - Z$
for LHA < 180° ... $Z_n = 180° + Z$

N. Lat.: for LHA > 180° ... $Z_n = Z$
for LHA < 180° ... $Z_n = 360° - Z$

© British Crown Copyright 2022. All rights reserved.

SIGHT REDUCTION TABLE

B: (−) for 90° < LHA < 270°
Dec:(−) for Lat. contrary name

Z₁: same sign as B
Z₂: (−) for F > 90°

LHA/F	Lat./A	84° A/H	84° B/P	84° Z_1/Z_2	85° A/H	85° B/P	85° Z_1/Z_2	86° A/H	86° B/P	86° Z_1/Z_2	87° A/H	87° B/P	87° Z_1/Z_2	88° A/H	88° B/P	88° Z_1/Z_2	89° A/H	89° B/P	89° Z_1/Z_2	Lat./A	LHA
0	180	0 00	6 00	90·0	0 00	5 00	90·0	0 00	4 00	90·0	0 00	3 00	90·0	0 00	2 00	90·0	0 00	1 00	90·0	180	360
1	179	0 06	6 00	89·0	0 05	5 00	89·0	0 04	4 00	89·0	0 03	3 00	89·0	0 02	2 00	89·0	0 01	1 00	89·0	181	359
2	178	0 13	6 00	88·0	0 10	5 00	88·0	0 08	4 00	88·0	0 06	3 00	88·0	0 04	2 00	88·0	0 02	1 00	88·0	182	358
3	177	0 19	6 00	87·0	0 16	5 00	87·0	0 13	4 00	87·0	0 09	3 00	87·0	0 06	2 00	87·0	0 03	1 00	87·0	183	357
4	176	0 25	5 59	86·0	0 21	4 59	86·0	0 17	3 59	86·0	0 13	3 00	86·0	0 08	2 00	86·0	0 04	1 00	86·0	184	356
5	175	0 31	5 59	85·0	0 26	4 59	85·0	0 21	3 59	85·0	0 16	2 59	85·0	0 10	2 00	85·0	0 05	1 00	85·0	185	355
6	174	0 38	5 58	84·0	0 31	4 58	84·0	0 25	3 59	84·0	0 19	2 59	84·0	0 13	1 59	84·0	0 06	1 00	84·0	186	354
7	173	0 44	5 57	83·0	0 37	4 58	83·0	0 29	3 58	83·0	0 22	2 59	83·0	0 15	1 59	83·0	0 07	1 00	83·0	187	353
8	172	0 50	5 57	82·0	0 42	4 57	82·0	0 33	3 58	82·0	0 25	2 58	82·0	0 17	1 59	82·0	0 08	0 59	82·0	188	352
9	171	0 56	5 56	81·0	0 47	4 56	81·0	0 38	3 57	81·0	0 28	2 58	81·0	0 19	1 59	81·0	0 09	0 59	81·0	189	351
10	170	1 02	5 55	80·1	0 52	4 55	80·0	0 42	3 56	80·0	0 31	2 57	80·0	0 21	1 58	80·0	0 10	0 59	80·0	190	350
11	169	1 09	5 53	79·1	0 57	4 55	79·1	0 46	3 56	79·0	0 34	2 57	79·0	0 23	1 58	79·0	0 11	0 59	79·0	191	349
12	168	1 15	5 52	78·1	1 02	4 53	78·1	0 50	3 55	78·0	0 37	2 56	78·0	0 25	1 57	78·0	0 12	0 59	78·0	192	348
13	167	1 21	5 51	77·1	1 07	4 52	77·1	0 54	3 54	77·0	0 40	2 55	77·0	0 27	1 57	77·0	0 13	0 58	77·0	193	347
14	166	1 27	5 49	76·1	1 12	4 51	76·1	0 58	3 53	76·0	0 44	2 55	76·0	0 29	1 56	76·0	0 15	0 58	76·0	194	346
15	165	1 33	5 48	75·1	1 18	4 50	75·1	1 02	3 51	75·0	0 47	2 54	75·0	0 31	1 56	75·0	0 16	0 58	75·0	195	345
16	164	1 39	5 46	74·1	1 23	4 48	74·1	1 06	3 50	74·0	0 50	2 53	74·0	0 33	1 55	74·0	0 17	0 58	74·0	196	344
17	163	1 45	5 44	73·1	1 28	4 47	73·1	1 10	3 48	73·0	0 53	2 52	73·0	0 35	1 55	73·0	0 18	0 57	73·0	197	343
18	162	1 51	5 42	72·1	1 33	4 45	72·1	1 14	3 47	72·0	0 56	2 51	72·0	0 37	1 54	72·0	0 19	0 57	72·0	198	342
19	161	1 57	5 41	71·1	1 38	4 44	71·1	1 18	3 46	71·0	0 59	2 50	71·0	0 39	1 53	71·0	0 20	0 57	71·0	199	341
20	160	2 03	5 38	70·1	1 42	4 42	70·1	1 22	3 44	70·0	1 02	2 49	70·0	0 41	1 53	70·0	0 21	0 56	70·0	200	340
21	159	2 09	5 36	69·1	1 47	4 40	69·1	1 26	3 43	69·0	1 04	2 48	69·0	0 43	1 52	69·0	0 22	0 56	69·0	201	339
22	158	2 15	5 34	68·1	1 52	4 38	68·1	1 30	3 41	68·0	1 07	2 47	68·0	0 45	1 51	68·0	0 22	0 56	68·0	202	338
23	157	2 20	5 32	67·1	1 57	4 36	67·1	1 34	3 39	67·1	1 10	2 46	67·0	0 47	1 50	67·0	0 23	0 55	67·0	203	337
24	156	2 26	5 29	66·1	2 02	4 34	66·1	1 38	3 38	66·1	1 13	2 44	66·0	0 49	1 50	66·0	0 24	0 55	66·0	204	336
25	155	2 32	5 26	65·1	2 07	4 32	65·1	1 41	3 36	65·1	1 16	2 43	65·0	0 51	1 49	65·0	0 25	0 54	65·0	205	335
26	154	2 38	5 24	64·1	2 11	4 30	64·1	1 45	3 34	64·1	1 19	2 42	64·0	0 53	1 48	64·0	0 26	0 54	64·0	206	334
27	153	2 43	5 21	63·1	2 16	4 27	63·1	1 49	3 32	63·1	1 22	2 40	63·0	0 54	1 47	63·0	0 27	0 53	63·0	207	333
28	152	2 49	5 18	62·1	2 21	4 25	62·1	1 53	3 30	62·1	1 24	2 39	62·0	0 56	1 46	62·0	0 28	0 53	62·0	208	332
29	151	2 54	5 15	61·1	2 25	4 23	61·1	1 56	3 28	61·1	1 27	2 37	61·0	0 58	1 45	61·0	0 29	0 52	61·0	209	331
30	150	3 00	5 12	60·1	2 30	4 20	60·1	2 00	3 26	60·1	1 30	2 36	60·0	1 00	1 44	60·0	0 30	0 52	60·0	210	330
31	149	3 05	5 09	59·1	2 34	4 17	59·1	2 04	3 24	59·1	1 33	2 34	59·0	1 02	1 43	59·0	0 31	0 51	59·0	211	329
32	148	3 11	5 06	58·1	2 39	4 15	58·1	2 07	3 21	58·1	1 35	2 33	58·0	1 04	1 42	58·0	0 32	0 51	58·0	212	328
33	147	3 16	5 02	57·1	2 43	4 12	57·1	2 11	3 19	57·1	1 38	2 31	57·0	1 05	1 41	57·0	0 33	0 50	57·0	213	327
34	146	3 21	4 59	56·1	2 48	4 09	56·1	2 14	3 17	56·1	1 41	2 29	56·0	1 07	1 39	56·0	0 34	0 50	56·0	214	326
35	145	3 26	4 55	55·1	2 52	4 06	55·1	2 18	3 14	55·1	1 43	2 27	55·0	1 09	1 38	55·0	0 34	0 49	55·0	215	325
36	144	3 31	4 52	54·1	2 56	4 03	54·1	2 21	3 12	54·1	1 46	2 26	54·0	1 11	1 37	54·0	0 35	0 49	54·0	216	324
37	143	3 36	4 48	53·2	3 00	4 00	53·1	2 24	3 09	53·1	1 48	2 24	53·0	1 12	1 36	53·0	0 36	0 48	53·0	217	323
38	142	3 41	4 44	52·2	3 05	3 57	52·1	2 28	3 07	52·1	1 51	2 22	52·0	1 14	1 35	52·0	0 37	0 47	52·0	218	322
39	141	3 46	4 40	51·2	3 09	3 53	51·1	2 31	3 04	51·1	1 53	2 20	51·0	1 16	1 33	51·0	0 38	0 46	51·0	219	321
40	140	3 51	4 36	50·2	3 13	3 50	50·1	2 34	3 01	50·1	1 56	2 18	50·0	1 17	1 32	50·0	0 39	0 45	50·0	220	320
41	139	3 56	4 32	49·2	3 17	3 47	49·1	2 37	2 58	49·1	1 58	2 16	49·0	1 19	1 31	49·0	0 39	0 45	49·0	221	319
42	138	4 01	4 28	48·2	3 21	3 43	48·1	2 41	2 56	48·1	2 00	2 14	48·0	1 20	1 29	48·0	0 40	0 45	48·0	222	318
43	137	4 05	4 24	47·2	3 24	3 40	47·1	2 44	2 53	47·1	2 03	2 12	47·0	1 22	1 28	47·0	0 41	0 44	47·0	223	317
44	136	4 10	4 19	46·2	3 28	3 36	46·1	2 47	2 50	46·1	2 05	2 10	46·0	1 23	1 26	46·0	0 42	0 43	46·0	224	316
45	135	4 14	4 15	45·2	3 32	3 32	45·1	2 50	2 47	45·1	2 07	2 07	45·0	1 25	1 25	45·0	0 42	0 42	45·0	225	315

© British Crown Copyright 2022. All rights reserved.

Lat./A LHA/F	F	84° A/H	84° B/P	84° Z₁/Z₂	85° A/H	85° B/P	85° Z₁/Z₂	86° A/H	86° B/P	86° Z₁/Z₂	87° A/H	87° B/P	87° Z₁/Z₂	88° A/H	88° B/P	88° Z₁/Z₂	89° A/H	89° B/P	89° Z₁/Z₂	Lat./A LHA
45	135	4 14	4 15	45·2	3 32	3 32	45·1	2 50	2 50	45·1	2 07	2 07	45·0	1 25	1 25	45·0	0 42	0 42	45·0	225
46	134	4 19	4 11	44·2	3 36	3 29	44·1	2 53	2 47	44·1	2 09	2 05	44·0	1 26	1 23	44·0	0 43	0 42	44·0	226
47	133	4 23	4 06	43·2	3 39	3 25	43·1	2 55	2 44	43·1	2 12	2 03	43·0	1 28	1 22	43·0	0 44	0 41	43·0	227
48	132	4 27	4 01	42·2	3 43	3 21	42·1	2 58	2 41	42·1	2 14	2 01	42·0	1 29	1 20	42·0	0 45	0 40	42·0	228
49	131	4 31	3 57	41·2	3 46	3 17	41·1	3 01	2 38	41·1	2 16	1 58	41·0	1 31	1 19	41·0	0 45	0 39	41·0	229
50	130	4 36	3 52	40·2	3 50	3 13	40·1	3 04	2 34	40·1	2 18	1 56	40·0	1 32	1 17	40·0	0 46	0 39	40·0	230
51	129	4 40	3 47	39·2	3 53	3 09	39·1	3 06	2 31	39·1	2 20	1 53	39·0	1 33	1 16	39·0	0 47	0 38	39·0	231
52	128	4 43	3 42	38·2	3 56	3 05	38·1	3 09	2 28	38·1	2 22	1 51	38·0	1 35	1 14	38·0	0 47	0 37	38·0	232
53	127	4 47	3 37	37·2	3 59	3 01	37·1	3 12	2 25	37·1	2 24	1 48	37·0	1 36	1 12	37·0	0 48	0 36	37·0	233
54	126	4 51	3 32	36·1	4 03	2 57	36·1	3 14	2 21	36·1	2 26	1 46	36·0	1 37	1 11	36·0	0 49	0 35	36·0	234
55	125	4 55	3 27	35·1	4 06	2 52	35·1	3 17	2 18	35·1	2 27	1 43	35·0	1 38	1 09	35·0	0 49	0 34	35·0	235
56	124	4 58	3 22	34·1	4 09	2 48	34·1	3 19	2 14	34·1	2 29	1 41	34·0	1 39	1 07	34·0	0 50	0 34	34·0	236
57	123	5 02	3 17	33·1	4 12	2 44	33·1	3 21	2 11	33·1	2 31	1 38	33·0	1 41	1 05	33·0	0 50	0 33	33·0	237
58	122	5 05	3 11	32·1	4 14	2 39	32·1	3 23	2 07	32·1	2 33	1 35	32·0	1 42	1 04	32·0	0 51	0 32	32·0	238
59	121	5 08	3 06	31·1	4 17	2 35	31·1	3 26	2 04	31·1	2 34	1 33	31·0	1 43	1 02	31·0	0 51	0 31	31·0	239
60	120	5 12	3 00	30·1	4 20	2 30	30·1	3 28	2 00	30·1	2 36	1 30	30·0	1 44	1 00	30·0	0 52	0 30	30·0	240
61	119	5 15	2 55	29·1	4 22	2 26	29·1	3 30	1 56	29·1	2 37	1 27	29·0	1 45	0 58	29·0	0 52	0 29	29·0	241
62	118	5 18	2 49	28·1	4 25	2 21	28·1	3 32	1 53	28·1	2 39	1 25	28·0	1 46	0 56	28·0	0 53	0 28	28·0	242
63	117	5 21	2 44	27·1	4 27	2 16	27·1	3 34	1 49	27·1	2 40	1 22	27·0	1 47	0 54	27·0	0 53	0 27	27·0	243
64	116	5 23	2 38	26·1	4 30	2 12	26·1	3 36	1 45	26·1	2 42	1 19	26·0	1 48	0 53	26·0	0 54	0 26	26·0	244
65	115	5 26	2 33	25·1	4 32	2 07	25·1	3 37	1 42	25·1	2 43	1 16	25·0	1 49	0 51	25·0	0 54	0 25	25·0	245
66	114	5 29	2 27	24·1	4 34	2 02	24·1	3 39	1 38	24·1	2 44	1 13	24·0	1 50	0 49	24·0	0 55	0 24	24·0	246
67	113	5 31	2 21	23·1	4 36	1 57	23·1	3 41	1 34	23·1	2 46	1 10	23·0	1 50	0 47	23·0	0 55	0 23	23·0	247
68	112	5 34	2 15	22·1	4 38	1 53	22·1	3 42	1 30	22·0	2 47	1 07	22·0	1 51	0 45	22·0	0 56	0 22	22·0	248
69	111	5 36	2 09	21·1	4 40	1 48	21·1	3 44	1 26	21·0	2 48	1 05	21·0	1 52	0 43	21·0	0 56	0 22	21·0	249
70	110	5 38	2 04	20·1	4 42	1 43	20·1	3 46	1 22	20·0	2 49	1 02	20·0	1 53	0 41	20·0	0 56	0 20	20·0	250
71	109	5 40	1 58	19·1	4 44	1 38	19·1	3 47	1 18	19·0	2 50	0 59	19·0	1 53	0 39	19·0	0 57	0 19	19·0	251
72	108	5 42	1 52	18·1	4 45	1 33	18·1	3 48	1 14	18·0	2 51	0 56	18·0	1 54	0 37	18·0	0 57	0 18	18·0	252
73	107	5 44	1 46	17·1	4 47	1 28	17·1	3 49	1 10	17·0	2 52	0 53	17·0	1 55	0 35	17·0	0 57	0 17	17·0	253
74	106	5 46	1 40	16·1	4 48	1 23	16·1	3 51	1 06	16·0	2 53	0 50	16·0	1 55	0 33	16·0	0 58	0 15	16·0	254
75	105	5 48	1 33	15·1	4 50	1 18	15·1	3 52	1 02	15·0	2 54	0 47	15·0	1 56	0 31	15·0	0 58	0 15	15·0	255
76	104	5 49	1 27	14·1	4 51	1 13	14·1	3 53	0 58	14·0	2 55	0 44	14·0	1 56	0 29	14·0	0 58	0 14	14·0	256
77	103	5 51	1 21	13·1	4 52	1 08	13·0	3 54	0 54	13·0	2 55	0 41	13·0	1 57	0 27	13·0	0 58	0 13	13·0	257
78	102	5 52	1 15	12·1	4 53	1 03	12·0	3 55	0 50	12·0	2 56	0 37	12·0	1 57	0 25	12·0	0 59	0 11	12·0	258
79	101	5 53	1 09	11·1	4 54	0 57	11·0	3 56	0 46	11·0	2 57	0 34	11·0	1 58	0 23	11·0	0 59	0 10	11·0	259
80	100	5 55	1 03	10·0	4 55	0 52	10·0	3 56	0 42	10·0	2 57	0 31	10·0	1 58	0 21	10·0	0 59	0 10	10·0	260
81	99	5 56	0 57	9·0	4 56	0 47	9·0	3 57	0 38	9·0	2 58	0 28	9·0	1 59	0 19	9·0	0 59	0 09	9·0	261
82	98	5 56	0 50	8·0	4 57	0 42	8·0	3 58	0 33	8·0	2 58	0 25	8·0	1 59	0 17	8·0	0 59	0 08	8·0	262
83	97	5 57	0 44	7·0	4 58	0 37	7·0	3 58	0 29	7·0	2 59	0 22	7·0	1 59	0 15	7·0	1 00	0 07	7·0	263
84	96	5 58	0 38	6·0	4 58	0 31	6·0	3 59	0 25	6·0	2 59	0 19	6·0	1 59	0 13	6·0	1 00	0 06	6·0	264
85	95	5 58	0 31	5·0	4 59	0 26	5·0	3 59	0 21	5·0	2 59	0 16	5·0	2 00	0 10	5·0	1 00	0 05	5·0	265
86	94	5 59	0 25	4·0	4 59	0 21	4·0	3 59	0 17	4·0	3 00	0 13	4·0	2 00	0 08	4·0	1 00	0 04	4·0	266
87	93	5 59	0 19	3·0	5 00	0 16	3·0	4 00	0 13	3·0	3 00	0 09	3·0	2 00	0 06	3·0	1 00	0 03	3·0	267
88	92	6 00	0 13	2·0	5 00	0 10	2·0	4 00	0 08	2·0	3 00	0 06	2·0	2 00	0 04	2·0	1 00	0 02	2·0	268
89	91	6 00	0 06	1·0	5 00	0 05	1·0	4 00	0 04	1·0	3 00	0 03	1·0	2 00	0 02	1·0	1 00	0 01	1·0	269
90	90	6 00	0 00	0·0	5 00	0 00	0·0	4 00	0 00	0·0	3 00	0 00	0·0	2 00	0 00	0·0	1 00	0 00	0·0	270

N. Lat: for LHA > 180° ... $Z_n = Z$
for LHA < 180° ... $Z_n = 360° − Z$

S. Lat.: for LHA > 180° ... $Z_n = 180° − Z$
for LHA < 180° ... $Z_n = 180° + Z$

© British Crown Copyright 2022. All rights reserved.

AUXILIARY TABLE

Right margin: *Sign for $corr_2$ for A'.*   → + / −

Left margin: *Sign of $corr_1$ for F'. Reverse sign if F > 90°.*

The table is entered with the top scale (A', and row argument Z_2) to obtain $corr_2$, and with the bottom scale (F', and row argument P°) to obtain $corr_1$. Each column carries a top label (A' / Z-side) and a bottom label (F'). The left index column lists Z°_2 (89 → 50); the bottom-left index lists P° (1 → 40).

Column top-labels (left → right): □30, 29/31, 28/32, 27/33, 26/34, 25/35, 24/36, 23/37, 22/38, 21/39, 20/40, 19/41, 18/42, 17/43, 16/44, 15/45, 14/46, 13/47, 12/48, 11/49, 10/50, 9/51, 8/52, 7/53, 6/54, 5/55, 4/56, 3/57, 2/58, 1/59.

Corresponding column bottom-labels (F', left → right): 1/59, 2/58, 3/57, 4/56, 5/55, 6/54, 7/53, 8/52, 9/51, 10/50, 11/49, 12/48, 13/47, 14/46, 15/45, 16/44, 17/43, 18/42, 19/41, 20/40, 21/39, 22/38, 23/37, 24/36, 25/35, 26/34, 27/33, 28/32, 29/31, □30.

Z°_2	P°	□30	29/31	28/32	27/33	26/34	25/35	24/36	23/37	22/38	21/39	20/40	19/41	18/42	17/43	16/44	15/45	14/46	13/47	12/48	11/49	10/50	9/51	8/52	7/53	6/54	5/55	4/56	3/57	2/58	1/59
89	1	~	~	~	~	~	~	~	~	~	~	~	~	~	0	0	0	0	0	0	0	0	0	0	0	0	0	0	0	0	0
88	2	1	1	0	0	0	0	0	0	0	0	0	0	0	1	0	0	0	0	0	0	0	0	0	0	0	0	0	0	0	0
87	3	1	1	1	1	1	1	1	1	1	1	1	1	1	1	1	1	0	0	0	0	0	0	0	0	0	0	0	0	0	0
86	4	2	2	1	1	1	1	1	1	1	1	1	1	1	1	1	1	1	1	1	1	1	1	1	1	1	1	0	0	0	0
85	5	2	2	2	2	2	2	2	2	2	2	1	1	2	1	1	1	1	1	1	1	1	1	1	1	1	1	1	1	1	1
84	6	3	3	3	3	3	3	3	2	2	2	2	2	2	2	2	2	1	1	1	1	2	2	2	1	1	1	1	1	1	1
83	7	4	3	3	3	3	3	3	3	3	3	3	2	2	2	2	2	2	2	2	2	2	2	2	2	2	1	1	1	1	1
82	8	4	4	4	4	4	3	3	3	3	3	3	3	3	2	3	2	2	2	2	2	2	2	2	2	2	2	2	1	1	1
81	9	5	4	4	4	4	4	4	4	4	3	3	3	3	3	3	3	2	2	2	2	3	2	2	2	2	2	2	2	2	1
80	10	5	5	5	5	5	4	4	4	4	4	3	4	3	3	3	3	3	3	3	3	3	3	3	2	2	2	2	2	2	1
79	11	6	6	5	5	5	5	5	4	4	4	4	4	4	4	4	4	3	3	3	3	3	3	3	3	2	2	2	2	2	1
78	12	6	6	6	6	5	5	5	5	5	5	4	4	4	4	4	4	4	4	3	3	3	3	3	3	3	2	2	2	2	1
77	13	7	7	7	6	5	6	5	5	5	5	5	5	4	4	4	4	4	4	4	4	3	3	3	3	3	3	3	2	2	2
76	14	7	7	7	6	6	6	6	6	6	5	5	5	5	5	4	4	4	4	4	4	4	3	3	3	3	3	3	2	2	2
75	15	8	8	8	7	6	6	6	6	6	6	5	5	5	5	5	4	4	4	4	5	4	4	3	3	3	3	3	2	2	2
74	16	8	8	7	7	7	7	7	6	6	6	7	6	5	5	5	5	5	5	4	4	4	4	4	3	3	3	3	3	2	2
73	17	9	8	8	8	8	7	7	7	7	7	7	6	6	6	6	5	5	5	5	5	4	4	4	4	3	3	3	3	2	2
72	18	9	9	9	8	8	8	7	7	7	7	8	7	6	7	6	6	5	5	5	5	5	4	4	4	4	4	3	3	3	2
71	19	10	10	9	9	8	8	8	8	7	8	8	7	7	7	7	6	6	5	5	5	5	5	4	4	4	4	3	3	3	3
70	20	10	10	10	9	9	9	8	8	8	8	8	8	7	7	7	6	6	6	6	5	5	5	4	4	4	4	4	3	3	3
69	21	11	10	10	10	9	9	9	8	8	9	9	8	8	7	7	7	6	6	6	5	5	5	4	4	4	4	4	3	3	3
68	22	11	11	10	10	10	9	9	10	9	10	9	8	8	8	8	7	7	6	6	6	5	5	5	4	4	4	4	3	3	3
67	23	12	11	11	11	10	10	9	10	10	10	10	9	9	8	8	7	7	7	6	6	6	5	5	5	4	4	4	4	3	3
66	24	12	12	11	11	11	11	10	11	10	10	10	10	9	9	9	8	7	7	7	6	6	5	5	5	4	4	4	4	3	3
65	25	13	12	12	11	11	11	11	11	11	10	10	10	9	9	9	8	8	7	7	6	6	6	5	5	5	4	4	4	4	3
64	26	13	13	12	12	11	11	12	12	11	12	11	11	10	9	9	9	8	8	7	7	6	6	6	5	5	5	4	4	4	3
63	27	14	13	13	12	12	13	13	12	12	12	12	11	10	10	10	9	9	8	8	7	7	6	6	5	5	5	4	4	4	3
62	28	14	14	13	13	13	14	13	13	12	13	12	12	11	10	10	9	9	9	8	7	7	6	6	6	5	5	5	4	4	4
61	29	15	14	14	13	13	14	13	13	13	13	13	12	11	11	10	9	9	9	8	7	7	6	6	6	5	5	5	4	4	4
60	30	15	14	14	14	13	14	14	14	13	13	13	12	12	11	10	10	9	9	8	7	7	7	6	6	5	5	5	4	4	4
59	31	15	15	14	14	15	15	14	14	14	14	14	13	12	11	11	10	10	9	8	8	7	7	6	6	5	5	5	4	4	4
58	32	16	15	15	15	16	16	15	15	14	14	14	13	13	12	11	10	10	9	8	8	7	7	6	6	6	5	5	5	4	4
57	33	16	16	15	16	16	16	15	16	15	15	14	14	13	12	11	11	10	9	9	8	8	7	6	6	6	5	5	5	4	4
56	34	17	16	16	16	16	16	16	16	15	15	15	14	13	13	12	11	10	9	9	8	8	7	7	6	6	6	5	5	4	4
55	35	17	17	16	17	17	16	16	16	16	16	15	15	14	13	12	12	11	10	9	9	8	8	7	6	6	6	5	5	4	4
54	36	18	17	16	17	17	17	16	17	16	16	15	15	14	13	13	12	11	10	10	9	8	8	7	7	6	6	5	5	5	4
53	37	18	17	17	17	17	18	17	17	17	16	16	15	15	14	13	12	11	11	10	9	8	8	7	7	6	6	5	5	5	4
52	38	18	18	17	18	18	18	17	18	17	17	16	16	15	14	13	12	11	11	10	9	8	8	7	7	6	6	5	5	5	4
51	39	19	18	18	18	18	18	18	18	18	17	17	16	15	14	14	13	12	11	10	9	9	8	7	7	6	6	5	5	5	4
50	40	19	19	18	18	18	18	18	18	18	18	17	16	16	15	14	13	12	11	10	10	9	8	7	7	6	6	6	5	5	4

© British Crown Copyright 2022. All rights reserved.

For $Z_2 < 10°$, use 10°

−/+ A′ → (top)	30	29	28	27	26	25	24	23	22	21	20	19	18	17	16	15	14	13	12	11	10	9	8	7	6	5	4	3	2	1		
+/− A′ → (bottom)	□	31	32	33	34	35	36	37	38	39	40	41	42	43	44	45	46	47	48	49	50	51	52	53	54	55	56	57	58	59		
$Z_2°$																															**F' ±**	**P°**
49	20	19	18	18	17	16	16	15	14	14	13	12	12	11	10	10	9	9	8	7	7	6	5	5	4	3	3	2	1	1		41
48	20	19	19	18	17	17	16	15	15	14	13	13	12	11	11	10	9	9	8	7	7	6	5	5	4	3	3	2	1	1		42
47	20	20	19	18	18	17	16	16	15	14	14	13	12	12	11	10	10	9	8	8	7	6	5	5	4	3	3	2	1	1		43
46	21	20	19	19	18	17	17	16	15	15	14	13	13	12	11	10	10	9	9	8	7	6	6	5	4	4	3	2	2	1		44
45	21	20	20	19	18	18	17	16	16	15	14	13	13	12	11	11	10	10	9	8	8	7	6	5	4	4	3	2	1	1		45
44	22	21	20	19	19	18	17	17	16	15	14	14	13	12	12	11	11	10	9	8	8	7	6	6	5	4	3	3	2	1		46
43	22	21	20	20	19	18	18	17	16	15	15	14	13	13	12	11	11	10	9	8	8	7	6	6	5	4	3	3	2	1		47
42	22	22	21	20	19	19	18	17	16	16	15	14	14	13	12	12	11	10	10	8	8	7	6	6	5	4	3	3	2	1		48
41	23	22	21	20	20	19	18	18	17	16	15	15	14	14	12	11	11	11	10	9	8	7	6	6	5	4	3	3	2	1		49
40	23	22	22	21	20	19	19	18	17	16	16	15	14	14	12	12	12	11	10	9	8	8	7	6	5	4	3	3	2	1		50
39	23	23	22	21	20	19	19	18	17	17	16	15	15	14	13	12	12	11	10	9	8	8	7	6	5	4	4	3	2	1		51
38	24	23	22	21	20	20	19	18	17	17	16	15	15	14	13	13	12	12	11	9	8	8	7	6	5	4	4	3	2	1		52
37	24	23	23	22	21	20	20	19	18	17	16	16	15	14	13	13	12	12	11	9	8	8	7	6	5	4	4	3	2	1		53
36	24	23	23	22	21	20	20	19	18	17	16	16	15	14	14	13	13	12	11	10	8	8	7	6	5	5	4	3	3	2		54
35	25	24	23	22	22	21	20	19	18	18	17	16	15	15	14	13	13	12	11	10	8	8	7	6	5	5	4	3	3	2		55
34	25	24	23	22	22	21	21	20	18	18	17	16	15	15	14	13	13	12	11	10	8	8	7	6	5	5	4	3	3	2		56
33	25	24	23	23	22	21	21	20	18	18	17	16	16	15	14	13	13	12	11	10	9	8	7	6	6	5	4	3	3	2		57
32	25	25	24	23	22	22	21	20	19	18	17	17	16	15	14	13	13	12	11	10	9	8	7	6	6	5	4	3	3	2		58
31	26	25	24	23	23	22	21	20	19	18	17	17	16	15	15	13	13	12	11	10	9	8	7	6	6	5	4	3	3	2		59
30	26	25	24	23	23	22	21	21	19	18	17	17	16	15	15	14	13	12	11	10	9	8	7	6	6	5	4	3	3	2		60
29	26	25	24	24	23	22	21	21	19	18	17	17	16	16	15	14	13	13	12	10	9	8	7	6	6	5	4	3	3	2		61
28	26	26	25	24	23	22	22	21	19	19	18	17	16	16	15	14	13	13	12	10	9	8	7	6	6	5	4	3	3	2		62
27	27	26	25	24	23	23	22	21	20	19	18	17	16	16	15	14	14	13	12	11	9	8	7	6	6	5	4	3	3	2		63
26	27	26	25	24	24	23	22	21	20	19	18	17	16	16	15	14	14	13	12	11	9	8	7	6	6	5	4	3	3	2		64
25	27	26	25	24	24	23	22	22	20	19	19	18	17	16	15	14	14	13	12	11	9	8	7	6	6	5	4	3	3	2		65
24	27	26	26	25	24	23	23	22	20	19	19	18	17	16	15	14	14	13	12	11	9	8	7	7	6	5	4	3	3	2		66
23	28	27	26	25	25	24	23	22	21	20	19	18	17	16	16	15	14	13	12	11	9	8	7	7	6	5	4	3	3	2		67
22	28	27	26	25	25	24	23	22	21	20	19	18	17	16	16	15	14	13	12	11	10	8	7	7	6	5	4	3	3	2		68
21	28	27	27	26	25	24	23	23	21	20	20	19	17	16	16	15	14	14	12	11	10	9	8	7	6	5	4	3	3	2		69
20	28	28	27	26	25	24	24	23	22	21	20	19	18	17	16	15	14	14	12	11	10	9	8	7	6	5	4	3	3	2		70
19	28	27	26	26	25	24	24	23	22	21	20	19	18	17	16	15	15	14	13	11	10	9	8	7	6	5	4	3	3	2		71
18	29	28	27	26	26	25	24	23	22	21	20	19	18	17	16	15	15	14	13	11	10	9	8	7	6	5	4	3	3	2		72
17	29	28	27	27	26	25	24	24	22	22	21	20	18	17	16	15	15	14	13	11	10	9	8	7	6	5	4	3	3	2		73
16	29	28	27	27	26	25	24	24	23	22	21	20	18	17	16	15	15	14	13	11	10	9	8	7	6	5	4	3	3	2		74
15	29	28	28	27	26	26	25	24	23	22	21	20	18	17	16	15	15	14	13	11	10	9	8	7	6	5	4	3	3	2		75
14	29	28	27	26	25	24	23	22	21	20	19	18	17	16	16	15	15	14	13	11	10	9	8	7	6	5	4	3	3	2		76
13	29	28	27	27	26	24	24	23	22	21	20	19	18	17	16	15	15	14	13	11	10	9	8	7	6	5	4	3	3	2		77
12	29	28	27	27	26	25	24	24	23	22	21	19	18	17	16	15	15	14	13	11	10	9	8	7	6	5	4	3	3	1		78
11	30	29	28	27	27	26	24	24	23	22	21	20	18	17	16	15	15	14	13	11	10	9	8	7	6	5	4	3	2	1		79
10	30	29	28	27	27	26	25	25	24	23	22	20	18	17	16	15	15	14	13	11	10	9	8	7	6	5	4	3	3	2		80

For P > 80°, use 80°

© British Crown Copyright 2022. All rights reserved.

USE OF CONCISE SIGHT REDUCTION TABLES (continued)

4. *Example.* (b) Required the altitude and azimuth of *Vega* on 2023 July 29 at UT 04^h 50^m from the estimated position S 15°, W 152°.

1. Assumed latitude $Lat =$ 15° S
   From the almanac $GHA =$ 99° 39′
   Assumed longitude   151° 39′ W
   Local hour angle $LHA =$ 308

2. Reduction table, 1st entry
   $(Lat, LHA) = (15, 308)$ $A =$ 49   34 $A° = 50$, $A' = 34$
                                $B = +66$ 29 $Z_1 = +71{\cdot}7$, $LHA > 270°$
3. From the almanac $Dec = -38$ 48   *Lat* and *Dec* contrary
   Sum $= B + Dec$ $F = +27$ 41 $F° = 28$, $F' = 41$

4. Reduction table, 2nd entry
   $(A°, F°) = (50, 28)$ $H =$ 17   34 $P° = 37$
                                               $Z_2 = 67{\cdot}8$, $Z_2° = 68$

5. Auxiliary table, 1st entry
   $(F', P°) = (41, 37)$ $corr_1 =$ -11 $F < 90°$, $F' > 29′$
   Sum   17   23
6. Auxiliary table, 2nd entry
   $(A', Z_2°) = (34, 68)$ $corr_2 =$ $+10$ $A' > 30′$
7. Sum $=$ computed altitude $H_C = +17°$ 33′ $F > 0°$

8. Azimuth,   first component $Z_1 = +71{\cdot}7$ same sign as B
            second component $Z_2 = +67{\cdot}8$ $F < 90°$, $F > 0°$
   Sum $=$ azimuth angle $Z =$ 139·5

   True azimuth $Z_n =$ 040°   S *Lat*, *LHA* > 180°

5. *Form for use with the Concise Sight Reduction Tables.* The form on the following page lays out the procedure explained on pages 284–285. Each step is shown, with notes and rules to ensure accuracy, rather than speed, throughout the calculation. The form is mainly intended for the calculation of star positions. It therefore includes the formation of the Greenwich hour of Aries (*GHA* Aries), and thus the Greenwich hour angle of the star (*GHA*) from its tabular sidereal hour angle (*SHA*). These calculations, included in step 1 of the form, can easily be replaced by the interpolation of *GHA* and *Dec* for the Sun, Moon or planets.

The form may be freely copied; however, acknowledgement of the source is requested.

© British Crown Copyright 2022. All rights reserved.

Date & UT of observation		Body	Estimated Latitude & Longitude
	h m s		° ' ° '

Step	Calculate Altitude & Azimuth		Summary of Rules & Notes
Assumed latitude	$Lat =$ °		Nearest estimated latitude, integral number of degrees.
Assumed longitude	$Long =$ ° '		Choose $Long$ so that LHA has integral number of degrees.
1. From the almanac:	$Dec =$ ° '		Record the Dec for use in Step 3.
GHA Aries h	$=$ ° '		Needed if using SHA. Tabular value.
Increment m s	$=$ ° '		for minutes and seconds of time.
SHA	$SHA =$ ° '		
$GHA = GHA\ Aries + SHA$	$GHA =$ ° '		Remove multiples of 360°.
Assumed longitude	$Long =$ ° '		West longitudes are negative.
$LHA = GHA + Long$	$LHA =$ °		Remove multiples of 360°.
2. Reduction table, 1ˢᵗ entry			
$(Lat, LHA) = ($ °, °$)$	$A =$ ° ' $A° =$ °		nearest whole degree of A.
record A, B and Z_1.	$A' =$ '		minutes part of A.
	$B =$ ° '		B is minus if $90° < LHA < 270°$.
	$Z_1 =$ °		Z_1 has the same sign as B.
3. From step 1	$Dec =$ ° '		Dec is minus if contrary to Lat.
$F = B + Dec$	$F =$ ° '		Regard F as positive until step 7.
	$F° =$ °		nearest whole degree of F.
	$F' =$ '		minutes part of F.
4. Reduction table, 2ⁿᵈ entry			
$(A°, F°) = ($ °, °$)$	$H =$ ° ' $P° =$ °		nearest whole degree of P.
record H, P and Z_2.	$Z_2 =$ °		
5. Auxiliary table, 1ˢᵗ entry			
$(F', P°) = ($ ', °$)$	$corr_1 =$ '		$corr_1$ is minus if $F < 90°$ & $F' > 29'$,
record $corr_1$			or if $F > 90°$ & $F' < 30'$.
6. Auxiliary table, 2ⁿᵈ entry			$Z_2°$ nearest whole degree of Z_2.
$(A', Z_2°) = ($ ', °$)$	$corr_2 =$ '		$corr_2$ is minus if $A' < 30'$.
record $corr_2$			
7. Calculated altitude $=$	$H_c =$ ° '		H_c is minus if F is negative, and
$H_c = H + corr_1 + corr_2$			object is below the horizon.
8. Azimuth, 1ˢᵗ component	$Z_1 =$ °		Z_1 has the same sign as B.
2ⁿᵈ component	$Z_2 =$ °		Z_2 is minus if $F > 90°$.
			If F is negative, $Z_2 = 180° - Z_2$
$Z = Z_1 + Z_2$	$Z =$ °		Ignore the sign of Z.
			N Lat: If $LHA > 180°$, $Z_n = Z$, or if $LHA < 180°$, $Z_n = 360° - Z$,
			S Lat: If $LHA > 180°$, $Z_n = 180° - Z$, or if $LHA < 180°$, $Z_n = 180° + Z$.
True azimuth	$Z_n =$ °		©HMNAO

For use with *The Nautical Almanac's* Concise Sight Reduction Tables pages 284-318.

© British Crown Copyright 2022. All rights reserved.

POLAR PHENOMENA

EXPLANATION

1. *Introduction.* The graphs on pages 322-325 give data concerning the rising and setting of the Sun and Moon and the duration of civil twilight for high latitudes. Graphs are given instead of tables for high latitudes because they give a clearer picture of the phenomena and of the attainable accuracy in any given case. In the regions of the graph that are difficult to read accurately, the phenomenon itself is generally uncertain.

2. *Semiduration of sunlight.* The graphs for the semiduration of sunlight (page 322) give for latitudes north of N 65° the number of hours from sunrise to meridian passage or from meridian passage to sunset. There is continuous daylight in an area marked "Sun above horizon", and no direct sunlight in an area marked "Sun below horizon". The figures near the top indicate, for several convenient dates, the local mean times of meridian passage; with the aid of the intermediate dots the LMT on any given day may be obtained to the nearest minute. The LMT of sunrise may be found by subtracting the semiduration from the time of meridian passage, and the time of sunset by adding. The equation of time is given by subtracting the time of meridian passage from noon.

Examples. (a) Estimate the time of sunrise and sunset on 2023 March 10 at latitude N 77°. The semiduration of sunlight (page 322) is about $5^h 00^m$. The time of meridian passage is $12^h 10^m$, and hence the LMT of sunrise is $07^h 10^m$, and of sunset $17^h 10^m$. (b) Estimate the dates, for the first half of 2023, when the Sun is continuously below and above the horizon at latitude N 80°. The semiduration of sunlight graph (page 322) indicates the Sun is continuously below the horizon until about February 21, and is continuously above the horizon after April 14.

3. *Duration of civil twilight.* The graphs for the duration of twilight (page 322) give the interval from the beginning of morning civil twilight (Sun 6° below the horizon) to the time of sunrise or from the time of sunset to the end of evening civil twilight. In a region marked "No twilight or sunlight", the Sun is continuously below the horizon by more than 6°. In a region marked "Continuous twilight or sunlight", the Sun never goes lower than 6° below the horizon.

Adjacent to a region marked "No twilight or sunlight" is a region in which the Sun is continuously below the horizon, but so near to the horizon during a portion of the day that there is twilight. This area is the shaded region. The value given by the graph in this shaded region is the interval from the beginning of morning twilight to meridian passage of the Sun, or from meridian passage to the end of evening twilight, the total duration of twilight being twice the value given by the graph. The border between this shaded region and the remainder of the graph indicates that the Sun only just rises at meridian passage at the date and latitude shown. The remainder of the graph gives the total duration of civil twilight.

Examples. (a) Estimate the time of the beginning of morning civil twilight at latitude N 77° on 2023 March 10. The duration of twilight (page 322) is about $1^h 38^m$. Applying this to the time of sunrise, $07^h 10^m$, found in the preceding example, the beginning of morning civil twilight is $05^h 40^m$ LMT. (b) Estimate, for the first half of 2023, the limiting dates of civil twilight and sunlight at latitude N 80°. The graphs (page 322) indicate there is no sunlight or twilight till about February 6, there is twilight but no sunlight from February 6 until February 21, sunlight and twilight till April 1, continuous twilight or sunlight till April 14, and then continuous sunlight. (c) Estimate the time of the beginning and end of civil twilight on 2023 February 14 at latitude N 80°. The graph (page 322) indicates there is no direct sunlight at this date and latitude, but three hours of twilight before and after meridian passage occurring at $12^h 14^m$. Thus civil twilight begins at about $09^h 14^m$ and ends at about $15^h 14^m$ LMT.

© British Crown Copyright 2022. All rights reserved.

4. *Semiduration of moonlight* The graphs, for each month, for the semiduration of moonlight give for the Moon the same data as the graphs for the semiduration of sunlight give for the Sun. The scale near the top gives the LMT of meridian passage. In addition, the phase symbols are placed on the graphs to show the day on which each phase occurs. Since the times of meridian passage and the semiduration change more rapidly from day to day for the Moon than for the Sun, special care will be required in reading the graphs accurately.

For most purposes, in these high latitudes, a rough idea of the time of moonrise or moonset is all that is required, and this may be obtained by a glance at the graph.

Example. Estimate the moon phase and the time of moonrise and moonset on 2023 January 15 at latitude N 73°. The phase is found from pages 323-325 to be near last quarter, and the Moon crosses the meridian at 06^h LMT. The semiduration of moonlight taken for the time of meridian passage is 4 hours, giving moonrise at 02^h LMT on January 15 and moonset at 10^h on January 15.

If greater accuracy is required, it is necessary to read the graph for the UT of each phenomenon at the desired meridian. The dates indicated on the graph are for 00^h UT, and intermediate values of the UT may be located by estimation.

Example. Required to improve the results obtained in the preceding example, assuming the observer to be in longitude W 90° (6^h) west.

The values found previously were:

		d	h			d	h	
Time of meridian passage	2023 Jan.	15	06	LMT	=	Jan.	15	12	UT
Semiduration of moonlight			4					
Time of moonrise		Jan.	15	02	LMT	=	Jan.	15	08	UT
Time of moonset		Jan.	15	10	LMT	=	Jan.	15	16	UT

Returning to the graphs (pages 323-325) with these three values of the UT, the following results are obtained:

		d	h	m			d	h	m	
Time of meridian passage	2023 Jan.	15	06	10	LMT	=	Jan.	15	12	10	UT
Semiduration for moonrise			03	50						
Time of moonrise		Jan.	15	02	20	LMT	=	Jan.	15	08	20	UT
Semiduration for moonset			03	20						
Time of moonset		Jan.	15	09	30	LMT	=	Jan.	15	15	30	UT

© British Crown Copyright 2022. All rights reserved.

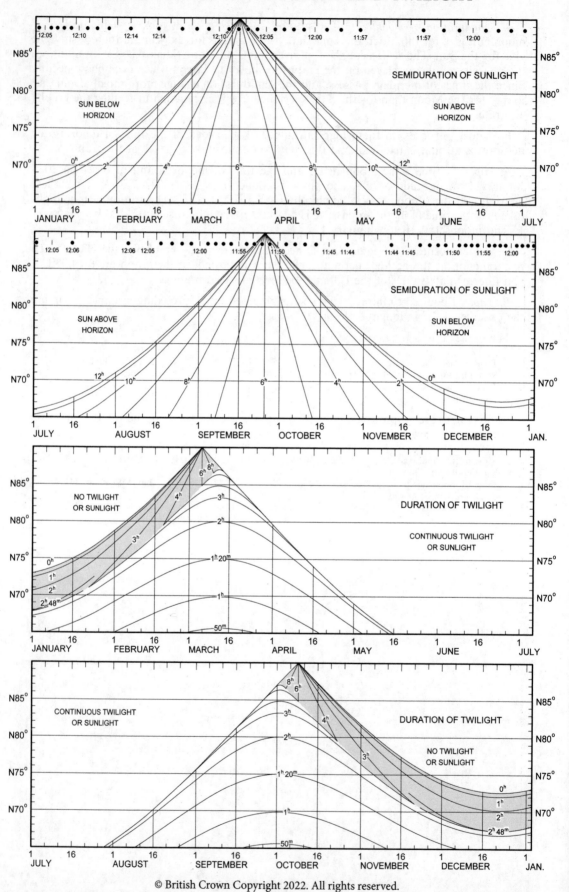

© British Crown Copyright 2022. All rights reserved.

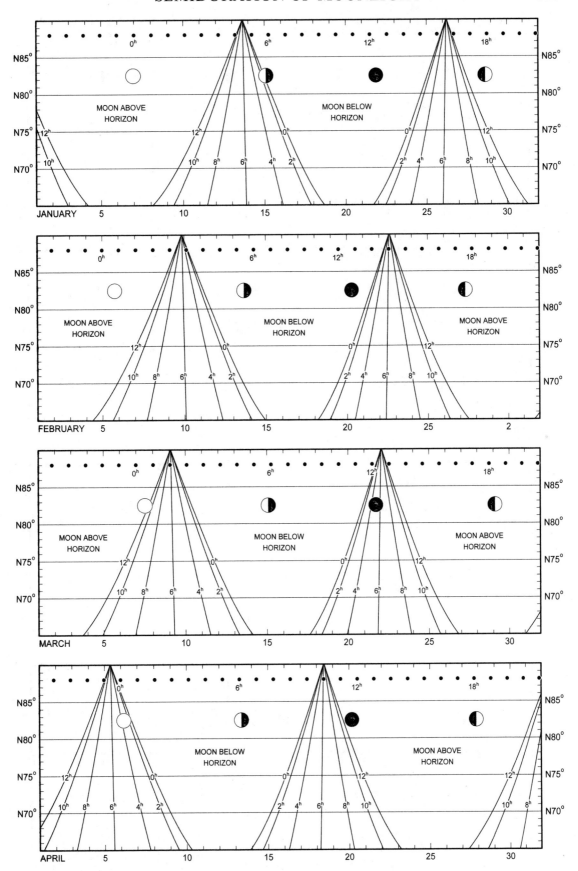

© British Crown Copyright 2022. All rights reserved.

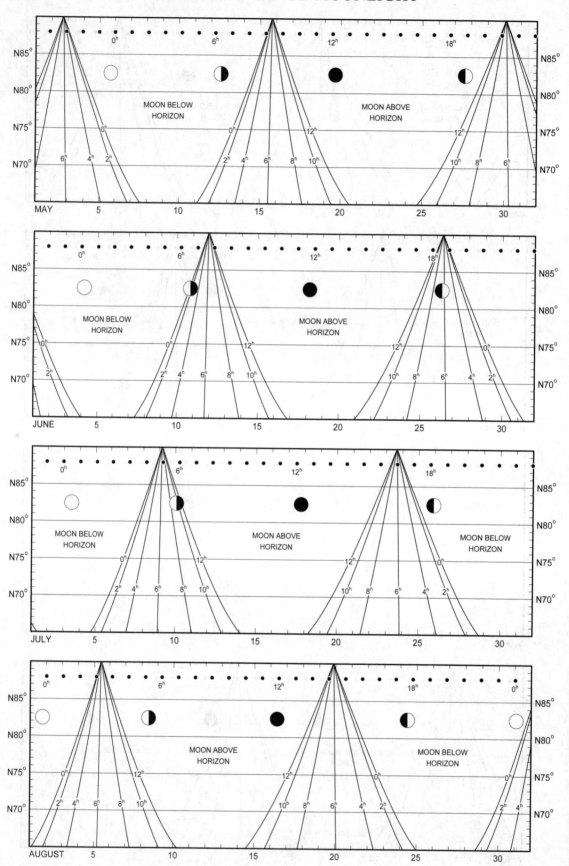

© British Crown Copyright 2022. All rights reserved.

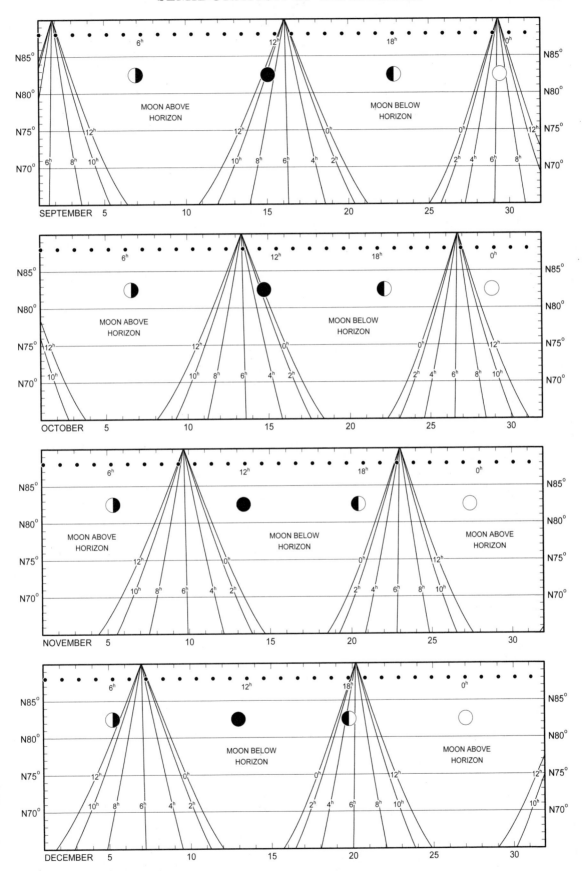

© British Crown Copyright 2022. All rights reserved.

NOTES

© British Crown Copyright 2022. All rights reserved.

CONVERSION OF ARC TO TIME

0°–59°		60°–119°		120°–179°		180°–239°		240°–299°		300°–359°			0′00	0′25	0′50	0′75
°	h m	°	h m	°	h m	°	h m	°	h m	°	h m	′	m s	m s	m s	m s
0	0 00	60	4 00	120	8 00	180	12 00	240	16 00	300	20 00	0	0 00	0 01	0 02	0 03
1	0 04	61	4 04	121	8 04	181	12 04	241	16 04	301	20 04	1	0 04	0 05	0 06	0 07
2	0 08	62	4 08	122	8 08	182	12 08	242	16 08	302	20 08	2	0 08	0 09	0 10	0 11
3	0 12	63	4 12	123	8 12	183	12 12	243	16 12	303	20 12	3	0 12	0 13	0 14	0 15
4	0 16	64	4 16	124	8 16	184	12 16	244	16 16	304	20 16	4	0 16	0 17	0 18	0 19
5	0 20	65	4 20	125	8 20	185	12 20	245	16 20	305	20 20	5	0 20	0 21	0 22	0 23
6	0 24	66	4 24	126	8 24	186	12 24	246	16 24	306	20 24	6	0 24	0 25	0 26	0 27
7	0 28	67	4 28	127	8 28	187	12 28	247	16 28	307	20 28	7	0 28	0 29	0 30	0 31
8	0 32	68	4 32	128	8 32	188	12 32	248	16 32	308	20 32	8	0 32	0 33	0 34	0 35
9	0 36	69	4 36	129	8 36	189	12 36	249	16 36	309	20 36	9	0 36	0 37	0 38	0 39
10	0 40	70	4 40	130	8 40	190	12 40	250	16 40	310	20 40	10	0 40	0 41	0 42	0 43
11	0 44	71	4 44	131	8 44	191	12 44	251	16 44	311	20 44	11	0 44	0 45	0 46	0 47
12	0 48	72	4 48	132	8 48	192	12 48	252	16 48	312	20 48	12	0 48	0 49	0 50	0 51
13	0 52	73	4 52	133	8 52	193	12 52	253	16 52	313	20 52	13	0 52	0 53	0 54	0 55
14	0 56	74	4 56	134	8 56	194	12 56	254	16 56	314	20 56	14	0 56	0 57	0 58	0 59
15	1 00	75	5 00	135	9 00	195	13 00	255	17 00	315	21 00	15	1 00	1 01	1 02	1 03
16	1 04	76	5 04	136	9 04	196	13 04	256	17 04	316	21 04	16	1 04	1 05	1 06	1 07
17	1 08	77	5 08	137	9 08	197	13 08	257	17 08	317	21 08	17	1 08	1 09	1 10	1 11
18	1 12	78	5 12	138	9 12	198	13 12	258	17 12	318	21 12	18	1 12	1 13	1 14	1 15
19	1 16	79	5 16	139	9 16	199	13 16	259	17 16	319	21 16	19	1 16	1 17	1 18	1 19
20	1 20	80	5 20	140	9 20	200	13 20	260	17 20	320	21 20	20	1 20	1 21	1 22	1 23
21	1 24	81	5 24	141	9 24	201	13 24	261	17 24	321	21 24	21	1 24	1 25	1 26	1 27
22	1 28	82	5 28	142	9 28	202	13 28	262	17 28	322	21 28	22	1 28	1 29	1 30	1 31
23	1 32	83	5 32	143	9 32	203	13 32	263	17 32	323	21 32	23	1 32	1 33	1 34	1 35
24	1 36	84	5 36	144	9 36	204	13 36	264	17 36	324	21 36	24	1 36	1 37	1 38	1 39
25	1 40	85	5 40	145	9 40	205	13 40	265	17 40	325	21 40	25	1 40	1 41	1 42	1 43
26	1 44	86	5 44	146	9 44	206	13 44	266	17 44	326	21 44	26	1 44	1 45	1 46	1 47
27	1 48	87	5 48	147	9 48	207	13 48	267	17 48	327	21 48	27	1 48	1 49	1 50	1 51
28	1 52	88	5 52	148	9 52	208	13 52	268	17 52	328	21 52	28	1 52	1 53	1 54	1 55
29	1 56	89	5 56	149	9 56	209	13 56	269	17 56	329	21 56	29	1 56	1 57	1 58	1 59
30	2 00	90	6 00	150	10 00	210	14 00	270	18 00	330	22 00	30	2 00	2 01	2 02	2 03
31	2 04	91	6 04	151	10 04	211	14 04	271	18 04	331	22 04	31	2 04	2 05	2 06	2 07
32	2 08	92	6 08	152	10 08	212	14 08	272	18 08	332	22 08	32	2 08	2 09	2 10	2 11
33	2 12	93	6 12	153	10 12	213	14 12	273	18 12	333	22 12	33	2 12	2 13	2 14	2 15
34	2 16	94	6 16	154	10 16	214	14 16	274	18 16	334	22 16	34	2 16	2 17	2 18	2 19
35	2 20	95	6 20	155	10 20	215	14 20	275	18 20	335	22 20	35	2 20	2 21	2 22	2 23
36	2 24	96	6 24	156	10 24	216	14 24	276	18 24	336	22 24	36	2 24	2 25	2 26	2 27
37	2 28	97	6 28	157	10 28	217	14 28	277	18 28	337	22 28	37	2 28	2 29	2 30	2 31
38	2 32	98	6 32	158	10 32	218	14 32	278	18 32	338	22 32	38	2 32	2 33	2 34	2 35
39	2 36	99	6 36	159	10 36	219	14 36	279	18 36	339	22 36	39	2 36	2 37	2 38	2 39
40	2 40	100	6 40	160	10 40	220	14 40	280	18 40	340	22 40	40	2 40	2 41	2 42	2 43
41	2 44	101	6 44	161	10 44	221	14 44	281	18 44	341	22 44	41	2 44	2 45	2 46	2 47
42	2 48	102	6 48	162	10 48	222	14 48	282	18 48	342	22 48	42	2 48	2 49	2 50	2 51
43	2 52	103	6 52	163	10 52	223	14 52	283	18 52	343	22 52	43	2 52	2 53	2 54	2 55
44	2 56	104	6 56	164	10 56	224	14 56	284	18 56	344	22 56	44	2 56	2 57	2 58	2 59
45	3 00	105	7 00	165	11 00	225	15 00	285	19 00	345	23 00	45	3 00	3 01	3 02	3 03
46	3 04	106	7 04	166	11 04	226	15 04	286	19 04	346	23 04	46	3 04	3 05	3 06	3 07
47	3 08	107	7 08	167	11 08	227	15 08	287	19 08	347	23 08	47	3 08	3 09	3 10	3 11
48	3 12	108	7 12	168	11 12	228	15 12	288	19 12	348	23 12	48	3 12	3 13	3 14	3 15
49	3 16	109	7 16	169	11 16	229	15 16	289	19 16	349	23 16	49	3 16	3 17	3 18	3 19
50	3 20	110	7 20	170	11 20	230	15 20	290	19 20	350	23 20	50	3 20	3 21	3 22	3 23
51	3 24	111	7 24	171	11 24	231	15 24	291	19 24	351	23 24	51	3 24	3 25	3 26	3 27
52	3 28	112	7 28	172	11 28	232	15 28	292	19 28	352	23 28	52	3 28	3 29	3 30	3 31
53	3 32	113	7 32	173	11 32	233	15 32	293	19 32	353	23 32	53	3 32	3 33	3 34	3 35
54	3 36	114	7 36	174	11 36	234	15 36	294	19 36	354	23 36	54	3 36	3 37	3 38	3 39
55	3 40	115	7 40	175	11 40	235	15 40	295	19 40	355	23 40	55	3 40	3 41	3 42	3 43
56	3 44	116	7 44	176	11 44	236	15 44	296	19 44	356	23 44	56	3 44	3 45	3 46	3 47
57	3 48	117	7 48	177	11 48	237	15 48	297	19 48	357	23 48	57	3 48	3 49	3 50	3 51
58	3 52	118	7 52	178	11 52	238	15 52	298	19 52	358	23 52	58	3 52	3 53	3 54	3 55
59	3 56	119	7 56	179	11 56	239	15 56	299	19 56	359	23 56	59	3 56	3 57	3 58	3 59

The above table is for converting expressions in arc to their equivalent in time; its main use in this Almanac is for the conversion of longitude for application to LMT (*added* if *west*, *subtracted* if *east*) to give UT or vice versa, particularly in the case of sunrise, sunset, etc.

i

0ᵐ	SUN PLANETS	ARIES	MOON	v or d Corrⁿ	v or d Corrⁿ	v or d Corrⁿ
s	° ′	° ′	° ′	′ ′	′ ′	′ ′
00	0 00·0	0 00·0	0 00·0	0·0 0·0	6·0 0·1	12·0 0·1
01	0 00·3	0 00·3	0 00·2	0·1 0·0	6·1 0·1	12·1 0·1
02	0 00·5	0 00·5	0 00·5	0·2 0·0	6·2 0·1	12·2 0·1
03	0 00·8	0 00·8	0 00·7	0·3 0·0	6·3 0·1	12·3 0·1
04	0 01·0	0 01·0	0 01·0	0·4 0·0	6·4 0·1	12·4 0·1
05	0 01·3	0 01·3	0 01·2	0·5 0·0	6·5 0·1	12·5 0·1
06	0 01·5	0 01·5	0 01·4	0·6 0·0	6·6 0·1	12·6 0·1
07	0 01·8	0 01·8	0 01·7	0·7 0·0	6·7 0·1	12·7 0·1
08	0 02·0	0 02·0	0 01·9	0·8 0·0	6·8 0·1	12·8 0·1
09	0 02·3	0 02·3	0 02·1	0·9 0·0	6·9 0·1	12·9 0·1
10	0 02·5	0 02·5	0 02·4	1·0 0·0	7·0 0·1	13·0 0·1
11	0 02·8	0 02·8	0 02·6	1·1 0·0	7·1 0·1	13·1 0·1
12	0 03·0	0 03·0	0 02·9	1·2 0·0	7·2 0·1	13·2 0·1
13	0 03·3	0 03·3	0 03·1	1·3 0·0	7·3 0·1	13·3 0·1
14	0 03·5	0 03·5	0 03·3	1·4 0·0	7·4 0·1	13·4 0·1
15	0 03·8	0 03·8	0 03·6	1·5 0·0	7·5 0·1	13·5 0·1
16	0 04·0	0 04·0	0 03·8	1·6 0·0	7·6 0·1	13·6 0·1
17	0 04·3	0 04·3	0 04·1	1·7 0·0	7·7 0·1	13·7 0·1
18	0 04·5	0 04·5	0 04·3	1·8 0·0	7·8 0·1	13·8 0·1
19	0 04·8	0 04·8	0 04·5	1·9 0·0	7·9 0·1	13·9 0·1
20	0 05·0	0 05·0	0 04·8	2·0 0·0	8·0 0·1	14·0 0·1
21	0 05·3	0 05·3	0 05·0	2·1 0·0	8·1 0·1	14·1 0·1
22	0 05·5	0 05·5	0 05·2	2·2 0·0	8·2 0·1	14·2 0·1
23	0 05·8	0 05·8	0 05·5	2·3 0·0	8·3 0·1	14·3 0·1
24	0 06·0	0 06·0	0 05·7	2·4 0·0	8·4 0·1	14·4 0·1
25	0 06·3	0 06·3	0 06·0	2·5 0·0	8·5 0·1	14·5 0·1
26	0 06·5	0 06·5	0 06·2	2·6 0·0	8·6 0·1	14·6 0·1
27	0 06·8	0 06·8	0 06·4	2·7 0·0	8·7 0·1	14·7 0·1
28	0 07·0	0 07·0	0 06·7	2·8 0·0	8·8 0·1	14·8 0·1
29	0 07·3	0 07·3	0 06·9	2·9 0·0	8·9 0·1	14·9 0·1
30	0 07·5	0 07·5	0 07·2	3·0 0·0	9·0 0·1	15·0 0·1
31	0 07·8	0 07·8	0 07·4	3·1 0·0	9·1 0·1	15·1 0·1
32	0 08·0	0 08·0	0 07·6	3·2 0·0	9·2 0·1	15·2 0·1
33	0 08·3	0 08·3	0 07·9	3·3 0·0	9·3 0·1	15·3 0·1
34	0 08·5	0 08·5	0 08·1	3·4 0·0	9·4 0·1	15·4 0·1
35	0 08·8	0 08·8	0 08·4	3·5 0·0	9·5 0·1	15·5 0·1
36	0 09·0	0 09·0	0 08·6	3·6 0·0	9·6 0·1	15·6 0·1
37	0 09·3	0 09·3	0 08·8	3·7 0·0	9·7 0·1	15·7 0·1
38	0 09·5	0 09·5	0 09·1	3·8 0·0	9·8 0·1	15·8 0·1
39	0 09·8	0 09·8	0 09·3	3·9 0·0	9·9 0·1	15·9 0·1
40	0 10·0	0 10·0	0 09·5	4·0 0·0	10·0 0·1	16·0 0·1
41	0 10·3	0 10·3	0 09·8	4·1 0·0	10·1 0·1	16·1 0·1
42	0 10·5	0 10·5	0 10·0	4·2 0·0	10·2 0·1	16·2 0·1
43	0 10·8	0 10·8	0 10·3	4·3 0·0	10·3 0·1	16·3 0·1
44	0 11·0	0 11·0	0 10·5	4·4 0·0	10·4 0·1	16·4 0·1
45	0 11·3	0 11·3	0 10·7	4·5 0·0	10·5 0·1	16·5 0·1
46	0 11·5	0 11·5	0 11·0	4·6 0·0	10·6 0·1	16·6 0·1
47	0 11·8	0 11·8	0 11·2	4·7 0·0	10·7 0·1	16·7 0·1
48	0 12·0	0 12·0	0 11·5	4·8 0·0	10·8 0·1	16·8 0·1
49	0 12·3	0 12·3	0 11·7	4·9 0·0	10·9 0·1	16·9 0·1
50	0 12·5	0 12·5	0 11·9	5·0 0·0	11·0 0·1	17·0 0·1
51	0 12·8	0 12·8	0 12·2	5·1 0·0	11·1 0·1	17·1 0·1
52	0 13·0	0 13·0	0 12·4	5·2 0·0	11·2 0·1	17·2 0·1
53	0 13·3	0 13·3	0 12·6	5·3 0·0	11·3 0·1	17·3 0·1
54	0 13·5	0 13·5	0 12·9	5·4 0·0	11·4 0·1	17·4 0·1
55	0 13·8	0 13·8	0 13·1	5·5 0·0	11·5 0·1	17·5 0·1
56	0 14·0	0 14·0	0 13·4	5·6 0·0	11·6 0·1	17·6 0·1
57	0 14·3	0 14·3	0 13·6	5·7 0·0	11·7 0·1	17·7 0·1
58	0 14·5	0 14·5	0 13·8	5·8 0·0	11·8 0·1	17·8 0·1
59	0 14·8	0 14·8	0 14·1	5·9 0·0	11·9 0·1	17·9 0·1
60	0 15·0	0 15·0	0 14·3	6·0 0·1	12·0 0·1	18·0 0·2

1ᵐ	SUN PLANETS	ARIES	MOON	v or d Corrⁿ	v or d Corrⁿ	v or d Corrⁿ
s	° ′	° ′	° ′	′ ′	′ ′	′ ′
00	0 15·0	0 15·0	0 14·3	0·0 0·0	6·0 0·2	12·0 0·3
01	0 15·3	0 15·3	0 14·6	0·1 0·0	6·1 0·2	12·1 0·3
02	0 15·5	0 15·5	0 14·8	0·2 0·0	6·2 0·2	12·2 0·3
03	0 15·8	0 15·8	0 15·0	0·3 0·0	6·3 0·2	12·3 0·3
04	0 16·0	0 16·0	0 15·3	0·4 0·0	6·4 0·2	12·4 0·3
05	0 16·3	0 16·3	0 15·5	0·5 0·0	6·5 0·2	12·5 0·3
06	0 16·5	0 16·5	0 15·7	0·6 0·0	6·6 0·2	12·6 0·3
07	0 16·8	0 16·8	0 16·0	0·7 0·0	6·7 0·2	12·7 0·3
08	0 17·0	0 17·0	0 16·2	0·8 0·0	6·8 0·2	12·8 0·3
09	0 17·3	0 17·3	0 16·5	0·9 0·0	6·9 0·2	12·9 0·3
10	0 17·5	0 17·5	0 16·7	1·0 0·0	7·0 0·2	13·0 0·3
11	0 17·8	0 17·8	0 16·9	1·1 0·0	7·1 0·2	13·1 0·3
12	0 18·0	0 18·0	0 17·2	1·2 0·0	7·2 0·2	13·2 0·3
13	0 18·3	0 18·3	0 17·4	1·3 0·0	7·3 0·2	13·3 0·3
14	0 18·5	0 18·6	0 17·7	1·4 0·0	7·4 0·2	13·4 0·3
15	0 18·8	0 18·8	0 17·9	1·5 0·0	7·5 0·2	13·5 0·3
16	0 19·0	0 19·1	0 18·1	1·6 0·0	7·6 0·2	13·6 0·3
17	0 19·3	0 19·3	0 18·4	1·7 0·0	7·7 0·2	13·7 0·3
18	0 19·5	0 19·6	0 18·6	1·8 0·0	7·8 0·2	13·8 0·3
19	0 19·8	0 19·8	0 18·9	1·9 0·0	7·9 0·2	13·9 0·3
20	0 20·0	0 20·1	0 19·1	2·0 0·1	8·0 0·2	14·0 0·4
21	0 20·3	0 20·3	0 19·3	2·1 0·1	8·1 0·2	14·1 0·4
22	0 20·5	0 20·6	0 19·6	2·2 0·1	8·2 0·2	14·2 0·4
23	0 20·8	0 20·8	0 19·8	2·3 0·1	8·3 0·2	14·3 0·4
24	0 21·0	0 21·1	0 20·0	2·4 0·1	8·4 0·2	14·4 0·4
25	0 21·3	0 21·3	0 20·3	2·5 0·1	8·5 0·2	14·5 0·4
26	0 21·5	0 21·6	0 20·5	2·6 0·1	8·6 0·2	14·6 0·4
27	0 21·8	0 21·8	0 20·8	2·7 0·1	8·7 0·2	14·7 0·4
28	0 22·0	0 22·1	0 21·0	2·8 0·1	8·8 0·2	14·8 0·4
29	0 22·3	0 22·3	0 21·2	2·9 0·1	8·9 0·2	14·9 0·4
30	0 22·5	0 22·6	0 21·5	3·0 0·1	9·0 0·2	15·0 0·4
31	0 22·8	0 22·8	0 21·7	3·1 0·1	9·1 0·2	15·1 0·4
32	0 23·0	0 23·1	0 22·0	3·2 0·1	9·2 0·2	15·2 0·4
33	0 23·3	0 23·3	0 22·2	3·3 0·1	9·3 0·2	15·3 0·4
34	0 23·5	0 23·6	0 22·4	3·4 0·1	9·4 0·2	15·4 0·4
35	0 23·8	0 23·8	0 22·7	3·5 0·1	9·5 0·2	15·5 0·4
36	0 24·0	0 24·1	0 22·9	3·6 0·1	9·6 0·2	15·6 0·4
37	0 24·3	0 24·3	0 23·1	3·7 0·1	9·7 0·2	15·7 0·4
38	0 24·5	0 24·6	0 23·4	3·8 0·1	9·8 0·2	15·8 0·4
39	0 24·8	0 24·8	0 23·6	3·9 0·1	9·9 0·2	15·9 0·4
40	0 25·0	0 25·1	0 23·9	4·0 0·1	10·0 0·3	16·0 0·4
41	0 25·3	0 25·3	0 24·1	4·1 0·1	10·1 0·3	16·1 0·4
42	0 25·5	0 25·6	0 24·3	4·2 0·1	10·2 0·3	16·2 0·4
43	0 25·8	0 25·8	0 24·6	4·3 0·1	10·3 0·3	16·3 0·4
44	0 26·0	0 26·1	0 24·8	4·4 0·1	10·4 0·3	16·4 0·4
45	0 26·3	0 26·3	0 25·1	4·5 0·1	10·5 0·3	16·5 0·4
46	0 26·5	0 26·6	0 25·3	4·6 0·1	10·6 0·3	16·6 0·4
47	0 26·8	0 26·8	0 25·5	4·7 0·1	10·7 0·3	16·7 0·4
48	0 27·0	0 27·1	0 25·8	4·8 0·1	10·8 0·3	16·8 0·4
49	0 27·3	0 27·3	0 26·0	4·9 0·1	10·9 0·3	16·9 0·4
50	0 27·5	0 27·6	0 26·2	5·0 0·1	11·0 0·3	17·0 0·4
51	0 27·8	0 27·8	0 26·5	5·1 0·1	11·1 0·3	17·1 0·4
52	0 28·0	0 28·1	0 26·7	5·2 0·1	11·2 0·3	17·2 0·4
53	0 28·3	0 28·3	0 27·0	5·3 0·1	11·3 0·3	17·3 0·4
54	0 28·5	0 28·6	0 27·2	5·4 0·1	11·4 0·3	17·4 0·4
55	0 28·8	0 28·8	0 27·4	5·5 0·1	11·5 0·3	17·5 0·4
56	0 29·0	0 29·1	0 27·7	5·6 0·1	11·6 0·3	17·6 0·4
57	0 29·3	0 29·3	0 27·9	5·7 0·1	11·7 0·3	17·7 0·4
58	0 29·5	0 29·6	0 28·2	5·8 0·1	11·8 0·3	17·8 0·4
59	0 29·8	0 29·8	0 28·4	5·9 0·1	11·9 0·3	17·9 0·4
60	0 30·0	0 30·1	0 28·6	6·0 0·2	12·0 0·3	18·0 0·5

m 2	SUN PLANETS	ARIES	MOON	v or Corrⁿ d		v or Corrⁿ d		v or Corrⁿ d	
s	° ′	° ′	° ′	′	′	′	′	′	′
00	0 30.0	0 30.1	0 28.6	0.0	0.0	6.0	0.3	12.0	0.5
01	0 30.3	0 30.3	0 28.9	0.1	0.0	6.1	0.3	12.1	0.5
02	0 30.5	0 30.6	0 29.1	0.2	0.0	6.2	0.3	12.2	0.5
03	0 30.8	0 30.8	0 29.3	0.3	0.0	6.3	0.3	12.3	0.5
04	0 31.0	0 31.1	0 29.6	0.4	0.0	6.4	0.3	12.4	0.5
05	0 31.3	0 31.3	0 29.8	0.5	0.0	6.5	0.3	12.5	0.5
06	0 31.5	0 31.6	0 30.1	0.6	0.0	6.6	0.3	12.6	0.5
07	0 31.8	0 31.8	0 30.3	0.7	0.0	6.7	0.3	12.7	0.5
08	0 32.0	0 32.1	0 30.5	0.8	0.0	6.8	0.3	12.8	0.5
09	0 32.3	0 32.3	0 30.8	0.9	0.0	6.9	0.3	12.9	0.5
10	0 32.5	0 32.6	0 31.0	1.0	0.0	7.0	0.3	13.0	0.5
11	0 32.8	0 32.8	0 31.3	1.1	0.0	7.1	0.3	13.1	0.5
12	0 33.0	0 33.1	0 31.5	1.2	0.1	7.2	0.3	13.2	0.6
13	0 33.3	0 33.3	0 31.7	1.3	0.1	7.3	0.3	13.3	0.6
14	0 33.5	0 33.6	0 32.0	1.4	0.1	7.4	0.3	13.4	0.6
15	0 33.8	0 33.8	0 32.2	1.5	0.1	7.5	0.3	13.5	0.6
16	0 34.0	0 34.1	0 32.5	1.6	0.1	7.6	0.3	13.6	0.6
17	0 34.3	0 34.3	0 32.7	1.7	0.1	7.7	0.3	13.7	0.6
18	0 34.5	0 34.6	0 32.9	1.8	0.1	7.8	0.3	13.8	0.6
19	0 34.8	0 34.8	0 33.2	1.9	0.1	7.9	0.3	13.9	0.6
20	0 35.0	0 35.1	0 33.4	2.0	0.1	8.0	0.3	14.0	0.6
21	0 35.3	0 35.3	0 33.6	2.1	0.1	8.1	0.3	14.1	0.6
22	0 35.5	0 35.6	0 33.9	2.2	0.1	8.2	0.3	14.2	0.6
23	0 35.8	0 35.8	0 34.1	2.3	0.1	8.3	0.3	14.3	0.6
24	0 36.0	0 36.1	0 34.4	2.4	0.1	8.4	0.4	14.4	0.6
25	0 36.3	0 36.3	0 34.6	2.5	0.1	8.5	0.4	14.5	0.6
26	0 36.5	0 36.6	0 34.8	2.6	0.1	8.6	0.4	14.6	0.6
27	0 36.8	0 36.9	0 35.1	2.7	0.1	8.7	0.4	14.7	0.6
28	0 37.0	0 37.1	0 35.3	2.8	0.1	8.8	0.4	14.8	0.6
29	0 37.3	0 37.4	0 35.6	2.9	0.1	8.9	0.4	14.9	0.6
30	0 37.5	0 37.6	0 35.8	3.0	0.1	9.0	0.4	15.0	0.6
31	0 37.8	0 37.9	0 36.0	3.1	0.1	9.1	0.4	15.1	0.6
32	0 38.0	0 38.1	0 36.3	3.2	0.1	9.2	0.4	15.2	0.6
33	0 38.3	0 38.4	0 36.5	3.3	0.1	9.3	0.4	15.3	0.6
34	0 38.5	0 38.6	0 36.7	3.4	0.1	9.4	0.4	15.4	0.6
35	0 38.8	0 38.9	0 37.0	3.5	0.1	9.5	0.4	15.5	0.6
36	0 39.0	0 39.1	0 37.2	3.6	0.2	9.6	0.4	15.6	0.7
37	0 39.3	0 39.4	0 37.5	3.7	0.2	9.7	0.4	15.7	0.7
38	0 39.5	0 39.6	0 37.7	3.8	0.2	9.8	0.4	15.8	0.7
39	0 39.8	0 39.9	0 37.9	3.9	0.2	9.9	0.4	15.9	0.7
40	0 40.0	0 40.1	0 38.2	4.0	0.2	10.0	0.4	16.0	0.7
41	0 40.3	0 40.4	0 38.4	4.1	0.2	10.1	0.4	16.1	0.7
42	0 40.5	0 40.6	0 38.7	4.2	0.2	10.2	0.4	16.2	0.7
43	0 40.8	0 40.9	0 38.9	4.3	0.2	10.3	0.4	16.3	0.7
44	0 41.0	0 41.1	0 39.1	4.4	0.2	10.4	0.4	16.4	0.7
45	0 41.3	0 41.4	0 39.4	4.5	0.2	10.5	0.4	16.5	0.7
46	0 41.5	0 41.6	0 39.6	4.6	0.2	10.6	0.4	16.6	0.7
47	0 41.8	0 41.9	0 39.8	4.7	0.2	10.7	0.4	16.7	0.7
48	0 42.0	0 42.1	0 40.1	4.8	0.2	10.8	0.5	16.8	0.7
49	0 42.3	0 42.4	0 40.3	4.9	0.2	10.9	0.5	16.9	0.7
50	0 42.5	0 42.6	0 40.6	5.0	0.2	11.0	0.5	17.0	0.7
51	0 42.8	0 42.9	0 40.8	5.1	0.2	11.1	0.5	17.1	0.7
52	0 43.0	0 43.1	0 41.0	5.2	0.2	11.2	0.5	17.2	0.7
53	0 43.3	0 43.4	0 41.3	5.3	0.2	11.3	0.5	17.3	0.7
54	0 43.5	0 43.6	0 41.5	5.4	0.2	11.4	0.5	17.4	0.7
55	0 43.8	0 43.9	0 41.8	5.5	0.2	11.5	0.5	17.5	0.7
56	0 44.0	0 44.1	0 42.0	5.6	0.2	11.6	0.5	17.6	0.7
57	0 44.3	0 44.4	0 42.2	5.7	0.2	11.7	0.5	17.7	0.7
58	0 44.5	0 44.6	0 42.5	5.8	0.2	11.8	0.5	17.8	0.7
59	0 44.8	0 44.9	0 42.7	5.9	0.2	11.9	0.5	17.9	0.7
60	0 45.0	0 45.1	0 43.0	6.0	0.3	12.0	0.5	18.0	0.8

m 3	SUN PLANETS	ARIES	MOON	v or Corrⁿ d		v or Corrⁿ d		v or Corrⁿ d	
s	° ′	° ′	° ′	′	′	′	′	′	′
00	0 45.0	0 45.1	0 43.0	0.0	0.0	6.0	0.4	12.0	0.7
01	0 45.3	0 45.4	0 43.2	0.1	0.0	6.1	0.4	12.1	0.7
02	0 45.5	0 45.6	0 43.4	0.2	0.0	6.2	0.4	12.2	0.7
03	0 45.8	0 45.9	0 43.7	0.3	0.0	6.3	0.4	12.3	0.7
04	0 46.0	0 46.1	0 43.9	0.4	0.0	6.4	0.4	12.4	0.7
05	0 46.3	0 46.4	0 44.1	0.5	0.0	6.5	0.4	12.5	0.7
06	0 46.5	0 46.6	0 44.4	0.6	0.0	6.6	0.4	12.6	0.7
07	0 46.8	0 46.9	0 44.6	0.7	0.0	6.7	0.4	12.7	0.7
08	0 47.0	0 47.1	0 44.9	0.8	0.0	6.8	0.4	12.8	0.7
09	0 47.3	0 47.4	0 45.1	0.9	0.1	6.9	0.4	12.9	0.8
10	0 47.5	0 47.6	0 45.3	1.0	0.1	7.0	0.4	13.0	0.8
11	0 47.8	0 47.9	0 45.6	1.1	0.1	7.1	0.4	13.1	0.8
12	0 48.0	0 48.1	0 45.8	1.2	0.1	7.2	0.4	13.2	0.8
13	0 48.3	0 48.4	0 46.1	1.3	0.1	7.3	0.4	13.3	0.8
14	0 48.5	0 48.6	0 46.3	1.4	0.1	7.4	0.4	13.4	0.8
15	0 48.8	0 48.9	0 46.5	1.5	0.1	7.5	0.4	13.5	0.8
16	0 49.0	0 49.1	0 46.8	1.6	0.1	7.6	0.4	13.6	0.8
17	0 49.3	0 49.4	0 47.0	1.7	0.1	7.7	0.4	13.7	0.8
18	0 49.5	0 49.6	0 47.2	1.8	0.1	7.8	0.5	13.8	0.8
19	0 49.8	0 49.9	0 47.5	1.9	0.1	7.9	0.5	13.9	0.8
20	0 50.0	0 50.1	0 47.7	2.0	0.1	8.0	0.5	14.0	0.8
21	0 50.3	0 50.4	0 48.0	2.1	0.1	8.1	0.5	14.1	0.8
22	0 50.5	0 50.6	0 48.2	2.2	0.1	8.2	0.5	14.2	0.8
23	0 50.8	0 50.9	0 48.4	2.3	0.1	8.3	0.5	14.3	0.8
24	0 51.0	0 51.1	0 48.7	2.4	0.1	8.4	0.5	14.4	0.8
25	0 51.3	0 51.4	0 48.9	2.5	0.1	8.5	0.5	14.5	0.8
26	0 51.5	0 51.6	0 49.2	2.6	0.2	8.6	0.5	14.6	0.9
27	0 51.8	0 51.9	0 49.4	2.7	0.2	8.7	0.5	14.7	0.9
28	0 52.0	0 52.1	0 49.6	2.8	0.2	8.8	0.5	14.8	0.9
29	0 52.3	0 52.4	0 49.9	2.9	0.2	8.9	0.5	14.9	0.9
30	0 52.5	0 52.6	0 50.1	3.0	0.2	9.0	0.5	15.0	0.9
31	0 52.8	0 52.9	0 50.3	3.1	0.2	9.1	0.5	15.1	0.9
32	0 53.0	0 53.1	0 50.6	3.2	0.2	9.2	0.5	15.2	0.9
33	0 53.3	0 53.4	0 50.8	3.3	0.2	9.3	0.5	15.3	0.9
34	0 53.5	0 53.6	0 51.1	3.4	0.2	9.4	0.5	15.4	0.9
35	0 53.8	0 53.9	0 51.3	3.5	0.2	9.5	0.6	15.5	0.9
36	0 54.0	0 54.1	0 51.5	3.6	0.2	9.6	0.6	15.6	0.9
37	0 54.3	0 54.4	0 51.8	3.7	0.2	9.7	0.6	15.7	0.9
38	0 54.5	0 54.6	0 52.0	3.8	0.2	9.8	0.6	15.8	0.9
39	0 54.8	0 54.9	0 52.3	3.9	0.2	9.9	0.6	15.9	0.9
40	0 55.0	0 55.2	0 52.5	4.0	0.2	10.0	0.6	16.0	0.9
41	0 55.3	0 55.4	0 52.7	4.1	0.2	10.1	0.6	16.1	0.9
42	0 55.5	0 55.7	0 53.0	4.2	0.2	10.2	0.6	16.2	0.9
43	0 55.8	0 55.9	0 53.2	4.3	0.3	10.3	0.6	16.3	1.0
44	0 56.0	0 56.2	0 53.4	4.4	0.3	10.4	0.6	16.4	1.0
45	0 56.3	0 56.4	0 53.7	4.5	0.3	10.5	0.6	16.5	1.0
46	0 56.5	0 56.7	0 53.9	4.6	0.3	10.6	0.6	16.6	1.0
47	0 56.8	0 56.9	0 54.2	4.7	0.3	10.7	0.6	16.7	1.0
48	0 57.0	0 57.2	0 54.4	4.8	0.3	10.8	0.6	16.8	1.0
49	0 57.3	0 57.4	0 54.6	4.9	0.3	10.9	0.6	16.9	1.0
50	0 57.5	0 57.7	0 54.9	5.0	0.3	11.0	0.6	17.0	1.0
51	0 57.8	0 57.9	0 55.1	5.1	0.3	11.1	0.6	17.1	1.0
52	0 58.0	0 58.2	0 55.4	5.2	0.3	11.2	0.7	17.2	1.0
53	0 58.3	0 58.4	0 55.6	5.3	0.3	11.3	0.7	17.3	1.0
54	0 58.5	0 58.7	0 55.8	5.4	0.3	11.4	0.7	17.4	1.0
55	0 58.8	0 58.9	0 56.1	5.5	0.3	11.5	0.7	17.5	1.0
56	0 59.0	0 59.2	0 56.3	5.6	0.3	11.6	0.7	17.6	1.0
57	0 59.3	0 59.4	0 56.6	5.7	0.3	11.7	0.7	17.7	1.0
58	0 59.5	0 59.7	0 56.8	5.8	0.3	11.8	0.7	17.8	1.0
59	0 59.8	0 59.9	0 57.0	5.9	0.3	11.9	0.7	17.9	1.0
60	1 00.0	1 00.2	0 57.3	6.0	0.4	12.0	0.7	18.0	1.1

4 m	SUN PLANETS	ARIES	MOON	v or d Corr^n	v or d Corr^n	v or d Corr^n
s	° ′	° ′	° ′	′ ′	′ ′	′ ′
00	1 00·0	1 00·2	0 57·3	0·0 0·0	6·0 0·5	12·0 0·9
01	1 00·3	1 00·4	0 57·5	0·1 0·0	6·1 0·5	12·1 0·9
02	1 00·5	1 00·7	0 57·7	0·2 0·0	6·2 0·5	12·2 0·9
03	1 00·8	1 00·9	0 58·0	0·3 0·0	6·3 0·5	12·3 0·9
04	1 01·0	1 01·2	0 58·2	0·4 0·0	6·4 0·5	12·4 0·9
05	1 01·3	1 01·4	0 58·5	0·5 0·0	6·5 0·5	12·5 0·9
06	1 01·5	1 01·7	0 58·7	0·6 0·0	6·6 0·5	12·6 0·9
07	1 01·8	1 01·9	0 58·9	0·7 0·1	6·7 0·5	12·7 1·0
08	1 02·0	1 02·2	0 59·2	0·8 0·1	6·8 0·5	12·8 1·0
09	1 02·3	1 02·4	0 59·4	0·9 0·1	6·9 0·5	12·9 1·0
10	1 02·5	1 02·7	0 59·7	1·0 0·1	7·0 0·5	13·0 1·0
11	1 02·8	1 02·9	0 59·9	1·1 0·1	7·1 0·5	13·1 1·0
12	1 03·0	1 03·2	1 00·1	1·2 0·1	7·2 0·5	13·2 1·0
13	1 03·3	1 03·4	1 00·4	1·3 0·1	7·3 0·5	13·3 1·0
14	1 03·5	1 03·7	1 00·6	1·4 0·1	7·4 0·6	13·4 1·0
15	1 03·8	1 03·9	1 00·8	1·5 0·1	7·5 0·6	13·5 1·0
16	1 04·0	1 04·2	1 01·1	1·6 0·1	7·6 0·6	13·6 1·0
17	1 04·3	1 04·4	1 01·3	1·7 0·1	7·7 0·6	13·7 1·0
18	1 04·5	1 04·7	1 01·6	1·8 0·1	7·8 0·6	13·8 1·0
19	1 04·8	1 04·9	1 01·8	1·9 0·1	7·9 0·6	13·9 1·0
20	1 05·0	1 05·2	1 02·0	2·0 0·2	8·0 0·6	14·0 1·1
21	1 05·3	1 05·4	1 02·3	2·1 0·2	8·1 0·6	14·1 1·1
22	1 05·5	1 05·7	1 02·5	2·2 0·2	8·2 0·6	14·2 1·1
23	1 05·8	1 05·9	1 02·8	2·3 0·2	8·3 0·6	14·3 1·1
24	1 06·0	1 06·2	1 03·0	2·4 0·2	8·4 0·6	14·4 1·1
25	1 06·3	1 06·4	1 03·2	2·5 0·2	8·5 0·6	14·5 1·1
26	1 06·5	1 06·7	1 03·5	2·6 0·2	8·6 0·6	14·6 1·1
27	1 06·8	1 06·9	1 03·7	2·7 0·2	8·7 0·7	14·7 1·1
28	1 07·0	1 07·2	1 03·9	2·8 0·2	8·8 0·7	14·8 1·1
29	1 07·3	1 07·4	1 04·2	2·9 0·2	8·9 0·7	14·9 1·1
30	1 07·5	1 07·7	1 04·4	3·0 0·2	9·0 0·7	15·0 1·1
31	1 07·8	1 07·9	1 04·7	3·1 0·2	9·1 0·7	15·1 1·1
32	1 08·0	1 08·2	1 04·9	3·2 0·2	9·2 0·7	15·2 1·1
33	1 08·3	1 08·4	1 05·1	3·3 0·2	9·3 0·7	15·3 1·1
34	1 08·5	1 08·7	1 05·4	3·4 0·3	9·4 0·7	15·4 1·2
35	1 08·8	1 08·9	1 05·6	3·5 0·3	9·5 0·7	15·5 1·2
36	1 09·0	1 09·2	1 05·9	3·6 0·3	9·6 0·7	15·6 1·2
37	1 09·3	1 09·4	1 06·1	3·7 0·3	9·7 0·7	15·7 1·2
38	1 09·5	1 09·7	1 06·3	3·8 0·3	9·8 0·7	15·8 1·2
39	1 09·8	1 09·9	1 06·6	3·9 0·3	9·9 0·7	15·9 1·2
40	1 10·0	1 10·2	1 06·8	4·0 0·3	10·0 0·8	16·0 1·2
41	1 10·3	1 10·4	1 07·0	4·1 0·3	10·1 0·8	16·1 1·2
42	1 10·5	1 10·7	1 07·3	4·2 0·3	10·2 0·8	16·2 1·2
43	1 10·8	1 10·9	1 07·5	4·3 0·3	10·3 0·8	16·3 1·2
44	1 11·0	1 11·2	1 07·8	4·4 0·3	10·4 0·8	16·4 1·2
45	1 11·3	1 11·4	1 08·0	4·5 0·3	10·5 0·8	16·5 1·2
46	1 11·5	1 11·7	1 08·2	4·6 0·3	10·6 0·8	16·6 1·2
47	1 11·8	1 11·9	1 08·5	4·7 0·4	10·7 0·8	16·7 1·3
48	1 12·0	1 12·2	1 08·7	4·8 0·4	10·8 0·8	16·8 1·3
49	1 12·3	1 12·4	1 09·0	4·9 0·4	10·9 0·8	16·9 1·3
50	1 12·5	1 12·7	1 09·2	5·0 0·4	11·0 0·8	17·0 1·3
51	1 12·8	1 12·9	1 09·4	5·1 0·4	11·1 0·8	17·1 1·3
52	1 13·0	1 13·2	1 09·7	5·2 0·4	11·2 0·8	17·2 1·3
53	1 13·3	1 13·5	1 09·9	5·3 0·4	11·3 0·8	17·3 1·3
54	1 13·5	1 13·7	1 10·2	5·4 0·4	11·4 0·9	17·4 1·3
55	1 13·8	1 14·0	1 10·4	5·5 0·4	11·5 0·9	17·5 1·3
56	1 14·0	1 14·2	1 10·6	5·6 0·4	11·6 0·9	17·6 1·3
57	1 14·3	1 14·5	1 10·9	5·7 0·4	11·7 0·9	17·7 1·3
58	1 14·5	1 14·7	1 11·1	5·8 0·4	11·8 0·9	17·8 1·3
59	1 14·8	1 15·0	1 11·3	5·9 0·4	11·9 0·9	17·9 1·3
60	1 15·0	1 15·2	1 11·6	6·0 0·5	12·0 0·9	18·0 1·4

5 m	SUN PLANETS	ARIES	MOON	v or d Corr^n	v or d Corr^n	v or d Corr^n
s	° ′	° ′	° ′	′ ′	′ ′	′ ′
00	1 15·0	1 15·2	1 11·6	0·0 0·0	6·0 0·6	12·0 1·1
01	1 15·3	1 15·5	1 11·8	0·1 0·0	6·1 0·6	12·1 1·1
02	1 15·5	1 15·7	1 12·1	0·2 0·0	6·2 0·6	12·2 1·1
03	1 15·8	1 16·0	1 12·3	0·3 0·0	6·3 0·6	12·3 1·1
04	1 16·0	1 16·2	1 12·5	0·4 0·0	6·4 0·6	12·4 1·1
05	1 16·3	1 16·5	1 12·8	0·5 0·0	6·5 0·6	12·5 1·1
06	1 16·5	1 16·7	1 13·0	0·6 0·1	6·6 0·6	12·6 1·2
07	1 16·8	1 17·0	1 13·3	0·7 0·1	6·7 0·6	12·7 1·2
08	1 17·0	1 17·2	1 13·5	0·8 0·1	6·8 0·6	12·8 1·2
09	1 17·3	1 17·5	1 13·7	0·9 0·1	6·9 0·6	12·9 1·2
10	1 17·5	1 17·7	1 14·0	1·0 0·1	7·0 0·6	13·0 1·2
11	1 17·8	1 18·0	1 14·2	1·1 0·1	7·1 0·7	13·1 1·2
12	1 18·0	1 18·2	1 14·4	1·2 0·1	7·2 0·7	13·2 1·2
13	1 18·3	1 18·5	1 14·7	1·3 0·1	7·3 0·7	13·3 1·2
14	1 18·5	1 18·7	1 14·9	1·4 0·1	7·4 0·7	13·4 1·2
15	1 18·8	1 19·0	1 15·2	1·5 0·1	7·5 0·7	13·5 1·2
16	1 19·0	1 19·2	1 15·4	1·6 0·1	7·6 0·7	13·6 1·2
17	1 19·3	1 19·5	1 15·6	1·7 0·2	7·7 0·7	13·7 1·3
18	1 19·5	1 19·7	1 15·9	1·8 0·2	7·8 0·7	13·8 1·3
19	1 19·8	1 20·0	1 16·1	1·9 0·2	7·9 0·7	13·9 1·3
20	1 20·0	1 20·2	1 16·4	2·0 0·2	8·0 0·7	14·0 1·3
21	1 20·3	1 20·5	1 16·6	2·1 0·2	8·1 0·7	14·1 1·3
22	1 20·5	1 20·7	1 16·8	2·2 0·2	8·2 0·8	14·2 1·3
23	1 20·8	1 21·0	1 17·1	2·3 0·2	8·3 0·8	14·3 1·3
24	1 21·0	1 21·2	1 17·3	2·4 0·2	8·4 0·8	14·4 1·3
25	1 21·3	1 21·5	1 17·5	2·5 0·2	8·5 0·8	14·5 1·3
26	1 21·5	1 21·7	1 17·8	2·6 0·2	8·6 0·8	14·6 1·3
27	1 21·8	1 22·0	1 18·0	2·7 0·2	8·7 0·8	14·7 1·3
28	1 22·0	1 22·2	1 18·3	2·8 0·3	8·8 0·8	14·8 1·4
29	1 22·3	1 22·5	1 18·5	2·9 0·3	8·9 0·8	14·9 1·4
30	1 22·5	1 22·7	1 18·7	3·0 0·3	9·0 0·8	15·0 1·4
31	1 22·8	1 23·0	1 19·0	3·1 0·3	9·1 0·8	15·1 1·4
32	1 23·0	1 23·2	1 19·2	3·2 0·3	9·2 0·8	15·2 1·4
33	1 23·3	1 23·5	1 19·5	3·3 0·3	9·3 0·9	15·3 1·4
34	1 23·5	1 23·7	1 19·7	3·4 0·3	9·4 0·9	15·4 1·4
35	1 23·8	1 24·0	1 19·9	3·5 0·3	9·5 0·9	15·5 1·4
36	1 24·0	1 24·2	1 20·2	3·6 0·3	9·6 0·9	15·6 1·4
37	1 24·3	1 24·5	1 20·4	3·7 0·3	9·7 0·9	15·7 1·4
38	1 24·5	1 24·7	1 20·7	3·8 0·3	9·8 0·9	15·8 1·4
39	1 24·8	1 25·0	1 20·9	3·9 0·4	9·9 0·9	15·9 1·5
40	1 25·0	1 25·2	1 21·1	4·0 0·4	10·0 0·9	16·0 1·5
41	1 25·3	1 25·5	1 21·4	4·1 0·4	10·1 0·9	16·1 1·5
42	1 25·5	1 25·7	1 21·6	4·2 0·4	10·2 0·9	16·2 1·5
43	1 25·8	1 26·0	1 21·8	4·3 0·4	10·3 0·9	16·3 1·5
44	1 26·0	1 26·2	1 22·1	4·4 0·4	10·4 1·0	16·4 1·5
45	1 26·3	1 26·5	1 22·3	4·5 0·4	10·5 1·0	16·5 1·5
46	1 26·5	1 26·7	1 22·6	4·6 0·4	10·6 1·0	16·6 1·5
47	1 26·8	1 27·0	1 22·8	4·7 0·4	10·7 1·0	16·7 1·5
48	1 27·0	1 27·2	1 23·0	4·8 0·4	10·8 1·0	16·8 1·5
49	1 27·3	1 27·5	1 23·3	4·9 0·4	10·9 1·0	16·9 1·5
50	1 27·5	1 27·7	1 23·5	5·0 0·5	11·0 1·0	17·0 1·6
51	1 27·8	1 28·0	1 23·8	5·1 0·5	11·1 1·0	17·1 1·6
52	1 28·0	1 28·2	1 24·0	5·2 0·5	11·2 1·0	17·2 1·6
53	1 28·3	1 28·5	1 24·2	5·3 0·5	11·3 1·0	17·3 1·6
54	1 28·5	1 28·7	1 24·5	5·4 0·5	11·4 1·0	17·4 1·6
55	1 28·8	1 29·0	1 24·7	5·5 0·5	11·5 1·1	17·5 1·6
56	1 29·0	1 29·2	1 24·9	5·6 0·5	11·6 1·1	17·6 1·6
57	1 29·3	1 29·5	1 25·2	5·7 0·5	11·7 1·1	17·7 1·6
58	1 29·5	1 29·7	1 25·4	5·8 0·5	11·8 1·1	17·8 1·6
59	1 29·8	1 30·0	1 25·7	5·9 0·5	11·9 1·1	17·9 1·6
60	1 30·0	1 30·2	1 25·9	6·0 0·6	12·0 1·1	18·0 1·7

m 6	SUN PLANETS	ARIES	MOON	v or Corrⁿ d		v or Corrⁿ d		v or Corrⁿ d	
s	° ′	° ′	° ′	′	′	′	′	′	′
00	1 30·0	1 30·2	1 25·9	0·0	0·0	6·0	0·7	12·0	1·3
01	1 30·3	1 30·5	1 26·1	0·1	0·0	6·1	0·7	12·1	1·3
02	1 30·5	1 30·7	1 26·4	0·2	0·0	6·2	0·7	12·2	1·3
03	1 30·8	1 31·0	1 26·6	0·3	0·0	6·3	0·7	12·3	1·3
04	1 31·0	1 31·2	1 26·9	0·4	0·0	6·4	0·7	12·4	1·3
05	1 31·3	1 31·5	1 27·1	0·5	0·1	6·5	0·7	12·5	1·4
06	1 31·5	1 31·8	1 27·3	0·6	0·1	6·6	0·7	12·6	1·4
07	1 31·8	1 32·0	1 27·6	0·7	0·1	6·7	0·7	12·7	1·4
08	1 32·0	1 32·3	1 27·8	0·8	0·1	6·8	0·7	12·8	1·4
09	1 32·3	1 32·5	1 28·0	0·9	0·1	6·9	0·7	12·9	1·4
10	1 32·5	1 32·8	1 28·3	1·0	0·1	7·0	0·8	13·0	1·4
11	1 32·8	1 33·0	1 28·5	1·1	0·1	7·1	0·8	13·1	1·4
12	1 33·0	1 33·3	1 28·8	1·2	0·1	7·2	0·8	13·2	1·4
13	1 33·3	1 33·5	1 29·0	1·3	0·1	7·3	0·8	13·3	1·4
14	1 33·5	1 33·8	1 29·2	1·4	0·2	7·4	0·8	13·4	1·5
15	1 33·8	1 34·0	1 29·5	1·5	0·2	7·5	0·8	13·5	1·5
16	1 34·0	1 34·3	1 29·7	1·6	0·2	7·6	0·8	13·6	1·5
17	1 34·3	1 34·5	1 30·0	1·7	0·2	7·7	0·8	13·7	1·5
18	1 34·5	1 34·8	1 30·2	1·8	0·2	7·8	0·8	13·8	1·5
19	1 34·8	1 35·0	1 30·4	1·9	0·2	7·9	0·9	13·9	1·5
20	1 35·0	1 35·3	1 30·7	2·0	0·2	8·0	0·9	14·0	1·5
21	1 35·3	1 35·5	1 30·9	2·1	0·2	8·1	0·9	14·1	1·5
22	1 35·5	1 35·8	1 31·1	2·2	0·2	8·2	0·9	14·2	1·5
23	1 35·8	1 36·0	1 31·4	2·3	0·2	8·3	0·9	14·3	1·5
24	1 36·0	1 36·3	1 31·6	2·4	0·3	8·4	0·9	14·4	1·6
25	1 36·3	1 36·5	1 31·9	2·5	0·3	8·5	0·9	14·5	1·6
26	1 36·5	1 36·8	1 32·1	2·6	0·3	8·6	0·9	14·6	1·6
27	1 36·8	1 37·0	1 32·3	2·7	0·3	8·7	0·9	14·7	1·6
28	1 37·0	1 37·3	1 32·6	2·8	0·3	8·8	1·0	14·8	1·6
29	1 37·3	1 37·5	1 32·8	2·9	0·3	8·9	1·0	14·9	1·6
30	1 37·5	1 37·8	1 33·1	3·0	0·3	9·0	1·0	15·0	1·6
31	1 37·8	1 38·0	1 33·3	3·1	0·3	9·1	1·0	15·1	1·6
32	1 38·0	1 38·3	1 33·5	3·2	0·3	9·2	1·0	15·2	1·6
33	1 38·3	1 38·5	1 33·8	3·3	0·4	9·3	1·0	15·3	1·7
34	1 38·5	1 38·8	1 34·0	3·4	0·4	9·4	1·0	15·4	1·7
35	1 38·8	1 39·0	1 34·3	3·5	0·4	9·5	1·0	15·5	1·7
36	1 39·0	1 39·3	1 34·5	3·6	0·4	9·6	1·0	15·6	1·7
37	1 39·3	1 39·5	1 34·7	3·7	0·4	9·7	1·1	15·7	1·7
38	1 39·5	1 39·8	1 35·0	3·8	0·4	9·8	1·1	15·8	1·7
39	1 39·8	1 40·0	1 35·2	3·9	0·4	9·9	1·1	15·9	1·7
40	1 40·0	1 40·3	1 35·4	4·0	0·4	10·0	1·1	16·0	1·7
41	1 40·3	1 40·5	1 35·7	4·1	0·4	10·1	1·1	16·1	1·7
42	1 40·5	1 40·8	1 35·9	4·2	0·5	10·2	1·1	16·2	1·8
43	1 40·8	1 41·0	1 36·2	4·3	0·5	10·3	1·1	16·3	1·8
44	1 41·0	1 41·3	1 36·4	4·4	0·5	10·4	1·1	16·4	1·8
45	1 41·3	1 41·5	1 36·6	4·5	0·5	10·5	1·1	16·5	1·8
46	1 41·5	1 41·8	1 36·9	4·6	0·5	10·6	1·1	16·6	1·8
47	1 41·8	1 42·0	1 37·1	4·7	0·5	10·7	1·2	16·7	1·8
48	1 42·0	1 42·3	1 37·4	4·8	0·5	10·8	1·2	16·8	1·8
49	1 42·3	1 42·5	1 37·6	4·9	0·5	10·9	1·2	16·9	1·8
50	1 42·5	1 42·8	1 37·8	5·0	0·5	11·0	1·2	17·0	1·8
51	1 42·8	1 43·0	1 38·1	5·1	0·6	11·1	1·2	17·1	1·9
52	1 43·0	1 43·3	1 38·3	5·2	0·6	11·2	1·2	17·2	1·9
53	1 43·3	1 43·5	1 38·5	5·3	0·6	11·3	1·2	17·3	1·9
54	1 43·5	1 43·8	1 38·8	5·4	0·6	11·4	1·2	17·4	1·9
55	1 43·8	1 44·0	1 39·0	5·5	0·6	11·5	1·2	17·5	1·9
56	1 44·0	1 44·3	1 39·3	5·6	0·6	11·6	1·3	17·6	1·9
57	1 44·3	1 44·5	1 39·5	5·7	0·6	11·7	1·3	17·7	1·9
58	1 44·5	1 44·8	1 39·7	5·8	0·6	11·8	1·3	17·8	1·9
59	1 44·8	1 45·0	1 40·0	5·9	0·6	11·9	1·3	17·9	1·9
60	1 45·0	1 45·3	1 40·2	6·0	0·7	12·0	1·3	18·0	2·0

m 7	SUN PLANETS	ARIES	MOON	v or Corrⁿ d		v or Corrⁿ d		v or Corrⁿ d	
s	° ′	° ′	° ′	′	′	′	′	′	′
00	1 45·0	1 45·3	1 40·2	0·0	0·0	6·0	0·8	12·0	1·5
01	1 45·3	1 45·5	1 40·5	0·1	0·0	6·1	0·8	12·1	1·5
02	1 45·5	1 45·8	1 40·7	0·2	0·0	6·2	0·8	12·2	1·5
03	1 45·8	1 46·0	1 40·9	0·3	0·0	6·3	0·8	12·3	1·5
04	1 46·0	1 46·3	1 41·2	0·4	0·1	6·4	0·8	12·4	1·6
05	1 46·3	1 46·5	1 41·4	0·5	0·1	6·5	0·8	12·5	1·6
06	1 46·5	1 46·8	1 41·6	0·6	0·1	6·6	0·8	12·6	1·6
07	1 46·8	1 47·0	1 41·9	0·7	0·1	6·7	0·8	12·7	1·6
08	1 47·0	1 47·3	1 42·1	0·8	0·1	6·8	0·9	12·8	1·6
09	1 47·3	1 47·5	1 42·4	0·9	0·1	6·9	0·9	12·9	1·6
10	1 47·5	1 47·8	1 42·6	1·0	0·1	7·0	0·9	13·0	1·6
11	1 47·8	1 48·0	1 42·8	1·1	0·1	7·1	0·9	13·1	1·6
12	1 48·0	1 48·3	1 43·1	1·2	0·2	7·2	0·9	13·2	1·7
13	1 48·3	1 48·5	1 43·3	1·3	0·2	7·3	0·9	13·3	1·7
14	1 48·5	1 48·8	1 43·6	1·4	0·2	7·4	0·9	13·4	1·7
15	1 48·8	1 49·0	1 43·8	1·5	0·2	7·5	0·9	13·5	1·7
16	1 49·0	1 49·3	1 44·0	1·6	0·2	7·6	1·0	13·6	1·7
17	1 49·3	1 49·5	1 44·3	1·7	0·2	7·7	1·0	13·7	1·7
18	1 49·5	1 49·8	1 44·5	1·8	0·2	7·8	1·0	13·8	1·7
19	1 49·8	1 50·1	1 44·8	1·9	0·2	7·9	1·0	13·9	1·7
20	1 50·0	1 50·3	1 45·0	2·0	0·3	8·0	1·0	14·0	1·8
21	1 50·3	1 50·6	1 45·2	2·1	0·3	8·1	1·0	14·1	1·8
22	1 50·5	1 50·8	1 45·5	2·2	0·3	8·2	1·0	14·2	1·8
23	1 50·8	1 51·1	1 45·7	2·3	0·3	8·3	1·0	14·3	1·8
24	1 51·0	1 51·3	1 45·9	2·4	0·3	8·4	1·1	14·4	1·8
25	1 51·3	1 51·6	1 46·2	2·5	0·3	8·5	1·1	14·5	1·8
26	1 51·5	1 51·8	1 46·4	2·6	0·3	8·6	1·1	14·6	1·8
27	1 51·8	1 52·1	1 46·7	2·7	0·3	8·7	1·1	14·7	1·8
28	1 52·0	1 52·3	1 46·9	2·8	0·4	8·8	1·1	14·8	1·9
29	1 52·3	1 52·6	1 47·1	2·9	0·4	8·9	1·1	14·9	1·9
30	1 52·5	1 52·8	1 47·4	3·0	0·4	9·0	1·1	15·0	1·9
31	1 52·8	1 53·1	1 47·6	3·1	0·4	9·1	1·1	15·1	1·9
32	1 53·0	1 53·3	1 47·9	3·2	0·4	9·2	1·2	15·2	1·9
33	1 53·3	1 53·6	1 48·1	3·3	0·4	9·3	1·2	15·3	1·9
34	1 53·5	1 53·8	1 48·3	3·4	0·4	9·4	1·2	15·4	1·9
35	1 53·8	1 54·1	1 48·6	3·5	0·4	9·5	1·2	15·5	1·9
36	1 54·0	1 54·3	1 48·8	3·6	0·5	9·6	1·2	15·6	2·0
37	1 54·3	1 54·6	1 49·0	3·7	0·5	9·7	1·2	15·7	2·0
38	1 54·5	1 54·8	1 49·3	3·8	0·5	9·8	1·2	15·8	2·0
39	1 54·8	1 55·1	1 49·5	3·9	0·5	9·9	1·2	15·9	2·0
40	1 55·0	1 55·3	1 49·8	4·0	0·5	10·0	1·3	16·0	2·0
41	1 55·3	1 55·6	1 50·0	4·1	0·5	10·1	1·3	16·1	2·0
42	1 55·5	1 55·8	1 50·2	4·2	0·5	10·2	1·3	16·2	2·0
43	1 55·8	1 56·1	1 50·5	4·3	0·5	10·3	1·3	16·3	2·0
44	1 56·0	1 56·3	1 50·7	4·4	0·6	10·4	1·3	16·4	2·1
45	1 56·3	1 56·6	1 51·0	4·5	0·6	10·5	1·3	16·5	2·1
46	1 56·5	1 56·8	1 51·2	4·6	0·6	10·6	1·3	16·6	2·1
47	1 56·8	1 57·1	1 51·4	4·7	0·6	10·7	1·3	16·7	2·1
48	1 57·0	1 57·3	1 51·7	4·8	0·6	10·8	1·4	16·8	2·1
49	1 57·3	1 57·6	1 51·9	4·9	0·6	10·9	1·4	16·9	2·1
50	1 57·5	1 57·8	1 52·1	5·0	0·6	11·0	1·4	17·0	2·1
51	1 57·8	1 58·1	1 52·4	5·1	0·6	11·1	1·4	17·1	2·1
52	1 58·0	1 58·3	1 52·6	5·2	0·7	11·2	1·4	17·2	2·2
53	1 58·3	1 58·6	1 52·9	5·3	0·7	11·3	1·4	17·3	2·2
54	1 58·5	1 58·8	1 53·1	5·4	0·7	11·4	1·4	17·4	2·2
55	1 58·8	1 59·1	1 53·3	5·5	0·7	11·5	1·4	17·5	2·2
56	1 59·0	1 59·3	1 53·6	5·6	0·7	11·6	1·5	17·6	2·2
57	1 59·3	1 59·6	1 53·8	5·7	0·7	11·7	1·5	17·7	2·2
58	1 59·5	1 59·8	1 54·1	5·8	0·7	11·8	1·5	17·8	2·2
59	1 59·8	2 00·1	1 54·3	5·9	0·7	11·9	1·5	17·9	2·2
60	2 00·0	2 00·3	1 54·5	6·0	0·8	12·0	1·5	18·0	2·3

8ᵐ

s	SUN PLANETS	ARIES	MOON	v or d	Corrⁿ	v or d	Corrⁿ	v or d	Corrⁿ
00	2 00·0	2 00·3	1 54·5	0·0	0·0	6·0	0·9	12·0	1·7
01	2 00·3	2 00·6	1 54·8	0·1	0·0	6·1	0·9	12·1	1·7
02	2 00·5	2 00·8	1 55·0	0·2	0·0	6·2	0·9	12·2	1·7
03	2 00·8	2 01·1	1 55·2	0·3	0·0	6·3	0·9	12·3	1·7
04	2 01·0	2 01·3	1 55·5	0·4	0·1	6·4	0·9	12·4	1·8
05	2 01·3	2 01·6	1 55·7	0·5	0·1	6·5	0·9	12·5	1·8
06	2 01·5	2 01·8	1 56·0	0·6	0·1	6·6	0·9	12·6	1·8
07	2 01·8	2 02·1	1 56·2	0·7	0·1	6·7	0·9	12·7	1·8
08	2 02·0	2 02·3	1 56·4	0·8	0·1	6·8	1·0	12·8	1·8
09	2 02·3	2 02·6	1 56·7	0·9	0·1	6·9	1·0	12·9	1·8
10	2 02·5	2 02·8	1 56·9	1·0	0·1	7·0	1·0	13·0	1·8
11	2 02·8	2 03·1	1 57·2	1·1	0·2	7·1	1·0	13·1	1·9
12	2 03·0	2 03·3	1 57·4	1·2	0·2	7·2	1·0	13·2	1·9
13	2 03·3	2 03·6	1 57·6	1·3	0·2	7·3	1·0	13·3	1·9
14	2 03·5	2 03·8	1 57·9	1·4	0·2	7·4	1·0	13·4	1·9
15	2 03·8	2 04·1	1 58·1	1·5	0·2	7·5	1·1	13·5	1·9
16	2 04·0	2 04·3	1 58·4	1·6	0·2	7·6	1·1	13·6	1·9
17	2 04·3	2 04·6	1 58·6	1·7	0·2	7·7	1·1	13·7	1·9
18	2 04·5	2 04·8	1 58·8	1·8	0·3	7·8	1·1	13·8	2·0
19	2 04·8	2 05·1	1 59·1	1·9	0·3	7·9	1·1	13·9	2·0
20	2 05·0	2 05·3	1 59·3	2·0	0·3	8·0	1·1	14·0	2·0
21	2 05·3	2 05·6	1 59·5	2·1	0·3	8·1	1·1	14·1	2·0
22	2 05·5	2 05·8	1 59·8	2·2	0·3	8·2	1·2	14·2	2·0
23	2 05·8	2 06·1	2 00·0	2·3	0·3	8·3	1·2	14·3	2·0
24	2 06·0	2 06·3	2 00·3	2·4	0·3	8·4	1·2	14·4	2·0
25	2 06·3	2 06·6	2 00·5	2·5	0·4	8·5	1·2	14·5	2·1
26	2 06·5	2 06·8	2 00·7	2·6	0·4	8·6	1·2	14·6	2·1
27	2 06·8	2 07·1	2 01·0	2·7	0·4	8·7	1·2	14·7	2·1
28	2 07·0	2 07·3	2 01·2	2·8	0·4	8·8	1·2	14·8	2·1
29	2 07·3	2 07·6	2 01·5	2·9	0·4	8·9	1·3	14·9	2·1
30	2 07·5	2 07·8	2 01·7	3·0	0·4	9·0	1·3	15·0	2·1
31	2 07·8	2 08·1	2 01·9	3·1	0·4	9·1	1·3	15·1	2·1
32	2 08·0	2 08·4	2 02·2	3·2	0·5	9·2	1·3	15·2	2·2
33	2 08·3	2 08·6	2 02·4	3·3	0·5	9·3	1·3	15·3	2·2
34	2 08·5	2 08·9	2 02·6	3·4	0·5	9·4	1·3	15·4	2·2
35	2 08·8	2 09·1	2 02·9	3·5	0·5	9·5	1·3	15·5	2·2
36	2 09·0	2 09·4	2 03·1	3·6	0·5	9·6	1·4	15·6	2·2
37	2 09·3	2 09·6	2 03·4	3·7	0·5	9·7	1·4	15·7	2·2
38	2 09·5	2 09·9	2 03·6	3·8	0·6	9·8	1·4	15·8	2·2
39	2 09·8	2 10·1	2 03·8	3·9	0·6	9·9	1·4	15·9	2·3
40	2 10·0	2 10·4	2 04·1	4·0	0·6	10·0	1·4	16·0	2·3
41	2 10·3	2 10·6	2 04·3	4·1	0·6	10·1	1·4	16·1	2·3
42	2 10·5	2 10·9	2 04·6	4·2	0·6	10·2	1·4	16·2	2·3
43	2 10·8	2 11·1	2 04·8	4·3	0·6	10·3	1·5	16·3	2·3
44	2 11·0	2 11·4	2 05·0	4·4	0·6	10·4	1·5	16·4	2·3
45	2 11·3	2 11·6	2 05·3	4·5	0·6	10·5	1·5	16·5	2·3
46	2 11·5	2 11·9	2 05·5	4·6	0·7	10·6	1·5	16·6	2·4
47	2 11·8	2 12·1	2 05·7	4·7	0·7	10·7	1·5	16·7	2·4
48	2 12·0	2 12·4	2 06·0	4·8	0·7	10·8	1·5	16·8	2·4
49	2 12·3	2 12·6	2 06·2	4·9	0·7	10·9	1·5	16·9	2·4
50	2 12·5	2 12·9	2 06·5	5·0	0·7	11·0	1·6	17·0	2·4
51	2 12·8	2 13·1	2 06·7	5·1	0·7	11·1	1·6	17·1	2·4
52	2 13·0	2 13·4	2 06·9	5·2	0·7	11·2	1·6	17·2	2·4
53	2 13·3	2 13·6	2 07·2	5·3	0·8	11·3	1·6	17·3	2·5
54	2 13·5	2 13·9	2 07·4	5·4	0·8	11·4	1·6	17·4	2·5
55	2 13·8	2 14·1	2 07·7	5·5	0·8	11·5	1·6	17·5	2·5
56	2 14·0	2 14·4	2 07·9	5·6	0·8	11·6	1·6	17·6	2·5
57	2 14·3	2 14·6	2 08·1	5·7	0·8	11·7	1·7	17·7	2·5
58	2 14·5	2 14·9	2 08·4	5·8	0·8	11·8	1·7	17·8	2·5
59	2 14·8	2 15·1	2 08·6	5·9	0·8	11·9	1·7	17·9	2·5
60	2 15·0	2 15·4	2 08·9	6·0	0·9	12·0	1·7	18·0	2·6

9ᵐ

s	SUN PLANETS	ARIES	MOON	v or d	Corrⁿ	v or d	Corrⁿ	v or d	Corrⁿ
00	2 15·0	2 15·4	2 08·9	0·0	0·0	6·0	1·0	12·0	1·9
01	2 15·3	2 15·6	2 09·1	0·1	0·0	6·1	1·0	12·1	1·9
02	2 15·5	2 15·9	2 09·3	0·2	0·0	6·2	1·0	12·2	1·9
03	2 15·8	2 16·1	2 09·6	0·3	0·0	6·3	1·0	12·3	1·9
04	2 16·0	2 16·4	2 09·8	0·4	0·1	6·4	1·0	12·4	2·0
05	2 16·3	2 16·6	2 10·0	0·5	0·1	6·5	1·0	12·5	2·0
06	2 16·5	2 16·9	2 10·3	0·6	0·1	6·6	1·0	12·6	2·0
07	2 16·8	2 17·1	2 10·5	0·7	0·1	6·7	1·1	12·7	2·0
08	2 17·0	2 17·4	2 10·8	0·8	0·1	6·8	1·1	12·8	2·0
09	2 17·3	2 17·6	2 11·0	0·9	0·1	6·9	1·1	12·9	2·0
10	2 17·5	2 17·9	2 11·2	1·0	0·2	7·0	1·1	13·0	2·1
11	2 17·8	2 18·1	2 11·5	1·1	0·2	7·1	1·1	13·1	2·1
12	2 18·0	2 18·4	2 11·7	1·2	0·2	7·2	1·1	13·2	2·1
13	2 18·3	2 18·6	2 12·0	1·3	0·2	7·3	1·2	13·3	2·1
14	2 18·5	2 18·9	2 12·2	1·4	0·2	7·4	1·2	13·4	2·1
15	2 18·8	2 19·1	2 12·4	1·5	0·2	7·5	1·2	13·5	2·1
16	2 19·0	2 19·4	2 12·7	1·6	0·3	7·6	1·2	13·6	2·2
17	2 19·3	2 19·6	2 12·9	1·7	0·3	7·7	1·2	13·7	2·2
18	2 19·5	2 19·9	2 13·1	1·8	0·3	7·8	1·2	13·8	2·2
19	2 19·8	2 20·1	2 13·4	1·9	0·3	7·9	1·3	13·9	2·2
20	2 20·0	2 20·4	2 13·6	2·0	0·3	8·0	1·3	14·0	2·2
21	2 20·3	2 20·6	2 13·9	2·1	0·3	8·1	1·3	14·1	2·2
22	2 20·5	2 20·9	2 14·1	2·2	0·3	8·2	1·3	14·2	2·2
23	2 20·8	2 21·1	2 14·3	2·3	0·4	8·3	1·3	14·3	2·3
24	2 21·0	2 21·4	2 14·6	2·4	0·4	8·4	1·3	14·4	2·3
25	2 21·3	2 21·6	2 14·8	2·5	0·4	8·5	1·3	14·5	2·3
26	2 21·5	2 21·9	2 15·1	2·6	0·4	8·6	1·4	14·6	2·3
27	2 21·8	2 22·1	2 15·3	2·7	0·4	8·7	1·4	14·7	2·3
28	2 22·0	2 22·4	2 15·5	2·8	0·4	8·8	1·4	14·8	2·3
29	2 22·3	2 22·6	2 15·8	2·9	0·5	8·9	1·4	14·9	2·4
30	2 22·5	2 22·9	2 16·0	3·0	0·5	9·0	1·4	15·0	2·4
31	2 22·8	2 23·1	2 16·2	3·1	0·5	9·1	1·4	15·1	2·4
32	2 23·0	2 23·4	2 16·5	3·2	0·5	9·2	1·5	15·2	2·4
33	2 23·3	2 23·6	2 16·7	3·3	0·5	9·3	1·5	15·3	2·4
34	2 23·5	2 23·9	2 17·0	3·4	0·5	9·4	1·5	15·4	2·4
35	2 23·8	2 24·1	2 17·2	3·5	0·6	9·5	1·5	15·5	2·5
36	2 24·0	2 24·4	2 17·4	3·6	0·6	9·6	1·5	15·6	2·5
37	2 24·3	2 24·6	2 17·7	3·7	0·6	9·7	1·5	15·7	2·5
38	2 24·5	2 24·9	2 17·9	3·8	0·6	9·8	1·6	15·8	2·5
39	2 24·8	2 25·1	2 18·2	3·9	0·6	9·9	1·6	15·9	2·5
40	2 25·0	2 25·4	2 18·4	4·0	0·6	10·0	1·6	16·0	2·5
41	2 25·3	2 25·6	2 18·6	4·1	0·6	10·1	1·6	16·1	2·5
42	2 25·5	2 25·9	2 18·9	4·2	0·7	10·2	1·6	16·2	2·6
43	2 25·8	2 26·1	2 19·1	4·3	0·7	10·3	1·6	16·3	2·6
44	2 26·0	2 26·4	2 19·3	4·4	0·7	10·4	1·6	16·4	2·6
45	2 26·3	2 26·7	2 19·6	4·5	0·7	10·5	1·7	16·5	2·6
46	2 26·5	2 26·9	2 19·8	4·6	0·7	10·6	1·7	16·6	2·6
47	2 26·8	2 27·2	2 20·1	4·7	0·7	10·7	1·7	16·7	2·6
48	2 27·0	2 27·4	2 20·3	4·8	0·8	10·8	1·7	16·8	2·7
49	2 27·3	2 27·7	2 20·5	4·9	0·8	10·9	1·7	16·9	2·7
50	2 27·5	2 27·9	2 20·8	5·0	0·8	11·0	1·7	17·0	2·7
51	2 27·8	2 28·2	2 21·0	5·1	0·8	11·1	1·8	17·1	2·7
52	2 28·0	2 28·4	2 21·3	5·2	0·8	11·2	1·8	17·2	2·7
53	2 28·3	2 28·7	2 21·5	5·3	0·8	11·3	1·8	17·3	2·7
54	2 28·5	2 28·9	2 21·7	5·4	0·9	11·4	1·8	17·4	2·8
55	2 28·8	2 29·2	2 22·0	5·5	0·9	11·5	1·8	17·5	2·8
56	2 29·0	2 29·4	2 22·2	5·6	0·9	11·6	1·8	17·6	2·8
57	2 29·3	2 29·7	2 22·5	5·7	0·9	11·7	1·9	17·7	2·8
58	2 29·5	2 29·9	2 22·7	5·8	0·9	11·8	1·9	17·8	2·8
59	2 29·8	2 30·2	2 22·9	5·9	0·9	11·9	1·9	17·9	2·8
60	2 30·0	2 30·4	2 23·2	6·0	1·0	12·0	1·9	18·0	2·9

10	SUN PLANETS	ARIES	MOON	v or Corrn d		v or Corrn d		v or Corrn d	
s	° ′	° ′	° ′	′	′	′	′	′	′
00	2 30·0	2 30·4	2 23·2	0·0	0·0	6·0	1·1	12·0	2·1
01	2 30·3	2 30·7	2 23·4	0·1	0·0	6·1	1·1	12·1	2·1
02	2 30·5	2 30·9	2 23·6	0·2	0·0	6·2	1·1	12·2	2·1
03	2 30·8	2 31·2	2 23·9	0·3	0·1	6·3	1·1	12·3	2·2
04	2 31·0	2 31·4	2 24·1	0·4	0·1	6·4	1·1	12·4	2·2
05	2 31·3	2 31·7	2 24·4	0·5	0·1	6·5	1·1	12·5	2·2
06	2 31·5	2 31·9	2 24·6	0·6	0·1	6·6	1·2	12·6	2·2
07	2 31·8	2 32·2	2 24·8	0·7	0·1	6·7	1·2	12·7	2·2
08	2 32·0	2 32·4	2 25·1	0·8	0·1	6·8	1·2	12·8	2·2
09	2 32·3	2 32·7	2 25·3	0·9	0·2	6·9	1·2	12·9	2·3
10	2 32·5	2 32·9	2 25·6	1·0	0·2	7·0	1·2	13·0	2·3
11	2 32·8	2 33·2	2 25·8	1·1	0·2	7·1	1·2	13·1	2·3
12	2 33·0	2 33·4	2 26·0	1·2	0·2	7·2	1·3	13·2	2·3
13	2 33·3	2 33·7	2 26·3	1·3	0·2	7·3	1·3	13·3	2·3
14	2 33·5	2 33·9	2 26·5	1·4	0·2	7·4	1·3	13·4	2·3
15	2 33·8	2 34·2	2 26·7	1·5	0·3	7·5	1·3	13·5	2·4
16	2 34·0	2 34·4	2 27·0	1·6	0·3	7·6	1·3	13·6	2·4
17	2 34·3	2 34·7	2 27·2	1·7	0·3	7·7	1·3	13·7	2·4
18	2 34·5	2 34·9	2 27·5	1·8	0·3	7·8	1·4	13·8	2·4
19	2 34·8	2 35·2	2 27·7	1·9	0·3	7·9	1·4	13·9	2·4
20	2 35·0	2 35·4	2 27·9	2·0	0·4	8·0	1·4	14·0	2·5
21	2 35·3	2 35·7	2 28·2	2·1	0·4	8·1	1·4	14·1	2·5
22	2 35·5	2 35·9	2 28·4	2·2	0·4	8·2	1·4	14·2	2·5
23	2 35·8	2 36·2	2 28·7	2·3	0·4	8·3	1·5	14·3	2·5
24	2 36·0	2 36·4	2 28·9	2·4	0·4	8·4	1·5	14·4	2·5
25	2 36·3	2 36·7	2 29·1	2·5	0·4	8·5	1·5	14·5	2·5
26	2 36·5	2 36·9	2 29·4	2·6	0·5	8·6	1·5	14·6	2·6
27	2 36·8	2 37·2	2 29·6	2·7	0·5	8·7	1·5	14·7	2·6
28	2 37·0	2 37·4	2 29·8	2·8	0·5	8·8	1·5	14·8	2·6
29	2 37·3	2 37·7	2 30·1	2·9	0·5	8·9	1·6	14·9	2·6
30	2 37·5	2 37·9	2 30·3	3·0	0·5	9·0	1·6	15·0	2·6
31	2 37·8	2 38·2	2 30·6	3·1	0·5	9·1	1·6	15·1	2·6
32	2 38·0	2 38·4	2 30·8	3·2	0·6	9·2	1·6	15·2	2·7
33	2 38·3	2 38·7	2 31·0	3·3	0·6	9·3	1·6	15·3	2·7
34	2 38·5	2 38·9	2 31·3	3·4	0·6	9·4	1·6	15·4	2·7
35	2 38·8	2 39·2	2 31·5	3·5	0·6	9·5	1·7	15·5	2·7
36	2 39·0	2 39·4	2 31·8	3·6	0·6	9·6	1·7	15·6	2·7
37	2 39·3	2 39·7	2 32·0	3·7	0·6	9·7	1·7	15·7	2·7
38	2 39·5	2 39·9	2 32·2	3·8	0·7	9·8	1·7	15·8	2·8
39	2 39·8	2 40·2	2 32·5	3·9	0·7	9·9	1·7	15·9	2·8
40	2 40·0	2 40·4	2 32·7	4·0	0·7	10·0	1·8	16·0	2·8
41	2 40·3	2 40·7	2 32·9	4·1	0·7	10·1	1·8	16·1	2·8
42	2 40·5	2 40·9	2 33·2	4·2	0·7	10·2	1·8	16·2	2·8
43	2 40·8	2 41·2	2 33·4	4·3	0·8	10·3	1·8	16·3	2·9
44	2 41·0	2 41·4	2 33·7	4·4	0·8	10·4	1·8	16·4	2·9
45	2 41·3	2 41·7	2 33·9	4·5	0·8	10·5	1·8	16·5	2·9
46	2 41·5	2 41·9	2 34·1	4·6	0·8	10·6	1·9	16·6	2·9
47	2 41·8	2 42·2	2 34·4	4·7	0·8	10·7	1·9	16·7	2·9
48	2 42·0	2 42·4	2 34·6	4·8	0·8	10·8	1·9	16·8	2·9
49	2 42·3	2 42·7	2 34·9	4·9	0·9	10·9	1·9	16·9	3·0
50	2 42·5	2 42·9	2 35·1	5·0	0·9	11·0	1·9	17·0	3·0
51	2 42·8	2 43·2	2 35·3	5·1	0·9	11·1	1·9	17·1	3·0
52	2 43·0	2 43·4	2 35·6	5·2	0·9	11·2	2·0	17·2	3·0
53	2 43·3	2 43·7	2 35·8	5·3	0·9	11·3	2·0	17·3	3·0
54	2 43·5	2 43·9	2 36·1	5·4	0·9	11·4	2·0	17·4	3·0
55	2 43·8	2 44·2	2 36·3	5·5	1·0	11·5	2·0	17·5	3·1
56	2 44·0	2 44·4	2 36·5	5·6	1·0	11·6	2·0	17·6	3·1
57	2 44·3	2 44·7	2 36·8	5·7	1·0	11·7	2·0	17·7	3·1
58	2 44·5	2 45·0	2 37·0	5·8	1·0	11·8	2·1	17·8	3·1
59	2 44·8	2 45·2	2 37·2	5·9	1·0	11·9	2·1	17·9	3·1
60	2 45·0	2 45·5	2 37·5	6·0	1·1	12·0	2·1	18·0	3·2

11	SUN PLANETS	ARIES	MOON	v or Corrn d		v or Corrn d		v or Corrn d	
s	° ′	° ′	° ′	′	′	′	′	′	′
00	2 45·0	2 45·5	2 37·5	0·0	0·0	6·0	1·2	12·0	2·3
01	2 45·3	2 45·7	2 37·7	0·1	0·0	6·1	1·2	12·1	2·3
02	2 45·5	2 46·0	2 38·0	0·2	0·0	6·2	1·2	12·2	2·3
03	2 45·8	2 46·2	2 38·2	0·3	0·1	6·3	1·2	12·3	2·4
04	2 46·0	2 46·5	2 38·4	0·4	0·1	6·4	1·2	12·4	2·4
05	2 46·3	2 46·7	2 38·7	0·5	0·1	6·5	1·2	12·5	2·4
06	2 46·5	2 47·0	2 38·9	0·6	0·1	6·6	1·3	12·6	2·4
07	2 46·8	2 47·2	2 39·2	0·7	0·1	6·7	1·3	12·7	2·4
08	2 47·0	2 47·5	2 39·4	0·8	0·2	6·8	1·3	12·8	2·5
09	2 47·3	2 47·7	2 39·6	0·9	0·2	6·9	1·3	12·9	2·5
10	2 47·5	2 48·0	2 39·9	1·0	0·2	7·0	1·3	13·0	2·5
11	2 47·8	2 48·2	2 40·1	1·1	0·2	7·1	1·4	13·1	2·5
12	2 48·0	2 48·5	2 40·3	1·2	0·2	7·2	1·4	13·2	2·5
13	2 48·3	2 48·7	2 40·6	1·3	0·2	7·3	1·4	13·3	2·5
14	2 48·5	2 49·0	2 40·8	1·4	0·3	7·4	1·4	13·4	2·6
15	2 48·8	2 49·2	2 41·1	1·5	0·3	7·5	1·4	13·5	2·6
16	2 49·0	2 49·5	2 41·3	1·6	0·3	7·6	1·5	13·6	2·6
17	2 49·3	2 49·7	2 41·5	1·7	0·3	7·7	1·5	13·7	2·6
18	2 49·5	2 50·0	2 41·8	1·8	0·3	7·8	1·5	13·8	2·6
19	2 49·8	2 50·2	2 42·0	1·9	0·4	7·9	1·5	13·9	2·7
20	2 50·0	2 50·5	2 42·3	2·0	0·4	8·0	1·5	14·0	2·7
21	2 50·3	2 50·7	2 42·5	2·1	0·4	8·1	1·6	14·1	2·7
22	2 50·5	2 51·0	2 42·7	2·2	0·4	8·2	1·6	14·2	2·7
23	2 50·8	2 51·2	2 43·0	2·3	0·4	8·3	1·6	14·3	2·7
24	2 51·0	2 51·5	2 43·2	2·4	0·5	8·4	1·6	14·4	2·8
25	2 51·3	2 51·7	2 43·4	2·5	0·5	8·5	1·6	14·5	2·8
26	2 51·5	2 52·0	2 43·7	2·6	0·5	8·6	1·6	14·6	2·8
27	2 51·8	2 52·2	2 43·9	2·7	0·5	8·7	1·7	14·7	2·8
28	2 52·0	2 52·5	2 44·2	2·8	0·5	8·8	1·7	14·8	2·8
29	2 52·3	2 52·7	2 44·4	2·9	0·6	8·9	1·7	14·9	2·9
30	2 52·5	2 53·0	2 44·6	3·0	0·6	9·0	1·7	15·0	2·9
31	2 52·8	2 53·2	2 44·9	3·1	0·6	9·1	1·7	15·1	2·9
32	2 53·0	2 53·5	2 45·1	3·2	0·6	9·2	1·8	15·2	2·9
33	2 53·3	2 53·7	2 45·4	3·3	0·6	9·3	1·8	15·3	2·9
34	2 53·5	2 54·0	2 45·6	3·4	0·7	9·4	1·8	15·4	3·0
35	2 53·8	2 54·2	2 45·8	3·5	0·7	9·5	1·8	15·5	3·0
36	2 54·0	2 54·5	2 46·1	3·6	0·7	9·6	1·8	15·6	3·0
37	2 54·3	2 54·7	2 46·3	3·7	0·7	9·7	1·9	15·7	3·0
38	2 54·5	2 55·0	2 46·6	3·8	0·7	9·8	1·9	15·8	3·0
39	2 54·8	2 55·2	2 46·8	3·9	0·7	9·9	1·9	15·9	3·0
40	2 55·0	2 55·5	2 47·0	4·0	0·8	10·0	1·9	16·0	3·1
41	2 55·3	2 55·7	2 47·3	4·1	0·8	10·1	1·9	16·1	3·1
42	2 55·5	2 56·0	2 47·5	4·2	0·8	10·2	2·0	16·2	3·1
43	2 55·8	2 56·2	2 47·7	4·3	0·8	10·3	2·0	16·3	3·1
44	2 56·0	2 56·5	2 48·0	4·4	0·8	10·4	2·0	16·4	3·1
45	2 56·3	2 56·7	2 48·2	4·5	0·9	10·5	2·0	16·5	3·2
46	2 56·5	2 57·0	2 48·5	4·6	0·9	10·6	2·0	16·6	3·2
47	2 56·8	2 57·2	2 48·7	4·7	0·9	10·7	2·1	16·7	3·2
48	2 57·0	2 57·5	2 48·9	4·8	0·9	10·8	2·1	16·8	3·2
49	2 57·3	2 57·7	2 49·2	4·9	0·9	10·9	2·1	16·9	3·2
50	2 57·5	2 58·0	2 49·4	5·0	1·0	11·0	2·1	17·0	3·3
51	2 57·8	2 58·2	2 49·7	5·1	1·0	11·1	2·1	17·1	3·3
52	2 58·0	2 58·5	2 49·9	5·2	1·0	11·2	2·1	17·2	3·3
53	2 58·3	2 58·7	2 50·1	5·3	1·0	11·3	2·2	17·3	3·3
54	2 58·5	2 59·0	2 50·4	5·4	1·0	11·4	2·2	17·4	3·3
55	2 58·8	2 59·2	2 50·6	5·5	1·1	11·5	2·2	17·5	3·4
56	2 59·0	2 59·5	2 50·8	5·6	1·1	11·6	2·2	17·6	3·4
57	2 59·3	2 59·7	2 51·1	5·7	1·1	11·7	2·2	17·7	3·4
58	2 59·5	3 00·0	2 51·3	5·8	1·1	11·8	2·3	17·8	3·4
59	2 59·8	3 00·2	2 51·6	5·9	1·1	11·9	2·3	17·9	3·4
60	3 00·0	3 00·5	2 51·8	6·0	1·2	12·0	2·3	18·0	3·5

12ᵐ

12	SUN PLANETS	ARIES	MOON	v or d	Corrⁿ	v or d	Corrⁿ	v or d	Corrⁿ
s	° ′	° ′	° ′	′	′	′	′	′	′
00	3 00·0	3 00·5	2 51·8	0·0	0·0	6·0	1·3	12·0	2·5
01	3 00·3	3 00·7	2 52·0	0·1	0·0	6·1	1·3	12·1	2·5
02	3 00·5	3 01·0	2 52·3	0·2	0·0	6·2	1·3	12·2	2·5
03	3 00·8	3 01·2	2 52·5	0·3	0·1	6·3	1·3	12·3	2·6
04	3 01·0	3 01·5	2 52·8	0·4	0·1	6·4	1·3	12·4	2·6
05	3 01·3	3 01·7	2 53·0	0·5	0·1	6·5	1·4	12·5	2·6
06	3 01·5	3 02·0	2 53·2	0·6	0·1	6·6	1·4	12·6	2·6
07	3 01·8	3 02·2	2 53·5	0·7	0·1	6·7	1·4	12·7	2·6
08	3 02·0	3 02·5	2 53·7	0·8	0·2	6·8	1·4	12·8	2·7
09	3 02·3	3 02·7	2 53·9	0·9	0·2	6·9	1·4	12·9	2·7
10	3 02·5	3 03·0	2 54·2	1·0	0·2	7·0	1·5	13·0	2·7
11	3 02·8	3 03·3	2 54·4	1·1	0·2	7·1	1·5	13·1	2·7
12	3 03·0	3 03·5	2 54·7	1·2	0·3	7·2	1·5	13·2	2·8
13	3 03·3	3 03·8	2 54·9	1·3	0·3	7·3	1·5	13·3	2·8
14	3 03·5	3 04·0	2 55·1	1·4	0·3	7·4	1·5	13·4	2·8
15	3 03·8	3 04·3	2 55·4	1·5	0·3	7·5	1·6	13·5	2·8
16	3 04·0	3 04·5	2 55·6	1·6	0·3	7·6	1·6	13·6	2·8
17	3 04·3	3 04·8	2 55·9	1·7	0·4	7·7	1·6	13·7	2·9
18	3 04·5	3 05·0	2 56·1	1·8	0·4	7·8	1·6	13·8	2·9
19	3 04·8	3 05·3	2 56·3	1·9	0·4	7·9	1·6	13·9	2·9
20	3 05·0	3 05·5	2 56·6	2·0	0·4	8·0	1·7	14·0	2·9
21	3 05·3	3 05·8	2 56·8	2·1	0·4	8·1	1·7	14·1	2·9
22	3 05·5	3 06·0	2 57·0	2·2	0·5	8·2	1·7	14·2	3·0
23	3 05·8	3 06·3	2 57·3	2·3	0·5	8·3	1·7	14·3	3·0
24	3 06·0	3 06·5	2 57·5	2·4	0·5	8·4	1·8	14·4	3·0
25	3 06·3	3 06·8	2 57·8	2·5	0·5	8·5	1·8	14·5	3·0
26	3 06·5	3 07·0	2 58·0	2·6	0·5	8·6	1·8	14·6	3·0
27	3 06·8	3 07·3	2 58·2	2·7	0·6	8·7	1·8	14·7	3·1
28	3 07·0	3 07·5	2 58·5	2·8	0·6	8·8	1·8	14·8	3·1
29	3 07·3	3 07·8	2 58·7	2·9	0·6	8·9	1·9	14·9	3·1
30	3 07·5	3 08·0	2 59·0	3·0	0·6	9·0	1·9	15·0	3·1
31	3 07·8	3 08·3	2 59·2	3·1	0·6	9·1	1·9	15·1	3·1
32	3 08·0	3 08·5	2 59·4	3·2	0·7	9·2	1·9	15·2	3·2
33	3 08·3	3 08·8	2 59·7	3·3	0·7	9·3	1·9	15·3	3·2
34	3 08·5	3 09·0	2 59·9	3·4	0·7	9·4	2·0	15·4	3·2
35	3 08·8	3 09·3	3 00·2	3·5	0·7	9·5	2·0	15·5	3·2
36	3 09·0	3 09·5	3 00·4	3·6	0·8	9·6	2·0	15·6	3·3
37	3 09·3	3 09·8	3 00·6	3·7	0·8	9·7	2·0	15·7	3·3
38	3 09·5	3 10·0	3 00·9	3·8	0·8	9·8	2·0	15·8	3·3
39	3 09·8	3 10·3	3 01·1	3·9	0·8	9·9	2·1	15·9	3·3
40	3 10·0	3 10·5	3 01·3	4·0	0·8	10·0	2·1	16·0	3·3
41	3 10·3	3 10·8	3 01·6	4·1	0·9	10·1	2·1	16·1	3·4
42	3 10·5	3 11·0	3 01·8	4·2	0·9	10·2	2·1	16·2	3·4
43	3 10·8	3 11·3	3 02·1	4·3	0·9	10·3	2·1	16·3	3·4
44	3 11·0	3 11·5	3 02·3	4·4	0·9	10·4	2·2	16·4	3·4
45	3 11·3	3 11·8	3 02·5	4·5	0·9	10·5	2·2	16·5	3·4
46	3 11·5	3 12·0	3 02·8	4·6	1·0	10·6	2·2	16·6	3·5
47	3 11·8	3 12·3	3 03·0	4·7	1·0	10·7	2·2	16·7	3·5
48	3 12·0	3 12·5	3 03·3	4·8	1·0	10·8	2·3	16·8	3·5
49	3 12·3	3 12·8	3 03·5	4·9	1·0	10·9	2·3	16·9	3·5
50	3 12·5	3 13·0	3 03·7	5·0	1·0	11·0	2·3	17·0	3·5
51	3 12·8	3 13·3	3 04·0	5·1	1·1	11·1	2·3	17·1	3·6
52	3 13·0	3 13·5	3 04·2	5·2	1·1	11·2	2·3	17·2	3·6
53	3 13·3	3 13·8	3 04·4	5·3	1·1	11·3	2·4	17·3	3·6
54	3 13·5	3 14·0	3 04·7	5·4	1·1	11·4	2·4	17·4	3·6
55	3 13·8	3 14·3	3 04·9	5·5	1·1	11·5	2·4	17·5	3·6
56	3 14·0	3 14·5	3 05·2	5·6	1·2	11·6	2·4	17·6	3·7
57	3 14·3	3 14·8	3 05·4	5·7	1·2	11·7	2·4	17·7	3·7
58	3 14·5	3 15·0	3 05·6	5·8	1·2	11·8	2·5	17·8	3·7
59	3 14·8	3 15·3	3 05·9	5·9	1·2	11·9	2·5	17·9	3·7
60	3 15·0	3 15·5	3 06·1	6·0	1·3	12·0	2·5	18·0	3·8

13ᵐ

13	SUN PLANETS	ARIES	MOON	v or d	Corrⁿ	v or d	Corrⁿ	v or d	Corrⁿ
s	° ′	° ′	° ′	′	′	′	′	′	′
00	3 15·0	3 15·5	3 06·1	0·0	0·0	6·0	1·4	12·0	2·7
01	3 15·3	3 15·8	3 06·4	0·1	0·0	6·1	1·4	12·1	2·7
02	3 15·5	3 16·0	3 06·6	0·2	0·0	6·2	1·4	12·2	2·7
03	3 15·8	3 16·3	3 06·8	0·3	0·1	6·3	1·4	12·3	2·8
04	3 16·0	3 16·5	3 07·1	0·4	0·1	6·4	1·4	12·4	2·8
05	3 16·3	3 16·8	3 07·3	0·5	0·1	6·5	1·5	12·5	2·8
06	3 16·5	3 17·0	3 07·5	0·6	0·1	6·6	1·5	12·6	2·8
07	3 16·8	3 17·3	3 07·8	0·7	0·2	6·7	1·5	12·7	2·9
08	3 17·0	3 17·5	3 08·0	0·8	0·2	6·8	1·5	12·8	2·9
09	3 17·3	3 17·8	3 08·3	0·9	0·2	6·9	1·6	12·9	2·9
10	3 17·5	3 18·0	3 08·5	1·0	0·2	7·0	1·6	13·0	2·9
11	3 17·8	3 18·3	3 08·7	1·1	0·2	7·1	1·6	13·1	2·9
12	3 18·0	3 18·5	3 09·0	1·2	0·3	7·2	1·6	13·2	3·0
13	3 18·3	3 18·8	3 09·2	1·3	0·3	7·3	1·6	13·3	3·0
14	3 18·5	3 19·0	3 09·5	1·4	0·3	7·4	1·7	13·4	3·0
15	3 18·8	3 19·3	3 09·7	1·5	0·3	7·5	1·7	13·5	3·0
16	3 19·0	3 19·5	3 09·9	1·6	0·4	7·6	1·7	13·6	3·1
17	3 19·3	3 19·8	3 10·2	1·7	0·4	7·7	1·7	13·7	3·1
18	3 19·5	3 20·0	3 10·4	1·8	0·4	7·8	1·8	13·8	3·1
19	3 19·8	3 20·3	3 10·7	1·9	0·4	7·9	1·8	13·9	3·1
20	3 20·0	3 20·5	3 10·9	2·0	0·5	8·0	1·8	14·0	3·2
21	3 20·3	3 20·8	3 11·1	2·1	0·5	8·1	1·8	14·1	3·2
22	3 20·5	3 21·0	3 11·4	2·2	0·5	8·2	1·8	14·2	3·2
23	3 20·8	3 21·3	3 11·6	2·3	0·5	8·3	1·9	14·3	3·2
24	3 21·0	3 21·6	3 11·8	2·4	0·5	8·4	1·9	14·4	3·2
25	3 21·3	3 21·8	3 12·1	2·5	0·6	8·5	1·9	14·5	3·3
26	3 21·5	3 22·1	3 12·3	2·6	0·6	8·6	1·9	14·6	3·3
27	3 21·8	3 22·3	3 12·6	2·7	0·6	8·7	2·0	14·7	3·3
28	3 22·0	3 22·6	3 12·8	2·8	0·6	8·8	2·0	14·8	3·3
29	3 22·3	3 22·8	3 13·0	2·9	0·7	8·9	2·0	14·9	3·4
30	3 22·5	3 23·1	3 13·3	3·0	0·7	9·0	2·0	15·0	3·4
31	3 22·8	3 23·3	3 13·5	3·1	0·7	9·1	2·0	15·1	3·4
32	3 23·0	3 23·6	3 13·8	3·2	0·7	9·2	2·1	15·2	3·4
33	3 23·3	3 23·8	3 14·0	3·3	0·7	9·3	2·1	15·3	3·4
34	3 23·5	3 24·1	3 14·2	3·4	0·8	9·4	2·1	15·4	3·5
35	3 23·8	3 24·3	3 14·5	3·5	0·8	9·5	2·1	15·5	3·5
36	3 24·0	3 24·6	3 14·7	3·6	0·8	9·6	2·2	15·6	3·5
37	3 24·3	3 24·8	3 14·9	3·7	0·8	9·7	2·2	15·7	3·5
38	3 24·5	3 25·1	3 15·2	3·8	0·9	9·8	2·2	15·8	3·6
39	3 24·8	3 25·3	3 15·4	3·9	0·9	9·9	2·2	15·9	3·6
40	3 25·0	3 25·6	3 15·7	4·0	0·9	10·0	2·3	16·0	3·6
41	3 25·3	3 25·8	3 15·9	4·1	0·9	10·1	2·3	16·1	3·6
42	3 25·5	3 26·1	3 16·1	4·2	0·9	10·2	2·3	16·2	3·6
43	3 25·8	3 26·3	3 16·4	4·3	1·0	10·3	2·3	16·3	3·7
44	3 26·0	3 26·6	3 16·6	4·4	1·0	10·4	2·3	16·4	3·7
45	3 26·3	3 26·8	3 16·9	4·5	1·0	10·5	2·4	16·5	3·7
46	3 26·5	3 27·1	3 17·1	4·6	1·0	10·6	2·4	16·6	3·7
47	3 26·8	3 27·3	3 17·3	4·7	1·1	10·7	2·4	16·7	3·8
48	3 27·0	3 27·6	3 17·6	4·8	1·1	10·8	2·4	16·8	3·8
49	3 27·3	3 27·8	3 17·8	4·9	1·1	10·9	2·5	16·9	3·8
50	3 27·5	3 28·1	3 18·0	5·0	1·1	11·0	2·5	17·0	3·8
51	3 27·8	3 28·3	3 18·3	5·1	1·1	11·1	2·5	17·1	3·8
52	3 28·0	3 28·6	3 18·5	5·2	1·2	11·2	2·5	17·2	3·9
53	3 28·3	3 28·8	3 18·8	5·3	1·2	11·3	2·5	17·3	3·9
54	3 28·5	3 29·1	3 19·0	5·4	1·2	11·4	2·6	17·4	3·9
55	3 28·8	3 29·3	3 19·2	5·5	1·2	11·5	2·6	17·5	3·9
56	3 29·0	3 29·6	3 19·5	5·6	1·3	11·6	2·6	17·6	4·0
57	3 29·3	3 29·8	3 19·7	5·7	1·3	11·7	2·6	17·7	4·0
58	3 29·5	3 30·1	3 20·0	5·8	1·3	11·8	2·7	17·8	4·0
59	3 29·8	3 30·3	3 20·2	5·9	1·3	11·9	2·7	17·9	4·0
60	3 30·0	3 30·6	3 20·4	6·0	1·4	12·0	2·7	18·0	4·1

14ᵐ	SUN PLANETS	ARIES	MOON	v or Corrⁿ d		v or Corrⁿ d		v or Corrⁿ d	
s	° ′	° ′	° ′	′	′	′	′	′	′
00	3 30·0	3 30·6	3 20·4	0·0	0·0	6·0	1·5	12·0	2·9
01	3 30·3	3 30·8	3 20·7	0·1	0·0	6·1	1·5	12·1	2·9
02	3 30·5	3 31·1	3 20·9	0·2	0·0	6·2	1·5	12·2	2·9
03	3 30·8	3 31·3	3 21·1	0·3	0·1	6·3	1·5	12·3	3·0
04	3 31·0	3 31·6	3 21·4	0·4	0·1	6·4	1·5	12·4	3·0
05	3 31·3	3 31·8	3 21·6	0·5	0·1	6·5	1·6	12·5	3·0
06	3 31·5	3 32·1	3 21·9	0·6	0·1	6·6	1·6	12·6	3·0
07	3 31·8	3 32·3	3 22·1	0·7	0·2	6·7	1·6	12·7	3·1
08	3 32·0	3 32·6	3 22·3	0·8	0·2	6·8	1·6	12·8	3·1
09	3 32·3	3 32·8	3 22·6	0·9	0·2	6·9	1·7	12·9	3·1
10	3 32·5	3 33·1	3 22·8	1·0	0·2	7·0	1·7	13·0	3·1
11	3 32·8	3 33·3	3 23·1	1·1	0·3	7·1	1·7	13·1	3·2
12	3 33·0	3 33·6	3 23·3	1·2	0·3	7·2	1·7	13·2	3·2
13	3 33·3	3 33·8	3 23·5	1·3	0·3	7·3	1·8	13·3	3·2
14	3 33·5	3 34·1	3 23·8	1·4	0·3	7·4	1·8	13·4	3·2
15	3 33·8	3 34·3	3 24·0	1·5	0·4	7·5	1·8	13·5	3·3
16	3 34·0	3 34·6	3 24·3	1·6	0·4	7·6	1·8	13·6	3·3
17	3 34·3	3 34·8	3 24·5	1·7	0·4	7·7	1·9	13·7	3·3
18	3 34·5	3 35·1	3 24·7	1·8	0·4	7·8	1·9	13·8	3·3
19	3 34·8	3 35·3	3 25·0	1·9	0·5	7·9	1·9	13·9	3·4
20	3 35·0	3 35·6	3 25·2	2·0	0·5	8·0	1·9	14·0	3·4
21	3 35·3	3 35·8	3 25·4	2·1	0·5	8·1	2·0	14·1	3·4
22	3 35·5	3 36·1	3 25·7	2·2	0·5	8·2	2·0	14·2	3·4
23	3 35·8	3 36·3	3 25·9	2·3	0·6	8·3	2·0	14·3	3·5
24	3 36·0	3 36·6	3 26·2	2·4	0·6	8·4	2·0	14·4	3·5
25	3 36·3	3 36·8	3 26·4	2·5	0·6	8·5	2·1	14·5	3·5
26	3 36·5	3 37·1	3 26·6	2·6	0·6	8·6	2·1	14·6	3·5
27	3 36·8	3 37·3	3 26·9	2·7	0·7	8·7	2·1	14·7	3·6
28	3 37·0	3 37·6	3 27·1	2·8	0·7	8·8	2·1	14·8	3·6
29	3 37·3	3 37·8	3 27·4	2·9	0·7	8·9	2·2	14·9	3·6
30	3 37·5	3 38·1	3 27·6	3·0	0·7	9·0	2·2	15·0	3·6
31	3 37·8	3 38·3	3 27·8	3·1	0·7	9·1	2·2	15·1	3·6
32	3 38·0	3 38·6	3 28·1	3·2	0·8	9·2	2·2	15·2	3·7
33	3 38·3	3 38·8	3 28·3	3·3	0·8	9·3	2·2	15·3	3·7
34	3 38·5	3 39·1	3 28·5	3·4	0·8	9·4	2·3	15·4	3·7
35	3 38·8	3 39·3	3 28·8	3·5	0·8	9·5	2·3	15·5	3·7
36	3 39·0	3 39·6	3 29·0	3·6	0·9	9·6	2·3	15·6	3·8
37	3 39·3	3 39·9	3 29·3	3·7	0·9	9·7	2·3	15·7	3·8
38	3 39·5	3 40·1	3 29·5	3·8	0·9	9·8	2·4	15·8	3·8
39	3 39·8	3 40·4	3 29·7	3·9	0·9	9·9	2·4	15·9	3·8
40	3 40·0	3 40·6	3 30·0	4·0	1·0	10·0	2·4	16·0	3·9
41	3 40·3	3 40·9	3 30·2	4·1	1·0	10·1	2·4	16·1	3·9
42	3 40·5	3 41·1	3 30·5	4·2	1·0	10·2	2·5	16·2	3·9
43	3 40·8	3 41·4	3 30·7	4·3	1·0	10·3	2·5	16·3	3·9
44	3 41·0	3 41·6	3 30·9	4·4	1·1	10·4	2·5	16·4	4·0
45	3 41·3	3 41·9	3 31·2	4·5	1·1	10·5	2·5	16·5	4·0
46	3 41·5	3 42·1	3 31·4	4·6	1·1	10·6	2·6	16·6	4·0
47	3 41·8	3 42·4	3 31·6	4·7	1·1	10·7	2·6	16·7	4·0
48	3 42·0	3 42·6	3 31·9	4·8	1·2	10·8	2·6	16·8	4·1
49	3 42·3	3 42·9	3 32·1	4·9	1·2	10·9	2·6	16·9	4·1
50	3 42·5	3 43·1	3 32·4	5·0	1·2	11·0	2·7	17·0	4·1
51	3 42·8	3 43·4	3 32·6	5·1	1·2	11·1	2·7	17·1	4·1
52	3 43·0	3 43·6	3 32·8	5·2	1·3	11·2	2·7	17·2	4·2
53	3 43·3	3 43·9	3 33·1	5·3	1·3	11·3	2·7	17·3	4·2
54	3 43·5	3 44·1	3 33·3	5·4	1·3	11·4	2·8	17·4	4·2
55	3 43·8	3 44·4	3 33·6	5·5	1·3	11·5	2·8	17·5	4·2
56	3 44·0	3 44·6	3 33·8	5·6	1·4	11·6	2·8	17·6	4·3
57	3 44·3	3 44·9	3 34·0	5·7	1·4	11·7	2·8	17·7	4·3
58	3 44·5	3 45·1	3 34·3	5·8	1·4	11·8	2·9	17·8	4·3
59	3 44·8	3 45·4	3 34·5	5·9	1·4	11·9	2·9	17·9	4·3
60	3 45·0	3 45·6	3 34·8	6·0	1·5	12·0	2·9	18·0	4·4

15ᵐ	SUN PLANETS	ARIES	MOON	v or Corrⁿ d		v or Corrⁿ d		v or Corrⁿ d	
s	° ′	° ′	° ′	′	′	′	′	′	′
00	3 45·0	3 45·6	3 34·8	0·0	0·0	6·0	1·6	12·0	3·1
01	3 45·3	3 45·9	3 35·0	0·1	0·0	6·1	1·6	12·1	3·1
02	3 45·5	3 46·1	3 35·2	0·2	0·1	6·2	1·6	12·2	3·2
03	3 45·8	3 46·4	3 35·5	0·3	0·1	6·3	1·6	12·3	3·2
04	3 46·0	3 46·6	3 35·7	0·4	0·1	6·4	1·7	12·4	3·2
05	3 46·3	3 46·9	3 35·9	0·5	0·1	6·5	1·7	12·5	3·2
06	3 46·5	3 47·1	3 36·2	0·6	0·2	6·6	1·7	12·6	3·3
07	3 46·8	3 47·4	3 36·4	0·7	0·2	6·7	1·7	12·7	3·3
08	3 47·0	3 47·6	3 36·7	0·8	0·2	6·8	1·8	12·8	3·3
09	3 47·3	3 47·9	3 36·9	0·9	0·2	6·9	1·8	12·9	3·3
10	3 47·5	3 48·1	3 37·1	1·0	0·3	7·0	1·8	13·0	3·4
11	3 47·8	3 48·4	3 37·4	1·1	0·3	7·1	1·8	13·1	3·4
12	3 48·0	3 48·6	3 37·6	1·2	0·3	7·2	1·9	13·2	3·4
13	3 48·3	3 48·9	3 37·9	1·3	0·3	7·3	1·9	13·3	3·4
14	3 48·5	3 49·1	3 38·1	1·4	0·4	7·4	1·9	13·4	3·5
15	3 48·8	3 49·4	3 38·3	1·5	0·4	7·5	1·9	13·5	3·5
16	3 49·0	3 49·6	3 38·6	1·6	0·4	7·6	2·0	13·6	3·5
17	3 49·3	3 49·9	3 38·8	1·7	0·4	7·7	2·0	13·7	3·5
18	3 49·5	3 50·1	3 39·0	1·8	0·5	7·8	2·0	13·8	3·6
19	3 49·8	3 50·4	3 39·3	1·9	0·5	7·9	2·0	13·9	3·6
20	3 50·0	3 50·6	3 39·5	2·0	0·5	8·0	2·1	14·0	3·6
21	3 50·3	3 50·9	3 39·8	2·1	0·5	8·1	2·1	14·1	3·6
22	3 50·5	3 51·1	3 40·0	2·2	0·6	8·2	2·1	14·2	3·7
23	3 50·8	3 51·4	3 40·2	2·3	0·6	8·3	2·1	14·3	3·7
24	3 51·0	3 51·6	3 40·5	2·4	0·6	8·4	2·2	14·4	3·7
25	3 51·3	3 51·9	3 40·7	2·5	0·6	8·5	2·2	14·5	3·7
26	3 51·5	3 52·1	3 41·0	2·6	0·7	8·6	2·2	14·6	3·8
27	3 51·8	3 52·4	3 41·2	2·7	0·7	8·7	2·2	14·7	3·8
28	3 52·0	3 52·6	3 41·4	2·8	0·7	8·8	2·3	14·8	3·8
29	3 52·3	3 52·9	3 41·7	2·9	0·7	8·9	2·3	14·9	3·8
30	3 52·5	3 53·1	3 41·9	3·0	0·8	9·0	2·3	15·0	3·9
31	3 52·8	3 53·4	3 42·1	3·1	0·8	9·1	2·4	15·1	3·9
32	3 53·0	3 53·6	3 42·4	3·2	0·8	9·2	2·4	15·2	3·9
33	3 53·3	3 53·9	3 42·6	3·3	0·9	9·3	2·4	15·3	4·0
34	3 53·5	3 54·1	3 42·9	3·4	0·9	9·4	2·4	15·4	4·0
35	3 53·8	3 54·4	3 43·1	3·5	0·9	9·5	2·5	15·5	4·0
36	3 54·0	3 54·6	3 43·3	3·6	0·9	9·6	2·5	15·6	4·0
37	3 54·3	3 54·9	3 43·6	3·7	1·0	9·7	2·5	15·7	4·1
38	3 54·5	3 55·1	3 43·8	3·8	1·0	9·8	2·5	15·8	4·1
39	3 54·8	3 55·4	3 44·1	3·9	1·0	9·9	2·6	15·9	4·1
40	3 55·0	3 55·6	3 44·3	4·0	1·0	10·0	2·6	16·0	4·1
41	3 55·3	3 55·9	3 44·5	4·1	1·1	10·1	2·6	16·1	4·2
42	3 55·5	3 56·1	3 44·8	4·2	1·1	10·2	2·6	16·2	4·2
43	3 55·8	3 56·4	3 45·0	4·3	1·1	10·3	2·7	16·3	4·2
44	3 56·0	3 56·6	3 45·2	4·4	1·1	10·4	2·7	16·4	4·2
45	3 56·3	3 56·9	3 45·5	4·5	1·2	10·5	2·7	16·5	4·3
46	3 56·5	3 57·1	3 45·7	4·6	1·2	10·6	2·7	16·6	4·3
47	3 56·8	3 57·4	3 46·0	4·7	1·2	10·7	2·8	16·7	4·3
48	3 57·0	3 57·6	3 46·2	4·8	1·2	10·8	2·8	16·8	4·3
49	3 57·3	3 57·9	3 46·4	4·9	1·3	10·9	2·8	16·9	4·4
50	3 57·5	3 58·2	3 46·7	5·0	1·3	11·0	2·8	17·0	4·4
51	3 57·8	3 58·4	3 46·9	5·1	1·3	11·1	2·9	17·1	4·4
52	3 58·0	3 58·7	3 47·2	5·2	1·3	11·2	2·9	17·2	4·4
53	3 58·3	3 58·9	3 47·4	5·3	1·4	11·3	2·9	17·3	4·5
54	3 58·5	3 59·2	3 47·6	5·4	1·4	11·4	2·9	17·4	4·5
55	3 58·8	3 59·4	3 47·9	5·5	1·4	11·5	3·0	17·5	4·5
56	3 59·0	3 59·7	3 48·1	5·6	1·4	11·6	3·0	17·6	4·5
57	3 59·3	3 59·9	3 48·4	5·7	1·5	11·7	3·0	17·7	4·6
58	3 59·5	4 00·2	3 48·6	5·8	1·5	11·8	3·0	17·8	4·6
59	3 59·8	4 00·4	3 48·8	5·9	1·5	11·9	3·1	17·9	4·6
60	4 00·0	4 00·7	3 49·1	6·0	1·6	12·0	3·1	18·0	4·7

16^m	SUN PLANETS	ARIES	MOON	v or Corrn d	v or Corrn d	v or Corrn d	17^m	SUN PLANETS	ARIES	MOON	v or Corrn d	v or Corrn d	v or Corrn d
s	° ′	° ′	° ′	′ ′	′ ′	′ ′	s	° ′	° ′	° ′	′ ′	′ ′	′ ′
00	4 00·0	4 00·7	3 49·1	0·0 0·0	6·0 1·7	12·0 3·3	00	4 15·0	4 15·7	4 03·4	0·0 0·0	6·0 1·8	12·0 3·5
01	4 00·3	4 00·9	3 49·3	0·1 0·0	6·1 1·7	12·1 3·3	01	4 15·3	4 15·9	4 03·6	0·1 0·0	6·1 1·8	12·1 3·5
02	4 00·5	4 01·2	3 49·5	0·2 0·1	6·2 1·7	12·2 3·4	02	4 15·5	4 16·2	4 03·9	0·2 0·1	6·2 1·8	12·2 3·6
03	4 00·8	4 01·4	3 49·8	0·3 0·1	6·3 1·7	12·3 3·4	03	4 15·8	4 16·5	4 04·1	0·3 0·1	6·3 1·8	12·3 3·6
04	4 01·0	4 01·7	3 50·0	0·4 0·1	6·4 1·8	12·4 3·4	04	4 16·0	4 16·7	4 04·3	0·4 0·1	6·4 1·9	12·4 3·6
05	4 01·3	4 01·9	3 50·3	0·5 0·1	6·5 1·8	12·5 3·4	05	4 16·3	4 17·0	4 04·6	0·5 0·1	6·5 1·9	12·5 3·6
06	4 01·5	4 02·2	3 50·5	0·6 0·2	6·6 1·8	12·6 3·5	06	4 16·5	4 17·2	4 04·8	0·6 0·2	6·6 1·9	12·6 3·7
07	4 01·8	4 02·4	3 50·7	0·7 0·2	6·7 1·8	12·7 3·5	07	4 16·8	4 17·5	4 05·1	0·7 0·2	6·7 2·0	12·7 3·7
08	4 02·0	4 02·7	3 51·0	0·8 0·2	6·8 1·9	12·8 3·5	08	4 17·0	4 17·7	4 05·3	0·8 0·2	6·8 2·0	12·8 3·7
09	4 02·3	4 02·9	3 51·2	0·9 0·2	6·9 1·9	12·9 3·5	09	4 17·3	4 18·0	4 05·5	0·9 0·3	6·9 2·0	12·9 3·8
10	4 02·5	4 03·2	3 51·5	1·0 0·3	7·0 1·9	13·0 3·6	10	4 17·5	4 18·2	4 05·8	1·0 0·3	7·0 2·0	13·0 3·8
11	4 02·8	4 03·4	3 51·7	1·1 0·3	7·1 2·0	13·1 3·6	11	4 17·8	4 18·5	4 06·0	1·1 0·3	7·1 2·1	13·1 3·8
12	4 03·0	4 03·7	3 51·9	1·2 0·3	7·2 2·0	13·2 3·6	12	4 18·0	4 18·7	4 06·2	1·2 0·4	7·2 2·1	13·2 3·9
13	4 03·3	4 03·9	3 52·2	1·3 0·4	7·3 2·0	13·3 3·7	13	4 18·3	4 19·0	4 06·5	1·3 0·4	7·3 2·1	13·3 3·9
14	4 03·5	4 04·2	3 52·4	1·4 0·4	7·4 2·0	13·4 3·7	14	4 18·5	4 19·2	4 06·7	1·4 0·4	7·4 2·2	13·4 3·9
15	4 03·8	4 04·4	3 52·6	1·5 0·4	7·5 2·1	13·5 3·7	15	4 18·8	4 19·5	4 07·0	1·5 0·4	7·5 2·2	13·5 3·9
16	4 04·0	4 04·7	3 52·9	1·6 0·4	7·6 2·1	13·6 3·7	16	4 19·0	4 19·7	4 07·2	1·6 0·5	7·6 2·2	13·6 4·0
17	4 04·3	4 04·9	3 53·1	1·7 0·5	7·7 2·1	13·7 3·8	17	4 19·3	4 20·0	4 07·4	1·7 0·5	7·7 2·2	13·7 4·0
18	4 04·5	4 05·2	3 53·4	1·8 0·5	7·8 2·1	13·8 3·8	18	4 19·5	4 20·2	4 07·7	1·8 0·5	7·8 2·3	13·8 4·0
19	4 04·8	4 05·4	3 53·6	1·9 0·5	7·9 2·2	13·9 3·8	19	4 19·8	4 20·5	4 07·9	1·9 0·6	7·9 2·3	13·9 4·1
20	4 05·0	4 05·7	3 53·8	2·0 0·6	8·0 2·2	14·0 3·9	20	4 20·0	4 20·7	4 08·2	2·0 0·6	8·0 2·3	14·0 4·1
21	4 05·3	4 05·9	3 54·1	2·1 0·6	8·1 2·2	14·1 3·9	21	4 20·3	4 21·0	4 08·4	2·1 0·6	8·1 2·4	14·1 4·1
22	4 05·5	4 06·2	3 54·3	2·2 0·6	8·2 2·3	14·2 3·9	22	4 20·5	4 21·2	4 08·6	2·2 0·6	8·2 2·4	14·2 4·1
23	4 05·8	4 06·4	3 54·6	2·3 0·6	8·3 2·3	14·3 3·9	23	4 20·8	4 21·5	4 08·9	2·3 0·7	8·3 2·4	14·3 4·2
24	4 06·0	4 06·7	3 54·8	2·4 0·7	8·4 2·3	14·4 4·0	24	4 21·0	4 21·7	4 09·1	2·4 0·7	8·4 2·5	14·4 4·2
25	4 06·3	4 06·9	3 55·0	2·5 0·7	8·5 2·3	14·5 4·0	25	4 21·3	4 22·0	4 09·3	2·5 0·7	8·5 2·5	14·5 4·2
26	4 06·5	4 07·2	3 55·3	2·6 0·7	8·6 2·4	14·6 4·0	26	4 21·5	4 22·2	4 09·6	2·6 0·8	8·6 2·5	14·6 4·3
27	4 06·8	4 07·4	3 55·5	2·7 0·7	8·7 2·4	14·7 4·0	27	4 21·8	4 22·5	4 09·8	2·7 0·8	8·7 2·5	14·7 4·3
28	4 07·0	4 07·7	3 55·7	2·8 0·8	8·8 2·4	14·8 4·1	28	4 22·0	4 22·7	4 10·1	2·8 0·8	8·8 2·6	14·8 4·3
29	4 07·3	4 07·9	3 56·0	2·9 0·8	8·9 2·4	14·9 4·1	29	4 22·3	4 23·0	4 10·3	2·9 0·8	8·9 2·6	14·9 4·3
30	4 07·5	4 08·2	3 56·2	3·0 0·8	9·0 2·5	15·0 4·1	30	4 22·5	4 23·2	4 10·5	3·0 0·9	9·0 2·6	15·0 4·4
31	4 07·8	4 08·4	3 56·5	3·1 0·9	9·1 2·5	15·1 4·2	31	4 22·8	4 23·5	4 10·8	3·1 0·9	9·1 2·7	15·1 4·4
32	4 08·0	4 08·7	3 56·7	3·2 0·9	9·2 2·5	15·2 4·2	32	4 23·0	4 23·7	4 11·0	3·2 0·9	9·2 2·7	15·2 4·4
33	4 08·3	4 08·9	3 56·9	3·3 0·9	9·3 2·6	15·3 4·2	33	4 23·3	4 24·0	4 11·3	3·3 1·0	9·3 2·7	15·3 4·5
34	4 08·5	4 09·2	3 57·2	3·4 0·9	9·4 2·6	15·4 4·2	34	4 23·5	4 24·2	4 11·5	3·4 1·0	9·4 2·7	15·4 4·5
35	4 08·8	4 09·4	3 57·4	3·5 1·0	9·5 2·6	15·5 4·3	35	4 23·8	4 24·5	4 11·7	3·5 1·0	9·5 2·8	15·5 4·5
36	4 09·0	4 09·7	3 57·7	3·6 1·0	9·6 2·6	15·6 4·3	36	4 24·0	4 24·7	4 12·0	3·6 1·1	9·6 2·8	15·6 4·6
37	4 09·3	4 09·9	3 57·9	3·7 1·0	9·7 2·7	15·7 4·3	37	4 24·3	4 25·0	4 12·2	3·7 1·1	9·7 2·8	15·7 4·6
38	4 09·5	4 10·2	3 58·1	3·8 1·0	9·8 2·7	15·8 4·3	38	4 24·5	4 25·2	4 12·5	3·8 1·1	9·8 2·9	15·8 4·6
39	4 09·8	4 10·4	3 58·4	3·9 1·1	9·9 2·7	15·9 4·4	39	4 24·8	4 25·5	4 12·7	3·9 1·1	9·9 2·9	15·9 4·6
40	4 10·0	4 10·7	3 58·6	4·0 1·1	10·0 2·8	16·0 4·4	40	4 25·0	4 25·7	4 12·9	4·0 1·2	10·0 2·9	16·0 4·7
41	4 10·3	4 10·9	3 58·8	4·1 1·1	10·1 2·8	16·1 4·4	41	4 25·3	4 26·0	4 13·2	4·1 1·2	10·1 2·9	16·1 4·7
42	4 10·5	4 11·2	3 59·1	4·2 1·2	10·2 2·8	16·2 4·5	42	4 25·5	4 26·2	4 13·4	4·2 1·2	10·2 3·0	16·2 4·7
43	4 10·8	4 11·4	3 59·3	4·3 1·2	10·3 2·8	16·3 4·5	43	4 25·8	4 26·5	4 13·6	4·3 1·3	10·3 3·0	16·3 4·8
44	4 11·0	4 11·7	3 59·6	4·4 1·2	10·4 2·9	16·4 4·5	44	4 26·0	4 26·7	4 13·9	4·4 1·3	10·4 3·0	16·4 4·8
45	4 11·3	4 11·9	3 59·8	4·5 1·2	10·5 2·9	16·5 4·5	45	4 26·3	4 27·0	4 14·1	4·5 1·3	10·5 3·1	16·5 4·8
46	4 11·5	4 12·2	4 00·0	4·6 1·3	10·6 2·9	16·6 4·6	46	4 26·5	4 27·2	4 14·4	4·6 1·3	10·6 3·1	16·6 4·8
47	4 11·8	4 12·4	4 00·3	4·7 1·3	10·7 2·9	16·7 4·6	47	4 26·8	4 27·5	4 14·6	4·7 1·4	10·7 3·1	16·7 4·9
48	4 12·0	4 12·7	4 00·5	4·8 1·3	10·8 3·0	16·8 4·6	48	4 27·0	4 27·7	4 14·8	4·8 1·4	10·8 3·2	16·8 4·9
49	4 12·3	4 12·9	4 00·8	4·9 1·3	10·9 3·0	16·9 4·6	49	4 27·3	4 28·0	4 15·1	4·9 1·4	10·9 3·2	16·9 4·9
50	4 12·5	4 13·2	4 01·0	5·0 1·4	11·0 3·0	17·0 4·7	50	4 27·5	4 28·2	4 15·3	5·0 1·5	11·0 3·2	17·0 5·0
51	4 12·8	4 13·4	4 01·2	5·1 1·4	11·1 3·1	17·1 4·7	51	4 27·8	4 28·5	4 15·6	5·1 1·5	11·1 3·2	17·1 5·0
52	4 13·0	4 13·7	4 01·5	5·2 1·4	11·2 3·1	17·2 4·7	52	4 28·0	4 28·7	4 15·8	5·2 1·5	11·2 3·3	17·2 5·0
53	4 13·3	4 13·9	4 01·7	5·3 1·5	11·3 3·1	17·3 4·8	53	4 28·3	4 29·0	4 16·0	5·3 1·5	11·3 3·3	17·3 5·0
54	4 13·5	4 14·2	4 02·0	5·4 1·5	11·4 3·1	17·4 4·8	54	4 28·5	4 29·2	4 16·3	5·4 1·6	11·4 3·3	17·4 5·1
55	4 13·8	4 14·4	4 02·2	5·5 1·5	11·5 3·2	17·5 4·8	55	4 28·8	4 29·5	4 16·5	5·5 1·6	11·5 3·4	17·5 5·1
56	4 14·0	4 14·7	4 02·4	5·6 1·5	11·6 3·2	17·6 4·8	56	4 29·0	4 29·7	4 16·7	5·6 1·6	11·6 3·4	17·6 5·1
57	4 14·3	4 14·9	4 02·7	5·7 1·6	11·7 3·2	17·7 4·9	57	4 29·3	4 30·0	4 17·0	5·7 1·7	11·7 3·4	17·7 5·2
58	4 14·5	4 15·2	4 02·9	5·8 1·6	11·8 3·2	17·8 4·9	58	4 29·5	4 30·2	4 17·2	5·8 1·7	11·8 3·4	17·8 5·2
59	4 14·8	4 15·4	4 03·1	5·9 1·6	11·9 3·3	17·9 4·9	59	4 29·8	4 30·5	4 17·5	5·9 1·7	11·9 3·5	17·9 5·2
60	4 15·0	4 15·7	4 03·4	6·0 1·7	12·0 3·3	18·0 5·0	60	4 30·0	4 30·7	4 17·7	6·0 1·8	12·0 3·5	18·0 5·3

18ᵐ

18 s	SUN PLANETS	ARIES	MOON	v or d Corrn	v or d Corrn	v or d Corrn
00	4 30.0	4 30.7	4 17.7	0.0 0.0	6.0 1.9	12.0 3.7
01	4 30.3	4 31.0	4 17.9	0.1 0.0	6.1 1.9	12.1 3.7
02	4 30.5	4 31.2	4 18.2	0.2 0.1	6.2 1.9	12.2 3.8
03	4 30.8	4 31.5	4 18.4	0.3 0.1	6.3 1.9	12.3 3.8
04	4 31.0	4 31.7	4 18.7	0.4 0.1	6.4 2.0	12.4 3.8
05	4 31.3	4 32.0	4 18.9	0.5 0.2	6.5 2.0	12.5 3.9
06	4 31.5	4 32.2	4 19.1	0.6 0.2	6.6 2.0	12.6 3.9
07	4 31.8	4 32.5	4 19.4	0.7 0.2	6.7 2.1	12.7 3.9
08	4 32.0	4 32.7	4 19.6	0.8 0.2	6.8 2.1	12.8 3.9
09	4 32.3	4 33.0	4 19.8	0.9 0.3	6.9 2.1	12.9 4.0
10	4 32.5	4 33.2	4 20.1	1.0 0.3	7.0 2.2	13.0 4.0
11	4 32.8	4 33.5	4 20.3	1.1 0.3	7.1 2.2	13.1 4.0
12	4 33.0	4 33.7	4 20.6	1.2 0.4	7.2 2.2	13.2 4.1
13	4 33.3	4 34.0	4 20.8	1.3 0.4	7.3 2.3	13.3 4.1
14	4 33.5	4 34.2	4 21.0	1.4 0.4	7.4 2.3	13.4 4.1
15	4 33.8	4 34.5	4 21.3	1.5 0.5	7.5 2.3	13.5 4.2
16	4 34.0	4 34.8	4 21.5	1.6 0.5	7.6 2.3	13.6 4.2
17	4 34.3	4 35.0	4 21.8	1.7 0.5	7.7 2.4	13.7 4.2
18	4 34.5	4 35.3	4 22.0	1.8 0.6	7.8 2.4	13.8 4.3
19	4 34.8	4 35.5	4 22.2	1.9 0.6	7.9 2.4	13.9 4.3
20	4 35.0	4 35.8	4 22.5	2.0 0.6	8.0 2.5	14.0 4.3
21	4 35.3	4 36.0	4 22.7	2.1 0.6	8.1 2.5	14.1 4.3
22	4 35.5	4 36.3	4 22.9	2.2 0.7	8.2 2.5	14.2 4.4
23	4 35.8	4 36.5	4 23.2	2.3 0.7	8.3 2.6	14.3 4.4
24	4 36.0	4 36.8	4 23.4	2.4 0.7	8.4 2.6	14.4 4.4
25	4 36.3	4 37.0	4 23.7	2.5 0.8	8.5 2.6	14.5 4.5
26	4 36.5	4 37.3	4 23.9	2.6 0.8	8.6 2.7	14.6 4.5
27	4 36.8	4 37.5	4 24.1	2.7 0.8	8.7 2.7	14.7 4.5
28	4 37.0	4 37.8	4 24.4	2.8 0.9	8.8 2.7	14.8 4.6
29	4 37.3	4 38.0	4 24.6	2.9 0.9	8.9 2.7	14.9 4.6
30	4 37.5	4 38.3	4 24.9	3.0 0.9	9.0 2.8	15.0 4.6
31	4 37.8	4 38.5	4 25.1	3.1 1.0	9.1 2.8	15.1 4.7
32	4 38.0	4 38.8	4 25.3	3.2 1.0	9.2 2.8	15.2 4.7
33	4 38.3	4 39.0	4 25.6	3.3 1.0	9.3 2.9	15.3 4.7
34	4 38.5	4 39.3	4 25.8	3.4 1.0	9.4 2.9	15.4 4.7
35	4 38.8	4 39.5	4 26.1	3.5 1.1	9.5 2.9	15.5 4.8
36	4 39.0	4 39.8	4 26.3	3.6 1.1	9.6 3.0	15.6 4.8
37	4 39.3	4 40.0	4 26.5	3.7 1.1	9.7 3.0	15.7 4.8
38	4 39.5	4 40.3	4 26.8	3.8 1.2	9.8 3.0	15.8 4.9
39	4 39.8	4 40.5	4 27.0	3.9 1.2	9.9 3.1	15.9 4.9
40	4 40.0	4 40.8	4 27.2	4.0 1.2	10.0 3.1	16.0 4.9
41	4 40.3	4 41.0	4 27.5	4.1 1.3	10.1 3.1	16.1 5.0
42	4 40.5	4 41.3	4 27.7	4.2 1.3	10.2 3.1	16.2 5.0
43	4 40.8	4 41.5	4 28.0	4.3 1.3	10.3 3.2	16.3 5.0
44	4 41.0	4 41.8	4 28.2	4.4 1.4	10.4 3.2	16.4 5.1
45	4 41.3	4 42.0	4 28.4	4.5 1.4	10.5 3.2	16.5 5.1
46	4 41.5	4 42.3	4 28.7	4.6 1.4	10.6 3.3	16.6 5.1
47	4 41.8	4 42.5	4 28.9	4.7 1.4	10.7 3.3	16.7 5.1
48	4 42.0	4 42.8	4 29.2	4.8 1.5	10.8 3.3	16.8 5.2
49	4 42.3	4 43.0	4 29.4	4.9 1.5	10.9 3.4	16.9 5.2
50	4 42.5	4 43.3	4 29.6	5.0 1.5	11.0 3.4	17.0 5.2
51	4 42.8	4 43.5	4 29.9	5.1 1.6	11.1 3.4	17.1 5.3
52	4 43.0	4 43.8	4 30.1	5.2 1.6	11.2 3.5	17.2 5.3
53	4 43.3	4 44.0	4 30.3	5.3 1.6	11.3 3.5	17.3 5.3
54	4 43.5	4 44.3	4 30.6	5.4 1.7	11.4 3.5	17.4 5.4
55	4 43.8	4 44.5	4 30.8	5.5 1.7	11.5 3.5	17.5 5.4
56	4 44.0	4 44.8	4 31.1	5.6 1.7	11.6 3.6	17.6 5.4
57	4 44.3	4 45.0	4 31.3	5.7 1.8	11.7 3.6	17.7 5.5
58	4 44.5	4 45.3	4 31.5	5.8 1.8	11.8 3.6	17.8 5.5
59	4 44.8	4 45.5	4 31.8	5.9 1.8	11.9 3.7	17.9 5.5
60	4 45.0	4 45.8	4 32.0	6.0 1.9	12.0 3.7	18.0 5.6

19ᵐ

19 s	SUN PLANETS	ARIES	MOON	v or d Corrn	v or d Corrn	v or d Corrn
00	4 45.0	4 45.8	4 32.0	0.0 0.0	6.0 2.0	12.0 3.9
01	4 45.3	4 46.0	4 32.3	0.1 0.0	6.1 2.0	12.1 3.9
02	4 45.5	4 46.3	4 32.5	0.2 0.1	6.2 2.0	12.2 4.0
03	4 45.8	4 46.5	4 32.7	0.3 0.1	6.3 2.0	12.3 4.0
04	4 46.0	4 46.8	4 33.0	0.4 0.1	6.4 2.1	12.4 4.0
05	4 46.3	4 47.0	4 33.2	0.5 0.2	6.5 2.1	12.5 4.1
06	4 46.5	4 47.3	4 33.4	0.6 0.2	6.6 2.1	12.6 4.1
07	4 46.8	4 47.5	4 33.7	0.7 0.2	6.7 2.2	12.7 4.1
08	4 47.0	4 47.8	4 33.9	0.8 0.3	6.8 2.2	12.8 4.2
09	4 47.3	4 48.0	4 34.2	0.9 0.3	6.9 2.2	12.9 4.2
10	4 47.5	4 48.3	4 34.4	1.0 0.3	7.0 2.3	13.0 4.2
11	4 47.8	4 48.5	4 34.6	1.1 0.4	7.1 2.3	13.1 4.3
12	4 48.0	4 48.8	4 34.9	1.2 0.4	7.2 2.3	13.2 4.3
13	4 48.3	4 49.0	4 35.1	1.3 0.4	7.3 2.4	13.3 4.3
14	4 48.5	4 49.3	4 35.4	1.4 0.5	7.4 2.4	13.4 4.4
15	4 48.8	4 49.5	4 35.6	1.5 0.5	7.5 2.4	13.5 4.4
16	4 49.0	4 49.8	4 35.8	1.6 0.5	7.6 2.5	13.6 4.4
17	4 49.3	4 50.0	4 36.1	1.7 0.6	7.7 2.5	13.7 4.5
18	4 49.5	4 50.3	4 36.3	1.8 0.6	7.8 2.5	13.8 4.5
19	4 49.8	4 50.5	4 36.6	1.9 0.6	7.9 2.6	13.9 4.5
20	4 50.0	4 50.8	4 36.8	2.0 0.7	8.0 2.6	14.0 4.6
21	4 50.3	4 51.0	4 37.0	2.1 0.7	8.1 2.6	14.1 4.6
22	4 50.5	4 51.3	4 37.3	2.2 0.7	8.2 2.7	14.2 4.6
23	4 50.8	4 51.5	4 37.5	2.3 0.7	8.3 2.7	14.3 4.6
24	4 51.0	4 51.8	4 37.7	2.4 0.8	8.4 2.7	14.4 4.7
25	4 51.3	4 52.0	4 38.0	2.5 0.8	8.5 2.8	14.5 4.7
26	4 51.5	4 52.3	4 38.2	2.6 0.8	8.6 2.8	14.6 4.7
27	4 51.8	4 52.5	4 38.5	2.7 0.9	8.7 2.8	14.7 4.8
28	4 52.0	4 52.8	4 38.7	2.8 0.9	8.8 2.9	14.8 4.8
29	4 52.3	4 53.1	4 38.9	2.9 0.9	8.9 2.9	14.9 4.8
30	4 52.5	4 53.3	4 39.2	3.0 1.0	9.0 2.9	15.0 4.9
31	4 52.8	4 53.6	4 39.4	3.1 1.0	9.1 3.0	15.1 4.9
32	4 53.0	4 53.8	4 39.7	3.2 1.0	9.2 3.0	15.2 4.9
33	4 53.3	4 54.1	4 39.9	3.3 1.1	9.3 3.0	15.3 5.0
34	4 53.5	4 54.3	4 40.1	3.4 1.1	9.4 3.1	15.4 5.0
35	4 53.8	4 54.6	4 40.4	3.5 1.1	9.5 3.1	15.5 5.0
36	4 54.0	4 54.8	4 40.6	3.6 1.2	9.6 3.1	15.6 5.1
37	4 54.3	4 55.1	4 40.8	3.7 1.2	9.7 3.2	15.7 5.1
38	4 54.5	4 55.3	4 41.1	3.8 1.2	9.8 3.2	15.8 5.1
39	4 54.8	4 55.6	4 41.3	3.9 1.3	9.9 3.2	15.9 5.2
40	4 55.0	4 55.8	4 41.6	4.0 1.3	10.0 3.3	16.0 5.2
41	4 55.3	4 56.1	4 41.8	4.1 1.3	10.1 3.3	16.1 5.2
42	4 55.5	4 56.3	4 42.0	4.2 1.4	10.2 3.3	16.2 5.3
43	4 55.8	4 56.6	4 42.3	4.3 1.4	10.3 3.4	16.3 5.3
44	4 56.0	4 56.8	4 42.5	4.4 1.4	10.4 3.4	16.4 5.3
45	4 56.3	4 57.1	4 42.8	4.5 1.5	10.5 3.4	16.5 5.4
46	4 56.5	4 57.3	4 43.0	4.6 1.5	10.6 3.4	16.6 5.4
47	4 56.8	4 57.6	4 43.2	4.7 1.5	10.7 3.5	16.7 5.4
48	4 57.0	4 57.8	4 43.5	4.8 1.6	10.8 3.5	16.8 5.5
49	4 57.3	4 58.1	4 43.7	4.9 1.6	10.9 3.5	16.9 5.5
50	4 57.5	4 58.3	4 43.9	5.0 1.6	11.0 3.6	17.0 5.5
51	4 57.8	4 58.6	4 44.2	5.1 1.7	11.1 3.6	17.1 5.6
52	4 58.0	4 58.8	4 44.4	5.2 1.7	11.2 3.6	17.2 5.6
53	4 58.3	4 59.1	4 44.7	5.3 1.7	11.3 3.7	17.3 5.6
54	4 58.5	4 59.3	4 44.9	5.4 1.8	11.4 3.7	17.4 5.7
55	4 58.8	4 59.6	4 45.1	5.5 1.8	11.5 3.7	17.5 5.7
56	4 59.0	4 59.8	4 45.4	5.6 1.8	11.6 3.8	17.6 5.7
57	4 59.3	5 00.1	4 45.6	5.7 1.9	11.7 3.8	17.7 5.8
58	4 59.5	5 00.3	4 45.9	5.8 1.9	11.8 3.8	17.8 5.8
59	4 59.8	5 00.6	4 46.1	5.9 1.9	11.9 3.9	17.9 5.8
60	5 00.0	5 00.8	4 46.3	6.0 2.0	12.0 3.9	18.0 5.9

20	SUN PLANETS	ARIES	MOON	v or d Corrⁿ	v or d Corrⁿ	v or d Corrⁿ
s	° ′	° ′	° ′	′ ′	′ ′	′ ′
00	5 00·0	5 00·8	4 46·3	0·0 0·0	6·0 2·1	12·0 4·1
01	5 00·3	5 01·1	4 46·6	0·1 0·0	6·1 2·1	12·1 4·1
02	5 00·5	5 01·3	4 46·8	0·2 0·1	6·2 2·1	12·2 4·2
03	5 00·8	5 01·6	4 47·0	0·3 0·1	6·3 2·2	12·3 4·2
04	5 01·0	5 01·8	4 47·3	0·4 0·1	6·4 2·2	12·4 4·2
05	5 01·3	5 02·1	4 47·5	0·5 0·2	6·5 2·2	12·5 4·3
06	5 01·5	5 02·3	4 47·8	0·6 0·2	6·6 2·3	12·6 4·3
07	5 01·8	5 02·6	4 48·0	0·7 0·2	6·7 2·3	12·7 4·3
08	5 02·0	5 02·8	4 48·2	0·8 0·3	6·8 2·3	12·8 4·4
09	5 02·3	5 03·1	4 48·5	0·9 0·3	6·9 2·4	12·9 4·4
10	5 02·5	5 03·3	4 48·7	1·0 0·3	7·0 2·4	13·0 4·4
11	5 02·8	5 03·6	4 49·0	1·1 0·4	7·1 2·4	13·1 4·5
12	5 03·0	5 03·8	4 49·2	1·2 0·4	7·2 2·5	13·2 4·5
13	5 03·3	5 04·1	4 49·4	1·3 0·4	7·3 2·5	13·3 4·5
14	5 03·5	5 04·3	4 49·7	1·4 0·5	7·4 2·5	13·4 4·6
15	5 03·8	5 04·6	4 49·9	1·5 0·5	7·5 2·6	13·5 4·6
16	5 04·0	5 04·8	4 50·2	1·6 0·5	7·6 2·6	13·6 4·6
17	5 04·3	5 05·1	4 50·4	1·7 0·6	7·7 2·6	13·7 4·7
18	5 04·5	5 05·3	4 50·6	1·8 0·6	7·8 2·7	13·8 4·7
19	5 04·8	5 05·6	4 50·9	1·9 0·6	7·9 2·7	13·9 4·7
20	5 05·0	5 05·8	4 51·1	2·0 0·7	8·0 2·7	14·0 4·8
21	5 05·3	5 06·1	4 51·3	2·1 0·7	8·1 2·8	14·1 4·8
22	5 05·5	5 06·3	4 51·6	2·2 0·8	8·2 2·8	14·2 4·9
23	5 05·8	5 06·6	4 51·8	2·3 0·8	8·3 2·8	14·3 4·9
24	5 06·0	5 06·8	4 52·1	2·4 0·8	8·4 2·9	14·4 4·9
25	5 06·3	5 07·1	4 52·3	2·5 0·9	8·5 2·9	14·5 5·0
26	5 06·5	5 07·3	4 52·5	2·6 0·9	8·6 2·9	14·6 5·0
27	5 06·8	5 07·6	4 52·8	2·7 0·9	8·7 3·0	14·7 5·0
28	5 07·0	5 07·8	4 53·0	2·8 1·0	8·8 3·0	14·8 5·1
29	5 07·3	5 08·1	4 53·3	2·9 1·0	8·9 3·0	14·9 5·1
30	5 07·5	5 08·3	4 53·5	3·0 1·0	9·0 3·1	15·0 5·1
31	5 07·8	5 08·6	4 53·7	3·1 1·1	9·1 3·1	15·1 5·2
32	5 08·0	5 08·8	4 54·0	3·2 1·1	9·2 3·1	15·2 5·2
33	5 08·3	5 09·1	4 54·2	3·3 1·1	9·3 3·2	15·3 5·2
34	5 08·5	5 09·3	4 54·4	3·4 1·2	9·4 3·2	15·4 5·3
35	5 08·8	5 09·6	4 54·7	3·5 1·2	9·5 3·2	15·5 5·3
36	5 09·0	5 09·8	4 54·9	3·6 1·2	9·6 3·3	15·6 5·3
37	5 09·3	5 10·1	4 55·2	3·7 1·3	9·7 3·3	15·7 5·4
38	5 09·5	5 10·3	4 55·4	3·8 1·3	9·8 3·3	15·8 5·4
39	5 09·8	5 10·6	4 55·6	3·9 1·3	9·9 3·4	15·9 5·4
40	5 10·0	5 10·8	4 55·9	4·0 1·4	10·0 3·4	16·0 5·5
41	5 10·3	5 11·1	4 56·1	4·1 1·4	10·1 3·5	16·1 5·5
42	5 10·5	5 11·4	4 56·4	4·2 1·4	10·2 3·5	16·2 5·5
43	5 10·8	5 11·6	4 56·6	4·3 1·5	10·3 3·5	16·3 5·6
44	5 11·0	5 11·9	4 56·8	4·4 1·5	10·4 3·6	16·4 5·6
45	5 11·3	5 12·1	4 57·1	4·5 1·5	10·5 3·6	16·5 5·6
46	5 11·5	5 12·4	4 57·3	4·6 1·6	10·6 3·6	16·6 5·7
47	5 11·8	5 12·6	4 57·5	4·7 1·6	10·7 3·7	16·7 5·7
48	5 12·0	5 12·9	4 57·8	4·8 1·6	10·8 3·7	16·8 5·7
49	5 12·3	5 13·1	4 58·0	4·9 1·7	10·9 3·7	16·9 5·8
50	5 12·5	5 13·4	4 58·3	5·0 1·7	11·0 3·8	17·0 5·8
51	5 12·8	5 13·6	4 58·5	5·1 1·7	11·1 3·8	17·1 5·8
52	5 13·0	5 13·9	4 58·7	5·2 1·8	11·2 3·8	17·2 5·9
53	5 13·3	5 14·1	4 59·0	5·3 1·8	11·3 3·9	17·3 5·9
54	5 13·5	5 14·4	4 59·2	5·4 1·8	11·4 3·9	17·4 5·9
55	5 13·8	5 14·6	4 59·5	5·5 1·9	11·5 3·9	17·5 6·0
56	5 14·0	5 14·9	4 59·7	5·6 1·9	11·6 4·0	17·6 6·0
57	5 14·3	5 15·1	4 59·9	5·7 1·9	11·7 4·0	17·7 6·0
58	5 14·5	5 15·4	5 00·2	5·8 2·0	11·8 4·0	17·8 6·1
59	5 14·8	5 15·6	5 00·4	5·9 2·0	11·9 4·1	17·9 6·1
60	5 15·0	5 15·9	5 00·7	6·0 2·1	12·0 4·1	18·0 6·2

21	SUN PLANETS	ARIES	MOON	v or d Corrⁿ	v or d Corrⁿ	v or d Corrⁿ
s	° ′	° ′	° ′	′ ′	′ ′	′ ′
00	5 15·0	5 15·9	5 00·7	0·0 0·0	6·0 2·2	12·0 4·3
01	5 15·3	5 16·1	5 00·9	0·1 0·0	6·1 2·2	12·1 4·3
02	5 15·5	5 16·4	5 01·1	0·2 0·1	6·2 2·2	12·2 4·4
03	5 15·8	5 16·6	5 01·4	0·3 0·1	6·3 2·3	12·3 4·4
04	5 16·0	5 16·9	5 01·6	0·4 0·1	6·4 2·3	12·4 4·4
05	5 16·3	5 17·1	5 01·8	0·5 0·2	6·5 2·3	12·5 4·5
06	5 16·5	5 17·4	5 02·1	0·6 0·2	6·6 2·4	12·6 4·5
07	5 16·8	5 17·6	5 02·3	0·7 0·3	6·7 2·4	12·7 4·6
08	5 17·0	5 17·9	5 02·6	0·8 0·3	6·8 2·4	12·8 4·6
09	5 17·3	5 18·1	5 02·8	0·9 0·3	6·9 2·5	12·9 4·6
10	5 17·5	5 18·4	5 03·0	1·0 0·4	7·0 2·5	13·0 4·7
11	5 17·8	5 18·6	5 03·3	1·1 0·4	7·1 2·5	13·1 4·7
12	5 18·0	5 18·9	5 03·5	1·2 0·4	7·2 2·6	13·2 4·7
13	5 18·3	5 19·1	5 03·8	1·3 0·5	7·3 2·6	13·3 4·8
14	5 18·5	5 19·4	5 04·0	1·4 0·5	7·4 2·7	13·4 4·8
15	5 18·8	5 19·6	5 04·2	1·5 0·5	7·5 2·7	13·5 4·8
16	5 19·0	5 19·9	5 04·5	1·6 0·6	7·6 2·7	13·6 4·9
17	5 19·3	5 20·1	5 04·7	1·7 0·6	7·7 2·8	13·7 4·9
18	5 19·5	5 20·4	5 04·9	1·8 0·6	7·8 2·8	13·8 4·9
19	5 19·8	5 20·6	5 05·2	1·9 0·7	7·9 2·8	13·9 5·0
20	5 20·0	5 20·9	5 05·4	2·0 0·7	8·0 2·9	14·0 5·0
21	5 20·3	5 21·1	5 05·7	2·1 0·8	8·1 2·9	14·1 5·1
22	5 20·5	5 21·4	5 05·9	2·2 0·8	8·2 2·9	14·2 5·1
23	5 20·8	5 21·6	5 06·1	2·3 0·8	8·3 3·0	14·3 5·1
24	5 21·0	5 21·9	5 06·4	2·4 0·9	8·4 3·0	14·4 5·2
25	5 21·3	5 22·1	5 06·6	2·5 0·9	8·5 3·0	14·5 5·2
26	5 21·5	5 22·4	5 06·9	2·6 0·9	8·6 3·1	14·6 5·2
27	5 21·8	5 22·6	5 07·1	2·7 1·0	8·7 3·1	14·7 5·3
28	5 22·0	5 22·9	5 07·3	2·8 1·0	8·8 3·2	14·8 5·3
29	5 22·3	5 23·1	5 07·6	2·9 1·0	8·9 3·2	14·9 5·3
30	5 22·5	5 23·4	5 07·8	3·0 1·1	9·0 3·2	15·0 5·4
31	5 22·8	5 23·6	5 08·0	3·1 1·1	9·1 3·3	15·1 5·4
32	5 23·0	5 23·9	5 08·3	3·2 1·1	9·2 3·3	15·2 5·4
33	5 23·3	5 24·1	5 08·5	3·3 1·2	9·3 3·3	15·3 5·5
34	5 23·5	5 24·4	5 08·8	3·4 1·2	9·4 3·4	15·4 5·5
35	5 23·8	5 24·6	5 09·0	3·5 1·3	9·5 3·4	15·5 5·6
36	5 24·0	5 24·9	5 09·2	3·6 1·3	9·6 3·4	15·6 5·6
37	5 24·3	5 25·1	5 09·5	3·7 1·3	9·7 3·5	15·7 5·6
38	5 24·5	5 25·4	5 09·7	3·8 1·4	9·8 3·5	15·8 5·7
39	5 24·8	5 25·6	5 10·0	3·9 1·4	9·9 3·5	15·9 5·7
40	5 25·0	5 25·9	5 10·2	4·0 1·4	10·0 3·6	16·0 5·7
41	5 25·3	5 26·1	5 10·4	4·1 1·5	10·1 3·6	16·1 5·8
42	5 25·5	5 26·4	5 10·7	4·2 1·5	10·2 3·7	16·2 5·8
43	5 25·8	5 26·6	5 10·9	4·3 1·5	10·3 3·7	16·3 5·8
44	5 26·0	5 26·9	5 11·1	4·4 1·6	10·4 3·7	16·4 5·9
45	5 26·3	5 27·1	5 11·4	4·5 1·6	10·5 3·8	16·5 5·9
46	5 26·5	5 27·4	5 11·6	4·6 1·6	10·6 3·8	16·6 5·9
47	5 26·8	5 27·6	5 11·9	4·7 1·7	10·7 3·8	16·7 6·0
48	5 27·0	5 27·9	5 12·1	4·8 1·7	10·8 3·9	16·8 6·0
49	5 27·3	5 28·1	5 12·3	4·9 1·8	10·9 3·9	16·9 6·1
50	5 27·5	5 28·4	5 12·6	5·0 1·8	11·0 3·9	17·0 6·1
51	5 27·8	5 28·6	5 12·8	5·1 1·8	11·1 4·0	17·1 6·1
52	5 28·0	5 28·9	5 13·1	5·2 1·9	11·2 4·0	17·2 6·2
53	5 28·3	5 29·1	5 13·3	5·3 1·9	11·3 4·0	17·3 6·2
54	5 28·5	5 29·4	5 13·5	5·4 1·9	11·4 4·1	17·4 6·2
55	5 28·8	5 29·7	5 13·8	5·5 2·0	11·5 4·1	17·5 6·3
56	5 29·0	5 29·9	5 14·0	5·6 2·0	11·6 4·2	17·6 6·3
57	5 29·3	5 30·2	5 14·3	5·7 2·0	11·7 4·2	17·7 6·3
58	5 29·5	5 30·4	5 14·5	5·8 2·1	11·8 4·2	17·8 6·4
59	5 29·8	5 30·7	5 14·7	5·9 2·1	11·9 4·3	17·9 6·4
60	5 30·0	5 30·9	5 15·0	6·0 2·2	12·0 4·3	18·0 6·5

22ᵐ	SUN PLANETS	ARIES	MOON	v or d Corrⁿ		v or d Corrⁿ		v or d Corrⁿ	
s	° ′	° ′	° ′	′	′	′	′	′	′
00	5 30·0	5 30·9	5 15·0	0·0	0·0	6·0	2·3	12·0	4·5
01	5 30·3	5 31·2	5 15·2	0·1	0·0	6·1	2·3	12·1	4·5
02	5 30·5	5 31·4	5 15·4	0·2	0·1	6·2	2·3	12·2	4·6
03	5 30·8	5 31·7	5 15·7	0·3	0·1	6·3	2·4	12·3	4·6
04	5 31·0	5 31·9	5 15·9	0·4	0·2	6·4	2·4	12·4	4·7
05	5 31·3	5 32·2	5 16·2	0·5	0·2	6·5	2·4	12·5	4·7
06	5 31·5	5 32·4	5 16·4	0·6	0·2	6·6	2·5	12·6	4·7
07	5 31·8	5 32·7	5 16·6	0·7	0·3	6·7	2·5	12·7	4·8
08	5 32·0	5 32·9	5 16·9	0·8	0·3	6·8	2·6	12·8	4·8
09	5 32·3	5 33·2	5 17·1	0·9	0·3	6·9	2·6	12·9	4·8
10	5 32·5	5 33·4	5 17·4	1·0	0·4	7·0	2·6	13·0	4·9
11	5 32·8	5 33·7	5 17·6	1·1	0·4	7·1	2·7	13·1	4·9
12	5 33·0	5 33·9	5 17·8	1·2	0·5	7·2	2·7	13·2	5·0
13	5 33·3	5 34·2	5 18·1	1·3	0·5	7·3	2·7	13·3	5·0
14	5 33·5	5 34·4	5 18·3	1·4	0·5	7·4	2·8	13·4	5·0
15	5 33·8	5 34·7	5 18·5	1·5	0·6	7·5	2·8	13·5	5·1
16	5 34·0	5 34·9	5 18·8	1·6	0·6	7·6	2·9	13·6	5·1
17	5 34·3	5 35·2	5 19·0	1·7	0·6	7·7	2·9	13·7	5·1
18	5 34·5	5 35·4	5 19·3	1·8	0·7	7·8	2·9	13·8	5·2
19	5 34·8	5 35·7	5 19·5	1·9	0·7	7·9	3·0	13·9	5·2
20	5 35·0	5 35·9	5 19·7	2·0	0·8	8·0	3·0	14·0	5·3
21	5 35·3	5 36·2	5 20·0	2·1	0·8	8·1	3·0	14·1	5·3
22	5 35·5	5 36·4	5 20·2	2·2	0·8	8·2	3·1	14·2	5·3
23	5 35·8	5 36·7	5 20·5	2·3	0·9	8·3	3·1	14·3	5·4
24	5 36·0	5 36·9	5 20·7	2·4	0·9	8·4	3·2	14·4	5·4
25	5 36·3	5 37·2	5 20·9	2·5	0·9	8·5	3·2	14·5	5·4
26	5 36·5	5 37·4	5 21·2	2·6	1·0	8·6	3·2	14·6	5·5
27	5 36·8	5 37·7	5 21·4	2·7	1·0	8·7	3·3	14·7	5·5
28	5 37·0	5 37·9	5 21·6	2·8	1·0	8·8	3·3	14·8	5·6
29	5 37·3	5 38·2	5 21·9	2·9	1·1	8·9	3·3	14·9	5·6
30	5 37·5	5 38·4	5 22·1	3·0	1·1	9·0	3·4	15·0	5·6
31	5 37·8	5 38·7	5 22·4	3·1	1·2	9·1	3·4	15·1	5·7
32	5 38·0	5 38·9	5 22·6	3·2	1·2	9·2	3·5	15·2	5·7
33	5 38·3	5 39·2	5 22·8	3·3	1·2	9·3	3·5	15·3	5·7
34	5 38·5	5 39·4	5 23·1	3·4	1·3	9·4	3·5	15·4	5·8
35	5 38·8	5 39·7	5 23·3	3·5	1·3	9·5	3·6	15·5	5·8
36	5 39·0	5 39·9	5 23·6	3·6	1·4	9·6	3·6	15·6	5·9
37	5 39·3	5 40·2	5 23·8	3·7	1·4	9·7	3·6	15·7	5·9
38	5 39·5	5 40·4	5 24·0	3·8	1·4	9·8	3·7	15·8	5·9
39	5 39·8	5 40·7	5 24·3	3·9	1·5	9·9	3·7	15·9	6·0
40	5 40·0	5 40·9	5 24·5	4·0	1·5	10·0	3·8	16·0	6·0
41	5 40·3	5 41·2	5 24·7	4·1	1·5	10·1	3·8	16·1	6·0
42	5 40·5	5 41·4	5 25·0	4·2	1·6	10·2	3·8	16·2	6·1
43	5 40·8	5 41·7	5 25·2	4·3	1·6	10·3	3·9	16·3	6·1
44	5 41·0	5 41·9	5 25·5	4·4	1·7	10·4	3·9	16·4	6·1
45	5 41·3	5 42·2	5 25·7	4·5	1·7	10·5	3·9	16·5	6·2
46	5 41·5	5 42·4	5 25·9	4·6	1·7	10·6	4·0	16·6	6·2
47	5 41·8	5 42·7	5 26·2	4·7	1·8	10·7	4·0	16·7	6·3
48	5 42·0	5 42·9	5 26·4	4·8	1·8	10·8	4·1	16·8	6·3
49	5 42·3	5 43·2	5 26·7	4·9	1·8	10·9	4·1	16·9	6·3
50	5 42·5	5 43·4	5 26·9	5·0	1·9	11·0	4·1	17·0	6·4
51	5 42·8	5 43·7	5 27·1	5·1	1·9	11·1	4·2	17·1	6·4
52	5 43·0	5 43·9	5 27·4	5·2	2·0	11·2	4·2	17·2	6·5
53	5 43·3	5 44·2	5 27·6	5·3	2·0	11·3	4·2	17·3	6·5
54	5 43·5	5 44·4	5 27·9	5·4	2·0	11·4	4·3	17·4	6·5
55	5 43·8	5 44·7	5 28·1	5·5	2·1	11·5	4·3	17·5	6·6
56	5 44·0	5 44·9	5 28·3	5·6	2·1	11·6	4·4	17·6	6·6
57	5 44·3	5 45·2	5 28·6	5·7	2·1	11·7	4·4	17·7	6·6
58	5 44·5	5 45·4	5 28·8	5·8	2·2	11·8	4·4	17·8	6·7
59	5 44·8	5 45·7	5 29·0	5·9	2·2	11·9	4·5	17·9	6·7
60	5 45·0	5 45·9	5 29·3	6·0	2·3	12·0	4·5	18·0	6·8

23ᵐ	SUN PLANETS	ARIES	MOON	v or d Corrⁿ		v or d Corrⁿ		v or d Corrⁿ	
s	° ′	° ′	° ′	′	′	′	′	′	′
00	5 45·0	5 45·9	5 29·3	0·0	0·0	6·0	2·4	12·0	4·7
01	5 45·3	5 46·2	5 29·5	0·1	0·0	6·1	2·4	12·1	4·7
02	5 45·5	5 46·4	5 29·8	0·2	0·1	6·2	2·4	12·2	4·8
03	5 45·8	5 46·7	5 30·0	0·3	0·1	6·3	2·5	12·3	4·8
04	5 46·0	5 46·9	5 30·2	0·4	0·2	6·4	2·5	12·4	4·9
05	5 46·3	5 47·2	5 30·5	0·5	0·2	6·5	2·5	12·5	4·9
06	5 46·5	5 47·4	5 30·7	0·6	0·2	6·6	2·6	12·6	4·9
07	5 46·8	5 47·7	5 31·0	0·7	0·3	6·7	2·6	12·7	5·0
08	5 47·0	5 48·0	5 31·2	0·8	0·3	6·8	2·7	12·8	5·0
09	5 47·3	5 48·2	5 31·4	0·9	0·4	6·9	2·7	12·9	5·1
10	5 47·5	5 48·5	5 31·7	1·0	0·4	7·0	2·7	13·0	5·1
11	5 47·8	5 48·7	5 31·9	1·1	0·4	7·1	2·8	13·1	5·1
12	5 48·0	5 49·0	5 32·1	1·2	0·5	7·2	2·8	13·2	5·2
13	5 48·3	5 49·2	5 32·4	1·3	0·5	7·3	2·9	13·3	5·2
14	5 48·5	5 49·5	5 32·6	1·4	0·5	7·4	2·9	13·4	5·2
15	5 48·8	5 49·7	5 32·9	1·5	0·6	7·5	2·9	13·5	5·3
16	5 49·0	5 50·0	5 33·1	1·6	0·6	7·6	3·0	13·6	5·3
17	5 49·3	5 50·2	5 33·3	1·7	0·7	7·7	3·0	13·7	5·4
18	5 49·5	5 50·5	5 33·6	1·8	0·7	7·8	3·1	13·8	5·4
19	5 49·8	5 50·7	5 33·8	1·9	0·7	7·9	3·1	13·9	5·4
20	5 50·0	5 51·0	5 34·1	2·0	0·8	8·0	3·1	14·0	5·5
21	5 50·3	5 51·2	5 34·3	2·1	0·8	8·1	3·2	14·1	5·5
22	5 50·5	5 51·5	5 34·5	2·2	0·9	8·2	3·2	14·2	5·6
23	5 50·8	5 51·7	5 34·8	2·3	0·9	8·3	3·3	14·3	5·6
24	5 51·0	5 52·0	5 35·0	2·4	0·9	8·4	3·3	14·4	5·6
25	5 51·3	5 52·2	5 35·2	2·5	1·0	8·5	3·3	14·5	5·7
26	5 51·5	5 52·5	5 35·5	2·6	1·0	8·6	3·4	14·6	5·7
27	5 51·8	5 52·7	5 35·7	2·7	1·1	8·7	3·4	14·7	5·8
28	5 52·0	5 53·0	5 36·0	2·8	1·1	8·8	3·4	14·8	5·8
29	5 52·3	5 53·2	5 36·2	2·9	1·1	8·9	3·5	14·9	5·8
30	5 52·5	5 53·5	5 36·4	3·0	1·2	9·0	3·5	15·0	5·9
31	5 52·8	5 53·7	5 36·7	3·1	1·2	9·1	3·6	15·1	5·9
32	5 53·0	5 54·0	5 36·9	3·2	1·3	9·2	3·6	15·2	6·0
33	5 53·3	5 54·2	5 37·2	3·3	1·3	9·3	3·6	15·3	6·0
34	5 53·5	5 54·5	5 37·4	3·4	1·3	9·4	3·7	15·4	6·0
35	5 53·8	5 54·7	5 37·6	3·5	1·4	9·5	3·7	15·5	6·1
36	5 54·0	5 55·0	5 37·9	3·6	1·4	9·6	3·8	15·6	6·1
37	5 54·3	5 55·2	5 38·1	3·7	1·4	9·7	3·8	15·7	6·1
38	5 54·5	5 55·5	5 38·4	3·8	1·5	9·8	3·8	15·8	6·2
39	5 54·8	5 55·7	5 38·6	3·9	1·5	9·9	3·9	15·9	6·2
40	5 55·0	5 56·0	5 38·8	4·0	1·6	10·0	3·9	16·0	6·3
41	5 55·3	5 56·2	5 39·1	4·1	1·6	10·1	4·0	16·1	6·3
42	5 55·5	5 56·5	5 39·3	4·2	1·6	10·2	4·0	16·2	6·3
43	5 55·8	5 56·7	5 39·5	4·3	1·7	10·3	4·0	16·3	6·4
44	5 56·0	5 57·0	5 39·8	4·4	1·7	10·4	4·1	16·4	6·4
45	5 56·3	5 57·2	5 40·0	4·5	1·8	10·5	4·1	16·5	6·5
46	5 56·5	5 57·5	5 40·3	4·6	1·8	10·6	4·2	16·6	6·5
47	5 56·8	5 57·7	5 40·5	4·7	1·8	10·7	4·2	16·7	6·5
48	5 57·0	5 58·0	5 40·7	4·8	1·9	10·8	4·2	16·8	6·6
49	5 57·3	5 58·2	5 41·0	4·9	1·9	10·9	4·3	16·9	6·6
50	5 57·5	5 58·5	5 41·2	5·0	2·0	11·0	4·3	17·0	6·7
51	5 57·8	5 58·7	5 41·5	5·1	2·0	11·1	4·3	17·1	6·7
52	5 58·0	5 59·0	5 41·7	5·2	2·0	11·2	4·4	17·2	6·7
53	5 58·3	5 59·2	5 41·9	5·3	2·1	11·3	4·4	17·3	6·8
54	5 58·5	5 59·5	5 42·2	5·4	2·1	11·4	4·5	17·4	6·8
55	5 58·8	5 59·7	5 42·4	5·5	2·2	11·5	4·5	17·5	6·9
56	5 59·0	6 00·0	5 42·6	5·6	2·2	11·6	4·5	17·6	6·9
57	5 59·3	6 00·2	5 42·9	5·7	2·2	11·7	4·6	17·7	6·9
58	5 59·5	6 00·5	5 43·1	5·8	2·3	11·8	4·6	17·8	7·0
59	5 59·8	6 00·7	5 43·4	5·9	2·3	11·9	4·7	17·9	7·0
60	6 00·0	6 01·0	5 43·6	6·0	2·4	12·0	4·7	18·0	7·1

24^m	SUN PLANETS	ARIES	MOON	v or d	Corrⁿ	v or d	Corrⁿ	v or d	Corrⁿ
s	° ′	° ′	° ′	′	′	′	′	′	′
00	6 00·0	6 01·0	5 43·6	0·0	0·0	6·0	2·5	12·0	4·9
01	6 00·3	6 01·2	5 43·8	0·1	0·0	6·1	2·5	12·1	4·9
02	6 00·5	6 01·5	5 44·1	0·2	0·1	6·2	2·5	12·2	5·0
03	6 00·8	6 01·7	5 44·3	0·3	0·1	6·3	2·6	12·3	5·0
04	6 01·0	6 02·0	5 44·6	0·4	0·2	6·4	2·6	12·4	5·1
05	6 01·3	6 02·2	5 44·8	0·5	0·2	6·5	2·7	12·5	5·1
06	6 01·5	6 02·5	5 45·0	0·6	0·2	6·6	2·7	12·6	5·1
07	6 01·8	6 02·7	5 45·3	0·7	0·3	6·7	2·7	12·7	5·2
08	6 02·0	6 03·0	5 45·5	0·8	0·3	6·8	2·8	12·8	5·2
09	6 02·3	6 03·2	5 45·7	0·9	0·4	6·9	2·8	12·9	5·3
10	6 02·5	6 03·5	5 46·0	1·0	0·4	7·0	2·9	13·0	5·3
11	6 02·8	6 03·7	5 46·2	1·1	0·4	7·1	2·9	13·1	5·3
12	6 03·0	6 04·0	5 46·5	1·2	0·5	7·2	2·9	13·2	5·4
13	6 03·3	6 04·2	5 46·7	1·3	0·5	7·3	3·0	13·3	5·4
14	6 03·5	6 04·5	5 46·9	1·4	0·6	7·4	3·0	13·4	5·5
15	6 03·8	6 04·7	5 47·2	1·5	0·6	7·5	3·1	13·5	5·5
16	6 04·0	6 05·0	5 47·4	1·6	0·7	7·6	3·1	13·6	5·6
17	6 04·3	6 05·2	5 47·7	1·7	0·7	7·7	3·1	13·7	5·6
18	6 04·5	6 05·5	5 47·9	1·8	0·7	7·8	3·2	13·8	5·6
19	6 04·8	6 05·7	5 48·1	1·9	0·8	7·9	3·2	13·9	5·7
20	6 05·0	6 06·0	5 48·4	2·0	0·8	8·0	3·3	14·0	5·7
21	6 05·3	6 06·3	5 48·6	2·1	0·9	8·1	3·3	14·1	5·8
22	6 05·5	6 06·5	5 48·8	2·2	0·9	8·2	3·3	14·2	5·8
23	6 05·8	6 06·8	5 49·1	2·3	0·9	8·3	3·4	14·3	5·8
24	6 06·0	6 07·0	5 49·3	2·4	1·0	8·4	3·4	14·4	5·9
25	6 06·3	6 07·3	5 49·6	2·5	1·0	8·5	3·5	14·5	5·9
26	6 06·5	6 07·5	5 49·8	2·6	1·1	8·6	3·5	14·6	6·0
27	6 06·8	6 07·8	5 50·0	2·7	1·1	8·7	3·6	14·7	6·0
28	6 07·0	6 08·0	5 50·3	2·8	1·1	8·8	3·6	14·8	6·0
29	6 07·3	6 08·3	5 50·5	2·9	1·2	8·9	3·6	14·9	6·1
30	6 07·5	6 08·5	5 50·8	3·0	1·2	9·0	3·7	15·0	6·1
31	6 07·8	6 08·8	5 51·0	3·1	1·3	9·1	3·7	15·1	6·2
32	6 08·0	6 09·0	5 51·2	3·2	1·3	9·2	3·8	15·2	6·2
33	6 08·3	6 09·3	5 51·5	3·3	1·3	9·3	3·8	15·3	6·2
34	6 08·5	6 09·5	5 51·7	3·4	1·4	9·4	3·8	15·4	6·3
35	6 08·8	6 09·8	5 52·0	3·5	1·4	9·5	3·9	15·5	6·3
36	6 09·0	6 10·0	5 52·2	3·6	1·5	9·6	3·9	15·6	6·4
37	6 09·3	6 10·3	5 52·4	3·7	1·5	9·7	4·0	15·7	6·4
38	6 09·5	6 10·5	5 52·7	3·8	1·6	9·8	4·0	15·8	6·5
39	6 09·8	6 10·8	5 52·9	3·9	1·6	9·9	4·0	15·9	6·5
40	6 10·0	6 11·0	5 53·1	4·0	1·6	10·0	4·1	16·0	6·5
41	6 10·3	6 11·3	5 53·4	4·1	1·7	10·1	4·1	16·1	6·6
42	6 10·5	6 11·5	5 53·6	4·2	1·7	10·2	4·2	16·2	6·6
43	6 10·8	6 11·8	5 53·9	4·3	1·8	10·3	4·2	16·3	6·7
44	6 11·0	6 12·0	5 54·1	4·4	1·8	10·4	4·2	16·4	6·7
45	6 11·3	6 12·3	5 54·3	4·5	1·8	10·5	4·3	16·5	6·7
46	6 11·5	6 12·5	5 54·6	4·6	1·9	10·6	4·3	16·6	6·8
47	6 11·8	6 12·8	5 54·8	4·7	1·9	10·7	4·4	16·7	6·8
48	6 12·0	6 13·0	5 55·1	4·8	2·0	10·8	4·4	16·8	6·9
49	6 12·3	6 13·3	5 55·3	4·9	2·0	10·9	4·5	16·9	6·9
50	6 12·5	6 13·5	5 55·5	5·0	2·0	11·0	4·5	17·0	6·9
51	6 12·8	6 13·8	5 55·8	5·1	2·1	11·1	4·5	17·1	7·0
52	6 13·0	6 14·0	5 56·0	5·2	2·1	11·2	4·6	17·2	7·0
53	6 13·3	6 14·3	5 56·2	5·3	2·2	11·3	4·6	17·3	7·1
54	6 13·5	6 14·5	5 56·5	5·4	2·2	11·4	4·7	17·4	7·1
55	6 13·8	6 14·8	5 56·7	5·5	2·2	11·5	4·7	17·5	7·1
56	6 14·0	6 15·0	5 57·0	5·6	2·3	11·6	4·7	17·6	7·2
57	6 14·3	6 15·3	5 57·2	5·7	2·3	11·7	4·8	17·7	7·2
58	6 14·5	6 15·5	5 57·4	5·8	2·4	11·8	4·8	17·8	7·3
59	6 14·8	6 15·8	5 57·7	5·9	2·4	11·9	4·9	17·9	7·3
60	6 15·0	6 16·0	5 57·9	6·0	2·5	12·0	4·9	18·0	7·4

25^m	SUN PLANETS	ARIES	MOON	v or d	Corrⁿ	v or d	Corrⁿ	v or d	Corrⁿ
s	° ′	° ′	° ′	′	′	′	′	′	′
00	6 15·0	6 16·0	5 57·9	0·0	0·0	6·0	2·6	12·0	5·1
01	6 15·3	6 16·3	5 58·2	0·1	0·0	6·1	2·6	12·1	5·1
02	6 15·5	6 16·5	5 58·4	0·2	0·1	6·2	2·6	12·2	5·2
03	6 15·8	6 16·8	5 58·6	0·3	0·1	6·3	2·7	12·3	5·2
04	6 16·0	6 17·0	5 58·9	0·4	0·2	6·4	2·7	12·4	5·3
05	6 16·3	6 17·3	5 59·1	0·5	0·2	6·5	2·8	12·5	5·3
06	6 16·5	6 17·5	5 59·3	0·6	0·3	6·6	2·8	12·6	5·4
07	6 16·8	6 17·8	5 59·6	0·7	0·3	6·7	2·8	12·7	5·4
08	6 17·0	6 18·0	5 59·8	0·8	0·3	6·8	2·9	12·8	5·4
09	6 17·3	6 18·3	6 00·1	0·9	0·4	6·9	2·9	12·9	5·5
10	6 17·5	6 18·5	6 00·3	1·0	0·4	7·0	3·0	13·0	5·5
11	6 17·8	6 18·8	6 00·5	1·1	0·5	7·1	3·0	13·1	5·6
12	6 18·0	6 19·0	6 00·8	1·2	0·5	7·2	3·1	13·2	5·6
13	6 18·3	6 19·3	6 01·0	1·3	0·6	7·3	3·1	13·3	5·7
14	6 18·5	6 19·5	6 01·3	1·4	0·6	7·4	3·1	13·4	5·7
15	6 18·8	6 19·8	6 01·5	1·5	0·6	7·5	3·2	13·5	5·7
16	6 19·0	6 20·0	6 01·7	1·6	0·7	7·6	3·2	13·6	5·8
17	6 19·3	6 20·3	6 02·0	1·7	0·7	7·7	3·3	13·7	5·8
18	6 19·5	6 20·5	6 02·2	1·8	0·8	7·8	3·3	13·8	5·9
19	6 19·8	6 20·8	6 02·5	1·9	0·8	7·9	3·4	13·9	5·9
20	6 20·0	6 21·0	6 02·7	2·0	0·9	8·0	3·4	14·0	6·0
21	6 20·3	6 21·3	6 02·9	2·1	0·9	8·1	3·4	14·1	6·0
22	6 20·5	6 21·5	6 03·2	2·2	0·9	8·2	3·5	14·2	6·0
23	6 20·8	6 21·8	6 03·4	2·3	1·0	8·3	3·5	14·3	6·1
24	6 21·0	6 22·0	6 03·6	2·4	1·0	8·4	3·6	14·4	6·1
25	6 21·3	6 22·3	6 03·9	2·5	1·1	8·5	3·6	14·5	6·2
26	6 21·5	6 22·5	6 04·1	2·6	1·1	8·6	3·7	14·6	6·2
27	6 21·8	6 22·8	6 04·4	2·7	1·1	8·7	3·7	14·7	6·2
28	6 22·0	6 23·0	6 04·6	2·8	1·2	8·8	3·7	14·8	6·3
29	6 22·3	6 23·3	6 04·8	2·9	1·2	8·9	3·8	14·9	6·3
30	6 22·5	6 23·5	6 05·1	3·0	1·3	9·0	3·8	15·0	6·4
31	6 22·8	6 23·8	6 05·3	3·1	1·3	9·1	3·9	15·1	6·4
32	6 23·0	6 24·0	6 05·6	3·2	1·4	9·2	3·9	15·2	6·5
33	6 23·3	6 24·3	6 05·8	3·3	1·4	9·3	4·0	15·3	6·5
34	6 23·5	6 24·5	6 06·0	3·4	1·4	9·4	4·0	15·4	6·5
35	6 23·8	6 24·8	6 06·3	3·5	1·5	9·5	4·0	15·5	6·6
36	6 24·0	6 25·1	6 06·5	3·6	1·5	9·6	4·1	15·6	6·6
37	6 24·3	6 25·3	6 06·7	3·7	1·6	9·7	4·1	15·7	6·7
38	6 24·5	6 25·6	6 07·0	3·8	1·6	9·8	4·2	15·8	6·7
39	6 24·8	6 25·8	6 07·2	3·9	1·7	9·9	4·2	15·9	6·8
40	6 25·0	6 26·1	6 07·5	4·0	1·7	10·0	4·3	16·0	6·8
41	6 25·3	6 26·3	6 07·7	4·1	1·7	10·1	4·3	16·1	6·8
42	6 25·5	6 26·6	6 07·9	4·2	1·8	10·2	4·3	16·2	6·9
43	6 25·8	6 26·8	6 08·2	4·3	1·8	10·3	4·4	16·3	6·9
44	6 26·0	6 27·1	6 08·4	4·4	1·9	10·4	4·4	16·4	7·0
45	6 26·3	6 27·3	6 08·7	4·5	1·9	10·5	4·5	16·5	7·0
46	6 26·5	6 27·6	6 08·9	4·6	2·0	10·6	4·5	16·6	7·1
47	6 26·8	6 27·8	6 09·1	4·7	2·0	10·7	4·5	16·7	7·1
48	6 27·0	6 28·1	6 09·4	4·8	2·0	10·8	4·6	16·8	7·1
49	6 27·3	6 28·3	6 09·6	4·9	2·1	10·9	4·6	16·9	7·2
50	6 27·5	6 28·6	6 09·8	5·0	2·1	11·0	4·7	17·0	7·2
51	6 27·8	6 28·8	6 10·1	5·1	2·2	11·1	4·7	17·1	7·3
52	6 28·0	6 29·1	6 10·3	5·2	2·2	11·2	4·8	17·2	7·3
53	6 28·3	6 29·3	6 10·6	5·3	2·3	11·3	4·8	17·3	7·4
54	6 28·5	6 29·6	6 10·8	5·4	2·3	11·4	4·8	17·4	7·4
55	6 28·8	6 29·8	6 11·0	5·5	2·3	11·5	4·9	17·5	7·4
56	6 29·0	6 30·1	6 11·3	5·6	2·4	11·6	4·9	17·6	7·5
57	6 29·3	6 30·3	6 11·5	5·7	2·4	11·7	5·0	17·7	7·5
58	6 29·5	6 30·6	6 11·8	5·8	2·5	11·8	5·0	17·8	7·6
59	6 29·8	6 30·8	6 12·0	5·9	2·5	11·9	5·1	17·9	7·6
60	6 30·0	6 31·1	6 12·2	6·0	2·6	12·0	5·1	18·0	7·7

m 26 s	SUN PLANETS ° '	ARIES ° '	MOON ° '	v or d '	Corrⁿ '	v or d '	Corrⁿ '	v or d '	Corrⁿ '
00	6 30·0	6 31·1	6 12·2	0·0	0·0	6·0	2·7	12·0	5·3
01	6 30·3	6 31·3	6 12·5	0·1	0·0	6·1	2·7	12·1	5·3
02	6 30·5	6 31·6	6 12·7	0·2	0·1	6·2	2·7	12·2	5·4
03	6 30·8	6 31·8	6 12·9	0·3	0·1	6·3	2·8	12·3	5·4
04	6 31·0	6 32·1	6 13·2	0·4	0·2	6·4	2·8	12·4	5·5
05	6 31·3	6 32·3	6 13·4	0·5	0·2	6·5	2·9	12·5	5·5
06	6 31·5	6 32·6	6 13·7	0·6	0·3	6·6	2·9	12·6	5·6
07	6 31·8	6 32·8	6 13·9	0·7	0·3	6·7	3·0	12·7	5·6
08	6 32·0	6 33·1	6 14·1	0·8	0·4	6·8	3·0	12·8	5·7
09	6 32·3	6 33·3	6 14·4	0·9	0·4	6·9	3·0	12·9	5·7
10	6 32·5	6 33·6	6 14·6	1·0	0·4	7·0	3·1	13·0	5·7
11	6 32·8	6 33·8	6 14·9	1·1	0·5	7·1	3·1	13·1	5·8
12	6 33·0	6 34·1	6 15·1	1·2	0·5	7·2	3·2	13·2	5·8
13	6 33·3	6 34·3	6 15·3	1·3	0·6	7·3	3·2	13·3	5·9
14	6 33·5	6 34·6	6 15·6	1·4	0·6	7·4	3·3	13·4	5·9
15	6 33·8	6 34·8	6 15·8	1·5	0·7	7·5	3·3	13·5	6·0
16	6 34·0	6 35·1	6 16·1	1·6	0·7	7·6	3·4	13·6	6·0
17	6 34·3	6 35·3	6 16·3	1·7	0·8	7·7	3·4	13·7	6·1
18	6 34·5	6 35·6	6 16·5	1·8	0·8	7·8	3·4	13·8	6·1
19	6 34·8	6 35·8	6 16·8	1·9	0·8	7·9	3·5	13·9	6·1
20	6 35·0	6 36·1	6 17·0	2·0	0·9	8·0	3·5	14·0	6·2
21	6 35·3	6 36·3	6 17·2	2·1	0·9	8·1	3·6	14·1	6·2
22	6 35·5	6 36·6	6 17·5	2·2	1·0	8·2	3·6	14·2	6·3
23	6 35·8	6 36·8	6 17·7	2·3	1·0	8·3	3·7	14·3	6·3
24	6 36·0	6 37·1	6 18·0	2·4	1·1	8·4	3·7	14·4	6·4
25	6 36·3	6 37·3	6 18·2	2·5	1·1	8·5	3·8	14·5	6·4
26	6 36·5	6 37·6	6 18·4	2·6	1·1	8·6	3·8	14·6	6·4
27	6 36·8	6 37·8	6 18·7	2·7	1·2	8·7	3·8	14·7	6·5
28	6 37·0	6 38·1	6 18·9	2·8	1·2	8·8	3·9	14·8	6·5
29	6 37·3	6 38·3	6 19·2	2·9	1·3	8·9	3·9	14·9	6·6
30	6 37·5	6 38·6	6 19·4	3·0	1·3	9·0	4·0	15·0	6·6
31	6 37·8	6 38·8	6 19·6	3·1	1·4	9·1	4·0	15·1	6·7
32	6 38·0	6 39·1	6 19·9	3·2	1·4	9·2	4·1	15·2	6·7
33	6 38·3	6 39·3	6 20·1	3·3	1·5	9·3	4·1	15·3	6·8
34	6 38·5	6 39·6	6 20·3	3·4	1·5	9·4	4·2	15·4	6·8
35	6 38·8	6 39·8	6 20·6	3·5	1·5	9·5	4·2	15·5	6·8
36	6 39·0	6 40·1	6 20·8	3·6	1·6	9·6	4·2	15·6	6·9
37	6 39·3	6 40·3	6 21·1	3·7	1·6	9·7	4·3	15·7	6·9
38	6 39·5	6 40·6	6 21·3	3·8	1·7	9·8	4·3	15·8	7·0
39	6 39·8	6 40·8	6 21·5	3·9	1·7	9·9	4·4	15·9	7·0
40	6 40·0	6 41·1	6 21·8	4·0	1·8	10·0	4·4	16·0	7·1
41	6 40·3	6 41·3	6 22·0	4·1	1·8	10·1	4·5	16·1	7·1
42	6 40·5	6 41·6	6 22·3	4·2	1·9	10·2	4·5	16·2	7·2
43	6 40·8	6 41·8	6 22·5	4·3	1·9	10·3	4·5	16·3	7·2
44	6 41·0	6 42·1	6 22·7	4·4	1·9	10·4	4·6	16·4	7·2
45	6 41·3	6 42·3	6 23·0	4·5	2·0	10·5	4·6	16·5	7·3
46	6 41·5	6 42·6	6 23·2	4·6	2·0	10·6	4·7	16·6	7·3
47	6 41·8	6 42·8	6 23·4	4·7	2·1	10·7	4·7	16·7	7·4
48	6 42·0	6 43·1	6 23·7	4·8	2·1	10·8	4·8	16·8	7·4
49	6 42·3	6 43·4	6 23·9	4·9	2·2	10·9	4·8	16·9	7·5
50	6 42·5	6 43·6	6 24·2	5·0	2·2	11·0	4·9	17·0	7·5
51	6 42·8	6 43·9	6 24·4	5·1	2·3	11·1	4·9	17·1	7·6
52	6 43·0	6 44·1	6 24·6	5·2	2·3	11·2	4·9	17·2	7·6
53	6 43·3	6 44·4	6 24·9	5·3	2·3	11·3	5·0	17·3	7·6
54	6 43·5	6 44·6	6 25·1	5·4	2·4	11·4	5·0	17·4	7·7
55	6 43·8	6 44·9	6 25·4	5·5	2·4	11·5	5·1	17·5	7·7
56	6 44·0	6 45·1	6 25·6	5·6	2·5	11·6	5·1	17·6	7·8
57	6 44·3	6 45·4	6 25·8	5·7	2·5	11·7	5·2	17·7	7·8
58	6 44·5	6 45·6	6 26·1	5·8	2·6	11·8	5·2	17·8	7·9
59	6 44·8	6 45·9	6 26·3	5·9	2·6	11·9	5·3	17·9	7·9
60	6 45·0	6 46·1	6 26·6	6·0	2·7	12·0	5·3	18·0	8·0

m 27 s	SUN PLANETS ° '	ARIES ° '	MOON ° '	v or d '	Corrⁿ '	v or d '	Corrⁿ '	v or d '	Corrⁿ '
00	6 45·0	6 46·1	6 26·6	0·0	0·0	6·0	2·8	12·0	5·5
01	6 45·3	6 46·4	6 26·8	0·1	0·0	6·1	2·8	12·1	5·5
02	6 45·5	6 46·6	6 27·0	0·2	0·1	6·2	2·8	12·2	5·6
03	6 45·8	6 46·9	6 27·3	0·3	0·1	6·3	2·9	12·3	5·6
04	6 46·0	6 47·1	6 27·5	0·4	0·2	6·4	2·9	12·4	5·7
05	6 46·3	6 47·4	6 27·7	0·5	0·2	6·5	3·0	12·5	5·7
06	6 46·5	6 47·6	6 28·0	0·6	0·3	6·6	3·0	12·6	5·8
07	6 46·8	6 47·9	6 28·2	0·7	0·3	6·7	3·1	12·7	5·8
08	6 47·0	6 48·1	6 28·5	0·8	0·4	6·8	3·1	12·8	5·9
09	6 47·3	6 48·4	6 28·7	0·9	0·4	6·9	3·2	12·9	5·9
10	6 47·5	6 48·6	6 28·9	1·0	0·5	7·0	3·2	13·0	6·0
11	6 47·8	6 48·9	6 29·2	1·1	0·5	7·1	3·3	13·1	6·0
12	6 48·0	6 49·1	6 29·4	1·2	0·6	7·2	3·3	13·2	6·1
13	6 48·3	6 49·4	6 29·7	1·3	0·6	7·3	3·3	13·3	6·1
14	6 48·5	6 49·6	6 29·9	1·4	0·6	7·4	3·4	13·4	6·1
15	6 48·8	6 49·9	6 30·1	1·5	0·7	7·5	3·4	13·5	6·2
16	6 49·0	6 50·1	6 30·4	1·6	0·7	7·6	3·5	13·6	6·2
17	6 49·3	6 50·4	6 30·6	1·7	0·8	7·7	3·5	13·7	6·3
18	6 49·5	6 50·6	6 30·8	1·8	0·8	7·8	3·6	13·8	6·3
19	6 49·8	6 50·9	6 31·1	1·9	0·9	7·9	3·6	13·9	6·4
20	6 50·0	6 51·1	6 31·3	2·0	0·9	8·0	3·7	14·0	6·4
21	6 50·3	6 51·4	6 31·6	2·1	1·0	8·1	3·7	14·1	6·5
22	6 50·5	6 51·6	6 31·8	2·2	1·0	8·2	3·8	14·2	6·5
23	6 50·8	6 51·9	6 32·0	2·3	1·1	8·3	3·8	14·3	6·6
24	6 51·0	6 52·1	6 32·3	2·4	1·1	8·4	3·9	14·4	6·6
25	6 51·3	6 52·4	6 32·5	2·5	1·1	8·5	3·9	14·5	6·6
26	6 51·5	6 52·6	6 32·8	2·6	1·2	8·6	3·9	14·6	6·7
27	6 51·8	6 52·9	6 33·0	2·7	1·2	8·7	4·0	14·7	6·7
28	6 52·0	6 53·1	6 33·2	2·8	1·3	8·8	4·0	14·8	6·8
29	6 52·3	6 53·4	6 33·5	2·9	1·3	8·9	4·1	14·9	6·8
30	6 52·5	6 53·6	6 33·7	3·0	1·4	9·0	4·1	15·0	6·9
31	6 52·8	6 53·9	6 33·9	3·1	1·4	9·1	4·2	15·1	6·9
32	6 53·0	6 54·1	6 34·2	3·2	1·5	9·2	4·2	15·2	7·0
33	6 53·3	6 54·4	6 34·4	3·3	1·5	9·3	4·3	15·3	7·0
34	6 53·5	6 54·6	6 34·7	3·4	1·6	9·4	4·3	15·4	7·1
35	6 53·8	6 54·9	6 34·9	3·5	1·6	9·5	4·4	15·5	7·1
36	6 54·0	6 55·1	6 35·1	3·6	1·7	9·6	4·4	15·6	7·2
37	6 54·3	6 55·4	6 35·4	3·7	1·7	9·7	4·4	15·7	7·2
38	6 54·5	6 55·6	6 35·6	3·8	1·7	9·8	4·5	15·8	7·2
39	6 54·8	6 55·9	6 35·9	3·9	1·8	9·9	4·5	15·9	7·3
40	6 55·0	6 56·1	6 36·1	4·0	1·8	10·0	4·6	16·0	7·3
41	6 55·3	6 56·4	6 36·3	4·1	1·9	10·1	4·6	16·1	7·4
42	6 55·5	6 56·6	6 36·6	4·2	1·9	10·2	4·7	16·2	7·4
43	6 55·8	6 56·9	6 36·8	4·3	2·0	10·3	4·7	16·3	7·5
44	6 56·0	6 57·1	6 37·0	4·4	2·0	10·4	4·8	16·4	7·5
45	6 56·3	6 57·4	6 37·3	4·5	2·1	10·5	4·8	16·5	7·6
46	6 56·5	6 57·6	6 37·5	4·6	2·1	10·6	4·9	16·6	7·6
47	6 56·8	6 57·9	6 37·8	4·7	2·2	10·7	4·9	16·7	7·7
48	6 57·0	6 58·1	6 38·0	4·8	2·2	10·8	5·0	16·8	7·7
49	6 57·3	6 58·4	6 38·2	4·9	2·2	10·9	5·0	16·9	7·7
50	6 57·5	6 58·6	6 38·5	5·0	2·3	11·0	5·0	17·0	7·8
51	6 57·8	6 58·9	6 38·7	5·1	2·3	11·1	5·1	17·1	7·8
52	6 58·0	6 59·1	6 39·0	5·2	2·4	11·2	5·1	17·2	7·9
53	6 58·3	6 59·4	6 39·2	5·3	2·4	11·3	5·2	17·3	7·9
54	6 58·5	6 59·6	6 39·4	5·4	2·5	11·4	5·2	17·4	8·0
55	6 58·8	6 59·9	6 39·7	5·5	2·5	11·5	5·3	17·5	8·0
56	6 59·0	7 00·1	6 39·9	5·6	2·6	11·6	5·3	17·6	8·1
57	6 59·3	7 00·4	6 40·2	5·7	2·6	11·7	5·4	17·7	8·1
58	6 59·5	7 00·6	6 40·4	5·8	2·7	11·8	5·4	17·8	8·2
59	6 59·8	7 00·9	6 40·6	5·9	2·7	11·9	5·5	17·9	8·2
60	7 00·0	7 01·1	6 40·9	6·0	2·8	12·0	5·5	18·0	8·3

28 m	SUN PLANETS	ARIES	MOON	v or Corrn d		v or Corrn d		v or Corrn d	
s	° ′	° ′	° ′	′	′	′	′	′	′
00	7 00·0	7 01·1	6 40·9	0·0	0·0	6·0	2·9	12·0	5·7
01	7 00·3	7 01·4	6 41·1	0·1	0·0	6·1	2·9	12·1	5·7
02	7 00·5	7 01·7	6 41·3	0·2	0·1	6·2	2·9	12·2	5·8
03	7 00·8	7 01·9	6 41·6	0·3	0·1	6·3	3·0	12·3	5·8
04	7 01·0	7 02·2	6 41·8	0·4	0·2	6·4	3·0	12·4	5·9
05	7 01·3	7 02·4	6 42·1	0·5	0·2	6·5	3·1	12·5	5·9
06	7 01·5	7 02·7	6 42·3	0·6	0·3	6·6	3·1	12·6	6·0
07	7 01·8	7 02·9	6 42·5	0·7	0·3	6·7	3·2	12·7	6·0
08	7 02·0	7 03·2	6 42·8	0·8	0·4	6·8	3·2	12·8	6·1
09	7 02·3	7 03·4	6 43·0	0·9	0·4	6·9	3·3	12·9	6·1
10	7 02·5	7 03·7	6 43·3	1·0	0·5	7·0	3·3	13·0	6·2
11	7 02·8	7 03·9	6 43·5	1·1	0·5	7·1	3·4	13·1	6·2
12	7 03·0	7 04·2	6 43·7	1·2	0·6	7·2	3·4	13·2	6·3
13	7 03·3	7 04·4	6 44·0	1·3	0·6	7·3	3·5	13·3	6·3
14	7 03·5	7 04·7	6 44·2	1·4	0·7	7·4	3·5	13·4	6·4
15	7 03·8	7 04·9	6 44·4	1·5	0·7	7·5	3·6	13·5	6·4
16	7 04·0	7 05·2	6 44·7	1·6	0·8	7·6	3·6	13·6	6·5
17	7 04·3	7 05·4	6 44·9	1·7	0·8	7·7	3·7	13·7	6·5
18	7 04·5	7 05·7	6 45·2	1·8	0·9	7·8	3·7	13·8	6·6
19	7 04·8	7 05·9	6 45·4	1·9	0·9	7·9	3·8	13·9	6·6
20	7 05·0	7 06·2	6 45·6	2·0	1·0	8·0	3·8	14·0	6·7
21	7 05·3	7 06·4	6 45·9	2·1	1·0	8·1	3·8	14·1	6·7
22	7 05·5	7 06·7	6 46·1	2·2	1·0	8·2	3·9	14·2	6·7
23	7 05·8	7 06·9	6 46·4	2·3	1·1	8·3	3·9	14·3	6·8
24	7 06·0	7 07·2	6 46·6	2·4	1·1	8·4	4·0	14·4	6·8
25	7 06·3	7 07·4	6 46·8	2·5	1·2	8·5	4·0	14·5	6·9
26	7 06·5	7 07·7	6 47·1	2·6	1·2	8·6	4·1	14·6	6·9
27	7 06·8	7 07·9	6 47·3	2·7	1·3	8·7	4·1	14·7	7·0
28	7 07·0	7 08·2	6 47·5	2·8	1·3	8·8	4·2	14·8	7·0
29	7 07·3	7 08·4	6 47·8	2·9	1·4	8·9	4·2	14·9	7·1
30	7 07·5	7 08·7	6 48·0	3·0	1·4	9·0	4·3	15·0	7·1
31	7 07·8	7 08·9	6 48·3	3·1	1·5	9·1	4·3	15·1	7·2
32	7 08·0	7 09·2	6 48·5	3·2	1·5	9·2	4·4	15·2	7·2
33	7 08·3	7 09·4	6 48·7	3·3	1·6	9·3	4·4	15·3	7·3
34	7 08·5	7 09·7	6 49·0	3·4	1·6	9·4	4·5	15·4	7·3
35	7 08·8	7 09·9	6 49·2	3·5	1·7	9·5	4·5	15·5	7·4
36	7 09·0	7 10·2	6 49·5	3·6	1·7	9·6	4·6	15·6	7·4
37	7 09·3	7 10·4	6 49·7	3·7	1·8	9·7	4·6	15·7	7·5
38	7 09·5	7 10·7	6 49·9	3·8	1·8	9·8	4·7	15·8	7·5
39	7 09·8	7 10·9	6 50·2	3·9	1·9	9·9	4·7	15·9	7·6
40	7 10·0	7 11·2	6 50·4	4·0	1·9	10·0	4·8	16·0	7·6
41	7 10·3	7 11·4	6 50·6	4·1	1·9	10·1	4·8	16·1	7·6
42	7 10·5	7 11·7	6 50·9	4·2	2·0	10·2	4·8	16·2	7·7
43	7 10·8	7 11·9	6 51·1	4·3	2·0	10·3	4·9	16·3	7·7
44	7 11·0	7 12·2	6 51·4	4·4	2·1	10·4	4·9	16·4	7·8
45	7 11·3	7 12·4	6 51·6	4·5	2·1	10·5	5·0	16·5	7·8
46	7 11·5	7 12·7	6 51·8	4·6	2·2	10·6	5·0	16·6	7·9
47	7 11·8	7 12·9	6 52·1	4·7	2·2	10·7	5·1	16·7	7·9
48	7 12·0	7 13·2	6 52·3	4·8	2·3	10·8	5·1	16·8	8·0
49	7 12·3	7 13·4	6 52·6	4·9	2·3	10·9	5·2	16·9	8·0
50	7 12·5	7 13·7	6 52·8	5·0	2·4	11·0	5·2	17·0	8·1
51	7 12·8	7 13·9	6 53·0	5·1	2·4	11·1	5·3	17·1	8·1
52	7 13·0	7 14·2	6 53·3	5·2	2·5	11·2	5·3	17·2	8·2
53	7 13·3	7 14·4	6 53·5	5·3	2·5	11·3	5·4	17·3	8·2
54	7 13·5	7 14·7	6 53·8	5·4	2·6	11·4	5·4	17·4	8·3
55	7 13·8	7 14·9	6 54·0	5·5	2·6	11·5	5·5	17·5	8·3
56	7 14·0	7 15·2	6 54·2	5·6	2·7	11·6	5·5	17·6	8·4
57	7 14·3	7 15·4	6 54·5	5·7	2·7	11·7	5·6	17·7	8·4
58	7 14·5	7 15·7	6 54·7	5·8	2·8	11·8	5·6	17·8	8·5
59	7 14·8	7 15·9	6 54·9	5·9	2·8	11·9	5·7	17·9	8·5
60	7 15·0	7 16·2	6 55·2	6·0	2·9	12·0	5·7	18·0	8·6

29 m	SUN PLANETS	ARIES	MOON	v or Corrn d		v or Corrn d		v or Corrn d	
s	° ′	° ′	° ′	′	′	′	′	′	′
00	7 15·0	7 16·2	6 55·2	0·0	0·0	6·0	3·0	12·0	5·9
01	7 15·3	7 16·4	6 55·4	0·1	0·0	6·1	3·0	12·1	5·9
02	7 15·5	7 16·7	6 55·7	0·2	0·1	6·2	3·0	12·2	6·0
03	7 15·8	7 16·9	6 55·9	0·3	0·1	6·3	3·1	12·3	6·0
04	7 16·0	7 17·2	6 56·1	0·4	0·2	6·4	3·1	12·4	6·1
05	7 16·3	7 17·4	6 56·4	0·5	0·2	6·5	3·2	12·5	6·1
06	7 16·5	7 17·7	6 56·6	0·6	0·3	6·6	3·2	12·6	6·2
07	7 16·8	7 17·9	6 56·9	0·7	0·3	6·7	3·3	12·7	6·2
08	7 17·0	7 18·2	6 57·1	0·8	0·4	6·8	3·3	12·8	6·3
09	7 17·3	7 18·4	6 57·3	0·9	0·4	6·9	3·4	12·9	6·3
10	7 17·5	7 18·7	6 57·6	1·0	0·5	7·0	3·4	13·0	6·4
11	7 17·8	7 18·9	6 57·8	1·1	0·5	7·1	3·5	13·1	6·4
12	7 18·0	7 19·2	6 58·0	1·2	0·6	7·2	3·5	13·2	6·5
13	7 18·3	7 19·4	6 58·3	1·3	0·6	7·3	3·6	13·3	6·5
14	7 18·5	7 19·7	6 58·5	1·4	0·7	7·4	3·6	13·4	6·6
15	7 18·8	7 20·0	6 58·8	1·5	0·7	7·5	3·7	13·5	6·6
16	7 19·0	7 20·2	6 59·0	1·6	0·8	7·6	3·7	13·6	6·7
17	7 19·3	7 20·5	6 59·2	1·7	0·8	7·7	3·8	13·7	6·7
18	7 19·5	7 20·7	6 59·5	1·8	0·9	7·8	3·8	13·8	6·8
19	7 19·8	7 21·0	6 59·7	1·9	0·9	7·9	3·9	13·9	6·8
20	7 20·0	7 21·2	7 00·0	2·0	1·0	8·0	3·9	14·0	6·9
21	7 20·3	7 21·5	7 00·2	2·1	1·0	8·1	4·0	14·1	6·9
22	7 20·5	7 21·7	7 00·4	2·2	1·1	8·2	4·0	14·2	7·0
23	7 20·8	7 22·0	7 00·7	2·3	1·1	8·3	4·1	14·3	7·0
24	7 21·0	7 22·2	7 00·9	2·4	1·2	8·4	4·1	14·4	7·1
25	7 21·3	7 22·5	7 01·1	2·5	1·2	8·5	4·2	14·5	7·1
26	7 21·5	7 22·7	7 01·4	2·6	1·3	8·6	4·2	14·6	7·2
27	7 21·8	7 23·0	7 01·6	2·7	1·3	8·7	4·3	14·7	7·2
28	7 22·0	7 23·2	7 01·9	2·8	1·4	8·8	4·3	14·8	7·3
29	7 22·3	7 23·5	7 02·1	2·9	1·4	8·9	4·4	14·9	7·3
30	7 22·5	7 23·7	7 02·3	3·0	1·5	9·0	4·4	15·0	7·4
31	7 22·8	7 24·0	7 02·6	3·1	1·5	9·1	4·5	15·1	7·4
32	7 23·0	7 24·2	7 02·8	3·2	1·6	9·2	4·5	15·2	7·5
33	7 23·3	7 24·5	7 03·1	3·3	1·6	9·3	4·6	15·3	7·5
34	7 23·5	7 24·7	7 03·3	3·4	1·7	9·4	4·6	15·4	7·6
35	7 23·8	7 25·0	7 03·5	3·5	1·7	9·5	4·7	15·5	7·6
36	7 24·0	7 25·2	7 03·8	3·6	1·8	9·6	4·7	15·6	7·7
37	7 24·3	7 25·5	7 04·0	3·7	1·8	9·7	4·8	15·7	7·7
38	7 24·5	7 25·7	7 04·3	3·8	1·9	9·8	4·8	15·8	7·8
39	7 24·8	7 26·0	7 04·5	3·9	1·9	9·9	4·9	15·9	7·8
40	7 25·0	7 26·2	7 04·7	4·0	2·0	10·0	4·9	16·0	7·9
41	7 25·3	7 26·5	7 05·0	4·1	2·0	10·1	5·0	16·1	7·9
42	7 25·5	7 26·7	7 05·2	4·2	2·1	10·2	5·0	16·2	8·0
43	7 25·8	7 27·0	7 05·4	4·3	2·1	10·3	5·1	16·3	8·0
44	7 26·0	7 27·2	7 05·7	4·4	2·2	10·4	5·1	16·4	8·1
45	7 26·3	7 27·5	7 05·9	4·5	2·2	10·5	5·2	16·5	8·1
46	7 26·5	7 27·7	7 06·2	4·6	2·3	10·6	5·2	16·6	8·2
47	7 26·8	7 28·0	7 06·4	4·7	2·3	10·7	5·3	16·7	8·2
48	7 27·0	7 28·2	7 06·6	4·8	2·4	10·8	5·3	16·8	8·3
49	7 27·3	7 28·5	7 06·9	4·9	2·4	10·9	5·4	16·9	8·3
50	7 27·5	7 28·7	7 07·1	5·0	2·5	11·0	5·4	17·0	8·4
51	7 27·8	7 29·0	7 07·4	5·1	2·5	11·1	5·5	17·1	8·4
52	7 28·0	7 29·2	7 07·6	5·2	2·6	11·2	5·5	17·2	8·5
53	7 28·3	7 29·5	7 07·8	5·3	2·6	11·3	5·6	17·3	8·5
54	7 28·5	7 29·7	7 08·1	5·4	2·7	11·4	5·6	17·4	8·6
55	7 28·8	7 30·0	7 08·3	5·5	2·7	11·5	5·7	17·5	8·6
56	7 29·0	7 30·2	7 08·5	5·6	2·8	11·6	5·7	17·6	8·7
57	7 29·3	7 30·5	7 08·8	5·7	2·8	11·7	5·8	17·7	8·7
58	7 29·5	7 30·7	7 09·0	5·8	2·9	11·8	5·8	17·8	8·8
59	7 29·8	7 31·0	7 09·3	5·9	2·9	11·9	5·9	17·9	8·8
60	7 30·0	7 31·2	7 09·5	6·0	3·0	12·0	5·9	18·0	8·9

30ᵐ

m 30 s	SUN PLANETS ° ′	ARIES ° ′	MOON ° ′	v or Corrⁿ d ′ ′	v or Corrⁿ d ′ ′	v or Corrⁿ d ′ ′
00	7 30·0	7 31·2	7 09·5	0·0 0·0	6·0 3·1	12·0 6·1
01	7 30·3	7 31·5	7 09·7	0·1 0·1	6·1 3·1	12·1 6·2
02	7 30·5	7 31·7	7 10·0	0·2 0·1	6·2 3·2	12·2 6·2
03	7 30·8	7 32·0	7 10·2	0·3 0·2	6·3 3·2	12·3 6·3
04	7 31·0	7 32·2	7 10·5	0·4 0·2	6·4 3·3	12·4 6·3
05	7 31·3	7 32·5	7 10·7	0·5 0·3	6·5 3·3	12·5 6·4
06	7 31·5	7 32·7	7 10·9	0·6 0·3	6·6 3·4	12·6 6·4
07	7 31·8	7 33·0	7 11·2	0·7 0·4	6·7 3·4	12·7 6·5
08	7 32·0	7 33·2	7 11·4	0·8 0·4	6·8 3·5	12·8 6·5
09	7 32·3	7 33·5	7 11·6	0·9 0·5	6·9 3·5	12·9 6·6
10	7 32·5	7 33·7	7 11·9	1·0 0·5	7·0 3·6	13·0 6·6
11	7 32·8	7 34·0	7 12·1	1·1 0·6	7·1 3·6	13·1 6·7
12	7 33·0	7 34·2	7 12·4	1·2 0·6	7·2 3·7	13·2 6·7
13	7 33·3	7 34·5	7 12·6	1·3 0·7	7·3 3·7	13·3 6·8
14	7 33·5	7 34·7	7 12·8	1·4 0·7	7·4 3·8	13·4 6·8
15	7 33·8	7 35·0	7 13·1	1·5 0·8	7·5 3·8	13·5 6·9
16	7 34·0	7 35·2	7 13·3	1·6 0·8	7·6 3·9	13·6 6·9
17	7 34·3	7 35·5	7 13·6	1·7 0·9	7·7 3·9	13·7 7·0
18	7 34·5	7 35·7	7 13·8	1·8 0·9	7·8 4·0	13·8 7·0
19	7 34·8	7 36·0	7 14·0	1·9 1·0	7·9 4·0	13·9 7·1
20	7 35·0	7 36·2	7 14·3	2·0 1·0	8·0 4·1	14·0 7·1
21	7 35·3	7 36·5	7 14·5	2·1 1·1	8·1 4·1	14·1 7·2
22	7 35·5	7 36·7	7 14·7	2·2 1·1	8·2 4·2	14·2 7·2
23	7 35·8	7 37·0	7 15·0	2·3 1·2	8·3 4·2	14·3 7·3
24	7 36·0	7 37·2	7 15·2	2·4 1·2	8·4 4·3	14·4 7·3
25	7 36·3	7 37·5	7 15·5	2·5 1·3	8·5 4·3	14·5 7·4
26	7 36·5	7 37·7	7 15·7	2·6 1·3	8·6 4·4	14·6 7·4
27	7 36·8	7 38·0	7 15·9	2·7 1·4	8·7 4·4	14·7 7·5
28	7 37·0	7 38·3	7 16·2	2·8 1·4	8·8 4·5	14·8 7·5
29	7 37·3	7 38·5	7 16·4	2·9 1·5	8·9 4·5	14·9 7·6
30	7 37·5	7 38·8	7 16·7	3·0 1·5	9·0 4·6	15·0 7·6
31	7 37·8	7 39·0	7 16·9	3·1 1·6	9·1 4·6	15·1 7·7
32	7 38·0	7 39·3	7 17·1	3·2 1·6	9·2 4·7	15·2 7·7
33	7 38·3	7 39·5	7 17·4	3·3 1·7	9·3 4·7	15·3 7·8
34	7 38·5	7 39·8	7 17·6	3·4 1·7	9·4 4·8	15·4 7·8
35	7 38·8	7 40·0	7 17·9	3·5 1·8	9·5 4·8	15·5 7·9
36	7 39·0	7 40·3	7 18·1	3·6 1·8	9·6 4·9	15·6 7·9
37	7 39·3	7 40·5	7 18·3	3·7 1·9	9·7 4·9	15·7 8·0
38	7 39·5	7 40·8	7 18·6	3·8 1·9	9·8 5·0	15·8 8·0
39	7 39·8	7 41·0	7 18·8	3·9 2·0	9·9 5·0	15·9 8·1
40	7 40·0	7 41·3	7 19·0	4·0 2·0	10·0 5·1	16·0 8·1
41	7 40·3	7 41·5	7 19·3	4·1 2·1	10·1 5·1	16·1 8·2
42	7 40·5	7 41·8	7 19·5	4·2 2·1	10·2 5·2	16·2 8·2
43	7 40·8	7 42·0	7 19·8	4·3 2·2	10·3 5·2	16·3 8·3
44	7 41·0	7 42·3	7 20·0	4·4 2·2	10·4 5·3	16·4 8·3
45	7 41·3	7 42·5	7 20·2	4·5 2·3	10·5 5·3	16·5 8·4
46	7 41·5	7 42·8	7 20·5	4·6 2·3	10·6 5·4	16·6 8·4
47	7 41·8	7 43·0	7 20·7	4·7 2·4	10·7 5·4	16·7 8·5
48	7 42·0	7 43·3	7 21·0	4·8 2·4	10·8 5·5	16·8 8·5
49	7 42·3	7 43·5	7 21·2	4·9 2·5	10·9 5·5	16·9 8·6
50	7 42·5	7 43·8	7 21·4	5·0 2·5	11·0 5·6	17·0 8·6
51	7 42·8	7 44·0	7 21·7	5·1 2·6	11·1 5·6	17·1 8·7
52	7 43·0	7 44·3	7 21·9	5·2 2·6	11·2 5·7	17·2 8·7
53	7 43·3	7 44·5	7 22·1	5·3 2·7	11·3 5·7	17·3 8·8
54	7 43·5	7 44·8	7 22·4	5·4 2·7	11·4 5·8	17·4 8·8
55	7 43·8	7 45·0	7 22·6	5·5 2·8	11·5 5·8	17·5 8·9
56	7 44·0	7 45·3	7 22·9	5·6 2·8	11·6 5·9	17·6 8·9
57	7 44·3	7 45·5	7 23·1	5·7 2·9	11·7 5·9	17·7 9·0
58	7 44·5	7 45·8	7 23·3	5·8 2·9	11·8 6·0	17·8 9·0
59	7 44·8	7 46·0	7 23·6	5·9 3·0	11·9 6·0	17·9 9·1
60	7 45·0	7 46·3	7 23·8	6·0 3·1	12·0 6·1	18·0 9·2

31ᵐ

m 31 s	SUN PLANETS ° ′	ARIES ° ′	MOON ° ′	v or Corrⁿ d ′ ′	v or Corrⁿ d ′ ′	v or Corrⁿ d ′ ′
00	7 45·0	7 46·3	7 23·8	0·0 0·0	6·0 3·2	12·0 6·3
01	7 45·3	7 46·5	7 24·1	0·1 0·1	6·1 3·2	12·1 6·4
02	7 45·5	7 46·8	7 24·3	0·2 0·1	6·2 3·3	12·2 6·4
03	7 45·8	7 47·0	7 24·5	0·3 0·2	6·3 3·3	12·3 6·5
04	7 46·0	7 47·3	7 24·8	0·4 0·2	6·4 3·4	12·4 6·5
05	7 46·3	7 47·5	7 25·0	0·5 0·3	6·5 3·4	12·5 6·6
06	7 46·5	7 47·8	7 25·2	0·6 0·3	6·6 3·5	12·6 6·6
07	7 46·8	7 48·0	7 25·5	0·7 0·4	6·7 3·5	12·7 6·7
08	7 47·0	7 48·3	7 25·7	0·8 0·4	6·8 3·6	12·8 6·7
09	7 47·3	7 48·5	7 26·0	0·9 0·5	6·9 3·6	12·9 6·8
10	7 47·5	7 48·8	7 26·2	1·0 0·5	7·0 3·7	13·0 6·8
11	7 47·8	7 49·0	7 26·4	1·1 0·6	7·1 3·7	13·1 6·9
12	7 48·0	7 49·3	7 26·7	1·2 0·6	7·2 3·8	13·2 6·9
13	7 48·3	7 49·5	7 26·9	1·3 0·7	7·3 3·8	13·3 7·0
14	7 48·5	7 49·8	7 27·2	1·4 0·7	7·4 3·9	13·4 7·0
15	7 48·8	7 50·0	7 27·4	1·5 0·8	7·5 3·9	13·5 7·1
16	7 49·0	7 50·3	7 27·6	1·6 0·8	7·6 4·0	13·6 7·1
17	7 49·3	7 50·5	7 27·9	1·7 0·9	7·7 4·0	13·7 7·2
18	7 49·5	7 50·8	7 28·1	1·8 0·9	7·8 4·1	13·8 7·2
19	7 49·8	7 51·0	7 28·4	1·9 1·0	7·9 4·1	13·9 7·3
20	7 50·0	7 51·3	7 28·6	2·0 1·1	8·0 4·2	14·0 7·4
21	7 50·3	7 51·5	7 28·8	2·1 1·1	8·1 4·3	14·1 7·4
22	7 50·5	7 51·8	7 29·1	2·2 1·2	8·2 4·3	14·2 7·5
23	7 50·8	7 52·0	7 29·3	2·3 1·2	8·3 4·4	14·3 7·5
24	7 51·0	7 52·3	7 29·5	2·4 1·3	8·4 4·4	14·4 7·6
25	7 51·3	7 52·5	7 29·8	2·5 1·3	8·5 4·5	14·5 7·6
26	7 51·5	7 52·8	7 30·0	2·6 1·4	8·6 4·5	14·6 7·7
27	7 51·8	7 53·0	7 30·3	2·7 1·4	8·7 4·6	14·7 7·7
28	7 52·0	7 53·3	7 30·5	2·8 1·5	8·8 4·6	14·8 7·8
29	7 52·3	7 53·5	7 30·7	2·9 1·5	8·9 4·7	14·9 7·8
30	7 52·5	7 53·8	7 31·0	3·0 1·6	9·0 4·7	15·0 7·9
31	7 52·8	7 54·0	7 31·2	3·1 1·6	9·1 4·8	15·1 7·9
32	7 53·0	7 54·3	7 31·5	3·2 1·7	9·2 4·8	15·2 8·0
33	7 53·3	7 54·5	7 31·7	3·3 1·7	9·3 4·9	15·3 8·0
34	7 53·5	7 54·8	7 31·9	3·4 1·8	9·4 4·9	15·4 8·1
35	7 53·8	7 55·0	7 32·2	3·5 1·8	9·5 5·0	15·5 8·1
36	7 54·0	7 55·3	7 32·4	3·6 1·9	9·6 5·0	15·6 8·2
37	7 54·3	7 55·5	7 32·6	3·7 1·9	9·7 5·1	15·7 8·2
38	7 54·5	7 55·8	7 32·9	3·8 2·0	9·8 5·1	15·8 8·3
39	7 54·8	7 56·0	7 33·1	3·9 2·0	9·9 5·2	15·9 8·3
40	7 55·0	7 56·3	7 33·4	4·0 2·1	10·0 5·3	16·0 8·4
41	7 55·3	7 56·6	7 33·6	4·1 2·2	10·1 5·3	16·1 8·5
42	7 55·5	7 56·8	7 33·8	4·2 2·2	10·2 5·4	16·2 8·5
43	7 55·8	7 57·1	7 34·1	4·3 2·3	10·3 5·4	16·3 8·6
44	7 56·0	7 57·3	7 34·3	4·4 2·3	10·4 5·5	16·4 8·6
45	7 56·3	7 57·6	7 34·6	4·5 2·4	10·5 5·5	16·5 8·7
46	7 56·5	7 57·8	7 34·8	4·6 2·4	10·6 5·6	16·6 8·7
47	7 56·8	7 58·1	7 35·0	4·7 2·5	10·7 5·6	16·7 8·8
48	7 57·0	7 58·3	7 35·3	4·8 2·5	10·8 5·7	16·8 8·8
49	7 57·3	7 58·6	7 35·5	4·9 2·6	10·9 5·7	16·9 8·9
50	7 57·5	7 58·8	7 35·7	5·0 2·6	11·0 5·8	17·0 8·9
51	7 57·8	7 59·1	7 36·0	5·1 2·7	11·1 5·8	17·1 9·0
52	7 58·0	7 59·3	7 36·2	5·2 2·7	11·2 5·9	17·2 9·0
53	7 58·3	7 59·6	7 36·5	5·3 2·8	11·3 5·9	17·3 9·1
54	7 58·5	7 59·8	7 36·7	5·4 2·8	11·4 6·0	17·4 9·1
55	7 58·8	8 00·1	7 36·9	5·5 2·9	11·5 6·0	17·5 9·2
56	7 59·0	8 00·3	7 37·2	5·6 2·9	11·6 6·1	17·6 9·2
57	7 59·3	8 00·6	7 37·4	5·7 3·0	11·7 6·1	17·7 9·3
58	7 59·5	8 00·8	7 37·7	5·8 3·0	11·8 6·2	17·8 9·3
59	7 59·8	8 01·1	7 37·9	5·9 3·1	11·9 6·2	17·9 9·4
60	8 00·0	8 01·3	7 38·1	6·0 3·2	12·0 6·3	18·0 9·5

32 m	SUN PLANETS	ARIES	MOON	v or d Corrⁿ		v or d Corrⁿ		v or d Corrⁿ	
s	° ′	° ′	° ′	′	′	′	′	′	′
00	8 00·0	8 01·3	7 38·1	0·0	0·0	6·0	3·3	12·0	6·5
01	8 00·3	8 01·6	7 38·4	0·1	0·1	6·1	3·3	12·1	6·6
02	8 00·5	8 01·8	7 38·6	0·2	0·1	6·2	3·4	12·2	6·6
03	8 00·8	8 02·1	7 38·8	0·3	0·2	6·3	3·4	12·3	6·7
04	8 01·0	8 02·3	7 39·1	0·4	0·2	6·4	3·5	12·4	6·7
05	8 01·3	8 02·6	7 39·3	0·5	0·3	6·5	3·5	12·5	6·8
06	8 01·5	8 02·8	7 39·6	0·6	0·3	6·6	3·6	12·6	6·8
07	8 01·8	8 03·1	7 39·8	0·7	0·4	6·7	3·6	12·7	6·9
08	8 02·0	8 03·3	7 40·0	0·8	0·4	6·8	3·7	12·8	6·9
09	8 02·3	8 03·6	7 40·3	0·9	0·5	6·9	3·7	12·9	7·0
10	8 02·5	8 03·8	7 40·5	1·0	0·5	7·0	3·8	13·0	7·0
11	8 02·8	8 04·1	7 40·8	1·1	0·6	7·1	3·8	13·1	7·1
12	8 03·0	8 04·3	7 41·0	1·2	0·7	7·2	3·9	13·2	7·2
13	8 03·3	8 04·6	7 41·2	1·3	0·7	7·3	4·0	13·3	7·2
14	8 03·5	8 04·8	7 41·5	1·4	0·8	7·4	4·0	13·4	7·3
15	8 03·8	8 05·1	7 41·7	1·5	0·8	7·5	4·1	13·5	7·3
16	8 04·0	8 05·3	7 42·0	1·6	0·9	7·6	4·1	13·6	7·4
17	8 04·3	8 05·6	7 42·2	1·7	0·9	7·7	4·2	13·7	7·4
18	8 04·5	8 05·8	7 42·4	1·8	1·0	7·8	4·2	13·8	7·5
19	8 04·8	8 06·1	7 42·7	1·9	1·0	7·9	4·3	13·9	7·5
20	8 05·0	8 06·3	7 42·9	2·0	1·1	8·0	4·3	14·0	7·6
21	8 05·3	8 06·6	7 43·1	2·1	1·1	8·1	4·4	14·1	7·6
22	8 05·5	8 06·8	7 43·4	2·2	1·2	8·2	4·4	14·2	7·7
23	8 05·8	8 07·1	7 43·6	2·3	1·2	8·3	4·5	14·3	7·7
24	8 06·0	8 07·3	7 43·9	2·4	1·3	8·4	4·6	14·4	7·8
25	8 06·3	8 07·6	7 44·1	2·5	1·4	8·5	4·6	14·5	7·9
26	8 06·5	8 07·8	7 44·3	2·6	1·4	8·6	4·7	14·6	7·9
27	8 06·8	8 08·1	7 44·6	2·7	1·5	8·7	4·7	14·7	8·0
28	8 07·0	8 08·3	7 44·8	2·8	1·5	8·8	4·8	14·8	8·0
29	8 07·3	8 08·6	7 45·1	2·9	1·6	8·9	4·8	14·9	8·1
30	8 07·5	8 08·8	7 45·3	3·0	1·6	9·0	4·9	15·0	8·1
31	8 07·8	8 09·1	7 45·5	3·1	1·7	9·1	4·9	15·1	8·2
32	8 08·0	8 09·3	7 45·8	3·2	1·7	9·2	5·0	15·2	8·2
33	8 08·3	8 09·6	7 46·0	3·3	1·8	9·3	5·0	15·3	8·3
34	8 08·5	8 09·8	7 46·2	3·4	1·8	9·4	5·1	15·4	8·3
35	8 08·8	8 10·1	7 46·5	3·5	1·9	9·5	5·1	15·5	8·4
36	8 09·0	8 10·3	7 46·7	3·6	2·0	9·6	5·2	15·6	8·5
37	8 09·3	8 10·6	7 47·0	3·7	2·0	9·7	5·3	15·7	8·5
38	8 09·5	8 10·8	7 47·2	3·8	2·1	9·8	5·3	15·8	8·6
39	8 09·8	8 11·1	7 47·4	3·9	2·1	9·9	5·4	15·9	8·6
40	8 10·0	8 11·3	7 47·7	4·0	2·2	10·0	5·4	16·0	8·7
41	8 10·3	8 11·6	7 47·9	4·1	2·2	10·1	5·5	16·1	8·7
42	8 10·5	8 11·8	7 48·2	4·2	2·3	10·2	5·5	16·2	8·8
43	8 10·8	8 12·1	7 48·4	4·3	2·3	10·3	5·6	16·3	8·8
44	8 11·0	8 12·3	7 48·6	4·4	2·4	10·4	5·6	16·4	8·9
45	8 11·3	8 12·6	7 48·9	4·5	2·4	10·5	5·7	16·5	8·9
46	8 11·5	8 12·8	7 49·1	4·6	2·5	10·6	5·7	16·6	9·0
47	8 11·8	8 13·1	7 49·3	4·7	2·5	10·7	5·8	16·7	9·0
48	8 12·0	8 13·3	7 49·6	4·8	2·6	10·8	5·9	16·8	9·1
49	8 12·3	8 13·6	7 49·8	4·9	2·7	10·9	5·9	16·9	9·2
50	8 12·5	8 13·8	7 50·1	5·0	2·7	11·0	6·0	17·0	9·2
51	8 12·8	8 14·1	7 50·3	5·1	2·8	11·1	6·0	17·1	9·3
52	8 13·0	8 14·3	7 50·5	5·2	2·8	11·2	6·1	17·2	9·3
53	8 13·3	8 14·6	7 50·8	5·3	2·9	11·3	6·1	17·3	9·4
54	8 13·5	8 14·9	7 51·0	5·4	2·9	11·4	6·2	17·4	9·4
55	8 13·8	8 15·1	7 51·3	5·5	3·0	11·5	6·2	17·5	9·5
56	8 14·0	8 15·4	7 51·5	5·6	3·0	11·6	6·3	17·6	9·5
57	8 14·3	8 15·6	7 51·7	5·7	3·1	11·7	6·3	17·7	9·6
58	8 14·5	8 15·9	7 52·0	5·8	3·1	11·8	6·4	17·8	9·6
59	8 14·8	8 16·1	7 52·2	5·9	3·2	11·9	6·4	17·9	9·7
60	8 15·0	8 16·4	7 52·5	6·0	3·3	12·0	6·5	18·0	9·8

33 m	SUN PLANETS	ARIES	MOON	v or d Corrⁿ		v or d Corrⁿ		v or d Corrⁿ	
s	° ′	° ′	° ′	′	′	′	′	′	′
00	8 15·0	8 16·4	7 52·5	0·0	0·0	6·0	3·4	12·0	6·7
01	8 15·3	8 16·6	7 52·7	0·1	0·1	6·1	3·4	12·1	6·8
02	8 15·5	8 16·9	7 52·9	0·2	0·1	6·2	3·5	12·2	6·8
03	8 15·8	8 17·1	7 53·2	0·3	0·2	6·3	3·5	12·3	6·9
04	8 16·0	8 17·4	7 53·4	0·4	0·2	6·4	3·6	12·4	6·9
05	8 16·3	8 17·6	7 53·6	0·5	0·3	6·5	3·6	12·5	7·0
06	8 16·5	8 17·9	7 53·9	0·6	0·3	6·6	3·7	12·6	7·0
07	8 16·8	8 18·1	7 54·1	0·7	0·4	6·7	3·7	12·7	7·1
08	8 17·0	8 18·4	7 54·4	0·8	0·4	6·8	3·8	12·8	7·1
09	8 17·3	8 18·6	7 54·6	0·9	0·5	6·9	3·9	12·9	7·2
10	8 17·5	8 18·9	7 54·8	1·0	0·6	7·0	3·9	13·0	7·3
11	8 17·8	8 19·1	7 55·1	1·1	0·6	7·1	4·0	13·1	7·3
12	8 18·0	8 19·4	7 55·3	1·2	0·7	7·2	4·0	13·2	7·4
13	8 18·3	8 19·6	7 55·5	1·3	0·7	7·3	4·1	13·3	7·4
14	8 18·5	8 19·9	7 55·8	1·4	0·8	7·4	4·1	13·4	7·5
15	8 18·8	8 20·1	7 56·0	1·5	0·8	7·5	4·2	13·5	7·5
16	8 19·0	8 20·4	7 56·3	1·6	0·9	7·6	4·2	13·6	7·6
17	8 19·3	8 20·6	7 56·5	1·7	0·9	7·7	4·3	13·7	7·6
18	8 19·5	8 20·9	7 56·7	1·8	1·0	7·8	4·4	13·8	7·7
19	8 19·8	8 21·1	7 57·0	1·9	1·1	7·9	4·4	13·9	7·8
20	8 20·0	8 21·4	7 57·2	2·0	1·1	8·0	4·5	14·0	7·8
21	8 20·3	8 21·6	7 57·5	2·1	1·2	8·1	4·5	14·1	7·9
22	8 20·5	8 21·9	7 57·7	2·2	1·2	8·2	4·6	14·2	7·9
23	8 20·8	8 22·1	7 57·9	2·3	1·3	8·3	4·6	14·3	8·0
24	8 21·0	8 22·4	7 58·2	2·4	1·3	8·4	4·7	14·4	8·0
25	8 21·3	8 22·6	7 58·4	2·5	1·4	8·5	4·7	14·5	8·1
26	8 21·5	8 22·9	7 58·7	2·6	1·5	8·6	4·8	14·6	8·2
27	8 21·8	8 23·1	7 58·9	2·7	1·5	8·7	4·9	14·7	8·2
28	8 22·0	8 23·4	7 59·1	2·8	1·6	8·8	4·9	14·8	8·3
29	8 22·3	8 23·6	7 59·4	2·9	1·6	8·9	5·0	14·9	8·3
30	8 22·5	8 23·9	7 59·6	3·0	1·7	9·0	5·0	15·0	8·4
31	8 22·8	8 24·1	7 59·8	3·1	1·7	9·1	5·1	15·1	8·4
32	8 23·0	8 24·4	8 00·1	3·2	1·8	9·2	5·1	15·2	8·5
33	8 23·3	8 24·6	8 00·3	3·3	1·8	9·3	5·2	15·3	8·5
34	8 23·5	8 24·9	8 00·6	3·4	1·9	9·4	5·2	15·4	8·6
35	8 23·8	8 25·1	8 00·8	3·5	2·0	9·5	5·3	15·5	8·7
36	8 24·0	8 25·4	8 01·0	3·6	2·0	9·6	5·4	15·6	8·7
37	8 24·3	8 25·6	8 01·3	3·7	2·1	9·7	5·4	15·7	8·8
38	8 24·5	8 25·9	8 01·5	3·8	2·1	9·8	5·5	15·8	8·8
39	8 24·8	8 26·1	8 01·8	3·9	2·2	9·9	5·5	15·9	8·9
40	8 25·0	8 26·4	8 02·0	4·0	2·2	10·0	5·6	16·0	8·9
41	8 25·3	8 26·6	8 02·2	4·1	2·3	10·1	5·6	16·1	9·0
42	8 25·5	8 26·9	8 02·5	4·2	2·3	10·2	5·7	16·2	9·0
43	8 25·8	8 27·1	8 02·7	4·3	2·4	10·3	5·8	16·3	9·1
44	8 26·0	8 27·4	8 02·9	4·4	2·5	10·4	5·8	16·4	9·2
45	8 26·3	8 27·6	8 03·2	4·5	2·5	10·5	5·9	16·5	9·2
46	8 26·5	8 27·9	8 03·4	4·6	2·6	10·6	5·9	16·6	9·3
47	8 26·8	8 28·1	8 03·7	4·7	2·6	10·7	6·0	16·7	9·3
48	8 27·0	8 28·4	8 03·9	4·8	2·7	10·8	6·0	16·8	9·4
49	8 27·3	8 28·6	8 04·1	4·9	2·7	10·9	6·1	16·9	9·4
50	8 27·5	8 28·9	8 04·4	5·0	2·8	11·0	6·1	17·0	9·5
51	8 27·8	8 29·1	8 04·6	5·1	2·8	11·1	6·2	17·1	9·5
52	8 28·0	8 29·4	8 04·9	5·2	2·9	11·2	6·3	17·2	9·6
53	8 28·3	8 29·6	8 05·1	5·3	3·0	11·3	6·3	17·3	9·7
54	8 28·5	8 29·9	8 05·3	5·4	3·0	11·4	6·4	17·4	9·7
55	8 28·8	8 30·1	8 05·6	5·5	3·1	11·5	6·4	17·5	9·8
56	8 29·0	8 30·4	8 05·8	5·6	3·1	11·6	6·5	17·6	9·8
57	8 29·3	8 30·6	8 06·1	5·7	3·2	11·7	6·5	17·7	9·9
58	8 29·5	8 30·9	8 06·3	5·8	3·2	11·8	6·6	17·8	9·9
59	8 29·8	8 31·1	8 06·5	5·9	3·3	11·9	6·6	17·9	10·0
60	8 30·0	8 31·4	8 06·8	6·0	3·4	12·0	6·7	18·0	10·1

34	SUN PLANETS	ARIES	MOON	v or d	Corrⁿ	v or d	Corrⁿ	v or d	Corrⁿ	35	SUN PLANETS	ARIES	MOON	v or d	Corrⁿ	v or d	Corrⁿ	v or d	Corrⁿ
s	° ′	° ′	° ′	′	′	′	′	′	′	s	° ′	° ′	° ′	′	′	′	′	′	′
00	8 30·0	8 31·4	8 06·8	0·0	0·0	6·0	3·5	12·0	6·9	00	8 45·0	8 46·4	8 21·1	0·0	0·0	6·0	3·6	12·0	7·1
01	8 30·3	8 31·6	8 07·0	0·1	0·1	6·1	3·5	12·1	7·0	01	8 45·3	8 46·7	8 21·3	0·1	0·1	6·1	3·6	12·1	7·2
02	8 30·5	8 31·9	8 07·2	0·2	0·1	6·2	3·6	12·2	7·0	02	8 45·5	8 46·9	8 21·6	0·2	0·1	6·2	3·7	12·2	7·2
03	8 30·8	8 32·1	8 07·5	0·3	0·2	6·3	3·6	12·3	7·1	03	8 45·8	8 47·2	8 21·8	0·3	0·2	6·3	3·7	12·3	7·3
04	8 31·0	8 32·4	8 07·7	0·4	0·2	6·4	3·7	12·4	7·1	04	8 46·0	8 47·4	8 22·0	0·4	0·2	6·4	3·8	12·4	7·3
05	8 31·3	8 32·6	8 08·0	0·5	0·3	6·5	3·7	12·5	7·2	05	8 46·3	8 47·7	8 22·3	0·5	0·3	6·5	3·8	12·5	7·4
06	8 31·5	8 32·9	8 08·2	0·6	0·3	6·6	3·8	12·6	7·2	06	8 46·5	8 47·9	8 22·5	0·6	0·4	6·6	3·9	12·6	7·5
07	8 31·8	8 33·2	8 08·4	0·7	0·4	6·7	3·9	12·7	7·3	07	8 46·8	8 48·2	8 22·8	0·7	0·4	6·7	4·0	12·7	7·5
08	8 32·0	8 33·4	8 08·7	0·8	0·5	6·8	3·9	12·8	7·4	08	8 47·0	8 48·4	8 23·0	0·8	0·5	6·8	4·0	12·8	7·6
09	8 32·3	8 33·7	8 08·9	0·9	0·5	6·9	4·0	12·9	7·4	09	8 47·3	8 48·7	8 23·2	0·9	0·5	6·9	4·1	12·9	7·6
10	8 32·5	8 33·9	8 09·2	1·0	0·6	7·0	4·0	13·0	7·5	10	8 47·5	8 48·9	8 23·5	1·0	0·6	7·0	4·1	13·0	7·7
11	8 32·8	8 34·2	8 09·4	1·1	0·6	7·1	4·1	13·1	7·5	11	8 47·8	8 49·2	8 23·7	1·1	0·7	7·1	4·2	13·1	7·8
12	8 33·0	8 34·4	8 09·6	1·2	0·7	7·2	4·1	13·2	7·6	12	8 48·0	8 49·4	8 23·9	1·2	0·7	7·2	4·3	13·2	7·8
13	8 33·3	8 34·7	8 09·9	1·3	0·7	7·3	4·2	13·3	7·6	13	8 48·3	8 49·7	8 24·2	1·3	0·8	7·3	4·3	13·3	7·9
14	8 33·5	8 34·9	8 10·1	1·4	0·8	7·4	4·3	13·4	7·7	14	8 48·5	8 49·9	8 24·4	1·4	0·8	7·4	4·4	13·4	7·9
15	8 33·8	8 35·2	8 10·3	1·5	0·9	7·5	4·3	13·5	7·8	15	8 48·8	8 50·2	8 24·7	1·5	0·9	7·5	4·4	13·5	8·0
16	8 34·0	8 35·4	8 10·6	1·6	0·9	7·6	4·4	13·6	7·8	16	8 49·0	8 50·4	8 24·9	1·6	0·9	7·6	4·5	13·6	8·0
17	8 34·3	8 35·7	8 10·8	1·7	1·0	7·7	4·4	13·7	7·9	17	8 49·3	8 50·7	8 25·1	1·7	1·0	7·7	4·6	13·7	8·1
18	8 34·5	8 35·9	8 11·1	1·8	1·0	7·8	4·5	13·8	7·9	18	8 49·5	8 50·9	8 25·4	1·8	1·1	7·8	4·6	13·8	8·2
19	8 34·8	8 36·2	8 11·3	1·9	1·1	7·9	4·5	13·9	8·0	19	8 49·8	8 51·2	8 25·6	1·9	1·1	7·9	4·7	13·9	8·2
20	8 35·0	8 36·4	8 11·5	2·0	1·2	8·0	4·6	14·0	8·1	20	8 50·0	8 51·5	8 25·9	2·0	1·2	8·0	4·7	14·0	8·3
21	8 35·3	8 36·7	8 11·8	2·1	1·2	8·1	4·7	14·1	8·1	21	8 50·3	8 51·7	8 26·1	2·1	1·2	8·1	4·8	14·1	8·3
22	8 35·5	8 36·9	8 12·0	2·2	1·3	8·2	4·7	14·2	8·2	22	8 50·5	8 52·0	8 26·3	2·2	1·3	8·2	4·9	14·2	8·4
23	8 35·8	8 37·2	8 12·3	2·3	1·3	8·3	4·8	14·3	8·2	23	8 50·8	8 52·2	8 26·6	2·3	1·4	8·3	4·9	14·3	8·5
24	8 36·0	8 37·4	8 12·5	2·4	1·4	8·4	4·8	14·4	8·3	24	8 51·0	8 52·5	8 26·8	2·4	1·4	8·4	5·0	14·4	8·5
25	8 36·3	8 37·7	8 12·7	2·5	1·4	8·5	4·9	14·5	8·3	25	8 51·3	8 52·7	8 27·0	2·5	1·5	8·5	5·0	14·5	8·6
26	8 36·5	8 37·9	8 13·0	2·6	1·5	8·6	4·9	14·6	8·4	26	8 51·5	8 53·0	8 27·3	2·6	1·5	8·6	5·1	14·6	8·6
27	8 36·8	8 38·2	8 13·2	2·7	1·6	8·7	5·0	14·7	8·5	27	8 51·8	8 53·2	8 27·5	2·7	1·6	8·7	5·1	14·7	8·7
28	8 37·0	8 38·4	8 13·4	2·8	1·6	8·8	5·1	14·8	8·5	28	8 52·0	8 53·5	8 27·8	2·8	1·7	8·8	5·2	14·8	8·8
29	8 37·3	8 38·7	8 13·7	2·9	1·7	8·9	5·1	14·9	8·6	29	8 52·3	8 53·7	8 28·0	2·9	1·7	8·9	5·3	14·9	8·8
30	8 37·5	8 38·9	8 13·9	3·0	1·7	9·0	5·2	15·0	8·6	30	8 52·5	8 54·0	8 28·2	3·0	1·8	9·0	5·3	15·0	8·9
31	8 37·8	8 39·2	8 14·2	3·1	1·8	9·1	5·2	15·1	8·7	31	8 52·8	8 54·2	8 28·5	3·1	1·8	9·1	5·4	15·1	8·9
32	8 38·0	8 39·4	8 14·4	3·2	1·8	9·2	5·3	15·2	8·7	32	8 53·0	8 54·5	8 28·7	3·2	1·9	9·2	5·4	15·2	9·0
33	8 38·3	8 39·7	8 14·6	3·3	1·9	9·3	5·3	15·3	8·8	33	8 53·3	8 54·7	8 29·0	3·3	2·0	9·3	5·5	15·3	9·1
34	8 38·5	8 39·9	8 14·9	3·4	2·0	9·4	5·4	15·4	8·9	34	8 53·5	8 55·0	8 29·2	3·4	2·0	9·4	5·6	15·4	9·1
35	8 38·8	8 40·2	8 15·1	3·5	2·0	9·5	5·5	15·5	8·9	35	8 53·8	8 55·2	8 29·4	3·5	2·1	9·5	5·6	15·5	9·2
36	8 39·0	8 40·4	8 15·4	3·6	2·1	9·6	5·5	15·6	9·0	36	8 54·0	8 55·5	8 29·7	3·6	2·1	9·6	5·7	15·6	9·2
37	8 39·3	8 40·7	8 15·6	3·7	2·1	9·7	5·6	15·7	9·0	37	8 54·3	8 55·7	8 29·9	3·7	2·2	9·7	5·7	15·7	9·3
38	8 39·5	8 40·9	8 15·8	3·8	2·2	9·8	5·6	15·8	9·1	38	8 54·5	8 56·0	8 30·2	3·8	2·2	9·8	5·8	15·8	9·3
39	8 39·8	8 41·2	8 16·1	3·9	2·2	9·9	5·7	15·9	9·1	39	8 54·8	8 56·2	8 30·4	3·9	2·3	9·9	5·9	15·9	9·4
40	8 40·0	8 41·4	8 16·3	4·0	2·3	10·0	5·8	16·0	9·2	40	8 55·0	8 56·5	8 30·6	4·0	2·4	10·0	5·9	16·0	9·5
41	8 40·3	8 41·7	8 16·5	4·1	2·4	10·1	5·8	16·1	9·3	41	8 55·3	8 56·7	8 30·9	4·1	2·4	10·1	6·0	16·1	9·5
42	8 40·5	8 41·9	8 16·8	4·2	2·4	10·2	5·9	16·2	9·3	42	8 55·5	8 57·0	8 31·1	4·2	2·5	10·2	6·0	16·2	9·6
43	8 40·8	8 42·2	8 17·0	4·3	2·5	10·3	5·9	16·3	9·4	43	8 55·8	8 57·2	8 31·3	4·3	2·5	10·3	6·1	16·3	9·6
44	8 41·0	8 42·4	8 17·3	4·4	2·5	10·4	6·0	16·4	9·4	44	8 56·0	8 57·5	8 31·6	4·4	2·6	10·4	6·2	16·4	9·7
45	8 41·3	8 42·7	8 17·5	4·5	2·6	10·5	6·0	16·5	9·5	45	8 56·3	8 57·7	8 31·8	4·5	2·7	10·5	6·2	16·5	9·8
46	8 41·5	8 42·9	8 17·7	4·6	2·6	10·6	6·1	16·6	9·5	46	8 56·5	8 58·0	8 32·1	4·6	2·7	10·6	6·3	16·6	9·8
47	8 41·8	8 43·2	8 18·0	4·7	2·7	10·7	6·2	16·7	9·6	47	8 56·8	8 58·2	8 32·3	4·7	2·8	10·7	6·3	16·7	9·9
48	8 42·0	8 43·4	8 18·2	4·8	2·8	10·8	6·2	16·8	9·7	48	8 57·0	8 58·5	8 32·5	4·8	2·8	10·8	6·4	16·8	9·9
49	8 42·3	8 43·7	8 18·5	4·9	2·8	10·9	6·3	16·9	9·7	49	8 57·3	8 58·7	8 32·8	4·9	2·9	10·9	6·4	16·9	10·0
50	8 42·5	8 43·9	8 18·7	5·0	2·9	11·0	6·3	17·0	9·8	50	8 57·5	8 59·0	8 33·0	5·0	3·0	11·0	6·5	17·0	10·1
51	8 42·8	8 44·2	8 18·9	5·1	2·9	11·1	6·4	17·1	9·8	51	8 57·8	8 59·2	8 33·3	5·1	3·0	11·1	6·6	17·1	10·1
52	8 43·0	8 44·4	8 19·2	5·2	3·0	11·2	6·4	17·2	9·9	52	8 58·0	8 59·5	8 33·5	5·2	3·1	11·2	6·6	17·2	10·2
53	8 43·3	8 44·7	8 19·4	5·3	3·0	11·3	6·5	17·3	9·9	53	8 58·3	8 59·7	8 33·7	5·3	3·1	11·3	6·7	17·3	10·2
54	8 43·5	8 44·9	8 19·7	5·4	3·1	11·4	6·6	17·4	10·0	54	8 58·5	9 00·0	8 34·0	5·4	3·2	11·4	6·7	17·4	10·3
55	8 43·8	8 45·2	8 19·9	5·5	3·2	11·5	6·6	17·5	10·1	55	8 58·8	9 00·2	8 34·2	5·5	3·3	11·5	6·8	17·5	10·4
56	8 44·0	8 45·4	8 20·1	5·6	3·2	11·6	6·7	17·6	10·1	56	8 59·0	9 00·5	8 34·4	5·6	3·3	11·6	6·9	17·6	10·4
57	8 44·3	8 45·7	8 20·4	5·7	3·3	11·7	6·7	17·7	10·2	57	8 59·3	9 00·7	8 34·7	5·7	3·4	11·7	6·9	17·7	10·5
58	8 44·5	8 45·9	8 20·6	5·8	3·3	11·8	6·8	17·8	10·2	58	8 59·5	9 01·0	8 34·9	5·8	3·4	11·8	7·0	17·8	10·5
59	8 44·8	8 46·2	8 20·8	5·9	3·4	11·9	6·8	17·9	10·3	59	8 59·8	9 01·2	8 35·2	5·9	3·5	11·9	7·0	17·9	10·6
60	8 45·0	8 46·4	8 21·1	6·0	3·5	12·0	6·9	18·0	10·4	60	9 00·0	9 01·5	8 35·4	6·0	3·6	12·0	7·1	18·0	10·7

36	SUN PLANETS	ARIES	MOON	v or d Corrⁿ	v or d Corrⁿ	v or d Corrⁿ
s	° ′	° ′	° ′	′ ′	′ ′	′ ′
00	9 00·0	9 01·5	8 35·4	0·0 0·0	6·0 3·7	12·0 7·3
01	9 00·3	9 01·7	8 35·6	0·1 0·1	6·1 3·7	12·1 7·4
02	9 00·5	9 02·0	8 35·9	0·2 0·1	6·2 3·8	12·2 7·4
03	9 00·8	9 02·2	8 36·1	0·3 0·2	6·3 3·8	12·3 7·5
04	9 01·0	9 02·5	8 36·4	0·4 0·2	6·4 3·9	12·4 7·5
05	9 01·3	9 02·7	8 36·6	0·5 0·3	6·5 4·0	12·5 7·6
06	9 01·5	9 03·0	8 36·8	0·6 0·4	6·6 4·0	12·6 7·7
07	9 01·8	9 03·2	8 37·1	0·7 0·4	6·7 4·1	12·7 7·7
08	9 02·0	9 03·5	8 37·3	0·8 0·5	6·8 4·1	12·8 7·8
09	9 02·3	9 03·7	8 37·5	0·9 0·5	6·9 4·2	12·9 7·8
10	9 02·5	9 04·0	8 37·8	1·0 0·6	7·0 4·3	13·0 7·9
11	9 02·8	9 04·2	8 38·0	1·1 0·7	7·1 4·3	13·1 8·0
12	9 03·0	9 04·5	8 38·3	1·2 0·7	7·2 4·4	13·2 8·0
13	9 03·3	9 04·7	8 38·5	1·3 0·8	7·3 4·4	13·3 8·1
14	9 03·5	9 05·0	8 38·7	1·4 0·9	7·4 4·5	13·4 8·2
15	9 03·8	9 05·2	8 39·0	1·5 0·9	7·5 4·6	13·5 8·2
16	9 04·0	9 05·5	8 39·2	1·6 1·0	7·6 4·6	13·6 8·3
17	9 04·3	9 05·7	8 39·5	1·7 1·0	7·7 4·7	13·7 8·3
18	9 04·5	9 06·0	8 39·7	1·8 1·1	7·8 4·7	13·8 8·4
19	9 04·8	9 06·2	8 39·9	1·9 1·2	7·9 4·8	13·9 8·5
20	9 05·0	9 06·5	8 40·2	2·0 1·2	8·0 4·9	14·0 8·5
21	9 05·3	9 06·7	8 40·4	2·1 1·3	8·1 4·9	14·1 8·6
22	9 05·5	9 07·0	8 40·6	2·2 1·3	8·2 5·0	14·2 8·6
23	9 05·8	9 07·2	8 40·9	2·3 1·4	8·3 5·0	14·3 8·7
24	9 06·0	9 07·5	8 41·1	2·4 1·5	8·4 5·1	14·4 8·8
25	9 06·3	9 07·7	8 41·4	2·5 1·5	8·5 5·2	14·5 8·8
26	9 06·5	9 08·0	8 41·6	2·6 1·6	8·6 5·2	14·6 8·9
27	9 06·8	9 08·2	8 41·8	2·7 1·6	8·7 5·3	14·7 8·9
28	9 07·0	9 08·5	8 42·1	2·8 1·7	8·8 5·4	14·8 9·0
29	9 07·3	9 08·7	8 42·3	2·9 1·8	8·9 5·4	14·9 9·1
30	9 07·5	9 09·0	8 42·6	3·0 1·8	9·0 5·5	15·0 9·1
31	9 07·8	9 09·2	8 42·8	3·1 1·9	9·1 5·5	15·1 9·2
32	9 08·0	9 09·5	8 43·0	3·2 1·9	9·2 5·6	15·2 9·2
33	9 08·3	9 09·8	8 43·3	3·3 2·0	9·3 5·7	15·3 9·3
34	9 08·5	9 10·0	8 43·5	3·4 2·1	9·4 5·7	15·4 9·4
35	9 08·8	9 10·3	8 43·8	3·5 2·1	9·5 5·8	15·5 9·4
36	9 09·0	9 10·5	8 44·0	3·6 2·2	9·6 5·8	15·6 9·5
37	9 09·3	9 10·8	8 44·2	3·7 2·3	9·7 5·9	15·7 9·6
38	9 09·5	9 11·0	8 44·5	3·8 2·3	9·8 6·0	15·8 9·6
39	9 09·8	9 11·3	8 44·7	3·9 2·4	9·9 6·0	15·9 9·7
40	9 10·0	9 11·5	8 44·9	4·0 2·4	10·0 6·1	16·0 9·7
41	9 10·3	9 11·8	8 45·2	4·1 2·5	10·1 6·1	16·1 9·8
42	9 10·5	9 12·0	8 45·4	4·2 2·6	10·2 6·2	16·2 9·9
43	9 10·8	9 12·3	8 45·7	4·3 2·6	10·3 6·3	16·3 9·9
44	9 11·0	9 12·5	8 45·9	4·4 2·7	10·4 6·3	16·4 10·0
45	9 11·3	9 12·8	8 46·1	4·5 2·7	10·5 6·4	16·5 10·0
46	9 11·5	9 13·0	8 46·4	4·6 2·8	10·6 6·4	16·6 10·1
47	9 11·8	9 13·3	8 46·6	4·7 2·9	10·7 6·5	16·7 10·2
48	9 12·0	9 13·5	8 46·9	4·8 2·9	10·8 6·6	16·8 10·2
49	9 12·3	9 13·8	8 47·1	4·9 3·0	10·9 6·6	16·9 10·3
50	9 12·5	9 14·0	8 47·3	5·0 3·0	11·0 6·7	17·0 10·3
51	9 12·8	9 14·3	8 47·6	5·1 3·1	11·1 6·8	17·1 10·4
52	9 13·0	9 14·5	8 47·8	5·2 3·2	11·2 6·8	17·2 10·5
53	9 13·3	9 14·8	8 48·0	5·3 3·2	11·3 6·9	17·3 10·5
54	9 13·5	9 15·0	8 48·3	5·4 3·3	11·4 6·9	17·4 10·6
55	9 13·8	9 15·3	8 48·5	5·5 3·3	11·5 7·0	17·5 10·6
56	9 14·0	9 15·5	8 48·8	5·6 3·4	11·6 7·1	17·6 10·7
57	9 14·3	9 15·8	8 49·0	5·7 3·5	11·7 7·1	17·7 10·8
58	9 14·5	9 16·0	8 49·2	5·8 3·5	11·8 7·2	17·8 10·8
59	9 14·8	9 16·3	8 49·5	5·9 3·6	11·9 7·2	17·9 10·9
60	9 15·0	9 16·5	8 49·7	6·0 3·7	12·0 7·3	18·0 11·0

37	SUN PLANETS	ARIES	MOON	v or d Corrⁿ	v or d Corrⁿ	v or d Corrⁿ
s	° ′	° ′	° ′	′ ′	′ ′	′ ′
00	9 15·0	9 16·5	8 49·7	0·0 0·0	6·0 3·8	12·0 7·5
01	9 15·3	9 16·8	8 50·0	0·1 0·1	6·1 3·8	12·1 7·6
02	9 15·5	9 17·0	8 50·2	0·2 0·1	6·2 3·9	12·2 7·6
03	9 15·8	9 17·3	8 50·4	0·3 0·2	6·3 3·9	12·3 7·7
04	9 16·0	9 17·5	8 50·7	0·4 0·3	6·4 4·0	12·4 7·8
05	9 16·3	9 17·8	8 50·9	0·5 0·3	6·5 4·1	12·5 7·8
06	9 16·5	9 18·0	8 51·1	0·6 0·4	6·6 4·1	12·6 7·9
07	9 16·8	9 18·3	8 51·4	0·7 0·4	6·7 4·2	12·7 7·9
08	9 17·0	9 18·5	8 51·6	0·8 0·5	6·8 4·3	12·8 8·0
09	9 17·3	9 18·8	8 51·9	0·9 0·6	6·9 4·3	12·9 8·1
10	9 17·5	9 19·0	8 52·1	1·0 0·6	7·0 4·4	13·0 8·1
11	9 17·8	9 19·3	8 52·3	1·1 0·7	7·1 4·4	13·1 8·2
12	9 18·0	9 19·5	8 52·6	1·2 0·8	7·2 4·5	13·2 8·3
13	9 18·3	9 19·8	8 52·8	1·3 0·8	7·3 4·6	13·3 8·3
14	9 18·5	9 20·0	8 53·1	1·4 0·9	7·4 4·6	13·4 8·4
15	9 18·8	9 20·3	8 53·3	1·5 0·9	7·5 4·7	13·5 8·4
16	9 19·0	9 20·5	8 53·5	1·6 1·0	7·6 4·8	13·6 8·5
17	9 19·3	9 20·8	8 53·8	1·7 1·1	7·7 4·8	13·7 8·6
18	9 19·5	9 21·0	8 54·0	1·8 1·1	7·8 4·9	13·8 8·6
19	9 19·8	9 21·3	8 54·3	1·9 1·2	7·9 4·9	13·9 8·7
20	9 20·0	9 21·5	8 54·5	2·0 1·3	8·0 5·0	14·0 8·8
21	9 20·3	9 21·8	8 54·7	2·1 1·3	8·1 5·1	14·1 8·8
22	9 20·5	9 22·0	8 55·0	2·2 1·4	8·2 5·1	14·2 8·9
23	9 20·8	9 22·3	8 55·2	2·3 1·4	8·3 5·2	14·3 8·9
24	9 21·0	9 22·5	8 55·4	2·4 1·5	8·4 5·3	14·4 9·0
25	9 21·3	9 22·8	8 55·7	2·5 1·6	8·5 5·3	14·5 9·1
26	9 21·5	9 23·0	8 55·9	2·6 1·6	8·6 5·4	14·6 9·1
27	9 21·8	9 23·3	8 56·2	2·7 1·7	8·7 5·4	14·7 9·2
28	9 22·0	9 23·5	8 56·4	2·8 1·8	8·8 5·5	14·8 9·3
29	9 22·3	9 23·8	8 56·6	2·9 1·8	8·9 5·6	14·9 9·3
30	9 22·5	9 24·0	8 56·9	3·0 1·9	9·0 5·6	15·0 9·4
31	9 22·8	9 24·3	8 57·1	3·1 1·9	9·1 5·7	15·1 9·4
32	9 23·0	9 24·5	8 57·4	3·2 2·0	9·2 5·8	15·2 9·5
33	9 23·3	9 24·8	8 57·6	3·3 2·1	9·3 5·8	15·3 9·6
34	9 23·5	9 25·0	8 57·8	3·4 2·1	9·4 5·9	15·4 9·6
35	9 23·8	9 25·3	8 58·1	3·5 2·2	9·5 5·9	15·5 9·7
36	9 24·0	9 25·5	8 58·3	3·6 2·3	9·6 6·0	15·6 9·8
37	9 24·3	9 25·8	8 58·5	3·7 2·3	9·7 6·1	15·7 9·8
38	9 24·5	9 26·0	8 58·8	3·8 2·4	9·8 6·1	15·8 9·9
39	9 24·8	9 26·3	8 59·0	3·9 2·4	9·9 6·2	15·9 9·9
40	9 25·0	9 26·5	8 59·3	4·0 2·5	10·0 6·3	16·0 10·0
41	9 25·3	9 26·8	8 59·5	4·1 2·6	10·1 6·3	16·1 10·1
42	9 25·5	9 27·0	8 59·7	4·2 2·6	10·2 6·4	16·2 10·1
43	9 25·8	9 27·3	9 00·0	4·3 2·7	10·3 6·4	16·3 10·2
44	9 26·0	9 27·5	9 00·2	4·4 2·8	10·4 6·5	16·4 10·3
45	9 26·3	9 27·8	9 00·5	4·5 2·8	10·5 6·6	16·5 10·3
46	9 26·5	9 28·1	9 00·7	4·6 2·9	10·6 6·6	16·6 10·4
47	9 26·8	9 28·3	9 00·9	4·7 2·9	10·7 6·7	16·7 10·4
48	9 27·0	9 28·6	9 01·2	4·8 3·0	10·8 6·8	16·8 10·5
49	9 27·3	9 28·8	9 01·4	4·9 3·1	10·9 6·8	16·9 10·6
50	9 27·5	9 29·1	9 01·6	5·0 3·1	11·0 6·9	17·0 10·6
51	9 27·8	9 29·3	9 01·9	5·1 3·2	11·1 6·9	17·1 10·7
52	9 28·0	9 29·6	9 02·1	5·2 3·3	11·2 7·0	17·2 10·8
53	9 28·3	9 29·8	9 02·4	5·3 3·3	11·3 7·1	17·3 10·8
54	9 28·5	9 30·1	9 02·6	5·4 3·4	11·4 7·1	17·4 10·9
55	9 28·8	9 30·3	9 02·8	5·5 3·4	11·5 7·2	17·5 10·9
56	9 29·0	9 30·6	9 03·1	5·6 3·5	11·6 7·3	17·6 11·0
57	9 29·3	9 30·8	9 03·3	5·7 3·6	11·7 7·3	17·7 11·1
58	9 29·5	9 31·1	9 03·6	5·8 3·6	11·8 7·4	17·8 11·1
59	9 29·8	9 31·3	9 03·8	5·9 3·7	11·9 7·4	17·9 11·2
60	9 30·0	9 31·6	9 04·0	6·0 3·8	12·0 7·5	18·0 11·3

38ᵐ

s	SUN PLANETS	ARIES	MOON	v or Corrⁿ d		v or Corrⁿ d		v or Corrⁿ d	
00	9 30·0	9 31·6	9 04·0	0·0	0·0	6·0	3·9	12·0	7·7
01	9 30·3	9 31·8	9 04·3	0·1	0·1	6·1	3·9	12·1	7·8
02	9 30·5	9 32·1	9 04·5	0·2	0·1	6·2	4·0	12·2	7·8
03	9 30·8	9 32·3	9 04·7	0·3	0·2	6·3	4·0	12·3	7·9
04	9 31·0	9 32·6	9 05·0	0·4	0·3	6·4	4·1	12·4	8·0
05	9 31·3	9 32·8	9 05·2	0·5	0·3	6·5	4·2	12·5	8·0
06	9 31·5	9 33·1	9 05·5	0·6	0·4	6·6	4·2	12·6	8·1
07	9 31·8	9 33·3	9 05·7	0·7	0·4	6·7	4·3	12·7	8·1
08	9 32·0	9 33·6	9 05·9	0·8	0·5	6·8	4·4	12·8	8·2
09	9 32·3	9 33·8	9 06·2	0·9	0·6	6·9	4·4	12·9	8·3
10	9 32·5	9 34·1	9 06·4	1·0	0·6	7·0	4·5	13·0	8·3
11	9 32·8	9 34·3	9 06·7	1·1	0·7	7·1	4·6	13·1	8·4
12	9 33·0	9 34·6	9 06·9	1·2	0·8	7·2	4·6	13·2	8·5
13	9 33·3	9 34·8	9 07·1	1·3	0·8	7·3	4·7	13·3	8·5
14	9 33·5	9 35·1	9 07·4	1·4	0·9	7·4	4·7	13·4	8·6
15	9 33·8	9 35·3	9 07·6	1·5	1·0	7·5	4·8	13·5	8·7
16	9 34·0	9 35·6	9 07·9	1·6	1·0	7·6	4·9	13·6	8·7
17	9 34·3	9 35·8	9 08·1	1·7	1·1	7·7	4·9	13·7	8·8
18	9 34·5	9 36·1	9 08·3	1·8	1·2	7·8	5·0	13·8	8·9
19	9 34·8	9 36·3	9 08·6	1·9	1·2	7·9	5·1	13·9	8·9
20	9 35·0	9 36·6	9 08·8	2·0	1·3	8·0	5·1	14·0	9·0
21	9 35·3	9 36·8	9 09·0	2·1	1·3	8·1	5·2	14·1	9·0
22	9 35·5	9 37·1	9 09·3	2·2	1·4	8·2	5·3	14·2	9·1
23	9 35·8	9 37·3	9 09·5	2·3	1·5	8·3	5·3	14·3	9·2
24	9 36·0	9 37·6	9 09·8	2·4	1·5	8·4	5·4	14·4	9·2
25	9 36·3	9 37·8	9 10·0	2·5	1·6	8·5	5·5	14·5	9·3
26	9 36·5	9 38·1	9 10·2	2·6	1·7	8·6	5·5	14·6	9·4
27	9 36·8	9 38·3	9 10·5	2·7	1·7	8·7	5·6	14·7	9·4
28	9 37·0	9 38·6	9 10·7	2·8	1·8	8·8	5·6	14·8	9·5
29	9 37·3	9 38·8	9 11·0	2·9	1·9	8·9	5·7	14·9	9·6
30	9 37·5	9 39·1	9 11·2	3·0	1·9	9·0	5·8	15·0	9·6
31	9 37·8	9 39·3	9 11·4	3·1	2·0	9·1	5·8	15·1	9·7
32	9 38·0	9 39·6	9 11·7	3·2	2·1	9·2	5·9	15·2	9·8
33	9 38·3	9 39·8	9 11·9	3·3	2·1	9·3	6·0	15·3	9·8
34	9 38·5	9 40·1	9 12·1	3·4	2·2	9·4	6·0	15·4	9·9
35	9 38·8	9 40·3	9 12·4	3·5	2·2	9·5	6·1	15·5	9·9
36	9 39·0	9 40·6	9 12·6	3·6	2·3	9·6	6·2	15·6	10·0
37	9 39·3	9 40·8	9 12·9	3·7	2·4	9·7	6·2	15·7	10·1
38	9 39·5	9 41·1	9 13·1	3·8	2·4	9·8	6·3	15·8	10·1
39	9 39·8	9 41·3	9 13·3	3·9	2·5	9·9	6·4	15·9	10·2
40	9 40·0	9 41·6	9 13·6	4·0	2·6	10·0	6·4	16·0	10·3
41	9 40·3	9 41·8	9 13·8	4·1	2·6	10·1	6·5	16·1	10·3
42	9 40·5	9 42·1	9 14·1	4·2	2·7	10·2	6·5	16·2	10·4
43	9 40·8	9 42·3	9 14·3	4·3	2·8	10·3	6·6	16·3	10·5
44	9 41·0	9 42·6	9 14·5	4·4	2·8	10·4	6·7	16·4	10·5
45	9 41·3	9 42·8	9 14·8	4·5	2·9	10·5	6·7	16·5	10·6
46	9 41·5	9 43·1	9 15·0	4·6	3·0	10·6	6·8	16·6	10·7
47	9 41·8	9 43·3	9 15·2	4·7	3·0	10·7	6·9	16·7	10·7
48	9 42·0	9 43·6	9 15·5	4·8	3·1	10·8	6·9	16·8	10·8
49	9 42·3	9 43·8	9 15·7	4·9	3·1	10·9	7·0	16·9	10·8
50	9 42·5	9 44·1	9 16·0	5·0	3·2	11·0	7·1	17·0	10·9
51	9 42·8	9 44·3	9 16·2	5·1	3·3	11·1	7·1	17·1	11·0
52	9 43·0	9 44·6	9 16·4	5·2	3·3	11·2	7·2	17·2	11·0
53	9 43·3	9 44·8	9 16·7	5·3	3·4	11·3	7·3	17·3	11·1
54	9 43·5	9 45·1	9 16·9	5·4	3·5	11·4	7·3	17·4	11·2
55	9 43·8	9 45·3	9 17·2	5·5	3·5	11·5	7·4	17·5	11·2
56	9 44·0	9 45·6	9 17·4	5·6	3·6	11·6	7·4	17·6	11·3
57	9 44·3	9 45·8	9 17·6	5·7	3·7	11·7	7·5	17·7	11·4
58	9 44·5	9 46·1	9 17·9	5·8	3·7	11·8	7·6	17·8	11·4
59	9 44·8	9 46·4	9 18·1	5·9	3·8	11·9	7·6	17·9	11·5
60	9 45·0	9 46·6	9 18·4	6·0	3·9	12·0	7·7	18·0	11·6

39ᵐ

s	SUN PLANETS	ARIES	MOON	v or Corrⁿ d		v or Corrⁿ d		v or Corrⁿ d	
00	9 45·0	9 46·6	9 18·4	0·0	0·0	6·0	4·0	12·0	7·9
01	9 45·3	9 46·9	9 18·6	0·1	0·1	6·1	4·0	12·1	8·0
02	9 45·5	9 47·1	9 18·8	0·2	0·1	6·2	4·1	12·2	8·0
03	9 45·8	9 47·4	9 19·1	0·3	0·2	6·3	4·1	12·3	8·1
04	9 46·0	9 47·6	9 19·3	0·4	0·3	6·4	4·2	12·4	8·2
05	9 46·3	9 47·9	9 19·5	0·5	0·3	6·5	4·3	12·5	8·2
06	9 46·5	9 48·1	9 19·8	0·6	0·4	6·6	4·3	12·6	8·3
07	9 46·8	9 48·4	9 20·0	0·7	0·5	6·7	4·4	12·7	8·4
08	9 47·0	9 48·6	9 20·3	0·8	0·5	6·8	4·5	12·8	8·4
09	9 47·3	9 48·9	9 20·5	0·9	0·6	6·9	4·5	12·9	8·5
10	9 47·5	9 49·1	9 20·7	1·0	0·7	7·0	4·6	13·0	8·6
11	9 47·8	9 49·4	9 21·0	1·1	0·7	7·1	4·7	13·1	8·6
12	9 48·0	9 49·6	9 21·2	1·2	0·8	7·2	4·7	13·2	8·7
13	9 48·3	9 49·9	9 21·5	1·3	0·9	7·3	4·8	13·3	8·8
14	9 48·5	9 50·1	9 21·7	1·4	0·9	7·4	4·9	13·4	8·8
15	9 48·8	9 50·4	9 21·9	1·5	1·0	7·5	4·9	13·5	8·9
16	9 49·0	9 50·6	9 22·2	1·6	1·1	7·6	5·0	13·6	9·0
17	9 49·3	9 50·9	9 22·4	1·7	1·1	7·7	5·1	13·7	9·0
18	9 49·5	9 51·1	9 22·6	1·8	1·2	7·8	5·1	13·8	9·1
19	9 49·8	9 51·4	9 22·9	1·9	1·3	7·9	5·2	13·9	9·2
20	9 50·0	9 51·6	9 23·1	2·0	1·3	8·0	5·3	14·0	9·2
21	9 50·3	9 51·9	9 23·4	2·1	1·4	8·1	5·3	14·1	9·3
22	9 50·5	9 52·1	9 23·6	2·2	1·4	8·2	5·4	14·2	9·3
23	9 50·8	9 52·4	9 23·8	2·3	1·5	8·3	5·5	14·3	9·4
24	9 51·0	9 52·6	9 24·1	2·4	1·6	8·4	5·5	14·4	9·5
25	9 51·3	9 52·9	9 24·3	2·5	1·6	8·5	5·6	14·5	9·5
26	9 51·5	9 53·1	9 24·6	2·6	1·7	8·6	5·7	14·6	9·6
27	9 51·8	9 53·4	9 24·8	2·7	1·8	8·7	5·7	14·7	9·7
28	9 52·0	9 53·6	9 25·0	2·8	1·8	8·8	5·8	14·8	9·7
29	9 52·3	9 53·9	9 25·3	2·9	1·9	8·9	5·9	14·9	9·8
30	9 52·5	9 54·1	9 25·5	3·0	2·0	9·0	5·9	15·0	9·9
31	9 52·8	9 54·4	9 25·7	3·1	2·0	9·1	6·0	15·1	9·9
32	9 53·0	9 54·6	9 26·0	3·2	2·1	9·2	6·1	15·2	10·0
33	9 53·3	9 54·9	9 26·2	3·3	2·2	9·3	6·1	15·3	10·1
34	9 53·5	9 55·1	9 26·5	3·4	2·2	9·4	6·2	15·4	10·1
35	9 53·8	9 55·4	9 26·7	3·5	2·3	9·5	6·3	15·5	10·2
36	9 54·0	9 55·6	9 26·9	3·6	2·4	9·6	6·3	15·6	10·3
37	9 54·3	9 55·9	9 27·2	3·7	2·4	9·7	6·4	15·7	10·3
38	9 54·5	9 56·1	9 27·4	3·8	2·5	9·8	6·5	15·8	10·4
39	9 54·8	9 56·4	9 27·7	3·9	2·6	9·9	6·5	15·9	10·5
40	9 55·0	9 56·6	9 27·9	4·0	2·6	10·0	6·6	16·0	10·5
41	9 55·3	9 56·9	9 28·1	4·1	2·7	10·1	6·6	16·1	10·6
42	9 55·5	9 57·1	9 28·4	4·2	2·8	10·2	6·7	16·2	10·7
43	9 55·8	9 57·4	9 28·6	4·3	2·8	10·3	6·8	16·3	10·7
44	9 56·0	9 57·6	9 28·8	4·4	2·9	10·4	6·8	16·4	10·8
45	9 56·3	9 57·9	9 29·1	4·5	3·0	10·5	6·9	16·5	10·9
46	9 56·5	9 58·1	9 29·3	4·6	3·0	10·6	7·0	16·6	10·9
47	9 56·8	9 58·4	9 29·6	4·7	3·1	10·7	7·0	16·7	11·0
48	9 57·0	9 58·6	9 29·8	4·8	3·2	10·8	7·1	16·8	11·1
49	9 57·3	9 58·9	9 30·0	4·9	3·2	10·9	7·2	16·9	11·1
50	9 57·5	9 59·1	9 30·3	5·0	3·3	11·0	7·2	17·0	11·2
51	9 57·8	9 59·4	9 30·5	5·1	3·4	11·1	7·3	17·1	11·3
52	9 58·0	9 59·6	9 30·8	5·2	3·4	11·2	7·4	17·2	11·3
53	9 58·3	9 59·9	9 31·0	5·3	3·5	11·3	7·4	17·3	11·4
54	9 58·5	10 00·1	9 31·2	5·4	3·6	11·4	7·5	17·4	11·5
55	9 58·8	10 00·4	9 31·5	5·5	3·6	11·5	7·6	17·5	11·5
56	9 59·0	10 00·6	9 31·7	5·6	3·7	11·6	7·6	17·6	11·6
57	9 59·3	10 00·9	9 32·0	5·7	3·8	11·7	7·7	17·7	11·7
58	9 59·5	10 01·1	9 32·2	5·8	3·8	11·8	7·8	17·8	11·7
59	9 59·8	10 01·4	9 32·4	5·9	3·9	11·9	7·8	17·9	11·8
60	10 00·0	10 01·6	9 32·7	6·0	4·0	12·0	7·9	18·0	11·9

40 s	SUN PLANETS	ARIES	MOON	v or d / Corrⁿ	v or d / Corrⁿ	v or d / Corrⁿ
00	10 00·0	10 01·6	9 32·7	0·0 0·0	6·0 4·1	12·0 8·1
01	10 00·3	10 01·9	9 32·9	0·1 0·1	6·1 4·1	12·1 8·2
02	10 00·5	10 02·1	9 33·1	0·2 0·1	6·2 4·2	12·2 8·2
03	10 00·8	10 02·4	9 33·4	0·3 0·2	6·3 4·3	12·3 8·3
04	10 01·0	10 02·6	9 33·6	0·4 0·3	6·4 4·3	12·4 8·4
05	10 01·3	10 02·9	9 33·9	0·5 0·3	6·5 4·4	12·5 8·4
06	10 01·5	10 03·1	9 34·1	0·6 0·4	6·6 4·5	12·6 8·5
07	10 01·8	10 03·4	9 34·3	0·7 0·5	6·7 4·5	12·7 8·6
08	10 02·0	10 03·6	9 34·6	0·8 0·5	6·8 4·6	12·8 8·6
09	10 02·3	10 03·9	9 34·8	0·9 0·6	6·9 4·7	12·9 8·7
10	10 02·5	10 04·1	9 35·1	1·0 0·7	7·0 4·7	13·0 8·8
11	10 02·8	10 04·4	9 35·3	1·1 0·7	7·1 4·8	13·1 8·8
12	10 03·0	10 04·7	9 35·5	1·2 0·8	7·2 4·9	13·2 8·9
13	10 03·3	10 04·9	9 35·8	1·3 0·9	7·3 4·9	13·3 9·0
14	10 03·5	10 05·2	9 36·0	1·4 0·9	7·4 5·0	13·4 9·0
15	10 03·8	10 05·4	9 36·2	1·5 1·0	7·5 5·1	13·5 9·1
16	10 04·0	10 05·7	9 36·5	1·6 1·1	7·6 5·1	13·6 9·2
17	10 04·3	10 05·9	9 36·7	1·7 1·1	7·7 5·2	13·7 9·2
18	10 04·5	10 06·2	9 37·0	1·8 1·2	7·8 5·3	13·8 9·3
19	10 04·8	10 06·4	9 37·2	1·9 1·3	7·9 5·3	13·9 9·4
20	10 05·0	10 06·7	9 37·4	2·0 1·4	8·0 5·4	14·0 9·5
21	10 05·3	10 06·9	9 37·7	2·1 1·4	8·1 5·5	14·1 9·5
22	10 05·5	10 07·2	9 37·9	2·2 1·5	8·2 5·5	14·2 9·6
23	10 05·8	10 07·4	9 38·2	2·3 1·6	8·3 5·6	14·3 9·7
24	10 06·0	10 07·7	9 38·4	2·4 1·6	8·4 5·7	14·4 9·7
25	10 06·3	10 07·9	9 38·6	2·5 1·7	8·5 5·7	14·5 9·8
26	10 06·5	10 08·2	9 38·9	2·6 1·8	8·6 5·8	14·6 9·9
27	10 06·8	10 08·4	9 39·1	2·7 1·8	8·7 5·9	14·7 9·9
28	10 07·0	10 08·7	9 39·3	2·8 1·9	8·8 5·9	14·8 10·0
29	10 07·3	10 08·9	9 39·6	2·9 2·0	8·9 6·0	14·9 10·1
30	10 07·5	10 09·2	9 39·8	3·0 2·0	9·0 6·1	15·0 10·1
31	10 07·8	10 09·4	9 40·1	3·1 2·1	9·1 6·1	15·1 10·2
32	10 08·0	10 09·7	9 40·3	3·2 2·2	9·2 6·2	15·2 10·3
33	10 08·3	10 09·9	9 40·5	3·3 2·2	9·3 6·3	15·3 10·3
34	10 08·5	10 10·2	9 40·8	3·4 2·3	9·4 6·3	15·4 10·4
35	10 08·8	10 10·4	9 41·0	3·5 2·4	9·5 6·4	15·5 10·5
36	10 09·0	10 10·7	9 41·3	3·6 2·4	9·6 6·5	15·6 10·5
37	10 09·3	10 10·9	9 41·5	3·7 2·5	9·7 6·5	15·7 10·6
38	10 09·5	10 11·2	9 41·7	3·8 2·6	9·8 6·6	15·8 10·7
39	10 09·8	10 11·4	9 42·0	3·9 2·6	9·9 6·7	15·9 10·7
40	10 10·0	10 11·7	9 42·2	4·0 2·7	10·0 6·8	16·0 10·8
41	10 10·3	10 11·9	9 42·4	4·1 2·8	10·1 6·8	16·1 10·9
42	10 10·5	10 12·2	9 42·7	4·2 2·8	10·2 6·9	16·2 10·9
43	10 10·8	10 12·4	9 42·9	4·3 2·9	10·3 7·0	16·3 11·0
44	10 11·0	10 12·7	9 43·2	4·4 3·0	10·4 7·0	16·4 11·1
45	10 11·3	10 12·9	9 43·4	4·5 3·0	10·5 7·1	16·5 11·1
46	10 11·5	10 13·2	9 43·6	4·6 3·1	10·6 7·2	16·6 11·2
47	10 11·8	10 13·4	9 43·9	4·7 3·2	10·7 7·2	16·7 11·3
48	10 12·0	10 13·7	9 44·1	4·8 3·2	10·8 7·3	16·8 11·3
49	10 12·3	10 13·9	9 44·4	4·9 3·3	10·9 7·4	16·9 11·4
50	10 12·5	10 14·2	9 44·6	5·0 3·4	11·0 7·4	17·0 11·5
51	10 12·8	10 14·4	9 44·8	5·1 3·4	11·1 7·5	17·1 11·5
52	10 13·0	10 14·7	9 45·1	5·2 3·5	11·2 7·6	17·2 11·6
53	10 13·3	10 14·9	9 45·3	5·3 3·6	11·3 7·6	17·3 11·7
54	10 13·5	10 15·2	9 45·6	5·4 3·6	11·4 7·7	17·4 11·7
55	10 13·8	10 15·4	9 45·8	5·5 3·7	11·5 7·8	17·5 11·8
56	10 14·0	10 15·7	9 46·0	5·6 3·8	11·6 7·8	17·6 11·9
57	10 14·3	10 15·9	9 46·3	5·7 3·8	11·7 7·9	17·7 11·9
58	10 14·5	10 16·2	9 46·5	5·8 3·9	11·8 8·0	17·8 12·0
59	10 14·8	10 16·4	9 46·7	5·9 4·0	11·9 8·0	17·9 12·1
60	10 15·0	10 16·7	9 47·0	6·0 4·1	12·0 8·1	18·0 12·2

41 s	SUN PLANETS	ARIES	MOON	v or d / Corrⁿ	v or d / Corrⁿ	v or d / Corrⁿ
00	10 15·0	10 16·7	9 47·0	0·0 0·0	6·0 4·2	12·0 8·3
01	10 15·3	10 16·9	9 47·2	0·1 0·1	6·1 4·2	12·1 8·4
02	10 15·5	10 17·2	9 47·5	0·2 0·1	6·2 4·3	12·2 8·4
03	10 15·8	10 17·4	9 47·7	0·3 0·2	6·3 4·4	12·3 8·5
04	10 16·0	10 17·7	9 47·9	0·4 0·3	6·4 4·4	12·4 8·6
05	10 16·3	10 17·9	9 48·2	0·5 0·3	6·5 4·5	12·5 8·6
06	10 16·5	10 18·2	9 48·4	0·6 0·4	6·6 4·6	12·6 8·7
07	10 16·8	10 18·4	9 48·7	0·7 0·5	6·7 4·6	12·7 8·8
08	10 17·0	10 18·7	9 48·9	0·8 0·6	6·8 4·7	12·8 8·9
09	10 17·3	10 18·9	9 49·1	0·9 0·6	6·9 4·8	12·9 8·9
10	10 17·5	10 19·2	9 49·4	1·0 0·7	7·0 4·8	13·0 9·0
11	10 17·8	10 19·4	9 49·6	1·1 0·8	7·1 4·9	13·1 9·1
12	10 18·0	10 19·7	9 49·8	1·2 0·8	7·2 5·0	13·2 9·1
13	10 18·3	10 19·9	9 50·1	1·3 0·9	7·3 5·0	13·3 9·2
14	10 18·5	10 20·2	9 50·3	1·4 1·0	7·4 5·1	13·4 9·3
15	10 18·8	10 20·4	9 50·6	1·5 1·0	7·5 5·2	13·5 9·3
16	10 19·0	10 20·7	9 50·8	1·6 1·1	7·6 5·3	13·6 9·4
17	10 19·3	10 20·9	9 51·0	1·7 1·2	7·7 5·3	13·7 9·5
18	10 19·5	10 21·2	9 51·3	1·8 1·2	7·8 5·4	13·8 9·5
19	10 19·8	10 21·4	9 51·5	1·9 1·3	7·9 5·5	13·9 9·6
20	10 20·0	10 21·7	9 51·8	2·0 1·4	8·0 5·5	14·0 9·7
21	10 20·3	10 21·9	9 52·0	2·1 1·5	8·1 5·6	14·1 9·8
22	10 20·5	10 22·2	9 52·2	2·2 1·5	8·2 5·7	14·2 9·8
23	10 20·8	10 22·4	9 52·5	2·3 1·6	8·3 5·7	14·3 9·9
24	10 21·0	10 22·7	9 52·7	2·4 1·7	8·4 5·8	14·4 10·0
25	10 21·3	10 23·0	9 52·9	2·5 1·7	8·5 5·9	14·5 10·0
26	10 21·5	10 23·2	9 53·2	2·6 1·8	8·6 5·9	14·6 10·1
27	10 21·8	10 23·5	9 53·4	2·7 1·9	8·7 6·0	14·7 10·2
28	10 22·0	10 23·7	9 53·7	2·8 1·9	8·8 6·1	14·8 10·2
29	10 22·3	10 24·0	9 53·9	2·9 2·0	8·9 6·2	14·9 10·3
30	10 22·5	10 24·2	9 54·1	3·0 2·1	9·0 6·2	15·0 10·4
31	10 22·8	10 24·5	9 54·4	3·1 2·1	9·1 6·3	15·1 10·4
32	10 23·0	10 24·7	9 54·6	3·2 2·2	9·2 6·4	15·2 10·5
33	10 23·3	10 25·0	9 54·9	3·3 2·3	9·3 6·4	15·3 10·6
34	10 23·5	10 25·2	9 55·1	3·4 2·4	9·4 6·5	15·4 10·7
35	10 23·8	10 25·5	9 55·3	3·5 2·4	9·5 6·6	15·5 10·7
36	10 24·0	10 25·7	9 55·6	3·6 2·5	9·6 6·6	15·6 10·8
37	10 24·3	10 26·0	9 55·8	3·7 2·6	9·7 6·7	15·7 10·9
38	10 24·5	10 26·2	9 56·1	3·8 2·6	9·8 6·8	15·8 10·9
39	10 24·8	10 26·5	9 56·3	3·9 2·7	9·9 6·8	15·9 11·0
40	10 25·0	10 26·7	9 56·5	4·0 2·8	10·0 6·9	16·0 11·1
41	10 25·3	10 27·0	9 56·8	4·1 2·8	10·1 7·0	16·1 11·1
42	10 25·5	10 27·2	9 57·0	4·2 2·9	10·2 7·1	16·2 11·2
43	10 25·8	10 27·5	9 57·2	4·3 3·0	10·3 7·1	16·3 11·3
44	10 26·0	10 27·7	9 57·5	4·4 3·0	10·4 7·2	16·4 11·3
45	10 26·3	10 28·0	9 57·7	4·5 3·1	10·5 7·3	16·5 11·4
46	10 26·5	10 28·2	9 58·0	4·6 3·2	10·6 7·3	16·6 11·5
47	10 26·8	10 28·5	9 58·2	4·7 3·3	10·7 7·4	16·7 11·6
48	10 27·0	10 28·7	9 58·4	4·8 3·3	10·8 7·5	16·8 11·6
49	10 27·3	10 29·0	9 58·7	4·9 3·4	10·9 7·5	16·9 11·7
50	10 27·5	10 29·2	9 58·9	5·0 3·5	11·0 7·6	17·0 11·8
51	10 27·8	10 29·5	9 59·2	5·1 3·5	11·1 7·7	17·1 11·8
52	10 28·0	10 29·7	9 59·4	5·2 3·6	11·2 7·7	17·2 11·9
53	10 28·3	10 30·0	9 59·6	5·3 3·7	11·3 7·8	17·3 12·0
54	10 28·5	10 30·2	9 59·9	5·4 3·7	11·4 7·9	17·4 12·0
55	10 28·8	10 30·5	10 00·1	5·5 3·8	11·5 8·0	17·5 12·1
56	10 29·0	10 30·7	10 00·3	5·6 3·9	11·6 8·0	17·6 12·2
57	10 29·3	10 31·0	10 00·6	5·7 3·9	11·7 8·1	17·7 12·2
58	10 29·5	10 31·2	10 00·8	5·8 4·0	11·8 8·2	17·8 12·3
59	10 29·8	10 31·5	10 01·1	5·9 4·1	11·9 8·2	17·9 12·4
60	10 30·0	10 31·7	10 01·3	6·0 4·2	12·0 8·3	18·0 12·5

42 s	SUN PLANETS	ARIES	MOON	v or Corrⁿ d		v or Corrⁿ d		v or Corrⁿ d	
	° ′	° ′	° ′	′	′	′	′	′	′
00	10 30·0	10 31·7	10 01·3	0·0	0·0	6·0	4·3	12·0	8·5
01	10 30·3	10 32·0	10 01·5	0·1	0·1	6·1	4·3	12·1	8·6
02	10 30·5	10 32·2	10 01·8	0·2	0·1	6·2	4·4	12·2	8·6
03	10 30·8	10 32·5	10 02·0	0·3	0·2	6·3	4·5	12·3	8·7
04	10 31·0	10 32·7	10 02·3	0·4	0·3	6·4	4·5	12·4	8·8
05	10 31·3	10 33·0	10 02·5	0·5	0·4	6·5	4·6	12·5	8·9
06	10 31·5	10 33·2	10 02·7	0·6	0·4	6·6	4·7	12·6	8·9
07	10 31·8	10 33·5	10 03·0	0·7	0·5	6·7	4·7	12·7	9·0
08	10 32·0	10 33·7	10 03·2	0·8	0·6	6·8	4·8	12·8	9·1
09	10 32·3	10 34·0	10 03·4	0·9	0·6	6·9	4·9	12·9	9·1
10	10 32·5	10 34·2	10 03·7	1·0	0·7	7·0	5·0	13·0	9·2
11	10 32·8	10 34·5	10 03·9	1·1	0·8	7·1	5·0	13·1	9·3
12	10 33·0	10 34·7	10 04·2	1·2	0·9	7·2	5·1	13·2	9·4
13	10 33·3	10 35·0	10 04·4	1·3	0·9	7·3	5·2	13·3	9·4
14	10 33·5	10 35·2	10 04·6	1·4	1·0	7·4	5·2	13·4	9·5
15	10 33·8	10 35·5	10 04·9	1·5	1·1	7·5	5·3	13·5	9·6
16	10 34·0	10 35·7	10 05·1	1·6	1·1	7·6	5·4	13·6	9·6
17	10 34·3	10 36·0	10 05·4	1·7	1·2	7·7	5·5	13·7	9·7
18	10 34·5	10 36·2	10 05·6	1·8	1·3	7·8	5·5	13·8	9·8
19	10 34·8	10 36·5	10 05·8	1·9	1·3	7·9	5·6	13·9	9·8
20	10 35·0	10 36·7	10 06·1	2·0	1·4	8·0	5·7	14·0	9·9
21	10 35·3	10 37·0	10 06·3	2·1	1·5	8·1	5·7	14·1	10·0
22	10 35·5	10 37·2	10 06·5	2·2	1·6	8·2	5·8	14·2	10·1
23	10 35·8	10 37·5	10 06·8	2·3	1·6	8·3	5·9	14·3	10·1
24	10 36·0	10 37·7	10 07·0	2·4	1·7	8·4	6·0	14·4	10·2
25	10 36·3	10 38·0	10 07·3	2·5	1·8	8·5	6·0	14·5	10·3
26	10 36·5	10 38·2	10 07·5	2·6	1·8	8·6	6·1	14·6	10·3
27	10 36·8	10 38·5	10 07·7	2·7	1·9	8·7	6·2	14·7	10·4
28	10 37·0	10 38·7	10 08·0	2·8	2·0	8·8	6·2	14·8	10·5
29	10 37·3	10 39·0	10 08·2	2·9	2·1	8·9	6·3	14·9	10·6
30	10 37·5	10 39·2	10 08·5	3·0	2·1	9·0	6·4	15·0	10·6
31	10 37·8	10 39·5	10 08·7	3·1	2·2	9·1	6·4	15·1	10·7
32	10 38·0	10 39·7	10 08·9	3·2	2·3	9·2	6·5	15·2	10·8
33	10 38·3	10 40·0	10 09·2	3·3	2·3	9·3	6·6	15·3	10·8
34	10 38·5	10 40·2	10 09·4	3·4	2·4	9·4	6·7	15·4	10·9
35	10 38·8	10 40·5	10 09·7	3·5	2·5	9·5	6·7	15·5	11·0
36	10 39·0	10 40·7	10 09·9	3·6	2·6	9·6	6·8	15·6	11·1
37	10 39·3	10 41·0	10 10·1	3·7	2·6	9·7	6·9	15·7	11·1
38	10 39·5	10 41·3	10 10·4	3·8	2·7	9·8	6·9	15·8	11·2
39	10 39·8	10 41·5	10 10·6	3·9	2·8	9·9	7·0	15·9	11·3
40	10 40·0	10 41·8	10 10·8	4·0	2·8	10·0	7·1	16·0	11·3
41	10 40·3	10 42·0	10 11·1	4·1	2·9	10·1	7·2	16·1	11·4
42	10 40·5	10 42·3	10 11·3	4·2	3·0	10·2	7·2	16·2	11·5
43	10 40·8	10 42·5	10 11·6	4·3	3·0	10·3	7·3	16·3	11·5
44	10 41·0	10 42·8	10 11·8	4·4	3·1	10·4	7·4	16·4	11·6
45	10 41·3	10 43·0	10 12·0	4·5	3·2	10·5	7·4	16·5	11·7
46	10 41·5	10 43·3	10 12·3	4·6	3·3	10·6	7·5	16·6	11·8
47	10 41·8	10 43·5	10 12·5	4·7	3·3	10·7	7·6	16·7	11·8
48	10 42·0	10 43·8	10 12·8	4·8	3·4	10·8	7·7	16·8	11·9
49	10 42·3	10 44·0	10 13·0	4·9	3·5	10·9	7·7	16·9	12·0
50	10 42·5	10 44·3	10 13·2	5·0	3·5	11·0	7·8	17·0	12·0
51	10 42·8	10 44·5	10 13·5	5·1	3·6	11·1	7·9	17·1	12·1
52	10 43·0	10 44·8	10 13·7	5·2	3·7	11·2	7·9	17·2	12·2
53	10 43·3	10 45·0	10 13·9	5·3	3·8	11·3	8·0	17·3	12·3
54	10 43·5	10 45·3	10 14·2	5·4	3·8	11·4	8·1	17·4	12·3
55	10 43·8	10 45·5	10 14·4	5·5	3·9	11·5	8·1	17·5	12·4
56	10 44·0	10 45·8	10 14·7	5·6	4·0	11·6	8·2	17·6	12·5
57	10 44·3	10 46·0	10 14·9	5·7	4·0	11·7	8·3	17·7	12·5
58	10 44·5	10 46·3	10 15·1	5·8	4·1	11·8	8·4	17·8	12·6
59	10 44·8	10 46·5	10 15·4	5·9	4·2	11·9	8·4	17·9	12·7
60	10 45·0	10 46·8	10 15·6	6·0	4·3	12·0	8·5	18·0	12·8

43 s	SUN PLANETS	ARIES	MOON	v or Corrⁿ d		v or Corrⁿ d		v or Corrⁿ d	
	° ′	° ′	° ′	′	′	′	′	′	′
00	10 45·0	10 46·8	10 15·6	0·0	0·0	6·0	4·4	12·0	8·7
01	10 45·3	10 47·0	10 15·9	0·1	0·1	6·1	4·4	12·1	8·8
02	10 45·5	10 47·3	10 16·1	0·2	0·1	6·2	4·5	12·2	8·8
03	10 45·8	10 47·5	10 16·3	0·3	0·2	6·3	4·6	12·3	8·9
04	10 46·0	10 47·8	10 16·6	0·4	0·3	6·4	4·6	12·4	9·0
05	10 46·3	10 48·0	10 16·8	0·5	0·4	6·5	4·7	12·5	9·1
06	10 46·5	10 48·3	10 17·0	0·6	0·4	6·6	4·8	12·6	9·1
07	10 46·8	10 48·5	10 17·3	0·7	0·5	6·7	4·9	12·7	9·2
08	10 47·0	10 48·8	10 17·5	0·8	0·6	6·8	4·9	12·8	9·3
09	10 47·3	10 49·0	10 17·8	0·9	0·7	6·9	5·0	12·9	9·4
10	10 47·5	10 49·3	10 18·0	1·0	0·7	7·0	5·1	13·0	9·4
11	10 47·8	10 49·5	10 18·2	1·1	0·8	7·1	5·1	13·1	9·5
12	10 48·0	10 49·8	10 18·5	1·2	0·9	7·2	5·2	13·2	9·6
13	10 48·3	10 50·0	10 18·7	1·3	0·9	7·3	5·3	13·3	9·6
14	10 48·5	10 50·3	10 19·0	1·4	1·0	7·4	5·4	13·4	9·7
15	10 48·8	10 50·5	10 19·2	1·5	1·1	7·5	5·4	13·5	9·8
16	10 49·0	10 50·8	10 19·4	1·6	1·2	7·6	5·5	13·6	9·9
17	10 49·3	10 51·0	10 19·7	1·7	1·2	7·7	5·6	13·7	9·9
18	10 49·5	10 51·3	10 19·9	1·8	1·3	7·8	5·7	13·8	10·0
19	10 49·8	10 51·5	10 20·2	1·9	1·4	7·9	5·7	13·9	10·1
20	10 50·0	10 51·8	10 20·4	2·0	1·5	8·0	5·8	14·0	10·2
21	10 50·3	10 52·0	10 20·6	2·1	1·5	8·1	5·9	14·1	10·2
22	10 50·5	10 52·3	10 20·9	2·2	1·6	8·2	5·9	14·2	10·3
23	10 50·8	10 52·5	10 21·1	2·3	1·7	8·3	6·0	14·3	10·4
24	10 51·0	10 52·8	10 21·3	2·4	1·7	8·4	6·1	14·4	10·4
25	10 51·3	10 53·0	10 21·6	2·5	1·8	8·5	6·2	14·5	10·5
26	10 51·5	10 53·3	10 21·8	2·6	1·9	8·6	6·2	14·6	10·6
27	10 51·8	10 53·5	10 22·1	2·7	2·0	8·7	6·3	14·7	10·7
28	10 52·0	10 53·8	10 22·3	2·8	2·0	8·8	6·4	14·8	10·7
29	10 52·3	10 54·0	10 22·5	2·9	2·1	8·9	6·5	14·9	10·8
30	10 52·5	10 54·3	10 22·8	3·0	2·2	9·0	6·5	15·0	10·9
31	10 52·8	10 54·5	10 23·0	3·1	2·2	9·1	6·6	15·1	10·9
32	10 53·0	10 54·8	10 23·3	3·2	2·3	9·2	6·7	15·2	11·0
33	10 53·3	10 55·0	10 23·5	3·3	2·4	9·3	6·7	15·3	11·1
34	10 53·5	10 55·3	10 23·7	3·4	2·5	9·4	6·8	15·4	11·2
35	10 53·8	10 55·5	10 24·0	3·5	2·5	9·5	6·9	15·5	11·2
36	10 54·0	10 55·8	10 24·2	3·6	2·6	9·6	7·0	15·6	11·3
37	10 54·3	10 56·0	10 24·4	3·7	2·7	9·7	7·0	15·7	11·4
38	10 54·5	10 56·3	10 24·7	3·8	2·8	9·8	7·1	15·8	11·5
39	10 54·8	10 56·5	10 24·9	3·9	2·8	9·9	7·2	15·9	11·5
40	10 55·0	10 56·8	10 25·2	4·0	2·9	10·0	7·3	16·0	11·6
41	10 55·3	10 57·0	10 25·4	4·1	3·0	10·1	7·3	16·1	11·7
42	10 55·5	10 57·3	10 25·6	4·2	3·0	10·2	7·4	16·2	11·7
43	10 55·8	10 57·5	10 25·9	4·3	3·1	10·3	7·5	16·3	11·8
44	10 56·0	10 57·8	10 26·1	4·4	3·2	10·4	7·5	16·4	11·9
45	10 56·3	10 58·0	10 26·4	4·5	3·3	10·5	7·6	16·5	12·0
46	10 56·5	10 58·3	10 26·6	4·6	3·3	10·6	7·7	16·6	12·0
47	10 56·8	10 58·5	10 26·8	4·7	3·4	10·7	7·8	16·7	12·1
48	10 57·0	10 58·8	10 27·1	4·8	3·5	10·8	7·8	16·8	12·2
49	10 57·3	10 59·0	10 27·3	4·9	3·6	10·9	7·9	16·9	12·3
50	10 57·5	10 59·3	10 27·5	5·0	3·6	11·0	8·0	17·0	12·3
51	10 57·8	10 59·6	10 27·8	5·1	3·7	11·1	8·0	17·1	12·4
52	10 58·0	10 59·8	10 28·0	5·2	3·8	11·2	8·1	17·2	12·5
53	10 58·3	11 00·1	10 28·3	5·3	3·8	11·3	8·2	17·3	12·5
54	10 58·5	11 00·3	10 28·5	5·4	3·9	11·4	8·3	17·4	12·6
55	10 58·8	11 00·6	10 28·7	5·5	4·0	11·5	8·3	17·5	12·7
56	10 59·0	11 00·8	10 29·0	5·6	4·1	11·6	8·4	17·6	12·8
57	10 59·3	11 01·1	10 29·2	5·7	4·1	11·7	8·5	17·7	12·8
58	10 59·5	11 01·3	10 29·5	5·8	4·2	11·8	8·6	17·8	12·9
59	10 59·8	11 01·6	10 29·7	5·9	4·3	11·9	8·6	17·9	13·0
60	11 00·0	11 01·8	10 29·9	6·0	4·4	12·0	8·7	18·0	13·1

44ᵐ	SUN PLANETS	ARIES	MOON	v or d / Corrⁿ	v or d / Corrⁿ	v or d / Corrⁿ
s	° ′	° ′	° ′	′ ′	′ ′	′ ′
00	11 00·0	11 01·8	10 29·9	0·0 0·0	6·0 4·5	12·0 8·9
01	11 00·3	11 02·1	10 30·2	0·1 0·1	6·1 4·5	12·1 9·0
02	11 00·5	11 02·3	10 30·4	0·2 0·1	6·2 4·6	12·2 9·0
03	11 00·8	11 02·6	10 30·6	0·3 0·2	6·3 4·7	12·3 9·1
04	11 01·0	11 02·8	10 30·9	0·4 0·3	6·4 4·7	12·4 9·2
05	11 01·3	11 03·1	10 31·1	0·5 0·4	6·5 4·8	12·5 9·3
06	11 01·5	11 03·3	10 31·4	0·6 0·4	6·6 4·9	12·6 9·3
07	11 01·8	11 03·6	10 31·6	0·7 0·5	6·7 5·0	12·7 9·4
08	11 02·0	11 03·8	10 31·8	0·8 0·6	6·8 5·0	12·8 9·5
09	11 02·3	11 04·1	10 32·1	0·9 0·7	6·9 5·1	12·9 9·6
10	11 02·5	11 04·3	10 32·3	1·0 0·7	7·0 5·2	13·0 9·6
11	11 02·8	11 04·6	10 32·6	1·1 0·8	7·1 5·3	13·1 9·7
12	11 03·0	11 04·8	10 32·8	1·2 0·9	7·2 5·3	13·2 9·8
13	11 03·3	11 05·1	10 33·0	1·3 1·0	7·3 5·4	13·3 9·9
14	11 03·5	11 05·3	10 33·3	1·4 1·0	7·4 5·5	13·4 9·9
15	11 03·8	11 05·6	10 33·5	1·5 1·1	7·5 5·6	13·5 10·0
16	11 04·0	11 05·8	10 33·8	1·6 1·2	7·6 5·6	13·6 10·1
17	11 04·3	11 06·1	10 34·0	1·7 1·3	7·7 5·7	13·7 10·2
18	11 04·5	11 06·3	10 34·2	1·8 1·3	7·8 5·8	13·8 10·2
19	11 04·8	11 06·6	10 34·5	1·9 1·4	7·9 5·9	13·9 10·3
20	11 05·0	11 06·8	10 34·7	2·0 1·5	8·0 5·9	14·0 10·4
21	11 05·3	11 07·1	10 34·9	2·1 1·6	8·1 6·0	14·1 10·5
22	11 05·5	11 07·3	10 35·2	2·2 1·6	8·2 6·1	14·2 10·5
23	11 05·8	11 07·6	10 35·4	2·3 1·7	8·3 6·2	14·3 10·6
24	11 06·0	11 07·8	10 35·7	2·4 1·8	8·4 6·2	14·4 10·7
25	11 06·3	11 08·1	10 35·9	2·5 1·9	8·5 6·3	14·5 10·8
26	11 06·5	11 08·3	10 36·1	2·6 1·9	8·6 6·4	14·6 10·8
27	11 06·8	11 08·6	10 36·4	2·7 2·0	8·7 6·5	14·7 10·9
28	11 07·0	11 08·8	10 36·6	2·8 2·1	8·8 6·5	14·8 11·0
29	11 07·3	11 09·1	10 36·9	2·9 2·2	8·9 6·6	14·9 11·1
30	11 07·5	11 09·3	10 37·1	3·0 2·2	9·0 6·7	15·0 11·1
31	11 07·8	11 09·6	10 37·3	3·1 2·3	9·1 6·7	15·1 11·2
32	11 08·0	11 09·8	10 37·6	3·2 2·4	9·2 6·8	15·2 11·3
33	11 08·3	11 10·1	10 37·8	3·3 2·4	9·3 6·9	15·3 11·3
34	11 08·5	11 10·3	10 38·0	3·4 2·5	9·4 7·0	15·4 11·4
35	11 08·8	11 10·6	10 38·3	3·5 2·6	9·5 7·0	15·5 11·5
36	11 09·0	11 10·8	10 38·5	3·6 2·7	9·6 7·1	15·6 11·6
37	11 09·3	11 11·1	10 38·8	3·7 2·7	9·7 7·2	15·7 11·6
38	11 09·5	11 11·3	10 39·0	3·8 2·8	9·8 7·3	15·8 11·7
39	11 09·8	11 11·6	10 39·2	3·9 2·9	9·9 7·3	15·9 11·8
40	11 10·0	11 11·8	10 39·5	4·0 3·0	10·0 7·4	16·0 11·9
41	11 10·3	11 12·1	10 39·7	4·1 3·0	10·1 7·5	16·1 11·9
42	11 10·5	11 12·3	10 40·0	4·2 3·1	10·2 7·6	16·2 12·0
43	11 10·8	11 12·6	10 40·2	4·3 3·2	10·3 7·6	16·3 12·1
44	11 11·0	11 12·8	10 40·4	4·4 3·3	10·4 7·7	16·4 12·2
45	11 11·3	11 13·1	10 40·7	4·5 3·3	10·5 7·8	16·5 12·2
46	11 11·5	11 13·3	10 40·9	4·6 3·4	10·6 7·9	16·6 12·3
47	11 11·8	11 13·6	10 41·1	4·7 3·5	10·7 7·9	16·7 12·4
48	11 12·0	11 13·8	10 41·4	4·8 3·6	10·8 8·0	16·8 12·5
49	11 12·3	11 14·1	10 41·6	4·9 3·6	10·9 8·1	16·9 12·5
50	11 12·5	11 14·3	10 41·9	5·0 3·7	11·0 8·2	17·0 12·6
51	11 12·8	11 14·6	10 42·1	5·1 3·8	11·1 8·2	17·1 12·7
52	11 13·0	11 14·8	10 42·3	5·2 3·9	11·2 8·3	17·2 12·8
53	11 13·3	11 15·1	10 42·6	5·3 3·9	11·3 8·4	17·3 12·8
54	11 13·5	11 15·3	10 42·8	5·4 4·0	11·4 8·5	17·4 12·9
55	11 13·8	11 15·6	10 43·1	5·5 4·1	11·5 8·5	17·5 13·0
56	11 14·0	11 15·8	10 43·3	5·6 4·2	11·6 8·6	17·6 13·1
57	11 14·3	11 16·1	10 43·5	5·7 4·2	11·7 8·7	17·7 13·1
58	11 14·5	11 16·3	10 43·8	5·8 4·3	11·8 8·8	17·8 13·2
59	11 14·8	11 16·6	10 44·0	5·9 4·4	11·9 8·8	17·9 13·3
60	11 15·0	11 16·8	10 44·3	6·0 4·5	12·0 8·9	18·0 13·4

45ᵐ	SUN PLANETS	ARIES	MOON	v or d / Corrⁿ	v or d / Corrⁿ	v or d / Corrⁿ
s	° ′	° ′	° ′	′ ′	′ ′	′ ′
00	11 15·0	11 16·8	10 44·3	0·0 0·0	6·0 4·6	12·0 9·1
01	11 15·3	11 17·1	10 44·5	0·1 0·1	6·1 4·6	12·1 9·2
02	11 15·5	11 17·3	10 44·7	0·2 0·2	6·2 4·7	12·2 9·3
03	11 15·8	11 17·6	10 45·0	0·3 0·2	6·3 4·8	12·3 9·3
04	11 16·0	11 17·9	10 45·2	0·4 0·3	6·4 4·9	12·4 9·4
05	11 16·3	11 18·1	10 45·4	0·5 0·4	6·5 4·9	12·5 9·5
06	11 16·5	11 18·4	10 45·7	0·6 0·5	6·6 5·0	12·6 9·6
07	11 16·8	11 18·6	10 45·9	0·7 0·5	6·7 5·1	12·7 9·6
08	11 17·0	11 18·9	10 46·2	0·8 0·6	6·8 5·2	12·8 9·7
09	11 17·3	11 19·1	10 46·4	0·9 0·7	6·9 5·2	12·9 9·8
10	11 17·5	11 19·4	10 46·6	1·0 0·8	7·0 5·3	13·0 9·9
11	11 17·8	11 19·6	10 46·9	1·1 0·8	7·1 5·4	13·1 9·9
12	11 18·0	11 19·9	10 47·1	1·2 0·9	7·2 5·5	13·2 10·0
13	11 18·3	11 20·1	10 47·4	1·3 1·0	7·3 5·5	13·3 10·1
14	11 18·5	11 20·4	10 47·6	1·4 1·1	7·4 5·6	13·4 10·2
15	11 18·8	11 20·6	10 47·8	1·5 1·1	7·5 5·7	13·5 10·2
16	11 19·0	11 20·9	10 48·1	1·6 1·2	7·6 5·8	13·6 10·3
17	11 19·3	11 21·1	10 48·3	1·7 1·3	7·7 5·8	13·7 10·4
18	11 19·5	11 21·4	10 48·5	1·8 1·4	7·8 5·9	13·8 10·5
19	11 19·8	11 21·6	10 48·8	1·9 1·4	7·9 6·0	13·9 10·5
20	11 20·0	11 21·9	10 49·0	2·0 1·5	8·0 6·1	14·0 10·6
21	11 20·3	11 22·1	10 49·3	2·1 1·6	8·1 6·1	14·1 10·7
22	11 20·5	11 22·4	10 49·5	2·2 1·7	8·2 6·2	14·2 10·8
23	11 20·8	11 22·6	10 49·7	2·3 1·7	8·3 6·3	14·3 10·8
24	11 21·0	11 22·9	10 50·0	2·4 1·8	8·4 6·4	14·4 10·9
25	11 21·3	11 23·1	10 50·2	2·5 1·9	8·5 6·4	14·5 11·0
26	11 21·5	11 23·4	10 50·5	2·6 2·0	8·6 6·5	14·6 11·1
27	11 21·8	11 23·6	10 50·7	2·7 2·0	8·7 6·6	14·7 11·1
28	11 22·0	11 23·9	10 50·9	2·8 2·1	8·8 6·7	14·8 11·2
29	11 22·3	11 24·1	10 51·2	2·9 2·2	8·9 6·7	14·9 11·3
30	11 22·5	11 24·4	10 51·4	3·0 2·3	9·0 6·8	15·0 11·4
31	11 22·8	11 24·6	10 51·6	3·1 2·4	9·1 6·9	15·1 11·5
32	11 23·0	11 24·9	10 51·9	3·2 2·4	9·2 7·0	15·2 11·5
33	11 23·3	11 25·1	10 52·1	3·3 2·5	9·3 7·1	15·3 11·6
34	11 23·5	11 25·4	10 52·4	3·4 2·6	9·4 7·1	15·4 11·7
35	11 23·8	11 25·6	10 52·6	3·5 2·7	9·5 7·2	15·5 11·8
36	11 24·0	11 25·9	10 52·8	3·6 2·7	9·6 7·3	15·6 11·8
37	11 24·3	11 26·1	10 53·1	3·7 2·8	9·7 7·4	15·7 11·9
38	11 24·5	11 26·4	10 53·3	3·8 2·9	9·8 7·4	15·8 12·0
39	11 24·8	11 26·6	10 53·6	3·9 3·0	9·9 7·5	15·9 12·1
40	11 25·0	11 26·9	10 53·8	4·0 3·0	10·0 7·6	16·0 12·1
41	11 25·3	11 27·1	10 54·0	4·1 3·1	10·1 7·7	16·1 12·2
42	11 25·5	11 27·4	10 54·3	4·2 3·2	10·2 7·7	16·2 12·3
43	11 25·8	11 27·6	10 54·5	4·3 3·3	10·3 7·8	16·3 12·3
44	11 26·0	11 27·9	10 54·7	4·4 3·3	10·4 7·9	16·4 12·4
45	11 26·3	11 28·1	10 55·0	4·5 3·4	10·5 8·0	16·5 12·5
46	11 26·5	11 28·4	10 55·2	4·6 3·5	10·6 8·0	16·6 12·6
47	11 26·8	11 28·6	10 55·5	4·7 3·6	10·7 8·1	16·7 12·7
48	11 27·0	11 28·9	10 55·7	4·8 3·6	10·8 8·2	16·8 12·7
49	11 27·3	11 29·1	10 55·9	4·9 3·7	10·9 8·3	16·9 12·8
50	11 27·5	11 29·4	10 56·2	5·0 3·8	11·0 8·3	17·0 12·9
51	11 27·8	11 29·6	10 56·4	5·1 3·9	11·1 8·4	17·1 13·0
52	11 28·0	11 29·9	10 56·7	5·2 3·9	11·2 8·5	17·2 13·0
53	11 28·3	11 30·1	10 56·9	5·3 4·0	11·3 8·6	17·3 13·1
54	11 28·5	11 30·4	10 57·1	5·4 4·1	11·4 8·6	17·4 13·2
55	11 28·8	11 30·6	10 57·4	5·5 4·2	11·5 8·7	17·5 13·3
56	11 29·0	11 30·9	10 57·6	5·6 4·2	11·6 8·8	17·6 13·3
57	11 29·3	11 31·1	10 57·9	5·7 4·3	11·7 8·9	17·7 13·4
58	11 29·5	11 31·4	10 58·1	5·8 4·4	11·8 8·9	17·8 13·5
59	11 29·8	11 31·6	10 58·3	5·9 4·5	11·9 9·0	17·9 13·6
60	11 30·0	11 31·9	10 58·6	6·0 4·6	12·0 9·1	18·0 13·7

46ᵐ	SUN PLANETS	ARIES	MOON	v or Corrⁿ d	v or Corrⁿ d	v or Corrⁿ d
s	° ′	° ′	° ′	′ ′	′ ′	′ ′
00	11 30·0	11 31·9	10 58·6	0·0 0·0	6·0 4·7	12·0 9·3
01	11 30·3	11 32·1	10 58·8	0·1 0·1	6·1 4·7	12·1 9·4
02	11 30·5	11 32·4	10 59·0	0·2 0·2	6·2 4·8	12·2 9·5
03	11 30·8	11 32·6	10 59·3	0·3 0·2	6·3 4·9	12·3 9·5
04	11 31·0	11 32·9	10 59·5	0·4 0·3	6·4 5·0	12·4 9·6
05	11 31·3	11 33·1	10 59·8	0·5 0·4	6·5 5·0	12·5 9·7
06	11 31·5	11 33·4	11 00·0	0·6 0·5	6·6 5·1	12·6 9·8
07	11 31·8	11 33·6	11 00·2	0·7 0·5	6·7 5·2	12·7 9·8
08	11 32·0	11 33·9	11 00·5	0·8 0·6	6·8 5·3	12·8 9·9
09	11 32·3	11 34·1	11 00·7	0·9 0·7	6·9 5·3	12·9 10·0
10	11 32·5	11 34·4	11 01·0	1·0 0·8	7·0 5·4	13·0 10·1
11	11 32·8	11 34·6	11 01·2	1·1 0·9	7·1 5·5	13·1 10·2
12	11 33·0	11 34·9	11 01·4	1·2 0·9	7·2 5·6	13·2 10·2
13	11 33·3	11 35·1	11 01·7	1·3 1·0	7·3 5·7	13·3 10·3
14	11 33·5	11 35·4	11 01·9	1·4 1·1	7·4 5·7	13·4 10·4
15	11 33·8	11 35·6	11 02·1	1·5 1·2	7·5 5·8	13·5 10·5
16	11 34·0	11 35·9	11 02·4	1·6 1·2	7·6 5·9	13·6 10·5
17	11 34·3	11 36·2	11 02·6	1·7 1·3	7·7 6·0	13·7 10·6
18	11 34·5	11 36·4	11 02·9	1·8 1·4	7·8 6·0	13·8 10·7
19	11 34·8	11 36·7	11 03·1	1·9 1·5	7·9 6·1	13·9 10·8
20	11 35·0	11 36·9	11 03·3	2·0 1·6	8·0 6·2	14·0 10·9
21	11 35·3	11 37·2	11 03·6	2·1 1·6	8·1 6·3	14·1 10·9
22	11 35·5	11 37·4	11 03·8	2·2 1·7	8·2 6·4	14·2 11·0
23	11 35·8	11 37·7	11 04·1	2·3 1·8	8·3 6·4	14·3 11·1
24	11 36·0	11 37·9	11 04·3	2·4 1·9	8·4 6·5	14·4 11·2
25	11 36·3	11 38·2	11 04·5	2·5 1·9	8·5 6·6	14·5 11·2
26	11 36·5	11 38·4	11 04·8	2·6 2·0	8·6 6·7	14·6 11·3
27	11 36·8	11 38·7	11 05·0	2·7 2·1	8·7 6·7	14·7 11·4
28	11 37·0	11 38·9	11 05·2	2·8 2·2	8·8 6·8	14·8 11·5
29	11 37·3	11 39·2	11 05·5	2·9 2·2	8·9 6·9	14·9 11·5
30	11 37·5	11 39·4	11 05·7	3·0 2·3	9·0 7·0	15·0 11·6
31	11 37·8	11 39·7	11 06·0	3·1 2·4	9·1 7·1	15·1 11·7
32	11 38·0	11 39·9	11 06·2	3·2 2·5	9·2 7·1	15·2 11·8
33	11 38·3	11 40·2	11 06·4	3·3 2·6	9·3 7·2	15·3 11·9
34	11 38·5	11 40·4	11 06·7	3·4 2·6	9·4 7·3	15·4 11·9
35	11 38·8	11 40·7	11 06·9	3·5 2·7	9·5 7·4	15·5 12·0
36	11 39·0	11 40·9	11 07·2	3·6 2·8	9·6 7·4	15·6 12·1
37	11 39·3	11 41·2	11 07·4	3·7 2·9	9·7 7·5	15·7 12·2
38	11 39·5	11 41·4	11 07·6	3·8 2·9	9·8 7·6	15·8 12·2
39	11 39·8	11 41·7	11 07·9	3·9 3·0	9·9 7·7	15·9 12·3
40	11 40·0	11 41·9	11 08·1	4·0 3·1	10·0 7·8	16·0 12·4
41	11 40·3	11 42·2	11 08·3	4·1 3·2	10·1 7·8	16·1 12·5
42	11 40·5	11 42·4	11 08·6	4·2 3·3	10·2 7·9	16·2 12·6
43	11 40·8	11 42·7	11 08·8	4·3 3·3	10·3 8·0	16·3 12·6
44	11 41·0	11 42·9	11 09·1	4·4 3·4	10·4 8·1	16·4 12·7
45	11 41·3	11 43·2	11 09·3	4·5 3·5	10·5 8·1	16·5 12·8
46	11 41·5	11 43·4	11 09·5	4·6 3·6	10·6 8·2	16·6 12·9
47	11 41·8	11 43·7	11 09·8	4·7 3·6	10·7 8·3	16·7 12·9
48	11 42·0	11 43·9	11 10·0	4·8 3·7	10·8 8·4	16·8 13·0
49	11 42·3	11 44·2	11 10·3	4·9 3·8	10·9 8·4	16·9 13·1
50	11 42·5	11 44·4	11 10·5	5·0 3·9	11·0 8·5	17·0 13·2
51	11 42·8	11 44·7	11 10·7	5·1 4·0	11·1 8·6	17·1 13·3
52	11 43·0	11 44·9	11 11·0	5·2 4·0	11·2 8·7	17·2 13·3
53	11 43·3	11 45·2	11 11·2	5·3 4·1	11·3 8·8	17·3 13·4
54	11 43·5	11 45·4	11 11·5	5·4 4·2	11·4 8·8	17·4 13·5
55	11 43·8	11 45·7	11 11·7	5·5 4·3	11·5 8·9	17·5 13·6
56	11 44·0	11 45·9	11 11·9	5·6 4·3	11·6 9·0	17·6 13·6
57	11 44·3	11 46·2	11 12·2	5·7 4·4	11·7 9·1	17·7 13·7
58	11 44·5	11 46·4	11 12·4	5·8 4·5	11·8 9·1	17·8 13·8
59	11 44·8	11 46·7	11 12·6	5·9 4·6	11·9 9·2	17·9 13·9
60	11 45·0	11 46·9	11 12·9	6·0 4·7	12·0 9·3	18·0 14·0

47ᵐ	SUN PLANETS	ARIES	MOON	v or Corrⁿ d	v or Corrⁿ d	v or Corrⁿ d
s	° ′	° ′	° ′	′ ′	′ ′	′ ′
00	11 45·0	11 46·9	11 12·9	0·0 0·0	6·0 4·8	12·0 9·5
01	11 45·3	11 47·2	11 13·1	0·1 0·1	6·1 4·8	12·1 9·6
02	11 45·5	11 47·4	11 13·4	0·2 0·2	6·2 4·9	12·2 9·7
03	11 45·8	11 47·7	11 13·6	0·3 0·2	6·3 5·0	12·3 9·7
04	11 46·0	11 47·9	11 13·8	0·4 0·3	6·4 5·1	12·4 9·8
05	11 46·3	11 48·2	11 14·1	0·5 0·4	6·5 5·1	12·5 9·9
06	11 46·5	11 48·4	11 14·3	0·6 0·5	6·6 5·2	12·6 10·0
07	11 46·8	11 48·7	11 14·6	0·7 0·6	6·7 5·3	12·7 10·1
08	11 47·0	11 48·9	11 14·8	0·8 0·6	6·8 5·4	12·8 10·1
09	11 47·3	11 49·2	11 15·0	0·9 0·7	6·9 5·5	12·9 10·2
10	11 47·5	11 49·4	11 15·3	1·0 0·8	7·0 5·5	13·0 10·3
11	11 47·8	11 49·7	11 15·5	1·1 0·9	7·1 5·6	13·1 10·4
12	11 48·0	11 49·9	11 15·7	1·2 1·0	7·2 5·7	13·2 10·5
13	11 48·3	11 50·2	11 16·0	1·3 1·0	7·3 5·8	13·3 10·5
14	11 48·5	11 50·4	11 16·2	1·4 1·1	7·4 5·9	13·4 10·6
15	11 48·8	11 50·7	11 16·5	1·5 1·2	7·5 5·9	13·5 10·7
16	11 49·0	11 50·9	11 16·7	1·6 1·3	7·6 6·0	13·6 10·8
17	11 49·3	11 51·2	11 16·9	1·7 1·3	7·7 6·1	13·7 10·8
18	11 49·5	11 51·4	11 17·2	1·8 1·4	7·8 6·2	13·8 10·9
19	11 49·8	11 51·7	11 17·4	1·9 1·5	7·9 6·3	13·9 11·0
20	11 50·0	11 51·9	11 17·7	2·0 1·6	8·0 6·3	14·0 11·1
21	11 50·3	11 52·2	11 17·9	2·1 1·7	8·1 6·4	14·1 11·2
22	11 50·5	11 52·4	11 18·1	2·2 1·7	8·2 6·5	14·2 11·2
23	11 50·8	11 52·7	11 18·4	2·3 1·8	8·3 6·6	14·3 11·3
24	11 51·0	11 52·9	11 18·6	2·4 1·9	8·4 6·7	14·4 11·4
25	11 51·3	11 53·2	11 18·8	2·5 2·0	8·5 6·7	14·5 11·5
26	11 51·5	11 53·4	11 19·1	2·6 2·1	8·6 6·8	14·6 11·6
27	11 51·8	11 53·7	11 19·3	2·7 2·1	8·7 6·9	14·7 11·6
28	11 52·0	11 53·9	11 19·6	2·8 2·2	8·8 7·0	14·8 11·7
29	11 52·3	11 54·2	11 19·8	2·9 2·3	8·9 7·0	14·9 11·8
30	11 52·5	11 54·5	11 20·0	3·0 2·4	9·0 7·1	15·0 11·9
31	11 52·8	11 54·7	11 20·3	3·1 2·5	9·1 7·2	15·1 12·0
32	11 53·0	11 55·0	11 20·5	3·2 2·5	9·2 7·3	15·2 12·0
33	11 53·3	11 55·2	11 20·8	3·3 2·6	9·3 7·4	15·3 12·1
34	11 53·5	11 55·5	11 21·0	3·4 2·7	9·4 7·4	15·4 12·2
35	11 53·8	11 55·7	11 21·2	3·5 2·8	9·5 7·5	15·5 12·3
36	11 54·0	11 56·0	11 21·5	3·6 2·9	9·6 7·6	15·6 12·4
37	11 54·3	11 56·2	11 21·7	3·7 2·9	9·7 7·7	15·7 12·4
38	11 54·5	11 56·5	11 22·0	3·8 3·0	9·8 7·8	15·8 12·5
39	11 54·8	11 56·7	11 22·2	3·9 3·1	9·9 7·8	15·9 12·6
40	11 55·0	11 57·0	11 22·4	4·0 3·2	10·0 7·9	16·0 12·7
41	11 55·3	11 57·2	11 22·7	4·1 3·2	10·1 8·0	16·1 12·7
42	11 55·5	11 57·5	11 22·9	4·2 3·3	10·2 8·1	16·2 12·8
43	11 55·8	11 57·7	11 23·1	4·3 3·4	10·3 8·2	16·3 12·9
44	11 56·0	11 58·0	11 23·4	4·4 3·5	10·4 8·2	16·4 13·0
45	11 56·3	11 58·2	11 23·6	4·5 3·6	10·5 8·3	16·5 13·1
46	11 56·5	11 58·5	11 23·9	4·6 3·6	10·6 8·4	16·6 13·1
47	11 56·8	11 58·7	11 24·1	4·7 3·7	10·7 8·5	16·7 13·2
48	11 57·0	11 59·0	11 24·3	4·8 3·8	10·8 8·6	16·8 13·3
49	11 57·3	11 59·2	11 24·6	4·9 3·9	10·9 8·6	16·9 13·4
50	11 57·5	11 59·5	11 24·8	5·0 4·0	11·0 8·7	17·0 13·5
51	11 57·8	11 59·7	11 25·1	5·1 4·0	11·1 8·8	17·1 13·5
52	11 58·0	12 00·0	11 25·3	5·2 4·1	11·2 8·9	17·2 13·6
53	11 58·3	12 00·2	11 25·5	5·3 4·2	11·3 8·9	17·3 13·7
54	11 58·5	12 00·5	11 25·8	5·4 4·3	11·4 9·0	17·4 13·8
55	11 58·8	12 00·7	11 26·0	5·5 4·4	11·5 9·1	17·5 13·9
56	11 59·0	12 01·0	11 26·2	5·6 4·4	11·6 9·2	17·6 13·9
57	11 59·3	12 01·2	11 26·5	5·7 4·5	11·7 9·3	17·7 14·0
58	11 59·5	12 01·5	11 26·7	5·8 4·6	11·8 9·3	17·8 14·1
59	11 59·8	12 01·7	11 27·0	5·9 4·7	11·9 9·4	17·9 14·2
60	12 00·0	12 02·0	11 27·2	6·0 4·8	12·0 9·5	18·0 14·3

48	SUN PLANETS	ARIES	MOON	v or d Corrⁿ	v or d Corrⁿ	v or d Corrⁿ	49	SUN PLANETS	ARIES	MOON	v or d Corrⁿ	v or d Corrⁿ	v or d Corrⁿ
s	° ′	° ′	° ′	′ ′	′ ′	′ ′	s	° ′	° ′	° ′	′ ′	′ ′	′ ′
00	12 00·0	12 02·0	11 27·2	0·0 0·0	6·0 4·9	12·0 9·7	00	12 15·0	12 17·0	11 41·5	0·0 0·0	6·0 5·0	12·0 9·9
01	12 00·3	12 02·2	11 27·4	0·1 0·1	6·1 4·9	12·1 9·8	01	12 15·3	12 17·3	11 41·8	0·1 0·1	6·1 5·0	12·1 10·0
02	12 00·5	12 02·5	11 27·7	0·2 0·2	6·2 5·0	12·2 9·9	02	12 15·5	12 17·5	11 42·0	0·2 0·2	6·2 5·1	12·2 10·1
03	12 00·8	12 02·7	11 27·9	0·3 0·2	6·3 5·1	12·3 9·9	03	12 15·8	12 17·8	11 42·2	0·3 0·2	6·3 5·2	12·3 10·1
04	12 01·0	12 03·0	11 28·2	0·4 0·3	6·4 5·2	12·4 10·0	04	12 16·0	12 18·0	11 42·5	0·4 0·3	6·4 5·3	12·4 10·2
05	12 01·3	12 03·2	11 28·4	0·5 0·4	6·5 5·3	12·5 10·1	05	12 16·3	12 18·3	11 42·7	0·5 0·4	6·5 5·4	12·5 10·3
06	12 01·5	12 03·5	11 28·6	0·6 0·5	6·6 5·3	12·6 10·2	06	12 16·5	12 18·5	11 42·9	0·6 0·5	6·6 5·4	12·6 10·4
07	12 01·8	12 03·7	11 28·9	0·7 0·6	6·7 5·4	12·7 10·3	07	12 16·8	12 18·8	11 43·2	0·7 0·6	6·7 5·5	12·7 10·5
08	12 02·0	12 04·0	11 29·1	0·8 0·6	6·8 5·5	12·8 10·3	08	12 17·0	12 19·0	11 43·4	0·8 0·7	6·8 5·6	12·8 10·6
09	12 02·3	12 04·2	11 29·3	0·9 0·7	6·9 5·6	12·9 10·4	09	12 17·3	12 19·3	11 43·7	0·9 0·7	6·9 5·7	12·9 10·6
10	12 02·5	12 04·5	11 29·6	1·0 0·8	7·0 5·7	13·0 10·5	10	12 17·5	12 19·5	11 43·9	1·0 0·8	7·0 5·8	13·0 10·7
11	12 02·8	12 04·7	11 29·8	1·1 0·9	7·1 5·7	13·1 10·6	11	12 17·8	12 19·8	11 44·1	1·1 0·9	7·1 5·9	13·1 10·8
12	12 03·0	12 05·0	11 30·1	1·2 1·0	7·2 5·8	13·2 10·7	12	12 18·0	12 20·0	11 44·4	1·2 1·0	7·2 5·9	13·2 10·9
13	12 03·3	12 05·2	11 30·3	1·3 1·1	7·3 5·9	13·3 10·8	13	12 18·3	12 20·3	11 44·6	1·3 1·1	7·3 6·0	13·3 11·0
14	12 03·5	12 05·5	11 30·5	1·4 1·1	7·4 6·0	13·4 10·8	14	12 18·5	12 20·5	11 44·9	1·4 1·2	7·4 6·1	13·4 11·1
15	12 03·8	12 05·7	11 30·8	1·5 1·2	7·5 6·1	13·5 10·9	15	12 18·8	12 20·8	11 45·1	1·5 1·2	7·5 6·2	13·5 11·1
16	12 04·0	12 06·0	11 31·0	1·6 1·3	7·6 6·1	13·6 11·0	16	12 19·0	12 21·0	11 45·3	1·6 1·3	7·6 6·3	13·6 11·2
17	12 04·3	12 06·2	11 31·3	1·7 1·4	7·7 6·2	13·7 11·1	17	12 19·3	12 21·3	11 45·6	1·7 1·4	7·7 6·4	13·7 11·3
18	12 04·5	12 06·5	11 31·5	1·8 1·5	7·8 6·3	13·8 11·2	18	12 19·5	12 21·5	11 45·8	1·8 1·5	7·8 6·4	13·8 11·4
19	12 04·8	12 06·7	11 31·7	1·9 1·5	7·9 6·4	13·9 11·2	19	12 19·8	12 21·8	11 46·1	1·9 1·6	7·9 6·5	13·9 11·5
20	12 05·0	12 07·0	11 32·0	2·0 1·6	8·0 6·5	14·0 11·3	20	12 20·0	12 22·0	11 46·3	2·0 1·7	8·0 6·6	14·0 11·6
21	12 05·3	12 07·2	11 32·2	2·1 1·7	8·1 6·5	14·1 11·4	21	12 20·3	12 22·3	11 46·5	2·1 1·7	8·1 6·7	14·1 11·6
22	12 05·5	12 07·5	11 32·4	2·2 1·8	8·2 6·6	14·2 11·5	22	12 20·5	12 22·5	11 46·8	2·2 1·8	8·2 6·8	14·2 11·7
23	12 05·8	12 07·7	11 32·7	2·3 1·9	8·3 6·7	14·3 11·6	23	12 20·8	12 22·8	11 47·0	2·3 1·9	8·3 6·8	14·3 11·8
24	12 06·0	12 08·0	11 32·9	2·4 1·9	8·4 6·8	14·4 11·6	24	12 21·0	12 23·0	11 47·2	2·4 2·0	8·4 6·9	14·4 11·9
25	12 06·3	12 08·2	11 33·2	2·5 2·0	8·5 6·9	14·5 11·7	25	12 21·3	12 23·3	11 47·5	2·5 2·1	8·5 7·0	14·5 12·0
26	12 06·5	12 08·5	11 33·4	2·6 2·1	8·6 7·0	14·6 11·8	26	12 21·5	12 23·5	11 47·7	2·6 2·1	8·6 7·1	14·6 12·0
27	12 06·8	12 08·7	11 33·6	2·7 2·2	8·7 7·0	14·7 11·9	27	12 21·8	12 23·8	11 48·0	2·7 2·2	8·7 7·2	14·7 12·1
28	12 07·0	12 09·0	11 33·9	2·8 2·3	8·8 7·1	14·8 12·0	28	12 22·0	12 24·0	11 48·2	2·8 2·3	8·8 7·3	14·8 12·2
29	12 07·3	12 09·2	11 34·1	2·9 2·3	8·9 7·2	14·9 12·0	29	12 22·3	12 24·3	11 48·4	2·9 2·4	8·9 7·3	14·9 12·3
30	12 07·5	12 09·5	11 34·4	3·0 2·4	9·0 7·3	15·0 12·1	30	12 22·5	12 24·5	11 48·7	3·0 2·5	9·0 7·4	15·0 12·4
31	12 07·8	12 09·7	11 34·6	3·1 2·5	9·1 7·4	15·1 12·2	31	12 22·8	12 24·8	11 48·9	3·1 2·6	9·1 7·5	15·1 12·5
32	12 08·0	12 10·0	11 34·8	3·2 2·6	9·2 7·4	15·2 12·3	32	12 23·0	12 25·0	11 49·2	3·2 2·6	9·2 7·6	15·2 12·5
33	12 08·3	12 10·2	11 35·1	3·3 2·7	9·3 7·5	15·3 12·4	33	12 23·3	12 25·3	11 49·4	3·3 2·7	9·3 7·7	15·3 12·6
34	12 08·5	12 10·5	11 35·3	3·4 2·7	9·4 7·6	15·4 12·4	34	12 23·5	12 25·5	11 49·6	3·4 2·8	9·4 7·8	15·4 12·7
35	12 08·8	12 10·7	11 35·6	3·5 2·8	9·5 7·7	15·5 12·5	35	12 23·8	12 25·8	11 49·9	3·5 2·9	9·5 7·8	15·5 12·8
36	12 09·0	12 11·0	11 35·8	3·6 2·9	9·6 7·8	15·6 12·6	36	12 24·0	12 26·0	11 50·1	3·6 3·0	9·6 7·9	15·6 12·9
37	12 09·3	12 11·2	11 36·0	3·7 3·0	9·7 7·8	15·7 12·7	37	12 24·3	12 26·3	11 50·3	3·7 3·1	9·7 8·0	15·7 13·0
38	12 09·5	12 11·5	11 36·3	3·8 3·1	9·8 7·9	15·8 12·8	38	12 24·5	12 26·5	11 50·6	3·8 3·1	9·8 8·1	15·8 13·0
39	12 09·8	12 11·7	11 36·5	3·9 3·2	9·9 8·0	15·9 12·9	39	12 24·8	12 26·8	11 50·8	3·9 3·2	9·9 8·2	15·9 13·1
40	12 10·0	12 12·0	11 36·7	4·0 3·2	10·0 8·1	16·0 12·9	40	12 25·0	12 27·0	11 51·1	4·0 3·3	10·0 8·3	16·0 13·2
41	12 10·3	12 12·2	11 37·0	4·1 3·3	10·1 8·2	16·1 13·0	41	12 25·3	12 27·3	11 51·3	4·1 3·4	10·1 8·3	16·1 13·3
42	12 10·5	12 12·5	11 37·2	4·2 3·4	10·2 8·2	16·2 13·1	42	12 25·5	12 27·5	11 51·5	4·2 3·5	10·2 8·4	16·2 13·4
43	12 10·8	12 12·8	11 37·5	4·3 3·5	10·3 8·3	16·3 13·2	43	12 25·8	12 27·8	11 51·8	4·3 3·5	10·3 8·5	16·3 13·4
44	12 11·0	12 13·0	11 37·7	4·4 3·6	10·4 8·4	16·4 13·3	44	12 26·0	12 28·0	11 52·0	4·4 3·6	10·4 8·6	16·4 13·5
45	12 11·3	12 13·3	11 37·9	4·5 3·6	10·5 8·5	16·5 13·3	45	12 26·3	12 28·3	11 52·3	4·5 3·7	10·5 8·7	16·5 13·6
46	12 11·5	12 13·5	11 38·2	4·6 3·7	10·6 8·6	16·6 13·4	46	12 26·5	12 28·5	11 52·5	4·6 3·8	10·6 8·7	16·6 13·7
47	12 11·8	12 13·8	11 38·4	4·7 3·8	10·7 8·6	16·7 13·5	47	12 26·8	12 28·8	11 52·7	4·7 3·9	10·7 8·8	16·7 13·8
48	12 12·0	12 14·0	11 38·7	4·8 3·9	10·8 8·7	16·8 13·6	48	12 27·0	12 29·0	11 53·0	4·8 4·0	10·8 8·9	16·8 13·9
49	12 12·3	12 14·3	11 38·9	4·9 4·0	10·9 8·8	16·9 13·7	49	12 27·3	12 29·3	11 53·2	4·9 4·0	10·9 9·0	16·9 13·9
50	12 12·5	12 14·5	11 39·1	5·0 4·0	11·0 8·9	17·0 13·7	50	12 27·5	12 29·5	11 53·4	5·0 4·1	11·0 9·1	17·0 14·0
51	12 12·8	12 14·8	11 39·4	5·1 4·1	11·1 9·0	17·1 13·8	51	12 27·8	12 29·8	11 53·7	5·1 4·2	11·1 9·2	17·1 14·1
52	12 13·0	12 15·0	11 39·6	5·2 4·2	11·2 9·1	17·2 13·9	52	12 28·0	12 30·0	11 53·9	5·2 4·3	11·2 9·2	17·2 14·2
53	12 13·3	12 15·3	11 39·8	5·3 4·3	11·3 9·1	17·3 14·0	53	12 28·3	12 30·3	11 54·2	5·3 4·4	11·3 9·3	17·3 14·3
54	12 13·5	12 15·5	11 40·1	5·4 4·4	11·4 9·2	17·4 14·1	54	12 28·5	12 30·5	11 54·4	5·4 4·5	11·4 9·4	17·4 14·4
55	12 13·8	12 15·8	11 40·3	5·5 4·4	11·5 9·3	17·5 14·1	55	12 28·8	12 30·8	11 54·6	5·5 4·5	11·5 9·5	17·5 14·4
56	12 14·0	12 16·0	11 40·6	5·6 4·5	11·6 9·4	17·6 14·2	56	12 29·0	12 31·1	11 54·9	5·6 4·6	11·6 9·6	17·6 14·5
57	12 14·3	12 16·3	11 40·8	5·7 4·6	11·7 9·5	17·7 14·3	57	12 29·3	12 31·3	11 55·1	5·7 4·7	11·7 9·7	17·7 14·6
58	12 14·5	12 16·5	11 41·0	5·8 4·7	11·8 9·5	17·8 14·4	58	12 29·5	12 31·6	11 55·4	5·8 4·8	11·8 9·7	17·8 14·7
59	12 14·8	12 16·8	11 41·3	5·9 4·8	11·9 9·6	17·9 14·5	59	12 29·8	12 31·8	11 55·6	5·9 4·9	11·9 9·8	17·9 14·8
60	12 15·0	12 17·0	11 41·5	6·0 4·9	12·0 9·7	18·0 14·6	60	12 30·0	12 32·1	11 55·8	6·0 5·0	12·0 9·9	18·0 14·9

50^m	SUN PLANETS	ARIES	MOON	v or Corr^n d	v or Corr^n d	v or Corr^n d
s	° ′	° ′	° ′	′ ′	′ ′	′ ′
00	12 30.0	12 32.1	11 55.8	0.0 0.0	6.0 5.1	12.0 10.1
01	12 30.3	12 32.3	11 56.1	0.1 0.1	6.1 5.1	12.1 10.2
02	12 30.5	12 32.6	11 56.3	0.2 0.2	6.2 5.2	12.2 10.3
03	12 30.8	12 32.8	11 56.5	0.3 0.3	6.3 5.3	12.3 10.4
04	12 31.0	12 33.1	11 56.8	0.4 0.3	6.4 5.4	12.4 10.4
05	12 31.3	12 33.3	11 57.0	0.5 0.4	6.5 5.5	12.5 10.5
06	12 31.5	12 33.6	11 57.3	0.6 0.5	6.6 5.6	12.6 10.6
07	12 31.8	12 33.8	11 57.5	0.7 0.6	6.7 5.6	12.7 10.7
08	12 32.0	12 34.1	11 57.7	0.8 0.7	6.8 5.7	12.8 10.8
09	12 32.3	12 34.3	11 58.0	0.9 0.8	6.9 5.8	12.9 10.9
10	12 32.5	12 34.6	11 58.2	1.0 0.8	7.0 5.9	13.0 10.9
11	12 32.8	12 34.8	11 58.5	1.1 0.9	7.1 6.0	13.1 11.0
12	12 33.0	12 35.1	11 58.7	1.2 1.0	7.2 6.1	13.2 11.1
13	12 33.3	12 35.3	11 58.9	1.3 1.1	7.3 6.1	13.3 11.2
14	12 33.5	12 35.6	11 59.2	1.4 1.2	7.4 6.2	13.4 11.3
15	12 33.8	12 35.8	11 59.4	1.5 1.3	7.5 6.3	13.5 11.4
16	12 34.0	12 36.1	11 59.7	1.6 1.3	7.6 6.4	13.6 11.4
17	12 34.3	12 36.3	11 59.9	1.7 1.4	7.7 6.5	13.7 11.5
18	12 34.5	12 36.6	12 00.1	1.8 1.5	7.8 6.6	13.8 11.6
19	12 34.8	12 36.8	12 00.4	1.9 1.6	7.9 6.6	13.9 11.7
20	12 35.0	12 37.1	12 00.6	2.0 1.7	8.0 6.7	14.0 11.8
21	12 35.3	12 37.3	12 00.8	2.1 1.8	8.1 6.8	14.1 11.9
22	12 35.5	12 37.6	12 01.1	2.2 1.9	8.2 6.9	14.2 12.0
23	12 35.8	12 37.8	12 01.3	2.3 1.9	8.3 7.0	14.3 12.0
24	12 36.0	12 38.1	12 01.6	2.4 2.0	8.4 7.1	14.4 12.1
25	12 36.3	12 38.3	12 01.8	2.5 2.1	8.5 7.2	14.5 12.2
26	12 36.5	12 38.6	12 02.0	2.6 2.2	8.6 7.2	14.6 12.3
27	12 36.8	12 38.8	12 02.3	2.7 2.3	8.7 7.3	14.7 12.4
28	12 37.0	12 39.1	12 02.5	2.8 2.4	8.8 7.4	14.8 12.5
29	12 37.3	12 39.3	12 02.8	2.9 2.4	8.9 7.5	14.9 12.5
30	12 37.5	12 39.6	12 03.0	3.0 2.5	9.0 7.6	15.0 12.6
31	12 37.8	12 39.8	12 03.2	3.1 2.6	9.1 7.7	15.1 12.7
32	12 38.0	12 40.1	12 03.5	3.2 2.7	9.2 7.7	15.2 12.8
33	12 38.3	12 40.3	12 03.7	3.3 2.8	9.3 7.8	15.3 12.9
34	12 38.5	12 40.6	12 03.9	3.4 2.9	9.4 7.9	15.4 13.0
35	12 38.8	12 40.8	12 04.2	3.5 2.9	9.5 8.0	15.5 13.0
36	12 39.0	12 41.1	12 04.4	3.6 3.0	9.6 8.1	15.6 13.1
37	12 39.3	12 41.3	12 04.7	3.7 3.1	9.7 8.2	15.7 13.2
38	12 39.5	12 41.6	12 04.9	3.8 3.2	9.8 8.2	15.8 13.3
39	12 39.8	12 41.8	12 05.1	3.9 3.3	9.9 8.3	15.9 13.4
40	12 40.0	12 42.1	12 05.4	4.0 3.4	10.0 8.4	16.0 13.5
41	12 40.3	12 42.3	12 05.6	4.1 3.5	10.1 8.5	16.1 13.6
42	12 40.5	12 42.6	12 05.9	4.2 3.5	10.2 8.6	16.2 13.6
43	12 40.8	12 42.8	12 06.1	4.3 3.6	10.3 8.7	16.3 13.7
44	12 41.0	12 43.1	12 06.3	4.4 3.7	10.4 8.8	16.4 13.8
45	12 41.3	12 43.3	12 06.6	4.5 3.8	10.5 8.8	16.5 13.9
46	12 41.5	12 43.6	12 06.8	4.6 3.9	10.6 8.9	16.6 14.0
47	12 41.8	12 43.8	12 07.0	4.7 4.0	10.7 9.0	16.7 14.1
48	12 42.0	12 44.1	12 07.3	4.8 4.0	10.8 9.1	16.8 14.1
49	12 42.3	12 44.3	12 07.5	4.9 4.1	10.9 9.2	16.9 14.2
50	12 42.5	12 44.6	12 07.8	5.0 4.2	11.0 9.3	17.0 14.3
51	12 42.8	12 44.8	12 08.0	5.1 4.3	11.1 9.3	17.1 14.4
52	12 43.0	12 45.1	12 08.2	5.2 4.4	11.2 9.4	17.2 14.5
53	12 43.3	12 45.3	12 08.5	5.3 4.5	11.3 9.5	17.3 14.6
54	12 43.5	12 45.6	12 08.7	5.4 4.5	11.4 9.6	17.4 14.6
55	12 43.8	12 45.8	12 09.0	5.5 4.6	11.5 9.7	17.5 14.7
56	12 44.0	12 46.1	12 09.2	5.6 4.7	11.6 9.8	17.6 14.8
57	12 44.3	12 46.3	12 09.4	5.7 4.8	11.7 9.8	17.7 14.9
58	12 44.5	12 46.6	12 09.7	5.8 4.9	11.8 9.9	17.8 15.0
59	12 44.8	12 46.8	12 09.9	5.9 5.0	11.9 10.0	17.9 15.1
60	12 45.0	12 47.1	12 10.2	6.0 5.1	12.0 10.1	18.0 15.2

51^m	SUN PLANETS	ARIES	MOON	v or Corr^n d	v or Corr^n d	v or Corr^n d
s	° ′	° ′	° ′	′ ′	′ ′	′ ′
00	12 45.0	12 47.1	12 10.2	0.0 0.0	6.0 5.2	12.0 10.3
01	12 45.3	12 47.3	12 10.4	0.1 0.1	6.1 5.2	12.1 10.4
02	12 45.5	12 47.6	12 10.6	0.2 0.2	6.2 5.3	12.2 10.5
03	12 45.8	12 47.8	12 10.9	0.3 0.3	6.3 5.4	12.3 10.6
04	12 46.0	12 48.1	12 11.1	0.4 0.3	6.4 5.5	12.4 10.6
05	12 46.3	12 48.3	12 11.3	0.5 0.4	6.5 5.6	12.5 10.7
06	12 46.5	12 48.6	12 11.6	0.6 0.5	6.6 5.7	12.6 10.8
07	12 46.8	12 48.8	12 11.8	0.7 0.6	6.7 5.8	12.7 10.9
08	12 47.0	12 49.1	12 12.1	0.8 0.7	6.8 5.8	12.8 11.0
09	12 47.3	12 49.4	12 12.3	0.9 0.8	6.9 5.9	12.9 11.1
10	12 47.5	12 49.6	12 12.5	1.0 0.9	7.0 6.0	13.0 11.2
11	12 47.8	12 49.9	12 12.8	1.1 0.9	7.1 6.1	13.1 11.2
12	12 48.0	12 50.1	12 13.0	1.2 1.0	7.2 6.2	13.2 11.3
13	12 48.3	12 50.4	12 13.3	1.3 1.1	7.3 6.3	13.3 11.4
14	12 48.5	12 50.6	12 13.5	1.4 1.2	7.4 6.4	13.4 11.5
15	12 48.8	12 50.9	12 13.7	1.5 1.3	7.5 6.4	13.5 11.6
16	12 49.0	12 51.1	12 14.0	1.6 1.4	7.6 6.5	13.6 11.7
17	12 49.3	12 51.4	12 14.2	1.7 1.5	7.7 6.6	13.7 11.8
18	12 49.5	12 51.6	12 14.4	1.8 1.5	7.8 6.7	13.8 11.8
19	12 49.8	12 51.9	12 14.7	1.9 1.6	7.9 6.8	13.9 11.9
20	12 50.0	12 52.1	12 14.9	2.0 1.7	8.0 6.9	14.0 12.0
21	12 50.3	12 52.4	12 15.2	2.1 1.8	8.1 7.0	14.1 12.1
22	12 50.5	12 52.6	12 15.4	2.2 1.9	8.2 7.0	14.2 12.2
23	12 50.8	12 52.9	12 15.6	2.3 2.0	8.3 7.1	14.3 12.3
24	12 51.0	12 53.1	12 15.9	2.4 2.1	8.4 7.2	14.4 12.4
25	12 51.3	12 53.4	12 16.1	2.5 2.1	8.5 7.3	14.5 12.4
26	12 51.5	12 53.6	12 16.4	2.6 2.2	8.6 7.4	14.6 12.5
27	12 51.8	12 53.9	12 16.6	2.7 2.3	8.7 7.5	14.7 12.6
28	12 52.0	12 54.1	12 16.8	2.8 2.4	8.8 7.6	14.8 12.7
29	12 52.3	12 54.4	12 17.1	2.9 2.5	8.9 7.6	14.9 12.8
30	12 52.5	12 54.6	12 17.3	3.0 2.6	9.0 7.7	15.0 12.9
31	12 52.8	12 54.9	12 17.5	3.1 2.7	9.1 7.8	15.1 13.0
32	12 53.0	12 55.1	12 17.8	3.2 2.7	9.2 7.9	15.2 13.0
33	12 53.3	12 55.4	12 18.0	3.3 2.8	9.3 8.0	15.3 13.1
34	12 53.5	12 55.6	12 18.3	3.4 2.9	9.4 8.1	15.4 13.2
35	12 53.8	12 55.9	12 18.5	3.5 3.0	9.5 8.2	15.5 13.3
36	12 54.0	12 56.1	12 18.7	3.6 3.1	9.6 8.2	15.6 13.4
37	12 54.3	12 56.4	12 19.0	3.7 3.2	9.7 8.3	15.7 13.5
38	12 54.5	12 56.6	12 19.2	3.8 3.3	9.8 8.4	15.8 13.6
39	12 54.8	12 56.9	12 19.5	3.9 3.3	9.9 8.5	15.9 13.6
40	12 55.0	12 57.1	12 19.7	4.0 3.4	10.0 8.6	16.0 13.7
41	12 55.3	12 57.4	12 19.9	4.1 3.5	10.1 8.7	16.1 13.8
42	12 55.5	12 57.6	12 20.2	4.2 3.6	10.2 8.8	16.2 13.9
43	12 55.8	12 57.9	12 20.4	4.3 3.7	10.3 8.8	16.3 14.0
44	12 56.0	12 58.1	12 20.6	4.4 3.8	10.4 8.9	16.4 14.1
45	12 56.3	12 58.4	12 20.9	4.5 3.9	10.5 9.0	16.5 14.2
46	12 56.5	12 58.6	12 21.1	4.6 3.9	10.6 9.1	16.6 14.2
47	12 56.8	12 58.9	12 21.4	4.7 4.0	10.7 9.2	16.7 14.3
48	12 57.0	12 59.1	12 21.6	4.8 4.1	10.8 9.3	16.8 14.4
49	12 57.3	12 59.4	12 21.8	4.9 4.2	10.9 9.4	16.9 14.5
50	12 57.5	12 59.6	12 22.1	5.0 4.3	11.0 9.4	17.0 14.6
51	12 57.8	12 59.9	12 22.3	5.1 4.4	11.1 9.5	17.1 14.7
52	12 58.0	13 00.1	12 22.6	5.2 4.5	11.2 9.6	17.2 14.8
53	12 58.3	13 00.4	12 22.8	5.3 4.5	11.3 9.7	17.3 14.8
54	12 58.5	13 00.6	12 23.0	5.4 4.6	11.4 9.8	17.4 14.9
55	12 58.8	13 00.9	12 23.3	5.5 4.7	11.5 9.9	17.5 15.0
56	12 59.0	13 01.1	12 23.5	5.6 4.8	11.6 10.0	17.6 15.1
57	12 59.3	13 01.4	12 23.8	5.7 4.9	11.7 10.0	17.7 15.2
58	12 59.5	13 01.6	12 24.0	5.8 5.0	11.8 10.1	17.8 15.3
59	12 59.8	13 01.9	12 24.2	5.9 5.1	11.9 10.2	17.9 15.4
60	13 00.0	13 02.1	12 24.5	6.0 5.2	12.0 10.3	18.0 15.5

52 (m)	SUN PLANETS	ARIES	MOON	v or d Corrn	v or d Corrn	v or d Corrn
s	° '	° '	° '	' '	' '	' '
00	13 00.0	13 02.1	12 24.5	0.0 0.0	6.0 5.3	12.0 10.5
01	13 00.3	13 02.4	12 24.7	0.1 0.1	6.1 5.3	12.1 10.6
02	13 00.5	13 02.6	12 24.9	0.2 0.2	6.2 5.4	12.2 10.7
03	13 00.8	13 02.9	12 25.2	0.3 0.3	6.3 5.5	12.3 10.8
04	13 01.0	13 03.1	12 25.4	0.4 0.4	6.4 5.6	12.4 10.9
05	13 01.3	13 03.4	12 25.7	0.5 0.4	6.5 5.7	12.5 10.9
06	13 01.5	13 03.6	12 25.9	0.6 0.5	6.6 5.8	12.6 11.0
07	13 01.8	13 03.9	12 26.1	0.7 0.6	6.7 5.9	12.7 11.1
08	13 02.0	13 04.1	12 26.4	0.8 0.7	6.8 6.0	12.8 11.2
09	13 02.3	13 04.4	12 26.6	0.9 0.8	6.9 6.0	12.9 11.3
10	13 02.5	13 04.6	12 26.9	1.0 0.9	7.0 6.1	13.0 11.4
11	13 02.8	13 04.9	12 27.1	1.1 1.0	7.1 6.2	13.1 11.5
12	13 03.0	13 05.1	12 27.3	1.2 1.1	7.2 6.3	13.2 11.6
13	13 03.3	13 05.4	12 27.6	1.3 1.1	7.3 6.4	13.3 11.6
14	13 03.5	13 05.6	12 27.8	1.4 1.2	7.4 6.5	13.4 11.7
15	13 03.8	13 05.9	12 28.0	1.5 1.3	7.5 6.6	13.5 11.8
16	13 04.0	13 06.1	12 28.3	1.6 1.4	7.6 6.7	13.6 11.9
17	13 04.3	13 06.4	12 28.5	1.7 1.5	7.7 6.7	13.7 12.0
18	13 04.5	13 06.6	12 28.8	1.8 1.6	7.8 6.8	13.8 12.1
19	13 04.8	13 06.9	12 29.0	1.9 1.7	7.9 6.9	13.9 12.2
20	13 05.0	13 07.1	12 29.2	2.0 1.8	8.0 7.0	14.0 12.3
21	13 05.3	13 07.4	12 29.5	2.1 1.8	8.1 7.1	14.1 12.3
22	13 05.5	13 07.7	12 29.7	2.2 1.9	8.2 7.2	14.2 12.4
23	13 05.8	13 07.9	12 30.0	2.3 2.0	8.3 7.3	14.3 12.5
24	13 06.0	13 08.2	12 30.2	2.4 2.1	8.4 7.4	14.4 12.6
25	13 06.3	13 08.4	12 30.4	2.5 2.2	8.5 7.4	14.5 12.7
26	13 06.5	13 08.7	12 30.7	2.6 2.3	8.6 7.5	14.6 12.8
27	13 06.8	13 08.9	12 30.9	2.7 2.4	8.7 7.6	14.7 12.9
28	13 07.0	13 09.2	12 31.1	2.8 2.5	8.8 7.7	14.8 13.0
29	13 07.3	13 09.4	12 31.4	2.9 2.5	8.9 7.8	14.9 13.0
30	13 07.5	13 09.7	12 31.6	3.0 2.6	9.0 7.9	15.0 13.1
31	13 07.8	13 09.9	12 31.9	3.1 2.7	9.1 8.0	15.1 13.2
32	13 08.0	13 10.2	12 32.1	3.2 2.8	9.2 8.0	15.2 13.3
33	13 08.3	13 10.4	12 32.3	3.3 2.9	9.3 8.1	15.3 13.4
34	13 08.5	13 10.7	12 32.6	3.4 3.0	9.4 8.2	15.4 13.5
35	13 08.8	13 10.9	12 32.8	3.5 3.1	9.5 8.3	15.5 13.6
36	13 09.0	13 11.2	12 33.1	3.6 3.2	9.6 8.4	15.6 13.7
37	13 09.3	13 11.4	12 33.3	3.7 3.2	9.7 8.5	15.7 13.7
38	13 09.5	13 11.7	12 33.5	3.8 3.3	9.8 8.6	15.8 13.8
39	13 09.8	13 11.9	12 33.8	3.9 3.4	9.9 8.7	15.9 13.9
40	13 10.0	13 12.2	12 34.0	4.0 3.5	10.0 8.8	16.0 14.0
41	13 10.3	13 12.4	12 34.2	4.1 3.6	10.1 8.8	16.1 14.1
42	13 10.5	13 12.7	12 34.5	4.2 3.7	10.2 8.9	16.2 14.2
43	13 10.8	13 12.9	12 34.7	4.3 3.8	10.3 9.0	16.3 14.3
44	13 11.0	13 13.2	12 35.0	4.4 3.9	10.4 9.1	16.4 14.3
45	13 11.3	13 13.4	12 35.2	4.5 3.9	10.5 9.2	16.5 14.4
46	13 11.5	13 13.7	12 35.4	4.6 4.0	10.6 9.3	16.6 14.5
47	13 11.8	13 13.9	12 35.7	4.7 4.1	10.7 9.4	16.7 14.6
48	13 12.0	13 14.2	12 35.9	4.8 4.2	10.8 9.5	16.8 14.7
49	13 12.3	13 14.4	12 36.2	4.9 4.3	10.9 9.5	16.9 14.8
50	13 12.5	13 14.7	12 36.4	5.0 4.4	11.0 9.6	17.0 14.9
51	13 12.8	13 14.9	12 36.6	5.1 4.5	11.1 9.7	17.1 15.0
52	13 13.0	13 15.2	12 36.9	5.2 4.6	11.2 9.8	17.2 15.1
53	13 13.3	13 15.4	12 37.1	5.3 4.6	11.3 9.9	17.3 15.1
54	13 13.5	13 15.7	12 37.4	5.4 4.7	11.4 10.0	17.4 15.2
55	13 13.8	13 15.9	12 37.6	5.5 4.8	11.5 10.1	17.5 15.3
56	13 14.0	13 16.2	12 37.8	5.6 4.9	11.6 10.2	17.6 15.4
57	13 14.3	13 16.4	12 38.1	5.7 5.0	11.7 10.2	17.7 15.5
58	13 14.5	13 16.7	12 38.3	5.8 5.1	11.8 10.3	17.8 15.6
59	13 14.8	13 16.9	12 38.5	5.9 5.2	11.9 10.4	17.9 15.7
60	13 15.0	13 17.2	12 38.8	6.0 5.3	12.0 10.5	18.0 15.8

53 (m)	SUN PLANETS	ARIES	MOON	v or d Corrn	v or d Corrn	v or d Corrn
s	° '	° '	° '	' '	' '	' '
00	13 15.0	13 17.2	12 38.8	0.0 0.0	6.0 5.4	12.0 10.7
01	13 15.3	13 17.4	12 39.0	0.1 0.1	6.1 5.4	12.1 10.8
02	13 15.5	13 17.7	12 39.3	0.2 0.2	6.2 5.5	12.2 10.9
03	13 15.8	13 17.9	12 39.5	0.3 0.3	6.3 5.6	12.3 11.0
04	13 16.0	13 18.2	12 39.7	0.4 0.4	6.4 5.7	12.4 11.1
05	13 16.3	13 18.4	12 40.0	0.5 0.4	6.5 5.8	12.5 11.1
06	13 16.5	13 18.7	12 40.2	0.6 0.5	6.6 5.9	12.6 11.2
07	13 16.8	13 18.9	12 40.5	0.7 0.6	6.7 6.0	12.7 11.3
08	13 17.0	13 19.2	12 40.7	0.8 0.7	6.8 6.1	12.8 11.4
09	13 17.3	13 19.4	12 40.9	0.9 0.8	6.9 6.2	12.9 11.5
10	13 17.5	13 19.7	12 41.2	1.0 0.9	7.0 6.2	13.0 11.6
11	13 17.8	13 19.9	12 41.4	1.1 1.0	7.1 6.3	13.1 11.7
12	13 18.0	13 20.2	12 41.6	1.2 1.1	7.2 6.4	13.2 11.8
13	13 18.3	13 20.4	12 41.9	1.3 1.2	7.3 6.5	13.3 11.9
14	13 18.5	13 20.7	12 42.1	1.4 1.2	7.4 6.6	13.4 11.9
15	13 18.8	13 20.9	12 42.4	1.5 1.3	7.5 6.7	13.5 12.0
16	13 19.0	13 21.2	12 42.6	1.6 1.4	7.6 6.8	13.6 12.1
17	13 19.3	13 21.4	12 42.8	1.7 1.5	7.7 6.9	13.7 12.2
18	13 19.5	13 21.7	12 43.1	1.8 1.6	7.8 7.0	13.8 12.3
19	13 19.8	13 21.9	12 43.3	1.9 1.7	7.9 7.0	13.9 12.4
20	13 20.0	13 22.2	12 43.6	2.0 1.8	8.0 7.1	14.0 12.5
21	13 20.3	13 22.4	12 43.8	2.1 1.9	8.1 7.2	14.1 12.6
22	13 20.5	13 22.7	12 44.0	2.2 2.0	8.2 7.3	14.2 12.7
23	13 20.8	13 22.9	12 44.3	2.3 2.1	8.3 7.4	14.3 12.7
24	13 21.0	13 23.2	12 44.5	2.4 2.1	8.4 7.5	14.4 12.8
25	13 21.3	13 23.4	12 44.7	2.5 2.2	8.5 7.6	14.5 12.9
26	13 21.5	13 23.7	12 45.0	2.6 2.3	8.6 7.7	14.6 13.0
27	13 21.8	13 23.9	12 45.2	2.7 2.4	8.7 7.8	14.7 13.1
28	13 22.0	13 24.2	12 45.5	2.8 2.5	8.8 7.8	14.8 13.2
29	13 22.3	13 24.4	12 45.7	2.9 2.6	8.9 7.9	14.9 13.3
30	13 22.5	13 24.7	12 45.9	3.0 2.7	9.0 8.0	15.0 13.4
31	13 22.8	13 24.9	12 46.2	3.1 2.8	9.1 8.1	15.1 13.5
32	13 23.0	13 25.2	12 46.4	3.2 2.9	9.2 8.2	15.2 13.6
33	13 23.3	13 25.4	12 46.7	3.3 2.9	9.3 8.3	15.3 13.6
34	13 23.5	13 25.7	12 46.9	3.4 3.0	9.4 8.4	15.4 13.7
35	13 23.8	13 26.0	12 47.1	3.5 3.1	9.5 8.5	15.5 13.8
36	13 24.0	13 26.2	12 47.4	3.6 3.2	9.6 8.6	15.6 13.9
37	13 24.3	13 26.5	12 47.6	3.7 3.3	9.7 8.6	15.7 14.0
38	13 24.5	13 26.7	12 47.9	3.8 3.4	9.8 8.7	15.8 14.1
39	13 24.8	13 27.0	12 48.1	3.9 3.5	9.9 8.8	15.9 14.2
40	13 25.0	13 27.2	12 48.3	4.0 3.6	10.0 8.9	16.0 14.3
41	13 25.3	13 27.5	12 48.6	4.1 3.7	10.1 9.0	16.1 14.4
42	13 25.5	13 27.7	12 48.8	4.2 3.7	10.2 9.1	16.2 14.4
43	13 25.8	13 28.0	12 49.0	4.3 3.8	10.3 9.2	16.3 14.5
44	13 26.0	13 28.2	12 49.3	4.4 3.9	10.4 9.3	16.4 14.6
45	13 26.3	13 28.5	12 49.5	4.5 4.0	10.5 9.4	16.5 14.7
46	13 26.5	13 28.7	12 49.8	4.6 4.1	10.6 9.5	16.6 14.8
47	13 26.8	13 29.0	12 50.0	4.7 4.2	10.7 9.5	16.7 14.9
48	13 27.0	13 29.2	12 50.2	4.8 4.3	10.8 9.6	16.8 15.0
49	13 27.3	13 29.5	12 50.5	4.9 4.4	10.9 9.7	16.9 15.1
50	13 27.5	13 29.7	12 50.7	5.0 4.5	11.0 9.8	17.0 15.2
51	13 27.8	13 30.0	12 51.0	5.1 4.5	11.1 9.9	17.1 15.2
52	13 28.0	13 30.2	12 51.2	5.2 4.6	11.2 10.0	17.2 15.3
53	13 28.3	13 30.5	12 51.4	5.3 4.7	11.3 10.1	17.3 15.4
54	13 28.5	13 30.7	12 51.7	5.4 4.8	11.4 10.2	17.4 15.5
55	13 28.8	13 31.0	12 51.9	5.5 4.9	11.5 10.3	17.5 15.6
56	13 29.0	13 31.2	12 52.1	5.6 5.0	11.6 10.3	17.6 15.7
57	13 29.3	13 31.5	12 52.4	5.7 5.1	11.7 10.4	17.7 15.8
58	13 29.5	13 31.7	12 52.6	5.8 5.2	11.8 10.5	17.8 15.9
59	13 29.8	13 32.0	12 52.9	5.9 5.3	11.9 10.6	17.9 16.0
60	13 30.0	13 32.2	12 53.1	6.0 5.4	12.0 10.7	18.0 16.1

54ᵐ s	SUN PLANETS	ARIES	MOON	v or d	Corrⁿ	v or d	Corrⁿ	v or d	Corrⁿ
00	13 30.0	13 32.2	12 53.1	0.0	0.0	6.0	5.5	12.0	10.9
01	13 30.3	13 32.5	12 53.3	0.1	0.1	6.1	5.5	12.1	11.0
02	13 30.5	13 32.7	12 53.6	0.2	0.2	6.2	5.6	12.2	11.1
03	13 30.8	13 33.0	12 53.8	0.3	0.3	6.3	5.7	12.3	11.2
04	13 31.0	13 33.2	12 54.1	0.4	0.4	6.4	5.8	12.4	11.3
05	13 31.3	13 33.5	12 54.3	0.5	0.5	6.5	5.9	12.5	11.4
06	13 31.5	13 33.7	12 54.5	0.6	0.5	6.6	6.0	12.6	11.4
07	13 31.8	13 34.0	12 54.8	0.7	0.6	6.7	6.1	12.7	11.5
08	13 32.0	13 34.2	12 55.0	0.8	0.7	6.8	6.2	12.8	11.6
09	13 32.3	13 34.5	12 55.2	0.9	0.8	6.9	6.3	12.9	11.7
10	13 32.5	13 34.7	12 55.5	1.0	0.9	7.0	6.4	13.0	11.8
11	13 32.8	13 35.0	12 55.7	1.1	1.0	7.1	6.4	13.1	11.9
12	13 33.0	13 35.2	12 56.0	1.2	1.1	7.2	6.5	13.2	12.0
13	13 33.3	13 35.5	12 56.2	1.3	1.2	7.3	6.6	13.3	12.1
14	13 33.5	13 35.7	12 56.4	1.4	1.3	7.4	6.7	13.4	12.2
15	13 33.8	13 36.0	12 56.7	1.5	1.4	7.5	6.8	13.5	12.3
16	13 34.0	13 36.2	12 56.9	1.6	1.5	7.6	6.9	13.6	12.4
17	13 34.3	13 36.5	12 57.2	1.7	1.5	7.7	7.0	13.7	12.4
18	13 34.5	13 36.7	12 57.4	1.8	1.6	7.8	7.1	13.8	12.5
19	13 34.8	13 37.0	12 57.6	1.9	1.7	7.9	7.2	13.9	12.6
20	13 35.0	13 37.2	12 57.9	2.0	1.8	8.0	7.3	14.0	12.7
21	13 35.3	13 37.5	12 58.1	2.1	1.9	8.1	7.4	14.1	12.8
22	13 35.5	13 37.7	12 58.3	2.2	2.0	8.2	7.4	14.2	12.9
23	13 35.8	13 38.0	12 58.6	2.3	2.1	8.3	7.5	14.3	13.0
24	13 36.0	13 38.2	12 58.8	2.4	2.2	8.4	7.6	14.4	13.1
25	13 36.3	13 38.5	12 59.1	2.5	2.3	8.5	7.7	14.5	13.2
26	13 36.5	13 38.7	12 59.3	2.6	2.4	8.6	7.8	14.6	13.3
27	13 36.8	13 39.0	12 59.5	2.7	2.5	8.7	7.9	14.7	13.4
28	13 37.0	13 39.2	12 59.8	2.8	2.5	8.8	8.0	14.8	13.4
29	13 37.3	13 39.5	13 00.0	2.9	2.6	8.9	8.1	14.9	13.5
30	13 37.5	13 39.7	13 00.3	3.0	2.7	9.0	8.2	15.0	13.6
31	13 37.8	13 40.0	13 00.5	3.1	2.8	9.1	8.3	15.1	13.7
32	13 38.0	13 40.2	13 00.7	3.2	2.9	9.2	8.4	15.2	13.8
33	13 38.3	13 40.5	13 01.0	3.3	3.0	9.3	8.4	15.3	13.9
34	13 38.5	13 40.7	13 01.2	3.4	3.1	9.4	8.5	15.4	14.0
35	13 38.8	13 41.0	13 01.5	3.5	3.2	9.5	8.6	15.5	14.1
36	13 39.0	13 41.2	13 01.7	3.6	3.3	9.6	8.7	15.6	14.2
37	13 39.3	13 41.5	13 01.9	3.7	3.4	9.7	8.8	15.7	14.3
38	13 39.5	13 41.7	13 02.2	3.8	3.5	9.8	8.9	15.8	14.4
39	13 39.8	13 42.0	13 02.4	3.9	3.5	9.9	9.0	15.9	14.4
40	13 40.0	13 42.2	13 02.6	4.0	3.6	10.0	9.1	16.0	14.5
41	13 40.3	13 42.5	13 02.9	4.1	3.7	10.1	9.2	16.1	14.6
42	13 40.5	13 42.7	13 03.1	4.2	3.8	10.2	9.3	16.2	14.7
43	13 40.8	13 43.0	13 03.4	4.3	3.9	10.3	9.4	16.3	14.8
44	13 41.0	13 43.2	13 03.6	4.4	4.0	10.4	9.4	16.4	14.9
45	13 41.3	13 43.5	13 03.8	4.5	4.1	10.5	9.5	16.5	15.0
46	13 41.5	13 43.7	13 04.1	4.6	4.2	10.6	9.6	16.6	15.1
47	13 41.8	13 44.0	13 04.3	4.7	4.3	10.7	9.7	16.7	15.2
48	13 42.0	13 44.3	13 04.6	4.8	4.4	10.8	9.8	16.8	15.3
49	13 42.3	13 44.5	13 04.8	4.9	4.5	10.9	9.9	16.9	15.4
50	13 42.5	13 44.8	13 05.0	5.0	4.5	11.0	10.0	17.0	15.4
51	13 42.8	13 45.0	13 05.3	5.1	4.6	11.1	10.1	17.1	15.5
52	13 43.0	13 45.3	13 05.5	5.2	4.7	11.2	10.2	17.2	15.6
53	13 43.3	13 45.5	13 05.7	5.3	4.8	11.3	10.3	17.3	15.7
54	13 43.5	13 45.8	13 06.0	5.4	4.9	11.4	10.4	17.4	15.8
55	13 43.8	13 46.0	13 06.2	5.5	5.0	11.5	10.4	17.5	15.9
56	13 44.0	13 46.3	13 06.5	5.6	5.1	11.6	10.5	17.6	16.0
57	13 44.3	13 46.5	13 06.7	5.7	5.2	11.7	10.6	17.7	16.1
58	13 44.5	13 46.8	13 06.9	5.8	5.3	11.8	10.7	17.8	16.2
59	13 44.8	13 47.0	13 07.2	5.9	5.4	11.9	10.8	17.9	16.3
60	13 45.0	13 47.3	13 07.4	6.0	5.5	12.0	10.9	18.0	16.4

55ᵐ s	SUN PLANETS	ARIES	MOON	v or d	Corrⁿ	v or d	Corrⁿ	v or d	Corrⁿ
00	13 45.0	13 47.3	13 07.4	0.0	0.0	6.0	5.6	12.0	11.1
01	13 45.3	13 47.5	13 07.7	0.1	0.1	6.1	5.6	12.1	11.2
02	13 45.5	13 47.8	13 07.9	0.2	0.2	6.2	5.7	12.2	11.3
03	13 45.8	13 48.0	13 08.1	0.3	0.3	6.3	5.8	12.3	11.4
04	13 46.0	13 48.3	13 08.4	0.4	0.4	6.4	5.9	12.4	11.5
05	13 46.3	13 48.5	13 08.6	0.5	0.5	6.5	6.0	12.5	11.6
06	13 46.5	13 48.8	13 08.8	0.6	0.6	6.6	6.1	12.6	11.7
07	13 46.8	13 49.0	13 09.1	0.7	0.6	6.7	6.2	12.7	11.7
08	13 47.0	13 49.3	13 09.3	0.8	0.7	6.8	6.3	12.8	11.8
09	13 47.3	13 49.5	13 09.6	0.9	0.8	6.9	6.4	12.9	11.9
10	13 47.5	13 49.8	13 09.8	1.0	0.9	7.0	6.5	13.0	12.0
11	13 47.8	13 50.0	13 10.0	1.1	1.0	7.1	6.6	13.1	12.1
12	13 48.0	13 50.3	13 10.3	1.2	1.1	7.2	6.7	13.2	12.2
13	13 48.3	13 50.5	13 10.5	1.3	1.2	7.3	6.8	13.3	12.3
14	13 48.5	13 50.8	13 10.8	1.4	1.3	7.4	6.8	13.4	12.4
15	13 48.8	13 51.0	13 11.0	1.5	1.4	7.5	6.9	13.5	12.5
16	13 49.0	13 51.3	13 11.2	1.6	1.5	7.6	7.0	13.6	12.6
17	13 49.3	13 51.5	13 11.5	1.7	1.6	7.7	7.1	13.7	12.7
18	13 49.5	13 51.8	13 11.7	1.8	1.7	7.8	7.2	13.8	12.8
19	13 49.8	13 52.0	13 12.0	1.9	1.8	7.9	7.3	13.9	12.9
20	13 50.0	13 52.3	13 12.2	2.0	1.9	8.0	7.4	14.0	13.0
21	13 50.3	13 52.5	13 12.4	2.1	1.9	8.1	7.5	14.1	13.0
22	13 50.5	13 52.8	13 12.7	2.2	2.0	8.2	7.6	14.2	13.1
23	13 50.8	13 53.0	13 12.9	2.3	2.1	8.3	7.7	14.3	13.2
24	13 51.0	13 53.3	13 13.1	2.4	2.2	8.4	7.8	14.4	13.3
25	13 51.3	13 53.5	13 13.4	2.5	2.3	8.5	7.9	14.5	13.4
26	13 51.5	13 53.8	13 13.6	2.6	2.4	8.6	8.0	14.6	13.5
27	13 51.8	13 54.0	13 13.9	2.7	2.5	8.7	8.0	14.7	13.6
28	13 52.0	13 54.3	13 14.1	2.8	2.6	8.8	8.1	14.8	13.7
29	13 52.3	13 54.5	13 14.3	2.9	2.7	8.9	8.2	14.9	13.8
30	13 52.5	13 54.8	13 14.6	3.0	2.8	9.0	8.3	15.0	13.9
31	13 52.8	13 55.0	13 14.8	3.1	2.9	9.1	8.4	15.1	14.0
32	13 53.0	13 55.3	13 15.1	3.2	3.0	9.2	8.5	15.2	14.1
33	13 53.3	13 55.5	13 15.3	3.3	3.1	9.3	8.6	15.3	14.2
34	13 53.5	13 55.8	13 15.5	3.4	3.1	9.4	8.7	15.4	14.3
35	13 53.8	13 56.0	13 15.8	3.5	3.2	9.5	8.8	15.5	14.3
36	13 54.0	13 56.3	13 16.0	3.6	3.3	9.6	8.9	15.6	14.4
37	13 54.3	13 56.5	13 16.2	3.7	3.4	9.7	9.0	15.7	14.5
38	13 54.5	13 56.8	13 16.5	3.8	3.5	9.8	9.1	15.8	14.6
39	13 54.8	13 57.0	13 16.7	3.9	3.6	9.9	9.2	15.9	14.7
40	13 55.0	13 57.3	13 17.0	4.0	3.7	10.0	9.3	16.0	14.8
41	13 55.3	13 57.5	13 17.2	4.1	3.8	10.1	9.3	16.1	14.9
42	13 55.5	13 57.8	13 17.4	4.2	3.9	10.2	9.4	16.2	15.0
43	13 55.8	13 58.0	13 17.7	4.3	4.0	10.3	9.5	16.3	15.1
44	13 56.0	13 58.3	13 17.9	4.4	4.1	10.4	9.6	16.4	15.2
45	13 56.3	13 58.5	13 18.2	4.5	4.2	10.5	9.7	16.5	15.3
46	13 56.5	13 58.8	13 18.4	4.6	4.3	10.6	9.8	16.6	15.4
47	13 56.8	13 59.0	13 18.6	4.7	4.3	10.7	9.9	16.7	15.4
48	13 57.0	13 59.3	13 18.9	4.8	4.4	10.8	10.0	16.8	15.5
49	13 57.3	13 59.5	13 19.1	4.9	4.5	10.9	10.1	16.9	15.6
50	13 57.5	13 59.8	13 19.3	5.0	4.6	11.0	10.2	17.0	15.7
51	13 57.8	14 00.0	13 19.6	5.1	4.7	11.1	10.3	17.1	15.8
52	13 58.0	14 00.3	13 19.8	5.2	4.8	11.2	10.4	17.2	15.9
53	13 58.3	14 00.5	13 20.1	5.3	4.9	11.3	10.5	17.3	16.0
54	13 58.5	14 00.8	13 20.3	5.4	5.0	11.4	10.5	17.4	16.1
55	13 58.8	14 01.0	13 20.5	5.5	5.1	11.5	10.6	17.5	16.2
56	13 59.0	14 01.3	13 20.8	5.6	5.2	11.6	10.7	17.6	16.3
57	13 59.3	14 01.5	13 21.0	5.7	5.3	11.7	10.8	17.7	16.4
58	13 59.5	14 01.8	13 21.3	5.8	5.4	11.8	10.9	17.8	16.5
59	13 59.8	14 02.0	13 21.5	5.9	5.5	11.9	11.0	17.9	16.6
60	14 00.0	14 02.3	13 21.7	6.0	5.6	12.0	11.1	18.0	16.7

56	SUN PLANETS	ARIES	MOON	v or d	Corrⁿ	v or d	Corrⁿ	v or d	Corrⁿ	57	SUN PLANETS	ARIES	MOON	v or d	Corrⁿ	v or d	Corrⁿ	v or d	Corrⁿ
s	° ′	° ′	° ′	′	′	′	′	′	′	s	° ′	° ′	° ′	′	′	′	′	′	′
00	14 00·0	14 02·3	13 21·7	0·0	0·0	6·0	5·7	12·0	11·3	00	14 15·0	14 17·3	13 36·1	0·0	0·0	6·0	5·8	12·0	11·5
01	14 00·3	14 02·6	13 22·0	0·1	0·1	6·1	5·7	12·1	11·4	01	14 15·3	14 17·6	13 36·3	0·1	0·1	6·1	5·8	12·1	11·6
02	14 00·5	14 02·8	13 22·2	0·2	0·2	6·2	5·8	12·2	11·5	02	14 15·5	14 17·8	13 36·5	0·2	0·2	6·2	5·9	12·2	11·7
03	14 00·8	14 03·1	13 22·4	0·3	0·3	6·3	5·9	12·3	11·6	03	14 15·8	14 18·1	13 36·8	0·3	0·3	6·3	6·0	12·3	11·8
04	14 01·0	14 03·3	13 22·7	0·4	0·4	6·4	6·0	12·4	11·7	04	14 16·0	14 18·3	13 37·0	0·4	0·4	6·4	6·1	12·4	11·9
05	14 01·3	14 03·6	13 22·9	0·5	0·5	6·5	6·1	12·5	11·8	05	14 16·3	14 18·6	13 37·2	0·5	0·5	6·5	6·2	12·5	12·0
06	14 01·5	14 03·8	13 23·2	0·6	0·6	6·6	6·2	12·6	11·9	06	14 16·5	14 18·8	13 37·5	0·6	0·6	6·6	6·3	12·6	12·1
07	14 01·8	14 04·1	13 23·4	0·7	0·7	6·7	6·3	12·7	12·0	07	14 16·8	14 19·1	13 37·7	0·7	0·7	6·7	6·4	12·7	12·2
08	14 02·0	14 04·3	13 23·6	0·8	0·8	6·8	6·4	12·8	12·1	08	14 17·0	14 19·3	13 38·0	0·8	0·8	6·8	6·5	12·8	12·3
09	14 02·3	14 04·6	13 23·9	0·9	0·8	6·9	6·5	12·9	12·1	09	14 17·3	14 19·6	13 38·2	0·9	0·9	6·9	6·6	12·9	12·4
10	14 02·5	14 04·8	13 24·1	1·0	0·9	7·0	6·6	13·0	12·2	10	14 17·5	14 19·8	13 38·4	1·0	1·0	7·0	6·7	13·0	12·5
11	14 02·8	14 05·1	13 24·4	1·1	1·0	7·1	6·7	13·1	12·3	11	14 17·8	14 20·1	13 38·7	1·1	1·1	7·1	6·8	13·1	12·6
12	14 03·0	14 05·3	13 24·6	1·2	1·1	7·2	6·8	13·2	12·4	12	14 18·0	14 20·3	13 38·9	1·2	1·2	7·2	6·9	13·2	12·7
13	14 03·3	14 05·6	13 24·8	1·3	1·2	7·3	6·9	13·3	12·5	13	14 18·3	14 20·6	13 39·2	1·3	1·2	7·3	7·0	13·3	12·7
14	14 03·5	14 05·8	13 25·1	1·4	1·3	7·4	7·0	13·4	12·6	14	14 18·5	14 20·9	13 39·4	1·4	1·3	7·4	7·1	13·4	12·8
15	14 03·8	14 06·1	13 25·3	1·5	1·4	7·5	7·1	13·5	12·7	15	14 18·8	14 21·1	13 39·6	1·5	1·4	7·5	7·2	13·5	12·9
16	14 04·0	14 06·3	13 25·6	1·6	1·5	7·6	7·2	13·6	12·8	16	14 19·0	14 21·4	13 39·9	1·6	1·5	7·6	7·3	13·6	13·0
17	14 04·3	14 06·6	13 25·8	1·7	1·6	7·7	7·3	13·7	12·9	17	14 19·3	14 21·6	13 40·1	1·7	1·6	7·7	7·4	13·7	13·1
18	14 04·5	14 06·8	13 26·0	1·8	1·7	7·8	7·3	13·8	13·0	18	14 19·5	14 21·9	13 40·3	1·8	1·7	7·8	7·5	13·8	13·2
19	14 04·8	14 07·1	13 26·3	1·9	1·8	7·9	7·4	13·9	13·1	19	14 19·8	14 22·1	13 40·6	1·9	1·8	7·9	7·6	13·9	13·3
20	14 05·0	14 07·3	13 26·5	2·0	1·9	8·0	7·5	14·0	13·2	20	14 20·0	14 22·4	13 40·8	2·0	1·9	8·0	7·7	14·0	13·4
21	14 05·3	14 07·6	13 26·7	2·1	2·0	8·1	7·6	14·1	13·3	21	14 20·3	14 22·6	13 41·1	2·1	2·0	8·1	7·8	14·1	13·5
22	14 05·5	14 07·8	13 27·0	2·2	2·1	8·2	7·7	14·2	13·4	22	14 20·5	14 22·9	13 41·3	2·2	2·1	8·2	7·9	14·2	13·6
23	14 05·8	14 08·1	13 27·2	2·3	2·2	8·3	7·8	14·3	13·5	23	14 20·8	14 23·1	13 41·5	2·3	2·2	8·3	8·0	14·3	13·7
24	14 06·0	14 08·3	13 27·5	2·4	2·3	8·4	7·9	14·4	13·6	24	14 21·0	14 23·4	13 41·8	2·4	2·3	8·4	8·1	14·4	13·8
25	14 06·3	14 08·6	13 27·7	2·5	2·4	8·5	8·0	14·5	13·7	25	14 21·3	14 23·6	13 42·0	2·5	2·4	8·5	8·1	14·5	13·9
26	14 06·5	14 08·8	13 27·9	2·6	2·4	8·6	8·1	14·6	13·7	26	14 21·5	14 23·9	13 42·3	2·6	2·5	8·6	8·2	14·6	14·0
27	14 06·8	14 09·1	13 28·2	2·7	2·5	8·7	8·2	14·7	13·8	27	14 21·8	14 24·1	13 42·5	2·7	2·6	8·7	8·3	14·7	14·1
28	14 07·0	14 09·3	13 28·4	2·8	2·6	8·8	8·3	14·8	13·9	28	14 22·0	14 24·4	13 42·7	2·8	2·7	8·8	8·4	14·8	14·2
29	14 07·3	14 09·6	13 28·7	2·9	2·7	8·9	8·4	14·9	14·0	29	14 22·3	14 24·6	13 43·0	2·9	2·8	8·9	8·5	14·9	14·3
30	14 07·5	14 09·8	13 28·9	3·0	2·8	9·0	8·5	15·0	14·1	30	14 22·5	14 24·9	13 43·2	3·0	2·9	9·0	8·6	15·0	14·4
31	14 07·8	14 10·1	13 29·1	3·1	2·9	9·1	8·6	15·1	14·2	31	14 22·8	14 25·1	13 43·4	3·1	3·0	9·1	8·7	15·1	14·5
32	14 08·0	14 10·3	13 29·4	3·2	3·0	9·2	8·7	15·2	14·3	32	14 23·0	14 25·4	13 43·7	3·2	3·1	9·2	8·8	15·2	14·6
33	14 08·3	14 10·6	13 29·6	3·3	3·1	9·3	8·8	15·3	14·4	33	14 23·3	14 25·6	13 43·9	3·3	3·2	9·3	8·9	15·3	14·7
34	14 08·5	14 10·8	13 29·8	3·4	3·2	9·4	8·9	15·4	14·5	34	14 23·5	14 25·9	13 44·2	3·4	3·3	9·4	9·0	15·4	14·8
35	14 08·8	14 11·1	13 30·1	3·5	3·3	9·5	8·9	15·5	14·6	35	14 23·8	14 26·1	13 44·4	3·5	3·4	9·5	9·1	15·5	14·9
36	14 09·0	14 11·3	13 30·3	3·6	3·4	9·6	9·0	15·6	14·7	36	14 24·0	14 26·4	13 44·6	3·6	3·5	9·6	9·2	15·6	15·0
37	14 09·3	14 11·6	13 30·6	3·7	3·5	9·7	9·1	15·7	14·8	37	14 24·3	14 26·6	13 44·9	3·7	3·5	9·7	9·3	15·7	15·0
38	14 09·5	14 11·8	13 30·8	3·8	3·6	9·8	9·2	15·8	14·9	38	14 24·5	14 26·9	13 45·1	3·8	3·6	9·8	9·4	15·8	15·1
39	14 09·8	14 12·1	13 31·0	3·9	3·7	9·9	9·3	15·9	15·0	39	14 24·8	14 27·1	13 45·4	3·9	3·7	9·9	9·5	15·9	15·2
40	14 10·0	14 12·3	13 31·3	4·0	3·8	10·0	9·4	16·0	15·1	40	14 25·0	14 27·4	13 45·6	4·0	3·8	10·0	9·6	16·0	15·3
41	14 10·3	14 12·6	13 31·5	4·1	3·9	10·1	9·5	16·1	15·2	41	14 25·3	14 27·6	13 45·8	4·1	3·9	10·1	9·7	16·1	15·4
42	14 10·5	14 12·8	13 31·8	4·2	4·0	10·2	9·6	16·2	15·3	42	14 25·5	14 27·9	13 46·1	4·2	4·0	10·2	9·8	16·2	15·5
43	14 10·8	14 13·1	13 32·0	4·3	4·0	10·3	9·7	16·3	15·3	43	14 25·8	14 28·1	13 46·3	4·3	4·1	10·3	9·9	16·3	15·6
44	14 11·0	14 13·3	13 32·2	4·4	4·1	10·4	9·8	16·4	15·4	44	14 26·0	14 28·4	13 46·5	4·4	4·2	10·4	10·0	16·4	15·7
45	14 11·3	14 13·6	13 32·5	4·5	4·2	10·5	9·9	16·5	15·5	45	14 26·3	14 28·6	13 46·8	4·5	4·3	10·5	10·1	16·5	15·8
46	14 11·5	14 13·8	13 32·7	4·6	4·3	10·6	10·0	16·6	15·6	46	14 26·5	14 28·9	13 47·0	4·6	4·4	10·6	10·2	16·6	15·9
47	14 11·8	14 14·1	13 32·9	4·7	4·4	10·7	10·1	16·7	15·7	47	14 26·8	14 29·1	13 47·3	4·7	4·5	10·7	10·3	16·7	16·0
48	14 12·0	14 14·3	13 33·2	4·8	4·5	10·8	10·2	16·8	15·8	48	14 27·0	14 29·4	13 47·5	4·8	4·6	10·8	10·4	16·8	16·1
49	14 12·3	14 14·6	13 33·4	4·9	4·6	10·9	10·3	16·9	15·9	49	14 27·3	14 29·6	13 47·7	4·9	4·7	10·9	10·4	16·9	16·2
50	14 12·5	14 14·8	13 33·7	5·0	4·7	11·0	10·4	17·0	16·0	50	14 27·5	14 29·9	13 48·0	5·0	4·8	11·0	10·5	17·0	16·3
51	14 12·8	14 15·1	13 33·9	5·1	4·8	11·1	10·5	17·1	16·1	51	14 27·8	14 30·1	13 48·2	5·1	4·9	11·1	10·6	17·1	16·4
52	14 13·0	14 15·3	13 34·1	5·2	4·9	11·2	10·5	17·2	16·2	52	14 28·0	14 30·4	13 48·5	5·2	5·0	11·2	10·7	17·2	16·5
53	14 13·3	14 15·6	13 34·4	5·3	5·0	11·3	10·6	17·3	16·3	53	14 28·3	14 30·6	13 48·7	5·3	5·1	11·3	10·8	17·3	16·6
54	14 13·5	14 15·8	13 34·6	5·4	5·1	11·4	10·7	17·4	16·4	54	14 28·5	14 30·9	13 48·9	5·4	5·2	11·4	10·9	17·4	16·7
55	14 13·8	14 16·1	13 34·9	5·5	5·2	11·5	10·8	17·5	16·5	55	14 28·8	14 31·1	13 49·2	5·5	5·3	11·5	11·0	17·5	16·8
56	14 14·0	14 16·3	13 35·1	5·6	5·3	11·6	10·9	17·6	16·6	56	14 29·0	14 31·4	13 49·4	5·6	5·4	11·6	11·1	17·6	16·9
57	14 14·3	14 16·6	13 35·3	5·7	5·4	11·7	11·0	17·7	16·7	57	14 29·3	14 31·6	13 49·7	5·7	5·5	11·7	11·2	17·7	17·0
58	14 14·5	14 16·8	13 35·6	5·8	5·5	11·8	11·1	17·8	16·8	58	14 29·5	14 31·9	13 49·9	5·8	5·6	11·8	11·3	17·8	17·1
59	14 14·8	14 17·1	13 35·8	5·9	5·6	11·9	11·2	17·9	16·9	59	14 29·8	14 32·1	13 50·1	5·9	5·7	11·9	11·4	17·9	17·2
60	14 15·0	14 17·3	13 36·1	6·0	5·7	12·0	11·3	18·0	17·0	60	14 30·0	14 32·4	13 50·4	6·0	5·8	12·0	11·5	18·0	17·3

58ᵐ

58 s	SUN PLANETS	ARIES	MOON	v or Corrⁿ d	v or Corrⁿ d	v or Corrⁿ d
	° ′	° ′	° ′	′ ′	′ ′	′ ′
00	14 30·0	14 32·4	13 50·4	0·0 0·0	6·0 5·9	12·0 11·7
01	14 30·3	14 32·6	13 50·6	0·1 0·1	6·1 5·9	12·1 11·8
02	14 30·5	14 32·9	13 50·8	0·2 0·2	6·2 6·0	12·2 11·9
03	14 30·8	14 33·1	13 51·1	0·3 0·3	6·3 6·1	12·3 12·0
04	14 31·0	14 33·4	13 51·3	0·4 0·4	6·4 6·2	12·4 12·1
05	14 31·3	14 33·6	13 51·6	0·5 0·5	6·5 6·3	12·5 12·2
06	14 31·5	14 33·9	13 51·8	0·6 0·6	6·6 6·4	12·6 12·3
07	14 31·8	14 34·1	13 52·0	0·7 0·7	6·7 6·5	12·7 12·4
08	14 32·0	14 34·4	13 52·3	0·8 0·8	6·8 6·6	12·8 12·5
09	14 32·3	14 34·6	13 52·5	0·9 0·9	6·9 6·7	12·9 12·6
10	14 32·5	14 34·9	13 52·8	1·0 1·0	7·0 6·8	13·0 12·7
11	14 32·8	14 35·1	13 53·0	1·1 1·1	7·1 6·9	13·1 12·8
12	14 33·0	14 35·4	13 53·2	1·2 1·2	7·2 7·0	13·2 12·9
13	14 33·3	14 35·6	13 53·5	1·3 1·3	7·3 7·1	13·3 13·0
14	14 33·5	14 35·9	13 53·7	1·4 1·4	7·4 7·2	13·4 13·1
15	14 33·8	14 36·1	13 53·9	1·5 1·5	7·5 7·3	13·5 13·2
16	14 34·0	14 36·4	13 54·2	1·6 1·6	7·6 7·4	13·6 13·3
17	14 34·3	14 36·6	13 54·4	1·7 1·7	7·7 7·5	13·7 13·4
18	14 34·5	14 36·9	13 54·7	1·8 1·8	7·8 7·6	13·8 13·5
19	14 34·8	14 37·1	13 54·9	1·9 1·9	7·9 7·7	13·9 13·6
20	14 35·0	14 37·4	13 55·1	2·0 2·0	8·0 7·8	14·0 13·7
21	14 35·3	14 37·6	13 55·4	2·1 2·0	8·1 7·9	14·1 13·7
22	14 35·5	14 37·9	13 55·6	2·2 2·1	8·2 8·0	14·2 13·8
23	14 35·8	14 38·1	13 55·9	2·3 2·2	8·3 8·1	14·3 13·9
24	14 36·0	14 38·4	13 56·1	2·4 2·3	8·4 8·2	14·4 14·0
25	14 36·3	14 38·6	13 56·3	2·5 2·4	8·5 8·3	14·5 14·1
26	14 36·5	14 38·9	13 56·6	2·6 2·5	8·6 8·4	14·6 14·2
27	14 36·8	14 39·2	13 56·8	2·7 2·6	8·7 8·5	14·7 14·3
28	14 37·0	14 39·4	13 57·0	2·8 2·7	8·8 8·6	14·8 14·4
29	14 37·3	14 39·7	13 57·3	2·9 2·8	8·9 8·7	14·9 14·5
30	14 37·5	14 39·9	13 57·5	3·0 2·9	9·0 8·8	15·0 14·6
31	14 37·8	14 40·2	13 57·8	3·1 3·0	9·1 8·9	15·1 14·7
32	14 38·0	14 40·4	13 58·0	3·2 3·1	9·2 9·0	15·2 14·8
33	14 38·3	14 40·7	13 58·2	3·3 3·2	9·3 9·1	15·3 14·9
34	14 38·5	14 40·9	13 58·5	3·4 3·3	9·4 9·2	15·4 15·0
35	14 38·8	14 41·2	13 58·7	3·5 3·4	9·5 9·3	15·5 15·1
36	14 39·0	14 41·4	13 59·0	3·6 3·5	9·6 9·4	15·6 15·2
37	14 39·3	14 41·7	13 59·2	3·7 3·6	9·7 9·5	15·7 15·3
38	14 39·5	14 41·9	13 59·4	3·8 3·7	9·8 9·6	15·8 15·4
39	14 39·8	14 42·2	13 59·7	3·9 3·8	9·9 9·7	15·9 15·5
40	14 40·0	14 42·4	13 59·9	4·0 3·9	10·0 9·8	16·0 15·6
41	14 40·3	14 42·7	14 00·1	4·1 4·0	10·1 9·8	16·1 15·7
42	14 40·5	14 42·9	14 00·4	4·2 4·1	10·2 9·9	16·2 15·8
43	14 40·8	14 43·2	14 00·6	4·3 4·2	10·3 10·0	16·3 15·9
44	14 41·0	14 43·4	14 00·9	4·4 4·3	10·4 10·1	16·4 16·0
45	14 41·3	14 43·7	14 01·1	4·5 4·4	10·5 10·2	16·5 16·1
46	14 41·5	14 43·9	14 01·3	4·6 4·5	10·6 10·3	16·6 16·2
47	14 41·8	14 44·2	14 01·6	4·7 4·6	10·7 10·4	16·7 16·3
48	14 42·0	14 44·4	14 01·8	4·8 4·7	10·8 10·5	16·8 16·4
49	14 42·3	14 44·7	14 02·1	4·9 4·8	10·9 10·6	16·9 16·5
50	14 42·5	14 44·9	14 02·3	5·0 4·9	11·0 10·7	17·0 16·6
51	14 42·8	14 45·2	14 02·5	5·1 5·0	11·1 10·8	17·1 16·7
52	14 43·0	14 45·4	14 02·8	5·2 5·1	11·2 10·9	17·2 16·8
53	14 43·3	14 45·7	14 03·0	5·3 5·2	11·3 11·0	17·3 16·9
54	14 43·5	14 45·9	14 03·3	5·4 5·3	11·4 11·1	17·4 17·0
55	14 43·8	14 46·2	14 03·5	5·5 5·4	11·5 11·2	17·5 17·1
56	14 44·0	14 46·4	14 03·7	5·6 5·5	11·6 11·3	17·6 17·2
57	14 44·3	14 46·7	14 04·0	5·7 5·6	11·7 11·4	17·7 17·3
58	14 44·5	14 46·9	14 04·2	5·8 5·7	11·8 11·5	17·8 17·4
59	14 44·8	14 47·2	14 04·4	5·9 5·8	11·9 11·6	17·9 17·5
60	14 45·0	14 47·4	14 04·7	6·0 5·9	12·0 11·7	18·0 17·6

59ᵐ

59 s	SUN PLANETS	ARIES	MOON	v or Corrⁿ d	v or Corrⁿ d	v or Corrⁿ d
	° ′	° ′	° ′	′ ′	′ ′	′ ′
00	14 45·0	14 47·4	14 04·7	0·0 0·0	6·0 6·0	12·0 11·9
01	14 45·3	14 47·7	14 04·9	0·1 0·1	6·1 6·0	12·1 12·0
02	14 45·5	14 47·9	14 05·2	0·2 0·2	6·2 6·1	12·2 12·1
03	14 45·8	14 48·2	14 05·4	0·3 0·3	6·3 6·2	12·3 12·2
04	14 46·0	14 48·4	14 05·6	0·4 0·4	6·4 6·3	12·4 12·3
05	14 46·3	14 48·7	14 05·9	0·5 0·5	6·5 6·4	12·5 12·4
06	14 46·5	14 48·9	14 06·1	0·6 0·6	6·6 6·5	12·6 12·5
07	14 46·8	14 49·2	14 06·4	0·7 0·7	6·7 6·6	12·7 12·6
08	14 47·0	14 49·4	14 06·6	0·8 0·8	6·8 6·7	12·8 12·7
09	14 47·3	14 49·7	14 06·8	0·9 0·9	6·9 6·8	12·9 12·8
10	14 47·5	14 49·9	14 07·1	1·0 1·0	7·0 6·9	13·0 12·9
11	14 47·8	14 50·2	14 07·3	1·1 1·1	7·1 7·0	13·1 13·0
12	14 48·0	14 50·4	14 07·5	1·2 1·2	7·2 7·1	13·2 13·1
13	14 48·3	14 50·7	14 07·8	1·3 1·3	7·3 7·2	13·3 13·2
14	14 48·5	14 50·9	14 08·0	1·4 1·4	7·4 7·3	13·4 13·3
15	14 48·8	14 51·2	14 08·3	1·5 1·5	7·5 7·4	13·5 13·4
16	14 49·0	14 51·4	14 08·5	1·6 1·6	7·6 7·5	13·6 13·5
17	14 49·3	14 51·7	14 08·7	1·7 1·7	7·7 7·6	13·7 13·6
18	14 49·5	14 51·9	14 09·0	1·8 1·8	7·8 7·7	13·8 13·7
19	14 49·8	14 52·2	14 09·2	1·9 1·9	7·9 7·8	13·9 13·8
20	14 50·0	14 52·4	14 09·5	2·0 2·0	8·0 7·9	14·0 13·9
21	14 50·3	14 52·7	14 09·7	2·1 2·1	8·1 8·0	14·1 14·0
22	14 50·5	14 52·9	14 09·9	2·2 2·2	8·2 8·1	14·2 14·1
23	14 50·8	14 53·2	14 10·2	2·3 2·3	8·3 8·2	14·3 14·2
24	14 51·0	14 53·4	14 10·4	2·4 2·4	8·4 8·3	14·4 14·3
25	14 51·3	14 53·7	14 10·6	2·5 2·5	8·5 8·4	14·5 14·4
26	14 51·5	14 53·9	14 10·9	2·6 2·6	8·6 8·5	14·6 14·5
27	14 51·8	14 54·2	14 11·1	2·7 2·7	8·7 8·6	14·7 14·6
28	14 52·0	14 54·4	14 11·4	2·8 2·8	8·8 8·7	14·8 14·7
29	14 52·3	14 54·7	14 11·6	2·9 2·9	8·9 8·8	14·9 14·8
30	14 52·5	14 54·9	14 11·8	3·0 3·0	9·0 8·9	15·0 14·9
31	14 52·8	14 55·2	14 12·1	3·1 3·1	9·1 9·0	15·1 15·0
32	14 53·0	14 55·4	14 12·3	3·2 3·2	9·2 9·1	15·2 15·1
33	14 53·3	14 55·7	14 12·6	3·3 3·3	9·3 9·2	15·3 15·2
34	14 53·5	14 55·9	14 12·8	3·4 3·4	9·4 9·3	15·4 15·3
35	14 53·8	14 56·2	14 13·0	3·5 3·5	9·5 9·4	15·5 15·4
36	14 54·0	14 56·4	14 13·3	3·6 3·6	9·6 9·5	15·6 15·5
37	14 54·3	14 56·7	14 13·5	3·7 3·7	9·7 9·6	15·7 15·6
38	14 54·5	14 56·9	14 13·8	3·8 3·8	9·8 9·7	15·8 15·7
39	14 54·8	14 57·2	14 14·0	3·9 3·9	9·9 9·8	15·9 15·8
40	14 55·0	14 57·5	14 14·2	4·0 4·0	10·0 9·9	16·0 15·9
41	14 55·3	14 57·7	14 14·5	4·1 4·1	10·1 10·0	16·1 16·0
42	14 55·5	14 58·0	14 14·7	4·2 4·2	10·2 10·1	16·2 16·1
43	14 55·8	14 58·2	14 14·9	4·3 4·3	10·3 10·2	16·3 16·2
44	14 56·0	14 58·5	14 15·2	4·4 4·4	10·4 10·3	16·4 16·3
45	14 56·3	14 58·7	14 15·4	4·5 4·5	10·5 10·4	16·5 16·4
46	14 56·5	14 59·0	14 15·7	4·6 4·6	10·6 10·5	16·6 16·5
47	14 56·8	14 59·2	14 15·9	4·7 4·7	10·7 10·6	16·7 16·6
48	14 57·0	14 59·5	14 16·1	4·8 4·8	10·8 10·7	16·8 16·7
49	14 57·3	14 59·7	14 16·4	4·9 4·9	10·9 10·8	16·9 16·8
50	14 57·5	15 00·0	14 16·6	5·0 5·0	11·0 10·9	17·0 16·9
51	14 57·8	15 00·2	14 16·9	5·1 5·1	11·1 11·0	17·1 17·0
52	14 58·0	15 00·5	14 17·1	5·2 5·2	11·2 11·1	17·2 17·1
53	14 58·3	15 00·7	14 17·3	5·3 5·3	11·3 11·2	17·3 17·2
54	14 58·5	15 01·0	14 17·6	5·4 5·4	11·4 11·3	17·4 17·3
55	14 58·8	15 01·2	14 17·8	5·5 5·5	11·5 11·4	17·5 17·4
56	14 59·0	15 01·5	14 18·0	5·6 5·6	11·6 11·5	17·6 17·5
57	14 59·3	15 01·7	14 18·3	5·7 5·7	11·7 11·6	17·7 17·6
58	14 59·5	15 02·0	14 18·5	5·8 5·8	11·8 11·7	17·8 17·7
59	14 59·8	15 02·2	14 18·8	5·9 5·9	11·9 11·8	17·9 17·8
60	15 00·0	15 02·5	14 19·0	6·0 6·0	12·0 11·9	18·0 17·9

TABLES FOR INTERPOLATING SUNRISE, MOONRISE, ETC.

TABLE I—FOR LATITUDE

Tabular Interval 10°	5°	2°	5ᵐ	10ᵐ	15ᵐ	20ᵐ	25ᵐ	30ᵐ	35ᵐ	40ᵐ	45ᵐ	50ᵐ	55ᵐ	60ᵐ	1ʰ05ᵐ	1ʰ10ᵐ	1ʰ15ᵐ	1ʰ20ᵐ
0 30	0 15	0 06	0	0	1	1	1	1	1	2	2	2	2	2	0 02	0 02	0 02	0 02
1 00	0 30	0 12	0	1	1	2	2	3	3	3	4	4	5	5	05	05	05	05
1 30	0 45	0 18	1	1	2	3	3	4	4	5	5	6	7	7	07	07	07	07
2 00	1 00	0 24	1	2	3	4	5	5	6	7	7	8	9	10	10	10	10	10
2 30	1 15	0 30	1	2	4	5	6	7	8	9	9	10	11	12	12	13	13	13
3 00	1 30	0 36	1	3	4	6	7	8	9	10	11	12	13	14	0 15	0 15	0 16	0 16
3 30	1 45	0 42	2	3	5	7	8	10	11	12	13	14	16	17	18	18	19	19
4 00	2 00	0 48	2	4	6	8	9	11	13	14	15	16	18	19	20	21	22	22
4 30	2 15	0 54	2	4	7	9	11	13	15	16	18	19	21	22	23	24	25	26
5 00	2 30	1 00	2	5	7	10	12	14	16	18	20	22	23	25	26	27	28	29
5 30	2 45	1 06	3	5	8	11	13	16	18	20	22	24	26	28	0 29	0 30	0 31	0 32
6 00	3 00	1 12	3	6	9	12	14	17	20	22	24	26	29	31	32	33	34	36
6 30	3 15	1 18	3	6	10	13	16	19	22	24	26	29	31	34	36	37	38	40
7 00	3 30	1 24	3	7	10	14	17	20	23	26	29	31	34	37	39	41	42	44
7 30	3 45	1 30	4	7	11	15	18	22	25	28	31	34	37	40	43	44	46	48
8 00	4 00	1 36	4	8	12	16	20	23	27	30	34	37	41	44	0 47	0 48	0 51	0 53
8 30	4 15	1 42	4	8	13	17	21	25	29	33	36	40	44	48	0 51	0 53	0 56	0 58
9 00	4 30	1 48	4	9	13	18	22	27	31	35	39	43	47	52	0 55	0 58	1 01	1 04
9 30	4 45	1 54	5	9	14	19	24	28	33	38	42	47	51	56	1 00	1 04	1 08	1 12
10 00	5 00	2 00	5	10	15	20	25	30	35	40	45	50	55	60	1 05	1 10	1 15	1 20

Table I is for interpolating the LMT of sunrise, twilight, moonrise, etc., for latitude. It is to be entered, in the appropriate column on the left, with the difference between true latitude and the nearest tabular latitude which is *less* than the true latitude; and with the argument at the top which is the nearest value of the difference between the times for the tabular latitude and the next higher one; the correction so obtained is applied to the time for the tabular latitude; the sign of the correction can be seen by inspection. It is to be noted that the interpolation is not linear, so that when using this table it is essential to take out the tabular phenomenon for the latitude *less* than the true latitude.

TABLE II—FOR LONGITUDE

Long. East or West	Difference between the times for given date and preceding date (for east longitude) or for given date and following date (for west longitude)																	
	10ᵐ	20ᵐ	30ᵐ	40ᵐ	50ᵐ	60ᵐ	1ʰ+ 10ᵐ	20ᵐ	30ᵐ	1ʰ+ 40ᵐ	50ᵐ	60ᵐ	2ʰ10ᵐ	2ʰ20ᵐ	2ʰ30ᵐ	2ʰ40ᵐ	2ʰ50ᵐ	3ʰ00ᵐ
0	0	0	0	0	0	0	0	0	0	0	0	0	0 00	0 00	0 00	0 00	0 00	0 00
10	0	1	1	1	1	2	2	2	2	3	3	3	04	04	04	04	05	05
20	1	1	2	2	3	3	4	4	5	6	6	7	07	08	08	09	09	10
30	1	2	2	3	4	5	6	7	7	8	9	10	11	12	12	13	14	15
40	1	2	3	4	6	7	8	9	10	11	12	13	14	16	17	18	19	20
50	1	3	4	6	7	8	10	11	12	14	15	17	0 18	0 19	0 21	0 22	0 24	0 25
60	2	3	5	7	8	10	12	13	15	17	18	20	22	23	25	27	28	30
70	2	4	6	8	10	12	14	16	17	19	21	23	25	27	29	31	33	35
80	2	4	7	9	11	13	16	18	20	22	24	27	29	31	33	36	38	40
90	2	5	7	10	12	15	17	20	22	25	27	30	32	35	37	40	42	45
100	3	6	8	11	14	17	19	22	25	28	31	33	0 36	0 39	0 42	0 44	0 47	0 50
110	3	6	9	12	15	18	21	24	27	31	34	37	40	43	46	49	0 52	0 55
120	3	7	10	13	17	20	23	27	30	33	37	40	43	47	50	53	0 57	1 00
130	4	7	11	14	18	22	25	29	32	36	40	43	47	51	54	0 58	1 01	1 05
140	4	8	12	16	19	23	27	31	35	39	43	47	51	54	0 58	1 02	1 06	1 10
150	4	8	13	17	21	25	29	33	38	42	46	50	0 54	0 58	1 03	1 07	1 11	1 15
160	4	9	13	18	22	27	31	36	40	44	49	53	0 58	1 02	1 07	1 11	1 16	1 20
170	5	9	14	19	24	28	33	38	42	47	52	57	1 01	1 06	1 11	1 16	1 20	1 25
180	5	10	15	20	25	30	35	40	45	50	55	60	1 05	1 10	1 15	1 20	1 25	1 30

Table II is for interpolating the LMT of moonrise, moonset and the Moon's meridian passage for longitude. It is entered with longitude and with the difference between the times for the given date and for the preceding date (in east longitudes) or following date (in west longitudes). The correction is normally *added* for west longitudes and *subtracted* for east longitudes, but if, as occasionally happens, the times become earlier each day instead of later, the signs of the corrections must be reversed.

INDEX TO SELECTED STARS, 2023

Name	No	Mag	SHA	Dec
Acamar	7	3·2	315	S 40
Achernar	5	0·5	335	S 57
Acrux	30	1·3	173	S 63
Adhara	19	1·5	255	S 29
Aldebaran	10	0·9	291	N 17
Alioth	32	1·8	166	N 56
Alkaid	34	1·9	153	N 49
Alnair	55	1·7	28	S 47
Alnilam	15	1·7	276	S 1
Alphard	25	2·0	218	S 9
Alphecca	41	2·2	126	N 27
Alpheratz	1	2·1	358	N 29
Altair	51	0·8	62	N 9
Ankaa	2	2·4	353	S 42
Antares	42	1·0	112	S 26
Arcturus	37	0·0	146	N 19
Atria	43	1·9	107	S 69
Avior	22	1·9	234	S 60
Bellatrix	13	1·6	278	N 6
Betelgeuse	16	Var.*	271	N 7
Canopus	17	−0·7	264	S 53
Capella	12	0·1	280	N 46
Deneb	53	1·3	49	N 45
Denebola	28	2·1	182	N 14
Diphda	4	2·0	349	S 18
Dubhe	27	1·8	194	N 62
Elnath	14	1·7	278	N 29
Eltanin	47	2·2	91	N 51
Enif	54	2·4	34	N 10
Fomalhaut	56	1·2	15	S 29
Gacrux	31	1·6	172	S 57
Gienah	29	2·6	176	S 18
Hadar	35	0·6	149	S 60
Hamal	6	2·0	328	N 24
Kaus Australis	48	1·9	84	S 34
Kochab	40	2·1	137	N 74
Markab	57	2·5	14	N 15
Menkar	8	2·5	314	N 4
Menkent	36	2·1	148	S 36
Miaplacidus	24	1·7	222	S 70
Mirfak	9	1·8	309	N 50
Nunki	50	2·0	76	S 26
Peacock	52	1·9	53	S 57
Pollux	21	1·1	243	N 28
Procyon	20	0·4	245	N 5
Rasalhague	46	2·1	96	N 13
Regulus	26	1·4	208	N 12
Rigel	11	0·1	281	S 8
Rigil Kentaurus	38	−0·3	140	S 61
Sabik	44	2·4	102	S 16
Schedar	3	2·2	350	N 57
Shaula	45	1·6	96	S 37
Sirius	18	−1·5	258	S 17
Spica	33	1·0	158	S 11
Suhail	23	2·2	223	S 44
Vega	49	0·0	81	N 39
Zubenelgenubi	39	2·8	137	S 16

No	Name	Mag	SHA	Dec
1	Alpheratz	2·1	358	N 29
2	Ankaa	2·4	353	S 42
3	Schedar	2·2	350	N 57
4	Diphda	2·0	349	S 18
5	Achernar	0·5	335	S 57
6	Hamal	2·0	328	N 24
7	Acamar	3·2	315	S 40
8	Menkar	2·5	314	N 4
9	Mirfak	1·8	309	N 50
10	Aldebaran	0·9	291	N 17
11	Rigel	0·1	281	S 8
12	Capella	0·1	280	N 46
13	Bellatrix	1·6	278	N 6
14	Elnath	1·7	278	N 29
15	Alnilam	1·7	276	S 1
16	Betelgeuse	Var.*	271	N 7
17	Canopus	−0·7	264	S 53
18	Sirius	−1·5	258	S 17
19	Adhara	1·5	255	S 29
20	Procyon	0·4	245	N 5
21	Pollux	1·1	243	N 28
22	Avior	1·9	234	S 60
23	Suhail	2·2	223	S 44
24	Miaplacidus	1·7	222	S 70
25	Alphard	2·0	218	S 9
26	Regulus	1·4	208	N 12
27	Dubhe	1·8	194	N 62
28	Denebola	2·1	182	N 14
29	Gienah	2·6	176	S 18
30	Acrux	1·3	173	S 63
31	Gacrux	1·6	172	S 57
32	Alioth	1·8	166	N 56
33	Spica	1·0	158	S 11
34	Alkaid	1·9	153	N 49
35	Hadar	0·6	149	S 60
36	Menkent	2·1	148	S 36
37	Arcturus	0·0	146	N 19
38	Rigil Kentaurus	−0·3	140	S 61
39	Zubenelgenubi	2·8	137	S 16
40	Kochab	2·1	137	N 74
41	Alphecca	2·2	126	N 27
42	Antares	1·0	112	S 26
43	Atria	1·9	107	S 69
44	Sabik	2·4	102	S 16
45	Shaula	1·6	96	S 37
46	Rasalhague	2·1	96	N 13
47	Eltanin	2·2	91	N 51
48	Kaus Australis	1·9	84	S 34
49	Vega	0·0	81	N 39
50	Nunki	2·0	76	S 26
51	Altair	0·8	62	N 9
52	Peacock	1·9	53	S 57
53	Deneb	1·3	49	N 45
54	Enif	2·4	34	N 10
55	Alnair	1·7	28	S 47
56	Fomalhaut	1·2	15	S 29
57	Markab	2·5	14	N 15

*0·1 — 1·2

© British Crown Copyright 2022. All rights reserved.

ALTITUDE CORRECTION TABLES 0°–35°— MOON

App. Alt.	0°–4° Corrn	5°–9° Corrn	10°–14° Corrn	15°–19° Corrn	20°–24° Corrn	25°–29° Corrn	30°–34° Corrn	App. Alt.
00	0° 34.5	5° 58.2	10° 62.1	15° 62.8	20° 62.2	25° 60.8	30° 58.9	00
10	36.5	58.5	62.2	62.8	62.2	60.8	58.8	10
20	38.3	58.7	62.2	62.8	62.1	60.7	58.8	20
30	40.0	58.9	62.3	62.8	62.1	60.7	58.7	30
40	41.5	59.1	62.3	62.8	62.0	60.6	58.6	40
50	42.9	59.3	62.4	62.7	62.0	60.6	58.5	50
00	1° 44.2	6° 59.5	11° 62.4	16° 62.7	21° 62.0	26° 60.5	31° 58.5	00
10	45.4	59.7	62.4	62.7	61.9	60.4	58.4	10
20	46.5	59.9	62.5	62.7	61.9	60.4	58.3	20
30	47.5	60.0	62.5	62.7	61.9	60.3	58.2	30
40	48.4	60.2	62.5	62.7	61.8	60.3	58.2	40
50	49.3	60.3	62.6	62.7	61.8	60.2	58.1	50
00	2° 50.1	7° 60.5	12° 62.6	17° 62.7	22° 61.7	27° 60.1	32° 58.0	00
10	50.8	60.6	62.6	62.6	61.7	60.1	57.9	10
20	51.5	60.7	62.6	62.6	61.6	60.0	57.8	20
30	52.2	60.9	62.7	62.6	61.6	59.9	57.8	30
40	52.8	61.0	62.7	62.6	61.6	59.9	57.7	40
50	53.4	61.1	62.7	62.6	61.5	59.8	57.6	50
00	3° 53.9	8° 61.2	13° 62.7	18° 62.5	23° 61.5	28° 59.7	33° 57.5	00
10	54.4	61.3	62.7	62.5	61.4	59.7	57.4	10
20	54.9	61.4	62.7	62.5	61.4	59.6	57.4	20
30	55.3	61.5	62.8	62.5	61.3	59.5	57.3	30
40	55.7	61.6	62.8	62.4	61.3	59.5	57.2	40
50	56.1	61.6	62.8	62.4	61.2	59.4	57.1	50
00	4° 56.4	9° 61.7	14° 62.8	19° 62.4	24° 61.2	29° 59.3	34° 57.0	00
10	56.8	61.8	62.8	62.4	61.1	59.3	56.9	10
20	57.1	61.9	62.8	62.3	61.1	59.2	56.9	20
30	57.4	61.9	62.8	62.3	61.0	59.1	56.8	30
40	57.7	62.0	62.8	62.3	61.0	59.1	56.7	40
50	58.0	62.1	62.8	62.2	60.9	59.0	56.6	50

HP	L U	L U	L U	L U	L U	L U	L U	HP
54.0	0.3 0.9	0.3 0.9	0.4 1.0	0.5 1.1	0.6 1.2	0.7 1.3	0.9 1.5	54.0
54.3	0.7 1.1	0.7 1.2	0.8 1.2	0.8 1.3	0.9 1.4	1.1 1.5	1.2 1.7	54.3
54.6	1.1 1.4	1.1 1.4	1.1 1.4	1.2 1.5	1.3 1.6	1.4 1.7	1.5 1.8	54.6
54.9	1.4 1.6	1.5 1.6	1.5 1.6	1.6 1.7	1.6 1.8	1.8 1.9	1.9 2.0	54.9
55.2	1.8 1.8	1.8 1.8	1.9 1.8	1.9 1.9	2.0 2.0	2.1 2.1	2.2 2.2	55.2
55.5	2.2 2.0	2.2 2.0	2.3 2.1	2.3 2.1	2.4 2.2	2.4 2.3	2.5 2.4	55.5
55.8	2.6 2.2	2.6 2.2	2.6 2.3	2.7 2.3	2.7 2.4	2.8 2.4	2.9 2.5	55.8
56.1	3.0 2.4	3.0 2.5	3.0 2.5	3.0 2.5	3.1 2.6	3.1 2.6	3.2 2.7	56.1
56.4	3.3 2.7	3.4 2.7	3.4 2.7	3.4 2.7	3.4 2.8	3.5 2.8	3.5 2.9	56.4
56.7	3.7 2.9	3.7 2.9	3.8 2.9	3.8 2.9	3.8 3.0	3.8 3.0	3.9 3.0	56.7
57.0	4.1 3.1	4.1 3.1	4.1 3.1	4.1 3.1	4.2 3.2	4.2 3.2	4.2 3.2	57.0
57.3	4.5 3.3	4.5 3.3	4.5 3.3	4.5 3.3	4.5 3.3	4.5 3.4	4.6 3.4	57.3
57.6	4.9 3.5	4.9 3.5	4.9 3.5	4.9 3.5	4.9 3.5	4.9 3.5	4.9 3.6	57.6
57.9	5.3 3.8	5.3 3.8	5.2 3.8	5.2 3.7	5.2 3.7	5.2 3.7	5.3 3.7	57.9
58.2	5.6 4.0	5.6 4.0	5.6 4.0	5.6 4.0	5.6 3.9	5.6 3.9	5.6 3.9	58.2
58.5	6.0 4.2	6.0 4.2	6.0 4.2	6.0 4.2	6.0 4.1	5.9 4.1	5.9 4.1	58.5
58.8	6.4 4.4	6.4 4.4	6.4 4.4	6.3 4.4	6.3 4.3	6.3 4.3	6.2 4.2	58.8
59.1	6.8 4.6	6.8 4.6	6.7 4.6	6.7 4.6	6.7 4.5	6.6 4.5	6.6 4.4	59.1
59.4	7.2 4.8	7.1 4.8	7.1 4.8	7.1 4.8	7.0 4.7	7.0 4.7	6.9 4.6	59.4
59.7	7.5 5.1	7.5 5.0	7.5 5.0	7.5 5.0	7.4 4.9	7.3 4.8	7.2 4.8	59.7
60.0	7.9 5.3	7.9 5.3	7.9 5.2	7.8 5.2	7.8 5.1	7.7 5.0	7.6 4.9	60.0
60.3	8.3 5.5	8.3 5.5	8.2 5.4	8.2 5.4	8.1 5.3	8.0 5.2	7.9 5.1	60.3
60.6	8.7 5.7	8.7 5.7	8.6 5.7	8.6 5.6	8.5 5.5	8.4 5.4	8.2 5.3	60.6
60.9	9.1 5.9	9.0 5.9	9.0 5.9	8.9 5.8	8.8 5.7	8.7 5.6	8.6 5.4	60.9
61.2	9.5 6.2	9.4 6.1	9.4 6.1	9.3 6.0	9.2 5.9	9.1 5.8	8.9 5.6	61.2
61.5	9.8 6.4	9.8 6.3	9.7 6.3	9.7 6.2	9.5 6.1	9.4 5.9	9.2 5.8	61.5

DIP

Ht. of Eye	Corrn	Ht. of Eye	Ht. of Eye	Corrn	Ht. of Eye
m		ft.	m		ft.
2.4	-2.8	8.0	9.5	-5.5	31.5
2.6	-2.9	8.6	9.9	-5.6	32.7
2.8	-3.0	9.2	10.3	-5.7	33.9
3.0	-3.1	9.8	10.6	-5.8	35.1
3.2	-3.2	10.5	11.0	-5.9	36.3
3.4	-3.3	11.2	11.4	-6.0	37.6
3.6	-3.4	11.9	11.8	-6.1	38.9
3.8	-3.5	12.6	12.2	-6.2	40.1
4.0	-3.6	13.3	12.6	-6.3	41.5
4.3	-3.7	14.1	13.0	-6.4	42.8
4.5	-3.8	14.9	13.4	-6.5	44.2
4.7	-3.9	15.7	13.8	-6.6	45.5
5.0	-4.0	16.5	14.2	-6.7	46.9
5.2	-4.1	17.4	14.7	-6.8	48.4
5.5	-4.2	18.3	15.1	-6.9	49.8
5.8	-4.3	19.1	15.5	-7.0	51.3
6.1	-4.4	20.1	16.0	-7.1	52.8
6.3	-4.5	21.0	16.5	-7.2	54.3
6.6	-4.6	22.0	16.9	-7.3	55.8
6.9	-4.7	22.9	17.4	-7.4	57.4
7.2	-4.8	23.9	17.9	-7.5	58.9
7.5	-4.9	24.9	18.4	-7.6	60.5
7.9	-5.0	26.0	18.8	-7.7	62.1
8.2	-5.1	27.1	19.3	-7.8	63.8
8.5	-5.2	28.1	19.8	-7.9	65.4
8.8	-5.3	29.2	20.4	-8.0	67.1
9.2	-5.4	30.4	20.9	-8.1	68.8
9.5		31.5	21.4		70.5

MOON CORRECTION TABLE

The correction is in two parts; the first correction is taken from the upper part of the table with argument apparent altitude, and the second from the lower part, with argument HP, in the same column as that from which the first correction was taken. Separate corrections are given in the lower part for lower (L) and upper (U) limbs. All corrections are to be **added** to apparent altitude, *but 30' is to be subtracted from the altitude of the upper limb.*

For corrections for pressure and temperature see page A4.

For bubble sextant observations ignore dip, take the mean of upper and lower limb corrections and subtract 15' from the altitude.

App. Alt. = Apparent altitude = Sextant altitude corrected for index error and dip.

© British Crown Copyright 2022. All rights reserved.

ALTITUDE CORRECTION TABLES 35°–90°— MOON

App. Alt.	35°–39° Corrn	40°–44° Corrn	45°–49° Corrn	50°–54° Corrn	55°–59° Corrn	60°–64° Corrn	65°–69° Corrn	70°–74° Corrn	75°–79° Corrn	80°–84° Corrn	85°–89° Corrn	App. Alt.
00	35 56·5	40 53·7	45 50·5	50 46·9	55 43·1	60 38·9	65 34·6	70 30·0	75 25·3	80 20·5	85 15·6	00
10	56·4	53·6	50·4	46·8	42·9	38·8	34·4	29·9	25·2	20·4	15·5	10
20	56·3	53·5	50·2	46·7	42·8	38·7	34·3	29·7	25·0	20·2	15·3	20
30	56·2	53·4	50·1	46·5	42·7	38·5	34·1	29·6	24·9	20·0	15·1	30
40	56·2	53·3	50·0	46·4	42·5	38·4	34·0	29·4	24·7	19·9	15·0	40
50	56·1	53·2	49·9	46·3	42·4	38·2	33·8	29·3	24·5	19·7	14·8	50
00	36 56·0	41 53·1	46 49·8	51 46·2	56 42·3	61 38·1	66 33·7	71 29·1	76 24·4	81 19·6	86 14·6	00
10	55·9	53·0	49·7	46·0	42·1	37·9	33·5	29·0	24·2	19·4	14·5	10
20	55·8	52·9	49·5	45·9	42·0	37·8	33·4	28·8	24·1	19·2	14·3	20
30	55·7	52·8	49·4	45·8	41·9	37·7	33·2	28·7	23·9	19·1	14·2	30
40	55·6	52·6	49·3	45·7	41·7	37·5	33·1	28·5	23·8	18·9	14·0	40
50	55·5	52·5	49·2	45·5	41·6	37·4	32·9	28·3	23·6	18·7	13·8	50
00	37 55·4	42 52·4	47 49·1	52 45·4	57 41·4	62 37·2	67 32·8	72 28·2	77 23·4	82 18·6	87 13·7	00
10	55·3	52·3	49·0	45·3	41·3	37·1	32·6	28·0	23·3	18·4	13·5	10
20	55·2	52·2	48·8	45·2	41·2	36·9	32·5	27·9	23·1	18·2	13·3	20
30	55·1	52·1	48·7	45·0	41·0	36·8	32·3	27·7	22·9	18·1	13·2	30
40	55·0	52·0	48·6	44·9	40·9	36·6	32·2	27·6	22·8	17·9	13·0	40
50	55·0	51·9	48·5	44·8	40·8	36·5	32·0	27·4	22·6	17·8	12·8	50
00	38 54·9	43 51·8	48 48·4	53 44·6	58 40·6	63 36·4	68 31·9	73 27·2	78 22·5	83 17·6	88 12·7	00
10	54·8	51·7	48·3	44·5	40·5	36·2	31·7	27·1	22·3	17·4	12·5	10
20	54·7	51·6	48·1	44·4	40·3	36·1	31·6	26·9	22·1	17·3	12·3	20
30	54·6	51·5	48·0	44·2	40·2	35·9	31·4	26·8	22·0	17·1	12·2	30
40	54·5	51·4	47·9	44·1	40·1	35·8	31·3	26·6	21·8	16·9	12·0	40
50	54·4	51·2	47·8	44·0	39·9	35·6	31·1	26·5	21·7	16·8	11·8	50
00	39 54·3	44 51·1	49 47·7	54 43·9	59 39·8	64 35·5	69 31·0	74 26·3	79 21·5	84 16·6	89 11·7	00
10	54·2	51·0	47·5	43·7	39·6	35·3	30·8	26·1	21·3	16·4	11·5	10
20	54·1	50·9	47·4	43·6	39·5	35·2	30·7	26·0	21·2	16·3	11·4	20
30	54·0	50·8	47·3	43·5	39·4	35·0	30·5	25·8	21·0	16·1	11·2	30
40	53·9	50·7	47·2	43·3	39·2	34·9	30·4	25·7	20·9	16·0	11·0	40
50	53·8	50·6	47·0	43·2	39·1	34·7	30·2	25·5	20·7	15·8	10·9	50

HP	L	U	L	U	L	U	L	U	L	U	L	U	L	U	L	U	L	U	L	U	L	U	HP
54·0	1·1	1·7	1·3	1·9	1·5	2·1	1·7	2·4	2·0	2·6	2·3	2·9	2·6	3·2	2·9	3·5	3·2	3·8	3·5	4·1	3·8	4·5	54·0
54·3	1·4	1·8	1·6	2·0	1·8	2·2	2·0	2·5	2·2	2·7	2·5	3·0	2·8	3·2	3·1	3·5	3·3	3·8	3·6	4·1	3·9	4·4	54·3
54·6	1·7	2·0	1·9	2·2	2·1	2·4	2·3	2·6	2·5	2·8	2·7	3·0	3·0	3·3	3·2	3·5	3·5	3·8	3·8	4·0	4·0	4·3	54·6
54·9	2·0	2·2	2·2	2·3	2·3	2·5	2·5	2·7	2·7	2·9	2·9	3·1	3·2	3·3	3·4	3·5	3·6	3·8	3·9	4·0	4·1	4·3	54·9
55·2	2·3	2·3	2·5	2·4	2·6	2·6	2·8	2·8	3·0	2·9	3·2	3·1	3·4	3·3	3·6	3·5	3·8	3·7	4·0	4·0	4·2	4·2	55·2
55·5	2·7	2·5	2·8	2·6	2·9	2·7	3·1	2·9	3·2	3·0	3·4	3·2	3·6	3·4	3·7	3·5	3·9	3·7	4·1	3·9	4·3	4·1	55·5
55·8	3·0	2·6	3·1	2·7	3·2	2·8	3·3	3·0	3·5	3·1	3·6	3·3	3·8	3·4	3·9	3·6	4·1	3·7	4·2	3·9	4·4	4·0	55·8
56·1	3·3	2·8	3·4	2·9	3·5	3·0	3·6	3·1	3·7	3·2	3·8	3·3	4·0	3·4	4·1	3·6	4·2	3·7	4·4	3·8	4·5	4·0	56·1
56·4	3·6	2·9	3·7	3·0	3·8	3·1	3·9	3·2	3·9	3·3	4·0	3·4	4·1	3·5	4·3	3·6	4·4	3·7	4·5	3·8	4·6	3·9	56·4
56·7	3·9	3·1	4·0	3·1	4·1	3·2	4·1	3·3	4·2	3·3	4·3	3·4	4·3	3·5	4·4	3·6	4·5	3·7	4·6	3·8	4·7	3·8	56·7
57·0	4·3	3·2	4·3	3·3	4·3	3·3	4·4	3·4	4·4	3·4	4·5	3·5	4·5	3·5	4·6	3·6	4·7	3·6	4·7	3·7	4·8	3·8	57·0
57·3	4·6	3·4	4·6	3·4	4·6	3·4	4·6	3·5	4·7	3·5	4·7	3·5	4·7	3·6	4·8	3·6	4·8	3·6	4·8	3·7	4·9	3·7	57·3
57·6	4·9	3·6	4·9	3·6	4·9	3·6	4·9	3·6	4·9	3·6	4·9	3·6	4·9	3·6	4·9	3·6	5·0	3·6	5·0	3·6	5·0	3·6	57·6
57·9	5·2	3·7	5·2	3·7	5·2	3·7	5·2	3·7	5·2	3·7	5·1	3·6	5·1	3·6	5·1	3·6	5·1	3·6	5·1	3·6	5·1	3·6	57·9
58·2	5·5	3·9	5·5	3·8	5·5	3·8	5·4	3·8	5·4	3·7	5·4	3·7	5·3	3·7	5·3	3·6	5·2	3·6	5·2	3·5	5·2	3·5	58·2
58·5	5·9	4·0	5·8	4·0	5·8	3·9	5·7	3·9	5·6	3·8	5·6	3·8	5·5	3·7	5·5	3·6	5·4	3·6	5·3	3·4	5·3	3·4	58·5
58·8	6·2	4·2	6·1	4·1	6·0	4·1	6·0	4·0	5·9	3·9	5·8	3·8	5·7	3·7	5·6	3·6	5·5	3·5	5·4	3·5	5·3	3·4	58·8
59·1	6·5	4·3	6·4	4·3	6·3	4·2	6·2	4·1	6·1	4·0	6·0	3·9	5·9	3·8	5·8	3·6	5·7	3·5	5·6	3·4	5·4	3·3	59·1
59·4	6·8	4·5	6·7	4·4	6·6	4·3	6·5	4·2	6·4	4·1	6·2	3·9	6·1	3·8	6·0	3·7	5·8	3·5	5·7	3·4	5·5	3·2	59·4
59·7	7·1	4·7	7·0	4·5	6·9	4·4	6·8	4·3	6·6	4·1	6·5	4·0	6·3	3·8	6·1	3·7	6·0	3·5	5·8	3·3	5·6	3·2	59·7
60·0	7·5	4·8	7·3	4·7	7·2	4·5	7·0	4·4	6·9	4·2	6·7	4·0	6·5	3·9	6·3	3·7	6·1	3·5	5·9	3·3	5·7	3·1	60·0
60·3	7·8	5·0	7·6	4·8	7·5	4·7	7·3	4·5	7·1	4·3	6·9	4·1	6·7	3·9	6·5	3·7	6·3	3·5	6·0	3·2	5·8	3·0	60·3
60·6	8·1	5·1	7·9	5·0	7·7	4·8	7·6	4·6	7·3	4·4	7·1	4·2	6·9	3·9	6·7	3·7	6·4	3·4	6·2	3·2	5·9	2·9	60·6
60·9	8·4	5·3	8·2	5·1	8·0	4·9	7·8	4·7	7·6	4·5	7·3	4·2	7·1	4·0	6·8	3·7	6·6	3·4	6·3	3·2	6·0	2·9	60·9
61·2	8·7	5·4	8·5	5·2	8·3	5·0	8·1	4·8	7·8	4·5	7·6	4·3	7·3	4·0	7·0	3·7	6·7	3·4	6·4	3·1	6·1	2·8	61·2
61·5	9·1	5·6	8·8	5·4	8·6	5·1	8·3	4·9	8·1	4·6	7·8	4·3	7·5	4·0	7·2	3·7	6·9	3·4	6·5	3·1	6·2	2·7	61·5

XXXV

© British Crown Copyright 2022. All rights reserved.

LIST OF CONTENTS

© British Crown Copyright 2022. All rights reserved.

SUBSCRIBE TO
CRUISING WORLD
TODAY!

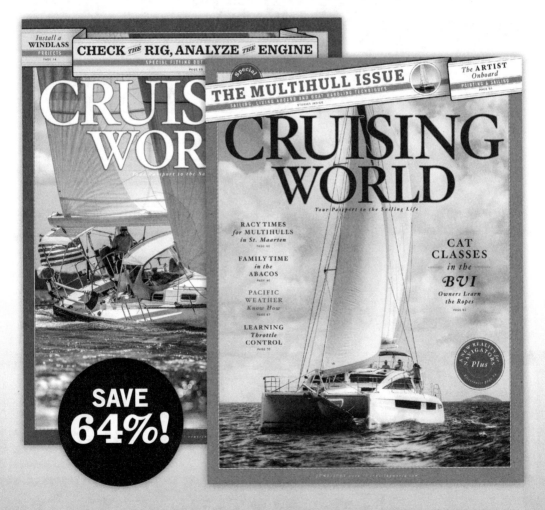

SAVE 64%!

1 year for only $19.97 – that's 64% off the cover price!

ORDER NOW: CRUISINGWORLD.COM/ALMANAC

Your Source For Nautical Books and Charts

Almanacs
Building and Upkeep
Celestial Navigation
Coast Pilots and Light Lists
Cruising Guides
Exam Preparation
Federal Regulations
Ship Knowledge
Navigation
Sailing Directions
Seamanship
Ship Handling
Tides and Currents
Tug and Barge

www.PilothouseCharts.com

Pilothouse

1-800-40-PILOT

and so much more...

PROFESSIONAL
MARINER
JOURNAL OF THE MARITIME INDUSTRY

ake control

ofessional Mariner provides all you need to know to
y informed about regulations, casualties, legislation,
d technologies to take your career to the next level.

bscribe Today www.professionalmariner.com/Subscribe/

PROFESSIONAL
MARINER
JOURNAL OF THE MARITIME INDUSTRY

LITTORAL
COMBAT SHIPS

HULL COATINGS

ICEBERGS?

INDUMAR

ADMIRALTY
CHART AGENT
DIGITAL DISTRIBUTOR

The only place to cover all your maritime needs!

Charts & Publications

Paper and electronic format, Print On Demand service, CNITA active member.

- ADMIRALTY
- OceanGrafix
- SEMAR Mexico

- IMO
- Witherbys
- Marisec

- Shipping Guides LTD
- I.C. Brindle & Co.
- ITU

Electronic Services

Installation and maintenance of navigation & communication equipment.

Class inspections approved by: ABS • BV • CCS • DNV GL • LR • RINA • NKK

- Sperry Marine
- Terma
- JRC

- Wärtsilä
- Consilium
- Entel

- Cobham Sailor
- Kelvin Hughes
- Tokyo Keiki

- Simrad
- Danelec
- Yokogawa

Maritime Products

SOLAS signage, safety equipment, nautical instruments & marine training software.

- DHR lights
- Annin Flags

- PC Maritime
- Videotel

- Maritime Progress
- Weems & Plath

Veracruz, Ver. | MX
Cd. del Carmen, Camp. | MX
Manzanillo, Col. | MX
Lima | PE

info@indumarver.com   www.indumarver.com

ISO 9001 2015 CERTIFIED

Captain

Deck Hand

Qualified Assessor

Engineer

Gain the professional maritime training you need for the level of success you want to achieve.

MPT is the most complete full-service private maritime school in the country. Our training programs are internationally acclaimed and are utilized by government agencies, global maritime businesses and individual crew members. Our campuses boast over 61,000 sq ft of classrooms, deck and engineering training labs, student service facilities and several off-site training facilites. Whether it's captaining a vessel, safeguarding marine environments, designing advanced ocean engineering structures, crewing a luxury megayacht or keeping the world's goods moving; MPT can provide the training you need.

USCG | MCA | RYA | PYA | NI | MARSHALL ISLANDS

YACHTING | MERCHANT | COMMERCIAL | PASSENGER VESSEL

To get started, call or email us today! info@mptusa.com

954.525.1014 | 1915 South Andrews Avenue, Fort Lauderdale, FL 33316 | mptusa.com

EST. 1983

MPT
MARITIME PROFESSIONAL TRAINING
Fort Lauderdale, Florida

Sea The World

SEATTLE MARINE & FISHING SUPPLY CO.

Four Locations to Meet Your Needs

Seattle
206-285-5010

Bellingham
360-734-2400

Kodiak
907-486-5752

Naknek
907-246-4230
(Seasonal, April - August)

b2b.seamar.com • seamar.com

**Clothing – Electrical – Fishing Gear
Engine Controls – Steering Equipment
Hydraulics – Hardware – Netting
Knives and Cutlery – Safety Gear
Maintenance – Paints and Solvents
Plumbing – Rope and Twine**

Islamorada

NAVIGATIONAL SUPPLIES & SERVICE I TELS: (507)228-4348 / 228-6069

Business Office: Bldg 808 Balboa Road, (former Canal Zone), Republic of Panama

Business Hours: 0800 - 1700 hours (Local) or 1300 - 2200 hours (UTC). Fax: 507-228-1234

Islamorada is the appointed Admiralty chart agent in the Republic of Panama, and the largest nautical bookstore in Latin America. Located in Balboa, and on the Panama Canal, Islamorada is ideally positioned to provide products and services to ships in transit through the Isthmus, as well as to other countries throughout the region.

Digital Charts   Paper Charts   Nautical Publications   Maritime Software   Instruments   Flags & Pennants   IMO Signs

Nautical Books

Navigation, Seamanship

Towing & Salvage

Ship Design & Naval Architecture

Yachting & Leisure

Marine Engineering

Cargo Work

Log Books

Maritime Business, Maritime Law

Publications

Almanacs & Sight Reduction Tables

ITU - Call Signs, Ship Stations,
Coastal Stations, MMS

Shipping Guides - Atlas, Guide to Port Entry

IMO - Solas, Marpol, STCW95
(Wide Range of Stock)

Plotting Instrument

Binoculars & Magnifying Glasses

Sextants

Weather Instruments

Clocks & Chronometers

Global Positioning Systems (GPS)

Iridium Satellite Telephones

Brands

C. Plath

B. Cooke & Sons

Blundell Harley

ACR

Admiralty

Oceangrafix

Maui Jim

Reactor Watches

Davis Instruments

and more.

Software For:

Electronic Chart Viewers and ECDIS
Software/Hardware

Interactive Diesel Engine Training

Tide Tables & Tidal Current Tables

Electronic Charts

Port Guides

Vessel Traffic Services

Superyacht operations

Fleet Tracking

Nautical Surveys

Because of our strategic location, we are able to provide fast delivery of charts and other important products to ships calling on ports throughout Latin America and the Caribbean Basin.

SAFE IN SAFETY
SAVE IN SAFETY

Meeting Point of All Routes

TUNA SHIP SUPPLY LTD. CO.

Your Safety Partner in TURKEY

- Admiralty Charts & Publications
- IMO/ITU/ICS/TSO   Publications
- Safety & Fire Equipment
- Bridge & Navigational Equipment
- Communication Equipment
- Oil Pollution Equipment
- Security Equipment (ISPS)
- Pilot & Embarkation Ladders
- IMO Symbols & Safety Posters, Flags
- Measurement Equipment

TUNA GEMI IKMAL SAN.TIC.LTD.STI.
Evliya Celebi Mah. Genc Osman Cad. No.44 A/1
Tuzla , 34944 ISTANBUL / TURKEY
Tel : +90 (216) 446 7403 - Fax : +90 (216) 446 76 08
supply@tunashipping.com / www.tunashipping.com

Nautical Charts

NOAA
Print on
Demand
Charts

Order online at paracay.com

or call (707) 822-9063

NGA
Print on
Demand
Charts

NOAA BookletCharts™

A reduced-scale nautical chart for small boaters

Made to help recreational boaters locate themselves on the water. It has been reduced in scale for convenience, but otherwise contains all the information of the full-scale nautical chart. The bar scales have also been reduced, and are accurate when used to measure distances in these BookletCharts™.

- Professionally printed and staple-bound
- High quality, durable paper
- Includes Notices to Mariners
- Printed on-demand with the latest data from NOAA
- Handy 8.5" x 11" size

Full-Scale NOAA Charts

Always current. Always printed on-demand

- Charts ship rolled in a sturdy cardboard tube
- Choose Traditional paper or Waterproof material

Small-Format NOAA Charts

Scaled down versions of the full-sized charts

- Handy for small craft and recreational use
- Choose Traditional paper or Waterproof material

NOAA Booklet & Folio Charts

Multi-page charts that cover rivers and other waterways that are too extensive to fit onto one full-scale chart.

- 12 x 18" Booklets are spiral-bound
- 36 x 12" Folios are staple bound

Canadian
Hydrographic
Super Dealer

Local Ownership • Expert Service

- Anchoring & Docking
- Sailboat Hardware
- Safety Equipment
- Techincal Clothing & Footwear
- Electrical & Plumbing Supplies
- Navigation Instruments & Publications
- Rigging Supplies
- Honda &Yamaha Outboard Sales & Service
- Inflatable Boat Sales & Service

919 Bay Ridge Rd.   Annapolis, MD
P: 410 267 8681 • www.fawcettboat.com

STORM TACTICS HANDBOOK THIRD EDITION

...n Tactics
...book, 3rd Ed.
...1 • 9781929214471
...ages

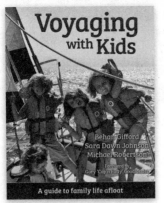

Voyaging With Kids:
A Guide to Family Life Afloat
PDB019 • 9781929214334
320 pages
$35.95

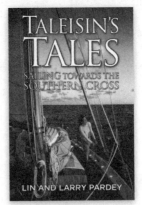

Taleisin's Tales:
Sailing towards the Southern Cross
PDB021 • 9781929214112
220 pages
$18.95

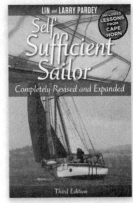

Self Sufficient Sailor, 3rd Edition
PDB101 • 9781929214877
320 pages
$29.95

The Real Deal:Larry Pardey,
Sailor & Adventurer DVD
PDV012
32 minutes
$22.95

Details of Classic Boat
Construction: The Hull
PDB020 • 9781929214440
452 pages
$49.95

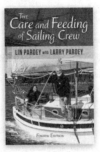

The Care and Feeding
of Sailing Crew, 4th Ed.
PDB017 • 9781929214341
416 pages
$24.95

Cruising in Seraffyn,
Tribute Edition
PDB100 • 9781929214150
224 pages
$18.95

...ost Control While You
...ruise DVD
...DV011 • 9781929214242
...0 minutes
...4.95

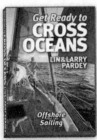

Get Ready to
CROSS OCEANS DVD
PDV008 • 9781929214228
90 minutes
$29.95

Get Ready to
CRUISE DVD
PDV007 • 9781929214198
90 minutes
$29.95

Cruising has
NO LIMITS DVD
PDV009 • 718122916429
74 minutes
$22.95

Storm Tactics,
Cape Horn Tested DVD
PDV006 • 9781929214105
84 minutes
$29.95

...eraffyn's
...Oriental Adventure
...DB006 • 9780964603639
...56 pages
...6.95

Seraffyn's
European Adventure
PDB007 • 9780964603646
319 pages
$16.95

Seraffyn's
Mediterranean Adventure
PDB015 • 9781929214167
256 pages
$16.95

Lin and Larry Pardey are a longtime cruising couple who have been dubbed "The Enablers" because of their enthusiasm and willingness to share their secrets for exploring the far corners of the world on a limited budget.

L&L

for sailing stories & cruising tips
landlpardey.com

BUY PARDEY BOOKS AND DVD'S at www.paracay.com

World Cruising Routes:
9th Edition
1000 Sailing Routes in All Oceans of The World

Long established as the bible for long-distance cruisers and a bestseller since its first publication in 1987, World Cruising Routes is a comprehensive guide to over 1,000 routes covering all the oceans of the world from the tropical South Seas to the high-latitudes of the Arctic and Antarctic.

This edition has been fully updated to reflect the recent changes in global weather conditions. Geared specifically to the needs of offshore navigators, this ninth edition assesses the consequences of climate change on sailing routes and provides over 6,000 waypoints to facilitate the planning of individual passages. Much of the information contained in the book was gathered during the author's three circumnavigations and voyages to Antarctica and the Northwest Passage.

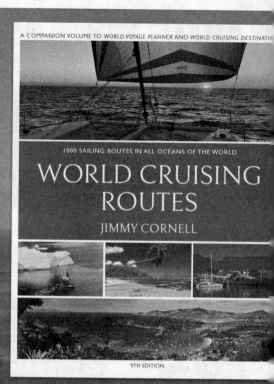

A COMPANION VOLUME TO WORLD VOYAGE PLANNER AND WORLD CRUISING DESTINATIONS

1000 SAILING ROUTES IN ALL OCEANS OF THE WORLD

WORLD CRUISING ROUTES
JIMMY CORNELL

9TH EDITION

 CORNELL SAILING

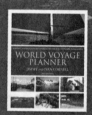
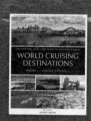

Jimmy Cornell books available from
PARADISE CAY PUBLICATIONS
Buy online at
www.paracay.com

Thousands of sailors have fulfilled their dream of blue water cruising with the help of Jimmy Cornell's books, among them the international bestseller World Cruising Routes. Now in its 7th edition, and with 200,000 copies sold to date, this is one of the best selling nautical publications in the world.

GET THE LATEST NEWS O
CORNELL SAILING EVENT

SUBSCRIBE TO THE NEWSLETTER
at **CORNELLSAILING.COM**

ISLANDS ODYSSEY

PACIFIC ODYSSEY

ATLANTIC ODYSSEY
CARIBBEAN ODYSSEY

Boat Books
Australia

Australia's Leading Nautical
Booksellers, Chart Agency and
one stop Navigation Centre

**Order securely online
all our titles and Charts**

Sydney
Ground Floor, 38 Oxley St,
St Leonards, NSW 2065.
Phone; 02 94391133
Fax; 02 94398517
charts@boatbooks-aust.com.au

www.boatbooks-aust.com.au

- Worldwide coverage of British Admiralty Charts
- Full Range of Australian and NZ Charts
- Complete Library of Marine Technical
  Publications –IMO, ITU, HMSO,
  Seamanship, Lloyds, Fairplay etc.
- Bridgewatch – Chart Correcting & Folio
  Management System
- Electronic Charts – AVCS & AUS ENC
- Over 5000 Marine Titles for every boating aspect

Fast and reliable service throughout Australia and the Asia Pacific Region

Commercial

Boat Books has a wide range of commercial
charts, software and services, including
BridgeWatch and more.

Recreational

Check out online shopping for a great range of
products for all recreational interests; sailing,
fishing, diving, rowing and more.

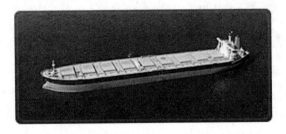

"PROUDLY TRAINING PROFESSIONAL MARINERS FOR MORE THAN 25 YEARS."

Visit our website for complete course listings,

including Celestial Navigation,

license prep programs, Able Seaman, Tankerman,

STCW, Radar, ECDIS and more.

FOR MORE INFORMATION
Call 800-642-CMTI

(800) 642-CMTI (2684) | www.chesapeakemarineinst.com | 3566 George Washington Memorial Hwy Hayes, VA 23072

TRUST THE EXPERTS

or more than 30 years our staff's trans-ocean pedigree has developed andfall into the industry source for expertise and product knowledge. lue-water sailors and professional mariners know and trust Landfall to outfit help guide their ships away from shore and across the sea.

Print On Demand Charts | Electronic Navigation Software | Chart Chips | Sextants | | Liferafts | PFDs | Flares | VHF | Tethers | EPIRBs | Satelite Phones | PLBs | AIS | Traditional Navigation Tools | First Aid Kits | Foul Weather Gear | Damage Control |

Landfall
YOUR JOURNEY STARTS HERE

151 Harvard Ave | Stamford, CT | 1800.941.2219 | LandfallNav.com

CHARTWATCH BY EW LINER
UKHO VERIFIED BACK-OF-BRIDGE SOFTWARE
The Ideal Replacement for Admiralty Gateway

- ChartWatch has been developed with one main objective: to provide Mariners with an **effective yet user friendly application** for the maintenance of ENCs and Paper Chart outfits on-board vessels.
- The ChartWatch software facilitates efficient inventory management including ordering and updating through three main modules:
  PAPER CHART MODULE | DIGITAL MODULE | DIGITAL CATALOGUE
- The Digital and Paper Modules allow for easy maintenance of both digital and paper chart holdings of vessels ensuring navigational safety and compliance.
- ChartWatch works on vessels with fleet broadband as well as on vessels with restricted email connectivity.

Digital Catalogue
- A comprehensive, multi-functional digital catalogue
- View, browse and select for purchase of all Admiralty digital products
- Automated port-to-port routing
- Highlights the existing on-board Admiralty digital product holdings
- Request & receive automated quotations in real time with our B2B application

Digital Module
- Maintain & update ENCs
- Download base data for AVCS & AIO, reducing the need to send AVCS DVDs on-board
- All base ENC & AIO data is backed up on-board reducing weekly data size and resulting in significant air time costs savings
- Generate complete base and updates for ENCs & AIO if ECDIS is corrupted
- Integrated Admiralty e-NP reader

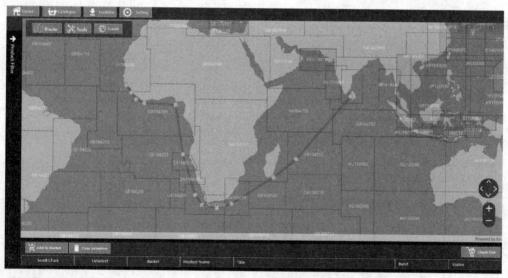

Paper Chart Module
- Vessel can maintain & update its own inventory
- Check updated status of inventory
- Download weekly corrections complete with Tracings
- Download weekly publication corrections
- Maintain an up-to-date Chart Correction Log
- Request and download historical chart corrections

Support
- Video tutorials for set-up, installation and training mariners. This saves time & eliminates the need to review detailed user guides.
- Further training through video conferencing or a suitable location.
- 24/7 technical support through email or remote access using Team Viewer or similar

Contact digitalsales@ewliner.com for a free 3-month trial
Subscribe to the full version Chartwatch on a quarterly or annual basis

WE'VE ALWAYS BEEN THANKFUL FOR LUCKY STARS.

Through calm and choppy waters, count on The Binnacle for all your navigational needs.
As an authorized print-on-demand chart dealer, we can print and ship NOAA
and Canadian nautical charts to wherever your lucky stars lead you.
Find us onshore and online at **binnacle.com**.

binnacle.com
a part of *The* BINNACLE

binnacle.com 1065 PURCELL'S COVE ROAD, HALIFAX, NOVA SCOTIA **1.800.665.6464**

Cruising Canada's Atlantic Provinces?

Nova Scotia
Newfoundland
Labrador
Gulf of St. Lawrence
New Brunswick
Quebec Shore
Prince Edward Island
Magdalens
Sable Island

The CRUISING CLUB OF AMERICA now publishes these definitive cruising guides available since 1952. All are updated regularly.

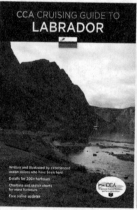

New editions are on chandlery shelves and available online at:
Paradise Cay (800) 736-4509 www.parcay.com
For more information: www.cruisingclub.org/book/ccaguides